Patterns of Economic Change by State and Area

INCOME, EMPLOYMENT, & GROSS DOMESTIC PRODUCT

Fourth Edition
2016

Patterns of Economic Change by State and Area

INCOME, EMPLOYMENT, & GROSS DOMESTIC PRODUCT

Fourth Edition
2015

Patterns of Economic Change by State and Area

INCOME, EMPLOYMENT, & GROSS DOMESTIC PRODUCT

Fourth Edition
2016

EDITED BY HANNAH M. ANDERSON

Lanham, MD

Published in the United States of America
by Bernan Press, a wholly owned subsidiary of
The Rowman & Littlefield Publishing Group, Inc.
4501 Forbes Boulevard, Suite 200
Lanham, Maryland 20706

Bernan Press
800-462-6420
www.rowman.com

ISBN-13: 978-1-59888-876-8
E-ISBN: 978-1-59888-877-5

∞™ The paper used in this publication meets the minimum requirements of
American National Standard for Information Sciences—Permanence of
Paper for Printed Library Materials, ANSI/NISO Z39.48-1992.
Manufactured in the United States of America.

Contents

Preface

Bernan Press is pleased to present the fourth edition of *Patterns of Economic Change by State and Area*. It is a special edition of *Business Statistics of the United States: Patterns of Economic Change,* bringing together measurements for regions, states, and metropolitan areas of some of the time trends that are displayed at the national level in *Business Statistics*. The title was added to the Bernan Press library of reference books in 2013. It includes some state indicators that were formerly shown in earlier editions of *Business Statistics*, which have been expanded to cover many more geographical entities including 381 metropolitan statistical areas.

This volume also complements such titles as *State and Metropolitan Area Data Book* and *County and City Extra*. In contrast to their predominantly current and detailed cross-section data on states and metropolitan areas, this book contributes historical time-series measurements of key aggregates that show how the economies of regions, states, and metropolitan areas have responded over time to cyclical currents and long-term trends.

All these data are compiled and published by U.S. government professional statistical agencies—the Bureau of Economic Analysis and the Census Bureau. Specific references to publications and web sites, along with definitions of terms and other essential information, are shown following each data series. With this information, the user can properly interpret and use the data and can update it, if desired, as the source agencies release new information over the course of the year.

The largest body of data included is "Personal Income and Employment by Region, State, and Metropolitan Area." These tables provide annual data, going far back as 1960, for farm and nonfarm earnings of persons; payments to persons of dividends, interest, and rent; personal current transfer receipts, which are income sources such as Social Security; total personal income; population; per capita personal income and disposable (after income taxes) personal income (that is, total income divided by the size of the population); and the total number of jobs in the state or area. Using these data, the performance of any given state or area, whether at one moment in time or over a span of years, can be studied, and compared and contrasted with that of the nation and other states or areas.

Even more comprehensive than personal income is gross domestic product (GDP), the measure of total U.S. economic activity, available and published here at the state level both in current dollar values and in the form of an index of quantities produced (that is to say, change in real output, corrected to remove the effects of inflation).

Moving from indicators of aggregate economic trends to effects on individuals and households, the third section shows data on median household incomes (the income of the "typical" household in the exact middle of the income distribution), corrected for inflation, and the poverty rate.

Hannah M. Anderson, editor of the past two editions of *State Profiles*, has edited this fourth edition of *Patterns of Economic Change by State and Area*. Cornelia J. Strawser provided assistance in planning the first edition.

PART A
PERSONAL INCOME AND EMPLOYMENT BY REGION, STATE, AND AREA

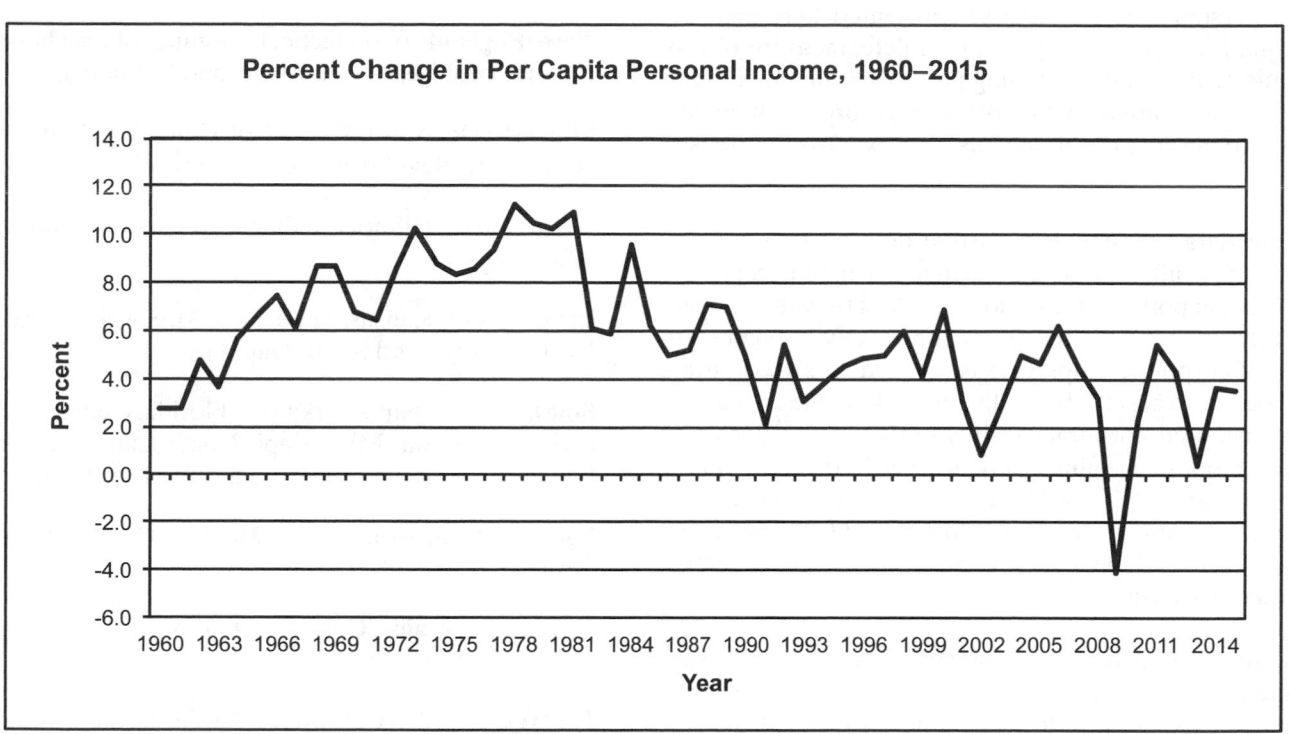

Percent Change in Per Capita Personal Income, 1960–2015

HIGHLIGHTS:

- In 2015, personal income per capita increased 3.5 percent after increasing 3.6 percent in 2014 and 0.4 percent in 2013. From 1960 through 2015, per capita personal income only declined once dropping from $41,082 in 2008 to $39,376 in 2009.

- Per capita personal income provides one measure of the affluence of the states and regions, and it varies widely. Among all states in 2015, Connecticut again had the highest per capita income at $66,972 followed by Massachusetts at $61,032 and New Jersey at $59,782. Mississippi had the lowest per capita income at $35,444. Nationally, per capita income was $47,669.

- Employment growth also differs significantly by state and metropolitan area. Although employment continued to increase in 2014, it declined by -0.1 or more in 31 MSAs. Greeley, CO, and Midland, TX, experienced the fastest growth in employment at 6.6 percent and 6.2 percent respectively.

- The value of total earnings by place of work in the United States increased 4.2 percent in 2015. These earnings include wages and salaries, supplements, and proprietors' income.

PART A NOTES AND DEFINITIONS: PERSONAL INCOME AND EMPLOYMENT BY REGION, STATE, AND METROPOLITAN AREA

Source: U.S. Department of Commerce, Bureau of Economic Analysis (BEA), <http://www.bea.gov>

The personal income data set presented here provides a comprehensive, though not complete, measure of economic activity and purchasing power for individual states and smaller areas, with historical records that enable users to observe developments over extensive periods of time.

These data are stated in current-dollar terms not corrected for inflation, so that changes over time represent changes in both quantity and price. And they do not completely represent corporate economic activity: compensation of corporate employees is covered, as are corporate dividends received by individuals, but the remaining undistributed corporate profits—difficult to allocate to small geographical units—are not. See Part B that follows for measures of Gross Domestic Product by state, which provide a complete allocation to states of GDP in current dollars and include inflation-corrected indexes of growth in quantity terms.

The summary definitions of personal income and its components in the next section are taken from a recent BEA press release. In a following section, further detail and explanation of the concepts is provided.

BEA definitions

Personal income is the income received by all persons from all sources. Personal income is the sum of net earnings by place of residence, property income, and personal current transfer receipts. **Property income** is rental income of persons, personal dividend income, and personal interest income. **Net earnings** is earnings by place of work (the sum of wage and salary disbursements, supplements to wages and salaries, and proprietors' income) less contributions for government social insurance, plus an adjustment to convert earnings by place of work to a place-of-residence basis. Personal income is measured before the deduction of personal income taxes and other personal taxes and is reported in current dollars (no adjustment is made for price changes).

The estimate of personal income in the United States is derived as the sum of the state estimates and the estimate for the District of Columbia; it differs from the estimate of personal income in the national income and product accounts (NIPAs) because of differences in coverage, in the methodologies used to prepare the estimates, and in the timing of the availability of source data.

BEA groups all 50 states and the District of Columbia into eight distinct regions for purposes of data collecting and analyses:

New England (Connecticut, Maine, Massachusetts, New Hampshire, Rhode Island, and Vermont);

Mideast (Delaware, District of Columbia, Maryland, New Jersey, New York, and Pennsylvania);

Great Lakes (Illinois, Indiana, Michigan, Ohio, and Wisconsin);

Plains (Iowa, Kansas, Minnesota, Missouri, Nebraska, North Dakota, and South Dakota);

Southeast (Alabama, Arkansas, Florida, Georgia, Kentucky, Louisiana, Mississippi, North Carolina, South Carolina, Tennessee, Virginia, and West Virginia);

Southwest (Arizona, New Mexico, Oklahoma, and Texas);

Rocky Mountain (Colorado, Idaho, Montana, Utah, and Wyoming); and

Far West (Alaska, California, Hawaii, Nevada, Oregon, and Washington).

State personal income statistics provide a framework for analyzing current economic conditions in each state and can serve as a basis for decision-making.

For example:

- Federal government agencies use the statistics as a basis for allocating funds and determining matching grants to states. The statistics are also used in forecasting models to project energy and water use.

- State governments use the statistics to project tax revenues and the need for public services.

- Academic regional economists use the statistics for applied research.

- Businesses, trade associations, and labor organizations use the statistics for market research.

BEA's national, international, regional, and industry estimates; the Survey of Current Business; and BEA news releases are available without charge on BEA's Web site at www.bea.gov. By visiting the site, you can also subscribe to receive free e-mail summaries of BEA releases and announcements.

More about income concepts

For the sake of simplicity, the following definitions and clarifications are written in terms of states, but all statements about "states" apply equally to regions and metropolitan areas.

The sum of state personal incomes for the United States (50 states and the District of Columbia) is somewhat smaller than U.S. personal income as shown in the national income and product accounts (NIPAs), due to slightly different definitions. The national total of the state estimates consists only of the income earned by persons who live in the United States and of foreign residents who work in the United States. The measure of personal income in the NIPAs is broader. It includes the earnings of federal civilian and military personnel stationed abroad and of U.S. residents on foreign assignment for less than a year. It also includes the investment income received by federal retirement plans for federal workers stationed abroad. NIPA personal income includes all income earned by U.S. citizens living abroad for less than a year; state personal income excludes the portion earned while the individual lives abroad. Earnings of foreign residents are included in the NIPAs only if they live and work in the United States for a year or more; state personal income, on the other hand, includes income paid to foreign nationals working in the United States regardless of length of residency. There are also statistical differences that reflect different timing of the availability of source data.

As in the NIPAs, personal income is defined to exclude capital gains.

Earnings by place of work consists of payments, to persons who work in the state, of wages and salaries; all supplements to wages and salaries (including employer contributions for government social insurance and all other benefits); and farm and nonfarm proprietors' income. Proprietor's income includes inventory valuation and capital consumption adjustments.

Contributions for government social insurance, which is subtracted from total earnings, includes both the employer and the employee contributions, on behalf of persons working in the state, for Social Security, Medicare, unemployment insurance, and other government social insurance, but does not include contributions to government employee retirement plans. Hence, personal income is defined as net of all contributions for government social insurance, which are commonly referred to as "Social Security taxes." Personal income is not net of other taxes on wages or other income such as Federal and state income taxes. These taxes are subtracted, however, to yield *"disposable personal income."*

Adjustment for residence. BEA adjusts earnings by place of work to a place-of-residence basis, to account for interstate and international commuting. The difference between earnings by place of residence and earnings by place of work is shown in the "Adjustment for residence" column. This adjustment is a net figure, equaling income received by state residents from employment outside the state minus income paid to persons residing outside the state but working in the state.

The effect of interstate commuting can be seen in its most extreme form in the District of Columbia. Its large negative adjustment for residence says that roughly half of total earnings by people working there are paid to persons living outside D.C. In comparison, Maryland and Virginia have substantial positive adjustments, representing income flowing from the District of Columbia and other employment sources outside the state. There is also a large negative adjustment for New York, associated with positive adjustments for New Jersey and Connecticut.

Dividends, interest, and rent. The rental income component of personal income, like that in the NIPAs, includes imputed rent on owner-occupied homes, net of capital consumption with capital consumption adjustment.

Personal current transfer receipts are aggregates for state residents of benefits from Social Security, Medicare, Medicaid, unemployment insurance, veterans' benefits, and other government benefits including the earned income credit. It does not include payments from government employee retirement plans, which are accounted for in supplements to wages and salaries.

It should be noted that in both the personal income and the NIPA accounts, the value of Medicare and Medicaid spending, even though in practice it is usually paid directly from the government to the health care provider, is treated as if it were cash income to the consumer, which is then expended in personal consumption expenditures.

Population is the U.S. Census Bureau estimate for the middle of the year. Note that because Hurricane Katrina occurred in August 2005, the population decline in Louisiana caused by that event does not appear until the entry for 2006.

Total employment is the total number of jobs, full-time plus part-time; each job that any person holds is counted at full weight. The employment estimates are on a place-of-work basis. Both wage and salary employment and self-employment are included. The main source for the wage and salary employment estimates is Bureau of Labor Statistics (BLS) estimates from unemployment insurance data (the ES-202 data), which also provides benchmarks for the widely-followed BLS payroll employment measures. Self-employment is estimated mainly from individual and partnership federal income tax returns. Therefore, this definition of employment is broader than BLS "total nonfarm payroll employment."

This concept of employment also differs from the concept of employment in the Current Population Survey (CPS), another BLS monthly survey, which is derived from a monthly count of persons employed; any individual will appear only once in the CPS in a given month, no matter how many different jobs he or she might hold. In addition, a self-employed individual who files more than one Schedule C income-tax filing will be counted more than once in the state figures. Finally, the state figures include members of the armed forces, who are not covered in the CPS. Due to these differences and other possible reporting inconsistencies, the BEA employment estimates are different from, and usually larger than, state employment estimates from the CPS.

The employment estimates correspond closely in coverage to the earnings estimates by place of work. However, the earnings estimates include the income of limited partnerships and of tax-exempt cooperatives, for which there are no corresponding employment estimates.

Per capita income is total income divided by the state's midyear population. This is an important tool for "scaling" income data to the size of the state, so that meaningful comparisons of economic performance among states can be made. Per capita income provides a useful gauge of economic strength, purchasing power, and fiscal capacity.

Users should not, however, assume that per capita income well represents the income of a typical state resident. Per capita incomes are averages—"means" in the technical language of statistics. Income of a typical person is better represented by the "median," which is the income of a person at the middle of the income distribution; half the population has higher income and half has lower. Where income is distributed so unequally that a relatively small number of persons have extremely high incomes, the mean will be higher than the median; and if the income distribution is becoming more unequal, the mean will rise faster than the median. Both of these conditions have been present for the U.S. economy as a whole in recent decades. Median household (not personal) incomes by state are presented in Part C.

UNITED STATES

Personal Income and Employment by Region and State: United States

(Millions of dollars, except as noted.)

Year	Personal income, total	Earnings by place of work			Less: Contributions for government social insurance	Plus: Adjustment for residence	Equals: Net earnings by place of residence	Plus: Dividends, interest, and rent	Plus: Personal current transfer receipts	Per capita (dollars)		Population (thousands)	Total employment (thousands)
		Nonfarm	Farm	Total						Personal income	Disposable personal income		
1960	418,095	335,061	13,734	348,795	16,358	-260	332,177	60,178	25,740	2,323	2,068	179,972	...
1961	436,553	346,111	14,467	360,578	16,916	-250	343,412	63,691	29,450	2,386	2,128	182,976	...
1962	464,248	369,606	14,526	384,132	19,023	-202	364,907	68,949	30,392	2,499	2,223	185,739	...
1963	487,847	388,985	14,414	403,399	21,559	-173	381,667	73,971	32,209	2,589	2,300	188,434	...
1964	522,796	418,041	13,227	431,268	22,258	-170	408,840	80,452	33,504	2,736	2,464	191,085	...
1965	564,631	449,105	15,576	464,681	23,278	-111	441,292	87,161	36,178	2,919	2,621	193,460	...
1966	612,945	494,927	16,631	511,558	31,136	-99	480,323	93,005	39,617	3,135	2,797	195,499	...
1967	656,851	529,362	15,259	544,621	34,600	-96	509,925	98,912	48,014	3,328	2,959	197,375	...
1968	720,704	581,688	15,420	597,108	38,392	-119	558,597	106,013	56,094	3,616	3,183	199,312	...
1969	791,150	637,792	17,430	655,222	43,791	-107	611,324	117,504	62,322	3,930	3,415	201,298	91,053
1970	855,078	677,462	17,660	695,122	46,012	-112	648,998	131,347	74,733	4,196	3,693	203,799	91,278
1971	923,964	725,987	18,142	744,129	50,859	-122	693,148	142,568	88,248	4,468	3,978	206,818	91,581
1972	1,015,526	800,006	21,947	821,953	58,897	-145	762,911	154,485	98,130	4,853	4,264	209,275	94,312
1973	1,131,213	886,446	34,875	921,321	75,183	-153	845,985	172,380	112,848	5,352	4,728	211,349	98,428
1974	1,242,433	966,418	30,097	996,515	84,872	-163	911,480	197,314	133,639	5,824	5,118	213,334	100,112
1975	1,359,998	1,033,304	29,132	1,062,436	88,974	-199	973,263	216,311	170,424	6,312	5,629	215,457	98,901
1976	1,491,506	1,150,940	25,218	1,176,158	100,987	-211	1,074,960	231,701	184,845	6,856	6,064	217,554	101,591
1977	1,646,968	1,282,436	24,491	1,306,927	112,699	-235	1,193,993	257,864	195,111	7,494	6,596	219,761	105,042
1978	1,851,867	1,451,175	28,384	1,479,559	130,827	-257	1,348,475	292,831	210,561	8,338	7,307	222,098	109,687
1979	2,068,806	1,621,969	30,221	1,652,190	152,273	-231	1,499,686	332,744	236,376	9,212	8,018	224,569	113,147
1980	2,307,005	1,767,869	20,738	1,788,607	165,670	-255	1,622,682	403,449	280,874	10,153	8,838	227,225	113,983
1981	2,584,340	1,936,479	27,476	1,963,955	195,066	-208	1,768,681	495,897	319,762	11,262	9,759	229,466	114,914
1982	2,767,657	2,030,291	24,766	2,055,057	208,173	-255	1,846,629	564,887	356,141	11,947	10,420	231,664	114,163
1983	2,957,901	2,171,992	17,450	2,189,442	225,143	-212	1,964,087	609,143	384,671	12,652	11,146	233,792	115,646
1984	3,268,535	2,401,770	32,159	2,433,929	256,550	-254	2,177,125	690,178	401,232	13,860	12,261	235,825	120,528
1985	3,501,927	2,585,178	32,255	2,617,433	280,379	-257	2,336,797	739,369	425,761	14,719	12,967	237,924	123,797
1986	3,712,243	2,755,283	33,394	2,788,677	302,389	228	2,486,516	774,016	451,711	15,459	13,640	240,133	126,232
1987	3,940,859	2,958,316	39,588	2,997,904	322,006	259	2,676,157	796,608	468,094	16,265	14,249	242,289	129,548
1988	4,260,753	3,223,118	39,231	3,262,349	360,285	226	2,902,290	861,053	497,410	17,426	15,362	244,499	133,564
1989	4,603,969	3,424,632	46,169	3,470,801	384,001	236	3,087,036	972,747	544,186	18,653	16,358	246,819	136,178
1990	4,890,453	3,635,438	47,615	3,683,053	408,676	313	3,274,690	1,018,532	597,231	19,591	17,215	249,623	138,331
1991	5,055,766	3,750,226	42,481	3,792,707	428,555	367	3,364,519	1,023,199	668,048	19,985	17,663	252,981	137,613
1992	5,402,109	4,013,404	50,716	4,064,120	453,768	478	3,610,830	1,043,340	747,939	21,060	18,675	256,514	138,166
1993	5,639,780	4,195,756	47,600	4,243,356	476,331	493	3,767,518	1,079,356	792,906	21,698	19,206	259,919	140,774
1994	5,930,316	4,412,747	51,008	4,463,755	507,188	533	3,957,100	1,144,336	828,880	22,538	19,907	263,126	144,197
1995	6,275,761	4,642,890	39,809	4,682,699	531,874	703	4,151,528	1,240,859	883,374	23,568	20,761	266,278	147,916
1996	6,661,697	4,909,590	55,361	4,964,951	554,150	675	4,411,476	1,321,093	929,128	24,728	21,624	269,394	151,056
1997	7,075,132	5,246,524	51,311	5,297,835	586,295	672	4,712,212	1,408,123	954,797	25,950	22,536	272,647	154,541
1998	7,588,703	5,668,776	49,045	5,717,821	623,685	755	5,094,891	1,509,934	983,878	27,510	23,771	275,854	158,481
1999	7,988,183	6,060,018	49,661	6,109,679	660,310	2,515	5,451,884	1,510,155	1,026,144	28,627	24,646	279,040	161,531
2000	8,634,847	6,558,532	52,714	6,611,246	704,849	2,587	5,908,984	1,638,583	1,087,280	30,602	26,224	282,162	165,371
2001	8,987,890	6,823,390	55,165	6,878,555	732,117	2,692	6,149,130	1,646,195	1,192,565	31,540	27,195	284,969	165,519
2002	9,150,761	6,965,616	43,340	7,008,956	750,341	2,656	6,261,271	1,604,837	1,284,653	31,815	28,151	287,625	165,159
2003	9,484,225	7,197,757	59,316	7,257,073	777,980	2,678	6,481,771	1,655,158	1,347,296	32,692	29,230	290,108	166,027
2004	10,047,876	7,619,625	76,299	7,695,924	827,766	2,659	6,870,817	1,755,766	1,421,293	34,316	30,731	292,805	169,037
2005	10,610,320	7,989,175	72,166	8,061,341	871,944	2,613	7,192,010	1,901,610	1,516,700	35,904	31,803	295,517	172,557
2006	11,381,350	8,487,352	55,439	8,542,791	921,187	2,617	7,624,221	2,142,567	1,614,562	38,144	33,600	298,380	176,124
2007	11,995,419	8,805,243	66,891	8,872,134	959,996	2,597	7,914,735	2,352,625	1,728,059	39,821	34,869	301,231	179,886
2008	12,492,705	9,023,719	70,735	9,094,454	986,781	2,649	8,110,322	2,425,839	1,956,544	41,082	36,128	304,094	179,640
2009	12,079,444	8,686,298	57,424	8,743,722	962,864	3,019	7,783,877	2,148,084	2,147,483	39,376	35,624	306,772	174,234
2010	12,459,613	8,908,900	66,926	8,975,826	982,431	3,067	7,996,462	2,138,496	2,324,655	40,277	36,275	309,347	173,035
2011	13,233,436	9,297,351	93,889	9,391,240	916,209	3,200	8,478,231	2,394,775	2,360,430	42,453	37,796	311,722	176,279
2012	13,904,485	9,745,876	94,357	9,840,233	950,002	3,410	8,893,641	2,644,535	2,366,309	44,266	39,459	314,112	179,082
2013	14,064,468	9,992,309	127,720	10,120,029	1,105,003	3,759	9,018,785	2,619,077	2,426,606	44,438	39,158	316,498	182,390
2014	14,683,147	10,471,756	112,282	10,584,038	1,157,138	3,820	9,430,720	2,723,288	2,529,139	46,049	40,471	318,857	185,799
2015	15,324,109	10,937,919	87,652	11,025,572	1,200,752	3,746	9,828,565	2,832,432	2,663,111	47,669	41,624	321,467	...

... = Not available.

REGION

Personal Income and Employment by Region and State: Far West

(Millions of dollars, except as noted.)

Year	Personal income, total	Derivation of personal income								Per capita (dollars)		Population (thousands)	Total employment (thousands)
		Earnings by place of work			Less: Contributions for government social insurance	Plus: Adjustment for residence	Equals: Net earnings by place of residence	Plus: Dividends, interest, and rent	Plus: Personal current transfer receipts	Personal income	Disposable personal income		
		Nonfarm	Farm	Total									
1960	60,982	48,258	1,965	50,223	2,357	-1	47,865	9,604	3,513	2,816	2,500	21,659	...
1961	64,546	50,969	1,866	52,835	2,496	-2	50,338	10,159	4,049	2,884	2,564	22,378	...
1962	69,551	55,320	1,975	57,294	2,978	-3	54,313	10,988	4,250	3,009	2,672	23,114	...
1963	74,000	59,144	1,914	61,058	3,461	-5	57,592	11,768	4,640	3,108	2,757	23,811	...
1964	79,847	63,554	2,018	65,572	3,582	-6	61,984	12,871	4,992	3,274	2,953	24,389	...
1965	85,530	67,798	2,009	69,806	3,732	-7	66,068	13,989	5,474	3,434	3,098	24,908	...
1966	93,233	74,920	2,259	77,178	4,926	-8	72,243	14,994	5,996	3,684	3,302	25,311	...
1967	100,395	80,342	2,125	82,467	5,452	-10	77,005	16,020	7,370	3,894	3,479	25,779	...
1968	110,330	88,601	2,383	90,983	6,123	-12	84,849	16,986	8,496	4,219	3,729	26,151	...
1969	121,614	96,749	2,481	99,229	6,626	-211	92,393	19,529	9,693	4,566	4,002	26,635	12,295
1970	131,426	102,202	2,440	104,642	6,894	-197	97,550	21,909	11,967	4,849	4,321	27,101	12,313
1971	140,461	108,127	2,470	110,597	7,515	-212	102,869	23,747	13,844	5,095	4,590	27,570	12,300
1972	154,141	119,222	3,114	122,336	8,729	-215	113,392	25,776	14,973	5,521	4,897	27,918	12,742
1973	170,173	131,569	4,254	135,822	11,058	-215	124,550	28,771	16,852	6,007	5,362	28,328	13,405
1974	190,691	145,306	5,389	150,695	12,600	-296	137,799	32,958	19,933	6,621	5,889	28,801	13,865
1975	212,219	160,170	4,811	164,981	13,656	-486	150,839	36,325	25,054	7,232	6,506	29,346	14,103
1976	235,797	180,567	4,813	185,380	15,727	-598	169,054	39,099	27,644	7,878	7,021	29,929	14,625
1977	261,470	202,188	4,684	206,872	17,862	-402	188,608	43,485	29,377	8,558	7,577	30,553	15,287
1978	298,381	232,596	4,757	237,353	21,059	-320	215,974	50,606	31,801	9,537	8,390	31,285	16,248
1979	338,430	264,399	5,909	270,308	25,060	-297	244,951	58,392	35,087	10,588	9,248	31,965	17,133
1980	383,701	292,510	7,355	299,864	27,354	-418	272,093	70,477	41,131	11,705	10,225	32,780	17,523
1981	429,247	321,386	5,852	327,238	32,526	-169	294,542	86,418	48,287	12,839	11,227	33,434	17,693
1982	458,008	338,477	5,929	344,406	34,875	-205	309,326	95,054	53,628	13,437	11,854	34,086	17,564
1983	494,015	364,933	5,969	370,902	38,249	-230	332,422	104,365	57,228	14,230	12,610	34,716	17,989
1984	545,001	403,974	6,614	410,588	43,877	-303	366,408	118,802	59,792	15,430	13,681	35,321	18,767
1985	586,908	437,419	6,383	443,802	48,006	-363	395,434	126,896	64,578	16,286	14,368	36,037	19,392
1986	628,745	472,154	7,290	479,444	52,251	-375	426,818	132,881	69,046	17,078	15,080	36,815	19,959
1987	674,634	513,938	8,487	522,425	56,781	-448	465,197	137,332	72,106	17,923	15,670	37,641	20,793
1988	733,923	564,044	8,996	573,040	64,107	-540	508,393	148,155	77,375	19,042	16,782	38,542	21,790
1989	796,054	603,271	9,003	612,273	69,060	-638	542,575	168,528	84,950	20,136	17,570	39,534	22,453
1990	857,059	650,642	9,490	660,132	74,731	-752	584,648	178,900	93,511	21,104	18,447	40,610	23,122
1991	892,213	678,468	8,641	687,109	78,399	-749	607,961	180,013	104,240	21,536	18,996	41,428	23,124
1992	946,821	717,876	9,397	727,273	82,247	-737	644,290	183,239	119,293	22,423	19,912	42,226	22,825
1993	977,870	736,325	10,709	747,034	84,534	-729	661,771	189,612	126,487	22,849	20,296	42,798	22,934
1994	1,016,045	764,009	10,055	774,064	88,381	-756	684,927	200,787	130,331	23,481	20,826	43,271	23,380
1995	1,071,607	798,816	9,667	808,482	91,651	-788	716,043	217,766	137,797	24,497	21,636	43,745	23,938
1996	1,141,289	848,668	11,191	859,859	95,355	-858	763,645	232,869	144,775	25,754	22,517	44,314	24,580
1997	1,216,589	912,158	11,489	923,648	101,059	-935	821,653	248,112	146,824	27,003	23,403	45,054	25,149
1998	1,321,435	998,016	11,138	1,009,153	108,701	-1,026	899,426	267,503	154,506	28,854	24,855	45,798	26,106
1999	1,409,428	1,082,656	11,660	1,094,316	116,480	-1,096	976,741	269,690	162,998	30,307	25,753	46,506	26,691
2000	1,546,211	1,197,943	11,823	1,209,765	127,413	-1,198	1,081,154	294,207	170,850	32,767	27,446	47,188	27,292
2001	1,600,031	1,235,325	11,209	1,246,534	132,590	-1,181	1,112,763	297,249	190,020	33,410	28,533	47,891	27,434
2002	1,631,992	1,258,735	11,806	1,270,541	136,598	943	1,134,887	293,145	203,960	33,654	29,672	48,493	27,454
2003	1,703,115	1,307,201	13,790	1,320,991	143,112	1,154	1,179,033	309,508	214,573	34,720	30,902	49,053	27,709
2004	1,815,692	1,390,721	16,110	1,406,831	155,433	2,052	1,253,450	338,447	223,796	36,605	32,622	49,602	28,262
2005	1,918,270	1,458,126	15,824	1,473,949	163,439	1,629	1,312,140	370,096	236,034	38,296	33,651	50,090	28,928
2006	2,062,464	1,545,774	14,045	1,559,819	170,460	692	1,390,051	418,953	253,460	40,784	35,660	50,571	29,596
2007	2,164,250	1,601,297	16,812	1,618,109	174,721	-628	1,442,761	451,327	270,161	42,410	36,889	51,031	30,242
2008	2,227,773	1,618,227	14,429	1,632,656	177,405	-2,296	1,452,955	466,059	308,760	43,167	37,786	51,609	30,017
2009	2,140,380	1,545,098	15,418	1,560,516	172,434	-2,228	1,385,854	412,624	341,902	41,029	36,964	52,168	28,868
2010	2,200,116	1,574,474	16,241	1,590,716	174,123	-2,298	1,414,295	408,123	377,698	41,751	37,352	52,696	28,499
2011	2,340,034	1,648,352	19,088	1,667,440	163,588	-2,381	1,501,470	457,840	380,723	43,976	38,874	53,211	28,981
2012	2,500,036	1,753,257	21,213	1,774,471	170,228	-2,571	1,601,672	514,797	383,567	46,524	41,116	53,737	29,808
2013	2,545,124	1,810,213	24,069	1,834,283	199,314	-2,599	1,632,370	516,166	396,588	46,897	40,862	54,271	30,634
2014	2,674,315	1,906,400	24,052	1,930,452	210,298	-2,814	1,717,339	538,557	418,419	48,775	42,367	54,830	31,396
2015	2,832,956	2,022,748	25,208	2,047,957	221,831	-3,062	1,823,064	561,658	448,234	51,124	44,079	55,414	...

... = Not available.

Personal Income and Employment by Area: Great Lakes

(Millions of dollars, except as noted.)

Year	Derivation of personal income									Per capita (dollars)		Population (thousands)	Total employment (thousands)
	Personal income, total	Earnings by place of work			Less: Contributions for government social insurance	Plus: Adjustment for residence	Equals: Net earnings by place of residence	Plus: Dividends, interest, and rent	Plus: Personal current transfer receipts	Personal income	Disposable personal income		
		Nonfarm	Farm	Total									
1960	89,057	73,836	2,014	75,850	3,657	-124	72,070	11,730	5,257	2,454	2,176	36,290	...
1961	91,256	74,024	2,446	76,470	3,618	-112	72,741	12,385	6,130	2,492	2,223	36,616	...
1962	96,745	79,020	2,352	81,373	4,044	-116	77,213	13,378	6,154	2,620	2,325	36,927	...
1963	101,264	82,950	2,365	85,315	4,562	-114	80,639	14,282	6,343	2,711	2,402	37,357	...
1964	108,845	89,682	2,045	91,726	4,763	-122	86,841	15,529	6,474	2,874	2,580	37,868	...
1965	118,836	97,504	2,631	100,135	4,947	-133	95,055	16,846	6,935	3,094	2,767	38,405	...
1966	129,264	107,613	2,972	110,585	6,742	-146	103,697	18,038	7,529	3,319	2,947	38,951	...
1967	135,968	112,828	2,535	115,363	7,274	-134	107,954	19,004	9,009	3,456	3,059	39,347	...
1968	148,309	123,287	2,431	125,718	7,989	-144	117,585	20,311	10,413	3,741	3,274	39,645	...
1969	161,929	135,103	2,870	137,973	9,311	272	128,934	21,661	11,334	4,058	3,493	39,904	17,785
1970	170,494	139,890	2,518	142,408	9,503	243	133,148	23,798	13,548	4,229	3,683	40,320	17,630
1971	183,427	148,982	2,899	151,881	10,424	317	141,774	25,550	16,102	4,515	3,986	40,622	17,549
1972	200,394	163,542	3,168	166,710	12,095	367	154,982	27,440	17,972	4,909	4,272	40,824	17,933
1973	223,875	182,407	5,213	187,620	15,631	418	172,408	30,529	20,938	5,467	4,781	40,947	18,710
1974	243,200	195,668	4,661	200,329	17,400	513	183,442	34,826	24,932	5,926	5,164	41,037	18,911
1975	262,732	203,836	5,818	209,654	17,669	591	192,576	38,124	32,031	6,392	5,645	41,105	18,399
1976	288,823	228,673	4,816	233,488	20,242	723	213,969	40,605	34,248	7,013	6,130	41,187	18,891
1977	320,539	256,830	4,818	261,647	22,758	904	239,793	44,977	35,769	7,751	6,739	41,353	19,508
1978	355,697	287,882	4,506	292,388	26,286	1,110	267,211	50,044	38,442	8,569	7,411	41,510	20,190
1979	391,885	315,546	5,223	320,769	29,932	1,326	292,163	56,257	43,465	9,418	8,110	41,611	20,491
1980	424,668	328,223	3,317	331,540	30,928	1,595	302,207	67,857	54,603	10,185	8,830	41,694	19,978
1981	463,297	349,945	3,683	353,628	35,439	1,332	319,521	83,073	60,703	11,124	9,603	41,648	19,795
1982	484,668	354,138	2,926	357,064	36,377	1,207	321,894	94,660	68,113	11,681	10,218	41,492	19,248
1983	510,529	374,261	-119	374,142	38,845	1,202	336,499	101,261	72,769	12,342	10,840	41,366	19,265
1984	563,598	414,054	4,409	418,463	44,260	1,328	375,530	113,535	74,532	13,616	12,014	41,393	20,028
1985	598,791	443,195	4,964	448,159	48,192	1,390	401,357	119,181	78,253	14,457	12,709	41,418	20,492
1986	631,279	470,783	4,488	475,270	51,647	1,466	425,089	124,256	81,934	15,228	13,409	41,455	20,934
1987	663,818	500,646	5,012	505,658	54,318	1,523	452,863	126,771	84,183	15,961	13,960	41,590	21,516
1988	711,154	543,700	3,363	547,063	60,614	1,645	488,093	135,147	87,914	17,046	14,974	41,721	22,070
1989	765,358	576,714	7,032	583,746	64,605	1,666	520,806	150,241	94,311	18,278	15,980	41,873	22,556
1990	808,453	608,741	6,005	614,746	68,950	1,927	547,722	157,672	103,058	19,207	16,821	42,091	22,928
1991	828,075	625,565	3,606	629,170	72,225	1,913	558,859	156,950	112,267	19,486	17,134	42,496	22,845
1992	889,436	671,689	6,123	677,812	76,663	2,030	603,179	162,260	123,996	20,732	18,316	42,903	22,971
1993	929,375	705,082	5,204	710,285	81,158	2,102	631,229	167,833	130,313	21,476	18,893	43,275	23,359
1994	985,774	749,949	6,083	756,032	87,642	2,279	670,670	180,741	134,363	22,615	19,830	43,590	24,060
1995	1,038,940	788,062	3,336	791,398	92,242	2,438	701,594	195,690	141,656	23,653	20,683	43,924	24,713
1996	1,096,975	825,551	6,936	832,488	95,305	2,683	739,865	208,928	148,182	24,796	21,553	44,239	25,105
1997	1,158,529	873,827	6,589	880,416	99,864	2,986	783,538	221,906	153,085	26,038	22,516	44,494	25,513
1998	1,230,225	932,788	5,585	938,373	104,858	3,025	836,539	238,146	155,539	27,505	23,671	44,728	25,943
1999	1,280,251	986,588	4,565	991,153	110,200	3,453	884,406	234,186	161,659	28,469	24,502	44,969	26,311
2000	1,363,017	1,045,265	5,402	1,050,667	114,562	3,795	939,900	251,887	171,229	30,145	25,978	45,216	26,800
2001	1,399,057	1,069,638	5,655	1,075,293	116,267	4,008	963,034	248,094	187,930	30,815	26,682	45,402	26,509
2002	1,417,345	1,090,524	3,752	1,094,275	117,881	2,106	978,500	239,252	199,593	31,116	27,490	45,550	26,241
2003	1,453,514	1,118,108	6,277	1,124,385	121,238	1,265	1,004,412	240,724	208,379	31,800	28,404	45,708	26,193
2004	1,516,178	1,166,114	10,208	1,176,322	127,508	2,413	1,051,227	247,780	217,172	33,072	29,649	45,844	26,406
2005	1,567,448	1,201,302	6,863	1,208,164	132,695	2,235	1,077,704	256,252	233,492	34,113	30,358	45,949	26,648
2006	1,653,854	1,252,018	6,462	1,258,480	138,389	3,709	1,123,800	284,502	245,552	35,897	31,807	46,072	26,850
2007	1,723,628	1,279,829	9,030	1,288,860	142,462	5,807	1,152,205	305,984	265,439	37,318	32,885	46,188	27,117
2008	1,779,417	1,294,345	11,442	1,305,787	145,210	6,389	1,166,966	313,425	299,026	38,453	33,984	46,275	26,863
2009	1,713,481	1,231,511	7,659	1,239,169	138,999	5,689	1,105,859	274,975	332,647	36,964	33,563	46,356	25,788
2010	1,752,729	1,253,773	8,833	1,262,606	141,100	5,668	1,127,174	269,585	355,970	37,745	34,101	46,436	25,592
2011	1,856,544	1,310,930	16,942	1,327,872	132,152	5,731	1,201,451	301,875	353,217	39,922	35,610	46,505	26,065
2012	1,932,394	1,367,929	11,904	1,379,833	137,272	6,191	1,248,751	330,056	353,587	41,493	37,006	46,572	26,336
2013	1,955,680	1,395,168	22,557	1,417,726	157,885	6,238	1,266,079	327,474	362,127	41,900	37,045	46,674	26,640
2014	2,022,590	1,450,244	15,610	1,465,853	164,371	6,589	1,308,071	339,419	375,100	43,274	38,185	46,739	27,036
2015	2,097,044	1,507,738	7,600	1,515,338	169,921	6,847	1,352,263	353,368	391,412	44,815	39294	46,793	...

... = Not available.

Personal Income and Employment by Region and State: Mideast

(Millions of dollars, except as noted.)

Year	Personal income, total	Earnings by place of work			Less: Contributions for government social insurance	Plus: Adjustment for residence	Equals: Net earnings by place of residence	Plus: Dividends, interest, and rent	Plus: Personal current transfer receipts	Per capita (dollars)		Population (thousands)	Total employment (thousands)
		Nonfarm	Farm	Total						Personal income	Disposable personal income		
1960	102,576	85,762	901	86,664	4,355	-761	81,547	14,910	6,119	2,658	2,333	38,597	...
1961	106,830	88,615	906	89,521	4,582	-791	84,148	15,688	6,994	2,730	2,397	39,133	...
1962	112,938	93,819	733	94,552	5,118	-804	88,630	17,158	7,150	2,855	2,501	39,552	...
1963	118,010	97,583	799	98,382	5,644	-841	91,898	18,519	7,593	2,944	2,578	40,083	...
1964	126,392	104,036	802	104,838	5,693	-902	98,243	20,288	7,861	3,117	2,767	40,555	...
1965	135,185	110,816	896	111,713	5,940	-932	104,841	21,939	8,405	3,295	2,915	41,025	...
1966	145,684	121,035	917	121,952	7,891	-1,011	113,050	23,233	9,401	3,522	3,097	41,360	...
1967	156,842	129,421	972	130,393	8,614	-1,183	120,596	24,644	11,602	3,769	3,297	41,617	...
1968	172,050	141,357	920	142,277	9,400	-1,301	131,576	26,602	13,872	4,104	3,558	41,924	...
1969	185,263	153,554	1,105	154,658	11,072	-1,738	141,848	28,157	15,257	4,399	3,762	42,111	19,432
1970	200,277	163,857	1,063	164,920	11,658	-1,662	151,600	30,572	18,105	4,711	4,085	42,517	19,465
1971	214,940	174,125	970	175,096	12,772	-1,759	160,564	32,638	21,738	5,014	4,406	42,870	19,299
1972	232,423	188,781	966	189,747	14,535	-1,945	173,267	34,737	24,419	5,406	4,685	42,992	19,521
1973	250,880	204,629	1,387	206,016	18,195	-2,080	185,740	37,838	27,301	5,857	5,101	42,837	19,968
1974	272,391	219,279	1,292	220,571	20,160	-2,297	198,115	42,468	31,808	6,378	5,531	42,709	19,954
1975	295,144	231,542	1,198	232,739	20,837	-2,642	209,261	45,416	40,467	6,908	6,082	42,728	19,480
1976	317,192	249,880	1,278	251,158	22,890	-2,963	225,305	48,139	43,748	7,434	6,507	42,667	19,563
1977	344,781	272,705	1,097	273,802	24,858	-3,356	245,589	53,112	46,080	8,104	7,052	42,547	19,848
1978	378,807	302,037	1,311	303,349	28,208	-3,932	271,209	58,735	48,863	8,930	7,743	42,421	20,411
1979	416,648	332,623	1,523	334,145	32,254	-4,582	297,310	65,715	53,623	9,836	8,467	42,358	20,871
1980	462,431	361,363	1,140	362,503	35,164	-5,392	321,948	78,739	61,744	10,939	9,403	42,272	20,911
1981	513,576	393,314	1,499	394,813	40,993	-5,868	347,952	96,002	69,621	12,133	10,346	42,329	20,978
1982	554,162	415,508	1,458	416,966	43,999	-6,064	366,903	109,953	77,306	13,075	11,175	42,382	20,858
1983	593,173	445,475	1,092	446,567	47,849	-6,161	392,557	117,042	83,575	13,943	12,088	42,544	21,045
1984	652,854	490,515	1,904	492,419	54,383	-6,569	431,468	134,422	86,965	15,294	13,288	42,687	21,766
1985	699,220	528,951	2,016	530,967	59,564	-6,951	464,451	143,374	91,394	16,339	14,133	42,794	22,333
1986	744,899	568,142	2,200	570,342	64,798	-6,861	498,682	149,637	96,579	17,327	14,986	42,991	22,837
1987	796,335	616,910	2,286	619,196	69,479	-7,207	542,510	154,611	99,214	18,438	15,806	43,190	23,321
1988	871,732	679,679	2,187	681,866	77,653	-7,980	596,232	170,131	105,368	20,070	17,373	43,435	23,927
1989	941,654	720,618	2,579	723,197	81,572	-8,366	633,260	194,397	113,997	21,605	18,628	43,585	24,201
1990	998,789	762,452	2,519	764,971	84,116	-8,624	672,230	201,675	124,884	22,823	19,786	43,762	24,260
1991	1,017,712	767,862	2,052	769,914	86,917	-9,011	673,986	202,345	141,381	23,093	20,133	44,071	23,703
1992	1,078,194	817,733	2,646	820,379	91,293	-10,681	718,405	202,986	156,803	24,288	21,212	44,392	23,597
1993	1,112,960	844,236	2,516	846,753	94,558	-10,448	741,746	205,665	165,549	24,889	21,688	44,717	23,714
1994	1,151,638	872,963	2,305	875,268	99,384	-10,164	765,721	214,427	171,491	25,609	22,268	44,970	23,879
1995	1,212,299	910,351	1,759	912,110	102,991	-10,957	798,162	232,806	181,331	26,829	23,291	45,186	24,157
1996	1,276,069	954,638	2,698	957,336	106,056	-11,411	839,869	245,882	190,318	28,117	24,229	45,384	24,387
1997	1,347,899	1,014,712	1,845	1,016,556	110,906	-11,768	893,883	261,598	192,419	29,572	25,275	45,580	24,763
1998	1,425,420	1,077,646	2,318	1,079,963	116,434	-13,018	950,512	275,910	198,998	31,108	26,407	45,822	25,150
1999	1,496,797	1,147,382	2,312	1,149,694	122,349	-13,290	1,014,054	276,146	206,597	32,464	27,429	46,106	25,669
2000	1,613,740	1,236,143	2,773	1,238,916	130,696	-11,997	1,096,223	299,563	217,955	34,789	29,286	46,386	26,347
2001	1,673,043	1,287,738	2,840	1,290,577	136,829	-11,593	1,142,155	296,253	234,635	35,887	30,114	46,619	26,411
2002	1,700,398	1,310,577	1,955	1,312,531	140,462	-7,625	1,164,444	283,116	252,838	36,301	31,480	46,841	26,362
2003	1,752,991	1,348,577	2,903	1,351,479	144,486	-7,048	1,199,945	290,331	262,715	37,270	32,677	47,035	26,454
2004	1,851,167	1,427,416	3,646	1,431,063	152,287	-11,683	1,267,093	307,425	276,650	39,251	34,405	47,162	26,840
2005	1,936,416	1,488,073	3,484	1,491,557	159,739	-16,805	1,315,013	335,282	286,122	40,992	35,500	47,239	27,247
2006	2,073,430	1,579,731	2,918	1,582,649	168,306	-22,733	1,391,609	378,992	302,829	43,804	37,642	47,334	27,653
2007	2,198,474	1,657,221	3,460	1,660,682	177,057	-29,810	1,453,815	424,985	319,675	46,309	39,354	47,474	28,200
2008	2,278,982	1,701,395	3,552	1,704,946	183,307	-27,043	1,494,596	429,498	354,888	47,793	40,802	47,685	28,334
2009	2,230,728	1,662,380	2,575	1,664,955	179,831	-25,513	1,459,612	382,681	388,436	46,528	41,117	47,944	27,748
2010	2,303,447	1,720,259	3,408	1,723,666	185,593	-29,486	1,508,587	378,875	415,985	47,781	42,044	48,209	27,679
2011	2,425,871	1,782,689	4,409	1,787,097	171,871	-32,541	1,582,686	420,614	422,572	50,038	43,483	48,480	28,198
2012	2,521,990	1,836,387	4,714	1,841,102	176,166	-34,435	1,630,501	470,281	421,208	51,790	45,176	48,697	28,473
2013	2,534,020	1,875,921	6,100	1,882,021	205,064	-32,575	1,644,382	461,974	427,663	51,819	44,492	48,902	28,874
2014	2,635,988	1,960,148	6,508	1,966,656	213,926	-37,081	1,715,648	480,530	439,811	53,749	45,991	49,043	29,271
2015	2,738,136	2,035,570	5,721	2,041,291	220,406	-39,152	1,781,733	499,084	457,320	55,667	47,282	49,188	...

... = Not available.

Personal Income and Employment by Region and State: New England

(Millions of dollars, except as noted.)

Year	Personal income, total	Derivation of personal income									Per capita (dollars)		Population (thousands)	Total employment (thousands)
		Earnings by place of work			Less: Contributions for government social insurance	Plus: Adjustment for residence	Equals: Net earnings by place of residence	Plus: Dividends, interest, and rent	Plus: Personal current transfer receipts		Personal income	Disposable personal income		
		Nonfarm	Farm	Total										
1960	26,551	21,393	318	21,711	1,025	27	20,713	4,077	1,761		2,521	2,220	10,532	...
1961	27,878	22,323	269	22,592	1,073	28	21,547	4,354	1,977		2,614	2,313	10,666	...
1962	29,568	23,695	259	23,954	1,216	32	22,770	4,791	2,007		2,738	2,416	10,800	...
1963	30,869	24,633	251	24,885	1,358	37	23,564	5,179	2,126		2,810	2,475	10,986	...
1964	33,047	26,186	289	26,475	1,400	42	25,117	5,723	2,207		2,954	2,644	11,186	...
1965	35,439	27,935	340	28,276	1,451	44	26,869	6,240	2,330		3,128	2,792	11,329	...
1966	38,495	30,807	345	31,151	1,937	51	29,265	6,718	2,512		3,368	2,981	11,430	...
1967	41,828	33,230	239	33,469	2,135	59	31,393	7,353	3,082		3,618	3,191	11,562	...
1968	45,296	36,072	266	36,338	2,370	71	34,040	7,574	3,682		3,892	3,383	11,637	...
1969	50,092	39,286	294	39,580	2,639	851	37,792	8,190	4,111		4,269	3,664	11,735	5,516
1970	54,011	41,806	306	42,112	2,775	857	40,194	8,913	4,903		4,547	3,970	11,878	5,518
1971	57,526	43,991	283	44,274	3,015	896	42,156	9,495	5,876		4,795	4,245	11,996	5,454
1972	62,322	47,959	288	48,247	3,456	960	45,751	10,164	6,408		5,156	4,498	12,088	5,573
1973	67,890	52,638	398	53,036	4,364	1,005	49,678	11,016	7,197		5,589	4,902	12,148	5,783
1974	73,620	56,129	430	56,559	4,833	1,092	52,818	12,271	8,531		6,056	5,302	12,157	5,843
1975	79,341	58,617	313	58,930	4,922	1,192	55,201	13,004	11,136		6,516	5,793	12,176	5,685
1976	86,191	64,455	428	64,883	5,524	1,295	60,654	13,847	11,690		7,061	6,221	12,207	5,811
1977	94,397	71,233	385	71,617	6,136	1,445	66,926	15,340	12,131		7,701	6,770	12,257	6,007
1978	104,910	80,159	397	80,556	7,102	1,638	75,091	16,998	12,821		8,527	7,447	12,303	6,276
1979	117,291	90,000	380	90,380	8,296	1,870	83,955	19,057	14,279		9,501	8,231	12,345	6,503
1980	132,577	99,574	368	99,943	9,177	2,192	92,958	23,179	16,439		10,716	9,249	12,372	6,623
1981	148,166	108,825	471	109,296	10,790	2,357	100,863	28,499	18,804		11,914	10,218	12,436	6,666
1982	161,319	116,276	513	116,789	11,780	2,520	107,530	33,238	20,552		12,939	11,161	12,468	6,667
1983	174,311	127,237	480	127,716	13,047	2,671	117,341	35,027	21,944		13,896	12,115	12,544	6,799
1984	195,597	143,667	568	144,235	15,176	2,866	131,925	40,679	22,992		15,472	13,555	12,642	7,159
1985	211,379	157,378	558	157,936	16,770	3,126	144,292	42,901	24,186		16,591	14,440	12,741	7,400
1986	228,359	171,526	576	172,102	18,495	3,243	156,850	46,113	25,396		17,795	15,409	12,833	7,638
1987	248,434	189,273	638	189,910	20,166	3,433	173,177	49,145	26,112		19,182	16,494	12,951	7,771
1988	273,462	208,896	653	209,549	22,629	3,700	190,620	54,757	28,085		20,900	18,177	13,085	8,018
1989	292,878	219,381	609	219,990	23,628	3,753	200,115	61,401	31,362		22,218	19,289	13,182	8,005
1990	301,162	223,413	702	224,115	24,142	3,442	203,415	62,678	35,069		22,764	19,796	13,230	7,853
1991	305,443	224,034	645	224,679	24,627	3,438	203,490	61,395	40,558		23,056	20,149	13,248	7,526
1992	323,283	237,138	794	237,932	25,840	4,696	216,789	62,514	43,980		24,360	21,273	13,271	7,566
1993	335,382	246,886	731	247,617	27,034	4,125	224,708	65,119	45,555		25,152	21,903	13,334	7,689
1994	349,543	258,208	678	258,886	28,609	3,919	234,197	67,481	47,866		26,092	22,678	13,396	7,782
1995	369,066	270,807	602	271,409	30,150	4,686	245,946	72,201	50,920		27,394	23,685	13,473	7,875
1996	389,875	286,239	688	286,927	31,550	5,444	260,822	76,628	52,426		28,763	24,583	13,555	8,004
1997	414,735	306,871	593	307,465	33,589	5,075	278,950	81,404	54,380		30,401	25,708	13,642	8,165
1998	443,057	328,775	658	329,433	35,668	6,567	300,332	87,629	55,096		32,260	27,019	13,734	8,359
1999	468,441	354,175	703	354,877	37,881	6,526	323,522	88,031	56,888		33,853	28,224	13,838	8,512
2000	514,797	390,641	777	391,418	41,128	6,779	357,069	97,682	60,046		36,904	30,312	13,950	8,734
2001	536,670	406,873	713	407,585	42,479	6,074	371,180	100,278	65,212		38,222	31,790	14,041	8,761
2002	541,551	410,368	657	411,025	43,130	6,646	374,541	96,818	70,192		38,347	33,122	14,122	8,706
2003	557,767	420,376	704	421,080	44,066	7,754	384,768	99,609	73,390		39,328	34,362	14,182	8,691
2004	588,652	445,540	799	446,339	47,120	7,540	406,759	104,563	77,330		41,435	36,232	14,207	8,786
2005	613,545	459,818	764	460,582	49,083	8,320	419,818	111,665	82,061		43,157	37,285	14,217	8,880
2006	659,151	483,791	652	484,444	51,050	9,450	442,844	129,909	86,399		46,271	39,805	14,246	8,986
2007	693,510	503,814	812	504,626	53,405	10,033	461,254	140,729	91,526		48,568	41,249	14,279	9,157
2008	716,672	513,540	639	514,179	55,058	10,873	469,994	142,151	104,527		49,977	42,780	14,340	9,168
2009	699,795	501,801	473	502,274	54,136	10,266	458,404	126,960	114,431		48,585	43,054	14,404	8,942
2010	723,225	517,628	617	518,245	54,989	12,348	475,604	127,055	120,565		49,994	44,005	14,466	8,875
2011	762,140	537,511	646	538,157	51,085	12,910	499,982	140,600	121,557		52,463	45,511	14,527	8,990
2012	798,856	556,873	814	557,687	52,604	14,752	519,834	156,548	122,474		54,796	47,765	14,579	9,092
2013	799,062	568,529	992	569,521	61,213	13,550	521,858	153,047	124,156		54,582	46,734	14,640	9,244
2014	833,832	593,659	996	594,655	63,962	15,500	546,193	159,346	128,293		56,798	48,487	14,681	9,378
2015	867,005	617,203	936	618,139	65,960	16,209	568,389	165,724	132,892		58,863	49,879	14,729	...

... = Not available.

Personal Income and Employment by Region and State: Plains

(Millions of dollars, except as noted.)

Year	Personal income, total	Earnings by place of work			Less: Contributions for government social insurance	Plus: Adjustment for residence	Equals: Net earnings by place of residence	Plus: Dividends, interest, and rent	Plus: Personal current transfer receipts	Per capita (dollars)		Population (thousands)	Total employment (thousands)
		Nonfarm	Farm	Total						Personal income	Disposable personal income		
1960	33,312	24,148	3,122	27,270	1,157	8	26,120	4,974	2,218	2,160	1,940	15,424	...
1961	34,562	25,066	3,042	28,109	1,212	6	26,903	5,195	2,464	2,220	1,994	15,570	...
1962	36,881	26,582	3,542	30,124	1,317	7	28,813	5,509	2,560	2,356	2,114	15,657	...
1963	38,368	27,823	3,487	31,310	1,493	4	29,820	5,853	2,696	2,442	2,188	15,715	...
1964	40,011	29,733	2,795	32,528	1,555	5	30,978	6,244	2,788	2,534	2,301	15,787	...
1965	43,915	31,684	4,110	35,794	1,632	4	34,165	6,728	3,021	2,776	2,514	15,819	...
1966	47,248	34,776	4,310	39,086	2,197	-0	36,889	7,096	3,263	2,974	2,673	15,888	...
1967	49,574	37,244	3,678	40,921	2,551	-5	38,365	7,315	3,894	3,110	2,787	15,942	...
1968	54,071	40,765	3,670	44,435	2,839	-14	41,581	7,984	4,505	3,370	2,998	16,047	...
1969	59,312	44,778	4,220	48,998	3,160	-396	45,441	8,930	4,940	3,661	3,210	16,202	7,506
1970	64,275	47,752	4,443	52,196	3,338	-341	48,516	9,967	5,792	3,931	3,485	16,350	7,506
1971	69,189	51,132	4,611	55,742	3,693	-339	51,711	10,825	6,653	4,200	3,767	16,475	7,506
1972	76,424	55,776	6,161	61,937	4,221	-343	57,373	11,799	7,252	4,614	4,087	16,563	7,506
1973	89,096	61,767	11,294	73,061	5,396	-379	67,285	13,360	8,450	5,358	4,780	16,628	7,506
1974	94,314	67,962	7,686	75,648	6,185	-415	69,048	15,416	9,850	5,657	4,965	16,672	7,506
1975	103,657	73,662	7,499	81,161	6,595	-411	74,155	17,380	12,122	6,191	5,506	16,743	7,506
1976	110,975	82,780	4,408	87,187	7,513	-503	79,172	18,609	13,194	6,581	5,811	16,864	7,506
1977	122,639	91,540	5,192	96,732	8,271	-635	87,826	20,871	13,943	7,236	6,375	16,950	7,506
1978	138,812	102,900	7,837	110,737	9,610	-788	100,339	23,296	15,177	8,152	7,161	17,028	7,506
1979	153,094	115,381	6,613	121,994	11,215	-954	109,825	26,274	16,996	8,954	7,799	17,097	7,506
1980	165,391	124,302	1,879	126,182	12,037	-1,104	113,041	32,029	20,321	9,612	8,366	17,208	7,506
1981	187,050	134,045	5,447	139,492	13,885	-1,304	124,302	39,591	23,157	10,835	9,410	17,264	7,506
1982	199,323	138,875	4,004	142,879	14,670	-1,301	126,909	46,617	25,797	11,527	10,030	17,292	7,506
1983	208,978	147,652	1,577	149,229	15,668	-1,385	132,175	49,058	27,745	12,062	10,651	17,325	7,506
1984	232,624	162,527	6,545	169,072	17,707	-1,550	149,815	53,903	28,906	13,383	11,926	17,382	7,506
1985	245,605	171,939	7,464	179,403	19,108	-1,666	158,629	56,367	30,609	14,114	12,554	17,402	7,506
1986	257,212	181,084	8,061	189,145	20,469	-1,789	166,886	58,236	32,090	14,788	13,193	17,393	7,506
1987	270,884	193,186	9,777	202,963	21,690	-1,898	179,374	58,498	33,012	15,543	13,778	17,428	7,506
1988	284,015	207,069	7,383	214,451	24,079	-2,060	188,312	61,045	34,659	16,199	14,367	17,533	7,506
1989	306,274	220,768	9,207	229,975	25,698	-2,139	202,138	66,532	37,604	17,407	15,379	17,595	7,506
1990	324,426	233,581	10,544	244,124	27,917	-2,415	213,793	69,978	40,655	18,332	16,182	17,698	7,506
1991	335,765	243,245	8,117	251,361	29,420	-2,433	219,508	71,465	44,792	18,817	16,690	17,843	7,506
1992	360,319	261,289	10,635	271,925	31,222	-2,550	238,153	73,637	48,529	19,989	17,770	18,026	7,506
1993	372,338	274,010	6,237	280,247	32,831	-2,646	244,770	76,085	51,484	20,447	18,129	18,210	7,506
1994	397,332	290,857	10,482	301,340	35,227	-2,807	263,306	80,249	53,778	21,617	19,150	18,381	7,506
1995	416,503	307,428	5,742	313,170	37,055	-3,040	273,075	86,391	57,037	22,454	19,803	18,550	7,506
1996	448,190	325,192	13,572	338,763	38,591	-3,303	296,870	91,626	59,694	23,961	21,035	18,705	7,506
1997	471,141	346,141	9,882	356,023	41,154	-3,693	311,176	98,352	61,614	24,992	21,810	18,851	7,506
1998	502,740	372,404	9,203	381,607	43,755	-3,933	333,919	105,256	63,566	26,477	23,052	18,988	7,506
1999	523,849	395,200	7,943	403,143	46,125	-4,240	352,777	104,561	66,511	27,382	23,883	19,131	7,506
2000	561,645	421,461	9,613	431,073	48,642	-4,541	377,890	112,585	71,169	29,138	25,374	19,275	7,506
2001	582,578	437,626	9,072	446,698	50,180	-4,647	391,871	112,440	78,268	30,069	26,276	19,375	7,506
2002	594,582	451,078	6,244	457,322	51,460	-5,478	400,384	110,057	84,142	30,541	27,206	19,468	7,506
2003	621,279	467,046	12,630	479,676	53,402	-5,627	420,648	113,354	87,278	31,748	28,604	19,569	7,506
2004	655,466	492,636	16,790	509,427	56,029	-5,218	448,180	115,901	91,385	33,293	30,097	19,688	7,506
2005	679,088	511,804	15,861	527,665	58,723	-5,485	463,456	118,658	96,974	34,293	30,701	19,803	7,506
2006	719,895	538,885	10,790	549,675	62,091	-5,121	482,462	132,494	104,939	36,072	32,101	19,957	7,506
2007	765,707	561,239	15,368	576,606	64,925	-4,829	506,852	146,109	112,746	38,084	33,700	20,106	7,506
2008	814,322	585,410	21,413	606,823	67,534	-6,502	532,787	154,040	127,495	40,216	35,664	20,249	7,506
2009	787,592	568,402	15,361	583,763	66,204	-5,389	512,170	137,733	137,688	38,621	35,099	20,393	7,506
2010	810,935	580,956	18,120	599,076	67,343	-5,161	526,572	137,060	147,303	39,488	35,751	20,536	7,506
2011	871,048	606,740	30,638	637,378	62,841	-5,172	569,365	151,897	149,786	42,192	37,824	20,645	7,506
2012	915,588	636,090	28,737	664,826	65,071	-5,359	594,397	170,935	150,255	44,105	39,504	20,759	7,506
2013	927,867	650,631	35,866	686,497	75,731	-5,535	605,232	169,095	153,541	44,409	39,435	20,893	7,506
2014	959,235	680,238	28,930	709,168	78,891	-6,031	624,247	175,789	159,199	45,665	40,432	21,006	7,506
2015	982,540	706,934	14,262	721,196	81,326	-6,286	633,585	183,016	165,939	46,515	40,871	21,123	...

... = Not available.

Personal Income and Employment by Region and State: Rocky Mountain

(Millions of dollars, except as noted.)

Year	Personal income, total	Derivation of personal income									Per capita (dollars)		Population (thousands)	Total employment (thousands)
		Earnings by place of work			Less: Contributions for government social insurance	Plus: Adjustment for residence	Equals: Net earnings by place of residence	Plus: Dividends, interest, and rent	Plus: Personal current transfer receipts		Personal income	Disposable personal income		
		Nonfarm	Farm	Total										
1960	9,731	7,384	590	7,974	354	-2	7,617	1,490	624		2,237	2,001	4,350	...
1961	10,318	7,898	536	8,434	382	-3	8,050	1,578	690		2,294	2,052	4,497	...
1962	11,119	8,382	721	9,103	412	-3	8,689	1,709	721		2,428	2,179	4,580	...
1963	11,482	8,777	636	9,413	478	-2	8,933	1,792	758		2,479	2,220	4,632	...
1964	12,010	9,287	520	9,806	491	-2	9,314	1,920	777		2,570	2,341	4,673	...
1965	12,900	9,769	736	10,505	499	-2	10,005	2,055	840		2,743	2,495	4,703	...
1966	13,686	10,531	706	11,237	646	-1	10,590	2,194	902		2,890	2,614	4,735	...
1967	14,544	11,153	717	11,870	722	-1	11,147	2,328	1,069		3,041	2,740	4,783	...
1968	15,796	12,198	754	12,953	805	-1	12,147	2,434	1,215		3,245	2,900	4,868	...
1969	17,681	13,475	889	14,364	881	17	13,499	2,837	1,345		3,577	3,152	4,943	2,216
1970	19,781	14,841	1,003	15,843	962	16	14,898	3,282	1,601		3,927	3,500	5,038	2,271
1971	22,014	16,595	966	17,562	1,102	18	16,478	3,666	1,871		4,238	3,802	5,194	2,343
1972	24,946	18,847	1,269	20,116	1,320	22	18,818	4,039	2,090		4,647	4,138	5,368	2,482
1973	28,497	21,388	1,751	23,140	1,728	22	21,434	4,622	2,442		5,156	4,586	5,527	2,646
1974	32,099	24,051	1,836	25,887	2,002	24	23,909	5,352	2,838		5,681	5,027	5,650	2,740
1975	35,411	26,654	1,385	28,039	2,179	35	25,895	5,986	3,530		6,125	5,485	5,782	2,778
1976	39,141	30,193	1,026	31,218	2,512	40	28,747	6,505	3,889		6,617	5,883	5,916	2,912
1977	43,635	34,292	685	34,977	2,870	42	32,149	7,331	4,154		7,178	6,348	6,079	3,060
1978	50,520	39,874	956	40,830	3,411	52	37,472	8,506	4,542		8,074	7,128	6,257	3,257
1979	57,113	45,468	748	46,215	4,090	53	42,179	9,778	5,157		8,870	7,771	6,439	3,402
1980	64,818	50,529	964	51,493	4,596	78	46,975	11,787	6,056		9,832	8,622	6,592	3,474
1981	73,772	56,681	1,053	57,734	5,564	51	52,221	14,477	7,074		10,941	9,542	6,743	3,559
1982	79,644	60,231	824	61,055	6,033	52	55,074	16,522	8,048		11,536	10,087	6,904	3,596
1983	84,860	63,477	1,144	64,621	6,397	54	58,278	17,737	8,845		12,063	10,732	7,035	3,642
1984	91,954	69,118	1,042	70,160	7,175	74	63,059	19,664	9,231		12,935	11,555	7,109	3,801
1985	96,902	72,929	844	73,773	7,730	91	66,133	20,980	9,789		13,519	12,050	7,168	3,861
1986	100,406	75,029	1,242	76,271	8,019	112	68,363	21,535	10,508		13,946	12,482	7,200	3,854
1987	103,883	77,351	1,578	78,929	8,209	135	70,854	21,882	11,147		14,417	12,853	7,206	3,885
1988	109,757	82,356	1,625	83,981	9,123	173	75,032	22,971	11,755		15,238	13,599	7,203	4,021
1989	119,200	87,706	2,216	89,923	9,870	209	80,262	25,961	12,976		16,477	14,623	7,234	4,114
1990	127,353	94,297	2,514	96,811	10,976	245	86,081	27,240	14,032		17,433	15,407	7,305	4,230
1991	135,141	100,927	2,466	103,393	12,004	275	91,663	28,007	15,470		18,074	16,024	7,477	4,335
1992	146,514	110,349	2,543	112,892	12,992	307	100,207	29,087	17,221		19,037	16,872	7,696	4,434
1993	158,590	119,544	3,220	122,764	14,206	342	108,900	31,150	18,539		19,977	17,679	7,939	4,626
1994	169,886	128,850	2,094	130,944	15,410	394	115,928	34,466	19,492		20,790	18,343	8,171	4,886
1995	183,629	137,577	1,995	139,571	16,397	454	123,628	38,540	21,461		21,913	19,317	8,380	5,046
1996	197,211	147,542	2,190	149,731	17,263	526	132,994	41,753	22,464		23,024	20,164	8,565	5,249
1997	210,999	158,877	2,053	160,930	18,380	603	143,153	44,814	23,032		24,125	20,995	8,746	5,440
1998	231,223	175,139	2,398	177,537	19,325	701	158,913	48,560	23,750		25,927	22,508	8,918	5,624
1999	247,739	190,714	2,746	193,459	20,641	801	173,619	49,147	24,972		27,241	23,583	9,094	5,752
2000	272,209	210,821	2,387	213,209	22,509	860	191,559	53,851	26,798		29,368	25,314	9,269	5,953
2001	286,782	221,548	3,060	224,608	23,609	944	201,943	55,487	29,352		30,409	26,484	9,431	6,005
2002	291,728	224,773	2,317	227,090	24,373	1,803	204,520	54,968	32,241		30,492	27,184	9,567	6,000
2003	300,666	230,208	2,386	232,595	25,135	1,675	209,134	57,504	34,028		31,076	27,992	9,675	6,022
2004	318,427	243,643	3,374	247,018	26,920	1,796	221,894	60,622	35,910		32,468	29,286	9,808	6,167
2005	341,851	259,600	3,431	263,031	28,874	1,674	235,831	67,297	38,723		34,281	30,529	9,972	6,367
2006	372,442	282,402	2,292	284,694	31,442	1,232	254,484	76,181	41,776		36,550	32,265	10,190	6,588
2007	396,562	295,640	3,257	298,898	33,412	1,419	266,905	84,722	44,936		38,108	33,433	10,406	6,846
2008	416,466	306,608	3,327	309,935	34,508	904	276,331	87,838	52,297		39,254	34,730	10,610	6,896
2009	400,744	295,886	2,187	298,072	33,427	951	265,597	77,490	57,656		37,127	33,735	10,794	6,688
2010	411,961	301,516	3,252	304,768	33,981	1,017	271,803	75,915	64,243		37,627	34,066	10,948	6,618
2011	441,834	313,551	4,740	318,292	32,087	1,203	287,408	88,689	65,737		39,862	35,699	11,084	6,743
2012	468,668	330,807	4,415	335,222	33,567	1,445	303,101	99,397	66,171		41,754	37,327	11,225	6,859
2013	479,672	344,051	5,544	349,595	39,140	1,425	311,880	99,340	68,451		42,129	37,341	11,386	7,031
2014	505,347	363,675	5,756	369,431	41,407	1,534	329,558	103,829	71,959		43,787	38,709	11,541	7,207
2015	529,246	381,554	4,577	386,132	43,233	1,602	344,500	108,330	76,416		45,126	39637	11,728	...

... = Not available.

Personal Income and Employment by Region and State: Southeast

(Millions of dollars, except as noted.)

Year	Personal income, total	Earnings by place of work			Less: Contributions for government social insurance	Plus: Adjustment for residence	Equals: Net earnings by place of residence	Plus: Dividends, interest, and rent	Plus: Personal current transfer receipts	Per capita (dollars)		Population (thousands)	Total employment (thousands)
		Nonfarm	Farm	Total						Personal income	Disposable personal income		
1960	67,090	51,972	3,350	55,322	2,447	589	53,464	9,023	4,603	1,725	1,569	38,885	...
1961	70,752	53,865	3,773	57,638	2,513	616	55,741	9,716	5,295	1,789	1,631	39,544	...
1962	75,497	57,975	3,533	61,509	2,806	676	59,379	10,562	5,556	1,879	1,702	40,179	...
1963	80,550	62,008	3,765	65,773	3,287	737	63,223	11,425	5,901	1,977	1,790	40,742	...
1964	86,981	67,477	3,625	71,102	3,444	801	68,459	12,364	6,158	2,104	1,923	41,349	...
1965	94,563	73,632	3,505	77,137	3,677	899	74,358	13,482	6,723	2,259	2,058	41,857	...
1966	103,717	82,104	3,714	85,818	4,914	1,000	81,903	14,474	7,340	2,454	2,220	42,257	...
1967	112,424	88,862	3,700	92,561	5,668	1,160	88,054	15,625	8,746	2,638	2,385	42,611	...
1968	124,491	98,949	3,572	102,521	6,410	1,258	97,369	17,022	10,100	2,892	2,588	43,042	...
1969	138,941	109,696	4,060	113,755	7,214	1,171	107,712	19,839	11,390	3,198	2,826	43,440	19,085
1970	152,513	118,246	4,050	122,296	7,779	1,059	115,576	23,159	13,778	3,468	3,094	43,974	19,254
1971	168,281	129,715	4,262	133,977	8,837	1,049	126,188	25,814	16,279	3,738	3,360	45,013	19,635
1972	189,053	146,425	4,964	151,389	10,454	1,118	142,053	28,580	18,420	4,108	3,650	46,019	20,523
1973	214,605	165,226	7,279	172,506	13,506	1,197	160,197	32,579	21,829	4,567	4,077	46,992	21,636
1974	239,133	182,211	6,663	188,874	15,479	1,299	174,694	38,049	26,391	4,987	4,432	47,955	22,069
1975	262,142	194,263	5,996	200,259	16,286	1,571	185,543	42,346	34,253	5,373	4,861	48,788	21,642
1976	290,859	218,149	6,366	224,516	18,675	1,774	207,615	45,792	37,453	5,874	5,269	49,514	22,351
1977	322,756	244,540	5,766	250,306	20,914	1,991	231,383	51,497	39,876	6,415	5,736	50,312	23,208
1978	366,893	278,737	6,931	285,667	24,375	2,345	263,637	59,604	43,652	7,178	6,386	51,113	24,305
1979	411,993	312,310	6,844	319,154	28,418	2,706	293,441	68,216	50,337	7,927	7,006	51,977	24,987
1980	464,066	344,347	4,173	348,520	31,420	3,247	320,348	83,620	60,098	8,776	7,745	52,881	25,324
1981	524,661	379,834	6,634	386,467	37,261	3,563	352,769	103,161	68,731	9,783	8,604	53,627	25,594
1982	562,473	399,291	6,759	406,049	39,941	3,764	369,872	116,347	76,254	10,368	9,163	54,249	25,499
1983	607,217	431,874	4,899	436,773	43,698	3,795	396,871	127,298	83,049	11,069	9,862	54,856	26,030
1984	674,332	480,044	8,400	488,443	49,934	4,058	442,567	144,257	87,508	12,147	10,888	55,515	27,280
1985	726,846	518,656	7,444	526,100	54,899	4,239	475,439	157,986	93,421	12,933	11,527	56,199	28,090
1986	774,421	555,430	6,952	562,382	59,997	4,440	506,825	167,985	99,611	13,620	12,148	56,861	28,826
1987	826,632	599,428	8,292	607,721	64,249	4,635	548,107	174,807	103,718	14,367	12,755	57,536	29,529
1988	898,737	652,391	10,868	663,258	72,102	5,106	596,262	191,177	111,298	15,463	13,798	58,120	30,527
1989	978,126	694,652	11,406	706,058	77,510	5,485	634,033	220,361	123,732	16,654	14,799	58,733	31,251
1990	1,039,643	738,262	10,875	749,137	83,396	6,130	671,871	231,947	135,825	17,468	15,557	59,516	31,840
1991	1,087,709	768,773	12,420	781,193	87,898	6,616	699,911	234,201	153,597	17,978	16,098	60,501	31,724
1992	1,168,824	830,006	13,206	843,212	94,074	7,053	756,191	239,286	173,347	19,003	17,050	61,508	32,180
1993	1,235,395	878,850	12,804	891,654	100,058	7,335	798,932	250,776	185,688	19,757	17,699	62,531	33,186
1994	1,309,932	932,442	14,006	946,447	107,408	7,236	846,275	266,394	197,262	20,605	18,409	63,574	34,135
1995	1,394,805	986,975	12,430	999,405	113,546	7,498	893,357	288,756	212,692	21,591	19,245	64,602	35,254
1996	1,479,936	1,044,403	14,181	1,058,584	118,968	7,168	946,784	307,800	225,352	22,556	19,982	65,611	36,087
1997	1,570,492	1,111,999	13,860	1,125,859	126,228	7,984	1,007,615	328,973	233,903	23,561	20,753	66,655	37,050
1998	1,688,998	1,207,863	12,938	1,220,801	135,207	8,007	1,093,600	354,807	240,590	24,975	21,911	67,627	38,028
1999	1,774,740	1,288,611	13,090	1,301,701	143,370	9,818	1,168,149	355,478	251,113	25,882	22,684	68,569	38,834
2000	1,903,741	1,381,529	14,412	1,395,941	151,849	8,278	1,252,371	383,173	268,197	27,393	23,990	69,497	39,746
2001	1,994,224	1,442,468	16,278	1,458,745	158,517	8,601	1,308,829	389,819	295,576	28,360	24,907	70,318	39,702
2002	2,046,819	1,490,878	10,346	1,501,224	163,464	5,488	1,343,248	384,436	319,135	28,767	25,787	71,152	39,745
2003	2,131,158	1,554,013	13,256	1,567,269	170,428	5,096	1,401,938	393,896	335,324	29,615	26,819	71,962	40,142
2004	2,281,092	1,655,936	16,851	1,672,787	181,864	7,771	1,498,695	423,214	359,183	31,240	28,326	73,019	41,182
2005	2,439,239	1,754,456	17,724	1,772,180	193,150	10,502	1,589,531	460,592	389,116	32,897	29,522	74,148	42,256
2006	2,619,166	1,864,013	13,076	1,877,088	206,595	15,120	1,685,613	520,170	413,383	34,892	31,172	75,066	43,300
2007	2,761,147	1,926,972	12,073	1,939,045	215,101	19,060	1,743,004	576,130	442,013	36,272	32,314	76,123	44,255
2008	2,857,195	1,959,122	11,976	1,971,099	220,560	19,370	1,769,908	585,136	502,150	37,079	33,201	77,058	43,924
2009	2,777,752	1,899,184	11,865	1,911,049	216,194	18,464	1,713,319	517,555	546,878	35,697	32,720	77,815	42,460
2010	2,868,222	1,939,924	10,969	1,950,894	220,584	20,245	1,750,554	525,134	592,534	36,504	33,367	78,573	42,194
2011	3,027,428	2,001,450	10,677	2,012,127	204,081	22,868	1,830,914	586,410	610,105	38,190	34,579	79,274	43,015
2012	3,157,759	2,094,872	15,497	2,110,368	211,282	22,837	1,921,923	623,491	612,346	39,476	35,784	79,991	43,558
2013	3,182,995	2,134,153	23,755	2,157,908	244,381	22,769	1,936,296	617,109	629,590	39,466	35,451	80,651	44,279
2014	3,319,079	2,229,570	20,342	2,249,912	255,197	25,457	2,020,173	640,652	658,254	40,792	36,572	81,366	45,119
2015	3,472,776	2,331,346	20,613	2,351,958	265,167	26,856	2,113,648	665,148	693,980	42,252	37681	82,191	...

... = Not available.

Personal Income and Employment by Region and State: Southwest

(Millions of dollars, except as noted.)

Year	Personal income, total	Earnings by place of work			Less: Contributions for government social insurance	Plus: Adjustment for residence	Equals: Net earnings by place of residence	Plus: Dividends, interest, and rent	Plus: Personal current transfer receipts	Per capita (dollars)		Population (thousands)	Total employment (thousands)
		Nonfarm	Farm	Total						Personal income	Disposable personal income		
1960	28,796	22,307	1,474	23,781	1,006	5	22,780	4,371	1,645	2,023	1,824	14,235	...
1961	30,411	23,350	1,628	24,979	1,040	6	23,944	4,616	1,851	2,087	1,882	14,572	...
1962	31,948	24,813	1,411	26,223	1,132	9	25,100	4,853	1,995	2,140	1,924	14,930	...
1963	33,304	26,067	1,197	27,264	1,277	12	25,999	5,152	2,152	2,204	1,981	15,108	...
1964	35,662	28,088	1,132	29,220	1,330	14	27,903	5,512	2,247	2,334	2,129	15,278	...
1965	38,264	29,966	1,349	31,315	1,400	16	29,931	5,882	2,451	2,482	2,259	15,414	...
1966	41,618	33,141	1,409	34,551	1,882	17	32,686	6,257	2,674	2,673	2,414	15,567	...
1967	45,276	36,283	1,294	37,577	2,185	19	35,411	6,623	3,242	2,878	2,592	15,734	...
1968	50,362	40,460	1,423	41,883	2,456	24	39,451	7,099	3,812	3,148	2,807	15,998	...
1969	56,318	45,152	1,513	46,665	2,887	-73	43,705	8,361	4,252	3,449	3,041	16,328	7,219
1970	62,299	48,868	1,837	50,706	3,104	-87	47,514	9,747	5,038	3,748	3,342	16,621	7,311
1971	68,127	53,319	1,681	55,000	3,501	-91	51,408	10,834	5,885	3,989	3,599	17,077	7,457
1972	75,821	59,453	2,017	61,470	4,085	-108	57,277	11,950	6,594	4,332	3,865	17,503	7,807
1973	86,198	66,822	3,298	70,120	5,306	-121	64,693	13,666	7,839	4,804	4,303	17,943	8,215
1974	96,985	75,812	2,139	77,951	6,213	-83	71,655	15,973	9,357	5,284	4,688	18,354	8,511
1975	109,352	84,560	2,112	86,672	6,831	-49	79,792	17,729	11,831	5,820	5,238	18,789	8,633
1976	122,530	96,244	2,083	98,327	7,904	22	90,445	19,105	12,980	6,359	5,679	19,270	9,001
1977	136,751	109,110	1,864	110,974	9,030	-224	101,720	21,251	13,781	6,938	6,149	19,710	9,466
1978	157,846	126,991	1,689	128,681	10,776	-362	117,542	25,041	15,263	7,822	6,918	20,180	10,046
1979	182,352	146,242	2,982	149,224	13,007	-354	135,863	29,055	17,433	8,777	7,686	20,777	10,528
1980	209,354	167,020	1,542	168,562	14,995	-453	153,113	35,761	20,480	9,771	8,523	21,426	10,923
1981	244,571	192,449	2,837	195,286	18,608	-168	176,510	44,676	23,385	11,124	9,596	21,985	11,449
1982	268,060	207,495	2,353	209,848	20,499	-229	189,120	52,497	26,443	11,762	10,219	22,791	11,682
1983	284,818	217,084	2,409	219,493	21,389	-159	197,945	57,356	29,517	12,169	10,786	23,405	11,712
1984	312,575	237,871	2,677	240,548	24,038	-157	216,353	64,917	31,305	13,146	11,715	23,776	12,259
1985	336,277	254,712	2,582	257,294	26,109	-124	231,061	71,686	33,530	13,915	12,395	24,166	12,617
1986	346,922	261,136	2,586	263,721	26,713	-6	237,002	73,373	36,548	14,111	12,707	24,585	12,483
1987	356,239	267,583	3,519	271,103	27,114	86	244,075	73,561	38,602	14,395	12,897	24,748	12,785
1988	377,972	284,983	4,156	289,140	29,977	183	259,346	77,670	40,956	15,204	13,685	24,860	13,055
1989	404,425	301,522	4,117	305,639	32,059	266	273,847	85,325	45,253	16,123	14,432	25,083	13,241
1990	433,569	324,050	4,967	329,017	34,447	360	294,930	88,441	50,198	17,062	15,246	25,411	13,553
1991	453,709	341,351	4,535	345,886	37,064	318	309,140	88,824	55,744	17,506	15,722	25,917	13,759
1992	488,717	367,323	5,371	372,694	39,437	360	333,617	90,331	64,769	18,448	16,645	26,491	13,885
1993	517,871	390,823	6,179	397,002	41,953	413	355,462	93,117	69,292	19,098	17,213	27,116	14,332
1994	550,166	415,470	5,304	420,773	45,127	432	376,077	99,792	74,297	19,810	17,829	27,772	14,845
1995	588,912	442,874	4,279	447,153	47,841	412	399,724	108,709	80,480	20,722	18,622	28,420	15,396
1996	632,152	477,358	3,905	481,264	51,061	425	430,627	115,608	85,918	21,784	19,440	29,020	15,883
1997	684,748	521,938	5,000	526,938	55,115	422	472,245	122,964	89,539	23,114	20,496	29,625	16,482
1998	745,605	576,146	4,809	580,955	59,737	433	521,650	132,121	91,833	24,657	21,790	30,240	17,037
1999	786,939	614,693	6,643	621,336	63,263	544	558,616	132,917	95,406	25,527	22,565	30,827	17,360
2000	859,487	674,729	5,527	680,257	68,049	611	612,818	145,634	101,035	27,389	24,134	31,381	17,903
2001	915,504	722,176	6,338	728,514	71,645	486	657,355	146,576	111,573	28,706	25,436	31,892	18,112
2002	926,345	728,683	6,264	734,947	72,973	-1,226	660,748	143,044	122,553	28,564	25,876	32,431	18,137
2003	963,735	752,228	7,370	759,597	76,113	-1,591	681,894	150,232	131,609	29,272	26,758	32,924	18,296
2004	1,021,201	797,618	8,520	806,138	80,606	-2,012	723,520	157,815	139,866	30,506	27,946	33,475	18,726
2005	1,114,463	855,997	8,216	864,213	86,240	544	778,517	181,769	154,177	32,684	29,601	34,098	19,371
2006	1,220,947	940,738	5,205	945,943	92,854	268	853,357	201,366	166,224	34,939	31,441	34,945	20,101
2007	1,292,142	979,230	6,078	985,308	98,915	1,546	887,938	222,639	181,564	36,272	32,551	35,624	20,798
2008	1,401,879	1,045,071	3,957	1,049,029	103,200	956	946,785	247,693	207,401	38,652	34,615	36,269	21,144
2009	1,328,972	982,037	1,886	983,923	101,640	778	883,062	218,065	227,845	36,016	33,245	36,899	20,741
2010	1,388,977	1,020,369	5,486	1,025,855	104,718	735	921,872	216,748	250,358	37,057	34,080	37,482	20,692
2011	1,508,538	1,096,128	6,750	1,102,877	98,504	581	1,004,955	246,849	256,733	39,703	36,063	37,995	21,215
2012	1,609,195	1,169,661	7,063	1,176,724	103,811	550	1,073,463	279,030	256,702	41,741	37,974	38,552	21,731
2013	1,640,048	1,213,641	8,836	1,222,478	122,276	486	1,100,688	274,871	264,490	41,966	37,831	39,081	22,287
2014	1,732,761	1,287,823	10,088	1,297,911	129,086	666	1,169,491	285,167	278,103	43,699	39,286	39,652	22,808
2015	1,804,406	1,334,825	8,735	1,343,561	132,909	732	1,211,383	296,104	296,918	44,774	40048	40,301	...

... = Not available.

STATE

Personal Income and Employment by Region and State: Alabama

(Millions of dollars, except as noted.)

Year	Personal income, total	Earnings by place of work			Less: Contributions for government social insurance	Plus: Adjustment for residence	Equals: Net earnings by place of residence	Plus: Dividends, interest, and rent	Plus: Personal current transfer receipts	Per capita (dollars)		Population (thousands)	Total employment (thousands)
		Nonfarm	Farm	Total						Personal income	Disposable personal income		
1960	5,216	4,175	257	4,432	187	2	4,247	584	385	1,593	1,457	3,274	...
1961	5,388	4,284	247	4,532	194	3	4,340	618	429	1,625	1,492	3,316	...
1962	5,657	4,517	227	4,744	219	4	4,529	660	468	1,702	1,552	3,323	...
1963	6,009	4,785	275	5,060	260	7	4,807	706	496	1,790	1,633	3,358	...
1964	6,521	5,251	247	5,498	265	8	5,241	767	513	1,921	1,762	3,395	...
1965	7,079	5,712	257	5,969	273	11	5,707	821	551	2,056	1,881	3,443	...
1966	7,592	6,255	244	6,499	376	17	6,140	853	599	2,192	1,989	3,464	...
1967	8,015	6,623	209	6,831	429	23	6,425	900	690	2,318	2,103	3,458	...
1968	8,753	7,195	229	7,425	473	27	6,978	974	801	2,540	2,287	3,446	...
1969	9,726	7,845	280	8,125	550	130	7,704	1,131	892	2,827	2,511	3,440	1,411
1970	10,605	8,392	250	8,642	590	125	8,178	1,330	1,097	3,074	2,774	3,450	1,413
1971	11,671	9,140	279	9,419	655	132	8,896	1,490	1,285	3,337	3,024	3,497	1,423
1972	12,964	10,166	348	10,514	765	165	9,914	1,619	1,431	3,662	3,293	3,540	1,471
1973	14,583	11,345	535	11,880	983	183	11,080	1,822	1,681	4,073	3,661	3,581	1,526
1974	16,176	12,641	340	12,981	1,136	195	12,039	2,126	2,011	4,459	4,001	3,628	1,552
1975	18,038	13,654	414	14,069	1,222	201	13,048	2,390	2,600	4,901	4,443	3,681	1,543
1976	20,229	15,522	479	16,001	1,422	215	14,794	2,586	2,849	5,413	4,871	3,737	1,594
1977	22,282	17,359	383	17,742	1,596	247	16,392	2,884	3,005	5,890	5,294	3,783	1,651
1978	25,197	19,686	509	20,196	1,840	267	18,622	3,306	3,269	6,572	5,891	3,834	1,713
1979	27,992	21,717	521	22,239	2,103	296	20,431	3,752	3,809	7,234	6,450	3,869	1,736
1980	30,864	23,536	211	23,747	2,277	328	21,798	4,587	4,479	7,913	7,038	3,900	1,732
1981	34,264	25,350	490	25,840	2,644	421	23,617	5,621	5,025	8,744	7,759	3,919	1,719
1982	36,198	26,232	411	26,643	2,783	444	24,305	6,340	5,553	9,222	8,265	3,925	1,687
1983	38,772	28,304	293	28,597	3,053	436	25,980	6,780	6,012	9,855	8,834	3,934	1,717
1984	42,649	31,168	482	31,650	3,427	465	28,688	7,609	6,352	10,792	9,716	3,952	1,780
1985	45,942	33,730	467	34,197	3,739	474	30,932	8,303	6,708	11,565	10,348	3,973	1,822
1986	48,627	35,896	458	36,354	3,972	503	32,885	8,762	6,980	12,183	10,903	3,992	1,858
1987	51,486	38,306	541	38,847	4,194	514	35,166	9,187	7,133	12,823	11,412	4,015	1,912
1988	55,388	41,196	802	41,998	4,668	517	37,847	10,090	7,451	13,765	12,348	4,024	1,970
1989	60,313	43,719	941	44,660	4,970	539	40,229	11,661	8,422	14,965	13,356	4,030	2,006
1990	64,070	46,621	849	47,470	5,366	533	42,637	12,158	9,275	15,820	14,133	4,050	2,048
1991	67,662	49,018	1,124	50,142	5,681	563	45,024	12,382	10,257	16,506	14,802	4,099	2,060
1992	72,847	52,863	1,003	53,866	6,062	614	48,418	12,777	11,652	17,537	15,775	4,154	2,097
1993	76,199	55,311	1,018	56,329	6,419	666	50,575	13,258	12,366	18,082	16,247	4,214	2,159
1994	80,681	58,273	1,069	59,342	6,849	759	53,251	14,309	13,120	18,938	16,956	4,260	2,180
1995	85,362	61,017	788	61,806	7,217	840	55,429	15,740	14,194	19,866	17,746	4,297	2,242
1996	89,084	63,613	917	64,530	7,464	846	57,913	16,171	15,000	20,569	18,303	4,331	2,275
1997	93,822	66,660	954	67,614	7,830	950	60,734	17,411	15,678	21,480	19,050	4,368	2,321
1998	100,253	71,620	1,076	72,696	8,228	1,066	65,534	18,732	15,987	22,760	20,212	4,405	2,362
1999	104,177	75,239	1,245	76,484	8,593	1,133	69,025	18,500	16,653	23,516	20,867	4,430	2,380
2000	109,741	78,656	960	79,616	8,886	1,259	71,989	20,002	17,750	24,649	21,916	4,452	2,395
2001	114,234	81,305	1,391	82,696	9,189	1,280	74,787	20,240	19,207	25,569	22,766	4,468	2,379
2002	116,899	83,994	987	84,980	9,480	946	76,446	19,908	20,545	26,093	23,608	4,480	2,370
2003	121,798	86,961	1,315	88,276	9,829	931	79,378	20,606	21,814	27,045	24,670	4,503	2,378
2004	130,495	92,242	1,802	94,044	10,326	1,102	84,820	22,567	23,109	28,802	26,376	4,531	2,437
2005	138,019	97,432	1,693	99,125	10,985	1,479	89,619	23,555	24,845	30,202	27,385	4,570	2,499
2006	146,661	103,514	995	104,510	11,673	1,745	94,582	25,297	26,782	31,683	28,506	4,629	2,556
2007	153,788	106,712	806	107,518	12,222	2,101	97,397	27,584	28,807	32,911	29,543	4,673	2,616
2008	159,994	108,664	882	109,546	12,608	1,950	98,888	28,908	32,197	33,910	30,530	4,718	2,595
2009	157,141	106,064	1,032	107,097	12,338	1,784	96,543	25,924	34,674	33,027	30,411	4,758	2,495
2010	163,067	108,278	851	109,129	12,751	1,844	98,221	26,906	37,940	34,073	31,310	4,786	2,469
2011	169,030	111,849	468	112,317	11,710	1,976	102,583	27,741	38,707	35,202	32,068	4,802	2,501
2012	173,601	114,274	873	115,147	11,942	2,208	105,413	29,306	38,882	36,036	32,950	4,817	2,513
2013	174,877	115,146	2,254	117,400	13,715	2,294	105,979	29,155	39,743	36,176	32,846	4,834	2,532
2014	181,909	120,322	1,837	122,159	14,147	2,365	110,376	30,267	41,265	37,512	34,026	4,849	2,560
2015	189,357	124,678	2,129	126,807	14,505	2,487	114,789	31,421	43,147	38,965	35213	4860	...

... = Not available.

Personal Income and Employment by Region and State: Alaska

(Millions of dollars, except as noted.)

Year	Personal income, total	Earnings by place of work			Less: Contributions for government social insurance	Plus: Adjustment for residence	Equals: Net earnings by place of residence	Plus: Dividends, interest, and rent	Plus: Personal current transfer receipts	Per capita (dollars)		Population (thousands)	Total employment (thousands)
		Nonfarm	Farm	Total						Personal income	Disposable personal income		
1960	807	721	2	723	28	-2	694	91	22	3,525	3,166	229	...
1961	797	708	2	709	28	-3	678	91	27	3,347	3,026	238	...
1962	830	740	1	741	29	-5	707	96	26	3,372	3,024	246	...
1963	898	804	1	805	33	-9	764	107	27	3,508	3,135	256	...
1964	1,006	904	1	905	37	-13	854	122	29	3,823	3,486	263	...
1965	1,085	981	1	982	41	-18	923	131	31	4,003	3,598	271	...
1966	1,154	1,051	1	1,052	48	-23	981	139	34	4,258	3,836	271	...
1967	1,257	1,152	1	1,153	54	-31	1,069	150	39	4,523	4,068	278	...
1968	1,357	1,258	2	1,260	67	-39	1,153	156	48	4,762	4,265	285	...
1969	1,565	1,436	1	1,438	94	-26	1,318	194	53	5,288	4,590	296	144
1970	1,787	1,624	2	1,626	105	-46	1,474	241	72	5,873	5,183	304	149
1971	1,969	1,789	2	1,790	118	-60	1,612	267	91	6,222	5,522	316	153
1972	2,148	1,959	2	1,961	134	-75	1,752	293	104	6,580	5,765	326	158
1973	2,483	2,163	2	2,165	165	-93	1,906	330	246	7,452	6,607	333	167
1974	3,012	2,868	2	2,870	241	-209	2,419	384	208	8,738	7,554	345	189
1975	4,117	4,433	4	4,437	408	-611	3,419	462	237	11,099	9,470	371	227
1976	4,843	5,496	4	5,499	526	-881	4,093	517	234	12,320	10,473	393	243
1977	5,026	5,086	5	5,090	463	-453	4,174	573	278	12,649	10,797	397	237
1978	5,176	4,971	5	4,976	435	-325	4,216	660	299	12,869	11,185	402	238
1979	5,470	5,191	4	5,195	468	-290	4,437	740	293	13,555	11,627	404	241
1980	6,205	5,866	3	5,870	511	-329	5,029	832	344	15,309	13,388	405	244
1981	7,057	6,781	2	6,783	653	-458	5,673	977	407	16,863	14,419	418	252
1982	8,610	7,845	3	7,848	766	-548	6,533	1,213	864	19,150	16,661	450	277
1983	9,368	8,776	2	8,778	852	-607	7,320	1,415	633	19,181	16,874	488	297
1984	9,961	9,289	2	9,291	952	-621	7,718	1,561	683	19,391	17,263	514	309
1985	10,772	9,772	2	9,774	976	-617	8,181	1,704	887	20,230	18,092	532	316
1986	10,869	9,602	7	9,609	925	-562	8,122	1,749	998	19,969	18,100	544	310
1987	10,431	9,036	9	9,046	871	-526	7,648	1,743	1,039	19,340	17,355	539	310
1988	10,875	9,450	11	9,461	949	-553	7,959	1,798	1,118	20,066	18,128	542	317
1989	11,939	10,324	6	10,330	1,048	-619	8,663	2,037	1,239	21,820	19,418	547	329
1990	12,650	10,938	8	10,947	1,169	-652	9,126	2,154	1,371	22,863	20,200	553	339
1991	13,200	11,460	9	11,469	1,239	-698	9,533	2,194	1,473	23,149	20,648	570	347
1992	14,093	12,126	9	12,135	1,307	-732	10,096	2,362	1,635	23,938	21,465	589	351
1993	14,838	12,576	11	12,587	1,387	-752	10,448	2,569	1,821	24,753	22,232	599	358
1994	15,326	12,897	12	12,910	1,442	-772	10,696	2,765	1,865	25,404	22,749	603	363
1995	15,739	13,090	13	13,104	1,455	-778	10,871	2,912	1,956	26,041	23,347	604	365
1996	16,167	13,301	14	13,315	1,459	-805	11,051	3,010	2,105	26,565	23,749	609	369
1997	17,048	13,897	16	13,913	1,505	-808	11,600	3,175	2,273	27,812	24,803	613	374
1998	17,824	14,490	17	14,507	1,548	-862	12,097	3,256	2,471	28,751	25,576	620	383
1999	18,395	14,854	19	14,873	1,570	-860	12,443	3,236	2,715	29,442	26,260	625	382
2000	19,769	15,801	21	15,822	1,644	-918	13,259	3,432	3,077	31,481	28,042	628	390
2001	20,830	16,891	20	16,911	1,738	-982	14,191	3,420	3,219	32,870	29,211	634	395
2002	21,825	17,839	19	17,859	1,827	-890	15,142	3,377	3,307	33,978	30,802	642	403
2003	22,868	18,761	12	18,773	1,891	-723	16,160	3,463	3,246	35,268	32,304	648	406
2004	24,114	19,773	15	19,788	2,015	-552	17,222	3,685	3,208	36,577	33,717	659	415
2005	25,692	20,908	14	20,922	2,155	-384	18,383	3,918	3,391	38,521	35,299	667	423
2006	27,380	22,100	10	22,110	2,362	-342	19,406	4,382	3,593	40,545	36,966	675	432
2007	29,517	23,157	9	23,167	2,461	-281	20,424	5,018	4,075	43,388	39,288	680	440
2008	32,497	24,277	3	24,280	2,543	-175	21,562	5,484	5,451	47,271	42,670	687	444
2009	32,284	25,137	8	25,145	2,587	-181	22,377	5,168	4,739	46,192	42,662	699	444
2010	34,103	26,104	10	26,115	2,680	-183	23,252	5,561	5,290	47,773	44,022	714	444
2011	36,527	27,584	9	27,593	2,540	-201	24,852	6,140	5,536	50,552	46,277	723	451
2012	38,213	29,069	17	29,086	2,691	-216	26,180	6,626	5,407	52,269	48,086	731	459
2013	37,791	29,252	16	29,268	3,122	-216	25,929	6,448	5,414	51,259	46,674	737	462
2014	39,793	30,050	9	30,059	3,134	-230	26,695	6,644	6,454	54,012	49,170	737	465
2015	41,312	30,894	20	30,914	3,168	-236	27,510	6,899	6,904	55,940	50,742	739	...

... = Not available.

Personal Income and Employment by Region and State: Arizona

(Millions of dollars, except as noted.)

Year	Personal income, total	Earnings by place of work			Less: Contributions for government social insurance	Plus: Adjustment for residence	Equals: Net earnings by place of residence	Plus: Dividends, interest, and rent	Plus: Personal current transfer receipts	Per capita (dollars)		Population (thousands)	Total employment (thousands)
		Nonfarm	Farm	Total						Personal income	Disposable personal income		
1960	2,833	2,208	128	2,337	118	-2	2,217	451	166	2,145	1,923	1,321	...
1961	3,086	2,374	135	2,509	125	-2	2,382	510	194	2,194	1,978	1,407	...
1962	3,322	2,572	138	2,710	139	-2	2,569	541	212	2,258	2,027	1,471	...
1963	3,493	2,730	113	2,842	162	-0	2,680	582	231	2,297	2,063	1,521	...
1964	3,747	2,904	130	3,035	167	-0	2,867	630	250	2,408	2,200	1,556	...
1965	3,978	3,067	128	3,195	174	1	3,022	674	282	2,511	2,294	1,584	...
1966	4,337	3,434	121	3,555	232	0	3,323	709	305	2,687	2,441	1,614	...
1967	4,720	3,689	149	3,838	266	0	3,572	770	377	2,867	2,592	1,646	...
1968	5,414	4,171	192	4,363	313	2	4,053	925	435	3,219	2,888	1,682	...
1969	6,310	4,787	203	4,990	322	-26	4,642	1,176	492	3,633	3,208	1,737	711
1970	7,180	5,392	180	5,572	362	-30	5,181	1,407	592	4,000	3,550	1,795	747
1971	8,206	6,155	201	6,356	430	-29	5,897	1,599	710	4,328	3,886	1,896	786
1972	9,404	7,144	205	7,349	525	-32	6,793	1,796	816	4,681	4,162	2,009	850
1973	10,860	8,292	240	8,531	695	-31	7,806	2,071	983	5,110	4,590	2,125	925
1974	12,242	9,096	384	9,480	791	-41	8,648	2,406	1,188	5,504	4,914	2,224	955
1975	13,162	9,486	217	9,704	816	-47	8,840	2,661	1,660	5,757	5,256	2,286	935
1976	14,662	10,583	330	10,912	916	-47	9,949	2,885	1,828	6,244	5,658	2,348	976
1977	16,480	12,139	267	12,406	1,061	-57	11,288	3,265	1,928	6,789	6,107	2,427	1,048
1978	19,438	14,402	318	14,720	1,292	-70	13,359	3,907	2,172	7,720	6,887	2,518	1,150
1979	22,886	17,084	399	17,483	1,606	-72	15,806	4,608	2,472	8,674	7,684	2,639	1,240
1980	26,363	19,140	477	19,617	1,822	-81	17,715	5,673	2,976	9,629	8,560	2,738	1,283
1981	30,119	21,383	414	21,797	2,191	-16	19,590	7,033	3,496	10,718	9,443	2,810	1,313
1982	31,885	22,200	396	22,596	2,315	-9	20,272	7,711	3,902	11,033	9,764	2,890	1,315
1983	35,030	24,381	328	24,708	2,580	2	22,130	8,628	4,271	11,799	10,536	2,969	1,379
1984	39,699	27,760	526	28,287	3,018	6	25,274	9,847	4,578	12,943	11,580	3,067	1,504
1985	44,054	31,039	492	31,531	3,435	19	28,115	10,971	4,968	13,838	12,316	3,184	1,622
1986	48,295	34,192	472	34,664	3,805	39	30,898	11,946	5,450	14,598	13,019	3,308	1,701
1987	52,226	36,918	634	37,552	4,075	65	33,543	12,730	5,954	15,195	13,530	3,437	1,765
1988	56,265	40,019	760	40,779	4,563	108	36,323	13,406	6,536	15,916	14,254	3,535	1,833
1989	60,487	41,571	690	42,262	4,873	166	37,554	15,353	7,580	16,699	14,886	3,622	1,865
1990	63,383	43,761	642	44,403	5,269	226	39,361	15,619	8,403	17,204	15,321	3,684	1,894
1991	66,575	46,466	739	47,204	5,627	222	41,800	15,392	9,383	17,573	15,682	3,789	1,903
1992	70,988	50,065	673	50,738	6,016	250	44,971	15,333	10,684	18,129	16,249	3,916	1,925
1993	76,431	53,965	789	54,754	6,488	266	48,532	16,374	11,525	18,800	16,824	4,065	2,011
1994	83,860	59,529	577	60,106	7,169	278	53,214	18,340	12,306	19,755	17,637	4,245	2,141
1995	91,283	64,610	824	65,434	7,483	295	58,246	19,920	13,117	20,594	18,366	4,432	2,258
1996	98,949	70,862	737	71,599	8,373	326	63,551	21,428	13,969	21,572	19,036	4,587	2,388
1997	107,437	77,149	740	77,889	8,976	361	69,274	23,586	14,577	22,680	19,956	4,737	2,497
1998	117,999	85,958	872	86,830	9,785	410	77,454	25,414	15,130	24,164	21,180	4,883	2,619
1999	125,530	92,820	848	93,668	10,486	470	83,652	25,762	16,116	24,987	21,882	5,024	2,701
2000	137,031	102,273	807	103,080	11,417	529	92,192	27,811	17,028	26,553	23,213	5,161	2,809
2001	143,546	107,259	747	108,006	11,946	581	96,642	27,590	19,315	27,220	23,943	5,273	2,841
2002	148,882	110,631	764	111,395	12,350	588	99,632	27,755	21,495	27,590	24,830	5,396	2,861
2003	156,750	115,380	727	116,107	12,831	586	103,862	29,410	23,478	28,446	25,795	5,510	2,934
2004	170,829	125,156	1,024	126,180	13,898	623	112,906	32,222	25,701	30,222	27,364	5,652	3,064
2005	189,358	137,304	995	138,299	15,254	710	123,755	36,865	28,737	32,429	29,006	5,839	3,239
2006	210,103	152,785	709	153,495	16,729	814	137,580	41,098	31,425	34,848	31,062	6,029	3,401
2007	221,597	159,091	837	159,928	17,696	1,059	143,292	44,187	34,118	35,929	32,043	6,168	3,494
2008	226,574	159,145	660	159,806	17,901	1,294	143,198	43,619	39,756	36,077	32,528	6,280	3,434
2009	216,065	149,328	416	149,744	17,067	1,231	133,907	37,736	44,422	34,063	31,488	6,343	3,264
2010	219,196	149,174	538	149,712	17,129	1,251	133,834	37,046	48,316	34,185	31,470	6,412	3,208
2011	230,920	155,714	987	156,701	15,873	1,244	142,071	40,526	48,323	35,675	32,421	6,473	3,268
2012	241,192	162,855	838	163,693	16,423	1,334	148,605	44,516	48,071	36,788	33,495	6,556	3,323
2013	243,657	166,562	1,265	167,827	19,166	1,282	149,944	44,511	49,202	36,723	33,132	6,635	3,399
2014	255,093	174,211	1,156	175,367	20,056	1,365	156,676	46,310	52,107	37,895	34,142	6,731	3,462
2015	266,756	181,212	1,305	182,517	20,749	1,454	163,222	48,083	55,451	39,060	35033	6829	...

... = Not available.

Personal Income and Employment by Region and State: Arkansas

(Millions of dollars, except as noted.)

Year	Personal income, total	Earnings by place of work			Less: Contributions for government social insurance	Plus: Adjustment for residence	Equals: Net earnings by place of residence	Plus: Dividends, interest, and rent	Plus: Personal current transfer receipts	Per capita (dollars)		Population (thousands)	Total employment (thousands)
		Nonfarm	Farm	Total						Personal income	Disposable personal income		
1960	2,558	1,808	313	2,121	92	-1	2,027	291	240	1,430	1,320	1,789	...
1961	2,782	1,922	368	2,290	95	-2	2,193	320	269	1,540	1,424	1,806	...
1962	2,973	2,115	324	2,439	109	-3	2,327	358	288	1,604	1,468	1,853	...
1963	3,149	2,258	322	2,580	127	-4	2,450	389	310	1,680	1,537	1,875	...
1964	3,418	2,446	360	2,806	137	-4	2,665	427	326	1,802	1,671	1,897	...
1965	3,606	2,626	288	2,914	147	-6	2,761	488	357	1,904	1,757	1,894	...
1966	4,007	2,881	393	3,275	191	-4	3,079	536	391	2,110	1,926	1,899	...
1967	4,249	3,130	301	3,431	221	-5	3,205	576	468	2,235	2,040	1,901	...
1968	4,595	3,445	337	3,782	252	-7	3,524	546	525	2,416	2,181	1,902	...
1969	5,130	3,784	346	4,130	278	32	3,883	662	584	2,681	2,399	1,913	800
1970	5,636	4,037	415	4,452	296	23	4,179	773	684	2,920	2,628	1,930	805
1971	6,273	4,516	407	4,923	340	22	4,605	866	802	3,181	2,898	1,972	831
1972	7,082	5,137	482	5,619	405	22	5,236	953	893	3,509	3,183	2,018	867
1973	8,381	5,787	914	6,701	524	18	6,194	1,104	1,083	4,072	3,679	2,058	902
1974	9,362	6,483	833	7,316	609	11	6,719	1,327	1,315	4,457	3,997	2,100	927
1975	10,317	6,955	795	7,749	638	9	7,120	1,528	1,669	4,780	4,366	2,158	905
1976	11,389	8,007	641	8,648	745	-1	7,902	1,657	1,829	5,251	4,731	2,169	941
1977	12,667	8,985	725	9,710	847	-7	8,856	1,869	1,942	5,739	5,185	2,207	981
1978	14,683	10,222	1,176	11,398	987	-11	10,399	2,152	2,132	6,552	5,918	2,241	1,021
1979	16,090	11,341	995	12,336	1,134	-13	11,188	2,457	2,444	7,091	6,356	2,269	1,031
1980	17,371	12,297	372	12,668	1,220	-4	11,445	3,027	2,900	7,590	6,765	2,289	1,032
1981	19,657	13,207	851	14,058	1,422	-23	12,613	3,764	3,280	8,572	7,649	2,293	· 1,026
1982	20,676	13,653	642	14,295	1,498	-20	12,777	4,333	3,567	9,012	7,995	2,294	1,011
1983	21,988	14,827	417	15,244	1,638	-50	13,555	4,574	3,859	9,536	8,561	2,306	1,039
1984	24,475	16,432	883	17,315	1,869	-69	15,377	5,054	4,044	10,551	9,541	2,320	1,079
1985	26,083	17,444	865	18,309	2,005	-75	16,228	5,573	4,282	11,208	10,108	2,327	1,098
1986	27,400	18,543	805	19,348	2,141	-101	17,106	5,781	4,512	11,750	10,629	2,332	1,110
1987	28,476	19,605	935	20,540	2,251	-124	18,165	5,668	4,644	12,157	10,951	2,342	1,137
1988	30,546	20,934	1,344	22,278	2,507	-157	19,614	6,048	4,885	13,039	11,771	2,343	1,170
1989	32,777	22,262	1,238	23,500	2,675	-161	20,664	6,714	5,399	13,969	12,574	2,346	1,189
1990	34,487	23,777	1,048	24,825	2,965	-220	21,639	7,001	5,847	14,635	13,150	2,357	1,204
1991	36,434	25,263	1,128	26,390	3,149	-248	22,994	6,958	6,483	15,288	13,777	2,383	1,230
1992	39,745	27,598	1,430	29,028	3,409	-271	25,347	7,208	7,189	16,451	14,850	2,416	1,255
1993	41,723	29,154	1,336	30,490	3,619	-308	26,564	7,572	7,587	16,986	15,331	2,456	1,301
1994	44,298	31,113	1,466	32,579	3,908	-334	28,336	7,998	7,963	17,762	15,961	2,494	1,329
1995	47,105	32,876	1,481	34,357	4,110	-304	29,943	8,571	8,590	18,579	16,650	2,535	1,382
1996	50,013	34,318	1,922	36,240	4,251	-301	31,688	9,223	9,102	19,444	17,411	2,572	1,405
1997	52,409	36,138	1,811	37,949	4,460	-305	33,184	9,723	9,502	20,149	17,954	2,601	1,427
1998	55,652	38,892	1,596	40,488	4,734	-306	35,448	10,386	9,818	21,190	18,823	2,626	1,444
1999	57,958	41,017	1,807	42,823	4,962	-322	37,539	10,297	10,121	21,856	19,447	2,652	1,461
2000	61,080	43,254	1,704	44,958	5,196	-360	39,403	10,936	10,741	22,803	20,240	2,679	1,483
2001	64,257	44,927	2,010	46,938	5,350	-349	41,239	11,107	11,911	23,873	21,234	2,692	1,484
2002	65,585	46,515	1,274	47,789	5,514	-446	41,829	10,936	12,820	24,237	21,899	2,706	1,480
2003	69,380	48,641	2,414	51,055	5,715	-508	44,831	11,158	13,391	25,462	23,252	2,725	1,483
2004	73,844	51,674	2,768	54,442	6,001	-544	47,897	11,596	14,351	26,855	24,569	2,750	1,505
2005	77,635	54,333	1,878	56,211	6,353	-567	49,290	12,931	15,413	27,915	25,336	2,781	1,536
2006	83,182	57,493	1,500	58,993	6,819	-439	51,735	14,615	16,832	29,479	26,697	2,822	1,569
2007	88,820	59,476	1,873	61,350	7,099	-372	53,878	16,741	18,200	31,180	28,057	2,849	1,586
2008	93,233	60,557	1,699	62,256	7,393	-106	54,757	18,177	20,299	32,434	29,189	2,875	1,583
2009	91,625	59,635	1,154	60,789	7,393	-115	53,281	16,334	22,010	31,629	29,013	2,897	1,549
2010	93,486	60,938	778	61,716	7,555	-143	54,018	15,856	23,612	31,991	29,328	2,922	1,544
2011	99,792	63,069	883	63,953	7,067	-131	56,754	18,940	24,097	33,961	30,876	2,938	1,564
2012	107,033	65,820	1,468	67,288	7,208	-183	59,896	22,806	24,330	36,291	33,074	2,949	1,567
2013	108,081	66,669	2,906	69,574	8,223	-209	61,143	22,192	24,746	36,529	33,042	2,959	1,571
2014	112,076	69,095	2,802	71,897	8,577	-264	63,056	22,819	26,201	37,782	34,136	2,966	1,588
2015	116,485	71,592	2,629	74,221	8,836	-267	65,118	23,824	27,544	39,107	35187	2979	...

... = Not available.

Personal Income and Employment by Region and State: California

(Millions of dollars, except as noted.)

Year	Personal income, total	Earnings by place of work			Less: Contributions for government social insurance	Plus: Adjustment for residence	Equals: Net earnings by place of residence	Plus: Dividends, interest, and rent	Plus: Personal current transfer receipts	Per capita (dollars)		Population (thousands)	Total employment (thousands)
		Nonfarm	Farm	Total						Personal income	Disposable personal income		
1960	46,333	36,582	1,437	38,019	1,720	-5	36,294	7,455	2,584	2,920	2,590	15,870	...
1961	49,147	38,749	1,369	40,118	1,832	-5	38,281	7,867	2,999	2,979	2,647	16,497	...
1962	52,939	42,069	1,433	43,502	2,249	-6	41,247	8,512	3,179	3,101	2,751	17,072	...
1963	56,605	45,194	1,367	46,562	2,625	-6	43,931	9,157	3,517	3,204	2,843	17,668	...
1964	61,292	48,640	1,517	50,157	2,731	-7	47,420	10,060	3,812	3,377	3,047	18,151	...
1965	65,446	51,704	1,464	53,168	2,846	-8	50,314	10,919	4,213	3,521	3,178	18,585	...
1966	71,123	56,955	1,583	58,538	3,740	-11	54,787	11,683	4,653	3,772	3,384	18,858	...
1967	76,482	60,941	1,496	62,436	4,100	-12	58,324	12,403	5,755	3,988	3,565	19,176	...
1968	83,787	67,002	1,720	68,722	4,587	-14	64,121	13,022	6,643	4,320	3,818	19,394	...
1969	92,174	72,892	1,705	74,597	4,827	-142	69,628	14,930	7,616	4,676	4,105	19,711	9,033
1970	99,441	76,944	1,709	78,653	5,018	-108	73,527	16,613	9,301	4,966	4,431	20,023	9,057
1971	106,005	81,216	1,707	82,924	5,449	-119	77,356	17,954	10,696	5,210	4,702	20,346	9,036
1972	116,356	89,613	2,173	91,786	6,333	-121	85,331	19,503	11,522	5,653	5,013	20,585	9,368
1973	127,637	98,343	2,931	101,274	7,973	-105	93,196	21,682	12,758	6,116	5,471	20,868	9,844
1974	142,322	107,902	3,645	111,547	9,013	-102	102,431	24,773	15,118	6,722	5,989	21,173	10,163
1975	157,356	117,516	3,273	120,788	9,600	14	111,203	27,158	18,994	7,306	6,589	21,537	10,286
1976	174,493	131,741	3,477	135,218	10,978	118	124,358	29,123	21,012	7,955	7,101	21,935	10,633
1977	193,588	148,077	3,543	151,620	12,560	-22	139,038	32,243	22,307	8,662	7,679	22,350	11,119
1978	220,523	170,369	3,489	173,858	14,806	-22	159,030	37,387	24,105	9,656	8,504	22,839	11,816
1979	250,027	193,563	4,573	198,136	17,663	1	180,473	43,068	26,486	10,752	9,403	23,255	12,461
1980	283,852	214,661	5,582	220,243	19,262	-73	200,908	52,161	30,784	11,926	10,415	23,801	12,762
1981	318,834	236,862	4,354	241,216	23,093	293	218,416	64,207	36,211	13,128	11,488	24,286	12,935
1982	340,837	250,811	4,600	255,410	24,994	302	230,718	70,431	39,688	13,732	12,104	24,820	12,863
1983	368,675	271,905	4,235	276,140	27,641	307	248,806	77,494	42,376	14,538	12,851	25,360	13,182
1984	409,989	303,777	4,910	308,687	32,061	250	276,876	88,896	44,216	15,864	14,015	25,844	13,797
1985	443,346	330,780	4,950	335,730	35,323	199	300,607	94,937	47,803	16,767	14,727	26,441	14,285
1986	476,272	358,738	5,390	364,128	38,688	160	325,601	99,318	51,353	17,573	15,452	27,102	14,710
1987	513,637	393,060	6,591	399,651	42,355	82	357,378	102,679	53,579	18,491	16,082	27,777	15,300
1988	558,066	430,530	6,936	437,466	47,729	43	389,780	110,936	57,351	19,606	17,206	28,464	16,022
1989	601,184	456,908	6,839	463,748	51,065	23	412,706	125,663	62,814	20,576	17,884	29,218	16,426
1990	643,955	488,844	7,216	496,060	54,273	-35	441,751	133,031	69,173	21,494	18,720	29,960	16,835
1991	665,002	505,941	6,316	512,257	56,411	-25	455,820	132,457	76,725	21,824	19,220	30,471	16,750
1992	701,387	530,812	6,825	537,636	58,517	-32	479,087	133,665	88,635	22,644	20,101	30,975	16,391
1993	718,212	539,560	7,769	547,328	59,531	35	487,832	136,776	93,604	22,964	20,388	31,275	16,367
1994	740,998	556,091	7,547	563,638	61,692	49	501,994	143,179	95,824	23,535	20,867	31,484	16,541
1995	779,582	580,551	7,227	587,778	63,539	37	524,277	154,962	100,343	24,595	21,681	31,697	16,940
1996	828,822	615,679	8,129	623,808	65,645	28	558,191	165,368	105,264	25,885	22,566	32,019	17,342
1997	881,904	660,931	8,693	669,624	69,728	-57	599,839	176,240	105,825	27,147	23,430	32,486	17,667
1998	961,026	725,558	8,217	733,775	75,085	-59	658,631	190,670	111,725	29,133	24,995	32,988	18,450
1999	1,027,199	789,637	8,987	798,624	81,356	-69	717,199	192,614	117,385	30,663	25,903	33,499	18,888
2000	1,134,894	883,668	8,893	892,562	90,069	-241	802,251	210,466	122,178	33,391	27,639	33,988	19,281
2001	1,175,423	911,994	8,429	920,422	94,915	-226	825,281	214,566	135,576	34,091	28,852	34,479	19,411
2002	1,196,318	927,067	8,958	936,025	97,817	1,903	840,111	210,502	145,705	34,306	30,088	34,872	19,437
2003	1,247,297	961,949	10,149	972,099	102,878	2,139	871,359	222,008	153,929	35,381	31,325	35,253	19,573
2004	1,324,948	1,022,336	12,322	1,034,659	112,446	2,517	924,730	238,881	161,337	37,244	32,997	35,575	19,877
2005	1,398,953	1,066,732	12,294	1,079,026	117,534	1,851	963,343	266,008	169,602	39,046	34,076	35,828	20,256
2006	1,501,831	1,126,901	10,503	1,137,404	120,861	1,111	1,017,654	301,894	182,283	41,693	36,200	36,021	20,645
2007	1,565,343	1,160,665	12,862	1,173,527	122,663	-331	1,050,533	322,015	192,794	43,182	37,236	36,250	21,040
2008	1,602,749	1,169,547	10,766	1,180,314	124,914	-1,767	1,053,632	330,904	218,213	43,786	37,991	36,604	20,819
2009	1,537,136	1,113,194	11,973	1,125,168	120,968	-1,719	1,002,482	293,529	241,125	41,588	37,210	36,961	20,038
2010	1,583,447	1,135,502	12,433	1,147,935	121,461	-1,856	1,024,618	291,961	266,868	42,411	37,630	37,336	19,804
2011	1,691,003	1,193,396	14,373	1,207,769	114,122	-2,024	1,091,622	330,633	268,747	44,852	39,313	37,702	20,172
2012	1,812,315	1,274,614	15,953	1,290,568	118,736	-2,109	1,169,723	371,014	271,578	47,614	41,704	38,063	20,850
2013	1,849,505	1,317,897	18,767	1,336,665	139,632	-2,172	1,194,862	372,654	281,990	48,125	41,535	38,431	21,496
2014	1,939,528	1,388,050	18,561	1,406,611	147,645	-2,292	1,256,674	389,198	293,656	49,985	42,993	38,803	22,040
2015	2,061,337	1,477,723	19,722	1,497,445	156,456	-2,526	1,338,463	406,282	316,593	52,651	44,933	39,151	...

... = Not available.

Personal Income and Employment by Region and State: Colorado

(Millions of dollars, except as noted.)

Year	Personal income, total	Earnings by place of work			Less: Contributions for government social insurance	Plus: Adjustment for residence	Equals: Net earnings by place of residence	Plus: Dividends, interest, and rent	Plus: Personal current transfer receipts	Per capita (dollars)		Population (thousands)	Total employment (thousands)
		Nonfarm	Farm	Total						Personal income	Disposable personal income		
1960	4,303	3,293	174	3,468	133	1	3,336	691	275	2,432	2,156	1,769	...
1961	4,634	3,565	176	3,740	150	1	3,591	741	302	2,513	2,228	1,844	...
1962	4,886	3,763	156	3,919	163	1	3,756	811	319	2,573	2,284	1,899	...
1963	5,117	3,969	140	4,109	191	0	3,919	859	339	2,643	2,348	1,936	...
1964	5,413	4,216	137	4,354	197	0	4,156	913	343	2,748	2,489	1,970	...
1965	5,780	4,419	213	4,633	198	-0	4,435	970	375	2,912	2,633	1,985	...
1966	6,220	4,844	192	5,036	263	-1	4,773	1,040	407	3,099	2,784	2,007	...
1967	6,707	5,204	186	5,390	295	-1	5,094	1,130	483	3,267	2,923	2,053	...
1968	7,449	5,785	244	6,029	334	-2	5,693	1,207	549	3,514	3,112	2,120	...
1969	8,363	6,474	251	6,725	387	2	6,340	1,417	605	3,861	3,373	2,166	1,001
1970	9,448	7,206	289	7,495	427	1	7,069	1,648	730	4,248	3,758	2,224	1,032
1971	10,654	8,173	301	8,475	499	3	7,978	1,826	850	4,625	4,114	2,304	1,072
1972	12,057	9,370	333	9,702	606	4	9,100	2,014	943	5,014	4,402	2,405	1,149
1973	13,775	10,710	440	11,150	798	3	10,355	2,312	1,108	5,519	4,863	2,496	1,243
1974	15,431	11,849	535	12,384	905	4	11,483	2,665	1,283	6,072	5,326	2,541	1,276
1975	17,008	12,944	464	13,407	967	8	12,448	2,949	1,610	6,576	5,845	2,586	1,285
1976	18,711	14,523	336	14,860	1,105	8	13,763	3,186	1,762	7,108	6,282	2,632	1,340
1977	20,872	16,422	266	16,688	1,261	11	15,438	3,565	1,869	7,742	6,792	2,696	1,411
1978	24,077	19,179	209	19,387	1,507	19	17,900	4,144	2,033	8,702	7,611	2,767	1,506
1979	27,640	22,179	218	22,397	1,839	19	20,577	4,778	2,284	9,701	8,430	2,849	1,593
1980	31,667	25,002	290	25,292	2,106	27	23,212	5,802	2,653	10,887	9,458	2,909	1,651
1981	36,459	28,468	306	28,774	2,598	3	26,179	7,166	3,114	12,243	10,571	2,978	1,717
1982	39,984	31,079	185	31,263	2,908	0	28,355	8,101	3,528	13,060	11,259	3,062	1,760
1983	42,969	33,001	361	33,361	3,130	-2	30,229	8,837	3,903	13,712	12,122	3,134	1,788
1984	46,899	36,091	426	36,518	3,539	6	32,985	9,800	4,113	14,795	13,126	3,170	1,883
1985	49,560	38,186	396	38,582	3,835	15	34,763	10,493	4,305	15,446	13,667	3,209	1,915
1986	51,513	39,608	398	40,006	4,021	20	36,006	10,886	4,621	15,912	14,133	3,237	1,914
1987	53,463	40,963	477	41,440	4,121	31	37,350	11,132	4,981	16,397	14,512	3,260	1,903
1988	56,575	43,477	578	44,055	4,530	46	39,571	11,755	5,249	17,342	15,392	3,262	1,968
1989	61,209	46,014	621	46,635	4,888	63	41,810	13,549	5,850	18,685	16,470	3,276	2,003
1990	64,866	49,056	713	49,768	5,334	86	44,520	14,077	6,269	19,611	17,228	3,308	2,040
1991	68,711	52,513	640	53,152	5,856	97	47,393	14,355	6,963	20,286	17,858	3,387	2,087
1992	74,732	57,635	679	58,313	6,359	112	52,067	14,846	7,819	21,377	18,829	3,496	2,135
1993	80,953	62,586	815	63,401	6,987	124	56,539	16,033	8,382	22,402	19,685	3,614	2,234
1994	87,222	67,244	584	67,828	7,557	142	60,413	17,916	8,893	23,420	20,528	3,724	2,345
1995	94,818	72,203	544	72,747	8,075	163	64,836	20,007	9,975	24,778	21,713	3,827	2,425
1996	102,272	78,010	671	78,681	8,626	182	70,237	21,700	10,335	26,090	22,679	3,920	2,519
1997	110,052	84,696	676	85,372	9,300	205	76,277	23,274	10,501	27,388	23,593	4,018	2,629
1998	122,406	95,015	808	95,823	9,709	231	86,346	25,342	10,719	29,734	25,498	4,117	2,735
1999	132,659	104,895	940	105,835	10,549	261	95,548	25,707	11,403	31,391	26,833	4,226	2,812
2000	148,128	118,182	780	118,962	11,703	289	107,548	28,532	12,049	34,234	29,101	4,327	2,924
2001	155,992	124,248	1,074	125,322	12,314	338	113,346	29,480	13,166	35,247	30,378	4,426	2,949
2002	157,173	124,278	714	124,992	12,726	1,259	113,524	28,805	14,844	35,002	30,907	4,490	2,923
2003	160,369	126,190	761	126,951	12,960	1,176	115,168	29,650	15,552	35,412	31,660	4,529	2,914
2004	167,794	132,202	956	133,158	13,831	1,291	120,618	30,933	16,243	36,676	32,825	4,575	2,964
2005	179,090	139,790	1,132	140,922	14,687	1,237	127,472	34,085	17,532	38,665	34,230	4,632	3,041
2006	192,162	148,880	799	149,679	15,591	794	134,881	38,477	18,803	40,709	35,708	4,720	3,112
2007	203,035	154,152	1,022	155,174	16,421	895	139,648	43,261	20,126	42,265	36,777	4,804	3,220
2008	213,342	161,475	784	162,259	17,107	522	145,674	44,173	23,495	43,631	38,249	4,890	3,256
2009	206,385	155,752	577	156,329	16,489	501	140,341	39,968	26,077	41,508	37,483	4,972	3,172
2010	211,420	158,586	911	159,497	16,660	527	143,365	38,528	29,528	41,877	37,568	5,049	3,142
2011	227,052	164,559	1,263	165,822	15,765	585	150,642	45,883	30,527	44,349	39,262	5,120	3,204
2012	240,905	174,193	1,153	175,346	16,534	625	159,437	50,754	30,714	46,402	41,153	5,192	3,260
2013	246,448	181,213	1,328	182,540	19,330	623	163,833	50,740	31,874	46,746	41,040	5,272	3,354
2014	261,735	193,463	1,399	194,861	20,700	637	174,799	52,895	34,042	48,869	42,791	5,356	3,452
2015	275,107	203,345	1,047	204,392	21,689	656	183,358	55,095	36,654	50,410	43835	5457	...

... = Not available.

Personal Income and Employment by Region and State: Connecticut

(Millions of dollars, except as noted.)

Year	Personal income, total	Derivation of personal income								Per capita (dollars)		Population (thousands)	Total employment (thousands)
		Earnings by place of work			Less: Contributions for government social insurance	Plus: Adjustment for residence	Equals: Net earnings by place of residence	Plus: Dividends, interest, and rent	Plus: Personal current transfer receipts	Personal income	Disposable personal income		
		Nonfarm	Farm	Total									
1960	7,267	5,838	63	5,901	278	3	5,626	1,252	389	2,856	2,495	2,544	...
1961	7,693	6,104	58	6,162	290	3	5,875	1,370	448	2,975	2,609	2,586	...
1962	8,218	6,527	59	6,587	320	3	6,270	1,508	441	3,105	2,719	2,647	...
1963	8,676	6,876	64	6,940	369	4	6,575	1,632	469	3,181	2,771	2,727	...
1964	9,318	7,349	62	7,411	379	5	7,037	1,786	495	3,330	2,957	2,798	...
1965	10,018	7,871	71	7,942	395	2	7,549	1,946	523	3,507	3,092	2,857	...
1966	11,007	8,809	73	8,883	553	-0	8,329	2,114	564	3,792	3,317	2,903	...
1967	12,064	9,520	58	9,578	602	2	8,977	2,385	701	4,110	3,567	2,935	...
1968	12,817	10,232	68	10,300	671	7	9,636	2,327	854	4,324	3,685	2,964	...
1969	14,693	11,172	67	11,238	753	729	11,215	2,531	947	4,898	4,145	3,000	1,417
1970	15,679	11,758	72	11,830	784	723	11,768	2,764	1,146	5,160	4,486	3,039	1,414
1971	16,512	12,173	69	12,243	841	755	12,157	2,931	1,424	5,393	4,763	3,061	1,388
1972	17,801	13,248	68	13,316	969	800	13,147	3,149	1,505	5,799	5,049	3,070	1,416
1973	19,366	14,666	81	14,747	1,236	811	14,322	3,414	1,630	6,310	5,528	3,069	1,480
1974	21,133	15,868	84	15,952	1,397	845	15,401	3,813	1,918	6,871	6,016	3,076	1,511
1975	22,706	16,527	75	16,603	1,424	937	16,116	4,045	2,546	7,361	6,541	3,085	1,468
1976	24,502	17,985	83	18,068	1,578	1,007	17,497	4,292	2,714	7,940	6,963	3,086	1,493
1977	27,002	20,021	84	20,104	1,779	1,114	19,440	4,726	2,837	8,742	7,668	3,089	1,546
1978	30,063	22,556	80	22,636	2,061	1,274	21,849	5,291	2,924	9,714	8,435	3,095	1,615
1979	33,794	25,440	79	25,519	2,421	1,454	24,552	5,988	3,254	10,902	9,390	3,100	1,673
1980	38,458	28,284	84	28,367	2,680	1,705	27,392	7,321	3,745	12,353	10,581	3,113	1,705
1981	43,174	30,989	82	31,071	3,155	1,902	29,818	9,036	4,320	13,799	11,766	3,129	1,727
1982	46,617	33,032	108	33,140	3,431	2,045	31,754	10,061	4,802	14,851	12,645	3,139	1,726
1983	49,859	35,647	106	35,753	3,737	2,183	34,199	10,475	5,185	15,766	13,768	3,162	1,743
1984	55,856	40,118	129	40,248	4,306	2,344	38,286	12,149	5,420	17,565	15,428	3,180	1,823
1985	59,951	43,698	128	43,826	4,742	2,583	41,667	12,536	5,748	18,728	16,304	3,201	1,879
1986	64,561	47,472	140	47,613	5,165	2,679	45,126	13,354	6,080	20,027	17,337	3,224	1,937
1987	70,595	52,768	142	52,910	5,653	2,829	50,085	14,226	6,284	21,740	18,640	3,247	1,984
1988	77,854	58,337	155	58,492	6,356	3,078	55,214	15,859	6,781	23,794	20,669	3,272	2,039
1989	84,526	61,554	141	61,695	6,676	3,095	58,113	18,810	7,602	25,743	22,384	3,283	2,032
1990	86,969	63,370	186	63,556	6,798	2,750	59,508	18,961	8,500	26,418	23,031	3,292	2,003
1991	87,600	64,251	165	64,416	7,011	2,713	60,118	17,961	9,521	26,522	23,133	3,303	1,923
1992	94,263	67,652	188	67,840	7,251	3,946	64,534	18,529	11,199	28,558	24,663	3,301	1,904
1993	97,514	70,330	210	70,540	7,515	3,353	66,378	19,454	11,683	29,468	25,348	3,309	1,925
1994	100,068	72,667	186	72,852	7,873	3,111	68,090	19,879	12,099	30,176	25,946	3,316	1,906
1995	105,447	75,963	173	76,136	8,269	3,837	71,705	20,789	12,953	31,722	27,085	3,324	1,944
1996	110,588	79,470	161	79,631	8,622	4,549	75,558	21,728	13,303	33,143	27,816	3,337	1,975
1997	117,944	86,149	158	86,307	9,146	4,086	81,247	23,029	13,668	35,214	29,178	3,349	2,000
1998	126,385	91,905	180	92,085	9,592	5,496	87,989	24,556	13,840	37,555	30,786	3,365	2,034
1999	132,613	97,962	193	98,155	10,053	5,378	93,480	24,962	14,171	39,160	31,965	3,386	2,066
2000	144,007	106,457	226	106,683	10,680	5,543	101,546	27,541	14,920	42,209	34,117	3,412	2,110
2001	149,999	112,007	200	112,207	11,047	4,789	105,948	28,211	15,841	43,696	35,322	3,433	2,114
2002	150,125	112,580	189	112,769	11,520	4,916	106,165	26,958	17,002	43,405	36,681	3,459	2,107
2003	153,963	115,019	189	115,208	11,765	5,430	108,874	27,766	17,323	44,187	37,843	3,484	2,103
2004	164,684	121,981	199	122,180	12,358	6,116	115,937	30,375	18,372	47,105	40,344	3,496	2,130
2005	173,529	126,837	190	127,027	12,782	6,752	120,997	33,585	18,947	49,481	41,682	3,507	2,159
2006	187,702	133,062	173	133,235	13,237	7,720	127,718	39,751	20,233	53,363	44,752	3,517	2,192
2007	200,077	138,928	214	139,142	13,839	8,898	134,202	44,419	21,456	56,723	46,909	3,527	2,238
2008	204,850	140,079	153	140,232	14,289	9,738	135,681	44,602	24,568	57,776	48,173	3,546	2,250
2009	197,697	136,178	141	136,319	13,927	9,199	131,591	38,867	27,239	55,505	48,252	3,562	2,193
2010	205,265	139,057	140	139,197	13,997	11,261	136,462	39,757	29,046	57,347	49,559	3,579	2,162
2011	215,017	144,035	124	144,159	12,969	11,710	142,900	42,962	29,155	59,884	51,002	3,591	2,197
2012	225,503	147,851	172	148,023	13,306	13,520	148,238	47,737	29,529	62,738	53,602	3,594	2,212
2013	223,561	150,458	228	150,686	15,571	12,300	147,414	46,326	29,821	62,112	51,955	3,599	2,235
2014	233,293	156,312	199	156,511	16,141	14,189	154,559	48,208	30,527	64,864	54,190	3,597	2,256
2015	240,519	160,258	228	160,486	16,365	14,918	159,038	50,089	31,392	66,972	55,568	3,591	...

... = Not available.

Personal Income and Employment by Region and State: Delaware

(Millions of dollars, except as noted.)

Year	Personal income, total	Earnings by place of work			Less: Contributions for government social insurance	Plus: Adjustment for residence	Equals: Net earnings by place of residence	Plus: Dividends, interest, and rent	Plus: Personal current transfer receipts	Per capita (dollars)		Population (thousands)	Total employment (thousands)
		Nonfarm	Farm	Total						Personal income	Disposable personal income		
1960	1,302	1,035	34	1,069	53	-51	966	282	54	2,901	2,441	449	...
1961	1,345	1,062	30	1,092	51	-51	990	290	65	2,917	2,471	461	...
1962	1,427	1,127	33	1,160	58	-52	1,050	310	67	3,043	2,547	469	...
1963	1,528	1,223	26	1,249	69	-56	1,124	335	70	3,164	2,671	483	...
1964	1,653	1,322	26	1,348	68	-58	1,222	357	74	3,326	2,812	497	...
1965	1,816	1,459	35	1,494	69	-65	1,361	375	80	3,581	3,024	507	...
1966	1,911	1,599	26	1,625	99	-69	1,458	365	88	3,703	3,138	516	...
1967	2,036	1,701	32	1,733	117	-68	1,548	379	108	3,878	3,299	525	...
1968	2,220	1,860	29	1,890	119	-70	1,701	393	127	4,158	3,513	534	...
1969	2,446	2,000	55	2,055	139	-28	1,888	419	139	4,529	3,761	540	271
1970	2,606	2,136	35	2,171	147	-30	1,993	448	165	4,736	3,960	550	275
1971	2,852	2,364	38	2,402	168	-46	2,188	470	194	5,047	4,263	565	280
1972	3,133	2,621	49	2,670	196	-54	2,420	498	215	5,460	4,599	574	293
1973	3,467	2,917	96	3,013	253	-75	2,684	535	248	5,988	5,028	579	305
1974	3,756	3,135	82	3,217	282	-80	2,856	597	303	6,441	5,427	583	302
1975	4,049	3,323	92	3,415	293	-90	3,032	609	408	6,878	5,883	589	292
1976	4,413	3,650	84	3,734	325	-99	3,310	664	439	7,445	6,273	593	296
1977	4,749	3,941	56	3,997	351	-114	3,532	740	477	7,984	6,735	595	296
1978	5,212	4,377	61	4,437	401	-138	3,898	814	500	8,713	7,352	598	304
1979	5,722	4,807	54	4,862	460	-155	4,246	903	573	9,555	7,991	599	312
1980	6,429	5,327	13	5,340	510	-192	4,638	1,096	695	10,806	9,025	595	312
1981	7,076	5,720	43	5,763	591	-211	4,961	1,333	782	11,874	9,839	596	314
1982	7,626	6,148	65	6,214	647	-243	5,323	1,472	831	12,727	10,696	599	317
1983	8,164	6,625	79	6,704	703	-289	5,711	1,567	886	13,483	11,483	605	325
1984	8,996	7,283	96	7,379	779	-328	6,272	1,774	949	14,709	12,607	612	340
1985	9,806	7,967	104	8,071	865	-370	6,837	1,971	998	15,860	13,606	618	357
1986	10,431	8,439	144	8,583	933	-398	7,251	2,100	1,080	16,622	14,231	628	370
1987	11,270	9,275	114	9,389	1,016	-467	7,906	2,239	1,125	17,693	15,225	637	387
1988	12,319	10,132	181	10,313	1,149	-525	8,639	2,443	1,237	19,021	16,455	648	403
1989	13,717	11,101	192	11,293	1,262	-618	9,413	2,963	1,342	20,838	18,000	658	415
1990	14,403	11,770	141	11,911	1,312	-688	9,911	3,051	1,441	21,511	18,557	670	420
1991	15,238	12,302	133	12,435	1,378	-682	10,376	3,188	1,674	22,308	19,435	683	414
1992	15,928	12,897	117	13,013	1,421	-725	10,867	3,238	1,822	22,920	20,010	695	413
1993	16,547	13,269	108	13,377	1,476	-681	11,220	3,379	1,948	23,426	20,424	706	421
1994	17,202	13,879	121	14,001	1,571	-722	11,707	3,425	2,070	23,973	20,777	718	424
1995	18,223	14,634	87	14,721	1,656	-848	12,217	3,743	2,262	24,972	21,655	730	442
1996	19,495	15,573	120	15,694	1,735	-1,049	12,910	4,078	2,507	26,310	22,638	741	453
1997	20,363	16,655	95	16,750	1,843	-1,346	13,561	4,267	2,535	27,097	23,032	751	464
1998	22,097	18,025	142	18,167	1,997	-1,457	14,714	4,684	2,699	28,948	24,612	763	477
1999	23,259	19,569	140	19,709	2,134	-1,697	15,878	4,566	2,814	30,012	25,563	775	490
2000	25,249	20,950	147	21,098	2,237	-1,791	17,070	5,109	3,070	32,109	27,516	786	501
2001	27,049	22,630	212	22,842	2,295	-1,883	18,665	5,017	3,367	33,994	29,188	796	501
2002	28,115	23,577	88	23,665	2,399	-1,913	19,352	5,136	3,626	34,875	30,715	806	499
2003	28,988	24,195	176	24,370	2,500	-1,974	19,896	5,198	3,894	35,438	31,504	818	503
2004	30,958	25,632	254	25,886	2,690	-2,035	21,161	5,604	4,193	37,263	33,120	831	516
2005	32,599	26,961	292	27,252	2,820	-2,124	22,308	5,771	4,519	38,571	33,841	845	527
2006	35,003	28,545	207	28,751	3,002	-2,181	23,569	6,540	4,894	40,735	35,780	859	536
2007	36,066	28,849	208	29,056	3,085	-2,114	23,858	6,903	5,306	41,372	36,243	872	544
2008	37,404	29,269	231	29,500	3,193	-2,054	24,252	7,029	6,123	42,319	37,319	884	545
2009	37,125	28,532	296	28,829	3,124	-1,568	24,137	6,338	6,650	41,633	37,644	892	526
2010	37,594	28,873	260	29,132	3,139	-1,763	24,230	6,142	7,221	41,783	37,712	900	521
2011	39,541	30,130	236	30,366	2,847	-2,194	25,325	6,669	7,547	43,555	38,808	908	529
2012	41,028	31,098	297	31,395	2,978	-2,208	26,210	7,085	7,733	44,747	40,069	917	533
2013	41,468	31,571	462	32,032	3,467	-2,170	26,395	6,966	8,108	44,819	39,871	925	543
2014	43,392	33,174	539	33,712	3,670	-2,332	27,711	7,255	8,427	46,378	41,251	936	554
2015	45,093	34,170	608	34,777	3,757	-2,371	28,649	7,546	8,898	47,662	42,229	946	...

... = Not available.

Personal Income and Employment by Region and State: District of Columbia

(Millions of dollars, except as noted.)

| Year | Personal income, total | Derivation of personal income | | | | | | | | | Per capita (dollars) | | Population (thousands) | Total employment (thousands) |
| | | Earnings by place of work | | | Less: Contributions for government social insurance | Plus: Adjustment for residence | Equals: Net earnings by place of residence | Plus: Dividends, interest, and rent | Plus: Personal current transfer receipts | | Personal income | Disposable personal income | | |
		Nonfarm	Farm	Total										
1960	2,379	3,253	0	3,253	102	-1,390	1,761	506	112		3,110	2,688	765	...
1961	2,502	3,450	0	3,450	108	-1,481	1,861	518	123		3,216	2,819	778	...
1962	2,691	3,716	0	3,716	115	-1,576	2,025	540	127		3,415	2,980	788	...
1963	2,861	4,001	0	4,001	139	-1,701	2,161	565	135		3,585	3,154	798	...
1964	3,035	4,292	0	4,292	136	-1,846	2,310	585	140		3,803	3,393	798	...
1965	3,269	4,628	0	4,628	141	-1,990	2,498	621	150		4,102	3,679	797	...
1966	3,409	4,991	0	4,991	186	-2,185	2,620	629	160		4,310	3,826	791	...
1967	3,648	5,647	0	5,647	215	-2,615	2,817	639	192		4,612	4,116	791	...
1968	3,829	6,075	0	6,075	237	-2,889	2,950	650	230		4,922	4,383	778	...
1969	3,725	6,453	0	6,453	254	-3,358	2,841	649	234		4,888	4,238	762	676
1970	4,129	7,057	0	7,057	276	-3,699	3,082	746	302		5,469	4,772	755	672
1971	4,597	7,737	0	7,737	301	-4,074	3,362	860	375		6,124	5,415	751	666
1972	4,991	8,381	0	8,381	346	-4,432	3,604	940	447		6,710	5,902	744	668
1973	5,251	8,903	0	8,903	417	-4,733	3,753	987	512		7,158	6,274	734	662
1974	5,697	9,612	0	9,612	475	-5,107	4,029	1,073	595		7,904	6,941	721	673
1975	6,187	10,581	0	10,581	524	-5,722	4,334	1,112	741		8,710	7,679	710	677
1976	6,550	11,443	0	11,443	576	-6,269	4,597	1,182	770		9,407	8,166	696	674
1977	7,032	12,387	0	12,387	612	-6,825	4,949	1,293	790		10,315	9,037	682	680
1978	7,491	13,558	0	13,558	674	-7,669	5,215	1,464	812		11,180	9,710	670	693
1979	7,905	14,694	0	14,694	777	-8,542	5,375	1,624	906		12,058	10,332	656	704
1980	8,355	15,983	0	15,983	866	-9,648	5,468	1,856	1,031		13,090	11,244	638	701
1981	8,971	17,087	0	17,087	1,010	-10,364	5,713	2,119	1,139		14,086	11,910	637	689
1982	9,568	18,017	0	18,017	1,077	-10,897	6,043	2,253	1,271		15,087	12,787	634	673
1983	9,977	18,895	0	18,895	1,298	-11,206	6,392	2,257	1,328		15,776	13,488	632	667
1984	10,899	20,603	0	20,603	1,472	-12,134	6,997	2,486	1,416		17,208	14,704	633	689
1985	11,548	22,030	0	22,030	1,687	-12,870	7,473	2,657	1,418		18,199	15,524	635	703
1986	12,134	23,232	0	23,232	1,867	-13,446	7,919	2,743	1,472		19,010	16,240	638	721
1987	12,781	24,718	0	24,718	2,031	-14,208	8,479	2,786	1,516		20,067	16,992	637	733
1988	14,042	27,353	0	27,353	2,320	-15,704	9,328	3,084	1,630		22,274	19,059	630	756
1989	14,971	28,961	0	28,961	2,556	-16,784	9,622	3,715	1,634		23,985	20,513	624	763
1990	15,576	30,956	0	30,956	2,759	-17,946	10,251	3,581	1,744		25,731	22,108	605	773
1991	16,272	32,640	0	32,640	2,940	-18,881	10,819	3,508	1,945		27,081	23,532	601	759
1992	17,188	34,493	0	34,493	3,124	-20,061	11,308	3,696	2,184		28,764	25,152	598	752
1993	17,910	35,623	0	35,623	3,273	-20,623	11,726	3,786	2,398		30,086	26,436	595	750
1994	18,320	36,413	0	36,413	3,414	-20,993	12,005	3,876	2,439		31,091	27,118	589	730
1995	18,434	36,690	0	36,690	3,484	-21,043	12,163	3,903	2,368		31,755	27,712	581	718
1996	19,195	37,288	0	37,288	3,521	-21,038	12,728	3,891	2,576		33,536	29,002	572	704
1997	20,209	38,594	0	38,594	3,666	-21,670	13,258	4,381	2,570		35,596	30,464	568	699
1998	21,472	40,642	0	40,642	3,743	-22,780	14,119	4,615	2,739		37,988	32,193	565	698
1999	22,473	44,081	0	44,081	4,083	-24,864	15,134	4,603	2,736		39,412	33,124	570	712
2000	24,725	46,759	0	46,759	4,309	-25,473	16,977	4,932	2,817		43,223	36,185	572	735
2001	25,906	50,022	0	50,022	4,922	-26,898	18,201	4,790	2,915		45,093	37,933	575	741
2002	26,435	52,864	0	52,864	5,230	-29,024	18,611	4,618	3,206		46,121	40,037	573	757
2003	27,191	55,596	0	55,596	5,446	-30,977	19,173	4,757	3,261		47,830	41,735	569	753
2004	28,925	59,509	0	59,509	5,815	-33,187	20,507	5,123	3,294		50,945	44,241	568	763
2005	30,570	62,693	0	62,693	6,150	-35,222	21,321	5,665	3,584		53,902	46,205	567	770
2006	32,945	66,349	0	66,349	6,515	-37,095	22,739	6,557	3,649		57,730	49,547	571	779
2007	35,100	69,727	0	69,727	6,870	-38,724	24,134	7,065	3,901		61,107	51,691	574	791
2008	38,423	74,346	0	74,346	7,399	-40,345	26,602	7,518	4,303		66,220	56,978	580	797
2009	37,205	74,915	0	74,915	7,623	-41,207	26,085	6,345	4,776		62,823	55,238	592	800
2010	38,577	78,632	0	78,632	8,084	-43,659	26,888	6,233	5,455		63,741	56,060	605	809
2011	41,791	82,110	0	82,110	7,416	-45,947	28,747	7,249	5,795		67,359	58,454	620	827
2012	43,801	83,505	0	83,505	7,666	-45,799	30,040	8,051	5,710		68,973	59,529	635	835
2013	44,533	84,646	0	84,646	8,889	-45,396	30,361	8,191	5,981		68,606	58,747	649	848
2014	46,016	88,173	0	88,173	9,277	-47,401	31,496	8,544	5,976		69,838	59,599	659	859
2015	48,070	92,821	0	92,821	9,678	-50,054	33,089	8,877	6,104		71,496	60,476	672	...

... = Not available.

Personal Income and Employment by Region and State: Florida

(Millions of dollars, except as noted.)

Year	Personal income, total	Derivation of personal income								Per capita (dollars)		Population (thousands)	Total employment (thousands)
		Earnings by place of work			Less: Contributions for government social insurance	Plus: Adjustment for residence	Equals: Net earnings by place of residence	Plus: Dividends, interest, and rent	Plus: Personal current transfer receipts	Personal income	Disposable personal income		
		Nonfarm	Farm	Total									
1960	10,480	7,683	381	8,064	329	-1	7,734	2,030	715	2,094	1,901	5,004	...
1961	11,106	7,978	440	8,418	344	-1	8,073	2,204	829	2,118	1,923	5,243	...
1962	11,986	8,604	454	9,058	389	-1	8,668	2,390	928	2,196	1,992	5,458	...
1963	12,880	9,285	436	9,721	449	-1	9,271	2,599	1,011	2,289	2,076	5,628	...
1964	14,112	10,223	492	10,715	481	-1	10,232	2,825	1,055	2,441	2,230	5,781	...
1965	15,452	11,203	466	11,669	516	-1	11,152	3,129	1,171	2,595	2,365	5,954	...
1966	16,978	12,456	476	12,932	680	-2	12,250	3,422	1,306	2,781	2,530	6,104	...
1967	18,786	13,661	515	14,176	809	-3	13,363	3,795	1,628	3,010	2,713	6,242	...
1968	21,612	15,580	528	16,109	966	-5	15,138	4,538	1,936	3,360	2,994	6,433	...
1969	25,165	17,935	636	18,571	1,132	-25	17,414	5,557	2,195	3,789	3,350	6,641	2,857
1970	28,474	20,003	546	20,550	1,272	-23	19,254	6,575	2,646	4,160	3,721	6,845	2,966
1971	31,975	22,199	639	22,838	1,473	-17	21,348	7,440	3,188	4,464	4,018	7,163	3,082
1972	36,786	25,738	738	26,477	1,798	-14	24,665	8,366	3,755	4,891	4,333	7,520	3,338
1973	42,791	30,118	837	30,954	2,422	-12	28,520	9,711	4,561	5,398	4,805	7,927	3,666
1974	48,155	33,103	908	34,011	2,782	-3	31,226	11,432	5,497	5,790	5,172	8,317	3,766
1975	52,615	34,576	998	35,575	2,860	-11	32,703	12,729	7,183	6,160	5,610	8,542	3,676
1976	57,334	37,656	1,035	38,691	3,170	8	35,529	13,827	7,978	6,594	5,961	8,695	3,730
1977	64,183	42,217	1,033	43,250	3,572	19	39,697	15,756	8,730	7,221	6,509	8,889	3,929
1978	74,170	48,871	1,234	50,105	4,251	22	45,875	18,596	9,698	8,122	7,275	9,132	4,239
1979	85,170	55,937	1,312	57,249	5,112	18	52,154	21,779	11,237	8,993	7,996	9,471	4,454
1980	100,175	64,095	1,667	65,762	5,909	12	59,866	26,930	13,379	10,181	9,008	9,840	4,688
1981	115,827	72,338	1,402	73,740	7,183	117	66,674	33,523	15,629	11,364	10,032	10,193	4,865
1982	125,266	77,148	1,777	78,925	7,887	141	71,179	36,399	17,689	11,963	10,481	10,471	4,954
1983	139,242	85,401	2,465	87,867	8,778	167	79,256	40,645	19,341	12,953	11,627	10,750	5,167
1984	154,952	96,042	1,828	97,870	10,141	208	87,937	46,418	20,597	14,036	12,706	11,040	5,502
1985	170,341	105,553	1,835	107,388	11,348	254	96,294	51,824	22,224	15,007	13,436	11,351	5,772
1986	184,230	114,970	1,972	116,943	12,681	317	104,579	55,706	23,945	15,790	14,089	11,668	6,015
1987	199,397	126,538	2,135	128,673	13,789	378	115,262	58,749	25,386	16,620	14,804	11,997	6,094
1988	218,710	139,112	2,687	141,799	15,631	454	126,622	64,283	27,805	17,772	15,895	12,306	6,390
1989	244,145	149,107	2,484	151,590	16,945	535	135,180	77,595	31,370	19,319	17,266	12,638	6,596
1990	260,094	159,233	2,084	161,317	17,936	633	144,014	81,697	34,382	19,956	17,907	13,033	6,740
1991	270,301	165,797	2,458	168,255	18,806	677	150,126	81,540	38,635	20,217	18,269	13,370	6,718
1992	286,473	177,892	2,460	180,352	20,071	744	161,025	81,103	44,345	20,986	18,970	13,651	6,763
1993	304,270	190,156	2,535	192,691	21,337	794	172,148	84,640	47,482	21,847	19,729	13,927	7,002
1994	320,445	201,307	2,165	203,472	22,867	855	181,460	88,366	50,619	22,504	20,277	14,239	7,234
1995	344,348	214,466	2,211	216,677	24,235	922	193,365	96,311	54,672	23,686	21,297	14,538	7,494
1996	366,382	228,979	1,953	230,932	25,571	995	206,356	102,179	57,847	24,667	21,951	14,853	7,740
1997	388,031	242,692	2,167	244,858	27,135	1,096	218,819	109,207	60,005	25,551	22,538	15,186	8,005
1998	418,883	264,216	2,651	266,867	29,132	1,222	238,958	118,556	61,369	27,048	23,765	15,487	8,329
1999	439,689	283,596	2,714	286,310	30,997	1,355	256,668	119,224	63,797	27,900	24,494	15,759	8,600
2000	474,962	308,110	2,590	310,700	33,265	1,518	278,953	127,999	68,010	29,597	25,889	16,048	8,918
2001	500,090	326,874	2,582	329,455	35,634	1,589	295,411	130,534	74,145	30,574	26,893	16,357	8,988
2002	517,901	342,547	2,511	345,058	37,216	874	308,715	129,360	79,826	31,032	27,900	16,689	9,109
2003	542,892	361,626	2,185	363,811	39,225	788	325,374	132,250	85,267	31,927	29,117	17,004	9,331
2004	592,858	390,422	2,294	392,716	42,621	1,108	351,203	149,978	91,677	34,042	30,870	17,415	9,714
2005	647,554	423,970	2,701	426,671	46,503	2,042	382,211	166,827	98,517	36,294	32,402	17,842	10,140
2006	705,089	452,269	2,644	454,912	50,378	3,107	407,641	192,308	105,140	38,812	34,639	18,167	10,471
2007	733,710	460,224	2,241	462,465	51,855	3,064	413,674	208,141	111,894	39,945	35,653	18,368	10,626
2008	741,430	453,276	2,235	455,510	51,676	2,827	406,661	207,581	127,188	40,018	36,049	18,527	10,357
2009	699,091	429,536	2,302	431,838	49,954	2,704	384,588	175,905	138,599	37,479	34,586	18,653	9,938
2010	729,923	436,374	2,578	438,952	50,742	2,816	391,026	187,293	151,603	38,718	35,619	18,852	9,877
2011	774,599	446,934	2,142	449,076	46,810	3,054	405,321	211,497	157,781	40,538	36,888	19,108	10,117
2012	798,388	468,161	2,540	470,700	48,939	3,151	424,912	217,193	156,283	41,249	37,447	19,355	10,325
2013	809,665	485,934	2,711	488,645	56,894	3,189	434,939	213,424	161,302	41,309	37,128	19,600	10,618
2014	850,178	511,292	2,558	513,850	59,959	3,378	457,269	221,757	171,152	42,737	38,286	19,893	10,911
2015	894,190	540,328	3,115	543,443	63,120	3,495	483,818	229,865	180,507	44,101	39,241	20,276	...

... = Not available.

Personal Income and Employment by Region and State: Georgia

(Millions of dollars, except as noted.)

Year	Personal income, total	Earnings by place of work Nonfarm	Farm	Total	Less: Contributions for government social insurance	Plus: Adjustment for residence	Equals: Net earnings by place of residence	Plus: Dividends, interest, and rent	Plus: Personal current transfer receipts	Per capita (dollars) Personal income	Disposable personal income	Population (thousands)	Total employment (thousands)
1960	6,949	5,611	326	5,937	262	-15	5,660	871	417	1,756	1,595	3,956	...
1961	7,250	5,774	347	6,121	266	-17	5,839	938	473	1,806	1,643	4,015	...
1962	7,794	6,290	312	6,602	298	-21	6,284	1,022	488	1,907	1,725	4,086	...
1963	8,474	6,809	400	7,209	349	-25	6,834	1,118	522	2,031	1,836	4,172	...
1964	9,180	7,470	334	7,804	377	-30	7,398	1,235	547	2,156	1,962	4,258	...
1965	10,133	8,229	377	8,606	408	-36	8,162	1,370	601	2,339	2,124	4,332	...
1966	11,174	9,227	389	9,616	546	-45	9,025	1,494	656	2,552	2,303	4,379	...
1967	12,140	10,037	386	10,423	626	-54	9,742	1,617	781	2,754	2,495	4,408	...
1968	13,400	11,224	343	11,567	684	-64	10,819	1,651	930	2,990	2,676	4,482	...
1969	14,944	12,502	420	12,921	786	-96	12,039	1,843	1,063	3,284	2,881	4,551	2,119
1970	16,272	13,355	398	13,752	837	-86	12,830	2,143	1,299	3,533	3,144	4,605	2,121
1971	17,970	14,625	456	15,082	952	-82	14,048	2,376	1,546	3,815	3,430	4,710	2,167
1972	20,160	16,529	471	17,000	1,128	-74	15,798	2,621	1,741	4,194	3,720	4,807	2,253
1973	22,773	18,504	788	19,292	1,445	-71	17,775	2,987	2,010	4,641	4,144	4,907	2,356
1974	24,986	20,061	672	20,733	1,628	-70	19,035	3,440	2,511	5,002	4,462	4,995	2,374
1975	27,003	21,042	638	21,680	1,680	-58	19,942	3,734	3,327	5,338	4,853	5,059	2,313
1976	29,997	23,847	629	24,477	1,946	-89	22,442	3,993	3,562	5,852	5,268	5,126	2,400
1977	33,160	26,968	365	27,333	2,190	-105	25,038	4,428	3,694	6,362	5,693	5,212	2,503
1978	37,626	30,610	568	31,178	2,552	-87	28,539	5,073	4,013	7,118	6,328	5,286	2,621
1979	42,114	34,261	598	34,858	2,974	-98	31,786	5,757	4,571	7,812	6,861	5,391	2,700
1980	46,931	37,797	40	37,837	3,302	-105	34,430	7,020	5,481	8,554	7,539	5,486	2,741
1981	53,091	41,683	523	42,206	3,919	-36	38,251	8,597	6,243	9,534	8,366	5,568	2,776
1982	57,499	44,484	683	45,167	4,272	-77	40,818	9,864	6,817	10,177	8,986	5,650	2,793
1983	63,101	49,120	476	49,595	4,793	-120	44,683	11,020	7,398	11,016	9,712	5,728	2,877
1984	71,483	55,860	956	56,816	5,611	-155	51,050	12,532	7,901	12,251	10,853	5,835	3,068
1985	78,389	61,869	787	62,656	6,361	-168	56,127	13,790	8,472	13,147	11,567	5,963	3,207
1986	85,539	68,045	828	68,872	7,085	-217	61,571	14,943	9,026	14,058	12,390	6,085	3,335
1987	92,052	73,690	895	74,585	7,617	-226	66,741	15,844	9,467	14,827	12,998	6,208	3,433
1988	100,335	80,171	1,151	81,322	8,521	-228	72,572	17,545	10,218	15,886	14,003	6,316	3,545
1989	108,166	84,693	1,357	86,050	9,070	-192	76,787	20,024	11,354	16,872	14,811	6,411	3,608
1990	115,538	90,277	1,261	91,538	9,696	-113	81,729	21,178	12,631	17,741	15,592	6,513	3,664
1991	121,118	93,666	1,565	95,231	10,179	-132	84,920	21,572	14,626	18,205	16,108	6,653	3,622
1992	131,312	102,210	1,640	103,850	10,960	-178	92,712	22,278	16,323	19,262	17,085	6,817	3,698
1993	139,468	108,838	1,475	110,313	11,712	-182	98,418	23,589	17,460	19,986	17,658	6,978	3,866
1994	150,307	116,491	1,941	118,432	12,670	-237	105,524	25,960	18,823	21,001	18,529	7,157	4,020
1995	162,223	125,556	1,764	127,320	13,607	-341	113,372	28,507	20,344	22,136	19,481	7,328	4,188
1996	175,284	135,696	1,857	137,554	14,539	-376	122,639	30,991	21,655	23,368	20,428	7,501	4,333
1997	186,660	145,183	1,813	146,996	15,463	-449	131,084	33,418	22,158	24,289	21,098	7,685	4,449
1998	204,709	161,270	1,803	163,073	16,839	-587	145,647	36,401	22,661	26,033	22,523	7,864	4,612
1999	218,195	174,839	1,945	176,784	18,151	-602	158,031	36,256	23,908	27,119	23,435	8,046	4,737
2000	236,062	188,533	1,845	190,378	19,382	-735	170,261	39,878	25,924	28,693	24,747	8,227	4,873
2001	247,909	196,781	2,218	198,999	20,151	-785	178,063	41,348	28,498	29,594	25,645	8,377	4,890
2002	254,127	201,182	1,644	202,826	20,550	-1,278	180,997	40,891	32,238	29,868	26,516	8,508	4,879
2003	262,760	207,395	2,051	209,446	21,157	-1,181	187,108	42,809	32,843	30,473	27,329	8,623	4,917
2004	276,470	218,960	2,168	221,128	23,010	-1,081	197,038	44,038	35,395	31,527	28,348	8,769	5,056
2005	294,532	230,621	2,469	233,090	23,996	-1,247	207,847	48,129	38,555	32,997	29,404	8,926	5,226
2006	315,144	245,034	1,570	246,605	25,480	-1,062	220,062	53,652	41,429	34,420	30,483	9,156	5,384
2007	332,915	254,065	1,838	255,904	26,201	-627	229,075	59,233	44,607	35,606	31,460	9,350	5,522
2008	341,180	256,314	2,166	258,479	27,306	-913	230,261	59,513	51,406	35,895	31,949	9,505	5,484
2009	330,916	246,005	1,807	247,812	26,545	-843	220,424	53,997	56,495	34,396	31,340	9,621	5,283
2010	335,021	246,790	1,565	248,355	27,118	-813	220,425	52,708	61,888	34,487	31,280	9,714	5,234
2011	359,047	256,439	1,427	257,866	24,926	-970	231,970	62,187	64,889	36,588	32,926	9,813	5,350
2012	369,520	266,804	2,643	269,447	25,871	-1,105	242,471	62,739	64,311	37,254	33,560	9,919	5,404
2013	375,758	275,579	3,078	278,657	30,326	-1,399	246,933	62,316	66,510	37,596	33,539	9,995	5,516
2014	393,594	290,183	2,619	292,802	31,868	-1,607	259,327	64,737	69,530	38,980	34,688	10,097	5,657
2015	414,274	305,332	3,050	308,382	33,318	-1,716	273,348	67,289	73,637	40,551	35880	10216	...

... = Not available.

Personal Income and Employment by Region and State: Hawaii

(Millions of dollars, except as noted.)

Year	Personal income, total	Earnings by place of work			Less: Contributions for government social insurance	Plus: Adjustment for residence	Equals: Net earnings by place of residence	Plus: Dividends, interest, and rent	Plus: Personal current transfer receipts	Per capita (dollars)		Population (thousands)	Total employment (thousands)
		Nonfarm	Farm	Total						Personal income	Disposable personal income		
1960	1,625	1,279	82	1,361	52	0	1,309	268	48	2,531	2,206	642	...
1961	1,761	1,384	75	1,459	57	0	1,402	300	59	2,673	2,328	659	...
1962	1,885	1,472	79	1,551	61	0	1,490	328	67	2,756	2,440	684	...
1963	2,014	1,581	88	1,669	76	0	1,593	351	70	2,953	2,618	682	...
1964	2,191	1,727	89	1,816	82	0	1,733	388	70	3,130	2,810	700	...
1965	2,406	1,889	91	1,980	85	0	1,895	430	81	3,418	3,082	704	...
1966	2,612	2,079	95	2,174	114	0	2,061	456	95	3,678	3,266	710	...
1967	2,831	2,242	98	2,340	131	0	2,209	502	121	3,916	3,469	723	...
1968	3,182	2,543	117	2,661	153	0	2,508	534	140	4,335	3,811	734	...
1969	3,647	2,926	119	3,045	182	0	2,863	624	160	4,908	4,258	743	416
1970	4,229	3,342	133	3,475	211	0	3,264	759	207	5,544	4,839	763	434
1971	4,589	3,584	131	3,715	236	0	3,479	840	270	5,798	5,137	792	437
1972	5,054	3,951	131	4,082	274	0	3,808	923	323	6,177	5,408	818	453
1973	5,594	4,385	138	4,523	348	0	4,175	1,050	370	6,645	5,830	842	473
1974	6,365	4,789	340	5,129	400	0	4,729	1,191	444	7,418	6,530	858	485
1975	6,936	5,296	202	5,497	442	0	5,055	1,304	577	7,926	7,130	875	499
1976	7,463	5,740	173	5,913	484	0	5,429	1,359	675	8,364	7,462	892	505
1977	8,075	6,229	184	6,413	522	0	5,891	1,476	708	8,818	7,830	916	509
1978	8,963	6,908	168	7,076	597	0	6,479	1,724	761	9,650	8,511	929	528
1979	10,051	7,764	193	7,958	700	0	7,257	1,953	840	10,579	9,289	950	556
1980	11,461	8,637	374	9,011	777	0	8,234	2,262	965	11,843	10,405	968	575
1981	12,391	9,327	199	9,526	896	0	8,630	2,627	1,134	12,667	11,130	978	568
1982	13,077	9,917	234	10,152	946	0	9,206	2,642	1,229	13,159	11,770	994	567
1983	14,420	10,669	338	11,008	1,036	0	9,971	3,097	1,351	14,239	12,739	1,013	577
1984	15,454	11,453	239	11,692	1,135	0	10,557	3,472	1,425	15,034	13,472	1,028	582
1985	16,453	12,250	222	12,472	1,237	0	11,235	3,707	1,511	15,825	14,125	1,040	598
1986	17,468	13,104	256	13,360	1,351	0	12,010	3,885	1,574	16,608	14,797	1,052	612
1987	18,623	14,212	239	14,451	1,477	0	12,975	4,019	1,629	17,439	15,325	1,068	643
1988	20,461	15,822	262	16,084	1,696	0	14,389	4,326	1,746	18,949	16,632	1,080	669
1989	22,865	17,607	248	17,856	1,887	0	15,969	4,960	1,937	20,890	18,152	1,095	696
1990	24,931	19,540	260	19,800	2,178	0	17,622	5,211	2,098	22,390	19,467	1,113	724
1991	26,366	20,787	232	21,018	2,345	0	18,673	5,389	2,304	23,194	20,061	1,137	745
1992	28,425	22,215	219	22,434	2,494	0	19,940	5,810	2,676	24,533	21,661	1,159	746
1993	29,472	22,741	216	22,957	2,543	0	20,414	6,128	2,930	25,129	22,222	1,173	742
1994	30,121	22,949	210	23,159	2,588	0	20,571	6,379	3,172	25,365	22,450	1,188	737
1995	30,777	22,967	199	23,166	2,586	0	20,581	6,609	3,587	25,715	22,889	1,197	734
1996	30,786	22,938	195	23,133	2,590	0	20,543	6,563	3,680	25,575	22,624	1,204	733
1997	31,792	23,573	205	23,778	2,630	0	21,147	6,951	3,694	26,239	23,202	1,212	734
1998	32,276	23,767	219	23,986	2,671	0	21,315	7,195	3,766	26,560	23,380	1,215	738
1999	33,253	24,480	246	24,726	2,740	0	21,986	7,345	3,922	27,475	24,140	1,210	737
2000	35,108	25,889	242	26,131	2,889	0	23,242	7,736	4,130	28,931	25,349	1,214	753
2001	36,347	27,005	237	27,242	3,048	0	24,194	7,702	4,450	29,648	26,001	1,226	757
2002	38,047	28,731	250	28,981	3,257	0	25,725	7,517	4,805	30,693	27,415	1,240	762
2003	39,849	30,617	251	30,868	3,503	0	27,364	7,522	4,963	31,850	28,641	1,251	778
2004	43,085	32,909	251	33,160	3,680	0	29,480	8,313	5,291	33,830	30,430	1,274	802
2005	46,111	35,127	262	35,388	3,948	0	31,440	8,969	5,702	35,669	31,701	1,293	827
2006	49,617	37,279	260	37,539	4,248	0	33,291	10,314	6,013	37,883	33,620	1,310	849
2007	52,659	38,865	248	39,114	4,441	0	34,673	11,385	6,600	40,024	35,525	1,316	872
2008	55,478	39,985	184	40,169	4,530	0	35,639	12,146	7,693	41,643	37,190	1,332	868
2009	55,340	39,408	192	39,600	4,474	0	35,127	11,954	8,260	41,093	37,542	1,347	840
2010	56,732	40,196	175	40,371	4,717	0	35,655	11,819	9,259	41,594	38,090	1,364	833
2011	59,179	41,993	170	42,164	4,497	0	37,667	11,874	9,639	42,938	38,989	1,378	844
2012	61,984	43,957	244	44,202	4,646	0	39,556	12,916	9,512	44,504	40,417	1,393	858
2013	62,437	44,817	269	45,086	5,409	0	39,677	12,921	9,839	44,314	39,800	1,409	877
2014	65,348	46,445	298	46,744	5,424	0	41,319	13,562	10,467	46,034	41,309	1,420	890
2015	68,373	48,576	344	48,920	5,579	0	43,341	14,096	10,936	47,753	42645	1432	...

... = Not available.

Personal Income and Employment by Region and State: Idaho

(Millions of dollars, except as noted.)

| Year | Personal income, total | Earnings by place of work | | | Less: Contributions for government social insurance | Plus: Adjustment for residence | Equals: Net earnings by place of residence | Plus: Dividends, interest, and rent | Plus: Personal current transfer receipts | Per capita (dollars) | | Population (thousands) | Total employment (thousands) |
		Nonfarm	Farm	Total						Personal income	Disposable personal income		
1960	1,301	926	159	1,085	50	-3	1,032	179	90	1,939	1,740	671	...
1961	1,378	986	159	1,144	56	-3	1,085	192	102	2,015	1,821	684	...
1962	1,475	1,060	167	1,227	62	-3	1,163	206	106	2,131	1,930	692	...
1963	1,508	1,078	175	1,253	69	-2	1,182	218	109	2,208	1,992	683	...
1964	1,558	1,157	135	1,292	70	-2	1,220	226	112	2,292	2,093	680	...
1965	1,779	1,260	232	1,493	76	-2	1,415	244	120	2,593	2,371	686	...
1966	1,803	1,332	180	1,512	93	-1	1,419	256	129	2,617	2,381	689	...
1967	1,917	1,397	207	1,603	107	-1	1,496	266	155	2,786	2,525	688	...
1968	2,047	1,525	186	1,710	122	-0	1,588	284	174	2,945	2,656	695	...
1969	2,370	1,692	253	1,945	126	13	1,831	345	194	3,352	3,001	707	315
1970	2,617	1,848	267	2,115	136	14	1,993	396	229	3,649	3,293	717	324
1971	2,860	2,027	249	2,277	154	16	2,139	452	269	3,872	3,495	739	332
1972	3,267	2,310	320	2,630	182	17	2,465	496	306	4,280	3,889	763	347
1973	3,779	2,610	453	3,063	239	19	2,844	585	351	4,832	4,355	782	365
1974	4,443	2,976	628	3,604	281	23	3,345	676	421	5,499	4,916	808	381
1975	4,778	3,380	387	3,767	314	28	3,480	774	524	5,743	5,181	832	393
1976	5,355	3,906	343	4,248	368	35	3,915	847	593	6,248	5,624	857	419
1977	5,851	4,393	240	4,633	416	35	4,253	970	628	6,623	5,945	883	435
1978	6,738	5,083	308	5,391	485	43	4,948	1,119	670	7,396	6,621	911	460
1979	7,390	5,611	233	5,843	564	48	5,327	1,281	783	7,924	7,077	933	469
1980	8,317	5,985	408	6,392	606	61	5,847	1,532	937	8,773	7,841	948	464
1981	9,172	6,447	427	6,873	703	53	6,223	1,874	1,074	9,532	8,439	962	462
1982	9,564	6,456	393	6,849	720	62	6,191	2,140	1,233	9,822	8,788	974	452
1983	10,363	6,965	584	7,549	779	63	6,833	2,226	1,303	10,554	9,514	982	463
1984	11,083	7,552	501	8,053	870	76	7,259	2,475	1,349	11,186	10,112	991	472
1985	11,634	7,938	458	8,396	929	85	7,552	2,637	1,445	11,704	10,551	994	474
1986	11,902	8,073	479	8,552	955	100	7,698	2,680	1,525	12,020	10,895	990	474
1987	12,491	8,517	594	9,111	988	108	8,231	2,690	1,570	12,681	11,472	985	487
1988	13,525	9,350	670	10,020	1,128	126	9,018	2,821	1,686	13,722	12,395	986	508
1989	14,924	10,138	881	11,019	1,243	142	9,918	3,172	1,834	15,008	13,414	994	525
1990	16,159	11,086	1,000	12,086	1,435	157	10,809	3,372	1,978	15,962	14,217	1,012	548
1991	16,985	11,850	829	12,678	1,564	178	11,292	3,478	2,214	16,311	14,550	1,041	566
1992	18,679	13,163	875	14,039	1,701	196	12,533	3,667	2,478	17,429	15,462	1,072	586
1993	20,487	14,367	1,085	15,452	1,863	217	13,806	4,014	2,667	18,477	16,430	1,109	612
1994	21,919	15,731	779	16,510	2,051	246	14,705	4,385	2,829	19,141	17,017	1,145	647
1995	23,555	16,595	844	17,439	2,180	286	15,545	4,897	3,114	20,008	17,769	1,177	667
1996	25,056	17,414	952	18,367	2,242	331	16,456	5,270	3,330	20,827	18,456	1,203	689
1997	26,167	18,285	756	19,041	2,337	378	17,083	5,629	3,455	21,300	18,803	1,229	708
1998	28,408	19,823	958	20,780	2,483	447	18,744	6,066	3,598	22,684	20,068	1,252	734
1999	30,267	21,459	1,007	22,466	2,616	512	20,361	6,082	3,823	23,726	20,910	1,276	748
2000	32,821	23,564	1,015	24,579	2,848	526	22,257	6,419	4,145	25,258	22,134	1,299	777
2001	34,419	24,348	1,126	25,474	2,894	554	23,134	6,649	4,635	26,075	23,010	1,320	783
2002	35,419	25,160	1,101	26,261	2,978	508	23,790	6,610	5,019	26,425	23,932	1,340	792
2003	36,853	26,127	870	26,998	3,100	493	24,390	7,127	5,336	27,031	24,659	1,363	801
2004	40,102	28,016	1,375	29,391	3,309	493	26,574	7,812	5,716	28,813	26,309	1,392	824
2005	42,583	29,907	1,202	31,109	3,588	504	28,024	8,384	6,175	29,815	26,783	1,428	860
2006	46,916	33,096	1,086	34,182	3,998	521	30,704	9,507	6,705	31,945	28,480	1,469	901
2007	49,596	34,081	1,591	35,672	4,190	590	32,072	10,247	7,278	32,952	29,341	1,505	931
2008	50,409	33,462	1,769	35,231	4,211	531	31,551	10,380	8,477	32,854	29,508	1,534	923
2009	48,797	32,729	1,126	33,854	4,122	606	30,338	9,141	9,318	31,392	28,896	1,554	883
2010	50,340	33,253	1,528	34,782	4,329	651	31,104	8,995	10,241	32,050	29,497	1,571	869
2011	53,127	33,581	2,146	35,727	3,970	755	32,512	10,318	10,297	33,544	30,594	1,584	878
2012	55,599	34,496	2,147	36,642	4,081	920	33,481	11,677	10,441	34,846	31,739	1,596	882
2013	57,484	36,121	2,461	38,582	4,693	885	34,774	11,928	10,782	35,641	32,243	1,613	902
2014	60,041	37,709	2,588	40,297	4,846	952	36,403	12,429	11,209	36,734	33,148	1,634	923
2015	62,083	39,369	1,979	41,347	5,014	1,003	37,336	12,975	11,772	37,509	33,646	1,655	...

... = Not available.

Personal Income and Employment by Region and State: Illinois

(Millions of dollars, except as noted.)

Year	Personal income, total	Derivation of personal income								Per capita (dollars)		Population (thousands)	Total employment (thousands)
		Earnings by place of work			Less: Contributions for government social insurance	Plus: Adjustment for residence	Equals: Net earnings by place of residence	Plus: Dividends, interest, and rent	Plus: Personal current transfer receipts	Personal income	Disposable personal income		
		Nonfarm	Farm	Total									
1960	27,344	22,661	647	23,308	1,073	-133	22,101	3,770	1,472	2,711	2,391	10,086	...
1961	28,412	23,099	814	23,912	1,089	-139	22,685	4,027	1,699	2,805	2,482	10,130	...
1962	29,980	24,382	798	25,179	1,196	-154	23,829	4,388	1,763	2,916	2,572	10,280	...
1963	31,164	25,297	821	26,118	1,329	-159	24,629	4,719	1,815	2,996	2,649	10,402	...
1964	33,306	27,148	665	27,813	1,337	-175	26,301	5,158	1,847	3,148	2,822	10,580	...
1965	36,124	29,150	903	30,052	1,356	-194	28,502	5,642	1,981	3,378	3,021	10,693	...
1966	39,162	32,091	976	33,067	1,821	-223	31,024	5,993	2,145	3,614	3,206	10,836	...
1967	41,645	34,077	936	35,012	1,988	-239	32,786	6,304	2,555	3,804	3,361	10,947	...
1968	44,614	36,770	691	37,461	2,193	-264	35,003	6,618	2,993	4,058	3,545	10,995	...
1969	48,574	40,140	913	41,053	2,715	63	38,400	6,937	3,236	4,400	3,773	11,039	5,179
1970	51,640	42,295	723	43,017	2,810	-18	40,190	7,613	3,837	4,642	4,002	11,125	5,144
1971	55,448	44,998	885	45,883	3,074	-60	42,750	8,108	4,590	4,948	4,333	11,206	5,104
1972	60,157	48,854	1,000	49,854	3,517	-83	46,254	8,736	5,167	5,343	4,619	11,258	5,155
1973	67,033	53,840	1,841	55,681	4,490	-100	51,091	9,795	6,147	5,953	5,178	11,260	5,351
1974	73,317	58,653	1,673	60,326	5,078	-117	55,130	11,178	7,008	6,503	5,630	11,274	5,441
1975	80,076	61,763	2,463	64,225	5,194	-140	58,891	12,201	8,984	7,082	6,221	11,306	5,342
1976	86,911	68,400	1,713	70,113	5,881	-130	64,102	12,882	9,927	7,650	6,649	11,360	5,458
1977	95,537	75,831	1,716	77,547	6,516	-68	70,963	14,189	10,384	8,376	7,259	11,406	5,587
1978	105,452	84,558	1,510	86,068	7,466	11	78,612	15,792	11,048	9,222	7,967	11,434	5,748
1979	115,663	92,461	1,838	94,298	8,484	90	85,904	17,726	12,032	10,126	8,682	11,423	5,803
1980	125,267	97,647	381	98,028	8,931	196	89,292	21,365	14,610	10,955	9,412	11,435	5,675
1981	138,798	104,430	1,522	105,953	10,249	114	95,817	26,199	16,782	12,129	10,401	11,443	5,664
1982	146,883	107,233	914	108,147	10,690	30	97,488	30,969	18,426	12,858	11,219	11,423	5,563
1983	153,272	112,332	-485	111,847	11,259	16	100,603	32,944	19,725	13,435	11,803	11,409	5,520
1984	168,780	123,452	1,227	124,678	12,810	-49	111,820	36,868	20,091	14,790	13,064	11,412	5,718
1985	177,588	130,570	1,718	132,287	13,763	-94	118,431	38,192	20,965	15,578	13,717	11,400	5,780
1986	186,842	138,997	1,426	140,423	14,681	-132	125,610	39,505	21,727	16,408	14,469	11,387	5,892
1987	197,671	149,575	1,431	151,007	15,562	-203	135,241	40,254	22,175	17,353	15,150	11,391	6,031
1988	212,991	163,901	856	164,757	17,396	-303	147,058	42,980	22,953	18,699	16,430	11,390	6,187
1989	226,785	172,814	2,174	174,988	18,513	-324	156,151	46,249	24,385	19,876	17,348	11,410	6,294
1990	240,750	183,572	1,763	185,336	19,273	-272	165,790	48,337	26,622	21,020	18,359	11,453	6,390
1991	245,974	187,870	977	188,847	20,215	-322	168,310	48,980	28,684	21,262	18,674	11,569	6,369
1992	266,536	202,207	2,056	204,263	21,320	-410	182,533	51,179	32,824	22,792	20,140	11,694	6,351
1993	275,770	210,627	1,712	212,338	22,492	-592	189,254	52,093	34,424	23,351	20,546	11,810	6,441
1994	290,485	221,803	2,306	224,110	24,002	-686	199,421	55,387	35,676	24,385	21,372	11,913	6,611
1995	308,424	234,627	604	235,231	25,277	-930	209,024	61,346	38,054	25,684	22,467	12,008	6,773
1996	328,069	246,950	2,501	249,451	26,332	-937	222,182	65,864	40,024	27,109	23,570	12,102	6,875
1997	346,358	262,448	2,135	264,583	27,787	-955	235,841	69,748	40,768	28,423	24,527	12,186	6,981
1998	366,677	278,823	1,539	280,362	29,387	-1,037	249,939	75,180	41,559	29,880	25,623	12,272	7,139
1999	381,400	296,171	1,086	297,257	30,785	-1,149	265,323	73,867	42,210	30,860	26,398	12,359	7,219
2000	409,650	315,460	1,812	317,272	32,341	-1,383	283,547	81,213	44,889	32,946	28,172	12,434	7,360
2001	421,549	326,065	1,691	327,756	33,140	-1,734	292,882	80,231	48,436	33,755	29,057	12,488	7,310
2002	426,753	332,249	996	333,245	33,642	-1,931	297,672	77,004	52,077	34,071	29,991	12,526	7,220
2003	434,774	338,478	1,940	340,419	34,503	-2,177	303,738	76,736	54,300	34,627	30,866	12,556	7,197
2004	454,822	353,479	3,709	357,188	36,555	-2,165	318,468	80,092	56,262	36,126	32,310	12,590	7,252
2005	475,288	367,358	1,731	369,089	38,640	-2,184	328,265	85,271	61,752	37,692	33,380	12,610	7,338
2006	508,525	388,615	1,907	390,522	40,444	-1,828	348,250	97,489	62,786	40,219	35,385	12,644	7,456
2007	537,796	403,004	3,110	406,114	42,264	-1,224	362,626	105,836	69,334	42,360	36,988	12,696	7,588
2008	556,032	410,357	4,688	415,045	43,051	-811	371,183	108,520	76,328	43,620	38,191	12,747	7,568
2009	531,433	392,410	2,705	395,115	41,164	-1,814	352,136	93,567	85,730	41,529	37,506	12,797	7,327
2010	541,261	397,147	2,683	399,830	41,819	-1,825	356,186	91,861	93,214	42,154	37,857	12,840	7,252
2011	569,681	414,601	5,532	420,134	39,281	-2,239	378,614	101,757	89,310	44,303	39,089	12,859	7,380
2012	593,049	431,524	3,210	434,734	40,979	-2,015	391,740	111,825	89,485	46,067	40,557	12,874	7,432
2013	599,119	437,665	8,298	445,963	47,218	-2,134	396,611	109,310	93,198	46,477	40,493	12,891	7,495
2014	613,672	453,039	4,119	457,157	48,951	-2,255	405,952	113,222	94,498	47,643	41,334	12,881	7,596
2015	636,281	472,003	1,738	473,741	50,735	-2,357	420,650	117,690	97,941	49,471	42583	12862	...

... = Not available.

Personal Income and Employment by Region and State: Indiana

(Millions of dollars, except as noted.)

Year	Personal income, total	Earnings by place of work			Less: Contributions for government social insurance	Plus: Adjustment for residence	Equals: Net earnings by place of residence	Plus: Dividends, interest, and rent	Plus: Personal current transfer receipts	Per capita (dollars)		Population (thousands)	Total employment (thousands)
		Nonfarm	Farm	Total						Personal income	Disposable personal income		
1960	10,410	8,580	366	8,946	415	41	8,571	1,235	604	2,227	1,990	4,674	...
1961	10,727	8,636	464	9,100	411	44	8,732	1,303	692	2,268	2,039	4,730	...
1962	11,481	9,337	452	9,788	461	49	9,376	1,408	697	2,424	2,167	4,736	...
1963	12,058	9,823	470	10,294	526	49	9,816	1,518	724	2,513	2,232	4,799	...
1964	12,837	10,647	301	10,948	545	47	10,450	1,639	749	2,644	2,372	4,856	...
1965	14,190	11,598	553	12,151	581	50	11,619	1,765	806	2,883	2,584	4,922	...
1966	15,317	12,847	480	13,327	818	56	12,565	1,886	866	3,064	2,720	4,999	...
1967	16,041	13,455	431	13,886	916	60	13,029	2,001	1,011	3,175	2,811	5,053	...
1968	17,415	14,658	379	15,037	993	69	14,113	2,121	1,180	3,419	3,002	5,093	...
1969	19,197	16,024	550	16,574	1,097	45	15,523	2,394	1,279	3,733	3,233	5,143	2,327
1970	19,958	16,458	381	16,838	1,115	78	15,802	2,656	1,501	3,835	3,363	5,204	2,291
1971	21,704	17,495	596	18,092	1,227	140	17,004	2,910	1,790	4,134	3,664	5,250	2,290
1972	23,748	19,404	507	19,910	1,440	179	18,649	3,129	1,970	4,484	3,931	5,296	2,367
1973	27,245	21,768	1,228	22,996	1,863	221	21,353	3,557	2,335	5,112	4,523	5,329	2,483
1974	29,138	23,356	735	24,091	2,089	282	22,284	4,098	2,757	5,447	4,743	5,350	2,493
1975	31,453	24,052	1,097	25,149	2,120	329	23,359	4,583	3,512	5,878	5,216	5,351	2,405
1976	34,953	27,314	1,076	28,391	2,438	387	26,340	4,940	3,674	6,507	5,709	5,372	2,489
1977	38,693	30,887	724	31,611	2,754	445	29,302	5,534	3,857	7,159	6,256	5,405	2,578
1978	43,179	34,762	731	35,493	3,190	500	32,803	6,134	4,242	7,928	6,898	5,446	2,670
1979	47,590	38,219	672	38,891	3,630	578	35,838	6,880	4,872	8,692	7,529	5,475	2,708
1980	51,177	39,339	379	39,718	3,714	691	36,695	8,383	6,099	9,321	8,132	5,491	2,626
1981	56,129	42,232	306	42,538	4,296	749	38,990	10,326	6,813	10,242	8,893	5,480	2,603
1982	58,057	42,264	307	42,571	4,390	810	38,992	11,474	7,592	10,618	9,302	5,468	2,522
1983	60,857	44,702	-260	44,442	4,660	838	40,620	12,064	8,172	11,166	9,851	5,450	2,542
1984	67,574	49,235	753	49,988	5,258	984	45,714	13,290	8,569	12,380	10,970	5,458	2,642
1985	71,325	52,242	682	52,924	5,686	1,058	48,296	14,011	9,019	13,065	11,535	5,459	2,695
1986	75,221	55,389	578	55,967	6,056	1,135	51,047	14,649	9,525	13,792	12,211	5,454	2,755
1987	79,856	59,702	763	60,465	6,434	1,186	55,216	14,931	9,709	14,591	12,871	5,473	2,849
1988	85,438	64,803	284	65,087	7,215	1,284	59,156	15,993	10,290	15,558	13,735	5,492	2,935
1989	93,123	69,243	965	70,208	7,737	1,350	63,821	18,113	11,188	16,859	14,814	5,524	3,010
1990	98,288	73,053	863	73,916	8,408	1,492	67,000	19,130	12,158	17,685	15,555	5,558	3,070
1991	101,120	76,168	242	76,409	8,884	1,501	69,026	18,716	13,378	18,005	15,879	5,616	3,072
1992	109,582	81,986	849	82,835	9,455	1,657	75,037	19,259	15,286	19,311	17,110	5,675	3,121
1993	115,567	86,657	866	87,523	10,062	1,877	79,338	20,092	16,138	20,137	17,797	5,739	3,197
1994	122,830	92,535	828	93,363	10,900	2,008	84,471	21,522	16,837	21,201	18,657	5,794	3,287
1995	128,384	96,561	349	96,910	11,416	2,289	87,783	23,450	17,151	21,940	19,275	5,851	3,379
1996	135,673	100,881	1,196	102,076	11,792	2,427	92,711	24,854	18,108	22,972	20,116	5,906	3,418
1997	142,738	106,555	1,161	107,716	12,409	2,555	97,862	26,285	18,590	23,968	20,891	5,955	3,476
1998	154,099	115,812	769	116,582	13,176	2,584	105,990	28,805	19,305	25,688	22,349	5,999	3,544
1999	160,523	122,709	473	123,182	13,815	2,836	112,203	28,118	20,202	26,555	23,133	6,045	3,595
2000	171,313	129,529	873	130,403	14,396	3,124	119,130	30,447	21,736	28,122	24,633	6,092	3,646
2001	175,575	131,375	1,068	132,443	14,582	3,384	121,246	30,309	24,021	28,652	25,120	6,128	3,585
2002	177,603	134,264	474	134,738	14,955	2,869	122,652	29,464	25,486	28,850	25,684	6,156	3,551
2003	182,388	138,076	1,266	139,342	15,468	2,772	126,645	29,235	26,508	29,433	26,453	6,197	3,551
2004	191,312	144,926	2,052	146,977	16,253	2,859	133,584	29,659	28,068	30,693	27,697	6,233	3,589
2005	196,346	149,424	1,332	150,756	16,986	2,677	136,447	29,333	30,565	31,272	28,018	6,279	3,630
2006	208,245	156,298	1,136	157,435	17,861	2,922	142,496	32,744	33,004	32,884	29,350	6,333	3,672
2007	216,066	159,437	1,507	160,945	18,374	3,646	146,217	35,244	34,605	33,868	30,050	6,380	3,719
2008	225,168	161,469	2,259	163,729	18,799	3,871	148,801	36,294	40,072	35,047	31,251	6,425	3,683
2009	216,953	151,865	1,494	153,359	18,032	4,479	139,805	32,874	44,274	33,588	30,639	6,459	3,526
2010	223,204	156,504	1,581	158,085	18,448	4,277	143,914	31,986	47,305	34,390	31,224	6,490	3,519
2011	236,923	164,071	2,698	166,770	17,110	4,455	154,114	35,428	47,381	36,357	32,668	6,517	3,585
2012	248,346	172,352	2,320	174,672	17,806	4,397	161,263	38,161	48,922	37,987	34,296	6,538	3,634
2013	251,599	175,100	5,258	180,358	20,679	4,731	164,410	37,920	49,269	38,291	34,287	6,571	3,675
2014	261,092	182,809	3,689	186,498	21,522	5,135	170,111	39,364	51,618	39,578	35,394	6,597	3,729
2015	271,426	190,617	2,233	192,850	22,266	5,315	175,899	40,951	54,575	40,998	36,471	6,620	...

... = Not available.

Personal Income and Employment by Region and State: Iowa

(Millions of dollars, except as noted.)

Year	Personal income, total	Earnings by place of work			Less: Contributions for government social insurance	Plus: Adjustment for residence	Equals: Net earnings by place of residence	Plus: Dividends, interest, and rent	Plus: Personal current transfer receipts	Per capita (dollars)		Population (thousands)	Total employment (thousands)
		Nonfarm	Farm	Total						Personal income	Disposable personal income		
1960	5,737	3,914	732	4,646	186	35	4,495	857	385	2,082	1,873	2,756	...
1961	6,077	4,029	852	4,881	189	38	4,730	922	424	2,205	1,994	2,756	...
1962	6,336	4,210	883	5,094	203	41	4,931	961	444	2,304	2,083	2,750	...
1963	6,739	4,433	1,001	5,434	233	43	5,244	1,031	464	2,453	2,220	2,747	...
1964	7,060	4,751	921	5,672	247	47	5,472	1,109	479	2,571	2,346	2,746	...
1965	7,827	5,080	1,247	6,328	261	50	6,118	1,188	522	2,855	2,599	2,742	...
1966	8,529	5,651	1,346	6,997	352	55	6,699	1,263	566	3,088	2,782	2,762	...
1967	8,691	6,040	1,080	7,120	418	59	6,762	1,255	675	3,112	2,797	2,793	...
1968	9,363	6,503	1,021	7,524	457	63	7,130	1,451	782	3,340	2,979	2,803	...
1969	10,412	7,130	1,238	8,368	543	90	7,914	1,642	856	3,712	3,280	2,805	1,289
1970	11,124	7,556	1,215	8,772	567	97	8,301	1,831	992	3,933	3,504	2,829	1,295
1971	11,668	8,066	1,012	9,078	626	97	8,549	1,993	1,127	4,091	3,686	2,852	1,297
1972	13,068	8,790	1,485	10,274	719	103	9,659	2,193	1,216	4,568	4,049	2,861	1,316
1973	15,673	9,844	2,732	12,576	930	98	11,744	2,525	1,404	5,472	4,887	2,864	1,374
1974	16,254	11,021	1,721	12,742	1,092	91	11,741	2,887	1,626	5,668	4,930	2,868	1,407
1975	18,218	12,005	1,970	13,975	1,167	107	12,915	3,286	2,017	6,323	5,592	2,881	1,407
1976	19,334	13,575	1,227	14,802	1,322	100	13,580	3,535	2,219	6,658	5,833	2,904	1,455
1977	21,325	15,132	1,226	16,358	1,459	74	14,973	4,007	2,345	7,317	6,412	2,914	1,488
1978	24,592	16,708	2,441	19,149	1,671	73	17,550	4,458	2,584	8,425	7,406	2,919	1,513
1979	26,338	18,714	1,575	20,289	1,955	81	18,415	5,027	2,895	9,030	7,855	2,917	1,554
1980	27,991	19,786	717	20,503	2,058	100	18,546	6,033	3,412	9,606	8,339	2,914	1,537
1981	31,667	20,948	1,639	22,587	2,315	127	20,399	7,386	3,882	10,890	9,462	2,908	1,507
1982	32,600	20,959	816	21,775	2,344	199	19,631	8,543	4,426	11,287	9,911	2,888	1,471
1983	33,320	21,851	6	21,857	2,426	213	19,644	8,933	4,743	11,608	10,282	2,871	1,474
1984	37,002	23,546	1,463	25,008	2,684	241	22,566	9,578	4,859	12,944	11,636	2,859	1,499
1985	38,315	24,209	1,752	25,961	2,810	279	23,430	9,729	5,156	13,541	12,172	2,830	1,495
1986	39,614	24,994	2,128	27,122	2,966	274	24,430	9,833	5,351	14,189	12,786	2,792	1,494
1987	41,467	26,830	2,459	29,290	3,174	268	26,384	9,618	5,466	14,986	13,377	2,767	1,514
1988	42,751	28,862	1,646	30,509	3,527	311	27,293	9,744	5,714	15,443	13,752	2,768	1,557
1989	46,533	30,894	2,400	33,294	3,765	322	29,850	10,581	6,101	16,795	14,901	2,771	1,600
1990	49,067	32,692	2,504	35,196	4,079	319	31,436	11,001	6,630	17,644	15,618	2,781	1,635
1991	50,203	34,168	1,780	35,949	4,285	373	32,037	11,039	7,127	17,945	15,918	2,798	1,654
1992	53,915	36,479	2,700	39,180	4,529	411	35,062	11,155	7,698	19,130	17,056	2,818	1,669
1993	54,138	38,279	889	39,168	4,773	401	34,796	11,284	8,058	19,083	16,949	2,837	1,692
1994	59,006	40,798	2,861	43,659	5,142	423	38,940	11,690	8,376	20,698	18,431	2,851	1,725
1995	61,476	42,830	1,818	44,647	5,400	484	39,731	12,921	8,824	21,440	19,055	2,867	1,785
1996	67,007	44,989	3,724	48,714	5,382	529	43,861	13,877	9,268	23,266	20,692	2,880	1,815
1997	70,118	47,640	3,397	51,037	5,908	604	45,734	14,854	9,530	24,253	21,408	2,891	1,841
1998	73,514	51,391	2,162	53,553	6,289	695	47,960	15,784	9,769	25,324	22,333	2,903	1,877
1999	75,472	54,164	1,603	55,767	6,557	796	50,006	15,333	10,133	25,868	22,813	2,918	1,893
2000	80,727	56,983	2,463	59,447	6,805	881	53,523	16,351	10,852	27,561	24,393	2,929	1,913
2001	83,172	58,737	2,273	61,010	6,967	925	54,968	16,459	11,746	28,367	25,164	2,932	1,899
2002	85,384	60,387	2,146	62,533	7,123	796	56,206	16,251	12,927	29,099	26,287	2,934	1,878
2003	87,371	62,879	2,343	65,222	7,447	730	58,505	15,989	12,877	29,698	27,029	2,942	1,872
2004	94,955	67,077	4,804	71,881	7,837	1,067	65,112	16,501	13,342	32,148	29,397	2,954	1,901
2005	97,440	70,278	3,852	74,131	8,247	1,067	66,951	16,241	14,248	32,869	29,805	2,964	1,935
2006	103,126	74,425	2,835	77,260	8,687	1,177	69,751	17,656	15,719	34,575	31,165	2,983	1,963
2007	110,415	77,853	3,840	81,692	9,119	1,279	73,853	19,846	16,716	36,815	32,935	2,999	1,991
2008	118,676	82,207	4,903	87,110	9,540	1,146	78,716	20,897	19,062	39,339	35,357	3,017	1,996
2009	115,623	80,591	3,357	83,949	9,422	1,158	75,684	19,553	20,386	38,123	34,911	3,033	1,959
2010	118,006	81,778	3,833	85,611	9,720	1,165	77,056	19,243	21,708	38,687	35,299	3,050	1,945
2011	128,905	85,351	7,594	92,945	9,111	1,283	85,116	21,715	22,073	42,058	38,069	3,065	1,971
2012	133,675	89,176	6,795	95,972	9,392	1,200	87,780	23,881	22,014	43,458	39,203	3,076	1,988
2013	135,242	89,913	8,893	98,806	10,759	1,196	89,243	23,720	22,279	43,735	39,235	3,092	2,012
2014	139,625	94,505	7,377	101,882	11,162	1,013	91,732	24,638	23,254	44,937	40,237	3,107	2,032
2015	140,501	98,193	2,654	100,848	11,475	1,080	90,453	25,674	24,374	44,971	39915	3124	...

... = Not available.

Personal Income and Employment by Region and State: Kansas

(Millions of dollars, except as noted.)

Year	Personal income, total	Earnings by place of work			Less: Contributions for government social insurance	Plus: Adjustment for residence	Equals: Net earnings by place of residence	Plus: Dividends, interest, and rent	Plus: Personal current transfer receipts	Per capita (dollars)		Population (thousands)	Total employment (thousands)
		Nonfarm	Farm	Total						Personal income	Disposable personal income		
1960	4,825	3,298	443	3,740	161	175	3,755	768	302	2,210	1,990	2,183	...
1961	5,040	3,457	451	3,908	177	178	3,909	796	335	2,275	2,052	2,215	...
1962	5,244	3,639	422	4,062	183	194	4,073	826	345	2,350	2,110	2,231	...
1963	5,365	3,739	404	4,143	206	215	4,151	847	366	2,420	2,163	2,217	...
1964	5,650	3,985	368	4,354	213	236	4,377	894	379	2,558	2,330	2,209	...
1965	6,025	4,160	462	4,623	222	259	4,660	951	413	2,731	2,486	2,206	...
1966	6,456	4,556	478	5,035	293	295	5,036	976	444	2,935	2,635	2,200	...
1967	6,760	4,846	407	5,253	340	325	5,239	990	532	3,077	2,757	2,197	...
1968	7,364	5,318	400	5,718	377	355	5,697	1,051	616	3,323	2,950	2,216	...
1969	8,203	5,789	465	6,254	421	448	6,280	1,234	689	3,669	3,230	2,236	1,029
1970	8,897	6,094	606	6,700	442	446	6,704	1,389	803	3,958	3,511	2,248	1,017
1971	9,657	6,570	706	7,276	492	439	7,223	1,518	916	4,299	3,868	2,246	1,022
1972	10,766	7,265	963	8,228	573	459	8,114	1,668	985	4,773	4,254	2,256	1,048
1973	12,261	8,107	1,386	9,493	734	473	9,232	1,878	1,151	5,415	4,812	2,264	1,090
1974	13,263	9,042	1,060	10,102	853	486	9,735	2,205	1,324	5,848	5,139	2,268	1,122
1975	14,515	10,027	807	10,834	936	501	10,398	2,503	1,613	6,370	5,668	2,279	1,133
1976	15,745	11,281	584	11,865	1,069	511	11,307	2,655	1,783	6,850	6,082	2,299	1,169
1977	17,174	12,418	498	12,916	1,175	555	12,295	2,949	1,929	7,409	6,533	2,318	1,208
1978	19,009	14,074	285	14,359	1,374	600	13,586	3,320	2,104	8,149	7,159	2,333	1,252
1979	21,700	15,888	706	16,594	1,615	646	15,625	3,754	2,321	9,244	8,041	2,347	1,296
1980	23,852	17,403	101	17,503	1,757	721	16,468	4,623	2,761	10,068	8,743	2,369	1,309
1981	27,024	19,048	345	19,393	2,055	743	18,081	5,762	3,181	11,332	9,745	2,385	1,322
1982	29,305	19,739	577	20,316	2,180	764	18,900	6,837	3,569	12,204	10,543	2,401	1,306
1983	30,570	20,774	384	21,157	2,288	741	19,611	7,154	3,804	12,655	11,161	2,416	1,323
1984	33,478	22,757	751	23,507	2,567	800	21,741	7,816	3,922	13,811	12,298	2,424	1,365
1985	35,289	23,854	811	24,664	2,732	853	22,786	8,368	4,136	14,538	12,896	2,427	1,368
1986	36,988	25,191	938	26,129	2,885	844	24,088	8,560	4,340	15,205	13,598	2,433	1,368
1987	38,670	26,499	1,173	27,672	3,003	915	25,584	8,624	4,462	15,813	14,030	2,445	1,421
1988	40,682	28,109	1,141	29,250	3,318	919	26,852	9,148	4,682	16,524	14,667	2,462	1,432
1989	42,989	29,959	831	30,790	3,510	976	28,257	9,591	5,142	17,385	15,319	2,473	1,454
1990	45,671	31,609	1,383	32,992	3,887	969	30,074	10,015	5,582	18,406	16,285	2,481	1,474
1991	47,311	32,991	1,035	34,025	4,119	948	30,854	10,393	6,064	18,934	16,818	2,499	1,489
1992	51,020	35,596	1,408	37,004	4,382	1,029	33,651	10,646	6,723	20,147	18,002	2,532	1,502
1993	53,383	37,402	1,346	38,748	4,591	1,117	35,274	10,987	7,122	20,881	18,612	2,557	1,525
1994	55,822	39,263	1,436	40,699	4,897	1,068	36,870	11,595	7,357	21,632	19,243	2,581	1,551
1995	58,154	41,255	794	42,050	5,091	1,160	38,119	12,283	7,752	22,358	19,780	2,601	1,600
1996	61,973	43,572	1,508	45,079	5,327	1,150	40,902	13,056	8,014	23,703	20,878	2,615	1,632
1997	65,845	46,708	1,421	48,129	5,697	1,047	43,479	13,956	8,410	24,986	21,851	2,635	1,677
1998	70,274	50,351	1,309	51,660	6,068	1,068	46,660	15,069	8,544	26,413	23,085	2,661	1,723
1999	72,968	53,228	1,403	54,631	6,343	1,022	49,310	14,756	8,902	27,244	23,811	2,678	1,740
2000	77,427	56,467	1,014	57,480	6,655	1,125	51,950	15,826	9,651	28,744	25,096	2,694	1,759
2001	80,494	58,948	1,164	60,111	6,870	1,110	54,352	15,593	10,549	29,789	26,139	2,702	1,767
2002	81,029	60,214	497	60,712	7,008	1,028	54,732	15,093	11,204	29,861	26,704	2,714	1,752
2003	83,791	61,557	1,679	63,236	7,172	1,024	57,088	14,994	11,709	30,772	27,816	2,723	1,739
2004	87,496	64,978	1,608	66,586	7,552	1,079	60,114	15,342	12,041	31,999	29,008	2,734	1,750
2005	91,920	67,813	1,931	69,743	7,906	1,157	62,995	16,243	12,682	33,483	30,044	2,745	1,763
2006	99,431	72,627	1,139	73,767	8,405	1,161	66,522	19,273	13,636	35,987	32,056	2,763	1,796
2007	106,124	75,849	1,591	77,440	8,802	1,355	69,993	21,463	14,667	38,122	33,702	2,784	1,846
2008	114,950	80,296	2,255	82,550	9,191	1,445	74,804	23,589	16,557	40,936	36,343	2,808	1,861
2009	110,161	76,975	1,967	78,942	8,995	1,801	71,748	20,393	18,020	38,889	35,379	2,833	1,818
2010	112,171	78,849	2,438	81,288	9,244	1,804	73,848	19,150	19,173	39,235	35,545	2,859	1,802
2011	121,695	83,112	3,873	86,985	8,549	1,402	79,837	22,228	19,630	42,403	38,119	2,870	1,819
2012	126,190	86,121	3,113	89,234	8,848	1,863	82,249	24,567	19,374	43,725	39,339	2,886	1,840
2013	128,315	87,990	5,126	93,116	10,231	1,593	84,479	24,217	19,619	44,311	39,601	2,896	1,867
2014	130,364	91,109	3,056	94,165	10,645	1,510	85,029	25,057	20,277	44,891	40,010	2,904	1,897
2015	133,591	93,520	2,233	95,754	10,860	1,658	86,552	26,030	21,009	45,876	40,640	2,912	...

... = Not available.

Personal Income and Employment by Region and State: Kentucky

(Millions of dollars, except as noted.)

Year	Personal income, total	Earnings by place of work			Less: Contributions for government social insurance	Plus: Adjustment for residence	Equals: Net earnings by place of residence	Plus: Dividends, interest, and rent	Plus: Personal current transfer receipts	Per capita (dollars)		Population (thousands)	Total employment (thousands)
		Nonfarm	Farm	Total						Personal income	Disposable personal income		
1960	5,034	3,743	323	4,066	184	89	3,971	634	429	1,655	1,498	3,041	...
1961	5,360	3,843	396	4,240	185	81	4,136	669	555	1,755	1,597	3,054	...
1962	5,688	4,183	396	4,579	209	84	4,454	730	504	1,847	1,669	3,079	...
1963	5,980	4,451	405	4,856	240	84	4,699	776	504	1,931	1,748	3,096	...
1964	6,238	4,742	297	5,039	245	91	4,885	823	530	1,994	1,815	3,129	...
1965	6,766	5,126	366	5,492	258	96	5,331	856	579	2,155	1,958	3,140	...
1966	7,397	5,714	382	6,096	339	104	5,862	908	627	2,350	2,113	3,147	...
1967	8,002	6,215	383	6,598	400	80	6,277	978	746	2,523	2,278	3,172	...
1968	8,737	6,869	372	7,242	446	86	6,882	1,012	843	2,735	2,446	3,195	...
1969	9,702	7,507	428	7,935	509	164	7,590	1,168	944	3,034	2,666	3,198	1,332
1970	10,517	8,073	393	8,466	547	153	8,072	1,341	1,105	3,256	2,890	3,231	1,336
1971	11,445	8,790	408	9,198	615	97	8,680	1,467	1,298	3,470	3,109	3,298	1,360
1972	12,655	9,727	507	10,234	713	91	9,611	1,602	1,441	3,793	3,354	3,336	1,392
1973	14,211	10,986	579	11,565	919	45	10,691	1,801	1,720	4,215	3,768	3,372	1,461
1974	16,007	12,226	665	12,891	1,060	18	11,849	2,107	2,051	4,685	4,108	3,417	1,496
1975	17,446	13,133	482	13,616	1,122	11	12,505	2,358	2,584	5,030	4,508	3,469	1,465
1976	19,489	14,842	557	15,399	1,291	-17	14,091	2,566	2,831	5,520	4,923	3,530	1,523
1977	21,868	16,777	683	17,460	1,451	6	16,015	2,886	2,968	6,117	5,407	3,575	1,579
1978	24,358	18,976	605	19,580	1,686	29	17,924	3,256	3,178	6,745	5,938	3,611	1,645
1979	27,352	21,198	679	21,877	1,944	26	19,958	3,690	3,704	7,507	6,603	3,644	1,665
1980	29,771	22,228	561	22,789	2,059	57	20,787	4,515	4,468	8,125	7,181	3,664	1,642
1981	33,115	23,947	939	24,885	2,392	16	22,510	5,566	5,039	9,022	7,928	3,670	1,634
1982	35,287	24,799	902	25,701	2,526	10	23,186	6,602	5,499	9,580	8,444	3,683	1,616
1983	36,630	26,076	232	26,308	2,653	33	23,687	6,989	5,953	9,915	8,793	3,694	1,624
1984	40,883	28,757	1,121	29,878	3,000	2	26,880	7,774	6,228	11,063	9,906	3,695	1,676
1985	42,685	30,265	876	31,141	3,218	-4	27,919	8,250	6,517	11,553	10,299	3,695	1,698
1986	43,905	31,247	648	31,895	3,453	22	28,463	8,617	6,824	11,905	10,613	3,688	1,733
1987	46,333	33,495	731	34,226	3,682	4	30,549	8,727	7,057	12,579	11,158	3,683	1,765
1988	50,390	36,852	778	37,631	4,098	-6	33,526	9,369	7,495	13,693	12,197	3,680	1,816
1989	54,151	38,980	1,142	40,121	4,407	-42	35,672	10,244	8,235	14,726	13,027	3,677	1,865
1990	57,483	41,304	1,123	42,426	4,818	-35	37,573	10,899	9,010	15,561	13,736	3,694	1,906
1991	60,643	43,201	1,123	44,324	5,093	-42	39,188	11,209	10,245	16,292	14,467	3,722	1,903
1992	65,372	47,018	1,309	48,326	5,520	-263	42,544	11,580	11,248	17,361	15,427	3,765	1,949
1993	67,907	49,336	1,115	50,451	5,886	-253	44,312	11,893	11,702	17,813	15,810	3,812	1,993
1994	71,377	52,018	1,166	53,184	6,331	-336	46,517	12,587	12,274	18,544	16,418	3,849	2,035
1995	74,799	54,302	708	55,011	6,635	-337	48,039	13,558	13,202	19,241	16,969	3,887	2,110
1996	79,386	56,963	1,138	58,101	6,898	-319	50,884	14,520	13,982	20,254	17,822	3,920	2,141
1997	84,294	60,649	1,139	61,788	7,299	-319	54,171	15,346	14,777	21,325	18,666	3,953	2,189
1998	89,446	64,607	1,011	65,619	7,748	-191	57,679	16,596	15,171	22,443	19,598	3,985	2,223
1999	93,434	69,087	784	69,871	8,258	-275	61,338	16,360	15,736	23,253	20,307	4,018	2,264
2000	101,038	73,453	1,493	74,945	8,525	-296	66,124	18,006	16,908	24,954	21,877	4,049	2,307
2001	104,686	76,334	1,082	77,417	8,743	-575	68,099	18,166	18,421	25,733	22,548	4,068	2,284
2002	107,073	78,979	680	79,659	9,025	-942	69,691	17,664	19,718	26,180	23,346	4,090	2,262
2003	109,914	82,042	703	82,745	9,283	-1,278	72,184	17,393	20,337	26,697	23,971	4,117	2,272
2004	116,280	86,665	1,246	87,911	9,671	-1,390	76,850	17,538	21,892	28,046	25,330	4,146	2,298
2005	122,015	90,916	1,577	92,493	10,150	-1,721	80,622	18,206	23,187	29,171	26,174	4,183	2,334
2006	129,094	94,922	1,236	96,159	10,690	-1,838	83,631	20,478	24,984	30,596	27,439	4,219	2,373
2007	134,862	97,891	773	98,663	11,168	-1,686	85,809	22,175	26,877	31,682	28,262	4,257	2,414
2008	141,364	100,773	443	101,217	11,640	-1,691	87,886	23,166	30,312	32,953	29,425	4,290	2,403
2009	139,231	97,279	708	97,987	11,512	-1,857	84,619	21,179	33,434	32,251	29,423	4,317	2,328
2010	143,444	100,773	377	101,150	11,829	-2,116	87,204	20,836	35,403	32,977	30,000	4,350	2,322
2011	151,109	104,896	921	105,817	10,943	-2,293	92,581	22,619	35,909	34,578	31,223	4,370	2,365
2012	156,990	108,710	926	109,635	11,301	-2,330	96,005	25,008	35,978	35,814	32,438	4,383	2,385
2013	158,238	109,516	2,118	111,634	12,949	-2,005	96,681	24,744	36,814	35,967	32,334	4,400	2,402
2014	165,044	113,748	1,268	115,016	13,527	-2,031	99,458	25,586	40,001	37,396	33,581	4,413	2,437
2015	172,550	118,177	1,489	119,666	13,992	-2,153	103,522	26,589	42,440	38,989	34,865	4,426	...

... = Not available.

Personal Income and Employment by Region and State: Louisiana

(Millions of dollars, except as noted.)

Year	Personal income, total	Derivation of personal income									Per capita (dollars)		Population (thousands)	Total employment (thousands)
		Earnings by place of work			Less: Contributions for government social insurance	Plus: Adjustment for residence	Equals: Net earnings by place of residence	Plus: Dividends, interest, and rent	Plus: Personal current transfer receipts		Personal income	Disposable personal income		
		Nonfarm	Farm	Total										
1960	5,596	4,388	186	4,574	185	-1	4,387	773	436		1,717	1,567	3,260	...
1961	5,825	4,507	218	4,725	187	-1	4,536	802	486		1,772	1,617	3,287	...
1962	6,159	4,798	204	5,003	208	-0	4,795	860	504		1,841	1,677	3,345	...
1963	6,567	5,094	261	5,355	246	-0	5,109	922	535		1,945	1,763	3,377	...
1964	7,018	5,539	226	5,765	262	-0	5,503	961	554		2,037	1,866	3,446	...
1965	7,607	6,062	198	6,260	286	-0	5,974	1,035	598		2,176	1,995	3,496	...
1966	8,415	6,823	239	7,062	389	3	6,676	1,097	642		2,371	2,142	3,550	...
1967	9,222	7,467	267	7,734	432	5	7,307	1,163	752		2,575	2,333	3,581	...
1968	10,091	8,213	299	8,512	489	4	8,027	1,213	850		2,801	2,517	3,603	...
1969	10,706	8,719	241	8,961	569	4	8,396	1,348	961		2,958	2,639	3,619	1,440
1970	11,584	9,217	283	9,500	592	4	8,912	1,518	1,154		3,174	2,872	3,650	1,429
1971	12,625	9,990	320	10,310	658	-8	9,644	1,663	1,318		3,402	3,082	3,711	1,445
1972	13,809	10,982	349	11,330	757	-21	10,553	1,806	1,450		3,671	3,302	3,762	1,488
1973	15,401	12,129	579	12,708	960	-37	11,711	2,004	1,686		4,065	3,668	3,789	1,550
1974	17,504	13,683	614	14,297	1,118	-54	13,125	2,405	1,975		4,581	4,096	3,821	1,598
1975	19,685	15,468	419	15,887	1,243	-83	14,561	2,684	2,440		5,064	4,578	3,887	1,641
1976	22,198	17,739	455	18,194	1,454	-112	16,628	2,872	2,698		5,617	5,022	3,952	1,702
1977	24,785	20,004	454	20,458	1,627	-138	18,693	3,189	2,903		6,172	5,501	4,016	1,756
1978	28,369	23,237	373	23,610	1,933	-184	21,493	3,719	3,157		6,965	6,162	4,073	1,849
1979	32,216	26,362	503	26,865	2,277	-229	24,359	4,264	3,592		7,783	6,833	4,139	1,897
1980	37,069	30,166	175	30,341	2,594	-331	27,417	5,360	4,292		8,778	7,676	4,223	1,964
1981	42,736	34,422	266	34,688	3,177	-351	31,160	6,786	4,790		9,977	8,654	4,283	2,030
1982	45,908	35,944	263	36,207	3,376	-331	32,500	7,882	5,525		10,547	9,291	4,353	2,023
1983	47,840	36,402	232	36,634	3,378	-312	32,944	8,610	6,285		10,884	9,701	4,395	1,984
1984	50,914	38,490	323	38,813	3,663	-302	34,848	9,522	6,544		11,570	10,365	4,400	2,023
1985	52,997	39,433	231	39,664	3,775	-273	35,616	10,333	7,048		12,023	10,759	4,408	2,009
1986	53,025	38,659	235	38,894	3,646	-218	35,029	10,258	7,737		12,032	10,911	4,407	1,928
1987	53,217	38,803	396	39,199	3,609	-185	35,405	9,977	7,834		12,250	11,088	4,344	1,904
1988	56,163	41,079	629	41,708	4,014	-166	37,528	10,414	8,221		13,095	11,900	4,289	1,935
1989	59,670	43,194	469	43,663	4,273	-133	39,257	11,422	8,991		14,030	12,667	4,253	1,953
1990	64,267	46,857	404	47,262	4,760	-111	42,391	11,971	9,905		15,224	13,730	4,222	2,005
1991	67,720	49,240	469	49,709	5,135	-127	44,448	11,947	11,325		15,922	14,392	4,253	2,030
1992	72,591	52,309	577	52,886	5,381	-125	47,381	12,215	12,995		16,909	15,360	4,293	2,038
1993	76,205	54,427	590	55,017	5,634	-129	49,254	12,644	14,307		17,655	16,019	4,316	2,086
1994	81,218	57,625	679	58,304	6,083	-148	52,072	13,322	15,824		18,682	16,925	4,347	2,126
1995	85,205	60,491	673	61,163	6,384	-177	54,603	14,598	16,005		19,459	17,587	4,379	2,194
1996	88,954	63,326	884	64,210	6,696	-204	57,310	15,352	16,292		20,222	18,099	4,399	2,239
1997	93,605	67,333	643	67,976	7,088	-219	60,670	16,348	16,587		21,173	18,837	4,421	2,290
1998	97,900	70,918	466	71,384	7,529	-237	63,618	17,469	16,813		22,048	19,637	4,440	2,337
1999	99,954	72,867	637	73,505	7,650	-217	65,637	17,066	17,251		22,407	20,023	4,461	2,351
2000	105,401	76,781	623	77,404	7,906	-231	69,268	18,445	17,688		23,570	21,054	4,472	2,387
2001	112,488	81,760	659	82,419	8,345	-206	73,868	18,336	20,283		25,121	22,424	4,478	2,396
2002	115,335	84,699	430	85,130	8,638	-414	76,078	17,894	21,363		25,646	23,286	4,497	2,398
2003	118,760	88,102	797	88,899	8,884	-701	79,314	18,023	21,422		26,268	24,093	4,521	2,417
2004	125,060	92,405	791	93,197	9,167	-821	83,208	18,201	23,651		27,472	25,319	4,552	2,431
2005	134,132	96,149	681	96,830	9,388	-636	86,807	19,616	27,709		29,308	26,943	4,577	2,396
2006	143,051	103,352	718	104,070	10,068	-28	93,974	23,506	25,571		33,247	30,188	4,303	2,409
2007	156,895	109,552	831	110,383	10,737	-106	99,541	30,746	26,608		35,857	32,261	4,376	2,499
2008	167,924	118,672	468	119,140	11,405	-460	107,275	30,335	30,314		37,858	33,968	4,436	2,550
2009	163,264	115,923	642	116,565	11,367	-473	104,725	26,416	32,123		36,348	33,410	4,492	2,533
2010	169,219	120,035	635	120,670	11,629	-495	108,546	26,179	34,495		37,227	34,280	4,546	2,532
2011	176,202	123,702	733	124,435	10,698	-378	113,359	27,860	34,983		38,506	35,278	4,576	2,562
2012	186,616	128,844	1,128	129,972	11,033	-299	118,641	32,392	35,583		40,527	36,957	4,605	2,598
2013	188,965	132,193	1,516	133,709	12,985	-319	120,405	31,916	36,644		40,819	36,970	4,629	2,638
2014	195,426	138,641	1,027	139,668	13,568	-459	125,641	33,142	36,644		42,030	37,965	4,650	2,678
2015	202,048	141,289	929	142,219	13,686	-434	128,099	34,468	39,481		43,252	38,954	4,671	...

... = Not available.

Personal Income and Employment by Region and State: Maine

(Millions of dollars, except as noted.)

Year	Personal income, total	Earnings by place of work			Less: Contributions for government social insurance	Plus: Adjustment for residence	Equals: Net earnings by place of residence	Plus: Dividends, interest, and rent	Plus: Personal current transfer receipts	Per capita (dollars)		Population (thousands)	Total employment (thousands)
		Nonfarm	Farm	Total						Personal income	Disposable personal income		
1960	1,936	1,509	103	1,612	70	-32	1,511	273	152	1,985	1,808	975	...
1961	1,962	1,551	67	1,618	73	-33	1,512	283	167	1,972	1,796	995	...
1962	2,040	1,611	66	1,678	78	-34	1,565	302	172	2,052	1,863	994	...
1963	2,106	1,662	59	1,722	87	-34	1,600	325	181	2,121	1,936	993	...
1964	2,274	1,769	90	1,859	92	-34	1,733	358	184	2,290	2,106	993	...
1965	2,457	1,867	126	1,993	93	-32	1,868	396	192	2,464	2,268	997	...
1966	2,612	2,035	107	2,142	119	-36	1,987	415	210	2,615	2,403	999	...
1967	2,742	2,180	55	2,234	138	-38	2,059	434	248	2,731	2,496	1,004	...
1968	2,921	2,357	55	2,412	157	-41	2,214	429	279	2,939	2,654	994	...
1969	3,217	2,539	74	2,614	181	-24	2,408	497	312	3,243	2,894	992	443
1970	3,530	2,739	78	2,816	193	-20	2,603	557	371	3,541	3,198	997	446
1971	3,791	2,909	66	2,976	211	-19	2,746	606	438	3,732	3,419	1,016	443
1972	4,151	3,198	65	3,263	242	-22	3,000	662	490	4,012	3,655	1,035	453
1973	4,663	3,521	148	3,669	302	-13	3,355	724	584	4,456	4,022	1,046	470
1974	5,178	3,804	195	4,000	338	-8	3,654	821	703	4,884	4,413	1,060	478
1975	5,580	4,085	82	4,167	357	-21	3,789	892	899	5,199	4,747	1,073	475
1976	6,378	4,715	163	4,878	422	-24	4,432	969	977	5,852	5,318	1,090	498
1977	6,932	5,155	129	5,284	461	-26	4,796	1,095	1,041	6,271	5,705	1,105	513
1978	7,663	5,783	90	5,873	531	-25	5,318	1,229	1,117	6,870	6,213	1,115	531
1979	8,517	6,425	76	6,500	607	-17	5,876	1,379	1,262	7,571	6,806	1,125	545
1980	9,585	7,086	49	7,135	668	-14	6,453	1,656	1,475	8,506	7,619	1,127	553
1981	10,586	7,592	118	7,710	771	-48	6,891	2,014	1,681	9,343	8,301	1,133	551
1982	11,464	8,049	104	8,153	831	-46	7,276	2,346	1,843	10,086	8,897	1,137	553
1983	12,294	8,742	72	8,814	910	-33	7,871	2,431	1,992	10,740	9,593	1,145	565
1984	13,639	9,674	118	9,792	1,043	-26	8,722	2,816	2,101	11,802	10,594	1,156	587
1985	14,708	10,531	103	10,634	1,132	-5	9,497	2,988	2,223	12,648	11,298	1,163	606
1986	15,971	11,483	93	11,576	1,239	35	10,372	3,292	2,306	13,649	12,129	1,170	630
1987	17,384	12,602	135	12,737	1,356	59	11,440	3,584	2,360	14,675	12,916	1,185	653
1988	19,127	14,045	117	14,162	1,543	73	12,692	3,929	2,506	15,889	14,026	1,204	686
1989	20,818	15,146	126	15,272	1,650	72	13,694	4,423	2,700	17,064	15,082	1,220	702
1990	21,655	15,644	173	15,817	1,788	71	14,100	4,541	3,014	17,581	15,584	1,232	701
1991	21,996	15,612	127	15,739	1,803	88	14,024	4,502	3,470	17,780	15,872	1,237	678
1992	23,023	16,266	178	16,443	1,905	132	14,671	4,520	3,832	18,589	16,670	1,239	681
1993	23,768	16,808	156	16,964	2,016	191	15,140	4,587	4,042	19,132	17,171	1,242	692
1994	24,763	17,475	148	17,623	2,130	251	15,744	4,790	4,229	19,927	17,822	1,243	703
1995	25,879	17,951	123	18,074	2,208	318	16,184	5,234	4,461	20,812	18,618	1,243	705
1996	27,358	18,735	151	18,886	2,273	372	16,984	5,602	4,772	21,903	19,479	1,249	714
1997	28,858	19,827	105	19,931	2,399	445	17,978	5,887	4,993	22,999	20,307	1,255	727
1998	30,792	21,184	178	21,362	2,544	519	19,337	6,314	5,141	24,455	21,415	1,259	749
1999	32,288	22,664	195	22,859	2,684	585	20,760	6,236	5,291	25,488	22,329	1,267	763
2000	34,620	24,118	208	24,326	2,815	702	22,213	6,785	5,622	27,109	23,623	1,277	784
2001	36,358	25,371	193	25,565	2,949	745	23,360	6,942	6,056	28,279	24,729	1,286	788
2002	37,657	26,450	157	26,607	2,977	696	24,326	6,872	6,459	29,057	25,946	1,296	790
2003	39,589	27,644	163	27,808	3,064	679	25,423	7,137	7,030	30,301	27,362	1,307	794
2004	41,726	29,219	178	29,397	3,222	694	26,868	7,368	7,490	31,762	28,753	1,314	808
2005	42,606	29,760	173	29,933	3,327	693	27,299	7,152	8,155	32,307	28,976	1,319	810
2006	45,029	31,420	168	31,588	3,540	706	28,755	7,919	8,355	34,019	30,439	1,324	818
2007	46,911	32,201	183	32,384	3,696	728	29,415	8,536	8,960	35,350	31,539	1,327	829
2008	48,824	32,844	132	32,976	3,802	706	29,881	8,601	10,342	36,695	32,800	1,331	825
2009	48,644	32,383	120	32,503	3,723	676	29,456	7,966	11,222	36,586	33,385	1,330	803
2010	49,248	32,793	179	32,972	3,808	709	29,873	8,041	11,334	37,102	33,805	1,327	791
2011	51,255	33,370	143	33,514	3,489	755	30,780	8,649	11,825	38,597	34,831	1,328	794
2012	52,598	34,163	191	34,354	3,585	777	31,546	9,281	11,770	39,589	35,791	1,329	796
2013	52,566	34,711	217	34,928	4,155	790	31,563	8,970	12,033	39,562	35,489	1,329	803
2014	54,195	35,727	226	35,953	4,278	846	32,521	9,323	12,351	40,745	36,521	1,330	811
2015	55,941	36,794	217	37,011	4,367	883	33,527	9,676	12,738	42,077	37544	1329	...

... = Not available.

Personal Income and Employment by Region and State: Maryland

(Millions of dollars, except as noted.)

Year	Personal income, total	Derivation of personal income									Per capita (dollars)		Population (thousands)	Total employment (thousands)
		Earnings by place of work			Less: Contributions for government social insurance	Plus: Adjustment for residence	Equals: Net earnings by place of residence	Plus: Dividends, interest, and rent	Plus: Personal current transfer receipts		Personal income	Disposable personal income		
		Nonfarm	Farm	Total										
1960	7,741	5,754	94	5,848	289	627	6,186	1,214	340		2,487	2,179	3,113	...
1961	8,240	6,090	90	6,179	312	689	6,556	1,293	391		2,595	2,289	3,176	...
1962	8,905	6,566	85	6,651	351	773	7,074	1,415	416		2,729	2,379	3,263	...
1963	9,541	7,009	67	7,077	381	864	7,560	1,546	436		2,818	2,448	3,386	...
1964	10,406	7,609	86	7,695	397	952	8,250	1,696	460		2,980	2,628	3,492	...
1965	11,347	8,217	98	8,315	399	1,065	8,981	1,863	504		3,152	2,770	3,600	...
1966	12,521	9,231	79	9,310	526	1,186	9,970	1,995	557		3,389	2,938	3,695	...
1967	13,632	9,820	95	9,915	587	1,450	10,778	2,163	691		3,628	3,139	3,757	...
1968	15,060	10,896	87	10,983	643	1,617	11,956	2,277	826		3,947	3,326	3,815	...
1969	17,270	12,156	133	12,289	751	2,320	13,859	2,467	944		4,465	3,751	3,868	1,679
1970	19,210	13,252	122	13,374	815	2,713	15,272	2,812	1,126		4,878	4,176	3,938	1,702
1971	21,174	14,456	94	14,550	917	3,023	16,657	3,144	1,373		5,264	4,571	4,023	1,729
1972	23,220	15,885	128	16,013	1,060	3,279	18,232	3,414	1,574		5,690	4,864	4,081	1,781
1973	25,572	17,611	209	17,820	1,354	3,478	19,944	3,811	1,816		6,223	5,345	4,109	1,846
1974	27,928	19,185	165	19,350	1,533	3,680	21,498	4,325	2,105		6,757	5,755	4,133	1,868
1975	30,272	20,318	204	20,522	1,624	4,057	22,955	4,670	2,647		7,282	6,307	4,157	1,846
1976	32,913	22,330	175	22,504	1,808	4,350	25,046	5,012	2,855		7,889	6,824	4,172	1,866
1977	35,683	24,270	130	24,400	1,974	4,691	27,117	5,524	3,042		8,507	7,292	4,195	1,919
1978	39,666	27,023	184	27,207	2,262	5,092	30,038	6,274	3,354		9,418	8,061	4,212	2,004
1979	43,607	29,803	160	29,964	2,611	5,462	32,814	6,987	3,805		10,325	8,777	4,223	2,059
1980	48,539	32,560	58	32,619	2,866	5,948	35,700	8,303	4,535		11,481	9,803	4,228	2,070
1981	53,952	35,730	129	35,860	3,381	6,285	38,763	9,994	5,195		12,659	10,684	4,262	2,095
1982	58,495	37,548	144	37,693	3,617	6,789	40,865	11,847	5,783		13,658	11,606	4,283	2,084
1983	62,780	40,853	90	40,943	4,071	7,134	44,006	12,471	6,303		14,555	12,529	4,313	2,151
1984	69,612	45,407	266	45,673	4,672	7,803	48,803	14,165	6,644		15,947	13,700	4,365	2,243
1985	75,637	49,830	278	50,108	5,284	8,406	53,229	15,385	7,023		17,139	14,790	4,413	2,342
1986	81,682	54,171	288	54,459	5,837	9,016	57,638	16,550	7,494		18,204	15,727	4,487	2,428
1987	88,109	59,288	300	59,587	6,331	9,641	62,898	17,432	7,780		19,299	16,468	4,566	2,553
1988	96,767	65,518	365	65,883	7,214	10,685	69,354	19,108	8,304		20,775	17,954	4,658	2,647
1989	104,490	70,022	366	70,388	7,758	11,494	74,124	21,320	9,045		22,103	18,922	4,727	2,704
1990	110,720	74,222	357	74,579	8,395	12,094	78,278	22,533	9,910		23,068	19,799	4,800	2,737
1991	114,751	75,956	310	76,266	8,671	12,639	80,235	23,355	11,162		23,574	20,398	4,868	2,662
1992	120,565	79,387	343	79,729	9,016	13,401	84,114	23,936	12,514		24,488	21,291	4,923	2,636
1993	125,465	82,625	320	82,945	9,364	13,624	87,205	25,204	13,056		25,235	21,912	4,972	2,659
1994	131,221	86,606	308	86,914	9,916	14,020	91,018	26,561	13,642		26,124	22,613	5,023	2,706
1995	136,888	90,277	215	90,492	10,287	13,991	94,195	28,391	14,302		26,999	23,266	5,070	2,765
1996	143,275	94,034	395	94,429	10,645	14,365	98,149	29,831	15,296		28,027	24,012	5,112	2,806
1997	151,292	100,458	280	100,738	11,307	14,299	103,731	31,952	15,610		29,335	24,740	5,157	2,870
1998	162,851	108,855	326	109,180	11,984	15,660	112,857	33,707	16,288		31,291	26,565	5,204	2,933
1999	172,886	116,539	350	116,889	12,726	16,739	120,902	34,722	17,262		32,902	27,904	5,255	3,003
2000	187,716	126,057	417	126,474	13,596	18,981	131,859	37,611	18,246		35,345	29,883	5,311	3,088
2001	197,891	133,824	417	134,241	14,646	20,016	139,611	38,381	19,899		36,819	31,195	5,375	3,113
2002	205,229	140,703	226	140,929	15,326	20,018	145,620	38,262	21,347		37,723	32,682	5,440	3,150
2003	214,374	147,694	315	148,008	16,030	20,190	152,169	39,279	22,927		39,004	34,111	5,496	3,187
2004	229,818	158,635	444	159,078	17,256	21,183	163,006	42,806	24,007		41,432	36,316	5,547	3,250
2005	242,155	167,355	392	167,747	18,183	21,628	171,192	45,018	25,945		43,301	37,593	5,592	3,316
2006	258,321	177,235	309	177,544	19,378	22,325	180,491	50,756	27,074		45,904	39,723	5,627	3,380
2007	269,714	183,323	299	183,622	20,234	22,793	186,181	54,221	29,311		47,708	40,977	5,653	3,445
2008	280,306	189,051	457	189,508	21,007	22,110	190,611	56,271	33,424		49,307	42,665	5,685	3,437
2009	279,294	189,251	341	189,593	20,983	23,381	191,990	51,307	35,997		48,739	43,217	5,730	3,368
2010	287,571	194,574	310	194,884	21,883	24,000	197,001	51,400	39,171		49,683	43,990	5,788	3,345
2011	302,712	202,876	442	203,318	20,338	23,688	206,667	55,675	40,370		51,800	45,327	5,844	3,395
2012	312,724	208,685	584	209,269	20,912	23,346	211,702	60,180	40,841		53,078	46,554	5,892	3,437
2013	312,054	210,323	802	211,125	23,720	23,460	210,865	58,960	42,229		52,545	45,560	5,939	3,491
2014	323,778	218,199	626	218,825	24,341	23,022	217,506	61,473	44,799		54,176	46,900	5,976	3,528
2015	337,174	227,129	634	227,762	25,087	24,236	226,911	63,737	46,525		56,127	48287	6007	...

... = Not available.

Personal Income and Employment by Region and State: Massachusetts

(Millions of dollars, except as noted.)

Year	Personal income, total	Earnings by place of work			Less: Contributions for government social insurance	Plus: Adjustment for residence	Equals: Net earnings by place of residence	Plus: Dividends, interest, and rent	Plus: Personal current transfer receipts	Per capita (dollars)		Population (thousands)	Total employment (thousands)
		Nonfarm	Farm	Total						Personal income	Disposable personal income		
1960	13,193	10,817	68	10,886	499	-75	10,311	1,962	921	2,557	2,238	5,160	...
1961	13,867	11,328	60	11,388	528	-83	10,778	2,063	1,027	2,657	2,345	5,219	...
1962	14,654	11,983	61	12,044	617	-92	11,335	2,268	1,051	2,784	2,446	5,263	...
1963	15,237	12,392	61	12,453	680	-98	11,675	2,453	1,110	2,851	2,504	5,344	...
1964	16,267	13,115	63	13,178	698	-108	12,372	2,745	1,151	2,986	2,664	5,448	...
1965	17,349	13,921	69	13,990	714	-122	13,154	2,982	1,212	3,153	2,809	5,502	...
1966	18,688	15,198	72	15,270	942	-141	14,187	3,201	1,300	3,376	2,981	5,535	...
1967	20,300	16,366	56	16,422	1,033	-157	15,231	3,464	1,605	3,629	3,197	5,594	...
1968	22,173	17,830	65	17,894	1,139	-175	16,580	3,657	1,936	3,947	3,424	5,618	...
1969	24,152	19,444	66	19,510	1,262	-126	18,122	3,873	2,157	4,275	3,646	5,650	2,679
1970	26,093	20,750	69	20,819	1,327	-105	19,387	4,156	2,551	4,575	3,964	5,704	2,679
1971	27,884	21,951	63	22,015	1,448	-105	20,462	4,403	3,020	4,859	4,268	5,739	2,644
1972	30,122	23,839	63	23,902	1,651	-104	22,146	4,662	3,314	5,228	4,517	5,762	2,697
1973	32,659	26,045	71	26,116	2,075	-124	23,917	5,026	3,716	5,647	4,911	5,784	2,787
1974	35,287	27,644	70	27,714	2,275	-142	25,297	5,586	4,405	6,108	5,297	5,777	2,811
1975	37,985	28,769	69	28,838	2,295	-153	26,390	5,863	5,732	6,592	5,811	5,762	2,728
1976	40,803	31,307	76	31,383	2,556	-173	28,654	6,203	5,946	7,098	6,205	5,749	2,756
1977	44,419	34,431	79	34,511	2,817	-219	31,474	6,837	6,108	7,733	6,731	5,744	2,833
1978	49,083	38,546	104	38,650	3,248	-279	35,122	7,484	6,476	8,547	7,413	5,743	2,958
1979	54,590	43,183	91	43,274	3,796	-364	39,113	8,307	7,169	9,500	8,165	5,746	3,074
1980	61,455	47,816	106	47,922	4,215	-483	43,224	10,043	8,188	10,695	9,145	5,746	3,134
1981	68,462	52,353	116	52,470	4,981	-622	46,866	12,291	9,304	11,868	10,055	5,769	3,142
1982	75,054	56,213	132	56,344	5,484	-747	50,113	14,885	10,056	13,005	11,145	5,771	3,143
1983	81,578	61,963	164	62,128	6,141	-918	55,068	15,855	10,655	14,067	12,113	5,799	3,215
1984	92,020	70,580	183	70,762	7,225	-1,176	62,361	18,454	11,204	15,755	13,634	5,841	3,402
1985	99,606	77,457	160	77,618	8,002	-1,371	68,244	19,640	11,722	16,938	14,571	5,881	3,510
1986	107,411	84,234	175	84,409	8,883	-1,495	74,031	21,048	12,332	18,197	15,580	5,903	3,605
1987	116,375	92,514	153	92,667	9,651	-1,666	81,350	22,346	12,679	19,608	16,692	5,935	3,632
1988	127,991	101,914	172	102,087	10,787	-1,883	89,417	24,914	13,661	21,403	18,472	5,980	3,739
1989	134,971	106,155	153	106,308	11,166	-2,034	93,108	26,457	15,406	22,437	19,269	6,015	3,710
1990	139,000	107,406	153	107,559	11,186	-2,076	94,297	27,440	17,264	23,080	19,827	6,023	3,615
1991	141,239	107,353	173	107,526	11,384	-2,238	93,904	27,539	19,796	23,468	20,302	6,018	3,451
1992	148,539	113,930	171	114,102	11,985	-2,348	99,769	28,113	20,658	24,639	21,377	6,029	3,482
1993	154,466	118,778	164	118,942	12,586	-2,564	103,792	29,418	21,256	25,487	22,051	6,061	3,548
1994	162,149	125,031	150	125,181	13,379	-2,767	109,035	30,628	22,486	26,603	22,932	6,095	3,616
1995	171,547	131,678	146	131,824	14,168	-2,830	114,826	32,897	23,824	27,933	23,923	6,141	3,649
1996	182,447	140,533	166	140,699	14,935	-3,098	122,666	35,214	24,567	29,523	25,019	6,180	3,713
1997	193,952	150,184	168	150,352	15,992	-3,407	130,953	37,571	25,428	31,152	26,141	6,226	3,802
1998	206,185	160,511	108	160,619	17,060	-3,607	139,952	40,681	25,552	32,875	27,251	6,272	3,898
1999	219,739	174,823	109	174,932	18,308	-4,191	152,432	40,848	26,458	34,783	28,671	6,317	3,968
2000	244,509	195,962	132	196,093	20,253	-5,058	170,783	45,842	27,884	38,438	31,002	6,361	4,078
2001	254,460	202,438	110	202,548	20,769	-5,089	176,690	47,285	30,486	39,774	32,817	6,398	4,087
2002	255,030	201,647	131	201,779	20,728	-4,473	176,578	45,382	33,071	39,742	34,166	6,417	4,032
2003	261,679	204,875	131	205,006	20,943	-3,878	180,186	46,544	34,949	40,744	35,392	6,423	4,001
2004	273,639	217,176	146	217,322	22,730	-5,131	189,460	47,812	36,367	42,674	37,076	6,412	4,024
2005	285,564	223,265	125	223,390	23,794	-5,139	194,458	52,030	39,076	44,596	38,326	6,403	4,064
2006	307,300	235,224	130	235,354	24,648	-5,225	205,481	60,918	40,902	47,940	41,030	6,410	4,112
2007	322,244	246,839	131	246,970	25,855	-6,054	215,061	64,560	42,622	50,103	42,194	6,432	4,202
2008	334,717	253,357	160	253,517	26,700	-5,972	220,845	65,145	48,727	51,742	44,003	6,469	4,217
2009	327,809	247,685	124	247,809	26,326	-5,419	216,064	58,380	53,364	50,296	44,323	6,518	4,123
2010	338,985	257,329	131	257,459	26,802	-5,676	224,981	57,833	56,171	51,643	45,097	6,564	4,113
2011	359,224	269,097	136	269,233	24,983	-6,305	237,945	64,806	56,473	54,327	46,679	6,612	4,175
2012	377,728	280,909	193	281,101	25,816	-6,898	248,387	72,437	56,905	56,752	49,064	6,656	4,250
2013	379,381	287,503	202	287,705	30,099	-6,771	250,835	71,197	57,349	56,549	47,895	6,709	4,349
2014	396,206	301,534	178	301,712	31,680	-6,922	263,111	74,156	58,939	58,737	49,522	6,745	4,428
2015	414,724	316,644	195	316,839	33,060	-7,424	276,355	77,253	61,115	61,032	50,993	6,795	...

... = Not available.

Personal Income and Employment by Region and State: Michigan

(Millions of dollars, except as noted.)

| | | Derivation of personal income | | | | | | | | Per capita (dollars) | | | |
| | | Earnings by place of work | | | Less: Contributions for government social insurance | Plus: Adjustment for residence | Equals: Net earnings by place of residence | Plus: Dividends, interest, and rent | Plus: Personal current transfer receipts | | | | |
Year	Personal income, total	Nonfarm	Farm	Total						Personal income	Disposable personal income	Population (thousands)	Total employment (thousands)
1960	18,838	15,858	240	16,097	824	37	15,309	2,416	1,112	2,405	2,142	7,834	...
1961	18,912	15,493	300	15,793	786	38	15,045	2,535	1,332	2,396	2,152	7,893	...
1962	20,273	16,794	275	17,070	888	42	16,223	2,745	1,304	2,555	2,275	7,933	...
1963	21,650	18,086	300	18,386	1,038	45	17,392	2,931	1,327	2,687	2,383	8,058	...
1964	23,750	19,872	295	20,167	1,077	49	19,139	3,245	1,366	2,901	2,606	8,187	...
1965	26,373	22,157	274	22,431	1,122	54	21,363	3,534	1,476	3,156	2,823	8,357	...
1966	28,754	24,464	349	24,814	1,572	63	23,305	3,832	1,617	3,378	3,005	8,512	...
1967	29,956	25,214	276	25,491	1,652	68	23,906	4,048	2,002	3,471	3,082	8,630	...
1968	33,115	28,009	304	28,313	1,854	77	26,535	4,268	2,312	3,808	3,319	8,696	...
1969	35,931	30,753	351	31,104	2,206	109	29,006	4,366	2,559	4,092	3,504	8,781	3,640
1970	37,166	30,932	341	31,272	2,196	112	29,189	4,762	3,216	4,178	3,634	8,897	3,558
1971	40,420	33,536	310	33,845	2,450	105	31,501	5,081	3,838	4,505	3,957	8,972	3,571
1972	44,882	37,462	427	37,888	2,905	114	35,097	5,468	4,318	4,973	4,292	9,025	3,687
1973	50,074	42,257	561	42,818	3,800	140	39,158	5,990	4,925	5,520	4,794	9,072	3,858
1974	53,567	43,884	649	44,534	4,082	140	40,591	6,823	6,153	5,880	5,132	9,109	3,854
1975	57,303	45,147	578	45,725	4,091	150	41,784	7,444	8,075	6,292	5,580	9,108	3,695
1976	64,002	51,787	478	52,264	4,794	191	47,662	8,017	8,323	7,020	6,126	9,117	3,844
1977	71,985	59,228	559	59,787	5,491	217	54,513	8,927	8,545	7,861	6,796	9,157	4,016
1978	80,264	66,852	510	67,361	6,391	261	61,231	9,949	9,083	8,722	7,472	9,202	4,186
1979	87,967	72,640	545	73,185	7,194	307	66,298	11,196	10,473	9,511	8,144	9,249	4,228
1980	94,143	73,319	536	73,856	7,174	353	67,035	13,281	13,826	10,171	8,839	9,256	4,030
1981	100,693	77,256	515	77,771	8,186	375	69,961	16,087	14,646	10,934	9,467	9,209	3,978
1982	103,938	76,718	410	77,127	8,241	378	69,264	18,325	16,349	11,403	10,008	9,115	3,823
1983	110,448	81,974	222	82,195	8,954	411	73,652	19,496	17,300	12,207	10,683	9,048	3,866
1984	122,144	91,601	551	92,152	10,356	476	82,272	22,381	17,491	13,497	11,844	9,049	4,040
1985	132,507	101,047	663	101,710	11,666	498	90,543	23,914	18,051	14,599	12,720	9,076	4,233
1986	141,065	108,439	493	108,932	12,551	486	96,867	25,269	18,929	15,455	13,488	9,128	4,349
1987	146,706	112,864	665	113,530	12,896	504	101,138	26,104	19,464	15,968	13,897	9,187	4,483
1988	156,539	121,688	585	122,273	14,305	513	108,481	27,756	20,302	16,982	14,853	9,218	4,582
1989	168,622	129,080	981	130,061	15,142	512	115,431	31,225	21,966	18,223	15,872	9,253	4,709
1990	176,444	134,618	776	135,394	16,053	458	119,799	32,842	23,803	18,949	16,593	9,311	4,791
1991	180,156	136,874	667	137,541	16,559	487	121,470	32,205	26,481	19,165	16,862	9,400	4,721
1992	191,165	146,250	757	147,007	17,547	552	130,012	33,103	28,050	20,167	17,862	9,479	4,751
1993	201,355	154,232	737	154,969	18,603	628	136,993	34,380	29,982	21,106	18,537	9,540	4,812
1994	216,514	166,147	563	166,710	20,421	754	147,042	39,196	30,276	22,559	19,746	9,598	4,985
1995	228,975	175,494	695	176,189	21,539	797	155,447	41,574	31,955	23,664	20,631	9,676	5,142
1996	241,001	183,897	618	184,515	22,020	823	163,318	44,126	33,556	24,696	21,417	9,759	5,247
1997	253,800	193,154	608	193,762	23,099	910	171,573	46,741	35,485	25,874	22,350	9,809	5,330
1998	268,247	206,213	631	206,844	24,261	994	183,576	49,424	35,247	27,239	23,381	9,848	5,377
1999	281,153	218,382	824	219,206	25,631	1,081	194,656	48,726	37,772	28,408	24,398	9,897	5,476
2000	298,801	232,596	610	233,206	26,849	1,099	207,456	52,303	39,043	30,023	25,903	9,952	5,608
2001	302,179	233,214	564	233,778	26,634	1,191	208,336	50,364	43,478	30,245	26,249	9,991	5,508
2002	303,809	235,288	601	235,889	26,929	1,009	209,969	48,799	45,041	30,333	26,903	10,016	5,449
2003	311,876	239,976	708	240,684	27,315	648	214,017	50,561	47,298	31,060	27,840	10,041	5,424
2004	322,744	246,957	1,146	248,103	28,254	1,127	220,976	52,448	49,319	32,097	28,937	10,055	5,446
2005	330,823	251,880	1,054	252,935	29,144	1,068	224,859	53,513	52,451	32,914	29,527	10,051	5,474
2006	339,674	254,984	1,138	256,122	29,869	1,446	227,699	55,952	56,023	33,845	30,291	10,036	5,440
2007	348,598	255,424	1,205	256,629	30,230	1,666	228,066	59,304	61,228	34,855	31,017	10,001	5,435
2008	356,375	252,898	1,480	254,378	30,279	1,752	225,850	60,767	69,759	35,828	31,940	9,947	5,316
2009	338,230	234,330	1,061	235,391	28,301	1,509	208,599	52,172	77,459	34,159	31,291	9,902	5,030
2010	347,646	239,202	1,490	240,693	28,694	1,581	213,579	51,393	82,674	35,199	32,040	9,876	5,008
2011	368,790	249,324	2,884	252,208	26,711	1,732	227,229	58,967	82,594	37,343	33,593	9,876	5,138
2012	382,065	260,571	1,713	262,284	27,808	1,904	236,380	63,434	82,251	38,652	34,679	9,885	5,204
2013	387,978	267,294	2,456	269,749	32,300	1,908	239,358	64,902	83,719	39,197	34,839	9,898	5,291
2014	403,726	279,128	1,923	281,051	33,555	2,087	249,582	67,245	86,899	40,740	36,149	9,910	5,391
2015	421,044	290,816	1,180	291,996	34,706	2,160	259,450	70,066	91,527	42,427	37,436	9,924	...

... = Not available.

Personal Income and Employment by Region and State: Minnesota

(Millions of dollars, except as noted.)

Year	Personal income, total	Derivation of personal income								Per capita (dollars)		Population (thousands)	Total employment (thousands)
		Earnings by place of work			Less: Contributions for government social insurance	Plus: Adjustment for residence	Equals: Net earnings by place of residence	Plus: Dividends, interest, and rent	Plus: Personal current transfer receipts	Personal income	Disposable personal income		
		Nonfarm	Farm	Total									
1960	7,435	5,605	514	6,119	260	-1	5,858	1,070	507	2,171	1,937	3,425	...
1961	7,820	5,852	540	6,393	269	-3	6,120	1,129	571	2,254	2,013	3,470	...
1962	8,241	6,292	467	6,759	303	-3	6,453	1,197	590	2,346	2,086	3,513	...
1963	8,742	6,552	621	7,173	339	-4	6,830	1,287	625	2,476	2,210	3,531	...
1964	9,098	7,010	402	7,412	348	-4	7,060	1,387	651	2,557	2,308	3,558	...
1965	10,057	7,561	652	8,213	372	-7	7,834	1,515	708	2,800	2,517	3,592	...
1966	10,904	8,338	733	9,071	522	-13	8,536	1,607	761	3,015	2,693	3,617	...
1967	11,716	9,051	643	9,695	602	-17	9,076	1,715	925	3,202	2,850	3,659	...
1968	12,897	10,002	680	10,682	683	-24	9,975	1,865	1,058	3,483	3,083	3,703	...
1969	14,345	11,195	720	11,915	781	-31	11,103	2,080	1,162	3,817	3,320	3,758	1,691
1970	15,640	11,961	876	12,836	825	-27	11,985	2,282	1,373	4,099	3,614	3,815	1,699
1971	16,681	12,755	796	13,551	910	-27	12,615	2,473	1,594	4,331	3,858	3,852	1,706
1972	18,132	13,831	959	14,790	1,036	-29	13,725	2,644	1,762	4,689	4,114	3,867	1,780
1973	21,241	15,392	2,179	17,571	1,333	-35	16,203	2,973	2,066	5,467	4,858	3,885	1,878
1974	22,866	16,928	1,644	18,572	1,525	-32	17,016	3,427	2,423	5,865	5,109	3,898	1,921
1975	24,736	18,350	1,264	19,614	1,613	-33	17,968	3,844	2,924	6,301	5,532	3,926	1,920
1976	26,720	20,496	782	21,279	1,845	-41	19,393	4,113	3,214	6,753	5,888	3,957	1,977
1977	30,082	22,697	1,501	24,198	2,043	-55	22,100	4,602	3,380	7,559	6,577	3,980	2,034
1978	33,749	25,860	1,625	27,484	2,409	-69	25,006	5,115	3,627	8,427	7,294	4,005	2,122
1979	37,547	29,422	1,245	30,667	2,855	-87	27,725	5,767	4,056	9,298	7,968	4,038	2,218
1980	41,697	32,062	959	33,021	3,107	-93	29,820	7,011	4,866	10,207	8,787	4,085	2,248
1981	46,203	34,664	1,040	35,704	3,604	-134	31,966	8,654	5,583	11,237	9,641	4,112	2,233
1982	49,470	36,163	819	36,982	3,838	-157	32,987	10,206	6,277	11,974	10,337	4,131	2,192
1983	52,086	38,711	119	38,830	4,161	-185	34,484	10,836	6,766	12,577	10,901	4,141	2,219
1984	59,084	43,467	1,444	44,911	4,796	-243	39,872	12,116	7,097	14,211	12,446	4,158	2,324
1985	62,698	46,585	1,343	47,927	5,234	-291	42,403	12,755	7,540	14,984	13,124	4,184	2,385
1986	66,395	49,472	1,641	51,113	5,701	-328	45,084	13,432	7,879	15,789	13,877	4,205	2,417
1987	70,827	53,340	2,138	55,478	6,107	-378	48,994	13,705	8,128	16,724	14,574	4,235	2,509
1988	74,630	57,696	1,253	58,949	6,828	-454	51,667	14,376	8,588	17,371	15,168	4,296	2,580
1989	81,662	61,800	2,051	63,852	7,303	-440	56,109	16,202	9,351	18,824	16,417	4,338	2,634
1990	86,896	65,860	1,956	67,816	7,829	-472	59,515	17,330	10,051	19,795	17,202	4,390	2,692
1991	89,548	68,812	1,207	70,019	8,278	-476	61,265	17,478	10,805	20,165	17,619	4,441	2,717
1992	96,321	74,663	1,401	76,063	8,869	-510	66,685	17,888	11,748	21,426	18,683	4,496	2,762
1993	99,216	78,056	187	78,243	9,313	-516	68,414	18,406	12,395	21,777	18,924	4,556	2,817
1994	106,426	82,716	1,340	84,056	9,990	-562	73,504	19,885	13,037	23,084	20,055	4,610	2,904
1995	112,631	87,444	519	87,963	10,530	-611	76,822	21,992	13,817	24,169	20,892	4,660	2,995
1996	121,487	93,433	1,921	95,354	11,136	-686	83,531	23,491	14,464	25,778	22,035	4,713	3,056
1997	128,315	99,874	898	100,772	11,836	-768	88,168	25,455	14,692	26,938	22,964	4,763	3,109
1998	139,769	109,171	1,399	110,570	12,712	-849	97,010	27,554	15,206	29,037	24,679	4,813	3,187
1999	147,129	116,508	1,264	117,772	13,570	-953	103,250	27,891	15,988	30,190	25,855	4,873	3,252
2000	159,518	126,334	1,455	127,789	14,525	-1,038	112,226	30,164	17,128	32,332	27,504	4,934	3,327
2001	166,059	131,599	1,029	132,629	15,034	-1,131	116,463	30,374	19,222	33,326	28,543	4,983	3,339
2002	170,137	135,088	1,017	136,105	15,408	-1,043	119,655	29,612	20,870	33,899	29,558	5,019	3,331
2003	178,171	140,132	1,880	142,012	16,097	-1,023	124,892	31,386	21,893	35,256	31,131	5,054	3,343
2004	187,860	147,929	2,448	150,377	17,008	-1,084	132,285	32,567	23,008	36,924	32,729	5,088	3,387
2005	193,454	151,899	2,997	154,896	17,748	-1,210	135,938	33,407	24,110	37,787	33,102	5,120	3,447
2006	204,654	157,743	2,542	160,286	18,560	-900	140,825	37,270	26,558	39,634	34,584	5,164	3,491
2007	216,410	165,214	2,515	167,729	19,329	-1,256	147,144	40,202	29,064	41,560	36,091	5,207	3,536
2008	226,968	170,161	4,060	174,220	19,932	-1,460	152,829	41,150	32,988	43,256	37,606	5,247	3,522
2009	216,866	162,128	2,224	164,353	19,269	-1,228	143,855	36,815	36,196	41,064	36,729	5,281	3,423
2010	226,049	167,223	3,288	170,510	19,537	-1,202	149,771	37,251	39,027	42,567	37,892	5,310	3,396
2011	241,807	176,133	4,497	180,630	18,321	-1,302	161,007	41,424	39,377	45,214	39,759	5,348	3,457
2012	254,468	182,790	6,235	189,025	19,048	-1,178	168,798	46,238	39,432	47,293	41,571	5,381	3,491
2013	257,058	188,092	6,053	194,145	22,383	-1,213	170,549	45,706	40,803	47,410	41,126	5,422	3,541
2014	267,389	197,180	4,360	201,540	23,183	-1,228	177,128	47,508	42,753	48,998	42,350	5,457	3,591
2015	277,483	206,753	2,009	208,762	24,082	-1,398	183,282	49,448	44,752	50,541	43,323	5,490	...

... = Not available.

Personal Income and Employment by Region and State: Mississippi

(Millions of dollars, except as noted.)

Year	Personal income, total	Derivation of personal income									Per capita (dollars)		Population (thousands)	Total employment (thousands)
		Earnings by place of work			Less: Contributions for government social insurance	Plus: Adjustment for residence	Equals: Net earnings by place of residence	Plus: Dividends, interest, and rent	Plus: Personal current transfer receipts		Personal income	Disposable personal income		
		Nonfarm	Farm	Total										
1960	2,775	2,035	281	2,316	101	12	2,227	315	233		1,272	1,179	2,182	...
1961	3,006	2,126	353	2,480	104	13	2,388	355	262		1,363	1,274	2,206	...
1962	3,136	2,281	297	2,579	115	15	2,479	385	273		1,398	1,296	2,243	...
1963	3,446	2,427	432	2,859	136	17	2,740	416	290		1,536	1,421	2,244	...
1964	3,566	2,593	370	2,963	143	20	2,839	424	303		1,591	1,484	2,241	...
1965	3,876	2,880	352	3,232	152	22	3,102	447	328		1,726	1,604	2,246	...
1966	4,229	3,226	347	3,572	197	23	3,398	471	360		1,884	1,737	2,245	...
1967	4,572	3,448	386	3,834	226	25	3,633	508	431		2,052	1,894	2,228	...
1968	4,998	3,832	364	4,196	253	31	3,975	535	489		2,253	2,068	2,219	...
1969	5,534	4,233	349	4,581	291	36	4,326	657	552		2,493	2,276	2,220	909
1970	6,064	4,498	394	4,892	310	37	4,619	756	689		2,730	2,483	2,221	917
1971	6,719	4,931	436	5,367	351	59	5,074	830	814		2,966	2,738	2,266	939
1972	7,654	5,669	494	6,163	421	74	5,816	920	918		3,317	3,019	2,307	979
1973	8,743	6,373	692	7,065	538	94	6,621	1,057	1,065		3,721	3,406	2,350	1,019
1974	9,610	7,034	515	7,549	615	123	7,056	1,241	1,312		4,040	3,661	2,379	1,031
1975	10,425	7,538	377	7,915	653	149	7,411	1,383	1,631		4,344	4,000	2,400	1,001
1976	11,820	8,556	576	9,132	757	180	8,555	1,480	1,786		4,864	4,437	2,430	1,039
1977	13,154	9,620	609	10,230	850	218	9,598	1,646	1,910		5,347	4,891	2,460	1,071
1978	14,648	10,904	455	11,359	982	272	10,649	1,899	2,100		5,887	5,325	2,488	1,101
1979	16,554	12,086	704	12,791	1,129	328	11,989	2,168	2,396		6,600	5,948	2,508	1,114
1980	17,998	13,041	185	13,226	1,210	413	12,429	2,690	2,879		7,127	6,419	2,525	1,111
1981	20,205	14,234	334	14,568	1,421	440	13,587	3,355	3,263		7,958	7,114	2,539	1,107
1982	21,340	14,619	425	15,044	1,497	458	14,004	3,748	3,588		8,347	7,596	2,557	1,079
1983	22,337	15,402	102	15,504	1,594	513	14,423	3,963	3,951		8,699	7,887	2,568	1,088
1984	24,401	16,666	480	17,146	1,773	572	15,945	4,371	4,085		9,465	8,624	2,578	1,117
1985	25,726	17,594	438	18,032	1,914	604	16,722	4,724	4,280		9,940	9,053	2,588	1,124
1986	26,679	18,511	204	18,715	2,032	592	17,275	4,869	4,535		10,286	9,410	2,594	1,131
1987	28,202	19,434	587	20,020	2,125	630	18,526	4,956	4,721		10,895	9,935	2,589	1,141
1988	30,162	20,806	733	21,538	2,374	672	19,837	5,296	5,029		11,689	10,699	2,580	1,169
1989	32,652	22,254	569	22,823	2,542	715	20,997	6,160	5,495		12,684	11,554	2,574	1,189
1990	34,268	23,688	493	24,181	2,803	749	22,128	6,178	5,962		13,288	12,097	2,579	1,203
1991	36,072	24,755	588	25,343	2,989	804	23,159	6,206	6,708		13,881	12,690	2,599	1,211
1992	38,903	26,733	671	27,404	3,192	823	25,035	6,353	7,515		14,827	13,573	2,624	1,234
1993	41,442	28,816	584	29,400	3,453	840	26,788	6,643	8,012		15,609	14,246	2,655	1,287
1994	44,848	31,268	844	32,113	3,779	838	29,172	7,176	8,500		16,678	15,173	2,689	1,335
1995	47,382	32,773	679	33,452	3,946	921	30,427	7,664	9,291		17,403	15,803	2,723	1,365
1996	50,291	34,198	1,078	35,276	4,069	963	32,169	8,163	9,959		18,300	16,570	2,748	1,389
1997	53,121	36,200	991	37,191	4,284	1,113	34,021	8,766	10,334		19,129	17,277	2,777	1,415
1998	56,302	38,768	967	39,734	4,579	1,189	36,345	9,538	10,419		20,073	18,096	2,805	1,446
1999	58,247	40,615	946	41,561	4,783	1,288	38,067	9,449	10,731		20,594	18,555	2,828	1,470
2000	61,474	42,425	792	43,217	4,926	1,480	39,772	10,176	11,526		21,582	19,494	2,848	1,477
2001	65,065	43,436	1,583	45,019	5,013	1,643	41,650	10,548	12,867		22,806	20,625	2,853	1,457
2002	66,245	45,190	642	45,832	5,217	1,544	42,158	10,277	13,809		23,173	21,270	2,859	1,456
2003	68,786	46,905	1,190	48,095	5,381	1,601	44,315	10,029	14,441		23,981	22,139	2,868	1,454
2004	72,967	49,628	1,804	51,432	5,702	1,803	47,533	9,909	15,524		25,257	23,526	2,889	1,473
2005	77,861	51,861	1,768	53,629	5,918	1,964	49,674	10,750	17,437		26,794	24,805	2,906	1,485
2006	81,484	54,940	812	55,752	6,401	2,204	51,555	12,323	17,607		28,050	25,721	2,905	1,511
2007	86,511	56,532	1,139	57,671	6,669	2,373	53,375	14,764	18,373		29,543	27,112	2,928	1,543
2008	90,505	58,720	944	59,664	6,886	2,423	55,201	14,504	20,800		30,703	28,064	2,948	1,542
2009	89,321	57,053	985	58,037	6,796	2,333	53,574	13,526	22,221		30,188	28,116	2,959	1,498
2010	91,451	57,976	922	58,898	6,895	2,363	54,365	13,024	24,061		30,783	28,460	2,971	1,492
2011	95,239	59,550	650	60,200	6,422	2,519	56,297	14,025	24,917		31,976	29,571	2,978	1,511
2012	98,921	61,958	1,301	63,259	6,632	2,653	59,279	14,728	24,914		33,127	30,593	2,986	1,521
2013	100,626	62,584	2,568	65,152	7,537	2,741	60,356	14,743	25,526		33,629	30,890	2,992	1,534
2014	103,091	64,402	2,063	66,466	7,751	2,794	61,509	15,214	26,367		34,431	31,594	2,994	1,554
2015	106,075	65,765	1,895	67,659	7,854	2,956	62,761	15,738	27,576		35,444	32,424	2,993	...

... = Not available.

Personal Income and Employment by Region and State: Missouri

(Millions of dollars, except as noted.)

Year	Personal income, total	Earnings by place of work			Less: Contributions for government social insurance	Plus: Adjustment for residence	Equals: Net earnings by place of residence	Plus: Dividends, interest, and rent	Plus: Personal current transfer receipts	Per capita (dollars)		Population (thousands)	Total employment (thousands)
		Nonfarm	Farm	Total						Personal income	Disposable personal income		
1960	9,638	7,707	443	8,150	358	-180	7,612	1,356	671	2,228	1,986	4,326	...
1961	9,967	7,888	484	8,372	375	-186	7,812	1,410	745	2,292	2,043	4,349	...
1962	10,495	8,359	486	8,845	408	-203	8,234	1,489	771	2,409	2,139	4,357	...
1963	11,013	8,868	440	9,309	469	-227	8,613	1,592	808	2,507	2,221	4,392	...
1964	11,632	9,501	335	9,836	491	-251	9,094	1,708	830	2,619	2,357	4,442	...
1965	12,651	10,188	533	10,721	517	-276	9,928	1,835	888	2,832	2,531	4,467	...
1966	13,552	11,213	417	11,630	695	-315	10,620	1,972	960	2,996	2,670	4,523	...
1967	14,416	11,973	404	12,377	797	-351	11,229	2,067	1,120	3,176	2,827	4,539	...
1968	15,951	13,158	478	13,636	898	-388	12,350	2,288	1,313	3,492	3,086	4,568	...
1969	16,884	14,290	450	14,740	954	-752	13,033	2,423	1,428	3,639	3,157	4,640	2,216
1970	18,437	15,203	525	15,728	1,005	-696	14,027	2,718	1,692	3,936	3,462	4,685	2,203
1971	19,898	16,221	571	16,792	1,109	-681	15,002	2,945	1,951	4,213	3,742	4,723	2,200
1972	21,643	17,587	714	18,301	1,261	-698	16,341	3,190	2,112	4,553	3,995	4,753	2,242
1973	24,038	19,125	1,215	20,340	1,584	-730	18,026	3,562	2,450	5,035	4,462	4,775	2,325
1974	25,725	20,618	640	21,258	1,767	-757	18,735	4,099	2,892	5,376	4,727	4,785	2,341
1975	28,178	21,905	698	22,603	1,842	-772	19,989	4,533	3,655	5,876	5,240	4,795	2,291
1976	30,858	24,547	471	25,018	2,097	-840	22,082	4,872	3,904	6,397	5,656	4,824	2,365
1977	34,196	27,264	717	27,981	2,332	-971	24,679	5,442	4,075	7,058	6,238	4,845	2,424
1978	38,083	30,461	920	31,381	2,697	-1,123	27,561	6,093	4,428	7,818	6,860	4,871	2,512
1979	42,467	33,758	1,179	34,937	3,090	-1,281	30,566	6,893	5,008	8,686	7,583	4,889	2,576
1980	46,091	36,064	242	36,306	3,279	-1,489	31,538	8,454	6,099	9,364	8,180	4,922	2,549
1981	51,467	38,822	773	39,594	3,789	-1,632	34,173	10,441	6,852	10,435	9,073	4,932	2,540
1982	54,991	40,595	347	40,942	4,044	-1,687	35,211	12,310	7,470	11,156	9,653	4,929	2,516
1983	58,675	43,704	-103	43,601	4,389	-1,711	37,501	13,153	8,022	11,869	10,494	4,944	2,562
1984	65,051	48,348	426	48,774	4,997	-1,860	41,917	14,762	8,372	13,075	11,617	4,975	2,667
1985	69,636	51,855	798	52,652	5,479	-1,991	45,183	15,623	8,830	13,926	12,327	5,000	2,738
1986	73,376	55,078	584	55,662	5,879	-2,056	47,728	16,351	9,298	14,608	12,948	5,023	2,801
1987	77,319	58,708	739	59,447	6,196	-2,172	51,079	16,666	9,574	15,290	13,515	5,057	2,836
1988	82,003	62,760	658	63,417	6,836	-2,254	54,327	17,567	10,109	16,137	14,306	5,082	2,885
1989	87,799	66,608	912	67,520	7,299	-2,388	57,833	18,994	10,972	17,230	15,210	5,096	2,938
1990	91,774	69,669	708	70,377	7,872	-2,602	59,903	19,980	11,890	17,894	15,795	5,129	2,972
1991	95,973	71,691	589	72,281	8,214	-2,593	61,474	20,604	13,895	18,560	16,511	5,171	2,942
1992	102,405	76,410	862	77,271	8,666	-2,718	65,887	21,682	14,836	19,629	17,511	5,217	2,957
1993	107,143	79,935	500	80,435	9,093	-2,837	68,505	22,709	15,928	20,326	18,109	5,271	3,041
1994	113,503	84,937	725	85,662	9,774	-2,863	73,024	23,777	16,701	21,317	18,925	5,324	3,113
1995	119,307	90,165	219	90,383	10,357	-3,114	76,912	24,592	17,803	22,183	19,621	5,378	3,196
1996	126,396	94,972	1,052	96,024	10,779	-3,214	82,031	25,760	18,605	23,271	20,481	5,432	3,255
1997	134,266	101,017	1,059	102,077	11,410	-3,393	87,273	27,685	19,308	24,496	21,461	5,481	3,328
1998	141,002	106,903	545	107,448	12,010	-3,556	91,881	29,184	19,937	25,536	22,277	5,522	3,384
1999	146,849	113,339	241	113,580	12,637	-3,687	97,256	28,718	20,875	26,402	23,034	5,562	3,425
2000	157,091	120,263	788	121,051	13,301	-3,971	103,779	31,014	22,298	28,015	24,446	5,607	3,474
2001	162,433	124,006	836	124,842	13,689	-3,951	107,202	30,637	24,595	28,794	25,139	5,641	3,454
2002	165,959	128,112	406	128,517	14,019	-4,569	109,930	29,784	26,246	29,245	26,100	5,675	3,440
2003	172,773	132,219	1,063	133,281	14,449	-4,579	114,254	31,105	27,415	30,261	27,326	5,709	3,447
2004	181,837	138,444	2,267	140,711	14,985	-4,452	121,274	31,639	28,924	31,636	28,699	5,748	3,483
2005	188,783	144,501	1,406	145,907	15,741	-4,681	125,484	32,353	30,946	32,603	29,300	5,790	3,536
2006	201,039	152,337	1,267	153,604	16,728	-4,685	132,191	35,930	32,917	34,408	30,771	5,843	3,590
2007	211,023	157,144	1,372	158,517	17,506	-4,369	136,642	39,212	35,169	35,842	31,860	5,888	3,642
2008	221,796	163,323	2,033	165,356	18,264	-5,796	141,296	40,963	39,538	37,441	33,278	5,924	3,632
2009	216,420	158,788	1,659	160,447	17,735	-5,336	137,376	36,189	42,855	36,306	33,122	5,961	3,532
2010	219,686	159,586	1,301	160,887	17,704	-5,157	138,026	36,055	45,605	36,638	33,364	5,996	3,474
2011	228,655	162,503	2,195	164,698	16,310	-4,568	143,820	38,361	46,474	38,042	34,275	6,011	3,508
2012	240,441	169,373	1,515	170,887	16,745	-5,137	149,005	44,394	47,041	39,905	36,012	6,025	3,529
2013	243,592	173,244	3,019	176,262	19,463	-4,993	151,806	43,775	48,011	40,297	36,068	6,045	3,564
2014	252,482	178,993	3,787	182,780	20,122	-5,087	157,571	45,678	49,233	41,639	37,202	6,064	3,602
2015	260,123	186,056	1,469	187,525	20,791	-5,372	161,361	47,596	51,165	42,752	37,949	6,084	...

... = Not available.

Personal Income and Employment by Region and State: Montana

(Millions of dollars, except as noted.)

Year	Personal income, total	Derivation of personal income								Per capita (dollars)		Population (thousands)	Total employment (thousands)
		Earnings by place of work			Less: Contributions for government social insurance	Plus: Adjustment for residence	Equals: Net earnings by place of residence	Plus: Dividends, interest, and rent	Plus: Personal current transfer receipts	Personal income	Disposable personal income		
		Nonfarm	Farm	Total									
1960	1,446	1,012	162	1,175	62	0	1,113	226	108	2,130	1,925	679	...
1961	1,450	1,061	110	1,171	63	0	1,108	224	117	2,083	1,871	696	...
1962	1,697	1,123	277	1,400	64	-0	1,336	241	119	2,431	2,216	698	...
1963	1,687	1,174	213	1,387	72	-0	1,315	251	121	2,400	2,174	703	...
1964	1,723	1,228	169	1,398	74	-0	1,323	274	126	2,440	2,239	706	...
1965	1,853	1,306	190	1,496	76	-0	1,420	298	134	2,624	2,393	706	...
1966	1,987	1,393	227	1,619	99	-0	1,520	324	143	2,810	2,552	707	...
1967	2,026	1,432	191	1,623	108	-0	1,514	342	169	2,890	2,615	701	...
1968	2,123	1,508	196	1,704	115	-1	1,588	343	191	3,033	2,742	700	...
1969	2,354	1,636	242	1,878	127	-1	1,750	394	210	3,391	2,985	694	298
1970	2,609	1,759	291	2,050	137	-1	1,912	455	241	3,742	3,345	697	301
1971	2,792	1,924	251	2,175	151	-1	2,023	489	280	3,927	3,556	711	307
1972	3,235	2,162	401	2,563	177	-0	2,385	540	310	4,498	4,029	719	319
1973	3,748	2,410	575	2,985	227	0	2,759	629	360	5,152	4,597	727	333
1974	4,074	2,711	466	3,177	262	1	2,916	735	423	5,526	4,915	737	344
1975	4,490	3,017	400	3,417	283	2	3,136	840	514	5,994	5,381	749	344
1976	4,815	3,426	225	3,651	324	3	3,331	915	570	6,348	5,650	759	359
1977	5,207	3,847	71	3,918	369	4	3,553	1,039	615	6,751	5,968	771	372
1978	6,106	4,370	303	4,673	433	3	4,243	1,188	675	7,788	6,927	784	390
1979	6,560	4,816	119	4,934	496	6	4,444	1,356	760	8,312	7,289	789	396
1980	7,210	5,118	120	5,238	542	13	4,709	1,606	895	9,141	8,036	789	393
1981	8,186	5,569	227	5,796	632	25	5,188	1,963	1,034	10,292	9,082	795	395
1982	8,627	5,718	172	5,889	664	17	5,243	2,227	1,158	10,731	9,576	804	391
1983	9,091	6,043	127	6,169	700	9	5,479	2,343	1,268	11,167	10,010	814	398
1984	9,613	6,396	44	6,440	758	6	5,687	2,573	1,353	11,711	10,532	821	408
1985	9,761	6,530	-84	6,445	790	3	5,659	2,672	1,431	11,871	10,678	822	406
1986	10,153	6,534	238	6,772	805	-2	5,965	2,660	1,528	12,477	11,335	814	402
1987	10,434	6,718	317	7,035	827	-3	6,204	2,629	1,601	12,960	11,680	805	406
1988	10,715	7,154	110	7,264	927	-1	6,337	2,685	1,693	13,390	12,006	800	416
1989	11,815	7,574	420	7,994	997	-3	6,995	2,965	1,856	14,776	13,170	800	424
1990	12,429	8,042	396	8,438	1,118	-4	7,315	3,081	2,033	15,533	13,870	800	433
1991	13,256	8,637	551	9,188	1,219	-11	7,958	3,159	2,140	16,372	14,699	810	444
1992	14,106	9,352	489	9,841	1,324	-2	8,516	3,269	2,321	17,082	15,320	826	456
1993	15,257	10,064	773	10,837	1,462	1	9,377	3,388	2,493	18,061	16,219	845	470
1994	15,672	10,653	390	11,043	1,547	6	9,501	3,582	2,589	18,195	16,262	861	494
1995	16,534	11,030	339	11,369	1,564	9	9,813	3,947	2,774	18,862	16,895	877	504
1996	17,309	11,519	310	11,829	1,563	12	10,278	4,151	2,880	19,530	17,445	886	519
1997	18,044	11,988	239	12,227	1,585	14	10,656	4,448	2,940	20,278	18,037	890	526
1998	19,377	12,898	300	13,198	1,643	19	11,574	4,751	3,052	21,713	19,300	892	537
1999	19,963	13,498	390	13,888	1,692	22	12,218	4,715	3,031	22,243	19,726	898	542
2000	21,324	14,393	262	14,655	1,793	27	12,889	5,045	3,389	23,594	20,888	904	553
2001	22,449	15,070	350	15,421	1,908	33	13,546	5,230	3,672	24,751	21,949	907	559
2002	23,062	15,848	199	16,047	2,022	29	14,055	5,204	3,802	25,296	22,824	912	564
2003	24,520	16,658	354	17,012	2,124	15	14,903	5,648	3,969	26,663	24,259	920	571
2004	26,207	17,701	556	18,257	2,259	29	16,028	5,932	4,248	28,180	25,664	930	584
2005	27,790	18,928	594	19,522	2,457	23	17,087	6,167	4,536	29,561	26,608	940	598
2006	29,995	20,504	164	20,668	2,656	20	18,033	7,044	4,918	31,484	28,160	953	615
2007	32,196	21,512	421	21,933	2,857	36	19,113	7,836	5,247	33,374	29,611	965	634
2008	34,089	22,265	505	22,771	2,925	28	19,873	8,246	5,970	34,912	31,149	976	635
2009	33,088	21,700	359	22,059	2,872	30	19,217	7,405	6,467	33,627	30,612	984	618
2010	34,410	22,335	542	22,877	2,929	46	19,994	7,359	7,058	34,737	31,667	991	614
2011	36,872	23,552	698	24,249	2,779	91	21,561	8,316	6,995	36,959	33,348	998	620
2012	39,304	24,832	743	25,575	2,865	150	22,861	9,246	7,197	39,102	35,157	1,005	629
2013	39,462	25,177	1,039	26,216	3,299	165	23,082	9,005	7,375	38,884	34,684	1,015	638
2014	40,844	26,213	833	27,045	3,448	191	23,788	9,360	7,696	39,903	35,504	1,024	643
2015	42,647	27,545	758	28,303	3,601	184	24,886	9,752	8,009	41,280	36,512	1,033	...

... = Not available.

Personal Income and Employment by Region and State: Nebraska

(Millions of dollars, except as noted.)

Year	Personal income, total	Earnings by place of work			Less: Contributions for government social insurance	Plus: Adjustment for residence	Equals: Net earnings by place of residence	Plus: Dividends, interest, and rent	Plus: Personal current transfer receipts	Per capita (dollars)		Population (thousands)	Total employment (thousands)
		Nonfarm	Farm	Total						Personal income	Disposable personal income		
1960	3,141	2,156	392	2,547	116	-11	2,420	536	185	2,217	2,006	1,417	...
1961	3,215	2,265	319	2,584	119	-11	2,454	556	205	2,223	1,996	1,446	...
1962	3,493	2,389	437	2,827	128	-10	2,689	588	216	2,386	2,165	1,464	...
1963	3,588	2,473	394	2,867	140	-10	2,718	642	229	2,431	2,199	1,476	...
1964	3,687	2,620	312	2,932	146	-9	2,777	673	236	2,488	2,279	1,482	...
1965	4,054	2,734	497	3,232	148	-8	3,076	720	258	2,756	2,532	1,471	...
1966	4,354	2,937	592	3,530	196	-8	3,326	748	280	2,990	2,725	1,456	...
1967	4,508	3,168	488	3,656	228	-8	3,420	747	341	3,094	2,806	1,457	...
1968	4,810	3,460	444	3,904	245	-8	3,651	766	394	3,279	2,949	1,467	...
1969	5,393	3,833	604	4,437	269	-102	4,067	897	429	3,658	3,229	1,474	704
1970	5,810	4,154	542	4,696	289	-110	4,298	1,015	498	3,905	3,476	1,488	715
1971	6,380	4,473	688	5,160	321	-113	4,727	1,091	562	4,241	3,841	1,504	728
1972	7,064	4,909	808	5,717	364	-121	5,232	1,213	620	4,653	4,139	1,518	748
1973	8,234	5,475	1,227	6,702	468	-125	6,110	1,383	741	5,387	4,803	1,529	775
1974	8,581	6,066	771	6,837	541	-133	6,163	1,571	847	5,580	4,916	1,538	793
1975	9,809	6,611	1,109	7,719	580	-142	6,998	1,775	1,036	6,364	5,721	1,541	790
1976	10,246	7,474	588	8,062	662	-149	7,251	1,889	1,105	6,615	5,920	1,549	811
1977	11,102	8,147	532	8,678	722	-148	7,808	2,117	1,177	7,142	6,310	1,554	831
1978	12,843	9,107	1,085	10,192	831	-171	9,191	2,347	1,305	8,228	7,308	1,561	854
1979	13,849	10,172	754	10,927	966	-198	9,762	2,633	1,453	8,853	7,760	1,564	876
1980	14,762	11,023	107	11,130	1,044	-214	9,871	3,193	1,697	9,389	8,241	1,572	877
1981	17,128	11,874	834	12,708	1,201	-254	11,253	3,919	1,956	10,851	9,607	1,579	871
1982	18,435	12,343	767	13,110	1,279	-262	11,569	4,712	2,154	11,655	10,172	1,582	861
1983	19,113	12,964	550	13,514	1,351	-276	11,887	4,895	2,331	12,064	10,801	1,584	867
1984	21,224	14,170	1,161	15,330	1,520	-316	13,495	5,285	2,444	13,360	12,095	1,589	886
1985	22,366	14,900	1,450	16,350	1,645	-342	14,363	5,408	2,596	14,114	12,770	1,585	898
1986	23,031	15,509	1,414	16,924	1,766	-344	14,814	5,503	2,715	14,629	13,236	1,574	898
1987	24,075	16,420	1,636	18,056	1,867	-343	15,845	5,453	2,777	15,368	13,854	1,567	925
1988	25,715	17,536	2,031	19,567	2,086	-379	17,102	5,718	2,896	16,364	14,745	1,571	947
1989	27,268	18,710	1,847	20,557	2,231	-392	17,935	6,214	3,119	17,315	15,505	1,575	965
1990	29,214	20,011	2,199	22,210	2,466	-391	19,353	6,479	3,383	18,471	16,510	1,582	988
1991	30,327	20,993	1,997	22,990	2,606	-427	19,958	6,730	3,640	19,003	17,036	1,596	992
1992	32,255	22,459	2,117	24,576	2,735	-471	21,370	6,934	3,952	20,013	17,985	1,612	999
1993	33,311	23,580	1,746	25,326	2,880	-486	21,959	7,132	4,219	20,491	18,389	1,626	1,021
1994	35,399	25,238	1,851	27,088	3,086	-502	23,500	7,497	4,401	21,598	19,352	1,639	1,061
1995	37,421	26,933	1,324	28,257	3,235	-547	24,474	8,259	4,688	22,583	20,127	1,657	1,071
1996	40,753	28,466	2,596	31,062	3,415	-599	27,048	8,717	4,987	24,348	21,681	1,674	1,097
1997	41,937	30,073	1,757	31,830	3,637	-677	27,517	9,249	5,171	24,868	21,921	1,686	1,111
1998	44,832	32,231	1,647	33,878	3,853	-714	29,311	10,010	5,511	26,437	23,270	1,696	1,137
1999	46,928	34,292	1,575	35,867	4,059	-800	31,009	10,093	5,826	27,527	24,224	1,705	1,155
2000	49,664	36,270	1,450	37,720	4,239	-867	32,613	10,941	6,110	28,978	25,438	1,714	1,172
2001	51,902	37,896	1,815	39,711	4,412	-899	34,400	10,782	6,720	30,178	26,650	1,720	1,172
2002	53,052	39,534	1,069	40,603	4,576	-928	35,100	10,809	7,144	30,696	27,644	1,728	1,164
2003	56,699	41,111	2,660	43,771	4,744	-956	38,071	11,174	7,454	32,611	29,732	1,739	1,167
2004	59,073	43,342	2,875	46,217	4,959	-976	40,282	10,982	7,809	33,768	30,794	1,749	1,179
2005	61,250	45,063	2,877	47,940	5,222	-989	41,729	11,253	8,269	34,772	31,458	1,761	1,192
2006	63,785	47,548	1,652	49,200	5,617	-1,008	42,575	12,276	8,933	35,982	32,251	1,773	1,205
2007	68,635	49,448	2,712	52,160	5,843	-990	45,326	13,884	9,424	38,484	34,334	1,783	1,228
2008	72,980	51,450	3,178	54,628	6,029	-968	47,630	14,759	10,591	40,626	36,429	1,796	1,234
2009	71,105	51,269	2,717	53,986	6,045	-955	46,986	13,062	11,057	39,226	35,912	1,813	1,222
2010	73,236	52,201	3,221	55,421	6,220	-883	48,318	13,053	11,866	40,023	36,431	1,830	1,214
2011	80,727	54,537	6,420	60,957	5,695	-938	54,324	14,301	12,102	43,820	39,683	1,842	1,227
2012	84,569	58,192	4,643	62,835	5,861	-954	56,020	16,344	12,205	45,578	41,111	1,855	1,245
2013	86,447	58,979	6,881	65,861	6,735	-924	58,202	15,886	12,359	46,254	41,504	1,869	1,259
2014	89,479	61,944	6,327	68,271	7,108	-941	60,221	16,457	12,800	47,557	42,564	1,882	1,276
2015	91,040	65,062	4,038	69,100	7,421	-1,001	60,678	17,126	13,236	48,006	42591	1896	...

... = Not available.

Personal Income and Employment by Region and State: Nevada

(Millions of dollars, except as noted.)

Year	Personal income, total	Earnings by place of work			Less: Contributions for government social insurance	Plus: Adjustment for residence	Equals: Net earnings by place of residence	Plus: Dividends, interest, and rent	Plus: Personal current transfer receipts	Per capita (dollars)		Population (thousands)	Total employment (thousands)
		Nonfarm	Farm	Total						Personal income	Disposable personal income		
1960	884	748	15	763	36	-2	724	119	41	3,036	2,687	291	...
1961	978	825	13	837	40	-3	795	134	49	3,106	2,724	315	...
1962	1,170	1,004	19	1,023	50	-4	969	150	51	3,324	2,931	352	...
1963	1,317	1,149	20	1,169	66	-6	1,097	162	58	3,317	2,907	397	...
1964	1,426	1,244	12	1,256	67	-5	1,184	177	65	3,346	2,999	426	...
1965	1,526	1,310	14	1,323	66	-5	1,253	201	72	3,436	3,087	444	...
1966	1,608	1,385	18	1,404	80	-4	1,320	210	78	3,605	3,228	446	...
1967	1,707	1,457	17	1,474	87	-3	1,385	227	95	3,801	3,395	449	...
1968	1,992	1,676	20	1,696	101	-4	1,591	288	113	4,292	3,754	464	...
1969	2,257	1,932	32	1,964	132	-34	1,798	334	125	4,702	4,023	480	244
1970	2,534	2,144	34	2,178	144	-39	1,995	392	148	5,138	4,562	493	256
1971	2,831	2,377	35	2,412	165	-41	2,206	441	184	5,445	4,889	520	267
1972	3,162	2,646	42	2,689	194	-44	2,450	493	218	5,783	5,161	547	280
1973	3,582	3,022	56	3,078	256	-54	2,768	560	254	6,296	5,618	569	304
1974	3,971	3,315	35	3,349	288	-56	3,005	650	315	6,654	5,915	597	317
1975	4,478	3,663	33	3,696	313	-58	3,325	716	438	7,225	6,586	620	326
1976	5,094	4,196	36	4,232	368	-68	3,796	809	490	7,876	7,066	647	349
1977	5,899	4,929	27	4,957	439	-84	4,433	931	535	8,699	7,757	678	384
1978	7,128	6,018	23	6,041	555	-117	5,369	1,155	604	9,909	8,747	719	432
1979	8,270	6,976	9	6,985	681	-132	6,173	1,385	712	10,809	9,460	765	468
1980	9,565	7,905	57	7,962	778	-160	7,024	1,676	866	11,806	10,402	810	489
1981	10,882	8,849	28	8,877	931	-167	7,779	2,048	1,055	12,838	11,275	848	500
1982	11,641	9,126	33	9,158	953	-168	8,037	2,429	1,175	13,206	11,702	882	494
1983	12,367	9,667	26	9,693	1,049	-177	8,467	2,615	1,285	13,711	12,245	902	499
1984	13,493	10,525	36	10,560	1,191	-190	9,179	2,938	1,376	14,589	13,048	925	523
1985	14,709	11,363	29	11,392	1,313	-201	9,879	3,318	1,512	15,467	13,759	951	545
1986	15,913	12,296	28	12,324	1,452	-218	10,654	3,574	1,685	16,227	14,401	981	570
1987	17,404	13,614	48	13,663	1,615	-240	11,807	3,798	1,798	17,006	15,018	1,023	616
1988	19,786	15,653	65	15,718	1,873	-282	13,563	4,248	1,975	18,405	16,197	1,075	662
1989	22,278	17,432	79	17,511	2,119	-326	15,066	4,933	2,280	19,587	17,232	1,137	710
1990	24,995	19,618	82	19,701	2,497	-377	16,827	5,559	2,609	20,476	17,987	1,221	756
1991	27,487	21,132	76	21,208	2,660	-346	18,202	6,065	3,221	21,206	18,819	1,296	769
1992	30,503	23,318	73	23,391	2,890	-305	20,196	6,663	3,645	22,572	20,005	1,351	776
1993	32,962	25,309	119	25,428	3,163	-344	21,921	7,192	3,849	23,357	20,624	1,411	819
1994	36,518	28,045	82	28,127	3,534	-354	24,239	8,243	4,037	24,357	21,592	1,499	898
1995	40,086	30,732	70	30,802	3,879	-349	26,574	9,134	4,379	25,346	22,454	1,582	953
1996	44,342	34,021	70	34,091	4,196	-369	29,526	10,101	4,714	26,611	23,311	1,666	1,024
1997	48,513	37,243	70	37,314	4,477	-328	32,508	10,979	5,025	27,500	24,149	1,764	1,089
1998	52,980	40,526	93	40,619	4,785	-350	35,484	12,145	5,352	28,589	24,888	1,853	1,131
1999	57,511	44,736	85	44,822	5,085	-382	39,354	12,575	5,583	29,726	25,877	1,935	1,190
2000	63,045	48,408	104	48,512	4,986	-339	43,188	13,857	6,001	31,230	27,114	2,019	1,253
2001	66,706	51,374	118	51,492	5,292	-293	45,907	14,010	6,788	31,789	27,810	2,098	1,285
2002	69,305	53,186	90	53,276	5,537	-322	47,417	14,241	7,647	31,882	28,457	2,174	1,301
2003	74,993	56,936	94	57,029	5,604	-355	51,071	15,704	8,218	33,347	30,063	2,249	1,356
2004	83,864	63,351	127	63,478	6,127	-377	56,975	18,014	8,875	35,744	32,061	2,346	1,447
2005	94,083	70,127	135	70,263	6,726	-385	63,151	21,337	9,595	38,683	34,329	2,432	1,539
2006	100,692	75,802	128	75,930	7,750	-411	67,769	22,555	10,368	39,915	35,429	2,523	1,613
2007	106,485	79,678	94	79,772	8,173	-440	71,159	23,997	11,329	40,939	36,437	2,601	1,653
2008	106,789	78,032	143	78,175	7,699	-403	70,072	23,326	13,391	40,243	36,296	2,654	1,629
2009	99,146	71,387	115	71,502	7,420	-283	63,799	20,062	15,285	36,931	33,901	2,685	1,524
2010	99,806	70,800	133	70,933	7,308	-195	63,430	19,539	16,838	36,918	33,827	2,703	1,484
2011	102,612	71,088	195	71,283	6,895	-56	64,332	21,213	17,068	37,745	34,345	2,719	1,508
2012	108,657	73,777	106	73,883	7,248	-33	66,602	24,835	17,219	39,436	35,834	2,755	1,524
2013	109,490	75,131	108	75,240	8,003	13	67,250	24,667	17,573	39,223	35,154	2,791	1,566
2014	115,672	79,820	222	80,042	8,836	-28	71,178	25,604	18,890	40,742	36,447	2,839	1,615
2015	121,973	84,113	189	84,302	9,367	-21	74,915	26,570	20,488	42,185	37,532	2,891	...

... = Not available.

Personal Income and Employment by Region and State: New Hampshire

(Millions of dollars, except as noted.)

Year	Personal income, total	Derivation of personal income								Per capita (dollars)		Population (thousands)	Total employment (thousands)
		Earnings by place of work			Less: Contributions for government social insurance	Plus: Adjustment for residence	Equals: Net earnings by place of residence	Plus: Dividends, interest, and rent	Plus: Personal current transfer receipts	Personal income	Disposable personal income		
		Nonfarm	Farm	Total									
1960	1,380	1,038	20	1,058	55	82	1,084	205	90	2,266	2,031	609	...
1961	1,454	1,082	21	1,103	56	89	1,135	217	102	2,353	2,116	618	...
1962	1,556	1,154	19	1,173	62	98	1,210	242	105	2,462	2,209	632	...
1963	1,623	1,199	18	1,216	68	104	1,252	258	113	2,500	2,232	649	...
1964	1,745	1,284	18	1,302	71	112	1,344	286	116	2,632	2,398	663	...
1965	1,883	1,379	21	1,400	75	122	1,448	312	123	2,785	2,525	676	...
1966	2,064	1,530	24	1,554	103	142	1,594	338	132	3,031	2,717	681	...
1967	2,255	1,679	17	1,697	116	157	1,738	362	155	3,235	2,897	697	...
1968	2,493	1,849	20	1,868	128	176	1,916	398	180	3,517	3,127	709	...
1969	2,788	2,006	21	2,027	129	235	2,133	452	203	3,851	3,410	724	334
1970	2,974	2,128	17	2,145	136	221	2,230	502	241	4,009	3,532	742	334
1971	3,228	2,287	15	2,301	151	231	2,382	554	292	4,236	3,799	762	336
1972	3,569	2,541	16	2,557	177	254	2,635	612	322	4,566	4,035	782	350
1973	4,016	2,888	21	2,908	230	282	2,961	675	380	5,008	4,478	802	374
1974	4,422	3,120	14	3,134	258	325	3,201	766	456	5,413	4,818	817	381
1975	4,815	3,285	17	3,302	267	358	3,393	837	586	5,801	5,243	830	370
1976	5,444	3,786	19	3,805	310	402	3,897	921	626	6,427	5,757	847	394
1977	6,155	4,303	18	4,321	354	475	4,441	1,052	661	7,060	6,294	872	418
1978	7,097	5,017	19	5,036	421	567	5,182	1,190	725	7,938	7,014	894	446
1979	8,110	5,734	22	5,755	504	683	5,934	1,347	829	8,893	7,845	912	468
1980	9,274	6,357	14	6,371	559	845	6,657	1,645	972	10,034	8,880	924	482
1981	10,506	7,025	23	7,048	667	953	7,334	2,034	1,138	11,217	9,896	937	492
1982	11,568	7,577	19	7,596	740	1,038	7,894	2,426	1,248	12,207	10,892	948	498
1983	12,714	8,500	17	8,517	841	1,155	8,831	2,550	1,333	13,270	11,835	958	518
1984	14,383	9,597	22	9,618	977	1,364	10,005	2,968	1,410	14,724	13,173	977	553
1985	15,893	10,768	24	10,792	1,126	1,499	11,165	3,251	1,476	15,944	14,146	997	586
1986	17,589	12,103	25	12,128	1,276	1,574	12,426	3,615	1,548	17,159	15,134	1,025	617
1987	19,464	13,668	43	13,711	1,420	1,686	13,976	3,907	1,581	18,462	16,266	1,054	635
1988	21,419	15,088	45	15,133	1,606	1,826	15,354	4,353	1,713	19,785	17,554	1,083	660
1989	22,925	15,730	35	15,765	1,677	1,945	16,032	4,974	1,919	20,756	18,432	1,105	660
1990	23,025	15,595	44	15,639	1,710	1,975	15,905	4,970	2,150	20,699	18,473	1,112	643
1991	23,789	15,578	45	15,623	1,730	2,121	16,014	4,893	2,882	21,433	19,267	1,110	616
1992	24,949	16,696	51	16,747	1,839	2,181	17,089	4,790	3,070	22,320	20,087	1,118	629
1993	25,787	17,447	42	17,489	1,919	2,307	17,877	4,938	2,973	22,832	20,464	1,129	642
1994	27,573	18,608	40	18,648	2,074	2,403	18,976	5,221	3,376	24,133	21,659	1,143	666
1995	29,300	19,741	35	19,776	2,224	2,396	19,948	5,710	3,641	25,312	22,644	1,158	679
1996	31,032	21,069	41	21,110	2,347	2,571	21,334	6,099	3,599	26,417	23,408	1,175	696
1997	33,336	22,836	38	22,874	2,521	2,809	23,162	6,434	3,741	28,027	24,524	1,189	717
1998	36,173	25,135	40	25,175	2,734	2,910	25,351	6,942	3,880	29,996	26,235	1,206	742
1999	38,145	26,813	45	26,858	2,904	3,383	27,336	6,851	3,958	31,215	27,100	1,222	760
2000	42,520	29,703	45	29,747	3,190	4,029	30,586	7,673	4,261	34,293	29,466	1,240	782
2001	44,127	30,974	42	31,016	3,324	4,071	31,763	7,711	4,653	35,147	30,628	1,256	788
2002	45,072	31,867	43	31,909	3,387	3,967	32,489	7,518	5,065	35,515	31,813	1,269	789
2003	46,329	33,140	49	33,189	3,553	3,963	33,600	7,534	5,195	36,199	32,793	1,280	798
2004	49,527	35,328	58	35,386	3,812	4,236	35,810	8,036	5,682	38,390	34,934	1,290	813
2005	51,431	36,859	50	36,908	3,979	4,397	37,326	8,177	5,928	39,609	35,735	1,298	827
2006	55,099	38,947	40	38,987	4,150	4,668	39,505	9,263	6,331	42,112	37,827	1,308	836
2007	57,276	39,754	42	39,796	4,323	4,800	40,274	10,132	6,870	43,638	38,942	1,313	849
2008	59,052	40,376	32	40,408	4,461	4,838	40,785	10,310	7,958	44,876	40,198	1,316	846
2009	57,824	39,807	18	39,825	4,434	4,285	39,676	9,572	8,577	43,936	40,415	1,316	823
2010	59,649	41,000	28	41,028	4,554	4,708	41,182	9,335	9,132	45,308	41,467	1,317	814
2011	63,276	42,144	27	42,171	4,229	5,252	43,193	11,003	9,081	48,005	43,476	1,318	820
2012	66,787	43,385	57	43,442	4,331	5,665	44,775	12,780	9,231	50,546	46,059	1,321	825
2013	66,839	44,034	81	44,115	4,964	5,507	44,658	12,616	9,565	50,535	45,586	1,323	835
2014	70,020	46,258	64	46,322	5,163	5,525	46,683	13,175	10,162	52,773	47,452	1,327	847
2015	72,948	47,826	78	47,904	5,281	5,853	48,476	13,673	10,799	54,817	49,069	1,331	...

... = Not available.

Personal Income and Employment by Region and State: New Jersey

(Millions of dollars, except as noted.)

Year	Personal income, total	Derivation of personal income								Per capita (dollars)		Population (thousands)	Total employment (thousands)
		Earnings by place of work			Less: Contributions for government social insurance	Plus: Adjustment for residence	Equals: Net earnings by place of residence	Plus: Dividends, interest, and rent	Plus: Personal current transfer receipts	Personal income	Disposable personal income		
		Nonfarm	Farm	Total									
1960	16,588	13,159	121	13,280	660	866	13,486	2,206	896	2,718	2,406	6,103	...
1961	17,446	13,711	120	13,831	695	924	14,061	2,361	1,024	2,785	2,465	6,265	...
1962	18,768	14,660	110	14,769	771	1,026	15,024	2,666	1,079	2,944	2,602	6,376	...
1963	19,691	15,295	108	15,403	869	1,101	15,635	2,897	1,159	3,015	2,662	6,531	...
1964	21,119	16,233	103	16,336	881	1,219	16,674	3,241	1,205	3,171	2,851	6,660	...
1965	22,698	17,371	119	17,490	935	1,330	17,885	3,527	1,285	3,354	2,993	6,767	...
1966	24,589	18,958	120	19,078	1,212	1,529	19,395	3,810	1,385	3,589	3,201	6,851	...
1967	26,498	20,305	105	20,410	1,346	1,695	20,759	4,097	1,642	3,825	3,387	6,928	...
1968	29,094	22,162	102	22,264	1,535	1,904	22,634	4,496	1,964	4,153	3,646	7,005	...
1969	32,546	24,101	105	24,206	1,829	3,189	25,566	4,768	2,212	4,587	3,988	7,095	3,061
1970	35,352	26,038	100	26,138	1,958	3,145	27,326	5,337	2,689	4,917	4,321	7,190	3,125
1971	38,133	27,851	93	27,944	2,170	3,241	29,015	5,842	3,277	5,237	4,666	7,282	3,119
1972	41,445	30,408	89	30,497	2,484	3,447	31,460	6,322	3,663	5,649	4,965	7,337	3,184
1973	45,038	33,463	127	33,590	3,131	3,543	34,002	6,905	4,131	6,140	5,438	7,335	3,288
1974	48,928	35,928	138	36,066	3,461	3,715	36,321	7,760	4,847	6,670	5,883	7,335	3,301
1975	52,917	37,713	97	37,811	3,544	3,922	38,189	8,390	6,338	7,208	6,450	7,341	3,191
1976	57,362	41,344	102	41,446	3,933	4,094	41,607	8,902	6,853	7,811	6,915	7,344	3,248
1977	62,757	45,502	112	45,614	4,316	4,455	45,754	9,774	7,229	8,548	7,484	7,342	3,325
1978	69,680	51,018	127	51,145	4,987	5,032	51,190	10,802	7,689	9,472	8,271	7,356	3,465
1979	77,343	56,539	127	56,666	5,748	5,769	56,687	12,106	8,550	10,490	9,066	7,373	3,552
1980	86,956	61,872	116	61,988	6,317	6,722	62,393	14,781	9,781	11,788	10,164	7,376	3,601
1981	97,057	67,681	150	67,831	7,368	7,308	67,771	18,306	10,980	13,103	11,264	7,407	3,631
1982	104,844	72,208	166	72,374	7,997	7,777	72,154	20,656	12,035	14,109	12,140	7,431	3,639
1983	113,452	78,823	192	79,015	8,983	8,118	78,150	22,311	12,992	15,192	13,223	7,468	3,739
1984	125,655	87,842	200	88,042	10,427	8,544	86,159	25,948	13,547	16,719	14,620	7,515	3,914
1985	134,894	95,299	227	95,525	11,395	8,971	93,101	27,594	14,199	17,830	15,449	7,566	4,026
1986	144,359	103,137	229	103,366	12,408	9,556	100,514	28,978	14,867	18,939	16,387	7,622	4,122
1987	155,776	113,073	258	113,331	13,525	10,090	109,897	30,520	15,360	20,308	17,409	7,671	4,220
1988	171,093	125,343	253	125,596	15,224	10,508	120,880	33,858	16,355	22,184	19,234	7,712	4,317
1989	183,705	132,145	246	132,391	15,871	10,364	126,884	39,294	17,527	23,777	20,639	7,726	4,351
1990	192,504	137,985	243	138,228	16,024	10,373	132,577	40,595	19,331	24,798	21,600	7,763	4,310
1991	196,000	139,552	228	139,780	16,533	10,323	133,571	40,181	22,249	25,081	21,927	7,815	4,172
1992	210,738	149,321	237	149,558	17,491	12,090	144,157	40,817	25,764	26,742	23,439	7,881	4,170
1993	217,232	155,319	265	155,584	18,116	12,278	149,746	40,564	26,922	27,328	23,858	7,949	4,197
1994	224,967	161,894	282	162,177	19,138	12,264	155,303	42,361	27,303	28,071	24,405	8,014	4,232
1995	239,340	169,696	277	169,973	19,894	13,400	163,480	46,689	29,170	29,609	25,816	8,083	4,296
1996	253,237	178,300	297	178,597	20,745	15,362	173,214	49,920	30,102	31,074	26,892	8,150	4,352
1997	269,821	188,842	247	189,089	21,524	18,129	185,694	53,262	30,865	32,830	28,179	8,219	4,412
1998	287,112	201,555	265	201,820	22,687	19,634	198,767	56,630	31,715	34,644	29,430	8,287	4,496
1999	300,286	212,727	232	212,959	23,766	21,540	210,733	56,514	33,039	35,921	30,296	8,360	4,562
2000	330,182	232,979	323	233,302	25,556	24,593	232,340	62,581	35,262	39,165	32,820	8,431	4,737
2001	341,631	240,088	269	240,357	26,593	26,547	240,311	62,130	39,190	40,227	33,844	8,493	4,758
2002	350,352	247,488	288	247,776	27,296	27,469	247,950	60,029	42,373	40,964	35,608	8,553	4,772
2003	360,066	254,496	308	254,804	27,721	29,104	256,187	61,023	42,857	41,861	36,830	8,601	4,807
2004	377,210	266,427	330	266,757	29,096	31,314	268,975	64,791	43,443	43,686	38,517	8,635	4,888
2005	392,286	277,140	340	277,480	30,532	33,305	280,253	66,302	45,731	45,341	39,441	8,652	4,971
2006	419,607	291,090	380	291,470	31,790	35,669	295,349	74,589	49,668	48,444	41,978	8,662	5,044
2007	439,837	300,727	395	301,121	33,659	37,920	305,382	82,437	52,018	50,685	43,319	8,678	5,119
2008	455,211	307,006	351	307,357	34,561	39,385	312,181	84,284	58,746	52,256	44,813	8,711	5,116
2009	440,404	299,989	360	300,350	33,760	31,987	298,577	76,570	65,258	50,300	44,680	8,756	4,991
2010	450,757	304,041	331	304,372	34,311	35,987	306,048	74,021	70,689	51,202	45,326	8,804	4,944
2011	473,577	311,583	349	311,932	31,598	39,775	320,109	81,977	71,491	53,556	46,788	8,843	5,000
2012	489,437	322,510	405	322,915	32,248	39,868	330,536	88,648	70,253	55,142	48,421	8,876	5,033
2013	491,865	329,626	418	330,044	37,501	40,989	333,533	87,436	70,896	55,194	47,677	8,912	5,110
2014	515,020	341,413	390	341,803	38,699	47,515	350,618	90,987	73,415	57,620	49,785	8,938	5,166
2015	535,604	354,934	471	355,405	39,934	49,267	364,738	94,646	76,220	59,782	51,295	8,959	...

... = Not available.

Personal Income and Employment by Region and State: New Mexico

(Millions of dollars, except as noted.)

Year	Personal income, total	Earnings by place of work			Less: Contributions for government social insurance	Plus: Adjustment for residence	Equals: Net earnings by place of residence	Plus: Dividends, interest, and rent	Plus: Personal current transfer receipts	Per capita (dollars)		Population (thousands)	Total employment (thousands)
		Nonfarm	Farm	Total						Personal income	Disposable personal income		
1960	1,905	1,538	86	1,624	61	-16	1,548	255	102	1,997	1,822	954	...
1961	1,993	1,576	102	1,678	61	-16	1,601	273	118	2,065	1,884	965	...
1962	2,069	1,665	83	1,748	66	-17	1,665	284	120	2,114	1,922	979	...
1963	2,140	1,717	87	1,804	74	-18	1,712	299	129	2,163	1,969	989	...
1964	2,261	1,832	66	1,898	78	-19	1,800	325	135	2,247	2,071	1,006	...
1965	2,398	1,929	78	2,007	81	-21	1,905	347	145	2,370	2,167	1,012	...
1966	2,520	2,019	100	2,120	104	-21	1,995	368	156	2,502	2,287	1,007	...
1967	2,603	2,090	90	2,180	121	-21	2,037	370	195	2,603	2,378	1,000	...
1968	2,818	2,235	102	2,337	125	-23	2,189	401	228	2,835	2,579	994	...
1969	3,125	2,464	107	2,571	152	-22	2,397	467	261	3,091	2,768	1,011	395
1970	3,478	2,661	131	2,792	163	-23	2,606	546	325	3,399	3,060	1,023	399
1971	3,847	2,935	130	3,065	188	-23	2,854	615	378	3,652	3,339	1,053	416
1972	4,322	3,314	137	3,450	220	-21	3,209	691	422	4,010	3,639	1,078	440
1973	4,842	3,685	180	3,865	282	-18	3,564	778	500	4,385	3,979	1,104	461
1974	5,438	4,132	147	4,279	328	-16	3,935	902	601	4,814	4,347	1,130	478
1975	6,195	4,641	177	4,818	366	-13	4,438	1,019	738	5,328	4,892	1,163	491
1976	6,905	5,270	124	5,393	420	-13	4,960	1,118	828	5,778	5,254	1,195	512
1977	7,728	5,958	135	6,093	481	-11	5,601	1,255	872	6,307	5,727	1,225	539
1978	8,852	6,831	168	6,999	565	-11	6,422	1,474	956	7,071	6,358	1,252	568
1979	9,992	7,675	207	7,883	667	-10	7,206	1,683	1,103	7,803	7,003	1,281	592
1980	11,219	8,439	180	8,620	736	-4	7,879	2,025	1,315	8,568	7,700	1,309	597
1981	12,688	9,477	129	9,606	888	-13	8,704	2,482	1,502	9,520	8,455	1,333	611
1982	13,849	10,102	116	10,218	966	-15	9,236	2,962	1,651	10,155	8,998	1,364	619
1983	14,837	10,738	127	10,865	1,035	-11	9,819	3,213	1,804	10,641	9,646	1,394	631
1984	16,219	11,729	147	11,876	1,164	-1	10,711	3,581	1,927	11,448	10,416	1,417	655
1985	17,534	12,568	208	12,776	1,271	6	11,511	3,960	2,064	12,191	11,065	1,438	674
1986	18,256	12,972	194	13,167	1,327	13	11,852	4,181	2,222	12,481	11,388	1,463	680
1987	19,052	13,517	241	13,757	1,371	28	12,415	4,287	2,350	12,886	11,631	1,479	699
1988	20,112	14,310	319	14,630	1,530	39	13,139	4,453	2,520	13,495	12,189	1,490	733
1989	21,546	15,201	383	15,584	1,648	48	13,984	4,766	2,796	14,327	12,876	1,504	749
1990	23,032	16,359	417	16,776	1,872	57	14,961	5,023	3,048	15,137	13,616	1,522	761
1991	24,676	17,575	403	17,978	2,032	70	16,016	5,243	3,417	15,865	14,316	1,555	784
1992	26,528	18,903	484	19,388	2,166	86	17,308	5,421	3,799	16,627	15,029	1,595	797
1993	28,523	20,408	530	20,938	2,341	105	18,702	5,702	4,118	17,430	15,713	1,636	825
1994	30,471	21,801	457	22,258	2,547	122	19,833	6,208	4,430	18,111	16,299	1,682	857
1995	32,748	23,257	391	23,648	2,718	134	21,064	6,806	4,878	19,035	17,153	1,720	898
1996	34,410	24,036	402	24,438	2,808	155	21,785	7,303	5,322	19,637	17,616	1,752	909
1997	36,128	25,226	543	25,769	2,931	178	23,016	7,675	5,437	20,356	18,160	1,775	923
1998	38,192	26,711	585	27,296	3,082	202	24,416	8,057	5,719	21,295	18,998	1,793	936
1999	39,358	27,734	679	28,413	3,202	232	25,443	7,864	6,051	21,768	19,387	1,808	941
2000	42,686	30,575	542	31,116	3,385	258	27,989	8,274	6,423	23,438	20,953	1,821	962
2001	46,276	32,843	789	33,632	3,624	243	30,251	8,856	7,169	25,264	22,550	1,832	975
2002	47,824	34,677	549	35,226	3,807	129	31,548	8,405	7,870	25,777	23,425	1,855	983
2003	49,287	35,865	573	36,438	3,997	36	32,477	8,379	8,431	26,250	24,019	1,878	1,002
2004	52,230	37,667	876	38,543	4,208	17	34,352	8,885	8,993	27,435	25,153	1,904	1,026
2005	56,045	39,971	883	40,854	4,471	4	36,387	9,953	9,705	29,005	26,375	1,932	1,050
2006	59,840	42,749	606	43,355	4,876	112	38,591	10,657	10,592	30,497	27,511	1,962	1,079
2007	63,349	44,311	861	45,172	5,133	158	40,197	11,634	11,517	31,832	28,628	1,990	1,105
2008	67,103	46,389	637	47,026	5,408	53	41,671	12,181	13,251	33,374	30,251	2,011	1,107
2009	65,773	44,979	313	45,292	5,355	55	39,993	11,119	14,662	32,293	29,685	2,037	1,075
2010	68,183	45,871	781	46,652	5,477	34	41,209	11,106	15,867	33,019	30,491	2,065	1,060
2011	71,821	47,358	1,051	48,408	5,070	28	43,367	12,394	16,061	34,556	31,659	2,078	1,064
2012	74,181	48,613	979	49,592	5,177	48	44,463	13,691	16,027	35,585	32,685	2,085	1,066
2013	73,571	48,701	970	49,671	5,940	51	43,782	13,601	16,188	35,254	32,084	2,087	1,073
2014	77,356	50,390	1,294	51,684	6,159	56	45,581	14,089	17,685	37,091	33,734	2,086	1,083
2015	80,201	51,574	1,030	52,604	6,251	81	46,434	14,652	19,114	38,457	34,871	2,085	...

... = Not available.

Personal Income and Employment by Region and State: New York

(Millions of dollars, except as noted.)

| Year | Personal income, total | Earnings by place of work | | | Less: Contributions for government social insurance | Plus: Adjustment for residence | Equals: Net earnings by place of residence | Plus: Dividends, interest, and rent | Plus: Personal current transfer receipts | Per capita (dollars) | | Population (thousands) | Total employment (thousands) |
		Nonfarm	Farm	Total						Personal income	Disposable personal income		
1960	48,288	40,578	353	40,931	2,041	-732	38,159	7,336	2,794	2,868	2,498	16,838	...
1961	50,449	42,125	364	42,489	2,191	-785	39,513	7,729	3,207	2,957	2,564	17,061	...
1962	53,148	44,458	287	44,745	2,490	-870	41,385	8,468	3,295	3,072	2,666	17,301	...
1963	55,349	45,964	336	46,300	2,712	-935	42,653	9,147	3,549	3,170	2,752	17,461	...
1964	59,121	48,730	318	49,048	2,681	-1,031	45,336	10,062	3,723	3,361	2,959	17,589	...
1965	62,757	51,434	366	51,800	2,803	-1,116	47,881	10,861	4,016	3,539	3,104	17,734	...
1966	67,355	55,805	427	56,232	3,720	-1,270	51,242	11,477	4,636	3,775	3,291	17,843	...
1967	72,615	59,699	380	60,079	4,032	-1,412	54,635	12,080	5,900	4,049	3,500	17,935	...
1968	80,125	65,492	388	65,880	4,446	-1,594	59,840	13,072	7,213	4,439	3,811	18,051	...
1969	83,913	70,681	440	71,121	5,291	-3,431	62,399	13,778	7,735	4,635	3,912	18,105	8,494
1970	90,165	75,134	420	75,554	5,534	-3,391	66,628	14,628	8,909	4,935	4,243	18,272	8,466
1971	96,393	79,519	410	79,929	6,030	-3,532	70,367	15,282	10,744	5,249	4,578	18,365	8,345
1972	103,115	85,345	353	85,698	6,796	-3,813	75,090	16,032	11,993	5,619	4,848	18,352	8,348
1973	109,639	90,960	470	91,430	8,413	-3,949	79,068	17,283	13,289	6,026	5,221	18,195	8,465
1974	118,078	96,263	444	96,707	9,188	-4,156	83,363	19,297	15,418	6,533	5,641	18,073	8,392
1975	127,412	101,016	379	101,395	9,452	-4,446	87,497	20,409	19,506	7,066	6,194	18,032	8,172
1976	134,872	107,223	401	107,624	10,248	-4,701	92,675	21,398	20,800	7,503	6,544	17,975	8,125
1977	145,586	116,201	331	116,532	11,010	-5,241	100,281	23,546	21,759	8,155	7,085	17,852	8,199
1978	158,660	127,911	433	128,344	12,375	-5,929	110,040	25,834	22,786	8,954	7,745	17,720	8,384
1979	173,525	140,625	539	141,164	14,082	-6,773	120,309	28,879	24,337	9,841	8,451	17,634	8,581
1980	193,182	154,019	530	154,550	15,430	-7,863	131,257	33,935	27,991	10,997	9,405	17,567	8,602
1981	215,239	168,765	543	169,308	18,083	-8,554	142,670	40,980	31,588	12,252	10,375	17,568	8,666
1982	233,470	180,922	518	181,440	19,681	-9,328	152,431	46,484	34,555	13,273	11,214	17,590	8,673
1983	251,848	195,326	371	195,697	21,224	-9,895	164,578	49,892	37,377	14,239	12,243	17,687	8,730
1984	279,012	215,299	494	215,793	23,937	-10,598	181,257	58,195	39,559	15,723	13,561	17,746	9,003
1985	298,868	232,976	561	233,537	26,272	-11,369	195,896	61,217	41,755	16,798	14,393	17,792	9,227
1986	318,950	251,868	654	252,522	28,844	-11,989	211,688	63,015	44,246	17,885	15,308	17,833	9,424
1987	340,487	273,211	732	273,943	30,680	-12,792	230,471	64,629	45,387	19,055	16,151	17,869	9,472
1988	373,993	301,156	645	301,801	34,031	-13,722	254,047	71,651	48,295	20,845	17,884	17,941	9,684
1989	404,343	318,130	777	318,907	35,481	-13,794	269,633	81,687	53,023	22,485	19,180	17,983	9,752
1990	432,392	338,348	775	339,123	35,787	-13,497	289,840	84,387	58,165	23,994	20,648	18,021	9,727
1991	432,624	333,148	647	333,795	36,733	-13,464	283,598	84,283	64,744	23,872	20,650	18,123	9,483
1992	457,407	356,041	749	356,790	38,353	-16,613	301,824	83,219	72,364	25,068	21,718	18,247	9,410
1993	469,767	364,388	793	365,181	39,223	-16,387	309,571	83,343	76,854	25,566	22,064	18,375	9,431
1994	484,813	373,579	672	374,250	40,889	-16,386	316,975	87,237	80,601	26,264	22,666	18,459	9,465
1995	511,630	391,089	538	391,627	42,381	-18,627	330,619	95,236	85,775	27,620	23,789	18,524	9,511
1996	538,197	413,178	767	413,945	43,658	-21,487	348,800	99,962	89,435	28,953	24,722	18,588	9,595
1997	568,314	441,952	456	442,408	45,606	-24,057	372,745	106,231	89,338	30,462	25,829	18,657	9,732
1998	596,673	466,887	690	467,576	47,877	-27,354	392,346	110,999	93,328	31,813	26,694	18,756	9,891
1999	628,080	498,673	771	499,444	50,239	-28,573	420,632	111,281	96,167	33,262	27,720	18,883	10,145
2000	671,290	537,160	780	537,940	54,133	-32,373	451,433	119,210	100,646	35,328	29,302	19,002	10,393
2001	692,858	557,594	930	558,524	56,439	-33,336	468,749	116,731	107,378	36,308	29,729	19,083	10,398
2002	694,348	554,679	712	555,391	57,392	-27,840	470,159	107,520	116,669	36,282	31,000	19,138	10,309
2003	713,332	565,995	865	566,859	59,174	-27,281	480,405	111,422	121,505	37,199	32,171	19,176	10,339
2004	754,248	599,544	1,083	600,627	62,095	-33,763	504,769	118,579	130,900	39,342	33,900	19,172	10,485
2005	791,723	624,109	1,072	625,181	64,922	-40,310	519,949	141,542	130,233	41,381	35,200	19,133	10,621
2006	849,616	669,114	915	670,029	68,610	-48,689	552,729	159,291	137,595	44,472	37,301	19,105	10,771
2007	914,147	715,909	1,275	717,184	72,636	-58,179	586,368	184,043	143,736	47,780	39,574	19,132	11,042
2008	942,015	732,028	1,303	733,331	75,341	-55,557	602,432	182,443	157,139	49,032	40,786	19,212	11,163
2009	920,076	707,095	791	707,886	73,058	-45,862	588,966	158,998	172,112	47,655	41,395	19,307	10,957
2010	956,132	741,331	1,326	742,657	75,675	-52,469	614,514	159,181	182,438	49,283	42,563	19,401	10,956
2011	1,007,280	767,442	1,727	769,169	69,994	-56,228	642,946	178,591	185,743	51,598	43,951	19,522	11,244
2012	1,050,369	789,399	1,594	790,993	71,806	-58,477	660,710	204,827	184,833	53,571	45,832	19,607	11,374
2013	1,055,803	808,688	2,160	810,848	84,510	-58,137	668,201	200,744	186,858	53,606	44,892	19,696	11,555
2014	1,098,103	853,230	2,253	855,482	89,240	-67,005	699,237	208,669	190,197	55,611	46,266	19,746	11,764
2015	1,142,485	886,957	1,789	888,747	92,052	-69,780	726,915	216,416	199,154	57,705	47,590	19,799	...

... = Not available.

Personal Income and Employment by Region and State: North Carolina

(Millions of dollars, except as noted.)

Year	Personal income, total	Earnings by place of work			Less: Contributions for government social insurance	Plus: Adjustment for residence	Equals: Net earnings by place of residence	Plus: Dividends, interest, and rent	Plus: Personal current transfer receipts	Per capita (dollars)		Population (thousands)	Total employment (thousands)
		Nonfarm	Farm	Total						Personal income	Disposable personal income		
1960	7,646	5,987	604	6,592	307	10	6,295	895	457	1,672	1,523	4,573	...
1961	8,093	6,260	645	6,905	314	10	6,601	968	524	1,735	1,582	4,663	...
1962	8,681	6,774	627	7,402	347	11	7,066	1,063	552	1,844	1,672	4,707	...
1963	9,129	7,193	606	7,799	412	11	7,399	1,135	595	1,925	1,741	4,742	...
1964	9,885	7,809	634	8,443	435	12	8,020	1,241	623	2,058	1,883	4,802	...
1965	10,689	8,594	532	9,126	467	11	8,670	1,339	679	2,198	1,992	4,863	...
1966	11,869	9,677	618	10,295	617	11	9,688	1,443	738	2,424	2,185	4,896	...
1967	12,821	10,527	607	11,134	716	10	10,429	1,533	859	2,589	2,336	4,952	...
1968	14,122	11,803	518	12,321	826	13	11,508	1,633	981	2,822	2,513	5,004	...
1969	15,814	13,049	673	13,722	900	20	12,842	1,865	1,107	3,143	2,763	5,031	2,458
1970	17,266	14,022	672	14,694	971	16	13,739	2,189	1,338	3,386	2,998	5,099	2,469
1971	18,796	15,312	627	15,939	1,102	13	14,851	2,376	1,569	3,614	3,227	5,201	2,490
1972	21,242	17,405	750	18,155	1,309	8	16,855	2,631	1,757	4,011	3,536	5,296	2,602
1973	24,058	19,536	1,162	20,698	1,678	7	19,027	2,992	2,038	4,470	3,965	5,382	2,720
1974	26,521	21,286	1,110	22,396	1,901	13	20,507	3,480	2,533	4,856	4,282	5,461	2,743
1975	28,819	22,339	1,066	23,404	1,978	15	21,442	3,855	3,522	5,207	4,701	5,535	2,647
1976	31,951	25,093	1,148	26,241	2,272	14	23,983	4,170	3,798	5,712	5,096	5,593	2,754
1977	35,004	27,937	857	28,794	2,513	19	26,300	4,697	4,007	6,175	5,484	5,668	2,851
1978	39,496	31,590	1,142	32,732	2,920	18	29,830	5,352	4,315	6,881	6,083	5,740	2,946
1979	43,638	35,300	757	36,056	3,390	13	32,679	6,026	4,933	7,522	6,592	5,802	3,046
1980	48,935	38,661	651	39,312	3,717	17	35,612	7,425	5,898	8,295	7,267	5,899	3,052
1981	55,094	42,478	1,049	43,527	4,380	-30	39,117	9,179	6,798	9,249	8,086	5,957	3,072
1982	59,016	44,554	1,064	45,618	4,635	-41	40,943	10,505	7,568	9,805	8,695	6,019	3,042
1983	64,310	49,241	635	49,875	5,173	-59	44,643	11,512	8,155	10,582	9,356	6,077	3,129
1984	72,718	55,506	1,292	56,798	5,969	-95	50,734	13,369	8,615	11,797	10,469	6,164	3,292
1985	78,721	60,424	1,161	61,584	6,589	-157	54,839	14,646	9,237	12,587	11,131	6,254	3,392
1986	84,797	65,558	1,145	66,703	7,294	-219	59,190	15,780	9,827	13,414	11,857	6,322	3,494
1987	91,334	71,644	1,141	72,785	7,869	-300	64,615	16,499	10,220	14,263	12,505	6,404	3,610
1988	100,022	78,192	1,477	79,669	8,838	-363	70,468	18,477	11,077	15,434	13,619	6,481	3,751
1989	109,071	83,879	1,722	85,601	9,490	-418	75,693	21,010	12,367	16,613	14,566	6,565	3,838
1990	115,755	88,393	2,135	90,528	10,257	-458	79,814	22,268	13,674	17,370	15,309	6,664	3,902
1991	120,936	91,390	2,394	93,784	10,747	-440	82,597	22,615	15,724	17,826	15,785	6,784	3,866
1992	131,825	100,361	2,340	102,702	11,649	-465	90,588	23,828	17,409	19,113	16,980	6,897	3,964
1993	140,621	106,455	2,613	109,067	12,435	-481	96,151	25,335	19,134	19,967	17,705	7,043	4,087
1994	149,735	113,612	2,826	116,437	13,399	-546	102,492	27,334	19,908	20,833	18,403	7,187	4,201
1995	160,530	120,656	2,710	123,365	14,228	-618	108,519	29,707	22,305	21,857	19,256	7,345	4,355
1996	171,935	127,749	2,996	130,745	14,926	-682	115,137	32,583	24,215	22,923	20,126	7,501	4,459
1997	184,820	137,656	3,064	140,720	15,978	-760	123,982	35,420	25,418	24,138	21,091	7,657	4,603
1998	198,910	149,672	2,409	152,081	17,207	-738	134,136	38,350	26,425	25,472	22,108	7,809	4,707
1999	210,373	160,472	2,240	162,712	18,336	-807	143,569	38,742	28,062	26,464	23,022	7,949	4,804
2000	225,286	171,821	2,965	174,786	19,428	-921	154,437	40,823	30,026	27,876	24,200	8,082	4,893
2001	233,860	177,049	3,122	180,171	20,100	-830	159,241	41,117	33,503	28,484	24,813	8,210	4,856
2002	237,355	181,012	1,514	182,525	20,361	-1,200	160,963	40,144	36,248	28,507	25,327	8,326	4,843
2003	244,934	186,593	1,598	188,191	21,370	-1,456	165,365	41,430	38,139	29,081	26,082	8,423	4,854
2004	263,311	197,885	2,374	200,259	22,457	-1,363	176,439	45,754	41,118	30,785	27,724	8,553	4,971
2005	280,702	208,870	3,169	212,039	24,015	-1,670	186,354	49,786	44,562	32,245	28,752	8,705	5,100
2006	301,182	224,121	2,615	226,736	25,774	-1,510	199,452	53,162	48,569	33,775	29,935	8,917	5,260
2007	320,003	234,809	2,251	237,059	27,518	-1,241	208,300	59,440	52,263	35,096	30,905	9,118	5,446
2008	334,365	240,315	2,259	242,574	28,284	-1,388	212,902	62,054	59,409	35,917	31,852	9,309	5,432
2009	330,202	234,430	2,250	236,680	27,503	-1,176	208,001	55,760	66,441	34,944	31,805	9,450	5,237
2010	340,018	241,918	2,474	244,392	27,473	-1,206	215,713	53,750	70,555	35,569	32,322	9,559	5,186
2011	353,462	245,874	2,162	248,036	25,652	-1,256	221,128	59,957	72,376	36,622	32,886	9,652	5,301
2012	376,817	263,657	3,026	266,683	26,667	-1,456	238,561	64,225	74,031	38,655	34,870	9,748	5,362
2013	372,031	261,019	3,773	264,792	30,687	-1,522	232,584	64,059	75,389	37,774	33,687	9,849	5,449
2014	389,513	274,868	4,326	279,194	32,293	-1,808	245,093	66,458	77,962	39,171	34,927	9,944	5,552
2015	408,364	289,603	3,452	293,055	33,794	-1,945	257,316	69,044	82,004	40,656	36049	10044	...

... = Not available.

Personal Income and Employment by Region and State: North Dakota

(Millions of dollars, except as noted.)

Year	Personal income, total	Derivation of personal income								Per capita (dollars)		Population (thousands)	Total employment (thousands)
		Earnings by place of work			Less: Contributions for government social insurance	Plus: Adjustment for residence	Equals: Net earnings by place of residence	Plus: Dividends, interest, and rent	Plus: Personal current transfer receipts	Personal income	Disposable personal income		
		Nonfarm	Farm	Total									
1960	1,212	717	273	991	41	-12	938	190	83	1,911	1,766	634	...
1961	1,111	751	145	896	43	-12	841	180	90	1,734	1,597	641	...
1962	1,557	814	478	1,292	47	-14	1,230	232	94	2,444	2,271	637	...
1963	1,450	867	328	1,195	56	-14	1,124	228	98	2,251	2,075	644	...
1964	1,441	934	241	1,175	59	-17	1,099	238	104	2,221	2,052	649	...
1965	1,678	996	382	1,379	62	-17	1,300	264	114	2,586	2,404	649	...
1966	1,698	1,050	349	1,399	74	-16	1,309	266	123	2,625	2,424	647	...
1967	1,699	1,079	310	1,389	89	-16	1,284	268	147	2,715	2,490	626	...
1968	1,775	1,149	285	1,433	95	-16	1,322	289	164	2,859	2,619	621	...
1969	1,994	1,253	385	1,638	102	-55	1,480	332	183	3,211	2,895	621	274
1970	2,105	1,394	306	1,700	115	-58	1,528	366	212	3,401	3,091	619	281
1971	2,427	1,528	434	1,962	129	-61	1,772	406	248	3,872	3,576	627	284
1972	2,890	1,708	668	2,376	147	-64	2,165	449	276	4,580	4,219	631	288
1973	4,039	1,923	1,529	3,452	189	-67	3,195	533	310	6,386	5,883	632	300
1974	4,003	2,166	1,164	3,330	224	-79	3,027	621	356	6,312	5,643	634	308
1975	4,200	2,443	945	3,388	256	-83	3,049	732	420	6,579	5,911	638	314
1976	4,117	2,776	478	3,254	294	-97	2,864	789	465	6,380	5,727	645	326
1977	4,276	3,007	274	3,281	303	-103	2,876	894	507	6,588	5,941	649	331
1978	5,371	3,423	865	4,288	354	-113	3,822	996	553	8,255	7,418	651	345
1979	5,514	3,827	502	4,329	412	-130	3,787	1,113	613	8,455	7,575	652	353
1980	5,280	4,154	-383	3,771	450	-145	3,175	1,380	725	8,068	7,092	654	355
1981	6,914	4,640	372	5,012	533	-166	4,313	1,770	831	10,484	9,240	660	359
1982	7,487	4,905	306	5,211	576	-168	4,466	2,090	932	11,192	10,083	669	360
1983	7,887	5,164	366	5,531	613	-171	4,746	2,105	1,036	11,656	10,586	677	365
1984	8,493	5,363	612	5,975	652	-171	5,152	2,230	1,111	12,480	11,373	680	366
1985	8,782	5,455	699	6,154	678	-170	5,306	2,296	1,180	12,973	11,836	677	364
1986	8,911	5,512	693	6,205	698	-168	5,339	2,285	1,287	13,309	12,202	670	357
1987	9,162	5,738	789	6,527	727	-168	5,631	2,184	1,346	13,857	12,644	661	363
1988	8,474	5,987	-61	5,927	794	-175	4,957	2,163	1,353	12,930	11,680	655	366
1989	9,507	6,238	442	6,680	840	-180	5,660	2,372	1,474	14,709	13,330	646	370
1990	10,290	6,595	773	7,368	933	-184	6,251	2,461	1,578	16,137	14,643	638	374
1991	10,410	6,941	614	7,555	1,002	-191	6,362	2,443	1,605	16,374	14,830	636	382
1992	11,411	7,380	1,074	8,454	1,064	-206	7,183	2,456	1,772	17,880	16,287	638	388
1993	11,563	7,884	624	8,508	1,146	-225	7,137	2,559	1,867	18,033	16,327	641	397
1994	12,545	8,373	1,059	9,432	1,221	-240	7,971	2,673	1,901	19,456	17,684	645	411
1995	12,579	8,797	429	9,226	1,270	-262	7,694	2,874	2,010	19,417	17,543	648	418
1996	14,071	9,292	1,308	10,600	1,327	-294	8,979	2,999	2,092	21,635	19,634	650	426
1997	13,809	9,779	304	10,083	1,374	-321	8,388	3,239	2,182	21,253	19,110	650	430
1998	15,134	10,325	972	11,297	1,438	-344	9,515	3,410	2,209	23,372	21,103	648	436
1999	15,270	10,777	692	11,469	1,478	-370	9,621	3,345	2,304	23,701	21,370	644	437
2000	16,609	11,411	1,100	12,511	1,550	-404	10,558	3,579	2,472	25,870	23,356	642	441
2001	16,960	12,004	801	12,805	1,591	-445	10,768	3,630	2,562	26,540	23,870	639	443
2002	17,332	12,566	603	13,169	1,649	-490	11,031	3,613	2,688	27,158	24,838	638	441
2003	18,843	13,269	1,495	14,765	1,738	-541	12,486	3,589	2,767	29,496	27,239	639	442
2004	19,159	14,154	945	15,098	1,840	-590	12,669	3,564	2,926	29,717	27,413	645	451
2005	20,306	14,873	1,190	16,062	1,919	-630	13,513	3,649	3,143	31,429	28,797	646	460
2006	21,318	16,027	738	16,765	2,012	-677	14,076	3,948	3,294	32,826	29,791	649	469
2007	23,607	16,781	1,621	18,401	2,113	-710	15,578	4,478	3,551	36,162	32,636	653	480
2008	26,910	18,045	2,637	20,681	2,259	-765	17,657	5,231	4,022	40,923	36,803	658	489
2009	26,214	18,558	1,679	20,237	2,420	-751	17,066	4,948	4,200	39,422	36,114	665	491
2010	28,973	20,142	2,291	22,433	2,494	-810	19,129	5,297	4,547	42,964	39,138	674	500
2011	32,796	23,085	2,283	25,369	2,628	-918	21,822	6,315	4,659	47,861	42,853	685	525
2012	38,866	26,971	3,837	30,809	2,848	-1,047	26,914	7,243	4,709	55,388	49,423	702	562
2013	39,358	29,049	2,332	31,382	3,497	-1,116	26,768	7,730	4,860	54,373	48,039	724	581
2014	41,265	31,855	1,358	33,214	3,850	-1,224	28,140	8,070	5,055	55,802	48,999	739	601
2015	41,166	31,593	700	32,292	3,768	-1,170	27,355	8,476	5,335	54,376	47,515	757	...

... = Not available.

Personal Income and Employment by Region and State: Ohio

(Millions of dollars, except as noted.)

Year	Personal income, total	Earnings by place of work			Less: Contributions for government social insurance	Plus: Adjustment for residence	Equals: Net earnings by place of residence	Plus: Dividends, interest, and rent	Plus: Personal current transfer receipts	Per capita (dollars)		Population (thousands)	Total employment (thousands)
		Nonfarm	Farm	Total						Personal income	Disposable personal income		
1960	23,510	19,713	334	20,047	1,003	-132	18,913	3,086	1,512	2,415	2,145	9,734	...
1961	23,960	19,690	373	20,063	984	-122	18,957	3,243	1,760	2,432	2,172	9,854	...
1962	25,243	20,934	336	21,270	1,125	-127	20,018	3,493	1,731	2,542	2,262	9,929	...
1963	26,288	21,844	334	22,179	1,236	-129	20,813	3,693	1,782	2,632	2,339	9,986	...
1964	28,064	23,496	305	23,802	1,355	-134	22,313	3,963	1,789	2,784	2,509	10,080	...
1965	30,357	25,436	358	25,794	1,409	-147	24,238	4,225	1,893	2,976	2,664	10,201	...
1966	33,135	28,106	496	28,602	1,864	-166	26,571	4,525	2,038	3,208	2,858	10,330	...
1967	34,709	29,371	329	29,700	1,958	-161	27,581	4,749	2,379	3,333	2,966	10,414	...
1968	38,275	32,297	412	32,710	2,134	-184	30,392	5,193	2,690	3,640	3,201	10,516	...
1969	41,815	35,504	417	35,921	2,360	-195	33,367	5,548	2,900	3,959	3,433	10,563	4,695
1970	44,121	36,824	435	37,259	2,408	-184	34,667	6,059	3,395	4,136	3,638	10,669	4,683
1971	46,947	38,736	415	39,151	2,603	-135	36,412	6,521	4,014	4,373	3,908	10,735	4,627
1972	50,934	42,156	506	42,662	2,985	-134	39,543	6,953	4,438	4,739	4,170	10,747	4,710
1973	56,459	46,968	667	47,634	3,864	-160	43,611	7,683	5,166	5,244	4,617	10,767	4,902
1974	61,841	50,559	798	51,357	4,310	-135	46,912	8,727	6,203	5,744	5,044	10,766	4,964
1975	66,119	52,331	814	53,145	4,336	-94	48,715	9,472	7,933	6,139	5,440	10,770	4,809
1976	72,484	58,174	787	58,962	4,942	-109	53,911	10,071	8,502	6,741	5,935	10,753	4,889
1977	80,273	65,198	675	65,872	5,554	-115	60,203	11,140	8,930	7,453	6,519	10,771	5,034
1978	88,756	72,674	628	73,301	6,397	-137	66,768	12,393	9,594	8,222	7,171	10,795	5,206
1979	98,037	79,861	762	80,623	7,322	-160	73,141	13,942	10,953	9,079	7,862	10,799	5,291
1980	107,028	83,522	575	84,096	7,612	-182	76,303	16,914	13,811	9,909	8,631	10,801	5,204
1981	116,356	89,294	167	89,461	8,708	-486	80,267	20,742	15,347	10,785	9,337	10,788	5,135
1982	121,687	90,116	270	90,386	8,900	-611	80,875	23,001	17,810	11,312	9,915	10,757	4,967
1983	129,000	95,370	-69	95,302	9,613	-714	84,975	24,979	19,045	12,014	10,548	10,738	4,960
1984	142,456	105,882	874	106,756	10,932	-845	94,979	27,828	19,649	13,267	11,718	10,738	5,160
1985	151,328	113,111	870	113,981	11,870	-921	101,190	29,194	20,944	14,097	12,414	10,735	5,287
1986	158,446	119,030	684	119,714	12,856	-954	105,904	30,357	22,185	14,766	13,030	10,730	5,401
1987	166,011	125,980	734	126,714	13,614	-997	112,103	30,857	23,052	15,428	13,503	10,760	5,548
1988	178,043	136,220	783	137,003	15,149	-1,044	120,810	33,000	24,233	16,488	14,498	10,799	5,682
1989	191,553	144,656	1,171	145,827	16,209	-1,107	128,511	37,211	25,831	17,689	15,480	10,829	5,803
1990	202,827	152,228	1,205	153,433	17,415	-1,095	134,923	39,165	28,740	18,669	16,366	10,864	5,863
1991	207,193	156,221	702	156,923	18,308	-1,116	137,499	38,705	30,988	18,929	16,646	10,946	5,842
1992	220,962	166,890	1,184	168,075	19,470	-1,232	147,373	39,555	34,034	20,034	17,673	11,029	5,854
1993	230,240	174,589	933	175,523	20,592	-1,330	153,601	41,250	35,389	20,740	18,248	11,101	5,960
1994	242,928	185,394	1,162	186,556	22,172	-1,453	162,930	43,253	36,744	21,782	19,129	11,152	6,136
1995	254,378	193,314	891	194,205	23,353	-1,494	169,358	46,246	38,774	22,707	19,873	11,203	6,300
1996	266,568	201,455	1,250	202,705	24,062	-1,550	177,093	49,266	40,209	23,710	20,590	11,243	6,395
1997	282,349	212,934	1,684	214,619	24,790	-1,648	188,181	52,745	41,423	25,037	21,672	11,277	6,500
1998	298,717	226,740	1,270	228,011	25,559	-1,825	200,627	55,907	42,182	26,408	22,780	11,312	6,597
1999	308,888	237,986	851	238,837	26,717	-1,795	210,325	55,042	43,521	27,250	23,540	11,335	6,675
2000	325,351	249,546	1,208	250,754	27,075	-1,755	221,924	57,160	46,267	28,631	24,681	11,364	6,780
2001	334,990	256,180	1,139	257,319	27,710	-1,684	227,925	56,599	50,466	29,418	25,446	11,387	6,713
2002	340,053	261,474	584	262,058	27,767	-2,495	231,796	54,425	53,832	29,809	26,245	11,408	6,636
2003	349,663	269,455	790	270,245	28,881	-2,549	238,814	54,430	56,419	30,579	27,223	11,435	6,617
2004	363,405	281,260	1,406	282,667	30,574	-2,324	249,769	54,670	58,967	31,732	28,299	11,452	6,661
2005	374,698	288,564	1,076	289,639	31,408	-2,417	255,814	56,471	62,413	32,687	28,973	11,463	6,707
2006	395,120	301,272	921	302,194	32,809	-2,197	267,187	62,116	65,817	34,415	30,422	11,481	6,745
2007	409,790	306,956	1,123	308,079	33,614	-1,977	272,488	67,270	70,032	35,632	31,374	11,500	6,798
2008	421,955	310,338	1,330	311,668	34,548	-2,193	274,927	68,051	78,977	36,643	32,414	11,515	6,731
2009	409,619	297,018	1,617	298,635	33,489	-1,872	263,274	60,347	85,998	35,530	32,235	11,529	6,466
2010	419,791	304,180	1,607	305,787	33,711	-1,794	270,282	58,770	90,740	36,377	32,842	11,540	6,400
2011	448,018	319,599	2,958	322,557	31,756	-1,858	288,943	65,822	93,253	38,807	34,693	11,545	6,503
2012	465,839	334,191	1,952	336,143	32,866	-1,764	301,513	72,873	91,452	40,329	36,095	11,551	6,584
2013	471,547	342,056	3,122	345,178	37,066	-2,021	306,092	71,909	93,546	40,749	36,253	11,572	6,658
2014	489,695	356,146	2,314	358,460	38,999	-2,308	317,153	74,485	98,057	42,236	37,558	11,594	6,753
2015	504,993	367,491	766	368,257	40,105	-2,389	325,763	77,674	101,557	43,478	38449	11615	...

... = Not available.

Personal Income and Employment by Region and State: Oklahoma

(Millions of dollars, except as noted.)

Year	Personal income, total	Earnings by place of work Nonfarm	Farm	Total	Less: Contributions for government social insurance	Plus: Adjustment for residence	Equals: Net earnings by place of residence	Plus: Dividends, interest, and rent	Plus: Personal current transfer receipts	Per capita (dollars) Personal income	Disposable personal income	Population (thousands)	Total employment (thousands)
1960	4,619	3,361	335	3,696	150	7	3,552	689	378	1,977	1,792	2,336	...
1961	4,779	3,495	301	3,796	159	8	3,646	717	416	2,008	1,813	2,380	...
1962	4,983	3,726	240	3,966	178	11	3,799	743	441	2,053	1,852	2,427	...
1963	5,151	3,893	214	4,107	208	12	3,911	769	471	2,112	1,907	2,439	...
1964	5,517	4,184	208	4,392	208	14	4,199	827	491	2,256	2,055	2,446	...
1965	5,912	4,420	278	4,697	216	17	4,499	888	526	2,423	2,208	2,440	...
1966	6,341	4,818	267	5,085	286	21	4,820	938	584	2,584	2,342	2,454	...
1967	6,924	5,281	276	5,557	337	25	5,246	979	700	2,782	2,517	2,489	...
1968	7,580	5,864	219	6,084	385	31	5,729	1,062	789	3,029	2,722	2,503	...
1969	8,440	6,409	275	6,685	401	63	6,347	1,238	855	3,329	2,948	2,535	1,107
1970	9,304	6,907	359	7,266	431	65	6,900	1,422	981	3,625	3,248	2,566	1,120
1971	10,138	7,496	335	7,831	484	64	7,411	1,596	1,131	3,872	3,512	2,618	1,132
1972	11,122	8,260	417	8,677	558	73	8,193	1,689	1,240	4,185	3,742	2,657	1,183
1973	12,610	9,156	734	9,889	720	83	9,252	1,952	1,406	4,680	4,221	2,694	1,221
1974	14,034	10,394	452	10,846	845	107	10,107	2,263	1,664	5,136	4,559	2,732	1,256
1975	15,692	11,503	404	11,907	928	142	11,121	2,519	2,052	5,661	5,100	2,772	1,269
1976	17,269	12,827	338	13,165	1,054	177	12,288	2,730	2,251	6,116	5,475	2,823	1,305
1977	19,197	14,609	183	14,792	1,198	153	13,747	3,057	2,393	6,698	5,958	2,866	1,359
1978	21,786	16,760	174	16,934	1,418	149	15,665	3,546	2,575	7,479	6,585	2,913	1,428
1979	25,286	19,151	634	19,786	1,688	164	18,262	4,069	2,955	8,514	7,474	2,970	1,481
1980	29,132	22,174	265	22,439	1,971	173	20,641	5,073	3,419	9,581	8,351	3,041	1,547
1981	34,025	25,640	330	25,970	2,450	198	23,718	6,425	3,882	10,989	9,435	3,096	1,625
1982	37,994	28,031	487	28,518	2,748	204	25,974	7,643	4,376	11,850	10,101	3,206	1,673
1983	38,869	28,154	214	28,368	2,739	241	25,870	8,198	4,801	11,813	10,407	3,290	1,638
1984	41,684	29,987	376	30,363	2,969	289	27,683	9,019	4,982	12,687	11,280	3,286	1,665
1985	43,419	30,839	382	31,221	3,109	331	28,443	9,655	5,322	13,273	11,812	3,271	1,648
1986	43,626	30,730	645	31,374	3,161	382	28,595	9,373	5,657	13,412	12,200	3,253	1,588
1987	43,451	30,697	564	31,261	3,181	429	28,508	9,056	5,886	13,536	12,147	3,210	1,599
1988	45,332	31,970	765	32,734	3,498	478	29,715	9,387	6,231	14,314	12,846	3,167	1,608
1989	48,330	33,812	802	34,614	3,731	505	31,388	10,313	6,629	15,341	13,693	3,150	1,623
1990	50,949	35,769	862	36,631	4,066	569	33,133	10,682	7,133	16,180	14,264	3,149	1,655
1991	52,474	37,149	623	37,772	4,324	597	34,046	10,625	7,804	16,525	14,710	3,175	1,668
1992	55,899	39,379	844	40,223	4,550	619	36,292	10,876	8,730	17,357	15,525	3,221	1,680
1993	58,123	41,171	867	42,038	4,798	657	37,897	11,046	9,180	17,872	15,994	3,252	1,716
1994	60,728	42,803	826	43,628	5,058	714	39,284	11,691	9,753	18,509	16,534	3,281	1,748
1995	63,398	44,490	286	44,777	5,276	747	40,248	12,617	10,533	19,164	17,110	3,308	1,800
1996	67,140	47,099	359	47,458	5,474	780	42,764	13,322	11,055	20,101	17,858	3,340	1,850
1997	70,868	50,042	662	50,704	5,734	859	45,830	13,680	11,359	21,011	18,529	3,373	1,897
1998	75,390	53,757	518	54,275	6,033	894	49,136	14,666	11,589	22,140	19,513	3,405	1,939
1999	78,356	55,868	839	56,706	6,218	940	51,428	14,823	12,105	22,797	20,098	3,437	1,954
2000	85,672	61,134	831	61,966	6,600	1,020	56,386	16,489	12,797	24,801	21,901	3,454	1,994
2001	92,129	66,453	815	67,269	7,047	1,015	61,236	16,765	14,128	26,572	23,515	3,467	2,011
2002	93,532	67,558	979	68,537	7,253	701	61,985	16,384	15,163	26,807	24,198	3,489	1,989
2003	96,554	70,043	968	71,011	7,471	605	64,145	16,434	15,975	27,548	25,069	3,505	1,973
2004	102,195	74,167	1,260	75,427	7,993	462	67,896	17,309	16,990	28,989	26,411	3,525	1,997
2005	109,855	79,791	1,321	81,112	8,471	382	73,023	18,527	18,305	30,957	27,919	3,549	2,041
2006	120,481	87,305	665	87,970	9,118	317	79,169	21,293	20,020	33,522	30,018	3,594	2,099
2007	125,613	88,383	637	89,020	9,592	797	80,225	23,921	21,467	34,563	30,804	3,634	2,155
2008	138,462	97,653	864	98,516	10,040	792	89,268	25,092	24,102	37,739	33,753	3,669	2,193
2009	128,546	89,180	41	89,221	9,851	727	80,097	22,486	25,962	34,578	31,722	3,718	2,145
2010	135,151	93,638	846	94,484	10,040	707	85,151	22,322	27,678	35,949	32,995	3,759	2,133
2011	147,813	102,013	1,388	103,401	9,689	718	94,429	25,335	28,049	39,037	35,402	3,787	2,163
2012	158,596	109,680	1,849	111,529	10,287	773	102,015	27,906	28,675	41,549	37,749	3,817	2,215
2013	161,686	114,038	1,910	115,948	11,924	742	104,766	27,665	29,255	41,962	37,911	3,853	2,251
2014	169,228	119,503	2,306	121,809	12,221	793	110,381	28,651	30,196	43,637	39,370	3,878	2,282
2015	173,187	121,426	2,197	123,623	12,281	842	112,185	29,771	31,231	44,272	39787	3912	...

... = Not available.

Personal Income and Employment by Region and State: Oregon

(Millions of dollars, except as noted.)

Year	Personal income, total	Earnings by place of work			Less: Contributions for government social insurance	Plus: Adjustment for residence	Equals: Net earnings by place of residence	Plus: Dividends, interest, and rent	Plus: Personal current transfer receipts	Per capita (dollars)		Population (thousands)	Total employment (thousands)
		Nonfarm	Farm	Total						Personal income	Disposable personal income		
1960	4,145	3,300	174	3,474	207	-18	3,249	592	304	2,339	2,057	1,772	...
1961	4,305	3,390	161	3,551	211	-19	3,321	632	352	2,409	2,137	1,787	...
1962	4,574	3,619	172	3,791	232	-23	3,536	679	359	2,516	2,223	1,818	...
1963	4,822	3,862	163	4,026	266	-27	3,732	719	371	2,602	2,279	1,853	...
1964	5,192	4,192	150	4,342	271	-33	4,039	769	384	2,750	2,427	1,888	...
1965	5,643	4,556	168	4,724	276	-39	4,410	818	414	2,913	2,590	1,937	...
1966	6,083	4,960	195	5,155	352	-43	4,760	875	447	3,089	2,729	1,969	...
1967	6,452	5,218	185	5,403	392	-47	4,964	955	533	3,260	2,881	1,979	...
1968	7,027	5,716	183	5,899	444	-55	5,400	1,027	600	3,506	3,067	2,004	...
1969	7,782	6,250	226	6,476	482	-92	5,903	1,217	662	3,774	3,248	2,062	920
1970	8,471	6,634	216	6,850	505	-66	6,279	1,387	805	4,033	3,533	2,100	926
1971	9,310	7,265	204	7,469	569	-53	6,848	1,530	932	4,330	3,827	2,150	951
1972	10,432	8,202	259	8,461	679	-46	7,736	1,674	1,022	4,752	4,161	2,195	1,001
1973	11,749	9,215	371	9,586	880	-51	8,656	1,881	1,213	5,248	4,610	2,239	1,058
1974	13,322	10,217	477	10,694	1,002	-59	9,633	2,194	1,496	5,841	5,096	2,281	1,089
1975	14,784	11,103	394	11,496	1,056	-32	10,408	2,475	1,901	6,360	5,640	2,325	1,105
1976	16,683	12,779	370	13,149	1,234	-16	11,898	2,714	2,071	7,033	6,175	2,372	1,156
1977	18,667	14,512	320	14,832	1,420	-75	13,336	3,091	2,239	7,652	6,624	2,439	1,223
1978	21,418	16,851	317	17,168	1,693	-129	15,347	3,627	2,444	8,534	7,360	2,510	1,296
1979	24,224	19,062	390	19,452	1,987	-204	17,261	4,222	2,740	9,395	8,070	2,578	1,350
1980	26,826	20,387	477	20,864	2,127	-251	18,486	5,083	3,256	10,157	8,773	2,641	1,350
1981	28,977	21,223	406	21,629	2,369	-269	18,990	6,219	3,767	10,861	9,421	2,668	1,319
1982	29,703	21,099	293	21,393	2,403	-258	18,732	6,725	4,247	11,146	9,696	2,665	1,270
1983	31,521	22,269	301	22,570	2,558	-247	19,765	7,193	4,564	11,881	10,440	2,653	1,295
1984	34,216	24,333	402	24,735	2,890	-287	21,558	7,945	4,713	12,831	11,329	2,667	1,342
1985	35,892	25,639	428	26,067	3,070	-317	22,680	8,281	4,931	13,429	11,807	2,673	1,370
1986	37,857	27,226	550	27,775	3,251	-373	24,152	8,685	5,020	14,107	12,343	2,684	1,406
1987	39,855	29,169	515	29,684	3,438	-436	25,810	8,849	5,197	14,756	12,911	2,701	1,455
1988	43,416	32,156	702	32,858	3,931	-505	28,422	9,462	5,531	15,838	14,029	2,741	1,522
1989	47,825	34,959	675	35,633	4,272	-563	30,799	10,943	6,083	17,138	14,915	2,791	1,574
1990	51,672	38,239	713	38,953	4,791	-614	33,547	11,510	6,615	18,065	15,871	2,860	1,626
1991	54,360	40,310	727	41,037	5,106	-678	35,252	11,783	7,325	18,562	16,242	2,929	1,636
1992	58,159	43,441	730	44,171	5,459	-776	37,936	12,072	8,151	19,440	17,010	2,992	1,654
1993	62,320	46,459	850	47,309	5,830	-872	40,607	13,009	8,704	20,364	17,780	3,060	1,698
1994	66,793	50,070	776	50,846	6,322	-938	43,587	14,170	9,036	21,399	18,615	3,121	1,781
1995	71,914	53,401	688	54,090	6,789	-1,116	46,184	15,718	10,011	22,583	19,668	3,184	1,845
1996	77,572	57,970	840	58,810	7,452	-1,351	50,007	16,913	10,652	23,889	20,707	3,247	1,920
1997	82,429	62,250	956	63,206	7,910	-1,538	53,758	17,708	10,963	24,946	21,445	3,304	1,986
1998	87,518	66,543	862	67,404	8,366	-1,661	57,378	18,742	11,399	26,106	22,498	3,352	2,021
1999	91,498	70,424	824	71,248	8,726	-1,756	60,765	18,326	12,406	26,959	23,121	3,394	2,049
2000	99,044	76,743	826	77,569	9,417	-1,998	66,154	19,841	13,049	28,878	24,681	3,430	2,090
2001	101,756	77,967	833	78,801	9,449	-2,089	67,262	19,702	14,791	29,342	25,397	3,468	2,077
2002	102,965	78,932	837	79,769	9,612	-2,241	67,916	19,276	15,773	29,306	25,857	3,513	2,069
2003	106,522	81,225	1,123	82,349	9,918	-2,380	70,050	20,214	16,258	30,028	26,694	3,547	2,085
2004	112,389	85,987	1,256	87,243	10,619	-2,455	74,169	21,539	16,681	31,486	28,002	3,569	2,139
2005	117,191	89,877	1,251	91,128	11,213	-2,593	77,322	22,117	17,752	32,434	28,396	3,613	2,201
2006	126,816	95,831	1,326	97,157	12,049	-2,841	82,267	25,591	18,958	34,546	30,126	3,671	2,262
2007	132,696	99,340	1,398	100,738	12,552	-3,125	85,062	27,197	20,437	35,648	31,265	3,722	2,311
2008	138,500	100,832	1,127	101,959	12,705	-3,409	85,845	28,909	23,747	36,750	32,173	3,769	2,300
2009	134,787	96,396	1,020	97,417	12,196	-3,299	81,922	25,762	27,103	35,390	31,875	3,809	2,203
2010	137,332	97,532	953	98,485	12,519	-3,139	82,826	25,204	29,301	35,791	32,087	3,837	2,171
2011	145,084	101,361	1,107	102,468	11,576	-3,432	87,460	27,890	29,734	37,512	33,219	3,868	2,200
2012	152,371	106,654	1,454	108,108	12,128	-3,592	92,389	30,257	29,725	39,083	34,657	3,899	2,216
2013	154,869	110,258	1,455	111,713	14,177	-3,615	93,921	30,129	30,820	39,426	34,481	3,928	2,254
2014	163,653	115,505	1,780	117,285	14,939	-3,617	98,730	31,399	33,524	41,220	35,956	3,970	2,310
2015	173,170	122,470	1,932	124,402	15,766	-3,861	104,775	32,644	35,751	42,974	37,222	4,030	...

... = Not available.

Personal Income and Employment by Region and State: Pennsylvania

(Millions of dollars, except as noted.)

Year	Personal income, total	Derivation of personal income									Per capita (dollars)		Population (thousands)	Total employment (thousands)
		Earnings by place of work			Less: Contributions for government social insurance	Plus: Adjustment for residence	Equals: Net earnings by place of residence	Plus: Dividends, interest, and rent	Plus: Personal current transfer receipts		Personal income	Disposable personal income		
		Nonfarm	Farm	Total										
1960	26,277	21,984	298	22,282	1,211	-81	20,990	3,365	1,922		2,319	2,063	11,329	...
1961	26,847	22,177	302	22,479	1,225	-87	21,167	3,497	2,183		2,357	2,109	11,392	...
1962	27,998	23,292	219	23,511	1,334	-104	22,073	3,759	2,167		2,466	2,193	11,355	...
1963	29,040	24,091	261	24,352	1,474	-113	22,765	4,029	2,245		2,542	2,258	11,424	...
1964	31,058	25,850	269	26,119	1,530	-137	24,452	4,347	2,259		2,696	2,424	11,519	...
1965	33,298	27,707	278	27,986	1,594	-156	26,236	4,692	2,370		2,866	2,568	11,620	...
1966	35,898	30,451	266	30,716	2,148	-202	28,366	4,957	2,575		3,078	2,738	11,664	...
1967	38,414	32,250	359	32,609	2,317	-232	30,060	5,286	3,068		3,289	2,928	11,681	...
1968	41,722	34,872	314	35,186	2,421	-269	32,495	5,714	3,512		3,553	3,139	11,741	...
1969	45,364	38,162	372	38,534	2,809	-430	35,295	6,077	3,992		3,864	3,365	11,741	5,250
1970	48,815	40,240	387	40,627	2,928	-400	37,299	6,602	4,914		4,133	3,627	11,812	5,226
1971	51,790	42,198	335	42,533	3,186	-371	38,976	7,039	5,775		4,358	3,868	11,884	5,159
1972	56,519	46,142	347	46,489	3,654	-373	42,462	7,531	6,527		4,748	4,127	11,905	5,247
1973	61,912	50,775	485	51,260	4,627	-343	46,290	8,317	7,305		5,209	4,555	11,885	5,402
1974	68,005	55,157	463	55,620	5,222	-349	50,049	9,416	8,539		5,732	4,986	11,864	5,419
1975	74,306	58,591	425	59,016	5,400	-362	53,254	10,225	10,828		6,245	5,521	11,898	5,302
1976	81,081	63,891	517	64,408	6,000	-338	58,070	10,981	12,030		6,821	6,004	11,887	5,353
1977	88,974	70,404	469	70,873	6,595	-321	63,957	12,235	12,783		7,488	6,554	11,882	5,429
1978	98,098	78,151	506	78,657	7,508	-320	70,829	13,546	13,722		8,268	7,209	11,865	5,562
1979	108,546	86,154	642	86,796	8,576	-342	77,878	15,217	15,452		9,142	7,929	11,874	5,664
1980	118,970	91,602	424	92,025	9,175	-359	82,492	18,768	17,711		10,024	8,707	11,868	5,624
1981	131,280	98,330	635	98,965	10,559	-332	88,074	23,269	19,937		11,070	9,549	11,859	5,584
1982	140,159	100,664	564	101,228	10,980	-161	90,087	27,241	22,831		11,833	10,296	11,845	5,474
1983	146,952	104,953	361	105,313	11,570	-23	93,720	28,544	24,688		12,414	10,937	11,838	5,433
1984	158,682	114,081	848	114,929	13,095	145	101,979	31,853	24,849		13,430	11,837	11,815	5,577
1985	168,466	120,848	846	121,695	14,060	281	107,915	34,550	26,001		14,312	12,602	11,771	5,679
1986	177,342	127,296	886	128,181	14,908	399	113,672	36,251	27,419		15,051	13,281	11,783	5,772
1987	187,912	137,345	883	138,228	15,896	528	122,859	37,006	28,046		15,910	13,953	11,811	5,957
1988	203,518	150,177	743	150,920	17,715	779	133,984	39,987	29,547		17,181	15,119	11,846	6,120
1989	220,429	160,259	998	161,257	18,645	972	143,584	45,418	31,426		18,577	16,302	11,866	6,216
1990	233,194	169,171	1,002	170,173	19,839	1,040	151,373	47,528	34,293		19,591	17,243	11,903	6,293
1991	242,826	174,264	734	174,998	20,662	1,053	155,389	47,830	39,607		20,266	17,942	11,982	6,212
1992	256,369	185,594	1,202	186,796	21,889	1,227	166,134	48,079	42,155		21,276	18,830	12,049	6,216
1993	266,038	193,012	1,030	194,042	23,105	1,341	172,278	49,390	44,371		21,951	19,441	12,120	6,256
1994	275,115	200,592	921	201,513	24,456	1,654	178,712	50,968	45,436		22,613	19,967	12,166	6,323
1995	287,784	207,965	642	208,607	25,290	2,170	185,487	54,844	47,453		23,592	20,759	12,198	6,423
1996	302,669	216,265	1,118	217,383	25,752	2,436	194,067	58,199	50,402		24,767	21,667	12,220	6,477
1997	317,900	228,211	767	228,978	26,960	2,877	204,894	61,505	51,501		25,998	22,602	12,228	6,585
1998	335,214	241,683	896	242,578	28,148	3,278	217,709	65,276	52,229		27,374	23,698	12,246	6,655
1999	349,812	255,793	819	256,612	29,402	3,565	230,775	64,459	54,579		28,524	24,675	12,264	6,757
2000	374,577	272,238	1,106	273,343	30,865	4,066	246,545	70,119	57,914		30,493	26,369	12,284	6,894
2001	387,708	283,580	1,011	284,591	31,934	3,962	256,619	69,203	61,886		31,524	27,359	12,299	6,901
2002	395,920	291,266	640	291,906	32,819	3,665	262,753	67,552	65,616		32,108	28,483	12,331	6,874
2003	409,038	300,601	1,240	301,841	33,614	3,889	272,115	68,652	68,271		33,055	29,597	12,375	6,864
2004	430,009	317,669	1,536	319,205	35,335	4,805	288,675	70,522	70,812		34,648	31,108	12,411	6,938
2005	447,084	329,815	1,389	331,204	37,131	5,918	299,991	70,983	76,110		35,910	31,906	12,450	7,042
2006	477,939	347,398	1,108	348,506	39,011	7,237	316,732	81,259	79,948		38,202	33,812	12,511	7,143
2007	503,611	358,687	1,284	359,971	40,573	8,493	327,891	90,317	85,403		40,084	35,201	12,564	7,258
2008	525,623	369,695	1,210	370,905	41,806	9,418	338,517	91,952	95,154		41,675	36,715	12,612	7,276
2009	516,623	362,597	787	363,383	41,282	7,756	329,857	83,123	103,644		40,785	36,865	12,667	7,107
2010	532,817	372,808	1,181	373,989	42,500	8,418	339,907	81,899	111,011		41,918	37,735	12,711	7,104
2011	560,971	388,548	1,656	390,203	39,676	8,365	358,892	90,453	111,625		44,018	39,232	12,744	7,202
2012	584,630	401,190	1,834	403,025	40,556	8,834	371,303	101,489	111,838		45,781	40,930	12,770	7,262
2013	588,296	411,067	2,259	413,325	46,978	8,681	375,028	99,677	113,591		46,028	40,768	12,781	7,326
2014	609,679	425,959	2,700	428,659	48,700	9,120	389,080	103,602	116,997		47,679	42,135	12,787	7,400
2015	629,710	439,560	2,219	441,780	49,899	9,549	401,430	107,861	120,419		49,180	43,206	12,804	...

... = Not available.

Personal Income and Employment by Region and State: Rhode Island

(Millions of dollars, except as noted.)

Year	Personal income, total	Derivation of personal income								Per capita (dollars)		Population (thousands)	Total employment (thousands)
		Earnings by place of work			Less: Contributions for government social insurance	Plus: Adjustment for residence	Equals: Net earnings by place of residence	Plus: Dividends, interest, and rent	Plus: Personal current transfer receipts	Personal income	Disposable personal income		
		Nonfarm	Farm	Total									
1960	2,015	1,617	8	1,625	96	54	1,582	283	150	2,357	2,107	855	...
1961	2,110	1,671	7	1,678	98	57	1,637	306	166	2,459	2,191	858	...
1962	2,269	1,791	7	1,798	108	62	1,753	347	169	2,605	2,330	871	...
1963	2,365	1,848	7	1,855	118	67	1,804	381	179	2,700	2,412	876	...
1964	2,519	1,972	8	1,980	122	73	1,931	404	184	2,846	2,576	885	...
1965	2,720	2,125	8	2,134	133	82	2,083	439	198	3,046	2,752	893	...
1966	2,972	2,348	9	2,357	162	96	2,290	464	218	3,306	2,965	899	...
1967	3,222	2,520	7	2,527	175	105	2,457	500	265	3,545	3,192	909	...
1968	3,521	2,753	8	2,761	200	116	2,677	536	308	3,818	3,401	922	...
1969	3,739	2,954	8	2,962	231	63	2,795	596	347	4,011	3,550	932	440
1970	4,085	3,170	9	3,180	245	64	2,999	663	423	4,298	3,846	951	440
1971	4,326	3,330	8	3,338	267	59	3,130	699	497	4,487	4,019	964	436
1972	4,709	3,664	8	3,671	307	53	3,418	745	546	4,823	4,270	976	447
1973	5,025	3,896	6	3,902	381	69	3,590	811	625	5,138	4,549	978	452
1974	5,263	3,964	9	3,973	410	88	3,651	879	734	5,520	4,871	954	439
1975	5,700	4,125	9	4,134	416	82	3,800	928	972	6,024	5,424	946	424
1976	6,224	4,615	9	4,624	473	88	4,239	991	995	6,550	5,840	950	442
1977	6,809	5,076	8	5,084	521	103	4,667	1,100	1,042	7,128	6,368	955	459
1978	7,472	5,639	9	5,648	597	102	5,152	1,208	1,112	7,806	6,875	957	474
1979	8,304	6,280	8	6,288	685	110	5,713	1,355	1,236	8,681	7,571	957	483
1980	9,335	6,835	8	6,843	745	124	6,222	1,683	1,431	9,839	8,637	949	484
1981	10,403	7,358	9	7,367	851	154	6,670	2,097	1,636	10,916	9,586	953	484
1982	11,169	7,705	27	7,732	902	208	7,038	2,335	1,796	11,705	10,334	954	475
1983	12,049	8,343	37	8,380	988	263	7,655	2,480	1,914	12,599	11,164	956	480
1984	13,280	9,228	32	9,260	1,136	332	8,456	2,857	1,967	13,806	12,283	962	504
1985	14,283	10,017	42	10,059	1,220	392	9,230	2,965	2,088	14,741	13,093	969	519
1986	15,348	10,879	43	10,922	1,330	417	10,009	3,167	2,172	15,704	13,874	977	537
1987	16,479	11,794	41	11,835	1,430	485	10,889	3,353	2,237	16,653	14,562	990	546
1988	18,173	13,004	42	13,046	1,595	559	12,010	3,765	2,398	18,239	16,056	996	560
1989	19,796	13,745	32	13,777	1,661	626	12,742	4,441	2,613	19,783	17,418	1,001	560
1990	20,308	14,086	31	14,117	1,790	672	12,998	4,420	2,890	20,187	17,814	1,006	550
1991	20,434	13,835	32	13,866	1,809	697	12,755	4,168	3,511	20,219	17,905	1,011	524
1992	21,391	14,698	29	14,727	1,923	719	13,523	4,206	3,661	21,125	18,794	1,013	529
1993	22,307	15,230	30	15,260	2,011	762	14,010	4,324	3,973	21,975	19,524	1,015	533
1994	22,867	15,765	25	15,790	2,109	831	14,512	4,404	3,951	22,508	19,957	1,016	533
1995	24,111	16,488	25	16,513	2,182	861	15,191	4,750	4,170	23,708	21,014	1,017	536
1996	24,982	16,981	23	17,004	2,229	930	15,706	5,023	4,253	24,471	21,564	1,021	540
1997	26,452	17,909	16	17,924	2,334	997	16,587	5,349	4,516	25,798	22,523	1,025	546
1998	28,277	19,376	15	19,391	2,471	1,076	17,995	5,716	4,566	27,423	23,849	1,031	555
1999	29,511	20,498	15	20,513	2,589	1,178	19,102	5,664	4,745	28,365	24,651	1,040	565
2000	31,733	22,057	16	22,074	2,756	1,338	20,656	6,155	4,922	30,214	26,056	1,050	579
2001	33,378	23,057	18	23,075	2,866	1,314	21,523	6,351	5,505	31,574	27,275	1,057	581
2002	34,855	24,298	22	24,320	2,964	1,299	22,655	6,458	5,742	32,698	28,944	1,066	584
2003	36,572	25,610	23	25,633	3,120	1,321	23,834	6,833	5,905	34,137	30,508	1,071	590
2004	38,214	26,937	25	26,961	3,287	1,362	25,036	6,880	6,298	35,562	31,807	1,075	598
2005	39,077	27,676	24	27,700	3,405	1,345	25,640	6,886	6,551	36,592	32,514	1,068	602
2006	41,225	29,160	22	29,183	3,590	1,289	26,881	7,551	6,793	38,779	34,330	1,063	607
2007	43,023	29,737	23	29,760	3,701	1,350	27,409	8,175	7,439	40,691	35,862	1,057	614
2008	44,193	30,035	15	30,050	3,752	1,261	27,559	8,364	8,270	41,889	37,111	1,055	605
2009	43,285	29,216	15	29,231	3,694	1,189	26,726	7,591	8,969	41,081	37,347	1,054	585
2010	45,005	30,525	15	30,540	3,771	999	27,769	7,701	9,534	42,737	38,746	1,053	581
2011	46,596	31,114	12	31,126	3,486	1,202	28,841	8,133	9,622	44,292	39,582	1,052	587
2012	48,509	32,250	19	32,269	3,564	1,375	30,080	8,923	9,506	46,084	41,415	1,053	588
2013	48,607	33,066	22	33,088	4,110	1,406	30,385	8,619	9,603	46,145	40,993	1,053	597
2014	51,027	34,528	21	34,549	4,292	1,519	31,776	8,966	10,285	48,359	42,910	1,055	607
2015	52,905	35,757	23	35,781	4,413	1,620	32,987	9,303	10,615	50,080	44201	1056	...

... = Not available.

Personal Income and Employment by Region and State: South Carolina

(Millions of dollars, except as noted.)

Year	Personal income, total	Derivation of personal income								Per capita (dollars)		Population (thousands)	Total employment (thousands)
		Earnings by place of work			Less: Contributions for government social insurance	Plus: Adjustment for residence	Equals: Net earnings by place of residence	Plus: Dividends, interest, and rent	Plus: Personal current transfer receipts	Personal income	Disposable personal income		
		Nonfarm	Farm	Total									
1960	3,587	2,902	169	3,071	135	18	2,954	424	210	1,500	1,378	2,392	...
1961	3,766	2,994	196	3,190	138	19	3,071	457	238	1,563	1,435	2,409	...
1962	4,034	3,231	185	3,417	153	23	3,286	495	253	1,665	1,518	2,423	...
1963	4,267	3,437	189	3,626	189	26	3,463	532	272	1,735	1,583	2,460	...
1964	4,583	3,727	180	3,907	203	30	3,734	564	284	1,852	1,704	2,475	...
1965	5,065	4,131	182	4,313	221	35	4,127	627	310	2,031	1,860	2,494	...
1966	5,690	4,726	196	4,922	290	44	4,676	672	342	2,258	2,050	2,520	...
1967	6,135	5,106	197	5,304	342	50	5,012	722	401	2,422	2,198	2,533	...
1968	6,804	5,737	155	5,892	387	58	5,563	770	471	2,659	2,394	2,559	...
1969	7,595	6,271	188	6,460	417	128	6,170	887	537	2,955	2,638	2,570	1,170
1970	8,364	6,767	189	6,956	449	126	6,633	1,062	669	3,219	2,905	2,598	1,196
1971	9,161	7,376	204	7,580	509	137	7,208	1,174	779	3,442	3,112	2,662	1,215
1972	10,283	8,329	214	8,543	600	154	8,097	1,309	876	3,783	3,359	2,718	1,262
1973	11,650	9,424	303	9,726	773	167	9,120	1,486	1,044	4,197	3,743	2,775	1,328
1974	13,188	10,527	342	10,869	898	180	10,152	1,718	1,318	4,638	4,127	2,843	1,365
1975	14,353	11,064	277	11,341	928	192	10,606	1,933	1,814	4,949	4,514	2,900	1,326
1976	16,032	12,634	234	12,868	1,089	226	12,005	2,099	1,927	5,450	4,904	2,941	1,376
1977	17,515	13,927	188	14,115	1,199	247	13,163	2,339	2,013	5,860	5,254	2,989	1,411
1978	19,787	15,777	246	16,023	1,389	265	14,900	2,677	2,210	6,507	5,818	3,041	1,466
1979	22,172	17,659	260	17,919	1,608	290	16,601	3,022	2,549	7,183	6,351	3,087	1,507
1980	24,831	19,487	36	19,524	1,774	322	18,072	3,657	3,102	7,922	7,020	3,135	1,523
1981	27,941	21,453	172	21,625	2,091	348	19,882	4,475	3,584	8,789	7,749	3,179	1,536
1982	29,708	22,223	195	22,418	2,196	381	20,603	5,170	3,935	9,262	8,249	3,208	1,514
1983	32,286	24,370	51	24,421	2,470	392	22,343	5,746	4,196	9,983	8,890	3,234	1,547
1984	35,967	27,199	270	27,469	2,850	425	25,044	6,498	4,425	10,993	9,834	3,272	1,625
1985	38,534	29,052	197	29,249	3,096	478	26,630	7,110	4,794	11,666	10,404	3,303	1,655
1986	41,173	31,254	91	31,346	3,425	543	28,464	7,651	5,058	12,317	10,993	3,343	1,697
1987	44,132	33,754	250	34,003	3,665	586	30,925	8,008	5,199	13,055	11,601	3,381	1,738
1988	47,967	36,894	348	37,241	4,151	611	33,702	8,717	5,549	14,058	12,567	3,412	1,809
1989	52,226	39,493	367	39,860	4,513	572	35,919	9,885	6,422	15,108	13,407	3,457	1,858
1990	56,082	42,594	300	42,895	4,974	508	38,429	10,537	7,116	16,018	14,208	3,501	1,913
1991	58,483	43,830	399	44,229	5,192	495	39,532	10,792	8,159	16,380	14,649	3,570	1,886
1992	62,318	46,558	377	46,935	5,480	504	41,959	11,183	9,177	17,213	15,435	3,620	1,897
1993	65,499	48,920	337	49,257	5,824	521	43,954	11,710	9,835	17,880	16,019	3,663	1,931
1994	69,488	51,320	491	51,811	6,195	637	46,253	12,548	10,688	18,753	16,760	3,705	1,979
1995	73,582	54,119	384	54,503	6,555	769	48,717	13,436	11,429	19,629	17,464	3,749	2,038
1996	78,254	56,860	463	57,324	6,771	879	51,432	14,519	12,303	20,614	18,255	3,796	2,080
1997	83,269	60,434	472	60,906	7,187	1,038	54,756	15,624	12,888	21,574	19,032	3,860	2,141
1998	89,467	65,243	334	65,577	7,735	1,117	58,959	16,961	13,548	22,828	20,085	3,919	2,189
1999	94,259	69,644	403	70,047	8,170	1,206	63,083	16,802	14,374	23,715	20,858	3,975	2,236
2000	101,181	74,022	526	74,548	8,624	1,432	67,357	18,372	15,452	25,143	22,209	4,024	2,276
2001	105,117	76,035	650	76,686	8,877	1,427	69,235	18,644	17,238	25,859	22,904	4,065	2,250
2002	107,883	78,195	230	78,425	9,138	1,349	70,636	18,525	18,722	26,263	23,696	4,108	2,241
2003	111,655	81,339	527	81,866	9,531	1,404	73,740	18,244	19,671	26,903	24,463	4,150	2,258
2004	118,473	85,497	643	86,140	10,016	1,713	77,838	19,362	21,274	28,135	25,631	4,211	2,304
2005	125,552	89,938	646	90,584	10,500	1,834	81,918	20,752	22,881	29,402	26,536	4,270	2,354
2006	135,891	96,018	458	96,476	11,437	2,155	87,194	23,949	24,748	31,183	28,013	4,358	2,417
2007	144,182	100,365	292	100,657	11,955	2,508	91,210	26,616	26,356	32,443	29,054	4,444	2,486
2008	151,491	103,192	424	103,616	12,282	2,769	94,103	26,989	30,400	33,449	30,215	4,529	2,476
2009	149,164	100,201	462	100,662	11,924	2,647	91,386	24,204	33,575	32,499	29,982	4,590	2,373
2010	152,314	101,342	407	101,749	12,076	2,626	92,298	23,691	36,325	32,853	30,232	4,636	2,357
2011	159,910	105,059	284	105,343	11,286	2,640	96,697	26,472	36,741	34,220	31,179	4,673	2,418
2012	167,468	110,346	515	110,860	11,621	2,990	102,230	28,321	36,917	35,461	32,331	4,723	2,453
2013	169,269	112,212	816	113,027	13,408	3,177	102,796	28,484	37,989	35,472	32,014	4,772	2,501
2014	177,242	117,777	361	118,138	14,111	3,520	107,548	29,557	40,138	36,677	33,058	4,832	2,556
2015	186,286	123,651	373	124,025	14,728	3,720	113,017	30,689	42,580	38,041	34,129	4,897	...

... = Not available.

Personal Income and Employment by Region and State: South Dakota

(Millions of dollars, except as noted.)

Year	Personal income, total	Earnings by place of work			Less: Contributions for government social insurance	Plus: Adjustment for residence	Equals: Net earnings by place of residence	Plus: Dividends, interest, and rent	Plus: Personal current transfer receipts	Per capita (dollars)		Population (thousands)	Total employment (thousands)
		Nonfarm	Farm	Total						Personal income	Disposable personal income		
1960	1,323	752	324	1,076	35	0	1,042	196	86	1,938	1,801	683	...
1961	1,332	823	251	1,075	39	0	1,036	201	94	1,922	1,772	693	...
1962	1,517	878	368	1,246	45	1	1,202	215	100	2,152	1,991	705	...
1963	1,471	890	299	1,189	51	1	1,139	226	106	2,078	1,913	708	...
1964	1,443	933	216	1,149	50	1	1,100	234	109	2,058	1,919	701	...
1965	1,623	964	334	1,299	51	2	1,249	255	119	2,346	2,195	692	...
1966	1,755	1,031	393	1,425	64	2	1,363	264	129	2,570	2,390	683	...
1967	1,783	1,085	344	1,430	77	3	1,355	273	154	2,657	2,467	671	...
1968	1,910	1,175	362	1,538	84	3	1,457	275	177	2,855	2,626	669	...
1969	2,080	1,289	357	1,646	90	6	1,563	323	194	3,114	2,844	668	303
1970	2,263	1,390	373	1,763	95	6	1,674	367	222	3,394	3,133	667	305
1971	2,478	1,520	404	1,923	106	6	1,823	400	255	3,691	3,449	671	306
1972	2,861	1,686	564	2,250	121	7	2,136	442	282	4,223	3,948	677	309
1973	3,610	1,900	1,027	2,927	158	7	2,776	506	327	5,317	4,935	679	323
1974	3,621	2,119	688	2,807	183	8	2,632	607	383	5,326	4,874	680	326
1975	4,001	2,321	707	3,028	200	10	2,838	707	456	5,871	5,453	681	326
1976	3,954	2,630	277	2,907	225	12	2,695	757	503	5,757	5,277	687	336
1977	4,485	2,875	445	3,320	238	13	3,095	860	530	6,510	6,043	689	342
1978	5,165	3,267	616	3,883	274	14	3,623	967	575	7,493	6,912	689	355
1979	5,680	3,599	652	4,251	322	15	3,944	1,086	649	8,243	7,582	689	359
1980	5,719	3,812	137	3,948	342	16	3,623	1,336	761	8,278	7,519	691	353
1981	6,647	4,049	444	4,493	388	13	4,118	1,658	872	9,640	8,783	690	348
1982	7,034	4,170	373	4,544	408	10	4,146	1,919	969	10,185	9,233	691	344
1983	7,327	4,484	255	4,739	440	4	4,302	1,982	1,042	10,572	9,751	693	353
1984	8,291	4,878	689	5,567	491	-2	5,073	2,116	1,102	11,891	11,075	697	362
1985	8,518	5,082	612	5,694	530	-5	5,159	2,187	1,171	12,196	11,338	698	365
1986	8,896	5,327	663	5,990	574	-12	5,404	2,273	1,220	12,782	11,893	696	366
1987	9,364	5,651	843	6,494	618	-19	5,857	2,248	1,260	13,454	12,451	696	381
1988	9,760	6,118	715	6,833	692	-27	6,114	2,328	1,318	13,980	12,926	698	388
1989	10,516	6,558	724	7,282	750	-37	6,494	2,577	1,445	15,094	13,898	697	396
1990	11,513	7,145	1,021	8,166	851	-54	7,261	2,713	1,540	16,516	15,157	697	409
1991	11,993	7,648	894	8,543	916	-68	7,558	2,778	1,656	17,044	15,655	704	420
1992	12,992	8,303	1,074	9,377	976	-85	8,315	2,876	1,800	18,226	16,746	713	431
1993	13,586	8,874	945	9,819	1,035	-100	8,684	3,007	1,895	18,813	17,196	722	442
1994	14,631	9,533	1,211	10,744	1,117	-131	9,496	3,130	2,005	20,021	18,393	731	464
1995	14,934	10,004	640	10,644	1,171	-150	9,323	3,470	2,142	20,238	18,495	738	472
1996	16,504	10,468	1,462	11,930	1,224	-189	10,517	3,726	2,262	22,237	20,390	742	479
1997	16,852	11,049	1,046	12,095	1,292	-186	10,617	3,914	2,321	22,644	20,523	744	485
1998	18,216	12,032	1,167	13,200	1,385	-233	11,582	4,245	2,389	24,416	22,161	746	490
1999	19,234	12,892	1,165	14,057	1,482	-250	12,325	4,425	2,483	25,631	23,159	750	500
2000	20,610	13,733	1,342	15,076	1,568	-267	13,241	4,711	2,658	27,267	24,707	756	509
2001	21,557	14,437	1,153	15,590	1,617	-256	13,717	4,966	2,874	28,440	25,810	758	510
2002	21,690	15,177	505	15,683	1,678	-273	13,731	4,895	3,063	28,538	26,277	760	508
2003	23,631	15,878	1,511	17,389	1,755	-283	15,351	5,117	3,162	30,941	28,877	764	508
2004	25,087	16,713	1,843	18,556	1,849	-263	16,445	5,306	3,336	32,564	30,366	770	517
2005	25,935	17,378	1,608	18,986	1,939	-199	16,847	5,513	3,575	33,443	30,915	775	527
2006	26,543	18,177	616	18,793	2,082	-189	16,522	6,140	3,882	33,898	30,963	783	537
2007	29,494	18,950	1,717	20,667	2,213	-138	18,316	7,023	4,154	37,257	34,000	792	549
2008	32,041	19,930	2,347	22,277	2,318	-105	19,854	7,450	4,737	40,095	36,703	799	559
2009	31,202	20,093	1,757	21,850	2,317	-77	19,455	6,773	4,974	38,661	36,103	807	555
2010	32,814	21,177	1,750	22,926	2,422	-79	20,425	7,012	5,377	40,204	37,442	816	555
2011	36,462	22,019	3,775	25,794	2,226	-131	23,438	7,553	5,471	44,241	40,879	824	563
2012	37,379	23,466	2,599	26,065	2,329	-105	23,630	8,268	5,480	44,792	41,153	835	571
2013	37,855	23,364	3,562	26,926	2,662	-78	24,185	8,061	5,608	44,772	40,895	846	577
2014	38,631	24,651	2,666	27,317	2,820	-74	24,423	8,381	5,827	45,279	41,147	853	584
2015	38,637	25,757	1,159	26,916	2,929	-83	23,904	8,666	6,068	45,002	40505	859	...

... = Not available.

Personal Income and Employment by Region and State: Tennessee

(Millions of dollars, except as noted.)

Year	Personal income, total	Earnings by place of work			Less: Contributions for government social insurance	Plus: Adjustment for residence	Equals: Net earnings by place of residence	Plus: Dividends, interest, and rent	Plus: Personal current transfer receipts	Per capita (dollars)		Population (thousands)	Total employment (thousands)
		Nonfarm	Farm	Total						Personal income	Disposable personal income		
1960	5,956	4,833	246	5,079	243	31	4,868	684	404	1,666	1,519	3,575	...
1961	6,304	5,034	294	5,328	247	31	5,112	733	459	1,741	1,591	3,622	...
1962	6,689	5,404	254	5,659	273	31	5,416	796	477	1,821	1,639	3,673	...
1963	7,095	5,759	278	6,036	323	31	5,744	849	502	1,908	1,736	3,718	...
1964	7,627	6,263	238	6,501	339	30	6,192	910	525	2,023	1,859	3,771	...
1965	8,312	6,834	254	7,087	363	32	6,756	977	578	2,188	2,003	3,798	...
1966	9,153	7,689	258	7,947	502	34	7,478	1,039	636	2,395	2,172	3,822	...
1967	9,795	8,224	219	8,442	564	51	7,929	1,104	763	2,538	2,308	3,859	...
1968	10,912	9,141	225	9,366	635	50	8,781	1,256	875	2,814	2,528	3,878	...
1969	11,817	10,000	256	10,255	659	-146	9,450	1,389	978	3,032	2,692	3,897	1,789
1970	12,844	10,630	269	10,899	696	-147	10,057	1,590	1,197	3,262	2,919	3,937	1,785
1971	14,183	11,697	267	11,963	789	-157	11,017	1,769	1,397	3,537	3,189	4,010	1,817
1972	15,960	13,258	326	13,584	938	-184	12,462	1,960	1,539	3,904	3,515	4,088	1,924
1973	18,114	14,951	493	15,444	1,211	-167	14,066	2,232	1,817	4,377	3,939	4,138	2,025
1974	20,047	16,452	318	16,770	1,384	-177	15,209	2,618	2,221	4,771	4,293	4,202	2,055
1975	21,881	17,357	250	17,607	1,431	-181	15,995	2,952	2,934	5,135	4,668	4,261	1,983
1976	24,475	19,539	371	19,910	1,640	-174	18,096	3,172	3,207	5,654	5,113	4,329	2,052
1977	27,121	21,987	300	22,286	1,847	-231	20,208	3,546	3,367	6,161	5,574	4,402	2,135
1978	30,915	25,304	319	25,623	2,152	-295	23,176	4,065	3,673	6,929	6,234	4,462	2,227
1979	34,461	28,050	342	28,392	2,482	-345	25,565	4,619	4,276	7,602	6,825	4,533	2,279
1980	38,000	30,084	197	30,281	2,668	-412	27,200	5,641	5,159	8,260	7,403	4,600	2,259
1981	42,288	32,734	360	33,094	3,136	-447	29,511	6,930	5,846	9,138	8,186	4,628	2,255
1982	44,963	33,946	302	34,249	3,331	-405	30,513	8,036	6,415	9,678	8,714	4,646	2,217
1983	48,000	36,677	-33	36,644	3,652	-418	32,575	8,538	6,888	10,301	9,300	4,660	2,239
1984	53,410	40,686	412	41,098	4,190	-444	36,464	9,735	7,211	11,396	10,347	4,687	2,344
1985	57,236	43,877	335	44,212	4,589	-469	39,154	10,419	7,664	12,138	10,978	4,715	2,399
1986	61,284	47,350	241	47,592	5,066	-505	42,020	11,036	8,228	12,933	11,713	4,739	2,477
1987	66,008	51,583	305	51,888	5,474	-534	45,880	11,461	8,667	13,801	12,444	4,783	2,578
1988	71,769	56,049	389	56,438	6,108	-546	49,784	12,669	9,317	14,882	13,485	4,822	2,663
1989	77,070	59,470	443	59,913	6,569	-571	52,773	14,040	10,257	15,876	14,333	4,854	2,735
1990	81,935	62,909	443	63,352	7,002	-629	55,721	14,859	11,354	16,740	15,160	4,894	2,777
1991	86,090	65,880	510	66,391	7,455	-622	58,313	14,863	12,914	17,334	15,752	4,967	2,778
1992	94,250	72,290	665	72,956	8,067	-483	64,406	15,314	14,529	18,664	16,969	5,050	2,837
1993	100,336	77,405	593	77,998	8,654	-596	68,748	16,006	15,582	19,530	17,739	5,138	2,943
1994	106,696	82,782	655	83,437	9,401	-687	73,348	17,000	16,348	20,395	18,468	5,231	3,061
1995	114,573	88,399	441	88,840	10,015	-768	78,057	18,590	17,926	21,508	19,445	5,327	3,145
1996	121,012	93,178	393	93,571	10,377	-785	82,408	19,728	18,876	22,341	20,091	5,417	3,195
1997	128,174	99,524	381	99,905	11,008	-1,031	87,866	20,685	19,624	23,308	20,896	5,499	3,269
1998	141,011	110,909	205	111,114	11,708	-1,176	98,230	22,289	20,492	25,316	22,756	5,570	3,343
1999	147,279	117,022	57	117,079	12,361	-1,360	103,358	22,545	21,377	26,119	23,494	5,639	3,401
2000	156,872	123,819	328	124,147	12,928	-1,551	109,667	24,009	23,195	27,503	24,804	5,704	3,464
2001	161,866	126,959	461	127,420	13,337	-1,642	112,441	24,135	25,289	28,147	25,377	5,751	3,428
2002	165,839	131,604	90	131,694	13,950	-1,942	115,802	22,923	27,114	28,613	26,256	5,796	3,414
2003	172,239	136,302	202	136,504	14,455	-2,016	120,033	23,414	28,792	29,454	27,223	5,848	3,440
2004	182,791	144,853	384	145,237	15,248	-1,786	128,202	23,965	30,624	30,925	28,672	5,911	3,520
2005	189,889	149,043	543	149,585	15,886	-1,725	131,974	25,134	32,780	31,695	29,178	5,991	3,586
2006	201,367	157,056	268	157,324	16,752	-1,763	138,808	27,925	34,633	33,072	30,194	6,089	3,656
2007	211,376	161,407	-146	161,261	17,528	-1,285	142,449	30,876	38,051	34,227	31,164	6,176	3,719
2008	220,580	164,222	217	164,439	17,989	-1,310	145,140	32,619	42,822	35,307	32,379	6,247	3,696
2009	217,354	159,552	323	159,875	17,644	-958	141,273	30,017	46,064	34,468	32,281	6,306	3,546
2010	226,302	163,499	179	163,678	18,093	-765	144,819	31,066	50,417	35,601	33,242	6,357	3,530
2011	238,810	171,111	491	171,602	16,810	-804	153,988	33,388	51,434	37,323	34,550	6,398	3,604
2012	252,636	182,480	513	182,993	17,313	-1,195	164,485	36,172	51,978	39,137	36,276	6,455	3,648
2013	255,422	185,900	1,199	187,099	20,000	-1,329	165,771	36,084	53,568	39,312	36,170	6,497	3,702
2014	264,965	193,891	749	194,640	20,795	-1,268	172,576	37,563	54,826	40,457	37,131	6,549	3,774
2015	277,707	203,727	597	204,324	21,698	-1,395	181,231	39,043	57,433	42,069	38423	6601	...

... = Not available.

Personal Income and Employment by Region and State: Texas

(Millions of dollars, except as noted.)

Year	Personal income, total	Derivation of personal income								Per capita (dollars)		Population (thousands)	Total employment (thousands)
		Earnings by place of work			Less: Contributions for government social insurance	Plus: Adjustment for residence	Equals: Net earnings by place of residence	Plus: Dividends, interest, and rent	Plus: Personal current transfer receipts	Personal income	Disposable personal income		
		Nonfarm	Farm	Total									
1960	19,438	15,200	924	16,124	677	16	15,464	2,976	998	2,020	1,819	9,624	...
1961	20,553	15,905	1,090	16,995	696	16	16,316	3,115	1,122	2,093	1,884	9,820	...
1962	21,574	16,850	950	17,799	749	17	17,068	3,285	1,222	2,146	1,927	10,053	...
1963	22,520	17,728	783	18,511	832	18	17,696	3,502	1,321	2,217	1,988	10,159	...
1964	24,137	19,167	728	19,895	877	18	19,036	3,730	1,371	2,350	2,141	10,270	...
1965	25,976	20,551	865	21,416	930	19	20,505	3,973	1,498	2,503	2,274	10,378	...
1966	28,420	22,871	920	23,791	1,259	17	22,548	4,242	1,630	2,709	2,439	10,492	...
1967	31,029	25,224	778	26,002	1,461	15	24,555	4,505	1,969	2,928	2,630	10,599	...
1968	34,550	28,190	910	29,099	1,634	14	27,479	4,711	2,360	3,193	2,835	10,819	...
1969	38,444	31,492	927	32,419	2,012	-87	30,319	5,480	2,644	3,481	3,061	11,045	5,005
1970	42,338	33,908	1,168	35,076	2,149	-100	32,827	6,371	3,139	3,768	3,356	11,237	5,045
1971	45,936	36,733	1,015	37,748	2,399	-103	35,246	7,024	3,667	3,991	3,595	11,510	5,123
1972	50,972	40,735	1,257	41,993	2,783	-128	39,082	7,774	4,116	4,335	3,863	11,759	5,334
1973	57,886	45,690	2,145	47,835	3,608	-155	44,071	8,865	4,950	4,816	4,301	12,019	5,608
1974	65,271	52,190	1,157	53,347	4,249	-133	48,965	10,401	5,904	5,320	4,707	12,268	5,822
1975	74,303	58,931	1,314	60,245	4,721	-131	55,393	11,530	7,380	5,912	5,296	12,568	5,938
1976	83,694	67,565	1,292	68,857	5,513	-95	63,249	12,372	8,073	6,486	5,767	12,903	6,207
1977	93,346	76,404	1,280	77,683	6,290	-309	71,084	13,674	8,588	7,076	6,237	13,192	6,521
1978	107,770	88,998	1,030	90,028	7,501	-430	82,097	16,114	9,560	7,984	7,047	13,498	6,900
1979	124,188	102,331	1,741	104,073	9,047	-437	94,589	18,696	10,903	8,943	7,795	13,887	7,215
1980	142,639	117,266	620	117,886	10,466	-542	106,878	22,991	12,770	9,948	8,627	14,338	7,496
1981	167,739	135,950	1,963	137,913	13,078	-337	124,498	28,736	14,505	11,375	9,763	14,746	7,900
1982	184,332	147,163	1,354	148,517	14,470	-409	133,638	34,181	16,513	12,023	10,438	15,331	8,074
1983	196,082	153,812	1,741	155,552	15,035	-392	140,126	37,316	18,640	12,448	11,014	15,752	8,064
1984	214,973	168,395	1,628	170,023	16,887	-450	152,685	42,469	19,818	13,430	11,945	16,007	8,434
1985	231,269	180,266	1,500	181,766	18,295	-479	162,992	47,100	21,176	14,212	12,645	16,273	8,674
1986	236,746	183,241	1,275	184,516	18,420	-440	165,656	47,872	23,217	14,295	12,861	16,561	8,514
1987	241,510	186,451	2,081	188,533	18,487	-436	169,609	47,488	24,412	14,530	13,023	16,622	8,723
1988	256,262	198,684	2,312	200,996	20,385	-442	180,170	50,424	25,669	15,375	13,857	16,667	8,880
1989	274,062	210,937	2,242	213,179	21,806	-452	190,921	54,893	28,248	16,307	14,611	16,807	9,005
1990	296,205	228,160	3,047	231,207	23,239	-492	207,475	57,117	31,613	17,366	15,557	17,057	9,243
1991	309,983	240,161	2,770	242,931	25,081	-572	217,279	57,565	35,140	17,817	16,041	17,398	9,404
1992	335,302	258,975	3,370	262,345	26,705	-595	235,045	58,701	41,556	18,880	17,080	17,760	9,483
1993	354,794	275,279	3,993	279,272	28,325	-616	250,331	59,995	44,468	19,535	17,653	18,162	9,781
1994	375,107	291,337	3,444	294,781	30,353	-682	263,746	63,553	47,808	20,206	18,240	18,564	10,098
1995	401,483	310,517	2,778	313,295	32,365	-764	280,166	69,366	51,952	21,177	19,079	18,959	10,440
1996	431,653	335,362	2,408	337,769	34,406	-836	302,527	73,555	55,571	22,319	19,974	19,340	10,738
1997	470,315	369,521	3,055	372,576	37,474	-976	334,126	78,024	58,166	23,825	21,172	19,740	11,165
1998	514,024	409,720	2,835	412,554	40,837	-1,073	370,644	83,984	59,396	25,500	22,571	20,158	11,542
1999	543,695	438,271	4,277	442,548	43,357	-1,098	398,093	84,468	61,135	26,447	23,424	20,558	11,764
2000	594,097	480,747	3,347	484,094	46,647	-1,196	436,251	93,059	64,787	28,365	25,006	20,944	12,139
2001	633,553	515,620	3,987	519,607	49,028	-1,352	469,227	93,366	70,961	29,717	26,366	21,320	12,285
2002	636,108	515,818	3,973	519,790	49,563	-2,644	467,583	90,500	78,025	29,327	26,616	21,690	12,304
2003	661,144	530,941	5,101	536,042	51,814	-2,817	481,411	96,009	83,724	30,010	27,501	22,031	12,387
2004	695,947	560,628	5,359	565,988	54,508	-3,114	508,366	99,399	88,182	31,077	28,572	22,394	12,638
2005	759,204	598,930	5,018	603,948	58,044	-552	545,352	116,424	97,429	33,330	30,290	22,778	13,041
2006	830,523	657,898	3,225	661,123	62,131	-975	598,018	128,318	104,187	35,554	32,088	23,360	13,522
2007	881,583	687,445	3,743	691,187	66,495	-468	624,224	142,897	114,462	36,992	33,277	23,832	14,045
2008	969,740	741,884	1,796	743,681	69,850	-1,183	672,648	166,801	130,292	39,892	35,645	24,309	14,410
2009	918,587	698,550	1,116	699,667	69,367	-1,234	629,065	146,724	142,799	37,037	34,215	24,802	14,257
2010	966,448	731,686	3,321	735,007	72,072	-1,257	661,678	146,274	158,496	38,282	35,198	25,246	14,291
2011	1,057,983	791,043	3,325	794,368	67,872	-1,408	725,088	168,594	164,301	41,235	37,436	25,657	14,719
2012	1,135,226	848,512	3,398	851,910	71,925	-1,606	778,380	192,918	163,928	43,505	39,554	26,094	15,127
2013	1,161,134	884,340	4,691	889,031	85,246	-1,590	802,196	189,094	169,844	43,807	39,449	26,506	15,563
2014	1,231,085	943,718	5,333	949,051	90,650	-1,548	856,853	196,117	178,115	45,669	40,988	26,957	15,982
2015	1,284,262	980,614	4,203	984,816	93,628	-1,645	889,543	203,597	191,122	46,745	41725	27474	...

... = Not available.

Personal Income and Employment by Region and State: Utah

(Millions of dollars, except as noted.)

Year	Personal income, total	Derivation of personal income									Per capita (dollars)		Population (thousands)	Total employment (thousands)
		Earnings by place of work			Less: Contributions for government social insurance	Plus: Adjustment for residence	Equals: Net earnings by place of residence	Plus: Dividends, interest, and rent	Plus: Personal current transfer receipts		Personal income	Disposable personal income		
		Nonfarm	Farm	Total										
1960.............	1,900	1,548	44	1,592	75	1	1,518	276	105		2,111	1,906	900	...
1961.............	2,034	1,668	35	1,703	79	1	1,625	292	117		2,173	1,958	936	...
1962.............	2,210	1,808	54	1,862	87	1	1,775	312	122		2,307	2,085	958	...
1963.............	2,299	1,908	41	1,949	105	1	1,845	322	132		2,360	2,129	974	...
1964.............	2,418	1,994	30	2,025	106	1	1,920	358	141		2,473	2,261	978	...
1965.............	2,561	2,085	47	2,132	109	1	2,024	385	152		2,577	2,359	994	...
1966.............	2,726	2,247	49	2,296	144	1	2,153	411	162		2,702	2,463	1,009	...
1967.............	2,878	2,363	63	2,426	159	1	2,268	419	191		2,825	2,567	1,019	...
1968.............	3,092	2,549	67	2,616	175	1	2,442	430	220		3,005	2,701	1,029	...
1969.............	3,383	2,760	74	2,834	175	2	2,661	473	248		3,231	2,872	1,047	444
1970.............	3,767	3,034	78	3,112	190	1	2,923	545	299		3,535	3,178	1,066	455
1971.............	4,219	3,375	77	3,452	218	1	3,236	630	352		3,833	3,473	1,101	467
1972.............	4,713	3,778	88	3,866	260	4	3,611	700	402		4,154	3,743	1,135	494
1973.............	5,240	4,213	130	4,343	338	7	4,012	757	472		4,483	4,034	1,169	523
1974.............	5,863	4,741	97	4,837	395	10	4,452	873	538		4,891	4,390	1,199	545
1975.............	6,542	5,252	67	5,319	432	13	4,900	969	673		5,302	4,815	1,234	553
1976.............	7,393	6,012	74	6,087	502	16	5,600	1,061	732		5,810	5,206	1,272	580
1977.............	8,358	6,866	64	6,930	575	20	6,375	1,194	788		6,349	5,670	1,316	613
1978.............	9,601	7,907	72	7,979	678	25	7,326	1,397	878		7,037	6,273	1,364	651
1979.............	10,849	8,940	82	9,023	810	34	8,247	1,603	999		7,661	6,791	1,416	678
1980.............	12,172	9,882	60	9,942	902	51	9,091	1,902	1,179		8,266	7,346	1,473	687
1981.............	13,725	11,047	42	11,089	1,088	53	10,054	2,291	1,381		9,056	8,005	1,515	697
1982.............	14,916	11,736	46	11,782	1,176	53	10,658	2,670	1,587		9,572	8,448	1,558	707
1983.............	15,956	12,491	36	12,527	1,267	43	11,303	2,923	1,729		10,004	8,935	1,595	719
1984.............	17,598	13,884	57	13,941	1,448	39	12,532	3,284	1,782		10,847	9,739	1,622	761
1985.............	18,880	14,858	57	14,915	1,578	40	13,378	3,566	1,936		11,492	10,290	1,643	789
1986.............	19,817	15,532	87	15,619	1,658	35	13,997	3,726	2,094		11,918	10,665	1,663	801
1987.............	20,741	16,199	130	16,329	1,723	25	14,632	3,865	2,244		12,360	11,021	1,678	830
1988.............	22,052	17,326	208	17,535	1,936	24	15,623	4,084	2,344		13,053	11,660	1,689	865
1989.............	23,701	18,564	205	18,769	2,115	22	16,676	4,436	2,588		13,894	12,428	1,706	897
1990.............	25,737	20,305	252	20,558	2,390	17	18,185	4,712	2,840		14,866	13,143	1,731	938
1991.............	27,624	21,926	233	22,159	2,619	11	19,551	4,935	3,137		15,521	13,806	1,780	961
1992.............	29,925	23,862	279	24,141	2,832	7	21,316	5,129	3,480		16,292	14,500	1,837	979
1993.............	32,312	25,805	300	26,105	3,077	7	23,035	5,502	3,775		17,021	15,114	1,898	1,026
1994.............	35,051	28,137	219	28,357	3,388	7	24,976	6,185	3,889		17,879	15,786	1,960	1,102
1995.............	38,230	30,473	166	30,639	3,687	0	26,952	7,060	4,219		18,981	16,699	2,014	1,150
1996.............	41,619	33,054	173	33,227	3,920	0	29,307	7,846	4,467		20,126	17,666	2,068	1,218
1997.............	45,005	35,903	198	36,100	4,202	-0	31,898	8,463	4,644		21,231	18,593	2,120	1,270
1998.............	48,551	38,951	232	39,183	4,484	-4	34,696	9,008	4,847		22,416	19,630	2,166	1,309
1999.............	51,530	41,903	240	42,143	4,729	-1	37,412	8,999	5,119		23,386	20,469	2,203	1,336
2000.............	55,621	45,028	207	45,235	5,046	5	40,195	9,927	5,499		24,781	21,707	2,245	1,377
2001.............	58,719	47,486	317	47,803	5,292	9	42,521	10,171	6,027		25,712	22,686	2,284	1,385
2002.............	60,353	48,560	201	48,760	5,420	4	43,344	10,417	6,592		25,960	23,358	2,325	1,389
2003.............	62,109	49,762	217	49,979	5,649	10	44,340	10,740	7,028		26,316	23,832	2,360	1,400
2004.............	66,152	53,469	307	53,775	6,124	27	47,678	11,038	7,436		27,545	24,987	2,402	1,452
2005.............	72,252	57,675	270	57,946	6,634	-9	51,303	12,856	8,094		29,398	26,272	2,458	1,515
2006.............	80,275	64,465	147	64,613	7,284	29	57,358	14,100	8,818		31,786	28,206	2,526	1,590
2007.............	87,395	69,215	183	69,398	7,832	51	61,617	16,184	9,594		33,643	29,730	2,598	1,673
2008.............	91,906	70,896	201	71,096	8,023	41	63,115	17,566	11,225		34,512	30,864	2,663	1,684
2009.............	88,314	68,387	93	68,480	7,769	6	60,716	15,184	12,414		32,428	29,582	2,723	1,629
2010.............	90,483	69,429	189	69,618	7,833	-11	61,773	14,939	13,771		32,614	29,788	2,774	1,611
2011.............	96,889	72,906	322	73,227	7,448	-26	65,754	16,884	14,250		34,415	31,152	2,815	1,654
2012.............	102,772	77,377	276	77,653	7,840	-33	69,779	18,838	14,155		35,995	32,440	2,855	1,695
2013.............	106,073	81,339	510	81,849	9,295	-47	72,508	18,926	14,639		36,542	32,666	2,903	1,741
2014.............	110,842	85,219	592	85,811	9,785	-46	75,980	19,749	15,113		37,664	33,586	2,943	1,785
2015.............	116,992	90,255	605	90,860	10,326	-56	80,477	20,603	15,912		39,045	34,599	2,996	...

... = Not available.

Personal Income and Employment by Region and State: Vermont

(Millions of dollars, except as noted.)

Year	Personal income, total	Derivation of personal income								Per capita (dollars)		Population (thousands)	Total employment (thousands)
		Earnings by place of work			Less: Contributions for government social insurance	Plus: Adjustment for residence	Equals: Net earnings by place of residence	Plus: Dividends, interest, and rent	Plus: Personal current transfer receipts	Personal income	Disposable personal income		
		Nonfarm	Farm	Total									
1960	760	574	56	631	27	-5	598	103	59	1,954	1,760	389	...
1961	792	588	56	643	28	-5	610	115	67	2,031	1,832	390	...
1962	831	628	46	674	31	-5	638	124	70	2,115	1,910	393	...
1963	862	656	43	699	36	-5	658	129	74	2,171	1,940	397	...
1964	923	695	49	744	38	-5	701	145	77	2,314	2,085	399	...
1965	1,013	771	45	817	41	-7	768	164	81	2,506	2,273	404	...
1966	1,151	886	59	945	58	-10	877	186	87	2,786	2,491	413	...
1967	1,246	965	46	1,011	71	-10	930	208	107	2,944	2,629	423	...
1968	1,371	1,051	51	1,102	74	-11	1,017	227	126	3,188	2,817	430	...
1969	1,504	1,172	58	1,229	83	-27	1,119	240	144	3,441	2,992	437	203
1970	1,649	1,260	62	1,322	89	-26	1,207	271	172	3,696	3,233	446	205
1971	1,786	1,340	61	1,402	98	-24	1,280	301	205	3,930	3,533	454	206
1972	1,970	1,469	68	1,538	111	-21	1,406	334	230	4,253	3,756	463	211
1973	2,160	1,621	72	1,693	141	-20	1,533	365	262	4,611	4,118	469	220
1974	2,337	1,728	59	1,787	155	-17	1,615	407	315	4,939	4,411	473	222
1975	2,554	1,826	61	1,887	162	-11	1,714	439	401	5,322	4,779	480	220
1976	2,839	2,047	78	2,125	184	-6	1,935	472	432	5,853	5,280	485	228
1977	3,080	2,247	66	2,314	203	-2	2,108	530	442	6,259	5,599	492	236
1978	3,532	2,618	95	2,713	244	-1	2,467	597	467	7,088	6,334	498	252
1979	3,976	2,938	105	3,043	284	6	2,765	680	530	7,862	6,979	506	261
1980	4,469	3,196	108	3,305	309	14	3,010	831	629	8,720	7,712	513	266
1981	5,035	3,507	123	3,631	364	17	3,284	1,027	725	9,766	8,604	516	270
1982	5,447	3,701	123	3,824	392	23	3,455	1,185	807	10,492	9,341	519	271
1983	5,816	4,041	83	4,124	430	22	3,715	1,236	864	11,114	9,917	523	277
1984	6,418	4,471	84	4,555	489	27	4,093	1,435	890	12,187	10,905	527	289
1985	6,937	4,907	101	5,008	548	29	4,489	1,520	929	13,088	11,647	530	300
1986	7,480	5,355	99	5,455	602	33	4,886	1,637	957	14,005	12,407	534	311
1987	8,137	5,927	124	6,051	656	41	5,436	1,729	971	15,060	13,236	540	320
1988	8,897	6,509	121	6,630	742	46	5,933	1,938	1,025	16,183	14,295	550	334
1989	9,842	7,051	123	7,174	798	50	6,425	2,296	1,121	17,648	15,543	558	341
1990	10,205	7,313	115	7,427	870	50	6,608	2,347	1,251	18,069	15,944	565	341
1991	10,386	7,405	104	7,509	890	58	6,677	2,331	1,379	18,266	16,223	569	334
1992	11,118	7,897	177	8,073	937	66	7,202	2,356	1,560	19,411	17,301	573	342
1993	11,538	8,294	128	8,422	986	76	7,512	2,398	1,629	19,971	17,788	578	349
1994	12,123	8,662	129	8,791	1,043	91	7,840	2,559	1,725	20,764	18,527	584	359
1995	12,782	8,987	100	9,087	1,100	104	8,092	2,821	1,870	21,702	19,379	589	362
1996	13,467	9,450	147	9,597	1,144	120	8,574	2,962	1,932	22,684	20,119	594	367
1997	14,192	9,966	110	10,076	1,197	145	9,023	3,135	2,034	23,763	20,900	597	373
1998	15,244	10,664	136	10,801	1,266	173	9,707	3,419	2,117	25,389	22,254	600	381
1999	16,145	11,415	146	11,561	1,343	194	10,412	3,469	2,264	26,700	23,379	605	390
2000	17,408	12,344	151	12,495	1,435	225	11,285	3,686	2,437	28,556	24,879	610	401
2001	18,347	13,026	149	13,175	1,523	245	11,897	3,778	2,673	29,968	26,267	612	404
2002	18,812	13,526	115	13,641	1,554	240	12,328	3,630	2,854	30,567	27,280	615	405
2003	19,635	14,087	148	14,235	1,622	238	12,851	3,795	2,989	31,779	28,764	618	405
2004	20,862	14,900	193	15,093	1,710	264	13,648	4,092	3,123	33,652	30,543	620	413
2005	21,337	15,422	202	15,623	1,796	271	14,098	3,835	3,403	34,347	30,814	621	417
2006	22,796	15,978	118	16,096	1,884	293	14,505	4,507	3,784	36,597	32,659	623	421
2007	23,979	16,355	218	16,574	1,991	311	14,893	4,907	4,179	38,460	34,130	623	425
2008	25,036	16,850	146	16,996	2,054	302	15,244	5,129	4,663	40,111	35,766	624	425
2009	24,535	16,533	55	16,587	2,032	337	14,892	4,584	5,060	39,268	35,940	625	415
2010	25,073	16,924	124	17,048	2,056	346	15,337	4,389	5,347	40,066	36,598	626	413
2011	26,771	17,752	204	17,955	1,929	298	16,324	5,047	5,400	42,735	38,580	626	417
2012	27,730	18,316	182	18,497	2,002	313	16,808	5,390	5,532	44,287	40,131	626	422
2013	28,108	18,757	242	18,999	2,314	318	17,004	5,319	5,785	44,839	40,244	627	425
2014	29,090	19,301	308	19,608	2,409	343	17,543	5,517	6,030	46,428	41,593	627	430
2015	29,968	19,925	194	20,119	2,474	360	18,005	5,730	6,233	47,864	42,654	626	...

... = Not available.

Personal Income and Employment by Region and State: Virginia

(Millions of dollars, except as noted.)

Year	Personal income, total	Earnings by place of work			Less: Contributions for government social insurance	Plus: Adjustment for residence	Equals: Net earnings by place of residence	Plus: Dividends, interest, and rent	Plus: Personal current transfer receipts	Per capita (dollars)		Population (thousands)	Total employment (thousands)
		Nonfarm	Farm	Total						Personal income	Disposable personal income		
1960	8,204	6,225	214	6,440	268	467	6,638	1,193	373	2,058	1,845	3,986	...
1961	8,742	6,566	225	6,791	284	499	7,006	1,308	428	2,135	1,920	4,095	...
1962	9,432	7,085	222	7,307	318	553	7,542	1,438	452	2,257	2,018	4,180	...
1963	10,144	7,698	136	7,834	370	610	8,074	1,585	485	2,372	2,106	4,276	...
1964	11,197	8,423	222	8,644	384	663	8,923	1,762	512	2,570	2,323	4,357	...
1965	12,091	9,042	208	9,250	403	747	9,594	1,937	560	2,741	2,466	4,411	...
1966	13,088	9,963	156	10,119	544	826	10,401	2,076	610	2,937	2,622	4,456	...
1967	14,317	10,776	201	10,977	633	987	11,331	2,251	734	3,176	2,830	4,508	...
1968	15,836	12,046	178	12,224	700	1,063	12,588	2,393	855	3,474	3,072	4,558	...
1969	17,871	13,702	213	13,915	799	999	14,114	2,778	979	3,873	3,366	4,614	2,148
1970	19,388	14,705	213	14,918	869	905	14,953	3,255	1,180	4,161	3,636	4,660	2,158
1971	21,429	16,202	193	16,395	999	943	16,339	3,677	1,413	4,509	3,979	4,753	2,196
1972	23,779	18,032	254	18,286	1,166	999	18,119	4,039	1,622	4,925	4,289	4,828	2,263
1973	26,599	20,180	355	20,535	1,483	1,076	20,128	4,533	1,938	5,421	4,749	4,907	2,384
1974	29,484	22,220	316	22,537	1,701	1,184	22,020	5,163	2,301	5,923	5,149	4,978	2,451
1975	32,413	23,900	266	24,166	1,822	1,451	23,794	5,671	2,948	6,410	5,694	5,056	2,425
1976	35,757	26,554	237	26,791	2,071	1,677	26,396	6,132	3,229	6,967	6,145	5,133	2,501
1977	39,623	29,530	169	29,700	2,302	1,900	29,297	6,864	3,462	7,611	6,673	5,206	2,585
1978	44,964	33,259	291	33,549	2,624	2,262	33,187	7,954	3,824	8,509	7,422	5,284	2,698
1979	50,089	37,031	157	37,187	3,054	2,646	36,779	8,922	4,388	9,407	8,186	5,325	2,767
1980	56,563	40,863	69	40,932	3,380	3,197	40,749	10,590	5,224	10,537	9,159	5,368	2,797
1981	63,483	45,193	271	45,464	4,013	3,334	44,785	12,669	6,029	11,661	10,067	5,444	2,812
1982	68,642	48,555	122	48,678	4,369	3,374	47,683	14,373	6,586	12,497	10,861	5,493	2,824
1983	74,262	53,066	45	53,111	4,945	3,357	51,523	15,619	7,120	13,345	11,716	5,565	2,897
1984	82,640	59,223	328	59,551	5,702	3,560	57,409	17,700	7,531	14,642	12,932	5,644	3,041
1985	89,531	64,861	231	65,092	6,436	3,684	62,340	19,143	8,048	15,666	13,756	5,715	3,181
1986	96,590	70,679	277	70,956	7,279	3,807	67,485	20,574	8,531	16,620	14,601	5,812	3,316
1987	104,294	77,416	371	77,787	7,981	3,917	73,724	21,710	8,860	17,581	15,321	5,932	3,480
1988	114,135	84,824	523	85,347	9,002	4,310	80,655	24,006	9,474	18,906	16,578	6,037	3,558
1989	123,358	90,663	643	91,306	9,746	4,545	86,105	26,876	10,376	20,156	17,594	6,120	3,655
1990	129,544	94,493	687	95,181	10,317	5,180	90,044	28,238	11,263	20,838	18,253	6,217	3,700
1991	135,045	97,976	622	98,598	10,808	5,613	93,402	29,201	12,442	21,432	18,873	6,301	3,642
1992	143,871	104,235	672	104,907	11,444	6,017	99,481	30,396	13,993	22,430	19,811	6,414	3,657
1993	151,327	109,308	544	109,852	12,027	6,332	104,158	32,369	14,800	23,247	20,495	6,510	3,730
1994	159,147	114,816	644	115,460	12,719	6,256	108,996	34,478	15,673	24,138	21,213	6,593	3,813
1995	166,956	119,883	567	120,450	13,264	6,366	113,552	36,429	16,975	25,028	21,965	6,671	3,903
1996	175,268	126,415	570	126,985	13,952	5,916	118,949	38,379	17,940	25,962	22,673	6,751	3,983
1997	186,788	135,523	425	135,948	14,948	6,477	127,476	40,748	18,564	27,351	23,773	6,829	4,082
1998	199,552	146,900	419	147,319	16,047	6,206	137,479	42,860	19,213	28,917	24,781	6,901	4,168
1999	213,357	158,458	326	158,784	17,283	7,917	149,418	43,690	20,249	30,479	25,902	7,000	4,260
2000	230,690	173,507	568	174,075	18,643	6,056	161,488	47,512	21,690	32,465	27,593	7,106	4,397
2001	242,666	182,829	488	183,318	19,664	6,300	169,954	48,580	24,131	33,711	28,715	7,198	4,415
2002	248,877	187,985	377	188,362	20,311	6,214	174,265	49,034	25,578	34,154	29,845	7,287	4,422
2003	263,332	198,303	287	198,590	21,344	6,707	183,953	51,936	27,443	35,745	31,541	7,367	4,469
2004	282,227	214,243	547	214,789	23,264	8,124	199,650	53,597	28,980	37,753	33,414	7,476	4,593
2005	303,359	228,288	589	228,877	24,884	9,745	213,738	58,158	31,463	40,036	35,106	7,577	4,710
2006	325,257	240,038	287	240,325	26,493	11,371	225,203	65,644	34,410	42,386	37,019	7,674	4,789
2007	344,318	250,274	238	250,512	27,639	13,014	235,886	71,784	36,648	44,422	38,722	7,751	4,881
2008	357,348	256,615	293	256,908	28,545	13,884	242,247	72,867	42,235	45,618	39,796	7,833	4,885
2009	352,368	256,198	262	256,460	28,617	13,038	240,880	66,214	45,274	44,458	39,819	7,926	4,778
2010	364,452	263,810	260	264,070	29,685	14,581	248,966	66,084	49,402	45,412	40,508	8,025	4,750
2011	386,767	272,290	525	272,815	27,329	16,892	262,378	73,093	51,296	47,689	42,053	8,110	4,811
2012	404,103	281,506	584	282,091	28,208	16,982	270,865	81,411	51,827	49,320	43,705	8,193	4,862
2013	404,886	285,340	787	286,127	32,572	16,749	270,304	80,825	53,757	48,956	42,962	8,270	4,902
2014	419,185	292,910	712	293,622	33,349	19,054	279,327	84,059	55,799	50,345	44,141	8,326	4,939
2015	437,111	304,593	895	305,488	34,374	20,130	291,244	87,301	58,566	52,136	45,453	8,384	...

... = Not available.

Personal Income and Employment by Region and State: Washington

(Millions of dollars, except as noted.)

Year	Personal income, total	Derivation of personal income								Per capita (dollars)		Population (thousands)	Total employment (thousands)
		Earnings by place of work			Less: Contributions for government social insurance	Plus: Adjustment for residence	Equals: Net earnings by place of residence	Plus: Dividends, interest, and rent	Plus: Personal current transfer receipts	Personal income	Disposable personal income		
		Nonfarm	Farm	Total									
1960	7,189	5,628	256	5,884	313	26	5,596	1,078	514	2,518	2,264	2,855	...
1961	7,558	5,914	247	6,160	327	29	5,862	1,133	563	2,622	2,356	2,882	...
1962	8,153	6,415	271	6,686	358	35	6,363	1,224	567	2,771	2,485	2,942	...
1963	8,345	6,553	275	6,827	395	43	6,475	1,272	598	2,824	2,528	2,955	...
1964	8,741	6,846	251	7,096	394	52	6,755	1,356	631	2,952	2,695	2,961	...
1965	9,425	7,357	271	7,628	418	63	7,273	1,488	663	3,177	2,891	2,967	...
1966	10,654	8,490	366	8,856	593	72	8,335	1,631	689	3,485	3,136	3,057	...
1967	11,667	9,332	327	9,659	688	83	9,054	1,784	829	3,676	3,293	3,174	...
1968	12,986	10,406	341	10,746	770	100	10,076	1,959	951	3,971	3,534	3,270	...
1969	14,189	11,312	398	11,709	909	83	10,883	2,229	1,077	4,244	3,741	3,343	1,539
1970	14,964	11,514	346	11,860	911	62	11,011	2,518	1,435	4,379	3,936	3,417	1,491
1971	15,756	11,896	391	12,287	979	61	11,369	2,716	1,671	4,571	4,147	3,447	1,457
1972	16,990	12,851	507	13,358	1,115	71	12,314	2,891	1,784	4,929	4,426	3,447	1,481
1973	19,127	14,441	756	15,197	1,435	87	13,849	3,267	2,011	5,501	4,922	3,477	1,558
1974	21,699	16,216	891	17,107	1,656	130	15,581	3,766	2,352	6,116	5,476	3,548	1,622
1975	24,548	18,160	906	19,066	1,837	200	17,429	4,211	2,907	6,783	6,098	3,619	1,659
1976	27,220	20,615	754	21,369	2,137	249	19,481	4,577	3,162	7,376	6,607	3,691	1,739
1977	30,215	23,355	604	23,959	2,457	232	21,734	5,171	3,310	8,009	7,154	3,772	1,815
1978	35,173	27,479	754	28,233	2,973	273	25,533	6,053	3,588	9,051	8,002	3,886	1,939
1979	40,388	31,843	740	32,582	3,561	329	29,350	7,024	4,015	10,065	8,818	4,013	2,058
1980	45,792	35,054	861	35,915	3,898	395	32,412	8,463	4,916	11,022	9,674	4,155	2,105
1981	51,106	38,345	863	39,207	4,585	432	35,055	10,340	5,712	12,066	10,563	4,236	2,119
1982	54,140	39,678	767	40,445	4,812	468	36,101	11,613	6,425	12,660	11,294	4,277	2,094
1983	57,663	41,647	1,066	42,713	5,114	495	38,093	12,551	7,019	13,409	12,089	4,300	2,140
1984	61,887	44,598	1,024	45,622	5,647	544	40,520	13,990	7,378	14,248	12,902	4,344	2,214
1985	65,734	47,614	753	48,367	6,087	572	42,852	14,947	7,935	14,939	13,499	4,400	2,277
1986	70,366	51,188	1,060	52,247	6,585	617	46,279	15,671	8,416	15,803	14,312	4,453	2,351
1987	74,684	54,847	1,084	55,931	7,025	672	49,578	16,244	8,862	16,480	14,813	4,532	2,470
1988	81,319	60,433	1,020	61,453	7,929	756	54,280	17,385	9,654	17,526	15,818	4,640	2,600
1989	89,962	66,040	1,156	67,196	8,669	847	59,373	19,993	10,596	18,954	16,932	4,746	2,718
1990	98,856	73,462	1,210	74,672	9,823	925	65,774	21,436	11,646	20,162	17,967	4,903	2,842
1991	105,798	78,839	1,281	80,120	10,637	998	70,481	22,126	13,192	21,052	18,858	5,026	2,877
1992	114,254	85,964	1,542	87,506	11,580	1,109	77,035	22,667	14,552	22,139	19,865	5,161	2,907
1993	120,066	89,681	1,744	91,425	12,079	1,204	80,549	23,939	15,578	22,745	20,469	5,279	2,951
1994	126,289	93,956	1,429	95,385	12,804	1,259	83,840	26,052	16,396	23,495	21,078	5,375	3,060
1995	133,509	98,074	1,468	99,543	13,404	1,418	87,557	28,431	17,521	24,358	21,819	5,481	3,101
1996	143,601	104,760	1,943	106,703	14,014	1,639	94,327	30,915	18,360	25,782	22,899	5,570	3,192
1997	154,904	114,264	1,549	115,814	14,810	1,797	102,800	33,059	19,044	27,297	24,052	5,675	3,298
1998	169,810	127,131	1,730	128,862	16,246	1,906	114,521	35,495	19,794	29,432	25,647	5,770	3,382
1999	181,572	138,526	1,498	140,024	17,003	1,972	124,993	35,593	20,986	31,077	26,655	5,843	3,444
2000	194,351	147,433	1,737	149,171	18,408	2,297	133,060	38,876	22,415	32,882	28,415	5,911	3,525
2001	198,970	150,094	1,573	151,666	18,149	2,410	135,927	37,848	25,195	33,241	29,215	5,986	3,509
2002	203,533	152,979	1,652	154,631	18,548	2,493	138,576	38,233	26,725	33,629	30,266	6,052	3,483
2003	211,587	157,712	2,161	159,874	19,317	2,473	143,030	40,597	27,960	34,663	31,526	6,104	3,510
2004	227,293	166,364	2,138	168,503	20,547	2,919	150,875	48,015	28,403	36,787	33,685	6,179	3,582
2005	236,240	175,354	1,868	177,222	21,862	3,141	158,501	47,747	29,992	37,754	34,211	6,257	3,683
2006	256,128	187,861	1,818	189,679	23,189	3,175	169,665	54,218	32,245	40,204	36,168	6,371	3,795
2007	277,551	199,591	2,200	201,790	24,431	3,550	180,910	61,715	34,925	42,954	38,388	6,462	3,924
2008	291,760	205,554	2,206	207,760	25,013	3,458	186,205	65,291	40,265	44,460	40,074	6,562	3,957
2009	281,687	199,575	2,109	201,684	24,789	3,253	180,148	56,149	45,390	42,248	39,024	6,667	3,820
2010	288,695	204,341	2,536	206,877	25,438	3,074	184,513	54,040	50,142	42,821	39,371	6,742	3,763
2011	305,628	212,929	3,233	216,163	23,958	3,332	195,537	60,092	49,999	44,800	40,649	6,822	3,806
2012	326,497	225,184	3,440	228,624	24,781	3,379	207,223	69,148	50,127	47,344	43,032	6,896	3,899
2013	331,031	232,859	3,453	236,311	28,972	3,391	210,731	69,348	50,953	47,468	42,634	6,974	3,978
2014	350,322	246,530	3,181	249,711	30,320	3,353	222,745	72,149	55,427	49,610	44,412	7,062	4,076
2015	366,790	258,972	3,001	261,973	31,495	3,582	234,060	75,168	57,562	51,146	45,511	7,171	...

... = Not available.

Personal Income and Employment by Region and State: West Virginia

(Millions of dollars, except as noted.)

| | | Derivation of personal income | | | | | | | | Per capita (dollars) | | | |
| | | Earnings by place of work | | | Less: Contributions for government social insurance | Plus: Adjustment for residence | Equals: Net earnings by place of residence | Plus: Dividends, interest, and rent | Plus: Personal current transfer receipts | | | Population (thousands) | Total employment (thousands) |
Year	Personal income, total	Nonfarm	Farm	Total						Personal income	Disposable personal income		
1960	3,090	2,581	50	2,631	155	-20	2,456	330	304	1,667	1,499	1,853	...
1961	3,132	2,575	43	2,618	153	-20	2,445	343	344	1,713	1,541	1,828	...
1962	3,267	2,690	32	2,722	168	-19	2,535	365	367	1,806	1,625	1,809	...
1963	3,410	2,812	25	2,837	186	-18	2,634	397	379	1,899	1,702	1,796	...
1964	3,636	2,992	23	3,015	173	-17	2,825	426	385	2,024	1,836	1,797	...
1965	3,887	3,194	25	3,219	184	-13	3,022	454	411	2,177	1,978	1,786	...
1966	4,125	3,468	15	3,483	244	-10	3,228	463	434	2,324	2,097	1,775	...
1967	4,369	3,648	29	3,677	268	-8	3,401	477	492	2,470	2,232	1,769	...
1968	4,629	3,861	23	3,883	298	2	3,587	499	544	2,626	2,348	1,763	...
1969	4,938	4,149	31	4,180	323	-72	3,784	555	599	2,828	2,483	1,746	652
1970	5,499	4,549	26	4,575	350	-75	4,150	627	722	3,148	2,793	1,747	660
1971	6,034	4,937	26	4,962	395	-90	4,477	686	871	3,408	3,038	1,770	670
1972	6,678	5,453	31	5,484	455	-102	4,927	754	997	3,717	3,299	1,797	684
1973	7,302	5,893	45	5,938	568	-105	5,265	850	1,186	4,045	3,614	1,805	700
1974	8,093	6,494	29	6,524	648	-119	5,757	992	1,344	4,461	3,939	1,814	711
1975	9,145	7,237	15	7,251	711	-124	6,417	1,128	1,601	4,969	4,401	1,841	717
1976	10,188	8,161	4	8,165	819	-152	7,194	1,236	1,758	5,427	4,777	1,877	739
1977	11,394	9,228	-1	9,227	918	-185	8,125	1,394	1,875	5,979	5,273	1,906	758
1978	12,681	10,302	13	10,315	1,058	-214	9,043	1,555	2,083	6,603	5,842	1,920	781
1979	14,146	11,368	18	11,386	1,212	-224	9,949	1,759	2,438	7,295	6,410	1,939	790
1980	15,558	12,092	9	12,102	1,311	-247	10,544	2,177	2,836	7,973	6,981	1,951	782
1981	16,962	12,794	-22	12,772	1,484	-226	11,062	2,696	3,203	8,680	7,615	1,954	762
1982	17,970	13,131	-28	13,103	1,572	-170	11,362	3,096	3,512	9,217	8,133	1,950	740
1983	18,449	12,988	-15	12,974	1,571	-145	11,258	3,300	3,891	9,485	8,423	1,945	722
1984	19,840	14,016	24	14,040	1,737	-112	12,191	3,675	3,975	10,292	9,185	1,928	732
1985	20,661	14,553	22	14,575	1,828	-107	12,640	3,873	4,149	10,835	9,667	1,907	732
1986	21,170	14,717	48	14,765	1,921	-86	12,758	4,006	4,406	11,247	10,073	1,882	731
1987	21,701	15,160	7	15,167	1,992	-26	13,150	4,023	4,528	11,683	10,455	1,858	738
1988	23,150	16,282	6	16,288	2,190	8	14,106	4,265	4,779	12,649	11,403	1,830	751
1989	24,529	16,937	34	16,971	2,310	95	14,757	4,728	5,043	13,577	12,151	1,807	757
1990	26,120	18,115	47	18,161	2,502	92	15,751	4,962	5,407	14,571	13,036	1,793	778
1991	27,205	18,759	37	18,796	2,663	74	16,208	4,917	6,079	15,124	13,575	1,799	779
1992	29,317	19,939	62	20,001	2,840	134	17,296	5,051	6,970	16,229	14,652	1,806	789
1993	30,400	20,725	65	20,789	3,059	132	17,863	5,116	7,420	16,726	15,105	1,818	801
1994	31,693	21,817	61	21,878	3,205	182	18,854	5,315	7,524	17,410	15,670	1,820	822
1995	32,740	22,437	24	22,461	3,352	225	19,334	5,647	7,759	17,953	16,134	1,824	838
1996	34,072	23,109	9	23,118	3,454	236	19,899	5,991	8,182	18,692	16,769	1,823	847
1997	35,499	24,008	-0	24,007	3,548	394	20,853	6,277	8,368	19,514	17,452	1,819	858
1998	36,911	24,848	1	24,849	3,721	441	21,568	6,670	8,673	20,330	18,155	1,816	868
1999	37,818	25,755	-13	25,741	3,827	503	22,418	6,547	8,853	20,873	18,638	1,812	869
2000	39,953	27,146	19	27,165	4,141	628	23,652	7,014	9,287	22,110	19,737	1,807	875
2001	41,985	28,179	30	28,209	4,115	748	24,842	7,062	10,082	23,306	20,756	1,801	874
2002	43,702	28,977	-33	28,945	4,061	784	25,668	6,880	11,154	24,206	21,945	1,805	873
2003	44,707	29,804	-13	29,791	4,254	805	26,342	6,603	11,763	24,669	22,538	1,812	870
2004	46,315	31,462	30	31,492	4,381	906	28,017	6,710	11,588	25,498	23,387	1,816	881
2005	47,989	33,036	11	33,047	4,571	1,002	29,477	6,747	11,765	26,360	23,931	1,820	891
2006	51,764	35,253	-27	35,226	4,630	1,179	31,776	7,310	12,678	28,319	25,680	1,828	905
2007	53,767	35,663	-63	35,601	4,508	1,317	32,409	8,029	13,328	29,316	26,449	1,834	917
2008	57,780	37,802	-52	37,750	4,547	1,385	34,588	8,422	14,770	31,397	28,205	1,840	921
2009	58,074	37,310	-62	37,247	4,600	1,379	34,026	8,081	15,967	31,429	28,764	1,848	902
2010	59,526	38,189	-55	38,135	4,736	1,553	34,951	7,742	16,833	32,104	29,347	1,854	900
2011	63,461	40,676	-10	40,667	4,430	1,620	37,857	8,630	16,975	34,211	30,941	1,855	910
2012	65,665	42,314	-21	42,293	4,548	1,419	39,164	9,190	17,311	35,374	32,231	1,856	919
2013	65,178	42,062	29	42,091	5,087	1,402	38,406	9,169	17,603	35,163	31,841	1,854	914
2014	66,857	42,441	20	42,461	5,252	1,784	38,993	9,493	18,371	36,132	32,686	1,850	914
2015	68,329	42,611	60	42,670	5,262	1,977	39,386	9,876	19,066	37,047	33426	1844	...

... = Not available.

Personal Income and Employment by Region and State: Wisconsin

(Millions of dollars, except as noted.)

Year	Personal income, total	Earnings by place of work			Less: Contributions for government social insurance	Plus: Adjustment for residence	Equals: Net earnings by place of residence	Plus: Dividends, interest, and rent	Plus: Personal current transfer receipts	Per capita (dollars)		Population (thousands)	Total employment (thousands)
		Nonfarm	Farm	Total						Personal income	Disposable personal income		
1960	8,955	7,024	428	7,452	341	64	7,175	1,223	557	2,260	1,993	3,962	...
1961	9,245	7,106	496	7,602	348	67	7,321	1,278	646	2,306	2,051	4,009	...
1962	9,769	7,574	492	8,065	374	75	7,766	1,344	658	2,413	2,136	4,049	...
1963	10,104	7,900	439	8,339	433	81	7,988	1,421	695	2,457	2,166	4,112	...
1964	10,889	8,519	478	8,997	449	92	8,639	1,525	724	2,614	2,331	4,165	...
1965	11,793	9,163	545	9,708	479	104	9,333	1,681	779	2,787	2,476	4,232	...
1966	12,896	10,105	670	10,775	668	124	10,231	1,803	862	3,017	2,656	4,274	...
1967	13,616	10,710	564	11,274	760	138	10,652	1,902	1,063	3,164	2,762	4,303	...
1968	14,890	11,552	645	12,197	815	159	11,541	2,111	1,237	3,427	2,989	4,345	...
1969	16,413	12,683	638	13,321	934	250	12,637	2,417	1,359	3,749	3,215	4,378	1,944
1970	17,609	13,381	639	14,021	974	255	13,301	2,709	1,599	3,979	3,460	4,426	1,954
1971	18,907	14,217	693	14,910	1,070	268	14,107	2,929	1,870	4,239	3,737	4,460	1,957
1972	20,673	15,666	729	16,396	1,248	291	15,439	3,154	2,079	4,596	4,006	4,498	2,014
1973	23,064	17,575	916	18,491	1,614	317	17,194	3,505	2,365	5,104	4,457	4,518	2,116
1974	25,336	19,216	806	20,022	1,840	343	18,525	4,000	2,811	5,583	4,848	4,538	2,159
1975	27,780	20,543	867	21,409	1,927	346	19,828	4,425	3,528	6,079	5,338	4,570	2,148
1976	30,473	22,997	762	23,759	2,188	383	21,955	4,695	3,823	6,647	5,798	4,585	2,211
1977	34,052	25,686	1,144	26,830	2,443	424	24,811	5,187	4,054	7,381	6,417	4,613	2,293
1978	38,047	29,036	1,128	30,164	2,843	476	27,797	5,775	4,475	8,214	7,082	4,632	2,380
1979	42,628	32,365	1,407	33,773	3,302	511	30,982	6,513	5,134	9,136	7,895	4,666	2,460
1980	47,053	34,396	1,446	35,842	3,497	536	32,882	7,914	6,257	9,986	8,664	4,712	2,443
1981	51,321	36,733	1,172	37,905	3,999	580	34,486	9,720	7,115	10,858	9,362	4,726	2,415
1982	54,103	37,808	1,024	38,832	4,156	600	35,276	10,891	7,936	11,441	9,958	4,729	2,373
1983	56,952	39,883	473	40,356	4,359	651	36,647	11,778	8,527	12,062	10,620	4,721	2,376
1984	62,644	43,885	1,003	44,889	4,904	760	40,745	13,168	8,732	13,228	11,682	4,736	2,467
1985	66,042	46,225	1,031	47,256	5,208	849	42,896	13,870	9,275	13,910	12,288	4,748	2,495
1986	69,705	48,928	1,307	50,235	5,503	930	45,662	14,475	9,568	14,657	12,950	4,756	2,537
1987	73,574	52,525	1,418	53,943	5,811	1,033	49,165	14,625	9,784	15,399	13,523	4,778	2,605
1988	78,143	57,088	855	57,943	6,549	1,194	52,588	15,419	10,136	16,204	14,247	4,822	2,684
1989	85,276	60,921	1,741	62,662	7,004	1,234	56,892	17,443	10,942	17,559	15,411	4,857	2,740
1990	90,143	65,270	1,397	66,667	7,801	1,343	60,210	18,198	11,735	18,379	16,103	4,905	2,814
1991	93,632	68,432	1,018	69,450	8,259	1,363	62,554	18,343	12,735	18,861	16,557	4,964	2,840
1992	101,191	74,357	1,276	75,633	8,872	1,463	68,224	19,165	13,802	20,136	17,699	5,025	2,894
1993	106,443	78,976	956	79,932	9,408	1,520	72,044	20,018	14,380	20,933	18,364	5,085	2,950
1994	113,018	84,069	1,224	85,293	10,146	1,657	76,804	21,383	14,830	22,015	19,261	5,134	3,040
1995	118,779	88,066	797	88,863	10,657	1,777	79,983	23,074	15,722	22,909	19,992	5,185	3,120
1996	125,663	92,369	1,372	93,741	11,100	1,920	84,561	24,818	16,283	24,027	20,832	5,230	3,171
1997	133,284	98,736	1,000	99,736	11,780	2,123	90,080	26,387	16,818	25,309	21,814	5,266	3,226
1998	142,485	105,199	1,376	106,575	12,476	2,309	96,408	28,830	17,247	26,896	23,088	5,298	3,285
1999	148,287	111,340	1,331	112,671	13,252	2,480	101,899	28,433	17,954	27,807	23,896	5,333	3,346
2000	157,901	118,134	899	119,032	13,901	2,711	107,842	30,764	19,294	29,382	25,310	5,374	3,407
2001	164,765	122,803	1,192	123,996	14,202	2,851	112,645	30,591	21,529	30,473	26,372	5,407	3,392
2002	169,128	127,249	1,097	128,346	14,588	2,653	116,411	29,561	23,157	31,060	27,464	5,445	3,385
2003	174,812	132,124	1,572	133,696	15,070	2,571	121,197	29,762	23,853	31,905	28,468	5,479	3,404
2004	183,895	139,492	1,895	141,387	15,873	2,915	128,429	30,911	24,555	33,350	29,883	5,514	3,458
2005	190,293	144,076	1,669	145,745	16,517	3,091	132,319	31,663	26,311	34,311	30,505	5,546	3,499
2006	202,289	150,848	1,359	152,207	17,407	3,366	138,166	36,201	27,921	36,268	32,062	5,578	3,537
2007	211,378	155,009	2,085	157,093	17,981	3,696	142,808	38,331	30,239	37,674	33,250	5,611	3,576
2008	219,886	159,284	1,684	160,968	18,533	3,769	146,204	39,792	33,889	38,980	34,397	5,641	3,565
2009	217,247	155,889	781	156,670	18,013	3,387	142,045	36,015	39,187	38,320	34,661	5,669	3,440
2010	220,826	156,739	1,473	158,212	18,428	3,429	143,213	35,576	42,037	38,815	35,042	5,689	3,412
2011	233,132	163,335	2,869	166,203	17,294	3,642	152,551	39,901	40,679	40,837	36,480	5,709	3,460
2012	243,096	169,291	2,709	172,000	17,814	3,670	157,856	43,764	41,477	42,463	37,968	5,725	3,482
2013	245,438	173,054	3,424	176,477	20,622	3,754	159,609	43,433	42,396	42,737	37,857	5,743	3,521
2014	254,405	179,121	3,566	182,687	21,345	3,931	165,273	45,104	44,028	44,186	39,104	5,758	3,567
2015	263,301	186,811	1,682	188,493	22,109	4,118	170,501	46,987	45,812	45,617	40,095	5,772	...

... = Not available.

Personal Income and Employment by Region and State: Wyoming

(Millions of dollars, except as noted.)

Year	Personal income, total	Earnings by place of work			Less: Contributions for government social insurance	Plus: Adjustment for residence	Equals: Net earnings by place of residence	Plus: Dividends, interest, and rent	Plus: Personal current transfer receipts	Per capita (dollars)		Population (thousands)	Total employment (thousands)
		Nonfarm	Farm	Total						Personal income	Disposable personal income		
1960	781	604	51	654	34	-2	619	118	45	2,360	2,116	331	...
1961	822	619	57	676	34	-1	641	129	53	2,440	2,202	337	...
1962	851	628	67	694	35	-1	659	138	54	2,555	2,295	333	...
1963	871	647	67	714	40	-1	672	142	56	2,592	2,303	336	...
1964	898	691	47	738	43	-1	695	148	55	2,649	2,420	339	...
1965	927	699	53	752	41	-1	711	158	58	2,792	2,547	332	...
1966	950	715	58	773	48	-0	725	164	61	2,941	2,666	323	...
1967	1,016	757	70	828	53	-0	774	171	71	3,157	2,843	322	...
1968	1,085	832	62	894	59	0	835	169	81	3,349	3,003	324	...
1969	1,212	912	70	982	66	0	917	207	89	3,683	3,265	329	158
1970	1,341	993	79	1,072	71	0	1,001	238	103	4,017	3,579	334	159
1971	1,490	1,095	88	1,183	81	-1	1,102	269	119	4,381	3,930	340	165
1972	1,675	1,228	126	1,354	95	-3	1,256	289	129	4,829	4,380	347	172
1973	1,955	1,445	153	1,598	127	-7	1,464	339	152	5,533	4,949	353	182
1974	2,288	1,774	111	1,885	158	-14	1,713	403	172	6,276	5,513	365	194
1975	2,593	2,061	67	2,128	181	-16	1,931	454	208	6,815	6,079	380	203
1976	2,867	2,325	48	2,373	213	-22	2,138	497	232	7,250	6,406	395	214
1977	3,347	2,763	45	2,808	249	-29	2,530	563	254	8,133	7,184	412	231
1978	3,999	3,335	65	3,400	309	-38	3,054	659	286	9,280	8,172	431	250
1979	4,674	3,922	96	4,018	380	-54	3,584	759	331	10,344	8,962	452	266
1980	5,451	4,543	86	4,629	441	-74	4,114	944	393	11,496	9,992	474	279
1981	6,231	5,150	51	5,201	541	-83	4,577	1,183	471	12,672	10,947	492	289
1982	6,553	5,244	29	5,273	565	-80	4,628	1,383	542	12,940	11,353	506	287
1983	6,482	4,978	36	5,014	522	-58	4,434	1,407	641	12,701	11,317	510	274
1984	6,760	5,195	14	5,209	560	-53	4,596	1,531	633	13,390	12,020	505	276
1985	7,066	5,417	18	5,434	599	-52	4,783	1,611	672	14,141	12,693	500	277
1986	7,021	5,282	40	5,321	581	-42	4,699	1,582	741	14,166	12,854	496	264
1987	6,754	4,954	59	5,013	550	-27	4,437	1,566	751	14,161	12,782	477	258
1988	6,891	5,048	59	5,108	602	-22	4,484	1,625	782	14,816	13,357	465	264
1989	7,550	5,416	90	5,506	628	-15	4,864	1,838	849	16,472	14,755	458	265
1990	8,161	5,808	153	5,961	699	-11	5,252	1,997	912	17,989	16,127	454	271
1991	8,565	6,002	213	6,215	745	-1	5,469	2,081	1,015	18,649	16,776	459	277
1992	9,072	6,336	221	6,558	777	-6	5,774	2,175	1,123	19,457	17,533	466	280
1993	9,580	6,721	247	6,969	817	-8	6,144	2,214	1,223	20,250	18,190	473	285
1994	10,023	7,084	122	7,206	866	-7	6,332	2,397	1,293	20,868	18,725	480	298
1995	10,492	7,276	102	7,378	891	-5	6,482	2,630	1,380	21,626	19,418	485	301
1996	10,954	7,544	83	7,628	913	0	6,715	2,786	1,453	22,440	19,707	488	304
1997	11,731	8,006	184	8,190	957	5	7,238	3,000	1,492	23,967	20,949	489	307
1998	12,481	8,452	99	8,551	1,006	8	7,554	3,393	1,534	25,430	22,188	491	310
1999	13,320	8,959	168	9,127	1,054	7	8,080	3,644	1,596	27,085	23,578	492	314
2000	14,315	9,653	124	9,777	1,121	14	8,670	3,928	1,716	28,959	24,997	494	322
2001	15,204	10,395	192	10,587	1,202	10	9,395	3,956	1,853	30,736	26,772	495	329
2002	15,722	10,928	102	11,030	1,226	3	9,806	3,932	1,984	31,442	28,208	500	333
2003	16,815	11,470	184	11,654	1,303	-18	10,333	4,339	2,143	33,400	30,350	503	336
2004	18,171	12,255	181	12,436	1,396	-44	10,996	4,908	2,267	35,692	32,516	509	343
2005	20,136	13,300	232	13,532	1,508	-80	11,944	5,805	2,387	39,164	35,119	514	354
2006	23,095	15,456	97	15,553	1,912	-132	13,509	7,053	2,533	44,186	38,895	523	369
2007	24,340	16,681	40	16,721	2,112	-153	14,456	7,194	2,690	45,505	39,801	535	387
2008	26,720	18,511	68	18,579	2,242	-218	16,118	7,473	3,129	48,934	43,145	546	397
2009	24,159	17,318	32	17,350	2,173	-193	14,984	5,794	3,381	43,153	39,566	560	386
2010	25,309	17,913	81	17,995	2,230	-197	15,568	6,094	3,647	44,846	40,697	564	382
2011	27,893	18,954	312	19,267	2,125	-203	16,939	7,288	3,666	49,140	44,480	568	387
2012	30,087	19,909	95	20,005	2,247	-217	17,542	8,882	3,663	52,154	46,317	577	393
2013	30,206	20,201	206	20,407	2,523	-200	17,684	8,741	3,782	51,791	45,884	583	396
2014	31,885	21,071	344	21,415	2,627	-199	18,588	9,397	3,900	54,584	48,264	584	403
2015	32,417	21,040	189	21,229	2,602	-184	18,443	9,905	4,069	55,303	48,725	586	...

... = Not available.

Personal Income and Employment by Area: Abilene, TX

(Thousands of dollars, except as noted.)

Year	Personal income, total	Earnings by place of work			Less: Contributions for government social insurance	Plus: Adjustment for residence	Equals: Net earnings by place of residence	Plus: Dividends, interest, and rent	Plus: Personal current transfer receipts	Per capita personal income (dollars)	Population (persons)	Total employment
		Nonfarm	Farm	Total								
1970	443,495	322,920	23,059	345,979	19,934	1,863	327,908	73,938	41,649	3,620	122,505	56,215
1971	474,162	347,558	20,798	368,356	22,303	2,003	348,056	78,915	47,191	3,798	124,841	56,614
1972	539,218	393,394	28,946	422,340	26,147	2,373	398,566	88,372	52,280	4,196	128,517	59,092
1973	579,226	419,671	27,728	447,399	31,846	2,458	418,011	98,238	62,977	4,542	127,533	60,359
1974	653,223	488,284	8,813	497,097	38,282	1,630	460,445	118,961	73,817	5,079	128,625	63,366
1975	767,218	562,703	21,367	584,070	44,278	1,702	541,494	137,034	88,690	5,855	131,031	65,822
1976	847,559	633,523	17,641	651,164	50,603	2,096	602,657	147,947	96,955	6,355	133,379	68,298
1977	920,573	695,985	12,946	708,931	55,793	2,173	655,311	162,328	102,934	6,919	133,052	69,994
1978	1,057,525	806,540	9,999	816,539	65,480	1,512	752,571	190,791	114,163	7,865	134,462	72,932
1979	1,205,694	916,826	20,602	937,428	78,599	1,126	859,955	218,885	126,854	8,826	136,601	75,773
1980	1,392,677	1,054,774	10,764	1,065,538	91,347	448	974,639	273,241	144,797	9,941	140,098	78,280
1981	1,678,262	1,247,820	46,280	1,294,100	116,795	-3,092	1,174,213	341,320	162,729	11,711	143,310	84,737
1982	1,795,083	1,318,408	23,155	1,341,563	125,452	-1,662	1,214,449	399,580	181,054	12,056	148,899	86,685
1983	1,872,242	1,371,725	8,428	1,380,153	129,737	-2,141	1,248,275	426,504	197,463	12,242	152,939	86,693
1984	1,994,522	1,447,943	10,327	1,458,270	140,379	-2,560	1,315,331	468,596	210,595	12,986	153,587	87,720
1985	2,118,488	1,531,208	308	1,531,516	150,084	-2,358	1,379,074	514,260	225,154	13,804	153,470	88,722
1986	2,110,118	1,496,445	10,951	1,507,396	144,782	-274	1,362,340	501,209	246,569	13,611	155,031	83,720
1987	2,080,373	1,430,601	28,279	1,458,880	138,648	1,559	1,321,791	498,299	260,283	13,539	153,655	82,965
1988	2,172,606	1,521,509	15,165	1,536,674	152,195	3,369	1,387,848	513,193	271,565	14,480	150,042	83,645
1989	2,259,631	1,523,106	18,571	1,541,677	154,717	7,498	1,394,458	574,822	290,351	15,132	149,324	82,367
1990	2,313,227	1,558,463	38,433	1,596,896	156,668	10,283	1,450,511	541,740	320,976	15,647	147,834	80,942
1991	2,372,735	1,626,082	14,310	1,640,392	168,262	5,066	1,477,196	537,674	357,865	16,097	147,400	82,259
1992	2,532,171	1,722,397	36,748	1,759,145	176,727	6,192	1,588,610	535,313	408,248	16,890	149,917	82,277
1993	2,655,273	1,803,704	30,802	1,834,506	184,213	6,245	1,656,538	569,623	429,112	17,365	152,909	84,362
1994	2,711,191	1,875,607	19,614	1,895,221	193,361	4,630	1,706,490	545,007	459,694	17,630	153,779	85,682
1995	2,904,312	1,977,979	17,649	1,995,628	203,789	3,561	1,795,400	607,755	501,157	18,606	156,097	88,181
1996	3,093,095	2,124,671	6,377	2,131,048	214,107	3,165	1,920,106	637,606	535,383	19,783	156,351	89,587
1997	3,307,392	2,303,426	22,943	2,326,369	227,052	4,426	2,103,743	642,563	561,086	21,012	157,405	91,934
1998	3,462,019	2,424,399	8,464	2,432,863	232,301	6,403	2,206,965	688,312	566,742	21,875	158,264	92,579
1999	3,606,422	2,549,245	30,364	2,579,609	240,171	7,632	2,347,070	673,354	585,998	22,575	159,755	91,440
2000	3,704,390	2,591,074	7,821	2,598,895	244,306	10,171	2,364,760	732,390	607,240	23,111	160,288	91,030
2001	3,778,557	2,587,380	37,105	2,624,485	250,336	13,140	2,387,289	735,204	656,064	23,777	158,917	89,515
2002	3,911,534	2,719,593	15,655	2,735,248	265,072	7,504	2,477,680	727,336	706,518	24,599	159,012	90,398
2003	4,115,222	2,850,090	31,335	2,881,425	281,431	-7,116	2,592,878	767,730	754,614	25,913	158,810	91,995
2004	4,293,244	3,012,636	36,986	3,049,622	297,861	-10,829	2,740,932	757,139	795,173	26,807	160,156	93,423
2005	4,491,803	3,117,970	31,086	3,149,056	310,484	-13,903	2,824,669	806,171	860,963	27,941	160,761	94,657
2006	4,747,075	3,363,715	8,097	3,371,812	329,193	-15,379	3,027,240	812,963	906,872	29,414	161,389	95,582
2007	5,073,971	3,497,707	31,167	3,528,874	350,929	-5,427	3,172,518	911,452	990,001	31,316	162,023	97,671
2008	5,610,330	3,813,620	-1,699	3,811,921	372,140	-3,711	3,436,070	1,088,515	1,085,745	34,523	162,508	99,720
2009	5,329,176	3,573,947	-4,965	3,568,982	370,766	-5,170	3,193,046	971,221	1,164,909	32,517	163,888	97,837
2010	5,558,649	3,683,085	24,652	3,707,737	378,918	-1,390	3,327,429	961,515	1,269,705	33,558	165,642	97,131
2011	5,961,234	3,886,895	23,304	3,910,199	351,807	7,062	3,565,454	1,092,958	1,302,822	35,774	166,637	98,576
2012	6,349,442	4,198,270	5,773	4,204,043	372,575	16,558	3,848,026	1,199,522	1,301,894	37,901	167,529	100,325
2013	6,465,992	4,337,848	40,795	4,378,643	431,915	18,388	3,965,116	1,149,882	1,350,994	38,614	167,452	101,535
2014	6,779,927	4,579,042	25,250	4,604,292	452,806	23,692	4,175,178	1,195,334	1,409,415	40,215	168,592	103,112

Personal Income and Employment by Metropolitan Statistical Area: Akron, OH

(Thousands of dollars, except as noted.)

Year	Personal income, total	Earnings by place of work			Less: Contributions for government social insurance	Plus: Adjustment for residence	Equals: Net earnings by place of residence	Plus: Dividends, interest, and rent	Plus: Personal current transfer receipts	Per capita personal income (dollars)	Population (persons)	Total employment
		Nonfarm	Farm	Total								
1970	2,837,126	2,332,623	6,504	2,339,127	158,576	98,417	2,278,968	350,602	207,556	4,178	679,077	279,931
1971	2,987,986	2,426,891	8,998	2,435,889	169,666	102,226	2,368,449	376,369	243,168	4,399	679,231	274,958
1972	3,260,687	2,670,858	9,046	2,679,904	197,372	105,344	2,587,876	401,406	271,405	4,816	677,046	283,207
1973	3,561,357	2,920,428	11,556	2,931,984	250,765	126,907	2,808,126	434,872	318,359	5,267	676,196	292,971
1974	3,875,437	3,122,414	14,191	3,136,605	276,803	144,574	3,004,376	492,363	378,698	5,782	670,284	296,332
1975	4,109,115	3,177,405	12,512	3,189,917	270,258	165,287	3,084,946	528,922	495,247	6,107	672,844	285,325
1976	4,414,340	3,401,972	11,154	3,413,126	295,638	209,155	3,326,643	557,765	529,932	6,609	667,910	284,907
1977	4,933,029	3,867,551	8,387	3,875,938	337,775	240,019	3,778,182	610,799	544,048	7,449	662,233	297,537
1978	5,461,092	4,295,362	2,354	4,297,716	387,518	290,828	4,201,026	679,683	580,383	8,293	658,517	305,459
1979	6,002,453	4,676,680	2,036	4,678,716	438,962	341,037	4,580,791	763,343	658,319	9,090	660,364	307,763
1980	6,594,106	4,918,915	136	4,919,051	458,075	381,426	4,842,402	925,016	826,688	9,986	660,334	300,754
1981	7,220,323	5,271,556	885	5,272,441	526,076	407,212	5,153,577	1,147,530	919,216	10,959	658,870	297,681
1982	7,545,390	5,348,491	3,026	5,351,517	538,767	395,945	5,208,695	1,292,268	1,044,427	11,500	656,126	289,691
1983	7,971,454	5,632,378	608	5,632,986	579,166	394,415	5,448,235	1,399,714	1,123,505	12,189	653,968	285,981
1984	8,681,663	6,159,456	10,113	6,169,569	647,822	435,852	5,957,599	1,567,680	1,156,384	13,317	651,917	296,150
1985	9,195,244	6,517,358	5,841	6,523,199	693,342	464,838	6,294,695	1,663,650	1,236,899	14,180	648,457	303,855
1986	9,622,295	6,869,273	5,499	6,874,772	748,895	462,604	6,588,481	1,726,564	1,307,250	14,880	646,647	308,919
1987	10,079,467	7,242,806	5,481	7,248,287	787,366	485,196	6,946,117	1,758,623	1,374,727	15,559	647,810	316,920
1988	10,747,708	7,730,225	3,746	7,733,971	868,905	529,913	7,394,979	1,899,391	1,453,338	16,464	652,814	325,266
1989	11,722,479	8,318,500	6,396	8,324,896	941,017	566,514	7,950,393	2,204,127	1,567,959	17,880	655,626	333,052
1990	12,374,755	8,709,420	5,510	8,714,930	1,005,927	627,923	8,336,926	2,275,404	1,762,425	18,788	658,654	337,124
1991	12,660,736	8,983,998	4,478	8,988,476	1,062,753	614,170	8,539,893	2,253,155	1,867,688	19,054	664,478	337,813
1992	13,552,405	9,649,938	9,294	9,659,232	1,140,104	644,407	9,163,535	2,341,354	2,047,516	20,235	669,752	341,070
1993	14,163,377	10,209,691	9,975	10,219,666	1,217,361	600,610	9,602,915	2,403,081	2,157,381	21,010	674,114	350,680
1994	15,035,676	10,864,735	12,657	10,877,392	1,316,338	662,291	10,223,345	2,546,822	2,265,509	22,174	678,063	364,299
1995	15,949,577	11,367,656	8,600	11,376,256	1,390,839	687,368	10,672,785	2,863,709	2,413,083	23,381	682,146	374,193
1996	16,781,997	11,993,670	14,035	12,007,705	1,454,193	734,418	11,287,930	2,995,029	2,499,038	24,419	687,264	380,965
1997	17,746,438	12,552,630	15,526	12,568,156	1,480,989	883,348	11,970,515	3,192,174	2,583,749	25,740	689,461	387,561
1998	18,876,588	13,401,380	11,111	13,412,491	1,527,836	973,680	12,858,335	3,423,176	2,595,077	27,316	691,039	385,609
1999	19,552,704	13,841,109	9,566	13,850,675	1,567,056	1,246,570	13,530,189	3,353,962	2,668,553	28,209	693,125	393,201
2000	20,720,930	14,531,353	7,362	14,538,715	1,585,332	1,357,193	14,310,576	3,559,117	2,851,237	29,774	695,946	396,767
2001	20,914,847	14,713,552	7,183	14,720,735	1,580,602	1,304,760	14,444,893	3,381,823	3,088,131	29,959	698,108	392,627
2002	21,314,782	15,224,199	6,912	15,231,111	1,609,794	1,195,835	14,817,152	3,194,406	3,303,224	30,470	699,533	392,574
2003	22,127,329	15,912,068	6,584	15,918,652	1,695,407	1,098,722	15,321,967	3,337,398	3,467,964	31,559	701,139	393,637
2004	22,768,493	16,774,167	7,477	16,781,644	1,825,157	998,228	15,954,715	3,205,991	3,607,787	32,442	701,811	401,028
2005	23,582,252	17,371,397	8,823	17,380,220	1,897,765	899,432	16,381,887	3,425,983	3,774,382	33,569	702,498	408,944
2006	24,752,362	18,207,545	5,398	18,212,943	1,986,364	782,967	17,009,546	3,775,448	3,967,368	35,238	702,433	413,970
2007	25,767,222	18,753,041	8,216	18,761,257	2,055,274	646,698	17,352,681	4,206,660	4,207,881	36,631	703,423	419,724
2008	26,598,737	19,227,292	6,570	19,233,862	2,138,350	498,219	17,593,731	4,248,459	4,756,547	37,820	703,300	419,600
2009	25,801,543	18,412,359	8,550	18,420,909	2,059,244	482,668	16,844,333	3,759,632	5,197,578	36,683	703,361	400,446
2010	26,403,013	18,780,170	7,316	18,787,486	2,069,549	504,541	17,222,478	3,661,548	5,518,987	37,559	702,967	395,734
2011	27,883,852	19,586,994	17,812	19,604,806	1,931,536	583,142	18,256,412	4,001,877	5,625,563	39,671	702,881	401,051
2012	28,994,601	20,308,047	12,355	20,320,402	1,994,283	769,919	19,096,038	4,423,396	5,475,167	41,291	702,203	404,630
2013	29,481,082	20,739,988	12,931	20,752,919	2,233,146	949,719	19,469,492	4,427,349	5,584,241	41,924	703,210	406,595
2014	30,564,440	21,600,771	9,685	21,610,456	2,361,159	903,192	20,152,489	4,579,693	5,832,258	43,426	703,825	413,857

Personal Income and Employment by Metropolitan Statistical Area: Albany, GA

(Thousands of dollars, except as noted.)

| Year | Personal income, total | Derivation of personal income | | | | | Equals: Net earnings by place of residence | Plus: Dividends, interest, and rent | Plus: Personal current transfer receipts | Per capita personal income (dollars) | Population (persons) | Total employment |
| | | Earnings by place of work | | | Less: Contributions for government social insurance | Plus: Adjustment for residence | | | | | | |
		Nonfarm	Farm	Total								
1970	379,876	300,796	19,201	319,997	18,064	-11,424	290,509	53,930	35,437	2,981	127,420	55,527
1971	433,462	337,305	25,573	362,878	21,332	-11,948	329,598	61,291	42,573	3,307	131,064	57,139
1972	489,268	391,197	22,936	414,133	26,092	-14,591	373,450	67,632	48,186	3,611	135,481	60,656
1973	566,336	445,497	40,135	485,632	33,919	-17,310	434,403	77,731	54,202	4,111	137,763	64,136
1974	587,184	452,763	40,403	493,166	36,260	-17,462	439,444	80,436	67,304	4,378	134,109	61,360
1975	615,977	470,323	30,736	501,059	37,272	-18,463	445,324	84,738	85,915	4,543	135,587	59,212
1976	682,530	530,022	30,246	560,268	42,341	-20,707	497,220	91,181	94,129	4,941	138,131	59,886
1977	742,956	602,124	15,785	617,909	47,827	-24,614	545,468	101,955	95,533	5,258	141,309	61,621
1978	858,224	698,570	24,946	723,516	57,001	-29,539	636,976	117,247	104,001	6,041	142,070	64,454
1979	962,711	797,968	20,042	818,010	68,376	-34,555	715,079	130,837	116,795	6,663	144,480	66,510
1980	1,067,522	879,062	-8,766	870,296	75,763	-30,337	764,196	161,621	141,705	7,272	146,793	66,284
1981	1,221,404	963,514	28,242	991,756	89,744	-37,424	864,588	194,800	162,016	8,221	148,567	67,040
1982	1,290,934	1,002,728	24,404	1,027,132	94,880	-39,765	892,487	222,849	175,598	8,626	149,660	66,060
1983	1,375,988	1,067,655	20,128	1,087,783	102,460	-42,028	943,295	240,927	191,766	9,191	149,716	66,278
1984	1,540,839	1,172,512	61,678	1,234,190	115,267	-45,750	1,073,173	264,625	203,041	10,251	150,313	69,522
1985	1,616,969	1,247,521	44,877	1,292,398	125,679	-46,980	1,119,739	281,245	215,985	10,704	151,062	71,096
1986	1,685,158	1,281,555	45,601	1,327,156	130,292	-44,532	1,152,332	299,474	233,352	11,204	150,405	70,814
1987	1,741,530	1,313,553	49,300	1,362,853	132,851	-43,959	1,186,043	311,356	244,131	11,640	149,611	71,010
1988	1,870,923	1,402,152	67,038	1,469,190	146,216	-44,361	1,278,613	328,746	263,564	12,586	148,651	70,486
1989	2,000,884	1,473,995	53,026	1,527,021	155,228	-44,331	1,327,462	381,819	291,603	13,546	147,705	70,955
1990	2,125,966	1,580,716	49,756	1,630,472	166,212	-47,916	1,416,344	389,157	320,465	14,498	146,642	72,212
1991	2,267,274	1,660,267	72,623	1,732,890	177,460	-57,632	1,497,798	401,351	368,125	15,329	147,910	71,684
1992	2,385,133	1,729,316	78,943	1,808,259	183,592	-57,758	1,566,909	407,117	411,107	15,894	150,065	71,406
1993	2,497,211	1,823,249	65,440	1,888,689	195,109	-61,441	1,632,139	427,116	437,956	16,430	151,993	73,056
1994	2,733,619	1,987,293	106,393	2,093,686	214,938	-71,219	1,807,529	457,221	468,869	17,840	153,232	76,059
1995	2,885,451	2,114,871	99,771	2,214,642	227,328	-75,243	1,912,071	480,714	492,666	18,726	154,087	78,366
1996	3,064,071	2,259,374	91,318	2,350,692	240,644	-83,959	2,026,089	515,864	522,118	19,695	155,576	80,407
1997	3,152,786	2,314,998	89,293	2,404,291	245,036	-85,922	2,073,333	539,797	539,656	20,114	156,748	80,915
1998	3,279,491	2,423,211	76,547	2,499,758	251,954	-87,642	2,160,162	570,767	548,562	20,829	157,452	80,537
1999	3,370,220	2,485,935	88,315	2,574,250	255,632	-87,170	2,231,448	563,456	575,316	21,379	157,644	79,952
2000	3,504,756	2,573,702	90,826	2,664,528	263,439	-95,907	2,305,182	577,416	622,158	22,237	157,610	80,758
2001	3,716,420	2,706,561	100,383	2,806,944	275,905	-100,545	2,430,494	612,720	673,206	23,561	157,735	79,520
2002	3,833,055	2,744,828	106,065	2,850,893	282,328	-101,466	2,467,099	613,036	752,920	24,423	156,947	77,961
2003	3,968,531	2,843,058	118,354	2,961,412	291,851	-108,956	2,560,605	650,868	757,058	25,291	156,914	79,265
2004	4,072,964	2,957,992	90,582	3,048,574	312,080	-120,575	2,615,919	649,357	807,688	25,957	156,911	79,353
2005	4,225,725	3,068,089	119,375	3,187,464	322,374	-112,495	2,752,595	625,475	847,655	26,935	156,886	81,088
2006	4,354,328	3,147,985	101,584	3,249,569	332,720	-94,817	2,822,032	634,552	897,744	27,662	157,412	81,213
2007	4,550,664	3,200,319	103,140	3,303,459	335,893	-83,061	2,884,505	720,634	945,525	28,918	157,367	81,685
2008	4,698,216	3,183,366	114,779	3,298,145	353,095	-89,110	2,855,940	779,987	1,062,289	29,820	157,551	80,943
2009	4,692,603	3,161,048	95,016	3,256,064	351,751	-92,868	2,811,445	721,748	1,159,410	29,706	157,969	78,731
2010	4,810,358	3,167,508	92,738	3,260,246	358,487	-92,152	2,809,607	742,615	1,258,136	30,510	157,663	78,104
2011	5,161,771	3,209,752	116,946	3,326,698	322,424	-95,209	2,909,065	934,420	1,318,286	32,713	157,791	79,812
2012	5,180,356	3,267,754	181,861	3,449,615	328,363	-88,662	3,032,590	858,445	1,289,321	32,921	157,355	79,979
2013	5,160,245	3,319,389	169,654	3,489,043	374,826	-88,989	3,025,228	819,042	1,315,975	33,123	155,790	79,970
2014	5,219,676	3,365,409	101,150	3,466,559	379,472	-82,877	3,004,210	847,122	1,368,344	33,692	154,925	80,348

Personal Income and Employment by Metropolitan Statistical Area: Albany, OR

(Thousands of dollars, except as noted.)

| Year | Personal income, total | Derivation of personal income | | | | | | | | Per capita personal income (dollars) | Population (persons) | Total employment |
| | | Earnings by place of work | | | Less: Contributions for government social insurance | Plus: Adjustment for residence | Equals: Net earnings by place of residence | Plus: Dividends, interest, and rent | Plus: Personal current transfer receipts | | | |
		Nonfarm	Farm	Total								
1970	241,272	198,287	9,156	207,443	16,044	-10,338	181,061	35,477	24,734	3,324	72,587	29,190
1971	267,093	220,361	9,305	229,666	18,472	-12,348	198,846	39,285	28,962	3,535	75,547	30,345
1972	296,402	247,089	9,966	257,055	21,770	-14,463	220,822	43,512	32,068	3,876	76,467	31,600
1973	343,431	280,096	20,904	301,000	28,275	-18,030	254,695	49,394	39,342	4,395	78,150	33,577
1974	393,454	316,376	24,904	341,280	32,806	-22,606	285,868	57,693	49,893	4,980	79,006	34,924
1975	426,744	346,527	10,517	357,044	34,806	-26,774	295,464	66,524	64,756	5,272	80,942	35,650
1976	493,527	407,020	18,081	425,101	41,288	-33,051	350,762	73,349	69,416	5,988	82,420	37,031
1977	558,428	466,006	17,381	483,387	47,606	-38,271	397,510	85,320	75,598	6,591	84,723	38,988
1978	622,743	531,980	8,533	540,513	55,649	-43,517	441,347	98,923	82,473	7,213	86,334	40,485
1979	689,070	582,501	7,402	589,903	62,649	-47,609	479,645	116,530	92,895	7,742	88,999	41,045
1980	759,515	623,332	8,106	631,438	67,047	-54,844	509,547	139,689	110,279	8,470	89,668	40,737
1981	829,426	640,865	21,633	662,498	73,921	-54,732	533,845	167,286	128,295	9,198	90,173	39,457
1982	850,462	627,116	17,560	644,676	73,527	-47,147	524,002	182,041	144,419	9,476	89,748	37,614
1983	894,641	665,681	11,243	676,924	79,247	-46,933	550,744	190,042	153,855	10,005	89,415	38,353
1984	962,282	713,351	13,701	727,052	88,384	-46,028	592,640	208,353	161,289	10,782	89,253	39,132
1985	1,002,007	733,039	20,176	753,215	91,647	-43,980	617,588	213,052	171,367	11,384	88,019	39,314
1986	1,046,576	749,823	27,446	777,269	93,033	-35,817	648,419	221,455	176,702	11,889	88,026	39,908
1987	1,111,973	802,589	35,590	838,179	98,036	-33,006	707,137	222,387	182,449	12,626	88,069	40,842
1988	1,239,094	887,246	65,344	952,590	111,697	-31,933	808,960	236,657	193,477	13,888	89,223	42,853
1989	1,337,436	950,825	46,701	997,526	119,408	-25,205	852,913	271,826	212,697	14,879	89,890	44,288
1990	1,408,839	995,995	47,858	1,043,853	128,352	-18,231	897,270	281,565	230,004	15,365	91,690	44,792
1991	1,485,376	1,041,643	49,302	1,090,945	136,170	-21,666	933,109	290,187	262,080	15,947	93,145	44,656
1992	1,580,853	1,105,539	56,730	1,162,269	143,269	-20,667	998,333	288,780	293,740	16,798	94,112	44,762
1993	1,693,204	1,171,214	60,085	1,231,299	153,941	-12,365	1,064,993	311,721	316,490	17,731	95,496	46,076
1994	1,793,081	1,279,642	57,032	1,336,674	168,314	-13,231	1,155,129	320,619	317,333	18,501	96,919	48,997
1995	1,913,588	1,384,912	31,183	1,416,095	183,023	-17,320	1,215,752	350,524	347,312	19,358	98,853	51,874
1996	2,084,795	1,498,080	60,586	1,558,666	200,736	-16,531	1,341,399	379,165	364,231	20,727	100,582	54,263
1997	2,157,679	1,587,285	35,554	1,622,839	209,543	-12,201	1,401,095	383,080	373,504	21,143	102,054	55,265
1998	2,229,830	1,616,334	29,030	1,645,364	212,674	-8,120	1,424,570	400,407	404,853	21,697	102,770	54,804
1999	2,293,381	1,645,008	35,816	1,680,824	214,095	-2,136	1,464,593	380,568	448,220	22,166	103,462	53,145
2000	2,391,424	1,696,791	24,566	1,721,357	218,419	14,886	1,517,824	405,505	468,095	23,213	103,020	52,608
2001	2,511,393	1,740,752	45,245	1,785,997	223,775	-1,551	1,560,671	423,833	526,889	24,254	103,544	51,697
2002	2,554,173	1,752,504	57,010	1,809,514	226,275	5,933	1,589,172	408,524	556,477	24,428	104,561	51,212
2003	2,608,338	1,776,448	64,819	1,841,267	229,463	13,482	1,625,286	409,393	573,659	24,599	106,035	50,789
2004	2,765,951	1,857,907	85,811	1,943,718	243,208	21,988	1,722,498	440,653	602,800	25,899	106,799	51,568
2005	2,872,167	1,953,790	72,942	2,026,732	260,200	31,707	1,798,239	423,491	650,437	26,562	108,132	53,461
2006	3,096,883	2,079,825	92,244	2,172,069	280,358	42,972	1,934,683	461,264	700,936	27,959	110,764	54,528
2007	3,277,259	2,166,077	87,705	2,253,782	292,250	55,629	2,017,161	508,852	751,246	29,020	112,932	55,580
2008	3,411,054	2,191,660	46,280	2,237,940	297,591	67,461	2,007,810	560,608	842,636	29,670	114,967	55,760
2009	3,426,219	2,027,692	35,054	2,062,746	276,899	119,086	1,904,933	537,744	983,542	29,536	116,001	52,383
2010	3,508,808	2,037,118	29,031	2,066,149	282,835	124,282	1,907,596	530,598	1,070,614	30,023	116,871	51,774
2011	3,630,785	2,064,629	30,516	2,095,145	257,419	130,574	1,968,300	565,072	1,097,413	30,739	118,117	51,484
2012	3,761,778	2,173,360	47,942	2,221,302	270,277	134,364	2,085,389	573,512	1,102,877	31,783	118,360	51,811
2013	3,847,624	2,203,569	47,589	2,251,158	309,422	155,238	2,096,974	605,504	1,145,146	32,430	118,644	52,166
2014	4,086,613	2,295,643	51,211	2,346,854	324,620	168,831	2,191,065	632,697	1,262,851	34,239	119,356	53,569

Personal Income and Employment by Metropolitan Statistical Area: Albany-Schenectady-Troy, NY

(Thousands of dollars, except as noted.)

Year	Personal income, total	Earnings by place of work			Less: Contributions for government social insurance	Plus: Adjustment for residence	Equals: Net earnings by place of residence	Plus: Dividends, interest, and rent	Plus: Personal current transfer receipts	Per capita personal income (dollars)	Population (persons)	Total employment
		Nonfarm	Farm	Total								
1970	3,307,720	2,825,531	18,008	2,843,539	218,154	-99,418	2,525,967	483,234	298,519	4,412	749,695	338,712
1971	3,656,765	3,127,021	17,331	3,144,352	248,053	-111,851	2,784,448	521,383	350,934	4,803	761,289	347,216
1972	3,934,076	3,363,441	16,643	3,380,084	278,178	-113,445	2,988,461	559,105	386,510	5,093	772,468	350,334
1973	4,225,636	3,617,741	19,914	3,637,655	345,098	-119,406	3,173,151	610,816	441,669	5,456	774,486	358,789
1974	4,580,685	3,869,447	18,043	3,887,490	380,223	-136,415	3,370,852	691,145	518,688	5,928	772,691	359,694
1975	4,955,323	4,036,424	16,565	4,052,989	390,931	-148,120	3,513,938	755,920	685,465	6,399	774,345	354,340
1976	5,286,544	4,329,123	19,204	4,348,327	432,721	-181,502	3,734,104	794,973	757,467	6,840	772,927	357,485
1977	5,715,695	4,678,470	14,406	4,692,876	466,785	-211,383	4,014,708	879,529	821,458	7,379	774,635	366,349
1978	6,255,029	5,200,315	17,638	5,217,953	532,454	-247,142	4,438,357	949,275	867,397	8,054	776,648	378,544
1979	6,882,524	5,706,765	22,512	5,729,277	604,006	-274,459	4,850,812	1,080,993	950,719	8,867	776,196	385,189
1980	7,678,489	6,169,544	22,965	6,192,509	639,168	-303,001	5,250,340	1,308,284	1,119,865	9,949	771,823	385,427
1981	8,495,902	6,673,621	22,763	6,696,384	733,697	-311,716	5,650,971	1,589,646	1,255,285	10,998	772,505	383,685
1982	9,277,948	7,152,875	22,347	7,175,222	787,805	-324,340	6,063,077	1,839,311	1,375,560	11,992	773,678	384,637
1983	9,999,023	7,678,870	17,273	7,696,143	848,981	-330,175	6,516,987	2,002,853	1,479,183	12,858	777,649	387,575
1984	11,084,878	8,581,836	20,518	8,602,354	966,547	-348,308	7,287,499	2,279,925	1,517,454	14,215	779,804	404,423
1985	11,906,898	9,325,863	21,973	9,347,836	1,069,592	-366,787	7,911,457	2,387,557	1,607,884	15,192	783,736	419,617
1986	12,807,215	10,119,072	26,337	10,145,409	1,174,343	-373,894	8,597,172	2,534,624	1,675,419	16,237	788,761	435,382
1987	13,604,498	10,863,847	26,652	10,890,499	1,244,257	-379,186	9,267,056	2,637,951	1,699,491	17,189	791,466	442,103
1988	14,782,550	11,913,261	23,341	11,936,602	1,399,089	-391,666	10,145,847	2,835,780	1,800,923	18,522	798,121	457,684
1989	16,337,607	12,883,400	28,838	12,912,238	1,481,660	-421,974	11,008,604	3,387,161	1,941,842	20,322	803,919	468,296
1990	17,241,791	13,673,171	27,860	13,701,031	1,509,970	-437,977	11,753,084	3,390,790	2,097,917	21,251	811,352	477,904
1991	17,805,666	14,030,282	22,539	14,052,821	1,595,895	-440,537	12,016,389	3,446,308	2,342,969	21,760	818,272	474,065
1992	18,891,700	14,895,803	27,212	14,923,015	1,662,869	-478,041	12,782,105	3,450,164	2,659,431	22,919	824,285	476,931
1993	19,474,500	15,422,709	27,362	15,450,071	1,725,842	-517,828	13,206,401	3,464,371	2,803,728	23,525	827,812	483,377
1994	20,119,173	15,938,322	22,765	15,961,087	1,809,582	-530,709	13,620,796	3,588,754	2,909,623	24,216	830,817	491,282
1995	20,806,094	16,156,323	19,459	16,175,782	1,830,758	-531,024	13,814,000	3,916,699	3,075,395	25,054	830,439	484,903
1996	21,433,358	16,636,456	27,042	16,663,498	1,844,696	-579,783	14,239,019	3,993,957	3,200,382	25,885	828,007	482,555
1997	22,568,298	17,625,140	6,249	17,631,389	1,923,585	-627,804	15,080,000	4,240,039	3,248,259	27,365	824,711	487,706
1998	23,542,540	18,389,089	21,264	18,410,353	2,011,786	-693,256	15,705,311	4,361,395	3,475,834	28,581	823,712	499,918
1999	24,581,935	19,536,010	25,354	19,561,364	2,096,244	-723,297	16,741,823	4,254,203	3,585,909	29,828	824,119	511,386
2000	26,203,373	21,145,132	28,820	21,173,952	2,268,780	-857,351	18,047,821	4,497,970	3,657,582	31,670	827,399	522,609
2001	27,540,297	22,379,856	33,873	22,413,729	2,411,316	-935,894	19,066,519	4,509,886	3,963,892	33,140	831,034	519,204
2002	27,476,327	22,783,110	25,170	22,808,280	2,495,119	-1,047,252	19,265,909	3,949,852	4,260,566	32,837	836,753	518,159
2003	28,643,058	23,740,094	30,529	23,770,623	2,603,383	-1,151,661	20,015,579	4,231,575	4,395,904	33,912	844,619	522,682
2004	30,262,913	24,731,630	34,877	24,766,507	2,693,274	-1,055,576	21,017,657	4,614,079	4,631,177	35,587	850,384	528,842
2005	31,702,524	25,402,157	31,529	25,433,686	2,779,352	-942,838	21,711,496	5,173,699	4,817,329	37,096	854,604	535,003
2006	33,490,244	26,605,403	24,810	26,630,213	2,872,782	-897,964	22,859,467	5,523,824	5,106,953	38,926	860,365	537,507
2007	35,044,110	27,339,218	31,661	27,370,879	2,944,678	-733,124	23,693,077	6,057,558	5,293,475	40,604	863,068	542,425
2008	36,970,575	28,588,084	32,951	28,621,035	3,103,497	-764,866	24,752,672	6,228,686	5,989,217	42,677	866,282	547,726
2009	37,422,203	29,281,170	22,795	29,303,965	3,131,929	-868,924	25,303,112	5,534,000	6,585,091	43,046	869,361	539,512
2010	38,557,339	29,758,026	42,859	29,800,885	3,207,057	-793,015	25,800,813	5,722,410	7,034,116	44,270	870,954	533,007
2011	40,181,415	30,431,286	58,063	30,489,349	2,960,032	-794,810	26,734,507	6,091,157	7,355,751	46,029	872,966	536,667
2012	41,895,724	31,413,988	60,252	31,474,240	3,034,253	-737,282	27,702,705	6,938,981	7,254,038	47,866	875,270	542,156
2013	42,524,052	32,629,198	80,619	32,709,817	3,570,584	-866,502	28,272,731	6,866,824	7,384,497	48,406	878,479	547,531
2014	43,902,194	33,699,437	79,239	33,778,676	3,707,311	-863,581	29,207,784	7,071,299	7,623,111	49,879	880,167	553,399

Personal Income and Employment by Metropolitan Statistical Area: Albuquerque, NM

(Thousands of dollars, except as noted.)

| Year | Personal income, total | Derivation of personal income | | | | | | | | | Per capita personal income (dollars) | Population (persons) | Total employment |
| | | Earnings by place of work | | | Less: Contributions for government social insurance | Plus: Adjustment for residence | Equals: Net earnings by place of residence | Plus: Dividends, interest, and rent | Plus: Personal current transfer receipts | | | |
		Nonfarm	Farm	Total								
1970	1,406,626	1,102,399	8,526	1,110,925	69,248	14,697	1,056,374	227,304	122,948	3,682	382,076	152,994
1971	1,588,949	1,242,177	7,925	1,250,102	81,837	17,012	1,185,277	261,247	142,425	3,997	397,496	164,049
1972	1,823,000	1,436,808	9,518	1,446,326	98,796	19,175	1,366,705	296,670	159,625	4,471	407,732	177,980
1973	2,030,765	1,602,129	10,994	1,613,123	126,791	22,301	1,508,633	331,979	190,153	4,761	426,583	187,854
1974	2,274,156	1,758,704	11,608	1,770,312	142,552	32,499	1,660,259	385,800	228,097	5,161	440,633	193,502
1975	2,565,764	1,944,208	10,450	1,954,658	156,325	48,544	1,846,877	433,490	285,397	5,693	450,712	198,943
1976	2,905,580	2,209,926	8,613	2,218,539	180,604	66,775	2,104,710	479,036	321,834	6,254	464,570	210,271
1977	3,254,862	2,494,460	10,504	2,504,964	206,193	86,451	2,385,222	533,300	336,340	6,762	481,349	221,559
1978	3,774,732	2,901,138	16,512	2,917,650	247,261	108,686	2,779,075	631,124	364,533	7,658	492,914	237,762
1979	4,297,600	3,297,520	22,012	3,319,532	295,139	130,917	3,155,310	719,974	422,316	8,450	508,581	247,977
1980	4,823,362	3,614,695	25,181	3,639,876	322,760	128,934	3,446,050	864,639	512,673	9,177	525,593	248,765
1981	5,375,251	3,965,722	23,779	3,989,501	378,663	119,794	3,730,632	1,055,877	588,742	10,058	534,415	250,776
1982	5,663,667	4,129,114	21,598	4,150,712	400,925	60,872	3,810,659	1,235,552	617,456	11,080	511,169	248,041
1983	6,198,830	4,599,572	16,765	4,616,337	454,754	32,536	4,194,119	1,340,676	664,035	11,867	522,356	259,621
1984	6,898,199	5,125,561	22,804	5,148,365	522,520	33,407	4,659,252	1,514,339	724,608	12,929	533,544	275,851
1985	7,566,216	5,625,836	19,816	5,645,652	585,624	26,952	5,086,980	1,698,061	781,175	13,893	544,603	290,100
1986	8,075,752	5,993,333	17,588	6,010,921	631,203	27,859	5,407,577	1,827,681	840,494	14,450	558,859	300,497
1987	8,578,676	6,392,012	16,156	6,408,168	667,865	32,405	5,772,708	1,904,518	901,450	14,937	574,324	314,235
1988	9,112,007	6,837,429	22,915	6,860,344	739,907	32,414	6,152,851	1,986,968	972,188	15,603	583,976	330,259
1989	9,677,127	7,229,669	32,012	7,261,681	790,737	40,843	6,511,787	2,076,397	1,088,943	16,290	594,036	336,572
1990	10,381,138	7,742,313	31,253	7,773,566	899,476	49,603	6,923,693	2,263,069	1,194,376	17,228	602,588	341,067
1991	11,109,511	8,300,071	33,167	8,333,238	973,862	47,213	7,406,589	2,356,316	1,346,606	18,025	616,345	348,198
1992	11,933,969	8,987,553	26,268	9,013,821	1,045,200	42,572	8,011,193	2,434,972	1,487,804	18,852	633,032	355,488
1993	12,885,707	9,789,624	29,723	9,819,347	1,138,606	30,966	8,711,707	2,561,707	1,612,293	19,825	649,987	370,109
1994	14,018,931	10,709,124	23,835	10,732,959	1,270,721	30,909	9,493,147	2,826,450	1,699,334	20,932	669,734	389,822
1995	15,100,452	11,509,063	18,021	11,527,084	1,369,032	24,115	10,182,167	3,043,045	1,875,240	21,951	687,901	411,302
1996	15,919,211	12,002,087	24,087	12,026,174	1,425,874	9,919	10,610,219	3,268,335	2,040,657	22,737	700,161	418,022
1997	16,728,171	12,630,956	27,038	12,657,994	1,494,645	1,047	11,164,396	3,465,558	2,098,217	23,572	709,661	425,091
1998	17,572,197	13,361,187	27,423	13,388,610	1,568,733	4,571	11,824,448	3,604,318	2,143,431	24,494	717,406	430,755
1999	18,137,847	13,950,580	31,829	13,982,409	1,634,634	-5,524	12,342,251	3,506,830	2,288,766	25,098	722,692	433,312
2000	19,792,621	15,393,708	27,249	15,420,957	1,742,982	-15,421	13,662,554	3,681,740	2,448,327	27,031	732,220	445,334
2001	21,394,494	16,596,100	37,056	16,633,156	1,854,646	22,626	14,801,136	3,841,196	2,752,162	28,836	741,932	452,412
2002	21,954,832	17,157,784	22,215	17,179,999	1,916,848	-27,000	15,236,151	3,694,649	3,024,032	28,975	757,716	452,470
2003	22,562,165	17,643,160	35,448	17,678,608	2,000,165	-30,966	15,647,477	3,653,099	3,261,589	29,221	772,128	457,240
2004	23,753,358	18,464,573	53,134	18,517,707	2,091,210	4,313	16,430,810	3,823,218	3,499,330	30,097	789,237	470,201
2005	25,411,755	19,456,402	43,538	19,499,940	2,205,243	62,765	17,357,462	4,266,094	3,788,199	31,390	809,551	481,097
2006	27,403,545	20,759,117	26,020	20,785,137	2,397,737	168,958	18,556,358	4,677,686	4,169,501	32,967	831,252	498,812
2007	28,792,454	21,455,399	45,594	21,500,993	2,495,552	237,416	19,242,857	5,019,968	4,529,629	33,888	849,641	509,012
2008	30,228,228	22,063,205	25,805	22,089,010	2,588,215	242,413	19,743,208	5,218,210	5,266,810	35,011	863,383	509,621
2009	29,866,502	21,726,982	3,375	21,730,357	2,586,108	184,817	19,329,066	4,731,846	5,805,590	34,077	876,448	492,959
2010	30,410,627	21,750,620	11,661	21,762,281	2,612,549	186,025	19,335,757	4,731,912	6,342,958	34,183	889,649	482,565
2011	31,779,933	22,240,139	32,356	22,272,495	2,397,882	210,935	20,085,548	5,249,903	6,444,482	35,426	897,091	481,849
2012	32,520,090	22,658,089	31,515	22,689,604	2,438,355	187,132	20,438,381	5,624,607	6,457,102	36,093	901,016	481,043
2013	32,413,299	22,622,284	40,132	22,662,416	2,791,305	201,399	20,072,510	5,768,294	6,572,495	35,881	903,345	483,599
2014	33,781,875	23,331,324	63,139	23,394,463	2,885,947	132,992	20,641,508	5,979,553	7,160,814	37,345	904,587	487,905

Personal Income and Employment by Metropolitan Statistical Area: Alexandria, LA

(Thousands of dollars, except as noted.)

| Year | Personal income, total | Derivation of personal income | | | | | | | | Per capita personal income (dollars) | Population (persons) | Total employment |
| | | Earnings by place of work | | | Less: Contributions for government social insurance | Plus: Adjustment for residence | Equals: Net earnings by place of residence | Plus: Dividends, interest, and rent | Plus: Personal current transfer receipts | | | |
		Nonfarm	Farm	Total								
1970	395,471	294,488	7,270	301,758	17,442	2,352	286,668	58,846	49,957	2,989	132,287	50,427
1971	449,222	333,163	9,715	342,878	20,344	2,792	325,326	68,130	55,766	3,285	136,756	52,411
1972	490,112	364,519	10,548	375,067	22,986	2,888	354,969	74,195	60,948	3,566	137,425	52,809
1973	544,666	401,709	13,353	415,062	28,429	5,207	391,840	82,820	70,006	3,891	139,971	55,643
1974	590,985	431,429	9,874	441,303	31,787	4,380	413,896	93,945	83,144	4,216	140,176	55,277
1975	660,141	470,702	7,520	478,222	34,510	5,244	448,956	104,445	106,740	4,677	141,141	55,321
1976	742,238	528,245	15,920	544,165	39,761	7,171	511,575	113,209	117,454	5,162	143,786	57,332
1977	812,103	581,309	10,656	591,965	43,249	10,159	558,875	127,108	126,120	5,552	146,270	58,249
1978	922,484	656,325	14,608	670,933	49,095	15,222	637,060	148,389	137,035	6,249	147,614	60,432
1979	1,022,110	715,733	16,103	731,836	55,037	20,817	697,616	167,125	157,369	6,820	149,880	60,097
1980	1,165,648	811,747	3,030	814,777	62,753	24,184	776,208	203,692	185,748	7,659	152,197	61,010
1981	1,296,880	889,185	3,317	892,502	73,153	30,413	849,762	244,732	202,386	8,489	152,773	61,163
1982	1,392,234	926,881	2,289	929,170	76,196	25,662	878,636	276,082	237,516	9,107	152,877	61,401
1983	1,500,831	992,447	16,209	1,008,656	82,131	23,018	949,543	296,075	255,213	9,745	154,017	62,122
1984	1,592,293	1,060,452	8,389	1,068,841	90,312	19,170	997,699	321,342	273,252	10,305	154,515	63,636
1985	1,688,529	1,103,672	9,225	1,112,897	95,519	16,075	1,033,453	354,452	300,624	10,965	153,989	63,606
1986	1,751,921	1,145,056	8,769	1,153,825	99,624	7,976	1,062,177	367,087	322,657	11,351	154,335	63,566
1987	1,806,550	1,190,669	14,161	1,204,830	102,962	3,155	1,105,023	368,816	332,711	11,793	153,188	64,188
1988	1,906,923	1,258,296	22,823	1,281,119	113,969	1,240	1,168,390	388,520	350,013	12,597	151,377	64,413
1989	2,056,968	1,350,853	14,966	1,365,819	126,114	-8,053	1,231,652	439,092	386,224	13,697	150,180	65,261
1990	2,185,106	1,444,152	14,302	1,458,454	137,338	-8,739	1,312,377	440,937	431,792	14,667	148,982	65,706
1991	2,261,118	1,496,335	6,633	1,502,968	147,454	-7,321	1,348,193	431,635	481,290	15,171	149,046	65,863
1992	2,350,888	1,531,555	20,480	1,552,035	149,629	-3,466	1,398,940	418,872	533,076	15,925	147,621	64,337
1993	2,485,024	1,585,387	20,678	1,606,065	156,108	-5,706	1,444,251	427,047	613,726	17,472	142,225	65,441
1994	2,666,669	1,657,925	24,939	1,682,864	167,106	-6,229	1,509,529	457,639	699,501	18,637	143,086	66,500
1995	2,763,171	1,737,048	22,071	1,759,119	176,030	-5,580	1,577,509	497,870	687,792	19,167	144,162	69,293
1996	2,839,675	1,800,094	26,878	1,826,972	184,216	-5,172	1,637,584	520,054	682,037	19,724	143,970	69,670
1997	2,944,641	1,843,454	19,408	1,862,862	190,137	-3,260	1,669,465	564,658	710,518	20,451	143,986	70,362
1998	3,110,334	1,975,925	13,806	1,989,731	206,131	-7,692	1,775,908	607,568	726,858	21,550	144,330	72,299
1999	3,213,945	2,101,342	22,131	2,123,473	216,471	-12,771	1,894,231	594,391	725,323	22,195	144,803	74,471
2000	3,345,085	2,180,740	24,056	2,204,796	222,371	-12,499	1,969,926	634,314	740,845	23,041	145,179	74,969
2001	3,674,725	2,359,282	21,860	2,381,142	234,837	-11,667	2,134,638	639,731	900,356	25,325	145,102	74,011
2002	3,800,848	2,489,533	16,394	2,505,927	247,048	-18,170	2,240,709	629,318	930,821	26,138	145,416	74,597
2003	3,872,490	2,585,434	28,923	2,614,357	254,131	-26,131	2,334,095	633,737	904,658	26,521	146,017	74,874
2004	4,175,417	2,761,227	21,538	2,782,765	269,881	-34,481	2,478,403	658,257	1,038,757	28,409	146,973	76,357
2005	4,521,684	2,960,486	21,693	2,982,179	286,096	-47,059	2,649,024	729,499	1,143,161	30,566	147,930	78,117
2006	4,821,434	3,262,908	28,401	3,291,309	315,353	-68,201	2,907,755	740,533	1,173,146	31,900	151,142	82,276
2007	5,086,389	3,451,924	33,050	3,484,974	334,195	-80,564	3,070,215	789,155	1,227,019	33,572	151,506	84,217
2008	5,531,096	3,696,304	14,553	3,710,857	352,567	-87,595	3,270,695	920,987	1,339,414	36,283	152,442	84,131
2009	5,494,776	3,679,159	28,335	3,707,494	355,640	-83,743	3,268,111	825,491	1,401,174	35,875	153,164	82,174
2010	5,499,203	3,653,172	27,129	3,680,301	351,369	-62,559	3,266,373	780,248	1,452,582	35,680	154,127	80,383
2011	5,596,948	3,536,446	27,260	3,563,706	313,676	-47,755	3,202,275	919,250	1,475,423	36,245	154,419	80,877
2012	5,863,989	3,621,812	37,672	3,659,484	319,990	-33,053	3,306,441	1,027,533	1,530,015	37,958	154,487	80,031
2013	5,880,978	3,643,786	55,767	3,699,553	368,642	-32,593	3,298,318	990,368	1,592,292	37,966	154,903	79,733
2014	5,992,829	3,776,106	38,829	3,814,935	378,530	-28,257	3,408,148	1,027,272	1,557,409	38,695	154,872	80,562

Personal Income and Employment by Metropolitan Statistical Area: Allentown-Bethlehem-Easton, PA-NJ

(Thousands of dollars, except as noted.)

| Year | Personal income, total | Derivation of personal income | | | | | | | | | Per capita personal income (dollars) | Population (persons) | Total employment |
| | | Earnings by place of work | | | Less: Contributions for government social insurance | Plus: Adjustment for residence | Equals: Net earnings by place of residence | Plus: Dividends, interest, and rent | Plus: Personal current transfer receipts | | | |
		Nonfarm	Farm	Total								
1970	2,469,997	2,049,501	15,931	2,065,432	156,110	22,631	1,931,953	321,333	216,711	4,147	595,577	272,973
1971	2,632,989	2,154,629	12,596	2,167,225	170,707	31,958	2,028,476	350,170	254,343	4,375	601,892	271,090
1972	2,920,001	2,397,403	13,758	2,411,161	199,430	39,470	2,251,201	381,495	287,305	4,825	605,156	277,879
1973	3,288,541	2,717,273	19,656	2,736,929	260,552	49,861	2,526,238	437,294	325,009	5,383	610,947	292,047
1974	3,691,259	3,022,082	21,975	3,044,057	300,808	56,984	2,800,233	506,746	384,280	5,976	617,690	297,119
1975	4,057,618	3,211,197	19,496	3,230,693	312,336	68,050	2,986,407	562,282	508,929	6,522	622,114	290,754
1976	4,413,875	3,456,397	21,927	3,478,324	339,856	92,671	3,231,139	601,613	581,123	7,064	624,814	291,781
1977	4,879,796	3,829,468	21,206	3,850,674	371,459	121,171	3,600,386	672,142	607,268	7,775	627,598	296,393
1978	5,426,741	4,277,956	23,713	4,301,669	426,553	152,880	4,027,996	743,291	655,454	8,618	629,719	304,849
1979	6,055,873	4,763,943	31,467	4,795,410	490,484	184,890	4,489,816	836,888	729,169	9,566	633,073	310,781
1980	6,683,475	5,069,451	16,665	5,086,116	527,829	229,932	4,788,219	1,042,200	853,056	10,502	636,389	310,670
1981	7,397,767	5,426,088	23,287	5,449,375	604,899	273,407	5,117,883	1,298,075	981,809	11,582	638,748	310,155
1982	7,926,180	5,535,807	20,473	5,556,280	627,105	326,296	5,255,471	1,533,773	1,136,936	12,369	640,790	302,259
1983	8,294,923	5,699,894	3,954	5,703,848	651,724	392,457	5,444,581	1,602,370	1,247,972	12,928	641,637	298,035
1984	9,099,035	6,314,477	26,639	6,341,116	750,966	454,569	6,044,719	1,806,134	1,248,182	14,110	644,843	309,576
1985	9,754,428	6,691,337	27,471	6,718,808	802,490	527,839	6,444,157	1,986,366	1,323,905	15,047	648,256	314,763
1986	10,282,309	6,961,411	22,123	6,983,534	830,501	615,178	6,768,211	2,096,007	1,418,091	15,713	654,365	317,329
1987	10,997,416	7,552,288	21,949	7,574,237	891,013	690,886	7,374,110	2,173,568	1,449,738	16,577	663,413	329,686
1988	11,925,177	8,217,957	26,781	8,244,738	989,951	801,207	8,055,994	2,324,814	1,544,369	17,673	674,767	339,830
1989	13,013,556	8,767,840	36,413	8,804,253	1,043,682	890,874	8,651,445	2,708,375	1,653,736	19,063	682,657	345,404
1990	13,702,405	9,192,940	33,673	9,226,613	1,089,776	984,942	9,121,779	2,746,883	1,833,743	19,893	688,801	349,846
1991	14,358,147	9,469,215	20,150	9,489,365	1,137,149	999,247	9,351,463	2,871,750	2,134,934	20,625	696,168	345,339
1992	15,211,454	10,191,364	35,527	10,226,891	1,212,597	1,078,202	10,092,496	2,828,531	2,290,427	21,640	702,948	345,658
1993	15,760,988	10,644,664	26,975	10,671,639	1,287,943	1,163,968	10,547,664	2,815,786	2,397,538	22,237	708,776	347,081
1994	16,328,206	11,068,580	21,304	11,089,884	1,361,992	1,208,612	10,936,504	2,927,392	2,464,310	22,868	714,019	351,274
1995	17,022,854	11,476,843	15,864	11,492,707	1,406,919	1,272,423	11,358,211	3,071,654	2,592,989	23,719	717,685	355,394
1996	17,954,716	11,925,534	33,545	11,959,079	1,421,949	1,397,609	11,934,739	3,251,516	2,768,461	24,866	722,063	357,386
1997	18,912,039	12,497,338	14,314	12,511,652	1,482,965	1,535,231	12,563,918	3,484,046	2,864,075	26,033	726,464	365,995
1998	19,835,305	13,080,957	16,154	13,097,111	1,540,224	1,715,639	13,272,526	3,650,948	2,911,831	27,143	730,779	369,513
1999	20,953,752	14,080,203	8,024	14,088,227	1,627,694	1,831,142	14,291,675	3,588,691	3,073,386	28,457	736,327	377,396
2000	22,604,339	14,917,644	27,820	14,945,464	1,703,970	2,176,183	15,417,677	3,912,145	3,274,517	30,472	741,817	388,135
2001	23,437,070	15,736,381	17,931	15,754,312	1,803,009	2,047,625	15,998,928	3,865,000	3,573,142	31,303	748,705	390,939
2002	24,353,471	16,265,427	11,011	16,276,438	1,862,485	2,241,107	16,655,060	3,859,421	3,838,990	32,187	756,628	390,329
2003	25,401,770	16,823,867	28,812	16,852,679	1,909,558	2,509,766	17,452,887	4,006,584	3,942,299	33,121	766,938	393,643
2004	26,461,903	17,678,907	38,511	17,717,418	2,002,825	2,739,043	18,453,636	3,903,186	4,105,081	34,044	777,277	400,601
2005	27,809,608	18,517,928	25,626	18,543,554	2,124,825	3,077,640	19,496,369	3,861,217	4,452,022	35,303	787,738	410,746
2006	29,787,989	19,586,167	21,641	19,607,808	2,246,411	3,407,882	20,769,279	4,297,332	4,721,378	37,301	798,586	420,007
2007	31,669,877	20,352,886	31,178	20,384,064	2,343,334	3,735,407	21,776,137	4,823,113	5,070,627	39,216	807,578	427,287
2008	33,207,398	20,658,743	27,497	20,686,240	2,397,861	4,062,980	22,351,359	5,108,464	5,747,575	40,793	814,050	428,159
2009	32,149,377	20,146,029	22,714	20,168,743	2,349,444	3,265,302	21,084,601	4,745,641	6,319,135	39,313	817,779	417,511
2010	33,216,373	20,677,321	26,862	20,704,183	2,421,624	3,533,745	21,816,304	4,586,628	6,813,441	40,405	822,083	417,804
2011	34,514,535	21,441,879	41,664	21,483,543	2,266,336	3,411,300	22,628,507	5,054,631	6,831,397	41,824	825,229	424,933
2012	35,347,038	22,163,372	52,025	22,215,397	2,327,705	3,154,365	23,042,057	5,429,944	6,875,037	42,736	827,109	430,825
2013	35,801,104	22,702,168	59,966	22,762,134	2,704,887	3,175,974	23,233,221	5,610,730	6,957,153	43,288	827,044	437,184
2014	37,502,532	23,662,229	53,409	23,715,638	2,814,025	3,574,616	24,476,229	5,833,427	7,192,876	45,193	829,835	443,157

Personal Income and Employment by Metropolitan Statistical Area: Altoona, PA

(Thousands of dollars, except as noted.)

Year	Personal income, total	Earnings by place of work			Less: Contributions for government social insurance	Plus: Adjustment for residence	Equals: Net earnings by place of residence	Plus: Dividends, interest, and rent	Plus: Personal current transfer receipts	Per capita personal income (dollars)	Population (persons)	Total employment
		Nonfarm	Farm	Total								
1970	470,010	400,464	5,984	406,448	34,429	-18,687	353,332	47,987	68,691	3,468	135,538	57,438
1971	498,833	421,185	4,239	425,424	37,056	-19,265	369,103	51,375	78,355	3,641	136,999	56,621
1972	535,230	451,934	4,049	455,983	41,151	-21,098	393,734	54,841	86,655	3,887	137,687	57,144
1973	588,697	501,445	4,690	506,135	50,902	-24,347	430,886	61,193	96,618	4,311	136,556	59,254
1974	646,029	543,897	3,915	547,812	57,822	-26,687	463,303	69,498	113,228	4,717	136,956	58,969
1975	711,663	577,379	4,079	581,458	59,813	-27,768	493,877	76,656	141,130	5,209	136,611	57,981
1976	793,477	655,239	5,067	660,306	69,525	-33,256	557,525	83,074	152,878	5,833	136,023	59,523
1977	875,283	735,062	4,591	739,653	79,292	-39,361	621,000	93,427	160,856	6,388	137,015	60,379
1978	963,998	811,731	5,878	817,609	87,981	-45,242	684,386	103,516	176,096	7,000	137,705	61,616
1979	1,064,562	892,689	7,240	899,929	99,294	-50,576	750,059	115,353	199,150	7,716	137,966	61,945
1980	1,138,361	912,544	4,455	916,999	100,441	-53,568	762,990	147,561	227,810	8,343	136,443	60,840
1981	1,228,618	947,834	5,475	953,309	111,386	-53,497	788,426	183,889	256,303	9,070	135,457	59,371
1982	1,280,479	926,356	5,733	932,089	110,192	-46,944	774,953	215,880	289,646	9,443	135,600	56,566
1983	1,328,797	935,304	4,292	939,596	109,361	-44,990	785,245	227,995	315,557	9,887	134,397	55,220
1984	1,410,303	1,007,063	9,577	1,016,640	123,588	-48,323	844,729	253,241	312,333	10,610	132,925	56,874
1985	1,510,645	1,091,698	10,326	1,102,024	137,081	-57,148	907,795	274,874	327,976	11,422	132,253	58,346
1986	1,597,768	1,165,938	10,854	1,176,792	148,703	-62,390	965,699	293,587	338,482	12,145	131,556	59,616
1987	1,659,701	1,228,495	12,261	1,240,756	154,524	-63,594	1,022,638	295,693	341,370	12,601	131,712	60,857
1988	1,744,263	1,286,433	11,739	1,298,172	166,767	-60,763	1,070,642	314,838	358,783	13,274	131,408	62,323
1989	1,890,040	1,373,947	13,450	1,387,397	174,680	-61,460	1,151,257	362,347	376,436	14,478	130,546	63,201
1990	1,999,489	1,458,453	10,361	1,468,814	183,813	-65,519	1,219,482	363,690	416,317	15,311	130,593	64,824
1991	2,092,659	1,500,192	8,733	1,508,925	190,789	-68,356	1,249,780	368,759	474,120	15,955	131,160	63,975
1992	2,237,057	1,642,352	12,423	1,654,775	207,365	-80,667	1,366,743	372,595	497,719	17,042	131,270	65,472
1993	2,349,522	1,754,293	8,334	1,762,627	223,618	-91,595	1,447,414	382,612	519,496	17,845	131,661	67,208
1994	2,453,331	1,848,543	10,107	1,858,650	238,533	-99,074	1,521,043	400,004	532,284	18,568	132,124	68,011
1995	2,547,259	1,904,646	10,105	1,914,751	242,910	-103,203	1,568,638	427,371	551,250	19,326	131,802	69,263
1996	2,687,964	2,008,084	12,725	2,020,809	246,880	-112,119	1,661,810	442,496	583,658	20,506	131,080	70,018
1997	2,831,238	2,128,599	12,656	2,141,255	257,658	-118,619	1,764,978	468,038	598,222	21,624	130,931	70,970
1998	2,974,339	2,243,976	23,558	2,267,534	268,242	-132,064	1,867,228	487,309	619,802	22,790	130,509	71,011
1999	3,087,420	2,366,471	23,528	2,389,999	281,010	-144,838	1,964,151	479,437	643,832	23,794	129,757	72,342
2000	3,218,311	2,439,645	19,256	2,458,901	284,718	-150,997	2,023,186	513,300	681,825	24,952	128,981	72,234
2001	3,232,509	2,427,092	22,366	2,449,458	291,098	-154,013	2,004,347	497,093	731,069	25,161	128,471	71,975
2002	3,300,453	2,461,914	14,096	2,476,010	294,114	-158,823	2,023,073	501,698	775,682	25,859	127,631	72,065
2003	3,413,689	2,550,878	19,953	2,570,831	300,544	-165,860	2,104,427	507,891	801,371	26,805	127,353	72,574
2004	3,561,208	2,679,809	35,478	2,715,287	314,777	-172,453	2,228,057	492,155	840,996	27,998	127,194	73,558
2005	3,696,521	2,773,996	32,592	2,806,588	334,736	-176,895	2,294,957	507,064	894,500	29,168	126,730	74,402
2006	3,840,924	2,853,760	21,007	2,874,767	345,176	-178,260	2,351,331	549,847	939,746	30,243	127,002	74,624
2007	4,051,155	2,959,624	31,377	2,991,001	360,467	-182,894	2,447,640	606,620	996,895	31,887	127,048	75,269
2008	4,193,001	2,984,108	23,644	3,007,752	367,195	-182,877	2,457,680	635,568	1,099,753	32,987	127,112	74,397
2009	4,231,293	2,990,673	10,026	3,000,699	369,286	-187,396	2,444,017	609,983	1,177,293	33,275	127,161	73,229
2010	4,329,994	3,052,965	24,706	3,077,671	377,889	-184,684	2,515,098	597,922	1,216,974	34,086	127,030	72,530
2011	4,559,035	3,163,872	36,081	3,199,953	354,960	-196,184	2,648,809	666,424	1,243,802	35,849	127,175	73,251
2012	4,694,331	3,200,545	29,302	3,229,847	356,299	-199,399	2,674,149	757,965	1,262,217	36,964	126,999	73,310
2013	4,669,334	3,257,288	36,946	3,294,234	408,368	-207,166	2,678,700	715,034	1,275,600	36,947	126,379	73,723
2014	4,828,627	3,347,982	48,017	3,395,999	420,902	-210,771	2,764,326	743,668	1,320,633	38,336	125,955	73,905

Personal Income and Employment by Metropolitan Statistical Area: Amarillo, TX

(Thousands of dollars, except as noted.)

| Year | Personal income, total | Derivation of personal income | | | | | | | | Per capita personal income (dollars) | Population (persons) | Total employment |
| | | Earnings by place of work | | | Less: Contributions for government social insurance | Plus: Adjustment for residence | Equals: Net earnings by place of residence | Plus: Dividends, interest, and rent | Plus: Personal current transfer receipts | | | |
		Nonfarm	Farm	Total								
1970	600,852	462,971	34,855	497,826	30,161	-4,320	463,345	94,801	42,706	3,870	155,258	73,776
1971	654,638	503,924	35,705	539,629	33,600	-3,946	502,083	103,519	49,036	4,139	158,182	74,731
1972	699,449	546,380	26,606	572,986	38,300	-3,563	531,123	112,973	55,353	4,356	160,557	76,674
1973	816,333	611,461	61,278	672,739	49,703	-584	622,452	127,940	65,941	5,050	161,637	80,252
1974	887,983	719,079	5,605	724,684	60,173	-3,093	661,418	151,324	75,241	5,435	163,395	85,601
1975	1,094,368	848,905	57,335	906,240	69,359	-1,417	835,464	167,623	91,281	6,596	165,916	89,728
1976	1,197,594	971,145	30,894	1,002,039	80,048	-4,737	917,254	181,849	98,491	7,071	169,368	92,626
1977	1,321,461	1,073,903	33,243	1,107,146	89,765	-6,178	1,011,203	203,759	106,499	7,637	173,027	95,339
1978	1,498,210	1,222,840	28,581	1,251,421	104,114	-2,439	1,144,868	234,729	118,613	8,529	175,670	98,271
1979	1,687,039	1,368,375	38,566	1,406,941	122,572	-1,359	1,283,010	267,943	136,086	9,314	181,120	101,304
1980	1,849,859	1,503,790	-2,565	1,501,225	135,124	-823	1,365,278	327,343	157,238	9,970	185,546	102,188
1981	2,136,504	1,668,589	34,200	1,702,789	162,641	-730	1,539,418	416,602	180,484	11,328	188,598	104,700
1982	2,341,038	1,795,232	28,833	1,824,065	178,863	5,485	1,650,687	488,014	202,337	12,158	192,559	106,682
1983	2,602,783	1,943,921	113,847	2,057,768	192,822	-1,629	1,863,317	514,297	225,169	13,299	195,720	109,796
1984	2,768,320	2,083,932	74,321	2,158,253	213,771	2,355	1,946,837	577,141	244,342	13,917	198,910	113,248
1985	2,897,300	2,178,650	54,116	2,232,766	227,019	2,527	2,008,274	623,739	265,287	14,530	199,407	115,109
1986	2,933,834	2,193,876	62,145	2,256,021	226,562	-1,078	2,028,381	615,920	289,533	14,624	200,618	111,050
1987	2,986,821	2,249,330	39,110	2,288,440	227,335	-901	2,060,204	617,137	309,480	14,907	200,360	113,749
1988	3,030,185	2,217,598	49,748	2,267,346	234,504	27,487	2,060,329	635,420	334,436	15,070	201,069	112,617
1989	3,179,285	2,287,304	53,257	2,340,561	242,025	12,886	2,111,422	708,786	359,077	15,919	199,721	109,387
1990	3,320,340	2,390,968	81,987	2,472,955	246,418	17,138	2,243,675	685,844	390,821	16,728	198,488	110,406
1991	3,402,037	2,441,087	84,189	2,525,276	259,949	14,486	2,279,813	686,864	435,360	16,957	200,626	112,231
1992	3,660,759	2,654,086	90,477	2,744,563	277,660	7,604	2,474,507	680,111	506,141	18,000	203,371	113,046
1993	3,899,095	2,864,377	100,772	2,965,149	298,738	3,527	2,669,938	693,703	535,454	18,811	207,282	117,950
1994	4,130,680	3,083,734	58,101	3,141,835	325,511	-2,321	2,814,003	747,603	569,074	19,548	211,306	122,956
1995	4,380,387	3,295,771	49,618	3,345,389	346,914	-3,213	2,995,262	768,455	616,670	20,149	217,400	126,957
1996	4,578,798	3,428,693	49,137	3,477,830	355,720	-2,205	3,119,905	801,830	657,063	20,831	219,808	128,079
1997	4,881,707	3,652,402	63,534	3,715,936	374,066	-80	3,341,790	852,856	687,061	21,984	222,054	130,252
1998	5,122,823	3,825,706	67,525	3,893,231	389,941	2,538	3,505,828	921,810	695,185	22,916	223,545	141,019
1999	5,264,213	3,974,557	88,983	4,063,540	406,074	-2,987	3,654,479	893,630	716,104	23,229	226,621	141,751
2000	5,515,325	4,143,524	72,046	4,215,570	417,469	-4,523	3,793,578	968,126	753,621	24,062	229,215	144,582
2001	5,843,395	4,405,254	101,522	4,506,776	440,856	-8,625	4,057,295	962,472	823,628	25,367	230,351	136,415
2002	5,988,038	4,567,920	85,182	4,653,102	459,023	-3,631	4,190,448	914,427	883,163	25,774	232,326	137,388
2003	6,339,420	4,781,127	107,626	4,888,753	489,546	21,606	4,420,813	975,957	942,650	26,960	235,138	141,611
2004	6,632,136	5,071,288	101,469	5,172,757	516,392	33,541	4,689,906	948,067	994,163	27,917	237,566	145,301
2005	7,246,805	5,320,545	97,244	5,417,789	537,420	187,743	5,068,112	1,103,378	1,075,315	30,147	240,380	147,140
2006	7,698,479	5,793,606	77,034	5,870,640	570,893	142,607	5,442,354	1,114,207	1,141,918	31,726	242,656	150,557
2007	8,150,998	5,961,011	114,821	6,075,832	599,781	163,529	5,639,580	1,265,979	1,245,439	33,323	244,608	153,258
2008	8,856,851	6,486,216	82,941	6,569,157	636,557	100,372	6,032,972	1,428,973	1,394,906	35,937	246,458	156,413
2009	8,532,656	6,366,720	62,939	6,429,659	648,766	71,973	5,852,866	1,195,816	1,483,974	34,216	249,373	155,983
2010	9,089,117	6,588,842	155,673	6,744,515	665,809	98,740	6,177,446	1,275,181	1,636,490	35,969	252,696	153,856
2011	9,633,764	6,840,450	176,337	7,016,787	607,108	109,034	6,518,713	1,414,752	1,700,299	37,634	255,988	156,588
2012	10,074,878	7,197,470	133,285	7,330,755	629,777	132,736	6,833,714	1,559,061	1,682,103	39,087	257,755	158,453
2013	10,217,922	7,404,753	135,316	7,540,069	732,768	145,677	6,952,978	1,533,928	1,731,016	39,477	258,833	161,306
2014	10,787,744	7,714,663	197,681	7,912,344	758,649	234,055	7,387,750	1,589,856	1,810,138	41,510	259,885	163,567

Personal Income and Employment by Metropolitan Statistical Area: Ames, IA

(Thousands of dollars, except as noted.)

Year	Personal income, total	Earnings by place of work			Less: Contributions for government social insurance	Plus: Adjustment for residence	Equals: Net earnings by place of residence	Plus: Dividends, interest, and rent	Plus: Personal current transfer receipts	Per capita personal income (dollars)	Population (persons)	Total employment
		Nonfarm	Farm	Total								
1970	222,255	161,954	15,700	177,654	11,447	-157	166,050	41,007	15,198	3,534	62,885	28,559
1971	239,798	179,631	10,914	190,545	13,161	-476	176,908	45,712	17,178	3,767	63,651	29,140
1972	265,430	195,640	16,979	212,619	15,190	-1,681	195,748	50,993	18,689	4,108	64,612	30,331
1973	313,324	222,712	34,059	256,771	20,092	-3,216	233,463	58,027	21,834	4,721	66,375	32,103
1974	335,343	250,401	20,755	271,156	23,826	-4,324	243,006	66,954	25,383	4,956	67,669	33,140
1975	375,269	279,671	19,247	298,918	26,318	-5,852	266,748	77,167	31,354	5,518	68,014	33,849
1976	412,074	319,974	12,761	332,735	30,197	-8,251	294,287	83,136	34,651	5,966	69,071	35,772
1977	453,115	370,886	-3,110	367,776	34,371	-11,931	321,474	94,993	36,648	6,482	69,899	37,579
1978	536,483	420,781	24,041	444,822	40,785	-14,900	389,137	105,940	41,406	7,523	71,311	39,155
1979	585,831	469,182	13,252	482,434	47,392	-16,660	418,382	120,221	47,228	8,200	71,442	40,186
1980	646,169	501,896	15,415	517,311	50,488	-19,802	447,021	143,289	55,859	8,917	72,468	40,763
1981	711,885	528,769	20,826	549,595	56,844	-17,649	475,102	173,422	63,361	9,770	72,864	39,295
1982	758,619	551,082	14,919	566,001	59,804	-18,224	487,973	201,236	69,410	10,494	72,292	39,073
1983	807,132	584,358	11,120	595,478	62,991	-18,884	513,603	215,119	78,410	11,009	73,316	39,812
1984	888,087	647,345	20,908	668,253	71,024	-20,473	576,756	230,459	80,872	12,098	73,408	41,501
1985	944,637	692,315	22,178	714,493	77,553	-21,330	615,610	240,435	88,592	12,757	74,050	42,726
1986	979,759	716,146	28,768	744,914	82,313	-18,903	643,698	245,037	91,024	13,236	74,022	42,744
1987	1,025,773	758,335	30,112	788,447	87,119	-17,258	684,070	245,090	96,613	13,992	73,312	43,166
1988	1,062,590	814,862	13,091	827,953	98,163	-17,847	711,943	250,798	99,849	14,382	73,881	45,013
1989	1,170,230	887,494	31,276	918,770	105,469	-19,048	794,253	266,754	109,223	15,876	73,711	46,420
1990	1,239,033	939,082	22,564	961,646	113,310	-18,026	830,310	290,422	118,301	16,658	74,382	47,526
1991	1,295,353	982,595	19,915	1,002,510	117,896	-19,128	865,486	304,352	125,515	17,388	74,497	47,846
1992	1,367,086	1,041,514	32,604	1,074,118	123,239	-21,313	929,566	305,415	132,105	18,196	75,130	47,929
1993	1,410,672	1,106,840	6,480	1,113,320	129,804	-27,218	956,298	311,698	142,676	18,560	76,008	48,460
1994	1,523,371	1,169,160	33,163	1,202,323	138,002	-30,514	1,033,807	341,430	148,134	20,071	75,899	48,857
1995	1,606,895	1,218,146	30,095	1,248,241	143,316	-33,374	1,071,551	379,298	156,046	21,070	76,265	50,377
1996	1,724,650	1,291,940	42,044	1,333,984	146,289	-37,464	1,150,231	408,539	165,880	22,416	76,937	50,625
1997	1,835,422	1,384,380	40,002	1,424,382	161,806	-42,609	1,219,967	440,487	174,968	23,582	77,833	51,103
1998	1,931,544	1,494,583	26,161	1,520,744	172,231	-45,132	1,303,381	445,152	183,011	24,693	78,221	51,921
1999	2,010,357	1,599,433	20,839	1,620,272	183,405	-51,086	1,385,781	432,535	192,041	25,328	79,372	53,133
2000	2,106,613	1,670,803	26,554	1,697,357	189,624	-53,806	1,453,927	453,700	198,986	26,283	80,152	53,521
2001	2,212,429	1,775,061	22,095	1,797,156	195,613	-53,902	1,547,641	441,690	223,098	27,566	80,260	53,248
2002	2,275,799	1,830,767	30,067	1,860,834	202,130	-70,507	1,588,197	442,451	245,151	27,793	81,885	53,511
2003	2,377,306	1,942,786	28,905	1,971,691	214,251	-90,363	1,667,077	468,052	242,177	28,968	82,068	53,734
2004	2,557,188	2,075,979	54,179	2,130,158	225,186	-110,833	1,794,139	515,135	247,914	30,901	82,754	54,965
2005	2,643,554	2,171,958	47,838	2,219,796	233,992	-131,950	1,853,854	526,750	262,950	31,895	82,884	55,094
2006	2,905,617	2,383,467	38,988	2,422,455	250,519	-155,811	2,016,125	596,121	293,371	34,289	84,739	55,851
2007	3,122,452	2,547,370	57,705	2,605,075	267,146	-179,694	2,158,235	640,588	323,629	36,081	86,540	56,444
2008	3,785,142	3,227,119	45,776	3,272,895	307,295	-205,906	2,759,694	645,827	379,621	43,096	87,831	56,550
2009	3,386,750	2,891,837	40,889	2,932,726	291,031	-250,270	2,391,425	602,286	393,039	37,932	89,285	55,994
2010	3,416,694	2,946,814	27,705	2,974,519	297,017	-306,799	2,370,703	606,903	439,088	38,134	89,596	55,480
2011	3,615,070	2,955,211	57,027	3,012,238	268,924	-279,745	2,463,569	701,559	449,942	39,771	90,896	56,156
2012	3,558,553	2,816,114	57,221	2,873,335	265,460	-257,307	2,350,568	767,947	440,038	38,798	91,721	56,369
2013	3,417,536	2,823,644	37,131	2,860,775	306,048	-354,846	2,199,881	773,661	443,994	36,586	93,410	57,679
2014	3,573,861	3,019,335	37,139	3,056,474	327,536	-418,493	2,310,445	795,123	468,293	37,990	94,073	58,659

Personal Income and Employment by Area: Anchorage, AK

(Thousands of dollars, except as noted.)

| Year | Personal income, total | Derivation of personal income | | | | | | | | | Per capita personal income (dollars) | Population (persons) | Total employment |
| | | Earnings by place of work | | | Less: Contributions for government social insurance | Plus: Adjustment for residence | Equals: Net earnings by place of residence | Plus: Dividends, interest, and rent | Plus: Personal current transfer receipts | | | |
		Nonfarm	Farm	Total								
1970	905,376	783,746	1,403	785,149	49,509	14,636	750,276	130,313	24,787	6,745	134,230	70,329
1971	998,210	872,057	1,236	873,293	56,711	4,868	821,450	144,837	31,923	7,036	141,875	73,124
1972	1,102,437	967,792	1,442	969,234	65,356	-3,608	900,270	163,394	38,773	7,300	151,010	77,502
1973	1,215,079	1,057,155	1,218	1,058,373	78,992	-11,110	968,271	187,215	59,593	7,803	155,729	81,822
1974	1,497,046	1,342,105	1,222	1,343,327	108,558	-16,202	1,218,567	216,710	61,769	9,278	161,355	92,715
1975	1,999,371	1,803,824	2,448	1,806,272	156,793	21,873	1,671,352	254,765	73,254	11,410	175,236	106,942
1976	2,386,744	2,157,329	2,892	2,160,221	195,385	55,676	2,020,512	283,725	82,507	12,823	186,127	113,300
1977	2,656,495	2,423,444	3,230	2,426,674	218,903	20,636	2,228,407	322,235	105,853	14,005	189,680	117,650
1978	2,702,756	2,419,627	3,226	2,422,853	213,140	4,701	2,214,414	373,131	115,211	13,926	194,074	119,090
1979	2,806,305	2,510,199	3,340	2,513,539	227,737	13,434	2,299,236	393,552	113,517	14,389	195,031	119,439
1980	3,156,564	2,798,519	3,111	2,801,630	246,262	31,044	2,586,412	436,377	133,775	16,284	193,839	119,735
1981	3,687,461	3,238,597	1,537	3,240,134	312,783	85,989	3,013,340	510,088	164,033	18,453	199,831	123,606
1982	4,585,206	3,838,357	2,413	3,840,770	379,929	94,511	3,555,352	634,137	395,717	21,144	216,861	139,054
1983	5,071,128	4,343,653	2,824	4,346,477	440,008	135,887	4,042,356	748,990	279,782	21,369	237,309	150,798
1984	5,520,409	4,783,492	4,136	4,787,628	509,769	107,393	4,385,252	831,458	303,699	21,883	252,265	158,830
1985	5,878,689	5,034,286	5,421	5,039,707	527,266	58,545	4,570,986	913,464	394,239	22,257	264,128	163,306
1986	5,894,711	5,011,562	8,802	5,020,364	504,834	-7,997	4,507,533	935,979	451,199	21,826	270,074	158,789
1987	5,581,185	4,690,959	10,913	4,701,872	465,937	-45,955	4,189,980	912,582	478,623	21,044	265,211	157,016
1988	5,636,527	4,717,637	11,517	4,729,154	486,165	-57,779	4,185,210	931,192	520,125	21,379	263,645	156,200
1989	6,150,245	5,053,048	8,453	5,061,501	524,288	-1,467	4,535,746	1,039,150	575,349	23,300	263,958	159,968
1990	6,643,943	5,517,213	8,855	5,526,068	605,913	-51,429	4,868,726	1,126,000	649,217	24,813	267,762	166,968
1991	6,977,383	5,831,940	8,567	5,840,507	646,134	-70,136	5,124,237	1,153,707	699,439	25,152	277,407	172,470
1992	7,502,427	6,205,125	6,855	6,211,980	680,604	-71,071	5,460,305	1,262,677	779,445	25,843	290,307	173,979
1993	7,948,771	6,516,228	8,900	6,525,128	728,917	-82,636	5,713,575	1,371,158	864,038	26,807	296,514	177,780
1994	8,270,583	6,716,692	10,960	6,727,652	763,809	-74,304	5,889,539	1,497,252	883,792	27,551	300,188	181,242
1995	8,416,120	6,729,303	11,250	6,740,553	759,816	-64,851	5,915,886	1,561,050	939,184	27,879	301,878	182,105
1996	8,679,609	6,847,501	11,873	6,859,374	763,017	-57,036	6,039,321	1,627,718	1,012,570	28,683	302,606	183,521
1997	9,258,754	7,291,431	13,771	7,305,202	801,953	-72,892	6,430,357	1,726,325	1,102,072	30,210	306,480	187,454
1998	9,800,075	7,687,152	11,077	7,698,229	834,766	-52,602	6,810,861	1,784,645	1,204,569	31,321	312,895	194,099
1999	10,147,547	7,947,561	11,993	7,959,554	855,997	-77,864	7,025,693	1,788,593	1,333,261	31,994	317,172	194,367
2000	10,854,692	8,374,726	11,894	8,386,620	890,959	-64,553	7,431,108	1,902,537	1,521,047	33,856	320,618	198,093
2001	11,713,139	9,192,772	11,047	9,203,819	963,725	-47,753	8,192,341	1,919,226	1,601,572	35,921	326,081	201,679
2002	12,403,057	9,803,304	11,615	9,814,919	1,026,623	26,634	8,814,930	1,947,219	1,640,908	37,293	332,582	206,185
2003	13,028,314	10,388,454	8,881	10,397,335	1,069,541	122,296	9,450,090	1,972,271	1,605,953	38,576	337,730	209,894
2004	13,830,062	11,027,669	10,444	11,038,113	1,146,002	235,795	10,127,906	2,100,469	1,601,687	40,059	345,245	214,669
2005	14,722,834	11,624,583	9,913	11,634,496	1,221,262	358,648	10,771,882	2,265,878	1,685,074	41,957	350,903	219,256
2006	15,767,152	12,234,667	8,240	12,242,907	1,326,553	453,113	11,369,467	2,599,609	1,798,076	43,954	358,718	224,570
2007	16,973,026	12,771,466	7,466	12,778,932	1,377,904	575,529	11,976,557	2,937,845	2,058,624	47,122	360,194	228,795
2008	18,760,956	13,425,783	5,252	13,431,035	1,427,335	728,685	12,732,385	3,203,754	2,824,817	51,311	365,633	230,876
2009	18,605,585	13,925,097	7,054	13,932,151	1,455,128	771,780	13,248,803	2,943,428	2,413,354	49,673	374,562	231,301
2010	19,644,727	14,385,847	6,659	14,392,506	1,505,436	791,416	13,678,486	3,260,821	2,705,420	51,276	383,120	230,086
2011	20,852,213	15,057,156	4,904	15,062,060	1,414,707	893,812	14,541,165	3,483,381	2,827,667	53,723	388,140	231,978
2012	21,804,553	15,897,675	7,582	15,905,257	1,505,926	954,488	15,353,819	3,710,225	2,740,509	55,563	392,431	237,582
2013	21,587,776	15,981,829	7,675	15,989,504	1,743,790	975,620	15,221,334	3,603,024	2,763,418	54,306	397,521	239,399
2014	22,789,133	16,391,987	5,262	16,397,249	1,751,026	1,110,247	15,756,470	3,723,191	3,309,472	57,131	398,892	240,304

Personal Income and Employment by Area: Ann Arbor, MI

(Thousands of dollars, except as noted.)

Year	Personal income, total	Derivation of personal income								Per capita personal income (dollars)	Population (persons)	Total employment
		Earnings by place of work			Less: Contributions for government social insurance	Plus: Adjustment for residence	Equals: Net earnings by place of residence	Plus: Dividends, interest, and rent	Plus: Personal current transfer receipts			
		Nonfarm	Farm	Total								
1970	1,086,705	936,719	6,117	942,836	64,093	3,540	882,283	144,766	59,656	4,640	234,226	105,059
1971	1,201,269	1,064,269	5,067	1,069,336	74,950	-21,186	973,200	157,770	70,299	5,085	236,222	109,389
1972	1,337,254	1,191,254	9,904	1,201,158	89,223	-28,945	1,082,990	174,025	80,239	5,538	241,470	114,647
1973	1,501,401	1,378,129	12,572	1,390,701	120,110	-53,795	1,216,796	190,090	94,515	6,084	246,780	124,307
1974	1,618,877	1,437,461	6,577	1,444,038	129,203	-37,409	1,277,426	217,306	124,145	6,313	256,447	128,003
1975	1,782,199	1,525,263	12,638	1,537,901	133,228	-37,700	1,366,973	242,252	172,974	7,100	251,024	126,982
1976	2,010,121	1,842,265	7,804	1,850,069	164,904	-114,131	1,571,034	264,487	174,600	7,916	253,934	136,907
1977	2,267,105	2,159,532	9,577	2,169,109	192,960	-182,615	1,793,534	297,520	176,051	8,807	257,407	146,330
1978	2,581,672	2,553,800	4,964	2,558,764	236,617	-259,611	2,062,536	335,291	183,845	9,938	259,775	157,722
1979	2,866,633	2,861,649	5,136	2,866,785	272,261	-325,742	2,268,782	381,185	216,666	10,906	262,859	165,863
1980	3,149,399	2,999,275	3,921	3,003,196	277,809	-333,317	2,392,070	451,900	305,429	11,911	264,400	164,425
1981	3,389,193	3,210,428	7,135	3,217,563	322,787	-363,532	2,531,244	551,206	306,743	12,913	262,466	165,139
1982	3,577,528	3,271,330	3,102	3,274,432	334,386	-343,238	2,596,808	642,141	338,579	13,747	260,239	163,116
1983	3,851,694	3,571,119	-339	3,570,780	373,401	-397,824	2,799,555	694,584	357,555	14,802	260,212	167,452
1984	4,238,255	4,031,301	4,921	4,036,222	438,596	-497,927	3,099,699	785,564	352,992	16,255	260,737	174,759
1985	4,619,905	4,463,254	9,576	4,472,830	495,653	-567,204	3,409,973	848,144	361,788	17,595	262,568	181,371
1986	4,938,342	4,723,921	4,022	4,727,943	525,235	-543,845	3,658,863	910,451	369,028	18,559	266,087	187,119
1987	5,198,787	4,936,818	4,932	4,941,750	543,160	-546,245	3,852,345	965,886	380,556	19,275	269,717	195,094
1988	5,687,472	5,465,297	3,421	5,468,718	622,018	-627,241	4,219,459	1,070,886	397,127	20,807	273,346	202,667
1989	6,188,533	5,809,803	8,223	5,818,026	658,594	-659,911	4,499,521	1,253,248	435,764	22,155	279,329	207,606
1990	6,578,347	6,206,905	7,757	6,214,662	713,841	-697,552	4,803,269	1,297,460	477,618	23,164	283,987	213,654
1991	6,650,541	6,238,137	3,050	6,241,187	726,643	-688,524	4,826,020	1,294,599	529,922	23,162	287,126	210,795
1992	7,123,851	6,670,985	6,866	6,677,851	768,751	-706,761	5,202,339	1,359,918	561,594	24,538	290,323	213,642
1993	7,520,645	6,923,246	3,227	6,926,473	800,546	-663,592	5,462,335	1,454,752	603,558	25,789	291,617	217,534
1994	8,058,313	7,322,829	2,302	7,325,131	865,568	-667,671	5,791,892	1,647,799	618,622	27,440	293,671	220,460
1995	8,612,704	7,472,654	1,933	7,474,587	883,361	-439,905	6,151,321	1,763,467	697,916	28,909	297,926	221,177
1996	9,021,772	7,813,179	1,301	7,814,480	903,407	-457,843	6,453,230	1,813,037	755,505	29,762	303,133	224,214
1997	9,516,635	8,450,292	1,284	8,451,576	975,250	-660,360	6,815,966	1,953,244	747,425	30,858	308,398	228,650
1998	10,101,390	9,063,524	3,131	9,066,655	1,042,071	-732,174	7,292,410	2,066,723	742,257	32,314	312,601	229,824
1999	10,787,167	10,009,618	6,691	10,016,309	1,141,130	-1,010,386	7,864,793	2,090,184	832,190	33,893	318,270	238,458
2000	11,588,409	10,709,388	1,924	10,711,312	1,201,574	-1,029,282	8,480,456	2,237,776	870,177	35,726	324,372	244,027
2001	11,806,147	10,991,423	853	10,992,276	1,205,239	-1,144,656	8,642,381	2,200,321	963,445	35,912	328,749	241,693
2002	12,268,534	11,379,950	1,485	11,381,435	1,259,103	-1,100,412	9,021,920	2,223,062	1,023,552	36,869	332,763	241,116
2003	12,813,140	11,600,323	6,172	11,606,495	1,270,627	-1,025,103	9,310,765	2,403,222	1,099,153	38,117	336,154	238,943
2004	13,486,375	11,975,289	12,636	11,987,925	1,313,065	-937,309	9,737,551	2,608,333	1,140,491	39,733	339,422	240,132
2005	13,814,641	12,197,954	11,171	12,209,125	1,342,500	-837,148	10,029,477	2,560,571	1,224,593	40,366	342,234	242,613
2006	14,527,819	12,434,350	11,953	12,446,303	1,375,146	-721,316	10,349,841	2,861,780	1,316,198	42,230	344,018	242,024
2007	15,027,334	12,709,702	11,060	12,720,762	1,408,919	-608,001	10,703,842	2,874,779	1,448,713	43,518	345,310	241,522
2008	15,189,265	12,478,159	8,769	12,486,928	1,392,727	-466,769	10,627,432	2,844,337	1,717,496	44,466	341,595	238,149
2009	14,018,484	12,076,216	9,617	12,085,833	1,352,750	-1,070,967	9,662,116	2,480,051	1,876,317	40,808	343,520	233,941
2010	15,339,868	12,456,259	13,057	12,469,316	1,382,521	-355,764	10,731,031	2,551,918	2,056,919	44,396	345,525	237,424
2011	15,376,496	12,651,799	37,398	12,689,197	1,241,174	-1,005,043	10,442,980	2,846,998	2,086,518	44,040	349,150	241,249
2012	16,210,608	13,187,719	13,004	13,200,723	1,291,095	-954,483	10,955,145	3,190,704	2,064,759	46,144	351,301	242,832
2013	16,536,318	13,600,621	37,893	13,638,514	1,509,286	-1,119,555	11,009,673	3,376,554	2,150,091	46,658	354,418	246,718
2014	17,260,080	14,107,552	17,145	14,124,697	1,559,219	-1,023,084	11,542,394	3,459,999	2,257,687	48,365	356,874	249,396

Personal Income and Employment by Area: Anniston-Oxford, AL

(Thousands of dollars, except as noted.)

Year	Personal income, total	Earnings by place of work			Less: Contributions for government social insurance	Plus: Adjustment for residence	Equals: Net earnings by place of residence	Plus: Dividends, interest, and rent	Plus: Personal current transfer receipts	Per capita personal income (dollars)	Population (persons)	Total employment
		Nonfarm	Farm	Total								
1970	313,313	279,133	2,076	281,209	17,108	-27,567	236,534	45,711	31,068	3,038	103,125	46,650
1971	352,809	313,907	2,099	316,006	19,851	-31,208	264,947	51,342	36,520	3,405	103,622	47,036
1972	395,520	351,869	2,782	354,651	23,011	-33,524	298,116	57,082	40,322	3,809	103,846	48,347
1973	432,119	377,161	5,683	382,844	28,220	-33,277	321,347	63,485	47,287	4,114	105,027	49,305
1974	483,711	414,470	2,398	416,868	32,063	-35,286	349,519	76,136	58,056	4,567	105,917	50,224
1975	555,543	459,517	5,713	465,230	35,211	-39,127	390,892	88,695	75,956	5,192	107,005	50,663
1976	621,947	522,895	4,806	527,701	41,974	-41,722	444,005	97,368	80,574	5,515	112,768	53,001
1977	699,210	590,038	4,940	594,978	46,902	-45,406	502,670	111,472	85,068	6,199	112,801	55,396
1978	772,896	643,636	5,394	649,030	51,361	-44,969	552,700	128,452	91,744	6,636	116,474	56,359
1979	845,438	694,389	5,118	699,507	58,250	-43,189	598,068	141,923	105,447	7,242	116,742	56,639
1980	968,248	787,119	4,448	791,567	64,661	-52,880	674,026	169,001	125,221	8,068	120,016	57,453
1981	1,064,214	854,897	3,916	858,813	75,631	-58,350	724,832	197,857	141,525	8,809	120,814	55,980
1982	1,139,524	899,661	4,605	904,266	78,852	-66,546	758,868	224,483	156,173	9,332	122,109	55,531
1983	1,214,006	961,290	2,359	963,649	89,775	-70,139	803,735	242,193	168,078	10,013	121,249	56,216
1984	1,335,689	1,066,588	2,759	1,069,347	101,706	-79,033	888,608	270,170	176,911	10,972	121,739	58,552
1985	1,399,517	1,119,392	2,982	1,122,374	109,242	-87,000	926,132	285,868	187,517	11,796	118,644	58,483
1986	1,466,499	1,171,186	3,899	1,175,085	114,975	-90,568	969,542	302,533	194,424	12,460	117,700	59,039
1987	1,521,451	1,223,775	360	1,224,135	120,758	-93,589	1,009,788	313,960	197,703	12,884	118,092	59,851
1988	1,603,107	1,291,099	3,502	1,294,601	133,514	-97,212	1,063,875	332,248	206,984	13,671	117,260	61,561
1989	1,701,501	1,327,620	14,589	1,342,209	139,596	-103,019	1,099,594	365,923	235,984	14,620	116,381	61,654
1990	1,754,407	1,357,759	17,407	1,375,166	146,927	-103,970	1,124,269	372,335	257,803	15,109	116,118	61,400
1991	1,843,918	1,426,126	22,715	1,448,841	155,902	-112,376	1,180,563	375,584	287,771	16,000	115,247	60,775
1992	1,946,403	1,490,884	12,187	1,503,071	163,388	-108,769	1,230,914	391,224	324,265	16,808	115,804	61,360
1993	1,999,818	1,511,790	15,986	1,527,776	170,059	-106,008	1,251,709	404,291	343,818	17,192	116,324	61,935
1994	2,068,151	1,548,381	12,121	1,560,502	175,668	-98,623	1,286,211	421,210	360,730	17,804	116,161	60,986
1995	2,179,901	1,599,292	12,631	1,611,923	183,008	-99,160	1,329,755	458,776	391,370	18,665	116,790	61,993
1996	2,241,476	1,611,802	15,864	1,627,666	185,003	-92,556	1,350,107	474,857	416,512	19,210	116,684	62,273
1997	2,320,590	1,679,821	17,029	1,696,850	193,510	-90,814	1,412,526	474,448	433,616	19,791	117,254	63,984
1998	2,467,395	1,775,174	14,094	1,789,268	201,921	-98,379	1,488,968	527,650	450,777	21,057	117,179	64,347
1999	2,482,340	1,802,864	7,763	1,810,627	205,195	-93,966	1,511,466	497,258	473,616	21,602	114,910	63,119
2000	2,476,600	1,734,812	4,921	1,739,733	198,748	-68,514	1,472,471	498,426	505,703	22,295	111,081	60,916
2001	2,599,783	1,787,805	10,174	1,797,979	205,699	-71,165	1,521,115	526,324	552,344	23,365	111,266	59,781
2002	2,702,385	1,884,914	5,877	1,890,791	216,128	-91,434	1,583,229	524,049	595,107	24,209	111,625	60,323
2003	2,842,306	1,995,857	7,514	2,003,371	228,809	-114,338	1,660,224	549,010	633,072	25,219	112,705	61,021
2004	3,026,352	2,162,762	10,795	2,173,557	244,576	-141,202	1,787,779	584,385	654,188	26,673	113,462	63,185
2005	3,146,580	2,289,636	16,281	2,305,917	259,969	-167,459	1,878,489	569,978	698,113	27,487	114,477	63,836
2006	3,305,921	2,418,190	7,196	2,425,386	273,804	-193,642	1,957,940	602,785	745,196	28,650	115,388	64,603
2007	3,518,325	2,586,061	7,081	2,593,142	296,581	-227,971	2,068,590	657,859	791,876	30,275	116,211	66,549
2008	3,634,437	2,636,545	7,970	2,644,515	307,604	-254,234	2,082,677	668,758	883,002	30,991	117,274	65,021
2009	3,589,919	2,567,645	13,272	2,580,917	299,295	-267,656	2,013,966	619,632	956,321	30,330	118,363	61957
2010	3,667,623	2,572,870	13,529	2,586,399	305,520	-258,496	2,022,383	614,350	1,030,890	30,965	118,443	60,423
2011	3,745,463	2,600,639	5,379	2,606,018	277,619	-264,184	2,064,215	638,141	1,043,107	31,806	117,760	60,683
2012	3,753,096	2,518,186	13,560	2,531,746	270,516	-218,170	2,043,060	660,348	1,049,688	32,006	117,264	60,148
2013	3,679,457	2,388,959	30,656	2,419,615	291,780	-153,128	1,974,707	644,612	1,060,138	31,571	116,547	58,476
2014	3,796,611	2,443,536	28,170	2,471,706	293,471	-133,309	2,044,926	669,862	1,081,823	32,753	115,916	58,318

Personal Income and Employment by Area: Appleton, WI

(Thousands of dollars, except as noted.)

| Year | Personal income, total | Derivation of personal income | | | | | | | | | Per capita personal income (dollars) | Population (persons) | Total employment |
| | | Earnings by place of work | | | Less: Contributions for government social insurance | Plus: Adjustment for residence | Equals: Net earnings by place of residence | Plus: Dividends, interest, and rent | Plus: Personal current transfer receipts | | | |
		Nonfarm	Farm	Total								
1970	550,048	431,862	21,585	453,447	31,605	3,476	425,318	84,785	39,945	3,734	147,307	65,092
1971	580,975	450,700	24,127	474,827	34,056	2,644	443,415	91,291	46,269	3,917	148,324	64,945
1972	637,065	497,687	27,064	524,751	39,697	2,009	487,063	98,074	51,928	4,269	149,228	66,928
1973	721,386	574,083	31,917	606,000	53,011	-2,255	550,734	109,609	61,043	4,842	148,989	71,600
1974	799,110	643,260	27,607	670,867	61,582	-8,035	601,250	125,188	72,672	5,308	150,556	74,056
1975	875,920	676,927	32,698	709,625	63,425	-6,268	639,932	140,263	95,725	5,706	153,496	72,298
1976	975,300	778,356	30,329	808,685	74,164	-10,420	724,101	149,033	102,166	6,404	152,296	74,840
1977	1,089,946	866,495	48,117	914,612	82,671	-13,693	818,248	164,769	106,929	7,065	154,282	77,570
1978	1,208,342	976,226	42,134	1,018,360	95,932	-19,533	902,895	186,065	119,382	7,766	155,590	80,387
1979	1,395,391	1,147,185	59,161	1,206,346	117,583	-39,991	1,048,772	210,639	135,980	8,900	156,784	86,376
1980	1,538,890	1,233,616	57,885	1,291,501	126,106	-48,030	1,117,365	254,729	166,796	9,625	159,892	86,329
1981	1,678,475	1,325,969	40,137	1,366,106	144,820	-43,337	1,177,949	314,499	186,027	10,446	160,685	86,079
1982	1,773,337	1,378,373	30,510	1,408,883	152,278	-38,907	1,217,698	342,632	213,007	10,984	161,454	84,927
1983	1,904,233	1,472,321	19,134	1,491,455	162,367	-33,772	1,295,316	381,037	227,880	11,748	162,093	85,443
1984	2,127,498	1,646,622	36,915	1,683,537	185,940	-28,620	1,468,977	428,530	229,991	13,029	163,293	89,336
1985	2,280,296	1,768,852	39,811	1,808,663	201,469	-23,558	1,583,636	453,781	242,879	13,848	164,668	91,393
1986	2,446,782	1,899,914	50,700	1,950,614	215,930	-17,549	1,717,135	474,069	255,578	14,699	166,459	94,148
1987	2,605,237	2,064,191	57,328	2,121,519	230,837	-20,926	1,869,756	474,517	260,964	15,459	168,530	98,260
1988	2,772,261	2,247,729	33,449	2,281,178	259,450	-20,367	2,001,361	501,237	269,663	16,170	171,443	100,937
1989	3,022,931	2,394,473	64,510	2,458,983	274,876	-16,357	2,167,750	562,293	292,888	17,446	173,276	102,137
1990	3,202,067	2,534,383	51,740	2,586,123	303,944	10,612	2,292,791	594,721	314,555	18,263	175,333	105,276
1991	3,362,736	2,702,424	41,255	2,743,679	328,248	11,162	2,426,593	598,616	337,527	18,994	177,039	107,722
1992	3,694,328	2,959,522	62,295	3,021,817	354,871	18,221	2,685,167	645,338	363,823	20,577	179,533	109,626
1993	3,894,234	3,131,385	45,837	3,177,222	374,974	57,415	2,859,663	659,355	375,216	21,360	182,315	112,232
1994	4,182,001	3,364,150	66,530	3,430,680	407,320	62,549	3,085,909	706,693	389,399	22,507	185,813	116,611
1995	4,420,648	3,506,924	42,794	3,549,718	424,528	101,582	3,226,772	773,667	420,209	23,432	188,656	120,299
1996	4,702,628	3,729,414	61,312	3,790,726	448,716	87,380	3,429,390	830,998	442,240	24,546	191,586	124,832
1997	4,921,738	3,881,036	43,848	3,924,884	465,281	122,111	3,581,714	879,369	460,655	25,363	194,050	126,560
1998	5,205,666	3,987,310	64,466	4,051,776	475,305	188,917	3,765,388	965,263	475,015	26,455	196,776	125,248
1999	5,573,459	4,297,466	65,099	4,362,565	513,046	259,320	4,108,839	961,277	503,343	27,938	199,495	128,392
2000	6,026,140	4,615,967	44,151	4,660,118	545,377	303,912	4,418,653	1,061,524	545,963	29,741	202,618	132,013
2001	6,306,577	4,995,894	48,602	5,044,496	582,417	194,990	4,657,069	1,051,270	598,238	30,663	205,676	138,373
2002	6,483,503	5,122,259	43,966	5,166,225	591,212	211,353	4,786,366	1,032,541	664,596	31,059	208,747	139,405
2003	6,839,764	5,428,869	72,373	5,501,242	618,035	240,487	5,123,694	1,026,863	689,207	32,362	211,350	141,659
2004	7,270,698	5,804,775	73,391	5,878,166	661,205	297,737	5,514,698	1,041,162	714,838	34,040	213,592	145,426
2005	7,579,066	5,989,094	74,775	6,063,869	689,478	336,540	5,710,931	1,096,071	772,064	35,100	215,925	146,668
2006	8,029,195	6,199,037	54,231	6,253,268	720,232	404,874	5,937,910	1,252,549	838,736	36,757	218,441	148,164
2007	8,439,020	6,471,210	91,497	6,562,707	753,183	424,233	6,233,757	1,287,203	918,060	38,295	220,368	151,030
2008	8,682,240	6,504,760	77,515	6,582,275	765,422	437,441	6,254,294	1,369,257	1,058,689	39,038	222,402	150,748
2009	8,579,305	6,454,024	21,320	6,475,344	750,904	425,451	6,149,891	1,229,593	1,199,821	38,193	224,632	146,679
2010	8,635,883	6,377,020	50,064	6,427,084	763,865	457,258	6,120,477	1,218,012	1,297,394	38,237	225,850	145,194
2011	9,163,311	6,664,376	108,926	6,773,302	722,038	521,769	6,573,033	1,316,403	1,273,875	40,294	227,411	148,115
2012	9,547,374	6,982,799	115,226	7,098,025	749,345	508,618	6,857,298	1,415,451	1,274,625	41,768	228,581	149,400
2013	9,736,899	7,085,542	130,257	7,215,799	856,503	606,109	6,965,405	1,470,229	1,301,265	42,358	229,869	150,322
2014	10,139,890	7,415,244	150,760	7,566,004	893,563	581,887	7,254,328	1,529,535	1,356,027	43,801	231,497	153,303

Personal Income and Employment by Area: Asheville, NC

(Thousands of dollars, except as noted.)

Year	Personal income, total	Earnings by place of work			Less: Contributions for government social insurance	Plus: Adjustment for residence	Equals: Net earnings by place of residence	Plus: Dividends, interest, and rent	Plus: Personal current transfer receipts	Per capita personal income (dollars)	Population (persons)	Total employment
		Nonfarm	Farm	Total								
1970	782,992	605,388	19,802	625,190	41,768	1,166	584,588	119,226	79,178	3,179	246,263	107,391
1971	858,946	666,067	17,192	683,259	47,442	835	636,652	131,167	91,127	3,421	251,104	108,988
1972	970,373	758,815	21,447	780,262	56,878	2,281	725,665	143,929	100,779	3,831	253,306	115,239
1973	1,106,180	876,605	20,034	896,639	75,821	2,041	822,859	164,877	118,444	4,299	257,291	122,493
1974	1,213,302	935,930	18,913	954,843	84,149	4,570	875,264	192,163	145,875	4,649	260,984	121,406
1975	1,314,167	952,474	23,361	975,835	84,222	8,343	899,956	212,539	201,672	4,963	264,807	115,701
1976	1,467,292	1,079,834	26,738	1,106,572	96,895	12,370	1,022,047	231,635	213,610	5,495	266,999	120,996
1977	1,645,723	1,212,687	37,511	1,250,198	108,165	15,814	1,157,847	262,751	225,125	6,078	270,770	126,497
1978	1,849,648	1,378,928	38,342	1,417,270	126,742	19,127	1,309,655	296,929	243,064	6,710	275,655	131,939
1979	2,053,064	1,519,668	38,992	1,558,660	144,801	26,045	1,439,904	336,069	277,091	7,341	279,654	134,546
1980	2,336,636	1,671,947	33,427	1,705,374	160,220	34,973	1,580,127	427,196	329,313	8,238	283,635	135,100
1981	2,632,205	1,812,812	49,471	1,862,283	186,898	38,196	1,713,581	534,733	383,891	9,204	285,988	136,135
1982	2,807,343	1,882,827	46,631	1,929,458	198,322	40,239	1,771,375	610,594	425,374	9,711	289,085	134,442
1983	3,085,966	2,064,983	54,479	2,119,462	219,368	41,098	1,941,192	681,058	463,716	10,648	289,822	138,779
1984	3,436,444	2,320,613	50,544	2,371,157	251,548	42,594	2,162,203	779,329	494,912	11,708	293,506	145,445
1985	3,680,461	2,488,175	41,163	2,529,338	274,382	39,449	2,294,405	854,222	531,834	12,409	296,586	149,776
1986	3,921,539	2,657,448	27,646	2,685,094	299,078	35,597	2,421,613	928,588	571,338	13,113	299,050	153,313
1987	4,206,865	2,875,451	36,167	2,911,618	319,888	37,143	2,628,873	974,782	603,210	14,012	300,229	156,232
1988	4,586,264	3,143,686	51,225	3,194,911	360,713	35,919	2,870,117	1,073,081	643,066	15,149	302,741	163,112
1989	5,017,655	3,342,711	38,993	3,381,704	386,398	35,017	3,030,323	1,271,938	715,394	16,425	305,480	167,964
1990	5,346,064	3,541,442	71,916	3,613,358	417,891	35,603	3,231,070	1,325,162	789,832	17,273	309,502	171,956
1991	5,622,067	3,717,613	70,075	3,787,688	443,852	32,904	3,376,740	1,343,271	902,056	17,839	315,160	172,486
1992	6,068,759	4,036,460	94,323	4,130,783	475,354	30,096	3,685,525	1,390,391	992,843	18,892	321,240	176,331
1993	6,493,418	4,304,601	112,821	4,417,422	510,769	22,633	3,929,286	1,475,776	1,088,356	19,784	328,220	181,752
1994	6,830,927	4,541,991	119,581	4,661,572	545,983	18,944	4,134,533	1,570,926	1,125,468	20,398	334,878	186,248
1995	7,353,039	4,779,360	123,208	4,902,568	576,465	16,804	4,342,907	1,751,991	1,258,141	21,517	341,739	191,577
1996	7,768,717	5,028,759	99,626	5,128,385	600,150	15,619	4,543,854	1,868,734	1,356,129	22,329	347,921	196,267
1997	8,403,014	5,449,539	96,290	5,545,829	642,957	14,889	4,917,761	2,062,476	1,422,777	23,734	354,052	203,879
1998	9,003,972	5,858,511	109,395	5,967,906	682,643	17,751	5,303,014	2,231,981	1,468,977	25,017	359,909	208,138
1999	9,399,621	6,215,196	129,994	6,345,190	718,068	15,266	5,642,388	2,192,867	1,564,366	25,741	365,159	212,011
2000	9,954,184	6,543,723	117,977	6,661,700	748,269	13,333	5,926,764	2,350,439	1,676,981	26,859	370,615	215,661
2001	10,147,774	6,679,884	94,007	6,773,891	774,192	1,413	6,001,112	2,296,429	1,850,233	27,068	374,904	214,467
2002	10,269,439	6,808,996	57,836	6,866,832	785,837	-18,375	6,062,620	2,226,003	1,980,816	27,038	379,818	215,013
2003	10,490,016	7,046,977	66,629	7,113,606	830,215	-42,516	6,240,875	2,179,729	2,069,412	27,234	385,178	218,515
2004	11,359,668	7,462,076	75,409	7,537,485	871,463	-52,825	6,613,197	2,507,234	2,239,237	29,074	390,713	224,424
2005	12,006,322	7,807,931	116,187	7,924,118	929,495	-79,918	6,914,705	2,692,852	2,398,765	30,288	396,408	229,990
2006	12,954,513	8,389,361	113,218	8,502,579	996,853	-90,379	7,415,347	2,928,554	2,610,612	32,022	404,546	237,850
2007	13,772,926	8,763,607	54,857	8,818,464	1,065,881	-97,852	7,654,731	3,334,884	2,783,311	33,442	411,842	247,771
2008	14,238,706	8,940,140	69,398	9,009,538	1,089,572	-117,568	7,802,398	3,337,243	3,099,065	34,108	417,457	246,214
2009	14,106,317	8,833,721	69,663	8,903,384	1,064,148	-121,615	7,717,621	2,949,450	3,439,246	33,426	422,014	236,393
2010	14,170,343	8,864,313	64,215	8,928,528	1,047,450	-131,940	7,749,138	2,813,288	3,607,917	33,306	425,465	234,575
2011	14,670,831	8,864,318	72,251	8,936,569	971,888	-152,134	7,812,547	3,140,028	3,718,256	34,243	428,436	239,224
2012	15,672,221	9,500,569	56,466	9,557,035	1,011,174	-154,413	8,391,448	3,454,749	3,826,024	36,266	432,142	241,491
2013	15,416,977	9,375,526	70,153	9,445,679	1,161,419	-150,658	8,133,602	3,392,698	3,890,677	35,226	437,661	246,309
2014	16,131,125	9,882,279	81,276	9,963,555	1,224,482	-157,811	8,581,262	3,524,249	4,025,614	36,470	442,316	250,549

Personal Income and Employment by Area: Athens-Clarke County, GA

(Thousands of dollars, except as noted.)

Year	Personal income, total	Earnings by place of work			Less: Contributions for government social insurance	Plus: Adjustment for residence	Equals: Net earnings by place of residence	Plus: Dividends, interest, and rent	Plus: Personal current transfer receipts	Per capita personal income (dollars)	Population (persons)	Total employment
		Nonfarm	Farm	Total								
1970	285,820	245,041	4,596	249,637	14,503	-10,747	224,387	39,750	21,683	3,019	94,672	42,435
1971	320,376	275,556	3,976	279,532	16,774	-11,994	250,764	44,171	25,441	3,296	97,214	44,721
1972	361,801	312,091	4,906	316,997	20,077	-14,083	282,837	49,671	29,293	3,583	100,987	47,189
1973	412,297	351,748	11,328	363,076	25,915	-16,738	320,423	57,073	34,801	3,906	105,560	48,552
1974	467,099	402,056	6,262	408,318	30,536	-20,900	356,882	67,192	43,025	4,338	107,666	50,427
1975	516,657	420,497	13,538	434,035	31,436	-18,954	383,645	75,254	57,758	4,775	108,211	49,988
1976	573,149	477,809	12,846	490,655	36,710	-23,393	430,552	81,125	61,472	5,401	106,120	51,555
1977	634,918	535,531	14,142	549,673	41,017	-28,726	479,930	90,782	64,206	5,917	107,309	54,049
1978	711,897	607,171	16,686	623,857	47,935	-36,175	539,747	101,451	70,699	6,564	108,452	56,422
1979	781,496	662,268	18,183	680,451	54,760	-36,825	588,866	112,208	80,422	7,160	109,148	57,722
1980	860,981	717,886	2,511	720,397	59,414	-39,181	621,802	141,642	97,537	7,531	114,324	57,313
1981	984,343	794,729	12,091	806,820	70,904	-39,630	696,286	176,564	111,493	8,412	117,011	58,812
1982	1,065,511	826,838	22,803	849,641	75,119	-38,894	735,628	206,772	123,111	9,008	118,289	58,163
1983	1,192,794	931,623	22,242	953,865	85,981	-42,483	825,401	232,160	135,233	9,910	120,365	60,122
1984	1,308,634	1,006,038	37,211	1,043,249	95,629	-41,526	906,094	257,659	144,881	10,685	122,473	63,350
1985	1,417,750	1,097,117	30,358	1,127,475	107,113	-42,653	977,709	282,441	157,600	11,403	124,327	65,645
1986	1,557,792	1,202,537	44,593	1,247,130	118,968	-44,564	1,083,598	304,974	169,220	12,419	125,434	68,018
1987	1,658,972	1,302,018	28,113	1,330,131	127,801	-44,502	1,157,828	321,932	179,212	12,961	128,002	70,290
1988	1,821,322	1,428,346	43,576	1,471,922	146,014	-44,223	1,281,685	348,938	190,699	13,947	130,586	72,042
1989	2,027,774	1,542,796	61,980	1,604,776	158,331	-45,413	1,401,032	416,370	210,372	15,145	133,894	73,601
1990	2,174,562	1,662,455	57,138	1,719,593	170,741	-46,660	1,502,192	434,577	237,793	15,883	136,914	74,955
1991	2,255,740	1,702,997	59,358	1,762,355	177,350	-45,701	1,539,304	443,344	273,092	16,187	139,359	73,882
1992	2,383,980	1,797,668	59,742	1,857,410	186,659	-38,988	1,631,763	448,993	303,224	16,801	141,899	74,262
1993	2,542,827	1,911,266	61,475	1,972,741	198,814	-32,984	1,740,943	480,515	321,369	17,547	144,916	78,030
1994	2,713,820	2,043,250	66,849	2,110,099	213,691	-39,920	1,856,488	517,650	339,682	18,219	148,953	80,774
1995	2,934,030	2,197,516	58,360	2,255,876	229,113	-37,702	1,989,061	575,403	369,566	19,339	151,718	85,085
1996	3,152,108	2,354,926	66,352	2,421,278	242,470	-39,318	2,139,490	619,257	393,361	20,339	154,977	88,923
1997	3,308,439	2,477,632	68,759	2,546,391	250,368	-50,235	2,245,788	666,661	395,990	20,901	158,291	90,120
1998	3,547,704	2,676,097	82,974	2,759,071	267,867	-49,848	2,441,356	704,183	402,165	22,128	160,330	92,204
1999	3,708,949	2,834,967	82,915	2,917,882	281,938	-59,332	2,576,612	703,374	428,963	22,691	163,456	93,924
2000	3,896,709	2,946,960	74,920	3,021,880	291,783	-63,205	2,666,892	755,223	474,594	23,367	166,763	95,804
2001	4,071,003	3,077,801	102,078	3,179,879	309,945	-96,431	2,773,503	777,118	520,382	24,093	168,973	96,218
2002	4,120,093	3,205,332	62,553	3,267,885	323,441	-183,537	2,760,907	776,377	582,809	24,117	170,838	96,684
2003	4,328,392	3,396,515	66,022	3,462,537	339,815	-228,109	2,894,613	845,455	588,324	24,898	173,847	98,984
2004	4,540,747	3,553,629	97,350	3,650,979	365,454	-220,247	3,065,278	842,522	632,947	25,495	178,106	101,280
2005	4,852,387	3,762,662	102,887	3,865,549	380,898	-199,628	3,285,023	871,695	695,669	27,112	178,974	105,705
2006	5,130,651	4,007,560	48,119	4,055,679	408,581	-235,546	3,411,552	982,423	736,676	28,010	183,171	109,048
2007	5,384,661	4,130,345	72,768	4,203,113	409,442	-296,111	3,497,560	1,087,382	799,719	28,829	186,781	112,735
2008	5,657,097	4,329,772	108,530	4,438,302	453,585	-370,521	3,614,196	1,111,460	931,441	29,782	189,948	112,976
2009	5,553,205	4,274,000	86,665	4,360,665	443,573	-467,967	3,449,125	1,091,167	1,012,913	28,920	192,021	110,225
2010	5,599,681	4,313,437	64,260	4,377,697	451,545	-522,663	3,403,489	1,077,456	1,118,736	28,943	193,476	109,092
2011	5,939,561	4,419,077	46,635	4,465,712	407,007	-520,528	3,538,177	1,207,138	1,194,246	30,513	194,658	109,395
2012	6,142,390	4,577,138	110,914	4,688,052	419,818	-530,469	3,737,765	1,225,378	1,179,247	31,274	196,405	110,716
2013	6,320,102	4,731,555	156,182	4,887,737	488,712	-543,531	3,855,494	1,248,970	1,215,638	31,938	197,884	113,092
2014	6,649,831	4,898,302	176,712	5,075,014	507,427	-478,440	4,089,147	1,286,233	1,274,451	33,414	199,016	113,965

Personal Income and Employment by Area: Atlanta-Sandy Springs-Roswell, GA

(Thousands of dollars, except as noted.)

Year	Personal income, total	Derivation of personal income								Per capita personal income (dollars)	Population (persons)	Total employment
		Earnings by place of work			Less: Contributions for government social insurance	Plus: Adjustment for residence	Equals: Net earnings by place of residence	Plus: Dividends, interest, and rent	Plus: Personal current transfer receipts			
		Nonfarm	Farm	Total								
1970	7,677,326	6,711,043	32,676	6,743,719	424,490	-84,614	6,234,615	970,863	471,848	4,123	1,862,083	924,492
1971	8,516,621	7,401,365	28,231	7,429,596	485,358	-88,275	6,855,963	1,095,597	565,061	4,427	1,923,687	956,707
1972	9,734,560	8,516,620	36,008	8,552,628	587,731	-104,882	7,860,015	1,232,046	642,499	4,900	1,986,477	1,013,051
1973	11,009,723	9,671,552	67,946	9,739,498	767,896	-124,040	8,847,562	1,410,702	751,459	5,357	2,055,233	1,078,478
1974	12,122,898	10,497,366	33,695	10,531,061	862,290	-134,131	9,534,640	1,640,234	948,024	5,747	2,109,395	1,089,091
1975	13,062,683	10,961,081	63,265	11,024,346	880,136	-138,394	10,005,816	1,740,731	1,316,136	6,139	2,127,779	1,049,087
1976	14,438,366	12,292,144	71,420	12,363,564	1,009,289	-149,893	11,204,382	1,837,304	1,396,680	6,706	2,152,893	1,087,337
1977	16,236,027	14,045,369	63,099	14,108,468	1,148,484	-164,364	12,795,620	2,005,015	1,435,392	7,399	2,194,331	1,147,650
1978	18,421,192	16,042,254	68,900	16,111,154	1,351,575	-177,735	14,581,844	2,285,664	1,553,684	8,242	2,234,980	1,217,960
1979	20,765,762	18,097,605	72,610	18,170,215	1,586,598	-206,106	16,377,511	2,617,006	1,771,245	9,045	2,295,738	1,273,760
1980	23,639,438	20,300,327	27,771	20,328,098	1,788,440	-240,463	18,299,195	3,217,195	2,123,048	10,050	2,352,155	1,312,418
1981	26,656,415	22,596,152	57,878	22,654,030	2,148,708	-278,066	20,227,256	4,025,165	2,403,994	11,091	2,403,406	1,337,201
1982	28,903,101	24,250,504	95,879	24,346,383	2,366,061	-297,188	21,683,134	4,590,002	2,629,965	11,780	2,453,618	1,357,118
1983	32,262,935	27,115,829	69,657	27,185,486	2,681,241	-334,056	24,170,189	5,230,267	2,862,479	12,820	2,516,569	1,418,357
1984	37,097,595	31,388,704	106,421	31,495,125	3,192,267	-374,547	27,928,311	6,109,288	3,059,996	14,302	2,593,856	1,541,244
1985	41,594,614	35,478,675	84,875	35,563,550	3,691,992	-410,214	31,461,344	6,856,348	3,276,922	15,466	2,689,442	1,644,282
1986	45,984,283	39,486,500	101,677	39,588,177	4,155,215	-428,171	35,004,791	7,479,036	3,500,456	16,512	2,784,902	1,737,089
1987	50,184,319	43,438,499	57,437	43,495,936	4,528,976	-500,395	38,466,565	8,062,102	3,655,652	17,414	2,881,787	1,799,907
1988	55,164,436	47,567,382	100,323	47,667,705	5,075,496	-517,906	42,074,303	9,138,222	3,951,911	18,603	2,965,367	1,869,917
1989	59,308,006	50,148,185	153,761	50,301,946	5,379,936	-511,444	44,410,566	10,476,484	4,420,956	19,553	3,033,139	1,902,034
1990	63,749,209	53,700,072	144,832	53,844,904	5,790,521	-526,954	47,527,429	11,234,389	4,987,391	20,536	3,104,221	1,936,224
1991	66,603,494	55,852,879	160,299	56,013,178	6,085,762	-540,620	49,386,796	11,396,272	5,820,426	20,844	3,195,398	1,917,337
1992	72,659,210	61,372,497	172,661	61,545,158	6,580,567	-607,657	54,356,934	11,737,104	6,565,172	22,072	3,291,991	1,962,091
1993	78,029,709	65,933,364	167,381	66,100,745	7,087,003	-663,967	58,349,775	12,591,234	7,088,700	22,935	3,402,250	2,072,915
1994	84,507,724	70,966,483	192,293	71,158,776	7,724,395	-723,656	62,710,725	14,069,903	7,727,096	23,983	3,523,718	2,172,516
1995	92,467,790	77,309,915	156,150	77,466,065	8,385,326	-802,701	68,278,038	15,730,230	8,459,522	25,370	3,644,699	2,273,047
1996	101,250,706	84,770,241	175,481	84,945,722	9,078,337	-915,094	74,952,291	17,287,939	9,010,476	26,887	3,765,817	2,380,579
1997	109,165,390	91,660,030	178,862	91,838,892	9,784,319	-1,025,906	81,028,667	18,928,641	9,208,082	28,075	3,888,398	2,460,237
1998	122,029,210	103,693,368	213,854	103,907,222	10,811,113	-1,198,932	91,897,177	20,692,305	9,439,728	30,345	4,021,410	2,586,886
1999	131,681,949	113,997,689	203,703	114,201,392	11,841,838	-1,360,034	100,999,520	20,742,769	9,939,660	31,671	4,157,862	2,681,623
2000	145,114,296	125,292,884	164,512	125,457,396	12,838,019	-1,555,726	111,063,651	23,160,224	10,890,421	33,799	4,293,475	2,778,147
2001	152,625,575	131,557,761	228,703	131,786,464	13,355,149	-1,602,747	116,828,568	23,653,923	12,143,084	34,668	4,402,455	2,812,469
2002	155,891,624	133,601,902	135,178	133,737,080	13,489,463	-1,671,760	118,575,857	23,508,922	13,806,845	34,725	4,489,288	2,798,847
2003	160,404,018	136,356,939	146,690	136,503,629	13,787,830	-1,227,805	121,487,994	24,667,061	14,248,963	35,080	4,572,541	2,807,681
2004	168,901,108	143,712,006	229,613	143,941,619	14,965,526	-978,706	127,997,387	25,521,956	15,381,765	36,248	4,659,574	2,890,010
2005	181,205,056	151,548,879	232,611	151,781,490	15,598,438	-1,045,153	135,137,899	28,961,990	17,105,167	37,982	4,770,870	2,999,687
2006	195,769,087	161,380,203	111,182	161,491,385	16,551,507	-853,740	144,086,138	33,183,898	18,499,051	39,695	4,931,848	3,115,127
2007	207,457,773	168,351,050	162,436	168,513,486	17,167,721	-387,120	150,958,645	36,394,942	20,104,186	40,948	5,066,356	3,220,807
2008	210,916,883	169,062,969	207,769	169,270,738	17,711,659	-150,178	151,408,901	35,835,507	23,672,475	40,796	5,170,099	3,204,933
2009	201,850,448	160,609,341	157,991	160,767,332	17,099,292	322,774	143,990,814	31,582,489	26,277,145	38,515	5,240,828	3,087,492
2010	203,519,728	160,472,205	126,687	160,598,892	17,413,058	467,470	143,653,304	30,737,129	29,129,295	38,369	5,304,207	3,058,343
2011	219,302,662	167,530,497	71,431	167,601,928	16,002,138	399,240	151,999,030	36,667,978	30,635,654	40,802	5,374,825	3,142,592
2012	227,590,427	175,228,552	230,087	175,458,639	16,670,063	399,776	159,188,352	38,039,391	30,362,684	41,710	5,456,472	3,184,392
2013	231,100,784	181,300,780	303,406	181,604,186	19,742,878	411,367	162,272,675	37,280,773	31,547,336	41,825	5,525,432	3,268,416
2014	244,065,812	192,577,908	352,095	192,930,003	20,941,218	75,780	172,064,565	38,794,895	33,206,352	43,472	5,614,323	3,374,779

Personal Income and Employment by Area: Atlantic City-Hammonton, NJ

(Thousands of dollars, except as noted.)

Year	Personal income, total	Earnings by place of work			Less: Contributions for government social insurance	Plus: Adjustment for residence	Equals: Net earnings by place of residence	Plus: Dividends, interest, and rent	Plus: Personal current transfer receipts	Per capita personal income (dollars)	Population (persons)	Total employment
		Nonfarm	Farm	Total								
1970	784,227	556,613	6,342	562,955	39,544	36,041	559,452	124,531	100,244	4,458	175,908	79,885
1971	873,283	594,975	6,399	601,374	43,679	57,876	615,571	137,484	120,228	4,856	179,824	79,392
1972	965,913	652,602	5,316	657,918	50,296	74,418	682,040	149,583	134,290	5,222	184,987	82,297
1973	1,081,184	730,287	8,073	738,360	63,328	89,182	764,214	164,652	152,318	5,776	187,199	85,385
1974	1,173,275	765,381	8,991	774,372	68,830	104,618	810,160	184,689	178,426	6,204	189,113	84,867
1975	1,284,620	805,837	8,100	813,937	70,338	118,154	861,753	198,787	224,080	6,777	189,544	82,280
1976	1,420,500	902,949	8,936	911,885	77,967	129,805	963,723	209,899	246,878	7,492	189,613	84,161
1977	1,573,731	1,010,916	11,534	1,022,450	85,302	144,865	1,082,013	230,899	260,819	8,313	189,311	85,095
1978	1,778,819	1,183,105	11,718	1,194,823	103,033	149,952	1,241,742	261,706	275,371	9,307	191,121	90,253
1979	2,068,679	1,489,693	9,673	1,499,366	142,968	114,711	1,471,109	295,301	302,269	10,714	193,082	99,716
1980	2,383,151	1,795,513	11,740	1,807,253	179,689	65,399	1,692,963	359,556	330,632	12,249	194,566	109,410
1981	2,729,848	2,161,855	10,799	2,172,654	237,775	-2,434	1,932,445	440,890	356,513	13,929	195,984	118,656
1982	2,913,926	2,305,500	14,457	2,319,957	254,824	-35,177	2,029,956	507,743	376,227	14,826	196,548	119,783
1983	3,176,186	2,600,551	20,497	2,621,048	294,840	-86,797	2,239,411	536,771	400,004	15,947	199,168	124,824
1984	3,586,376	3,024,284	15,085	3,039,369	352,555	-143,804	2,543,010	631,121	412,245	17,688	202,752	133,475
1985	3,836,637	3,297,175	20,107	3,317,282	390,134	-199,132	2,728,016	672,257	436,364	18,620	206,045	139,336
1986	4,103,066	3,610,360	21,519	3,631,879	426,729	-270,695	2,934,455	709,421	459,190	19,596	209,388	141,884
1987	4,351,478	3,927,030	18,435	3,945,465	466,000	-351,209	3,128,256	747,043	476,179	20,470	212,581	148,142
1988	4,757,473	4,368,713	18,427	4,387,140	521,551	-452,570	3,413,019	831,898	512,556	21,879	217,445	152,703
1989	4,959,986	4,516,513	18,262	4,534,775	540,333	-550,631	3,443,811	963,061	553,114	22,384	221,589	155,641
1990	5,069,532	4,706,721	17,135	4,723,856	549,692	-681,738	3,492,426	970,807	606,299	22,488	225,431	159,479
1991	4,793,815	4,310,454	20,486	4,330,940	527,251	-649,415	3,154,274	926,706	712,835	20,955	228,763	152,342
1992	5,392,380	4,851,767	22,501	4,874,268	572,163	-674,915	3,627,190	924,434	840,756	23,282	231,612	152,205
1993	5,645,440	5,132,725	26,421	5,159,146	595,398	-707,045	3,856,703	905,547	883,190	24,096	234,288	153,047
1994	5,787,626	5,268,808	26,756	5,295,564	627,015	-705,697	3,962,852	947,020	877,754	24,463	236,589	154,444
1995	6,261,554	5,626,599	28,932	5,655,531	656,733	-709,987	4,288,811	1,026,444	946,299	26,176	239,212	157,855
1996	6,677,666	5,987,169	31,538	6,018,707	688,462	-715,433	4,614,812	1,085,581	977,273	27,576	242,152	159,704
1997	7,022,924	6,304,756	30,222	6,334,978	705,025	-747,609	4,882,344	1,138,518	1,002,062	28,692	244,771	162,668
1998	7,313,542	6,582,868	27,005	6,609,873	725,611	-782,214	5,102,048	1,184,506	1,026,988	29,506	247,863	167,547
1999	7,510,180	6,789,521	22,567	6,812,088	736,734	-783,046	5,292,308	1,167,649	1,050,223	29,989	250,432	169,744
2000	7,939,227	7,088,702	31,353	7,120,055	762,017	-795,154	5,562,884	1,252,416	1,123,927	31,297	253,674	173,377
2001	8,188,997	7,242,163	29,657	7,271,820	785,383	-844,950	5,641,487	1,287,497	1,260,013	32,021	255,737	173,367
2002	8,471,218	7,508,447	36,805	7,545,252	818,149	-862,531	5,864,572	1,227,013	1,379,633	32,674	259,263	173,381
2003	8,832,399	7,846,515	35,273	7,881,788	845,303	-883,987	6,152,498	1,250,448	1,429,453	33,547	263,285	176,415
2004	9,267,147	8,233,346	34,948	8,268,294	885,799	-904,846	6,477,649	1,365,704	1,423,794	34,615	267,723	179,470
2005	9,661,120	8,643,497	45,844	8,689,341	945,739	-925,498	6,818,104	1,285,499	1,557,517	35,738	270,332	185,554
2006	10,108,963	8,931,688	67,208	8,998,896	976,595	-916,915	7,105,386	1,298,258	1,705,319	37,198	271,759	187,040
2007	10,377,593	8,928,122	71,935	9,000,057	1,006,682	-892,780	7,100,595	1,465,707	1,811,291	38,110	272,303	185,664
2008	10,676,594	8,821,618	60,483	8,882,101	1,022,983	-876,309	6,982,809	1,639,666	2,054,119	39,106	273,014	184,522
2009	10,729,823	8,331,794	62,209	8,394,003	969,586	-612,997	6,811,420	1,624,029	2,294,374	39,153	274,049	176,286
2010	10,865,497	8,368,945	53,102	8,422,047	981,746	-645,647	6,794,654	1,581,881	2,488,962	39,545	274,762	174,309
2011	11,364,859	8,481,853	61,014	8,542,867	905,351	-561,143	7,076,373	1,755,782	2,532,704	41,338	274,923	174,182
2012	11,553,537	8,671,609	71,819	8,743,428	912,926	-624,430	7,206,072	1,852,863	2,494,602	41,927	275,566	175,054
2013	11,504,811	8,602,872	59,590	8,662,462	1,024,355	-521,330	7,116,777	1,854,306	2,533,728	41,659	276,167	173,610
2014	11,926,549	8,751,689	63,528	8,815,217	1,035,218	-419,496	7,360,503	1,936,488	2,629,558	43,336	275,209	170,776

Personal Income and Employment by Area: Auburn-Opelika, AL

(Thousands of dollars, except as noted.)

Year	Personal income, total	Earnings by place of work			Less: Contributions for government social insurance	Plus: Adjustment for residence	Equals: Net earnings by place of residence	Plus: Dividends, interest, and rent	Plus: Personal current transfer receipts	Per capita personal income (dollars)	Population (persons)	Total employment
		Nonfarm	Farm	Total								
1970	168,756	135,548	2,208	137,756	10,502	7,579	134,833	20,613	13,310	2,755	61,262	25,031
1971	188,289	148,195	2,833	151,028	11,785	10,304	149,547	23,489	15,253	3,042	61,896	24,952
1972	212,798	168,957	3,307	172,264	14,043	11,486	169,707	25,984	17,107	3,424	62,158	26,173
1973	241,228	192,600	4,206	196,806	18,356	13,211	191,661	29,228	20,339	3,735	64,588	27,551
1974	270,356	213,169	1,937	215,106	20,983	16,430	210,553	34,577	25,226	3,928	68,823	27,763
1975	300,888	228,689	1,641	230,330	22,484	19,193	227,039	39,698	34,151	4,337	69,373	27,700
1976	340,316	258,133	3,543	261,676	25,925	23,724	259,475	44,188	36,653	4,863	69,980	28,875
1977	392,581	302,155	4,294	306,449	30,185	25,420	301,684	51,405	39,492	5,463	71,861	30,460
1978	451,924	347,957	6,677	354,634	35,197	29,332	348,769	60,243	42,912	6,101	74,069	32,087
1979	499,305	378,481	7,184	385,665	39,515	34,243	380,393	68,075	50,837	6,571	75,990	32,315
1980	564,563	422,779	6,441	429,220	44,732	36,668	421,156	81,689	61,718	7,369	76,610	32,917
1981	619,211	460,022	6,436	466,458	52,583	37,726	451,601	100,099	67,511	7,961	77,777	32,811
1982	656,628	474,237	6,100	480,337	54,923	41,147	466,561	116,239	73,828	8,312	79,001	32,816
1983	727,625	536,798	4,844	541,642	61,834	41,193	521,001	126,329	80,295	9,196	79,121	34,028
1984	808,206	609,871	3,601	613,472	70,998	41,828	584,302	140,442	83,462	10,066	80,289	36,719
1985	869,135	647,463	4,710	652,173	74,576	48,100	625,697	153,352	90,086	10,707	81,176	37,024
1986	921,580	679,423	3,796	683,219	77,162	54,294	660,351	165,759	95,470	11,133	82,776	37,444
1987	982,202	725,876	4,876	730,752	81,299	58,887	708,340	175,568	98,294	11,879	82,681	38,845
1988	1,062,450	795,047	5,176	800,223	92,555	58,501	766,169	192,057	104,224	12,558	84,601	40,675
1989	1,189,137	883,397	5,290	888,687	101,734	54,145	841,098	227,448	120,591	13,851	85,851	43,158
1990	1,250,651	925,144	6,036	931,180	107,168	61,246	885,258	230,039	135,354	14,255	87,735	43,140
1991	1,320,883	946,539	9,466	956,005	109,328	80,701	927,378	241,089	152,416	14,757	89,508	43,300
1992	1,447,030	1,033,147	6,649	1,039,796	117,463	98,850	1,021,183	253,925	171,922	15,802	91,572	44,434
1993	1,538,116	1,072,701	17,090	1,089,791	122,334	120,948	1,088,405	264,888	184,823	16,312	94,295	45,513
1994	1,641,598	1,135,955	8,893	1,144,848	130,330	143,817	1,158,335	283,279	199,984	17,090	96,057	46,095
1995	1,769,558	1,191,322	8,524	1,199,846	137,145	167,300	1,230,001	322,841	216,716	17,805	99,386	48,314
1996	1,854,482	1,229,122	5,676	1,234,798	140,354	196,671	1,291,115	333,179	230,188	18,148	102,185	49,880
1997	2,002,182	1,307,555	6,079	1,313,634	149,463	228,037	1,392,208	363,186	246,788	18,786	106,578	51,253
1998	2,162,310	1,396,549	5,168	1,401,717	154,718	266,410	1,513,409	392,025	256,876	19,669	109,936	51,954
1999	2,304,378	1,497,012	4,259	1,501,271	163,661	294,451	1,632,061	397,977	274,340	20,411	112,898	52,914
2000	2,434,242	1,548,372	3,725	1,552,097	169,732	322,299	1,704,664	432,698	296,880	21,088	115,430	54,761
2001	2,540,282	1,571,747	5,273	1,577,020	175,005	353,204	1,755,219	446,893	338,170	21,745	116,819	54,170
2002	2,686,502	1,689,875	7,257	1,697,132	186,824	365,692	1,876,000	451,225	359,277	22,692	118,392	56,169
2003	2,851,007	1,782,186	7,330	1,789,516	198,807	387,927	1,978,636	488,283	384,088	23,744	120,071	57,290
2004	3,133,725	1,973,024	9,608	1,982,632	218,437	431,233	2,195,428	526,121	412,176	25,629	122,274	60,874
2005	3,329,093	2,097,658	6,640	2,104,298	232,306	454,028	2,326,020	554,054	449,019	26,394	126,133	63,479
2006	3,598,918	2,253,121	8,004	2,261,125	249,739	486,582	2,497,968	608,891	492,059	27,845	129,247	66,240
2007	3,817,936	2,350,632	7,943	2,358,575	263,562	514,412	2,609,425	658,809	549,702	28,938	131,934	68,360
2008	4,067,490	2,430,148	3,770	2,433,918	274,270	529,271	2,688,919	741,527	637,044	30,236	134,524	68,576
2009	3,993,639	2,417,370	4,631	2,422,001	271,294	456,588	2,607,295	706,499	679,845	28,821	138,566	67,119
2010	4,184,407	2,458,911	3,267	2,462,178	279,105	519,107	2,702,180	713,150	769,077	29,719	140,799	66,820
2011	4,490,871	2,587,774	2,153	2,589,927	260,225	590,185	2,919,887	765,282	805,702	31,155	144,146	69,516
2012	4,735,931	2,682,181	3,251	2,685,432	268,778	672,754	3,089,408	827,389	819,134	31,991	148,040	71,541
2013	4,832,245	2,727,050	10,609	2,737,659	314,275	723,611	3,146,995	839,378	845,872	31,852	151,708	73,729
2014	5,100,260	2,919,532	10,431	2,929,963	332,746	739,562	3,336,779	864,101	899,380	33,064	154,255	76,038

Personal Income and Employment by Area: Augusta-Richmond County, GA-SC

(Thousands of dollars, except as noted.)

Year	Personal income, total	Earnings by place of work			Less: Contributions for government social insurance	Plus: Adjustment for residence	Equals: Net earnings by place of residence	Plus: Dividends, interest, and rent	Plus: Personal current transfer receipts	Per capita personal income (dollars)	Population (persons)	Total employment
		Nonfarm	Farm	Total								
1970	1,148,962	949,528	12,844	962,372	59,380	-18,283	884,709	172,085	92,168	3,481	330,105	149,954
1971	1,240,601	1,022,006	17,231	1,039,237	67,016	-28,348	943,873	183,440	113,288	3,756	330,340	149,885
1972	1,343,527	1,107,582	16,681	1,124,263	75,514	-28,192	1,020,557	193,527	129,443	4,091	328,410	151,635
1973	1,494,630	1,216,707	34,737	1,251,444	94,054	-28,079	1,129,311	215,663	149,656	4,495	332,508	157,074
1974	1,676,707	1,357,246	22,469	1,379,715	109,140	-30,608	1,239,967	249,912	186,828	4,920	340,794	160,613
1975	1,807,545	1,423,789	20,486	1,444,275	114,385	-30,752	1,299,138	270,677	237,730	5,181	348,901	157,238
1976	2,070,201	1,668,281	24,825	1,693,106	136,281	-43,613	1,513,212	299,853	257,136	5,765	359,074	165,293
1977	2,271,827	1,849,292	22,400	1,871,692	150,578	-47,916	1,673,198	331,519	267,110	6,228	364,786	172,285
1978	2,536,745	2,065,657	20,102	2,085,759	171,732	-53,431	1,860,596	383,229	292,920	6,778	374,244	178,197
1979	2,869,354	2,316,193	41,217	2,357,410	199,677	-62,862	2,094,871	439,969	334,514	7,485	383,370	184,512
1980	3,172,229	2,540,726	5,825	2,546,551	219,943	-72,456	2,254,152	517,617	400,460	8,124	390,476	186,358
1981	3,547,385	2,782,481	25,099	2,807,580	259,245	-64,900	2,483,435	600,397	463,553	9,017	393,411	187,332
1982	3,960,379	3,128,381	22,811	3,151,192	297,024	-82,596	2,771,572	686,420	502,387	9,948	398,117	191,980
1983	4,293,768	3,403,407	-1,782	3,401,625	330,052	-85,031	2,986,542	763,741	543,485	10,652	403,081	192,244
1984	4,864,592	3,882,670	26,619	3,909,289	388,635	-91,844	3,428,810	857,317	578,465	11,868	409,893	205,007
1985	5,363,793	4,317,635	28,328	4,345,963	440,626	-102,906	3,802,431	935,992	625,370	12,809	418,761	214,148
1986	5,816,779	4,689,475	21,646	4,711,121	487,627	-102,510	4,120,984	1,025,060	670,735	13,602	427,630	221,104
1987	6,016,124	4,812,482	28,808	4,841,290	495,899	-95,334	4,250,057	1,050,964	715,103	14,011	429,399	221,744
1988	6,454,708	5,147,074	44,131	5,191,205	549,924	-97,046	4,544,235	1,135,756	774,717	14,940	432,054	227,226
1989	7,106,415	5,614,463	47,243	5,661,706	608,658	-111,236	4,941,812	1,291,382	873,221	16,290	436,235	235,072
1990	7,757,981	6,215,789	28,140	6,243,929	683,727	-133,979	5,426,223	1,366,256	965,502	17,387	446,200	247,348
1991	8,100,938	6,376,281	45,798	6,422,079	712,566	-122,382	5,587,131	1,394,401	1,119,406	17,619	459,773	243,584
1992	8,700,746	6,830,454	43,057	6,873,511	756,503	-117,755	5,999,253	1,467,363	1,234,130	18,341	474,398	243,360
1993	8,963,493	7,004,759	26,637	7,031,396	782,282	-111,478	6,137,636	1,503,424	1,322,433	18,799	476,818	247,474
1994	9,364,999	7,182,029	46,644	7,228,673	810,717	-93,382	6,324,574	1,645,676	1,394,749	19,376	483,333	251,197
1995	9,736,801	7,358,407	38,406	7,396,813	828,559	-75,571	6,492,683	1,734,814	1,509,304	19,908	489,089	253,558
1996	10,165,309	7,483,562	36,765	7,520,327	830,912	-46,039	6,643,376	1,906,025	1,615,908	20,712	490,788	254,613
1997	10,611,051	7,787,111	37,575	7,824,686	857,519	-25,100	6,942,067	2,006,120	1,662,864	21,392	496,030	260,000
1998	11,346,125	8,332,333	34,547	8,366,880	908,839	5,786	7,463,827	2,170,778	1,711,520	22,663	500,636	264,875
1999	11,840,338	8,793,995	38,983	8,832,978	957,149	8,253	7,884,082	2,146,187	1,810,069	23,451	504,895	270,755
2000	12,484,527	9,150,674	48,318	9,198,992	993,468	15,554	8,221,078	2,317,310	1,946,139	24,533	508,896	274,436
2001	13,124,378	9,515,189	72,270	9,587,459	1,032,411	20,650	8,575,698	2,414,648	2,134,032	25,602	512,626	273,899
2002	13,612,431	9,873,307	54,658	9,927,965	1,078,516	-62,481	8,786,968	2,435,840	2,389,623	26,339	516,818	273,665
2003	14,149,789	10,426,942	62,626	10,489,568	1,124,965	-103,868	9,260,735	2,436,383	2,452,671	27,205	520,120	278,726
2004	14,826,531	10,950,272	86,800	11,037,072	1,203,637	-96,249	9,737,186	2,471,571	2,617,774	28,145	526,789	286,502
2005	15,594,814	11,401,998	97,494	11,499,492	1,241,772	-3,793	10,253,927	2,553,099	2,787,788	29,353	531,294	291,340
2006	16,418,054	11,837,520	71,005	11,908,525	1,303,534	-7,520	10,597,471	2,825,869	2,994,714	30,480	538,643	293,146
2007	17,193,490	12,190,269	54,652	12,244,921	1,329,299	-27,583	10,888,039	3,113,209	3,192,242	31,517	545,524	299,203
2008	17,843,285	12,638,446	45,837	12,684,283	1,419,016	-45,423	11,219,844	2,988,636	3,634,805	32,288	552,627	299,467
2009	18,108,359	12,625,129	51,160	12,676,289	1,421,706	-73,020	11,181,563	2,948,947	3,977,849	32,447	558,096	294,766
2010	18,694,727	12,995,123	49,533	13,044,656	1,478,101	-88,201	11,478,354	2,923,394	4,292,979	32,990	566,683	294,308
2011	19,848,824	13,439,739	28,123	13,467,862	1,365,732	-88,521	12,013,609	3,335,143	4,500,072	34,759	571,047	295,805
2012	20,119,075	13,814,838	54,878	13,869,716	1,400,469	-77,927	12,391,320	3,258,447	4,469,308	34,883	576,755	297,345
2013	20,344,420	13,925,112	84,269	14,009,381	1,581,011	-62,042	12,366,328	3,384,715	4,593,377	35,063	580,230	300,961
2014	21,079,003	14,408,700	61,263	14,469,963	1,633,689	-62,568	12,773,706	3,525,026	4,780,271	36,117	583,632	306,407

Personal Income and Employment by Area: Austin-Round Rock-San Marcos, TX

(Thousands of dollars, except as noted.)

Year	Personal income, total	Earnings by place of work			Less: Contributions for government social insurance	Plus: Adjustment for residence	Equals: Net earnings by place of residence	Plus: Dividends, interest, and rent	Plus: Personal current transfer receipts	Per capita personal income (dollars)	Population (persons)	Total employment
		Nonfarm	Farm	Total								
1970	1,464,833	1,158,673	13,108	1,171,781	69,396	-1,165	1,101,220	258,519	105,094	3,645	401,871	184,371
1971	1,659,801	1,315,035	11,680	1,326,715	82,025	-204	1,244,486	294,133	121,182	3,959	419,249	195,537
1972	1,916,298	1,513,798	25,787	1,539,585	98,461	777	1,441,901	338,100	136,297	4,278	447,971	210,710
1973	2,192,543	1,722,934	45,885	1,768,819	128,968	1,905	1,641,756	382,174	168,613	4,632	473,351	226,304
1974	2,474,333	1,939,262	25,287	1,964,549	149,877	1,649	1,816,321	451,482	206,530	5,092	485,969	235,030
1975	2,839,651	2,201,088	18,666	2,219,754	167,560	3,998	2,056,192	517,378	266,081	5,709	497,356	240,694
1976	3,249,957	2,556,780	30,898	2,587,678	195,426	2,297	2,394,549	561,995	293,413	6,278	517,680	255,068
1977	3,605,197	2,890,504	6,674	2,897,178	224,831	-432	2,671,915	627,420	305,862	6,776	532,052	272,296
1978	4,207,549	3,364,241	15,778	3,380,019	269,208	-4,337	3,106,474	758,554	342,521	7,811	538,668	290,687
1979	4,874,046	3,882,130	28,186	3,910,316	326,104	-1,888	3,582,324	896,456	395,266	8,528	571,520	308,207
1980	5,617,437	4,433,603	2,256	4,435,859	373,621	850	4,063,088	1,086,889	467,460	9,528	589,582	322,221
1981	6,563,308	5,112,653	25,653	5,138,306	467,038	5,736	4,677,004	1,349,451	536,853	10,831	605,961	342,388
1982	7,508,651	5,765,364	28,665	5,794,029	532,851	6,375	5,267,553	1,636,324	604,774	11,854	633,452	362,756
1983	8,641,055	6,737,160	12,928	6,750,088	616,451	-8,108	6,125,529	1,848,248	667,278	12,930	668,303	388,622
1984	10,150,053	8,037,122	13,370	8,050,492	758,728	-23,025	7,268,739	2,160,884	720,430	14,343	707,646	431,932
1985	11,478,718	9,152,969	-6,662	9,146,307	877,555	-34,122	8,234,630	2,452,831	791,257	15,133	758,510	468,315
1986	12,002,833	9,540,015	-2,221	9,537,794	911,319	-34,341	8,592,134	2,525,833	884,866	15,134	793,109	471,436
1987	12,197,738	9,660,970	2,914	9,663,884	901,106	-22,142	8,740,636	2,501,367	955,735	15,108	807,392	481,326
1988	12,930,122	10,187,424	807	10,188,231	988,496	-11,126	9,188,609	2,717,846	1,023,667	15,823	817,153	484,629
1989	13,905,858	10,683,035	11,448	10,694,483	1,052,817	-1,405	9,640,261	3,122,428	1,143,169	16,717	831,848	490,138
1990	15,377,092	11,884,582	7,443	11,892,025	1,162,456	2,927	10,732,496	3,372,589	1,272,007	18,050	851,898	512,913
1991	16,327,970	13,005,305	12,737	13,018,042	1,301,888	-19,903	11,696,251	3,216,383	1,415,336	18,540	880,678	536,269
1992	17,959,280	14,361,818	19,923	14,381,741	1,432,140	-42,168	12,907,433	3,391,959	1,659,888	19,674	912,833	554,727
1993	19,652,355	15,899,503	30,278	15,929,781	1,589,253	-76,160	14,264,368	3,620,129	1,767,858	20,691	949,788	591,053
1994	21,518,991	17,497,236	20,938	17,518,174	1,777,163	-109,586	15,631,425	3,989,851	1,897,715	21,760	988,925	624,671
1995	23,804,471	19,493,299	21,924	19,515,223	1,994,942	-158,152	17,362,129	4,385,633	2,056,709	23,076	1,031,557	663,975
1996	26,104,152	21,566,217	-12,971	21,553,246	2,197,105	-213,192	19,142,949	4,751,204	2,209,999	24,327	1,073,037	692,327
1997	29,016,608	24,133,481	15,227	24,148,708	2,457,286	-280,856	21,410,566	5,263,183	2,342,859	26,111	1,111,264	725,886
1998	33,851,221	28,895,632	-5,486	28,890,146	2,884,549	-411,373	25,594,224	5,818,542	2,438,455	29,294	1,155,579	766,677
1999	38,143,522	33,109,960	28,248	33,138,208	3,277,015	-561,875	29,299,318	6,217,040	2,627,164	31,631	1,205,898	805,295
2000	41,828,446	36,510,486	13,532	36,524,018	3,639,252	-667,697	32,217,069	6,786,515	2,824,862	33,067	1,264,950	849,776
2001	43,504,644	37,850,494	14,131	37,864,625	3,685,574	-660,087	33,518,964	6,819,542	3,166,138	32,925	1,321,316	864,421
2002	42,673,381	37,000,956	15,564	37,016,520	3,584,846	-977,547	32,454,127	6,677,448	3,541,806	31,661	1,347,822	857,143
2003	44,188,483	37,920,624	39,951	37,960,575	3,751,890	-915,580	33,293,105	7,065,562	3,829,816	32,113	1,376,030	863,080
2004	46,896,702	39,846,957	68,045	39,915,002	3,939,820	-931,091	35,044,091	7,767,450	4,085,161	33,259	1,410,058	886,470
2005	51,761,805	42,801,019	49,741	42,850,760	4,223,475	-756,125	37,871,160	9,397,906	4,492,739	35,615	1,453,358	932,803
2006	57,071,026	46,941,030	43,090	46,984,120	4,501,395	-975,874	41,506,851	10,699,143	4,865,032	37,659	1,515,485	977,222
2007	61,104,751	49,434,378	46,139	49,480,517	4,824,491	-469,593	44,186,433	11,521,573	5,396,745	38,726	1,577,856	1,033,523
2008	67,348,545	52,136,661	-7,240	52,129,421	5,005,750	-426,135	46,697,536	14,237,219	6,413,790	41,220	1,633,870	1,068,627
2009	65,448,950	51,143,861	-12,418	51,131,443	5,033,522	-424,904	45,673,017	12,602,025	7,173,908	38,904	1,682,338	1,064,298
2010	69,124,528	54,046,052	3,243	54,049,295	5,288,980	-471,572	48,288,743	12,656,705	8,179,080	40,009	1,727,743	1,076,924
2011	75,581,541	58,037,206	-2,956	58,034,250	5,002,957	-507,543	52,523,750	14,461,801	8,595,990	42,412	1,782,089	1,114,870
2012	83,215,532	62,110,479	17,837	62,128,316	5,329,296	-562,408	56,236,612	18,317,296	8,661,624	45,321	1,836,149	1,152,354
2013	85,628,710	65,606,297	29,127	65,635,424	6,431,188	-624,263	58,579,973	17,938,226	9,110,511	45,407	1,885,803	1,208,017
2014	91,385,667	70,720,208	30,825	70,751,033	6,922,196	-684,225	63,144,612	18,562,571	9,678,484	47,026	1,943,299	1,252,927

Personal Income and Employment by Area: Bakersfield-Delano, CA

(Thousands of dollars, except as noted.)

| Year | Personal income, total | Derivation of personal income | | | | | Equals: Net earnings by place of residence | Plus: Dividends, interest, and rent | Plus: Personal current transfer receipts | Per capita personal income (dollars) | Population (persons) | Total employment |
| | | Earnings by place of work | | | Less: Contributions for government social insurance | Plus: Adjustment for residence | | | | | | |
		Nonfarm	Farm	Total								
1970	1,356,435	1,009,543	118,613	1,128,156	62,598	-43,610	1,021,948	184,547	149,940	4,100	330,868	138,871
1971	1,464,105	1,083,386	130,600	1,213,986	69,095	-47,069	1,097,822	200,828	165,455	4,355	336,227	142,153
1972	1,592,117	1,171,391	149,304	1,320,695	77,995	-50,086	1,192,614	220,153	179,350	4,727	336,833	145,354
1973	1,815,118	1,312,708	203,198	1,515,906	99,706	-55,286	1,360,914	253,553	200,651	5,292	343,007	153,762
1974	2,152,111	1,491,923	316,347	1,808,270	117,906	-66,732	1,623,632	287,239	241,240	6,241	344,840	163,320
1975	2,337,539	1,679,085	255,472	1,934,557	129,759	-86,497	1,718,301	322,135	297,103	6,550	356,866	170,339
1976	2,755,229	1,897,636	418,562	2,316,198	149,765	-95,136	2,071,297	343,104	340,828	7,509	366,932	173,782
1977	2,911,878	2,105,889	334,713	2,440,602	169,934	-104,753	2,165,915	381,443	364,520	7,823	372,217	179,070
1978	3,210,154	2,393,952	276,117	2,670,069	195,935	-110,274	2,363,860	447,534	398,760	8,493	377,990	185,586
1979	3,823,827	2,738,552	473,541	3,212,093	233,037	-122,189	2,856,867	522,338	444,622	9,725	393,198	197,044
1980	4,488,004	3,083,116	641,573	3,724,689	259,937	-143,566	3,321,186	643,575	523,243	11,043	406,407	202,903
1981	4,804,726	3,464,000	398,604	3,862,604	321,457	-140,913	3,400,234	784,775	619,717	11,470	418,877	207,514
1982	5,225,068	3,733,378	447,822	4,181,200	358,405	-145,816	3,676,979	868,476	679,613	12,048	433,698	205,351
1983	5,442,616	3,926,286	346,178	4,272,464	388,511	-141,608	3,742,345	954,357	745,914	12,177	446,961	211,093
1984	6,004,689	4,351,360	367,679	4,719,039	448,453	-151,780	4,118,806	1,087,036	798,847	13,070	459,411	217,562
1985	6,441,974	4,736,141	335,570	5,071,711	496,649	-153,172	4,421,890	1,157,830	862,254	13,584	474,243	223,569
1986	6,878,521	4,980,538	428,057	5,408,595	529,879	-146,302	4,732,414	1,206,048	940,059	14,147	486,217	227,198
1987	7,139,426	5,145,401	464,962	5,610,363	549,651	-125,645	4,935,067	1,221,909	982,450	14,339	497,910	231,475
1988	7,825,063	5,713,581	503,156	6,216,737	632,336	-134,408	5,449,993	1,309,158	1,065,912	15,314	510,980	243,334
1989	8,344,297	5,997,309	483,707	6,481,016	669,729	-129,851	5,681,436	1,480,011	1,182,850	15,806	527,922	245,816
1990	9,059,529	6,528,793	567,906	7,096,699	727,997	-146,290	6,222,412	1,531,533	1,305,584	16,486	549,535	253,759
1991	9,658,432	7,137,676	440,670	7,578,346	799,104	-168,178	6,611,064	1,567,473	1,479,895	16,964	569,346	267,697
1992	10,142,185	7,315,933	502,880	7,818,813	813,302	-150,773	6,854,738	1,553,565	1,733,882	17,193	589,897	262,789
1993	10,626,091	7,482,058	695,604	8,177,662	836,513	-147,613	7,193,536	1,577,369	1,855,186	17,715	599,843	262,890
1994	10,868,451	7,625,759	650,492	8,276,251	849,749	-139,154	7,287,348	1,676,948	1,904,155	17,681	614,707	266,806
1995	11,267,528	7,952,229	566,500	8,518,729	874,038	-142,113	7,502,578	1,756,690	2,008,260	18,168	620,201	278,216
1996	11,882,401	8,270,695	647,960	8,918,655	876,902	-130,555	7,911,198	1,859,023	2,112,180	18,960	626,719	288,670
1997	12,218,841	8,620,381	560,139	9,180,520	901,940	-125,378	8,153,202	1,958,976	2,106,663	19,252	634,695	289,487
1998	12,997,099	9,382,790	427,924	9,810,714	960,039	-123,363	8,727,312	2,071,149	2,198,638	20,213	643,016	303,818
1999	13,363,023	9,604,997	406,462	10,011,459	982,156	-93,648	8,935,655	2,090,798	2,336,570	20,388	655,428	309,799
2000	14,184,531	10,275,930	506,144	10,782,074	1,052,978	-84,118	9,644,978	2,137,603	2,401,950	21,369	663,803	311,128
2001	15,297,565	11,090,750	510,962	11,601,712	1,205,382	-84,865	10,311,465	2,325,575	2,660,525	22,610	676,574	311,943
2002	16,388,965	11,846,377	725,157	12,571,534	1,302,453	-78,835	11,190,246	2,328,178	2,870,541	23,613	694,059	319,271
2003	17,449,701	12,620,841	638,076	13,258,917	1,401,591	-71,589	11,785,737	2,562,607	3,101,357	24,430	714,272	325,957
2004	18,949,790	13,523,690	1,078,572	14,602,262	1,543,535	-62,093	12,996,634	2,667,119	3,286,037	25,737	736,296	328,643
2005	20,208,590	14,547,698	1,160,129	15,707,827	1,671,192	-51,761	13,984,874	2,757,958	3,465,758	26,565	760,726	345,020
2006	21,610,247	15,926,824	901,437	16,828,261	1,768,139	-39,490	15,020,632	2,841,599	3,748,016	27,546	784,511	356,784
2007	23,261,884	16,692,884	1,250,723	17,943,607	1,818,993	-24,201	16,100,413	3,131,832	4,029,639	28,959	803,281	366,764
2008	24,345,002	17,541,266	848,305	18,389,571	1,899,447	-6,763	16,483,361	3,309,166	4,552,475	29,750	818,327	369,062
2009	23,932,706	16,753,997	946,623	17,700,620	1,859,239	-52,544	15,788,837	3,135,628	5,008,241	28,830	830,137	354,465
2010	25,446,517	17,485,232	1,269,228	18,754,460	1,887,045	-78,467	16,788,948	3,154,975	5,502,594	30,230	841,762	353,907
2011	27,234,090	18,714,516	1,372,792	20,087,308	1,825,510	-100,038	18,161,760	3,548,945	5,523,385	32,045	849,872	369,648
2012	29,451,811	20,383,724	1,618,906	22,002,630	1,947,779	-125,846	19,929,005	3,968,677	5,554,129	34,386	856,502	389,465
2013	30,477,931	20,943,658	1,994,266	22,937,924	2,247,805	-114,924	20,575,195	4,139,535	5,763,201	35,197	865,923	401,923
2014	31,629,281	22,074,757	1,757,961	23,832,718	2,362,295	-119,218	21,351,205	4,332,937	5,945,139	36,165	874,589	412,183

Personal Income and Employment by Area: Baltimore-Columbia-Towson, MD

(Thousands of dollars, except as noted.)

Year	Personal income, total	Earnings by place of work			Less: Contributions for government social insurance	Plus: Adjustment for residence	Equals: Net earnings by place of residence	Plus: Dividends, interest, and rent	Plus: Personal current transfer receipts	Per capita personal income (dollars)	Population (persons)	Total employment
		Nonfarm	Farm	Total								
1970	9,443,907	7,804,458	31,091	7,835,549	496,727	65,337	7,404,159	1,331,137	708,611	4,508	2,094,838	991,821
1971	10,338,891	8,404,807	23,419	8,428,226	552,062	144,092	8,020,256	1,454,854	863,781	4,849	2,132,113	994,410
1972	11,358,367	9,142,059	32,179	9,174,238	629,686	236,017	8,780,569	1,581,242	996,556	5,277	2,152,232	1,011,325
1973	12,540,289	10,069,361	47,689	10,117,050	797,680	317,719	9,637,089	1,761,482	1,141,718	5,785	2,167,899	1,041,876
1974	13,846,212	11,018,836	44,100	11,062,936	907,009	393,152	10,549,079	1,994,104	1,303,029	6,353	2,179,392	1,056,134
1975	15,019,160	11,660,926	50,531	11,711,457	956,010	484,515	11,239,962	2,146,735	1,632,463	6,876	2,184,332	1,038,096
1976	16,342,595	12,694,866	42,381	12,737,247	1,058,328	610,916	12,289,835	2,293,970	1,758,790	7,466	2,188,964	1,040,323
1977	17,824,765	13,787,110	32,102	13,819,212	1,154,071	752,162	13,417,303	2,531,768	1,875,694	8,095	2,201,877	1,068,371
1978	19,896,626	15,330,973	47,166	15,378,139	1,319,784	911,878	14,970,233	2,858,449	2,067,944	9,026	2,204,362	1,108,082
1979	21,950,391	16,792,917	44,409	16,837,326	1,515,579	1,113,341	16,435,088	3,177,798	2,337,505	9,936	2,209,160	1,139,209
1980	24,610,119	18,286,319	25,118	18,311,437	1,651,213	1,340,289	18,000,513	3,809,753	2,799,853	11,169	2,203,385	1,139,485
1981	27,190,506	19,993,352	36,098	20,029,450	1,938,378	1,316,416	19,407,488	4,623,790	3,159,228	12,279	2,214,413	1,146,005
1982	29,256,737	20,865,242	36,616	20,901,858	2,050,386	1,387,813	20,239,285	5,517,212	3,500,240	13,174	2,220,748	1,137,050
1983	31,302,515	22,535,022	29,743	22,564,765	2,279,282	1,451,043	21,736,526	5,769,500	3,796,489	14,047	2,228,439	1,164,025
1984	34,367,618	24,783,769	69,673	24,853,442	2,588,034	1,611,788	23,877,196	6,525,682	3,964,740	15,310	2,244,735	1,202,935
1985	37,110,853	26,937,906	68,515	27,006,421	2,895,298	1,771,307	25,882,430	7,057,208	4,171,215	16,450	2,255,970	1,243,523
1986	39,814,211	28,917,977	55,037	28,973,014	3,148,149	1,925,276	27,750,141	7,558,913	4,505,157	17,419	2,285,633	1,276,452
1987	42,504,614	31,251,717	67,075	31,318,792	3,371,142	2,090,181	30,037,831	7,897,766	4,569,017	18,403	2,309,719	1,332,191
1988	46,427,807	34,359,755	78,740	34,438,495	3,819,264	2,262,144	32,881,375	8,697,015	4,849,417	19,834	2,340,870	1,366,737
1989	49,616,761	36,474,927	78,618	36,553,545	4,076,335	2,396,400	34,873,610	9,499,968	5,243,183	21,019	2,360,610	1,393,176
1990	52,538,144	38,610,499	90,099	38,700,598	4,397,500	2,494,572	36,797,670	10,038,878	5,701,596	21,977	2,390,543	1,404,128
1991	54,503,172	39,593,229	77,117	39,670,346	4,548,811	2,580,267	37,701,802	10,387,562	6,413,808	22,539	2,418,136	1,358,484
1992	57,135,975	41,198,156	94,402	41,292,558	4,706,269	2,766,237	39,352,526	10,630,011	7,153,438	23,416	2,440,078	1,339,950
1993	59,133,677	42,582,711	96,257	42,678,968	4,858,715	2,908,614	40,728,867	10,985,142	7,419,668	24,057	2,458,038	1,347,488
1994	61,645,785	44,259,300	88,186	44,347,486	5,092,663	3,072,681	42,327,504	11,556,617	7,761,664	24,904	2,475,364	1,371,332
1995	64,494,100	46,091,028	78,522	46,169,550	5,271,529	3,169,837	44,067,858	12,357,817	8,068,425	25,897	2,490,370	1,394,314
1996	67,617,929	48,018,060	112,173	48,130,233	5,437,439	3,335,457	46,028,251	12,934,444	8,655,234	27,031	2,501,453	1,409,343
1997	71,657,552	50,794,923	91,119	50,886,042	5,714,625	3,596,585	48,768,002	14,099,110	8,790,440	28,509	2,513,492	1,436,116
1998	76,733,874	54,725,189	106,715	54,831,904	6,026,812	3,868,483	52,673,575	14,998,176	9,062,123	30,386	2,525,266	1,465,276
1999	81,678,347	59,046,539	106,814	59,153,353	6,436,335	4,206,829	56,923,847	15,192,392	9,562,108	32,153	2,540,307	1,507,673
2000	87,730,139	63,289,319	131,721	63,421,040	6,821,473	4,664,461	61,264,028	16,450,183	10,015,928	34,297	2,557,958	1,541,686
2001	92,518,088	67,199,193	110,311	67,309,504	7,382,128	4,829,516	64,756,892	16,951,162	10,810,034	35,923	2,575,471	1,545,739
2002	95,753,410	70,544,922	89,751	70,634,673	7,715,901	4,516,272	67,435,044	16,825,035	11,493,331	36,878	2,596,501	1,558,915
2003	99,589,946	73,721,986	75,215	73,797,201	8,032,211	4,151,710	69,916,700	17,385,451	12,287,795	38,095	2,614,232	1,568,784
2004	107,156,849	79,481,519	94,478	79,575,997	8,688,175	4,317,748	75,205,570	19,119,222	12,832,057	40,729	2,630,946	1,597,635
2005	112,364,166	83,903,049	78,470	83,981,519	9,156,826	4,089,888	78,914,581	19,573,621	13,875,964	42,494	2,644,231	1,630,588
2006	119,781,049	88,821,643	64,909	88,886,552	9,770,490	3,991,047	83,107,109	22,253,902	14,420,038	45,062	2,658,162	1,663,770
2007	124,884,380	91,947,036	58,780	92,005,816	10,201,028	3,665,962	85,470,750	23,830,484	15,583,146	46,815	2,667,619	1,696,184
2008	128,464,938	93,940,715	79,685	94,020,400	10,554,152	2,714,990	86,181,238	24,730,756	17,552,944	47,938	2,679,819	1,695,277
2009	128,344,783	93,677,088	78,487	93,755,575	10,499,720	3,571,103	86,826,958	22,554,221	18,963,604	47,605	2,696,018	1,659,209
2010	132,110,673	96,407,544	69,643	96,477,187	10,966,348	3,651,044	89,161,883	22,515,876	20,432,914	48,648	2,715,625	1,648,447
2011	139,380,349	100,912,604	94,838	101,007,442	10,233,253	3,024,892	93,799,081	24,580,988	21,000,280	50,958	2,735,205	1,679,773
2012	144,247,043	105,196,888	137,513	105,334,401	10,647,628	1,913,071	96,599,844	26,386,459	21,260,740	52,335	2,756,231	1,708,343
2013	144,266,217	106,577,145	165,361	106,742,506	12,144,386	1,701,228	96,299,348	26,062,403	21,904,466	52,006	2,774,050	1,736,857
2014	149,573,086	110,654,041	122,333	110,776,374	12,472,326	816,750	99,120,798	27,196,737	23,255,551	53,690	2,785,874	1,754,218

Personal Income and Employment by Area: Bangor, ME

(Thousands of dollars, except as noted.)

Year	Personal income, total	Earnings by place of work			Less: Contributions for government social insurance	Plus: Adjustment for residence	Equals: Net earnings by place of residence	Plus: Dividends, interest, and rent	Plus: Personal current transfer receipts	Per capita personal income (dollars)	Population (persons)	Total employment
		Nonfarm	Farm	Total								
1970	409,852	335,686	4,999	340,685	24,136	-2,926	313,623	53,819	42,410	3,258	125,812	53,058
1971	442,614	361,812	4,725	366,537	26,637	-5,337	334,563	57,651	50,400	3,460	127,935	53,213
1972	488,967	404,380	5,027	409,407	31,014	-8,180	370,213	62,087	56,667	3,789	129,035	54,697
1973	541,969	445,103	9,235	454,338	38,652	-9,049	406,637	68,507	66,825	4,144	130,797	57,117
1974	602,949	480,683	10,276	490,959	43,214	-4,799	442,946	78,771	81,232	4,566	132,038	58,222
1975	667,661	528,383	5,129	533,512	47,314	-8,251	477,947	86,177	103,537	5,004	133,434	59,000
1976	759,573	609,095	12,834	621,929	56,185	-10,573	555,171	92,575	111,827	5,604	135,542	61,770
1977	815,840	663,277	5,670	668,947	60,903	-14,979	593,065	103,355	119,420	5,993	136,134	63,665
1978	897,245	733,061	6,218	739,279	68,841	-18,847	651,591	117,174	128,480	6,553	136,912	65,596
1979	1,003,092	825,242	4,827	830,069	79,837	-23,470	726,762	131,560	144,770	7,313	137,157	67,939
1980	1,120,591	902,532	2,486	905,018	86,748	-27,601	790,669	158,425	171,497	8,166	137,228	68,884
1981	1,223,547	963,062	8,985	972,047	99,796	-34,209	838,042	191,056	194,449	8,869	137,952	68,180
1982	1,303,026	1,005,380	7,172	1,012,552	106,957	-35,827	869,768	221,480	211,778	9,441	138,020	67,853
1983	1,401,515	1,098,329	5,266	1,103,595	117,253	-41,603	944,739	228,292	228,484	10,148	138,101	69,290
1984	1,551,769	1,218,320	8,837	1,227,157	134,109	-45,254	1,047,794	262,729	241,246	11,205	138,488	71,880
1985	1,641,127	1,292,743	6,847	1,299,590	142,720	-46,526	1,110,344	277,161	253,622	11,836	138,654	73,522
1986	1,743,169	1,364,445	7,908	1,372,353	149,155	-46,079	1,177,119	302,867	263,183	12,526	139,169	74,368
1987	1,907,719	1,512,157	9,727	1,521,884	162,172	-53,512	1,306,200	331,403	270,116	13,606	140,207	76,675
1988	2,105,675	1,687,817	8,582	1,696,399	184,350	-61,775	1,450,274	368,276	287,125	14,762	142,639	80,867
1989	2,272,893	1,842,520	8,983	1,851,503	197,204	-66,937	1,587,362	375,119	310,412	15,632	145,402	82,915
1990	2,343,507	1,870,775	11,056	1,881,831	210,932	-62,362	1,608,537	386,179	348,791	15,937	147,046	82,886
1991	2,396,961	1,862,493	7,187	1,869,680	211,943	-65,622	1,592,115	405,890	398,956	16,271	147,315	80,019
1992	2,503,647	1,954,365	10,722	1,965,087	224,740	-70,749	1,669,598	396,722	437,327	17,097	146,435	80,228
1993	2,605,807	2,037,609	9,406	2,047,015	240,365	-74,729	1,731,921	403,516	470,370	17,757	146,752	82,174
1994	2,713,679	2,106,739	7,486	2,114,225	251,418	-77,337	1,785,470	436,231	491,978	18,460	147,000	82,635
1995	2,779,728	2,140,167	6,318	2,146,485	257,778	-79,578	1,809,129	452,544	518,055	19,075	145,724	82,741
1996	2,900,155	2,200,720	8,227	2,208,947	261,809	-79,131	1,868,007	479,287	552,861	19,952	145,356	83,203
1997	3,034,204	2,305,253	4,537	2,309,790	273,135	-83,652	1,953,003	502,160	579,041	20,939	144,910	83,642
1998	3,196,957	2,447,235	7,425	2,454,660	288,043	-92,957	2,073,660	523,777	599,520	22,113	144,574	85,954
1999	3,324,860	2,588,514	8,067	2,596,581	301,182	-101,915	2,193,484	513,008	618,368	22,946	144,902	86,800
2000	3,553,366	2,742,235	7,837	2,750,072	313,655	-107,640	2,328,777	571,305	653,284	24,517	144,937	89,379
2001	3,740,537	2,931,881	6,979	2,938,860	334,892	-124,075	2,479,893	563,219	697,425	25,601	146,110	89,861
2002	3,909,383	3,043,440	4,216	3,047,656	337,239	-132,897	2,577,520	589,318	742,545	26,541	147,298	90,175
2003	4,062,396	3,110,239	4,952	3,115,191	338,962	-137,781	2,638,448	607,866	816,082	27,309	148,759	89,511
2004	4,248,243	3,275,395	7,761	3,283,156	355,449	-146,677	2,781,030	588,304	878,909	28,547	148,814	90,773
2005	4,384,066	3,387,587	6,463	3,394,050	373,637	-154,553	2,865,860	564,823	953,383	29,281	149,726	91,976
2006	4,607,654	3,570,421	3,207	3,573,628	394,633	-163,524	3,015,471	611,720	980,463	30,424	151,446	92,915
2007	4,811,727	3,649,919	6,585	3,656,504	411,455	-168,865	3,076,184	678,931	1,056,612	31,608	152,232	94,169
2008	5,021,984	3,680,979	5,617	3,686,596	420,248	-174,722	3,091,626	713,098	1,217,260	32,744	153,372	93,873
2009	5,071,062	3,681,952	3,574	3,685,526	416,490	-187,592	3,081,444	672,916	1,316,702	32,978	153,770	91,575
2010	5,090,441	3,665,490	15,321	3,680,811	419,350	-177,295	3,084,166	677,817	1,328,458	33,091	153,831	89,447
2011	5,268,888	3,707,254	9,953	3,717,207	381,692	-182,910	3,152,605	729,923	1,386,360	34,258	153,799	89,491
2012	5,380,952	3,800,207	11,418	3,811,625	391,498	-187,626	3,232,501	766,601	1,381,850	35,030	153,612	89,568
2013	5,379,976	3,865,343	14,394	3,879,737	453,236	-190,879	3,235,622	733,625	1,410,729	35,053	153,479	90,047
2014	5,509,736	3,942,182	15,768	3,957,950	462,128	-193,182	3,302,640	760,860	1,446,236	35,914	153,414	90,509

Personal Income and Employment by Area: Barnstable Town, MA

(Thousands of dollars, except as noted.)

| Year | Personal income, total | Derivation of personal income | | | | | | | | | Per capita personal income (dollars) | Population (persons) | Total employment |
| | | Earnings by place of work | | | Less: Contributions for government social insurance | Plus: Adjustment for residence | Equals: Net earnings by place of residence | Plus: Dividends, interest, and rent | Plus: Personal current transfer receipts | | | | |
		Nonfarm	Farm	Total									
1970	471,314	296,414	1,016	297,430	17,483	-10,768	269,179	147,217	54,918		4,827	97,632	47,104
1971	542,895	332,632	942	333,574	20,635	-4,032	308,907	164,415	69,573		5,470	99,244	49,746
1972	620,289	372,718	1,042	373,760	24,040	3,773	353,493	183,405	83,391		6,251	99,237	52,776
1973	691,394	410,771	1,303	412,074	30,244	17,140	398,970	194,127	98,297		6,224	111,093	57,102
1974	762,377	430,557	1,271	431,828	32,765	29,334	428,397	214,870	119,110		6,157	123,816	57,828
1975	861,904	461,751	1,063	462,814	34,194	42,404	471,024	233,530	157,350		6,659	129,437	58,475
1976	974,867	531,662	1,205	532,867	39,344	54,956	548,479	257,521	168,867		7,322	133,142	61,244
1977	1,102,051	599,784	1,215	600,999	44,795	70,921	627,125	292,619	182,307		7,982	138,071	65,095
1978	1,251,618	687,919	1,853	689,772	52,316	90,996	728,452	324,053	199,113		8,879	140,966	69,572
1979	1,433,106	769,126	1,531	770,657	61,720	117,365	826,302	374,330	232,474		9,798	146,265	73,652
1980	1,658,724	849,685	2,161	851,846	69,045	148,346	931,147	453,806	273,771		11,144	148,847	76,419
1981	1,890,105	934,618	2,144	936,762	82,871	154,882	1,008,773	559,193	322,139		12,419	152,189	78,745
1982	2,116,559	997,077	2,902	999,979	91,500	166,022	1,074,501	685,541	356,517		13,703	154,460	81,237
1983	2,339,663	1,132,934	5,211	1,138,145	105,359	180,916	1,213,702	746,383	379,578		14,872	157,320	86,481
1984	2,688,667	1,336,141	4,481	1,340,622	128,140	202,622	1,415,104	864,188	409,375		16,583	162,135	92,174
1985	2,979,259	1,531,856	4,296	1,536,152	150,310	225,541	1,611,383	925,159	442,717		17,885	166,578	96,878
1986	3,277,681	1,720,250	4,405	1,724,655	174,084	248,258	1,798,829	1,001,393	477,459		19,097	171,633	101,045
1987	3,641,330	1,979,734	3,632	1,983,366	198,958	288,663	2,073,071	1,062,912	505,347		20,664	176,215	100,196
1988	3,959,741	2,164,950	4,838	2,169,788	221,023	321,600	2,270,365	1,154,913	534,463		21,860	181,137	104,357
1989	4,047,669	2,191,614	4,793	2,196,407	224,703	335,532	2,307,236	1,153,500	586,933		21,922	184,642	102,008
1990	4,328,474	2,170,996	4,460	2,175,456	219,874	391,021	2,346,603	1,314,088	667,783		23,106	187,335	100,006
1991	4,400,401	2,172,760	6,354	2,179,114	224,243	399,609	2,354,480	1,295,973	749,948		23,262	189,165	96,477
1992	4,712,886	2,329,433	6,365	2,335,798	237,616	425,192	2,523,374	1,377,624	811,888		24,598	191,595	99,683
1993	5,051,411	2,474,629	6,266	2,480,895	253,388	474,498	2,702,005	1,488,828	860,578		25,927	194,830	103,453
1994	5,363,800	2,648,216	5,500	2,653,716	273,854	528,747	2,908,609	1,551,579	903,612		27,017	198,533	107,427
1995	5,730,556	2,814,806	5,627	2,820,433	294,442	589,104	3,115,095	1,649,261	966,200		28,247	202,874	109,482
1996	6,164,640	3,006,397	9,896	3,016,293	308,868	625,695	3,333,120	1,805,240	1,026,280		29,802	206,852	112,108
1997	6,550,737	3,152,868	12,317	3,165,185	327,632	719,331	3,556,884	1,920,638	1,073,215		31,138	210,380	116,668
1998	7,119,465	3,450,800	3,033	3,453,833	355,166	807,410	3,906,077	2,110,615	1,102,773		33,191	214,497	121,433
1999	7,684,942	3,901,993	2,201	3,904,194	392,740	889,802	4,401,256	2,127,484	1,156,202		35,097	218,960	126,746
2000	8,122,505	4,031,895	3,596	4,035,491	408,128	1,012,499	4,639,862	2,251,782	1,230,861		36,419	223,031	131,585
2001	8,687,101	4,400,058	2,317	4,402,375	443,704	1,012,338	4,971,009	2,366,100	1,349,992		38,767	224,087	132,539
2002	8,785,554	4,641,144	3,133	4,644,277	473,733	1,007,421	5,177,965	2,178,812	1,428,777		38,974	225,421	134,167
2003	9,126,618	4,865,112	3,264	4,868,376	497,026	1,017,480	5,388,830	2,235,260	1,502,528		40,381	226,011	138,091
2004	9,753,290	5,151,654	4,230	5,155,884	546,770	1,037,376	5,646,490	2,544,690	1,562,110		43,490	224,264	141,166
2005	9,812,539	5,242,201	4,427	5,246,628	576,200	1,009,188	5,679,616	2,487,589	1,645,334		44,202	221,995	141,979
2006	10,273,228	5,395,600	4,584	5,400,184	583,928	1,007,219	5,823,475	2,698,100	1,751,653		46,689	220,037	141,814
2007	10,523,616	5,460,425	6,336	5,466,761	602,195	1,010,680	5,875,246	2,815,528	1,832,842		48,189	218,380	143,314
2008	10,887,205	5,513,030	10,084	5,523,114	612,109	988,732	5,899,737	2,950,532	2,036,936		50,156	217,066	141,810
2009	10,704,096	5,390,311	6,566	5,396,877	603,347	899,811	5,693,341	2,779,731	2,231,024		49,557	215,994	138,082
2010	10,992,573	5,502,242	7,739	5,509,981	604,674	898,933	5,804,240	2,853,415	2,334,918		50,914	215,903	137,572
2011	11,627,029	5,722,831	7,039	5,729,870	571,296	1,021,697	6,180,271	3,101,002	2,345,756		53,995	215,335	138,485
2012	12,238,270	6,036,694	7,659	6,044,353	590,563	1,057,319	6,511,109	3,349,581	2,377,580		56,963	214,845	141,149
2013	12,355,408	6,199,017	7,201	6,206,218	675,432	990,347	6,521,133	3,404,695	2,429,580		57,511	214,836	144,552
2014	12,871,729	6,425,718	4,289	6,430,007	705,701	1,087,706	6,812,012	3,569,997	2,489,720		59,892	214,914	146,688

Personal Income and Employment by Area: Baton Rouge, LA

(Thousands of dollars, except as noted.)

Year	Personal income, total	Earnings by place of work			Less: Contributions for government social insurance	Plus: Adjustment for residence	Equals: Net earnings by place of residence	Plus: Dividends, interest, and rent	Plus: Personal current transfer receipts	Per capita personal income (dollars)	Population (persons)	Total employment
		Nonfarm	Farm	Total								
1970	1,517,474	1,235,207	27,926	1,263,133	77,644	20,239	1,205,728	183,293	128,453	3,248	467,187	175,083
1971	1,657,863	1,343,492	29,516	1,373,008	86,480	21,882	1,308,410	203,161	146,292	3,481	476,302	179,120
1972	1,831,218	1,483,140	34,997	1,518,137	100,089	27,269	1,445,317	223,295	162,606	3,745	488,967	187,519
1973	2,034,306	1,646,562	51,347	1,697,909	128,175	25,396	1,595,130	247,025	192,151	4,089	497,516	197,959
1974	2,390,145	1,936,823	58,585	1,995,408	156,257	26,928	1,866,079	297,473	226,593	4,708	507,687	210,762
1975	2,737,706	2,227,401	32,065	2,259,466	175,628	31,358	2,115,196	337,709	284,801	5,285	517,996	221,963
1976	3,219,522	2,675,551	50,527	2,726,078	216,961	27,632	2,536,749	367,372	315,401	6,043	532,769	238,072
1977	3,631,353	3,047,397	39,029	3,086,426	242,233	30,101	2,874,294	408,508	348,551	6,613	549,090	244,790
1978	4,131,989	3,492,956	34,979	3,527,935	285,513	36,236	3,278,658	477,007	376,324	7,363	561,187	260,518
1979	4,700,873	3,957,279	37,084	3,994,363	333,758	53,060	3,713,665	553,542	433,666	8,138	577,630	268,260
1980	5,557,454	4,645,001	20,204	4,665,205	389,604	45,430	4,321,031	720,084	516,339	9,346	594,659	281,511
1981	6,265,751	5,171,097	24,461	5,195,558	465,610	39,691	4,769,639	914,757	581,355	10,328	606,705	289,146
1982	6,708,679	5,433,933	22,044	5,455,977	492,704	14,991	4,978,264	1,064,399	666,016	10,849	618,386	291,462
1983	7,084,773	5,593,299	26,311	5,619,610	498,738	26,002	5,146,874	1,170,660	767,239	11,275	628,340	291,172
1984	7,594,392	5,974,024	13,358	5,987,382	545,584	20,065	5,461,863	1,325,962	806,567	11,989	633,436	302,207
1985	7,956,109	6,176,354	18,578	6,194,932	564,852	7,807	5,637,887	1,448,466	869,756	12,491	636,971	302,128
1986	7,930,113	6,055,319	27,665	6,082,984	542,967	-4,524	5,535,493	1,433,387	961,233	12,454	636,761	295,628
1987	8,000,793	6,164,863	20,017	6,184,880	545,242	-17,477	5,622,161	1,403,874	974,758	12,720	629,017	296,915
1988	8,584,587	6,729,031	46,644	6,775,675	631,748	-33,156	6,110,771	1,445,018	1,028,798	13,732	625,135	303,980
1989	9,310,819	7,202,326	31,248	7,233,574	688,191	-29,702	6,515,681	1,681,152	1,113,986	14,936	623,372	309,087
1990	10,108,089	7,910,264	32,403	7,942,667	779,815	-27,854	7,134,998	1,737,916	1,235,175	16,165	625,305	321,133
1991	10,736,551	8,468,410	19,804	8,488,214	857,418	-62,970	7,567,826	1,760,445	1,408,280	16,903	635,197	329,966
1992	11,784,795	9,324,990	42,460	9,367,450	935,409	-98,293	8,333,748	1,821,863	1,629,184	18,209	647,179	340,665
1993	12,269,916	9,614,891	35,260	9,650,151	971,504	-90,325	8,588,322	1,891,049	1,790,545	18,669	657,226	347,916
1994	13,169,044	10,193,564	33,531	10,227,095	1,057,987	-101,440	9,067,668	2,088,314	2,013,062	19,819	664,462	356,542
1995	13,824,190	10,670,305	39,919	10,710,224	1,108,555	-99,847	9,501,822	2,261,213	2,061,155	20,595	671,247	368,168
1996	14,486,483	11,233,210	53,083	11,286,293	1,179,827	-109,566	9,996,900	2,384,530	2,105,053	21,351	678,500	377,415
1997	15,050,988	11,729,361	48,323	11,777,684	1,226,629	-102,733	10,448,322	2,465,050	2,137,616	21,940	686,021	381,499
1998	15,970,284	12,545,248	35,389	12,580,637	1,328,806	-128,443	11,123,388	2,685,350	2,161,546	23,043	693,072	395,663
1999	16,522,910	13,163,821	52,268	13,216,089	1,379,240	-155,747	11,681,102	2,629,452	2,212,356	23,578	700,767	405,493
2000	17,499,034	13,926,965	53,817	13,980,782	1,433,916	-172,284	12,374,582	2,823,251	2,301,201	24,731	707,589	415,591
2001	18,306,115	14,525,170	52,136	14,577,306	1,456,237	-199,223	12,921,846	2,746,682	2,637,587	25,757	710,731	413,370
2002	18,919,774	15,104,872	42,728	15,147,600	1,513,878	-229,340	13,404,382	2,688,635	2,826,757	26,447	715,379	414,417
2003	19,464,331	15,674,665	48,745	15,723,410	1,555,960	-295,900	13,871,550	2,732,659	2,860,122	26,949	722,274	418,542
2004	20,646,969	16,343,413	50,409	16,393,822	1,590,489	-282,016	14,521,317	2,920,712	3,204,940	28,292	729,774	421,918
2005	22,916,309	17,502,854	44,948	17,547,802	1,675,319	-206,061	15,666,422	3,095,866	4,154,021	31,157	735,507	434,020
2006	24,947,403	19,285,017	59,308	19,344,325	1,856,332	-212,385	17,275,608	3,669,831	4,001,964	32,318	771,940	456,112
2007	27,010,794	20,609,304	57,207	20,666,511	1,997,313	-89,735	18,579,463	4,294,840	4,136,491	34,638	779,796	470,880
2008	29,225,239	22,187,604	31,354	22,218,958	2,124,753	-36,743	20,057,462	4,390,291	4,777,486	37,099	787,767	481,296
2009	29,214,886	22,427,754	40,266	22,468,020	2,155,481	-193,324	20,119,215	4,079,147	5,016,524	36,707	795,897	481,210
2010	30,082,198	22,625,065	45,182	22,670,247	2,149,697	6,931	20,527,481	4,171,894	5,382,823	37,393	804,491	476,962
2011	31,694,106	23,251,148	57,780	23,308,928	1,976,062	210,197	21,543,063	4,665,618	5,485,425	39,194	808,657	482,737
2012	32,923,739	24,481,147	81,975	24,563,122	2,074,912	-147,853	22,340,357	5,002,153	5,581,229	40,398	814,993	490,087
2013	33,640,094	25,641,905	94,221	25,736,126	2,510,914	-518,148	22,707,064	5,205,996	5,727,034	41,004	820,409	502,842
2014	34,875,701	27,066,485	55,785	27,122,270	2,634,780	-766,001	23,721,489	5,399,137	5,755,075	42,249	825,478	514,246

Personal Income and Employment by Area: Battle Creek, MI

(Thousands of dollars, except as noted.)

| Year | Personal income, total | Derivation of personal income | | | | | | | | Per capita personal income (dollars) | Population (persons) | Total employment |
| | | Earnings by place of work | | | Less: Contributions for government social insurance | Plus: Adjustment for residence | Equals: Net earnings by place of residence | Plus: Dividends, interest, and rent | Plus: Personal current transfer receipts | | | |
		Nonfarm	Farm	Total								
1970	574,530	500,953	7,173	508,126	36,214	-26,569	445,343	71,142	58,045	4,059	141,561	62,407
1971	626,165	547,122	6,267	553,389	40,854	-33,288	479,247	77,705	69,213	4,452	140,647	63,123
1972	689,148	605,591	9,419	615,010	47,211	-40,083	527,716	84,769	76,663	4,854	141,963	64,437
1973	757,834	672,993	15,821	688,814	60,903	-47,773	580,138	91,550	86,146	5,324	142,349	66,077
1974	802,480	709,603	7,321	716,924	66,185	-53,995	596,744	102,453	103,283	5,611	143,021	66,005
1975	890,650	763,470	12,747	776,217	69,442	-64,124	642,651	112,653	135,346	6,244	142,640	64,320
1976	975,339	858,609	9,566	868,175	80,024	-77,473	710,678	122,219	142,442	6,851	142,359	66,464
1977	1,055,969	945,154	8,157	953,311	88,510	-89,161	775,640	136,958	143,371	7,396	142,772	67,485
1978	1,158,413	1,048,964	6,575	1,055,539	100,211	-103,831	851,497	151,153	155,763	8,075	143,463	68,846
1979	1,257,669	1,132,416	6,581	1,138,997	112,584	-117,600	908,813	170,793	178,063	8,836	142,341	69,077
1980	1,334,596	1,143,896	4,081	1,147,977	112,244	-124,518	911,215	200,775	222,606	9,418	141,701	65,129
1981	1,447,068	1,203,720	10,190	1,213,910	127,255	-126,777	959,878	241,165	246,025	10,199	141,880	62,898
1982	1,507,104	1,199,877	2,563	1,202,440	127,081	-125,268	950,091	276,863	280,150	10,774	139,886	59,788
1983	1,540,771	1,221,504	-5,022	1,216,482	133,201	-121,705	961,576	286,685	292,510	11,195	137,629	59,063
1984	1,628,191	1,276,065	7,011	1,283,076	143,995	-122,035	1,017,046	319,429	291,716	12,000	135,682	59,859
1985	1,744,874	1,400,532	7,368	1,407,900	162,003	-134,789	1,111,108	335,304	298,462	12,971	134,523	61,694
1986	1,838,888	1,474,077	8,658	1,482,735	172,267	-139,411	1,171,057	354,821	313,010	13,691	134,316	62,869
1987	1,969,960	1,621,577	9,943	1,631,520	186,783	-159,353	1,285,384	364,442	320,134	14,609	134,849	66,233
1988	2,054,110	1,732,582	6,745	1,739,327	207,464	-169,595	1,362,268	360,127	331,715	15,277	134,459	66,844
1989	2,202,264	1,822,979	16,229	1,839,208	216,946	-171,445	1,450,817	396,850	354,597	16,258	135,457	67,838
1990	2,312,015	1,933,608	13,863	1,947,471	232,874	-180,550	1,534,047	400,504	377,464	16,972	136,226	69,258
1991	2,422,971	2,040,385	9,803	2,050,188	248,912	-197,954	1,603,322	403,138	416,511	17,710	136,814	71,364
1992	2,577,952	2,200,613	10,524	2,211,137	266,635	-221,310	1,723,192	414,702	440,058	18,776	137,298	72,964
1993	2,664,336	2,255,771	11,144	2,266,915	276,241	-221,796	1,768,878	425,722	469,736	19,338	137,775	73,362
1994	2,824,757	2,402,284	10,077	2,412,361	299,051	-238,441	1,874,869	473,029	476,859	20,483	137,910	75,666
1995	2,920,506	2,508,704	8,068	2,516,772	313,032	-250,789	1,952,951	468,819	498,736	21,257	137,393	78,757
1996	3,023,330	2,580,064	7,857	2,587,921	314,813	-252,333	2,020,775	484,503	518,052	22,128	136,630	77,972
1997	3,229,624	2,769,627	10,019	2,779,646	334,718	-274,992	2,169,936	507,447	552,241	23,602	136,834	80,495
1998	3,328,409	2,864,948	9,098	2,874,046	340,394	-279,074	2,254,578	529,430	544,401	24,157	137,783	78,266
1999	3,381,218	2,841,692	8,076	2,849,768	337,565	-259,175	2,253,028	545,966	582,224	24,498	138,021	75,539
2000	3,446,986	2,876,398	10,211	2,886,609	340,872	-265,662	2,280,075	563,101	603,810	24,976	138,014	75,076
2001	3,549,989	2,882,028	14,323	2,896,351	342,346	-249,909	2,304,096	568,725	677,168	25,695	138,158	73,943
2002	3,666,872	3,026,409	7,472	3,033,881	359,276	-280,766	2,393,839	573,817	699,216	26,460	138,580	73,968
2003	3,727,525	3,052,907	9,460	3,062,367	360,088	-298,323	2,403,956	585,192	738,377	26,824	138,962	72,438
2004	3,848,631	3,168,679	22,098	3,190,777	373,934	-322,116	2,494,727	587,035	766,869	27,600	139,443	72,671
2005	3,927,454	3,216,252	15,450	3,231,702	380,978	-340,405	2,510,319	605,844	811,291	28,266	138,946	71,591
2006	3,974,266	3,268,803	7,074	3,275,877	394,138	-355,013	2,526,726	576,163	871,377	28,738	138,291	70,580
2007	4,097,933	3,305,818	12,207	3,318,025	397,865	-370,319	2,549,841	602,975	945,117	29,785	137,582	70,059
2008	4,312,660	3,388,454	9,713	3,398,167	411,276	-391,027	2,595,864	653,460	1,063,336	31,408	137,313	68,878
2009	4,212,755	3,283,753	15,098	3,298,851	402,235	-429,990	2,466,626	590,908	1,155,221	30,908	136,301	65,850
2010	4,302,398	3,346,562	25,051	3,371,613	407,555	-484,893	2,479,165	579,508	1,243,725	31,636	135,998	65,459
2011	4,426,922	3,336,823	49,492	3,386,315	366,533	-474,204	2,545,578	644,801	1,236,543	32,724	135,282	65,840
2012	4,508,596	3,479,057	12,643	3,491,700	383,637	-511,337	2,596,726	686,463	1,225,407	33,456	134,760	65,346
2013	4,610,772	3,549,483	58,027	3,607,510	438,880	-517,929	2,650,701	706,715	1,253,356	34,197	134,830	66,269
2014	4,732,090	3,691,580	20,762	3,712,342	453,661	-551,466	2,707,215	733,711	1,291,164	35,084	134,878	67,402

Personal Income and Employment by Area: Bay City, MI

(Thousands of dollars, except as noted.)

Year	Personal income, total	Earnings by place of work			Less: Contributions for government social insurance	Plus: Adjustment for residence	Equals: Net earnings by place of residence	Plus: Dividends, interest, and rent	Plus: Personal current transfer receipts	Per capita personal income (dollars)	Population (persons)	Total employment
		Nonfarm	Farm	Total								
1970	418,696	293,738	5,220	298,958	20,928	44,374	322,404	55,379	40,913	3,563	117,502	39,729
1971	461,978	320,598	4,167	324,765	23,426	52,919	354,258	59,729	47,991	3,898	118,513	39,422
1972	496,804	342,970	4,894	347,864	26,568	58,501	379,797	64,643	52,364	4,172	119,094	39,885
1973	558,288	386,719	11,092	397,811	34,621	65,518	428,708	71,120	58,460	4,659	119,824	41,851
1974	618,075	414,343	23,624	437,967	38,401	64,265	463,831	81,022	73,222	5,127	120,548	41,896
1975	658,091	429,780	10,222	440,002	39,024	70,468	471,446	91,532	95,113	5,464	120,441	40,211
1976	750,374	491,532	10,673	502,205	45,513	98,793	555,485	98,171	96,718	6,224	120,560	41,485
1977	857,602	563,120	10,968	574,088	52,335	124,852	646,605	110,301	100,696	7,058	121,500	43,222
1978	944,277	613,020	13,745	626,765	58,492	148,519	716,792	119,733	107,752	7,736	122,057	43,662
1979	1,032,513	654,589	17,957	672,546	64,790	164,954	772,710	135,200	124,603	8,528	121,074	43,509
1980	1,127,929	667,123	26,055	693,178	65,510	157,967	785,635	166,318	175,976	9,397	120,037	41,737
1981	1,215,137	735,462	4,991	740,453	78,205	171,014	833,262	203,661	178,214	10,092	120,401	42,279
1982	1,254,904	728,328	6,508	734,836	78,800	160,086	816,122	235,156	203,626	10,563	118,804	40,466
1983	1,316,536	754,174	5,011	759,185	82,139	174,696	851,742	246,823	217,971	11,221	117,330	40,371
1984	1,413,041	805,310	7,458	812,768	90,753	189,767	911,782	277,577	223,682	12,111	116,677	40,939
1985	1,488,830	848,328	13,314	861,642	98,160	207,814	971,296	288,657	228,877	12,944	115,017	41,442
1986	1,555,016	906,942	1,131	908,073	103,782	210,548	1,014,839	300,436	239,741	13,609	114,267	42,479
1987	1,613,935	935,857	10,654	946,511	105,920	220,662	1,061,253	302,486	250,196	14,162	113,959	43,197
1988	1,709,586	1,010,520	8,551	1,019,071	118,999	235,304	1,135,376	314,976	259,234	15,143	112,898	44,027
1989	1,790,620	1,029,284	16,004	1,045,288	121,084	252,894	1,177,098	330,465	283,057	15,979	112,061	44,282
1990	1,903,284	1,101,041	13,106	1,114,147	131,061	253,160	1,236,246	359,052	307,986	17,023	111,804	45,908
1991	1,964,531	1,133,686	11,929	1,145,615	137,290	264,302	1,272,627	356,962	334,942	17,571	111,803	45,846
1992	2,087,478	1,203,647	17,461	1,221,108	144,951	286,720	1,362,877	368,211	356,390	18,608	112,182	46,227
1993	2,172,622	1,282,371	14,293	1,296,664	155,430	273,133	1,414,367	377,953	380,302	19,330	112,397	46,432
1994	2,292,819	1,356,389	6,640	1,363,029	167,355	289,651	1,485,325	417,067	390,427	20,467	112,025	47,608
1995	2,374,944	1,434,488	17,518	1,452,006	177,855	274,447	1,548,598	421,604	404,742	21,266	111,680	49,673
1996	2,469,130	1,547,801	5,539	1,553,340	187,407	242,550	1,608,483	444,198	416,449	22,198	111,231	51,133
1997	2,587,131	1,610,695	7,438	1,618,133	194,336	249,886	1,673,683	474,574	438,874	23,299	111,040	52,171
1998	2,652,080	1,680,789	2,520	1,683,309	199,717	230,265	1,713,857	498,720	439,503	23,956	110,704	51,609
1999	2,757,674	1,730,994	8,547	1,739,541	204,036	270,356	1,805,861	478,560	473,253	25,003	110,295	51,982
2000	2,902,819	1,799,965	971	1,800,936	211,969	303,942	1,892,909	514,097	495,813	26,343	110,192	53,380
2001	2,911,938	1,773,411	-7,251	1,766,160	209,131	302,289	1,859,318	502,011	550,609	26,512	109,836	51,568
2002	2,927,795	1,787,867	8,402	1,796,269	211,451	290,940	1,875,758	484,058	567,979	26,650	109,861	51,055
2003	2,995,962	1,811,970	4,247	1,816,217	212,841	285,689	1,889,065	505,278	601,619	27,346	109,559	50,706
2004	3,045,340	1,847,780	12,122	1,859,902	218,866	285,116	1,926,152	488,244	630,944	27,823	109,453	50,923
2005	3,096,361	1,877,214	13,068	1,890,282	224,675	283,135	1,948,742	483,763	663,856	28,364	109,165	50,191
2006	3,194,124	1,938,886	15,224	1,954,110	234,744	287,535	2,006,901	474,826	712,397	29,382	108,711	49,729
2007	3,304,297	1,947,498	11,908	1,959,406	239,336	287,347	2,007,417	518,874	778,006	30,558	108,132	50,011
2008	3,497,908	1,980,676	26,974	2,007,650	245,197	286,199	2,048,652	572,020	877,236	32,292	108,320	49,145
2009	3,429,479	1,940,930	14,185	1,955,115	242,088	240,968	1,953,995	516,239	959,245	31,780	107,913	47,300
2010	3,550,644	1,947,528	24,274	1,971,802	242,233	280,467	2,010,036	499,583	1,041,025	32,969	107,695	46,757
2011	3,680,785	1,977,028	41,235	2,018,263	220,862	301,475	2,098,876	537,751	1,044,158	34,247	107,477	46,927
2012	3,722,133	2,031,026	36,685	2,067,711	227,929	291,338	2,131,120	556,708	1,034,305	34,759	107,084	47,322
2013	3,733,524	2,086,772	24,769	2,111,541	266,012	273,890	2,119,419	547,473	1,066,632	34,914	106,936	47,415
2014	3,866,902	2,102,592	16,981	2,119,573	268,706	341,740	2,192,607	567,213	1,107,082	36,419	106,179	47,459

Personal Income and Employment by Area: Beaumont-Port Arthur, TX

(Thousands of dollars, except as noted.)

| Year | Personal income, total | Derivation of personal income | | | | | | | | Per capita personal income (dollars) | Population (persons) | Total employment |
| | | Earnings by place of work | | | Less: Contributions for government social insurance | Plus: Adjustment for residence | Equals: Net earnings by place of residence | Plus: Dividends, interest, and rent | Plus: Personal current transfer receipts | | | |
		Nonfarm	Farm	Total								
1970	1,290,815	1,111,000	2,176	1,113,176	72,923	-13,396	1,026,857	158,587	105,371	3,593	359,291	139,079
1971	1,385,541	1,178,036	3,751	1,181,787	79,889	-11,957	1,089,941	172,322	123,278	3,836	361,233	140,072
1972	1,493,675	1,264,626	4,717	1,269,343	90,461	-11,072	1,167,810	187,314	138,551	4,118	362,681	141,566
1973	1,626,872	1,374,688	6,352	1,381,040	114,895	-10,270	1,255,875	206,959	164,038	4,551	357,512	146,460
1974	1,904,369	1,616,540	12,000	1,628,540	139,034	-17,393	1,472,113	241,404	190,852	5,312	358,506	153,311
1975	2,139,726	1,778,394	15,416	1,793,810	147,808	-12,059	1,633,943	268,899	236,884	5,885	363,590	153,637
1976	2,476,733	2,146,360	3,153	2,149,513	182,614	-36,495	1,930,404	291,345	254,984	6,707	369,268	163,590
1977	2,779,034	2,428,531	10,809	2,439,340	206,723	-47,872	2,184,745	322,952	271,337	7,404	375,363	169,957
1978	3,086,951	2,690,062	2,880	2,692,942	234,638	-47,541	2,410,763	374,334	301,854	8,182	377,286	173,977
1979	3,466,830	3,000,754	9,394	3,010,148	271,907	-48,936	2,689,305	433,570	343,955	9,032	383,832	179,197
1980	3,882,316	3,278,184	6,220	3,284,404	298,249	-43,460	2,942,695	539,735	399,886	10,004	388,072	177,396
1981	4,434,204	3,726,185	-1,830	3,724,355	363,444	-52,793	3,308,118	675,205	450,881	11,273	393,359	186,607
1982	4,679,338	3,796,405	-2,306	3,794,099	383,646	-56,363	3,354,090	798,176	527,072	11,719	399,300	179,648
1983	4,845,530	3,823,140	-21	3,823,119	380,754	-62,541	3,379,824	849,233	616,473	12,095	400,634	172,840
1984	5,029,087	3,869,498	-3,947	3,865,551	395,358	-61,363	3,408,830	964,252	656,005	12,620	398,516	172,570
1985	5,102,406	3,810,438	3,305	3,813,743	392,355	-57,432	3,363,956	1,054,366	684,084	12,957	393,786	168,736
1986	5,048,988	3,693,223	751	3,693,974	375,743	-54,753	3,263,478	1,043,563	741,947	13,237	381,420	160,923
1987	5,029,222	3,671,944	-2,137	3,669,807	371,899	-53,286	3,244,622	1,011,989	772,611	13,266	379,118	165,149
1988	5,317,968	3,922,157	13,434	3,935,591	414,439	-58,798	3,462,354	1,057,143	798,471	14,172	375,245	167,774
1989	5,645,101	4,053,719	11,139	4,064,858	432,120	-67,362	3,565,376	1,208,720	871,005	15,093	374,021	168,178
1990	5,956,438	4,392,048	10,633	4,402,681	460,792	-85,853	3,856,036	1,139,494	960,908	15,882	375,055	174,023
1991	6,440,406	4,857,196	15,972	4,873,168	519,316	-112,611	4,241,241	1,154,475	1,044,690	16,945	380,069	183,546
1992	6,925,062	5,185,360	12,654	5,198,014	550,140	-123,209	4,524,665	1,177,637	1,222,760	17,997	384,799	183,011
1993	6,929,274	5,181,222	12,148	5,193,370	549,864	-104,175	4,539,331	1,101,561	1,288,382	17,770	389,937	183,297
1994	7,219,870	5,377,714	8,869	5,386,583	579,146	-97,247	4,710,190	1,130,614	1,379,066	18,426	391,836	183,107
1995	7,541,381	5,496,309	8,961	5,505,270	599,028	-98,519	4,807,723	1,241,734	1,491,924	19,058	395,704	186,653
1996	7,734,278	5,584,686	4,727	5,589,413	603,708	-109,545	4,876,160	1,271,579	1,586,539	19,573	395,151	187,334
1997	8,388,726	6,216,828	6,022	6,222,850	661,350	-140,386	5,421,114	1,317,178	1,650,434	21,150	396,639	194,273
1998	8,920,442	6,755,935	5,800	6,761,735	704,930	-162,094	5,894,711	1,382,517	1,643,214	22,430	397,703	198,339
1999	8,891,205	6,767,156	6,560	6,773,716	700,020	-150,641	5,923,055	1,323,844	1,644,306	22,224	400,075	197,061
2000	9,405,958	7,165,895	3,107	7,169,002	717,166	-165,683	6,286,153	1,410,402	1,709,403	23,527	399,797	199,853
2001	9,707,230	7,335,585	2,636	7,338,221	730,944	-154,092	6,453,185	1,407,855	1,846,190	24,407	397,731	196,246
2002	9,708,686	7,319,362	3,516	7,322,878	741,925	-194,621	6,386,332	1,338,156	1,984,198	24,397	397,949	195,863
2003	10,045,956	7,605,397	14,946	7,620,343	783,002	-299,257	6,538,084	1,399,713	2,108,159	25,232	398,146	197,203
2004	10,227,115	7,795,057	21,761	7,816,818	798,261	-296,537	6,722,020	1,321,967	2,183,128	25,632	398,998	197,003
2005	10,965,675	8,236,313	26,755	8,263,068	849,837	-316,236	7,096,995	1,337,655	2,531,025	27,406	400,115	200,483
2006	11,830,658	9,164,656	32,805	9,197,461	933,350	-311,307	7,952,804	1,416,706	2,461,148	30,068	393,468	207,570
2007	12,520,067	9,519,579	31,184	9,550,763	986,607	-289,185	8,274,971	1,592,434	2,652,662	31,563	396,665	212,935
2008	13,454,209	10,056,488	-4,859	10,051,629	1,038,575	-346,596	8,666,458	1,861,241	2,926,510	33,666	399,641	214,574
2009	13,287,635	9,818,938	-3,318	9,815,620	1,029,235	-342,645	8,443,740	1,701,808	3,142,087	33,087	401,592	210,555
2010	13,813,371	10,061,727	-6,756	10,054,971	1,073,031	-374,881	8,607,059	1,798,351	3,407,961	34,213	403,748	209,047
2011	14,528,335	10,555,927	-11,308	10,544,619	1,001,118	-413,947	9,129,554	1,902,259	3,496,522	35,848	405,275	213,860
2012	15,322,268	11,061,439	-10,946	11,050,493	1,034,429	-421,012	9,595,052	2,247,446	3,479,770	37,942	403,832	213,387
2013	15,096,831	10,981,693	-6,275	10,975,418	1,161,643	-359,756	9,454,019	2,052,671	3,590,141	37,237	405,424	211,590
2014	16,116,634	11,830,279	-8,664	11,821,615	1,244,071	-314,121	10,263,423	2,133,349	3,719,862	39,752	405,427	217,441

Personal Income and Employment by Area: Beckley, WV

(Thousands of dollars, except as noted.)

| Year | Personal income, total | Derivation of personal income | | | | | | | | | Per capita personal income (dollars) | Population (persons) | Total employment |
| | | Earnings by place of work | | | Less: Contributions for government social insurance | Plus: Adjustment for residence | Equals: Net earnings by place of residence | Plus: Dividends, interest, and rent | Plus: Personal current transfer receipts | | | |
		Nonfarm	Farm	Total								
1970	341,667	252,090	140	252,230	18,662	10,843	244,411	33,917	63,339	2,852	119,794	34,722
1971	382,530	272,797	278	273,075	21,177	11,574	263,472	37,831	81,227	3,125	122,399	35,712
1972	441,729	314,516	381	314,897	25,404	13,148	302,641	42,610	96,478	3,491	126,518	38,148
1973	492,383	337,734	651	338,385	31,511	13,789	320,663	49,478	122,242	3,826	128,707	39,217
1974	544,722	376,208	526	376,734	36,347	13,043	353,430	58,365	132,927	4,211	129,362	40,310
1975	643,112	452,110	488	452,598	43,395	16,438	425,641	67,825	149,646	4,850	132,602	43,351
1976	743,702	543,292	276	543,568	54,034	14,820	504,354	75,700	163,648	5,374	138,390	46,063
1977	806,921	592,725	288	593,013	57,770	15,244	550,487	84,671	171,763	5,673	142,246	46,317
1978	908,266	667,970	372	668,342	66,952	13,660	615,050	94,211	199,005	6,302	144,129	47,908
1979	998,548	696,756	837	697,593	72,995	23,549	648,147	107,180	243,221	6,884	145,047	46,987
1980	1,089,901	732,951	789	733,740	78,397	26,628	681,971	132,633	275,297	7,535	144,639	46,598
1981	1,186,431	790,795	-344	790,451	91,020	25,755	725,186	163,277	297,968	8,221	144,324	46,263
1982	1,270,894	820,844	-259	820,585	97,721	36,218	759,082	190,025	321,787	8,805	144,345	45,744
1983	1,275,819	781,707	-333	781,374	93,195	32,666	720,845	199,102	355,872	8,855	144,081	43,320
1984	1,369,668	862,512	100	862,612	105,675	36,126	793,063	222,495	354,110	9,633	142,180	44,190
1985	1,413,602	898,078	-292	897,786	112,018	36,014	821,782	233,481	358,339	10,081	140,228	44,214
1986	1,435,230	891,567	-411	891,156	114,608	44,881	821,429	234,113	379,688	10,414	137,822	43,044
1987	1,456,997	904,411	-346	904,065	117,441	54,300	840,924	232,743	383,330	10,895	133,725	42,517
1988	1,508,174	935,945	-553	935,392	124,628	52,275	863,039	243,203	401,932	11,623	129,757	42,630
1989	1,576,343	947,074	274	947,348	129,105	61,481	879,724	272,542	424,077	12,525	125,854	42,806
1990	1,660,955	999,938	-85	999,853	138,156	77,410	939,107	271,781	450,067	13,321	124,685	43,965
1991	1,760,947	1,051,909	-406	1,051,503	150,790	79,187	979,900	276,851	504,196	14,092	124,959	44,633
1992	1,876,856	1,102,439	53	1,102,492	160,399	86,615	1,028,708	277,892	570,256	14,988	125,222	45,282
1993	1,953,246	1,164,225	-51	1,164,174	176,515	71,720	1,059,379	284,827	609,040	15,460	126,345	46,344
1994	2,062,834	1,238,017	-316	1,237,701	187,441	83,783	1,134,043	299,987	628,804	16,297	126,577	48,415
1995	2,174,865	1,328,563	-576	1,327,987	205,287	86,784	1,209,484	322,119	643,262	17,048	127,571	50,747
1996	2,283,279	1,395,874	-958	1,394,916	215,541	89,233	1,268,608	341,599	673,072	17,779	128,425	52,378
1997	2,370,568	1,448,644	-635	1,448,009	220,495	93,488	1,321,002	363,773	685,793	18,480	128,275	53,304
1998	2,485,605	1,510,657	-918	1,509,739	232,056	96,255	1,373,938	388,513	723,154	19,435	127,892	54,738
1999	2,519,780	1,548,040	-1,396	1,546,644	236,780	99,259	1,409,123	380,789	729,868	19,774	127,431	54,517
2000	2,615,302	1,593,164	-978	1,592,186	250,319	107,705	1,449,572	410,115	755,615	20,670	126,525	54,316
2001	2,758,660	1,687,699	-1,087	1,686,612	251,839	99,358	1,534,131	413,474	811,055	22,013	125,318	54,816
2002	2,877,638	1,743,838	-1,842	1,741,996	249,915	91,296	1,583,377	407,006	887,255	22,898	125,672	54,863
2003	2,904,937	1,755,483	-1,956	1,753,527	256,124	76,875	1,574,278	392,318	938,341	23,143	125,519	54,028
2004	3,005,936	1,881,847	-1,462	1,880,385	268,110	67,702	1,679,977	391,333	934,626	24,020	125,145	55,255
2005	3,103,252	2,009,227	-1,962	2,007,265	284,837	53,450	1,775,878	379,610	947,764	24,912	124,570	56,220
2006	3,323,515	2,151,748	-2,033	2,149,715	289,426	45,372	1,905,661	407,639	1,010,215	26,721	124,378	57,354
2007	3,457,889	2,172,874	-2,696	2,170,178	281,811	37,289	1,925,656	465,924	1,066,309	27,759	124,566	57,737
2008	3,733,994	2,345,750	-2,184	2,343,566	287,794	23,187	2,078,959	498,449	1,156,586	29,980	124,550	58,096
2009	3,777,166	2,308,130	-2,292	2,305,838	292,101	7,420	2,021,157	525,808	1,230,201	30,262	124,816	56,653
2010	3,861,972	2,435,600	-2,179	2,433,421	306,123	-6,634	2,120,664	464,290	1,277,018	30,920	124,902	56,768
2011	4,164,708	2,656,576	-1,629	2,654,947	293,496	1,930	2,363,381	521,242	1,280,085	33,268	125,187	58,044
2012	4,392,406	2,790,160	-1,445	2,788,715	300,586	-7,177	2,480,952	597,175	1,314,279	35,134	125,020	58,187
2013	4,169,994	2,653,150	-1,122	2,652,028	324,561	-21,076	2,306,391	540,957	1,322,646	33,576	124,196	56,875
2014	4,198,863	2,589,739	-1,441	2,588,298	324,770	-12,517	2,251,011	558,756	1,389,096	34,034	123,373	56,318

Personal Income and Employment by Area: Bellingham, WA

(Thousands of dollars, except as noted.)

Year	Personal income, total	Earnings by place of work			Less: Contributions for government social insurance	Plus: Adjustment for residence	Equals: Net earnings by place of residence	Plus: Dividends, interest, and rent	Plus: Personal current transfer receipts	Per capita personal income (dollars)	Population (persons)	Total employment
		Nonfarm	Farm	Total								
1970	319,460	237,137	15,801	252,938	19,139	-310	233,489	52,223	33,748	3,867	82,606	34,551
1971	367,072	279,076	17,662	296,738	23,859	-2,188	270,691	57,692	38,689	4,284	85,688	37,206
1972	387,039	288,131	20,011	308,142	25,342	-1,104	281,696	61,943	43,400	4,327	89,443	36,628
1973	431,945	319,354	24,205	343,559	32,310	-346	310,903	71,217	49,825	4,815	89,700	38,054
1974	487,588	356,970	25,038	382,008	37,079	-848	344,081	82,675	60,832	5,356	91,043	39,342
1975	553,652	403,597	25,466	429,063	41,778	-1,765	385,520	92,998	75,134	5,932	93,332	41,368
1976	631,524	465,339	32,419	497,758	48,448	-1,386	447,924	103,549	80,051	6,574	96,070	44,257
1977	698,873	523,375	29,485	552,860	55,259	-2,959	494,642	120,608	83,623	7,099	98,453	46,132
1978	794,625	605,190	26,584	631,774	65,007	-3,378	563,389	140,656	90,580	7,830	101,482	48,497
1979	903,991	685,358	32,817	718,175	76,119	-4,097	637,959	163,253	102,779	8,661	104,380	50,544
1980	987,260	723,836	24,518	748,354	80,749	-2,887	664,718	196,364	126,178	9,208	107,222	50,074
1981	1,072,021	752,898	28,200	781,098	91,221	46	689,923	237,942	144,156	9,826	109,096	50,010
1982	1,122,299	774,372	26,531	800,903	96,332	952	705,523	256,682	160,094	10,213	109,885	49,658
1983	1,227,721	832,254	36,157	868,411	103,961	2,041	766,491	285,231	175,999	11,098	110,630	51,784
1984	1,314,660	881,648	35,699	917,347	113,542	2,926	806,731	320,429	187,500	11,812	111,294	52,881
1985	1,404,066	933,163	42,527	975,690	120,523	5,456	860,623	342,977	200,466	12,487	112,441	53,901
1986	1,511,275	1,014,299	53,521	1,067,820	131,482	6,430	942,768	357,184	211,323	13,343	113,262	56,022
1987	1,613,065	1,092,534	60,023	1,152,557	142,081	5,642	1,016,118	373,103	223,844	13,983	115,361	58,864
1988	1,746,281	1,186,973	57,470	1,244,443	157,060	11,114	1,098,497	406,972	240,812	14,674	119,002	62,798
1989	1,972,301	1,344,659	66,655	1,411,314	178,573	14,247	1,246,988	467,378	257,935	15,997	123,294	67,307
1990	2,256,618	1,593,753	75,914	1,669,667	213,532	14,184	1,470,319	501,005	285,294	17,478	129,111	73,036
1991	2,445,492	1,704,471	69,168	1,773,639	231,294	21,924	1,564,269	555,155	326,068	18,274	133,823	74,567
1992	2,597,760	1,818,303	89,406	1,907,709	246,567	29,447	1,690,589	552,190	354,981	18,695	138,957	77,046
1993	2,707,268	1,895,449	76,300	1,971,749	259,140	35,291	1,747,900	577,027	382,341	18,844	143,669	78,697
1994	2,891,158	2,017,116	75,184	2,092,300	277,227	41,487	1,856,560	622,142	412,456	19,589	147,593	82,327
1995	3,056,007	2,119,674	67,442	2,187,116	290,767	50,130	1,946,479	660,050	449,478	20,189	151,369	83,655
1996	3,306,261	2,245,410	95,281	2,340,691	300,370	57,577	2,097,898	729,750	478,613	21,312	155,134	86,113
1997	3,495,087	2,367,972	77,362	2,445,334	303,396	71,339	2,213,277	777,513	504,297	22,102	158,133	88,181
1998	3,770,945	2,525,535	104,979	2,630,514	320,375	86,394	2,396,533	844,359	530,053	23,424	160,988	89,489
1999	3,963,398	2,649,749	108,236	2,757,985	327,997	105,614	2,535,602	852,095	575,701	24,084	164,566	91,502
2000	4,194,977	2,760,670	89,499	2,850,169	347,099	123,027	2,626,097	938,629	630,251	25,015	167,696	93,366
2001	4,483,837	2,966,071	109,552	3,075,623	371,434	123,965	2,828,154	938,270	717,413	26,195	171,172	93,656
2002	4,602,032	3,150,045	91,117	3,241,162	391,712	122,439	2,971,889	872,814	757,329	26,312	174,904	95,976
2003	4,982,877	3,398,011	116,597	3,514,608	422,958	125,952	3,217,602	962,318	802,957	28,017	177,851	98,620
2004	5,351,537	3,651,961	124,756	3,776,717	457,166	131,118	3,450,669	1,065,449	835,419	29,444	181,756	102,454
2005	5,690,732	3,952,604	123,606	4,076,210	503,613	138,166	3,710,763	1,097,096	882,873	30,686	185,450	107,143
2006	6,152,396	4,203,671	86,694	4,290,365	527,303	142,989	3,906,051	1,296,086	950,259	32,565	188,926	109,678
2007	6,770,438	4,448,228	109,271	4,557,499	556,363	151,134	4,152,270	1,585,000	1,033,168	35,110	192,837	113,887
2008	7,204,198	4,602,421	78,070	4,680,491	576,143	155,006	4,259,354	1,745,025	1,199,819	36,624	196,708	114,709
2009	7,073,008	4,580,225	59,150	4,639,375	584,350	156,797	4,211,822	1,517,144	1,344,042	35,389	199,865	110,456
2010	7,265,303	4,644,512	98,339	4,742,851	596,568	162,971	4,309,254	1,465,067	1,490,982	36,053	201,518	108,543
2011	7,682,270	4,771,025	144,712	4,915,737	562,108	185,025	4,538,654	1,649,697	1,493,919	37,782	203,329	109,692
2012	8,092,042	5,026,196	136,501	5,162,697	579,300	203,778	4,787,175	1,810,009	1,494,858	39,507	204,827	112,257
2013	8,161,636	5,190,922	152,027	5,342,949	666,627	203,634	4,879,956	1,755,756	1,525,924	39,572	206,248	114,288
2014	8,509,074	5,285,074	188,066	5,473,140	678,553	226,984	5,021,571	1,826,337	1,661,166	40,840	208,351	116,419

Personal Income and Employment by Area: Bend-Redmond, OR

(Thousands of dollars, except as noted.)

| Year | Personal income, total | Derivation of personal income | | | | | | | | Per capita personal income (dollars) | Population (persons) | Total employment |
| | | Earnings by place of work | | | Less: Contributions for government social insurance | Plus: Adjustment for residence | Equals: Net earnings by place of residence | Plus: Dividends, interest, and rent | Plus: Personal current transfer receipts | | | |
		Nonfarm	Farm	Total								
1970	123,584	90,820	1,419	92,239	6,623	2,325	87,941	23,314	12,329	4,002	30,882	13,667
1971	142,201	104,850	1,428	106,278	7,921	2,605	100,962	26,842	14,397	4,331	32,835	15,106
1972	167,426	123,803	3,740	127,543	9,891	2,944	120,596	30,395	16,435	4,811	34,804	16,767
1973	194,368	144,312	4,286	148,598	13,282	3,090	138,406	36,062	19,900	5,158	37,682	18,403
1974	219,085	157,486	3,468	160,954	14,878	3,653	149,729	43,669	25,687	5,456	40,155	18,902
1975	254,172	177,362	3,663	181,025	16,127	5,729	170,627	50,127	33,418	5,992	42,422	19,706
1976	306,383	222,139	3,277	225,416	20,214	4,395	209,597	59,056	37,730	6,856	44,686	22,354
1977	366,871	270,166	2,384	272,550	25,185	4,468	251,833	71,392	43,646	7,648	47,969	25,288
1978	441,000	329,904	132	330,036	31,690	4,341	302,687	89,084	49,229	8,266	53,349	28,444
1979	522,652	391,357	894	392,251	39,375	3,581	356,457	107,336	58,859	8,942	58,452	30,620
1980	570,462	403,841	1,159	405,000	40,276	4,215	368,939	127,840	73,683	9,147	62,365	30,066
1981	614,562	407,797	1,658	409,455	43,436	6,110	372,129	153,959	88,474	9,735	63,130	29,334
1982	634,464	401,095	901	401,996	43,503	6,744	365,237	166,423	102,804	10,066	63,031	27,771
1983	700,818	447,900	6,098	453,998	49,112	7,815	412,701	178,819	109,298	11,210	62,516	29,659
1984	783,073	509,320	6,702	516,022	57,380	9,030	467,672	200,209	115,192	12,266	63,839	31,566
1985	847,603	556,516	5,061	561,577	63,842	10,413	508,148	215,241	124,214	13,048	64,959	33,037
1986	905,976	597,152	1,660	598,812	68,210	12,472	543,074	234,984	127,918	13,694	66,160	34,685
1987	971,380	644,691	373	645,064	72,643	14,396	586,817	252,038	132,525	14,528	66,862	35,621
1988	1,083,544	729,868	2,340	732,208	85,024	17,340	664,524	273,182	145,838	15,730	68,882	38,234
1989	1,221,548	797,469	3,178	800,647	95,285	18,900	724,262	336,685	160,601	17,105	71,415	41,660
1990	1,387,554	942,117	1,483	943,600	114,548	18,011	847,063	365,421	175,070	18,245	76,053	45,455
1991	1,533,947	1,054,408	743	1,055,151	128,482	18,228	944,897	391,031	198,019	19,066	80,456	46,995
1992	1,674,820	1,147,649	-1,148	1,146,501	137,688	24,281	1,033,094	416,117	225,609	19,891	84,199	48,397
1993	1,844,226	1,267,231	-2,400	1,264,831	150,783	23,402	1,137,450	463,120	243,656	20,943	88,061	51,071
1994	1,979,324	1,362,959	-2,878	1,360,081	164,055	25,537	1,221,563	495,565	262,196	21,657	91,393	54,760
1995	2,147,140	1,430,911	-2,694	1,428,217	174,057	26,027	1,280,187	571,899	295,054	22,485	95,491	57,626
1996	2,350,276	1,559,874	-2,979	1,556,895	190,652	27,030	1,393,273	635,331	321,672	23,654	99,362	60,831
1997	2,515,523	1,658,888	-2,219	1,656,669	201,419	27,814	1,483,064	688,407	344,052	24,522	102,581	64,237
1998	2,777,539	1,823,361	187	1,823,548	219,253	27,870	1,632,165	784,748	360,626	26,002	106,820	66,568
1999	2,988,225	2,021,545	-4,353	2,017,192	240,429	26,604	1,803,367	781,729	403,129	26,697	111,933	70,484
2000	3,301,352	2,249,806	-5,968	2,243,838	266,098	26,406	2,004,146	863,676	433,530	28,322	116,566	74,674
2001	3,516,101	2,399,589	-4,569	2,395,020	278,780	23,474	2,139,714	877,073	499,314	29,173	120,526	77,172
2002	3,693,754	2,578,841	-4,708	2,574,133	299,310	21,253	2,296,076	846,078	551,600	29,492	125,247	78,672
2003	3,935,473	2,766,350	-3,043	2,763,307	323,575	19,716	2,459,448	895,689	580,336	30,485	129,094	80,901
2004	4,311,036	3,042,001	1,268	3,043,269	362,719	18,444	2,698,994	1,012,052	599,990	32,231	133,756	86,166
2005	4,714,503	3,339,972	-3,747	3,336,225	408,869	16,737	2,944,093	1,115,555	654,855	33,539	140,567	92,162
2006	5,369,287	3,772,646	-5,178	3,767,468	462,381	14,786	3,319,873	1,331,716	717,698	36,242	148,149	98,206
2007	5,670,756	3,869,303	-11,295	3,858,008	480,814	11,188	3,388,382	1,490,855	791,519	37,153	152,633	101,576
2008	6,029,162	3,891,635	-15,127	3,876,508	475,965	6,564	3,407,107	1,643,507	978,548	38,446	156,820	99,343
2009	5,655,432	3,567,117	-14,024	3,553,093	440,357	9,073	3,121,809	1,359,876	1,173,747	35,943	157,345	92,688
2010	5,695,970	3,509,225	-13,802	3,495,423	440,356	15,366	3,070,433	1,339,002	1,286,535	36,090	157,828	90,930
2011	6,015,853	3,580,403	-11,625	3,568,778	406,352	24,772	3,187,198	1,509,602	1,319,053	37,649	159,786	92,313
2012	6,313,477	3,745,819	-2,667	3,743,152	423,918	45,677	3,364,911	1,622,073	1,326,493	39,033	161,746	93,864
2013	6,636,813	3,980,605	-6,616	3,973,989	509,428	41,508	3,506,069	1,736,291	1,394,453	39,992	165,955	98,264
2014	7,100,843	4,300,939	103	4,301,042	558,527	28,576	3,771,091	1,810,289	1,519,463	41,675	170,388	103,090

Personal Income and Employment by Area: Billings, MT

(Thousands of dollars, except as noted.)

Year	Personal income, total	Earnings by place of work			Less: Contributions for government social insurance	Plus: Adjustment for residence	Equals: Net earnings by place of residence	Plus: Dividends, interest, and rent	Plus: Personal current transfer receipts	Per capita personal income (dollars)	Population (persons)	Total employment
		Nonfarm	Farm	Total								
1970	373,718	279,227	21,119	300,346	21,611	-584	278,151	64,697	30,870	3,901	95,810	43,329
1971	412,852	311,585	19,473	331,058	24,478	-420	306,160	70,525	36,167	4,202	98,257	44,885
1972	475,197	352,401	33,796	386,197	29,206	-408	356,583	78,037	40,577	4,740	100,254	47,205
1973	526,952	394,863	32,842	427,705	37,863	-561	389,281	90,216	47,455	5,167	101,991	50,349
1974	599,120	451,488	29,474	480,962	44,203	-437	436,322	106,539	56,259	5,695	105,198	52,867
1975	671,720	510,273	13,919	524,192	48,184	1,850	477,858	125,139	68,723	6,240	107,654	53,779
1976	755,613	595,120	4,887	600,007	57,135	935	543,807	136,433	75,373	6,846	110,368	57,467
1977	858,865	683,743	3,628	687,371	66,290	1,308	622,389	154,855	81,621	7,616	112,764	60,302
1978	980,646	782,888	8,724	791,612	78,780	1,336	714,168	175,778	90,700	8,434	116,271	64,090
1979	1,093,823	878,530	3,293	881,823	92,405	1,006	790,424	201,909	101,490	9,318	117,391	65,442
1980	1,211,931	932,653	5,962	938,615	99,612	10,771	849,774	241,188	120,969	10,294	117,733	64,651
1981	1,373,633	1,033,929	3,939	1,037,868	118,482	8,062	927,448	306,866	139,319	11,481	119,645	66,183
1982	1,490,316	1,100,805	4,625	1,105,430	129,309	7,943	984,064	349,022	157,230	12,168	122,475	67,078
1983	1,583,298	1,170,710	5,439	1,176,149	137,993	4,801	1,042,957	365,183	175,158	12,602	125,635	68,542
1984	1,702,197	1,245,926	9,641	1,255,567	151,242	-945	1,103,380	409,318	189,499	13,267	128,301	70,868
1985	1,756,006	1,276,814	10,451	1,287,265	157,990	-1,839	1,127,436	426,161	202,409	13,613	128,999	70,516
1986	1,759,965	1,273,705	10,786	1,284,491	160,248	-2,253	1,121,990	420,523	217,452	13,745	128,041	69,709
1987	1,796,329	1,282,952	20,444	1,303,396	159,795	45	1,143,646	421,791	230,892	14,296	125,649	69,468
1988	1,859,136	1,339,174	18,826	1,358,000	174,570	1,287	1,184,717	425,794	248,625	15,044	123,581	71,737
1989	2,015,267	1,418,948	23,378	1,442,326	186,024	3,072	1,259,374	483,071	272,822	16,416	122,761	73,107
1990	2,114,749	1,504,906	22,084	1,526,990	209,624	4,833	1,322,199	488,959	303,591	17,257	122,545	73,868
1991	2,259,540	1,638,694	28,195	1,666,889	232,246	5,822	1,440,465	499,044	320,031	18,179	124,295	75,939
1992	2,416,214	1,770,368	33,817	1,804,185	252,659	2,641	1,554,167	517,956	344,091	18,941	127,568	78,363
1993	2,564,778	1,907,071	37,464	1,944,535	278,603	1,393	1,667,325	525,081	372,372	19,617	130,744	80,093
1994	2,708,134	2,017,478	25,776	2,043,254	295,284	1,633	1,749,603	566,103	392,428	20,325	133,239	83,702
1995	2,854,431	2,089,778	13,238	2,103,016	298,041	1,756	1,806,731	628,142	419,558	21,094	135,318	84,768
1996	2,977,570	2,168,644	14,053	2,182,697	296,115	1,217	1,887,799	655,840	433,931	21,763	136,818	87,037
1997	3,123,307	2,262,966	10,961	2,273,927	299,257	1,441	1,976,111	702,243	444,953	22,686	137,674	87,651
1998	3,348,954	2,426,454	13,653	2,440,107	310,902	2,525	2,131,730	754,256	462,968	24,257	138,062	90,397
1999	3,462,220	2,558,678	16,744	2,575,422	322,881	6,547	2,259,088	744,248	458,884	24,851	139,319	91,771
2000	3,705,499	2,719,420	15,214	2,734,634	341,218	12,942	2,406,358	787,926	511,215	26,440	140,150	93,485
2001	3,931,071	2,911,638	26,888	2,938,526	371,565	9,630	2,576,591	798,049	556,431	27,790	141,458	94,679
2002	4,027,198	3,054,283	10,026	3,064,309	397,150	3,169	2,670,328	783,173	573,697	28,184	142,891	95,850
2003	4,203,118	3,177,158	24,000	3,201,158	413,080	-2,942	2,785,136	820,051	597,931	29,099	144,443	96,881
2004	4,507,605	3,376,306	43,421	3,419,727	440,217	-7,726	2,971,784	889,222	646,599	30,824	146,238	99,512
2005	4,819,403	3,648,767	38,560	3,687,327	478,680	-14,975	3,193,672	934,777	690,954	32,441	148,558	102,016
2006	5,214,118	3,927,103	2,582	3,929,685	513,010	-19,924	3,396,751	1,058,942	758,425	34,652	150,471	104,041
2007	5,597,901	4,189,365	6,015	4,195,380	559,892	-28,527	3,606,961	1,176,783	814,157	36,718	152,455	107,877
2008	5,965,932	4,350,411	9,816	4,360,227	572,745	-36,710	3,750,772	1,288,469	926,691	38,463	155,110	107,951
2009	5,709,215	4,204,110	4,031	4,208,141	562,308	-24,719	3,621,114	1,101,936	986,165	36,273	157,395	105,745
2010	5,966,558	4,320,861	11,087	4,331,948	572,532	-15,289	3,744,127	1,135,427	1,087,004	37,446	159,338	104,886
2011	6,417,601	4,606,465	26,076	4,632,541	547,163	-4,743	4,080,635	1,262,932	1,074,034	39,920	160,761	106,200
2012	6,918,228	4,871,810	29,635	4,901,445	568,066	17,008	4,350,387	1,460,120	1,107,721	42,485	162,839	108,056
2013	6,818,366	4,948,869	39,183	4,988,052	652,305	38,135	4,373,882	1,316,922	1,127,562	41,268	165,222	108,303
2014	7,110,250	5,152,292	51,082	5,203,374	681,004	39,735	4,562,105	1,371,620	1,176,525	42,606	166,885	109,441

Personal Income and Employment by Area: Binghamton, NY

(Thousands of dollars, except as noted.)

Year	Personal income, total	Earnings by place of work			Less: Contributions for government social insurance	Plus: Adjustment for residence	Equals: Net earnings by place of residence	Plus: Dividends, interest, and rent	Plus: Personal current transfer receipts	Per capita personal income (dollars)	Population (persons)	Total employment
		Nonfarm	Farm	Total								
1970	1,097,994	953,304	8,644	961,948	71,901	-32,676	857,371	136,228	104,395	4,084	268,851	117,119
1971	1,171,497	1,001,693	8,709	1,010,402	78,160	-36,152	896,090	146,763	128,644	4,327	270,746	116,349
1972	1,237,846	1,060,220	8,840	1,069,060	87,343	-36,752	944,965	158,225	134,656	4,627	267,509	117,444
1973	1,332,154	1,142,418	10,063	1,152,481	108,690	-37,722	1,006,069	173,999	152,086	4,980	267,518	120,927
1974	1,440,060	1,217,612	7,005	1,224,617	119,004	-38,475	1,067,138	195,569	177,353	5,421	265,630	121,541
1975	1,580,788	1,299,177	6,632	1,305,809	124,685	-44,965	1,136,159	214,674	229,955	5,884	268,656	119,091
1976	1,690,030	1,396,017	8,396	1,404,413	137,684	-49,284	1,217,445	228,263	244,322	6,281	269,063	120,675
1977	1,844,248	1,537,013	4,869	1,541,882	151,332	-59,898	1,330,652	253,532	260,064	6,864	268,668	124,414
1978	2,026,625	1,708,578	7,722	1,716,300	172,170	-68,242	1,475,888	270,918	279,819	7,570	267,705	128,940
1979	2,223,364	1,875,723	9,421	1,885,144	194,532	-77,045	1,613,567	307,427	302,370	8,328	266,989	130,555
1980	2,450,295	2,025,532	9,728	2,035,260	209,227	-86,011	1,740,022	364,795	345,478	9,294	263,639	129,633
1981	2,725,535	2,216,011	7,811	2,223,822	243,390	-97,142	1,883,290	447,165	395,080	10,330	263,859	129,925
1982	3,000,764	2,400,644	14,097	2,414,741	266,749	-110,723	2,037,269	519,739	443,756	11,366	264,005	129,662
1983	3,210,935	2,557,513	7,900	2,565,413	287,485	-113,933	2,163,995	571,814	475,126	12,187	263,473	128,801
1984	3,571,002	2,859,547	8,857	2,868,404	328,436	-125,327	2,414,641	662,312	494,049	13,569	263,182	135,188
1985	3,781,218	3,068,180	9,830	3,078,010	355,797	-136,874	2,585,339	678,494	517,385	14,284	264,719	139,580
1986	3,952,926	3,181,245	10,358	3,191,603	375,398	-133,464	2,682,741	718,519	551,666	14,993	263,651	140,401
1987	4,165,680	3,386,890	10,639	3,397,529	390,613	-136,924	2,869,992	732,130	563,558	15,883	262,266	140,900
1988	4,418,807	3,601,883	7,672	3,609,555	424,416	-138,747	3,046,392	774,619	597,796	16,751	263,797	145,553
1989	4,747,530	3,759,828	12,087	3,771,915	437,574	-135,718	3,198,623	901,554	647,353	17,957	264,388	143,469
1990	4,918,478	3,847,721	13,620	3,861,341	429,027	-137,509	3,294,805	919,131	704,542	18,579	264,731	142,457
1991	5,079,172	3,968,840	9,602	3,978,442	452,179	-142,188	3,384,075	926,556	768,541	19,121	265,632	139,936
1992	5,273,418	4,078,476	13,779	4,092,255	457,065	-149,147	3,486,043	923,772	863,603	19,782	266,571	138,396
1993	5,258,423	4,075,871	14,745	4,090,616	463,676	-153,298	3,473,642	869,498	915,283	19,769	265,993	137,687
1994	5,297,989	4,056,916	13,015	4,069,931	464,806	-146,052	3,459,073	885,310	953,606	20,062	264,082	136,661
1995	5,423,480	4,086,608	9,727	4,096,335	463,522	-145,632	3,487,181	932,798	1,003,501	20,853	260,079	134,001
1996	5,575,222	4,173,662	16,315	4,189,977	465,062	-139,759	3,585,156	947,964	1,042,102	21,719	256,702	132,577
1997	5,777,112	4,338,280	5,366	4,343,646	479,294	-135,976	3,728,376	1,011,414	1,037,322	22,725	254,213	134,726
1998	5,857,142	4,393,752	8,907	4,402,659	486,556	-141,959	3,774,144	1,005,711	1,077,287	23,129	253,235	134,290
1999	6,104,765	4,661,488	6,475	4,667,963	505,577	-153,190	4,009,196	990,211	1,105,358	24,151	252,773	137,801
2000	6,438,117	4,977,641	4,297	4,981,938	539,674	-172,656	4,269,608	1,034,561	1,133,948	25,529	252,189	140,731
2001	6,573,630	5,052,667	4,485	5,057,152	559,793	-160,058	4,337,301	1,020,769	1,215,560	26,026	252,580	138,783
2002	6,608,392	5,058,375	271	5,058,646	565,674	-171,888	4,321,084	967,067	1,320,241	26,076	253,430	135,871
2003	6,654,057	5,030,779	6,918	5,037,697	560,319	-162,152	4,315,226	973,012	1,365,819	26,308	252,932	134,677
2004	6,985,287	5,182,593	15,234	5,197,827	575,278	-139,325	4,483,224	1,070,304	1,431,759	27,653	252,605	135,281
2005	7,131,050	5,372,440	19,109	5,391,549	603,656	-129,401	4,658,492	975,347	1,497,211	28,288	252,088	135,538
2006	7,580,958	5,694,618	17,277	5,711,895	632,330	-100,192	4,979,373	1,007,784	1,593,801	30,031	252,441	136,798
2007	8,036,539	5,933,882	15,987	5,949,869	655,048	-91,321	5,203,500	1,148,183	1,684,856	31,835	252,442	138,905
2008	8,542,846	6,201,628	12,221	6,213,849	690,870	-88,666	5,434,313	1,232,862	1,875,671	33,829	252,527	138,507
2009	8,637,061	6,159,940	5,069	6,165,009	681,898	-100,409	5,382,702	1,168,753	2,085,606	34,251	252,171	134,609
2010	8,784,474	6,179,598	10,188	6,189,786	689,282	-62,475	5,438,029	1,122,438	2,224,007	34,933	251,469	132,879
2011	9,059,405	6,234,896	17,087	6,251,983	629,528	-33,057	5,589,398	1,221,166	2,248,841	36,201	250,251	132,260
2012	9,280,955	6,295,746	11,848	6,307,594	630,072	7,920	5,685,442	1,357,300	2,238,213	37,272	249,005	131,530
2013	9,274,074	6,331,510	19,747	6,351,257	712,935	45,335	5,683,657	1,326,516	2,263,901	37,341	248,362	129,982
2014	9,406,696	6,404,042	20,815	6,424,857	727,066	47,717	5,745,508	1,372,350	2,288,838	38,050	247,219	129,471

Personal Income and Employment by Area: Birmingham-Hoover, AL

(Thousands of dollars, except as noted.)

Year	Personal income, total	Derivation of personal income									Per capita personal income (dollars)	Population (persons)	Total employment
		Earnings by place of work			Less: Contributions for government social insurance	Plus: Adjustment for residence	Equals: Net earnings by place of residence	Plus: Dividends, interest, and rent	Plus: Personal current transfer receipts				
		Nonfarm	Farm	Total									
1970	2,846,114	2,382,825	17,346	2,400,171	173,738	-8,205	2,218,228	336,909	290,977		3,411	834,280	356,195
1971	3,124,980	2,592,585	19,381	2,611,966	192,855	-18,701	2,400,410	373,207	351,363		3,696	845,548	360,430
1972	3,475,298	2,907,007	25,868	2,932,875	227,028	-33,777	2,672,070	406,513	396,715		4,076	852,711	373,689
1973	3,908,058	3,264,298	43,422	3,307,720	294,270	-39,654	2,973,796	455,699	478,563		4,523	864,085	388,783
1974	4,400,207	3,686,015	18,811	3,704,826	342,915	-44,824	3,317,087	530,973	552,147		5,056	870,341	398,688
1975	4,935,346	4,028,260	36,095	4,064,355	369,784	-46,999	3,647,572	594,580	693,194		5,588	883,172	399,287
1976	5,480,190	4,496,913	36,100	4,533,013	421,303	-43,083	4,068,627	640,911	770,652		6,119	895,598	407,393
1977	6,050,140	5,007,915	40,289	5,048,204	470,235	-43,792	4,534,177	707,836	808,127		6,658	908,642	421,750
1978	6,801,735	5,669,969	35,593	5,705,562	542,754	-42,623	5,120,185	798,548	883,002		7,399	919,252	435,995
1979	7,605,957	6,295,409	42,940	6,338,349	624,297	-42,937	5,671,115	909,271	1,025,571		8,199	927,712	445,633
1980	8,360,350	6,714,567	28,813	6,743,380	664,144	-36,015	6,043,221	1,113,065	1,204,064		8,983	930,680	438,371
1981	9,083,094	7,127,190	29,113	7,156,303	761,085	-50,070	6,345,148	1,395,061	1,342,885		9,764	930,227	430,843
1982	9,611,093	7,395,663	33,312	7,428,975	805,117	-50,931	6,572,927	1,570,694	1,467,472		10,377	926,197	423,068
1983	10,209,031	7,847,560	28,481	7,876,041	862,930	-59,056	6,954,055	1,670,943	1,584,033		11,012	927,062	425,578
1984	11,206,269	8,636,067	36,137	8,672,204	967,766	-58,091	7,646,347	1,891,785	1,668,137		12,032	931,399	442,199
1985	12,116,967	9,396,673	40,217	9,436,890	1,061,632	-67,708	8,307,550	2,080,885	1,728,532		12,933	936,926	457,464
1986	12,810,941	10,003,942	25,798	10,029,740	1,130,344	-76,092	8,823,304	2,199,218	1,788,419		13,607	941,503	471,914
1987	13,588,190	10,645,292	37,999	10,683,291	1,188,957	-89,684	9,404,650	2,352,069	1,831,471		14,326	948,471	485,505
1988	14,739,154	11,554,379	62,445	11,616,824	1,327,582	-113,403	10,175,839	2,675,448	1,887,867		15,498	951,042	500,481
1989	16,084,105	12,274,861	88,893	12,363,754	1,408,124	-121,219	10,834,411	3,129,712	2,119,982		16,852	954,416	507,055
1990	17,237,312	13,215,920	86,432	13,302,352	1,532,422	-129,268	11,640,662	3,285,421	2,311,229		17,980	958,709	518,079
1991	18,099,433	13,848,008	109,684	13,957,692	1,617,462	-137,398	12,202,832	3,374,119	2,522,482		18,669	969,491	519,983
1992	19,385,664	14,903,847	96,330	15,000,177	1,717,648	-150,969	13,131,560	3,404,540	2,849,564		19,781	980,037	528,501
1993	20,298,587	15,546,273	111,156	15,657,429	1,809,071	-146,366	13,701,992	3,597,659	2,998,936		20,465	991,884	542,304
1994	21,660,040	16,521,202	84,611	16,605,813	1,947,552	-153,729	14,504,532	3,986,882	3,168,626		21,591	1,003,186	549,975
1995	23,141,590	17,552,237	83,420	17,635,657	2,080,193	-162,409	15,393,055	4,333,688	3,414,847		22,830	1,013,634	566,345
1996	24,366,079	18,620,955	76,686	18,697,641	2,182,000	-174,609	16,341,032	4,431,443	3,593,604		23,831	1,022,434	578,023
1997	25,737,145	19,488,504	88,902	19,577,406	2,287,542	-179,651	17,110,213	4,897,861	3,729,071		24,977	1,030,425	590,779
1998	27,641,004	21,129,189	107,953	21,237,142	2,417,057	-182,019	18,638,066	5,277,212	3,725,726		26,590	1,039,523	603,670
1999	28,985,241	22,566,973	94,327	22,661,300	2,557,770	-196,124	19,907,406	5,213,242	3,864,593		27,672	1,047,440	612,593
2000	31,213,441	24,253,239	65,470	24,318,709	2,685,104	-212,033	21,421,572	5,685,486	4,106,383		29,634	1,053,306	619,397
2001	32,334,651	25,178,255	104,870	25,283,125	2,784,934	-231,223	22,266,968	5,724,330	4,343,353		30,531	1,059,082	622,286
2002	33,300,719	26,226,509	73,639	26,300,148	2,895,606	-381,258	23,023,284	5,625,249	4,652,186		31,328	1,062,966	621,560
2003	34,449,370	26,906,612	99,728	27,006,340	2,979,867	-433,527	23,592,946	5,930,198	4,926,226		32,169	1,070,886	621,316
2004	37,156,136	28,514,740	118,975	28,633,715	3,118,017	-453,812	25,061,886	6,908,353	5,185,897		34,461	1,078,204	635,429
2005	39,476,744	29,873,489	99,246	29,972,735	3,279,228	-185,817	26,507,690	7,425,088	5,543,966		36,340	1,086,318	650,376
2006	42,081,657	31,458,642	45,217	31,503,859	3,444,860	-106,166	27,952,833	8,130,038	5,998,786		38,297	1,098,818	663,732
2007	43,841,425	32,425,829	33,899	32,459,728	3,610,118	59,447	28,909,057	8,507,999	6,424,369		39,595	1,107,256	678,147
2008	45,236,939	32,921,096	35,777	32,956,873	3,704,166	-20,655	29,232,052	8,763,111	7,241,776		40,495	1,117,101	674,421
2009	43,017,836	31,531,575	51,212	31,582,787	3,557,925	3,139	28,028,001	7,307,191	7,682,644		38,229	1,125,271	645,802
2010	44,413,804	31,717,104	45,433	31,762,537	3,610,393	77,451	28,229,595	7,769,742	8,414,467		39,338	1,129,034	636,261
2011	46,406,160	33,198,137	8,392	33,206,529	3,324,230	51,521	29,933,820	7,752,393	8,719,947		41,031	1,131,010	644,358
2012	48,594,518	34,745,405	31,191	34,776,596	3,466,029	19,799	31,330,366	8,509,768	8,754,384		42,841	1,134,297	655,605
2013	48,405,157	35,064,946	111,466	35,176,412	3,999,327	-8,086	31,168,999	8,271,790	8,964,368		42,477	1,139,556	662,082
2014	50,618,572	36,710,988	94,378	36,805,366	4,137,499	33,120	32,700,987	8,586,617	9,330,968		44,256	1,143,772	668,144

Personal Income and Employment by Area: Bismarck, ND

(Thousands of dollars, except as noted.)

| Year | Personal income, total | Derivation of personal income | | | | | | | | Per capita personal income (dollars) | Population (persons) | Total employment |
| | | Earnings by place of work | | | Less: Contributions for government social insurance | Plus: Adjustment for residence | Equals: Net earnings by place of residence | Plus: Dividends, interest, and rent | Plus: Personal current transfer receipts | | | |
		Nonfarm	Farm	Total								
1970	236,199	174,811	19,530	194,341	14,005	-1,554	178,782	36,730	20,687	3,519	67,114	30,677
1971	266,630	191,121	26,517	217,638	15,628	-1,299	200,711	41,026	24,893	3,919	68,027	30,842
1972	310,235	215,332	40,442	255,774	18,163	-945	236,666	45,568	28,001	4,493	69,047	31,964
1973	370,203	247,061	63,093	310,154	24,380	-764	285,010	53,207	31,986	5,198	71,215	33,892
1974	403,186	286,604	43,830	330,434	29,821	1,918	302,531	63,422	37,233	5,517	73,082	35,517
1975	456,419	333,227	35,926	369,153	34,764	4,446	338,835	72,591	44,993	6,033	75,660	37,555
1976	508,022	397,852	21,483	419,335	41,802	-219	377,314	80,486	50,222	6,505	78,103	40,157
1977	571,424	447,014	17,503	464,517	44,847	3,986	423,656	92,962	54,806	7,132	80,117	42,079
1978	670,476	500,480	39,405	539,885	51,417	13,125	501,593	108,231	60,652	8,207	81,696	44,053
1979	748,381	573,407	26,722	600,129	61,512	16,597	555,214	124,856	68,311	8,885	84,232	46,483
1980	803,015	631,495	-12,474	619,021	68,504	16,608	567,125	152,492	83,398	9,302	86,328	46,997
1981	942,507	672,935	37,449	710,384	76,741	18,730	652,373	193,623	96,511	10,829	87,039	46,555
1982	1,022,075	714,856	21,043	735,899	82,943	29,899	682,855	232,063	107,157	11,584	88,228	46,654
1983	1,091,309	754,406	15,437	769,843	87,850	55,529	737,522	232,453	121,334	12,131	89,961	47,560
1984	1,137,307	798,002	20,450	818,452	95,770	35,042	757,724	245,233	134,350	12,448	91,367	48,441
1985	1,163,160	825,463	18,564	844,027	102,064	20,767	762,730	256,452	143,978	12,695	91,624	48,697
1986	1,209,332	846,198	34,382	880,580	106,830	14,174	787,924	260,343	161,065	13,232	91,397	48,760
1987	1,258,676	890,631	42,197	932,828	112,261	15,445	836,012	252,979	169,685	13,923	90,400	50,050
1988	1,252,891	937,559	362	937,921	123,486	12,599	827,034	251,969	173,888	13,919	90,011	50,981
1989	1,369,911	993,053	18,557	1,011,610	132,067	11,849	891,392	282,494	196,025	15,223	89,992	52,751
1990	1,455,854	1,065,341	18,746	1,084,087	149,760	11,619	945,946	298,168	211,740	16,157	90,106	54,138
1991	1,511,715	1,129,263	18,326	1,147,589	161,548	9,946	995,987	297,193	218,535	16,630	90,902	55,794
1992	1,656,928	1,223,448	39,129	1,262,577	174,667	10,015	1,097,925	311,478	247,525	17,920	92,461	57,107
1993	1,761,695	1,312,436	38,413	1,350,849	188,640	9,609	1,171,818	327,030	262,847	18,741	94,002	58,940
1994	1,843,083	1,399,233	24,811	1,424,044	203,411	8,956	1,229,589	346,823	266,671	19,402	94,993	61,673
1995	1,935,372	1,471,749	5,617	1,477,366	213,379	10,641	1,274,628	375,663	285,081	20,086	96,355	62,530
1996	2,055,981	1,531,059	23,807	1,554,866	220,012	16,203	1,351,057	401,160	303,764	21,032	97,755	63,482
1997	2,139,266	1,616,447	-12,555	1,603,892	229,792	9,138	1,383,238	433,652	322,376	21,682	98,667	64,878
1998	2,306,557	1,726,527	24,895	1,751,422	243,703	8,124	1,515,843	459,854	330,860	23,119	99,769	66,974
1999	2,393,945	1,817,634	23,973	1,841,607	252,416	9,019	1,598,210	453,969	341,766	23,867	100,303	68,714
2000	2,593,518	1,932,503	52,224	1,984,727	265,971	7,718	1,726,474	492,262	374,782	25,673	101,020	69,693
2001	2,733,152	2,067,995	43,284	2,111,279	275,679	10,064	1,845,664	495,724	391,764	26,984	101,289	70,293
2002	2,811,529	2,188,961	7,864	2,196,825	287,710	6,957	1,916,072	483,747	411,710	27,472	102,340	70,734
2003	3,008,684	2,323,877	47,618	2,371,495	306,783	8,328	2,073,040	506,194	429,450	29,154	103,201	71,736
2004	3,208,401	2,474,533	46,166	2,520,699	323,881	10,307	2,207,125	540,187	461,089	30,788	104,211	73,808
2005	3,385,882	2,581,752	72,280	2,654,032	336,272	15,908	2,333,668	548,444	503,770	31,960	105,942	75,795
2006	3,608,051	2,767,989	25,279	2,793,268	352,995	29,787	2,470,060	610,597	527,394	33,451	107,861	78,145
2007	3,908,922	2,912,104	59,988	2,972,092	368,363	37,211	2,640,940	690,693	577,289	35,619	109,742	80,119
2008	4,206,735	3,058,540	59,764	3,118,304	384,521	44,783	2,778,566	765,509	662,660	37,802	111,282	81,834
2009	4,303,195	3,172,055	56,875	3,228,930	417,086	60,792	2,872,636	738,166	692,393	38,033	113,143	82,701
2010	4,647,750	3,391,403	74,091	3,465,494	422,991	59,889	3,102,392	783,544	761,814	40,333	115,233	83,424
2011	5,138,015	3,668,633	77,117	3,745,750	423,305	69,365	3,391,810	956,695	789,510	43,768	117,393	85,704
2012	5,753,913	4,027,206	194,331	4,221,537	431,963	87,459	3,877,033	1,074,653	802,227	47,832	120,293	89,008
2013	6,004,675	4,353,356	93,020	4,446,376	533,026	98,572	4,011,922	1,162,071	830,682	48,428	123,993	92,034
2014	6,351,812	4,702,126	35,254	4,737,380	576,349	110,657	4,271,688	1,207,005	873,119	50,173	126,597	94,003

Personal Income and Employment by Area: Blacksburg-Christiansburg-Radford, VA

(Thousands of dollars, except as noted.)

Year	Personal income, total	Earnings by place of work			Less: Contributions for government social insurance	Plus: Adjustment for residence	Equals: Net earnings by place of residence	Plus: Dividends, interest, and rent	Plus: Personal current transfer receipts	Per capita personal income (dollars)	Population (persons)	Total employment
		Nonfarm	Farm	Total								
1970	334,831	292,238	3,517	295,755	18,674	-9,780	267,301	37,534	29,996	2,910	115,045	49,602
1971	358,689	305,181	3,480	308,661	20,368	-7,416	280,877	41,864	35,948	3,039	118,015	49,332
1972	404,165	343,920	5,497	349,417	24,187	-7,825	317,405	46,403	40,357	3,340	120,995	51,367
1973	461,227	390,666	5,989	396,655	31,566	-6,607	358,482	53,426	49,319	3,701	124,637	54,208
1974	511,085	425,476	3,673	429,149	35,812	-4,115	389,222	62,496	59,367	3,950	129,374	55,589
1975	564,135	447,599	2,466	450,065	36,957	-880	412,228	71,757	80,150	4,255	132,569	54,664
1976	628,609	499,850	4,474	504,324	41,894	156	462,586	78,053	87,970	4,678	134,388	56,066
1977	704,779	567,626	3,143	570,769	47,710	-64	522,995	88,410	93,374	5,140	137,116	58,455
1978	805,071	649,204	5,140	654,344	55,965	576	598,955	102,843	103,273	5,752	139,973	61,737
1979	902,024	718,924	7,963	726,887	64,393	-518	661,976	119,468	120,580	6,381	141,368	63,660
1980	1,011,339	777,708	7,021	784,729	70,302	3,443	717,870	149,445	144,024	7,131	141,822	64,487
1981	1,109,559	835,125	4,556	839,681	81,279	4,330	762,732	180,549	166,278	7,733	143,481	63,247
1982	1,194,520	882,132	2,145	884,277	87,722	2,338	798,893	214,739	180,888	8,302	143,876	62,976
1983	1,310,979	976,357	5,436	981,793	98,504	-4,243	879,046	235,776	196,157	9,108	143,941	64,508
1984	1,463,569	1,113,361	6,653	1,120,014	115,917	-11,715	992,382	266,725	204,462	10,081	145,187	68,180
1985	1,568,084	1,200,394	5,447	1,205,841	126,974	-16,059	1,062,808	288,162	217,114	10,746	145,916	70,289
1986	1,666,504	1,282,086	7,149	1,289,235	139,607	-20,128	1,129,500	308,461	228,543	11,333	147,046	71,382
1987	1,777,838	1,390,232	16,600	1,406,832	149,787	-26,402	1,230,643	315,081	232,114	12,003	148,117	73,880
1988	1,918,754	1,521,601	18,940	1,540,541	168,841	-36,881	1,334,819	337,528	246,407	12,762	150,354	76,291
1989	2,056,187	1,602,316	21,935	1,624,251	177,757	-42,411	1,404,083	385,488	266,616	13,573	151,489	77,183
1990	2,131,012	1,652,472	22,893	1,675,365	183,292	-41,329	1,450,744	387,960	292,308	13,913	153,166	77,391
1991	2,162,769	1,636,011	18,421	1,654,432	183,661	-32,605	1,438,166	408,103	316,500	14,050	153,932	75,259
1992	2,283,376	1,728,598	16,396	1,744,994	192,717	-33,725	1,518,552	414,687	350,137	14,714	155,188	75,068
1993	2,377,462	1,799,558	13,579	1,813,137	200,436	-31,748	1,580,953	429,522	366,987	15,231	156,096	76,456
1994	2,512,785	1,915,508	13,357	1,928,865	211,220	-32,488	1,685,157	442,931	384,697	15,943	157,612	78,109
1995	2,641,263	1,977,779	11,046	1,988,825	217,256	-26,767	1,744,802	481,896	414,565	16,677	158,380	80,647
1996	2,731,753	2,035,359	9,239	2,044,598	221,187	-24,919	1,798,492	498,355	434,906	17,163	159,164	81,325
1997	2,925,625	2,187,006	7,357	2,194,363	235,846	-27,840	1,930,677	543,840	451,108	18,260	160,219	82,437
1998	3,075,869	2,309,765	9,796	2,319,561	245,364	-24,751	2,049,446	558,447	467,976	18,935	162,444	82,892
1999	3,263,921	2,505,396	8,746	2,514,142	265,461	-34,676	2,214,005	562,012	487,904	19,856	164,379	86,750
2000	3,452,722	2,603,939	18,706	2,622,645	274,518	-25,479	2,322,648	611,320	518,754	20,867	165,462	87,689
2001	3,600,835	2,676,217	15,403	2,691,620	295,085	-20,643	2,375,892	647,825	577,118	21,506	167,434	85,228
2002	3,679,955	2,778,337	17,071	2,795,408	308,514	-30,469	2,456,425	620,836	602,694	21,970	167,498	85,691
2003	3,893,770	2,922,220	10,954	2,933,174	321,544	-21,719	2,589,911	647,524	656,335	23,140	168,270	86,846
2004	4,115,127	3,082,583	14,284	3,096,867	342,013	-16,197	2,738,657	679,792	696,678	24,347	169,018	87,690
2005	4,356,511	3,253,071	13,960	3,267,031	367,483	-15,224	2,884,324	715,767	756,420	25,478	170,990	88,936
2006	4,632,495	3,399,359	3,478	3,402,837	390,801	-10,105	3,001,931	807,356	823,208	26,771	173,039	89,603
2007	4,870,095	3,516,546	-1,955	3,514,591	404,046	-16,345	3,094,200	895,593	880,302	27,844	174,908	90,355
2008	5,042,900	3,524,085	-882	3,523,203	408,883	-10,765	3,103,555	934,052	1,005,293	28,596	176,348	90,587
2009	5,108,342	3,467,211	698	3,467,909	401,410	3,121	3,069,620	969,049	1,069,673	28,774	177,535	87,888
2010	5,114,128	3,481,471	1,375	3,482,846	409,970	581	3,073,457	890,399	1,150,272	28,649	178,512	86,132
2011	5,400,171	3,606,218	7,948	3,614,166	382,012	-10,594	3,221,560	1,011,505	1,167,106	30,184	178,911	87,473
2012	5,656,006	3,790,746	10,138	3,800,884	400,256	-21,616	3,379,012	1,104,087	1,172,907	31,500	179,558	88,876
2013	5,698,334	3,869,716	13,518	3,883,234	458,452	-28,264	3,396,518	1,102,167	1,199,649	31,491	180,952	89,787
2014	5,925,193	4,039,496	17,733	4,057,229	476,787	-38,435	3,542,007	1,144,390	1,238,796	32,627	181,605	90,723

Personal Income and Employment by Area: Bloomington, IL

(Thousands of dollars, except as noted.)

Year	Personal income, total	Earnings by place of work			Less: Contributions for government social insurance	Plus: Adjustment for residence	Equals: Net earnings by place of residence	Plus: Dividends, interest, and rent	Plus: Personal current transfer receipts	Per capita personal income (dollars)	Population (persons)	Total employment
		Nonfarm	Farm	Total								
1970	491,651	366,584	29,630	396,214	23,520	5,780	378,474	77,150	36,027	4,029	122,030	55,784
1971	547,829	405,250	39,221	444,471	26,753	5,819	423,537	83,352	40,940	4,384	124,949	57,171
1972	593,523	450,191	28,618	478,809	31,363	5,662	453,108	94,452	45,963	4,552	130,387	59,551
1973	703,589	499,306	71,492	570,798	40,161	6,606	537,243	112,797	53,549	5,338	131,804	62,641
1974	784,258	554,471	79,086	633,557	46,806	8,361	595,112	127,377	61,769	5,926	132,331	64,356
1975	919,779	619,830	115,397	735,227	50,512	9,076	693,791	146,007	79,981	6,987	131,642	64,245
1976	981,118	695,543	92,531	788,074	57,886	7,132	737,320	155,981	87,817	7,370	133,130	65,859
1977	1,075,569	787,033	85,863	872,896	66,262	662	807,296	175,952	92,321	7,981	134,758	68,361
1978	1,147,620	879,807	50,209	930,016	75,943	1,524	855,597	192,585	99,438	8,459	135,673	71,369
1979	1,289,513	992,621	67,792	1,060,413	90,113	-9,296	961,004	218,217	110,292	9,463	136,266	73,714
1980	1,369,151	1,067,577	13,240	1,080,817	96,731	-10,718	973,368	258,902	136,881	9,959	137,480	72,290
1981	1,566,076	1,177,802	53,382	1,231,184	115,975	-19,454	1,095,755	312,125	158,196	11,338	138,131	73,541
1982	1,674,278	1,240,439	31,970	1,272,409	123,132	-31,875	1,117,402	380,896	175,980	12,111	138,240	73,521
1983	1,714,386	1,339,070	-28,814	1,310,256	133,345	-52,059	1,124,852	400,134	189,400	12,308	139,295	74,776
1984	1,929,934	1,518,506	48,744	1,567,250	158,542	-112,002	1,296,706	438,907	194,321	13,797	139,879	77,336
1985	2,016,981	1,617,298	63,185	1,680,483	171,195	-137,613	1,371,675	437,970	207,336	14,370	140,360	76,738
1986	2,044,820	1,507,746	56,875	1,564,621	156,364	-36,134	1,372,123	457,735	214,962	14,629	139,774	74,708
1987	2,128,084	1,598,181	44,850	1,643,031	163,611	-20,237	1,459,183	446,588	222,313	15,087	141,058	76,745
1988	2,269,967	1,801,158	21,887	1,823,045	188,933	-53,107	1,581,005	454,390	234,572	15,914	142,641	81,146
1989	2,551,607	2,007,278	60,313	2,067,591	213,134	-78,699	1,775,758	529,206	246,643	17,699	144,167	85,475
1990	2,727,589	2,227,871	58,264	2,286,135	231,696	-100,455	1,953,984	506,818	266,787	18,648	146,269	87,860
1991	2,801,226	2,334,135	19,548	2,353,683	249,665	-110,177	1,993,841	522,131	285,254	18,824	148,813	89,538
1992	3,088,935	2,568,040	55,349	2,623,389	270,416	-129,126	2,223,847	546,404	318,684	20,473	150,875	92,071
1993	3,193,435	2,690,066	33,397	2,723,463	284,836	-135,810	2,302,817	556,575	334,043	20,796	153,557	93,063
1994	3,462,475	2,941,997	74,024	3,016,021	313,951	-155,113	2,546,957	573,936	341,582	22,271	155,467	96,956
1995	3,633,797	3,141,505	-3,723	3,137,782	332,327	-175,525	2,629,930	636,510	367,357	23,032	157,769	99,502
1996	3,908,743	3,271,721	91,253	3,362,974	340,465	-182,629	2,839,880	678,812	390,051	24,568	159,099	101,224
1997	4,110,488	3,447,139	77,821	3,524,960	354,331	-191,590	2,979,039	728,122	403,327	25,515	161,099	104,868
1998	4,352,225	3,744,696	24,884	3,769,580	380,142	-225,047	3,164,391	766,520	421,314	26,651	163,307	110,006
1999	4,674,324	4,126,244	28,170	4,154,414	410,269	-260,967	3,483,178	757,096	434,050	28,176	165,899	115,160
2000	4,951,104	4,327,476	65,681	4,393,157	425,600	-279,422	3,688,135	803,385	459,584	29,533	167,644	116,734
2001	5,232,999	4,612,880	68,513	4,681,393	466,783	-292,510	3,922,100	816,297	494,602	30,872	169,505	116,753
2002	5,383,284	4,874,799	57,560	4,932,359	494,846	-313,886	4,123,627	731,006	528,651	31,197	172,555	117,759
2003	5,613,831	5,071,942	72,024	5,143,966	513,253	-323,523	4,307,190	755,390	551,251	32,174	174,481	117,553
2004	5,884,877	5,193,616	138,389	5,332,005	533,177	-320,404	4,478,424	825,102	581,351	33,481	175,767	116,566
2005	5,932,597	5,305,840	63,206	5,369,046	543,227	-322,914	4,502,905	786,835	642,857	33,515	177,015	117,694
2006	6,412,055	5,655,113	86,902	5,742,015	571,976	-332,566	4,837,473	904,894	669,688	35,679	179,717	118,707
2007	6,716,807	5,784,900	151,820	5,936,720	589,809	-327,684	5,019,227	964,649	732,931	36,913	181,965	120,627
2008	7,160,557	6,062,544	213,307	6,275,851	620,302	-330,293	5,325,256	1,005,932	829,369	39,010	183,558	121,429
2009	7,142,276	6,090,639	130,154	6,220,793	620,615	-379,062	5,221,116	1,004,074	917,086	38,552	185,265	119,928
2010	7,300,304	6,190,923	132,385	6,323,308	631,217	-401,536	5,290,555	995,547	1,014,202	39,160	186,421	118,987
2011	7,802,879	6,413,051	265,798	6,678,849	582,268	-384,117	5,712,464	1,093,724	996,691	41,664	187,282	119,746
2012	8,030,117	6,678,777	163,458	6,842,235	609,335	-379,435	5,853,465	1,180,118	996,534	42,508	188,910	120,650
2013	8,317,191	6,839,714	355,602	7,195,316	712,276	-400,032	6,083,008	1,200,887	1,033,296	43,479	191,294	118,858
2014	8,196,953	6,778,753	168,507	6,947,260	707,583	-336,955	5,902,722	1,237,603	1,056,628	43,064	190,345	118,277

Personal Income and Employment by Area: Bloomington, IN

(Thousands of dollars, except as noted.)

Year	Personal income, total	Earnings by place of work			Less: Contributions for government social insurance	Plus: Adjustment for residence	Equals: Net earnings by place of residence	Plus: Dividends, interest, and rent	Plus: Personal current transfer receipts	Per capita personal income (dollars)	Population (persons)	Total employment
		Nonfarm	Farm	Total								
1970	293,271	246,291	1,772	248,063	16,732	-2,417	228,914	43,274	21,083	3,003	97,656	40,115
1971	336,407	285,633	2,718	288,351	20,166	-4,300	263,885	48,503	24,019	3,374	99,712	43,719
1972	368,822	308,727	3,263	311,990	23,115	-775	288,100	53,364	27,358	3,562	103,553	45,422
1973	412,427	340,630	6,908	347,538	29,379	1,043	319,202	59,714	33,511	3,954	104,311	47,027
1974	444,029	358,872	4,027	362,899	32,425	4,179	334,653	68,932	40,444	4,180	106,218	46,825
1975	480,068	361,993	3,663	365,656	32,416	12,081	345,321	79,171	55,576	4,618	103,965	44,564
1976	543,722	420,468	5,377	425,845	37,758	13,206	401,293	86,581	55,848	5,132	105,944	47,509
1977	610,988	472,859	3,593	476,452	42,021	17,949	452,380	98,391	60,217	5,563	109,821	48,817
1978	696,890	537,416	3,150	540,566	49,020	23,865	515,411	113,145	68,334	6,210	112,226	50,475
1979	767,553	580,941	2,958	583,899	54,893	33,900	562,906	125,946	78,701	6,790	113,041	51,520
1980	862,969	637,267	-424	636,843	59,704	37,315	614,454	156,253	92,262	7,500	115,057	53,462
1981	969,551	702,244	3	702,247	71,211	38,733	669,769	194,490	105,292	8,320	116,537	54,013
1982	1,031,950	737,889	27	737,916	76,225	36,129	697,820	216,929	117,201	8,781	117,520	54,716
1983	1,105,448	803,130	-6,533	796,597	82,352	31,859	746,104	233,321	126,023	9,365	118,037	55,528
1984	1,215,378	880,907	-150	880,757	91,264	36,207	825,700	256,756	132,922	10,305	117,945	57,620
1985	1,300,733	948,571	-1,712	946,859	99,460	38,590	885,989	273,425	141,319	11,010	118,146	59,678
1986	1,410,661	1,046,669	-2,662	1,044,007	110,086	35,169	969,090	295,128	146,443	11,850	119,043	61,907
1987	1,516,805	1,152,538	-1,707	1,150,831	118,969	27,999	1,059,861	302,675	154,269	12,588	120,497	65,078
1988	1,637,106	1,252,885	-4,104	1,248,781	135,487	25,728	1,139,022	331,363	166,721	13,407	122,111	67,474
1989	1,807,396	1,355,995	1,960	1,357,955	146,850	26,266	1,237,371	385,702	184,323	14,476	124,856	68,835
1990	1,937,049	1,452,690	6	1,452,696	161,911	28,557	1,319,342	415,469	202,238	15,280	126,773	70,276
1991	2,037,226	1,544,868	-1,831	1,543,037	173,933	27,490	1,396,594	415,412	225,220	15,918	127,983	70,628
1992	2,203,126	1,677,315	2,602	1,679,917	187,555	19,101	1,511,463	439,127	252,536	16,930	130,131	72,264
1993	2,303,194	1,765,537	2,007	1,767,544	198,453	6,915	1,576,006	458,979	268,209	17,396	132,395	74,141
1994	2,416,946	1,859,513	2,090	1,861,603	213,631	-9,389	1,638,583	499,894	278,469	17,946	134,678	75,988
1995	2,544,748	1,954,036	50	1,954,086	224,497	-13,336	1,716,253	539,880	288,615	18,674	136,275	78,167
1996	2,703,390	2,065,273	2,885	2,068,158	235,628	-23,745	1,808,785	578,860	315,745	19,619	137,794	80,732
1997	2,878,042	2,213,578	2,638	2,216,216	251,722	-36,749	1,927,745	620,524	329,773	20,665	139,271	82,095
1998	3,070,836	2,349,418	-566	2,348,852	262,654	-43,628	2,042,570	666,181	362,085	21,852	140,527	82,590
1999	3,220,907	2,489,312	-1,511	2,487,801	275,205	-52,005	2,160,591	671,983	388,333	22,719	141,770	84,282
2000	3,433,864	2,642,603	792	2,643,395	289,399	-62,372	2,291,624	725,139	417,101	24,062	142,709	85,427
2001	3,496,697	2,644,463	1,579	2,646,042	284,627	-69,435	2,291,980	746,673	458,044	24,342	143,650	84,486
2002	3,535,280	2,723,181	-304	2,722,877	295,247	-70,840	2,356,790	694,963	483,527	24,431	144,707	84,592
2003	3,720,780	2,879,182	3,620	2,882,802	312,720	-76,297	2,493,785	721,682	505,313	25,340	146,835	86,920
2004	3,964,894	2,997,553	7,722	3,005,275	325,911	-71,919	2,607,445	822,971	534,478	26,691	148,549	87,887
2005	4,081,341	3,105,153	5,312	3,110,465	343,176	-72,201	2,695,088	801,071	585,182	27,192	150,096	88,696
2006	4,360,169	3,227,166	2,763	3,229,929	359,615	-69,689	2,800,625	921,851	637,693	28,582	152,548	89,825
2007	4,578,732	3,363,307	4,379	3,367,686	376,342	-62,112	2,929,232	976,900	672,600	29,664	154,352	92,060
2008	4,893,248	3,484,004	8,123	3,492,127	393,141	-60,922	3,038,064	1,068,224	786,960	31,334	156,164	92,219
2009	4,750,298	3,498,653	7,580	3,506,233	398,503	-128,636	2,979,094	920,800	850,404	30,096	157,840	91,953
2010	4,837,572	3,525,678	9,095	3,534,773	399,195	-125,243	3,010,335	897,901	929,336	30,215	160,107	90,556
2011	5,090,521	3,652,524	11,445	3,663,969	362,255	-128,495	3,173,219	983,903	933,399	31,451	161,855	90,975
2012	5,288,568	3,768,363	4,896	3,773,259	372,945	-125,655	3,274,659	1,050,768	963,141	32,515	162,652	90,493
2013	5,306,971	3,781,752	14,366	3,796,118	428,985	-128,897	3,238,236	1,105,442	963,293	32,520	163,190	90,259
2014	5,533,026	3,932,050	10,485	3,942,535	443,583	-129,782	3,369,170	1,142,714	1,021,142	33,675	164,308	90,897

Personal Income and Employment by Area: Bloomsberg-Berwick, PA

(Thousands of dollars, except as noted.)

Year	Personal income, total	Earnings by place of work			Less: Contributions for government social insurance	Plus: Adjustment for residence	Equals: Net earnings by place of residence	Plus: Dividends, interest, and rent	Plus: Personal current transfer receipts	Per capita personal income (dollars)	Population (persons)	Total employment
		Nonfarm	Farm	Total								
1970	250,511	206,898	6,163	213,061	15,627	-11,271	186,163	29,280	35,068	3,485	71,882	33,766
1971	267,364	219,898	4,975	224,873	17,361	-8,924	198,588	31,560	37,216	3,651	73,233	33,943
1972	303,565	250,321	4,873	255,194	20,463	-9,297	225,434	35,111	43,020	4,074	74,511	35,339
1973	343,352	283,239	7,632	290,871	26,299	-9,691	254,881	40,162	48,309	4,565	75,213	37,183
1974	381,478	314,930	7,241	322,171	30,729	-15,111	276,331	46,121	59,026	5,009	76,162	37,830
1975	411,594	310,636	7,075	317,711	28,978	-5,838	282,895	50,579	78,120	5,351	76,926	35,596
1976	449,306	333,903	8,236	342,139	31,763	-3,466	306,910	54,518	87,878	5,830	77,069	35,569
1977	488,394	370,289	7,012	377,301	35,346	-5,316	336,639	61,575	90,180	6,306	77,452	36,182
1978	544,828	422,852	7,769	430,621	41,398	-8,360	380,863	68,301	95,664	7,004	77,789	37,911
1979	609,649	477,616	10,442	488,058	48,245	-15,028	424,785	75,647	109,217	7,777	78,394	38,953
1980	658,039	504,124	5,215	509,339	51,415	-19,769	438,155	94,061	125,823	8,352	78,787	38,905
1981	732,217	543,260	9,826	553,086	59,321	-20,135	473,630	115,611	142,976	9,244	79,211	38,916
1982	782,783	559,866	8,196	568,062	61,708	-20,271	486,083	134,780	161,920	9,881	79,223	37,763
1983	834,282	608,206	-1,411	606,795	67,718	-28,337	510,740	150,253	173,289	10,471	79,674	38,203
1984	899,178	664,555	7,281	671,836	76,995	-37,428	557,413	166,091	175,674	11,363	79,135	39,057
1985	964,421	726,311	8,420	734,731	85,549	-48,309	600,873	181,771	181,777	12,258	78,679	40,396
1986	1,015,432	759,288	6,188	765,476	89,560	-46,160	629,756	193,992	191,684	12,898	78,729	40,797
1987	1,072,050	814,867	7,788	822,655	94,964	-49,754	677,937	199,337	194,776	13,619	78,718	41,605
1988	1,156,139	888,402	9,295	897,697	106,272	-51,337	740,088	210,270	205,781	14,553	79,446	43,282
1989	1,262,958	953,789	12,390	966,179	112,265	-57,384	796,530	240,176	226,252	15,743	80,226	44,433
1990	1,317,344	1,020,005	11,032	1,031,037	120,232	-68,454	842,351	240,651	234,342	16,241	81,113	45,090
1991	1,384,978	1,064,371	3,361	1,067,732	126,957	-77,817	862,958	248,560	273,460	16,958	81,669	44,976
1992	1,474,151	1,155,570	18,069	1,173,639	137,562	-100,342	935,735	251,629	286,787	17,894	82,381	45,346
1993	1,526,041	1,213,415	15,083	1,228,498	146,613	-111,230	970,655	258,749	296,637	18,430	82,802	45,742
1994	1,563,193	1,293,530	15,604	1,309,134	159,473	-135,053	1,014,608	258,873	289,712	18,879	82,801	46,889
1995	1,615,705	1,259,433	5,784	1,265,217	154,373	-83,386	1,027,458	285,453	302,794	19,464	83,012	46,421
1996	1,673,480	1,265,931	15,878	1,281,809	151,951	-66,563	1,063,295	288,947	321,238	20,159	83,013	45,448
1997	1,728,580	1,349,968	14,226	1,364,194	161,202	-108,387	1,094,605	306,686	327,289	20,848	82,914	45,712
1998	1,806,124	1,483,590	12,439	1,496,029	173,076	-163,678	1,159,275	321,617	325,232	21,860	82,623	47,631
1999	1,850,472	1,549,950	8,482	1,558,432	177,296	-174,631	1,206,505	306,167	337,800	22,444	82,449	47,851
2000	1,977,090	1,597,909	15,522	1,613,431	180,227	-141,897	1,291,307	324,642	361,141	24,049	82,211	48,515
2001	2,098,832	1,652,438	10,948	1,663,386	183,293	-104,981	1,375,112	334,746	388,974	25,412	82,592	49,796
2002	2,228,120	1,778,929	5,955	1,784,884	193,697	-121,004	1,470,183	339,398	418,539	26,897	82,838	50,876
2003	2,278,430	1,818,092	15,691	1,833,783	195,727	-136,472	1,501,584	335,805	441,041	27,372	83,240	50,516
2004	2,398,763	1,954,569	23,419	1,977,988	209,711	-155,774	1,612,503	326,308	459,952	28,724	83,511	51,811
2005	2,443,169	2,015,320	18,046	2,033,366	221,461	-169,337	1,642,568	305,710	494,891	29,183	83,718	53,439
2006	2,559,936	2,140,519	15,826	2,156,345	232,946	-206,445	1,716,954	327,123	515,859	30,477	83,996	54,889
2007	2,734,836	2,269,844	18,285	2,288,129	251,011	-228,653	1,808,465	372,377	553,994	32,441	84,303	56,504
2008	2,903,882	2,375,408	12,074	2,387,482	264,014	-261,014	1,862,454	417,505	623,923	34,270	84,735	56,891
2009	2,905,771	2,374,615	9,455	2,384,070	266,116	-301,459	1,816,495	402,370	686,906	34,031	85,385	56,392
2010	3,060,014	2,505,471	17,001	2,522,472	278,875	-289,683	1,953,914	398,756	707,344	35,724	85,656	56,766
2011	3,225,419	2,655,647	16,411	2,672,058	262,233	-340,570	2,069,255	434,046	722,118	37,809	85,309	57,817
2012	3,315,417	2,747,850	23,290	2,771,140	267,809	-363,361	2,139,970	458,672	716,775	38,815	85,415	58,858
2013	3,362,318	2,883,786	22,527	2,906,313	316,547	-427,969	2,161,797	472,220	728,301	39,245	85,674	59,921
2014	3,446,717	2,849,099	24,377	2,873,476	318,014	-355,616	2,199,846	489,197	757,674	40,189	85,763	58,785

Personal Income and Employment by Area: Boise City, ID

(Thousands of dollars, except as noted.)

Year	Personal income, total	Derivation of personal income								Per capita personal income (dollars)	Population (persons)	Total employment
		Earnings by place of work			Less: Contributions for government social insurance	Plus: Adjustment for residence	Equals: Net earnings by place of residence	Plus: Dividends, interest, and rent	Plus: Personal current transfer receipts			
		Nonfarm	Farm	Total								
1970	770,269	576,133	42,703	618,836	40,945	4,082	581,973	122,593	65,703	3,993	192,885	93,530
1971	864,876	647,451	42,222	689,673	47,174	3,995	646,494	140,592	77,790	4,270	202,549	97,869
1972	984,504	746,700	49,919	796,619	57,213	3,488	742,894	152,720	88,890	4,653	211,579	103,513
1973	1,133,609	852,566	74,955	927,521	76,192	3,116	854,445	176,829	102,335	5,155	219,916	110,066
1974	1,301,996	968,535	87,151	1,055,686	88,942	3,536	970,280	206,007	125,709	5,659	230,081	114,790
1975	1,483,278	1,121,929	64,001	1,185,930	101,179	6,663	1,091,414	237,412	154,452	6,264	236,798	119,885
1976	1,677,265	1,306,279	52,111	1,358,390	120,033	8,012	1,246,369	262,257	168,639	6,809	246,322	128,647
1977	1,890,272	1,494,855	39,297	1,534,152	138,147	10,284	1,406,289	303,506	180,477	7,384	255,984	136,175
1978	2,195,480	1,750,952	47,195	1,798,147	163,952	12,076	1,646,271	349,951	199,258	8,218	267,147	146,795
1979	2,423,167	1,919,146	42,590	1,961,736	190,026	15,306	1,787,016	398,930	237,221	8,781	275,953	150,083
1980	2,689,722	2,051,225	62,521	2,113,746	205,087	15,652	1,924,311	476,817	288,594	9,559	281,376	148,453
1981	2,971,786	2,210,717	64,806	2,275,523	239,179	18,816	2,055,160	586,516	330,110	10,394	285,918	146,355
1982	3,159,821	2,282,287	66,400	2,348,687	252,351	15,713	2,112,049	672,085	375,687	10,920	289,363	145,330
1983	3,397,397	2,451,687	93,734	2,545,421	271,882	16,575	2,290,114	705,236	402,047	11,619	292,391	148,415
1984	3,700,758	2,703,793	84,064	2,787,857	307,614	14,466	2,494,709	790,890	415,159	12,458	297,051	154,103
1985	3,943,080	2,888,881	76,445	2,965,326	334,317	12,042	2,643,051	853,353	446,676	13,094	301,145	156,609
1986	4,075,665	2,982,296	77,450	3,059,746	347,902	12,815	2,724,659	879,080	471,926	13,462	302,755	158,446
1987	4,304,320	3,178,199	89,486	3,267,685	361,845	12,368	2,918,208	898,746	487,366	14,172	303,727	163,218
1988	4,730,596	3,564,649	100,905	3,665,554	422,206	9,367	3,252,715	956,472	521,409	15,437	306,455	172,597
1989	5,220,069	3,903,474	135,821	4,039,295	468,800	6,995	3,577,490	1,077,294	565,285	16,680	312,962	181,032
1990	5,691,977	4,278,397	145,370	4,423,767	543,912	11,609	3,891,464	1,192,798	607,715	17,660	322,316	190,433
1991	6,118,839	4,659,874	149,546	4,809,420	605,821	9,645	4,213,244	1,220,631	684,964	18,245	335,378	198,902
1992	6,859,297	5,305,591	143,780	5,449,371	674,565	9,611	4,784,417	1,305,968	768,912	19,731	347,646	207,984
1993	7,671,710	5,963,646	192,678	6,156,324	758,925	5,471	5,402,870	1,440,700	828,140	21,069	364,123	220,250
1994	8,514,211	6,689,407	134,865	6,824,272	855,550	10,447	5,979,169	1,654,106	880,936	22,396	380,160	236,337
1995	9,263,777	7,231,932	132,566	7,364,498	931,140	15,209	6,448,567	1,842,429	972,781	23,430	395,382	245,882
1996	9,805,443	7,577,869	135,754	7,713,623	957,173	16,096	6,772,546	1,984,218	1,048,679	23,947	409,471	255,743
1997	10,339,375	7,965,848	121,237	8,087,085	999,286	19,154	7,106,953	2,142,312	1,090,110	24,455	422,797	266,539
1998	11,375,264	8,726,912	155,419	8,882,331	1,075,222	20,513	7,827,622	2,369,933	1,177,709	25,946	438,421	280,220
1999	12,418,766	9,697,339	150,560	9,847,899	1,159,432	24,384	8,712,851	2,443,782	1,262,133	27,424	452,837	288,308
2000	13,942,742	11,121,342	147,589	11,268,931	1,317,920	26,256	9,977,267	2,597,452	1,368,023	29,728	469,017	304,474
2001	14,429,488	11,348,361	181,107	11,529,468	1,328,438	28,487	10,229,517	2,673,182	1,526,789	29,686	486,078	310,960
2002	14,957,845	11,659,836	168,174	11,828,010	1,347,680	1,024	10,481,354	2,788,397	1,688,094	29,916	499,994	313,002
2003	15,587,506	12,085,881	140,777	12,226,658	1,393,626	-11,523	10,821,509	2,956,390	1,809,607	30,415	512,491	316,010
2004	16,982,227	13,043,663	215,397	13,259,060	1,497,903	-8,810	11,752,347	3,294,522	1,935,358	32,287	525,975	327,198
2005	18,067,956	13,927,101	193,228	14,120,329	1,631,267	1,631	12,490,693	3,455,123	2,122,140	33,032	546,980	344,123
2006	20,473,754	15,676,092	164,137	15,840,229	1,846,757	24,488	14,017,960	4,149,602	2,306,192	35,882	570,583	366,248
2007	21,222,326	15,940,204	236,276	16,176,480	1,909,975	55,674	14,322,179	4,356,841	2,543,306	35,950	590,330	378,753
2008	20,903,634	15,282,115	222,611	15,504,726	1,878,527	72,267	13,698,466	4,148,584	3,056,584	34,654	603,218	373,954
2009	20,378,915	15,012,473	100,167	15,112,640	1,829,226	127,910	13,411,324	3,527,968	3,439,623	33,335	611,341	354,103
2010	21,086,632	15,321,347	220,770	15,542,117	1,925,768	144,439	13,760,788	3,517,072	3,808,772	34,125	617,923	348,959
2011	21,931,560	15,410,254	288,343	15,698,597	1,768,224	160,699	14,091,072	4,009,333	3,831,155	34,944	627,627	355,653
2012	23,111,455	15,858,501	308,073	16,166,574	1,823,616	172,788	14,515,746	4,672,088	3,923,621	36,245	637,651	360,429
2013	23,953,114	16,797,509	284,960	17,082,469	2,130,022	183,619	15,136,066	4,723,308	4,093,740	36,825	650,457	371,423
2014	25,242,080	17,752,300	330,761	18,083,061	2,222,684	178,451	16,038,828	4,927,167	4,276,085	37,991	664,422	381,426

Personal Income and Employment by Area: Boston-Cambridge-Newton, MA-NH

(Thousands of dollars, except as noted.)

| Year | Personal income, total | Derivation of personal income | | | | | | | | | Per capita personal income (dollars) | Population (persons) | Total employment |
| | | Earnings by place of work | | | Less: Contributions for government social insurance | Plus: Adjustment for residence | Equals: Net earnings by place of residence | Plus: Dividends, interest, and rent | Plus: Personal current transfer receipts | | | |
		Nonfarm	Farm	Total								
1970	18,833,860	15,280,424	28,963	15,309,387	969,109	-246,108	14,094,170	3,004,173	1,735,517	4,794	3,928,508	1,906,572
1971	20,120,287	16,228,157	27,487	16,255,644	1,061,528	-304,127	14,889,989	3,183,576	2,046,722	5,089	3,953,760	1,880,515
1972	21,694,357	17,633,330	29,773	17,663,103	1,211,526	-373,403	16,078,174	3,369,039	2,247,144	5,450	3,980,347	1,918,584
1973	23,427,883	19,202,180	32,016	19,234,196	1,515,854	-462,516	17,255,826	3,649,374	2,522,683	5,882	3,982,918	1,976,758
1974	25,289,635	20,385,348	30,843	20,416,191	1,663,210	-549,589	18,203,392	4,079,914	3,006,329	6,371	3,969,705	1,995,376
1975	27,084,928	21,322,196	32,501	21,354,697	1,692,392	-635,195	19,027,110	4,261,906	3,795,912	6,851	3,953,504	1,943,843
1976	29,066,041	23,153,226	36,941	23,190,167	1,878,742	-746,111	20,565,314	4,524,582	3,976,145	7,365	3,946,719	1,961,507
1977	31,657,808	25,568,063	39,821	25,607,884	2,078,220	-934,149	22,595,515	4,997,190	4,065,103	8,020	3,947,472	2,021,580
1978	34,971,230	28,721,904	50,711	28,772,615	2,404,024	-1,183,540	25,185,051	5,491,549	4,294,630	8,866	3,944,294	2,118,025
1979	38,913,685	32,362,865	49,871	32,412,736	2,826,669	-1,452,367	28,133,700	6,082,768	4,697,217	9,870	3,942,625	2,213,716
1980	43,963,071	36,183,419	59,301	36,242,720	3,172,323	-1,781,943	31,288,454	7,330,258	5,344,359	11,141	3,946,114	2,271,006
1981	49,250,824	39,886,218	61,881	39,948,099	3,786,086	-1,983,926	34,178,087	9,002,681	6,070,056	12,416	3,966,836	2,288,684
1982	54,264,121	43,205,966	71,846	43,277,812	4,217,874	-2,183,666	36,876,272	10,884,073	6,503,776	13,644	3,977,211	2,304,308
1983	59,295,391	47,962,991	93,378	48,056,369	4,762,616	-2,451,592	40,842,161	11,563,453	6,889,777	14,799	4,006,648	2,364,109
1984	67,088,160	54,657,693	96,576	54,754,269	5,601,867	-2,808,463	46,343,939	13,494,806	7,249,415	16,611	4,038,686	2,509,018
1985	72,890,626	60,183,929	83,269	60,267,198	6,241,202	-3,103,991	50,922,005	14,421,324	7,547,297	17,901	4,071,845	2,591,649
1986	78,702,561	65,462,373	88,426	65,550,799	6,932,105	-3,316,832	55,301,862	15,501,695	7,899,004	19,249	4,088,650	2,660,368
1987	85,322,797	71,748,158	79,340	71,827,498	7,518,153	-3,593,673	60,715,672	16,535,788	8,071,337	20,786	4,104,797	2,682,717
1988	94,210,625	79,108,887	94,044	79,202,931	8,407,380	-3,951,130	66,844,421	18,636,476	8,729,728	22,837	4,125,293	2,758,108
1989	99,179,965	82,321,175	80,238	82,401,413	8,689,875	-4,066,574	69,644,964	19,712,118	9,822,883	23,959	4,139,484	2,735,161
1990	102,135,172	83,375,246	78,374	83,453,620	8,743,167	-4,223,066	70,487,387	20,635,064	11,012,721	24,686	4,137,302	2,665,144
1991	103,937,879	83,527,064	95,748	83,622,812	8,918,557	-4,178,291	70,525,964	20,759,871	12,652,044	25,178	4,128,150	2,541,026
1992	109,801,833	88,820,289	97,012	88,917,301	9,416,093	-4,309,068	75,192,140	21,370,388	13,239,305	26,537	4,137,692	2,555,157
1993	114,229,782	92,506,465	96,751	92,603,216	9,866,980	-4,453,157	78,283,079	22,346,268	13,600,435	27,435	4,163,698	2,603,207
1994	119,886,776	97,422,232	85,358	97,507,590	10,519,477	-4,831,606	82,156,507	23,318,173	14,412,096	28,618	4,189,180	2,655,650
1995	127,389,009	103,460,970	89,064	103,550,034	11,225,961	-5,323,961	87,000,112	25,070,652	15,318,245	30,110	4,230,795	2,685,848
1996	135,905,411	110,741,624	93,865	110,835,489	11,888,425	-5,664,239	93,282,825	26,851,722	15,770,864	31,861	4,265,564	2,740,663
1997	144,717,466	119,036,582	91,918	119,128,500	12,809,869	-6,635,484	99,683,147	28,720,522	16,313,797	33,634	4,302,696	2,813,151
1998	154,721,922	127,963,344	60,904	128,024,248	13,742,095	-7,307,428	106,974,725	31,358,057	16,389,140	35,669	4,337,751	2,890,553
1999	165,552,777	140,208,407	54,229	140,262,636	14,843,324	-8,460,758	116,958,554	31,660,129	16,934,094	37,886	4,369,743	2,944,512
2000	186,192,118	158,900,166	65,029	158,965,195	16,566,243	-10,027,851	132,371,101	35,966,607	17,854,410	42,304	4,401,256	3,031,999
2001	192,963,118	164,050,173	54,833	164,105,006	16,883,859	-10,906,443	136,314,704	37,126,917	19,521,497	43,537	4,432,132	3,041,324
2002	192,429,979	162,021,870	69,051	162,090,921	16,708,889	-10,228,942	135,153,090	36,136,552	21,140,337	43,340	4,440,034	2,987,194
2003	196,625,852	163,843,118	72,750	163,915,868	16,812,317	-9,727,905	137,375,646	37,002,790	22,247,416	44,338	4,434,723	2,953,209
2004	205,832,867	174,160,472	78,754	174,239,226	18,240,862	-11,087,662	144,910,702	37,730,092	23,192,073	46,516	4,424,956	2,966,396
2005	216,206,684	179,359,454	63,631	179,423,085	19,055,218	-11,001,514	149,366,353	42,037,210	24,803,121	48,937	4,418,046	3,002,701
2006	234,494,325	189,707,755	75,483	189,783,238	19,790,709	-11,175,569	158,816,960	49,712,874	25,964,491	52,965	4,427,356	3,046,396
2007	246,223,179	199,828,559	77,971	199,906,530	20,857,269	-12,287,556	166,761,705	52,317,814	27,143,660	55,358	4,447,838	3,125,061
2008	255,246,153	205,274,156	103,402	205,377,558	21,580,695	-12,345,142	171,451,721	52,619,323	31,175,109	56,935	4,483,141	3,147,405
2009	248,646,435	200,988,684	75,322	201,064,006	21,306,527	-11,692,517	168,064,962	46,567,759	34,013,714	54,923	4,527,220	3,082,890
2010	257,931,552	209,586,943	77,324	209,664,267	21,793,061	-12,118,124	175,753,082	46,296,681	35,881,789	56,506	4,564,659	3,078,150
2011	274,620,984	219,311,750	102,147	219,413,897	20,246,277	-12,538,285	186,629,335	51,938,462	36,053,187	59,586	4,608,848	3,128,624
2012	289,693,363	229,240,820	152,863	229,393,683	20,975,966	-13,465,538	194,952,179	58,564,381	36,176,803	62,291	4,650,668	3,184,001
2013	290,726,759	234,463,338	161,935	234,625,273	24,518,623	-13,065,505	197,041,145	57,154,075	36,531,539	61,882	4,698,049	3,260,551
2014	304,328,805	246,863,853	145,378	247,009,231	25,867,330	-14,008,815	207,133,086	59,517,115	37,678,604	64,311	4,732,161	3,322,513

Personal Income and Employment by Area: Boulder, CO

(Thousands of dollars, except as noted.)

Year	Personal income, total	Derivation of personal income									Per capita personal income (dollars)	Population (persons)	Total employment
		Earnings by place of work			Less: Contributions for government social insurance	Plus: Adjustment for residence	Equals: Net earnings by place of residence	Plus: Dividends, interest, and rent	Plus: Personal current transfer receipts				
		Nonfarm	Farm	Total									
1970	593,943	395,895	5,052	400,947	21,172	79,073	458,848	102,510	32,585		4,454	133,342	55,395
1971	673,474	454,144	474	454,618	24,881	88,975	518,712	116,040	38,722		4,783	140,808	59,121
1972	760,243	514,559	4,041	518,600	30,157	100,215	588,658	127,797	43,788		5,024	151,309	64,116
1973	853,792	576,367	2,914	579,281	39,837	115,280	654,724	144,451	54,617		5,353	159,509	69,942
1974	966,687	663,524	2,695	666,219	46,970	115,764	735,013	168,532	63,142		5,808	166,449	75,635
1975	1,092,114	752,521	6,510	759,031	52,425	114,286	820,892	190,509	80,713		6,553	166,670	78,961
1976	1,224,516	862,802	7,921	870,723	61,907	116,252	925,068	211,073	88,375		7,241	169,117	85,236
1977	1,411,190	1,023,996	7,292	1,031,288	74,657	119,723	1,076,354	239,109	95,727		7,923	178,121	92,627
1978	1,657,698	1,226,848	6,797	1,233,645	92,236	130,597	1,272,006	280,875	104,817		9,037	183,432	102,720
1979	1,932,299	1,433,614	5,149	1,438,763	114,316	162,357	1,486,804	326,499	118,996		10,326	187,125	110,002
1980	2,187,629	1,561,420	9,224	1,570,644	127,270	209,651	1,653,025	397,567	137,037		11,457	190,935	112,861
1981	2,522,729	1,777,374	12,943	1,790,317	156,444	227,463	1,861,336	501,289	160,104		12,890	195,705	117,528
1982	2,781,899	1,989,725	8,662	1,998,387	181,654	226,300	2,043,033	561,562	177,304		13,852	200,827	121,300
1983	3,041,675	2,224,707	9,338	2,234,045	208,132	212,083	2,237,996	609,956	193,723		14,734	206,440	128,223
1984	3,395,037	2,531,866	10,185	2,542,051	247,455	202,863	2,497,459	696,364	201,214		16,075	211,206	141,199
1985	3,551,682	2,599,127	5,064	2,604,191	258,111	241,934	2,588,014	749,350	214,318		16,601	213,942	140,650
1986	3,722,146	2,727,934	4,846	2,732,780	273,381	244,992	2,704,391	784,976	232,779		17,234	215,971	141,908
1987	3,948,807	2,959,587	5,572	2,965,159	294,035	210,821	2,881,945	815,036	251,826		18,112	218,024	143,586
1988	4,260,496	3,219,908	8,427	3,228,335	332,841	225,008	3,120,502	873,730	266,264		19,373	219,915	152,086
1989	4,673,624	3,427,910	10,222	3,438,132	361,917	224,898	3,301,113	1,065,419	307,092		20,910	223,507	155,495
1990	5,006,361	3,728,766	11,309	3,740,075	403,653	217,724	3,554,146	1,127,887	324,328		22,115	226,374	160,076
1991	5,314,194	4,077,760	12,648	4,090,408	452,879	166,418	3,803,947	1,157,975	352,272		22,823	232,846	164,862
1992	5,885,373	4,593,527	7,319	4,600,846	503,546	142,497	4,239,797	1,255,206	390,370		24,479	240,430	169,291
1993	6,353,617	5,023,719	9,237	5,032,956	555,170	93,128	4,570,914	1,365,299	417,404		25,681	247,405	178,775
1994	6,897,928	5,455,627	9,281	5,464,908	609,706	-20,268	4,834,934	1,621,308	441,686		27,123	254,324	186,270
1995	7,471,003	5,878,968	9,403	5,888,371	-658,239	-72,566	5,157,566	1,829,526	483,911		28,788	259,520	192,888
1996	8,071,776	6,363,670	11,385	6,375,055	707,622	-78,977	5,588,456	1,974,781	508,539		30,502	264,630	198,754
1997	8,770,948	7,011,397	11,363	7,022,760	779,673	-134,155	6,108,932	2,151,387	510,629		32,396	270,744	207,295
1998	9,692,163	8,217,375	10,422	8,227,797	867,582	-517,018	6,843,197	2,340,342	508,624		34,919	277,562	213,640
1999	10,634,875	9,049,077	9,262	9,058,339	944,641	-452,082	7,661,616	2,435,367	537,892		37,198	285,901	221,367
2000	12,243,083	11,186,539	8,277	11,194,816	1,144,861	-1,146,406	8,903,549	2,762,740	576,794		41,734	293,358	237,793
2001	12,372,850	11,275,436	10,105	11,285,541	1,157,368	-1,164,165	8,964,008	2,770,655	638,187		41,224	300,137	244,639
2002	10,948,016	9,751,747	9,444	9,761,191	1,011,498	-1,041,826	7,707,867	2,557,139	683,010		39,174	279,468	213,502
2003	11,105,562	9,889,367	6,072	9,895,439	1,021,422	-1,101,613	7,772,404	2,602,464	730,694		39,838	278,768	213,165
2004	11,651,164	10,357,621	10,413	10,368,034	1,089,750	-1,191,963	8,086,321	2,816,805	748,038		41,652	279,728	217,185
2005	12,552,129	10,779,345	8,726	10,788,071	1,129,792	-1,291,568	8,366,711	3,339,150	846,268		44,790	280,241	221,461
2006	13,451,640	11,345,274	6,976	11,352,250	1,182,955	-1,383,701	8,785,594	3,821,315	844,731		47,324	284,243	225,621
2007	14,107,944	11,760,691	6,335	11,767,026	1,245,568	-1,476,547	9,044,911	4,135,629	927,404		49,083	287,428	233,605
2008	14,711,118	12,226,080	4,719	12,230,799	1,291,385	-1,552,025	9,387,389	4,162,481	1,161,248		50,578	290,859	238,106
2009	14,076,894	11,721,369	7,551	11,728,920	1,222,237	-1,326,854	9,179,829	3,647,575	1,249,490		48,013	293,190	232,430
2010	14,997,719	11,991,353	7,609	11,998,962	1,241,828	-787,490	9,969,644	3,600,066	1,428,009		50,674	295,967	230,594
2011	15,844,186	12,447,906	14,025	12,461,931	1,178,305	-944,931	10,338,695	4,041,180	1,464,311		52,700	300,650	237,400
2012	16,851,388	13,136,047	7,929	13,143,976	1,232,241	-978,690	10,933,045	4,450,046	1,468,297		55,163	305,483	242,367
2013	17,396,723	13,645,846	10,011	13,655,857	1,451,949	-1,089,171	11,114,737	4,741,119	1,540,867		56,047	310,396	248,403
2014	18,369,741	14,422,502	9,827	14,432,329	1,540,782	-1,086,361	11,805,186	4,920,066	1,644,489		58,627	313,333	254,361

Personal Income and Employment by Area: Bowling Green, KY

(Thousands of dollars, except as noted.)

Year	Personal income, total	Earnings by place of work			Less: Contributions for government social insurance	Plus: Adjustment for residence	Equals: Net earnings by place of residence	Plus: Dividends, interest, and rent	Plus: Personal current transfer receipts	Per capita personal income (dollars)	Population (persons)	Total employment
		Nonfarm	Farm	Total								
1970	237,356	175,948	15,726	191,674	11,945	683	180,412	28,686	28,258	2,648	89,652	37,297
1971	264,388	195,668	17,127	212,795	13,712	729	199,812	32,245	32,331	2,827	93,520	38,393
1972	302,312	225,289	21,037	246,326	16,575	742	230,493	36,388	35,431	3,172	95,307	40,228
1973	348,655	260,067	25,936	286,003	21,794	2,331	266,540	40,662	41,453	3,652	95,464	42,648
1974	386,089	287,363	22,853	310,216	25,070	3,153	288,299	47,578	50,212	3,984	96,904	43,625
1975	426,463	311,990	15,600	327,590	26,799	3,139	303,930	55,707	66,826	4,336	98,351	43,179
1976	483,572	359,898	14,572	374,470	31,446	4,996	348,020	61,353	74,199	4,809	100,546	45,371
1977	539,220	398,210	22,342	420,552	34,784	7,949	393,717	70,186	75,317	5,269	102,335	46,883
1978	617,159	466,369	21,200	487,569	41,834	8,746	454,481	81,115	81,563	5,922	104,207	50,148
1979	703,415	524,147	26,878	551,025	48,699	12,401	514,727	93,460	95,228	6,659	105,640	50,732
1980	772,493	552,746	16,764	569,510	51,615	13,525	531,420	120,104	120,969	7,182	107,557	49,865
1981	898,420	630,619	27,548	658,167	63,699	15,635	610,103	150,874	137,443	8,198	109,593	50,960
1982	958,624	649,475	23,333	672,808	66,817	23,718	629,709	175,895	153,020	8,345	114,875	50,359
1983	994,593	696,998	-5,907	691,091	71,491	21,750	641,350	189,258	163,985	8,511	116,854	51,861
1984	1,128,766	780,612	26,201	806,813	81,520	19,734	745,027	212,929	170,810	9,918	113,805	53,904
1985	1,190,212	848,542	13,813	862,355	90,459	20,062	791,958	219,911	178,343	10,517	113,170	54,825
1986	1,203,164	846,999	13,792	860,791	93,862	22,480	789,409	224,877	188,878	10,693	112,523	55,198
1987	1,268,807	894,910	21,528	916,438	98,646	25,651	843,443	227,675	197,689	11,306	112,227	55,910
1988	1,397,741	996,141	24,017	1,020,158	110,515	23,962	933,605	252,050	212,086	12,444	112,325	57,594
1989	1,528,393	1,071,075	36,531	1,107,606	121,280	19,310	1,005,636	287,154	235,603	13,564	112,679	59,974
1990	1,601,178	1,115,244	36,270	1,151,514	129,979	20,235	1,041,770	296,213	263,195	14,012	114,270	61,201
1991	1,716,386	1,198,152	37,618	1,235,770	141,902	18,906	1,112,774	305,417	298,195	14,850	115,583	62,846
1992	1,874,665	1,340,205	43,313	1,383,518	158,802	16,750	1,241,466	310,364	322,835	15,954	117,502	65,051
1993	1,984,879	1,432,065	37,730	1,469,795	172,045	20,277	1,318,027	326,453	340,399	16,496	120,327	66,995
1994	2,129,890	1,575,920	34,123	1,610,043	192,987	16,242	1,433,298	339,677	356,915	17,360	122,686	69,464
1995	2,240,383	1,672,506	14,256	1,686,762	205,612	13,587	1,494,737	361,721	383,925	17,874	125,345	72,461
1996	2,405,969	1,770,547	31,371	1,801,918	215,457	9,297	1,595,758	393,386	416,825	18,834	127,749	73,893
1997	2,581,980	1,907,102	32,931	1,940,033	229,466	10,179	1,720,746	418,234	443,000	19,848	130,090	75,666
1998	2,706,701	2,016,629	12,190	2,028,819	240,260	13,650	1,802,209	447,287	457,205	20,468	132,238	75,609
1999	2,851,041	2,179,770	3,829	2,183,599	257,539	12,487	1,938,547	438,921	473,573	21,317	133,747	77,329
2000	3,099,308	2,315,687	34,045	2,349,732	263,311	14,813	2,101,234	490,177	507,897	22,896	135,367	78,818
2001	3,165,796	2,330,438	31,734	2,362,172	263,913	13,058	2,111,317	492,662	561,817	23,125	136,901	77,568
2002	3,293,080	2,472,297	22,257	2,494,554	277,724	13,738	2,230,568	455,093	607,419	23,775	138,510	77,442
2003	3,420,122	2,606,956	24,137	2,631,093	289,439	5,087	2,346,741	447,315	626,066	24,270	140,921	78,556
2004	3,690,681	2,771,342	46,273	2,817,615	303,563	8,515	2,522,567	490,976	677,138	25,801	143,044	80,345
2005	3,916,641	2,954,661	61,845	3,016,506	327,567	10,000	2,698,939	497,798	719,904	26,841	145,918	83,217
2006	4,147,942	3,107,328	54,351	3,161,679	347,091	17,080	2,831,668	534,733	781,541	27,778	149,324	85,117
2007	4,359,850	3,220,188	24,256	3,244,444	363,212	21,944	2,903,176	605,444	851,230	28,738	151,710	87,782
2008	4,614,541	3,329,830	16,620	3,346,450	380,864	29,307	2,994,893	643,291	976,357	29,865	154,513	87,266
2009	4,512,384	3,126,112	21,568	3,147,680	366,782	5,206	2,786,104	626,085	1,100,195	28,745	156,978	83,413
2010	4,748,051	3,292,228	25,388	3,317,616	381,108	17,451	2,953,959	621,016	1,173,076	29,828	159,181	83,929
2011	5,029,799	3,436,671	55,585	3,492,256	352,575	9,328	3,149,009	683,250	1,197,540	31,338	160,504	86,740
2012	5,201,801	3,595,522	57,161	3,652,683	366,479	14,875	3,301,079	703,962	1,196,760	32,040	162,352	88,219
2013	5,313,549	3,699,244	99,643	3,798,887	429,318	1,935	3,371,504	719,633	1,222,412	32,431	163,841	89,331
2014	5,568,600	3,894,226	73,151	3,967,377	456,009	-17,752	3,493,616	746,364	1,328,620	33,600	165,732	90,980

Personal Income and Employment by Area: Bremerton-Silverdale, WA

(Thousands of dollars, except as noted.)

Year	Personal income, total	Derivation of personal income									Per capita personal income (dollars)	Population (persons)	Total employment
		Earnings by place of work			Less: Contributions for government social insurance	Plus: Adjustment for residence	Equals: Net earnings by place of residence	Plus: Dividends, interest, and rent	Plus: Personal current transfer receipts			
		Nonfarm	Farm	Total								
1970	484,215	392,399	1,502	393,901	17,268	-42,293	334,340	115,181	34,694	4,765	101,617	45,195
1971	505,417	402,041	1,060	403,101	18,254	-46,751	338,096	125,441	41,880	4,974	101,606	41,911
1972	547,809	433,089	1,156	434,245	20,733	-47,939	365,573	135,406	46,830	5,359	102,225	41,798
1973	626,216	490,168	2,012	492,180	26,640	-49,802	415,738	156,803	53,675	5,578	112,257	45,114
1974	739,144	583,248	1,568	584,816	32,475	-59,784	492,557	185,002	61,585	6,602	111,965	49,047
1975	853,307	674,309	1,237	675,546	40,020	-66,078	569,448	207,427	76,432	7,164	119,117	51,652
1976	950,154	752,863	1,182	754,045	47,753	-67,065	639,227	225,603	85,324	7,854	120,976	54,063
1977	1,095,810	870,131	1,259	871,390	56,003	-73,278	742,109	260,512	93,189	8,704	125,902	58,694
1978	1,254,697	971,606	1,744	973,350	63,907	-66,048	843,395	309,872	101,430	9,459	132,640	61,793
1979	1,435,898	1,100,331	1,980	1,102,311	74,979	-61,019	966,313	356,723	112,862	10,203	140,733	65,222
1980	1,607,702	1,182,180	1,577	1,183,757	82,672	-41,707	1,059,378	406,738	141,586	10,807	148,762	67,650
1981	1,777,759	1,276,175	1,644	1,277,819	97,426	-40,312	1,140,081	469,165	168,513	11,476	154,907	68,860
1982	1,968,024	1,411,838	1,663	1,413,501	105,653	-59,469	1,248,379	534,612	185,033	12,692	155,059	70,104
1983	2,189,441	1,601,484	1,159	1,602,643	131,219	-65,712	1,405,712	587,326	196,403	13,640	160,515	73,806
1984	2,307,241	1,659,376	406	1,659,782	141,762	-54,581	1,463,439	631,753	212,049	14,265	161,742	75,920
1985	2,431,375	1,709,334	133	1,709,467	155,676	-30,543	1,523,248	678,611	229,516	14,867	163,546	77,990
1986	2,506,847	1,709,375	-354	1,709,021	162,310	3,046	1,549,757	711,102	245,988	15,258	164,293	77,909
1987	2,700,488	1,844,813	1,287	1,846,100	179,383	27,645	1,694,362	743,965	262,161	15,908	169,760	83,191
1988	2,987,872	2,086,552	577	2,087,129	211,614	24,726	1,900,241	808,278	279,353	16,699	178,929	90,373
1989	3,251,787	2,208,328	3,607	2,211,935	231,971	55,973	2,035,937	905,698	310,152	17,822	182,461	92,716
1990	3,776,382	2,520,233	2,237	2,522,470	274,094	217,533	2,465,909	966,571	343,902	19,681	191,879	99,487
1991	4,146,364	2,791,199	3,826	2,795,025	308,906	220,338	2,706,457	1,039,229	400,678	20,770	199,636	103,816
1992	4,486,902	3,011,158	3,536	3,014,694	340,130	267,014	2,941,578	1,094,886	450,438	21,411	209,562	105,396
1993	4,724,985	3,013,222	3,068	3,016,290	347,167	391,807	3,060,930	1,164,709	499,346	22,366	211,262	103,073
1994	4,941,239	3,108,379	3,211	3,111,590	362,329	419,442	3,168,703	1,242,461	530,075	23,044	214,422	106,538
1995	5,209,945	3,224,669	1,691	3,226,360	377,135	431,144	3,280,369	1,354,951	574,625	23,322	223,391	108,268
1996	5,475,088	3,336,951	1,399	3,338,350	385,053	421,449	3,374,746	1,493,647	606,695	24,164	226,584	112,627
1997	5,923,653	3,498,236	2,134	3,500,370	396,145	599,274	3,703,499	1,577,515	642,639	25,822	229,403	111,977
1998	6,182,415	3,543,418	720	3,544,138	401,553	746,846	3,889,431	1,623,370	669,614	27,012	228,878	110,014
1999	6,481,008	3,708,542	917	3,709,459	414,233	835,724	4,130,950	1,643,557	706,501	28,253	229,393	110,332
2000	7,096,262	3,954,702	1,281	3,955,983	444,725	1,069,958	4,581,216	1,737,003	778,043	30,493	232,720	112,512
2001	7,413,302	4,168,337	890	4,169,227	467,808	1,084,335	4,785,754	1,744,588	882,960	31,611	234,513	112,896
2002	7,892,778	4,651,717	1,068	4,652,785	526,221	1,122,561	5,249,125	1,708,871	934,782	33,145	238,129	116,511
2003	8,331,921	4,939,596	2,584	4,942,180	561,930	1,115,148	5,495,398	1,846,296	990,227	34,751	239,758	119,238
2004	8,777,289	5,228,109	1,930	5,230,039	604,780	1,105,835	5,731,094	2,022,791	1,023,404	36,276	241,960	122,230
2005	9,216,065	5,529,401	801	5,530,202	643,064	1,086,999	5,974,137	2,146,456	1,095,472	38,431	239,806	125,301
2006	9,755,317	5,804,578	2,158	5,806,736	677,728	1,065,210	6,194,218	2,372,036	1,189,063	39,809	245,054	127,378
2007	10,134,724	5,943,336	1,401	5,944,737	696,473	1,025,244	6,273,508	2,579,102	1,282,114	41,518	244,105	128,048
2008	10,663,393	6,096,384	-2,497	6,093,887	716,142	977,550	6,355,295	2,822,641	1,485,457	43,187	246,912	127,529
2009	10,254,852	6,050,936	-1,525	6,049,411	729,064	801,821	6,122,168	2,480,213	1,652,471	41,217	248,800	123,317
2010	10,441,430	6,206,712	-2,406	6,204,306	750,721	748,000	6,201,585	2,404,799	1,835,046	41,492	251,650	120,460
2011	10,810,421	6,314,653	-451	6,314,202	698,263	692,987	6,308,926	2,654,434	1,847,061	42,498	254,372	120,243
2012	11,193,801	6,423,712	-1,506	6,422,206	705,450	710,487	6,427,243	2,900,148	1,866,410	43,956	254,659	120,784
2013	11,195,488	6,390,928	-2,252	6,388,676	784,763	816,008	6,419,921	2,876,142	1,899,425	44,215	253,205	120,795
2014	11,838,125	6,675,428	-767	6,674,661	813,949	908,910	6,769,622	3,011,416	2,057,087	46,573	254,183	123,572

Personal Income and Employment by Area: Bridgeport-Stamford-Norwalk, CT

(Thousands of dollars, except as noted.)

Year	Personal income, total	Earnings by place of work			Less: Contributions for government social insurance	Plus: Adjustment for residence	Equals: Net earnings by place of residence	Plus: Dividends, interest, and rent	Plus: Personal current transfer receipts	Per capita personal income (dollars)	Population (persons)	Total employment
		Nonfarm	Farm	Total								
1970	4,866,731	3,152,682	3,681	3,156,363	208,962	669,820	3,617,221	966,033	283,477	6,138	792,934	366,252
1971	5,106,426	3,257,323	3,673	3,260,996	223,363	684,667	3,722,300	1,033,311	350,815	6,441	792,758	358,267
1972	5,489,362	3,544,710	3,649	3,548,359	258,000	708,383	3,998,742	1,116,530	374,090	6,966	788,034	364,054
1973	5,883,600	3,919,506	4,252	3,923,758	330,354	704,072	4,297,476	1,179,462	406,662	7,481	786,524	379,191
1974	6,354,695	4,238,181	4,041	4,242,222	374,258	724,284	4,592,248	1,287,354	475,093	8,061	788,324	383,909
1975	6,818,311	4,473,819	3,695	4,477,514	386,283	782,427	4,873,658	1,321,743	622,910	8,581	794,554	374,936
1976	7,450,347	4,979,739	3,072	4,982,811	437,127	818,255	5,363,939	1,415,950	670,458	9,343	797,444	385,892
1977	8,293,136	5,652,661	3,313	5,655,974	498,579	880,326	6,037,721	1,552,676	702,739	10,233	810,423	403,360
1978	9,318,883	6,437,605	3,316	6,440,921	585,428	975,241	6,830,734	1,749,632	738,517	11,610	802,642	425,460
1979	10,533,496	7,307,975	2,917	7,310,892	692,806	1,092,550	7,710,636	2,001,994	820,866	13,123	802,656	442,700
1980	12,122,310	8,297,944	2,688	8,300,632	789,350	1,244,916	8,756,198	2,416,121	949,991	14,990	808,703	455,859
1981	13,778,395	9,258,136	2,181	9,260,317	949,492	1,362,438	9,673,263	3,031,537	1,073,595	16,944	813,186	470,540
1982	14,891,260	9,928,666	3,067	9,931,733	1,048,044	1,448,019	10,331,708	3,366,172	1,193,380	18,206	817,943	474,803
1983	15,790,510	10,616,278	2,425	10,618,703	1,128,848	1,562,163	11,052,018	3,451,979	1,286,513	19,213	821,854	476,184
1984	17,777,694	12,036,702	2,881	12,039,583	1,308,932	1,666,068	12,396,719	4,036,203	1,344,772	21,546	825,107	495,194
1985	19,151,850	13,150,989	2,624	13,153,613	1,448,341	1,850,358	13,555,630	4,166,378	1,429,842	23,064	830,396	509,468
1986	20,539,078	14,295,130	2,965	14,298,095	1,579,604	1,889,598	14,608,089	4,415,632	1,515,357	24,692	831,797	519,808
1987	22,430,024	15,831,067	3,085	15,834,152	1,717,306	2,009,131	16,125,977	4,738,084	1,565,963	27,080	828,277	525,397
1988	25,112,468	17,760,079	2,656	17,762,735	1,932,961	2,181,177	18,010,951	5,411,075	1,690,442	30,380	826,605	537,634
1989	27,289,901	18,569,647	2,065	18,571,712	2,015,088	2,200,988	18,757,612	6,646,944	1,885,345	32,978	827,517	532,086
1990	28,049,644	19,206,694	3,099	19,209,793	2,057,995	1,820,255	18,972,053	6,969,200	2,108,391	33,841	828,860	521,951
1991	28,267,439	19,509,007	3,962	19,512,969	2,126,995	1,798,547	19,184,521	6,727,286	2,355,632	33,931	833,094	503,321
1992	31,798,790	21,088,464	5,910	21,094,374	2,232,532	2,930,508	21,792,350	7,230,951	2,775,489	38,111	834,372	501,927
1993	32,834,451	22,207,842	8,461	22,216,303	2,333,813	2,293,118	22,175,608	7,752,498	2,906,345	39,138	838,945	512,679
1994	33,599,508	22,954,600	9,607	22,964,207	2,452,080	2,040,991	22,553,118	8,042,635	3,003,755	39,882	842,482	508,287
1995	36,487,564	24,771,768	10,395	24,782,163	2,636,561	2,602,533	24,748,135	8,514,840	3,224,589	43,025	848,057	518,746
1996	39,098,290	26,380,982	5,162	26,386,144	2,785,708	3,173,215	26,773,651	9,014,362	3,310,277	45,760	854,421	528,175
1997	42,152,965	29,346,889	4,646	29,351,535	3,007,277	2,491,458	28,835,716	9,914,092	3,403,157	48,957	861,020	537,529
1998	46,449,589	31,653,138	6,922	31,660,060	3,184,333	3,690,774	32,166,501	10,870,254	3,412,834	53,473	868,651	550,327
1999	49,114,833	34,109,969	10,122	34,120,091	3,372,305	3,379,682	34,127,468	11,487,570	3,499,795	56,000	877,043	561,741
2000	54,013,570	37,801,395	11,396	37,812,791	3,622,348	3,230,598	37,421,041	12,892,566	3,699,963	61,076	884,364	575,098
2001	56,123,616	40,122,245	11,820	40,134,065	3,712,498	2,493,663	38,915,230	13,285,957	3,922,429	63,127	889,063	572,844
2002	54,963,055	39,131,137	11,776	39,142,913	3,779,167	2,671,385	38,035,131	12,728,795	4,199,129	61,556	892,900	569,579
2003	55,861,362	39,723,502	11,415	39,734,917	3,857,283	3,082,593	38,960,227	12,650,994	4,250,141	62,321	896,342	570,077
2004	61,358,135	42,121,390	12,643	42,134,033	4,043,397	3,673,660	41,764,296	15,032,748	4,561,091	68,368	897,472	577,370
2005	66,463,695	43,943,535	14,874	43,958,409	4,175,387	4,284,022	44,067,044	17,781,559	4,615,092	74,042	897,653	585,367
2006	74,334,504	46,816,283	16,179	46,832,462	4,370,936	5,019,028	47,480,554	21,959,040	4,894,910	82,939	896,254	596,312
2007	79,709,854	49,079,034	19,799	49,098,833	4,596,837	5,952,317	50,454,313	24,107,121	5,148,420	88,813	897,498	616,084
2008	80,188,743	49,100,116	10,973	49,111,089	4,703,693	6,416,708	50,824,104	23,480,474	5,884,165	88,722	903,824	616,803
2009	75,018,211	46,812,181	10,203	46,822,384	4,504,087	6,809,975	49,128,272	19,390,317	6,499,622	82,399	910,421	603,708
2010	80,759,800	48,718,142	9,008	48,727,150	4,578,093	8,744,362	52,893,419	20,958,571	6,907,810	87,830	919,506	598,022
2011	85,336,794	51,255,212	5,814	51,261,026	4,227,123	8,962,649	55,996,552	22,425,249	6,914,993	91,886	928,722	615,463
2012	91,090,080	52,741,115	10,695	52,751,810	4,335,666	10,776,770	59,192,914	24,891,960	7,005,206	97,392	935,290	621,876
2013	88,929,427	53,721,762	15,528	53,737,290	5,147,544	9,801,184	58,390,930	23,459,599	7,078,898	94,393	942,119	632,584
2014	93,303,580	55,828,902	10,948	55,839,850	5,357,254	11,202,333	61,684,929	24,370,584	7,248,067	98,688	945,438	640,232

Personal Income and Employment by Area: Brownsville-Harlingen, TX

(Thousands of dollars, except as noted.)

Year	Personal income, total	Earnings by place of work			Less: Contributions for government social insurance	Plus: Adjustment for residence	Equals: Net earnings by place of residence	Plus: Dividends, interest, and rent	Plus: Personal current transfer receipts	Per capita personal income (dollars)	Population (persons)	Total employment
		Nonfarm	Farm	Total								
1970	311,957	236,452	12,535	248,987	15,000	-8,983	225,004	48,167	38,786	2,209	141,196	48,384
1971	363,113	265,911	24,210	290,121	17,408	-9,845	262,868	54,501	45,744	2,458	147,753	50,443
1972	411,579	312,056	20,676	332,732	21,566	-12,392	298,774	61,545	51,260	2,613	157,489	54,936
1973	482,079	367,883	15,921	383,804	29,725	-15,446	338,633	72,193	71,253	2,888	166,939	59,244
1974	567,740	423,254	25,565	448,819	35,323	-17,792	395,704	86,811	85,225	3,297	172,211	62,830
1975	648,243	487,124	17,041	504,165	40,246	-21,544	442,375	100,145	105,723	3,546	182,806	64,977
1976	722,739	548,933	16,964	565,897	45,664	-23,538	496,695	107,661	118,383	3,816	189,415	67,457
1977	792,156	594,767	25,495	620,262	49,589	-25,294	545,379	120,401	126,376	4,068	194,722	69,508
1978	936,964	708,788	33,308	742,096	60,254	-27,948	653,894	142,943	140,127	4,710	198,941	74,442
1979	1,068,799	817,734	13,414	831,148	72,680	-28,388	730,080	170,912	167,807	5,200	205,544	77,871
1980	1,227,643	923,036	3,944	926,980	82,787	-28,038	816,155	209,020	202,468	5,792	211,944	81,655
1981	1,447,038	1,049,900	39,017	1,088,917	101,802	-22,863	964,252	257,100	225,686	6,572	220,184	84,935
1982	1,546,421	1,108,878	15,480	1,124,358	108,940	-24,156	991,262	303,736	251,423	6,703	230,718	85,599
1983	1,649,464	1,123,349	30,554	1,153,903	107,925	-22,682	1,023,296	331,473	294,695	6,905	238,878	83,585
1984	1,752,153	1,170,871	28,770	1,199,641	114,124	-22,715	1,062,802	368,186	321,165	7,230	242,355	83,931
1985	1,898,625	1,252,200	43,113	1,295,313	122,365	-23,008	1,149,940	403,142	345,543	7,721	245,894	85,022
1986	1,955,320	1,296,449	15,734	1,312,183	124,438	-22,823	1,164,922	415,454	374,944	7,790	250,996	83,543
1987	2,016,547	1,319,798	41,152	1,360,950	125,588	-23,023	1,212,339	413,857	390,351	7,948	253,714	85,358
1988	2,178,419	1,437,863	50,888	1,488,751	143,189	-21,716	1,323,846	439,052	415,521	8,563	254,410	88,741
1989	2,354,628	1,560,247	28,628	1,588,875	160,255	-23,126	1,405,494	484,233	464,901	9,179	256,512	93,483
1990	2,626,386	1,758,644	39,592	1,798,236	177,536	-27,032	1,593,668	491,500	541,218	10,035	261,728	98,639
1991	2,833,541	1,883,753	30,741	1,914,494	194,118	-27,270	1,693,106	510,011	630,424	10,523	269,261	101,267
1992	3,179,786	2,068,908	38,156	2,107,064	211,568	-30,823	1,864,673	539,203	775,910	11,466	277,322	104,646
1993	3,448,124	2,258,027	57,997	2,316,024	232,090	-32,609	2,051,325	543,679	853,120	11,960	288,297	109,851
1994	3,671,027	2,410,238	51,942	2,462,180	251,641	-33,623	2,176,916	564,876	929,235	12,347	297,316	115,588
1995	3,841,261	2,485,786	25,422	2,511,208	260,821	-31,987	2,218,400	619,820	1,003,041	12,597	304,928	117,889
1996	4,054,082	2,589,523	48,255	2,637,778	269,177	-27,924	2,340,677	625,096	1,088,309	12,990	312,086	121,253
1997	4,329,055	2,818,090	44,581	2,862,671	289,749	-27,283	2,545,639	643,666	1,139,750	13,601	318,281	124,620
1998	4,622,899	3,059,130	69,785	3,128,915	308,607	-28,091	2,792,217	683,072	1,147,610	14,244	324,556	127,628
1999	4,795,593	3,216,762	73,285	3,290,047	321,028	-23,490	2,945,529	674,316	1,175,748	14,520	330,277	132,144
2000	5,172,335	3,462,689	67,296	3,529,985	342,424	-21,906	3,165,655	739,827	1,266,853	15,388	336,123	139,359
2001	5,584,259	3,746,889	62,748	3,809,637	365,198	-10,164	3,434,275	759,161	1,390,823	16,311	342,368	143,308
2002	6,017,682	4,055,798	55,212	4,111,010	392,595	-9,947	3,708,468	751,006	1,558,208	17,184	350,194	148,381
2003	6,371,052	4,222,434	92,504	4,314,938	415,339	-8,847	3,890,752	815,582	1,664,718	17,772	358,492	149,488
2004	6,593,135	4,415,517	81,712	4,497,229	434,440	-6,891	4,055,898	790,623	1,746,614	17,999	366,299	153,071
2005	6,951,818	4,537,227	81,196	4,618,423	456,368	-4,825	4,157,230	846,814	1,947,774	18,616	373,429	155,539
2006	7,461,335	4,929,707	65,097	4,994,804	491,721	-2,017	4,501,066	888,429	2,071,840	19,626	380,169	162,580
2007	7,944,165	5,116,275	65,391	5,181,666	524,284	1,399	4,658,781	968,949	2,316,435	20,564	386,306	167,526
2008	8,474,342	5,314,220	41,577	5,355,797	545,216	4,838	4,815,419	1,073,005	2,585,918	21,563	393,000	170,810
2009	8,752,637	5,410,225	35,955	5,446,180	560,898	-2,099	4,883,183	1,005,166	2,864,288	21,865	400,303	171,252
2010	9,245,009	5,636,323	45,754	5,682,077	591,139	-4,087	5,086,851	1,008,124	3,150,034	22,678	407,672	172,333
2011	9,625,983	5,811,255	41,844	5,853,099	543,618	-10,418	5,299,063	1,100,635	3,226,285	23,297	413,188	179,034
2012	9,952,491	6,079,793	50,363	6,130,156	566,286	-5,734	5,558,136	1,216,018	3,178,337	23,921	416,048	181,447
2013	10,169,819	6,220,565	58,791	6,279,356	651,225	5,717	5,633,848	1,266,617	3,269,354	24,317	418,217	185,747
2014	10,598,668	6,490,625	46,347	6,536,972	676,503	13,147	5,873,616	1,310,198	3,414,854	25,211	420,392	188,784

Personal Income and Employment by Area: Brunswick, GA

(Thousands of dollars, except as noted.)

| Year | Personal income, total | Derivation of personal income | | | | | | | | | Per capita personal income (dollars) | Population (persons) | Total employment |
| | | Earnings by place of work | | | Less: Contributions for government social insurance | Plus: Adjustment for residence | Equals: Net earnings by place of residence | Plus: Dividends, interest, and rent | Plus: Personal current transfer receipts | | | |
		Nonfarm	Farm	Total								
1970	216,856	171,207	2,545	173,752	10,952	2,528	165,328	34,030	17,498	3,383	64,102	27,191
1971	248,379	197,293	2,304	199,597	13,264	2,748	189,081	38,598	20,700	3,774	65,809	28,897
1972	275,078	217,984	2,732	220,716	15,250	3,837	209,303	42,484	23,291	4,073	67,537	29,346
1973	296,327	230,377	4,341	234,718	18,125	4,839	221,432	47,112	27,783	4,329	68,446	29,715
1974	313,164	236,624	4,817	241,441	19,641	6,216	228,016	50,604	34,544	4,622	67,760	29,309
1975	319,756	227,962	5,782	233,744	18,695	7,268	222,317	51,022	46,417	4,823	66,301	27,827
1976	365,776	267,658	5,543	273,201	22,053	7,789	258,937	57,067	49,772	5,473	66,832	29,663
1977	410,029	303,721	4,017	307,738	24,900	8,857	291,695	65,079	53,255	6,007	68,260	31,063
1978	467,421	343,686	5,484	349,170	28,580	10,409	330,999	77,737	58,685	6,827	68,464	32,995
1979	528,639	386,215	3,838	390,053	33,403	12,779	369,429	92,015	67,195	7,521	70,289	33,871
1980	597,174	426,170	2,186	428,356	37,008	16,975	408,323	108,913	79,938	8,300	71,952	34,773
1981	661,985	454,928	3,723	458,651	42,747	19,981	435,885	134,240	91,860	9,103	72,718	34,166
1982	700,873	465,342	4,853	470,195	44,653	21,615	447,157	152,376	101,340	9,519	73,627	33,888
1983	752,233	498,009	3,778	501,787	48,038	22,249	475,998	166,472	109,763	10,108	74,420	34,276
1984	833,682	553,461	5,345	558,806	54,688	25,750	529,868	184,628	119,186	11,040	75,513	35,831
1985	916,073	618,562	4,013	622,575	62,484	24,508	584,599	204,047	127,427	11,972	76,517	37,907
1986	989,153	666,794	4,978	671,772	68,210	27,902	631,464	221,143	136,546	12,701	77,877	38,823
1987	1,049,290	708,223	3,121	711,344	72,101	29,301	668,544	235,641	145,105	13,274	79,049	39,594
1988	1,144,574	773,641	5,119	778,760	81,220	28,986	726,526	258,750	159,298	14,259	80,269	41,522
1989	1,265,222	824,877	8,088	832,965	87,378	30,910	776,497	317,158	171,567	15,541	81,414	42,364
1990	1,347,782	872,383	6,950	879,333	91,812	33,886	821,407	336,372	190,003	16,349	82,437	42,569
1991	1,415,310	901,474	7,553	909,027	96,000	43,050	856,077	338,059	221,174	16,990	83,303	42,130
1992	1,528,837	974,830	8,274	983,104	102,506	43,041	923,639	359,947	245,251	18,144	84,259	42,703
1993	1,614,542	1,028,516	7,183	1,035,699	109,032	42,334	969,001	380,628	264,913	18,856	85,624	44,165
1994	1,722,143	1,081,671	6,499	1,088,170	116,267	47,814	1,019,717	413,946	288,480	19,912	86,487	45,056
1995	1,860,304	1,163,500	5,703	1,169,203	124,503	51,020	1,095,720	453,606	310,978	21,255	87,522	47,089
1996	2,012,881	1,244,172	5,420	1,249,592	131,582	53,360	1,171,370	506,573	334,938	22,734	88,541	48,188
1997	2,124,972	1,307,287	4,864	1,312,151	135,853	58,240	1,234,538	543,913	346,521	23,604	90,027	48,883
1998	2,269,931	1,411,304	5,060	1,416,364	143,857	68,988	1,341,495	575,697	352,739	24,901	91,160	50,398
1999	2,342,180	1,470,740	5,340	1,476,080	148,562	73,781	1,401,299	574,643	366,238	25,343	92,420	51,007
2000	2,480,511	1,545,400	4,867	1,550,267	155,616	65,806	1,460,457	630,460	389,594	26,574	93,344	52,165
2001	2,546,076	1,576,631	5,619	1,582,250	163,616	56,742	1,475,376	654,837	415,863	26,786	95,052	52,147
2002	2,635,603	1,654,589	3,544	1,658,133	172,201	51,261	1,537,193	633,729	464,681	27,280	96,612	52,308
2003	2,748,907	1,760,761	3,688	1,764,449	184,386	31,798	1,611,861	662,365	474,681	27,999	98,180	52,743
2004	2,986,746	1,906,992	3,928	1,910,920	205,657	22,124	1,727,387	740,631	518,728	29,904	99,879	54,683
2005	3,127,038	1,988,890	3,700	1,992,590	212,362	15,480	1,795,708	790,081	541,249	30,799	101,532	56,678
2006	3,376,420	2,156,223	1,119	2,157,342	234,138	5,533	1,928,737	869,469	578,214	32,244	104,715	58,329
2007	3,510,323	2,195,170	1,604	2,196,774	232,406	637	1,965,005	926,518	618,800	32,705	107,334	59,413
2008	3,610,369	2,257,706	1,173	2,258,879	249,429	-6,689	2,002,761	907,895	699,713	32,948	109,579	58,580
2009	3,457,882	2,156,904	908	2,157,812	239,225	1,813	1,920,400	778,286	759,196	31,056	111,343	55,176
2010	3,439,996	2,098,929	1,285	2,100,214	236,939	11,417	1,874,692	743,860	821,444	30,558	112,574	53,282
2011	3,680,350	2,132,899	1,019	2,133,918	214,378	16,735	1,936,275	883,091	860,984	32,560	113,034	53,147
2012	3,744,492	2,205,058	2,843	2,207,901	222,865	17,600	2,002,636	879,335	862,521	33,009	113,437	53,500
2013	3,811,599	2,254,512	2,449	2,256,961	255,753	20,692	2,021,900	900,189	889,510	33,432	114,012	54,128
2014	3,925,729	2,282,623	3,129	2,285,752	258,068	35,672	2,063,356	931,211	931,162	34,194	114,806	54,415

Personal Income and Employment by Area: Buffalo-Cheektowaga-Niagara Falls, NY

(Thousands of dollars, except as noted.)

Year	Personal income, total	Earnings by place of work			Less: Contributions for government social insurance	Plus: Adjustment for residence	Equals: Net earnings by place of residence	Plus: Dividends, interest, and rent	Plus: Personal current transfer receipts	Per capita personal income (dollars)	Population (persons)	Total employment
		Nonfarm	Farm	Total								
1970	5,681,714	4,751,295	22,870	4,774,165	357,861	-65,632	4,350,672	781,476	549,566	4,204	1,351,513	568,934
1971	6,121,779	5,074,295	22,715	5,097,010	392,449	-72,552	4,632,009	816,504	673,266	4,519	1,354,743	567,469
1972	6,477,529	5,390,469	18,241	5,408,710	439,976	-76,041	4,892,693	851,468	733,368	4,807	1,347,603	566,533
1973	7,018,568	5,906,886	26,612	5,933,498	559,600	-79,854	5,294,044	925,583	798,941	5,262	1,333,861	585,656
1974	7,572,143	6,272,045	25,992	6,298,037	613,643	-79,643	5,604,751	1,045,772	921,620	5,742	1,318,687	586,402
1975	8,177,988	6,504,139	23,307	6,527,446	623,846	-80,403	5,823,197	1,141,910	1,212,881	6,229	1,312,980	568,364
1976	8,806,255	7,060,201	23,390	7,083,591	691,508	-88,344	6,303,739	1,200,133	1,302,383	6,758	1,303,095	569,298
1977	9,600,788	7,734,157	22,196	7,756,353	753,883	-98,524	6,903,946	1,325,814	1,371,028	7,444	1,289,794	577,315
1978	10,369,829	8,427,137	27,648	8,454,785	840,374	-105,446	7,508,965	1,434,858	1,426,006	8,126	1,276,092	585,744
1979	11,389,493	9,246,798	31,775	9,278,573	949,644	-111,569	8,217,360	1,617,937	1,554,196	9,014	1,263,570	597,758
1980	12,352,237	9,636,954	31,575	9,668,529	985,941	-110,199	8,572,389	1,931,755	1,848,093	9,951	1,241,275	583,672
1981	13,457,206	10,307,990	34,392	10,342,382	1,125,826	-113,553	9,103,003	2,311,749	2,042,454	10,917	1,232,720	575,313
1982	14,143,513	10,375,358	32,821	10,408,179	1,144,119	-105,443	9,158,617	2,639,099	2,345,797	11,559	1,223,579	552,973
1983	14,844,248	10,745,865	24,781	10,770,646	1,191,178	-102,494	9,476,974	2,829,555	2,537,719	12,263	1,210,449	542,712
1984	16,251,796	11,804,766	31,688	11,836,454	1,329,736	-104,267	10,402,451	3,208,579	2,640,766	13,571	1,197,531	560,459
1985	17,191,450	12,639,948	34,497	12,674,445	1,447,002	-108,570	11,118,873	3,340,266	2,732,311	14,424	1,191,856	572,233
1986	18,082,364	13,373,036	39,283	13,412,319	1,548,370	-106,959	11,756,990	3,436,513	2,888,861	15,265	1,184,555	585,218
1987	18,839,183	14,068,942	45,235	14,114,177	1,606,660	-101,953	12,405,564	3,475,716	2,957,903	15,969	1,179,756	593,226
1988	20,200,808	15,296,806	39,417	15,336,223	1,777,759	-106,183	13,452,281	3,602,274	3,146,253	17,102	1,181,174	611,066
1989	21,641,387	16,221,811	43,670	16,265,481	1,869,988	-104,837	14,290,656	3,989,440	3,361,291	18,248	1,185,954	623,408
1990	23,034,812	17,113,713	42,119	17,155,832	1,890,016	-107,957	15,157,859	4,224,028	3,652,925	19,342	1,190,943	630,513
1991	23,501,076	17,425,659	35,470	17,461,129	1,994,522	-110,345	15,356,262	4,161,334	3,983,480	19,666	1,194,992	622,358
1992	24,658,488	18,372,061	36,249	18,408,310	2,068,492	-115,177	16,224,641	4,060,503	4,373,344	20,575	1,198,490	619,834
1993	25,141,523	18,720,881	37,038	18,757,919	2,125,442	-117,665	16,514,812	4,048,351	4,578,360	20,938	1,200,744	620,260
1994	26,078,814	19,395,517	31,806	19,427,323	2,223,142	-120,946	17,083,235	4,169,527	4,826,052	21,724	1,200,479	633,711
1995	27,221,478	20,013,849	26,445	20,040,294	2,294,801	-129,946	17,615,547	4,549,531	5,056,400	22,725	1,197,885	626,083
1996	28,006,991	20,558,358	31,638	20,589,996	2,313,895	-145,419	18,130,682	4,629,159	5,247,150	23,453	1,194,167	626,699
1997	29,017,251	21,335,271	26,443	21,361,714	2,362,260	-150,993	18,848,461	4,877,448	5,291,342	24,463	1,186,175	631,833
1998	29,801,285	21,948,311	33,657	21,981,968	2,419,878	-171,853	19,390,237	4,946,304	5,464,744	25,288	1,178,462	626,564
1999	30,847,534	23,121,653	43,761	23,165,414	2,507,833	-186,624	20,470,957	4,796,981	5,579,596	26,296	1,173,102	637,327
2000	32,273,968	24,255,515	48,044	24,303,559	2,625,586	-205,131	21,472,842	5,055,981	5,745,145	27,607	1,169,060	644,807
2001	32,827,827	24,415,093	52,046	24,467,139	2,705,608	-166,675	21,594,856	5,106,337	6,126,634	28,177	1,165,067	635,219
2002	33,289,245	24,933,325	46,340	24,979,665	2,806,632	-170,929	22,002,104	4,825,268	6,461,873	28,656	1,161,678	632,064
2003	34,478,816	25,760,164	52,187	25,812,351	2,899,878	-173,884	22,738,589	5,101,999	6,638,228	29,725	1,159,918	635,399
2004	35,858,145	27,054,389	57,392	27,111,781	3,039,015	-178,980	23,893,786	4,950,075	7,014,284	31,017	1,156,070	641,850
2005	36,600,338	27,391,319	53,512	27,444,831	3,114,757	-133,015	24,197,059	5,119,211	7,284,068	31,866	1,148,563	642,704
2006	38,323,827	28,587,403	48,975	28,636,378	3,223,912	-90,978	25,321,488	5,296,164	7,706,175	33,567	1,141,712	641,920
2007	40,201,299	29,501,870	69,601	29,571,471	3,309,125	-56,447	26,205,899	5,946,767	8,048,633	35,336	1,137,678	646,095
2008	42,089,641	30,475,188	77,628	30,552,816	3,439,250	-57,287	27,056,279	6,123,959	8,909,403	37,039	1,136,364	650,050
2009	42,571,645	30,501,405	50,088	30,551,493	3,428,336	-26,352	27,096,805	5,771,837	9,703,003	37,496	1,135,377	637,576
2010	43,965,788	31,446,172	77,127	31,523,299	3,536,138	-7,877	27,979,284	5,753,365	10,233,139	38,725	1,135,342	636,997
2011	46,203,989	32,812,130	88,371	32,900,501	3,323,357	-12,703	29,564,441	6,270,082	10,369,466	40,694	1,135,411	645,875
2012	47,797,540	33,728,948	87,458	33,816,406	3,388,021	-10,695	30,417,690	7,003,337	10,376,513	42,110	1,135,067	649,569
2013	48,179,435	34,537,895	120,431	34,658,326	3,912,783	12,548	30,758,091	6,866,512	10,554,832	42,406	1,136,153	654,091
2014	49,631,417	35,690,310	106,020	35,796,330	4,069,872	-13,278	31,713,180	7,139,030	10,779,207	43,676	1,136,360	659,430

Personal Income and Employment by Area: Burlington, NC

(Thousands of dollars, except as noted.)

Year	Personal income, total	Earnings by place of work			Less: Contributions for government social insurance	Plus: Adjustment for residence	Equals: Net earnings by place of residence	Plus: Dividends, interest, and rent	Plus: Personal current transfer receipts	Per capita personal income (dollars)	Population (persons)	Total employment
		Nonfarm	Farm	Total								
1970	349,411	293,245	6,208	299,453	21,451	9,038	287,040	38,761	23,610	3,608	96,843	51,242
1971	380,057	315,000	5,430	320,430	24,016	12,669	309,083	42,238	28,736	3,858	98,499	51,105
1972	422,798	349,143	6,033	355,176	27,936	17,342	344,582	46,016	32,200	4,239	99,740	52,100
1973	468,094	383,752	9,782	393,534	35,009	21,356	379,881	50,636	37,577	4,684	99,940	53,563
1974	502,504	398,579	9,484	408,063	37,926	27,796	397,933	57,642	46,929	5,062	99,272	52,836
1975	535,167	403,610	6,373	409,983	37,596	33,159	405,546	63,876	65,745	5,447	98,243	49,823
1976	587,334	434,296	11,436	445,732	41,198	40,924	445,458	68,845	73,031	5,949	98,721	49,923
1977	625,684	454,047	9,621	463,668	42,848	53,056	473,876	76,690	75,118	6,352	98,505	49,601
1978	694,426	497,172	8,532	505,704	48,507	72,975	530,172	85,262	78,992	7,047	98,540	50,016
1979	778,245	553,340	6,792	560,132	55,701	88,850	593,281	95,141	89,823	7,857	99,048	53,068
1980	867,645	593,825	4,996	598,821	60,008	102,324	641,137	119,375	107,133	8,717	99,532	52,664
1981	974,431	662,695	9,242	671,937	71,609	100,449	700,777	149,913	123,741	9,736	100,083	53,335
1982	1,044,613	686,401	9,436	695,837	74,489	99,775	721,123	180,469	143,021	10,343	101,000	52,891
1983	1,129,573	760,337	4,830	765,167	82,845	100,909	783,231	196,099	150,243	11,122	101,559	53,988
1984	1,249,177	848,980	10,577	859,557	94,675	103,162	868,044	226,609	154,524	12,282	101,706	56,603
1985	1,332,255	908,461	6,762	915,223	102,634	104,519	917,108	247,893	167,254	12,995	102,524	57,844
1986	1,444,779	1,005,075	7,089	1,012,164	116,026	99,032	995,170	271,244	178,365	13,957	103,515	59,960
1987	1,541,982	1,104,807	5,294	1,110,101	125,289	95,434	1,080,246	273,607	188,129	14,675	105,072	62,866
1988	1,676,142	1,216,487	8,774	1,225,261	140,611	89,274	1,173,924	297,632	204,586	15,764	106,327	66,241
1989	1,822,022	1,296,789	14,869	1,311,658	150,087	83,157	1,244,728	350,873	226,421	16,961	107,425	67,397
1990	1,891,928	1,352,690	19,328	1,372,018	160,377	75,071	1,286,712	360,002	245,214	17,406	108,695	68,152
1991	1,969,383	1,409,294	18,350	1,427,644	170,160	70,265	1,327,749	361,713	279,921	17,780	110,762	66,347
1992	2,101,031	1,501,091	18,130	1,519,221	178,542	80,879	1,421,558	372,951	306,522	18,622	112,825	67,347
1993	2,235,573	1,601,496	16,625	1,618,121	192,222	81,055	1,506,954	399,587	329,032	19,494	114,678	68,752
1994	2,369,895	1,698,341	15,536	1,713,877	206,111	88,316	1,596,082	426,201	347,612	20,292	116,788	69,706
1995	2,534,463	1,782,525	10,378	1,792,903	216,596	100,772	1,677,079	471,544	385,840	21,335	118,796	71,463
1996	2,686,267	1,873,306	10,954	1,884,260	226,640	103,950	1,761,570	509,983	414,714	22,152	121,263	73,122
1997	2,891,965	2,034,364	10,023	2,044,387	242,913	107,628	1,909,102	549,433	433,430	23,345	123,877	74,821
1998	3,127,700	2,200,027	9,317	2,209,344	260,538	135,208	2,084,014	597,279	446,407	24,777	126,232	78,562
1999	3,319,880	2,406,436	12,115	2,418,551	282,328	126,942	2,263,165	587,892	468,823	25,787	128,743	80,206
2000	3,503,719	2,511,966	16,135	2,528,101	292,759	141,749	2,377,091	624,306	502,322	26,660	131,423	81,263
2001	3,581,500	2,541,869	16,481	2,558,350	297,944	128,306	2,388,712	626,014	566,774	26,859	133,346	79,653
2002	3,666,775	2,592,530	5,166	2,597,696	296,960	153,309	2,454,045	606,082	606,648	27,113	135,239	78,211
2003	3,731,887	2,585,590	10,739	2,596,329	302,557	177,602	2,471,374	619,839	640,674	27,439	136,009	77,280
2004	3,925,205	2,707,645	11,184	2,718,829	314,718	214,847	2,618,958	617,091	689,156	28,522	137,619	78,523
2005	4,080,277	2,777,631	14,507	2,792,138	330,239	247,764	2,709,663	630,266	740,348	29,289	139,311	79,364
2006	4,428,317	2,942,281	12,598	2,954,879	349,130	293,018	2,898,767	701,758	827,792	31,304	141,462	80,015
2007	4,691,488	3,009,945	11,448	3,021,393	364,584	338,568	2,995,377	819,012	877,099	32,419	144,712	83,101
2008	4,871,778	3,044,432	5,661	3,050,093	372,320	379,168	3,056,941	811,425	1,003,412	32,983	147,704	81,724
2009	4,786,807	2,844,943	3,180	2,848,123	348,039	442,200	2,942,284	733,131	1,111,392	31,922	149,954	77,710
2010	4,868,085	2,910,521	2,862	2,913,383	345,632	440,465	3,008,216	693,577	1,166,292	32,122	151,551	76,834
2011	5,030,123	2,965,166	147	2,965,313	326,515	436,724	3,075,522	783,107	1,171,494	32,905	152,866	78,724
2012	5,283,136	3,211,449	5,941	3,217,390	341,177	399,248	3,275,461	803,735	1,203,940	34,379	153,672	80,012
2013	5,199,787	3,128,540	7,172	3,135,712	387,618	438,128	3,186,222	795,121	1,218,444	33,615	154,685	80,344
2014	5,421,753	3,205,334	9,818	3,215,152	396,815	533,195	3,351,532	825,490	1,244,731	34,801	155,792	81,138

Personal Income and Employment by Area: Burlington-South Burlington, VT

(Thousands of dollars, except as noted.)

| Year | Personal income, total | Derivation of personal income | | | | | | | | Per capita personal income (dollars) | Population (persons) | Total employment |
| | | Earnings by place of work | | | Less: Contributions for government social insurance | Plus: Adjustment for residence | Equals: Net earnings by place of residence | Plus: Dividends, interest, and rent | Plus: Personal current transfer receipts | | | |
		Nonfarm	Farm	Total								
1970	512,561	423,104	17,722	440,826	29,444	-13,440	397,942	67,938	46,681	3,806	134,673	62,022
1971	552,383	447,956	17,720	465,676	31,994	-12,744	420,938	74,985	56,460	4,016	137,553	62,103
1972	601,300	485,095	19,304	504,399	36,122	-13,164	455,113	82,057	64,130	4,277	140,585	62,800
1973	648,327	522,042	20,573	542,615	44,911	-12,936	484,768	90,149	73,410	4,602	140,865	64,201
1974	698,514	553,834	16,913	570,747	49,146	-12,323	509,278	101,206	88,030	4,931	141,657	64,786
1975	780,610	605,120	17,982	623,102	52,565	-13,588	556,949	113,455	110,206	5,436	143,608	64,467
1976	870,194	682,987	22,301	705,288	60,602	-15,128	629,558	122,308	118,328	5,993	145,209	67,585
1977	948,986	756,822	18,942	775,764	67,583	-16,692	691,489	137,239	120,258	6,433	147,509	70,446
1978	1,101,817	894,757	27,525	922,282	82,639	-21,619	818,024	157,337	126,456	7,394	149,023	76,185
1979	1,253,621	1,025,608	29,838	1,055,446	98,499	-26,176	930,771	179,330	143,520	8,272	151,554	80,057
1980	1,417,110	1,136,648	30,079	1,166,727	109,727	-29,041	1,027,959	220,223	168,928	9,117	155,430	82,463
1981	1,611,127	1,285,079	32,918	1,317,997	133,162	-36,114	1,148,721	270,731	191,675	10,261	157,017	85,578
1982	1,751,178	1,390,621	31,780	1,422,401	147,354	-42,566	1,232,481	311,105	207,592	11,037	158,663	87,158
1983	1,886,351	1,524,518	21,355	1,545,873	163,393	-49,531	1,332,949	332,570	220,832	11,769	160,287	89,680
1984	2,082,550	1,688,634	22,047	1,710,681	186,031	-56,200	1,468,450	387,194	226,906	12,877	161,724	94,035
1985	2,282,585	1,867,903	27,639	1,895,542	209,699	-64,930	1,620,913	423,169	238,503	13,939	163,751	98,992
1986	2,466,767	2,030,483	27,935	2,058,418	228,907	-71,760	1,757,751	463,326	245,690	14,875	165,834	103,108
1987	2,682,771	2,234,111	36,515	2,270,626	247,883	-80,447	1,942,296	489,133	251,342	15,992	167,755	107,321
1988	2,964,418	2,492,200	34,060	2,526,260	284,100	-97,553	2,144,607	552,598	267,213	17,288	171,477	113,250
1989	3,321,762	2,741,203	35,548	2,776,751	309,473	-108,811	2,358,467	666,769	296,526	18,984	174,979	117,499
1990	3,491,486	2,897,631	33,930	2,931,561	346,099	-117,366	2,468,096	693,831	329,559	19,642	177,757	117,930
1991	3,577,674	2,966,636	28,614	2,995,250	357,372	-118,595	2,519,283	695,632	362,759	19,937	179,447	115,960
1992	3,812,096	3,136,669	49,875	3,186,544	373,108	-123,589	2,689,847	712,247	410,002	21,041	181,178	117,796
1993	3,977,874	3,299,633	39,987	3,339,620	394,254	-129,470	2,815,896	728,795	433,183	21,630	183,909	120,276
1994	4,143,973	3,392,561	40,336	3,432,897	409,133	-129,957	2,893,807	795,903	454,263	22,138	187,186	123,280
1995	4,424,735	3,564,596	31,957	3,596,553	434,510	-142,056	3,019,987	909,364	495,384	23,374	189,300	125,287
1996	4,701,019	3,815,439	46,011	3,861,450	460,097	-159,336	3,242,017	946,265	512,737	24,607	191,043	128,300
1997	4,953,547	4,012,469	34,235	4,046,704	480,695	-169,497	3,396,512	1,013,998	543,037	25,661	193,040	130,011
1998	5,345,090	4,342,316	44,223	4,386,539	513,747	-185,267	3,687,525	1,094,091	563,474	27,454	194,691	133,186
1999	5,726,848	4,715,649	48,024	4,763,673	552,694	-201,319	4,009,660	1,110,739	606,449	29,066	197,026	136,934
2000	6,219,280	5,146,245	51,256	5,197,501	595,655	-223,070	4,378,776	1,178,621	661,883	31,159	199,600	141,938
2001	6,565,298	5,448,926	52,174	5,501,100	635,150	-233,315	4,632,635	1,206,567	726,096	32,605	201,361	143,936
2002	6,743,029	5,597,234	39,726	5,636,960	640,202	-237,589	4,759,169	1,206,407	777,453	33,208	203,052	143,437
2003	7,070,454	5,805,129	48,902	5,854,031	664,570	-243,061	4,946,400	1,308,892	815,162	34,625	204,201	143,693
2004	7,459,192	6,112,226	65,146	6,177,372	698,682	-235,501	5,243,189	1,368,582	847,421	36,271	205,652	146,213
2005	7,655,189	6,317,340	67,671	6,385,011	728,610	-243,667	5,412,734	1,316,634	925,821	37,047	206,637	147,224
2006	8,196,308	6,572,728	40,239	6,612,967	764,226	-249,681	5,599,060	1,578,375	1,018,873	39,514	207,426	148,105
2007	8,601,545	6,741,875	71,646	6,813,521	804,684	-246,305	5,762,532	1,699,686	1,139,327	41,308	208,232	150,108
2008	9,001,447	6,968,954	47,471	7,016,425	833,373	-249,406	5,933,646	1,777,490	1,290,311	43,001	209,332	151,294
2009	8,825,735	6,923,304	20,128	6,943,432	833,888	-257,721	5,851,823	1,577,261	1,396,651	41,940	210,435	149,067
2010	9,035,668	7,142,566	41,629	7,184,195	853,026	-284,426	6,046,743	1,500,092	1,488,833	42,720	211,508	150,432
2011	9,795,197	7,523,224	67,152	7,590,376	800,676	-286,170	6,503,530	1,771,402	1,520,265	46,022	212,837	153,750
2012	10,192,926	7,836,567	57,392	7,893,959	839,000	-317,326	6,737,633	1,899,844	1,555,449	47,659	213,874	156,273
2013	10,336,611	8,041,879	79,169	8,121,048	973,927	-323,823	6,823,298	1,893,767	1,619,546	48,061	215,072	157,917
2014	10,698,034	8,268,647	101,194	8,369,841	1,011,490	-321,558	7,036,793	1,967,097	1,694,144	49,490	216,167	160,322

Personal Income and Employment by Area: California-Lexington Park, MD

(Thousands of dollars, except as noted.)

Year	Personal income, total	Earnings by place of work			Less: Contributions for government social insurance	Plus: Adjustment for residence	Equals: Net earnings by place of residence	Plus: Dividends, interest, and rent	Plus: Personal current transfer receipts	Per capita personal income (dollars)	Population (persons)	Total employment
		Nonfarm	Farm	Total								
1970	205,255	147,810	5,694	153,504	7,478	9,200	155,226	40,679	9,350	4,290	47,840	19,164
1971	230,562	162,689	4,453	167,142	8,459	16,495	175,178	44,135	11,249	4,600	50,127	19,026
1972	259,746	180,707	5,240	185,947	9,625	21,365	197,687	49,129	12,930	5,113	50,805	19,653
1973	278,596	184,762	8,012	192,774	10,637	28,359	210,496	52,944	15,156	5,580	49,928	19,221
1974	315,002	206,442	7,933	214,375	12,701	34,137	235,811	60,946	18,245	6,097	51,667	20,064
1975	313,939	195,162	6,410	201,572	12,572	40,664	229,664	61,366	22,909	5,953	52,738	18,610
1976	347,807	213,617	7,717	221,334	14,073	48,775	256,036	66,555	25,216	6,474	53,724	18,852
1977	383,769	229,748	7,698	237,446	15,214	58,662	280,894	75,200	27,675	7,039	54,522	19,582
1978	430,137	248,338	10,702	259,040	16,768	71,031	313,303	86,294	30,540	7,580	56,744	20,556
1979	465,106	266,171	7,430	273,601	19,870	84,402	338,133	91,887	35,086	7,945	58,541	20,935
1980	527,520	300,090	3,785	303,875	22,922	98,586	379,539	105,404	42,577	8,766	60,176	21,211
1981	635,906	360,576	11,537	372,113	26,509	114,874	460,478	125,603	49,825	10,394	61,182	22,032
1982	693,679	388,859	18,623	407,482	29,106	116,980	495,356	142,927	55,396	11,243	61,697	22,268
1983	735,682	422,734	9,533	432,267	34,543	123,760	521,484	154,043	60,155	11,780	62,450	23,501
1984	806,572	466,122	8,430	474,552	39,891	133,607	568,268	172,775	65,529	12,753	63,245	24,650
1985	881,156	509,227	12,874	522,101	45,530	146,612	623,183	187,691	70,282	13,636	64,618	25,721
1986	952,008	564,245	4,446	568,691	52,568	159,589	675,712	202,448	73,848	14,301	66,570	27,230
1987	1,043,104	628,994	5,201	634,195	59,506	169,875	744,564	216,352	82,188	15,099	69,083	29,457
1988	1,178,149	736,579	6,935	743,514	73,915	182,869	852,468	236,434	89,247	16,412	71,785	32,351
1989	1,292,781	810,159	3,530	813,689	83,118	195,765	926,336	264,327	102,118	17,439	74,130	34,042
1990	1,393,172	883,634	5,634	889,268	93,086	206,240	1,002,422	276,434	114,316	18,245	76,361	35,990
1991	1,473,548	947,069	6,380	953,449	101,079	194,607	1,046,977	294,602	131,969	18,903	77,952	36,785
1992	1,553,117	995,795	4,799	1,000,594	106,975	195,114	1,088,733	309,992	154,392	19,706	78,815	36,686
1993	1,583,702	1,005,194	4,259	1,009,453	108,684	201,261	1,102,030	320,012	161,660	20,305	77,994	35,928
1994	1,634,987	1,040,544	5,236	1,045,780	114,623	200,875	1,132,032	336,258	166,697	20,765	78,737	36,940
1995	1,708,730	1,092,861	-5,492	1,087,369	119,644	196,326	1,164,051	366,175	178,504	21,569	79,222	38,098
1996	1,836,602	1,193,867	14,510	1,208,377	130,378	184,403	1,262,402	385,556	188,644	22,777	80,633	40,147
1997	2,107,341	1,461,876	7,330	1,469,206	159,123	149,326	1,459,409	450,731	197,201	25,339	83,165	44,464
1998	2,345,137	1,708,117	1,123	1,709,240	183,824	116,430	1,641,846	500,366	202,925	27,601	84,967	47,321
1999	2,431,853	1,767,523	2,628	1,770,151	190,550	121,168	1,700,769	514,328	216,756	28,401	85,627	48,049
2000	2,617,744	1,931,709	10,803	1,942,512	206,174	105,910	1,842,248	541,493	234,003	30,264	86,498	49,409
2001	2,707,616	2,043,971	10,929	2,054,900	216,470	85,143	1,923,573	523,133	260,910	30,960	87,455	50,212
2002	2,965,138	2,254,578	-4,702	2,249,876	238,834	126,304	2,137,346	537,583	290,209	33,012	89,819	52,425
2003	3,277,824	2,485,696	6,194	2,491,890	263,783	176,335	2,404,442	565,246	308,136	35,500	92,333	54,856
2004	3,525,568	2,662,603	8,146	2,670,749	284,802	229,370	2,615,317	576,347	333,904	37,150	94,900	56,313
2005	3,722,819	2,767,423	5,178	2,772,601	295,277	280,734	2,758,058	599,185	365,576	38,431	96,871	56,998
2006	4,098,086	3,023,852	3,183	3,027,035	323,697	353,138	3,056,476	652,225	389,385	41,458	98,849	59,011
2007	4,428,555	3,182,388	2,299	3,184,687	344,824	429,345	3,269,208	730,973	428,374	44,022	100,599	61,342
2008	4,725,977	3,258,148	2,921	3,261,069	357,799	493,665	3,396,935	825,746	503,296	46,369	101,921	61,533
2009	4,748,457	3,482,634	2,247	3,484,881	384,162	314,000	3,414,719	797,071	536,667	45,980	103,273	61,592
2010	4,976,952	3,784,731	-1,181	3,783,550	425,851	219,222	3,576,921	806,143	593,888	47,068	105,740	62,723
2011	5,250,673	4,032,540	3,135	4,035,675	405,541	120,873	3,751,007	872,657	627,009	48,727	107,757	63,634
2012	5,351,906	4,065,313	266	4,065,579	410,756	126,340	3,781,163	921,113	649,630	49,101	108,999	63,825
2013	5,348,798	4,068,355	-42	4,068,313	463,232	112,686	3,717,767	957,870	673,161	48,855	109,484	64,551
2014	5,544,902	4,146,803	-1,917	4,144,886	468,906	158,354	3,834,334	997,032	713,536	50,234	110,382	65,076

Personal Income and Employment by Area: Canton-Massillon, OH

(Thousands of dollars, except as noted.)

Year	Personal income, total	Earnings by place of work			Less: Contributions for government social insurance	Plus: Adjustment for residence	Equals: Net earnings by place of residence	Plus: Dividends, interest, and rent	Plus: Personal current transfer receipts	Per capita personal income (dollars)	Population (persons)	Total employment
		Nonfarm	Farm	Total								
1970	1,538,652	1,259,692	6,263	1,265,955	86,403	32,767	1,212,319	201,541	124,792	3,901	394,389	166,024
1971	1,594,186	1,268,744	7,849	1,276,593	89,495	43,683	1,230,781	215,087	148,318	4,017	396,830	160,591
1972	1,767,097	1,419,460	7,807	1,427,267	105,412	52,572	1,374,427	228,725	163,945	4,478	394,589	163,820
1973	1,988,813	1,616,473	9,499	1,625,972	139,857	59,363	1,545,478	252,923	190,412	4,913	404,798	173,392
1974	2,226,197	1,794,884	10,639	1,805,523	161,136	66,165	1,710,552	290,137	225,508	5,479	406,348	179,109
1975	2,392,910	1,857,014	14,869	1,871,883	162,465	73,647	1,783,065	315,481	294,364	5,946	402,470	173,184
1976	2,605,301	2,030,005	15,741	2,045,746	180,923	82,558	1,947,381	336,247	321,673	6,504	400,573	173,726
1977	2,887,504	2,253,566	13,768	2,267,334	200,669	112,931	2,179,596	373,481	334,427	7,195	401,304	177,260
1978	3,218,718	2,533,892	8,722	2,542,614	233,670	134,521	2,443,465	418,927	356,326	7,965	404,117	184,559
1979	3,617,995	2,841,434	7,293	2,848,727	272,784	155,260	2,731,203	477,740	409,052	8,980	402,887	189,646
1980	3,958,272	2,953,714	297	2,954,011	282,431	175,740	2,847,320	589,093	521,859	9,789	404,365	186,051
1981	4,371,458	3,215,404	2,760	3,218,164	329,515	177,492	3,066,141	726,842	578,475	10,841	403,233	184,686
1982	4,511,670	3,146,031	4,582	3,150,613	326,647	188,516	3,012,482	807,953	691,235	11,234	401,616	177,193
1983	4,672,576	3,196,079	-311	3,195,768	334,666	205,135	3,066,237	865,913	740,426	11,689	399,727	172,450
1984	5,080,026	3,515,274	10,183	3,525,457	378,965	221,134	3,367,626	957,822	754,578	12,728	399,131	179,713
1985	5,310,894	3,662,073	12,457	3,674,530	400,955	236,157	3,509,732	1,001,460	799,702	13,394	396,527	183,119
1986	5,459,182	3,705,648	12,327	3,717,975	417,024	263,599	3,564,550	1,035,285	859,347	13,871	393,569	185,112
1987	5,719,614	3,942,778	14,925	3,957,703	443,742	265,461	3,779,422	1,042,828	897,364	14,586	392,135	191,292
1988	6,114,089	4,262,791	14,230	4,277,021	494,460	278,580	4,061,141	1,113,301	939,647	15,528	393,752	194,561
1989	6,557,242	4,487,999	19,738	4,507,737	522,313	304,343	4,289,767	1,265,168	1,002,307	16,622	394,481	198,003
1990	6,931,822	4,728,152	17,440	4,745,592	560,478	312,232	4,497,346	1,308,385	1,126,091	17,566	394,606	201,081
1991	7,031,371	4,817,628	9,328	4,826,956	582,376	322,289	4,566,869	1,272,630	1,191,872	17,710	397,025	200,722
1992	7,528,022	5,166,138	20,514	5,186,652	617,527	341,368	4,910,493	1,309,016	1,308,513	18,848	399,399	199,451
1993	7,863,031	5,431,635	16,229	5,447,864	661,052	365,322	5,152,134	1,359,254	1,351,643	19,555	402,098	202,448
1994	8,288,913	5,774,264	25,708	5,799,972	711,120	391,900	5,480,752	1,443,937	1,364,224	20,537	403,612	207,012
1995	8,665,373	6,004,290	27,036	6,031,326	749,400	417,736	5,699,662	1,532,648	1,433,063	21,400	404,924	212,418
1996	9,039,010	6,196,797	26,678	6,223,475	762,440	453,427	5,914,462	1,622,927	1,501,621	22,268	405,915	215,591
1997	9,417,048	6,422,993	27,659	6,450,652	772,726	477,358	6,155,284	1,722,225	1,539,539	23,181	406,235	218,984
1998	10,105,556	6,969,618	54,886	7,024,504	807,235	501,435	6,718,704	1,788,848	1,598,004	24,879	406,189	224,728
1999	10,412,357	7,195,872	46,528	7,242,400	824,670	534,158	6,951,888	1,805,926	1,654,543	25,584	406,983	226,613
2000	10,984,647	7,579,639	35,205	7,614,844	837,711	561,581	7,338,714	1,878,610	1,767,323	26,997	406,887	231,852
2001	11,170,769	7,748,070	33,110	7,781,180	860,041	526,668	7,447,807	1,810,373	1,912,589	27,497	406,256	228,976
2002	11,249,921	7,736,090	26,119	7,762,209	845,603	572,775	7,489,381	1,717,850	2,042,690	27,707	406,039	225,070
2003	11,488,120	7,816,872	25,331	7,842,203	866,890	629,749	7,605,062	1,738,618	2,144,440	28,293	406,046	222,066
2004	11,813,218	8,090,044	29,694	8,119,738	912,770	712,879	7,919,847	1,700,218	2,193,153	29,099	405,960	223,210
2005	12,274,126	8,357,553	31,731	8,389,284	949,203	805,209	8,245,290	1,695,648	2,333,188	30,294	405,168	225,351
2006	12,780,895	8,504,064	25,076	8,529,140	968,162	888,778	8,449,756	1,862,356	2,468,783	31,531	405,343	221,588
2007	13,373,749	8,623,955	31,312	8,655,267	989,297	986,422	8,652,392	2,086,281	2,635,076	32,945	405,939	222,865
2008	13,982,382	8,847,849	36,352	8,884,201	1,026,445	1,066,623	8,924,379	2,105,449	2,952,554	34,427	406,140	220,532
2009	13,467,986	8,279,825	41,977	8,321,802	983,542	1,028,420	8,366,680	1,870,517	3,230,789	33,244	405,127	211,338
2010	13,876,200	8,507,776	47,067	8,554,843	986,364	1,103,583	8,672,062	1,799,912	3,404,226	34,330	404,202	209,064
2011	14,858,014	9,077,681	61,054	9,138,735	951,901	1,127,460	9,314,294	2,057,158	3,486,562	36,858	403,119	213,933
2012	15,437,776	9,462,244	49,612	9,511,856	981,222	1,202,368	9,733,002	2,274,450	3,430,324	38,269	403,404	218,094
2013	15,574,198	9,797,989	63,291	9,861,280	1,108,106	1,065,204	9,818,378	2,202,719	3,553,101	38,598	403,493	221,595
2014	16,184,794	10,220,830	63,957	10,284,787	1,162,712	1,062,988	10,185,063	2,287,073	3,712,658	40,069	403,923	225,199

Personal Income and Employment by Area: Cape Coral-Fort Myers, FL

(Thousands of dollars, except as noted.)

Year	Personal income, total	Derivation of personal income								Per capita personal income (dollars)	Population (persons)	Total employment
		Earnings by place of work			Less: Contributions for government social insurance	Plus: Adjustment for residence	Equals: Net earnings by place of residence	Plus: Dividends, interest, and rent	Plus: Personal current transfer receipts			
		Nonfarm	Farm	Total								
1970	429,291	256,160	7,788	263,948	16,301	5,693	253,340	126,375	49,576	3,996	107,430	42,485
1971	486,382	282,727	8,448	291,175	18,792	5,900	278,283	145,996	62,103	4,159	116,946	44,589
1972	572,491	338,447	9,099	347,546	23,700	6,897	330,743	165,793	75,955	4,484	127,672	49,836
1973	705,982	420,068	10,076	430,144	33,844	9,882	406,182	203,597	96,203	5,143	137,276	58,032
1974	830,374	485,193	9,569	494,762	41,155	10,604	464,211	249,558	116,605	5,656	146,825	61,830
1975	929,016	505,504	15,192	520,696	42,100	8,476	487,072	287,767	154,177	5,997	154,905	61,397
1976	1,055,848	580,127	17,346	597,473	48,458	8,410	557,425	324,749	173,674	6,614	159,632	65,373
1977	1,235,467	682,712	18,233	700,945	57,763	10,729	653,911	385,189	196,367	7,100	173,998	73,310
1978	1,500,668	836,319	23,175	859,494	72,566	14,181	801,109	470,837	228,722	8,204	182,920	83,121
1979	1,778,853	989,141	24,644	1,013,785	90,397	14,949	938,337	568,103	272,413	9,236	192,597	90,770
1980	2,164,526	1,149,411	25,998	1,175,409	106,373	17,382	1,086,418	744,606	333,502	10,404	208,050	96,755
1981	2,578,511	1,316,015	22,103	1,338,118	131,787	19,001	1,225,332	949,639	403,540	11,785	218,795	103,581
1982	2,757,706	1,365,192	27,149	1,392,341	142,832	16,972	1,266,481	1,018,452	472,773	11,942	230,932	106,186
1983	3,136,182	1,543,711	39,899	1,583,610	160,655	14,588	1,437,543	1,175,441	523,198	12,983	241,554	113,430
1984	3,572,981	1,775,959	39,545	1,815,504	189,367	16,477	1,642,614	1,360,716	569,651	13,995	255,299	121,575
1985	4,062,778	2,005,264	43,315	2,048,579	218,359	18,905	1,849,125	1,575,334	638,319	15,210	267,107	129,854
1986	4,522,852	2,255,149	50,847	2,305,996	252,185	18,727	2,072,538	1,744,282	706,032	16,125	280,483	136,443
1987	5,009,318	2,558,806	58,630	2,617,436	282,950	19,800	2,354,286	1,890,114	764,918	16,966	295,262	138,260
1988	5,573,956	2,884,658	58,449	2,943,107	329,699	23,552	2,636,960	2,095,949	841,047	18,166	306,842	149,455
1989	6,508,435	3,202,106	61,650	3,263,756	372,331	24,710	2,916,135	2,635,648	956,652	20,197	322,253	159,512
1990	6,912,581	3,431,530	41,827	3,473,357	394,912	29,988	3,108,433	2,751,829	1,052,319	20,390	339,012	164,024
1991	7,142,053	3,621,112	48,490	3,669,602	417,707	33,276	3,285,171	2,684,928	1,171,954	20,344	351,069	163,361
1992	7,586,470	3,878,432	46,252	3,924,684	445,102	38,340	3,517,922	2,731,348	1,337,200	21,092	359,679	162,757
1993	8,025,561	4,142,414	49,101	4,191,515	472,611	48,985	3,767,889	2,828,133	1,429,539	21,753	368,938	170,194
1994	8,565,887	4,477,767	39,826	4,517,593	518,294	53,797	4,053,096	2,982,252	1,530,539	22,487	380,928	178,317
1995	9,350,009	4,779,625	41,282	4,820,907	549,601	64,268	4,335,574	3,359,328	1,655,107	23,863	391,823	186,043
1996	9,858,311	5,148,660	30,688	5,179,348	582,229	76,390	4,673,509	3,422,965	1,761,837	24,601	400,723	191,718
1997	10,428,608	5,305,750	33,445	5,339,195	604,113	106,495	4,841,577	3,746,311	1,840,720	25,384	410,841	196,507
1998	11,353,388	5,913,446	43,416	5,956,862	656,668	119,025	5,419,219	4,073,411	1,860,758	26,911	421,889	206,126
1999	11,963,149	6,489,055	45,843	6,534,898	709,860	137,297	5,962,335	4,050,062	1,950,752	27,694	431,981	211,813
2000	13,025,264	7,014,775	43,903	7,058,678	764,156	169,914	6,464,436	4,462,266	2,098,562	29,316	444,311	221,094
2001	14,385,929	7,988,096	42,924	8,031,020	876,789	157,926	7,312,157	4,791,314	2,282,458	31,203	461,037	234,742
2002	15,146,690	8,779,631	45,517	8,825,148	946,976	144,743	8,022,915	4,662,261	2,461,514	31,629	478,889	242,577
2003	16,160,125	9,608,184	43,697	9,651,881	1,041,991	137,405	8,747,295	4,767,998	2,644,832	32,472	497,662	260,556
2004	18,440,975	10,665,274	42,673	10,707,947	1,178,734	129,775	9,658,988	5,910,997	2,870,990	35,298	522,431	278,201
2005	20,662,247	12,022,428	45,862	12,068,290	1,334,006	118,130	10,852,414	6,713,264	3,096,569	37,227	555,029	298,673
2006	23,122,129	13,030,999	35,471	13,066,470	1,465,866	96,866	11,697,470	8,049,074	3,375,585	39,683	582,678	315,544
2007	23,691,172	12,934,201	25,063	12,959,264	1,475,363	66,281	11,550,182	8,464,639	3,676,351	39,177	604,716	315,741
2008	24,371,579	12,257,328	26,470	12,283,798	1,412,884	32,113	10,903,027	9,212,381	4,256,171	39,889	610,984	300,539
2009	23,472,334	11,326,700	28,776	11,355,476	1,342,971	-12,998	9,999,507	8,759,662	4,713,165	38,335	612,297	287,087
2010	23,036,697	11,323,406	36,699	11,360,105	1,352,883	-192,906	9,814,316	8,040,991	5,181,390	37,125	620,521	285,904
2011	25,414,282	11,827,572	34,522	11,862,094	1,276,795	-96,318	10,488,981	9,464,362	5,460,939	40,250	631,412	294,449
2012	25,959,494	12,557,440	45,820	12,603,260	1,344,863	-313,146	10,945,251	9,435,950	5,578,293	40,248	644,988	303,567
2013	27,116,736	13,398,475	51,401	13,449,876	1,597,146	-236,412	11,616,318	9,658,513	5,841,905	41,003	661,336	316,440
2014	28,704,773	14,419,284	40,575	14,459,859	1,726,200	-326,173	12,407,486	10,022,379	6,274,908	42,243	679,513	332,902

Personal Income and Employment by Area: Cape Girardeau-Jackson, MO-IL

(Thousands of dollars, except as noted.)

Year	Personal income, total	Earnings by place of work			Less: Contributions for government social insurance	Plus: Adjustment for residence	Equals: Net earnings by place of residence	Plus: Dividends, interest, and rent	Plus: Personal current transfer receipts	Per capita personal income (dollars)	Population (persons)	Total employment
		Nonfarm	Farm	Total								
1970	221,486	170,084	9,171	179,255	11,405	-6,546	161,304	32,022	28,160	3,144	70,436	30,842
1971	241,892	186,397	8,250	194,647	12,963	-7,088	174,596	35,453	31,843	3,364	71,899	31,125
1972	261,855	199,096	10,466	209,562	14,450	-6,606	188,506	39,158	34,191	3,556	73,647	31,770
1973	295,835	218,313	18,539	236,852	18,254	-6,104	212,494	44,325	39,016	4,036	73,297	33,247
1974	329,622	251,495	10,119	261,614	21,944	-7,726	231,944	51,364	46,314	4,419	74,588	34,420
1975	378,851	274,996	17,405	292,401	23,478	-8,795	260,128	59,003	59,720	5,078	74,605	34,141
1976	421,878	318,112	15,432	333,544	27,451	-11,026	295,067	64,304	62,507	5,492	76,817	36,445
1977	462,350	350,853	14,501	365,354	30,208	-11,248	323,898	73,185	65,267	5,958	77,598	37,517
1978	525,431	401,976	19,953	421,929	35,866	-13,024	373,039	81,603	70,789	6,665	78,829	39,115
1979	588,877	445,762	24,964	470,726	41,160	-14,585	414,981	93,452	80,444	7,366	79,941	39,912
1980	631,886	467,234	2,883	470,117	43,073	-11,146	415,898	118,067	97,921	7,747	81,562	39,014
1981	719,329	497,746	16,547	514,293	49,323	-11,291	453,679	145,321	120,329	8,768	82,038	39,055
1982	754,080	514,291	10,882	525,173	51,882	-12,571	460,720	173,919	119,441	9,244	81,576	39,480
1983	800,970	561,745	-1,820	559,925	56,354	-16,844	486,727	185,471	128,772	9,822	81,546	40,586
1984	890,512	616,695	13,170	629,865	63,602	-17,596	548,667	208,076	133,769	10,896	81,732	41,905
1985	947,136	656,635	16,431	673,066	68,883	-18,408	585,775	219,712	141,649	11,521	82,211	43,356
1986	995,976	714,620	2,341	716,961	75,566	-22,025	619,370	228,622	147,984	12,092	82,368	44,845
1987	1,062,744	776,447	9,625	786,072	81,133	-23,327	681,612	229,278	151,854	12,878	82,524	46,098
1988	1,112,708	827,442	4,319	831,761	89,026	-23,969	718,766	234,339	159,603	13,443	82,775	46,557
1989	1,200,008	878,704	12,982	891,686	95,487	-25,708	770,491	253,397	176,120	14,504	82,734	47,610
1990	1,234,970	912,786	9,411	922,197	102,288	-30,331	789,578	255,737	189,655	14,873	83,037	49,146
1991	1,300,671	948,168	6,612	954,780	108,023	-33,472	813,285	272,138	215,248	15,504	83,892	48,247
1992	1,406,008	1,032,264	14,305	1,046,569	116,489	-44,252	885,828	286,928	233,252	16,518	85,118	49,450
1993	1,477,745	1,086,416	10,172	1,096,588	123,262	-49,193	924,133	305,715	247,897	17,223	85,803	50,713
1994	1,559,997	1,167,077	8,418	1,175,495	133,146	-53,297	989,052	311,976	258,969	18,083	86,267	52,387
1995	1,657,907	1,251,084	3,121	1,254,205	142,368	-63,033	1,048,804	331,602	277,501	19,038	87,084	54,098
1996	1,731,601	1,288,781	9,210	1,297,991	144,811	-67,166	1,086,014	352,777	292,810	19,683	87,975	54,280
1997	1,825,776	1,353,980	8,961	1,362,941	150,824	-72,038	1,140,079	378,376	307,321	20,684	88,270	54,484
1998	1,928,607	1,452,088	3,279	1,455,367	161,166	-82,042	1,212,159	393,622	322,826	21,747	88,682	56,827
1999	2,035,809	1,588,052	2,342	1,590,394	175,453	-100,318	1,314,623	391,505	329,681	22,616	90,016	58,795
2000	2,176,576	1,673,281	10,136	1,683,417	181,461	-108,077	1,393,879	426,886	355,811	24,043	90,527	59,554
2001	2,245,956	1,701,108	13,124	1,714,232	186,093	-112,756	1,415,383	434,811	395,762	24,620	91,226	58,714
2002	2,356,147	1,812,886	7,318	1,820,204	195,291	-123,751	1,501,162	423,554	431,431	25,696	91,694	58,753
2003	2,446,369	1,866,780	22,287	1,889,067	201,148	-130,023	1,557,896	435,779	452,694	26,637	91,840	59,130
2004	2,560,446	1,935,388	37,731	1,973,119	207,731	-129,875	1,635,513	442,569	482,364	27,611	92,734	58,967
2005	2,615,954	2,024,683	18,733	2,043,416	218,896	-136,068	1,688,452	406,576	520,926	28,076	93,173	60,526
2006	2,772,091	2,141,234	11,963	2,153,197	233,334	-141,817	1,778,046	443,277	550,768	29,438	94,167	61,625
2007	2,966,308	2,253,312	5,377	2,258,689	249,021	-149,628	1,860,040	513,669	592,599	31,351	94,616	63,049
2008	3,106,665	2,279,981	29,845	2,309,826	252,957	-143,161	1,913,708	536,748	656,209	32,691	95,031	63,003
2009	3,143,405	2,327,938	11,907	2,339,845	257,547	-146,566	1,935,732	497,945	709,728	32,869	95,634	61,786
2010	3,184,843	2,331,245	15,467	2,346,712	256,717	-142,116	1,947,879	479,839	757,125	33,031	96,421	60,374
2011	3,331,329	2,371,975	23,747	2,395,722	235,104	-120,890	2,039,728	524,734	766,867	34,334	97,027	60,549
2012	3,547,062	2,495,569	17,932	2,513,501	242,756	-107,550	2,163,195	608,227	775,640	36,479	97,235	60,989
2013	3,569,458	2,533,673	40,055	2,573,728	279,981	-108,271	2,185,476	591,287	792,695	36,566	97,617	61,831
2014	3,672,994	2,577,071	45,100	2,622,171	284,726	-89,166	2,248,279	617,418	807,297	37,507	97,929	61,320

Personal Income and Employment by Area: Carbondale-Marion, IL

(Thousands of dollars, except as noted.)

Year	Personal income, total	Nonfarm	Farm	Total	Less: Contributions for government social insurance	Plus: Adjustment for residence	Equals: Net earnings by place of residence	Plus: Dividends, interest, and rent	Plus: Personal current transfer receipts	Per capita personal income (dollars)	Population (persons)	Total employment
1970	324,328	259,942	2,145	262,087	15,052	-2,289	244,746	40,656	38,926	3,106	104,404	40,154
1971	364,142	288,507	2,871	291,378	17,188	-2,687	271,503	44,754	47,885	3,409	106,828	41,453
1972	400,364	313,662	3,009	316,671	19,471	-1,415	295,785	49,492	55,087	3,696	108,334	42,454
1973	454,351	344,159	9,466	353,625	24,400	-1,370	327,855	56,375	70,121	4,250	106,903	43,396
1974	492,871	366,288	9,510	375,798	27,065	1,115	349,848	65,203	77,820	4,593	107,320	44,408
1975	585,214	419,905	12,813	432,718	29,669	2,637	405,686	76,662	102,866	5,305	110,316	44,949
1976	655,924	487,370	8,797	496,167	36,115	1,381	461,433	82,778	111,713	5,752	114,039	47,991
1977	716,493	532,984	11,370	544,354	40,062	4,627	508,919	93,509	114,065	6,190	115,743	49,432
1978	781,133	588,474	8,304	596,778	45,110	4,623	556,291	103,718	121,124	6,705	116,505	50,217
1979	879,524	645,058	11,013	656,071	51,396	15,817	620,492	119,777	139,255	7,459	117,908	51,476
1980	966,250	686,491	2,196	688,687	54,271	19,015	653,431	147,752	165,067	8,141	118,692	51,285
1981	1,066,037	729,775	7,504	737,279	61,069	17,767	693,977	182,296	189,764	8,846	120,509	51,216
1982	1,170,878	779,981	3,490	783,471	66,357	24,309	741,423	229,289	200,166	9,732	120,316	51,051
1983	1,244,831	837,893	-520	837,373	71,714	15,402	781,061	246,720	217,050	10,318	120,650	52,036
1984	1,347,834	913,499	2,643	916,142	80,827	14,869	850,184	274,855	222,795	11,245	119,864	53,250
1985	1,404,032	929,457	11,698	941,155	83,347	25,168	882,976	290,824	230,232	11,701	119,997	53,361
1986	1,438,456	964,059	-4,184	959,875	86,303	25,361	898,933	305,518	234,005	12,025	119,619	54,938
1987	1,503,314	1,013,482	6,915	1,020,397	89,066	19,919	951,250	307,453	244,611	12,536	119,923	55,376
1988	1,555,242	1,051,814	8,316	1,060,130	96,661	23,835	987,304	310,023	257,915	13,041	119,255	55,452
1989	1,673,786	1,105,015	21,601	1,126,616	103,009	27,256	1,050,863	347,488	275,435	14,074	118,928	56,439
1990	1,738,478	1,189,999	9,269	1,199,268	109,133	23,760	1,113,895	333,427	291,156	14,637	118,770	58,256
1991	1,799,197	1,248,448	6,273	1,254,721	119,032	9,310	1,144,999	343,584	310,614	15,173	118,578	58,784
1992	1,950,256	1,344,056	12,146	1,356,202	126,134	5,016	1,235,084	357,272	357,900	16,286	119,749	59,722
1993	1,990,368	1,374,394	13,889	1,388,283	130,849	-1,796	1,255,638	362,169	372,561	16,462	120,909	60,133
1994	2,103,291	1,473,992	16,030	1,490,022	143,722	769	1,347,069	378,302	377,920	17,320	121,436	62,968
1995	2,217,664	1,539,036	8,874	1,547,910	150,424	-4,792	1,392,694	421,898	403,072	18,248	121,529	63,549
1996	2,305,285	1,579,577	14,467	1,594,044	152,865	-6,883	1,434,296	447,308	423,681	18,973	121,503	63,587
1997	2,396,417	1,639,923	14,443	1,654,366	156,971	-9,872	1,487,523	470,334	438,560	19,675	121,801	64,237
1998	2,499,453	1,713,400	14,538	1,727,938	164,477	-15,325	1,548,136	497,788	453,529	20,542	121,676	65,029
1999	2,596,701	1,846,291	7,930	1,854,221	173,441	-26,747	1,654,033	485,983	456,685	21,372	121,502	67,490
2000	2,718,876	1,939,054	11,003	1,950,057	179,146	-31,236	1,739,675	498,810	480,391	22,486	120,912	69,036
2001	2,887,738	2,052,954	6,777	2,059,731	189,772	-30,870	1,839,089	536,346	512,303	23,813	121,267	69,437
2002	2,995,678	2,198,618	-1,404	2,197,214	204,301	-46,218	1,946,695	501,784	547,199	24,740	121,086	69,597
2003	3,088,709	2,256,433	3,609	2,260,042	211,271	-59,885	1,988,886	530,563	569,260	25,361	121,792	69,574
2004	3,229,816	2,355,823	17,806	2,373,629	220,688	-71,551	2,081,390	544,972	603,454	26,293	122,841	70,098
2005	3,371,604	2,502,214	7,582	2,509,796	242,532	-85,484	2,181,780	524,294	665,530	27,216	123,881	71,812
2006	3,522,539	2,634,593	8,894	2,643,487	253,863	-92,719	2,296,905	549,552	676,082	28,272	124,594	72,819
2007	3,657,315	2,703,544	5,371	2,708,915	262,708	-104,855	2,341,352	571,964	743,999	29,324	124,719	73,139
2008	3,861,866	2,794,304	23,228	2,817,532	271,251	-125,789	2,420,492	628,119	813,255	30,826	125,279	72,554
2009	3,998,662	2,851,290	6,996	2,858,286	274,848	-138,537	2,444,901	653,211	900,550	31,762	125,893	72,359
2010	4,163,678	2,963,618	14,783	2,978,401	287,759	-147,819	2,542,823	644,641	976,214	32,832	126,819	72,397
2011	4,303,882	3,048,214	25,650	3,073,864	267,956	-159,418	2,646,490	704,274	953,118	33,860	127,107	72,940
2012	4,398,236	3,127,708	16,147	3,143,855	276,506	-168,001	2,699,348	752,090	946,798	34,636	126,984	72,686
2013	4,494,011	3,186,410	57,010	3,243,420	315,864	-189,912	2,737,644	764,260	992,107	35,367	127,069	71,618
2014	4,559,602	3,258,705	34,731	3,293,436	326,571	-201,038	2,765,827	785,672	1,008,103	35,992	126,685	72,081

Personal Income and Employment by Area: Carson City, NV

(Thousands of dollars, except as noted.)

Year	Personal income, total	Earnings by place of work			Less: Contributions for government social insurance	Plus: Adjustment for residence	Equals: Net earnings by place of residence	Plus: Dividends, interest, and rent	Plus: Personal current transfer receipts	Per capita personal income (dollars)	Population (persons)	Total employment
		Nonfarm	Farm	Total								
1970	85,034	66,887	47	66,934	2,301	700	65,333	14,586	5,115	5,301	16,041	8,194
1971	103,023	79,374	305	79,679	2,907	2,279	79,051	17,396	6,576	5,587	18,439	9,095
1972	120,448	91,872	155	92,027	3,824	4,252	92,455	20,082	7,911	6,025	19,991	9,860
1973	139,866	107,288	460	107,748	5,579	6,345	108,514	22,029	9,323	6,312	22,158	11,152
1974	160,643	123,272	96	123,368	6,755	6,973	123,586	25,328	11,729	6,747	23,808	12,036
1975	186,353	140,037	137	140,174	7,117	7,408	140,465	28,990	16,898	7,313	25,484	12,528
1976	216,649	164,981	143	165,124	8,899	7,010	163,235	34,379	19,035	8,303	26,094	13,820
1977	251,681	193,453	134	193,587	11,001	5,882	188,468	41,221	21,992	9,209	27,331	15,384
1978	305,913	240,851	116	240,967	14,851	1,593	227,709	52,520	25,684	10,207	29,972	17,838
1979	346,414	274,291	122	274,413	18,744	-3,226	252,443	64,394	29,577	10,900	31,782	19,081
1980	390,784	299,281	234	299,515	20,592	-769	278,154	75,869	36,761	12,090	32,323	19,360
1981	443,447	340,510	153	340,663	24,862	-8,393	307,408	91,816	44,223	13,247	33,475	19,536
1982	466,580	342,526	164	342,690	25,085	-7,269	310,336	109,061	47,183	13,593	34,324	18,960
1983	492,310	363,575	163	363,738	29,896	-12,435	321,407	117,458	53,445	14,206	34,654	19,392
1984	541,244	398,777	274	399,051	35,190	-13,376	350,485	133,889	56,870	15,350	35,260	20,535
1985	592,621	439,529	115	439,644	41,267	-21,452	376,925	152,800	62,896	16,286	36,389	21,622
1986	638,398	471,920	104	472,024	45,552	-26,796	399,676	169,384	69,338	17,214	37,086	22,495
1987	664,764	510,688	221	510,909	49,982	-36,135	424,792	165,699	74,273	17,773	37,403	24,244
1988	729,136	566,367	116	566,483	57,171	-41,645	467,667	181,487	79,982	18,998	38,379	25,165
1989	800,669	608,570	153	608,723	62,181	-50,419	496,123	211,762	92,784	20,190	39,657	25,785
1990	864,225	660,423	190	660,613	69,062	-41,830	549,721	212,298	102,206	21,227	40,714	26,766
1991	932,404	707,385	152	707,537	73,328	-50,560	583,649	225,884	122,871	22,239	41,926	27,173
1992	1,018,376	780,064	140	780,204	79,209	-59,398	641,597	241,876	134,903	23,557	43,231	27,073
1993	1,072,178	838,015	176	838,191	86,047	-81,327	670,817	260,042	141,319	24,055	44,572	28,566
1994	1,155,584	920,918	79	920,997	96,962	-100,361	723,674	288,803	143,107	25,063	46,108	30,498
1995	1,248,377	1,007,083	-8	1,007,075	106,936	-120,418	779,721	312,234	156,422	26,134	47,768	32,941
1996	1,324,649	1,081,779	-105	1,081,674	110,691	-148,473	822,510	339,151	162,988	26,875	49,290	34,369
1997	1,417,456	1,178,179	-179	1,178,000	116,711	-174,112	887,177	359,118	171,161	28,089	50,463	35,519
1998	1,472,477	1,247,759	-7	1,247,752	122,451	-185,361	939,940	353,333	179,204	28,949	50,864	36,240
1999	1,543,597	1,351,645	117	1,351,762	128,605	-214,225	1,008,932	353,702	180,963	29,711	51,953	37,614
2000	1,694,338	1,456,980	139	1,457,119	122,045	-223,424	1,111,650	387,559	195,129	32,231	52,568	39,196
2001	1,735,646	1,502,749	315	1,503,064	126,334	-232,754	1,143,976	375,697	215,973	32,459	53,472	39,493
2002	1,731,475	1,543,672	563	1,544,235	130,463	-265,879	1,147,893	344,376	239,206	31,768	54,503	39,746
2003	1,861,934	1,654,432	305	1,654,737	132,892	-307,841	1,214,004	395,171	252,759	33,710	55,234	40,265
2004	1,977,971	1,778,172	304	1,778,476	138,976	-357,601	1,281,899	432,554	263,518	35,324	55,995	41,217
2005	2,071,549	1,897,307	302	1,897,609	147,143	-405,298	1,345,168	446,101	280,280	37,004	55,982	41,967
2006	2,114,630	1,980,813	324	1,981,137	154,841	-439,167	1,387,129	436,712	290,789	38,163	55,410	42,128
2007	2,180,706	2,045,206	173	2,045,379	160,618	-482,694	1,402,067	469,441	309,198	39,443	55,288	42,932
2008	2,134,750	1,994,819	748	1,995,567	159,478	-499,187	1,336,902	449,941	347,907	38,428	55,552	40,643
2009	2,039,730	1,896,395	880	1,897,275	151,894	-523,568	1,221,813	426,503	391,414	36,818	55,401	39,063
2010	2,042,647	1,928,053	1,786	1,929,839	152,632	-550,371	1,226,836	388,591	427,220	36,964	55,260	37,772
2011	2,066,710	1,887,611	2,531	1,890,142	141,434	-552,905	1,195,803	437,986	432,921	37,750	54,747	37,690
2012	2,083,783	1,910,859	2,338	1,913,197	145,868	-553,364	1,213,965	428,347	441,471	38,180	54,578	36,833
2013	2,115,316	1,917,171	2,768	1,919,939	160,084	-555,312	1,204,543	463,150	447,623	39,128	54,061	36,763
2014	2,237,917	1,971,060	3,816	1,974,876	168,986	-535,744	1,270,146	476,490	491,281	41,046	54,522	37,123

Personal Income and Employment by Area: Casper, WY

(Thousands of dollars, except as noted.)

Year	Personal income, total	Earnings by place of work			Less: Contributions for government social insurance	Plus: Adjustment for residence	Equals: Net earnings by place of residence	Plus: Dividends, interest, and rent	Plus: Personal current transfer receipts	Per capita personal income (dollars)	Population (persons)	Total employment
		Nonfarm	Farm	Total								
1970.............	240,412	188,428	4,641	193,069	12,904	6,644	186,809	38,026	15,577	4,679	51,381	25,733
1971.............	258,286	202,170	2,614	204,784	14,304	7,414	197,894	42,619	17,773	4,956	52,121	26,453
1972.............	275,437	215,893	4,135	220,028	16,194	7,387	211,221	45,268	18,948	5,187	53,106	27,009
1973.............	315,938	248,214	7,885	256,099	21,425	6,152	240,826	52,973	22,139	5,982	52,814	28,431
1974.............	387,510	312,974	5,375	318,349	26,848	6,857	298,358	64,064	25,088	7,243	53,504	30,410
1975.............	466,838	389,422	2,302	391,724	32,946	7,296	366,074	70,559	30,205	8,323	56,088	33,334
1976.............	514,759	434,854	1,994	436,848	39,067	5,608	403,389	78,550	32,820	8,789	58,567	35,183
1977.............	628,131	545,402	1,847	547,249	47,380	3,965	503,834	88,981	35,316	10,209	61,526	39,229
1978.............	764,284	679,052	1,662	680,714	61,393	-596	618,725	105,794	39,765	11,666	65,515	44,060
1979.............	877,581	786,956	2,593	789,549	75,562	-5,847	708,140	122,846	46,595	12,839	68,354	46,821
1980.............	1,008,129	897,255	1,898	899,153	86,058	-13,176	799,919	153,094	55,116	13,901	72,523	48,294
1981.............	1,171,319	1,026,830	1,174	1,028,004	106,676	-10,568	910,760	194,855	65,704	15,609	75,042	51,043
1982.............	1,198,480	1,003,643	3,855	1,007,498	107,639	-7,796	892,063	229,583	76,834	15,546	77,094	49,117
1983.............	1,110,348	878,702	7,597	886,299	92,206	-3,795	790,298	229,022	91,028	14,554	76,292	44,001
1984.............	1,136,572	899,393	3,260	902,653	97,199	-1,054	804,400	242,801	89,371	15,534	73,166	44,094
1985.............	1,123,004	864,705	2,436	867,141	95,245	2,319	774,215	250,053	98,736	15,691	71,569	42,169
1986.............	1,018,483	748,850	839	749,689	83,057	5,499	672,131	238,677	107,675	14,723	69,177	37,710
1987.............	1,024,232	752,876	1,434	754,310	80,841	6,046	679,515	235,292	109,425	15,867	64,552	36,574
1988.............	1,035,840	750,618	988	751,606	87,737	8,310	672,179	248,954	114,707	16,572	62,507	37,519
1989.............	1,167,390	845,022	-123	844,899	91,644	11,764	765,019	275,787	126,584	18,914	61,722	37,111
1990.............	1,293,901	935,101	-415	934,686	105,507	13,562	842,741	311,208	139,952	21,109	61,296	38,058
1991.............	1,300,445	884,068	3,403	887,471	107,689	12,193	791,975	355,455	153,015	20,870	62,312	38,809
1992.............	1,381,819	925,468	2,646	928,114	110,743	12,035	829,406	380,245	172,168	21,903	63,087	38,045
1993.............	1,452,103	974,270	2,716	976,986	115,008	11,636	873,614	388,173	190,316	22,696	63,981	38,759
1994.............	1,493,842	1,002,371	1,633	1,004,004	119,060	11,899	896,843	404,639	192,360	22,871	65,316	39,738
1995.............	1,517,067	1,025,908	1,098	1,027,006	121,353	10,883	916,536	393,947	206,584	23,095	65,687	40,383
1996.............	1,576,694	1,072,386	782	1,073,168	123,359	10,407	960,216	399,622	216,856	23,940	65,859	40,551
1997.............	1,713,543	1,197,285	2,625	1,199,910	131,862	10,072	1,078,120	413,544	221,879	25,841	66,311	41,280
1998.............	1,783,033	1,233,203	1,421	1,234,624	137,071	8,862	1,106,415	447,003	229,615	26,956	66,146	41,533
1999.............	1,881,875	1,317,899	2,591	1,320,490	144,025	7,167	1,183,632	462,240	236,003	28,392	66,282	42,093
2000.............	2,126,348	1,530,585	2,137	1,532,722	163,696	2,573	1,371,599	499,783	254,966	31,926	66,603	43,298
2001.............	2,191,895	1,599,291	3,642	1,602,933	174,670	627	1,428,890	492,930	270,075	32,726	66,978	44,632
2002.............	2,271,772	1,674,732	3,262	1,677,994	177,132	568	1,501,430	477,964	292,378	33,629	67,554	44,984
2003.............	2,397,271	1,763,467	5,582	1,769,049	188,298	524	1,581,275	498,647	317,349	35,127	68,246	45,923
2004.............	2,579,642	1,935,973	4,540	1,940,513	209,515	502	1,731,500	515,890	332,252	37,367	69,035	47,653
2005.............	2,933,222	2,169,358	7,632	2,176,990	230,602	466	1,946,854	641,463	344,905	41,950	69,922	49,267
2006.............	3,357,536	2,542,384	1,228	2,543,612	292,080	440	2,251,972	752,914	352,650	47,419	70,806	51,488
2007.............	3,444,930	2,673,476	-722	2,672,754	318,694	373	2,354,433	717,010	373,487	47,605	72,365	53,522
2008.............	4,055,801	3,212,427	-2,422	3,210,005	347,383	283	2,862,905	752,284	440,612	55,045	73,682	54,386
2009.............	3,463,708	2,710,447	-1,403	2,709,044	320,096	5,701	2,394,649	593,975	475,084	46,037	75,238	52,037
2010.............	3,680,609	2,829,356	-153	2,829,203	332,211	1,421	2,498,413	672,752	509,444	48,772	75,466	51,956
2011.............	4,071,810	3,092,896	6,048	3,098,944	326,866	-9,004	2,763,074	800,727	508,009	53,285	76,416	53,448
2012.............	4,407,304	3,318,366	-477	3,317,889	356,267	-13,061	2,948,561	957,966	500,777	56,011	78,686	55,556
2013.............	4,588,385	3,358,191	4,086	3,362,277	401,610	-15,182	2,945,485	1,121,643	521,257	56,547	81,143	56,612
2014.............	4,888,491	3,572,606	11,766	3,584,372	425,235	-17,035	3,142,102	1,210,067	536,322	59,890	81,624	57,869

Personal Income and Employment by Area: Cedar Rapids, IA

(Thousands of dollars, except as noted.)

| Year | Personal income, total | Derivation of personal income | | | | | | | | Per capita personal income (dollars) | Population (persons) | Total employment |
| | | Earnings by place of work | | | Less: Contributions for government social insurance | Plus: Adjustment for residence | Equals: Net earnings by place of residence | Plus: Dividends, interest, and rent | Plus: Personal current transfer receipts | | | |
		Nonfarm	Farm	Total								
1970	870,099	680,214	45,908	726,122	51,334	-2,862	671,926	135,654	62,519	4,220	206,165	96,649
1971	909,413	708,528	41,325	749,853	55,651	-4,351	689,851	146,361	73,201	4,382	207,532	94,803
1972	984,148	761,089	52,935	814,024	63,501	-5,201	745,322	158,445	80,381	4,732	207,990	96,324
1973	1,119,280	855,100	84,216	939,316	82,738	-6,996	849,582	177,503	92,195	5,408	206,982	100,990
1974	1,222,904	955,695	61,195	1,016,890	95,619	-8,200	913,071	202,615	107,218	5,883	207,881	104,894
1975	1,367,572	1,045,303	68,297	1,113,600	102,083	-8,930	1,002,587	231,048	133,937	6,511	210,055	105,550
1976	1,489,451	1,180,076	42,148	1,222,224	116,619	-11,111	1,094,494	247,311	147,646	7,043	211,491	108,639
1977	1,628,968	1,298,956	39,153	1,338,109	127,413	-13,127	1,197,569	277,083	154,316	7,726	210,846	110,943
1978	1,847,467	1,462,066	77,545	1,539,611	148,920	-18,563	1,372,128	308,015	167,324	8,754	211,033	114,026
1979	2,055,289	1,681,722	40,486	1,722,208	178,273	-25,920	1,518,015	348,781	188,493	9,698	211,937	121,050
1980	2,208,214	1,767,934	4,504	1,772,438	185,620	-25,811	1,561,007	418,038	229,169	10,335	213,666	119,634
1981	2,434,348	1,851,326	45,517	1,896,843	206,607	-29,133	1,661,103	515,029	258,216	11,454	212,534	116,231
1982	2,525,540	1,833,136	14,324	1,847,460	206,424	-30,307	1,610,729	613,024	301,787	12,005	210,374	111,314
1983	2,583,885	1,896,204	-19,506	1,876,698	213,291	-26,165	1,637,242	626,069	320,574	12,408	208,238	110,835
1984	2,833,879	2,037,083	51,007	2,088,090	234,825	-24,358	1,828,907	683,535	321,437	13,626	207,969	113,084
1985	2,976,741	2,186,256	35,174	2,221,430	255,289	-32,135	1,934,006	704,500	338,235	14,381	206,995	115,476
1986	3,131,297	2,312,150	59,524	2,371,674	274,778	-35,335	2,061,561	715,312	354,424	15,210	205,865	117,488
1987	3,324,349	2,507,905	71,887	2,579,792	296,097	-38,261	2,245,434	716,882	362,033	16,171	205,577	119,721
1988	3,489,838	2,713,527	22,352	2,735,879	329,957	-40,542	2,365,380	743,090	381,368	16,825	207,415	125,116
1989	3,860,998	2,936,337	81,773	3,018,110	354,022	-41,987	2,622,101	830,964	407,933	18,427	209,528	129,901
1990	4,048,209	3,115,461	83,721	3,199,182	386,921	-47,268	2,764,993	833,438	449,778	19,168	211,200	131,540
1991	4,173,275	3,239,429	48,500	3,287,929	405,898	-46,174	2,835,857	855,724	481,694	19,551	213,453	132,831
1992	4,427,576	3,435,942	87,268	3,523,210	427,003	-50,085	3,046,122	857,649	523,805	20,421	216,818	133,978
1993	4,599,277	3,649,356	35,798	3,685,154	457,550	-56,023	3,171,581	882,379	545,317	20,911	219,948	136,563
1994	4,946,046	3,931,705	85,138	4,016,843	498,317	-63,332	3,455,194	917,268	573,584	22,208	222,711	140,427
1995	5,244,916	4,169,394	44,740	4,214,134	528,399	-77,494	3,608,241	1,026,441	610,234	23,171	226,357	146,630
1996	5,609,875	4,357,109	115,314	4,472,423	532,634	-87,088	3,852,701	1,111,754	645,420	24,611	227,938	149,382
1997	5,937,550	4,624,993	100,181	4,725,174	580,129	-98,806	4,046,239	1,221,802	669,509	25,761	230,490	152,680
1998	6,484,312	5,225,396	67,631	5,293,027	645,806	-132,771	4,514,450	1,280,883	688,979	27,901	232,402	157,141
1999	6,828,800	5,620,279	60,474	5,680,753	684,581	-150,505	4,845,667	1,258,240	724,893	29,014	235,365	161,523
2000	7,301,846	5,989,118	78,456	6,067,574	721,361	-180,711	5,165,502	1,359,301	777,043	30,686	237,950	164,719
2001	7,406,552	5,994,503	93,973	6,088,476	719,734	-181,789	5,186,953	1,358,026	861,573	30,842	240,145	163,103
2002	7,503,452	5,924,135	87,830	6,011,965	710,121	-178,080	5,123,764	1,411,288	968,400	30,993	242,099	159,845
2003	7,643,649	6,100,778	86,811	6,187,589	735,075	-182,963	5,269,551	1,394,984	979,114	31,420	243,272	158,254
2004	8,075,493	6,486,896	139,175	6,626,071	769,148	-169,257	5,687,666	1,372,972	1,014,855	32,947	245,108	161,155
2005	8,391,234	6,821,459	91,506	6,912,965	811,539	-179,888	5,921,538	1,370,686	1,099,010	33,936	247,265	164,082
2006	8,950,380	7,179,242	69,324	7,248,566	851,325	-169,651	6,227,590	1,518,411	1,204,379	35,870	249,524	167,570
2007	9,637,071	7,632,055	102,350	7,734,405	910,510	-174,898	6,648,997	1,700,128	1,287,946	38,135	252,709	171,370
2008	10,323,616	8,047,206	117,637	8,164,843	963,467	-176,623	7,024,753	1,816,938	1,481,925	40,405	255,503	173,517
2009	10,291,016	7,926,770	82,593	8,009,363	949,204	-87,957	6,972,202	1,718,447	1,600,367	40,059	256,896	171,917
2010	10,614,109	8,168,002	90,665	8,258,667	984,840	-64,246	7,209,581	1,695,198	1,709,330	41,083	258,360	171,149
2011	11,200,601	8,475,927	195,702	8,671,629	918,163	-135,814	7,617,652	1,837,648	1,745,301	42,937	260,862	173,681
2012	11,701,512	8,763,376	147,323	8,910,699	935,131	-120,765	7,854,803	2,099,623	1,747,086	44,716	261,686	174,671
2013	11,809,642	8,862,808	249,903	9,112,711	1,069,008	-65,118	7,978,585	2,068,233	1,762,824	45,015	262,348	175,367
2014	12,232,532	9,314,948	139,769	9,454,717	1,111,797	-120,355	8,222,565	2,150,047	1,859,920	46,356	263,885	177,053

Personal Income and Employment by Area: Chambersburg-Waynesboro, PA

(Thousands of dollars, except as noted.)

Year	Personal income, total	Earnings by place of work			Less: Contributions for government social insurance	Plus: Adjustment for residence	Equals: Net earnings by place of residence	Plus: Dividends, interest, and rent	Plus: Personal current transfer receipts	Per capita personal income (dollars)	Population (persons)	Total employment
		Nonfarm	Farm	Total								
1970	401,633	309,882	16,046	325,928	18,784	5,791	312,935	54,783	33,915	3,972	101,127	45,763
1971	424,959	325,168	13,591	338,759	20,346	5,929	324,342	61,190	39,427	4,123	103,082	44,890
1972	476,738	366,293	15,581	381,874	24,028	6,803	364,649	67,751	44,338	4,624	103,103	46,239
1973	535,288	413,738	17,730	431,468	31,392	7,079	407,155	78,813	49,320	5,133	104,285	48,655
1974	597,051	455,584	20,778	476,362	36,378	8,343	448,327	89,809	58,915	5,599	106,640	50,542
1975	655,667	499,327	13,610	512,937	38,922	5,505	479,520	99,442	76,705	6,068	108,052	50,373
1976	714,084	535,404	17,185	552,589	42,775	8,535	518,349	108,063	87,672	6,481	110,183	50,555
1977	777,668	573,386	15,349	588,735	45,380	18,205	561,560	122,442	93,666	7,056	110,218	50,537
1978	877,402	648,324	19,434	667,758	52,338	21,227	636,647	141,279	99,476	7,893	111,166	51,634
1979	962,466	699,859	23,399	723,258	59,353	31,117	695,022	157,605	109,839	8,580	112,172	52,438
1980	1,058,562	770,065	15,522	785,587	66,285	20,207	739,509	193,365	125,688	9,301	113,810	53,620
1981	1,178,219	830,911	24,183	855,094	76,659	21,881	800,316	232,366	145,537	10,308	114,302	53,452
1982	1,243,116	813,352	25,195	838,547	75,731	28,321	791,137	272,754	179,225	10,839	114,688	52,664
1983	1,298,207	827,129	21,758	848,887	79,810	37,721	806,798	291,332	200,077	11,260	115,293	51,891
1984	1,413,543	900,094	40,751	940,845	91,682	54,726	903,889	320,079	189,575	12,135	116,482	52,342
1985	1,525,405	970,315	43,945	1,014,260	100,362	59,469	973,367	353,125	198,913	13,051	116,882	53,479
1986	1,610,639	1,004,606	52,853	1,057,459	106,610	71,963	1,022,812	376,144	211,683	13,712	117,464	54,682
1987	1,705,865	1,085,721	40,582	1,126,303	114,975	83,847	1,095,175	394,001	216,689	14,479	117,819	56,100
1988	1,825,354	1,171,620	40,010	1,211,630	128,876	99,857	1,182,611	413,818	228,925	15,345	118,953	58,222
1989	1,966,869	1,269,132	46,972	1,316,104	139,385	113,666	1,290,385	432,032	244,452	16,421	119,780	60,503
1990	2,109,912	1,338,293	39,001	1,377,294	148,841	130,634	1,359,087	479,141	271,684	17,365	121,503	62,343
1991	2,198,508	1,382,463	29,346	1,411,809	156,037	134,908	1,390,680	488,595	319,233	17,868	123,039	61,587
1992	2,319,006	1,447,605	53,088	1,500,693	165,185	151,490	1,486,998	496,515	335,493	18,687	124,095	61,679
1993	2,418,952	1,510,369	44,271	1,554,640	176,983	163,672	1,541,329	525,010	352,613	19,343	125,056	62,013
1994	2,508,189	1,586,880	39,805	1,626,685	189,106	181,601	1,619,180	527,017	361,992	19,906	126,002	62,399
1995	2,596,499	1,636,532	27,916	1,664,448	194,858	202,927	1,672,517	546,161	377,821	20,529	126,479	63,732
1996	2,778,378	1,726,332	47,791	1,774,123	200,979	218,024	1,791,168	582,688	404,522	21,895	126,897	65,054
1997	2,884,969	1,779,030	42,297	1,821,327	207,475	241,937	1,855,789	608,441	420,739	22,592	127,696	66,252
1998	3,069,400	1,878,638	55,057	1,933,695	215,632	267,367	1,985,430	644,493	439,477	23,888	128,492	65,485
1999	3,171,148	1,909,238	57,905	1,967,143	217,416	306,201	2,055,928	644,474	470,746	24,606	128,875	64,420
2000	3,353,664	1,986,041	61,565	2,047,606	224,751	335,483	2,158,338	692,895	502,431	25,848	129,745	65,039
2001	3,460,529	1,998,571	71,433	2,070,004	230,059	376,965	2,216,910	688,893	554,726	26,496	130,604	64,646
2002	3,536,300	2,085,024	32,127	2,117,151	240,484	381,357	2,258,024	690,609	587,667	26,791	131,998	65,084
2003	3,722,989	2,202,939	65,700	2,268,639	252,473	393,803	2,409,969	697,744	615,276	27,870	133,583	66,394
2004	4,014,088	2,419,161	95,162	2,514,323	277,822	428,141	2,664,642	693,683	655,763	29,571	135,742	69,118
2005	4,266,404	2,619,376	94,867	2,714,243	306,484	459,413	2,867,172	685,462	713,770	30,710	138,927	71,911
2006	4,564,567	2,806,154	70,484	2,876,638	328,533	488,411	3,036,516	751,702	776,349	32,050	142,421	74,345
2007	4,916,381	2,942,532	97,341	3,039,873	346,587	520,726	3,214,012	869,357	833,012	33,944	144,840	76,610
2008	5,113,745	3,017,762	94,794	3,112,556	354,798	534,914	3,292,672	899,121	921,952	34,780	147,032	77,237
2009	5,181,896	2,910,188	51,453	2,961,641	347,840	648,545	3,262,346	851,323	1,068,227	34,857	148,662	73,738
2010	5,324,731	2,972,071	78,977	3,051,048	359,706	689,432	3,380,774	815,443	1,128,514	35,520	149,908	73,484
2011	5,647,631	3,075,473	108,726	3,184,199	338,142	771,229	3,617,286	884,575	1,145,770	37,401	151,004	74,326
2012	5,771,629	3,156,205	106,249	3,262,454	345,046	770,328	3,687,736	923,550	1,160,343	38,074	151,589	74,868
2013	5,877,025	3,235,824	127,124	3,362,948	398,076	755,263	3,720,135	950,383	1,206,507	38,616	152,191	75,714
2014	6,111,371	3,344,129	162,885	3,507,014	413,118	764,507	3,858,403	986,368	1,266,600	39,972	152,892	76,654

Personal Income and Employment by Area: Champaign-Urbana, IL

(Thousands of dollars, except as noted.)

Year	Personal income, total	Derivation of personal income									Per capita personal income (dollars)	Population (persons)	Total employment
		Earnings by place of work			Less: Contributions for government social insurance	Plus: Adjustment for residence	Equals: Net earnings by place of residence	Plus: Dividends, interest, and rent	Plus: Personal current transfer receipts				
		Nonfarm	Farm	Total									
1970	797,174	608,062	38,946	647,008	32,629	-6,455	607,924	144,248	45,002	4,088	195,003	92,168
1971	891,675	667,629	59,975	727,604	37,394	-6,634	683,576	154,880	53,219	4,559	195,599	94,618
1972	946,799	714,935	47,080	762,015	41,835	-5,399	714,781	171,195	60,823	4,859	194,839	95,753
1973	1,090,941	773,338	103,088	876,426	51,561	-4,407	820,458	198,383	72,100	5,487	198,829	99,841
1974	1,173,717	836,890	98,889	935,779	59,138	-4,412	872,229	218,529	82,959	5,886	199,411	101,332
1975	1,381,875	957,558	146,278	1,103,836	66,143	-6,795	1,030,898	245,557	105,420	6,985	197,848	103,387
1976	1,451,074	1,042,161	116,436	1,158,597	74,742	-3,834	1,080,021	257,277	113,776	7,225	200,853	104,608
1977	1,550,727	1,113,426	116,575	1,230,001	80,335	819	1,150,485	282,211	118,031	7,669	202,220	106,004
1978	1,656,071	1,219,129	85,953	1,305,082	90,163	2,139	1,217,058	312,018	126,995	8,149	203,216	107,412
1979	1,826,481	1,319,435	112,465	1,431,900	102,411	5,511	1,335,000	352,010	139,471	9,144	199,739	109,443
1980	1,912,348	1,389,345	39,793	1,429,138	106,373	11,970	1,334,735	409,090	168,523	9,523	200,808	108,626
1981	2,155,707	1,499,378	82,765	1,582,143	123,365	13,948	1,472,726	483,495	199,486	10,633	202,737	108,357
1982	2,303,728	1,583,746	54,692	1,638,438	131,302	8,998	1,516,134	571,149	216,445	11,327	203,390	108,510
1983	2,378,488	1,683,514	-10,191	1,673,323	141,172	6,768	1,538,919	599,885	239,684	11,778	201,935	107,989
1984	2,676,663	1,826,150	85,634	1,911,784	158,361	15,892	1,769,315	658,014	249,334	13,240	202,158	110,746
1985	2,816,680	1,936,459	108,823	2,045,282	171,638	8,552	1,882,196	677,660	256,824	13,912	202,468	113,254
1986	2,950,342	2,096,597	90,222	2,186,819	186,822	-20,320	1,979,677	707,460	263,205	14,459	204,047	118,091
1987	3,089,024	2,252,592	70,748	2,323,340	198,396	-33,095	2,091,849	723,858	273,317	15,118	204,329	120,675
1988	3,251,649	2,434,963	47,518	2,482,481	225,641	-37,486	2,219,354	749,719	282,576	15,879	204,777	123,729
1989	3,504,109	2,529,576	99,706	2,629,282	237,273	-42,743	2,349,266	849,883	304,960	17,252	203,114	123,578
1990	3,682,664	2,754,581	97,719	2,852,300	257,130	-56,549	2,538,621	816,436	327,607	18,131	203,117	125,903
1991	3,714,851	2,816,399	44,233	2,860,632	270,873	-55,785	2,533,974	825,436	355,441	18,109	205,133	124,402
1992	4,004,142	3,004,982	90,344	3,095,326	285,716	-64,625	2,744,985	859,619	399,538	19,263	207,870	124,588
1993	4,018,379	2,971,948	103,642	3,075,590	285,674	-57,390	2,732,526	862,122	423,731	19,649	204,513	120,796
1994	4,157,040	3,078,955	134,730	3,213,685	301,781	-58,815	2,853,089	873,088	430,863	20,514	202,646	123,137
1995	4,308,844	3,223,685	32,677	3,256,362	317,013	-63,643	2,875,706	973,190	459,948	21,212	203,128	125,336
1996	4,598,055	3,346,303	127,332	3,473,635	327,310	-63,845	3,082,480	1,029,224	486,351	22,386	205,401	126,882
1997	4,831,724	3,497,841	107,009	3,604,850	339,175	-70,438	3,195,237	1,131,850	504,637	23,318	207,211	128,334
1998	5,043,319	3,688,430	59,324	3,747,754	355,052	-68,323	3,324,379	1,198,173	520,767	24,310	207,458	130,762
1999	5,272,525	3,966,251	44,250	4,010,501	375,001	-77,158	3,558,342	1,170,628	543,555	25,191	209,300	133,642
2000	5,694,036	4,255,862	85,656	4,341,518	394,921	-93,139	3,853,458	1,270,399	570,179	27,034	210,623	136,775
2001	6,009,330	4,534,200	87,722	4,621,922	416,929	-82,540	4,122,453	1,267,900	618,977	28,284	212,461	137,126
2002	6,096,359	4,773,940	67,430	4,841,370	440,669	-136,505	4,264,196	1,164,535	667,628	28,417	214,532	135,953
2003	6,332,690	4,913,805	92,298	5,006,103	456,315	-156,079	4,393,709	1,238,235	700,746	29,118	217,483	136,874
2004	6,693,883	5,112,732	177,254	5,289,986	472,592	-180,065	4,637,329	1,320,684	735,870	30,536	219,215	138,256
2005	6,749,747	5,251,554	80,011	5,331,565	493,951	-197,689	4,639,925	1,298,191	811,631	30,487	221,400	138,309
2006	7,125,828	5,478,633	113,089	5,591,722	507,547	-209,952	4,874,223	1,410,950	840,655	31,724	224,622	139,256
2007	7,547,124	5,712,142	186,493	5,898,635	534,123	-227,029	5,137,483	1,490,577	919,064	33,174	227,498	141,805
2008	8,074,362	5,969,835	284,456	6,254,291	559,637	-242,089	5,452,565	1,578,043	1,043,754	35,355	228,381	142,026
2009	8,240,316	5,986,210	166,332	6,152,542	552,216	-306,427	5,293,899	1,787,417	1,159,000	35,699	230,826	139,497
2010	8,304,219	6,112,599	181,031	6,293,630	563,123	-339,975	5,390,532	1,636,338	1,277,349	35,756	232,250	137,315
2011	8,567,007	6,159,409	302,357	6,461,766	512,490	-328,873	5,620,403	1,711,526	1,235,078	36,716	233,332	136,757
2012	8,785,229	6,406,377	202,039	6,608,416	535,445	-317,480	5,755,491	1,805,252	1,224,486	37,461	234,514	136,669
2013	9,065,046	6,603,879	383,093	6,986,972	616,896	-320,002	6,050,074	1,738,430	1,276,542	38,409	236,015	137,083
2014	9,309,054	6,807,025	259,834	7,066,859	638,418	-220,379	6,208,062	1,784,695	1,316,297	39,237	237,252	138,546

Personal Income and Employment by Area: Charleston, WV

(Thousands of dollars, except as noted.)

Year	Personal income, total	Earnings by place of work			Less: Contributions for government social insurance	Plus: Adjustment for residence	Equals: Net earnings by place of residence	Plus: Dividends, interest, and rent	Plus: Personal current transfer receipts	Per capita personal income (dollars)	Population (persons)	Total employment
		Nonfarm	Farm	Total								
1970	991,459	875,317	234	875,551	65,362	-37,123	773,066	116,671	101,722	3,756	263,984	112,925
1971	1,068,528	935,684	192	935,876	72,695	-42,227	820,954	126,039	121,535	4,029	265,194	113,601
1972	1,167,498	1,034,831	240	1,035,071	84,627	-59,092	891,352	136,394	139,752	4,406	264,953	116,423
1973	1,273,572	1,140,975	262	1,141,237	108,477	-76,452	956,308	152,359	164,905	4,844	262,931	119,946
1974	1,406,346	1,267,843	139	1,267,982	124,719	-101,250	1,042,013	178,397	185,936	5,378	261,523	123,324
1975	1,578,556	1,422,457	164	1,422,621	138,115	-124,684	1,159,822	200,149	218,585	5,951	265,278	125,757
1976	1,748,602	1,594,730	195	1,594,925	158,063	-147,500	1,289,362	217,809	241,431	6,557	266,697	129,397
1977	1,939,901	1,789,576	292	1,789,868	175,948	-173,134	1,440,786	243,208	255,907	7,204	269,295	132,961
1978	2,153,254	2,021,530	335	2,021,865	204,935	-214,083	1,602,847	268,304	282,103	7,920	271,875	138,957
1979	2,403,925	2,274,198	448	2,274,646	240,654	-263,017	1,770,975	301,896	331,054	8,816	272,681	142,342
1980	2,591,056	2,399,818	356	2,400,174	259,227	-292,373	1,848,574	363,384	379,098	9,484	273,195	138,180
1981	2,824,379	2,511,935	133	2,512,068	290,164	-295,976	1,925,928	451,130	447,321	10,343	273,065	131,513
1982	3,028,188	2,666,027	284	2,666,311	317,090	-326,638	2,022,583	515,257	490,348	11,140	271,826	128,902
1983	3,093,568	2,630,946	447	2,631,393	315,041	-317,558	1,998,794	545,154	549,620	11,472	269,657	124,483
1984	3,299,699	2,787,307	1,038	2,788,345	339,576	-327,095	2,121,674	605,017	573,008	12,357	267,030	125,051
1985	3,444,074	2,911,547	701	2,912,248	357,693	-341,787	2,212,768	636,194	595,112	13,108	262,742	125,298
1986	3,495,532	2,944,585	819	2,945,404	377,669	-359,952	2,207,783	653,507	634,242	13,507	258,796	125,037
1987	3,518,720	2,947,177	12	2,947,189	381,504	-358,610	2,207,075	657,569	654,076	13,740	256,091	124,011
1988	3,809,271	3,163,365	134	3,163,499	412,898	-339,351	2,411,250	703,710	694,311	15,211	250,433	125,278
1989	4,023,090	3,290,546	221	3,290,767	435,333	-353,828	2,501,606	792,710	728,774	16,331	246,351	125,964
1990	4,286,720	3,542,804	677	3,543,481	477,023	-402,146	2,664,312	844,897	777,511	17,632	243,124	129,747
1991	4,461,880	3,717,314	622	3,717,936	514,964	-432,733	2,770,239	811,018	880,623	18,352	243,125	130,517
1992	4,754,858	3,933,284	928	3,934,212	548,655	-483,101	2,902,456	839,797	1,012,605	19,480	244,084	132,244
1993	4,942,672	4,087,561	450	4,088,011	588,139	-494,265	3,005,607	855,210	1,081,855	20,257	244,001	134,391
1994	5,172,726	4,320,739	338	4,321,077	618,858	-534,500	3,167,719	909,217	1,095,790	21,279	243,093	138,091
1995	5,322,674	4,494,727	70	4,494,797	653,959	-583,225	3,257,613	946,842	1,118,219	21,920	242,822	140,818
1996	5,511,041	4,656,858	-819	4,656,039	678,621	-639,811	3,337,607	1,001,692	1,171,742	22,746	242,282	142,338
1997	5,669,111	4,830,190	-1,130	4,829,060	697,089	-685,644	3,446,327	1,027,710	1,195,074	23,518	241,059	144,325
1998	5,966,506	5,072,830	-1,142	5,071,688	737,749	-700,096	3,633,843	1,108,052	1,224,611	24,941	239,229	145,676
1999	6,094,572	5,295,098	-1,166	5,293,932	764,647	-735,157	3,794,128	1,060,615	1,239,829	25,682	237,312	147,705
2000	6,423,472	5,564,551	-726	5,563,825	823,375	-785,589	3,954,861	1,161,757	1,306,854	27,274	235,518	148,772
2001	6,688,743	5,762,642	-822	5,761,820	811,300	-818,840	4,131,680	1,148,122	1,408,941	28,655	233,423	147,359
2002	6,896,928	5,840,359	-1,188	5,839,171	787,528	-871,391	4,180,252	1,137,138	1,579,538	29,716	232,093	146,229
2003	6,992,754	5,937,131	-566	5,936,565	815,232	-921,191	4,200,142	1,134,079	1,658,533	30,198	231,566	145,000
2004	7,060,056	6,223,835	-114	6,223,721	831,137	-986,316	4,406,268	1,048,595	1,605,193	30,580	230,874	145,304
2005	7,356,211	6,547,320	-424	6,546,896	860,939	-1,059,378	4,626,579	1,109,967	1,619,665	32,117	229,041	145,587
2006	7,944,181	6,980,774	-844	6,979,930	866,095	-1,149,681	4,964,154	1,245,985	1,734,042	34,881	227,750	147,077
2007	8,062,395	6,983,006	-1,339	6,981,667	842,237	-1,200,600	4,938,830	1,300,652	1,822,913	35,491	227,165	147,915
2008	8,648,349	7,457,599	-849	7,456,750	851,364	-1,284,817	5,320,569	1,316,638	2,011,142	38,130	226,811	147,200
2009	8,431,691	7,267,744	-698	7,267,046	856,358	-1,343,822	5,066,866	1,201,894	2,162,931	37,075	227,421	145,180
2010	8,556,988	7,316,310	-929	7,315,381	867,339	-1,342,429	5,105,613	1,186,923	2,264,452	37,696	227,000	143,876
2011	9,115,478	7,806,238	-447	7,805,791	803,937	-1,419,079	5,582,775	1,279,405	2,253,298	40,356	225,879	144,524
2012	9,341,090	7,915,154	-19	7,915,135	807,747	-1,436,465	5,670,923	1,358,232	2,311,935	41,369	225,800	144,307
2013	9,160,039	7,687,410	237	7,687,647	885,399	-1,377,780	5,424,468	1,371,618	2,363,953	40,769	224,683	142,314
2014	9,371,149	7,731,504	-209	7,731,295	910,903	-1,345,955	5,474,437	1,417,958	2,478,754	42,046	222,878	142,223

Personal Income and Employment by Area: Charleston-North Charleston, SC

(Thousands of dollars, except as noted.)

Year	Personal income, total	Earnings by place of work			Less: Contributions for government social insurance	Plus: Adjustment for residence	Equals: Net earnings by place of residence	Plus: Dividends, interest, and rent	Plus: Personal current transfer receipts	Per capita personal income (dollars)	Population (persons)	Total employment
		Nonfarm	Farm	Total								
1970	1,277,027	1,058,887	7,639	1,066,526	59,898	-11,787	994,841	212,383	69,803	3,793	336,669	152,101
1971	1,380,875	1,132,743	7,446	1,140,189	66,798	-11,564	1,061,827	233,495	85,553	4,002	345,034	151,142
1972	1,513,886	1,235,313	9,813	1,245,126	75,438	-10,960	1,158,728	257,118	98,040	4,275	354,123	153,558
1973	1,673,681	1,366,864	10,318	1,377,182	94,055	-12,635	1,270,492	286,099	117,090	4,617	362,524	162,266
1974	1,952,307	1,579,889	15,077	1,594,966	113,060	-14,089	1,467,817	336,873	147,617	5,170	377,614	172,300
1975	2,206,936	1,759,936	19,661	1,779,597	128,328	-16,981	1,634,288	378,254	194,394	5,674	388,945	176,227
1976	2,449,364	1,981,406	12,311	1,993,717	148,863	-21,237	1,823,617	410,564	215,183	6,086	402,464	183,691
1977	2,639,414	2,140,722	8,786	2,149,508	159,554	-24,376	1,965,578	447,774	226,062	6,482	407,216	188,099
1978	2,995,726	2,413,398	15,418	2,428,816	181,834	-28,429	2,218,553	527,199	249,974	7,176	417,483	197,797
1979	3,356,172	2,703,576	20,159	2,723,735	212,054	-34,183	2,477,498	591,026	287,648	7,894	425,158	204,605
1980	3,789,471	3,026,164	6,976	3,033,140	237,871	-40,360	2,754,909	681,242	353,320	8,739	433,615	209,543
1981	4,299,464	3,411,702	10,642	3,422,344	287,607	-45,388	3,089,349	803,172	406,943	9,656	445,278	217,214
1982	4,649,270	3,628,429	23,524	3,651,953	308,623	-46,412	3,296,918	907,977	444,375	10,257	453,298	217,116
1983	5,014,207	3,911,521	10,127	3,921,648	349,967	-40,133	3,531,548	1,006,786	475,873	10,879	460,906	222,685
1984	5,541,424	4,342,002	19,015	4,361,017	403,264	-50,077	3,907,676	1,124,230	509,518	11,858	467,325	236,807
1985	5,908,004	4,637,942	8,199	4,646,141	444,899	-56,871	4,144,371	1,217,122	546,511	12,588	469,353	246,759
1986	6,330,807	4,966,817	7,302	4,974,119	493,245	-59,877	4,420,997	1,326,560	583,250	13,163	480,947	255,473
1987	6,761,377	5,326,117	11,954	5,338,071	528,764	-62,606	4,746,701	1,412,476	602,200	13,788	490,378	263,378
1988	7,288,813	5,791,313	17,965	5,809,278	601,080	-69,598	5,138,600	1,507,856	642,357	14,791	492,783	270,818
1989	7,914,619	6,154,421	13,890	6,168,311	653,841	-75,452	5,439,018	1,676,179	799,422	15,740	502,823	275,672
1990	8,612,819	6,736,491	12,967	6,749,458	739,620	-85,319	5,924,519	1,814,123	874,177	16,926	508,851	289,036
1991	8,974,082	6,966,428	19,060	6,985,488	777,910	-77,661	6,129,917	1,889,673	954,492	17,131	523,852	287,878
1992	9,434,879	7,245,020	16,418	7,261,438	813,488	-64,277	6,383,673	1,951,195	1,100,011	17,789	530,382	283,152
1993	9,792,005	7,411,198	23,960	7,435,158	843,837	-58,348	6,532,973	2,061,167	1,197,865	18,409	531,913	282,830
1994	10,023,776	7,426,863	34,106	7,460,969	861,533	-42,750	6,556,686	2,165,804	1,301,286	18,935	529,376	280,828
1995	10,233,045	7,446,727	31,774	7,478,501	869,584	-27,543	6,581,374	2,242,047	1,409,624	19,596	522,192	281,375
1996	10,732,661	7,704,883	27,846	7,732,729	889,686	-19,437	6,823,606	2,390,820	1,518,235	20,721	517,970	282,824
1997	11,487,733	8,264,651	28,077	8,292,728	958,508	-16,124	7,318,096	2,573,627	1,596,010	21,742	528,354	293,859
1998	12,521,133	9,111,957	20,573	9,132,530	1,053,610	-12,743	8,066,177	2,786,525	1,668,431	23,375	535,674	304,546
1999	13,433,277	9,976,663	24,118	10,000,781	1,143,369	-10,452	8,846,960	2,821,723	1,764,594	24,595	546,169	316,202
2000	14,604,579	10,854,907	25,267	10,880,174	1,228,420	-1,606	9,650,148	3,062,045	1,892,386	26,510	550,916	323,269
2001	15,168,706	11,218,296	26,859	11,245,155	1,279,660	6,776	9,972,271	3,096,827	2,099,608	27,238	556,901	329,250
2002	15,853,817	11,902,621	16,056	11,918,677	1,362,928	-55,548	10,500,201	3,074,949	2,278,667	28,051	565,179	334,599
2003	16,553,918	12,592,824	25,948	12,618,772	1,449,238	-113,300	11,056,234	3,092,642	2,405,042	28,871	573,376	341,087
2004	17,815,041	13,454,539	21,939	13,476,478	1,545,408	-110,510	11,820,560	3,398,687	2,595,794	30,337	587,231	353,739
2005	19,350,321	14,482,653	23,924	14,506,577	1,650,355	-171,185	12,685,037	3,860,515	2,804,769	32,341	598,313	364,466
2006	21,186,890	15,537,710	15,579	15,553,289	1,801,004	-81,890	13,670,395	4,512,924	3,003,571	34,480	614,463	373,935
2007	22,768,636	16,677,981	14,723	16,692,704	1,929,878	-99,965	14,662,861	4,922,640	3,183,135	36,234	628,384	389,868
2008	24,214,917	17,664,848	6,758	17,671,606	2,026,426	-61,723	15,583,457	4,909,086	3,722,374	37,623	643,613	398,328
2009	24,255,390	17,842,761	12,076	17,854,837	2,007,144	-58,140	15,789,553	4,345,587	4,120,250	37,006	655,447	385,581
2010	25,246,520	18,303,138	11,745	18,314,883	2,054,585	-64,068	16,196,230	4,545,468	4,504,822	37,810	667,724	387,330
2011	26,606,842	19,011,234	10,139	19,021,373	1,928,462	-77,181	17,015,730	4,972,795	4,618,317	39,043	681,482	401,513
2012	28,680,648	20,635,079	17,521	20,652,600	2,017,186	-83,296	18,552,118	5,463,467	4,665,063	41,123	697,435	411,077
2013	28,488,763	20,495,825	26,107	20,521,932	2,319,668	-91,375	18,110,889	5,521,376	4,856,498	40,008	712,081	421,288
2014	30,057,328	21,676,693	18,090	21,694,783	2,468,008	-104,494	19,122,281	5,743,650	5,191,397	41,305	727,689	433,062

Personal Income and Employment by Area: Charlotte-Concord-Gastonia, NC-SC

(Thousands of dollars, except as noted.)

| Year | Personal income, total | Derivation of personal income | | | | | | | | Per capita personal income (dollars) | Population (persons) | Total employment |
| | | Earnings by place of work | | | Less: Contributions for government social insurance | Plus: Adjustment for residence | Equals: Net earnings by place of residence | Plus: Dividends, interest, and rent | Plus: Personal current transfer receipts | | | |
		Nonfarm	Farm	Total								
1970	3,561,684	3,186,687	23,102	3,209,789	225,700	-51,981	2,932,108	384,353	245,223	3,603	988,444	503,563
1971	3,894,478	3,463,692	27,218	3,490,910	254,522	-55,627	3,180,761	424,585	289,132	3,865	1,007,583	511,003
1972	4,390,798	3,931,041	32,679	3,963,720	303,176	-64,339	3,596,205	468,961	325,632	4,271	1,027,951	534,518
1973	4,893,407	4,376,391	64,193	4,440,584	387,915	-69,884	3,982,785	525,514	385,108	4,692	1,042,990	557,073
1974	5,323,388	4,684,925	51,734	4,736,659	429,910	-72,712	4,234,037	606,798	482,553	5,051	1,054,007	556,610
1975	5,734,250	4,842,512	43,467	4,885,979	434,093	-78,241	4,373,645	669,961	690,644	5,417	1,058,573	531,234
1976	6,399,183	5,492,239	48,150	5,540,389	504,519	-87,723	4,948,147	726,087	724,949	6,005	1,065,660	552,899
1977	7,093,028	6,149,664	44,271	6,193,935	562,819	-101,532	5,529,584	811,023	752,421	6,590	1,076,317	576,425
1978	8,036,938	7,026,090	58,283	7,084,373	662,281	-120,818	6,301,274	925,660	810,004	7,339	1,095,051	604,651
1979	9,083,325	7,969,113	66,030	8,035,143	778,268	-146,685	7,110,190	1,057,061	916,074	8,144	1,115,330	631,747
1980	10,217,182	8,799,952	33,877	8,833,829	859,393	-173,816	7,800,620	1,325,350	1,091,212	8,941	1,142,703	636,966
1981	11,490,034	9,749,967	40,927	9,790,894	1,021,767	-208,899	8,560,228	1,672,039	1,257,767	9,907	1,159,800	644,468
1982	12,315,626	10,201,762	58,007	10,259,769	1,081,665	-223,426	8,954,678	1,944,563	1,416,385	10,466	1,176,768	634,435
1983	13,515,133	11,254,914	47,855	11,302,769	1,203,729	-244,247	9,854,793	2,135,301	1,525,039	11,390	1,186,619	648,334
1984	15,329,114	12,772,184	134,902	12,907,086	1,399,933	-274,590	11,232,563	2,495,243	1,601,308	12,703	1,206,699	687,850
1985	16,660,757	13,861,209	155,607	14,016,816	1,538,805	-300,054	12,177,957	2,751,581	1,731,219	13,547	1,229,877	711,901
1986	18,044,472	15,143,517	144,780	15,288,297	1,717,076	-331,016	13,240,205	2,969,499	1,834,768	14,462	1,247,714	738,057
1987	19,701,628	16,829,227	85,527	16,914,754	1,881,794	-379,203	14,653,757	3,143,402	1,904,469	15,486	1,272,213	768,719
1988	21,789,689	18,563,539	124,151	18,687,690	2,116,213	-420,969	16,150,508	3,575,003	2,064,178	16,798	1,297,129	803,761
1989	23,791,895	20,086,260	161,528	20,247,788	2,287,185	-461,882	17,498,721	3,981,891	2,311,283	18,016	1,320,598	826,270
1990	25,524,655	21,580,929	206,836	21,787,765	2,521,588	-507,264	18,758,913	4,208,740	2,557,002	18,909	1,349,847	844,984
1991	26,454,449	22,053,725	237,338	22,291,063	2,611,390	-496,650	19,183,023	4,313,139	2,958,287	19,157	1,380,932	830,828
1992	28,690,995	23,944,508	233,381	24,177,889	2,794,437	-520,888	20,862,564	4,547,206	3,281,225	20,416	1,405,306	844,448
1993	30,726,756	25,553,036	246,803	25,799,839	2,995,693	-541,411	22,262,735	4,888,128	3,575,893	21,402	1,435,716	873,760
1994	33,228,614	27,691,511	245,601	27,937,112	3,279,927	-585,024	24,072,161	5,408,491	3,747,962	22,599	1,470,366	909,458
1995	36,123,340	29,966,867	275,626	30,242,493	3,542,791	-637,200	26,062,502	5,927,854	4,132,984	23,938	1,509,023	948,911
1996	39,062,753	32,118,628	258,514	32,377,142	3,751,921	-664,692	27,960,529	6,612,969	4,489,255	25,190	1,550,697	975,193
1997	42,098,108	34,795,637	237,600	35,033,237	4,042,308	-721,674	30,269,255	7,137,303	4,691,550	26,396	1,594,838	1,014,492
1998	46,446,262	38,613,521	268,750	38,882,271	4,426,543	-783,909	33,671,819	7,857,758	4,916,685	28,322	1,639,936	1,044,737
1999	49,892,310	41,910,794	305,796	42,216,590	4,778,364	-868,320	36,569,906	8,110,438	5,211,966	29,581	1,686,617	1,084,033
2000	53,833,097	45,264,082	291,813	45,555,895	5,099,611	-937,304	39,518,980	8,678,253	5,635,864	31,142	1,728,616	1,115,557
2001	56,076,275	47,083,458	329,867	47,413,325	5,323,683	-1,019,647	41,069,995	8,663,465	6,342,815	31,691	1,769,476	1,115,551
2002	58,104,184	49,201,531	205,524	49,407,055	5,492,080	-1,194,673	42,720,302	8,448,602	6,935,280	32,161	1,806,638	1,118,829
2003	59,842,840	50,558,439	244,218	50,802,657	5,742,137	-1,273,363	43,787,157	8,710,901	7,344,782	32,497	1,841,489	1,119,026
2004	64,401,203	53,752,647	279,773	54,032,420	6,059,204	-1,259,576	46,713,640	9,773,059	7,914,504	34,256	1,880,010	1,146,453
2005	69,356,365	57,475,580	312,818	57,788,398	6,512,800	-1,411,097	49,864,501	10,926,968	8,564,896	35,859	1,934,168	1,186,735
2006	75,519,034	62,456,728	279,617	62,736,345	7,067,016	-1,434,727	54,234,602	11,882,449	9,401,983	37,586	2,009,239	1,238,687
2007	80,268,377	65,447,502	229,818	65,677,320	7,548,523	-1,247,697	56,881,100	13,190,912	10,196,365	38,477	2,086,153	1,293,758
2008	84,231,384	66,943,731	153,180	67,096,911	7,752,642	-1,107,976	58,236,293	14,128,495	11,866,596	39,145	2,151,756	1,302,011
2009	81,044,995	63,461,839	140,706	63,602,545	7,362,366	-1,082,456	55,157,723	12,303,404	13,583,868	36,908	2,195,856	1,249,371
2010	84,024,963	65,906,315	150,876	66,057,191	7,394,966	-1,107,540	57,554,685	11,816,388	14,653,890	37,783	2,223,894	1,241,068
2011	88,711,058	68,687,455	155,407	68,842,862	7,017,790	-1,195,840	60,629,232	13,195,610	14,886,216	39,302	2,257,149	1,296,795
2012	96,367,219	75,201,564	244,220	75,445,784	7,422,715	-1,334,791	66,688,278	14,549,043	15,129,898	41,974	2,295,879	1,327,159
2013	95,149,825	75,150,776	355,390	75,506,166	8,684,079	-1,354,947	65,467,140	14,238,910	15,443,775	40,709	2,337,339	1,364,160
2014	100,985,034	80,642,382	354,532	80,996,914	9,328,732	-1,559,077	70,109,105	14,818,814	16,057,115	42,425	2,380,314	1,409,063

Personal Income and Employment by Area: Charlottesville, VA

(Thousands of dollars, except as noted.)

Year	Personal income, total	Derivation of personal income									Per capita personal income (dollars)	Population (persons)	Total employment
		Earnings by place of work			Less: Contributions for government social insurance	Plus: Adjustment for residence	Equals: Net earnings by place of residence	Plus: Dividends, interest, and rent	Plus: Personal current transfer receipts				
		Nonfarm	Farm	Total									
1970	381,704	307,534	7,606	315,140	19,212	-19,632	276,296	75,825	29,583		3,413	111,846	51,870
1971	418,418	333,995	7,062	341,057	21,688	-19,151	300,218	83,041	35,159		3,680	113,689	52,468
1972	478,475	368,137	7,473	375,610	25,221	-3,505	346,884	91,459	40,132		4,025	118,870	54,890
1973	550,150	422,288	11,906	434,194	32,841	-3,810	397,543	104,501	48,106		4,499	122,296	58,728
1974	615,027	466,281	11,765	478,046	37,815	-3,969	436,262	120,128	58,637		4,902	125,476	60,912
1975	680,397	503,002	7,047	510,049	39,984	2,516	472,581	130,006	77,810		5,204	130,734	60,189
1976	757,824	559,072	5,038	564,110	44,944	10,363	529,529	142,572	85,723		5,721	132,458	62,508
1977	832,426	615,665	4,325	619,990	50,026	10,831	580,795	160,008	91,623		6,236	133,491	64,427
1978	952,208	711,717	10,296	722,013	58,754	5,200	668,459	184,640	99,109		7,053	135,000	68,132
1979	1,055,702	814,849	9,895	824,744	70,191	-9,717	744,836	197,690	113,176		7,713	136,881	71,979
1980	1,198,615	913,765	5,051	918,816	79,955	-17,755	821,106	242,782	134,727		8,683	138,046	74,348
1981	1,358,155	993,048	3,310	996,358	93,685	-12,088	890,585	311,745	155,825		9,709	139,886	74,591
1982	1,488,327	1,066,264	1,726	1,067,990	102,224	-14,664	951,102	366,143	171,082		10,568	140,835	75,162
1983	1,625,809	1,186,314	308	1,186,622	116,121	-21,812	1,048,689	390,409	186,711		11,423	142,328	77,404
1984	1,809,796	1,312,419	4,960	1,317,379	132,138	-21,717	1,163,524	447,742	198,530		12,598	143,655	80,110
1985	1,965,770	1,427,570	3,726	1,431,296	146,738	-24,153	1,260,405	494,661	210,704		13,459	146,056	82,356
1986	2,122,944	1,554,379	4,783	1,559,162	165,238	-23,958	1,369,966	532,870	220,108		14,535	146,055	86,235
1987	2,294,505	1,687,892	9,041	1,696,933	178,297	-21,720	1,496,916	569,807	227,782		15,437	148,641	90,858
1988	2,598,606	1,923,007	9,720	1,932,727	206,941	-23,681	1,702,105	654,240	242,261		17,175	151,301	91,623
1989	2,846,870	2,066,464	14,215	2,080,679	223,853	-21,891	1,834,935	741,525	270,410		18,437	154,409	94,636
1990	3,057,191	2,195,450	16,958	2,212,408	240,888	-20,828	1,950,692	815,713	290,786		19,362	157,899	95,934
1991	3,233,477	2,301,264	16,746	2,318,010	253,536	-19,724	2,044,750	866,344	322,383		20,139	160,559	95,320
1992	3,489,960	2,441,371	15,763	2,457,134	267,840	-20,576	2,168,718	948,992	372,250		21,391	163,154	96,170
1993	3,749,960	2,618,875	13,869	2,632,744	284,848	-26,801	2,321,095	1,028,942	399,923		22,496	166,695	99,792
1994	3,950,849	2,757,993	14,130	2,772,123	299,973	-30,459	2,441,691	1,093,204	415,954		23,208	170,234	101,956
1995	4,215,319	2,879,077	15,150	2,894,227	311,426	-34,788	2,548,013	1,209,865	457,441		24,329	173,261	104,722
1996	4,460,681	3,060,094	15,355	3,075,449	329,988	-44,556	2,700,905	1,273,134	486,642		25,276	176,481	107,633
1997	4,798,780	3,304,689	9,436	3,314,125	352,469	-47,925	2,913,731	1,374,494	510,555		26,688	179,813	110,980
1998	5,160,691	3,596,567	8,989	3,605,556	382,172	-63,580	3,159,804	1,481,460	519,427		28,165	183,230	115,734
1999	5,421,278	3,806,154	7,827	3,813,981	405,899	-68,539	3,339,543	1,533,026	548,709		28,969	187,141	118,584
2000	5,874,375	4,133,808	13,873	4,147,681	435,802	-84,985	3,626,894	1,649,553	597,928		30,818	190,613	122,061
2001	6,191,591	4,344,706	8,720	4,353,426	463,993	-77,496	3,811,937	1,720,839	658,815		31,980	193,611	123,039
2002	6,350,733	4,545,512	5,292	4,550,804	485,379	-90,781	3,974,644	1,687,390	688,699		32,344	196,350	124,006
2003	6,692,000	4,715,830	1,503	4,717,333	504,860	-151,310	4,061,163	1,893,740	737,097		33,696	198,602	125,115
2004	7,142,278	5,078,422	7,682	5,086,104	545,130	-200,624	4,340,350	2,027,074	774,854		35,536	200,985	129,500
2005	7,720,930	5,480,186	5,219	5,485,405	592,502	-246,460	4,646,443	2,229,337	845,150		37,668	204,975	133,677
2006	8,475,953	5,813,129	-5,897	5,807,232	632,717	-252,276	4,922,239	2,630,948	922,766		40,648	208,519	137,441
2007	9,041,125	6,108,397	-12,763	6,095,634	671,051	-260,546	5,164,037	2,894,930	982,158		42,771	211,383	141,481
2008	9,381,667	6,333,670	-2,346	6,331,324	694,951	-252,501	5,383,872	2,883,051	1,114,744		43,702	214,672	142,965
2009	9,115,160	6,374,041	2,740	6,376,781	696,414	-258,590	5,421,777	2,496,681	1,196,702		41,971	217,176	140,505
2010	9,433,722	6,579,942	5,485	6,585,427	727,419	-256,414	5,601,594	2,536,870	1,295,258		43,061	219,076	139,682
2011	10,148,563	6,898,097	10,648	6,908,745	674,345	-269,818	5,964,582	2,850,353	1,333,628		45,851	221,339	141,605
2012	10,969,167	7,258,751	22,168	7,280,919	701,953	-284,416	6,294,550	3,313,985	1,360,632		49,156	223,151	143,580
2013	11,072,432	7,408,212	18,765	7,426,977	819,218	-288,166	6,319,593	3,334,942	1,417,897		49,259	224,778	145,162
2014	11,568,703	7,784,098	14,779	7,798,877	858,573	-306,269	6,634,035	3,444,445	1,490,223		50,971	226,968	148,377

Personal Income and Employment by Area: Chattanooga, TN-GA

(Thousands of dollars, except as noted.)

| Year | Personal income, total | Derivation of personal income | | | | | | | | Per capita personal income (dollars) | Population (persons) | Total employment |
| | | Earnings by place of work | | | Less: Contributions for government social insurance | Plus: Adjustment for residence | Equals: Net earnings by place of residence | Plus: Dividends, interest, and rent | Plus: Personal current transfer receipts | | | |
		Nonfarm	Farm	Total								
1970	1,329,175	1,172,018	4,311	1,176,329	76,760	-43,659	1,055,910	161,021	112,244	3,572	372,113	172,095
1971	1,473,559	1,289,241	3,807	1,293,048	86,418	-47,128	1,159,502	182,071	131,986	3,874	380,419	174,934
1972	1,672,876	1,474,421	5,289	1,479,710	103,374	-52,802	1,323,534	202,275	147,067	4,322	387,034	186,173
1973	1,868,990	1,648,485	9,097	1,657,582	133,722	-56,162	1,467,698	226,482	174,810	4,731	395,063	196,966
1974	2,051,653	1,782,676	4,370	1,787,046	149,824	-59,495	1,577,727	263,424	210,502	5,146	398,683	197,405
1975	2,228,106	1,869,933	7,212	1,877,145	152,748	-55,033	1,669,364	286,169	272,573	5,549	401,552	190,016
1976	2,486,635	2,096,630	9,431	2,106,061	174,051	-52,002	1,880,008	308,219	298,408	6,126	405,890	196,745
1977	2,748,662	2,331,589	6,532	2,338,121	191,994	-62,200	2,083,927	345,694	319,041	6,687	411,025	201,417
1978	3,138,496	2,688,416	5,564	2,693,980	222,836	-75,243	2,395,901	396,198	346,397	7,545	415,992	211,442
1979	3,420,690	2,898,784	7,112	2,905,896	250,372	-79,903	2,575,621	443,889	401,180	8,074	423,664	214,637
1980	3,713,844	3,043,308	5,674	3,048,982	263,229	-80,270	2,705,483	523,804	484,557	8,689	427,429	208,292
1981	4,073,285	3,255,491	8,296	3,263,787	304,253	-83,956	2,875,578	645,605	552,102	9,461	430,519	206,190
1982	4,317,495	3,352,877	9,992	3,362,869	319,349	-79,304	2,964,216	754,696	598,583	10,106	427,203	199,884
1983	4,549,074	3,518,244	4,627	3,522,871	343,115	-71,158	3,108,598	800,143	640,333	10,748	423,243	199,125
1984	4,942,114	3,817,603	10,868	3,828,471	385,049	-72,359	3,371,063	898,437	672,614	11,652	424,137	206,887
1985	5,274,414	4,066,751	9,024	4,075,775	420,743	-69,656	3,585,376	972,769	716,269	12,424	424,535	211,855
1986	5,640,739	4,386,269	9,036	4,395,305	464,410	-85,184	3,845,711	1,033,525	761,503	13,278	424,816	218,811
1987	6,116,638	4,832,210	6,719	4,838,929	507,109	-89,680	4,242,140	1,077,646	796,852	14,247	429,335	229,011
1988	6,672,854	5,259,904	9,993	5,269,897	566,691	-95,005	4,608,201	1,212,169	852,484	15,403	433,218	235,200
1989	7,085,175	5,452,902	15,959	5,468,861	598,982	-98,541	4,771,338	1,371,408	942,429	16,325	434,018	240,365
1990	7,505,668	5,754,881	15,581	5,770,462	637,020	-89,837	5,043,605	1,436,887	1,025,176	17,305	433,718	243,572
1991	7,746,123	5,898,091	18,198	5,916,289	664,462	-91,591	5,160,236	1,417,935	1,167,952	17,689	437,902	243,018
1992	8,346,566	6,291,128	19,817	6,310,945	701,306	-64,715	5,544,924	1,480,097	1,321,545	18,902	441,576	245,510
1993	8,935,189	6,771,250	20,399	6,791,649	757,313	-68,506	5,965,830	1,555,582	1,413,777	19,971	447,416	254,759
1994	9,353,478	7,132,380	22,557	7,154,937	810,877	-93,121	6,250,939	1,615,635	1,486,904	20,655	452,845	261,969
1995	9,931,815	7,530,213	14,640	7,544,853	857,440	-106,156	6,581,257	1,745,377	1,605,181	21,681	458,090	266,963
1996	10,514,551	7,957,645	16,684	7,974,329	893,108	-93,733	6,987,488	1,848,510	1,678,553	22,754	462,090	273,762
1997	11,063,941	8,525,480	17,224	8,542,704	943,647	-113,434	7,485,623	1,834,867	1,743,451	23,704	466,756	276,491
1998	11,877,247	9,202,398	21,914	9,224,312	983,540	-101,488	8,139,284	1,981,926	1,756,037	25,264	470,131	283,193
1999	12,650,761	9,954,793	19,584	9,974,377	1,058,973	-118,931	8,796,473	2,013,690	1,840,598	26,700	473,820	291,928
2000	13,449,847	10,573,280	16,626	10,589,906	1,113,751	-134,644	9,341,511	2,129,722	1,978,614	28,160	477,630	299,220
2001	13,656,344	10,686,764	30,395	10,717,159	1,136,167	-189,884	9,391,108	2,112,597	2,152,639	28,345	481,798	296,902
2002	13,987,500	10,983,818	12,836	10,996,654	1,170,903	-190,812	9,634,939	2,029,101	2,323,460	28,783	485,957	294,768
2003	14,489,792	11,433,177	12,600	11,445,777	1,221,472	-222,091	10,002,214	2,065,821	2,421,757	29,566	490,089	297,250
2004	15,113,772	11,875,713	24,941	11,900,654	1,264,798	-195,316	10,440,540	2,093,407	2,579,825	30,551	494,709	300,975
2005	15,798,384	12,353,887	29,468	12,383,355	1,325,691	-198,975	10,858,689	2,188,239	2,751,456	31,624	499,564	306,450
2006	16,972,394	13,045,893	8,098	13,053,991	1,399,266	-156,563	11,498,162	2,530,587	2,943,645	33,511	506,473	312,322
2007	17,810,958	13,450,215	10,260	13,460,475	1,458,770	-149,526	11,852,179	2,744,314	3,214,465	34,712	513,100	317,900
2008	18,225,115	13,479,521	24,055	13,503,576	1,494,770	-156,261	11,852,545	2,774,689	3,597,881	35,131	518,778	313,729
2009	17,560,309	12,781,954	18,659	12,800,613	1,443,704	-146,333	11,210,576	2,532,985	3,816,748	33,507	524,082	295,572
2010	18,414,259	13,290,361	13,228	13,303,589	1,507,558	-185,324	11,610,707	2,648,681	4,154,871	34,803	529,103	293,587
2011	19,324,642	13,823,594	5,387	13,828,981	1,394,180	-167,398	12,267,403	2,795,286	4,261,953	36,245	533,162	299,982
2012	20,411,434	14,585,243	41,606	14,626,849	1,432,973	-183,701	13,010,175	3,110,316	4,290,943	37,940	537,997	302,205
2013	20,559,164	14,801,821	57,405	14,859,226	1,643,530	-218,726	12,996,970	3,118,697	4,443,497	37,921	542,161	305,137
2014	21,379,356	15,265,251	61,215	15,326,466	1,688,630	-79,510	13,558,326	3,260,505	4,560,525	39,260	544,559	305,485

Personal Income and Employment by Area: Cheyenne, WY

(Thousands of dollars, except as noted.)

Year	Personal income, total	Earnings by place of work			Less: Contributions for government social insurance	Plus: Adjustment for residence	Equals: Net earnings by place of residence	Plus: Dividends, interest, and rent	Plus: Personal current transfer receipts	Per capita personal income (dollars)	Population (persons)	Total employment
		Nonfarm	Farm	Total								
1970	251,235	194,510	4,016	198,526	14,212	-937	183,377	48,989	18,869	4,437	56,619	28,563
1971	277,173	215,234	3,692	218,926	16,164	-1,573	201,189	54,508	21,476	4,783	57,944	29,358
1972	314,333	248,943	5,405	254,348	19,435	-2,897	232,016	59,320	22,997	5,239	59,997	31,164
1973	366,191	299,568	2,699	302,267	26,358	-4,933	270,976	68,600	26,615	5,863	62,458	33,858
1974	418,405	339,797	5,972	345,769	30,392	-6,064	309,313	78,775	30,317	6,458	64,789	34,558
1975	457,177	369,924	3,179	373,103	32,738	-7,198	333,167	87,363	36,647	7,071	64,656	34,715
1976	494,494	402,574	2,462	405,036	37,177	-8,825	359,034	94,690	40,770	7,538	65,603	35,707
1977	540,404	440,387	1,956	442,343	40,521	-10,280	391,542	104,195	44,667	8,149	66,313	36,652
1978	627,233	514,777	3,702	518,479	48,371	-13,288	456,820	120,660	49,753	9,362	67,001	39,071
1979	706,341	583,592	3,925	587,517	57,616	-16,399	513,502	135,190	57,649	10,212	69,168	41,258
1980	805,758	655,546	5,503	661,049	63,994	-19,474	577,581	161,049	67,128	11,679	68,994	42,593
1981	900,829	721,608	4,130	725,738	75,197	-19,811	630,730	190,803	79,296	12,837	70,176	42,834
1982	974,458	764,276	2,479	766,755	80,704	-20,808	665,243	220,548	88,667	13,700	71,129	43,159
1983	1,001,844	771,306	3,502	774,808	80,500	-20,529	673,779	226,047	102,018	13,741	72,907	41,915
1984	1,062,321	819,679	1,091	820,770	87,568	-21,400	711,802	245,453	105,066	14,484	73,345	42,415
1985	1,110,399	853,388	828	854,216	92,828	-22,131	739,257	260,238	110,904	15,190	73,102	42,570
1986	1,153,488	879,042	4,623	883,665	96,753	-21,692	765,220	268,161	120,107	15,502	74,411	42,461
1987	1,170,267	882,125	8,265	890,390	98,059	-20,769	771,562	274,213	124,492	15,583	75,101	43,181
1988	1,204,025	908,068	7,579	915,647	107,834	-21,308	786,505	286,933	130,587	16,156	74,523	43,939
1989	1,291,535	955,045	8,791	963,836	112,897	-21,765	829,174	319,293	143,068	17,532	73,667	44,287
1990	1,386,714	998,571	14,182	1,012,753	122,601	-22,129	868,023	364,659	154,032	18,951	73,175	44,257
1991	1,448,162	1,054,646	14,714	1,069,360	130,928	-21,644	916,788	360,570	170,804	19,576	73,978	45,286
1992	1,536,996	1,130,781	16,041	1,146,822	139,826	-22,022	984,974	362,445	189,577	20,270	75,826	46,097
1993	1,614,907	1,201,007	19,740	1,220,747	147,894	-20,673	1,052,180	357,828	204,899	20,839	77,495	47,556
1994	1,705,353	1,261,353	9,595	1,270,948	155,019	-17,724	1,098,205	387,805	219,343	21,618	78,885	48,911
1995	1,788,652	1,288,472	15,818	1,304,290	157,386	-14,337	1,132,567	426,807	229,278	22,495	79,513	49,370
1996	1,846,057	1,307,204	12,029	1,319,233	159,500	-11,391	1,148,342	458,294	239,421	23,022	80,186	49,791
1997	1,935,499	1,339,888	24,662	1,364,550	165,561	-9,478	1,189,511	499,094	246,894	24,095	80,328	50,275
1998	2,083,213	1,446,241	16,566	1,462,807	175,633	-8,293	1,278,881	552,963	251,369	25,871	80,522	50,833
1999	2,200,031	1,536,791	13,622	1,550,413	186,542	-6,991	1,356,880	580,243	262,908	27,158	81,009	51,585
2000	2,349,091	1,640,372	15,282	1,655,654	195,763	-2,792	1,457,099	605,831	286,161	28,709	81,825	53,178
2001	2,466,436	1,740,502	19,801	1,760,303	207,336	-4,177	1,548,790	601,307	316,339	29,877	82,554	52,897
2002	2,647,854	1,905,041	5,639	1,910,680	219,356	-9,739	1,681,585	625,558	340,711	31,815	83,226	54,740
2003	2,836,079	2,025,291	13,248	2,038,539	236,478	-15,940	1,786,121	679,821	370,137	33,729	84,084	55,838
2004	2,992,549	2,141,767	13,401	2,155,168	251,256	-22,579	1,881,333	710,976	400,240	35,030	85,427	57,059
2005	3,150,419	2,253,610	18,804	2,272,414	261,945	-30,016	1,980,453	743,039	426,927	36,747	85,732	58,202
2006	3,441,772	2,519,163	12,948	2,532,111	321,159	-39,411	2,171,541	810,024	460,207	39,643	86,819	59,268
2007	3,583,289	2,616,818	18,408	2,635,226	337,963	-48,073	2,249,190	842,820	491,279	40,880	87,654	61,232
2008	3,911,136	2,752,376	27,041	2,779,417	347,821	-57,952	2,373,644	961,659	575,833	43,907	89,077	62,801
2009	3,802,078	2,798,899	18,427	2,817,326	355,926	-63,119	2,398,281	779,113	624,684	42,044	90,430	62,194
2010	3,934,881	2,838,578	28,245	2,866,823	363,159	-62,818	2,440,846	813,555	680,480	42,678	92,199	61,578
2011	4,346,882	2,957,842	64,782	3,022,624	345,047	-67,629	2,609,948	1,046,163	690,771	46,939	92,607	62,977
2012	4,527,399	3,151,699	33,020	3,184,719	371,664	-73,851	2,739,204	1,097,247	690,948	47,733	94,849	63,695
2013	4,566,540	3,259,763	35,459	3,295,222	425,199	-75,605	2,794,418	1,068,426	703,696	47,561	96,015	65,813
2014	4,744,712	3,348,442	45,590	3,394,032	434,938	-69,923	2,889,171	1,130,660	724,881	49,225	96,389	66,692

Personal Income and Employment by Area: Chicago-Naperville-Elgin, IL-IN-WI

(Thousands of dollars, except as noted.)

Year	Personal income, total	Earnings by place of work			Less: Contributions for government social insurance	Plus: Adjustment for residence	Equals: Net earnings by place of residence	Plus: Dividends, interest, and rent	Plus: Personal current transfer receipts	Per capita personal income (dollars)	Population (persons)	Total employment
		Nonfarm	Farm	Total								
1970	39,117,196	33,289,538	86,734	33,376,272	2,242,085	-221,975	30,912,212	5,570,603	2,634,381	4,954	7,895,845	3,748,330
1971	41,776,482	35,226,087	126,592	35,352,679	2,443,040	-245,315	32,664,324	5,930,278	3,181,880	5,251	7,955,398	3,702,932
1972	45,203,334	38,270,832	88,392	38,359,224	2,799,518	-282,547	35,277,159	6,326,082	3,600,093	5,670	7,972,491	3,731,149
1973	49,767,713	42,200,874	182,890	42,383,764	3,579,992	-323,853	38,479,919	7,003,233	4,284,561	6,247	7,966,188	3,874,673
1974	54,610,935	45,905,879	148,968	46,054,847	4,034,979	-355,618	41,664,250	8,038,791	4,907,894	6,849	7,973,418	3,934,993
1975	58,555,797	47,889,345	229,126	48,118,471	4,091,563	-371,083	43,655,825	8,623,474	6,276,498	7,330	7,988,641	3,831,128
1976	64,218,013	52,995,860	158,417	53,154,277	4,622,553	-383,248	48,148,476	9,108,355	6,961,182	8,012	8,014,978	3,918,359
1977	71,036,623	59,165,183	161,840	59,327,023	5,147,532	-417,000	53,762,491	9,980,844	7,293,288	8,827	8,047,518	4,032,483
1978	78,759,116	66,071,479	168,100	66,239,579	5,908,887	-467,667	59,863,025	11,114,181	7,781,910	9,762	8,067,880	4,165,078
1979	86,335,448	72,538,929	198,815	72,737,744	6,739,277	-535,486	65,462,981	12,444,432	8,428,035	10,718	8,055,256	4,212,288
1980	94,162,521	76,456,892	73,393	76,530,285	7,075,545	-532,371	68,922,369	14,976,826	10,263,326	11,693	8,052,943	4,122,105
1981	103,515,944	81,802,210	171,801	81,974,011	8,119,333	-534,104	73,320,574	18,483,254	11,712,116	12,878	8,038,127	4,108,351
1982	109,395,378	83,863,721	126,959	83,990,680	8,481,571	-537,341	74,971,768	21,641,535	12,782,075	13,594	8,047,477	4,025,482
1983	115,119,544	88,009,529	-55,778	87,953,751	8,964,223	-523,874	78,465,654	23,010,275	13,643,615	14,310	8,044,580	3,992,825
1984	126,059,797	96,658,511	128,843	96,787,354	10,162,988	-550,836	86,073,530	25,986,916	13,999,351	15,625	8,067,923	4,150,208
1985	133,134,084	102,715,086	184,891	102,899,977	10,958,616	-560,800	91,380,561	27,168,391	14,585,132	16,493	8,072,070	4,206,304
1986	140,925,456	109,845,304	169,806	110,015,110	11,741,284	-593,647	97,680,179	28,110,270	15,135,007	17,445	8,078,098	4,297,096
1987	150,341,810	118,981,237	208,759	119,189,996	12,511,093	-687,761	105,991,142	28,986,197	15,364,471	18,563	8,099,059	4,429,471
1988	163,860,875	131,062,994	127,766	131,190,760	14,014,960	-769,605	116,406,195	31,572,421	15,882,259	20,188	8,116,756	4,560,934
1989	173,455,150	138,340,455	323,630	138,664,085	14,916,186	-824,896	122,923,003	33,626,980	16,905,167	21,275	8,153,134	4,646,403
1990	185,603,988	146,808,833	253,715	147,062,548	15,585,582	-888,473	130,588,493	36,489,633	18,525,862	22,626	8,203,210	4,719,223
1991	190,254,106	150,499,206	96,837	150,596,043	16,336,006	-930,194	133,329,843	36,939,891	19,984,372	22,910	8,304,560	4,690,670
1992	205,709,815	162,341,287	181,171	162,522,458	17,251,412	-1,051,912	144,219,134	38,542,092	22,948,589	24,452	8,412,788	4,668,331
1993	213,635,012	169,114,440	167,898	169,282,338	18,167,410	-1,148,787	149,966,141	39,476,803	24,192,068	25,095	8,512,911	4,745,984
1994	225,126,232	177,648,018	258,907	177,906,925	19,346,700	-1,260,962	157,299,263	42,519,960	25,307,009	26,160	8,605,735	4,860,416
1995	240,970,377	188,536,884	115,890	188,652,774	20,441,219	-1,378,645	166,832,910	47,279,933	26,857,534	27,719	8,693,383	4,989,418
1996	255,962,866	199,421,346	251,170	199,672,516	21,398,756	-1,525,572	176,748,188	50,904,584	28,310,094	29,145	8,782,253	5,072,565
1997	271,380,395	212,797,851	226,612	213,024,463	22,676,290	-1,681,625	188,666,548	53,947,099	28,766,748	30,620	8,862,719	5,159,787
1998	289,229,532	227,190,036	164,991	227,355,027	24,082,377	-1,894,003	201,378,647	58,601,942	29,248,943	32,319	8,949,190	5,291,157
1999	302,359,194	241,929,828	138,238	242,068,066	25,314,950	-2,084,063	214,669,053	57,924,786	29,765,355	33,463	9,035,654	5,357,659
2000	326,319,283	258,870,700	171,539	259,042,239	26,722,556	-2,297,503	230,022,180	64,433,410	31,863,693	35,807	9,113,234	5,463,703
2001	335,092,306	266,897,000	186,933	267,083,933	27,191,461	-2,419,110	237,473,362	63,126,752	34,492,192	36,544	9,169,580	5,449,869
2002	338,624,846	270,321,763	140,353	270,462,116	27,458,762	-2,818,198	240,185,156	61,288,156	37,151,534	36,783	9,206,032	5,389,339
2003	343,361,031	275,329,524	193,297	275,522,821	28,188,420	-3,216,814	244,117,587	60,584,878	38,658,566	37,187	9,233,303	5,378,496
2004	358,692,110	287,876,234	387,699	288,263,933	29,885,780	-3,364,986	255,013,167	63,718,450	39,960,493	38,733	9,260,676	5,438,430
2005	377,634,098	298,872,846	234,482	299,107,328	31,493,855	-3,654,861	263,958,612	69,758,489	43,916,997	40,710	9,276,302	5,514,034
2006	405,710,177	316,540,968	229,376	316,770,344	32,991,475	-3,709,401	280,069,468	81,124,957	44,515,752	43,635	9,297,749	5,617,762
2007	428,700,489	328,282,207	430,440	328,712,647	34,463,389	-3,580,507	290,668,751	88,885,739	49,145,999	45,913	9,337,140	5,726,410
2008	440,229,833	333,886,097	447,646	334,333,743	35,042,416	-3,430,933	295,860,394	89,929,405	54,440,034	46,910	9,384,555	5,719,998
2009	415,835,242	316,381,528	209,516	316,591,044	33,252,140	-3,021,913	280,316,991	74,099,462	61,418,789	44,099	9,429,498	5,525,347
2010	423,231,547	320,256,897	234,373	320,491,270	33,719,721	-3,072,738	283,698,811	72,560,541	66,972,195	44,691	9,470,069	5,460,898
2011	445,027,116	334,458,582	503,812	334,962,394	31,601,083	-3,248,382	300,112,929	80,719,404	64,194,783	46,877	9,493,464	5,575,021
2012	467,491,704	349,851,655	338,322	350,189,977	33,121,088	-3,442,259	313,626,630	89,359,053	64,506,021	49,110	9,519,316	5,631,380
2013	468,864,947	356,027,303	672,576	356,699,879	38,398,221	-3,428,839	314,872,819	87,024,302	66,967,826	49,123	9,544,796	5,716,193
2014	484,322,292	369,171,751	358,600	369,530,351	39,863,689	-3,488,307	326,178,355	90,101,296	68,042,641	50,690	9,554,598	5,802,279

Personal Income and Employment by Area: Chico, CA

(Thousands of dollars, except as noted.)

Year	Personal income, total	Earnings by place of work			Less: Contributions for government social insurance	Plus: Adjustment for residence	Equals: Net earnings by place of residence	Plus: Dividends, interest, and rent	Plus: Personal current transfer receipts	Per capita personal income (dollars)	Population (persons)	Total employment
		Nonfarm	Farm	Total								
1970	381,020	227,858	24,434	252,292	15,039	6,627	243,880	74,037	63,103	3,711	102,682	36,830
1971	415,039	247,543	24,962	272,505	16,892	7,444	263,057	81,430	70,552	3,919	105,916	38,010
1972	460,815	275,618	28,920	304,538	19,710	8,670	293,498	90,297	77,020	4,086	112,775	40,361
1973	535,262	310,597	46,152	356,749	25,329	10,261	341,681	104,693	88,888	4,728	113,223	42,508
1974	628,228	344,291	70,657	414,948	29,016	12,230	398,162	121,640	108,426	5,356	117,295	44,300
1975	697,407	388,472	52,089	440,561	31,905	15,118	423,774	139,786	133,847	5,734	121,626	45,985
1976	763,106	451,481	29,862	481,343	37,428	17,966	461,881	151,902	149,323	6,086	125,377	48,998
1977	857,595	507,746	38,057	545,803	42,883	21,218	524,138	173,187	160,270	6,624	129,470	51,665
1978	973,056	582,367	31,548	613,915	49,917	25,812	589,810	206,406	176,840	7,383	131,797	54,807
1979	1,129,607	657,244	56,369	713,613	59,391	29,669	683,891	243,744	201,972	8,154	138,531	58,299
1980	1,317,930	745,724	61,407	807,131	65,508	32,571	774,194	303,580	240,156	9,100	144,828	60,482
1981	1,461,437	791,596	56,521	848,117	76,547	33,390	804,960	368,651	287,826	9,845	148,451	61,097
1982	1,521,337	804,960	42,256	847,216	80,400	34,858	801,674	397,418	322,245	10,015	151,913	59,921
1983	1,637,385	876,856	16,628	893,484	88,959	34,989	839,514	447,122	350,749	10,614	154,263	62,688
1984	1,795,369	966,681	31,211	997,892	102,365	37,534	933,061	489,605	372,703	11,451	156,791	64,197
1985	1,938,708	1,057,558	33,846	1,091,404	113,242	39,745	1,017,907	519,658	401,143	12,066	160,680	66,863
1986	2,072,311	1,151,972	27,616	1,179,588	125,374	44,563	1,098,777	540,780	432,754	12,695	163,233	68,099
1987	2,253,058	1,272,882	64,147	1,337,029	140,489	47,339	1,243,879	552,502	456,677	13,494	166,970	71,391
1988	2,462,872	1,413,271	80,281	1,493,552	161,144	51,141	1,383,549	587,416	491,907	14,327	171,909	76,545
1989	2,661,253	1,528,597	43,753	1,572,350	177,189	54,481	1,449,642	668,684	542,927	15,071	176,583	79,880
1990	2,867,576	1,675,467	63,550	1,739,017	190,636	59,989	1,608,370	677,940	581,266	15,614	183,652	84,276
1991	3,040,933	1,777,362	64,187	1,841,549	203,586	63,747	1,701,710	689,543	649,680	16,203	187,678	85,153
1992	3,227,217	1,863,624	80,716	1,944,340	212,767	67,859	1,799,432	694,154	733,631	16,949	190,409	84,849
1993	3,325,103	1,910,260	83,170	1,993,430	218,249	71,188	1,846,369	710,815	767,919	17,244	192,831	84,708
1994	3,464,786	2,047,776	64,102	2,111,878	232,132	73,541	1,953,287	722,585	788,914	17,800	194,648	88,262
1995	3,576,281	2,081,886	46,513	2,128,399	233,397	82,019	1,977,021	773,780	825,480	18,239	196,083	89,235
1996	3,785,585	2,201,530	58,420	2,259,950	237,017	86,375	2,109,308	816,001	860,276	19,282	196,327	91,583
1997	4,020,514	2,362,246	75,495	2,437,741	247,586	93,238	2,283,393	872,606	864,515	20,306	197,994	93,148
1998	4,216,734	2,516,430	14,484	2,530,914	258,779	101,831	2,373,966	932,476	910,292	21,084	199,993	94,720
1999	4,391,860	2,675,952	44,962	2,720,914	274,793	111,285	2,557,406	895,802	938,652	21,819	201,282	97,399
2000	4,723,076	2,912,062	59,814	2,971,876	295,105	123,854	2,800,625	946,463	975,988	23,174	203,807	98,928
2001	4,966,841	3,047,588	59,444	3,107,032	329,331	134,295	2,911,996	985,678	1,069,167	24,088	206,193	99,755
2002	5,139,878	3,280,396	65,932	3,346,328	358,008	140,132	3,128,452	889,164	1,122,262	24,579	209,120	101,854
2003	5,401,198	3,416,907	91,760	3,508,667	376,024	144,528	3,277,171	937,810	1,186,217	25,540	211,481	101,989
2004	5,813,951	3,640,659	102,286	3,742,945	417,876	154,317	3,479,386	1,075,207	1,259,358	27,287	213,065	104,178
2005	6,060,980	3,819,302	114,618	3,933,920	444,312	163,969	3,653,577	1,083,921	1,323,482	28,223	214,752	106,671
2006	6,444,113	4,019,173	79,518	4,098,691	448,968	177,045	3,826,768	1,182,993	1,434,352	29,720	216,824	107,455
2007	6,748,928	4,119,200	104,460	4,223,660	452,338	190,195	3,961,517	1,268,113	1,519,298	31,034	217,469	108,407
2008	6,936,284	4,052,534	144,355	4,196,889	454,096	191,962	3,934,755	1,304,811	1,696,718	31,668	219,034	105,697
2009	6,846,855	3,867,851	210,951	4,078,802	450,155	175,560	3,804,207	1,194,668	1,847,980	31,154	219,777	101,038
2010	7,000,427	3,879,064	197,572	4,076,636	446,472	179,967	3,810,131	1,184,794	2,005,502	31,831	219,924	99,642
2011	7,345,144	4,035,815	215,791	4,251,606	420,811	180,494	4,011,289	1,321,283	2,012,572	33,383	220,025	99,681
2012	7,662,810	4,234,502	229,391	4,463,893	433,889	176,377	4,206,381	1,405,596	2,050,833	34,630	221,279	102,571
2013	8,057,223	4,392,282	363,869	4,756,151	505,321	179,859	4,430,689	1,498,424	2,128,110	36,225	222,420	106,145
2014	8,298,110	4,563,278	283,568	4,846,846	527,000	192,977	4,512,823	1,568,305	2,216,982	37,005	224,241	109,017

Personal Income and Employment by Area: Cincinnati-Middletown, OH-KY-IN

(Thousands of dollars, except as noted.)

Year	Personal income, total	Earnings by place of work			Less: Contributions for government social insurance	Plus: Adjustment for residence	Equals: Net earnings by place of residence	Plus: Dividends, interest, and rent	Plus: Personal current transfer receipts	Per capita personal income (dollars)	Population (persons)	Total employment
		Nonfarm	Farm	Total								
1970	6,909,150	5,640,636	40,395	5,681,031	375,829	49,525	5,354,727	1,025,551	528,872	4,104	1,683,357	717,838
1971	7,221,153	5,820,793	34,064	5,854,857	398,814	43,991	5,500,034	1,095,245	625,874	4,271	1,690,881	706,103
1972	7,850,553	6,354,909	41,085	6,395,994	459,114	54,985	5,991,865	1,164,881	693,807	4,647	1,689,419	719,327
1973	8,686,038	7,075,256	51,828	7,127,084	590,318	59,006	6,595,772	1,282,242	808,024	5,111	1,699,443	749,255
1974	9,543,141	7,654,929	68,025	7,722,954	662,115	55,340	7,116,179	1,458,837	968,125	5,622	1,697,582	757,725
1975	10,282,746	8,055,315	68,008	8,123,323	679,411	52,669	7,496,581	1,580,267	1,205,898	6,066	1,695,118	742,023
1976	11,358,590	8,996,582	67,242	9,063,824	776,392	63,409	8,350,841	1,689,909	1,317,840	6,663	1,704,762	759,472
1977	12,629,944	10,098,503	63,076	10,161,579	873,120	72,896	9,361,355	1,872,933	1,395,656	7,365	1,714,809	787,208
1978	14,105,665	11,438,020	46,675	11,484,695	1,020,929	74,895	10,538,661	2,079,532	1,487,472	8,161	1,728,350	824,603
1979	15,703,906	12,723,950	42,197	12,766,147	1,186,960	78,043	11,657,230	2,346,838	1,699,838	9,047	1,735,736	843,934
1980	17,398,761	13,579,681	39,232	13,618,913	1,260,328	71,877	12,430,462	2,867,265	2,101,034	9,982	1,743,032	840,256
1981	19,106,885	14,489,374	40,325	14,529,699	1,436,896	79,059	13,171,862	3,590,152	2,344,871	10,937	1,747,031	829,486
1982	20,207,612	14,896,100	70,631	14,966,731	1,504,010	89,221	13,551,942	3,970,725	2,684,945	11,540	1,751,052	812,056
1983	21,522,330	15,849,733	654	15,850,387	1,628,333	100,366	14,322,420	4,312,378	2,887,532	12,286	1,751,730	815,951
1984	23,698,845	17,508,609	58,149	17,566,758	1,833,247	126,041	15,859,552	4,808,942	3,030,351	13,468	1,759,676	850,061
1985	25,375,771	18,890,597	56,936	18,947,533	2,009,271	147,872	17,086,134	5,054,875	3,234,762	14,340	1,769,618	880,814
1986	26,949,187	20,267,154	18,728	20,285,882	2,225,351	155,640	18,216,171	5,334,809	3,398,207	15,116	1,782,790	909,075
1987	28,665,073	21,847,181	21,856	21,869,037	2,400,246	155,633	19,624,424	5,516,558	3,524,091	15,921	1,800,487	939,655
1988	30,848,837	23,475,880	28,797	23,504,677	2,651,033	189,978	21,043,622	6,067,265	3,737,950	17,029	1,811,516	970,621
1989	33,419,230	25,124,390	55,762	25,180,152	2,852,727	202,194	22,529,619	6,910,592	3,979,019	18,354	1,820,832	995,454
1990	36,025,506	27,030,854	52,890	27,083,744	3,132,678	202,346	24,153,412	7,464,003	4,408,091	19,609	1,837,214	1,015,267
1991	37,025,646	28,046,906	47,051	28,093,957	3,329,568	222,303	24,986,692	7,230,030	4,808,924	19,918	1,858,915	1,016,454
1992	39,834,847	30,296,566	69,950	30,366,516	3,576,139	221,222	27,011,599	7,543,664	5,279,584	21,205	1,878,558	1,026,671
1993	41,617,854	31,620,600	49,054	31,669,654	3,756,456	249,441	28,162,639	7,930,517	5,524,698	21,903	1,900,124	1,043,171
1994	43,762,625	33,332,145	60,742	33,392,887	4,029,069	279,407	29,643,225	8,382,918	5,736,482	22,871	1,913,442	1,071,538
1995	46,087,847	35,006,892	15,287	35,022,179	4,268,068	299,646	31,053,757	8,945,277	6,088,813	23,919	1,926,822	1,101,936
1996	49,080,843	37,134,830	40,972	37,175,802	4,476,518	293,163	32,992,447	9,755,269	6,333,127	25,302	1,939,779	1,131,097
1997	52,463,216	39,857,078	65,864	39,922,942	4,708,803	303,620	35,517,759	10,413,496	6,531,961	26,818	1,956,236	1,158,927
1998	56,477,944	43,244,107	45,624	43,289,731	4,968,306	282,357	38,603,782	11,258,544	6,615,618	28,653	1,971,116	1,194,007
1999	58,892,252	46,023,095	18,177	46,041,272	5,284,742	279,043	41,035,573	11,025,489	6,831,190	29,676	1,984,493	1,213,950
2000	62,244,607	48,379,246	79,070	48,458,316	5,406,837	294,458	43,345,937	11,586,831	7,311,839	31,129	1,999,554	1,234,488
2001	64,952,503	50,531,413	59,916	50,591,329	5,539,349	325,962	45,377,942	11,544,091	8,030,470	32,279	2,012,228	1,227,491
2002	66,057,709	51,810,351	14,411	51,824,762	5,626,115	-87,943	46,110,704	11,353,941	8,593,064	32,695	2,020,396	1,223,431
2003	68,011,044	53,595,739	25,255	53,620,994	5,849,946	-228,583	47,542,465	11,528,654	8,939,925	33,478	2,031,529	1,226,420
2004	72,036,576	56,477,496	77,873	56,555,369	6,198,137	-75,812	50,281,420	12,345,611	9,409,545	35,264	2,042,753	1,239,563
2005	74,911,771	58,554,322	56,291	58,610,613	6,418,731	-109,670	52,082,212	12,822,393	10,007,166	36,456	2,054,879	1,256,979
2006	79,758,014	60,783,067	45,715	60,828,782	6,675,896	331,170	54,484,056	14,631,232	10,642,726	38,531	2,069,960	1,268,510
2007	82,563,818	62,570,371	29,436	62,599,807	6,919,894	512,122	56,192,035	15,029,141	11,342,642	39,617	2,084,042	1,287,869
2008	84,910,961	63,639,985	21,421	63,661,406	7,164,662	212,343	56,709,087	15,245,915	12,955,959	40,530	2,095,040	1,285,468
2009	81,588,315	61,625,080	43,482	61,668,562	7,021,522	68,059	54,715,099	12,809,098	14,064,118	38,711	2,107,649	1,242,886
2010	83,438,509	62,955,342	26,691	62,982,033	7,079,369	-41,028	55,861,636	12,601,374	14,975,499	39,398	2,117,863	1,227,465
2011	88,974,812	65,882,398	71,082	65,953,480	6,587,960	-87,389	59,278,131	14,345,685	15,350,996	41,903	2,123,332	1,242,992
2012	93,039,705	69,098,683	51,224	69,149,907	6,826,964	-150,947	62,171,996	15,764,442	15,103,267	43,685	2,129,786	1,253,811
2013	94,394,971	70,511,380	130,448	70,641,828	7,786,238	-159,309	62,696,281	16,163,730	15,534,960	44,140	2,138,536	1,268,622
2014	98,613,244	73,836,123	67,232	73,903,355	8,226,874	-181,037	65,495,444	16,737,388	16,380,412	45,878	2,149,449	1,290,564

Personal Income and Employment by Area: Clarksville, TN-KY

(Thousands of dollars, except as noted.)

Year	Personal income, total	Derivation of personal income								Per capita personal income (dollars)	Population (persons)	Total employment
		Earnings by place of work			Less: Contributions for government social insurance	Plus: Adjustment for residence	Equals: Net earnings by place of residence	Plus: Dividends, interest, and rent	Plus: Personal current transfer receipts			
		Nonfarm	Farm	Total								
1970	462,881	354,764	15,890	370,654	21,775	1,587	350,466	77,954	34,461	3,608	128,304	62,242
1971	520,811	398,342	20,030	418,372	25,845	1,765	394,292	86,158	40,361	3,942	132,120	63,181
1972	558,200	429,557	23,281	452,838	28,838	-1,518	422,482	91,054	44,664	4,277	130,523	62,873
1973	733,437	571,093	31,550	602,643	41,057	-7,162	554,424	126,227	52,786	5,050	145,221	74,314
1974	819,119	638,012	26,176	664,188	48,129	-7,925	608,134	147,640	63,345	5,442	150,507	75,527
1975	856,613	659,789	17,110	676,899	52,597	-6,411	617,891	159,150	79,572	5,783	148,128	73,152
1976	993,709	773,496	21,803	795,299	63,869	-7,868	723,562	184,224	85,923	6,550	151,709	79,719
1977	1,065,310	812,586	36,406	848,992	65,767	-4,147	779,078	194,664	91,568	6,804	156,582	78,755
1978	1,169,830	894,702	27,245	921,947	71,696	-6,384	843,867	226,085	99,878	7,438	157,269	80,086
1979	1,300,662	980,932	41,820	1,022,752	81,232	-4,792	936,728	248,324	115,610	8,138	159,822	80,031
1980	1,368,487	1,015,105	17,832	1,032,937	85,368	1,595	949,164	278,945	140,378	8,553	159,999	78,851
1981	1,542,119	1,142,478	34,486	1,176,964	101,188	-15,744	1,060,032	322,183	159,904	9,565	161,222	79,659
1982	1,654,309	1,203,602	28,822	1,232,424	104,253	-13,745	1,114,426	361,980	177,903	9,962	166,069	78,823
1983	1,715,563	1,288,568	-14,518	1,274,050	115,463	-13,287	1,145,300	381,816	188,447	10,303	166,510	79,185
1984	1,877,025	1,369,848	31,278	1,401,126	127,470	-6,399	1,267,257	411,280	198,488	11,227	167,189	81,128
1985	2,007,153	1,461,058	28,672	1,489,730	137,774	1,389	1,353,345	442,749	211,059	11,706	171,467	82,547
1986	2,116,609	1,547,229	21,627	1,568,856	149,810	6,113	1,425,159	468,613	222,837	12,382	170,942	83,901
1987	2,269,121	1,661,595	25,809	1,687,404	161,872	14,619	1,540,151	496,276	232,694	13,193	171,998	86,982
1988	2,429,273	1,783,199	24,288	1,807,487	181,359	21,841	1,647,969	529,115	252,189	13,959	174,027	88,495
1989	2,584,805	1,841,394	37,711	1,879,105	192,353	29,821	1,716,573	586,298	281,934	14,642	176,531	90,093
1990	2,584,434	1,824,272	32,107	1,856,379	196,307	40,838	1,700,910	567,151	316,373	14,290	180,857	87,447
1991	2,771,461	1,961,762	28,318	1,990,080	214,457	41,946	1,817,569	589,865	364,027	15,389	180,093	87,685
1992	3,302,603	2,396,969	43,760	2,440,729	265,243	35,358	2,210,844	686,337	405,422	17,386	189,963	97,180
1993	3,433,449	2,487,637	33,852	2,521,489	280,041	36,335	2,277,783	731,334	424,332	17,918	191,616	99,926
1994	3,612,112	2,590,491	43,322	2,633,813	290,403	42,071	2,385,481	778,937	447,694	18,363	196,709	102,624
1995	3,890,199	2,774,542	30,410	2,804,952	306,002	40,995	2,539,945	852,335	497,919	19,350	201,040	107,625
1996	4,130,911	2,926,646	49,821	2,976,467	320,710	43,025	2,698,782	905,822	526,307	19,831	208,307	109,895
1997	4,284,580	3,061,852	43,952	3,105,804	335,237	52,733	2,823,300	901,029	560,251	20,160	212,526	112,425
1998	4,572,821	3,237,153	23,058	3,260,211	348,567	62,562	2,974,206	1,013,715	584,900	21,270	214,986	113,467
1999	4,863,604	3,505,774	5,353	3,511,127	376,621	60,866	3,195,372	1,045,751	622,481	22,384	217,276	118,319
2000	5,372,102	3,871,236	47,727	3,918,963	405,264	65,589	3,579,288	1,111,865	680,949	24,317	220,923	121,113
2001	5,504,569	3,898,845	47,337	3,946,182	420,543	85,605	3,611,244	1,134,958	758,367	24,684	223,001	121,576
2002	5,796,835	4,178,836	30,295	4,209,131	451,093	35,844	3,793,882	1,178,833	824,120	25,868	224,096	122,577
2003	6,232,321	4,581,317	41,039	4,622,356	483,193	-24,745	4,114,418	1,230,279	887,624	27,836	223,891	124,166
2004	6,650,032	4,870,235	71,076	4,941,311	517,462	49,809	4,473,658	1,218,301	958,073	29,052	228,899	128,082
2005	7,274,527	5,584,084	94,092	5,678,176	589,617	-159,652	4,928,907	1,307,510	1,038,110	30,612	237,633	134,686
2006	7,840,090	6,048,806	69,849	6,118,655	641,272	-182,826	5,294,557	1,414,335	1,131,198	33,021	237,426	137,463
2007	8,297,808	6,233,955	31,648	6,265,603	663,472	-37,561	5,564,570	1,503,238	1,230,000	33,479	247,849	140,519
2008	8,797,199	6,635,122	47,822	6,682,944	711,098	-172,991	5,798,855	1,572,617	1,425,727	35,425	248,331	140,978
2009	9,056,632	6,745,678	48,097	6,793,775	736,671	-174,527	5,882,577	1,623,782	1,550,273	35,302	256,545	138,970
2010	9,454,590	7,021,654	17,835	7,039,489	775,083	-186,791	6,077,615	1,665,387	1,711,588	36,112	261,814	140,308
2011	10,267,916	7,513,151	70,056	7,583,207	751,353	-207,900	6,623,954	1,834,082	1,809,880	38,804	264,611	143,791
2012	10,480,507	7,631,732	74,340	7,706,072	757,986	-168,590	6,779,496	1,869,578	1,831,433	38,039	275,522	144,001
2013	10,473,535	7,456,343	160,210	7,616,553	821,765	-129,671	6,665,117	1,898,206	1,910,212	38,301	273,453	143,711
2014	10,649,620	7,541,229	48,225	7,589,454	826,764	-98,165	6,664,525	1,956,620	2,028,475	38,259	278,353	144,980

Personal Income and Employment by Area: Cleveland, TN

(Thousands of dollars, except as noted.)

Year	Personal income, total	Earnings by place of work			Less: Contributions for government social insurance	Plus: Adjustment for residence	Equals: Net earnings by place of residence	Plus: Dividends, interest, and rent	Plus: Personal current transfer receipts	Per capita personal income (dollars)	Population (persons)	Total employment
		Nonfarm	Farm	Total								
1970	194,792	162,350	1,834	164,184	10,907	2,890	156,167	21,457	17,168	3,100	62,840	28,344
1971	219,013	182,656	1,642	184,298	12,691	3,610	175,217	23,909	19,887	3,351	65,350	29,244
1972	249,955	210,093	2,478	212,571	15,388	4,587	201,770	26,420	21,765	3,717	67,241	31,705
1973	288,949	242,249	4,671	246,920	20,176	5,578	232,322	30,680	25,947	4,149	69,648	34,135
1974	306,128	248,670	1,718	250,388	21,519	7,394	236,263	35,926	33,939	4,270	71,692	32,962
1975	328,648	257,258	1,754	259,012	21,615	5,197	242,594	41,347	44,707	4,539	72,406	30,714
1976	372,542	294,191	2,363	296,554	25,427	10,668	281,795	43,448	47,299	5,039	73,937	32,387
1977	404,550	307,883	3,381	311,264	26,937	20,917	305,244	47,700	51,606	5,331	75,881	33,401
1978	462,193	361,915	1,083	362,998	32,219	21,903	352,682	53,768	55,743	5,952	77,652	35,414
1979	523,195	405,127	2,423	407,550	37,619	26,547	396,478	60,739	65,978	6,570	79,631	36,135
1980	599,220	452,619	4,438	457,057	41,941	26,420	441,536	75,031	82,653	7,365	81,363	36,047
1981	678,196	508,249	7,806	516,055	50,809	27,821	493,067	93,579	91,550	8,265	82,061	36,618
1982	723,298	528,690	7,029	535,719	53,899	29,813	511,633	110,414	101,251	8,806	82,139	36,932
1983	797,111	594,926	3,427	598,353	60,906	29,214	566,661	122,186	108,264	9,668	82,449	37,384
1984	884,229	654,532	11,349	665,881	69,126	33,538	630,293	138,788	115,148	10,570	83,652	39,385
1985	947,508	705,067	7,979	713,046	75,125	35,672	673,593	151,514	122,401	11,215	84,486	39,808
1986	1,012,602	737,083	12,234	749,317	80,203	47,586	716,700	164,102	131,800	11,932	84,865	40,542
1987	1,100,104	809,584	6,728	816,312	86,928	54,107	783,491	178,784	137,829	12,891	85,340	42,402
1988	1,185,369	859,709	7,790	867,499	94,423	71,313	844,389	191,307	149,673	13,703	86,505	43,780
1989	1,299,723	916,914	18,674	935,588	100,873	80,268	914,983	219,180	165,560	14,956	86,902	44,308
1990	1,364,544	963,736	16,411	980,147	106,454	81,289	954,982	224,435	185,127	15,562	87,684	43,815
1991	1,437,338	1,014,582	20,118	1,034,700	114,228	77,415	997,887	223,612	215,839	16,158	88,954	43,128
1992	1,589,080	1,124,539	19,717	1,144,256	124,999	82,897	1,102,154	233,186	253,740	17,594	90,317	44,380
1993	1,650,697	1,152,551	20,987	1,173,538	129,003	98,039	1,142,574	236,986	271,137	17,946	91,979	45,808
1994	1,760,363	1,240,561	17,079	1,257,640	140,271	99,032	1,216,401	262,935	281,027	18,896	93,161	46,481
1995	1,856,338	1,302,479	10,124	1,312,603	146,305	101,321	1,267,619	281,475	307,244	19,513	95,133	48,418
1996	1,997,659	1,409,373	13,214	1,422,587	154,757	100,734	1,368,564	301,418	327,677	20,627	96,848	50,123
1997	2,159,767	1,560,493	5,690	1,566,183	166,490	97,712	1,497,405	317,750	344,612	21,594	100,019	51,829
1998	2,346,287	1,704,818	10,176	1,714,994	173,039	107,982	1,649,937	341,833	354,517	23,058	101,755	51,889
1999	2,423,290	1,766,008	8,715	1,774,723	182,617	111,247	1,703,353	349,882	370,055	23,531	102,982	52,500
2000	2,479,533	1,755,799	6,425	1,762,224	182,986	128,835	1,708,073	372,503	398,957	23,764	104,338	52,592
2001	2,621,050	1,812,070	25,895	1,837,965	189,747	143,248	1,791,466	383,993	445,591	24,892	105,295	51,687
2002	2,669,796	1,858,608	4,510	1,863,118	197,311	168,588	1,834,395	359,309	476,092	25,192	105,979	51,574
2003	2,810,178	1,938,847	6,225	1,945,072	205,420	189,916	1,929,568	371,495	509,115	26,324	106,754	52,094
2004	3,010,264	2,066,863	19,697	2,086,560	219,588	222,710	2,089,682	371,950	548,632	27,847	108,099	53,387
2005	3,106,999	2,084,463	21,918	2,106,381	223,971	253,929	2,136,339	379,954	590,706	28,398	109,410	53,587
2006	3,223,873	2,117,206	6,114	2,123,320	229,512	280,710	2,174,518	407,614	641,741	28,998	111,177	53,760
2007	3,414,431	2,160,141	2,463	2,162,604	237,425	318,781	2,243,960	462,934	707,537	30,234	112,935	53,623
2008	3,629,867	2,199,899	13,304	2,213,203	242,493	348,429	2,319,139	510,214	800,514	31,756	114,306	53,022
2009	3,576,857	2,149,726	24,531	2,174,257	243,001	297,686	2,228,942	485,048	862,867	31,079	115,090	51,613
2010	3,661,706	2,185,731	33,430	2,219,161	247,494	303,669	2,275,336	430,898	955,472	31,576	115,965	51,287
2011	3,940,940	2,362,213	34,568	2,396,781	238,329	312,148	2,470,600	502,909	967,431	33,782	116,657	52,689
2012	4,253,281	2,680,155	33,751	2,713,906	255,250	271,244	2,729,900	546,740	976,641	36,127	117,730	54,590
2013	4,403,691	2,773,805	61,256	2,835,061	295,075	291,781	2,831,767	575,396	996,528	37,150	118,537	56,891
2014	4,601,591	2,935,451	65,382	3,000,833	311,076	289,407	2,979,164	601,811	1,020,616	38,441	119,705	58,996

Personal Income and Employment by Area: Cleveland-Elyria, OH

(Thousands of dollars, except as noted.)

Year	Personal income, total	Derivation of personal income								Per capita personal income (dollars)	Population (persons)	Total employment
		Earnings by place of work			Less: Contributions for government social insurance	Plus: Adjustment for residence	Equals: Net earnings by place of residence	Plus: Dividends, interest, and rent	Plus: Personal current transfer receipts			
		Nonfarm	Farm	Total								
1970	10,736,339	9,284,613	19,843	9,304,456	615,025	-287,318	8,402,113	1,541,542	792,684	4,630	2,318,811	1,076,814
1971	11,253,267	9,601,345	26,837	9,628,182	653,378	-306,356	8,668,448	1,635,679	949,140	4,866	2,312,528	1,044,149
1972	12,116,980	10,401,531	28,586	10,430,117	747,243	-334,075	9,348,799	1,722,554	1,045,627	5,320	2,277,630	1,053,824
1973	13,302,162	11,536,345	20,630	11,556,975	964,373	-386,917	10,205,685	1,892,554	1,203,923	5,870	2,266,062	1,095,299
1974	14,600,115	12,520,175	27,215	12,547,390	1,082,844	-438,821	11,025,725	2,159,926	1,414,464	6,496	2,247,641	1,114,246
1975	15,453,435	12,952,585	37,515	12,990,100	1,088,512	-479,237	11,422,351	2,288,861	1,742,223	6,906	2,237,565	1,077,447
1976	16,748,506	14,245,155	39,604	14,284,759	1,227,678	-557,150	12,499,931	2,400,969	1,847,606	7,545	2,219,936	1,088,064
1977	18,561,186	16,004,280	35,760	16,040,040	1,377,706	-656,322	14,006,012	2,614,490	1,940,684	8,385	2,213,651	1,114,106
1978	20,515,121	17,819,510	35,968	17,855,478	1,585,566	-767,250	15,502,662	2,918,792	2,093,667	9,296	2,206,866	1,148,501
1979	22,399,652	19,405,437	28,215	19,433,652	1,799,238	-878,507	16,755,907	3,276,113	2,367,632	10,253	2,184,615	1,159,618
1980	24,290,091	20,120,020	27,342	20,147,362	1,851,713	-944,312	17,351,337	3,914,065	3,024,689	11,181	2,172,438	1,133,733
1981	26,449,182	21,430,552	31,574	21,462,126	2,110,018	-1,027,886	18,324,222	4,804,147	3,320,813	12,233	2,162,129	1,112,891
1982	27,646,646	21,601,031	29,419	21,630,450	2,157,804	-1,022,460	18,450,186	5,338,784	3,857,676	12,855	2,150,690	1,072,341
1983	29,105,865	22,554,972	29,722	22,584,694	2,293,980	-1,054,160	19,236,554	5,718,686	4,150,625	13,559	2,146,550	1,058,826
1984	31,902,900	24,872,137	34,010	24,906,147	2,586,673	-1,157,088	21,162,386	6,420,404	4,320,110	14,899	2,141,290	1,090,297
1985	33,876,990	26,518,914	30,694	26,549,608	2,793,441	-1,229,382	22,526,785	6,769,341	4,580,864	15,895	2,131,240	1,106,952
1986	35,216,194	27,658,246	28,348	27,686,594	2,998,393	-1,261,919	23,426,282	6,918,121	4,871,791	16,607	2,120,606	1,123,074
1987	36,939,843	29,273,279	43,283	29,316,562	3,175,125	-1,320,592	24,820,845	7,070,664	5,048,334	17,475	2,113,892	1,145,205
1988	39,884,181	31,902,590	72,163	31,974,753	3,540,966	-1,428,788	27,004,999	7,600,828	5,278,354	18,974	2,102,075	1,171,445
1989	42,419,660	33,695,532	92,851	33,788,383	3,777,622	-1,527,622	28,483,139	8,309,449	5,627,072	20,164	2,103,702	1,194,435
1990	45,323,856	35,567,737	91,401	35,659,138	4,077,759	-1,659,929	29,921,450	9,207,393	6,195,013	21,539	2,104,288	1,206,598
1991	45,819,469	36,000,623	64,799	36,065,422	4,222,531	-1,661,329	30,181,562	8,978,643	6,659,264	21,638	2,117,512	1,192,489
1992	48,112,955	38,023,178	120,349	38,143,527	4,431,392	-1,782,611	31,929,524	8,952,896	7,230,535	22,577	2,131,036	1,181,133
1993	50,032,086	39,354,214	115,739	39,469,953	4,636,216	-1,808,580	33,025,157	9,451,466	7,555,463	23,375	2,140,398	1,195,585
1994	52,473,569	41,870,969	110,591	41,981,560	4,994,770	-1,967,424	35,019,366	9,652,352	7,801,851	24,448	2,146,303	1,223,705
1995	54,980,672	43,495,873	111,046	43,606,919	5,246,504	-2,077,057	36,283,358	10,452,219	8,245,095	25,570	2,150,203	1,251,048
1996	57,258,938	44,994,075	110,572	45,104,647	5,370,276	-2,210,965	37,523,406	11,237,628	8,497,904	26,588	2,153,598	1,268,542
1997	60,242,972	47,539,724	111,744	47,651,468	5,550,528	-2,500,294	39,600,646	11,886,248	8,756,078	27,985	2,152,676	1,290,060
1998	63,507,980	50,105,169	118,656	50,223,825	5,696,496	-2,707,892	41,819,437	12,906,894	8,781,649	29,517	2,151,568	1,305,464
1999	65,368,147	52,572,051	123,576	52,695,627	5,940,479	-3,067,745	43,687,403	12,663,612	9,017,132	30,405	2,149,943	1,322,916
2000	68,647,360	55,200,486	97,698	55,298,184	6,023,251	-3,323,833	45,951,100	13,160,280	9,535,980	31,966	2,147,532	1,340,015
2001	69,665,251	55,716,764	103,652	55,820,416	6,055,994	-3,221,889	46,542,533	12,890,913	10,231,805	32,527	2,141,787	1,318,948
2002	69,785,542	55,730,287	94,226	55,824,513	5,944,592	-3,377,908	46,502,013	12,471,704	10,811,825	32,668	2,136,201	1,291,357
2003	71,030,783	57,574,313	71,594	57,645,907	6,201,697	-3,515,673	47,928,537	11,757,615	11,344,631	33,330	2,131,150	1,288,733
2004	74,132,193	60,183,408	116,261	60,299,669	6,563,360	-3,605,357	50,130,952	12,207,484	11,793,757	34,920	2,122,934	1,295,337
2005	76,670,306	61,333,331	125,555	61,458,886	6,705,175	-3,471,673	51,282,038	13,050,304	12,337,964	36,307	2,111,699	1,299,134
2006	81,008,732	64,171,314	85,656	64,256,970	7,003,199	-3,594,158	53,659,613	14,494,375	12,854,744	38,586	2,099,415	1,307,888
2007	83,882,473	65,252,030	97,967	65,349,997	7,157,167	-3,587,730	54,605,100	15,674,452	13,602,921	40,105	2,091,596	1,315,009
2008	86,311,311	66,356,226	83,288	66,439,514	7,348,735	-3,483,539	55,607,240	15,573,687	15,130,384	41,394	2,085,110	1,301,441
2009	82,066,770	62,764,749	89,174	62,853,923	7,054,711	-3,341,586	52,457,626	13,447,704	16,161,440	39,435	2,081,063	1,250,887
2010	84,015,899	64,611,408	84,798	64,696,206	7,136,677	-3,426,185	54,133,344	12,925,719	16,956,836	40,479	2,075,558	1,237,431
2011	89,620,349	68,136,889	99,654	68,236,543	6,724,723	-3,671,609	57,840,211	14,408,724	17,371,414	43,328	2,068,399	1,255,016
2012	93,453,491	71,132,564	102,869	71,235,433	6,975,113	-3,993,426	60,266,894	16,101,650	17,084,947	45,265	2,064,570	1,272,270
2013	93,474,395	72,230,456	107,092	72,337,548	7,859,821	-4,063,224	60,414,503	15,576,046	17,483,846	45,259	2,065,328	1,285,047
2014	96,907,131	74,581,967	101,477	74,683,444	8,186,044	-4,054,772	62,442,628	16,155,859	18,308,644	46,960	2,063,598	1,294,529

Personal Income and Employment by Area: Coeur d'Alene, ID

(Thousands of dollars, except as noted.)

Year	Personal income, total	Nonfarm	Farm	Total	Less: Contributions for government social insurance	Plus: Adjustment for residence	Equals: Net earnings by place of residence	Plus: Dividends, interest, and rent	Plus: Personal current transfer receipts	Per capita personal income (dollars)	Population (persons)	Total employment
1970	126,644	73,929	2,621	76,550	5,381	19,452	90,621	21,804	14,219	3,560	35,579	12,625
1971	142,973	83,600	2,309	85,909	6,311	21,578	101,176	24,829	16,968	3,902	36,644	13,312
1972	165,775	100,236	3,474	103,710	7,992	23,590	119,308	27,184	19,283	4,229	39,195	14,772
1973	187,340	120,075	-2,546	117,529	11,145	26,473	132,857	31,549	22,934	4,406	42,519	16,223
1974	223,292	133,369	5,892	139,261	12,506	31,219	157,974	37,165	28,153	5,007	44,600	17,126
1975	253,854	147,044	4,059	151,103	13,391	36,181	173,893	43,450	36,511	5,360	47,365	17,382
1976	295,169	176,475	4,336	180,811	16,255	41,257	205,813	49,194	40,162	6,045	48,828	19,043
1977	340,306	210,031	2,752	212,783	19,534	45,864	239,113	58,245	42,948	6,600	51,565	20,572
1978	408,754	254,482	4,235	258,717	23,770	55,285	290,232	70,842	47,680	7,380	55,386	22,466
1979	470,442	289,983	3,523	293,506	28,596	64,410	329,320	84,301	56,821	8,011	58,728	24,047
1980	522,881	303,297	3,992	307,289	29,744	73,288	350,833	102,757	69,291	8,715	59,996	23,469
1981	571,538	315,867	2,922	318,789	33,338	79,627	365,078	126,425	80,035	9,396	60,827	23,099
1982	591,171	310,715	2,918	313,633	33,498	71,692	351,827	143,172	96,172	9,468	62,436	22,576
1983	662,525	362,534	5,631	368,165	39,518	76,489	405,136	156,296	101,093	10,518	62,987	24,041
1984	733,191	408,332	4,995	413,327	46,351	83,828	450,804	178,626	103,761	11,195	65,494	26,144
1985	771,557	427,039	3,827	430,866	49,274	85,520	467,112	192,212	112,233	11,553	66,783	26,831
1986	806,656	446,684	3,458	450,142	52,293	87,921	485,770	201,608	119,278	12,083	66,761	27,960
1987	838,887	476,278	147	476,425	54,613	94,325	516,137	199,133	123,617	12,680	66,160	29,674
1988	923,710	527,894	3,150	531,044	63,210	106,998	574,832	214,306	134,572	13,816	66,859	31,474
1989	1,032,186	592,168	3,829	595,997	72,138	117,333	641,192	242,768	148,226	15,238	67,738	33,071
1990	1,135,719	668,846	5,524	674,370	85,509	127,361	716,222	256,681	162,816	16,123	70,443	35,431
1991	1,231,885	738,437	2,405	740,842	96,754	127,468	771,556	274,560	185,769	16,659	73,946	38,117
1992	1,403,725	862,584	4,753	867,337	110,936	138,672	895,073	300,478	208,174	18,095	77,577	41,164
1993	1,558,452	970,621	5,297	975,918	125,379	143,423	993,962	335,406	229,084	18,855	82,654	44,016
1994	1,716,090	1,090,855	570	1,091,425	141,171	157,758	1,108,012	364,607	243,471	19,491	88,046	48,249
1995	1,844,731	1,135,051	339	1,135,390	148,655	170,485	1,157,220	417,154	270,357	19,905	92,677	50,172
1996	1,988,343	1,209,397	1,380	1,210,777	154,831	192,853	1,248,799	445,807	293,737	20,585	96,590	51,999
1997	2,112,634	1,278,838	-898	1,277,940	163,797	214,959	1,329,102	473,542	309,990	21,104	100,108	54,341
1998	2,306,921	1,410,331	1,096	1,411,427	175,762	245,239	1,480,904	499,297	326,720	22,459	102,717	55,769
1999	2,444,363	1,519,309	1,908	1,521,217	183,858	268,193	1,605,552	487,314	351,497	22,985	106,346	57,901
2000	2,640,880	1,683,817	2,876	1,686,693	198,582	240,712	1,728,823	525,870	386,187	24,120	109,487	59,984
2001	2,809,262	1,792,802	3,530	1,796,332	209,000	239,866	1,827,198	536,454	445,610	25,186	111,542	60,257
2002	2,846,698	1,834,792	4,056	1,838,848	219,141	234,957	1,854,664	509,371	482,663	25,044	113,667	61,884
2003	3,019,551	1,931,929	3,225	1,935,154	233,061	235,599	1,937,692	567,221	514,638	25,916	116,512	63,100
2004	3,330,903	2,141,715	4,170	2,145,885	258,282	250,542	2,138,145	634,321	558,437	27,528	121,002	67,185
2005	3,672,880	2,345,624	3,333	2,348,957	288,526	259,286	2,319,717	743,885	609,278	29,156	125,972	71,426
2006	4,046,258	2,621,282	1,695	2,622,977	324,973	275,564	2,573,568	818,893	653,797	31,243	129,510	75,547
2007	4,299,935	2,742,932	1,915	2,744,847	344,828	281,366	2,681,385	907,923	710,627	32,376	132,811	78,477
2008	4,401,206	2,722,138	-1,359	2,720,779	348,755	268,059	2,640,083	932,307	828,816	32,451	135,627	79,052
2009	4,356,029	2,614,272	672	2,614,944	339,452	309,166	2,584,658	856,341	915,030	31,702	137,407	75,459
2010	4,431,413	2,626,020	-3,784	2,622,236	356,966	331,650	2,596,920	824,301	1,010,192	31,906	138,890	73,921
2011	4,722,639	2,652,063	3,180	2,655,243	328,266	412,545	2,739,522	959,410	1,023,707	33,483	141,045	74,677
2012	4,956,497	2,662,522	4,993	2,667,515	331,364	543,413	2,879,564	1,028,775	1,048,158	34,832	142,297	73,999
2013	5,144,468	2,835,611	3,164	2,838,775	384,586	521,849	2,976,038	1,088,181	1,080,249	35,637	144,357	76,531
2014	5,400,382	2,948,081	1,996	2,950,077	395,020	567,234	3,122,291	1,134,670	1,143,421	36,656	147,326	78,837

Personal Income and Employment by Area: College Station-Bryan, TX

(Thousands of dollars, except as noted.)

| Year | Personal income, total | Derivation of personal income | | | | | | | | | Per capita personal income (dollars) | Population (persons) | Total employment |
| | | Earnings by place of work | | | Less: Contributions for government social insurance | Plus: Adjustment for residence | Equals: Net earnings by place of residence | Plus: Dividends, interest, and rent | Plus: Personal current transfer receipts | | | |
		Nonfarm	Farm	Total								
1970	237,051	176,634	9,198	185,832	11,227	42	174,647	37,066	25,338	2,874	82,495	33,470
1971	271,224	205,509	8,439	213,948	13,554	-442	199,952	42,062	29,210	3,198	84,820	35,764
1972	310,623	229,214	17,136	246,350	15,656	-181	230,513	47,966	32,144	3,448	90,094	37,801
1973	345,703	254,714	14,939	269,653	19,832	865	250,686	56,579	38,438	3,642	94,934	39,127
1974	379,676	278,196	7,244	285,440	22,472	2,331	265,299	67,837	46,540	3,812	99,612	39,846
1975	432,285	318,661	-2,657	316,004	25,202	3,501	294,303	79,458	58,524	4,380	98,699	41,325
1976	499,896	372,086	3,632	375,718	29,612	4,290	350,396	85,814	63,686	4,895	102,118	44,451
1977	569,178	426,538	6,122	432,660	34,291	5,707	404,076	97,258	67,844	5,389	105,615	48,208
1978	661,276	498,532	7,202	505,734	40,972	6,729	471,491	114,001	75,784	5,903	112,021	51,286
1979	753,478	567,872	7,896	575,768	48,901	9,156	536,023	131,730	85,725	6,435	117,089	53,353
1980	891,668	670,315	194	670,509	57,432	11,548	624,625	167,227	99,816	7,268	122,685	57,181
1981	1,129,098	873,818	14,397	888,215	81,533	-5,461	801,221	214,846	113,031	8,629	130,852	63,834
1982	1,274,649	958,995	9,929	968,924	90,480	-3,488	874,956	271,319	128,374	8,947	142,471	66,877
1983	1,380,013	1,032,142	5,877	1,038,019	94,658	-5,091	938,270	301,054	140,689	9,387	147,011	68,500
1984	1,520,087	1,124,675	4,258	1,128,933	103,557	-814	1,024,562	345,356	150,169	10,151	149,749	70,778
1985	1,586,484	1,150,955	2,369	1,153,324	105,487	2,810	1,050,647	375,637	160,200	10,388	152,724	71,201
1986	1,589,363	1,156,173	-8,884	1,147,289	104,172	4,800	1,047,917	368,035	173,411	10,325	153,931	69,985
1987	1,629,384	1,173,453	5,750	1,179,203	103,761	6,130	1,081,572	365,310	182,502	10,701	152,259	71,753
1988	1,729,822	1,273,891	3,305	1,277,196	119,754	2,499	1,159,941	377,884	191,997	11,465	150,882	74,831
1989	1,890,800	1,377,492	11,017	1,388,509	131,463	-3,161	1,253,885	422,969	213,946	12,574	150,375	77,282
1990	2,005,554	1,482,941	13,272	1,496,213	139,619	-1,281	1,355,313	414,308	235,933	13,238	151,495	79,083
1991	2,124,072	1,572,297	14,666	1,586,963	152,141	1,765	1,436,587	429,340	258,145	13,787	154,062	81,933
1992	2,279,457	1,694,595	20,737	1,715,332	163,031	97	1,552,398	430,242	296,817	14,399	158,308	83,359
1993	2,445,500	1,823,596	18,552	1,842,148	175,008	-4,125	1,663,015	471,316	311,169	14,844	164,742	87,560
1994	2,558,716	1,930,249	18,169	1,948,418	188,508	-6,696	1,753,214	479,642	325,860	15,239	167,911	90,558
1995	2,699,565	1,996,150	11,857	2,008,007	195,985	-8,060	1,803,962	533,450	362,153	15,823	170,608	92,132
1996	2,842,372	2,100,407	-883	2,099,524	204,183	-9,436	1,885,905	568,311	388,156	16,493	172,341	93,646
1997	3,111,976	2,328,988	8,985	2,337,973	224,080	-10,347	2,103,546	599,421	409,009	17,672	176,098	97,342
1998	3,302,396	2,520,008	-1,659	2,518,349	240,593	-14,307	2,263,449	614,927	424,020	18,398	179,498	100,946
1999	3,480,200	2,680,989	27,165	2,708,154	252,806	-16,840	2,438,508	606,259	435,433	19,088	182,327	100,855
2000	3,741,022	2,886,432	11,517	2,897,949	269,393	-20,084	2,608,472	667,765	464,785	20,139	185,760	104,086
2001	3,912,517	3,022,569	26,826	3,049,395	280,845	-21,803	2,746,747	659,134	506,636	20,776	188,315	105,527
2002	4,019,149	3,079,857	45,652	3,125,509	287,562	-28,564	2,809,383	655,056	554,710	20,931	192,016	106,487
2003	4,385,276	3,315,945	60,436	3,376,381	314,542	-32,108	3,029,731	747,327	608,218	22,347	196,234	108,435
2004	4,575,034	3,488,620	60,916	3,549,536	330,127	-37,304	3,182,105	755,127	637,802	22,947	199,374	110,529
2005	4,881,845	3,717,682	49,674	3,767,356	350,352	-41,103	3,375,901	809,212	696,732	23,989	203,500	114,221
2006	5,294,447	4,031,008	28,956	4,059,964	370,886	-32,471	3,656,607	895,559	742,281	25,331	209,014	118,492
2007	5,626,700	4,181,507	28,802	4,210,309	391,849	-21,762	3,796,698	1,011,283	818,719	26,416	213,000	118,297
2008	6,243,620	4,461,077	-59	4,461,018	413,603	-10,421	4,036,994	1,261,130	945,496	28,554	218,658	120,808
2009	6,286,561	4,615,208	-2,088	4,613,120	433,336	-60,590	4,119,194	1,136,531	1,030,836	27,926	225,114	124,046
2010	6,634,028	4,805,783	20,088	4,825,871	449,705	-62,731	4,313,435	1,171,741	1,148,852	28,909	229,478	125,615
2011	7,010,284	4,966,875	8,769	4,975,644	410,193	-23,463	4,541,988	1,283,776	1,184,520	30,272	231,578	125,181
2012	7,505,075	5,282,910	23,962	5,306,872	430,323	-19,992	4,856,557	1,461,338	1,187,180	32,022	234,373	128,599
2013	7,777,737	5,546,397	49,100	5,595,497	511,193	-12,747	5,071,557	1,476,307	1,229,873	32,646	238,245	134,219
2014	8,269,533	5,945,166	62,709	6,007,875	547,985	-56	5,459,834	1,521,714	1,287,985	34,044	242,905	138,932

Personal Income and Employment by Area: Colorado Springs, CO

(Thousands of dollars, except as noted.)

Year	Personal income, total	Earnings by place of work			Less: Contributions for government social insurance	Plus: Adjustment for residence	Equals: Net earnings by place of residence	Plus: Dividends, interest, and rent	Plus: Personal current transfer receipts	Per capita personal income (dollars)	Population (persons)	Total employment
		Nonfarm	Farm	Total								
1970	1,064,136	799,230	2,787	802,017	44,176	-1,434	756,407	246,333	61,396	4,406	241,543	116,502
1971	1,162,236	875,898	2,542	878,440	50,659	732	828,513	258,620	75,103	4,578	253,897	117,553
1972	1,362,196	1,039,027	2,983	1,042,010	63,176	3,845	982,679	291,679	87,838	4,981	273,474	128,822
1973	1,567,419	1,194,755	5,401	1,200,156	80,698	10,210	1,129,668	333,084	104,667	5,313	294,996	140,951
1974	1,720,475	1,296,940	3,687	1,300,627	91,168	15,864	1,225,323	375,605	119,547	5,741	299,705	142,577
1975	1,848,008	1,361,035	4,571	1,365,606	97,001	21,704	1,290,309	405,871	151,828	6,165	299,777	139,515
1976	1,993,695	1,467,274	5,370	1,472,644	106,204	29,891	1,396,331	434,104	163,260	6,699	297,633	143,093
1977	2,162,732	1,576,654	5,306	1,581,960	114,467	39,878	1,507,371	482,598	172,763	7,034	307,449	147,428
1978	2,498,807	1,813,584	4,390	1,817,974	132,674	50,425	1,735,725	573,396	189,686	8,007	312,072	154,227
1979	2,857,674	2,087,772	1,307	2,089,079	161,856	64,010	1,991,233	652,128	214,313	9,011	317,132	164,283
1980	3,247,237	2,341,186	2,454	2,343,640	185,717	81,576	2,239,499	753,827	253,911	10,142	320,180	170,287
1981	3,810,800	2,741,529	471	2,742,000	233,888	85,326	2,593,438	914,024	303,338	11,538	330,278	178,535
1982	4,211,989	3,018,575	2,944	3,021,519	259,813	88,494	2,850,200	1,020,009	341,780	12,337	341,418	185,178
1983	4,607,233	3,319,541	2,039	3,321,580	295,714	87,948	3,113,814	1,111,835	381,584	13,031	353,551	192,322
1984	5,224,664	3,806,239	1,309	3,807,548	353,241	86,926	3,541,233	1,264,568	418,863	14,325	364,735	209,639
1985	5,731,999	4,207,509	70	4,207,579	402,736	87,105	3,891,948	1,389,762	450,289	15,040	381,127	220,895
1986	6,178,443	4,559,767	-280	4,559,487	442,102	85,623	4,203,008	1,487,456	487,979	15,672	394,224	226,673
1987	6,561,408	4,841,058	1,600	4,842,658	467,635	85,460	4,460,483	1,567,035	533,890	16,129	406,810	229,718
1988	6,951,667	5,189,073	289	5,189,362	520,170	87,381	4,756,573	1,625,294	569,800	17,026	408,302	236,180
1989	7,328,490	5,332,068	467	5,332,535	551,518	90,739	4,871,756	1,818,715	638,019	17,885	409,747	238,697
1990	7,529,107	5,441,588	-297	5,441,291	578,744	104,895	4,967,442	1,864,803	696,862	18,363	410,017	235,412
1991	8,004,399	5,855,325	380	5,855,705	637,896	106,773	5,324,582	1,891,831	787,986	19,185	417,227	241,791
1992	8,747,860	6,433,081	2,367	6,435,448	703,765	108,633	5,840,316	2,018,580	888,964	20,078	435,686	250,936
1993	9,309,087	6,846,843	1,656	6,848,499	760,643	112,161	6,200,017	2,157,643	951,427	20,602	451,855	262,001
1994	10,104,424	7,438,455	-983	7,437,472	830,835	109,909	6,716,546	2,370,114	1,017,764	21,364	472,965	279,017
1995	11,060,241	8,050,467	-1,140	8,049,327	890,427	110,217	7,269,117	2,646,409	1,144,715	22,717	486,869	291,270
1996	11,909,529	8,719,332	-1,053	8,718,279	958,234	113,272	7,873,317	2,845,256	1,190,956	23,985	496,543	303,895
1997	12,607,048	9,343,074	-285	9,342,789	1,023,593	124,206	8,443,402	2,932,176	1,231,470	24,910	506,107	315,465
1998	14,084,464	10,567,005	335	10,567,340	1,084,668	136,542	9,619,214	3,188,002	1,277,248	27,201	517,799	326,735
1999	15,250,769	11,637,805	1,574	11,639,379	1,170,674	156,547	10,625,252	3,251,994	1,373,523	28,811	529,338	334,926
2000	16,741,725	12,876,059	4,035	12,880,094	1,281,096	177,889	11,776,887	3,507,695	1,457,143	30,969	540,593	345,904
2001	17,518,598	13,431,366	5,866	13,437,232	1,351,333	194,589	12,280,488	3,628,720	1,609,390	31,448	557,057	348,915
2002	17,819,252	13,604,323	3,867	13,608,190	1,412,949	198,019	12,393,260	3,596,888	1,829,104	31,500	565,688	346,556
2003	18,414,116	14,025,053	1,161	14,026,214	1,456,722	200,304	12,769,796	3,699,938	1,944,382	32,349	569,231	346,368
2004	19,255,348	14,705,682	8,395	14,714,077	1,562,322	213,122	13,364,877	3,843,555	2,046,916	33,294	578,345	353,803
2005	20,511,021	15,731,102	4,961	15,736,063	1,676,749	225,430	14,284,744	4,012,776	2,213,501	34,896	587,778	364,636
2006	21,699,894	16,443,239	934	16,444,173	1,753,100	243,515	14,934,588	4,366,074	2,399,232	36,015	602,532	370,461
2007	22,786,561	16,865,886	-2,524	16,863,362	1,808,662	262,717	15,317,417	4,860,332	2,608,812	37,386	609,490	378,032
2008	23,575,791	17,062,679	-7,048	17,055,631	1,856,055	280,252	15,479,828	4,941,844	3,154,119	37,986	620,644	377,762
2009	23,867,369	17,225,087	-6,601	17,218,486	1,873,135	262,582	15,607,933	4,687,132	3,572,304	37,825	630,998	371,383
2010	24,944,093	17,876,003	-4,152	17,871,851	1,941,087	262,841	16,193,605	4,619,499	4,130,989	38,355	650,351	370,220
2011	26,380,352	18,392,828	-1,028	18,391,800	1,841,529	288,758	16,839,029	5,216,195	4,325,128	39,953	660,278	376,441
2012	27,180,204	18,884,634	-3,521	18,881,113	1,891,807	312,012	17,301,318	5,494,551	4,384,335	40,622	669,100	377,198
2013	27,529,966	19,096,022	735	19,096,757	2,137,594	340,569	17,299,732	5,688,302	4,541,932	40,562	678,711	384,404
2014	28,830,216	19,889,849	1,854	19,891,703	2,224,548	372,261	18,039,416	5,959,016	4,831,784	41,971	686,908	391,773

Personal Income and Employment by Area: Columbia, MO

(Thousands of dollars, except as noted.)

Year	Personal income, total	Earnings by place of work			Less: Contributions for government social insurance	Plus: Adjustment for residence	Equals: Net earnings by place of residence	Plus: Dividends, interest, and rent	Plus: Personal current transfer receipts	Per capita personal income (dollars)	Population (persons)	Total employment
		Nonfarm	Farm	Total								
1970	282,962	242,429	3,792	246,221	14,721	-7,791	223,709	41,881	17,372	3,490	81,073	39,470
1971	313,824	266,859	4,649	271,508	16,668	-7,565	247,275	46,529	20,020	3,800	82,578	40,284
1972	348,491	295,940	4,267	300,207	18,832	-7,695	273,680	52,522	22,289	4,146	84,046	41,917
1973	396,442	329,436	11,501	340,937	24,222	-7,543	309,172	60,108	27,162	4,475	88,593	44,491
1974	447,773	370,524	8,518	379,042	28,234	-7,588	343,220	71,794	32,759	4,923	90,958	45,535
1975	507,910	417,872	2,514	420,386	31,481	-7,838	381,067	83,920	42,923	5,722	88,769	46,649
1976	578,607	478,030	3,918	481,948	36,313	-6,986	438,649	91,763	48,195	6,253	92,528	49,134
1977	646,446	531,459	6,431	537,890	40,445	-4,687	492,758	102,867	50,821	6,867	94,134	51,203
1978	731,113	602,717	5,950	608,667	47,635	-1,732	559,300	116,038	55,775	7,546	96,886	53,672
1979	828,816	678,077	10,408	688,485	55,730	-707	632,048	132,473	64,295	8,488	97,649	56,890
1980	930,950	748,768	758	749,526	60,654	884	689,756	162,763	78,431	9,238	100,776	57,601
1981	1,019,788	788,574	6,557	795,131	68,617	2,164	728,678	199,898	91,212	9,982	102,163	56,917
1982	1,104,195	829,959	3,079	833,038	73,046	986	760,978	243,552	99,665	10,718	103,024	56,723
1983	1,218,738	930,269	-574	929,695	82,481	-5,067	842,147	264,956	111,635	11,768	103,564	59,821
1984	1,313,380	1,002,226	1,682	1,003,908	91,460	-11,032	901,416	294,171	117,793	12,565	104,531	62,097
1985	1,405,759	1,083,796	9,767	1,093,563	101,030	-20,373	972,160	309,089	124,510	13,414	104,800	64,693
1986	1,499,850	1,171,462	608	1,172,070	110,932	-24,318	1,036,820	330,698	132,332	14,144	106,045	67,855
1987	1,604,849	1,268,413	1,953	1,270,366	119,102	-30,086	1,121,178	343,497	140,174	14,945	107,382	69,530
1988	1,705,774	1,371,924	1,682	1,373,606	136,521	-38,513	1,198,572	357,938	149,264	15,602	109,331	72,316
1989	1,837,286	1,476,542	6,610	1,483,152	148,002	-43,074	1,292,076	377,148	168,062	16,527	111,171	73,951
1990	1,984,646	1,603,909	4,558	1,608,467	165,779	-53,857	1,388,831	411,069	184,746	17,590	112,827	76,763
1991	2,141,942	1,731,006	4,930	1,735,936	181,302	-63,013	1,491,621	434,460	215,861	18,598	115,171	78,338
1992	2,332,052	1,907,767	2,660	1,910,427	197,728	-72,795	1,639,904	460,838	231,310	19,822	117,651	80,387
1993	2,492,443	2,003,033	5,222	2,008,255	208,164	-79,265	1,720,826	511,500	260,117	20,714	120,329	83,169
1994	2,659,064	2,167,548	1,758	2,169,306	226,727	-98,305	1,844,274	541,865	272,925	21,651	122,817	86,022
1995	2,818,739	2,279,909	-1,921	2,277,988	237,824	-106,179	1,933,985	586,920	297,834	22,456	125,520	89,182
1996	3,016,908	2,446,376	5,949	2,452,325	251,608	-120,515	2,080,202	624,002	312,704	23,502	128,366	92,799
1997	3,235,122	2,568,389	3,168	2,571,557	262,941	-128,120	2,180,496	728,943	325,683	24,699	130,981	94,940
1998	3,381,168	2,755,041	2,182	2,757,223	280,502	-142,970	2,333,751	704,720	342,697	25,499	132,601	96,094
1999	3,538,973	2,933,354	-2,740	2,930,614	294,439	-153,116	2,483,059	692,971	362,943	26,394	134,081	96,997
2000	3,778,877	3,120,388	4,004	3,124,392	310,645	-171,084	2,642,663	734,706	401,508	27,798	135,940	100,597
2001	3,931,531	3,243,684	4,296	3,247,980	325,977	-158,341	2,763,662	716,342	451,527	28,452	138,181	100,760
2002	4,004,005	3,348,510	2,519	3,351,029	337,825	-159,789	2,853,415	668,750	481,840	28,459	140,695	101,698
2003	4,359,049	3,616,771	8,205	3,624,976	354,176	-157,347	3,113,453	739,526	506,070	30,479	143,019	102,004
2004	4,735,462	3,860,850	19,172	3,880,022	375,248	-159,435	3,345,339	853,453	536,670	32,580	145,348	104,393
2005	4,966,139	4,065,435	3,568	4,069,003	398,848	-159,671	3,510,484	870,938	584,717	33,378	148,786	107,333
2006	5,353,741	4,332,358	4,851	4,337,209	422,747	-157,348	3,757,114	969,549	627,078	35,041	152,784	109,817
2007	5,666,085	4,479,588	4,363	4,483,951	442,569	-151,488	3,889,894	1,100,849	675,342	36,399	155,666	111,917
2008	5,910,368	4,507,996	7,272	4,515,268	454,088	-143,650	3,917,530	1,191,334	801,504	37,386	158,089	111,473
2009	6,097,268	4,558,567	10,183	4,568,750	456,525	-189,203	3,923,022	1,304,177	870,069	37,974	160,565	109,282
2010	6,030,944	4,705,876	8,835	4,714,711	468,819	-224,165	4,021,727	1,043,884	965,333	36,958	163,182	110,028
2011	6,324,318	4,892,420	16,091	4,908,511	438,214	-237,426	4,232,871	1,085,485	1,005,962	38,116	165,922	113,098
2012	6,721,507	5,211,368	6,190	5,217,558	461,671	-279,220	4,476,667	1,219,988	1,024,852	39,868	168,592	116,241
2013	6,952,092	5,453,170	22,538	5,475,708	548,732	-300,522	4,626,454	1,281,291	1,044,347	40,672	170,929	119,172
2014	7,153,637	5,600,907	28,436	5,629,343	565,051	-304,819	4,759,473	1,317,242	1,076,922	41,418	172,717	120,536

Personal Income and Employment by Area: Columbia, SC

(Thousands of dollars, except as noted.)

| Year | Personal income, total | Derivation of personal income | | | | | Equals: Net earnings by place of residence | Plus: Dividends, interest, and rent | Plus: Personal current transfer receipts | Per capita personal income (dollars) | Population (persons) | Total employment |
| | | Earnings by place of work | | | Less: Contributions for government social insurance | Plus: Adjustment for residence | | | | | | |
		Nonfarm	Farm	Total								
1970	1,453,738	1,205,024	16,335	1,221,359	75,700	3,168	1,148,827	207,505	97,406	3,586	405,343	198,370
1971	1,611,049	1,333,426	18,059	1,351,485	87,312	-286	1,263,887	232,200	114,962	3,830	420,632	204,042
1972	1,816,970	1,509,494	19,471	1,528,965	102,692	-2,241	1,424,032	259,843	133,095	4,249	427,654	213,386
1973	2,055,465	1,713,975	30,056	1,744,031	133,028	-7,967	1,603,036	291,703	160,726	4,687	438,518	225,415
1974	2,353,467	1,958,707	27,300	1,986,007	157,478	-17,963	1,810,566	342,206	200,695	5,169	455,302	237,022
1975	2,596,856	2,114,052	20,220	2,134,272	168,366	-23,294	1,942,612	381,973	272,271	5,623	461,809	235,356
1976	2,845,381	2,347,534	22,657	2,370,191	192,250	-31,291	2,146,650	405,967	292,764	6,090	467,203	240,094
1977	3,103,666	2,583,048	17,681	2,600,729	210,735	-38,124	2,351,870	446,937	304,859	6,499	477,566	247,405
1978	3,459,527	2,889,945	22,598	2,912,543	240,838	-46,442	2,625,263	499,888	334,376	7,158	483,307	255,079
1979	3,885,887	3,244,288	38,056	3,282,344	280,476	-59,449	2,942,419	558,781	384,687	7,901	491,796	263,946
1980	4,325,405	3,560,463	11,064	3,571,527	308,873	-68,140	3,194,514	665,015	465,876	8,654	499,796	267,308
1981	4,833,730	3,899,157	20,223	3,919,380	362,580	-67,563	3,489,237	806,572	537,921	9,566	505,283	268,434
1982	5,176,252	4,107,306	23,009	4,130,315	389,853	-66,647	3,673,815	923,774	578,663	10,197	507,615	268,213
1983	5,666,920	4,540,096	5,736	4,545,832	445,301	-72,407	4,028,124	1,017,291	621,505	11,039	513,337	276,269
1984	6,284,843	5,054,654	39,351	5,094,005	513,530	-76,022	4,504,453	1,124,913	655,477	12,116	518,709	289,340
1985	6,784,444	5,469,912	24,303	5,494,215	567,218	-75,185	4,851,812	1,226,453	706,179	13,014	521,313	298,320
1986	7,302,652	5,926,615	22,745	5,949,360	633,376	-77,979	5,238,005	1,321,008	743,639	13,821	528,371	308,968
1987	7,812,941	6,396,772	22,246	6,419,018	679,178	-76,167	5,663,673	1,383,336	765,932	14,663	532,846	314,930
1988	8,444,500	6,950,870	30,612	6,981,482	773,401	-82,167	6,125,914	1,498,926	819,660	15,710	537,516	327,808
1989	9,157,516	7,413,165	36,732	7,449,897	833,636	-75,265	6,540,996	1,676,393	940,127	16,836	543,917	335,359
1990	9,732,492	7,855,844	30,645	7,886,489	907,036	-101,527	6,877,926	1,805,217	1,049,349	17,643	551,633	341,316
1991	10,195,870	8,097,602	49,811	8,147,413	945,462	-75,788	7,126,163	1,852,147	1,217,560	18,102	563,238	336,460
1992	10,806,721	8,587,368	44,069	8,631,437	995,842	-92,449	7,543,146	1,907,646	1,355,929	18,882	572,323	340,420
1993	11,318,884	8,945,488	34,259	8,979,747	1,046,067	-55,783	7,877,897	1,989,896	1,451,091	19,450	581,956	344,577
1994	12,044,399	9,473,125	53,843	9,526,968	1,124,681	-77,854	8,324,433	2,151,574	1,568,392	20,418	589,879	356,921
1995	12,840,936	10,056,551	48,331	10,104,882	1,195,161	-73,902	8,835,819	2,331,989	1,673,128	21,432	599,158	369,402
1996	13,792,405	10,760,841	60,899	10,821,740	1,257,024	-86,060	9,478,656	2,516,214	1,797,535	22,650	608,946	382,266
1997	14,628,914	11,463,026	64,606	11,527,632	1,338,109	-84,925	10,104,598	2,648,378	1,875,938	23,604	619,752	393,077
1998	15,950,613	12,541,296	78,087	12,619,383	1,454,880	-87,735	11,076,768	2,899,761	1,974,084	25,280	630,966	404,855
1999	16,752,540	13,367,718	73,991	13,441,709	1,534,432	-116,015	11,791,262	2,866,651	2,094,627	26,171	640,126	412,486
2000	18,015,562	14,301,081	69,284	14,370,365	1,623,777	-99,899	12,646,689	3,110,592	2,258,281	27,735	649,567	421,846
2001	18,586,557	14,619,425	86,135	14,705,560	1,665,066	-87,502	12,952,992	3,098,936	2,534,629	28,199	659,125	415,538
2002	19,026,417	15,005,253	48,393	15,053,646	1,714,217	-181,021	13,158,408	3,106,333	2,761,676	28,564	666,087	414,775
2003	19,755,849	15,679,273	84,519	15,763,792	1,797,751	-216,047	13,749,994	3,097,210	2,908,645	29,221	676,083	417,903
2004	21,035,858	16,613,988	115,593	16,729,581	1,902,823	-176,345	14,650,413	3,242,164	3,143,281	30,468	690,421	426,052
2005	22,155,382	17,501,551	101,501	17,603,052	1,990,400	-257,735	15,354,917	3,412,612	3,387,853	31,689	699,160	434,774
2006	24,027,210	18,878,273	85,261	18,963,534	2,174,036	-336,908	16,452,590	3,906,812	3,667,808	33,600	715,091	448,647
2007	25,384,615	19,719,931	54,459	19,774,390	2,267,952	-312,298	17,194,140	4,269,429	3,921,046	34,747	730,546	461,416
2008	26,515,204	20,413,015	61,779	20,474,794	2,347,662	-355,316	17,771,816	4,184,238	4,559,150	35,556	745,740	461,137
2009	26,314,426	19,993,518	75,737	20,069,255	2,302,210	-338,915	17,428,130	3,933,390	4,952,906	34,652	759,400	445,213
2010	26,674,915	19,885,121	82,070	19,967,191	2,292,554	-307,147	17,367,490	3,863,197	5,444,228	34,658	769,661	439,952
2011	27,801,487	20,438,181	37,887	20,476,068	2,104,779	-306,021	18,065,268	4,228,587	5,507,632	35,798	776,630	445,864
2012	28,879,434	21,250,663	99,696	21,350,359	2,161,940	-281,887	18,906,532	4,476,845	5,496,057	36,823	784,279	454,699
2013	29,470,287	21,839,988	171,664	22,011,652	2,516,893	-300,635	19,194,124	4,591,095	5,685,068	37,190	792,422	464,290
2014	30,794,502	22,947,023	65,546	23,012,569	2,662,138	-351,653	19,998,778	4,750,397	6,045,327	38,469	800,495	475,365

Personal Income and Employment by Area: Columbus, GA-AL

(Thousands of dollars, except as noted.)

Year	Personal income, total	Derivation of personal income					Equals: Net earnings by place of residence	Plus: Dividends, interest, and rent	Plus: Personal current transfer receipts	Per capita personal income (dollars)	Population (persons)	Total employment
		Earnings by place of work			Less: Contributions for government social insurance	Plus: Adjustment for residence						
		Nonfarm	Farm	Total								
1970	965,533	777,678	3,997	781,675	48,177	-9,693	723,805	172,461	69,267	3,791	254,664	122,623
1971	1,019,345	821,687	4,129	825,816	53,641	-11,081	761,094	176,694	81,557	4,019	253,660	120,026
1972	1,058,009	849,912	4,756	854,668	57,423	-11,398	785,847	179,046	93,116	4,284	246,940	115,160
1973	1,143,748	913,269	6,869	920,138	68,631	-12,871	838,636	196,127	108,985	4,814	237,599	116,481
1974	1,253,996	985,464	5,792	991,256	77,488	-16,993	896,775	222,041	135,180	5,133	244,309	117,043
1975	1,339,712	1,040,336	4,544	1,044,880	82,812	-23,823	938,245	234,121	167,346	5,369	249,515	114,971
1976	1,478,729	1,164,256	7,064	1,171,320	95,249	-33,629	1,042,442	253,649	182,638	5,798	255,031	119,819
1977	1,618,071	1,294,892	3,966	1,298,858	105,422	-44,258	1,149,178	279,259	189,634	6,382	253,528	124,514
1978	1,800,364	1,434,402	6,433	1,440,835	117,710	-55,192	1,267,933	325,556	206,875	6,933	259,685	127,399
1979	1,922,276	1,516,593	8,641	1,525,234	130,304	-57,697	1,337,233	349,667	235,376	7,390	260,109	126,043
1980	2,108,083	1,628,875	5,831	1,634,706	140,753	-59,486	1,434,467	398,755	274,861	8,110	259,921	125,648
1981	2,348,708	1,762,813	11,671	1,774,484	161,549	-34,066	1,578,869	456,746	313,093	9,058	259,295	123,547
1982	2,567,580	1,901,857	10,761	1,912,618	172,529	-39,874	1,700,215	528,552	338,813	9,751	263,318	126,188
1983	2,721,595	2,026,206	6,895	2,033,101	191,025	-44,343	1,797,733	561,117	362,745	10,394	261,838	126,279
1984	3,026,331	2,278,405	8,984	2,287,389	220,938	-54,466	2,011,985	631,310	383,036	11,508	262,983	133,890
1985	3,255,122	2,460,692	5,799	2,466,491	242,822	-65,878	2,157,791	689,214	408,117	12,304	264,556	136,899
1986	3,480,788	2,647,865	4,482	2,652,347	264,403	-72,844	2,315,100	739,609	426,079	13,066	266,407	139,494
1987	3,687,026	2,835,702	7,097	2,842,799	283,897	-81,818	2,477,084	772,100	437,842	13,780	267,567	141,956
1988	3,922,702	3,001,862	9,422	3,011,284	312,127	-85,682	2,613,475	847,862	461,365	14,715	266,586	144,303
1989	4,060,978	3,075,413	9,688	3,085,101	325,526	-92,892	2,666,683	880,995	513,300	15,288	265,634	142,868
1990	4,284,288	3,240,757	7,902	3,248,659	345,931	-94,638	2,808,090	910,921	565,277	16,050	266,931	142,037
1991	4,478,605	3,363,843	11,981	3,375,824	363,116	-108,789	2,903,919	942,891	631,795	16,817	266,314	138,678
1992	4,876,393	3,656,590	11,533	3,668,123	395,433	-134,709	3,137,981	1,036,714	701,698	17,686	275,715	142,086
1993	5,024,382	3,758,134	12,340	3,770,474	409,946	-153,882	3,206,646	1,080,593	737,143	18,096	277,655	144,549
1994	5,252,689	3,902,957	15,542	3,918,499	426,663	-172,533	3,319,303	1,141,850	791,536	18,700	280,889	145,839
1995	5,472,048	4,049,008	10,178	4,059,186	439,992	-185,117	3,434,077	1,187,931	850,040	19,567	279,663	147,697
1996	5,675,706	4,242,682	14,706	4,257,388	458,774	-215,799	3,582,815	1,199,004	893,887	20,290	279,725	152,880
1997	6,034,472	4,568,257	13,875	4,582,132	490,039	-257,389	3,834,704	1,278,082	921,686	21,483	280,896	157,278
1998	6,495,733	4,934,281	16,595	4,950,876	521,682	-293,312	4,135,882	1,416,545	943,306	23,142	280,686	162,449
1999	6,754,331	5,207,651	22,518	5,230,169	549,138	-327,309	4,353,722	1,409,664	990,945	24,045	280,899	163,940
2000	7,107,584	5,444,958	15,268	5,460,226	569,970	-357,708	4,532,548	1,521,332	1,053,704	25,166	282,431	166,636
2001	7,497,861	5,645,462	20,006	5,665,468	591,539	-359,377	4,714,552	1,625,225	1,158,084	26,434	283,646	163,415
2002	7,678,640	5,777,436	15,850	5,793,286	605,755	-478,503	4,709,028	1,699,822	1,269,790	26,905	285,398	161,608
2003	7,961,545	6,056,345	19,966	6,076,311	628,484	-574,636	4,873,191	1,781,144	1,307,210	28,539	278,969	161,868
2004	8,305,277	6,314,126	19,056	6,333,182	669,831	-675,511	4,987,840	1,917,810	1,399,627	29,153	284,887	165,270
2005	8,761,192	6,735,135	19,003	6,754,138	708,684	-886,570	5,158,884	2,097,341	1,504,967	30,595	286,358	168,415
2006	9,295,717	7,121,479	13,902	7,135,381	748,245	-969,401	5,417,735	2,284,134	1,593,848	32,151	289,129	170,927
2007	9,611,927	7,374,355	9,140	7,383,495	768,970	-1,027,127	5,587,398	2,309,845	1,714,684	33,576	286,274	170,760
2008	9,777,673	7,656,685	15,101	7,671,786	824,402	-1,239,482	5,607,902	2,231,495	1,938,276	34,070	286,985	172,884
2009	9,575,229	7,699,680	14,767	7,714,447	840,589	-1,499,225	5,374,633	2,120,469	2,080,127	32,684	292,968	172,130
2010	9,930,025	7,909,905	12,660	7,922,565	878,037	-1,497,452	5,547,076	2,111,556	2,271,393	33,496	296,454	173,840
2011	10,819,249	8,319,504	9,778	8,329,282	825,090	-1,508,851	5,995,341	2,421,350	2,402,558	35,765	302,513	179,694
2012	11,057,824	8,687,131	20,519	8,707,650	860,676	-1,646,165	6,200,809	2,450,445	2,406,570	35,475	311,711	181,693
2013	11,155,031	8,768,721	34,636	8,803,357	972,248	-1,737,713	6,093,396	2,565,528	2,496,107	35,175	317,126	183,161
2014	11,518,629	8,820,450	22,232	8,842,682	972,071	-1,577,780	6,292,831	2,624,241	2,601,557	36,683	314,005	182,879

Personal Income and Employment by Area: Columbus, IN

(Thousands of dollars, except as noted.)

		Derivation of personal income										
		Earnings by place of work			Less: Contributions for government social insurance	Plus: Adjustment for residence	Equals: Net earnings by place of residence	Plus: Dividends, interest, and rent	Plus: Personal current transfer receipts	Per capita personal income (dollars)	Population (persons)	Total employment
Year	Personal income, total	Nonfarm	Farm	Total								
1970	238,081	4,171	57,080	265,223	3,416	268,639	17,850	-58,944	191,845	32,278	13,958	32,082
1971	260,604	4,520	57,662	282,578	5,698	288,276	19,784	-60,552	207,940	36,048	16,616	32,179
1972	284,028	4,826	58,851	308,055	4,624	312,679	22,947	-63,937	225,795	39,418	18,815	32,600
1973	330,905	5,541	59,716	356,413	12,215	368,628	30,828	-73,932	263,868	44,854	22,183	35,298
1974	372,034	6,175	60,249	404,184	10,806	414,990	36,163	-84,433	294,394	51,838	25,802	36,323
1975	378,965	6,228	60,844	390,846	7,833	398,679	34,116	-77,024	287,539	56,915	34,511	33,996
1976	435,424	7,101	61,316	463,142	12,561	475,703	41,400	-96,378	337,925	61,794	35,705	35,623
1977	493,517	7,913	62,371	539,829	7,900	547,729	47,605	-113,719	386,405	69,288	37,824	37,582
1978	548,544	8,672	63,254	610,015	7,443	617,458	55,638	-130,888	430,932	75,706	41,906	39,086
1979	605,763	9,448	64,113	687,709	4,795	692,504	65,182	-152,278	475,044	83,245	47,474	40,753
1980	620,530	9,552	64,960	659,332	1,774	661,106	62,493	-143,536	455,077	104,994	60,459	37,946
1981	700,534	10,895	64,301	729,248	4,143	733,391	74,793	-159,302	499,296	133,482	67,756	38,067
1982	708,696	11,075	63,992	695,479	3,942	699,421	72,517	-142,013	484,891	143,553	80,252	35,323
1983	755,037	11,841	63,765	743,285	-1,617	741,668	78,199	-145,876	517,593	152,697	84,747	35,344
1984	912,137	14,349	63,567	912,051	13,083	925,134	98,989	-182,914	643,231	181,566	87,340	37,712
1985	926,787	14,619	63,398	898,398	9,932	908,330	98,711	-164,027	645,592	188,266	92,929	37,442
1986	918,806	14,598	62,940	879,621	6,887	886,508	97,528	-150,770	638,210	182,900	97,696	37,657
1987	1,015,098	16,004	63,427	1,002,800	5,872	1,008,672	108,090	-171,168	729,414	186,014	99,670	38,972
1988	1,072,728	16,921	63,395	1,052,345	1,467	1,053,812	115,962	-166,388	771,462	195,301	105,965	40,195
1989	1,144,748	18,063	63,375	1,060,919	8,580	1,069,499	116,697	-148,909	803,893	225,733	115,122	40,871
1990	1,197,957	18,761	63,855	1,096,298	7,761	1,104,059	124,520	-140,711	838,828	234,651	124,478	42,137
1991	1,214,857	18,735	64,843	1,129,420	400	1,129,820	131,025	-151,067	847,728	231,785	135,344	42,105
1992	1,351,487	20,644	65,467	1,277,882	8,547	1,286,429	147,203	-184,536	954,690	240,078	156,719	44,050
1993	1,464,919	22,076	66,357	1,421,834	7,836	1,429,670	165,337	-223,932	1,040,401	259,086	165,432	46,277
1994	1,562,874	23,232	67,273	1,525,218	4,260	1,529,478	178,444	-238,645	1,112,389	278,772	171,713	48,419
1995	1,687,701	24,670	68,410	1,615,837	2,103	1,617,940	189,198	-252,343	1,176,399	331,571	179,731	49,868
1996	1,762,295	25,529	69,031	1,657,633	15,960	1,673,593	191,465	-267,327	1,214,801	352,433	195,061	50,171
1997	1,851,139	26,609	69,568	1,755,411	9,042	1,764,453	201,100	-285,175	1,278,178	373,838	199,123	51,045
1998	2,014,605	28,667	70,275	1,911,747	4,959	1,916,706	213,197	-312,191	1,391,318	412,446	210,841	52,874
1999	2,090,364	29,592	70,639	2,013,099	720	2,013,819	223,313	-319,017	1,471,489	400,260	218,615	52,928
2000	2,234,978	31,144	71,763	2,131,412	10,554	2,141,966	231,656	-342,811	1,567,499	432,047	235,432	52,816
2001	2,158,285	29,930	72,110	1,968,615	11,863	1,980,478	218,937	-288,908	1,472,633	420,515	265,137	50,692
2002	2,154,751	29,973	71,890	1,985,852	1,424	1,987,276	221,654	-307,056	1,458,566	412,116	284,069	49,593
2003	2,224,487	30,768	72,299	2,059,094	13,167	2,072,261	232,134	-333,431	1,506,696	419,500	298,291	49,331
2004	2,346,156	32,191	72,882	2,217,579	22,229	2,239,808	251,007	-372,029	1,616,772	410,864	318,520	50,997
2005	2,393,787	32,498	73,660	2,312,793	12,807	2,325,600	262,021	-402,340	1,661,239	384,562	347,986	52,251
2006	2,603,305	34,940	74,508	2,481,471	10,178	2,491,649	284,030	-439,941	1,767,678	459,387	376,240	53,192
2007	2,724,679	36,201	75,265	2,614,920	10,376	2,625,296	297,556	-473,555	1,854,185	472,851	397,643	54,640
2008	2,899,810	38,115	76,080	2,752,301	22,404	2,774,705	313,628	-511,866	1,949,211	489,901	460,698	55,056
2009	2,759,815	36,045	76,566	2,442,904	26,551	2,469,455	287,423	-370,077	1,811,955	438,340	509,520	51,711
2010	2,895,469	37,678	76,848	2,576,326	7,833	2,584,159	301,239	-358,401	1,924,519	428,767	542,183	51,452
2011	3,130,697	40,333	77,621	2,843,154	21,771	2,864,925	297,459	-461,846	2,105,620	482,450	542,627	54,610
2012	3,403,612	43,137	78,903	3,196,101	26,931	3,223,032	329,625	-598,101	2,295,306	544,003	564,303	57,851
2013	3,420,482	42,998	79,549	3,200,008	62,711	3,262,719	374,729	-570,237	2,317,753	532,334	570,395	57,812
2014	3,539,888	44,129	80,217	3,406,023	40,547	3,446,570	397,232	-654,285	2,395,053	551,894	592,941	59,447

Personal Income and Employment by Area: Columbus, OH

(Thousands of dollars, except as noted.)

Year	Personal income, total	Derivation of personal income								Per capita personal income (dollars)	Population (persons)	Total employment
		Earnings by place of work			Less: Contributions for government social insurance	Plus: Adjustment for residence	Equals: Net earnings by place of residence	Plus: Dividends, interest, and rent	Plus: Personal current transfer receipts			
		Nonfarm	Farm	Total								
1970	4,964,183	4,173,668	53,117	4,226,785	255,499	-13,574	3,957,712	657,345	349,126	4,057	1,223,517	547,892
1971	5,451,605	4,574,650	45,568	4,620,218	286,905	-18,998	4,314,315	725,893	411,397	4,372	1,246,879	559,807
1972	5,981,385	5,032,654	58,579	5,091,233	332,507	-23,399	4,735,327	786,375	459,683	4,753	1,258,508	585,094
1973	6,632,419	5,595,866	69,628	5,665,494	427,157	-25,790	5,212,547	874,659	545,213	5,217	1,271,417	610,863
1974	7,292,278	6,030,574	100,605	6,131,179	477,150	-27,226	5,626,803	999,532	665,943	5,667	1,286,905	619,395
1975	7,831,878	6,302,250	95,947	6,398,197	487,253	-31,152	5,879,792	1,088,089	863,997	6,026	1,299,613	608,330
1976	8,591,555	6,986,620	91,912	7,078,532	554,547	-33,708	6,490,277	1,160,721	940,557	6,596	1,302,532	620,404
1977	9,561,597	7,855,927	90,878	7,946,805	625,734	-39,832	7,281,239	1,289,583	990,775	7,267	1,315,830	642,252
1978	10,582,248	8,759,993	85,091	8,845,084	721,267	-46,420	8,077,397	1,445,053	1,059,798	7,993	1,323,883	669,335
1979	11,767,585	9,720,774	123,960	9,844,734	837,183	-52,166	8,955,385	1,615,932	1,196,268	8,845	1,330,412	687,708
1980	12,929,019	10,415,830	66,247	10,482,077	900,504	-63,045	9,518,528	1,950,953	1,459,538	9,727	1,329,236	695,825
1981	14,163,426	11,220,318	6,487	11,226,805	1,037,963	-67,948	10,120,894	2,369,420	1,673,112	10,565	1,340,612	689,230
1982	15,157,696	11,739,673	25,071	11,764,744	1,093,306	-88,758	10,582,680	2,661,220	1,913,796	11,278	1,343,981	680,904
1983	16,407,460	12,741,308	-10,765	12,730,543	1,220,698	-110,146	11,399,699	2,938,984	2,068,777	12,136	1,351,988	690,537
1984	18,264,327	14,263,660	107,378	14,371,038	1,398,990	-140,977	12,831,071	3,282,715	2,150,541	13,409	1,362,111	726,332
1985	19,771,767	15,621,231	114,542	15,735,773	1,565,680	-185,094	13,984,999	3,480,562	2,306,206	14,385	1,374,432	760,496
1986	21,023,783	16,796,635	93,278	16,889,913	1,734,416	-224,666	14,930,831	3,659,960	2,432,992	15,146	1,388,054	787,782
1987	22,311,003	18,077,336	71,251	18,148,587	1,872,917	-262,612	16,013,058	3,766,584	2,531,361	15,873	1,405,633	823,595
1988	24,215,485	19,795,608	86,205	19,881,813	2,098,434	-331,826	17,451,553	4,069,324	2,694,608	16,933	1,430,091	848,911
1989	26,505,154	21,396,132	99,899	21,496,031	2,280,706	-399,952	18,815,373	4,796,923	2,892,858	18,306	1,447,914	876,674
1990	28,152,464	22,817,748	104,717	22,922,465	2,493,666	-450,569	19,978,230	4,977,313	3,196,921	19,174	1,468,263	894,479
1991	29,237,356	23,779,819	42,654	23,822,473	2,670,017	-463,261	20,689,195	5,001,649	3,546,512	19,589	1,492,559	898,033
1992	31,629,116	25,732,552	118,915	25,851,467	2,899,501	-508,400	22,443,566	5,250,754	3,934,796	20,841	1,517,612	909,049
1993	33,415,300	27,149,842	111,147	27,260,989	3,083,884	-537,220	23,639,885	5,652,558	4,122,857	21,690	1,540,611	930,524
1994	35,676,222	29,012,231	141,493	29,153,724	3,359,275	-577,248	25,217,201	6,154,226	4,304,795	22,866	1,560,222	964,490
1995	37,394,114	30,592,308	104,343	30,696,651	3,583,733	-630,771	26,482,147	6,330,288	4,581,679	23,676	1,579,412	1,001,985
1996	39,278,832	32,238,502	147,669	32,386,171	3,743,956	-679,107	27,963,108	6,626,395	4,689,329	24,655	1,593,111	1,023,195
1997	42,285,277	34,585,618	204,551	34,790,169	3,916,247	-765,416	30,108,506	7,342,558	4,834,213	26,213	1,613,135	1,044,212
1998	45,478,482	37,791,886	142,349	37,934,235	4,130,753	-863,425	32,940,057	7,556,486	4,981,939	27,787	1,636,690	1,074,075
1999	48,026,871	40,399,099	106,769	40,505,868	4,419,714	-943,162	35,142,992	7,622,175	5,261,704	28,963	1,658,194	1,095,650
2000	52,022,418	43,936,593	156,435	44,093,028	4,623,423	-1,048,500	38,421,105	7,946,967	5,654,346	30,928	1,682,068	1,130,519
2001	54,545,323	46,024,840	150,075	46,174,915	4,811,315	-1,070,460	40,293,140	7,990,474	6,261,709	31,958	1,706,779	1,139,746
2002	56,391,542	47,721,409	80,258	47,801,667	4,889,376	-1,180,730	41,731,561	7,847,020	6,812,961	32,665	1,726,352	1,135,078
2003	58,510,655	49,028,976	100,728	49,129,704	5,065,991	-869,278	43,194,435	8,096,813	7,219,407	33,449	1,749,262	1,132,676
2004	61,169,179	51,320,958	178,142	51,499,100	5,368,439	-793,512	45,337,149	8,170,484	7,661,546	34,567	1,769,572	1,146,994
2005	63,642,982	53,048,661	96,358	53,145,019	5,524,816	-930,788	46,689,415	8,685,001	8,268,566	35,532	1,791,126	1,161,996
2006	67,514,255	55,744,736	90,437	55,835,173	5,804,568	-959,543	49,071,062	9,588,337	8,854,856	37,157	1,816,992	1,178,365
2007	70,244,095	57,520,680	123,852	57,644,532	6,026,277	-1,144,190	50,474,065	10,269,499	9,500,531	38,144	1,841,539	1,204,070
2008	72,236,308	58,245,540	135,093	58,380,633	6,228,214	-1,270,774	50,881,645	10,412,863	10,941,800	38,719	1,865,647	1,206,052
2009	71,323,717	57,192,106	189,406	57,381,512	6,177,686	-1,356,981	49,846,845	9,550,503	11,926,369	37,786	1,887,548	1,178,595
2010	73,666,662	58,895,718	187,377	59,083,095	6,222,262	-1,367,893	51,492,940	9,353,936	12,819,786	38,646	1,906,177	1,170,675
2011	79,420,789	62,349,817	350,587	62,700,404	5,875,873	-1,435,954	55,388,577	10,655,274	13,376,938	41,246	1,925,540	1,198,454
2012	84,450,430	66,329,194	220,370	66,549,564	6,139,994	-1,639,775	58,769,795	12,589,596	13,091,039	43,405	1,945,659	1,225,937
2013	85,923,198	68,630,369	418,352	69,048,721	7,033,253	-1,661,277	60,354,191	12,151,024	13,417,983	43,637	1,969,032	1,255,213
2014	89,559,301	71,802,203	229,934	72,032,137	7,448,337	-1,720,425	62,863,375	12,537,309	14,158,617	44,902	1,994,536	1,281,565

Personal Income and Employment by Area: Corpus Christi, TX

(Thousands of dollars, except as noted.)

Year	Personal income, total	Earnings by place of work			Less: Contributions for government social insurance	Plus: Adjustment for residence	Equals: Net earnings by place of residence	Plus: Dividends, interest, and rent	Plus: Personal current transfer receipts	Per capita personal income (dollars)	Population (persons)	Total employment
		Nonfarm	Farm	Total								
1970	1,068,933	886,514	14,784	901,298	51,642	-14,079	835,577	160,291	73,065	3,622	295,082	126,000
1971	1,169,621	967,416	14,510	981,926	58,101	-14,794	909,031	173,861	86,729	3,851	303,749	128,721
1972	1,271,740	1,043,741	20,263	1,064,004	65,233	-16,130	982,641	188,518	100,581	4,070	312,437	129,292
1973	1,416,977	1,145,953	40,995	1,186,948	82,891	-18,194	1,085,863	208,276	122,838	4,544	311,819	134,114
1974	1,612,980	1,298,271	40,590	1,338,861	96,621	-21,298	1,220,942	242,319	149,719	5,188	310,879	137,156
1975	1,823,859	1,476,005	29,555	1,505,560	107,771	-24,850	1,372,939	266,692	184,228	5,755	316,939	138,280
1976	2,082,845	1,716,119	33,517	1,749,636	125,053	-30,095	1,594,488	285,369	202,988	6,448	323,036	142,172
1977	2,203,174	1,815,620	21,713	1,837,333	134,752	-29,266	1,673,315	313,178	216,681	6,780	324,964	145,244
1978	2,547,522	2,125,085	18,406	2,143,491	161,523	-38,780	1,943,188	366,946	237,388	7,776	327,620	154,230
1979	2,933,312	2,464,501	21,507	2,486,008	198,186	-48,466	2,239,356	422,971	270,985	8,761	334,805	162,460
1980	3,282,390	2,753,483	-14,783	2,738,700	225,898	-51,890	2,460,912	505,883	315,595	9,592	342,213	166,236
1981	3,813,740	3,113,829	44,999	3,158,828	280,185	-49,577	2,829,066	634,794	349,880	10,956	348,104	175,453
1982	4,095,358	3,314,878	12,212	3,327,090	309,970	-64,479	2,952,641	749,351	393,366	11,376	359,988	180,014
1983	4,241,313	3,311,990	18,277	3,330,267	308,004	-57,560	2,964,703	815,155	461,455	11,535	367,695	176,099
1984	4,491,481	3,463,094	24,334	3,487,428	331,130	-54,304	3,101,994	901,176	488,311	12,143	369,879	178,794
1985	4,734,895	3,601,999	32,145	3,634,144	349,986	-49,306	3,234,852	989,302	510,741	12,777	370,569	180,370
1986	4,699,050	3,484,079	13,963	3,498,042	333,115	-43,238	3,121,689	1,005,205	572,156	12,549	374,442	170,111
1987	4,665,843	3,394,347	40,530	3,434,877	320,232	-32,060	3,082,585	974,701	608,557	12,622	369,672	171,076
1988	4,886,481	3,575,635	36,296	3,611,931	352,966	-34,642	3,224,323	1,025,187	636,971	13,316	366,973	172,794
1989	5,147,787	3,701,709	-1,111	3,700,598	372,375	-32,979	3,295,244	1,155,503	697,040	14,052	366,328	173,076
1990	5,570,495	4,096,881	2,719	4,099,600	407,487	-30,997	3,661,116	1,142,038	767,341	15,127	368,255	178,082
1991	5,938,062	4,338,842	43,331	4,382,173	443,257	-38,251	3,900,665	1,165,547	871,850	15,909	373,245	181,527
1992	6,428,621	4,635,251	30,655	4,665,906	470,390	-43,719	4,151,797	1,246,758	1,030,066	17,004	378,071	182,760
1993	6,718,667	4,938,224	39,245	4,977,469	502,521	-45,494	4,429,454	1,214,682	1,074,531	17,416	385,768	188,525
1994	7,109,101	5,202,073	53,812	5,255,885	534,801	-51,590	4,669,494	1,278,586	1,161,021	18,133	392,050	193,248
1995	7,438,528	5,338,652	72,122	5,410,774	552,532	-58,690	4,799,552	1,376,518	1,262,458	18,846	394,701	197,179
1996	7,930,970	5,778,977	5,115	5,784,092	591,131	-67,234	5,125,727	1,453,041	1,352,202	19,901	398,529	203,672
1997	8,417,245	6,141,109	41,118	6,182,227	622,733	-69,715	5,489,779	1,519,334	1,408,132	20,912	402,504	209,271
1998	8,899,911	6,546,556	33,993	6,580,549	656,294	-73,892	5,850,363	1,596,160	1,453,388	22,039	403,818	213,233
1999	9,170,863	6,810,874	102,846	6,913,720	670,089	-79,345	6,164,286	1,543,907	1,462,670	22,691	404,155	212,874
2000	9,558,959	7,064,322	71,904	7,136,226	694,169	-83,865	6,358,192	1,672,676	1,528,091	23,693	403,458	216,479
2001	10,076,870	7,537,826	14,794	7,552,620	732,885	-104,047	6,715,688	1,711,965	1,649,217	25,027	402,647	217,994
2002	10,225,323	7,687,852	15,739	7,703,591	760,410	-185,270	6,757,911	1,675,587	1,791,825	25,205	405,692	218,975
2003	10,806,206	8,156,168	94,342	8,250,510	813,771	-268,143	7,168,596	1,722,391	1,915,219	26,556	406,915	222,628
2004	11,245,223	8,599,250	121,681	8,720,931	850,754	-382,269	7,487,908	1,734,016	2,023,299	27,298	411,936	225,638
2005	11,940,694	9,098,016	51,513	9,149,529	905,114	-504,660	7,739,755	1,986,277	2,214,662	28,682	416,308	230,072
2006	12,847,269	10,016,859	588	10,017,447	976,295	-622,606	8,418,546	2,067,342	2,361,381	30,623	419,530	234,560
2007	13,558,105	10,397,799	62,838	10,460,637	1,037,302	-745,785	8,677,550	2,290,136	2,590,419	32,250	420,407	239,524
2008	14,647,211	11,185,761	65,821	11,251,582	1,100,910	-890,381	9,260,291	2,509,032	2,877,888	34,613	423,168	244,625
2009	14,375,529	10,665,234	56,794	10,722,028	1,084,513	-627,561	9,009,954	2,252,337	3,113,238	33,646	427,262	240,941
2010	15,329,854	11,114,542	173,932	11,288,474	1,130,030	-571,870	9,586,574	2,314,459	3,428,821	35,815	428,026	239,026
2011	16,581,718	11,830,686	185,891	12,016,577	1,055,409	-495,371	10,465,797	2,586,366	3,529,555	38,468	431,051	242,656
2012	17,615,056	12,909,674	72,927	12,982,601	1,134,102	-640,796	11,207,703	2,910,888	3,496,465	40,308	437,012	249,401
2013	17,923,570	13,362,810	152,604	13,515,414	1,320,087	-737,263	11,458,064	2,868,500	3,597,006	40,419	443,448	255,093
2014	18,803,037	14,210,726	117,700	14,328,426	1,397,722	-868,392	12,062,312	2,986,094	3,754,631	41,961	448,108	260,265

Personal Income and Employment by Area: Corvallis, OR

(Thousands of dollars, except as noted.)

Year	Personal income, total	Earnings by place of work			Less: Contributions for government social insurance	Plus: Adjustment for residence	Equals: Net earnings by place of residence	Plus: Dividends, interest, and rent	Plus: Personal current transfer receipts	Per capita personal income (dollars)	Population (persons)	Total employment
		Nonfarm	Farm	Total								
1970	181,521	135,955	3,433	139,388	9,350	3,552	133,590	35,308	12,623	3,365	53,943	19,498
1971	203,036	151,552	3,253	154,805	10,653	4,447	148,599	39,729	14,708	3,696	54,929	20,207
1972	229,694	171,177	4,151	175,328	12,614	6,204	168,918	44,305	16,471	3,820	60,135	21,016
1973	260,067	190,583	7,172	197,755	16,164	8,717	190,308	49,645	20,114	4,385	59,313	22,257
1974	294,981	210,461	8,217	218,678	18,409	11,813	212,082	58,001	24,898	4,818	61,230	23,381
1975	333,076	237,064	4,033	241,097	20,124	14,590	235,563	65,760	31,753	5,405	61,618	24,344
1976	383,212	275,239	5,906	281,145	23,621	18,366	275,890	72,443	34,879	6,151	62,299	25,929
1977	440,213	322,420	5,389	327,809	28,481	20,320	319,648	82,661	37,904	6,714	65,569	28,314
1978	507,951	376,034	5,090	381,124	34,732	23,238	369,630	96,812	41,509	7,586	66,955	30,807
1979	563,010	410,374	6,139	416,513	39,681	28,140	404,972	110,630	47,408	8,259	68,171	30,922
1980	621,797	439,477	6,890	446,367	43,078	32,272	435,561	130,789	55,447	9,081	68,471	30,495
1981	697,121	483,327	9,536	492,863	51,101	33,312	475,074	160,120	61,927	10,049	69,369	30,876
1982	732,393	511,745	8,591	520,336	55,909	26,404	490,831	171,225	70,337	10,544	69,461	31,071
1983	782,803	543,728	10,905	554,633	60,004	26,204	520,833	185,997	75,973	11,470	68,245	31,395
1984	843,307	581,809	14,585	596,394	65,980	27,815	558,229	205,146	79,932	12,498	67,474	32,566
1985	870,993	591,932	15,656	607,588	66,999	30,313	570,902	214,856	85,235	12,947	67,275	33,707
1986	921,019	637,343	19,477	656,820	72,524	26,429	610,725	227,037	83,257	13,759	66,940	35,204
1987	974,485	686,344	16,704	703,048	76,909	25,859	651,998	234,097	88,390	14,418	67,590	36,280
1988	1,046,694	754,367	23,404	777,771	89,034	25,646	714,383	239,872	92,439	15,421	67,876	37,645
1989	1,157,095	823,323	18,932	842,255	96,679	23,719	769,295	288,536	99,264	16,559	69,879	38,457
1990	1,212,282	870,664	17,570	888,234	104,846	24,895	808,283	295,329	108,670	17,060	71,059	39,188
1991	1,263,364	911,502	15,276	926,778	110,005	25,629	842,402	304,940	116,022	17,668	71,507	39,115
1992	1,352,253	990,825	12,485	1,003,310	118,561	21,989	906,738	318,487	127,028	18,621	72,618	39,372
1993	1,464,515	1,096,981	17,297	1,114,278	131,750	8,707	991,235	340,253	133,027	19,792	73,997	41,016
1994	1,577,087	1,204,487	21,742	1,226,229	146,440	1,179	1,080,968	352,440	143,679	20,894	75,481	42,864
1995	1,729,918	1,303,426	18,212	1,321,638	159,999	-7,819	1,153,820	414,809	161,289	22,608	76,517	44,979
1996	1,913,388	1,447,179	25,420	1,472,599	180,491	-21,936	1,270,172	471,260	171,956	24,601	77,776	48,096
1997	2,060,241	1,582,945	25,086	1,608,031	194,761	-35,330	1,377,940	505,434	176,867	26,225	78,560	49,568
1998	2,166,060	1,653,734	24,295	1,678,029	201,528	-33,946	1,442,555	536,380	187,125	27,438	78,943	50,731
1999	2,196,191	1,667,785	30,909	1,698,694	199,709	-30,183	1,468,802	522,412	204,977	28,065	78,254	50,416
2000	2,314,242	1,767,080	28,555	1,795,635	212,582	-45,563	1,537,490	563,722	213,030	29,580	78,236	51,339
2001	2,382,958	1,805,069	38,241	1,843,310	209,642	-27,407	1,606,261	539,578	237,119	30,360	78,491	52,225
2002	2,432,513	1,856,660	38,230	1,894,890	214,902	-38,755	1,641,233	543,185	248,095	30,329	80,203	51,243
2003	2,578,354	1,920,770	42,926	1,963,696	222,032	-51,139	1,690,525	624,197	263,632	32,100	80,322	52,555
2004	2,666,915	1,988,258	45,171	2,033,429	230,156	-63,638	1,739,635	659,414	267,866	33,274	80,149	53,707
2005	2,682,479	2,061,680	35,740	2,097,420	242,994	-77,479	1,776,947	611,017	294,515	33,140	80,943	54,473
2006	2,778,095	2,128,595	37,701	2,166,296	255,922	-90,184	1,820,190	642,072	315,833	33,897	81,957	54,926
2007	2,883,854	2,188,360	31,872	2,220,232	265,312	-103,911	1,851,009	693,455	339,390	34,447	83,718	55,070
2008	3,045,831	2,247,056	23,813	2,270,869	271,336	-117,118	1,882,415	765,240	398,176	36,195	84,150	55,004
2009	2,932,979	2,226,767	22,364	2,249,131	267,163	-180,138	1,801,830	690,491	440,658	34,348	85,390	54,308
2010	2,998,060	2,187,451	18,598	2,206,049	268,786	-114,450	1,822,813	694,952	480,295	35,052	85,531	50,060
2011	3,217,932	2,262,972	22,091	2,285,063	245,228	-124,703	1,915,132	821,932	480,868	37,425	85,983	51,214
2012	3,254,364	2,368,650	31,000	2,399,650	255,227	-145,954	1,998,469	786,384	469,511	37,675	86,380	51,058
2013	3,283,247	2,393,795	30,824	2,424,619	290,952	-138,458	1,995,209	797,038	491,000	38,195	85,960	50,711
2014	3,426,549	2,468,594	38,167	2,506,761	300,639	-119,784	2,086,338	827,198	513,013	39,698	86,316	51,720

Personal Income and Employment by Area: Crestview-Fort Walton Beach-Destin, FL

(Thousands of dollars, except as noted.)

Year	Personal income, total	Earnings by place of work			Less: Contributions for government social insurance	Plus: Adjustment for residence	Equals: Net earnings by place of residence	Plus: Dividends, interest, and rent	Plus: Personal current transfer receipts	Per capita personal income (dollars)	Population (persons)	Total employment
		Nonfarm	Farm	Total								
1970	398,131	321,223	1,010	322,233	17,638	-22,495	282,100	92,845	23,186	3,802	104,708	43,341
1971	452,341	366,514	2,955	369,469	21,210	-25,119	323,140	101,807	27,394	4,200	107,706	45,369
1972	513,128	414,291	3,357	417,648	24,411	-27,878	365,359	114,951	32,818	4,553	112,702	46,894
1973	559,760	441,713	7,473	449,186	28,184	-27,350	393,652	126,190	39,918	4,873	114,864	49,238
1974	618,181	479,881	9,103	488,984	32,799	-26,358	429,827	141,184	47,170	5,306	116,509	51,718
1975	692,930	522,309	9,441	531,750	36,987	-27,474	467,289	161,820	63,821	5,594	123,878	51,954
1976	757,902	575,134	5,722	580,856	41,822	-31,394	507,640	179,993	70,269	6,103	124,190	53,408
1977	831,332	628,273	2,592	630,865	45,680	-32,273	552,912	202,437	75,983	6,526	127,380	55,208
1978	951,440	704,300	6,354	710,654	51,189	-33,712	625,753	242,743	82,944	7,387	128,807	58,497
1979	1,044,218	764,587	8,298	772,885	58,529	-35,645	678,711	268,244	97,263	7,930	131,677	60,253
1980	1,158,897	829,771	3,131	832,902	62,925	-36,614	733,363	309,190	116,344	8,773	132,104	60,453
1981	1,354,844	975,612	1,404	977,016	79,429	-43,885	853,702	363,019	138,123	10,007	135,394	63,432
1982	1,482,761	1,060,951	2,488	1,063,439	87,829	-46,593	929,017	394,926	158,818	10,646	139,276	65,789
1983	1,638,466	1,165,349	1,356	1,166,705	102,149	-46,635	1,017,921	443,985	176,560	11,336	144,536	69,831
1984	1,840,528	1,306,049	3,932	1,309,981	118,650	-50,462	1,140,869	506,821	192,838	12,317	149,428	75,701
1985	2,000,326	1,400,756	2,645	1,403,401	131,934	-47,889	1,223,578	563,021	213,727	12,929	154,718	79,525
1986	2,176,269	1,532,313	3,898	1,536,211	149,316	-51,282	1,335,613	609,886	230,770	13,649	159,450	84,261
1987	2,366,045	1,674,404	3,871	1,678,275	163,337	-53,063	1,461,875	658,667	245,503	14,424	164,034	86,072
1988	2,569,686	1,804,127	7,717	1,811,844	183,805	-65,463	1,562,576	737,491	269,619	15,382	167,059	88,777
1989	2,818,320	1,933,650	8,849	1,942,499	200,429	-62,347	1,679,723	834,176	304,421	16,595	169,832	91,122
1990	3,062,539	2,049,134	7,352	2,056,486	216,137	-14,624	1,825,725	900,201	336,613	17,775	172,290	91,622
1991	3,268,364	2,193,414	7,569	2,200,983	234,358	-33,662	1,932,963	951,231	384,170	18,381	177,811	94,263
1992	3,567,349	2,361,677	8,806	2,370,483	254,874	-3,572	2,112,037	1,018,977	436,335	19,462	183,299	96,788
1993	3,813,352	2,508,812	7,412	2,516,224	272,059	-31,386	2,212,779	1,129,500	471,073	20,204	188,744	100,240
1994	4,003,717	2,608,707	7,325	2,616,032	285,678	-31,447	2,298,907	1,201,173	503,637	20,675	193,649	105,827
1995	4,331,430	2,821,684	7,071	2,828,755	304,730	-99,231	2,424,794	1,331,907	574,729	21,933	197,484	109,725
1996	4,608,801	3,045,048	10,114	3,055,162	327,754	-134,064	2,593,344	1,425,762	589,695	22,910	201,172	114,103
1997	4,901,666	3,202,738	9,292	3,212,030	347,886	-120,919	2,743,225	1,531,285	627,156	23,932	204,814	118,905
1998	5,197,831	3,404,091	4,898	3,408,989	368,050	-163,301	2,877,638	1,672,789	647,404	25,146	206,708	122,451
1999	5,536,607	3,603,204	7,237	3,610,441	386,726	-158,811	3,064,904	1,775,157	696,546	26,501	208,918	125,251
2000	5,836,419	3,871,760	3,357	3,875,117	413,849	-216,140	3,245,128	1,826,641	764,650	27,536	211,955	129,607
2001	6,194,792	4,111,705	3,174	4,114,879	437,143	-203,711	3,474,025	1,862,864	857,903	28,819	214,955	124,244
2002	6,855,888	4,753,060	-4,630	4,748,430	493,608	-266,241	3,988,581	1,931,129	936,178	31,136	220,192	128,956
2003	7,365,944	5,186,633	223	5,186,856	541,331	-330,675	4,314,850	2,039,615	1,011,479	32,998	223,227	136,042
2004	7,893,716	5,681,181	2,489	5,683,670	603,033	-387,785	4,692,852	2,112,927	1,087,937	34,317	230,024	147,081
2005	8,685,787	6,349,763	2,431	6,352,194	666,124	-424,396	5,261,674	2,276,645	1,147,468	37,208	233,437	152,677
2006	9,375,151	6,753,745	4,306	6,758,051	719,151	-454,188	5,584,712	2,571,264	1,219,175	39,858	235,216	158,628
2007	9,706,922	6,801,578	3,284	6,804,862	732,355	-490,713	5,581,794	2,837,007	1,288,121	41,300	235,032	159,149
2008	9,784,098	6,616,792	4,187	6,620,979	724,945	-532,944	5,363,090	2,946,518	1,474,490	41,579	235,315	152,495
2009	9,474,140	6,492,098	4,389	6,496,487	729,374	-535,110	5,232,003	2,633,670	1,608,467	40,198	235,687	148,518
2010	9,793,720	6,503,616	6,771	6,510,387	737,011	-542,657	5,230,719	2,746,034	1,816,967	41,498	236,006	145,840
2011	10,309,266	6,796,066	7,702	6,803,768	700,427	-570,694	5,532,647	2,887,583	1,889,036	43,143	238,954	150,413
2012	10,873,789	7,186,520	11,170	7,197,690	748,824	-629,565	5,819,301	3,201,475	1,853,013	43,897	247,712	153,367
2013	11,119,029	7,405,309	8,102	7,413,411	852,379	-638,415	5,922,617	3,250,997	1,945,415	43,895	253,309	157,911
2014	11,598,877	7,625,144	11,831	7,636,975	876,001	-643,259	6,117,715	3,394,197	2,086,965	44,950	258,042	159,574

Personal Income and Employment by Area: Cumberland, MD-WV

(Thousands of dollars, except as noted.)

Year	Personal income, total	Derivation of personal income									Per capita personal income (dollars)	Population (persons)	Total employment
		Earnings by place of work			Less: Contributions for government social insurance	Plus: Adjustment for residence	Equals: Net earnings by place of residence	Plus: Dividends, interest, and rent	Plus: Personal current transfer receipts				
		Nonfarm	Farm	Total									
1970	357,330	313,556	927	314,483	24,342	-17,013	273,128	37,900	46,302		3,335	107,140	42,280
1971	386,022	330,990	911	331,901	26,475	-15,078	290,348	40,773	54,901		3,583	107,735	41,720
1972	417,355	352,904	1,034	353,938	29,385	-13,306	311,247	43,681	62,427		3,812	109,483	41,890
1973	454,112	382,910	1,507	384,417	36,229	-13,159	335,029	48,836	70,247		4,186	108,476	42,897
1974	492,719	409,225	1,269	410,494	40,100	-16,808	353,586	56,535	82,598		4,517	109,091	42,044
1975	531,805	413,882	1,056	414,938	39,740	-14,356	360,842	63,783	107,180		4,910	108,304	40,012
1976	571,892	449,261	568	449,829	43,766	-15,681	390,382	68,928	112,582		5,288	108,148	39,976
1977	635,265	507,417	561	507,978	49,281	-18,547	440,150	77,515	117,600		5,889	107,873	40,722
1978	698,000	561,730	1,506	563,236	56,213	-19,629	487,394	85,159	125,447		6,515	107,138	42,694
1979	772,494	614,037	1,558	615,595	63,670	-17,860	534,065	94,014	144,415		7,156	107,955	42,382
1980	859,854	656,045	1,299	657,344	68,487	-16,674	572,183	117,971	169,700		7,971	107,868	42,213
1981	937,259	688,279	590	688,869	77,975	-11,709	599,185	143,713	194,361		8,676	108,027	41,782
1982	995,659	693,611	703	694,314	80,802	-7,692	605,820	173,222	216,617		9,279	107,298	40,498
1983	1,052,447	719,136	2,040	721,176	84,752	-5,005	631,419	185,381	235,647		9,915	106,147	40,484
1984	1,114,457	760,146	2,909	763,055	93,196	-5,467	664,392	204,962	245,103		10,665	104,497	40,688
1985	1,173,723	795,455	2,419	797,874	99,367	-4,065	694,442	220,113	259,168		11,352	103,396	41,264
1986	1,198,845	803,117	2,684	805,801	103,360	-169	702,272	232,013	264,560		11,677	102,668	40,906
1987	1,266,989	855,376	1,439	856,815	108,253	-98	748,464	232,792	285,733		12,389	102,270	42,300
1988	1,342,209	928,964	1,185	930,149	123,070	-1,850	805,229	236,089	300,891		13,135	102,187	43,808
1989	1,432,793	969,088	1,388	970,476	128,925	-1,068	840,483	271,033	321,277		14,035	102,086	44,253
1990	1,504,654	1,008,029	1,622	1,009,651	132,329	8,415	885,737	274,076	344,841		14,805	101,634	44,793
1991	1,554,926	1,017,454	967	1,018,421	133,759	10,168	894,830	280,493	379,603		15,229	102,101	44,400
1992	1,605,077	1,025,714	1,954	1,027,668	134,115	13,195	906,748	275,092	423,237		15,688	102,312	43,742
1993	1,657,777	1,068,042	2,083	1,070,125	139,819	11,627	941,933	278,850	436,994		16,196	102,359	43,705
1994	1,720,217	1,109,646	2,166	1,111,812	144,814	9,907	976,905	295,415	447,897		16,781	102,508	44,034
1995	1,771,908	1,134,324	823	1,135,147	148,127	9,501	996,521	305,101	470,286		17,253	102,704	44,466
1996	1,836,322	1,174,929	992	1,175,921	153,051	7,382	1,030,252	318,850	487,220		17,929	102,424	45,200
1997	1,919,218	1,230,913	-525	1,230,388	158,815	3,192	1,074,765	347,349	497,104		18,732	102,457	45,957
1998	1,967,638	1,265,325	109	1,265,434	160,812	3,964	1,108,586	355,584	503,468		19,156	102,718	46,237
1999	2,032,670	1,316,849	129	1,316,978	166,318	6,021	1,156,681	348,202	527,787		19,839	102,458	46,416
2000	2,130,713	1,380,114	1,056	1,381,170	173,907	7,162	1,214,425	369,253	547,035		20,918	101,858	47,325
2001	2,252,730	1,452,746	298	1,453,044	183,575	12,255	1,281,724	381,913	589,093		22,173	101,596	46,980
2002	2,336,186	1,533,029	326	1,533,355	190,449	10,070	1,352,976	356,489	626,721		23,025	101,462	46,826
2003	2,420,151	1,586,643	2,042	1,588,685	197,064	4,640	1,396,261	353,352	670,538		23,854	101,457	46,962
2004	2,523,608	1,659,739	3,920	1,663,659	205,183	6,861	1,465,337	377,041	681,230		24,824	101,658	47,678
2005	2,610,448	1,733,493	3,239	1,736,732	217,069	2,909	1,522,572	364,574	723,302		25,802	101,172	48,598
2006	2,726,696	1,822,192	1,038	1,823,230	229,136	9,540	1,603,634	370,909	752,153		26,916	101,304	49,093
2007	2,848,551	1,850,262	-966	1,849,296	232,063	19,867	1,637,100	413,292	798,159		27,932	101,981	48,903
2008	3,047,744	1,912,115	-190	1,911,925	238,804	23,462	1,696,583	466,488	884,673		29,745	102,462	48,516
2009	3,154,701	1,961,091	-538	1,960,553	246,107	14,088	1,728,534	468,311	957,856		30,574	103,181	48,451
2010	3,259,000	2,021,037	-444	2,020,593	257,989	4,952	1,767,556	470,686	1,020,758		31,568	103,236	48,734
2011	3,385,220	2,074,095	334	2,074,429	237,522	2,969	1,839,876	512,563	1,032,781		32,988	102,620	48,792
2012	3,439,269	2,081,321	-2,029	2,079,292	237,205	9,093	1,851,180	538,521	1,049,568		33,779	101,816	48,601
2013	3,485,691	2,104,449	-556	2,103,893	267,456	12,946	1,849,383	555,738	1,080,570		34,431	101,238	48,286
2014	3,603,884	2,133,692	-741	2,132,951	271,800	24,830	1,885,981	579,604	1,138,299		35,849	100,530	48,352

Personal Income and Employment by Area: Dallas-Fort Worth-Arlington, TX

(Thousands of dollars, except as noted.)

		Derivation of personal income										
		Earnings by place of work			Less: Contributions for government social insurance	Plus: Adjustment for residence	Equals: Net earnings by place of residence	Plus: Dividends, interest, and rent	Plus: Personal current transfer receipts	Per capita personal income (dollars)	Population (persons)	Total employment
Year	Personal income, total	Nonfarm	Farm	Total								
1970	10,511,291	8,991,019	39,410	9,030,429	588,164	-20,425	8,421,840	1,471,623	617,828	4,318	2,434,181	1,192,710
1971	11,239,285	9,463,439	34,789	9,498,228	634,413	10,895	8,874,710	1,625,061	739,514	4,534	2,478,739	1,193,666
1972	12,455,784	10,497,611	47,357	10,544,968	739,267	30,506	9,836,207	1,789,362	830,215	4,993	2,494,430	1,251,641
1973	13,976,469	11,793,607	81,724	11,875,331	960,442	40,588	10,955,477	2,035,664	985,328	5,483	2,549,156	1,329,267
1974	15,821,526	13,257,074	30,445	13,287,519	1,104,244	58,352	12,241,627	2,407,505	1,172,394	6,035	2,621,429	1,373,955
1975	17,611,412	14,571,197	33,749	14,604,946	1,183,094	77,215	13,499,067	2,600,086	1,512,259	6,600	2,668,519	1,372,695
1976	19,670,248	16,556,353	57,461	16,613,814	1,377,182	57,838	15,294,470	2,753,136	1,622,642	7,182	2,738,645	1,432,668
1977	22,007,259	18,949,196	16,900	18,966,096	1,595,697	-65,291	17,305,108	3,001,251	1,700,900	7,881	2,792,291	1,514,786
1978	25,620,928	22,175,300	38,316	22,213,616	1,912,937	-140,901	20,159,778	3,564,254	1,896,896	8,958	2,860,247	1,621,566
1979	29,749,066	25,913,972	41,806	25,955,778	2,339,737	-175,337	23,440,704	4,172,725	2,135,637	10,103	2,944,580	1,722,152
1980	34,599,858	29,926,923	-1,690	29,925,233	2,720,561	-217,414	26,987,258	5,122,917	2,489,683	11,317	3,057,465	1,795,112
1981	39,912,245	34,218,828	49,945	34,268,773	3,347,388	-230,713	30,690,672	6,375,176	2,846,397	12,706	3,141,226	1,877,705
1982	44,303,821	37,408,108	51,598	37,459,706	3,739,342	-287,246	33,433,118	7,622,245	3,248,458	13,611	3,255,044	1,927,039
1983	48,979,684	41,492,403	51,241	41,543,644	4,156,712	-354,335	37,032,597	8,394,276	3,552,811	14,549	3,366,597	1,997,325
1984	55,896,899	47,630,198	46,326	47,676,524	4,904,822	-419,009	42,352,693	9,775,748	3,768,458	16,045	3,483,781	2,168,499
1985	62,016,917	52,845,025	25,465	52,870,490	5,523,559	-496,966	46,849,965	11,089,819	4,077,133	17,108	3,624,952	2,297,002
1986	65,664,776	55,984,715	-844	55,983,871	5,798,886	-554,322	49,630,663	11,584,783	4,449,330	17,455	3,762,028	2,325,559
1987	68,067,834	58,182,218	10,756	58,192,974	5,929,767	-598,463	51,664,744	11,694,022	4,709,068	17,696	3,846,478	2,400,673
1988	72,026,117	61,583,951	13,230	61,597,181	6,426,905	-632,226	54,538,050	12,492,812	4,995,255	18,501	3,893,126	2,433,185
1989	76,860,713	65,434,819	43,067	65,477,886	6,835,323	-703,238	57,939,325	13,406,993	5,514,395	19,443	3,953,105	2,465,294
1990	83,106,694	70,393,508	53,108	70,446,616	7,245,126	-757,957	62,443,533	14,503,529	6,159,632	20,552	4,043,744	2,522,308
1991	86,281,528	73,166,752	48,648	73,215,400	7,719,174	-822,359	64,673,867	14,706,182	6,901,479	20,817	4,144,813	2,546,010
1992	92,784,369	78,494,569	72,152	78,566,721	8,201,799	-896,725	69,468,197	15,152,422	8,163,750	21,929	4,231,065	2,558,964
1993	98,467,989	83,860,032	65,492	83,925,524	8,733,909	-948,968	74,242,647	15,442,634	8,782,708	22,785	4,321,701	2,631,521
1994	105,111,453	89,431,105	76,248	89,507,353	9,447,719	-1,030,340	79,029,294	16,614,206	9,467,953	23,748	4,426,050	2,723,712
1995	113,163,551	96,073,065	33,318	96,106,383	10,164,004	-1,137,528	84,804,851	18,085,287	10,273,413	24,947	4,536,179	2,830,895
1996	123,330,185	104,990,937	25,250	105,016,187	10,969,462	-1,274,388	92,772,337	19,565,643	10,992,205	26,441	4,664,290	2,940,089
1997	135,167,633	116,255,135	67,224	116,322,359	12,087,904	-1,496,661	102,737,794	20,907,664	11,522,175	28,111	4,808,429	3,074,940
1998	150,218,596	130,602,748	42,344	130,645,092	13,346,315	-1,707,077	115,591,700	22,680,505	11,946,391	30,300	4,957,705	3,194,321
1999	159,928,710	140,886,548	97,573	140,984,121	14,395,356	-1,892,416	124,696,349	22,986,338	12,246,023	31,350	5,101,405	3,303,031
2000	177,728,911	156,677,209	41,566	156,718,775	15,682,226	-2,148,765	138,887,784	25,708,859	13,132,268	33,948	5,235,385	3,436,642
2001	187,399,213	165,727,357	69,054	165,796,411	16,237,356	-2,257,325	147,301,730	25,559,835	14,537,648	34,856	5,376,413	3,473,961
2002	188,558,277	166,566,927	64,870	166,631,797	16,274,084	-2,603,703	147,754,010	24,643,159	16,161,108	34,390	5,482,944	3,444,118
2003	193,234,640	168,715,090	123,322	168,838,412	16,803,475	-2,402,012	149,632,925	26,346,892	17,254,823	34,656	5,575,785	3,436,927
2004	203,082,574	177,460,580	141,326	177,601,906	17,649,833	-2,532,469	157,419,604	27,479,214	18,183,756	35,840	5,666,333	3,526,614
2005	221,753,494	188,012,110	119,114	188,131,224	18,632,577	-1,180,064	168,318,583	33,270,646	20,164,265	38,389	5,776,543	3,641,304
2006	242,818,670	204,954,491	111,177	205,065,668	19,721,295	-1,267,995	184,076,378	36,893,820	21,848,472	40,860	5,942,755	3,787,102
2007	256,874,978	213,001,291	115,032	213,116,323	20,868,184	-1,363,727	190,884,412	41,920,197	24,070,369	42,236	6,081,907	3,926,342
2008	277,616,418	224,355,324	4,088	224,359,412	21,532,029	-2,003,231	200,824,152	48,671,864	28,120,402	44,697	6,211,115	4,022,529
2009	260,761,727	211,993,249	-6,082	211,987,167	21,233,083	-1,806,658	188,947,426	40,750,913	31,063,388	41,118	6,341,740	3,946,223
2010	272,203,734	220,356,599	20,780	220,377,379	21,933,517	-1,656,280	196,787,582	40,713,221	34,702,931	42,184	6,452,725	3,948,869
2011	299,389,488	235,273,705	23,665	235,297,370	20,403,933	-1,691,805	213,201,632	50,129,566	36,058,290	45,535	6,574,866	4,088,782
2012	318,533,833	251,779,926	101,613	251,881,539	21,537,944	-1,829,153	228,514,442	53,798,578	36,220,813	47,471	6,710,066	4,209,496
2013	325,011,065	262,591,376	136,813	262,728,189	25,604,181	-1,817,984	235,306,024	52,078,482	37,626,559	47,634	6,823,113	4,338,058
2014	344,279,922	279,693,117	144,416	279,837,533	27,185,559	-2,013,763	250,638,211	54,072,932	39,568,779	49,506	6,954,330	4,464,571

Personal Income and Employment by Area: Dalton, GA

(Thousands of dollars, except as noted.)

Year	Personal income, total	Derivation of personal income									Per capita personal income (dollars)	Population (persons)	Total employment
		Earnings by place of work			Less: Contributions for government social insurance	Plus: Adjustment for residence	Equals: Net earnings by place of residence	Plus: Dividends, interest, and rent	Plus: Personal current transfer receipts				
		Nonfarm	Farm	Total									
1970	226,038	216,417	1,961	218,378	14,777	-17,329	186,272	22,790	16,976		3,297	68,569	35,168
1971	261,056	250,908	1,661	252,569	17,866	-19,887	214,816	27,032	19,208		3,662	71,282	37,695
1972	307,741	298,636	2,312	300,948	22,166	-23,809	254,973	31,440	21,328		4,175	73,703	41,452
1973	351,630	339,453	6,935	346,388	28,752	-26,439	291,197	35,120	25,313		4,562	77,080	43,738
1974	368,071	351,318	2,108	353,426	30,881	-27,086	295,459	40,137	32,475		4,630	79,491	42,486
1975	390,028	346,698	7,050	353,748	29,680	-25,264	298,804	43,887	47,337		4,925	79,193	39,069
1976	447,754	413,770	6,373	420,143	36,331	-30,496	353,316	47,336	47,102		5,608	79,835	42,562
1977	505,934	478,441	5,544	483,985	41,985	-36,925	405,075	52,712	48,147		6,180	81,872	45,560
1978	567,440	535,958	7,840	543,798	48,285	-40,432	455,081	60,463	51,896		6,800	83,444	47,923
1979	635,113	598,974	6,303	605,277	55,821	-44,595	504,861	70,093	60,159		7,483	84,874	49,185
1980	684,021	634,165	1,856	636,021	59,510	-49,266	527,245	83,815	72,961		7,977	85,754	48,891
1981	748,925	683,774	3,224	686,998	68,680	-56,413	561,905	103,004	84,016		8,631	86,771	48,672
1982	784,002	698,633	4,025	702,658	70,769	-61,839	570,050	120,894	93,058		8,993	87,177	46,909
1983	892,268	818,123	3,407	821,530	84,276	-79,006	658,248	135,034	98,986		10,180	87,649	50,744
1984	996,226	928,804	6,665	935,469	98,633	-94,583	742,253	148,165	105,808		11,155	89,307	54,398
1985	1,074,424	1,006,168	5,828	1,011,996	108,630	-108,145	795,221	165,443	113,760		11,851	90,663	56,119
1986	1,180,494	1,126,066	7,744	1,133,810	123,034	-128,915	881,861	177,787	120,846		12,808	92,171	58,945
1987	1,296,515	1,263,670	4,010	1,267,680	136,072	-153,904	977,704	193,360	125,451		13,741	94,353	62,232
1988	1,403,234	1,370,428	8,831	1,379,259	150,178	-173,035	1,056,046	213,298	133,890		14,571	96,302	65,112
1989	1,519,940	1,448,797	13,693	1,462,490	159,679	-189,703	1,113,108	256,210	150,622		15,536	97,831	66,708
1990	1,589,524	1,518,432	12,135	1,530,567	167,186	-205,633	1,157,748	263,207	168,569		16,063	98,957	67,995
1991	1,645,500	1,552,202	13,775	1,565,977	173,148	-216,728	1,176,101	273,494	195,905		16,392	100,385	66,329
1992	1,803,305	1,740,209	13,431	1,753,640	190,828	-254,870	1,307,942	274,850	220,513		17,712	101,814	69,845
1993	1,935,414	1,899,486	15,688	1,915,174	209,087	-289,852	1,416,235	284,672	234,507		18,692	103,540	73,741
1994	2,078,201	2,028,838	18,282	2,047,120	224,843	-318,773	1,503,504	317,740	256,957		19,573	106,177	76,724
1995	2,183,745	2,101,340	16,696	2,118,036	231,754	-334,325	1,551,957	349,837	281,951		20,077	108,771	78,552
1996	2,338,680	2,231,865	21,771	2,253,636	243,654	-364,032	1,645,950	386,169	306,561		21,056	111,071	80,144
1997	2,448,154	2,358,682	21,618	2,380,300	254,299	-390,200	1,735,801	399,900	312,453		21,539	113,661	81,060
1998	2,625,286	2,547,244	28,778	2,576,022	272,815	-427,076	1,876,131	430,778	318,377		22,746	115,417	82,165
1999	2,706,674	2,653,742	28,180	2,681,922	283,010	-447,507	1,951,405	414,557	340,712		22,938	118,000	83,292
2000	2,886,974	2,860,620	23,481	2,884,101	305,732	-507,487	2,070,882	446,446	369,646		23,867	120,959	87,141
2001	3,038,817	2,944,446	32,936	2,977,382	317,563	-519,386	2,140,433	483,194	415,190		24,504	124,015	85,390
2002	3,112,153	3,025,246	22,622	3,047,868	324,435	-571,666	2,151,767	484,817	475,569		24,659	126,208	85,991
2003	3,223,995	3,169,766	19,076	3,188,842	340,112	-635,391	2,213,339	524,440	486,216		25,094	128,476	86,474
2004	3,401,565	3,403,839	24,740	3,428,579	381,776	-689,511	2,357,292	523,249	521,024		25,905	131,307	88,466
2005	3,489,601	3,528,335	22,388	3,550,723	389,513	-726,150	2,435,060	494,417	560,124		26,064	133,885	89,460
2006	3,617,343	3,642,839	-629	3,642,210	397,021	-761,613	2,483,576	521,311	612,456		26,485	136,581	90,607
2007	3,821,490	3,748,534	7,545	3,756,079	401,223	-783,551	2,571,305	583,500	666,685		27,534	138,792	90,162
2008	3,763,235	3,505,029	19,086	3,524,115	391,260	-755,775	2,377,080	617,570	768,585		26,801	140,415	84,656
2009	3,707,223	3,330,288	14,431	3,344,719	371,458	-659,250	2,314,011	539,947	853,265		26,312	140,897	77,015
2010	3,705,251	3,258,020	10,307	3,268,327	368,210	-637,807	2,262,310	514,021	928,920		26,035	142,317	75,971
2011	3,931,876	3,377,015	1,423	3,378,438	346,983	-679,589	2,351,866	619,985	960,025		27,591	142,504	76,785
2012	4,030,117	3,462,456	30,686	3,493,142	353,855	-634,012	2,505,275	577,459	947,383		28,265	142,581	75,273
2013	4,221,101	3,626,483	43,961	3,670,444	410,284	-647,941	2,612,219	636,839	972,043		29,646	142,385	74,828
2014	4,385,260	3,863,111	52,584	3,915,695	438,149	-759,595	2,717,951	663,881	1,003,428		30,676	142,952	77,674

Personal Income and Employment by Area: Danville, IL

(Thousands of dollars, except as noted.)

Year	Personal income, total	Earnings by place of work			Less: Contributions for government social insurance	Plus: Adjustment for residence	Equals: Net earnings by place of residence	Plus: Dividends, interest, and rent	Plus: Personal current transfer receipts	Per capita personal income (dollars)	Population (persons)	Total employment
		Nonfarm	Farm	Total								
1970	374,159	304,895	13,951	318,846	20,397	-10,227	288,222	48,523	37,414	3,853	97,100	43,790
1971	415,351	333,958	21,318	355,276	22,802	-14,785	317,689	52,373	45,289	4,263	97,441	43,260
1972	449,839	371,181	17,581	388,762	26,546	-19,706	342,510	57,653	49,676	4,599	97,815	44,707
1973	530,307	427,060	39,440	466,500	35,525	-26,148	404,827	67,223	58,257	5,408	98,058	46,897
1974	558,978	445,859	38,951	484,810	38,523	-29,030	417,257	75,568	66,153	5,720	97,719	46,993
1975	624,682	473,651	54,161	527,812	39,974	-32,474	455,364	83,809	85,509	6,399	97,623	45,416
1976	675,901	538,529	44,156	582,685	46,452	-40,473	495,760	88,889	91,252	6,885	98,166	46,632
1977	721,739	584,743	41,993	626,736	50,321	-47,375	529,040	98,831	93,868	7,377	97,842	46,973
1978	781,477	651,625	31,194	682,819	57,774	-56,362	568,683	113,335	99,459	7,993	97,772	47,926
1979	842,992	682,689	48,559	731,248	62,548	-62,338	606,362	126,952	109,678	8,697	96,928	47,142
1980	867,180	688,176	14,957	703,133	62,509	-65,463	575,161	156,248	135,771	9,116	95,130	44,925
1981	965,848	727,089	30,391	757,480	71,108	-69,193	617,179	189,952	158,717	10,210	94,596	44,283
1982	1,002,493	724,992	18,848	743,840	72,098	-62,879	608,863	221,293	172,337	10,780	92,998	42,605
1983	1,011,723	753,636	-1,949	751,687	75,918	-61,665	614,104	217,409	180,210	10,907	92,758	42,368
1984	1,133,021	828,976	34,545	863,521	87,063	-66,041	710,417	241,928	180,676	12,297	92,141	42,881
1985	1,164,396	842,196	39,563	881,759	89,976	-63,663	728,120	247,007	189,269	12,714	91,584	42,021
1986	1,189,820	858,734	33,487	892,221	92,516	-59,730	739,975	252,565	197,280	12,996	91,551	42,054
1987	1,226,423	903,545	21,977	925,522	95,654	-58,087	771,781	251,232	203,410	13,491	90,909	42,017
1988	1,271,826	941,710	16,305	958,015	102,025	-53,139	802,851	257,059	211,916	14,158	89,831	42,051
1989	1,358,998	961,611	44,448	1,006,059	105,251	-48,582	852,226	285,756	221,016	15,314	88,740	41,546
1990	1,379,733	969,004	39,532	1,008,536	103,485	-36,871	868,180	269,188	242,365	15,651	88,155	41,527
1991	1,404,109	1,001,116	18,429	1,019,545	109,806	-37,268	872,471	270,764	260,874	15,958	87,986	41,296
1992	1,527,262	1,063,468	42,431	1,105,899	114,270	-39,243	952,386	279,046	295,830	17,366	87,944	41,311
1993	1,556,035	1,079,095	48,604	1,127,699	118,952	-37,000	971,747	278,430	305,858	17,735	87,738	40,834
1994	1,648,538	1,152,704	60,617	1,213,321	128,418	-39,518	1,045,385	290,862	312,291	18,750	87,922	42,042
1995	1,623,288	1,129,884	18,415	1,148,299	126,039	-30,149	992,111	303,464	327,713	18,751	86,570	41,796
1996	1,707,094	1,148,754	47,654	1,196,408	127,040	-27,146	1,042,222	323,698	341,174	20,013	85,298	42,425
1997	1,724,502	1,172,571	32,364	1,204,935	129,080	-23,409	1,052,446	326,836	345,220	20,223	85,274	42,515
1998	1,777,603	1,220,067	15,138	1,235,205	133,626	-25,266	1,076,313	347,442	353,848	20,914	84,996	42,323
1999	1,803,902	1,258,059	10,295	1,268,354	134,923	-18,972	1,114,459	332,275	357,168	21,405	84,276	42,218
2000	1,871,147	1,269,767	29,733	1,299,500	133,823	-9,403	1,156,274	342,103	372,770	22,323	83,821	42,357
2001	1,932,979	1,287,789	30,901	1,318,690	136,784	-11,308	1,170,598	365,154	397,227	23,109	83,646	40,598
2002	1,970,107	1,322,171	19,104	1,341,275	138,890	-6,257	1,196,128	349,925	424,054	23,651	83,299	39,995
2003	2,111,872	1,415,433	36,856	1,452,289	148,610	-851	1,302,828	360,694	448,350	25,445	82,996	40,712
2004	2,184,232	1,468,624	61,734	1,530,358	155,726	4,984	1,379,616	337,117	467,499	26,330	82,955	40,340
2005	2,190,932	1,511,097	21,103	1,532,200	166,582	11,082	1,376,700	310,753	503,479	26,484	82,728	40,538
2006	2,265,634	1,552,030	39,697	1,591,727	170,078	17,634	1,439,283	303,391	522,960	27,391	82,715	40,181
2007	2,326,871	1,531,948	59,225	1,591,173	170,013	24,286	1,445,446	314,971	566,454	28,287	82,258	40,117
2008	2,508,150	1,582,428	103,217	1,685,645	175,590	31,578	1,541,633	361,208	605,309	30,613	81,930	39,308
2009	2,497,632	1,539,586	61,392	1,600,978	171,458	27,683	1,457,203	359,533	680,896	30,567	81,710	37,941
2010	2,570,233	1,555,553	76,090	1,631,643	174,946	32,784	1,489,481	357,090	723,662	31,500	81,595	37,321
2011	2,699,514	1,621,988	127,789	1,749,777	165,610	26,886	1,611,053	383,963	704,498	33,181	81,358	37,985
2012	2,725,998	1,685,416	79,572	1,764,988	171,766	32,656	1,625,878	404,320	695,800	33,753	80,764	38,106
2013	2,818,464	1,668,319	179,273	1,847,592	191,171	33,952	1,690,373	400,823	727,268	35,048	80,418	37,199
2014	2,791,196	1,709,673	95,418	1,805,091	196,716	37,038	1,645,413	416,681	729,102	35,009	79,728	37,711

Personal Income and Employment by Area: Daphne-Fairhope-Foley, AL

(Thousands of dollars, except as noted.)

| Year | Personal income, total | Derivation of personal income | | | | | | | | | Per capita personal income (dollars) | Population (persons) | Total employment |
| | | Earnings by place of work | | | Less: Contributions for government social insurance | Plus: Adjustment for residence | Equals: Net earnings by place of residence | Plus: Dividends, interest, and rent | Plus: Personal current transfer receipts | | | | |
		Nonfarm	Farm	Total									
1970	172,451	79,420	5,789	85,209	6,114	47,294	126,389	28,296	17,766	2,900	59,474	19,749
1971	196,330	89,393	8,786	98,179	6,919	51,607	142,867	32,688	20,775	3,264	60,142	20,505
1972	223,337	104,363	9,606	113,969	8,432	57,577	163,114	36,691	23,532	3,577	62,435	21,727
1973	267,249	121,339	20,473	141,812	11,236	63,969	194,545	44,421	28,283	4,163	64,196	23,015
1974	304,840	137,836	17,877	155,713	13,293	73,169	215,589	54,474	34,777	4,614	66,072	23,738
1975	344,509	152,186	16,280	168,466	14,691	83,695	237,470	62,200	44,839	5,077	67,861	24,458
1976	404,670	180,559	27,854	208,413	17,619	94,807	285,601	69,357	49,712	5,761	70,244	25,750
1977	433,311	202,648	9,603	212,251	19,938	107,341	299,654	80,239	53,418	5,985	72,399	26,965
1978	494,105	219,074	20,914	239,988	21,698	124,355	342,645	92,304	59,156	6,628	74,550	27,291
1979	539,522	244,833	4,309	249,142	25,020	138,393	362,515	105,808	71,199	7,044	76,594	27,875
1980	612,860	263,959	1,749	265,708	26,899	159,392	398,201	130,926	83,733	7,765	78,931	27,777
1981	714,444	291,753	10,495	302,248	32,488	184,680	454,440	164,161	95,843	8,899	80,287	28,722
1982	756,544	306,512	438	306,950	34,874	192,752	464,828	184,994	106,722	9,189	82,331	29,388
1983	841,646	350,037	6,907	356,944	39,552	203,282	520,674	202,821	118,151	10,022	83,978	31,306
1984	937,423	395,644	4,842	400,486	45,773	224,511	579,224	229,427	128,772	10,806	86,752	33,057
1985	1,047,199	438,156	14,040	452,196	50,457	250,919	652,658	254,705	139,836	11,714	89,401	33,969
1986	1,114,484	469,686	9,187	478,873	53,058	270,828	696,643	270,157	147,684	12,205	91,311	34,674
1987	1,181,292	499,382	14,112	513,494	56,032	289,787	747,249	282,223	151,820	12,673	93,214	36,081
1988	1,280,528	529,339	14,640	543,979	61,784	315,531	797,726	314,411	168,391	13,529	94,649	37,654
1989	1,438,814	569,633	18,028	587,661	67,238	347,698	868,121	378,149	192,544	14,957	96,198	38,889
1990	1,565,529	632,358	11,511	643,869	74,867	390,347	959,349	395,734	210,446	15,821	98,955	40,545
1991	1,732,487	698,403	17,516	715,919	82,626	448,826	1,082,119	409,877	240,491	16,916	102,420	42,388
1992	1,929,046	775,139	20,742	795,881	90,355	506,456	1,211,982	439,000	278,064	18,097	106,595	44,246
1993	2,127,710	862,330	26,233	888,563	101,564	564,674	1,351,673	475,157	300,880	19,097	111,416	47,280
1994	2,347,195	966,920	21,661	988,581	116,179	601,968	1,474,370	537,233	335,592	20,136	116,565	50,770
1995	2,560,353	1,075,311	22,922	1,098,233	129,353	622,569	1,591,449	600,283	368,621	21,178	120,896	54,511
1996	2,799,545	1,197,168	23,839	1,221,007	140,649	670,361	1,750,719	646,804	402,022	22,323	125,412	56,932
1997	3,051,979	1,302,318	23,367	1,325,685	154,450	740,844	1,912,079	712,243	427,657	23,447	130,164	60,806
1998	3,327,140	1,517,708	4,983	1,522,691	171,534	746,474	2,097,631	780,060	449,449	24,747	134,444	64,772
1999	3,521,274	1,663,685	20,737	1,684,422	187,356	761,740	2,258,806	790,905	471,563	25,599	137,555	67,537
2000	3,840,678	1,810,871	15,223	1,826,094	199,934	817,599	2,443,759	875,921	520,998	27,173	141,342	69,551
2001	3,962,300	1,836,065	10,662	1,846,727	208,657	836,896	2,474,966	896,202	591,132	27,350	144,875	71,119
2002	4,101,353	1,931,802	3,441	1,935,243	221,574	849,655	2,563,324	887,018	651,011	27,720	147,957	72,063
2003	4,295,837	2,058,412	16,796	2,075,208	236,839	879,827	2,718,196	866,925	710,716	28,354	151,509	74,723
2004	4,805,315	2,256,485	19,159	2,275,644	258,335	949,483	2,966,792	1,055,292	783,231	30,751	156,266	78,332
2005	5,252,121	2,480,518	9,695	2,490,213	288,735	1,030,462	3,231,940	1,171,478	848,703	32,384	162,183	82,656
2006	5,866,389	2,752,453	17,075	2,769,528	319,346	1,126,897	3,577,079	1,359,237	930,073	34,894	168,121	87,256
2007	6,268,520	2,899,795	15,584	2,915,379	343,575	1,202,445	3,774,249	1,486,021	1,008,250	36,359	172,404	92,477
2008	6,415,310	2,935,011	10,885	2,945,896	353,826	1,211,720	3,803,790	1,468,449	1,143,071	36,486	175,827	93,628
2009	6,312,840	2,821,072	18,111	2,839,183	341,795	1,246,918	3,744,306	1,312,174	1,256,360	35,187	179,406	90,298
2010	6,697,447	2,877,911	5,536	2,883,447	353,426	1,364,648	3,894,669	1,362,728	1,440,050	36,555	183,216	89,570
2011	7,123,699	3,018,768	8,803	3,027,571	331,382	1,521,388	4,217,577	1,421,842	1,484,280	38,157	186,694	92,199
2012	7,284,777	3,100,728	15,791	3,116,519	339,871	1,551,827	4,328,475	1,452,119	1,504,183	38,228	190,561	93,644
2013	7,411,631	3,214,828	39,049	3,253,877	400,118	1,523,020	4,376,779	1,460,174	1,574,678	37,922	195,443	96,946
2014	7,812,413	3,424,296	22,138	3,446,434	422,246	1,600,749	4,624,937	1,518,672	1,668,804	39,040	200,111	99,809

Personal Income and Employment by Area: Davenport-Moline-Rock Island, IA-IL

(Thousands of dollars, except as noted.)

| Year | Personal income, total | Derivation of personal income | | | | | | | | | Per capita personal income (dollars) | Population (persons) | Total employment |
| | | Earnings by place of work | | | Less: Contributions for government social insurance | Plus: Adjustment for residence | Equals: Net earnings by place of residence | Plus: Dividends, interest, and rent | Plus: Personal current transfer receipts | | | | |
		Nonfarm	Farm	Total									
1970	1,625,992	1,316,965	48,364	1,365,329	86,009	-24,042	1,255,278	249,970	120,744	4,281	379,817	169,173
1971	1,721,687	1,389,245	39,893	1,429,138	93,458	-24,680	1,311,000	269,772	140,915	4,515	381,302	167,145
1972	1,891,929	1,525,647	59,947	1,585,594	108,874	-27,349	1,449,371	289,892	152,666	4,953	382,010	171,157
1973	2,174,843	1,745,649	100,802	1,846,451	145,158	-34,594	1,666,699	330,150	177,994	5,655	384,562	183,158
1974	2,437,357	1,997,345	80,378	2,077,723	173,786	-45,510	1,858,427	378,621	200,309	6,241	390,568	193,442
1975	2,706,693	2,139,126	126,030	2,265,156	182,626	-50,080	2,032,450	423,356	250,887	6,833	396,120	192,380
1976	2,904,331	2,361,747	83,964	2,445,711	206,986	-61,988	2,176,737	446,425	281,169	7,282	398,850	194,882
1977	3,194,877	2,647,658	69,582	2,717,240	233,113	-79,894	2,404,233	492,079	298,565	7,981	400,292	199,126
1978	3,510,847	2,906,926	91,583	2,998,509	265,345	-93,775	2,639,389	548,593	322,865	8,727	402,294	202,184
1979	3,921,540	3,297,772	77,154	3,374,926	315,315	-111,065	2,948,546	613,299	359,695	9,716	403,603	207,010
1980	4,262,007	3,544,100	-3,913	3,540,187	335,077	-123,751	3,081,359	746,923	433,725	10,539	404,420	202,488
1981	4,743,841	3,760,774	68,794	3,829,568	380,316	-124,793	3,324,459	910,606	508,776	11,709	405,162	201,299
1982	4,908,876	3,643,896	38,353	3,682,249	362,166	-109,010	3,211,073	1,092,194	605,609	12,210	402,024	190,760
1983	4,898,016	3,612,334	-51,993	3,560,341	361,772	-102,645	3,095,924	1,135,546	666,546	12,338	396,986	186,120
1984	5,387,379	3,915,877	80,114	3,995,991	403,808	-110,705	3,481,478	1,247,878	658,023	13,712	392,904	190,977
1985	5,586,812	4,059,006	106,178	4,165,184	426,120	-111,881	3,627,183	1,274,721	684,908	14,443	386,807	191,204
1986	5,597,506	4,039,270	73,382	4,112,652	428,583	-101,808	3,582,261	1,305,935	709,310	14,729	380,036	188,955
1987	5,869,829	4,330,970	95,775	4,426,745	455,506	-108,308	3,862,931	1,289,641	717,257	15,680	374,353	191,033
1988	6,043,922	4,509,652	53,648	4,563,300	489,641	-103,721	3,969,938	1,323,336	750,648	16,314	370,464	194,882
1989	6,479,697	4,770,730	78,925	4,849,655	524,235	-105,385	4,220,035	1,466,650	793,012	17,567	368,854	199,096
1990	6,803,832	5,092,450	80,068	5,172,518	563,266	-110,858	4,498,394	1,448,791	856,647	18,473	368,316	203,953
1991	6,986,020	5,233,483	66,233	5,299,716	591,533	-114,780	4,593,403	1,472,767	919,850	18,832	370,975	207,790
1992	7,448,352	5,544,369	105,292	5,649,661	618,887	-119,949	4,910,825	1,510,697	1,026,830	19,939	373,565	207,908
1993	7,543,628	5,626,164	65,738	5,691,902	641,018	-114,287	4,936,597	1,537,190	1,069,841	20,159	374,198	206,295
1994	7,866,536	5,939,367	92,223	6,031,590	686,347	-125,042	5,220,201	1,562,351	1,083,984	21,010	374,425	209,569
1995	8,297,634	6,239,425	16,812	6,256,237	720,545	-130,527	5,405,165	1,731,042	1,161,427	22,128	374,979	214,131
1996	8,869,704	6,557,809	117,691	6,675,500	739,240	-128,070	5,808,190	1,862,155	1,199,359	23,671	374,708	218,500
1997	9,338,243	6,976,896	96,402	7,073,298	794,611	-147,512	6,131,175	1,998,610	1,208,458	24,902	375,006	223,429
1998	9,854,305	7,369,072	70,673	7,439,745	836,527	-148,836	6,454,382	2,138,539	1,261,384	26,240	375,549	229,654
1999	9,936,116	7,507,593	36,263	7,543,856	844,465	-140,550	6,558,841	2,062,222	1,315,053	26,378	376,678	229,807
2000	10,446,674	7,826,111	69,716	7,895,827	871,902	-141,525	6,882,400	2,167,264	1,397,010	27,801	375,763	231,646
2001	10,698,132	7,980,997	59,323	8,040,320	888,368	-122,534	7,029,418	2,154,037	1,514,677	28,562	374,561	227,874
2002	10,971,325	8,262,520	45,875	8,308,395	911,156	-138,301	7,258,938	2,071,687	1,640,700	29,356	373,740	224,393
2003	11,314,711	8,525,901	127,978	8,653,879	940,214	-160,493	7,553,172	2,084,252	1,677,287	30,336	372,975	224,208
2004	12,036,141	9,103,567	170,248	9,273,815	1,002,999	-175,675	8,095,141	2,191,197	1,749,803	32,291	372,740	227,964
2005	12,425,704	9,533,588	71,488	9,605,076	1,065,429	-152,443	8,387,204	2,145,374	1,893,126	33,324	372,876	231,790
2006	13,165,449	10,036,721	67,357	10,104,078	1,104,108	-173,130	8,826,840	2,313,329	2,025,280	35,224	373,762	232,372
2007	13,978,012	10,490,268	134,296	10,624,564	1,160,773	-151,036	9,312,755	2,476,659	2,188,598	37,263	375,121	234,085
2008	14,941,611	10,958,201	203,893	11,162,094	1,214,139	-141,858	9,806,097	2,663,039	2,472,475	39,689	376,467	234,716
2009	14,591,862	10,664,852	101,494	10,766,346	1,184,363	-163,533	9,418,450	2,408,878	2,764,534	38,592	378,108	226,282
2010	15,027,322	10,955,766	90,901	11,046,667	1,232,816	-207,847	9,606,004	2,378,953	3,042,365	39,521	380,241	223,698
2011	16,034,624	11,494,279	258,116	11,752,395	1,164,597	-246,044	10,341,754	2,720,480	2,972,390	42,094	380,926	227,391
2012	16,353,073	11,857,828	146,841	12,004,669	1,195,447	-266,292	10,542,930	2,890,583	2,919,560	42,794	382,139	228,484
2013	16,416,695	11,837,502	301,008	12,138,510	1,358,083	-263,961	10,516,466	2,956,682	2,943,547	42,838	383,230	228,350
2014	16,734,644	12,053,014	141,792	12,194,806	1,373,559	-202,609	10,618,638	3,069,444	3,046,562	43,690	383,030	229,544

Personal Income and Employment by Area: Dayton, OH

(Thousands of dollars, except as noted.)

Year	Personal income, total	Earnings by place of work			Less: Contributions for government social insurance	Plus: Adjustment for residence	Equals: Net earnings by place of residence	Plus: Dividends, interest, and rent	Plus: Personal current transfer receipts	Per capita personal income (dollars)	Population (persons)	Total employment
		Nonfarm	Farm	Total								
1970	3,722,924	3,396,597	19,936	3,416,533	206,990	-243,317	2,966,226	536,049	220,649	4,554	817,533	388,647
1971	3,848,361	3,431,466	18,705	3,450,171	213,624	-234,452	3,002,095	577,264	269,002	4,714	816,329	370,912
1972	4,196,348	3,771,169	22,439	3,793,608	249,182	-253,053	3,291,373	607,553	297,422	5,155	813,964	380,981
1973	4,550,710	4,094,938	38,039	4,132,977	313,612	-272,078	3,547,287	657,539	345,884	5,644	806,273	389,418
1974	4,874,518	4,270,747	41,241	4,311,988	335,862	-267,535	3,708,591	734,418	431,509	6,102	798,827	389,620
1975	5,256,852	4,455,420	35,020	4,490,440	342,172	-253,345	3,894,923	807,026	554,903	6,590	797,720	377,791
1976	5,770,798	4,981,218	30,386	5,011,604	397,541	-287,948	4,326,115	860,498	584,185	7,267	794,070	386,876
1977	6,345,040	5,522,333	24,938	5,547,271	443,501	-322,226	4,781,544	954,775	608,721	8,047	788,517	399,513
1978	6,961,871	6,073,110	24,825	6,097,935	502,416	-354,765	5,240,754	1,065,943	655,174	8,829	788,528	414,200
1979	7,674,110	6,649,276	42,521	6,691,797	573,379	-396,368	5,722,050	1,188,317	763,743	9,699	791,260	421,805
1980	8,288,774	6,910,741	27,641	6,938,382	592,645	-404,794	5,940,943	1,400,448	947,383	10,466	792,002	412,506
1981	8,903,451	7,474,435	2,936	7,477,371	684,596	-625,812	6,166,963	1,682,924	1,053,564	11,258	790,829	408,425
1982	9,295,183	7,541,173	14,243	7,555,416	698,140	-623,174	6,234,102	1,838,349	1,222,732	11,823	786,167	394,889
1983	9,938,022	8,065,780	-10,541	8,055,239	778,279	-648,902	6,628,058	2,013,083	1,296,881	12,686	783,366	397,786
1984	11,002,922	9,015,183	36,095	9,051,278	897,233	-721,361	7,432,684	2,231,469	1,338,769	14,002	785,813	418,017
1985	11,791,148	9,740,531	49,998	9,790,529	998,701	-773,609	8,018,219	2,345,186	1,427,743	14,947	788,847	431,975
1986	12,435,384	10,287,642	35,647	10,323,289	1,092,539	-796,906	8,433,844	2,481,007	1,520,533	15,720	791,049	443,823
1987	12,914,929	10,678,207	29,137	10,707,344	1,134,955	-798,753	8,773,636	2,557,435	1,583,858	16,221	796,181	455,751
1988	13,940,536	11,655,954	35,824	11,691,778	1,283,795	-867,861	9,540,122	2,726,773	1,673,641	17,368	802,640	464,150
1989	14,957,113	12,285,353	47,404	12,332,757	1,363,771	-888,406	10,080,580	3,112,298	1,764,235	18,641	802,358	471,695
1990	15,587,365	12,722,368	45,026	12,767,394	1,450,070	-915,250	10,402,074	3,199,579	1,985,712	19,379	804,335	473,295
1991	16,174,964	13,092,593	27,917	13,120,510	1,529,416	-940,940	10,650,154	3,403,238	2,121,572	19,974	809,809	470,098
1992	16,885,932	13,735,105	53,109	13,788,214	1,603,403	-951,953	11,232,858	3,318,702	2,334,372	20,732	814,480	464,432
1993	17,555,532	14,375,400	41,646	14,417,046	1,695,606	-1,044,629	11,676,811	3,475,959	2,402,762	21,490	816,922	469,215
1994	18,377,710	15,135,699	45,918	15,181,617	1,812,080	-1,140,711	12,228,826	3,641,036	2,507,848	22,553	814,885	481,730
1995	19,453,961	15,885,212	30,974	15,916,186	1,915,624	-1,231,761	12,768,801	4,036,546	2,648,614	23,852	815,608	491,268
1996	20,192,146	16,427,436	44,535	16,471,971	1,962,614	-1,283,914	13,225,443	4,226,066	2,740,637	24,800	814,188	492,909
1997	21,198,024	17,255,638	66,260	17,321,898	2,022,000	-1,397,282	13,902,616	4,462,743	2,832,665	26,130	811,250	499,170
1998	22,047,212	17,873,663	46,723	17,920,386	2,030,258	-1,357,014	14,533,114	4,632,455	2,881,643	27,180	811,168	502,399
1999	22,554,593	18,448,890	26,549	18,475,439	2,092,661	-1,393,005	14,989,773	4,598,713	2,966,107	27,914	808,010	496,794
2000	23,692,043	19,231,770	42,183	19,273,953	2,113,431	-1,482,615	15,677,907	4,836,707	3,177,429	29,397	805,938	502,378
2001	24,294,071	19,558,119	48,764	19,606,883	2,146,773	-1,425,525	16,034,585	4,751,026	3,508,460	30,199	804,479	496,090
2002	24,611,814	19,817,531	25,554	19,843,085	2,142,873	-1,436,355	16,263,857	4,603,112	3,744,845	30,601	804,286	487,419
2003	25,140,751	20,374,862	38,461	20,413,323	2,217,942	-1,481,082	16,714,299	4,507,384	3,919,068	31,234	804,926	484,066
2004	25,707,773	21,070,391	53,523	21,123,914	2,321,192	-1,460,765	17,341,957	4,267,108	4,098,708	31,898	805,930	484,093
2005	26,434,674	21,513,557	41,233	21,554,790	2,369,230	-1,456,847	17,728,713	4,369,036	4,336,925	32,848	804,766	483,208
2006	27,989,467	22,413,370	38,857	22,452,227	2,475,592	-1,448,402	18,528,233	4,831,505	4,629,729	34,835	803,498	481,929
2007	28,723,114	22,345,944	44,013	22,389,957	2,475,722	-1,365,320	18,548,915	5,221,255	4,952,944	35,821	801,852	480,711
2008	29,321,877	22,220,206	30,037	22,250,243	2,504,264	-1,313,683	18,432,296	5,264,666	5,624,915	36,643	800,209	470,722
2009	28,531,937	21,297,370	52,204	21,349,574	2,420,954	-1,322,561	17,606,059	4,797,221	6,128,657	35,714	798,895	449,999
2010	29,219,105	21,800,556	39,921	21,840,477	2,449,161	-1,426,767	17,964,549	4,717,463	6,537,093	36,513	800,245	446,434
2011	31,001,862	22,807,335	69,151	22,876,486	2,299,182	-1,489,286	19,088,018	5,220,172	6,693,672	38,688	801,334	452,902
2012	31,737,772	23,414,498	43,531	23,458,029	2,355,513	-1,465,771	19,636,745	5,543,505	6,557,522	39,562	802,234	455,204
2013	31,949,042	23,619,494	117,973	23,737,467	2,609,990	-1,380,805	19,746,672	5,528,754	6,673,616	39,854	801,645	455,691
2014	33,143,730	24,490,019	52,328	24,542,347	2,729,770	-1,381,387	20,431,190	5,747,338	6,965,202	41,386	800,836	462,191

Personal Income and Employment by Area: Decatur, AL

(Thousands of dollars, except as noted.)

Year	Personal income, total	Earnings by place of work			Less: Contributions for government social insurance	Plus: Adjustment for residence	Equals: Net earnings by place of residence	Plus: Dividends, interest, and rent	Plus: Personal current transfer receipts	Per capita personal income (dollars)	Population (persons)	Total employment
		Nonfarm	Farm	Total								
1970	350,240	251,236	13,280	264,516	18,344	38,830	285,002	33,852	31,386	3,335	105,018	41,444
1971	375,168	259,855	13,605	273,460	19,308	44,366	298,518	38,772	37,878	3,485	107,661	41,034
1972	406,812	286,009	15,993	302,002	22,367	43,653	323,288	41,884	41,640	3,709	109,678	42,354
1973	452,237	322,760	25,527	348,287	29,339	39,669	358,617	46,362	47,258	4,094	110,455	44,291
1974	490,482	372,222	10,504	382,726	35,236	34,378	381,868	53,372	55,242	4,346	112,864	46,325
1975	562,630	418,008	22,106	440,114	39,306	28,305	429,113	59,722	73,795	4,931	114,103	46,956
1976	620,918	458,101	28,380	486,481	43,639	31,900	474,742	64,972	81,204	5,368	115,667	47,493
1977	688,494	514,776	27,274	542,050	49,012	38,248	531,286	73,092	84,116	5,879	117,115	49,637
1978	777,804	601,331	21,239	622,570	58,621	39,780	603,729	84,546	89,529	6,520	119,287	52,721
1979	888,487	682,596	26,101	708,697	68,680	48,773	688,790	96,434	103,263	7,354	120,822	53,931
1980	954,025	695,623	10,421	706,044	69,876	70,292	706,460	120,461	127,104	7,921	120,435	51,505
1981	1,069,570	753,288	20,057	773,345	81,159	85,362	777,548	148,956	143,066	8,887	120,351	51,147
1982	1,127,295	771,530	14,944	786,474	85,271	92,556	793,759	172,219	161,317	9,309	121,091	49,815
1983	1,217,778	831,594	5,425	837,019	92,425	114,533	859,127	183,902	174,749	9,988	121,928	50,679
1984	1,392,047	928,052	26,803	954,855	104,725	144,698	994,828	210,030	187,189	11,270	123,522	53,337
1985	1,525,469	1,000,432	19,773	1,020,205	113,028	185,384	1,092,561	233,076	199,832	12,196	125,076	54,919
1986	1,626,421	1,054,588	25,274	1,079,862	118,461	207,349	1,168,750	247,401	210,270	12,854	126,532	56,295
1987	1,718,101	1,132,563	27,374	1,159,937	125,489	211,203	1,245,651	257,538	214,912	13,407	128,146	58,491
1988	1,872,583	1,210,641	41,230	1,251,871	138,353	249,422	1,362,940	284,367	225,276	14,514	129,017	60,490
1989	2,035,906	1,301,529	45,530	1,347,059	149,201	254,475	1,452,333	322,472	261,101	15,641	130,162	62,258
1990	2,170,813	1,405,622	33,469	1,439,091	163,235	260,963	1,536,819	342,590	291,404	16,431	132,118	65,211
1991	2,298,585	1,505,454	46,433	1,551,887	176,513	245,359	1,620,733	354,108	323,744	17,126	134,218	65,427
1992	2,469,532	1,599,398	43,713	1,643,111	184,644	293,271	1,751,738	352,162	365,632	18,164	135,959	65,640
1993	2,560,422	1,684,128	36,775	1,720,903	197,412	288,661	1,812,152	363,021	385,249	18,552	138,014	67,205
1994	2,725,988	1,743,467	51,368	1,794,835	205,850	323,485	1,912,470	402,994	410,524	19,619	138,947	67,605
1995	2,855,051	1,826,307	25,330	1,851,637	217,009	335,000	1,969,628	441,748	443,675	20,335	140,404	69,872
1996	2,964,086	1,914,177	40,469	1,954,646	224,534	300,324	2,030,436	464,539	469,111	20,935	141,587	71,005
1997	3,089,298	2,021,256	42,605	2,063,861	235,839	274,562	2,102,584	491,705	495,009	21,610	142,959	72,474
1998	3,314,881	2,192,504	57,988	2,250,492	251,513	276,111	2,275,090	529,979	509,812	22,989	144,192	74,079
1999	3,434,585	2,313,872	61,957	2,375,829	265,226	260,002	2,370,605	524,963	539,017	23,653	145,207	75,092
2000	3,538,641	2,352,960	43,622	2,396,582	269,690	265,723	2,392,615	564,585	581,441	24,222	146,095	75,879
2001	3,614,135	2,420,585	64,564	2,485,149	281,352	246,840	2,450,637	564,193	599,305	24,661	146,552	75,461
2002	3,592,438	2,417,136	33,732	2,450,868	276,138	216,341	2,391,071	563,994	637,373	24,528	146,464	72,965
2003	3,737,492	2,465,664	54,197	2,519,861	282,093	221,881	2,459,649	597,367	680,476	25,359	147,386	72,060
2004	3,955,113	2,626,536	87,245	2,713,781	298,061	219,521	2,635,241	612,488	707,384	26,846	147,324	73,994
2005	4,093,635	2,716,783	72,208	2,788,991	311,223	227,031	2,704,799	623,433	765,403	27,585	148,399	74,755
2006	4,257,593	2,829,542	16,694	2,846,236	324,461	230,827	2,752,602	666,243	838,748	28,475	149,519	75,301
2007	4,487,772	2,945,476	32,417	2,977,893	342,415	240,534	2,876,012	704,641	907,119	29,781	150,690	77,379
2008	4,714,457	2,968,468	44,774	3,013,242	349,852	248,357	2,911,747	789,772	1,012,938	31,039	151,890	76,321
2009	4,703,136	2,803,475	47,154	2,850,629	333,193	383,284	2,900,720	687,660	1,114,756	30,686	153,269	72,061
2010	4,838,045	2,880,709	32,409	2,913,118	349,081	351,912	2,915,949	719,672	1,202,424	31,444	153,863	71,058
2011	4,919,169	2,962,568	2,556	2,965,124	322,954	340,231	2,982,401	728,295	1,208,473	31,961	153,914	72,512
2012	5,037,961	3,029,386	25,563	3,054,949	328,900	339,144	3,065,193	746,667	1,226,101	32,750	153,833	72,726
2013	5,114,180	3,040,915	94,351	3,135,266	376,317	341,904	3,100,853	755,090	1,258,237	33,383	153,199	73,060
2014	5,268,904	3,155,975	75,227	3,231,202	382,168	334,098	3,183,132	784,482	1,301,290	34,418	153,084	72,818

Personal Income and Employment by Area: Decatur, IL

(Thousands of dollars, except as noted.)

Year	Personal income, total	Earnings by place of work			Less: Contributions for government social insurance	Plus: Adjustment for residence	Equals: Net earnings by place of residence	Plus: Dividends, interest, and rent	Plus: Personal current transfer receipts	Per capita personal income (dollars)	Population (persons)	Total employment
		Nonfarm	Farm	Total								
1970	535,509	489,476	10,288	499,764	34,906	-46,468	418,390	73,080	44,039	4,287	124,905	61,590
1971	574,294	517,514	12,685	530,199	37,852	-49,197	443,150	78,322	52,822	4,584	125,278	60,980
1972	621,979	569,313	10,017	579,330	43,869	-56,918	478,543	85,585	57,851	4,966	125,241	62,469
1973	695,367	626,257	23,435	649,692	55,686	-63,841	530,165	96,019	69,183	5,479	126,910	65,047
1974	770,903	699,521	25,338	724,859	64,811	-74,799	585,249	108,127	77,527	6,034	127,752	66,355
1975	844,448	731,588	37,107	768,695	66,126	-78,777	623,792	121,217	99,439	6,535	129,218	65,268
1976	921,709	821,666	28,793	850,459	75,820	-90,536	684,103	127,804	109,802	7,106	129,701	66,311
1977	1,004,527	905,752	28,199	933,951	83,754	-101,504	748,693	140,710	115,124	7,647	131,366	68,395
1978	1,104,695	1,019,169	21,022	1,040,191	96,485	-117,813	825,893	157,693	121,109	8,343	132,404	69,932
1979	1,179,169	1,075,183	26,143	1,101,326	105,044	-122,336	873,946	172,542	132,681	8,909	132,364	69,000
1980	1,295,283	1,154,349	7,733	1,162,082	112,300	-136,997	912,785	219,063	163,435	9,872	131,205	67,250
1981	1,447,272	1,232,702	25,701	1,258,403	128,901	-143,284	986,218	272,394	188,660	11,108	130,295	67,071
1982	1,489,775	1,200,225	17,011	1,217,236	126,890	-127,235	963,111	311,398	215,266	11,595	128,485	63,475
1983	1,484,880	1,195,830	-9,713	1,186,117	127,257	-116,695	942,165	314,834	227,881	11,698	126,932	60,376
1984	1,650,507	1,340,296	19,603	1,359,899	148,894	-127,427	1,083,578	346,112	220,817	13,096	126,033	62,722
1985	1,729,993	1,400,784	24,463	1,425,247	158,147	-130,544	1,136,556	361,328	232,109	13,843	124,970	62,271
1986	1,773,258	1,441,262	21,468	1,462,730	163,100	-147,581	1,152,049	374,664	246,545	14,443	122,775	62,625
1987	1,847,429	1,524,060	18,364	1,542,424	169,262	-158,207	1,214,955	380,261	252,213	15,328	120,527	62,642
1988	1,923,853	1,602,567	11,177	1,613,744	183,046	-152,549	1,278,149	384,031	261,673	16,164	119,024	63,093
1989	2,080,812	1,681,912	25,595	1,707,507	192,222	-159,333	1,355,952	444,274	280,586	17,675	117,723	64,147
1990	2,152,966	1,774,763	18,461	1,793,224	197,029	-159,743	1,436,452	412,133	304,381	18,359	117,271	64,900
1991	2,192,263	1,807,790	10,554	1,818,344	206,415	-158,593	1,453,336	409,633	329,294	18,581	117,984	65,857
1992	2,361,618	1,881,317	30,313	1,911,630	209,510	-161,055	1,541,065	449,772	370,781	19,963	118,297	65,119
1993	2,401,846	1,945,464	21,164	1,966,628	220,566	-169,073	1,576,989	434,511	390,346	20,366	117,933	65,228
1994	2,472,588	2,007,118	35,406	2,042,524	229,876	-175,667	1,636,981	440,799	394,808	21,045	117,490	65,479
1995	2,550,671	2,035,011	4,948	2,039,959	232,692	-173,827	1,633,440	499,531	417,700	21,747	117,289	65,836
1996	2,724,202	2,198,539	35,233	2,233,772	248,948	-199,861	1,784,963	500,515	438,724	23,369	116,573	68,553
1997	2,784,941	2,248,002	30,525	2,278,527	253,983	-206,577	1,817,967	517,397	449,577	24,069	115,706	68,850
1998	2,931,932	2,385,113	12,526	2,397,639	267,296	-221,300	1,909,043	560,295	462,594	25,395	115,453	68,930
1999	3,095,498	2,605,710	13,402	2,619,112	285,900	-247,559	2,085,653	538,175	471,670	26,884	115,142	71,559
2000	3,176,668	2,620,895	22,787	2,643,682	286,002	-251,709	2,105,971	577,851	492,846	27,744	114,499	71,821
2001	3,265,994	2,654,121	24,597	2,678,718	288,353	-240,402	2,149,963	584,712	531,319	28,749	113,604	68,120
2002	3,214,633	2,626,882	17,701	2,644,583	281,280	-235,095	2,128,208	506,576	579,849	28,558	112,564	65,577
2003	3,302,249	2,709,576	21,361	2,730,937	291,224	-238,893	2,200,820	502,309	599,120	29,597	111,572	65,563
2004	3,558,611	2,901,064	50,906	2,951,970	315,130	-249,021	2,387,819	554,661	616,131	32,007	111,181	65,618
2005	3,686,826	3,056,951	23,584	3,080,535	335,745	-256,834	2,487,956	537,432	661,438	33,190	111,083	65,934
2006	3,850,080	3,170,216	30,436	3,200,652	344,737	-257,473	2,598,442	572,024	679,614	34,746	110,808	66,486
2007	4,107,087	3,348,429	50,780	3,399,209	366,988	-263,268	2,768,953	593,928	744,206	37,084	110,751	67,945
2008	4,313,609	3,412,038	69,259	3,481,297	375,798	-261,172	2,844,327	665,908	803,374	39,006	110,588	67,240
2009	4,316,568	3,260,512	49,834	3,310,346	360,614	-187,056	2,762,676	656,108	897,784	38,982	110,732	64,968
2010	4,300,087	3,214,732	46,004	3,260,736	359,311	-198,259	2,703,166	632,618	964,303	38,825	110,757	64,143
2011	4,546,066	3,375,022	83,584	3,458,606	340,534	-197,311	2,920,761	697,737	927,568	41,110	110,582	65,196
2012	4,537,015	3,428,323	42,989	3,471,312	346,066	-269,919	2,855,327	740,242	941,446	41,229	110,043	64,597
2013	4,632,913	3,409,163	139,550	3,548,713	387,845	-255,967	2,904,901	743,736	984,276	42,335	109,435	62,872
2014	4,703,812	3,646,366	77,573	3,723,939	409,024	-376,374	2,938,541	775,433	989,838	43,413	108,350	62,883

Personal Income and Employment by Area: Deltona-Daytona Beach-Ormond Beach, FL

(Thousands of dollars, except as noted.)

Year	Personal income, total	Derivation of personal income									Per capita personal income (dollars)	Population (persons)	Total employment
		Earnings by place of work			Less: Contributions for government social insurance	Plus: Adjustment for residence	Equals: Net earnings by place of residence	Plus: Dividends, interest, and rent	Plus: Personal current transfer receipts				
		Nonfarm	Farm	Total									
1970	646,019	361,251	9,803	371,054	23,287	19,770	367,537	181,426	97,056	3,694	174,894	64,013
1971	721,257	401,811	11,223	413,034	27,196	20,515	406,353	201,470	113,434	3,965	181,923	67,875
1972	824,740	470,648	13,503	484,151	33,731	21,930	472,350	222,571	129,819	4,348	189,672	74,167
1973	974,987	565,830	17,467	583,297	46,286	24,595	561,606	257,056	156,325	4,780	203,993	82,359
1974	1,106,157	633,137	16,556	649,693	54,411	24,954	620,236	302,068	183,853	5,095	217,106	86,169
1975	1,233,758	670,832	21,824	692,656	56,789	26,976	662,843	338,972	231,943	5,483	225,008	85,659
1976	1,350,069	734,447	21,117	755,564	62,502	29,717	722,779	371,097	256,193	5,864	230,241	86,843
1977	1,511,330	814,863	19,171	834,034	69,862	33,309	797,481	428,200	285,649	6,355	237,833	91,275
1978	1,755,442	952,878	21,542	974,420	83,901	41,547	932,066	507,432	315,944	7,112	246,836	98,192
1979	2,042,397	1,103,165	20,979	1,124,144	102,201	48,858	1,070,801	602,607	368,989	7,830	260,852	104,567
1980	2,441,158	1,252,082	27,051	1,279,133	117,822	57,612	1,218,923	776,711	445,524	8,954	272,648	110,011
1981	2,862,264	1,400,184	27,496	1,427,680	142,423	77,446	1,362,703	974,072	525,489	10,077	284,026	114,209
1982	3,122,221	1,484,486	40,034	1,524,520	156,730	98,586	1,466,376	1,059,594	596,251	10,585	294,958	117,353
1983	3,533,238	1,659,085	44,242	1,703,327	174,334	122,494	1,651,487	1,219,126	662,625	11,571	305,348	123,065
1984	3,949,944	1,899,047	42,595	1,941,642	204,642	151,982	1,888,982	1,361,758	699,204	12,501	315,969	131,569
1985	4,391,745	2,126,891	40,643	2,167,534	233,859	181,042	2,114,717	1,517,888	759,140	13,395	327,855	140,900
1986	4,794,608	2,336,208	44,216	2,380,424	263,237	217,027	2,334,214	1,637,563	822,831	14,090	340,285	148,201
1987	5,190,472	2,598,851	41,088	2,639,939	288,771	257,742	2,608,910	1,703,648	877,914	14,639	354,554	149,553
1988	5,725,082	2,842,418	48,483	2,890,901	327,681	305,264	2,868,484	1,871,718	984,880	15,485	369,706	156,611
1989	6,315,766	2,988,469	47,893	3,036,362	355,333	356,354	3,037,383	2,189,867	1,088,516	16,431	384,379	156,972
1990	6,723,095	3,159,307	47,618	3,206,925	369,847	415,422	3,252,500	2,275,406	1,195,189	16,655	403,674	155,591
1991	6,923,185	3,276,330	56,995	3,333,325	387,571	429,678	3,375,432	2,211,319	1,336,434	16,658	415,595	155,691
1992	7,337,111	3,500,346	64,726	3,565,072	412,273	472,400	3,625,199	2,196,581	1,515,331	17,234	425,733	156,162
1993	7,771,312	3,745,544	61,361	3,806,905	440,756	510,016	3,876,165	2,260,596	1,634,551	17,845	435,486	162,045
1994	8,241,386	3,954,628	62,090	4,016,718	474,970	547,697	4,089,445	2,398,787	1,753,154	18,506	445,335	166,426
1995	8,854,389	4,229,682	59,703	4,289,385	508,047	583,923	4,365,261	2,595,381	1,893,747	19,527	453,432	173,778
1996	9,423,585	4,478,586	59,170	4,537,756	529,476	643,802	4,652,082	2,767,965	2,003,538	20,461	460,565	177,992
1997	9,990,837	4,690,279	67,347	4,757,626	554,799	724,999	4,927,826	2,965,979	2,097,032	21,217	470,889	180,114
1998	10,565,539	4,900,774	65,012	4,965,786	575,456	820,109	5,210,439	3,189,764	2,165,336	22,058	478,995	183,660
1999	11,067,128	5,282,420	67,841	5,350,261	610,521	907,716	5,647,456	3,172,094	2,247,578	22,739	486,692	187,769
2000	11,875,083	5,624,489	66,013	5,690,502	646,397	1,019,739	6,063,844	3,432,624	2,378,615	23,965	495,514	192,852
2001	12,694,509	6,159,349	66,948	6,226,297	706,071	1,071,911	6,592,137	3,486,506	2,615,866	25,135	505,047	199,894
2002	13,268,608	6,470,833	61,682	6,532,515	748,580	1,204,603	6,988,538	3,481,105	2,798,965	25,707	516,153	206,150
2003	14,173,079	6,970,661	56,301	7,026,962	806,041	1,396,503	7,617,424	3,576,293	2,979,362	26,791	529,021	214,266
2004	15,677,202	7,605,505	62,775	7,668,280	888,471	1,628,775	8,408,584	4,013,828	3,254,790	28,701	546,232	223,458
2005	16,924,306	8,196,704	75,445	8,272,149	969,100	1,887,282	9,190,331	4,176,059	3,557,916	30,045	563,305	234,675
2006	18,351,212	8,765,865	66,411	8,832,276	1,063,097	2,148,255	9,917,434	4,572,769	3,861,009	31,690	579,087	244,471
2007	19,436,159	8,896,832	67,495	8,964,327	1,090,691	2,347,350	10,220,986	5,116,784	4,098,389	32,973	589,451	245,828
2008	19,821,289	8,650,737	61,470	8,712,207	1,080,687	2,448,090	10,079,610	5,155,434	4,586,245	33,544	590,912	235,682
2009	18,742,064	8,134,461	59,848	8,194,309	1,040,724	2,261,446	9,415,031	4,334,334	4,992,699	31,799	589,388	223,003
2010	19,466,828	8,285,723	53,215	8,338,938	1,066,240	2,246,690	9,519,388	4,545,150	5,402,290	32,957	590,678	220,054
2011	20,156,186	8,337,276	37,643	8,374,919	981,049	2,215,200	9,609,070	4,959,129	5,587,987	34,062	591,753	222,768
2012	20,561,067	8,685,244	35,418	8,720,662	1,025,368	2,358,109	10,053,403	4,886,538	5,621,126	34,521	595,602	225,629
2013	20,973,787	8,873,228	40,134	8,913,362	1,170,023	2,406,326	10,149,665	4,981,952	5,842,170	34,889	601,151	229,206
2014	22,060,823	9,297,149	40,079	9,337,228	1,227,877	2,568,289	10,677,640	5,187,567	6,195,616	36,169	609,939	235,006

Personal Income and Employment by Area: Denver-Aurora-Broomfield, CO

(Thousands of dollars, except as noted.)

		Derivation of personal income										
		Earnings by place of work			Less: Contributions for government social insurance	Plus: Adjustment for residence	Equals: Net earnings by place of residence	Plus: Dividends, interest, and rent	Plus: Personal current transfer receipts	Per capita personal income (dollars)	Population (persons)	Total employment
Year	Personal income, total	Nonfarm	Farm	Total								
1970	5,302,191	4,712	1,125,162	4,414,245	26,626	4,440,871	270,949	-111,392	4,058,530	874,132	369,529	567,136
1971	6,038,318	5,193	1,162,772	5,066,428	23,366	5,089,794	320,688	-133,500	4,635,606	974,910	427,802	597,433
1972	6,790,412	5,632	1,205,736	5,777,079	25,378	5,802,457	387,316	-158,080	5,257,061	1,062,317	471,034	638,174
1973	7,660,058	6,139	1,247,871	6,584,221	24,903	6,609,124	508,353	-191,689	5,909,082	1,202,367	548,609	688,969
1974	8,485,776	6,720	1,262,795	7,201,184	32,259	7,233,443	566,765	-208,879	6,457,799	1,388,415	639,562	697,029
1975	9,371,415	7,290	1,285,565	7,812,839	37,955	7,850,794	597,161	-224,816	7,028,817	1,526,827	815,771	696,348
1976	10,360,493	7,870	1,316,528	8,729,610	20,824	8,750,434	680,395	-254,766	7,815,273	1,651,279	893,941	721,876
1977	11,639,057	8,662	1,343,631	9,919,435	23,133	9,942,568	779,024	-299,294	8,864,250	1,835,016	939,791	763,237
1978	13,477,044	9,694	1,390,221	11,617,675	23,197	11,640,872	936,019	-358,723	10,346,130	2,114,400	1,016,514	821,600
1979	15,390,251	10,747	1,432,057	13,406,382	13,171	13,419,553	1,137,696	-449,532	11,832,325	2,424,218	1,133,708	870,090
1980	17,657,153	12,086	1,460,960	15,249,265	25,601	15,274,866	1,310,693	-555,643	13,408,530	2,949,469	1,299,154	901,316
1981	20,356,426	13,589	1,497,985	17,397,513	11,188	17,408,701	1,620,340	-625,263	15,163,098	3,670,391	1,522,937	939,574
1982	22,567,114	14,642	1,541,261	19,161,640	6,212	19,167,852	1,831,815	-651,383	16,684,654	4,163,007	1,719,453	968,403
1983	24,221,953	15,343	1,578,689	20,358,985	26,176	20,385,161	1,974,064	-642,795	17,768,302	4,564,889	1,888,762	980,047
1984	26,450,156	16,529	1,600,224	22,259,709	14,552	22,274,261	2,229,228	-643,043	19,401,990	5,061,369	1,986,797	1,034,156
1985	28,056,753	17,286	1,623,121	23,614,842	19,681	23,634,523	2,418,292	-673,353	20,542,878	5,435,459	2,078,416	1,054,857
1986	29,023,089	17,727	1,637,259	24,329,446	19,923	24,349,369	2,515,287	-663,771	21,170,311	5,620,388	2,232,390	1,047,201
1987	29,823,690	18,134	1,644,586	24,811,683	29,466	24,841,149	2,545,953	-615,043	21,680,153	5,723,293	2,420,244	1,033,523
1988	31,325,908	19,121	1,638,280	26,017,810	28,334	26,046,144	2,755,195	-606,476	22,684,473	6,082,249	2,559,186	1,053,281
1989	33,958,427	20,714	1,639,407	27,534,532	22,435	27,556,967	2,951,817	-592,385	24,012,765	7,091,412	2,854,250	1,065,789
1990	36,039,557	21,736	1,658,024	29,372,241	14,816	29,387,057	3,221,655	-583,608	25,581,794	7,390,444	3,067,319	1,084,091
1991	38,224,665	22,455	1,702,298	31,379,483	10,303	31,389,786	3,524,060	-567,311	27,298,415	7,541,594	3,384,656	1,108,061
1992	41,337,201	23,474	1,760,945	34,289,681	29,343	34,319,024	3,808,348	-593,661	29,917,015	7,624,425	3,795,761	1,129,013
1993	44,830,647	24,642	1,819,298	37,255,932	43,203	37,299,135	4,179,066	-586,872	32,533,197	8,216,842	4,080,608	1,174,291
1994	48,143,329	25,843	1,862,948	39,582,273	16,130	39,598,403	4,464,308	-496,104	34,637,991	9,177,636	4,327,702	1,223,582
1995	52,319,871	27,383	1,910,680	42,480,853	30,701	42,511,554	4,763,894	-484,666	37,262,994	10,212,798	4,844,079	1,259,599
1996	56,453,768	28,810	1,959,552	45,939,855	20,003	45,959,858	5,092,701	-533,713	40,333,444	11,095,242	5,025,082	1,304,522
1997	60,781,761	30,206	2,012,227	49,844,680	27,672	49,872,352	5,494,675	-567,243	43,810,434	11,908,114	5,063,213	1,362,615
1998	67,894,297	32,941	2,061,091	55,825,794	24,786	55,850,580	5,730,749	-321,803	49,798,028	12,995,621	5,100,648	1,422,883
1999	73,790,888	34,831	2,118,555	62,134,421	29,177	62,163,598	6,277,361	-523,326	55,362,911	13,039,553	5,388,424	1,467,480
2000	83,150,979	38,301	2,170,977	69,833,580	25,050	69,858,630	6,951,818	-58,185	62,848,627	14,610,255	5,692,097	1,526,010
2001	87,814,662	39,578	2,218,759	73,766,390	36,317	73,802,707	7,296,309	-57,468	66,448,930	15,163,745	6,201,987	1,526,943
2002	89,516,440	39,491	2,266,781	74,181,211	32,773	74,213,984	7,587,112	698,940	67,325,812	15,089,048	7,101,580	1,530,760
2003	90,840,721	39,757	2,284,876	75,043,239	20,232	75,063,471	7,693,370	636,444	68,006,545	15,408,093	7,426,083	1,517,677
2004	94,772,802	41,119	2,304,818	78,610,926	49,943	78,660,869	8,183,155	732,875	71,210,589	15,840,360	7,721,853	1,537,435
2005	100,982,951	43,289	2,332,749	83,120,432	51,912	83,172,344	8,659,906	671,172	75,183,610	17,533,485	8,265,856	1,574,535
2006	108,649,293	45,763	2,374,194	88,548,299	38,597	88,586,896	9,193,315	156,978	79,550,559	20,206,081	8,892,653	1,611,167
2007	113,819,351	47,058	2,418,686	91,290,194	54,025	91,344,219	9,647,553	174,202	81,870,868	22,432,505	9,515,978	1,668,243
2008	119,788,248	48,616	2,463,971	96,328,821	27,369	96,356,190	10,062,931	-275,037	86,018,222	22,430,338	11,339,688	1,686,986
2009	115,164,563	45,893	2,509,417	92,692,621	31,358	92,723,979	9,722,919	-543,235	82,457,825	20,071,666	12,635,072	1,648,371
2010	117,673,725	46,068	2,554,335	94,724,120	30,599	94,754,719	9,835,143	-1,002,293	83,917,283	19,396,270	14,360,172	1,636,520
2011	127,319,100	48,953	2,600,843	98,477,046	64,033	98,541,079	9,262,365	-884,974	88,393,740	24,103,534	14,821,826	1,673,341
2012	136,424,788	51,524	2,647,780	105,282,263	34,904	105,317,167	9,782,662	-898,350	94,636,155	26,913,546	14,875,087	1,715,370
2013	139,315,183	51,603	2,699,750	110,219,217	47,590	110,266,807	11,560,149	-828,281	97,878,377	25,990,453	15,446,353	1,777,179
2014	148,684,245	53,983	2,754,258	118,229,758	61,456	118,291,214	12,439,366	-770,974	105,080,874	27,100,820	16,502,551	1,837,288

Personal Income and Employment by Area: Des Moines-West Des Moines, IA

(Thousands of dollars, except as noted.)

Year	Personal income, total	Derivation of personal income								Per capita personal income (dollars)	Population (persons)	Total employment
		Earnings by place of work			Less: Contributions for government social insurance	Plus: Adjustment for residence	Equals: Net earnings by place of residence	Plus: Dividends, interest, and rent	Plus: Personal current transfer receipts			
		Nonfarm	Farm	Total								
1970	1,606,275	1,321,631	51,333	1,372,964	96,859	-41,385	1,234,720	244,479	127,076	4,407	364,467	187,011
1971	1,731,205	1,428,413	40,576	1,468,989	108,259	-44,766	1,315,964	268,749	146,492	4,681	369,809	189,174
1972	1,917,114	1,581,973	58,300	1,640,273	126,616	-50,523	1,463,134	294,296	159,684	5,136	373,239	195,315
1973	2,164,328	1,754,211	112,447	1,866,658	162,979	-55,750	1,647,929	329,746	186,653	5,708	379,164	203,486
1974	2,367,930	1,957,432	64,587	2,022,019	189,351	-62,641	1,770,027	379,565	218,338	6,178	383,309	207,989
1975	2,659,157	2,158,184	73,588	2,231,772	203,688	-68,754	1,959,330	424,282	275,545	6,885	386,229	211,349
1976	2,916,768	2,391,208	65,152	2,456,360	226,760	-73,717	2,155,883	454,669	306,216	7,501	388,848	218,073
1977	3,214,951	2,689,927	31,862	2,721,789	252,881	-83,193	2,385,715	508,898	320,338	8,281	388,226	226,273
1978	3,618,206	2,995,792	80,810	3,076,602	291,525	-91,253	2,693,824	571,689	352,693	9,274	390,158	234,444
1979	4,038,497	3,392,773	49,838	3,442,611	344,884	-101,409	2,996,318	648,467	393,712	10,345	390,395	241,384
1980	4,365,763	3,581,664	15,720	3,597,384	361,661	-107,889	3,127,834	771,269	466,660	11,118	392,658	241,141
1981	4,832,465	3,825,379	53,719	3,879,098	411,680	-115,526	3,351,892	945,103	535,470	12,279	393,561	236,774
1982	5,149,432	3,950,966	32,174	3,983,140	427,680	-118,009	3,437,451	1,104,687	607,294	13,115	392,625	233,881
1983	5,408,680	4,198,348	-8,792	4,189,556	454,509	-126,494	3,608,553	1,150,441	649,686	13,741	393,623	236,788
1984	5,879,143	4,585,372	28,443	4,613,815	510,009	-137,976	3,965,830	1,253,300	660,013	14,889	394,875	244,988
1985	6,168,520	4,822,247	41,488	4,863,735	544,317	-146,673	4,172,745	1,294,632	701,143	15,577	395,994	249,172
1986	6,454,316	5,075,540	59,709	5,135,249	586,402	-156,861	4,391,986	1,335,018	727,312	16,258	397,004	252,303
1987	6,844,366	5,469,251	79,243	5,548,494	629,331	-172,032	4,747,131	1,359,181	738,054	17,111	399,998	259,847
1988	7,383,643	6,025,848	39,021	6,064,869	711,419	-193,614	5,159,836	1,444,660	779,147	18,238	404,844	270,261
1989	8,032,637	6,488,063	93,387	6,581,450	762,746	-208,456	5,610,248	1,599,231	823,158	19,556	410,759	279,484
1990	8,680,688	6,986,585	72,630	7,059,215	847,489	-230,335	5,981,391	1,795,302	903,995	20,764	418,062	290,422
1991	8,969,867	7,355,292	55,449	7,410,741	899,795	-240,944	6,270,002	1,718,518	981,347	21,137	424,368	295,382
1992	9,613,624	7,930,203	87,279	8,017,482	964,088	-262,630	6,790,764	1,759,180	1,063,680	22,253	432,014	300,284
1993	9,984,551	8,334,995	17,551	8,352,546	1,014,802	-275,006	7,062,738	1,804,703	1,117,110	22,738	439,105	305,489
1994	10,685,072	8,873,202	97,543	8,970,745	1,094,386	-289,769	7,586,590	1,938,069	1,160,413	24,029	444,671	313,372
1995	11,413,099	9,434,388	56,275	9,490,663	1,161,292	-309,999	8,019,372	2,167,407	1,226,320	25,285	451,372	326,428
1996	12,199,451	9,989,120	132,079	10,121,199	1,190,667	-327,677	8,602,855	2,297,164	1,299,432	26,677	457,294	333,775
1997	12,907,529	10,623,564	107,054	10,730,618	1,290,980	-349,900	9,089,738	2,487,973	1,329,818	27,922	462,263	338,246
1998	13,963,117	11,561,361	69,533	11,630,894	1,381,115	-379,638	9,870,141	2,711,020	1,381,956	29,825	468,172	346,398
1999	14,666,442	12,440,151	41,380	12,481,531	1,478,844	-408,276	10,594,411	2,647,136	1,424,895	30,817	475,924	352,645
2000	15,612,798	13,113,349	59,766	13,173,115	1,535,149	-423,894	11,214,072	2,858,963	1,539,763	32,308	483,243	357,779
2001	16,334,495	13,829,854	45,554	13,875,408	1,611,940	-451,409	11,812,059	2,837,113	1,685,323	33,352	489,761	358,966
2002	17,158,844	14,686,806	57,632	14,744,438	1,696,118	-543,108	12,505,212	2,798,944	1,854,688	34,575	496,276	358,200
2003	17,873,288	15,539,747	69,733	15,609,480	1,794,192	-596,876	13,218,412	2,800,443	1,854,433	35,505	503,406	359,024
2004	19,646,085	16,670,637	174,349	16,844,986	1,901,494	-358,978	14,584,514	3,147,960	1,913,611	38,427	511,257	368,993
2005	20,510,263	17,470,349	133,189	17,603,538	1,996,564	-391,111	15,215,863	3,227,604	2,066,796	39,323	521,578	377,513
2006	21,943,131	18,490,281	104,279	18,594,560	2,098,291	-467,473	16,028,796	3,625,312	2,289,023	41,189	532,738	388,790
2007	23,470,411	19,527,537	167,405	19,694,942	2,230,377	-450,872	17,013,693	3,993,831	2,462,887	43,177	543,590	400,247
2008	24,469,448	20,231,004	219,138	20,450,142	2,312,674	-620,039	17,517,429	4,037,431	2,914,588	44,197	553,644	406,061
2009	24,280,016	20,231,076	162,110	20,393,186	2,315,460	-559,039	17,518,687	3,616,699	3,144,630	43,157	562,601	401,294
2010	25,007,906	20,651,708	121,541	20,773,249	2,384,865	-508,465	17,879,919	3,693,383	3,434,604	43,729	571,883	399,544
2011	26,378,115	21,201,167	258,096	21,459,263	2,211,478	-606,446	18,641,339	4,207,113	3,529,663	45,421	580,741	406,251
2012	28,229,462	22,662,286	213,659	22,875,945	2,315,567	-660,635	19,899,743	4,770,393	3,559,326	47,891	589,453	414,102
2013	28,249,496	22,894,565	260,784	23,155,349	2,688,991	-568,534	19,897,824	4,705,984	3,645,688	47,076	600,086	423,568
2014	29,841,639	24,245,841	225,794	24,471,635	2,814,936	-565,007	21,091,692	4,887,749	3,862,198	48,797	611,549	433,140

Personal Income and Employment by Area: Detroit-Warren-Dearborn, MI

(Thousands of dollars, except as noted.)

Year	Personal income, total	Earnings by place of work			Less: Contributions for government social insurance	Plus: Adjustment for residence	Equals: Net earnings by place of residence	Plus: Dividends, interest, and rent	Plus: Personal current transfer receipts	Per capita personal income (dollars)	Population (persons)	Total employment
		Nonfarm	Farm	Total								
1970	20,374,344	17,632,804	34,095	17,666,899	1,256,732	-160,431	16,249,736	2,527,233	1,597,375	4,589	4,439,498	1,819,813
1971	21,945,609	18,867,570	31,718	18,899,288	1,384,176	-165,181	17,349,931	2,674,304	1,921,374	4,921	4,459,793	1,803,088
1972	24,315,290	21,076,020	41,104	21,117,124	1,647,001	-195,495	19,274,628	2,842,956	2,197,706	5,460	4,453,517	1,854,501
1973	27,102,996	23,830,092	46,739	23,876,831	2,162,977	-206,306	21,507,548	3,085,789	2,509,659	6,110	4,435,796	1,939,903
1974	28,715,202	24,611,749	46,143	24,657,892	2,307,355	-274,162	22,076,375	3,517,690	3,121,137	6,494	4,422,090	1,926,974
1975	30,109,414	24,735,544	48,695	24,784,239	2,257,459	-277,941	22,248,839	3,765,277	4,095,298	6,852	4,394,458	1,808,270
1976	33,585,706	28,237,070	46,030	28,283,100	2,634,598	-248,684	25,399,818	4,040,710	4,145,178	7,700	4,361,574	1,876,295
1977	37,827,938	32,384,996	54,020	32,439,016	3,025,529	-260,599	29,152,888	4,443,636	4,231,414	8,692	4,351,973	1,960,763
1978	42,155,846	36,418,701	37,866	36,456,567	3,511,594	-273,277	32,671,696	4,967,026	4,517,124	9,676	4,356,619	2,043,005
1979	45,892,205	39,271,729	42,807	39,314,536	3,917,301	-286,408	35,110,827	5,546,616	5,234,762	10,533	4,356,811	2,045,908
1980	48,589,034	39,167,440	42,303	39,209,743	3,863,007	-285,764	35,060,972	6,523,498	7,004,564	11,196	4,339,778	1,921,891
1981	51,156,828	40,471,005	42,368	40,513,373	4,317,843	-223,088	35,972,442	7,882,590	7,301,796	11,964	4,275,732	1,876,138
1982	52,534,309	40,024,050	38,997	40,063,047	4,330,097	-218,130	35,514,820	8,934,890	8,084,599	12,440	4,223,098	1,789,482
1983	55,695,569	42,424,937	28,272	42,453,209	4,666,625	-164,196	37,622,388	9,489,979	8,583,202	13,308	4,185,050	1,798,974
1984	62,002,092	47,935,081	43,472	47,978,553	5,454,814	-176,159	42,347,580	10,998,196	8,656,316	14,823	4,182,763	1,897,635
1985	68,117,203	53,810,967	47,716	53,858,683	6,254,816	-206,965	47,396,902	11,863,983	8,856,318	16,234	4,195,986	2,012,186
1986	72,716,353	57,977,137	32,547	58,009,684	6,757,969	-273,413	50,978,302	12,478,371	9,259,680	17,232	4,219,771	2,067,378
1987	75,204,428	60,086,040	43,870	60,129,910	6,922,493	-326,729	52,880,688	12,879,958	9,443,782	17,731	4,241,494	2,118,647
1988	80,605,895	64,913,481	43,872	64,957,353	7,645,427	-373,988	56,937,938	13,836,399	9,831,558	19,037	4,234,083	2,168,474
1989	86,535,177	68,635,303	58,979	68,694,282	8,080,689	-364,240	60,249,353	15,734,097	10,551,727	20,419	4,237,904	2,227,089
1990	90,176,443	71,092,181	53,028	71,145,209	8,530,458	-376,733	62,238,018	16,577,951	11,360,474	21,213	4,250,986	2,244,909
1991	90,694,440	71,325,768	52,748	71,378,516	8,683,410	-391,982	62,303,124	15,864,662	12,526,654	21,162	4,285,663	2,181,991
1992	95,899,447	76,413,632	50,528	76,464,160	9,228,883	-559,332	66,675,945	15,963,351	13,260,151	22,200	4,319,806	2,182,305
1993	101,041,690	80,769,828	49,252	80,819,080	9,788,206	-779,435	70,251,439	16,620,845	14,169,406	23,256	4,344,712	2,209,546
1994	108,638,320	86,915,379	47,119	86,962,498	10,725,777	-941,848	75,294,873	19,059,027	14,284,420	24,886	4,365,423	2,279,342
1995	115,251,985	92,307,481	50,486	92,357,967	11,339,600	-1,320,982	79,697,385	20,494,618	15,059,982	26,195	4,399,746	2,339,032
1996	121,417,339	96,835,308	44,670	96,879,978	11,578,415	-1,528,491	83,773,072	21,858,924	15,785,343	27,389	4,433,102	2,391,801
1997	127,727,804	101,490,235	46,255	101,536,490	12,118,953	-1,584,172	87,833,365	23,014,454	16,879,985	28,765	4,440,400	2,425,583
1998	136,077,181	109,529,143	45,461	109,574,604	12,818,886	-1,899,380	94,856,338	24,606,548	16,614,295	30,636	4,441,717	2,460,908
1999	142,291,107	116,059,222	55,667	116,114,889	13,573,005	-1,987,265	100,554,619	24,153,075	17,583,413	31,992	4,447,649	2,508,007
2000	152,778,998	125,246,298	36,347	125,282,645	14,323,481	-2,455,539	108,503,625	26,298,731	17,976,642	34,290	4,455,503	2,575,515
2001	153,182,206	124,816,710	32,098	124,848,808	14,264,884	-2,072,008	108,511,916	24,799,609	19,870,681	34,332	4,461,855	2,527,930
2002	152,821,824	124,489,978	32,971	124,522,949	14,284,314	-2,207,822	108,030,813	24,325,907	20,465,104	34,292	4,456,433	2,491,093
2003	156,225,388	127,133,687	40,163	127,173,850	14,488,999	-2,679,300	110,005,551	24,853,761	21,366,076	35,080	4,453,371	2,471,561
2004	159,669,450	130,143,438	63,947	130,207,385	14,899,660	-2,710,190	112,597,535	24,877,760	22,194,155	35,914	4,445,887	2,466,487
2005	164,070,912	132,970,869	64,875	133,035,744	15,354,794	-2,981,104	114,699,846	25,762,507	23,608,559	37,028	4,431,048	2,483,625
2006	166,643,316	132,955,202	78,346	133,033,548	15,505,842	-2,902,614	114,625,092	26,995,577	25,022,647	37,790	4,409,697	2,454,080
2007	170,343,288	133,101,102	65,040	133,166,142	15,670,905	-3,045,652	114,449,585	28,607,422	27,286,281	38,917	4,377,116	2,445,366
2008	171,181,956	130,761,234	76,115	130,837,349	15,592,692	-3,167,012	112,077,645	28,056,387	31,047,924	39,447	4,339,504	2,393,616
2009	160,890,324	118,229,788	55,059	118,284,847	14,230,690	-1,875,785	102,178,372	23,926,180	34,785,772	37,315	4,311,728	2,237,792
2010	163,185,565	119,919,697	62,751	119,982,448	14,375,507	-2,447,462	103,159,479	23,041,580	36,984,506	38,028	4,291,176	2,230,406
2011	174,305,119	126,804,868	114,212	126,919,080	13,498,163	-2,156,385	111,264,532	26,143,755	36,896,832	40,658	4,287,145	2,302,999
2012	181,745,277	133,499,805	93,655	133,593,460	14,105,017	-2,458,099	117,030,344	27,957,711	36,757,222	42,336	4,292,912	2,345,608
2013	183,592,294	136,592,340	95,631	136,687,971	16,393,876	-2,212,002	118,082,093	28,587,385	36,922,816	42,742	4,295,394	2,387,622
2014	191,199,038	142,645,379	78,228	142,723,607	17,030,430	-2,421,908	123,271,269	29,678,020	38,249,749	44,500	4,296,611	2,429,818

Personal Income and Employment by Area: Dothan, AL

(Thousands of dollars, except as noted.)

Year	Personal income, total	Earnings by place of work			Less: Contributions for government social insurance	Plus: Adjustment for residence	Equals: Net earnings by place of residence	Plus: Dividends, interest, and rent	Plus: Personal current transfer receipts	Per capita personal income (dollars)	Population (persons)	Total employment
		Nonfarm	Farm	Total								
1970	278,317	176,717	18,077	194,794	13,410	33,701	215,085	33,866	29,366	3,021	92,122	41,593
1971	308,866	202,903	18,535	221,438	15,620	30,277	236,095	38,855	33,916	3,281	94,147	43,039
1972	348,428	237,135	26,184	263,319	19,290	24,189	268,218	42,463	37,747	3,560	97,881	45,497
1973	426,276	299,676	42,225	341,901	28,113	18,943	332,731	49,634	43,911	4,245	100,409	49,519
1974	475,592	343,593	34,200	377,793	33,309	18,531	363,015	59,642	52,935	4,513	105,391	51,163
1975	518,564	350,582	40,273	390,855	33,482	21,299	378,672	70,227	69,665	4,799	108,046	49,593
1976	596,296	426,049	38,312	464,361	41,752	21,826	444,435	75,681	76,180	5,432	109,777	51,727
1977	640,429	473,923	24,878	498,801	46,462	22,864	475,203	84,259	80,967	5,771	110,966	53,046
1978	724,970	537,742	33,225	570,967	53,693	22,532	539,806	96,930	88,234	6,429	112,772	54,447
1979	789,063	573,477	31,322	604,799	59,092	30,431	576,138	110,066	102,859	6,944	113,631	54,259
1980	866,284	656,721	-14,240	642,481	67,832	32,796	607,445	138,199	120,640	7,565	114,505	55,050
1981	1,033,751	692,195	44,870	737,065	76,922	64,446	724,589	171,157	138,005	8,944	115,576	54,328
1982	1,059,681	701,019	24,051	725,070	78,952	73,501	719,619	187,237	152,825	9,130	116,060	52,319
1983	1,116,355	749,479	9,441	758,920	84,530	76,187	750,577	199,456	166,322	9,626	115,974	52,832
1984	1,261,587	820,590	55,594	876,184	94,704	78,948	860,428	225,214	175,945	10,829	116,501	54,538
1985	1,326,805	884,454	28,328	912,782	102,271	81,177	891,688	245,898	189,219	11,309	117,318	55,398
1986	1,413,241	956,730	22,117	978,847	109,452	82,540	951,935	261,745	199,561	12,014	117,628	56,956
1987	1,514,427	1,038,312	35,133	1,073,445	117,653	82,718	1,038,510	268,381	207,536	12,728	118,980	59,215
1988	1,653,247	1,127,892	59,962	1,187,854	131,994	80,118	1,135,978	294,544	222,725	13,858	119,302	61,390
1989	1,839,169	1,235,505	75,457	1,310,962	144,222	71,948	1,238,688	349,333	251,148	15,396	119,455	64,645
1990	1,884,198	1,320,484	53,615	1,374,099	155,000	29,330	1,248,429	367,715	268,054	15,594	120,826	66,534
1991	1,977,400	1,377,489	82,868	1,460,357	163,316	19,541	1,316,582	371,231	289,587	16,141	122,507	67,078
1992	2,150,915	1,508,302	76,357	1,584,659	176,485	35,036	1,443,210	378,564	329,141	17,397	123,636	68,384
1993	2,190,343	1,556,876	62,167	1,619,043	184,225	23,581	1,458,399	386,410	345,534	17,526	124,976	69,447
1994	2,324,932	1,625,894	79,605	1,705,499	194,603	20,677	1,531,573	422,872	370,487	18,594	125,036	69,704
1995	2,475,727	1,721,174	76,707	1,797,881	207,126	19,181	1,609,936	461,726	404,065	19,669	125,872	71,949
1996	2,540,226	1,780,042	63,168	1,843,210	211,223	11,920	1,643,907	466,910	429,409	19,992	127,060	72,959
1997	2,660,691	1,858,612	46,335	1,904,947	220,356	26,877	1,711,468	498,486	450,737	20,777	128,062	74,932
1998	2,856,320	1,997,765	55,486	2,053,251	231,909	41,590	1,862,932	539,947	453,441	22,155	128,927	75,264
1999	2,993,912	2,073,049	78,790	2,151,839	239,328	64,700	1,977,211	538,218	478,483	23,035	129,970	75,404
2000	3,089,798	2,138,124	38,684	2,176,808	247,002	70,823	2,000,629	577,786	511,383	23,582	131,024	75,351
2001	3,323,267	2,200,504	94,752	2,295,256	252,430	91,749	2,134,575	608,240	580,452	25,289	131,413	73,774
2002	3,449,882	2,299,380	94,572	2,393,952	262,070	103,201	2,235,083	591,126	623,673	26,142	131,967	73,557
2003	3,565,023	2,387,872	86,149	2,474,021	273,120	118,084	2,318,985	578,446	667,592	26,687	133,586	74,531
2004	3,841,799	2,549,409	85,694	2,635,103	290,049	139,835	2,484,889	628,691	728,219	28,446	135,057	76,519
2005	4,116,000	2,696,744	90,115	2,786,859	307,149	173,597	2,653,307	679,141	783,552	30,122	136,643	78,240
2006	4,341,954	2,844,224	56,770	2,900,994	328,021	210,600	2,783,573	704,836	853,545	31,221	139,070	79,655
2007	4,587,205	2,905,248	54,615	2,959,863	340,247	228,294	2,847,910	813,997	925,298	32,497	141,157	81,477
2008	4,710,662	2,879,160	61,923	2,941,083	342,907	244,577	2,842,753	840,549	1,027,360	32,951	142,958	79,896
2009	4,733,692	2,834,857	61,910	2,896,767	338,557	301,194	2,859,404	758,583	1,115,705	32,783	144,396	76,665
2010	4,972,174	2,889,400	51,460	2,940,860	349,982	336,472	2,927,350	820,193	1,224,631	34,087	145,867	75,704
2011	5,111,138	2,925,572	42,746	2,968,318	316,614	338,011	2,989,715	862,875	1,258,548	34,851	146,655	75,890
2012	5,156,769	2,945,383	64,714	3,010,097	318,776	349,725	3,041,046	844,300	1,271,423	34,933	147,618	75,730
2013	5,175,896	2,982,166	123,164	3,105,330	365,842	290,984	3,030,472	842,558	1,302,866	35,069	147,592	75,777
2014	5,341,760	3,089,729	96,346	3,186,075	373,471	283,099	3,095,703	876,469	1,369,588	36,070	148,095	75894

Personal Income and Employment by Area: Dover, DE

(Thousands of dollars, except as noted.)

Year	Personal income, total	Earnings by place of work			Less: Contributions for government social insurance	Plus: Adjustment for residence	Equals: Net earnings by place of residence	Plus: Dividends, interest, and rent	Plus: Personal current transfer receipts	Per capita personal income (dollars)	Population (persons)	Total employment
		Nonfarm	Farm	Total								
1970	329,033	278,889	9,441	288,330	18,575	-15,599	254,156	53,435	21,442	3,982	82,633	42,223
1971	367,127	310,763	9,377	320,140	21,322	-15,983	282,835	58,681	25,611	4,238	86,628	43,110
1972	408,628	344,455	11,098	355,553	24,323	-15,651	315,579	64,603	28,446	4,565	89,512	45,268
1973	455,873	371,742	24,117	395,859	29,554	-14,169	352,136	70,684	33,053	5,049	90,286	46,076
1974	509,349	407,677	29,191	436,868	33,776	-14,664	388,428	80,771	40,150	5,596	91,026	45,692
1975	563,053	444,116	21,485	465,601	37,052	-14,372	414,177	91,286	57,590	6,086	92,521	44,751
1976	606,161	478,816	20,993	499,809	41,024	-13,111	445,674	97,753	62,734	6,417	94,465	44,883
1977	647,083	517,708	11,058	528,766	43,991	-13,230	471,545	107,638	67,900	6,722	96,264	45,851
1978	713,914	555,998	18,542	574,540	48,484	-7,297	518,759	121,843	73,312	7,266	98,251	45,902
1979	768,096	589,877	14,983	604,860	53,413	-2,376	549,071	134,800	84,225	7,746	99,166	46,424
1980	838,095	633,792	-63	633,729	58,556	3,916	579,089	158,850	100,156	8,528	98,280	46,321
1981	942,119	697,737	10,271	708,008	69,248	7,492	646,252	182,453	113,414	9,582	98,317	46,451
1982	1,018,692	748,781	9,497	758,278	74,883	11,769	695,164	201,623	121,905	10,266	99,225	47,096
1983	1,087,062	785,972	10,206	796,178	79,384	20,588	737,382	218,451	131,229	10,768	100,953	47,036
1984	1,188,082	860,371	15,794	876,165	87,901	24,651	812,915	239,352	135,815	11,733	101,261	48,525
1985	1,286,004	932,037	12,394	944,431	95,516	31,107	880,022	261,982	144,000	12,508	102,818	51,069
1986	1,387,137	1,011,731	12,461	1,024,192	105,128	32,097	951,161	281,424	154,552	13,247	104,713	52,893
1987	1,492,768	1,094,736	9,590	1,104,326	112,217	38,665	1,030,774	300,282	161,712	14,048	106,263	54,198
1988	1,632,851	1,186,873	26,827	1,213,700	128,407	45,180	1,130,473	323,588	178,790	15,265	106,965	55,677
1989	1,796,538	1,293,653	25,551	1,319,204	140,249	48,678	1,227,633	373,944	194,961	16,474	109,052	57,099
1990	1,902,385	1,405,820	21,541	1,427,361	150,355	50,428	1,327,434	362,063	212,888	17,041	111,638	58,224
1991	2,020,914	1,469,596	24,819	1,494,415	159,056	42,520	1,377,879	394,619	248,416	17,683	114,288	59,918
1992	2,136,521	1,562,108	28,902	1,591,010	168,611	32,970	1,455,369	405,267	275,885	18,469	115,682	61,604
1993	2,198,920	1,627,994	20,250	1,648,244	177,808	22,257	1,492,693	406,725	299,502	18,637	117,987	62,713
1994	2,299,580	1,712,638	24,506	1,737,144	188,586	14,302	1,562,860	436,123	300,597	19,318	119,039	63,944
1995	2,452,555	1,825,283	13,066	1,838,349	202,186	-50	1,636,113	475,276	341,166	20,317	120,715	65,999
1996	2,630,924	1,918,421	25,237	1,943,658	209,958	-5,518	1,728,182	513,431	389,311	21,663	121,447	67,066
1997	2,688,653	1,946,652	15,958	1,962,610	211,276	5,962	1,757,296	533,590	397,767	21,963	122,419	66,499
1998	2,863,987	2,079,306	25,618	2,104,924	224,727	3,200	1,883,397	547,504	433,086	23,086	124,056	67,720
1999	3,017,716	2,240,597	25,467	2,266,064	236,571	-2,229	2,027,264	550,394	440,058	24,024	125,611	69,932
2000	3,231,922	2,397,609	30,733	2,428,342	245,839	-4,044	2,178,459	576,222	477,241	25,402	127,229	71,384
2001	3,380,904	2,515,798	33,580	2,549,378	249,675	-25,964	2,273,739	587,280	519,885	26,162	129,228	73,820
2002	3,621,849	2,744,413	12,706	2,757,119	286,556	-9,048	2,461,515	594,448	565,886	27,475	131,824	75,439
2003	3,872,663	2,893,006	24,246	2,917,252	302,186	10,636	2,625,702	627,774	619,187	28,771	134,605	77,003
2004	4,192,957	3,121,339	45,589	3,166,928	329,963	32,714	2,869,679	646,478	676,800	30,091	139,342	79,893
2005	4,498,127	3,339,409	52,975	3,392,384	352,058	57,675	3,098,001	652,581	747,545	31,111	144,585	83,267
2006	4,792,092	3,509,734	45,781	3,555,515	371,206	84,630	3,268,939	703,981	819,172	32,010	149,704	84,479
2007	5,112,843	3,633,994	51,578	3,685,572	391,950	115,449	3,409,071	801,143	902,629	33,207	153,969	86,461
2008	5,477,785	3,762,636	55,859	3,818,495	406,046	143,082	3,555,531	863,341	1,058,913	34,686	157,925	86,557
2009	5,671,846	3,899,383	81,351	3,980,734	408,187	104,291	3,676,838	822,311	1,172,697	35,431	160,081	83,638
2010	5,693,778	3,884,192	70,815	3,955,007	407,614	15,816	3,563,209	829,313	1,301,256	34,941	162,954	84,349
2011	5,976,342	3,983,211	87,967	4,071,178	372,099	5,314	3,704,393	898,333	1,373,616	36,173	165,214	86,643
2012	6,153,524	4,100,769	105,697	4,206,466	391,521	-15,754	3,799,191	938,651	1,415,682	36,701	167,666	87,389
2013	6,253,852	4,125,387	138,370	4,263,757	452,716	17,123	3,828,164	942,313	1,483,375	36,882	169,562	89,281
2014	6,555,078	4,311,029	146,538	4,457,567	477,545	38,680	4,018,702	978,757	1,557,619	38,114	171,987	90,392

Personal Income and Employment by Area: Dubuque, IA

(Thousands of dollars, except as noted.)

Year	Personal income, total	Earnings by place of work			Less: Contributions for government social insurance	Plus: Adjustment for residence	Equals: Net earnings by place of residence	Plus: Dividends, interest, and rent	Plus: Personal current transfer receipts	Per capita personal income (dollars)	Population (persons)	Total employment
		Nonfarm	Farm	Total								
1970	338,936	307,840	17,404	325,244	23,291	-44,350	257,603	54,288	27,045	3,733	90,790	43,244
1971	360,196	331,453	14,793	346,246	26,066	-49,449	270,731	58,479	30,986	3,926	91,739	42,981
1972	396,201	372,020	15,811	387,831	30,892	-57,811	299,128	63,102	33,971	4,273	92,731	44,134
1973	448,150	422,750	22,897	445,647	40,709	-67,620	337,318	71,244	39,588	4,783	93,700	47,239
1974	498,239	487,298	13,798	501,096	48,829	-83,111	369,156	82,587	46,496	5,313	93,779	48,892
1975	549,289	517,285	20,357	537,642	50,614	-88,553	398,475	91,287	59,527	5,803	94,655	48,652
1976	597,694	574,411	13,839	588,250	57,048	-99,407	431,795	99,443	66,456	6,246	95,687	49,568
1977	674,884	665,595	12,712	678,307	65,783	-121,804	490,720	113,235	70,929	7,159	94,270	51,642
1978	750,497	731,559	27,794	759,353	74,826	-137,327	547,200	125,442	77,855	8,008	93,716	52,499
1979	809,949	808,700	15,871	824,571	85,847	-156,082	582,642	140,369	86,938	8,670	93,425	53,560
1980	857,874	847,390	-3,233	844,157	89,565	-169,577	585,015	167,876	104,983	9,155	93,701	52,948
1981	945,673	862,759	16,276	879,035	96,839	-161,501	620,695	206,116	118,862	10,135	93,307	50,728
1982	958,303	794,529	5,392	799,921	90,003	-132,006	577,912	237,670	142,721	10,417	91,992	47,472
1983	988,633	817,303	-12,104	805,199	92,792	-127,877	584,530	252,666	151,437	10,949	90,296	47,693
1984	1,108,749	898,500	30,820	929,320	105,242	-138,372	685,706	273,925	149,118	12,372	89,616	49,513
1985	1,150,463	932,931	27,501	960,432	110,615	-139,577	710,240	286,012	154,211	12,913	89,096	49,643
1986	1,177,864	924,305	38,284	962,589	111,192	-127,194	724,203	296,540	157,121	13,420	87,771	49,358
1987	1,272,647	1,040,777	46,379	1,087,156	123,784	-144,596	818,776	295,451	158,420	14,607	87,125	51,309
1988	1,308,839	1,083,148	29,898	1,113,046	132,633	-144,532	835,881	307,056	165,902	14,984	87,351	52,579
1989	1,409,996	1,131,388	50,926	1,182,314	137,136	-144,719	900,459	330,131	179,406	16,273	86,644	53,836
1990	1,473,910	1,189,733	49,245	1,238,978	148,358	-151,912	938,708	341,265	193,937	17,047	86,462	55,086
1991	1,522,485	1,246,156	35,645	1,281,801	156,993	-156,865	967,943	347,643	206,899	17,502	86,988	56,048
1992	1,653,587	1,354,302	55,414	1,409,716	169,295	-169,814	1,070,607	359,563	223,417	18,861	87,672	56,773
1993	1,705,528	1,419,319	36,742	1,456,061	178,350	-171,591	1,106,120	363,317	236,091	19,324	88,261	57,566
1994	1,827,921	1,544,528	48,326	1,592,854	196,177	-182,289	1,214,388	369,000	244,533	20,619	88,654	58,805
1995	1,936,984	1,636,039	29,762	1,665,801	207,539	-195,251	1,263,011	416,434	257,539	21,779	88,938	60,614
1996	2,022,186	1,624,367	58,676	1,683,043	198,750	-197,456	1,286,837	458,386	276,963	22,696	89,097	60,234
1997	2,096,137	1,705,153	48,299	1,753,452	214,752	-209,702	1,328,998	482,162	284,977	23,553	88,996	61,363
1998	2,227,455	1,783,205	41,147	1,824,352	223,456	-217,983	1,382,913	539,639	304,903	25,091	88,775	61,295
1999	2,244,721	1,833,712	29,395	1,863,107	227,417	-218,623	1,417,067	512,194	315,460	25,240	88,934	61,770
2000	2,380,831	1,903,143	48,407	1,951,550	233,079	-225,452	1,493,019	553,517	334,295	26,691	89,201	62,192
2001	2,419,776	1,902,641	43,056	1,945,697	230,808	-213,444	1,501,445	554,475	363,856	27,209	88,932	60,943
2002	2,493,520	1,986,944	31,725	2,018,669	239,577	-218,959	1,560,133	538,695	394,692	27,976	89,132	60,916
2003	2,578,994	2,100,262	36,296	2,136,558	254,268	-227,261	1,655,029	526,905	397,060	28,652	90,012	61,557
2004	2,764,376	2,259,799	56,763	2,316,562	268,942	-237,383	1,810,237	541,367	412,772	30,558	90,462	62,915
2005	2,884,929	2,389,947	44,468	2,434,415	284,854	-244,234	1,905,327	542,106	437,496	31,783	90,769	64,383
2006	3,114,885	2,523,787	29,052	2,552,839	298,492	-246,520	2,007,827	618,837	488,221	34,133	91,258	66,093
2007	3,329,232	2,607,062	39,975	2,647,037	309,322	-246,960	2,090,755	707,186	531,291	36,136	92,130	66,793
2008	3,532,167	2,750,612	39,615	2,790,227	324,818	-247,255	2,218,154	714,935	599,078	38,178	92,519	66,311
2009	3,420,855	2,694,811	13,494	2,708,305	326,051	-242,898	2,139,356	667,302	614,197	36,804	92,948	65,515
2010	3,470,790	2,757,341	30,824	2,788,165	348,348	-268,300	2,171,517	642,451	656,822	36,965	93,893	66,669
2011	3,722,195	2,901,270	62,706	2,963,976	331,507	-291,752	2,340,717	719,375	662,103	39,385	94,507	68,642
2012	3,925,257	3,118,409	70,808	3,189,217	347,090	-342,758	2,499,369	763,003	662,885	41,255	95,147	69,877
2013	3,997,256	3,125,774	97,396	3,223,170	393,614	-310,135	2,519,421	788,197	689,638	41,676	95,912	70,161
2014	4,159,988	3,272,202	73,000	3,345,202	403,074	-323,510	2,618,618	821,657	719,713	43,167	96,370	70,778

Personal Income and Employment by Area: Duluth, MN-WI

(Thousands of dollars, except as noted.)

Year	Personal income, total	Derivation of personal income								Per capita personal income (dollars)	Population (persons)	Total employment
		Earnings by place of work			Less: Contributions for government social insurance	Plus: Adjustment for residence	Equals: Net earnings by place of residence	Plus: Dividends, interest, and rent	Plus: Personal current transfer receipts			
		Nonfarm	Farm	Total								
1970	1,044,777	831,023	3,931	834,954	60,088	-6,921	767,945	149,352	127,480	3,554	293,960	115,741
1971	1,126,961	892,918	3,502	896,420	66,901	-7,575	821,944	159,185	145,832	3,804	296,224	116,412
1972	1,217,456	965,748	3,989	969,737	76,060	-8,233	885,444	167,881	164,131	4,120	295,529	118,378
1973	1,330,368	1,054,784	6,388	1,061,172	94,972	-8,302	957,898	186,362	186,108	4,552	292,286	121,637
1974	1,460,825	1,139,606	4,775	1,144,381	107,630	-7,313	1,029,438	214,735	216,652	5,059	288,748	123,186
1975	1,702,363	1,329,627	3,549	1,333,176	124,602	-2,578	1,205,996	240,668	255,699	5,858	290,582	126,320
1976	1,914,218	1,509,712	4,370	1,514,082	142,497	2,231	1,373,816	256,004	284,398	6,489	294,985	130,460
1977	1,980,973	1,531,644	6,518	1,538,162	144,800	-5,791	1,387,571	282,192	311,210	6,713	295,109	128,310
1978	2,273,826	1,802,795	7,071	1,809,866	173,075	-1,674	1,635,117	307,853	330,856	7,719	294,586	133,882
1979	2,512,370	1,989,221	7,888	1,997,109	197,885	4,100	1,803,324	341,988	367,058	8,482	296,193	137,174
1980	2,746,562	2,090,067	7,481	2,097,548	206,539	-10,844	1,880,165	416,655	449,742	9,266	296,407	135,992
1981	3,027,757	2,263,525	8,649	2,272,174	242,547	-17,203	2,012,424	514,189	501,144	10,263	295,015	133,167
1982	3,004,828	2,067,600	6,837	2,074,437	227,149	-18,668	1,828,620	575,550	600,658	10,284	292,192	122,580
1983	3,025,988	2,004,589	4,722	2,009,311	221,818	-14,313	1,773,180	607,661	645,147	10,559	286,582	117,782
1984	3,226,089	2,164,346	4,884	2,169,230	247,187	-13,793	1,908,250	665,812	652,027	11,480	281,016	120,193
1985	3,317,154	2,207,306	6,222	2,213,528	256,484	-14,794	1,942,250	691,062	683,842	12,019	275,987	120,332
1986	3,429,164	2,279,533	11,792	2,291,325	270,970	-19,330	2,001,025	725,616	702,523	12,634	271,434	121,403
1987	3,544,369	2,410,107	3,552	2,413,659	283,103	-23,820	2,106,736	722,805	714,828	13,172	269,076	123,967
1988	3,720,737	2,601,206	2,386	2,603,592	320,564	-23,576	2,259,452	738,245	723,040	13,911	267,468	127,214
1989	4,089,870	2,845,360	5,961	2,851,321	352,733	-22,954	2,475,634	841,479	772,757	15,245	268,268	131,705
1990	4,363,673	3,046,721	3,747	3,050,468	376,405	25,629	2,699,692	848,441	815,540	16,177	269,746	134,052
1991	4,529,954	3,237,300	1,700	3,239,000	403,334	-27,664	2,808,002	855,431	866,521	16,700	271,256	137,205
1992	4,804,776	3,460,829	4,799	3,465,628	423,800	-33,312	3,008,516	856,436	939,824	17,604	272,939	139,402
1993	4,909,203	3,546,255	4,697	3,550,952	438,077	-37,923	3,074,952	863,694	970,557	17,955	273,424	139,020
1994	5,141,403	3,721,149	5,411	3,726,560	464,397	-43,968	3,218,195	912,305	1,010,903	18,776	273,834	141,956
1995	5,462,352	3,919,545	2,895	3,922,440	487,304	-43,942	3,391,194	1,013,859	1,057,299	20,099	271,777	145,458
1996	5,754,580	4,118,581	2,958	4,121,539	506,279	-47,896	3,567,364	1,088,389	1,098,827	21,123	272,433	148,086
1997	5,967,192	4,301,849	2,008	4,303,857	530,309	-53,622	3,719,926	1,131,097	1,116,169	21,809	273,609	150,364
1998	6,406,386	4,660,673	3,512	4,664,185	564,606	-63,927	4,035,652	1,215,396	1,155,338	23,419	273,552	153,032
1999	6,667,724	4,943,442	3,294	4,946,736	596,210	-71,915	4,278,611	1,199,701	1,189,412	24,274	274,682	155,832
2000	7,098,055	5,256,267	2,362	5,258,629	624,950	-77,967	4,555,712	1,288,090	1,254,253	25,739	275,775	158,846
2001	7,246,980	5,240,527	2,729	5,243,256	628,319	-82,132	4,532,805	1,298,395	1,415,780	26,167	276,946	156,395
2002	7,638,502	5,570,781	1,820	5,572,601	656,726	-89,638	4,826,237	1,287,876	1,524,389	27,591	276,852	156,281
2003	7,888,916	5,694,934	4,356	5,699,290	672,632	-93,769	4,932,889	1,374,090	1,581,937	28,458	277,209	156,522
2004	8,197,961	5,983,267	4,502	5,987,769	703,369	-101,813	5,182,587	1,354,926	1,660,448	29,586	277,087	157,399
2005	8,276,409	6,101,961	3,260	6,105,221	732,651	-97,839	5,274,731	1,274,758	1,726,920	29,913	276,682	159,206
2006	8,679,392	6,301,059	4,106	6,305,165	762,499	-98,330	5,444,336	1,368,916	1,866,140	31,366	276,710	161,046
2007	9,178,111	6,566,413	5,153	6,571,566	795,638	-96,066	5,679,862	1,484,052	2,014,197	33,109	277,209	163,057
2008	9,621,210	6,800,716	218	6,800,934	827,819	-90,829	5,882,286	1,537,751	2,201,173	34,539	278,561	162,642
2009	9,442,729	6,467,466	-1,986	6,465,480	797,912	-94,262	5,573,306	1,425,560	2,443,863	33,789	279,465	157,187
2010	9,750,696	6,661,531	3,011	6,664,542	816,553	-85,098	5,762,891	1,416,897	2,570,908	34,850	279,789	156,365
2011	10,382,761	7,086,917	3,699	7,090,616	776,680	-89,768	6,224,168	1,582,505	2,576,088	37,094	279,907	157,286
2012	10,575,611	7,169,830	2,407	7,172,237	787,562	-85,730	6,298,945	1,695,278	2,581,388	37,822	279,614	157,629
2013	10,801,680	7,381,917	6,117	7,388,034	921,033	-92,615	6,374,386	1,761,590	2,665,704	38,585	279,942	159,583
2014	11,255,223	7,676,003	7,725	7,683,728	943,992	-96,397	6,643,339	1,832,937	2,778,947	40,166	280,218	161,342

Personal Income and Employment by Area: Durham-Chapel Hill, NC

(Thousands of dollars, except as noted.)

Year	Personal income, total	Derivation of personal income									Per capita personal income (dollars)	Population (persons)	Total employment
		Earnings by place of work			Less: Contributions for government social insurance	Plus: Adjustment for residence	Equals: Net earnings by place of residence	Plus: Dividends, interest, and rent	Plus: Personal current transfer receipts				
		Nonfarm	Farm	Total									
1970	891,876	760,309	22,672	782,981	50,259	-21,754	710,968	111,867	69,041		3,618	246,517	120,512
1971	1,005,236	865,415	24,128	889,543	59,151	-32,209	798,183	125,116	81,937		3,979	252,666	125,379
1972	1,111,782	961,911	26,764	988,675	68,592	-39,553	880,530	139,484	91,768		4,257	261,180	130,456
1973	1,223,401	1,049,825	45,351	1,095,176	86,838	-46,199	962,139	155,998	105,264		4,586	266,750	133,616
1974	1,351,127	1,161,803	36,434	1,198,237	99,818	-57,917	1,040,502	181,212	129,413		4,975	271,564	136,334
1975	1,515,010	1,283,152	42,026	1,325,178	109,791	-75,970	1,139,417	205,501	170,092		5,595	270,769	134,827
1976	1,673,097	1,426,881	47,767	1,474,648	124,369	-88,015	1,262,264	222,756	188,077		6,080	275,162	139,310
1977	1,855,481	1,606,022	46,880	1,652,902	138,761	-110,691	1,403,450	250,772	201,259		6,600	281,149	145,598
1978	2,086,004	1,843,272	45,608	1,888,880	165,451	-136,762	1,586,667	284,239	215,098		7,340	284,208	152,779
1979	2,315,219	2,067,000	33,060	2,100,060	193,578	-159,721	1,746,761	324,056	244,402		8,001	289,360	159,411
1980	2,612,343	2,291,396	29,054	2,320,450	215,340	-185,717	1,919,393	403,674	289,276		8,921	292,831	161,496
1981	2,958,025	2,553,474	49,217	2,602,691	259,568	-220,954	2,122,169	507,146	328,710		10,000	295,796	164,424
1982	3,230,105	2,792,081	46,400	2,838,481	285,480	-265,233	2,287,768	589,040	353,297		10,813	298,730	165,394
1983	3,510,617	3,085,648	29,439	3,115,087	319,465	-309,197	2,486,425	642,299	381,893		11,613	302,298	169,000
1984	4,011,623	3,558,712	57,383	3,616,095	375,208	-389,609	2,851,278	756,772	403,573		13,069	306,946	181,343
1985	4,443,928	4,040,531	39,559	4,080,090	433,856	-478,273	3,167,961	847,517	428,450		14,205	312,842	194,306
1986	4,803,669	4,405,000	45,407	4,450,407	484,101	-539,153	3,427,153	926,767	449,749		14,968	320,939	202,479
1987	5,182,997	4,838,797	41,562	4,880,359	523,175	-626,405	3,730,779	979,390	472,828		15,833	327,345	210,424
1988	5,683,986	5,311,265	50,485	5,361,750	593,448	-700,919	4,067,383	1,101,864	514,739		17,055	333,279	219,599
1989	6,344,316	5,843,935	73,992	5,917,927	652,382	-827,377	4,438,168	1,335,693	570,455		18,674	339,747	227,827
1990	6,813,738	6,385,750	76,802	6,462,552	732,497	-940,387	4,789,668	1,389,829	634,241		19,641	346,907	234,238
1991	7,211,313	6,943,077	81,031	7,024,108	806,869	-1,153,522	5,063,717	1,417,713	729,883		20,335	354,625	240,084
1992	7,883,040	7,675,618	70,716	7,746,334	877,737	-1,330,150	5,538,447	1,538,725	805,868		21,731	362,754	246,553
1993	8,396,092	8,144,926	82,794	8,227,720	932,899	-1,431,074	5,863,747	1,640,471	891,874		22,560	372,169	253,905
1994	8,852,996	8,597,275	75,492	8,672,767	1,002,171	-1,535,639	6,134,957	1,785,044	932,995		23,293	380,071	259,586
1995	9,412,287	9,233,470	77,519	9,310,989	1,078,060	-1,747,480	6,485,449	1,889,952	1,036,886		24,247	388,187	269,469
1996	10,064,292	9,886,022	78,209	9,964,231	1,149,886	-1,928,141	6,886,204	2,062,456	1,115,632		25,417	395,974	279,035
1997	10,728,749	10,730,614	74,928	10,805,542	1,241,277	-2,269,474	7,294,791	2,264,543	1,169,415		26,485	405,085	288,450
1998	11,533,460	11,717,950	83,862	11,801,812	1,346,270	-2,541,369	7,914,173	2,427,520	1,191,767		27,929	412,954	299,984
1999	12,330,420	12,949,131	80,230	13,029,361	1,474,687	-2,938,981	8,615,693	2,474,040	1,240,687		29,342	420,226	309,022
2000	13,294,240	14,541,158	80,181	14,621,339	1,626,560	-3,629,333	9,365,446	2,592,194	1,336,600		31,199	426,116	316,199
2001	13,907,610	14,770,091	96,644	14,866,735	1,664,975	-3,368,413	9,833,347	2,580,749	1,493,514		31,955	435,229	323,048
2002	14,043,374	14,828,937	38,549	14,867,486	1,655,311	-3,334,023	9,878,152	2,540,519	1,624,703		31,788	441,780	320,504
2003	14,527,653	15,285,110	46,869	15,331,979	1,727,208	-3,383,046	10,221,725	2,603,061	1,702,867		32,544	446,402	322,279
2004	15,966,908	16,384,658	68,146	16,452,804	1,817,236	-3,577,601	11,057,967	3,086,183	1,822,758		35,378	451,323	332,768
2005	16,822,530	16,907,043	74,042	16,981,085	1,891,378	-3,666,495	11,423,212	3,408,627	1,990,691		36,707	458,287	339,120
2006	18,317,183	18,411,116	74,083	18,485,199	2,053,941	-3,932,423	12,498,835	3,680,940	2,137,408		39,119	468,238	350,670
2007	19,842,551	19,886,390	66,087	19,952,477	2,245,971	-4,312,976	13,393,530	4,121,362	2,327,659		41,451	478,699	366,257
2008	20,790,010	20,576,432	48,298	20,624,730	2,341,051	-4,392,479	13,891,200	4,215,002	2,683,808		42,436	489,919	369,000
2009	20,588,778	20,686,386	48,645	20,735,031	2,339,431	-4,528,916	13,866,684	3,756,238	2,965,856		41,198	499,753	364,631
2010	21,278,104	21,442,687	53,982	21,496,669	2,330,624	-4,740,865	14,425,180	3,658,647	3,194,277		41,881	508,063	361,787
2011	22,290,645	20,988,490	26,782	21,015,272	2,059,884	-4,182,043	14,773,345	4,203,780	3,313,520		43,213	515,828	363,514
2012	23,948,202	22,616,113	57,994	22,674,107	2,158,386	-4,530,463	15,985,258	4,563,075	3,399,869		45,613	525,026	371,092
2013	23,811,042	22,846,875	73,190	22,920,065	2,544,482	-4,749,989	15,625,594	4,703,333	3,482,115		44,622	533,622	379,625
2014	24,892,430	24,075,989	95,097	24,171,086	2,691,208	-5,104,787	16,375,091	4,862,559	3,654,780		45,867	542,710	388,743

Personal Income and Employment by Area: East Stroudsburg, PA

(Thousands of dollars, except as noted.)

Year	Personal income, total	Earnings by place of work			Less: Contributions for government social insurance	Plus: Adjustment for residence	Equals: Net earnings by place of residence	Plus: Dividends, interest, and rent	Plus: Personal current transfer receipts	Per capita personal income (dollars)	Population (persons)	Total employment
		Nonfarm	Farm	Total								
1970	193,821	182,766	827	183,593	10,715	-31,854	141,024	34,704	18,093	4,265	45,441	25,965
1971	212,854	197,241	428	197,669	12,257	-32,213	153,199	38,375	21,280	4,597	46,302	26,505
1972	248,334	226,104	371	226,475	14,780	-30,212	181,483	42,232	24,619	5,077	48,917	27,900
1973	287,714	256,503	1,253	257,756	19,290	-27,558	210,908	47,910	28,896	5,564	51,711	30,353
1974	331,572	285,035	444	285,479	22,923	-21,832	240,724	55,368	35,480	6,042	54,877	31,305
1975	375,652	310,977	1,209	312,186	24,286	-22,028	265,872	61,229	48,551	6,518	57,637	31,147
1976	417,978	341,654	1,441	343,095	27,013	-20,393	295,689	66,872	55,417	6,924	60,370	31,868
1977	464,737	375,855	1,261	377,116	29,933	-18,541	328,642	76,252	59,843	7,395	62,848	33,116
1978	525,710	429,885	605	430,490	34,743	-20,507	375,240	85,108	65,362	8,022	65,535	34,888
1979	592,714	465,155	1,693	466,848	39,493	-7,482	419,873	98,326	74,515	8,728	67,911	35,265
1980	669,989	504,042	847	504,889	43,763	-1,083	460,043	121,477	88,469	9,620	69,649	35,960
1981	746,442	544,495	1,354	545,849	50,517	-2,191	493,141	151,188	102,113	10,592	70,470	36,945
1982	817,805	576,330	628	576,958	53,316	-3,430	520,212	180,798	116,795	11,408	71,688	37,363
1983	884,083	621,706	-703	621,003	60,457	3,848	564,394	190,104	129,585	12,202	72,455	38,614
1984	994,297	705,841	127	705,968	71,377	12,169	646,760	212,969	134,568	13,518	73,556	41,607
1985	1,101,592	773,186	490	773,676	80,585	20,453	713,544	243,042	145,006	14,639	75,250	43,899
1986	1,226,331	859,486	-310	859,176	91,341	34,890	802,725	267,460	156,146	15,697	78,127	46,679
1987	1,360,863	976,153	-184	975,969	104,780	38,141	909,330	288,757	162,776	16,668	81,647	49,932
1988	1,522,739	1,078,614	258	1,078,872	119,860	64,943	1,023,955	320,877	177,907	17,469	87,169	52,588
1989	1,664,412	1,174,058	307	1,174,365	129,279	80,771	1,125,857	345,393	193,162	18,003	92,452	54,322
1990	1,754,892	1,199,535	1,230	1,200,765	134,268	91,784	1,158,281	375,324	221,287	18,112	96,889	54,242
1991	1,825,425	1,192,347	805	1,193,152	134,808	142,696	1,201,040	362,727	261,658	17,990	101,469	51,670
1992	1,954,338	1,225,601	652	1,226,253	139,658	219,601	1,306,196	358,528	289,614	18,498	105,649	51,456
1993	2,098,558	1,274,725	376	1,275,101	148,263	274,281	1,401,119	388,252	309,187	19,067	110,062	52,129
1994	2,238,082	1,345,131	813	1,345,944	159,841	308,462	1,494,565	405,589	337,928	19,504	114,752	54,504
1995	2,384,942	1,414,895	221	1,415,116	168,190	333,336	1,580,262	444,275	360,405	20,030	119,070	55,406
1996	2,551,561	1,488,624	874	1,489,498	172,658	377,729	1,694,569	466,209	390,783	20,693	123,307	56,753
1997	2,744,454	1,560,336	300	1,560,636	179,586	449,896	1,830,946	499,809	413,699	21,530	127,470	58,180
1998	2,970,983	1,669,015	70	1,669,085	189,500	515,418	1,995,003	536,257	439,723	22,678	131,007	59,523
1999	3,179,319	1,799,956	-415	1,799,541	202,171	591,033	2,188,403	524,818	466,098	23,562	134,936	61,473
2000	3,549,875	2,012,083	950	2,013,033	222,748	678,660	2,468,945	575,020	505,910	25,409	139,710	65,493
2001	3,779,638	2,154,202	-112	2,154,090	238,928	716,477	2,631,639	592,478	555,521	26,289	143,775	67,379
2002	3,974,232	2,302,691	-560	2,302,131	258,370	733,637	2,777,398	584,326	612,508	26,703	148,833	69,040
2003	4,176,803	2,453,751	844	2,454,595	273,745	750,996	2,931,846	590,042	654,915	27,117	154,027	70,790
2004	4,492,768	2,707,652	2,159	2,709,811	300,275	802,860	3,212,396	572,992	707,380	28,403	158,181	72,933
2005	4,722,499	2,878,245	1,290	2,879,535	324,101	823,460	3,378,894	595,021	748,584	29,143	162,045	75,031
2006	5,029,025	3,100,117	1,058	3,101,175	345,695	863,037	3,618,517	612,989	797,519	30,445	165,185	77,718
2007	5,302,547	3,212,664	-1,175	3,211,489	365,980	884,838	3,730,347	710,189	862,011	31,685	167,352	80,446
2008	5,569,142	3,291,680	682	3,292,362	378,733	891,895	3,805,524	750,306	1,013,312	33,036	168,576	80,772
2009	5,414,796	3,222,369	1,498	3,223,867	372,152	729,611	3,581,326	724,962	1,108,508	31,966	169,390	77,981
2010	5,360,746	3,320,155	2,177	3,322,332	384,972	542,012	3,479,372	683,068	1,198,306	31,545	169,940	77,246
2011	5,639,557	3,357,471	1,884	3,359,355	353,280	636,285	3,642,360	772,968	1,224,229	33,201	169,860	76,812
2012	5,574,837	3,351,148	3,153	3,354,301	352,044	573,467	3,575,724	783,429	1,215,684	33,092	168,465	76,013
2013	5,792,186	3,277,058	3,772	3,280,830	390,326	837,785	3,728,289	807,123	1,256,774	34,657	167,130	75,225
2014	6036762	3277259	2425	3279684	392071	1007780	3895393	835493	1305876	36297	166314	74681

Personal Income and Employment by Area: Eau Claire, WI

(Thousands of dollars, except as noted.)

Year	Personal income, total	Earnings by place of work			Less: Contributions for government social insurance	Plus: Adjustment for residence	Equals: Net earnings by place of residence	Plus: Dividends, interest, and rent	Plus: Personal current transfer receipts	Per capita personal income (dollars)	Population (persons)	Total employment
		Nonfarm	Farm	Total								
1970	418,536	339,072	18,916	357,988	24,606	-15,243	318,139	58,457	41,940	3,622	115,555	51,672
1971	457,011	367,187	19,437	386,624	27,578	-15,096	343,950	64,159	48,902	3,853	118,617	52,507
1972	496,981	397,392	21,232	418,624	31,497	-14,998	372,129	69,665	55,187	4,100	121,204	53,066
1973	541,871	422,402	27,307	449,709	38,435	-13,778	397,496	78,771	65,604	4,507	120,238	53,548
1974	590,509	449,677	23,743	473,420	42,635	-12,403	418,382	91,118	81,009	4,872	121,193	53,903
1975	651,355	479,434	23,005	502,439	44,802	-10,876	446,761	101,510	103,084	5,252	124,012	54,581
1976	713,552	523,632	22,471	546,103	49,332	-8,480	488,291	108,902	116,359	5,732	124,496	55,598
1977	804,703	593,021	33,334	626,355	55,755	-8,938	561,662	122,240	120,801	6,336	127,012	58,235
1978	897,731	665,368	32,358	697,726	64,252	-8,098	625,376	138,481	133,874	6,964	128,912	60,913
1979	995,731	722,834	39,869	762,703	73,061	-5,196	684,446	155,903	155,382	7,701	129,293	62,962
1980	1,127,299	789,721	38,953	828,674	80,069	-3,627	744,978	194,403	187,918	8,579	131,405	63,315
1981	1,248,006	868,657	28,946	897,603	94,693	-6,408	796,502	242,042	209,462	9,384	132,986	63,776
1982	1,324,080	898,433	31,085	929,518	98,771	-5,618	825,129	271,984	226,967	9,901	133,738	63,651
1983	1,409,097	963,085	17,044	980,129	104,736	-6,106	869,287	294,267	245,543	10,553	133,527	63,838
1984	1,531,270	1,037,415	36,546	1,073,961	114,793	-6,791	952,377	323,071	255,822	11,411	134,188	65,777
1985	1,615,890	1,092,665	38,545	1,131,210	121,819	-6,894	1,002,497	339,240	274,153	12,048	134,120	66,855
1986	1,729,924	1,189,307	46,202	1,235,509	132,621	-9,486	1,093,402	356,288	280,234	12,886	134,252	69,351
1987	1,827,310	1,281,543	46,161	1,327,704	140,459	-8,540	1,178,705	357,704	290,901	13,512	135,233	71,536
1988	1,920,011	1,383,820	35,469	1,419,289	158,021	-8,116	1,253,152	366,473	300,386	14,105	136,125	73,958
1989	2,093,496	1,460,401	58,235	1,518,636	168,018	-6,230	1,344,388	427,393	321,715	15,260	137,187	74,933
1990	2,199,634	1,550,894	45,879	1,596,773	184,659	-3,906	1,408,208	445,227	346,199	15,966	137,771	75,588
1991	2,277,992	1,635,490	29,109	1,664,599	196,411	-5,918	1,462,270	443,351	372,371	16,350	139,325	77,150
1992	2,464,561	1,772,589	39,166	1,811,755	210,433	-6,088	1,595,234	466,945	402,382	17,527	140,614	78,688
1993	2,546,610	1,851,741	28,959	1,880,700	219,142	-4,457	1,657,101	483,858	405,651	17,936	141,985	79,787
1994	2,718,666	1,996,463	39,188	2,035,651	238,979	-8,665	1,788,007	515,874	414,785	19,012	142,998	83,136
1995	2,873,373	2,125,898	23,168	2,149,066	256,323	-13,870	1,878,873	558,194	436,306	19,961	143,950	87,319
1996	3,056,103	2,263,987	48,049	2,312,036	271,153	-19,613	2,021,270	584,096	450,737	21,100	144,842	90,392
1997	3,272,618	2,467,206	27,624	2,494,830	293,360	-29,131	2,172,339	636,590	463,689	22,441	145,834	92,863
1998	3,535,918	2,678,759	41,835	2,720,594	316,325	-34,792	2,369,477	687,676	478,765	24,141	146,470	95,088
1999	3,697,832	2,866,124	40,433	2,906,557	339,264	-36,601	2,530,692	675,446	491,694	25,091	147,378	98,773
2000	3,950,564	3,063,773	23,401	3,087,174	358,715	-42,135	2,686,324	733,678	530,562	26,575	148,656	99,703
2001	4,101,094	3,081,786	30,283	3,112,069	349,815	-35,952	2,726,302	780,550	594,242	27,404	149,655	96,802
2002	4,203,036	3,197,507	26,972	3,224,479	360,108	-45,088	2,819,283	745,786	637,967	27,863	150,846	96,782
2003	4,347,014	3,325,132	39,691	3,364,823	372,134	-46,974	2,945,715	743,339	657,960	28,633	151,816	97,569
2004	4,522,819	3,510,891	56,721	3,567,612	392,238	-47,664	3,127,710	715,850	679,259	29,480	153,419	99,605
2005	4,729,732	3,671,031	44,190	3,715,221	416,955	-48,335	3,249,931	746,820	732,981	30,552	154,809	101,493
2006	5,050,478	3,905,568	30,486	3,936,054	445,109	-55,135	3,435,810	846,337	768,331	32,340	156,167	104,406
2007	5,326,242	4,043,197	49,559	4,092,756	464,153	-46,014	3,582,589	905,638	838,015	33,784	157,654	106,232
2008	5,616,495	4,169,879	50,752	4,220,631	478,981	-25,092	3,716,558	961,778	938,159	35,391	158,700	106,385
2009	5,678,269	4,153,788	14,768	4,168,556	473,801	-26,694	3,668,061	933,954	1,076,254	35,429	160,271	103,732
2010	5,814,428	4,244,191	46,121	4,290,312	492,007	-30,260	3,768,045	887,718	1,158,665	35,973	161,633	104,267
2011	6,170,289	4,406,962	94,025	4,500,987	458,325	-22,927	4,019,735	1,011,633	1,138,921	37,892	162,838	106,545
2012	6,552,617	4,726,939	80,892	4,807,831	488,423	-47,444	4,271,964	1,115,794	1,164,859	39,982	163,891	108,851
2013	6,632,414	4,765,181	84,186	4,849,367	558,460	-41,903	4,249,004	1,181,246	1,202,164	40,220	164,903	108,856
2014	6,945,834	4,997,988	99,259	5,097,247	586,408	-41,662	4,469,177	1,228,530	1,248,127	42,090	165,024	110,298

Personal Income and Employment by Area: El Centro, CA

(Thousands of dollars, except as noted.)

| Year | Personal income, total | Derivation of personal income | | | | | | | | Per capita personal income (dollars) | Population (persons) | Total employment |
| | | Earnings by place of work | | | Less: Contributions for government social insurance | Plus: Adjustment for residence | Equals: Net earnings by place of residence | Plus: Dividends, interest, and rent | Plus: Personal current transfer receipts | | | |
		Nonfarm	Farm	Total								
1970	296,353	176,547	102,809	279,356	12,198	-42,085	225,073	33,783	37,497	3,962	74,795	34,273
1971	298,824	188,648	88,107	276,755	13,492	-40,905	222,358	36,473	39,993	3,988	74,931	34,377
1972	381,823	204,628	148,542	353,170	15,357	-40,154	297,659	40,554	43,610	5,033	75,869	35,499
1973	422,949	233,922	155,052	388,974	20,080	-41,299	327,595	48,400	46,954	5,310	79,648	37,260
1974	484,973	270,553	177,654	448,207	23,946	-49,961	374,300	54,836	55,837	5,949	81,526	39,718
1975	518,339	307,390	168,146	475,536	25,971	-61,274	388,291	61,176	68,872	6,246	82,989	42,553
1976	574,912	345,652	181,160	526,812	29,805	-69,288	427,719	62,318	84,875	6,743	85,264	44,782
1977	596,124	376,060	166,362	542,422	32,377	-75,835	434,210	67,593	94,321	6,853	86,981	44,503
1978	649,034	417,406	168,076	585,482	36,382	-83,103	465,997	79,174	103,863	7,336	88,474	44,679
1979	922,004	469,299	371,339	840,638	43,317	-81,412	715,909	91,658	114,437	10,235	90,086	46,745
1980	883,073	504,817	271,261	776,078	46,341	-92,491	637,246	112,461	133,366	9,538	92,584	45,523
1981	929,643	536,250	203,896	740,146	52,664	-56,926	630,556	140,412	158,675	9,858	94,301	43,663
1982	1,027,874	550,190	267,565	817,755	54,739	-64,909	698,107	155,559	174,208	10,742	95,688	43,260
1983	1,090,257	552,002	290,123	842,125	56,120	-63,598	722,407	176,478	191,372	11,253	96,890	42,970
1984	1,115,779	601,472	255,088	856,560	63,559	-69,006	723,995	180,842	210,942	11,447	97,475	42,308
1985	1,110,792	636,966	200,804	837,770	67,003	-68,633	702,134	181,076	227,582	11,198	99,199	41,051
1986	1,148,458	701,546	174,015	875,561	75,209	-66,651	733,701	184,749	230,008	11,614	98,885	42,325
1987	1,350,425	769,504	303,976	1,073,480	82,622	-66,346	924,512	187,287	238,626	13,494	100,077	43,579
1988	1,554,791	883,538	393,506	1,277,044	98,598	-69,166	1,109,280	193,292	252,219	15,261	101,881	47,530
1989	1,677,297	968,805	385,739	1,354,544	110,905	-70,910	1,172,729	224,188	280,380	15,949	105,166	52,145
1990	1,772,151	1,047,786	369,225	1,417,011	118,698	-72,012	1,226,301	229,565	316,285	15,989	110,839	52,121
1991	1,853,242	1,096,279	359,154	1,455,433	123,810	-64,863	1,266,760	228,832	357,650	15,820	117,143	51,265
1992	1,991,194	1,235,650	297,403	1,533,053	135,580	-70,839	1,326,634	229,313	435,247	16,081	123,823	52,634
1993	2,237,288	1,319,767	431,050	1,750,817	143,996	-69,731	1,537,090	240,124	460,074	16,852	132,758	55,335
1994	2,258,093	1,376,686	382,693	1,759,379	150,506	-72,121	1,536,752	257,742	463,599	16,812	134,315	56,933
1995	2,333,699	1,378,219	396,911	1,775,130	148,969	-67,528	1,558,633	282,209	492,857	17,036	136,986	58,101
1996	2,317,299	1,412,603	306,694	1,719,297	146,868	-63,143	1,509,286	288,765	519,248	16,794	137,987	58,050
1997	2,412,828	1,499,860	312,060	1,811,920	151,822	-61,036	1,599,062	303,826	509,940	17,406	138,624	59,914
1998	2,601,221	1,612,701	353,416	1,966,117	159,969	-56,695	1,749,453	312,801	538,967	18,631	139,615	61,436
1999	2,690,311	1,690,540	337,246	2,027,786	169,976	-49,755	1,808,055	315,501	566,755	19,073	141,056	63,174
2000	2,697,945	1,771,963	257,015	2,028,978	177,859	-40,613	1,810,506	314,748	572,691	18,945	142,410	60,429
2001	2,944,662	1,925,379	263,773	2,189,152	201,960	-15,854	1,971,338	350,904	622,420	20,491	143,707	59,985
2002	3,307,874	2,081,878	420,516	2,502,394	221,883	-28,285	2,252,226	363,797	691,851	22,713	145,640	62,113
2003	3,427,432	2,227,568	331,911	2,559,479	242,591	-42,081	2,274,807	417,873	734,752	23,005	148,984	63,886
2004	3,542,513	2,343,349	338,057	2,681,406	260,678	-56,483	2,364,245	422,980	755,288	23,266	152,259	63,188
2005	3,719,161	2,490,838	355,822	2,846,660	278,782	-73,725	2,494,153	426,057	798,951	23,824	156,113	64,742
2006	4,002,565	2,697,421	365,484	3,062,905	293,884	-94,324	2,674,697	437,896	889,972	24,937	160,505	68,927
2007	4,220,056	2,849,060	337,727	3,186,787	301,690	-116,040	2,769,057	472,379	978,620	25,639	164,596	70,468
2008	4,624,400	2,953,513	534,439	3,487,952	314,496	-138,387	3,035,069	504,069	1,085,262	27,540	167,917	71,750
2009	4,667,494	2,918,899	462,000	3,380,899	316,545	-143,931	2,920,423	516,471	1,230,600	27,135	172,008	69,698
2010	4,858,656	2,961,210	441,710	3,402,920	312,678	-147,313	2,942,929	537,812	1,377,915	27,799	174,779	69,874
2011	5,314,670	3,099,710	685,800	3,785,510	295,575	-153,633	3,336,302	601,427	1,376,941	30,146	176,300	71,503
2012	5,425,321	3,238,425	597,293	3,835,718	309,934	-154,081	3,371,703	666,876	1,386,742	30,575	177,443	75,939
2013	5,591,488	3,308,103	670,756	3,978,859	351,022	-154,541	3,473,296	686,946	1,431,246	31,498	177,517	78,355
2014	5,802,217	3,415,375	721,563	4,136,938	366,591	-152,811	3,617,536	710,165	1,474,516	32,398	179,091	81,499

Personal Income and Employment by Area: Elizabethtown-Fort Knox, KY

(Thousands of dollars, except as noted.)

Year	Personal income, total	Derivation of personal income									Per capita personal income (dollars)	Population (persons)	Total employment
		Earnings by place of work			Less: Contributions for government social insurance	Plus: Adjustment for residence	Equals: Net earnings by place of residence	Plus: Dividends, interest, and rent	Plus: Personal current transfer receipts				
		Nonfarm	Farm	Total									
1970	491,615	398,703	12,529	411,232	23,039	-14,469	373,724	98,241	19,650		4,567	107,652	63,118
1971	505,655	410,432	12,972	423,404	25,386	-13,149	384,869	98,237	22,549		4,689	107,830	58,437
1972	542,107	437,030	15,160	452,190	27,167	-11,212	413,811	103,133	25,163		5,116	105,967	55,176
1973	559,396	437,831	20,332	458,163	28,728	-7,017	422,418	106,722	30,256		5,643	99,133	53,229
1974	651,676	507,925	21,922	529,847	35,205	-8,139	486,503	127,476	37,697		6,213	104,885	56,273
1975	671,298	528,303	8,542	536,845	39,119	-9,763	487,963	134,174	49,161		6,080	110,417	55,211
1976	705,191	550,944	11,074	562,018	41,609	-7,873	512,536	137,498	55,157		5,974	118,037	54,863
1977	812,581	631,361	15,044	646,405	47,522	-5,185	593,698	162,127	56,756		6,828	118,999	58,950
1978	868,224	663,928	13,202	677,130	49,187	-841	627,102	180,485	60,637		7,425	116,940	58,530
1979	961,283	727,507	18,573	746,080	55,912	1,967	692,135	197,695	71,453		8,081	118,949	58,857
1980	1,041,783	775,337	12,994	788,331	60,353	6,677	734,655	220,053	87,075		8,452	123,258	59,302
1981	1,117,968	825,026	23,285	848,311	67,596	-1,699	779,016	236,393	102,559		9,222	121,230	55,951
1982	1,223,157	902,488	19,247	921,735	73,092	-6,471	842,172	268,594	112,391		10,125	120,805	57,731
1983	1,299,068	970,567	-4,977	965,590	82,238	-4,478	878,874	298,188	122,006		10,665	121,809	59,250
1984	1,415,768	1,040,726	20,621	1,061,347	89,965	-6,184	965,198	318,611	131,959		11,583	122,225	59,602
1985	1,504,095	1,115,432	13,121	1,128,553	98,762	-7,494	1,022,297	340,289	141,509		12,247	122,818	61,588
1986	1,567,670	1,159,473	10,639	1,170,112	107,212	-4,034	1,058,866	357,732	151,072		12,723	123,219	62,886
1987	1,642,277	1,216,960	15,614	1,232,574	114,431	-1,049	1,117,094	367,876	157,307		13,346	123,053	63,165
1988	1,735,800	1,288,564	13,949	1,302,513	127,116	3,629	1,179,026	383,910	172,864		13,901	124,869	64,064
1989	1,862,408	1,357,656	27,634	1,385,290	137,221	1,991	1,250,060	415,239	197,109		14,962	124,472	65,539
1990	1,948,721	1,418,662	27,448	1,446,110	149,829	-1,497	1,294,784	436,346	217,591		15,532	125,466	66,277
1991	2,020,080	1,466,587	26,767	1,493,354	157,435	3,645	1,339,564	430,760	249,756		16,627	121,495	63,642
1992	2,215,557	1,602,564	31,941	1,634,505	174,928	13,013	1,472,590	462,972	279,995		18,454	120,059	64,628
1993	2,254,926	1,618,004	28,089	1,646,093	179,628	26,963	1,493,428	471,766	289,732		17,825	126,505	64,846
1994	2,345,919	1,652,746	29,606	1,682,352	185,252	42,933	1,540,033	503,116	302,770		18,282	128,321	65,357
1995	2,419,050	1,679,148	12,002	1,691,150	187,469	58,197	1,561,878	527,837	329,335		18,691	129,423	66,847
1996	2,543,183	1,740,313	25,435	1,765,748	193,965	70,510	1,642,293	548,484	352,406		19,731	128,895	67,246
1997	2,649,377	1,824,695	13,987	1,838,682	203,643	87,906	1,722,945	547,568	378,864		20,351	130,182	67,884
1998	2,844,263	1,923,533	2,078	1,925,611	213,826	112,637	1,824,422	622,061	397,780		21,641	131,428	69,400
1999	2,975,550	2,039,292	-17,686	2,021,606	226,441	138,669	1,933,834	628,483	413,233		22,447	132,558	70,619
2000	3,299,590	2,236,718	10,403	2,247,121	241,342	158,927	2,164,706	683,731	451,153		24,531	134,506	72,663
2001	3,422,684	2,275,149	12,327	2,287,476	249,658	179,487	2,217,305	703,040	502,339		25,230	135,657	73,430
2002	3,521,822	2,412,239	-8,224	2,404,015	262,076	143,955	2,285,894	685,321	550,607		25,784	136,591	72,231
2003	3,705,455	2,604,188	-488	2,603,700	280,454	123,695	2,446,941	685,628	572,886		27,179	136,333	73,737
2004	3,877,497	2,766,983	11,992	2,778,975	295,843	90,170	2,573,302	677,805	626,390		28,051	138,230	75,171
2005	4,002,788	2,869,560	29,401	2,898,961	305,803	53,933	2,647,091	687,487	668,210		28,555	140,177	74,347
2006	4,237,139	3,071,109	18,544	3,089,653	330,839	28,510	2,787,324	719,019	730,796		30,078	140,870	76,935
2007	4,405,418	3,120,322	6,601	3,126,923	338,598	16,282	2,804,607	805,411	795,400		31,058	141,844	77,628
2008	4,629,072	3,253,285	-3,592	3,249,693	357,691	2,542	2,894,544	823,605	910,923		32,374	142,988	76,908
2009	4,669,519	3,269,256	2,540	3,271,796	368,274	-104,187	2,799,335	853,244	1,016,940		32,466	143,829	75,179
2010	4,955,041	3,736,238	-5,262	3,730,976	417,083	-360,478	2,953,415	900,896	1,100,730		33,056	149,897	78,881
2011	5,179,697	4,012,051	14,799	4,026,850	405,609	-573,991	3,047,250	1,011,227	1,121,220		34,236	151,295	80,717
2012	5,387,211	3,973,420	16,639	3,990,059	400,216	-343,677	3,246,166	1,008,638	1,132,407		35,816	150,413	78,536
2013	5,447,423	4,001,619	58,193	4,059,812	447,689	-349,931	3,262,192	1,019,639	1,165,592		35,982	151,395	78,388
2014	5,604,695	3,917,970	5,118	3,923,088	439,175	-147,663	3,336,250	1,012,600	1,255,845		36,974	151,585	76,921

Personal Income and Employment by Area: Elkhart-Goshen, IN

(Thousands of dollars, except as noted.)

Year	Personal income, total	Derivation of personal income									Per capita personal income (dollars)	Population (persons)	Total employment
		Earnings by place of work			Less: Contributions for government social insurance	Plus: Adjustment for residence	Equals: Net earnings by place of residence	Plus: Dividends, interest, and rent	Plus: Personal current transfer receipts				
		Nonfarm	Farm	Total									
1970	550,867	559,218	6,678	565,896	39,107	-84,896	441,893	74,174	34,800		4,350	126,624	71,287
1971	600,059	610,982	8,364	619,346	44,415	-97,340	477,591	81,532	40,936		4,724	127,025	73,110
1972	681,087	714,425	8,090	722,515	55,043	-120,029	547,443	88,227	45,417		5,255	129,596	80,429
1973	756,918	797,153	15,797	812,950	70,119	-137,570	605,261	98,258	53,399		5,722	132,290	84,783
1974	746,800	758,774	8,299	767,073	69,608	-128,835	568,630	111,479	66,691		5,636	132,510	77,343
1975	782,734	763,423	14,151	777,574	68,709	-132,205	576,660	119,365	86,709		5,953	131,484	73,077
1976	905,413	943,107	15,240	958,347	86,525	-176,686	695,136	128,803	81,474		6,890	131,402	82,175
1977	1,017,123	1,089,354	10,433	1,099,787	101,518	-211,213	787,056	143,522	86,545		7,615	133,567	87,444
1978	1,137,922	1,248,307	4,913	1,253,220	119,592	-252,035	881,593	162,018	94,311		8,398	135,493	93,129
1979	1,199,422	1,287,381	3,826	1,291,207	126,331	-260,659	904,217	182,318	112,887		8,775	136,687	89,398
1980	1,222,110	1,224,887	8,290	1,233,177	118,426	-245,500	869,251	211,231	141,628		8,902	137,292	80,021
1981	1,349,026	1,333,124	6,274	1,339,398	137,810	-264,180	937,408	256,433	155,185		9,859	136,836	81,375
1982	1,436,873	1,403,825	2,142	1,405,967	148,234	-281,943	975,790	289,044	172,039		10,399	138,179	82,288
1983	1,638,622	1,695,439	-736	1,694,703	179,196	-355,318	1,160,189	304,068	174,365		11,681	140,286	91,798
1984	1,878,213	1,950,475	14,866	1,965,341	212,635	-409,357	1,343,349	350,111	184,753		12,980	144,701	100,401
1985	1,985,487	2,051,015	14,229	2,065,244	228,276	-427,169	1,409,799	372,818	202,870		13,480	147,287	101,827
1986	2,154,153	2,242,465	14,300	2,256,765	250,771	-465,789	1,540,205	396,787	217,161		14,458	148,990	106,079
1987	2,349,196	2,477,147	17,339	2,494,486	273,523	-514,503	1,706,460	420,114	222,622		15,540	151,167	112,993
1988	2,535,632	2,707,394	9,082	2,716,476	306,591	-563,066	1,846,819	450,143	238,670		16,474	153,917	118,921
1989	2,726,187	2,808,368	24,021	2,832,389	319,493	-572,333	1,940,563	532,007	253,617		17,497	155,813	119,871
1990	2,797,773	2,823,711	20,457	2,844,168	330,839	-558,340	1,954,989	562,577	280,207		17,875	156,517	117,792
1991	2,843,314	2,855,679	11,015	2,866,694	336,297	-557,418	1,972,979	555,232	315,103		17,980	158,141	113,810
1992	3,132,936	3,180,487	18,894	3,199,381	369,889	-627,557	2,201,935	568,057	362,944		19,525	160,454	117,964
1993	3,343,138	3,433,026	18,421	3,451,447	399,069	-673,939	2,378,439	584,779	379,920		20,446	163,510	123,339
1994	3,612,468	3,767,934	16,011	3,783,945	444,647	-743,919	2,595,379	620,187	396,902		21,697	166,498	129,440
1995	3,803,432	3,945,319	10,087	3,955,406	468,164	-765,545	2,721,697	670,363	411,372		22,390	169,869	134,046
1996	3,966,487	4,049,833	21,687	4,071,520	480,126	-779,834	2,811,560	711,001	443,926		22,983	172,582	133,328
1997	4,128,738	4,183,599	26,012	4,209,611	495,176	-799,623	2,914,812	757,484	456,442		23,556	175,274	134,160
1998	4,489,905	4,589,265	25,812	4,615,077	534,712	-880,479	3,199,886	802,037	487,982		25,240	177,885	140,583
1999	4,793,027	5,007,551	12,761	5,020,312	576,060	-968,629	3,475,623	804,130	513,274		26,533	180,645	146,199
2000	5,045,440	5,224,226	16,832	5,241,058	593,735	-1,011,721	3,635,602	857,086	552,752		27,509	183,412	147,694
2001	5,055,793	5,028,429	27,500	5,055,929	562,277	-924,297	3,569,355	861,414	625,024		27,372	184,708	140,235
2002	5,222,462	5,351,827	21,740	5,373,567	598,215	-1,042,206	3,733,146	830,740	658,576		28,299	184,543	140,301
2003	5,430,050	5,646,781	37,959	5,684,740	632,105	-1,155,812	3,896,823	848,959	684,268		29,015	187,149	142,988
2004	5,786,840	6,238,623	50,819	6,289,442	696,296	-1,330,540	4,262,606	797,185	727,049		30,567	189,316	150,880
2005	5,989,047	6,521,389	36,026	6,557,415	736,093	-1,453,306	4,368,016	820,711	800,320		31,154	192,242	153,912
2006	6,275,170	6,742,754	26,571	6,769,325	766,404	-1,541,382	4,461,539	941,565	872,066		32,173	195,047	156,318
2007	6,400,449	6,753,632	34,914	6,788,546	768,057	-1,592,868	4,427,621	1,053,925	918,903		32,605	196,304	155,182
2008	6,127,876	6,141,460	35,037	6,176,497	712,118	-1,489,519	3,974,860	1,054,404	1,098,612		30,986	197,762	144,563
2009	5,777,130	5,096,228	9,468	5,105,696	607,289	-908,568	3,589,839	898,379	1,288,912		29,249	197,514	123,873
2010	6,094,339	5,563,971	34,263	5,598,234	663,405	-1,068,511	3,866,318	911,554	1,316,467		30,867	197,441	129,274
2011	6,543,177	5,856,083	60,108	5,916,191	629,075	-1,100,043	4,187,073	1,045,413	1,310,691		32,966	198,480	133,234
2012	6,882,397	6,420,723	64,668	6,485,391	679,581	-1,288,234	4,517,576	1,023,251	1,341,570		34,544	199,236	138,897
2013	7,113,265	6,821,438	96,539	6,917,977	819,793	-1,416,676	4,681,508	1,089,837	1,341,920		35,462	200,591	144,896
2014	7,542,382	7,442,909	110,304	7,553,213	884,976	-1,667,056	5,001,181	1,138,322	1,402,879		37,344	201,971	150412

Personal Income and Employment by Area: Elmira, NY

(Thousands of dollars, except as noted.)

Year	Personal income, total	Earnings by place of work			Less: Contributions for government social insurance	Plus: Adjustment for residence	Equals: Net earnings by place of residence	Plus: Dividends, interest, and rent	Plus: Personal current transfer receipts	Per capita personal income (dollars)	Population (persons)	Total employment
		Nonfarm	Farm	Total								
1970	397,483	336,957	2,368	339,325	25,373	-12,412	301,540	52,371	43,572	3,918	101,457	45,446
1971	418,601	349,458	2,230	351,688	27,192	-12,313	312,183	54,558	51,860	4,141	101,080	44,720
1972	451,342	377,201	2,196	379,397	30,787	-12,138	336,472	58,969	55,901	4,440	101,665	44,763
1973	493,397	415,616	2,892	418,508	39,391	-11,815	367,302	64,549	61,546	4,912	100,452	47,207
1974	533,555	433,563	2,210	435,773	42,454	-7,592	385,727	73,776	74,052	5,339	99,936	46,263
1975	573,004	443,859	1,974	445,833	42,399	-4,956	398,478	79,552	94,974	5,702	100,497	44,186
1976	617,840	482,301	2,702	485,003	47,320	-5,924	431,759	84,171	101,910	6,178	100,008	44,018
1977	662,653	503,249	2,167	505,416	49,351	602	456,667	92,744	113,242	6,671	99,335	43,206
1978	713,374	549,374	2,186	551,560	55,145	3,886	500,301	97,759	115,314	7,229	98,689	43,898
1979	773,920	588,822	2,967	591,789	60,779	8,598	539,608	106,969	127,343	7,791	99,339	44,018
1980	865,166	641,373	3,316	644,689	65,977	12,023	590,735	128,161	146,270	8,879	97,443	43,155
1981	946,917	690,086	3,108	693,194	75,556	7,786	625,424	155,530	165,963	9,822	96,406	43,073
1982	993,210	685,394	3,010	688,404	75,753	10,368	623,019	181,377	188,814	10,342	96,032	40,676
1983	1,041,159	707,587	2,736	710,323	78,723	11,483	643,083	190,186	207,890	10,999	94,659	39,693
1984	1,126,028	767,452	3,740	771,192	86,977	11,185	695,400	210,034	220,594	12,083	93,190	40,900
1985	1,156,241	779,871	4,238	784,109	89,739	18,763	713,133	217,285	225,823	12,541	92,200	41,191
1986	1,216,869	822,183	5,105	827,288	96,525	21,761	752,524	228,972	235,373	13,346	91,179	42,328
1987	1,297,028	915,275	5,771	921,046	105,457	10,302	825,891	234,045	237,092	14,126	91,819	44,422
1988	1,392,867	1,003,169	4,398	1,007,567	118,303	11,877	901,141	243,240	248,486	14,954	93,142	46,262
1989	1,533,921	1,096,474	4,544	1,101,018	127,681	9,016	982,353	290,029	261,539	16,198	94,701	47,884
1990	1,607,862	1,149,487	4,132	1,153,619	127,222	10,548	1,036,945	290,624	280,293	16,873	95,292	48,188
1991	1,660,486	1,180,485	3,035	1,183,520	133,598	8,760	1,058,682	294,571	307,233	17,479	95,001	47,118
1992	1,724,350	1,227,927	3,014	1,230,941	136,941	-292	1,093,708	290,434	340,208	18,160	94,954	46,818
1993	1,751,328	1,254,749	3,197	1,257,946	142,315	-9,026	1,106,605	291,844	352,879	18,491	94,711	46,964
1994	1,815,536	1,310,240	2,784	1,313,024	150,604	-19,645	1,142,775	301,932	370,829	19,287	94,132	47,823
1995	1,886,083	1,360,539	2,175	1,362,714	156,193	-23,874	1,182,647	317,112	386,324	20,134	93,675	47,762
1996	1,951,613	1,409,498	3,161	1,412,659	160,241	-28,117	1,224,301	324,742	402,570	20,991	92,972	48,771
1997	2,016,989	1,478,629	1,506	1,480,135	165,208	-41,993	1,272,934	334,080	409,975	21,885	92,162	49,516
1998	2,075,861	1,544,178	2,636	1,546,814	172,134	-50,994	1,323,686	332,864	419,311	22,615	91,791	50,920
1999	2,150,317	1,605,834	2,635	1,608,469	174,985	-45,453	1,388,031	323,289	438,997	23,556	91,284	51,476
2000	2,265,743	1,651,068	2,714	1,653,782	180,544	8,420	1,481,658	340,728	443,357	24,873	91,094	51,228
2001	2,282,261	1,677,400	3,073	1,680,473	186,850	-30,361	1,463,262	342,436	476,563	25,141	90,780	50,787
2002	2,269,594	1,663,164	1,240	1,664,404	188,540	-26,410	1,449,454	298,750	521,390	25,047	90,613	49,228
2003	2,328,718	1,700,587	2,097	1,702,684	192,436	-22,892	1,487,356	302,394	538,968	25,830	90,154	48,346
2004	2,428,244	1,751,679	2,740	1,754,419	198,589	-18,942	1,536,888	317,710	573,646	27,048	89,777	47,449
2005	2,552,110	1,855,697	2,361	1,858,058	214,189	-15,248	1,628,621	327,143	596,346	28,721	88,860	47,828
2006	2,648,543	1,931,523	1,371	1,932,894	221,727	-10,778	1,700,389	322,495	625,659	29,849	88,732	48,301
2007	2,792,858	2,006,777	1,777	2,008,554	228,478	-6,017	1,774,059	363,493	655,306	31,510	88,634	49,113
2008	3,008,842	2,129,333	1,425	2,130,758	243,840	-932	1,885,986	401,353	721,503	33,997	88,503	49,173
2009	2,980,918	2,081,599	-379	2,081,220	235,476	-26,723	1,819,021	371,102	790,795	33,550	88,849	47,307
2010	3,097,371	2,222,079	1,280	2,223,359	252,523	-63,200	1,907,636	357,918	831,817	34,823	88,947	47,319
2011	3,241,398	2,310,968	2,613	2,313,581	238,331	-59,847	2,015,403	396,609	829,386	36,431	88,973	47,805
2012	3,307,433	2,369,008	2,259	2,371,267	240,384	-76,322	2,054,561	423,852	829,020	37,066	89,231	47,356
2013	3,321,098	2,384,319	1,670	2,385,989	273,526	-58,810	2,053,653	416,523	850,922	37,533	88,485	46,530
2014	3,407,233	2,451,739	1,934	2,453,673	282,602	-58,072	2,112,999	432,636	861,598	38,820	87,770	46,691

Personal Income and Employment by Area: El Paso, TX

(Thousands of dollars, except as noted.)

Year	Personal income, total	Earnings by place of work			Less: Contributions for government social insurance	Plus: Adjustment for residence	Equals: Net earnings by place of residence	Plus: Dividends, interest, and rent	Plus: Personal current transfer receipts	Per capita personal income (dollars)	Population (persons)	Total employment
		Nonfarm	Farm	Total								
1970	1,198,212	975,055	9,345	984,400	62,026	-23,301	899,073	212,730	86,409	3,302	362,854	150,442
1971	1,310,182	1,074,573	7,844	1,082,417	71,639	-33,013	977,765	229,397	103,020	3,526	371,562	155,024
1972	1,420,075	1,170,152	13,411	1,183,563	81,214	-50,028	1,052,321	248,057	119,697	3,729	380,771	158,645
1973	1,622,038	1,349,835	10,984	1,360,819	105,969	-65,380	1,189,470	289,223	143,345	4,048	400,736	172,265
1974	1,821,070	1,506,967	11,675	1,518,642	122,106	-78,479	1,318,057	334,456	168,557	4,397	414,149	178,186
1975	1,920,367	1,653,431	11,999	1,665,430	135,057	-186,579	1,343,794	361,741	214,832	4,466	430,008	183,213
1976	2,139,061	1,847,723	16,226	1,863,949	153,446	-205,631	1,504,872	389,873	244,316	4,828	443,031	189,986
1977	2,354,886	2,039,855	20,615	2,060,470	168,057	-232,223	1,660,190	431,721	262,975	5,203	452,639	194,248
1978	2,643,659	2,293,694	12,779	2,306,473	192,179	-258,390	1,855,904	494,952	292,803	5,708	463,126	200,883
1979	3,012,766	2,587,310	10,812	2,598,122	227,863	-256,445	2,113,814	556,184	342,768	6,344	474,925	208,458
1980	3,343,503	2,855,498	6,588	2,862,086	253,028	-322,014	2,287,044	649,666	406,793	6,873	486,485	214,832
1981	4,040,460	3,241,928	20,461	3,262,389	308,726	-132,348	2,821,315	767,625	451,520	8,073	500,476	223,237
1982	4,351,610	3,444,419	6,794	3,451,213	326,341	-162,929	2,961,943	884,787	504,880	8,451	514,949	222,683
1983	4,672,567	3,636,929	17,879	3,654,808	343,899	-157,638	3,153,271	951,216	568,080	8,918	523,973	219,571
1984	5,042,498	3,936,835	15,534	3,952,369	383,119	-187,924	3,381,326	1,046,191	614,981	9,472	532,385	227,764
1985	5,437,941	4,240,017	17,161	4,257,178	416,452	-205,297	3,635,429	1,145,825	656,687	10,042	541,534	232,617
1986	5,742,648	4,472,764	8,031	4,480,795	438,314	-201,887	3,840,594	1,188,813	713,241	10,398	552,279	235,285
1987	5,966,748	4,647,426	19,333	4,666,759	453,731	-221,868	3,991,160	1,218,539	757,049	10,613	562,186	245,513
1988	6,390,718	5,020,173	18,127	5,038,300	508,262	-239,153	4,290,885	1,288,862	810,971	11,180	571,624	254,501
1989	7,002,148	5,380,893	16,492	5,397,385	554,064	-250,803	4,592,518	1,474,353	935,277	11,993	583,850	264,114
1990	7,576,208	5,719,119	12,285	5,731,404	581,943	-277,114	4,872,347	1,641,249	1,062,612	12,664	598,255	269,064
1991	7,880,652	6,045,625	7,748	6,053,373	624,968	-307,217	5,121,188	1,542,367	1,217,097	12,896	611,092	271,145
1992	8,708,294	6,667,559	26,917	6,694,476	688,722	-329,024	5,676,730	1,561,078	1,470,486	14,000	622,040	281,367
1993	9,171,120	7,015,243	23,325	7,038,568	731,024	-342,027	5,965,517	1,612,527	1,593,076	14,398	636,952	288,491
1994	9,677,167	7,438,745	31,411	7,470,156	774,093	-379,779	6,316,284	1,657,836	1,703,047	14,909	649,075	295,015
1995	10,162,249	7,729,546	27,551	7,757,097	802,131	-395,371	6,559,595	1,750,267	1,852,387	15,459	657,359	299,334
1996	10,552,196	7,901,671	25,758	7,927,429	813,917	-407,339	6,706,173	1,812,383	2,033,640	15,997	659,655	298,829
1997	11,283,074	8,472,703	31,215	8,503,918	865,888	-449,304	7,188,726	1,957,254	2,137,094	16,883	668,300	307,305
1998	11,938,481	9,044,935	37,464	9,082,399	913,788	-479,105	7,689,506	2,122,516	2,126,459	17,700	674,484	313,512
1999	12,245,179	9,424,719	32,290	9,457,009	943,127	-494,690	8,019,192	2,059,649	2,166,338	18,042	678,720	318,009
2000	13,106,853	10,138,745	28,707	10,167,452	985,164	-516,293	8,665,995	2,157,260	2,283,598	19,132	685,086	325,093
2001	14,270,783	11,258,843	29,458	11,288,301	1,039,441	-526,347	9,722,513	2,067,595	2,480,675	20,606	692,568	324,593
2002	15,138,116	11,866,023	31,439	11,897,462	1,090,195	-509,681	10,297,586	2,097,270	2,743,260	21,631	699,844	332,012
2003	15,563,634	12,183,411	40,850	12,224,261	1,146,282	-486,307	10,591,672	2,034,151	2,937,811	21,966	708,545	335,910
2004	16,175,393	12,607,267	36,806	12,644,073	1,199,350	-457,283	10,987,440	2,156,794	3,031,159	22,435	720,997	340,807
2005	17,155,179	13,122,380	36,633	13,159,013	1,261,676	-426,030	11,471,307	2,357,776	3,326,096	23,452	731,511	348,423
2006	18,637,493	14,268,950	20,121	14,289,071	1,343,648	-401,295	12,544,128	2,558,605	3,534,760	24,908	748,254	360,277
2007	20,033,450	15,041,515	26,419	15,067,934	1,441,137	-367,891	13,258,906	2,877,254	3,897,290	26,393	759,040	372,504
2008	21,274,400	15,569,009	19,135	15,588,144	1,496,047	-323,781	13,768,316	3,100,653	4,405,431	27,511	773,304	384,114
2009	21,961,187	15,899,979	13,303	15,913,282	1,572,013	-365,736	13,975,533	3,115,408	4,870,246	27,793	790,182	384,782
2010	23,270,704	16,686,548	20,714	16,707,262	1,675,093	-378,860	14,653,309	3,178,643	5,438,752	28,833	807,089	390,742
2011	24,611,884	17,362,666	18,106	17,380,772	1,571,326	-392,978	15,416,468	3,555,478	5,639,938	29,900	823,134	403,939
2012	25,851,473	18,148,880	14,344	18,163,224	1,646,737	-427,856	16,088,631	4,170,124	5,592,718	30,979	834,477	407,347
2013	25,692,455	18,264,875	13,903	18,278,778	1,855,436	-398,357	16,024,985	3,908,513	5,758,957	30,783	834,630	411,902
2014	26,606,169	18,888,023	18,230	18,906,253	1,906,509	-414,396	16,585,348	4,026,244	5,994,577	31,799	836,698	416354

Personal Income and Employment by Area: Erie, PA

(Thousands of dollars, except as noted.)

Year	Personal income, total	Earnings by place of work			Less: Contributions for government social insurance	Plus: Adjustment for residence	Equals: Net earnings by place of residence	Plus: Dividends, interest, and rent	Plus: Personal current transfer receipts	Per capita personal income (dollars)	Population (persons)	Total employment
		Nonfarm	Farm	Total								
1970	1,032,059	876,132	9,693	885,825	65,451	-14,829	805,545	126,841	99,673	3,905	264,315	117,410
1971	1,113,613	947,849	7,669	955,518	73,696	-17,249	864,573	134,022	115,018	4,145	268,634	118,885
1972	1,214,888	1,043,182	6,961	1,050,143	85,357	-19,595	945,191	141,352	128,345	4,460	272,384	121,771
1973	1,354,693	1,174,841	13,611	1,188,452	110,177	-22,338	1,055,937	156,738	142,018	4,935	274,509	128,972
1974	1,516,520	1,313,499	13,040	1,326,539	128,119	-26,452	1,171,968	177,604	166,948	5,508	275,306	133,424
1975	1,647,724	1,380,816	12,089	1,392,905	130,633	-28,763	1,233,509	193,859	220,356	5,900	279,275	131,019
1976	1,758,807	1,455,971	13,712	1,469,683	140,390	-28,411	1,300,882	206,318	251,607	6,250	281,390	128,968
1977	1,923,096	1,606,537	15,839	1,622,376	157,429	-31,428	1,433,519	228,386	261,191	6,868	280,019	131,617
1978	2,131,120	1,797,821	19,266	1,817,087	181,303	-35,759	1,600,025	251,954	279,141	7,654	278,420	136,329
1979	2,348,088	1,980,287	15,477	1,995,764	205,530	-38,964	1,751,270	283,707	313,111	8,422	278,792	137,775
1980	2,570,372	2,095,382	10,104	2,105,486	214,290	-41,057	1,850,139	351,529	368,704	9,178	280,043	134,200
1981	2,824,698	2,242,121	16,432	2,258,553	244,875	-45,649	1,968,029	436,820	419,849	10,069	280,529	131,270
1982	2,978,971	2,290,847	10,085	2,300,932	254,517	-49,400	1,997,015	499,656	482,300	10,589	281,320	128,148
1983	3,076,706	2,320,363	7,358	2,327,721	260,836	-49,895	2,016,990	527,165	532,551	10,923	281,683	124,998
1984	3,306,320	2,539,181	10,711	2,549,892	298,656	-56,046	2,195,190	589,011	522,119	11,769	280,928	128,793
1985	3,481,132	2,669,750	13,588	2,683,338	317,618	-61,873	2,303,847	632,055	545,230	12,541	277,584	130,880
1986	3,610,665	2,743,118	15,076	2,758,194	325,786	-66,231	2,366,177	663,154	581,334	13,029	277,123	131,407
1987	3,762,372	2,879,948	21,354	2,901,302	336,674	-70,485	2,494,143	674,771	593,458	13,644	275,759	133,889
1988	4,023,975	3,131,218	14,988	3,146,206	373,063	-78,716	2,694,427	706,655	622,893	14,647	274,732	138,424
1989	4,411,488	3,382,289	21,128	3,403,417	393,717	-87,699	2,922,001	826,298	663,189	16,014	275,474	141,704
1990	4,661,300	3,608,152	23,708	3,631,860	423,353	-97,116	3,111,391	821,637	728,272	16,894	275,911	145,501
1991	4,913,873	3,782,020	23,928	3,805,948	449,016	-104,728	3,252,204	829,431	832,238	17,678	277,973	145,836
1992	5,236,336	4,036,359	36,226	4,072,585	477,397	-115,203	3,479,985	865,269	891,082	18,731	279,548	146,388
1993	5,487,254	4,235,873	25,935	4,261,808	508,457	-122,819	3,630,532	916,274	940,448	19,542	280,796	148,918
1994	5,712,900	4,375,204	21,488	4,396,692	536,906	-125,922	3,733,864	1,016,290	962,746	20,284	281,649	149,803
1995	5,875,774	4,534,444	15,063	4,549,507	557,152	-133,764	3,858,591	1,008,074	1,009,109	20,827	282,127	153,226
1996	6,184,772	4,646,948	28,540	4,675,488	562,103	-138,971	3,974,414	1,133,538	1,076,820	21,887	282,582	154,003
1997	6,474,746	4,853,870	19,469	4,873,339	582,948	-146,578	4,143,813	1,229,458	1,101,475	22,911	282,609	155,708
1998	6,636,295	5,001,408	23,464	5,024,872	594,420	-152,625	4,277,827	1,245,680	1,112,788	23,553	281,764	156,241
1999	6,834,976	5,278,272	31,997	5,310,269	617,535	-165,628	4,527,106	1,150,977	1,156,893	24,298	281,294	160,244
2000	7,142,178	5,437,662	29,465	5,467,127	629,878	-175,124	4,662,125	1,255,828	1,224,225	25,435	280,803	163,204
2001	7,247,758	5,502,464	25,505	5,527,969	633,529	-186,349	4,708,091	1,212,408	1,327,259	25,825	280,647	159,685
2002	7,380,570	5,513,360	17,093	5,530,453	635,369	-185,286	4,709,798	1,242,473	1,428,299	26,324	280,379	157,549
2003	7,524,694	5,584,467	26,318	5,610,785	636,780	-183,535	4,790,470	1,226,038	1,508,186	26,859	280,153	156,547
2004	7,875,003	5,927,482	19,644	5,947,126	672,099	-188,094	5,086,933	1,231,384	1,556,686	28,341	277,864	158,595
2005	8,106,404	6,162,115	19,266	6,181,381	716,414	-189,572	5,275,395	1,165,601	1,665,408	29,243	277,211	160,914
2006	8,590,972	6,409,128	16,443	6,425,571	744,442	-189,108	5,492,021	1,344,562	1,754,389	30,860	278,389	161,678
2007	9,110,683	6,638,909	15,955	6,654,864	773,200	-188,820	5,692,844	1,539,377	1,878,462	32,705	278,573	162,896
2008	9,458,339	6,747,057	12,938	6,759,995	786,539	-185,847	5,787,609	1,541,345	2,129,385	33,939	278,686	162,022
2009	9,350,360	6,478,787	7,672	6,486,459	763,246	-192,593	5,530,620	1,390,890	2,428,850	33,413	279,838	156,229
2010	9,595,114	6,589,420	11,502	6,600,922	782,454	-196,096	5,622,372	1,384,938	2,587,804	34,180	280,720	156,260
2011	10,217,506	7,039,315	20,111	7,059,426	755,290	-229,181	6,074,955	1,543,177	2,599,374	36,369	280,938	159,139
2012	10,517,500	7,144,375	27,126	7,171,501	761,432	-238,714	6,171,355	1,839,095	2,507,050	37,455	280,801	160,095
2013	10,428,430	7,210,285	23,059	7,233,344	864,239	-228,348	6,140,757	1,650,558	2,637,115	37,276	279,760	160,018
2014	10,636,535	7,349,232	21,660	7,370,892	877,520	-226,449	6,266,923	1,711,692	2,657,920	38,200	278,443	160,785

Personal Income and Employment by Area: Eugene-Springfield, OR

(Thousands of dollars, except as noted.)

Year	Personal income, total	Earnings by place of work			Less: Contributions for government social insurance	Plus: Adjustment for residence	Equals: Net earnings by place of residence	Plus: Dividends, interest, and rent	Plus: Personal current transfer receipts	Per capita personal income (dollars)	Population (persons)	Total employment
		Nonfarm	Farm	Total								
1970.............	784,294	624,274	6,452	630,726	49,259	8,550	590,017	122,545	71,732	3,624	216,409	85,936
1971.............	872,838	696,211	5,215	701,426	56,290	9,530	654,666	135,123	83,049	3,953	220,797	90,186
1972.............	990,586	802,061	6,534	808,595	68,255	10,158	750,498	147,331	92,757	4,364	227,016	96,964
1973.............	1,121,015	910,234	11,626	921,860	88,722	10,999	844,137	166,285	110,593	4,858	230,743	103,424
1974.............	1,249,742	983,046	15,718	998,764	98,024	12,712	913,452	195,014	141,276	5,283	236,565	105,876
1975.............	1,388,017	1,058,886	9,081	1,067,967	101,333	14,590	981,224	222,311	184,482	5,776	240,324	106,648
1976.............	1,609,056	1,257,337	12,309	1,269,646	122,087	16,824	1,164,383	247,762	196,911	6,543	245,932	114,312
1977.............	1,846,126	1,461,828	9,812	1,471,640	144,512	19,047	1,346,175	284,313	215,638	7,328	251,925	122,378
1978.............	2,124,506	1,691,176	7,703	1,698,879	170,596	21,838	1,550,121	338,073	236,312	8,164	260,240	130,003
1979.............	2,386,427	1,882,313	10,665	1,892,978	195,854	26,053	1,723,177	396,690	266,560	8,910	267,827	133,161
1980.............	2,582,092	1,954,321	5,590	1,959,911	203,446	31,829	1,788,294	472,576	321,222	9,365	275,708	131,154
1981.............	2,754,954	1,988,901	13,181	2,002,082	222,567	24,780	1,804,295	577,578	373,081	9,943	277,068	126,204
1982.............	2,745,081	1,903,531	9,777	1,913,308	217,298	24,284	1,720,294	608,574	416,213	10,079	272,346	118,130
1983.............	2,920,264	2,031,458	4,847	2,036,305	233,172	26,034	1,829,167	647,214	443,883	10,878	268,453	121,237
1984.............	3,162,537	2,223,745	14,399	2,238,144	263,752	25,685	2,000,077	705,428	457,032	11,806	267,878	127,016
1985.............	3,303,710	2,329,074	15,078	2,344,152	278,457	25,773	2,091,468	729,574	482,668	12,371	267,051	129,177
1986.............	3,457,234	2,445,890	20,513	2,466,403	292,120	25,704	2,199,987	765,113	492,134	12,985	266,239	132,737
1987.............	3,693,288	2,665,751	18,942	2,684,693	315,104	25,029	2,394,618	787,521	511,149	13,748	268,636	139,567
1988.............	4,053,304	2,937,802	31,426	2,969,228	361,121	26,100	2,634,207	874,066	545,031	14,847	273,014	146,319
1989.............	4,468,164	3,165,600	30,636	3,196,236	390,738	24,963	2,830,461	1,040,892	596,811	16,034	278,665	151,322
1990.............	4,719,393	3,368,255	33,135	3,401,390	422,889	27,315	3,005,816	1,063,506	650,071	16,602	284,261	154,526
1991.............	4,907,919	3,481,108	25,783	3,506,891	440,052	29,418	3,096,257	1,091,414	720,248	17,012	288,490	152,184
1992.............	5,217,397	3,712,890	26,624	3,739,514	466,026	29,909	3,303,397	1,107,116	806,884	17,838	292,482	153,541
1993.............	5,594,714	3,960,405	39,806	4,000,211	494,180	28,911	3,534,942	1,193,848	865,924	18,820	297,281	156,357
1994.............	6,009,871	4,304,910	35,161	4,340,071	538,189	29,261	3,831,143	1,271,714	907,014	19,912	301,819	164,297
1995.............	6,425,740	4,479,159	27,241	4,506,400	562,766	34,548	3,978,182	1,436,545	1,011,013	20,951	306,704	167,644
1996.............	6,842,005	4,747,782	25,572	4,773,354	605,435	37,233	4,205,152	1,567,401	1,069,452	22,000	311,004	173,379
1997.............	7,253,941	5,093,862	25,440	5,119,302	640,342	37,510	4,516,470	1,634,308	1,103,163	22,914	316,579	177,912
1998.............	7,731,354	5,435,421	15,209	5,450,630	677,246	32,873	4,806,257	1,724,831	1,200,266	24,187	319,646	181,071
1999.............	7,983,358	5,669,651	15,739	5,685,390	697,185	30,282	5,018,487	1,666,342	1,298,529	24,810	321,778	184,347
2000.............	8,506,900	6,030,398	15,238	6,045,636	731,972	29,653	5,343,317	1,799,531	1,364,052	26,297	323,492	186,579
2001.............	8,762,622	6,088,097	18,503	6,106,600	739,724	34,632	5,401,508	1,829,783	1,531,331	26,974	324,855	182,443
2002.............	8,790,366	6,182,990	18,104	6,201,094	763,068	18,940	5,456,966	1,765,237	1,568,163	26,840	327,506	184,593
2003.............	9,004,583	6,416,993	29,501	6,446,494	792,134	3,272	5,657,632	1,712,345	1,634,606	27,217	330,845	186,168
2004.............	9,562,268	6,806,542	31,938	6,838,480	851,013	-14,580	5,972,887	1,887,837	1,701,544	28,774	332,327	191,656
2005.............	10,082,587	7,172,107	29,720	7,201,827	911,767	-34,680	6,255,380	2,017,169	1,810,038	30,023	335,831	197,092
2006.............	10,919,089	7,564,776	39,036	7,603,812	968,212	-56,059	6,579,541	2,405,324	1,934,224	32,122	339,926	201,739
2007.............	11,272,793	7,801,136	41,810	7,842,946	1,003,116	-78,711	6,761,119	2,444,264	2,067,410	32,690	344,844	205,478
2008.............	11,690,848	7,895,534	33,029	7,928,563	1,013,037	-100,002	6,815,524	2,540,608	2,334,716	33,577	348,176	202,342
2009.............	11,385,410	7,376,118	34,144	7,410,262	951,533	-80,754	6,377,975	2,298,987	2,708,448	32,451	350,850	190,409
2010.............	11,547,065	7,376,751	29,001	7,405,752	969,053	-77,760	6,358,939	2,302,517	2,885,609	32,818	351,852	183,682
2011.............	12,047,023	7,627,489	31,809	7,659,298	892,783	-81,243	6,685,272	2,444,751	2,917,000	34,080	353,491	185,632
2012.............	12,545,269	7,980,537	47,515	8,028,052	929,032	-85,279	7,013,741	2,611,875	2,919,653	35,391	354,481	185,788
2013.............	12,724,475	8,241,587	42,739	8,284,326	1,078,675	-85,978	7,119,673	2,585,415	3,019,387	35,777	355,661	187,213
2014.............	13,392,647	8,560,985	58,255	8,619,240	1,129,966	-86,452	7,402,822	2,696,857	3,292,968	37,374	358,337	191,372

Personal Income and Employment by Area: Evansville, IN-KY

(Thousands of dollars, except as noted.)

Year	Personal income, total	Derivation of personal income									Per capita personal income (dollars)	Population (persons)	Total employment
		Earnings by place of work			Less: Contributions for government social insurance	Plus: Adjustment for residence	Equals: Net earnings by place of residence	Plus: Dividends, interest, and rent	Plus: Personal current transfer receipts			
		Nonfarm	Farm	Total								
1970	946,635	832,039	6,874	838,913	57,264	-58,029	723,620	136,885	86,130	3,714	254,890	118,647
1971	1,038,781	898,059	16,810	914,869	64,130	-61,578	789,161	149,814	99,806	4,030	257,776	121,245
1972	1,127,761	984,840	15,568	1,000,408	74,477	-69,283	856,648	161,190	109,923	4,369	258,125	124,254
1973	1,287,580	1,109,063	33,292	1,142,355	96,499	-73,864	971,992	182,659	132,929	4,951	260,065	130,416
1974	1,410,585	1,201,176	25,662	1,226,838	108,186	-77,598	1,041,054	212,558	156,973	5,414	260,547	129,898
1975	1,552,031	1,283,171	24,500	1,307,671	113,155	-72,965	1,121,551	234,731	195,749	5,947	260,965	127,384
1976	1,738,224	1,461,623	29,192	1,490,815	131,133	-86,948	1,272,734	258,253	207,237	6,622	262,498	133,259
1977	2,004,654	1,715,224	26,138	1,741,362	151,081	-100,215	1,490,066	293,776	220,812	7,535	266,046	139,775
1978	2,243,938	1,951,061	16,816	1,967,877	177,541	-118,911	1,671,425	332,477	240,036	8,300	270,348	146,579
1979	2,492,895	2,153,966	26,957	2,180,923	203,196	-132,211	1,845,516	372,744	274,635	9,136	272,865	148,866
1980	2,725,146	2,268,827	18,288	2,287,115	215,759	-140,422	1,930,934	468,046	326,166	9,857	276,466	146,600
1981	3,007,154	2,418,697	14,470	2,433,167	248,251	-140,392	2,044,524	587,262	375,368	10,868	276,701	145,853
1982	3,186,912	2,501,046	11,966	2,513,012	263,673	-136,989	2,112,350	660,639	413,923	11,472	277,792	144,080
1983	3,323,672	2,622,766	-24,714	2,598,052	275,498	-139,889	2,182,665	694,701	446,306	11,942	278,314	143,145
1984	3,718,254	2,924,783	22,230	2,947,013	315,667	-155,807	2,475,539	771,331	471,384	13,306	279,451	148,687
1985	3,905,175	3,059,249	15,490	3,074,739	337,196	-156,157	2,581,386	824,839	498,950	13,936	280,221	149,820
1986	4,051,416	3,154,804	16,298	3,171,102	352,470	-153,595	2,665,037	856,078	530,301	14,480	279,786	150,742
1987	4,185,159	3,282,934	11,856	3,294,790	360,659	-147,816	2,786,315	855,629	543,215	14,982	279,347	152,301
1988	4,485,180	3,537,248	10,569	3,547,817	398,862	-160,320	2,988,635	921,405	575,140	16,080	278,923	155,991
1989	4,812,077	3,689,615	33,366	3,722,981	419,195	-160,346	3,143,440	1,039,547	629,090	17,252	278,930	158,985
1990	5,101,106	3,924,843	10,152	3,934,995	457,801	-168,221	3,308,973	1,103,477	688,656	18,258	279,384	161,461
1991	5,245,933	4,108,295	-6,760	4,101,535	484,655	-174,918	3,441,962	1,049,017	754,954	18,651	281,270	161,774
1992	5,676,149	4,430,780	28,439	4,459,219	515,557	-198,179	3,745,483	1,082,910	847,756	19,974	284,179	164,642
1993	5,961,686	4,678,843	16,998	4,695,841	550,693	-217,189	3,927,959	1,135,281	898,446	20,792	286,723	169,312
1994	6,224,833	4,882,665	18,122	4,900,787	584,389	-238,743	4,077,655	1,215,556	931,622	21,563	288,681	174,356
1995	6,429,089	5,015,992	6,702	5,022,694	602,788	-245,449	4,174,457	1,293,175	961,457	22,173	289,950	177,218
1996	6,845,456	5,318,962	52,924	5,371,886	633,376	-278,802	4,459,708	1,369,982	1,015,766	23,432	292,136	179,775
1997	7,168,378	5,664,062	23,574	5,687,636	670,545	-310,259	4,706,832	1,427,916	1,033,630	24,391	293,894	182,816
1998	7,730,425	6,101,148	12,251	6,113,399	710,733	-299,809	5,102,857	1,557,580	1,069,988	26,248	294,517	183,219
1999	7,930,962	6,361,319	4,680	6,365,999	741,718	-315,341	5,308,940	1,509,894	1,112,128	26,829	295,610	185,594
2000	8,419,389	6,651,479	41,242	6,692,721	763,363	-315,151	5,614,207	1,617,189	1,187,993	28,398	296,480	188,284
2001	8,756,864	6,925,573	45,299	6,970,872	778,769	-335,348	5,856,755	1,605,904	1,294,205	29,482	297,027	185,120
2002	8,958,694	7,171,541	14,990	7,186,531	806,011	-365,369	6,015,151	1,570,426	1,373,117	30,024	298,383	184,498
2003	9,146,776	7,342,377	49,005	7,391,382	827,629	-421,791	6,141,962	1,585,694	1,419,120	30,426	300,628	184,122
2004	9,477,675	7,562,065	78,188	7,640,253	851,164	-419,190	6,369,899	1,603,577	1,504,199	31,351	302,310	182,839
2005	9,801,761	7,847,516	77,246	7,924,762	894,100	-454,286	6,576,376	1,606,177	1,619,208	32,259	303,844	183,997
2006	10,387,918	8,229,573	62,680	8,292,253	943,522	-466,523	6,882,208	1,748,807	1,756,903	33,998	305,549	184,747
2007	10,539,875	8,135,889	51,678	8,187,567	944,377	-422,079	6,821,111	1,872,270	1,846,494	34,280	307,468	184,922
2008	11,240,975	8,535,536	93,282	8,628,818	996,616	-429,263	7,202,939	1,932,808	2,105,228	36,424	308,614	183,910
2009	10,807,100	8,109,628	85,279	8,194,907	969,553	-391,049	6,834,305	1,723,427	2,249,368	34,843	310,170	178,541
2010	11,197,949	8,422,422	34,629	8,457,051	997,841	-394,662	7,064,548	1,749,119	2,384,282	35,916	311,778	178,347
2011	11,958,603	8,858,153	112,660	8,970,813	919,521	-404,022	7,647,270	1,919,385	2,391,948	38,257	312,589	182,081
2012	12,529,111	9,083,230	57,312	9,140,542	929,268	-346,481	7,864,793	2,195,389	2,468,929	39,991	313,298	181,740
2013	12,328,397	8,929,096	245,345	9,174,441	1,053,002	-294,670	7,826,769	2,003,800	2,497,828	39,209	314,429	180,403
2014	12,848,433	9,427,935	119,759	9,547,694	1,110,358	-311,167	8,126,169	2,086,430	2,635,834	40,768	315,162	183,286

Personal Income and Employment by Area: Fairbanks, AK

(Thousands of dollars, except as noted.)

Year	Personal income, total	Earnings by place of work			Less: Contributions for government social insurance	Plus: Adjustment for residence	Equals: Net earnings by place of residence	Plus: Dividends, interest, and rent	Plus: Personal current transfer receipts	Per capita personal income (dollars)	Population (persons)	Total employment
		Nonfarm	Farm	Total								
1970	276,178	252,190	204	252,394	16,119	-10,854	225,421	42,835	7,922	6,012	45,940	23,571
1971	288,446	270,863	203	271,066	17,603	-20,903	232,560	45,469	10,417	6,103	47,260	23,042
1972	307,440	296,804	334	297,138	19,822	-30,138	247,178	48,335	11,927	6,447	47,690	23,612
1973	324,299	313,476	325	313,801	23,162	-36,014	254,625	51,787	17,887	6,805	47,654	23,221
1974	449,000	510,259	560	510,819	45,534	-94,314	370,971	61,143	16,886	9,262	48,480	28,366
1975	802,653	935,387	905	936,292	92,452	-136,630	707,210	75,399	20,044	15,506	51,765	38,163
1976	845,859	946,561	943	947,504	94,808	-114,400	738,296	83,561	24,002	15,109	55,983	36,768
1977	757,245	820,894	704	821,598	76,786	-118,131	626,681	93,517	37,047	13,661	55,433	34,246
1978	728,844	709,038	884	709,922	62,570	-65,836	581,516	106,217	41,111	13,174	55,325	31,953
1979	745,055	731,024	438	731,462	66,193	-68,274	596,995	111,496	36,564	13,569	54,910	32,015
1980	814,990	789,688	272	789,960	67,982	-71,038	650,940	124,686	39,364	14,948	54,520	31,780
1981	926,801	896,675	30	896,705	82,633	-81,727	732,345	145,229	49,227	16,382	56,576	33,124
1982	1,174,505	1,070,690	5	1,070,695	99,124	-91,418	880,153	179,741	114,611	19,606	59,905	36,850
1983	1,249,600	1,171,140	-237	1,170,903	108,734	-102,399	959,770	204,713	85,117	19,021	65,695	38,748
1984	1,304,968	1,248,069	-879	1,247,190	122,346	-135,416	989,428	224,588	90,952	19,106	68,300	41,113
1985	1,398,002	1,324,131	-1,903	1,322,228	129,228	-152,994	1,040,006	245,239	112,757	19,571	71,433	42,878
1986	1,370,482	1,246,128	-943	1,245,185	115,737	-139,505	989,943	250,668	129,871	18,641	73,520	41,269
1987	1,341,377	1,186,568	527	1,187,095	109,799	-130,023	947,273	258,482	135,622	18,243	73,528	42,080
1988	1,379,694	1,201,887	848	1,202,735	117,058	-128,230	957,447	275,568	146,679	18,307	75,364	42,911
1989	1,511,000	1,255,240	-338	1,254,902	122,990	-89,039	1,042,873	305,095	163,032	19,593	77,121	43,488
1990	1,567,606	1,319,816	777	1,320,593	134,292	-118,726	1,067,575	314,498	185,533	20,080	78,067	43,739
1991	1,633,294	1,380,818	1,557	1,382,375	142,544	-127,752	1,112,079	323,531	197,684	20,295	80,479	44,917
1992	1,767,303	1,495,350	2,452	1,497,802	156,634	-145,229	1,195,939	350,825	220,539	21,420	82,506	45,630
1993	1,846,979	1,526,580	1,486	1,528,066	161,907	-147,875	1,218,284	385,542	243,153	22,258	82,979	46,493
1994	1,861,316	1,530,091	312	1,530,403	164,475	-141,184	1,224,744	389,439	247,133	22,288	83,512	46,423
1995	1,938,086	1,588,027	1,216	1,589,243	170,524	-151,885	1,266,834	415,124	256,128	23,652	81,941	46,681
1996	1,989,866	1,623,430	111	1,623,541	173,814	-160,069	1,289,658	426,524	273,684	24,009	82,880	47,330
1997	2,083,405	1,699,690	271	1,699,961	182,277	-173,293	1,344,391	443,770	295,244	25,259	82,483	48,611
1998	2,194,491	1,779,327	650	1,779,977	189,319	-177,286	1,413,372	459,516	321,603	26,345	83,299	49,592
1999	2,267,518	1,828,666	577	1,829,243	191,582	-186,774	1,450,887	469,432	347,199	27,192	83,390	49,427
2000	2,435,861	1,949,279	404	1,949,683	201,863	-203,157	1,544,663	500,298	390,900	29,346	83,005	50,501
2001	2,513,678	2,043,339	2,036	2,045,375	209,584	-222,923	1,612,868	488,459	412,351	29,638	84,814	51,965
2002	2,686,760	2,210,436	2,276	2,212,712	226,316	-202,119	1,784,277	483,621	418,862	31,207	86,095	53,192
2003	2,868,541	2,366,445	3,963	2,370,408	239,575	-171,570	1,959,263	502,496	406,782	33,015	86,885	53,609
2004	3,058,665	2,518,418	3,965	2,522,383	257,643	-131,575	2,133,165	527,971	397,529	34,350	89,043	54,995
2005	3,358,139	2,731,035	5,643	2,736,678	280,959	-87,959	2,367,760	569,548	420,831	37,135	90,431	56,246
2006	3,678,651	2,960,925	4,760	2,965,685	314,409	-35,116	2,616,160	616,172	446,319	40,628	90,545	57,751
2007	3,975,444	3,044,507	4,896	3,049,403	319,539	24,168	2,754,032	713,367	508,045	42,498	93,545	59,043
2008	4,409,232	3,184,839	1,085	3,185,924	330,940	88,157	2,943,141	772,284	693,807	46,633	94,552	58,751
2009	4,400,420	3,289,196	3,455	3,292,651	337,774	94,198	3,049,075	753,931	597,414	46,204	95,238	58,022
2010	4,574,089	3,374,278	3,840	3,378,118	346,314	94,938	3,126,742	777,790	669,557	46,592	98,174	57,292
2011	4,976,795	3,612,522	3,229	3,615,751	335,296	105,606	3,386,061	888,736	701,998	50,769	98,029	58,995
2012	5,111,243	3,717,649	5,193	3,722,842	348,682	109,251	3,483,411	950,479	677,353	50,997	100,227	59,347
2013	4,947,504	3,621,188	3,400	3,624,588	382,454	115,163	3,357,297	920,568	669,639	49,079	100,807	58,458
2014	5,145,900	3,637,694	2,912	3,640,606	377,239	132,284	3,395,651	944,418	805,831	51,792	99,357	58,007

Personal Income and Employment by Area: Fargo, ND-MN

(Thousands of dollars, except as noted.)

Year	Personal income, total	Earnings by place of work			Less: Contributions for government social insurance	Plus: Adjustment for residence	Equals: Net earnings by place of residence	Plus: Dividends, interest, and rent	Plus: Personal current transfer receipts	Per capita personal income (dollars)	Population (persons)	Total employment
		Nonfarm	Farm	Total								
1970	461,921	362,542	26,901	389,443	28,348	-5,550	355,545	70,298	36,078	3,827	120,690	57,963
1971	508,477	392,748	32,997	425,745	31,523	-6,398	387,824	77,533	43,120	4,118	123,471	58,638
1972	565,239	433,362	43,016	476,378	36,305	-7,410	432,663	83,886	48,690	4,505	125,464	60,388
1973	738,932	494,002	148,456	642,458	47,657	-8,735	586,066	96,667	56,199	5,853	126,247	64,939
1974	774,820	553,340	107,712	661,052	55,300	-10,032	595,720	113,677	65,423	6,076	127,527	66,730
1975	805,511	614,847	53,703	668,550	60,545	-11,105	596,900	131,654	76,957	6,247	128,935	68,868
1976	954,014	712,814	100,034	812,848	71,960	-13,696	727,192	141,938	84,884	7,240	131,761	72,986
1977	965,436	793,850	13,485	807,335	78,082	-16,720	712,533	160,652	92,251	7,233	133,484	75,490
1978	1,163,112	901,208	90,175	991,383	91,267	-20,502	879,614	180,814	102,684	8,537	136,239	78,760
1979	1,238,880	997,930	47,748	1,045,678	105,121	-23,682	916,875	205,262	116,743	9,042	137,013	80,905
1980	1,279,793	1,032,849	-10,742	1,022,107	108,371	-25,678	888,058	253,095	138,640	9,275	137,979	78,475
1981	1,477,077	1,111,935	34,643	1,146,578	123,868	-27,984	994,726	323,957	158,394	10,615	139,144	77,415
1982	1,589,813	1,160,215	29,562	1,189,777	131,226	-27,431	1,031,120	382,111	176,582	11,338	140,221	76,983
1983	1,689,505	1,241,154	37,578	1,278,732	142,297	-27,960	1,108,475	385,528	195,502	11,866	142,387	79,004
1984	1,841,558	1,354,542	55,770	1,410,312	160,412	-29,603	1,220,297	411,575	209,686	12,773	144,178	82,450
1985	1,923,175	1,433,914	39,665	1,473,579	174,605	-30,304	1,268,670	430,772	223,733	13,161	146,132	84,299
1986	2,050,093	1,525,948	65,203	1,591,151	190,012	-30,040	1,371,099	439,416	239,578	13,922	147,258	85,952
1987	2,169,763	1,625,432	87,881	1,713,313	202,064	-30,121	1,481,128	431,818	256,817	14,604	148,578	89,329
1988	2,229,630	1,728,651	43,833	1,772,484	222,888	-30,971	1,518,625	443,659	267,346	14,817	150,478	92,213
1989	2,413,499	1,844,528	40,085	1,884,613	240,369	-31,458	1,612,786	503,569	297,144	15,896	151,829	94,155
1990	2,608,036	1,983,318	80,174	2,063,492	271,881	-32,466	1,759,145	522,077	326,814	16,963	153,752	96,333
1991	2,707,245	2,102,008	64,604	2,166,612	294,376	-36,991	1,835,245	538,753	333,247	17,406	155,533	100,109
1992	2,941,602	2,254,517	97,922	2,352,439	313,894	-40,254	1,998,291	575,022	368,289	18,596	158,182	102,535
1993	3,043,079	2,396,309	30,961	2,427,270	336,104	-43,730	2,047,436	602,222	393,421	18,963	160,472	104,841
1994	3,293,157	2,575,563	91,129	2,666,692	362,862	-48,216	2,255,614	636,993	400,550	20,213	162,919	109,730
1995	3,472,077	2,710,083	51,556	2,761,639	378,924	-53,028	2,329,687	719,929	422,461	21,033	165,081	113,090
1996	3,767,556	2,893,814	136,773	3,030,587	400,551	-57,588	2,572,448	754,161	440,947	22,602	166,691	115,991
1997	3,955,292	3,091,808	65,393	3,157,201	421,830	-64,474	2,670,897	827,535	456,860	23,439	168,747	118,867
1998	4,290,291	3,382,966	71,964	3,454,930	454,239	-74,556	2,926,135	882,209	481,947	25,105	170,893	121,797
1999	4,527,992	3,594,461	96,658	3,691,119	477,293	-81,345	3,132,481	882,212	513,299	26,190	172,892	123,831
2000	4,955,481	3,926,227	98,631	4,024,858	512,259	-89,353	3,423,246	978,638	553,597	28,322	174,970	126,369
2001	5,083,883	4,063,078	90,341	4,153,419	523,373	-97,246	3,532,800	965,648	585,435	28,717	177,033	127,625
2002	5,304,550	4,230,879	90,027	4,320,906	544,400	-100,988	3,675,518	1,007,282	621,750	29,652	178,891	128,512
2003	5,608,421	4,490,045	140,941	4,630,986	577,481	-105,130	3,948,375	1,011,354	648,692	30,894	181,539	130,056
2004	5,924,344	4,815,122	118,535	4,933,657	614,097	-118,327	4,201,233	1,033,344	689,767	31,775	186,448	133,649
2005	6,236,784	5,048,387	115,900	5,164,287	640,098	-129,478	4,394,711	1,097,397	744,676	32,946	189,303	137,565
2006	6,738,999	5,413,964	122,796	5,536,760	671,722	-140,664	4,724,374	1,222,659	791,966	34,843	193,412	141,934
2007	7,241,642	5,706,766	140,938	5,847,704	705,106	-137,004	5,005,594	1,366,284	869,764	36,737	197,121	146,316
2008	8,044,690	6,078,271	210,626	6,288,897	745,625	-133,444	5,409,828	1,617,352	1,017,510	39,955	201,346	149,389
2009	7,905,449	6,202,824	63,310	6,266,134	788,288	-154,801	5,323,045	1,489,515	1,092,889	38,334	206,223	149,244
2010	8,509,522	6,461,340	163,637	6,624,977	782,505	-152,353	5,690,119	1,621,413	1,197,990	40,633	209,423	149,365
2011	9,338,294	7,047,188	175,760	7,222,948	779,709	-168,112	6,275,127	1,827,326	1,235,841	43,876	212,835	153,526
2012	10,334,390	7,698,430	303,587	8,002,017	797,731	-170,250	7,034,036	2,048,709	1,251,645	47,613	217,052	158,473
2013	10,702,297	8,107,884	246,265	8,354,149	957,306	-177,122	7,219,721	2,176,555	1,306,021	47,809	223,853	163,419
2014	11,166,605	8,677,802	78,874	8,756,676	1,026,165	-201,655	7,528,856	2,267,442	1,370,307	48,914	228,291	168,229

Personal Income and Employment by Area: Farmington, NM

(Thousands of dollars, except as noted.)

Year	Personal income, total	Derivation of personal income								Per capita personal income (dollars)	Population (persons)	Total employment
		Earnings by place of work			Less: Contributions for government social insurance	Plus: Adjustment for residence	Equals: Net earnings by place of residence	Plus: Dividends, interest, and rent	Plus: Personal current transfer receipts			
		Nonfarm	Farm	Total								
1970	142,172	114,520	1,940	116,460	7,015	1,491	110,936	15,961	15,275	2,694	52,779	16,564
1971	168,332	138,306	1,434	139,740	8,874	1,100	131,966	18,471	17,895	3,122	53,916	17,929
1972	195,098	159,610	1,861	161,471	10,557	1,120	152,034	21,320	21,744	3,499	55,756	18,919
1973	230,412	191,358	2,493	193,851	14,961	637	179,527	24,307	26,578	3,924	58,722	21,634
1974	279,706	232,400	2,617	235,017	18,932	-81	216,004	29,341	34,361	4,576	61,123	24,337
1975	327,717	270,206	2,067	272,273	21,833	-466	249,974	36,142	41,601	5,070	64,638	26,037
1976	385,225	323,417	1,509	324,926	26,842	-1,808	296,276	41,421	47,528	5,652	68,161	27,389
1977	460,992	398,902	2,605	401,507	33,905	-6,501	361,101	48,595	51,296	6,459	71,376	30,699
1978	542,863	485,529	-835	484,694	42,910	-11,790	429,994	56,907	55,962	7,225	75,134	33,028
1979	599,140	535,784	-1,030	534,754	48,919	-17,271	468,564	65,552	65,024	7,592	78,915	34,065
1980	700,734	634,038	-2,554	631,484	57,992	-27,042	546,450	80,615	73,669	8,513	82,318	36,207
1981	822,185	744,765	-277	744,488	73,413	-33,587	637,488	103,544	81,153	9,583	85,794	38,634
1982	856,615	757,164	-2,089	755,075	75,962	-33,129	645,984	125,536	85,095	9,643	88,833	37,760
1983	842,055	706,484	2,322	708,806	70,334	-27,341	611,131	132,772	98,152	9,283	90,708	35,488
1984	877,923	727,468	2,359	729,827	74,216	-24,932	630,679	144,639	102,605	9,612	91,339	35,364
1985	932,088	768,055	4,056	772,111	79,346	-26,180	666,585	158,251	107,252	10,171	91,644	36,677
1986	937,671	753,700	5,969	759,669	78,176	-24,872	656,621	163,115	117,935	10,020	93,577	35,730
1987	916,457	716,838	13,662	730,500	72,747	-21,286	636,467	159,447	120,543	9,930	92,289	34,608
1988	965,946	759,966	23,430	783,396	81,894	-22,880	678,622	161,128	126,196	10,496	92,031	36,149
1989	1,065,899	835,686	29,476	865,162	91,183	-25,575	748,404	175,382	142,113	11,534	92,413	37,919
1990	1,182,398	961,999	29,246	991,245	111,588	-29,933	849,724	181,632	151,042	12,913	91,567	40,164
1991	1,282,017	1,037,299	25,319	1,062,618	121,371	-31,749	909,498	198,549	173,970	13,674	93,755	42,648
1992	1,370,090	1,102,523	31,061	1,133,584	127,329	-32,135	974,120	203,110	192,860	14,387	95,233	43,061
1993	1,483,672	1,190,103	38,632	1,228,735	137,673	-34,409	1,056,653	215,829	211,190	15,167	97,821	44,491
1994	1,594,827	1,271,351	38,871	1,310,222	148,593	-36,451	1,125,178	233,026	236,623	15,931	100,106	46,604
1995	1,710,762	1,356,808	42,618	1,399,426	157,750	-38,236	1,203,440	252,287	255,035	16,873	101,390	49,846
1996	1,787,194	1,383,471	37,394	1,420,865	159,974	-35,839	1,225,052	271,541	290,601	17,199	103,911	50,807
1997	1,896,308	1,440,701	70,613	1,511,314	165,344	-36,749	1,309,221	293,198	293,889	17,974	105,501	52,569
1998	1,988,605	1,520,740	54,905	1,575,645	173,873	-37,609	1,364,163	303,230	321,212	18,317	108,565	53,506
1999	2,055,163	1,593,497	44,523	1,638,020	181,852	-35,709	1,420,459	290,954	343,750	18,256	112,574	54,176
2000	2,213,216	1,742,781	31,986	1,774,767	188,947	-33,969	1,551,851	297,500	363,865	19,392	114,131	54,282
2001	2,424,561	1,926,586	18,884	1,945,470	214,548	-44,771	1,686,151	333,906	404,504	20,947	115,745	56,869
2002	2,503,941	1,985,010	9,199	1,994,209	220,022	-37,218	1,736,969	323,465	443,507	20,966	119,430	57,184
2003	2,609,008	2,052,086	7,821	2,059,907	229,032	-29,408	1,801,467	333,059	474,482	21,464	121,553	57,958
2004	2,812,968	2,221,165	7,256	2,228,421	248,375	-21,366	1,958,680	357,887	496,401	22,836	123,179	60,174
2005	3,101,477	2,413,098	6,833	2,419,931	266,505	-11,203	2,142,223	420,943	538,311	24,850	124,809	62,321
2006	3,393,926	2,674,681	142	2,674,823	298,613	788	2,376,998	441,504	575,424	27,145	125,028	64,291
2007	3,645,627	2,833,825	10,172	2,843,997	322,256	14,669	2,536,410	487,000	622,217	28,899	126,149	65,875
2008	4,086,114	3,175,326	6,842	3,182,168	358,294	31,172	2,855,046	515,181	715,887	32,198	126,905	67,695
2009	3,866,137	2,879,989	9,873	2,889,862	334,985	32,398	2,587,275	486,205	792,657	29,887	129,359	64,711
2010	3,935,970	2,886,287	8,600	2,894,887	334,856	32,705	2,592,736	479,105	864,129	30,241	130,155	62,377
2011	4,207,365	3,073,671	28,524	3,102,195	319,205	30,868	2,813,858	520,407	873,100	32,861	128,035	63,237
2012	4,331,349	3,175,623	20,197	3,195,820	327,412	32,619	2,901,027	565,988	864,334	33,742	128,367	64,169
2013	4,265,395	3,148,958	30,519	3,179,477	374,082	33,723	2,839,118	565,093	861,184	33,732	126,448	64,239
2014	4,480,693	3,275,750	37,223	3,312,973	391,322	35,271	2,956,922	584,647	939,124	36,197	123,785	65,343

Personal Income and Employment by Area: Fayetteville, NC

(Thousands of dollars, except as noted.)

Year	Personal income, total	Earnings by place of work			Less: Contributions for government social insurance	Plus: Adjustment for residence	Equals: Net earnings by place of residence	Plus: Dividends, interest, and rent	Plus: Personal current transfer receipts	Per capita personal income (dollars)	Population (persons)	Total employment
		Nonfarm	Farm	Total								
1970	893,891	756,997	12,471	769,468	46,776	-44,677	678,015	174,357	41,519	3,913	228,446	112,945
1971	941,761	803,191	12,250	815,441	53,127	-46,790	715,524	175,973	50,264	4,073	231,237	109,455
1972	1,076,814	924,943	14,413	939,356	62,149	-55,330	821,877	196,087	58,850	4,625	232,815	113,149
1973	1,214,039	1,042,332	16,664	1,058,996	75,642	-61,688	921,666	224,447	67,926	5,085	238,764	119,544
1974	1,400,786	1,191,207	17,555	1,208,762	90,462	-67,167	1,051,133	265,547	84,106	5,584	250,874	124,799
1975	1,510,760	1,259,829	13,314	1,273,143	100,659	-66,120	1,106,364	289,580	114,816	5,972	252,984	123,017
1976	1,612,718	1,338,828	17,565	1,356,393	110,252	-69,138	1,177,003	303,864	131,851	6,258	257,713	123,376
1977	1,718,913	1,412,568	14,753	1,427,321	114,407	-67,292	1,245,622	333,166	140,125	6,550	262,434	123,810
1978	1,883,369	1,520,565	13,994	1,534,559	122,616	-65,474	1,346,469	386,149	150,751	7,104	265,132	123,934
1979	2,023,823	1,643,528	9,296	1,652,824	138,588	-70,462	1,443,774	411,010	169,039	7,672	263,783	126,562
1980	2,336,974	1,877,609	6,546	1,884,155	156,816	-72,948	1,654,391	479,601	202,982	8,708	268,372	132,509
1981	2,587,098	2,075,595	11,003	2,086,598	182,868	-75,498	1,828,232	527,708	231,158	9,551	270,877	131,023
1982	2,792,193	2,223,489	16,299	2,239,788	192,186	-81,364	1,966,238	573,885	252,070	10,248	272,471	130,296
1983	3,060,882	2,444,826	7,674	2,452,500	220,950	-87,695	2,143,855	640,479	276,548	11,081	276,236	134,692
1984	3,361,147	2,681,734	15,688	2,697,422	248,824	-96,358	2,352,240	712,266	296,641	11,985	280,454	140,886
1985	3,571,298	2,843,366	12,212	2,855,578	268,890	-100,256	2,486,432	766,060	318,806	12,607	283,286	143,770
1986	3,793,994	3,009,503	18,349	3,027,852	291,300	-103,774	2,632,778	827,482	333,734	13,355	284,080	145,243
1987	3,995,286	3,190,377	17,097	3,207,474	311,027	-111,043	2,785,404	866,061	343,821	13,872	288,001	149,275
1988	4,241,541	3,417,865	22,814	3,440,679	350,797	-120,543	2,969,339	895,164	377,038	14,782	286,942	151,677
1989	4,517,521	3,577,536	26,197	3,603,733	372,503	-119,182	3,112,048	977,718	427,755	15,319	294,889	155,228
1990	4,655,856	3,683,452	38,352	3,721,804	397,073	-136,688	3,188,043	990,833	476,980	15,583	298,784	153,724
1991	4,883,333	3,872,187	30,448	3,902,635	423,655	-155,820	3,323,160	1,018,878	541,295	16,119	302,956	152,205
1992	5,854,885	4,739,520	28,091	4,767,611	523,867	-218,398	4,025,346	1,229,376	600,163	19,185	305,176	169,016
1993	6,102,033	4,867,532	28,512	4,896,044	549,440	-226,162	4,120,442	1,313,962	667,629	19,377	314,917	172,380
1994	6,241,748	4,942,957	29,614	4,972,571	550,403	-233,491	4,188,677	1,356,055	697,016	19,586	318,691	174,463
1995	6,565,388	5,113,868	18,412	5,132,280	560,183	-249,432	4,322,665	1,458,205	784,518	20,355	322,543	178,702
1996	6,837,797	5,249,931	35,109	5,285,040	573,486	-259,948	4,451,606	1,528,560	857,631	21,048	324,870	179,262
1997	7,078,915	5,500,076	41,694	5,541,770	598,707	-278,427	4,664,636	1,501,563	912,716	21,473	329,662	181,817
1998	7,475,959	5,782,099	15,792	5,797,891	626,104	-296,215	4,875,572	1,652,195	948,192	22,580	331,086	185,962
1999	7,842,799	6,076,298	14,775	6,091,073	656,144	-320,118	5,114,811	1,699,015	1,028,973	23,450	334,441	189,098
2000	8,289,398	6,431,560	40,231	6,471,791	689,341	-356,191	5,426,259	1,757,249	1,105,890	24,548	337,678	191,304
2001	8,632,875	6,625,575	44,661	6,670,236	716,896	-347,594	5,605,746	1,794,600	1,232,529	25,463	339,038	187,251
2002	9,079,994	7,230,570	8,814	7,239,384	778,785	-631,036	5,829,563	1,898,646	1,351,785	26,590	341,482	191,172
2003	9,464,846	7,830,306	7,541	7,837,847	846,624	-964,811	6,026,412	1,986,158	1,452,276	27,852	339,823	195,992
2004	9,765,795	8,292,024	39,870	8,331,894	898,811	-1,291,819	6,141,264	2,051,252	1,573,279	28,245	345,748	200,111
2005	10,363,320	9,130,306	38,059	9,168,365	988,084	-1,738,303	6,441,978	2,180,578	1,740,764	30,170	343,493	206,445
2006	10,656,160	9,686,728	55,599	9,742,327	1,049,987	-2,122,881	6,569,459	2,201,043	1,885,658	30,557	348,725	209,419
2007	11,185,383	10,370,788	25,609	10,396,397	1,133,326	-2,584,168	6,678,903	2,446,776	2,059,704	31,887	350,780	215,682
2008	11,582,132	11,090,662	39,934	11,130,596	1,217,754	-3,128,480	6,784,362	2,457,135	2,340,635	32,560	355,712	219,115
2009	11,888,729	11,515,973	31,799	11,547,772	1,280,862	-3,551,637	6,715,273	2,630,201	2,543,255	32,782	362,658	220,132
2010	12,384,901	12,038,058	38,988	12,077,046	1,327,981	-3,845,950	6,903,115	2,715,132	2,766,654	33,680	367,727	220,439
2011	12,958,090	12,391,664	44,406	12,436,070	1,258,442	-4,112,783	7,064,845	2,957,184	2,936,061	34,710	373,329	222,665
2012	13,338,111	12,537,625	61,147	12,598,772	1,266,355	-4,021,700	7,310,717	2,990,399	3,036,995	35,705	373,566	220,660
2013	13,313,952	12,186,992	76,132	12,263,124	1,379,029	-3,757,169	7,126,926	3,081,115	3,105,911	35,258	377,619	219,277
2014	13,753,137	12,104,267	80,016	12,184,283	1,359,469	-3,465,769	7,359,045	3,174,313	3,219,779	36,390	377,939	217188

Personal Income and Employment by Area: Fayetteville-Springdale-Rogers, AR-MO

(Thousands of dollars, except as noted.)

Year	Personal income, total	Earnings by place of work			Less: Contributions for government social insurance	Plus: Adjustment for residence	Equals: Net earnings by place of residence	Plus: Dividends, interest, and rent	Plus: Personal current transfer receipts	Per capita personal income (dollars)	Population (persons)	Total employment
		Nonfarm	Farm	Total								
1970	413,500	316,034	11,894	327,928	22,812	-10,839	294,277	68,419	50,804	2,748	150,488	70,807
1971	469,256	349,104	18,310	367,414	25,755	-10,400	331,259	78,029	59,968	3,015	155,659	71,683
1972	555,070	402,124	39,992	442,116	31,077	-10,402	400,637	87,563	66,870	3,373	164,587	75,556
1973	664,697	458,152	72,183	530,335	40,696	-10,507	479,132	105,718	79,847	3,919	169,595	78,403
1974	705,444	511,420	23,347	534,767	47,146	-10,593	477,028	129,992	98,424	4,020	175,478	80,412
1975	838,319	542,057	75,475	617,532	48,945	-10,860	557,727	152,467	128,125	4,702	178,301	78,703
1976	944,512	643,431	61,328	704,759	58,721	-12,285	633,753	169,206	141,553	5,148	183,484	83,760
1977	1,058,817	741,029	51,710	792,739	68,496	-13,664	710,579	196,475	151,763	5,554	190,629	88,950
1978	1,228,468	854,296	73,510	927,806	81,127	-16,110	830,569	230,218	167,681	6,283	195,519	93,869
1979	1,371,131	963,848	59,363	1,023,211	94,495	-19,478	909,238	269,367	192,526	6,826	200,858	97,375
1980	1,542,312	1,058,650	42,790	1,101,440	103,799	-22,671	974,970	336,738	230,604	7,510	205,371	99,074
1981	1,763,261	1,171,804	60,434	1,232,238	125,196	-30,189	1,076,853	419,136	267,272	8,526	206,809	101,476
1982	1,882,490	1,215,378	61,102	1,276,480	131,870	-32,449	1,112,161	478,017	292,312	9,045	208,135	101,411
1983	2,076,706	1,354,375	67,759	1,422,134	148,333	-38,403	1,235,398	521,169	320,139	9,842	211,010	104,781
1984	2,378,801	1,550,778	137,228	1,688,006	174,083	-46,576	1,467,347	573,150	338,304	11,068	214,918	110,511
1985	2,605,017	1,684,589	163,140	1,847,729	190,645	-52,776	1,604,308	640,147	360,562	11,927	218,411	114,621
1986	2,879,110	1,861,114	230,081	2,091,195	211,461	-60,774	1,818,960	679,421	380,729	12,979	221,825	119,025
1987	3,020,650	2,068,017	169,772	2,237,789	233,366	-68,059	1,936,364	685,131	399,155	13,304	227,055	125,866
1988	3,287,108	2,299,487	163,036	2,462,523	269,760	-82,593	2,110,170	755,281	421,657	14,236	230,907	132,435
1989	3,621,740	2,510,503	205,230	2,715,733	294,318	-94,544	2,326,871	830,684	464,185	15,442	234,537	136,787
1990	3,861,749	2,717,351	161,597	2,878,948	332,716	-115,993	2,430,239	926,036	505,474	15,992	241,478	139,593
1991	4,164,932	2,937,329	154,255	3,091,584	360,901	-116,190	2,614,493	990,648	559,791	16,616	250,665	146,715
1992	4,671,355	3,303,921	178,397	3,482,318	403,539	-115,051	2,963,728	1,087,366	620,261	17,957	260,143	153,194
1993	5,072,256	3,596,614	163,215	3,759,829	440,861	-124,205	3,194,763	1,214,612	662,881	18,575	273,070	163,449
1994	5,566,402	3,979,984	180,065	4,160,049	493,466	-146,762	3,519,821	1,336,946	709,635	19,493	285,563	172,371
1995	6,105,793	4,329,985	180,164	4,510,149	533,315	-156,843	3,819,991	1,512,501	773,301	20,376	299,657	183,452
1996	6,607,923	4,573,053	223,540	4,796,593	559,343	-171,487	4,065,763	1,713,774	828,386	21,178	312,015	189,353
1997	7,111,599	4,889,836	234,173	5,124,009	598,205	-196,748	4,329,056	1,900,159	882,384	22,110	321,648	193,813
1998	7,795,419	5,387,131	240,646	5,627,777	653,206	-197,350	4,777,221	2,084,046	934,152	23,663	329,438	196,865
1999	8,384,116	5,914,930	271,439	6,186,369	715,656	-209,863	5,260,850	2,147,609	975,657	24,745	338,827	203,117
2000	9,089,616	6,425,585	225,074	6,650,659	773,633	-225,033	5,651,993	2,388,168	1,049,455	26,005	349,532	209,646
2001	9,883,287	7,026,948	278,416	7,305,364	820,343	-255,734	6,229,287	2,478,708	1,175,292	27,580	358,350	218,496
2002	10,437,972	7,605,964	188,928	7,794,892	887,229	-264,533	6,643,130	2,530,618	1,264,224	28,392	367,634	225,455
2003	11,242,244	8,207,332	199,193	8,406,525	946,082	-263,687	7,196,756	2,713,198	1,332,290	29,627	379,457	230,493
2004	12,563,312	8,952,286	336,543	9,288,829	1,016,746	-266,718	8,005,365	3,122,956	1,434,991	31,993	392,694	238,571
2005	13,833,787	9,623,235	248,528	9,871,763	1,102,347	-262,873	8,506,543	3,762,944	1,564,300	33,907	407,987	250,905
2006	15,439,476	10,365,104	121,825	10,486,929	1,200,778	-249,358	9,036,793	4,659,273	1,743,410	36,412	424,016	261,047
2007	16,972,134	10,788,667	170,309	10,958,976	1,254,202	-216,969	9,487,805	5,566,410	1,917,919	38,879	436,539	265,722
2008	18,302,007	11,151,944	174,273	11,326,217	1,323,871	-174,891	9,827,455	6,258,291	2,216,261	40,981	446,592	266,303
2009	17,384,426	11,041,751	41,993	11,083,744	1,323,127	-165,663	9,594,954	5,335,250	2,454,222	38,196	455,143	258,825
2010	17,959,662	11,473,774	39,580	11,513,354	1,368,627	-180,696	9,964,031	5,292,519	2,703,112	38,565	465,699	259,104
2011	20,485,924	12,011,286	298	12,011,584	1,296,644	-194,785	10,520,155	7,170,288	2,795,481	43,199	474,222	266,230
2012	23,740,015	12,879,780	105,375	12,985,155	1,350,198	-214,954	11,420,003	9,463,382	2,856,630	49,148	483,029	272,731
2013	24,237,451	13,652,279	248,187	13,900,466	1,614,569	-228,400	12,057,497	9,214,038	2,965,916	49,226	492,375	279,710
2014	25,426,622	14,439,541	379,580	14,819,121	1,722,754	-253,126	12,843,241	9,422,098	3,161,283	50,686	501,653	289,917

Personal Income and Employment by Area: Flagstaff, AZ

(Thousands of dollars, except as noted.)

Year	Personal income, total	Earnings by place of work			Less: Contributions for government social insurance	Plus: Adjustment for residence	Equals: Net earnings by place of residence	Plus: Dividends, interest, and rent	Plus: Personal current transfer receipts	Per capita personal income (dollars)	Population (persons)	Total employment
		Nonfarm	Farm	Total								
1970	160,786	133,353	2,083	135,436	7,929	-8,971	118,536	26,648	15,602	3,269	49,180	20,148
1971	190,255	162,914	2,268	165,182	10,419	-13,565	141,198	29,571	19,486	3,568	53,330	21,705
1972	230,656	207,832	3,051	210,883	14,192	-21,497	175,194	33,239	22,223	3,963	58,203	24,041
1973	272,445	249,303	4,013	253,316	19,668	-25,725	207,923	38,499	26,023	4,419	61,654	26,189
1974	293,990	262,806	150	262,956	21,044	-21,610	220,302	43,666	30,022	4,535	64,831	26,719
1975	332,192	276,857	5,866	282,723	21,637	-16,253	244,833	46,964	40,395	4,757	69,825	26,902
1976	357,832	293,574	1,493	295,067	22,768	-10,204	262,095	50,672	45,065	5,389	66,403	27,565
1977	393,449	322,936	1,148	324,084	25,138	-5,975	292,971	58,045	42,433	5,707	68,939	29,570
1978	466,270	380,902	6,516	387,418	30,620	-6,774	350,024	69,125	47,121	6,584	70,815	32,397
1979	516,661	422,057	646	422,703	35,957	-6,120	380,626	81,113	54,922	7,043	73,357	33,879
1980	595,453	475,951	2,285	478,236	41,461	-5,714	431,061	97,989	66,403	7,879	75,579	35,165
1981	659,683	514,553	666	515,219	48,110	-2,142	464,967	120,530	74,186	8,480	77,794	35,739
1982	701,570	530,934	3,444	534,378	50,961	178	483,595	137,269	80,706	8,863	79,156	35,849
1983	768,838	574,391	3,431	577,822	57,080	-866	519,876	158,136	90,826	9,478	81,118	37,242
1984	858,999	642,766	5,768	648,534	64,982	-4,044	579,508	181,827	97,664	10,270	83,640	39,790
1985	938,931	708,153	935	709,088	73,183	-5,917	629,988	200,863	108,080	11,121	84,431	41,603
1986	1,037,025	789,721	3,307	793,028	82,627	-8,353	702,048	220,481	114,496	11,842	87,575	43,483
1987	1,108,883	844,946	1,538	846,484	88,022	-9,833	748,629	234,386	125,868	12,269	90,380	45,220
1988	1,188,590	912,141	678	912,819	99,814	-14,662	798,343	252,837	137,410	12,732	93,355	46,586
1989	1,266,057	929,779	-305	929,474	104,392	-15,764	809,318	292,870	163,869	13,300	95,194	47,115
1990	1,371,049	1,008,081	775	1,008,856	116,572	-20,256	872,028	316,580	182,441	14,119	97,106	48,543
1991	1,463,580	1,080,240	1,751	1,081,991	126,056	-22,479	933,456	327,177	202,947	14,688	99,647	49,766
1992	1,605,770	1,186,652	2,163	1,188,815	138,435	-25,517	1,024,863	349,232	231,675	15,666	102,498	51,643
1993	1,701,264	1,255,058	107	1,255,165	147,039	-24,822	1,083,304	371,433	246,527	16,115	105,570	53,787
1994	1,851,243	1,350,494	-1,110	1,349,384	157,844	-23,884	1,167,656	422,822	260,765	17,034	108,680	56,507
1995	1,975,886	1,419,451	-1,248	1,418,203	158,661	-23,453	1,236,089	475,515	264,282	17,808	110,954	58,867
1996	2,122,460	1,525,590	899	1,526,489	174,578	-23,168	1,328,743	509,329	284,388	18,835	112,686	61,574
1997	2,279,480	1,623,016	734	1,623,750	181,721	-18,928	1,423,101	562,025	294,354	19,918	114,444	62,567
1998	2,459,508	1,736,960	4,580	1,741,540	190,724	-15,957	1,534,859	614,453	310,196	21,410	114,874	65,508
1999	2,607,034	1,852,019	9,547	1,861,566	200,175	-13,843	1,647,548	628,529	330,957	22,610	115,307	66,909
2000	2,819,250	2,007,152	4,264	2,011,416	213,591	-11,279	1,786,546	683,938	348,766	24,143	116,773	70,054
2001	2,948,827	2,061,988	9,274	2,071,262	225,488	9,456	1,855,230	683,101	410,496	24,930	118,283	70,371
2002	3,099,317	2,188,178	614	2,188,792	239,766	12,574	1,961,600	681,961	455,756	25,549	121,308	71,378
2003	3,245,548	2,319,251	-92	2,319,159	251,360	16,211	2,084,010	658,604	502,934	26,412	122,882	73,727
2004	3,501,321	2,496,182	1,723	2,497,905	269,905	20,603	2,248,603	731,716	521,002	27,984	125,117	77,953
2005	3,806,400	2,694,459	78	2,694,537	292,472	25,685	2,427,750	802,062	576,588	29,966	127,025	80,212
2006	4,209,190	2,955,762	-31	2,955,731	311,841	32,007	2,675,897	917,825	615,468	32,707	128,695	82,928
2007	4,497,402	3,186,113	17,914	3,204,027	341,406	39,776	2,902,397	928,223	666,782	34,478	130,442	86,446
2008	4,741,258	3,225,362	9,741	3,235,103	349,528	45,480	2,931,055	1,034,428	775,775	35,959	131,853	85,414
2009	4,595,269	3,145,242	2,476	3,147,718	344,079	37,940	2,841,579	887,113	866,577	34,427	133,477	82,871
2010	4,603,037	3,155,203	1,595	3,156,798	344,504	35,112	2,847,406	803,440	952,191	34,197	134,603	83,135
2011	4,819,660	3,221,815	2,503	3,224,318	310,799	40,101	2,953,620	918,993	947,047	35,925	134,159	82,517
2012	4,978,754	3,310,145	492	3,310,637	318,057	45,050	3,037,630	1,022,744	918,380	36,622	135,949	83,273
2013	5,127,921	3,458,721	2,427	3,461,148	376,856	40,785	3,125,077	1,070,712	932,132	37,515	136,690	85,047
2014	5,399,899	3,615,640	7,206	3,622,846	397,096	40,643	3,266,393	1,107,577	1,025,929	39,220	137,682	86,398

Personal Income and Employment by Area: Flint, MI

(Thousands of dollars, except as noted.)

| Year | Personal income, total | Derivation of personal income | | | | | | | | Per capita personal income (dollars) | Population (persons) | Total employment |
| | | Earnings by place of work | | | Less: Contributions for government social insurance | Plus: Adjustment for residence | Equals: Net earnings by place of residence | Plus: Dividends, interest, and rent | Plus: Personal current transfer receipts | | | |
		Nonfarm	Farm	Total								
1970	1,762,611	1,620,865	3,749	1,624,614	113,439	-119,458	1,391,717	207,274	163,620	3,952	446,058	169,418
1971	2,041,037	1,929,435	3,188	1,932,623	138,409	-154,878	1,639,336	219,702	181,999	4,553	448,310	180,597
1972	2,221,341	2,119,051	5,044	2,124,095	164,610	-175,150	1,784,335	233,044	203,962	4,951	448,656	181,540
1973	2,439,165	2,372,043	6,331	2,378,374	213,069	-200,173	1,965,132	247,060	226,973	5,399	451,762	190,536
1974	2,460,327	2,269,345	6,992	2,276,337	211,254	-185,391	1,879,692	274,176	306,459	5,466	450,155	181,085
1975	2,677,745	2,422,486	7,264	2,429,750	222,103	-204,935	2,002,712	289,470	385,563	5,992	446,850	172,646
1976	3,186,929	3,029,418	6,365	3,035,783	283,603	-283,512	2,468,668	324,246	394,015	7,164	444,880	184,610
1977	3,673,112	3,594,231	5,861	3,600,092	336,765	-356,363	2,906,964	368,561	397,587	8,226	446,546	197,459
1978	4,022,100	3,980,051	1,933	3,981,984	387,416	-396,476	3,198,092	407,832	416,176	8,946	449,607	205,560
1979	4,391,486	4,296,807	4,071	4,300,878	427,340	-427,330	3,446,208	457,509	487,769	9,735	451,082	209,373
1980	4,620,254	4,182,343	3,704	4,186,047	408,258	-412,989	3,364,800	532,874	722,580	10,287	449,131	193,291
1981	5,038,499	4,632,447	4,682	4,637,129	493,230	-464,188	3,679,711	645,772	713,016	11,377	442,878	196,257
1982	5,001,400	4,341,303	-159	4,341,144	468,809	-409,007	3,463,328	736,724	801,348	11,442	437,115	180,848
1983	5,443,275	4,830,924	2,642	4,833,566	531,404	-467,013	3,835,149	779,942	828,184	12,583	432,600	184,486
1984	6,065,488	5,471,133	5,904	5,477,037	624,808	-524,533	4,327,696	901,238	836,554	14,097	430,254	194,055
1985	6,590,014	6,010,228	4,895	6,015,123	705,066	-561,694	4,748,363	971,276	870,375	15,281	431,268	202,416
1986	6,919,610	6,239,061	3,838	6,242,899	732,763	-554,885	4,955,251	1,045,728	918,631	15,979	433,037	205,863
1987	6,623,107	5,700,879	4,050	5,704,929	661,344	-421,690	4,621,895	1,035,042	966,170	15,284	433,335	202,507
1988	6,851,908	5,772,692	3,977	5,776,669	685,436	-378,319	4,712,914	1,100,397	1,038,597	15,931	430,096	194,226
1989	7,183,841	5,986,789	6,405	5,993,194	714,199	-370,649	4,908,346	1,139,926	1,135,569	16,748	428,946	198,317
1990	7,519,345	6,132,024	5,372	6,137,396	741,868	-353,731	5,041,797	1,255,999	1,221,549	17,449	430,938	201,117
1991	7,876,808	6,397,986	1,817	6,399,803	786,257	-356,601	5,256,945	1,229,556	1,390,307	18,268	431,184	196,856
1992	8,137,606	6,504,498	1,331	6,505,829	789,813	-290,858	5,425,158	1,246,995	1,465,453	18,883	430,944	195,695
1993	8,495,450	6,722,381	1,467	6,723,848	823,066	-248,234	5,652,548	1,287,452	1,555,450	19,725	430,702	195,165
1994	9,371,228	7,562,842	-1,445	7,561,397	930,484	-287,302	6,343,611	1,464,992	1,562,625	21,756	430,742	205,760
1995	9,876,975	7,828,423	1,510	7,829,933	957,531	-235,088	6,637,314	1,555,508	1,684,153	22,850	432,261	214,744
1996	10,311,363	7,863,004	-1,952	7,861,052	933,462	-128,179	6,799,411	1,631,045	1,880,907	23,797	433,302	218,418
1997	10,482,217	7,917,620	-2,213	7,915,407	937,397	-17,314	6,960,696	1,735,365	1,786,156	24,210	432,978	218,542
1998	10,784,698	8,113,994	-2,741	8,111,253	942,698	120,670	7,289,225	1,753,557	1,741,916	24,898	433,160	217,088
1999	11,099,280	8,180,443	2,658	8,183,101	956,733	248,684	7,475,052	1,755,066	1,869,162	25,550	434,409	214,175
2000	11,615,761	8,412,742	-2,056	8,410,686	970,747	392,285	7,832,224	1,826,536	1,957,001	26,583	436,965	214,909
2001	11,506,866	8,298,640	-5,569	8,293,071	962,426	296,311	7,626,956	1,723,743	2,156,167	26,236	438,584	211,243
2002	11,733,371	8,367,652	-903	8,366,749	970,204	387,326	7,783,871	1,709,517	2,239,983	26,663	440,062	209,508
2003	12,112,111	8,427,879	2,251	8,430,130	970,934	484,718	7,943,914	1,789,884	2,378,313	27,422	441,689	208,064
2004	12,377,216	8,652,854	6,529	8,659,383	1,007,180	598,877	8,251,080	1,657,570	2,468,566	27,969	442,534	211,275
2005	12,358,407	8,371,229	7,814	8,379,043	982,628	674,655	8,071,070	1,669,991	2,617,346	27,928	442,508	206,146
2006	12,842,798	8,570,103	8,425	8,578,528	1,022,876	793,658	8,349,310	1,721,654	2,771,834	29,111	441,164	205,756
2007	13,044,632	8,320,823	8,013	8,328,836	1,003,460	881,522	8,206,898	1,791,086	3,046,648	29,775	438,109	204,141
2008	13,142,696	7,906,210	11,631	7,917,841	968,789	935,771	7,884,823	1,766,878	3,490,995	30,347	433,082	193,422
2009	12,690,870	7,427,784	5,844	7,433,628	922,899	682,067	7,192,796	1,601,881	3,896,193	29,652	427,989	185,987
2010	12,855,255	7,449,596	9,325	7,458,921	917,967	534,052	7,075,006	1,563,945	4,216,304	30,249	424,976	183,431
2011	13,418,960	7,688,462	23,208	7,711,670	850,517	620,167	7,481,320	1,753,295	4,184,345	31,820	421,716	186,821
2012	13,686,157	7,871,090	20,215	7,891,305	869,321	771,723	7,793,707	1,763,861	4,128,589	32,737	418,058	186,228
2013	13,945,189	7,988,768	25,311	8,014,079	1,015,252	786,727	7,785,554	1,878,850	4,280,785	33,552	415,623	189,274
2014	14,400,945	8,277,590	21,432	8,299,022	1,043,216	812,644	8,068,450	1,946,377	4,386,118	34,878	412,895	192,136

Personal Income and Employment by Area: Florence, SC

(Thousands of dollars, except as noted.)

| Year | Personal income, total | Derivation of personal income | | | | | | | | Per capita personal income (dollars) | Population (persons) | Total employment |
| | | Earnings by place of work | | | Less: Contributions for government social insurance | Plus: Adjustment for residence | Equals: Net earnings by place of residence | Plus: Dividends, interest, and rent | Plus: Personal current transfer receipts | | | |
		Nonfarm	Farm	Total								
1970	405,461	336,115	23,087	359,202	23,637	-14,705	320,860	43,415	41,186	2,833	143,122	68,218
1971	444,431	368,062	23,811	391,873	26,699	-15,721	349,453	47,913	47,065	3,052	145,616	69,457
1972	500,450	420,694	24,895	445,589	31,941	-18,496	395,152	53,068	52,230	3,404	147,002	72,381
1973	575,196	486,703	30,377	517,080	42,491	-22,120	452,469	60,820	61,907	3,786	151,937	76,728
1974	672,952	557,855	43,467	601,322	50,584	-27,239	523,499	68,793	80,660	4,269	157,632	78,964
1975	712,562	563,221	31,022	594,243	49,699	-24,208	520,336	79,118	113,108	4,429	160,899	74,439
1976	790,031	648,441	23,012	671,453	58,461	-27,531	585,461	85,469	119,101	4,867	162,337	76,550
1977	867,618	720,543	20,706	741,249	65,020	-29,970	646,259	95,685	125,674	5,213	166,445	77,460
1978	990,783	817,931	32,603	850,534	75,495	-32,226	742,813	107,039	140,931	5,858	169,123	79,149
1979	1,095,078	917,168	21,030	938,198	87,479	-37,873	812,846	119,814	162,418	6,374	171,805	80,572
1980	1,217,871	1,015,550	1,734	1,017,284	96,820	-44,159	876,305	149,060	192,506	7,030	173,231	81,883
1981	1,392,491	1,128,927	25,746	1,154,673	115,644	-52,500	986,529	187,053	218,909	8,000	174,072	82,700
1982	1,454,639	1,134,347	33,593	1,167,940	119,110	-48,222	1,000,608	217,248	236,783	8,341	174,401	79,678
1983	1,550,477	1,220,982	11,315	1,232,297	130,065	-45,527	1,056,705	241,491	252,281	8,920	173,824	80,119
1984	1,727,813	1,371,869	23,390	1,395,259	151,219	-53,949	1,190,091	272,125	265,597	9,879	174,898	83,677
1985	1,824,120	1,422,851	22,453	1,445,304	158,687	-51,844	1,234,773	297,944	291,403	10,398	175,430	82,212
1986	1,918,730	1,528,047	-3,836	1,524,211	174,548	-49,328	1,300,335	313,471	304,924	10,951	175,210	83,463
1987	2,055,989	1,622,427	28,369	1,650,796	182,753	-46,700	1,421,343	322,679	311,967	11,762	174,806	84,803
1988	2,242,064	1,774,477	39,132	1,813,609	207,126	-50,821	1,555,662	353,824	332,578	12,831	174,734	88,568
1989	2,468,410	1,899,077	37,198	1,936,275	225,134	-51,176	1,659,965	423,565	384,880	14,052	175,658	91,566
1990	2,640,737	2,059,639	23,238	2,082,877	247,473	-52,714	1,782,690	429,910	428,137	14,944	176,706	93,814
1991	2,810,391	2,168,214	33,573	2,201,787	262,966	-60,023	1,878,798	437,843	493,750	15,655	179,519	94,063
1992	3,006,203	2,306,281	36,008	2,342,289	277,060	-61,115	2,004,114	443,436	558,653	16,514	182,044	95,003
1993	3,167,572	2,441,637	29,036	2,470,673	296,509	-64,972	2,109,192	461,686	596,694	17,198	184,186	96,466
1994	3,344,698	2,544,262	43,427	2,587,689	312,172	-64,327	2,211,190	497,764	635,744	18,007	185,744	98,121
1995	3,505,468	2,692,905	23,097	2,716,002	329,940	-72,061	2,314,001	518,847	672,620	18,668	187,778	100,459
1996	3,752,435	2,861,167	44,991	2,906,158	344,323	-82,481	2,479,354	554,154	718,927	19,862	188,929	102,855
1997	3,928,008	3,010,178	40,799	3,050,977	360,923	-88,563	2,601,491	582,053	744,464	20,601	190,674	106,126
1998	4,167,158	3,221,120	17,350	3,238,470	384,816	-94,824	2,758,830	630,462	777,866	21,740	191,680	107,057
1999	4,324,051	3,355,289	20,787	3,376,076	395,368	-94,375	2,886,333	613,809	823,909	22,446	192,641	107,733
2000	4,620,308	3,553,687	50,162	3,603,849	416,600	-101,426	3,085,823	669,296	865,189	23,904	193,290	108,486
2001	4,822,248	3,647,865	67,434	3,715,299	427,370	-112,777	3,175,152	697,262	949,834	24,826	194,240	106,886
2002	4,950,094	3,782,910	-7,344	3,775,566	442,626	-120,238	3,212,702	697,967	1,039,425	25,309	195,590	107,597
2003	5,118,531	3,873,336	47,419	3,920,755	452,908	-122,408	3,345,439	690,923	1,082,169	25,975	197,053	106,436
2004	5,377,311	4,026,888	37,816	4,064,704	471,295	-126,732	3,466,677	737,991	1,172,643	27,157	198,010	107,151
2005	5,591,264	4,161,421	24,671	4,186,092	485,153	-123,264	3,577,675	761,684	1,251,905	28,073	199,167	108,231
2006	6,029,775	4,436,627	22,161	4,458,788	527,388	-120,913	3,810,487	886,989	1,332,299	30,012	200,913	110,032
2007	6,303,802	4,605,604	7,496	4,613,100	548,271	-120,760	3,944,069	957,127	1,402,606	31,169	202,246	113,049
2008	6,551,185	4,649,684	14,832	4,664,516	555,267	-118,219	3,991,030	965,901	1,594,254	32,144	203,805	112,542
2009	6,404,180	4,468,668	12,082	4,480,750	538,378	-129,903	3,812,469	870,869	1,720,842	31,267	204,825	108,124
2010	6,524,012	4,491,782	5,051	4,496,833	540,457	-127,354	3,829,022	849,445	1,845,545	31,714	205,713	107,836
2011	6,805,976	4,576,263	11,594	4,587,857	493,193	-91,982	4,002,682	953,440	1,849,854	33,080	205,746	109,502
2012	6,959,798	4,727,393	33,792	4,761,185	503,809	-91,608	4,165,768	947,723	1,846,307	33,749	206,225	110,575
2013	7,083,017	4,870,850	51,291	4,922,141	586,904	-99,980	4,235,257	980,213	1,867,547	34,320	206,380	111,861
2014	7,291,681	5,001,902	16,467	5,018,369	602,566	-92,998	4,322,805	1,013,943	1,954,933	35,220	207,030	112,643

Personal Income and Employment by Area: Florence-Muscle Shoals, AL

(Thousands of dollars, except as noted.)

| Year | Personal income, total | Derivation of personal income | | | | | | | | | Per capita personal income (dollars) | Population (persons) | Total employment |
| | | Earnings by place of work | | | Less: Contributions for government social insurance | Plus: Adjustment for residence | Equals: Net earnings by place of residence | Plus: Dividends, interest, and rent | Plus: Personal current transfer receipts | | | | |
		Nonfarm	Farm	Total									
1970	363,952	287,623	11,269	298,892	19,098	2,547	282,341	44,947	36,664	3,082	118,093	45,574
1971	406,915	319,140	13,503	332,643	21,253	1,523	312,913	51,268	42,734	3,376	120,545	46,466
1972	444,389	359,137	14,600	373,737	25,604	-4,412	343,721	54,301	46,367	3,655	121,579	48,921
1973	489,526	396,276	19,485	415,761	33,191	-7,029	375,541	60,502	53,483	3,962	123,562	50,449
1974	544,751	445,488	13,243	458,731	38,994	-9,071	410,666	70,095	63,990	4,388	124,134	51,771
1975	597,618	471,080	11,781	482,861	40,926	-9,284	432,651	79,447	85,520	4,727	126,431	50,742
1976	689,141	555,105	23,631	578,736	48,725	-22,400	507,611	87,388	94,142	5,389	127,873	53,503
1977	759,867	631,422	17,434	648,856	55,100	-32,383	561,373	99,802	98,692	5,836	130,206	55,877
1978	871,268	734,654	18,412	753,066	64,548	-39,887	648,631	116,388	106,249	6,607	131,868	59,286
1979	970,479	792,728	28,891	821,619	72,331	-34,239	715,049	133,419	122,011	7,212	134,560	59,603
1980	1,072,902	857,196	12,059	869,255	78,019	-37,720	753,516	168,340	151,046	7,929	135,322	58,791
1981	1,188,523	903,473	22,282	925,755	89,404	-20,571	815,780	205,346	167,397	8,732	136,104	57,118
1982	1,235,048	912,357	22,328	934,685	92,281	-18,256	824,148	224,948	185,952	9,139	135,139	55,778
1983	1,283,380	944,161	1,285	945,446	99,153	-6,234	840,059	237,097	206,224	9,574	134,050	56,395
1984	1,388,206	993,743	13,187	1,006,930	107,165	4,448	904,213	263,957	220,036	10,399	133,488	57,561
1985	1,470,393	1,029,739	12,687	1,042,426	113,220	24,331	953,537	284,986	231,870	11,027	133,350	57,338
1986	1,550,151	1,078,451	7,737	1,086,188	118,286	40,305	1,008,207	299,634	242,310	11,686	132,653	57,115
1987	1,630,753	1,124,798	13,778	1,138,576	122,477	57,376	1,073,475	308,451	248,827	12,369	131,839	58,321
1988	1,772,907	1,217,467	18,618	1,236,085	137,899	80,075	1,178,261	338,095	256,551	13,520	131,132	60,565
1989	1,892,327	1,277,379	14,515	1,291,894	147,400	82,290	1,226,784	378,134	287,409	14,472	130,762	62,347
1990	2,074,754	1,397,822	9,946	1,407,768	161,987	111,445	1,357,226	402,889	314,639	15,737	131,838	64,761
1991	2,166,071	1,461,701	19,772	1,481,473	170,877	107,954	1,418,550	398,414	349,107	16,197	133,733	66,343
1992	2,316,382	1,566,928	23,991	1,590,919	180,401	112,923	1,523,441	402,884	390,057	17,136	135,174	67,141
1993	2,408,403	1,635,522	16,628	1,652,150	192,102	120,284	1,580,332	417,031	411,040	17,583	136,971	68,977
1994	2,550,262	1,727,331	32,016	1,759,347	204,809	117,490	1,672,028	441,125	437,109	18,509	137,786	69,508
1995	2,700,100	1,809,531	3,344	1,812,875	217,006	129,142	1,725,011	501,746	473,343	19,430	138,962	72,519
1996	2,811,318	1,868,993	25,920	1,894,913	221,563	124,846	1,798,196	512,638	500,484	20,035	140,318	73,172
1997	2,904,690	1,916,287	15,974	1,932,261	226,908	129,976	1,835,329	542,360	527,001	20,551	141,339	73,294
1998	2,978,827	1,909,522	15,576	1,925,098	222,547	148,050	1,850,601	578,623	549,603	20,972	142,041	71,757
1999	3,057,409	1,979,672	11,394	1,991,066	229,262	157,269	1,919,073	568,401	569,935	21,485	142,305	71,540
2000	3,188,727	2,021,395	18,261	2,039,656	231,968	163,340	1,971,028	614,651	603,048	22,293	143,036	72,009
2001	3,283,937	2,031,542	20,577	2,052,119	235,630	178,154	1,994,643	619,794	669,500	23,032	142,584	70,279
2002	3,288,774	2,018,256	6,638	2,024,894	233,707	165,778	1,956,965	615,427	716,382	23,134	142,163	67,716
2003	3,408,058	2,083,445	32,801	2,116,246	241,844	165,763	2,040,165	612,504	755,389	23,936	142,382	67,493
2004	3,603,009	2,202,111	49,745	2,251,856	254,981	180,536	2,177,411	613,415	812,183	25,176	143,112	69,442
2005	3,806,245	2,321,049	48,853	2,369,902	273,431	196,681	2,293,152	648,147	864,946	26,484	143,717	71,736
2006	4,021,940	2,476,729	38,276	2,515,005	292,272	215,218	2,437,951	650,639	933,350	27,794	144,707	74,252
2007	4,279,977	2,543,238	29,356	2,572,594	305,020	240,867	2,508,441	776,935	994,601	29,397	145,593	75,339
2008	4,413,954	2,551,658	32,177	2,583,835	312,606	252,750	2,523,979	796,994	1,092,981	30,093	146,675	74,049
2009	4,397,262	2,536,004	29,400	2,565,404	311,087	230,398	2,484,715	732,033	1,180,514	29,923	146,952	72,359
2010	4,595,021	2,658,016	255	2,658,271	330,939	243,633	2,570,965	746,685	1,277,371	31,210	147,231	72,192
2011	4,740,074	2,709,381	1,516	2,710,897	304,135	257,824	2,664,586	803,763	1,271,725	32,236	147,042	73,261
2012	4,799,282	2,724,117	6,934	2,731,051	304,406	273,789	2,700,434	819,543	1,279,305	32,611	147,167	73,049
2013	4,843,319	2,762,633	58,759	2,821,392	348,751	261,472	2,734,113	813,478	1,295,728	32,887	147,273	73,315
2014	5,047,108	2,923,921	40,791	2,964,712	362,550	263,107	2,865,269	847,843	1,333,996	34,185	147,639	74,663

Personal Income and Employment by Area: Fond du Lac, WI

(Thousands of dollars, except as noted.)

Year	Personal income, total	Earnings by place of work			Less: Contributions for government social insurance	Plus: Adjustment for residence	Equals: Net earnings by place of residence	Plus: Dividends, interest, and rent	Plus: Personal current transfer receipts	Per capita personal income (dollars)	Population (persons)	Total employment
		Nonfarm	Farm	Total								
1970	321,764	245,756	18,456	264,212	18,807	-2,938	242,467	50,806	28,491	3,813	84,380	39,020
1971	343,227	256,550	21,497	278,047	20,238	-428	257,381	53,522	32,324	4,107	83,569	38,765
1972	374,798	283,715	20,008	303,723	23,510	2,250	282,463	56,563	35,772	4,396	85,264	40,118
1973	421,559	320,915	21,909	342,824	30,581	4,099	316,342	63,719	41,498	4,873	86,518	41,920
1974	461,480	342,799	21,018	363,817	33,885	9,186	339,118	72,699	49,663	5,331	86,561	42,694
1975	508,912	358,986	25,368	384,354	34,687	14,050	363,717	80,662	64,533	5,840	87,138	41,961
1976	563,495	406,870	22,955	429,825	39,852	17,975	407,948	85,201	70,346	6,490	86,830	42,917
1977	634,781	448,168	39,691	487,859	44,127	23,441	467,173	94,435	73,173	7,241	87,670	44,071
1978	699,514	500,700	32,151	532,851	50,575	32,295	514,571	104,361	80,582	7,974	87,720	44,857
1979	791,456	562,167	40,505	602,672	59,087	40,588	584,173	115,537	91,746	8,976	88,172	46,299
1980	860,102	585,508	35,167	620,675	61,496	45,557	604,736	142,006	113,360	9,672	88,924	45,661
1981	943,940	648,891	24,762	673,653	73,081	43,465	644,037	174,968	124,935	10,659	88,556	46,334
1982	994,624	663,337	21,333	684,670	75,710	43,962	652,922	199,470	142,232	11,256	88,361	45,665
1983	1,037,359	698,700	6,129	704,829	79,161	49,126	674,794	212,627	149,938	11,750	88,289	45,170
1984	1,156,967	779,851	23,085	802,936	90,274	52,581	765,243	240,333	151,391	13,065	88,552	46,517
1985	1,211,479	812,553	25,336	837,889	94,159	55,602	799,332	249,896	162,251	13,621	88,942	46,739
1986	1,274,369	848,358	33,960	882,318	98,070	65,597	849,845	257,702	166,822	14,333	88,909	45,908
1987	1,361,624	929,867	41,385	971,252	105,180	70,470	936,542	256,628	168,454	15,293	89,038	46,598
1988	1,423,621	1,006,014	20,739	1,026,753	117,346	76,969	986,376	262,402	174,843	15,856	89,787	47,180
1989	1,602,958	1,143,595	45,809	1,189,404	132,900	66,732	1,123,236	288,701	191,021	17,861	89,748	50,119
1990	1,683,822	1,206,357	39,054	1,245,411	145,118	81,412	1,181,705	296,262	205,855	18,648	90,296	51,402
1991	1,719,254	1,236,762	34,829	1,271,591	151,295	80,681	1,200,977	298,564	219,713	18,838	91,265	51,910
1992	1,851,998	1,349,348	37,534	1,386,882	163,381	85,024	1,308,525	304,386	239,087	20,120	92,049	52,863
1993	1,954,486	1,442,926	27,400	1,470,326	175,223	86,933	1,382,036	323,497	248,953	21,044	92,876	54,466
1994	2,097,530	1,550,665	42,564	1,593,229	189,842	93,702	1,497,089	343,146	257,295	22,382	93,717	55,863
1995	2,188,455	1,601,174	26,664	1,627,838	196,590	100,798	1,532,046	385,350	271,059	23,156	94,509	56,839
1996	2,308,158	1,661,176	43,435	1,704,611	202,365	107,038	1,609,284	414,472	284,402	24,162	95,529	57,633
1997	2,416,040	1,735,579	27,387	1,762,966	211,526	111,403	1,662,843	459,572	293,625	25,168	95,998	57,950
1998	2,559,135	1,845,592	41,879	1,887,471	224,855	115,852	1,778,468	475,646	305,021	26,516	96,512	59,467
1999	2,621,584	1,898,535	37,113	1,935,648	232,480	126,568	1,829,736	478,443	313,405	27,031	96,985	59,810
2000	2,769,493	2,007,950	22,249	2,030,199	241,590	133,497	1,922,106	505,309	342,078	28,437	97,390	60,695
2001	2,864,385	2,039,684	29,470	2,069,154	239,421	161,538	1,991,271	491,921	381,193	29,271	97,856	59,067
2002	2,963,467	2,112,864	23,969	2,136,833	245,231	168,890	2,060,492	491,333	411,642	30,210	98,097	59,440
2003	3,054,837	2,166,343	42,976	2,209,319	251,049	177,476	2,135,746	493,592	425,499	31,023	98,470	58,935
2004	3,183,684	2,293,715	48,697	2,342,412	264,281	191,705	2,269,836	481,235	432,613	32,182	98,929	58,973
2005	3,287,070	2,371,738	45,874	2,417,612	275,565	202,772	2,344,819	478,929	463,322	33,103	99,297	59,261
2006	3,440,021	2,458,721	33,760	2,492,481	287,085	214,964	2,420,360	527,634	492,027	34,428	99,920	59,588
2007	3,634,336	2,527,265	65,013	2,592,278	298,260	233,828	2,527,846	573,332	533,158	36,155	100,520	60,230
2008	3,820,516	2,607,531	64,807	2,672,338	309,381	251,074	2,614,031	611,509	594,976	37,781	101,122	60,414
2009	3,657,475	2,425,229	19,051	2,444,280	291,132	244,170	2,397,318	560,654	699,503	36,080	101,370	57,502
2010	3,705,201	2,390,642	58,108	2,448,750	294,344	255,493	2,409,899	543,027	752,275	36,452	101,645	56,964
2011	3,913,029	2,497,022	110,097	2,607,119	279,087	275,032	2,603,064	591,860	718,105	38,441	101,792	57,810
2012	4,097,097	2,626,283	105,757	2,732,040	291,559	275,114	2,715,595	653,447	728,055	40,285	101,702	57,945
2013	4,129,887	2,674,792	121,422	2,796,214	333,596	269,313	2,731,931	649,019	748,937	40,629	101,648	59,284
2014	4,318,062	2,778,723	153,774	2,932,497	344,894	277,025	2,864,628	673,899	779,535	42,434	101,759	60,127

Personal Income and Employment by Area: Fort Collins-Loveland, CO

(Thousands of dollars, except as noted.)

Year	Personal income, total	Earnings by place of work			Less: Contributions for government social insurance	Plus: Adjustment for residence	Equals: Net earnings by place of residence	Plus: Dividends, interest, and rent	Plus: Personal current transfer receipts	Per capita personal income (dollars)	Population (persons)	Total employment
		Nonfarm	Farm	Total								
1970	309,032	210,467	6,352	216,819	10,780	10,517	216,556	65,016	27,460	3,392	91,095	35,982
1971	363,001	242,805	11,168	253,973	12,652	15,136	256,457	74,743	31,801	3,737	97,125	37,219
1972	421,836	289,652	8,067	297,719	16,568	20,977	302,128	83,723	35,985	3,942	106,999	41,926
1973	491,789	335,407	9,374	344,781	22,325	28,157	350,613	97,870	43,306	4,374	112,441	45,809
1974	567,932	381,264	8,603	389,867	26,294	37,152	400,725	116,008	51,199	4,735	119,945	48,576
1975	662,526	435,538	12,393	447,931	29,156	45,638	464,413	132,820	65,293	5,494	120,593	51,021
1976	766,345	515,729	9,461	525,190	35,067	57,959	548,082	146,779	71,484	6,221	123,187	55,630
1977	881,046	604,650	5,331	609,981	42,418	68,831	636,394	167,781	76,871	6,676	131,973	60,594
1978	1,045,796	726,473	6,673	733,146	52,744	84,446	764,848	195,699	85,249	7,590	137,780	66,489
1979	1,234,578	868,063	399	868,462	66,507	102,032	903,987	233,639	96,952	8,487	145,474	71,512
1980	1,413,318	962,399	127	962,526	75,088	119,917	1,007,355	289,637	116,326	9,416	150,091	73,957
1981	1,605,082	1,056,828	7,402	1,064,230	88,905	132,062	1,107,387	356,829	140,866	10,467	153,347	74,913
1982	1,754,591	1,137,673	5,147	1,142,820	97,245	151,964	1,197,539	396,198	160,854	11,147	157,410	76,547
1983	1,932,274	1,251,302	10,291	1,261,593	109,134	166,978	1,319,437	436,184	176,653	11,941	161,816	80,642
1984	2,125,657	1,395,818	8,358	1,404,176	126,427	181,121	1,458,870	480,004	186,783	12,877	165,073	86,194
1985	2,280,450	1,497,468	6,159	1,503,627	139,172	194,263	1,558,718	521,117	200,615	13,439	169,687	88,750
1986	2,442,774	1,619,865	5,133	1,624,998	153,186	201,996	1,673,808	550,582	218,384	14,017	174,271	91,424
1987	2,612,375	1,741,448	4,839	1,746,287	162,522	213,349	1,797,114	575,174	240,087	14,708	177,612	92,603
1988	2,793,810	1,878,390	8,116	1,886,506	184,099	232,202	1,934,609	605,932	253,269	15,469	180,610	98,006
1989	3,080,909	2,040,367	13,274	2,053,641	205,907	249,741	2,097,475	698,952	284,482	16,789	183,507	101,762
1990	3,312,931	2,230,878	13,687	2,244,565	232,185	268,057	2,280,437	726,316	306,178	17,688	187,299	105,353
1991	3,528,483	2,400,455	13,097	2,413,552	256,406	292,065	2,449,211	740,697	338,575	18,268	193,154	110,094
1992	3,860,011	2,659,017	17,321	2,676,338	280,347	307,722	2,703,713	774,185	382,113	19,280	200,212	113,837
1993	4,227,697	2,930,787	21,225	2,952,012	314,947	322,212	2,959,277	859,329	409,091	20,312	208,143	121,231
1994	4,597,005	3,231,825	16,963	3,248,788	352,302	334,010	3,230,496	932,464	434,045	21,197	216,868	128,209
1995	5,012,090	3,473,100	13,973	3,487,073	378,998	352,880	3,460,955	1,064,363	486,772	22,501	222,750	134,280
1996	5,490,046	3,867,878	22,078	3,889,956	417,305	363,561	3,836,212	1,145,581	508,253	24,042	228,350	143,321
1997	5,943,783	4,180,982	22,625	4,203,607	445,415	396,275	4,154,467	1,271,323	517,993	25,428	233,746	148,781
1998	6,468,270	4,568,784	21,322	4,590,106	454,295	452,981	4,588,792	1,345,834	533,644	26,865	240,765	155,107
1999	6,933,157	4,937,516	17,857	4,955,373	485,191	503,965	4,974,147	1,388,407	570,603	28,083	246,884	159,372
2000	7,831,719	5,623,583	13,871	5,637,454	547,172	592,968	5,683,250	1,539,856	608,613	30,947	253,072	167,271
2001	8,450,452	6,216,740	17,855	6,234,595	594,906	589,636	6,229,325	1,548,438	672,689	32,434	260,541	170,581
2002	8,590,546	6,396,701	7,457	6,404,158	635,641	576,747	6,345,264	1,485,084	760,198	32,372	265,372	171,477
2003	8,589,109	6,396,488	2,659	6,399,147	643,991	562,638	6,317,794	1,478,004	793,311	31,995	268,448	171,809
2004	8,976,059	6,626,432	18,512	6,644,944	684,630	570,267	6,530,581	1,613,131	832,347	33,060	271,510	177,619
2005	9,482,905	6,925,316	20,089	6,945,405	725,116	582,560	6,802,849	1,764,546	915,510	34,469	275,116	182,253
2006	10,163,681	7,295,803	14,260	7,310,063	761,299	595,654	7,144,418	2,015,507	1,003,756	36,207	280,713	185,701
2007	10,821,112	7,539,362	24,375	7,563,737	797,902	610,665	7,376,500	2,354,051	1,090,561	37,821	286,112	192,140
2008	11,160,358	7,654,055	17,180	7,671,235	818,815	608,302	7,460,722	2,377,032	1,322,604	38,266	291,650	192,395
2009	10,974,876	7,521,127	11,968	7,533,095	797,409	563,031	7,298,717	2,188,103	1,488,056	36,990	296,696	188,943
2010	11,218,645	7,658,002	22,355	7,680,357	813,695	563,027	7,429,689	2,117,734	1,671,222	37,335	300,484	188,412
2011	11,996,355	7,954,297	25,194	7,979,491	777,518	612,219	7,814,192	2,451,778	1,730,385	39,301	305,241	192,251
2012	12,644,658	8,367,545	27,598	8,395,143	815,851	634,231	8,213,523	2,685,707	1,745,428	40,680	310,835	195,469
2013	13,237,112	8,748,707	32,742	8,781,449	931,785	656,199	8,505,863	2,901,439	1,829,810	41,824	316,494	201,852
2014	14,126,667	9,425,717	42,787	9,468,504	1,009,189	684,833	9,144,148	3,015,708	1,966,811	43,584	324,122	207,650

Personal Income and Employment by Area: Fort Smith, AR-OK

(Thousands of dollars, except as noted.)

Year	Personal income, total	Nonfarm	Farm	Total	Less: Contributions for government social insurance	Plus: Adjustment for residence	Equals: Net earnings by place of residence	Plus: Dividends, interest, and rent	Plus: Personal current transfer receipts	Per capita personal income (dollars)	Population (persons)	Total employment
1970	466,712	359,356	10,804	370,160	26,257	-5,343	338,560	64,036	64,116	2,893	161,302	63,978
1971	523,554	397,090	12,403	409,493	29,933	-3,059	376,501	71,489	75,564	3,142	166,652	66,079
1972	585,671	447,192	16,324	463,516	35,379	-4,941	423,196	77,899	84,576	3,432	170,641	69,301
1973	668,285	504,802	25,669	530,471	46,121	-6,005	478,345	90,550	99,390	3,862	173,030	72,952
1974	765,468	582,212	19,627	601,839	54,915	-7,344	539,580	108,383	117,505	4,279	178,875	76,608
1975	856,290	633,137	19,367	652,504	58,104	-7,881	586,519	121,683	148,088	4,122	207,746	76,082
1976	963,185	725,992	18,936	744,928	68,361	-7,724	668,843	132,050	162,292	5,117	188,214	79,870
1977	1,087,643	839,541	16,361	855,902	79,970	-9,832	766,100	149,875	171,668	5,596	194,364	84,651
1978	1,230,036	961,536	11,478	973,014	94,147	-12,537	866,330	176,194	187,512	6,202	198,313	89,078
1979	1,377,584	1,055,617	21,150	1,076,767	106,792	-13,114	956,861	202,425	218,298	6,826	201,812	89,789
1980	1,545,361	1,150,110	9,011	1,159,121	114,137	-12,358	1,032,626	251,925	260,810	7,588	203,668	89,678
1981	1,752,498	1,276,853	22,295	1,299,148	136,486	-18,760	1,143,902	313,647	294,949	8,596	203,878	92,299
1982	1,834,952	1,296,727	12,381	1,309,108	141,865	-19,332	1,147,911	362,281	324,760	8,991	204,078	89,608
1983	1,975,620	1,419,235	11,829	1,431,064	157,205	-24,371	1,249,488	379,519	346,613	9,531	207,278	93,043
1984	2,192,229	1,605,965	13,707	1,619,672	182,941	-29,676	1,407,055	426,156	359,018	10,417	210,446	98,057
1985	2,351,896	1,717,634	16,340	1,733,974	197,098	-32,894	1,503,982	466,804	381,110	11,082	212,229	100,810
1986	2,500,503	1,850,511	24,613	1,875,124	212,533	-37,106	1,625,485	477,364	397,654	11,664	214,383	103,742
1987	2,650,967	2,015,592	20,187	2,035,779	228,643	-43,472	1,763,664	475,390	411,913	12,212	217,078	108,679
1988	2,823,919	2,151,079	24,423	2,175,502	253,140	-48,215	1,874,147	511,152	438,620	12,951	218,039	112,329
1989	2,994,301	2,247,622	37,611	2,285,233	263,535	-58,510	1,963,188	549,019	482,094	13,674	218,975	113,097
1990	3,134,642	2,373,768	24,139	2,397,907	289,451	-66,752	2,041,704	565,779	527,159	14,261	219,804	114,149
1991	3,285,282	2,480,454	26,621	2,507,075	303,298	-55,267	2,148,510	551,770	585,002	14,743	222,842	116,211
1992	3,611,506	2,734,893	35,627	2,770,520	331,416	-60,070	2,379,034	570,894	661,578	15,958	226,308	118,602
1993	3,758,072	2,856,480	45,470	2,901,950	350,117	-63,092	2,488,741	574,669	694,662	16,260	231,118	124,499
1994	4,053,340	3,097,485	60,742	3,158,227	384,469	-71,002	2,702,756	616,007	734,577	17,320	234,032	128,786
1995	4,280,685	3,256,529	39,525	3,296,054	401,123	-74,718	2,820,213	665,607	794,865	17,876	239,471	133,767
1996	4,496,957	3,382,920	53,384	3,436,304	411,639	-71,330	2,953,335	703,879	839,743	18,466	243,520	136,556
1997	4,727,577	3,566,966	60,439	3,627,405	430,823	-71,899	3,124,683	740,042	862,852	19,152	246,842	138,117
1998	5,027,719	3,831,285	59,760	3,891,045	455,422	-77,056	3,358,567	789,029	880,123	20,154	249,460	139,946
1999	5,252,347	4,041,052	78,430	4,119,482	478,840	-76,887	3,563,755	771,681	916,911	20,799	252,529	142,503
2000	5,633,533	4,353,184	69,392	4,422,576	505,931	-75,426	3,841,219	825,978	966,336	21,995	256,126	144,565
2001	5,926,818	4,492,318	83,666	4,575,984	519,510	-64,374	3,992,100	852,641	1,082,077	22,964	258,087	144,289
2002	5,976,839	4,500,939	77,511	4,578,450	521,130	-91,323	3,965,997	820,195	1,190,647	22,978	260,117	143,028
2003	6,201,360	4,714,179	58,195	4,772,374	540,278	-104,737	4,127,359	815,547	1,258,454	23,678	261,903	143,183
2004	6,573,621	4,984,819	93,454	5,078,273	566,674	-122,373	4,389,226	825,140	1,359,255	24,897	264,035	144,952
2005	7,012,784	5,365,413	84,194	5,449,607	610,171	-138,593	4,700,843	869,245	1,442,696	26,294	266,708	149,031
2006	7,577,117	5,774,823	37,947	5,812,770	662,161	-132,124	5,018,485	971,732	1,586,900	27,952	271,075	153,017
2007	7,916,978	5,825,906	31,134	5,857,040	678,717	-84,979	5,093,344	1,121,446	1,702,188	28,862	274,305	156,549
2008	8,376,702	5,929,374	52,281	5,981,655	702,851	-87,394	5,191,410	1,260,388	1,924,904	30,315	276,322	154,783
2009	8,127,262	5,558,849	11,358	5,570,207	679,657	-74,436	4,816,114	1,205,785	2,105,363	29,140	278,908	149,388
2010	8,339,983	5,677,859	82,057	5,759,916	699,727	-76,765	4,983,424	1,101,663	2,254,896	29,708	280,729	146,389
2011	8,732,310	5,779,246	100,259	5,879,505	644,071	-86,767	5,148,667	1,273,590	2,310,053	31,075	281,012	144,821
2012	9,072,887	5,956,457	128,092	6,084,549	651,097	-82,507	5,350,945	1,375,418	2,346,524	32,322	280,704	144,541
2013	9,111,615	5,943,109	164,752	6,107,861	731,240	-76,442	5,300,179	1,406,415	2,405,021	32,550	279,930	144,034
2014	9,478,220	6,169,801	167,885	6,337,686	758,646	-86,638	5,492,402	1,456,471	2,529,347	33,900	279,592	145,340

Personal Income and Employment by Area: Fort Wayne, IN

(Thousands of dollars, except as noted.)

| Year | Personal income, total | Derivation of personal income | | | | | | | | Per capita personal income (dollars) | Population (persons) | Total employment |
| | | Earnings by place of work | | | Less: Contributions for government social insurance | Plus: Adjustment for residence | Equals: Net earnings by place of residence | Plus: Dividends, interest, and rent | Plus: Personal current transfer receipts | | | |
		Nonfarm	Farm	Total								
1970	1,340,608	1,231,065	16,694	1,247,759	84,534	-105,974	1,057,251	196,488	86,869	4,079	328,656	161,511
1971	1,451,564	1,313,963	25,182	1,339,145	93,298	-111,412	1,134,435	213,000	104,129	4,357	333,164	161,889
1972	1,603,582	1,474,889	20,761	1,495,650	111,541	-124,291	1,259,818	227,946	115,818	4,769	336,249	169,353
1973	1,807,822	1,641,651	48,325	1,689,976	143,480	-134,650	1,411,846	258,089	137,887	5,342	338,398	177,766
1974	1,963,406	1,787,341	29,248	1,816,589	162,478	-146,608	1,507,503	298,111	157,792	5,778	339,819	181,183
1975	2,059,002	1,791,196	37,895	1,829,091	160,154	-140,318	1,528,619	325,942	204,441	6,064	339,555	171,717
1976	2,304,610	2,044,742	37,029	2,081,771	185,573	-156,999	1,739,199	352,853	212,558	6,804	338,719	178,522
1977	2,586,935	2,328,994	33,271	2,362,265	211,259	-178,532	1,972,474	394,628	219,833	7,619	339,540	186,924
1978	2,892,160	2,638,997	21,395	2,660,392	246,446	-199,281	2,214,665	435,901	241,594	8,416	343,658	194,996
1979	3,215,451	2,924,234	27,928	2,952,162	282,399	-218,269	2,451,494	487,698	276,259	9,304	345,596	198,262
1980	3,419,803	2,967,086	24,654	2,991,740	284,910	-209,792	2,497,038	581,055	341,710	9,899	345,480	188,701
1981	3,728,023	3,158,576	3,073	3,161,649	326,300	-219,645	2,615,704	717,143	395,176	10,874	342,832	187,540
1982	3,808,718	3,091,308	9,876	3,101,184	324,805	-204,756	2,571,623	794,328	442,767	11,181	340,642	179,724
1983	3,940,331	3,211,105	-10,192	3,200,913	339,241	-199,428	2,662,244	804,065	474,022	11,652	338,181	179,245
1984	4,390,010	3,582,687	22,941	3,605,628	388,068	-211,073	3,006,487	892,440	491,083	13,001	337,671	188,092
1985	4,737,355	3,919,674	11,685	3,931,359	432,651	-232,117	3,266,591	955,797	514,967	13,891	341,030	196,048
1986	5,185,062	4,341,056	18,399	4,359,455	481,318	-260,070	3,618,067	1,023,470	543,525	15,005	345,561	205,357
1987	5,581,769	4,746,648	23,661	4,770,309	519,846	-283,650	3,966,813	1,064,511	550,445	15,900	351,063	214,510
1988	6,111,006	5,183,759	13,141	5,196,900	582,591	-309,951	4,304,358	1,202,034	604,614	17,312	352,986	222,312
1989	6,654,985	5,573,905	20,838	5,594,743	626,466	-325,836	4,642,441	1,363,763	648,781	18,792	354,134	229,759
1990	6,949,880	5,804,801	34,492	5,839,293	672,047	-342,534	4,824,712	1,428,215	696,953	19,557	355,358	230,671
1991	6,995,820	5,879,328	15,755	5,895,083	693,978	-360,385	4,840,720	1,378,919	776,181	19,512	358,547	229,542
1992	7,618,478	6,360,509	25,215	6,385,724	740,403	-377,428	5,267,893	1,439,578	911,007	21,061	361,726	233,513
1993	7,921,101	6,689,399	30,087	6,719,486	782,071	-397,109	5,540,306	1,440,942	939,853	21,698	365,059	237,212
1994	8,399,401	7,079,752	27,727	7,107,479	838,449	-402,625	5,866,405	1,538,287	994,709	22,841	367,729	242,100
1995	8,864,324	7,418,501	15,027	7,433,528	877,667	-391,396	6,164,465	1,681,333	1,018,526	23,897	370,934	247,340
1996	9,300,177	7,709,451	40,260	7,749,711	900,964	-411,503	6,437,244	1,797,991	1,064,942	24,811	374,837	249,925
1997	9,763,742	8,118,571	59,087	8,177,658	945,144	-456,456	6,776,058	1,904,364	1,083,320	25,785	378,663	255,042
1998	10,522,243	8,749,765	30,911	8,780,676	997,140	-458,352	7,325,184	2,057,115	1,139,944	27,459	383,203	259,634
1999	10,935,716	9,273,384	1,203	9,274,587	1,044,181	-487,325	7,743,081	2,007,527	1,185,108	28,270	386,827	260,124
2000	11,543,009	9,655,091	19,435	9,674,526	1,075,181	-528,413	8,070,932	2,166,708	1,305,369	29,519	391,039	262,700
2001	11,847,570	9,873,240	30,052	9,903,292	1,095,180	-521,583	8,286,529	2,116,284	1,444,757	30,102	393,580	255,936
2002	12,000,211	9,943,159	5,139	9,948,298	1,111,965	-504,735	8,331,598	2,134,416	1,534,197	30,292	396,147	253,123
2003	11,997,460	9,948,679	42,912	9,991,591	1,123,432	-463,558	8,404,601	1,999,007	1,593,852	30,069	398,993	249,964
2004	12,523,341	10,226,015	71,710	10,297,725	1,158,024	-443,754	8,695,947	2,132,593	1,694,801	31,263	400,583	251,923
2005	12,848,955	10,517,630	38,831	10,556,461	1,205,977	-404,023	8,946,461	2,045,236	1,857,258	31,864	403,240	254,310
2006	13,785,746	11,033,857	41,021	11,074,878	1,273,616	-375,485	9,425,777	2,350,494	2,009,475	33,890	406,783	258,936
2007	14,295,847	11,235,939	45,916	11,281,855	1,308,392	-328,725	9,644,738	2,548,795	2,102,314	34,849	410,223	262,086
2008	14,715,268	11,289,963	71,803	11,361,766	1,323,782	-278,608	9,759,376	2,498,822	2,457,070	35,711	412,062	258,870
2009	14,037,118	10,696,258	68,875	10,765,133	1,284,442	-374,172	9,106,519	2,215,846	2,714,753	33,870	414,438	247,336
2010	14,354,729	10,930,306	41,713	10,972,019	1,305,706	-379,861	9,286,452	2,163,711	2,904,566	34,436	416,850	245,720
2011	15,282,336	11,465,916	87,618	11,553,534	1,216,187	-390,911	9,946,436	2,422,694	2,913,206	36,408	419,757	251,077
2012	16,046,827	11,886,511	124,968	12,011,479	1,242,230	-393,852	10,375,397	2,634,866	3,036,564	38,045	421,780	253,533
2013	16,122,962	11,972,435	212,810	12,185,245	1,420,364	-313,480	10,451,401	2,611,785	3,059,776	37,975	424,570	253,687
2014	16,863,876	12,540,602	140,937	12,681,539	1,481,967	-267,611	10,931,961	2,715,402	3,216,513	39,477	427,183	257,444

Personal Income and Employment by Area: Fresno, CA

(Thousands of dollars, except as noted.)

Year	Personal income, total	Derivation of personal income								Per capita personal income (dollars)	Population (persons)	Total employment
		Earnings by place of work			Less: Contributions for government social insurance	Plus: Adjustment for residence	Equals: Net earnings by place of residence	Plus: Dividends, interest, and rent	Plus: Personal current transfer receipts			
		Nonfarm	Farm	Total								
1970	1,652,657	1,115,852	163,187	1,279,039	76,000	-4,659	1,198,380	227,043	227,234	3,983	414,886	180,330
1971	1,799,513	1,232,134	164,215	1,396,349	85,668	-7,642	1,303,039	248,298	248,176	4,237	424,697	185,808
1972	2,035,429	1,397,611	213,278	1,610,889	100,605	-11,602	1,498,682	277,151	259,596	4,713	431,918	198,065
1973	2,336,200	1,578,672	293,372	1,872,044	129,421	-16,692	1,725,931	324,841	285,428	5,311	439,865	206,954
1974	2,736,168	1,772,154	430,003	2,202,157	149,793	-24,202	2,028,162	376,262	331,744	6,082	449,886	216,106
1975	2,957,347	1,974,295	335,593	2,309,888	162,007	-33,472	2,114,409	429,144	413,794	6,371	464,183	222,296
1976	3,387,959	2,237,141	456,376	2,693,517	187,139	-43,998	2,462,380	464,924	460,655	7,100	477,162	231,059
1977	3,618,410	2,506,948	367,290	2,874,238	213,963	-55,049	2,605,226	524,662	488,522	7,399	489,016	239,078
1978	4,035,414	2,876,336	324,389	3,200,725	249,553	-69,132	2,882,040	615,838	537,536	8,110	497,564	249,946
1979	4,787,737	3,325,269	539,229	3,864,498	302,874	-89,416	3,472,208	722,523	593,006	9,456	506,332	267,295
1980	5,529,740	3,642,170	717,272	4,359,442	326,555	-107,707	3,925,180	901,607	702,953	10,682	517,679	275,120
1981	5,789,241	3,888,737	444,440	4,333,177	379,847	-94,169	3,859,161	1,090,891	839,189	10,946	528,891	275,530
1982	6,087,889	4,014,654	471,836	4,486,490	400,855	-100,595	3,985,040	1,166,467	936,382	11,243	541,500	277,400
1983	6,410,514	4,307,372	347,771	4,655,143	436,840	-102,852	4,115,451	1,269,208	1,025,855	11,532	555,873	284,985
1984	7,089,714	4,692,890	487,089	5,179,979	495,585	-110,273	4,574,121	1,410,599	1,104,994	12,393	572,091	289,156
1985	7,614,794	4,991,704	583,227	5,574,931	533,216	-115,715	4,926,000	1,479,504	1,209,290	13,037	584,070	292,647
1986	8,132,396	5,341,214	634,627	5,975,841	580,017	-118,376	5,277,448	1,543,984	1,310,964	13,700	593,621	296,092
1987	8,891,993	5,879,971	806,603	6,686,574	642,391	-127,492	5,916,691	1,605,259	1,370,043	14,605	608,831	308,325
1988	9,548,499	6,382,059	855,872	7,237,931	719,454	-139,408	6,379,069	1,683,911	1,485,519	15,213	627,658	320,730
1989	10,360,717	6,879,476	832,276	7,711,752	786,010	-158,545	6,767,197	1,955,213	1,638,307	15,921	650,755	328,682
1990	11,277,596	7,608,905	880,645	8,489,550	861,878	-182,360	7,445,312	1,975,754	1,856,530	16,775	672,302	342,583
1991	11,804,630	8,148,899	690,165	8,839,064	924,041	-185,502	7,729,521	1,986,142	2,088,967	17,069	691,569	351,296
1992	12,566,945	8,536,049	743,824	9,279,873	960,772	-179,838	8,139,263	1,980,856	2,446,826	17,693	710,263	347,643
1993	13,303,020	8,977,027	890,254	9,867,281	1,004,318	-190,972	8,671,991	2,039,773	2,591,256	18,302	726,859	356,938
1994	13,619,111	9,319,356	828,600	10,147,956	1,039,840	-192,799	8,915,317	2,125,156	2,578,638	18,408	739,835	364,559
1995	14,173,048	9,645,937	725,940	10,371,877	1,058,975	-191,017	9,121,885	2,360,781	2,690,382	18,909	749,534	377,757
1996	14,812,681	9,969,724	834,813	10,804,537	1,061,324	-188,175	9,555,038	2,435,525	2,822,118	19,454	761,409	384,048
1997	15,214,370	10,329,668	829,925	11,159,593	1,082,367	-170,217	9,907,009	2,505,072	2,802,289	19,723	771,391	379,588
1998	16,168,866	11,142,444	707,882	11,850,326	1,136,545	-166,372	10,547,409	2,597,600	3,023,857	20,766	778,615	392,681
1999	17,068,093	11,729,802	901,329	12,631,131	1,195,794	-160,822	11,274,515	2,610,050	3,183,528	21,621	789,405	396,268
2000	18,456,944	13,138,732	809,646	13,948,378	1,303,449	-152,925	12,492,004	2,691,658	3,273,282	23,034	801,288	401,007
2001	19,695,559	14,173,720	610,845	14,784,565	1,484,446	-186,194	13,113,925	2,890,683	3,690,951	24,225	813,021	401,094
2002	21,053,632	15,178,553	822,681	16,001,234	1,618,823	-203,167	14,179,244	2,936,203	3,938,185	25,373	829,762	412,320
2003	22,288,243	15,688,545	1,182,827	16,871,372	1,716,775	-216,856	14,937,741	3,133,851	4,216,651	26,308	847,193	414,090
2004	23,580,860	16,688,835	1,365,678	18,054,513	1,894,938	-232,017	15,927,558	3,211,019	4,442,283	27,387	861,035	419,080
2005	24,448,492	17,361,814	1,273,284	18,635,098	1,991,490	-244,256	16,399,352	3,380,873	4,668,267	28,022	872,470	428,516
2006	25,816,612	18,401,513	1,215,018	19,616,531	2,045,716	-258,816	17,311,999	3,503,756	5,000,857	29,209	883,862	439,167
2007	27,098,519	19,040,784	1,216,165	20,256,949	2,076,381	-271,542	17,909,026	3,820,867	5,368,626	30,246	895,933	449,672
2008	28,087,217	19,194,401	1,001,968	20,196,369	2,112,384	-277,475	17,806,510	4,264,186	6,016,521	30,878	909,630	446,835
2009	28,138,041	18,496,838	1,394,108	19,890,946	2,070,555	-234,457	17,585,934	3,895,886	6,656,221	30,536	921,478	430,696
2010	29,112,907	18,630,185	1,461,357	20,091,542	2,049,165	-243,486	17,798,891	3,914,622	7,399,394	31,216	932,642	425,816
2011	30,921,664	19,370,449	1,810,902	21,181,351	1,919,740	-239,450	19,022,161	4,450,534	7,448,969	32,851	941,260	431,511
2012	32,374,913	20,218,921	1,797,721	22,016,642	1,979,027	-172,602	19,865,013	4,909,366	7,600,534	34,142	948,240	444,612
2013	33,354,677	20,933,285	1,743,016	22,676,301	2,308,210	-150,599	20,217,492	5,188,708	7,948,477	34,886	956,102	460,035
2014	34,567,706	21,846,785	1,562,746	23,409,531	2,411,647	-139,014	20,858,870	5,437,502	8,271,334	35,785	965,974	468,804

Personal Income and Employment by Area: Gadsden, AL

(Thousands of dollars, except as noted.)

Year	Personal income, total	Earnings by place of work			Less: Contributions for government social insurance	Plus: Adjustment for residence	Equals: Net earnings by place of residence	Plus: Dividends, interest, and rent	Plus: Personal current transfer receipts	Per capita personal income (dollars)	Population (persons)	Total employment
		Nonfarm	Farm	Total								
1970	282,865	229,538	2,232	231,770	16,799	6,371	221,342	28,645	32,878	3,005	94,134	35,044
1971	310,937	242,664	2,771	245,435	18,185	11,378	238,628	32,000	40,309	3,277	94,887	35,388
1972	349,047	275,126	3,487	278,613	21,681	13,074	270,006	35,086	43,955	3,645	95,758	36,119
1973	386,527	304,679	5,490	310,169	27,982	14,151	296,338	39,943	50,246	4,023	96,072	37,400
1974	424,510	330,208	2,314	332,522	31,337	16,086	317,271	47,391	59,848	4,395	96,579	37,366
1975	470,669	347,080	5,355	352,435	32,702	19,250	338,983	54,598	77,088	4,806	97,936	36,837
1976	513,115	379,148	5,050	384,198	36,439	23,635	371,394	58,750	82,971	5,184	98,984	36,805
1977	587,106	449,492	5,004	454,496	43,343	23,641	434,794	65,635	86,677	5,861	100,171	39,116
1978	667,927	520,180	6,142	526,322	51,217	25,757	500,862	74,513	92,552	6,566	101,731	41,070
1979	749,170	584,945	5,449	590,394	59,483	27,508	558,419	84,276	106,475	7,278	102,937	42,239
1980	818,238	615,579	-41	615,538	62,277	35,432	588,693	103,120	126,425	7,935	103,112	41,418
1981	911,313	665,119	8,550	673,669	72,546	40,642	641,765	125,695	143,853	8,835	103,143	40,735
1982	924,410	638,544	4,786	643,330	71,545	46,907	618,692	142,316	163,402	9,017	102,524	38,726
1983	982,538	678,200	5,322	683,522	77,458	46,135	652,199	154,098	176,241	9,566	102,707	38,722
1984	1,074,112	744,804	4,324	749,128	87,107	50,716	712,737	174,904	186,471	10,499	102,307	40,376
1985	1,128,573	771,987	6,044	778,031	90,447	57,543	745,127	188,873	194,573	11,033	102,291	40,925
1986	1,175,517	789,666	8,419	798,085	91,110	62,193	769,168	202,351	203,998	11,563	101,664	40,944
1987	1,247,348	866,618	3,147	869,765	98,401	64,750	836,114	203,432	207,802	12,312	101,314	41,863
1988	1,327,576	921,419	8,917	930,336	107,870	73,377	895,843	217,356	214,377	13,180	100,728	42,754
1989	1,412,399	935,508	13,807	949,315	109,713	82,439	922,041	246,216	244,142	14,078	100,327	43,434
1990	1,456,218	948,218	12,087	960,305	111,742	86,920	935,483	255,216	265,519	14,590	99,809	43,565
1991	1,496,273	963,204	12,656	975,860	114,402	91,681	953,139	246,797	296,337	14,908	100,365	43,913
1992	1,612,458	1,051,949	13,248	1,065,197	123,013	92,158	1,034,342	248,176	329,940	15,973	100,950	44,463
1993	1,690,671	1,102,999	13,949	1,116,948	131,091	99,564	1,085,421	260,116	345,134	16,688	101,310	46,081
1994	1,792,289	1,184,261	17,652	1,201,913	141,431	87,867	1,148,349	271,604	372,336	17,535	102,213	46,709
1995	1,855,296	1,233,639	9,837	1,243,476	149,036	81,515	1,175,955	288,268	391,073	18,128	102,342	47,735
1996	1,940,370	1,230,959	16,302	1,247,261	147,524	129,092	1,228,829	294,657	416,884	18,827	103,063	48,513
1997	2,039,826	1,282,347	20,697	1,303,044	153,033	139,034	1,289,045	317,771	433,010	19,589	104,129	49,701
1998	2,128,519	1,344,224	20,007	1,364,231	157,480	142,068	1,348,819	330,626	449,074	20,395	104,367	49,736
1999	2,183,773	1,364,965	21,313	1,386,278	157,865	161,571	1,389,984	325,781	468,008	20,997	104,002	49,055
2000	2,275,045	1,408,186	17,883	1,426,069	160,987	167,285	1,432,367	346,839	495,839	22,027	103,286	49,505
2001	2,351,786	1,389,595	23,460	1,413,055	161,589	193,978	1,445,444	362,634	543,708	22,838	102,976	48,114
2002	2,418,702	1,432,279	16,872	1,449,151	168,283	198,160	1,479,028	360,920	578,754	23,485	102,988	48,655
2003	2,494,645	1,462,882	20,286	1,483,168	172,146	201,498	1,512,520	377,034	605,091	24,214	103,025	47,982
2004	2,618,013	1,546,073	30,965	1,577,038	181,401	215,766	1,611,403	379,267	627,343	25,398	103,080	49,352
2005	2,705,801	1,616,902	12,677	1,629,579	190,925	225,856	1,664,510	369,991	671,300	26,226	103,174	50,149
2006	2,797,078	1,672,527	-4,602	1,667,925	197,584	234,518	1,704,859	372,299	719,920	27,018	103,528	49,973
2007	2,951,425	1,694,816	2,536	1,697,352	203,498	245,027	1,738,881	436,713	775,831	28,408	103,893	49,698
2008	3,082,985	1,729,977	4,688	1,734,665	210,736	254,279	1,778,208	455,808	848,969	29,585	104,206	49,410
2009	3,074,647	1,697,303	6,009	1,703,312	206,791	233,151	1,729,672	426,177	918,798	29,496	104,239	46,800
2010	3,197,673	1,737,459	4,512	1,741,971	215,849	231,917	1,758,039	449,951	989,683	30,599	104,501	46,436
2011	3,260,049	1,788,235	-7,415	1,780,820	198,422	230,220	1,812,618	461,776	985,655	31,253	104,310	47,829
2012	3,325,302	1,809,229	-1,250	1,807,979	200,168	238,117	1,845,928	484,385	994,989	31,875	104,324	48,048
2013	3,312,362	1,797,212	16,409	1,813,621	226,900	239,933	1,826,654	464,241	1,021,467	31,861	103,962	48,163
2014	3,455,238	1,882,783	15,010	1,897,793	234,476	251,573	1,914,890	484,358	1,055,990	33,374	103,531	48,947

Personal Income and Employment by Area: Gainesville, FL

(Thousands of dollars, except as noted.)

Year	Personal income, total	Derivation of personal income								Per capita personal income (dollars)	Population (persons)	Total employment
		Earnings by place of work			Less: Contributions for government social insurance	Plus: Adjustment for residence	Equals: Net earnings by place of residence	Plus: Dividends, interest, and rent	Plus: Personal current transfer receipts			
		Nonfarm	Farm	Total								
1970	357,698	297,383	7,286	304,669	16,834	-12,883	274,952	56,240	26,506	3,289	108,745	50,213
1971	411,206	339,245	9,489	348,734	20,266	-15,783	312,685	65,036	33,485	3,650	112,666	52,801
1972	488,374	410,198	10,011	420,209	25,691	-20,969	373,549	75,817	39,008	3,942	123,894	58,353
1973	573,481	485,298	14,785	500,083	35,519	-25,684	438,880	88,475	46,126	4,400	130,322	63,584
1974	645,054	542,494	12,339	554,833	41,868	-28,467	484,498	104,684	55,872	4,744	135,976	66,040
1975	720,950	589,855	12,518	602,373	45,622	-29,463	527,288	119,873	73,789	5,243	137,514	66,766
1976	779,577	637,839	12,808	650,647	51,462	-32,067	567,118	127,689	84,770	5,659	137,769	66,895
1977	855,993	706,977	7,984	714,961	57,914	-35,762	621,285	142,068	92,640	6,002	142,625	70,025
1978	981,284	806,752	12,297	819,049	69,143	-40,490	709,416	167,426	104,442	6,626	148,102	74,708
1979	1,108,139	900,450	19,483	919,933	81,590	-43,878	794,465	190,010	123,664	7,304	151,718	78,191
1980	1,276,766	1,016,274	17,545	1,033,819	90,425	-50,398	892,996	235,986	147,784	8,075	158,113	81,820
1981	1,454,394	1,130,250	16,891	1,147,141	109,255	-48,858	989,028	293,317	172,049	8,993	161,727	83,589
1982	1,604,169	1,233,707	24,066	1,257,773	122,497	-55,936	1,079,340	335,161	189,668	9,667	165,951	86,074
1983	1,786,541	1,374,551	22,341	1,396,892	136,448	-65,770	1,194,674	379,907	211,960	10,578	168,900	88,731
1984	2,010,297	1,567,214	19,767	1,586,981	158,498	-79,812	1,348,671	433,068	228,558	11,630	172,859	94,216
1985	2,225,385	1,750,433	17,559	1,767,992	179,980	-91,777	1,496,235	479,409	249,741	12,556	177,239	99,763
1986	2,383,684	1,870,408	16,930	1,887,338	195,812	-99,519	1,592,007	522,541	269,136	13,269	179,646	104,449
1987	2,563,372	2,014,556	15,531	2,030,087	206,174	-108,235	1,715,678	559,391	288,303	14,034	182,650	105,549
1988	2,797,559	2,210,835	20,755	2,231,590	236,120	-122,628	1,872,842	610,105	314,612	15,070	185,638	109,865
1989	3,099,629	2,397,547	24,108	2,421,655	256,274	-137,833	2,027,548	708,861	363,220	16,424	188,728	112,555
1990	3,312,218	2,574,543	23,443	2,597,986	272,976	-153,303	2,171,707	740,270	400,241	17,209	192,474	116,385
1991	3,480,022	2,712,000	26,863	2,738,863	289,665	-163,660	2,285,538	743,773	450,711	17,524	198,591	117,284
1992	3,694,872	2,888,159	39,066	2,927,225	308,245	-179,927	2,439,053	744,491	511,328	18,114	203,980	117,689
1993	3,919,324	3,074,501	38,006	3,112,507	325,363	-194,015	2,593,129	777,684	548,511	18,789	208,594	122,951
1994	4,118,940	3,253,069	34,269	3,287,338	347,643	-220,817	2,718,878	821,800	578,262	19,528	210,925	126,720
1995	4,394,255	3,406,708	28,505	3,435,213	363,962	-232,954	2,838,297	929,477	626,481	20,335	216,093	130,710
1996	4,599,443	3,579,586	29,770	3,609,356	380,520	-262,448	2,966,388	971,924	661,131	20,939	219,654	134,282
1997	4,865,458	3,775,617	36,206	3,811,823	402,714	-289,683	3,119,426	1,063,949	682,083	21,775	223,439	135,691
1998	5,177,652	4,089,325	37,586	4,126,911	434,041	-329,553	3,363,317	1,126,804	687,531	22,842	226,674	141,153
1999	5,400,983	4,304,540	39,738	4,344,278	454,571	-310,031	3,579,676	1,112,008	709,299	23,492	229,909	144,720
2000	5,736,360	4,572,312	33,939	4,606,251	480,107	-342,952	3,783,192	1,172,407	780,761	24,614	233,054	149,069
2001	6,068,111	4,804,032	38,615	4,842,647	508,034	-344,251	3,990,362	1,205,892	871,857	25,712	236,001	152,265
2002	6,240,740	5,040,629	21,929	5,062,558	531,116	-373,949	4,157,493	1,138,936	944,311	26,099	239,116	151,553
2003	6,477,473	5,199,945	19,750	5,219,695	547,542	-387,956	4,284,197	1,180,033	1,013,243	26,763	242,033	152,563
2004	7,286,512	5,919,367	27,103	5,946,470	622,235	-452,640	4,871,595	1,418,928	995,989	29,724	245,138	161,138
2005	7,829,414	6,303,375	27,469	6,330,844	665,883	-488,169	5,176,792	1,535,640	1,116,982	31,373	249,557	164,143
2006	8,411,304	6,698,878	21,358	6,720,236	713,269	-509,602	5,497,365	1,756,448	1,157,491	32,891	255,729	167,305
2007	8,814,048	6,931,226	14,934	6,946,160	745,832	-531,907	5,668,421	1,911,798	1,233,829	33,992	259,295	169,822
2008	9,157,136	7,015,816	21,361	7,037,177	761,432	-540,173	5,735,572	1,992,125	1,429,439	34,993	261,685	167,443
2009	8,818,133	6,873,396	19,980	6,893,376	753,103	-569,041	5,571,232	1,716,642	1,530,259	33,467	263,486	161,075
2010	9,230,417	7,033,500	36,612	7,070,112	768,156	-571,048	5,730,908	1,797,842	1,701,667	34,876	264,667	158,811
2011	9,730,754	7,108,678	41,502	7,150,180	693,869	-584,539	5,871,772	2,068,568	1,790,414	36,487	266,691	159,819
2012	9,836,606	7,379,101	62,451	7,441,552	718,507	-618,331	6,104,714	1,974,952	1,756,940	36,624	268,585	161,243
2013	10,012,909	7,578,672	65,557	7,644,229	833,005	-628,241	6,182,983	1,997,304	1,832,622	37,055	270,216	162,977
2014	10,514,601	7,914,434	78,022	7,992,456	869,080	-647,901	6,475,475	2,060,236	1,978,890	38,462	273,377	166,583

Personal Income and Employment by Area: Gainesville, GA

(Thousands of dollars, except as noted.)

Year	Personal income, total	Derivation of personal income								Per capita personal income (dollars)	Population (persons)	Total employment
		Earnings by place of work			Less: Contributions for government social insurance	Plus: Adjustment for residence	Equals: Net earnings by place of residence	Plus: Dividends, interest, and rent	Plus: Personal current transfer receipts			
		Nonfarm	Farm	Total								
1970	195,703	166,446	3,899	170,345	10,560	-1,028	158,757	21,819	15,127	3,272	59,814	29,685
1971	211,538	176,913	3,140	180,053	11,564	214	168,703	24,768	18,067	3,412	62,007	30,211
1972	241,200	200,193	4,894	205,087	13,765	1,592	192,914	27,743	20,543	3,804	63,406	30,977
1973	274,668	218,120	12,623	230,743	17,172	3,442	217,013	33,177	24,478	4,172	65,831	31,482
1974	299,090	238,417	5,711	244,128	19,557	3,797	228,368	40,201	30,521	4,478	66,786	32,098
1975	336,301	246,511	15,535	262,046	19,800	5,232	247,478	45,656	43,167	4,869	69,063	31,241
1976	379,400	287,407	16,659	304,066	23,544	6,508	287,030	47,841	44,529	5,449	69,626	33,292
1977	429,417	332,673	15,914	348,587	27,087	8,018	329,518	52,447	47,452	6,032	71,185	35,486
1978	494,963	387,349	17,534	404,883	32,505	9,662	382,040	60,681	52,242	6,824	72,534	37,509
1979	556,999	445,864	9,311	455,175	39,116	11,184	427,243	70,462	59,294	7,499	74,275	39,816
1980	633,482	488,700	2,974	491,674	42,989	19,296	467,981	92,076	73,425	8,327	76,074	39,846
1981	711,312	534,639	5,942	540,581	50,546	20,327	510,362	117,336	83,614	9,163	77,629	40,631
1982	764,888	558,356	10,285	568,641	53,837	24,024	538,828	132,201	93,859	9,703	78,832	40,711
1983	841,192	614,665	9,698	624,363	59,650	26,534	591,247	148,619	101,326	10,478	80,278	42,095
1984	981,732	712,097	29,324	741,421	71,046	28,719	699,094	175,510	107,128	11,969	82,024	45,932
1985	1,081,134	800,420	24,107	824,527	81,984	29,599	772,142	195,533	113,459	12,844	84,174	48,216
1986	1,200,489	880,727	40,447	921,174	91,438	30,721	860,457	219,466	120,566	13,790	87,054	49,668
1987	1,276,398	975,308	25,526	1,000,834	101,462	25,469	924,841	225,465	126,092	14,327	89,092	51,538
1988	1,393,341	1,059,477	35,774	1,095,251	113,503	23,577	1,005,325	248,861	139,155	15,214	91,583	53,765
1989	1,517,683	1,124,368	49,850	1,174,218	121,111	17,593	1,070,700	293,346	153,637	16,169	93,865	55,176
1990	1,606,533	1,200,532	41,786	1,242,318	129,249	9,656	1,122,725	310,679	173,129	16,697	96,215	55,485
1991	1,682,272	1,240,574	41,418	1,281,992	135,419	16,967	1,163,540	316,654	202,078	16,903	99,525	55,068
1992	1,829,929	1,358,728	38,613	1,397,341	145,832	21,799	1,273,308	323,930	232,691	17,908	102,186	56,420
1993	1,984,094	1,499,701	40,924	1,540,625	161,354	10,800	1,390,071	343,889	250,134	18,735	105,903	60,311
1994	2,178,131	1,652,669	37,617	1,690,286	178,913	6,570	1,517,943	386,513	273,675	19,796	110,029	64,802
1995	2,328,279	1,763,984	33,533	1,797,517	190,092	13,373	1,620,798	405,693	301,788	20,341	114,464	67,737
1996	2,532,222	1,885,282	39,090	1,924,372	200,645	29,963	1,753,690	453,118	325,414	21,253	119,147	69,621
1997	2,687,976	2,019,874	34,976	2,054,850	212,011	30,177	1,873,016	480,310	334,650	21,639	124,219	71,817
1998	2,995,864	2,248,040	48,776	2,296,816	230,664	42,706	2,108,858	542,482	344,524	23,191	129,182	74,970
1999	3,284,798	2,511,754	46,582	2,558,336	254,072	50,174	2,354,438	566,139	364,221	24,371	134,781	77,471
2000	3,566,531	2,711,433	37,046	2,748,479	274,491	47,343	2,521,331	637,394	407,806	25,296	140,993	81,798
2001	3,748,504	2,848,758	53,698	2,902,456	291,657	26,421	2,637,220	659,528	451,756	25,649	146,148	81,883
2002	3,893,156	2,951,214	32,712	2,983,926	303,435	24,858	2,705,349	669,820	517,987	25,915	150,229	82,436
2003	4,072,234	3,088,455	32,636	3,121,091	316,864	23,567	2,827,794	713,950	530,490	26,519	153,561	84,537
2004	4,309,317	3,289,801	49,768	3,339,569	348,419	22,549	3,013,699	704,186	591,432	27,556	156,385	87,401
2005	4,822,984	3,635,454	46,549	3,682,003	374,205	22,475	3,330,273	834,376	658,335	29,960	160,979	90,298
2006	5,202,413	3,915,385	16,269	3,931,654	403,170	21,422	3,549,906	930,281	722,226	31,241	166,524	94,162
2007	5,446,514	4,061,727	14,744	4,076,471	416,714	19,886	3,679,643	984,751	782,120	31,584	172,446	98,733
2008	5,678,751	4,135,247	19,860	4,155,107	442,274	17,397	3,730,230	1,038,521	910,000	32,033	177,277	99,812
2009	5,562,510	3,889,880	12,214	3,902,094	418,036	67,169	3,551,227	992,846	1,018,437	31,162	178,503	94,296
2010	5,600,220	3,945,047	5,289	3,950,336	430,840	63,454	3,582,950	893,064	1,124,206	31,106	180,034	94,663
2011	5,966,473	4,214,806	-8,491	4,206,315	405,642	-37,213	3,763,460	1,018,995	1,184,018	32,612	182,954	97,997
2012	6,191,541	4,326,209	19,318	4,345,527	414,628	72,201	4,003,100	1,002,044	1,186,397	33,453	185,084	98,156
2013	6,439,532	4,600,308	23,661	4,623,969	498,198	49,787	4,175,558	1,022,617	1,241,357	34,297	187,759	102,008
2014	6,770,253	4,890,622	29,363	4,919,985	528,633	33,709	4,425,061	1,062,362	1,282,830	35,491	190,761	104,696

Personal Income and Employment by Area: Gettysburg, PA

(Thousands of dollars, except as noted.)

Year	Personal income, total	Earnings by place of work			Less: Contributions for government social insurance	Plus: Adjustment for residence	Equals: Net earnings by place of residence	Plus: Dividends, interest, and rent	Plus: Personal current transfer receipts	Per capita personal income (dollars)	Population (persons)	Total employment
		Nonfarm	Farm	Total								
1970	220,279	128,101	8,495	136,596	9,340	45,735	172,991	29,449	17,839	3,853	57,165	24,009
1971	237,007	136,176	6,958	143,134	10,344	51,549	184,339	32,150	20,518	4,043	58,628	23,992
1972	266,984	149,265	7,988	157,253	11,787	61,324	206,790	35,479	24,715	4,390	60,815	24,380
1973	300,435	164,718	11,039	175,757	14,854	70,870	231,773	41,350	27,312	4,797	62,627	25,256
1974	334,470	176,103	15,221	191,324	16,536	80,338	255,126	46,788	32,556	5,265	63,523	24,999
1975	362,842	184,927	9,788	194,715	16,850	87,708	265,573	53,974	43,295	5,684	63,834	24,443
1976	413,934	212,368	16,688	229,056	19,568	98,720	308,208	57,621	48,105	6,424	64,435	25,654
1977	457,621	230,661	18,720	249,381	21,206	114,364	342,539	64,650	50,432	6,997	65,398	26,298
1978	511,072	264,857	10,236	275,093	24,871	134,244	384,466	73,133	53,473	7,716	66,235	27,477
1979	573,715	290,611	10,133	300,744	28,216	155,908	428,436	85,904	59,375	8,511	67,409	28,152
1980	643,223	317,153	5,865	323,018	31,259	174,231	465,990	108,241	68,992	9,388	68,513	28,790
1981	709,760	345,970	6,185	352,155	36,658	182,295	497,792	132,073	79,895	10,211	69,506	28,581
1982	766,221	361,564	15,662	377,226	38,529	181,203	519,900	153,030	93,291	10,880	70,422	28,659
1983	803,548	394,355	8,998	403,353	42,342	185,461	546,472	155,589	101,487	11,369	70,679	29,204
1984	884,918	436,370	18,378	454,748	48,563	203,929	610,114	174,972	99,832	12,590	70,290	30,229
1985	950,789	472,832	17,063	489,895	53,532	217,602	653,965	190,079	106,745	13,383	71,043	31,718
1986	1,027,945	511,771	27,130	538,901	58,365	228,607	709,143	205,107	113,695	14,180	72,492	32,650
1987	1,099,434	567,433	21,028	588,461	64,276	246,588	770,773	210,601	118,060	14,862	73,976	34,638
1988	1,204,071	631,329	22,895	654,224	72,681	267,159	848,702	226,283	129,086	15,985	75,326	35,985
1989	1,310,249	692,335	19,197	711,532	78,199	279,193	912,526	257,264	140,459	17,103	76,609	36,964
1990	1,399,096	738,381	29,588	767,969	83,834	296,067	980,202	261,701	157,193	17,756	78,797	37,551
1991	1,450,322	754,206	31,501	785,707	87,710	297,659	995,656	271,319	183,347	18,009	80,531	37,987
1992	1,542,805	818,061	40,966	859,027	94,835	299,012	1,063,204	278,062	201,539	18,867	81,771	38,543
1993	1,591,621	861,886	33,922	895,808	101,859	302,511	1,096,460	283,199	211,962	19,173	83,013	38,395
1994	1,629,082	898,173	19,829	918,002	109,090	302,612	1,111,524	292,532	225,026	19,351	84,186	39,636
1995	1,729,312	920,464	29,863	950,327	112,377	311,541	1,149,491	341,946	237,875	20,330	85,063	40,120
1996	1,839,258	943,065	41,584	984,649	112,220	334,598	1,207,027	374,355	257,876	21,324	86,252	40,211
1997	1,970,734	979,752	33,758	1,013,510	114,458	394,952	1,294,004	410,004	266,726	22,458	87,751	40,491
1998	2,082,459	1,060,642	25,391	1,086,033	120,696	397,366	1,362,703	442,317	277,439	23,379	89,074	43,273
1999	2,227,219	1,175,879	32,859	1,208,738	129,648	412,078	1,491,168	440,193	295,858	24,647	90,363	44,683
2000	2,410,916	1,252,592	20,051	1,272,643	137,328	469,903	1,605,218	483,167	322,531	26,361	91,457	46,223
2001	2,554,745	1,284,005	32,258	1,316,263	144,658	515,844	1,687,449	507,783	359,513	27,592	92,591	46,253
2002	2,656,641	1,353,610	19,169	1,372,779	151,716	551,207	1,772,270	502,646	381,725	28,282	93,934	46,987
2003	2,807,051	1,436,454	33,129	1,469,583	159,417	591,045	1,901,211	505,850	399,990	29,392	95,503	47,552
2004	2,956,831	1,542,426	22,005	1,564,431	171,677	650,957	2,043,711	483,808	429,312	30,389	97,300	48,920
2005	3,101,284	1,637,466	19,394	1,656,860	184,864	708,417	2,180,413	453,537	467,334	31,451	98,606	50,642
2006	3,335,941	1,751,622	7,330	1,758,952	199,290	779,015	2,338,677	493,562	503,702	33,393	99,899	52,382
2007	3,555,120	1,792,025	16,340	1,808,365	207,403	847,236	2,448,198	560,990	545,932	35,374	100,502	53,400
2008	3,697,873	1,766,294	57,803	1,824,097	208,306	872,254	2,488,045	586,397	623,431	36,592	101,056	52,781
2009	3,740,488	1,706,097	61,158	1,767,255	203,091	884,413	2,448,577	522,487	769,424	36,942	101,252	50,903
2010	3,797,694	1,723,026	56,925	1,779,951	205,866	923,515	2,497,600	538,710	761,384	37,427	101,470	49,796
2011	3,952,284	1,767,544	57,087	1,824,631	191,667	975,973	2,608,937	594,294	749,053	38,882	101,649	49,459
2012	4,095,550	1,816,088	85,901	1,901,989	196,252	996,671	2,702,408	640,029	753,113	40,335	101,538	49,741
2013	4,204,191	1,906,466	81,622	1,988,088	231,867	992,311	2,748,532	682,712	772,947	41,438	101,457	51,811
2014	4,350,902	1,982,507	92,695	2,075,202	241,182	1,001,632	2,835,652	708,704	806,546	42,776	101,714	52,367

Personal Income and Employment by Area: Glens Falls, NY

(Thousands of dollars, except as noted.)

| Year | Personal income, total | Derivation of personal income | | | | | | | | Per capita personal income (dollars) | Population (persons) | Total employment |
| | | Earnings by place of work | | | Less: Contributions for government social insurance | Plus: Adjustment for residence | Equals: Net earnings by place of residence | Plus: Dividends, interest, and rent | Plus: Personal current transfer receipts | | | |
		Nonfarm	Farm	Total								
1970	371,511	298,068	9,468	307,536	22,577	-2,830	282,129	48,495	40,887	3,621	102,612	43,236
1971	399,191	315,636	9,831	325,467	24,786	-5,129	295,552	54,224	49,415	3,814	104,666	43,913
1972	427,549	337,893	10,127	348,020	27,754	-7,223	313,043	60,864	53,642	4,037	105,917	44,230
1973	465,351	367,892	11,125	379,017	34,816	-8,810	335,391	68,537	61,423	4,375	106,354	45,768
1974	506,740	395,485	9,488	404,973	38,663	-10,662	355,648	77,082	74,010	4,747	106,739	46,106
1975	550,021	408,256	7,154	415,410	39,089	-10,810	365,511	84,957	99,553	5,075	108,378	44,892
1976	599,037	453,583	9,186	462,769	44,431	-12,557	405,781	89,899	103,357	5,501	108,894	46,339
1977	646,109	494,747	6,145	500,892	48,256	-17,149	435,487	100,444	110,178	5,883	109,831	47,327
1978	710,811	554,755	10,298	565,053	55,170	-24,044	485,839	106,749	118,223	6,442	110,335	48,379
1979	779,194	608,981	14,680	623,661	62,393	-31,355	529,913	121,506	127,775	7,054	110,464	49,743
1980	867,878	656,479	15,690	672,169	67,336	-36,169	568,664	148,592	150,622	7,910	109,725	49,896
1981	961,361	707,585	15,255	722,840	77,390	-37,414	608,036	181,461	171,864	8,753	109,830	50,090
1982	1,042,082	747,338	16,038	763,376	82,735	-35,754	644,887	204,568	192,627	9,493	109,768	50,097
1983	1,122,883	798,343	14,578	812,921	88,645	-33,951	690,325	229,057	203,501	10,204	110,046	50,967
1984	1,258,987	907,672	14,725	922,397	102,388	-35,451	784,558	262,624	211,805	11,390	110,536	52,557
1985	1,349,389	966,649	15,939	982,588	110,118	-28,360	844,110	281,595	223,684	12,109	111,433	53,905
1986	1,467,563	1,072,240	17,836	1,090,076	123,438	-30,761	935,877	299,521	232,165	13,073	112,257	56,468
1987	1,598,801	1,185,134	18,413	1,203,547	134,970	-30,288	1,038,289	323,554	236,958	14,019	114,046	57,673
1988	1,754,966	1,319,177	14,952	1,334,129	153,028	-29,377	1,151,724	349,147	254,095	15,175	115,651	60,396
1989	1,906,223	1,373,877	19,982	1,393,859	158,087	-16,935	1,218,837	416,665	270,721	16,290	117,016	60,320
1990	1,994,238	1,421,450	22,262	1,443,712	157,428	-8,901	1,277,383	419,672	297,183	16,755	119,027	60,604
1991	2,049,392	1,449,637	16,786	1,466,423	164,916	-10	1,301,497	416,403	331,492	17,038	120,286	59,605
1992	2,210,114	1,555,184	22,557	1,577,741	172,986	6,749	1,411,504	419,827	378,783	18,222	121,290	59,655
1993	2,261,677	1,593,777	22,127	1,615,904	178,490	15,302	1,452,716	415,976	392,985	18,452	122,572	60,889
1994	2,347,648	1,659,287	17,571	1,676,858	188,805	17,542	1,505,595	423,868	418,185	19,120	122,783	63,236
1995	2,469,441	1,720,109	13,731	1,733,840	193,808	25,436	1,565,468	460,983	442,990	19,996	123,496	64,371
1996	2,563,678	1,760,418	23,186	1,783,604	194,754	37,310	1,626,160	472,107	465,411	20,739	123,615	63,799
1997	2,673,044	1,844,985	9,380	1,854,365	199,577	53,659	1,708,447	493,805	470,792	21,660	123,410	63,862
1998	2,780,975	1,881,369	24,231	1,905,600	204,643	70,730	1,771,687	513,315	495,973	22,530	123,436	62,074
1999	2,867,896	1,940,615	23,823	1,964,438	206,489	93,959	1,851,908	500,199	515,789	23,114	124,074	63,330
2000	3,064,075	2,095,132	20,381	2,115,513	222,131	114,957	2,008,339	520,284	535,452	24,661	124,250	64,376
2001	3,146,164	2,075,151	25,354	2,100,505	229,273	166,932	2,038,164	529,943	578,057	25,261	124,548	63,196
2002	3,184,526	2,135,782	16,185	2,151,967	241,585	158,875	2,069,257	491,296	623,973	25,491	124,926	63,079
2003	3,335,099	2,252,707	20,164	2,272,871	254,035	163,667	2,182,503	497,805	654,791	26,481	125,944	64,544
2004	3,559,468	2,405,797	29,042	2,434,839	270,814	175,682	2,339,707	519,682	700,079	28,060	126,854	66,431
2005	3,710,280	2,526,584	28,798	2,555,382	288,166	172,373	2,439,589	534,577	736,114	29,061	127,674	67,290
2006	3,848,910	2,632,688	17,413	2,650,101	297,357	183,818	2,536,562	519,565	792,783	29,993	128,325	67,879
2007	4,003,654	2,699,121	19,778	2,718,899	302,661	199,092	2,615,330	549,598	838,726	31,086	128,794	68,519
2008	4,358,714	2,839,732	19,124	2,858,856	321,687	209,037	2,746,206	675,661	936,847	33,762	129,100	70,314
2009	4,446,337	2,849,574	10,987	2,860,561	323,254	226,303	2,763,610	640,072	1,042,655	34,529	128,771	68,710
2010	4,594,274	2,929,648	27,764	2,957,412	334,425	210,476	2,833,463	648,459	1,112,352	35,617	128,991	67,770
2011	4,829,070	3,016,838	45,058	3,061,896	313,079	241,275	2,990,092	708,455	1,130,523	37,498	128,782	68,276
2012	4,957,485	3,138,137	42,902	3,181,039	322,846	206,195	3,064,388	758,006	1,135,091	38,587	128,476	68,255
2013	5,018,195	3,147,055	59,941	3,206,996	366,987	289,431	3,129,440	743,931	1,144,824	39,236	127,898	67,820
2014	5,180,850	3,266,472	71,923	3,338,395	384,334	270,118	3,224,179	773,274	1,183,397	40,684	127,345	68,459

Personal Income and Employment by Area: Goldsboro, NC

(Thousands of dollars, except as noted.)

Year	Personal income, total	Earnings by place of work			Less: Contributions for government social insurance	Plus: Adjustment for residence	Equals: Net earnings by place of residence	Plus: Dividends, interest, and rent	Plus: Personal current transfer receipts	Per capita personal income (dollars)	Population (persons)	Total employment
		Nonfarm	Farm	Total								
1970	286,445	231,982	16,522	248,504	15,680	-13,318	219,506	44,189	22,750	3,341	85,747	42,648
1971	313,658	254,254	17,910	272,164	17,999	-15,035	239,130	47,663	26,865	3,567	87,943	43,039
1972	353,811	283,420	23,683	307,103	20,513	-15,693	270,897	52,151	30,763	3,925	90,151	43,682
1973	391,003	304,603	35,177	339,780	24,689	-14,524	300,567	56,704	33,732	4,328	90,338	44,400
1974	443,705	341,319	40,079	381,398	28,817	-16,792	335,789	66,703	41,213	4,833	91,807	45,687
1975	476,560	358,138	36,633	394,771	31,216	-14,608	348,947	73,685	53,928	5,152	92,498	44,628
1976	517,370	391,273	35,703	426,976	35,037	-13,905	378,034	79,869	59,467	5,542	93,352	45,876
1977	547,373	422,384	21,812	444,196	37,333	-12,663	394,200	90,538	62,635	5,782	94,674	46,344
1978	614,024	466,020	33,578	499,598	41,876	-12,106	445,616	101,263	67,145	6,344	96,788	46,994
1979	665,895	520,761	18,240	539,001	48,700	-11,018	479,283	110,456	76,156	6,855	97,135	48,534
1980	733,416	562,862	13,743	576,605	52,559	-10,886	513,160	129,005	91,251	7,537	97,314	48,041
1981	807,485	601,400	26,141	627,541	60,103	-14,098	553,340	148,527	105,618	8,234	98,066	47,291
1982	867,979	635,920	28,662	664,582	63,595	-17,109	583,878	168,661	115,440	8,803	98,603	46,959
1983	928,343	691,544	16,564	708,108	70,066	-17,312	620,730	182,634	124,979	9,340	99,391	47,490
1984	1,053,611	752,144	61,483	813,627	78,344	-16,249	719,034	202,830	131,747	10,495	100,393	48,551
1985	1,100,090	787,314	55,857	843,171	83,299	-13,469	746,403	212,469	141,218	10,871	101,193	48,845
1986	1,145,543	821,788	53,196	874,984	88,997	-11,937	774,050	221,391	150,102	11,432	100,205	48,493
1987	1,190,916	883,297	28,753	912,050	95,038	-10,425	806,587	229,038	155,291	11,757	101,296	49,782
1988	1,290,069	960,995	30,270	991,265	107,844	-15,611	867,810	253,483	168,776	12,614	102,269	52,540
1989	1,416,509	1,019,993	46,259	1,066,252	114,808	-12,431	939,013	291,559	185,937	13,628	103,938	52,694
1990	1,530,023	1,075,207	56,241	1,131,448	123,205	17,308	1,025,551	296,328	208,144	14,586	104,896	53,244
1991	1,613,568	1,106,438	73,633	1,180,071	128,107	20,339	1,072,303	301,785	239,480	15,144	106,545	51,973
1992	1,756,107	1,187,986	69,324	1,257,310	136,880	50,720	1,171,150	320,286	264,671	16,319	107,614	52,502
1993	1,853,560	1,258,444	73,468	1,331,912	146,115	46,025	1,231,822	327,634	294,104	17,103	108,374	53,661
1994	1,969,663	1,311,175	79,421	1,390,596	152,634	71,899	1,309,861	352,343	307,459	17,995	109,459	55,617
1995	2,088,005	1,387,637	73,618	1,461,255	161,288	60,545	1,360,512	383,685	343,808	18,713	111,578	57,476
1996	2,198,814	1,440,435	82,389	1,522,824	165,815	62,876	1,419,885	407,078	371,851	19,476	112,898	57,498
1997	2,307,993	1,514,497	82,324	1,596,821	173,536	49,774	1,473,059	439,667	395,267	20,359	113,366	59,127
1998	2,389,116	1,596,348	59,431	1,655,779	182,320	36,041	1,509,500	474,422	405,194	21,063	113,429	58,366
1999	2,488,440	1,664,223	43,210	1,707,433	190,137	63,877	1,581,173	475,968	431,299	21,987	113,176	58,698
2000	2,627,023	1,748,448	50,595	1,799,043	198,272	72,652	1,673,423	498,050	455,550	23,115	113,648	59,853
2001	2,731,855	1,817,664	56,717	1,874,381	208,003	58,929	1,725,307	512,554	493,994	23,978	113,934	58,449
2002	2,806,171	1,874,804	36,674	1,911,478	215,469	64,988	1,760,997	512,734	532,440	24,550	114,305	58,480
2003	2,862,575	1,903,707	16,197	1,919,904	221,147	69,763	1,768,520	526,744	567,311	24,980	114,595	57,493
2004	3,050,312	2,014,208	34,207	2,048,415	233,044	78,872	1,894,243	548,129	607,940	26,187	116,484	57,973
2005	3,184,970	2,077,736	55,258	2,132,994	243,265	86,466	1,976,195	552,817	655,958	27,220	117,009	58,039
2006	3,335,077	2,177,914	37,459	2,215,373	257,930	96,612	2,054,055	562,872	718,150	28,375	117,534	58,889
2007	3,578,728	2,263,770	68,214	2,331,984	272,504	108,018	2,167,498	646,497	764,733	30,088	118,942	60,419
2008	3,740,735	2,294,357	108,460	2,402,817	277,031	116,182	2,241,968	652,346	846,421	31,196	119,910	59,428
2009	3,773,618	2,309,573	92,362	2,401,935	279,006	103,870	2,226,799	623,314	923,505	31,131	121,217	58,478
2010	3,876,317	2,345,293	114,263	2,459,556	275,806	112,254	2,296,004	605,230	975,083	31,543	122,888	57,394
2011	4,054,248	2,427,240	102,422	2,529,662	262,470	117,703	2,384,895	662,754	1,006,599	32,690	124,022	58,471
2012	4,293,347	2,550,904	147,343	2,698,247	270,062	126,008	2,554,193	708,012	1,031,142	34,484	124,504	58,342
2013	4,244,444	2,485,412	186,565	2,671,977	300,404	124,823	2,496,396	695,364	1,052,684	34,066	124,596	57,862
2014	4,378,472	2,508,291	218,207	2,726,498	300,713	143,052	2,568,837	722,027	1,087,608	35,181	124,456	57,409

Personal Income and Employment by Area: Grand Forks, ND-MN

(Thousands of dollars, except as noted.)

Year	Personal income, total	Earnings by place of work			Less: Contributions for government social insurance	Plus: Adjustment for residence	Equals: Net earnings by place of residence	Plus: Dividends, interest, and rent	Plus: Personal current transfer receipts	Per capita personal income (dollars)	Population (persons)	Total employment
		Nonfarm	Farm	Total								
1970	357,775	248,514	33,965	282,479	18,853	4,886	268,512	59,759	29,504	3,729	95,935	43,052
1971	391,461	270,169	34,767	304,936	21,288	7,820	291,468	65,432	34,561	3,999	97,885	43,405
1972	441,472	300,976	47,267	348,243	24,388	7,707	331,562	71,999	37,911	4,477	98,607	44,636
1973	578,737	339,822	142,350	482,172	30,746	1,065	452,491	83,569	42,677	5,799	99,795	46,958
1974	602,157	377,602	119,775	497,377	36,013	-4,437	456,927	95,042	50,188	6,016	100,100	48,256
1975	643,149	415,821	102,682	518,503	40,614	-4,346	473,543	109,394	60,212	6,549	98,203	48,980
1976	681,579	486,109	67,380	553,489	48,357	-7,481	497,651	118,084	65,844	6,774	100,617	51,544
1977	676,150	501,762	29,499	531,261	48,635	-7,216	475,410	129,774	70,966	6,633	101,935	51,571
1978	815,676	550,272	105,612	655,884	54,218	-8,036	593,630	143,373	78,673	8,058	101,225	52,678
1979	847,222	601,160	72,976	674,136	61,546	-9,212	603,378	156,831	87,013	8,357	101,383	52,989
1980	880,865	644,823	19,371	664,194	66,540	-9,987	587,667	189,553	103,645	8,715	101,074	53,483
1981	997,145	699,222	30,374	729,596	75,838	-9,531	644,227	233,966	118,952	9,837	101,367	52,972
1982	1,091,688	741,388	37,012	778,400	80,770	-9,051	688,579	271,340	131,769	10,718	101,851	53,099
1983	1,164,317	783,952	47,597	831,549	86,799	-7,852	736,898	278,817	148,602	11,293	103,104	54,018
1984	1,296,840	830,834	111,083	941,917	94,693	-8,090	839,134	297,574	160,132	12,501	103,741	54,465
1985	1,310,085	875,893	62,395	938,288	102,024	-8,290	827,974	310,529	171,582	12,632	103,712	55,684
1986	1,412,214	920,735	110,567	1,031,302	110,241	-8,954	912,107	320,414	179,693	13,665	103,349	55,969
1987	1,463,349	975,706	110,250	1,085,956	117,601	-9,365	958,990	314,517	189,842	14,149	103,422	57,658
1988	1,463,913	1,019,592	63,615	1,083,207	128,682	-8,154	946,371	321,071	196,471	14,030	104,341	58,645
1989	1,553,196	1,075,350	56,876	1,132,226	137,304	-7,757	987,165	353,170	212,861	14,921	104,094	59,627
1990	1,647,102	1,120,857	89,844	1,210,701	148,094	-7,862	1,054,745	363,937	228,420	15,964	103,177	59,698
1991	1,677,762	1,185,269	64,659	1,249,928	159,622	-10,701	1,079,605	365,286	232,871	16,284	103,034	61,249
1992	1,815,188	1,254,100	121,728	1,375,828	169,611	-14,027	1,192,190	363,767	259,231	17,423	104,181	61,836
1993	1,813,431	1,327,749	29,754	1,357,503	181,398	-17,537	1,158,568	383,989	270,874	17,363	104,443	63,139
1994	1,940,597	1,400,911	63,520	1,464,431	191,772	-20,816	1,251,843	416,046	272,708	18,377	105,601	65,108
1995	2,015,359	1,469,005	42,450	1,511,455	199,215	-25,675	1,286,565	440,973	287,821	19,076	105,650	66,896
1996	2,166,154	1,528,296	129,960	1,658,256	206,139	-28,994	1,423,123	445,904	297,127	20,543	105,443	67,548
1997	2,138,172	1,589,056	31,905	1,620,961	212,442	-33,056	1,375,463	464,376	298,333	20,630	103,643	65,519
1998	2,259,075	1,644,926	96,309	1,741,235	219,342	-36,735	1,485,158	478,881	295,036	22,605	99,938	65,346
1999	2,248,682	1,674,043	61,528	1,735,571	222,342	-38,448	1,474,781	462,737	311,164	22,965	97,919	64,671
2000	2,376,128	1,722,165	107,160	1,829,325	228,218	-41,416	1,559,691	480,850	335,587	24,394	97,405	64,420
2001	2,419,744	1,796,123	60,123	1,856,246	230,571	-43,338	1,582,337	477,255	360,152	25,033	96,663	64,564
2002	2,495,245	1,861,932	56,862	1,918,794	238,485	-52,437	1,627,872	485,290	382,083	25,893	96,367	64,897
2003	2,714,366	1,998,783	146,942	2,145,725	253,172	-58,660	1,833,893	482,942	397,531	28,196	96,267	65,706
2004	2,760,391	2,117,082	62,300	2,179,382	266,759	-65,701	1,846,922	493,636	419,833	28,120	98,164	67,015
2005	2,866,667	2,194,015	81,116	2,275,131	277,095	-72,526	1,925,510	488,227	452,930	29,318	97,777	68,456
2006	3,047,454	2,305,181	108,591	2,413,772	286,448	-78,402	2,048,922	522,108	476,424	31,012	98,266	69,089
2007	3,266,952	2,394,457	143,357	2,537,814	296,557	-81,507	2,159,750	593,257	513,945	33,471	97,606	69,783
2008	3,628,602	2,494,659	271,642	2,766,301	306,311	-82,388	2,377,602	669,820	581,180	36,992	98,092	69,044
2009	3,498,626	2,538,739	125,501	2,664,240	322,944	-84,929	2,256,367	624,999	617,260	35,722	97,941	68,646
2010	3,689,733	2,620,099	187,260	2,807,359	317,318	-86,230	2,403,811	623,162	662,760	37,419	98,605	67,895
2011	3,928,779	2,715,968	175,360	2,891,328	305,894	-87,413	2,498,021	750,499	680,259	40,010	98,195	67,964
2012	4,307,044	2,866,721	340,330	3,207,051	308,801	-94,085	2,804,165	818,779	684,100	43,412	99,214	69,949
2013	4,397,314	2,963,325	335,395	3,298,720	361,349	-91,067	2,846,304	847,716	703,294	43,532	101,014	70,561
2014	4,433,434	3,124,775	165,676	3,290,451	381,008	-94,939	2,814,504	880,305	738,625	43,532	101,842	71,275

Personal Income and Employment by Area: Grand Island, NE

(Thousands of dollars, except as noted.)

Year	Personal income, total	Earnings by place of work			Less: Contributions for government social insurance	Plus: Adjustment for residence	Equals: Net earnings by place of residence	Plus: Dividends, interest, and rent	Plus: Personal current transfer receipts	Per capita personal income (dollars)	Population (persons)	Total employment
		Nonfarm	Farm	Total								
1970	257,855	170,434	36,916	207,350	11,911	-5,113	190,326	44,823	22,706	3,836	67,211	31,910
1971	272,795	179,316	37,327	216,643	12,841	-4,889	198,913	48,561	25,321	4,048	67,395	31,655
1972	301,631	199,428	39,107	238,535	14,654	-5,340	218,541	55,162	27,928	4,443	67,890	33,218
1973	352,658	226,873	54,970	281,843	19,273	-6,082	256,488	62,969	33,201	5,135	68,678	35,148
1974	378,159	246,842	49,501	296,343	21,797	-6,208	268,338	71,436	38,385	5,503	68,715	35,595
1975	440,190	269,600	72,115	341,715	23,314	-6,879	311,522	83,133	45,535	6,295	69,925	35,293
1976	449,790	307,273	40,153	347,426	26,855	-7,314	313,257	88,314	48,219	6,423	70,033	36,625
1977	461,792	339,122	8,055	347,177	29,475	-8,269	309,433	99,990	52,369	6,484	71,220	37,764
1978	566,384	376,960	63,368	440,328	33,695	-9,083	397,550	111,102	57,732	7,926	71,462	39,141
1979	590,929	423,673	27,977	451,650	39,400	-10,611	401,639	124,361	64,929	8,162	72,400	39,560
1980	604,592	465,393	-33,537	431,856	43,359	-12,974	375,523	152,687	76,382	8,287	72,954	40,087
1981	759,490	505,446	39,462	544,908	50,049	-12,530	482,329	187,924	89,237	10,295	73,771	40,254
1982	779,578	507,552	10,899	518,451	51,424	-11,608	455,419	224,027	100,132	10,490	74,317	38,976
1983	809,373	522,607	11,381	533,988	53,185	-10,932	469,871	230,631	108,871	10,928	74,064	39,138
1984	929,681	558,713	81,854	640,567	58,537	-10,183	571,847	243,070	114,764	12,535	74,167	39,328
1985	935,945	567,431	71,892	639,323	61,318	-9,479	568,526	246,742	120,677	12,703	73,677	38,879
1986	979,721	592,237	91,630	683,867	65,846	-10,005	608,016	244,943	126,762	13,530	72,410	38,811
1987	1,015,363	619,204	106,083	725,287	68,955	-8,992	647,340	238,190	129,833	14,111	71,955	39,539
1988	1,083,545	653,793	133,897	787,690	75,952	-7,148	704,590	242,359	136,596	15,086	71,826	40,534
1989	1,155,435	692,486	127,812	820,298	80,723	-6,345	733,230	276,630	145,575	16,106	71,740	41,448
1990	1,210,882	748,714	134,690	883,404	89,960	-6,376	787,068	267,312	156,502	16,801	72,071	42,489
1991	1,284,891	794,194	142,669	936,863	96,200	-8,051	832,612	283,823	168,456	17,661	72,752	43,359
1992	1,339,319	849,795	127,794	977,589	101,326	-8,277	867,986	287,019	184,314	18,227	73,479	44,308
1993	1,366,619	909,677	85,512	995,189	108,969	-9,299	876,921	296,192	193,506	18,350	74,477	45,175
1994	1,481,904	988,355	111,096	1,099,451	118,562	-9,879	971,010	305,713	205,181	19,736	75,088	47,719
1995	1,547,325	1,035,312	94,093	1,129,405	122,433	-9,569	997,403	333,974	215,948	20,368	75,970	47,414
1996	1,689,006	1,082,877	155,638	1,238,515	127,484	-10,104	1,100,927	357,076	231,003	22,069	76,534	48,688
1997	1,709,807	1,141,195	102,854	1,244,049	135,455	-10,663	1,097,931	370,854	241,022	22,194	77,040	49,347
1998	1,800,356	1,202,259	92,069	1,294,328	140,918	-9,828	1,143,582	399,964	256,810	23,217	77,545	50,142
1999	1,852,967	1,255,170	78,710	1,333,880	145,587	-9,345	1,178,948	399,971	274,048	23,791	77,886	50,668
2000	1,941,859	1,308,943	80,460	1,389,403	150,569	-10,704	1,228,130	428,510	285,219	25,017	77,621	50,857
2001	2,048,693	1,390,151	85,435	1,475,586	159,023	-15,710	1,300,853	432,270	315,570	26,500	77,308	50,448
2002	2,130,353	1,500,048	59,551	1,559,599	167,477	-24,422	1,367,700	424,128	338,525	27,479	77,526	49,798
2003	2,283,538	1,550,658	131,021	1,681,679	173,272	-28,267	1,480,140	446,114	357,284	29,298	77,941	50,047
2004	2,323,596	1,619,927	138,307	1,758,234	179,572	-35,657	1,543,005	405,388	375,203	29,708	78,215	50,455
2005	2,404,593	1,712,507	153,423	1,865,930	193,492	-44,768	1,627,670	382,113	394,810	30,773	78,140	51,665
2006	2,491,704	1,817,895	94,279	1,912,174	209,946	-48,663	1,653,565	416,712	421,427	31,719	78,556	52,703
2007	2,726,756	1,924,168	154,225	2,078,393	223,473	-51,834	1,803,086	479,760	443,910	34,521	78,988	53,692
2008	2,937,565	1,989,803	156,614	2,146,417	231,371	-53,025	1,862,021	577,576	497,968	36,744	79,947	54,506
2009	2,886,825	1,993,962	145,283	2,139,245	233,068	-52,301	1,853,876	513,501	519,448	35,566	81,169	54,312
2010	2,906,966	2,007,233	144,148	2,151,381	240,931	-52,507	1,857,943	494,910	554,113	35,432	82,043	53,874
2011	3,211,078	2,068,577	295,106	2,363,683	218,844	-54,421	2,090,418	563,310	557,350	38,836	82,683	54,953
2012	3,372,063	2,207,982	259,266	2,467,248	224,811	-59,678	2,182,759	627,328	561,976	40,402	83,462	55,922
2013	3,407,382	2,249,740	314,615	2,564,355	258,570	-62,327	2,243,458	595,954	567,970	40,474	84,187	56,544
2014	3,447,271	2,366,505	212,143	2,578,648	274,133	-65,721	2,238,794	619,113	589,364	40,673	84,755	56,897

Personal Income and Employment by Area: Grand Junction, CO

(Thousands of dollars, except as noted.)

Year	Personal income, total	Earnings by place of work			Less: Contributions for government social insurance	Plus: Adjustment for residence	Equals: Net earnings by place of residence	Plus: Dividends, interest, and rent	Plus: Personal current transfer receipts	Per capita personal income (dollars)	Population (persons)	Total employment
		Nonfarm	Farm	Total								
1970	191,307	139,393	3,993	143,386	8,195	117	135,308	32,814	23,185	3,512	54,479	23,121
1971	211,974	149,831	7,157	156,988	8,932	451	148,507	36,439	27,028	3,832	55,311	23,077
1972	233,885	169,528	4,600	174,128	10,758	1,086	164,456	40,033	29,396	4,110	56,912	24,258
1973	272,075	194,057	8,130	202,187	14,205	2,066	190,048	47,651	34,376	4,694	57,962	26,242
1974	321,917	232,812	6,702	239,514	17,459	3,092	225,147	57,062	39,708	5,459	58,973	28,069
1975	377,967	276,135	7,304	283,439	20,538	3,692	266,593	64,188	47,186	5,975	63,261	30,541
1976	423,061	311,901	5,577	317,478	23,291	5,470	299,657	72,163	51,241	6,350	66,628	32,111
1977	508,567	387,870	3,986	391,856	28,908	6,582	369,530	84,271	54,766	7,415	68,585	35,299
1978	592,309	457,686	827	458,513	35,274	8,477	431,716	100,545	60,048	8,201	72,223	37,820
1979	684,618	525,405	4,395	529,800	43,288	10,878	497,390	118,918	68,310	8,897	76,946	40,671
1980	805,665	610,797	2,580	613,377	51,893	13,794	575,278	149,285	81,102	9,731	82,796	43,710
1981	977,055	744,831	2,350	747,181	69,526	15,818	693,473	188,054	95,528	11,146	87,659	48,937
1982	1,079,935	798,946	-1,789	797,157	76,842	21,089	741,404	224,618	113,913	11,470	94,152	50,531
1983	1,089,071	769,000	1,206	770,206	73,346	23,096	719,956	235,322	133,793	11,343	96,012	48,319
1984	1,086,549	749,522	1,610	751,132	72,847	21,458	699,743	245,201	141,605	11,498	94,496	46,669
1985	1,078,623	731,316	-854	730,462	73,140	21,682	679,004	251,772	147,847	12,069	89,368	44,600
1986	1,058,873	688,536	-4,408	684,128	71,250	22,483	635,361	260,441	163,071	12,117	87,386	42,603
1987	1,145,215	753,475	-1,131	752,344	75,766	22,280	698,858	267,262	179,095	13,097	87,443	42,211
1988	1,252,220	840,532	433	840,965	87,270	22,237	775,932	286,438	189,850	14,090	88,872	45,112
1989	1,350,483	883,101	2,537	885,638	96,135	23,702	813,205	326,109	211,169	14,803	91,231	47,556
1990	1,450,731	959,538	2,293	961,831	107,103	28,337	883,065	340,830	226,836	15,473	93,757	49,479
1991	1,547,055	1,035,607	4,680	1,040,287	119,167	26,540	947,660	346,182	253,213	16,057	96,348	50,610
1992	1,687,662	1,133,419	8,463	1,141,882	128,847	23,809	1,036,844	367,626	283,192	17,225	97,977	51,414
1993	1,803,560	1,213,838	10,155	1,223,993	139,318	25,438	1,110,113	385,771	307,676	17,932	100,579	53,284
1994	1,921,790	1,289,048	7,041	1,296,089	149,379	30,827	1,177,537	418,368	325,885	18,591	103,373	55,648
1995	2,093,919	1,368,562	6,204	1,374,766	158,716	32,075	1,248,125	480,264	365,530	19,760	105,968	58,004
1996	2,221,502	1,465,281	8,137	1,473,418	167,445	33,691	1,339,664	502,463	379,375	20,545	108,131	61,078
1997	2,414,238	1,617,346	8,572	1,625,918	181,526	36,172	1,480,564	544,277	389,397	21,835	110,566	63,850
1998	2,658,262	1,778,041	12,260	1,790,301	183,000	39,896	1,647,197	580,955	430,110	23,590	112,686	66,506
1999	2,801,758	1,906,463	8,094	1,914,557	193,483	42,530	1,763,604	581,011	457,143	24,400	114,827	68,199
2000	3,041,019	2,070,081	8,692	2,078,773	204,113	47,450	1,922,110	640,328	478,581	25,852	117,631	70,062
2001	3,159,144	2,142,307	12,979	2,155,286	219,482	48,201	1,984,005	654,633	520,506	26,437	119,496	71,047
2002	3,269,009	2,256,208	13,499	2,269,707	243,681	61,692	2,087,718	604,910	576,381	26,699	122,440	72,866
2003	3,391,152	2,338,038	9,229	2,347,267	254,281	75,938	2,168,924	627,671	594,557	27,131	124,994	73,781
2004	3,621,236	2,482,338	14,605	2,496,943	277,595	94,230	2,313,578	674,678	632,980	28,362	127,678	76,566
2005	3,912,936	2,679,484	18,082	2,697,566	304,464	116,070	2,509,172	716,749	687,015	30,055	130,194	79,241
2006	4,287,068	2,954,225	11,812	2,966,037	335,666	144,491	2,774,862	773,787	738,419	31,835	134,665	82,327
2007	4,758,410	3,229,555	9,268	3,238,823	371,773	181,380	3,048,430	930,948	779,032	34,127	139,434	87,525
2008	5,350,256	3,615,289	6,565	3,621,854	416,717	225,971	3,431,108	1,044,642	874,506	37,374	143,155	91,386
2009	4,994,845	3,378,241	3,255	3,381,496	386,656	174,597	3,169,437	915,644	909,764	33,783	147,851	86,350
2010	4,889,542	3,219,101	7,111	3,226,212	366,742	172,715	3,032,185	856,526	1,000,831	33,379	146,485	83,094
2011	5,147,866	3,336,747	13,372	3,350,119	350,852	186,432	3,185,699	944,550	1,017,617	34,929	147,380	83,606
2012	5,379,747	3,489,824	14,195	3,504,019	362,037	190,128	3,332,110	1,028,794	1,018,843	36,418	147,724	84,362
2013	5,376,625	3,520,872	10,922	3,531,794	405,691	191,984	3,318,087	1,009,647	1,048,891	36,403	147,699	84,292
2014	5,644,717	3,675,601	27,711	3,703,312	423,093	197,916	3,478,135	1,054,065	1,112,517	38,074	148,255	86,154

Personal Income and Employment by Area: Grand Rapids-Wyoming, MI

(Thousands of dollars, except as noted.)

Year	Personal income, total	Earnings by place of work			Less: Contributions for government social insurance	Plus: Adjustment for residence	Equals: Net earnings by place of residence	Plus: Dividends, interest, and rent	Plus: Personal current transfer receipts	Per capita personal income (dollars)	Population (persons)	Total employment
		Nonfarm	Farm	Total								
1970	2,406,765	1,997,842	34,693	2,032,535	144,453	-19,775	1,868,307	325,391	213,067	3,897	617,650	260,078
1971	2,600,804	2,147,674	31,639	2,179,313	160,305	-19,624	1,999,384	348,370	253,050	4,190	620,779	264,236
1972	2,896,674	2,409,960	39,810	2,449,770	189,300	-19,433	2,241,037	376,460	279,177	4,621	626,892	276,468
1973	3,235,764	2,729,175	50,705	2,779,880	248,822	-22,872	2,508,186	410,596	316,982	5,071	638,073	292,681
1974	3,542,445	2,937,600	55,816	2,993,416	277,431	-25,816	2,690,169	465,952	386,324	5,508	643,154	298,385
1975	3,827,084	3,041,899	50,408	3,092,307	277,745	-20,150	2,794,412	521,639	511,033	5,903	648,334	289,665
1976	4,275,967	3,488,015	48,437	3,536,452	327,765	-23,720	3,184,967	559,113	531,887	6,536	654,247	305,252
1977	4,825,520	4,010,577	64,106	4,074,683	378,367	-34,621	3,661,695	622,648	541,177	7,281	662,779	323,181
1978	5,507,842	4,664,116	74,469	4,738,585	453,517	-47,883	4,237,185	699,846	570,811	8,193	672,225	345,133
1979	6,166,535	5,258,346	76,263	5,334,609	535,810	-68,444	4,730,355	794,521	641,659	9,001	685,105	356,907
1980	6,729,506	5,510,942	80,761	5,591,703	559,568	-67,955	4,964,180	964,579	800,747	9,653	697,163	349,556
1981	7,368,903	5,931,891	77,555	6,009,446	648,341	-80,381	5,280,724	1,192,206	895,973	10,464	704,228	350,029
1982	7,792,526	6,055,460	92,839	6,148,299	670,446	-92,175	5,385,678	1,386,544	1,020,304	11,032	706,354	344,069
1983	8,385,389	6,626,901	60,933	6,687,834	747,007	-121,353	5,819,474	1,489,558	1,076,357	11,821	709,384	356,659
1984	9,420,110	7,561,122	97,112	7,658,234	882,329	-165,538	6,610,367	1,726,943	1,082,800	13,090	719,650	378,005
1985	10,208,531	8,250,987	125,919	8,376,906	973,045	-190,915	7,212,946	1,847,967	1,147,618	13,970	730,764	396,691
1986	10,900,838	8,841,847	94,631	8,936,478	1,040,299	-178,299	7,717,880	1,969,090	1,213,868	14,712	740,945	405,607
1987	11,718,890	9,581,701	110,195	9,691,896	1,105,433	-214,555	8,371,908	2,085,313	1,261,669	15,544	753,914	423,569
1988	12,694,959	10,539,213	98,368	10,637,581	1,256,809	-265,798	9,114,974	2,258,307	1,321,678	16,495	769,644	441,855
1989	13,805,385	11,385,954	149,788	11,535,742	1,341,167	-302,937	9,891,638	2,447,570	1,466,177	17,654	782,004	458,586
1990	14,801,578	12,088,640	133,568	12,222,208	1,451,921	-335,691	10,434,596	2,752,757	1,614,225	18,609	795,411	473,830
1991	15,402,695	12,417,918	141,032	12,558,950	1,510,579	-329,803	10,718,568	2,853,603	1,830,524	19,001	810,613	472,642
1992	16,697,486	13,421,079	138,874	13,559,953	1,619,271	-382,590	11,558,092	3,180,761	1,958,633	20,281	823,316	479,549
1993	17,583,460	14,386,850	127,202	14,514,052	1,748,983	-447,453	12,317,616	3,174,786	2,091,058	21,040	835,716	492,605
1994	19,155,351	15,800,724	112,139	15,912,863	1,964,863	-557,847	13,390,153	3,655,611	2,109,587	22,549	849,497	519,290
1995	20,444,988	17,019,940	117,484	17,137,424	2,121,871	-675,918	14,339,635	3,919,466	2,185,887	23,644	864,714	546,139
1996	21,770,026	18,063,645	123,971	18,187,616	2,213,624	-756,364	15,217,628	4,256,901	2,295,497	24,737	880,047	559,946
1997	23,229,553	19,214,431	127,828	19,342,259	2,363,733	-866,322	16,112,204	4,634,546	2,482,803	25,984	893,999	575,693
1998	24,877,377	20,710,974	135,089	20,846,063	2,511,971	-955,314	17,378,778	4,978,519	2,520,080	27,444	906,489	583,336
1999	26,045,545	21,929,188	153,265	22,082,453	2,650,132	-1,095,617	18,336,704	5,002,931	2,705,910	28,290	920,648	595,441
2000	27,820,710	23,525,850	125,504	23,651,354	2,790,652	-1,251,086	19,609,616	5,337,091	2,874,003	29,782	934,152	615,100
2001	28,214,592	23,502,386	127,413	23,629,799	2,694,526	-1,238,131	19,697,142	5,277,416	3,240,034	29,871	944,552	601,291
2002	28,451,039	24,006,160	129,529	24,135,689	2,735,103	-1,226,957	20,173,629	4,851,593	3,425,817	29,880	952,185	593,853
2003	29,488,784	24,386,706	136,909	24,523,615	2,771,534	-1,178,987	20,573,094	5,302,089	3,613,601	30,741	959,259	590,994
2004	31,819,204	25,451,859	186,453	25,638,312	2,910,627	-1,122,172	21,605,513	6,425,440	3,788,251	32,970	965,089	601,909
2005	32,962,432	26,317,645	173,349	26,490,994	3,038,616	-1,100,226	22,352,152	6,578,150	4,032,130	33,957	970,713	610,159
2006	34,687,622	27,020,551	198,297	27,218,848	3,163,383	-1,051,629	23,003,836	7,297,698	4,386,088	35,518	976,610	609,775
2007	35,625,038	26,935,890	209,727	27,145,617	3,193,205	-962,234	22,990,178	7,828,290	4,806,570	36,291	981,643	610,114
2008	37,006,597	26,738,246	237,665	26,975,911	3,206,079	-860,073	22,909,759	8,518,001	5,578,837	37,587	984,563	597,557
2009	33,999,040	25,244,095	223,558	25,467,653	3,032,169	-791,990	21,643,494	6,197,933	6,157,613	34,437	987,281	562,899
2010	35,760,889	26,017,116	234,297	26,251,413	3,098,393	-678,669	22,474,351	6,636,078	6,650,460	36,151	989,205	562,200
2011	39,022,607	27,243,838	391,939	27,635,777	2,907,039	-739,278	23,989,460	8,371,539	6,661,608	39,165	996,355	584,219
2012	41,399,491	28,875,989	230,942	29,106,931	3,071,823	-797,015	25,238,093	9,544,588	6,616,810	41,147	1,006,131	601,761
2013	42,112,667	30,082,054	387,725	30,469,779	3,600,946	-915,787	25,953,046	9,396,225	6,763,396	41,399	1,017,247	620,318
2014	44,317,379	32,076,269	334,726	32,410,995	3,814,364	-1,065,317	27,531,314	9,721,481	7,064,584	43,123	1,027,703	642,776

Personal Income and Employment by Area: Grant Pass, OR

(Thousands of dollars, except as noted.)

| Year | Personal income, total | Derivation of personal income | | | | | | | | Per capita personal income (dollars) | Population (persons) | Total employment |
| | | Earnings by place of work | | | Less: Contributions for government social insurance | Plus: Adjustment for residence | Equals: Net earnings by place of residence | Plus: Dividends, interest, and rent | Plus: Personal current transfer receipts | | | |
		Nonfarm	Farm	Total								
1970	126,382	85,122	1,526	86,648	6,304	431	80,775	25,995	19,612	3,481	36,304	12,674
1971	144,489	98,013	756	98,769	7,507	755	92,017	29,397	23,075	3,719	38,848	13,786
1972	163,138	112,660	246	112,906	9,217	1,154	104,843	32,562	25,733	4,048	40,305	14,944
1973	187,733	128,794	688	129,482	11,930	1,494	119,046	37,193	31,494	4,351	43,151	16,085
1974	208,732	132,469	2,143	134,612	12,576	2,473	124,509	43,644	40,579	4,559	45,787	15,850
1975	241,789	149,616	2,164	151,780	13,613	2,462	140,629	50,283	50,877	5,034	48,032	16,628
1976	285,967	184,912	2,857	187,769	17,001	2,491	173,259	57,794	54,914	5,639	50,710	18,506
1977	326,287	212,629	2,509	215,138	20,079	2,839	197,898	68,202	60,187	6,209	52,549	19,980
1978	376,300	248,119	1,869	249,988	23,949	3,300	229,339	80,961	66,000	6,748	55,762	21,235
1979	420,202	270,828	2,398	273,226	27,102	4,393	250,517	94,983	74,702	7,258	57,893	22,222
1980	467,053	279,051	3,929	282,980	28,014	5,253	260,219	116,634	90,200	7,923	58,948	22,300
1981	505,875	282,481	2,732	285,213	30,389	4,077	258,901	142,447	104,527	8,545	59,202	21,755
1982	520,851	273,902	2,478	276,380	30,290	3,899	249,989	155,220	115,642	8,956	58,154	21,089
1983	578,212	303,091	2,473	305,564	33,996	5,459	277,027	177,488	123,697	10,047	57,548	21,796
1984	631,149	333,131	2,819	335,950	38,447	7,611	305,114	196,208	129,827	10,682	59,083	22,691
1985	674,180	354,566	2,161	356,727	41,573	7,616	322,770	213,884	137,526	11,113	60,666	23,251
1986	711,291	374,251	1,591	375,842	43,644	9,300	341,498	227,499	142,294	11,718	60,702	23,778
1987	741,864	404,928	1,206	406,134	47,005	10,755	369,884	223,522	148,458	12,114	61,238	24,388
1988	798,958	448,656	1,426	450,082	54,412	11,931	407,601	230,739	160,618	12,945	61,721	25,684
1989	887,333	483,652	2,335	485,987	59,497	11,817	438,307	268,877	180,149	14,343	61,865	26,508
1990	933,303	512,701	2,100	514,801	63,477	14,419	465,743	268,927	198,633	14,818	62,985	26,838
1991	977,138	517,523	2,494	520,017	65,289	16,443	471,171	282,574	223,393	15,132	64,575	26,716
1992	1,034,330	545,971	1,564	547,535	68,861	20,269	498,943	288,947	246,440	15,790	65,507	27,206
1993	1,115,033	588,548	4,314	592,862	73,697	22,504	541,669	308,028	265,336	16,519	67,500	27,970
1994	1,194,232	628,816	5,559	634,375	79,320	27,227	582,282	323,083	288,867	17,206	69,406	29,344
1995	1,284,477	647,489	5,102	652,591	83,051	30,884	600,424	355,324	328,729	18,012	71,313	29,760
1996	1,367,879	694,745	3,890	698,635	88,810	35,069	644,894	373,912	349,073	18,917	72,310	30,589
1997	1,447,325	743,871	3,505	747,376	93,532	39,994	693,838	389,030	364,457	19,707	73,442	31,808
1998	1,545,084	806,307	4,325	810,632	99,060	45,167	756,739	400,020	388,325	20,752	74,455	32,325
1999	1,617,179	860,804	1,366	862,170	104,437	50,874	808,607	384,101	424,471	21,502	75,209	33,281
2000	1,716,482	900,875	694	901,569	108,731	60,805	853,643	418,859	443,980	22,630	75,851	33,674
2001	1,799,351	940,111	1,903	942,014	111,555	62,075	892,534	408,913	497,904	23,536	76,452	33,780
2002	1,834,376	989,768	958	990,726	119,717	65,866	936,875	379,434	518,067	23,605	77,712	34,158
2003	1,896,367	1,043,025	2,691	1,045,716	128,537	72,139	989,318	379,764	527,285	24,072	78,779	35,415
2004	2,027,474	1,125,193	4,682	1,129,875	141,877	80,590	1,068,588	419,808	539,078	25,430	79,729	37,148
2005	2,127,910	1,186,169	4,415	1,190,584	154,719	87,296	1,123,161	440,805	563,944	26,381	80,660	38,577
2006	2,289,207	1,258,305	2,282	1,260,587	164,414	94,603	1,190,776	499,754	598,677	28,054	81,601	39,547
2007	2,376,363	1,252,084	-151	1,251,933	167,259	99,541	1,184,215	553,142	639,006	29,070	81,746	39,621
2008	2,401,561	1,207,021	-3,535	1,203,486	164,187	101,258	1,140,557	547,311	713,693	29,149	82,389	38,352
2009	2,396,068	1,156,920	-1,731	1,155,189	159,736	95,322	1,090,775	491,966	813,327	29,109	82,315	36,475
2010	2,435,126	1,153,381	-1,239	1,152,142	162,928	92,821	1,082,035	472,706	880,385	29,397	82,835	35,316
2011	2,511,282	1,165,859	756	1,166,615	149,817	87,622	1,104,420	503,588	903,274	30,396	82,618	35,446
2012	2,600,951	1,197,013	4,675	1,201,688	153,316	114,012	1,162,384	528,952	909,615	31,419	82,782	35,422
2013	2,654,463	1,200,110	3,996	1,204,106	173,287	147,001	1,177,820	531,037	945,606	31,877	83,271	35,468
2014	2,806,979	1,268,291	7,132	1,275,423	184,475	135,424	1,226,372	555,788	1,024,819	33,577	83,599	36,616

Personal Income and Employment by Area: Great Falls, MT

(Thousands of dollars, except as noted.)

Year	Personal income, total	Derivation of personal income									Per capita personal income (dollars)	Population (persons)	Total employment
		Earnings by place of work			Less: Contributions for government social insurance	Plus: Adjustment for residence	Equals: Net earnings by place of residence	Plus: Dividends, interest, and rent	Plus: Personal current transfer receipts				
		Nonfarm	Farm	Total									
1970	358,327	275,060	13,037	288,097	20,138	-2,117	265,842	65,534	26,951		4,356	82,258	37,297
1971	385,359	294,343	13,295	307,638	21,982	-2,089	283,567	69,723	32,069		4,563	84,453	37,626
1972	430,610	329,003	17,116	346,119	25,407	-2,088	318,624	76,025	35,961		5,075	84,842	38,689
1973	468,875	356,077	17,888	373,965	30,802	-1,937	341,226	86,186	41,463		5,534	84,728	39,742
1974	516,841	390,369	17,376	407,745	34,694	-1,440	371,611	97,887	47,343		6,071	85,126	40,285
1975	559,811	418,179	16,120	434,299	37,319	427	397,407	106,082	56,322		6,610	84,693	39,860
1976	620,286	477,402	10,105	487,507	43,737	1,477	445,247	113,767	61,272		7,309	84,869	42,084
1977	672,063	524,171	3,862	528,033	48,578	3,179	482,634	124,581	64,848		7,792	86,247	43,274
1978	742,084	572,109	7,251	579,360	54,438	6,853	531,775	138,758	71,551		8,568	86,611	44,429
1979	799,743	610,083	5,506	615,589	60,509	10,229	565,309	152,936	81,498		9,467	84,475	44,026
1980	848,105	621,332	6,544	627,876	62,439	16,304	581,741	172,640	93,724		10,519	80,627	42,836
1981	910,912	654,883	4,250	659,133	70,056	9,550	598,627	205,195	107,090		11,360	80,183	42,087
1982	956,591	670,470	4,248	674,718	72,419	8,411	610,710	227,855	118,026		11,989	79,791	41,059
1983	1,021,491	710,659	10,537	721,196	77,767	7,238	650,667	240,213	130,611		12,670	80,621	41,553
1984	1,077,556	742,056	8,905	750,961	84,046	6,860	673,775	264,226	139,555		13,416	80,318	41,719
1985	1,088,160	743,254	1,261	744,515	85,621	6,031	664,925	276,685	146,550		13,672	79,591	40,524
1986	1,122,850	757,406	9,147	766,553	89,223	4,325	681,655	283,388	157,807		14,363	78,179	40,276
1987	1,156,274	777,848	9,394	787,242	91,849	3,834	699,227	289,199	167,848		14,875	77,733	40,260
1988	1,220,628	830,733	5,527	836,260	103,648	2,185	734,797	307,780	178,051		15,713	77,681	42,046
1989	1,309,211	876,194	20,390	896,584	109,807	2,015	788,792	331,173	189,246		16,764	78,098	42,690
1990	1,359,490	921,173	12,318	933,491	122,125	2,434	813,800	340,187	205,503		17,477	77,788	43,160
1991	1,429,354	979,364	18,455	997,819	132,082	959	866,696	344,853	217,805		18,173	78,651	44,293
1992	1,490,096	1,030,735	16,016	1,046,751	141,656	312	905,407	352,573	232,116		18,690	79,727	44,595
1993	1,584,164	1,081,196	35,116	1,116,312	151,704	-710	963,898	370,977	249,289		19,551	81,028	44,940
1994	1,605,538	1,109,263	12,336	1,121,599	155,314	-1,031	965,254	383,284	257,000		19,548	82,134	46,791
1995	1,690,409	1,143,862	15,472	1,159,334	156,309	-2,610	1,000,415	416,932	273,062		20,564	82,201	47,358
1996	1,743,245	1,185,583	7,935	1,193,518	156,318	-3,456	1,033,744	427,442	282,059		21,148	82,429	47,981
1997	1,793,705	1,200,897	9,215	1,210,112	154,218	-4,073	1,051,821	451,902	289,982		22,183	80,861	47,438
1998	1,893,610	1,276,149	8,546	1,284,695	159,095	-6,325	1,119,275	474,484	299,851		23,462	80,709	48,179
1999	1,929,137	1,319,548	9,723	1,329,271	161,541	-7,857	1,159,873	473,240	296,024		23,936	80,596	47,636
2000	2,018,983	1,364,141	2,256	1,366,397	166,578	-9,259	1,190,560	497,649	330,774		25,137	80,318	47,962
2001	2,109,954	1,425,498	4,962	1,430,460	175,704	-10,960	1,243,796	512,290	353,868		26,356	80,055	47,825
2002	2,189,239	1,503,100	1,806	1,504,906	185,917	-12,551	1,306,438	520,970	361,831		27,418	79,848	47,701
2003	2,268,928	1,571,441	4,819	1,576,260	193,669	-14,138	1,368,453	525,315	375,160		28,492	79,633	47,728
2004	2,396,024	1,664,703	16,504	1,681,207	206,463	-15,784	1,458,960	538,115	398,949		29,876	80,198	48,445
2005	2,482,235	1,739,727	18,233	1,757,960	218,634	-17,442	1,521,884	531,138	429,213		31,012	80,041	48,917
2006	2,708,630	1,877,414	9,998	1,887,412	235,747	-19,499	1,632,166	615,948	460,516		33,865	79,984	50,124
2007	2,821,437	1,931,208	14,533	1,945,741	247,284	-21,016	1,677,441	661,279	482,717		35,224	80,099	50,506
2008	2,957,671	2,006,650	15,990	2,022,640	256,252	-22,826	1,743,562	667,310	546,799		36,728	80,529	50,776
2009	2,947,056	2,029,557	9,768	2,039,325	262,047	-25,430	1,751,848	603,456	591,752		36,528	80,680	50,183
2010	3,083,041	2,103,194	15,532	2,118,726	269,695	-29,087	1,819,944	624,876	638,221		37,826	81,506	49,764
2011	3,186,844	2,141,121	21,046	2,162,167	250,195	-28,253	1,883,719	672,856	630,269		38,984	81,747	49,378
2012	3,277,715	2,178,454	19,256	2,197,710	251,029	-17,130	1,929,551	711,349	636,815		40,087	81,765	49,276
2013	3,256,594	2,163,031	24,414	2,187,445	279,235	-22,169	1,886,041	721,162	649,391		39,520	82,404	49,597
2014	3,389,496	2,260,473	25,050	2,285,523	292,544	-26,979	1,966,000	753,063	670,433		41,163	82,344	49,643

Personal Income and Employment by Area: Greeley, CO

(Thousands of dollars, except as noted.)

Year	Personal income, total	Earnings by place of work			Less: Contributions for government social insurance	Plus: Adjustment for residence	Equals: Net earnings by place of residence	Plus: Dividends, interest, and rent	Plus: Personal current transfer receipts	Per capita personal income (dollars)	Population (persons)	Total employment
		Nonfarm	Farm	Total								
1970	328,475	171,878	74,032	245,910	10,272	17,289	252,927	46,747	28,801	3,649	90,012	34,611
1971	364,323	198,186	70,784	268,970	12,225	21,567	278,312	52,258	33,753	3,885	93,779	35,647
1972	427,150	245,185	77,292	322,477	16,200	25,034	331,311	58,597	37,242	4,289	99,597	39,546
1973	508,340	294,524	93,932	388,456	22,619	28,709	394,546	69,317	44,477	4,869	104,411	44,129
1974	607,080	345,956	127,349	473,305	27,829	30,612	476,088	79,700	51,292	5,618	108,059	47,670
1975	661,330	377,735	120,928	498,663	29,231	38,144	507,576	91,369	62,385	6,096	108,479	47,671
1976	715,812	441,482	100,074	541,556	34,841	43,780	550,495	97,596	67,721	6,504	110,052	49,788
1977	733,830	480,256	49,520	529,776	38,072	59,129	550,833	109,849	73,148	6,520	112,555	51,346
1978	858,660	537,973	72,424	610,397	42,909	80,738	648,226	127,837	82,597	7,472	114,919	52,739
1979	964,715	607,003	59,800	666,803	50,846	103,170	719,127	152,858	92,730	8,026	120,194	53,520
1980	1,049,853	657,553	16,013	673,566	55,380	129,900	748,086	188,910	112,857	8,482	123,767	54,564
1981	1,216,039	711,161	68,999	780,160	63,899	140,601	856,862	228,644	130,533	9,745	124,780	55,002
1982	1,275,192	769,880	33,936	803,816	70,895	140,199	873,120	255,899	146,173	10,142	125,733	55,718
1983	1,378,635	846,675	40,986	887,661	78,878	131,374	940,157	277,564	160,914	10,642	129,542	58,126
1984	1,522,354	917,729	85,385	1,003,114	88,737	134,225	1,048,602	303,080	170,672	11,642	130,764	59,839
1985	1,572,494	997,758	56,504	1,054,262	99,499	117,823	1,072,586	321,245	178,663	11,967	131,402	60,864
1986	1,612,213	1,037,064	69,237	1,106,301	106,056	107,081	1,107,326	314,578	190,309	12,240	131,715	60,862
1987	1,684,250	1,076,062	93,869	1,169,931	108,873	96,791	1,157,849	324,616	201,785	12,787	131,713	61,351
1988	1,784,026	1,163,814	119,612	1,283,426	123,424	73,224	1,233,226	335,698	215,102	13,532	131,842	65,219
1989	1,954,141	1,262,323	150,496	1,412,819	136,554	61,361	1,337,626	382,985	233,530	14,781	132,202	66,292
1990	2,026,762	1,334,579	158,672	1,493,251	146,970	58,025	1,404,306	374,142	248,314	15,336	132,161	66,690
1991	2,129,678	1,429,131	140,126	1,569,257	163,699	70,506	1,476,064	380,943	272,671	15,862	134,262	68,491
1992	2,309,172	1,543,292	133,374	1,676,666	173,718	108,214	1,611,162	391,056	306,954	16,787	137,560	69,676
1993	2,563,061	1,691,178	180,102	1,871,280	193,206	133,628	1,811,702	422,757	328,602	17,976	142,586	73,905
1994	2,743,560	1,840,138	142,257	1,982,395	211,562	158,026	1,928,859	464,187	350,514	18,622	147,328	77,289
1995	2,913,895	1,946,851	114,611	2,061,462	221,985	185,157	2,024,634	491,210	398,051	19,153	152,140	79,705
1996	3,178,634	2,080,809	152,216	2,233,025	231,870	228,631	2,229,786	539,032	409,816	20,358	156,140	82,605
1997	3,434,326	2,223,587	188,080	2,411,667	243,968	281,054	2,448,753	566,762	418,811	21,262	161,525	86,239
1998	3,835,384	2,498,014	186,173	2,684,187	247,858	349,159	2,785,488	622,542	427,354	23,029	166,547	89,433
1999	4,236,515	2,786,883	209,137	2,996,020	271,193	416,089	3,140,916	633,973	461,626	24,300	174,342	92,186
2000	4,683,677	3,081,027	177,287	3,258,314	294,397	527,026	3,490,943	700,247	492,487	25,613	182,861	95,936
2001	5,106,767	3,357,236	270,794	3,628,030	329,051	542,152	3,841,131	722,018	543,618	26,548	192,360	100,768
2002	5,251,490	3,557,446	146,844	3,704,290	361,572	630,799	3,973,517	672,740	605,233	25,967	202,234	102,079
2003	5,452,093	3,612,787	147,007	3,759,794	373,535	717,281	4,103,540	707,594	640,959	26,104	208,858	103,418
2004	5,862,026	3,798,776	190,162	3,988,938	404,296	839,827	4,424,469	756,365	681,192	27,224	215,322	106,490
2005	6,397,440	4,013,708	239,816	4,253,524	430,110	975,222	4,798,636	851,154	747,650	28,704	222,879	109,735
2006	6,915,281	4,357,723	176,299	4,534,022	464,527	1,150,310	5,219,805	887,799	807,677	29,975	230,703	113,903
2007	7,538,578	4,592,123	197,631	4,789,754	499,370	1,351,546	5,641,930	1,030,247	866,401	31,716	237,692	117,983
2008	8,189,439	4,790,562	190,709	4,981,271	521,675	1,534,223	5,993,819	1,169,250	1,026,370	33,640	243,442	120,677
2009	8,048,673	4,572,186	131,299	4,703,485	490,070	1,584,127	5,797,542	1,085,071	1,166,060	32,429	248,193	116,949
2010	8,301,365	4,653,497	231,915	4,885,412	501,162	1,510,473	5,894,723	1,058,763	1,347,879	32,660	254,173	115,879
2011	8,869,944	4,958,377	262,483	5,220,860	492,729	1,529,011	6,257,142	1,207,654	1,405,148	34,282	258,737	120,311
2012	9,519,729	5,442,262	300,103	5,742,365	536,278	1,544,762	6,750,849	1,346,720	1,422,160	36,034	264,189	123,436
2013	9,966,945	5,928,751	339,018	6,267,769	652,818	1,517,443	7,132,394	1,358,670	1,475,881	36,838	270,560	129,908
2014	10,735,917	6,687,810	379,284	7,067,094	742,549	1,400,368	7,724,913	1,424,092	1,586,912	38,664	277,670	138,454

Personal Income and Employment by Area: Green Bay, WI

(Thousands of dollars, except as noted.)

Year	Personal income, total	Earnings by place of work			Less: Contributions for government social insurance	Plus: Adjustment for residence	Equals: Net earnings by place of residence	Plus: Dividends, interest, and rent	Plus: Personal current transfer receipts	Per capita personal income (dollars)	Population (persons)	Total employment
		Nonfarm	Farm	Total								
1970	722,285	569,590	26,951	596,541	42,146	-2,924	551,471	111,133	59,681	3,547	203,616	84,132
1971	786,140	617,397	28,725	646,122	47,141	-3,699	595,282	121,554	69,304	3,805	206,593	84,910
1972	870,161	691,928	29,312	721,240	55,645	-4,697	660,898	132,228	77,035	4,174	208,479	89,459
1973	968,852	772,015	33,593	805,608	71,346	-3,896	730,366	149,343	89,143	4,593	210,941	94,338
1974	1,094,024	869,519	31,139	900,658	83,458	-4,625	812,575	172,705	108,744	5,154	212,277	98,309
1975	1,218,831	952,339	32,090	984,429	89,570	-4,341	890,518	191,752	136,561	5,659	215,386	100,255
1976	1,356,320	1,065,376	36,830	1,102,206	101,874	-2,311	998,021	204,593	153,706	6,232	217,622	103,497
1977	1,535,618	1,208,997	52,286	1,261,283	114,792	-873	1,145,618	227,897	162,103	7,023	218,655	107,283
1978	1,729,859	1,374,568	48,825	1,423,393	133,934	1,709	1,291,168	257,656	181,035	7,854	220,260	112,205
1979	1,935,577	1,510,689	67,284	1,577,973	153,374	8,625	1,433,224	290,115	212,238	8,766	220,801	114,982
1980	2,156,297	1,627,060	70,215	1,697,275	165,303	10,027	1,541,999	358,523	255,775	9,612	224,345	115,673
1981	2,357,893	1,752,638	53,614	1,806,252	190,829	7,150	1,622,573	442,681	292,639	10,427	226,129	114,829
1982	2,517,917	1,852,370	49,943	1,902,313	204,176	-1,327	1,696,810	497,447	323,660	11,079	227,271	115,900
1983	2,697,251	2,014,147	28,352	2,042,499	221,114	-11,270	1,810,115	536,905	350,231	11,817	228,249	117,407
1984	2,997,160	2,253,845	46,873	2,300,718	254,312	-18,961	2,027,445	608,427	361,288	12,978	230,950	122,659
1985	3,221,339	2,436,592	56,057	2,492,649	277,836	-26,508	2,188,305	652,839	380,195	13,868	232,292	126,109
1986	3,425,158	2,634,279	55,903	2,690,182	299,488	-33,467	2,357,227	675,987	391,944	14,593	234,712	131,147
1987	3,584,145	2,797,503	62,502	2,860,005	312,667	-40,068	2,507,270	671,271	405,604	15,126	236,959	132,768
1988	3,781,252	2,989,646	38,158	3,027,804	344,452	-50,526	2,632,826	727,079	421,347	15,791	239,462	136,000
1989	4,169,018	3,189,240	96,220	3,285,460	364,293	-58,674	2,862,493	851,983	454,542	17,282	241,229	138,858
1990	4,464,632	3,532,262	76,628	3,608,890	420,240	-79,642	3,109,008	867,885	487,739	18,244	244,716	145,741
1991	4,680,007	3,720,521	56,536	3,777,057	447,195	-62,209	3,267,653	876,263	536,091	18,794	249,019	147,990
1992	5,073,776	4,066,301	73,858	4,140,159	482,356	-65,843	3,591,960	902,942	578,874	20,048	253,077	152,470
1993	5,391,310	4,377,521	57,581	4,435,102	517,202	-91,574	3,826,326	957,368	607,616	20,905	257,897	157,686
1994	5,754,456	4,721,174	72,490	4,793,664	565,261	-129,014	4,099,389	1,026,151	628,916	21,959	262,056	164,348
1995	6,096,735	4,985,310	46,735	5,032,045	601,023	-160,452	4,270,570	1,156,972	669,193	22,854	266,765	170,096
1996	6,522,262	5,277,978	72,413	5,350,391	631,805	-179,331	4,539,255	1,283,005	700,002	24,078	270,879	174,894
1997	7,031,310	5,764,844	54,416	5,819,260	685,185	-220,155	4,913,920	1,393,273	724,117	25,645	274,177	179,143
1998	7,505,933	6,137,801	90,579	6,228,380	725,323	-238,653	5,264,404	1,496,645	744,884	27,104	276,931	183,465
1999	7,845,534	6,615,148	94,534	6,709,682	784,256	-323,372	5,602,054	1,471,478	772,002	28,010	280,100	190,572
2000	8,383,412	7,099,176	68,521	7,167,697	833,301	-401,180	5,933,216	1,622,358	827,838	29,594	283,282	195,849
2001	8,727,681	7,228,506	87,080	7,315,586	830,043	-324,704	6,160,839	1,643,431	923,411	30,540	285,783	194,848
2002	8,989,199	7,498,688	80,127	7,578,815	860,156	-369,545	6,349,114	1,631,002	1,009,083	31,135	288,713	194,932
2003	9,306,349	7,841,812	120,111	7,961,923	893,374	-402,199	6,666,350	1,591,409	1,048,590	31,962	291,169	198,245
2004	9,857,419	8,311,213	138,287	8,449,500	943,890	-401,421	7,104,189	1,665,041	1,088,189	33,464	294,570	202,727
2005	10,145,629	8,536,872	122,334	8,659,206	979,170	-401,828	7,278,208	1,683,866	1,183,555	34,183	296,800	204,203
2006	10,734,007	8,880,335	97,911	8,978,246	1,026,709	-422,380	7,529,157	1,922,970	1,281,880	35,936	298,702	205,431
2007	11,260,154	9,141,024	160,369	9,301,393	1,060,581	-421,353	7,819,459	2,044,761	1,395,934	37,386	301,190	207,722
2008	11,832,792	9,468,499	153,499	9,621,998	1,100,949	-412,601	8,108,448	2,132,207	1,592,137	39,121	302,468	207,257
2009	11,644,131	9,355,741	54,908	9,410,649	1,085,649	-417,635	7,907,365	1,905,980	1,830,786	38,217	304,686	201,619
2010	12,094,568	9,551,274	121,500	9,672,774	1,117,948	-441,396	8,113,430	1,999,648	1,981,490	39,433	306,712	201,056
2011	12,725,732	9,958,880	217,743	10,176,623	1,043,318	-468,562	8,664,743	2,122,426	1,938,563	41,215	308,763	203,947
2012	13,337,693	10,318,643	234,683	10,553,326	1,076,450	-463,121	9,013,755	2,354,695	1,969,243	42,879	311,052	205,607
2013	13,538,161	10,634,117	266,083	10,900,200	1,248,691	-491,699	9,159,810	2,358,185	2,020,166	43,312	312,573	207,437
2014	14,078,656	10,951,232	329,600	11,280,832	1,288,718	-468,141	9,523,973	2,450,954	2,103,729	44,761	314,531	209,669

Personal Income and Employment by Area: Greensboro-High Point, NC

(Thousands of dollars, except as noted.)

Year	Personal income, total	Earnings by place of work			Less: Contributions for government social insurance	Plus: Adjustment for residence	Equals: Net earnings by place of residence	Plus: Dividends, interest, and rent	Plus: Personal current transfer receipts	Per capita personal income (dollars)	Population (persons)	Total employment
		Nonfarm	Farm	Total								
1970	1,727,320	1,585,044	25,267	1,610,311	112,594	-84,818	1,412,899	202,614	111,807	3,937	438,730	247,290
1971	1,893,389	1,737,911	29,467	1,767,378	128,225	-99,380	1,539,773	221,641	131,975	4,226	448,079	251,788
1972	2,105,957	1,953,984	29,637	1,983,621	151,619	-115,234	1,716,768	242,537	146,652	4,623	455,577	262,903
1973	2,334,489	2,164,091	48,538	2,212,629	192,675	-128,661	1,891,293	271,898	171,298	5,067	460,732	272,867
1974	2,542,342	2,334,517	42,217	2,376,734	215,681	-143,307	2,017,746	314,219	210,377	5,478	464,097	272,067
1975	2,720,706	2,395,711	46,541	2,442,252	216,506	-149,504	2,076,242	344,230	300,234	5,832	466,520	258,218
1976	2,985,231	2,654,835	47,890	2,702,725	245,749	-167,129	2,289,847	373,325	322,059	6,333	471,352	268,292
1977	3,306,032	2,964,536	46,006	3,010,542	273,013	-189,171	2,548,358	419,253	338,421	6,928	477,233	278,421
1978	3,762,472	3,438,150	49,194	3,487,344	326,691	-237,440	2,923,213	472,077	367,182	7,799	482,440	291,685
1979	4,149,579	3,808,404	32,284	3,840,688	375,104	-268,346	3,197,238	534,494	417,847	8,517	487,216	298,117
1980	4,596,505	4,117,721	23,149	4,140,870	406,218	-298,584	3,436,068	659,946	500,491	9,320	493,196	296,162
1981	5,138,524	4,495,827	43,888	4,539,715	475,054	-334,893	3,729,768	831,737	577,019	10,340	496,975	298,011
1982	5,460,254	4,690,433	47,363	4,737,796	500,111	-354,579	3,883,106	934,459	642,689	10,906	500,656	295,265
1983	5,949,528	5,148,890	33,403	5,182,293	552,305	-395,571	4,234,417	1,029,387	685,724	11,799	504,241	302,975
1984	6,679,883	5,801,164	32,881	5,834,045	639,045	-448,577	4,746,423	1,214,315	719,145	13,139	508,397	320,355
1985	7,166,536	6,208,994	32,460	6,241,454	692,214	-476,802	5,072,438	1,326,296	767,802	13,990	512,256	327,294
1986	7,677,330	6,668,887	37,953	6,706,840	757,438	-511,854	5,437,548	1,424,763	815,019	14,857	516,765	338,297
1987	8,341,441	7,389,953	34,186	7,424,139	825,923	-575,711	6,022,505	1,468,397	850,539	15,943	523,217	351,897
1988	9,112,426	7,995,038	51,903	8,046,941	914,109	-624,689	6,508,143	1,682,565	921,718	17,193	530,011	364,650
1989	9,772,763	8,477,216	81,424	8,558,640	967,590	-659,037	6,932,013	1,816,977	1,023,773	18,255	535,336	368,711
1990	10,409,534	8,874,867	94,276	8,969,143	1,040,312	-689,792	7,239,039	2,054,867	1,115,628	19,184	542,612	373,827
1991	10,692,693	8,991,479	100,492	9,091,971	1,067,441	-655,115	7,369,415	2,059,143	1,264,135	19,343	552,787	365,866
1992	11,527,300	9,758,429	100,651	9,859,080	1,141,838	-696,788	8,020,454	2,120,799	1,386,047	20,526	561,591	368,982
1993	12,225,576	10,311,894	113,315	10,425,209	1,216,309	-776,044	8,432,856	2,282,397	1,510,323	21,400	571,281	381,473
1994	12,999,017	11,026,346	120,599	11,146,945	1,313,292	-826,190	9,007,463	2,416,037	1,575,517	22,339	581,897	391,593
1995	13,784,694	11,717,625	118,868	11,836,493	1,397,499	-941,234	9,497,760	2,529,270	1,757,664	23,191	594,390	405,535
1996	14,712,347	12,364,116	137,178	12,501,294	1,458,883	-1,024,453	10,017,958	2,782,335	1,912,054	24,311	605,175	414,861
1997	15,769,184	13,151,848	139,871	13,291,719	1,537,512	-1,057,513	10,696,694	3,069,469	2,003,021	25,619	615,526	423,430
1998	16,957,388	14,201,808	140,740	14,342,548	1,645,755	-1,100,252	11,596,541	3,272,946	2,087,901	27,050	626,891	427,195
1999	17,664,799	15,124,919	146,895	15,271,814	1,741,306	-1,192,950	12,337,558	3,139,141	2,188,100	27,730	637,026	434,538
2000	18,584,863	15,782,803	129,925	15,912,728	1,798,764	-1,183,997	12,929,967	3,312,341	2,342,555	28,795	645,409	437,940
2001	19,128,162	16,136,605	136,387	16,272,992	1,847,146	-1,152,857	13,272,989	3,248,015	2,607,158	29,304	652,741	429,057
2002	19,236,818	16,242,358	63,948	16,306,306	1,839,618	-1,212,441	13,254,247	3,175,090	2,807,481	29,242	657,855	423,379
2003	19,670,312	16,665,496	72,601	16,738,097	1,928,586	-1,274,075	13,535,436	3,211,567	2,923,309	29,662	663,140	423,185
2004	20,890,723	17,427,353	99,708	17,527,061	1,997,319	-1,314,423	14,215,319	3,514,297	3,161,107	31,287	667,711	430,301
2005	21,964,491	18,141,933	112,690	18,254,623	2,110,046	-1,391,729	14,752,848	3,813,619	3,398,024	32,440	677,080	438,181
2006	23,399,119	19,156,158	110,114	19,266,272	2,229,813	-1,468,105	15,568,354	4,141,652	3,689,113	33,930	689,637	448,309
2007	24,426,199	19,711,445	77,843	19,789,288	2,335,872	-1,509,769	15,943,647	4,535,010	3,947,542	34,870	700,485	457,410
2008	24,717,788	19,520,444	57,418	19,577,862	2,351,363	-1,560,315	15,666,184	4,529,907	4,521,697	34,745	711,405	451,962
2009	24,439,270	18,944,519	67,978	19,012,497	2,254,934	-1,386,074	15,371,489	3,965,956	5,101,825	33,995	718,902	429,079
2010	24,869,502	19,142,025	75,716	19,217,741	2,228,530	-1,394,269	15,594,942	3,857,285	5,417,275	34,301	725,040	424,142
2011	25,783,178	19,446,658	35,708	19,482,366	2,079,485	-1,385,675	16,017,206	4,230,705	5,535,267	35,316	730,077	431,534
2012	27,151,355	20,410,163	79,077	20,489,240	2,141,442	-1,441,670	16,906,128	4,629,287	5,615,940	36,897	735,866	433,974
2013	26,959,542	20,635,898	103,381	20,739,279	2,481,414	-1,497,760	16,760,105	4,502,648	5,696,789	36,367	741,314	439,041
2014	28,207,761	21,511,505	137,792	21,649,297	2,580,813	-1,410,714	17,657,770	4,683,853	5,866,138	37,782	746,593	443,856

Personal Income and Employment by Area: Greenville, NC

(Thousands of dollars, except as noted.)

Year	Personal income, total	Earnings by place of work			Less: Contributions for government social insurance	Plus: Adjustment for residence	Equals: Net earnings by place of residence	Plus: Dividends, interest, and rent	Plus: Personal current transfer receipts	Per capita personal income (dollars)	Population (persons)	Total employment
		Nonfarm	Farm	Total								
1970	216,801	137,946	31,833	169,779	9,442	7,094	167,431	29,152	20,218	2,926	74,101	32,746
1971	235,560	158,817	25,375	184,192	11,293	7,836	180,735	31,700	23,125	3,128	75,306	33,622
1972	263,684	177,871	28,590	206,461	13,155	10,295	203,601	35,222	24,861	3,517	74,977	34,854
1973	308,016	200,814	42,623	243,437	17,074	12,144	238,507	40,852	28,657	4,064	75,787	36,126
1974	349,102	225,272	44,966	270,238	19,969	15,763	266,032	47,712	35,358	4,595	75,977	37,100
1975	402,502	259,835	47,129	306,964	23,147	17,234	301,051	54,959	46,492	5,102	78,887	37,475
1976	457,626	297,838	51,297	349,135	27,161	21,326	343,300	60,582	53,744	5,710	80,147	39,729
1977	481,661	335,970	24,155	360,125	30,283	24,324	354,166	69,199	58,296	5,950	80,948	40,727
1978	560,725	381,583	47,162	428,745	35,460	27,242	420,527	76,516	63,682	6,841	81,969	41,601
1979	597,525	428,220	20,821	449,041	41,457	30,481	438,065	85,617	73,843	7,215	82,819	43,563
1980	692,090	477,256	28,325	505,581	46,473	35,663	494,771	107,686	89,633	7,641	90,580	43,433
1981	784,089	526,923	35,185	562,108	55,352	38,056	544,812	136,386	102,891	8,518	92,047	44,149
1982	855,040	567,684	41,688	609,372	60,823	37,329	585,878	156,330	112,832	9,155	93,400	44,824
1983	915,394	630,257	21,149	651,406	67,871	40,267	623,802	169,046	122,546	9,661	94,750	46,159
1984	1,044,239	731,205	35,167	766,372	80,509	40,077	725,940	189,725	128,574	10,859	96,164	48,581
1985	1,114,929	782,630	34,765	817,395	86,971	43,442	773,866	204,014	137,049	11,408	97,730	49,206
1986	1,202,364	862,683	31,169	893,852	97,342	43,306	839,816	217,533	145,015	12,069	99,626	51,663
1987	1,304,196	953,876	32,498	986,374	105,837	45,988	926,525	227,636	150,035	12,786	102,001	53,714
1988	1,452,142	1,064,817	43,205	1,108,022	122,968	48,535	1,033,589	257,557	160,996	13,922	104,306	57,254
1989	1,641,725	1,198,380	47,865	1,246,245	137,500	43,814	1,152,559	306,816	182,350	15,419	106,474	59,652
1990	1,789,912	1,324,508	54,999	1,379,507	153,439	34,820	1,260,888	316,543	212,481	16,413	109,054	62,264
1991	1,893,833	1,372,717	56,497	1,429,214	160,933	53,924	1,322,205	324,506	247,122	16,915	111,965	61,864
1992	2,036,429	1,503,802	42,116	1,545,918	173,496	48,814	1,421,236	338,948	276,245	17,814	114,318	62,509
1993	2,186,097	1,622,192	41,781	1,663,973	186,632	42,960	1,520,301	358,504	307,292	18,728	116,728	64,747
1994	2,315,675	1,743,797	43,301	1,787,098	202,221	13,330	1,598,207	396,209	321,259	19,347	119,694	67,248
1995	2,499,953	1,852,359	28,171	1,880,530	214,195	31,133	1,697,468	434,721	367,764	20,404	122,525	71,899
1996	2,646,794	1,956,754	51,852	2,008,606	223,116	-19,281	1,766,209	478,804	401,781	21,198	124,861	72,840
1997	2,883,176	2,106,045	61,051	2,167,096	238,591	-1,708	1,926,797	535,285	421,094	22,558	127,812	73,994
1998	2,988,152	2,229,450	25,189	2,254,639	252,523	5,705	2,007,821	569,664	410,667	22,894	130,519	74,566
1999	3,131,924	2,410,584	16,643	2,427,227	272,414	-44,485	2,110,328	564,102	457,494	23,628	132,554	77,622
2000	3,388,094	2,645,680	36,590	2,682,270	293,438	-63,253	2,325,579	585,379	477,136	25,228	134,298	79,649
2001	3,489,372	2,648,328	29,737	2,678,065	294,638	11,385	2,394,812	575,575	518,985	25,544	136,605	78,087
2002	3,620,816	2,745,907	16,533	2,762,440	303,162	-177	2,459,101	591,091	570,624	26,025	139,128	78,507
2003	3,772,624	2,847,915	20,856	2,868,771	321,209	-12,962	2,534,600	630,389	607,635	26,641	141,610	78,881
2004	4,026,096	3,010,949	27,759	3,038,708	337,064	-27,443	2,674,201	693,723	658,172	27,865	144,486	81,497
2005	4,275,750	3,187,643	25,001	3,212,644	364,211	-43,440	2,804,993	742,735	728,022	28,904	147,929	84,150
2006	4,591,624	3,410,816	26,216	3,437,032	389,743	-61,029	2,986,260	789,188	816,176	30,024	152,934	87,060
2007	4,915,468	3,642,795	32,554	3,675,349	423,579	-81,443	3,170,327	852,471	892,670	31,213	157,479	91,490
2008	5,232,131	3,763,115	43,849	3,806,964	436,438	-100,871	3,269,655	940,751	1,021,725	32,274	162,116	92,220
2009	5,201,075	3,745,929	47,062	3,792,991	430,814	-122,567	3,239,610	856,590	1,104,875	31,411	165,581	89,386
2010	5,357,917	3,882,469	44,527	3,926,996	426,077	-151,687	3,349,232	831,417	1,177,268	31,736	168,826	89,194
2011	5,563,865	3,933,263	49,266	3,982,529	390,720	-156,761	3,435,048	908,778	1,220,039	32,582	170,763	90,938
2012	6,058,577	4,301,363	72,535	4,373,898	416,924	-192,153	3,764,821	1,028,485	1,265,271	35,042	172,895	92,738
2013	5,965,589	4,256,687	81,194	4,337,881	478,956	-199,187	3,659,738	1,010,782	1,295,069	34,216	174,351	93,344
2014	6,209,314	4,446,327	88,574	4,534,901	499,722	-216,753	3,818,426	1,034,947	1,355,941	35,410	175,354	94,807

Personal Income and Employment by Area: Greenville-Anderson-Mauldin, SC

(Thousands of dollars, except as noted.)

| Year | Personal income, total | Derivation of personal income | | | | | | | | Per capita personal income (dollars) | Population (persons) | Total employment |
| | | Earnings by place of work | | | Less: Contributions for government social insurance | Plus: Adjustment for residence | Equals: Net earnings by place of residence | Plus: Dividends, interest, and rent | Plus: Personal current transfer receipts | | | |
		Nonfarm	Farm	Total								
1970	1,515,572	1,295,666	8,982	1,304,648	91,249	15,347	1,228,746	169,771	117,055	3,321	456,342	218,306
1971	1,660,494	1,415,272	11,057	1,426,329	103,491	13,892	1,336,730	187,422	136,342	3,551	467,592	222,013
1972	1,878,303	1,626,242	9,444	1,635,686	124,784	8,816	1,519,718	206,640	151,945	3,911	480,222	236,053
1973	2,151,361	1,878,925	15,114	1,894,039	165,193	3,530	1,732,376	237,535	181,450	4,378	491,446	252,272
1974	2,424,484	2,106,861	12,242	2,119,103	191,998	-5,921	1,921,184	276,527	226,773	4,799	505,159	260,780
1975	2,579,020	2,131,827	10,248	2,142,075	188,404	-2,356	1,951,315	306,695	321,010	5,039	511,828	245,959
1976	2,900,252	2,445,751	11,286	2,457,037	222,212	-1,058	2,233,767	331,570	334,915	5,666	511,833	258,160
1977	3,211,750	2,733,527	11,405	2,744,932	248,827	-8,597	2,487,508	372,020	352,222	6,116	525,157	267,903
1978	3,616,854	3,107,451	14,667	3,122,118	290,594	-15,927	2,815,597	417,264	383,993	6,771	534,157	279,956
1979	4,076,030	3,502,913	18,593	3,521,506	338,065	-23,887	3,159,554	473,216	443,260	7,504	543,173	288,304
1980	4,611,088	3,872,293	4,404	3,876,697	372,658	-25,552	3,478,487	593,622	538,979	8,303	555,331	291,377
1981	5,139,192	4,223,541	5,059	4,228,600	436,152	-29,540	3,762,908	745,272	631,012	9,109	564,171	292,183
1982	5,430,341	4,306,388	10,036	4,316,424	451,197	-26,779	3,838,448	887,572	704,321	9,547	568,779	286,688
1983	5,894,823	4,672,204	4,206	4,676,410	497,912	-27,041	4,151,457	991,669	751,697	10,312	571,626	291,548
1984	6,518,729	5,182,225	11,794	5,194,019	569,765	-26,912	4,597,342	1,131,766	789,621	11,319	575,900	304,398
1985	7,009,136	5,556,068	8,695	5,564,763	618,437	-27,990	4,918,336	1,229,605	861,195	12,054	581,502	310,248
1986	7,524,665	6,012,358	6,087	6,018,445	686,336	-35,700	5,296,409	1,315,414	912,842	12,830	586,510	318,643
1987	8,120,109	6,571,226	13,879	6,585,105	739,784	-36,891	5,808,430	1,370,074	941,605	13,702	592,638	328,469
1988	8,955,936	7,312,152	18,862	7,331,014	844,692	-50,013	6,436,309	1,514,077	1,005,550	14,881	601,817	345,744
1989	9,682,500	7,816,226	21,905	7,838,131	913,487	-63,679	6,860,965	1,691,734	1,129,801	15,860	610,505	356,698
1990	10,455,049	8,420,850	22,059	8,442,909	1,001,794	-87,613	7,353,502	1,843,911	1,257,636	16,855	620,288	364,023
1991	10,788,900	8,604,455	21,967	8,626,422	1,038,663	-79,483	7,508,276	1,838,610	1,442,014	17,164	628,575	358,319
1992	11,497,947	9,029,089	28,135	9,057,224	1,079,693	10,734	7,988,265	1,901,982	1,607,700	18,040	637,366	358,466
1993	12,233,563	9,696,132	31,473	9,727,605	1,169,457	-29,906	8,528,242	1,990,557	1,714,764	18,902	647,208	372,522
1994	13,102,073	10,344,150	33,321	10,377,471	1,262,496	-5,698	9,109,277	2,132,325	1,860,471	19,935	657,228	383,788
1995	14,147,285	11,129,479	22,907	11,152,386	1,364,195	13,430	9,801,621	2,375,666	1,969,998	21,161	668,549	398,851
1996	15,063,222	11,794,626	10,759	11,805,385	1,420,055	-7,265	10,378,065	2,576,570	2,108,587	22,111	681,257	409,377
1997	15,960,705	12,449,786	18,703	12,468,489	1,498,581	20,201	10,990,109	2,772,058	2,198,538	23,013	693,566	418,744
1998	17,258,017	13,405,322	19,993	13,425,315	1,608,334	72,460	11,889,441	3,052,620	2,315,956	24,434	706,300	426,636
1999	18,021,637	14,255,830	27,818	14,283,648	1,692,581	15,282	12,606,349	2,964,121	2,451,167	25,117	717,514	436,596
2000	19,386,247	15,269,100	31,760	15,300,860	1,797,095	-46,731	13,457,034	3,275,282	2,653,931	26,639	727,743	447,875
2001	20,028,632	15,587,670	29,280	15,616,950	1,836,724	4,867	13,785,093	3,265,079	2,978,460	27,225	735,668	437,399
2002	20,150,392	15,478,915	20,981	15,499,896	1,828,660	-9,469	13,661,767	3,249,926	3,238,699	27,189	741,131	426,055
2003	20,619,442	15,967,759	14,631	15,982,390	1,891,645	-6,750	14,083,995	3,157,167	3,378,280	27,593	747,276	429,121
2004	21,544,199	16,533,308	26,278	16,559,586	1,956,723	27,585	14,630,448	3,240,059	3,673,692	28,566	754,196	435,169
2005	22,755,936	17,371,396	33,221	17,404,617	2,050,521	59,824	15,413,920	3,378,729	3,963,287	29,822	763,048	446,243
2006	24,608,839	18,426,358	10,596	18,436,954	2,223,775	111,887	16,325,066	3,969,983	4,313,790	31,651	777,494	457,848
2007	26,338,762	19,366,553	4,023	19,370,576	2,333,939	189,797	17,226,434	4,522,109	4,590,219	33,193	793,500	472,801
2008	27,638,061	20,009,477	-3,764	20,005,713	2,407,621	229,376	17,827,468	4,511,677	5,298,916	34,173	808,765	470,556
2009	26,742,666	19,100,791	11,593	19,112,384	2,302,166	160,785	16,971,003	3,871,924	5,899,739	32,642	819,279	445,469
2010	27,479,687	19,435,680	14,811	19,450,491	2,351,881	215,784	17,314,394	3,802,931	6,362,362	33,278	825,765	442,365
2011	28,832,374	20,363,621	734	20,364,355	2,232,226	142,928	18,275,057	4,168,034	6,389,283	34,595	833,417	459,052
2012	30,122,686	21,353,635	13,192	21,366,827	2,285,990	229,261	19,310,098	4,388,739	6,423,849	35,774	842,037	464,136
2013	30,582,769	21,823,074	30,854	21,853,928	2,650,081	305,798	19,509,645	4,508,569	6,564,555	35,963	850,406	474,271
2014	32,198,126	22,995,440	23,990	23,019,430	2,789,742	375,355	20,605,043	4,688,543	6,904,540	37,333	862,463	486,164

Personal Income and Employment by Area: Gulfport-Biloxi-Pascagoula, MS

(Thousands of dollars, except as noted.)

Year	Personal income, total	Earnings by place of work			Less: Contributions for government social insurance	Plus: Adjustment for residence	Equals: Net earnings by place of residence	Plus: Dividends, interest, and rent	Plus: Personal current transfer receipts	Per capita personal income (dollars)	Population (persons)	Total employment
		Nonfarm	Farm	Total								
1970	842,473	748,887	1,991	750,878	48,020	-56,745	646,113	141,182	55,178	3,489	241,495	109,735
1971	904,846	790,990	2,199	793,189	52,602	-51,477	689,110	149,867	65,869	3,600	251,347	111,651
1972	1,065,977	952,081	1,906	953,987	66,088	-63,643	824,256	166,508	75,213	4,120	258,728	120,441
1973	1,210,884	1,076,076	2,790	1,078,866	82,592	-67,992	928,282	192,296	90,306	4,462	271,384	128,013
1974	1,325,399	1,156,060	2,334	1,158,394	92,019	-69,921	996,454	216,846	112,099	4,811	275,483	128,526
1975	1,497,288	1,308,048	1,712	1,309,760	106,258	-82,810	1,120,692	237,821	138,775	5,407	276,941	131,617
1976	1,668,729	1,468,553	2,093	1,470,646	121,873	-91,434	1,257,339	255,476	155,914	5,851	285,195	137,857
1977	1,824,908	1,615,402	2,950	1,618,352	138,001	-104,292	1,376,059	278,490	170,359	6,262	291,439	142,534
1978	2,009,899	1,755,641	2,607	1,758,248	151,565	-108,401	1,498,282	320,537	191,080	6,774	296,689	142,259
1979	2,166,909	1,835,488	3,426	1,838,914	163,127	-94,801	1,580,986	356,031	229,892	7,255	298,661	138,800
1980	2,460,565	2,032,751	595	2,033,346	176,151	-94,788	1,762,407	426,156	272,002	8,171	301,117	142,303
1981	2,832,581	2,327,936	525	2,328,461	215,889	-114,419	1,998,153	517,903	316,525	9,307	304,337	144,575
1982	3,115,635	2,596,825	2,706	2,599,531	246,833	-156,177	2,196,521	567,787	351,327	10,019	310,986	148,783
1983	3,163,795	2,526,740	491	2,527,231	243,657	-125,343	2,158,231	601,934	403,630	10,031	315,399	141,240
1984	3,322,966	2,623,508	671	2,624,179	258,966	-123,585	2,241,628	660,284	421,054	10,573	314,280	143,148
1985	3,536,993	2,800,155	764	2,800,919	283,269	-144,880	2,372,770	718,201	446,022	11,124	317,972	147,352
1986	3,778,263	3,010,135	-564	3,009,571	308,351	-169,130	2,532,090	771,763	474,410	11,696	323,031	153,422
1987	3,882,770	3,092,727	837	3,093,564	316,701	-182,281	2,594,582	788,942	499,246	12,073	321,614	152,171
1988	4,100,369	3,258,201	1,467	3,259,668	349,141	-195,092	2,715,435	850,017	534,917	12,897	317,926	153,728
1989	4,355,745	3,368,205	1,603	3,369,808	362,300	-194,809	2,812,699	946,621	596,425	13,855	314,383	153,676
1990	4,548,998	3,545,423	1,563	3,546,986	399,763	-207,297	2,939,926	953,354	655,718	14,558	312,471	154,152
1991	4,817,884	3,783,188	1,477	3,784,665	434,238	-224,224	3,126,203	953,142	738,539	15,294	315,015	157,723
1992	5,234,664	4,117,559	2,913	4,120,472	471,418	-245,428	3,403,626	993,444	837,594	16,188	323,357	162,663
1993	5,813,979	4,651,248	1,236	4,652,484	536,149	-287,887	3,828,448	1,088,079	897,452	17,514	331,962	177,618
1994	6,282,804	5,044,298	26	5,044,324	596,905	-296,275	4,151,144	1,185,293	946,367	18,431	340,882	187,042
1995	6,565,675	5,152,678	-531	5,152,147	607,070	-295,041	4,250,036	1,264,928	1,050,711	18,977	345,981	185,900
1996	6,833,690	5,234,243	-2,101	5,232,142	617,576	-280,001	4,334,565	1,353,971	1,145,154	19,696	346,950	188,184
1997	7,212,673	5,528,868	-1,918	5,526,950	655,548	-299,730	4,571,672	1,435,082	1,205,919	20,545	351,065	194,086
1998	7,969,509	6,313,116	-1,417	6,311,699	753,671	-390,235	5,167,793	1,593,605	1,208,111	22,415	355,546	204,334
1999	8,363,178	6,709,308	186	6,709,494	798,614	-402,557	5,508,323	1,601,402	1,253,453	23,165	361,019	211,630
2000	8,888,044	7,040,298	1,232	7,041,530	823,890	-417,715	5,799,925	1,726,698	1,361,421	24,324	365,397	210,659
2001	9,158,665	7,035,088	3,469	7,038,557	791,868	-401,271	5,845,418	1,793,926	1,519,321	24,877	368,163	207,368
2002	9,241,385	7,120,829	1,830	7,122,659	809,595	-489,262	5,823,802	1,798,439	1,619,144	24,917	370,891	206,435
2003	9,576,527	7,498,487	1,914	7,500,401	850,865	-581,774	6,067,762	1,790,072	1,718,693	25,792	371,296	208,876
2004	9,865,837	7,820,846	2,241	7,823,087	888,912	-655,616	6,278,559	1,715,214	1,872,064	26,014	379,253	210,148
2005	10,931,604	8,155,194	1,420	8,156,614	925,256	-742,523	6,488,835	1,616,573	2,826,196	28,511	383,412	205,132
2006	10,491,198	8,278,901	1,334	8,280,235	951,874	-789,361	6,539,000	1,828,811	2,123,387	30,212	347,253	196,416
2007	12,738,027	8,974,207	-4,236	8,969,971	1,036,533	-924,791	7,008,647	3,718,462	2,010,918	35,702	356,789	208,425
2008	12,474,655	9,601,498	-5,867	9,595,631	1,092,045	-1,027,421	7,476,165	2,700,331	2,298,159	34,338	363,290	210,652
2009	12,446,572	9,563,746	-5,122	9,558,624	1,101,419	-1,066,541	7,390,664	2,608,295	2,447,613	33,861	367,577	206,365
2010	12,680,233	9,670,546	-7,627	9,662,919	1,114,070	-1,087,561	7,461,288	2,489,683	2,729,262	34,130	371,524	206,281
2011	12,769,769	9,568,775	-3,787	9,564,988	1,002,541	-1,061,811	7,500,636	2,403,734	2,865,399	33,984	375,762	204,578
2012	12,869,564	9,673,170	-1,801	9,671,369	1,020,743	-1,044,145	7,606,481	2,404,551	2,858,532	33,959	378,970	204,773
2013	12,990,049	9,810,226	3,425	9,813,651	1,171,333	-1,084,932	7,557,386	2,471,328	2,961,335	33,965	382,458	207,166
2014	13,385,359	9,965,323	-1,887	9,963,436	1,186,610	-1,048,718	7,728,108	2,564,477	3,092,774	34,664	386,144	207,241

Personal Income and Employment by Area: Hagerstown-Martinsburg, MD-WV

(Thousands of dollars, except as noted.)

Year	Personal income, total	Earnings by place of work			Less: Contributions for government social insurance	Plus: Adjustment for residence	Equals: Net earnings by place of residence	Plus: Dividends, interest, and rent	Plus: Personal current transfer receipts	Per capita personal income (dollars)	Population (persons)	Total employment
		Nonfarm	Farm	Total								
1970	530,574	417,406	11,573	428,979	30,006	21,674	420,647	63,423	46,504	3,780	140,356	61,187
1971	580,323	441,972	10,561	452,533	32,550	31,387	451,370	69,945	59,008	4,079	142,270	60,568
1972	643,850	496,537	12,910	509,447	38,553	35,078	505,972	76,858	61,020	4,449	144,718	62,605
1973	713,054	551,850	15,830	567,680	48,918	39,174	557,936	86,974	68,144	4,849	147,060	65,091
1974	800,193	615,576	17,050	632,626	56,559	42,477	618,544	101,571	80,078	5,351	149,552	66,441
1975	883,397	662,447	13,828	676,275	59,782	47,689	664,182	114,392	104,823	5,825	151,655	65,786
1976	960,599	718,534	10,573	729,107	65,495	58,457	722,069	122,884	115,646	6,246	153,782	66,479
1977	1,066,965	815,572	9,073	824,645	75,148	59,513	809,010	137,398	120,557	6,885	154,974	68,660
1978	1,203,493	919,908	18,477	938,385	85,635	67,450	920,200	155,564	127,729	7,677	156,758	71,340
1979	1,345,088	1,036,644	17,323	1,053,967	100,560	68,503	1,021,910	177,016	146,162	8,467	158,863	73,750
1980	1,448,403	1,064,794	10,237	1,075,031	103,211	86,932	1,058,752	212,299	177,352	9,053	159,999	71,741
1981	1,586,451	1,142,421	9,391	1,151,812	118,001	93,482	1,127,293	255,870	203,288	9,898	160,281	71,196
1982	1,689,261	1,149,736	9,169	1,158,905	120,861	102,713	1,140,757	309,932	238,572	10,507	160,772	69,372
1983	1,778,350	1,214,704	9,288	1,223,992	131,440	97,147	1,189,699	328,967	259,684	10,922	162,823	70,800
1984	1,989,393	1,381,050	17,047	1,398,097	154,420	102,108	1,345,785	375,180	268,428	12,069	164,837	73,953
1985	2,121,940	1,468,810	18,508	1,487,318	166,993	112,024	1,432,349	402,127	287,464	12,724	166,763	75,989
1986	2,258,663	1,549,803	24,866	1,574,669	178,749	135,408	1,531,328	428,391	298,944	13,378	168,834	78,736
1987	2,427,606	1,683,932	22,279	1,706,211	192,889	151,239	1,664,561	441,988	321,057	14,164	171,398	82,899
1988	2,620,314	1,820,924	22,460	1,843,384	214,711	177,652	1,806,325	469,077	344,912	15,078	173,783	86,869
1989	2,850,918	1,956,116	19,599	1,975,715	231,566	196,954	1,941,103	535,791	374,024	16,101	177,068	89,711
1990	2,976,972	2,080,267	23,169	2,103,436	250,302	173,209	2,026,343	546,740	403,889	16,376	181,790	91,971
1991	3,064,874	2,185,512	21,715	2,207,227	268,832	108,758	2,047,153	557,992	459,729	16,506	185,679	92,208
1992	3,227,231	2,300,364	31,988	2,332,352	283,424	92,808	2,141,736	562,078	523,417	17,069	189,071	91,949
1993	3,355,659	2,382,580	20,418	2,402,998	296,786	104,967	2,211,179	590,404	554,076	17,548	191,225	93,693
1994	3,573,710	2,535,810	17,635	2,553,445	317,111	124,742	2,361,076	635,430	577,204	18,473	193,451	95,211
1995	3,729,203	2,680,590	8,978	2,689,568	335,630	110,912	2,464,850	671,208	593,145	19,042	195,846	99,247
1996	3,960,341	2,802,458	14,789	2,817,247	348,519	141,630	2,610,358	713,413	636,570	19,997	198,049	101,073
1997	4,305,794	3,007,295	10,476	3,017,771	368,868	230,069	2,878,972	778,215	648,607	21,534	199,951	103,427
1998	4,476,362	3,188,411	15,319	3,203,730	386,002	157,176	2,974,904	820,346	681,112	22,077	202,761	105,106
1999	4,671,170	3,417,168	15,748	3,432,916	409,548	111,924	3,135,292	814,698	721,180	22,726	205,544	106,998
2000	5,097,008	3,614,175	16,220	3,630,395	433,660	266,043	3,462,778	870,927	763,303	24,457	208,408	109,185
2001	5,447,204	3,818,802	19,405	3,838,207	463,904	306,418	3,680,721	919,489	846,994	25,753	211,521	111,224
2002	5,730,164	3,952,578	8,789	3,961,367	474,342	374,902	3,861,927	918,938	949,299	26,565	215,706	111,311
2003	6,074,725	4,167,187	22,032	4,189,219	501,655	467,926	4,155,490	887,239	1,031,996	27,438	221,396	112,477
2004	6,516,870	4,441,023	32,171	4,473,194	534,086	568,439	4,507,547	965,735	1,043,588	28,623	227,681	114,346
2005	6,954,427	4,752,448	31,319	4,783,767	572,499	683,624	4,894,892	956,679	1,102,856	29,695	234,198	118,108
2006	7,555,310	5,059,125	25,892	5,085,017	604,263	826,733	5,307,487	1,058,126	1,189,697	31,401	240,604	120,871
2007	7,956,215	5,118,940	27,283	5,146,223	605,889	944,355	5,484,689	1,181,557	1,289,969	32,434	245,305	122,040
2008	8,454,498	5,209,292	32,087	5,241,379	615,224	1,073,298	5,699,453	1,259,484	1,495,561	34,049	248,303	122,017
2009	8,569,657	5,073,202	26,451	5,099,653	602,067	1,227,781	5,725,367	1,211,107	1,633,183	34,308	249,783	118,319
2010	8,810,763	5,132,538	30,395	5,162,933	624,845	1,303,870	5,841,958	1,185,168	1,783,637	34,907	252,408	117,699
2011	9,236,618	5,401,049	46,750	5,447,799	587,025	1,259,738	6,120,512	1,278,401	1,837,705	36,288	254,533	120,462
2012	9,511,470	5,606,109	61,429	5,667,538	612,846	1,225,913	6,280,605	1,361,421	1,869,444	37,122	256,224	124,043
2013	9,571,336	5,680,117	60,838	5,740,955	691,156	1,189,565	6,239,364	1,377,471	1,954,501	37,105	257,950	125,533
2014	9,925,785	5,817,780	60,384	5,878,164	704,763	1,259,299	6,432,700	1,436,993	2,056,092	38,166	260,070	126,682

Personal Income and Employment by Area: Hammond, LA

(Thousands of dollars, except as noted.)

Year	Personal income, total	Derivation of personal income									Per capita personal income (dollars)	Population (persons)	Total employment
		Earnings by place of work			Less: Contributions for government social insurance	Plus: Adjustment for residence	Equals: Net earnings by place of residence	Plus: Dividends, interest, and rent	Plus: Personal current transfer receipts				
		Nonfarm	Farm	Total									
1970	154,100	93,082	9,962	103,044	5,808	12,778	110,014	17,755	26,331	2,326	66,244	20,955
1971	170,812	99,807	12,708	112,515	6,320	14,806	121,001	19,347	30,464	2,496	68,421	21,042
1972	189,884	112,265	13,297	125,562	7,388	17,744	135,918	21,205	32,761	2,777	68,368	22,132
1973	218,752	127,634	17,087	144,721	9,546	20,790	155,965	24,867	37,920	3,173	68,944	23,356
1974	244,191	140,511	12,603	153,114	10,737	26,149	168,526	30,801	44,864	3,488	70,000	23,840
1975	283,762	152,275	16,710	168,985	11,233	34,287	192,039	34,880	56,843	3,939	72,031	23,535
1976	322,427	172,662	15,038	187,700	12,930	45,305	220,075	38,818	63,534	4,345	74,202	24,397
1977	363,532	194,392	15,626	210,018	14,430	53,721	249,309	44,698	69,525	4,765	76,299	24,835
1978	412,607	226,707	11,984	238,691	17,242	64,555	286,004	51,062	75,541	5,285	78,065	26,739
1979	470,674	252,400	9,122	261,522	19,426	83,218	325,314	58,028	87,332	5,900	79,771	26,121
1980	544,288	276,680	7,470	284,150	21,049	100,857	363,958	73,121	107,209	6,717	81,026	27,010
1981	615,329	307,746	7,413	315,159	24,519	114,898	405,538	90,128	119,663	7,486	82,194	27,882
1982	678,672	326,315	6,516	332,831	25,612	119,792	427,011	107,239	144,422	8,016	84,663	28,300
1983	734,168	349,924	7,721	357,645	26,796	116,819	447,668	124,837	161,663	8,481	86,562	28,974
1984	785,212	384,757	8,146	392,903	30,162	117,067	479,808	136,018	169,386	8,919	88,037	29,761
1985	831,581	408,294	13,146	421,440	32,175	111,156	500,421	148,292	182,868	9,357	88,876	30,136
1986	853,008	423,641	16,492	440,133	33,353	103,439	510,219	151,082	191,707	9,559	89,239	30,240
1987	856,393	425,508	20,654	446,162	33,584	100,035	512,613	144,556	199,224	9,735	87,971	29,887
1988	889,492	436,054	20,048	456,102	37,054	111,122	530,170	150,367	208,955	10,222	87,019	30,165
1989	952,780	463,158	22,992	486,150	41,367	115,941	560,724	160,580	231,476	11,024	86,429	30,880
1990	1,026,902	505,273	18,542	523,815	45,965	128,261	606,111	161,931	258,860	11,975	85,754	31,266
1991	1,119,453	566,287	15,416	581,703	52,908	133,252	662,047	165,275	292,131	12,944	86,485	32,005
1992	1,242,213	636,603	21,559	658,162	58,929	141,883	741,116	166,812	334,285	14,096	88,124	33,722
1993	1,354,031	698,051	21,192	719,243	64,390	143,442	798,295	176,253	379,483	15,064	89,885	35,685
1994	1,474,099	754,320	23,940	778,260	71,411	155,392	862,241	193,398	418,460	16,071	91,726	37,632
1995	1,545,768	802,895	25,547	828,442	76,855	165,872	917,459	205,185	423,124	16,484	93,775	39,337
1996	1,610,581	845,020	28,427	873,447	81,835	175,627	967,239	216,021	427,321	16,980	94,851	40,716
1997	1,704,473	899,452	20,373	919,825	86,394	194,308	1,027,739	231,080	445,654	17,660	96,515	41,476
1998	1,787,545	946,351	24,571	970,922	90,960	218,631	1,098,593	246,117	442,835	18,195	98,246	41,212
1999	1,846,123	1,010,085	25,357	1,035,442	96,605	222,635	1,161,472	244,317	440,334	18,527	99,643	42,733
2000	1,961,549	1,091,948	21,068	1,113,016	102,901	231,603	1,241,718	258,285	461,546	19,476	100,716	44,330
2001	2,161,652	1,201,171	21,916	1,223,087	112,630	237,020	1,347,477	256,334	557,841	21,264	101,657	45,196
2002	2,214,586	1,252,443	13,651	1,266,094	118,335	237,085	1,384,844	258,521	571,221	21,603	102,511	45,406
2003	2,299,421	1,332,946	11,887	1,344,833	125,231	246,606	1,466,208	268,026	565,187	22,156	103,782	47,040
2004	2,489,043	1,437,552	19,135	1,456,687	133,200	261,865	1,585,352	261,187	642,504	23,630	105,335	48,223
2005	2,707,953	1,551,027	12,619	1,563,646	143,536	275,487	1,695,597	271,575	740,781	25,311	106,987	49,756
2006	3,081,518	1,808,408	16,175	1,824,583	169,552	313,050	1,968,081	337,116	776,321	27,007	114,102	54,248
2007	3,364,417	1,915,779	17,879	1,933,658	179,876	328,047	2,081,829	463,823	818,765	28,807	116,792	56,966
2008	3,636,589	2,088,983	8,457	2,097,440	194,473	347,451	2,250,418	464,079	922,092	30,657	118,621	57,907
2009	3,665,335	2,047,636	3,239	2,050,875	190,297	381,877	2,242,455	441,006	981,874	30,542	120,009	57,592
2010	3,779,294	2,222,464	4,144	2,226,608	204,955	299,129	2,320,782	410,495	1,048,017	31,087	121,572	57,655
2011	3,942,736	2,321,280	4,997	2,326,277	194,365	285,355	2,417,267	450,512	1,074,957	32,126	122,727	57,775
2012	4,098,077	2,293,224	5,735	2,298,959	189,164	393,042	2,502,837	487,253	1,107,987	33,111	123,767	57,775
2013	4,191,231	2,276,954	10,223	2,287,177	217,294	466,768	2,536,651	510,608	1,143,972	33,394	125,508	57,700
2014	4,344,101	2,399,064	12,268	2,411,332	226,839	484,816	2,669,309	528,828	1,145,964	34,192	127,049	58,225

Personal Income and Employment by Area: Hanford-Corcoran, CA

(Thousands of dollars, except as noted.)

Year	Personal income, total	Earnings by place of work			Less: Contributions for government social insurance	Plus: Adjustment for residence	Equals: Net earnings by place of residence	Plus: Dividends, interest, and rent	Plus: Personal current transfer receipts	Per capita personal income (dollars)	Population (persons)	Total employment
		Nonfarm	Farm	Total								
1970	265,330	176,420	37,589	214,009	11,838	-8,604	193,567	43,275	28,488	3,986	66,570	28,533
1971	279,028	192,643	32,327	224,970	13,658	-8,483	202,829	45,671	30,528	4,199	66,450	29,151
1972	314,414	209,569	45,745	255,314	15,425	-8,004	231,885	49,894	32,635	4,613	68,161	29,839
1973	345,154	230,635	49,406	280,041	18,586	-7,895	253,560	56,959	34,635	5,053	68,308	30,582
1974	436,901	254,850	108,358	363,208	21,494	-7,657	334,057	62,501	40,343	6,326	69,067	31,905
1975	445,361	274,568	83,520	358,088	23,299	-7,956	326,833	67,978	50,550	6,309	70,590	32,738
1976	532,215	286,584	150,747	437,331	25,183	-6,213	405,935	69,382	56,898	7,422	71,708	32,207
1977	530,622	316,574	110,503	427,077	28,242	-6,675	392,160	77,716	60,746	7,322	72,467	33,077
1978	524,828	352,993	48,869	401,862	31,412	-6,331	364,119	92,136	68,573	7,135	73,556	33,605
1979	684,161	395,991	147,861	543,852	36,681	-5,502	501,669	106,149	76,343	9,300	73,562	35,517
1980	846,296	421,269	246,478	667,747	37,877	-3,813	626,057	126,879	93,360	11,396	74,265	35,016
1981	827,354	487,920	126,860	614,780	46,808	-3,111	564,861	153,888	108,605	10,854	76,229	35,983
1982	889,508	519,619	139,665	659,284	49,671	-2,431	607,182	166,921	115,405	11,373	78,213	34,679
1983	856,945	551,435	51,580	603,015	54,110	-2,724	546,181	189,027	121,737	10,562	81,138	35,641
1984	997,493	608,521	125,454	733,975	62,562	-5,932	665,481	204,363	127,649	12,017	83,004	36,754
1985	1,004,173	623,115	107,477	730,592	64,432	-5,371	660,789	206,095	137,289	11,785	85,205	36,258
1986	1,005,463	633,337	82,972	716,309	66,968	-4,521	644,820	210,394	150,249	11,641	86,372	36,047
1987	1,155,535	692,213	170,505	862,718	74,066	-11,804	776,848	222,034	156,653	13,126	88,032	36,612
1988	1,238,551	801,238	149,802	951,040	88,578	-24,550	837,912	231,663	168,976	13,105	94,510	39,367
1989	1,376,610	920,107	150,800	1,070,907	100,302	-40,728	929,877	261,496	185,237	13,787	99,850	41,267
1990	1,385,793	940,234	117,547	1,057,781	103,690	-36,729	917,362	262,501	205,930	13,602	101,885	40,087
1991	1,484,202	997,223	157,140	1,154,363	113,066	-43,872	997,425	254,080	232,697	14,225	104,334	41,203
1992	1,618,658	1,038,298	207,796	1,246,094	118,078	-41,440	1,086,576	256,265	275,817	15,069	107,414	41,535
1993	1,707,490	1,101,420	208,763	1,310,183	126,313	-42,344	1,141,526	271,457	294,507	15,642	109,161	43,577
1994	1,771,129	1,152,957	201,742	1,354,699	130,433	-43,671	1,180,595	296,883	293,651	15,875	111,565	44,229
1995	1,790,686	1,191,157	165,464	1,356,621	131,768	-43,405	1,181,448	302,274	306,964	15,730	113,840	45,163
1996	1,918,990	1,233,142	219,171	1,452,313	132,561	-40,200	1,279,552	317,045	322,393	16,627	115,411	47,583
1997	1,963,345	1,307,776	173,915	1,481,691	136,961	-40,117	1,304,613	337,664	321,068	16,814	116,769	48,573
1998	2,002,827	1,341,738	120,561	1,462,299	136,366	-24,144	1,301,789	350,692	350,346	16,490	121,457	48,028
1999	2,134,260	1,420,751	158,152	1,578,903	144,865	-22,565	1,411,473	353,184	369,603	16,885	126,402	48,374
2000	2,252,223	1,525,299	154,548	1,679,847	156,002	-23,700	1,500,145	370,822	381,256	17,347	129,835	49,602
2001	2,530,460	1,657,754	207,146	1,864,900	176,805	6,531	1,694,626	407,925	427,909	19,043	132,881	48,960
2002	2,714,250	1,835,524	183,347	2,018,871	196,750	-499	1,821,622	431,517	461,111	20,051	135,369	51,606
2003	3,088,489	2,031,229	300,437	2,331,666	220,645	-9,308	2,101,713	482,163	504,613	22,157	139,393	53,968
2004	3,383,803	2,204,552	417,642	2,622,194	247,542	-19,623	2,355,029	491,514	537,260	23,564	143,601	54,687
2005	3,478,661	2,305,712	385,285	2,690,997	257,721	-30,614	2,402,662	505,269	570,730	23,966	145,147	55,661
2006	3,489,648	2,478,042	200,610	2,678,652	269,058	-43,006	2,366,588	511,731	611,329	23,625	147,712	55,661
2007	3,968,492	2,601,145	494,894	3,096,039	272,820	-56,617	2,766,602	543,344	658,546	26,383	150,420	57,558
2008	3,978,531	2,708,500	293,295	3,001,795	286,575	-71,170	2,644,050	586,401	748,080	26,170	152,027	57,492
2009	3,792,920	2,624,286	108,437	2,732,723	285,834	-54,729	2,392,160	587,196	813,564	24,908	152,278	55,817
2010	4,051,300	2,646,593	246,168	2,892,761	284,363	-80,966	2,527,432	617,024	906,844	26,580	152,418	54,991
2011	4,516,364	2,727,536	590,483	3,318,019	266,768	-99,516	2,951,735	652,213	912,416	29,701	152,063	55,059
2012	4,491,688	2,760,753	487,522	3,248,275	268,975	-103,132	2,876,168	692,266	923,254	29,679	151,340	55,527
2013	4,533,297	2,779,219	438,612	3,217,831	299,220	-73,958	2,844,653	723,888	964,756	30,049	150,862	56,303
2014	4,864,335	2,950,461	596,477	3,546,938	312,538	-133,705	3,100,695	762,890	1,000,750	32,371	150,269	58,482

Personal Income and Employment by Area: Harrisburg-Carlisle, PA

(Thousands of dollars, except as noted.)

Year	Personal income, total	Earnings by place of work			Less: Contributions for government social insurance	Plus: Adjustment for residence	Equals: Net earnings by place of residence	Plus: Dividends, interest, and rent	Plus: Personal current transfer receipts	Per capita personal income (dollars)	Population (persons)	Total employment
		Nonfarm	Farm	Total								
1970	1,757,421	1,569,545	20,955	1,590,500	110,101	-107,690	1,372,709	235,877	148,835	4,272	411,421	212,257
1971	1,915,344	1,716,291	14,838	1,731,129	124,668	-127,808	1,478,653	261,644	175,047	4,594	416,883	214,199
1972	2,117,775	1,921,927	14,822	1,936,749	145,631	-158,654	1,632,464	288,197	197,114	5,022	421,671	223,174
1973	2,347,847	2,168,492	22,403	2,190,895	187,977	-192,795	1,810,123	321,072	216,652	5,499	426,925	233,699
1974	2,589,623	2,397,060	22,150	2,419,210	215,859	-236,930	1,966,421	367,678	255,524	6,045	428,390	239,598
1975	2,810,085	2,536,591	17,999	2,554,590	222,482	-258,675	2,073,433	409,183	327,469	6,549	429,067	235,721
1976	3,073,124	2,803,514	22,334	2,825,848	253,182	-304,279	2,268,387	445,271	359,466	7,139	430,488	239,343
1977	3,352,125	3,098,618	15,433	3,114,051	281,710	-361,594	2,470,747	501,319	380,059	7,707	434,923	244,658
1978	3,675,161	3,436,050	16,109	3,452,159	320,415	-423,455	2,708,289	559,435	407,437	8,415	436,716	251,930
1979	4,037,182	3,805,783	21,438	3,827,221	368,646	-504,879	2,953,696	624,565	458,921	9,139	441,734	257,914
1980	4,455,051	4,137,752	3,739	4,141,491	400,551	-592,001	3,148,939	775,346	530,766	9,928	448,717	260,074
1981	4,934,692	4,461,761	13,774	4,475,535	462,945	-627,937	3,384,653	946,036	604,003	10,916	452,040	259,996
1982	5,395,344	4,715,669	18,666	4,734,335	493,249	-651,306	3,589,780	1,118,078	687,486	11,965	450,941	259,191
1983	5,758,800	5,034,837	10,726	5,045,563	535,159	-679,718	3,830,686	1,189,502	738,612	12,710	453,087	260,817
1984	6,302,060	5,547,915	39,001	5,586,916	614,797	-739,252	4,232,867	1,322,837	746,356	13,843	455,244	271,598
1985	6,782,008	5,939,703	38,270	5,977,973	669,968	-763,177	4,544,828	1,436,883	800,297	14,858	456,461	279,915
1986	7,295,266	6,417,847	39,315	6,457,162	732,623	-823,608	4,900,931	1,538,264	856,071	15,867	459,787	288,050
1987	7,773,243	6,914,008	35,700	6,949,708	782,801	-861,227	5,305,680	1,588,173	879,390	16,805	462,555	299,738
1988	8,416,899	7,561,159	22,946	7,584,105	885,824	-913,953	5,784,328	1,694,211	938,360	18,053	466,243	310,881
1989	9,258,153	8,169,083	40,703	8,209,786	941,695	-964,680	6,303,411	1,948,732	1,006,010	19,671	470,638	320,922
1990	9,867,588	8,751,022	38,935	8,789,957	1,015,959	-996,422	6,777,576	1,964,343	1,125,669	20,736	475,860	327,398
1991	10,391,344	9,228,170	23,514	9,251,684	1,082,772	-1,093,820	7,075,092	2,022,843	1,293,409	21,560	481,975	329,899
1992	10,981,179	9,863,637	49,123	9,912,760	1,150,010	-1,203,481	7,559,269	2,050,465	1,371,445	22,573	486,480	332,619
1993	11,420,307	10,331,116	42,620	10,373,736	1,218,217	-1,296,414	7,859,105	2,121,696	1,439,506	23,219	491,859	336,584
1994	11,878,494	10,842,417	44,246	10,886,663	1,303,223	-1,387,279	8,196,161	2,201,550	1,480,783	23,941	496,159	345,672
1995	12,432,115	11,305,583	26,713	11,332,296	1,357,533	-1,506,428	8,468,335	2,407,410	1,556,370	24,924	498,803	353,789
1996	13,134,897	11,899,659	53,202	11,952,861	1,400,458	-1,643,302	8,909,101	2,567,294	1,658,502	26,166	501,990	360,378
1997	13,796,631	12,559,904	27,454	12,587,358	1,467,197	-1,736,798	9,383,363	2,704,253	1,709,015	27,395	503,624	364,360
1998	14,530,271	13,376,274	37,614	13,413,888	1,541,643	-1,903,072	9,969,173	2,803,985	1,757,113	28,687	506,506	370,749
1999	15,085,894	14,010,768	35,022	14,045,790	1,600,637	-1,990,788	10,454,365	2,774,146	1,857,383	29,686	508,176	373,502
2000	15,799,253	14,549,170	51,173	14,600,343	1,639,943	-2,047,359	10,913,041	2,920,237	1,965,975	31,012	509,451	377,224
2001	16,492,128	15,283,448	49,032	15,332,480	1,722,165	-2,157,705	11,452,610	2,889,594	2,149,924	32,250	511,391	374,021
2002	16,977,579	15,885,486	23,114	15,908,600	1,801,464	-2,329,941	11,777,195	2,897,117	2,303,267	32,931	515,553	376,034
2003	17,563,507	16,452,556	57,904	16,510,460	1,853,273	-2,455,011	12,202,176	2,956,754	2,404,577	33,831	519,152	377,593
2004	18,381,720	17,439,175	86,939	17,526,114	1,952,183	-2,584,771	12,989,160	2,899,283	2,493,277	35,222	521,882	382,926
2005	18,984,573	17,972,766	78,144	18,050,910	2,023,674	-2,660,250	13,366,986	2,889,573	2,728,014	36,108	525,775	386,068
2006	19,925,714	18,683,329	59,067	18,742,396	2,095,158	-2,755,093	13,892,145	3,129,815	2,903,754	37,435	532,268	392,899
2007	20,917,296	19,273,098	78,882	19,351,980	2,168,541	-2,826,149	14,357,290	3,498,491	3,061,515	38,933	537,268	396,375
2008	21,742,807	19,630,873	87,366	19,718,239	2,219,280	-2,850,298	14,648,661	3,599,452	3,494,694	40,094	542,301	395,575
2009	21,769,897	19,559,803	47,781	19,607,584	2,221,440	-2,948,974	14,437,170	3,431,385	3,901,342	39,808	546,874	387,882
2010	22,433,346	19,974,719	61,904	20,036,623	2,278,144	-2,945,700	14,812,779	3,379,918	4,240,649	40,769	550,258	383,776
2011	23,630,443	20,692,891	108,867	20,801,758	2,111,527	-3,066,068	15,624,163	3,689,383	4,316,897	42,814	551,935	387,222
2012	24,551,757	21,212,392	112,753	21,325,145	2,152,133	-3,035,874	16,137,138	4,040,995	4,373,624	44,251	554,827	389,185
2013	24,952,278	21,956,660	146,795	22,103,455	2,523,705	-3,188,533	16,391,217	4,062,068	4,498,993	44,725	557,906	393,556
2014	25,812,532	22,706,976	181,559	22,888,535	2,609,249	-3,320,678	16,958,608	4,203,298	4,650,626	46,024	560,849	397,566

Personal Income and Employment by Area: Harrisonburg, VA

(Thousands of dollars, except as noted.)

Year	Personal income, total	Earnings by place of work			Less: Contributions for government social insurance	Plus: Adjustment for residence	Equals: Net earnings by place of residence	Plus: Dividends, interest, and rent	Plus: Personal current transfer receipts	Per capita personal income (dollars)	Population (persons)	Total employment
		Nonfarm	Farm	Total								
1970	210,626	159,639	12,492	172,131	10,339	8,847	170,639	25,572	14,415	3,354	62,807	31,524
1971	230,223	177,045	12,350	189,395	11,932	7,317	184,780	28,646	16,797	3,537	65,099	32,660
1972	254,120	193,818	15,843	209,661	13,760	7,143	203,044	31,868	19,208	3,728	68,174	33,531
1973	294,569	222,683	23,025	245,708	18,182	6,364	233,890	38,058	22,621	4,250	69,311	35,796
1974	304,098	236,631	7,781	244,412	20,082	7,000	231,330	44,801	27,967	4,242	71,687	35,967
1975	334,705	250,652	11,408	262,060	20,724	2,544	243,880	50,125	40,700	4,556	73,459	35,112
1976	373,043	288,059	10,015	298,074	24,226	2,100	275,948	55,612	41,483	5,029	74,179	36,872
1977	413,526	319,844	11,996	331,840	26,990	558	305,408	64,281	43,837	5,505	75,123	37,960
1978	463,333	360,266	14,429	374,695	30,889	-1,664	342,142	72,674	48,517	6,050	76,581	38,530
1979	521,186	411,066	12,404	423,470	36,745	-7,793	378,932	87,436	54,818	6,780	76,866	40,432
1980	590,020	458,137	6,669	464,806	41,118	-9,563	414,125	110,304	65,591	7,653	77,093	41,367
1981	652,061	489,188	9,645	498,833	47,159	-12,113	439,561	134,153	78,347	8,308	78,483	40,603
1982	706,569	534,808	6,509	541,317	52,748	-16,804	471,765	151,261	83,543	8,934	79,086	41,535
1983	769,297	582,546	7,545	590,091	57,810	-18,359	513,922	163,751	91,624	9,668	79,575	43,301
1984	879,806	644,937	39,436	684,373	65,629	-18,836	599,908	182,640	97,258	11,036	79,725	44,841
1985	954,537	699,341	45,043	744,384	72,863	-22,628	648,893	198,818	106,826	11,870	80,416	46,105
1986	1,074,741	804,919	62,602	867,521	86,474	-32,836	748,211	215,120	111,410	13,199	81,428	48,414
1987	1,126,140	880,735	33,168	913,903	94,127	-33,781	785,995	224,562	115,583	13,590	82,868	49,974
1988	1,256,209	968,116	47,932	1,016,048	106,027	-38,944	871,077	255,039	130,093	14,792	84,927	51,531
1989	1,383,386	1,041,763	73,416	1,115,179	115,261	-43,462	956,456	288,661	138,269	15,985	86,545	52,875
1990	1,445,709	1,103,164	71,671	1,174,835	122,928	-50,651	1,001,256	289,047	155,406	16,270	88,857	54,138
1991	1,516,327	1,158,498	72,910	1,231,408	130,377	-60,459	1,040,572	303,852	171,903	16,677	90,921	54,601
1992	1,645,037	1,267,782	91,635	1,359,417	141,737	-74,008	1,143,672	310,245	191,120	17,672	93,087	56,747
1993	1,749,113	1,361,066	93,859	1,454,925	151,741	-85,847	1,217,337	330,047	201,729	18,347	95,333	58,861
1994	1,839,387	1,456,233	91,837	1,548,070	161,951	-96,453	1,289,666	341,014	208,707	18,840	97,631	60,901
1995	1,906,089	1,515,132	85,100	1,600,232	168,027	-106,562	1,325,643	353,530	226,916	19,059	100,011	62,815
1996	1,982,613	1,565,733	82,479	1,648,212	171,045	-110,059	1,367,108	375,324	240,181	19,314	102,652	63,643
1997	2,091,954	1,690,898	67,985	1,758,883	182,829	-123,537	1,452,517	392,898	246,539	20,073	104,218	65,073
1998	2,230,351	1,796,223	85,955	1,882,178	191,837	-137,082	1,553,259	420,360	256,732	21,138	105,512	65,517
1999	2,328,265	1,921,216	81,430	2,002,646	205,600	-157,269	1,639,777	417,464	271,024	21,696	107,311	67,995
2000	2,492,787	2,040,077	95,410	2,135,487	215,809	-173,351	1,746,327	455,174	291,286	22,993	108,414	69,365
2001	2,671,935	2,194,129	119,508	2,313,637	239,491	-198,730	1,875,416	473,053	323,466	24,221	110,317	70,522
2002	2,672,665	2,286,201	43,235	2,329,436	248,937	-214,983	1,865,516	459,150	347,999	23,831	112,152	71,125
2003	2,855,355	2,410,699	54,533	2,465,232	261,205	-238,900	1,965,127	520,734	369,494	25,235	113,151	72,224
2004	2,990,263	2,522,349	89,824	2,612,173	275,963	-256,034	2,080,176	505,999	404,088	26,106	114,542	73,314
2005	3,152,304	2,639,826	116,110	2,755,936	290,367	-274,837	2,190,732	515,194	446,378	27,035	116,602	73,590
2006	3,344,189	2,830,726	60,516	2,891,242	317,674	-298,031	2,275,537	578,884	489,768	28,136	118,858	75,844
2007	3,566,177	2,946,744	103,566	3,050,310	330,734	-319,627	2,399,949	645,113	521,115	29,515	120,825	77,288
2008	3,695,066	3,000,430	105,465	3,105,895	340,903	-339,573	2,425,419	677,133	592,514	30,198	122,361	77,917
2009	3,633,054	2,998,170	64,202	3,062,372	340,451	-373,700	2,348,221	651,808	633,025	29,265	124,144	76,143
2010	3,737,828	3,012,767	108,918	3,121,685	347,215	-369,818	2,404,652	650,797	682,379	29,801	125,426	75,954
2011	3,960,837	3,085,167	136,137	3,221,304	319,442	-391,104	2,510,758	732,646	717,433	31,207	126,920	77,399
2012	4,124,074	3,209,131	111,427	3,320,558	331,738	-403,573	2,585,247	806,380	732,447	32,069	128,599	77,836
2013	4,214,819	3,270,705	173,778	3,444,483	383,061	-393,740	2,667,682	808,719	738,418	32,614	129,233	78,476
2014	4,403,248	3,364,754	203,605	3,568,359	392,282	-389,255	2,786,822	841,926	774,500	33,703	130,649	79,386

Personal Income and Employment by Area: Hartford-West Hartford-East Hartford, CT

(Thousands of dollars, except as noted.)

| Year | Personal income, total | Derivation of personal income | | | | | | | | Per capita personal income (dollars) | Population (persons) | Total employment |
| | | Earnings by place of work | | | Less: Contributions for government social insurance | Plus: Adjustment for residence | Equals: Net earnings by place of residence | Plus: Dividends, interest, and rent | Plus: Personal current transfer receipts | | | |
		Nonfarm	Farm	Total								
1970	5,170,803	4,392,783	37,659	4,430,442	293,222	-178,102	3,959,118	825,999	385,686	4,983	1,037,762	515,814
1971	5,392,124	4,488,382	34,903	4,523,285	309,310	-172,841	4,041,134	863,969	487,021	5,151	1,046,710	504,925
1972	5,778,498	4,865,318	32,162	4,897,480	356,062	-185,853	4,355,565	913,476	509,457	5,498	1,050,940	514,795
1973	6,329,992	5,401,329	38,187	5,439,516	455,426	-211,431	4,772,659	1,010,776	546,557	6,019	1,051,711	538,925
1974	6,949,218	5,855,964	53,090	5,909,054	515,034	-239,393	5,154,627	1,150,978	643,613	6,589	1,054,609	551,581
1975	7,489,569	6,157,199	40,568	6,197,767	528,872	-268,346	5,400,549	1,240,411	848,609	7,128	1,050,706	539,442
1976	7,996,992	6,599,289	43,958	6,643,247	579,288	-287,485	5,776,474	1,311,520	908,998	7,632	1,047,780	544,412
1977	8,737,499	7,270,574	43,950	7,314,524	650,126	-316,435	6,347,963	1,443,485	946,051	8,392	1,041,160	560,291
1978	9,746,986	8,289,674	39,082	8,328,756	764,832	-379,951	7,183,973	1,603,645	959,368	9,311	1,046,844	589,554
1979	11,023,932	9,474,334	39,097	9,513,431	909,025	-476,694	8,127,712	1,815,486	1,080,734	10,516	1,048,331	614,832
1980	12,541,993	10,582,331	46,358	10,628,689	1,004,620	-574,290	9,049,779	2,244,053	1,248,161	11,906	1,053,458	629,793
1981	13,925,652	11,491,422	41,916	11,533,338	1,172,453	-634,164	9,726,721	2,758,481	1,440,450	13,155	1,058,562	632,664
1982	15,046,979	12,246,278	47,685	12,293,963	1,267,473	-688,689	10,337,801	3,108,876	1,600,302	14,194	1,060,120	629,064
1983	16,105,115	13,205,175	50,346	13,255,521	1,378,411	-757,795	11,119,315	3,252,527	1,733,273	15,078	1,068,101	636,326
1984	17,958,159	14,786,867	53,766	14,840,633	1,579,981	-880,968	12,379,684	3,758,658	1,819,817	16,717	1,074,268	666,698
1985	19,304,857	16,216,533	58,141	16,274,674	1,750,056	-1,026,843	13,497,775	3,869,937	1,937,145	17,849	1,081,595	692,320
1986	21,012,624	17,903,132	64,897	17,968,029	1,939,613	-1,199,437	14,828,979	4,132,168	2,051,477	19,236	1,092,348	723,469
1987	23,034,227	19,949,857	66,046	20,015,903	2,126,561	-1,377,083	16,512,259	4,395,433	2,126,535	20,819	1,106,430	745,697
1988	25,252,306	21,882,294	84,760	21,967,054	2,387,606	-1,531,160	18,048,288	4,904,478	2,299,540	22,523	1,121,183	767,174
1989	27,459,310	23,241,209	77,794	23,319,003	2,517,739	-1,693,711	19,107,553	5,759,827	2,591,930	24,445	1,123,307	766,227
1990	28,288,036	24,067,055	102,455	24,169,510	2,579,629	-1,915,352	19,674,529	5,717,182	2,896,325	25,144	1,125,047	758,360
1991	28,456,409	24,282,950	88,972	24,371,922	2,641,818	-1,872,900	19,857,204	5,347,155	3,252,050	25,239	1,127,479	724,845
1992	29,783,221	25,054,441	93,327	25,147,768	2,694,451	-1,888,073	20,565,244	5,403,650	3,814,327	26,472	1,125,083	709,988
1993	30,677,408	25,731,438	97,715	25,829,153	2,765,966	-1,905,072	21,158,115	5,548,220	3,971,073	27,253	1,125,634	710,405
1994	31,320,945	26,329,121	79,656	26,408,777	2,867,030	-1,893,662	21,648,085	5,564,610	4,108,250	27,817	1,125,949	698,042
1995	32,282,379	26,874,908	81,929	26,956,837	2,952,747	-1,783,522	22,220,568	5,663,985	4,397,826	28,707	1,124,531	708,359
1996	33,531,121	27,739,416	68,047	27,807,463	3,044,154	-1,621,081	23,142,228	5,878,042	4,510,851	29,769	1,126,396	715,650
1997	35,589,770	29,650,972	62,968	29,713,940	3,199,896	-1,610,901	24,903,143	6,055,832	4,630,795	31,523	1,128,992	722,220
1998	37,737,040	31,733,300	72,278	31,805,578	3,362,423	-1,724,911	26,718,244	6,310,518	4,708,278	33,267	1,134,353	732,477
1999	39,402,854	33,861,401	73,141	33,934,542	3,536,817	-1,951,679	28,446,046	6,150,241	4,806,567	34,524	1,141,318	744,548
2000	42,736,822	36,632,103	89,226	36,721,329	3,755,247	-1,948,730	31,017,352	6,667,621	5,051,849	37,134	1,150,872	759,681
2001	44,496,839	38,375,112	81,841	38,456,953	3,890,899	-2,275,751	32,290,303	6,851,784	5,354,752	38,409	1,158,513	762,575
2002	44,669,324	38,751,562	73,282	38,824,844	4,071,517	-2,244,040	32,509,287	6,413,072	5,746,965	38,212	1,169,000	756,035
2003	46,077,413	39,616,337	73,386	39,689,723	4,140,715	-2,193,313	33,355,695	6,858,458	5,863,260	39,069	1,179,394	752,038
2004	48,874,677	42,297,470	74,416	42,371,886	4,376,970	-2,253,699	35,741,217	6,966,642	6,166,818	41,328	1,182,605	760,070
2005	51,108,126	44,322,615	66,575	44,389,190	4,564,410	-2,297,402	37,527,378	7,189,047	6,391,701	43,023	1,187,929	772,534
2006	54,415,453	46,266,199	63,699	46,329,898	4,707,059	-2,219,376	39,403,463	8,158,153	6,853,837	45,585	1,193,725	784,941
2007	58,242,772	48,642,733	82,256	48,724,989	4,935,180	-2,181,152	41,608,657	9,340,364	7,293,751	48,601	1,198,395	799,995
2008	60,261,478	49,129,849	64,283	49,194,132	5,110,338	-1,918,305	42,165,489	9,735,468	8,360,521	50,033	1,204,436	807,287
2009	59,560,786	48,145,185	60,367	48,205,552	5,010,106	-1,777,772	41,417,674	8,869,773	9,273,339	49,240	1,209,604	786,178
2010	60,481,870	48,759,247	60,261	48,819,508	5,015,100	-1,773,494	42,030,914	8,556,059	9,894,897	49,819	1,214,021	774,284
2011	62,987,760	50,396,069	52,264	50,448,333	4,666,397	-2,009,753	43,772,183	9,286,801	9,928,776	51,782	1,216,393	785,969
2012	65,336,242	51,708,938	68,622	51,777,560	4,796,221	-2,081,093	44,900,246	10,389,603	10,046,393	53,768	1,215,143	790,726
2013	65,503,800	52,702,879	88,550	52,791,429	5,605,720	-2,215,597	44,970,112	10,361,945	10,171,743	53,871	1,215,943	797,446
2014	68,095,064	55,058,302	76,588	55,134,890	5,826,944	-2,454,633	46,853,313	10,810,672	10,431,079	56,078	1,214,295	807,246

Personal Income and Employment by Area: Hattiesburg, MS

(Thousands of dollars, except as noted.)

Year	Personal income, total	Derivation of personal income									Per capita personal income (dollars)	Population (persons)	Total employment
		Earnings by place of work			Less: Contributions for government social insurance	Plus: Adjustment for residence	Equals: Net earnings by place of residence	Plus: Dividends, interest, and rent	Plus: Personal current transfer receipts				
		Nonfarm	Farm	Total									
1970	224,912	177,872	4,196	182,068	12,383	-135	169,550	28,421	26,941	2,733	82,290	33,601
1971	249,595	196,136	4,164	200,300	13,978	30	186,352	32,076	31,167	2,972	83,983	35,050
1972	281,820	222,248	4,590	226,838	16,506	160	210,492	35,875	35,453	3,228	87,298	37,235
1973	318,035	246,574	8,399	254,973	20,913	819	234,879	41,494	41,662	3,566	89,186	38,607
1974	360,525	276,349	6,110	282,459	24,295	907	259,071	49,876	51,578	3,963	90,966	39,612
1975	400,399	301,969	5,691	307,660	26,179	1,760	283,241	53,783	63,375	4,350	92,048	39,716
1976	454,666	347,439	6,391	353,830	30,522	2,338	325,646	58,320	70,700	4,866	93,441	41,341
1977	514,218	396,760	7,741	404,501	34,591	3,231	373,141	65,069	76,008	5,391	95,376	43,243
1978	574,454	441,628	8,334	449,962	39,365	4,919	415,516	74,248	84,690	5,934	96,810	44,696
1979	639,518	484,186	11,511	495,697	44,782	7,361	458,276	83,390	97,852	6,504	98,328	45,088
1980	718,681	531,610	5,523	537,133	49,257	8,139	496,015	106,742	115,924	7,166	100,284	45,403
1981	805,405	583,216	5,230	588,446	58,512	6,094	536,028	136,860	132,517	7,863	102,434	45,484
1982	851,189	603,918	9,239	613,157	62,413	4,036	554,780	151,776	144,633	8,173	104,145	45,036
1983	921,566	683,359	4,944	688,303	71,411	-17,489	599,403	162,123	160,040	8,624	106,863	47,090
1984	991,710	720,827	6,410	727,237	76,966	-10,875	639,396	183,668	168,646	9,210	107,674	47,377
1985	1,038,761	728,826	7,722	736,548	79,176	4,700	662,072	201,776	174,913	9,639	107,761	47,057
1986	1,088,599	776,365	7,520	783,885	85,344	-1,081	697,460	210,797	180,342	10,054	108,276	47,970
1987	1,155,196	835,196	8,302	843,498	91,608	-5,240	746,650	216,419	192,127	10,657	108,400	49,468
1988	1,227,807	894,267	10,026	904,293	102,496	-6,486	795,311	226,098	206,398	11,367	108,015	50,464
1989	1,354,395	975,631	11,126	986,757	111,165	-10,120	865,472	261,581	227,342	12,398	109,245	51,867
1990	1,434,292	1,059,397	5,456	1,064,853	124,937	-13,434	926,482	258,731	249,079	13,086	109,601	52,390
1991	1,487,763	1,082,301	6,003	1,088,304	130,550	-11,002	946,752	262,443	278,568	13,463	110,509	52,773
1992	1,610,983	1,164,715	9,012	1,173,727	138,705	-15,770	1,019,252	280,110	311,621	14,483	111,229	53,563
1993	1,722,577	1,244,182	9,715	1,253,897	147,626	-15,230	1,091,041	301,147	330,389	15,320	112,437	55,796
1994	1,863,353	1,361,135	14,191	1,375,326	162,289	-19,302	1,193,735	321,870	347,748	16,354	113,942	58,389
1995	2,002,721	1,452,480	12,874	1,465,354	172,289	-24,535	1,268,530	352,762	381,429	17,231	116,231	61,030
1996	2,118,290	1,532,432	14,408	1,546,840	179,153	-24,098	1,343,589	368,842	405,859	17,929	118,152	62,103
1997	2,278,882	1,645,936	16,490	1,662,426	191,108	-23,612	1,447,706	408,123	423,053	19,051	119,618	64,061
1998	2,395,792	1,726,545	19,188	1,745,733	200,428	-20,398	1,524,907	446,882	424,003	19,744	121,340	66,662
1999	2,497,537	1,822,063	18,320	1,840,383	210,483	-24,238	1,605,662	451,597	440,278	20,372	122,598	68,856
2000	2,625,073	1,876,010	17,361	1,893,371	214,498	-24,291	1,654,582	497,213	473,278	21,112	124,342	69,455
2001	2,838,487	2,022,521	22,356	2,044,877	227,369	-14,610	1,802,898	500,431	535,158	22,689	125,102	69,946
2002	3,001,932	2,164,883	16,300	2,181,183	241,224	-25,367	1,914,592	499,520	587,820	23,788	126,193	70,623
2003	3,011,097	2,223,757	15,930	2,239,687	248,426	-51,517	1,939,744	459,071	612,282	23,640	127,371	71,220
2004	3,190,546	2,361,361	30,854	2,392,215	265,158	-70,894	2,056,163	474,949	659,434	24,739	128,966	72,299
2005	3,382,461	2,485,433	30,504	2,515,937	277,374	-93,874	2,144,689	491,219	746,553	25,857	130,815	74,688
2006	3,709,468	2,757,734	23,778	2,781,512	314,115	-88,444	2,378,953	583,217	747,298	27,648	134,167	78,831
2007	3,898,022	2,854,845	20,853	2,875,698	328,837	-80,130	2,466,731	643,375	787,916	28,392	137,293	81,378
2008	4,107,222	2,916,566	12,912	2,929,478	334,806	-84,179	2,510,493	703,746	892,983	29,484	139,305	81,231
2009	4,182,488	2,959,757	13,801	2,973,558	341,310	-85,921	2,546,327	674,267	961,894	29,607	141,266	79,942
2010	4,277,330	2,978,459	9,992	2,988,451	343,843	-82,702	2,561,906	657,660	1,057,764	29,841	143,336	79,656
2011	4,472,906	3,043,850	-361	3,043,489	316,703	-87,960	2,638,826	724,611	1,109,469	30,784	145,298	80,464
2012	4,679,952	3,193,576	6,473	3,200,049	331,144	-103,566	2,765,339	810,446	1,104,167	31,899	146,713	81,552
2013	4,717,152	3,220,438	35,373	3,255,811	376,415	-102,709	2,776,687	813,283	1,127,182	31,906	147,846	82,381
2014	4,873,947	3,348,034	23,634	3,371,668	391,948	-113,027	2,866,693	837,291	1,169,963	32,787	148,656	83,958

Personal Income and Employment by Area: Hickory-Lenoir-Morganton, NC

(Thousands of dollars, except as noted.)

Year	Personal income, total	Earnings by place of work			Less: Contributions for government social insurance	Plus: Adjustment for residence	Equals: Net earnings by place of residence	Plus: Dividends, interest, and rent	Plus: Personal current transfer receipts	Per capita personal income (dollars)	Population (persons)	Total employment
		Nonfarm	Farm	Total								
1970	782,149	714,704	5,822	720,526	51,357	-23,299	645,870	82,908	53,371	3,426	228,324	123,300
1971	863,685	786,885	7,418	794,303	58,880	-25,289	710,134	91,340	62,211	3,684	234,432	126,489
1972	977,358	903,191	4,440	907,631	70,924	-28,145	808,562	100,586	68,210	4,065	240,460	133,573
1973	1,101,510	1,010,596	17,369	1,027,965	90,692	-30,401	906,872	113,524	81,114	4,456	247,184	139,492
1974	1,181,601	1,065,364	12,392	1,077,756	99,690	-30,479	947,587	132,051	101,963	4,700	251,418	138,142
1975	1,252,117	1,058,830	12,323	1,071,153	97,494	-26,421	947,238	144,544	160,335	4,942	253,359	129,718
1976	1,407,581	1,227,919	15,129	1,243,048	116,385	-32,898	1,093,765	156,116	157,700	5,525	254,783	137,473
1977	1,585,264	1,398,025	18,542	1,416,567	132,099	-37,418	1,247,050	174,690	163,524	6,155	257,538	143,921
1978	1,750,481	1,553,692	15,989	1,569,681	151,127	-39,404	1,379,150	196,470	174,861	6,674	262,291	148,852
1979	1,925,806	1,696,696	15,718	1,712,414	170,929	-40,524	1,500,961	223,275	201,570	7,247	265,722	150,985
1980	2,145,886	1,833,217	11,711	1,844,928	183,352	-41,273	1,620,303	279,126	246,457	7,916	271,068	151,175
1981	2,414,570	2,030,613	20,220	2,050,833	217,563	-48,853	1,784,417	349,260	280,893	8,854	272,705	153,144
1982	2,558,938	2,090,748	17,859	2,108,607	224,665	-50,454	1,833,488	399,719	325,731	9,306	274,966	150,999
1983	2,839,924	2,355,239	16,805	2,372,044	255,634	-59,258	2,057,152	438,816	343,956	10,302	275,660	156,262
1984	3,181,091	2,643,047	30,453	2,673,500	295,026	-68,086	2,310,388	509,938	360,765	11,404	278,940	164,550
1985	3,377,482	2,795,417	29,010	2,824,427	315,256	-68,824	2,440,347	549,642	387,493	11,942	282,830	167,043
1986	3,671,564	3,052,958	33,545	3,086,503	350,071	-75,569	2,660,863	596,136	414,565	12,925	284,074	172,324
1987	3,959,196	3,350,132	22,195	3,372,327	377,613	-82,674	2,912,040	618,499	428,657	13,832	286,235	178,889
1988	4,337,956	3,656,016	23,866	3,679,882	420,870	-90,264	3,168,748	703,197	466,011	14,985	289,487	185,685
1989	4,718,369	3,864,299	44,579	3,908,878	443,268	-92,380	3,373,230	825,481	519,658	16,207	291,125	189,029
1990	4,935,638	4,034,904	54,256	4,089,160	474,204	-93,121	3,521,835	842,616	571,187	16,817	293,489	191,322
1991	5,088,230	4,083,798	64,011	4,147,809	485,909	-90,836	3,571,064	852,299	664,867	17,131	297,026	187,870
1992	5,526,083	4,496,660	71,782	4,568,442	526,799	-103,945	3,937,698	868,919	719,466	18,360	300,989	193,366
1993	5,881,382	4,784,853	77,439	4,862,292	566,702	-109,407	4,186,183	906,143	789,056	19,232	305,812	198,101
1994	6,265,065	5,102,252	78,139	5,180,391	610,972	-113,139	4,456,280	989,706	819,079	20,145	310,993	201,756
1995	6,580,803	5,231,660	75,032	5,306,692	628,502	-100,314	4,577,876	1,077,877	925,050	20,789	316,556	206,522
1996	6,954,794	5,444,255	80,034	5,524,289	648,959	-101,290	4,774,040	1,172,456	1,008,298	21,605	321,905	208,510
1997	7,405,665	5,775,135	83,910	5,859,045	681,435	-97,448	5,080,162	1,260,157	1,065,346	22,612	327,516	211,062
1998	7,939,655	6,202,583	92,049	6,294,632	730,011	-99,264	5,465,357	1,361,067	1,113,231	23,853	332,861	213,035
1999	8,394,601	6,608,769	96,134	6,704,903	768,357	-96,681	5,839,865	1,382,529	1,172,207	24,839	337,955	216,406
2000	8,826,856	6,951,200	89,655	7,040,855	801,953	-99,582	6,139,320	1,431,313	1,256,223	25,716	343,247	221,415
2001	9,081,786	6,983,956	92,276	7,076,232	812,099	-85,773	6,178,360	1,477,100	1,426,326	26,176	346,952	218,040
2002	9,044,376	6,882,183	54,211	6,936,394	787,193	-67,133	6,082,068	1,414,950	1,547,358	25,967	348,299	209,957
2003	9,168,339	6,844,552	56,390	6,900,942	800,239	-41,452	6,059,251	1,482,481	1,626,607	26,235	349,472	204,676
2004	9,618,310	7,185,244	65,512	7,250,756	832,249	-21,000	6,397,507	1,484,313	1,736,490	27,385	351,224	207,684
2005	10,031,030	7,300,338	99,495	7,399,833	867,235	-22,195	6,510,403	1,629,985	1,890,642	28,324	354,159	208,443
2006	10,533,229	7,677,086	89,236	7,766,322	914,398	-22,265	6,829,659	1,634,256	2,069,314	29,464	357,492	210,855
2007	10,899,414	7,746,504	57,390	7,803,894	940,505	1,141	6,864,530	1,814,909	2,219,975	30,210	360,791	211,335
2008	11,093,776	7,663,857	22,230	7,686,087	938,619	27,264	6,774,732	1,813,533	2,505,511	30,477	364,003	205,854
2009	10,931,059	7,140,244	44,298	7,184,542	869,227	79,872	6,395,187	1,649,135	2,886,737	29,896	365,639	191,094
2010	11,077,663	7,233,117	50,764	7,283,881	859,787	90,818	6,514,912	1,562,817	2,999,934	30,324	365,305	187,349
2011	11,341,627	7,312,435	19,293	7,331,728	813,224	98,234	6,616,738	1,718,747	3,006,142	31,125	364,392	190,064
2012	11,954,805	7,665,093	38,569	7,703,662	823,231	163,772	7,044,203	1,849,392	3,061,210	32,869	363,711	190,278
2013	11,681,185	7,503,391	62,670	7,566,061	934,050	164,492	6,796,503	1,807,904	3,076,778	32,147	363,373	191,463
2014	12,210,265	7,843,749	93,065	7,936,814	972,655	232,940	7,197,099	1,876,774	3,136,392	33,647	362,896	193,489

Personal Income and Employment by Area: Hilton Head Island-Bluffton-Beaufort, SC

(Thousands of dollars, except as noted.)

Year	Personal income, total	Earnings by place of work			Less: Contributions for government social insurance	Plus: Adjustment for residence	Equals: Net earnings by place of residence	Plus: Dividends, interest, and rent	Plus: Personal current transfer receipts	Per capita personal income (dollars)	Population (persons)	Total employment
		Nonfarm	Farm	Total								
1970	266,378	199,446	4,221	203,667	12,006	4,875	196,536	56,510	13,332	4,221	63,110	34,783
1971	269,951	202,515	4,282	206,797	13,002	4,723	198,518	55,703	15,730	4,175	64,658	32,961
1972	325,804	249,229	4,614	253,843	16,252	3,977	241,568	66,020	18,216	4,739	68,755	35,347
1973	364,596	280,338	3,754	284,092	20,026	2,990	267,056	75,929	21,611	5,313	68,623	37,134
1974	392,784	293,412	5,248	298,660	22,034	3,887	280,513	84,986	27,285	5,924	66,303	36,514
1975	434,437	313,285	6,507	319,792	24,645	5,302	300,449	95,777	38,211	5,786	75,090	36,956
1976	512,119	370,366	4,328	374,694	29,810	6,658	351,542	116,522	44,055	6,560	78,071	40,575
1977	556,651	402,116	3,417	405,533	32,099	6,425	379,859	131,148	45,644	7,261	76,668	41,908
1978	619,105	440,683	2,761	443,444	35,133	5,588	413,899	154,108	51,098	7,883	78,535	43,150
1979	697,114	495,925	3,202	499,127	41,307	3,647	461,467	174,057	61,590	8,744	79,724	44,712
1980	793,990	558,399	396	558,795	46,426	2,422	514,791	203,468	75,731	9,859	80,532	46,210
1981	954,676	663,574	579	664,153	58,587	6,617	612,183	253,939	88,554	11,512	82,926	46,448
1982	1,010,957	691,186	3,044	694,230	61,621	7,792	640,401	275,278	95,278	11,820	85,527	46,606
1983	1,067,672	729,837	6	729,843	67,731	8,034	670,146	293,789	103,737	12,219	87,375	47,483
1984	1,231,429	852,155	-714	851,441	82,141	4,781	774,081	343,182	114,166	13,643	90,263	51,207
1985	1,353,400	937,486	-1,446	936,040	93,582	2,578	845,036	384,525	123,839	14,699	92,077	54,742
1986	1,475,668	1,018,348	508	1,018,856	104,259	4,820	919,417	423,200	133,051	15,667	94,192	56,562
1987	1,559,682	1,056,152	2,219	1,058,371	108,382	9,437	959,426	460,250	140,006	16,210	96,218	57,567
1988	1,675,899	1,119,537	3,149	1,122,686	119,792	15,942	1,018,836	507,507	149,556	17,028	98,423	58,897
1989	1,836,198	1,182,206	3,522	1,185,728	128,927	18,857	1,075,658	587,289	173,251	18,335	100,147	60,252
1990	2,028,767	1,280,066	3,677	1,283,743	143,710	17,002	1,157,035	677,985	193,747	19,744	102,754	61,850
1991	2,113,025	1,310,072	5,364	1,315,436	149,814	18,092	1,183,714	704,360	224,951	19,941	105,964	60,325
1992	2,332,289	1,427,274	3,751	1,431,025	163,687	17,997	1,285,335	789,067	257,887	21,305	109,469	61,579
1993	2,488,680	1,500,015	13,358	1,513,373	174,901	19,858	1,358,330	846,913	283,437	21,910	113,587	63,720
1994	2,738,083	1,644,670	9,740	1,654,410	194,233	18,982	1,479,159	942,402	316,522	23,206	117,989	66,792
1995	2,933,360	1,807,159	8,815	1,815,974	213,245	8,371	1,611,100	976,173	346,087	24,002	122,214	71,135
1996	3,226,100	1,951,612	5,183	1,956,795	227,817	18,026	1,747,004	1,096,980	382,116	25,386	127,083	74,453
1997	3,560,132	2,119,397	5,582	2,124,979	247,887	8,403	1,885,495	1,262,255	412,382	26,972	131,994	78,311
1998	3,929,710	2,327,310	6,592	2,333,902	271,146	3,797	2,066,553	1,417,029	446,128	28,887	136,035	80,959
1999	4,213,113	2,570,007	9,810	2,579,817	294,778	-12,151	2,272,888	1,459,408	480,817	30,437	138,422	84,776
2000	4,525,675	2,740,893	8,601	2,749,494	314,332	-18,866	2,416,296	1,581,964	527,415	31,642	143,027	88,416
2001	4,760,098	2,914,730	9,910	2,924,640	332,163	-35,701	2,556,776	1,602,093	601,229	32,476	146,574	89,917
2002	4,991,832	3,107,844	10,830	3,118,674	351,249	-24,184	2,743,241	1,589,654	658,937	33,192	150,392	91,775
2003	5,251,935	3,305,282	21,224	3,326,506	377,837	-16,649	2,932,020	1,604,016	715,899	34,499	152,234	94,091
2004	5,805,995	3,561,112	28,258	3,589,370	410,190	-1,125	3,178,055	1,854,448	773,492	36,796	157,787	97,494
2005	6,318,133	3,812,308	24,846	3,837,154	437,873	14,633	3,413,914	2,055,981	848,238	38,680	163,343	100,955
2006	7,109,345	4,134,851	28,626	4,163,477	485,615	31,348	3,709,210	2,457,691	942,444	41,914	169,619	105,678
2007	7,515,924	4,314,837	12,516	4,327,353	510,689	38,559	3,855,223	2,633,127	1,027,574	43,100	174,382	110,066
2008	7,682,495	4,299,711	21,161	4,320,872	510,636	42,201	3,852,437	2,638,454	1,191,604	42,676	180,019	107,568
2009	7,494,131	4,090,474	18,220	4,108,694	489,049	47,603	3,667,248	2,484,713	1,342,170	40,735	183,971	102,323
2010	7,279,472	4,031,440	21,027	4,052,467	483,479	54,318	3,623,306	2,195,381	1,460,785	38,742	187,898	99,499
2011	7,739,865	4,116,519	16,910	4,133,429	446,897	66,110	3,752,642	2,458,696	1,528,527	40,838	189,524	99,913
2012	8,168,916	4,348,453	10,458	4,358,911	467,639	65,854	3,957,126	2,641,326	1,570,464	42,161	193,755	101,929
2013	8,392,944	4,470,966	12,739	4,483,705	536,485	69,235	4,016,455	2,711,762	1,664,727	42,329	198,279	103,591
2014	8,773,590	4,659,398	10,792	4,670,190	561,876	75,570	4,183,884	2,804,986	1,784,720	43,215	203,022	105,741

Personal Income and Employment by Area: Hinesville, GA

(Thousands of dollars, except as noted.)

| Year | Personal income, total | Derivation of personal income | | | | | | | | Per capita personal income (dollars) | Population (persons) | Total employment |
| | | Earnings by place of work | | | Less: Contributions for government social insurance | Plus: Adjustment for residence | Equals: Net earnings by place of residence | Plus: Dividends, interest, and rent | Plus: Personal current transfer receipts | | | |
		Nonfarm	Farm	Total								
1970	76,062	69,946	971	70,917	3,612	-15,226	52,079	18,816	5,167	3,570	21,303	9,248
1971	80,891	73,963	1,172	75,135	4,095	-15,097	55,943	18,558	6,390	3,747	21,587	9,029
1972	88,408	79,495	1,184	80,679	4,411	-14,082	62,186	19,229	6,993	4,038	21,894	8,729
1973	95,476	83,803	1,648	85,451	4,854	-14,324	66,273	21,128	8,075	4,504	21,198	8,747
1974	105,968	92,621	1,473	94,094	5,503	-15,534	73,057	22,761	10,150	5,001	21,188	9,148
1975	124,541	103,959	1,017	104,976	6,553	-12,674	85,749	25,665	13,127	4,994	24,937	9,529
1976	172,267	188,670	734	189,404	13,903	-64,590	110,911	47,266	14,090	5,962	28,894	15,280
1977	227,639	266,469	-512	265,957	19,864	-102,702	143,391	69,583	14,665	6,770	33,625	20,349
1978	267,245	305,153	1,463	306,616	21,728	-120,894	163,994	86,793	16,458	7,026	38,038	21,446
1979	308,541	352,306	1,416	353,722	25,705	-138,673	189,344	100,167	19,030	7,838	39,364	22,895
1980	355,884	398,754	986	399,740	29,189	-148,539	222,012	110,826	23,046	8,278	42,989	24,553
1981	397,270	443,656	940	444,596	33,385	-155,600	255,611	115,008	26,651	8,554	46,444	26,045
1982	448,491	490,361	1,455	491,816	36,015	-161,760	294,041	124,868	29,582	9,236	48,561	26,948
1983	453,807	487,970	1,604	489,574	38,682	-156,940	293,952	127,476	32,379	9,524	47,647	25,701
1984	487,522	517,619	1,431	519,050	41,864	-160,034	317,152	134,276	36,094	9,744	50,034	25,809
1985	527,444	558,099	599	558,698	46,189	-168,541	343,968	144,502	38,974	10,288	51,268	26,658
1986	557,080	584,611	770	585,381	49,627	-176,892	358,862	156,675	41,543	10,736	51,890	27,196
1987	591,446	612,813	366	613,179	53,134	-178,451	381,594	166,187	43,665	10,907	54,228	28,028
1988	614,602	642,886	800	643,686	59,924	-188,297	395,465	171,696	47,441	11,018	55,780	27,945
1989	655,675	666,454	1,200	667,654	63,613	-186,747	417,294	185,074	53,307	11,388	57,578	28,135
1990	658,805	597,192	743	597,935	58,718	-109,349	429,868	166,485	62,452	11,120	59,247	24,410
1991	719,239	688,738	1,200	689,938	69,660	-161,287	458,991	188,018	72,230	11,956	60,158	25,608
1992	861,162	871,759	1,504	873,263	92,266	-243,362	537,635	238,205	85,322	13,234	65,072	29,828
1993	903,876	850,043	1,405	851,448	91,634	-193,796	566,018	244,541	93,317	13,950	64,792	29,680
1994	950,466	876,973	1,744	878,717	91,284	-198,182	589,251	259,933	101,282	14,017	67,809	30,543
1995	1,022,300	931,628	1,482	933,110	93,857	-211,597	627,656	283,031	111,613	14,931	68,468	32,025
1996	1,074,906	954,217	1,722	955,939	95,815	-201,800	658,324	294,371	122,211	15,407	69,766	32,488
1997	1,114,168	1,010,389	1,817	1,012,206	100,400	-206,502	705,304	280,722	128,142	15,588	71,477	32,627
1998	1,155,925	1,037,778	2,479	1,040,257	102,767	-227,266	710,224	313,494	132,207	16,273	71,035	32,842
1999	1,228,435	1,069,311	3,137	1,072,448	105,073	-196,377	770,998	315,189	142,248	17,039	72,095	32,845
2000	1,287,749	1,160,697	3,118	1,163,815	114,190	-245,863	803,762	327,278	156,709	17,841	72,181	34,662
2001	1,361,927	1,237,877	4,471	1,242,348	124,087	-288,673	829,588	353,960	178,379	18,932	71,939	34,863
2002	1,428,289	1,319,140	3,433	1,322,573	131,940	-335,759	854,874	368,580	204,835	19,459	73,399	34,854
2003	1,573,229	1,532,825	3,834	1,536,659	150,869	-429,224	956,566	406,249	210,414	22,080	71,252	36,264
2004	1,663,278	1,657,119	4,249	1,661,368	167,339	-483,732	1,010,297	416,345	236,636	22,293	74,609	37,991
2005	1,813,786	1,872,842	3,883	1,876,725	184,722	-587,079	1,104,924	445,460	263,402	23,742	76,395	38,119
2006	1,866,357	1,973,080	2,413	1,975,493	196,043	-634,185	1,145,265	439,895	281,197	24,819	75,199	38,198
2007	1,983,238	2,098,870	2,941	2,101,811	205,867	-697,188	1,198,756	478,966	305,516	26,065	76,089	39,492
2008	2,143,687	2,366,195	3,694	2,369,889	239,546	-835,962	1,294,381	500,286	349,020	28,439	75,379	42,087
2009	2,178,390	2,377,954	2,819	2,380,773	246,081	-854,476	1,280,216	520,298	377,876	26,944	80,848	41,738
2010	2,222,731	2,572,123	3,409	2,575,532	271,924	-1,064,056	1,239,552	558,701	424,478	28,730	77,365	43,165
2011	2,412,096	2,712,114	2,834	2,714,948	263,404	-1,113,243	1,338,301	613,218	460,577	30,017	80,358	44,849
2012	2,393,918	2,661,281	4,423	2,665,704	262,420	-1,060,823	1,342,461	603,988	447,469	29,354	81,552	44,063
2013	2,419,518	2,634,172	6,459	2,640,631	284,518	-1,029,771	1,326,342	621,097	472,079	29,982	80,698	43,737
2014	2,495,794	2,552,841	6,187	2,559,028	272,246	-912,178	1,374,604	621,678	499,512	30,322	82,311	42,552

Personal Income and Employment by Area: Homosassa Springs, FL

(Thousands of dollars, except as noted.)

Year	Personal income, total	Earnings by place of work			Less: Contributions for government social insurance	Plus: Adjustment for residence	Equals: Net earnings by place of residence	Plus: Dividends, interest, and rent	Plus: Personal current transfer receipts	Per capita personal income (dollars)	Population (persons)	Total employment
		Nonfarm	Farm	Total								
1970	64,139	35,187	678	35,865	2,186	-1,264	32,415	19,767	11,957	3,240	19,799	6,020
1971	77,155	41,108	795	41,903	2,741	-1,248	37,914	23,734	15,507	3,402	22,680	6,864
1972	96,244	53,601	1,015	54,616	3,804	-2,130	48,682	27,688	19,874	3,577	26,906	8,318
1973	129,877	77,686	1,403	79,089	6,375	-4,758	67,956	35,828	26,093	3,860	33,646	10,406
1974	144,858	73,705	1,064	74,769	6,439	-1,996	66,334	45,112	33,412	3,890	37,239	10,038
1975	168,704	75,565	1,144	76,709	6,531	-1,582	68,596	51,870	48,238	4,233	39,855	9,797
1976	186,472	85,652	1,259	86,911	7,386	-1,662	77,863	58,300	50,309	4,519	41,261	10,225
1977	216,674	97,326	1,277	98,603	8,587	-745	89,271	69,786	57,617	4,769	45,432	11,298
1978	263,380	116,440	1,533	117,973	10,487	317	107,803	88,485	67,092	5,446	48,361	12,617
1979	320,983	140,764	1,520	142,284	13,412	-5	128,867	110,241	81,875	6,222	51,586	14,045
1980	398,615	171,666	1,412	173,078	16,575	-1,199	155,304	142,811	100,500	7,154	55,719	15,605
1981	486,575	209,198	669	209,867	21,753	-1,673	186,441	178,241	121,893	8,153	59,678	17,682
1982	549,105	239,616	1,306	240,922	26,216	-4,898	209,808	194,661	144,636	8,725	62,938	18,878
1983	627,155	255,507	743	256,250	27,762	1,707	230,195	228,175	168,785	9,382	66,850	19,846
1984	769,497	304,802	901	305,703	33,645	3,346	275,404	301,789	192,304	10,830	71,051	21,909
1985	910,213	381,809	223	382,032	43,101	-1,075	337,856	360,215	212,142	12,181	74,724	24,290
1986	985,607	378,149	266	378,415	44,255	10,212	344,372	407,461	233,774	12,460	79,104	25,542
1987	1,083,288	444,005	-472	443,533	50,824	13,847	406,556	424,213	252,519	13,034	83,112	26,811
1988	1,196,348	468,317	39	468,356	56,724	23,212	434,844	473,686	287,818	13,908	86,021	27,981
1989	1,359,499	520,403	242	520,645	65,526	27,166	482,285	561,406	315,808	15,172	89,607	29,039
1990	1,453,361	548,636	129	548,765	68,292	30,561	511,034	592,235	350,092	15,356	94,645	29,942
1991	1,532,421	607,442	692	608,134	75,405	32,457	565,186	569,005	398,230	15,706	97,569	30,207
1992	1,629,161	664,070	1,314	665,384	81,939	36,837	620,282	554,365	454,514	16,257	100,210	30,105
1993	1,721,515	713,128	999	714,127	87,648	43,935	670,414	567,237	483,864	16,881	101,978	31,764
1994	1,841,986	757,428	977	758,405	95,341	52,040	715,104	607,083	519,799	17,639	104,429	33,496
1995	1,920,012	780,477	617	781,094	99,307	62,356	744,143	609,766	566,103	17,847	107,581	34,117
1996	2,037,778	820,786	626	821,412	102,910	72,338	790,840	642,508	604,430	18,533	109,954	35,859
1997	2,198,414	891,330	1,288	892,618	111,376	78,135	859,377	706,881	632,156	19,634	111,972	36,610
1998	2,343,921	938,822	1,638	940,460	116,064	90,917	915,313	775,782	652,826	20,499	114,344	38,679
1999	2,507,527	1,029,578	2,965	1,032,543	123,922	99,697	1,008,318	822,342	676,867	21,499	116,634	40,314
2000	2,703,266	1,087,022	2,665	1,089,687	130,337	111,081	1,070,431	907,850	724,985	22,784	118,649	42,046
2001	2,824,122	1,166,564	2,970	1,169,534	140,120	118,432	1,147,846	890,334	785,942	23,302	121,197	43,191
2002	2,907,809	1,193,751	2,373	1,196,124	144,236	125,622	1,177,510	892,439	837,860	23,547	123,491	43,818
2003	3,067,916	1,291,479	1,717	1,293,196	155,515	141,232	1,278,913	897,140	891,863	24,307	126,215	45,415
2004	3,274,004	1,385,303	1,763	1,387,066	169,699	158,877	1,376,244	920,506	977,254	25,216	129,840	47,735
2005	3,608,143	1,563,286	1,701	1,564,987	194,129	186,251	1,557,109	973,173	1,077,861	26,969	133,791	50,555
2006	3,915,532	1,705,834	2,168	1,708,002	215,847	212,802	1,704,957	1,028,522	1,182,053	28,409	137,826	53,883
2007	4,160,675	1,712,830	1,729	1,714,559	223,172	227,592	1,718,979	1,169,448	1,272,248	29,514	140,974	54,764
2008	4,292,882	1,662,860	1,775	1,664,635	221,669	233,903	1,676,869	1,198,310	1,417,703	30,206	142,122	51,938
2009	4,196,119	1,656,672	1,884	1,658,556	225,677	211,729	1,644,608	1,026,630	1,524,881	29,680	141,381	49,865
2010	4,338,008	1,721,749	1,709	1,723,458	235,366	202,720	1,690,812	1,025,629	1,621,567	30,704	141,283	49,077
2011	4,439,627	1,700,988	1,069	1,702,057	216,156	213,347	1,699,248	1,064,697	1,675,682	31,763	139,773	49,079
2012	4,472,181	1,732,609	1,724	1,734,333	223,059	224,371	1,735,645	1,048,741	1,687,795	32,107	139,290	49,339
2013	4,618,959	1,735,922	2,402	1,738,324	248,837	235,991	1,725,478	1,165,789	1,727,692	33,198	139,134	49,384
2014	4,765,844	1,728,327	2,546	1,730,873	251,087	260,608	1,740,394	1,211,005	1,814,445	34,194	139,377	49,830

Personal Income and Employment by Area: Hot Springs, AR

(Thousands of dollars, except as noted.)

Year	Personal income, total	Earnings by place of work			Less: Contributions for government social insurance	Plus: Adjustment for residence	Equals: Net earnings by place of residence	Plus: Dividends, interest, and rent	Plus: Personal current transfer receipts	Per capita personal income (dollars)	Population (persons)	Total employment
		Nonfarm	Farm	Total								
1970	174,278	119,582	641	120,223	8,762	-1,586	109,875	38,076	26,327	3,191	54,620	23,344
1971	201,694	139,702	719	140,421	10,589	-1,726	128,106	42,893	30,695	3,526	57,207	25,542
1972	228,670	159,607	1,156	160,763	12,631	-1,451	146,681	47,451	34,538	3,862	59,206	26,849
1973	261,720	181,374	2,534	183,908	16,531	-1,699	165,678	54,445	41,597	4,266	61,347	28,786
1974	299,980	204,813	1,321	206,134	19,377	-938	185,819	64,425	49,736	4,710	63,691	29,920
1975	327,632	209,780	2,726	212,506	19,256	-2,403	190,847	73,055	63,730	5,115	64,058	27,808
1976	372,098	242,814	2,507	245,321	22,333	-948	222,040	81,464	68,594	5,661	65,728	29,099
1977	419,758	275,884	1,754	277,638	25,723	-272	251,643	94,279	73,836	6,217	67,520	30,813
1978	473,275	308,415	2,692	311,107	29,330	552	282,329	109,681	81,265	6,910	68,495	31,529
1979	527,955	338,312	2,588	340,900	33,365	760	308,295	126,428	93,232	7,539	70,026	31,939
1980	605,594	369,587	2,229	371,816	36,186	2,619	338,249	158,373	108,972	8,585	70,545	31,739
1981	681,615	391,767	2,699	394,466	41,789	1,366	354,043	199,870	127,702	9,676	70,445	31,654
1982	734,442	413,549	2,682	416,231	45,082	-3,477	367,672	226,516	140,254	10,413	70,534	31,979
1983	772,900	438,725	1,524	440,249	48,177	-276	391,796	229,371	151,733	10,817	71,455	32,719
1984	843,015	473,733	1,806	475,539	53,759	2,863	424,643	258,213	160,159	11,681	72,172	33,519
1985	902,595	498,022	1,429	499,451	57,652	2,260	444,059	287,972	170,564	12,500	72,209	34,063
1986	948,886	519,777	2,412	522,189	60,434	1,644	463,399	302,140	183,347	13,090	72,487	34,160
1987	983,748	546,948	863	547,811	63,590	1,980	486,201	303,560	193,987	13,431	73,244	34,459
1988	1,036,868	571,932	1,125	573,057	69,364	4,131	507,824	320,667	208,377	14,239	72,821	34,781
1989	1,147,714	605,536	2,193	607,729	74,205	6,233	539,757	378,755	229,202	15,680	73,195	35,525
1990	1,211,818	639,221	1,272	640,493	81,093	9,278	568,678	393,380	249,760	16,473	73,563	35,662
1991	1,278,339	683,351	1,532	684,883	86,843	6,743	604,783	390,990	282,566	17,080	74,844	36,928
1992	1,394,549	746,329	1,842	748,171	94,628	6,101	659,644	418,173	316,732	18,217	76,553	38,245
1993	1,504,755	810,554	4,640	815,194	103,034	3,773	715,933	452,627	336,195	19,152	78,568	40,364
1994	1,589,224	872,979	5,867	878,846	113,502	2,225	767,569	471,898	349,757	19,700	80,673	41,171
1995	1,687,604	939,033	7,341	946,374	121,723	472	825,123	486,321	376,160	20,577	82,015	43,164
1996	1,774,389	974,470	7,369	981,839	125,848	842	856,833	521,346	396,210	21,221	83,615	43,870
1997	1,869,037	1,020,860	8,089	1,028,949	132,075	-428	896,446	552,763	419,828	21,983	85,021	45,357
1998	1,979,588	1,101,801	7,695	1,109,496	140,596	-1,617	967,283	575,465	436,840	22,973	86,172	45,789
1999	2,014,406	1,157,992	6,923	1,164,915	147,071	-3,396	1,014,448	554,251	445,707	23,107	87,177	46,335
2000	2,109,235	1,216,521	3,928	1,220,449	153,089	-3,539	1,063,821	574,881	470,533	23,884	88,311	47,228
2001	2,172,833	1,269,769	3,438	1,273,207	156,538	-7,303	1,109,366	544,384	519,083	24,405	89,032	48,295
2002	2,196,829	1,296,523	1,614	1,298,137	160,680	5,753	1,143,210	507,673	545,946	24,510	89,630	48,046
2003	2,282,711	1,359,661	2,438	1,362,099	168,317	19,721	1,213,503	501,641	567,567	25,228	90,483	48,952
2004	2,423,045	1,429,468	3,609	1,433,077	176,298	35,041	1,291,820	531,946	599,279	26,602	91,084	50,063
2005	2,593,533	1,492,923	3,766	1,496,689	187,185	51,509	1,361,013	588,044	644,476	28,161	92,096	51,313
2006	2,815,011	1,578,882	4,432	1,583,314	198,415	70,592	1,455,491	650,055	709,465	29,922	94,077	52,845
2007	2,942,050	1,600,848	7,363	1,608,211	204,506	90,043	1,493,748	692,063	756,239	31,050	94,753	53,682
2008	3,007,214	1,624,976	5,166	1,630,142	211,375	108,641	1,527,408	645,280	834,526	31,444	95,636	52,806
2009	3,008,550	1,608,605	3,007	1,611,612	211,742	103,841	1,503,711	596,496	908,343	31,391	95,840	51,987
2010	3,052,616	1,637,185	1,700	1,638,885	215,878	105,346	1,528,353	566,854	957,409	31,746	96,156	51,147
2011	3,218,191	1,702,361	912	1,703,273	204,051	124,098	1,623,320	618,956	975,915	33,300	96,641	51,775
2012	3,388,577	1,789,819	2,158	1,791,977	208,353	130,946	1,714,570	685,728	988,279	34,993	96,837	52,158
2013	3,380,179	1,794,938	6,196	1,801,134	236,468	116,239	1,680,905	690,481	1,008,793	34,824	97,065	52,390
2014	3,524,851	1,846,770	7,257	1,854,027	244,934	128,467	1,737,560	715,661	1,071,630	36,218	97,322	52,922

Personal Income and Employment by Area: Houma-Thibodaux, LA

(Thousands of dollars, except as noted.)

Year	Personal income, total	Earnings by place of work			Less: Contributions for government social insurance	Plus: Adjustment for residence	Equals: Net earnings by place of residence	Plus: Dividends, interest, and rent	Plus: Personal current transfer receipts	Per capita personal income (dollars)	Population (persons)	Total employment
		Nonfarm	Farm	Total								
1970	420,915	329,431	9,719	339,150	21,274	29,127	347,003	44,714	29,198	2,894	145,445	50,412
1971	465,270	364,039	10,296	374,335	24,071	30,696	380,960	50,047	34,263	3,144	147,993	51,619
1972	513,363	403,422	11,561	414,983	28,022	32,705	419,666	55,115	38,582	3,391	151,395	53,708
1973	579,456	456,928	20,999	477,927	36,898	31,276	472,305	61,538	45,613	3,789	152,931	56,711
1974	681,213	526,904	34,047	560,951	43,757	35,530	552,724	75,078	53,411	4,401	154,770	59,281
1975	785,563	625,196	15,974	641,170	51,256	41,812	631,726	88,945	64,892	4,943	158,910	62,632
1976	915,510	736,448	24,000	760,448	61,058	44,659	744,049	98,080	73,381	5,625	162,751	66,030
1977	1,036,225	841,513	26,866	868,379	70,733	47,515	845,161	110,669	80,395	6,231	166,289	69,860
1978	1,220,529	1,023,575	11,096	1,034,671	88,373	57,357	1,003,655	126,415	90,459	7,194	169,656	75,915
1979	1,408,376	1,196,553	10,196	1,206,749	107,246	60,774	1,160,277	144,605	103,494	8,094	173,998	79,997
1980	1,675,742	1,404,520	7,637	1,412,157	124,425	70,115	1,357,847	192,066	125,829	9,398	178,317	84,311
1981	1,969,344	1,623,168	12,222	1,635,390	154,750	92,039	1,572,679	250,445	146,220	10,717	183,763	88,068
1982	2,082,436	1,648,758	12,443	1,661,201	160,941	101,489	1,601,749	305,926	174,761	11,055	188,371	87,004
1983	2,003,427	1,478,430	7,082	1,485,512	140,742	104,651	1,449,421	332,023	221,983	10,553	189,850	78,980
1984	2,089,806	1,529,255	1,389	1,530,644	150,224	114,555	1,494,975	368,521	226,310	11,027	189,525	79,729
1985	2,137,599	1,542,555	1,402	1,543,957	151,877	120,094	1,512,174	382,835	242,590	11,270	189,669	79,101
1986	2,018,333	1,373,742	2,912	1,376,654	131,002	113,023	1,358,675	370,644	289,014	10,698	188,665	71,653
1987	1,956,745	1,320,250	5,552	1,325,802	124,085	108,704	1,310,421	354,788	291,536	10,581	184,936	70,421
1988	2,080,406	1,406,768	8,702	1,415,470	140,681	127,022	1,401,811	379,360	299,235	11,312	183,916	71,686
1989	2,220,488	1,461,416	9,953	1,471,369	147,344	140,912	1,464,937	426,264	329,287	12,119	183,230	71,631
1990	2,427,433	1,639,859	5,470	1,645,329	170,146	161,099	1,636,282	428,628	362,523	13,275	182,852	75,007
1991	2,566,479	1,721,016	6,979	1,727,995	182,081	166,882	1,712,796	429,704	423,979	13,914	184,458	75,913
1992	2,683,726	1,744,703	9,646	1,754,349	180,380	164,524	1,738,493	444,161	501,072	14,463	185,561	73,772
1993	2,835,636	1,864,291	11,240	1,875,531	196,269	154,407	1,833,669	450,073	551,894	15,239	186,083	77,661
1994	3,039,008	1,998,011	9,383	2,007,394	215,175	158,319	1,950,538	474,097	614,373	16,245	187,077	79,935
1995	3,182,888	2,077,198	10,704	2,087,902	223,948	166,387	2,030,341	527,529	625,018	16,933	187,973	82,540
1996	3,406,471	2,264,516	8,758	2,273,274	243,695	166,144	2,195,723	569,936	640,812	17,997	189,283	86,114
1997	3,789,146	2,610,941	9,871	2,620,812	278,714	166,088	2,508,186	631,259	649,701	19,803	191,339	92,368
1998	4,009,619	2,815,889	8,719	2,824,608	301,187	170,058	2,693,479	677,429	638,711	20,704	193,664	97,225
1999	3,942,791	2,755,142	10,351	2,765,493	291,798	153,455	2,627,150	658,382	657,259	20,264	194,569	95,814
2000	4,273,082	3,017,347	9,137	3,026,484	311,862	138,281	2,852,903	737,475	682,704	21,966	194,531	98,915
2001	4,748,836	3,469,997	9,210	3,479,207	362,571	115,656	3,232,292	730,311	786,233	24,308	195,360	101,499
2002	4,832,024	3,553,040	8,239	3,561,279	375,335	102,045	3,287,989	720,605	823,430	24,566	196,692	103,268
2003	4,981,093	3,715,296	8,089	3,723,385	388,987	85,676	3,420,074	714,189	846,830	25,137	198,156	105,356
2004	5,127,110	3,825,008	8,804	3,833,812	393,369	64,913	3,505,356	683,054	938,700	25,717	199,363	105,252
2005	5,651,762	4,154,784	11,088	4,165,872	420,609	45,735	3,790,998	815,700	1,045,064	28,193	200,467	107,980
2006	6,664,258	5,001,833	28,304	5,030,137	509,103	21,300	4,542,334	1,036,505	1,085,419	32,607	204,379	116,068
2007	7,436,288	5,626,018	24,664	5,650,682	573,542	10,944	5,088,084	1,204,195	1,144,009	36,204	205,401	122,431
2008	8,311,698	6,262,747	12,004	6,274,751	621,330	-19,304	5,634,117	1,381,973	1,295,608	40,142	207,056	124,223
2009	8,198,164	6,125,458	14,664	6,140,122	610,899	-11,577	5,517,646	1,327,243	1,353,275	39,458	207,769	120,885
2010	8,410,420	6,472,002	18,598	6,490,600	631,779	-4,853	5,853,968	1,086,149	1,470,303	40,392	208,221	120,280
2011	8,560,048	6,515,626	23,241	6,538,867	565,365	13,641	5,987,143	1,097,819	1,475,086	41,031	208,626	119,098
2012	9,402,313	7,171,524	27,629	7,199,153	608,029	-46,525	6,544,599	1,379,635	1,478,079	45,018	208,856	122,489
2013	9,980,819	7,879,830	25,393	7,905,223	768,583	-160,718	6,975,922	1,468,045	1,536,852	47,536	209,963	127,153
2014	10,400,169	8,346,414	17,066	8,363,480	810,927	-213,882	7,338,671	1,526,393	1,535,105	49,209	211,348	129,835

Personal Income and Employment by Area: Houston-The Woodlands-Sugar Land, TX

(Thousands of dollars, except as noted.)

Year	Personal income, total	Derivation of personal income									Per capita personal income (dollars)	Population (persons)	Total employment
		Earnings by place of work			Less: Contributions for government social insurance	Plus: Adjustment for residence	Equals: Net earnings by place of residence	Plus: Dividends, interest, and rent	Plus: Personal current transfer receipts				
		Nonfarm	Farm	Total									
1970	9,327,716	8,138,052	28,654	8,166,706	527,413	-74,893	7,564,400	1,265,067	498,249		4,226	2,207,116	1,022,725
1971	10,231,247	8,905,616	28,463	8,934,079	594,467	-118,039	8,221,573	1,411,651	598,023		4,497	2,275,020	1,053,329
1972	11,347,481	9,913,346	32,560	9,945,906	697,119	-154,219	9,094,568	1,568,694	684,219		4,864	2,333,148	1,105,219
1973	12,856,797	11,339,615	64,053	11,403,668	931,233	-205,614	10,266,821	1,774,248	815,728		5,353	2,401,849	1,187,670
1974	15,281,661	13,517,657	60,173	13,577,830	1,140,478	-216,647	12,220,705	2,098,639	962,317		6,162	2,479,921	1,264,423
1975	18,059,336	15,979,801	60,526	16,040,327	1,320,396	-165,954	14,553,977	2,310,029	1,195,330		6,979	2,587,627	1,336,396
1976	20,698,711	18,563,694	27,670	18,591,364	1,570,081	-118,556	16,902,727	2,469,075	1,326,909		7,677	2,696,239	1,417,454
1977	23,610,909	21,431,885	67,965	21,499,850	1,816,811	-185,066	19,497,973	2,699,712	1,413,224		8,431	2,800,536	1,511,549
1978	27,948,475	25,526,190	32,374	25,558,564	2,223,125	-231,454	23,103,985	3,257,679	1,586,811		9,586	2,915,493	1,631,614
1979	32,653,908	29,907,915	67,348	29,975,263	2,726,076	-282,798	26,966,389	3,878,506	1,809,013		10,767	3,032,641	1,734,505
1980	38,236,748	34,837,265	44,589	34,881,854	3,205,119	-341,672	31,335,063	4,762,196	2,139,489		12,051	3,172,859	1,823,264
1981	45,479,851	41,401,944	37,608	41,439,552	4,104,376	-364,429	36,970,747	6,049,474	2,459,630		13,743	3,309,381	1,961,475
1982	50,328,318	45,124,092	17,728	45,141,820	4,584,155	-387,283	40,170,382	7,250,355	2,907,581		14,359	3,504,930	2,009,330
1983	51,170,072	44,707,507	43,932	44,751,439	4,497,421	-366,636	39,887,382	7,820,654	3,462,036		14,193	3,605,388	1,927,450
1984	54,566,042	47,272,487	21,480	47,293,967	4,858,734	-382,133	42,053,100	8,876,292	3,636,650		15,063	3,622,633	1,979,788
1985	57,280,586	48,948,323	91,236	49,039,559	5,058,357	-308,288	43,672,914	9,741,854	3,865,818		15,786	3,628,588	1,979,670
1986	57,143,429	48,129,909	49,160	48,179,069	4,916,134	-272,407	42,990,528	9,785,887	4,367,014		15,578	3,668,133	1,894,904
1987	57,962,219	48,761,974	42,192	48,804,166	4,881,212	-224,149	43,698,805	9,712,125	4,551,289		15,985	3,626,052	1,925,079
1988	62,584,699	52,810,662	112,518	52,923,180	5,486,534	-289,471	47,147,175	10,710,239	4,727,285		17,311	3,615,294	2,000,883
1989	68,274,442	58,001,520	87,195	58,088,715	6,026,364	-345,411	51,716,940	11,411,124	5,146,378		18,603	3,670,089	2,075,840
1990	75,483,855	64,280,987	70,910	64,351,897	6,578,636	-430,874	57,342,387	12,384,229	5,757,239		19,992	3,775,620	2,171,989
1991	79,893,958	68,273,918	95,407	68,369,325	7,166,989	-488,513	60,713,823	12,707,341	6,472,794		20,565	3,884,885	2,231,824
1992	86,694,974	73,943,851	86,891	74,030,742	7,594,965	-517,460	65,918,317	12,968,755	7,807,902		21,729	3,989,770	2,228,085
1993	90,904,066	77,484,608	80,701	77,565,309	7,899,743	-540,377	69,125,189	13,228,071	8,550,806		22,305	4,075,564	2,271,445
1994	94,892,827	80,467,476	100,474	80,567,950	8,337,143	-571,876	71,658,931	13,997,396	9,236,500		22,847	4,153,355	2,333,616
1995	102,296,403	86,004,428	109,662	86,114,090	8,851,917	-621,923	76,640,250	15,580,313	10,075,840		24,197	4,227,574	2,402,453
1996	111,401,224	94,194,439	86,489	94,280,928	9,450,816	-699,584	84,130,528	16,581,288	10,689,408		25,820	4,314,589	2,471,047
1997	123,114,018	105,308,962	103,190	105,412,152	10,346,003	-812,974	94,253,175	17,703,299	11,157,544		27,935	4,407,210	2,579,858
1998	135,915,134	117,126,746	96,725	117,223,471	11,307,121	-915,448	105,000,902	19,514,772	11,399,460		30,110	4,513,913	2,704,119
1999	143,467,269	124,718,143	119,358	124,837,501	11,888,901	-966,089	111,982,511	19,624,848	11,859,910		31,034	4,622,857	2,736,379
2000	158,381,336	137,533,163	86,636	137,619,799	12,816,838	-1,116,263	123,686,698	22,092,638	12,602,000		33,573	4,717,507	2,818,059
2001	174,192,394	153,533,073	91,010	153,624,083	13,801,898	-1,522,080	138,300,105	22,032,940	13,859,349		36,156	4,817,815	2,886,232
2002	171,346,851	150,016,550	98,439	150,114,989	13,899,141	-1,923,620	134,292,228	21,700,329	15,354,294		34,706	4,937,081	2,910,089
2003	177,632,974	154,227,887	138,678	154,366,565	14,412,146	-2,242,139	137,712,280	23,456,503	16,464,191		35,270	5,036,393	2,924,032
2004	188,844,455	164,241,312	159,954	164,401,266	15,158,652	-2,543,431	146,699,183	24,797,893	17,347,379		36,793	5,132,602	2,972,563
2005	209,838,823	178,218,273	151,227	178,369,500	16,287,651	-1,804,622	160,277,227	30,150,593	19,411,003		40,094	5,233,729	3,075,178
2006	234,583,811	198,566,772	154,638	198,721,410	17,641,730	-2,106,205	178,973,475	34,865,976	20,744,360		43,252	5,423,615	3,207,607
2007	247,328,430	208,318,087	118,292	208,436,379	19,187,844	-2,424,540	186,823,995	37,745,424	22,759,011		44,637	5,540,882	3,368,562
2008	280,129,728	232,075,425	74,541	232,149,966	20,448,987	-2,701,147	208,999,832	44,816,515	26,313,381		49,350	5,676,381	3,472,250
2009	254,588,924	208,628,406	61,399	208,689,805	20,004,302	-2,476,106	186,209,397	39,454,167	28,925,360		43,698	5,826,108	3,450,341
2010	267,524,283	218,755,635	46,853	218,802,488	20,565,006	-2,367,043	195,870,439	38,921,239	32,732,605		44,969	5,949,076	3,446,871
2011	295,695,119	241,805,921	39,274	241,845,195	19,578,353	-2,674,472	219,592,370	41,923,863	34,178,886		48,789	6,060,721	3,560,330
2012	323,933,105	261,509,709	87,118	261,596,827	20,937,136	-3,050,284	237,609,407	52,279,448	34,044,250		52,358	6,186,923	3,687,067
2013	333,437,118	274,762,685	116,933	274,879,618	25,263,336	-3,228,030	246,388,252	51,718,904	35,329,962		52,644	6,333,809	3,823,933
2014	355,790,380	295,200,428	108,824	295,309,252	27,076,014	-3,318,156	264,915,082	53,649,817	37,225,481		54,820	6,490,180	3,945,191

Personal Income and Employment by Area: Huntington-Ashland, WV-KY-OH

(Thousands of dollars, except as noted.)

Year	Personal income, total	Earnings by place of work			Less: Contributions for government social insurance	Plus: Adjustment for residence	Equals: Net earnings by place of residence	Plus: Dividends, interest, and rent	Plus: Personal current transfer receipts	Per capita personal income (dollars)	Population (persons)	Total employment
		Nonfarm	Farm	Total								
1970	1,059,483	858,618	4,535	863,153	66,999	9,329	805,483	123,505	130,495	3,169	334,330	119,730
1971	1,157,847	924,956	3,869	928,825	73,953	14,313	869,185	134,881	153,781	3,404	340,145	121,125
1972	1,242,798	980,444	5,675	986,119	81,687	22,439	926,871	145,484	170,443	3,618	343,475	120,225
1973	1,373,123	1,081,987	7,086	1,089,073	102,949	27,191	1,013,315	163,379	196,429	4,003	342,989	123,834
1974	1,546,785	1,195,269	6,952	1,202,221	117,003	41,938	1,127,156	190,919	228,710	4,491	344,384	126,438
1975	1,728,608	1,299,357	7,304	1,306,661	125,815	53,255	1,234,101	215,372	279,135	4,980	347,122	126,903
1976	1,952,728	1,494,657	6,858	1,501,515	147,512	57,908	1,411,911	237,341	303,476	5,496	355,311	131,120
1977	2,187,841	1,688,042	5,480	1,693,522	165,477	69,766	1,597,811	269,972	320,058	6,061	360,951	136,556
1978	2,457,423	1,922,081	4,395	1,926,476	194,916	82,018	1,813,578	295,214	348,631	6,739	364,651	141,485
1979	2,762,950	2,160,396	2,983	2,163,379	226,166	96,843	2,034,056	329,683	399,211	7,467	370,018	143,365
1980	3,039,255	2,271,370	1,439	2,272,809	238,617	110,845	2,145,037	405,071	489,147	8,143	373,228	141,228
1981	3,286,398	2,402,781	2,632	2,405,413	271,413	104,015	2,238,015	497,148	551,235	8,817	372,735	138,629
1982	3,429,638	2,403,818	4,214	2,408,032	280,021	122,565	2,250,576	570,243	608,819	9,248	370,867	132,782
1983	3,535,018	2,410,437	-247	2,410,190	283,358	129,430	2,256,262	605,701	673,055	9,504	371,942	129,173
1984	3,807,038	2,587,893	6,685	2,594,578	311,280	150,465	2,433,763	676,527	696,748	10,319	368,941	131,431
1985	4,010,062	2,720,918	3,597	2,724,515	331,973	166,328	2,558,870	708,196	742,996	10,970	365,559	132,535
1986	4,131,239	2,788,428	1,026	2,789,454	353,825	176,871	2,612,500	737,425	781,314	11,440	361,118	133,493
1987	4,301,201	2,950,389	-1,505	2,948,884	371,417	177,432	2,754,899	731,864	814,438	12,013	358,041	135,685
1988	4,559,264	3,171,724	-1,587	3,170,137	414,366	179,889	2,935,660	767,323	856,281	12,844	354,959	139,421
1989	4,867,055	3,347,749	447	3,348,196	441,148	187,001	3,094,049	858,390	914,616	13,769	353,470	142,984
1990	5,185,712	3,592,143	3,579	3,595,722	481,096	204,329	3,318,955	873,652	993,105	14,710	352,539	148,238
1991	5,408,731	3,700,910	5,010	3,705,920	503,021	217,783	3,420,682	879,975	1,108,074	15,242	354,853	148,269
1992	5,869,237	4,021,992	6,060	4,028,052	538,780	238,708	3,727,980	898,745	1,242,512	16,442	356,976	151,101
1993	6,072,420	4,133,538	3,146	4,136,684	571,443	262,833	3,828,074	926,282	1,318,064	16,856	360,258	152,539
1994	6,317,935	4,326,645	5,192	4,331,837	599,514	265,309	3,997,632	957,642	1,362,661	17,469	361,659	156,273
1995	6,526,679	4,367,908	1,321	4,369,229	614,519	313,311	4,068,021	1,017,672	1,440,986	17,995	362,701	159,781
1996	6,786,407	4,462,841	-24	4,462,817	631,307	350,762	4,182,272	1,089,342	1,514,793	18,694	363,025	161,222
1997	7,148,161	4,693,536	2,050	4,695,586	655,381	375,682	4,415,887	1,159,519	1,572,755	19,679	363,240	163,757
1998	7,394,391	4,834,514	679	4,835,193	681,577	381,521	4,535,137	1,235,308	1,623,946	20,384	362,749	165,780
1999	7,548,925	4,974,323	-2,956	4,971,367	701,406	401,045	4,671,006	1,196,162	1,681,757	20,836	362,305	166,935
2000	7,913,718	5,180,813	1,267	5,182,080	739,671	415,196	4,857,605	1,275,649	1,780,464	21,850	362,183	167,369
2001	8,290,321	5,365,577	-2,104	5,363,473	743,013	437,089	5,057,549	1,293,027	1,939,745	22,973	360,868	166,234
2002	8,577,962	5,552,214	-5,951	5,546,263	750,913	389,059	5,184,409	1,271,185	2,122,368	23,787	360,609	165,091
2003	8,837,332	5,795,996	-1,497	5,794,499	788,695	362,715	5,368,519	1,234,737	2,234,076	24,418	361,922	166,583
2004	9,105,254	6,094,470	-64	6,094,406	815,866	393,110	5,671,650	1,170,701	2,262,903	25,168	361,774	168,828
2005	9,408,705	6,350,335	-945	6,349,390	848,909	398,849	5,899,330	1,165,034	2,344,341	26,001	361,864	169,837
2006	10,045,278	6,737,599	-4,267	6,733,332	871,243	414,927	6,277,016	1,256,976	2,511,286	27,683	362,868	172,164
2007	10,623,551	6,991,464	-8,718	6,982,746	882,323	449,156	6,549,579	1,419,517	2,654,455	29,246	363,249	176,223
2008	11,361,167	7,363,987	-8,990	7,354,997	905,861	444,003	6,893,139	1,524,358	2,943,670	31,221	363,898	175,955
2009	11,429,055	7,257,821	-6,429	7,251,392	907,525	442,241	6,786,108	1,459,092	3,183,855	31,336	364,731	170,482
2010	11,677,983	7,404,212	-6,916	7,397,296	926,055	496,486	6,967,727	1,377,791	3,332,465	31,980	365,170	168,972
2011	12,200,084	7,676,286	-4,448	7,671,838	849,299	457,021	7,279,560	1,543,296	3,377,228	33,431	364,937	169,468
2012	12,549,339	7,927,461	-1,048	7,926,413	874,512	474,002	7,525,903	1,613,125	3,410,311	34,387	364,944	170,357
2013	12,496,192	7,982,790	444	7,983,234	982,612	442,912	7,443,534	1,588,017	3,464,641	34,312	364,189	169,691
2014	12,815,640	8,127,458	-2,094	8,125,364	1,021,033	418,065	7,522,396	1,648,177	3,645,067	35,273	363,325	170,380

Personal Income and Employment by Area: Huntsville, AL

(Thousands of dollars, except as noted.)

Year	Personal income, total	Derivation of personal income					Equals: Net earnings by place of residence	Plus: Dividends, interest, and rent	Plus: Personal current transfer receipts	Per capita personal income (dollars)	Population (persons)	Total employment
		Earnings by place of work			Less: Contributions for government social insurance	Plus: Adjustment for residence						
		Nonfarm	Farm	Total								
1970	903,116	874,715	19,625	894,340	43,608	-126,729	724,003	130,902	48,211	3,956	228,314	107,133
1971	997,241	956,321	26,234	982,555	48,042	-144,780	789,733	151,954	55,554	4,326	230,509	106,235
1972	1,081,014	1,030,177	26,466	1,056,643	55,275	-147,689	853,679	165,133	62,202	4,653	232,339	109,439
1973	1,163,615	1,088,098	35,145	1,123,243	68,262	-147,457	907,524	181,690	74,401	4,989	233,247	111,439
1974	1,253,519	1,155,823	29,060	1,184,883	76,269	-151,043	957,571	204,615	91,333	5,406	231,872	112,513
1975	1,335,683	1,207,411	21,649	1,229,060	81,735	-154,833	992,492	221,562	121,629	5,752	232,194	110,559
1976	1,480,995	1,334,492	31,163	1,365,655	95,163	-159,356	1,111,136	237,703	132,156	6,312	234,646	113,836
1977	1,619,760	1,484,503	18,543	1,503,046	108,945	-172,844	1,221,257	262,467	136,036	6,836	236,952	119,368
1978	1,821,699	1,664,409	24,866	1,689,275	125,973	-188,118	1,375,184	300,395	146,120	7,651	238,094	125,751
1979	2,009,710	1,833,668	33,993	1,867,661	144,815	-216,365	1,506,481	333,210	170,019	8,375	239,958	126,654
1980	2,221,207	2,014,573	6,819	2,021,392	157,311	-251,774	1,612,307	398,898	210,002	9,118	243,620	126,604
1981	2,494,709	2,239,428	29,027	2,268,455	190,238	-292,326	1,785,891	476,114	232,704	10,151	245,771	128,803
1982	2,732,151	2,443,534	28,965	2,472,499	212,983	-323,575	1,935,941	539,053	257,157	10,965	249,166	131,353
1983	3,013,748	2,810,015	-7,338	2,802,677	261,989	-385,174	2,155,514	578,849	279,385	11,871	253,867	139,295
1984	3,450,486	3,245,042	23,922	3,268,964	310,637	-460,531	2,497,796	657,552	295,138	13,353	258,407	149,177
1985	3,836,663	3,678,235	18,660	3,696,895	362,934	-545,988	2,787,973	730,324	318,366	14,501	264,588	158,683
1986	4,162,637	4,039,602	10,465	4,050,067	407,722	-603,504	3,038,841	786,086	337,710	15,404	270,237	166,030
1987	4,542,687	4,421,897	13,831	4,435,728	445,998	-646,456	3,343,274	854,145	345,268	16,418	276,697	174,660
1988	4,976,910	4,880,679	28,462	4,909,141	508,594	-740,804	3,659,743	950,971	366,196	17,539	283,769	182,016
1989	5,409,592	5,182,022	20,431	5,202,453	546,314	-765,763	3,890,376	1,098,364	420,852	18,680	289,588	186,585
1990	5,775,810	5,563,280	14,241	5,577,521	604,330	-830,088	4,143,103	1,167,589	465,118	19,622	294,353	191,461
1991	6,134,496	5,843,691	30,927	5,874,618	640,791	-832,721	4,401,106	1,201,265	532,125	20,309	302,052	192,008
1992	6,681,146	6,383,264	32,797	6,416,061	699,801	-918,927	4,797,333	1,278,907	604,906	21,471	311,170	195,615
1993	6,858,307	6,543,449	18,591	6,562,040	726,486	-942,097	4,893,457	1,316,552	648,298	21,366	320,998	200,042
1994	7,092,402	6,697,029	42,729	6,739,758	762,923	-986,505	4,990,330	1,424,035	678,037	21,781	325,620	196,887
1995	7,436,854	6,947,699	6,460	6,954,159	796,018	-1,037,690	5,120,451	1,575,788	740,615	22,842	325,571	200,903
1996	7,737,187	7,054,634	37,511	7,092,145	811,715	-990,292	5,290,138	1,652,894	794,155	23,623	327,532	204,454
1997	8,254,249	7,440,423	8,422	7,448,845	861,786	-949,968	5,637,091	1,780,313	836,845	24,992	330,281	209,852
1998	8,869,921	7,993,906	24,733	8,018,639	917,195	-989,945	6,111,499	1,895,283	863,139	26,357	336,527	216,793
1999	9,114,348	8,247,413	27,607	8,275,020	952,281	-1,000,222	6,322,517	1,873,583	918,248	26,841	339,572	219,065
2000	9,859,538	8,859,091	31,351	8,890,442	1,015,400	-1,060,850	6,814,192	2,042,316	1,003,030	28,664	343,972	224,649
2001	10,100,172	9,159,988	26,206	9,186,194	1,035,182	-1,173,591	6,977,421	1,994,452	1,128,299	28,986	348,453	226,403
2002	10,474,711	9,565,738	-4,569	9,561,169	1,081,678	-1,208,932	7,270,559	1,972,917	1,231,235	29,580	354,116	225,887
2003	11,183,825	10,174,289	55,434	10,229,723	1,151,650	-1,229,058	7,849,015	1,999,888	1,334,922	31,073	359,920	230,542
2004	11,957,805	10,720,779	78,074	10,798,853	1,202,532	-1,245,316	8,351,005	2,173,290	1,433,510	32,739	365,248	237,842
2005	12,926,558	11,451,646	61,649	11,513,295	1,289,117	-1,253,579	8,970,599	2,388,370	1,567,589	34,676	372,777	245,126
2006	14,078,332	12,329,119	53,739	12,382,858	1,386,638	-1,247,139	9,749,081	2,600,344	1,728,907	36,775	382,821	253,144
2007	15,041,724	12,964,522	34,662	12,999,184	1,472,417	-1,289,601	10,237,166	2,905,598	1,898,960	38,379	391,922	263,400
2008	15,966,368	13,536,226	55,494	13,591,720	1,558,205	-1,350,165	10,683,350	3,095,609	2,187,409	39,682	402,361	267,542
2009	16,019,129	13,841,239	40,801	13,882,040	1,591,643	-1,535,954	10,754,443	2,878,967	2,385,719	38,864	412,182	263,952
2010	16,862,173	14,353,547	4,079	14,357,626	1,668,393	-1,531,390	11,157,843	3,029,479	2,674,851	40,204	419,418	263,041
2011	17,709,752	14,800,318	29,837	14,830,155	1,523,697	-1,566,697	11,739,761	3,169,074	2,800,917	41,646	425,248	266,830
2012	18,154,211	15,004,654	46,507	15,051,161	1,553,829	-1,557,495	11,939,837	3,369,434	2,844,940	42,196	430,231	268,881
2013	18,239,961	15,181,442	100,116	15,281,558	1,800,135	-1,562,023	11,919,400	3,366,493	2,954,068	41,835	435,997	272,623
2014	18,992,753	15,799,448	57,282	15,856,730	1,862,470	-1,582,221	12,412,039	3,490,886	3,089,828	43,059	441,086	275,342

Personal Income and Employment by Area: Idaho Falls, ID

(Thousands of dollars, except as noted.)

Year	Personal income, total	Earnings by place of work			Less: Contributions for government social insurance	Plus: Adjustment for residence	Equals: Net earnings by place of residence	Plus: Dividends, interest, and rent	Plus: Personal current transfer receipts	Per capita personal income (dollars)	Population (persons)	Total employment
		Nonfarm	Farm	Total								
1970	246,774	198,949	24,705	223,654	14,927	-10,930	197,797	32,108	16,869	3,670	67,248	31,286
1971	266,710	213,212	23,431	236,643	16,559	-10,160	209,924	36,836	19,950	3,963	67,297	31,832
1972	301,294	241,627	26,886	268,513	19,582	-10,964	237,967	40,419	22,908	4,330	69,575	33,559
1973	348,533	266,790	44,126	310,916	24,925	-11,692	274,299	48,262	25,972	4,964	70,208	34,784
1974	406,260	303,440	57,679	361,119	29,228	-11,977	319,914	56,246	30,100	5,552	73,174	36,116
1975	437,641	348,358	34,227	382,585	33,247	-13,884	335,454	64,483	37,704	5,819	75,210	37,509
1976	494,259	409,549	27,596	437,145	39,932	-18,320	378,893	70,612	44,754	6,410	77,106	40,884
1977	546,595	469,935	20,883	490,818	46,295	-23,836	420,687	79,677	46,231	6,859	79,685	43,056
1978	610,055	536,969	21,740	558,709	53,797	-32,335	472,577	90,357	47,121	7,364	82,839	45,361
1979	659,579	584,990	15,097	600,087	61,177	-37,127	501,783	102,047	55,749	7,838	84,150	44,826
1980	743,135	628,936	31,508	660,444	65,989	-37,615	556,840	120,264	66,031	8,746	84,969	44,180
1981	814,873	668,390	40,290	708,680	74,874	-41,890	591,916	146,577	76,380	9,448	86,247	42,968
1982	852,145	687,465	38,654	726,119	78,757	-45,076	602,286	167,328	82,531	9,914	85,951	42,575
1983	917,598	742,134	50,722	792,856	85,383	-53,791	653,682	174,269	89,647	10,569	86,820	43,606
1984	998,526	817,487	41,824	859,311	96,249	-53,446	709,616	194,720	94,190	11,386	87,700	44,662
1985	1,083,120	897,870	41,031	938,901	107,543	-58,416	772,942	208,723	101,455	12,290	88,130	46,059
1986	1,128,950	949,746	40,198	989,944	114,285	-67,273	808,386	211,760	108,804	12,724	88,724	46,656
1987	1,189,333	1,003,567	46,630	1,050,197	118,797	-71,224	860,176	215,088	114,069	13,232	89,885	47,643
1988	1,267,098	1,067,672	41,180	1,108,852	125,814	-66,515	916,523	226,008	124,567	14,030	90,313	49,146
1989	1,394,744	1,140,213	62,426	1,202,639	136,728	-67,315	998,596	260,397	135,751	15,386	90,651	50,522
1990	1,510,607	1,257,492	76,906	1,334,398	162,005	-81,133	1,091,260	269,489	149,858	16,400	92,109	53,055
1991	1,578,111	1,346,496	56,415	1,402,911	176,973	-96,324	1,129,614	280,977	167,520	16,652	94,772	55,402
1992	1,712,161	1,445,583	65,525	1,511,108	187,529	-100,506	1,223,073	298,328	190,760	17,579	97,397	56,340
1993	1,813,664	1,522,635	76,074	1,598,709	197,823	-107,873	1,293,013	312,556	208,095	18,327	98,961	58,099
1994	1,877,729	1,578,980	49,431	1,628,411	209,699	-101,340	1,317,372	338,524	221,833	18,715	100,332	59,318
1995	1,957,647	1,604,234	59,956	1,664,190	217,302	-99,121	1,347,767	365,565	244,315	19,423	100,789	58,985
1996	2,017,191	1,664,355	64,420	1,728,775	224,564	-139,064	1,365,147	391,003	261,041	20,010	100,809	60,883
1997	2,107,518	1,746,668	48,598	1,795,266	234,733	-143,204	1,417,329	417,423	272,766	20,763	101,505	62,038
1998	2,246,714	1,867,836	62,775	1,930,611	248,374	-151,100	1,531,137	438,194	277,383	21,935	102,425	63,294
1999	2,379,515	1,966,855	72,907	2,039,762	258,122	-146,275	1,635,365	445,473	298,677	23,002	103,450	65,060
2000	2,545,267	2,100,310	80,334	2,180,644	274,280	-158,290	1,748,074	468,026	329,167	24,228	105,055	66,606
2001	2,730,889	2,207,134	76,805	2,283,939	264,866	-154,157	1,864,916	501,371	364,602	25,743	106,082	67,165
2002	2,868,766	2,318,631	110,192	2,428,823	277,355	-159,205	1,992,263	486,844	389,659	26,620	107,768	67,966
2003	3,052,628	2,444,968	62,898	2,507,866	293,027	-135,229	2,079,610	557,232	415,786	27,767	109,937	69,995
2004	3,296,265	2,586,323	102,721	2,689,044	308,444	-148,378	2,232,222	609,162	454,881	29,127	113,168	72,152
2005	3,565,130	2,760,143	73,181	2,833,324	330,027	-153,539	2,349,758	718,751	496,621	30,679	116,208	75,254
2006	3,923,116	3,036,250	89,803	3,126,053	364,208	-167,533	2,594,312	778,738	550,066	32,698	119,981	78,423
2007	4,269,719	3,207,450	128,607	3,336,057	386,879	-126,656	2,822,522	863,012	584,185	34,377	124,203	81,910
2008	4,512,498	3,301,149	163,057	3,464,206	406,502	-137,332	2,920,372	916,957	675,169	35,157	128,353	82,742
2009	4,319,602	3,333,993	124,472	3,458,465	410,036	-147,490	2,900,939	694,237	724,426	32,818	131,621	80,040
2010	4,413,678	3,414,949	106,194	3,521,143	434,433	-171,504	2,915,206	703,882	794,590	32,989	133,791	79,582
2011	4,741,540	3,468,208	149,546	3,617,754	393,561	-172,863	3,051,330	888,780	801,430	35,143	134,922	79,592
2012	4,933,478	3,508,163	120,802	3,628,965	395,139	-135,953	3,097,873	1,009,632	825,973	36,207	136,259	79,210
2013	4,954,804	3,589,942	144,765	3,734,707	446,309	-130,077	3,158,321	941,177	855,306	36,154	137,046	80,287
2014	5,087,873	3,686,215	124,668	3,810,883	455,505	-117,348	3,238,030	980,085	869,758	36,798	138,266	81,956

Personal Income and Employment by Area: Indianapolis-Carmel-Anderson, IN

(Thousands of dollars, except as noted.)

Year	Personal income, total	Earnings by place of work			Less: Contributions for government social insurance	Plus: Adjustment for residence	Equals: Net earnings by place of residence	Plus: Dividends, interest, and rent	Plus: Personal current transfer receipts	Per capita personal income (dollars)	Population (persons)	Total employment
		Nonfarm	Farm	Total								
1970	5,342,177	4,627,205	39,661	4,666,866	310,573	-85,025	4,271,268	716,304	354,605	4,149	1,287,512	599,216
1971	5,816,065	4,983,933	70,109	5,054,042	346,518	-95,894	4,611,630	783,260	421,175	4,488	1,295,884	600,061
1972	6,339,022	5,488,885	56,661	5,545,546	404,591	-106,142	5,034,813	838,380	465,829	4,852	1,306,519	616,990
1973	7,151,500	6,144,759	152,176	6,296,935	522,040	-121,342	5,653,553	940,138	557,809	5,453	1,311,545	646,904
1974	7,743,577	6,622,732	91,430	6,714,162	584,815	-131,204	5,998,143	1,082,226	663,208	5,864	1,320,524	656,064
1975	8,345,570	6,907,962	137,348	7,045,310	599,376	-139,152	6,306,782	1,193,465	845,323	6,330	1,318,435	637,432
1976	9,218,979	7,737,168	139,556	7,876,724	683,115	-153,932	7,039,677	1,279,137	900,165	6,973	1,322,178	654,608
1977	10,230,523	8,715,680	91,621	8,807,301	771,125	-171,824	7,864,352	1,418,076	948,095	7,706	1,327,653	676,374
1978	11,402,614	9,746,717	100,568	9,847,285	887,910	-191,740	8,767,635	1,592,339	1,042,640	8,528	1,337,003	701,877
1979	12,603,264	10,768,095	91,570	10,859,665	1,017,331	-210,525	9,631,809	1,776,605	1,194,850	9,390	1,342,252	718,694
1980	13,794,027	11,295,389	71,980	11,367,369	1,059,244	-214,859	10,093,266	2,174,685	1,526,076	10,227	1,348,738	706,615
1981	15,110,480	12,141,048	55,427	12,196,475	1,227,322	-226,591	10,742,562	2,694,515	1,673,403	11,188	1,350,644	699,352
1982	15,615,472	12,259,344	47,358	12,306,702	1,262,594	-209,215	10,834,893	2,937,802	1,842,777	11,555	1,351,396	681,888
1983	16,626,845	13,096,774	-12,281	13,084,493	1,354,195	-201,459	11,528,839	3,106,607	1,991,399	12,293	1,352,538	690,577
1984	18,470,906	14,639,405	91,586	14,730,991	1,547,881	-261,007	12,922,103	3,457,982	2,090,821	13,572	1,360,966	724,435
1985	19,840,650	15,843,410	91,139	15,934,549	1,707,527	-284,965	13,942,057	3,690,704	2,207,889	14,512	1,367,229	748,013
1986	21,166,415	17,036,644	52,965	17,089,609	1,846,264	-312,790	14,930,555	3,895,122	2,340,738	15,390	1,375,291	774,534
1987	22,610,552	18,368,924	78,028	18,446,952	1,969,893	-321,745	16,155,314	4,065,171	2,390,067	16,284	1,388,481	801,322
1988	24,458,464	19,985,621	34,077	20,019,698	2,210,830	-335,189	17,473,679	4,435,916	2,548,869	17,492	1,398,243	826,484
1989	26,760,182	21,497,129	107,608	21,604,737	2,383,424	-369,770	18,851,543	5,131,492	2,777,147	18,953	1,411,888	856,717
1990	28,679,339	22,994,874	102,593	23,097,467	2,636,286	-398,015	20,063,166	5,595,183	3,020,990	20,037	1,431,307	881,268
1991	29,931,711	24,352,162	23,006	24,375,168	2,823,502	-409,236	21,142,430	5,430,456	3,358,825	20,537	1,457,442	887,840
1992	32,436,739	26,187,539	93,135	26,280,674	3,012,846	-360,998	22,906,830	5,665,980	3,863,929	21,902	1,481,005	898,464
1993	34,402,350	27,735,848	120,286	27,856,134	3,201,071	-359,950	24,295,113	6,007,347	4,099,890	22,851	1,505,485	922,306
1994	36,797,671	29,649,910	94,716	29,744,626	3,476,898	-356,831	25,910,897	6,590,988	4,295,786	24,060	1,529,405	948,056
1995	38,498,659	30,904,913	43,899	30,948,812	3,642,371	-346,138	26,960,303	7,177,384	4,360,972	24,814	1,551,504	975,060
1996	40,754,029	32,649,968	137,691	32,787,659	3,801,790	-371,119	28,614,750	7,602,974	4,536,305	25,898	1,573,626	992,151
1997	43,075,830	34,741,850	135,600	34,877,450	4,032,520	-395,431	30,449,499	7,929,180	4,697,151	27,010	1,594,815	1,015,309
1998	47,451,116	38,335,664	82,285	38,417,949	4,339,912	-478,255	33,599,782	9,014,722	4,836,612	29,374	1,615,438	1,044,114
1999	49,941,199	41,040,497	52,780	41,093,277	4,606,669	-511,253	35,975,355	8,866,302	5,099,542	30,461	1,639,509	1,070,471
2000	54,533,851	44,633,391	99,294	44,732,685	4,924,756	-560,976	39,246,953	9,737,210	5,549,688	32,773	1,663,995	1,098,696
2001	56,601,274	46,310,062	116,763	46,426,825	5,048,065	-585,160	40,793,600	9,665,749	6,141,925	33,547	1,687,209	1,093,517
2002	57,328,325	47,150,728	55,852	47,206,580	5,161,316	-820,275	41,224,989	9,529,869	6,573,467	33,564	1,708,018	1,088,150
2003	58,642,830	48,224,117	141,683	48,365,800	5,324,304	-849,168	42,192,328	9,556,896	6,893,606	33,911	1,729,297	1,091,691
2004	61,845,170	50,900,803	233,989	51,134,792	5,626,241	-839,385	44,669,166	9,883,311	7,292,693	35,327	1,750,639	1,109,564
2005	63,882,997	52,736,252	147,368	52,883,620	5,900,436	-1,018,357	45,964,827	9,971,013	7,947,157	36,032	1,772,959	1,127,927
2006	68,511,088	55,747,457	127,293	55,874,750	6,251,814	-984,142	48,638,794	11,302,278	8,570,016	38,046	1,800,724	1,148,398
2007	70,806,286	56,970,570	161,739	57,132,309	6,446,171	-637,123	50,049,015	11,700,952	9,056,319	38,766	1,826,515	1,172,340
2008	73,616,124	58,157,488	253,371	58,410,859	6,641,477	-677,033	51,092,349	11,865,259	10,658,516	39,786	1,850,321	1,178,799
2009	71,127,120	55,623,529	269,149	55,892,678	6,454,988	-861,293	48,576,397	10,684,746	11,865,977	37,966	1,873,460	1,141,460
2010	73,139,390	57,081,131	189,542	57,270,673	6,554,517	-954,738	49,761,418	10,447,681	12,930,291	38,647	1,892,508	1,138,769
2011	77,841,647	59,822,349	285,598	60,107,947	6,048,130	-900,111	53,159,706	11,617,924	13,064,017	40,750	1,910,206	1,163,674
2012	82,058,189	63,118,971	175,556	63,294,527	6,346,014	-801,162	56,147,351	12,546,728	13,364,110	42,544	1,928,783	1,187,447
2013	83,472,732	64,903,784	719,683	65,623,467	7,474,272	-837,101	57,312,094	12,577,405	13,583,233	42,738	1,953,146	1,211,366
2014	86,769,196	67,545,174	394,527	67,939,701	7,768,935	-719,788	59,450,978	13,040,920	14,277,298	44,017	1,971,274	1,233,169

Personal Income and Employment by Area: Iowa City, IA

(Thousands of dollars, except as noted.)

Year	Personal income, total	Earnings by place of work			Less: Contributions for government social insurance	Plus: Adjustment for residence	Equals: Net earnings by place of residence	Plus: Dividends, interest, and rent	Plus: Personal current transfer receipts	Per capita personal income (dollars)	Population (persons)	Total employment
		Nonfarm	Farm	Total								
1970	343,646	253,878	28,880	282,758	18,405	-4,162	260,191	61,463	21,992	3,767	91,237	44,389
1971	372,724	280,750	25,278	306,028	21,175	-4,551	280,302	66,455	25,967	4,026	92,581	45,252
1972	407,088	297,656	35,247	332,903	23,487	-1,745	307,671	72,172	27,245	4,399	92,551	45,759
1973	472,501	333,685	55,593	389,278	30,370	-179	358,729	81,923	31,849	5,013	94,258	48,094
1974	506,211	376,164	33,921	410,085	36,076	568	374,577	94,343	37,291	5,298	95,544	50,462
1975	601,009	423,025	61,549	484,574	40,020	2,469	447,023	108,368	45,618	6,262	95,973	52,099
1976	652,666	485,217	39,319	524,536	45,784	4,361	483,113	119,157	50,396	6,607	98,784	54,408
1977	734,912	558,181	33,628	591,809	51,730	3,650	543,729	137,782	53,401	7,409	99,194	56,853
1978	848,722	631,428	60,378	691,806	61,179	4,599	635,226	154,512	58,984	8,519	99,624	59,367
1979	929,213	699,370	47,130	746,500	70,908	9,116	684,708	177,735	66,770	9,133	101,738	60,040
1980	1,011,509	765,868	19,130	784,998	77,533	11,946	719,411	213,296	78,802	9,887	102,308	61,267
1981	1,154,689	822,204	52,002	874,206	88,949	17,360	802,617	260,903	91,169	11,116	103,873	60,386
1982	1,234,380	872,700	39,792	912,492	95,657	13,652	830,487	302,240	101,653	11,790	104,697	61,469
1983	1,311,933	957,077	15,720	972,797	104,077	8,239	876,959	324,946	110,028	12,391	105,874	62,017
1984	1,461,889	1,036,216	63,644	1,099,860	115,033	5,704	990,531	357,522	113,836	13,646	107,132	64,839
1985	1,524,790	1,091,206	53,494	1,144,700	123,179	7,814	1,029,335	371,114	124,341	14,079	108,304	65,524
1986	1,603,386	1,160,876	51,982	1,212,858	134,748	6,733	1,084,843	388,501	130,042	14,707	109,024	66,717
1987	1,687,638	1,242,597	58,387	1,300,984	143,026	8,284	1,166,242	384,982	136,414	15,340	110,013	67,957
1988	1,780,489	1,368,654	28,662	1,397,316	163,850	6,126	1,239,592	395,114	145,783	15,869	112,201	70,554
1989	2,007,865	1,516,667	54,196	1,570,863	179,342	-338	1,391,183	457,193	159,489	17,619	113,962	73,114
1990	2,124,969	1,621,573	58,582	1,680,155	194,937	-1,257	1,483,961	467,332	173,676	18,285	116,212	75,272
1991	2,226,492	1,724,731	43,157	1,767,888	206,706	-5,889	1,555,293	484,656	186,543	18,979	117,311	77,243
1992	2,391,173	1,845,332	58,207	1,903,539	217,348	-6,078	1,680,113	510,818	200,242	20,021	119,436	78,669
1993	2,511,119	1,948,293	32,319	1,980,612	227,465	-10,419	1,742,728	554,529	213,862	20,747	121,037	81,316
1994	2,723,250	2,111,923	63,227	2,175,150	249,096	-19,711	1,906,343	591,183	225,724	22,125	123,084	84,043
1995	2,848,329	2,218,296	27,996	2,246,292	260,285	-24,538	1,961,469	645,617	241,243	22,835	124,733	87,281
1996	3,050,495	2,327,994	72,285	2,400,279	263,875	-28,043	2,108,361	684,326	257,808	24,267	125,704	88,742
1997	3,221,152	2,456,254	77,451	2,533,705	285,925	-29,160	2,218,620	732,383	270,149	25,353	127,050	90,147
1998	3,422,154	2,669,556	38,219	2,707,775	307,887	-27,794	2,372,094	772,724	277,336	26,668	128,325	93,836
1999	3,626,386	2,908,517	24,260	2,932,777	331,771	-36,401	2,564,605	767,253	294,528	27,811	130,392	95,286
2000	3,982,548	3,232,161	43,105	3,275,266	361,413	-52,656	2,861,197	796,843	324,508	30,131	132,173	97,751
2001	4,123,127	3,352,538	46,197	3,398,735	372,134	-72,949	2,953,652	816,385	353,090	30,630	134,610	100,398
2002	4,233,576	3,462,548	35,051	3,497,599	386,876	-99,482	3,011,241	830,931	391,404	31,116	136,056	102,601
2003	4,394,904	3,654,118	38,517	3,692,635	408,217	-128,237	3,156,181	848,389	390,334	31,879	137,863	104,109
2004	4,705,434	3,873,780	91,408	3,965,188	428,033	-164,145	3,373,010	918,752	413,672	33,575	140,149	106,027
2005	4,833,444	4,041,115	65,836	4,106,951	446,771	-193,050	3,467,130	914,775	451,539	34,122	141,650	107,863
2006	5,181,344	4,283,234	70,767	4,354,001	472,536	-217,959	3,663,506	1,020,324	497,514	36,057	143,698	110,061
2007	5,573,636	4,551,327	80,466	4,631,793	505,216	-246,462	3,880,115	1,142,996	550,525	38,142	146,129	112,906
2008	5,955,624	4,820,348	102,409	4,922,757	533,402	-282,862	4,106,493	1,189,276	659,855	40,025	148,799	114,644
2009	5,941,005	4,924,708	69,099	4,993,807	539,068	-383,403	4,071,336	1,182,367	687,302	39,200	151,556	114,590
2010	6,052,404	5,040,193	79,081	5,119,274	557,290	-409,839	4,152,145	1,152,217	748,042	39,568	152,963	114,497
2011	6,634,451	5,230,227	180,319	5,410,546	517,142	-361,228	4,532,176	1,322,779	779,496	42,649	155,560	117,615
2012	6,969,794	5,510,958	168,189	5,679,147	539,110	-383,851	4,756,186	1,422,243	791,365	43,881	158,834	119,793
2013	7,173,286	5,712,920	223,645	5,936,565	629,213	-446,002	4,861,350	1,499,983	811,953	44,326	161,829	122,206
2014	7,483,942	5,960,224	187,892	6,148,116	648,271	-412,319	5,087,526	1,540,100	856,316	45,535	164,357	123,116

Personal Income and Employment by Area: Ithaca, NY

(Thousands of dollars, except as noted.)

Year	Personal income, total	Earnings by place of work			Less: Contributions for government social insurance	Plus: Adjustment for residence	Equals: Net earnings by place of residence	Plus: Dividends, interest, and rent	Plus: Personal current transfer receipts	Per capita personal income (dollars)	Population (persons)	Total employment
		Nonfarm	Farm	Total								
1970	271,990	237,189	4,196	241,385	16,309	-20,675	204,401	45,347	22,242	3,532	77,008	31,858
1971	294,845	252,665	4,118	256,783	17,878	-20,896	218,009	49,148	27,688	3,815	77,277	32,074
1972	323,582	278,732	4,935	283,667	20,756	-23,959	238,952	53,720	30,910	4,040	80,102	33,322
1973	362,693	315,174	9,405	324,579	27,404	-28,356	268,819	59,637	34,237	4,353	83,324	35,318
1974	403,374	354,057	6,680	360,737	32,015	-33,511	295,211	67,344	40,819	4,713	85,580	37,573
1975	431,867	364,684	7,334	372,018	33,070	-34,687	304,261	72,693	54,913	5,053	85,471	36,913
1976	455,764	385,245	7,249	392,494	35,377	-35,473	321,644	76,721	57,399	5,295	86,067	37,712
1977	473,709	391,980	6,288	398,268	36,238	-34,621	327,409	85,060	61,240	5,490	86,287	38,255
1978	518,309	435,284	7,527	442,811	42,019	-38,457	362,335	90,481	65,493	5,995	86,457	39,942
1979	568,003	477,204	9,980	487,184	47,948	-43,813	395,423	101,305	71,275	6,517	87,161	41,218
1980	652,039	542,526	8,416	550,942	54,902	-51,888	444,152	124,077	83,810	7,466	87,331	41,835
1981	754,251	617,612	9,996	627,608	66,918	-57,305	503,385	155,983	94,883	8,556	88,150	43,881
1982	838,758	695,868	9,818	705,686	73,620	-66,867	565,199	169,274	104,285	9,482	88,458	45,648
1983	949,504	796,365	8,255	804,620	83,920	-78,195	642,505	192,900	114,099	10,689	88,828	48,064
1984	1,063,403	901,260	10,705	911,965	95,917	-86,570	729,478	214,096	119,829	11,938	89,080	50,756
1985	1,138,556	974,375	13,415	987,790	105,424	-96,508	785,858	225,406	127,292	12,680	89,791	52,407
1986	1,218,461	1,048,949	12,947	1,061,896	115,514	-102,547	843,835	241,106	133,520	13,586	89,687	54,502
1987	1,299,405	1,136,926	10,312	1,147,238	123,762	-111,053	912,423	251,079	135,903	14,396	90,264	55,893
1988	1,393,482	1,227,683	11,747	1,239,430	138,424	-121,930	979,076	269,854	144,552	15,165	91,888	58,258
1989	1,561,451	1,348,080	15,043	1,363,123	150,636	-133,164	1,079,323	327,166	154,962	16,743	93,262	60,237
1990	1,621,732	1,396,999	16,417	1,413,416	149,889	-141,149	1,122,378	330,506	168,848	17,208	94,241	60,340
1991	1,665,249	1,436,957	16,652	1,453,609	158,268	-150,067	1,145,274	332,234	187,741	17,477	95,283	60,526
1992	1,747,944	1,490,462	25,689	1,516,151	160,008	-156,343	1,199,800	337,145	210,999	18,268	95,685	59,647
1993	1,777,691	1,505,154	33,802	1,538,956	162,169	-164,642	1,212,145	346,210	219,336	18,494	96,122	59,660
1994	1,847,797	1,589,201	24,187	1,613,388	175,117	-181,405	1,256,866	363,629	227,302	19,166	96,409	60,253
1995	1,933,738	1,639,328	23,837	1,663,165	181,551	-193,777	1,287,837	396,093	249,808	19,962	96,870	60,082
1996	1,957,819	1,638,632	25,893	1,664,525	181,412	-196,308	1,286,805	414,712	256,302	20,331	96,298	58,651
1997	2,024,637	1,742,034	10,029	1,752,063	192,824	-216,327	1,342,912	420,862	260,863	21,043	96,216	58,558
1998	2,096,287	1,792,889	13,385	1,806,274	200,128	-236,333	1,369,813	449,770	276,704	21,828	96,036	57,840
1999	2,221,884	1,969,755	13,608	1,983,363	216,347	-275,845	1,491,171	445,410	285,303	22,988	96,656	61,373
2000	2,330,953	2,050,616	17,282	2,067,898	226,597	-291,349	1,549,952	481,459	299,542	24,128	96,608	62,330
2001	2,432,137	2,132,794	18,594	2,151,388	242,633	-300,667	1,608,088	497,446	326,603	24,956	97,458	62,274
2002	2,471,044	2,234,688	10,075	2,244,763	260,239	-324,223	1,660,301	456,044	354,699	25,156	98,227	62,599
2003	2,624,018	2,402,292	12,398	2,414,690	280,440	-352,346	1,781,904	473,892	368,222	26,492	99,049	64,100
2004	2,761,183	2,505,538	16,050	2,521,588	288,785	-368,581	1,864,222	505,149	391,812	27,742	99,531	65,495
2005	2,807,575	2,563,393	14,711	2,578,104	297,906	-378,708	1,901,490	500,030	406,055	28,236	99,433	66,208
2006	2,937,451	2,692,779	10,164	2,702,943	309,117	-396,254	1,997,572	510,342	429,537	29,477	99,651	66,241
2007	3,100,371	2,793,876	18,079	2,811,955	318,480	-410,238	2,083,237	564,510	452,624	31,032	99,910	67,216
2008	3,374,347	2,998,507	16,558	3,015,065	346,108	-435,975	2,232,982	631,634	509,731	33,615	100,383	68,125
2009	3,394,296	3,053,974	8,143	3,062,117	350,228	-458,578	2,253,311	581,655	559,330	33,442	101,497	66,655
2010	3,461,886	3,084,831	15,861	3,100,692	353,095	-456,118	2,291,479	566,794	603,613	34,031	101,726	65,962
2011	3,645,858	3,159,306	21,015	3,180,321	325,937	-461,169	2,393,215	638,368	614,275	35,721	102,066	65,504
2012	3,790,993	3,297,967	19,233	3,317,200	337,980	-492,063	2,487,157	701,098	602,738	36,790	103,044	66,211
2013	3,826,057	3,341,790	24,432	3,366,222	386,558	-472,431	2,507,233	701,149	617,675	36,659	104,368	66,713
2014	3,945,360	3,416,880	28,252	3,445,132	394,522	-467,988	2,582,622	728,193	634,545	37,686	104,691	65,510

Personal Income and Employment by Area: Jackson, MI

(Thousands of dollars, except as noted.)

Year	Personal income, total	Earnings by place of work			Less: Contributions for government social insurance	Plus: Adjustment for residence	Equals: Net earnings by place of residence	Plus: Dividends, interest, and rent	Plus: Personal current transfer receipts	Per capita personal income (dollars)	Population (persons)	Total employment
		Nonfarm	Farm	Total								
1970	582,063	481,769	6,320	488,089	34,559	7,296	460,826	70,977	50,260	4,064	143,227	58,293
1971	607,370	489,930	5,032	494,962	36,270	12,969	471,661	74,484	61,225	4,230	143,589	56,632
1972	683,240	561,285	6,598	567,883	44,160	15,431	539,154	79,624	64,462	4,732	144,372	59,352
1973	769,000	635,855	9,711	645,566	58,182	20,896	608,280	88,258	72,462	5,286	145,481	62,549
1974	824,143	673,587	3,531	677,118	63,956	21,414	634,576	100,993	88,574	5,610	146,903	62,188
1975	901,472	705,209	8,532	713,741	65,210	22,618	671,149	111,778	118,545	6,095	147,902	60,080
1976	975,324	752,318	6,588	758,906	70,800	38,505	726,611	119,935	128,778	6,568	148,498	60,290
1977	1,084,919	843,043	6,622	849,665	79,826	51,685	821,524	134,237	129,158	7,218	150,313	62,569
1978	1,223,141	964,075	4,487	968,562	93,660	64,811	939,713	147,057	136,371	8,073	151,502	65,436
1979	1,341,568	1,044,801	3,241	1,048,042	105,633	78,202	1,020,611	165,216	155,741	8,838	151,789	65,967
1980	1,429,470	1,060,360	1,934	1,062,294	105,607	81,796	1,038,483	196,727	194,260	9,432	151,554	62,760
1981	1,542,985	1,120,884	5,662	1,126,546	120,698	81,108	1,086,956	238,915	217,114	10,187	151,459	62,048
1982	1,578,403	1,100,255	3,562	1,103,817	120,194	76,737	1,060,360	270,261	247,782	10,509	150,195	58,972
1983	1,635,068	1,120,360	-6,602	1,113,758	123,429	85,220	1,075,549	293,983	265,536	11,053	147,930	57,854
1984	1,749,868	1,183,550	5,205	1,188,755	135,043	99,254	1,152,966	332,159	264,743	12,037	145,374	58,403
1985	1,827,805	1,224,558	7,805	1,232,363	142,157	114,029	1,204,235	347,696	275,874	12,640	144,602	59,140
1986	1,929,812	1,297,461	5,415	1,302,876	150,672	113,218	1,265,422	370,542	293,848	13,277	145,355	60,642
1987	2,075,034	1,438,176	11,410	1,449,586	164,651	103,120	1,388,055	383,130	303,849	14,043	147,758	62,691
1988	2,181,392	1,514,924	7,773	1,522,697	180,076	116,749	1,459,370	400,504	321,518	14,704	148,357	63,018
1989	2,365,197	1,627,457	15,571	1,643,028	191,220	112,978	1,564,786	454,883	345,528	15,893	148,816	65,309
1990	2,441,891	1,687,695	9,843	1,697,538	200,410	113,871	1,610,999	456,502	374,390	16,265	150,128	65,679
1991	2,488,269	1,700,863	5,075	1,705,938	204,988	118,894	1,619,844	447,808	420,617	16,474	151,039	64,640
1992	2,636,291	1,797,165	4,868	1,802,033	214,691	137,049	1,724,391	461,036	450,864	17,405	151,465	65,537
1993	2,785,216	1,898,161	2,106	1,900,267	228,257	142,917	1,814,927	487,101	483,188	18,270	152,445	66,378
1994	2,958,187	2,022,190	1,032	2,023,222	248,591	161,655	1,936,286	535,875	486,026	19,425	152,288	68,008
1995	3,136,309	2,139,390	1,839	2,141,229	264,250	167,270	2,044,249	583,931	508,129	20,457	153,313	70,813
1996	3,278,574	2,235,208	1,558	2,236,766	269,764	181,771	2,148,773	600,836	528,965	21,250	154,289	72,489
1997	3,452,617	2,334,079	471	2,334,550	282,426	206,312	2,258,436	637,604	556,577	22,227	155,331	73,186
1998	3,577,780	2,417,276	1,065	2,418,341	290,922	239,041	2,366,460	651,076	560,244	22,936	155,991	72,657
1999	3,811,251	2,624,850	4,601	2,629,451	314,969	260,994	2,575,476	630,167	605,608	24,262	157,085	75,459
2000	4,010,448	2,739,276	4,324	2,743,600	326,537	290,751	2,707,814	678,333	624,301	25,274	158,679	77,608
2001	4,056,467	2,790,510	880	2,791,390	321,660	233,027	2,702,757	656,675	697,035	25,389	159,772	76,246
2002	4,103,584	2,837,634	148	2,837,782	326,561	229,007	2,740,228	636,353	727,003	25,505	160,893	75,674
2003	4,142,808	2,817,432	-1,053	2,816,379	323,715	223,433	2,716,097	659,159	767,552	25,554	162,119	74,785
2004	4,288,808	2,968,911	7,146	2,976,057	342,139	234,327	2,868,245	628,602	791,961	26,451	162,140	75,828
2005	4,411,495	3,057,056	5,934	3,062,990	357,832	239,239	2,944,397	624,843	842,255	27,057	163,047	76,049
2006	4,498,291	3,087,618	8,056	3,095,674	364,044	240,029	2,971,659	619,031	907,601	27,532	163,387	74,751
2007	4,636,603	3,100,612	6,871	3,107,483	370,019	243,652	2,981,116	665,513	989,974	28,390	163,316	74,040
2008	4,760,496	3,093,955	-344	3,093,611	373,506	243,039	2,963,144	678,747	1,118,605	29,600	160,825	73,122
2009	4,681,612	2,908,253	1,724	2,909,977	354,545	214,773	2,770,205	662,270	1,249,137	29,239	160,114	69,441
2010	4,822,311	2,979,237	11,952	2,991,189	359,074	218,868	2,850,983	634,506	1,336,822	30,111	160,149	68,487
2011	5,071,452	3,129,323	27,560	3,156,883	342,423	218,792	3,033,252	702,821	1,335,379	31,760	159,678	71,567
2012	5,187,249	3,223,790	6,079	3,229,869	354,740	227,194	3,102,323	742,670	1,342,256	32,389	160,156	71,521
2013	5,353,621	3,384,705	39,087	3,423,792	417,589	196,112	3,202,315	775,466	1,375,840	33,479	159,909	73,156
2014	5,509,407	3,481,713	8,630	3,490,343	427,850	217,190	3,279,683	803,376	1,426,348	34,490	159,741	73,890

Personal Income and Employment by Area: Jackson, MS

(Thousands of dollars, except as noted.)

Year	Personal income, total	Derivation of personal income								Per capita personal income (dollars)	Population (persons)	Total employment
		Earnings by place of work			Less: Contributions for government social insurance	Plus: Adjustment for residence	Equals: Net earnings by place of residence	Plus: Dividends, interest, and rent	Plus: Personal current transfer receipts			
		Nonfarm	Farm	Total								
1970	1,166,000	943,064	50,369	993,433	63,915	-12,626	916,892	144,238	104,870	3,226	361,473	170,261
1971	1,297,227	1,042,388	57,412	1,099,800	73,056	-13,665	1,013,079	159,571	124,577	3,509	369,687	175,421
1972	1,460,362	1,179,962	64,881	1,244,843	86,602	-15,760	1,142,481	175,449	142,432	3,861	378,229	182,347
1973	1,677,568	1,353,418	90,830	1,444,248	114,495	-20,168	1,309,585	201,359	166,624	4,356	385,151	194,536
1974	1,902,935	1,531,214	76,358	1,607,572	133,895	-16,574	1,457,103	239,994	205,838	4,794	396,911	200,851
1975	2,046,716	1,617,456	44,671	1,662,127	139,323	-5,171	1,517,633	270,236	258,847	5,059	404,561	194,047
1976	2,305,549	1,808,088	74,095	1,882,183	159,022	2,227	1,725,388	289,625	290,536	5,608	411,149	198,388
1977	2,588,489	2,067,800	61,160	2,128,960	180,875	6,008	1,954,093	321,878	312,518	6,198	417,649	207,091
1978	2,966,979	2,385,476	62,119	2,447,595	214,810	17,141	2,249,926	373,281	343,772	6,946	427,123	219,759
1979	3,395,750	2,701,891	87,364	2,789,255	253,438	38,816	2,574,633	434,016	387,101	7,821	434,186	226,855
1980	3,708,180	2,937,645	26,842	2,964,487	274,623	15,673	2,705,537	540,839	461,804	8,417	440,574	225,694
1981	4,120,141	3,164,029	34,497	3,198,526	318,814	28,254	2,907,966	682,313	529,862	9,268	444,541	224,409
1982	4,339,994	3,256,054	62,076	3,318,130	335,421	20,207	3,002,916	765,279	571,799	9,683	448,195	219,440
1983	4,612,486	3,492,817	20,107	3,512,924	362,829	27,182	3,177,277	806,502	628,707	10,200	452,220	222,590
1984	5,061,545	3,834,152	86,329	3,920,481	409,134	11,193	3,522,540	890,199	648,806	11,081	456,787	230,375
1985	5,341,387	4,090,924	46,240	4,137,164	446,933	-3,036	3,687,195	970,548	683,644	11,488	464,955	234,972
1986	5,593,541	4,315,210	39,452	4,354,662	476,306	-17,941	3,860,415	1,005,187	727,939	11,959	467,741	238,293
1987	5,937,321	4,574,309	70,985	4,645,294	501,189	-25,714	4,118,391	1,045,983	772,947	12,654	469,189	241,648
1988	6,364,076	4,904,351	85,723	4,990,074	557,804	-25,270	4,407,000	1,127,569	829,507	13,579	468,678	248,098
1989	7,000,832	5,270,655	77,521	5,348,176	595,516	-31,976	4,720,684	1,374,252	905,896	14,897	469,951	253,316
1990	7,338,984	5,599,905	67,312	5,667,217	657,583	-32,844	4,976,790	1,369,143	993,051	15,496	473,615	255,177
1991	7,721,440	5,878,272	74,803	5,953,075	705,001	-39,777	5,208,297	1,396,284	1,116,859	16,170	477,502	257,780
1992	8,312,935	6,325,951	74,220	6,400,171	749,204	-42,105	5,608,862	1,450,317	1,253,756	17,231	482,440	262,586
1993	8,836,703	6,745,309	73,656	6,818,965	797,755	-50,020	5,971,190	1,513,097	1,352,416	18,146	486,974	272,370
1994	9,547,119	7,265,179	102,556	7,367,735	865,583	-57,389	6,444,763	1,647,416	1,454,940	19,369	492,911	281,002
1995	10,241,567	7,803,007	73,314	7,876,321	923,057	-69,309	6,883,955	1,775,104	1,582,508	20,559	498,145	289,786
1996	10,850,314	8,183,602	120,867	8,304,469	955,558	-79,977	7,268,934	1,899,503	1,681,877	21,474	505,267	295,891
1997	11,556,211	8,708,688	104,279	8,812,967	1,011,510	-96,987	7,704,470	2,109,145	1,742,596	22,614	511,024	302,489
1998	12,287,550	9,374,954	115,026	9,489,980	1,079,326	-108,364	8,302,290	2,236,484	1,748,776	23,734	517,713	309,693
1999	12,682,700	9,833,834	109,093	9,942,927	1,130,875	-121,325	8,690,727	2,194,952	1,797,021	24,319	521,516	313,337
2000	13,481,570	10,381,459	83,831	10,465,290	1,176,667	-139,352	9,149,271	2,391,316	1,940,983	25,614	526,339	316,472
2001	14,032,672	10,658,659	137,842	10,796,501	1,205,971	-154,303	9,436,227	2,405,735	2,190,710	26,562	528,292	317,804
2002	14,466,858	11,176,407	48,291	11,224,698	1,257,213	-230,129	9,737,356	2,366,072	2,363,430	27,248	530,930	318,334
2003	15,280,987	11,797,775	116,823	11,914,598	1,314,398	-127,004	10,473,196	2,338,379	2,469,412	28,531	535,600	321,580
2004	16,436,213	12,661,526	194,607	12,856,133	1,408,979	-45,986	11,401,168	2,394,970	2,640,075	30,317	542,144	329,941
2005	17,516,657	13,189,275	194,448	13,383,723	1,446,205	-61,321	11,876,197	2,818,538	2,821,922	31,997	547,444	332,715
2006	19,039,671	14,165,900	85,655	14,251,555	1,578,662	-94,782	12,578,111	3,454,770	3,006,790	34,190	556,877	341,284
2007	19,415,108	14,362,441	108,344	14,470,785	1,628,376	-147,173	12,695,236	3,536,142	3,183,730	34,722	559,153	347,740
2008	20,655,744	15,174,407	100,503	15,274,910	1,701,258	-176,735	13,396,917	3,619,857	3,638,970	36,766	561,812	352,483
2009	20,085,640	14,751,240	116,172	14,867,412	1,682,927	-237,144	12,947,341	3,230,172	3,908,127	35,589	564,376	347,158
2010	20,722,924	15,127,951	105,879	15,233,830	1,709,237	-217,864	13,306,729	3,161,129	4,255,066	36,426	568,905	344,609
2011	22,039,898	15,815,925	56,936	15,872,861	1,591,745	-247,828	14,033,288	3,574,612	4,431,998	38,370	574,402	351,151
2012	22,962,414	16,482,426	123,162	16,605,588	1,642,426	-227,302	14,735,860	3,811,519	4,415,035	39,803	576,899	352,503
2013	23,084,102	16,735,648	226,133	16,961,781	1,893,687	-299,367	14,768,727	3,774,035	4,541,340	39,992	577,219	358,249
2014	23,844,391	17,323,201	203,603	17,526,804	1,964,221	-320,809	15,241,774	3,887,091	4,715,526	41,284	577,564	364,147

Personal Income and Employment by Area: Jackson, TN

(Thousands of dollars, except as noted.)

Year	Personal income, total	Earnings by place of work			Less: Contributions for government social insurance	Plus: Adjustment for residence	Equals: Net earnings by place of residence	Plus: Dividends, interest, and rent	Plus: Personal current transfer receipts	Per capita personal income (dollars)	Population (persons)	Total employment
		Nonfarm	Farm	Total								
1970	269,682	209,763	13,008	222,771	14,425	1,438	209,784	29,834	30,064	2,982	90,439	41,609
1971	300,940	232,418	17,810	250,228	16,233	-897	233,098	33,743	34,099	3,260	92,319	42,190
1972	334,656	268,123	14,517	282,640	19,475	-3,653	259,512	37,648	37,496	3,528	94,860	45,340
1973	379,789	300,928	22,036	322,964	24,814	-6,349	291,801	42,966	45,022	3,972	95,609	47,469
1974	417,311	346,584	8,372	354,956	30,102	-12,374	312,480	50,221	54,610	4,323	96,538	48,962
1975	462,062	372,145	8,638	380,783	31,703	-15,640	333,440	57,903	70,719	4,732	97,641	47,350
1976	511,544	419,512	9,335	428,847	36,392	-20,579	371,876	62,138	77,530	5,190	98,570	48,158
1977	567,541	478,164	8,000	486,164	41,703	-28,119	416,342	69,928	81,271	5,700	99,563	49,487
1978	627,251	528,657	10,746	539,403	46,912	-32,102	460,389	78,910	87,952	6,300	99,563	49,960
1979	681,821	580,054	5,172	585,226	53,566	-39,450	492,210	88,819	100,792	6,740	101,162	50,542
1980	735,883	606,945	-3,475	603,470	56,056	-46,035	501,379	111,400	123,104	7,189	102,369	49,086
1981	808,742	637,095	4,408	641,503	62,639	-44,754	534,110	137,242	137,390	7,868	102,788	47,615
1982	856,883	644,824	4,601	649,425	64,169	-44,748	540,508	165,739	150,636	8,341	102,728	46,149
1983	920,692	711,503	-7,837	703,666	71,432	-47,525	584,709	174,995	160,988	9,002	102,276	47,546
1984	1,043,701	803,180	12,393	815,573	84,022	-52,595	678,956	198,908	165,837	10,151	102,820	51,276
1985	1,099,103	850,662	1,621	852,283	90,239	-53,910	708,134	213,911	177,058	10,586	103,826	51,084
1986	1,176,443	920,402	4,848	925,250	99,596	-59,692	765,962	219,969	190,512	11,351	103,639	52,206
1987	1,276,448	986,380	30,992	1,017,372	105,690	-60,841	850,841	224,598	201,009	12,337	103,462	53,337
1988	1,375,282	1,072,535	24,912	1,097,447	118,913	-60,437	918,097	242,418	214,767	13,263	103,695	55,784
1989	1,473,334	1,172,370	19,309	1,191,679	131,705	-71,129	988,845	251,729	232,760	14,177	103,923	58,447
1990	1,599,843	1,272,638	16,924	1,289,562	143,303	-81,376	1,064,883	282,187	252,773	15,297	104,582	59,632
1991	1,677,063	1,333,485	27,594	1,361,079	152,483	-86,282	1,122,314	273,676	281,073	15,803	106,123	60,230
1992	1,863,615	1,500,795	40,605	1,541,400	168,540	-101,749	1,271,111	277,827	314,677	17,279	107,853	63,184
1993	1,962,108	1,598,987	27,732	1,626,719	180,258	-113,082	1,333,379	286,975	341,754	17,872	109,784	65,375
1994	2,131,006	1,755,131	45,076	1,800,207	200,519	-130,964	1,468,724	303,675	358,607	19,111	111,509	69,405
1995	2,255,430	1,866,723	29,647	1,896,370	213,596	-144,975	1,537,799	320,198	397,433	19,857	113,582	71,076
1996	2,384,462	1,971,124	37,090	2,008,214	221,727	-160,159	1,626,328	343,488	414,646	20,680	115,301	71,865
1997	2,552,895	2,167,455	25,704	2,193,159	242,154	-189,621	1,761,384	360,759	430,752	21,827	116,961	75,450
1998	2,770,152	2,393,747	9,550	2,403,297	257,982	-213,448	1,931,867	390,497	447,788	23,276	119,013	77,328
1999	2,895,577	2,539,154	2,557	2,541,711	273,624	-236,420	2,031,667	398,366	465,544	23,962	120,842	79,327
2000	3,132,554	2,736,266	19,311	2,755,577	288,075	-260,191	2,207,311	421,345	503,898	25,647	122,142	80,805
2001	3,110,455	2,672,279	14,380	2,686,659	287,320	-267,109	2,132,230	428,200	550,025	25,209	123,387	78,726
2002	3,184,097	2,763,957	-220	2,763,737	299,061	-288,936	2,175,740	410,539	597,818	25,701	123,890	77,742
2003	3,323,078	2,862,654	21,058	2,883,712	308,868	-313,488	2,261,356	420,844	640,878	26,824	123,886	78,211
2004	3,459,318	3,001,280	18,040	3,019,320	322,856	-340,454	2,356,010	426,851	676,457	27,597	125,351	79,672
2005	3,592,048	3,095,463	33,266	3,128,729	334,871	-355,286	2,438,572	428,909	724,567	28,465	126,192	80,875
2006	3,737,848	3,206,311	34,564	3,240,875	347,805	-360,649	2,532,421	442,150	763,277	29,293	127,602	81,684
2007	3,902,004	3,279,865	7,262	3,287,127	360,353	-372,176	2,554,598	502,988	844,418	30,453	128,134	83,339
2008	4,075,269	3,318,599	36,776	3,355,375	369,064	-382,690	2,603,621	538,366	933,282	31,728	128,445	82,385
2009	4,057,744	3,184,417	35,119	3,219,536	360,089	-341,479	2,517,968	533,525	1,006,251	31,415	129,164	78,631
2010	4,183,746	3,252,968	15,684	3,268,652	368,439	-357,502	2,542,711	533,530	1,107,505	32,172	130,043	78,660
2011	4,451,019	3,425,368	41,107	3,466,475	342,323	-396,166	2,727,986	594,699	1,128,334	34,291	129,803	80,639
2012	4,633,464	3,676,671	8,216	3,684,887	353,614	-442,086	2,889,187	610,941	1,133,336	35,539	130,378	82,128
2013	4,665,071	3,725,393	52,104	3,777,497	404,453	-482,413	2,890,631	618,031	1,156,409	35,688	130,718	82,582
2014	4,734,886	3,824,949	13,659	3,838,608	413,371	-507,185	2,918,052	638,046	1,178,788	36,359	130,225	83,688

Personal Income and Employment by Area: Jacksonville, FL

(Thousands of dollars, except as noted.)

Year	Personal income, total	Derivation of personal income					Equals: Net earnings by place of residence	Plus: Dividends, interest, and rent	Plus: Personal current transfer receipts	Per capita personal income (dollars)	Population (persons)	Total employment
		Earnings by place of work			Less: Contributions for government social insurance	Plus: Adjustment for residence						
		Nonfarm	Farm	Total								
1970	2,573,330	2,120,730	13,021	2,133,751	135,388	-12,212	1,986,151	409,749	177,430	4,128	623,388	295,684
1971	2,846,773	2,339,574	15,481	2,355,055	155,780	-13,826	2,185,449	452,553	208,771	4,485	634,713	301,891
1972	3,195,429	2,633,503	17,939	2,651,442	183,196	-15,425	2,452,821	496,751	245,857	4,944	646,275	313,941
1973	3,579,442	2,959,237	22,872	2,982,109	235,105	-17,618	2,729,386	555,200	294,856	5,425	659,829	332,075
1974	4,041,589	3,312,885	26,398	3,339,283	272,986	-20,794	3,045,503	652,485	343,601	5,877	687,746	345,616
1975	4,432,569	3,550,536	33,133	3,583,669	290,668	-22,642	3,270,359	721,900	440,310	6,417	690,714	341,634
1976	4,739,580	3,796,284	32,329	3,828,613	319,292	-25,005	3,484,316	760,007	495,257	6,785	698,553	340,298
1977	5,173,729	4,156,291	25,448	4,181,739	350,583	-29,534	3,801,622	837,103	535,004	7,340	704,888	349,448
1978	5,787,302	4,649,631	17,301	4,666,932	401,184	-31,287	4,234,461	967,685	585,156	8,085	715,770	368,161
1979	6,361,499	5,091,425	14,875	5,106,300	460,712	-31,643	4,613,945	1,080,069	667,485	8,814	721,782	371,167
1980	7,252,287	5,702,093	20,702	5,722,795	517,785	-32,345	5,172,665	1,294,789	784,833	9,782	741,394	381,950
1981	8,259,249	6,414,319	34,314	6,448,633	624,302	-36,238	5,788,093	1,565,869	905,287	10,933	755,420	390,199
1982	9,046,558	6,951,736	53,584	7,005,320	690,891	-24,455	6,289,974	1,744,421	1,012,163	11,773	768,427	397,586
1983	9,905,498	7,617,418	48,983	7,666,401	769,182	-31,111	6,866,108	1,932,696	1,106,694	12,645	783,354	411,897
1984	11,158,388	8,647,852	45,034	8,692,886	897,080	-35,582	7,760,224	2,229,081	1,169,083	13,876	804,178	442,276
1985	12,288,486	9,549,072	41,498	9,590,570	1,005,112	-37,083	8,548,375	2,490,896	1,249,215	14,846	827,746	470,849
1986	13,354,672	10,433,153	46,883	10,480,036	1,129,350	-32,088	9,318,598	2,709,210	1,326,864	15,652	853,211	493,439
1987	14,418,107	11,303,375	48,872	11,352,247	1,211,438	-10,603	10,130,206	2,893,595	1,394,306	16,482	874,757	503,658
1988	15,586,378	12,199,904	55,776	12,255,680	1,355,019	-4,802	10,895,859	3,162,843	1,527,676	17,387	896,417	519,933
1989	17,087,919	12,986,213	51,174	13,037,387	1,448,318	10,200	11,599,269	3,756,992	1,731,658	18,897	904,284	536,809
1990	18,392,171	13,928,260	59,205	13,987,465	1,553,226	32,359	12,466,598	4,023,988	1,901,585	19,731	932,169	555,661
1991	19,057,476	14,459,196	60,202	14,519,398	1,627,249	36,358	12,928,507	3,986,241	2,142,728	19,944	955,572	555,630
1992	20,197,453	15,379,367	56,741	15,436,108	1,733,722	44,422	13,746,808	3,985,940	2,464,705	20,658	977,699	555,070
1993	21,401,250	16,272,605	55,119	16,327,724	1,823,866	43,329	14,547,187	4,204,042	2,650,021	21,606	990,520	568,743
1994	22,579,162	17,147,088	51,594	17,198,682	1,928,865	42,214	15,312,031	4,491,291	2,775,840	22,479	1,004,478	582,196
1995	24,282,223	18,285,357	48,373	18,333,730	2,042,846	34,824	16,325,708	4,954,212	3,002,303	23,791	1,020,631	603,371
1996	26,074,204	19,646,408	54,202	19,700,610	2,176,148	20,982	17,545,444	5,354,573	3,174,187	24,777	1,052,363	630,841
1997	27,741,796	21,006,186	61,165	21,067,351	2,327,389	5,942	18,745,904	5,696,605	3,299,287	25,757	1,077,069	648,513
1998	30,150,640	22,854,005	69,637	22,923,642	2,492,595	-5,269	20,425,778	6,383,621	3,341,241	27,538	1,094,889	672,188
1999	31,476,022	23,942,485	71,522	24,014,007	2,603,613	-23	21,410,371	6,579,690	3,485,961	28,358	1,109,951	689,566
2000	34,338,108	26,257,664	71,717	26,329,381	2,810,600	-19,132	23,499,649	7,076,731	3,761,728	30,488	1,126,282	718,792
2001	35,461,534	26,904,252	85,413	26,989,665	2,942,853	-21,931	24,024,881	7,293,760	4,142,893	30,887	1,148,091	708,339
2002	36,814,317	28,140,380	72,548	28,212,928	3,073,424	-165,741	24,973,763	7,285,127	4,555,427	31,429	1,171,363	712,231
2003	39,075,349	30,229,331	62,282	30,291,613	3,280,712	-324,046	26,686,855	7,494,440	4,894,054	32,753	1,193,042	733,693
2004	42,146,347	32,259,282	72,019	32,331,301	3,511,337	-377,338	28,442,626	8,415,839	5,287,882	34,465	1,222,866	760,709
2005	45,905,445	34,617,804	71,995	34,689,799	3,766,300	-336,355	30,587,144	9,568,109	5,750,192	36,752	1,249,072	785,323
2006	50,605,687	37,438,755	61,365	37,500,120	4,138,697	-164,404	33,197,019	11,140,132	6,268,536	39,464	1,282,311	817,359
2007	52,526,342	38,348,356	63,321	38,411,677	4,267,791	-212,933	33,930,953	11,839,266	6,756,123	40,195	1,306,788	833,342
2008	53,298,906	37,655,481	57,758	37,713,239	4,256,172	-193,161	33,263,906	12,190,644	7,844,356	40,295	1,322,728	819,292
2009	50,745,076	36,111,197	47,292	36,158,489	4,140,228	-115,952	31,902,309	10,142,215	8,700,552	38,012	1,334,972	787,632
2010	52,864,767	37,029,822	52,560	37,082,382	4,234,247	-68,013	32,780,122	10,380,621	9,704,024	39,184	1,349,137	782,791
2011	55,742,248	37,642,950	34,002	37,676,952	3,897,618	-35,414	33,743,920	11,863,283	10,135,045	40,932	1,361,833	800,044
2012	58,110,532	39,427,266	33,239	39,460,505	4,088,662	-58,720	35,313,123	12,746,846	10,050,563	42,145	1,378,834	809,090
2013	58,703,318	40,460,027	39,962	40,499,989	4,705,136	-70,617	35,724,236	12,540,822	10,438,260	42,050	1,396,046	825,920
2014	61,608,676	42,365,827	39,010	42,404,837	4,930,645	-54,208	37,419,984	13,025,694	11,162,998	43,413	1,419,127	844,261

Personal Income and Employment by Area: Jacksonville, NC

(Thousands of dollars, except as noted.)

Year	Personal income, total	Earnings by place of work			Less: Contributions for government social insurance	Plus: Adjustment for residence	Equals: Net earnings by place of residence	Plus: Dividends, interest, and rent	Plus: Personal current transfer receipts	Per capita personal income (dollars)	Population (persons)	Total employment
		Nonfarm	Farm	Total								
1970	469,029	388,113	6,832	394,945	23,178	-10,641	361,126	96,085	11,818	4,572	102,582	63,781
1971	454,193	381,294	5,501	386,795	24,401	-11,203	351,191	88,927	14,075	4,504	100,831	56,615
1972	503,949	422,516	6,898	429,414	27,138	-11,986	390,290	97,489	16,170	5,323	94,669	55,778
1973	547,020	452,175	12,176	464,351	30,157	-12,831	421,363	107,303	18,354	5,870	93,193	55,913
1974	637,819	526,324	11,996	538,320	37,150	-14,711	486,459	129,229	22,131	6,619	96,362	59,332
1975	715,949	586,995	14,622	601,617	45,481	-15,508	540,628	145,394	29,927	6,351	112,734	62,166
1976	756,439	619,700	11,994	631,694	49,730	-15,680	566,284	155,698	34,457	6,562	115,272	62,032
1977	798,491	652,302	6,364	658,666	51,230	-16,899	590,537	171,238	36,716	6,861	116,382	62,822
1978	880,531	703,806	8,889	712,695	54,031	-18,126	640,538	200,452	39,541	7,433	118,455	63,952
1979	904,078	725,229	4,673	729,902	57,850	-18,343	653,709	204,334	46,035	7,990	113,156	61,681
1980	953,904	757,817	7,614	765,431	60,076	-18,936	686,419	211,140	56,345	8,403	113,515	60,235
1981	1,227,741	987,533	7,606	995,139	81,794	-17,667	895,678	266,527	65,536	10,575	116,100	62,778
1982	1,330,442	1,059,501	11,799	1,071,300	85,350	-16,683	969,267	286,715	74,460	11,191	118,881	62,899
1983	1,431,610	1,145,374	4,867	1,150,241	97,164	-17,212	1,035,865	314,053	81,692	11,525	124,216	66,943
1984	1,603,347	1,283,476	3,660	1,287,136	112,447	-16,607	1,158,082	355,892	89,373	12,497	128,297	69,653
1985	1,768,675	1,418,697	1,713	1,420,410	125,829	-17,714	1,276,867	394,562	97,246	13,274	133,240	72,992
1986	1,855,176	1,474,351	2,639	1,476,990	134,088	-15,485	1,327,417	422,406	105,353	13,429	138,143	73,307
1987	1,983,772	1,570,964	7,133	1,578,097	144,848	-15,076	1,418,173	455,383	110,216	14,053	141,166	77,154
1988	2,069,524	1,644,297	4,219	1,648,516	161,756	-12,425	1,474,335	473,212	121,977	14,503	142,695	77,449
1989	2,232,088	1,752,738	4,745	1,757,483	175,342	-11,868	1,570,273	523,333	138,482	14,963	149,174	80,413
1990	2,117,584	1,625,411	18,608	1,644,019	169,454	-1,040	1,473,525	490,995	153,064	14,108	150,098	73,735
1991	2,164,655	1,643,205	27,745	1,670,950	174,542	2,960	1,499,368	489,589	175,698	14,303	151,342	71,053
1992	2,553,416	1,964,271	24,415	1,988,686	214,924	-3,097	1,770,665	588,414	194,337	17,445	146,370	78,921
1993	2,552,779	1,914,118	32,473	1,946,591	214,637	1,370	1,733,324	602,384	217,071	17,273	147,789	79,122
1994	2,740,975	2,043,473	32,768	2,076,241	222,585	-1,756	1,851,900	656,456	232,619	18,677	146,760	80,724
1995	2,867,730	2,103,131	31,653	2,134,784	222,558	-784	1,911,442	689,782	266,506	19,474	147,258	83,029
1996	2,995,022	2,166,344	35,414	2,201,758	229,258	4,159	1,976,659	722,622	295,741	20,147	148,658	84,330
1997	3,199,053	2,300,526	35,197	2,335,723	243,953	3,939	2,095,709	791,319	312,025	21,622	147,955	86,093
1998	3,343,371	2,427,266	13,744	2,441,010	255,615	7,313	2,192,708	818,018	332,645	22,175	150,773	86,096
1999	3,524,709	2,557,648	16,338	2,573,986	268,327	7,936	2,313,595	852,567	358,547	23,556	149,628	87,806
2000	3,650,210	2,621,688	33,097	2,654,785	275,436	13,411	2,392,760	874,272	383,178	24,225	150,678	87,523
2001	3,841,458	2,734,769	35,247	2,770,016	290,067	16,849	2,496,798	916,042	428,618	25,429	151,068	87,606
2002	3,870,706	2,766,081	12,972	2,779,053	292,265	2,409	2,489,197	914,908	466,601	25,233	153,397	89,515
2003	4,263,536	3,105,741	7,035	3,112,776	327,521	-14,156	2,771,099	991,961	500,476	28,333	150,481	91,170
2004	4,755,464	3,540,112	11,429	3,551,541	375,852	-35,598	3,140,091	1,058,157	557,216	29,939	158,837	94,362
2005	5,186,185	3,884,001	26,708	3,910,709	412,260	-60,507	3,437,942	1,136,403	611,840	32,990	157,205	98,048
2006	5,463,469	4,141,521	8,633	4,150,154	450,309	-86,085	3,613,760	1,175,555	674,154	33,896	161,185	100,352
2007	6,073,321	4,623,522	22,377	4,645,899	501,959	-120,916	4,023,024	1,318,547	731,750	37,201	163,256	103,214
2008	6,850,492	5,191,958	38,301	5,230,259	561,595	-164,066	4,504,598	1,498,587	847,307	40,521	169,059	108,480
2009	7,420,484	5,722,790	34,181	5,756,971	629,753	-210,890	4,916,328	1,575,754	928,402	42,877	173,064	112,434
2010	7,954,641	6,153,210	56,677	6,209,887	666,216	-241,156	5,302,515	1,622,511	1,029,615	44,300	179,563	113,215
2011	8,190,336	6,233,224	51,980	6,285,204	625,502	-254,330	5,405,372	1,697,947	1,087,017	46,040	177,895	113,043
2012	8,325,881	6,259,142	68,466	6,327,608	636,619	-247,852	5,443,137	1,754,449	1,128,295	45,277	183,888	111,951
2013	8,192,468	6,091,934	84,658	6,176,592	678,305	-237,859	5,260,428	1,756,950	1,175,090	44,124	185,669	111,902
2014	8,354,931	6,112,257	93,988	6,206,245	669,958	-234,093	5,302,194	1,815,822	1,236,915	44,538	187,589	110,968

Personal Income and Employment by Area: Janesville-Beloit, WI

(Thousands of dollars, except as noted.)

| Year | Personal income, total | Derivation of personal income | | | | | | | | Per capita personal income (dollars) | Population (persons) | Total employment |
| | | Earnings by place of work | | | Less: Contributions for government social insurance | Plus: Adjustment for residence | Equals: Net earnings by place of residence | Plus: Dividends, interest, and rent | Plus: Personal current transfer receipts | | | |
		Nonfarm	Farm	Total								
1970	508,279	376,021	15,862	391,883	27,547	26,825	391,161	72,693	44,425	3,854	131,872	53,249
1971	553,372	406,272	18,858	425,130	30,633	26,222	420,719	78,598	54,055	4,184	132,257	53,167
1972	596,921	439,054	18,644	457,698	35,424	29,294	451,568	84,351	61,002	4,480	133,253	53,902
1973	673,934	503,258	27,163	530,421	46,955	30,945	514,411	92,637	66,886	5,007	134,603	57,505
1974	730,826	544,024	20,932	564,956	52,883	31,889	543,962	104,022	82,842	5,374	135,984	59,092
1975	787,694	564,752	24,949	589,701	53,851	30,112	565,962	114,319	107,413	5,721	137,680	58,336
1976	884,675	673,837	11,494	685,331	64,971	26,324	646,684	122,475	115,516	6,439	137,402	60,119
1977	1,000,186	777,562	22,736	800,298	74,572	24,855	750,581	135,868	113,737	7,255	137,859	62,999
1978	1,110,594	869,430	21,388	890,818	86,392	32,365	836,791	149,618	124,185	8,044	138,065	64,619
1979	1,231,902	956,752	28,106	984,858	98,137	34,002	920,723	164,827	146,352	8,811	139,809	66,458
1980	1,316,009	933,874	28,814	962,688	94,885	41,549	909,352	197,373	209,284	9,449	139,269	63,602
1981	1,463,160	1,043,333	26,676	1,070,009	113,731	40,449	996,727	241,487	224,946	10,577	138,336	64,284
1982	1,478,219	1,014,909	13,209	1,028,118	112,561	41,643	957,200	276,408	244,611	10,720	137,893	61,023
1983	1,601,437	1,145,160	-1,542	1,143,618	126,634	39,409	1,056,393	300,790	244,254	11,643	137,549	62,519
1984	1,784,248	1,280,969	12,983	1,293,952	145,659	52,741	1,201,034	333,367	249,847	12,974	137,523	65,192
1985	1,883,956	1,350,652	18,198	1,368,850	156,866	62,988	1,274,972	344,085	264,899	13,680	137,713	65,868
1986	1,954,511	1,360,366	23,452	1,383,818	156,925	85,149	1,312,042	364,813	277,656	14,209	137,555	66,699
1987	2,029,259	1,401,018	36,795	1,437,813	158,400	99,628	1,379,041	361,955	288,263	14,961	135,641	68,104
1988	2,199,737	1,583,140	16,307	1,599,447	184,089	115,226	1,530,584	375,829	293,324	16,105	136,588	70,857
1989	2,349,981	1,650,872	35,354	1,686,226	193,405	130,785	1,623,606	413,573	312,802	17,009	138,161	71,522
1990	2,488,082	1,765,788	30,483	1,796,271	214,282	140,211	1,722,200	429,333	336,549	17,790	139,859	73,269
1991	2,541,670	1,761,695	22,044	1,783,739	215,681	145,238	1,713,296	445,160	383,214	17,998	141,219	71,991
1992	2,814,123	2,029,273	31,349	2,060,622	245,808	128,430	1,943,244	465,550	405,329	19,692	142,904	75,226
1993	2,937,968	2,134,166	19,344	2,153,510	258,685	135,968	2,030,793	490,977	416,198	20,350	144,372	76,394
1994	3,115,768	2,288,397	29,048	2,317,445	277,869	152,038	2,191,614	504,229	419,925	21,344	145,982	78,980
1995	3,302,627	2,437,908	23,590	2,461,498	295,925	152,842	2,318,415	540,399	443,813	22,288	148,179	82,349
1996	3,431,493	2,503,852	34,925	2,538,777	299,104	160,081	2,399,754	572,509	459,230	22,886	149,937	82,642
1997	3,609,869	2,659,257	22,985	2,682,242	313,932	166,396	2,534,706	606,851	468,312	24,043	150,145	84,076
1998	3,790,853	2,763,458	27,132	2,790,590	323,434	185,230	2,652,386	661,738	476,729	25,134	150,827	83,547
1999	3,887,753	2,854,465	28,576	2,883,041	335,048	202,987	2,750,980	639,491	497,282	25,655	151,541	84,545
2000	4,056,769	2,928,031	21,468	2,949,499	340,704	226,373	2,835,168	676,608	544,993	26,608	152,464	84,802
2001	4,149,594	2,949,493	27,152	2,976,645	350,798	221,198	2,847,045	693,032	609,517	27,091	153,174	82,871
2002	4,280,318	3,071,324	19,721	3,091,045	361,170	217,890	2,947,765	677,850	654,703	27,862	153,628	82,137
2003	4,435,020	3,209,967	34,091	3,244,058	375,686	217,248	3,085,620	673,858	675,542	28,749	154,268	82,575
2004	4,532,143	3,282,488	48,847	3,331,335	384,403	213,788	3,160,720	673,717	697,706	29,111	155,685	83,629
2005	4,640,207	3,362,237	37,771	3,400,008	399,513	209,978	3,210,473	679,139	750,595	29,601	156,761	84,881
2006	5,004,024	3,644,501	31,637	3,676,138	437,712	220,122	3,458,548	754,335	791,141	31,564	158,538	86,136
2007	5,122,927	3,616,747	43,853	3,660,600	436,458	213,200	3,437,342	832,664	852,921	32,036	159,912	85,764
2008	5,184,870	3,527,164	25,098	3,552,262	430,153	200,382	3,322,491	878,300	984,079	32,275	160,647	83,203
2009	5,229,946	3,245,056	21,216	3,266,272	394,596	393,214	3,264,890	808,987	1,156,069	32,603	160,411	77,088
2010	5,345,072	3,223,655	30,754	3,254,409	396,825	369,420	3,227,004	891,974	1,226,094	33,359	160,230	76,044
2011	5,633,800	3,373,936	70,612	3,444,548	373,249	450,152	3,521,451	928,863	1,183,486	35,211	160,001	75,706
2012	5,905,089	3,602,047	36,964	3,639,011	395,697	397,670	3,640,984	1,054,879	1,209,226	36,844	160,271	77,205
2013	6,122,245	3,893,668	95,033	3,988,701	476,920	305,531	3,817,312	1,071,790	1,233,143	38,113	160,633	78,604
2014	6,240,143	3,822,066	62,442	3,884,508	478,671	454,015	3,859,852	1,109,131	1,271,160	38,713	161,188	79,862

Personal Income and Employment by Area: Jefferson City, MO

(Thousands of dollars, except as noted.)

Year	Personal income, total	Earnings by place of work			Less: Contributions for government social insurance	Plus: Adjustment for residence	Equals: Net earnings by place of residence	Plus: Dividends, interest, and rent	Plus: Personal current transfer receipts	Per capita personal income (dollars)	Population (persons)	Total employment
		Nonfarm	Farm	Total								
1970	340,482	267,715	17,635	285,350	16,832	-8,787	259,731	49,419	31,332	3,621	94,027	47,791
1971	369,536	293,896	14,825	308,721	19,137	-10,846	278,738	55,057	35,741	3,907	94,588	48,879
1972	404,741	318,467	19,926	338,393	21,652	-12,098	304,643	61,396	38,702	4,145	97,637	50,046
1973	462,256	352,754	35,029	387,783	27,702	-13,805	346,276	70,749	45,231	4,693	98,495	52,912
1974	510,394	396,343	25,828	422,171	32,363	-15,925	373,883	83,465	53,046	5,107	99,942	54,087
1975	557,014	425,295	19,171	444,466	33,845	-17,797	392,824	95,349	68,841	5,459	102,037	53,159
1976	622,971	494,857	14,904	509,761	39,834	-24,799	445,128	103,366	74,477	6,006	103,718	55,939
1977	696,826	564,493	19,949	584,442	45,955	-35,742	502,745	116,772	77,309	6,632	105,067	59,122
1978	802,879	669,199	27,687	696,886	57,196	-51,150	588,540	130,078	84,261	7,419	108,217	63,595
1979	889,907	743,388	30,741	774,129	66,049	-60,387	647,693	146,773	95,441	8,111	109,714	64,788
1980	984,481	820,969	3,830	824,799	71,753	-71,872	681,174	186,965	116,342	8,687	113,330	65,774
1981	1,119,603	900,782	16,658	917,440	85,063	-77,700	754,677	231,668	133,258	9,785	114,422	66,216
1982	1,223,328	968,077	12,608	980,685	93,981	-86,217	800,487	274,621	148,220	10,618	115,211	65,896
1983	1,312,721	1,034,184	3,568	1,037,752	100,137	-84,439	853,176	298,749	160,796	11,272	116,456	67,159
1984	1,424,322	1,087,055	19,960	1,107,015	106,525	-74,569	925,921	330,252	168,149	12,138	117,342	68,046
1985	1,477,458	1,097,210	22,559	1,119,769	107,857	-61,722	950,190	349,655	177,613	12,628	117,000	67,660
1986	1,590,275	1,199,202	21,281	1,220,483	119,473	-67,512	1,033,498	369,639	187,138	13,436	118,360	69,180
1987	1,658,743	1,263,231	23,077	1,286,308	124,791	-69,419	1,092,098	376,932	189,713	13,912	119,231	69,132
1988	1,730,295	1,344,706	15,683	1,360,389	140,417	-67,824	1,152,148	380,410	197,737	14,462	119,646	70,870
1989	1,896,860	1,451,700	23,913	1,475,613	152,246	-72,392	1,250,975	428,721	217,164	15,774	120,250	73,463
1990	1,993,617	1,563,415	21,113	1,584,528	167,205	-83,404	1,333,919	421,308	238,390	16,462	121,107	75,568
1991	2,119,243	1,647,046	18,083	1,665,129	178,157	-88,769	1,398,203	444,271	276,769	17,216	123,100	76,650
1992	2,271,369	1,778,451	17,008	1,795,459	190,252	-96,323	1,508,884	459,101	303,384	18,200	124,802	77,896
1993	2,387,974	1,862,559	16,679	1,879,238	199,701	-100,965	1,578,572	486,190	323,212	18,853	126,662	79,861
1994	2,524,889	1,989,698	4,921	1,994,619	214,580	-107,368	1,672,671	507,537	344,681	19,650	128,490	82,641
1995	2,674,821	2,126,600	-4,155	2,122,445	229,149	-119,015	1,774,281	532,705	367,835	20,395	131,148	85,679
1996	2,863,341	2,268,982	19,850	2,288,832	240,979	-130,942	1,916,911	565,904	380,526	21,432	133,601	88,188
1997	3,067,757	2,435,977	21,067	2,457,044	256,542	-145,427	2,055,075	615,362	397,320	22,606	135,707	90,574
1998	3,198,454	2,558,264	8,890	2,567,154	268,519	-153,525	2,145,110	639,086	414,258	23,301	137,268	92,080
1999	3,370,349	2,773,560	-4,585	2,768,975	287,742	-174,498	2,306,735	630,098	433,516	24,293	138,736	93,763
2000	3,569,274	2,914,403	10,394	2,924,797	300,926	-186,352	2,437,519	672,597	459,158	25,443	140,285	95,566
2001	3,770,800	3,119,224	13,394	3,132,618	316,876	-221,683	2,594,059	665,774	510,967	26,745	140,991	96,822
2002	3,808,607	3,193,359	4,581	3,197,940	323,821	-242,863	2,631,256	632,294	545,057	26,785	142,190	96,005
2003	4,006,684	3,362,849	17,890	3,380,739	339,170	-268,430	2,773,139	662,811	570,734	27,985	143,171	98,119
2004	4,261,793	3,545,497	80,343	3,625,840	354,103	-277,367	2,994,370	655,212	612,211	29,879	142,637	98,606
2005	4,395,901	3,670,673	56,064	3,726,737	370,443	-280,832	3,075,462	660,817	659,622	30,432	144,450	98,955
2006	4,606,886	3,828,371	49,402	3,877,773	384,331	-292,938	3,200,504	703,716	702,666	31,629	145,654	99,514
2007	4,889,962	3,952,031	50,997	4,003,028	400,736	-274,527	3,327,765	803,110	759,087	33,389	146,455	100,716
2008	5,161,303	4,054,502	80,525	4,135,027	417,010	-282,414	3,435,603	864,478	861,222	34,923	147,792	101,674
2009	5,169,078	4,076,247	49,233	4,125,480	416,377	-291,915	3,417,188	819,096	932,794	34,720	148,880	100,180
2010	5,250,548	4,133,389	55,645	4,189,034	422,611	-298,173	3,468,250	777,256	1,005,042	35,015	149,950	99,396
2011	5,366,577	4,105,139	78,609	4,183,748	379,397	-287,222	3,517,129	829,532	1,019,916	35,687	150,377	98,571
2012	5,546,722	4,137,945	51,577	4,189,522	378,812	-269,918	3,540,792	968,011	1,037,919	36,888	150,366	97,692
2013	5,629,253	4,260,266	94,742	4,355,008	440,521	-283,527	3,630,960	930,044	1,068,249	37,369	150,638	98,046
2014	5,802,782	4,332,583	142,596	4,475,179	451,061	-283,400	3,740,718	957,122	1,104,942	38,463	150,866	98,363

Personal Income and Employment by Area: Johnson City, TN

(Thousands of dollars, except as noted.)

| Year | Personal income, total | Derivation of personal income | | | | | | | | | | |
| | | Earnings by place of work | | | Less: Contributions for government social insurance | Plus: Adjustment for residence | Equals: Net earnings by place of residence | Plus: Dividends, interest, and rent | Plus: Personal current transfer receipts | Per capita personal income (dollars) | Population (persons) | Total employment |
		Nonfarm	Farm	Total								
1970	398,991	283,979	7,417	291,396	18,568	36,437	309,265	45,802	43,924	3,000	132,997	51,412
1971	441,788	318,051	6,578	324,629	21,424	36,637	339,842	51,620	50,326	3,239	136,401	53,402
1972	494,120	356,330	10,656	366,986	25,215	39,934	381,705	57,384	55,031	3,526	140,121	56,559
1973	559,960	410,724	13,635	424,359	33,261	40,420	431,518	64,651	63,791	3,973	140,947	60,518
1974	617,840	446,757	10,492	457,249	37,493	44,515	464,271	74,980	78,589	4,313	143,257	60,850
1975	655,699	439,019	7,022	446,041	35,459	51,467	462,049	84,994	108,656	4,506	145,524	55,431
1976	726,588	493,107	11,555	504,662	40,948	59,516	523,230	89,644	113,714	4,855	149,645	57,109
1977	800,100	547,568	9,283	556,851	45,671	71,497	582,677	99,669	117,754	5,356	149,374	59,709
1978	916,229	631,367	9,013	640,380	53,515	88,348	675,213	114,733	126,283	6,077	150,780	62,719
1979	1,030,296	708,632	4,474	713,106	63,248	102,095	751,953	133,012	145,331	6,709	153,562	64,552
1980	1,169,288	785,755	7,798	793,553	70,751	109,885	832,687	164,903	171,698	7,499	155,925	66,128
1981	1,312,428	859,240	14,605	873,845	83,424	121,606	912,027	201,554	198,847	8,305	158,024	65,685
1982	1,373,502	878,965	13,403	892,368	86,848	119,005	924,525	227,273	221,704	8,670	158,424	64,173
1983	1,468,366	946,646	4,682	951,328	94,516	124,995	981,807	247,215	239,344	9,235	158,995	64,560
1984	1,600,387	1,037,299	10,254	1,047,553	107,358	127,377	1,067,572	281,370	251,445	10,019	159,742	67,109
1985	1,688,747	1,090,698	10,028	1,100,726	114,429	142,918	1,129,215	295,107	264,425	10,593	159,422	67,936
1986	1,807,941	1,177,398	5,215	1,182,613	126,535	152,599	1,208,677	317,506	281,758	11,347	159,326	69,445
1987	1,917,508	1,272,000	7,170	1,279,170	136,009	155,785	1,298,946	322,155	296,407	12,034	159,337	72,376
1988	2,060,813	1,362,836	10,211	1,373,047	152,083	169,557	1,390,521	352,309	317,983	12,946	159,181	75,181
1989	2,229,464	1,437,761	11,320	1,449,081	162,953	193,826	1,479,954	397,160	352,350	13,984	159,430	77,238
1990	2,403,427	1,568,707	17,634	1,586,341	178,341	207,240	1,615,240	400,197	387,990	14,933	160,942	80,870
1991	2,530,815	1,647,709	19,679	1,667,388	190,434	208,683	1,685,637	407,624	437,554	15,519	163,079	80,820
1992	2,745,349	1,821,767	22,254	1,844,021	208,268	207,464	1,843,217	412,684	489,448	16,655	164,834	83,910
1993	2,871,881	1,886,507	22,440	1,908,947	215,761	230,281	1,923,467	422,078	526,336	17,187	167,100	85,376
1994	2,977,416	1,998,449	21,143	2,019,592	233,660	194,705	1,980,637	445,645	551,134	17,585	169,319	88,631
1995	3,170,266	2,107,933	14,908	2,122,841	248,129	206,541	2,081,253	485,941	603,072	18,469	171,654	91,968
1996	3,354,409	2,211,856	7,894	2,219,750	257,747	230,514	2,192,517	522,714	639,178	19,245	174,296	93,587
1997	3,554,777	2,381,066	12,082	2,393,148	273,736	219,233	2,338,645	544,899	671,233	20,100	176,853	95,673
1998	3,788,165	2,562,115	10,983	2,573,098	287,394	213,430	2,499,134	577,253	711,778	21,213	178,581	96,179
1999	3,862,526	2,675,349	7,567	2,682,916	298,795	155,212	2,539,333	583,270	739,923	21,441	180,145	97,573
2000	4,127,394	2,893,768	13,319	2,907,087	318,489	106,394	2,694,992	616,917	815,485	22,685	181,944	99,445
2001	4,285,861	2,905,369	7,002	2,912,371	325,378	178,234	2,765,227	639,392	881,242	23,525	182,187	98,124
2002	4,397,021	2,984,484	3,107	2,987,591	336,234	174,871	2,826,228	603,364	967,429	23,900	183,973	96,232
2003	4,552,968	3,100,535	3,948	3,104,483	346,876	167,150	2,924,757	615,607	1,012,604	24,473	186,040	97,206
2004	4,903,282	3,351,044	5,240	3,356,284	372,812	175,680	3,159,152	655,165	1,088,965	26,176	187,317	100,527
2005	5,103,935	3,501,766	6,739	3,508,505	392,867	186,076	3,301,714	638,986	1,163,235	26,979	189,182	102,763
2006	5,375,504	3,658,447	2,384	3,660,831	412,877	192,604	3,440,558	698,810	1,236,136	28,006	191,943	104,128
2007	5,725,323	3,800,457	-3,625	3,796,832	434,973	204,422	3,566,281	800,502	1,358,540	29,540	193,819	106,955
2008	5,982,426	3,877,855	-2,093	3,875,762	451,202	199,667	3,624,227	843,096	1,515,103	30,485	196,242	106,364
2009	5,984,214	3,831,502	6,246	3,837,748	453,223	145,572	3,530,097	835,437	1,618,680	30,269	197,698	102,171
2010	6,235,355	3,862,805	1,827	3,864,632	459,273	206,231	3,611,590	854,271	1,769,494	31,337	198,976	101,353
2011	6,594,359	4,051,408	500	4,051,908	429,594	256,998	3,879,312	901,344	1,813,703	33,006	199,794	103,631
2012	6,798,152	4,243,031	3,674	4,246,705	434,927	227,521	4,039,299	935,249	1,823,604	33,902	200,524	103,737
2013	6,809,626	4,215,637	8,623	4,224,260	488,067	251,825	3,988,018	967,820	1,853,788	33,884	200,969	101,616
2014	6,989,274	4,290,575	13,361	4,303,936	495,276	269,464	4,078,124	1,005,599	1,905,551	34,757	201,091	102,171

Personal Income and Employment by Area: Johnstown, PA

(Thousands of dollars, except as noted.)

Year	Personal income, total	Earnings by place of work			Less: Contributions for government social insurance	Plus: Adjustment for residence	Equals: Net earnings by place of residence	Plus: Dividends, interest, and rent	Plus: Personal current transfer receipts	Per capita personal income (dollars)	Population (persons)	Total employment
		Nonfarm	Farm	Total								
1970	606,634	521,845	2,913	524,758	39,131	-33,446	452,181	62,649	91,804	3,243	187,061	70,524
1971	651,431	547,900	2,272	550,172	42,709	-35,193	472,270	66,640	112,521	3,450	188,837	70,619
1972	728,397	620,787	1,235	622,022	50,029	-41,099	530,894	70,957	126,546	3,843	189,521	71,565
1973	808,792	688,392	4,001	692,393	63,793	-45,385	583,215	79,683	145,894	4,273	189,286	73,454
1974	913,903	783,250	3,920	787,170	75,704	-54,473	656,993	92,278	164,632	4,849	188,475	74,173
1975	1,049,839	889,389	3,081	892,470	83,580	-63,823	745,067	107,179	197,593	5,560	188,819	76,041
1976	1,146,489	960,567	3,689	964,256	91,481	-66,100	806,675	115,801	224,013	6,031	190,087	76,121
1977	1,259,746	1,043,649	3,134	1,046,783	98,398	-69,302	879,083	130,805	249,858	6,620	190,302	76,013
1978	1,359,156	1,101,794	6,242	1,108,036	105,791	-68,510	933,735	148,357	277,064	7,224	188,155	74,653
1979	1,518,628	1,242,326	7,715	1,250,041	122,559	-85,124	1,042,358	171,177	305,093	8,148	186,373	76,327
1980	1,593,495	1,213,392	9,740	1,223,132	120,236	-78,939	1,023,957	217,900	351,638	8,708	182,986	71,866
1981	1,713,422	1,248,402	13,143	1,261,545	133,237	-73,128	1,055,180	268,260	389,982	9,440	181,509	69,018
1982	1,759,783	1,190,724	4,771	1,195,495	129,013	-53,799	1,012,683	305,555	441,545	9,853	178,601	65,149
1983	1,793,087	1,147,438	2,825	1,150,263	124,334	-42,450	983,479	334,755	474,853	10,131	176,996	62,516
1984	1,897,947	1,230,795	6,383	1,237,178	140,893	-40,068	1,056,217	372,475	469,255	10,800	175,730	63,475
1985	1,938,249	1,245,406	4,915	1,250,321	144,650	-35,808	1,069,863	390,490	477,896	11,217	172,797	64,019
1986	1,959,626	1,227,072	4,333	1,231,405	146,281	-31,281	1,053,843	405,981	499,802	11,500	170,400	64,855
1987	2,021,239	1,289,414	3,779	1,293,193	151,811	-24,572	1,116,810	397,077	507,352	11,993	168,535	66,371
1988	2,210,851	1,483,590	574	1,484,164	173,542	-27,352	1,283,270	404,782	522,799	13,318	166,006	68,288
1989	2,363,215	1,572,305	3,398	1,575,703	183,132	-31,048	1,361,523	457,534	544,158	14,412	163,970	69,263
1990	2,485,791	1,657,474	5,587	1,663,061	193,548	-26,814	1,442,699	451,533	591,559	15,256	162,938	71,269
1991	2,630,251	1,719,890	5,359	1,725,249	202,551	-22,257	1,500,441	447,719	682,091	16,189	162,473	70,635
1992	2,730,190	1,781,249	8,837	1,790,086	209,164	-6,206	1,574,716	445,536	709,938	16,827	162,247	70,141
1993	2,798,977	1,817,610	8,520	1,826,130	218,872	5,365	1,612,623	445,926	740,428	17,302	161,770	70,383
1994	2,883,892	1,887,003	7,006	1,894,009	233,172	12,648	1,673,485	460,253	750,154	17,938	160,766	71,846
1995	2,992,529	1,943,275	5,389	1,948,664	240,980	10,080	1,717,764	504,473	770,292	18,716	159,892	73,380
1996	3,071,817	1,944,114	8,967	1,953,081	237,214	20,551	1,736,418	523,123	812,276	19,370	158,588	73,457
1997	3,165,516	1,997,160	2,679	1,999,839	243,537	26,477	1,782,779	555,456	827,281	20,112	157,396	73,397
1998	3,299,319	2,124,200	2,260	2,126,460	251,250	28,003	1,903,213	566,289	829,817	21,193	155,677	74,134
1999	3,428,092	2,240,888	643	2,241,531	262,828	30,008	2,008,711	555,112	864,269	22,273	153,911	74,990
2000	3,522,913	2,237,911	3,133	2,241,044	260,824	46,964	2,027,184	590,470	905,259	23,161	152,107	74,960
2001	3,669,896	2,284,351	-1,257	2,283,094	266,063	62,151	2,079,182	619,930	970,784	24,320	150,902	73,963
2002	3,711,409	2,303,359	-2,524	2,300,835	269,481	62,873	2,094,227	592,788	1,024,394	24,771	149,831	72,876
2003	3,843,733	2,402,386	4,133	2,406,519	277,664	66,149	2,195,004	598,977	1,049,752	25,825	148,836	72,852
2004	3,970,184	2,528,367	2,445	2,530,812	292,169	70,707	2,309,350	565,585	1,095,249	26,846	147,886	73,645
2005	4,113,515	2,643,835	5,407	2,649,242	314,422	75,282	2,410,102	543,169	1,160,244	27,988	146,975	74,252
2006	4,323,940	2,772,537	6,941	2,779,478	329,268	81,166	2,531,376	581,059	1,211,505	29,597	146,093	75,976
2007	4,577,618	2,866,912	4,337	2,871,249	343,446	87,366	2,615,169	671,364	1,291,085	31,508	145,283	76,657
2008	4,771,102	2,921,650	7,210	2,928,860	353,102	92,311	2,668,069	696,376	1,406,657	32,985	144,646	76,895
2009	4,765,413	2,888,769	2,286	2,891,055	353,384	86,068	2,623,739	692,539	1,449,135	33,050	144,186	74,523
2010	4,698,216	2,950,921	1,695	2,952,616	363,889	-47,439	2,541,288	646,979	1,509,949	32,753	143,444	73,796
2011	5,035,482	3,032,023	10,328	3,042,351	337,318	107,821	2,812,854	705,870	1,516,758	35,320	142,566	73,715
2012	5,070,248	3,022,359	11,377	3,033,736	334,370	126,738	2,826,104	739,513	1,504,631	35,824	141,531	73,159
2013	5,062,599	2,999,084	10,294	3,009,378	372,682	142,583	2,779,279	752,030	1,531,290	36,448	138,900	71,985
2014	5,169,960	3,034,831	6,618	3,041,449	386,304	163,001	2,818,146	782,294	1,569,520	37,536	137,732	71,579

Personal Income and Employment by Area: Jonesboro, AR

(Thousands of dollars, except as noted.)

Year	Personal income, total	Earnings by place of work			Less: Contributions for government social insurance	Plus: Adjustment for residence	Equals: Net earnings by place of residence	Plus: Dividends, interest, and rent	Plus: Personal current transfer receipts	Per capita personal income (dollars)	Population (persons)	Total employment
		Nonfarm	Farm	Total								
1970	232,414	146,815	43,150	189,965	11,136	3,787	182,616	25,344	24,454	2,922	79,540	34,569
1971	251,845	165,082	38,960	204,042	12,866	3,752	194,928	28,481	28,436	3,053	82,495	35,576
1972	278,994	189,559	37,116	226,675	15,373	3,711	215,013	31,514	32,467	3,333	83,698	36,928
1973	340,650	208,170	72,099	280,269	19,394	3,973	264,848	36,962	38,840	4,010	84,953	37,486
1974	382,837	228,173	78,869	307,042	21,956	4,149	289,235	45,377	48,225	4,465	85,734	37,982
1975	409,457	258,462	54,099	312,561	24,362	3,839	292,038	55,138	62,281	4,743	86,332	38,045
1976	438,459	301,148	36,526	337,674	28,746	3,038	311,966	58,855	67,638	4,971	88,200	39,374
1977	490,819	338,522	44,679	383,201	32,614	1,788	352,375	65,377	73,067	5,475	89,644	41,014
1978	630,233	387,483	126,999	514,482	38,343	1,374	477,513	73,319	79,401	6,981	90,272	42,812
1979	628,997	432,361	67,534	499,895	44,209	312	455,998	83,334	89,665	6,925	90,835	42,949
1980	649,094	456,853	28,711	485,564	46,459	182	439,287	101,005	108,802	7,190	90,274	42,267
1981	736,763	475,058	67,706	542,764	52,321	-328	490,115	125,664	120,984	8,178	90,094	40,797
1982	766,726	490,844	51,517	542,361	54,932	174	487,603	148,141	130,982	8,586	89,303	40,231
1983	788,061	527,757	25,220	552,977	59,214	87	493,850	151,042	143,169	8,848	89,065	40,737
1984	906,815	594,400	64,617	659,017	68,381	209	590,845	164,863	151,107	10,141	89,417	42,557
1985	950,821	630,386	51,211	681,597	73,061	500	609,036	182,054	159,731	10,595	89,745	43,490
1986	969,364	677,993	17,228	695,221	78,652	129	616,698	187,664	165,002	10,791	89,832	44,766
1987	1,060,130	745,511	50,416	795,927	85,954	-744	709,229	181,034	169,867	11,643	91,051	46,963
1988	1,158,948	805,885	78,456	884,341	96,411	580	788,510	192,330	178,108	12,606	91,939	48,776
1989	1,221,900	864,064	46,661	910,725	103,622	1,077	808,180	214,624	199,096	13,179	92,714	49,447
1990	1,288,781	907,624	43,599	951,223	112,976	4,868	843,115	227,103	218,563	13,711	93,999	49,752
1991	1,375,607	952,780	67,661	1,020,441	118,918	7,368	908,891	222,354	244,362	14,601	94,210	49,788
1992	1,514,082	1,049,829	89,017	1,138,846	130,022	6,744	1,015,568	229,336	269,178	15,773	95,994	51,479
1993	1,578,124	1,116,779	74,143	1,190,922	138,930	5,846	1,057,838	238,909	281,377	16,113	97,939	52,981
1994	1,654,868	1,184,674	81,584	1,266,258	148,863	6,375	1,123,770	243,905	287,193	16,737	98,872	53,314
1995	1,792,233	1,266,013	98,035	1,364,048	158,287	4,575	1,210,336	270,959	310,938	17,775	100,831	56,015
1996	1,899,387	1,323,661	113,473	1,437,134	164,198	5,287	1,278,223	292,927	328,237	18,503	102,652	56,986
1997	1,987,367	1,400,585	108,787	1,509,372	172,907	5,335	1,341,800	303,447	342,120	19,085	104,130	57,997
1998	2,100,327	1,512,160	90,008	1,602,168	182,674	5,657	1,425,151	317,990	357,186	19,888	105,607	59,040
1999	2,211,936	1,633,548	79,816	1,713,364	194,317	2,138	1,521,185	316,967	373,784	20,757	106,563	60,497
2000	2,335,582	1,713,583	90,538	1,804,121	202,419	2,067	1,603,769	336,007	395,806	21,599	108,136	61,282
2001	2,420,818	1,716,822	93,165	1,809,987	202,477	7,189	1,614,699	354,239	451,880	22,255	108,774	60,660
2002	2,495,369	1,800,200	43,861	1,844,061	210,510	-1,105	1,632,446	358,260	504,663	22,853	109,191	60,762
2003	2,739,425	1,892,909	184,642	2,077,551	219,722	-10,234	1,847,595	363,341	528,489	24,864	110,177	61,301
2004	2,830,277	2,021,286	166,195	2,187,481	232,064	-13,389	1,942,028	313,099	575,150	25,413	111,370	62,572
2005	2,918,024	2,118,306	102,559	2,220,865	246,187	-20,115	1,954,563	341,267	622,194	25,922	112,570	63,303
2006	3,076,022	2,209,725	113,601	2,323,326	261,169	-32,635	2,029,522	371,021	675,479	26,835	114,629	64,836
2007	3,213,461	2,252,002	107,428	2,359,430	269,290	-44,234	2,045,906	432,737	734,818	27,663	116,163	64,809
2008	3,393,504	2,335,682	110,195	2,445,877	285,741	-58,655	2,101,481	458,391	833,632	28,779	117,915	64,705
2009	3,428,168	2,309,343	115,989	2,425,332	287,911	-70,693	2,066,728	445,437	916,003	28,541	120,114	64,335
2010	3,534,681	2,408,426	104,595	2,513,021	299,340	-85,689	2,127,992	423,327	983,362	29,147	121,270	64,995
2011	3,774,881	2,533,534	121,855	2,655,389	284,749	-84,972	2,285,668	474,173	1,015,040	30,730	122,840	67,521
2012	3,967,306	2,658,918	127,732	2,786,650	291,628	-80,835	2,414,187	525,615	1,027,504	31,936	124,228	67,684
2013	4,088,176	2,740,330	226,973	2,967,303	335,455	-99,900	2,531,948	508,632	1,047,596	32,480	125,869	68,735
2014	4,186,277	2,864,158	133,981	2,998,139	352,686	-109,026	2,536,427	526,386	1,123,464	33,024	126,764	70,029

Personal Income and Employment by Area: Joplin, MO
(Thousands of dollars, except as noted.)

Year	Personal income, total	Earnings by place of work			Less: Contributions for government social insurance	Plus: Adjustment for residence	Equals: Net earnings by place of residence	Plus: Dividends, interest, and rent	Plus: Personal current transfer receipts	Per capita personal income (dollars)	Population (persons)	Total employment
		Nonfarm	Farm	Total								
1970	353,956	274,034	10,341	284,375	18,399	-6,364	259,612	49,256	45,088	3,132	113,028	48,807
1971	378,277	291,854	9,671	301,525	20,308	-8,304	272,913	53,692	51,672	3,306	114,407	49,252
1972	427,562	332,208	15,571	347,779	24,322	-9,881	313,576	58,841	55,145	3,643	117,364	52,210
1973	484,239	369,418	26,756	396,174	31,341	-10,992	353,841	66,527	63,871	4,056	119,399	55,584
1974	522,502	408,465	9,893	418,358	35,911	-12,999	369,448	78,012	75,042	4,320	120,962	55,905
1975	567,734	424,410	10,444	434,854	36,445	-12,722	385,687	86,551	95,496	4,687	121,126	53,422
1976	631,223	475,534	14,454	489,988	41,337	-14,269	434,382	95,415	101,426	5,183	121,777	55,436
1977	701,014	535,205	13,728	548,933	46,634	-15,984	486,315	109,632	105,067	5,666	123,716	57,532
1978	785,368	608,968	14,860	623,828	54,953	-19,981	548,894	122,480	113,994	6,288	124,905	59,753
1979	878,918	679,764	16,617	696,381	63,378	-21,235	611,768	138,935	128,215	6,934	126,753	61,872
1980	979,553	725,795	17,943	743,738	67,466	-23,675	652,597	172,213	154,743	7,662	127,845	61,478
1981	1,099,355	802,547	15,893	818,440	79,874	-27,381	711,185	211,329	176,841	8,529	128,894	62,909
1982	1,176,797	839,305	6,326	845,631	84,985	-32,271	728,375	249,765	198,657	9,107	129,226	62,312
1983	1,268,190	905,752	6,240	911,992	91,712	-35,751	784,529	271,950	211,711	9,783	129,634	64,321
1984	1,401,745	1,014,506	5,248	1,019,754	105,788	-42,024	871,942	309,975	219,828	10,727	130,678	67,177
1985	1,492,355	1,092,857	7,212	1,100,069	116,190	-47,776	936,103	323,326	232,926	11,348	131,504	69,624
1986	1,590,254	1,170,475	14,388	1,184,863	124,873	-55,292	1,004,698	338,718	246,838	12,032	132,165	71,862
1987	1,672,082	1,264,651	7,274	1,271,925	132,982	-61,680	1,077,263	337,720	257,099	12,545	133,284	73,545
1988	1,782,108	1,341,897	12,251	1,354,148	145,717	-64,641	1,143,790	359,368	278,950	13,332	133,670	74,700
1989	1,893,986	1,417,369	20,801	1,438,170	155,491	-67,058	1,215,621	384,052	294,313	14,092	134,404	75,726
1990	1,998,131	1,501,133	14,731	1,515,864	169,119	-74,172	1,272,573	406,704	318,854	14,777	135,219	77,595
1991	2,117,025	1,590,743	12,284	1,603,027	181,051	-79,881	1,342,095	405,155	369,775	15,486	136,705	78,870
1992	2,321,123	1,733,386	14,248	1,747,634	195,108	-87,461	1,465,065	455,149	400,909	16,715	138,865	81,177
1993	2,465,157	1,848,263	13,136	1,861,399	209,233	-95,664	1,556,502	474,531	434,124	17,414	141,558	84,247
1994	2,650,376	2,017,422	11,926	2,029,348	230,113	-109,326	1,689,909	505,108	455,359	18,378	144,212	88,024
1995	2,797,922	2,145,844	7,933	2,153,777	245,998	-116,718	1,791,061	516,132	490,729	19,065	146,755	90,789
1996	2,961,731	2,262,297	21,944	2,284,241	256,495	-123,653	1,904,093	531,731	525,907	19,817	149,456	93,362
1997	3,157,715	2,418,182	22,213	2,440,395	274,231	-136,890	2,029,274	570,824	557,617	20,795	151,852	95,844
1998	3,313,749	2,551,686	22,394	2,574,080	289,630	-144,854	2,139,596	597,816	576,337	21,509	154,066	98,483
1999	3,465,229	2,692,981	15,780	2,708,761	303,436	-148,263	2,257,062	599,461	608,706	22,238	155,822	99,499
2000	3,659,893	2,815,111	8,374	2,823,485	313,439	-152,122	2,357,924	650,936	651,033	23,213	157,665	100,362
2001	3,804,000	2,912,830	21,161	2,933,991	325,459	-159,832	2,448,700	623,298	732,002	23,990	158,567	98,949
2002	3,832,247	2,947,127	15,319	2,962,446	328,499	-162,399	2,471,548	573,981	786,718	23,938	160,092	97,829
2003	4,004,247	3,081,314	30,070	3,111,384	341,400	-172,382	2,597,602	579,645	827,000	24,712	162,037	98,226
2004	4,298,126	3,247,419	67,536	3,314,955	358,063	-178,484	2,778,408	654,979	864,739	26,209	163,997	98,945
2005	4,443,626	3,372,216	63,658	3,435,874	373,986	-184,660	2,877,228	633,700	932,698	26,743	166,160	100,399
2006	4,726,437	3,599,816	42,142	3,641,958	403,164	-189,528	3,049,266	698,929	978,242	28,017	168,701	102,929
2007	4,997,435	3,756,833	39,537	3,796,370	426,075	-195,092	3,175,203	768,587	1,053,645	29,187	171,224	105,814
2008	5,330,072	3,875,772	83,295	3,959,067	448,193	-185,462	3,325,412	827,871	1,176,789	30,855	172,744	105,346
2009	5,319,817	3,847,524	47,926	3,895,450	443,392	-188,043	3,264,015	779,403	1,276,399	30,505	174,394	102,270
2010	5,394,283	3,872,433	55,904	3,928,337	443,575	-180,010	3,304,752	739,404	1,350,127	30,663	175,922	99,888
2011	5,679,096	3,991,860	61,662	4,053,522	414,622	-175,247	3,463,653	828,077	1,387,366	32,143	176,680	101,010
2012	5,915,596	4,109,771	60,244	4,170,015	418,889	-167,931	3,583,195	985,814	1,346,587	33,911	174,445	101,870
2013	5,881,478	4,169,192	84,739	4,253,931	480,094	-150,827	3,623,010	892,598	1,365,870	33,568	175,209	101,655
2014	6,059,293	4,211,121	131,320	4,342,441	486,103	-128,178	3,728,160	931,725	1,399,408	34,400	176,141	101,493

Personal Income and Employment by Area: Kahului-Wailuku-Lahaina, HI

(Thousands of dollars, except as noted.)

Year	Personal income, total	Earnings by place of work			Less: Contributions for government social insurance	Plus: Adjustment for residence	Equals: Net earnings by place of residence	Plus: Dividends, interest, and rent	Plus: Personal current transfer receipts	Per capita personal income (dollars)	Population (persons)	Total employment
		Nonfarm	Farm	Total								
1970	199,671	124,707	37,343	162,050	9,259	32	152,823	31,386	15,462	4,341	45,995	22,016
1971	220,331	136,165	37,904	174,069	10,635	-58	163,376	36,603	20,352	4,255	51,784	22,664
1972	242,474	148,728	39,733	188,461	12,183	-109	176,169	41,138	25,167	4,709	51,488	23,264
1973	268,607	165,459	38,686	204,145	15,878	-225	188,042	49,886	30,679	5,098	52,693	24,568
1974	357,733	192,435	89,294	281,729	19,580	-729	261,420	58,739	37,574	6,667	53,661	26,464
1975	380,832	234,224	54,923	289,147	21,968	-2,381	264,798	67,337	48,697	6,720	56,669	29,157
1976	423,068	269,955	54,157	324,112	25,324	-3,096	295,692	71,647	55,729	7,031	60,173	31,192
1977	474,847	316,351	55,733	372,084	29,810	-4,035	338,239	79,946	56,662	7,566	62,763	33,058
1978	530,786	366,650	47,483	414,133	36,293	-4,790	373,050	96,445	61,291	8,048	65,950	35,880
1979	613,371	425,813	53,938	479,751	43,393	-5,657	430,701	115,236	67,434	8,821	69,537	37,847
1980	732,152	470,538	97,238	567,776	47,270	-6,091	514,415	136,648	81,089	10,222	71,624	39,255
1981	766,654	516,202	51,457	567,659	55,584	-4,136	507,939	162,976	95,739	10,354	74,043	38,790
1982	831,226	570,277	58,659	628,936	62,351	-4,245	562,340	162,097	106,789	10,781	77,103	40,711
1983	978,195	634,414	103,443	737,857	68,462	-3,696	665,699	194,608	117,888	12,218	80,060	43,194
1984	1,037,636	706,159	69,577	775,736	77,922	-3,753	694,061	220,788	122,787	12,506	82,969	44,749
1985	1,127,852	788,657	63,316	851,973	88,160	-4,536	759,277	239,139	129,436	13,246	85,147	48,048
1986	1,230,071	865,585	73,511	939,096	97,650	-4,756	836,690	258,540	134,841	14,076	87,389	50,149
1987	1,331,397	962,446	73,277	1,035,723	108,359	-4,903	922,461	269,980	138,956	14,706	90,532	53,953
1988	1,500,176	1,124,654	66,870	1,191,524	128,163	-5,474	1,057,887	294,375	147,914	15,999	93,767	58,381
1989	1,748,558	1,325,250	60,850	1,386,100	149,805	-8,240	1,228,055	356,568	163,935	18,060	96,819	62,829
1990	1,951,822	1,504,296	67,682	1,571,978	177,003	-9,774	1,385,201	386,213	180,408	19,190	101,709	66,255
1991	2,074,855	1,619,724	67,274	1,686,998	192,436	-10,156	1,484,406	387,374	203,075	19,648	105,599	69,643
1992	2,302,017	1,761,892	97,223	1,859,115	208,876	-9,971	1,640,268	416,123	245,626	21,200	108,585	72,764
1993	2,443,441	1,863,845	57,066	1,920,911	215,201	-9,408	1,696,302	484,979	262,160	21,827	111,944	72,912
1994	2,536,001	1,945,204	58,477	2,003,681	228,246	-10,553	1,764,882	490,276	280,843	22,099	114,754	73,468
1995	2,612,437	1,975,940	59,511	2,035,451	229,713	-9,459	1,796,279	494,791	321,367	22,159	117,895	73,984
1996	2,642,791	1,991,240	56,091	2,047,331	233,397	-10,597	1,803,337	497,755	341,699	21,898	120,689	74,645
1997	2,734,190	2,046,358	57,536	2,103,894	238,101	-11,001	1,854,792	541,666	337,732	22,270	122,772	75,979
1998	2,845,422	2,110,168	65,456	2,175,624	245,738	-12,100	1,917,786	574,397	353,239	22,828	124,648	78,169
1999	3,050,934	2,277,918	71,152	2,349,070	264,026	-14,857	2,070,187	602,599	378,148	24,183	126,160	80,249
2000	3,255,020	2,430,777	62,666	2,493,443	281,300	-16,704	2,195,439	661,031	398,550	25,217	129,078	82,690
2001	3,419,178	2,576,000	66,466	2,642,466	297,721	-16,310	2,328,435	669,697	421,046	25,819	132,428	85,519
2002	3,617,057	2,750,517	72,036	2,822,553	319,797	-14,690	2,488,066	670,202	458,789	26,876	134,583	87,046
2003	3,794,377	2,934,511	73,758	3,008,269	345,769	-12,786	2,649,714	665,470	479,193	27,576	137,596	88,748
2004	4,166,729	3,176,315	78,894	3,255,209	362,372	-10,721	2,882,116	764,107	520,506	29,630	140,625	92,607
2005	4,510,885	3,449,410	85,401	3,534,811	396,237	-8,343	3,130,231	816,737	563,917	31,446	143,448	96,948
2006	4,947,834	3,724,568	95,119	3,819,687	432,710	-5,250	3,381,727	973,566	592,541	33,941	145,776	99,798
2007	5,272,925	3,896,684	99,491	3,996,175	455,900	-1,665	3,538,610	1,077,858	656,457	35,600	148,117	103,357
2008	5,529,610	3,913,336	77,324	3,990,660	453,039	2,354	3,539,975	1,209,048	780,587	36,517	151,424	101,942
2009	5,256,613	3,674,872	71,998	3,746,870	423,026	5,267	3,329,111	1,062,048	865,454	34,269	153,393	96,050
2010	5,428,448	3,660,993	69,217	3,730,210	440,568	7,364	3,297,006	1,150,261	981,181	35,006	155,072	94,903
2011	5,677,219	3,832,109	66,295	3,898,404	421,609	8,567	3,485,362	1,170,055	1,021,802	36,194	156,854	95,982
2012	6,061,880	4,060,100	95,646	4,155,746	438,814	6,726	3,723,658	1,337,543	1,000,679	38,240	158,521	98,080
2013	6,086,180	4,184,670	93,447	4,278,117	520,685	7,375	3,764,807	1,291,352	1,030,021	37,831	160,880	101,031
2014	6,432,812	4,383,139	96,854	4,479,993	521,981	7,705	3,965,717	1,357,134	1,109,961	39,439	163,108	103,153

Personal Income and Employment by Area: Kalamazoo-Portage, MI

(Thousands of dollars, except as noted.)

Year	Personal income, total	Earnings by place of work			Less: Contributions for government social insurance	Plus: Adjustment for residence	Equals: Net earnings by place of residence	Plus: Dividends, interest, and rent	Plus: Personal current transfer receipts	Per capita personal income (dollars)	Population (persons)	Total employment
		Nonfarm	Farm	Total								
1970	1,017,960	836,364	18,026	854,390	59,929	-3,277	791,184	141,542	85,234	3,947	257,900	108,004
1971	1,076,900	875,082	17,465	892,547	64,642	-1,998	825,907	148,492	102,501	4,146	259,747	106,654
1972	1,180,271	963,566	20,557	984,123	74,874	-692	908,557	158,388	113,326	4,486	263,099	110,715
1973	1,321,306	1,081,459	29,593	1,111,052	97,611	-2,839	1,010,602	178,929	131,775	5,040	262,173	115,785
1974	1,460,293	1,180,646	27,751	1,208,397	110,553	-9,201	1,088,643	208,186	163,464	5,523	264,388	118,408
1975	1,604,587	1,261,321	28,432	1,289,753	114,779	-12,678	1,162,296	224,130	218,161	6,010	266,969	117,797
1976	1,760,903	1,416,154	20,303	1,436,457	131,604	-17,273	1,287,580	241,889	231,434	6,531	269,631	121,403
1977	1,970,362	1,602,177	29,010	1,631,187	147,877	-21,316	1,461,994	271,009	237,359	7,243	272,051	126,334
1978	2,197,427	1,801,891	30,743	1,832,634	170,622	-25,176	1,636,836	301,814	258,777	8,014	274,191	131,628
1979	2,431,091	2,021,375	21,330	2,042,705	200,012	-42,788	1,799,905	338,256	292,930	8,799	276,290	134,464
1980	2,655,789	2,142,806	12,626	2,155,432	211,258	-57,559	1,886,615	406,740	362,434	9,498	279,626	132,685
1981	2,937,357	2,319,175	21,181	2,340,356	246,051	-56,241	2,038,064	503,593	395,700	10,462	280,754	132,264
1982	3,065,340	2,349,796	20,089	2,369,885	253,826	-50,092	2,065,967	562,346	437,027	10,922	280,662	129,119
1983	3,265,710	2,502,054	15,861	2,517,915	274,339	-48,888	2,194,688	602,357	468,665	11,693	279,280	129,086
1984	3,560,060	2,718,015	28,677	2,746,692	308,601	-46,878	2,391,213	687,297	481,550	12,737	279,510	132,514
1985	3,813,398	2,935,879	43,510	2,979,389	338,590	-54,225	2,586,574	717,261	509,563	13,587	280,675	136,989
1986	4,098,407	3,161,849	35,216	3,197,065	365,172	-39,314	2,792,579	769,244	536,584	14,476	283,122	141,796
1987	4,392,047	3,404,471	51,943	3,456,414	386,888	-35,799	3,033,727	808,074	550,246	15,339	286,324	148,346
1988	4,725,566	3,743,009	44,055	3,787,064	436,954	-37,913	3,312,197	841,212	572,157	16,302	289,882	153,749
1989	5,170,238	3,984,157	60,902	4,045,059	461,157	-35,986	3,547,916	997,356	624,966	17,700	292,105	159,164
1990	5,349,970	4,124,577	51,771	4,176,348	487,083	-27,924	3,661,341	1,008,407	680,222	18,182	294,251	161,538
1991	5,612,715	4,333,992	57,279	4,391,271	517,849	-23,625	3,849,797	1,005,976	756,942	18,951	296,165	163,402
1992	5,933,357	4,586,851	57,236	4,644,087	544,712	-8,808	4,090,567	1,035,893	806,897	19,817	299,414	164,582
1993	6,272,017	4,828,611	50,729	4,879,340	576,255	2,912	4,305,997	1,094,442	871,578	20,723	302,658	167,830
1994	6,644,088	5,047,390	47,794	5,095,184	614,937	31,632	4,511,879	1,258,679	873,530	21,830	304,355	170,650
1995	6,976,316	5,307,207	54,012	5,361,219	648,377	38,229	4,751,071	1,277,629	947,616	22,761	306,504	175,650
1996	7,337,221	5,595,041	49,406	5,644,447	669,041	38,416	5,013,822	1,357,751	965,648	23,741	309,056	177,475
1997	7,619,991	5,747,525	55,568	5,803,093	688,365	77,041	5,191,769	1,404,150	1,024,072	24,547	310,425	178,617
1998	7,976,677	6,035,477	58,736	6,094,213	716,489	89,577	5,467,301	1,496,135	1,013,241	25,571	311,947	177,167
1999	8,201,156	6,234,173	62,193	6,296,366	736,400	105,272	5,665,238	1,428,755	1,107,163	26,149	313,627	177,824
2000	8,527,873	6,407,445	67,806	6,475,251	752,803	124,255	5,846,703	1,531,911	1,149,259	27,051	315,250	180,141
2001	8,791,481	6,601,848	68,032	6,669,880	748,631	110,001	6,031,250	1,470,077	1,290,154	27,776	316,512	176,252
2002	9,066,803	6,841,670	64,995	6,906,665	777,410	116,255	6,245,510	1,483,345	1,337,948	28,448	318,714	175,451
2003	9,417,291	7,127,666	66,174	7,193,840	803,956	109,543	6,499,427	1,511,139	1,406,725	29,351	320,856	175,147
2004	9,776,141	7,232,592	93,603	7,326,195	824,635	139,972	6,641,532	1,649,176	1,485,433	30,575	319,746	176,953
2005	10,014,471	7,334,869	80,968	7,415,837	848,590	141,830	6,709,077	1,723,519	1,581,875	31,269	320,268	178,841
2006	10,475,331	7,560,654	95,656	7,656,310	888,371	167,400	6,935,339	1,841,514	1,698,478	32,613	321,197	179,724
2007	10,863,764	7,753,160	99,282	7,852,442	920,328	195,428	7,127,542	1,873,497	1,862,725	33,731	322,070	181,734
2008	11,401,444	7,944,609	101,538	8,046,147	953,865	209,987	7,302,269	1,969,883	2,129,292	35,259	323,363	178,292
2009	11,113,304	7,617,318	101,045	7,718,363	917,804	150,482	6,951,041	1,830,067	2,332,196	34,131	325,604	171,542
2010	11,303,231	7,669,494	112,133	7,781,627	916,554	211,238	7,076,311	1,732,393	2,494,527	34,575	326,920	167,896
2011	12,033,675	7,835,052	185,283	8,020,335	837,958	223,815	7,406,192	2,110,950	2,516,533	36,640	328,432	168,421
2012	12,322,635	8,159,464	92,164	8,251,628	873,231	241,284	7,619,681	2,226,034	2,476,920	37,311	330,270	169,239
2013	12,770,372	8,409,079	169,029	8,578,108	1,015,647	273,765	7,836,226	2,379,776	2,554,370	38,401	332,557	171,328
2014	13,221,277	8,717,756	135,286	8,853,042	1,046,927	298,021	8,104,136	2,454,976	2,662,165	39,583	334,017	174,477

Personal Income and Employment by Area: Kankakee-Bradley, IL

(Thousands of dollars, except as noted.)

Year	Personal income, total	Earnings by place of work			Less: Contributions for government social insurance	Plus: Adjustment for residence	Equals: Net earnings by place of residence	Plus: Dividends, interest, and rent	Plus: Personal current transfer receipts	Per capita personal income (dollars)	Population (persons)	Total employment
		Nonfarm	Farm	Total								
1970	374,741	287,814	11,263	299,077	19,044	13,014	293,047	50,317	31,377	3,850	97,342	39,706
1971	414,995	311,499	18,119	329,618	21,318	14,684	322,984	54,208	37,803	4,206	98,659	40,376
1972	449,633	342,594	12,309	354,903	24,795	16,906	347,014	59,694	42,925	4,510	99,695	40,906
1973	513,248	374,349	30,151	404,500	31,456	19,713	392,757	67,509	52,982	5,166	99,351	42,692
1974	554,108	406,095	23,455	429,550	35,238	22,274	416,586	76,227	61,295	5,553	99,787	43,581
1975	609,231	413,314	36,404	449,718	34,949	26,503	441,272	87,315	80,644	6,093	99,990	42,589
1976	653,987	446,748	30,555	477,303	38,528	32,989	471,764	91,391	90,832	6,510	100,458	42,763
1977	719,417	492,571	30,958	523,529	42,611	39,868	520,786	100,996	97,635	7,080	101,619	44,000
1978	791,919	546,734	27,246	573,980	48,497	49,393	574,876	111,893	105,150	7,687	103,025	45,063
1979	865,073	586,329	33,924	620,253	54,028	59,097	625,322	124,303	115,448	8,299	104,238	44,868
1980	924,319	608,735	10,574	619,309	55,847	65,127	628,589	155,771	139,959	8,984	102,886	43,027
1981	1,037,308	652,831	27,418	680,249	64,401	66,461	682,309	192,320	162,679	10,116	102,544	43,280
1982	1,080,062	655,367	18,876	674,243	65,026	67,427	676,644	222,306	181,112	10,671	101,218	41,632
1983	1,093,287	667,831	-1,245	666,586	66,316	69,013	669,283	225,652	198,352	10,981	99,560	40,857
1984	1,181,138	698,649	24,129	722,778	71,530	79,489	730,737	250,092	200,309	11,990	98,513	41,023
1985	1,220,112	724,515	29,777	754,292	75,637	83,484	762,139	252,477	205,496	12,573	97,039	41,045
1986	1,267,865	758,844	28,807	787,651	79,429	87,236	795,458	260,399	212,008	13,217	95,926	41,221
1987	1,328,429	816,028	25,452	841,480	84,303	91,839	849,016	263,032	216,381	13,882	95,692	42,154
1988	1,406,675	867,915	33,595	901,510	92,654	99,573	908,429	270,144	228,102	14,733	95,481	42,337
1989	1,505,976	912,180	43,751	955,931	98,323	105,561	963,169	300,050	242,757	15,751	95,611	42,756
1990	1,639,831	1,013,349	60,016	1,073,365	106,981	104,045	1,070,429	304,367	265,035	16,983	96,560	45,566
1991	1,661,063	1,056,319	38,170	1,094,489	114,440	107,292	1,087,341	288,755	284,967	17,019	97,598	47,700
1992	1,790,945	1,123,893	42,895	1,166,788	119,928	115,132	1,161,992	303,905	325,048	18,051	99,215	45,999
1993	1,894,368	1,217,408	50,451	1,267,859	131,719	114,680	1,250,820	305,745	337,803	18,800	100,766	47,610
1994	1,994,229	1,296,862	53,546	1,350,408	142,625	120,455	1,328,238	319,742	346,249	19,602	101,736	50,134
1995	2,127,658	1,389,704	35,545	1,425,249	153,522	121,002	1,392,729	361,314	373,615	20,875	101,923	52,190
1996	2,226,543	1,420,596	52,412	1,473,008	154,895	134,093	1,452,206	382,757	391,580	21,766	102,296	51,612
1997	2,289,085	1,467,795	30,408	1,498,203	159,395	148,792	1,487,600	400,052	401,433	22,235	102,951	52,245
1998	2,369,471	1,512,775	21,905	1,534,680	163,151	169,475	1,541,004	419,359	409,108	22,955	103,222	53,005
1999	2,446,009	1,589,490	18,608	1,608,098	168,857	189,982	1,629,223	401,175	415,611	23,593	103,675	53,246
2000	2,610,393	1,681,079	28,694	1,709,773	175,927	208,713	1,742,559	432,053	435,781	25,138	103,842	54,132
2001	2,702,045	1,726,304	23,880	1,750,184	182,826	225,756	1,793,114	440,421	468,510	25,859	104,490	53,428
2002	2,783,112	1,792,463	15,592	1,808,055	189,091	242,023	1,860,987	415,573	506,552	26,523	104,932	52,421
2003	2,868,209	1,816,797	16,835	1,833,632	191,764	255,355	1,897,223	436,528	534,458	27,111	105,794	52,088
2004	2,966,901	1,878,480	50,235	1,928,715	201,365	278,255	2,005,605	404,513	556,783	27,795	106,744	52,453
2005	3,068,581	1,940,206	34,547	1,974,753	214,331	300,537	2,060,959	389,124	618,498	28,435	107,917	53,634
2006	3,244,080	2,030,561	37,639	2,068,200	225,023	331,311	2,174,488	426,571	643,021	29,563	109,735	54,950
2007	3,459,705	2,093,980	74,778	2,168,758	234,586	364,501	2,298,673	455,667	705,365	31,029	111,499	55,459
2008	3,690,227	2,150,198	106,346	2,256,544	240,388	393,593	2,409,749	506,767	773,711	32,756	112,658	54,948
2009	3,620,293	2,124,301	76,500	2,200,801	234,538	298,139	2,264,402	483,773	872,118	32,008	113,107	54,012
2010	3,673,783	2,109,177	64,788	2,173,965	235,278	330,199	2,268,886	467,833	937,064	32,379	113,462	53,475
2011	3,786,954	2,172,062	101,057	2,273,119	220,339	334,419	2,387,199	496,017	903,738	33,379	113,453	53,325
2012	3,840,939	2,304,750	67,453	2,372,203	234,395	280,348	2,418,156	519,230	903,553	34,013	112,926	54,459
2013	3,943,207	2,343,346	133,326	2,476,672	267,671	291,074	2,500,075	515,266	927,866	35,147	112,193	54,696
2014	3,971,295	2,416,910	67,689	2,484,599	277,179	289,629	2,497,049	534,613	939,633	35,657	111,375	55,037

Personal Income and Employment by Area: Kansas City, MO-KS

(Thousands of dollars, except as noted.)

Year	Personal income, total	Derivation of personal income								Per capita personal income (dollars)	Population (persons)	Total employment
		Earnings by place of work			Less: Contributions for government social insurance	Plus: Adjustment for residence	Equals: Net earnings by place of residence	Plus: Dividends, interest, and rent	Plus: Personal current transfer receipts			
		Nonfarm	Farm	Total								
1970	6,162,982	5,165,929	69,514	5,235,443	347,962	-33,460	4,854,021	865,150	443,811	4,341	1,419,593	674,424
1971	6,718,469	5,604,219	73,673	5,677,892	390,806	-34,427	5,252,659	950,176	515,634	4,691	1,432,356	679,124
1972	7,365,221	6,150,177	96,596	6,246,773	452,442	-35,169	5,759,162	1,038,096	567,963	5,115	1,439,848	697,223
1973	8,088,707	6,748,774	139,328	6,888,102	574,782	-36,218	6,277,102	1,147,561	664,044	5,561	1,454,634	727,985
1974	8,761,103	7,251,741	70,030	7,321,771	637,906	-33,569	6,650,296	1,331,883	778,924	6,038	1,450,974	734,327
1975	9,648,769	7,838,414	73,351	7,911,765	677,428	-37,829	7,196,508	1,459,856	992,405	6,683	1,443,816	727,345
1976	10,598,381	8,756,143	50,836	8,806,979	772,971	-44,818	7,989,190	1,550,642	1,058,549	7,299	1,452,126	751,366
1977	11,802,813	9,812,073	83,989	9,896,062	861,914	-54,997	8,979,151	1,710,472	1,113,190	8,111	1,455,117	776,160
1978	13,113,726	10,971,092	94,470	11,065,562	996,230	-61,948	10,007,384	1,914,606	1,191,736	8,928	1,468,792	807,453
1979	14,661,090	12,211,735	153,550	12,365,285	1,149,435	-66,596	11,149,254	2,165,337	1,346,499	9,935	1,475,676	828,859
1980	16,036,159	13,040,343	7,307	13,047,650	1,224,137	-72,354	11,751,159	2,648,415	1,636,585	10,804	1,484,234	821,393
1981	17,630,948	13,889,179	99,884	13,989,063	1,399,849	-83,934	12,505,280	3,247,547	1,878,121	11,835	1,489,775	814,405
1982	18,899,200	14,526,021	34,995	14,561,016	1,495,497	-87,897	12,977,622	3,858,049	2,063,529	12,645	1,494,551	808,137
1983	19,996,789	15,488,973	-19,609	15,469,364	1,612,417	-92,819	13,764,128	4,070,561	2,162,100	13,308	1,502,652	812,620
1984	22,193,542	17,276,906	12,963	17,289,869	1,846,369	-93,780	15,349,720	4,585,746	2,258,076	14,613	1,518,797	856,338
1985	24,050,310	18,824,704	107,515	18,932,219	2,056,544	-138,082	16,737,593	4,915,906	2,396,811	15,654	1,536,347	889,683
1986	25,599,256	20,201,394	68,334	20,269,728	2,220,942	-159,762	17,889,024	5,158,247	2,551,985	16,468	1,554,473	916,814
1987	27,190,846	21,630,390	75,366	21,705,756	2,345,522	-174,362	19,185,872	5,341,198	2,663,776	17,247	1,576,591	941,024
1988	28,897,272	22,935,217	69,250	23,004,467	2,566,565	-181,635	20,256,267	5,775,136	2,865,869	18,129	1,593,958	960,486
1989	30,700,242	24,243,825	103,879	24,347,704	2,711,478	-182,512	21,453,714	6,160,040	3,086,488	19,155	1,602,744	975,387
1990	32,163,371	25,400,257	55,057	25,455,314	2,964,635	-225,919	22,264,760	6,547,710	3,350,901	19,867	1,618,905	985,056
1991	33,746,201	26,448,581	23,415	26,471,996	3,126,479	-242,326	23,103,191	6,839,002	3,804,008	20,621	1,636,516	981,595
1992	36,305,733	28,580,807	103,864	28,684,671	3,342,086	-286,907	25,055,678	7,094,217	4,155,838	21,959	1,653,327	988,989
1993	38,156,612	30,161,492	34,715	30,196,207	3,523,708	-308,695	26,363,804	7,342,702	4,450,106	22,794	1,673,964	1,013,149
1994	40,398,584	31,981,500	89,670	32,071,170	3,772,853	-361,305	27,937,012	7,782,726	4,678,846	23,849	1,693,952	1,037,813
1995	42,653,826	33,787,530	7,622	33,795,152	3,955,820	-392,195	29,447,137	8,196,763	5,009,926	24,935	1,710,587	1,069,637
1996	45,287,586	35,859,479	121,449	35,980,928	4,151,629	-442,846	31,386,453	8,634,412	5,266,721	26,126	1,733,398	1,093,386
1997	48,081,857	38,232,319	111,615	38,343,934	4,413,129	-498,132	33,432,673	9,268,326	5,380,858	27,373	1,756,537	1,131,838
1998	51,734,294	41,341,003	64,378	41,405,381	4,717,954	-557,183	36,130,244	10,065,203	5,538,847	29,114	1,776,976	1,162,007
1999	54,723,068	44,626,450	36,660	44,663,110	5,062,782	-635,544	38,964,784	9,962,480	5,795,804	30,457	1,796,711	1,182,796
2000	58,955,347	48,066,426	61,223	48,127,649	5,397,857	-720,128	42,009,664	10,732,655	6,213,028	32,430	1,817,929	1,202,490
2001	60,950,111	49,926,860	91,953	50,018,813	5,621,881	-753,677	43,643,255	10,469,986	6,836,870	33,169	1,837,551	1,209,812
2002	62,339,408	51,392,771	20,595	51,413,366	5,746,446	-913,335	44,753,585	10,307,270	7,278,553	33,538	1,858,778	1,203,170
2003	63,932,417	52,568,915	77,777	52,646,692	5,891,085	-888,896	45,866,711	10,449,670	7,616,036	34,095	1,875,142	1,199,426
2004	66,820,361	55,222,449	241,330	55,463,779	6,159,081	-895,751	48,408,947	10,436,762	7,974,652	35,316	1,892,097	1,215,667
2005	69,553,067	57,538,920	132,305	57,671,225	6,430,448	-985,933	50,254,844	10,804,710	8,493,513	36,426	1,909,428	1,233,107
2006	74,832,189	60,923,047	81,187	61,004,234	6,811,546	-1,046,723	53,145,965	12,549,143	9,137,081	38,738	1,931,764	1,256,700
2007	79,463,089	63,535,731	114,108	63,649,839	7,142,069	-868,244	55,639,526	13,961,894	9,861,669	40,653	1,954,688	1,288,582
2008	84,286,926	65,806,473	165,652	65,972,125	7,419,164	-877,664	57,675,297	15,257,810	11,353,819	42,701	1,973,888	1,293,861
2009	81,771,855	64,265,146	169,297	64,434,443	7,267,332	-716,786	56,450,325	13,019,175	12,302,355	40,992	1,994,834	1,260,901
2010	83,326,376	65,218,629	102,689	65,321,318	7,334,574	-713,990	57,272,754	12,794,585	13,259,037	41,381	2,013,651	1,237,241
2011	87,849,734	67,194,763	204,828	67,399,591	6,734,818	-711,655	59,953,118	14,398,101	13,498,515	43,383	2,025,003	1,255,345
2012	91,407,209	70,235,145	109,035	70,344,180	6,986,865	-702,607	62,654,708	15,178,566	13,573,935	44,825	2,039,213	1,269,726
2013	92,399,487	71,749,253	327,582	72,076,835	8,140,879	-692,922	63,243,034	15,248,677	13,907,776	44,956	2,055,351	1,289,076
2014	95,932,257	74,620,804	308,011	74,928,815	8,497,313	-727,653	65,703,849	15,854,184	14,374,224	46,319	2,071,133	1,314,078

Personal Income and Employment by Area: Kennewick-Pasco-Richland, WA

(Thousands of dollars, except as noted.)

Year	Personal income, total	Earnings by place of work			Less: Contributions for government social insurance	Plus: Adjustment for residence	Equals: Net earnings by place of residence	Plus: Dividends, interest, and rent	Plus: Personal current transfer receipts	Per capita personal income (dollars)	Population (persons)	Total employment
		Nonfarm	Farm	Total								
1970	380,821	298,166	25,178	323,344	24,115	471	299,700	47,187	33,934	4,073	93,499	40,817
1971	401,790	309,125	26,738	335,863	26,085	84	309,862	52,523	39,405	4,271	94,080	40,315
1972	450,004	342,762	38,957	381,719	30,826	-1,475	349,418	58,322	42,264	4,734	95,067	41,832
1973	521,205	393,504	57,633	451,137	41,352	-4,871	404,914	69,488	46,803	5,474	95,211	44,867
1974	631,239	472,953	84,601	557,554	51,670	-8,915	496,969	79,882	54,388	6,398	98,666	49,005
1975	760,300	596,372	84,272	680,644	65,038	-16,391	599,215	94,683	66,402	7,238	105,045	54,232
1976	852,496	686,413	79,488	765,901	75,583	-18,389	671,929	105,889	74,678	7,555	112,838	58,982
1977	995,892	870,562	50,060	920,622	96,883	-33,604	790,135	126,501	79,256	8,325	119,629	64,042
1978	1,222,722	1,086,240	72,695	1,158,935	124,589	-49,948	984,398	152,280	86,044	9,463	129,214	71,236
1979	1,411,679	1,284,134	58,472	1,342,606	152,526	-59,659	1,130,421	182,134	99,124	10,235	137,929	77,504
1980	1,585,039	1,351,486	107,312	1,458,798	159,895	-62,309	1,236,594	220,161	128,284	10,893	145,515	78,001
1981	1,870,505	1,677,700	95,127	1,772,827	217,248	-104,809	1,450,770	270,864	148,871	12,519	149,418	82,905
1982	1,934,884	1,664,398	87,982	1,752,380	216,889	-89,354	1,446,137	305,969	182,778	12,640	153,079	77,676
1983	1,969,928	1,633,013	93,703	1,726,716	210,908	-68,535	1,447,273	321,698	200,957	13,188	149,371	74,772
1984	1,960,988	1,514,328	126,040	1,640,368	199,586	-45,429	1,395,353	352,806	212,829	13,301	147,429	71,264
1985	1,986,484	1,579,732	71,484	1,651,216	210,827	-47,830	1,392,559	369,935	223,990	13,569	146,400	72,013
1986	2,085,849	1,630,907	98,519	1,729,426	218,866	-46,011	1,464,549	383,600	237,700	14,233	146,551	72,890
1987	2,163,212	1,682,830	105,728	1,788,558	225,286	-45,280	1,517,992	394,697	250,523	14,661	147,547	76,282
1988	2,226,376	1,712,300	123,261	1,835,561	236,351	-44,815	1,554,395	395,493	276,488	15,171	146,750	76,763
1989	2,382,578	1,787,754	123,374	1,911,128	246,958	-40,686	1,623,484	460,293	298,801	16,306	146,117	78,677
1990	2,618,609	2,032,415	127,930	2,160,345	286,226	-48,287	1,825,832	464,186	328,591	17,304	151,331	84,264
1991	2,861,006	2,212,075	116,961	2,329,036	315,117	-22,010	1,991,909	487,742	381,355	18,341	155,993	86,871
1992	3,185,207	2,472,455	144,861	2,617,316	349,838	-23,385	2,244,093	520,687	420,427	19,701	161,680	89,400
1993	3,534,696	2,718,048	217,013	2,935,061	377,535	-24,287	2,533,239	551,112	450,345	21,030	168,075	93,769
1994	3,802,086	3,012,588	186,200	3,198,788	429,446	-30,268	2,739,074	587,863	475,149	21,732	174,957	100,015
1995	3,883,182	2,975,427	215,708	3,191,135	428,019	-22,321	2,740,795	626,279	516,108	21,513	180,501	97,934
1996	4,026,941	2,952,458	281,136	3,233,594	416,240	-14,083	2,803,271	668,310	555,360	22,174	181,605	97,910
1997	4,126,232	3,030,270	226,829	3,257,099	411,766	-10,047	2,835,286	711,774	579,172	22,436	183,909	98,810
1998	4,341,278	3,190,899	244,469	3,435,368	433,351	1,006	3,003,023	731,897	606,358	23,304	186,290	98,085
1999	4,558,996	3,399,322	221,051	3,620,373	446,738	8,895	3,182,530	721,857	654,609	24,118	189,025	101,033
2000	4,904,123	3,593,524	263,407	3,856,931	481,777	16,107	3,391,261	776,322	736,540	25,450	192,696	102,414
2001	5,284,418	3,897,832	252,573	4,150,405	508,572	19,657	3,661,490	794,624	828,304	26,904	196,420	105,605
2002	5,625,128	4,280,240	279,392	4,559,632	563,119	21,148	4,017,661	756,251	851,216	27,753	202,688	108,554
2003	5,998,362	4,523,419	352,865	4,876,284	594,019	22,175	4,304,440	774,265	919,657	28,694	209,043	111,174
2004	6,311,958	4,845,875	314,403	5,160,278	640,049	25,151	4,545,380	820,891	945,687	29,515	213,854	112,768
2005	6,586,821	5,060,353	318,817	5,379,170	669,666	26,831	4,736,335	830,571	1,019,915	30,065	219,086	115,120
2006	6,840,023	5,122,643	355,040	5,477,683	671,243	31,415	4,837,855	900,715	1,101,453	30,516	224,149	116,133
2007	7,534,516	5,538,654	393,214	5,931,868	726,550	36,277	5,241,595	1,088,326	1,204,595	32,865	229,255	121,399
2008	8,268,791	5,902,927	377,628	6,280,555	770,287	50,915	5,561,183	1,295,811	1,411,797	34,838	237,348	125,641
2009	8,678,842	6,256,125	393,282	6,649,407	829,864	37,119	5,856,662	1,256,187	1,565,993	35,337	245,600	128,235
2010	9,293,632	6,760,856	434,381	7,195,237	886,706	25,577	6,334,108	1,226,475	1,733,049	36,363	255,578	133,222
2011	9,972,592	7,061,227	533,835	7,595,062	835,956	17,585	6,776,691	1,425,943	1,769,958	37,827	263,639	135,781
2012	10,050,159	6,883,455	578,836	7,462,291	801,771	37,317	6,697,837	1,524,859	1,827,463	37,469	268,227	136819
2013	10,000,744	6,960,737	575,397	7,536,134	919,485	21,947	6,638,596	1,506,139	1,856,009	36,894	271,067	136,996
2014	10,379,756	7,226,585	485,227	7,711,812	956,162	22,002	6,777,652	1,563,810	2,038,294	37,842	274,295	139,332

Personal Income and Employment by Area: Killeen-Temple, TX

(Thousands of dollars, except as noted.)

Year	Personal income, total	Earnings by place of work			Less: Contributions for government social insurance	Plus: Adjustment for residence	Equals: Net earnings by place of residence	Plus: Dividends, interest, and rent	Plus: Personal current transfer receipts	Per capita personal income (dollars)	Population (persons)	Total employment
		Nonfarm	Farm	Total								
1970	746,636	597,781	6,948	604,729	36,662	-13,448	554,619	151,793	40,224	4,400	169,695	89,828
1971	808,021	650,851	5,616	656,467	42,553	-12,190	601,724	159,491	46,806	4,633	174,387	90,083
1972	981,840	791,447	10,687	802,134	51,897	-13,052	737,185	191,038	53,617	5,071	193,630	97,294
1973	1,135,046	889,555	26,109	915,664	62,086	-3,549	850,029	221,400	63,617	5,237	216,716	102,623
1974	1,254,822	990,722	5,656	996,378	72,599	850	924,629	255,510	74,683	5,657	221,833	106,605
1975	1,406,044	1,101,937	6,746	1,108,683	85,600	-2,324	1,020,759	291,726	93,559	6,359	221,119	110,740
1976	1,561,836	1,226,036	4,861	1,230,897	97,634	4,656	1,137,919	319,682	104,235	6,794	229,880	115,223
1977	1,662,698	1,300,398	-4,065	1,296,333	102,590	5,301	1,199,044	350,892	112,762	7,151	232,517	117,302
1978	1,856,889	1,428,225	2,093	1,430,318	111,551	-158	1,318,609	412,569	125,711	7,836	236,961	120,403
1979	1,894,405	1,443,844	2,644	1,446,488	118,080	3,722	1,332,130	415,322	146,953	8,140	232,714	114,795
1980	2,151,448	1,622,895	-3,352	1,619,543	132,995	8,556	1,495,104	481,582	174,762	9,438	227,951	117,723
1981	2,444,148	1,859,753	8,900	1,868,653	159,975	-13,452	1,695,226	550,496	198,426	10,503	232,715	121,283
1982	2,663,721	2,019,213	6,046	2,025,259	170,762	-14,711	1,839,786	605,255	218,680	11,143	239,048	121,716
1983	2,864,690	2,163,944	-2,144	2,161,800	188,938	-13,931	1,958,931	664,803	240,956	11,825	242,252	122,761
1984	3,101,334	2,336,362	439	2,336,801	209,963	-11,905	2,114,933	728,072	258,329	12,674	244,697	126,897
1985	3,332,769	2,498,890	-5,052	2,493,838	228,543	-12,560	2,252,735	796,714	283,320	13,192	252,645	131,716
1986	3,514,378	2,634,660	-6,190	2,628,470	243,038	-18,895	2,366,537	840,319	307,522	13,870	253,385	133,296
1987	3,636,993	2,714,173	2,846	2,717,019	250,254	-23,714	2,443,051	864,512	329,430	14,004	259,706	137,444
1988	3,865,468	2,904,777	442	2,905,219	283,667	-28,206	2,593,346	914,638	357,484	14,733	262,373	139,949
1989	4,027,980	2,967,475	7,253	2,974,728	296,527	-27,992	2,650,209	981,197	396,574	15,116	266,463	140,155
1990	4,148,131	3,072,729	4,510	3,077,239	310,507	-32,716	2,734,016	966,898	447,217	15,391	269,515	139,118
1991	4,043,930	2,946,433	9,484	2,955,917	303,482	-21,522	2,630,913	924,554	488,463	15,222	265,657	128,838
1992	4,696,839	3,453,778	9,043	3,462,821	361,663	-26,910	3,074,248	1,038,236	584,355	17,349	270,722	139,350
1993	5,223,581	3,877,713	9,453	3,887,166	411,515	-31,382	3,444,269	1,157,122	622,190	18,226	286,593	151,294
1994	5,680,524	4,242,782	7,485	4,250,267	444,099	-32,610	3,773,558	1,262,132	644,834	18,450	307,884	162,733
1995	6,014,340	4,458,337	-73	4,458,264	458,481	-26,158	3,973,625	1,339,619	701,096	19,202	313,222	169,153
1996	6,288,492	4,605,953	2,812	4,608,765	473,084	-10,878	4,124,803	1,411,728	751,961	19,737	318,613	170,885
1997	6,447,056	4,783,262	2,363	4,785,625	487,425	13,506	4,311,706	1,338,583	796,767	20,033	321,821	172,991
1998	6,921,051	5,038,104	-5,193	5,032,911	506,716	47,230	4,573,425	1,509,515	838,111	21,274	325,335	176,097
1999	7,417,170	5,383,400	10,188	5,393,588	535,276	90,449	4,948,761	1,585,038	883,371	22,789	325,473	179,612
2000	7,848,445	5,682,085	5,480	5,687,565	560,999	118,069	5,244,635	1,627,654	976,156	23,570	332,989	182,510
2001	8,264,850	5,948,193	4,920	5,953,113	595,893	125,482	5,482,702	1,694,258	1,087,890	24,568	336,409	182,501
2002	8,757,889	6,372,033	8,900	6,380,933	637,320	87,169	5,830,782	1,735,701	1,191,406	25,666	341,231	184,853
2003	9,427,760	6,933,198	23,132	6,956,330	694,929	63,785	6,325,186	1,770,581	1,331,993	27,497	342,865	187,184
2004	9,942,474	7,312,302	27,834	7,340,136	738,456	59,434	6,661,114	1,866,641	1,414,719	28,428	349,745	189,914
2005	10,951,016	8,132,741	23,757	8,156,498	810,077	36,518	7,382,939	2,022,037	1,546,040	30,629	357,533	197,292
2006	11,987,648	9,100,068	19,940	9,120,008	893,340	-21,613	8,205,055	2,116,328	1,666,265	32,802	365,460	205,833
2007	13,173,112	9,904,984	4,363	9,909,347	976,414	-50,714	8,882,219	2,433,593	1,857,300	34,593	380,804	215,933
2008	14,426,948	10,765,587	-32,669	10,732,918	1,071,801	-88,541	9,572,576	2,708,011	2,146,361	36,781	392,237	224,177
2009	14,897,357	11,158,129	-40,030	11,118,099	1,141,319	-101,522	9,875,258	2,756,820	2,265,279	37,679	395,375	222,760
2010	15,212,049	11,174,199	-24,566	11,149,633	1,160,552	-92,158	9,896,923	2,708,567	2,606,559	37,265	408,217	217,956
2011	16,078,670	11,539,581	-25,823	11,513,758	1,088,039	-90,864	10,334,855	2,961,201	2,782,614	38,958	412,715	221,316
2012	16,332,169	11,592,600	2,761	11,595,361	1,094,002	-62,797	10,438,562	3,057,784	2,835,823	38,852	420,364	220,767
2013	16,181,083	11,416,880	-4,533	11,412,347	1,196,159	-49,066	10,167,122	3,010,544	3,003,417	38,228	423,282	220,047
2014	16,576,889	11,555,091	10,624	11,565,715	1,198,519	-47,788	10,319,408	3,085,558	3,171,923	39,017	424,858	220,075

Personal Income and Employment by Area: Kingsport-Bristol-Bristol, TN-VA

(Thousands of dollars, except as noted.)

Year	Personal income, total	Earnings by place of work			Less: Contributions for government social insurance	Plus: Adjustment for residence	Equals: Net earnings by place of residence	Plus: Dividends, interest, and rent	Plus: Personal current transfer receipts	Per capita personal income (dollars)	Population (persons)	Total employment
		Nonfarm	Farm	Total								
1970	756,492	658,435	19,281	677,716	43,978	-29,279	604,459	82,534	69,499	3,129	241,800	103,480
1971	815,869	701,033	16,521	717,554	48,661	-25,509	643,384	91,674	80,811	3,303	247,013	103,817
1972	905,586	771,125	23,320	794,445	56,042	-24,614	713,789	101,094	90,703	3,627	249,683	106,749
1973	1,019,775	865,375	27,630	893,005	72,613	-23,493	796,899	114,373	108,503	4,027	253,233	112,348
1974	1,142,344	969,154	21,652	990,806	84,923	-27,963	877,920	132,762	131,662	4,439	257,350	115,905
1975	1,246,922	1,039,406	12,733	1,052,139	88,947	-41,956	921,236	153,588	172,098	4,783	260,702	114,222
1976	1,396,732	1,173,458	19,217	1,192,675	101,998	-48,127	1,042,550	167,216	186,966	5,281	264,479	119,484
1977	1,556,211	1,331,620	13,402	1,345,022	115,508	-60,034	1,169,480	189,748	196,983	5,818	267,499	124,891
1978	1,764,985	1,534,500	16,489	1,550,989	133,630	-86,116	1,331,243	216,690	217,052	6,496	271,688	131,666
1979	1,941,932	1,695,294	6,596	1,701,890	151,086	-110,040	1,440,764	247,328	253,840	7,061	275,007	133,425
1980	2,124,562	1,782,540	9,212	1,791,752	159,005	-117,373	1,515,374	308,388	300,800	7,621	278,763	130,586
1981	2,416,923	1,988,706	23,148	2,011,854	191,421	-133,887	1,686,546	381,891	348,486	8,632	279,993	131,108
1982	2,562,512	2,036,559	19,381	2,055,940	206,451	-101,001	1,748,488	431,756	382,268	9,138	280,418	128,310
1983	2,710,283	2,132,818	7,064	2,139,882	218,001	-98,187	1,823,694	473,228	413,361	9,710	279,113	127,756
1984	2,915,821	2,247,659	13,856	2,261,515	235,450	-87,707	1,938,358	538,692	438,771	10,470	278,485	129,086
1985	3,148,960	2,458,040	14,105	2,472,145	261,926	-97,043	2,113,176	570,162	465,622	11,332	277,884	132,126
1986	3,328,275	2,606,077	4,864	2,610,941	285,255	-97,732	2,227,954	603,591	496,730	12,021	276,878	133,598
1987	3,499,624	2,746,347	14,931	2,761,278	298,286	-93,654	2,369,338	608,740	521,546	12,624	277,217	136,288
1988	3,777,079	2,963,090	18,197	2,981,287	330,066	-104,229	2,546,992	671,132	558,955	13,694	275,824	139,584
1989	4,049,997	3,178,774	21,918	3,200,692	358,456	-117,285	2,724,951	709,675	615,371	14,692	275,656	143,467
1990	4,367,329	3,381,413	28,262	3,409,675	383,977	-117,071	2,908,627	784,356	674,346	15,812	276,205	147,539
1991	4,614,892	3,567,527	29,767	3,597,294	410,766	-125,322	3,061,206	799,362	754,324	16,550	278,847	148,554
1992	4,922,279	3,792,804	39,437	3,832,241	431,845	-119,943	3,280,453	795,555	846,271	17,437	282,292	151,184
1993	5,080,355	3,914,189	31,123	3,945,312	448,578	-132,461	3,364,273	814,216	901,866	17,817	285,142	153,439
1994	5,237,056	3,964,064	27,311	3,991,375	458,288	-95,785	3,437,302	851,138	948,616	18,271	286,625	153,499
1995	5,567,563	4,188,005	15,043	4,203,048	483,661	-110,820	3,608,567	925,874	1,033,122	19,214	289,762	158,102
1996	5,872,704	4,420,022	2,027	4,422,049	500,827	-139,414	3,781,808	1,006,104	1,084,792	20,101	292,153	158,808
1997	6,101,510	4,511,246	6,655	4,517,901	505,902	-111,413	3,900,586	1,058,521	1,142,403	20,736	294,250	160,258
1998	6,408,713	4,666,645	8,216	4,674,861	512,533	-92,702	4,069,626	1,150,839	1,188,248	21,627	296,333	158,495
1999	6,716,381	4,852,424	9,370	4,861,794	527,335	-21,651	4,312,808	1,170,904	1,232,669	22,549	297,863	159,447
2000	7,095,441	4,961,636	24,282	4,985,918	537,392	28,680	4,477,206	1,288,268	1,329,967	23,768	298,534	158,724
2001	7,379,339	5,241,820	16,945	5,258,765	578,617	-50,829	4,629,319	1,295,692	1,454,328	24,709	298,648	157,615
2002	7,538,348	5,356,793	10,942	5,367,735	596,963	-65,697	4,705,075	1,269,675	1,563,598	25,189	299,267	157,444
2003	7,786,530	5,546,476	303	5,546,779	620,267	-73,011	4,853,501	1,297,218	1,635,811	25,923	300,370	157,896
2004	8,100,469	5,781,405	8,669	5,790,074	645,229	-73,223	5,071,622	1,280,614	1,748,233	26,942	300,668	157,017
2005	8,339,068	5,920,973	8,085	5,929,058	670,696	-84,092	5,174,270	1,273,922	1,890,876	27,565	302,519	158,166
2006	8,931,674	6,252,217	-8,899	6,243,318	719,304	-102,088	5,421,926	1,459,318	2,050,430	29,329	304,535	161,157
2007	9,417,235	6,435,937	-18,306	6,417,631	747,955	-116,855	5,552,821	1,640,454	2,223,960	30,695	306,805	162,934
2008	9,849,994	6,564,020	-17,040	6,546,980	776,517	-127,980	5,642,483	1,722,637	2,484,874	31,973	308,069	162,450
2009	9,709,677	6,357,360	-15,060	6,342,300	760,820	-73,659	5,507,821	1,521,232	2,680,624	31,393	309,293	156,262
2010	9,831,920	6,421,476	-14,630	6,406,846	780,670	-118,319	5,507,857	1,457,296	2,866,767	31,758	309,584	153,499
2011	10,512,217	6,905,617	-8,710	6,896,907	744,206	-183,859	5,968,842	1,620,046	2,923,329	34,008	309,107	156,522
2012	10,891,132	7,100,262	-11,675	7,088,587	748,641	-170,547	6,169,399	1,784,963	2,936,770	35,261	308,872	155,222
2013	10,783,044	7,057,375	-7,621	7,049,754	837,835	-186,906	6,025,013	1,752,428	3,005,603	34,969	308,356	154,897
2014	11,063,653	7,213,898	2,132	7,216,030	852,481	-196,282	6,167,267	1,824,292	3,072,094	35,912	308,079	155,683

Personal Income and Employment by Area: Kingston, NY

(Thousands of dollars, except as noted.)

Year	Personal income, total	Earnings by place of work			Less: Contributions for government social insurance	Plus: Adjustment for residence	Equals: Net earnings by place of residence	Plus: Dividends, interest, and rent	Plus: Personal current transfer receipts	Per capita personal income (dollars)	Population (persons)	Total employment
		Nonfarm	Farm	Total								
1970	575,708	411,345	6,869	418,214	31,226	43,041	430,029	90,412	55,267	4,047	142,242	52,414
1971	624,762	437,574	6,704	444,278	34,452	51,998	461,824	97,182	65,756	4,259	146,705	53,640
1972	676,291	467,437	4,043	471,480	38,536	62,670	495,614	104,740	75,937	4,505	150,111	54,890
1973	754,031	517,772	7,123	524,895	49,347	71,399	546,947	118,752	88,332	4,929	152,980	57,237
1974	827,029	547,361	8,995	556,356	53,684	81,872	584,544	136,446	106,039	5,368	154,057	57,453
1975	911,998	568,775	9,644	578,419	54,755	93,670	617,334	149,995	144,669	5,845	156,022	55,738
1976	964,921	597,523	8,456	605,979	58,960	104,547	651,566	155,607	157,748	6,115	157,793	55,635
1977	1,036,515	638,288	9,387	647,675	62,659	121,025	706,041	169,873	160,601	6,579	157,559	56,665
1978	1,142,048	712,702	10,910	723,612	71,437	140,418	792,593	181,181	168,274	7,200	158,617	58,794
1979	1,270,298	797,326	13,556	810,882	82,280	162,165	890,767	197,431	182,100	7,959	159,606	61,376
1980	1,417,489	860,320	12,069	872,389	89,455	186,693	969,627	235,131	212,731	8,965	158,111	61,668
1981	1,568,548	928,046	10,227	938,273	102,508	204,575	1,040,340	285,076	243,132	9,951	157,625	61,536
1982	1,757,311	1,047,384	12,650	1,060,034	116,493	219,673	1,163,214	327,563	266,534	11,138	157,770	63,222
1983	1,932,478	1,195,281	6,514	1,201,795	134,108	222,499	1,290,186	359,523	282,769	12,199	158,414	66,330
1984	2,176,418	1,367,479	8,563	1,376,042	156,527	242,501	1,462,016	419,806	294,596	13,640	159,557	69,296
1985	2,340,089	1,470,361	11,961	1,482,322	170,522	267,003	1,578,803	451,649	309,637	14,637	159,880	71,174
1986	2,516,678	1,629,916	12,194	1,642,110	191,321	276,082	1,726,871	469,470	320,337	15,753	159,760	74,612
1987	2,643,345	1,706,793	15,992	1,722,785	196,061	300,550	1,827,274	489,336	326,735	16,331	161,865	73,866
1988	2,820,351	1,798,613	18,746	1,817,359	211,746	334,116	1,939,729	530,155	350,467	17,315	162,889	76,380
1989	3,079,744	1,908,903	19,024	1,927,927	220,622	354,857	2,062,162	632,767	384,815	18,738	164,359	76,774
1990	3,199,919	1,981,855	18,161	2,000,016	219,515	377,415	2,157,916	618,138	423,865	19,271	166,049	77,348
1991	3,367,813	2,101,545	23,424	2,124,969	238,891	377,158	2,263,236	632,101	472,476	19,943	168,869	77,826
1992	3,578,337	2,197,900	18,949	2,216,849	244,835	404,589	2,376,603	660,941	540,793	20,942	170,872	78,504
1993	3,505,915	2,079,163	18,762	2,097,925	232,371	444,763	2,310,317	624,823	570,775	20,313	172,594	76,404
1994	3,515,570	2,012,694	16,512	2,029,206	226,596	467,445	2,270,055	631,909	613,606	20,409	172,252	76,405
1995	3,597,135	1,951,444	16,993	1,968,437	219,587	519,991	2,268,841	682,073	646,221	20,870	172,362	74,331
1996	3,695,647	1,950,190	14,804	1,964,994	215,026	574,577	2,324,545	692,321	678,781	21,337	173,205	74,388
1997	3,870,596	2,060,383	13,923	2,074,306	222,365	608,289	2,460,230	718,097	692,269	22,226	174,148	75,635
1998	4,144,477	2,204,499	12,134	2,216,633	238,111	675,411	2,653,933	751,154	739,390	23,671	175,085	77,655
1999	4,358,586	2,360,175	19,304	2,379,479	250,647	747,748	2,876,580	727,965	754,041	24,691	176,526	80,685
2000	4,645,629	2,502,126	18,412	2,520,538	267,928	829,860	3,082,470	769,231	793,928	26,127	177,810	82,748
2001	4,893,080	2,565,516	19,102	2,584,618	276,596	953,787	3,261,809	773,888	857,383	27,421	178,440	82,634
2002	4,893,091	2,638,547	7,957	2,646,504	291,527	954,315	3,309,292	670,482	913,317	27,165	180,128	83,384
2003	5,068,041	2,756,555	15,108	2,771,663	303,932	977,349	3,445,080	671,065	951,896	28,009	180,942	84,368
2004	5,323,226	2,865,925	12,633	2,878,558	315,618	1,004,241	3,567,181	753,445	1,002,600	29,273	181,847	85,067
2005	5,590,700	2,981,449	8,279	2,989,728	331,830	1,034,528	3,692,426	850,736	1,047,538	30,644	182,438	85,704
2006	6,081,123	3,278,418	13,288	3,291,706	362,172	1,136,834	4,066,368	899,752	1,115,003	33,258	182,845	86,578
2007	6,362,199	3,379,469	25,737	3,405,206	374,610	1,185,124	4,215,720	964,846	1,181,633	34,801	182,818	87,374
2008	6,749,894	3,469,263	25,973	3,495,236	387,282	1,218,518	4,326,472	1,106,967	1,316,455	36,850	183,174	86,742
2009	6,622,520	3,447,750	23,951	3,471,701	380,974	997,262	4,087,989	1,077,743	1,456,788	36,260	182,638	84,563
2010	6,755,525	3,551,810	25,315	3,577,125	394,461	981,755	4,164,419	1,028,463	1,562,643	37,042	182,374	84,342
2011	7,022,501	3,579,015	20,973	3,599,988	361,139	1,037,167	4,276,016	1,139,110	1,607,375	38,456	182,613	84,066
2012	7,191,507	3,650,988	16,722	3,667,710	366,466	994,282	4,295,526	1,252,598	1,643,383	39,577	181,708	83,757
2013	7,209,701	3,716,528	28,127	3,744,655	420,234	999,283	4,323,704	1,218,294	1,667,703	39,866	180,848	84,147
2014	7,515,195	3,819,116	22,143	3,841,259	436,038	1,114,295	4,519,516	1,256,067	1,739,612	41,648	180,445	85,717

Personal Income and Employment by Area: Knoxville, TN

(Thousands of dollars, except as noted.)

Year	Personal income, total	Earnings by place of work			Less: Contributions for government social insurance	Plus: Adjustment for residence	Equals: Net earnings by place of residence	Plus: Dividends, interest, and rent	Plus: Personal current transfer receipts	Per capita personal income (dollars)	Population (persons)	Total employment
		Nonfarm	Farm	Total								
1970	1,679,179	1,390,376	10,161	1,400,537	89,115	-12,262	1,299,160	208,191	171,828	3,178	528,426	214,863
1971	1,851,167	1,521,201	9,787	1,530,988	100,676	-11,443	1,418,869	230,401	201,897	3,421	541,129	218,824
1972	2,049,381	1,686,594	14,737	1,701,331	117,150	-8,957	1,575,224	251,857	222,300	3,734	548,773	227,791
1973	2,304,790	1,889,882	21,507	1,911,389	150,269	-11,184	1,749,936	288,479	266,375	4,163	553,697	239,669
1974	2,588,291	2,098,597	17,094	2,115,691	172,065	-13,881	1,929,745	341,031	317,515	4,618	560,437	243,085
1975	2,912,975	2,290,110	11,946	2,302,056	184,289	-12,145	2,105,622	401,723	405,630	5,102	570,915	242,890
1976	3,293,139	2,609,779	24,786	2,634,565	213,154	-13,307	2,408,104	438,333	446,702	5,644	583,484	255,754
1977	3,689,507	2,969,462	17,342	2,986,804	241,560	-18,716	2,726,528	494,782	468,197	6,208	594,330	266,898
1978	4,216,902	3,417,189	16,052	3,433,241	280,965	-16,105	3,136,171	564,279	516,452	7,007	601,788	279,856
1979	4,733,477	3,822,430	13,358	3,835,788	327,653	-21,375	3,486,760	640,997	605,720	7,729	612,421	290,671
1980	5,266,847	4,122,694	20,384	4,143,078	353,824	-29,060	3,760,194	789,368	717,285	8,444	623,731	291,449
1981	5,885,095	4,510,730	28,817	4,539,547	420,463	-21,745	4,097,339	970,875	816,881	9,337	630,304	295,737
1982	6,329,120	4,787,578	25,314	4,812,892	461,203	-30,832	4,320,857	1,122,818	885,445	9,944	636,499	299,009
1983	6,684,490	5,035,833	12,007	5,047,840	493,333	-23,522	4,530,985	1,187,789	965,716	10,472	638,326	291,743
1984	7,301,959	5,488,517	23,314	5,511,831	560,310	-27,261	4,924,260	1,366,145	1,011,554	11,470	636,588	301,274
1985	7,732,727	5,826,573	16,093	5,842,666	607,134	-26,117	5,209,415	1,452,032	1,071,280	12,142	636,844	306,615
1986	8,170,665	6,178,962	13,926	6,192,888	661,427	-36,880	5,494,581	1,521,501	1,154,583	12,893	633,710	314,957
1987	8,826,373	6,763,318	14,322	6,777,640	714,866	-39,694	6,023,080	1,582,532	1,220,761	13,864	636,657	327,828
1988	9,698,812	7,507,998	13,375	7,521,373	815,407	-54,377	6,651,589	1,743,282	1,303,941	15,099	642,344	344,316
1989	10,252,071	7,902,774	20,362	7,923,136	874,217	-51,495	6,997,424	1,808,730	1,445,917	15,827	647,744	351,772
1990	11,038,304	8,371,590	22,419	8,394,009	933,743	-35,580	7,424,686	2,018,905	1,594,713	16,890	653,537	358,570
1991	11,616,129	8,808,384	24,568	8,832,952	1,002,645	-73,043	7,757,264	2,054,109	1,804,756	17,464	665,146	360,963
1992	12,602,311	9,664,668	30,375	9,695,043	1,086,650	-105,141	8,503,252	2,072,951	2,026,108	18,590	677,924	371,887
1993	13,442,216	10,349,788	30,355	10,380,143	1,167,114	-119,437	9,093,592	2,180,317	2,168,307	19,510	688,984	385,921
1994	14,098,929	10,853,586	24,992	10,878,578	1,256,250	-128,102	9,494,226	2,332,375	2,272,328	20,098	701,511	398,164
1995	14,996,045	11,430,834	21,094	11,451,928	1,327,502	-148,660	9,975,766	2,551,970	2,468,309	20,993	714,347	407,652
1996	15,683,560	11,920,852	10,497	11,931,349	1,364,048	-169,088	10,398,213	2,699,942	2,585,405	21,640	724,741	411,103
1997	16,548,036	12,582,379	15,120	12,597,499	1,431,114	-206,072	10,960,313	2,901,762	2,685,961	22,602	732,158	415,188
1998	18,093,239	13,926,416	18,686	13,945,102	1,522,807	-204,755	12,217,540	3,095,462	2,780,237	24,538	737,355	425,836
1999	18,611,959	14,370,059	23,996	14,394,055	1,582,853	-179,150	12,632,052	3,078,747	2,901,160	25,033	743,499	431,313
2000	20,165,093	15,498,634	30,978	15,529,612	1,674,502	-192,733	13,662,377	3,315,252	3,187,464	26,892	749,847	441,545
2001	20,699,929	15,815,094	40,254	15,855,348	1,700,284	-230,056	13,925,008	3,339,473	3,435,448	27,364	756,459	440,866
2002	21,205,996	16,380,836	40,373	16,421,209	1,796,139	-299,641	14,325,429	3,187,669	3,692,898	27,780	763,352	443,073
2003	22,013,239	17,080,115	25,441	17,105,556	1,874,641	-330,003	14,900,912	3,270,681	3,841,646	28,510	772,111	449,153
2004	23,231,546	18,163,631	20,415	18,184,046	1,983,324	-342,725	15,857,997	3,300,168	4,073,381	29,779	780,124	464,110
2005	24,281,985	18,911,273	15,831	18,927,104	2,072,481	-352,206	16,502,417	3,433,186	4,346,382	30,711	790,669	473,135
2006	25,889,712	20,024,478	3,300	20,027,778	2,189,683	-372,279	17,465,816	3,778,205	4,645,691	32,167	804,860	484,452
2007	27,157,121	20,624,619	-13,273	20,611,346	2,293,834	-391,796	17,925,716	4,169,991	5,061,414	33,261	816,480	494,871
2008	28,597,169	21,178,664	-11,840	21,166,824	2,378,225	-437,127	18,351,472	4,560,054	5,685,643	34,575	827,099	497,087
2009	28,093,241	20,687,921	-6,932	20,680,989	2,358,168	-506,810	17,816,011	4,161,301	6,115,929	33,691	833,862	477,792
2010	29,185,515	21,312,978	-1,400	21,311,578	2,438,167	-479,727	18,393,684	4,174,627	6,617,204	34,799	838,687	474,319
2011	31,056,689	22,436,562	-3,276	22,433,286	2,277,514	-609,899	19,545,873	4,771,702	6,739,114	36,850	842,785	481,973
2012	32,689,610	23,441,423	6,234	23,447,657	2,299,724	-491,848	20,656,085	5,173,481	6,860,044	38,557	847,817	480,660
2013	32,679,709	23,781,470	19,103	23,800,573	2,649,366	-520,065	20,631,142	4,988,619	7,059,948	38,359	851,951	483,259
2014	33,900,697	24,719,769	23,012	24,742,781	2,741,874	-542,772	21,458,135	5,200,053	7,242,509	39,530	857,585	491,733

Personal Income and Employment by Area: Kokomo, IN

(Thousands of dollars, except as noted.)

Year	Personal income, total	Derivation of personal income								Per capita personal income (dollars)	Population (persons)	Total employment
		Earnings by place of work			Less: Contributions for government social insurance	Plus: Adjustment for residence	Equals: Net earnings by place of residence	Plus: Dividends, interest, and rent	Plus: Personal current transfer receipts			
		Nonfarm	Farm	Total								
1970	330,942	339,403	5,101	344,504	22,733	-52,938	268,833	39,985	22,124	3,970	83,353	42,282
1971	383,343	400,345	7,664	408,009	27,903	-65,977	314,129	43,703	25,511	4,569	83,904	44,735
1972	427,688	460,789	5,807	466,596	34,537	-78,906	353,153	46,444	28,091	5,042	84,832	46,840
1973	496,910	536,224	17,916	554,140	46,926	-94,934	412,280	52,922	31,708	5,795	85,745	50,105
1974	504,914	533,791	9,731	543,522	48,464	-94,199	400,859	60,778	43,277	5,789	87,215	47,441
1975	527,853	521,184	17,570	538,754	46,757	-92,547	399,450	67,979	60,424	6,074	86,906	43,959
1976	600,848	646,542	10,822	657,364	58,907	-124,762	473,695	74,606	52,547	6,930	86,700	47,377
1977	669,691	746,452	5,793	752,245	67,991	-152,605	531,649	84,007	54,035	7,687	87,123	49,509
1978	736,493	827,814	9,483	837,297	77,815	-174,369	585,113	90,896	60,484	8,441	87,248	50,886
1979	780,039	868,697	7,452	876,149	84,319	-185,580	606,250	98,857	74,932	8,935	87,305	49,709
1980	836,283	862,930	1,444	864,374	83,180	-187,595	593,599	119,470	123,214	9,637	86,774	45,809
1981	883,986	922,338	85	922,423	95,940	-197,350	629,133	145,625	109,228	10,267	86,098	46,275
1982	877,951	866,039	2,790	868,829	91,592	-176,972	600,265	156,297	121,389	10,328	85,004	42,641
1983	968,777	993,458	-1,920	991,538	106,423	-208,101	677,014	166,387	125,376	11,460	84,532	43,455
1984	1,108,256	1,165,151	7,157	1,172,308	128,577	-250,111	793,620	186,649	127,987	13,089	84,671	47,020
1985	1,203,393	1,285,290	8,624	1,293,914	143,969	-278,604	871,341	198,989	133,063	14,248	84,459	47,707
1986	1,228,258	1,289,373	6,711	1,296,084	143,515	-271,684	880,885	206,918	140,455	14,663	83,768	47,674
1987	1,250,968	1,302,502	9,828	1,312,330	143,223	-267,132	901,975	203,928	145,065	15,199	82,308	48,068
1988	1,360,533	1,450,783	5,576	1,456,359	163,395	-302,538	990,426	214,491	155,616	16,798	80,994	48,902
1989	1,466,304	1,534,774	10,431	1,545,205	173,296	-317,414	1,054,495	240,604	171,205	18,158	80,751	49,968
1990	1,509,489	1,542,136	13,107	1,555,243	180,307	-304,179	1,070,757	248,883	189,849	18,641	80,976	50,562
1991	1,542,351	1,588,429	8,786	1,597,215	187,804	-319,785	1,089,626	242,725	210,000	18,827	81,924	50,375
1992	1,654,522	1,716,279	12,379	1,728,658	199,092	-359,688	1,169,878	243,835	240,809	20,046	82,537	52,015
1993	1,763,844	1,858,615	15,884	1,874,499	218,365	-404,750	1,251,384	260,661	251,799	21,182	83,271	53,683
1994	1,876,452	2,044,467	16,630	2,061,097	240,030	-467,682	1,353,385	265,286	257,781	22,450	83,584	53,788
1995	1,970,165	2,130,441	8,025	2,138,466	236,695	-506,087	1,395,684	310,258	264,223	23,481	83,905	56,546
1996	2,032,988	2,164,131	21,936	2,186,067	229,036	-525,903	1,431,128	320,014	281,846	24,015	84,656	56,874
1997	2,070,159	2,177,135	20,605	2,197,740	227,438	-528,561	1,441,741	339,125	289,293	24,450	84,669	56,082
1998	2,198,357	2,329,922	11,951	2,341,873	232,288	-568,980	1,540,605	360,442	297,310	26,059	84,361	56,600
1999	2,309,325	2,504,341	7,155	2,511,496	245,574	-628,054	1,637,868	355,467	315,990	27,242	84,772	57,196
2000	2,403,844	2,562,243	13,580	2,575,823	248,848	-648,326	1,678,649	384,660	340,535	28,300	84,940	57,367
2001	2,342,701	2,446,656	15,228	2,461,884	281,275	-597,189	1,583,420	374,767	384,514	27,591	84,909	54,724
2002	2,396,186	2,515,461	9,719	2,525,180	288,513	-603,557	1,633,110	360,154	402,922	28,336	84,563	54,137
2003	2,454,868	2,545,458	14,966	2,560,424	292,938	-598,723	1,668,763	364,199	421,906	29,039	84,538	52,861
2004	2,545,915	2,646,279	24,697	2,670,976	300,284	-604,645	1,766,047	328,522	451,346	30,204	84,291	52,468
2005	2,591,572	2,640,576	15,455	2,656,031	300,958	-584,829	1,770,244	328,812	492,516	30,712	84,382	52,031
2006	2,712,300	2,694,645	10,515	2,705,160	311,369	-572,056	1,821,735	352,500	538,065	32,311	83,943	51,743
2007	2,821,308	2,721,422	11,343	2,732,765	315,629	-555,241	1,861,895	394,086	565,327	33,690	83,743	51,257
2008	2,721,871	2,420,200	24,414	2,444,614	287,455	-474,172	1,682,987	395,309	643,575	32,608	83,472	48,679
2009	2,541,836	2,023,135	10,845	2,033,980	248,085	-326,602	1,459,293	371,177	711,366	30,735	82,701	43,728
2010	2,572,023	2,036,919	5,396	2,042,315	247,795	-326,203	1,468,317	357,401	746,305	31,076	82,766	44,910
2011	2,729,374	2,168,456	21,422	2,189,878	235,324	-368,709	1,585,845	394,763	748,766	32,928	82,888	45,904
2012	2,836,417	2,253,678	26,366	2,280,044	242,569	-385,678	1,651,797	410,906	773,714	34,185	82,973	46,741
2013	2,868,562	2,333,400	48,408	2,381,808	293,985	-415,748	1,672,075	409,165	787,322	34,577	82,961	47,916
2014	2,964,748	2,444,495	21,809	2,466,304	307,318	-433,943	1,725,043	426,551	813,154	35,728	82,982	48,843

Personal Income and Employment by Area: La Crosse-Onalaska, WI-MN

(Thousands of dollars, except as noted.)

Year	Personal income, total	Earnings by place of work			Less: Contributions for government social insurance	Plus: Adjustment for residence	Equals: Net earnings by place of residence	Plus: Dividends, interest, and rent	Plus: Personal current transfer receipts	Per capita personal income (dollars)	Population (persons)	Total employment
		Nonfarm	Farm	Total								
1970	350,940	265,650	18,975	284,625	19,719	-7,003	257,903	57,443	35,594	3,572	98,260	42,995
1971	378,509	284,947	19,289	304,236	21,845	-7,223	275,168	61,439	41,902	3,812	99,301	43,907
1972	411,990	312,922	21,855	334,777	25,281	-8,417	301,079	65,159	45,752	4,173	98,738	45,533
1973	465,818	353,354	31,478	384,832	32,705	-9,951	342,176	71,080	52,562	4,651	100,165	48,430
1974	511,746	392,276	24,873	417,149	37,822	-11,763	367,564	80,214	63,968	5,026	101,810	49,921
1975	564,166	429,483	19,890	449,373	40,610	-13,112	395,651	89,980	78,535	5,393	104,618	50,747
1976	634,011	493,766	19,442	513,208	47,636	-16,114	449,458	99,095	85,458	6,113	103,720	53,331
1977	714,762	553,197	30,107	583,304	53,355	-19,506	510,443	113,160	91,159	6,723	106,314	55,192
1978	799,610	633,322	28,734	662,056	62,648	-24,041	575,367	123,892	100,351	7,302	109,509	57,889
1979	894,673	713,379	27,666	741,045	73,651	-26,424	640,970	136,300	117,403	8,035	111,346	60,200
1980	1,016,031	793,095	25,165	818,260	81,539	-31,130	705,591	170,424	140,016	9,262	109,696	61,582
1981	1,132,427	869,814	25,271	895,085	95,804	-38,119	761,162	211,988	159,277	10,251	110,473	62,428
1982	1,210,277	904,286	24,697	928,983	100,726	-38,828	789,429	245,356	175,492	10,903	111,000	61,655
1983	1,287,107	972,848	9,211	982,059	107,946	-42,081	832,032	263,652	191,423	11,583	111,122	62,200
1984	1,409,363	1,060,038	25,696	1,085,734	120,446	-45,509	919,779	291,904	197,680	12,559	112,222	64,086
1985	1,485,249	1,111,139	30,350	1,141,489	127,277	-47,845	966,367	305,674	213,208	13,151	112,937	64,642
1986	1,563,120	1,162,301	41,491	1,203,792	133,262	-49,440	1,021,090	323,825	218,205	13,820	113,108	65,626
1987	1,667,898	1,255,016	46,390	1,301,406	141,399	-53,685	1,106,322	337,184	224,392	14,608	114,178	67,341
1988	1,762,016	1,376,242	26,650	1,402,892	161,277	-60,714	1,180,901	347,375	233,740	15,324	114,981	70,751
1989	1,936,142	1,480,702	45,117	1,525,819	174,225	-64,340	1,287,254	395,341	253,547	16,735	115,693	70,706
1990	2,085,969	1,563,608	47,337	1,610,945	190,349	-65,676	1,354,920	460,341	270,708	17,864	116,769	72,019
1991	2,133,306	1,635,318	34,342	1,669,660	201,251	-69,304	1,399,105	446,818	287,383	18,125	117,700	73,440
1992	2,275,972	1,762,919	33,911	1,796,830	213,582	-74,460	1,508,788	454,825	312,359	19,093	119,207	75,248
1993	2,414,555	1,880,504	23,131	1,903,635	226,964	-79,108	1,597,563	494,534	322,458	20,022	120,597	77,177
1994	2,555,144	2,007,064	25,708	2,032,772	244,263	-83,968	1,704,541	521,358	329,245	20,969	121,856	79,874
1995	2,627,393	2,054,632	12,051	2,066,683	251,075	-83,869	1,731,739	543,605	352,049	21,377	122,910	81,628
1996	2,780,050	2,195,930	26,283	2,222,213	266,815	-90,508	1,864,890	555,720	359,440	22,434	123,920	83,209
1997	2,932,227	2,354,003	19,722	2,373,725	283,335	-98,635	1,991,755	569,651	370,821	23,548	124,521	85,030
1998	3,149,745	2,511,724	29,481	2,541,205	299,955	-103,801	2,137,449	634,218	378,078	25,123	125,371	86,832
1999	3,257,428	2,611,840	24,275	2,636,115	311,735	-97,361	2,227,019	632,688	397,721	25,844	126,041	87,151
2000	3,432,071	2,723,400	14,998	2,738,398	322,799	-99,208	2,316,391	681,989	433,691	27,020	127,021	88,456
2001	3,612,809	2,863,102	17,959	2,881,061	334,273	-115,856	2,430,932	695,714	486,163	28,308	127,624	88,810
2002	3,680,537	2,933,515	14,479	2,947,994	341,315	-121,185	2,485,494	660,885	534,158	28,696	128,261	87,975
2003	3,866,369	3,095,808	27,088	3,122,896	355,758	-126,897	2,640,241	676,744	549,384	30,023	128,780	89,144
2004	4,011,150	3,194,469	38,067	3,232,536	366,039	-127,923	2,738,574	706,923	565,653	31,096	128,992	89,278
2005	4,156,174	3,311,586	37,231	3,348,817	382,914	-140,137	2,825,766	729,368	601,040	32,082	129,549	90,461
2006	4,391,934	3,481,541	27,160	3,508,701	406,084	-157,527	2,945,090	811,085	635,759	33,746	130,147	92,380
2007	4,623,826	3,586,736	26,384	3,613,120	422,626	-157,381	3,033,113	901,373	689,340	35,245	131,190	93,393
2008	4,943,686	3,770,269	31,299	3,801,568	442,562	-166,732	3,192,274	980,355	771,057	37,475	131,920	93,207
2009	4,979,986	3,780,082	12,649	3,792,731	442,712	-170,979	3,179,040	918,383	882,563	37,423	133,072	91,355
2010	5,022,664	3,831,475	26,830	3,858,305	458,936	-172,103	3,227,266	837,449	957,949	37,523	133,856	91,409
2011	5,371,511	3,967,143	52,653	4,019,796	427,253	-173,052	3,419,491	1,024,528	927,492	40,015	134,238	92,351
2012	5,626,535	4,118,372	59,814	4,178,186	440,330	-182,956	3,554,900	1,119,644	951,991	41,479	135,647	93,954
2013	5,621,488	4,232,549	50,516	4,283,065	511,250	-182,046	3,589,769	1,051,422	980,297	41,287	136,156	94,857
2014	5,832,793	4,389,243	54,484	4,443,727	529,202	-195,818	3,718,707	1,092,781	1,021,305	42,653	136,749	95,192

Personal Income and Employment by Area: Lafayette, LA

(Thousands of dollars, except as noted.)

Year	Personal income, total	Earnings by place of work			Less: Contributions for government social insurance	Plus: Adjustment for residence	Equals: Net earnings by place of residence	Plus: Dividends, interest, and rent	Plus: Personal current transfer receipts	Per capita personal income (dollars)	Population (persons)	Total employment
		Nonfarm	Farm	Total								
1970	799,475	585,891	39,652	625,543	36,957	24,871	613,457	102,561	83,457	2,688	297,437	106,400
1971	878,013	647,316	38,897	686,213	41,721	23,460	667,952	114,108	95,953	2,910	301,678	108,662
1972	977,604	731,156	45,181	776,337	49,714	21,076	747,699	125,606	104,299	3,176	307,819	113,843
1973	1,142,966	826,792	101,536	928,328	65,085	17,236	880,479	141,631	120,856	3,658	312,430	119,859
1974	1,336,227	954,515	122,915	1,077,430	77,644	17,881	1,017,667	174,291	144,269	4,213	317,134	124,542
1975	1,547,626	1,130,713	105,665	1,236,378	91,074	18,537	1,163,841	206,444	177,341	4,797	322,597	130,569
1976	1,707,048	1,336,024	42,940	1,378,964	109,380	13,891	1,283,475	226,431	197,142	5,159	330,873	137,893
1977	1,972,686	1,577,379	50,850	1,628,229	128,516	6,329	1,506,042	256,717	209,927	5,840	337,770	147,120
1978	2,360,594	1,963,989	35,423	1,999,412	164,968	-2,716	1,831,728	299,968	228,898	6,856	344,306	161,185
1979	2,767,296	2,324,040	53,177	2,377,217	204,852	-15,503	2,156,862	350,101	260,333	7,867	351,776	170,540
1980	3,311,333	2,777,554	27,202	2,804,756	244,515	-32,427	2,527,814	473,474	310,045	9,161	361,450	181,105
1981	4,069,789	3,459,631	16,031	3,475,662	329,428	-61,591	3,084,643	641,847	343,299	10,966	371,133	199,253
1982	4,535,509	3,753,607	42,429	3,796,036	370,924	-77,190	3,347,922	784,546	403,041	11,759	385,710	205,964
1983	4,503,675	3,530,064	27,416	3,557,480	341,351	-63,432	3,152,697	847,921	503,057	11,438	393,737	193,845
1984	4,654,310	3,653,169	12,044	3,665,213	364,278	-57,313	3,243,622	906,125	504,563	11,844	392,956	193,564
1985	4,864,472	3,749,852	28,171	3,778,023	379,562	-57,415	3,341,046	990,091	533,335	12,299	395,505	192,643
1986	4,591,673	3,371,808	16,568	3,388,376	334,428	-35,430	3,018,518	938,546	634,609	11,564	397,056	174,850
1987	4,345,373	3,145,323	22,222	3,167,545	306,254	-15,111	2,846,180	866,595	632,598	11,167	389,109	164,848
1988	4,699,332	3,437,197	79,750	3,516,947	352,178	-16,715	3,148,054	905,032	646,246	12,243	383,841	171,932
1989	5,058,003	3,649,805	65,716	3,715,521	376,284	-11,225	3,328,012	1,017,702	712,289	13,179	383,800	177,407
1990	5,502,100	4,083,473	36,132	4,119,605	432,145	-18,655	3,668,805	1,052,894	780,401	14,351	383,397	186,879
1991	5,782,893	4,276,106	43,202	4,319,308	464,819	-21,780	3,832,709	1,053,534	896,650	14,893	388,299	191,220
1992	6,084,108	4,411,039	61,344	4,472,383	470,247	-1,984	4,000,152	1,055,261	1,028,695	15,500	392,531	188,119
1993	6,474,152	4,682,443	72,349	4,754,792	503,980	-5,465	4,245,347	1,107,635	1,121,170	16,270	397,922	195,210
1994	6,962,373	5,043,457	54,811	5,098,268	554,587	-24,064	4,519,617	1,184,005	1,258,751	17,303	402,385	201,325
1995	7,366,197	5,301,924	89,238	5,391,162	582,132	-47,273	4,761,757	1,304,803	1,299,637	18,114	406,658	208,746
1996	7,947,136	5,814,050	99,344	5,913,394	636,478	-76,557	5,200,359	1,420,986	1,325,791	19,325	411,228	217,292
1997	8,745,578	6,530,592	85,973	6,616,565	707,932	-100,202	5,808,431	1,574,326	1,362,821	20,995	416,562	228,667
1998	9,269,309	6,975,849	78,228	7,054,077	751,563	-126,020	6,176,494	1,690,656	1,402,159	22,013	421,081	237,221
1999	9,206,107	6,788,239	73,061	6,861,300	723,511	-93,127	6,044,662	1,689,619	1,471,826	21,707	424,114	232,328
2000	9,795,806	7,236,007	71,574	7,307,581	761,001	-116,453	6,430,127	1,849,451	1,516,228	23,040	425,158	235,868
2001	10,685,730	8,002,510	76,068	8,078,578	862,900	-154,977	7,060,701	1,872,944	1,752,085	25,040	426,750	242,178
2002	10,876,904	8,250,644	45,341	8,295,985	882,222	-207,905	7,205,858	1,814,869	1,856,177	25,274	430,358	242,726
2003	11,263,271	8,643,953	90,029	8,733,982	904,401	-238,672	7,590,909	1,814,167	1,858,195	26,018	432,900	244,233
2004	11,750,146	9,042,785	75,804	9,118,589	931,191	-251,847	7,935,551	1,772,517	2,042,078	26,949	436,018	245,222
2005	13,027,378	9,911,719	55,699	9,967,418	999,439	-299,649	8,668,330	2,085,603	2,273,445	29,612	439,936	251,706
2006	14,909,702	11,396,295	65,219	11,461,514	1,140,305	-409,058	9,912,151	2,613,714	2,383,837	33,078	450,740	267,223
2007	15,969,288	12,191,979	81,374	12,273,353	1,228,531	-452,432	10,592,390	2,881,622	2,495,276	35,150	454,315	276,773
2008	18,403,409	13,632,381	120,730	13,753,111	1,325,275	-406,195	12,021,641	3,508,200	2,873,568	40,085	459,111	282,147
2009	17,309,058	12,976,579	103,208	13,079,787	1,290,797	-365,909	11,423,081	2,875,201	3,010,776	37,304	463,998	278,581
2010	18,278,913	13,572,881	97,625	13,670,506	1,326,615	-355,320	11,988,571	3,080,515	3,209,827	39,087	467,650	278,751
2011	19,173,652	14,453,525	101,947	14,555,472	1,240,949	-359,237	12,955,286	2,944,448	3,273,918	40,736	470,677	285,761
2012	20,988,440	15,426,811	124,579	15,551,390	1,310,864	-414,395	13,826,131	3,856,595	3,305,714	44,259	474,220	293,965
2013	20,985,402	16,036,907	179,262	16,216,169	1,558,921	-380,116	14,277,132	3,294,168	3,414,102	43,741	479,763	300,515
2014	21,847,615	16,879,894	111,758	16,991,652	1,630,407	-387,778	14,973,467	3,431,295	3,442,853	45,049	484,974	303,795

Personal Income and Employment by Area: Lafayette-West Lafayette, IN

(Thousands of dollars, except as noted.)

| Year | Personal income, total | Derivation of personal income | | | | | | | | | Per capita personal income (dollars) | Population (persons) | Total employment |
| | | Earnings by place of work | | | Less: Contributions for government social insurance | Plus: Adjustment for residence | Equals: Net earnings by place of residence | Plus: Dividends, interest, and rent | Plus: Personal current transfer receipts | | | |
		Nonfarm	Farm	Total								
1970	503,973	413,708	20,631	434,339	28,045	-14,855	391,439	79,097	33,437	3,636	138,617	62,709
1971	558,408	440,110	35,303	475,413	30,892	-13,936	430,585	87,864	39,959	3,966	140,794	63,225
1972	599,417	480,817	27,485	508,302	35,671	-14,439	458,192	95,613	45,612	4,152	144,368	64,982
1973	710,502	532,372	75,074	607,446	45,500	-15,103	546,843	109,864	53,795	4,968	143,014	67,510
1974	749,300	582,988	49,767	632,755	52,537	-18,267	561,951	126,176	61,173	5,160	145,206	68,865
1975	845,947	612,536	87,733	700,269	54,672	-18,654	626,943	141,222	77,782	5,832	145,041	68,001
1976	898,689	680,637	62,857	743,494	61,149	-17,392	664,953	151,896	81,840	6,117	146,905	70,142
1977	977,305	772,112	37,801	809,913	68,649	-21,203	720,061	171,209	86,035	6,578	148,579	72,763
1978	1,108,953	881,694	47,200	928,894	80,449	-25,419	823,026	190,077	95,850	7,377	150,334	75,536
1979	1,232,887	976,723	53,338	1,030,061	92,420	-28,307	909,334	214,684	108,869	8,126	151,718	75,825
1980	1,321,274	1,038,421	19,870	1,058,291	97,674	-30,210	930,407	261,155	129,712	8,698	151,907	76,075
1981	1,482,797	1,110,934	41,251	1,152,185	113,096	-29,032	1,010,057	322,853	149,887	9,715	152,637	75,590
1982	1,556,737	1,140,627	38,427	1,179,054	118,701	-31,514	1,028,839	359,656	168,242	10,126	153,738	74,541
1983	1,597,760	1,189,393	-2,527	1,186,866	123,193	-29,726	1,033,947	380,185	183,628	10,379	153,944	74,681
1984	1,776,629	1,300,144	48,005	1,348,149	137,269	-31,208	1,179,672	404,072	192,885	11,570	153,552	77,450
1985	1,877,009	1,373,319	52,368	1,425,687	147,204	-34,514	1,243,969	429,231	203,809	12,171	154,225	78,778
1986	1,971,491	1,471,806	36,502	1,508,308	158,406	-41,344	1,308,558	447,884	215,049	12,780	154,265	80,336
1987	2,085,262	1,584,952	45,674	1,630,626	167,220	-50,211	1,413,195	453,711	218,356	13,468	154,829	82,628
1988	2,185,349	1,720,095	11,447	1,731,542	189,749	-51,453	1,490,340	464,635	230,374	13,968	156,458	85,370
1989	2,443,925	1,878,033	55,990	1,934,023	207,584	-61,220	1,665,219	528,816	249,890	15,378	158,926	87,860
1990	2,595,592	2,037,048	50,175	2,087,223	231,033	-76,425	1,779,765	546,648	269,179	16,317	159,075	90,758
1991	2,669,061	2,180,009	-3,015	2,176,994	250,304	-89,697	1,836,993	541,804	290,264	16,514	161,622	92,258
1992	2,892,888	2,331,659	38,090	2,369,749	264,547	-101,380	2,003,822	562,054	327,012	17,646	163,942	93,614
1993	3,039,217	2,443,825	41,225	2,485,050	278,886	-105,513	2,100,651	594,522	344,044	18,216	166,846	95,426
1994	3,228,044	2,600,330	52,280	2,652,610	299,856	-117,644	2,235,110	634,432	358,502	19,126	168,780	97,690
1995	3,407,108	2,782,954	3,352	2,786,306	320,352	-139,459	2,326,495	713,250	367,363	19,903	171,187	101,510
1996	3,601,247	2,899,299	77,639	2,976,938	328,711	-157,170	2,491,057	723,146	387,044	20,776	173,337	103,302
1997	3,825,667	3,100,008	69,596	3,169,604	350,340	-184,045	2,635,219	788,627	401,821	21,926	174,481	105,842
1998	4,097,444	3,367,857	27,745	3,395,602	369,632	-203,757	2,822,213	839,419	435,812	23,307	175,806	109,954
1999	4,223,612	3,533,219	21,321	3,554,540	384,551	-221,492	2,948,497	817,252	457,863	23,816	177,346	112,295
2000	4,550,931	3,795,748	25,859	3,821,607	404,838	-244,949	3,171,820	881,684	497,427	25,435	178,921	113,622
2001	4,727,769	3,927,718	39,892	3,967,610	422,458	-237,492	3,307,660	879,330	540,779	26,163	180,706	111,550
2002	4,745,461	3,946,654	30,018	3,976,672	426,417	-252,325	3,297,930	870,225	577,306	26,105	181,781	110,875
2003	4,794,974	4,005,866	47,404	4,053,270	435,199	-256,415	3,361,656	828,402	604,916	26,113	183,621	108,505
2004	5,060,752	4,228,610	88,905	4,317,515	459,130	-278,630	3,579,755	837,590	643,407	27,356	184,996	109,470
2005	5,288,654	4,462,713	62,098	4,524,811	488,518	-293,675	3,742,618	841,995	704,041	28,128	188,023	111,504
2006	5,569,176	4,614,070	55,032	4,669,102	509,364	-286,048	3,873,690	932,174	763,312	28,997	192,060	113,917
2007	5,837,620	4,751,352	84,336	4,835,688	527,992	-278,649	4,029,047	999,418	809,155	29,914	195,149	115,929
2008	6,245,255	4,918,035	135,629	5,053,664	551,479	-279,901	4,222,284	1,069,146	953,825	31,549	197,954	115,922
2009	6,008,613	4,700,771	75,046	4,775,817	537,201	-290,369	3,948,247	1,018,827	1,041,539	29,927	200,775	112,212
2010	6,194,562	4,799,517	92,825	4,892,342	546,331	-284,203	4,061,808	988,614	1,144,140	30,658	202,055	111,642
2011	6,653,552	5,079,683	171,735	5,251,418	510,712	-308,173	4,432,533	1,092,689	1,128,330	32,546	204,434	115,252
2012	6,901,888	5,326,632	116,876	5,443,508	532,276	-329,406	4,581,826	1,166,770	1,153,292	33,325	207,110	118,420
2013	6,998,495	5,323,833	269,390	5,593,223	608,466	-307,220	4,677,537	1,159,783	1,161,175	33,363	209,769	118,756
2014	7,249,868	5,604,683	178,952	5,783,635	638,446	-310,821	4,834,368	1,191,751	1,223,749	34,246	211,697	120,808

Personal Income and Employment by Area: Lake Charles, LA

(Thousands of dollars, except as noted.)

Year	Personal income, total	Earnings by place of work			Less: Contributions for government social insurance	Plus: Adjustment for residence	Equals: Net earnings by place of residence	Plus: Dividends, interest, and rent	Plus: Personal current transfer receipts	Per capita personal income (dollars)	Population (persons)	Total employment
		Nonfarm	Farm	Total								
1970	488,499	408,772	8,433	417,205	26,515	-3,097	387,593	55,747	45,159	3,181	153,590	57,589
1971	525,817	440,452	8,758	449,210	29,222	-5,744	414,244	61,166	50,407	3,400	154,666	57,881
1972	552,356	458,693	8,903	467,596	31,780	-5,961	429,855	66,117	56,384	3,515	157,151	57,794
1973	621,987	516,555	18,047	534,602	41,616	-10,345	482,641	72,285	67,061	3,915	158,870	60,991
1974	707,094	591,280	16,504	607,784	49,209	-15,480	543,095	86,443	77,556	4,438	159,343	62,986
1975	804,282	670,831	15,228	686,059	54,433	-21,368	610,258	97,833	96,191	5,015	160,391	65,067
1976	911,375	791,524	2,070	793,594	65,168	-28,958	699,468	105,546	106,361	5,601	162,731	68,125
1977	1,027,317	895,936	8,560	904,496	73,112	-36,962	794,422	116,940	115,955	6,206	165,539	71,271
1978	1,214,218	1,091,786	10,762	1,102,548	91,950	-59,544	951,054	139,469	123,695	7,243	167,630	78,314
1979	1,397,832	1,285,678	11,753	1,297,431	112,962	-85,552	1,098,917	162,334	136,581	8,131	171,913	82,909
1980	1,629,846	1,494,999	8,637	1,503,636	130,913	-112,200	1,260,523	202,409	166,914	9,185	177,456	86,336
1981	1,885,294	1,723,896	3,871	1,727,767	162,348	-127,897	1,437,522	262,240	185,532	10,432	180,724	89,401
1982	1,925,536	1,645,077	5,670	1,650,747	157,870	-105,383	1,387,494	308,958	229,084	10,473	183,865	82,812
1983	2,016,893	1,662,420	4,750	1,667,170	157,302	-108,287	1,401,581	342,603	272,709	10,921	184,681	80,277
1984	2,037,267	1,631,345	2,356	1,633,701	156,757	-94,502	1,382,442	379,982	274,843	11,055	184,287	78,899
1985	2,099,066	1,659,893	4,615	1,664,508	160,808	-95,647	1,408,053	409,832	281,181	11,468	183,031	78,558
1986	2,104,169	1,644,435	61	1,644,496	158,069	-95,059	1,391,368	403,813	308,988	11,606	181,297	76,259
1987	2,166,564	1,713,408	1,930	1,715,338	162,760	-95,271	1,457,307	395,092	314,165	12,022	180,214	77,853
1988	2,299,594	1,797,755	13,651	1,811,406	179,495	-95,531	1,536,380	436,589	326,625	12,850	178,955	79,865
1989	2,443,213	1,921,995	2,519	1,924,514	195,459	-106,586	1,622,469	452,981	367,763	13,743	177,773	82,655
1990	2,725,887	2,171,880	4,960	2,176,840	227,866	-125,719	1,823,255	495,036	407,596	15,355	177,524	87,736
1991	2,881,469	2,308,158	2,286	2,310,444	247,093	-131,871	1,931,480	495,665	454,324	16,058	179,439	89,353
1992	3,030,106	2,406,489	4,581	2,411,070	254,461	-133,956	2,022,653	501,148	506,305	16,765	180,736	88,809
1993	3,179,028	2,486,069	5,344	2,491,413	264,066	-143,348	2,083,999	538,561	556,468	17,458	182,093	89,641
1994	3,429,084	2,668,194	1,629	2,669,823	287,657	-157,254	2,224,912	582,196	621,976	18,618	184,181	93,804
1995	3,645,969	2,835,969	6,465	2,842,434	305,110	-169,232	2,368,092	635,478	642,399	19,538	186,607	97,914
1996	3,864,813	3,065,443	2,306	3,067,749	330,253	-187,416	2,550,080	661,575	653,158	20,413	189,335	102,120
1997	4,078,639	3,291,466	3,640	3,295,106	353,288	-199,857	2,741,961	664,124	672,554	21,346	191,076	105,423
1998	4,203,304	3,372,206	6,897	3,379,103	369,828	-214,189	2,795,086	732,340	675,878	21,839	192,470	107,857
1999	4,264,451	3,418,507	6,219	3,424,726	370,393	-217,066	2,837,267	715,620	711,564	22,049	193,408	107,714
2000	4,421,033	3,522,384	5,305	3,527,689	374,452	-217,725	2,935,512	753,207	732,314	22,849	193,491	108,566
2001	4,725,753	3,741,452	11,315	3,752,767	387,210	-239,776	3,125,781	769,562	830,410	24,464	193,171	107,188
2002	4,767,084	3,778,307	5,451	3,783,758	396,509	-247,656	3,139,593	760,506	866,985	24,659	193,321	107,093
2003	4,805,657	3,852,890	10,679	3,863,569	398,748	-257,041	3,207,780	711,186	886,691	24,701	194,552	106,748
2004	5,009,403	4,022,922	11,197	4,034,119	410,450	-269,038	3,354,631	686,886	967,886	25,631	195,444	106,227
2005	5,444,903	4,295,254	4,397	4,299,651	430,690	-292,129	3,576,832	719,012	1,149,059	27,743	196,263	107,708
2006	5,875,313	4,609,150	13,411	4,622,561	456,227	-314,172	3,852,162	939,721	1,083,430	30,431	193,069	109,689
2007	6,513,034	4,866,284	4,034	4,870,318	485,299	-336,069	4,048,950	1,342,417	1,121,667	33,469	194,598	113,185
2008	7,019,237	5,320,856	2,263	5,323,119	521,633	-368,560	4,432,926	1,299,884	1,286,427	35,746	196,362	115,073
2009	6,705,803	5,116,725	5,138	5,121,863	506,629	-323,736	4,291,498	1,062,895	1,351,410	33,866	198,010	111,944
2010	6,859,930	5,150,570	6,361	5,156,931	501,056	-297,963	4,357,912	1,048,839	1,453,179	34,288	200,069	109,758
2011	7,154,135	5,335,550	8,983	5,344,533	467,674	-321,607	4,555,252	1,116,121	1,482,762	35,665	200,592	111,471
2012	7,596,170	5,612,786	15,236	5,628,022	486,444	-326,713	4,814,865	1,256,931	1,524,374	37,740	201,276	113,619
2013	7,636,134	5,748,180	32,625	5,780,805	578,212	-359,552	4,843,041	1,226,118	1,566,975	37,717	202,461	116,063
2014	8,178,960	6,540,296	26,402	6,566,698	659,934	-574,768	5,331,996	1,282,989	1,563,975	40,116	203,883	122,455

Personal Income and Employment by Area: Lake Havasu City-Kingman, AZ

(Thousands of dollars, except as noted.)

Year	Personal income, total	Derivation of personal income								Per capita personal income (dollars)	Population (persons)	Total employment
		Earnings by place of work			Less: Contributions for government social insurance	Plus: Adjustment for residence	Equals: Net earnings by place of residence	Plus: Dividends, interest, and rent	Plus: Personal current transfer receipts			
		Nonfarm	Farm	Total								
1970	102,056	66,236	1,274	67,510	4,225	11,261	74,546	17,814	9,696	3,875	26,338	9,297
1971	118,068	74,097	2,040	76,137	4,937	13,623	84,823	20,732	12,513	4,109	28,736	9,969
1972	135,205	83,543	3,489	87,032	5,873	14,827	95,986	23,743	15,476	4,350	31,084	10,832
1973	162,506	97,982	5,483	103,465	7,882	18,543	114,126	28,846	19,534	4,775	34,030	11,853
1974	180,926	115,479	686	116,165	9,800	16,214	122,579	34,597	23,750	4,947	36,572	13,269
1975	209,221	125,990	9,382	135,372	10,576	16,045	140,841	39,270	29,110	5,312	39,388	13,882
1976	228,511	141,745	54	141,799	11,874	18,151	148,076	44,306	36,129	5,382	42,458	14,593
1977	266,750	160,950	2,912	163,862	13,812	21,997	172,047	52,812	41,891	6,159	43,312	15,773
1978	327,165	196,749	3,876	200,625	17,289	26,888	210,224	66,808	50,133	7,110	46,017	17,606
1979	396,233	247,642	1,930	249,572	23,306	27,787	254,053	81,914	60,266	7,652	51,783	20,022
1980	459,465	269,102	4,924	274,026	25,668	32,120	280,478	103,069	75,918	8,143	56,423	21,285
1981	513,947	282,891	3,578	286,469	29,311	36,856	294,014	126,110	93,823	8,769	58,607	21,566
1982	543,441	270,934	4,562	275,496	28,949	42,189	288,736	144,274	110,431	8,690	62,539	20,609
1983	607,164	290,203	7,597	297,800	31,045	50,006	316,761	167,107	123,296	9,486	64,005	21,081
1984	710,206	342,002	5,857	347,859	37,252	56,931	367,538	205,835	136,833	10,543	67,364	23,340
1985	805,919	389,386	2,387	391,773	43,430	66,537	414,880	234,932	156,107	11,388	70,769	25,423
1986	902,925	432,296	1,266	433,562	48,416	78,090	463,236	265,270	174,419	11,981	75,366	26,881
1987	997,913	486,175	1,456	487,631	54,319	92,441	525,753	276,575	195,585	12,907	77,314	29,243
1988	1,113,113	536,706	3,910	540,616	62,328	112,613	590,901	301,420	220,792	13,512	82,381	31,315
1989	1,253,224	596,226	6,951	603,177	72,844	136,251	666,584	336,927	249,713	14,398	87,040	33,410
1990	1,437,986	702,966	8,192	711,158	86,981	165,038	789,215	365,939	282,832	15,059	95,491	36,930
1991	1,535,005	760,729	7,829	768,558	94,308	170,651	844,901	366,993	323,111	15,010	102,263	38,893
1992	1,639,791	812,716	7,696	820,412	100,658	183,161	902,915	370,489	366,387	15,093	108,644	39,206
1993	1,786,202	877,372	6,157	883,529	109,043	198,768	973,254	411,423	401,525	15,437	115,706	40,507
1994	1,982,444	959,323	5,223	964,546	120,219	217,220	1,061,547	477,514	443,383	16,130	122,906	43,326
1995	2,028,116	984,314	1,863	986,177	120,797	234,432	1,099,812	444,433	483,871	15,568	130,274	43,977
1996	2,182,134	1,048,851	3,450	1,052,301	131,001	256,134	1,177,434	477,588	527,112	15,994	136,436	46,030
1997	2,372,782	1,160,996	2,951	1,163,947	139,899	277,657	1,301,705	511,203	559,874	16,838	140,922	47,793
1998	2,594,884	1,266,663	4,027	1,270,690	148,963	303,433	1,425,160	558,125	611,599	17,877	145,155	49,398
1999	2,784,826	1,387,850	6,183	1,394,033	160,337	333,283	1,566,979	565,746	652,101	18,522	150,351	51,364
2000	3,030,207	1,532,383	7,874	1,540,257	174,372	355,812	1,721,697	605,923	702,587	19,398	156,215	54,489
2001	3,228,149	1,632,335	7,447	1,639,782	191,125	365,784	1,814,441	630,137	783,571	20,137	160,312	56,336
2002	3,430,058	1,774,985	5,191	1,780,176	209,036	395,783	1,966,923	600,735	862,400	20,644	166,155	58,534
2003	3,669,332	1,897,301	8,670	1,905,971	224,724	429,003	2,110,250	619,136	939,946	21,255	172,633	62,234
2004	3,989,468	2,056,036	11,952	2,067,988	246,491	473,201	2,294,698	672,346	1,022,424	22,100	180,521	66,452
2005	4,446,321	2,292,513	11,337	2,303,850	279,096	534,419	2,559,173	754,528	1,132,620	23,554	188,773	71,384
2006	4,877,000	2,562,759	9,535	2,572,294	304,124	604,003	2,872,173	755,132	1,249,695	24,861	196,168	75,016
2007	5,146,815	2,594,780	6,157	2,600,937	315,662	634,359	2,919,634	872,660	1,354,521	25,765	199,760	75,036
2008	5,273,167	2,523,525	7,766	2,531,291	315,452	637,658	2,853,497	897,957	1,521,713	26,356	200,078	69,771
2009	5,093,873	2,292,413	364	2,292,777	296,565	582,456	2,578,668	819,123	1,696,082	25,508	199,696	64,395
2010	5,143,789	2,282,890	394	2,283,284	300,203	576,543	2,559,624	789,964	1,794,201	25,670	200,380	62,845
2011	5,219,541	2,302,591	11,861	2,314,452	276,996	509,493	2,546,949	846,510	1,826,082	25,757	202,642	62,827
2012	5,347,552	2,348,442	9,011	2,357,453	280,861	532,454	2,609,046	882,044	1,856,462	26,320	203,174	61,827
2013	5,396,628	2,399,898	12,352	2,412,250	323,027	500,178	2,589,401	895,061	1,912,166	26,603	202,855	62,630
2014	5,633,946	2,491,717	11,255	2,502,972	336,631	536,719	2,703,060	935,629	1,995,257	27,704	203,361	63,834

Personal Income and Employment by Area: Lakeland-Winter Haven, FL

(Thousands of dollars, except as noted.)

| Year | Personal income, total | Derivation of personal income | | | | | | | | | Per capita personal income (dollars) | Population (persons) | Total employment |
| | | Earnings by place of work | | | Less: Contributions for government social insurance | Plus: Adjustment for residence | Equals: Net earnings by place of residence | Plus: Dividends, interest, and rent | Plus: Personal current transfer receipts | | | |
		Nonfarm	Farm	Total								
1970	808,988	586,079	54,769	640,848	38,981	-22,644	579,223	148,163	81,602	3,512	230,334	97,281
1971	900,473	646,702	62,637	709,339	44,615	-23,629	641,095	161,872	97,506	3,729	241,479	100,888
1972	1,034,359	749,062	76,593	825,655	54,268	-27,619	743,768	177,836	112,755	4,098	252,394	107,814
1973	1,202,878	894,543	73,763	968,306	74,503	-34,655	859,148	209,338	134,392	4,590	262,049	118,069
1974	1,387,786	1,047,451	75,436	1,122,887	91,301	-44,418	987,168	245,948	154,670	5,064	274,042	125,364
1975	1,572,971	1,174,172	79,911	1,254,083	100,928	-57,044	1,096,111	277,727	199,133	5,531	284,417	128,059
1976	1,695,612	1,248,391	91,047	1,339,438	108,871	-58,012	1,172,555	298,908	224,149	5,856	289,562	128,195
1977	1,909,675	1,399,934	116,831	1,516,765	122,456	-68,408	1,325,901	338,155	245,619	6,451	296,048	134,567
1978	2,207,581	1,604,217	156,694	1,760,911	143,986	-80,617	1,536,308	400,402	270,871	7,330	301,183	142,680
1979	2,519,656	1,847,583	154,007	2,001,590	173,781	-98,532	1,729,277	472,640	317,739	8,057	312,723	149,427
1980	2,989,670	2,138,590	203,370	2,341,960	202,950	-117,805	2,021,205	591,285	377,180	9,226	324,038	156,846
1981	3,305,041	2,362,726	135,209	2,497,935	241,458	-125,696	2,130,781	731,569	442,691	9,926	332,973	160,268
1982	3,450,107	2,360,130	132,440	2,492,570	247,168	-112,000	2,133,402	804,559	512,146	10,149	339,930	155,026
1983	3,770,421	2,510,579	171,774	2,682,353	263,157	-99,437	2,319,759	894,326	556,336	10,895	346,080	157,947
1984	4,129,098	2,807,197	122,032	2,929,229	301,586	-91,049	2,536,594	1,013,367	579,137	11,650	354,414	165,687
1985	4,480,338	3,012,407	127,755	3,140,162	329,542	-83,691	2,726,929	1,121,847	631,562	12,315	363,802	173,302
1986	4,785,149	3,180,932	117,296	3,298,228	356,930	-68,491	2,872,807	1,222,321	690,021	12,861	372,057	176,446
1987	5,186,439	3,486,244	136,969	3,623,213	383,942	-65,291	3,173,980	1,285,035	727,424	13,645	380,106	178,789
1988	5,726,086	3,823,537	190,740	4,014,277	434,125	-59,567	3,520,585	1,384,215	821,286	14,714	389,160	188,505
1989	6,307,831	4,137,089	148,850	4,285,939	475,179	-61,624	3,749,136	1,651,277	907,418	15,840	398,231	195,457
1990	6,597,182	4,308,232	120,957	4,429,189	489,586	-25,746	3,913,857	1,677,914	1,005,411	16,179	407,756	194,693
1991	6,838,644	4,403,365	134,981	4,538,346	504,108	61,875	4,096,113	1,617,719	1,124,812	16,473	415,136	191,941
1992	7,233,217	4,655,664	78,279	4,733,943	530,097	99,711	4,303,557	1,634,820	1,294,840	17,093	423,171	188,240
1993	7,635,244	4,896,756	84,171	4,980,927	553,995	183,208	4,610,140	1,620,100	1,405,004	17,788	429,224	192,484
1994	8,258,091	5,288,919	87,382	5,376,301	604,923	234,815	5,006,193	1,743,577	1,508,321	18,833	438,480	199,641
1995	8,887,957	5,595,537	96,626	5,692,163	636,280	339,307	5,395,190	1,873,285	1,619,482	19,875	447,182	205,287
1996	9,425,416	5,988,981	80,402	6,069,383	670,561	338,787	5,737,609	1,965,990	1,721,817	20,737	454,512	210,699
1997	9,773,380	6,140,565	89,533	6,230,098	692,675	440,659	5,978,082	2,000,598	1,794,700	21,085	463,519	214,741
1998	10,721,622	6,718,326	132,670	6,850,996	746,296	506,938	6,611,638	2,237,779	1,872,205	22,742	471,450	223,509
1999	11,273,726	7,153,417	116,156	7,269,573	781,492	675,290	7,163,371	2,176,444	1,933,911	23,583	478,047	227,665
2000	11,773,436	7,305,105	121,160	7,426,265	808,636	761,460	7,379,089	2,340,745	2,053,602	24,249	485,515	235,518
2001	12,372,437	7,882,918	102,568	7,985,486	874,987	606,672	7,717,171	2,423,789	2,231,477	25,100	492,917	233,584
2002	12,614,280	8,155,157	118,420	8,273,577	899,823	586,333	7,960,087	2,239,684	2,414,509	25,155	501,469	236,225
2003	13,340,055	8,631,323	93,797	8,725,120	947,495	587,935	8,365,560	2,365,117	2,609,378	26,001	513,058	240,591
2004	14,700,148	9,409,459	93,508	9,502,967	1,031,704	607,191	9,078,454	2,755,516	2,866,178	27,858	527,685	252,395
2005	16,109,932	10,310,750	135,249	10,445,999	1,144,324	640,543	9,942,218	3,082,975	3,084,739	29,431	547,373	267,297
2006	17,218,068	11,018,090	150,695	11,168,785	1,244,149	649,153	10,573,789	3,300,232	3,344,047	30,296	568,324	276,418
2007	17,889,005	11,178,538	89,147	11,267,685	1,275,437	638,780	10,631,028	3,582,962	3,675,015	30,528	585,982	278,610
2008	18,310,640	10,942,883	83,299	11,026,182	1,275,523	611,575	10,362,234	3,746,941	4,201,465	30,784	594,801	269,239
2009	17,548,745	10,452,746	106,355	10,559,101	1,246,204	543,668	9,856,565	3,169,663	4,522,517	29,312	598,683	259,322
2010	18,604,007	10,496,441	125,066	10,621,507	1,252,443	559,537	9,928,601	3,769,716	4,905,690	30,834	603,359	255,722
2011	19,716,102	10,539,443	124,077	10,663,520	1,145,410	609,065	10,127,175	4,456,320	5,132,607	32,338	609,696	258,186
2012	19,491,446	10,821,694	113,271	10,934,965	1,184,208	671,093	10,421,850	3,919,110	5,150,486	31,654	615,764	261,707
2013	19,776,904	11,256,020	112,575	11,368,595	1,376,408	683,439	10,675,626	3,752,481	5,348,797	31,737	623,159	266,695
2014	20,722,081	11,715,794	102,463	11,818,257	1,433,857	778,409	11,162,809	3,887,624	5,671,648	32,652	634,638	272,117

Personal Income and Employment by Area: Lancaster, PA

(Thousands of dollars, except as noted.)

Year	Personal income, total	Derivation of personal income									Per capita personal income (dollars)	Population (persons)	Total employment
		Earnings by place of work			Less: Contributions for government social insurance	Plus: Adjustment for residence	Equals: Net earnings by place of residence	Plus: Dividends, interest, and rent	Plus: Personal current transfer receipts			
		Nonfarm	Farm	Total								
1970	1,390,862	1,061,433	84,767	1,146,200	78,563	42,944	1,110,581	179,647	100,634	4,329	321,290	156,017
1971	1,454,086	1,119,018	66,208	1,185,226	86,287	49,117	1,148,056	190,328	115,702	4,445	327,155	156,834
1972	1,615,395	1,261,340	65,432	1,326,772	102,540	57,182	1,281,414	204,709	129,272	4,863	332,160	163,540
1973	1,828,991	1,431,511	87,805	1,519,316	134,168	65,718	1,450,866	234,584	143,541	5,430	336,819	172,896
1974	1,973,916	1,535,988	68,078	1,604,066	149,336	78,743	1,533,473	265,852	174,591	5,803	340,170	173,356
1975	2,124,883	1,598,341	62,793	1,661,134	150,550	89,512	1,600,096	293,687	231,100	6,162	344,814	168,983
1976	2,342,173	1,793,490	51,857	1,845,347	172,580	102,191	1,774,958	319,031	248,184	6,742	347,407	173,386
1977	2,591,489	2,016,158	28,510	2,044,668	193,513	116,814	1,967,969	361,222	262,298	7,381	351,084	179,617
1978	2,970,248	2,303,297	70,842	2,374,139	226,062	134,580	2,282,657	404,145	283,446	8,375	354,667	187,604
1979	3,335,892	2,567,308	90,470	2,657,778	261,659	157,037	2,553,156	457,755	324,981	9,284	359,329	192,732
1980	3,610,486	2,711,859	46,456	2,758,315	279,918	182,740	2,661,137	571,253	378,096	9,935	363,420	194,330
1981	3,998,909	2,905,297	83,261	2,988,558	320,438	195,934	2,864,054	701,654	433,201	10,897	366,979	193,300
1982	4,299,337	3,027,354	69,015	3,096,369	338,229	198,900	2,957,040	836,439	505,858	11,589	370,992	191,675
1983	4,603,719	3,284,197	52,440	3,336,637	370,797	199,872	3,165,712	894,453	543,554	12,236	376,234	194,960
1984	5,153,650	3,664,356	147,665	3,812,021	430,942	211,594	3,592,673	1,008,806	552,171	13,530	380,892	203,704
1985	5,558,637	3,977,179	116,493	4,093,672	471,757	217,336	3,839,251	1,120,666	598,720	14,429	385,245	210,863
1986	6,065,962	4,347,281	167,565	4,514,846	515,635	220,051	4,219,262	1,205,309	641,391	15,461	392,339	218,827
1987	6,555,162	4,776,929	168,649	4,945,578	560,143	231,861	4,617,296	1,266,411	671,455	16,316	401,773	228,379
1988	7,078,111	5,284,962	81,846	5,366,808	626,838	245,243	4,985,213	1,363,400	729,498	17,257	410,152	237,036
1989	7,916,737	5,732,291	178,115	5,910,406	666,532	260,357	5,504,231	1,616,697	795,809	18,958	417,585	244,037
1990	8,278,345	6,104,816	110,193	6,215,009	717,197	265,127	5,762,939	1,651,580	863,826	19,481	424,947	250,269
1991	8,518,399	6,240,575	83,396	6,323,971	740,609	275,750	5,859,112	1,663,377	995,910	19,754	431,229	247,396
1992	9,111,417	6,678,766	146,879	6,825,645	787,121	288,909	6,327,433	1,718,813	1,065,171	20,903	435,886	249,064
1993	9,685,067	7,059,127	148,174	7,207,301	844,916	288,918	6,651,303	1,913,091	1,120,673	21,959	441,056	251,472
1994	9,892,020	7,354,100	123,479	7,477,579	894,869	299,633	6,882,343	1,840,508	1,169,169	22,167	446,254	255,573
1995	10,293,690	7,680,513	77,836	7,758,349	929,394	306,953	7,135,908	1,918,701	1,239,081	22,783	451,817	263,269
1996	10,942,631	8,007,911	183,834	8,191,745	946,082	320,907	7,566,570	2,043,041	1,333,020	24,008	455,783	266,835
1997	11,615,874	8,562,298	149,084	8,711,382	996,180	338,089	8,053,291	2,182,158	1,380,425	25,247	460,085	273,421
1998	12,169,168	8,945,816	141,196	9,087,012	1,034,928	360,244	8,412,328	2,307,461	1,449,379	26,211	464,272	272,471
1999	12,698,231	9,441,015	114,924	9,555,939	1,077,824	377,541	8,855,656	2,304,041	1,538,534	27,140	467,879	276,666
2000	13,779,828	10,208,362	167,626	10,375,988	1,146,655	394,379	9,623,712	2,504,606	1,651,510	29,197	471,955	282,337
2001	14,123,373	10,430,251	179,171	10,609,422	1,183,859	422,829	9,848,392	2,452,257	1,822,724	29,703	475,483	284,726
2002	14,200,822	10,685,356	97,428	10,782,784	1,216,949	430,356	9,996,191	2,240,887	1,963,744	29,578	480,118	285,200
2003	14,882,889	11,076,865	180,757	11,257,622	1,253,618	444,763	10,448,767	2,341,053	2,093,069	30,679	485,119	285,367
2004	15,735,371	11,650,657	263,496	11,914,153	1,318,895	469,924	11,065,182	2,481,685	2,188,504	32,115	489,977	291,857
2005	16,433,101	12,183,530	267,320	12,450,850	1,385,879	494,281	11,559,252	2,454,236	2,419,613	33,217	494,722	297,439
2006	17,155,974	12,634,745	199,205	12,833,950	1,435,704	517,027	11,915,273	2,649,359	2,591,342	34,249	500,922	300,219
2007	18,017,473	12,821,180	301,903	13,123,083	1,467,085	541,158	12,197,156	3,039,049	2,781,268	35,563	506,639	304,665
2008	18,823,191	13,046,784	236,960	13,283,744	1,504,917	562,081	12,340,908	3,295,061	3,187,222	36,767	511,957	304,578
2009	18,468,686	12,599,031	129,756	12,728,787	1,465,935	566,354	11,829,206	3,086,990	3,552,490	35,752	516,577	296,529
2010	18,970,748	12,854,798	272,555	13,127,353	1,500,270	590,837	12,217,920	2,943,213	3,809,615	36,460	520,317	294,474
2011	20,021,134	13,247,491	343,324	13,590,815	1,389,076	647,915	12,849,654	3,317,094	3,854,386	38,232	523,670	296,642
2012	20,766,240	13,704,387	340,887	14,045,274	1,420,386	632,836	13,257,724	3,605,352	3,903,164	39,422	526,766	300,916
2013	21,268,985	14,184,337	430,418	14,614,755	1,646,414	627,621	13,595,962	3,671,582	4,001,441	40,121	530,122	304,365
2014	22,245,595	14,807,650	561,032	15,368,682	1,723,428	636,586	14,281,840	3,824,305	4,139,450	41,712	533,320	310,808

Personal Income and Employment by Area: Lansing-East Lansing, MI

(Thousands of dollars, except as noted.)

Year	Personal income, total	Derivation of personal income								Per capita personal income (dollars)	Population (persons)	Total employment
		Earnings by place of work			Less: Contributions for government social insurance	Plus: Adjustment for residence	Equals: Net earnings by place of residence	Plus: Dividends, interest, and rent	Plus: Personal current transfer receipts			
		Nonfarm	Farm	Total								
1970	1,483,180	1,274,895	22,940	1,297,835	86,343	-34,417	1,177,075	191,410	114,695	3,913	379,047	158,585
1971	1,678,713	1,472,879	20,531	1,493,410	102,438	-55,762	1,335,210	208,295	135,208	4,389	382,476	163,734
1972	1,856,017	1,637,490	27,688	1,665,178	121,231	-67,290	1,476,657	228,936	150,424	4,804	386,369	169,358
1973	2,053,812	1,842,313	31,672	1,873,985	157,845	-80,358	1,635,782	249,627	168,403	5,226	392,980	176,554
1974	2,161,701	1,842,419	35,555	1,877,974	162,471	-58,268	1,657,235	283,711	220,755	5,442	397,253	176,321
1975	2,404,628	2,014,871	33,314	2,048,185	174,693	-72,222	1,801,270	320,026	283,332	6,032	398,619	177,812
1976	2,692,533	2,341,218	24,793	2,366,011	207,138	-105,413	2,053,460	344,838	294,235	6,721	400,590	184,014
1977	3,030,841	2,655,243	29,327	2,684,570	234,369	-131,333	2,318,868	387,340	324,633	7,495	404,394	190,769
1978	3,345,940	3,008,289	20,992	3,029,281	274,162	-158,569	2,596,550	431,536	317,854	8,162	409,950	200,143
1979	3,736,504	3,356,494	28,336	3,384,830	315,533	-181,742	2,887,555	489,922	359,027	9,033	413,652	206,975
1980	4,086,640	3,519,650	25,126	3,544,776	322,550	-190,086	3,032,140	582,947	471,553	9,728	420,109	204,514
1981	4,482,802	3,865,291	33,643	3,898,934	387,823	-228,460	3,282,651	697,289	502,862	10,657	420,637	203,789
1982	4,638,879	3,890,020	14,054	3,904,074	393,485	-225,390	3,285,199	798,756	554,924	11,181	414,906	196,333
1983	5,046,420	4,314,379	6,816	4,321,195	446,673	-275,224	3,599,298	865,401	581,721	12,229	412,647	200,932
1984	5,468,504	4,632,774	24,922	4,657,696	492,443	-281,611	3,883,642	977,656	607,206	13,245	412,862	204,494
1985	5,895,523	5,077,831	28,171	5,106,002	559,288	-312,129	4,234,585	1,036,478	624,460	14,185	415,612	215,819
1986	6,286,825	5,404,844	22,605	5,427,449	598,253	-315,027	4,514,169	1,109,065	663,591	14,888	422,282	222,907
1987	6,490,981	5,501,098	31,248	5,532,346	602,002	-284,891	4,645,453	1,145,440	700,088	15,214	426,652	232,298
1988	6,882,782	5,904,964	23,640	5,928,604	672,781	-301,943	4,953,880	1,202,383	726,519	16,019	429,673	237,230
1989	7,445,368	6,305,384	51,818	6,357,202	714,991	-312,440	5,329,771	1,322,465	793,132	17,294	430,527	243,788
1990	7,786,402	6,572,454	40,127	6,612,581	754,900	-316,786	5,540,895	1,383,210	862,297	17,965	433,414	248,011
1991	8,126,623	6,889,686	25,930	6,915,616	803,646	-334,902	5,777,068	1,385,369	964,186	18,597	436,979	248,866
1992	8,582,748	7,290,012	29,953	7,319,965	842,607	-349,103	6,128,255	1,449,504	1,004,989	19,545	439,128	249,680
1993	8,849,269	7,406,629	28,731	7,435,360	857,339	-324,267	6,253,754	1,505,083	1,090,432	20,056	441,234	249,094
1994	9,456,840	7,924,594	25,464	7,950,058	934,929	-347,751	6,667,378	1,681,749	1,107,713	21,363	442,671	256,015
1995	9,872,866	8,294,560	27,552	8,322,112	980,291	-358,057	6,983,764	1,735,859	1,153,243	22,267	443,395	268,156
1996	10,366,452	8,660,011	33,210	8,693,221	997,635	-368,295	7,327,291	1,832,433	1,206,728	23,189	447,043	272,297
1997	10,861,327	8,970,970	31,741	9,002,711	1,033,673	-367,522	7,601,516	1,964,782	1,295,029	24,250	447,895	271,236
1998	11,181,164	9,267,539	35,191	9,302,730	1,056,583	-357,364	7,888,783	1,983,656	1,308,725	24,992	447,384	271,794
1999	11,784,162	9,923,407	48,459	9,971,866	1,133,157	-387,641	8,451,068	1,934,646	1,398,448	26,357	447,095	275,791
2000	12,343,274	10,410,610	27,415	10,438,025	1,177,515	-404,555	8,855,955	2,024,250	1,463,069	27,507	448,735	279,114
2001	12,777,171	10,740,036	27,441	10,767,477	1,197,543	-406,630	9,163,304	1,981,189	1,632,678	28,265	452,051	278,230
2002	12,791,232	10,971,216	24,586	10,995,802	1,230,640	-499,057	9,266,105	1,834,161	1,690,966	28,087	455,420	277,328
2003	13,083,969	11,098,513	34,331	11,132,844	1,240,209	-543,710	9,348,925	1,953,954	1,781,090	28,544	458,376	278,535
2004	13,387,980	11,195,065	70,289	11,265,354	1,252,417	-499,553	9,513,384	2,012,436	1,862,160	28,996	461,724	276,307
2005	13,673,812	11,348,552	51,362	11,399,914	1,280,420	-497,626	9,621,868	2,057,403	1,994,541	29,549	462,743	273,916
2006	14,167,695	11,761,155	58,001	11,819,156	1,339,483	-579,653	9,900,020	2,117,083	2,150,592	30,577	463,349	275,028
2007	14,582,113	11,864,966	65,159	11,930,125	1,361,486	-612,382	9,956,257	2,258,167	2,367,689	31,440	463,804	276,430
2008	15,216,132	12,026,582	71,145	12,097,727	1,393,487	-623,478	10,080,762	2,396,251	2,739,119	32,819	463,638	271,541
2009	14,750,603	11,430,883	39,625	11,470,508	1,336,354	-596,953	9,537,201	2,167,959	3,045,443	31,849	463,147	259,109
2010	15,389,126	11,908,469	85,977	11,994,446	1,376,941	-637,597	9,979,908	2,133,932	3,275,286	33,155	464,158	258,880
2011	15,946,646	11,985,217	185,109	12,170,326	1,235,472	-617,369	10,317,485	2,352,814	3,276,347	34,222	465,980	261,779
2012	16,356,353	12,208,880	109,977	12,318,857	1,258,494	-572,506	10,487,857	2,600,115	3,268,381	35,049	466,666	260,375
2013	16,639,900	12,630,258	149,849	12,780,107	1,478,465	-623,121	10,678,521	2,600,730	3,360,649	35,529	468,348	262,495
2014	17,246,456	13,088,442	118,957	13,207,399	1,521,737	-621,975	11,063,687	2,679,781	3,502,988	36,659	470,458	266,477

Personal Income and Employment by Area: Laredo, TX

(Thousands of dollars, except as noted.)

Year	Personal income, total	Earnings by place of work			Less: Contributions for government social insurance	Plus: Adjustment for residence	Equals: Net earnings by place of residence	Plus: Dividends, interest, and rent	Plus: Personal current transfer receipts	Per capita personal income (dollars)	Population (persons)	Total employment
		Nonfarm	Farm	Total								
1970	181,593	149,190	3,057	152,247	9,355	-6,698	136,194	25,996	19,403	2,469	73,536	27,042
1971	196,729	160,445	4,055	164,500	10,408	-8,002	146,090	28,208	22,431	2,537	77,556	26,710
1972	219,753	180,440	3,804	184,244	12,054	-9,804	162,386	31,842	25,525	2,712	81,025	27,421
1973	235,421	193,610	4,793	198,403	14,681	-11,960	171,762	33,268	30,391	2,834	83,080	28,534
1974	241,046	195,900	3,075	198,975	16,009	-13,675	169,291	29,933	41,822	3,117	77,327	28,206
1975	278,240	225,997	2,604	228,601	18,440	-17,034	193,127	32,181	52,932	3,352	83,006	29,172
1976	311,957	258,381	1,274	259,655	21,264	-18,652	219,739	34,181	58,037	3,526	88,481	30,810
1977	349,748	294,226	895	295,121	24,151	-20,834	250,136	37,716	61,896	3,821	91,535	32,558
1978	400,684	335,869	753	336,622	27,980	-22,442	286,200	46,237	68,247	4,273	93,776	34,251
1979	466,961	386,222	4,058	390,280	33,811	-23,984	332,485	55,535	78,941	4,822	96,844	36,084
1980	553,808	462,396	-189	462,207	41,358	-29,977	390,872	69,067	93,869	5,512	100,481	38,920
1981	668,445	549,923	82	550,005	53,540	-21,510	474,955	89,667	103,823	6,361	105,077	42,261
1982	720,592	572,274	3,387	575,661	56,014	-23,629	496,018	105,161	119,413	6,486	111,106	42,033
1983	713,445	527,477	-2,178	525,299	49,979	-21,441	453,879	112,558	147,008	6,181	115,419	37,681
1984	770,616	578,911	-2,660	576,251	56,077	-25,131	495,043	126,650	148,923	6,611	116,566	39,429
1985	834,786	645,084	-6,055	639,029	63,528	-29,273	546,228	135,358	153,200	7,065	118,164	42,213
1986	870,340	663,323	-5,409	657,914	64,312	-27,909	565,693	137,182	167,465	7,133	122,011	41,857
1987	915,467	700,550	-1,422	699,128	66,954	-29,486	602,688	137,739	175,040	7,351	124,528	43,947
1988	1,017,314	793,127	-1,595	791,532	78,923	-30,800	681,809	150,080	185,425	8,037	126,575	46,882
1989	1,152,111	887,955	-482	887,473	89,320	-32,938	765,215	169,717	217,179	8,866	129,943	50,230
1990	1,301,710	1,013,164	1,399	1,014,563	99,840	-36,213	878,510	174,076	249,124	9,683	134,430	53,910
1991	1,466,825	1,149,040	1,924	1,150,964	116,071	-40,914	993,979	185,155	287,691	10,471	140,082	57,729
1992	1,698,769	1,306,319	1,666	1,307,985	130,193	-45,098	1,132,694	214,088	351,987	11,554	147,026	60,857
1993	1,869,946	1,457,629	-406	1,457,223	144,729	-49,928	1,262,566	233,411	373,969	12,100	154,536	65,418
1994	2,053,691	1,617,643	-1,622	1,616,021	162,665	-54,913	1,398,443	238,279	416,969	12,747	161,107	69,329
1995	2,145,220	1,619,703	-803	1,618,900	162,391	-52,261	1,404,248	272,917	468,055	12,810	167,466	68,700
1996	2,312,809	1,734,780	-2,648	1,732,132	172,941	-55,279	1,503,912	291,360	517,537	13,479	171,583	70,431
1997	2,534,995	1,928,394	-390	1,928,004	193,219	-61,011	1,673,774	316,598	544,623	14,311	177,140	75,384
1998	2,688,123	2,061,133	2,566	2,063,699	205,966	-60,800	1,796,933	343,718	547,472	14,690	182,994	78,708
1999	2,804,817	2,170,108	8,200	2,178,308	218,043	-62,913	1,897,352	349,232	558,233	14,839	189,014	81,228
2000	3,061,243	2,372,806	9,208	2,382,014	235,771	-67,817	2,078,426	389,759	593,058	15,733	194,576	85,584
2001	3,495,708	2,719,855	14,027	2,733,882	256,468	-67,102	2,410,312	434,409	650,987	17,448	200,347	88,299
2002	3,721,728	2,903,274	14,800	2,918,074	275,282	-72,916	2,569,876	415,412	736,440	18,067	206,001	93,272
2003	3,983,833	3,069,627	22,933	3,092,560	297,260	-78,247	2,717,053	471,554	795,226	18,811	211,786	95,570
2004	4,191,645	3,275,119	20,778	3,295,897	316,424	-83,985	2,895,488	467,273	828,884	19,240	217,858	99,644
2005	4,629,819	3,569,882	10,092	3,579,974	344,560	-92,224	3,143,190	548,419	938,210	20,696	223,703	104,228
2006	4,993,750	3,813,243	12,533	3,825,776	362,263	-97,149	3,366,364	623,796	1,003,590	21,778	229,307	107,864
2007	5,276,760	3,954,375	2,158	3,956,533	383,128	-102,249	3,471,156	680,677	1,124,927	22,493	234,594	112,325
2008	5,896,156	4,295,844	-1,924	4,293,920	399,645	-105,445	3,788,830	813,284	1,294,042	24,538	240,287	114,991
2009	5,785,806	4,072,970	-4,601	4,068,369	395,964	-102,148	3,570,257	757,567	1,457,982	23,528	245,908	113,095
2010	6,137,287	4,323,478	-4,926	4,318,552	423,012	-102,169	3,793,371	725,931	1,617,985	24,421	251,308	114,128
2011	6,689,784	4,703,275	2,676	4,705,951	405,445	-103,496	4,197,010	834,028	1,658,746	26,171	255,618	120,669
2012	7,060,919	4,980,347	2,085	4,982,432	427,475	-99,546	4,455,411	955,214	1,650,294	27,159	259,986	122,815
2013	7,247,549	5,128,189	6,101	5,134,290	493,463	-95,976	4,544,851	1,008,274	1,694,424	27,477	263,772	125,806
2014	7,561,382	5,351,998	8,465	5,360,463	513,113	-91,446	4,755,904	1,039,171	1,766,307	28,355	266,673	128,384

Personal Income and Employment by Area: Las Cruces, NM

(Thousands of dollars, except as noted.)

Year	Personal income, total	Derivation of personal income								Per capita personal income (dollars)	Population (persons)	Total employment
		Earnings by place of work			Less: Contributions for government social insurance	Plus: Adjustment for residence	Equals: Net earnings by place of residence	Plus: Dividends, interest, and rent	Plus: Personal current transfer receipts			
		Nonfarm	Farm	Total								
1970	227,435	180,614	12,396	193,010	8,393	-6,926	177,691	31,840	17,904	3,237	70,254	27,080
1971	257,147	202,533	14,117	216,650	9,841	-8,705	198,104	37,144	21,899	3,536	72,726	28,316
1972	280,452	217,345	15,179	232,524	11,044	-6,950	214,530	41,273	24,649	3,664	76,553	29,477
1973	309,351	237,872	16,334	254,206	14,266	-6,305	233,635	46,731	28,985	4,022	76,909	30,621
1974	356,233	259,949	28,036	287,985	16,312	-5,816	265,857	54,815	35,561	4,516	78,888	31,045
1975	387,703	279,112	16,500	295,612	17,752	1,478	279,338	63,917	44,448	4,729	81,979	31,211
1976	438,821	317,141	22,899	340,040	20,374	-1,250	318,416	70,124	50,281	5,147	85,259	32,448
1977	488,766	364,197	20,042	384,239	24,369	-3,654	356,216	78,950	53,600	5,535	88,302	35,175
1978	561,767	415,491	24,856	440,347	28,803	-4,103	407,441	94,486	59,840	6,093	92,193	37,771
1979	615,002	456,844	14,132	470,976	33,333	-2,628	435,015	109,462	70,525	6,561	93,741	39,643
1980	695,428	488,720	21,677	510,397	35,824	2,191	476,764	132,318	86,346	7,168	97,012	39,628
1981	805,344	545,663	35,568	581,231	43,145	7,163	545,249	161,509	98,586	8,084	99,623	40,165
1982	894,203	597,042	32,691	629,733	48,468	11,568	592,833	190,875	110,495	8,644	103,448	41,829
1983	1,011,117	674,670	46,103	720,773	57,163	12,659	676,269	211,346	123,502	9,395	107,627	44,305
1984	1,111,239	741,744	41,180	782,924	64,306	16,920	735,538	238,591	137,110	9,880	112,474	46,879
1985	1,216,021	799,388	49,585	848,973	71,816	23,055	800,212	268,299	147,510	10,454	116,321	48,564
1986	1,315,342	847,771	67,614	915,385	78,524	31,518	868,379	289,310	157,653	10,918	120,474	49,986
1987	1,407,467	904,144	65,169	969,313	84,078	40,329	925,564	309,730	172,173	11,257	125,032	52,506
1988	1,481,360	947,274	66,638	1,013,912	94,931	50,073	969,054	324,633	187,673	11,394	130,016	55,774
1989	1,643,102	1,023,581	93,269	1,116,850	104,886	51,851	1,063,815	367,233	212,054	12,358	132,957	57,095
1990	1,767,888	1,100,451	103,630	1,204,081	118,716	60,921	1,146,286	380,028	241,574	12,943	136,593	57,771
1991	1,894,914	1,191,467	87,239	1,278,706	130,353	73,753	1,222,106	397,612	275,196	13,417	141,228	59,961
1992	2,081,885	1,303,934	102,692	1,406,626	141,766	88,747	1,353,607	416,281	311,997	14,163	146,995	60,744
1993	2,219,926	1,387,966	86,376	1,474,342	151,674	104,050	1,426,718	445,646	347,562	14,505	153,049	61,738
1994	2,310,600	1,419,483	75,878	1,495,361	159,768	120,335	1,455,928	473,270	381,402	14,668	157,530	62,238
1995	2,519,135	1,515,529	100,397	1,615,926	170,318	130,333	1,575,941	512,585	430,609	15,645	161,014	65,557
1996	2,633,601	1,573,102	76,986	1,650,088	177,394	140,040	1,612,734	551,852	469,015	15,902	165,618	67,010
1997	2,769,025	1,637,050	104,121	1,741,171	185,516	156,487	1,712,142	574,288	482,595	16,377	169,081	68,290
1998	2,985,461	1,784,771	112,490	1,897,261	201,410	169,874	1,865,725	603,387	516,349	17,352	172,057	69,866
1999	3,090,771	1,872,533	112,266	1,984,799	213,484	188,367	1,959,682	581,534	549,555	17,774	173,889	72,182
2000	3,282,416	2,036,949	80,173	2,117,122	223,578	204,166	2,097,710	592,778	591,928	18,746	175,098	74,606
2001	3,638,442	2,209,225	112,816	2,322,041	236,770	205,363	2,290,634	667,606	680,202	20,615	176,496	76,107
2002	3,847,692	2,429,810	94,716	2,524,526	258,755	190,222	2,455,993	630,908	760,791	21,560	178,464	78,272
2003	3,987,720	2,540,912	116,229	2,657,141	278,039	170,138	2,549,240	621,637	816,843	21,905	182,045	80,383
2004	4,229,199	2,681,366	152,558	2,833,924	295,740	148,489	2,686,673	668,667	873,859	22,868	184,939	82,511
2005	4,583,228	2,900,232	172,705	3,072,937	323,353	123,321	2,872,905	760,014	950,309	24,224	189,199	85,918
2006	4,810,645	3,102,077	123,005	3,225,082	351,918	90,785	2,963,949	805,669	1,041,027	24,835	193,701	87,929
2007	5,167,837	3,257,589	175,132	3,432,721	375,013	53,093	3,110,801	907,350	1,149,686	26,120	197,853	90,022
2008	5,428,332	3,459,847	100,946	3,560,793	402,129	8,865	3,167,529	931,812	1,328,991	27,026	200,855	91,583
2009	5,658,905	3,542,981	116,085	3,659,066	417,077	22,025	3,264,014	892,038	1,502,853	27,551	205,401	90,645
2010	5,965,697	3,654,825	205,805	3,860,630	432,940	17,881	3,445,571	889,850	1,630,276	28,376	210,237	90,929
2011	6,187,245	3,728,782	186,256	3,915,038	396,964	21,278	3,539,352	992,034	1,655,859	29,063	212,890	92,322
2012	6,412,252	3,804,355	126,259	3,930,614	403,787	60,483	3,587,310	1,176,245	1,648,697	29,935	214,208	92,097
2013	6,227,731	3,825,088	122,381	3,947,469	464,422	29,963	3,513,010	1,065,161	1,649,560	29,143	213,697	93,671
2014	6,537,004	3,935,398	138,359	4,073,757	480,224	34,206	3,627,739	1,100,293	1,808,972	30,593	213,676	94,333

Personal Income and Employment by Area: Las Vegas-Henderson-Paradise, NV

(Thousands of dollars, except as noted.)

Year	Personal income, total	Derivation of personal income								Per capita personal income (dollars)	Population (persons)	Total employment
		Earnings by place of work			Less: Contributions for government social insurance	Plus: Adjustment for residence	Equals: Net earnings by place of residence	Plus: Dividends, interest, and rent	Plus: Personal current transfer receipts			
		Nonfarm	Farm	Total								
1970.............	1,416,939	1,184,879	1,732	1,186,611	82,314	41,365	1,145,662	195,309	75,968	5,132	276,079	134,095
1971.............	1,569,318	1,306,675	1,334	1,308,009	93,505	37,342	1,251,846	219,961	97,511	5,356	293,008	138,801
1972.............	1,731,195	1,452,939	1,318	1,454,257	109,842	26,189	1,370,604	243,338	117,253	5,631	307,426	145,742
1973.............	1,961,591	1,683,415	1,418	1,684,833	146,925	12,694	1,550,602	273,606	137,383	6,142	319,399	160,282
1974.............	2,195,758	1,852,647	2,006	1,854,653	164,868	13,834	1,703,619	318,344	173,795	6,517	336,930	168,726
1975.............	2,484,227	2,046,423	2,074	2,048,497	180,969	14,999	1,882,527	359,566	242,134	7,071	351,339	174,218
1976.............	2,826,937	2,343,704	2,783	2,346,487	213,203	8,992	2,142,276	409,452	275,209	7,650	369,529	186,546
1977.............	3,257,999	2,732,975	2,580	2,735,555	251,966	889	2,484,478	470,151	303,370	8,355	389,965	204,806
1978.............	3,912,315	3,304,455	2,496	3,306,951	314,392	-3,022	2,989,537	584,193	338,585	9,475	412,913	228,609
1979.............	4,580,596	3,868,379	1,518	3,869,897	388,226	-10,578	3,471,093	701,638	407,865	10,378	441,358	251,535
1980.............	5,301,315	4,380,338	3,213	4,383,551	443,251	-3,497	3,936,803	861,352	503,160	11,299	469,185	265,076
1981.............	6,098,001	4,930,300	1,887	4,932,187	530,878	19,457	4,420,766	1,054,928	622,307	12,376	492,747	272,538
1982.............	6,568,414	5,108,310	2,477	5,110,787	541,265	40,716	4,610,238	1,261,415	696,761	12,786	513,708	269,949
1983.............	7,010,736	5,448,252	926	5,449,178	597,931	43,553	4,894,800	1,359,160	756,776	13,223	530,195	274,043
1984.............	7,605,157	5,874,785	2,951	5,877,736	670,344	52,385	5,259,777	1,527,361	818,019	13,957	544,893	286,101
1985.............	8,330,031	6,362,745	2,478	6,365,223	739,665	69,674	5,695,232	1,728,371	906,428	14,846	561,081	300,096
1986.............	9,102,317	6,943,776	1,535	6,945,311	825,195	64,123	6,184,239	1,894,313	1,023,765	15,673	580,775	316,982
1987.............	10,028,979	7,773,825	2,128	7,775,953	930,044	46,202	6,892,111	2,032,922	1,103,946	16,394	611,763	345,999
1988.............	11,473,425	8,979,720	2,161	8,981,881	1,086,945	42,501	7,937,437	2,304,565	1,231,423	17,722	647,410	375,496
1989.............	13,156,801	10,232,051	2,945	10,234,996	1,263,165	13,714	8,985,545	2,743,534	1,427,722	19,027	691,467	412,843
1990.............	15,068,765	11,854,862	3,280	11,858,142	1,541,955	-15,902	10,300,285	3,108,851	1,659,629	19,928	756,170	452,016
1991.............	16,712,965	12,890,544	3,501	12,894,045	1,653,815	-2,914	11,237,316	3,406,081	2,069,568	20,479	816,085	465,549
1992.............	18,686,167	14,348,944	4,769	14,353,713	1,812,172	-11,869	12,529,672	3,790,588	2,365,907	21,795	857,357	472,519
1993.............	20,551,065	15,911,220	5,733	15,916,953	2,021,745	-83,112	13,812,096	4,210,532	2,528,437	22,775	902,338	504,060
1994.............	23,067,196	17,953,830	5,450	17,959,280	2,295,750	-143,455	15,520,075	4,850,098	2,697,023	23,716	972,624	567,840
1995.............	25,563,139	19,920,429	5,574	19,926,003	2,551,331	-189,440	17,185,232	5,456,386	2,921,521	24,678	1,035,847	606,312
1996.............	28,600,183	22,401,311	6,320	22,407,631	2,809,594	-279,398	19,318,639	6,112,507	3,169,037	26,003	1,099,894	662,190
1997.............	31,651,322	24,803,401	6,527	24,809,928	3,033,850	-303,324	21,472,754	6,776,583	3,401,985	26,886	1,177,230	713,369
1998.............	35,054,456	27,378,365	6,873	27,385,238	3,280,589	-317,941	23,786,708	7,620,222	3,647,526	28,015	1,251,258	749,040
1999.............	38,440,364	30,575,180	6,434	30,581,614	3,531,346	-351,142	26,699,126	7,914,398	3,826,840	29,094	1,321,254	804,030
2000.............	42,322,385	33,343,669	5,112	33,348,781	3,489,339	-372,281	29,487,161	8,714,167	4,121,057	30,362	1,393,909	852,405
2001.............	45,147,653	35,908,571	5,103	35,913,674	3,748,613	-428,924	31,736,137	8,724,493	4,687,023	30,912	1,460,500	882,717
2002.............	47,406,076	37,463,485	3,947	37,467,432	3,959,707	-440,072	33,067,653	9,034,532	5,303,891	31,128	1,522,962	895,579
2003.............	51,400,682	40,056,794	3,450	40,060,244	3,999,618	-470,118	35,590,508	10,095,791	5,714,383	32,447	1,584,166	939,492
2004.............	57,703,673	44,972,015	3,472	44,975,487	4,419,000	-513,270	40,043,217	11,510,364	6,150,092	34,703	1,662,773	1,011,193
2005.............	65,606,440	50,194,868	3,143	50,198,011	4,895,203	-554,724	44,748,084	14,198,388	6,659,968	37,933	1,729,522	1,084,733
2006.............	70,802,847	54,524,564	3,872	54,528,436	5,705,574	-568,440	48,254,422	15,354,297	7,194,128	39,253	1,803,774	1,143,479
2007.............	74,630,629	57,015,899	2,517	57,018,416	6,013,141	-576,187	50,429,088	16,321,993	7,879,548	39,956	1,867,817	1,172,674
2008.............	75,494,913	56,543,252	2,236	56,545,488	5,665,533	-558,856	50,321,099	15,785,348	9,388,466	39,478	1,912,349	1,163,809
2009.............	70,129,464	51,868,225	2,708	51,870,933	5,471,807	-418,325	45,980,801	13,412,338	10,736,325	36,160	1,939,407	1,086,009
2010.............	70,428,593	51,007,428	2,632	51,010,060	5,342,646	-303,720	45,363,694	13,189,206	11,875,693	36,057	1,953,263	1,057,759
2011.............	71,777,369	51,140,880	3,331	51,144,211	5,022,800	-161,607	45,959,804	13,812,150	12,005,415	36,488	1,967,159	1,078,835
2012.............	77,373,382	53,368,359	1,146	53,369,505	5,301,650	-149,856	47,917,999	17,347,411	12,107,972	38,713	1,998,646	1,093,543
2013.............	77,298,937	54,330,787	1,554	54,332,341	5,829,648	-108,465	48,394,228	16,569,597	12,335,112	38,091	2,029,316	1,126,440
2014.............	81,821,005	57,980,701	2,204	57,982,905	6,500,453	-148,812	51,333,640	17,219,447	13,267,918	39,533	2,069,681	1,166,051

Personal Income and Employment by Area: Lawrence, KS

(Thousands of dollars, except as noted.)

Year	Personal income, total	Earnings by place of work			Less: Contributions for government social insurance	Plus: Adjustment for residence	Equals: Net earnings by place of residence	Plus: Dividends, interest, and rent	Plus: Personal current transfer receipts	Per capita personal income (dollars)	Population (persons)	Total employment
		Nonfarm	Farm	Total								
1970	188,577	142,505	2,913	145,418	10,193	8,564	143,789	31,233	13,555	3,238	58,233	23,010
1971	212,249	162,044	4,306	166,350	12,103	7,842	162,089	34,582	15,578	3,560	59,621	24,197
1972	228,770	169,413	5,104	174,517	13,315	11,345	172,547	38,075	18,148	3,765	60,767	24,524
1973	252,995	187,454	6,280	193,734	17,182	12,723	189,275	41,795	21,925	4,091	61,848	25,994
1974	282,919	214,801	2,360	217,161	20,658	11,401	207,904	48,730	26,285	4,502	62,844	27,633
1975	321,714	238,085	4,435	242,520	22,712	12,298	232,106	57,426	32,182	5,311	60,580	27,762
1976	361,577	275,723	3,491	279,214	26,556	12,643	265,301	60,477	35,799	5,879	61,498	29,598
1977	414,181	317,243	7,089	324,332	30,394	13,456	307,394	66,278	40,509	6,581	62,932	31,544
1978	461,040	356,141	4,192	360,333	35,431	16,757	341,659	74,654	44,727	7,019	65,685	33,135
1979	513,435	397,584	4,206	401,790	41,165	19,420	380,045	85,637	47,753	7,697	66,710	34,211
1980	565,611	420,573	-20	420,553	43,725	23,843	400,671	107,028	57,912	8,312	68,045	34,501
1981	635,462	452,146	2,407	454,553	50,291	30,099	434,361	134,173	66,928	9,134	69,569	33,622
1982	665,872	461,303	353	461,656	51,836	35,496	445,316	151,139	69,417	9,520	69,948	33,433
1983	715,958	493,344	-3,135	490,209	54,363	40,759	476,605	164,310	75,043	10,236	69,947	33,914
1984	789,048	537,609	1,966	539,575	59,561	48,670	528,684	183,637	76,727	11,173	70,618	35,192
1985	856,752	569,979	7,741	577,720	63,298	56,931	571,353	202,586	82,813	11,874	72,151	36,131
1986	924,970	626,997	5,794	632,791	69,329	62,865	626,327	215,741	82,902	12,409	74,538	37,149
1987	974,898	658,463	8,028	666,491	72,255	69,050	663,286	222,971	88,641	12,803	76,148	39,566
1988	1,058,234	721,842	10,187	732,029	83,157	76,150	725,022	235,856	97,356	13,433	78,779	42,190
1989	1,168,801	795,452	8,100	803,552	90,618	82,093	795,027	265,020	108,754	14,593	80,092	43,552
1990	1,230,365	850,102	5,626	855,728	102,001	88,549	842,276	265,631	122,458	14,963	82,229	44,906
1991	1,307,632	900,787	4,465	905,252	109,468	98,480	894,264	275,542	137,826	15,626	83,683	46,550
1992	1,428,702	975,575	11,483	987,058	117,095	110,541	980,504	292,997	155,201	16,734	85,379	47,328
1993	1,518,184	1,039,884	2,834	1,042,718	124,410	124,761	1,043,069	307,659	167,456	17,267	87,926	48,723
1994	1,639,148	1,111,029	5,717	1,116,746	135,055	137,138	1,118,829	347,530	172,789	18,277	89,683	49,946
1995	1,737,680	1,175,691	1,989	1,177,680	141,406	151,112	1,187,386	366,640	183,654	19,010	91,408	53,006
1996	1,846,642	1,235,077	9,201	1,244,278	146,671	168,453	1,266,060	389,958	190,624	19,775	93,381	54,732
1997	2,021,494	1,358,642	8,054	1,366,696	161,081	182,492	1,388,107	430,649	202,738	21,122	95,706	57,637
1998	2,202,188	1,489,775	504	1,490,279	173,287	206,260	1,523,252	463,964	214,972	22,571	97,566	59,930
1999	2,303,472	1,576,137	-2,401	1,573,736	182,303	234,526	1,625,959	451,643	225,870	23,153	99,490	62,113
2000	2,499,247	1,702,290	-5,719	1,696,571	196,736	260,745	1,760,580	489,932	248,735	24,931	100,247	63,698
2001	2,656,158	1,817,366	-3,140	1,814,226	210,656	295,292	1,898,862	483,177	274,119	26,229	101,269	65,641
2002	2,752,230	1,884,920	-7,085	1,877,835	217,088	300,732	1,961,479	498,235	292,516	26,837	102,552	65,474
2003	2,832,259	1,917,575	-1,761	1,915,814	222,035	306,094	1,999,873	525,079	307,307	27,346	103,570	65,653
2004	2,933,163	2,007,898	8,077	2,015,975	232,491	324,448	2,107,932	505,346	319,885	27,981	104,826	65,107
2005	3,068,396	2,079,439	1,688	2,081,127	241,635	339,108	2,178,600	552,656	337,140	29,035	105,681	65,278
2006	3,314,533	2,180,800	-3,054	2,177,746	252,572	361,496	2,286,670	669,415	358,448	30,923	107,187	65,776
2007	3,454,331	2,238,291	1,455	2,239,746	257,527	384,090	2,366,309	693,888	394,134	32,017	107,892	66,419
2008	3,613,530	2,308,354	5,774	2,314,128	263,809	404,798	2,455,117	686,100	472,313	33,149	109,010	65,254
2009	3,599,243	2,299,773	15,032	2,314,805	267,292	344,161	2,391,674	695,588	511,981	32,709	110,039	64,533
2010	3,626,822	2,304,100	9,057	2,313,157	271,144	387,963	2,429,976	634,509	562,337	32,587	111,296	63,388
2011	3,827,825	2,369,096	17,670	2,386,766	244,628	387,328	2,529,466	714,701	583,658	34,028	112,491	62,894
2012	3,990,739	2,430,597	12,519	2,443,116	250,860	457,904	2,650,160	762,171	578,408	35,211	113,339	62,693
2013	4,116,749	2,515,896	38,640	2,554,536	293,284	461,759	2,723,011	798,609	595,129	35,859	114,803	64,079
2014	4,277,044	2,607,672	20,496	2,628,168	305,429	508,727	2,831,466	821,705	623,873	36,686	116,585	65,461

Personal Income and Employment by Area: Lawton, OK

(Thousands of dollars, except as noted.)

Year	Personal income, total	Earnings by place of work			Less: Contributions for government social insurance	Plus: Adjustment for residence	Equals: Net earnings by place of residence	Plus: Dividends, interest, and rent	Plus: Personal current transfer receipts	Per capita personal income (dollars)	Population (persons)	Total employment
		Nonfarm	Farm	Total								
1970	473,491	374,503	6,559	381,062	21,692	-8,107	351,263	96,996	25,232	4,123	114,835	57,235
1971	477,014	377,293	5,259	382,552	23,342	-8,442	350,768	96,858	29,388	4,158	114,717	53,368
1972	487,393	382,959	7,874	390,833	23,936	-8,857	358,040	96,643	32,710	4,551	107,106	50,475
1973	545,729	417,859	18,630	436,489	28,238	-9,686	398,565	109,395	37,769	4,991	109,334	51,921
1974	600,122	462,039	11,260	473,299	32,850	-10,405	430,044	124,483	45,595	5,416	110,808	53,070
1975	642,416	490,486	9,177	499,663	37,042	-10,539	452,082	134,199	56,135	5,706	112,591	53,108
1976	744,011	572,061	10,070	582,131	44,720	-10,780	526,631	154,835	62,545	6,141	121,157	56,963
1977	789,560	612,403	1,099	613,502	47,460	-11,201	554,841	168,497	66,222	6,447	122,462	57,631
1978	873,990	679,331	1,598	680,929	53,308	-15,432	612,189	191,425	70,376	7,025	124,413	58,416
1979	969,602	730,790	18,862	749,652	59,447	-11,836	678,369	209,258	81,975	7,935	122,200	58,783
1980	1,058,728	794,607	5,723	800,330	64,973	-8,816	726,541	236,565	95,622	8,806	120,234	59,943
1981	1,220,559	906,252	13,931	920,183	77,698	-6,092	836,393	276,326	107,840	10,023	121,777	60,159
1982	1,381,824	1,036,112	9,655	1,045,767	87,837	-10,698	947,232	314,236	120,356	10,931	126,418	63,838
1983	1,454,417	1,075,558	8,504	1,084,062	93,866	-10,192	980,004	343,510	130,903	11,267	129,084	63,134
1984	1,546,035	1,149,635	4,486	1,154,121	102,427	-11,493	1,040,201	367,924	137,910	12,074	128,046	64,339
1985	1,651,410	1,224,461	12,685	1,237,146	111,421	-13,850	1,111,875	392,615	146,920	12,977	127,261	65,425
1986	1,713,977	1,273,228	24,740	1,297,968	118,538	-16,187	1,163,243	397,169	153,565	13,614	125,897	64,430
1987	1,766,946	1,332,156	12,310	1,344,466	125,431	-19,133	1,199,902	404,012	163,032	14,102	125,301	65,717
1988	1,784,493	1,335,426	22,196	1,357,622	134,686	-16,014	1,206,922	401,067	176,504	14,474	123,289	64,438
1989	1,821,674	1,344,796	17,241	1,362,037	138,496	-14,945	1,208,596	422,169	190,909	15,303	119,044	63,133
1990	1,893,315	1,387,280	27,272	1,414,552	147,994	-14,094	1,252,464	430,271	210,580	16,030	118,112	62,529
1991	1,943,740	1,437,780	13,199	1,450,979	157,105	-15,012	1,278,862	432,456	232,422	16,487	117,896	60,909
1992	2,198,231	1,643,258	20,012	1,663,270	181,849	-22,205	1,459,216	477,185	261,830	17,253	127,413	65,370
1993	2,189,594	1,613,496	19,351	1,632,847	182,537	-18,441	1,431,869	485,478	272,247	17,449	125,485	64,545
1994	2,216,170	1,625,561	11,813	1,637,374	183,414	-16,867	1,437,093	489,097	289,980	17,684	125,323	63,353
1995	2,292,335	1,648,516	2,162	1,650,678	185,112	-16,553	1,449,013	526,633	316,689	18,575	123,412	64,135
1996	2,351,635	1,666,757	9,673	1,676,430	185,857	-13,921	1,476,652	542,540	332,443	19,064	123,357	64,864
1997	2,380,798	1,705,301	12,275	1,717,576	189,191	-10,727	1,517,658	522,972	340,168	19,436	122,497	64,740
1998	2,499,747	1,784,162	11,403	1,795,565	195,273	-11,708	1,588,584	564,445	346,718	20,477	122,076	64,175
1999	2,584,765	1,831,709	17,240	1,848,949	199,685	-11,124	1,638,140	574,151	372,474	21,093	122,542	64,436
2000	2,721,598	1,920,066	19,278	1,939,344	206,091	-8,435	1,724,818	602,615	394,165	22,364	121,695	64,729
2001	2,875,783	2,001,831	10,597	2,012,428	217,373	-3,462	1,791,593	641,817	442,373	23,974	119,955	64,741
2002	2,994,528	2,107,367	18,628	2,125,995	229,953	-19,102	1,876,940	644,236	473,352	24,978	119,889	64,904
2003	3,185,677	2,286,431	19,970	2,306,401	247,552	-33,898	2,024,951	647,158	513,568	27,116	117,484	65,425
2004	3,311,883	2,417,516	31,670	2,449,186	265,936	-43,510	2,139,740	633,880	538,263	27,071	122,341	66,614
2005	3,462,572	2,530,501	36,111	2,566,612	273,944	-55,883	2,236,785	635,678	590,109	28,504	121,475	65,015
2006	3,773,303	2,814,931	13,626	2,828,557	301,353	-79,894	2,447,310	688,418	637,575	30,682	122,980	67,867
2007	3,956,149	2,913,645	3,061	2,916,706	313,821	-90,340	2,512,545	752,674	690,930	31,444	125,814	69,408
2008	4,178,048	3,052,121	23,030	3,075,151	330,287	-115,602	2,629,262	771,638	777,148	33,649	124,166	69,959
2009	4,300,492	3,167,431	-9,374	3,158,057	351,596	-128,721	2,677,740	790,779	831,973	34,095	126,131	70,139
2010	4,620,217	3,438,683	-2,808	3,435,875	377,442	-150,649	2,907,784	816,515	895,918	35,101	131,625	72,035
2011	4,772,416	3,442,265	17,098	3,459,363	345,952	-144,482	2,968,929	876,512	926,975	36,082	132,267	70,070
2012	4,786,519	3,400,923	31,653	3,432,576	341,907	-132,259	2,958,410	876,395	951,714	36,054	132,758	68,643
2013	4,814,894	3,429,738	24,080	3,453,818	386,705	-134,163	2,932,950	909,253	972,691	36,702	131,188	69,240
2014	4,900,986	3,440,836	39,623	3,480,459	382,186	-129,320	2,968,953	925,014	1,007,019	37,360	131,183	69,048

Personal Income and Employment by Area: Lebanon, PA

(Thousands of dollars, except as noted.)

| Year | Personal income, total | Derivation of personal income | | | | | | | | | Per capita personal income (dollars) | Population (persons) | Total employment |
| | | Earnings by place of work | | | Less: Contributions for government social insurance | Plus: Adjustment for residence | Equals: Net earnings by place of residence | Plus: Dividends, interest, and rent | Plus: Personal current transfer receipts | | | |
		Nonfarm	Farm	Total								
1970	391,012	299,456	11,617	311,073	20,759	20,039	310,353	46,619	34,040	3,903	100,193	44,662
1971	403,635	307,171	9,638	316,809	21,967	18,475	313,317	50,643	39,675	3,922	102,907	43,469
1972	446,408	343,394	9,890	353,284	25,787	19,621	347,118	55,063	44,227	4,317	103,414	44,721
1973	495,611	380,027	12,642	392,669	33,035	23,706	383,340	62,634	49,637	4,717	105,069	45,978
1974	551,427	420,886	10,251	431,137	38,229	26,981	419,889	72,028	59,510	5,236	105,311	46,696
1975	606,579	454,216	8,655	462,871	39,642	20,584	443,813	80,634	82,132	4,880	124,289	46,734
1976	661,832	495,428	9,602	505,030	43,853	26,733	487,910	87,285	86,637	6,116	108,206	46,955
1977	734,795	550,904	8,027	558,931	48,559	33,882	544,254	98,597	91,944	6,800	108,055	47,783
1978	813,340	604,704	10,665	615,369	54,533	43,615	604,451	111,542	97,347	7,441	109,308	48,272
1979	915,938	672,700	14,272	686,972	62,616	57,650	682,006	125,365	108,567	8,319	110,096	49,036
1980	1,001,611	705,967	8,178	714,145	66,213	71,145	719,077	157,940	124,594	9,203	108,839	48,871
1981	1,106,376	740,681	12,109	752,790	74,753	91,181	769,218	193,113	144,045	10,091	109,645	48,150
1982	1,169,853	727,958	10,790	738,748	74,059	110,872	775,561	225,855	168,437	10,580	110,574	46,129
1983	1,238,300	758,335	10,838	769,173	79,392	124,069	813,850	242,746	181,704	11,237	110,199	45,813
1984	1,342,841	802,783	24,989	827,772	88,197	152,995	892,570	269,566	180,705	12,180	110,250	46,912
1985	1,426,282	840,626	25,334	865,960	93,846	167,728	939,842	293,758	192,682	12,921	110,382	47,415
1986	1,517,538	874,609	32,066	906,675	98,039	192,263	1,000,899	310,284	206,355	13,701	110,764	47,688
1987	1,615,466	950,729	28,399	979,128	106,583	216,158	1,088,703	317,694	209,069	14,470	111,646	50,000
1988	1,753,367	1,056,272	14,420	1,070,692	121,044	241,819	1,191,467	335,805	226,095	15,566	112,643	52,423
1989	1,929,610	1,131,058	23,680	1,154,738	127,605	276,305	1,303,438	382,715	243,457	17,075	113,009	52,792
1990	2,030,651	1,171,983	31,606	1,203,589	133,391	290,412	1,360,610	399,155	270,886	17,796	114,109	52,552
1991	2,132,516	1,197,105	26,362	1,223,467	138,595	323,982	1,408,854	408,275	315,387	18,504	115,248	52,326
1992	2,250,907	1,278,729	28,901	1,307,630	147,886	351,957	1,511,701	408,168	331,038	19,393	116,066	52,293
1993	2,344,679	1,316,468	24,837	1,341,305	155,972	388,064	1,573,397	418,460	352,822	20,080	116,764	51,088
1994	2,452,665	1,402,428	23,340	1,425,768	166,646	410,820	1,669,942	423,398	359,325	20,889	117,415	51,472
1995	2,530,689	1,383,877	16,045	1,399,922	166,464	471,214	1,704,672	445,407	380,610	21,481	117,809	52,277
1996	2,666,049	1,401,069	28,451	1,429,520	164,990	527,291	1,791,821	466,337	407,891	22,519	118,391	52,193
1997	2,804,102	1,476,628	26,696	1,503,324	172,786	557,453	1,887,991	495,610	420,501	23,613	118,753	53,347
1998	2,979,372	1,547,904	29,297	1,577,201	179,219	610,227	2,008,209	534,490	436,673	24,913	119,590	51,899
1999	3,091,138	1,644,343	20,712	1,665,055	187,965	615,285	2,092,375	531,572	467,191	25,772	119,944	52,831
2000	3,246,694	1,741,813	38,442	1,780,255	198,674	607,369	2,188,950	562,920	494,824	26,986	120,309	54,476
2001	3,400,737	1,851,473	40,987	1,892,460	212,423	635,423	2,315,460	550,400	534,877	28,116	120,954	55,020
2002	3,401,812	1,869,639	21,018	1,890,657	216,262	632,600	2,306,995	520,306	574,511	27,953	121,698	55,409
2003	3,528,530	1,953,874	48,065	2,001,939	224,969	648,003	2,424,973	504,187	599,370	28,651	123,154	56,120
2004	3,813,784	2,092,513	73,200	2,165,713	241,063	682,545	2,607,195	567,675	638,914	30,597	124,644	57,409
2005	3,951,217	2,180,038	68,761	2,248,799	255,084	700,225	2,693,940	554,541	702,736	31,310	126,197	58,811
2006	4,196,052	2,337,645	42,910	2,380,555	272,487	741,296	2,849,364	604,719	741,969	32,704	128,302	61,123
2007	4,441,636	2,410,260	59,999	2,470,259	283,223	771,538	2,958,574	695,911	787,151	34,119	130,182	63,019
2008	4,684,285	2,489,765	65,538	2,555,303	293,633	784,254	3,045,924	735,312	903,049	35,602	131,574	63,367
2009	4,710,493	2,483,471	51,466	2,534,937	294,495	747,474	2,987,916	707,855	1,014,722	35,428	132,959	62,592
2010	4,885,089	2,605,912	58,584	2,664,496	310,477	768,873	3,122,892	688,439	1,073,758	36,530	133,728	63,039
2011	5,136,917	2,728,735	89,043	2,817,778	294,019	769,168	3,292,927	753,838	1,090,152	38,180	134,544	64,262
2012	5,267,437	2,823,213	91,586	2,914,799	302,256	740,453	3,352,996	814,270	1,100,171	38,851	135,582	65,730
2013	5,400,271	2,852,908	131,621	2,984,529	341,628	789,872	3,432,773	831,081	1,136,417	39,794	135,707	65,619
2014	5,595,392	2,874,155	155,914	3,030,069	347,148	876,410	3,559,331	864,637	1,171,424	41,034	136,359	65,179

Personal Income and Employment by Area: Lewiston, ID-WA

(Thousands of dollars, except as noted.)

Year	Personal income, total	Earnings by place of work			Less: Contributions for government social insurance	Plus: Adjustment for residence	Equals: Net earnings by place of residence	Plus: Dividends, interest, and rent	Plus: Personal current transfer receipts	Per capita personal income (dollars)	Population (persons)	Total employment
		Nonfarm	Farm	Total								
1970	164,532	115,962	8,313	124,275	9,095	4,861	120,041	26,251	18,240	3,722	44,211	17,980
1971	179,845	127,368	8,214	135,582	10,329	4,329	129,582	29,692	20,571	4,015	44,792	18,651
1972	201,468	143,177	11,849	155,026	12,020	3,294	146,300	32,046	23,122	4,342	46,404	18,905
1973	225,898	162,426	15,283	177,709	15,830	890	162,769	36,750	26,379	4,863	46,454	20,121
1974	262,182	183,464	25,104	208,568	18,365	-1,609	188,594	42,140	31,448	5,619	46,658	20,911
1975	285,701	207,234	13,662	220,896	20,154	-1,026	199,716	47,708	38,277	6,112	46,744	21,367
1976	313,142	233,343	12,210	245,553	23,000	-1,723	220,830	50,608	41,704	6,576	47,617	22,040
1977	341,111	260,206	10,087	270,293	25,749	-4,143	240,401	56,520	44,190	7,122	47,898	22,824
1978	383,724	296,530	10,330	306,860	29,545	-5,897	271,418	63,613	48,693	7,905	48,543	23,861
1979	425,166	334,530	8,658	343,188	35,020	-10,983	297,185	72,212	55,769	8,672	49,026	24,620
1980	476,671	359,202	15,518	374,720	37,639	-12,953	324,128	86,586	65,957	9,518	50,082	24,405
1981	517,073	372,981	18,414	391,395	42,011	-12,391	336,993	105,576	74,504	10,307	50,169	23,670
1982	540,268	368,891	19,741	388,632	42,465	-10,416	335,751	120,872	83,645	10,837	49,856	22,989
1983	589,909	399,512	27,815	427,327	46,124	-9,347	371,856	129,676	88,377	11,876	49,673	23,660
1984	616,403	420,119	16,212	436,331	50,195	-8,237	377,899	145,629	92,875	12,263	50,264	23,775
1985	625,320	423,846	4,636	428,482	51,026	-6,546	370,910	153,495	100,915	12,442	50,257	23,403
1986	649,866	434,710	11,266	445,976	52,988	-4,821	388,167	155,970	105,729	13,026	49,891	23,465
1987	671,670	457,512	8,254	465,766	55,791	-4,989	404,986	155,558	111,126	13,416	50,063	24,138
1988	719,682	494,565	12,478	507,043	62,664	-2,218	442,161	158,600	118,921	14,395	49,995	25,462
1989	786,157	530,251	18,246	548,497	67,867	-365	480,265	179,334	126,558	15,426	50,964	26,044
1990	845,907	579,300	21,540	600,840	77,583	1,339	524,596	183,569	137,742	16,417	51,526	26,983
1991	893,239	617,382	10,877	628,259	83,610	378	545,027	190,383	157,829	17,018	52,487	27,518
1992	975,937	690,728	9,824	700,552	92,283	-1,637	606,632	197,668	171,637	18,198	53,629	28,639
1993	1,056,966	743,438	23,147	766,585	99,583	-2,467	664,535	209,407	183,024	19,305	54,750	29,620
1994	1,106,790	798,128	7,128	805,256	107,177	-3,597	694,482	217,100	195,208	19,769	55,987	31,132
1995	1,150,746	797,829	10,704	808,533	107,803	-2,777	697,953	241,232	211,561	20,289	56,718	31,384
1996	1,220,828	839,940	13,468	853,408	111,092	-5,349	736,967	260,207	223,654	21,294	57,332	32,113
1997	1,280,611	896,616	426	897,042	116,075	-7,881	773,086	276,324	231,201	22,128	57,874	33,058
1998	1,363,145	958,636	6,472	965,108	121,627	-9,784	833,697	284,846	244,602	23,456	58,116	33,483
1999	1,422,503	1,017,915	8,585	1,026,500	124,742	-11,619	890,139	278,358	254,006	24,508	58,042	33,610
2000	1,486,343	1,049,424	19,707	1,069,131	129,406	-12,605	927,120	285,939	273,284	25,651	57,944	34,314
2001	1,541,347	1,077,372	19,933	1,097,305	133,031	-16,230	948,044	293,325	299,978	26,831	57,446	33,501
2002	1,552,537	1,104,887	16,602	1,121,489	136,393	-19,953	965,143	273,555	313,839	26,953	57,601	33,352
2003	1,611,482	1,136,570	18,587	1,155,157	141,207	-20,339	993,611	287,613	330,258	27,697	58,183	33,678
2004	1,682,431	1,171,500	23,458	1,194,958	144,879	-18,943	1,031,136	301,012	350,283	28,720	58,581	33,770
2005	1,728,581	1,204,694	22,086	1,226,780	151,224	-15,090	1,060,466	300,896	367,219	29,308	58,979	34,260
2006	1,839,065	1,279,647	16,271	1,295,918	161,565	-12,904	1,121,449	320,440	397,176	30,833	59,646	34,819
2007	1,962,400	1,334,775	20,648	1,355,423	169,597	-15,184	1,170,642	361,416	430,342	32,757	59,908	35,644
2008	2,058,934	1,350,164	22,556	1,372,720	173,430	-12,779	1,186,511	400,059	472,364	34,200	60,203	35,162
2009	2,035,072	1,314,153	16,866	1,331,019	171,763	-11,524	1,147,732	380,122	507,218	33,658	60,464	34,133
2010	2,092,652	1,350,803	21,657	1,372,460	181,030	-11,278	1,180,152	366,781	545,719	34,296	61,018	34,034
2011	2,173,463	1,356,654	24,945	1,381,599	163,357	-10,842	1,207,400	418,830	547,233	35,432	61,342	33,906
2012	2,216,527	1,371,150	19,429	1,390,579	164,749	-6,488	1,219,342	453,122	544,063	36,070	61,450	33,337
2013	2,265,307	1,433,112	20,611	1,453,723	190,553	-13,095	1,250,075	452,476	562,756	36,512	62,042	34,247
2014	2,346,563	1,481,662	-1,067	1,480,595	196,240	-11,391	1,272,964	471,884	601,715	37,729	62,196	34,865

Personal Income and Employment by Area: Lewiston-Auburn, ME

(Thousands of dollars, except as noted.)

| Year | Personal income, total | Derivation of personal income | | | | | | | | Per capita personal income (dollars) | Population (persons) | Total employment |
| | | Earnings by place of work | | | Less: Contributions for government social insurance | Plus: Adjustment for residence | Equals: Net earnings by place of residence | Plus: Dividends, interest, and rent | Plus: Personal current transfer receipts | | | |
		Nonfarm	Farm	Total								
1970	337,302	245,744	6,907	252,651	19,291	22,063	255,423	43,522	38,357	3,688	91,463	42,844
1971	347,840	241,251	7,099	248,350	19,477	26,149	255,022	46,545	46,273	3,745	92,881	40,634
1972	370,743	256,283	9,495	265,778	21,738	27,731	271,771	49,780	49,192	3,954	93,756	40,343
1973	419,798	288,531	18,096	306,627	27,820	29,359	308,166	54,407	57,225	4,415	95,076	42,562
1974	455,986	309,309	13,975	323,284	30,844	32,700	325,140	62,446	68,400	4,756	95,870	43,143
1975	500,318	329,626	14,041	343,667	32,268	35,395	346,794	67,744	85,780	5,237	95,535	42,320
1976	573,766	381,644	23,386	405,030	38,489	43,480	410,021	72,356	91,389	5,907	97,130	44,591
1977	616,486	417,042	18,291	435,333	42,096	46,696	439,933	80,602	95,951	6,279	98,181	46,014
1978	677,580	466,086	15,016	481,102	48,555	54,621	487,168	88,540	101,872	6,856	98,837	47,120
1979	745,626	510,537	12,901	523,438	54,493	63,767	532,712	96,829	116,085	7,482	99,656	47,810
1980	838,756	554,202	11,128	565,330	59,010	78,354	584,674	117,696	136,386	8,427	99,531	47,774
1981	916,533	584,286	13,423	597,709	66,270	86,090	617,529	142,639	156,365	9,209	99,522	47,298
1982	986,247	600,404	15,140	615,544	68,408	100,597	647,733	167,701	170,813	9,976	98,860	45,953
1983	1,062,868	655,516	13,366	668,882	74,858	107,526	701,550	176,025	185,293	10,708	99,262	46,577
1984	1,170,464	730,043	20,067	750,110	85,417	111,881	776,574	200,147	193,743	11,703	100,018	48,103
1985	1,229,887	773,540	17,568	791,108	90,215	113,043	813,936	211,160	204,791	12,285	100,114	48,570
1986	1,326,826	837,435	14,671	852,106	97,136	127,824	882,794	231,907	212,125	13,241	100,204	50,078
1987	1,449,008	939,415	14,137	953,552	107,058	139,271	985,765	247,313	215,930	14,293	101,378	51,603
1988	1,586,288	1,028,934	12,437	1,041,371	119,791	164,431	1,086,011	269,711	230,566	15,318	103,559	53,611
1989	1,721,082	1,098,545	10,731	1,109,276	126,141	184,805	1,167,940	307,003	246,139	16,348	105,276	54,122
1990	1,772,087	1,114,320	17,088	1,131,408	134,137	195,675	1,192,946	301,141	278,000	16,811	105,412	53,181
1991	1,772,870	1,115,967	16,841	1,132,808	136,422	167,499	1,163,885	290,005	318,980	16,889	104,973	50,918
1992	1,842,471	1,156,558	16,732	1,173,290	142,774	181,084	1,211,600	278,233	352,638	17,659	104,335	50,835
1993	1,905,560	1,218,378	22,212	1,240,590	154,004	172,566	1,259,152	277,193	369,215	18,241	104,464	52,166
1994	1,995,846	1,288,846	27,361	1,316,207	164,818	168,734	1,320,123	288,371	387,352	19,170	104,112	53,466
1995	2,052,702	1,328,645	10,621	1,339,266	171,013	162,913	1,331,166	316,778	404,758	19,781	103,769	53,265
1996	2,148,518	1,380,351	21,502	1,401,853	174,536	153,700	1,381,017	335,243	432,258	20,866	102,966	53,134
1997	2,252,908	1,450,437	14,203	1,464,640	182,904	174,900	1,456,636	346,991	449,281	21,976	102,518	53,271
1998	2,351,559	1,550,892	13,724	1,564,616	194,452	161,799	1,531,963	359,653	459,943	22,804	103,120	55,713
1999	2,468,260	1,690,676	23,918	1,714,594	208,774	146,477	1,652,297	349,914	466,049	23,870	103,403	58,681
2000	2,614,280	1,808,394	23,628	1,832,022	220,032	130,997	1,742,987	380,928	490,365	25,173	103,852	60,400
2001	2,789,516	1,906,416	24,369	1,930,785	230,675	174,267	1,874,377	387,481	527,658	26,755	104,260	61,316
2002	2,958,175	2,046,529	23,291	2,069,820	240,101	163,491	1,993,210	401,688	563,277	28,156	105,063	62,112
2003	3,088,122	2,131,152	30,986	2,162,138	246,594	146,467	2,062,011	407,782	618,329	29,095	106,140	62,026
2004	3,133,930	2,212,873	23,188	2,236,061	253,417	130,019	2,112,663	369,321	651,946	29,326	106,867	62,635
2005	3,188,820	2,260,048	9,054	2,269,102	261,280	110,155	2,117,977	352,322	718,521	29,704	107,352	62,932
2006	3,336,388	2,402,634	10,548	2,413,182	280,791	93,748	2,226,139	386,635	723,614	30,912	107,932	63,716
2007	3,478,415	2,482,888	17,416	2,500,304	294,750	73,545	2,279,099	429,090	770,226	32,286	107,739	65,118
2008	3,605,902	2,522,211	19,819	2,542,030	301,496	49,538	2,290,072	426,168	889,662	33,300	108,284	64,980
2009	3,644,579	2,478,742	14,776	2,493,518	295,496	55,077	2,253,099	415,924	975,556	33,799	107,830	62,953
2010	3,646,485	2,502,621	14,800	2,517,421	302,943	16,962	2,231,440	445,706	969,339	33,870	107,661	62,571
2011	3,756,227	2,549,050	15,646	2,564,696	277,290	-11,327	2,276,079	464,983	1,015,165	34,989	107,353	62,791
2012	3,818,327	2,618,070	25,687	2,643,757	284,988	-25,886	2,332,883	482,915	1,002,529	35,517	107,506	62,856
2013	3,788,208	2,646,039	28,593	2,674,632	328,940	-36,937	2,308,755	466,023	1,013,430	35,275	107,391	62,797
2014	3,900,024	2,758,002	35,490	2,793,492	341,677	-67,887	2,383,928	486,792	1,029,304	36,300	107,440	63,961

Personal Income and Employment by Area: Lexington-Fayette, KY

(Thousands of dollars, except as noted.)

Year	Personal income, total	Derivation of personal income									Per capita personal income (dollars)	Population (persons)	Total employment
		Earnings by place of work			Less: Contributions for government social insurance	Plus: Adjustment for residence	Equals: Net earnings by place of residence	Plus: Dividends, interest, and rent	Plus: Personal current transfer receipts				
		Nonfarm	Farm	Total									
1970	1,014,633	859,877	42,124	902,001	54,163	-49,999	797,839	142,565	74,229	3,793	267,481	140,584
1971	1,123,531	952,088	39,006	991,094	61,436	-52,234	877,424	159,183	86,924	4,105	273,697	143,669
1972	1,247,354	1,057,838	51,243	1,109,081	72,088	-61,984	975,009	176,165	96,180	4,425	281,894	148,727
1973	1,393,612	1,199,599	54,506	1,254,105	94,851	-71,651	1,087,603	195,284	110,725	4,845	287,662	158,535
1974	1,553,529	1,328,797	56,972	1,385,769	108,738	-83,371	1,193,660	226,200	133,669	5,245	296,218	162,910
1975	1,703,757	1,421,417	60,952	1,482,369	115,190	-84,922	1,282,257	246,466	175,034	5,724	297,670	157,519
1976	1,924,166	1,631,319	71,845	1,703,164	135,761	-104,716	1,462,687	271,237	190,242	6,342	303,393	166,412
1977	2,138,653	1,807,150	94,260	1,901,410	150,367	-118,216	1,632,827	302,141	203,685	6,933	308,473	170,538
1978	2,429,422	2,033,991	148,323	2,182,314	175,832	-139,275	1,867,207	343,083	219,132	7,793	311,728	180,152
1979	2,714,031	2,303,061	141,902	2,444,963	206,600	-165,646	2,072,717	393,988	247,326	8,567	316,817	184,649
1980	3,015,671	2,443,011	193,405	2,636,416	221,253	-172,998	2,242,165	476,876	296,630	9,478	318,175	183,059
1981	3,416,733	2,668,913	258,179	2,927,092	260,843	-186,564	2,479,685	600,187	336,861	10,681	319,884	183,889
1982	3,673,936	2,824,810	231,382	3,056,192	281,232	-195,401	2,579,559	731,440	362,937	11,400	322,286	185,181
1983	3,999,716	3,085,798	280,225	3,366,023	310,274	-218,665	2,837,084	768,535	394,097	12,336	324,231	191,185
1984	4,526,303	3,504,266	364,345	3,868,611	359,216	-258,054	3,251,341	859,792	415,170	13,921	325,133	200,185
1985	4,825,819	3,794,890	341,328	4,136,218	396,859	-285,101	3,454,258	927,151	444,410	14,602	330,485	205,232
1986	4,966,855	3,990,839	253,497	4,244,336	433,192	-295,698	3,515,446	984,390	467,019	14,819	335,169	212,210
1987	5,254,389	4,282,536	238,901	4,521,437	463,752	-322,575	3,735,110	1,027,911	491,368	15,499	339,008	216,098
1988	5,846,039	4,831,768	245,711	5,077,479	520,275	-352,187	4,205,017	1,107,763	533,259	17,035	343,186	223,962
1989	6,282,315	5,214,617	233,857	5,448,474	570,758	-400,988	4,476,728	1,208,937	596,650	18,215	344,891	230,602
1990	6,855,463	5,743,621	242,676	5,986,297	652,388	-465,742	4,868,167	1,330,553	656,743	19,578	350,161	235,619
1991	7,279,058	6,064,091	248,903	6,312,994	692,104	-469,437	5,151,453	1,381,651	745,954	20,455	355,861	237,345
1992	7,799,420	6,492,754	314,329	6,807,083	739,906	-507,766	5,559,411	1,416,425	823,584	21,474	363,195	242,428
1993	8,107,399	6,768,332	281,970	7,050,302	778,884	-510,836	5,760,582	1,470,633	876,184	21,921	369,839	248,440
1994	8,428,793	7,010,027	278,514	7,288,541	825,453	-546,833	5,916,255	1,599,563	912,975	22,448	375,478	251,588
1995	8,982,286	7,425,357	279,784	7,705,141	878,581	-602,377	6,224,183	1,774,154	983,949	23,632	380,096	264,124
1996	9,615,334	8,007,520	321,845	8,329,365	937,874	-699,183	6,692,308	1,874,685	1,048,341	24,903	386,117	272,024
1997	10,265,666	8,559,934	387,127	8,947,061	999,013	-776,829	7,171,219	1,985,583	1,108,864	26,251	391,065	279,832
1998	11,049,098	9,190,962	448,365	9,639,327	1,069,700	-812,194	7,757,433	2,150,805	1,140,860	27,777	397,775	286,458
1999	11,730,975	9,847,071	547,133	10,394,204	1,148,677	-846,516	8,399,011	2,157,621	1,174,343	29,009	404,393	293,935
2000	12,685,185	10,486,174	643,026	11,129,200	1,192,653	-920,727	9,015,820	2,375,778	1,293,587	30,945	409,924	300,614
2001	12,955,077	10,869,093	402,457	11,271,550	1,223,409	-939,852	9,108,289	2,398,021	1,448,767	31,253	414,520	296,591
2002	13,249,325	11,268,051	390,442	11,658,493	1,266,079	-987,952	9,404,462	2,270,737	1,574,126	31,663	418,448	292,314
2003	13,585,758	11,690,520	287,630	11,978,150	1,301,343	-1,028,808	9,647,999	2,308,958	1,628,801	31,970	424,953	295,360
2004	14,354,455	12,284,281	341,976	12,626,257	1,345,240	-1,070,638	10,210,379	2,396,936	1,747,140	33,365	430,229	298,347
2005	15,057,387	12,793,284	293,097	13,086,381	1,394,667	-1,113,488	10,578,226	2,619,265	1,859,896	34,464	436,898	304,314
2006	16,231,116	13,457,532	298,780	13,756,312	1,473,968	-1,148,752	11,133,592	3,086,967	2,010,557	36,418	445,685	313,664
2007	16,997,399	14,042,790	234,501	14,277,291	1,550,360	-1,189,328	11,537,603	3,278,724	2,181,072	37,593	452,138	321,019
2008	17,514,308	14,434,637	30,954	14,465,591	1,608,126	-1,191,277	11,666,188	3,298,154	2,549,966	38,065	460,112	320,675
2009	17,048,945	13,837,243	47,495	13,884,738	1,575,153	-1,143,398	11,166,187	3,054,049	2,828,709	36,482	467,328	310,953
2010	17,595,882	14,195,147	58,162	14,253,309	1,597,107	-1,084,879	11,571,323	2,898,749	3,125,810	37,169	473,402	309,916
2011	18,725,215	14,855,381	62,408	14,917,789	1,467,299	-1,126,716	12,323,774	3,220,001	3,181,440	39,137	478,459	314,964
2012	19,595,405	15,531,862	103,050	15,634,912	1,524,147	-1,169,550	12,941,215	3,467,742	3,186,448	40,435	484,616	319,410
2013	19,955,545	15,925,066	138,023	16,063,089	1,786,087	-1,180,546	13,096,456	3,568,718	3,290,371	40,782	489,324	325,232
2014	20,869,902	16,693,094	85,086	16,778,180	1,881,786	-1,257,857	13,638,537	3,688,966	3,542,399	42,231	494,189	333,239

Personal Income and Employment by Area: Lima, OH

(Thousands of dollars, except as noted.)

Year	Personal income, total	Earnings by place of work			Less: Contributions for government social insurance	Plus: Adjustment for residence	Equals: Net earnings by place of residence	Plus: Dividends, interest, and rent	Plus: Personal current transfer receipts	Per capita personal income (dollars)	Population (persons)	Total employment
		Nonfarm	Farm	Total								
1970	439,215	420,720	4,748	425,468	28,588	-51,216	345,664	58,459	35,092	3,954	111,084	56,153
1971	465,599	434,336	4,889	439,225	30,076	-47,578	361,571	61,681	42,347	4,178	111,437	54,945
1972	489,032	453,456	6,580	460,036	33,227	-48,003	378,806	64,859	45,367	4,420	110,643	54,610
1973	553,497	524,524	9,359	533,883	44,576	-59,326	429,981	71,324	52,192	5,021	110,245	57,847
1974	607,199	572,417	10,743	583,160	50,375	-67,385	465,400	80,138	61,661	5,488	110,637	58,786
1975	646,967	594,239	8,751	602,990	50,985	-71,366	480,639	86,671	79,657	5,839	110,806	56,340
1976	698,769	643,331	10,327	653,658	56,239	-76,648	520,771	93,131	84,867	6,361	109,853	56,613
1977	774,576	734,824	6,671	741,495	64,248	-96,065	581,182	104,743	88,651	7,012	110,465	58,352
1978	861,263	839,325	6,315	845,640	76,299	-117,213	652,128	115,353	93,782	7,842	109,828	60,165
1979	953,162	933,137	7,214	940,351	88,075	-137,532	714,744	129,459	108,959	8,568	111,247	61,611
1980	1,034,351	956,194	7,039	963,233	88,646	-145,786	728,801	161,379	144,171	9,220	112,188	58,688
1981	1,096,308	981,669	-194	981,475	97,348	-147,110	737,017	198,012	161,279	9,812	111,726	57,444
1982	1,144,674	1,007,903	-1,951	1,005,952	101,638	-155,809	748,505	216,225	179,944	10,423	109,826	55,345
1983	1,223,588	1,080,837	-5,489	1,075,348	110,331	-169,271	795,746	234,764	193,078	11,232	108,936	55,927
1984	1,384,885	1,238,026	14,176	1,252,202	129,461	-199,680	923,061	263,505	198,319	12,631	109,642	58,993
1985	1,466,460	1,342,175	12,473	1,354,648	142,609	-222,182	989,857	272,560	204,043	13,380	109,601	61,057
1986	1,548,329	1,450,232	10,201	1,460,433	158,698	-246,697	1,055,038	281,160	212,131	14,107	109,755	62,105
1987	1,584,915	1,495,111	10,926	1,506,037	164,129	-250,900	1,091,008	279,965	213,942	14,392	110,123	62,506
1988	1,665,526	1,564,917	12,609	1,577,526	176,828	-259,139	1,141,559	292,075	231,892	15,070	110,518	64,316
1989	1,749,133	1,598,809	22,643	1,621,452	182,532	-261,755	1,177,165	324,080	247,888	15,862	110,270	65,527
1990	1,813,963	1,637,408	26,710	1,664,118	190,920	-265,565	1,207,633	329,718	276,612	16,514	109,841	65,107
1991	1,847,669	1,677,999	16,968	1,694,967	199,574	-269,808	1,225,585	326,213	295,871	16,810	109,916	64,909
1992	1,977,725	1,752,271	18,530	1,770,801	207,497	-263,852	1,299,452	336,952	341,321	17,940	110,242	63,879
1993	1,992,300	1,793,252	12,010	1,805,262	213,804	-273,925	1,317,533	340,630	334,137	18,069	110,262	64,648
1994	2,109,381	1,886,555	14,207	1,900,762	227,168	-285,732	1,387,862	366,116	355,403	19,152	110,138	65,381
1995	2,160,864	1,880,991	4,325	1,885,316	227,671	-264,410	1,393,235	392,575	375,054	19,673	109,841	66,147
1996	2,219,317	1,899,312	6,756	1,906,068	226,168	-260,352	1,419,548	413,976	385,793	20,254	109,573	66,212
1997	2,291,551	1,936,739	20,069	1,956,808	224,798	-269,842	1,462,168	434,219	395,164	20,995	109,150	66,563
1998	2,436,093	2,061,684	7,448	2,069,132	230,512	-288,217	1,550,403	475,472	410,218	22,432	108,599	67,708
1999	2,559,655	2,255,332	875	2,256,207	249,284	-350,930	1,655,993	479,374	424,288	23,658	108,192	71,093
2000	2,686,542	2,382,052	13,401	2,395,453	252,301	-380,731	1,762,421	477,419	446,702	24,740	108,589	72,881
2001	2,782,507	2,470,094	12,328	2,482,422	264,274	-394,233	1,823,915	474,408	484,184	25,640	108,523	70,453
2002	2,839,462	2,519,481	-2,058	2,517,423	265,419	-385,593	1,866,411	466,715	506,336	26,166	108,518	69,791
2003	2,906,129	2,578,363	3,685	2,582,048	275,522	-375,377	1,931,149	444,211	530,769	27,054	107,418	69,338
2004	3,006,435	2,675,868	19,141	2,695,009	292,009	-360,618	2,042,382	408,906	555,147	28,143	106,826	69,670
2005	3,084,650	2,726,691	12,946	2,739,637	301,877	-344,405	2,093,355	398,943	592,352	28,866	106,861	69,850
2006	3,242,189	2,811,251	14,345	2,825,596	309,232	-325,292	2,191,072	418,210	632,907	30,381	106,716	68,954
2007	3,374,336	2,829,124	13,772	2,842,896	312,282	-298,195	2,232,419	466,318	675,599	31,619	106,717	67,950
2008	3,418,320	2,759,378	14,794	2,774,172	311,223	-264,542	2,198,407	474,139	745,774	32,015	106,773	66,209
2009	3,363,067	2,731,050	20,008	2,751,058	310,916	-339,250	2,100,892	437,589	824,586	31,573	106,518	63,821
2010	3,426,222	2,774,697	31,977	2,806,674	311,058	-365,630	2,129,986	426,296	869,940	32,212	106,364	63,111
2011	3,578,898	2,848,553	47,787	2,896,340	289,081	-393,092	2,214,167	469,068	895,663	33,793	105,907	63,630
2012	3,709,846	2,931,071	27,097	2,958,168	299,001	-384,068	2,275,099	547,502	887,245	35,237	105,283	63,945
2013	3,691,381	2,995,031	48,681	3,043,712	334,416	-420,553	2,288,743	496,204	906,434	35,085	105,214	64,185
2014	3,799,150	3,060,313	25,255	3,085,568	343,877	-386,804	2,354,887	513,659	930,604	36,169	105,040	63,862

Personal Income and Employment by Area: Lincoln, NE

(Thousands of dollars, except as noted.)

Year	Personal income, total	Earnings by place of work Nonfarm	Farm	Total	Less: Contributions for government social insurance	Plus: Adjustment for residence	Equals: Net earnings by place of residence	Plus: Dividends, interest, and rent	Plus: Personal current transfer receipts	Per capita personal income (dollars)	Population (persons)	Total employment
1970	760,334	609,182	15,182	624,364	40,790	-6,182	577,392	128,056	54,886	4,149	183,265	94,866
1971	833,411	665,494	18,341	683,835	45,895	-7,448	630,492	140,096	62,823	4,439	187,741	98,445
1972	916,668	734,460	19,078	753,538	52,849	-9,002	691,687	154,653	70,328	4,698	195,133	102,842
1973	1,032,723	825,288	30,980	856,268	69,063	-11,160	776,045	172,296	84,382	5,265	196,134	107,748
1974	1,146,335	926,894	21,704	948,598	81,359	-14,039	853,200	197,244	95,891	5,743	199,608	111,765
1975	1,302,929	1,019,889	45,582	1,065,471	87,628	-16,075	961,768	221,472	119,689	6,551	198,905	112,328
1976	1,417,933	1,152,559	19,752	1,172,311	100,169	-18,551	1,053,591	236,204	128,138	7,124	199,025	116,047
1977	1,549,271	1,265,606	14,912	1,280,518	110,723	-19,969	1,149,826	263,691	135,754	7,719	200,719	119,912
1978	1,762,868	1,417,504	55,099	1,472,603	128,277	-23,124	1,321,202	290,573	151,093	8,684	203,010	123,341
1979	1,923,881	1,572,386	26,032	1,598,418	147,910	-26,822	1,423,686	331,199	168,996	9,413	204,382	127,203
1980	2,084,872	1,691,375	-10,358	1,681,017	158,154	-29,332	1,493,531	391,991	199,350	9,957	209,378	127,424
1981	2,352,613	1,831,428	23,553	1,854,981	184,336	-33,925	1,636,720	483,346	232,547	11,112	211,713	125,565
1982	2,559,289	1,909,084	44,769	1,953,853	196,722	-35,357	1,721,774	581,931	255,584	12,025	212,839	123,845
1983	2,678,045	2,026,196	18,131	2,044,327	209,412	-38,520	1,796,395	604,511	277,139	12,502	214,209	124,320
1984	2,906,636	2,224,822	22,541	2,247,363	236,591	-43,968	1,966,804	653,519	286,313	13,442	216,231	128,322
1985	3,105,366	2,376,038	36,630	2,412,668	259,391	-46,445	2,106,832	686,706	311,828	14,268	217,648	132,780
1986	3,244,391	2,505,442	45,520	2,550,962	283,776	-51,530	2,215,656	704,967	323,768	14,819	218,934	134,997
1987	3,430,894	2,704,280	41,939	2,746,219	306,228	-57,611	2,382,380	714,827	333,687	15,566	220,410	140,194
1988	3,703,485	2,901,538	61,759	2,963,297	343,757	-62,917	2,556,623	792,479	354,383	16,599	223,119	146,113
1989	3,966,301	3,123,735	59,010	3,182,745	368,858	-69,456	2,744,431	836,257	385,613	17,517	226,420	149,477
1990	4,278,028	3,381,689	63,057	3,444,746	412,494	-77,477	2,954,775	902,508	420,745	18,588	230,144	155,589
1991	4,491,170	3,549,183	45,534	3,594,717	434,958	-83,083	3,076,676	958,130	456,364	19,241	233,419	156,858
1992	4,819,639	3,805,201	59,416	3,864,617	456,950	-92,434	3,315,233	1,005,809	498,597	20,265	237,827	158,269
1993	5,059,420	4,033,330	31,059	4,064,389	484,031	-102,433	3,477,925	1,041,988	539,507	20,840	242,779	162,253
1994	5,450,789	4,318,447	58,159	4,376,606	520,714	-112,516	3,743,376	1,147,472	559,941	22,164	245,933	169,247
1995	5,852,162	4,618,254	17,899	4,636,153	546,448	-119,339	3,970,366	1,279,880	601,916	23,362	250,498	172,577
1996	6,253,859	4,857,489	94,383	4,951,872	577,491	-128,746	4,245,635	1,362,940	645,284	24,631	253,904	177,454
1997	6,535,639	5,128,948	53,369	5,182,317	615,521	-139,333	4,427,463	1,439,000	669,176	25,391	257,404	180,195
1998	7,100,697	5,599,482	54,298	5,653,780	663,376	-158,125	4,832,279	1,533,938	734,480	27,204	261,021	184,660
1999	7,480,951	5,953,058	47,648	6,000,706	697,899	-170,455	5,132,352	1,576,060	772,539	28,350	263,880	189,256
2000	8,141,539	6,472,784	43,776	6,516,560	741,124	-187,117	5,588,319	1,733,995	819,225	30,374	268,042	193,177
2001	8,401,231	6,837,928	45,303	6,883,231	774,251	-225,750	5,883,230	1,599,513	918,488	30,974	271,237	197,326
2002	8,739,319	7,140,372	14,504	7,154,876	808,254	-237,007	6,109,615	1,637,225	992,479	31,783	274,972	198,430
2003	9,182,208	7,402,392	61,008	7,463,400	836,473	-238,956	6,387,971	1,747,562	1,046,675	32,888	279,194	201,187
2004	9,576,230	7,790,412	90,402	7,880,814	873,252	-239,606	6,767,956	1,700,555	1,107,719	33,986	281,768	204,796
2005	9,913,206	8,094,174	55,675	8,149,849	918,689	-233,437	6,997,723	1,732,444	1,183,039	34,726	285,469	208,199
2006	10,460,159	8,429,031	30,129	8,459,160	972,634	-222,249	7,264,277	1,932,790	1,263,092	36,202	288,940	210,124
2007	10,992,086	8,687,495	67,847	8,755,342	1,000,553	-212,171	7,542,618	2,099,675	1,349,793	37,580	292,502	213,547
2008	11,495,855	8,848,986	101,992	8,950,978	1,018,036	-201,450	7,731,492	2,227,217	1,537,146	38,804	296,258	212,713
2009	11,293,455	8,826,463	91,706	8,918,169	1,017,287	-201,365	7,699,517	1,978,778	1,615,160	37,691	299,633	209,837
2010	11,505,461	8,894,978	94,674	8,989,652	1,043,781	-202,051	7,743,820	2,006,839	1,754,802	37,982	302,922	207,342
2011	12,286,583	9,171,216	186,831	9,358,047	953,173	-228,153	8,176,721	2,317,704	1,792,158	40,064	306,673	209,108
2012	13,099,357	9,775,475	103,523	9,878,998	981,651	-236,247	8,661,100	2,615,683	1,822,574	42,197	310,434	213,492
2013	13,317,647	9,991,801	216,357	10,208,158	1,142,714	-220,367	8,845,077	2,612,960	1,859,610	42,366	314,349	217,177
2014	13,841,972	10,458,628	154,565	10,613,193	1,201,629	-213,121	9,198,443	2,702,188	1,941,341	43,399	318,945	220,588

Personal Income and Employment by Area: Little Rock-North Little Rock-Conway, AR

(Thousands of dollars, except as noted.)

| Year | Personal income, total | Derivation of personal income | | | | | | | | Per capita personal income (dollars) | Population (persons) | Total employment |
| | | Earnings by place of work | | | Less: Contributions for government social insurance | Plus: Adjustment for residence | Equals: Net earnings by place of residence | Plus: Dividends, interest, and rent | Plus: Personal current transfer receipts | | | |
		Nonfarm	Farm	Total								
1970	1,451,569	1,198,834	28,284	1,227,118	85,462	-22,808	1,118,848	210,407	122,314	3,639	398,923	189,395
1971	1,638,928	1,355,557	29,033	1,384,590	99,363	-27,509	1,257,718	236,352	144,858	3,992	410,511	196,544
1972	1,856,646	1,547,042	36,863	1,583,905	119,038	-29,235	1,435,632	258,835	162,179	4,400	421,948	209,206
1973	2,126,742	1,755,798	68,368	1,824,166	155,333	-35,367	1,633,466	290,565	202,711	4,899	434,101	221,631
1974	2,413,965	1,968,952	72,021	2,040,973	180,073	-35,666	1,825,234	340,620	248,111	5,362	450,208	229,229
1975	2,688,037	2,149,769	53,257	2,203,026	192,768	-35,257	1,975,001	392,939	320,097	5,910	454,800	226,577
1976	2,983,373	2,430,114	40,363	2,470,477	221,591	-36,678	2,212,208	420,634	350,531	6,443	463,036	234,682
1977	3,290,717	2,708,478	41,072	2,749,550	249,469	-37,885	2,462,196	462,397	366,124	6,988	470,916	243,509
1978	3,755,808	3,072,560	70,406	3,142,966	290,242	-36,529	2,816,195	532,994	406,619	7,834	479,418	254,644
1979	4,176,941	3,412,388	49,201	3,461,589	334,368	-13,675	3,113,546	597,738	465,657	8,605	485,427	260,249
1980	4,645,221	3,725,516	28,470	3,753,986	364,058	-19,966	3,369,962	720,197	555,062	9,370	495,743	259,470
1981	5,107,081	4,010,376	38,154	4,048,530	423,958	-34,359	3,590,213	887,197	629,671	10,245	498,489	257,023
1982	5,468,931	4,250,591	21,921	4,272,512	457,671	-47,283	3,767,558	1,016,395	684,978	10,909	501,306	256,891
1983	5,915,597	4,629,018	18,750	4,647,768	504,405	-54,305	4,089,058	1,079,163	747,376	11,710	505,195	264,519
1984	6,463,229	5,067,837	35,275	5,103,112	567,820	-60,949	4,474,343	1,203,940	784,946	12,657	510,658	275,936
1985	7,004,147	5,495,999	35,424	5,531,423	623,358	-72,872	4,835,193	1,328,933	840,021	13,565	516,324	284,898
1986	7,452,225	5,857,730	26,615	5,884,345	669,379	-72,495	5,142,471	1,414,727	895,027	14,273	522,119	289,743
1987	7,748,133	6,153,785	45,518	6,199,303	700,160	-87,075	5,412,068	1,409,918	926,147	14,685	527,622	295,390
1988	8,205,596	6,499,244	75,779	6,575,023	770,340	-94,719	5,709,964	1,520,466	975,166	15,519	528,733	304,689
1989	8,872,025	6,907,693	63,311	6,971,004	818,999	-105,985	6,046,020	1,733,171	1,092,834	16,663	532,436	312,014
1990	9,420,411	7,423,808	50,965	7,474,773	917,205	-122,207	6,435,361	1,798,086	1,186,964	17,561	536,444	317,357
1991	9,979,252	7,940,372	49,661	7,990,033	980,041	-149,033	6,860,959	1,793,019	1,325,274	18,381	542,913	324,532
1992	10,839,565	8,666,214	64,548	8,730,762	1,060,473	-173,886	7,496,403	1,878,574	1,464,588	19,626	552,311	331,121
1993	11,374,767	9,108,839	57,578	9,166,417	1,111,557	-195,237	7,859,623	1,965,393	1,549,751	20,244	561,887	341,004
1994	11,976,712	9,619,952	63,673	9,683,625	1,191,716	-221,815	8,270,094	2,082,618	1,624,000	21,053	568,889	347,270
1995	12,748,959	10,217,841	59,899	10,277,740	1,260,005	-252,508	8,765,227	2,224,497	1,759,235	22,120	576,345	361,633
1996	13,579,689	10,790,930	83,088	10,874,018	1,319,935	-281,730	9,272,353	2,390,703	1,916,633	23,219	584,861	370,043
1997	14,216,804	11,378,315	73,912	11,452,227	1,388,627	-310,658	9,752,942	2,489,650	1,974,212	24,027	591,707	376,359
1998	15,195,790	12,251,962	60,985	12,312,947	1,476,266	-347,928	10,488,753	2,695,901	2,011,136	25,418	597,826	382,150
1999	15,830,908	12,892,590	66,956	12,959,546	1,543,186	-384,495	11,031,865	2,695,536	2,103,507	26,154	605,291	387,631
2000	16,767,658	13,622,758	71,601	13,694,359	1,612,609	-419,480	11,662,270	2,819,491	2,285,897	27,384	612,313	392,229
2001	17,513,115	14,220,582	76,119	14,296,701	1,666,180	-462,305	12,168,216	2,798,183	2,546,716	28,333	618,126	393,780
2002	18,118,325	14,695,072	50,882	14,745,954	1,710,165	-531,574	12,504,215	2,862,966	2,751,144	29,028	624,166	391,912
2003	18,929,004	15,352,756	105,011	15,457,767	1,780,520	-628,611	13,048,636	2,975,926	2,904,442	29,997	631,032	394,882
2004	19,926,029	16,242,062	109,099	16,351,161	1,860,225	-722,925	13,768,011	3,030,072	3,127,946	31,156	639,558	401,510
2005	21,176,951	17,016,750	57,258	17,074,008	1,946,002	-755,675	14,372,331	3,416,507	3,388,113	32,641	648,784	410,123
2006	22,845,235	18,117,249	66,524	18,183,773	2,093,961	-721,084	15,368,728	3,781,922	3,694,585	34,524	661,719	421,532
2007	24,607,738	19,336,472	76,523	19,412,995	2,222,691	-804,290	16,386,014	4,189,829	4,031,895	36,649	671,441	430,614
2008	25,531,770	19,308,407	64,621	19,373,028	2,286,437	-648,078	16,438,513	4,554,899	4,538,358	37,443	681,888	431,401
2009	25,539,669	19,536,103	52,731	19,588,834	2,322,087	-663,234	16,603,513	4,031,288	4,904,868	36,912	691,903	424,951
2010	25,912,415	19,558,648	29,599	19,588,247	2,328,224	-636,173	16,623,850	3,954,549	5,334,016	36,896	702,305	423,752
2011	27,437,051	20,353,668	30,194	20,383,862	2,181,795	-689,632	17,512,435	4,444,040	5,480,576	38,602	710,759	431,646
2012	29,152,433	21,189,023	52,009	21,241,032	2,225,983	-663,838	18,351,211	5,215,170	5,586,052	40,619	717,703	432,132
2013	28,886,709	21,349,901	140,429	21,490,330	2,540,346	-743,217	18,206,767	4,963,502	5,716,440	39,880	724,335	435,220
2014	29,840,060	21,927,454	88,598	22,016,052	2,625,985	-755,199	18,634,868	5,100,730	6,104,462	40,925	729,135	437,379

Personal Income and Employment by Area: Logan, UT-ID

(Thousands of dollars, except as noted.)

Year	Personal income, total	Derivation of personal income									Per capita personal income (dollars)	Population (persons)	Total employment
		Earnings by place of work			Less: Contributions for government social insurance	Plus: Adjustment for residence	Equals: Net earnings by place of residence	Plus: Dividends, interest, and rent	Plus: Personal current transfer receipts				
		Nonfarm	Farm	Total									
1970	141,399	86,706	14,685	101,391	5,819	10,331	105,903	22,819	12,677		2,839	49,811	19,220
1971	157,759	95,725	15,313	111,038	6,628	11,957	116,367	26,445	14,947		3,106	50,796	19,811
1972	179,052	108,874	18,233	127,107	7,903	13,299	132,503	29,733	16,816		3,385	52,893	20,828
1973	199,904	123,325	21,084	144,409	10,481	13,893	147,821	32,329	19,754		3,674	54,413	22,111
1974	225,159	138,831	23,551	162,382	12,370	15,869	165,881	36,963	22,315		4,036	55,792	23,183
1975	249,129	157,980	17,379	175,359	13,729	18,542	180,172	41,631	27,326		4,334	57,480	23,664
1976	285,768	187,226	17,899	205,125	16,419	21,011	209,717	45,695	30,356		4,846	58,974	25,332
1977	313,608	209,229	13,463	222,692	18,121	24,270	228,841	52,006	32,761		5,155	60,841	26,351
1978	357,933	241,397	14,333	255,730	21,308	28,307	262,729	59,293	35,911		5,734	62,424	27,771
1979	406,704	277,568	11,630	289,198	25,753	33,727	297,172	68,631	40,901		6,342	64,124	29,228
1980	460,350	306,820	12,162	318,982	29,480	39,110	328,612	83,269	48,469		6,898	66,734	30,090
1981	508,888	332,276	7,358	339,634	34,407	44,985	350,212	100,595	58,081		7,349	69,244	29,973
1982	547,981	340,940	11,617	352,557	35,436	49,546	366,667	117,135	64,179		7,666	71,482	29,880
1983	598,017	376,675	9,287	385,962	38,861	54,277	401,378	127,532	69,107		8,123	73,620	30,808
1984	655,440	414,396	12,819	427,215	43,782	59,929	443,362	138,508	73,570		8,766	74,772	31,754
1985	704,900	440,986	15,646	456,632	47,165	67,184	476,651	147,979	80,270		9,366	75,261	32,227
1986	764,578	486,695	21,073	507,768	52,725	71,245	526,288	155,164	83,126		10,107	75,651	33,320
1987	831,560	523,241	33,077	556,318	56,726	78,976	578,568	161,421	91,571		10,877	76,454	34,995
1988	881,164	568,334	34,688	603,022	65,303	83,498	621,217	165,660	94,287		11,349	77,643	36,896
1989	970,443	627,316	40,451	667,767	73,151	87,137	681,753	183,270	105,420		12,303	78,881	39,229
1990	1,035,739	685,564	45,831	731,395	81,411	89,126	739,110	181,747	114,882		12,992	79,719	40,769
1991	1,103,759	744,290	42,607	786,897	89,444	91,459	788,912	189,780	125,067		13,401	82,362	41,907
1992	1,199,890	815,125	50,395	865,520	96,617	96,857	865,760	193,885	140,245		14,067	85,299	42,939
1993	1,300,783	886,544	51,483	938,027	105,471	98,493	931,049	216,482	153,252		14,752	88,175	44,894
1994	1,385,883	973,484	44,482	1,017,966	116,911	99,635	1,000,690	229,092	156,101		15,196	91,202	48,049
1995	1,480,683	1,025,861	39,471	1,065,332	123,620	104,294	1,046,006	262,518	172,159		15,719	94,198	50,269
1996	1,592,351	1,095,837	47,950	1,143,787	128,601	108,700	1,123,886	288,685	179,780		16,449	96,807	52,531
1997	1,718,988	1,189,528	46,597	1,236,125	137,296	116,820	1,215,649	317,161	186,178		17,403	98,774	54,389
1998	1,846,745	1,267,242	65,911	1,333,153	145,366	125,199	1,312,986	338,390	195,369		18,300	100,916	55,942
1999	1,919,950	1,338,562	64,901	1,403,463	152,674	122,365	1,373,154	338,970	207,826		18,910	101,532	57,052
2000	2,003,678	1,391,748	43,216	1,434,964	157,569	131,373	1,408,768	368,234	226,676		19,413	103,211	58,432
2001	2,137,146	1,465,359	68,348	1,533,707	166,337	134,622	1,501,992	383,992	251,162		20,492	104,294	58,655
2002	2,201,669	1,560,386	34,997	1,595,383	176,340	135,207	1,554,250	376,931	270,488		20,542	107,180	59,625
2003	2,325,847	1,675,278	35,315	1,710,593	191,681	134,813	1,653,725	386,717	285,405		21,374	108,819	61,729
2004	2,544,956	1,826,150	60,071	1,886,221	209,880	139,140	1,815,481	421,592	307,883		22,966	110,813	63,944
2005	2,646,656	1,919,255	38,677	1,957,932	220,566	143,672	1,881,038	432,275	333,343		23,509	112,580	65,118
2006	2,814,566	2,068,479	23,223	2,091,702	234,064	146,394	2,004,032	448,673	361,861		24,837	113,321	67,017
2007	3,057,404	2,189,644	45,868	2,235,512	249,968	151,685	2,137,229	520,580	399,595		26,379	115,901	70,244
2008	3,317,509	2,313,335	50,394	2,363,729	264,344	148,831	2,248,216	597,061	472,232		27,786	119,394	72,701
2009	3,254,262	2,268,704	28,174	2,296,878	259,347	131,006	2,168,537	570,544	515,181		26,447	123,048	71,611
2010	3,397,912	2,372,490	47,737	2,420,227	270,512	115,892	2,265,607	556,134	576,171		26,951	126,076	73,667
2011	3,623,456	2,494,131	65,337	2,559,468	252,078	103,004	2,410,394	620,498	592,564		28,386	127,648	72,779
2012	3,765,966	2,536,120	64,731	2,600,851	254,183	99,029	2,445,697	737,037	583,232		29,246	128,769	73,422
2013	3,808,706	2,668,675	80,004	2,748,679	301,627	104,975	2,552,027	660,755	595,924		29,258	130,175	74,307
2014	3,990,765	2,789,117	94,545	2,883,662	318,582	110,763	2,675,843	688,274	626,648		30,379	131,364	76,303

Personal Income and Employment by Area: Longview, TX

(Thousands of dollars, except as noted.)

Year	Personal income, total	Earnings by place of work			Less: Contributions for government social insurance	Plus: Adjustment for residence	Equals: Net earnings by place of residence	Plus: Dividends, interest, and rent	Plus: Personal current transfer receipts	Per capita personal income (dollars)	Population (persons)	Total employment
		Nonfarm	Farm	Total								
1970	430,471	308,789	3,621	312,410	19,889	24,534	317,055	64,231	49,185	3,285	131,055	53,026
1971	471,396	340,531	2,366	342,897	22,565	25,076	345,408	70,010	55,978	3,528	133,616	54,346
1972	524,734	377,004	7,382	384,386	26,067	27,446	385,765	76,675	62,294	3,811	137,697	56,603
1973	594,167	426,823	12,755	439,578	34,476	28,952	434,054	86,399	73,714	4,239	140,153	59,291
1974	692,559	502,180	12,161	514,341	41,875	30,498	502,964	102,227	87,368	4,841	143,059	62,300
1975	790,943	569,740	3,785	573,525	46,219	35,610	562,916	120,387	107,640	5,379	147,050	64,378
1976	917,990	686,086	4,128	690,214	56,627	34,276	667,863	132,189	117,938	6,111	150,221	68,830
1977	1,020,063	763,848	2,988	766,836	63,446	40,071	743,461	149,647	126,955	6,565	155,386	71,742
1978	1,182,938	891,718	5,108	896,826	75,591	45,972	867,207	174,674	141,057	7,402	159,818	76,038
1979	1,355,100	1,036,909	4,321	1,041,230	92,299	44,043	992,974	202,313	159,813	8,178	165,709	79,930
1980	1,567,210	1,172,418	-372	1,172,046	105,502	51,618	1,118,162	262,833	186,215	9,181	170,696	82,526
1981	1,865,221	1,389,484	797	1,390,281	135,515	53,791	1,308,557	343,073	213,591	10,653	175,096	89,406
1982	2,071,448	1,481,248	12,637	1,493,885	148,512	52,561	1,397,934	423,708	249,806	11,251	184,111	91,268
1983	2,142,054	1,490,562	4,438	1,495,000	147,543	40,349	1,387,806	471,364	282,884	11,452	187,045	88,609
1984	2,293,958	1,585,494	5,936	1,591,430	160,976	53,356	1,483,810	516,435	293,713	12,307	186,400	90,541
1985	2,440,659	1,651,765	4,222	1,655,987	169,884	67,142	1,553,245	576,970	310,444	13,162	185,436	91,871
1986	2,460,005	1,644,167	4,911	1,649,078	167,096	58,669	1,540,651	577,224	342,130	13,376	183,911	88,573
1987	2,457,552	1,651,535	-138	1,651,397	165,730	61,613	1,547,280	553,348	356,924	13,522	181,744	91,065
1988	2,598,139	1,760,605	200	1,760,805	183,535	66,438	1,643,708	584,072	370,359	14,382	180,657	92,809
1989	2,755,937	1,805,995	13,548	1,819,543	190,397	68,109	1,697,255	659,353	399,329	15,370	179,308	91,708
1990	2,907,065	1,934,112	16,475	1,950,587	199,401	79,208	1,830,394	636,616	440,055	16,132	180,206	94,053
1991	3,030,848	2,024,719	18,908	2,043,627	214,380	77,538	1,906,785	642,001	482,062	16,603	182,550	95,739
1992	3,235,716	2,184,126	28,511	2,212,637	228,364	63,434	2,047,707	633,059	554,950	17,609	183,757	96,484
1993	3,309,641	2,219,931	25,190	2,245,121	232,013	83,845	2,096,953	621,042	591,646	17,892	184,979	98,115
1994	3,472,674	2,352,242	23,536	2,375,778	248,598	58,587	2,185,767	658,767	628,140	18,646	186,238	100,672
1995	3,674,025	2,453,697	11,758	2,465,455	261,970	68,354	2,271,839	720,039	682,147	19,476	188,646	102,590
1996	3,907,330	2,636,770	10,242	2,647,012	277,748	68,675	2,437,939	746,748	722,643	20,505	190,556	105,595
1997	4,159,079	2,871,694	20,789	2,892,483	298,682	42,886	2,636,687	766,061	756,331	21,646	192,139	109,323
1998	4,358,964	3,059,794	22,168	3,081,962	315,526	17,219	2,783,655	803,590	771,719	22,572	193,114	110,874
1999	4,470,795	3,153,270	34,084	3,187,354	321,560	13,824	2,879,618	804,903	786,274	23,023	194,184	111,133
2000	4,862,139	3,422,370	27,092	3,449,462	338,585	18,910	3,129,787	908,337	824,015	25,048	194,113	113,718
2001	5,065,595	3,708,892	40,258	3,749,150	372,459	-133,181	3,243,510	923,865	898,220	25,928	195,374	115,383
2002	5,116,961	3,728,861	44,805	3,773,666	375,433	-147,595	3,250,638	885,650	980,673	25,876	197,750	114,447
2003	5,363,737	3,903,888	43,837	3,947,725	397,158	-168,174	3,382,393	952,662	1,028,682	26,880	199,547	115,164
2004	5,504,234	4,112,673	42,964	4,155,637	417,142	-191,202	3,547,293	879,636	1,077,305	27,353	201,231	116,343
2005	5,943,748	4,478,738	32,973	4,511,711	456,535	-237,901	3,817,275	962,944	1,163,529	29,271	203,062	120,522
2006	6,477,703	4,979,346	16,041	4,995,387	491,930	-302,395	4,201,062	1,047,214	1,229,427	31,516	205,537	124,197
2007	6,994,328	5,273,110	18,042	5,291,152	533,266	-314,449	4,443,437	1,215,495	1,335,396	33,657	207,813	129,204
2008	8,208,974	6,123,085	-99	6,122,986	583,239	-338,800	5,200,947	1,523,813	1,484,214	39,080	210,058	132,342
2009	7,675,228	5,521,495	-3,814	5,517,681	565,839	-321,519	4,630,323	1,426,687	1,618,218	36,013	213,121	129,398
2010	7,888,466	5,956,734	13,250	5,969,984	611,982	-365,667	4,992,335	1,146,011	1,750,120	36,736	214,732	131,359
2011	8,864,716	6,355,684	4,501	6,360,185	570,477	-244,968	5,544,740	1,532,137	1,787,839	41,046	215,968	131,973
2012	9,076,368	6,777,912	21,683	6,799,595	606,692	-246,062	5,946,841	1,351,301	1,778,226	41,522	218,591	136,182
2013	9,094,780	6,959,185	32,387	6,991,572	708,307	-272,147	6,011,118	1,248,995	1,834,667	41,920	216,957	138,554
2014	9,500,484	7,308,357	48,595	7,356,952	737,839	-321,713	6,297,400	1,298,726	1,904,358	43,684	217,481	140,857

Personal Income and Employment by Area: Longview, WA

(Thousands of dollars, except as noted.)

					Derivation of personal income								
		Earnings by place of work			Less: Contributions for government social insurance	Plus: Adjustment for residence	Equals: Net earnings by place of residence	Plus: Dividends, interest, and rent	Plus: Personal current transfer receipts	Per capita personal income (dollars)	Population (persons)	Total employment
Year	Personal income, total	Nonfarm	Farm	Total								
1970	272,907	244,361	2,108	246,469	22,330	-12,183	211,956	33,598	27,353	3,967	68,799	29,467
1971	283,845	247,567	2,301	249,868	23,414	-11,702	214,752	36,343	32,750	4,065	69,830	28,695
1972	320,623	287,121	3,030	290,151	28,573	-14,473	247,105	39,272	34,246	4,640	69,102	30,465
1973	363,108	326,177	6,572	332,749	37,278	-17,087	278,384	45,064	39,660	5,102	71,174	32,414
1974	413,726	371,266	6,439	377,705	43,530	-21,106	313,069	53,432	47,225	5,746	72,006	33,292
1975	473,268	423,100	5,023	428,123	48,366	-25,002	354,755	60,456	58,057	6,357	74,445	34,143
1976	536,032	499,639	5,355	504,994	58,514	-39,489	406,991	65,741	63,300	7,211	74,340	35,416
1977	576,251	530,819	3,537	534,356	61,768	-39,367	433,221	73,692	69,338	7,718	74,659	35,411
1978	638,620	582,495	6,920	589,415	69,021	-43,009	477,385	85,025	76,210	8,455	75,532	35,985
1979	712,249	640,624	8,125	648,749	77,342	-47,537	523,870	99,082	89,297	9,118	78,118	36,487
1980	797,155	707,805	4,568	712,373	85,927	-58,844	567,602	118,567	110,986	10,014	79,601	37,129
1981	851,647	732,643	6,468	739,111	95,066	-56,325	587,720	142,174	121,753	10,691	79,657	36,029
1982	870,249	706,585	7,424	714,009	93,703	-49,039	571,267	157,819	141,163	11,015	79,006	34,093
1983	938,167	759,302	7,525	766,827	102,389	-53,286	611,152	175,063	151,952	11,889	78,908	34,630
1984	991,131	796,134	7,438	803,572	111,335	-50,001	642,236	189,038	159,857	12,524	79,138	35,602
1985	1,011,535	789,375	8,431	797,806	110,318	-43,759	643,729	198,339	169,467	12,865	78,627	35,058
1986	1,056,381	818,021	8,571	826,592	114,439	-40,582	671,571	207,729	177,081	13,608	77,632	35,534
1987	1,106,613	872,706	5,495	878,201	121,803	-43,134	713,264	208,659	184,690	14,110	78,428	37,670
1988	1,192,322	955,649	6,574	962,223	136,437	-43,386	782,400	220,594	189,328	14,992	79,531	39,451
1989	1,308,386	1,026,926	9,732	1,036,658	145,867	-43,842	846,949	256,126	205,311	16,157	80,982	40,985
1990	1,406,632	1,119,694	10,582	1,130,276	161,250	-44,711	924,315	256,488	225,829	17,055	82,478	42,731
1991	1,524,873	1,211,550	12,040	1,223,590	176,574	-56,395	990,621	276,050	258,202	18,109	84,207	43,637
1992	1,567,539	1,206,141	13,060	1,219,201	172,426	-41,056	1,005,719	276,974	284,846	18,373	85,316	42,176
1993	1,632,784	1,253,143	13,214	1,266,357	181,553	-43,174	1,041,630	280,162	310,992	18,875	86,506	42,678
1994	1,717,438	1,330,503	11,345	1,341,848	192,804	-54,123	1,094,921	294,547	327,970	19,563	87,791	44,279
1995	1,787,345	1,373,944	10,264	1,384,208	198,975	-52,077	1,133,156	309,072	345,117	20,019	89,284	45,260
1996	1,860,482	1,413,770	8,959	1,422,729	197,846	-47,146	1,177,737	330,691	352,054	20,598	90,325	46,179
1997	1,933,883	1,440,565	7,117	1,447,682	192,887	-40,694	1,214,101	355,009	364,773	21,166	91,367	46,315
1998	2,037,750	1,509,322	7,488	1,516,810	200,337	-38,589	1,277,884	373,049	386,817	22,077	92,301	46,454
1999	2,133,192	1,592,522	7,662	1,600,184	205,271	-42,145	1,352,768	370,103	410,321	22,982	92,820	47,738
2000	2,223,287	1,648,076	4,851	1,652,927	218,033	-37,905	1,396,989	392,367	433,931	23,910	92,984	48,313
2001	2,379,221	1,755,124	4,953	1,760,077	229,631	-45,490	1,484,956	400,428	493,837	25,417	93,608	46,972
2002	2,410,477	1,762,103	3,632	1,765,735	226,118	-21,573	1,518,044	368,976	523,457	25,555	94,325	45,503
2003	2,460,129	1,770,933	7,454	1,778,387	229,902	2,256	1,550,741	366,188	543,200	26,029	94,516	45,362
2004	2,557,732	1,836,663	7,303	1,843,966	241,686	26,433	1,628,713	370,534	558,485	26,771	95,541	45,646
2005	2,685,349	1,921,335	2,012	1,923,347	258,168	53,028	1,718,207	374,529	592,613	27,817	96,536	46,660
2006	2,847,805	2,003,743	53	2,003,796	267,482	82,127	1,818,441	381,537	647,827	28,719	99,162	47,366
2007	3,136,494	2,123,186	-1,058	2,122,128	280,428	118,225	1,959,925	472,606	703,963	31,133	100,744	48,419
2008	3,346,976	2,135,634	-1,698	2,133,936	278,709	150,700	2,005,927	532,626	808,423	32,914	101,688	47,410
2009	3,357,480	2,025,593	544	2,026,137	272,722	166,364	1,919,779	516,555	921,146	32,876	102,126	45,062
2010	3,404,152	2,111,566	2,860	2,114,426	288,796	89,325	1,914,955	494,164	995,033	33,246	102,392	44,497
2011	3,521,115	2,129,582	6,208	2,135,790	267,191	122,778	1,991,377	549,982	979,756	34,410	102,329	44,348
2012	3,649,759	2,245,788	5,138	2,250,926	274,375	107,420	2,083,971	570,334	995,454	35,860	101,777	44,185
2013	3,699,379	2,321,346	4,990	2,326,336	316,826	89,909	2,099,419	585,477	1,014,483	36,365	101,729	44,768
2014	3,894,794	2,460,286	4,455	2,464,741	331,994	55,896	2,188,643	614,679	1,091,472	38,135	102,133	46,596

Personal Income and Employment by Area: Los Angeles-Long Beach-Anaheim, CA

(Thousands of dollars, except as noted.)

Year	Personal income, total	Earnings by place of work			Less: Contributions for government social insurance	Plus: Adjustment for residence	Equals: Net earnings by place of residence	Plus: Dividends, interest, and rent	Plus: Personal current transfer receipts	Per capita personal income (dollars)	Population (persons)	Total employment
		Nonfarm	Farm	Total								
1970	42,927,657	35,594,640	66,565	35,661,205	2,390,551	-786,757	32,483,897	6,501,858	3,941,902	5,065	8,475,377	3,938,904
1971	44,986,936	36,891,996	64,606	36,956,602	2,544,776	-976,991	33,434,835	6,960,181	4,591,920	5,238	8,587,868	3,890,306
1972	49,004,474	40,718,457	78,966	40,797,423	2,968,436	-1,212,536	36,616,451	7,469,067	4,918,956	5,703	8,593,421	4,034,431
1973	53,150,745	44,634,041	94,016	44,728,057	3,752,102	-1,413,864	39,562,091	8,199,656	5,388,998	6,146	8,647,592	4,258,523
1974	58,712,518	48,748,619	111,613	48,860,232	4,209,086	-1,633,638	43,017,508	9,349,942	6,345,068	6,706	8,754,864	4,372,383
1975	64,504,096	52,578,113	102,827	52,680,940	4,416,099	-1,805,239	46,459,602	10,133,511	7,910,983	7,295	8,842,499	4,367,984
1976	71,398,764	58,976,371	124,366	59,100,737	5,063,085	-2,015,790	52,021,862	10,709,334	8,667,568	7,947	8,984,368	4,520,496
1977	79,276,288	66,588,178	139,889	66,728,067	5,814,293	-2,422,522	58,491,252	11,660,485	9,124,551	8,746	9,063,784	4,733,736
1978	90,403,435	76,826,462	133,347	76,959,809	6,887,204	-2,869,680	67,202,925	13,411,188	9,789,322	9,821	9,204,893	5,044,872
1979	102,102,863	87,566,429	187,217	87,753,646	8,227,958	-3,398,157	76,127,531	15,455,646	10,519,686	10,987	9,292,983	5,314,599
1980	115,146,067	97,197,322	267,554	97,464,876	8,973,877	-4,110,405	84,380,594	18,744,983	12,020,490	12,179	9,454,611	5,404,030
1981	129,816,151	107,711,954	228,530	107,940,484	10,780,386	-4,600,947	92,559,151	23,227,148	14,029,852	13,503	9,613,602	5,490,043
1982	137,869,112	113,073,951	253,341	113,327,292	11,558,891	-5,011,669	96,756,732	25,699,494	15,412,886	14,049	9,813,347	5,398,676
1983	148,188,066	121,607,737	310,139	121,917,876	12,615,426	-5,615,233	103,687,217	28,103,514	16,397,335	14,804	10,009,841	5,496,333
1984	164,101,988	135,431,554	318,906	135,750,460	14,556,908	-6,475,678	114,717,874	32,481,150	16,902,964	16,144	10,165,047	5,772,337
1985	177,173,660	147,342,784	316,614	147,659,398	16,004,290	-7,386,619	124,268,489	34,694,494	18,210,677	17,110	10,354,836	5,967,933
1986	189,833,438	159,714,079	301,198	160,015,277	17,476,291	-8,329,983	134,209,003	36,187,583	19,436,852	17,871	10,622,535	6,154,066
1987	205,188,893	176,283,150	299,373	176,582,523	19,214,108	-9,579,643	147,788,772	37,291,919	20,108,202	18,937	10,835,330	6,389,935
1988	220,727,713	191,251,019	325,423	191,576,442	21,395,491	-10,683,942	159,497,009	40,072,197	21,158,507	20,065	11,000,781	6,660,585
1989	234,364,942	201,158,356	345,310	201,503,666	22,650,224	-11,823,512	167,029,930	44,427,419	22,907,593	20,967	11,177,630	6,773,734
1990	251,700,060	214,365,987	377,725	214,743,712	23,917,328	-13,679,533	177,146,851	49,389,402	25,163,807	22,280	11,297,143	6,881,721
1991	255,603,270	216,259,159	310,597	216,569,756	24,222,184	-13,209,555	179,138,017	48,635,891	27,829,362	22,420	11,400,816	6,700,497
1992	267,768,303	224,102,898	277,269	224,380,167	24,728,026	-12,928,454	186,723,687	48,700,006	32,344,610	23,179	11,552,438	6,471,123
1993	270,368,400	224,944,366	282,541	225,226,907	24,778,313	-13,034,778	187,413,816	48,807,009	34,147,575	23,242	11,632,798	6,397,429
1994	277,321,956	229,282,488	274,942	229,557,430	25,424,207	-12,836,566	191,296,657	50,675,745	35,349,554	23,778	11,663,207	6,402,534
1995	289,419,017	236,244,841	319,223	236,564,064	25,869,091	-12,883,166	197,811,807	54,774,157	36,833,053	24,752	11,692,693	6,550,063
1996	306,167,971	248,085,477	323,988	248,409,465	26,466,435	-12,780,381	209,162,649	58,350,463	38,654,859	26,010	11,771,038	6,656,417
1997	323,352,231	263,466,740	364,919	263,831,659	27,809,295	-13,922,628	222,099,736	62,485,560	38,766,935	27,136	11,915,815	6,736,278
1998	352,178,848	287,134,236	413,740	287,547,976	29,774,338	-14,145,799	243,627,839	67,543,837	41,007,172	29,138	12,086,776	7,027,231
1999	369,933,610	305,125,188	444,681	305,569,869	31,513,552	-14,231,270	259,825,047	66,906,821	43,201,742	30,191	12,253,223	7,135,043
2000	395,896,075	326,163,778	465,406	326,629,184	33,555,712	-14,941,070	278,132,402	72,825,535	44,938,138	31,946	12,392,704	7,236,774
2001	419,543,977	345,355,186	393,147	345,748,333	35,734,075	-15,615,907	294,398,351	74,992,966	50,152,660	33,533	12,511,491	7,286,003
2002	430,494,601	355,275,539	409,587	355,685,126	37,265,752	-16,322,618	302,096,756	74,672,309	53,725,536	34,128	12,614,158	7,279,707
2003	448,803,239	368,957,558	459,551	369,417,109	39,297,384	-16,924,599	313,195,126	78,922,431	56,685,682	35,349	12,696,521	7,326,998
2004	472,307,944	390,882,966	420,018	391,302,984	42,855,139	-17,792,209	330,655,636	82,298,401	59,353,907	37,087	12,734,974	7,426,691
2005	500,331,127	404,981,253	420,332	405,401,585	44,570,694	-18,458,366	342,372,525	95,986,313	61,972,289	39,314	12,726,428	7,542,949
2006	539,107,154	427,670,177	463,841	428,134,018	45,862,184	-19,388,427	362,883,407	110,273,629	65,950,118	42,549	12,670,216	7,687,080
2007	556,735,701	437,187,893	404,027	437,591,920	46,398,612	-20,160,301	371,033,007	116,602,060	69,100,634	44,073	12,631,988	7,822,651
2008	573,639,303	442,821,107	327,508	443,148,615	47,269,863	-20,322,499	375,556,253	120,426,398	77,656,652	45,194	12,692,740	7,694,300
2009	548,440,931	418,650,638	301,658	418,952,296	45,401,334	-18,549,393	355,001,569	107,964,867	85,474,495	42,932	12,774,577	7,389,426
2010	562,935,039	424,367,774	236,615	424,604,389	45,463,798	-18,156,805	360,983,786	107,435,058	94,516,195	43,824	12,845,311	7,310,481
2011	596,210,411	442,906,519	187,554	443,094,073	42,527,504	-19,193,102	381,373,467	119,636,813	95,200,131	46,023	12,954,525	7,465,902
2012	640,902,580	470,284,224	207,661	470,491,885	43,886,620	-19,892,879	406,712,386	137,957,283	96,232,911	49,056	13,064,761	7,749,112
2013	644,229,231	482,836,305	204,830	483,041,135	51,236,388	-19,964,738	411,840,009	132,597,678	99,791,544	48,895	13,175,849	7,989,280
2014	673,073,539	505,040,757	178,898	505,219,655	53,897,723	-20,829,376	430,492,556	138,697,644	103,883,339	50,751	13,262,220	8,158,392

Personal Income and Employment by Area: Louisville/Jefferson County, KY-IN

(Thousands of dollars, except as noted.)

Year	Personal income, total	Derivation of personal income								Per capita personal income (dollars)	Population (persons)	Total employment
		Earnings by place of work			Less: Contributions for government social insurance	Plus: Adjustment for residence	Equals: Net earnings by place of residence	Plus: Dividends, interest, and rent	Plus: Personal current transfer receipts			
		Nonfarm	Farm	Total								
1970	3,813,969	3,215,353	41,471	3,256,824	223,314	-15,204	3,018,306	503,482	292,181	3,945	966,908	446,276
1971	4,091,087	3,413,097	43,840	3,456,937	244,722	-19,714	3,192,501	547,451	351,135	4,170	981,174	447,479
1972	4,497,958	3,786,724	48,027	3,834,751	287,478	-28,871	3,518,402	588,162	391,394	4,571	983,998	459,721
1973	5,018,335	4,249,464	60,149	4,309,613	371,632	-39,434	3,898,547	655,371	464,417	5,036	996,523	481,524
1974	5,501,290	4,572,007	68,263	4,640,270	413,747	-42,259	4,184,264	758,818	558,208	5,472	1,005,432	489,621
1975	5,877,710	4,723,887	54,950	4,778,837	417,596	-40,470	4,320,771	831,127	725,812	5,827	1,008,789	470,167
1976	6,454,534	5,236,265	60,122	5,296,387	471,191	-42,534	4,782,662	890,615	781,257	6,367	1,013,771	477,680
1977	7,179,345	5,896,192	63,950	5,960,142	529,935	-46,145	5,384,062	992,015	803,268	7,069	1,015,639	494,112
1978	7,997,026	6,645,841	50,516	6,696,357	611,688	-47,117	6,037,552	1,100,505	858,969	7,820	1,022,668	516,166
1979	8,813,691	7,276,099	50,623	7,326,722	693,242	-51,907	6,581,573	1,244,351	987,767	8,583	1,026,904	521,237
1980	9,659,391	7,667,431	48,608	7,716,039	729,738	-54,366	6,931,935	1,518,480	1,208,976	9,431	1,024,218	512,145
1981	10,700,017	8,259,751	76,117	8,335,868	846,518	-56,384	7,432,966	1,901,382	1,365,669	10,455	1,023,428	508,363
1982	11,321,929	8,388,181	89,059	8,477,240	875,073	-39,790	7,562,377	2,245,846	1,513,706	11,043	1,025,301	492,030
1983	11,977,858	8,936,797	33,528	8,970,325	938,500	-43,868	7,987,957	2,376,096	1,613,805	11,691	1,024,512	493,381
1984	13,154,608	9,821,201	118,551	9,939,752	1,055,205	-66,284	8,818,263	2,655,171	1,681,174	12,862	1,022,721	509,674
1985	13,865,427	10,351,287	112,848	10,464,135	1,128,342	-74,405	9,261,388	2,826,823	1,777,216	13,581	1,020,967	518,551
1986	14,537,229	10,859,667	103,562	10,963,229	1,220,063	-78,103	9,665,063	2,996,240	1,875,926	14,253	1,019,913	531,916
1987	15,342,096	11,585,897	117,671	11,703,568	1,295,341	-85,098	10,323,129	3,083,255	1,935,712	15,035	1,020,403	543,749
1988	16,770,725	12,747,362	119,520	12,866,882	1,441,140	-95,688	11,330,054	3,383,588	2,057,083	16,447	1,019,654	564,610
1989	18,079,625	13,553,947	196,800	13,750,747	1,537,587	-94,790	12,118,370	3,700,655	2,260,600	17,709	1,020,953	577,251
1990	19,171,999	14,320,875	172,686	14,493,561	1,677,159	-93,573	12,722,829	3,991,357	2,457,813	18,696	1,025,448	592,058
1991	19,963,183	14,866,028	156,551	15,022,579	1,766,063	-107,463	13,149,053	4,078,865	2,735,265	19,277	1,035,577	589,956
1992	21,520,258	16,160,184	113,191	16,273,375	1,907,350	-133,842	14,232,183	4,285,465	3,002,610	20,575	1,045,950	600,441
1993	22,504,938	17,059,782	98,241	17,158,023	2,032,338	-166,533	14,959,152	4,414,919	3,130,867	21,293	1,056,941	616,676
1994	23,699,777	18,068,787	87,372	18,156,159	2,192,089	-201,657	15,762,413	4,659,173	3,278,191	22,219	1,066,643	634,530
1995	25,031,935	18,983,970	45,519	19,029,489	2,305,461	-215,003	16,509,025	5,039,469	3,483,441	23,250	1,076,646	655,893
1996	26,415,491	19,845,675	74,027	19,919,702	2,389,302	-236,934	17,293,466	5,435,258	3,686,767	24,341	1,085,228	665,467
1997	27,850,336	20,989,498	58,311	21,047,809	2,516,578	-257,546	18,273,685	5,699,494	3,877,157	25,457	1,094,013	681,426
1998	30,128,532	22,904,648	60,058	22,964,706	2,717,047	-312,042	19,935,617	6,224,462	3,968,453	27,318	1,102,866	695,622
1999	31,513,131	24,570,392	28,394	24,598,786	2,909,679	-376,296	21,312,811	6,134,592	4,065,728	28,293	1,113,813	709,794
2000	33,898,818	26,227,642	89,719	26,317,361	3,015,125	-431,565	22,870,671	6,666,370	4,361,777	30,157	1,124,086	724,386
2001	35,446,550	27,711,351	72,425	27,783,776	3,140,687	-478,328	24,164,761	6,531,049	4,750,740	31,308	1,132,204	716,229
2002	36,222,212	28,333,391	30,758	28,364,149	3,213,781	-580,619	24,569,749	6,557,300	5,095,163	31,766	1,140,281	707,095
2003	36,985,679	29,135,727	57,222	29,192,949	3,282,663	-650,526	25,259,760	6,453,217	5,272,702	32,113	1,151,726	704,680
2004	39,145,820	31,004,025	84,847	31,088,872	3,436,409	-667,628	26,984,835	6,538,127	5,622,858	33,691	1,161,921	714,510
2005	40,733,842	32,072,973	49,734	32,122,707	3,553,411	-697,667	27,871,629	6,857,756	6,004,457	34,738	1,172,611	725,648
2006	43,529,774	33,544,932	46,085	33,591,017	3,742,910	-767,128	29,080,979	8,006,185	6,442,610	36,666	1,187,190	740,628
2007	45,427,510	34,695,949	39,258	34,735,207	3,930,253	-637,507	30,167,447	8,344,805	6,915,258	37,771	1,202,720	754,368
2008	47,166,241	35,270,836	41,503	35,312,339	4,051,357	-454,700	30,806,282	8,499,030	7,860,929	38,761	1,216,853	751,054
2009	45,717,423	33,892,274	23,888	33,916,162	3,981,798	-394,025	29,540,339	7,469,722	8,707,362	37,230	1,227,965	728,216
2010	47,288,858	34,736,170	21,563	34,757,733	4,042,433	-185,447	30,529,853	7,453,503	9,305,502	38,205	1,237,778	720,528
2011	49,471,194	35,901,021	58,440	35,959,461	3,702,125	-15,975	32,241,361	7,791,584	9,438,249	39,738	1,244,938	731,715
2012	52,640,483	37,789,156	66,349	37,855,505	3,882,543	-255,959	33,717,003	9,405,154	9,518,326	42,049	1,251,870	745,765
2013	52,137,383	38,299,350	176,457	38,475,807	4,516,195	-295,178	33,664,434	8,802,788	9,670,161	41,305	1,262,244	760,480
2014	54,591,529	40,271,776	125,818	40,397,594	4,768,247	-534,348	35,094,999	9,114,833	10,381,697	42,996	1,269,702	777,074

Personal Income and Employment by Area: Lubbock, TX

(Thousands of dollars, except as noted.)

Year	Personal income, total	Derivation of personal income								Per capita personal income (dollars)	Population (persons)	Total employment
		Earnings by place of work			Less: Contributions for government social insurance	Plus: Adjustment for residence	Equals: Net earnings by place of residence	Plus: Dividends, interest, and rent	Plus: Personal current transfer receipts			
		Nonfarm	Farm	Total								
1970	723,786	534,920	72,755	607,675	32,937	-1,714	573,024	105,449	45,313	3,649	198,372	89,704
1971	740,495	574,172	36,994	611,166	36,625	-1,627	572,914	114,357	53,224	3,639	203,502	90,946
1972	831,983	647,544	42,473	690,017	43,026	-2,381	644,610	127,139	60,234	3,960	210,117	96,524
1973	1,011,976	728,455	128,140	856,595	56,164	-3,897	796,534	142,327	73,115	4,815	210,167	102,204
1974	1,056,621	837,410	39,322	876,732	66,753	-5,206	804,773	166,977	84,871	4,942	213,786	106,461
1975	1,154,712	921,838	16,898	938,736	72,294	-5,497	860,945	189,743	104,024	5,343	216,123	107,353
1976	1,342,249	1,051,794	64,733	1,116,527	84,120	-6,842	1,025,565	204,273	112,411	6,152	218,179	112,458
1977	1,520,087	1,185,337	91,656	1,276,993	95,619	-8,948	1,172,426	228,125	119,536	6,865	221,434	118,015
1978	1,675,577	1,338,669	61,042	1,399,711	110,060	-10,407	1,279,244	261,949	134,384	7,448	224,976	121,963
1979	1,888,412	1,500,156	76,650	1,576,806	129,659	-13,593	1,433,554	298,375	156,483	8,314	227,137	122,321
1980	2,073,542	1,664,314	23,238	1,687,552	145,428	-13,034	1,529,090	362,552	181,900	9,033	229,562	124,241
1981	2,403,027	1,795,398	128,361	1,923,759	168,020	-12,479	1,743,260	451,999	207,768	10,418	230,672	124,379
1982	2,550,256	1,920,375	53,595	1,973,970	181,998	-9,454	1,782,518	534,562	233,176	10,969	232,493	125,658
1983	2,807,254	2,102,573	79,715	2,182,288	197,026	-13,528	1,971,734	573,784	261,736	11,902	235,862	126,896
1984	2,929,848	2,171,606	66,769	2,238,375	205,249	-7,658	2,025,468	618,940	285,440	12,347	237,294	126,165
1985	3,100,039	2,296,775	59,799	2,356,574	219,087	-7,875	2,129,612	660,813	309,614	13,164	235,499	127,720
1986	3,149,378	2,349,605	34,368	2,383,973	222,947	-12,247	2,148,779	662,639	337,960	13,350	235,917	125,110
1987	3,283,737	2,345,508	142,163	2,487,671	222,187	-1,735	2,263,749	654,371	365,617	13,947	235,440	129,492
1988	3,473,688	2,521,612	145,844	2,667,456	247,889	-3,929	2,415,638	667,669	390,381	14,695	236,385	131,935
1989	3,609,645	2,628,603	79,322	2,707,925	262,524	-9,785	2,435,616	742,016	432,013	15,219	237,184	131,633
1990	3,880,412	2,828,995	131,118	2,960,113	277,251	-2,079	2,680,783	716,378	483,251	16,360	237,193	134,323
1991	3,955,904	2,961,423	47,069	3,008,492	296,459	-2,717	2,709,316	712,171	534,417	16,512	239,584	135,650
1992	4,246,411	3,110,679	115,664	3,226,343	308,704	-13,037	2,904,602	706,851	634,958	17,607	241,180	134,968
1993	4,511,943	3,295,124	169,934	3,465,058	326,178	-15,071	3,123,809	717,784	670,350	18,408	245,109	139,393
1994	4,750,000	3,497,208	134,153	3,631,361	349,420	-18,992	3,262,949	758,206	728,845	19,037	249,516	141,802
1995	4,952,035	3,622,619	91,851	3,714,470	364,714	-24,756	3,325,000	839,695	787,340	19,635	252,199	146,373
1996	5,256,413	3,799,207	139,585	3,938,792	378,063	-29,979	3,530,750	878,266	847,397	20,731	253,555	147,374
1997	5,456,389	3,991,364	128,863	4,120,227	393,843	-32,898	3,693,486	877,096	885,807	21,467	254,178	150,419
1998	5,710,654	4,331,193	74,900	4,406,093	416,915	-41,429	3,947,749	928,030	834,875	22,527	253,502	151,108
1999	5,869,752	4,486,899	90,275	4,577,174	423,321	-46,007	4,107,846	893,573	868,333	23,063	254,507	151,992
2000	6,243,658	4,822,035	41,838	4,863,873	448,424	-55,406	4,360,043	964,256	919,359	24,327	256,651	155,683
2001	6,264,136	4,739,298	56,871	4,796,169	458,423	-49,640	4,288,106	979,782	996,248	24,091	260,015	157,316
2002	6,536,679	4,991,494	54,896	5,046,390	480,963	-47,690	4,517,737	945,563	1,073,379	24,885	262,680	157,033
2003	6,945,273	5,151,633	119,655	5,271,288	503,741	-40,399	4,727,148	1,065,449	1,152,676	26,077	266,338	157,016
2004	7,188,257	5,379,756	189,335	5,569,091	524,186	-35,547	5,009,358	980,725	1,198,174	26,775	268,466	160,081
2005	7,624,985	5,578,079	208,791	5,786,870	548,251	-27,583	5,211,036	1,105,453	1,308,496	28,191	270,478	162,958
2006	8,026,285	6,007,583	74,148	6,081,731	578,551	-25,007	5,478,173	1,136,462	1,411,650	29,248	274,419	165,871
2007	8,551,715	6,124,655	176,166	6,300,821	597,252	-15,331	5,688,238	1,332,875	1,530,602	30,821	277,466	167,892
2008	9,135,499	6,462,133	86,530	6,548,663	625,992	-3,804	5,918,867	1,518,306	1,698,326	32,589	280,321	170,879
2009	9,147,189	6,489,589	106,814	6,596,403	643,879	-48,137	5,904,387	1,409,565	1,833,237	31,957	286,236	171,757
2010	9,622,215	6,725,387	177,286	6,902,673	665,480	-37,879	6,199,314	1,421,168	2,001,733	32,936	292,152	170,941
2011	10,073,563	6,926,750	80,074	7,006,824	604,949	7,331	6,409,206	1,583,399	2,080,958	34,105	295,366	174,742
2012	10,747,714	7,388,779	59,402	7,448,181	636,454	54,130	6,865,857	1,826,921	2,054,936	36,070	297,972	177,045
2013	11,034,893	7,694,898	239,230	7,934,128	753,326	65,904	7,246,706	1,673,004	2,115,183	36,568	301,760	181,781
2014	11,441,626	8,146,780	38,832	8,185,612	792,929	105,916	7,498,599	1,734,821	2,208,206	37,434	305,644	185,103

Personal Income and Employment by Area: Lynchburg, VA

(Thousands of dollars, except as noted.)

Year	Personal income, total	Earnings by place of work Nonfarm	Earnings by place of work Farm	Earnings by place of work Total	Less: Contributions for government social insurance	Plus: Adjustment for residence	Equals: Net earnings by place of residence	Plus: Dividends, interest, and rent	Plus: Personal current transfer receipts	Per capita personal income (dollars)	Population (persons)	Total employment
1970	548,352	473,066	9,319	482,385	31,116	-26,498	424,771	75,395	48,186	3,294	166,469	79,441
1971	588,447	505,436	8,535	513,971	34,589	-30,864	448,518	82,802	57,127	3,434	171,359	79,326
1972	658,682	576,507	9,656	586,163	41,585	-40,558	504,020	90,603	64,059	3,770	174,732	82,093
1973	737,353	645,415	13,386	658,801	53,726	-45,150	559,925	102,421	75,007	4,178	176,483	86,237
1974	823,516	715,824	13,987	729,811	61,975	-51,491	616,345	118,413	88,758	4,620	178,257	88,455
1975	896,797	747,411	7,790	755,201	62,991	-42,691	649,519	129,019	118,259	4,867	184,275	85,436
1976	1,005,349	848,592	6,035	854,627	72,634	-45,772	736,221	140,417	128,711	5,421	185,470	89,082
1977	1,122,209	947,684	3,417	951,101	81,181	-47,311	822,609	158,808	140,792	6,010	186,723	91,298
1978	1,277,364	1,085,678	4,841	1,090,519	95,045	-55,184	940,290	179,947	157,127	6,680	191,211	95,509
1979	1,444,578	1,225,909	5,991	1,231,900	111,791	-61,016	1,059,093	205,615	179,870	7,452	193,855	99,044
1980	1,607,019	1,311,673	1,023	1,312,696	119,808	-63,400	1,129,488	257,052	220,479	8,257	194,636	97,473
1981	1,779,059	1,402,890	3,913	1,406,803	138,455	-64,917	1,203,431	318,611	257,017	9,072	196,102	96,671
1982	1,897,212	1,441,043	-3,295	1,437,748	144,672	-54,198	1,238,878	370,614	287,720	9,623	197,158	95,302
1983	2,074,874	1,553,473	953	1,554,426	158,174	-45,627	1,350,625	410,551	313,698	10,526	197,122	95,745
1984	2,301,014	1,721,341	3,257	1,724,598	180,864	-38,753	1,504,981	466,263	329,770	11,606	198,260	99,984
1985	2,466,183	1,818,002	803	1,818,805	194,439	-22,141	1,602,225	502,395	361,563	12,388	199,074	102,302
1986	2,633,150	1,939,593	916	1,940,509	213,488	-9,385	1,717,636	524,347	391,167	13,141	200,383	103,804
1987	2,853,957	2,090,078	7,842	2,097,920	227,523	5,719	1,876,116	560,543	417,298	14,164	201,487	108,094
1988	3,072,829	2,222,935	8,971	2,231,906	248,829	20,067	2,003,144	622,202	447,483	15,125	203,166	109,641
1989	3,357,637	2,373,516	13,715	2,387,231	268,218	37,330	2,156,343	723,486	477,808	16,394	204,803	112,967
1990	3,506,124	2,501,632	14,603	2,516,235	284,303	57,574	2,289,506	705,771	510,847	16,945	206,913	115,259
1991	3,612,841	2,570,781	11,071	2,581,852	295,243	62,827	2,349,436	719,426	543,979	17,289	208,971	114,238
1992	3,839,737	2,706,691	12,641	2,719,332	306,734	77,177	2,489,775	741,744	608,218	18,036	212,888	114,404
1993	4,067,807	2,903,141	5,357	2,908,498	329,660	87,435	2,666,273	778,025	623,509	18,930	214,890	117,353
1994	4,270,500	3,053,218	9,034	3,062,252	346,479	99,061	2,814,834	800,567	655,099	19,614	217,728	120,192
1995	4,446,940	3,138,724	4,530	3,143,254	355,677	115,973	2,903,550	838,589	704,801	20,249	219,612	122,217
1996	4,641,923	3,242,115	3,755	3,245,870	365,272	128,436	3,009,034	892,187	740,702	20,922	221,872	123,775
1997	4,866,576	3,424,931	685	3,425,616	382,495	142,042	3,185,163	915,433	765,980	21,711	224,156	125,140
1998	5,179,637	3,626,608	3,750	3,630,358	400,576	164,876	3,394,658	982,104	802,875	22,952	225,675	125,582
1999	5,444,790	3,871,906	-1,829	3,870,077	426,793	178,396	3,621,680	968,757	854,353	23,950	227,337	128,941
2000	5,786,706	4,054,015	10,690	4,064,705	440,832	201,332	3,825,205	1,046,782	914,719	25,285	228,855	131,075
2001	5,976,130	4,118,510	2,515	4,121,025	463,809	190,296	3,847,512	1,103,141	1,025,477	26,040	229,499	129,293
2002	6,075,228	4,165,176	-575	4,164,601	468,604	187,110	3,883,107	1,104,675	1,087,446	26,373	230,356	128,331
2003	6,309,867	4,301,357	-8,787	4,292,570	483,196	204,548	4,013,922	1,130,832	1,165,113	27,124	232,634	127,954
2004	6,629,164	4,549,686	-3,008	4,546,678	517,598	200,723	4,229,803	1,176,345	1,223,016	28,260	234,574	129,933
2005	6,911,245	4,806,347	-3,880	4,802,467	555,830	167,080	4,413,717	1,188,715	1,308,813	28,976	238,515	134,168
2006	7,403,113	5,071,985	-22,291	5,049,694	594,464	173,904	4,629,134	1,317,762	1,456,217	30,439	243,213	137,155
2007	7,802,593	5,283,655	-25,344	5,258,311	620,338	191,469	4,829,442	1,423,301	1,549,850	31,612	246,827	140,196
2008	8,204,839	5,376,517	-19,605	5,356,912	637,734	231,207	4,950,385	1,476,803	1,777,651	32,912	249,299	140,294
2009	8,139,840	5,290,307	-15,030	5,275,277	630,269	224,488	4,869,496	1,348,745	1,921,599	32,373	251,441	136,604
2010	8,284,260	5,326,747	-14,067	5,312,680	644,958	219,243	4,886,965	1,309,601	2,087,694	32,741	253,024	134,488
2011	8,661,295	5,393,169	-4,331	5,388,838	589,314	234,932	5,034,456	1,426,025	2,200,814	34,088	254,086	134,545
2012	8,989,205	5,538,813	208	5,539,021	601,329	253,158	5,190,850	1,616,140	2,182,215	35,178	255,534	135,073
2013	9,039,966	5,640,913	940	5,641,853	694,804	250,216	5,197,265	1,582,773	2,259,928	35,213	256,724	135,396
2014	9,343,092	5,854,757	3,656	5,858,413	717,555	251,295	5,392,153	1,650,368	2,300,571	36,237	257,835	136,962

Personal Income and Employment by Area: Macon, GA

(Thousands of dollars, except as noted.)

Year	Personal income, total	Earnings by place of work			Less: Contributions for government social insurance	Plus: Adjustment for residence	Equals: Net earnings by place of residence	Plus: Dividends, interest, and rent	Plus: Personal current transfer receipts	Per capita personal income (dollars)	Population (persons)	Total employment
		Nonfarm	Farm	Total								
1970	663,245	455,174	5,480	460,654	29,751	92,351	523,254	82,378	57,613	3,660	181,228	78,317
1971	730,771	496,558	6,314	502,872	33,500	98,935	568,307	93,575	68,889	3,932	185,839	79,907
1972	793,334	547,412	6,403	553,815	38,739	98,260	613,336	101,677	78,321	4,210	188,436	81,664
1973	853,676	597,736	9,270	607,006	48,637	95,214	653,583	111,790	88,303	4,525	188,667	83,070
1974	942,924	665,223	6,565	671,788	56,266	92,993	708,515	126,913	107,496	4,981	189,318	85,187
1975	1,044,429	728,758	6,406	735,164	60,628	92,715	767,251	141,436	135,742	5,444	191,852	85,941
1976	1,133,400	805,314	7,557	812,871	68,332	90,238	834,777	150,641	147,982	5,895	192,268	87,195
1977	1,225,611	873,163	5,885	879,048	73,582	98,660	904,126	167,550	153,935	6,263	195,693	87,585
1978	1,335,133	961,993	7,626	969,619	83,090	95,629	982,158	187,094	165,881	6,760	197,518	88,125
1979	1,481,475	1,085,335	8,213	1,093,548	97,897	89,474	1,085,125	208,789	187,561	7,462	198,531	89,341
1980	1,651,814	1,213,766	3,215	1,216,981	109,783	73,663	1,180,861	250,195	220,758	8,309	198,810	91,031
1981	1,864,770	1,337,221	4,189	1,341,410	130,634	97,319	1,308,095	306,265	250,410	9,336	199,746	91,575
1982	2,000,981	1,415,663	6,712	1,422,375	140,826	100,793	1,382,342	348,107	270,532	9,961	200,885	91,762
1983	2,157,188	1,529,118	4,380	1,533,498	152,985	94,084	1,474,597	387,014	295,577	10,656	202,440	92,018
1984	2,365,485	1,700,444	7,142	1,707,586	175,195	89,532	1,621,923	430,357	313,205	11,625	203,490	95,941
1985	2,519,078	1,827,848	7,939	1,835,787	192,199	82,715	1,726,303	455,454	337,321	12,330	204,300	97,593
1986	2,684,056	1,983,004	8,443	1,991,447	210,655	58,650	1,839,442	486,345	358,269	13,133	204,377	99,644
1987	2,862,833	2,153,168	11,064	2,164,232	226,332	24,238	1,962,138	522,919	377,776	13,962	205,043	101,989
1988	3,091,444	2,332,646	15,057	2,347,703	253,820	10,098	2,103,981	571,797	415,666	15,000	206,097	105,223
1989	3,329,823	2,460,513	17,966	2,478,479	268,612	7,392	2,217,259	664,137	448,427	16,101	206,803	106,740
1990	3,464,316	2,599,287	19,002	2,618,289	282,424	-43,744	2,292,121	681,222	490,973	16,720	207,190	108,636
1991	3,631,014	2,689,917	20,952	2,710,869	296,445	-50,105	2,364,319	698,356	568,339	17,344	209,358	106,541
1992	3,868,286	2,881,002	20,696	2,901,698	313,038	-39,550	2,549,110	692,727	626,449	18,358	210,716	107,456
1993	4,034,121	2,992,017	23,445	3,015,462	326,646	-48,392	2,640,424	724,689	669,008	18,895	213,497	111,132
1994	4,275,511	3,166,868	24,655	3,191,523	347,432	-63,250	2,780,841	775,843	718,827	19,848	215,416	113,744
1995	4,576,681	3,381,445	19,344	3,400,789	370,204	-54,627	2,975,958	846,216	754,507	21,093	216,979	118,082
1996	4,902,566	3,549,789	16,840	3,566,629	389,880	21,820	3,198,569	903,066	800,931	22,417	218,702	121,131
1997	5,057,121	3,734,024	17,764	3,751,788	408,021	-41,295	3,302,472	930,534	824,115	22,897	220,860	122,871
1998	5,365,045	3,950,437	20,479	3,970,916	424,464	-15,108	3,531,344	1,005,129	828,572	24,196	221,736	124,025
1999	5,539,671	4,129,946	26,544	4,156,490	439,762	-5,705	3,711,023	964,726	863,922	24,949	222,038	125,507
2000	5,802,093	4,206,007	23,908	4,229,915	446,316	39,821	3,823,420	1,060,144	918,529	26,088	222,407	126,793
2001	6,038,843	4,349,893	30,298	4,380,191	457,243	49,783	3,972,731	1,086,012	980,100	27,096	222,869	124,898
2002	6,269,564	4,508,217	21,415	4,529,632	473,760	-16,560	4,039,312	1,103,036	1,127,216	27,907	224,661	124,791
2003	6,300,124	4,573,011	23,479	4,596,490	481,461	-26,348	4,088,681	1,077,036	1,134,407	27,878	225,987	126,087
2004	6,516,438	4,804,633	26,724	4,831,357	518,351	-80,750	4,232,256	1,089,483	1,194,699	28,657	227,394	129,221
2005	6,716,200	4,922,242	29,017	4,951,259	528,588	-112,206	4,310,465	1,106,916	1,298,819	29,441	228,125	130,711
2006	7,037,126	5,102,006	14,164	5,116,170	547,927	-112,426	4,455,817	1,198,126	1,383,183	30,642	229,655	131,449
2007	7,240,329	5,042,499	17,626	5,060,125	540,033	-81,605	4,438,487	1,316,130	1,485,712	31,418	230,452	132,248
2008	7,500,881	5,189,476	23,010	5,212,486	576,412	-136,961	4,499,113	1,339,958	1,661,810	32,427	231,314	134,067
2009	7,467,516	5,067,835	20,555	5,088,390	568,835	-73,339	4,446,216	1,238,518	1,782,782	32,179	232,065	129,176
2010	7,596,339	5,083,724	24,840	5,108,564	577,798	-67,205	4,463,561	1,196,348	1,936,430	32,700	232,307	128,436
2011	8,039,615	5,211,749	28,062	5,239,811	524,563	-92,158	4,623,090	1,417,105	1,999,420	34,527	232,851	130,643
2012	7,985,601	5,342,833	43,019	5,385,852	535,861	-158,180	4,691,811	1,320,139	1,973,651	34,297	232,840	131,642
2013	8,094,003	5,561,489	50,952	5,612,441	630,834	-239,815	4,741,792	1,351,093	2,001,118	34,989	231,332	132,742
2014	8,361,285	5,793,999	56,579	5,850,578	655,637	-312,225	4,882,716	1,406,364	2,072,205	36,282	230,450	135,917

Personal Income and Employment by Area: Madera-Chowchilla, CA

(Thousands of dollars, except as noted.)

Year	Personal income, total	Earnings by place of work			Less: Contributions for government social insurance	Plus: Adjustment for residence	Equals: Net earnings by place of residence	Plus: Dividends, interest, and rent	Plus: Personal current transfer receipts	Per capita personal income (dollars)	Population (persons)	Total employment
		Nonfarm	Farm	Total								
1970	157,432	78,082	31,793	109,875	5,668	4,196	108,403	23,515	25,514	3,775	41,707	16,486
1971	172,855	88,260	31,328	119,588	6,585	6,021	119,024	25,811	28,020	4,043	42,754	17,136
1972	203,290	101,910	42,466	144,376	7,902	8,579	145,053	29,471	28,766	4,703	43,223	18,531
1973	252,325	115,344	67,670	183,014	10,197	11,703	184,520	35,792	32,013	5,676	44,458	19,251
1974	288,209	130,473	76,193	206,666	11,941	14,871	209,596	40,688	37,925	6,256	46,071	20,413
1975	303,524	147,955	57,037	204,992	13,104	17,223	209,111	46,570	47,843	6,334	47,917	21,108
1976	350,803	170,316	69,799	240,115	15,289	21,289	246,115	50,370	54,318	7,059	49,699	22,320
1977	403,985	193,382	84,098	277,480	17,627	26,937	286,790	57,565	59,630	7,655	52,777	23,161
1978	443,986	225,418	68,117	293,535	20,769	35,230	307,996	70,809	65,181	7,965	55,741	24,123
1979	600,041	272,318	149,895	422,213	25,614	43,840	440,439	86,871	72,731	9,973	60,169	26,794
1980	679,045	297,963	158,035	455,998	27,402	52,113	480,709	110,473	87,863	10,617	63,961	27,854
1981	664,807	319,225	81,551	400,776	32,156	57,160	425,780	133,745	105,282	9,891	67,214	28,249
1982	684,433	324,510	77,066	401,576	33,558	59,547	427,565	143,611	113,257	9,885	69,240	28,791
1983	697,139	351,878	40,329	392,207	37,101	63,865	418,971	153,651	124,517	9,750	71,504	30,018
1984	777,912	394,675	59,288	453,963	43,037	70,401	481,327	167,178	129,407	10,657	72,996	29,837
1985	827,656	424,458	53,885	478,343	46,706	75,296	506,933	172,177	148,546	11,018	75,118	30,233
1986	919,604	471,553	78,828	550,381	52,657	78,946	576,670	180,600	162,334	11,949	76,960	30,149
1987	1,047,561	541,267	125,140	666,407	61,030	81,790	687,167	191,480	168,914	13,260	79,003	32,257
1988	1,132,165	586,714	120,682	707,396	68,729	90,034	728,701	210,376	193,088	13,847	81,762	33,655
1989	1,221,069	616,747	111,293	728,040	72,550	109,949	765,439	245,661	209,969	14,400	84,797	34,542
1990	1,328,247	681,177	111,716	792,893	79,043	122,543	836,393	259,954	231,900	14,903	89,125	35,423
1991	1,412,447	763,744	90,776	854,520	88,680	121,334	887,174	258,389	266,884	14,872	94,973	38,461
1992	1,596,637	828,901	164,280	993,181	95,962	122,245	1,019,464	263,154	314,019	16,041	99,536	38,949
1993	1,657,616	888,995	129,811	1,018,806	101,933	126,162	1,043,035	274,835	339,746	15,933	104,039	39,682
1994	1,692,503	943,787	94,313	1,038,100	107,496	126,526	1,057,130	290,245	345,128	15,759	107,396	41,256
1995	1,722,809	958,823	66,891	1,025,714	110,197	125,925	1,041,442	314,124	367,243	15,762	109,300	44,780
1996	1,880,309	1,002,649	136,248	1,138,897	111,214	124,066	1,151,749	333,757	394,803	16,619	113,143	46,793
1997	2,023,176	1,095,786	176,901	1,272,687	117,732	117,250	1,272,205	351,294	399,677	17,375	116,442	48,055
1998	2,121,892	1,249,913	92,249	1,342,162	129,639	110,018	1,322,541	373,156	426,195	17,810	119,143	52,160
1999	2,242,426	1,313,413	132,312	1,445,725	138,427	114,149	1,421,447	368,875	452,104	18,398	121,883	52,501
2000	2,345,725	1,354,339	152,537	1,506,876	144,086	130,445	1,493,235	387,580	464,910	18,980	123,587	51,585
2001	2,511,091	1,543,634	105,362	1,648,996	167,995	114,986	1,595,987	401,260	513,844	19,996	125,581	50,975
2002	2,702,417	1,665,552	149,689	1,815,241	183,985	114,468	1,745,724	405,738	550,955	21,052	128,369	52,401
2003	2,913,210	1,799,694	152,045	1,951,739	202,696	120,112	1,869,155	457,194	586,861	21,947	132,738	54,532
2004	3,260,174	1,944,616	354,488	2,299,104	226,155	125,035	2,197,984	453,626	608,564	23,778	137,106	56,825
2005	3,400,751	2,064,823	342,340	2,407,163	242,311	128,954	2,293,806	465,128	641,817	24,237	140,313	58,244
2006	3,602,477	2,260,552	254,354	2,514,906	253,825	137,457	2,398,538	506,872	697,067	25,083	143,622	60,020
2007	3,912,309	2,348,964	356,777	2,705,741	257,399	141,282	2,589,624	575,886	746,799	26,784	146,067	60,293
2008	3,945,625	2,343,192	287,598	2,630,790	257,919	139,751	2,512,622	589,929	843,074	26,595	148,359	59,306
2009	3,741,308	2,282,856	133,622	2,416,478	260,312	96,606	2,252,772	559,167	929,369	25,070	149,234	58,020
2010	4,100,878	2,264,098	379,125	2,643,223	253,844	118,331	2,507,710	570,553	1,022,615	27,130	151,154	57,226
2011	4,393,948	2,367,858	492,763	2,860,621	239,794	113,570	2,734,397	627,863	1,031,688	28,879	152,148	57,005
2012	4,686,820	2,517,120	676,277	3,193,397	252,992	44,530	2,984,935	653,323	1,048,562	30,785	152,244	59,356
2013	4,971,069	2,657,690	818,604	3,476,294	296,899	10,528	3,189,923	706,407	1,074,739	32,669	152,165	61,252
2014	5,106,586	2,785,275	770,259	3,555,534	310,632	7,186	3,252,088	739,501	1,114,997	33,042	154,548	63,296

Personal Income and Employment by Area: Madison, WI

(Thousands of dollars, except as noted.)

Year	Personal income, total	Earnings by place of work			Less: Contributions for government social insurance	Plus: Adjustment for residence	Equals: Net earnings by place of residence	Plus: Dividends, interest, and rent	Plus: Personal current transfer receipts	Per capita personal income (dollars)	Population (persons)	Total employment
		Nonfarm	Farm	Total								
1970	1,697,760	1,321,928	87,386	1,409,314	90,597	-19,154	1,299,563	277,846	120,351	4,496	377,631	191,581
1971	1,841,156	1,427,703	91,918	1,519,621	101,500	-19,907	1,398,214	303,873	139,069	4,812	382,627	194,234
1972	1,982,178	1,536,435	94,778	1,631,213	115,366	-18,426	1,497,421	329,792	154,965	5,180	382,656	200,459
1973	2,202,391	1,700,663	119,509	1,820,172	147,243	-16,643	1,656,286	364,727	181,378	5,707	385,942	208,252
1974	2,398,439	1,860,054	97,909	1,957,963	169,979	-16,995	1,770,989	414,214	213,236	6,108	392,653	212,493
1975	2,684,612	2,038,983	115,196	2,154,179	184,359	-17,331	1,952,489	464,141	267,982	6,855	391,644	216,816
1976	2,935,265	2,288,745	90,258	2,379,003	209,710	-14,065	2,155,228	498,270	281,767	7,400	396,665	227,364
1977	3,266,693	2,535,149	116,541	2,651,690	232,485	-9,224	2,409,981	556,316	300,396	8,137	401,437	235,127
1978	3,671,990	2,866,098	123,377	2,989,475	270,539	-5,435	2,713,501	629,346	329,143	9,039	406,224	243,149
1979	4,066,377	3,144,267	146,018	3,290,285	311,040	1,558	2,980,803	705,104	380,470	9,930	409,524	250,720
1980	4,530,879	3,425,610	147,235	3,572,845	341,201	-2,277	3,229,367	847,115	454,397	10,849	417,638	255,057
1981	4,931,023	3,654,186	135,612	3,789,798	391,202	-251	3,398,345	1,027,293	505,385	11,716	420,874	253,625
1982	5,308,234	3,901,787	109,991	4,011,778	417,110	-11,203	3,583,465	1,173,462	551,307	12,557	422,726	253,833
1983	5,647,632	4,172,735	31,920	4,204,655	438,106	-12,359	3,754,190	1,287,690	605,752	13,275	425,420	257,282
1984	6,188,146	4,562,457	92,057	4,654,514	482,639	-14,151	4,157,724	1,407,225	623,197	14,397	429,829	267,580
1985	6,647,948	4,943,050	104,018	5,047,068	525,882	-26,529	4,494,657	1,485,716	667,575	15,302	434,452	276,651
1986	7,113,200	5,317,685	144,315	5,462,000	565,268	-39,659	4,857,073	1,559,629	696,498	16,192	439,308	283,663
1987	7,635,959	5,806,904	168,547	5,975,451	607,559	-53,567	5,314,325	1,603,538	718,096	17,168	444,766	295,146
1988	7,996,680	6,256,815	76,938	6,333,753	688,813	-62,155	5,582,785	1,662,857	751,038	17,695	451,906	305,036
1989	8,900,157	6,812,372	178,065	6,990,437	753,182	-76,693	6,160,562	1,918,455	821,140	19,500	456,408	315,061
1990	9,549,047	7,430,565	140,059	7,570,624	855,605	-93,525	6,621,494	2,038,078	889,475	20,572	464,185	326,175
1991	10,052,209	7,928,786	105,479	8,034,265	923,286	-119,868	6,991,111	2,087,448	973,650	21,202	474,124	332,549
1992	10,996,872	8,669,408	140,284	8,809,692	996,870	-141,766	7,671,056	2,252,196	1,073,620	22,735	483,693	340,984
1993	11,645,945	9,294,155	94,381	9,388,536	1,061,193	-163,325	8,164,018	2,353,709	1,128,218	23,555	494,411	349,725
1994	12,394,363	9,912,245	121,567	10,033,812	1,149,868	-183,818	8,700,126	2,530,755	1,163,482	24,672	502,367	359,601
1995	13,139,062	10,426,737	76,177	10,502,914	1,211,728	-201,438	9,089,748	2,801,005	1,248,309	25,778	509,694	367,663
1996	13,864,671	10,880,479	133,845	11,014,324	1,263,849	-225,088	9,525,387	3,022,614	1,316,670	26,857	516,235	374,687
1997	14,764,577	11,701,181	87,598	11,788,779	1,351,136	-260,137	10,177,506	3,208,199	1,378,872	28,188	523,795	381,856
1998	15,867,262	12,557,244	128,166	12,685,410	1,442,036	-300,149	10,943,225	3,551,637	1,372,400	30,104	527,073	389,787
1999	16,604,241	13,407,379	142,407	13,549,786	1,549,427	-351,322	11,649,037	3,516,077	1,439,127	31,247	531,380	399,208
2000	17,976,071	14,566,248	100,200	14,666,448	1,664,897	-413,701	12,587,850	3,825,243	1,562,978	33,445	537,485	408,605
2001	18,875,354	15,510,883	138,054	15,648,937	1,740,595	-469,071	13,439,271	3,707,851	1,728,232	34,648	544,773	415,031
2002	19,736,364	16,476,298	118,611	16,594,909	1,839,309	-522,503	14,233,097	3,642,597	1,860,670	35,735	552,305	418,880
2003	20,572,359	17,222,817	161,593	17,384,410	1,913,825	-591,059	14,879,526	3,754,564	1,938,269	36,793	559,138	423,670
2004	21,751,974	18,285,159	220,210	18,505,369	2,024,082	-628,097	15,853,190	3,890,001	2,008,783	38,406	566,363	433,466
2005	22,719,737	19,054,217	192,626	19,246,843	2,112,552	-666,359	16,467,932	4,077,572	2,174,233	39,648	573,036	441,971
2006	24,325,411	19,967,424	166,395	20,133,819	2,224,376	-710,122	17,199,321	4,801,017	2,325,073	41,919	580,296	447,709
2007	25,537,760	20,663,168	234,706	20,897,874	2,312,345	-727,143	17,858,386	5,076,458	2,602,916	43,453	587,711	455,061
2008	26,267,546	21,165,618	147,836	21,313,454	2,378,937	-753,024	18,181,493	5,140,860	2,945,193	44,188	594,452	456,186
2009	25,987,567	21,155,407	83,119	21,238,526	2,347,832	-947,958	17,942,736	4,781,430	3,263,401	43,189	601,715	446,370
2010	26,391,063	21,245,949	153,855	21,399,804	2,404,335	-954,690	18,040,779	4,769,623	3,580,661	43,520	606,409	445,419
2011	28,253,761	22,439,474	309,754	22,749,228	2,269,453	-1,087,470	19,392,305	5,349,388	3,512,068	46,033	613,773	455,900
2012	29,711,805	23,548,907	232,693	23,781,600	2,361,765	-1,059,958	20,359,877	5,758,142	3,593,786	47,891	620,401	464,098
2013	30,760,219	24,570,692	387,943	24,958,635	2,814,053	-1,034,017	21,110,565	5,950,194	3,699,460	49,023	627,466	471,142
2014	31,669,729	25,403,287	342,302	25,745,589	2,905,430	-1,191,954	21,648,205	6,147,424	3,874,100	49,969	633,787	479,466

Personal Income and Employment by Area: Manchester-Nashua, NH

(Thousands of dollars, except as noted.)

| Year | Personal income, total | Derivation of personal income | | | | | | | | Per capita personal income (dollars) | Population (persons) | Total employment |
| | | Earnings by place of work | | | Less: Contributions for government social insurance | Plus: Adjustment for residence | Equals: Net earnings by place of residence | Plus: Dividends, interest, and rent | Plus: Personal current transfer receipts | | | |
		Nonfarm	Farm	Total								
1970	964,302	791,495	3,474	794,969	51,606	1,121	744,484	147,011	72,807	4,259	226,390	115,787
1971	1,030,877	830,216	3,064	833,280	56,139	5,661	782,802	159,973	88,102	4,341	237,461	114,427
1972	1,122,826	900,365	3,113	903,478	64,221	14,238	853,495	173,801	95,530	4,760	235,887	115,341
1973	1,259,751	1,016,901	4,381	1,021,282	83,627	20,997	958,652	188,865	112,234	5,258	239,589	122,872
1974	1,387,906	1,098,535	2,685	1,101,220	93,381	31,780	1,039,619	213,569	134,718	5,697	243,605	125,196
1975	1,514,390	1,159,617	3,301	1,162,918	96,173	39,039	1,105,784	234,204	174,402	6,101	248,215	121,735
1976	1,722,466	1,331,559	3,868	1,335,427	111,678	56,378	1,280,127	256,630	185,709	6,733	255,826	129,826
1977	1,969,874	1,516,133	4,452	1,520,585	127,409	89,766	1,482,942	292,204	194,728	7,492	262,922	137,799
1978	2,303,391	1,762,433	5,581	1,768,014	151,020	142,529	1,759,523	330,946	212,922	8,573	268,671	147,386
1979	2,642,732	2,029,572	4,870	2,034,442	181,677	174,103	2,026,868	374,244	241,620	9,603	275,208	155,080
1980	3,043,277	2,279,218	2,559	2,281,777	204,182	219,804	2,297,399	463,153	282,725	10,940	278,189	159,785
1981	3,437,168	2,531,067	3,425	2,534,492	243,930	242,190	2,532,752	574,770	329,646	12,110	283,833	162,816
1982	3,803,258	2,775,030	4,012	2,779,042	274,341	253,209	2,757,910	687,936	357,412	13,236	287,334	166,065
1983	4,217,296	3,162,046	3,488	3,165,534	317,734	262,284	3,110,084	726,173	381,039	14,501	290,819	174,012
1984	4,827,513	3,665,980	3,817	3,669,797	380,778	287,071	3,576,090	852,191	399,232	16,195	298,089	189,171
1985	5,336,216	4,093,216	5,022	4,098,238	435,028	310,548	3,973,758	943,770	418,688	17,354	307,490	199,943
1986	5,891,717	4,568,288	5,080	4,573,368	489,177	311,147	4,395,338	1,054,667	441,712	18,629	316,260	208,594
1987	6,468,540	5,124,567	9,013	5,133,580	541,236	296,909	4,889,253	1,129,103	450,184	19,951	324,218	214,561
1988	7,014,825	5,555,895	10,442	5,566,337	600,716	324,035	5,289,656	1,235,015	490,154	21,301	329,319	220,131
1989	7,395,450	5,700,648	6,849	5,707,497	617,692	354,780	5,444,585	1,395,580	555,285	22,072	335,057	215,952
1990	7,360,584	5,666,745	7,989	5,674,734	631,777	304,044	5,347,001	1,389,670	623,913	21,857	336,768	208,783
1991	7,633,214	5,689,276	8,088	5,697,364	642,207	342,124	5,397,281	1,397,552	838,381	22,646	337,066	199,944
1992	7,969,388	6,109,073	7,564	6,116,637	684,290	296,499	5,728,846	1,349,967	890,575	23,365	341,078	202,042
1993	8,218,306	6,225,695	6,256	6,231,951	696,541	411,799	5,947,209	1,407,384	863,713	23,825	344,944	204,282
1994	8,785,819	6,538,329	5,723	6,544,052	740,156	501,233	6,305,129	1,522,367	958,323	25,161	349,190	209,544
1995	9,379,951	6,905,490	5,160	6,910,650	785,396	559,148	6,684,402	1,661,304	1,034,245	26,523	353,651	212,713
1996	10,081,802	7,494,175	5,126	7,499,301	841,909	587,229	7,244,621	1,807,271	1,029,910	28,112	358,624	218,719
1997	10,951,579	8,135,288	4,700	8,139,988	903,787	680,992	7,917,193	1,964,344	1,070,042	30,065	364,261	225,406
1998	11,932,349	8,947,352	3,978	8,951,330	978,985	701,491	8,673,836	2,143,410	1,115,103	32,198	370,595	233,118
1999	12,763,910	9,635,747	6,428	9,642,175	1,049,943	875,663	9,467,895	2,155,111	1,140,904	33,910	376,407	238,108
2000	14,372,525	10,730,238	6,031	10,736,269	1,162,888	1,137,775	10,711,156	2,443,532	1,217,837	37,608	382,162	245,727
2001	14,756,077	10,962,374	5,176	10,967,550	1,184,712	1,171,001	10,953,839	2,474,164	1,328,074	38,089	387,414	244,885
2002	14,827,198	11,047,640	5,732	11,053,372	1,183,603	1,080,623	10,950,392	2,432,918	1,443,888	38,051	389,665	242,497
2003	15,340,045	11,593,584	5,908	11,599,492	1,253,693	1,050,090	11,395,889	2,467,980	1,476,176	39,187	391,461	246,181
2004	16,351,742	12,331,974	5,887	12,337,861	1,342,205	1,035,597	12,031,253	2,722,772	1,597,717	41,457	394,428	250,269
2005	16,777,778	12,873,764	3,304	12,877,068	1,396,466	1,003,167	12,483,769	2,630,262	1,663,747	42,327	396,381	255,141
2006	17,748,912	13,444,597	2,788	13,447,385	1,444,237	965,991	12,969,139	3,006,601	1,773,172	44,576	398,169	256,334
2007	18,666,536	13,954,614	692	13,955,306	1,520,209	936,164	13,371,261	3,369,163	1,926,112	46,802	398,843	260,147
2008	19,127,195	14,162,672	-194	14,162,478	1,563,659	865,734	13,464,553	3,419,190	2,243,452	47,871	399,556	259,587
2009	18,845,365	13,797,300	-2,204	13,795,096	1,537,030	823,763	13,081,829	3,327,965	2,435,571	47,096	400,148	252,583
2010	19,164,921	14,049,513	-2,575	14,046,938	1,566,150	1,111,406	13,592,194	2,962,156	2,610,571	47,795	400,982	248,313
2011	20,393,594	14,660,922	-3,824	14,657,098	1,462,314	1,007,787	14,202,571	3,619,434	2,571,589	50,766	401,716	251,139
2012	21,548,729	15,012,474	-536	15,011,938	1,493,085	1,107,304	14,626,157	4,309,459	2,613,113	53,524	402,600	251,977
2013	21,367,669	15,270,069	3,294	15,273,363	1,716,808	1,073,435	14,629,990	4,032,873	2,704,806	52,969	403,398	255,784
2014	22,438,346	16,222,006	-1,411	16,220,595	1,801,991	921,418	15,340,022	4,228,363	2,869,961	55,378	405,184	260,371

Personal Income and Employment by Area: Manhattan, KS

(Thousands of dollars, except as noted.)

Year	Personal income, total	Derivation of personal income								Per capita personal income (dollars)	Population (persons)	Total employment
		Earnings by place of work			Less: Contributions for government social insurance	Plus: Adjustment for residence	Equals: Net earnings by place of residence	Plus: Dividends, interest, and rent	Plus: Personal current transfer receipts			
		Nonfarm	Farm	Total								
1970	289,535	119,899	6,205	126,104	7,980	111,438	229,562	46,272	13,701	4,208	68,809	21,881
1971	317,813	138,883	5,617	144,500	9,592	116,208	251,116	51,103	15,594	4,532	70,127	23,477
1972	339,251	149,970	8,926	158,896	10,975	119,370	267,291	54,337	17,623	4,869	69,674	23,827
1973	367,336	159,945	12,980	172,925	13,580	126,038	285,383	61,174	20,779	5,048	72,765	24,363
1974	406,259	179,599	11,472	191,071	16,209	135,205	310,067	71,583	24,609	5,478	74,161	25,624
1975	445,618	204,769	10,758	215,527	18,551	140,118	337,094	78,436	30,088	5,950	74,899	26,460
1976	480,237	231,416	7,675	239,091	21,194	145,497	363,394	82,822	34,021	6,205	77,389	27,641
1977	524,347	262,206	3,182	265,388	23,924	152,048	393,512	93,373	37,462	6,949	75,461	29,291
1978	579,713	296,030	7,468	303,498	28,062	156,495	431,931	106,337	41,445	7,531	76,980	30,448
1979	629,093	316,115	5,094	321,209	31,057	174,117	464,269	119,053	45,771	8,138	77,305	30,601
1980	705,466	341,438	-3,482	337,956	33,768	206,931	511,119	139,296	55,051	8,970	78,646	30,601
1981	802,025	375,267	10,916	386,183	39,956	227,921	574,148	165,555	62,322	10,028	79,976	30,908
1982	865,074	397,352	9,603	406,955	42,754	242,103	606,304	191,687	67,083	10,716	80,726	31,468
1983	908,835	416,490	7,266	423,756	43,923	250,353	630,186	203,800	74,849	10,993	82,675	31,585
1984	965,838	454,290	8,182	462,472	48,262	251,827	666,037	221,700	78,101	11,807	81,804	32,746
1985	1,042,245	481,353	17,971	499,324	51,750	270,418	717,992	238,147	86,106	12,946	80,504	33,518
1986	1,079,823	506,312	13,479	519,791	54,185	277,794	743,400	251,241	85,182	13,464	80,200	33,800
1987	1,118,018	537,356	15,618	552,974	57,329	277,530	773,175	255,260	89,583	13,841	80,773	35,862
1988	1,163,436	572,547	14,442	586,989	64,382	283,260	805,867	263,686	93,883	14,246	81,667	37,095
1989	1,243,323	620,231	9,033	629,264	68,951	287,475	847,788	291,281	104,254	15,020	82,780	37,881
1990	1,251,663	648,648	13,690	662,338	75,230	271,534	858,642	281,455	111,566	15,018	83,343	38,985
1991	1,280,300	692,852	8,561	701,413	81,733	247,193	866,873	290,578	122,849	15,746	81,311	40,004
1992	1,456,741	764,962	17,072	782,034	89,294	305,637	998,377	322,082	136,282	17,184	84,774	40,430
1993	1,456,422	775,707	12,293	788,000	89,952	290,597	988,645	325,420	142,357	17,278	84,291	41,564
1994	1,547,047	834,236	15,603	849,839	98,486	304,567	1,055,920	347,146	143,981	18,098	85,482	42,235
1995	1,566,328	875,812	3,304	879,116	102,753	287,830	1,064,193	348,640	153,495	18,267	85,748	43,743
1996	1,569,777	922,889	17,937	940,826	107,216	224,315	1,057,925	353,338	158,514	18,944	82,862	44,143
1997	1,613,663	958,683	10,659	969,342	112,129	222,785	1,079,998	366,996	166,669	19,765	81,644	44,564
1998	1,682,168	1,001,137	6,640	1,007,777	115,707	227,268	1,119,338	394,695	168,135	20,746	81,084	45,013
1999	1,767,736	1,071,382	9,971	1,081,353	122,530	233,528	1,192,351	398,462	176,923	21,834	80,961	45,613
2000	1,903,668	1,174,687	8,240	1,182,927	134,342	233,385	1,281,970	427,620	194,078	23,347	81,539	46,851
2001	2,024,805	1,282,521	13,834	1,296,355	145,267	243,224	1,394,312	418,809	211,684	24,883	81,374	47,492
2002	2,089,986	1,328,443	3,664	1,332,107	150,349	258,890	1,440,648	424,844	224,494	25,737	81,205	47,424
2003	2,213,789	1,390,049	14,526	1,404,575	157,802	279,807	1,526,580	449,488	237,721	27,048	81,847	48,043
2004	2,313,589	1,452,585	22,211	1,474,796	165,494	308,235	1,617,537	450,293	245,759	27,737	83,411	47,705
2005	2,435,668	1,526,223	17,189	1,543,412	174,467	343,004	1,711,949	464,383	259,336	28,929	84,195	48,559
2006	2,653,834	1,638,492	5,977	1,644,469	187,050	387,017	1,844,436	532,465	276,933	30,628	86,648	49,739
2007	2,899,709	1,733,613	9,662	1,743,275	197,609	440,401	1,986,067	613,414	300,228	33,055	87,724	51,767
2008	3,209,823	1,871,206	13,625	1,884,831	211,554	503,085	2,176,362	678,995	354,466	35,535	90,328	53,324
2009	3,288,441	1,848,966	25,353	1,874,319	210,826	558,341	2,221,834	690,576	376,031	36,057	91,201	52,646
2010	3,532,100	1,892,724	19,409	1,912,133	218,589	724,097	2,417,641	700,900	413,559	37,840	93,344	52,056
2011	3,736,909	1,962,764	44,140	2,006,904	198,996	743,876	2,551,784	751,010	434,115	39,161	95,424	51,545
2012	3,799,261	2,048,050	37,198	2,085,248	208,246	690,038	2,567,040	801,085	431,136	38,513	98,648	52,559
2013	3,731,224	2,051,510	68,108	2,119,618	234,370	609,888	2,495,136	790,815	445,273	37,852	98,575	53,211
2014	3,795,291	2,133,173	40,096	2,173,269	245,163	586,619	2,514,725	814,547	466,019	38,692	98,091	53,548

Personal Income and Employment by Area: Mankato-North Mankato, MN

(Thousands of dollars, except as noted.)

Year	Personal income, total	Derivation of personal income									Per capita personal income (dollars)	Population (persons)	Total employment
		Earnings by place of work			Less: Contributions for government social insurance	Plus: Adjustment for residence	Equals: Net earnings by place of residence	Plus: Dividends, interest, and rent	Plus: Personal current transfer receipts				
		Nonfarm	Farm	Total									
1970	263,085	181,698	29,959	211,657	12,252	-980	198,425	43,085	21,575		3,415	77,037	32,324
1971	278,491	199,916	23,124	223,040	14,015	-2,169	206,856	46,824	24,811		3,570	78,012	32,665
1972	303,084	214,023	29,059	243,082	15,686	-2,045	225,351	50,203	27,530		3,911	77,494	34,258
1973	377,354	241,617	69,116	310,733	20,598	-3,171	286,964	58,209	32,181		4,910	76,854	36,352
1974	403,085	272,426	53,774	326,200	24,431	-4,725	297,044	67,784	38,257		5,202	77,488	37,064
1975	435,091	299,371	44,128	343,499	26,495	-6,526	310,478	77,748	46,865		5,627	77,328	37,194
1976	448,210	331,585	19,745	351,330	29,938	-8,088	313,304	82,905	52,001		5,760	77,818	37,739
1977	534,447	365,682	62,841	428,523	33,056	-9,775	385,692	93,282	55,473		6,845	78,073	39,224
1978	593,131	415,382	65,510	480,892	38,944	-12,161	429,787	103,093	60,251		7,613	77,906	40,917
1979	634,194	462,411	47,155	509,566	45,017	-14,617	449,932	116,192	68,070		8,082	78,471	42,687
1980	682,878	491,356	32,905	524,261	47,553	-16,391	460,317	140,694	81,867		8,603	79,381	42,871
1981	757,958	530,617	34,659	565,276	55,025	-16,583	493,668	171,886	92,404		9,504	79,753	43,218
1982	802,312	553,020	19,326	572,346	58,109	-16,551	497,686	201,663	102,963		10,034	79,958	43,012
1983	829,135	590,339	-6,280	584,059	62,631	-16,810	504,618	213,161	111,356		10,391	79,795	43,112
1984	948,292	637,492	42,219	679,711	69,110	-13,681	596,920	235,209	116,163		11,886	79,784	43,684
1985	986,488	657,882	47,123	705,005	72,838	-11,050	621,117	240,768	124,603		12,301	80,198	44,449
1986	1,028,757	690,747	45,184	735,931	78,541	-9,803	647,587	250,349	130,821		12,813	80,288	44,537
1987	1,130,682	748,940	80,606	829,546	84,844	-10,707	733,995	258,514	138,173		14,067	80,379	45,846
1988	1,143,122	810,169	42,856	853,025	95,149	-9,554	748,322	250,487	144,313		14,049	81,366	47,128
1989	1,272,905	866,116	73,909	940,025	101,571	-6,989	831,465	287,892	153,548		15,608	81,555	47,596
1990	1,341,523	932,847	59,515	992,362	109,679	-4,800	877,883	299,609	164,031		16,304	82,283	48,587
1991	1,373,983	990,956	29,459	1,020,415	118,050	-11,168	891,197	309,029	173,757		16,602	82,758	49,463
1992	1,489,240	1,096,732	44,590	1,141,322	128,820	-16,652	995,850	307,306	186,084		17,953	82,954	51,307
1993	1,525,770	1,160,466	-331	1,160,135	136,851	-22,642	1,000,642	329,941	195,187		18,320	83,283	52,620
1994	1,664,356	1,241,678	51,008	1,292,686	148,154	-26,647	1,117,885	341,826	204,645		19,881	83,717	54,719
1995	1,732,207	1,297,323	22,553	1,319,876	154,359	-29,182	1,136,335	378,528	217,344		20,489	84,545	55,982
1996	1,868,497	1,362,863	81,129	1,443,992	160,183	-31,367	1,252,442	391,820	224,235		22,005	84,912	56,419
1997	1,910,788	1,417,056	51,682	1,468,738	166,294	-34,664	1,267,780	415,013	227,995		22,507	84,897	56,660
1998	2,095,090	1,589,388	53,104	1,642,492	182,577	-47,229	1,412,686	450,809	231,595		24,715	84,771	60,091
1999	2,166,986	1,661,820	43,248	1,705,068	192,062	-52,763	1,460,243	462,821	243,922		25,462	85,105	61,228
2000	2,269,288	1,751,684	59,198	1,810,882	200,849	-58,802	1,551,231	455,684	262,373		26,420	85,892	61,906
2001	2,422,656	1,862,645	48,419	1,911,064	211,241	-63,976	1,635,847	487,013	299,796		27,813	87,105	61,937
2002	2,447,170	1,929,396	41,766	1,971,162	219,711	-83,497	1,667,954	455,264	323,952		27,775	88,107	62,729
2003	2,611,640	2,024,312	62,421	2,086,733	231,606	-96,464	1,758,663	507,656	345,321		29,234	89,336	62,894
2004	2,735,043	2,116,929	124,863	2,241,792	243,343	-107,805	1,890,644	483,543	360,856		30,338	90,152	63,921
2005	2,835,318	2,228,339	148,837	2,377,176	259,788	-121,420	1,995,968	461,514	377,836		31,119	91,111	65,637
2006	3,015,966	2,376,606	131,716	2,508,322	280,181	-137,683	2,090,458	504,290	421,218		32,472	92,879	67,298
2007	3,104,159	2,407,538	93,791	2,501,329	283,930	-134,606	2,082,793	561,716	459,650		33,036	93,963	68,138
2008	3,318,816	2,462,445	159,890	2,622,335	291,580	-142,603	2,188,152	603,739	526,925		34,890	95,121	67,585
2009	3,170,490	2,366,947	102,198	2,469,145	283,963	-143,013	2,042,169	543,317	585,004		32,988	96,111	66,082
2010	3,359,683	2,466,868	146,626	2,613,494	290,075	-155,431	2,167,988	548,398	643,297		34,704	96,809	65,651
2011	3,660,736	2,592,814	223,771	2,816,585	274,577	-174,112	2,367,896	654,308	638,532		37,632	97,276	66,974
2012	3,893,461	2,739,926	263,049	3,002,975	287,653	-190,745	2,524,577	729,075	639,809		39,755	97,936	67,104
2013	3,955,150	2,814,197	264,121	3,078,318	337,163	-175,687	2,565,468	731,192	658,490		40,475	97,718	68,345
2014	4,072,894	2,972,016	195,573	3,167,589	350,985	-194,593	2,622,011	760,332	690,551		41,358	98,478	69,017

Personal Income and Employment by Area: Mansfield, OH

(Thousands of dollars, except as noted.)

Year	Personal income, total	Derivation of personal income									Per capita personal income (dollars)	Population (persons)	Total employment
		Earnings by place of work			Less: Contributions for government social insurance	Plus: Adjustment for residence	Equals: Net earnings by place of residence	Plus: Dividends, interest, and rent	Plus: Personal current transfer receipts				
		Nonfarm	Farm	Total									
1970	516,155	470,892	2,941	473,833	31,347	-27,315	415,171	64,441	36,543		3,975	129,838	60,931
1971	567,491	519,504	1,989	521,493	36,010	-30,564	454,919	69,297	43,275		4,385	129,411	63,089
1972	605,822	555,712	3,572	559,284	40,680	-33,442	485,162	73,587	47,073		4,630	130,847	63,607
1973	669,543	619,441	4,793	624,234	53,147	-37,487	533,600	81,417	54,526		5,114	130,923	66,236
1974	706,631	631,079	5,918	636,997	56,036	-34,534	546,427	92,412	67,792		5,421	130,356	64,297
1975	746,313	638,382	7,033	645,415	55,070	-33,343	557,002	99,276	90,035		5,702	130,887	60,904
1976	822,126	718,277	8,277	726,554	63,706	-39,160	623,688	105,613	92,825		6,268	131,160	61,493
1977	923,677	825,296	6,640	831,936	74,107	-48,224	709,605	117,116	96,956		7,077	130,524	64,527
1978	1,001,612	894,890	4,947	899,837	82,483	-50,001	767,353	129,264	104,995		7,654	130,866	65,594
1979	1,096,542	971,471	4,548	976,019	92,464	-52,410	831,145	146,099	119,298		8,423	130,178	65,972
1980	1,189,228	1,011,247	153	1,011,400	95,333	-55,799	860,268	180,674	148,286		9,070	131,116	65,230
1981	1,324,794	1,114,758	327	1,115,085	112,650	-69,158	933,277	223,354	168,163		10,154	130,465	65,158
1982	1,344,614	1,066,706	3,203	1,069,909	107,859	-64,749	897,301	244,052	203,261		10,412	129,141	61,624
1983	1,481,540	1,209,513	-2,432	1,207,081	126,327	-83,098	997,656	269,365	214,519		11,569	128,066	63,435
1984	1,613,889	1,321,436	6,262	1,327,698	141,117	-89,546	1,097,035	298,977	217,877		12,561	128,485	66,715
1985	1,715,283	1,422,114	7,323	1,429,437	154,326	-101,767	1,173,344	308,792	233,147		13,382	128,181	67,043
1986	1,788,979	1,477,432	5,310	1,482,742	164,713	-104,391	1,213,638	321,938	253,403		14,040	127,418	68,043
1987	1,841,140	1,532,143	6,927	1,539,070	170,131	-106,013	1,262,926	320,888	257,326		14,458	127,345	69,183
1988	1,936,923	1,637,185	6,640	1,643,825	187,832	-113,213	1,342,780	327,321	266,822		15,231	127,167	70,397
1989	2,049,152	1,704,558	10,767	1,715,325	196,549	-118,161	1,400,615	361,150	287,387		16,187	126,590	71,654
1990	2,108,528	1,721,773	9,376	1,731,149	201,886	-114,151	1,415,112	370,988	322,428		16,713	126,160	70,803
1991	2,106,463	1,705,631	1,482	1,707,113	202,508	-103,260	1,401,345	356,849	348,269		16,581	127,040	68,169
1992	2,208,896	1,753,366	14,244	1,767,610	204,692	-95,702	1,467,216	363,233	378,447		17,328	127,475	68,884
1993	2,335,932	1,889,070	5,787	1,894,857	225,176	-102,045	1,567,636	373,558	394,738		18,279	127,792	71,627
1994	2,446,899	1,963,323	11,829	1,975,152	236,861	-88,848	1,649,443	384,785	412,671		19,075	128,281	72,358
1995	2,521,720	2,027,308	14,140	2,041,448	246,503	-93,498	1,701,447	386,601	433,672		19,668	128,217	74,128
1996	2,643,556	2,114,472	16,478	2,130,950	253,674	-99,979	1,777,297	411,299	454,960		20,510	128,894	74,963
1997	2,783,186	2,219,008	17,427	2,236,435	258,857	-102,851	1,874,727	440,343	468,116		21,597	128,868	75,038
1998	2,864,434	2,258,821	14,627	2,273,448	256,869	-94,019	1,922,560	461,647	480,227		22,284	128,540	72,761
1999	2,951,497	2,352,412	9,902	2,362,314	264,023	-96,770	2,001,521	448,143	501,833		22,839	129,233	73,276
2000	3,079,724	2,436,663	10,519	2,447,182	264,511	-95,348	2,087,323	468,169	524,232		23,901	128,853	73,901
2001	3,197,305	2,504,128	11,061	2,515,189	275,184	-95,261	2,144,744	467,708	584,853		24,943	128,187	72,629
2002	3,295,832	2,590,598	3,803	2,594,401	278,755	-98,175	2,217,471	456,002	622,359		25,676	128,363	71,876
2003	3,392,262	2,646,498	4,203	2,650,701	287,881	-99,334	2,263,486	466,907	661,869		26,438	128,312	71,020
2004	3,468,722	2,721,940	9,603	2,731,543	302,289	-99,264	2,329,990	446,785	691,947		27,080	128,094	70,677
2005	3,515,157	2,740,011	6,700	2,746,711	304,507	-97,599	2,344,605	446,487	724,065		27,522	127,724	70,446
2006	3,635,164	2,809,196	6,559	2,815,755	315,093	-96,483	2,404,179	461,412	769,573		28,558	127,292	70,356
2007	3,701,202	2,747,377	6,969	2,754,346	307,148	-91,308	2,355,890	525,557	819,755		29,144	126,995	69,310
2008	3,823,622	2,741,906	10,525	2,752,431	315,734	-88,397	2,348,300	563,339	911,983		30,315	126,128	68,023
2009	3,702,321	2,522,677	10,193	2,532,870	295,743	-57,037	2,180,090	519,158	1,003,073		29,546	125,308	63,939
2010	3,720,609	2,500,747	22,168	2,522,915	290,449	-49,207	2,183,259	497,868	1,039,482		29,963	124,175	62,702
2011	3,926,008	2,569,231	35,329	2,604,560	271,125	-45,360	2,288,075	568,989	1,068,944		31,901	123,070	63,818
2012	3,984,867	2,604,131	23,420	2,627,551	273,735	-6,038	2,347,778	575,982	1,061,107		32,506	122,588	62,738
2013	4,020,339	2,629,583	46,798	2,676,381	300,610	-13,585	2,362,186	584,730	1,073,423		32,875	122,292	62,584
2014	4,167,918	2,732,432	40,915	2,773,347	316,264	-14,081	2,443,002	606,719	1,118,197		34,180	121,942	63,423

Personal Income and Employment by Area: McAllen-Edinburg-Mission, TX

(Thousands of dollars, except as noted.)

Year	Personal income, total	Earnings by place of work			Less: Contributions for government social insurance	Plus: Adjustment for residence	Equals: Net earnings by place of residence	Plus: Dividends, interest, and rent	Plus: Personal current transfer receipts	Per capita personal income (dollars)	Population (persons)	Total employment
		Nonfarm	Farm	Total								
1970	361,760	261,656	22,601	284,257	15,860	-9,278	259,119	56,852	45,789	1,976	183,040	55,167
1971	425,729	297,861	37,595	335,456	18,581	-8,767	308,108	64,240	53,381	2,201	193,397	58,147
1972	476,627	347,654	25,965	373,619	22,664	-9,109	341,846	72,936	61,845	2,326	204,904	64,427
1973	567,118	406,992	26,895	433,887	31,119	-9,522	393,246	86,560	87,312	2,613	217,004	69,841
1974	666,751	476,756	30,438	507,194	37,482	-11,646	458,066	104,568	104,117	2,979	223,800	74,338
1975	784,422	556,615	34,284	590,899	42,731	-12,912	535,256	121,620	127,546	3,286	238,746	77,588
1976	893,823	660,225	22,947	683,172	51,002	-14,268	617,902	134,065	141,856	3,590	249,003	82,908
1977	1,040,005	736,851	70,547	807,398	57,494	-15,727	734,177	153,247	152,581	4,020	258,732	87,780
1978	1,174,844	833,909	64,062	897,971	66,294	-15,009	816,668	182,570	175,606	4,415	266,103	90,869
1979	1,316,343	937,510	39,547	977,057	78,510	-13,788	884,759	214,977	216,607	4,778	275,488	93,698
1980	1,539,247	1,080,883	28,323	1,109,206	92,606	-14,984	1,001,616	269,482	268,149	5,372	286,540	99,240
1981	1,836,401	1,236,761	86,461	1,323,222	116,678	-8,076	1,198,468	337,220	300,713	6,151	298,559	106,048
1982	2,002,327	1,337,820	67,723	1,405,543	128,049	-9,145	1,268,349	399,022	334,956	6,392	313,256	110,680
1983	2,128,606	1,388,693	48,611	1,437,304	129,299	-9,803	1,298,202	429,964	400,440	6,520	326,453	108,973
1984	2,324,211	1,503,781	52,377	1,556,158	142,003	-9,105	1,405,050	480,007	439,154	6,947	334,571	110,090
1985	2,549,610	1,650,137	44,532	1,694,669	156,625	-8,570	1,529,474	532,012	488,124	7,474	341,145	113,109
1986	2,648,092	1,715,614	30,958	1,746,572	160,769	-8,847	1,576,956	547,007	524,129	7,555	350,514	112,319
1987	2,758,170	1,783,259	53,465	1,836,724	166,031	-9,046	1,661,647	549,803	546,720	7,698	358,307	117,858
1988	3,036,386	2,003,338	65,415	2,068,753	193,316	-8,276	1,867,161	573,467	595,758	8,308	365,499	124,638
1989	3,333,497	2,155,703	46,903	2,202,606	214,558	-5,042	1,983,006	664,529	685,962	8,840	377,106	131,460
1990	3,651,169	2,346,428	60,723	2,407,151	229,548	-3,798	2,173,805	675,360	802,004	9,430	387,200	134,822
1991	4,029,788	2,567,671	81,093	2,648,764	256,871	-4,029	2,387,864	720,504	921,420	9,985	403,571	138,175
1992	4,474,757	2,793,788	83,404	2,877,192	276,612	-1,604	2,598,976	724,125	1,151,656	10,546	424,312	142,423
1993	4,846,469	3,061,784	113,222	3,175,006	304,283	-2,291	2,868,432	736,392	1,241,645	10,830	447,508	148,166
1994	5,269,018	3,343,682	100,392	3,444,074	337,830	-5,965	3,100,279	784,572	1,384,167	11,237	468,906	155,816
1995	5,601,220	3,503,458	83,306	3,586,764	355,902	-6,227	3,224,635	845,926	1,530,659	11,487	487,593	163,571
1996	6,035,541	3,781,234	60,367	3,841,601	378,066	-8,082	3,455,453	892,028	1,688,060	11,989	503,411	171,626
1997	6,531,412	4,198,311	60,429	4,258,740	413,114	-11,467	3,834,159	924,263	1,772,990	12,563	519,903	182,919
1998	7,049,213	4,596,308	111,076	4,707,384	443,570	-11,736	4,252,078	962,815	1,834,320	13,104	537,929	188,246
1999	7,403,876	4,921,561	122,059	5,043,620	472,318	-16,472	4,554,830	965,631	1,883,415	13,319	555,875	199,744
2000	8,120,718	5,495,499	111,149	5,606,648	512,574	-19,027	5,075,047	1,041,273	2,004,398	14,167	573,216	212,045
2001	8,982,766	6,141,239	126,783	6,268,022	556,457	-15,979	5,695,586	1,082,921	2,204,259	15,223	590,067	221,448
2002	9,579,016	6,494,993	110,783	6,605,776	596,605	-10,321	5,998,850	1,066,678	2,513,488	15,690	610,520	231,403
2003	10,258,281	6,944,023	153,020	7,097,043	653,922	-2,736	6,440,385	1,075,641	2,742,255	16,219	632,475	239,945
2004	11,024,928	7,541,405	140,874	7,682,279	710,408	7,733	6,979,604	1,155,107	2,890,217	16,863	653,779	254,381
2005	12,069,123	8,095,140	159,252	8,254,392	777,453	19,661	7,496,600	1,294,610	3,277,913	17,881	674,982	269,161
2006	13,024,520	8,880,215	105,888	8,986,103	844,155	35,213	8,177,161	1,312,855	3,534,504	18,731	695,352	281,225
2007	14,034,725	9,397,677	98,782	9,496,459	914,027	53,218	8,635,650	1,439,616	3,959,459	19,622	715,264	297,625
2008	15,353,037	9,968,681	58,841	10,027,522	958,781	71,350	9,140,091	1,711,029	4,501,917	20,840	736,694	307,270
2009	15,979,708	10,222,336	49,765	10,272,101	1,004,817	48,168	9,315,452	1,662,544	5,001,712	21,096	757,468	309,064
2010	16,886,696	10,714,321	95,850	10,810,171	1,051,477	38,881	9,797,575	1,631,143	5,457,978	21,672	779,194	312,839
2011	17,761,750	11,269,642	58,559	11,328,201	980,017	46,370	10,394,554	1,776,675	5,590,521	22,333	795,303	325,920
2012	18,301,724	11,699,096	88,034	11,787,130	1,012,164	56,415	10,831,381	1,992,299	5,478,044	22,658	807,725	330,937
2013	18,810,847	12,266,846	71,438	12,338,284	1,180,294	49,379	11,207,369	2,006,844	5,596,634	22,970	818,942	338,127
2014	19,740,566	12,906,216	85,006	12,991,222	1,239,449	59,938	11,811,711	2,074,839	5,854,016	23,753	831,073	345,300

Personal Income and Employment by Area: Medford, OR

(Thousands of dollars, except as noted.)

Year	Personal income, total	Earnings by place of work			Less: Contributions for government social insurance	Plus: Adjustment for residence	Equals: Net earnings by place of residence	Plus: Dividends, interest, and rent	Plus: Personal current transfer receipts	Per capita personal income (dollars)	Population (persons)	Total employment
		Nonfarm	Farm	Total								
1970	329,733	236,403	5,186	241,589	18,016	4,495	228,068	62,972	38,693	3,457	95,374	36,133
1971	377,829	271,994	8,211	280,205	21,443	4,934	263,696	69,958	44,175	3,798	99,487	39,058
1972	428,532	316,455	6,464	322,919	26,338	5,544	302,125	77,195	49,212	4,226	101,396	41,785
1973	489,140	359,354	9,492	368,846	34,228	5,736	340,354	88,656	60,130	4,561	107,245	44,421
1974	554,089	394,461	10,847	405,308	38,393	5,172	372,087	104,464	77,538	4,995	110,926	45,606
1975	625,921	433,403	9,193	442,596	40,680	5,691	407,607	118,779	99,535	5,446	114,924	46,756
1976	714,314	505,852	10,334	516,186	47,733	7,225	475,678	129,496	109,140	6,070	117,683	49,250
1977	815,390	587,914	8,841	596,755	56,268	8,191	548,678	146,916	119,796	6,666	122,329	52,964
1978	948,114	687,993	11,085	699,078	67,432	9,037	640,683	176,569	130,862	7,499	126,435	57,334
1979	1,067,439	764,086	16,388	780,474	77,611	9,135	711,998	207,675	147,766	8,216	129,918	58,937
1980	1,189,455	813,524	20,498	834,022	83,028	9,372	760,366	252,718	176,371	8,948	132,929	58,583
1981	1,275,011	826,822	12,612	839,434	90,124	11,269	760,579	310,775	203,657	9,476	134,546	57,391
1982	1,304,229	809,448	10,891	820,339	90,009	11,811	742,141	334,113	227,975	9,744	133,847	54,859
1983	1,415,649	891,691	5,080	896,771	100,092	12,210	808,889	366,397	240,363	10,634	133,130	57,463
1984	1,580,084	1,019,146	11,081	1,030,227	117,621	11,724	924,330	407,200	248,554	11,719	134,830	60,553
1985	1,668,706	1,076,657	12,473	1,089,130	125,208	12,442	976,364	426,095	266,247	12,230	136,444	61,517
1986	1,766,531	1,150,545	13,786	1,164,331	133,867	11,861	1,042,325	454,257	269,949	12,857	137,397	63,925
1987	1,885,844	1,264,991	6,955	1,271,946	146,275	11,684	1,137,355	465,162	283,327	13,506	139,626	67,656
1988	2,060,829	1,382,422	9,246	1,391,668	165,594	12,523	1,238,597	517,205	305,027	14,630	140,860	71,400
1989	2,270,607	1,476,311	13,546	1,489,857	176,766	14,303	1,327,394	603,700	339,513	15,818	143,549	72,786
1990	2,422,277	1,599,989	10,885	1,610,874	195,762	13,919	1,429,031	622,243	371,003	16,434	147,392	75,872
1991	2,559,416	1,656,943	16,701	1,673,644	205,921	13,457	1,481,180	658,864	419,372	16,955	150,956	76,214
1992	2,750,342	1,812,097	16,851	1,828,948	224,257	11,886	1,616,577	676,227	457,538	17,747	154,975	78,291
1993	2,968,485	1,961,923	19,986	1,981,909	240,025	11,506	1,753,390	725,263	489,832	18,663	159,054	80,714
1994	3,230,935	2,161,079	15,642	2,176,721	264,507	9,556	1,921,770	786,986	522,179	19,758	163,527	85,896
1995	3,437,712	2,231,476	14,502	2,245,978	276,437	9,879	1,979,420	877,265	581,027	20,539	167,378	88,260
1996	3,661,494	2,355,049	20,101	2,375,150	295,221	10,116	2,090,045	948,694	622,755	21,448	170,715	91,601
1997	3,829,665	2,477,500	19,388	2,496,888	309,399	9,895	2,197,384	992,304	639,977	22,070	173,523	95,490
1998	4,114,019	2,681,123	15,018	2,696,141	329,994	9,465	2,375,612	1,049,860	688,547	23,290	176,645	97,258
1999	4,409,894	2,946,608	14,364	2,960,972	353,114	8,982	2,616,840	1,040,013	753,041	24,600	179,264	99,916
2000	4,718,828	3,140,218	10,269	3,150,487	376,791	7,719	2,781,415	1,137,021	800,392	25,960	181,775	103,169
2001	5,067,572	3,381,238	12,986	3,394,224	392,617	14,546	3,016,153	1,147,118	904,301	27,566	183,835	104,473
2002	5,195,708	3,567,083	11,071	3,578,154	417,656	10,802	3,171,300	1,073,317	951,091	27,829	186,704	105,258
2003	5,562,734	3,785,188	16,723	3,801,911	445,748	7,139	3,363,302	1,191,116	1,008,316	29,303	189,838	108,511
2004	5,857,258	4,048,847	18,475	4,067,322	484,258	3,010	3,586,074	1,230,702	1,040,482	30,477	192,185	112,420
2005	6,158,175	4,241,143	17,894	4,259,037	517,865	-1,840	3,739,332	1,303,870	1,114,973	31,629	194,701	115,799
2006	6,714,721	4,502,085	17,085	4,519,170	547,496	-7,283	3,964,391	1,555,555	1,194,775	34,109	196,858	117,740
2007	6,922,850	4,571,743	17,932	4,589,675	567,366	-13,074	4,009,235	1,634,362	1,279,253	34,762	199,152	119,936
2008	6,981,633	4,421,090	14,258	4,435,348	556,382	-18,318	3,860,648	1,670,582	1,450,403	34,707	201,162	116,787
2009	6,783,171	4,209,686	21,748	4,231,434	533,886	-20,003	3,677,545	1,457,409	1,648,217	33,530	202,301	110,725
2010	6,819,499	4,171,002	17,896	4,188,898	542,196	-16,923	3,629,779	1,412,050	1,777,670	33,524	203,421	109,020
2011	7,117,888	4,191,562	20,883	4,212,445	491,636	-7,685	3,713,124	1,583,089	1,821,675	34,763	204,754	109,346
2012	7,382,454	4,378,682	29,356	4,408,038	512,487	-31,357	3,864,194	1,664,260	1,854,000	35,774	206,363	110,027
2013	7,481,426	4,535,000	28,146	4,563,146	601,730	-65,686	3,895,730	1,653,400	1,932,296	35,953	208,091	112,631
2014	7,914,576	4,731,103	39,821	4,770,924	634,298	-52,366	4,084,260	1,724,453	2,105,863	37,637	210,287	115,201

Personal Income and Employment by Area: Memphis, TN-MS-AR

(Thousands of dollars, except as noted.)

| Year | Personal income, total | Derivation of personal income | | | | | | | | | Per capita personal income (dollars) | Population (persons) | Total employment |
| | | Earnings by place of work | | | Less: Contributions for government social insurance | Plus: Adjustment for residence | Equals: Net earnings by place of residence | Plus: Dividends, interest, and rent | Plus: Personal current transfer receipts | | | |
		Nonfarm	Farm	Total								
1970	3,228,107	2,685,260	62,006	2,747,266	175,962	-19,079	2,552,225	418,386	257,496	3,508	920,140	414,524
1971	3,622,577	3,022,517	62,028	3,084,545	205,060	-26,545	2,852,940	463,029	306,608	3,896	929,937	429,167
1972	4,108,550	3,463,729	65,820	3,529,549	244,395	-34,155	3,250,999	514,223	343,328	4,350	944,488	455,373
1973	4,570,547	3,855,629	95,319	3,950,948	312,264	-40,997	3,597,687	570,018	402,842	4,820	948,225	472,452
1974	5,062,857	4,231,385	62,031	4,293,416	354,055	-44,455	3,894,906	667,659	500,292	5,271	960,477	479,924
1975	5,494,253	4,451,671	57,072	4,508,743	367,248	-46,938	4,094,557	733,286	666,410	5,702	963,646	463,926
1976	5,972,367	4,840,079	74,410	4,914,489	409,053	-45,609	4,459,827	765,208	747,332	6,161	969,411	466,956
1977	6,557,517	5,368,531	87,727	5,456,258	455,179	-47,670	4,953,409	828,053	776,055	6,724	975,249	481,178
1978	7,405,923	6,106,272	87,774	6,194,046	526,033	-47,367	5,620,646	938,392	846,885	7,530	983,532	500,999
1979	8,278,303	6,814,702	95,662	6,910,364	612,009	-56,580	6,241,775	1,060,522	976,006	8,308	996,459	513,957
1980	9,161,981	7,445,711	13,508	7,459,219	667,951	-66,245	6,725,023	1,273,103	1,163,855	9,110	1,005,686	514,719
1981	10,022,438	7,954,463	53,659	8,008,122	768,297	-75,606	7,164,219	1,549,521	1,308,698	10,001	1,002,176	503,394
1982	10,579,823	8,248,426	43,806	8,292,232	812,081	-99,949	7,380,202	1,798,353	1,401,268	10,524	1,005,293	491,268
1983	11,357,622	8,932,604	-600	8,932,004	889,537	-116,287	7,926,180	1,913,300	1,518,142	11,248	1,009,767	501,064
1984	12,589,396	9,926,103	55,925	9,982,028	1,019,561	-129,407	8,833,060	2,174,744	1,581,592	12,424	1,013,317	522,360
1985	13,483,957	10,697,032	56,140	10,753,172	1,115,344	-140,689	9,497,139	2,322,153	1,664,665	13,165	1,024,191	533,858
1986	14,341,002	11,480,065	18,234	11,498,299	1,222,958	-151,485	10,123,856	2,441,332	1,775,814	13,868	1,034,093	551,772
1987	15,504,133	12,497,484	79,696	12,577,180	1,324,233	-148,355	11,104,592	2,545,189	1,854,352	14,806	1,047,141	573,250
1988	16,796,098	13,503,188	103,910	13,607,098	1,475,295	-137,581	11,994,222	2,828,363	1,973,513	15,822	1,061,590	595,468
1989	18,274,092	14,520,590	65,713	14,586,303	1,597,355	-171,724	12,817,224	3,321,671	2,135,197	17,061	1,071,132	616,435
1990	19,344,580	15,488,787	68,692	15,557,479	1,725,551	-203,394	13,628,534	3,397,531	2,318,515	17,935	1,078,598	623,835
1991	20,166,211	16,187,792	73,987	16,261,779	1,829,268	-219,226	14,213,285	3,366,940	2,585,986	18,472	1,091,735	618,879
1992	21,797,654	17,558,361	102,131	17,660,492	1,954,509	-243,684	15,462,299	3,460,489	2,874,866	19,737	1,104,416	620,945
1993	23,187,981	18,745,183	73,792	18,818,975	2,081,817	-275,343	16,461,815	3,613,504	3,112,662	20,754	1,117,303	638,087
1994	24,959,061	20,315,562	116,421	20,431,983	2,283,523	-325,654	17,822,806	3,857,296	3,278,959	22,030	1,132,959	671,106
1995	26,823,100	21,752,269	75,325	21,827,594	2,433,561	-369,952	19,024,081	4,183,838	3,615,181	23,361	1,148,208	688,368
1996	28,476,322	23,035,899	140,308	23,176,207	2,537,181	-416,491	20,222,535	4,437,888	3,815,899	24,514	1,161,613	702,296
1997	30,041,351	24,487,363	94,099	24,581,462	2,691,291	-468,452	21,421,719	4,712,742	3,906,890	25,622	1,172,495	721,454
1998	33,653,860	27,959,911	48,009	28,007,920	2,929,901	-542,175	24,535,844	5,012,591	4,105,425	28,351	1,187,032	741,209
1999	34,814,896	29,228,284	52,658	29,280,942	3,081,985	-596,398	25,602,559	4,976,247	4,236,090	28,944	1,202,822	751,679
2000	36,262,585	30,265,706	46,490	30,312,196	3,175,104	-648,968	26,488,124	5,267,186	4,507,275	29,815	1,216,257	764,311
2001	38,667,718	32,438,282	147,416	32,585,698	3,385,765	-685,624	28,514,309	5,236,801	4,916,608	31,575	1,224,627	763,816
2002	39,421,890	33,414,045	32,809	33,446,854	3,538,942	-826,065	29,081,847	5,071,422	5,268,621	31,917	1,235,125	759,821
2003	40,730,934	34,351,124	158,881	34,510,005	3,635,627	-913,954	29,960,424	5,172,161	5,598,349	32,652	1,247,414	759,311
2004	42,611,865	36,090,902	181,540	36,272,442	3,793,936	-996,443	31,482,063	5,283,742	5,846,060	33,847	1,258,948	769,925
2005	43,972,315	36,767,942	153,610	36,921,552	3,889,500	-984,836	32,047,216	5,671,730	6,253,369	34,570	1,271,965	782,884
2006	46,493,593	38,426,769	122,794	38,549,563	4,090,763	-959,397	33,499,403	6,450,684	6,543,506	35,989	1,291,868	802,196
2007	48,445,318	39,511,203	111,260	39,622,463	4,273,898	-891,505	34,457,060	6,850,290	7,137,968	37,201	1,302,273	816,878
2008	49,418,521	39,424,449	108,671	39,533,120	4,307,346	-854,615	34,371,159	6,980,870	8,066,492	37,700	1,310,829	811,520
2009	48,144,360	38,039,369	107,701	38,147,070	4,205,626	-774,774	33,166,670	6,340,040	8,637,650	36,536	1,317,719	782,187
2010	49,608,299	38,503,853	34,832	38,538,685	4,246,819	-763,545	33,528,321	6,530,296	9,549,682	37,396	1,326,580	777,818
2011	51,866,467	39,688,302	104,249	39,792,551	3,890,537	-800,582	35,101,432	6,990,933	9,774,102	38,916	1,332,790	795,705
2012	54,837,709	42,050,619	99,971	42,150,590	3,977,504	-831,967	37,341,119	7,601,839	9,894,751	40,901	1,340,755	801,396
2013	54,987,023	42,325,221	323,046	42,648,267	4,562,467	-807,818	37,277,982	7,533,496	10,175,545	40,983	1,341,710	808,320
2014	56,327,800	43,451,180	135,038	43,586,218	4,688,753	-803,258	38,094,207	7,823,399	10,410,194	41,935	1,343,230	818,450

Personal Income and Employment by Area: Merced, CA

(Thousands of dollars, except as noted.)

Year	Personal income, total	Earnings by place of work			Less: Contributions for government social insurance	Plus: Adjustment for residence	Equals: Net earnings by place of residence	Plus: Dividends, interest, and rent	Plus: Personal current transfer receipts	Per capita personal income (dollars)	Population (persons)	Total employment
		Nonfarm	Farm	Total								
1970	434,855	252,157	78,531	330,688	17,348	3,914	317,254	68,196	49,405	4,131	105,275	45,456
1971	460,215	277,621	69,534	347,155	19,997	4,047	331,205	73,780	55,230	4,260	108,032	47,188
1972	517,508	307,064	88,135	395,199	22,971	4,852	377,080	82,251	58,177	4,681	110,548	49,741
1973	612,189	343,468	130,956	474,424	28,474	4,962	450,912	96,655	64,622	5,350	114,436	51,449
1974	685,053	387,089	137,450	524,539	33,375	5,514	496,678	111,134	77,241	5,808	117,949	54,411
1975	782,144	429,122	167,674	596,796	36,925	4,160	564,031	122,506	95,607	6,440	121,456	56,336
1976	876,639	489,213	186,623	675,836	43,212	3,285	635,909	131,128	109,602	6,938	126,358	58,502
1977	962,447	548,398	191,997	740,395	48,921	3,912	695,386	147,096	119,965	7,603	126,591	60,515
1978	1,016,259	623,647	134,596	758,243	55,636	5,885	708,492	174,088	133,679	7,913	128,435	61,473
1979	1,169,300	696,251	179,664	875,915	63,495	9,408	821,828	198,159	149,313	8,873	131,775	64,328
1980	1,329,573	750,425	223,498	973,923	67,517	10,730	917,136	234,044	178,393	9,803	135,625	64,044
1981	1,358,459	804,211	127,573	931,784	77,881	16,101	870,004	276,350	212,105	9,729	139,632	62,729
1982	1,453,746	862,670	118,986	981,656	84,534	18,970	916,092	301,219	236,435	10,183	142,766	62,096
1983	1,520,857	917,804	83,605	1,001,409	91,814	22,201	931,796	327,048	262,013	10,300	147,657	62,975
1984	1,766,068	1,032,124	167,318	1,199,442	107,368	26,640	1,118,714	362,799	284,555	11,668	151,357	64,798
1985	1,904,185	1,119,615	171,155	1,290,770	117,430	32,535	1,205,875	379,784	318,526	12,211	155,939	66,196
1986	2,052,932	1,196,194	202,346	1,398,540	127,043	40,249	1,311,746	397,244	343,942	12,912	158,988	67,501
1987	2,278,776	1,320,170	271,136	1,591,306	138,797	53,514	1,506,023	415,002	357,751	13,984	162,956	70,309
1988	2,387,707	1,411,633	258,992	1,670,625	155,939	66,097	1,580,783	422,076	384,848	14,234	167,749	73,220
1989	2,604,439	1,500,672	283,848	1,784,520	168,168	76,834	1,693,186	486,967	424,286	15,056	172,988	74,815
1990	2,777,602	1,610,063	285,166	1,895,229	180,400	90,941	1,805,770	500,637	471,195	15,435	179,953	76,728
1991	2,897,170	1,682,009	275,569	1,957,578	191,595	96,845	1,862,828	502,914	531,428	15,569	186,091	78,038
1992	3,093,288	1,755,615	298,703	2,054,318	199,586	107,031	1,961,763	500,184	631,341	16,324	189,489	76,943
1993	3,190,092	1,800,751	308,550	2,109,301	206,694	118,030	2,020,637	504,080	665,375	16,517	193,137	78,232
1994	3,268,282	1,824,576	326,879	2,151,455	208,000	132,484	2,075,939	513,458	678,885	16,523	197,798	77,678
1995	3,156,077	1,758,184	218,588	1,976,772	199,383	157,856	1,935,245	508,949	711,883	16,161	195,291	77,043
1996	3,469,219	1,805,344	399,358	2,204,702	196,701	185,224	2,193,225	528,346	747,648	17,807	194,819	77,229
1997	3,582,106	1,929,808	358,554	2,288,362	204,895	220,187	2,303,654	541,927	736,525	18,063	198,312	77,931
1998	3,809,341	2,112,579	300,280	2,412,859	216,560	256,429	2,452,728	580,229	776,384	18,834	202,264	82,567
1999	4,001,087	2,225,707	293,176	2,518,883	230,468	305,479	2,593,894	587,544	819,649	19,354	206,734	83,973
2000	4,225,124	2,367,715	247,684	2,615,399	245,910	386,462	2,755,951	623,283	845,890	19,906	212,258	83,240
2001	4,601,710	2,555,788	298,828	2,854,616	273,919	391,317	2,972,014	672,138	957,558	21,030	218,816	82,802
2002	4,923,549	2,790,077	315,187	3,105,264	305,630	420,079	3,219,713	670,321	1,033,515	21,848	225,351	87,531
2003	5,368,289	2,996,842	436,174	3,433,016	334,531	445,473	3,543,958	722,491	1,101,840	23,166	231,735	87,965
2004	5,882,047	3,196,670	682,654	3,879,324	368,264	472,211	3,983,271	731,137	1,167,639	24,800	237,180	88,445
2005	5,983,236	3,318,386	601,898	3,920,284	384,898	489,401	4,024,787	729,456	1,228,993	24,668	242,554	88,256
2006	6,204,942	3,556,195	417,115	3,973,310	394,523	528,025	4,106,812	767,864	1,330,266	25,291	245,338	91,097
2007	6,958,047	3,641,366	858,471	4,499,837	396,981	563,325	4,666,181	864,956	1,426,910	27,996	248,540	94,354
2008	6,869,132	3,629,906	560,352	4,190,258	401,345	583,014	4,371,927	887,181	1,610,024	27,418	250,538	92,851
2009	6,747,116	3,577,138	469,331	4,046,469	403,937	468,745	4,111,277	847,613	1,788,226	26,742	252,302	90,960
2010	7,104,887	3,615,308	570,841	4,186,149	396,127	460,068	4,250,090	864,294	1,990,503	27,674	256,731	90,679
2011	7,858,717	3,769,602	962,849	4,732,451	371,704	533,367	4,894,114	968,463	1,996,140	30,261	259,698	90,904
2012	8,060,966	3,956,961	895,218	4,852,179	388,492	488,302	4,951,989	1,073,762	2,035,215	30,793	261,783	94,716
2013	8,635,380	4,084,616	1,201,690	5,286,306	446,302	499,803	5,339,807	1,166,655	2,128,918	32,774	263,481	97,399
2014	9,020,129	4,276,301	1,250,133	5,526,434	465,128	521,262	5,582,568	1,221,891	2,215,670	33,865	266,353	100,466

Personal Income and Employment by Area: Miami-Fort Lauderdale-Pompano Beach, FL

(Thousands of dollars, except as noted.)

Year	Personal income, total	Derivation of personal income									Per capita personal income (dollars)	Population (persons)	Total employment
		Earnings by place of work			Less: Contributions for government social insurance	Plus: Adjustment for residence	Equals: Net earnings by place of residence	Plus: Dividends, interest, and rent	Plus: Personal current transfer receipts			
		Nonfarm	Farm	Total									
1970	10,819,880	7,591,813	105,059	7,696,872	490,761	-12,415	7,193,696	2,734,498	891,686		4,798	2,255,202	1,054,067
1971	12,082,256	8,333,921	122,138	8,456,059	560,807	-16,601	7,878,651	3,115,976	1,087,629		5,109	2,364,750	1,087,984
1972	13,860,883	9,628,363	131,527	9,759,890	685,284	-20,633	9,053,973	3,512,379	1,294,531		5,592	2,478,824	1,178,470
1973	16,183,471	11,356,837	139,634	11,496,471	933,948	-29,300	10,533,223	4,078,065	1,572,183		6,213	2,604,637	1,304,027
1974	18,258,008	12,400,627	201,117	12,601,744	1,064,125	-29,297	11,508,322	4,810,852	1,938,834		6,649	2,745,960	1,330,500
1975	19,651,664	12,620,540	226,346	12,846,886	1,059,036	-29,269	11,758,581	5,296,863	2,596,220		6,926	2,837,578	1,275,484
1976	21,350,671	13,720,951	233,926	13,954,877	1,168,205	-26,294	12,760,378	5,725,278	2,865,015		7,403	2,884,080	1,292,596
1977	23,889,248	15,418,006	208,539	15,626,545	1,322,007	-32,409	14,272,129	6,507,980	3,109,139		8,132	2,937,632	1,367,587
1978	27,546,120	17,930,226	195,555	18,125,781	1,585,493	-48,141	16,492,147	7,610,224	3,443,749		9,173	3,002,966	1,485,993
1979	31,804,449	20,673,433	210,600	20,884,033	1,919,378	-67,331	18,897,324	8,953,392	3,953,733		10,187	3,121,950	1,567,870
1980	37,472,266	23,971,282	291,109	24,262,391	2,247,862	-90,238	21,924,291	10,885,920	4,662,055		11,512	3,254,936	1,663,461
1981	43,420,898	26,944,106	323,739	27,267,845	2,720,704	-39,285	24,507,856	13,520,826	5,392,216		12,822	3,386,317	1,715,798
1982	46,254,003	28,341,182	422,817	28,763,999	2,943,142	-48,366	25,772,491	14,449,483	6,032,029		13,408	3,449,745	1,720,145
1983	50,895,255	31,060,572	715,874	31,776,446	3,233,549	-70,056	28,472,841	15,870,052	6,552,362		14,514	3,506,541	1,771,008
1984	56,107,229	34,411,544	450,907	34,862,451	3,677,992	-90,862	31,093,597	17,995,743	7,017,889		15,759	3,560,292	1,862,036
1985	61,180,554	37,529,188	454,282	37,983,470	4,075,773	-111,821	33,795,876	19,921,003	7,463,675		16,841	3,632,834	1,921,376
1986	65,515,351	40,567,378	537,808	41,105,186	4,520,079	-120,066	36,465,041	21,081,469	7,968,841		17,663	3,709,283	1,976,279
1987	71,001,097	44,877,705	590,313	45,468,018	4,932,983	-140,519	40,394,516	22,228,417	8,378,164		18,699	3,797,118	1,983,981
1988	77,261,114	49,170,289	621,712	49,792,001	5,554,435	-157,715	44,079,851	24,093,055	9,088,208		19,852	3,891,758	2,077,107
1989	85,919,438	51,787,934	555,191	52,343,125	5,905,466	-157,726	46,279,933	29,406,816	10,232,689		21,566	3,984,047	2,124,442
1990	91,598,177	54,927,437	431,771	55,359,208	6,200,302	-183,884	48,975,022	31,481,552	11,141,603		22,458	4,078,578	2,151,815
1991	95,390,473	56,982,071	512,637	57,494,708	6,462,550	-177,329	50,854,829	31,937,746	12,597,898		22,839	4,176,731	2,129,237
1992	100,641,080	61,054,880	600,067	61,654,947	6,856,552	-166,852	54,631,543	31,417,889	14,591,648		23,608	4,262,995	2,133,944
1993	107,030,633	65,953,882	661,304	66,615,186	7,360,268	-170,090	59,084,828	32,485,186	15,460,619		24,660	4,340,175	2,221,343
1994	111,992,319	69,431,899	484,294	69,916,193	7,836,302	-175,369	61,904,522	33,722,818	16,364,979		25,194	4,445,162	2,289,282
1995	120,203,576	73,773,480	516,285	74,289,765	8,275,302	-174,724	65,839,739	36,613,145	17,750,692		26,435	4,547,191	2,367,458
1996	127,739,455	78,614,595	417,206	79,031,801	8,695,322	-180,144	70,156,335	38,778,128	18,804,992		27,457	4,652,414	2,423,829
1997	133,721,078	82,381,887	450,641	82,832,528	9,113,262	-168,112	73,551,154	40,866,849	19,303,075		28,150	4,750,249	2,495,838
1998	144,404,544	89,790,061	550,442	90,340,503	9,751,110	-173,847	80,415,546	44,339,006	19,649,992		29,855	4,836,853	2,584,242
1999	151,121,099	96,146,025	633,878	96,779,903	10,378,780	-178,057	86,223,066	44,536,230	20,361,803		30,641	4,932,004	2,675,874
2000	164,157,830	105,655,530	576,295	106,231,825	11,202,775	-197,069	94,831,981	47,659,227	21,666,622		32,662	5,025,895	2,770,994
2001	173,267,271	113,448,661	629,770	114,078,431	12,192,986	-257,617	101,627,828	48,163,521	23,475,922		33,902	5,110,780	2,870,972
2002	179,531,077	118,441,483	616,327	119,057,810	12,634,647	-623,949	105,799,214	48,657,320	25,074,543		34,544	5,197,205	2,902,518
2003	185,042,653	122,976,578	547,192	123,523,770	13,130,020	-767,921	109,625,829	48,683,857	26,732,967		35,168	5,261,713	2,952,020
2004	200,643,353	131,090,716	524,419	131,615,135	14,082,186	-974,286	116,558,663	55,557,343	28,527,347		37,599	5,336,368	3,036,493
2005	219,589,958	142,209,790	595,387	142,805,177	15,345,522	-1,040,885	126,418,770	62,603,151	30,568,037		40,581	5,411,148	3,169,202
2006	238,722,083	151,079,698	594,829	151,674,527	16,574,756	-1,224,277	133,875,494	73,008,229	31,838,360		43,966	5,429,748	3,253,418
2007	248,386,768	153,643,602	562,505	154,206,107	17,078,345	-1,421,753	135,706,009	79,435,368	33,245,391		45,803	5,422,987	3,318,451
2008	248,921,194	152,123,297	555,209	152,678,506	17,066,365	-1,741,580	133,870,561	77,484,281	37,566,352		45,635	5,454,633	3,267,313
2009	230,793,387	143,374,285	592,462	143,966,747	16,412,257	-1,686,501	125,867,989	64,225,457	40,699,941		41,927	5,504,624	3,141,630
2010	242,333,210	146,090,857	580,380	146,671,237	16,662,085	-1,206,296	128,802,856	69,257,350	44,273,004		43,378	5,586,506	3,141,700
2011	256,722,762	150,972,311	454,598	151,426,909	15,403,838	-1,406,794	134,616,277	76,413,371	45,693,114		44,985	5,706,892	3,254,933
2012	270,018,210	159,133,749	499,556	159,633,305	16,109,282	-2,043,033	141,480,990	83,967,121	44,570,099		46,641	5,789,346	3,339,122
2013	272,261,505	166,585,851	600,277	167,186,128	18,896,346	-2,285,400	146,004,382	80,652,084	45,605,039		46,434	5,863,458	3,458,389
2014	285,960,690	176,159,860	510,444	176,670,304	20,025,308	-2,497,565	154,147,431	83,818,690	47,994,569		48,224	5,929,819	3,554,117

Personal Income and Employment by Area: Michigan City-La Porte, IN

(Thousands of dollars, except as noted.)

Year	Personal income, total	Derivation of personal income			Less: Contributions for government social insurance	Plus: Adjustment for residence	Equals: Net earnings by place of residence	Plus: Dividends, interest, and rent	Plus: Personal current transfer receipts	Per capita personal income (dollars)	Population (persons)	Total employment
		Earnings by place of work										
		Nonfarm	Farm	Total								
1970	404,382	320,178	5,729	325,907	22,456	20,808	324,259	50,597	29,526	3,834	105,461	45,672
1971	428,508	327,144	10,528	337,672	23,782	24,128	338,018	54,910	35,580	4,031	106,310	44,103
1972	470,905	363,316	7,144	370,460	27,838	31,284	373,906	58,648	38,351	4,412	106,744	45,366
1973	537,218	404,498	16,325	420,823	35,558	40,110	425,375	67,332	44,511	5,014	107,134	47,958
1974	586,083	437,230	8,392	445,622	40,261	50,728	456,089	78,662	51,332	5,468	107,180	48,730
1975	637,178	445,544	17,067	462,611	40,208	59,437	481,840	87,550	67,788	5,935	107,353	46,388
1976	702,676	493,689	16,159	509,848	45,038	71,792	536,602	94,459	71,615	6,530	107,604	47,203
1977	779,800	552,402	8,926	561,328	50,054	88,921	600,195	105,566	74,039	7,187	108,496	48,332
1978	885,243	624,907	13,976	638,883	58,176	106,999	687,706	116,474	81,063	8,136	108,807	50,502
1979	976,686	679,490	9,852	689,342	65,577	128,491	752,256	130,837	93,593	8,949	109,142	50,703
1980	1,058,048	719,867	4,803	724,670	69,332	127,134	782,472	160,871	114,705	9,738	108,657	49,332
1981	1,148,454	752,036	5,889	757,925	77,837	135,946	816,034	198,372	134,048	10,583	108,515	48,011
1982	1,158,446	748,808	886	749,694	79,295	125,532	795,931	209,164	153,351	10,712	108,140	46,152
1983	1,173,145	766,964	-8,369	758,595	81,529	108,938	786,004	217,637	169,504	10,940	107,230	45,219
1984	1,268,730	820,629	10,149	830,778	89,348	111,643	853,073	243,700	171,957	11,860	106,976	46,096
1985	1,325,757	871,183	8,641	879,824	96,368	111,859	895,315	251,312	179,130	12,427	106,680	47,280
1986	1,380,789	917,767	7,760	925,527	102,005	103,412	926,934	261,686	192,169	13,064	105,696	48,106
1987	1,459,529	982,423	14,118	996,541	107,304	108,757	997,994	264,346	197,189	13,794	105,806	49,835
1988	1,556,871	1,075,400	4,993	1,080,393	123,643	113,246	1,069,996	281,595	205,280	14,696	105,941	51,945
1989	1,698,799	1,140,666	22,362	1,163,028	131,127	119,534	1,151,435	325,982	221,382	15,951	106,502	53,294
1990	1,770,483	1,194,760	20,991	1,215,751	139,608	119,441	1,195,584	336,388	238,511	16,507	107,257	53,683
1991	1,804,890	1,237,751	2,954	1,240,705	146,180	118,627	1,213,152	333,090	258,648	16,689	108,151	53,728
1992	1,947,378	1,321,152	19,383	1,340,535	154,983	126,126	1,311,678	338,958	296,742	17,878	108,928	53,920
1993	2,020,670	1,376,148	14,238	1,390,386	162,405	128,044	1,356,025	348,829	315,816	18,460	109,461	54,837
1994	2,125,526	1,447,742	19,164	1,466,906	172,870	142,059	1,436,095	364,399	325,032	19,390	109,620	55,637
1995	2,217,682	1,495,730	13,892	1,509,622	179,301	144,746	1,475,067	411,727	330,888	20,240	109,571	57,043
1996	2,320,103	1,534,944	22,259	1,557,203	182,095	154,681	1,529,789	439,121	351,193	21,134	109,783	56,722
1997	2,456,750	1,635,299	23,965	1,659,264	192,651	154,317	1,620,930	474,286	361,534	22,380	109,774	57,371
1998	2,585,657	1,743,279	18,885	1,762,164	200,609	164,099	1,725,654	489,312	370,691	23,516	109,954	58,253
1999	2,620,195	1,794,430	9,345	1,803,775	206,144	163,824	1,761,455	474,335	384,405	23,814	110,028	58,939
2000	2,779,106	1,901,572	13,320	1,914,892	216,551	156,390	1,854,731	518,452	405,923	25,237	110,121	59,868
2001	2,774,878	1,904,878	19,422	1,924,300	219,502	121,782	1,826,580	503,822	444,476	25,209	110,077	59,766
2002	2,798,837	1,920,041	10,805	1,930,846	223,159	129,687	1,837,374	489,804	471,659	25,547	109,555	59,057
2003	2,865,497	1,935,788	23,442	1,959,230	225,073	138,082	1,872,239	503,013	490,245	26,282	109,027	58,012
2004	2,946,554	2,004,347	41,231	2,045,578	233,982	152,727	1,964,323	464,297	517,934	27,054	108,914	58,240
2005	3,029,883	2,080,378	22,386	2,102,764	246,371	167,987	2,024,380	442,825	562,678	27,660	109,541	59,093
2006	3,181,149	2,141,525	26,211	2,167,736	255,457	183,293	2,095,572	483,751	601,826	29,014	109,641	59,076
2007	3,324,610	2,198,018	25,203	2,223,221	264,766	202,864	2,161,319	532,231	631,060	29,993	110,846	59,411
2008	3,485,379	2,224,920	32,438	2,257,358	270,245	218,532	2,205,645	557,621	722,113	31,324	111,267	58,420
2009	3,368,805	2,084,205	17,018	2,101,223	258,485	229,395	2,072,133	493,432	803,240	30,223	111,465	55,873
2010	3,474,949	2,098,567	34,925	2,133,492	259,093	281,620	2,156,019	463,984	854,946	31,188	111,421	54,457
2011	3,693,546	2,174,601	53,658	2,228,259	238,657	334,234	2,323,836	521,939	847,771	33,219	111,187	55,049
2012	3,893,168	2,242,609	57,363	2,299,972	242,960	369,541	2,426,553	593,717	872,898	35,024	111,158	54,747
2013	3,872,611	2,256,692	81,016	2,337,708	278,685	365,481	2,424,504	563,959	884,148	34,808	111,256	54,512
2014	3,998,834	2,320,323	59,030	2,379,353	286,027	395,758	2,489,084	585,156	924,594	35,882	111,444	54,725

Personal Income and Employment by Area: Midland, MI

(Thousands of dollars, except as noted.)

| Year | Personal income, total | Derivation of personal income | | | | | Equals: Net earnings by place of residence | Plus: Dividends, interest, and rent | Plus: Personal current transfer receipts | Per capita personal income (dollars) | Population (persons) | Total employment |
| | | Earnings by place of work | | | Less: Contributions for government social insurance | Plus: Adjustment for residence | | | | | | |
		Nonfarm	Farm	Total								
1970	275,913	285,981	1,613	287,594	20,219	-51,061	216,314	44,423	15,176	4,314	63,956	28,920
1971	297,604	301,581	1,394	302,975	22,121	-49,504	231,350	46,959	19,295	4,575	65,050	27,915
1972	319,796	318,060	2,621	320,681	24,578	-48,271	247,832	50,364	21,600	4,898	65,286	27,970
1973	350,404	351,135	3,187	354,322	31,828	-50,788	271,706	53,840	24,858	5,278	66,390	29,341
1974	408,571	406,825	7,733	414,558	38,416	-61,338	314,804	59,744	34,023	6,083	67,168	28,737
1975	446,191	438,683	4,214	442,897	40,362	-64,964	337,571	67,057	41,563	6,502	68,626	30,639
1976	508,680	509,381	2,797	512,178	47,602	-73,038	391,538	74,147	42,995	7,338	69,324	32,404
1977	591,421	604,047	4,500	608,547	56,695	-89,592	462,260	83,351	45,810	8,343	70,888	35,226
1978	660,440	673,243	3,989	677,232	64,444	-92,887	519,901	91,557	48,982	9,186	71,900	35,972
1979	727,557	738,827	3,508	742,335	74,550	-99,207	568,578	103,974	55,005	9,945	73,158	36,279
1980	770,036	735,976	2,014	737,990	73,494	-89,594	574,902	122,467	72,667	10,423	73,882	34,846
1981	851,324	792,478	2,026	794,504	85,842	-91,300	617,362	156,904	77,058	11,361	74,936	34,356
1982	898,592	823,581	1,165	824,746	92,225	-99,984	632,537	179,096	86,959	12,016	74,784	33,960
1983	945,369	841,574	-235	841,339	94,247	-89,079	658,013	192,602	94,754	12,572	75,198	33,798
1984	1,015,104	851,391	2,194	853,585	96,306	-62,399	694,880	217,620	102,604	13,386	75,835	33,330
1985	1,085,684	881,860	2,030	883,890	100,225	-41,811	741,854	236,041	107,789	14,977	72,492	33,734
1986	1,167,922	959,828	1,050	960,878	108,944	-43,347	808,587	243,528	115,807	16,088	72,598	34,691
1987	1,266,560	1,037,321	2,758	1,040,079	115,912	-47,210	876,957	268,151	121,452	17,337	73,054	36,329
1988	1,394,143	1,155,209	4,046	1,159,255	132,012	-48,391	978,852	288,697	126,594	18,823	74,065	37,224
1989	1,545,100	1,231,785	7,238	1,239,023	141,271	-52,083	1,045,669	358,900	140,531	20,666	74,767	39,737
1990	1,638,994	1,307,337	2,919	1,310,256	153,520	-48,716	1,108,020	376,808	154,166	21,565	76,002	41,424
1991	1,690,094	1,331,154	2,997	1,334,151	157,915	-28,526	1,147,710	370,696	171,688	22,026	76,733	41,784
1992	1,819,111	1,470,442	3,582	1,474,024	173,186	-49,472	1,251,366	383,426	184,319	23,366	77,853	43,653
1993	1,906,036	1,506,766	4,413	1,511,179	178,711	-25,278	1,307,190	396,604	202,242	24,246	78,614	43,354
1994	1,985,367	1,526,974	1,693	1,528,667	185,902	-4,622	1,338,143	440,297	206,927	25,020	79,352	43,013
1995	2,102,356	1,630,414	2,723	1,633,137	197,828	-12,573	1,422,736	463,606	216,014	26,332	79,841	43,166
1996	2,243,092	1,738,237	1,452	1,739,689	206,769	11,229	1,544,149	476,068	222,875	27,728	80,897	44,035
1997	2,308,675	1,799,728	1,115	1,800,843	212,924	-6,126	1,581,793	480,517	246,365	28,276	81,648	44,500
1998	2,475,368	1,874,696	866	1,875,562	219,696	32,187	1,688,053	535,775	251,540	30,158	82,081	44,381
1999	2,509,353	1,892,232	2,749	1,894,981	222,724	44,132	1,716,389	517,860	275,104	30,380	82,599	45,697
2000	2,622,828	2,071,295	2,108	2,073,403	244,414	-30,887	1,798,102	530,111	294,615	31,633	82,913	47,028
2001	2,634,869	2,069,812	1,332	2,071,144	227,661	-49,426	1,794,057	512,352	328,460	31,527	83,576	46,748
2002	2,618,351	2,035,628	1,645	2,037,273	224,960	-40,915	1,771,398	502,165	344,788	31,296	83,664	46,368
2003	2,696,745	2,091,009	1,370	2,092,379	228,449	-34,126	1,829,804	505,161	361,780	32,100	84,012	45,909
2004	3,043,437	2,314,495	4,392	2,318,887	253,027	-28,515	2,037,345	624,718	381,374	36,206	84,058	45,522
2005	3,002,044	2,279,450	5,663	2,285,113	253,105	-18,808	2,013,200	578,769	410,075	35,768	83,930	46,102
2006	3,120,957	2,325,023	2,855	2,327,878	263,417	-9,746	2,054,715	631,965	434,277	37,291	83,693	46,755
2007	3,259,752	2,421,980	5,041	2,427,021	276,950	-517	2,149,554	633,093	477,105	38,992	83,600	47,917
2008	3,562,597	2,579,463	9,657	2,589,120	294,689	9,596	2,304,027	713,053	545,517	42,612	83,605	48,093
2009	3,351,208	2,423,272	3,612	2,426,884	282,432	57,388	2,201,840	558,986	590,382	40,068	83,639	46,729
2010	3,399,101	2,511,523	7,519	2,519,042	286,714	17,794	2,250,122	517,596	631,383	40,628	83,664	46,618
2011	3,685,293	2,666,300	20,811	2,687,111	268,339	56,183	2,474,955	578,446	631,892	43,996	83,765	47,567
2012	3,706,983	2,597,367	15,317	2,612,684	266,317	79,200	2,425,567	646,716	634,700	44,316	83,649	47,519
2013	3,701,701	2,606,144	14,034	2,620,178	307,510	81,079	2,393,747	655,700	652,254	44,282	83,593	48,106
2014	3,850,272	2,804,174	5,767	2,809,941	326,736	5,493	2,488,698	678,715	682,859	46,151	83,427	49,234

Personal Income and Employment by Area: Midland, TX

(Thousands of dollars, except as noted.)

Year	Personal income, total	Earnings by place of work			Less: Contributions for government social insurance	Plus: Adjustment for residence	Equals: Net earnings by place of residence	Plus: Dividends, interest, and rent	Plus: Personal current transfer receipts	Per capita personal income (dollars)	Population (persons)	Total employment
		Nonfarm	Farm	Total								
1970	327,906	277,820	8,502	286,322	16,115	-7,795	262,412	51,778	13,716	4,665	70,297	34,454
1971	354,538	302,113	7,968	310,081	17,843	-8,551	283,687	54,873	15,978	4,972	71,302	35,324
1972	382,901	326,581	7,542	334,123	19,843	-8,855	305,425	59,303	18,173	5,357	71,477	35,958
1973	436,754	360,804	20,683	381,487	25,760	-10,122	345,605	69,008	22,141	6,129	71,259	37,635
1974	489,963	417,576	2,960	420,536	30,516	-11,582	378,438	84,690	26,835	6,683	73,313	39,497
1975	592,713	523,019	-1,933	521,086	37,720	-17,061	466,305	94,593	31,815	7,836	75,637	43,247
1976	685,254	593,517	13,799	607,316	42,464	-18,378	546,474	103,247	35,533	8,792	77,943	43,997
1977	772,860	677,813	17,684	695,497	50,590	-25,653	619,254	115,730	37,876	9,756	79,216	48,808
1978	926,118	829,590	7,603	837,193	62,781	-34,494	739,918	142,864	43,336	11,443	80,934	52,831
1979	1,082,037	942,293	32,756	975,049	74,353	-39,783	860,913	171,610	49,514	12,951	83,546	54,875
1980	1,284,931	1,178,444	-11,224	1,167,220	96,272	-59,539	1,011,409	215,879	57,643	14,486	88,700	61,483
1981	1,656,261	1,454,246	33,403	1,487,649	131,837	-69,430	1,286,382	305,289	64,590	17,627	93,964	71,676
1982	1,863,075	1,635,142	21,385	1,656,527	157,802	-75,688	1,423,037	366,025	74,013	17,921	103,959	77,759
1983	1,800,629	1,526,723	3,763	1,530,486	148,806	-64,687	1,316,993	390,756	92,880	16,049	112,195	73,906
1984	1,879,709	1,562,594	-6,629	1,555,965	157,124	-57,663	1,341,178	437,429	101,102	16,795	111,919	74,561
1985	2,038,387	1,660,474	1,141	1,661,615	171,287	-54,509	1,435,819	491,644	110,924	17,881	113,997	76,826
1986	1,949,743	1,538,419	6,383	1,544,802	154,851	-49,117	1,340,834	476,407	132,502	16,627	117,265	68,942
1987	1,892,984	1,457,303	30,395	1,487,698	145,530	-37,409	1,304,759	449,313	138,912	16,858	112,287	69,786
1988	2,086,874	1,600,824	26,466	1,627,290	164,594	-37,671	1,425,025	516,605	145,244	18,727	111,439	71,380
1989	2,202,772	1,669,355	4,013	1,673,368	167,597	-27,478	1,478,293	561,058	163,421	19,757	111,494	68,991
1990	2,410,385	1,734,574	20,527	1,755,101	170,702	-18,663	1,565,736	664,814	179,835	21,594	111,624	68,901
1991	2,401,801	1,705,753	2,682	1,708,435	178,553	-15,766	1,514,116	683,304	204,381	21,175	113,427	70,299
1992	2,582,530	1,826,992	20,668	1,847,660	185,285	-14,003	1,648,372	687,197	246,961	22,393	115,325	68,743
1993	2,751,028	1,954,995	28,854	1,983,849	195,576	-9,021	1,779,252	705,967	265,809	23,623	116,456	71,541
1994	2,814,996	1,945,812	11,153	1,956,965	195,530	87	1,761,522	761,590	291,884	23,911	117,728	72,932
1995	2,887,022	2,047,695	8,911	2,056,606	202,016	3,501	1,858,091	714,413	314,518	24,364	118,493	73,505
1996	3,141,272	2,259,276	170	2,259,446	212,205	5,577	2,052,818	750,679	337,775	26,355	119,192	74,051
1997	3,567,441	2,647,706	21,220	2,668,926	237,930	1,443	2,432,439	781,687	353,315	29,316	121,691	78,960
1998	3,644,399	2,699,140	-6,554	2,692,586	238,486	16,064	2,470,164	817,537	356,698	29,582	123,197	79,652
1999	3,533,972	2,526,019	19,973	2,545,992	223,352	17,783	2,340,423	821,994	371,555	28,863	122,440	76,954
2000	3,910,665	2,767,694	-1,134	2,766,560	236,673	31,139	2,561,026	958,339	391,300	32,513	120,280	77,726
2001	4,413,910	3,288,064	5,752	3,293,816	275,938	53,555	3,071,433	923,090	419,387	36,516	120,877	79,299
2002	4,171,955	3,084,030	617	3,084,647	270,347	51,364	2,865,664	848,134	458,157	34,093	122,371	78,860
2003	4,514,658	3,316,672	34,446	3,351,118	288,867	52,791	3,115,042	912,956	486,660	36,492	123,717	82,814
2004	4,984,000	3,709,846	23,944	3,733,790	318,341	57,350	3,472,799	999,545	511,656	39,826	125,144	84,114
2005	5,836,278	4,334,451	34,338	4,368,789	364,771	60,256	4,064,274	1,224,988	547,016	45,968	126,963	88,209
2006	6,704,878	5,028,297	13,230	5,041,527	412,778	67,107	4,695,856	1,423,512	585,510	51,462	130,287	93,623
2007	7,121,341	5,280,206	45,863	5,326,069	458,967	72,160	4,939,262	1,523,174	658,905	53,364	133,448	98,742
2008	9,667,186	7,538,342	-1,680	7,536,662	560,949	80,602	7,056,315	1,887,651	723,220	70,533	137,060	106,199
2009	7,777,693	5,976,265	15,248	5,991,513	512,432	47,750	5,526,831	1,481,044	769,818	55,181	140,948	103,493
2010	8,982,961	7,102,765	41,667	7,144,432	584,975	4,690	6,564,147	1,580,250	838,564	63,350	141,798	108,316
2011	11,435,536	9,352,647	18,610	9,371,257	623,330	57,956	8,805,883	1,778,297	851,356	78,868	144,996	113,808
2012	13,680,588	11,117,832	11,723	11,129,555	720,285	34,024	10,443,294	2,400,213	837,081	89,949	152,092	126,341
2013	13,968,522	11,848,021	32,225	11,880,246	888,199	-2,386	10,989,661	2,125,773	853,088	88,836	157,240	134,269
2014	15,300,461	13,345,859	8,883	13,354,742	1,021,190	-149,789	12,183,763	2,224,109	892,589	94,863	161,290	142,583

Personal Income and Employment by Area: Milwaukee-Waukesha-West Allis, WI

(Thousands of dollars, except as noted.)

Year	Personal income, total	Derivation of personal income									Per capita personal income (dollars)	Population (persons)	Total employment
		Earnings by place of work			Less: Contributions for government social insurance	Plus: Adjustment for residence	Equals: Net earnings by place of residence	Plus: Dividends, interest, and rent	Plus: Personal current transfer receipts				
		Nonfarm	Farm	Total									
1970	6,407,962	5,372,563	22,593	5,395,156	393,284	-108,499	4,893,373	977,773	536,816		4,562	1,404,488	659,946
1971	6,809,792	5,648,100	26,072	5,674,172	428,350	-119,584	5,126,238	1,048,744	634,810		4,846	1,405,231	655,077
1972	7,424,196	6,215,370	23,554	6,238,924	499,766	-138,615	5,600,543	1,117,798	705,855		5,243	1,416,024	671,565
1973	8,185,338	6,956,293	28,048	6,984,341	648,379	-162,423	6,173,539	1,220,918	790,881		5,808	1,409,344	707,070
1974	8,989,911	7,575,007	23,235	7,598,242	731,201	-187,408	6,679,633	1,395,084	915,194		6,378	1,409,473	721,019
1975	9,705,776	7,991,720	29,193	8,020,913	752,534	-201,830	7,066,549	1,505,697	1,133,530		6,956	1,395,236	705,141
1976	10,542,472	8,801,207	27,862	8,829,069	844,519	-233,318	7,751,232	1,580,478	1,210,762		7,532	1,399,726	718,806
1977	11,626,236	9,806,007	40,202	9,846,209	940,487	-273,630	8,632,092	1,715,160	1,278,984		8,340	1,394,089	744,641
1978	12,937,697	11,006,636	39,093	11,045,729	1,087,913	-320,270	9,637,546	1,877,092	1,423,059		9,313	1,389,196	773,376
1979	14,373,962	12,219,522	47,736	12,267,258	1,256,825	-373,230	10,637,203	2,120,518	1,616,241		10,302	1,395,212	794,684
1980	15,801,347	12,958,565	52,592	13,011,157	1,324,228	-412,888	11,274,041	2,573,528	1,953,778		11,314	1,396,659	783,371
1981	17,304,835	13,763,397	46,335	13,809,732	1,504,611	-442,089	11,863,032	3,192,052	2,249,751		12,435	1,391,672	769,054
1982	18,276,477	14,155,705	39,592	14,195,297	1,561,049	-442,268	12,191,980	3,550,576	2,533,921		13,133	1,391,628	746,855
1983	18,996,675	14,541,610	21,344	14,562,954	1,603,592	-437,888	12,521,474	3,740,813	2,734,388		13,693	1,387,307	735,233
1984	20,812,506	16,064,222	30,560	16,094,782	1,816,823	-481,363	13,796,596	4,241,450	2,774,460		15,028	1,384,897	771,524
1985	21,917,019	16,919,931	34,538	16,954,469	1,928,278	-502,893	14,523,298	4,460,936	2,932,785		15,775	1,389,361	782,599
1986	23,019,621	17,840,497	38,849	17,879,346	2,031,939	-524,855	15,322,552	4,633,734	3,063,335		16,545	1,391,362	794,602
1987	24,331,148	19,089,107	40,547	19,129,654	2,134,088	-546,243	16,449,323	4,748,993	3,132,832		17,403	1,398,088	815,518
1988	26,265,120	20,814,981	28,981	20,843,962	2,401,152	-585,758	17,857,052	5,146,772	3,261,296		18,633	1,409,602	847,896
1989	28,445,820	22,194,711	54,825	22,249,536	2,557,500	-618,184	19,073,852	5,879,312	3,492,656		20,009	1,421,621	867,258
1990	29,965,884	23,552,064	38,823	23,590,887	2,830,207	-638,424	20,122,256	6,102,094	3,741,534		20,878	1,435,303	881,288
1991	30,940,473	24,356,896	35,545	24,392,441	2,955,610	-672,533	20,764,298	6,123,045	4,053,130		21,342	1,449,760	874,176
1992	33,169,291	26,259,103	47,706	26,306,809	3,155,663	-766,084	22,385,062	6,385,302	4,398,927		22,676	1,462,728	882,783
1993	34,753,851	27,653,183	37,627	27,690,810	3,318,791	-851,688	23,520,331	6,627,272	4,606,248		23,630	1,470,728	893,226
1994	36,580,527	29,138,933	38,932	29,177,865	3,551,459	-952,206	24,674,200	7,121,718	4,784,609		24,779	1,476,272	915,146
1995	38,410,390	30,493,472	30,041	30,523,513	3,723,671	-1,048,256	25,751,586	7,624,018	5,034,786		25,929	1,481,347	932,863
1996	40,395,808	32,014,895	36,415	32,051,310	3,875,314	-1,127,486	27,048,510	8,205,445	5,141,853		27,183	1,486,045	942,951
1997	42,775,096	34,144,110	26,294	34,170,404	4,114,384	-1,254,029	28,801,991	8,663,728	5,309,377		28,758	1,487,435	959,068
1998	45,739,354	36,512,841	34,738	36,547,579	4,364,239	-1,363,470	30,819,870	9,485,472	5,434,012		30,678	1,490,926	977,473
1999	47,546,510	38,491,127	35,974	38,527,101	4,619,602	-1,377,389	32,530,110	9,345,207	5,671,193		31,777	1,496,255	988,845
2000	50,415,593	40,502,027	30,587	40,532,614	4,805,074	-1,559,150	34,168,390	10,180,030	6,067,173		33,556	1,502,420	1,002,892
2001	52,301,141	42,165,131	42,544	42,207,675	4,893,288	-1,696,864	35,617,523	9,892,047	6,791,571		34,700	1,507,257	992,212
2002	53,253,625	43,203,157	43,805	43,246,962	4,974,424	-1,887,740	36,384,798	9,613,397	7,255,430		35,168	1,514,251	978,376
2003	54,327,188	44,455,983	61,870	44,517,853	5,090,956	-2,061,986	37,364,911	9,537,719	7,424,558		35,748	1,519,746	975,620
2004	56,791,926	46,570,711	66,552	46,637,263	5,318,291	-2,144,128	39,174,844	10,067,046	7,550,036		37,307	1,522,302	985,273
2005	58,903,231	47,895,792	51,677	47,947,469	5,496,399	-2,175,011	40,276,059	10,625,781	8,001,391		38,691	1,522,391	992,410
2006	63,366,797	50,556,414	46,677	50,603,091	5,829,012	-2,198,552	42,575,527	12,411,980	8,379,290		41,582	1,523,907	1,003,815
2007	65,511,169	51,906,925	57,445	51,964,370	6,001,852	-2,251,551	43,710,967	12,820,840	8,979,362		42,804	1,530,492	1,015,795
2008	67,746,295	53,552,943	44,252	53,597,195	6,194,609	-2,433,052	44,969,534	12,839,016	9,937,745		44,042	1,538,232	1,012,751
2009	66,924,919	52,304,197	31,413	52,335,610	5,987,101	-2,405,495	43,943,014	11,297,745	11,684,160		43,188	1,549,613	971,720
2010	67,720,376	52,406,333	42,579	52,448,912	6,097,772	-2,283,440	44,067,700	11,090,595	12,562,081		43,507	1,556,535	959,138
2011	71,050,979	54,459,354	63,898	54,523,252	5,710,274	-2,432,678	46,380,300	12,650,323	12,020,356		45,512	1,561,141	972,460
2012	74,154,635	56,081,408	62,294	56,143,702	5,843,401	-2,317,011	47,983,290	13,904,268	12,267,077		47,330	1,566,755	979,360
2013	73,982,660	57,092,110	74,407	57,166,517	6,749,271	-2,417,558	47,999,688	13,506,275	12,476,697		47,118	1,570,167	992,547
2014	76,470,112	58,807,375	78,864	58,886,239	6,958,622	-2,412,288	49,515,329	14,043,650	12,911,133		48,638	1,572,245	1,003,705

Personal Income and Employment by Area: Minneapolis-St. Paul-Bloomington, MN-WI

(Thousands of dollars, except as noted.)

Year	Personal income, total	Derivation of personal income								Per capita personal income (dollars)	Population (persons)	Total employment
		Earnings by place of work			Less: Contributions for government social insurance	Plus: Adjustment for residence	Equals: Net earnings by place of residence	Plus: Dividends, interest, and rent	Plus: Personal current transfer receipts			
		Nonfarm	Farm	Total								
1970	9,759,847	8,131,412	119,802	8,251,214	562,908	-54,944	7,633,362	1,385,157	741,328	4,682	2,084,574	1,001,143
1971	10,411,899	8,602,642	110,803	8,713,445	615,651	-53,021	8,044,773	1,498,740	868,386	4,948	2,104,296	997,890
1972	11,207,881	9,277,473	126,846	9,404,319	698,206	-55,481	8,650,632	1,598,665	958,584	5,317	2,107,895	1,038,036
1973	12,486,852	10,334,351	220,351	10,554,702	901,524	-62,315	9,590,863	1,760,848	1,135,141	5,874	2,125,921	1,097,783
1974	13,747,932	11,324,805	176,524	11,501,329	1,021,370	-65,931	10,414,028	2,019,417	1,314,487	6,409	2,145,063	1,123,468
1975	14,945,269	12,105,797	156,192	12,261,989	1,062,096	-71,440	11,128,453	2,216,651	1,600,165	6,937	2,154,275	1,115,829
1976	16,354,838	13,453,676	93,501	13,547,177	1,213,136	-82,183	12,251,858	2,352,957	1,750,023	7,544	2,167,976	1,147,906
1977	18,298,608	15,144,310	220,262	15,364,572	1,364,717	-101,146	13,898,709	2,601,021	1,798,878	8,396	2,179,319	1,198,787
1978	20,542,022	17,220,889	203,531	17,424,420	1,605,920	-117,565	15,700,935	2,914,760	1,926,327	9,337	2,200,167	1,259,054
1979	23,320,238	19,789,821	179,973	19,969,794	1,922,843	-141,410	17,905,541	3,277,594	2,137,103	10,482	2,224,748	1,330,627
1980	26,206,726	21,862,162	134,141	21,996,303	2,123,744	-156,288	19,716,271	3,955,066	2,535,389	11,576	2,263,881	1,360,454
1981	29,067,996	23,737,554	143,873	23,881,427	2,470,430	-182,861	21,228,136	4,927,089	2,912,771	12,683	2,291,962	1,357,542
1982	31,443,924	25,083,387	128,051	25,211,438	2,663,778	-188,979	22,358,681	5,840,185	3,245,058	13,570	2,317,206	1,336,848
1983	33,660,799	27,109,498	22,122	27,131,620	2,917,886	-205,854	24,007,880	6,164,334	3,488,585	14,435	2,331,850	1,356,281
1984	37,913,743	30,735,216	164,108	30,899,324	3,395,249	-244,743	27,259,332	7,008,927	3,645,484	16,099	2,354,976	1,445,106
1985	40,956,070	33,376,468	166,120	33,542,588	3,745,159	-274,910	29,522,519	7,512,747	3,920,804	17,130	2,390,959	1,497,630
1986	43,680,370	35,717,233	183,657	35,900,890	4,109,624	-292,238	31,499,028	8,051,849	4,129,493	17,989	2,428,147	1,533,116
1987	46,940,368	38,751,344	235,882	38,987,226	4,420,030	-316,026	34,251,170	8,398,551	4,290,647	19,013	2,468,889	1,602,851
1988	50,512,605	41,975,938	130,610	42,106,548	4,930,671	-346,288	36,829,589	9,084,706	4,598,310	20,016	2,523,553	1,654,072
1989	54,773,810	44,814,117	271,369	45,085,486	5,246,250	-343,781	39,495,455	10,267,917	5,010,438	21,376	2,562,410	1,689,977
1990	58,397,654	47,462,195	229,560	47,691,755	5,611,932	-333,777	41,746,046	11,215,158	5,436,450	22,408	2,606,156	1,721,797
1991	60,572,818	49,484,101	159,429	49,643,530	5,917,275	-356,133	43,370,122	11,300,345	5,902,351	22,889	2,646,336	1,728,757
1992	65,235,448	53,770,751	174,768	53,945,519	6,352,884	-411,976	47,180,659	11,620,473	6,434,316	24,263	2,688,729	1,756,753
1993	68,018,042	56,188,798	86,016	56,274,814	6,662,195	-445,511	49,167,108	12,019,353	6,831,581	24,876	2,734,239	1,794,801
1994	72,518,503	59,592,894	168,202	59,761,096	7,156,727	-507,663	52,096,706	13,231,050	7,190,747	26,117	2,776,675	1,853,150
1995	77,546,273	63,274,008	90,313	63,364,321	7,570,544	-567,100	55,226,677	14,672,191	7,647,405	27,506	2,819,211	1,911,772
1996	82,879,248	67,623,408	187,685	67,811,093	8,021,386	-645,863	59,143,844	15,709,937	8,025,467	28,964	2,861,505	1,951,582
1997	88,877,419	72,646,024	119,595	72,765,619	8,562,941	-727,006	63,475,672	17,248,716	8,153,031	30,615	2,903,107	1,989,738
1998	97,032,397	79,671,747	190,964	79,862,711	9,229,696	-827,836	69,805,179	18,770,355	8,456,863	32,931	2,946,520	2,045,926
1999	102,694,076	85,408,053	181,118	85,589,171	9,900,581	-986,311	74,702,279	19,097,294	8,894,503	34,292	2,994,735	2,093,413
2000	112,276,082	93,502,657	171,999	93,674,656	10,690,656	-1,164,475	81,819,525	20,860,516	9,596,041	36,879	3,044,425	2,149,236
2001	116,454,140	97,211,226	152,195	97,363,421	11,041,021	-1,276,444	85,045,956	20,655,732	10,752,452	37,728	3,086,645	2,160,424
2002	118,752,002	98,905,748	169,972	99,075,720	11,228,316	-1,188,220	86,659,184	20,362,695	11,730,123	38,108	3,116,197	2,150,566
2003	123,739,955	102,496,745	234,479	102,731,224	11,726,269	-1,171,702	89,833,253	21,647,396	12,259,306	39,365	3,143,413	2,157,226
2004	131,075,751	108,427,338	314,081	108,741,419	12,402,494	-1,252,821	95,086,104	23,125,650	12,863,997	41,324	3,171,902	2,191,025
2005	135,693,994	111,603,633	328,765	111,932,398	12,952,518	-1,327,395	97,652,485	24,490,724	13,550,785	42,417	3,199,046	2,234,659
2006	144,417,416	115,963,520	289,067	116,252,587	13,518,104	-996,414	101,738,069	27,743,937	14,935,410	44,651	3,234,367	2,269,356
2007	152,746,225	122,095,272	284,804	122,380,076	14,099,945	-1,422,843	106,857,288	29,407,992	16,480,945	46,717	3,269,613	2,302,066
2008	158,315,511	125,782,422	374,939	126,157,361	14,516,671	-1,706,355	109,934,335	29,434,111	18,947,065	47,956	3,301,252	2,295,430
2009	150,342,525	118,969,445	252,203	119,221,648	13,922,629	-1,299,011	104,000,008	25,648,146	20,694,371	45,141	3,330,508	2,222,857
2010	156,093,746	122,638,076	297,701	122,935,777	14,115,533	-1,320,441	107,499,803	26,102,748	22,491,195	46,524	3,355,105	2,207,744
2011	167,030,693	129,855,057	395,076	130,250,133	13,275,210	-1,472,717	115,502,206	28,852,881	22,675,606	49,284	3,389,149	2,260,339
2012	175,741,553	135,191,402	519,848	135,711,250	13,835,183	-1,514,848	120,361,219	32,593,901	22,786,433	51,340	3,423,070	2,287,819
2013	177,151,430	139,005,882	452,223	139,458,105	16,297,543	-1,532,744	121,627,818	31,883,377	23,640,235	51,179	3,461,434	2,328,724
2014	185,824,874	146,073,093	343,807	146,416,900	16,950,455	-1,584,546	127,881,899	33,106,501	24,836,474	53,166	3,495,176	2,369,366

Personal Income and Employment by Area: Missoula, MT

(Thousands of dollars, except as noted.)

Year	Personal income, total	Earnings by place of work			Less: Contributions for government social insurance	Plus: Adjustment for residence	Equals: Net earnings by place of residence	Plus: Dividends, interest, and rent	Plus: Personal current transfer receipts	Per capita personal income (dollars)	Population (persons)	Total employment
		Nonfarm	Farm	Total								
1970	209,108	174,404	696	175,100	13,535	-5,121	156,444	34,558	18,106	3,576	58,472	25,139
1971	233,819	194,508	977	195,485	15,269	-5,788	174,428	37,968	21,423	3,898	59,990	26,508
1972	263,378	222,052	1,412	223,464	18,329	-8,040	197,095	41,932	24,351	4,254	61,918	28,195
1973	290,283	243,927	2,012	245,939	23,012	-9,306	213,621	47,777	28,885	4,506	64,424	29,798
1974	329,079	272,632	1,830	274,462	26,113	-10,968	237,381	56,430	35,268	4,911	67,007	30,952
1975	367,586	295,743	1,130	296,873	26,809	-11,732	258,332	66,003	43,251	5,482	67,056	31,090
1976	421,418	347,664	1,104	348,768	32,426	-14,969	301,373	72,634	47,411	6,060	69,539	33,780
1977	491,707	416,264	176	416,440	39,930	-20,141	356,369	84,043	51,295	6,928	70,970	36,648
1978	573,088	491,640	1,716	493,356	48,972	-25,279	419,105	98,138	55,845	7,935	72,226	40,008
1979	639,238	545,956	1,559	547,515	56,986	-30,897	459,632	113,748	65,858	8,628	74,088	40,389
1980	693,336	573,984	1,393	575,377	61,324	-33,588	480,465	133,429	79,442	9,109	76,115	39,442
1981	734,958	576,824	435	577,259	65,004	-22,865	489,390	153,877	91,691	9,626	76,352	37,592
1982	768,655	586,582	309	586,891	67,402	-26,005	493,484	177,100	98,071	10,216	75,242	36,696
1983	826,004	645,804	1,154	646,958	75,130	-29,392	542,436	178,254	105,314	10,930	75,571	38,399
1984	906,571	710,831	155	710,986	84,485	-31,958	594,543	200,423	111,605	11,793	76,875	40,726
1985	951,648	743,731	-522	743,209	89,956	-32,171	621,082	210,110	120,456	12,236	77,774	41,567
1986	985,277	767,134	955	768,089	94,262	-31,599	642,228	212,703	130,346	12,640	77,949	41,942
1987	1,026,052	797,926	-243	797,683	97,936	-31,770	667,977	218,604	139,471	13,209	77,680	43,048
1988	1,086,601	845,041	-516	844,525	109,216	-33,760	701,549	235,224	149,828	14,009	77,564	44,555
1989	1,163,858	903,302	369	903,671	118,660	-36,901	748,110	248,636	167,112	14,922	77,995	45,814
1990	1,257,315	981,074	197	981,271	137,268	-40,358	803,645	268,437	185,233	15,899	79,080	47,616
1991	1,336,982	1,046,477	284	1,046,761	148,125	-43,353	855,283	286,815	194,884	16,486	81,098	49,299
1992	1,470,906	1,170,171	293	1,170,464	165,648	-50,994	953,822	305,549	211,535	17,605	83,549	51,852
1993	1,579,969	1,270,176	700	1,270,876	184,308	-56,107	1,030,461	325,623	223,885	18,320	86,243	54,021
1994	1,673,876	1,334,606	-1,778	1,332,828	191,728	-58,349	1,082,751	360,680	230,445	19,013	88,037	56,003
1995	1,791,197	1,402,962	-2,871	1,400,091	196,343	-64,103	1,139,645	401,894	249,658	19,811	90,413	58,094
1996	1,896,346	1,483,070	-4,343	1,478,727	198,807	-71,078	1,208,842	428,345	259,159	20,624	91,947	60,152
1997	2,003,809	1,554,851	-4,406	1,550,445	202,650	-75,237	1,272,558	468,004	263,247	21,511	93,151	61,250
1998	2,156,403	1,674,811	-2,575	1,672,236	210,452	-82,863	1,378,921	505,014	272,468	22,978	93,847	63,020
1999	2,249,192	1,788,019	-1,455	1,786,564	221,070	-92,328	1,473,166	509,220	266,806	23,728	94,791	64,702
2000	2,459,368	1,934,022	-1,751	1,932,271	238,346	-102,850	1,591,075	565,641	302,652	25,571	96,178	66,225
2001	2,607,752	2,083,834	632	2,084,466	258,771	-112,242	1,713,453	555,357	338,942	26,764	97,435	68,015
2002	2,751,511	2,224,271	3,101	2,227,372	278,568	-129,206	1,819,598	581,077	350,836	27,802	98,968	69,135
2003	2,884,549	2,329,244	143	2,329,387	291,333	-145,838	1,892,216	627,289	365,044	28,852	99,976	70,443
2004	3,014,602	2,418,442	774	2,419,216	302,374	-159,315	1,957,527	672,277	384,798	29,867	100,934	71,959
2005	3,165,981	2,541,724	434	2,542,158	323,389	-177,086	2,041,683	710,442	413,856	30,949	102,298	73,366
2006	3,443,652	2,699,129	-1,625	2,697,504	342,530	-194,992	2,159,982	834,702	448,968	32,994	104,372	75,178
2007	3,642,218	2,800,439	-798	2,799,641	365,354	-215,627	2,218,660	942,537	481,021	34,325	106,110	77,642
2008	3,817,396	2,836,949	-4,908	2,832,041	369,796	-231,027	2,231,218	1,019,261	566,917	35,429	107,747	76,642
2009	3,857,165	2,808,444	-2,707	2,805,737	368,101	-240,236	2,197,400	1,039,549	620,216	35,479	108,717	75,408
2010	3,690,677	2,809,931	-3,057	2,806,874	366,955	-229,217	2,210,702	791,204	688,771	33,728	109,425	73,885
2011	3,938,895	2,898,428	3,744	2,902,172	341,125	-257,938	2,303,109	954,959	680,827	35,769	110,121	75,063
2012	4,221,450	2,994,328	-5,125	2,989,203	345,722	-264,285	2,379,196	1,137,174	705,080	38,013	111,054	75,554
2013	4,155,239	3,026,653	-1,284	3,025,369	397,593	-263,652	2,364,124	1,069,454	721,661	37,177	111,769	76,639
2014	4,329,548	3,157,115	-2,813	3,154,302	416,273	-275,151	2,462,878	1,110,764	755,906	38,422	112,684	77,655

Personal Income and Employment by Area: Mobile, AL

(Thousands of dollars, except as noted.)

| Year | Personal income, total | Derivation of personal income | | | | | | | | Per capita personal income (dollars) | Population (persons) | Total employment |
| | | Earnings by place of work | | | Less: Contributions for government social insurance | Plus: Adjustment for residence | Equals: Net earnings by place of residence | Plus: Dividends, interest, and rent | Plus: Personal current transfer receipts | | | |
		Nonfarm	Farm	Total								
1970	948,701	778,189	6,544	784,733	58,018	-2,463	724,252	128,884	95,565	2,980	318,311	121,223
1971	1,025,486	826,721	7,528	834,249	62,798	-3,022	768,429	144,367	112,690	3,172	323,278	121,416
1972	1,133,908	915,921	8,338	924,259	72,892	-44	851,323	157,547	125,038	3,496	324,325	126,180
1973	1,270,750	1,037,554	11,743	1,049,297	94,645	-2,884	951,768	174,526	144,456	3,916	324,541	133,484
1974	1,452,125	1,180,020	13,415	1,193,435	110,620	-7,678	1,075,137	202,965	174,023	4,408	329,414	137,961
1975	1,663,165	1,329,978	12,485	1,342,463	123,488	-5,390	1,213,585	228,620	220,960	4,961	335,235	141,132
1976	1,884,747	1,531,406	12,637	1,544,043	145,117	-8,591	1,390,335	246,806	247,606	5,465	344,892	147,159
1977	2,098,142	1,716,518	12,734	1,729,252	163,405	-3,720	1,562,127	273,429	262,586	5,941	353,134	153,854
1978	2,365,070	1,966,015	17,104	1,983,119	189,710	-26,859	1,766,550	312,122	286,398	6,568	360,079	162,577
1979	2,607,497	2,148,573	9,494	2,158,067	214,248	-40,535	1,903,284	357,450	346,763	7,208	361,747	163,160
1980	2,970,557	2,426,000	17,588	2,443,588	240,300	-58,029	2,145,259	439,921	385,377	8,112	366,205	167,983
1981	3,291,749	2,644,618	22,705	2,667,323	283,050	-65,402	2,318,871	533,674	439,204	8,886	370,432	168,136
1982	3,448,944	2,670,745	29,045	2,699,790	292,608	-48,992	2,358,190	598,039	492,715	9,203	374,782	161,111
1983	3,582,811	2,766,074	31,713	2,797,787	305,498	-71,300	2,420,989	615,141	546,681	9,507	376,842	159,696
1984	3,849,676	2,976,799	20,464	2,997,263	334,641	-87,840	2,574,782	690,094	584,800	10,233	376,211	164,970
1985	4,156,256	3,239,663	23,788	3,263,451	365,351	-110,483	2,787,617	748,229	620,410	10,971	378,847	169,061
1986	4,344,717	3,380,469	23,981	3,404,450	379,534	-118,045	2,906,871	788,900	648,946	11,382	381,729	169,068
1987	4,508,031	3,525,176	25,781	3,550,957	390,640	-132,971	3,027,346	813,332	667,353	11,749	383,696	171,067
1988	4,775,200	3,745,430	33,858	3,779,288	429,412	-143,784	3,206,092	875,152	693,956	12,517	381,501	175,349
1989	5,189,416	3,993,092	36,765	4,029,857	457,732	-172,537	3,399,588	1,001,417	788,411	13,697	378,869	177,801
1990	5,515,161	4,263,230	36,842	4,300,072	496,100	-191,738	3,612,234	1,038,660	864,267	14,545	379,167	181,716
1991	5,895,198	4,643,303	43,056	4,686,359	543,554	-254,843	3,887,962	1,044,348	962,888	15,393	382,978	188,154
1992	6,339,017	4,986,815	33,632	5,020,447	577,620	-304,855	4,137,972	1,098,942	1,102,103	16,334	388,097	191,637
1993	6,622,090	5,258,291	26,390	5,284,681	612,971	-355,251	4,316,459	1,138,913	1,166,718	16,818	393,740	199,587
1994	6,929,168	5,523,911	18,733	5,542,644	652,875	-396,012	4,493,757	1,198,935	1,236,476	17,512	395,685	201,086
1995	7,250,228	5,659,151	19,287	5,678,438	674,471	-420,641	4,583,326	1,323,987	1,342,915	18,324	395,664	204,219
1996	7,538,445	5,955,035	19,882	5,974,917	706,197	-474,565	4,794,155	1,333,395	1,410,895	19,029	396,163	208,206
1997	7,882,407	6,284,739	25,674	6,310,413	745,208	-551,043	5,014,162	1,403,526	1,464,719	19,809	397,917	213,334
1998	8,509,942	6,783,764	20,700	6,804,464	782,922	-512,390	5,509,152	1,507,344	1,493,446	21,356	398,479	216,463
1999	8,594,211	6,894,373	24,415	6,918,788	796,357	-539,709	5,582,722	1,474,240	1,537,249	21,522	399,323	216,211
2000	8,918,556	7,065,244	24,531	7,089,775	810,338	-590,473	5,688,964	1,593,027	1,636,565	22,292	400,073	217,342
2001	9,139,594	7,268,961	20,773	7,289,734	831,102	-609,752	5,848,880	1,495,444	1,795,270	22,842	400,129	215,030
2002	9,247,393	7,344,364	20,241	7,364,605	845,698	-610,222	5,908,685	1,479,231	1,859,477	23,203	398,549	213,121
2003	9,488,724	7,430,240	28,525	7,458,765	855,921	-611,644	5,991,200	1,549,654	1,947,870	23,836	398,082	212,164
2004	10,013,657	7,785,653	35,361	7,821,014	886,965	-622,463	6,311,586	1,634,387	2,067,684	25,163	397,959	214,694
2005	10,703,000	8,345,523	25,272	8,370,795	963,178	-654,876	6,752,741	1,621,615	2,328,644	26,828	398,942	221,206
2006	11,636,427	9,133,421	38,121	9,171,542	1,043,470	-689,947	7,438,125	1,813,922	2,384,380	28,881	402,916	227,710
2007	12,107,724	9,430,157	28,310	9,458,467	1,097,729	-690,728	7,670,010	1,950,529	2,487,185	29,843	405,715	234,735
2008	12,830,488	9,784,635	22,900	9,807,535	1,147,394	-695,556	7,964,585	2,037,621	2,828,282	31,355	409,196	234,619
2009	12,688,922	9,716,969	26,475	9,743,444	1,134,689	-745,331	7,863,424	1,861,916	2,963,582	30,799	411,994	226,683
2010	13,206,877	9,966,571	21,620	9,988,191	1,180,246	-878,056	7,929,889	1,983,941	3,293,047	31,944	413,432	226,542
2011	13,711,782	10,431,644	21,645	10,453,289	1,101,371	-1,071,437	8,280,481	2,066,200	3,365,101	33,188	413,154	232,248
2012	13,771,023	10,482,378	23,512	10,505,890	1,101,057	-1,082,088	8,322,745	2,090,313	3,357,965	33,267	413,955	229,080
2013	13,964,602	10,547,428	38,814	10,586,242	1,258,546	-1,038,439	8,289,257	2,262,532	3,412,813	33,685	414,560	228,594
2014	14,542,254	10,993,217	36,264	11,029,481	1,294,132	-1,101,343	8,634,006	2,351,734	3,556,514	35,031	415,123	231,390

Personal Income and Employment by Area: Modesto, CA

(Thousands of dollars, except as noted.)

Year	Personal income, total	Derivation of personal income								Per capita personal income (dollars)	Population (persons)	Total employment
		Earnings by place of work			Less: Contributions for government social insurance	Plus: Adjustment for residence	Equals: Net earnings by place of residence	Plus: Dividends, interest, and rent	Plus: Personal current transfer receipts			
		Nonfarm	Farm	Total								
1970	790,022	504,942	62,878	567,820	36,064	30,124	561,880	114,455	113,687	4,039	195,578	83,872
1971	854,092	552,697	59,022	611,719	40,601	32,599	603,717	125,527	124,848	4,277	199,698	85,423
1972	963,328	625,455	78,807	704,262	48,303	34,681	690,640	139,086	133,602	4,777	201,644	90,511
1973	1,100,761	696,814	121,303	818,117	61,399	38,250	794,968	160,847	144,946	5,116	215,178	93,856
1974	1,253,219	786,199	136,115	922,314	71,069	43,311	894,556	185,560	173,103	5,633	222,484	98,381
1975	1,386,612	880,426	98,255	978,681	76,936	48,828	950,573	214,038	222,001	6,041	229,518	100,774
1976	1,553,422	1,004,429	91,410	1,095,839	88,944	55,194	1,062,089	236,300	255,033	6,574	236,293	104,388
1977	1,802,205	1,154,722	146,629	1,301,351	103,959	61,888	1,259,280	270,480	272,445	7,297	246,995	110,136
1978	2,020,520	1,322,489	136,991	1,459,480	121,270	70,082	1,408,292	316,990	295,238	8,171	247,280	116,129
1979	2,298,411	1,510,317	154,380	1,664,697	145,809	78,131	1,597,019	371,782	329,610	8,808	260,933	122,698
1980	2,589,026	1,640,870	157,655	1,798,525	155,616	87,397	1,730,306	464,152	394,568	9,666	267,852	123,136
1981	2,868,888	1,787,368	117,691	1,905,059	184,443	105,113	1,825,729	575,593	467,566	10,427	275,137	124,323
1982	3,085,248	1,888,219	120,912	2,009,131	197,822	123,750	1,935,059	632,215	517,974	10,990	280,737	124,463
1983	3,278,954	2,004,319	95,376	2,099,695	212,862	145,857	2,032,690	690,382	555,882	11,365	288,504	125,566
1984	3,662,983	2,232,015	136,281	2,368,296	245,015	183,210	2,306,491	765,770	590,722	12,464	293,879	128,705
1985	4,011,275	2,430,603	189,065	2,619,668	269,392	216,882	2,567,158	801,256	642,861	13,314	301,285	134,089
1986	4,333,669	2,652,460	188,103	2,840,563	296,545	249,192	2,793,210	843,513	696,946	13,928	311,154	137,844
1987	4,766,783	2,961,187	259,365	3,220,552	332,116	278,316	3,166,752	868,534	731,497	14,741	323,380	146,944
1988	5,197,707	3,261,763	256,249	3,518,012	376,049	321,094	3,463,057	939,584	795,066	15,466	336,063	156,458
1989	5,745,063	3,581,557	246,647	3,828,204	414,775	362,730	3,776,159	1,105,243	863,661	16,274	353,017	165,120
1990	6,268,942	3,917,741	288,259	4,206,000	451,539	405,527	4,159,988	1,143,859	965,095	16,703	375,312	171,839
1991	6,599,522	4,085,334	301,706	4,387,040	473,361	435,478	4,349,157	1,162,593	1,087,772	17,090	386,163	174,223
1992	6,960,495	4,307,798	292,584	4,600,382	496,414	456,191	4,560,159	1,136,687	1,263,649	17,634	394,725	173,045
1993	7,249,533	4,503,504	279,017	4,782,521	519,160	471,908	4,735,269	1,163,333	1,350,931	18,042	401,805	174,101
1994	7,432,037	4,640,047	252,861	4,892,908	532,335	505,834	4,866,407	1,202,897	1,362,733	18,293	406,274	174,328
1995	7,662,562	4,730,318	192,942	4,923,260	533,053	549,841	4,940,048	1,291,321	1,431,193	18,674	410,337	177,970
1996	8,193,247	4,961,567	332,517	5,294,084	541,016	585,823	5,338,891	1,355,028	1,499,328	19,735	415,159	183,775
1997	8,763,841	5,427,787	362,751	5,790,538	579,294	643,883	5,855,127	1,416,321	1,492,393	20,804	421,264	187,933
1998	9,534,739	6,002,923	385,908	6,388,831	624,483	691,452	6,455,800	1,504,474	1,574,465	22,238	428,754	198,159
1999	10,000,540	6,450,924	258,084	6,709,008	669,935	786,942	6,826,015	1,505,030	1,669,495	22,801	438,609	203,079
2000	10,912,444	7,122,284	217,476	7,339,760	723,888	950,878	7,566,750	1,575,234	1,770,460	24,278	449,471	205,738
2001	11,516,890	7,436,153	316,260	7,752,413	813,669	928,970	7,867,714	1,652,163	1,997,013	24,834	463,761	208,016
2002	12,244,552	7,997,672	321,892	8,319,564	884,886	959,587	8,394,265	1,669,677	2,180,610	25,645	477,469	212,596
2003	12,845,823	8,424,368	366,506	8,790,874	949,207	1,001,206	8,842,873	1,710,986	2,291,964	26,358	487,357	214,853
2004	13,792,927	8,935,856	645,488	9,581,344	1,043,809	1,056,531	9,594,066	1,820,551	2,378,310	28,000	492,613	217,091
2005	14,451,614	9,428,947	591,228	10,020,175	1,110,892	1,116,518	10,025,801	1,959,204	2,466,609	28,902	500,020	222,238
2006	14,975,003	9,671,529	571,259	10,242,788	1,104,266	1,155,441	10,293,963	2,049,980	2,631,060	29,674	504,651	222,590
2007	15,650,586	9,837,863	629,868	10,467,731	1,098,877	1,210,333	10,579,187	2,254,040	2,817,359	30,818	507,834	226,110
2008	15,740,550	9,696,474	448,741	10,145,215	1,101,291	1,229,368	10,273,292	2,252,617	3,214,641	30,923	509,032	221,586
2009	15,461,589	9,274,838	479,127	9,753,965	1,083,373	1,173,849	9,844,441	2,070,766	3,546,382	30,226	511,536	211,158
2010	16,035,859	9,397,534	515,795	9,913,329	1,077,023	1,182,149	10,018,455	2,114,563	3,902,841	31,120	515,283	209,191
2011	16,814,528	9,687,651	658,856	10,346,507	1,006,229	1,227,844	10,568,122	2,357,154	3,889,252	32,444	518,270	210,269
2012	17,767,475	10,162,304	727,011	10,889,315	1,040,450	1,369,189	11,218,054	2,589,213	3,960,208	34,029	522,134	216,241
2013	18,399,577	10,447,505	887,115	11,334,620	1,202,338	1,430,670	11,562,952	2,711,660	4,124,965	34,961	526,286	221,897
2014	19,341,120	10,904,077	1,042,934	11,947,011	1,258,247	1,534,597	12,223,361	2,845,303	4,272,456	36,356	531,997	227,971

Personal Income and Employment by Area: Monroe, LA

(Thousands of dollars, except as noted.)

Year	Personal income, total	Earnings by place of work			Less: Contributions for government social insurance	Plus: Adjustment for residence	Equals: Net earnings by place of residence	Plus: Dividends, interest, and rent	Plus: Personal current transfer receipts	Per capita personal income (dollars)	Population (persons)	Total employment
		Nonfarm	Farm	Total								
1970	366,885	287,904	5,537	293,441	18,552	-4,250	270,639	50,302	45,944	2,737	134,052	49,954
1971	414,470	325,210	7,137	332,347	21,650	-4,075	306,622	55,836	52,012	3,035	136,572	52,109
1972	461,699	365,348	6,923	372,271	25,623	-3,432	343,216	61,128	57,355	3,289	140,389	54,220
1973	516,539	410,200	9,969	420,169	33,180	-3,239	383,750	67,124	65,665	3,627	142,397	58,132
1974	575,985	451,874	4,903	456,777	37,586	-1,338	417,853	80,157	77,975	3,983	144,601	58,242
1975	650,258	495,244	6,719	501,963	40,178	-158	461,627	90,266	98,365	4,377	148,558	57,979
1976	758,552	593,609	10,866	604,475	49,545	-1,042	553,888	97,347	107,317	4,970	152,634	61,479
1977	845,914	664,034	13,048	677,082	54,637	3,141	625,586	108,034	112,294	5,477	154,446	63,178
1978	985,191	782,976	11,131	794,107	66,187	6,966	734,886	126,908	123,397	6,332	155,598	66,282
1979	1,097,677	857,410	14,055	871,465	74,866	13,893	810,492	146,590	140,595	6,963	157,646	66,963
1980	1,221,938	919,124	5,210	924,334	79,986	23,439	867,787	183,025	171,126	7,597	160,840	67,917
1981	1,368,803	1,016,267	7,587	1,023,854	93,632	19,890	950,112	228,191	190,500	8,435	162,278	68,401
1982	1,462,206	1,052,337	7,714	1,060,051	98,181	17,143	979,013	264,723	218,470	8,980	162,833	68,211
1983	1,578,412	1,136,580	7,129	1,143,709	105,205	14,483	1,052,987	285,122	240,303	9,586	164,650	69,765
1984	1,707,816	1,231,326	16,330	1,247,656	116,967	9,823	1,140,512	316,818	250,486	10,290	165,968	71,694
1985	1,820,150	1,312,551	10,285	1,322,836	126,095	3,648	1,200,389	349,224	270,537	10,906	166,887	73,963
1986	1,905,365	1,367,350	17,834	1,385,184	130,745	-1,927	1,252,512	359,825	293,028	11,274	169,012	73,356
1987	1,924,890	1,394,304	20,690	1,414,994	131,335	-3,917	1,279,742	345,755	299,393	11,491	167,513	73,825
1988	2,025,367	1,474,394	23,833	1,498,227	144,227	-6,808	1,347,192	359,764	318,411	12,213	165,842	73,947
1989	2,178,169	1,560,902	27,526	1,588,428	154,608	-8,678	1,425,142	406,038	346,989	13,273	164,107	74,432
1990	2,316,882	1,680,323	21,941	1,702,264	169,682	-10,134	1,522,448	411,749	382,685	14,219	162,944	75,648
1991	2,441,451	1,760,070	24,938	1,785,008	182,438	-11,007	1,591,563	415,680	434,208	14,876	164,119	76,682
1992	2,640,881	1,903,224	34,992	1,938,216	194,168	-13,960	1,730,088	418,195	492,598	15,882	166,280	78,203
1993	2,788,340	1,987,731	45,266	2,032,997	204,446	-17,180	1,811,371	435,409	541,560	16,665	167,314	81,017
1994	2,968,893	2,100,844	52,565	2,153,409	220,475	-23,099	1,909,835	460,478	598,580	17,691	167,822	81,542
1995	3,152,665	2,249,007	47,290	2,296,297	236,940	-32,025	2,027,332	523,257	602,076	18,676	168,806	84,945
1996	3,319,390	2,343,014	60,329	2,403,343	247,955	-38,176	2,117,212	537,184	664,994	19,610	169,266	86,982
1997	3,338,442	2,401,784	42,549	2,444,333	253,919	-40,663	2,149,751	556,611	632,080	19,646	169,934	87,893
1998	3,495,591	2,499,235	32,148	2,531,383	266,676	-43,391	2,221,316	627,013	647,262	20,544	170,152	90,049
1999	3,639,236	2,669,061	30,359	2,699,420	281,959	-56,833	2,360,628	625,409	653,199	21,416	169,927	92,350
2000	3,903,096	2,888,705	28,356	2,917,061	295,452	-62,662	2,558,947	662,190	681,959	22,955	170,033	95,053
2001	4,104,285	3,008,103	40,596	3,048,699	307,089	-74,078	2,667,532	647,062	789,691	24,204	169,572	96,225
2002	4,247,060	3,147,662	27,643	3,175,305	323,167	-75,691	2,776,447	633,018	837,595	24,931	170,352	97,970
2003	4,335,163	3,221,376	36,961	3,258,337	324,126	-79,605	2,854,606	639,657	840,900	25,307	171,306	97,121
2004	4,543,128	3,335,950	62,657	3,398,607	330,141	-76,011	2,992,455	614,048	936,625	26,418	171,969	97,301
2005	4,805,623	3,490,871	55,403	3,546,274	339,014	-84,365	3,122,895	674,361	1,008,367	27,901	172,241	96,075
2006	5,185,644	3,693,095	36,052	3,729,147	358,301	-86,094	3,284,752	814,235	1,086,657	29,785	174,102	98,461
2007	5,397,609	3,835,515	31,095	3,866,610	369,829	-84,391	3,412,390	839,649	1,145,570	31,034	173,927	99,119
2008	5,707,800	3,921,474	21,425	3,942,899	375,995	-80,291	3,486,613	930,104	1,291,083	32,724	174,425	98,717
2009	5,730,788	3,914,192	28,752	3,942,944	381,919	-100,863	3,460,162	905,265	1,365,361	32,623	175,667	97,502
2010	5,784,361	4,005,425	30,187	4,035,612	388,142	-109,627	3,537,843	808,137	1,438,381	32,720	176,785	97,087
2011	6,018,907	4,051,860	20,904	4,072,764	350,204	-105,989	3,616,571	930,233	1,472,103	33,930	177,390	99,061
2012	6,236,857	4,220,279	35,497	4,255,776	363,519	-123,315	3,768,942	967,526	1,500,389	35,061	177,885	99,888
2013	6,371,223	4,315,764	54,024	4,369,788	428,237	-110,633	3,830,918	1,001,859	1,538,446	35,670	178,618	101,265
2014	6,515,194	4,445,091	49,664	4,494,755	439,772	-101,422	3,953,561	1,035,341	1,526,292	36,425	178,864	101,805

Personal Income and Employment by Area: Monroe, MI

(Thousands of dollars, except as noted.)

| Year | Personal income, total | Derivation of personal income | | | | | | | | Per capita personal income (dollars) | Population (persons) | Total employment |
| | | Earnings by place of work | | | Less: Contributions for government social insurance | Plus: Adjustment for residence | Equals: Net earnings by place of residence | Plus: Dividends, interest, and rent | Plus: Personal current transfer receipts | | | |
		Nonfarm	Farm	Total								
1970	446,061	210,646	9,339	219,985	14,721	157,348	362,612	51,961	31,488	3,728	119,640	28,386
1971	488,772	234,197	7,299	241,496	16,779	169,362	394,079	56,949	37,744	4,020	121,589	29,043
1972	558,706	274,590	12,706	287,296	20,988	187,294	453,602	63,370	41,734	4,527	123,422	30,768
1973	634,896	316,846	13,417	330,263	28,072	213,311	515,502	71,388	48,006	5,108	124,301	32,201
1974	678,434	331,571	8,861	340,432	30,754	225,302	534,980	81,184	62,270	5,432	124,906	32,581
1975	729,345	340,318	16,178	356,496	30,582	225,946	551,860	89,008	88,477	5,775	126,297	31,334
1976	825,674	388,838	9,801	398,639	35,212	276,011	639,438	95,271	90,965	6,494	127,148	32,540
1977	940,933	450,179	12,484	462,663	40,796	319,993	741,860	107,034	92,039	7,238	129,995	33,950
1978	1,053,792	502,590	10,288	512,878	46,921	370,489	836,446	117,454	99,892	7,956	132,450	34,920
1979	1,169,412	534,120	16,792	550,912	51,719	417,408	916,601	134,018	118,793	8,708	134,285	34,884
1980	1,270,396	545,933	20,439	566,372	52,494	426,808	940,686	160,707	169,003	9,429	134,732	33,246
1981	1,374,503	639,837	13,626	653,463	68,849	414,236	998,850	197,250	178,403	10,202	134,729	34,698
1982	1,434,989	685,646	6,945	692,591	75,038	389,001	1,006,554	223,033	205,402	10,844	132,334	34,361
1983	1,537,962	755,749	3,366	759,115	82,542	406,775	1,083,348	240,923	213,691	11,750	130,888	35,020
1984	1,649,679	708,263	18,996	727,259	78,043	511,438	1,160,654	275,694	213,331	12,607	130,851	33,976
1985	1,747,773	729,343	15,385	744,728	81,723	577,118	1,240,123	290,907	216,743	13,405	130,386	35,020
1986	1,912,072	883,545	13,375	896,920	99,617	575,361	1,372,664	311,151	228,257	14,579	131,150	37,893
1987	1,984,822	941,567	13,857	955,424	105,040	580,228	1,430,612	318,810	235,400	15,053	131,852	39,715
1988	2,146,061	1,055,273	14,276	1,069,549	121,541	619,319	1,567,327	334,181	244,553	16,253	132,040	40,868
1989	2,272,017	1,149,507	16,162	1,165,669	134,626	624,232	1,655,275	350,513	266,229	17,121	132,700	43,343
1990	2,343,180	1,209,969	17,769	1,227,738	143,891	594,194	1,678,041	371,511	293,628	17,501	133,892	45,406
1991	2,387,202	1,246,537	8,131	1,254,668	150,623	582,309	1,686,354	366,656	334,192	17,727	134,664	46,113
1992	2,585,615	1,360,945	12,379	1,373,324	162,837	645,901	1,856,388	376,766	352,461	19,113	135,277	46,355
1993	2,752,643	1,419,508	11,056	1,430,564	171,030	723,757	1,983,291	393,250	376,102	20,296	135,623	46,938
1994	3,068,038	1,542,697	12,100	1,554,797	187,904	839,848	2,206,741	474,589	386,708	22,430	136,783	48,731
1995	3,228,487	1,620,968	17,231	1,638,199	196,616	882,848	2,324,431	503,081	400,975	23,288	138,631	50,033
1996	3,380,977	1,681,684	14,046	1,695,730	199,212	933,757	2,430,275	533,634	417,068	24,129	140,123	50,605
1997	3,578,946	1,787,181	19,730	1,806,911	210,011	978,668	2,575,568	555,893	447,485	25,253	141,725	52,094
1998	3,809,205	1,910,526	20,821	1,931,347	221,262	1,071,119	2,781,204	580,398	447,603	26,636	143,009	53,704
1999	4,090,444	2,096,444	21,801	2,118,245	243,178	1,166,395	3,041,462	569,207	479,775	28,303	144,525	56,262
2000	4,311,514	2,203,728	20,343	2,224,071	253,575	1,209,650	3,180,146	620,546	510,822	29,457	146,364	58,548
2001	4,358,097	2,209,851	14,945	2,224,796	258,013	1,233,509	3,200,292	588,580	569,225	29,525	147,605	58,335
2002	4,529,710	2,340,989	18,784	2,359,773	273,184	1,285,843	3,372,432	570,880	586,398	30,491	148,561	59,062
2003	4,681,967	2,416,081	18,538	2,434,619	279,190	1,314,233	3,469,662	594,038	618,267	31,266	149,747	59,041
2004	4,767,288	2,467,688	23,411	2,491,099	286,929	1,342,434	3,546,604	575,212	645,472	31,547	151,117	59,079
2005	4,881,813	2,500,809	21,110	2,521,919	293,289	1,360,073	3,588,703	597,109	696,001	32,038	152,374	59,391
2006	5,112,861	2,613,519	26,806	2,640,325	310,642	1,437,222	3,766,905	588,053	757,903	33,317	153,460	59,920
2007	5,208,558	2,565,267	26,273	2,591,540	308,588	1,448,285	3,731,237	650,715	826,606	33,949	153,424	59,505
2008	5,296,675	2,483,471	20,785	2,504,256	302,986	1,423,553	3,624,823	701,450	970,402	34,663	152,806	58,217
2009	5,012,789	2,278,464	25,652	2,304,116	280,547	1,291,035	3,314,604	615,219	1,082,966	32,915	152,296	54,281
2010	5,127,490	2,310,933	29,071	2,340,004	283,002	1,317,946	3,374,948	602,970	1,149,572	33,753	151,911	53,181
2011	5,422,631	2,366,853	53,205	2,420,058	258,786	1,462,419	3,623,691	648,774	1,150,166	35,793	151,499	54,095
2012	5,554,239	2,486,005	27,631	2,513,636	274,355	1,494,213	3,733,494	676,830	1,143,915	36,822	150,840	55,187
2013	5,672,801	2,600,792	55,347	2,656,139	324,592	1,458,899	3,790,446	699,223	1,183,132	37,774	150,179	57,073
2014	5,885,705	2,724,671	34,824	2,759,495	339,352	1,497,291	3,917,434	726,717	1,241,554	39,284	149,824	58,518

Personal Income and Employment by Area: Montgomery, AL

(Thousands of dollars, except as noted.)

Year	Personal income, total	Derivation of personal income									Per capita personal income (dollars)	Population (persons)	Total employment
		Earnings by place of work			Less: Contributions for government social insurance	Plus: Adjustment for residence	Equals: Net earnings by place of residence	Plus: Dividends, interest, and rent	Plus: Personal current transfer receipts				
		Nonfarm	Farm	Total									
1970	819,374	650,128	20,376	670,504	45,296	-3,075	622,133	125,963	71,278	3,425	239,239	109,720
1971	929,647	736,486	23,155	759,641	52,137	-3,913	703,591	143,065	82,991	3,834	242,500	112,842
1972	1,078,193	856,535	32,191	888,726	63,004	-5,009	820,713	164,433	93,047	4,273	252,309	119,422
1973	1,218,038	964,908	42,950	1,007,858	80,874	-7,015	919,969	187,738	110,331	4,720	258,064	124,450
1974	1,351,914	1,074,789	25,326	1,100,115	93,246	-10,088	996,781	219,157	135,976	5,123	263,893	126,242
1975	1,462,166	1,139,727	21,515	1,161,242	100,315	-11,613	1,049,314	238,833	174,019	5,497	265,984	124,938
1976	1,635,763	1,274,217	42,584	1,316,801	114,952	-15,650	1,186,199	255,954	193,610	6,055	270,156	127,870
1977	1,780,114	1,416,650	19,548	1,436,198	128,178	-21,262	1,286,758	284,407	208,949	6,524	272,860	132,672
1978	2,025,691	1,609,999	33,859	1,643,858	147,474	-29,961	1,466,423	327,777	231,491	7,319	276,789	139,055
1979	2,253,602	1,789,695	40,331	1,830,026	171,143	-41,086	1,617,797	365,644	270,161	7,996	281,831	142,495
1980	2,489,266	1,950,365	18,150	1,968,515	187,794	-43,874	1,736,847	435,418	317,001	8,688	286,531	142,176
1981	2,739,136	2,077,109	17,490	2,094,599	214,726	-29,591	1,850,282	531,379	357,475	9,498	288,378	139,589
1982	2,922,923	2,166,763	27,443	2,194,206	227,135	-31,487	1,935,584	588,576	398,763	10,104	289,284	137,511
1983	3,193,608	2,404,410	19,706	2,424,116	255,205	-42,479	2,126,432	639,227	427,949	11,022	289,744	141,881
1984	3,511,103	2,663,247	21,969	2,685,216	286,771	-51,993	2,346,452	711,270	453,381	12,008	292,394	147,345
1985	3,799,403	2,901,295	29,648	2,930,943	314,478	-62,840	2,553,625	769,104	476,674	12,905	294,421	150,916
1986	4,058,525	3,138,014	23,556	3,161,570	339,756	-71,977	2,749,837	811,938	496,750	13,623	297,919	156,125
1987	4,346,634	3,368,765	43,316	3,412,081	359,967	-83,888	2,968,226	869,386	509,022	14,423	301,371	160,694
1988	4,676,690	3,614,603	53,144	3,667,747	403,539	-95,328	3,168,880	968,838	538,972	15,448	302,729	166,464
1989	5,087,301	3,812,274	49,481	3,861,755	426,324	-104,234	3,331,197	1,143,159	612,945	16,680	305,003	169,489
1990	5,339,060	4,007,366	50,701	4,058,067	455,458	-111,759	3,490,850	1,162,097	686,113	17,446	306,042	170,900
1991	5,618,028	4,211,255	63,503	4,274,758	481,979	-117,070	3,675,709	1,185,891	756,428	18,057	311,129	171,043
1992	6,056,609	4,529,294	43,101	4,572,395	513,121	-126,707	3,932,567	1,264,944	859,098	19,107	316,981	175,249
1993	6,342,311	4,766,714	29,227	4,795,941	541,797	-134,991	4,119,153	1,300,778	922,380	19,653	322,707	179,984
1994	6,765,219	5,099,527	29,287	5,128,814	583,258	-144,590	4,400,966	1,392,678	971,575	20,647	327,654	183,466
1995	7,164,405	5,311,434	13,297	5,324,731	609,465	-153,338	4,561,928	1,546,602	1,055,875	21,603	331,647	189,986
1996	7,486,077	5,564,306	23,807	5,588,113	634,898	-165,623	4,787,592	1,584,823	1,113,662	22,346	335,014	194,046
1997	7,908,123	5,827,364	38,983	5,866,347	667,339	-179,955	5,019,053	1,721,640	1,167,430	23,334	338,906	197,762
1998	8,413,538	6,286,985	34,682	6,321,667	703,226	-197,755	5,420,686	1,798,940	1,193,912	24,592	342,120	201,475
1999	8,807,039	6,689,493	50,162	6,739,655	741,311	-217,493	5,780,851	1,780,874	1,245,314	25,562	344,540	205,499
2000	9,321,004	7,024,220	42,542	7,066,762	770,616	-231,153	6,064,993	1,934,075	1,321,936	26,855	347,080	207,081
2001	9,765,997	7,452,576	53,726	7,506,302	814,525	-261,789	6,429,988	1,937,959	1,398,050	28,005	348,725	208,177
2002	10,182,343	7,862,105	34,756	7,896,861	858,776	-339,075	6,699,010	1,953,939	1,529,394	29,011	350,984	208,967
2003	10,708,356	8,238,543	61,609	8,300,152	897,978	-355,223	7,046,951	2,022,175	1,639,230	30,386	352,411	209,881
2004	11,388,323	8,672,134	103,179	8,775,313	935,517	-390,962	7,448,834	2,217,006	1,722,483	32,079	355,009	214,503
2005	11,868,534	9,096,852	107,040	9,203,892	985,882	-452,494	7,765,516	2,250,826	1,852,192	33,091	358,659	220,590
2006	12,625,528	9,688,868	95,409	9,784,277	1,048,660	-485,139	8,250,478	2,367,698	2,007,352	34,497	365,989	226,642
2007	13,048,421	9,862,628	60,125	9,922,753	1,086,497	-436,878	8,399,378	2,478,384	2,170,659	35,324	369,390	233,290
2008	13,478,321	9,977,877	53,223	10,031,100	1,122,785	-453,854	8,454,461	2,598,117	2,425,743	36,403	370,249	230,985
2009	13,221,830	9,842,482	64,878	9,907,360	1,111,146	-449,518	8,346,696	2,276,594	2,598,540	35,556	371,860	223,388
2010	13,562,244	9,918,384	63,526	9,981,910	1,133,836	-441,255	8,406,819	2,281,184	2,874,241	36,146	375,208	219,713
2011	14,114,961	10,107,922	53,058	10,160,980	1,028,729	-456,181	8,676,070	2,473,423	2,965,468	37,345	377,960	220,408
2012	14,169,361	10,074,612	76,854	10,151,466	1,028,315	-445,762	8,677,389	2,547,957	2,944,015	37,697	375,874	217,958
2013	14,148,450	10,047,927	136,635	10,184,562	1,173,706	-446,017	8,564,839	2,567,637	3,015,974	37,836	373,945	218,655
2014	14,632,563	10,373,058	125,363	10,498,421	1,194,432	-456,157	8,847,832	2,657,609	3,127,122	39,215	373,141	220,003

Personal Income and Employment by Area: Morgantown, WV

(Thousands of dollars, except as noted.)

Year	Personal income, total	Earnings by place of work			Less: Contributions for government social insurance	Plus: Adjustment for residence	Equals: Net earnings by place of residence	Plus: Dividends, interest, and rent	Plus: Personal current transfer receipts	Per capita personal income (dollars)	Population (persons)	Total employment
		Nonfarm	Farm	Total								
1970	264,642	213,890	847	214,737	14,864	4,498	204,371	31,936	28,335	2,966	89,219	34,394
1971	294,692	237,404	952	238,356	17,315	3,268	224,309	35,408	34,975	3,250	90,684	35,273
1972	338,235	278,067	870	278,937	21,296	-417	257,224	39,745	41,266	3,596	94,067	37,872
1973	360,660	294,157	1,016	295,173	25,961	-3,500	265,712	44,665	50,283	3,754	96,069	38,107
1974	399,583	327,230	47	327,277	29,918	-7,287	290,072	52,328	57,183	4,065	98,296	38,804
1975	453,700	372,144	-100	372,044	33,555	-11,287	327,202	58,594	67,904	4,639	97,808	40,252
1976	505,050	421,134	-102	421,032	38,650	-18,308	364,074	65,462	75,514	5,072	99,573	42,073
1977	567,201	474,034	-184	473,850	42,227	-20,069	411,554	74,817	80,830	5,585	101,553	43,083
1978	636,300	534,673	905	535,578	48,968	-27,654	458,956	85,613	91,731	6,170	103,131	44,710
1979	687,189	571,940	312	572,252	55,473	-32,995	483,784	96,627	106,778	6,586	104,338	43,728
1980	765,324	625,303	32	625,335	63,757	-41,531	520,047	122,174	123,103	7,232	105,829	43,877
1981	860,400	680,506	-2,339	678,167	73,808	-38,178	566,181	152,534	141,685	8,032	107,115	43,092
1982	940,433	755,345	-2,007	753,338	85,550	-49,401	618,387	172,674	149,372	8,761	107,348	43,856
1983	1,004,701	787,241	-461	786,780	90,595	-51,664	644,521	193,556	166,624	9,308	107,934	44,249
1984	1,084,065	855,150	1,748	856,898	100,426	-54,673	701,799	208,964	173,302	10,016	108,233	45,127
1985	1,139,851	900,471	1,867	902,338	107,846	-58,880	735,612	221,323	182,916	10,674	106,785	46,436
1986	1,179,572	928,016	2,476	930,492	117,075	-66,122	747,295	235,061	197,216	11,112	106,152	47,850
1987	1,233,811	986,175	-576	985,599	125,455	-71,516	788,628	240,917	204,266	11,660	105,816	49,184
1988	1,374,355	1,098,308	-372	1,097,936	140,715	-64,197	893,024	260,572	220,759	13,034	105,441	50,388
1989	1,445,820	1,131,300	1,329	1,132,629	148,822	-56,763	927,044	281,565	237,211	13,771	104,993	51,305
1990	1,556,083	1,222,688	178	1,222,866	162,962	-58,223	1,001,681	299,490	254,912	14,863	104,696	53,460
1991	1,647,556	1,288,873	-1,523	1,287,350	175,059	-59,829	1,052,462	304,341	290,753	15,509	106,229	54,423
1992	1,804,783	1,386,193	638	1,386,831	191,375	-69,704	1,125,752	332,457	346,574	16,794	107,468	56,208
1993	1,858,021	1,423,596	814	1,424,410	202,956	-72,098	1,149,356	339,259	369,406	17,112	108,582	56,446
1994	1,952,878	1,524,878	1,007	1,525,885	217,818	-80,450	1,227,617	352,612	372,649	17,835	109,494	58,961
1995	2,011,623	1,535,265	-1,598	1,533,667	223,573	-76,413	1,233,681	392,352	385,590	18,247	110,247	59,587
1996	2,085,190	1,556,724	48	1,556,772	224,494	-73,723	1,258,555	415,599	411,036	18,861	110,553	59,610
1997	2,140,271	1,569,891	-2,136	1,567,755	223,571	-63,711	1,280,473	435,684	424,114	19,320	110,781	59,184
1998	2,225,801	1,648,243	-2,359	1,645,884	238,981	-78,898	1,328,005	463,274	434,522	20,067	110,918	59,848
1999	2,313,773	1,753,085	-3,453	1,749,632	253,014	-88,838	1,407,780	462,930	443,063	20,866	110,888	60,779
2000	2,502,261	1,938,472	-603	1,937,869	285,778	-107,190	1,544,901	488,206	469,154	22,474	111,338	62,289
2001	2,741,804	2,123,332	-1,144	2,122,188	291,847	-97,640	1,732,701	493,481	515,622	24,315	112,764	63,294
2002	2,895,468	2,234,505	-4,372	2,230,133	289,256	-112,834	1,828,043	489,555	577,870	25,323	114,343	64,154
2003	2,984,937	2,346,788	-6,888	2,339,900	313,484	-137,289	1,889,127	479,817	615,993	25,629	116,466	64,627
2004	3,104,597	2,495,235	-4,111	2,491,124	324,366	-150,851	2,015,907	491,183	597,507	26,296	118,062	66,827
2005	3,301,942	2,669,767	-4,855	2,664,912	343,578	-155,424	2,165,910	532,564	603,468	27,531	119,937	68,698
2006	3,603,717	2,876,898	-5,251	2,871,647	353,114	-165,590	2,352,943	601,996	648,778	29,564	121,894	69,900
2007	3,766,690	2,988,002	-6,654	2,981,348	352,926	-185,142	2,443,280	637,748	685,662	30,498	123,507	73,054
2008	4,098,100	3,275,483	-6,343	3,269,140	367,605	-211,538	2,689,997	647,990	760,113	32,715	125,267	75,300
2009	4,195,684	3,425,130	-7,756	3,417,374	392,108	-263,400	2,761,866	618,063	815,755	32,908	127,498	76,008
2010	4,475,626	3,656,969	-9,182	3,647,787	424,701	-282,439	2,940,647	638,164	896,815	34,341	130,328	77,443
2011	4,834,344	3,806,068	-5,646	3,800,422	384,821	-212,395	3,203,206	721,525	909,613	36,537	132,314	77,943
2012	5,044,026	3,972,611	-7,279	3,965,332	397,162	-217,093	3,351,077	772,735	920,214	37,519	134,441	80,095
2013	5,090,183	4,065,295	-5,504	4,059,791	459,438	-233,887	3,366,466	782,497	941,220	37,448	135,925	81,336
2014	5,282,314	4,227,868	-6,558	4,221,310	485,725	-259,841	3,475,744	806,682	999,888	38,487	137,251	82,394

Personal Income and Employment by Area: Morristown, TN

(Thousands of dollars, except as noted.)

Year	Personal income, total	Earnings by place of work			Less: Contributions for government social insurance	Plus: Adjustment for residence	Equals: Net earnings by place of residence	Plus: Dividends, interest, and rent	Plus: Personal current transfer receipts	Per capita personal income (dollars)	Population (persons)	Total employment
		Nonfarm	Farm	Total								
1970	179,260	173,605	5,207	178,812	11,370	-25,117	142,325	19,230	17,705	2,798	64,065	33,308
1971	204,359	200,743	4,924	205,667	13,742	-29,457	162,468	21,984	19,907	3,072	66,514	34,956
1972	238,047	234,509	7,545	242,054	16,982	-34,438	190,634	24,986	22,427	3,465	68,704	38,430
1973	270,911	262,012	10,577	272,589	21,721	-36,367	214,501	28,606	27,804	3,843	70,499	39,656
1974	293,681	280,735	7,171	287,906	24,229	-37,794	225,883	33,372	34,426	4,049	72,527	38,744
1975	310,062	276,882	3,538	280,420	23,614	-33,926	222,880	36,978	50,204	4,252	72,914	34,813
1976	350,495	317,935	8,141	326,076	27,710	-38,374	259,992	39,983	50,520	4,699	74,589	37,232
1977	391,297	365,372	4,401	369,773	32,177	-45,369	292,227	45,283	53,787	5,098	76,762	39,929
1978	448,740	420,607	5,354	425,961	37,669	-50,537	337,755	52,591	58,394	5,693	78,827	42,110
1979	500,873	462,146	4,013	466,159	42,794	-51,793	371,572	60,377	68,924	6,293	79,591	42,332
1980	546,804	472,907	2,456	475,363	43,459	-47,926	383,978	76,624	86,202	6,760	80,893	40,018
1981	603,168	500,855	5,204	506,059	49,754	-45,215	411,090	95,246	96,832	7,358	81,970	38,986
1982	644,907	524,018	3,537	527,555	52,848	-49,809	424,898	112,120	107,889	7,725	83,487	38,391
1983	699,448	577,173	-2,351	574,822	58,734	-55,473	460,615	121,808	117,025	8,083	86,535	39,955
1984	780,259	650,698	2,817	653,515	68,632	-62,961	521,922	135,617	122,720	9,038	86,327	41,739
1985	818,403	669,448	4,029	673,477	71,304	-58,462	543,711	144,318	130,374	9,796	83,544	41,597
1986	869,332	709,257	2,150	711,407	77,163	-57,074	577,170	150,332	141,830	10,453	83,162	42,533
1987	937,832	771,320	2,867	774,187	83,417	-59,062	631,708	156,336	149,788	11,364	82,524	43,935
1988	1,030,884	847,262	2,661	849,923	94,372	-59,226	696,325	171,949	162,610	12,390	83,204	45,919
1989	1,142,919	940,076	4,338	944,414	105,373	-72,218	766,823	198,392	177,704	13,758	83,074	48,607
1990	1,237,757	1,017,512	5,154	1,022,666	114,538	-67,961	840,167	198,826	198,764	14,772	83,791	50,379
1991	1,296,511	1,049,832	5,660	1,055,492	119,909	-75,619	859,964	200,704	235,843	15,294	84,770	49,816
1992	1,429,510	1,157,268	7,254	1,164,522	130,645	-76,885	956,992	200,485	272,033	16,557	86,338	51,670
1993	1,524,841	1,237,072	6,078	1,243,150	141,173	-80,491	1,021,486	210,187	293,168	17,231	88,492	53,277
1994	1,592,952	1,279,905	5,285	1,285,190	149,202	-72,649	1,063,339	224,375	305,238	17,659	90,206	53,805
1995	1,709,926	1,348,845	1,844	1,350,689	157,114	-62,732	1,130,843	249,886	329,197	18,449	92,682	54,986
1996	1,805,994	1,415,386	-2,300	1,413,086	163,214	-62,793	1,187,079	268,893	350,022	18,974	95,181	55,998
1997	1,958,107	1,519,867	2,026	1,521,893	172,478	-50,612	1,298,803	287,093	372,211	20,062	97,602	56,824
1998	2,143,846	1,666,931	4,145	1,671,076	182,928	-36,637	1,451,511	304,088	388,247	21,546	99,503	58,046
1999	2,237,720	1,779,791	3,892	1,783,683	195,029	-68,837	1,519,817	310,673	407,230	22,069	101,395	60,046
2000	2,341,055	1,847,839	8,022	1,855,861	203,920	-92,094	1,559,847	331,773	449,435	22,774	102,796	61,511
2001	2,467,438	1,898,769	9,093	1,907,862	207,943	-72,147	1,627,772	344,035	495,631	23,766	103,821	59,048
2002	2,465,791	1,892,423	6,216	1,898,639	211,749	-89,022	1,597,868	326,215	541,708	23,728	103,919	58,100
2003	2,580,104	1,983,188	7,295	1,990,483	222,692	-84,420	1,683,371	330,737	565,996	24,505	105,291	59,026
2004	2,698,678	2,115,961	7,921	2,123,882	236,533	-86,184	1,801,165	305,838	591,675	25,384	106,314	60,483
2005	2,718,307	2,102,772	9,939	2,112,711	236,477	-96,884	1,779,350	298,583	640,374	25,239	107,703	60,200
2006	2,839,791	2,158,975	6,472	2,165,447	242,361	-86,683	1,836,403	320,959	682,429	25,885	109,708	60,726
2007	3,013,344	2,206,504	1,111	2,207,615	251,202	-62,566	1,893,847	365,605	753,892	26,959	111,776	61,090
2008	3,146,020	2,187,982	1,135	2,189,117	254,170	-57,184	1,877,763	410,128	858,129	27,813	113,115	60,391
2009	3,172,250	2,040,331	4,475	2,044,806	243,066	26,715	1,828,455	408,214	935,581	27,920	113,618	56,226
2010	3,253,004	2,096,382	7,637	2,104,019	252,700	-6,179	1,845,140	402,431	1,005,433	28,481	114,217	55,597
2011	3,455,878	2,146,459	4,960	2,151,419	232,994	80,432	1,998,857	430,549	1,026,472	30,103	114,800	55,920
2012	3,481,792	2,240,522	5,256	2,245,778	236,985	1,907	2,010,700	443,739	1,027,353	30,265	115,042	56,063
2013	3,536,993	2,256,330	7,191	2,263,521	268,604	27,664	2,022,581	457,724	1,056,688	30,657	115,374	56,235
2014	3,655,749	2,341,294	11,903	2,353,197	275,989	20,652	2,097,860	477,287	1,080,602	31,593	115,713	57,263

Personal Income and Employment by Area: Mount Vernon-Anacortes, WA

(Thousands of dollars, except as noted.)

Year	Personal income, total	Derivation of personal income									Per capita personal income (dollars)	Population (persons)	Total employment
		Earnings by place of work			Less: Contributions for government social insurance	Plus: Adjustment for residence	Equals: Net earnings by place of residence	Plus: Dividends, interest, and rent	Plus: Personal current transfer receipts				
		Nonfarm	Farm	Total									
1970	209,595	141,719	11,282	153,001	11,412	7,270	148,859	35,815	24,921	3,998	52,419	21,242
1971	228,841	154,016	13,347	167,363	12,966	6,661	161,058	39,482	28,301	4,343	52,694	21,537
1972	251,451	172,955	14,626	187,581	15,490	5,484	177,575	43,399	30,477	4,731	53,145	22,736
1973	293,402	205,293	21,565	226,858	21,484	3,736	209,110	49,308	34,984	5,511	53,244	24,711
1974	324,123	216,488	26,573	243,061	22,871	4,981	225,171	56,047	42,905	5,986	54,151	24,990
1975	361,348	239,233	25,179	264,412	24,749	4,915	244,578	64,424	52,346	6,763	53,431	25,161
1976	412,229	289,215	23,491	312,706	30,573	1,051	283,184	71,655	57,390	7,300	56,468	26,771
1977	442,263	304,443	20,725	325,168	32,150	4,183	297,201	83,178	61,884	7,662	57,722	26,893
1978	503,048	353,102	18,807	371,909	37,624	5,519	339,804	97,032	66,212	8,452	59,516	28,633
1979	580,842	399,945	26,152	426,097	43,649	8,605	391,053	114,324	75,465	9,453	61,443	29,681
1980	654,964	430,465	24,671	455,136	47,239	8,284	416,181	142,940	95,843	10,156	64,491	29,998
1981	725,621	466,073	21,994	488,067	56,258	7,353	439,162	175,643	110,816	11,031	65,779	30,968
1982	776,534	482,638	22,382	505,020	59,947	7,337	452,410	198,535	125,589	11,623	66,812	30,991
1983	851,178	528,900	31,270	560,170	66,188	4,971	498,953	214,092	138,133	12,500	68,094	32,337
1984	896,816	538,438	28,703	567,141	69,957	8,800	505,984	243,512	147,320	13,036	68,795	32,176
1985	948,857	565,244	28,368	593,612	72,868	12,605	533,349	260,667	154,841	13,724	69,139	32,600
1986	1,011,206	601,730	35,546	637,276	78,055	18,401	577,622	270,564	163,020	14,373	70,353	33,374
1987	1,044,689	607,104	47,568	654,672	78,676	26,363	602,359	271,513	170,817	14,671	71,206	34,918
1988	1,162,103	689,596	53,987	743,583	91,066	30,679	683,196	295,080	183,827	15,816	73,477	37,811
1989	1,333,799	792,497	55,908	848,405	106,385	33,520	775,540	359,349	198,910	17,538	76,054	40,078
1990	1,458,883	896,944	55,632	952,576	122,253	39,447	869,770	373,130	215,983	18,132	80,457	42,865
1991	1,578,828	985,321	55,087	1,040,408	135,812	38,944	943,540	392,106	243,182	18,849	83,761	44,137
1992	1,704,799	1,058,179	66,374	1,124,553	145,823	45,673	1,024,403	401,182	279,214	19,721	86,445	44,728
1993	1,806,064	1,113,360	76,876	1,190,236	152,711	51,743	1,089,268	415,027	301,769	20,173	89,530	45,889
1994	1,932,468	1,198,835	74,805	1,273,640	166,433	45,177	1,152,384	455,216	324,868	21,044	91,829	48,619
1995	2,069,075	1,262,987	81,677	1,344,664	176,353	45,495	1,213,806	503,437	351,832	21,999	94,053	49,832
1996	2,215,644	1,305,012	84,985	1,389,997	175,793	57,390	1,271,594	567,336	376,714	23,142	95,743	51,671
1997	2,350,304	1,403,699	82,817	1,486,516	180,821	72,852	1,378,547	585,936	385,821	24,096	97,539	52,910
1998	2,566,057	1,544,004	87,614	1,631,618	193,733	89,006	1,526,891	634,436	404,730	25,684	99,909	53,835
1999	2,738,824	1,721,556	92,672	1,814,228	210,631	78,475	1,682,072	626,077	430,675	26,930	101,701	56,151
2000	2,922,828	1,860,517	83,351	1,943,868	231,440	69,669	1,782,097	678,783	461,948	28,262	103,420	58,459
2001	3,089,975	1,964,869	93,837	2,058,706	240,238	83,339	1,901,807	672,491	515,677	29,560	104,534	58,619
2002	3,165,346	2,059,055	80,190	2,139,245	251,848	87,735	1,975,132	646,275	543,939	29,985	105,563	58,733
2003	3,305,346	2,154,615	100,047	2,254,662	265,099	93,785	2,083,348	655,775	566,223	30,785	107,369	59,803
2004	3,461,031	2,256,394	84,242	2,340,636	278,340	100,911	2,163,207	710,348	587,476	31,744	109,030	61,005
2005	3,682,178	2,441,324	87,162	2,528,486	307,125	113,382	2,334,743	723,093	624,342	33,268	110,683	63,488
2006	4,031,802	2,588,824	90,730	2,679,554	322,077	125,944	2,483,421	879,898	668,483	35,800	112,621	65,190
2007	4,316,401	2,700,895	91,443	2,792,338	339,720	141,086	2,593,704	1,004,415	718,282	37,841	114,066	67,145
2008	4,478,559	2,669,811	87,585	2,757,396	339,775	154,093	2,571,714	1,082,583	824,262	38,672	115,808	66,295
2009	4,402,417	2,535,309	97,209	2,632,518	330,303	179,083	2,481,298	994,235	926,884	37,771	116,557	63,204
2010	4,365,292	2,547,704	98,817	2,646,521	335,783	147,758	2,458,496	889,726	1,017,070	37,321	116,967	62,159
2011	4,573,128	2,571,032	97,596	2,668,628	311,703	190,919	2,547,844	998,879	1,026,405	38,841	117,740	62,169
2012	4,802,894	2,693,432	96,258	2,789,690	321,200	183,028	2,651,518	1,118,808	1,032,568	40,701	118,005	62,338
2013	4,857,028	2,796,291	104,305	2,900,596	375,185	165,885	2,691,296	1,110,876	1,054,856	40,904	118,742	64,591
2014	5,155,069	2,949,676	96,372	3,046,048	393,230	204,131	2,856,949	1,153,263	1,144,857	42,829	120,365	65,994

Personal Income and Employment by Area: Muncie, IN

(Thousands of dollars, except as noted.)

Year	Personal income, total	Earnings by place of work			Less: Contributions for government social insurance	Plus: Adjustment for residence	Equals: Net earnings by place of residence	Plus: Dividends, interest, and rent	Plus: Personal current transfer receipts	Per capita personal income (dollars)	Population (persons)	Total employment
		Nonfarm	Farm	Total								
1970	451,666	398,619	4,642	403,261	26,965	-19,108	357,188	61,674	32,804	3,490	129,415	54,161
1971	493,329	422,612	8,306	430,918	29,576	-15,071	386,271	67,236	39,822	3,780	130,524	53,900
1972	522,193	445,192	5,567	450,759	33,280	-11,582	405,897	71,669	44,627	3,916	133,342	54,086
1973	592,569	497,623	14,805	512,428	42,844	-8,998	460,586	79,708	52,275	4,455	133,005	55,918
1974	643,834	542,236	7,282	549,518	48,890	-9,950	490,678	91,232	61,924	4,905	131,273	56,276
1975	681,830	539,574	12,836	552,410	48,237	-6,236	497,937	101,136	82,757	5,232	130,324	53,413
1976	747,169	599,134	9,773	608,907	53,908	-1,711	553,288	108,866	85,015	5,725	130,508	54,644
1977	835,487	679,187	6,761	685,948	60,869	-1,499	623,580	121,508	90,399	6,419	130,160	57,114
1978	923,249	746,251	8,060	754,311	68,838	2,427	687,900	135,244	100,105	7,118	129,712	57,799
1979	1,019,367	823,551	6,886	830,437	78,526	-359	751,552	153,165	114,650	7,926	128,611	59,035
1980	1,117,335	859,642	2,578	862,220	81,171	-3,095	777,954	188,561	150,820	8,702	128,394	57,729
1981	1,209,661	901,806	1,571	903,377	92,243	465	811,599	234,729	163,333	9,500	127,338	56,902
1982	1,222,547	874,813	4,049	878,862	91,568	5,838	793,132	248,765	180,650	9,711	125,887	54,123
1983	1,297,606	939,482	-4,074	935,408	98,405	9,046	846,049	258,752	192,805	10,459	124,068	54,000
1984	1,417,376	1,026,518	8,332	1,034,850	109,770	15,093	940,173	276,656	200,547	11,470	123,569	55,565
1985	1,479,351	1,072,956	5,784	1,078,740	116,765	18,312	980,287	291,357	207,707	12,121	122,044	56,476
1986	1,559,285	1,146,049	5,656	1,151,705	125,155	13,420	1,039,970	302,142	217,173	12,911	120,770	57,543
1987	1,623,818	1,208,989	9,926	1,218,915	130,697	11,116	1,099,334	302,602	221,882	13,411	121,082	58,948
1988	1,734,669	1,307,312	4,447	1,311,759	145,694	16,694	1,182,759	318,239	233,671	14,376	120,662	60,820
1989	1,870,543	1,374,779	9,547	1,384,326	154,616	23,483	1,253,193	362,195	255,155	15,593	119,962	61,574
1990	1,990,143	1,462,604	9,279	1,471,883	168,665	21,417	1,324,635	383,168	282,340	16,616	119,774	62,976
1991	2,055,165	1,538,746	4,990	1,543,736	179,241	10,099	1,374,594	374,466	306,105	17,130	119,973	62,840
1992	2,152,463	1,665,977	8,886	1,674,863	191,084	-47,668	1,436,111	374,007	342,345	17,885	120,352	65,363
1993	2,223,880	1,723,423	11,760	1,735,183	199,661	-52,605	1,482,917	378,698	362,265	18,389	120,935	65,781
1994	2,348,830	1,839,567	15,737	1,855,304	215,603	-72,366	1,567,335	403,649	377,846	19,490	120,514	67,867
1995	2,443,864	1,917,268	8,157	1,925,425	224,657	-83,918	1,616,850	447,117	379,897	20,246	120,707	69,973
1996	2,516,348	1,921,009	11,212	1,932,221	222,557	-58,192	1,651,472	464,207	400,669	20,868	120,582	68,253
1997	2,592,241	2,011,178	16,568	2,027,746	232,241	-71,294	1,724,211	460,373	407,657	21,505	120,539	68,126
1998	2,736,643	2,055,049	13,412	2,068,461	232,568	-32,012	1,803,881	507,190	425,572	22,902	119,495	68,311
1999	2,817,079	2,103,873	10,358	2,114,231	236,193	-10,074	1,867,964	495,620	453,495	23,718	118,772	68,732
2000	2,983,775	2,207,717	12,916	2,220,633	245,069	-5,885	1,969,679	530,764	483,332	25,121	118,776	69,057
2001	3,029,573	2,214,907	14,706	2,229,613	249,984	-41,516	1,938,113	553,883	537,577	25,187	120,281	68,460
2002	3,017,671	2,222,158	4,722	2,226,880	250,708	-51,989	1,924,183	533,928	559,560	25,158	119,949	65,935
2003	3,078,045	2,259,359	13,031	2,272,390	255,997	-63,802	1,952,591	548,713	576,741	25,664	119,935	64,863
2004	3,049,713	2,271,159	23,005	2,294,164	257,725	-74,241	1,962,198	482,180	605,335	25,641	118,938	63,738
2005	3,065,885	2,290,949	14,669	2,305,618	264,968	-85,262	1,955,388	451,914	658,583	25,945	118,170	62,815
2006	3,137,784	2,322,330	10,660	2,332,990	270,082	-95,389	1,967,519	463,261	707,004	26,744	117,326	63,598
2007	3,221,351	2,357,006	8,751	2,365,757	275,919	-106,727	1,983,111	510,474	727,766	27,479	117,229	63,885
2008	3,370,773	2,383,361	17,472	2,400,833	280,635	-117,299	2,002,899	537,638	830,236	28,808	117,007	62,176
2009	3,319,898	2,280,535	11,223	2,291,758	274,540	-120,202	1,897,016	503,623	919,259	28,257	117,490	59,325
2010	3,369,933	2,251,597	9,042	2,260,639	268,991	-101,394	1,890,254	493,216	986,463	28,638	117,672	57,534
2011	3,491,486	2,312,503	22,348	2,334,851	246,002	-113,855	1,974,994	534,815	981,677	29,640	117,797	58,293
2012	3,629,323	2,416,277	19,047	2,435,324	255,782	-142,170	2,037,372	570,394	1,021,557	30,938	117,309	58,711
2013	3,636,201	2,442,508	43,813	2,486,321	296,667	-154,790	2,034,864	574,091	1,027,246	30,985	117,355	58,674
2014	3,738,515	2,523,427	19,273	2,542,700	305,303	-165,557	2,071,840	595,417	1,071,258	31,933	117,074	58,603

Personal Income and Employment by Area: Muskegon-Norton Shores, MI

(Thousands of dollars, except as noted.)

Year	Personal income, total	Derivation of personal income			Less: Contributions for government social insurance	Plus: Adjustment for residence	Equals: Net earnings by place of residence	Plus: Dividends, interest, and rent	Plus: Personal current transfer receipts	Per capita personal income (dollars)	Population (persons)	Total employment
		Earnings by place of work										
		Nonfarm	Farm	Total								
1970	578,102	503,286	3,319	506,605	36,139	-23,873	446,593	64,370	67,139	3,668	157,595	61,851
1971	598,472	500,209	3,304	503,513	37,037	-19,147	447,329	68,080	83,063	3,780	158,338	59,280
1972	664,756	563,232	3,743	566,975	44,138	-22,323	500,514	72,813	91,429	4,204	158,137	61,124
1973	723,405	622,576	3,694	626,270	56,776	-26,788	542,706	78,967	101,732	4,604	157,135	63,037
1974	800,296	680,454	5,755	686,209	63,978	-31,511	590,720	90,351	119,225	5,120	156,315	64,536
1975	874,131	713,629	4,593	718,222	65,004	-33,353	619,865	100,100	154,166	5,594	156,266	63,935
1976	952,682	788,878	4,627	793,505	73,762	-34,166	685,577	105,077	162,028	6,053	157,395	65,187
1977	1,044,811	873,821	5,573	879,394	81,465	-33,871	764,058	114,548	166,205	6,634	157,496	66,515
1978	1,172,340	984,185	7,285	991,470	95,122	-35,338	861,010	129,672	181,658	7,455	157,258	68,481
1979	1,287,916	1,074,787	5,242	1,080,029	108,592	-35,214	936,223	147,725	203,968	8,148	158,067	68,649
1980	1,387,398	1,110,446	5,379	1,115,825	110,521	-38,587	966,717	177,961	242,720	8,789	157,850	66,135
1981	1,497,125	1,163,882	7,758	1,171,640	125,075	-41,507	1,005,058	216,498	275,569	9,443	158,550	64,362
1982	1,562,590	1,154,847	9,653	1,164,500	125,615	-35,008	1,003,877	247,805	310,908	10,009	156,114	61,143
1983	1,624,142	1,192,949	7,477	1,200,426	131,908	-27,141	1,041,377	253,498	329,267	10,513	154,496	60,591
1984	1,794,744	1,336,460	8,729	1,345,189	154,387	-25,856	1,164,946	297,513	332,285	11,591	154,844	64,284
1985	1,901,008	1,421,078	12,683	1,433,761	166,241	-24,056	1,243,464	308,750	348,794	12,213	155,654	66,520
1986	1,971,195	1,475,588	8,086	1,483,674	172,581	-30,118	1,280,975	324,324	365,896	12,651	155,812	67,445
1987	2,063,277	1,512,594	8,319	1,520,913	173,494	-14,726	1,332,693	355,095	375,489	13,197	156,345	67,252
1988	2,151,663	1,588,513	7,751	1,596,264	188,960	-651	1,406,653	354,790	390,220	13,649	157,643	68,222
1989	2,299,170	1,670,993	10,877	1,681,870	197,412	6,231	1,490,689	387,377	421,104	14,518	158,365	69,448
1990	2,417,730	1,739,866	7,588	1,747,454	208,189	8,222	1,547,487	410,745	459,498	15,169	159,384	70,361
1991	2,481,756	1,747,782	9,589	1,757,371	211,795	17,714	1,563,290	408,154	510,312	15,426	160,885	68,332
1992	2,625,138	1,858,283	10,002	1,868,285	223,688	35,987	1,680,584	414,901	529,653	16,191	162,135	68,157
1993	2,736,269	1,919,668	8,785	1,928,453	233,846	54,233	1,748,840	432,630	554,799	16,778	163,082	67,576
1994	2,920,628	2,036,045	8,135	2,044,180	254,701	86,505	1,875,984	489,287	555,357	17,844	163,678	69,480
1995	3,062,975	2,134,320	9,654	2,143,974	270,894	98,877	1,971,957	510,431	580,587	18,625	164,457	71,863
1996	3,228,550	2,233,118	8,884	2,242,002	279,187	121,874	2,084,689	532,710	611,151	19,477	165,763	73,599
1997	3,446,325	2,382,283	9,540	2,391,823	297,185	144,463	2,239,101	565,111	642,113	20,627	167,077	75,236
1998	3,640,471	2,563,813	11,327	2,575,140	317,124	159,219	2,417,235	576,697	646,539	21,651	168,147	77,572
1999	3,854,508	2,726,152	11,966	2,738,118	335,469	171,293	2,573,942	573,947	706,619	22,763	169,331	80,845
2000	4,051,993	2,849,318	7,809	2,857,127	350,566	198,645	2,705,206	612,235	734,552	23,780	170,396	82,838
2001	4,209,534	2,912,279	8,372	2,920,651	335,189	198,843	2,784,305	597,183	828,046	24,609	171,055	81,283
2002	4,178,111	2,882,295	6,170	2,888,465	334,794	175,172	2,728,843	582,213	867,055	24,353	171,563	80,902
2003	4,300,085	2,949,045	9,445	2,958,490	341,788	157,148	2,773,850	613,176	913,059	24,961	172,269	82,030
2004	4,406,788	3,076,013	13,884	3,089,897	360,145	143,052	2,872,804	594,625	939,359	25,507	172,771	83,875
2005	4,476,372	3,130,907	13,827	3,144,734	377,183	123,962	2,891,513	586,899	997,960	25,784	173,608	84,308
2006	4,621,535	3,214,139	14,701	3,228,840	394,920	106,174	2,940,094	611,317	1,070,124	26,605	173,710	84,877
2007	4,723,586	3,207,640	19,171	3,226,811	398,836	85,612	2,913,587	641,887	1,168,112	27,188	173,738	84,164
2008	4,877,487	3,214,998	20,375	3,235,373	403,529	63,854	2,895,698	666,659	1,315,130	28,056	173,846	83,088
2009	4,801,335	2,986,006	18,694	3,004,700	376,226	104,677	2,733,151	607,904	1,460,280	27,793	172,755	78,366
2010	4,946,412	3,064,303	22,888	3,087,191	383,370	81,822	2,785,643	605,677	1,555,092	28,772	171,916	77,525
2011	5,174,692	3,171,364	44,636	3,216,000	358,419	85,585	2,943,166	697,176	1,534,350	30,442	169,986	79,603
2012	5,311,020	3,294,125	16,557	3,310,682	372,550	93,583	3,031,715	747,823	1,531,482	31,214	170,146	80,528
2013	5,415,758	3,355,508	40,711	3,396,219	423,978	108,206	3,080,447	759,971	1,575,340	31,442	172,246	81,004
2014	5,662,490	3,513,607	34,683	3,548,290	441,239	133,458	3,240,509	789,992	1,631,989	32,856	172,344	83,044

Personal Income and Employment by Area: Myrtle Beach-North Myrtle Beach-Conway, SC-NC

(Thousands of dollars, except as noted.)

Year	Personal income, total	Earnings by place of work			Less: Contributions for government social insurance	Plus: Adjustment for residence	Equals: Net earnings by place of residence	Plus: Dividends, interest, and rent	Plus: Personal current transfer receipts	Per capita personal income (dollars)	Population (persons)	Total employment
		Nonfarm	Farm	Total								
1970	284,778	204,895	19,298	224,193	13,478	6,031	216,746	41,295	26,737	2,988	95,303	42,155
1971	334,454	241,054	18,453	259,507	16,402	9,088	252,193	51,113	31,148	3,306	101,165	45,218
1972	391,202	289,297	22,502	311,799	20,303	6,175	297,671	58,470	35,061	3,645	107,339	48,709
1973	449,596	333,803	27,197	361,000	26,458	6,007	340,549	67,649	41,398	3,966	113,376	52,009
1974	511,710	373,268	36,788	410,056	31,109	2,352	381,299	77,392	53,019	4,325	118,307	53,860
1975	577,611	423,313	28,498	451,811	35,517	-2,481	413,813	89,965	73,833	4,735	121,997	55,574
1976	640,061	480,438	22,519	502,957	40,806	-4,407	457,744	98,629	83,688	5,020	127,490	58,366
1977	706,060	541,171	17,141	558,312	45,663	-8,552	504,097	114,256	87,707	5,515	128,032	62,138
1978	826,686	620,948	36,238	657,186	53,200	-11,294	592,692	137,049	96,945	6,257	132,125	66,349
1979	911,287	699,116	15,134	714,250	62,065	-15,732	636,453	160,266	114,568	6,773	134,546	68,739
1980	1,038,270	772,972	12,589	785,561	68,908	-20,065	696,588	199,218	142,464	7,494	138,543	70,280
1981	1,201,933	865,043	27,210	892,253	83,236	-22,806	786,211	246,345	169,377	8,377	143,488	72,021
1982	1,330,778	945,513	17,925	963,438	93,370	-24,529	845,539	291,084	194,155	8,993	147,977	75,532
1983	1,538,440	1,102,598	14,018	1,116,616	109,956	-18,338	988,322	336,935	213,183	9,908	155,270	80,547
1984	1,754,416	1,267,356	10,611	1,277,967	131,306	-20,966	1,125,695	398,420	230,301	10,725	163,585	88,239
1985	1,955,304	1,392,510	18,514	1,411,024	147,079	-21,651	1,242,294	456,718	256,292	11,412	171,336	91,199
1986	2,112,604	1,488,620	-2,657	1,485,963	161,192	1,213	1,325,984	506,021	280,599	11,899	177,546	93,765
1987	2,311,863	1,622,404	21,732	1,644,136	173,473	11,276	1,481,939	533,190	296,734	12,608	183,363	95,855
1988	2,533,410	1,763,245	24,547	1,787,792	195,416	24,787	1,617,163	592,363	323,884	13,541	187,091	100,892
1989	2,803,079	1,889,440	27,082	1,916,522	213,940	39,826	1,742,408	674,144	386,527	14,695	190,746	103,297
1990	3,015,794	2,032,750	28,366	2,061,116	235,651	56,892	1,882,357	697,024	436,413	15,352	196,448	107,397
1991	3,194,717	2,170,033	37,160	2,207,193	256,764	31,736	1,982,165	717,183	495,369	15,770	202,583	108,714
1992	3,411,628	2,285,109	39,524	2,324,633	268,816	46,940	2,102,757	738,143	570,728	16,378	208,302	109,888
1993	3,569,200	2,363,123	36,261	2,399,384	281,331	45,787	2,163,840	779,888	625,472	17,125	208,415	111,547
1994	3,899,098	2,581,337	35,349	2,616,686	313,925	41,807	2,344,568	852,863	701,667	18,079	215,675	118,839
1995	4,328,554	2,877,380	23,808	2,901,188	349,624	37,771	2,589,335	962,430	776,789	19,258	224,765	128,781
1996	4,786,610	3,152,831	33,975	3,186,806	373,954	52,190	2,865,042	1,070,275	851,293	20,365	235,041	135,319
1997	5,265,019	3,475,942	39,667	3,515,609	411,647	63,820	3,167,782	1,186,512	910,725	21,482	245,090	144,171
1998	5,727,144	3,830,271	1,543	3,831,814	451,274	85,208	3,465,748	1,277,922	983,474	22,492	254,627	149,636
1999	6,164,071	4,215,170	13,676	4,228,846	489,884	94,764	3,833,726	1,279,202	1,051,143	23,420	263,200	154,911
2000	6,630,645	4,447,806	42,355	4,490,161	518,117	101,005	4,073,049	1,413,913	1,143,683	24,401	271,736	158,101
2001	6,956,332	4,628,933	60,989	4,689,922	540,159	66,838	4,216,601	1,456,068	1,283,663	25,024	277,987	156,603
2002	7,087,743	4,757,168	-10,733	4,746,435	560,265	63,109	4,249,279	1,425,579	1,412,885	24,881	284,862	158,269
2003	7,586,738	5,124,798	22,485	5,147,283	609,174	82,037	4,620,146	1,433,713	1,532,879	25,955	292,309	163,169
2004	8,266,132	5,514,524	24,125	5,538,649	657,982	115,081	4,995,748	1,559,488	1,710,896	27,333	302,421	171,731
2005	9,001,307	5,942,873	22,990	5,965,863	713,768	137,656	5,389,751	1,720,779	1,890,777	28,329	317,745	180,803
2006	9,990,674	6,569,740	11,829	6,581,569	808,252	169,943	5,943,260	1,942,860	2,104,554	29,722	336,132	192,643
2007	10,676,084	6,745,885	6,721	6,752,606	840,166	215,076	6,127,516	2,260,037	2,288,531	30,375	351,472	198,562
2008	11,258,026	6,717,348	30,403	6,747,751	838,024	263,830	6,173,557	2,411,344	2,673,125	30,940	363,866	194,339
2009	11,197,081	6,386,556	37,471	6,424,027	801,232	336,725	5,959,520	2,184,247	3,053,314	30,147	371,417	184,023
2010	11,441,798	6,446,569	36,379	6,482,948	807,529	358,044	6,033,463	2,068,286	3,340,049	30,218	378,644	182,281
2011	11,953,478	6,576,537	32,243	6,608,780	756,808	336,476	6,188,448	2,299,518	3,465,512	30,991	385,705	186,152
2012	12,517,846	6,920,746	46,381	6,967,127	782,475	311,320	6,495,972	2,422,994	3,598,880	31,761	394,128	189,007
2013	12,932,308	7,125,930	62,302	7,188,232	913,211	344,943	6,619,964	2,489,092	3,823,252	31,948	404,789	194,312
2014	13,746,904	7,469,335	56,740	7,526,075	964,418	455,232	7,016,889	2,602,121	4,127,894	32,913	417,668	198,468

Personal Income and Employment by Area: Napa, CA

(Thousands of dollars, except as noted.)

Year	Personal income, total	Derivation of personal income									Per capita personal income (dollars)	Population (persons)	Total employment
		Earnings by place of work			Less: Contributions for government social insurance	Plus: Adjustment for residence	Equals: Net earnings by place of residence	Plus: Dividends, interest, and rent	Plus: Personal current transfer receipts				
		Nonfarm	Farm	Total									
1970	381,122	202,052	6,511	208,563	12,292	65,768	262,039	80,484	38,599		4,790	79,562	27,680
1971	416,513	219,581	6,258	225,839	13,833	71,073	283,079	90,670	42,764		5,094	81,771	28,531
1972	447,853	234,393	7,762	242,155	15,459	76,008	302,704	99,341	45,808		5,382	83,208	29,297
1973	507,165	269,398	13,400	282,798	20,318	80,673	343,153	111,545	52,467		5,782	87,718	31,552
1974	577,179	304,612	9,589	314,201	23,987	95,996	386,210	128,521	62,448		6,359	90,759	33,495
1975	672,761	349,463	15,444	364,907	27,125	111,502	449,284	144,821	78,656		7,186	93,627	35,667
1976	742,054	382,503	16,148	398,651	29,663	127,074	496,062	157,104	88,888		7,814	94,964	36,033
1977	823,991	415,361	21,533	436,894	32,771	145,041	549,164	177,033	97,794		8,537	96,521	36,858
1978	941,351	475,234	26,011	501,245	38,553	166,576	629,268	207,502	104,581		9,761	96,437	38,852
1979	1,054,048	545,916	20,588	566,504	47,032	176,327	695,799	237,053	121,196		10,670	98,789	41,207
1980	1,163,733	585,568	20,909	606,477	50,093	188,381	744,765	280,323	138,645		11,716	99,331	43,047
1981	1,321,371	664,724	22,664	687,388	62,901	197,774	822,261	339,047	160,063		13,259	99,662	44,376
1982	1,417,820	691,593	37,653	729,246	67,362	215,270	877,154	366,430	174,236		14,013	101,178	44,528
1983	1,511,583	734,302	19,871	754,173	72,930	235,609	916,852	406,023	188,708		14,885	101,549	45,542
1984	1,651,720	830,468	19,956	850,424	86,003	245,461	1,009,882	447,336	194,502		16,209	101,902	47,379
1985	1,782,964	902,017	21,142	923,159	94,672	261,836	1,090,323	482,098	210,543		17,308	103,014	49,000
1986	1,916,647	996,897	30,221	1,027,118	106,515	270,944	1,191,547	501,796	223,304		18,387	104,237	51,024
1987	2,007,894	1,070,637	23,722	1,094,359	114,649	281,234	1,260,944	516,890	230,060		19,121	105,010	52,434
1988	2,184,240	1,197,479	28,504	1,225,983	133,416	293,250	1,385,817	553,228	245,195		20,581	106,130	54,863
1989	2,419,363	1,267,960	59,217	1,327,177	142,910	308,404	1,492,671	656,422	270,270		22,265	108,662	56,480
1990	2,571,082	1,393,212	45,325	1,438,537	156,586	339,733	1,621,684	659,561	289,837		23,104	111,284	59,343
1991	2,712,956	1,490,512	54,906	1,545,418	167,885	345,186	1,722,719	670,573	319,664		24,173	112,233	60,173
1992	2,839,602	1,598,320	44,668	1,642,988	178,472	326,332	1,790,848	684,765	363,989		24,839	114,322	60,221
1993	2,956,121	1,669,007	33,636	1,702,643	186,186	321,142	1,837,599	733,705	384,817		25,712	114,972	60,849
1994	3,087,247	1,760,359	35,649	1,796,008	195,370	334,342	1,934,980	761,799	390,468		26,597	116,077	62,499
1995	3,224,773	1,869,008	40,338	1,909,346	205,533	301,388	2,005,201	812,163	407,409		27,634	116,697	64,022
1996	3,462,028	2,017,022	53,432	2,070,454	214,578	289,486	2,145,362	888,266	428,400		29,340	117,996	67,250
1997	3,719,134	2,200,730	98,409	2,299,139	233,103	253,246	2,319,282	961,647	438,205		31,042	119,808	70,898
1998	4,017,388	2,455,451	64,220	2,519,671	254,154	249,505	2,515,022	1,036,677	465,689		33,042	121,583	77,117
1999	4,368,691	2,820,651	77,608	2,898,259	289,103	228,909	2,838,065	1,065,377	465,249		35,510	123,026	81,487
2000	4,818,829	3,105,989	140,396	3,246,385	317,518	232,374	3,161,241	1,169,612	487,976		38,685	124,565	82,590
2001	4,912,255	3,292,744	136,469	3,429,213	358,970	190,300	3,260,543	1,128,175	523,537		38,735	126,818	84,371
2002	5,026,307	3,486,972	149,145	3,636,117	385,838	143,403	3,393,682	1,077,849	554,776		39,041	128,744	85,786
2003	5,237,331	3,698,855	117,395	3,816,250	415,033	96,698	3,497,915	1,153,672	585,744		40,244	130,138	86,743
2004	5,543,407	3,991,456	95,837	4,087,293	460,043	46,642	3,673,892	1,252,248	617,267		42,515	130,387	88,296
2005	5,806,212	4,137,357	151,651	4,289,008	474,525	-12,557	3,801,926	1,350,213	654,073		44,533	130,381	89,231
2006	6,072,045	4,302,985	89,390	4,392,375	478,237	-79,095	3,835,043	1,529,699	707,303		46,196	131,440	89,124
2007	6,300,933	4,528,786	67,723	4,596,509	494,857	-156,184	3,945,468	1,607,735	747,730		47,524	132,583	91,648
2008	6,411,722	4,624,273	40,169	4,664,442	507,477	-232,957	3,924,008	1,646,427	841,287		47,815	134,093	91,828
2009	6,118,444	4,398,585	110,389	4,508,974	489,883	-246,682	3,772,409	1,438,884	907,151		45,228	135,280	89,013
2010	6,138,781	4,399,191	86,509	4,485,700	479,712	-278,139	3,727,849	1,420,715	990,217		44,865	136,829	88,562
2011	6,590,991	4,589,060	58,359	4,647,419	446,655	-267,669	3,933,095	1,650,132	1,007,764		47,741	138,056	89,544
2012	7,227,213	4,893,076	204,191	5,097,267	467,637	-306,111	4,323,519	1,886,120	1,017,574		51,944	139,135	92,617
2013	7,400,483	5,186,550	204,360	5,390,910	559,278	-313,284	4,518,348	1,836,586	1,045,549		52,643	140,580	96,230
2014	7,734,502	5,468,536	135,455	5,603,991	592,883	-271,759	4,739,349	1,910,718	1,084,435		54,596	141,667	99,435

Personal Income and Employment by Area: Naples-Immokalee-Marco Island, FL

(Thousands of dollars, except as noted.)

Year	Personal income, total	Derivation of personal income									Per capita personal income (dollars)	Population (persons)	Total employment
		Earnings by place of work			Less: Contributions for government social insurance	Plus: Adjustment for residence	Equals: Net earnings by place of residence	Plus: Dividends, interest, and rent	Plus: Personal current transfer receipts				
		Nonfarm	Farm	Total									
1970	210,997	126,546	9,560	136,106	7,829	-11,901	116,376	79,885	14,736	5,428	38,874	19,784
1971	251,099	142,771	12,446	155,217	9,157	-11,258	134,802	96,059	20,238	5,883	42,683	21,385
1972	294,132	163,290	15,182	178,472	11,053	-11,549	155,870	113,861	24,401	5,985	49,144	22,959
1973	372,071	215,183	16,135	231,318	16,968	-14,982	199,368	141,474	31,229	6,795	54,757	28,113
1974	432,018	236,628	18,908	255,536	19,697	-15,311	220,528	172,638	38,852	7,398	58,396	30,121
1975	463,997	233,581	21,777	255,358	18,884	-10,971	225,503	185,705	52,789	7,295	63,602	28,974
1976	530,453	265,781	22,891	288,672	20,883	-9,283	258,506	212,507	59,440	8,022	66,125	29,334
1977	627,730	325,076	21,698	346,774	26,089	-10,657	310,028	250,135	67,567	9,045	69,404	34,304
1978	767,292	405,611	25,432	431,043	33,747	-13,386	383,910	305,035	78,347	10,252	74,844	40,053
1979	902,435	477,570	35,609	513,179	41,994	-13,138	458,047	350,734	93,654	11,020	81,890	44,215
1980	1,090,445	556,627	37,864	594,491	49,835	-13,204	531,452	444,467	114,526	12,462	87,504	46,868
1981	1,348,824	646,842	37,397	684,239	63,122	-13,309	607,808	601,941	139,075	14,430	93,473	50,278
1982	1,458,148	657,925	49,704	707,629	67,559	-8,955	631,115	659,467	167,566	14,596	99,902	51,225
1983	1,678,933	722,843	84,208	807,051	73,794	-6,628	726,629	764,363	187,941	16,103	104,265	55,623
1984	1,936,152	832,816	78,778	911,594	87,495	-9,322	814,777	913,749	207,626	17,585	110,105	61,169
1985	2,170,071	949,458	88,742	1,038,200	102,725	-11,860	923,615	1,016,373	230,083	18,775	115,584	65,543
1986	2,455,872	1,070,233	104,993	1,175,226	119,764	-11,800	1,043,662	1,154,998	257,212	20,244	121,311	71,756
1987	2,844,371	1,286,028	122,892	1,408,920	141,862	-15,836	1,251,222	1,312,486	280,663	22,235	127,921	74,893
1988	3,467,338	1,492,521	142,264	1,634,785	169,089	-21,501	1,444,195	1,700,479	322,664	25,606	135,413	83,812
1989	3,948,931	1,699,311	177,436	1,876,747	196,280	-25,905	1,654,562	1,931,591	362,778	27,274	144,790	89,342
1990	4,234,849	1,838,404	114,906	1,953,310	211,536	-29,184	1,712,590	2,107,715	414,544	27,398	154,568	92,101
1991	4,596,290	1,968,478	163,669	2,132,147	226,356	-25,654	1,880,137	2,239,103	477,050	28,028	163,988	94,434
1992	5,145,671	2,139,435	207,357	2,346,792	243,319	-23,516	2,079,957	2,502,549	563,165	29,903	172,077	96,093
1993	5,671,193	2,341,381	204,490	2,545,871	264,512	-30,496	2,250,863	2,806,284	614,046	31,283	181,288	101,102
1994	6,257,950	2,588,056	154,108	2,742,164	295,029	-31,119	2,416,016	3,168,211	673,723	32,742	191,132	104,131
1995	6,810,865	2,827,798	147,719	2,975,517	316,757	-33,737	2,625,023	3,453,468	732,374	34,116	199,639	107,407
1996	7,434,153	3,099,486	134,526	3,234,012	342,644	-41,717	2,849,651	3,795,207	789,295	35,535	209,205	113,188
1997	8,385,417	3,507,850	142,932	3,650,782	386,804	-63,440	3,200,538	4,345,731	839,148	37,956	220,923	119,660
1998	9,269,384	3,841,013	164,924	4,005,937	417,175	-68,818	3,519,944	4,872,331	877,109	39,720	233,371	128,261
1999	10,001,395	4,283,873	154,799	4,438,672	457,312	-82,304	3,899,056	5,158,163	944,176	40,806	245,094	133,959
2000	10,864,987	4,763,953	156,565	4,920,518	507,190	-110,033	4,303,295	5,524,394	1,037,298	42,773	254,015	144,102
2001	11,920,829	5,344,900	147,768	5,492,668	577,244	-112,469	4,802,955	5,968,453	1,149,421	45,114	264,240	154,441
2002	12,450,282	5,549,137	164,071	5,713,208	609,632	-77,656	5,025,920	6,185,998	1,238,364	45,193	275,490	160,642
2003	13,404,436	6,206,278	142,374	6,348,652	676,637	-37,537	5,634,478	6,435,258	1,334,700	46,980	285,321	171,528
2004	15,935,447	6,811,469	145,617	6,957,086	752,961	13,232	6,217,357	8,270,320	1,447,770	53,832	296,021	180,930
2005	18,220,930	7,593,085	178,498	7,771,583	834,538	73,191	7,010,236	9,603,980	1,606,714	59,264	307,452	186,932
2006	20,898,631	8,086,110	167,147	8,253,257	904,195	140,268	7,489,330	11,675,224	1,734,077	66,850	312,621	195,896
2007	22,002,557	8,034,761	154,984	8,189,745	908,590	207,915	7,489,070	12,653,165	1,860,322	69,974	314,437	193,091
2008	22,094,705	7,464,734	155,432	7,620,166	861,216	253,985	7,012,935	12,948,728	2,133,042	69,778	316,641	182,182
2009	18,850,405	6,798,226	159,159	6,957,385	805,908	303,580	6,455,057	10,022,239	2,373,109	59,188	318,485	174,001
2010	20,320,655	7,021,437	143,984	7,165,421	828,007	495,110	6,832,524	10,891,794	2,596,337	62,969	322,710	173,860
2011	21,758,888	7,245,740	118,642	7,364,382	770,335	412,572	7,006,619	12,042,707	2,709,562	66,358	327,903	180,710
2012	24,129,288	7,689,559	131,154	7,820,713	812,974	644,374	7,652,113	13,749,130	2,728,045	72,488	332,873	187,218
2013	24,571,667	8,250,255	150,911	8,401,166	968,130	572,642	8,005,678	13,741,228	2,824,761	72,247	340,106	194,758
2014	25,763,656	8,793,993	113,830	8,907,823	1,041,116	650,768	8,517,475	14,236,337	3,009,844	73,869	348,777	202,939

Personal Income and Employment by Area: Nashville-Davidson—Murfreesboro—Franklin, TN

(Thousands of dollars, except as noted.)

Year	Personal income, total	Derivation of personal income					Equals: Net earnings by place of residence	Plus: Dividends, interest, and rent	Plus: Personal current transfer receipts	Per capita personal income (dollars)	Population (persons)	Total employment
		Earnings by place of work			Less: Contributions for government social insurance	Plus: Adjustment for residence						
		Nonfarm	Farm	Total								
1970	2,871,920	2,384,626	54,080	2,438,706	155,235	-4,482	2,278,989	371,931	221,000	3,613	794,960	388,326
1971	3,126,955	2,584,980	49,397	2,634,377	173,003	-2,952	2,458,422	408,820	259,713	3,876	806,661	390,781
1972	3,517,251	2,936,297	59,226	2,995,523	207,389	-7,610	2,780,524	450,645	286,082	4,233	831,002	414,671
1973	4,010,013	3,356,858	84,658	3,441,516	272,313	-10,169	3,159,034	513,325	337,654	4,762	842,119	441,535
1974	4,470,713	3,725,669	62,857	3,788,526	315,214	-13,584	3,459,728	601,954	409,031	5,199	859,921	454,143
1975	4,838,237	3,926,707	37,484	3,964,191	325,367	-13,883	3,624,941	670,533	542,763	5,502	879,430	437,309
1976	5,457,389	4,477,586	62,377	4,539,963	377,132	-21,451	4,141,380	722,417	593,592	6,123	891,221	457,484
1977	6,139,287	5,094,104	65,171	5,159,275	427,494	-30,404	4,701,377	815,107	622,803	6,747	909,992	481,268
1978	7,033,484	5,896,055	67,651	5,963,706	502,365	-45,811	5,415,530	935,445	682,509	7,560	930,403	503,047
1979	7,895,799	6,606,100	63,285	6,669,385	587,718	-49,168	6,032,499	1,068,637	794,663	8,321	948,910	520,756
1980	8,725,940	7,086,170	45,449	7,131,619	632,400	-53,541	6,445,678	1,301,983	978,279	9,030	966,369	516,142
1981	9,837,249	7,882,875	72,860	7,955,735	761,086	-86,882	7,107,767	1,615,957	1,113,525	10,091	974,846	523,293
1982	10,528,581	8,249,140	71,894	8,321,034	818,066	-65,617	7,437,351	1,854,237	1,236,993	10,734	980,868	519,035
1983	11,356,836	9,057,212	-3,235	9,053,977	911,747	-66,510	8,075,720	1,962,350	1,318,766	11,468	990,291	530,629
1984	12,852,038	10,267,657	72,091	10,339,748	1,064,235	-88,856	9,186,657	2,276,944	1,388,437	12,785	1,005,226	566,641
1985	14,124,333	11,433,722	53,779	11,487,501	1,201,456	-123,163	10,162,882	2,476,036	1,485,415	13,839	1,020,620	597,123
1986	15,457,511	12,677,816	15,911	12,693,727	1,359,711	-155,413	11,178,603	2,680,820	1,598,088	14,845	1,041,249	628,746
1987	16,762,535	13,882,702	14,390	13,897,092	1,475,492	-197,422	12,224,178	2,844,401	1,693,956	15,728	1,065,808	657,288
1988	18,159,850	14,965,732	18,111	14,983,843	1,621,149	-215,584	13,147,110	3,170,999	1,841,741	16,803	1,080,719	672,526
1989	19,352,536	15,878,188	31,653	15,909,841	1,740,013	-260,507	13,909,321	3,412,001	2,031,214	17,689	1,094,048	684,522
1990	20,551,292	16,635,543	37,556	16,673,099	1,841,021	-303,940	14,528,138	3,748,075	2,275,079	18,539	1,108,523	692,179
1991	21,784,765	17,729,533	51,092	17,780,625	1,990,437	-364,606	15,425,582	3,757,725	2,601,458	19,265	1,130,775	699,011
1992	24,154,852	19,847,272	67,458	19,914,730	2,191,639	-429,561	17,293,530	3,943,133	2,918,189	20,898	1,155,871	715,870
1993	26,042,764	21,544,957	64,248	21,609,205	2,376,207	-482,674	18,750,324	4,181,216	3,111,224	21,957	1,186,057	752,674
1994	28,132,620	23,489,182	60,778	23,549,960	2,629,670	-538,563	20,381,727	4,487,928	3,262,965	23,076	1,219,138	796,197
1995	30,739,568	25,570,235	43,113	25,613,348	2,847,787	-608,580	22,156,981	4,993,794	3,588,793	24,573	1,250,936	825,158
1996	32,674,619	27,239,973	-13,087	27,226,886	2,977,184	-648,062	23,601,640	5,297,798	3,775,181	25,484	1,282,177	849,563
1997	34,879,114	29,288,708	26,655	29,315,363	3,201,903	-710,973	25,402,487	5,550,233	3,926,394	26,564	1,313,031	879,964
1998	39,037,345	32,967,626	-6,726	32,960,900	3,419,082	-751,152	28,790,666	6,110,411	4,136,268	29,154	1,338,997	911,372
1999	41,353,662	35,270,594	-39,382	35,231,212	3,643,998	-824,585	30,762,629	6,267,415	4,323,618	30,350	1,362,545	931,947
2000	45,040,718	38,356,480	22,294	38,378,774	3,887,075	-905,843	33,585,856	6,739,821	4,715,041	32,464	1,387,417	955,226
2001	46,213,939	39,340,140	3,007	39,343,147	3,999,930	-932,460	34,410,757	6,603,514	5,199,668	32,795	1,409,191	947,418
2002	47,762,628	41,210,980	-41,020	41,169,960	4,193,813	-1,043,894	35,932,253	6,244,127	5,586,248	33,450	1,427,867	946,147
2003	49,636,601	42,673,370	-47,694	42,625,676	4,352,332	-1,050,509	37,222,835	6,446,126	5,967,640	34,232	1,450,015	955,915
2004	53,663,872	46,079,855	-9,057	46,070,798	4,640,195	-930,960	40,499,643	6,770,289	6,393,940	36,297	1,478,449	988,263
2005	55,877,941	47,475,515	-6,517	47,468,998	4,868,222	-909,816	41,690,960	7,300,996	6,885,985	36,973	1,511,310	1,019,501
2006	60,147,479	50,917,306	-32,987	50,884,319	5,206,501	-1,068,620	44,609,198	8,249,344	7,288,937	38,720	1,553,397	1,048,402
2007	63,304,796	52,403,508	-83,540	52,319,968	5,482,479	-773,937	46,063,552	9,200,043	8,041,201	39,755	1,592,365	1,072,982
2008	66,920,052	54,423,756	-17,307	54,406,449	5,694,153	-895,818	47,816,478	9,877,680	9,225,894	41,133	1,626,925	1,071,324
2009	65,702,511	53,633,148	-47,455	53,585,693	5,586,061	-848,338	47,151,294	8,614,923	9,936,294	39,718	1,654,243	1,034,075
2010	69,056,777	55,304,238	-49,347	55,254,891	5,740,094	-834,676	48,680,121	9,344,209	11,032,447	41,205	1,675,913	1,034,080
2011	73,089,183	58,237,269	-16,918	58,220,351	5,345,846	-860,408	52,014,097	9,808,156	11,266,930	43,037	1,698,288	1,064,235
2012	79,090,471	63,306,696	60,706	63,367,402	5,631,790	-1,020,571	56,715,041	11,025,111	11,350,319	45,792	1,727,153	1,097,230
2013	80,586,660	65,567,736	96,457	65,664,193	6,634,986	-1,062,695	57,966,512	10,844,063	11,776,085	45,825	1,758,577	1,134,618
2014	84,957,372	69,619,461	50,980	69,670,441	7,041,410	-1,119,760	61,509,271	11,300,701	12,147,400	47,392	1,792,649	1,172,081

Personal Income and Employment by Area: New Bern, NC

(Thousands of dollars, except as noted.)

| Year | Personal income, total | Derivation of personal income | | | | | | | | Per capita personal income (dollars) | Population (persons) | Total employment |
| | | Earnings by place of work | | | Less: Contributions for government social insurance | Plus: Adjustment for residence | Equals: Net earnings by place of residence | Plus: Dividends, interest, and rent | Plus: Personal current transfer receipts | | | |
		Nonfarm	Farm	Total								
1970	285,670	229,807	15,138	244,945	12,390	-13,283	219,272	46,715	19,683	3,480	82,081	40,058
1971	300,194	248,162	11,597	259,759	13,749	-16,730	229,280	48,076	22,838	3,578	83,889	38,574
1972	333,261	270,075	18,626	288,701	15,358	-18,815	254,528	52,069	26,664	3,915	85,129	38,318
1973	392,668	313,250	26,311	339,561	19,658	-21,154	298,749	63,951	29,968	4,486	87,526	40,884
1974	433,209	344,824	26,683	371,507	23,207	-22,843	325,457	71,607	36,145	5,002	86,605	41,460
1975	473,281	370,739	25,448	396,187	26,471	-23,760	345,956	80,333	46,992	5,328	88,837	41,185
1976	461,660	357,684	24,001	381,685	25,898	-21,930	333,857	74,573	53,230	5,070	91,051	37,864
1977	514,970	405,592	14,147	419,739	29,647	-22,935	367,157	89,841	57,972	5,658	91,010	40,592
1978	615,021	480,156	24,300	504,456	35,161	-29,395	439,900	112,148	62,973	6,719	91,529	43,032
1979	671,514	534,559	10,629	545,188	41,013	-30,215	473,960	126,286	71,268	7,408	90,650	44,787
1980	783,110	605,264	16,815	622,079	46,284	-32,221	543,574	154,006	85,530	8,564	91,445	46,872
1981	833,368	644,988	16,948	661,936	51,043	-49,532	561,361	173,993	98,014	9,023	92,365	43,576
1982	937,390	717,455	26,122	743,577	56,875	-56,962	629,740	198,003	109,647	9,959	94,122	45,190
1983	985,741	771,222	6,322	777,544	65,449	-58,576	653,519	214,249	117,973	10,341	95,328	46,894
1984	1,131,529	879,352	20,643	899,995	76,938	-63,450	759,607	245,419	126,503	11,635	97,256	49,839
1985	1,223,035	958,648	13,553	972,201	86,660	-70,560	814,981	270,250	137,804	12,247	99,860	51,285
1986	1,310,210	1,022,283	15,701	1,037,984	95,177	-74,935	867,872	294,197	148,141	13,062	100,306	52,168
1987	1,367,813	1,052,743	23,782	1,076,525	100,713	-70,137	905,675	304,588	157,550	13,678	99,999	52,819
1988	1,464,085	1,128,051	25,509	1,153,560	113,404	-77,604	962,552	328,262	173,271	14,454	101,292	53,217
1989	1,592,164	1,191,774	25,672	1,217,446	122,442	-81,116	1,013,888	383,007	195,269	15,647	101,757	54,451
1990	1,623,902	1,213,652	26,557	1,240,209	129,662	-90,351	1,020,196	388,038	215,668	15,779	102,918	54,413
1991	1,716,011	1,261,076	35,313	1,296,389	136,845	-95,689	1,063,855	400,686	251,470	16,459	104,258	53,677
1992	1,897,895	1,415,520	29,937	1,445,457	154,766	-111,362	1,179,329	441,046	277,520	17,963	105,655	55,701
1993	1,956,126	1,417,173	31,525	1,448,698	157,551	-104,467	1,186,680	461,625	307,821	18,477	105,871	55,763
1994	2,061,989	1,486,718	31,139	1,517,857	165,790	-106,493	1,245,574	494,516	321,899	19,372	106,443	56,340
1995	2,199,549	1,559,383	29,094	1,588,477	173,312	-108,125	1,307,040	530,359	362,150	20,339	108,147	58,223
1996	2,376,016	1,660,764	44,778	1,705,542	184,523	-112,365	1,408,654	576,815	390,547	21,630	109,848	60,554
1997	2,540,516	1,747,043	52,150	1,799,193	193,807	-106,492	1,498,894	633,091	408,531	22,788	111,484	62,242
1998	2,673,765	1,890,248	21,825	1,912,073	208,664	-112,218	1,591,191	658,226	424,348	23,748	112,591	64,013
1999	2,815,676	1,996,863	20,620	2,017,483	219,903	-111,635	1,685,945	670,202	459,529	24,679	114,091	64,824
2000	3,027,712	2,134,704	66,499	2,201,203	232,706	-117,340	1,851,157	689,955	486,600	26,292	115,156	65,829
2001	3,107,331	2,167,919	80,082	2,248,001	237,707	-135,623	1,874,671	696,116	536,544	26,698	116,388	65,379
2002	3,086,630	2,190,819	28,707	2,219,526	240,573	-140,465	1,838,488	677,501	570,641	26,686	115,664	64,925
2003	3,253,282	2,345,087	28,785	2,373,872	261,408	-166,376	1,946,088	704,620	602,574	28,100	115,776	65,843
2004	3,513,026	2,529,358	55,679	2,585,037	281,204	-180,927	2,122,906	742,133	647,987	30,150	116,520	67,676
2005	3,750,099	2,675,614	91,741	2,767,355	300,852	-198,629	2,267,874	785,693	696,532	31,838	117,787	69,085
2006	3,912,110	2,799,769	64,143	2,863,912	318,683	-197,737	2,347,492	812,984	751,634	32,624	119,915	70,245
2007	4,203,038	2,972,196	40,890	3,013,086	342,064	-216,117	2,454,905	937,232	810,901	34,772	120,873	71,308
2008	4,430,419	3,056,792	43,135	3,099,927	351,441	-215,343	2,533,143	988,836	908,440	36,169	122,491	70,462
2009	4,537,624	3,164,401	43,077	3,207,478	360,920	-222,796	2,623,762	920,486	993,376	36,242	125,202	68,745
2010	4,634,276	3,217,386	53,085	3,270,471	360,734	-234,127	2,675,610	898,741	1,059,925	36,460	127,105	67,806
2011	4,743,637	3,188,617	58,664	3,247,281	332,650	-253,952	2,660,679	989,412	1,093,546	36,990	128,241	67,298
2012	4,956,178	3,341,090	79,666	3,420,756	345,037	-266,742	2,808,977	1,019,318	1,127,883	38,530	128,630	67,508
2013	4,845,495	3,204,107	82,337	3,286,444	376,131	-244,238	2,666,075	1,025,486	1,153,934	37,977	127,589	67,456
2014	5,004,713	3,303,609	78,094	3,381,703	385,505	-248,605	2,747,593	1,065,169	1,191,951	39,242	127,534	68,030

Personal Income and Employment by Area: New Haven-Milford, CT

(Thousands of dollars, except as noted.)

Year	Personal income, total	Earnings by place of work			Less: Contributions for government social insurance	Plus: Adjustment for residence	Equals: Net earnings by place of residence	Plus: Dividends, interest, and rent	Plus: Personal current transfer receipts	Per capita personal income (dollars)	Population (persons)	Total employment
		Nonfarm	Farm	Total								
1970	3,590,585	2,765,539	7,183	2,772,722	188,141	97,319	2,681,900	588,884	319,801	4,804	747,435	341,697
1971	3,808,608	2,888,247	7,292	2,895,539	203,266	99,848	2,792,121	621,174	395,313	5,031	757,031	335,504
1972	4,110,230	3,145,262	7,069	3,152,331	234,151	114,841	3,033,021	660,917	416,292	5,422	758,131	342,677
1973	4,475,302	3,450,342	8,267	3,458,609	296,384	135,465	3,297,690	727,117	450,495	5,914	756,777	357,175
1974	4,881,868	3,692,940	7,802	3,700,742	330,304	158,632	3,529,070	824,036	528,762	6,430	759,277	364,298
1975	5,238,078	3,773,748	8,099	3,781,847	329,632	190,705	3,642,920	885,097	710,061	6,895	759,648	349,425
1976	5,605,941	4,048,129	7,787	4,055,916	359,127	223,453	3,920,242	934,749	750,950	7,393	758,263	351,258
1977	6,142,698	4,447,317	9,735	4,457,052	396,063	265,628	4,326,617	1,030,455	785,626	8,105	757,917	361,753
1978	6,793,914	4,949,450	11,701	4,961,151	452,783	328,369	4,836,737	1,151,525	805,652	8,973	757,121	374,218
1979	7,565,106	5,488,975	10,419	5,499,394	524,191	406,809	5,382,012	1,293,813	889,281	9,951	760,219	385,300
1980	8,474,424	5,901,681	11,139	5,912,820	563,729	522,112	5,871,203	1,599,463	1,003,758	11,120	762,066	386,193
1981	9,449,408	6,326,905	8,176	6,335,081	648,154	623,136	6,310,063	1,956,724	1,182,621	12,378	763,373	385,348
1982	10,120,328	6,644,564	12,366	6,656,930	692,012	697,039	6,661,957	2,144,416	1,313,955	13,231	764,877	381,104
1983	10,894,630	7,221,399	12,025	7,233,424	757,949	743,113	7,218,588	2,258,919	1,417,123	14,131	770,970	385,388
1984	12,205,245	8,152,021	12,890	8,164,911	877,892	836,314	8,123,333	2,610,256	1,471,656	15,723	776,264	406,456
1985	13,053,020	8,820,661	12,253	8,832,914	961,245	935,537	8,807,206	2,695,476	1,550,338	16,669	783,092	416,819
1986	14,064,501	9,538,886	13,458	9,552,344	1,042,786	1,039,193	9,548,751	2,882,234	1,633,516	17,814	789,528	428,205
1987	15,359,850	10,659,455	12,641	10,672,096	1,151,944	1,120,836	10,640,988	3,035,141	1,683,721	19,285	796,486	441,230
1988	16,950,221	11,861,384	13,924	11,875,308	1,306,442	1,230,513	11,799,379	3,338,151	1,812,691	21,152	801,339	455,617
1989	18,282,597	12,465,966	11,670	12,477,636	1,368,838	1,329,831	12,438,629	3,811,040	2,032,928	22,740	804,000	453,175
1990	18,766,380	12,741,739	13,039	12,754,778	1,381,413	1,382,731	12,756,096	3,739,617	2,270,667	23,302	805,366	445,131
1991	18,914,449	12,993,976	11,418	13,005,394	1,436,124	1,335,563	12,904,833	3,473,316	2,536,300	23,424	807,490	426,841
1992	19,941,637	13,653,670	13,825	13,667,495	1,486,998	1,314,572	13,495,069	3,448,826	2,997,742	24,660	808,659	424,565
1993	20,743,414	14,160,726	17,019	14,177,745	1,540,077	1,374,657	14,012,325	3,604,804	3,126,285	25,642	808,977	429,976
1994	21,325,827	14,546,184	15,310	14,561,494	1,597,601	1,454,619	14,418,512	3,647,276	3,260,039	26,355	809,178	425,475
1995	22,265,070	15,016,489	16,502	15,032,991	1,665,622	1,550,843	14,918,212	3,863,131	3,483,727	27,516	809,157	432,879
1996	22,974,601	15,691,280	13,890	15,705,170	1,738,809	1,468,198	15,434,559	3,975,885	3,564,157	28,329	811,000	442,172
1997	24,225,560	16,749,043	13,178	16,762,221	1,831,397	1,525,582	16,456,406	4,109,420	3,659,734	29,779	813,505	446,766
1998	25,426,744	17,810,832	15,450	17,826,282	1,915,854	1,594,539	17,504,967	4,220,810	3,700,967	31,110	817,313	454,473
1999	26,600,753	18,691,242	17,586	18,708,828	1,982,318	1,874,257	18,600,767	4,211,846	3,788,140	32,424	820,396	459,758
2000	28,609,030	20,181,610	20,230	20,201,840	2,097,636	1,877,289	19,981,493	4,630,391	3,997,146	34,681	824,911	468,887
2001	29,784,274	21,033,980	20,368	21,054,348	2,187,256	2,091,273	20,958,365	4,588,965	4,236,944	35,890	829,875	471,244
2002	30,435,188	21,740,262	23,653	21,763,915	2,330,125	2,047,307	21,481,097	4,405,990	4,548,101	36,445	835,099	472,129
2003	31,151,751	22,230,560	23,435	22,253,995	2,386,916	2,036,749	21,903,828	4,625,424	4,622,499	37,000	841,939	469,696
2004	32,654,791	23,486,632	25,782	23,512,414	2,504,797	2,103,410	23,111,027	4,626,400	4,917,364	38,667	844,505	479,040
2005	33,522,578	24,058,112	27,959	24,086,071	2,562,944	2,098,320	23,621,447	4,806,629	5,094,502	39,570	847,162	482,559
2006	35,310,599	24,932,089	27,423	24,959,512	2,632,758	2,127,572	24,454,326	5,439,779	5,416,494	41,532	850,207	488,643
2007	37,252,761	25,750,374	32,487	25,782,861	2,731,654	2,192,855	25,244,062	6,286,971	5,721,728	43,642	853,598	495,676
2008	38,393,258	26,085,973	22,518	26,108,491	2,833,809	2,199,940	25,474,622	6,381,934	6,536,702	44,819	856,622	496,234
2009	37,620,201	25,716,037	21,735	25,737,772	2,790,836	1,466,950	24,413,886	5,964,736	7,241,579	43,743	860,025	483,305
2010	38,324,213	26,072,753	21,756	26,094,509	2,797,413	1,550,287	24,847,383	5,773,903	7,702,927	44,389	863,367	475,735
2011	39,954,880	26,591,451	15,251	26,606,702	2,590,017	1,816,643	25,833,328	6,377,741	7,743,811	46,241	864,049	481,376
2012	41,350,921	27,404,365	22,443	27,426,808	2,664,621	1,732,185	26,494,372	6,989,014	7,867,535	47,858	864,031	485,762
2013	41,533,240	27,973,897	27,925	28,001,822	3,093,248	1,555,645	26,464,219	7,171,317	7,897,704	48,126	863,016	490,248
2014	43,288,478	28,893,837	27,599	28,921,436	3,183,217	1,989,880	27,728,099	7,490,187	8,070,192	50,261	861,277	493,753

Personal Income and Employment by Area: New Orleans-Metairie-Kenner, LA

(Thousands of dollars, except as noted.)

Year	Personal income, total	Derivation of personal income									Per capita personal income (dollars)	Population (persons)	Total employment
		Earnings by place of work			Less: Contributions for government social insurance	Plus: Adjustment for residence	Equals: Net earnings by place of residence	Plus: Dividends, interest, and rent	Plus: Personal current transfer receipts				
		Nonfarm	Farm	Total									
1970	4,272,879	3,692,470	10,681	3,703,151	241,315	-113,029	3,348,807	569,052	355,020		3,726	1,146,894	504,994
1971	4,615,407	3,969,856	11,797	3,981,653	266,323	-133,283	3,582,047	622,114	411,246		3,957	1,166,467	508,631
1972	5,042,212	4,361,987	14,514	4,376,501	307,439	-155,355	3,913,707	670,234	458,271		4,247	1,187,285	526,614
1973	5,549,742	4,809,394	22,938	4,832,332	390,737	-172,691	4,268,904	740,672	540,166		4,636	1,197,218	548,458
1974	6,254,476	5,355,977	31,416	5,387,393	446,765	-204,045	4,736,583	887,357	630,536		5,200	1,202,899	563,281
1975	7,039,302	6,028,637	13,862	6,042,499	493,477	-243,614	5,305,408	961,137	772,757		5,783	1,217,164	581,071
1976	7,900,881	6,859,159	15,927	6,875,086	572,554	-289,836	6,012,696	1,029,672	858,513		6,372	1,239,970	600,729
1977	8,766,571	7,661,993	14,610	7,676,603	636,449	-329,913	6,710,241	1,128,580	927,750		6,984	1,255,289	617,879
1978	9,948,950	8,744,368	11,747	8,756,115	740,630	-387,772	7,627,713	1,310,322	1,010,915		7,832	1,270,252	640,835
1979	11,224,283	9,910,212	11,342	9,921,554	872,300	-470,010	8,579,244	1,499,760	1,145,279		8,731	1,285,635	657,374
1980	12,883,835	11,269,017	9,160	11,278,177	985,674	-584,669	9,707,834	1,820,042	1,355,959		9,847	1,308,411	679,099
1981	14,768,547	12,783,936	12,294	12,796,230	1,201,115	-622,462	10,972,653	2,275,204	1,520,690		11,166	1,322,669	695,393
1982	15,882,748	13,473,067	13,603	13,486,670	1,291,861	-645,270	11,549,539	2,610,258	1,722,951		11,844	1,340,939	692,756
1983	16,588,465	13,751,098	14,467	13,765,565	1,312,453	-659,564	11,793,548	2,854,250	1,940,667		12,276	1,351,273	679,426
1984	17,693,629	14,551,917	8,367	14,560,284	1,420,914	-676,950	12,462,420	3,198,448	2,032,761		13,102	1,350,467	693,125
1985	18,378,464	14,751,398	11,223	14,762,621	1,445,102	-638,613	12,678,906	3,501,079	2,198,479		13,615	1,349,897	681,199
1986	18,685,014	14,778,323	12,490	14,790,813	1,430,585	-577,788	12,782,440	3,520,769	2,381,805		13,868	1,347,337	660,295
1987	18,852,015	14,926,704	11,818	14,938,522	1,421,105	-560,089	12,957,328	3,474,293	2,420,394		14,203	1,327,369	650,890
1988	19,735,007	15,650,340	17,881	15,668,221	1,557,727	-571,033	13,539,461	3,627,907	2,567,639		15,061	1,310,318	664,408
1989	20,895,409	16,379,333	17,963	16,397,296	1,638,472	-581,587	14,177,237	3,923,303	2,794,869		16,112	1,296,918	668,800
1990	22,359,194	17,575,895	8,413	17,584,308	1,807,209	-640,392	15,136,707	4,148,522	3,073,965		17,400	1,285,014	681,627
1991	23,459,692	18,386,076	9,733	18,395,809	1,937,666	-646,328	15,811,815	4,110,329	3,537,548		18,116	1,294,966	685,564
1992	25,102,097	19,414,024	14,708	19,428,732	2,014,172	-647,390	16,767,170	4,260,779	4,074,148		19,205	1,307,069	683,945
1993	26,219,381	20,079,661	19,104	20,098,765	2,088,600	-639,561	17,370,604	4,394,014	4,454,763		19,935	1,315,265	695,199
1994	27,717,140	21,204,412	14,246	21,218,658	2,243,435	-665,206	18,310,017	4,536,420	4,870,703		20,944	1,323,418	705,084
1995	29,266,092	22,329,398	15,692	22,345,090	2,357,523	-706,371	19,281,196	5,038,005	4,946,891		22,001	1,330,188	724,157
1996	30,215,555	23,013,598	13,828	23,027,426	2,427,219	-725,615	19,874,592	5,307,931	5,033,032		22,699	1,331,131	732,972
1997	31,892,499	24,372,804	15,079	24,387,883	2,564,260	-766,658	21,056,965	5,721,563	5,113,971		23,916	1,333,525	747,596
1998	33,279,131	25,642,296	16,582	25,658,878	2,723,636	-803,670	22,131,572	6,022,325	5,125,234		24,918	1,335,520	756,834
1999	33,914,611	26,385,315	17,153	26,402,468	2,776,672	-780,797	22,844,999	5,832,529	5,237,083		25,340	1,338,370	760,101
2000	35,768,382	27,617,340	15,391	27,632,731	2,841,641	-786,750	24,004,340	6,395,120	5,368,922		26,707	1,339,280	769,597
2001	37,770,125	29,162,054	15,637	29,177,691	2,963,245	-789,250	25,425,196	6,245,390	6,099,539		28,092	1,344,528	775,121
2002	38,711,387	30,168,836	14,902	30,183,738	3,060,775	-964,067	26,158,896	6,186,520	6,365,971		28,577	1,354,638	774,675
2003	39,435,940	31,184,982	16,125	31,201,107	3,142,099	-1,198,746	26,860,262	6,260,665	6,315,013		28,888	1,365,146	780,031
2004	41,263,991	32,743,892	16,673	32,760,565	3,245,680	-1,414,255	28,100,630	6,275,524	6,887,837		29,951	1,377,699	783,510
2005	42,951,472	32,276,871	17,268	32,294,139	3,144,984	-1,279,613	27,869,542	6,471,898	8,610,032		30,980	1,386,429	719,260
2006	43,099,648	32,516,295	36,836	32,553,131	3,140,854	-655,978	28,756,299	8,253,082	6,090,267		41,434	1,040,195	653,602
2007	49,868,434	34,542,819	31,671	34,574,490	3,355,445	-996,697	30,222,348	13,421,508	6,224,578		45,485	1,096,365	691,538
2008	50,267,308	37,162,681	13,041	37,175,722	3,542,587	-1,606,443	32,026,692	10,982,118	7,258,498		44,256	1,135,831	716,514
2009	47,851,887	36,170,761	16,377	36,187,138	3,547,991	-1,500,780	31,138,367	8,920,885	7,792,635		40,975	1,167,842	717,582
2010	49,966,225	37,698,316	19,120	37,717,436	3,660,635	-1,635,409	32,421,392	8,832,524	8,712,309		41,785	1,195,794	723,468
2011	51,158,841	38,625,440	21,851	38,647,291	3,344,286	-1,824,989	33,478,016	8,819,271	8,861,554		42,133	1,214,235	728,895
2012	54,935,998	39,924,107	20,450	39,944,557	3,407,042	-1,524,882	35,012,633	10,942,074	8,981,291		44,722	1,228,375	744,079
2013	55,715,566	40,657,629	31,161	40,688,790	3,991,521	-1,235,522	35,461,747	10,961,808	9,292,011		44,861	1,241,949	760,391
2014	57,937,472	42,416,613	20,954	42,437,567	4,157,139	-1,113,439	37,166,989	11,409,555	9,360,928		46,282	1,251,849	772,620

Personal Income and Employment by Area: New York-Northern New Jersey-Long Island, NY-NJ-PA

(Thousands of dollars, except as noted.)

Year	Personal income, total	Derivation of personal income								Per capita personal income (dollars)	Population (persons)	Total employment
		Earnings by place of work			Less: Contributions for government social insurance	Plus: Adjustment for residence	Equals: Net earnings by place of residence	Plus: Dividends, interest, and rent	Plus: Personal current transfer receipts			
		Nonfarm	Farm	Total								
1970	92,591,113	75,195,183	80,494	75,275,677	5,549,743	-931,037	68,794,897	15,314,248	8,481,968	5,280	17,535,718	8,260,820
1971	98,811,403	79,432,869	74,998	79,507,867	6,045,993	-1,035,389	72,426,485	16,130,130	10,254,788	5,608	17,619,521	8,111,649
1972	106,055,987	85,549,959	64,414	85,614,373	6,835,480	-1,225,313	77,553,580	16,991,276	11,511,131	6,031	17,585,345	8,136,244
1973	112,680,150	91,399,671	94,357	91,494,028	8,462,653	-1,397,048	81,634,327	18,270,247	12,775,576	6,460	17,443,567	8,246,386
1974	121,247,126	96,701,791	97,091	96,798,882	9,225,748	-1,568,103	86,005,031	20,398,374	14,843,721	6,995	17,332,549	8,154,035
1975	130,740,315	101,725,601	88,016	101,813,617	9,494,198	-1,777,671	90,541,748	21,554,301	18,644,266	7,574	17,261,678	7,918,534
1976	138,906,245	108,481,663	86,510	108,568,173	10,309,619	-1,996,216	96,262,338	22,665,801	19,978,106	8,078	17,196,345	7,896,024
1977	150,448,513	117,971,088	102,110	118,073,198	11,113,141	-2,317,369	104,642,688	24,907,966	20,897,859	8,812	17,073,947	7,982,339
1978	164,905,175	130,524,298	116,896	130,641,194	12,580,451	-2,633,294	115,427,449	27,558,364	21,919,362	9,721	16,964,428	8,203,566
1979	180,676,383	143,607,075	132,263	143,739,338	14,352,884	-2,967,028	126,419,426	30,738,432	23,518,525	10,690	16,902,176	8,399,502
1980	201,962,461	157,831,154	156,082	157,987,236	15,826,664	-3,359,072	138,801,500	36,346,902	26,814,059	11,962	16,883,742	8,473,331
1981	225,775,914	173,309,174	165,378	173,474,552	18,585,836	-3,589,303	151,299,413	44,232,706	30,243,795	13,349	16,912,851	8,561,737
1982	244,933,810	186,395,999	162,255	186,558,254	20,357,846	-3,938,706	162,261,702	49,874,868	32,797,240	14,448	16,953,181	8,600,498
1983	265,582,155	202,927,388	159,125	203,086,513	22,305,693	-4,225,648	176,555,172	53,536,154	35,490,829	15,546	17,083,867	8,726,253
1984	294,681,178	224,103,563	185,807	224,289,370	25,379,118	-4,611,971	194,298,281	62,838,850	37,544,047	17,148	17,184,801	9,029,518
1985	316,322,995	242,968,796	187,526	243,156,322	27,842,623	-5,046,985	210,266,714	66,411,323	39,644,958	18,324	17,262,804	9,249,556
1986	338,616,483	263,880,163	193,640	264,073,803	30,633,114	-5,165,033	228,275,656	68,452,860	41,887,967	19,519	17,348,462	9,445,159
1987	364,610,530	288,980,160	229,365	289,209,525	32,993,048	-5,549,419	250,667,058	70,830,908	43,112,564	20,947	17,406,126	9,529,663
1988	402,702,938	319,888,188	228,646	320,116,834	36,717,077	-6,080,299	277,319,458	79,535,181	45,848,299	23,072	17,454,527	9,698,726
1989	433,303,842	336,615,787	226,323	336,842,110	38,130,451	-6,243,573	292,468,086	90,561,473	50,274,283	24,842	17,442,709	9,725,398
1990	462,390,874	357,168,670	210,587	357,379,257	38,473,693	-6,044,187	312,861,377	94,147,381	55,382,116	26,486	17,457,943	9,624,264
1991	461,869,728	351,097,493	193,045	351,290,538	39,291,617	-6,093,776	305,905,145	93,679,208	62,285,375	26,313	17,552,994	9,303,754
1992	491,249,950	376,525,927	188,399	376,714,326	41,277,145	-7,688,043	327,749,138	93,259,366	70,241,446	27,762	17,695,120	9,228,347
1993	506,121,196	387,601,544	211,418	387,812,962	42,351,338	-7,396,978	338,064,646	93,488,670	74,567,880	28,342	17,857,808	9,250,792
1994	523,425,324	399,221,414	191,598	399,413,012	44,358,121	-7,350,991	347,703,900	98,304,018	77,417,406	29,091	17,992,928	9,259,764
1995	557,117,762	420,627,898	186,999	420,814,897	46,189,399	-8,414,611	366,210,887	108,192,356	82,714,519	30,721	18,134,488	9,388,188
1996	590,640,582	447,180,504	180,839	447,361,343	48,041,978	-9,740,806	389,578,559	114,977,081	86,084,942	32,317	18,276,694	9,523,904
1997	628,431,348	479,443,498	155,638	479,599,136	50,263,830	-9,874,606	419,460,700	122,668,716	86,301,932	34,088	18,435,323	9,678,437
1998	665,578,325	511,299,746	186,552	511,486,298	53,148,417	-12,113,325	446,224,556	129,713,525	89,640,244	35,757	18,613,907	9,879,697
1999	701,490,538	545,827,189	199,873	546,027,062	55,974,232	-11,947,073	478,105,757	130,548,055	92,836,726	37,300	18,806,645	10,117,341
2000	761,298,684	594,754,391	247,932	595,002,323	60,640,163	-13,323,607	521,038,553	142,379,513	97,880,618	40,111	18,980,010	10,447,522
2001	785,637,492	616,546,550	220,332	616,766,882	62,984,128	-12,733,864	541,048,890	139,127,258	105,461,344	41,113	19,109,150	10,496,110
2002	791,682,598	616,276,849	224,190	616,501,039	63,908,737	-6,069,064	546,523,238	130,567,627	114,591,733	41,244	19,195,261	10,435,642
2003	810,910,266	627,241,137	230,482	627,471,619	65,399,889	-3,902,798	558,168,932	134,063,602	118,677,732	42,129	19,248,311	10,457,533
2004	856,557,962	663,402,815	229,730	663,632,545	68,705,867	-8,565,987	586,360,691	143,495,542	126,701,729	44,488	19,253,664	10,617,027
2005	899,260,219	691,429,110	232,258	691,661,368	71,913,174	-13,427,607	606,320,587	166,932,503	126,007,129	46,769	19,227,714	10,778,138
2006	969,970,851	740,354,299	250,001	740,604,300	75,938,828	-19,736,595	644,928,877	191,171,090	133,870,884	50,518	19,200,372	10,971,464
2007	1,041,447,145	790,395,196	239,591	790,634,787	80,964,871	-27,490,824	682,179,092	219,460,726	139,807,327	54,140	19,236,108	11,281,469
2008	1,068,110,531	805,382,199	232,201	805,614,400	83,511,494	-23,539,472	698,563,434	216,268,634	153,278,463	55,231	19,338,823	11,394,356
2009	1,029,811,322	774,284,670	234,360	774,519,030	80,682,328	-20,648,825	673,187,877	188,268,018	168,355,427	52,895	19,469,123	11,172,371
2010	1,067,371,531	807,189,369	247,548	807,436,917	83,131,890	-23,003,911	701,301,116	186,729,673	179,340,742	54,459	19,599,534	11,163,663
2011	1,126,298,908	835,242,435	229,295	835,471,730	76,721,634	-24,016,589	734,733,507	209,401,099	182,164,302	57,010	19,756,128	11,481,114
2012	1,173,865,512	860,763,555	275,637	861,039,192	78,668,896	-25,680,070	756,690,226	237,007,154	180,168,132	59,064	19,874,606	11,630,572
2013	1,180,592,340	882,372,627	347,403	882,720,030	92,795,657	-24,081,068	765,843,305	233,135,207	181,613,828	59,023	20,002,086	11,866,010
2014	1,234,505,553	931,409,398	282,420	931,691,818	97,815,569	-27,433,012	806,443,237	242,606,195	185,456,121	61,440	20,092,883	12,094,064

Personal Income and Employment by Area: Niles-Benton Harbor, MI

(Thousands of dollars, except as noted.)

| Year | Personal income, total | Derivation of personal income | | | | | | | | | Per capita personal income (dollars) | Population (persons) | Total employment |
| | | Earnings by place of work | | | Less: Contributions for government social insurance | Plus: Adjustment for residence | Equals: Net earnings by place of residence | Plus: Dividends, interest, and rent | Plus: Personal current transfer receipts | | | | |
		Nonfarm	Farm	Total									
1970	663,481	546,792	13,052	559,844	39,687	-10,882	509,275	89,382	64,824		4,046	163,981	74,168
1971	713,940	587,579	12,290	599,869	43,922	-12,976	542,971	94,089	76,880		4,321	165,230	73,938
1972	804,662	680,051	11,695	691,746	53,707	-17,217	620,822	100,784	83,056		4,787	168,102	78,406
1973	890,799	755,229	15,564	770,793	69,060	-17,975	683,758	110,670	96,371		5,220	170,653	81,115
1974	969,345	797,510	22,494	820,004	75,629	-18,226	726,149	125,895	117,301		5,636	172,002	80,618
1975	1,024,983	806,235	15,667	821,902	74,539	-15,135	732,228	135,572	157,183		5,911	173,395	76,020
1976	1,095,597	861,138	13,170	874,308	80,940	-9,889	783,479	145,050	167,068		6,265	174,881	77,131
1977	1,221,730	974,534	20,099	994,633	91,954	-12,532	890,147	161,907	169,676		6,987	174,870	80,061
1978	1,336,959	1,064,631	22,766	1,087,397	103,327	-8,073	975,997	177,415	183,547		7,709	173,427	81,369
1979	1,427,689	1,122,892	10,930	1,133,822	113,332	-3,144	1,017,346	198,461	211,882		8,222	173,635	80,344
1980	1,518,165	1,129,096	10,910	1,140,006	113,486	-424	1,026,096	238,104	253,965		8,863	171,288	75,636
1981	1,651,886	1,192,278	14,545	1,206,823	129,067	530	1,078,286	291,131	282,469		9,662	170,961	73,651
1982	1,713,339	1,190,251	16,173	1,206,424	130,946	2,365	1,077,843	327,576	307,920		10,269	166,840	70,908
1983	1,773,693	1,233,145	10,889	1,244,034	137,640	5,073	1,111,467	335,722	326,504		10,794	164,326	70,184
1984	1,920,603	1,343,008	15,670	1,358,678	155,332	8,515	1,211,861	379,707	329,035		11,761	163,308	71,984
1985	2,021,390	1,416,246	24,911	1,441,157	165,932	8,917	1,284,142	392,781	344,467		12,405	162,945	73,946
1986	2,146,160	1,537,397	16,730	1,554,127	180,070	4,411	1,378,468	406,702	360,990		13,214	162,415	75,938
1987	2,299,055	1,667,283	28,463	1,695,746	191,830	5,722	1,509,638	417,557	371,860		14,107	162,973	78,673
1988	2,416,746	1,755,082	20,933	1,776,015	208,736	13,658	1,580,937	448,945	386,864		14,827	163,001	80,352
1989	2,579,937	1,846,773	30,772	1,877,545	218,200	14,238	1,673,583	497,760	408,594		15,911	162,143	81,954
1990	2,667,463	1,924,997	18,952	1,943,949	231,037	13,330	1,726,242	498,768	442,453		16,525	161,415	82,670
1991	2,740,584	1,963,617	22,914	1,986,531	238,957	16,894	1,764,468	488,137	487,979		16,957	161,622	81,364
1992	2,949,067	2,122,586	24,690	2,147,276	255,655	18,777	1,910,398	518,030	520,639		18,206	161,982	81,260
1993	3,126,628	2,286,597	19,862	2,306,459	278,217	19,993	2,048,235	522,013	556,380		19,269	162,266	81,681
1994	3,302,098	2,405,103	20,202	2,425,305	300,933	25,113	2,149,485	593,381	559,232		20,339	162,353	85,310
1995	3,474,207	2,519,967	22,834	2,542,801	314,856	34,925	2,262,870	636,087	575,250		21,311	163,022	88,048
1996	3,593,916	2,581,375	19,748	2,601,123	316,430	42,588	2,327,281	672,240	594,395		22,066	162,873	88,373
1997	3,829,043	2,738,414	24,180	2,762,594	334,147	42,542	2,470,989	712,885	645,169		23,577	162,407	88,512
1998	3,951,990	2,833,113	24,163	2,857,276	340,596	61,806	2,578,486	739,363	634,141		24,388	162,046	90,362
1999	4,164,355	3,031,233	29,642	3,060,875	360,291	63,801	2,764,385	712,319	687,651		25,701	162,028	89,339
2000	4,342,846	3,145,683	26,051	3,171,734	370,409	73,292	2,874,617	755,515	712,714		26,730	162,471	90,166
2001	4,419,549	3,105,699	33,411	3,139,110	354,230	80,619	2,865,499	745,529	808,521		27,425	161,153	86,966
2002	4,486,133	3,173,328	26,100	3,199,428	360,580	101,492	2,940,340	722,161	823,632		27,933	160,604	85,404
2003	4,589,529	3,168,460	34,557	3,203,017	360,811	120,916	2,963,122	759,279	867,128		28,628	160,314	84,474
2004	4,786,207	3,298,531	46,956	3,345,487	376,444	147,192	3,116,235	774,340	895,632		29,962	159,742	85,104
2005	4,886,640	3,367,369	39,519	3,406,888	389,630	171,596	3,188,854	755,999	941,787		30,829	158,510	85,794
2006	5,114,002	3,492,707	48,155	3,540,862	406,509	202,208	3,336,561	769,285	1,008,156		32,462	157,537	85,400
2007	5,434,559	3,621,227	58,308	3,679,535	425,767	239,193	3,492,961	847,681	1,093,917		34,532	157,378	87,792
2008	5,706,627	3,631,440	53,153	3,684,593	434,946	265,782	3,515,429	952,280	1,238,918		36,260	157,380	85,756
2009	5,346,996	3,450,957	49,374	3,500,331	414,916	99,963	3,185,378	819,971	1,341,647		34,045	157,059	80,791
2010	5,588,564	3,592,826	47,860	3,640,686	425,971	110,070	3,324,785	832,022	1,431,757		35,641	156,803	80,626
2011	5,858,724	3,575,439	82,135	3,657,574	384,337	144,863	3,418,100	1,011,479	1,429,145		37,425	156,544	80,878
2012	5,852,885	3,604,381	46,928	3,651,309	389,268	205,968	3,468,009	964,017	1,420,859		37,505	156,057	80,747
2013	5,946,548	3,776,349	63,861	3,840,210	455,797	156,615	3,541,028	966,585	1,438,935		38,286	155,321	81,013
2014	6,226,934	3,946,904	52,877	3,999,781	477,128	213,913	3,736,566	1,003,310	1,487,058		40,113	155,233	82,848

Personal Income and Employment by Area: North Port-Bradenton-Sarasota, FL

(Thousands of dollars, except as noted.)

| Year | Personal income, total | Derivation of personal income | | | | | | | | | Per capita personal income (dollars) | Population (persons) | Total employment |
| | | Earnings by place of work | | | Less: Contributions for government social insurance | Plus: Adjustment for residence | Equals: Net earnings by place of residence | Plus: Dividends, interest, and rent | Plus: Personal current transfer receipts | | | | |
		Nonfarm	Farm	Total									
1970	993,586	506,230	18,012	524,242	33,169	-5,797	485,276	375,397	132,913	4,518	219,936	86,898
1971	1,127,568	568,333	21,641	589,974	38,956	-5,096	545,922	420,585	161,061	4,849	232,523	91,869
1972	1,299,541	669,072	25,314	694,386	48,314	-4,823	641,249	468,550	189,742	5,311	244,710	99,827
1973	1,548,683	815,769	27,042	842,811	67,612	-7,451	767,748	547,859	233,076	5,850	264,738	113,242
1974	1,768,157	905,491	28,319	933,810	79,394	-8,058	846,358	646,439	275,360	6,266	282,181	117,686
1975	1,939,637	928,033	30,883	958,916	79,931	-6,233	872,752	719,738	347,147	6,714	288,894	114,242
1976	2,180,943	1,050,530	33,441	1,083,971	89,893	-5,446	988,632	809,887	382,424	7,352	296,666	119,612
1977	2,520,520	1,218,739	32,209	1,250,948	105,433	-6,540	1,138,975	954,211	427,334	8,218	306,701	130,788
1978	2,996,524	1,470,350	37,440	1,507,790	130,343	-8,229	1,369,218	1,144,983	482,323	9,303	322,092	144,674
1979	3,495,108	1,695,710	51,405	1,747,115	157,614	-11,231	1,578,270	1,351,663	565,175	10,322	338,608	153,849
1980	4,174,648	1,922,067	71,451	1,993,518	180,928	-11,986	1,800,604	1,698,588	675,456	11,769	354,724	160,146
1981	4,961,288	2,155,896	62,577	2,218,473	218,919	8,799	2,008,353	2,155,899	797,036	13,403	370,172	166,835
1982	5,329,018	2,265,077	91,159	2,356,236	241,096	28,604	2,143,744	2,277,066	908,208	13,852	384,723	172,913
1983	6,074,655	2,569,631	140,496	2,710,127	272,030	53,153	2,491,250	2,584,395	999,010	15,204	399,556	183,463
1984	6,796,738	2,930,226	94,846	3,025,072	319,317	86,074	2,791,829	2,946,610	1,058,299	16,434	413,582	196,895
1985	7,538,742	3,169,730	94,367	3,264,097	353,652	126,577	3,037,022	3,347,066	1,154,654	17,670	426,636	204,184
1986	8,199,135	3,457,878	102,700	3,560,578	396,180	171,268	3,335,666	3,608,962	1,254,507	18,696	438,539	213,336
1987	8,919,204	3,907,531	111,600	4,019,131	441,934	221,567	3,798,764	3,779,695	1,340,745	19,810	450,241	215,825
1988	9,770,523	4,253,793	129,257	4,383,050	499,477	285,301	4,168,874	4,131,771	1,469,878	21,110	462,830	227,771
1989	11,451,385	4,626,725	127,372	4,754,097	554,799	348,462	4,547,760	5,298,411	1,605,214	24,046	476,235	237,209
1990	12,151,517	5,026,970	100,338	5,127,308	589,907	408,947	4,946,348	5,466,416	1,738,753	24,633	493,311	246,876
1991	12,346,318	5,339,335	120,688	5,460,023	630,498	337,497	5,167,022	5,286,383	1,892,913	24,443	505,103	251,512
1992	13,116,197	5,829,103	136,436	5,965,539	680,412	381,473	5,666,600	5,350,138	2,099,459	25,658	511,201	257,502
1993	13,699,713	6,283,632	139,204	6,422,836	728,539	295,477	5,989,774	5,480,850	2,229,089	26,300	520,892	269,675
1994	14,677,626	6,802,098	117,265	6,919,363	802,290	286,036	6,403,109	5,897,281	2,377,236	27,577	532,241	286,866
1995	15,604,830	7,595,622	117,902	7,713,524	892,232	122,901	6,944,193	6,133,960	2,526,677	28,804	541,758	309,665
1996	16,547,266	7,782,006	107,746	7,889,752	898,128	411,272	7,402,896	6,481,394	2,662,976	30,031	551,004	304,542
1997	17,637,738	8,323,702	132,073	8,455,775	962,962	451,526	7,944,339	6,933,955	2,759,444	31,423	561,309	317,015
1998	19,291,365	8,988,128	159,302	9,147,430	1,025,200	654,118	8,776,348	7,650,141	2,864,876	33,667	573,004	322,552
1999	20,165,446	9,683,965	160,548	9,844,513	1,085,245	882,351	9,641,619	7,561,690	2,962,137	34,655	581,892	330,193
2000	21,735,760	10,696,447	163,632	10,860,079	1,180,474	702,028	10,381,633	8,233,851	3,120,276	36,666	592,809	355,395
2001	22,632,083	10,945,336	169,717	11,115,053	1,202,910	1,120,616	11,032,759	8,240,944	3,358,380	37,347	605,988	329,951
2002	23,357,249	11,825,791	178,500	12,004,291	1,307,014	1,083,054	11,780,331	8,013,861	3,563,057	37,640	620,540	349,562
2003	24,196,406	12,413,745	161,797	12,575,542	1,369,003	983,515	12,190,054	8,256,525	3,749,827	38,113	634,862	355,407
2004	26,618,070	13,591,618	168,128	13,759,746	1,520,505	927,074	13,166,315	9,469,254	3,982,501	40,705	653,934	375,114
2005	29,206,264	15,049,754	216,968	15,266,722	1,694,967	874,458	14,446,213	10,503,189	4,256,862	43,284	674,757	398,146
2006	31,630,247	16,117,360	204,264	16,321,624	1,829,404	771,061	15,263,281	11,764,264	4,602,702	46,167	685,132	413,589
2007	32,447,771	15,968,806	185,425	16,154,231	1,840,962	604,036	14,917,305	12,624,762	4,905,704	46,908	691,735	414,045
2008	31,778,331	14,949,428	179,992	15,129,420	1,748,023	371,294	13,752,691	12,498,610	5,527,030	45,662	695,944	392,338
2009	29,247,743	13,931,382	183,563	14,114,945	1,678,139	380,441	12,817,247	10,389,346	6,041,150	41,904	697,973	377,656
2010	30,167,757	13,798,053	186,652	13,984,705	1,671,141	468,645	12,782,209	10,914,712	6,470,836	42,885	703,462	367,259
2011	32,264,956	14,093,333	145,128	14,238,461	1,549,734	539,430	13,228,157	12,320,099	6,716,700	45,510	708,971	376,050
2012	32,769,247	14,752,004	152,728	14,904,732	1,617,555	566,889	13,854,066	12,144,663	6,770,518	45,505	720,121	385,464
2013	34,101,192	15,463,272	169,443	15,632,715	1,898,231	543,266	14,277,750	12,775,635	7,047,807	46,544	732,659	400,640
2014	35,878,708	16,448,947	148,463	16,597,410	2,022,546	527,430	15,102,294	13,271,908	7,504,506	47,921	748,708	415,988

Personal Income and Employment by Area: Norwich-New London, CT

(Thousands of dollars, except as noted.)

Year	Personal income, total	Derivation of personal income			Less: Contributions for government social insurance	Plus: Adjustment for residence	Equals: Net earnings by place of residence	Plus: Dividends, interest, and rent	Plus: Personal current transfer receipts	Per capita personal income (dollars)	Population (persons)	Total employment
		Earnings by place of work										
		Nonfarm	Farm	Total								
1970	1,008,400	826,451	8,094	834,545	52,910	-39,010	742,625	194,466	71,309	4,358	231,405	102,499
1971	1,088,311	891,562	8,046	899,608	60,164	-44,696	794,748	208,285	85,278	4,651	233,975	103,331
1972	1,197,185	978,217	8,926	987,143	69,019	-48,295	869,829	231,852	95,504	5,012	238,857	104,979
1973	1,320,703	1,096,880	11,330	1,108,210	86,485	-57,794	963,931	252,425	104,347	5,546	238,138	109,925
1974	1,473,761	1,240,325	6,002	1,246,327	102,790	-73,649	1,069,888	281,272	122,601	6,183	238,362	115,819
1975	1,575,158	1,275,480	10,476	1,285,956	105,536	-71,651	1,108,769	307,058	159,331	6,519	241,627	112,930
1976	1,705,644	1,397,189	11,625	1,408,814	118,516	-77,870	1,212,428	319,700	173,516	7,049	241,968	116,012
1977	1,892,938	1,572,047	13,141	1,585,188	138,790	-91,830	1,354,568	355,389	182,981	7,846	241,265	122,050
1978	2,046,849	1,659,674	8,360	1,668,034	147,775	-81,603	1,438,656	409,454	198,739	8,433	242,732	121,499
1979	2,257,135	1,830,542	9,990	1,840,532	168,617	-83,409	1,588,506	452,936	215,693	9,373	240,812	123,476
1980	2,561,530	2,036,416	11,647	2,048,063	183,291	-90,411	1,774,361	539,417	247,752	10,707	239,228	126,114
1981	2,919,227	2,312,184	18,060	2,330,244	223,217	-115,359	1,991,668	641,759	285,800	12,064	241,985	129,103
1982	3,204,864	2,550,755	22,255	2,573,010	251,097	-141,333	2,180,580	709,870	314,414	13,186	243,051	131,160
1983	3,521,060	2,857,517	24,081	2,881,598	288,556	-163,743	2,429,299	753,298	338,463	14,267	246,802	135,782
1984	3,916,839	3,146,510	38,287	3,184,797	326,082	-166,568	2,692,147	863,849	360,843	15,731	248,990	140,610
1985	4,149,952	3,333,665	37,036	3,370,701	348,267	-155,236	2,867,198	897,516	385,238	16,720	248,201	143,521
1986	4,300,531	3,354,930	38,619	3,393,549	346,231	-110,545	2,936,773	953,214	410,544	17,288	248,765	144,825
1987	4,659,012	3,638,739	43,265	3,682,004	372,044	-92,851	3,217,109	1,016,330	425,573	18,595	250,549	149,270
1988	4,947,502	3,862,525	38,843	3,901,368	407,835	-77,866	3,415,667	1,072,804	459,031	19,564	252,893	151,325
1989	5,383,377	4,110,883	36,125	4,147,008	433,531	-86,447	3,627,030	1,239,392	516,955	21,211	253,805	152,415
1990	5,591,983	4,126,764	44,215	4,170,979	433,964	52,772	3,789,787	1,220,693	581,503	21,889	255,474	149,439
1991	5,665,287	4,245,434	40,538	4,285,972	454,985	10,944	3,841,931	1,169,502	653,854	22,151	255,761	143,950
1992	6,019,093	4,416,613	42,499	4,459,112	470,077	83,480	4,072,515	1,178,260	768,318	23,856	252,306	141,923
1993	6,250,531	4,620,527	54,397	4,674,924	491,002	28,909	4,212,831	1,232,299	805,401	24,619	253,886	143,783
1994	6,552,089	5,010,021	48,516	5,058,537	542,941	-77,739	4,437,857	1,286,531	827,701	25,632	255,618	145,989
1995	6,834,760	5,330,948	34,773	5,365,721	581,631	-196,167	4,587,923	1,360,551	886,286	26,509	257,828	151,338
1996	7,073,608	5,545,348	37,243	5,582,591	604,401	-237,426	4,740,764	1,415,623	917,221	27,339	258,741	153,594
1997	7,516,398	5,976,857	35,484	6,012,341	636,423	-278,527	5,097,391	1,472,929	946,078	29,059	258,662	157,056
1998	7,903,707	6,183,644	37,569	6,221,213	649,305	-200,695	5,371,213	1,556,451	976,043	30,799	256,626	157,045
1999	8,203,053	6,495,008	38,211	6,533,219	664,542	-204,658	5,664,019	1,537,937	1,001,097	31,848	257,568	158,687
2000	8,638,199	6,750,984	41,910	6,792,894	682,707	-133,116	5,977,071	1,613,921	1,047,207	33,243	259,848	161,570
2001	9,134,679	7,126,594	45,595	7,172,189	709,258	-103,379	6,359,552	1,654,313	1,120,814	34,946	261,396	163,089
2002	9,554,916	7,504,482	51,549	7,556,031	767,629	-114,515	6,673,887	1,673,622	1,207,407	36,097	264,698	166,746
2003	10,024,188	7,836,595	48,504	7,885,099	792,093	-126,518	6,966,488	1,814,485	1,243,215	37,602	266,584	167,983
2004	10,513,561	8,268,154	46,398	8,314,552	827,407	-139,192	7,347,953	1,854,231	1,311,377	39,143	268,595	168,495
2005	10,781,027	8,515,959	41,746	8,557,705	852,057	-149,568	7,556,080	1,858,288	1,366,659	39,979	269,664	171,278
2006	11,267,298	8,774,496	38,060	8,812,556	874,453	-157,998	7,780,105	2,013,134	1,474,059	41,605	270,814	171,902
2007	11,837,588	9,077,270	44,072	9,121,342	906,732	-169,572	8,045,038	2,206,998	1,585,552	43,735	270,669	173,475
2008	12,410,372	9,313,037	42,329	9,355,366	949,386	-181,225	8,224,755	2,364,214	1,821,403	45,520	272,634	175,900
2009	12,289,798	9,227,841	42,110	9,269,951	948,887	-289,348	8,031,716	2,227,195	2,030,887	44,914	273,630	170,888
2010	12,407,845	9,249,593	37,181	9,286,774	939,510	-301,993	8,045,271	2,167,526	2,195,048	45,267	274,102	167,864
2011	12,938,597	9,358,127	36,397	9,394,524	859,007	-195,735	8,339,782	2,386,199	2,212,616	47,212	274,056	167,206
2012	13,332,090	9,392,360	48,608	9,440,968	869,139	-139,691	8,432,138	2,669,992	2,229,960	48,561	274,544	165,815
2013	13,282,930	9,364,140	60,074	9,424,214	987,951	21,789	8,458,052	2,562,121	2,262,757	48,482	273,976	165,097
2014	13,758,048	9,578,265	62,421	9,640,686	1,008,850	162,466	8,794,302	2,646,804	2,316,942	50,271	273,676	163944

Personal Income and Employment by Area: Ocala, FL

(Thousands of dollars, except as noted.)

Year	Personal income, total	Earnings by place of work			Less: Contributions for government social insurance	Plus: Adjustment for residence	Equals: Net earnings by place of residence	Plus: Dividends, interest, and rent	Plus: Personal current transfer receipts	Per capita personal income (dollars)	Population (persons)	Total employment
		Nonfarm	Farm	Total								
1970	229,271	152,248	10,838	163,086	9,942	5,220	158,364	44,092	26,815	3,260	70,320	28,119
1971	266,170	175,732	11,581	187,313	12,020	6,183	181,476	51,679	33,015	3,471	76,690	30,308
1972	316,034	209,498	13,638	223,136	15,029	8,424	216,531	59,892	39,611	3,898	81,072	32,968
1973	383,862	253,500	15,795	269,295	20,854	10,573	259,014	74,750	50,098	4,279	89,718	36,754
1974	426,575	272,449	9,833	282,282	23,546	11,936	270,672	91,131	64,772	4,378	97,426	37,392
1975	466,287	282,054	8,011	290,065	24,147	14,316	280,234	102,691	83,362	4,676	99,728	36,675
1976	516,356	310,237	6,790	317,027	27,176	17,057	306,908	110,496	98,952	4,906	105,252	37,671
1977	578,269	346,362	6,406	352,768	30,542	19,467	341,693	125,722	110,854	5,268	109,765	39,712
1978	672,209	403,138	6,772	409,910	36,357	22,154	395,707	152,399	124,103	5,968	112,629	43,276
1979	789,123	474,422	5,470	479,892	44,930	23,877	458,839	183,121	147,163	6,699	117,793	46,365
1980	961,057	549,417	9,789	559,206	52,422	27,768	534,552	244,637	181,868	7,737	124,218	50,295
1981	1,133,378	625,460	1,985	627,445	64,198	39,206	602,453	313,254	217,671	8,658	130,907	52,796
1982	1,277,392	677,606	14,606	692,212	71,612	50,756	671,356	351,835	254,201	9,298	137,381	54,974
1983	1,455,612	768,474	17,815	786,289	80,556	59,007	764,740	408,324	282,548	10,034	145,069	58,774
1984	1,650,474	887,412	20,324	907,736	95,426	72,380	884,690	466,132	299,652	10,893	151,521	63,433
1985	1,885,472	999,760	25,105	1,024,865	109,924	89,921	1,004,862	540,774	339,836	11,824	159,464	68,511
1986	2,102,678	1,123,252	30,358	1,153,610	126,021	103,110	1,130,699	593,556	378,423	12,578	167,170	73,388
1987	2,309,506	1,249,169	27,728	1,276,897	138,434	121,421	1,259,884	634,584	415,038	13,245	174,370	74,876
1988	2,558,165	1,374,793	33,223	1,408,016	157,496	145,043	1,395,563	697,872	464,730	14,190	180,277	77,900
1989	2,871,826	1,490,162	32,666	1,522,828	174,986	169,390	1,517,232	818,070	536,524	15,312	187,560	79,822
1990	3,113,308	1,586,473	33,303	1,619,776	184,248	200,129	1,635,657	873,275	604,376	15,796	197,095	81,784
1991	3,194,117	1,653,915	32,379	1,686,294	193,637	133,355	1,626,012	872,472	695,633	15,675	203,775	81,874
1992	3,426,667	1,774,575	45,330	1,819,905	207,277	139,610	1,752,238	879,381	795,048	16,365	209,388	82,420
1993	3,689,645	1,930,510	53,045	1,983,555	225,315	154,549	1,912,789	920,219	856,637	17,176	214,818	86,980
1994	3,982,217	2,073,199	54,190	2,127,389	245,865	182,980	2,064,504	984,548	933,165	17,816	223,523	89,626
1995	4,300,885	2,223,793	55,084	2,278,877	261,688	173,628	2,190,817	1,100,226	1,009,842	18,650	230,611	92,766
1996	4,637,462	2,435,601	55,140	2,490,741	280,098	156,611	2,367,254	1,194,619	1,075,589	19,597	236,637	98,351
1997	4,940,419	2,560,581	66,722	2,627,303	295,990	199,110	2,530,423	1,272,566	1,137,430	20,309	243,264	102,369
1998	5,393,486	2,782,278	63,155	2,845,433	317,186	245,866	2,774,113	1,402,899	1,216,474	21,567	250,086	107,391
1999	5,701,025	2,991,489	57,076	3,048,565	336,316	285,380	2,997,629	1,425,659	1,277,737	22,360	254,964	110,685
2000	6,111,455	3,132,298	33,152	3,165,450	350,111	388,124	3,203,463	1,545,587	1,362,405	23,486	260,221	113,998
2001	6,384,527	3,253,346	36,351	3,289,697	377,477	407,732	3,319,952	1,572,728	1,491,847	24,133	264,553	112,490
2002	6,506,555	3,423,319	37,295	3,460,614	397,793	384,420	3,447,241	1,454,879	1,604,435	23,946	271,716	115,655
2003	6,950,329	3,750,258	20,968	3,771,226	434,310	375,049	3,711,965	1,518,620	1,719,744	24,815	280,091	121,426
2004	7,657,010	4,104,398	24,059	4,128,457	481,878	362,856	4,009,435	1,752,533	1,895,042	26,298	291,164	128,768
2005	8,500,856	4,517,276	13,328	4,530,604	537,001	348,470	4,342,073	2,040,668	2,118,115	28,004	303,558	135,886
2006	9,451,120	5,000,425	17,698	5,018,123	604,533	329,539	4,743,129	2,376,462	2,331,529	29,879	316,310	144,690
2007	9,859,462	5,041,637	-17,772	5,023,865	618,023	280,550	4,686,392	2,653,950	2,519,120	30,278	325,634	147,778
2008	9,991,332	4,926,315	-40,324	4,885,991	615,875	220,026	4,490,142	2,648,683	2,852,507	30,272	330,052	143,328
2009	9,714,269	4,541,754	-37,776	4,503,978	585,689	248,040	4,166,329	2,410,624	3,137,316	29,359	330,880	133,977
2010	10,024,540	4,550,580	-12,605	4,537,975	590,960	278,336	4,225,351	2,423,738	3,375,451	30,237	331,527	130,350
2011	10,524,447	4,587,557	-55,406	4,532,151	547,759	311,352	4,295,744	2,725,535	3,503,168	31,652	332,507	131,783
2012	10,600,769	4,737,590	-13,600	4,723,990	567,759	323,547	4,479,778	2,582,455	3,538,536	31,692	334,495	133,789
2013	10,606,178	4,884,522	-35,861	4,848,661	650,972	350,916	4,548,605	2,421,046	3,636,527	31,551	336,159	136,470
2014	11,047,141	5,049,599	-13,652	5,035,947	677,045	378,880	4,737,782	2,494,420	3,814,939	32,571	339,167	140101

Personal Income and Employment by Area: Ocean City, NJ

(Thousands of dollars, except as noted.)

Year	Personal income, total	Earnings by place of work			Less: Contributions for government social insurance	Plus: Adjustment for residence	Equals: Net earnings by place of residence	Plus: Dividends, interest, and rent	Plus: Personal current transfer receipts	Per capita personal income (dollars)	Population (persons)	Total employment
		Nonfarm	Farm	Total								
1970	261,758	151,745	1,101	152,846	11,161	25,701	167,386	60,259	34,113	4,344	60,259	25,672
1971	292,902	168,600	962	169,562	12,868	26,854	183,548	67,790	41,564	4,614	63,485	26,985
1972	334,503	190,882	1,019	191,901	15,158	33,338	210,081	75,508	48,914	5,044	66,321	28,236
1973	393,148	228,251	1,460	229,711	20,343	39,316	248,684	87,018	57,446	5,765	68,194	30,935
1974	441,691	246,806	1,582	248,388	22,757	47,002	272,633	100,940	68,118	6,141	71,929	30,751
1975	504,097	271,468	1,387	272,855	24,934	55,646	303,567	113,404	87,126	6,811	74,014	31,385
1976	567,899	306,493	1,313	307,806	27,946	65,333	345,193	122,809	99,897	7,391	76,838	32,553
1977	630,921	339,744	883	340,627	31,201	75,229	384,655	138,789	107,477	8,063	78,248	34,569
1978	710,467	384,266	1,093	385,359	35,913	89,326	438,772	154,437	117,258	8,896	79,862	36,393
1979	789,808	415,148	981	416,129	40,718	111,327	486,738	171,965	131,105	9,664	81,725	37,189
1980	913,979	454,497	557	455,054	44,608	138,302	548,748	214,897	150,334	11,045	82,754	38,264
1981	1,034,898	486,113	1,037	487,150	51,639	167,589	603,100	260,600	171,198	12,240	84,550	39,013
1982	1,119,123	510,175	1,647	511,822	54,942	178,504	635,384	293,216	190,523	13,150	85,104	39,669
1983	1,216,113	566,172	2,287	568,459	62,741	192,029	697,747	312,476	205,890	14,196	85,665	42,138
1984	1,336,085	626,998	2,308	629,306	72,461	208,932	765,777	355,873	214,435	15,341	87,092	43,146
1985	1,443,657	690,350	2,381	692,731	80,195	223,312	835,848	387,800	220,009	16,285	88,647	43,532
1986	1,554,787	755,715	2,461	758,176	89,144	235,112	904,144	420,138	230,505	17,250	90,130	44,391
1987	1,662,708	827,194	1,996	829,190	98,534	250,826	981,482	441,670	239,556	18,065	92,038	44,431
1988	1,812,581	929,417	2,216	931,633	113,409	268,112	1,086,336	470,737	255,508	19,498	92,961	46,515
1989	1,952,313	981,491	2,274	983,765	119,460	279,733	1,144,038	533,966	274,309	20,588	94,830	47,087
1990	2,043,491	1,016,866	2,425	1,019,291	120,117	310,128	1,209,302	534,326	299,863	21,427	95,368	47,010
1991	2,089,324	1,032,647	2,088	1,034,735	125,118	314,438	1,224,055	517,377	347,892	21,538	97,006	46,586
1992	2,240,087	1,108,000	2,240	1,110,240	133,066	328,909	1,306,083	523,055	410,949	22,830	98,121	47,721
1993	2,339,577	1,149,848	2,833	1,152,681	136,129	358,883	1,375,435	528,034	436,108	23,751	98,504	47,462
1994	2,409,778	1,198,220	3,379	1,201,599	144,341	360,908	1,418,166	543,545	448,067	24,204	99,561	47,835
1995	2,551,364	1,246,551	2,923	1,249,474	149,382	376,904	1,476,996	594,846	479,522	25,411	100,405	48,319
1996	2,671,791	1,295,968	2,485	1,298,453	155,746	391,284	1,533,991	634,923	502,877	26,490	100,861	49,078
1997	2,886,683	1,401,204	2,297	1,403,501	161,637	441,914	1,683,778	680,726	522,179	28,474	101,380	50,322
1998	3,038,129	1,448,739	3,617	1,452,356	167,025	498,958	1,784,289	717,320	536,520	29,820	101,883	51,249
1999	3,150,923	1,540,947	4,327	1,545,274	174,305	511,200	1,882,169	715,616	553,138	30,851	102,135	51,877
2000	3,364,418	1,627,838	5,617	1,633,455	182,950	543,601	1,994,106	789,030	581,282	32,883	102,314	53,971
2001	3,551,353	1,724,730	5,651	1,730,381	197,023	581,726	2,115,084	806,481	629,788	34,809	102,023	56,793
2002	3,625,041	1,803,744	6,229	1,809,973	209,313	553,879	2,154,539	761,786	708,716	35,647	101,694	57,680
2003	3,681,296	1,916,227	6,035	1,922,262	218,776	524,870	2,228,356	767,941	684,999	36,194	101,710	59,017
2004	3,860,770	2,046,022	6,120	2,052,142	235,527	504,521	2,321,136	856,016	683,618	38,423	100,482	61,025
2005	3,927,644	2,157,453	6,405	2,163,858	256,473	464,500	2,371,885	826,402	729,357	39,566	99,269	63,304
2006	3,996,861	2,203,575	7,110	2,210,685	262,119	405,615	2,354,181	844,271	798,409	40,497	98,695	63,334
2007	4,040,831	2,205,043	7,411	2,212,454	269,397	345,445	2,288,502	908,281	844,048	41,366	97,686	63,129
2008	4,197,162	2,286,975	6,393	2,293,368	278,652	285,527	2,300,243	972,833	924,086	43,026	97,550	62,678
2009	4,280,080	2,289,321	5,771	2,295,092	278,997	248,344	2,264,439	988,580	1,027,061	44,017	97,238	62,080
2010	4,374,105	2,298,167	5,170	2,303,337	282,700	255,878	2,276,515	1,006,683	1,090,907	44,965	97,278	61,808
2011	4,597,442	2,327,621	4,368	2,331,989	261,808	298,983	2,369,164	1,120,573	1,107,705	47,611	96,562	61,889
2012	4,753,111	2,406,385	4,874	2,411,259	265,156	327,110	2,473,213	1,177,910	1,101,988	49,307	96,398	61,644
2013	4,765,211	2,440,730	6,144	2,446,874	301,439	313,263	2,458,698	1,197,010	1,109,503	49,716	95,849	62,374
2014	4,940,006	2,536,507	5,895	2,542,402	312,570	311,203	2,541,035	1,258,502	1,140,469	51,812	95,344	63531

Personal Income and Employment by Area: Odessa, TX

(Thousands of dollars, except as noted.)

Year	Personal income, total	Derivation of personal income									Per capita personal income (dollars)	Population (persons)	Total employment
		Earnings by place of work			Less: Contributions for government social insurance	Plus: Adjustment for residence	Equals: Net earnings by place of residence	Plus: Dividends, interest, and rent	Plus: Personal current transfer receipts				
		Nonfarm	Farm	Total									
1970	341,589	301,571	460	302,031	18,409	7,050	290,672	33,863	17,054		3,685	92,704	38,555
1971	366,186	322,172	99	322,271	20,093	7,266	309,444	36,709	20,033		3,912	93,609	39,295
1972	403,986	357,488	-680	356,808	23,239	7,708	341,277	39,993	22,716		4,275	94,500	40,684
1973	449,534	398,466	225	398,691	30,713	8,158	376,136	45,978	27,420		4,820	93,264	43,432
1974	540,718	479,764	610	480,374	37,996	9,548	451,926	56,191	32,601		5,594	96,667	46,851
1975	650,369	572,578	55	572,633	44,309	15,327	543,651	66,956	39,762		6,529	99,614	49,230
1976	791,801	710,308	298	710,606	52,843	16,432	674,195	73,680	43,926		7,733	102,392	51,191
1977	892,511	801,975	74	802,049	61,468	21,620	762,201	83,235	47,075		8,524	104,702	54,572
1978	1,027,754	921,573	743	922,316	73,925	29,161	877,552	96,873	53,329		9,500	108,189	58,659
1979	1,123,294	999,167	221	999,388	85,385	34,828	948,831	112,245	62,218		10,081	111,422	59,768
1980	1,345,438	1,175,235	72	1,175,307	102,391	54,830	1,127,746	145,358	72,334		11,494	117,052	64,450
1981	1,747,053	1,546,834	1,095	1,547,929	144,618	59,924	1,463,235	201,310	82,508		14,156	123,418	73,670
1982	1,880,958	1,620,590	1,234	1,621,824	158,107	64,618	1,528,335	255,986	96,637		13,882	135,501	74,922
1983	1,738,536	1,431,658	383	1,432,041	139,207	52,276	1,345,110	270,588	122,838		12,594	138,041	67,260
1984	1,745,164	1,407,656	475	1,408,131	142,278	51,933	1,317,786	298,682	128,696		13,023	134,006	66,031
1985	1,795,170	1,445,220	696	1,445,916	150,025	46,610	1,342,501	316,862	135,807		13,475	133,225	67,259
1986	1,600,108	1,216,315	509	1,216,824	123,137	44,240	1,137,927	297,410	164,771		11,978	133,588	57,894
1987	1,530,490	1,154,837	598	1,155,435	116,067	33,581	1,072,949	290,634	166,907		12,226	125,180	55,809
1988	1,587,536	1,201,093	232	1,201,325	126,055	33,476	1,108,746	308,771	170,019		13,005	122,067	57,518
1989	1,651,598	1,222,736	127	1,222,863	127,453	27,309	1,122,719	332,524	196,355		13,795	119,722	55,919
1990	1,697,215	1,269,531	-158	1,269,373	131,685	23,861	1,161,549	317,072	218,594		14,304	118,652	57,211
1991	1,800,015	1,358,512	-590	1,357,922	143,786	17,976	1,232,112	314,534	253,369		15,006	119,955	58,006
1992	1,850,992	1,366,452	-233	1,366,219	142,361	15,832	1,239,690	308,926	302,376		15,294	121,027	56,475
1993	1,917,577	1,426,738	-532	1,426,206	149,040	9,582	1,286,748	304,098	326,731		15,845	121,018	56,906
1994	1,981,492	1,475,326	-185	1,475,141	155,738	663	1,320,066	310,029	351,397		16,341	121,258	58,224
1995	2,044,847	1,502,268	-1,185	1,501,083	158,991	-2,009	1,340,083	330,459	374,305		16,897	121,017	58,734
1996	2,129,943	1,567,763	-2,232	1,565,531	163,408	-6,843	1,395,280	340,367	394,296		17,528	121,519	59,531
1997	2,326,811	1,756,396	-1,810	1,754,586	179,062	-9,780	1,565,744	354,073	406,994		19,112	121,749	61,867
1998	2,503,838	1,955,831	-1,613	1,954,218	196,920	-30,474	1,726,824	371,518	405,496		20,267	123,544	64,991
1999	2,380,648	1,814,884	-1,468	1,813,416	177,730	-25,072	1,610,614	344,730	425,304		19,442	122,450	60,939
2000	2,578,329	1,995,957	-852	1,995,105	190,319	-38,832	1,765,954	373,478	438,897		21,363	120,694	62,664
2001	2,692,296	2,106,696	-575	2,106,121	212,600	-57,169	1,836,352	383,613	472,331		22,287	120,802	63,948
2002	2,755,638	2,136,142	445	2,136,587	215,132	-60,578	1,860,877	371,997	522,764		22,550	122,199	63,948
2003	2,867,516	2,203,684	963	2,204,647	225,806	-64,777	1,914,064	394,642	558,810		23,363	122,739	64,545
2004	2,966,971	2,329,294	1,002	2,330,296	238,217	-70,427	2,021,652	369,853	575,466		23,896	124,163	65,896
2005	3,291,124	2,589,510	855	2,590,365	266,919	-80,762	2,242,684	424,780	623,660		26,250	125,378	68,390
2006	3,759,008	3,053,805	541	3,054,346	307,939	-97,617	2,648,790	462,495	647,723		29,488	127,476	72,910
2007	4,176,773	3,434,944	865	3,435,809	348,800	-113,920	2,973,089	508,875	694,809		32,016	130,459	76,019
2008	4,697,306	3,871,425	-1,834	3,869,591	389,989	-130,374	3,349,228	591,124	756,954		35,301	133,064	81,338
2009	4,375,307	3,452,341	-2,071	3,450,270	356,058	-84,167	3,010,045	545,845	819,417		31,953	136,930	77,236
2010	4,711,883	3,699,439	-2,330	3,697,109	382,053	-41,256	3,273,800	528,000	910,083		34,369	137,098	77,913
2011	5,511,805	4,519,904	-2,237	4,517,667	417,441	-143,512	3,956,714	656,060	899,031		39,457	139,690	85,363
2012	6,327,190	5,307,777	-2,267	5,305,510	480,931	-155,229	4,669,350	783,791	874,049		43,804	144,444	91,748
2013	6,503,220	5,672,587	-1,792	5,670,795	575,660	-130,760	4,964,375	659,406	879,439		43,493	149,522	93,987
2014	7,244,097	6,295,130	-1,557	6,293,573	637,001	-18,057	5,638,515	692,689	912,893		47,069	153,904	98968

Personal Income and Employment by Area: Ogden-Clearfield, UT

(Thousands of dollars, except as noted.)

Year	Personal income, total	Derivation of personal income											
		Earnings by place of work			Less: Contributions for government social insurance	Plus: Adjustment for residence	Equals: Net earnings by place of residence	Plus: Dividends, interest, and rent	Plus: Personal current transfer receipts	Per capita personal income (dollars)	Population (persons)	Total employment
		Nonfarm	Farm	Total								
1970	963,647	738,134	19,328	757,462	36,595	23,939	744,806	154,240	64,601	3,726	258,652	101,375
1971	1,100,203	851,154	18,875	870,029	42,032	9,696	837,693	186,215	76,295	4,144	265,466	102,505
1972	1,181,748	899,827	21,518	921,345	49,285	22,504	894,564	201,530	85,654	4,356	271,286	106,947
1973	1,279,243	959,557	29,967	989,524	61,191	32,861	961,194	216,182	101,867	4,642	275,564	109,681
1974	1,418,924	1,061,785	25,577	1,087,362	71,464	42,341	1,058,239	244,764	115,921	5,073	279,691	112,270
1975	1,562,663	1,171,076	15,280	1,186,356	79,865	45,780	1,152,271	268,152	142,240	5,451	286,672	114,043
1976	1,748,515	1,322,239	15,401	1,337,640	92,699	54,530	1,299,471	294,367	154,677	5,962	293,292	118,620
1977	1,938,568	1,462,468	10,038	1,472,506	104,226	73,364	1,441,644	329,892	167,032	6,433	301,368	123,292
1978	2,221,374	1,661,580	13,471	1,675,051	121,620	94,230	1,647,661	387,909	185,804	7,144	310,926	130,121
1979	2,498,308	1,858,951	15,558	1,874,509	145,163	116,920	1,846,266	439,766	212,276	7,789	320,746	136,040
1980	2,803,524	2,037,840	12,117	2,049,957	159,248	150,701	2,041,410	512,435	249,679	8,453	331,666	137,885
1981	3,146,100	2,276,847	6,066	2,282,913	190,343	158,039	2,250,609	602,447	293,044	9,242	340,400	140,230
1982	3,436,497	2,435,014	7,952	2,442,966	206,927	179,018	2,415,057	687,870	333,570	9,853	348,770	141,296
1983	3,704,310	2,598,164	5,019	2,603,183	232,532	221,729	2,592,380	750,233	361,697	10,410	355,842	143,806
1984	4,087,115	2,897,189	7,831	2,905,020	269,072	240,416	2,876,364	836,141	374,610	11,305	361,527	152,784
1985	4,466,989	3,195,782	5,909	3,201,691	310,562	253,506	3,144,635	910,801	411,553	12,168	367,103	161,151
1986	4,722,499	3,376,761	12,637	3,389,398	334,104	267,762	3,323,056	959,888	439,555	12,673	372,647	166,082
1987	4,915,932	3,455,080	35,064	3,490,144	343,673	317,593	3,464,064	992,612	459,256	12,961	379,274	171,824
1988	5,206,808	3,667,856	52,004	3,719,860	384,820	347,105	3,682,145	1,038,162	486,501	13,658	381,216	178,142
1989	5,583,558	3,927,506	47,140	3,974,646	421,983	374,945	3,927,608	1,121,018	534,932	14,498	385,120	184,178
1990	6,064,145	4,219,302	60,135	4,279,437	471,418	498,411	4,306,430	1,167,860	589,855	15,556	389,815	190,389
1991	6,431,484	4,500,835	54,339	4,555,174	511,109	522,387	4,566,452	1,222,355	642,677	16,142	398,436	192,203
1992	6,919,669	4,784,959	73,622	4,858,581	544,893	630,520	4,944,208	1,262,585	712,876	16,929	408,757	193,998
1993	7,387,694	5,062,325	75,662	5,137,987	583,895	720,422	5,274,514	1,332,815	780,365	17,594	419,888	199,000
1994	7,894,505	5,368,801	55,777	5,424,578	630,690	811,675	5,605,563	1,482,726	806,216	18,317	430,988	213,802
1995	8,549,961	5,758,440	44,342	5,802,782	679,336	888,308	6,011,754	1,667,112	871,095	19,399	440,732	220,335
1996	9,233,460	6,171,681	49,938	6,221,619	723,710	995,675	6,493,584	1,813,440	926,436	20,485	450,737	233,975
1997	9,951,345	6,608,625	53,417	6,662,042	766,365	1,159,709	7,055,386	1,927,628	968,331	21,600	460,703	244,207
1998	10,685,361	7,034,721	54,214	7,088,935	806,095	1,318,787	7,601,627	2,067,652	1,016,082	22,725	470,206	248,079
1999	11,209,942	7,371,247	48,196	7,419,443	836,266	1,497,012	8,080,189	2,055,392	1,074,361	23,404	478,978	251,197
2000	12,013,813	7,851,884	34,992	7,886,876	884,793	1,617,430	8,619,513	2,246,160	1,148,140	24,623	487,906	256,649
2001	12,693,698	8,310,300	46,887	8,357,187	936,309	1,711,750	9,132,628	2,291,660	1,269,410	25,620	495,459	258,859
2002	13,299,879	8,785,944	23,886	8,809,830	986,740	1,823,912	9,647,002	2,268,049	1,384,828	26,376	504,247	262,870
2003	13,931,372	9,163,114	29,324	9,192,438	1,046,614	1,937,509	10,083,333	2,362,713	1,485,326	27,156	513,021	266,675
2004	14,750,056	9,796,342	42,046	9,838,388	1,127,145	2,113,933	10,825,176	2,371,820	1,553,060	28,237	522,374	276,422
2005	15,751,068	10,342,501	38,527	10,381,028	1,191,545	2,242,550	11,432,033	2,643,334	1,675,701	29,584	532,425	284,623
2006	17,281,841	11,399,039	30,425	11,429,464	1,296,170	2,504,270	12,637,564	2,822,408	1,821,869	31,666	545,746	296,050
2007	18,758,144	11,983,352	39,157	12,022,509	1,365,738	2,742,933	13,399,704	3,365,395	1,993,045	33,391	561,767	310,097
2008	19,614,738	12,253,785	38,825	12,292,610	1,398,722	2,838,627	13,732,515	3,519,029	2,363,194	33,992	577,040	311,773
2009	19,107,251	11,985,325	23,569	12,008,894	1,366,936	2,730,391	13,372,349	3,147,340	2,587,562	32,453	588,773	302,891
2010	19,482,686	12,125,832	32,800	12,158,632	1,376,135	2,787,838	13,570,335	3,024,308	2,888,043	32,494	599,569	297,330
2011	20,684,616	12,564,890	68,020	12,632,910	1,297,328	3,022,641	14,358,223	3,340,427	2,985,966	34,140	605,878	304,187
2012	21,675,198	13,107,420	54,337	13,161,757	1,344,793	3,254,216	15,071,180	3,628,761	2,975,257	35,381	612,629	308,565
2013	22,255,834	13,636,526	77,824	13,714,350	1,573,068	3,403,470	15,544,752	3,654,148	3,056,934	35,767	622,238	315,418
2014	23,300,405	14,271,494	89,807	14,361,301	1,655,096	3,610,361	16,316,566	3,822,003	3,161,836	36,851	632,293	322847

Personal Income and Employment by Area: Oklahoma City, OK

(Thousands of dollars, except as noted.)

Year	Personal income, total	Derivation of personal income					Equals: Net earnings by place of residence	Plus: Dividends, interest, and rent	Plus: Personal current transfer receipts	Per capita personal income (dollars)	Population (persons)	Total employment
		Earnings by place of work			Less: Contributions for government social insurance	Plus: Adjustment for residence						
		Nonfarm	Farm	Total								
1970	3,010,242	2,488,199	27,488	2,515,687	143,758	-51,914	2,320,015	454,313	235,914	4,134	728,165	354,356
1971	3,355,990	2,745,984	26,904	2,772,888	164,431	-50,684	2,557,773	521,188	277,029	4,468	751,178	364,970
1972	3,683,138	3,056,123	24,884	3,081,007	194,150	-70,482	2,816,375	556,795	309,968	4,782	770,165	385,385
1973	4,074,302	3,354,071	61,343	3,415,414	249,832	-77,370	3,088,212	629,554	356,536	5,191	784,927	398,352
1974	4,554,901	3,732,519	40,620	3,773,139	288,038	-77,071	3,408,030	724,863	422,008	5,746	792,748	407,075
1975	5,008,898	4,027,776	34,624	4,062,400	309,340	-64,674	3,688,386	789,162	531,350	6,275	798,210	406,103
1976	5,482,615	4,422,025	30,336	4,452,361	347,102	-60,191	4,045,068	856,580	580,967	6,783	808,238	411,197
1977	6,159,364	5,064,040	17,862	5,081,902	398,459	-95,539	4,587,904	962,648	608,812	7,504	820,775	432,760
1978	7,072,536	5,887,225	13,197	5,900,422	480,958	-126,406	5,293,058	1,127,136	652,342	8,449	837,101	465,144
1979	8,147,208	6,788,678	37,811	6,826,489	580,145	-145,659	6,100,685	1,297,301	749,222	9,563	851,930	488,083
1980	9,550,879	7,959,540	23,121	7,982,661	688,884	-182,748	7,111,029	1,576,073	863,777	10,886	877,354	513,837
1981	11,125,317	9,225,346	5,797	9,231,143	861,510	-181,478	8,188,155	1,959,732	977,430	12,393	897,677	543,150
1982	12,540,141	10,249,788	16,888	10,266,676	981,046	-173,861	9,111,769	2,336,846	1,091,526	13,379	937,318	568,698
1983	12,968,109	10,451,074	4,078	10,455,152	1,000,019	-203,896	9,251,237	2,528,654	1,188,218	13,342	971,970	562,358
1984	13,925,407	11,176,280	10,990	11,187,270	1,089,785	-213,394	9,884,091	2,803,166	1,238,150	14,157	983,657	574,026
1985	14,457,231	11,405,139	26,215	11,431,354	1,130,774	-200,177	10,100,403	3,010,120	1,346,708	14,634	987,888	562,905
1986	14,437,964	11,319,358	49,383	11,368,741	1,144,357	-185,947	10,038,437	2,950,956	1,448,571	14,673	983,997	542,698
1987	14,435,794	11,331,672	42,464	11,374,136	1,153,140	-171,596	10,049,400	2,865,748	1,520,646	14,882	970,003	543,299
1988	15,110,037	11,858,117	57,831	11,915,948	1,271,503	-181,191	10,463,254	3,009,552	1,637,231	15,635	966,423	549,865
1989	16,268,202	12,580,718	64,905	12,645,623	1,357,681	-166,712	11,121,230	3,403,310	1,743,662	16,772	969,976	557,627
1990	16,944,655	13,138,476	51,645	13,190,121	1,467,297	-181,990	11,540,834	3,512,306	1,891,515	17,424	972,512	567,554
1991	17,472,916	13,580,482	41,302	13,621,784	1,554,089	-183,130	11,884,565	3,499,342	2,089,009	17,758	983,942	568,264
1992	18,615,899	14,442,893	61,647	14,504,540	1,644,896	-197,406	12,662,238	3,593,335	2,360,326	18,646	998,407	574,498
1993	19,528,057	15,216,958	54,227	15,271,185	1,749,776	-212,390	13,309,019	3,754,736	2,464,302	19,240	1,014,998	586,259
1994	20,524,108	15,851,994	63,012	15,915,006	1,853,379	-226,138	13,835,489	4,027,624	2,660,995	19,939	1,029,338	599,649
1995	21,513,519	16,551,214	7,759	16,558,973	1,943,717	-242,471	14,372,785	4,267,164	2,873,570	20,699	1,039,343	621,260
1996	22,855,818	17,589,270	19,233	17,608,503	2,028,027	-240,876	15,339,600	4,502,308	3,013,910	21,728	1,051,886	640,572
1997	23,837,227	18,417,005	27,930	18,444,935	2,099,327	-250,591	16,095,017	4,624,223	3,117,987	22,375	1,065,333	652,676
1998	25,565,719	19,800,773	13,887	19,814,660	2,209,221	-258,629	17,346,810	4,981,176	3,237,733	23,777	1,075,233	667,218
1999	26,907,741	20,973,483	36,648	21,010,131	2,314,772	-300,314	18,395,045	5,100,183	3,412,513	24,723	1,088,347	679,606
2000	30,011,716	23,415,690	34,231	23,449,921	2,498,520	-343,850	20,607,551	5,688,270	3,715,895	27,330	1,098,132	697,801
2001	32,361,523	25,407,299	42,071	25,449,370	2,647,728	-378,553	22,423,089	5,789,592	4,148,842	29,184	1,108,860	704,740
2002	33,074,925	26,200,666	61,093	26,261,759	2,759,969	-544,624	22,957,166	5,846,819	4,270,940	29,472	1,122,241	700,207
2003	34,360,251	27,460,578	49,256	27,509,834	2,884,871	-630,813	23,994,150	5,871,620	4,494,481	30,289	1,134,419	698,567
2004	36,583,626	29,265,191	86,251	29,351,442	3,098,078	-710,574	25,542,790	6,278,638	4,762,198	31,936	1,145,524	711,979
2005	39,537,058	31,279,333	99,302	31,378,635	3,234,035	-715,687	27,428,913	6,836,025	5,272,120	34,045	1,161,308	724,849
2006	43,949,910	34,332,003	42,892	34,374,895	3,472,221	-740,241	30,162,433	8,002,959	5,784,518	37,162	1,182,668	742,048
2007	45,437,956	34,459,452	55,091	34,514,543	3,630,445	-385,293	30,498,805	8,704,867	6,234,284	37,876	1,199,665	757,894
2008	50,171,672	38,244,933	74,654	38,319,587	3,812,520	-345,690	34,161,377	8,886,573	7,123,722	41,238	1,216,645	773,659
2009	46,435,001	34,805,686	-5,904	34,799,782	3,761,883	-363,144	30,674,755	8,060,482	7,699,764	37,515	1,237,780	761,202
2010	48,703,350	36,550,586	39,132	36,589,718	3,852,821	-369,126	32,367,771	8,038,375	8,297,204	38,718	1,257,888	762,817
2011	53,676,596	40,180,363	89,912	40,270,275	3,736,461	-402,455	36,131,359	9,076,472	8,468,765	42,038	1,276,858	781,295
2012	57,501,721	43,216,262	123,923	43,340,185	3,965,993	-400,364	38,973,828	9,840,781	8,687,112	44,304	1,297,886	803,153
2013	59,496,011	45,514,943	123,956	45,638,899	4,649,059	-420,627	40,569,213	9,963,313	8,963,485	45,053	1,320,585	821,239
2014	62,394,052	47,810,327	139,913	47,950,240	4,790,971	-425,500	42,733,769	10,329,277	9,331,006	46,675	1,336,767	834526

Personal Income and Employment by Area: Olympia-Tumwater, WA

(Thousands of dollars, except as noted.)

Year	Personal income, total	Derivation of personal income									Per capita personal income (dollars)	Population (persons)	Total employment
		Earnings by place of work			Less: Contributions for government social insurance	Plus: Adjustment for residence	Equals: Net earnings by place of residence	Plus: Dividends, interest, and rent	Plus: Personal current transfer receipts				
		Nonfarm	Farm	Total									
1970	353,899	259,608	5,347	264,955	19,590	8,879	254,244	69,153	30,502		4,567	77,498	34,767
1971	391,528	284,652	4,690	289,342	22,570	11,785	278,557	76,202	36,769		4,899	79,920	35,873
1972	422,854	305,241	6,506	311,747	25,336	12,312	298,723	81,772	42,359		5,159	81,970	36,700
1973	481,145	339,233	15,247	354,480	32,489	19,213	341,204	91,166	48,775		5,665	84,930	37,999
1974	547,116	381,973	14,107	396,080	38,280	24,001	381,801	105,774	59,541		6,115	89,466	39,450
1975	623,749	431,926	11,846	443,772	42,959	26,811	427,624	122,711	73,414		6,653	93,760	41,096
1976	715,265	498,092	12,270	510,362	50,440	35,300	495,222	137,858	82,185		7,314	97,798	43,594
1977	810,372	562,848	11,627	574,475	57,128	45,744	563,091	159,206	88,075		7,607	106,529	45,440
1978	967,504	676,393	17,035	693,428	71,083	56,887	679,232	190,224	98,048		8,579	112,782	49,562
1979	1,112,201	761,852	18,956	780,808	81,440	76,564	775,932	224,272	111,997		9,332	119,176	53,380
1980	1,280,773	838,650	19,121	857,771	92,880	102,772	867,663	270,225	142,885		10,220	125,325	55,242
1981	1,444,715	908,396	19,848	928,244	108,596	134,223	953,871	325,356	165,488		11,171	129,326	55,939
1982	1,524,160	918,227	21,445	939,672	112,255	151,436	978,853	361,527	183,780		11,537	132,109	55,768
1983	1,644,210	1,002,466	19,571	1,022,037	124,859	140,166	1,037,344	404,959	201,907		12,279	133,899	58,575
1984	1,808,336	1,125,521	17,246	1,142,767	142,948	139,701	1,139,520	454,562	214,254		13,324	135,721	61,228
1985	1,981,650	1,233,950	17,362	1,251,312	158,993	155,483	1,247,802	495,441	238,407		14,294	138,632	63,934
1986	2,149,747	1,342,583	16,932	1,359,515	176,564	173,668	1,356,619	532,239	260,889		15,139	141,998	67,550
1987	2,297,340	1,448,423	12,531	1,460,954	189,590	194,883	1,466,247	551,398	279,695		15,755	145,813	71,492
1988	2,499,951	1,579,200	12,051	1,591,251	215,743	225,177	1,600,685	590,948	308,318		16,618	150,439	75,337
1989	2,811,148	1,747,720	19,838	1,767,558	236,833	241,119	1,771,844	692,173	347,131		18,094	155,365	79,332
1990	3,116,930	1,965,556	19,785	1,985,341	265,620	309,602	2,029,323	710,139	377,468		19,121	163,014	83,933
1991	3,455,853	2,219,130	21,606	2,240,736	299,050	325,144	2,266,830	759,371	429,652		20,402	169,388	87,571
1992	3,807,167	2,455,188	25,923	2,481,111	326,308	380,431	2,535,234	785,968	485,965		21,582	176,407	90,233
1993	4,078,286	2,643,109	26,964	2,670,073	348,416	395,081	2,716,738	834,486	527,062		22,279	183,054	92,374
1994	4,283,922	2,753,624	28,357	2,781,981	368,276	415,108	2,828,813	896,009	559,100		22,909	186,997	96,701
1995	4,524,380	2,873,771	26,118	2,899,889	384,235	448,625	2,964,279	951,861	608,240		23,563	192,013	97,945
1996	4,783,013	2,996,723	28,790	3,025,513	386,723	490,110	3,128,900	1,014,465	639,648		24,372	196,247	101,394
1997	5,119,560	3,184,511	29,377	3,213,888	394,406	590,606	3,410,088	1,049,931	659,541		25,660	199,512	103,918
1998	5,484,669	3,450,385	34,681	3,485,066	428,229	620,249	3,677,086	1,117,463	690,120		27,145	202,050	106,513
1999	5,733,454	3,711,814	33,051	3,744,865	447,210	587,172	3,884,827	1,110,035	738,592		27,985	204,873	108,578
2000	6,352,025	4,037,865	22,703	4,060,568	489,655	783,495	4,354,408	1,194,485	803,132		30,497	208,287	110,923
2001	6,768,411	4,210,045	24,902	4,234,947	504,897	931,870	4,661,920	1,201,425	905,066		31,863	212,421	111,517
2002	6,927,476	4,416,483	18,999	4,435,482	537,392	909,535	4,807,625	1,162,628	957,223		32,025	216,313	114,564
2003	7,288,242	4,651,222	32,744	4,683,966	566,989	899,924	5,016,901	1,259,916	1,011,425		33,204	219,499	117,660
2004	7,689,995	4,930,139	29,711	4,959,850	598,961	897,240	5,258,129	1,374,385	1,057,481		34,487	222,985	120,204
2005	8,114,376	5,269,356	22,295	5,291,651	643,310	899,479	5,547,820	1,437,362	1,129,194		35,743	227,023	123,435
2006	8,698,713	5,615,970	22,827	5,638,797	679,400	906,983	5,866,380	1,597,548	1,234,785		37,384	232,688	127,648
2007	9,416,356	6,005,974	22,725	6,028,699	723,956	928,907	6,233,650	1,834,234	1,348,472		39,602	237,772	132,354
2008	9,913,852	6,204,440	23,818	6,228,258	740,441	907,634	6,395,451	1,964,578	1,553,823		40,575	244,332	134,624
2009	9,802,516	6,121,036	23,687	6,144,723	750,042	802,705	6,197,386	1,861,779	1,743,351		39,220	249,936	130,580
2010	9,979,805	6,183,968	26,958	6,210,926	759,971	745,420	6,196,375	1,847,159	1,936,271		39,439	253,046	128,204
2011	10,310,693	6,232,156	31,792	6,263,948	695,096	743,668	6,312,520	2,034,363	1,963,810		40,201	256,481	128,564
2012	10,619,373	6,397,236	37,161	6,434,397	700,875	764,944	6,498,466	2,144,384	1,976,523		41,047	258,713	130,463
2013	10,783,721	6,619,810	43,492	6,663,302	825,458	702,964	6,540,808	2,201,844	2,041,069		41,071	262,561	133,633
2014	11,430,070	6,916,092	47,527	6,963,619	858,725	848,175	6,953,069	2,264,244	2,212,757		42,994	265,851	137281

Personal Income and Employment by Area: Omaha-Council Bluffs, NE-IA

(Thousands of dollars, except as noted.)

Year	Personal income, total	Derivation of personal income			Less: Contributions for government social insurance	Plus: Adjustment for residence	Equals: Net earnings by place of residence	Plus: Dividends, interest, and rent	Plus: Personal current transfer receipts	Per capita personal income (dollars)	Population (persons)	Total employment
		Earnings by place of work										
		Nonfarm	Farm	Total								
1970	2,662,128	2,118,166	83,142	2,201,308	148,476	-19,832	2,033,000	423,273	205,855	4,281	621,778	297,197
1971	2,868,526	2,281,003	85,385	2,366,388	165,260	-20,688	2,180,440	454,220	233,866	4,526	633,774	301,792
1972	3,148,177	2,494,720	111,595	2,606,315	188,058	-20,514	2,397,743	492,842	257,592	4,890	643,739	308,000
1973	3,541,582	2,759,983	180,756	2,940,739	237,937	-19,672	2,683,130	550,568	307,884	5,463	648,329	318,343
1974	3,810,605	3,021,481	96,778	3,118,259	270,557	-15,216	2,832,486	623,209	354,910	5,837	652,850	324,237
1975	4,219,538	3,251,069	128,980	3,380,049	285,951	-9,356	3,084,742	688,942	445,854	6,500	649,131	321,665
1976	4,591,751	3,630,461	80,493	3,710,954	324,424	-5,885	3,380,645	736,515	474,591	6,996	656,376	330,324
1977	5,036,764	3,979,940	103,766	4,083,706	355,442	-3,427	3,724,837	816,689	495,238	7,688	655,126	339,330
1978	5,655,097	4,425,971	172,349	4,598,320	405,439	1,260	4,194,141	910,114	550,842	8,589	658,391	350,508
1979	6,190,164	4,921,673	97,417	5,019,090	469,203	4,636	4,554,523	1,017,689	617,952	9,411	657,736	359,581
1980	6,828,493	5,348,409	41,975	5,390,384	507,665	13,287	4,896,006	1,209,540	722,947	10,426	654,969	356,972
1981	7,638,738	5,794,541	125,271	5,919,812	586,703	-5,191	5,327,918	1,487,495	823,325	11,617	657,562	357,821
1982	8,294,491	6,154,540	105,617	6,260,157	635,310	-10,475	5,614,372	1,779,013	901,106	12,554	660,724	356,924
1983	8,708,672	6,554,684	44,620	6,599,304	685,649	-13,339	5,900,316	1,840,131	968,225	13,124	663,573	363,321
1984	9,606,239	7,212,029	122,261	7,334,290	774,541	-16,174	6,543,575	2,037,951	1,024,713	14,368	668,605	375,618
1985	10,244,768	7,683,167	209,689	7,892,856	844,222	-17,463	7,031,171	2,120,012	1,093,585	15,261	671,289	386,904
1986	10,671,684	8,087,142	163,430	8,250,572	913,550	-19,772	7,317,250	2,210,357	1,144,077	15,871	672,408	392,455
1987	11,203,904	8,575,280	156,780	8,732,060	961,734	-18,652	7,751,674	2,275,762	1,176,468	16,660	672,505	405,568
1988	11,883,815	9,153,120	145,083	9,298,203	1,067,331	-20,774	8,210,098	2,436,153	1,237,564	17,553	677,009	416,931
1989	12,649,173	9,752,408	149,828	9,902,236	1,136,376	-23,036	8,742,824	2,587,873	1,318,476	18,578	680,885	428,864
1990	13,692,049	10,486,950	161,014	10,647,964	1,272,820	-24,848	9,350,296	2,897,090	1,444,663	19,904	687,913	439,366
1991	14,319,186	10,977,845	159,207	11,137,052	1,344,448	-31,463	9,761,141	2,987,225	1,570,820	20,560	696,443	440,334
1992	15,237,531	11,690,134	200,167	11,890,301	1,412,509	-38,329	10,439,463	3,087,529	1,710,539	21,633	704,360	442,339
1993	15,743,158	12,172,522	87,622	12,260,144	1,473,220	-39,308	10,747,616	3,174,714	1,820,828	22,234	708,077	450,793
1994	16,882,938	13,034,032	185,663	13,219,695	1,581,818	-45,836	11,592,041	3,378,691	1,912,206	23,609	715,120	466,628
1995	18,197,756	14,115,953	62,935	14,178,888	1,687,161	-60,030	12,431,697	3,738,591	2,027,468	25,104	724,894	477,507
1996	19,647,251	15,140,908	249,890	15,390,798	1,798,580	-77,493	13,514,725	3,990,941	2,141,585	26,661	736,937	491,378
1997	20,710,459	16,056,209	188,442	16,244,651	1,935,011	-96,372	14,213,268	4,269,541	2,227,650	27,749	746,356	499,983
1998	22,246,053	17,223,319	127,982	17,351,301	2,052,769	-107,885	15,190,647	4,723,952	2,331,454	29,510	753,844	515,664
1999	23,660,733	18,546,742	120,873	18,667,615	2,192,395	-131,034	16,344,186	4,846,404	2,470,143	31,067	761,603	527,035
2000	25,265,018	19,656,088	151,303	19,807,391	2,295,419	-148,114	17,363,858	5,294,824	2,606,336	32,842	769,291	538,046
2001	26,310,510	20,566,226	154,642	20,720,868	2,370,994	-161,000	18,188,874	5,262,066	2,859,570	33,898	776,165	536,093
2002	27,386,858	21,411,125	111,568	21,522,693	2,457,502	-177,255	18,887,936	5,418,200	3,080,722	34,952	783,567	532,047
2003	28,452,879	22,327,916	174,546	22,502,462	2,556,971	-217,791	19,727,700	5,516,388	3,208,791	35,921	792,086	533,465
2004	30,206,908	23,639,555	330,760	23,970,315	2,680,251	-208,396	21,081,668	5,763,890	3,361,350	37,608	803,214	541,887
2005	31,592,648	24,565,928	244,748	24,810,676	2,820,269	-201,738	21,788,669	6,203,709	3,600,270	38,797	814,309	549,045
2006	33,924,530	26,289,149	156,178	26,445,327	3,062,350	-194,506	23,188,471	6,826,433	3,909,626	41,123	824,961	559,998
2007	35,832,994	27,140,867	224,426	27,365,293	3,152,213	-244,135	23,968,945	7,713,851	4,150,198	42,937	834,554	571,521
2008	37,708,744	28,413,022	298,588	28,711,610	3,267,402	-272,033	25,172,175	7,770,752	4,765,817	44,619	845,119	577,518
2009	36,587,292	28,124,258	342,108	28,466,366	3,262,221	-270,477	24,933,668	6,665,435	4,988,189	42,731	856,233	569,284
2010	37,433,978	28,361,448	274,999	28,636,447	3,335,711	-248,841	25,051,895	6,964,609	5,417,474	43,121	868,113	562,749
2011	39,514,381	29,535,994	500,304	30,036,298	3,047,160	-257,762	26,731,376	7,198,934	5,584,071	45,057	876,979	569,206
2012	42,231,728	31,430,805	327,260	31,758,065	3,145,368	-262,906	28,349,791	8,260,709	5,621,228	47,681	885,707	577,680
2013	42,523,902	31,912,032	684,108	32,596,140	3,625,176	-301,653	28,669,311	8,124,659	5,729,932	47,482	895,573	587,048
2014	44,154,343	33,519,534	372,702	33,892,236	3,812,940	-310,334	29,768,962	8,421,720	5,963,661	48,821	904,421	598336

Personal Income and Employment by Area: Orlando-Kissimmee-Sanford, FL

(Thousands of dollars, except as noted.)

Year	Personal income, total	Derivation of personal income					Equals: Net earnings by place of residence	Plus: Dividends, interest, and rent	Plus: Personal current transfer receipts	Per capita personal income (dollars)	Population (persons)	Total employment
		Earnings by place of work			Less: Contributions for government social insurance	Plus: Adjustment for residence						
		Nonfarm	Farm	Total								
1970	2,101,709	1,480,157	96,216	1,576,373	95,062	20,977	1,502,288	416,195	183,226	3,979	528,201	232,835
1971	2,449,134	1,746,193	108,392	1,854,585	117,558	18,958	1,755,985	471,580	221,569	4,384	558,715	252,062
1972	2,904,039	2,111,040	129,052	2,240,092	149,361	18,079	2,108,810	541,105	254,124	4,842	599,794	289,075
1973	3,424,575	2,569,235	130,585	2,699,820	208,780	12,779	2,503,819	617,883	302,873	5,317	644,122	323,363
1974	3,752,389	2,767,014	128,252	2,895,266	233,515	11,804	2,673,555	710,739	368,095	5,514	680,514	326,248
1975	4,032,553	2,834,421	150,953	2,985,374	235,913	6,354	2,755,815	784,263	492,475	5,848	689,597	315,687
1976	4,444,413	3,146,445	168,736	3,315,181	268,006	-2,918	3,044,257	853,944	546,212	6,305	704,932	327,025
1977	4,945,983	3,507,935	193,055	3,700,990	301,156	-6,859	3,392,975	962,234	590,774	6,816	725,644	344,104
1978	5,790,451	4,126,733	248,997	4,375,730	363,424	-17,637	3,994,669	1,145,746	650,036	7,730	749,095	375,240
1979	6,675,623	4,796,171	244,634	5,040,805	441,872	-24,523	4,574,410	1,338,633	762,580	8,549	780,907	396,668
1980	7,933,082	5,569,383	327,856	5,897,239	516,163	-36,932	5,344,144	1,669,439	919,499	9,755	813,225	418,551
1981	9,158,631	6,450,860	237,729	6,688,589	640,439	-53,374	5,994,776	2,084,907	1,078,948	10,832	845,498	441,015
1982	10,209,945	7,249,375	280,905	7,530,280	736,135	-95,177	6,698,968	2,285,742	1,225,235	11,637	877,348	463,274
1983	11,525,733	8,268,369	351,236	8,619,605	845,668	-136,542	7,637,395	2,550,780	1,337,558	12,580	916,199	494,692
1984	12,959,837	9,567,986	229,751	9,797,737	1,004,967	-189,259	8,603,511	2,936,897	1,419,429	13,533	957,644	537,857
1985	14,405,731	10,769,914	210,047	10,979,961	1,151,298	-247,719	9,580,944	3,284,234	1,540,553	14,459	996,347	573,928
1986	15,848,401	12,072,646	202,627	12,275,273	1,323,854	-324,188	10,627,231	3,560,055	1,661,115	15,262	1,038,445	615,381
1987	17,266,100	13,369,523	188,910	13,558,433	1,451,403	-416,274	11,690,756	3,805,831	1,769,513	15,955	1,082,164	636,135
1988	19,239,672	15,041,254	217,068	15,258,322	1,671,725	-502,346	13,084,251	4,193,271	1,962,150	17,179	1,119,977	672,874
1989	21,489,212	16,541,693	193,250	16,734,943	1,850,611	-604,734	14,279,598	4,954,903	2,254,711	18,345	1,171,413	713,886
1990	23,155,736	17,994,629	163,502	18,158,131	2,002,404	-715,821	15,439,906	5,198,525	2,517,305	18,663	1,240,724	739,630
1991	24,166,822	18,668,242	199,941	18,868,183	2,093,963	-656,165	16,118,055	5,192,770	2,855,997	18,832	1,283,301	737,044
1992	25,766,757	20,124,964	184,609	20,309,573	2,247,477	-719,319	17,342,777	5,079,734	3,344,246	19,537	1,318,902	755,421
1993	27,497,326	21,551,951	184,234	21,736,185	2,389,447	-795,580	18,551,158	5,282,573	3,663,595	20,262	1,357,101	788,146
1994	28,999,977	22,807,569	164,982	22,972,551	2,568,551	-881,666	19,522,334	5,541,658	3,935,985	20,799	1,394,315	813,296
1995	31,170,586	24,382,100	177,566	24,559,666	2,723,279	-924,936	20,911,451	5,988,125	4,271,010	21,822	1,428,415	840,455
1996	33,598,637	26,380,270	159,583	26,539,853	2,922,087	-1,003,246	22,614,520	6,419,252	4,564,865	22,862	1,469,619	885,718
1997	36,179,696	28,646,330	186,603	28,832,933	3,176,979	-1,157,284	24,498,670	6,884,060	4,796,966	23,800	1,520,145	935,200
1998	39,515,302	31,766,937	198,540	31,965,477	3,493,809	-1,354,295	27,117,373	7,465,467	4,932,462	25,203	1,567,910	988,587
1999	42,344,708	34,724,129	199,055	34,923,184	3,771,267	-1,525,126	29,626,791	7,580,766	5,137,151	26,334	1,607,993	1,034,704
2000	45,921,267	37,785,495	197,869	37,983,364	4,065,861	-1,768,341	32,149,162	8,218,613	5,553,492	27,715	1,656,890	1,075,452
2001	48,612,927	40,132,651	195,950	40,328,601	4,350,734	-1,833,509	34,144,358	8,311,791	6,156,778	28,423	1,710,359	1,078,665
2002	50,450,627	41,889,499	180,733	42,070,232	4,527,738	-2,125,218	35,417,276	8,207,317	6,826,034	28,660	1,760,345	1,077,705
2003	53,299,395	44,507,625	150,859	44,658,484	4,801,770	-2,454,626	37,402,088	8,494,252	7,403,055	29,422	1,811,544	1,113,228
2004	58,014,588	48,726,163	174,966	48,901,129	5,291,566	-2,675,287	40,934,276	9,077,167	8,003,145	30,890	1,878,077	1,173,745
2005	64,021,200	53,749,591	191,933	53,941,524	5,866,852	-2,747,261	45,327,411	10,035,123	8,658,666	32,734	1,955,794	1,240,257
2006	69,726,752	57,487,921	187,208	57,675,129	6,342,501	-2,873,838	48,458,790	11,929,423	9,338,539	34,517	2,020,057	1,292,086
2007	72,491,425	59,078,296	168,436	59,246,732	6,585,256	-3,149,835	49,511,641	12,949,552	10,030,232	35,227	2,057,865	1,326,528
2008	73,526,299	58,810,915	167,492	58,978,407	6,622,733	-3,304,754	49,050,920	12,834,868	11,640,511	35,222	2,087,489	1,311,408
2009	69,882,570	54,836,781	172,865	55,009,646	6,286,556	-2,951,043	45,772,047	11,238,903	12,871,620	33,090	2,111,917	1,249,386
2010	72,793,248	55,731,010	175,008	55,906,018	6,397,783	-2,927,083	46,581,152	11,696,417	14,515,679	34,021	2,139,686	1,247,769
2011	76,936,649	56,980,135	147,817	57,127,952	5,871,300	-2,941,566	48,315,086	13,334,497	15,287,066	35,355	2,176,088	1,287,595
2012	79,405,797	60,189,760	161,507	60,351,267	6,208,923	-3,235,145	50,907,199	13,300,581	15,198,017	35,674	2,225,901	1,326,570
2013	81,354,562	62,572,327	183,187	62,755,514	7,268,658	-3,351,880	52,134,976	13,462,946	15,756,640	35,822	2,271,083	1,366,358
2014	86,133,623	66,527,245	181,585	66,708,830	7,739,431	-3,732,636	55,236,763	14,037,471	16,859,389	37,104	2,321,418	1416050

Personal Income and Employment by Area: Oshkosh-Neenah, WI

(Thousands of dollars, except as noted.)

Year	Personal income, total	Derivation of personal income									Per capita personal income (dollars)	Population (persons)	Total employment
		Earnings by place of work			Less: Contributions for government social insurance	Plus: Adjustment for residence	Equals: Net earnings by place of residence	Plus: Dividends, interest, and rent	Plus: Personal current transfer receipts				
		Nonfarm	Farm	Total									
1970	506,387	427,380	8,094	435,474	31,107	-23,923	380,444	84,370	41,573		3,889	130,213	58,052
1971	531,334	442,234	8,734	450,968	33,318	-25,025	392,625	89,421	49,288		4,049	131,228	57,187
1972	574,052	484,545	9,278	493,823	38,654	-30,023	425,146	94,626	54,280		4,362	131,616	58,727
1973	636,244	543,954	10,572	554,526	50,124	-34,268	470,134	103,336	62,774		4,874	130,530	61,323
1974	702,288	593,486	11,118	604,604	56,715	-38,674	509,215	116,930	76,143		5,439	129,132	62,563
1975	775,674	646,469	11,649	658,118	60,727	-44,415	552,976	127,887	94,811		5,947	130,425	62,538
1976	852,241	724,578	8,554	733,132	69,024	-50,986	613,122	136,655	102,464		6,527	130,569	64,799
1977	954,245	815,450	15,525	830,975	76,947	-59,874	694,154	151,523	108,568		7,305	130,632	66,556
1978	1,059,183	919,028	12,376	931,404	89,300	-69,223	772,881	167,117	119,185		8,152	129,936	68,792
1979	1,184,353	1,023,729	16,827	1,040,556	103,272	-74,209	863,075	187,080	134,198		9,052	130,845	71,146
1980	1,303,363	1,084,553	17,305	1,101,858	109,167	-77,520	915,171	225,021	163,171		9,893	131,746	69,583
1981	1,421,332	1,158,187	12,466	1,170,653	124,390	-84,148	962,115	276,787	182,430		10,822	131,335	68,777
1982	1,511,758	1,207,086	10,160	1,217,246	131,822	-88,810	996,614	309,227	205,917		11,511	131,330	68,279
1983	1,625,407	1,304,333	1,762	1,306,095	142,548	-99,675	1,063,872	338,820	222,715		12,357	131,539	68,795
1984	1,782,605	1,441,903	8,571	1,450,474	161,739	-112,148	1,176,587	378,070	227,948		13,392	133,106	72,636
1985	1,896,729	1,542,626	7,785	1,550,411	174,897	-120,707	1,254,807	401,885	240,037		14,132	134,219	74,641
1986	2,001,123	1,643,355	9,520	1,652,875	186,159	-131,647	1,335,069	418,757	247,297		14,782	135,372	76,626
1987	2,114,494	1,763,946	11,760	1,775,706	197,085	-142,423	1,436,198	424,296	254,000		15,511	136,319	78,525
1988	2,243,393	1,897,567	5,323	1,902,890	218,357	-153,505	1,531,028	447,835	264,530		16,238	138,161	80,578
1989	2,444,758	1,992,015	14,624	2,006,639	228,126	-145,560	1,632,953	525,965	285,840		17,588	139,004	81,836
1990	2,626,925	2,185,268	12,963	2,198,231	261,184	-166,988	1,770,059	549,549	307,317		18,648	140,871	86,195
1991	2,744,730	2,334,107	9,998	2,344,105	280,843	-194,239	1,869,023	545,187	330,520		19,159	143,263	88,504
1992	2,995,566	2,580,953	13,232	2,594,185	306,477	-234,134	2,053,574	583,719	358,273		20,595	145,449	90,993
1993	3,097,445	2,708,802	5,775	2,714,577	323,820	-261,000	2,129,757	593,198	374,490		20,924	148,031	92,431
1994	3,305,830	2,858,528	15,263	2,873,791	343,771	-266,877	2,263,143	653,550	389,137		22,207	148,867	94,352
1995	3,500,857	3,061,325	6,186	3,067,511	367,889	-301,890	2,397,732	691,549	411,576		23,227	150,725	97,363
1996	3,671,725	3,159,966	12,232	3,172,198	377,150	-290,726	2,504,322	741,835	425,568		24,123	152,206	98,410
1997	3,845,597	3,340,949	7,138	3,348,087	396,055	-318,028	2,634,004	772,288	439,305		25,049	153,525	99,045
1998	4,126,330	3,639,356	12,896	3,652,252	429,635	-409,582	2,813,035	864,229	449,066		26,717	154,444	101,678
1999	4,275,818	3,885,754	12,291	3,898,045	455,398	-479,124	2,963,523	848,107	464,188		27,444	155,801	103,808
2000	4,529,869	4,109,482	7,373	4,116,855	478,847	-476,102	3,161,906	870,283	497,680		28,834	157,103	106,157
2001	4,670,070	4,215,219	6,496	4,221,715	492,184	-490,975	3,238,556	881,301	550,213		29,527	158,163	104,589
2002	4,803,737	4,361,975	8,792	4,370,767	505,373	-528,891	3,336,503	872,028	595,206		30,187	159,134	105,212
2003	4,955,841	4,459,714	16,013	4,475,727	514,990	-560,400	3,400,337	946,261	609,243		31,083	159,440	104,210
2004	5,145,844	4,706,482	16,087	4,722,569	542,599	-603,792	3,576,178	941,292	628,374		32,135	160,130	104,522
2005	5,295,097	4,847,970	17,315	4,865,285	561,250	-636,967	3,667,068	955,728	672,301		32,797	161,451	105,731
2006	5,628,749	4,974,883	11,681	4,986,564	582,633	-659,122	3,744,809	1,164,705	719,235		34,590	162,727	106,445
2007	5,833,916	5,189,279	21,151	5,210,430	602,846	-697,958	3,909,626	1,153,319	770,971		35,565	164,037	107,574
2008	6,037,610	5,359,190	25,762	5,384,952	629,326	-733,462	4,022,164	1,131,569	883,877		36,612	164,910	109,242
2009	5,976,107	5,247,095	7,381	5,254,476	615,223	-696,364	3,942,889	1,014,675	1,018,543		35,908	166,429	105,959
2010	6,174,175	5,457,094	11,069	5,468,163	650,839	-748,020	4,069,304	1,020,014	1,084,857		36,970	167,004	106,530
2011	6,519,074	5,659,029	27,754	5,686,783	603,134	-830,669	4,252,980	1,211,016	1,055,078		38,906	167,558	108,478
2012	6,678,893	5,786,665	24,412	5,811,077	613,321	-823,810	4,373,946	1,237,305	1,067,642		39,606	168,634	108,102
2013	6,631,285	5,930,749	30,320	5,961,069	713,384	-921,543	4,326,142	1,207,466	1,097,677		39,155	169,360	109,058
2014	6,864,790	6,075,170	32,420	6,107,590	729,749	-906,959	4,470,882	1,253,442	1,140,466		40,498	169,511	109770

Personal Income and Employment by Area: Owensboro, KY

(Thousands of dollars, except as noted.)

Year	Personal income, total	Earnings by place of work			Less: Contributions for government social insurance	Plus: Adjustment for residence	Equals: Net earnings by place of residence	Plus: Dividends, interest, and rent	Plus: Personal current transfer receipts	Per capita personal income (dollars)	Population (persons)	Total employment
		Nonfarm	Farm	Total								
1970	320,041	256,202	11,629	267,831	17,575	-1,263	248,993	40,427	30,621	3,342	95,768	42,800
1971	346,028	271,049	12,931	283,980	19,049	727	265,658	43,990	36,380	3,569	96,960	42,627
1972	385,010	296,874	15,826	312,700	22,120	6,028	296,608	47,937	40,465	3,960	97,215	43,642
1973	426,878	326,205	25,247	351,452	28,023	3,226	326,655	52,374	47,849	4,352	98,090	45,008
1974	475,252	360,416	24,164	384,580	32,271	3,155	355,464	60,531	59,257	4,801	98,996	46,164
1975	517,520	385,871	16,717	402,588	34,050	5,515	374,053	68,742	74,725	5,185	99,816	44,188
1976	575,742	433,976	18,542	452,518	38,732	8,008	421,794	75,671	78,277	5,735	100,389	45,399
1977	646,552	482,321	26,841	509,162	42,776	13,435	479,821	86,096	80,635	6,417	100,759	46,935
1978	724,323	561,522	15,482	577,004	51,356	14,564	540,212	98,240	85,871	7,102	101,985	49,522
1979	819,776	626,817	19,612	646,429	59,521	21,479	608,387	112,755	98,634	7,943	103,209	49,610
1980	911,057	692,168	3,400	695,568	66,050	19,931	649,449	144,326	117,282	8,766	103,927	49,868
1981	1,023,626	749,383	22,733	772,116	76,964	15,072	710,224	180,192	133,210	9,819	104,247	49,877
1982	1,078,582	764,429	15,520	779,949	79,631	19,432	719,750	212,270	146,562	10,299	104,731	49,194
1983	1,119,348	831,286	-22,117	809,169	86,159	17,898	740,908	221,387	157,053	10,618	105,422	50,297
1984	1,249,579	877,119	34,038	911,157	93,698	20,465	837,924	243,178	168,477	11,730	106,527	51,708
1985	1,281,328	897,821	21,806	919,627	97,176	20,497	842,948	259,083	179,297	12,066	106,197	51,751
1986	1,308,455	923,836	17,374	941,210	103,153	16,495	854,552	264,135	189,768	12,374	105,746	52,395
1987	1,349,077	963,654	15,413	979,067	106,507	15,735	888,295	263,942	196,840	12,842	105,054	52,141
1988	1,443,787	1,048,726	17,796	1,066,522	116,804	14,203	963,921	271,256	208,610	13,813	104,527	52,711
1989	1,561,765	1,096,936	47,480	1,144,416	124,637	14,294	1,034,073	296,878	230,814	14,937	104,559	54,131
1990	1,645,868	1,159,595	42,261	1,201,856	136,173	14,071	1,079,754	315,551	250,563	15,717	104,716	54,954
1991	1,708,496	1,199,437	33,325	1,232,762	142,423	11,558	1,101,897	323,824	282,775	16,241	105,194	54,878
1992	1,833,614	1,280,013	56,361	1,336,374	149,957	7,761	1,194,178	331,960	307,476	17,295	106,017	55,861
1993	1,896,208	1,357,671	45,428	1,403,099	162,106	4,913	1,245,906	335,721	314,581	17,780	106,646	57,276
1994	2,019,259	1,446,474	53,978	1,500,452	176,060	1,523	1,325,915	360,173	333,171	18,777	107,539	59,266
1995	2,086,788	1,505,373	31,868	1,537,241	184,351	-1,123	1,351,767	376,719	358,302	19,280	108,234	60,800
1996	2,190,649	1,536,812	64,763	1,601,575	187,130	-1,849	1,412,596	401,419	376,634	20,177	108,573	60,962
1997	2,330,846	1,676,157	43,614	1,719,771	202,596	-10,678	1,506,497	426,202	398,147	21,413	108,851	62,246
1998	2,414,398	1,745,863	29,201	1,775,064	211,963	-8,030	1,555,071	452,269	407,058	22,135	109,075	62,917
1999	2,498,215	1,848,215	26,715	1,874,930	222,758	-7,028	1,645,144	426,468	426,603	22,808	109,533	63,698
2000	2,692,409	1,939,333	62,273	2,001,606	226,117	-9,426	1,766,063	470,822	455,524	24,462	110,064	64,188
2001	2,711,454	1,942,868	63,219	2,006,087	226,920	-20,977	1,758,190	458,379	494,885	24,652	109,991	63,028
2002	2,783,607	2,009,513	19,670	2,029,183	231,736	-15,031	1,782,416	468,432	532,759	25,262	110,190	61,698
2003	2,879,136	2,063,778	35,627	2,099,405	235,246	-4,329	1,859,830	471,825	547,481	26,000	110,735	62,085
2004	3,027,453	2,138,672	81,335	2,220,007	240,654	9,030	1,988,383	451,335	587,735	27,275	110,999	62,640
2005	3,196,682	2,225,365	113,314	2,338,679	250,677	20,091	2,108,093	459,380	629,209	28,678	111,469	62,919
2006	3,361,922	2,332,755	86,424	2,419,179	264,441	18,588	2,173,326	505,283	683,313	29,976	112,152	64,088
2007	3,536,166	2,420,146	64,877	2,485,023	277,664	31,575	2,238,934	558,535	738,697	31,321	112,900	65,252
2008	3,810,174	2,527,803	79,613	2,607,416	290,705	43,590	2,360,301	614,403	835,470	33,525	113,651	64,460
2009	3,787,988	2,440,887	109,019	2,549,906	287,451	32,421	2,294,876	568,420	924,692	33,116	114,385	62,614
2010	3,875,797	2,532,631	71,737	2,604,368	295,506	35,675	2,344,537	550,881	980,379	33,764	114,791	62,504
2011	4,153,082	2,643,505	124,281	2,767,786	273,650	39,474	2,533,610	623,966	995,506	36,001	115,361	64,256
2012	4,275,582	2,776,268	98,148	2,874,416	291,778	13,974	2,596,612	688,217	990,753	36,885	115,918	65,775
2013	4,416,191	2,855,491	194,505	3,049,996	339,878	8,986	2,719,104	684,600	1,012,487	37,940	116,399	65,471
2014	4,573,925	2,968,885	147,209	3,116,094	354,955	8,658	2,769,797	709,195	1,094,933	39,259	116,506	65797

Personal Income and Employment by Area: Oxnard-Thousand Oaks-Ventura, CA

(Thousands of dollars, except as noted.)

Year	Personal income, total	Earnings by place of work			Less: Contributions for government social insurance	Plus: Adjustment for residence	Equals: Net earnings by place of residence	Plus: Dividends, interest, and rent	Plus: Personal current transfer receipts	Per capita personal income (dollars)	Population (persons)	Total employment
		Nonfarm	Farm	Total								
1970	1,673,166	997,954	70,144	1,068,098	60,380	267,571	1,275,289	270,049	127,828	4,390	381,174	135,394
1971	1,844,484	1,092,586	77,954	1,170,540	67,405	288,851	1,391,986	301,438	151,060	4,661	395,691	140,085
1972	2,083,420	1,227,239	91,278	1,318,517	79,649	342,191	1,581,059	332,571	169,790	5,100	408,523	147,656
1973	2,362,312	1,358,648	129,273	1,487,921	99,728	402,985	1,791,178	378,059	193,075	5,632	419,461	155,861
1974	2,690,182	1,515,375	139,016	1,654,391	115,204	474,838	2,014,025	438,619	237,538	6,200	433,885	164,301
1975	3,058,264	1,705,121	143,245	1,848,366	128,314	536,303	2,256,355	493,450	308,459	6,813	448,918	171,738
1976	3,402,490	1,903,017	110,060	2,013,077	145,971	637,687	2,504,793	541,418	356,279	7,389	460,485	176,285
1977	3,911,617	2,178,853	148,233	2,327,086	172,328	766,796	2,921,554	611,817	378,246	8,171	478,695	188,053
1978	4,624,040	2,541,561	191,946	2,733,507	206,565	943,883	3,470,825	735,500	417,715	9,359	494,086	202,771
1979	5,225,016	2,870,774	153,355	3,024,129	245,912	1,155,918	3,934,135	827,178	463,703	10,201	512,189	213,342
1980	6,062,617	3,223,780	161,842	3,385,622	270,932	1,381,209	4,495,899	1,019,304	547,414	11,378	532,827	221,151
1981	6,866,663	3,593,132	155,419	3,748,551	329,440	1,550,620	4,969,731	1,246,062	650,870	12,567	546,389	225,479
1982	7,459,596	3,912,046	206,124	4,118,170	369,622	1,618,106	5,366,654	1,375,025	717,917	13,270	562,142	229,893
1983	8,098,933	4,260,586	213,837	4,474,423	416,881	1,743,026	5,800,568	1,539,470	758,895	14,071	575,586	237,557
1984	9,046,382	4,814,283	238,127	5,052,410	492,894	1,918,094	6,477,610	1,760,728	808,044	15,364	588,790	248,225
1985	9,851,856	5,330,776	217,602	5,548,378	554,793	2,085,924	7,079,509	1,891,007	881,340	16,343	602,819	260,105
1986	10,794,280	5,886,888	317,243	6,204,131	621,422	2,258,054	7,840,763	2,001,534	951,983	17,540	615,422	270,559
1987	11,783,983	6,533,104	387,110	6,920,214	700,533	2,495,192	8,714,873	2,082,686	986,424	18,644	632,062	287,425
1988	12,926,679	7,324,491	445,607	7,770,098	811,225	2,650,492	9,609,365	2,261,235	1,056,079	19,861	650,851	305,846
1989	13,961,374	7,815,652	427,647	8,243,299	875,359	2,813,681	10,181,621	2,630,585	1,149,168	21,004	664,692	317,976
1990	14,954,713	8,464,279	465,101	8,929,380	943,815	3,082,774	11,068,339	2,639,386	1,246,988	22,317	670,117	327,267
1991	15,581,903	8,935,743	438,537	9,374,280	998,843	3,159,834	11,535,271	2,649,792	1,396,840	23,060	675,706	332,915
1992	16,163,309	9,497,375	285,341	9,782,716	1,054,217	3,194,115	11,922,614	2,649,001	1,591,694	23,626	684,143	332,193
1993	16,933,627	9,821,702	414,090	10,235,792	1,088,981	3,314,406	12,461,217	2,787,791	1,684,619	24,544	689,943	335,316
1994	17,620,145	10,317,679	358,400	10,676,079	1,149,271	3,377,934	12,904,742	3,002,755	1,712,648	25,225	698,509	344,984
1995	18,806,068	10,610,404	441,879	11,052,283	1,168,432	3,647,571	13,531,422	3,471,463	1,803,183	26,733	703,486	352,089
1996	19,571,880	11,150,358	332,740	11,483,098	1,198,256	3,727,166	14,012,008	3,655,325	1,904,547	27,558	710,215	358,399
1997	20,992,887	11,812,577	413,120	12,225,697	1,256,990	4,159,993	15,128,700	3,919,488	1,944,699	29,112	721,107	357,142
1998	21,997,407	12,690,357	408,398	13,098,755	1,342,124	4,092,820	15,849,451	4,102,960	2,044,996	30,101	730,779	371,983
1999	23,565,276	13,918,669	464,355	14,383,024	1,453,182	4,198,896	17,128,738	4,275,325	2,161,213	31,701	743,357	386,579
2000	25,788,869	15,655,355	426,597	16,081,952	1,612,604	4,385,141	18,854,489	4,648,036	2,286,344	34,089	756,506	396,576
2001	26,641,359	16,558,949	305,737	16,864,686	1,776,193	4,457,110	19,545,603	4,559,900	2,535,856	34,749	766,689	399,927
2002	27,299,010	17,190,502	369,614	17,560,116	1,875,892	4,446,792	20,131,016	4,452,761	2,715,233	35,022	779,489	407,979
2003	29,284,479	18,533,121	367,885	18,901,006	2,043,598	4,699,648	21,557,056	4,836,719	2,890,704	37,160	788,070	417,008
2004	31,493,474	20,023,630	525,264	20,548,894	2,278,602	5,012,331	23,282,623	5,195,666	3,015,185	39,665	793,994	422,023
2005	33,357,516	21,128,197	508,854	21,637,051	2,407,147	5,239,499	24,469,403	5,690,654	3,197,459	42,002	794,197	430,960
2006	35,584,729	21,884,287	652,815	22,537,102	2,441,305	5,384,163	25,479,960	6,660,890	3,443,879	44,582	798,183	436,761
2007	37,081,090	22,465,837	634,208	23,100,045	2,458,201	5,604,048	26,245,892	7,181,144	3,654,054	46,350	800,027	442,627
2008	36,669,201	21,647,334	633,232	22,280,566	2,409,787	5,373,118	25,243,897	7,197,362	4,227,942	45,475	806,353	435,959
2009	35,123,778	20,943,345	810,871	21,754,216	2,384,204	4,610,242	23,980,254	6,451,913	4,691,611	43,090	815,130	422,095
2010	36,032,516	21,430,388	855,717	22,286,105	2,397,670	4,613,942	24,502,377	6,319,982	5,210,157	43,657	825,353	418,321
2011	38,195,055	22,378,338	722,124	23,100,462	2,245,192	4,754,280	25,609,550	7,306,304	5,279,201	45,964	830,973	423,530
2012	40,391,098	23,368,849	872,526	24,241,375	2,294,535	5,300,762	27,247,602	7,848,834	5,294,662	48,345	835,476	431,486
2013	40,940,858	23,562,678	1,071,007	24,633,685	2,630,182	5,226,268	27,229,771	8,219,325	5,491,762	48,683	840,972	439,056
2014	42,651,306	24,491,701	990,667	25,482,368	2,736,480	5,616,676	28,362,564	8,574,672	5,714,070	50,405	846,178	447252

Personal Income and Employment by Area: Palm Bay-Melbourne-Titusville, FL

(Thousands of dollars, except as noted.)

Year	Personal income, total	Earnings by place of work			Less: Contributions for government social insurance	Plus: Adjustment for residence	Equals: Net earnings by place of residence	Plus: Dividends, interest, and rent	Plus: Personal current transfer receipts	Per capita personal income (dollars)	Population (persons)	Total employment
		Nonfarm	Farm	Total								
1970	963,400	826,415	3,649	830,064	48,418	-25,184	756,462	151,260	55,678	4,195	229,660	96,024
1971	1,000,654	819,100	5,158	824,258	49,360	-19,317	755,581	174,536	70,537	4,319	231,701	92,542
1972	1,101,472	885,102	7,339	892,441	56,797	-17,404	818,240	197,389	85,843	4,779	230,503	95,402
1973	1,217,475	960,278	9,272	969,550	71,295	-13,412	884,843	228,138	104,494	5,111	238,222	101,054
1974	1,292,657	976,188	8,879	985,067	75,325	-11,013	898,729	264,902	129,026	5,421	238,464	99,316
1975	1,433,017	1,050,772	6,844	1,057,616	80,238	-13,502	963,876	301,862	167,279	5,940	241,241	97,287
1976	1,550,558	1,123,404	6,191	1,129,595	87,661	-10,492	1,031,442	333,422	185,694	6,439	240,791	98,836
1977	1,728,008	1,253,338	6,385	1,259,723	100,298	-9,636	1,149,789	378,069	200,150	7,157	241,451	103,907
1978	2,021,233	1,462,001	7,983	1,469,984	120,935	-9,211	1,339,838	456,429	224,966	8,052	251,031	113,104
1979	2,371,954	1,728,048	10,283	1,738,331	150,984	-10,083	1,577,264	533,704	260,986	9,018	263,038	121,837
1980	2,830,083	2,019,081	13,200	2,032,281	178,073	-8,209	1,845,999	671,712	312,372	10,266	275,664	129,188
1981	3,260,602	2,276,198	9,240	2,285,438	216,346	-8,173	2,060,919	828,964	370,719	11,402	285,963	133,908
1982	3,584,642	2,481,019	12,079	2,493,098	243,013	-9,925	2,240,160	919,999	424,483	11,985	299,098	138,412
1983	4,008,258	2,774,462	13,416	2,787,878	277,932	-13,184	2,496,762	1,042,534	468,962	12,930	310,006	147,424
1984	4,555,169	3,189,665	10,245	3,199,910	330,120	-16,082	2,853,708	1,190,922	510,539	14,112	322,780	159,722
1985	5,062,166	3,546,940	10,256	3,557,196	375,182	-15,676	3,166,338	1,333,756	562,072	15,024	336,935	170,814
1986	5,397,579	3,736,704	9,107	3,745,811	407,335	-9,306	3,329,170	1,445,983	622,426	15,458	349,183	175,694
1987	5,818,789	4,051,143	9,653	4,060,796	437,498	-5,638	3,617,660	1,532,353	668,776	16,180	359,628	176,540
1988	6,419,159	4,504,595	15,615	4,520,210	500,037	-4,020	4,016,153	1,662,105	740,901	17,277	371,547	187,777
1989	7,217,707	4,920,373	14,347	4,934,720	551,197	-553	4,382,970	1,976,925	857,812	18,775	384,423	196,440
1990	7,679,768	5,240,654	14,051	5,254,705	585,849	791	4,669,647	2,044,715	965,406	19,047	403,209	202,232
1991	8,061,329	5,536,719	16,213	5,552,932	624,168	-2,656	4,926,108	2,032,261	1,102,960	19,401	415,512	203,022
1992	8,603,546	5,924,736	14,610	5,939,346	666,016	5,283	5,278,613	2,043,601	1,281,332	20,216	425,584	203,939
1993	8,976,799	6,115,806	13,347	6,129,153	685,359	23,446	5,467,240	2,124,895	1,384,664	20,576	436,282	206,630
1994	9,347,231	6,259,533	12,453	6,271,986	725,784	44,879	5,591,081	2,253,532	1,502,618	21,043	444,198	209,999
1995	9,842,082	6,416,285	11,076	6,427,361	745,828	68,284	5,749,817	2,462,694	1,629,571	21,808	451,310	211,373
1996	10,268,230	6,560,380	8,958	6,569,338	766,054	98,877	5,902,161	2,618,907	1,747,162	22,524	455,889	215,068
1997	10,982,716	6,993,051	10,210	7,003,261	816,791	123,281	6,309,751	2,830,526	1,842,439	23,788	461,686	223,138
1998	11,610,945	7,413,269	14,038	7,427,307	859,715	163,354	6,730,946	2,971,037	1,908,962	24,830	467,624	231,153
1999	12,080,423	7,782,691	15,838	7,798,529	894,888	205,694	7,109,335	2,952,365	2,018,723	25,587	472,138	234,839
2000	13,299,767	8,680,750	16,580	8,697,330	983,041	233,250	7,947,539	3,200,423	2,151,805	27,834	477,819	243,415
2001	13,942,503	9,079,448	16,267	9,095,715	1,012,627	255,512	8,338,600	3,240,885	2,363,018	28,663	486,429	248,733
2002	14,469,014	9,466,350	17,667	9,484,017	1,052,244	269,846	8,701,619	3,208,113	2,559,282	29,205	495,425	248,195
2003	15,418,777	10,118,780	14,727	10,133,507	1,128,002	297,362	9,302,867	3,364,608	2,751,302	30,541	504,847	257,115
2004	16,613,651	11,097,230	14,234	11,111,464	1,242,854	336,253	10,204,863	3,411,351	2,997,437	32,028	518,722	269,122
2005	17,740,726	11,901,513	18,493	11,920,006	1,341,951	374,663	10,952,718	3,603,958	3,184,050	33,479	529,907	279,577
2006	18,932,332	12,501,040	16,276	12,517,316	1,427,803	405,849	11,495,362	4,002,217	3,434,753	35,378	535,138	287,537
2007	19,601,958	12,529,436	11,228	12,540,664	1,448,749	429,127	11,521,042	4,423,385	3,657,531	36,319	539,719	286,686
2008	20,011,172	12,401,632	9,232	12,410,864	1,455,429	447,204	11,402,639	4,477,103	4,131,430	36,895	542,378	275,860
2009	19,427,383	12,174,704	9,092	12,183,796	1,443,206	404,060	11,144,650	3,860,523	4,422,210	35,837	542,109	265,150
2010	19,826,418	12,243,635	15,281	12,258,916	1,462,445	402,884	11,199,355	3,886,866	4,740,197	36,444	544,029	262,161
2011	20,699,703	12,242,452	11,638	12,254,090	1,324,649	429,750	11,359,191	4,372,006	4,968,506	38,021	544,431	263,521
2012	20,698,424	12,292,247	14,920	12,307,167	1,340,183	472,282	11,439,266	4,271,584	4,987,574	37,794	547,669	264,281
2013	20,913,021	12,368,105	14,769	12,382,874	1,510,641	492,797	11,365,030	4,416,914	5,131,077	37,924	551,440	266,809
2014	21,647,137	12,562,045	18,696	12,580,741	1,540,567	552,083	11,592,257	4,598,137	5,456,743	38,872	556,885	270517

Personal Income and Employment by Area: Panama City-Lynn Haven-Panama City Beach, FL

(Thousands of dollars, except as noted.)

Year	Personal income, total	Derivation of personal income					Equals: Net earnings by place of residence	Plus: Dividends, interest, and rent	Plus: Personal current transfer receipts	Per capita personal income (dollars)	Population (persons)	Total employment
		Earnings by place of work			Less: Contributions for government social insurance	Plus: Adjustment for residence						
		Nonfarm	Farm	Total								
1970	296,679	239,594	174	239,768	14,055	-1,965	223,748	50,388	22,543	3,458	85,792	35,240
1971	323,845	257,410	210	257,620	15,682	-1,933	240,005	57,027	26,813	3,668	88,300	35,430
1972	359,567	284,335	210	284,545	18,042	-2,103	264,400	63,062	32,105	4,012	89,621	36,514
1973	411,823	325,730	439	326,169	23,516	-2,670	299,983	72,581	39,259	4,489	91,744	39,716
1974	471,221	370,034	796	370,830	28,237	-3,756	338,837	84,723	47,661	4,873	96,694	42,168
1975	528,729	403,520	793	404,313	30,812	-4,700	368,801	97,254	62,674	5,312	99,527	42,716
1976	596,355	461,216	656	461,872	36,025	-7,151	418,696	107,460	70,199	5,828	102,320	45,048
1977	645,236	492,754	448	493,202	38,689	-7,057	447,456	120,332	77,448	6,208	103,944	46,176
1978	741,541	562,376	341	562,717	44,703	-8,598	509,416	147,070	85,055	7,046	105,250	48,370
1979	819,097	613,669	277	613,946	51,796	-10,616	551,534	169,749	97,814	7,581	108,048	49,098
1980	930,225	676,386	301	676,687	57,183	-9,264	610,240	203,113	116,872	8,537	108,965	50,033
1981	1,062,722	768,782	170	768,952	70,068	-10,406	688,478	238,944	135,300	9,572	111,027	51,966
1982	1,166,168	827,176	304	827,480	76,994	-12,482	738,004	273,133	155,031	10,169	114,679	53,880
1983	1,283,815	910,429	275	910,704	86,226	-13,865	810,613	302,651	170,551	10,985	116,871	56,082
1984	1,446,855	1,040,386	321	1,040,707	101,135	-17,870	921,702	342,536	182,617	12,037	120,204	60,969
1985	1,581,445	1,137,041	375	1,137,416	113,154	-19,160	1,005,102	379,140	197,203	12,663	124,892	65,284
1986	1,709,859	1,226,291	537	1,226,828	125,384	-19,357	1,082,087	414,250	213,522	13,214	129,400	67,908
1987	1,787,678	1,280,076	621	1,280,697	129,866	-18,308	1,132,523	427,986	227,169	13,467	132,748	67,445
1988	1,934,902	1,388,494	565	1,389,059	145,910	-17,562	1,225,587	460,195	249,120	14,296	135,342	69,027
1989	2,096,053	1,448,398	279	1,448,677	154,754	-16,524	1,277,399	530,571	288,083	15,273	137,241	70,569
1990	2,269,340	1,571,061	138	1,571,199	168,697	-18,851	1,383,651	564,537	321,152	16,349	138,809	73,233
1991	2,433,925	1,698,172	-25	1,698,147	183,471	-22,113	1,492,563	576,731	364,631	17,210	141,422	74,997
1992	2,605,128	1,807,595	-263	1,807,332	196,083	-25,521	1,585,728	604,041	415,359	17,988	144,829	76,244
1993	2,794,472	1,920,442	-32	1,920,410	208,335	-28,986	1,683,089	664,402	446,981	18,726	149,232	78,539
1994	2,907,572	2,003,101	372	2,003,473	219,331	-31,390	1,752,752	671,212	483,608	19,092	152,295	79,835
1995	3,148,856	2,119,687	653	2,120,340	229,649	-33,422	1,857,269	750,073	541,514	20,328	154,905	81,750
1996	3,313,303	2,244,033	1,170	2,245,203	241,830	-37,590	1,965,783	796,405	551,115	21,013	157,681	84,598
1997	3,476,490	2,355,883	1,766	2,357,649	254,651	-40,110	2,062,888	835,342	578,260	21,807	159,420	85,586
1998	3,642,883	2,468,881	1,465	2,470,346	267,687	-42,438	2,160,221	897,164	585,498	22,812	159,691	87,126
1999	3,765,717	2,561,524	1,362	2,562,886	275,123	-42,502	2,245,261	897,546	622,910	23,411	160,855	87,558
2000	3,919,183	2,614,876	1,072	2,615,948	280,179	-42,817	2,292,952	957,691	668,540	24,050	162,959	88,162
2001	4,243,748	2,857,362	1,064	2,858,426	308,443	-52,576	2,497,407	1,006,942	739,399	25,708	165,075	89,812
2002	4,456,780	3,065,025	861	3,065,886	330,355	-57,449	2,678,082	965,618	813,080	26,586	167,638	91,886
2003	4,790,332	3,333,510	581	3,334,091	357,144	-61,008	2,915,939	1,001,889	872,504	28,127	170,310	94,971
2004	5,200,359	3,612,656	730	3,613,386	391,489	-63,918	3,157,979	1,106,604	935,776	29,843	174,259	100,791
2005	5,677,895	3,992,438	827	3,993,265	433,563	-68,110	3,491,592	1,188,086	998,217	31,774	178,698	105,148
2006	6,065,782	4,258,658	754	4,259,412	469,645	-68,080	3,721,687	1,289,532	1,054,563	33,420	181,500	108,492
2007	6,310,364	4,274,696	654	4,275,350	475,463	-65,249	3,734,638	1,463,750	1,111,976	34,815	181,253	108,598
2008	6,511,641	4,258,613	657	4,259,270	479,684	-62,035	3,717,551	1,525,629	1,268,461	35,755	182,118	106,873
2009	6,321,150	4,129,481	566	4,130,047	475,230	-54,680	3,600,137	1,345,716	1,375,297	34,467	183,397	104,063
2010	6,608,483	4,249,990	641	4,250,631	491,317	-66,986	3,692,328	1,371,469	1,544,686	35,700	185,111	103,647
2011	6,857,979	4,274,779	745	4,275,524	446,907	-58,070	3,770,547	1,493,233	1,594,199	36,996	185,370	104,255
2012	6,831,274	4,293,809	718	4,294,527	454,133	-41,321	3,799,073	1,466,595	1,565,606	36,402	187,664	104,517
2013	6,922,682	4,394,643	892	4,395,535	518,961	-46,537	3,830,037	1,483,566	1,609,079	36,288	190,771	106,598
2014	7,328,599	4,667,012	1,035	4,668,047	551,154	-56,060	4,060,833	1,565,236	1,702,530	37,596	194,929	109920

Personal Income and Employment by Area: Parkersburg-Marietta-Vienna, WV-OH

(Thousands of dollars, except as noted.)

		Derivation of personal income										
		Earnings by place of work			Less: Contributions for government social insurance	Plus: Adjustment for residence	Equals: Net earnings by place of residence	Plus: Dividends, interest, and rent	Plus: Personal current transfer receipts	Per capita personal income (dollars)	Population (persons)	Total employment
Year	Personal income, total	Nonfarm	Farm	Total								
1970	317,786	266,066	716	266,782	20,162	2,015	248,635	38,980	30,171	3,504	90,698	37,759
1971	336,514	281,465	831	282,296	22,081	-874	259,341	41,787	35,386	3,734	90,111	38,352
1972	368,806	314,949	1,037	315,986	26,269	-5,742	283,975	45,593	39,238	4,053	91,003	39,746
1973	405,697	350,001	1,456	351,457	33,776	-7,815	309,866	50,647	45,184	4,416	91,866	42,037
1974	461,692	397,723	819	398,542	40,232	-10,273	348,037	58,988	54,667	5,008	92,182	43,648
1975	494,187	401,964	280	402,244	39,454	-7,856	354,934	66,014	73,239	5,305	93,160	41,134
1976	545,715	449,922	-144	449,778	44,953	-7,991	396,834	71,379	77,502	5,798	94,121	42,127
1977	619,521	515,300	-243	515,057	51,319	-8,167	455,571	79,511	84,439	6,524	94,964	44,102
1978	698,745	586,412	151	586,563	60,451	-5,605	520,507	88,161	90,077	7,224	96,719	46,028
1979	768,932	649,431	219	649,650	69,301	-13,893	566,456	99,555	102,921	7,893	97,422	46,895
1980	846,336	697,127	344	697,471	75,171	-22,735	599,565	121,648	125,123	8,588	98,551	46,059
1981	927,867	758,083	-821	757,262	87,222	-31,673	638,367	149,320	140,180	9,421	98,486	45,220
1982	962,259	776,995	-1,633	775,362	91,943	-41,390	642,029	165,402	154,828	9,869	97,500	44,032
1983	1,019,379	814,902	-1,352	813,550	97,825	-47,159	668,566	182,373	168,440	10,469	97,368	44,220
1984	1,102,133	880,602	-197	880,405	108,095	-48,792	723,518	202,991	175,624	11,367	96,959	45,190
1985	1,167,476	930,569	103	930,672	115,381	-53,242	762,049	216,096	189,331	12,107	96,427	45,545
1986	1,197,383	953,719	-393	953,326	122,683	-55,023	775,620	220,475	201,288	12,479	95,949	45,461
1987	1,235,887	998,395	-848	997,547	130,717	-66,022	800,808	225,154	209,925	13,081	94,480	47,158
1988	1,339,209	1,101,563	-690	1,100,873	147,162	-76,335	877,376	237,115	224,718	14,263	93,892	47,850
1989	1,407,152	1,124,103	-473	1,123,630	152,119	-70,827	900,684	267,355	239,113	15,187	92,654	48,408
1990	1,493,039	1,183,743	109	1,183,852	162,086	-77,499	944,267	289,372	259,400	16,201	92,156	48,937
1991	1,534,824	1,208,923	-631	1,208,292	170,145	-81,747	956,400	287,076	291,348	16,584	92,547	48,290
1992	1,642,979	1,300,451	-114	1,300,337	183,199	-86,339	1,030,799	276,374	335,806	17,638	93,148	49,325
1993	1,717,729	1,360,685	-88	1,360,597	195,215	-89,598	1,075,784	282,115	359,830	18,319	93,766	50,279
1994	1,775,298	1,414,267	48	1,414,315	201,174	-91,565	1,121,576	292,967	360,755	18,848	94,190	51,179
1995	1,841,282	1,459,345	-335	1,459,010	208,384	-95,538	1,155,088	314,484	371,710	19,499	94,428	51,896
1996	1,917,070	1,527,302	-135	1,527,167	218,300	-116,611	1,192,256	328,929	395,885	20,328	94,308	52,966
1997	1,985,851	1,584,872	-543	1,584,329	224,583	-118,629	1,241,117	336,769	407,965	21,075	94,229	53,811
1998	2,038,673	1,596,849	-1,698	1,595,151	228,679	-104,828	1,261,644	355,262	421,767	21,680	94,035	53,300
1999	2,119,700	1,655,451	-2,112	1,653,339	235,235	-112,725	1,305,379	383,248	431,073	22,560	93,958	53,406
2000	2,206,422	1,748,021	-1,867	1,746,154	255,502	-133,565	1,357,087	394,740	454,595	23,545	93,711	54,195
2001	2,257,669	1,758,630	-2,472	1,756,158	249,774	-118,401	1,387,983	376,853	492,833	24,137	93,536	53,485
2002	2,356,422	1,784,047	-3,627	1,780,420	249,236	-109,438	1,421,746	379,418	555,258	25,223	93,424	52,507
2003	2,405,464	1,804,342	-2,580	1,801,762	255,987	-100,078	1,445,697	377,039	582,728	25,872	92,974	52,143
2004	2,504,649	1,898,372	-2,116	1,896,256	264,663	-94,780	1,536,813	394,770	573,066	27,017	92,705	52,541
2005	2,496,082	1,892,236	-2,971	1,889,265	262,745	-82,485	1,544,035	363,267	588,780	26,940	92,655	52,167
2006	2,685,502	1,998,090	-4,092	1,993,998	266,157	-73,632	1,654,209	391,225	640,068	29,082	92,343	52,837
2007	2,793,573	1,999,680	-5,319	1,994,361	254,409	-57,148	1,682,804	432,886	677,883	30,268	92,295	52,758
2008	2,927,390	2,025,029	-4,802	2,020,227	247,241	-43,209	1,729,777	445,738	751,875	31,638	92,528	51,879
2009	2,907,874	1,975,044	-5,286	1,969,758	245,879	-70,297	1,653,582	422,108	832,184	31,422	92,544	50,462
2010	2,933,172	1,985,289	-5,290	1,979,999	248,411	-84,660	1,646,928	408,731	877,513	31,636	92,715	49,908
2011	3,089,724	2,064,019	-3,398	2,060,621	230,285	-90,573	1,739,763	457,558	892,403	33,371	92,587	50,546
2012	3,223,408	2,158,950	-4,233	2,154,717	237,765	-94,700	1,822,252	499,005	902,151	34,898	92,367	50,861
2013	3,224,787	2,165,307	-2,671	2,162,636	266,415	-66,901	1,829,320	481,334	914,133	34,948	92,275	50,314
2014	3,356,897	2,193,612	-3,209	2,190,403	275,259	-7,671	1,907,473	501,305	948,119	36,456	92,082	50340

Personal Income and Employment by Area: Pensacola-Ferry Pass-Brent, FL

(Thousands of dollars, except as noted.)

Year	Personal income, total	Earnings by place of work			Less: Contributions for government social insurance	Plus: Adjustment for residence	Equals: Net earnings by place of residence	Plus: Dividends, interest, and rent	Plus: Personal current transfer receipts	Per capita personal income (dollars)	Population (persons)	Total employment
		Nonfarm	Farm	Total								
1970	973,870	796,834	3,947	800,781	44,344	-3,018	753,419	162,004	58,447	3,989	244,134	104,526
1971	1,102,537	897,648	5,392	903,040	52,591	-2,605	847,844	186,418	68,275	4,390	251,153	107,815
1972	1,235,071	1,005,598	5,444	1,011,042	61,568	-224	949,250	205,917	79,904	4,731	261,051	111,779
1973	1,323,454	1,062,394	12,847	1,075,241	73,602	1,451	1,003,090	222,500	97,864	5,005	264,441	114,005
1974	1,480,119	1,175,301	15,565	1,190,866	85,207	836	1,106,495	256,282	117,342	5,532	267,551	117,846
1975	1,641,824	1,279,573	16,176	1,295,749	93,858	699	1,202,590	287,202	152,032	5,956	275,666	119,341
1976	1,737,825	1,350,987	9,495	1,360,482	101,929	7,879	1,266,432	299,816	171,577	6,156	282,287	118,547
1977	1,897,272	1,471,656	5,051	1,476,707	111,237	10,062	1,375,532	336,454	185,286	6,648	285,381	121,814
1978	2,132,806	1,622,724	11,976	1,634,700	124,900	13,712	1,523,512	403,020	206,274	7,446	286,428	126,124
1979	2,379,185	1,807,154	9,538	1,816,692	146,096	15,140	1,685,736	455,214	238,235	8,228	289,161	128,844
1980	2,626,574	1,949,746	2,698	1,952,444	160,743	22,597	1,814,298	531,125	281,151	9,000	291,830	131,667
1981	3,004,369	2,216,557	4,358	2,220,915	195,341	26,259	2,051,833	624,065	328,471	10,032	299,477	135,907
1982	3,269,158	2,388,170	3,212	2,391,382	215,098	32,583	2,208,867	694,791	365,500	10,757	303,905	136,941
1983	3,557,001	2,588,135	3,495	2,591,630	241,151	32,495	2,382,974	772,678	401,349	11,390	312,280	140,353
1984	3,903,066	2,815,535	9,967	2,825,502	269,943	38,808	2,594,367	878,259	430,440	12,381	315,257	148,279
1985	4,167,876	2,980,082	8,145	2,988,227	292,900	41,453	2,736,780	967,119	463,977	12,994	320,743	154,423
1986	4,458,934	3,182,882	7,457	3,190,339	322,615	48,579	2,916,303	1,046,851	495,780	13,614	327,528	161,370
1987	4,718,650	3,359,171	12,090	3,371,261	338,530	56,258	3,088,989	1,102,644	527,017	14,091	334,873	161,606
1988	5,031,318	3,557,669	15,904	3,573,573	373,384	76,663	3,276,852	1,179,844	574,622	15,068	333,905	162,727
1989	5,454,689	3,745,057	13,018	3,758,075	399,145	81,862	3,440,792	1,348,082	665,815	15,966	341,654	165,545
1990	5,786,856	3,982,904	16,662	3,999,566	426,936	50,213	3,622,843	1,430,815	733,198	16,739	345,706	167,249
1991	6,090,400	4,159,765	17,949	4,177,714	451,017	83,007	3,809,704	1,450,868	829,828	17,254	352,981	168,899
1992	6,494,042	4,481,565	22,207	4,503,772	489,554	55,188	4,069,406	1,472,953	951,683	17,941	361,975	172,885
1993	6,787,286	4,618,991	23,817	4,642,808	505,620	94,737	4,231,925	1,537,345	1,018,016	18,459	367,689	174,170
1994	7,095,327	4,792,875	21,746	4,814,621	529,859	108,188	4,392,950	1,613,195	1,089,182	18,982	373,790	178,056
1995	7,540,682	4,954,154	12,332	4,966,486	546,166	189,655	4,609,975	1,747,272	1,183,435	19,833	380,205	183,511
1996	8,130,329	5,311,600	21,581	5,333,181	579,626	235,193	4,988,748	1,902,402	1,239,179	20,929	388,477	190,014
1997	8,611,864	5,639,534	15,609	5,655,143	616,173	238,927	5,277,897	2,038,931	1,295,036	21,534	399,925	198,535
1998	9,155,845	5,976,882	10,259	5,987,141	647,269	299,338	5,639,210	2,214,779	1,301,856	22,390	408,930	205,241
1999	9,501,048	6,216,782	16,177	6,232,959	670,485	311,412	5,873,886	2,238,859	1,388,303	23,172	410,026	208,458
2000	10,134,938	6,550,020	21,807	6,571,827	704,174	388,038	6,255,691	2,375,679	1,503,568	24,535	413,085	213,458
2001	10,791,228	6,900,578	16,454	6,917,032	749,941	400,590	6,567,681	2,538,061	1,685,486	25,752	419,037	209,329
2002	11,103,996	7,074,330	13,091	7,087,421	771,240	396,265	6,712,446	2,543,687	1,847,863	26,127	425,006	209,417
2003	11,692,296	7,472,195	23,596	7,495,791	811,686	455,799	7,139,904	2,545,911	2,006,481	27,314	428,066	213,496
2004	12,667,600	8,180,045	16,089	8,196,134	889,658	539,644	7,846,120	2,618,680	2,202,800	29,090	435,466	222,139
2005	13,392,610	8,595,192	18,305	8,613,497	946,240	670,487	8,337,744	2,768,750	2,286,116	30,474	439,471	226,314
2006	14,546,183	9,234,332	24,102	9,258,434	1,032,281	804,142	9,030,295	3,080,010	2,435,878	32,808	443,378	231,982
2007	15,047,099	9,387,566	9,960	9,397,526	1,056,110	764,330	9,105,746	3,321,157	2,620,196	33,924	443,551	234,510
2008	15,349,778	9,295,895	15,404	9,311,299	1,060,496	728,176	8,978,979	3,386,082	2,984,717	34,464	445,392	226,942
2009	15,135,798	9,136,938	10,283	9,147,221	1,060,775	724,230	8,810,676	3,092,178	3,232,944	33,894	446,559	219,202
2010	15,661,210	9,290,323	21,313	9,311,636	1,082,514	745,858	8,974,980	3,137,399	3,548,831	34,727	450,980	219,137
2011	16,406,600	9,534,905	24,627	9,559,532	1,012,098	780,149	9,327,583	3,383,185	3,695,832	36,032	455,339	221,293
2012	16,770,149	9,757,155	30,654	9,787,809	1,044,071	836,595	9,580,333	3,532,522	3,657,294	36,251	462,612	222,100
2013	16,902,334	9,909,271	30,570	9,939,841	1,179,934	853,120	9,613,027	3,499,805	3,789,502	36,064	468,682	225,887
2014	17,526,288	10,206,076	9,737	10,215,813	1,213,472	882,945	9,885,286	3,628,884	4,012,118	36,969	474,081	228567

Personal Income and Employment by Area: Peoria, IL

(Thousands of dollars, except as noted.)

Year	Personal income, total	Derivation of personal income								Per capita personal income (dollars)	Population (persons)	Total employment
		Earnings by place of work			Less: Contributions for government social insurance	Plus: Adjustment for residence	Equals: Net earnings by place of residence	Plus: Dividends, interest, and rent	Plus: Personal current transfer receipts			
		Nonfarm	Farm	Total								
1970	1,570,940	1,313,878	39,905	1,353,783	88,889	-36,033	1,228,861	227,054	115,025	4,316	363,968	164,383
1971	1,714,235	1,427,716	45,525	1,473,241	99,872	-38,814	1,334,555	243,771	135,909	4,641	369,391	164,742
1972	1,844,146	1,540,029	39,836	1,579,865	113,722	-41,422	1,424,721	265,246	154,179	4,937	373,551	165,245
1973	2,125,570	1,755,643	88,311	1,843,954	151,297	-50,316	1,642,341	303,166	180,063	5,677	374,401	175,153
1974	2,389,308	1,993,880	89,396	2,083,276	178,108	-62,709	1,842,459	346,248	200,601	6,351	376,199	181,638
1975	2,732,306	2,216,840	132,393	2,349,233	193,838	-74,418	2,080,977	397,792	253,537	7,223	378,257	186,144
1976	2,940,538	2,432,080	103,506	2,535,586	217,688	-82,784	2,235,114	421,218	284,206	7,711	381,346	190,624
1977	3,197,155	2,661,506	97,330	2,758,836	237,167	-95,987	2,425,682	469,117	302,356	8,367	382,124	191,841
1978	3,565,515	3,047,278	78,840	3,126,118	281,109	-122,802	2,722,207	519,458	323,850	9,296	383,538	197,934
1979	3,821,788	3,210,609	92,214	3,302,823	306,869	-127,328	2,868,626	587,320	365,842	9,953	384,001	194,459
1980	4,162,757	3,499,029	12,668	3,511,697	335,921	-158,724	3,017,052	698,568	447,137	10,735	387,782	192,228
1981	4,597,429	3,665,879	105,728	3,771,607	378,117	-160,673	3,232,817	846,216	518,396	11,870	387,307	188,890
1982	4,654,760	3,459,407	75,482	3,534,889	360,299	-127,985	3,046,605	998,544	609,611	12,136	383,564	175,891
1983	4,496,853	3,220,105	-30,363	3,189,742	334,538	-89,567	2,765,637	1,055,661	675,555	11,886	378,344	166,495
1984	4,919,234	3,515,434	74,008	3,589,442	379,187	-97,437	3,112,818	1,159,622	646,794	13,229	371,853	172,623
1985	5,073,122	3,595,530	117,205	3,712,735	391,886	-91,935	3,228,914	1,172,266	671,942	13,920	364,457	171,203
1986	5,210,659	3,709,940	85,667	3,795,607	404,254	-97,648	3,293,705	1,212,409	704,545	14,562	357,835	172,056
1987	5,406,082	3,935,569	71,899	4,007,468	421,471	-104,943	3,481,054	1,196,001	729,027	15,231	354,936	174,514
1988	5,850,130	4,437,864	30,787	4,468,651	488,523	-123,586	3,856,542	1,235,499	758,089	16,493	354,697	181,969
1989	6,325,863	4,746,678	73,465	4,820,143	524,844	-121,515	4,173,784	1,341,167	810,912	17,707	357,249	187,671
1990	6,685,104	5,031,113	78,385	5,109,498	541,460	-109,793	4,458,245	1,351,517	875,342	18,608	359,269	191,515
1991	6,717,910	5,015,691	51,657	5,067,348	554,844	-99,028	4,413,476	1,368,291	936,143	18,583	361,500	191,716
1992	7,169,185	5,259,447	101,801	5,361,248	569,527	-98,174	4,693,547	1,413,999	1,061,639	19,792	362,223	190,752
1993	7,466,926	5,586,144	77,400	5,663,544	616,566	-122,772	4,924,206	1,448,204	1,094,516	20,599	362,492	194,442
1994	7,925,394	5,940,105	128,785	6,068,890	660,417	-115,796	5,292,677	1,512,087	1,120,630	21,842	362,843	199,927
1995	8,171,160	6,065,046	33,904	6,098,950	672,712	-96,839	5,329,399	1,646,696	1,195,065	22,302	366,385	202,647
1996	8,716,500	6,399,366	149,453	6,548,819	708,637	-125,085	5,715,097	1,738,161	1,263,242	23,782	366,521	210,524
1997	9,177,407	6,784,290	125,888	6,910,178	748,438	-141,652	6,020,088	1,875,122	1,282,197	25,032	366,624	214,200
1998	9,680,925	7,251,440	91,948	7,343,388	792,948	-146,078	6,404,362	1,981,275	1,295,288	26,379	366,997	218,474
1999	9,904,344	7,560,664	65,170	7,625,834	813,057	-136,387	6,676,390	1,906,156	1,321,798	26,945	367,581	218,298
2000	10,336,564	7,725,057	106,940	7,831,997	822,246	-132,410	6,877,341	2,064,829	1,394,394	28,191	366,659	220,662
2001	10,574,459	8,019,755	90,727	8,110,482	864,082	-149,834	7,096,566	1,994,529	1,483,364	28,924	365,600	216,820
2002	10,668,104	8,240,467	56,813	8,297,280	882,719	-153,682	7,260,879	1,817,391	1,589,834	29,123	366,312	212,706
2003	11,042,074	8,476,958	103,182	8,580,140	906,748	-149,363	7,524,029	1,858,003	1,660,042	30,149	366,256	211,056
2004	11,802,192	9,108,090	188,503	9,296,593	992,082	-162,217	8,142,294	1,929,830	1,730,068	32,074	367,962	215,421
2005	12,444,110	9,884,453	75,648	9,960,101	1,083,293	-200,167	8,676,641	1,894,861	1,872,608	33,653	369,772	219,108
2006	13,463,666	10,721,007	84,493	10,805,500	1,154,378	-239,337	9,411,785	2,119,623	1,932,258	36,223	371,687	224,365
2007	14,200,263	11,136,142	186,461	11,322,603	1,204,445	-250,876	9,867,282	2,216,445	2,116,536	37,950	374,179	228,753
2008	14,981,922	11,515,258	275,791	11,791,049	1,251,990	-260,480	10,278,579	2,379,593	2,323,750	39,847	375,982	229,013
2009	14,763,993	11,027,144	178,908	11,206,052	1,198,114	-195,876	9,812,062	2,337,762	2,614,169	38,917	379,373	218,326
2010	14,894,680	11,049,514	130,159	11,179,673	1,227,388	-195,922	9,756,363	2,324,575	2,813,742	39,305	378,954	218,319
2011	16,322,841	12,197,242	310,499	12,507,741	1,203,899	-277,023	11,026,819	2,583,251	2,712,771	42,991	379,677	222,727
2012	17,041,659	13,041,718	175,348	13,217,066	1,288,694	-335,889	11,592,483	2,744,743	2,704,433	44,793	380,450	225,860
2013	16,589,336	12,301,318	377,841	12,679,159	1,401,671	-236,304	11,041,184	2,709,844	2,838,308	43,419	382,079	220,077
2014	16,679,535	12,486,491	170,349	12,656,840	1,418,031	-248,734	10,990,075	2,813,578	2,875,882	43,889	380,040	219836

Personal Income and Employment by Area: Philadelphia-Camden-Wilmington, PA-NJ-DE-MD

(Thousands of dollars, except as noted.)

Year	Personal income, total	Derivation of personal income			Less: Contributions for government social insurance	Plus: Adjustment for residence	Equals: Net earnings by place of residence	Plus: Dividends, interest, and rent	Plus: Personal current transfer receipts	Per capita personal income (dollars)	Population (persons)	Total employment
		Earnings by place of work										
		Nonfarm	Farm	Total								
1970	24,517,823	20,082,492	94,448	20,176,940	1,437,186	57,889	18,797,643	3,632,496	2,087,684	4,599	5,331,133	2,424,294
1971	26,115,721	21,166,250	99,205	21,265,455	1,572,289	76,972	19,770,138	3,880,603	2,464,980	4,870	5,362,194	2,392,220
1972	28,323,593	22,982,602	91,533	23,074,135	1,794,052	127,089	21,407,172	4,134,833	2,781,588	5,290	5,353,850	2,424,493
1973	30,572,933	24,916,622	135,537	25,052,159	2,244,167	191,928	22,999,920	4,478,299	3,094,714	5,749	5,317,951	2,467,445
1974	33,257,348	26,707,785	135,103	26,842,888	2,493,914	249,381	24,598,355	4,999,927	3,659,066	6,280	5,295,959	2,453,221
1975	35,931,515	28,088,496	110,152	28,198,648	2,558,809	283,064	25,922,903	5,318,007	4,690,605	6,794	5,288,609	2,376,788
1976	39,096,194	30,529,171	139,511	30,668,682	2,832,970	363,388	28,199,100	5,698,557	5,198,537	7,403	5,280,969	2,398,310
1977	42,524,159	33,169,570	132,403	33,301,973	3,070,800	438,269	30,669,442	6,276,292	5,578,425	8,077	5,264,778	2,415,937
1978	46,718,663	36,723,751	134,332	36,858,083	3,492,893	518,076	33,883,266	6,903,908	5,931,489	8,903	5,247,420	2,480,533
1979	51,469,188	40,312,163	136,126	40,448,289	3,984,647	611,147	37,074,789	7,729,095	6,665,304	9,807	5,248,348	2,531,977
1980	57,024,112	43,618,108	89,436	43,707,544	4,332,737	751,817	40,126,624	9,332,620	7,564,868	10,874	5,244,018	2,533,311
1981	63,109,519	47,094,277	127,745	47,222,022	5,006,641	850,542	43,065,923	11,521,849	8,521,747	12,020	5,250,278	2,530,893
1982	68,189,902	49,729,805	151,116	49,880,921	5,382,760	907,387	45,405,548	13,298,490	9,485,864	12,971	5,257,004	2,524,306
1983	72,878,419	53,458,375	143,538	53,601,913	5,879,901	982,358	48,704,370	13,993,406	10,180,643	13,851	5,261,664	2,558,593
1984	79,407,197	58,556,035	202,459	58,758,494	6,684,493	1,105,142	53,179,143	15,731,828	10,496,226	15,042	5,279,124	2,645,844
1985	85,661,906	63,397,792	225,204	63,622,996	7,333,331	1,184,224	57,473,889	17,122,030	11,065,987	16,180	5,294,461	2,722,101
1986	91,154,215	67,819,364	214,907	68,034,271	7,911,720	1,315,118	61,437,669	18,039,746	11,676,800	17,085	5,335,416	2,785,227
1987	97,761,879	73,902,649	199,920	74,102,569	8,543,817	1,448,270	67,007,022	18,758,854	11,996,003	18,160	5,383,434	2,876,967
1988	106,127,808	80,627,407	182,308	80,809,715	9,546,249	1,577,232	72,840,698	20,549,655	12,737,455	19,576	5,421,382	2,951,624
1989	114,841,643	85,914,355	185,138	86,099,493	10,056,767	1,644,040	77,686,766	23,408,404	13,746,473	21,132	5,434,490	2,987,983
1990	121,404,601	90,304,607	213,732	90,518,339	10,575,762	1,714,242	81,656,819	24,939,282	14,808,500	22,296	5,445,186	2,986,306
1991	125,471,290	92,090,921	204,036	92,294,957	10,908,821	1,911,169	83,297,305	24,961,225	17,212,760	22,897	5,479,918	2,912,895
1992	132,380,107	97,431,175	225,644	97,656,819	11,461,633	2,004,976	88,200,162	25,400,367	18,779,578	24,053	5,503,640	2,891,738
1993	137,006,410	100,766,858	239,650	101,006,508	11,912,838	2,126,908	91,220,578	26,043,984	19,741,848	24,761	5,533,081	2,910,168
1994	141,508,377	104,345,002	244,090	104,589,092	12,571,747	2,234,069	94,251,414	27,010,492	20,246,471	25,440	5,562,336	2,922,050
1995	149,045,667	108,789,276	233,869	109,023,145	13,034,135	2,411,534	98,400,544	29,335,859	21,309,264	26,681	5,586,177	2,963,541
1996	157,162,634	114,184,733	281,357	114,466,090	13,476,912	2,379,674	103,368,852	31,212,002	22,581,780	28,054	5,602,154	2,998,593
1997	165,579,903	120,982,078	273,455	121,255,533	14,151,771	2,644,719	109,748,481	32,876,291	22,955,131	29,486	5,615,600	3,061,561
1998	177,061,009	130,279,215	279,053	130,558,268	15,025,387	2,659,943	118,192,824	35,528,932	23,339,253	31,394	5,640,015	3,126,541
1999	184,922,637	137,920,672	260,535	138,181,207	15,731,452	2,674,060	125,123,815	35,519,980	24,278,842	32,642	5,665,210	3,175,279
2000	199,936,453	148,270,364	307,803	148,578,167	16,681,383	3,007,971	134,904,755	38,879,777	26,151,921	35,126	5,691,968	3,244,168
2001	208,572,311	156,104,682	269,347	156,374,029	17,274,343	3,309,433	142,409,119	38,298,754	27,864,438	36,502	5,713,954	3,257,877
2002	214,591,170	162,009,929	265,675	162,275,604	17,903,661	2,947,630	147,319,573	37,421,320	29,850,277	37,363	5,743,383	3,254,913
2003	221,984,776	167,979,761	274,273	168,254,034	18,483,276	2,950,510	152,721,268	38,348,603	30,914,905	38,446	5,773,864	3,265,967
2004	234,004,289	177,760,324	318,507	178,078,831	19,498,224	3,373,100	161,953,707	40,489,311	31,561,271	40,314	5,804,535	3,308,038
2005	244,544,922	185,039,244	300,658	185,339,902	20,411,696	3,826,508	168,754,714	41,857,892	33,932,316	41,952	5,829,139	3,368,213
2006	262,735,308	195,370,926	283,044	195,653,970	21,484,043	4,383,480	178,553,407	48,584,316	35,597,585	44,865	5,856,125	3,418,977
2007	275,275,158	201,332,184	299,727	201,631,911	22,359,755	4,964,648	184,236,804	52,898,580	38,139,774	46,799	5,882,126	3,471,263
2008	286,824,736	208,530,993	274,694	208,805,687	23,134,147	5,155,850	190,827,390	53,347,803	42,649,543	48,557	5,906,917	3,489,665
2009	281,094,528	205,127,026	318,440	205,445,466	22,829,563	4,757,110	187,373,013	47,180,120	46,541,395	47,310	5,941,539	3,407,488
2010	288,766,933	208,807,847	304,534	209,112,381	23,228,807	5,046,962	190,930,536	46,791,190	51,045,207	48,359	5,971,276	3,390,756
2011	302,959,352	215,758,040	324,766	216,082,806	21,383,909	5,267,957	199,966,854	51,340,147	51,652,351	50,518	5,997,083	3,434,016
2012	317,569,134	223,885,677	413,868	224,299,545	21,968,911	5,777,341	208,107,975	57,719,893	51,741,266	52,744	6,020,925	3,457,365
2013	319,686,131	229,678,299	470,789	230,149,088	25,583,065	5,696,778	210,262,801	56,751,834	52,671,496	52,961	6,036,228	3,512,290
2014	332,426,085	239,024,050	522,087	239,546,137	26,610,010	5,942,535	218,878,662	59,006,969	54,540,454	54,936	6,051,170	3564216

Personal Income and Employment by Area: Phoenix-Mesa-Glendale, AZ

(Thousands of dollars, except as noted.)

Year	Personal income, total	Earnings by place of work			Less: Contributions for government social insurance	Plus: Adjustment for residence	Equals: Net earnings by place of residence	Plus: Dividends, interest, and rent	Plus: Personal current transfer receipts	Per capita personal income (dollars)	Population (persons)	Total employment
		Nonfarm	Farm	Total								
1970	4,413,209	3,383,773	105,153	3,488,926	230,632	-21,610	3,236,684	840,612	335,913	4,204	1,049,680	456,574
1971	5,007,476	3,827,346	120,929	3,948,275	272,161	-21,623	3,654,491	952,886	400,099	4,551	1,100,219	478,419
1972	5,748,335	4,469,159	98,528	4,567,687	335,218	-14,641	4,217,828	1,070,500	460,007	4,939	1,163,970	522,280
1973	6,662,330	5,214,294	106,777	5,321,071	448,512	-11,608	4,860,951	1,242,514	558,865	5,383	1,237,668	574,470
1974	7,556,984	5,693,287	247,112	5,940,399	506,663	-20,048	5,413,688	1,456,702	686,594	5,804	1,301,957	592,448
1975	8,044,061	5,878,340	94,831	5,973,171	515,861	-28,660	5,428,650	1,627,509	987,902	6,013	1,337,680	573,360
1976	9,034,117	6,619,944	206,113	6,826,057	585,353	-38,899	6,201,805	1,770,795	1,061,517	6,612	1,366,423	603,064
1977	10,251,290	7,689,999	159,414	7,849,413	686,978	-39,577	7,122,858	2,003,645	1,124,787	7,235	1,416,931	654,968
1978	12,203,141	9,273,523	162,453	9,435,976	851,039	-37,077	8,547,860	2,394,768	1,260,513	8,265	1,476,485	728,998
1979	14,539,953	11,130,690	246,899	11,377,589	1,067,111	-42,428	10,268,050	2,835,083	1,436,820	9,403	1,546,348	792,672
1980	16,832,545	12,554,018	296,437	12,850,455	1,214,376	-55,351	11,580,728	3,518,134	1,733,683	10,441	1,612,182	820,853
1981	19,266,457	14,081,778	256,213	14,337,991	1,466,097	-52,778	12,819,116	4,401,565	2,045,776	11,613	1,658,988	843,575
1982	20,468,561	14,744,872	222,721	14,967,593	1,559,860	-43,499	13,364,234	4,832,731	2,271,596	11,979	1,708,649	847,957
1983	22,659,467	16,359,089	175,169	16,534,258	1,751,677	-31,642	14,750,939	5,425,559	2,482,969	12,861	1,761,819	895,053
1984	25,952,467	18,838,187	320,170	19,158,357	2,069,986	-33,930	17,054,441	6,219,351	2,678,675	14,124	1,837,457	988,892
1985	29,114,077	21,344,321	288,071	21,632,392	2,383,883	-41,856	19,206,653	6,981,508	2,925,916	15,070	1,931,978	1,074,363
1986	32,055,320	23,614,825	286,319	23,901,144	2,650,089	-45,009	21,206,046	7,610,529	3,238,745	15,922	2,013,320	1,130,847
1987	34,792,318	25,603,139	356,798	25,959,937	2,847,742	-37,093	23,075,102	8,184,139	3,533,077	16,548	2,102,571	1,175,415
1988	37,538,662	27,929,421	389,911	28,319,332	3,196,897	-51,414	25,071,021	8,588,834	3,878,807	17,358	2,162,647	1,224,682
1989	40,344,707	29,044,598	423,994	29,468,592	3,409,809	-16,175	26,042,608	9,830,741	4,471,358	18,194	2,217,530	1,247,064
1990	42,207,940	30,617,924	384,406	31,002,330	3,695,377	-13,230	27,293,723	9,992,118	4,922,099	18,766	2,249,116	1,266,338
1991	44,062,066	32,295,183	443,627	32,738,810	3,916,468	-5,571	28,816,771	9,761,215	5,484,080	18,999	2,319,206	1,263,249
1992	46,924,045	34,806,352	386,057	35,192,409	4,180,062	2,126	31,014,473	9,681,071	6,228,501	19,562	2,398,760	1,271,798
1993	50,353,482	37,528,404	422,391	37,950,795	4,508,571	13,273	33,455,497	10,200,907	6,697,078	20,208	2,491,818	1,328,795
1994	55,654,217	41,577,625	367,401	41,945,026	4,998,511	11,679	36,958,194	11,558,846	7,137,177	21,295	2,613,502	1,416,403
1995	61,261,242	45,799,230	406,849	46,206,079	5,289,088	-22,941	40,894,050	12,732,061	7,635,131	22,325	2,744,046	1,508,585
1996	67,085,906	50,928,034	443,806	51,371,840	5,996,757	-56,304	45,318,779	13,650,432	8,116,695	23,492	2,855,711	1,614,248
1997	73,545,398	55,839,047	422,315	56,261,362	6,482,787	-38,079	49,740,496	15,337,419	8,467,483	24,815	2,963,714	1,702,231
1998	81,239,066	62,843,697	456,300	63,299,997	7,128,875	-33,573	56,137,549	16,380,096	8,721,421	26,423	3,074,532	1,793,413
1999	86,796,626	68,106,184	444,049	68,550,233	7,661,943	-15,294	60,872,996	16,636,210	9,287,420	27,309	3,178,349	1,860,012
2000	95,606,604	75,685,390	362,492	76,047,882	8,420,368	-1,505	67,626,009	18,123,335	9,857,260	29,206	3,273,477	1,933,698
2001	100,211,898	79,758,575	352,525	80,111,100	8,817,900	-5,502	71,287,698	17,753,873	11,170,327	29,792	3,363,736	1,960,289
2002	103,863,497	81,739,714	334,981	82,074,695	9,051,546	-23,288	72,999,861	18,401,479	12,462,157	30,084	3,452,470	1,974,195
2003	109,207,058	84,928,999	380,744	85,309,743	9,375,050	-46,249	75,888,444	19,696,232	13,622,382	30,881	3,536,388	2,023,506
2004	118,998,397	92,340,973	541,300	92,882,273	10,169,885	-50,447	82,661,941	21,357,130	14,979,326	32,716	3,637,332	2,112,466
2005	132,291,554	101,758,726	475,066	102,233,792	11,188,863	-23,566	91,021,363	24,468,931	16,801,260	35,047	3,774,696	2,249,814
2006	147,810,181	113,606,512	373,402	113,979,914	12,315,456	7,703	101,672,161	27,758,313	18,379,707	37,762	3,914,212	2,367,648
2007	155,493,071	117,949,019	415,823	118,364,842	12,987,439	232,071	105,609,474	29,897,222	19,986,375	38,698	4,018,128	2,427,390
2008	157,244,946	117,398,091	346,942	117,745,033	13,046,276	521,738	105,220,495	28,516,118	23,508,333	38,293	4,106,372	2,396,656
2009	148,837,502	109,311,899	168,072	109,479,971	12,350,622	504,992	97,634,341	24,842,415	26,360,746	35,833	4,153,609	2,269,307
2010	151,301,118	109,176,478	195,042	109,371,520	12,392,321	531,203	97,510,402	24,751,646	29,039,070	35,944	4,209,347	2,226,822
2011	160,086,328	114,878,657	381,029	115,259,686	11,538,698	551,043	104,272,031	26,740,120	29,074,177	37,631	4,254,149	2,284,790
2012	168,757,726	120,879,689	405,723	121,285,412	11,995,286	576,821	109,866,947	29,975,173	28,915,606	38,965	4,330,974	2,329,701
2013	170,239,926	123,921,339	519,732	124,441,071	14,076,429	598,251	110,962,893	29,673,184	29,603,849	38,655	4,404,129	2,395,853
2014	178,871,199	130,259,316	620,729	130,880,045	14,806,532	635,697	116,709,210	30,901,958	31,260,031	39,846	4,489,109	2448608

Personal Income and Employment by Area: Pine Bluff, AR

(Thousands of dollars, except as noted.)

Year	Personal income, total	Earnings by place of work			Less: Contributions for government social insurance	Plus: Adjustment for residence	Equals: Net earnings by place of residence	Plus: Dividends, interest, and rent	Plus: Personal current transfer receipts	Per capita personal income (dollars)	Population (persons)	Total employment
		Nonfarm	Farm	Total								
1970	291,282	216,629	19,611	236,240	16,562	1,788	221,466	35,675	34,141	2,788	104,477	38,872
1971	320,839	234,414	24,064	258,478	18,270	1,706	241,914	39,658	39,267	3,093	103,719	39,197
1972	347,911	256,593	24,640	281,233	21,138	1,541	261,636	43,247	43,028	3,317	104,888	39,993
1973	405,187	286,674	44,097	330,771	27,314	1,082	304,539	49,024	51,624	3,887	104,231	41,117
1974	434,142	317,734	27,289	345,023	31,299	120	313,844	57,880	62,418	4,125	105,251	42,161
1975	477,449	333,108	34,207	367,315	31,913	-1,413	333,989	64,815	78,645	4,533	105,335	40,227
1976	535,306	375,578	39,947	415,525	36,522	-1,179	377,824	70,464	87,018	5,047	106,074	40,529
1977	591,865	424,054	39,313	463,367	41,774	-1,264	420,329	79,430	92,106	5,552	106,613	42,336
1978	679,547	505,048	48,248	553,296	50,778	-11,846	490,672	88,123	100,752	6,262	108,520	45,097
1979	757,706	588,653	44,581	633,234	61,539	-24,884	546,811	97,984	112,911	6,854	110,555	46,194
1980	823,922	658,397	14,601	672,998	68,113	-33,585	571,300	120,480	132,142	7,357	111,988	46,894
1981	905,900	662,269	39,133	701,402	73,591	-22,552	605,259	148,039	152,602	8,097	111,883	44,628
1982	917,417	647,072	23,206	670,278	74,269	-14,989	581,020	172,452	163,945	8,300	110,538	42,054
1983	965,009	692,043	11,379	703,422	80,028	-15,620	607,774	180,392	176,843	8,776	109,954	42,484
1984	1,049,925	745,403	28,861	774,264	89,511	-16,926	667,827	199,696	182,402	9,583	109,561	42,993
1985	1,102,074	784,381	26,203	810,584	95,465	-19,905	695,214	215,807	191,053	10,121	108,892	43,590
1986	1,184,612	883,476	23,889	907,365	108,926	-37,300	761,139	223,811	199,662	10,924	108,437	45,357
1987	1,207,973	872,918	39,024	911,942	105,889	-24,178	781,875	219,339	206,759	11,118	108,653	44,835
1988	1,308,201	934,426	66,385	1,000,811	119,357	-26,518	854,936	238,459	214,806	12,050	108,561	46,386
1989	1,364,643	969,538	42,115	1,011,653	125,894	-28,541	857,218	267,939	239,486	12,637	107,985	47,039
1990	1,424,492	1,039,512	34,870	1,074,382	137,679	-35,577	901,126	265,278	258,088	13,318	106,958	47,603
1991	1,458,577	1,028,507	46,134	1,074,641	132,871	-22,354	919,416	257,235	281,926	13,598	107,267	47,185
1992	1,571,671	1,100,309	66,146	1,166,455	139,970	-21,593	1,004,892	253,071	313,708	14,608	107,590	47,356
1993	1,636,324	1,148,016	52,152	1,200,168	146,763	-20,830	1,032,575	276,882	326,867	15,253	107,282	48,353
1994	1,706,017	1,176,444	83,601	1,260,045	150,939	-15,832	1,093,274	268,646	344,097	15,827	107,791	47,473
1995	1,764,889	1,229,721	54,941	1,284,662	157,250	-14,819	1,112,593	283,880	368,416	16,385	107,714	48,926
1996	1,851,312	1,257,193	94,248	1,351,441	159,871	-11,441	1,180,129	293,939	377,244	17,188	107,707	49,406
1997	1,892,736	1,302,800	83,386	1,386,186	165,900	-9,347	1,210,939	290,511	391,286	17,571	107,720	49,381
1998	1,978,165	1,369,390	76,279	1,445,669	172,868	-8,150	1,264,651	307,314	406,200	18,412	107,440	49,233
1999	2,014,079	1,415,240	84,910	1,500,150	177,122	-7,394	1,315,634	292,851	405,594	18,781	107,241	49,256
2000	2,102,878	1,495,504	73,583	1,569,087	184,699	-8,101	1,376,287	300,304	426,287	19,619	107,184	49,453
2001	2,199,651	1,529,213	86,656	1,615,869	189,407	5,880	1,432,342	300,826	466,483	20,661	106,464	49,105
2002	2,235,322	1,574,286	52,211	1,626,497	193,423	-12,737	1,420,337	306,934	508,051	21,095	105,965	48,185
2003	2,351,547	1,644,219	115,418	1,759,637	199,782	-29,751	1,530,104	292,561	528,882	22,297	105,465	48,629
2004	2,474,157	1,745,411	132,043	1,877,454	210,196	-49,552	1,617,706	290,032	566,419	23,639	104,665	49,461
2005	2,490,972	1,786,188	95,338	1,881,526	214,431	-65,910	1,601,185	296,481	593,306	23,971	103,917	49,239
2006	2,555,587	1,846,102	67,391	1,913,493	226,263	-77,031	1,610,199	303,733	641,655	24,782	103,121	49,060
2007	2,636,958	1,839,862	92,014	1,931,876	227,271	-82,943	1,621,662	331,382	683,914	25,873	101,921	48,287
2008	2,682,129	1,847,660	89,840	1,937,500	232,099	-112,539	1,592,862	337,645	751,622	26,476	101,305	47,781
2009	2,738,014	1,855,076	68,761	1,923,837	236,114	-99,297	1,588,426	336,271	813,317	27,219	100,593	47,469
2010	2,754,072	1,902,849	47,162	1,950,011	240,733	-133,178	1,576,100	318,237	859,735	27,520	100,076	47,160
2011	2,822,147	1,897,502	59,692	1,957,194	217,208	-124,733	1,615,253	345,239	861,655	28,506	99,001	47,100
2012	2,884,948	1,933,053	110,267	2,043,320	218,349	-173,238	1,651,733	374,554	858,661	29,637	97,344	46,520
2013	2,919,033	1,851,411	184,011	2,035,422	236,195	-114,195	1,685,032	368,096	865,905	30,505	95,689	44,974
2014	2,934,900	1,848,529	143,137	1,991,666	238,472	-100,294	1,652,900	376,791	905,209	30,986	94,716	43896

Personal Income and Employment by Area: Pittsburgh, PA

(Thousands of dollars, except as noted.)

Year	Personal income, total	Derivation of personal income					Equals: Net earnings by place of residence	Plus: Dividends, interest, and rent	Plus: Personal current transfer receipts	Per capita personal income (dollars)	Population (persons)	Total employment
		Earnings by place of work			Less: Contributions for government social insurance	Plus: Adjustment for residence						
		Nonfarm	Farm	Total								
1970	11,280,435	9,301,752	33,266	9,335,018	683,635	-29,232	8,622,151	1,492,488	1,165,796	4,089	2,758,743	1,132,359
1971	11,878,331	9,687,871	35,548	9,723,419	738,906	-37,494	8,947,019	1,563,998	1,367,314	4,302	2,760,937	1,113,813
1972	12,847,662	10,507,630	41,854	10,549,484	840,895	-45,805	9,662,784	1,649,279	1,535,599	4,669	2,751,873	1,124,028
1973	14,001,204	11,558,427	40,406	11,598,833	1,065,963	-57,824	10,475,046	1,808,649	1,717,509	5,129	2,730,057	1,154,111
1974	15,551,869	12,792,945	43,833	12,836,778	1,226,950	-85,019	11,524,809	2,055,023	1,972,037	5,753	2,703,028	1,167,040
1975	17,175,433	13,856,151	46,381	13,902,532	1,299,014	-100,897	12,502,621	2,224,090	2,448,722	6,360	2,700,715	1,159,949
1976	18,713,711	15,067,384	57,588	15,124,972	1,434,009	-105,313	13,585,650	2,390,055	2,738,006	6,947	2,693,955	1,169,981
1977	20,609,480	16,713,470	59,236	16,772,706	1,585,810	-128,485	15,058,411	2,655,237	2,895,832	7,680	2,683,597	1,185,498
1978	22,664,651	18,495,441	53,682	18,549,123	1,802,874	-153,571	16,592,678	2,944,994	3,126,979	8,474	2,674,747	1,210,116
1979	25,115,547	20,498,117	59,775	20,557,892	2,070,691	-180,131	18,307,070	3,318,550	3,489,927	9,443	2,659,625	1,231,366
1980	27,581,326	21,700,364	42,172	21,742,536	2,199,143	-187,555	19,355,838	4,160,621	4,064,867	10,422	2,646,406	1,214,171
1981	30,392,315	23,276,832	62,251	23,339,083	2,531,332	-204,494	20,603,257	5,226,069	4,562,989	11,553	2,630,712	1,200,978
1982	31,986,867	23,096,473	55,200	23,151,673	2,558,140	-97,488	20,496,045	6,097,279	5,393,543	12,207	2,620,312	1,156,673
1983	32,689,553	23,164,998	34,791	23,199,789	2,589,793	-43,842	20,566,154	6,285,876	5,837,523	12,540	2,606,777	1,121,342
1984	34,709,776	24,643,167	66,774	24,709,941	2,856,225	-26,320	21,827,396	7,012,318	5,870,062	13,443	2,581,947	1,133,457
1985	36,145,320	25,586,292	63,081	25,649,373	3,003,581	-7,943	22,637,849	7,476,679	6,030,792	14,215	2,542,677	1,144,718
1986	37,286,077	26,222,398	54,693	26,277,091	3,100,969	2,976	23,179,098	7,729,785	6,377,194	14,816	2,516,600	1,149,933
1987	38,813,755	27,769,021	50,953	27,819,974	3,234,617	10,947	24,596,304	7,691,211	6,526,240	15,558	2,494,837	1,176,201
1988	42,054,921	30,443,426	44,317	30,487,743	3,579,936	14,180	26,921,987	8,319,643	6,813,291	16,959	2,479,863	1,207,101
1989	45,098,644	32,280,897	56,804	32,337,701	3,754,294	16,983	28,600,390	9,374,221	7,124,033	18,259	2,469,921	1,228,910
1990	48,214,473	34,346,779	85,280	34,432,059	4,036,280	-5,502	30,390,277	9,947,326	7,876,870	19,523	2,469,681	1,257,869
1991	50,423,926	35,776,922	64,794	35,841,716	4,255,381	-36,817	31,549,518	9,881,790	8,992,618	20,357	2,476,980	1,250,192
1992	53,049,119	38,390,640	79,522	38,470,162	4,546,236	-84,654	33,839,272	9,760,125	9,449,722	21,339	2,486,034	1,259,326
1993	54,820,928	39,866,333	61,947	39,928,280	4,797,237	-121,130	35,009,913	9,807,224	10,003,791	22,008	2,490,949	1,267,305
1994	56,506,170	41,366,104	39,116	41,405,220	5,068,827	-138,141	36,198,252	10,059,869	10,248,049	22,721	2,486,989	1,282,644
1995	58,732,169	42,577,357	23,790	42,601,147	5,224,939	-158,867	37,217,341	10,837,084	10,677,744	23,681	2,480,098	1,296,271
1996	61,409,236	44,069,125	42,879	44,112,004	5,300,031	-184,652	38,627,321	11,543,839	11,238,076	24,850	2,471,209	1,303,923
1997	64,687,172	46,692,281	11,972	46,704,253	5,543,862	-214,479	40,945,912	12,300,147	11,441,113	26,293	2,460,208	1,320,252
1998	67,185,902	48,977,489	21,096	48,998,585	5,728,720	-243,271	43,026,594	12,693,290	11,466,018	27,426	2,449,747	1,331,795
1999	70,501,187	52,606,800	19,113	52,625,913	6,058,232	-311,060	46,256,621	12,351,492	11,893,074	28,911	2,438,518	1,352,954
2000	74,872,221	55,610,297	44,350	55,654,647	6,300,329	-353,101	49,001,217	13,453,345	12,417,659	30,833	2,428,303	1,378,771
2001	77,899,330	58,449,316	21,415	58,470,731	6,570,336	-431,996	51,468,399	13,243,112	13,187,819	32,223	2,417,480	1,387,113
2002	79,067,574	59,597,310	22,955	59,620,265	6,703,594	-551,795	52,364,876	12,877,943	13,824,755	32,831	2,408,348	1,379,393
2003	80,832,671	60,819,177	55,707	60,874,884	6,785,192	-645,568	53,444,124	13,007,465	14,381,082	33,664	2,401,168	1,370,279
2004	84,121,399	63,783,569	53,069	63,836,638	7,079,326	-642,359	56,114,953	13,155,944	14,850,502	35,210	2,389,107	1,378,420
2005	86,633,924	65,645,448	37,717	65,683,165	7,400,280	-587,214	57,695,671	12,996,384	15,941,869	36,485	2,374,483	1,386,529
2006	93,014,249	69,284,880	48,242	69,333,122	7,797,840	-537,965	60,997,317	15,187,686	16,829,246	39,345	2,364,039	1,398,010
2007	97,230,663	71,325,384	9,049	71,334,433	8,121,416	-574,584	62,638,433	16,694,785	17,897,445	41,218	2,358,914	1,418,393
2008	101,471,604	74,088,613	-4,042	74,084,571	8,420,907	-423,734	65,239,930	16,690,145	19,541,529	43,055	2,356,802	1,418,814
2009	98,913,500	71,957,259	-10,066	71,947,193	8,286,904	-494,265	63,166,024	15,108,497	20,638,979	41,994	2,355,432	1,391,913
2010	102,225,815	74,698,036	3,168	74,701,204	8,586,424	-553,554	65,561,226	14,773,620	21,890,969	43,377	2,356,678	1,391,240
2011	108,264,243	78,829,870	19,567	78,849,437	8,097,003	-678,431	70,074,003	16,430,534	21,759,706	45,881	2,359,680	1,415,066
2012	113,042,143	81,785,642	37,543	81,823,185	8,317,543	-686,361	72,819,281	18,446,478	21,776,384	47,878	2,361,068	1,431,978
2013	112,846,030	83,479,885	58,180	83,538,065	9,621,926	-745,639	73,170,500	17,808,026	21,867,504	47,805	2,360,565	1,439,608
2014	116,265,059	85,915,467	53,731	85,969,198	9,907,504	-775,552	75,286,142	18,515,175	22,463,742	49,349	2,355,968	1445889

Personal Income and Employment by Area: Pittsfield, MA

(Thousands of dollars, except as noted.)

| Year | Personal income, total | Derivation of personal income | | | | | | | | Per capita personal income (dollars) | Population (persons) | Total employment |
| | | Earnings by place of work | | | Less: Contributions for government social insurance | Plus: Adjustment for residence | Equals: Net earnings by place of residence | Plus: Dividends, interest, and rent | Plus: Personal current transfer receipts | | | |
		Nonfarm	Farm	Total								
1970	620,487	484,314	3,850	488,164	32,373	-3,302	452,489	99,341	68,657	4,140	149,893	66,119
1971	661,273	511,872	3,674	515,546	35,381	-2,891	477,274	105,538	78,461	4,380	150,987	65,091
1972	710,526	551,844	3,487	555,331	40,377	-2,074	512,880	112,877	84,769	4,773	148,869	65,585
1973	781,900	616,944	3,547	620,491	52,376	-1,604	566,511	119,582	95,807	5,228	149,573	69,449
1974	849,368	666,651	3,067	669,718	58,309	-546	610,863	130,211	108,294	5,676	149,649	70,334
1975	912,231	680,409	3,696	684,105	57,405	2,135	628,835	137,571	145,825	6,131	148,788	67,804
1976	962,583	718,296	3,568	721,864	61,743	5,097	665,218	143,772	153,593	6,577	146,360	66,846
1977	1,023,255	759,940	3,476	763,416	65,540	8,403	706,279	157,603	159,373	7,065	144,826	67,029
1978	1,124,991	842,735	4,563	847,298	75,018	11,699	783,979	172,115	168,897	7,687	146,354	68,925
1979	1,240,217	921,523	4,285	925,808	85,047	16,298	857,059	190,983	192,175	8,528	145,437	71,249
1980	1,381,782	995,504	4,098	999,602	91,459	20,747	928,890	233,413	219,479	9,524	145,081	71,264
1981	1,523,685	1,073,113	3,527	1,076,640	106,361	17,407	987,686	286,485	249,514	10,535	144,629	70,426
1982	1,653,463	1,133,174	4,247	1,137,421	114,762	12,802	1,035,461	343,859	274,143	11,631	142,162	69,487
1983	1,764,476	1,215,191	5,004	1,220,195	124,006	8,231	1,104,420	364,930	295,126	12,429	141,969	69,795
1984	1,955,392	1,361,637	6,718	1,368,355	142,937	2,760	1,228,178	416,190	311,024	13,793	141,767	72,759
1985	2,077,203	1,469,106	6,393	1,475,499	154,863	-4,485	1,316,151	436,679	324,373	14,738	140,938	74,546
1986	2,218,455	1,584,797	7,153	1,591,950	169,895	-11,735	1,410,320	468,816	339,319	15,801	140,396	77,067
1987	2,340,146	1,692,786	5,607	1,698,393	178,957	-19,214	1,500,222	489,768	350,156	16,683	140,268	76,319
1988	2,520,775	1,824,880	4,308	1,829,188	196,152	-28,529	1,604,507	537,425	378,843	18,033	139,787	78,504
1989	2,696,207	1,923,973	4,253	1,928,226	207,653	-41,217	1,679,356	598,052	418,799	19,288	139,790	79,087
1990	2,772,387	1,954,255	4,723	1,958,978	206,800	-50,856	1,701,322	610,216	460,849	19,885	139,423	77,748
1991	2,799,173	1,886,264	4,606	1,890,870	203,878	-43,996	1,642,996	628,122	528,055	20,187	138,661	73,552
1992	2,831,577	1,950,027	6,006	1,956,033	208,414	-38,631	1,708,988	575,728	546,861	20,547	137,809	73,706
1993	2,946,273	2,001,972	3,839	2,005,811	216,245	-35,813	1,753,753	628,685	563,835	21,484	137,139	75,102
1994	3,045,304	2,055,118	3,836	2,058,954	222,327	-31,053	1,805,574	643,267	596,463	22,200	137,176	75,643
1995	3,167,524	2,130,533	2,251	2,132,784	231,994	-28,928	1,871,862	668,983	626,679	23,140	136,885	75,632
1996	3,352,269	2,245,547	3,080	2,248,627	239,526	-25,703	1,983,398	725,249	643,622	24,531	136,657	76,886
1997	3,522,309	2,376,754	3,455	2,380,209	251,705	-24,047	2,104,457	751,799	666,053	25,785	136,602	77,231
1998	3,686,765	2,485,624	3,993	2,489,617	261,997	-18,675	2,208,945	821,821	655,999	27,156	135,763	78,372
1999	3,837,917	2,641,224	4,708	2,645,932	271,994	-13,354	2,360,584	798,036	679,297	28,381	135,227	79,183
2000	4,095,800	2,790,264	4,801	2,795,065	284,373	-2,882	2,507,810	880,707	707,283	30,391	134,769	79,575
2001	4,281,539	2,903,724	3,854	2,907,578	300,680	-1,664	2,605,234	907,830	768,475	31,969	133,928	80,672
2002	4,365,223	3,052,209	3,471	3,055,680	318,006	-9,008	2,728,666	810,605	825,952	32,691	133,529	80,940
2003	4,395,009	3,059,388	3,437	3,062,825	316,926	-16,439	2,729,460	784,769	880,780	32,940	133,423	81,037
2004	4,665,643	3,216,497	5,363	3,221,860	345,532	-25,033	2,851,295	893,620	920,728	35,060	133,076	81,490
2005	4,791,171	3,327,824	3,781	3,331,605	367,599	-34,234	2,929,772	870,274	991,125	36,143	132,563	83,197
2006	4,989,338	3,422,895	1,349	3,424,244	374,255	-43,416	3,006,573	939,612	1,043,153	37,805	131,977	84,061
2007	5,158,394	3,476,320	742	3,477,062	383,259	-53,196	3,040,607	1,035,744	1,082,043	39,113	131,883	84,966
2008	5,363,047	3,525,542	951	3,526,493	391,976	-62,726	3,071,791	1,074,165	1,217,091	40,823	131,372	84,756
2009	5,275,123	3,418,301	1,147	3,419,448	382,059	-64,784	2,972,605	985,306	1,317,212	40,187	131,264	82,833
2010	5,351,621	3,451,337	2,075	3,453,412	378,032	-59,904	3,015,476	951,237	1,384,908	40,756	131,310	81,975
2011	5,647,040	3,579,772	2,231	3,582,003	355,449	-60,733	3,165,821	1,077,952	1,403,267	43,247	130,575	81,855
2012	5,894,287	3,719,200	5,590	3,724,790	361,975	-60,395	3,302,420	1,154,939	1,436,928	45,261	130,230	83,108
2013	5,916,304	3,775,327	9,446	3,784,773	413,220	-58,308	3,313,245	1,158,210	1,444,849	45,690	129,489	84,035
2014	6,108,507	3,887,840	5,834	3,893,674	427,951	-54,497	3,411,226	1,204,861	1,492,420	47,458	128,715	84559

Personal Income and Employment by Area: Pocatello, ID

(Thousands of dollars, except as noted.)

Year	Personal income, total	Earnings by place of work			Less: Contributions for government social insurance	Plus: Adjustment for residence	Equals: Net earnings by place of residence	Plus: Dividends, interest, and rent	Plus: Personal current transfer receipts	Per capita personal income (dollars)	Population (persons)	Total employment
		Nonfarm	Farm	Total								
1970	178,517	133,828	3,631	137,459	11,199	12,399	138,659	23,316	16,542	3,413	52,301	21,284
1971	195,453	146,280	3,624	149,904	12,336	11,719	149,287	26,477	19,689	3,672	53,234	21,673
1972	218,976	164,487	4,820	169,307	14,415	13,030	167,922	28,857	22,197	4,036	54,256	22,338
1973	242,803	189,049	1,123	190,172	19,082	14,367	185,457	32,244	25,102	4,445	54,619	23,949
1974	285,332	219,467	7,129	226,596	22,900	15,581	219,277	37,066	28,989	5,077	56,204	25,253
1975	326,774	252,106	3,668	255,774	25,495	17,803	248,082	42,517	36,175	5,725	57,076	26,556
1976	384,377	306,209	4,574	310,783	31,431	18,680	298,032	46,553	39,792	6,401	60,045	28,815
1977	422,574	336,756	2,607	339,363	34,826	22,703	327,240	52,560	42,774	6,774	62,378	30,488
1978	477,979	381,230	3,615	384,845	39,846	24,281	369,280	60,934	47,765	7,489	63,821	31,826
1979	528,267	423,355	2,156	425,511	46,323	23,431	402,619	70,519	55,129	8,143	64,871	32,145
1980	572,352	445,771	4,848	450,619	49,240	26,149	427,528	78,776	66,048	8,718	65,650	30,930
1981	619,640	469,155	5,630	474,785	55,897	33,261	452,149	93,691	73,800	9,320	66,486	30,178
1982	656,371	482,057	5,353	487,410	59,787	37,451	465,074	108,424	82,873	9,785	67,081	29,433
1983	695,680	502,274	6,435	508,709	62,289	46,595	493,015	114,164	88,501	10,336	67,307	29,207
1984	731,753	525,618	3,059	528,677	68,115	53,508	514,070	125,678	92,005	10,903	67,114	29,669
1985	787,263	566,507	4,749	571,256	74,743	57,533	554,046	134,516	98,701	11,741	67,051	30,216
1986	783,408	547,225	5,512	552,737	73,232	62,543	542,048	138,493	102,867	11,685	67,043	28,847
1987	801,705	553,041	3,786	556,827	71,438	74,925	560,314	135,797	105,594	12,121	66,140	28,462
1988	835,210	580,975	2,416	583,391	80,078	81,131	584,444	138,798	111,968	12,734	65,588	29,680
1989	897,286	617,567	5,353	622,920	86,943	84,483	620,460	154,660	122,166	13,622	65,869	30,423
1990	947,582	653,832	7,369	661,201	95,650	91,626	657,177	158,314	132,091	14,301	66,258	30,888
1991	1,012,527	686,419	6,828	693,247	100,821	110,209	702,635	162,671	147,221	15,036	67,338	31,624
1992	1,100,369	751,826	10,965	762,791	106,527	107,990	764,254	168,373	167,742	15,907	69,173	32,944
1993	1,183,916	815,245	10,158	825,403	115,189	110,405	820,619	184,393	178,904	16,729	70,770	34,329
1994	1,244,252	859,858	6,749	866,607	120,592	112,321	858,336	197,283	188,633	17,170	72,468	35,875
1995	1,307,942	888,704	9,322	898,026	125,308	111,976	884,694	219,115	204,133	17,770	73,603	36,418
1996	1,375,797	949,915	8,287	958,202	131,525	105,795	932,472	228,794	214,531	18,585	74,026	38,085
1997	1,436,229	990,727	4,435	995,162	135,580	111,771	971,353	243,020	221,856	19,243	74,635	38,859
1998	1,519,737	1,068,629	6,684	1,075,313	141,673	112,238	1,045,878	249,461	224,398	20,300	74,864	40,007
1999	1,568,057	1,129,037	9,063	1,138,100	146,115	96,385	1,088,370	246,410	233,277	20,762	75,527	41,237
2000	1,638,415	1,181,856	8,953	1,190,809	151,640	100,003	1,139,172	251,903	247,340	21,636	75,728	42,449
2001	1,735,189	1,225,516	8,532	1,234,048	154,226	111,397	1,191,219	264,120	279,850	22,743	76,296	42,874
2002	1,817,019	1,274,635	12,120	1,286,755	158,063	106,460	1,235,152	275,271	306,596	23,756	76,487	42,816
2003	1,904,020	1,341,951	8,453	1,350,404	164,537	106,007	1,291,874	291,228	320,918	24,950	76,312	43,893
2004	2,040,991	1,457,309	11,192	1,468,501	177,620	110,064	1,400,945	293,694	346,352	26,564	76,834	45,528
2005	2,143,672	1,551,741	8,750	1,560,491	190,745	110,958	1,480,704	296,277	366,691	27,689	77,419	47,014
2006	2,264,358	1,631,209	8,628	1,639,837	200,420	109,905	1,549,322	317,680	397,356	28,849	78,491	47,905
2007	2,349,488	1,665,847	10,011	1,675,858	207,408	108,325	1,576,775	346,729	425,984	29,614	79,338	48,571
2008	2,382,285	1,643,503	14,368	1,657,871	208,793	103,367	1,552,445	341,286	488,554	29,554	80,609	46,711
2009	2,351,333	1,556,039	9,698	1,565,737	203,788	122,098	1,484,047	339,678	527,608	28,677	81,994	44,806
2010	2,399,735	1,569,307	11,455	1,580,762	214,599	119,015	1,485,178	330,426	584,131	28,912	83,000	43,757
2011	2,502,473	1,591,526	17,786	1,609,312	197,744	130,108	1,541,676	365,211	595,586	29,948	83,562	43,940
2012	2,533,585	1,597,522	14,293	1,611,815	198,067	135,691	1,549,439	381,852	602,294	30,255	83,741	43,824
2013	2,580,665	1,624,619	17,351	1,641,970	219,820	135,130	1,557,280	411,214	612,171	30,972	83,322	44,394
2014	2,672,358	1,681,338	16,947	1,698,285	225,691	142,778	1,615,372	428,454	628,532	32,063	83,347	45338

Personal Income and Employment by Area: Portland-South Portland-Biddeford, ME

(Thousands of dollars, except as noted.)

Year	Personal income, total	Earnings by place of work			Less: Contributions for government social insurance	Plus: Adjustment for residence	Equals: Net earnings by place of residence	Plus: Dividends, interest, and rent	Plus: Personal current transfer receipts	Per capita personal income (dollars)	Population (persons)	Total employment
		Nonfarm	Farm	Total								
1970	1,299,346	1,054,298	7,804	1,062,102	71,698	-38,271	952,133	227,925	119,288	3,954	328,590	156,769
1971	1,400,620	1,121,097	7,885	1,128,982	78,837	-36,798	1,013,347	246,472	140,801	4,166	336,169	155,953
1972	1,551,184	1,249,789	8,971	1,258,760	92,402	-42,218	1,124,140	268,352	158,692	4,523	342,955	160,994
1973	1,699,821	1,355,261	14,673	1,369,934	114,173	-39,503	1,216,258	293,994	189,569	4,864	349,490	165,759
1974	1,858,175	1,461,087	12,171	1,473,258	127,325	-50,524	1,295,409	332,608	230,158	5,218	356,106	169,317
1975	2,049,180	1,586,223	10,744	1,596,967	135,312	-65,919	1,395,736	357,995	295,449	5,678	360,891	170,259
1976	2,311,675	1,811,808	17,917	1,829,725	157,854	-75,688	1,596,183	391,724	323,768	6,330	365,186	177,404
1977	2,545,999	2,007,381	8,929	2,016,310	175,222	-84,775	1,756,313	444,358	345,328	6,834	372,562	184,124
1978	2,854,717	2,268,195	10,650	2,278,845	204,215	-95,751	1,978,879	505,051	370,787	7,555	377,860	193,643
1979	3,168,514	2,519,284	6,276	2,525,560	234,416	-104,257	2,186,887	563,271	418,356	8,269	383,159	200,253
1980	3,597,722	2,811,378	4,152	2,815,530	260,393	-116,759	2,438,378	674,222	485,122	9,326	385,753	204,838
1981	4,001,240	3,090,234	6,089	3,096,323	305,905	-169,238	2,621,180	824,537	555,523	10,231	391,072	207,150
1982	4,403,387	3,357,168	8,144	3,365,312	338,426	-192,565	2,834,321	963,611	605,455	11,165	394,395	210,235
1983	4,747,952	3,657,439	2,920	3,660,359	377,092	-191,586	3,091,681	1,003,843	652,428	11,891	399,275	217,658
1984	5,339,154	4,095,465	9,110	4,104,575	438,249	-191,058	3,475,268	1,174,609	689,277	13,168	405,463	228,798
1985	5,854,180	4,508,819	6,880	4,515,699	484,748	-169,963	3,860,988	1,257,585	735,607	14,216	411,789	239,590
1986	6,481,475	5,018,357	9,923	5,028,280	547,026	-163,800	4,317,454	1,396,153	767,868	15,506	417,991	254,199
1987	7,118,525	5,566,932	8,278	5,575,210	606,622	-161,444	4,807,144	1,521,624	789,757	16,756	424,840	265,537
1988	7,915,522	6,254,838	7,575	6,262,413	694,911	-183,565	5,383,937	1,692,144	839,441	18,254	433,634	281,206
1989	8,559,104	6,716,229	5,378	6,721,607	738,717	-212,287	5,770,603	1,885,671	902,830	19,508	438,759	287,046
1990	8,928,987	6,955,519	13,093	6,968,612	807,292	-222,842	5,938,478	1,984,103	1,006,406	20,165	442,790	285,041
1991	9,018,768	6,889,807	10,943	6,900,750	807,401	-179,641	5,913,708	1,948,779	1,156,281	20,248	445,414	273,772
1992	9,443,648	7,201,635	15,223	7,216,858	854,240	-152,575	6,210,043	1,961,215	1,272,390	21,131	446,901	274,413
1993	9,780,086	7,390,151	12,704	7,402,855	895,274	-94,749	6,412,832	2,025,912	1,341,342	21,751	449,643	276,688
1994	10,270,014	7,735,700	10,031	7,745,731	956,241	-47,964	6,741,526	2,126,852	1,401,636	22,636	453,695	283,211
1995	10,875,073	8,017,373	11,513	8,028,886	997,818	6,878	7,037,946	2,353,963	1,483,164	23,770	457,522	285,360
1996	11,591,413	8,416,339	10,943	8,427,282	1,035,159	60,081	7,452,204	2,549,609	1,589,600	24,988	463,883	290,659
1997	12,379,165	9,021,810	9,895	9,031,705	1,106,313	90,026	8,015,418	2,697,505	1,666,242	26,329	470,167	299,375
1998	13,300,305	9,682,470	11,100	9,693,570	1,180,157	146,818	8,660,231	2,931,433	1,708,641	27,974	475,444	307,664
1999	14,076,004	10,442,467	11,772	10,454,239	1,256,404	193,213	9,391,048	2,917,029	1,767,927	29,205	481,966	313,401
2000	15,168,642	11,091,502	15,882	11,107,384	1,316,278	303,510	10,094,616	3,176,548	1,897,478	31,008	489,179	322,959
2001	15,943,453	11,706,182	14,888	11,721,070	1,374,672	281,310	10,627,708	3,265,192	2,050,553	32,211	494,975	327,152
2002	16,392,928	12,181,833	14,472	12,196,305	1,384,981	242,152	11,053,476	3,153,045	2,186,407	32,774	500,178	327,860
2003	17,377,078	12,856,960	14,499	12,871,459	1,438,528	218,485	11,651,416	3,355,408	2,370,254	34,420	504,858	332,440
2004	18,554,637	13,748,099	14,552	13,762,651	1,529,145	228,592	12,462,098	3,571,272	2,521,267	36,494	508,428	340,187
2005	18,889,886	13,929,491	11,151	13,940,642	1,563,153	228,211	12,605,700	3,546,254	2,737,932	37,018	510,287	340,377
2006	20,187,937	14,754,372	10,566	14,764,938	1,666,988	233,664	13,331,614	4,052,357	2,803,966	39,537	510,614	345,035
2007	20,977,439	15,176,933	9,245	15,186,178	1,741,631	234,694	13,679,241	4,292,380	3,005,818	40,950	512,265	350,587
2008	21,721,852	15,583,628	5,435	15,589,063	1,797,446	211,138	14,002,755	4,214,917	3,504,180	42,245	514,191	350,526
2009	21,306,495	15,319,675	7,519	15,327,194	1,761,831	185,001	13,750,364	3,766,516	3,789,615	41,394	514,728	341,361
2010	21,758,209	15,622,355	12,912	15,635,267	1,807,322	239,723	14,067,668	3,810,584	3,879,957	42,347	513,807	338,361
2011	22,802,443	16,019,432	11,790	16,031,222	1,658,724	296,607	14,669,105	4,106,861	4,026,477	44,191	515,995	341,896
2012	23,578,207	16,466,663	18,549	16,485,212	1,712,078	316,908	15,090,042	4,461,190	4,026,975	45,499	518,219	343,965
2013	23,599,505	16,745,166	23,210	16,768,376	1,993,989	338,344	15,112,731	4,329,258	4,157,516	45,352	520,363	347,309
2014	24,448,512	17,270,254	23,718	17,293,972	2,057,553	414,858	15,651,277	4,499,266	4,297,969	46,697	523,552	350946

Personal Income and Employment by Area: Portland-Vancouver-Hillsboro, OR-WA

(Thousands of dollars, except as noted.)

Year	Personal income, total	Earnings by place of work Nonfarm	Earnings by place of work Farm	Earnings by place of work Total	Less: Contributions for government social insurance	Plus: Adjustment for residence	Equals: Net earnings by place of residence	Plus: Dividends, interest, and rent	Plus: Personal current transfer receipts	Per capita personal income (dollars)	Population (persons)	Total employment
1970	4,805,505	3,853,964	48,010	3,901,974	294,374	7,136	3,614,736	763,271	427,498	4,429	1,085,025	497,091
1971	5,251,969	4,174,531	44,528	4,219,059	328,026	22,332	3,913,365	841,464	497,140	4,751	1,105,374	506,310
1972	5,852,769	4,706,905	48,379	4,755,284	392,279	37,900	4,400,905	912,176	539,688	5,160	1,134,259	535,293
1973	6,552,659	5,286,974	83,122	5,370,096	510,759	47,752	4,907,089	1,012,237	633,333	5,660	1,157,768	564,082
1974	7,417,574	5,922,913	79,239	6,002,152	586,768	58,349	5,473,733	1,177,011	766,830	6,314	1,174,809	583,002
1975	8,226,510	6,385,882	72,248	6,458,130	616,976	99,307	5,940,461	1,310,064	975,985	6,898	1,192,510	587,075
1976	9,222,407	7,241,324	70,781	7,312,105	712,908	125,959	6,725,156	1,431,973	1,065,278	7,602	1,213,090	609,841
1977	10,267,690	8,190,276	71,689	8,261,965	813,974	78,812	7,526,803	1,608,234	1,132,653	8,264	1,242,430	640,432
1978	11,821,409	9,561,597	69,748	9,631,345	977,647	49,226	8,702,924	1,886,852	1,231,633	9,270	1,275,246	683,210
1979	13,430,225	10,935,169	82,997	11,018,166	1,162,884	13,530	9,868,812	2,191,317	1,370,096	10,234	1,312,315	719,013
1980	15,031,438	11,965,353	81,851	12,047,204	1,272,567	2,265	10,776,902	2,646,089	1,608,447	11,162	1,346,705	728,447
1981	16,456,011	12,664,770	83,103	12,747,873	1,436,597	14,330	11,325,606	3,269,433	1,860,972	12,060	1,364,523	717,025
1982	17,039,912	12,728,015	69,321	12,797,336	1,470,701	40,787	11,367,422	3,555,748	2,116,742	12,408	1,373,347	694,891
1983	17,950,317	13,272,270	74,090	13,346,360	1,550,685	61,290	11,856,965	3,794,563	2,298,789	13,093	1,371,007	703,207
1984	19,623,849	14,628,925	109,744	14,738,669	1,768,828	57,842	13,027,683	4,233,159	2,363,007	14,217	1,380,339	734,223
1985	20,651,350	15,495,738	109,246	15,604,984	1,885,163	49,870	13,769,691	4,429,204	2,452,455	14,842	1,391,424	754,432
1986	21,948,911	16,571,728	158,946	16,730,674	2,010,221	50,054	14,770,507	4,665,515	2,512,889	15,570	1,409,733	775,492
1987	23,216,426	17,739,771	150,209	17,889,980	2,121,464	47,874	15,816,390	4,797,448	2,602,588	16,312	1,423,238	803,521
1988	25,458,941	19,750,884	182,506	19,933,390	2,435,521	47,537	17,545,406	5,163,800	2,749,735	17,508	1,454,141	845,832
1989	28,233,308	21,625,225	187,842	21,813,067	2,663,644	58,008	19,207,431	6,007,510	3,018,367	18,984	1,487,217	883,562
1990	30,981,326	23,981,678	240,900	24,222,578	3,033,481	61,076	21,250,173	6,461,408	3,269,745	20,171	1,535,965	918,239
1991	32,687,692	25,413,205	267,345	25,680,550	3,253,609	70,336	22,497,277	6,557,834	3,632,581	20,626	1,584,767	929,685
1992	35,110,011	27,496,827	246,867	27,743,694	3,492,390	64,674	24,315,978	6,758,480	4,035,553	21,596	1,625,751	941,423
1993	37,729,172	29,534,306	249,269	29,783,575	3,752,651	55,145	26,086,069	7,335,441	4,307,662	22,596	1,669,701	969,806
1994	40,716,935	31,803,293	230,689	32,033,982	4,077,633	48,812	28,005,161	8,264,361	4,447,413	23,836	1,708,216	1,022,108
1995	44,196,631	34,357,111	238,680	34,595,791	4,428,385	12,116	30,179,522	9,134,072	4,883,037	25,266	1,749,224	1,065,398
1996	48,235,255	37,736,849	268,174	38,005,023	4,895,455	-24,432	33,085,136	9,934,662	5,215,457	26,841	1,797,066	1,112,001
1997	51,962,522	41,044,511	318,191	41,362,702	5,236,440	-61,658	36,064,604	10,539,424	5,358,494	28,243	1,839,867	1,160,405
1998	55,281,940	43,930,786	320,597	44,251,383	5,547,173	-66,289	38,637,921	11,214,288	5,429,731	29,478	1,875,365	1,187,911
1999	57,836,840	46,434,561	328,869	46,763,430	5,774,322	-68,774	40,920,334	11,046,558	5,869,948	30,340	1,906,262	1,202,587
2000	63,658,330	51,372,779	299,534	51,672,313	6,333,615	-118,056	45,220,642	12,097,319	6,340,369	32,902	1,934,792	1,229,668
2001	65,292,254	52,374,237	327,285	52,701,522	6,354,259	-108,057	46,239,206	11,813,006	7,240,042	33,124	1,971,152	1,228,381
2002	65,417,319	52,127,559	320,638	52,448,197	6,340,680	-200,769	45,906,748	11,658,203	7,852,368	32,661	2,002,918	1,214,165
2003	67,242,943	53,153,655	406,874	53,560,529	6,498,374	-206,833	46,855,322	12,330,149	8,057,472	33,221	2,024,115	1,215,716
2004	71,160,521	56,390,292	424,479	56,814,771	6,972,298	-33,593	49,808,880	13,157,156	8,194,485	34,895	2,039,297	1,247,324
2005	74,859,874	59,193,088	435,445	59,628,533	7,322,374	83,190	52,389,349	13,775,149	8,695,376	36,211	2,067,325	1,286,486
2006	81,122,054	63,307,992	487,793	63,795,785	7,878,436	88,693	56,006,042	15,847,870	9,268,142	38,571	2,103,164	1,329,069
2007	85,542,797	66,082,901	476,059	66,558,960	8,220,756	113,507	58,451,711	17,018,453	10,072,633	40,014	2,137,828	1,364,628
2008	89,874,570	67,376,359	375,118	67,751,477	8,349,299	60,969	59,463,147	18,557,285	11,854,138	41,362	2,172,853	1,369,794
2009	86,819,125	64,471,657	388,483	64,860,140	8,046,841	244,783	57,058,082	16,167,562	13,593,481	39,343	2,206,737	1,313,566
2010	88,687,837	65,652,473	343,424	65,995,897	8,307,914	389,885	58,077,868	15,756,660	14,853,309	39,733	2,232,079	1,303,101
2011	94,577,916	68,978,649	346,479	69,325,128	7,775,633	335,396	61,884,891	17,726,487	14,966,538	41,845	2,260,178	1,331,840
2012	100,469,629	73,293,382	405,725	73,699,107	8,191,739	329,802	65,837,170	19,703,941	14,928,518	43,898	2,288,729	1,355,439
2013	101,893,020	75,978,245	444,451	76,422,696	9,617,959	371,618	67,176,355	19,296,129	15,420,536	44,019	2,314,747	1,387,458
2014	107,536,731	79,883,898	510,438	80,394,336	10,142,089	441,568	70,693,815	20,117,217	16,725,699	45,794	2,348,247	1425453

Personal Income and Employment by Area: Port St. Lucie, FL

(Thousands of dollars, except as noted.)

Year	Personal income, total	Derivation of personal income								Per capita personal income (dollars)	Population (persons)	Total employment
		Earnings by place of work			Less: Contributions for government social insurance	Plus: Adjustment for residence	Equals: Net earnings by place of residence	Plus: Dividends, interest, and rent	Plus: Personal current transfer receipts			
		Nonfarm	Farm	Total								
1970	317,669	186,073	23,641	209,714	12,412	298	197,600	85,036	35,033	3,984	79,741	33,285
1971	368,659	210,040	28,337	238,377	14,601	2,422	226,198	99,320	43,141	4,358	84,589	35,253
1972	445,192	258,052	34,881	292,933	18,903	2,429	276,459	115,893	52,840	4,940	90,118	39,752
1973	543,336	319,835	34,460	354,295	26,816	3,961	331,440	144,355	67,541	5,276	102,977	44,659
1974	623,397	357,010	35,234	392,244	31,474	4,824	365,594	175,101	82,702	5,527	112,792	46,293
1975	701,060	381,458	38,997	420,455	33,146	5,611	392,920	201,030	107,110	5,954	117,754	46,049
1976	797,848	435,505	46,111	481,616	37,833	7,789	451,572	225,153	121,123	6,538	122,024	48,072
1977	918,154	490,527	58,524	549,051	43,123	11,920	517,848	263,444	136,862	7,233	126,939	51,647
1978	1,098,004	580,753	77,889	658,642	51,937	16,374	623,079	319,774	155,151	8,197	133,944	56,962
1979	1,315,828	706,014	80,958	786,972	66,063	17,310	738,219	391,296	186,313	9,188	143,206	62,851
1980	1,673,498	885,017	122,384	1,007,401	83,903	3,204	926,702	518,958	227,838	10,883	153,770	68,854
1981	1,939,836	980,630	85,659	1,066,289	99,992	20,658	986,955	682,759	270,122	11,844	163,782	71,320
1982	2,154,105	1,052,124	98,310	1,150,434	111,108	31,770	1,071,096	766,378	316,631	12,408	173,600	74,297
1983	2,440,358	1,141,287	154,046	1,295,333	119,742	56,799	1,232,390	853,230	354,738	13,452	181,413	77,623
1984	2,668,134	1,237,831	101,719	1,339,550	132,984	90,562	1,297,128	983,860	387,146	14,052	189,879	81,858
1985	3,003,434	1,346,794	110,120	1,456,914	148,160	118,945	1,427,699	1,142,554	433,181	15,185	197,784	86,119
1986	3,332,730	1,509,244	110,034	1,619,278	170,297	139,957	1,588,938	1,262,466	481,326	16,103	206,964	90,815
1987	3,710,144	1,725,630	135,300	1,860,930	192,185	159,616	1,828,361	1,358,319	523,464	17,032	217,839	93,920
1988	4,327,071	1,943,219	220,566	2,163,785	223,815	187,169	2,127,139	1,607,773	592,159	19,008	227,640	101,218
1989	4,968,130	2,144,032	167,524	2,311,556	252,133	208,784	2,268,207	2,011,500	688,423	20,767	239,233	107,262
1990	5,424,417	2,280,872	124,563	2,405,435	264,583	238,094	2,378,946	2,272,545	772,926	21,297	254,702	109,748
1991	5,612,853	2,344,992	149,173	2,494,165	273,644	248,813	2,469,334	2,255,932	887,587	21,330	263,143	108,584
1992	5,913,203	2,533,962	106,874	2,640,836	292,540	267,563	2,615,859	2,263,074	1,034,270	21,924	269,716	108,447
1993	6,287,998	2,690,047	103,939	2,793,986	308,989	280,853	2,765,850	2,402,361	1,119,787	22,681	277,235	111,244
1994	6,620,203	2,811,389	88,625	2,900,014	330,634	304,332	2,873,712	2,538,867	1,207,624	23,228	285,006	113,621
1995	7,263,031	2,965,483	97,094	3,062,577	349,115	325,264	3,038,726	2,914,833	1,309,472	25,000	290,527	117,523
1996	7,758,953	3,148,054	59,515	3,207,569	365,916	363,576	3,205,229	3,150,673	1,403,051	26,041	297,947	122,505
1997	8,268,141	3,315,519	61,224	3,376,743	386,018	395,068	3,385,793	3,396,841	1,485,507	27,116	304,912	126,227
1998	8,945,941	3,536,884	105,857	3,642,741	407,970	447,329	3,682,100	3,715,629	1,548,212	28,748	311,185	133,328
1999	9,401,071	3,798,564	90,135	3,888,699	430,764	497,099	3,955,034	3,835,973	1,610,064	29,720	316,323	137,118
2000	10,038,971	4,051,062	83,928	4,134,990	458,183	568,346	4,245,153	4,072,881	1,720,937	31,292	320,819	142,560
2001	10,597,137	4,434,887	67,306	4,502,193	501,597	601,134	4,601,730	4,145,168	1,850,239	32,277	328,315	146,878
2002	10,879,026	4,769,194	66,418	4,835,612	538,568	725,518	5,022,562	3,875,937	1,980,527	32,116	338,741	151,278
2003	11,598,011	5,131,819	51,042	5,182,861	580,523	864,346	5,466,684	4,023,451	2,107,876	32,994	351,522	158,075
2004	13,473,103	5,840,842	64,662	5,905,504	659,336	1,109,722	6,355,890	4,814,760	2,302,453	36,584	368,277	169,958
2005	14,839,874	6,475,718	102,282	6,578,000	742,122	1,355,201	7,191,079	5,263,110	2,385,685	38,658	383,877	182,591
2006	16,475,405	6,978,848	95,957	7,074,805	812,608	1,590,107	7,852,304	6,054,796	2,568,305	41,494	397,053	190,964
2007	17,476,595	7,242,761	67,119	7,309,880	851,270	1,789,227	8,247,837	6,477,862	2,750,896	42,584	410,402	193,325
2008	17,784,222	6,965,193	64,566	7,029,759	833,011	1,868,360	8,065,108	6,590,606	3,128,508	42,595	417,520	187,933
2009	16,221,628	6,526,946	60,612	6,587,558	798,747	1,780,989	7,569,800	5,232,409	3,419,419	38,637	419,850	180,985
2010	16,458,433	6,621,588	67,101	6,688,689	812,405	1,504,122	7,380,406	5,372,175	3,705,852	38,703	425,246	182,519
2011	17,694,858	6,719,252	76,013	6,795,265	749,794	1,629,836	7,675,307	6,152,654	3,866,897	41,307	428,374	184,081
2012	19,124,774	6,917,553	84,618	7,002,171	776,138	2,193,966	8,419,999	6,855,054	3,849,721	44,229	432,405	186,959
2013	19,011,374	7,086,406	86,179	7,172,585	889,102	2,297,203	8,580,686	6,422,059	4,008,629	43,426	437,785	191,116
2014	19,987,336	7,463,721	71,549	7,535,270	938,173	2,467,292	9,064,389	6,659,378	4,263,569	44,974	444,420	197574

Personal Income and Employment by Area: Prescott, AZ

(Thousands of dollars, except as noted.)

Year	Personal income, total	Derivation of personal income								Per capita personal income (dollars)	Population (persons)	Total employment
		Earnings by place of work			Less: Contributions for government social insurance	Plus: Adjustment for residence	Equals: Net earnings by place of residence	Plus: Dividends, interest, and rent	Plus: Personal current transfer receipts			
		Nonfarm	Farm	Total								
1970	143,442	80,957	2,618	83,575	5,139	2,451	80,887	43,136	19,419	3,818	37,570	12,550
1971	170,003	95,964	3,448	99,412	6,313	4,222	97,321	49,276	23,406	4,208	40,403	13,909
1972	201,901	114,626	5,913	120,539	7,929	6,253	118,863	55,558	27,480	4,500	44,864	15,086
1973	239,502	135,115	8,017	143,132	10,487	8,526	141,171	66,083	32,248	4,995	47,951	16,708
1974	261,283	148,500	552	149,052	12,164	8,437	145,325	78,094	37,864	5,201	50,233	17,382
1975	295,455	159,576	7,979	167,555	12,876	8,078	162,757	84,539	48,159	5,886	50,194	17,370
1976	329,258	184,742	2,119	186,861	14,689	7,257	179,429	94,079	55,750	5,906	55,746	18,441
1977	380,641	213,436	4,211	217,647	17,527	8,164	208,284	110,146	62,211	6,371	59,742	20,271
1978	447,611	239,106	7,945	247,051	19,845	14,508	241,714	134,601	71,296	7,176	62,377	21,755
1979	516,016	277,458	1,932	279,390	24,174	17,397	272,613	161,806	81,597	7,837	65,842	23,433
1980	616,543	313,693	5,298	318,991	28,012	19,107	310,086	205,770	100,687	8,974	68,705	24,767
1981	712,487	344,573	1,853	346,426	33,682	21,075	333,819	258,171	120,497	10,052	70,883	25,230
1982	753,789	347,764	3,847	351,611	35,049	22,086	338,648	277,171	137,970	10,185	74,009	25,227
1983	830,463	384,461	4,085	388,546	39,454	26,992	376,084	303,848	150,531	10,818	76,769	26,696
1984	940,151	421,100	6,213	427,313	44,122	35,214	418,405	357,295	164,451	11,806	79,633	28,552
1985	1,053,712	476,425	1,593	478,018	51,314	41,703	468,407	404,766	180,539	12,750	82,642	31,802
1986	1,176,918	533,768	3,059	536,827	57,507	49,969	529,289	448,856	198,773	13,220	89,025	34,400
1987	1,271,479	583,372	2,537	585,909	62,972	55,996	578,933	471,264	221,282	13,554	93,811	36,621
1988	1,400,368	640,942	327	641,269	72,278	63,509	632,500	519,420	248,448	14,075	99,493	38,956
1989	1,538,674	672,682	3,236	675,918	81,396	69,320	663,842	595,112	279,720	14,845	103,651	40,422
1990	1,648,994	729,809	5,446	735,255	89,819	77,914	723,350	611,481	314,163	15,154	108,818	42,267
1991	1,757,034	807,981	5,430	813,411	98,980	82,526	796,957	607,737	352,340	15,533	113,119	44,202
1992	1,898,072	903,729	6,620	910,349	110,218	91,671	891,802	608,226	398,044	16,027	118,427	46,644
1993	2,069,473	1,005,038	2,783	1,007,821	123,138	99,473	984,156	656,092	429,225	16,534	125,164	49,463
1994	2,367,092	1,161,071	-296	1,160,775	141,596	109,370	1,128,549	771,924	466,619	17,934	131,986	55,718
1995	2,516,026	1,230,031	-765	1,229,266	145,686	123,022	1,206,602	800,675	508,749	17,984	139,901	57,666
1996	2,732,719	1,321,740	4,724	1,326,464	158,302	137,026	1,305,188	877,912	549,619	18,664	146,414	60,672
1997	2,983,057	1,474,035	6,124	1,480,159	171,423	150,397	1,459,133	946,857	577,067	19,635	151,924	64,787
1998	3,279,063	1,591,714	12,725	1,604,439	182,105	168,545	1,590,879	1,060,914	627,270	20,795	157,686	67,614
1999	3,463,269	1,719,409	24,233	1,743,642	193,375	185,423	1,735,690	1,065,047	662,532	21,254	162,943	66,760
2000	3,725,022	1,837,785	17,691	1,855,476	206,548	207,148	1,856,076	1,148,143	720,803	22,093	168,608	70,265
2001	3,847,382	1,897,038	24,930	1,921,968	220,178	211,036	1,912,826	1,136,905	797,651	22,286	172,636	71,477
2002	3,998,337	2,035,519	10,701	2,046,220	238,393	214,266	2,022,093	1,093,904	882,340	22,543	177,362	73,645
2003	4,247,170	2,169,594	14,426	2,184,020	253,384	217,968	2,148,604	1,148,195	950,371	23,325	182,090	76,086
2004	4,721,404	2,360,205	16,085	2,376,290	278,181	230,147	2,328,256	1,328,406	1,064,742	25,138	187,822	80,342
2005	5,317,891	2,621,954	16,668	2,638,622	313,847	246,250	2,571,025	1,564,760	1,182,106	27,212	195,424	85,630
2006	5,879,466	2,979,983	11,745	2,991,728	352,585	268,967	2,908,110	1,641,261	1,330,095	28,809	204,082	91,724
2007	6,354,093	3,125,581	10,291	3,135,872	377,396	277,453	3,035,929	1,865,566	1,452,598	30,435	208,773	94,930
2008	6,393,358	3,055,210	7,585	3,062,795	379,340	265,951	2,949,406	1,802,062	1,641,890	30,270	211,211	89,050
2009	6,072,603	2,793,190	1,479	2,794,669	358,306	246,294	2,682,657	1,557,504	1,832,442	28,757	211,172	83,516
2010	6,077,340	2,717,985	-2,278	2,715,707	354,989	248,730	2,609,448	1,505,304	1,962,588	28,869	210,517	80,860
2011	6,345,155	2,716,902	888	2,717,790	324,184	265,845	2,659,451	1,655,869	2,029,835	30,045	211,185	80,354
2012	6,591,170	2,817,876	1,801	2,819,677	335,177	275,958	2,760,458	1,744,248	2,086,464	31,016	212,509	81,640
2013	6,811,155	2,914,520	7,715	2,922,235	390,696	282,232	2,813,771	1,808,447	2,188,937	31,623	215,389	83,296
2014	7,172,392	3,095,294	7,943	3,103,237	414,346	290,025	2,978,916	1,884,465	2,309,011	32,774	218,844	85992

Personal Income and Employment by Area: Providence-Warwick, RI-MA

(Thousands of dollars, except as noted.)

Year	Personal income, total	Derivation of personal income								Per capita personal income (dollars)	Population (persons)	Total employment
		Earnings by place of work			Less: Contributions for government social insurance	Plus: Adjustment for residence	Equals: Net earnings by place of residence	Plus: Dividends, interest, and rent	Plus: Personal current transfer receipts			
		Nonfarm	Farm	Total								
1970	5,814,008	4,396,885	16,934	4,413,819	328,715	190,432	4,275,536	909,667	628,805	4,164	1,396,129	629,664
1971	6,198,530	4,623,024	15,023	4,638,047	358,216	213,129	4,492,960	963,259	742,311	4,386	1,413,149	623,177
1972	6,764,478	5,085,892	14,154	5,100,046	411,755	237,176	4,925,467	1,027,843	811,168	4,730	1,430,040	639,853
1973	7,268,365	5,464,574	12,997	5,477,571	514,209	273,054	5,236,416	1,112,061	919,888	5,057	1,437,274	652,677
1974	7,689,040	5,612,380	13,930	5,626,310	553,187	320,828	5,393,951	1,211,097	1,083,992	5,443	1,412,609	640,670
1975	8,336,065	5,808,998	14,558	5,823,556	556,877	352,317	5,618,996	1,283,788	1,433,281	5,929	1,406,082	615,617
1976	9,137,790	6,514,921	15,516	6,530,437	636,881	393,707	6,287,263	1,365,906	1,484,621	6,454	1,415,810	641,578
1977	10,017,357	7,175,173	14,737	7,189,910	701,293	458,258	6,946,875	1,515,848	1,554,634	7,044	1,422,032	665,492
1978	11,037,099	7,980,470	19,317	7,999,787	803,514	528,962	7,725,235	1,659,943	1,651,921	7,742	1,425,662	687,471
1979	12,273,908	8,854,036	17,291	8,871,327	921,195	615,528	8,565,660	1,859,166	1,849,082	8,583	1,430,055	699,681
1980	13,740,526	9,561,995	18,875	9,580,870	996,188	725,051	9,309,733	2,292,083	2,138,710	9,649	1,424,092	699,678
1981	15,218,259	10,271,079	23,193	10,294,272	1,140,405	805,181	9,959,048	2,822,529	2,436,682	10,643	1,429,942	696,826
1982	16,410,311	10,816,420	42,156	10,858,576	1,215,934	882,715	10,525,357	3,219,097	2,665,857	11,465	1,431,288	687,087
1983	17,741,536	11,770,612	54,607	11,825,219	1,337,787	989,934	11,477,366	3,432,420	2,831,750	12,370	1,434,222	697,303
1984	19,609,754	13,058,181	54,689	13,112,870	1,540,711	1,144,278	12,716,437	3,964,156	2,929,161	13,601	1,441,812	730,198
1985	21,113,071	14,211,993	60,588	14,272,581	1,660,354	1,251,892	13,864,119	4,142,710	3,106,242	14,544	1,451,669	752,699
1986	22,676,181	15,398,727	65,343	15,464,070	1,810,674	1,338,711	14,992,107	4,429,890	3,254,184	15,505	1,462,482	774,732
1987	24,320,642	16,666,238	60,720	16,726,958	1,943,190	1,515,270	16,299,038	4,664,071	3,357,533	16,444	1,478,976	783,574
1988	26,743,581	18,375,653	60,575	18,436,228	2,170,330	1,681,082	17,946,980	5,185,397	3,611,204	17,906	1,493,594	804,366
1989	28,849,860	19,409,470	50,346	19,459,816	2,266,863	1,766,551	18,959,504	5,898,094	3,992,262	19,185	1,503,781	805,887
1990	29,657,669	19,766,259	47,613	19,813,872	2,389,118	1,876,062	19,300,816	5,903,549	4,453,304	19,599	1,513,216	786,517
1991	29,933,439	19,466,061	50,386	19,516,447	2,411,286	1,865,988	18,971,149	5,634,565	5,327,725	19,703	1,519,234	749,079
1992	31,359,790	20,700,348	45,545	20,745,893	2,560,911	1,937,752	20,122,734	5,668,739	5,568,317	20,599	1,522,392	760,306
1993	32,679,566	21,641,379	46,008	21,687,387	2,707,000	1,977,803	20,958,190	5,810,948	5,910,428	21,386	1,528,117	772,176
1994	33,876,700	22,565,721	40,456	22,606,177	2,849,013	2,137,151	21,894,315	5,970,302	6,012,083	22,112	1,532,065	778,499
1995	35,651,200	23,574,978	40,440	23,615,418	2,957,763	2,222,876	22,880,531	6,428,039	6,342,630	23,213	1,535,833	784,811
1996	37,054,612	24,462,686	44,400	24,507,086	3,032,164	2,317,885	23,792,807	6,775,779	6,486,026	24,035	1,541,702	791,039
1997	39,248,117	25,765,013	35,823	25,800,836	3,177,135	2,610,808	25,234,509	7,190,244	6,823,364	25,339	1,548,897	802,598
1998	41,661,073	27,547,712	30,382	27,578,094	3,348,753	2,889,855	27,119,196	7,640,967	6,900,910	26,734	1,558,350	815,527
1999	43,685,406	29,286,932	31,434	29,318,366	3,514,029	3,152,217	28,956,554	7,563,199	7,165,653	27,797	1,571,610	831,953
2000	47,096,855	31,430,817	35,491	31,466,308	3,732,044	3,670,252	31,404,516	8,221,888	7,470,451	29,694	1,586,085	852,137
2001	49,774,374	32,887,436	35,881	32,923,317	3,898,665	3,970,663	32,995,315	8,482,242	8,296,817	31,198	1,595,424	851,130
2002	51,752,660	34,468,061	43,649	34,511,710	4,029,875	3,928,730	34,410,565	8,540,384	8,801,711	32,170	1,608,716	853,901
2003	54,061,543	36,152,251	43,475	36,195,726	4,218,923	3,962,475	35,939,278	8,987,713	9,134,552	33,420	1,617,623	860,703
2004	56,340,654	38,120,456	46,779	38,167,235	4,488,403	4,092,432	37,771,264	8,919,137	9,650,253	34,766	1,620,567	872,072
2005	57,713,651	39,141,216	42,154	39,183,370	4,674,614	4,080,005	38,588,761	8,952,931	10,171,959	35,772	1,613,353	878,457
2006	60,878,375	41,164,968	43,262	41,208,230	4,903,584	4,103,095	40,407,741	9,880,136	10,590,498	37,870	1,607,583	884,911
2007	63,415,919	42,001,705	40,164	42,041,869	5,045,588	4,239,460	41,235,741	10,804,749	11,375,429	39,571	1,602,603	893,488
2008	65,546,577	42,626,256	33,304	42,659,560	5,129,807	4,175,721	41,705,474	11,041,991	12,799,112	40,929	1,601,459	881,741
2009	64,459,075	41,360,053	30,600	41,390,653	5,042,827	4,033,631	40,381,457	10,081,710	13,995,908	40,263	1,600,970	852,056
2010	66,688,902	42,931,393	29,371	42,960,764	5,127,538	3,919,029	41,752,255	10,108,410	14,828,237	41,625	1,602,154	846,162
2011	69,352,886	44,186,793	19,875	44,206,668	4,783,579	4,133,915	43,557,004	10,857,902	14,937,980	43,315	1,601,145	855,741
2012	72,150,312	45,810,117	30,525	45,840,642	4,889,711	4,446,344	45,397,275	11,854,932	14,898,105	44,998	1,603,402	860,080
2013	72,459,301	46,884,144	35,025	46,919,169	5,622,922	4,528,722	45,824,969	11,593,394	15,040,938	45,131	1,605,521	876,055
2014	75,869,760	48,943,768	41,157	48,984,925	5,880,204	4,859,667	47,964,388	12,068,721	15,836,651	47,143	1,609,367	891739

Personal Income and Employment by Area: Provo-Orem, UT

(Thousands of dollars, except as noted.)

Year	Personal income, total	Derivation of personal income									Per capita personal income (dollars)	Population (persons)	Total employment
		Earnings by place of work			Less: Contributions for government social insurance	Plus: Adjustment for residence	Equals: Net earnings by place of residence	Plus: Dividends, interest, and rent	Plus: Personal current transfer receipts				
		Nonfarm	Farm	Total									
1970	395,806	297,865	9,575	307,440	20,247	24,817	312,010	48,520	35,276		2,756	143,630	52,365
1971	439,533	326,041	9,460	335,501	22,891	28,831	341,441	55,396	42,696		2,918	150,643	54,182
1972	508,978	382,830	7,560	390,390	28,013	34,722	397,099	63,040	48,839		3,185	159,828	58,707
1973	584,719	437,418	17,429	454,847	37,403	40,136	457,580	69,421	57,718		3,494	167,341	63,657
1974	657,737	492,262	12,655	504,917	43,894	46,820	507,843	82,105	67,789		3,771	174,411	66,614
1975	731,925	538,592	8,587	547,179	47,786	55,013	554,406	91,728	85,791		4,082	179,319	66,238
1976	851,062	632,533	10,408	642,941	55,472	68,306	655,775	102,384	92,903		4,595	185,213	70,264
1977	983,074	738,299	8,495	746,794	64,506	82,283	764,571	117,854	100,649		5,011	196,202	75,348
1978	1,134,320	857,371	6,739	864,110	77,072	93,201	880,239	139,287	114,794		5,545	204,554	80,873
1979	1,302,860	989,309	10,277	999,586	94,196	101,998	1,007,388	164,004	131,468		6,040	215,721	84,123
1980	1,449,820	1,074,397	7,749	1,082,146	102,125	113,878	1,093,899	197,723	158,198		6,431	225,440	83,779
1981	1,625,269	1,192,440	6,033	1,198,473	122,784	128,769	1,204,458	237,354	183,457		7,001	232,150	84,370
1982	1,714,105	1,190,044	7,346	1,197,390	122,681	144,798	1,219,507	277,159	217,439		7,190	238,395	85,064
1983	1,826,085	1,252,912	8,125	1,261,037	128,847	153,785	1,285,975	305,886	234,224		7,502	243,424	87,034
1984	2,024,280	1,405,716	9,736	1,415,452	147,731	171,271	1,438,992	342,676	242,612		8,193	247,068	92,533
1985	2,168,713	1,501,991	10,980	1,512,971	160,485	185,807	1,538,293	372,065	258,355		8,648	250,774	95,049
1986	2,289,048	1,593,159	9,930	1,603,089	170,807	182,576	1,614,858	389,684	284,506		9,039	253,249	97,302
1987	2,421,564	1,658,178	14,360	1,672,538	177,161	180,886	1,676,263	403,621	341,680		9,452	256,199	101,692
1988	2,665,232	1,894,440	22,414	1,916,854	214,750	178,864	1,880,968	430,833	353,431		10,250	260,016	110,799
1989	2,929,169	2,087,984	21,389	2,109,373	241,905	186,406	2,053,874	485,510	389,785		11,005	266,166	117,040
1990	3,245,823	2,393,664	23,080	2,416,744	285,760	191,559	2,322,543	498,184	425,096		11,990	270,713	125,706
1991	3,574,339	2,667,066	28,856	2,695,922	324,902	199,211	2,570,231	533,949	470,159		12,814	278,950	131,672
1992	3,895,413	2,919,593	31,985	2,951,578	351,574	220,666	2,820,670	552,985	521,758		13,435	289,947	133,739
1993	4,242,998	3,166,567	27,338	3,193,905	381,572	240,859	3,053,192	620,597	569,209		14,049	302,004	138,561
1994	4,668,178	3,511,857	23,570	3,535,427	427,535	263,373	3,371,265	713,368	583,545		14,823	314,918	151,987
1995	5,154,617	3,896,285	19,596	3,915,881	480,669	279,618	3,714,830	813,075	626,712		15,850	325,204	161,158
1996	5,657,709	4,258,709	23,519	4,282,228	512,062	313,010	4,083,176	909,275	665,258		16,755	337,667	172,108
1997	6,017,537	4,525,972	25,750	4,551,722	537,912	355,026	4,368,836	967,021	681,680		17,298	347,876	180,366
1998	6,682,034	5,075,024	33,353	5,108,377	587,461	384,406	4,905,322	1,059,173	717,539		18,500	361,197	188,461
1999	7,143,745	5,491,587	26,291	5,517,878	627,439	412,725	5,303,164	1,082,079	758,502		19,323	369,707	195,232
2000	7,778,049	5,928,037	29,690	5,957,727	673,982	448,715	5,732,460	1,225,314	820,275		20,464	380,079	202,884
2001	8,107,891	6,167,267	27,558	6,194,825	697,370	460,501	5,957,956	1,235,695	914,240		20,575	394,059	205,612
2002	8,566,849	6,431,666	20,090	6,451,756	712,021	526,975	6,266,710	1,284,635	1,015,504		21,118	405,672	206,808
2003	9,065,563	6,760,579	30,018	6,790,597	752,155	611,703	6,650,145	1,328,981	1,086,437		21,856	414,780	209,032
2004	9,710,010	7,329,016	43,485	7,372,501	823,694	743,155	7,291,962	1,264,809	1,153,239		22,846	425,023	221,674
2005	10,844,739	7,921,352	44,468	7,965,820	897,912	891,439	7,959,347	1,623,048	1,262,344		24,668	439,623	233,846
2006	12,249,394	8,960,852	24,213	8,985,065	999,910	1,104,829	9,089,984	1,796,907	1,362,503		26,776	457,471	247,287
2007	13,769,736	9,780,716	46,265	9,826,981	1,093,293	1,334,607	10,068,295	2,203,638	1,497,803		28,736	479,181	262,850
2008	14,728,093	10,030,775	32,906	10,063,681	1,117,241	1,496,955	10,443,395	2,482,585	1,802,113		29,596	497,639	265,237
2009	14,088,778	9,602,789	25,048	9,627,837	1,076,069	1,518,704	10,070,472	2,030,001	1,988,305		27,356	515,010	258,550
2010	14,512,892	9,729,275	38,176	9,767,451	1,082,581	1,646,400	10,331,270	1,950,391	2,231,231		27,392	529,830	254,626
2011	15,659,636	10,326,991	58,160	10,385,151	1,039,934	1,748,728	11,093,945	2,255,906	2,309,785		28,978	540,396	265,018
2012	16,941,501	11,181,967	61,832	11,243,799	1,114,835	1,886,338	12,015,302	2,641,637	2,284,562		30,807	549,930	273,957
2013	17,555,173	11,958,871	81,628	12,040,499	1,349,788	1,840,000	12,530,711	2,668,890	2,355,572		31,223	562,253	285,194
2014	18,418,348	12,647,084	98,449	12,745,533	1,433,858	1,903,390	13,215,065	2,786,062	2,417,221		32,230	571,460	295063

Personal Income and Employment by Area: Pueblo, CO

(Thousands of dollars, except as noted.)

Year	Personal income, total	Earnings by place of work Nonfarm	Farm	Total	Less: Contributions for government social insurance	Plus: Adjustment for residence	Equals: Net earnings by place of residence	Plus: Dividends, interest, and rent	Plus: Personal current transfer receipts	Per capita personal income (dollars)	Population (persons)	Total employment
1970	413,138	327,403	2,799	330,202	18,433	-8,445	303,324	61,504	48,310	3,484	118,574	46,458
1971	455,683	356,850	2,040	358,890	20,388	-8,474	330,028	68,793	56,862	3,774	120,746	46,902
1972	505,395	399,631	3,621	403,252	24,406	-8,881	369,965	74,178	61,252	4,141	122,032	49,018
1973	572,752	458,574	3,679	462,253	33,443	-11,736	417,074	84,178	71,500	4,594	124,680	51,840
1974	640,259	509,103	3,556	512,659	38,730	-13,429	460,500	97,690	82,069	5,138	124,611	52,526
1975	705,149	544,713	5,049	549,762	41,357	-12,314	496,091	109,466	99,592	5,568	126,644	51,414
1976	763,670	590,536	5,562	596,098	46,026	-12,212	537,860	114,994	110,816	6,077	125,675	52,192
1977	818,205	633,126	3,157	636,283	50,559	-11,395	574,329	124,376	119,500	6,565	124,638	51,961
1978	906,895	705,231	2,408	707,639	58,442	-12,490	636,707	139,078	131,110	7,316	123,963	53,178
1979	1,013,757	791,038	2,784	793,822	68,723	-14,255	710,844	157,016	145,897	8,053	125,884	54,608
1980	1,110,217	831,055	3,717	834,772	72,490	-13,738	748,544	189,374	172,299	8,810	126,012	53,070
1981	1,233,005	894,241	6,589	900,830	83,788	-14,014	803,028	226,510	203,467	9,796	125,863	51,665
1982	1,260,347	854,709	4,088	858,797	81,074	-10,347	767,376	254,812	238,159	10,059	125,299	49,099
1983	1,273,658	807,415	6,344	813,759	76,284	-4,772	732,703	272,927	268,028	10,130	125,737	47,022
1984	1,352,076	848,253	6,076	854,329	83,176	-2,358	768,795	306,631	276,650	10,888	124,183	47,903
1985	1,419,913	895,218	4,593	899,811	89,995	-329	809,487	328,995	281,431	11,465	123,851	48,921
1986	1,480,586	923,987	6,196	930,183	93,809	1,298	837,672	344,521	298,393	11,930	124,111	49,175
1987	1,503,473	923,542	7,908	931,450	92,412	2,811	841,849	344,550	317,074	12,094	124,312	48,884
1988	1,588,899	992,014	8,405	1,000,419	105,236	3,299	898,482	351,300	339,117	12,840	123,745	51,235
1989	1,712,067	1,068,053	7,117	1,075,170	117,185	1,434	959,419	383,171	369,477	13,847	123,639	52,619
1990	1,793,515	1,137,478	5,452	1,142,930	126,027	887	1,017,790	382,525	393,200	14,566	123,134	55,119
1991	1,877,409	1,181,728	4,628	1,186,356	135,038	3,790	1,055,108	373,712	448,589	15,208	123,447	54,874
1992	2,002,271	1,256,299	5,394	1,261,693	141,535	9,553	1,129,711	366,850	505,710	16,097	124,387	55,461
1993	2,122,802	1,331,693	7,188	1,338,881	153,974	13,814	1,198,721	380,462	543,619	16,762	126,644	56,530
1994	2,282,476	1,454,404	2,425	1,456,829	168,608	17,491	1,305,712	404,660	572,104	17,723	128,787	59,435
1995	2,493,726	1,545,464	-547	1,544,917	178,535	21,771	1,388,153	447,099	658,474	19,056	130,865	61,533
1996	2,606,523	1,622,615	186	1,622,801	187,794	28,539	1,463,546	481,338	661,639	19,644	132,686	64,066
1997	2,791,628	1,775,720	-37	1,775,683	201,946	32,587	1,606,324	504,638	680,666	20,711	134,792	66,762
1998	2,977,359	1,904,218	-379	1,903,839	200,684	41,755	1,744,910	536,244	696,205	21,624	137,690	69,455
1999	3,158,726	2,033,254	-679	2,032,575	207,012	52,176	1,877,739	530,303	750,684	22,533	140,184	70,098
2000	3,373,575	2,171,407	1,181	2,172,588	215,098	68,188	2,025,678	560,603	787,294	23,791	141,800	70,915
2001	3,603,625	2,321,356	5,526	2,326,882	236,162	71,359	2,162,079	591,888	849,658	25,023	144,014	71,304
2002	3,724,101	2,379,176	-2,707	2,376,469	252,943	66,541	2,190,067	594,206	939,828	25,414	146,537	70,974
2003	3,816,947	2,399,905	621	2,400,526	257,402	62,666	2,205,790	633,085	978,072	25,806	147,907	71,005
2004	3,908,018	2,520,535	10,088	2,530,623	276,443	61,316	2,315,496	569,647	1,022,875	26,289	148,654	71,142
2005	3,978,791	2,538,117	7,843	2,545,960	284,376	56,414	2,317,998	561,951	1,098,842	26,556	149,825	72,211
2006	4,138,092	2,661,252	3,993	2,665,245	299,571	53,656	2,419,330	565,098	1,153,664	27,220	152,026	73,599
2007	4,446,472	2,802,004	9,439	2,811,443	321,915	51,996	2,541,524	686,155	1,218,793	28,665	155,121	76,038
2008	4,483,750	2,917,134	1,830	2,918,964	336,564	48,495	2,630,895	726,858	1,125,997	28,605	156,748	76,519
2009	4,578,153	2,928,783	1,184	2,929,967	334,198	33,841	2,629,610	715,078	1,233,465	29,004	157,846	75,234
2010	4,742,210	2,974,182	5,583	2,979,765	338,761	33,791	2,674,795	702,816	1,364,599	29,725	159,536	74,674
2011	5,017,016	3,131,404	13,093	3,144,497	327,789	24,564	2,841,272	765,090	1,410,654	31,315	160,213	75,421
2012	5,142,024	3,185,556	5,201	3,190,757	336,294	21,688	2,876,151	835,620	1,430,253	31,970	160,840	75,204
2013	5,167,317	3,187,814	7,417	3,195,231	375,272	29,255	2,849,214	838,738	1,479,365	32,031	161,320	75,225
2014	5,449,642	3,349,547	9,416	3,358,963	398,067	21,617	2,982,513	876,471	1,590,658	33,666	161,875	76,411

Personal Income and Employment by Area: Punta Gorda, FL

(Thousands of dollars, except as noted.)

| Year | Personal income, total | Derivation of personal income | | | | | | | | Per capita personal income (dollars) | Population (persons) | Total employment |
| | | Earnings by place of work | | | Less: Contributions for government social insurance | Plus: Adjustment for residence | Equals: Net earnings by place of residence | Plus: Dividends, interest, and rent | Plus: Personal current transfer receipts | | | |
		Nonfarm	Farm	Total								
1970	106,240	50,088	1,445	51,533	3,282	628	48,879	38,236	19,125	3,797	27,977	8,072
1971	125,453	58,166	1,667	59,833	4,050	526	56,309	45,893	23,251	4,175	30,046	8,996
1972	155,968	77,760	1,915	79,675	5,624	120	74,171	53,510	28,287	4,819	32,364	10,711
1973	190,008	92,883	1,975	94,858	7,591	1,079	88,346	66,495	35,167	5,167	36,771	12,355
1974	218,779	99,557	2,118	101,675	8,688	1,912	94,899	81,797	42,083	5,276	41,468	12,512
1975	246,206	101,298	2,556	103,854	8,787	2,484	97,551	96,543	52,112	5,622	43,796	12,707
1976	282,953	119,086	3,428	122,514	10,214	2,502	114,802	108,922	59,229	6,387	44,299	13,487
1977	335,159	143,344	3,963	147,307	12,511	2,435	137,231	128,904	69,024	7,122	47,062	15,343
1978	407,584	177,292	5,226	182,518	15,797	2,382	169,103	158,488	79,993	8,000	50,945	17,656
1979	477,016	197,334	6,258	203,592	18,416	4,914	190,090	190,774	96,152	8,626	55,299	18,195
1980	585,333	232,900	8,615	241,515	22,005	6,148	225,658	238,691	120,984	9,842	59,472	19,577
1981	699,588	269,993	4,781	274,774	27,682	8,712	255,804	295,529	148,255	11,032	63,412	21,295
1982	755,183	271,701	6,998	278,699	29,458	13,507	262,748	318,152	174,283	11,112	67,961	21,403
1983	860,951	307,338	9,099	316,437	33,087	17,219	300,569	370,221	190,161	12,037	71,524	22,702
1984	1,003,394	344,067	6,478	350,545	37,893	23,186	335,838	460,991	206,565	13,171	76,183	24,000
1985	1,146,872	384,558	6,489	391,047	43,555	28,743	376,235	540,428	230,209	14,179	80,886	26,318
1986	1,276,367	435,539	6,475	442,014	50,794	32,412	423,632	598,496	254,239	14,828	86,079	28,995
1987	1,413,291	502,868	6,934	509,802	57,694	39,316	491,424	646,458	275,409	15,405	91,745	30,055
1988	1,611,297	589,227	12,578	601,805	69,738	44,229	576,296	726,069	308,932	16,569	97,247	32,981
1989	1,920,418	667,930	10,764	678,694	81,956	49,821	646,559	911,292	362,567	18,457	104,050	36,229
1990	2,062,381	726,990	10,902	737,892	87,584	57,281	707,589	948,385	406,407	18,280	112,821	38,654
1991	2,124,169	757,169	16,356	773,525	92,119	63,325	744,731	918,903	460,535	18,030	117,813	39,216
1992	2,258,860	826,932	13,367	840,299	100,349	67,318	807,268	922,898	528,694	18,690	120,861	39,827
1993	2,388,598	881,202	13,998	895,200	106,622	74,131	862,709	951,862	574,027	19,242	124,134	41,205
1994	2,570,320	940,946	11,591	952,537	116,547	80,801	916,791	1,021,388	632,141	20,170	127,434	43,349
1995	2,748,063	992,333	11,731	1,004,064	123,535	92,711	973,240	1,092,584	682,239	21,021	130,731	44,270
1996	2,919,349	1,069,689	8,462	1,078,151	130,437	95,466	1,043,180	1,154,425	721,744	22,018	132,587	46,679
1997	3,123,617	1,113,614	10,933	1,124,547	135,545	110,296	1,099,298	1,271,540	752,779	23,145	134,959	48,085
1998	3,350,242	1,223,193	15,746	1,238,939	145,457	123,177	1,216,659	1,342,977	790,606	24,348	137,598	51,952
1999	3,497,293	1,350,168	13,324	1,363,492	156,755	135,775	1,342,512	1,334,426	820,355	24,938	140,240	54,477
2000	3,757,705	1,478,364	13,598	1,491,962	168,344	153,123	1,476,741	1,410,281	870,683	26,413	142,266	56,799
2001	3,875,964	1,604,019	8,565	1,612,584	185,414	155,188	1,582,358	1,350,274	943,332	26,491	146,311	58,590
2002	3,849,476	1,638,015	10,711	1,648,726	192,465	165,689	1,621,950	1,233,230	994,296	25,642	150,123	58,315
2003	3,991,986	1,722,086	11,809	1,733,895	201,410	179,773	1,712,258	1,233,571	1,046,157	26,051	153,235	59,234
2004	4,571,474	2,002,624	13,859	2,016,483	230,675	207,177	1,992,985	1,410,168	1,168,321	28,978	157,755	62,081
2005	4,754,960	2,092,290	23,459	2,115,749	249,729	237,546	2,103,566	1,494,074	1,157,320	30,625	155,262	65,019
2006	5,204,913	2,323,768	30,823	2,354,591	282,088	273,344	2,345,847	1,605,186	1,253,880	33,131	157,099	70,607
2007	5,407,368	2,262,769	21,466	2,284,235	281,804	283,834	2,286,265	1,784,384	1,336,719	33,851	159,742	70,490
2008	5,432,811	2,133,361	26,568	2,159,929	276,177	286,571	2,170,323	1,762,813	1,499,675	33,856	160,467	66,657
2009	5,124,759	2,003,509	34,603	2,038,112	268,465	262,870	2,032,517	1,457,341	1,634,901	32,104	159,629	64,256
2010	5,174,988	2,042,271	45,043	2,087,314	276,025	190,026	2,001,315	1,423,090	1,750,583	32,358	159,927	64,651
2011	5,425,752	2,089,995	43,697	2,133,692	260,150	148,877	2,022,419	1,597,876	1,805,457	33,993	159,613	66,235
2012	5,546,791	2,157,975	58,199	2,216,174	270,904	153,366	2,098,636	1,591,887	1,856,268	34,073	162,792	67,076
2013	5,798,591	2,272,015	56,847	2,328,862	315,880	173,006	2,185,988	1,686,036	1,926,567	35,154	164,948	68,630
2014	6,123,958	2,348,586	49,274	2,397,860	328,771	236,327	2,305,416	1,755,788	2,062,754	36,350	168,474	69,995

Personal Income and Employment by Area: Racine, WI

(Thousands of dollars, except as noted.)

| Year | Personal income, total | Derivation of personal income | | | | | | | | | Per capita personal income (dollars) | Population (persons) | Total employment |
| | | Earnings by place of work | | | Less: Contributions for government social insurance | Plus: Adjustment for residence | Equals: Net earnings by place of residence | Plus: Dividends, interest, and rent | Plus: Personal current transfer receipts | | | |
		Nonfarm	Farm	Total								
1970	702,939	507,589	8,788	516,377	36,912	61,060	540,525	103,254	59,160	4,114	170,861	65,523
1971	743,757	530,467	10,607	541,074	40,077	62,166	563,163	109,490	71,104	4,366	170,371	64,391
1972	823,284	595,724	9,099	604,823	47,589	68,154	625,388	115,972	81,924	4,834	170,296	67,536
1973	919,370	677,670	12,091	689,761	62,908	74,986	701,839	125,760	91,771	5,388	170,642	72,370
1974	1,027,254	758,576	9,860	768,436	73,325	81,482	776,593	142,039	108,622	5,982	171,715	74,830
1975	1,134,114	823,003	17,565	840,568	77,691	77,965	840,842	158,881	134,391	6,522	173,903	74,659
1976	1,239,447	921,043	14,053	935,096	88,352	80,412	927,156	166,542	145,749	7,195	172,264	76,731
1977	1,368,624	1,023,001	24,379	1,047,380	97,927	86,331	1,035,784	179,931	152,909	7,978	171,543	78,866
1978	1,540,790	1,165,407	18,325	1,183,732	115,034	103,166	1,171,864	200,947	167,979	8,970	171,762	81,566
1979	1,727,768	1,304,468	17,773	1,322,241	133,883	126,677	1,315,035	223,332	189,401	10,030	172,266	84,225
1980	1,879,400	1,355,173	16,142	1,371,315	138,305	143,097	1,376,107	270,881	232,412	10,865	172,979	81,694
1981	2,039,145	1,425,390	16,407	1,441,797	156,343	148,449	1,433,903	337,547	267,695	11,859	171,952	79,864
1982	2,087,748	1,380,094	9,325	1,389,419	152,944	167,363	1,403,838	375,609	308,301	12,203	171,080	76,027
1983	2,183,220	1,428,602	-897	1,427,705	157,879	175,671	1,445,497	408,176	329,547	12,862	169,741	75,330
1984	2,406,007	1,590,791	11,588	1,602,379	180,511	191,225	1,613,093	463,799	329,115	14,185	169,619	79,329
1985	2,493,181	1,634,897	11,683	1,646,580	186,383	202,459	1,662,656	480,757	349,768	14,643	170,270	78,935
1986	2,625,155	1,755,491	13,822	1,769,313	199,841	199,378	1,768,850	492,722	363,583	15,473	169,655	80,809
1987	2,782,699	1,868,702	17,342	1,886,044	208,179	230,993	1,908,858	505,010	368,831	16,351	170,181	82,839
1988	3,005,042	2,022,506	15,401	2,037,907	233,498	265,532	2,069,941	555,152	379,949	17,478	171,934	85,849
1989	3,233,958	2,194,757	14,220	2,208,977	253,177	265,815	2,221,615	601,555	410,788	18,623	173,657	87,306
1990	3,444,854	2,343,819	11,249	2,355,068	281,741	296,361	2,369,688	634,230	440,936	19,627	175,518	89,786
1991	3,610,056	2,444,498	12,447	2,456,945	296,608	304,809	2,465,146	664,036	480,874	20,294	177,885	89,881
1992	3,800,983	2,560,190	26,826	2,587,016	306,654	356,503	2,636,865	647,367	516,751	21,087	180,251	89,115
1993	3,996,659	2,682,996	22,638	2,705,634	322,587	410,012	2,793,059	674,368	529,232	21,987	181,776	90,045
1994	4,230,063	2,810,483	23,509	2,833,992	342,973	463,040	2,954,059	738,410	537,594	23,072	183,338	91,293
1995	4,419,114	2,859,106	21,941	2,881,047	351,129	514,633	3,044,551	808,918	565,645	23,912	184,808	93,148
1996	4,644,855	2,992,674	19,427	3,012,101	363,022	538,101	3,187,180	873,124	584,551	25,018	185,658	94,284
1997	4,955,041	3,250,510	16,886	3,267,396	389,885	573,473	3,450,984	904,484	599,573	26,551	186,621	94,788
1998	5,186,395	3,376,493	15,508	3,392,001	404,264	620,907	3,608,644	971,291	606,460	27,633	187,689	95,320
1999	5,249,847	3,507,104	15,114	3,522,218	422,250	575,369	3,675,337	943,663	630,847	27,871	188,361	94,045
2000	5,527,919	3,535,110	15,177	3,550,287	420,648	705,415	3,835,054	1,003,921	688,944	29,263	188,904	94,452
2001	5,834,596	3,670,558	18,496	3,689,054	426,862	790,933	4,053,125	1,014,473	766,998	30,863	189,047	92,486
2002	5,973,273	3,784,874	17,450	3,802,324	435,580	787,615	4,154,359	999,707	819,207	31,466	189,833	91,518
2003	6,222,891	3,957,245	24,808	3,982,053	452,162	807,359	4,337,250	1,039,539	846,102	32,607	190,845	91,500
2004	6,549,838	4,168,150	25,320	4,193,470	474,334	842,385	4,561,521	1,131,323	856,994	34,148	191,808	93,206
2005	6,596,067	4,234,859	19,210	4,254,069	486,411	851,788	4,619,446	1,052,888	923,733	34,132	193,251	93,483
2006	6,955,683	4,372,337	26,043	4,398,380	507,257	879,233	4,770,356	1,209,183	976,144	35,870	193,915	93,814
2007	7,240,087	4,501,742	28,281	4,530,023	521,505	917,073	4,925,591	1,256,342	1,058,154	37,244	194,395	93,858
2008	7,599,009	4,555,756	17,453	4,573,209	530,685	925,658	4,968,182	1,434,283	1,196,544	39,023	194,730	92,672
2009	7,356,610	4,329,154	16,281	4,345,435	505,808	951,045	4,790,672	1,154,792	1,411,146	37,701	195,130	88,302
2010	7,379,343	4,359,164	13,486	4,372,650	517,105	863,977	4,719,522	1,154,038	1,505,783	37,756	195,446	87,877
2011	7,698,519	4,554,693	21,605	4,576,298	487,160	893,092	4,982,230	1,259,114	1,457,175	39,484	194,979	89,338
2012	8,018,422	4,709,047	18,096	4,727,143	502,767	839,356	5,063,732	1,466,749	1,487,941	41,187	194,683	90,374
2013	7,828,142	4,678,821	24,168	4,702,989	567,971	881,244	5,016,262	1,286,532	1,525,348	40,160	194,922	89,420
2014	8,079,455	4,846,614	15,510	4,862,124	586,567	885,729	5,161,286	1,337,448	1,580,721	41,398	195,163	90,932

Personal Income and Employment by Area: Raleigh-Cary, NC

(Thousands of dollars, except as noted.)

Year	Personal income, total	Earnings by place of work			Less: Contributions for government social insurance	Plus: Adjustment for residence	Equals: Net earnings by place of residence	Plus: Dividends, interest, and rent	Plus: Personal current transfer receipts	Per capita personal income (dollars)	Population (persons)	Total employment
		Nonfarm	Farm	Total								
1970	1,190,771	960,608	50,778	1,011,386	63,442	17,970	965,914	146,475	78,382	3,731	319,135	165,563
1971	1,312,160	1,052,632	48,736	1,101,368	71,831	26,058	1,055,595	164,178	92,387	3,993	328,641	168,259
1972	1,485,755	1,195,301	59,681	1,254,982	86,153	30,147	1,198,976	183,392	103,387	4,398	337,793	177,550
1973	1,687,610	1,369,253	71,393	1,440,646	114,504	33,206	1,359,348	208,543	119,719	4,864	346,989	188,533
1974	1,916,704	1,530,427	86,463	1,616,890	133,023	40,043	1,523,910	244,427	148,367	5,374	356,680	195,217
1975	2,140,715	1,654,348	95,251	1,749,599	142,702	54,362	1,661,259	276,590	202,866	5,900	362,809	190,837
1976	2,360,078	1,841,330	89,164	1,930,494	162,059	64,632	1,833,067	301,065	225,946	6,398	368,858	197,595
1977	2,612,161	2,070,530	64,738	2,135,268	180,758	79,193	2,033,703	340,278	238,180	6,925	377,230	205,674
1978	2,984,559	2,370,458	92,034	2,462,492	214,033	89,938	2,338,397	387,312	258,850	7,752	385,013	214,810
1979	3,382,735	2,766,350	40,794	2,807,144	260,627	94,684	2,641,201	444,142	297,392	8,599	393,407	229,255
1980	3,851,992	3,086,166	45,642	3,131,808	293,787	104,701	2,942,722	552,860	356,410	9,527	404,305	233,851
1981	4,340,446	3,353,617	75,283	3,428,900	344,406	146,009	3,230,503	692,840	417,103	10,536	411,982	236,605
1982	4,760,142	3,632,069	74,247	3,706,316	380,184	178,613	3,504,745	798,009	457,388	11,339	419,800	239,666
1983	5,361,794	4,149,216	47,984	4,197,200	438,319	201,794	3,960,675	901,715	499,404	12,429	431,398	252,652
1984	6,299,899	4,876,943	81,770	4,958,713	523,564	248,503	4,683,652	1,081,378	534,869	14,059	448,113	273,343
1985	7,221,873	5,660,998	82,595	5,743,593	616,390	295,397	5,422,600	1,222,797	576,476	15,440	467,729	294,465
1986	7,908,956	6,240,714	49,645	6,290,359	691,844	346,600	5,945,115	1,345,484	618,357	16,369	483,172	307,223
1987	8,620,109	6,777,142	69,832	6,846,974	736,800	433,593	6,543,767	1,427,394	648,948	17,432	494,491	320,160
1988	9,575,532	7,449,231	96,170	7,545,401	834,331	490,416	7,201,486	1,663,938	710,108	18,731	511,200	336,952
1989	10,613,433	8,072,590	107,346	8,179,936	901,821	591,639	7,869,754	1,937,376	806,303	20,126	527,344	350,715
1990	11,466,660	8,717,106	137,296	8,854,402	998,554	672,051	8,527,899	2,038,826	899,935	20,891	548,874	361,542
1991	12,163,082	9,074,329	151,425	9,225,754	1,054,473	863,913	9,035,194	2,099,981	1,027,907	21,409	568,119	361,975
1992	13,484,619	10,105,831	154,988	10,260,819	1,153,126	1,002,943	10,110,636	2,218,474	1,155,509	22,904	588,751	373,756
1993	14,692,610	11,016,373	162,058	11,178,431	1,253,743	1,067,167	10,991,855	2,414,817	1,285,938	23,985	612,576	394,846
1994	15,909,559	11,954,072	160,415	12,114,487	1,380,844	1,131,978	11,865,621	2,697,532	1,346,406	24,931	638,140	413,368
1995	17,394,588	12,908,257	140,888	13,049,145	1,491,561	1,294,982	12,852,566	3,017,138	1,524,884	26,106	666,317	433,235
1996	19,073,613	14,115,478	148,754	14,264,232	1,623,547	1,406,039	14,046,724	3,389,933	1,636,956	27,464	694,496	456,366
1997	21,211,834	15,576,287	197,289	15,773,576	1,794,732	1,654,261	15,633,105	3,845,073	1,733,656	29,398	721,528	484,256
1998	23,386,203	17,396,789	166,500	17,563,289	1,986,603	1,828,603	17,405,289	4,162,679	1,818,235	31,178	750,079	512,242
1999	25,202,540	18,871,327	160,949	19,032,276	2,154,736	2,114,779	18,992,319	4,288,669	1,921,552	32,445	776,786	521,191
2000	27,898,186	20,763,593	209,877	20,973,470	2,357,359	2,647,122	21,263,233	4,566,540	2,068,413	34,692	804,157	539,505
2001	29,432,460	22,398,860	191,043	22,589,903	2,507,264	2,385,523	22,468,162	4,589,306	2,374,992	35,329	833,100	540,014
2002	30,010,088	22,744,147	77,026	22,821,173	2,540,077	2,589,641	22,870,737	4,492,775	2,646,576	34,931	859,117	544,745
2003	31,236,078	23,380,794	68,159	23,448,953	2,669,135	2,895,870	23,675,688	4,734,172	2,826,218	35,362	883,333	549,185
2004	33,917,922	24,927,874	113,832	25,041,706	2,810,967	3,318,597	25,549,336	5,334,479	3,034,107	37,293	909,510	568,926
2005	37,475,936	26,849,930	111,517	26,961,447	3,049,015	3,792,560	27,704,992	6,388,129	3,382,815	39,669	944,725	594,031
2006	41,548,908	29,385,740	96,767	29,482,507	3,333,053	4,414,857	30,564,311	7,247,927	3,736,670	42,002	989,219	628,281
2007	45,041,757	31,255,961	85,530	31,341,491	3,618,916	5,158,337	32,880,912	8,070,727	4,090,118	43,541	1,034,476	666,996
2008	47,680,889	32,402,356	125,860	32,528,216	3,760,841	5,496,698	34,264,073	8,557,537	4,859,279	44,265	1,077,163	673,699
2009	46,952,203	31,735,727	130,504	31,866,231	3,659,202	5,873,059	34,080,088	7,342,212	5,529,903	42,297	1,110,061	654,985
2010	49,629,333	33,579,545	105,951	33,685,496	3,715,235	6,314,192	36,284,453	7,277,480	6,067,400	43,636	1,137,346	654,036
2011	51,621,926	34,617,752	116,147	34,733,899	3,513,636	5,798,143	37,018,406	8,299,772	6,303,748	44,379	1,163,203	676,474
2012	56,005,914	38,061,011	141,220	38,202,231	3,709,330	6,105,612	40,598,513	8,979,711	6,427,690	47,100	1,189,075	696,028
2013	55,121,255	37,760,836	171,331	37,932,167	4,342,007	5,974,419	39,564,579	8,987,306	6,569,370	45,356	1,215,299	717,004
2014	57,967,189	40,249,394	199,996	40,449,390	4,636,666	5,946,566	41,759,290	9,309,688	6,898,211	46,636	1,242,974	740,176

Personal Income and Employment by Area: Rapid City, SD

(Thousands of dollars, except as noted.)

Year	Personal income, total	Derivation of personal income									Per capita personal income (dollars)	Population (persons)	Total employment
		Earnings by place of work			Less: Contributions for government social insurance	Plus: Adjustment for residence	Equals: Net earnings by place of residence	Plus: Dividends, interest, and rent	Plus: Personal current transfer receipts				
		Nonfarm	Farm	Total									
1970	321,858	237,952	12,570	250,522	15,427	4,015	239,110	58,580	24,168		3,941	81,667	37,761
1971	362,677	272,391	13,455	285,846	18,244	2,291	269,893	65,071	27,713		4,285	84,645	39,342
1972	416,667	314,155	18,840	332,995	21,475	2,421	313,941	72,102	30,624		4,726	88,158	41,056
1973	475,219	350,302	32,633	382,935	27,099	2,276	358,112	83,074	34,033		5,401	87,982	43,482
1974	506,326	381,205	14,705	395,910	30,697	3,250	368,463	97,505	40,358		5,669	89,308	43,651
1975	566,752	415,513	19,374	434,887	34,279	4,765	405,373	111,572	49,807		6,315	89,744	44,004
1976	621,664	466,024	11,385	477,409	38,464	6,245	445,190	121,258	55,216		6,632	93,739	45,978
1977	687,651	514,065	10,741	524,806	40,910	8,108	492,004	137,794	57,853		7,118	96,608	48,360
1978	796,005	590,696	18,138	608,834	47,425	10,564	571,973	161,587	62,445		8,067	98,670	51,590
1979	886,761	652,176	22,537	674,713	55,530	13,435	632,618	181,389	72,754		8,865	100,024	52,967
1980	940,404	670,650	14,881	685,531	57,159	15,801	644,173	210,311	85,920		9,672	97,234	51,844
1981	1,030,667	710,710	16,466	727,176	64,237	15,835	678,774	249,572	102,321		10,555	97,645	50,991
1982	1,113,213	757,170	13,588	770,758	69,082	12,655	714,331	283,181	115,701		11,259	98,875	51,796
1983	1,192,765	828,464	12,515	840,979	77,075	10,717	774,621	291,285	126,859		11,886	100,353	54,204
1984	1,315,111	922,967	19,837	942,804	87,847	8,781	863,738	316,629	134,744		12,728	103,323	58,045
1985	1,364,495	965,414	6,798	972,212	94,902	7,382	884,692	334,871	144,932		12,975	105,166	58,311
1986	1,442,865	1,017,167	15,237	1,032,404	103,590	5,801	934,615	353,359	154,891		13,556	106,441	59,737
1987	1,528,746	1,094,957	11,223	1,106,180	113,141	4,152	997,191	370,113	161,442		14,053	108,783	63,586
1988	1,607,321	1,165,858	6,051	1,171,909	124,710	2,163	1,049,362	387,355	170,604		14,698	109,358	62,921
1989	1,726,535	1,237,870	10,028	1,247,898	134,167	1,179	1,114,910	421,361	190,264		15,882	108,707	64,630
1990	1,864,894	1,348,126	15,712	1,363,838	153,795	-8,889	1,201,154	457,480	206,260		16,981	109,825	67,637
1991	1,974,093	1,432,283	7,924	1,440,207	165,039	-8,023	1,267,145	483,150	223,798		17,548	112,499	69,532
1992	2,128,892	1,530,071	14,180	1,544,251	175,289	-5,145	1,363,817	518,544	246,531		18,555	114,732	70,921
1993	2,239,995	1,609,023	20,354	1,629,377	183,493	-3,764	1,442,120	531,826	266,049		19,283	116,165	72,557
1994	2,326,251	1,665,369	5,715	1,671,084	191,344	349	1,480,089	557,307	288,855		19,879	117,020	75,111
1995	2,460,901	1,718,503	14,584	1,733,087	196,499	929	1,537,517	608,527	314,857		20,856	117,995	75,455
1996	2,534,963	1,744,792	2,759	1,747,551	200,529	2,646	1,549,668	649,157	336,138		21,506	117,871	75,634
1997	2,642,434	1,812,393	7,235	1,819,628	208,799	1,418	1,612,247	687,035	343,152		22,433	117,790	76,299
1998	2,859,211	1,962,512	13,491	1,976,003	223,306	-917	1,751,780	750,015	357,416		24,180	118,245	78,819
1999	3,048,231	2,099,598	30,614	2,130,212	239,912	-4,563	1,885,737	785,633	376,861		25,576	119,182	81,438
2000	3,232,251	2,210,761	32,306	2,243,067	252,560	-5,020	1,985,487	839,041	407,723		26,831	120,469	83,386
2001	3,429,059	2,344,906	36,123	2,381,029	262,531	-4,836	2,113,662	863,190	452,207		28,178	121,692	77,918
2002	3,599,525	2,519,422	15,948	2,535,370	279,285	-13,848	2,242,237	872,834	484,454		29,307	122,822	79,911
2003	3,816,591	2,657,204	47,720	2,704,924	293,523	-15,474	2,395,927	914,909	505,755		30,959	123,278	81,042
2004	4,069,843	2,787,173	38,948	2,826,121	308,928	-11,846	2,505,347	1,021,015	543,481		32,450	125,419	82,098
2005	4,224,325	2,872,354	56,200	2,928,554	321,104	-2,798	2,604,652	1,036,245	583,428		33,527	125,998	83,351
2006	4,441,195	2,979,959	11,861	2,991,820	341,388	4,603	2,655,035	1,154,825	631,335		34,841	127,471	84,665
2007	4,736,966	3,098,933	19,095	3,118,028	359,200	3,567	2,762,395	1,287,894	686,677		36,744	128,918	86,176
2008	5,022,068	3,253,230	36,587	3,289,817	376,839	-173	2,912,805	1,307,113	802,150		38,302	131,119	89,139
2009	5,024,587	3,301,915	4,254	3,306,169	381,442	-9,609	2,915,118	1,256,459	853,010		37,707	133,254	88,490
2010	5,309,790	3,470,731	12,827	3,483,558	399,416	-15,423	3,068,719	1,284,523	956,548		39,317	135,052	88,326
2011	5,571,925	3,585,974	51,963	3,637,937	367,577	-28,718	3,241,642	1,346,830	983,453		40,864	136,354	89,844
2012	5,844,499	3,763,672	42,700	3,806,372	381,123	-44,316	3,380,933	1,465,949	997,617		42,110	138,791	90,483
2013	5,763,557	3,769,389	26,168	3,795,557	434,632	-43,519	3,317,406	1,410,152	1,035,999		40,771	141,363	91,907
2014	6,077,188	3,941,313	84,328	4,025,641	456,814	-33,628	3,535,199	1,466,070	1,075,919		42,309	143,638	93,202

Personal Income and Employment by Area: Reading, PA

(Thousands of dollars, except as noted.)

Year	Personal income, total	Derivation of personal income								Per capita personal income (dollars)	Population (persons)	Total employment
		Earnings by place of work			Less: Contributions for government social insurance	Plus: Adjustment for residence	Equals: Net earnings by place of residence	Plus: Dividends, interest, and rent	Plus: Personal current transfer receipts			
		Nonfarm	Farm	Total								
1970	1,252,191	1,030,143	18,618	1,048,761	79,002	5,003	974,762	162,836	114,593	4,219	296,772	146,430
1971	1,331,368	1,089,631	13,346	1,102,977	86,780	9,594	1,025,791	172,374	133,203	4,446	299,474	145,699
1972	1,477,324	1,204,609	20,067	1,224,676	100,840	18,145	1,141,981	184,768	150,575	4,910	300,891	148,292
1973	1,643,504	1,343,229	23,025	1,366,254	129,077	29,109	1,266,286	208,090	169,128	5,388	305,011	154,355
1974	1,808,580	1,445,980	21,103	1,467,083	143,747	42,608	1,365,944	237,805	204,831	5,916	305,720	155,151
1975	1,952,951	1,489,406	19,342	1,508,748	144,415	56,363	1,420,696	261,596	270,659	6,364	306,891	149,308
1976	2,165,822	1,658,282	25,018	1,683,300	163,067	66,805	1,587,038	285,241	293,543	7,022	308,452	153,056
1977	2,411,813	1,856,815	23,147	1,879,962	181,730	82,171	1,780,403	323,708	307,702	7,865	306,642	156,627
1978	2,695,572	2,085,152	22,645	2,107,797	209,603	104,525	2,002,719	360,518	332,335	8,720	309,110	161,553
1979	3,021,394	2,325,587	25,717	2,351,304	241,628	129,708	2,239,384	412,032	369,978	9,682	312,055	164,360
1980	3,364,884	2,497,989	23,303	2,521,292	260,503	157,015	2,417,804	514,358	432,722	10,750	313,016	165,898
1981	3,725,713	2,716,881	34,842	2,751,723	303,546	153,611	2,601,788	636,065	487,860	11,850	314,414	165,448
1982	3,974,619	2,811,084	34,229	2,845,313	319,571	154,997	2,680,739	732,345	561,535	12,634	314,597	163,637
1983	4,279,827	3,043,416	40,381	3,083,797	349,732	147,404	2,881,469	792,276	606,082	13,579	315,184	164,855
1984	4,665,958	3,376,550	62,824	3,439,374	405,209	143,008	3,177,173	883,845	604,940	14,686	317,711	171,552
1985	4,908,938	3,522,215	53,764	3,575,979	427,168	151,543	3,300,354	961,030	647,554	15,432	318,105	172,691
1986	5,162,989	3,708,217	51,486	3,759,703	449,554	153,254	3,463,403	1,013,714	685,872	16,114	320,394	173,929
1987	5,482,244	4,004,999	60,684	4,065,683	478,845	153,838	3,740,676	1,039,367	702,201	16,927	323,871	179,717
1988	5,932,154	4,390,677	48,387	4,439,064	534,082	152,792	4,057,774	1,130,041	744,339	18,087	327,977	184,644
1989	6,555,851	4,834,508	63,531	4,898,039	575,104	130,802	4,453,737	1,307,165	794,949	19,632	333,938	189,338
1990	6,758,768	4,989,097	68,319	5,057,416	597,325	127,052	4,587,143	1,295,921	875,704	20,007	337,812	190,057
1991	7,005,430	5,064,401	63,660	5,128,061	610,832	153,930	4,671,159	1,313,626	1,020,645	20,446	342,637	185,735
1992	7,519,190	5,494,510	84,278	5,578,788	654,923	170,928	5,094,793	1,329,057	1,095,340	21,729	346,050	186,648
1993	7,873,807	5,794,211	72,384	5,866,595	704,757	195,096	5,356,934	1,376,819	1,140,054	22,485	350,186	188,584
1994	8,248,150	6,135,295	81,336	6,216,631	753,130	209,291	5,672,792	1,409,649	1,165,709	23,294	354,092	190,821
1995	8,615,632	6,315,141	60,382	6,375,523	772,617	246,743	5,849,649	1,544,195	1,221,788	24,120	357,193	194,899
1996	9,058,008	6,517,214	69,451	6,586,665	777,689	301,139	6,110,115	1,645,466	1,302,427	25,135	360,380	197,093
1997	9,473,435	6,788,908	61,859	6,850,767	808,391	358,536	6,400,912	1,736,129	1,336,394	26,045	363,739	202,003
1998	9,926,262	7,008,098	67,360	7,075,458	828,920	438,310	6,684,848	1,868,942	1,372,472	27,041	367,082	206,132
1999	10,364,569	7,314,735	65,889	7,380,624	848,988	519,769	7,051,405	1,859,868	1,453,296	27,941	370,942	211,207
2000	11,112,215	7,715,976	87,965	7,803,941	884,835	611,888	7,530,994	2,026,069	1,555,152	29,668	374,546	215,363
2001	11,419,947	7,906,775	90,747	7,997,522	914,643	636,862	7,719,741	1,990,056	1,710,150	30,253	377,487	211,691
2002	11,789,320	8,154,877	65,288	8,220,165	932,635	654,771	7,942,301	1,992,449	1,854,570	30,916	381,338	208,984
2003	12,087,686	8,332,665	88,801	8,421,466	941,068	673,244	8,153,642	2,013,142	1,920,902	31,328	385,846	206,962
2004	12,507,094	8,676,447	104,395	8,780,842	978,380	716,049	8,518,511	1,970,731	2,017,852	32,000	390,848	211,076
2005	13,003,126	9,026,799	93,183	9,119,982	1,029,000	760,948	8,851,930	1,941,161	2,210,035	32,842	395,933	215,075
2006	14,180,418	9,742,788	66,715	9,809,503	1,107,386	848,205	9,550,322	2,262,243	2,367,853	35,289	401,834	221,770
2007	14,897,219	10,058,381	69,683	10,128,064	1,149,551	921,614	9,900,127	2,516,196	2,480,896	36,763	405,223	225,132
2008	15,241,997	9,993,638	69,354	10,062,992	1,160,938	959,439	9,861,493	2,561,491	2,819,013	37,382	407,737	224,444
2009	15,163,472	9,806,747	60,294	9,867,041	1,136,885	999,333	9,729,489	2,261,895	3,172,088	36,993	409,904	217,094
2010	15,647,783	10,015,877	84,195	10,100,072	1,170,744	1,095,276	10,024,604	2,206,929	3,416,250	37,989	411,905	217,678
2011	16,440,851	10,451,871	107,986	10,559,857	1,096,198	1,119,962	10,583,621	2,418,280	3,438,950	39,849	412,580	220,238
2012	17,273,224	10,767,941	124,899	10,892,840	1,120,207	1,115,704	10,888,337	2,911,129	3,473,758	41,798	413,252	221,085
2013	17,088,283	10,918,263	168,463	11,086,726	1,282,753	1,123,066	10,927,039	2,634,286	3,526,958	41,311	413,652	222,702
2014	17,729,322	11,418,753	200,104	11,618,857	1,342,318	1,088,703	11,365,242	2,743,691	3,620,389	42,856	413,691	226,019

Personal Income and Employment by Area: Redding, CA

(Thousands of dollars, except as noted.)

Year	Personal income, total	Earnings by place of work			Less: Contributions for government social insurance	Plus: Adjustment for residence	Equals: Net earnings by place of residence	Plus: Dividends, interest, and rent	Plus: Personal current transfer receipts	Per capita personal income (dollars)	Population (persons)	Total employment
		Nonfarm	Farm	Total								
1970	314,924	231,359	2,632	233,991	14,441	4,022	223,572	45,779	45,573	4,039	77,980	29,369
1971	347,868	255,486	2,018	257,504	16,494	3,857	244,867	51,388	51,613	4,379	79,434	30,699
1972	381,723	283,698	664	284,362	19,471	4,044	268,935	57,083	55,705	4,733	80,656	32,031
1973	433,330	322,128	4,603	326,731	25,246	3,587	305,072	67,018	61,240	5,143	84,249	34,817
1974	496,661	355,137	7,558	362,695	28,249	2,686	337,132	79,977	79,552	5,732	86,651	35,762
1975	561,099	395,486	6,204	401,690	30,408	2,039	373,321	91,424	96,354	6,093	92,082	37,593
1976	643,701	466,842	5,855	472,697	36,514	1,562	437,745	101,880	104,076	6,782	94,909	40,685
1977	726,005	527,552	6,150	533,702	42,177	814	492,339	118,301	115,365	7,249	100,157	43,503
1978	850,265	622,559	7,998	630,557	50,784	-704	579,069	143,652	127,544	8,209	103,572	47,369
1979	973,332	703,850	9,184	713,034	60,603	-2,301	650,130	170,706	152,496	8,675	112,199	49,477
1980	1,080,871	741,652	12,312	753,964	63,175	-3,542	687,247	206,651	186,973	9,271	116,590	50,551
1981	1,173,965	762,504	11,264	773,768	71,178	-2,398	700,192	246,682	227,091	9,761	120,270	50,078
1982	1,251,216	796,587	12,814	809,401	76,268	-2,297	730,836	270,884	249,496	10,297	121,513	49,830
1983	1,362,772	864,926	10,392	875,318	84,296	-416	790,606	309,276	262,890	11,097	122,807	51,243
1984	1,506,622	966,037	10,951	976,988	98,420	-525	878,043	345,697	282,882	12,022	125,322	53,517
1985	1,609,293	1,017,635	10,711	1,028,346	105,523	1,617	924,440	375,416	309,437	12,527	128,461	54,432
1986	1,738,678	1,110,513	8,259	1,118,772	117,433	1,875	1,003,214	399,367	336,097	13,362	130,119	56,501
1987	1,893,855	1,255,463	8,784	1,264,247	134,171	120	1,130,196	407,188	356,471	14,244	132,958	60,612
1988	2,088,799	1,410,952	9,280	1,420,232	155,642	-2,837	1,261,753	439,149	387,897	15,288	136,627	64,192
1989	2,321,293	1,548,174	10,319	1,558,493	172,436	-4,591	1,381,466	510,667	429,160	16,463	140,997	66,910
1990	2,538,679	1,698,492	10,535	1,709,027	187,385	-6,564	1,515,078	548,461	475,140	17,083	148,606	71,727
1991	2,704,641	1,815,975	9,100	1,825,075	200,303	-6,805	1,617,967	556,469	530,205	17,592	153,746	73,820
1992	2,887,132	1,918,916	9,719	1,928,635	209,941	-2,571	1,716,123	558,679	612,330	18,413	156,800	73,116
1993	2,999,842	1,983,312	10,573	1,993,885	217,846	-149	1,775,890	574,779	649,173	19,018	157,735	73,197
1994	3,124,985	2,096,580	12,873	2,109,453	228,554	3,402	1,884,301	586,681	654,003	19,701	158,621	75,586
1995	3,241,128	2,148,744	8,563	2,157,307	230,708	10,035	1,936,634	614,215	690,279	20,359	159,198	75,741
1996	3,371,196	2,212,740	9,557	2,222,297	229,467	15,220	2,008,050	633,153	729,993	21,105	159,737	77,057
1997	3,555,404	2,342,795	13,056	2,355,851	239,406	19,690	2,136,135	678,697	740,572	22,116	160,761	78,613
1998	3,763,913	2,444,038	11,221	2,455,259	244,467	27,053	2,237,845	710,779	815,289	23,229	162,034	79,091
1999	3,934,600	2,582,935	12,572	2,595,507	258,018	35,055	2,372,544	701,623	860,433	24,290	161,987	81,190
2000	4,188,884	2,743,785	12,532	2,756,317	274,731	43,193	2,524,779	751,560	912,545	25,602	163,615	83,788
2001	4,510,840	2,938,179	14,316	2,952,495	310,799	47,897	2,689,593	796,996	1,024,251	27,107	166,408	85,938
2002	4,706,431	3,195,038	14,970	3,210,008	343,403	31,960	2,898,565	716,418	1,091,448	27,653	170,198	88,890
2003	4,887,539	3,362,481	17,781	3,380,262	367,310	14,047	3,026,999	749,356	1,111,184	28,219	173,202	90,509
2004	5,169,241	3,536,705	18,053	3,554,758	402,051	-5,944	3,146,763	857,423	1,165,055	29,561	174,867	92,228
2005	5,350,904	3,686,223	17,734	3,703,957	426,788	-28,596	3,248,573	876,538	1,225,793	30,470	175,615	93,546
2006	5,685,630	3,849,426	11,953	3,861,379	431,038	-53,353	3,376,988	969,433	1,339,209	32,274	176,166	95,039
2007	5,890,625	3,922,646	7,776	3,930,422	434,788	-80,099	3,415,535	1,049,366	1,425,724	33,366	176,548	95,982
2008	5,900,117	3,760,722	10,898	3,771,620	424,551	-101,715	3,245,354	1,066,533	1,588,230	33,288	177,247	91,880
2009	5,804,772	3,539,888	18,336	3,558,224	412,423	-91,251	3,054,550	998,185	1,752,037	32,744	177,279	87,368
2010	5,938,481	3,507,123	28,506	3,535,629	405,493	-83,141	3,046,995	994,119	1,897,367	33,497	177,286	85,727
2011	6,188,095	3,627,294	29,850	3,657,144	381,532	-100,984	3,174,628	1,103,377	1,910,090	34,774	177,950	86,073
2012	6,379,918	3,695,198	40,208	3,735,406	382,247	-99,790	3,253,369	1,166,940	1,959,609	35,758	178,421	86,825
2013	6,514,113	3,725,843	33,399	3,759,242	431,988	-66,880	3,260,374	1,219,916	2,033,823	36,364	179,137	87,542
2014	6,815,459	3,911,964	35,881	3,947,845	454,010	-68,228	3,425,607	1,282,079	2,107,773	37,905	179,804	90,076

Personal Income and Employment by Area: Reno, NV

(Thousands of dollars, except as noted.)

Year	Personal income, total	Earnings by place of work			Less: Contributions for government social insurance	Plus: Adjustment for residence	Equals: Net earnings by place of residence	Plus: Dividends, interest, and rent	Plus: Personal current transfer receipts	Per capita personal income (dollars)	Population (persons)	Total employment
		Nonfarm	Farm	Total								
1970	663,474	540,385	1,110	541,495	36,240	-5,384	499,871	121,731	41,872	5,401	122,838	68,813
1971	749,461	613,543	1,099	614,642	42,479	-9,835	562,328	136,421	50,712	5,799	129,234	73,393
1972	840,359	692,543	1,411	693,954	51,278	-13,424	629,252	151,795	59,312	6,172	136,146	77,256
1973	945,020	788,422	1,992	790,414	67,580	-18,431	704,403	173,289	67,328	6,663	141,828	83,477
1974	1,042,271	851,525	896	852,421	74,021	-20,707	757,693	202,735	81,843	7,028	148,306	85,698
1975	1,184,643	956,045	1,284	957,329	80,698	-24,569	852,062	219,418	113,163	7,737	153,109	89,100
1976	1,369,476	1,129,380	1,588	1,130,968	98,386	-31,696	1,000,886	246,036	122,554	8,577	159,670	96,622
1977	1,620,704	1,370,098	1,022	1,371,120	122,155	-42,126	1,206,839	280,067	133,798	9,602	168,795	108,044
1978	2,007,458	1,718,845	773	1,719,618	159,462	-48,444	1,511,712	344,342	151,404	11,234	178,694	124,884
1979	2,334,021	2,001,948	-679	2,001,269	196,099	-57,840	1,747,330	412,225	174,466	12,381	188,511	134,856
1980	2,623,533	2,202,278	3,015	2,205,293	215,531	-64,211	1,925,551	492,364	205,618	13,324	196,906	135,996
1981	2,923,421	2,376,269	2,127	2,378,396	247,641	-60,453	2,070,302	607,476	245,643	14,352	203,693	136,031
1982	3,106,493	2,429,592	2,459	2,432,051	253,427	-58,773	2,119,851	713,728	272,914	14,767	210,363	133,990
1983	3,292,360	2,559,119	1,746	2,560,865	276,750	-51,464	2,232,651	755,256	304,453	15,460	212,962	133,936
1984	3,610,096	2,812,526	1,057	2,813,583	317,274	-54,288	2,442,021	846,238	321,837	16,544	218,215	141,249
1985	3,916,499	3,011,438	333	3,011,771	346,641	-53,690	2,611,440	957,742	347,317	17,508	223,695	145,142
1986	4,200,545	3,251,248	86	3,251,334	385,249	-55,651	2,810,434	1,010,593	379,518	18,249	230,182	151,010
1987	4,536,449	3,541,329	1,571	3,542,900	420,097	-60,632	3,062,171	1,076,597	397,681	19,121	237,251	160,239
1988	4,981,614	3,929,762	1,742	3,931,504	467,725	-68,357	3,395,422	1,163,999	422,193	20,383	244,395	167,081
1989	5,386,913	4,172,091	1,999	4,174,090	501,851	-65,522	3,606,717	1,297,717	482,479	21,486	250,718	170,932
1990	5,958,472	4,563,022	1,341	4,564,363	570,298	-101,078	3,892,987	1,527,671	537,814	22,990	259,178	175,220
1991	6,457,111	4,839,973	1,789	4,841,762	598,456	-96,706	4,146,600	1,657,623	652,888	24,215	266,660	174,711
1992	7,104,975	5,302,569	591	5,303,160	647,726	-108,640	4,546,794	1,834,618	723,563	25,973	273,556	175,503
1993	7,383,257	5,555,796	9,233	5,565,029	687,326	-102,146	4,775,557	1,869,791	737,909	26,248	281,288	182,728
1994	8,013,298	5,975,573	3,433	5,979,006	743,288	-110,355	5,125,363	2,154,498	733,437	27,514	291,248	192,012
1995	8,678,072	6,428,484	3,957	6,432,441	799,511	-118,329	5,514,601	2,363,338	800,133	28,903	300,246	200,861
1996	9,359,578	6,931,825	5,137	6,936,962	838,502	-125,264	5,973,196	2,546,959	839,423	30,176	310,169	209,606
1997	9,971,701	7,439,231	3,325	7,442,556	872,068	-123,487	6,447,001	2,651,255	873,445	31,218	319,425	218,118
1998	10,662,355	7,924,559	4,103	7,928,662	915,297	-148,292	6,865,073	2,893,164	904,118	32,509	327,980	224,911
1999	11,504,450	8,658,029	4,195	8,662,224	954,880	-140,120	7,567,224	3,015,675	921,551	34,217	336,225	227,738
2000	12,667,406	9,352,405	5,651	9,358,056	937,955	-142,752	8,277,349	3,407,815	982,242	36,740	344,782	237,577
2001	13,395,479	9,912,086	4,324	9,916,410	1,004,716	-177,041	8,734,653	3,562,466	1,098,360	37,698	355,341	240,711
2002	13,680,496	10,070,662	3,828	10,074,490	1,024,381	-164,038	8,886,071	3,577,365	1,217,060	37,408	365,706	242,117
2003	14,724,381	10,818,331	3,515	10,821,846	1,045,178	-158,492	9,618,176	3,815,229	1,290,976	39,191	375,713	249,521
2004	16,335,317	11,802,240	4,888	11,807,128	1,109,848	-149,545	10,547,735	4,392,264	1,395,318	42,286	386,308	261,058
2005	17,836,366	12,806,790	4,572	12,811,362	1,180,844	-138,889	11,491,629	4,850,395	1,494,342	44,979	396,546	272,020
2006	18,715,207	13,623,869	6,223	13,630,092	1,314,837	-125,304	12,189,951	4,911,028	1,614,228	46,283	404,366	282,553
2007	20,116,458	14,705,401	2,767	14,708,168	1,389,688	-120,242	13,198,238	5,160,000	1,758,220	48,741	412,724	288,260
2008	19,309,337	13,558,037	3,910	13,561,947	1,281,924	-104,606	12,175,417	5,061,370	2,072,550	46,096	418,892	277,141
2009	17,532,414	11,961,109	6,207	11,967,316	1,203,058	-33,751	10,730,507	4,419,064	2,382,843	41,567	421,787	258,375
2010	17,578,488	11,923,847	6,378	11,930,225	1,193,249	32,542	10,769,518	4,186,508	2,622,462	41,261	426,032	246,892
2011	18,453,620	11,831,187	8,400	11,839,587	1,119,872	71,694	10,791,409	4,977,151	2,685,060	43,030	428,858	249,227
2012	18,639,683	12,002,424	6,945	12,009,369	1,159,255	82,434	10,932,548	5,001,890	2,705,245	43,048	433,001	249,325
2013	19,381,848	12,268,123	8,633	12,276,756	1,303,080	114,497	11,088,173	5,501,857	2,791,818	44,280	437,713	257,492
2014	20,476,660	13,105,928	14,176	13,120,104	1,423,951	67,285	11,763,438	5,705,129	3,008,093	46,120	443,990	265,449

Personal Income and Employment by Area: Richmond, VA

(Thousands of dollars, except as noted.)

| Year | Personal income, total | Derivation of personal income | | | | | | | | | Per capita personal income (dollars) | Population (persons) | Total employment |
| | | Earnings by place of work | | | Less: Contributions for government social insurance | Plus: Adjustment for residence | Equals: Net earnings by place of residence | Plus: Dividends, interest, and rent | Plus: Personal current transfer receipts | | | |
		Nonfarm	Farm	Total								
1970	2,891,074	2,496,155	16,378	2,512,533	157,625	-86,004	2,268,904	426,390	195,780	4,030	717,320	363,604
1971	3,191,666	2,720,816	15,031	2,735,847	178,873	-70,776	2,486,198	469,015	236,453	4,378	729,032	368,947
1972	3,504,093	2,996,854	19,800	3,016,654	206,223	-91,272	2,719,159	509,343	275,591	4,787	731,939	378,331
1973	3,918,286	3,370,557	30,585	3,401,142	267,295	-114,259	3,019,588	574,287	324,411	5,285	741,343	401,104
1974	4,401,541	3,766,288	30,463	3,796,751	308,978	-131,956	3,355,817	667,258	378,466	5,885	747,915	417,651
1975	4,916,053	4,086,820	24,993	4,111,813	329,345	-84,929	3,697,539	735,724	482,790	6,479	758,781	413,944
1976	5,402,694	4,519,210	21,381	4,540,591	372,334	-92,234	4,076,023	793,103	533,568	6,993	772,532	424,700
1977	5,998,664	5,034,738	9,842	5,044,580	413,127	-90,292	4,541,161	885,940	571,563	7,624	786,806	438,435
1978	6,802,983	5,709,632	27,261	5,736,893	476,683	-106,554	5,153,656	1,021,625	627,702	8,560	794,750	457,990
1979	7,680,051	6,410,456	574	6,411,030	559,694	-74,519	5,776,817	1,185,240	717,994	9,554	803,835	471,434
1980	8,626,635	7,065,254	-9,013	7,056,241	620,379	-103,164	6,332,698	1,436,070	857,867	10,649	810,116	472,830
1981	9,672,902	7,733,241	25,268	7,758,509	728,564	-117,781	6,912,164	1,768,391	992,347	11,829	817,739	470,744
1982	10,438,666	8,238,816	9,663	8,248,479	787,999	-118,341	7,342,139	2,009,282	1,087,245	12,673	823,713	469,070
1983	11,250,343	8,865,029	-5,256	8,859,773	865,206	-111,279	7,883,288	2,195,077	1,171,978	13,553	830,095	475,270
1984	12,385,892	9,687,120	38,965	9,726,085	971,997	-106,859	8,647,229	2,495,369	1,243,294	14,805	836,596	489,234
1985	13,391,329	10,532,805	21,982	10,554,787	1,084,788	-111,272	9,358,727	2,701,238	1,331,364	15,836	845,645	509,452
1986	14,401,518	11,367,576	23,463	11,391,039	1,210,734	-112,729	10,067,576	2,915,996	1,417,946	16,797	857,407	529,695
1987	15,748,321	12,597,690	27,226	12,624,916	1,330,296	-130,251	11,164,369	3,104,986	1,478,966	18,035	873,222	556,131
1988	17,319,511	13,867,530	45,223	13,912,753	1,506,074	-147,306	12,259,373	3,471,070	1,589,068	19,485	888,857	568,478
1989	18,925,450	14,930,307	54,279	14,984,586	1,629,281	-157,594	13,197,711	3,990,044	1,737,695	20,954	903,206	583,119
1990	19,864,842	15,575,957	59,009	15,634,966	1,716,904	-166,602	13,751,460	4,243,019	1,870,363	21,598	919,735	589,433
1991	20,321,817	15,975,989	46,424	16,022,413	1,780,781	-188,017	14,053,615	4,207,169	2,061,033	21,762	933,839	578,586
1992	21,586,319	16,915,269	51,478	16,966,747	1,872,197	-215,021	14,879,529	4,387,800	2,318,990	22,701	950,908	579,119
1993	22,654,111	17,672,778	37,840	17,710,618	1,961,629	-246,715	15,502,274	4,670,735	2,481,102	23,461	965,604	587,075
1994	23,939,472	18,720,432	57,663	18,778,095	2,067,568	-288,400	16,422,127	4,940,736	2,576,609	24,452	979,035	605,263
1995	25,089,549	19,631,798	54,871	19,686,669	2,164,347	-327,362	17,194,960	5,100,970	2,793,619	25,293	991,943	621,056
1996	26,336,743	20,609,185	73,411	20,682,596	2,256,603	-362,978	18,063,015	5,325,818	2,947,910	26,229	1,004,116	632,125
1997	28,086,813	22,228,507	44,214	22,272,721	2,414,993	-433,822	19,423,906	5,621,581	3,041,326	27,590	1,017,990	650,624
1998	29,934,927	23,781,811	26,578	23,808,389	2,552,685	-463,746	20,791,958	6,026,646	3,116,323	29,026	1,031,320	662,083
1999	31,391,385	25,334,649	25,459	25,360,108	2,730,423	-510,735	22,118,950	6,009,458	3,262,977	30,018	1,045,761	677,616
2000	33,814,101	27,166,977	44,685	27,211,662	2,888,348	-564,942	23,758,372	6,568,291	3,487,438	31,931	1,058,966	694,400
2001	35,690,783	28,673,840	30,720	28,704,560	3,091,920	-591,910	25,020,730	6,803,259	3,866,794	33,330	1,070,817	693,994
2002	36,688,158	29,518,932	26,427	29,545,359	3,192,679	-730,975	25,621,705	7,018,839	4,047,614	33,833	1,084,389	692,791
2003	38,455,525	30,567,996	27,418	30,595,414	3,299,561	-770,524	26,525,329	7,606,056	4,324,140	35,003	1,098,631	695,080
2004	40,989,768	32,832,800	39,643	32,872,443	3,578,315	-757,120	28,537,008	7,926,654	4,526,106	36,732	1,115,900	709,534
2005	43,898,425	34,949,878	34,697	34,984,575	3,832,709	-675,847	30,476,019	8,496,896	4,925,510	38,675	1,135,074	728,792
2006	47,130,258	36,431,846	17,274	36,449,120	4,044,111	-471,781	31,933,228	9,802,708	5,394,322	40,725	1,157,286	742,080
2007	49,805,184	38,390,053	12,720	38,402,773	4,251,498	-356,289	33,794,986	10,218,859	5,791,339	42,411	1,174,344	758,368
2008	51,799,407	39,326,546	28,859	39,355,405	4,367,960	-252,735	34,734,710	10,373,593	6,691,104	43,561	1,189,113	763,902
2009	50,008,097	38,065,528	30,551	38,096,079	4,243,509	-218,537	33,634,033	9,078,410	7,295,654	41,649	1,200,712	741,470
2010	51,212,300	38,833,463	19,181	38,852,644	4,368,718	-196,237	34,287,689	8,997,736	7,926,875	42,322	1,210,063	734,947
2011	54,077,676	40,012,417	66,069	40,078,486	4,035,350	-222,434	35,820,702	10,032,977	8,223,997	44,341	1,219,592	747,057
2012	57,015,404	41,438,129	72,534	41,510,663	4,189,052	-249,209	37,072,402	11,622,514	8,320,488	46,214	1,233,722	759,154
2013	57,246,515	42,504,434	90,580	42,595,014	4,906,109	-269,095	37,419,810	11,159,569	8,667,136	45,912	1,246,867	770,453
2014	59,326,150	44,061,713	47,409	44,109,122	5,066,539	-279,816	38,762,767	11,570,693	8,992,690	47,083	1,260,029	780,955

Personal Income and Employment by Area: Riverside-San Bernardino-Ontario, CA

(Thousands of dollars, except as noted.)

Year	Personal income, total	Earnings by place of work			Less: Contributions for government social insurance	Plus: Adjustment for residence	Equals: Net earnings by place of residence	Plus: Dividends, interest, and rent	Plus: Personal current transfer receipts	Per capita personal income (dollars)	Population (persons)	Total employment
		Nonfarm	Farm	Total								
1970	4,907,137	3,151,293	112,771	3,264,064	207,830	441,162	3,497,396	838,029	571,712	4,291	1,143,539	418,790
1971	5,322,079	3,359,766	94,990	3,454,756	228,306	543,577	3,770,027	905,230	646,822	4,544	1,171,161	422,980
1972	5,941,974	3,703,684	144,267	3,847,951	264,172	676,302	4,260,081	980,764	701,129	4,995	1,189,476	436,775
1973	6,598,529	4,067,374	168,227	4,235,601	327,699	813,331	4,721,233	1,087,553	789,743	5,489	1,202,185	458,353
1974	7,406,590	4,437,314	167,136	4,604,450	368,936	963,244	5,198,758	1,244,509	963,323	6,023	1,229,743	468,665
1975	8,389,400	4,805,791	224,490	5,030,281	394,264	1,134,916	5,770,933	1,393,389	1,225,078	6,719	1,248,571	473,347
1976	9,471,311	5,409,961	257,788	5,667,749	447,018	1,340,054	6,560,785	1,526,849	1,383,677	7,385	1,282,517	491,513
1977	10,660,538	6,117,721	259,954	6,377,675	516,353	1,575,513	7,436,835	1,716,864	1,506,839	7,911	1,347,627	524,096
1978	12,348,594	7,153,156	255,381	7,408,537	616,607	1,878,077	8,670,007	2,026,400	1,652,187	8,601	1,435,733	566,072
1979	14,001,511	8,114,804	197,276	8,312,080	732,243	2,204,667	9,784,504	2,358,903	1,858,104	9,354	1,496,847	596,581
1980	16,133,155	8,925,656	263,796	9,189,452	783,375	2,600,113	11,006,190	2,891,610	2,235,355	10,260	1,572,429	609,845
1981	18,493,878	9,793,363	284,213	10,077,576	937,702	3,128,217	12,268,091	3,516,616	2,709,171	11,373	1,626,183	618,273
1982	19,934,097	10,218,679	335,822	10,554,501	1,005,149	3,493,848	13,043,200	3,898,285	2,992,612	11,819	1,686,602	618,248
1983	21,935,695	11,167,263	389,914	11,557,177	1,128,266	3,972,451	14,401,362	4,340,474	3,193,859	12,582	1,743,463	645,466
1984	24,739,934	12,702,469	434,226	13,136,695	1,334,489	4,647,461	16,449,667	4,898,758	3,391,509	13,661	1,811,019	685,286
1985	27,645,990	14,327,341	459,539	14,786,880	1,523,351	5,354,608	18,618,137	5,303,283	3,724,570	14,566	1,897,927	736,046
1986	30,747,890	16,076,373	519,696	16,596,069	1,737,856	6,077,927	20,936,140	5,733,111	4,078,639	15,410	1,995,378	781,634
1987	34,103,502	18,184,669	513,690	18,698,359	1,977,297	6,990,045	23,711,107	6,042,318	4,350,077	16,069	2,122,256	829,482
1988	37,971,184	20,328,786	586,423	20,915,209	2,289,920	7,918,691	26,543,980	6,613,267	4,813,937	16,748	2,267,166	889,223
1989	42,577,436	22,410,291	558,642	22,968,933	2,547,931	8,877,085	29,298,087	7,917,712	5,361,637	17,468	2,437,479	947,954
1990	47,045,889	24,528,202	610,184	25,138,386	2,768,008	10,444,913	32,815,291	8,217,585	6,013,013	17,885	2,630,471	1,003,046
1991	48,668,452	26,023,375	527,988	26,551,363	2,946,018	10,007,868	33,613,213	8,227,703	6,827,536	17,768	2,739,150	1,037,939
1992	51,022,484	27,741,789	530,221	28,272,010	3,113,800	9,739,456	34,897,666	8,211,257	7,913,561	18,084	2,821,341	1,035,249
1993	52,350,571	28,340,070	516,656	28,856,726	3,202,012	9,796,254	35,450,968	8,390,419	8,509,184	18,276	2,864,517	1,039,281
1994	53,815,597	29,636,433	562,443	30,198,876	3,356,445	9,590,881	36,433,312	8,648,270	8,734,015	18,522	2,905,505	1,065,322
1995	55,830,391	30,992,649	550,028	31,542,677	3,448,697	9,424,751	37,518,731	9,097,402	9,214,258	18,927	2,949,807	1,099,819
1996	58,511,859	32,618,466	668,841	33,287,307	3,509,281	9,299,677	39,077,703	9,694,268	9,739,888	19,567	2,990,316	1,132,225
1997	62,032,956	34,995,710	558,232	35,553,942	3,696,144	10,078,222	41,936,020	10,248,770	9,848,166	20,390	3,042,372	1,168,111
1998	67,489,887	39,056,662	743,489	39,800,151	4,035,995	10,422,545	46,186,701	10,872,393	10,430,793	21,713	3,108,220	1,245,906
1999	71,462,967	42,694,493	700,439	43,394,932	4,413,588	10,543,737	49,525,081	10,971,740	10,966,146	22,406	3,189,513	1,314,500
2000	76,950,152	46,678,790	451,362	47,130,152	4,804,372	11,298,904	53,624,684	11,811,498	11,513,970	23,482	3,277,022	1,359,557
2001	83,542,991	50,892,386	584,214	51,476,600	5,467,459	11,814,709	57,823,850	12,941,769	12,777,372	24,736	3,377,365	1,407,349
2002	88,200,654	54,896,577	502,476	55,399,053	5,993,256	12,329,228	61,735,025	12,741,747	13,723,882	25,295	3,486,938	1,461,049
2003	95,235,652	59,515,234	619,694	60,134,928	6,602,545	13,108,975	66,641,358	13,835,684	14,758,610	26,324	3,617,771	1,511,837
2004	103,450,765	66,019,925	744,382	66,764,307	7,640,093	14,440,362	73,564,576	14,204,706	15,681,483	27,546	3,755,607	1,598,258
2005	110,790,295	71,111,840	649,444	71,761,284	8,257,309	15,430,075	78,934,050	15,166,167	16,690,078	28,586	3,875,709	1,682,196
2006	119,033,139	75,999,427	476,681	76,476,108	8,543,426	16,591,605	84,524,287	16,371,490	18,137,362	29,859	3,986,510	1,743,161
2007	124,018,895	77,232,071	713,239	77,945,310	8,475,144	17,188,624	86,658,790	17,873,490	19,486,615	30,491	4,067,344	1,772,141
2008	126,595,580	76,166,272	543,214	76,709,486	8,391,438	16,879,564	85,197,612	18,886,969	22,510,999	30,776	4,113,447	1,747,808
2009	122,813,670	71,875,708	345,025	72,220,733	8,084,089	15,974,273	80,110,917	17,703,755	24,998,998	29,518	4,160,685	1,668,668
2010	125,382,262	72,224,989	403,113	72,628,102	8,020,582	15,622,668	80,230,188	17,336,734	27,815,340	29,542	4,244,242	1,641,034
2011	132,483,826	75,471,588	599,315	76,070,903	7,603,271	16,655,628	85,123,260	19,238,914	28,121,652	30,793	4,302,359	1,690,202
2012	136,936,870	78,621,121	476,675	79,097,796	7,772,802	17,013,005	88,337,999	20,122,046	28,476,825	31,489	4,348,670	1,738,578
2013	140,979,258	81,475,250	412,609	81,887,859	9,035,515	17,209,973	90,062,317	21,471,062	29,445,879	32,112	4,390,262	1,799,101
2014	147,727,265	85,994,864	471,836	86,466,700	9,600,817	17,759,281	94,625,164	22,502,137	30,599,964	33,258	4,441,890	1,866,302

Personal Income and Employment by Area: Roanoke, VA

(Thousands of dollars, except as noted.)

Year	Personal income, total	Earnings by place of work			Less: Contributions for government social insurance	Plus: Adjustment for residence	Equals: Net earnings by place of residence	Plus: Dividends, interest, and rent	Plus: Personal current transfer receipts	Per capita personal income (dollars)	Population (persons)	Total employment
		Nonfarm	Farm	Total								
1970	860,339	731,821	5,166	736,987	51,639	-17,389	667,959	114,740	77,640	3,715	231,596	113,547
1971	940,525	795,543	5,124	800,667	57,676	-19,906	723,085	126,958	90,482	3,946	238,357	115,420
1972	1,038,329	886,374	6,865	893,239	67,325	-28,193	797,721	138,918	101,690	4,265	243,439	120,323
1973	1,167,893	1,003,197	8,755	1,011,952	86,635	-34,349	890,968	158,462	118,463	4,707	248,131	128,106
1974	1,296,920	1,096,483	10,001	1,106,484	97,675	-37,708	971,101	185,794	140,025	5,160	251,318	131,119
1975	1,427,299	1,162,803	7,237	1,170,040	100,252	-27,987	1,041,801	204,120	181,378	5,632	253,423	128,335
1976	1,584,411	1,299,733	6,213	1,305,946	114,726	-25,359	1,165,861	219,766	198,784	6,199	255,587	131,459
1977	1,738,392	1,429,202	5,681	1,434,883	127,564	-22,524	1,284,795	239,861	213,736	6,721	258,644	135,493
1978	1,974,375	1,613,179	7,666	1,620,845	145,076	-9,098	1,466,671	269,380	238,324	7,593	260,021	140,517
1979	2,155,549	1,767,383	6,158	1,773,541	165,451	-27,075	1,581,015	308,035	266,499	8,231	261,869	141,562
1980	2,372,978	1,905,280	148	1,905,428	178,693	-46,365	1,680,370	380,060	312,548	9,109	260,501	140,251
1981	2,616,922	2,050,016	3,461	2,053,477	207,136	-51,754	1,794,587	466,953	355,382	10,000	261,693	138,411
1982	2,779,457	2,128,003	1,017	2,129,020	220,821	-57,174	1,851,025	542,528	385,904	10,619	261,751	138,094
1983	3,028,762	2,331,666	4,006	2,335,672	245,691	-62,094	2,027,887	586,321	414,554	11,575	261,672	140,118
1984	3,397,810	2,623,173	7,535	2,630,708	286,004	-73,845	2,270,859	694,288	432,663	12,937	262,643	146,364
1985	3,673,062	2,859,358	8,502	2,867,860	317,600	-85,204	2,465,056	745,257	462,749	13,955	263,208	152,702
1986	3,898,250	3,040,040	10,437	3,050,477	348,615	-90,263	2,611,599	794,155	492,496	14,786	263,645	155,869
1987	4,156,435	3,279,714	12,646	3,292,360	371,674	-98,523	2,822,163	820,778	513,494	15,683	265,026	160,150
1988	4,396,444	3,435,916	15,906	3,451,822	399,155	-106,686	2,945,981	914,786	535,677	16,540	265,805	159,825
1989	4,774,313	3,667,541	21,315	3,688,856	425,188	-121,026	3,142,642	1,048,709	582,962	17,898	266,749	164,203
1990	5,037,403	3,906,941	25,411	3,932,352	457,662	-140,303	3,334,387	1,076,406	626,610	18,696	269,440	166,966
1991	5,175,881	4,011,278	22,642	4,033,920	474,459	-151,815	3,407,646	1,085,290	682,945	18,966	272,906	164,617
1992	5,471,461	4,291,055	22,515	4,313,570	499,942	-174,349	3,639,279	1,078,305	753,877	19,972	273,951	166,401
1993	5,763,377	4,553,863	17,606	4,571,469	530,205	-198,538	3,842,726	1,128,538	792,113	20,833	276,643	169,750
1994	6,040,705	4,764,024	18,740	4,782,764	551,813	-221,303	4,009,648	1,181,995	849,062	21,638	279,176	175,063
1995	6,338,465	4,999,917	14,725	5,014,642	582,235	-247,535	4,184,872	1,250,942	902,651	22,562	280,938	179,737
1996	6,647,349	5,203,428	12,302	5,215,730	601,512	-269,030	4,345,188	1,359,999	942,162	23,496	282,915	183,486
1997	6,919,399	5,434,140	6,988	5,441,128	625,354	-288,426	4,527,348	1,421,104	970,947	24,313	284,593	183,985
1998	7,355,887	5,863,918	9,715	5,873,633	664,699	-329,480	4,879,454	1,467,900	1,008,533	25,741	285,762	191,086
1999	7,607,655	6,111,437	4,446	6,115,883	693,612	-357,268	5,065,003	1,490,267	1,052,385	26,490	287,193	190,872
2000	7,987,059	6,356,090	9,934	6,366,024	713,106	-395,386	5,257,532	1,611,830	1,117,697	27,666	288,699	194,470
2001	8,438,228	6,657,028	7,804	6,664,832	754,927	-388,238	5,521,667	1,688,669	1,227,892	29,143	289,547	191,456
2002	8,640,058	6,852,585	2,790	6,855,375	781,403	-469,093	5,604,879	1,728,448	1,306,731	29,746	290,466	190,072
2003	8,917,379	7,052,257	-3,236	7,049,021	798,903	-481,108	5,769,010	1,754,173	1,394,196	30,530	292,082	188,267
2004	9,425,490	7,508,424	9,768	7,518,192	854,010	-544,274	6,119,908	1,826,020	1,479,562	32,087	293,745	190,901
2005	9,906,906	7,802,710	9,854	7,812,564	897,467	-459,114	6,455,983	1,849,829	1,601,094	33,424	296,405	196,533
2006	10,440,393	8,172,197	231	8,172,428	956,508	-469,992	6,745,928	1,945,960	1,748,505	34,809	299,930	202,247
2007	11,103,740	8,541,041	2,661	8,543,702	998,138	-501,772	7,043,792	2,186,628	1,873,320	36,663	302,858	206,049
2008	11,504,980	8,740,618	5,614	8,746,232	1,026,331	-576,772	7,143,129	2,258,512	2,103,339	37,648	305,596	201,892
2009	11,380,223	8,627,181	2,872	8,630,053	1,015,301	-564,662	7,050,090	2,047,824	2,282,309	36,971	307,816	194,583
2010	11,453,282	8,505,540	7,296	8,512,836	1,015,165	-549,510	6,948,161	2,057,621	2,447,500	37,092	308,781	190,746
2011	11,960,620	8,731,100	16,780	8,747,880	942,049	-573,302	7,232,529	2,234,989	2,493,102	38,659	309,390	192,368
2012	12,624,187	9,020,767	19,283	9,040,050	972,944	-590,540	7,476,566	2,592,469	2,555,152	40,630	310,710	193,635
2013	12,569,191	9,170,234	19,705	9,189,939	1,119,257	-581,752	7,488,930	2,451,111	2,629,150	40,234	312,404	193,781
2014	12,968,988	9,425,334	24,225	9,449,559	1,147,178	-598,875	7,703,506	2,557,271	2,708,211	41,383	313,388	195,666

Personal Income and Employment by Area: Rochester, MN

(Thousands of dollars, except as noted.)

Year	Personal income, total	Earnings by place of work			Less: Contributions for government social insurance	Plus: Adjustment for residence	Equals: Net earnings by place of residence	Plus: Dividends, interest, and rent	Plus: Personal current transfer receipts	Per capita personal income (dollars)	Population (persons)	Total employment
		Nonfarm	Farm	Total								
1970	529,011	387,699	54,160	441,859	26,598	-3,591	411,670	76,103	41,238	3,871	136,645	61,810
1971	563,745	416,238	51,141	467,379	29,647	-4,488	433,244	82,979	47,522	4,085	138,020	62,584
1972	621,945	458,379	61,672	520,051	34,157	-5,685	480,209	89,391	52,345	4,456	139,574	66,413
1973	737,598	517,583	108,372	625,955	44,716	-7,641	573,598	102,024	61,976	5,259	140,244	70,682
1974	777,550	563,456	81,076	644,532	50,508	-8,545	585,479	117,837	74,234	5,497	141,439	72,619
1975	860,711	635,020	68,272	703,292	55,511	-11,942	635,839	136,114	88,758	6,054	142,168	73,701
1976	938,788	720,333	52,250	772,583	64,229	-14,873	693,481	147,989	97,318	6,525	143,886	76,699
1977	1,092,376	803,807	106,467	910,274	71,851	-18,558	819,865	168,683	103,828	7,508	145,499	78,691
1978	1,231,227	930,688	112,323	1,043,011	86,719	-25,264	931,028	186,367	113,832	8,434	145,983	81,851
1979	1,324,315	1,038,954	72,670	1,111,624	100,475	-28,367	982,782	211,733	129,800	8,965	147,713	84,728
1980	1,478,638	1,143,921	64,120	1,208,041	110,485	-32,283	1,065,273	257,886	155,479	9,960	148,456	86,430
1981	1,645,220	1,239,161	70,431	1,309,592	128,063	-33,637	1,147,892	316,305	181,023	10,985	149,775	86,334
1982	1,823,847	1,343,976	74,810	1,418,786	143,134	-38,447	1,237,205	385,263	201,379	12,124	150,427	86,370
1983	1,875,170	1,450,135	-5,787	1,444,348	156,269	-42,398	1,245,681	407,841	221,648	12,343	151,922	88,143
1984	2,183,856	1,638,323	89,078	1,727,401	181,227	-50,104	1,496,070	449,114	238,672	14,262	153,128	91,755
1985	2,287,655	1,735,919	77,798	1,813,717	195,256	-54,873	1,563,588	470,215	253,852	14,789	154,688	92,865
1986	2,407,742	1,816,975	107,005	1,923,980	209,000	-57,520	1,657,460	484,266	266,016	15,554	154,797	92,206
1987	2,557,135	1,935,064	146,085	2,081,149	220,219	-64,282	1,796,648	484,965	275,522	16,447	155,475	94,618
1988	2,654,048	2,103,481	87,019	2,190,500	247,633	-72,328	1,870,539	491,161	292,348	16,708	158,849	98,326
1989	2,970,544	2,293,927	135,285	2,429,212	269,735	-82,037	2,077,440	571,299	321,805	18,451	160,993	101,567
1990	3,176,070	2,507,855	126,270	2,634,125	296,813	-93,356	2,243,956	590,231	341,883	19,434	163,427	104,645
1991	3,296,823	2,651,724	96,584	2,748,308	318,122	-96,488	2,333,698	598,283	364,842	19,840	166,169	106,918
1992	3,512,153	2,840,753	76,200	2,916,953	337,125	-99,965	2,479,863	637,363	394,927	20,886	168,159	108,570
1993	3,563,300	2,962,138	41,748	3,003,886	352,453	-102,654	2,548,779	603,004	411,517	20,797	171,334	110,560
1994	3,738,122	3,025,998	101,797	3,127,795	364,228	-101,021	2,662,546	636,000	439,576	21,675	172,466	110,937
1995	3,882,057	3,117,424	49,006	3,166,430	375,713	-100,592	2,690,125	719,476	472,456	22,473	172,741	113,113
1996	4,219,711	3,350,234	107,306	3,457,540	400,008	-107,522	2,950,010	769,564	500,137	24,229	174,161	114,704
1997	4,419,389	3,573,916	68,056	3,641,972	426,907	-118,859	3,096,206	813,138	510,045	25,074	176,251	118,626
1998	4,903,565	3,993,341	100,151	4,093,492	470,007	-137,201	3,486,284	897,286	519,995	27,320	179,488	123,753
1999	5,234,661	4,344,887	78,092	4,422,979	510,733	-154,259	3,757,987	918,119	558,555	28,683	182,498	127,721
2000	5,570,640	4,610,768	57,614	4,668,382	539,086	-163,942	3,965,354	1,000,422	604,864	30,019	185,573	131,396
2001	6,072,105	5,080,227	40,062	5,120,289	575,085	-179,010	4,366,194	1,026,652	679,259	32,332	187,803	133,511
2002	6,367,428	5,388,775	21,061	5,409,836	607,027	-183,591	4,619,218	1,003,449	744,761	33,399	190,646	134,779
2003	6,781,145	5,744,405	55,507	5,799,912	652,494	-222,523	4,924,895	1,057,306	798,944	35,123	193,067	137,492
2004	7,049,114	6,006,176	117,318	6,123,494	683,449	-208,964	5,231,081	973,363	844,670	36,094	195,300	139,279
2005	7,116,019	6,059,636	149,570	6,209,206	700,358	-213,055	5,295,793	942,552	877,674	36,087	197,188	140,420
2006	7,508,277	6,313,603	103,288	6,416,891	735,999	-207,854	5,473,038	1,078,721	956,518	37,586	199,763	142,267
2007	7,977,760	6,589,102	117,949	6,707,051	768,448	-219,346	5,719,257	1,223,138	1,035,365	39,537	201,782	144,180
2008	8,275,785	6,653,403	159,318	6,812,721	783,658	-210,115	5,818,948	1,294,767	1,162,070	40,532	204,181	143,421
2009	8,175,391	6,615,696	72,166	6,687,862	787,639	-214,259	5,685,964	1,213,115	1,276,312	39,668	206,097	140,668
2010	8,773,980	7,045,382	137,762	7,183,144	819,992	-177,063	6,186,089	1,201,486	1,386,405	42,358	207,140	138,513
2011	9,055,981	6,944,952	248,737	7,193,689	723,852	-166,385	6,303,452	1,355,277	1,397,252	43,422	208,556	140,079
2012	9,463,791	7,202,087	315,320	7,517,407	752,420	-172,354	6,592,633	1,471,183	1,399,975	45,128	209,709	142,858
2013	9,537,376	7,427,849	220,757	7,648,606	887,671	-181,043	6,579,892	1,514,236	1,443,248	45,022	211,838	144,756
2014	9,917,802	7,642,833	242,707	7,885,540	910,903	-153,970	6,820,667	1,576,073	1,521,062	46,611	212,778	145,337

Personal Income and Employment by Area: Rochester, NY

(Thousands of dollars, except as noted.)

Year	Personal income, total	Earnings by place of work			Less: Contributions for government social insurance	Plus: Adjustment for residence	Equals: Net earnings by place of residence	Plus: Dividends, interest, and rent	Plus: Personal current transfer receipts	Per capita personal income (dollars)	Population (persons)	Total employment
		Nonfarm	Farm	Total								
1970	4,554,160	3,791,267	64,553	3,855,820	276,964	-46,035	3,532,821	650,440	370,899	4,634	982,845	439,999
1971	4,881,161	4,032,063	61,581	4,093,644	304,319	-50,141	3,739,184	687,488	454,489	4,939	988,371	440,497
1972	5,256,165	4,392,616	41,128	4,433,744	352,229	-52,061	4,029,454	731,844	494,867	5,304	991,017	447,820
1973	5,759,741	4,819,656	72,803	4,892,459	448,781	-54,697	4,388,981	813,699	557,061	5,810	991,293	464,379
1974	6,305,084	5,243,981	84,056	5,328,037	507,725	-58,875	4,761,437	920,242	623,405	6,374	989,197	475,220
1975	6,815,217	5,508,838	65,112	5,573,950	521,206	-61,606	4,991,138	986,049	838,030	6,841	996,288	464,343
1976	7,257,498	5,918,531	57,078	5,975,609	572,254	-62,088	5,341,267	1,037,411	878,820	7,277	997,313	468,201
1977	7,871,205	6,448,341	60,062	6,508,403	622,054	-71,597	5,814,752	1,140,128	916,325	7,874	999,583	477,239
1978	8,537,037	7,071,068	66,337	7,137,405	698,906	-75,674	6,362,825	1,204,613	969,599	8,574	995,677	489,129
1979	9,471,813	7,873,332	80,471	7,953,803	805,638	-80,961	7,067,204	1,361,602	1,043,007	9,508	996,204	501,248
1980	10,644,554	8,679,386	68,504	8,747,890	886,640	-88,193	7,773,057	1,639,050	1,232,447	10,707	994,186	499,705
1981	11,935,934	9,583,434	83,508	9,666,942	1,041,775	-97,139	8,528,028	2,023,201	1,384,705	11,956	998,299	504,102
1982	12,982,803	10,313,149	71,042	10,384,191	1,137,881	-124,103	9,122,207	2,326,612	1,533,984	12,931	1,003,975	508,477
1983	13,582,654	10,662,559	35,353	10,697,912	1,181,442	-130,639	9,385,831	2,513,694	1,683,129	13,489	1,006,962	504,266
1984	14,907,941	11,635,722	57,621	11,693,343	1,312,840	-149,888	10,230,615	2,888,359	1,788,967	14,866	1,002,789	522,629
1985	15,998,219	12,632,869	69,579	12,702,448	1,444,272	-183,391	11,074,785	3,028,461	1,894,973	15,956	1,002,633	541,363
1986	16,842,203	13,316,360	83,299	13,399,659	1,549,087	-201,331	11,649,241	3,148,183	2,044,779	16,787	1,003,295	549,723
1987	17,490,212	13,891,065	100,828	13,991,893	1,589,925	-224,583	12,177,385	3,217,034	2,095,793	17,436	1,003,095	552,418
1988	18,985,537	15,201,776	102,315	15,304,091	1,774,323	-257,167	13,272,601	3,437,994	2,274,942	18,802	1,009,766	575,050
1989	20,823,654	16,293,837	107,259	16,401,096	1,881,939	-289,153	14,230,004	4,125,288	2,468,362	20,422	1,019,683	585,517
1990	21,617,139	16,894,654	103,722	16,998,376	1,870,996	-344,798	14,782,582	4,125,342	2,709,215	21,031	1,027,880	589,401
1991	22,473,297	17,620,812	92,143	17,712,955	1,998,595	-364,261	15,350,099	4,106,658	3,016,540	21,687	1,036,248	591,189
1992	23,562,336	18,520,111	101,400	18,621,511	2,061,091	-377,496	16,182,924	3,995,771	3,383,641	22,484	1,047,976	592,760
1993	24,160,756	19,036,484	110,352	19,146,836	2,131,981	-402,470	16,612,385	3,956,200	3,592,171	22,896	1,055,228	601,469
1994	24,865,140	19,520,189	91,886	19,612,075	2,216,695	-417,675	16,977,705	4,053,759	3,833,676	23,516	1,057,376	607,597
1995	26,030,877	20,294,721	73,772	20,368,493	2,297,161	-450,683	17,620,649	4,370,543	4,039,685	24,605	1,057,933	606,742
1996	26,947,758	20,847,744	92,886	20,940,630	2,341,807	-417,959	18,180,864	4,550,678	4,216,216	25,430	1,059,684	607,448
1997	28,035,951	21,702,865	89,680	21,792,545	2,402,551	-430,975	18,959,019	4,838,558	4,238,374	26,449	1,060,003	611,491
1998	29,130,833	22,439,224	98,922	22,538,146	2,451,649	-468,745	19,617,752	5,015,304	4,497,777	27,488	1,059,773	617,160
1999	30,032,790	23,421,851	128,971	23,550,822	2,507,475	-468,376	20,574,971	4,777,578	4,680,241	28,325	1,060,310	626,479
2000	31,384,224	24,370,633	132,118	24,502,751	2,601,042	-462,391	21,439,318	5,025,588	4,919,318	29,428	1,066,482	635,998
2001	32,269,268	25,116,080	150,023	25,266,103	2,737,718	-518,654	22,009,731	5,023,967	5,235,570	30,209	1,068,215	627,469
2002	32,295,713	25,177,365	114,733	25,292,098	2,784,338	-540,471	21,967,289	4,677,912	5,650,512	30,173	1,070,355	616,178
2003	33,001,540	25,943,118	142,818	26,085,936	2,862,480	-544,233	22,679,223	4,514,780	5,807,537	30,787	1,071,918	618,295
2004	34,539,386	27,017,918	150,944	27,168,862	2,972,680	-502,280	23,693,902	4,633,225	6,212,259	32,205	1,072,494	624,485
2005	35,659,050	27,813,217	122,885	27,936,102	3,096,114	-504,898	24,335,090	4,944,900	6,379,060	33,313	1,070,418	630,866
2006	37,067,438	28,744,111	131,158	28,875,269	3,184,430	-481,710	25,209,129	5,102,142	6,756,167	34,630	1,070,370	629,361
2007	38,762,455	29,551,069	243,271	29,794,340	3,275,834	-428,433	26,090,073	5,574,730	7,097,652	36,158	1,072,040	634,834
2008	41,078,668	30,501,912	274,900	30,776,812	3,414,416	-373,661	26,988,735	6,107,056	7,982,877	38,202	1,075,302	636,031
2009	40,982,606	30,309,331	172,248	30,481,579	3,373,693	-380,476	26,727,410	5,553,142	8,702,054	38,019	1,077,941	623,488
2010	42,084,357	31,094,402	258,043	31,352,445	3,463,594	-347,099	27,541,752	5,287,096	9,255,509	38,964	1,080,082	620,605
2011	44,285,294	32,212,561	302,272	32,514,833	3,239,036	-366,900	28,908,897	5,985,742	9,390,655	40,919	1,082,269	629,613
2012	46,243,083	33,222,751	254,974	33,477,725	3,306,860	-341,018	29,829,847	6,945,759	9,467,477	42,697	1,083,059	631,887
2013	46,263,990	34,134,990	347,566	34,482,556	3,816,503	-329,051	30,337,002	6,313,783	9,613,205	42,675	1,084,094	634,132
2014	47,493,982	34,966,710	323,856	35,290,566	3,939,690	-242,278	31,108,598	6,538,430	9,846,954	43,838	1,083,393	638,623

Personal Income and Employment by Area: Rockford, IL

(Thousands of dollars, except as noted.)

Year	Personal income, total	Derivation of personal income									Per capita personal income (dollars)	Population (persons)	Total employment
		Earnings by place of work			Less: Contributions for government social insurance	Plus: Adjustment for residence	Equals: Net earnings by place of residence	Plus: Dividends, interest, and rent	Plus: Personal current transfer receipts				
		Nonfarm	Farm	Total									
1970	1,159,537	1,037,134	7,477	1,044,611	70,694	-47,119	926,798	152,106	80,633		4,268	271,661	127,617
1971	1,225,662	1,078,154	10,151	1,088,305	75,477	-49,244	963,584	161,845	100,233		4,520	271,149	123,947
1972	1,347,906	1,197,538	10,445	1,207,983	89,405	-54,132	1,064,446	173,515	109,945		4,971	271,136	129,119
1973	1,514,022	1,357,586	17,225	1,374,811	117,718	-61,989	1,195,104	193,615	125,303		5,542	273,201	137,581
1974	1,648,813	1,471,989	7,638	1,479,627	132,750	-65,013	1,281,864	221,266	145,683		6,001	274,734	139,257
1975	1,771,977	1,506,373	20,025	1,526,398	130,653	-64,216	1,331,529	247,273	193,175		6,461	274,255	133,933
1976	1,954,262	1,680,951	14,558	1,695,509	148,983	-67,769	1,478,757	262,739	212,766		7,142	273,627	136,512
1977	2,147,121	1,867,418	12,755	1,880,173	167,649	-73,700	1,638,824	289,416	218,881		7,844	273,731	140,705
1978	2,411,618	2,151,444	12,304	2,163,748	200,479	-97,260	1,866,009	323,704	221,905		8,736	276,063	147,308
1979	2,670,822	2,380,236	18,108	2,398,344	228,962	-107,380	2,062,002	362,670	246,150		9,644	276,951	150,437
1980	2,879,211	2,460,167	-577	2,459,590	233,655	-110,797	2,115,138	449,904	314,169		10,289	279,829	144,840
1981	3,197,369	2,647,797	16,659	2,664,456	268,965	-116,032	2,279,459	557,943	359,967		11,395	280,591	144,654
1982	3,296,116	2,566,700	12,458	2,579,158	262,571	-91,246	2,225,341	646,454	424,321		11,818	278,911	137,928
1983	3,418,103	2,658,681	-11,555	2,647,126	274,372	-90,876	2,281,878	691,373	444,852		12,324	277,354	136,046
1984	3,821,742	3,015,012	24,062	3,039,074	324,914	-112,102	2,602,058	788,929	430,755		13,796	277,028	143,578
1985	4,047,623	3,217,149	40,072	3,257,221	353,131	-125,680	2,778,410	814,119	455,094		14,527	278,623	147,717
1986	4,275,432	3,442,237	30,056	3,472,293	377,817	-144,776	2,949,700	844,819	480,913		15,344	278,638	151,509
1987	4,496,418	3,652,881	27,066	3,679,947	393,105	-148,052	3,138,790	852,522	505,106		16,113	279,051	154,960
1988	4,900,117	4,082,793	15,656	4,098,449	449,313	-169,677	3,479,459	893,922	526,736		17,515	279,763	161,185
1989	5,232,014	4,252,510	28,887	4,281,397	468,940	-162,782	3,649,675	1,015,552	566,787		18,582	281,563	163,402
1990	5,410,360	4,430,812	30,072	4,460,884	476,472	-165,574	3,818,838	974,064	617,458		19,004	284,702	167,347
1991	5,503,581	4,451,916	12,533	4,464,449	489,171	-128,098	3,847,180	977,499	678,902		18,985	289,895	165,457
1992	5,956,294	4,696,544	21,945	4,718,489	506,653	-108,352	4,103,484	1,063,965	788,845		20,239	294,298	165,482
1993	6,184,415	4,897,481	12,180	4,909,661	536,299	-100,525	4,272,837	1,082,168	829,410		20,713	298,582	168,660
1994	6,655,062	5,373,938	27,611	5,401,549	594,036	-123,319	4,684,194	1,136,571	834,297		22,024	302,172	175,923
1995	7,119,982	5,743,297	18,000	5,761,297	632,098	-119,271	5,009,928	1,214,523	895,531		23,293	305,671	184,417
1996	7,468,546	5,937,939	42,600	5,980,539	646,241	-115,150	5,219,148	1,306,256	943,142		24,120	309,644	186,765
1997	7,790,303	6,163,299	28,260	6,191,559	666,793	-99,844	5,424,922	1,394,158	971,223		24,942	312,342	188,652
1998	8,178,106	6,473,651	27,935	6,501,586	694,561	-106,901	5,700,124	1,459,582	1,018,400		25,960	315,025	191,094
1999	8,456,830	6,754,650	20,167	6,774,817	714,422	-75,886	5,984,509	1,430,369	1,041,952		26,628	317,596	192,207
2000	8,833,567	6,965,899	23,190	6,989,089	726,847	-66,346	6,195,896	1,531,692	1,105,979		27,516	321,033	194,309
2001	8,895,297	6,963,916	18,446	6,982,362	744,770	-49,998	6,187,594	1,469,096	1,238,607		27,520	323,229	190,211
2002	9,142,811	7,160,683	10,518	7,171,201	761,573	-16,441	6,393,187	1,398,250	1,351,374		28,067	325,747	188,282
2003	9,425,418	7,283,079	11,240	7,294,319	776,965	16,979	6,534,333	1,462,786	1,428,299		28,608	329,472	187,496
2004	9,679,509	7,490,968	28,295	7,519,263	811,631	59,490	6,767,122	1,412,038	1,500,349		29,135	332,230	189,037
2005	10,128,713	7,819,803	10,663	7,830,466	873,332	131,752	7,088,886	1,397,122	1,642,705		30,154	335,903	189,309
2006	11,054,355	8,335,312	9,214	8,344,526	922,879	301,613	7,723,260	1,598,798	1,732,297		32,398	341,202	192,709
2007	11,671,717	8,640,349	33,774	8,674,123	956,914	385,445	8,102,654	1,648,444	1,920,619		33,587	347,503	196,107
2008	11,914,483	8,630,815	35,278	8,666,093	954,349	366,529	8,078,273	1,672,304	2,163,906		34,048	349,937	193,940
2009	11,607,353	7,994,230	7,049	8,001,279	879,951	369,862	7,491,190	1,627,579	2,488,584		33,186	349,766	180,909
2010	11,821,395	8,052,852	5,391	8,058,243	899,424	333,037	7,491,856	1,626,787	2,702,752		33,844	349,295	178,790
2011	12,313,076	8,469,257	58,203	8,527,460	860,455	325,562	7,992,567	1,750,880	2,569,629		35,394	347,890	181,883
2012	12,685,422	8,820,375	16,518	8,836,893	903,240	318,419	8,252,072	1,871,485	2,561,865		36,684	345,803	183,484
2013	12,806,710	8,879,601	95,792	8,975,393	1,026,168	314,020	8,263,245	1,858,478	2,684,987		37,147	344,755	182,716
2014	13,091,627	9,152,299	17,107	9,169,406	1,051,429	326,838	8,444,815	1,936,108	2,710,704		38,234	342,411	185,897

Personal Income and Employment by Area: Rocky Mount, NC

(Thousands of dollars, except as noted.)

Year	Personal income, total	Earnings by place of work			Less: Contributions for government social insurance	Plus: Adjustment for residence	Equals: Net earnings by place of residence	Plus: Dividends, interest, and rent	Plus: Personal current transfer receipts	Per capita personal income (dollars)	Population (persons)	Total employment
		Nonfarm	Farm	Total								
1970	332,160	242,960	32,529	275,489	17,855	4,063	261,697	37,991	32,472	2,977	111,571	53,924
1971	363,181	272,750	28,080	300,830	20,676	4,255	284,409	41,583	37,189	3,234	112,296	54,910
1972	419,728	317,697	36,223	353,920	25,068	3,018	331,870	46,552	41,306	3,696	113,571	58,004
1973	490,175	370,396	52,346	422,742	33,369	615	389,988	52,965	47,222	4,261	115,045	61,874
1974	550,861	415,104	56,786	471,890	39,137	404	433,157	60,483	57,221	4,733	116,381	63,125
1975	593,716	435,805	53,180	488,985	40,477	190	448,698	67,204	77,814	5,023	118,189	60,327
1976	670,338	500,918	61,036	561,954	47,479	-2,679	511,796	73,812	84,730	5,604	119,609	62,983
1977	712,214	555,157	37,517	592,674	52,255	-4,103	536,316	84,175	91,723	5,866	121,414	64,333
1978	804,557	624,743	53,060	677,803	60,064	-7,067	610,672	94,448	99,437	6,573	122,406	65,387
1979	850,950	691,137	13,722	704,859	68,664	-7,586	628,609	107,125	115,216	6,904	123,247	66,769
1980	943,365	741,854	15,654	757,508	73,744	-8,763	675,001	131,300	137,064	7,641	123,463	65,511
1981	1,100,202	830,197	51,760	881,957	88,646	-13,337	779,974	162,610	157,618	8,845	124,388	66,742
1982	1,177,266	864,974	57,823	922,797	93,013	-14,701	815,083	186,993	175,190	9,379	125,524	64,937
1983	1,255,415	956,154	34,109	990,263	103,210	-18,223	868,830	198,041	188,544	9,926	126,478	66,048
1984	1,416,542	1,064,731	66,167	1,130,898	118,052	-24,679	988,167	229,067	199,308	11,144	127,115	68,538
1985	1,511,824	1,145,798	62,735	1,208,533	129,135	-28,222	1,051,176	248,056	212,592	11,738	128,799	69,053
1986	1,600,915	1,257,225	47,421	1,304,646	144,462	-39,790	1,120,394	258,710	221,811	12,331	129,830	71,452
1987	1,708,266	1,358,312	60,304	1,418,616	153,734	-51,461	1,213,421	265,284	229,561	13,029	131,116	71,862
1988	1,884,671	1,502,040	81,572	1,583,612	174,782	-63,498	1,345,332	293,001	246,338	14,297	131,826	75,005
1989	2,030,764	1,583,780	82,267	1,666,047	184,173	-71,747	1,410,127	348,628	272,009	15,343	132,358	76,775
1990	2,112,436	1,647,157	96,111	1,743,268	196,221	-90,293	1,456,754	351,457	304,225	15,804	133,668	76,391
1991	2,193,346	1,720,496	96,229	1,816,725	207,524	-111,285	1,497,916	349,216	346,214	16,270	134,810	76,478
1992	2,336,456	1,831,629	90,608	1,922,237	218,040	-110,455	1,593,742	358,291	384,423	17,193	135,899	77,279
1993	2,470,021	1,911,553	94,901	2,006,454	228,571	-103,070	1,674,813	377,817	417,391	17,996	137,253	77,560
1994	2,589,091	1,999,545	109,109	2,108,654	241,277	-102,540	1,764,837	392,840	431,414	18,628	138,990	77,617
1995	2,748,669	2,109,736	112,631	2,222,367	254,933	-127,108	1,840,326	424,433	483,910	19,562	140,508	80,590
1996	2,968,562	2,188,906	117,978	2,306,884	261,395	-77,186	1,968,303	470,549	529,710	20,969	141,570	81,061
1997	3,179,138	2,286,353	148,423	2,434,776	270,265	-36,055	2,128,456	500,161	550,521	22,262	142,807	79,237
1998	3,294,341	2,375,839	127,184	2,503,023	279,965	-35,801	2,187,257	539,577	567,507	23,053	142,903	78,711
1999	3,376,830	2,474,629	70,097	2,544,726	290,478	-28,104	2,226,144	531,894	618,792	23,559	143,333	78,754
2000	3,550,475	2,580,439	122,547	2,702,986	301,353	-37,755	2,363,878	557,674	628,923	24,804	143,139	79,552
2001	3,695,655	2,682,925	112,087	2,795,012	311,283	-52,711	2,431,018	572,475	692,162	25,658	144,034	78,461
2002	3,695,103	2,704,788	48,530	2,753,318	310,601	-41,580	2,401,137	542,389	751,577	25,537	144,698	77,541
2003	3,779,249	2,752,242	50,330	2,802,572	322,681	-28,571	2,451,320	547,670	780,259	25,977	145,487	76,838
2004	4,020,787	2,875,800	77,667	2,953,467	333,682	-14,698	2,605,087	587,181	828,519	27,478	146,326	77,512
2005	4,179,485	2,932,708	106,538	3,039,246	346,119	3,124	2,696,251	585,027	898,207	28,427	147,027	77,579
2006	4,395,710	3,074,097	82,634	3,156,731	365,676	24,323	2,815,378	612,082	968,250	29,649	148,256	79,916
2007	4,606,974	3,165,744	61,343	3,227,087	383,776	46,768	2,890,079	691,982	1,024,913	30,786	149,644	81,910
2008	4,877,012	3,194,521	85,127	3,279,648	388,974	66,410	2,957,084	747,152	1,172,776	32,269	151,138	80,194
2009	4,936,826	3,143,013	92,623	3,235,636	377,683	65,382	2,923,335	722,000	1,291,491	32,537	151,729	76,260
2010	4,939,297	3,110,585	79,338	3,189,923	365,901	103,738	2,927,760	657,775	1,353,762	32,392	152,484	74,975
2011	5,003,835	3,021,094	75,295	3,096,389	331,650	114,854	2,879,593	741,172	1,383,070	32,954	151,845	76,255
2012	5,243,866	3,181,585	90,386	3,271,971	338,716	118,998	3,052,253	763,636	1,427,977	34,720	151,034	74,291
2013	5,113,802	3,002,408	95,542	3,097,950	371,592	150,599	2,876,957	803,926	1,432,919	34,066	150,114	73,587
2014	5,306,397	3,072,911	113,500	3,186,411	379,840	184,737	2,991,308	832,258	1,482,831	35,544	149,290	73,736

Personal Income and Employment by Area: Rome, GA

(Thousands of dollars, except as noted.)

| Year | Personal income, total | Derivation of personal income | | | | | | | | | Per capita personal income (dollars) | Population (persons) | Total employment |
| | | Earnings by place of work | | | Less: Contributions for government social insurance | Plus: Adjustment for residence | Equals: Net earnings by place of residence | Plus: Dividends, interest, and rent | Plus: Personal current transfer receipts | | | |
		Nonfarm	Farm	Total								
1970	249,262	214,446	1,300	215,746	14,268	-1,948	199,530	27,718	22,014	3,366	74,051	34,937
1971	271,710	232,316	1,480	233,796	16,110	-2,704	214,982	30,971	25,757	3,587	75,747	35,869
1972	303,353	262,057	1,752	263,809	19,108	-4,207	240,494	34,309	28,550	3,978	76,267	37,626
1973	341,924	296,880	2,816	299,696	24,839	-4,275	270,582	38,075	33,267	4,431	77,161	39,299
1974	377,310	323,667	1,544	325,211	28,021	-5,108	292,082	43,661	41,567	4,838	77,988	39,874
1975	401,672	326,718	1,467	328,185	27,711	-5,320	295,154	49,564	56,954	5,090	78,917	37,308
1976	445,055	368,650	1,443	370,093	31,912	-6,190	331,991	53,086	59,978	5,598	79,499	38,135
1977	487,092	406,113	1,192	407,305	35,013	-6,534	365,758	58,663	62,671	6,049	80,526	38,921
1978	530,609	442,837	1,222	444,059	39,348	-5,752	398,959	64,655	66,995	6,617	80,194	39,774
1979	589,254	490,334	3,957	494,291	45,262	-7,289	441,740	72,705	74,809	7,406	79,565	40,267
1980	649,889	523,376	925	524,301	48,203	-6,324	469,774	90,523	89,592	8,138	79,860	39,476
1981	712,480	556,262	2,734	558,996	54,995	-6,796	497,205	111,999	103,276	8,912	79,948	39,772
1982	741,824	564,404	4,178	568,582	56,719	-10,506	501,357	125,839	114,628	9,285	79,897	38,189
1983	795,976	605,330	1,948	607,278	61,168	-12,477	533,633	139,309	123,034	10,055	79,163	37,795
1984	863,462	656,117	2,528	658,645	68,094	-11,140	579,411	153,894	130,157	10,899	79,223	39,730
1985	919,692	701,310	1,250	702,560	74,220	-10,825	617,515	163,062	139,115	11,566	79,520	40,092
1986	994,470	761,781	583	762,364	81,288	-12,087	668,989	177,971	147,510	12,461	79,804	41,120
1987	1,069,671	829,592	-317	829,275	87,534	-13,587	728,154	187,284	154,233	13,324	80,281	42,515
1988	1,150,375	889,781	2,433	892,214	96,776	-14,080	781,358	199,091	169,926	14,194	81,046	43,653
1989	1,233,541	938,577	3,481	942,058	102,938	-15,860	823,260	229,867	180,414	15,175	81,290	44,055
1990	1,319,542	1,010,425	3,517	1,013,942	110,075	-23,154	880,713	239,582	199,247	16,194	81,483	44,628
1991	1,392,621	1,071,310	4,878	1,076,188	118,413	-33,229	924,546	242,060	226,015	16,927	82,274	44,515
1992	1,500,316	1,167,092	6,001	1,173,093	126,865	-42,205	1,004,023	246,277	250,016	18,054	83,100	45,569
1993	1,557,505	1,208,448	5,358	1,213,806	131,717	-43,115	1,038,974	251,444	267,087	18,521	84,094	47,211
1994	1,659,190	1,295,516	6,647	1,302,163	142,393	-51,416	1,108,354	268,511	282,325	19,540	84,911	49,360
1995	1,714,868	1,303,839	5,181	1,309,020	143,174	-43,791	1,122,055	289,986	302,827	19,926	86,063	49,299
1996	1,826,206	1,381,555	7,193	1,388,748	149,583	-50,128	1,189,037	316,971	320,198	20,976	87,061	49,613
1997	1,893,489	1,423,403	6,980	1,430,383	151,216	-47,895	1,231,272	333,979	328,238	21,519	87,991	50,251
1998	1,972,718	1,469,772	7,916	1,477,688	156,810	-40,300	1,280,578	352,500	339,640	22,207	88,833	50,002
1999	2,070,893	1,572,389	7,629	1,580,018	164,873	-41,390	1,373,755	334,256	362,882	23,097	89,659	49,926
2000	2,162,122	1,600,423	6,027	1,606,450	168,088	-34,770	1,403,592	373,642	384,888	23,802	90,837	50,477
2001	2,304,619	1,704,518	9,422	1,713,940	179,627	-47,118	1,487,195	392,360	425,064	25,275	91,181	50,971
2002	2,405,718	1,790,104	4,634	1,794,738	187,756	-62,322	1,544,660	385,165	475,893	25,981	92,597	50,885
2003	2,488,508	1,865,474	6,361	1,871,835	194,361	-78,710	1,598,764	413,994	475,750	26,604	93,539	51,854
2004	2,624,608	2,000,357	10,672	2,011,029	215,562	-97,765	1,697,702	397,471	529,435	27,917	94,014	53,242
2005	2,612,335	1,921,017	11,941	1,932,958	208,652	-106,547	1,617,759	424,082	570,494	27,693	94,332	53,147
2006	2,737,259	2,052,526	5,453	2,057,979	222,952	-126,320	1,708,707	434,273	594,279	28,763	95,165	54,622
2007	2,825,268	2,055,554	10,013	2,065,567	219,968	-139,320	1,706,279	497,016	621,973	29,644	95,308	54,116
2008	2,912,689	2,111,886	11,026	2,122,912	233,641	-155,173	1,734,098	505,255	673,336	30,365	95,922	52,534
2009	2,856,115	2,059,786	9,354	2,069,140	229,539	-178,290	1,661,311	451,541	743,263	29,633	96,383	50,805
2010	2,922,413	2,074,967	6,680	2,081,647	236,379	-183,155	1,662,113	449,169	811,131	30,318	96,393	50,320
2011	3,032,931	2,081,953	3,463	2,085,416	211,829	-182,546	1,691,041	488,551	853,339	31,533	96,182	50,192
2012	3,062,655	2,126,125	16,249	2,142,374	217,111	-183,539	1,741,724	481,635	839,296	31,881	96,066	50,245
2013	3,115,810	2,170,114	22,030	2,192,144	248,464	-171,784	1,771,896	491,344	852,570	32,448	96,025	50,492
2014	3,237,764	2,253,900	24,373	2,278,273	257,053	-168,082	1,853,138	511,120	873,506	33,705	96,063	51,762

Personal Income and Employment by Area: Sacramento-Arden-Arcade-Roseville, CA

(Thousands of dollars, except as noted.)

Year	Personal income, total	Derivation of personal income								Per capita personal income (dollars)	Population (persons)	Total employment
		Earnings by place of work			Less: Contributions for government social insurance	Plus: Adjustment for residence	Equals: Net earnings by place of residence	Plus: Dividends, interest, and rent	Plus: Personal current transfer receipts			
		Nonfarm	Farm	Total								
1970	4,049,580	3,044,572	78,526	3,123,098	168,077	45,970	3,000,991	636,687	411,902	4,753	852,036	360,459
1971	4,454,738	3,342,347	79,496	3,421,843	189,969	46,108	3,277,982	709,829	466,927	5,085	876,053	368,520
1972	4,918,294	3,707,128	99,494	3,806,622	223,277	48,386	3,631,731	781,566	504,997	5,449	902,647	385,583
1973	5,419,529	4,065,899	137,550	4,203,449	277,681	52,583	3,978,351	882,187	558,991	5,983	905,830	400,639
1974	6,105,583	4,480,402	192,552	4,672,954	315,345	58,423	4,416,032	1,022,949	666,602	6,584	927,304	417,125
1975	6,847,440	4,972,881	162,706	5,135,587	346,833	72,741	4,861,495	1,150,639	835,306	7,217	948,850	431,998
1976	7,560,735	5,587,045	109,773	5,696,818	400,782	77,025	5,373,061	1,253,796	933,878	7,786	971,060	450,281
1977	8,455,970	6,275,382	134,273	6,409,655	460,961	85,669	6,034,363	1,411,746	1,009,861	8,455	1,000,056	471,705
1978	9,703,076	7,213,350	141,698	7,355,048	546,840	102,761	6,910,969	1,672,083	1,120,024	9,323	1,040,724	504,114
1979	11,001,747	8,169,952	160,588	8,330,540	655,928	107,427	7,782,039	1,936,566	1,283,142	10,268	1,071,481	532,619
1980	12,342,296	8,807,178	214,973	9,022,151	690,741	132,483	8,463,893	2,338,237	1,540,166	11,150	1,106,955	544,041
1981	13,638,072	9,530,081	150,893	9,680,974	819,362	117,156	8,978,768	2,805,891	1,853,413	12,033	1,133,346	557,728
1982	14,592,605	10,123,980	117,568	10,241,548	891,663	124,934	9,474,819	3,090,371	2,027,415	12,488	1,168,540	565,530
1983	15,791,853	10,995,423	70,342	11,065,765	1,007,967	131,727	10,189,525	3,452,872	2,149,456	13,226	1,193,993	586,240
1984	17,734,095	12,467,971	159,386	12,627,357	1,188,698	135,767	11,574,426	3,886,538	2,273,131	14,555	1,218,388	613,520
1985	19,629,719	14,009,135	158,081	14,167,216	1,356,568	130,886	12,941,534	4,210,463	2,477,722	15,694	1,250,764	649,028
1986	21,442,082	15,539,688	154,651	15,694,339	1,532,953	132,540	14,293,926	4,463,864	2,684,292	16,685	1,285,092	678,664
1987	23,266,522	17,158,953	194,126	17,353,079	1,705,368	130,215	15,777,926	4,647,552	2,841,044	17,477	1,331,264	718,562
1988	25,355,890	18,876,199	194,123	19,070,322	1,951,752	139,723	17,258,293	5,000,056	3,097,541	18,389	1,378,887	756,390
1989	28,134,518	20,739,965	199,257	20,939,222	2,156,022	122,235	18,905,435	5,801,063	3,428,020	19,695	1,428,491	791,265
1990	30,775,461	23,002,882	219,420	23,222,302	2,374,162	116,592	20,964,732	5,980,147	3,830,582	20,228	1,521,462	837,598
1991	32,538,098	24,450,668	189,703	24,640,371	2,540,277	74,195	22,174,289	6,086,801	4,277,008	20,765	1,566,994	846,203
1992	34,537,828	25,846,004	192,455	26,038,459	2,667,131	18,142	23,389,470	6,178,214	4,970,144	21,703	1,591,373	838,258
1993	35,404,269	26,386,325	236,163	26,622,488	2,737,823	36,250	23,920,915	6,264,983	5,218,371	22,017	1,608,074	837,172
1994	37,409,617	28,147,438	232,174	28,379,612	2,918,571	-11,273	25,449,768	6,647,801	5,312,048	23,072	1,621,444	870,499
1995	39,917,590	29,929,343	215,440	30,144,783	3,055,333	-82,731	27,006,719	7,303,311	5,607,560	24,265	1,645,098	886,610
1996	41,851,933	31,302,371	236,265	31,538,636	3,128,674	-102,301	28,307,661	7,633,327	5,910,945	25,022	1,672,583	914,825
1997	44,616,670	33,658,181	224,093	33,882,274	3,324,374	-164,495	30,393,405	8,265,040	5,958,225	26,238	1,700,488	938,908
1998	48,139,119	36,798,122	198,992	36,997,114	3,591,860	-191,762	33,213,492	8,604,915	6,320,712	27,796	1,731,847	974,802
1999	51,742,834	40,076,463	274,838	40,351,301	3,918,258	-171,543	36,261,500	8,800,313	6,681,021	29,279	1,767,237	1,019,481
2000	56,520,568	44,431,283	234,096	44,665,379	4,281,641	-152,310	40,231,428	9,300,935	6,988,205	31,262	1,807,949	1,044,442
2001	60,552,964	47,901,697	203,322	48,105,019	4,772,113	-227,778	43,105,128	9,649,147	7,798,689	32,445	1,866,310	1,086,307
2002	63,274,211	50,744,445	202,883	50,947,328	5,114,218	-343,292	45,489,818	9,500,383	8,284,010	32,895	1,923,508	1,104,691
2003	67,512,263	53,986,128	219,412	54,205,540	5,500,060	-422,276	48,283,204	10,462,824	8,766,235	34,261	1,970,542	1,123,527
2004	72,418,897	57,767,086	254,010	58,021,096	6,038,794	-329,075	51,653,227	11,441,355	9,324,315	36,053	2,008,663	1,158,564
2005	76,133,465	61,136,842	231,933	61,368,775	6,414,895	-401,293	54,552,587	11,679,749	9,901,129	37,415	2,034,850	1,192,995
2006	80,990,667	64,166,056	218,542	64,384,598	6,528,788	-252,432	57,603,378	12,551,395	10,835,894	39,356	2,057,885	1,216,935
2007	84,493,872	65,855,979	312,641	66,168,620	6,553,105	-153,142	59,462,373	13,459,749	11,571,750	40,579	2,082,217	1,235,982
2008	87,408,600	66,299,622	298,148	66,597,770	6,617,131	-274,985	59,705,654	14,542,871	13,160,075	41,459	2,108,310	1,216,844
2009	85,777,065	63,900,277	368,096	64,268,373	6,444,163	-253,120	57,571,090	13,568,866	14,637,109	40,221	2,132,657	1,172,441
2010	87,541,827	63,941,488	263,799	64,205,287	6,348,573	-162,073	57,694,641	13,473,617	16,373,569	40,634	2,154,382	1,146,862
2011	92,604,093	66,762,521	303,307	67,065,828	5,933,029	-175,321	60,957,478	15,102,557	16,544,058	42,562	2,175,727	1,153,817
2012	98,002,289	70,778,642	380,175	71,158,817	6,165,189	-83,956	64,909,672	16,268,590	16,824,027	44,646	2,195,087	1,189,777
2013	100,936,181	72,804,198	419,053	73,223,251	7,181,725	-40,647	66,000,879	17,295,108	17,640,194	45,518	2,217,515	1,224,713
2014	105,153,710	75,876,783	330,457	76,207,240	7,517,250	-5,623	68,684,367	17,985,339	18,484,004	46,852	2,244,397	1,251,881

Personal Income and Employment by Area: Saginaw-Saginaw Township North, MI

(Thousands of dollars, except as noted.)

Year	Personal income, total	Earnings by place of work			Less: Contributions for government social insurance	Plus: Adjustment for residence	Equals: Net earnings by place of residence	Plus: Dividends, interest, and rent	Plus: Personal current transfer receipts	Per capita personal income (dollars)	Population (persons)	Total employment
		Nonfarm	Farm	Total								
1970	829,218	726,446	9,119	735,565	51,926	-38,433	645,206	107,518	76,494	3,763	220,370	84,309
1971	963,089	866,735	7,978	874,713	63,632	-52,805	758,276	114,803	90,010	4,315	223,170	89,057
1972	1,068,550	965,439	11,033	976,472	75,246	-58,760	842,466	123,294	102,790	4,769	224,074	92,541
1973	1,195,899	1,088,095	19,860	1,107,955	98,608	-66,049	943,298	134,543	118,058	5,310	225,199	96,459
1974	1,261,894	1,085,560	39,378	1,124,938	101,700	-56,938	966,300	151,239	144,355	5,586	225,920	95,113
1975	1,364,600	1,159,011	19,777	1,178,788	106,544	-58,189	1,014,055	166,695	183,850	6,045	225,723	92,153
1976	1,561,238	1,395,292	13,623	1,408,915	130,291	-84,199	1,194,425	180,193	186,620	6,905	226,118	96,864
1977	1,747,856	1,597,476	14,954	1,612,430	148,983	-110,380	1,353,067	202,695	192,094	7,705	226,861	100,874
1978	1,940,543	1,796,710	14,664	1,811,374	172,866	-129,188	1,509,320	220,797	210,426	8,544	227,115	104,515
1979	2,097,808	1,918,160	16,481	1,934,641	190,933	-140,449	1,603,259	248,399	246,150	9,252	226,732	105,175
1980	2,220,706	1,870,944	19,111	1,890,055	183,724	-132,976	1,573,355	296,569	350,782	9,767	227,373	98,304
1981	2,366,525	2,019,409	14,596	2,034,005	214,908	-157,069	1,662,028	357,736	346,761	10,559	224,132	98,329
1982	2,359,930	1,903,069	3,440	1,906,509	205,352	-137,795	1,563,362	401,841	394,727	10,682	220,925	91,223
1983	2,508,481	2,059,745	-1,869	2,057,876	227,716	-163,106	1,667,054	428,792	412,635	11,518	217,784	91,228
1984	2,739,644	2,274,646	10,295	2,284,941	260,828	-199,170	1,824,943	489,166	425,535	12,642	216,710	94,924
1985	2,919,217	2,493,043	8,707	2,501,750	291,692	-243,656	1,966,402	515,279	437,536	13,575	215,040	98,880
1986	3,003,009	2,557,099	2,888	2,559,987	300,357	-257,043	2,002,587	539,433	460,989	13,969	214,972	99,967
1987	3,069,027	2,635,933	16,687	2,652,620	304,617	-292,872	2,055,131	541,979	471,917	14,335	214,098	103,044
1988	3,211,469	2,802,993	13,870	2,816,863	332,058	-329,930	2,154,875	564,470	492,124	15,040	213,522	105,620
1989	3,406,247	2,911,766	23,482	2,935,248	345,748	-357,820	2,231,680	637,920	536,647	16,044	212,303	107,071
1990	3,507,939	2,978,446	15,114	2,993,560	358,916	-352,156	2,282,488	639,989	585,462	16,541	212,071	106,622
1991	3,601,667	3,058,692	14,911	3,073,603	373,654	-368,210	2,331,739	623,084	646,844	16,958	212,384	105,668
1992	3,782,519	3,235,415	13,108	3,248,523	388,938	-394,198	2,465,387	635,962	681,170	17,807	212,421	107,274
1993	3,975,339	3,380,082	16,127	3,396,209	412,584	-408,097	2,575,528	669,494	730,317	18,737	212,165	107,006
1994	4,210,698	3,626,976	1,699	3,628,675	446,685	-445,488	2,736,502	730,817	743,379	19,837	212,262	109,557
1995	4,391,642	3,741,053	11,843	3,752,896	460,296	-433,046	2,859,554	766,353	765,735	20,708	212,076	112,965
1996	4,593,760	3,904,880	7,989	3,912,869	466,413	-440,031	3,006,425	799,337	787,998	21,676	211,927	115,285
1997	4,827,298	4,063,331	6,680	4,070,011	481,095	-441,282	3,147,634	829,827	849,837	22,834	211,406	116,361
1998	4,926,915	4,214,435	2,248	4,216,683	491,038	-492,266	3,233,379	842,920	850,616	23,368	210,839	114,772
1999	5,151,913	4,484,706	19,921	4,504,627	518,355	-573,126	3,413,146	809,374	929,393	24,486	210,400	116,650
2000	5,375,719	4,637,239	8,487	4,645,726	530,033	-550,464	3,565,229	844,900	965,590	25,611	209,899	118,132
2001	5,504,463	4,700,933	-1,232	4,699,701	547,377	-535,006	3,617,318	826,416	1,060,729	26,279	209,460	115,904
2002	5,366,363	4,589,865	14,368	4,604,233	536,160	-533,812	3,534,261	734,417	1,097,685	25,637	209,323	113,510
2003	5,467,894	4,677,132	12,194	4,689,326	542,872	-550,342	3,596,112	720,821	1,150,961	26,193	208,755	113,532
2004	5,607,105	4,694,564	18,262	4,712,826	549,106	-549,302	3,614,418	797,162	1,195,525	26,894	208,489	112,305
2005	5,652,610	4,674,881	17,956	4,692,837	551,110	-545,421	3,596,306	792,941	1,263,363	27,259	207,368	111,714
2006	5,775,428	4,781,650	23,398	4,805,048	576,104	-550,290	3,678,654	774,880	1,321,894	28,060	205,822	110,626
2007	5,890,306	4,664,460	27,170	4,691,630	566,137	-530,297	3,595,196	853,163	1,441,947	28,996	203,144	109,750
2008	5,971,334	4,478,166	41,625	4,519,791	549,160	-504,627	3,466,004	888,368	1,616,962	29,566	201,966	105,576
2009	5,883,670	4,358,113	21,661	4,379,774	540,259	-537,794	3,301,721	809,643	1,772,306	29,296	200,835	101,778
2010	6,047,505	4,420,688	25,793	4,446,481	543,710	-534,160	3,368,611	781,857	1,897,037	30,255	199,882	101,219
2011	6,277,336	4,597,482	62,447	4,659,929	505,834	-613,390	3,540,705	859,009	1,877,622	31,574	198,815	104,544
2012	6,323,352	4,639,958	62,176	4,702,134	513,616	-622,243	3,566,275	885,528	1,871,549	31,893	198,268	105,084
2013	6,419,235	4,715,194	47,148	4,762,342	592,536	-608,432	3,561,374	922,791	1,935,070	32,641	196,660	105,523
2014	6,640,133	4,860,084	29,334	4,889,418	609,762	-603,588	3,676,068	958,066	2,005,999	34,050	195,012	106,463

Personal Income and Employment by Area: St. Cloud, MN

(Thousands of dollars, except as noted.)

Year	Personal income, total	Earnings by place of work			Less: Contributions for government social insurance	Plus: Adjustment for residence	Equals: Net earnings by place of residence	Plus: Dividends, interest, and rent	Plus: Personal current transfer receipts	Per capita personal income (dollars)	Population (persons)	Total employment
		Nonfarm	Farm	Total								
1970	356,022	259,632	33,599	293,231	17,712	-2,262	273,257	48,607	34,158	3,049	116,762	45,611
1971	384,842	282,379	29,727	312,106	19,811	-891	291,404	53,288	40,150	3,235	118,978	46,936
1972	424,396	310,391	34,216	344,607	22,669	914	322,852	57,385	44,159	3,547	119,660	49,580
1973	500,958	352,544	60,194	412,738	29,713	1,779	384,804	64,810	51,344	4,108	121,957	53,110
1974	552,992	403,787	48,200	451,987	35,883	925	417,029	74,897	61,066	4,472	123,661	55,774
1975	606,489	448,155	35,997	484,152	38,868	-138	445,146	86,438	74,905	4,803	126,283	56,483
1976	667,316	500,060	29,564	529,624	44,340	589	485,873	94,757	86,686	5,235	127,477	57,890
1977	758,747	550,516	54,897	605,413	48,945	1,875	558,343	109,172	91,232	5,837	129,994	59,900
1978	847,350	634,342	48,700	683,042	58,620	1,655	626,077	123,008	98,265	6,461	131,145	62,454
1979	955,881	732,108	42,507	774,615	70,525	-384	703,706	141,395	110,780	7,219	132,420	66,254
1980	1,058,823	799,573	29,890	829,463	76,943	-2,115	750,405	175,072	133,346	7,915	133,782	67,330
1981	1,193,304	883,482	42,718	926,200	91,716	-10,480	824,004	214,907	154,393	8,825	135,211	67,644
1982	1,291,413	927,175	45,042	972,217	98,108	-15,018	859,091	258,366	173,956	9,488	136,115	67,216
1983	1,341,993	988,257	6,554	994,811	105,252	-17,188	872,371	280,109	189,513	9,792	137,048	68,777
1984	1,519,438	1,094,607	49,024	1,143,631	118,888	-16,531	1,008,212	309,965	201,261	11,007	138,037	71,557
1985	1,611,585	1,157,430	58,156	1,215,586	127,546	-16,352	1,071,688	327,239	212,658	11,562	139,387	73,891
1986	1,737,440	1,264,339	69,841	1,334,180	142,823	-22,204	1,169,153	348,286	220,001	12,332	140,892	77,336
1987	1,846,455	1,374,390	70,479	1,444,869	155,225	-28,731	1,260,913	357,661	227,881	12,975	142,314	81,199
1988	1,960,356	1,521,053	46,186	1,567,239	178,234	-39,435	1,349,570	371,395	239,391	13,532	144,873	85,778
1989	2,178,218	1,658,595	89,932	1,748,527	194,523	-48,628	1,505,376	408,411	264,431	14,809	147,087	89,177
1990	2,312,652	1,766,381	86,059	1,852,440	208,382	-57,809	1,586,249	445,306	281,097	15,410	150,078	90,903
1991	2,395,405	1,867,696	54,334	1,922,030	223,180	-62,860	1,635,990	454,027	305,388	15,779	151,812	93,550
1992	2,590,247	2,041,382	64,252	2,105,634	240,983	-65,188	1,799,463	461,111	329,673	16,882	153,430	95,350
1993	2,694,769	2,170,676	43,475	2,214,151	258,125	-72,897	1,883,129	466,352	345,288	17,330	155,495	97,771
1994	2,852,839	2,299,229	59,763	2,358,992	276,659	-72,813	2,009,520	482,380	360,939	18,140	157,264	100,598
1995	2,994,723	2,419,789	24,637	2,444,426	290,980	-81,030	2,072,416	536,430	385,877	18,808	159,224	105,687
1996	3,252,536	2,583,516	80,604	2,664,120	306,918	-84,848	2,272,354	569,352	410,830	20,257	160,563	108,022
1997	3,366,387	2,708,628	40,355	2,748,983	321,418	-88,103	2,339,462	606,526	420,399	20,750	162,234	107,758
1998	3,774,246	3,061,935	88,794	3,150,729	360,874	-121,522	2,668,333	665,564	440,349	23,105	163,352	110,630
1999	3,957,159	3,194,161	86,496	3,280,657	375,626	-82,340	2,822,691	671,266	463,202	23,916	165,463	112,358
2000	4,244,023	3,418,013	69,156	3,487,169	398,110	-75,340	3,013,719	729,833	500,471	25,241	168,139	115,324
2001	4,556,981	3,708,187	67,566	3,775,753	425,312	-112,112	3,238,329	755,250	563,402	26,714	170,587	118,630
2002	4,827,166	3,977,791	64,578	4,042,369	451,868	-125,089	3,465,412	743,069	618,685	27,883	173,123	119,743
2003	5,057,190	4,063,018	106,409	4,169,427	467,956	-101,352	3,600,119	801,204	655,867	28,872	175,161	119,866
2004	5,280,685	4,293,672	150,943	4,444,615	497,864	-102,008	3,844,743	739,880	696,062	29,858	176,860	121,846
2005	5,418,362	4,398,783	155,992	4,554,775	516,326	-100,294	3,938,155	739,571	740,636	30,233	179,222	124,669
2006	5,760,652	4,609,202	139,805	4,749,007	549,047	-102,000	4,097,960	835,956	826,736	31,674	181,873	126,815
2007	6,146,634	4,805,429	132,451	4,937,880	574,144	-100,136	4,263,600	962,551	920,483	33,297	184,598	129,447
2008	6,494,276	4,882,243	224,360	5,106,603	587,463	-107,135	4,412,005	1,001,799	1,080,472	34,821	186,507	129,584
2009	6,234,959	4,807,529	112,257	4,919,786	584,081	-268,582	4,067,123	972,469	1,195,367	33,145	188,114	126,215
2010	6,496,215	4,899,763	172,674	5,072,437	588,585	-251,067	4,232,785	933,065	1,330,365	34,337	189,188	124,401
2011	6,981,332	5,171,401	214,978	5,386,379	556,094	-276,204	4,554,081	1,063,379	1,363,872	36,730	190,072	127,262
2012	7,272,403	5,357,475	298,057	5,655,532	581,352	-282,996	4,791,184	1,138,695	1,342,524	38,173	190,513	129,020
2013	7,397,179	5,556,072	222,516	5,778,588	683,536	-275,546	4,819,506	1,186,367	1,391,306	38,658	191,348	130,899
2014	7,772,999	5,853,106	256,856	6,109,962	705,885	-324,420	5,079,657	1,235,827	1,457,515	40,396	192,418	133,375

Personal Income and Employment by Area: St. George, UT

(Thousands of dollars, except as noted.)

Year	Personal income, total	Earnings by place of work			Less: Contributions for government social insurance	Plus: Adjustment for residence	Equals: Net earnings by place of residence	Plus: Dividends, interest, and rent	Plus: Personal current transfer receipts	Per capita personal income (dollars)	Population (persons)	Total employment
		Nonfarm	Farm	Total								
1970	40,503	27,422	2,048	29,470	1,684	873	28,659	7,223	4,621	2,912	13,907	4,819
1971	45,014	29,906	1,736	31,642	1,903	1,208	30,947	8,527	5,540	2,994	15,037	5,015
1972	51,918	34,823	1,700	36,523	2,345	1,365	35,543	9,939	6,436	3,344	15,526	5,512
1973	60,014	39,387	2,851	42,238	3,041	1,653	40,850	11,311	7,853	3,664	16,379	5,916
1974	65,756	42,323	1,988	44,311	3,364	2,044	42,991	13,460	9,305	3,635	18,092	5,985
1975	76,363	48,009	1,533	49,542	3,693	2,441	48,290	16,260	11,813	4,127	18,504	6,192
1976	90,902	58,771	1,635	60,406	4,506	2,874	58,774	18,600	13,528	4,580	19,846	6,898
1977	105,767	68,044	1,709	69,753	5,261	3,557	68,049	22,186	15,532	5,066	20,877	7,443
1978	127,327	80,778	1,976	82,754	6,373	4,504	80,885	28,172	18,270	5,701	22,335	8,170
1979	153,061	98,582	2,130	100,712	8,500	5,181	97,393	34,048	21,620	6,372	24,019	9,054
1980	174,998	107,353	1,285	108,638	9,509	6,048	105,177	43,302	26,519	6,609	26,478	9,442
1981	194,629	113,397	611	114,008	11,006	6,566	109,568	52,206	32,855	6,934	28,070	9,582
1982	212,748	119,807	250	120,057	11,822	6,663	114,898	60,173	37,677	7,219	29,472	9,772
1983	239,397	136,596	-19	136,577	13,208	6,856	130,225	66,283	42,889	7,732	30,963	10,358
1984	291,357	173,752	228	173,980	16,853	6,883	164,010	79,663	47,684	8,879	32,816	11,851
1985	337,577	206,446	321	206,767	20,649	6,333	192,451	90,494	54,632	9,440	35,761	13,471
1986	386,985	240,059	578	240,637	24,226	5,963	222,374	102,183	62,428	9,796	39,503	14,907
1987	427,193	260,464	51	260,515	26,301	6,603	240,817	113,703	72,673	9,986	42,781	16,230
1988	466,931	282,215	811	283,026	30,569	7,717	260,174	126,223	80,534	10,463	44,627	17,503
1989	527,523	312,119	1,128	313,247	35,776	8,669	286,140	149,989	91,394	11,285	46,744	18,975
1990	607,619	378,324	1,938	380,262	43,610	8,738	345,390	156,792	105,437	12,354	49,183	21,258
1991	694,080	442,329	638	442,967	51,360	7,268	398,875	170,687	124,518	13,143	52,811	22,774
1992	773,935	489,194	1,521	490,715	56,974	8,985	442,726	187,760	143,449	13,735	56,349	24,084
1993	906,306	575,507	1,774	577,281	67,564	9,477	519,194	219,525	167,587	14,942	60,656	27,249
1994	1,054,943	698,874	203	699,077	83,211	7,912	623,778	249,841	181,324	15,865	66,493	33,162
1995	1,172,766	775,280	-872	774,408	93,859	9,236	689,785	276,299	206,682	16,230	72,261	35,711
1996	1,305,588	855,787	-1,000	854,787	101,009	12,298	766,076	308,819	230,693	16,814	77,647	38,801
1997	1,416,091	917,223	-480	916,743	106,487	15,633	825,889	337,614	252,588	17,371	81,520	40,701
1998	1,558,008	1,012,144	-314	1,011,830	115,874	18,035	913,991	375,491	268,526	18,365	84,837	42,665
1999	1,667,548	1,094,080	-682	1,093,398	123,190	21,511	991,719	388,440	287,389	18,939	88,049	44,720
2000	1,796,313	1,151,511	-626	1,150,885	131,483	24,904	1,044,306	431,345	320,662	19,695	91,206	47,117
2001	1,951,053	1,272,330	715	1,273,045	145,159	23,460	1,151,346	443,909	355,798	20,643	94,512	49,206
2002	2,058,581	1,385,739	-1,992	1,383,747	159,537	23,757	1,247,967	418,811	391,803	20,736	99,274	51,822
2003	2,196,038	1,483,186	112	1,483,298	175,728	24,378	1,331,948	435,653	428,437	21,078	104,188	54,093
2004	2,464,830	1,683,602	1,142	1,684,744	203,702	26,569	1,507,611	471,231	485,988	22,365	110,207	59,780
2005	2,853,691	1,949,955	894	1,950,849	238,029	29,186	1,742,006	571,611	540,074	23,981	119,000	65,603
2006	3,247,928	2,289,319	-1,638	2,287,681	274,247	32,517	2,045,951	611,090	590,887	25,615	126,796	71,114
2007	3,568,510	2,418,902	-4,465	2,414,437	289,945	33,199	2,157,691	753,766	657,053	26,978	132,277	74,922
2008	3,718,464	2,368,353	-4,117	2,364,236	285,173	30,792	2,109,855	846,407	762,202	27,432	135,552	74,794
2009	3,633,271	2,229,629	-3,377	2,226,252	268,940	29,263	1,986,575	780,954	865,742	26,503	137,088	71,047
2010	3,673,266	2,176,245	-2,954	2,173,291	264,132	24,228	1,933,387	792,553	947,326	26,540	138,406	68,855
2011	3,847,546	2,266,052	-466	2,265,586	253,021	18,897	2,031,462	838,928	977,156	27,191	141,502	70,968
2012	4,061,031	2,397,593	-1,127	2,396,466	265,660	17,939	2,148,745	915,092	997,194	28,076	144,643	73,481
2013	4,255,580	2,568,277	2,266	2,570,543	317,327	15,069	2,268,285	943,928	1,043,367	28,809	147,719	76,783
2014	4,506,565	2,745,094	2,690	2,747,784	341,355	14,241	2,420,670	988,292	1,097,603	29,659	151,948	80,218

Personal Income and Employment by Area: St. Joseph, MO-KS

(Thousands of dollars, except as noted.)

Year	Personal income, total	Earnings by place of work			Less: Contributions for government social insurance	Plus: Adjustment for residence	Equals: Net earnings by place of residence	Plus: Dividends, interest, and rent	Plus: Personal current transfer receipts	Per capita personal income (dollars)	Population (persons)	Total employment
		Nonfarm	Farm	Total								
1970	412,527	289,210	28,192	317,402	19,881	3,497	301,018	63,949	47,560	3,573	115,462	49,904
1971	445,397	311,174	27,784	338,958	22,133	4,876	321,701	69,119	54,577	3,805	117,065	50,202
1972	487,780	334,663	37,538	372,201	24,893	6,153	353,461	74,711	59,608	4,115	118,538	50,712
1973	542,678	360,349	53,986	414,335	31,136	7,792	390,991	82,724	68,963	4,588	118,278	51,864
1974	569,030	391,081	31,642	422,723	35,070	8,081	395,734	94,244	79,052	4,819	118,091	52,490
1975	625,007	421,077	30,026	451,103	36,835	11,373	425,641	103,497	95,869	5,255	118,925	52,020
1976	675,490	476,502	15,865	492,367	42,255	12,396	462,508	109,887	103,095	5,637	119,830	53,138
1977	746,111	519,404	25,614	545,018	46,062	15,930	514,886	122,632	108,593	6,213	120,097	53,528
1978	824,757	569,565	35,404	604,969	52,061	20,700	573,608	135,335	115,814	6,874	119,976	54,529
1979	922,220	625,569	45,851	671,420	59,164	25,508	637,764	153,455	131,001	7,711	119,604	55,845
1980	1,000,286	685,407	7,578	692,985	64,792	25,688	653,881	190,023	156,382	8,388	119,251	56,082
1981	1,135,436	730,467	37,359	767,826	74,086	27,900	721,640	234,802	178,994	9,575	118,583	55,596
1982	1,215,369	773,509	20,054	793,563	80,240	25,554	738,877	281,745	194,747	10,314	117,842	55,548
1983	1,254,453	804,934	-5,093	799,841	83,608	26,883	743,116	302,614	208,723	10,669	117,584	56,265
1984	1,368,100	871,983	9,717	881,700	92,793	26,479	815,386	332,864	219,850	11,657	117,358	57,192
1985	1,458,243	909,332	47,897	957,229	98,336	27,973	886,866	341,423	229,954	12,491	116,748	57,089
1986	1,497,212	940,599	34,300	974,899	101,853	28,889	901,935	351,572	243,705	12,852	116,500	56,485
1987	1,535,531	988,467	30,352	1,018,819	106,092	28,760	941,487	347,206	246,838	13,223	116,125	56,308
1988	1,601,482	1,072,257	16,741	1,088,998	119,702	26,183	995,479	354,741	251,262	13,891	115,289	57,352
1989	1,733,976	1,157,760	19,612	1,177,372	130,067	22,583	1,069,888	387,627	276,461	14,959	115,917	59,405
1990	1,775,061	1,204,585	25,060	1,229,645	137,542	16,310	1,108,413	377,123	289,525	15,301	116,008	60,198
1991	1,869,928	1,250,392	22,232	1,272,624	145,062	16,401	1,143,963	391,115	334,850	16,046	116,534	59,704
1992	1,982,355	1,308,015	38,199	1,346,214	149,135	22,543	1,219,622	406,761	355,972	16,889	117,377	59,547
1993	2,037,048	1,361,040	15,992	1,377,032	156,545	22,052	1,242,539	411,821	382,688	17,241	118,153	60,305
1994	2,151,164	1,436,466	41,352	1,477,818	166,285	27,149	1,338,682	415,024	397,458	18,212	118,119	60,738
1995	2,202,837	1,510,549	9,551	1,520,100	174,648	28,763	1,374,215	411,004	417,618	18,524	118,915	62,607
1996	2,345,251	1,545,081	62,340	1,607,421	176,031	35,248	1,466,638	441,489	437,124	19,677	119,187	62,179
1997	2,486,250	1,666,975	55,857	1,722,832	187,013	35,431	1,571,250	477,486	437,514	20,717	120,013	63,975
1998	2,578,634	1,778,540	35,276	1,813,816	198,537	36,751	1,652,030	477,666	448,938	21,312	120,992	65,431
1999	2,714,732	1,917,788	15,250	1,933,038	211,516	39,492	1,761,014	476,017	477,701	22,323	121,611	67,164
2000	2,918,051	2,053,121	26,882	2,080,003	223,846	43,616	1,899,773	504,748	513,530	23,515	124,091	68,383
2001	2,977,383	2,085,482	19,830	2,105,312	230,550	35,690	1,910,452	506,459	560,472	24,024	123,936	68,558
2002	3,005,398	2,149,399	-1,539	2,147,860	237,313	16,663	1,927,210	481,888	596,300	24,258	123,894	68,032
2003	3,088,888	2,209,659	12,109	2,221,768	243,758	-635	1,977,375	495,982	615,531	24,926	123,923	68,737
2004	3,241,587	2,323,384	70,965	2,394,349	255,457	-6,502	2,132,390	461,018	648,179	26,276	123,366	69,654
2005	3,325,903	2,429,269	44,255	2,473,524	269,801	-26,777	2,176,946	454,924	694,033	26,934	123,484	70,242
2006	3,531,470	2,626,158	31,221	2,657,379	294,035	-46,461	2,316,883	481,369	733,218	28,429	124,222	72,379
2007	3,791,159	2,772,316	59,601	2,831,917	314,037	-43,263	2,474,617	540,485	776,057	30,213	125,483	75,356
2008	4,021,945	2,871,132	67,606	2,938,738	326,850	-60,266	2,551,622	602,996	867,327	31,901	126,077	75,606
2009	4,033,839	2,878,391	77,167	2,955,558	326,431	-130,505	2,498,622	589,911	945,306	31,762	127,001	73,699
2010	4,022,076	2,906,924	36,088	2,943,012	325,793	-132,377	2,484,842	540,885	996,349	31,601	127,278	71,396
2011	4,286,456	2,986,541	87,195	3,073,736	301,361	-114,120	2,658,255	614,192	1,014,009	33,554	127,747	71,428
2012	4,337,533	3,117,509	43,893	3,161,402	310,015	-191,354	2,660,033	651,651	1,025,849	33,900	127,950	71,776
2013	4,439,933	3,172,459	126,721	3,299,180	357,996	-200,717	2,740,467	676,024	1,023,442	34,747	127,779	72,530
2014	4,544,413	3,277,329	104,844	3,382,173	369,667	-223,397	2,789,109	706,797	1,048,507	35,662	127,431	72,657

Personal Income and Employment by Area: St. Louis, MO-IL

(Thousands of dollars, except as noted.)

Year	Personal income, total	Earnings by place of work			Less: Contributions for government social insurance	Plus: Adjustment for residence	Equals: Net earnings by place of residence	Plus: Dividends, interest, and rent	Plus: Personal current transfer receipts	Per capita personal income (dollars)	Population (persons)	Total employment
		Nonfarm	Farm	Total								
1970	10,988,577	9,021,316	63,227	9,084,543	597,235	-16,432	8,470,876	1,635,928	881,773	4,360	2,520,475	1,119,503
1971	11,725,698	9,537,056	68,615	9,605,671	652,043	-17,389	8,936,239	1,745,506	1,043,953	4,664	2,514,268	1,108,632
1972	12,578,028	10,248,742	82,504	10,331,246	737,233	-19,435	9,574,578	1,870,402	1,133,048	5,019	2,506,053	1,120,309
1973	13,672,576	11,083,473	167,605	11,251,078	922,267	-41,886	10,286,925	2,059,392	1,326,259	5,483	2,493,703	1,155,750
1974	14,851,559	11,911,396	139,496	12,050,892	1,025,821	-65,076	10,959,995	2,350,687	1,540,877	5,981	2,483,293	1,165,071
1975	16,148,521	12,591,149	174,401	12,765,550	1,065,530	-78,476	11,621,544	2,562,774	1,964,203	6,503	2,483,274	1,144,591
1976	17,623,152	14,008,164	114,400	14,122,564	1,205,364	-129,363	12,787,837	2,743,843	2,091,472	7,097	2,483,161	1,174,761
1977	19,434,227	15,625,922	117,394	15,743,316	1,348,283	-178,030	14,217,003	3,051,056	2,166,168	7,848	2,476,457	1,208,780
1978	21,566,771	17,487,092	120,904	17,607,996	1,558,154	-230,226	15,819,616	3,398,093	2,349,062	8,697	2,479,899	1,251,667
1979	23,846,752	19,280,055	155,522	19,435,577	1,777,353	-280,272	17,377,952	3,833,890	2,634,910	9,598	2,484,555	1,285,355
1980	26,145,707	20,436,269	27,574	20,463,843	1,870,047	-309,713	18,284,083	4,631,681	3,229,943	10,513	2,486,989	1,260,871
1981	29,029,445	22,163,072	109,614	22,272,686	2,175,703	-386,800	19,710,183	5,765,300	3,553,962	11,671	2,487,360	1,257,134
1982	31,238,906	23,236,086	44,461	23,280,547	2,326,902	-375,827	20,577,818	6,802,594	3,858,494	12,589	2,481,504	1,247,588
1983	33,507,829	25,010,325	-17,801	24,992,524	2,531,847	-368,954	22,091,723	7,256,638	4,159,468	13,485	2,484,786	1,260,590
1984	36,943,649	27,699,488	77,105	27,776,593	2,894,145	-392,545	24,489,903	8,123,920	4,329,826	14,795	2,496,966	1,314,730
1985	39,376,007	29,694,911	26,835	29,721,746	3,167,919	-394,630	26,159,197	8,658,542	4,558,268	15,664	2,513,864	1,347,519
1986	41,648,018	31,514,382	67,476	31,581,858	3,395,482	-399,401	27,786,975	9,129,531	4,731,512	16,468	2,529,039	1,385,583
1987	43,983,395	33,539,151	101,578	33,640,729	3,567,501	-390,706	29,682,522	9,431,935	4,868,938	17,291	2,543,754	1,403,758
1988	46,900,239	35,998,160	77,380	36,075,540	3,937,066	-386,807	31,751,667	10,042,831	5,105,741	18,372	2,552,771	1,427,738
1989	50,076,352	38,127,789	207,195	38,334,984	4,186,354	-389,915	33,758,715	10,786,528	5,531,109	19,600	2,554,879	1,452,169
1990	52,805,818	39,871,140	125,746	39,996,886	4,493,645	-371,482	35,131,759	11,667,777	6,006,282	20,587	2,565,020	1,464,298
1991	54,130,033	40,362,148	77,097	40,439,245	4,633,523	-368,322	35,437,400	11,863,759	6,828,874	20,986	2,579,363	1,442,695
1992	57,404,463	42,572,438	181,608	42,754,046	4,825,152	-374,629	37,554,265	12,461,927	7,388,271	22,160	2,590,410	1,439,015
1993	59,777,266	44,151,995	130,440	44,282,435	5,027,816	-386,490	38,868,129	13,079,955	7,829,182	22,939	2,605,968	1,468,529
1994	62,865,847	46,652,371	147,419	46,799,790	5,400,710	-422,919	40,976,161	13,744,684	8,145,002	24,024	2,616,756	1,496,005
1995	66,454,332	49,526,332	47,068	49,573,400	5,725,912	-455,472	43,392,016	14,442,301	8,620,015	25,273	2,629,433	1,529,685
1996	69,636,024	51,906,974	178,404	52,085,378	5,942,875	-492,132	45,650,371	15,140,646	8,845,007	26,376	2,640,161	1,555,249
1997	73,978,283	55,279,806	166,447	55,446,253	6,303,315	-532,749	48,610,189	16,194,709	9,173,385	27,904	2,651,165	1,579,818
1998	77,718,570	58,122,125	136,112	58,258,237	6,599,416	-555,189	51,103,632	17,148,637	9,466,301	29,250	2,657,031	1,603,099
1999	80,504,567	61,283,228	104,008	61,387,236	6,894,417	-603,972	53,888,847	16,797,427	9,818,293	30,192	2,666,413	1,621,303
2000	85,846,588	65,008,331	150,154	65,158,485	7,252,497	-652,310	57,253,678	18,176,989	10,415,921	32,046	2,678,822	1,643,729
2001	87,723,130	66,533,650	155,461	66,689,111	7,399,221	-653,906	58,635,984	17,733,903	11,353,243	32,609	2,690,131	1,642,050
2002	90,628,993	69,266,288	72,474	69,338,762	7,614,087	-883,138	60,841,537	17,794,124	11,993,332	33,565	2,700,121	1,636,515
2003	94,159,470	71,315,689	194,341	71,510,030	7,845,997	-726,159	62,937,874	18,780,259	12,441,337	34,732	2,711,031	1,637,479
2004	98,236,161	74,192,138	361,294	74,553,432	8,087,209	-408,168	66,058,055	19,183,573	12,994,533	36,091	2,721,868	1,645,645
2005	102,568,097	77,199,355	178,461	77,377,816	8,458,190	-314,699	68,604,927	19,997,030	13,966,140	37,566	2,730,316	1,666,784
2006	109,549,506	81,051,310	175,216	81,226,526	8,938,846	-73,379	72,214,301	22,582,084	14,753,121	39,919	2,744,265	1,686,975
2007	114,212,092	83,375,197	180,916	83,556,113	9,323,363	391,681	74,624,431	23,713,731	15,873,930	41,448	2,755,581	1,708,496
2008	119,373,642	87,872,657	308,887	88,181,544	9,785,064	-750,459	77,646,021	24,007,372	17,720,249	43,130	2,767,776	1,712,171
2009	113,793,886	83,795,184	208,413	84,003,597	9,347,193	-530,524	74,125,880	20,460,478	19,207,528	40,942	2,779,404	1,658,857
2010	116,506,411	83,877,566	225,986	84,103,552	9,327,005	-339,594	74,436,953	21,517,981	20,551,477	41,760	2,789,886	1,637,064
2011	120,566,896	86,189,832	381,319	86,571,151	8,625,616	-361,293	77,584,242	22,334,938	20,647,716	43,156	2,793,725	1,659,124
2012	128,206,034	89,439,401	217,841	89,657,242	8,847,914	-481,061	80,328,267	27,040,460	20,837,307	45,832	2,797,281	1,663,318
2013	128,534,909	91,465,792	578,622	92,044,414	10,299,656	-551,313	81,193,445	25,889,913	21,451,551	45,879	2,801,587	1,681,115
2014	132,988,974	94,790,639	391,847	95,182,486	10,667,774	-595,576	83,919,136	27,064,146	22,005,692	47,391	2,806,207	1,702,859

Personal Income and Employment by Area: Salem, OR

(Thousands of dollars, except as noted.)

Year	Personal income, total	Earnings by place of work			Less: Contributions for government social insurance	Plus: Adjustment for residence	Equals: Net earnings by place of residence	Plus: Dividends, interest, and rent	Plus: Personal current transfer receipts	Per capita personal income (dollars)	Population (persons)	Total employment
		Nonfarm	Farm	Total								
1970	700,241	501,960	23,467	525,427	36,554	8,491	497,364	127,092	75,785	3,732	187,645	76,935
1971	775,967	556,301	23,671	579,972	42,020	11,541	549,493	139,322	87,152	4,017	193,158	78,983
1972	866,988	629,036	21,463	650,499	50,028	16,130	616,601	152,840	97,547	4,400	197,027	82,993
1973	998,577	706,866	48,661	755,527	64,980	21,709	712,256	171,974	114,347	5,003	199,576	88,074
1974	1,142,828	792,775	55,197	847,972	75,685	28,173	800,460	200,888	141,480	5,526	206,796	91,136
1975	1,276,911	877,378	43,561	920,939	81,630	32,924	872,233	231,127	173,551	6,039	211,453	93,710
1976	1,467,592	1,022,184	49,548	1,071,732	95,898	42,497	1,018,331	256,654	192,607	6,712	218,659	99,232
1977	1,654,358	1,163,035	43,377	1,206,412	110,810	53,534	1,149,136	296,567	208,655	7,242	228,455	106,818
1978	1,893,629	1,339,250	38,807	1,378,057	131,790	70,815	1,317,082	345,960	230,587	7,988	237,065	113,216
1979	2,148,618	1,509,840	43,798	1,553,638	154,503	89,163	1,488,298	399,540	260,780	8,820	243,606	118,107
1980	2,397,236	1,590,794	60,347	1,651,141	164,441	112,759	1,599,459	484,230	313,547	9,556	250,849	117,287
1981	2,602,152	1,671,529	54,163	1,725,692	185,419	110,502	1,650,775	588,838	362,539	10,239	254,150	115,262
1982	2,667,955	1,650,211	49,451	1,699,662	185,816	105,142	1,618,988	644,198	404,769	10,469	254,850	111,166
1983	2,815,801	1,731,493	43,087	1,774,580	194,488	104,065	1,684,157	695,335	436,309	11,025	255,400	113,893
1984	3,027,209	1,876,968	53,676	1,930,644	216,849	104,570	1,818,365	757,975	450,869	11,800	256,540	117,372
1985	3,205,778	2,016,223	58,153	2,074,376	235,002	97,008	1,936,382	790,748	478,648	12,413	258,250	121,772
1986	3,394,065	2,139,602	88,334	2,227,936	249,493	92,756	2,071,199	826,002	496,864	13,032	260,438	125,261
1987	3,586,722	2,325,858	88,904	2,414,762	267,136	85,948	2,233,574	834,041	519,107	13,636	263,037	132,049
1988	3,926,033	2,568,050	142,866	2,710,916	310,080	87,651	2,488,487	880,590	556,956	14,636	268,239	137,126
1989	4,336,345	2,840,205	126,180	2,966,385	343,332	84,722	2,707,775	1,011,985	616,585	15,849	273,600	141,107
1990	4,690,989	3,143,426	141,187	3,284,613	386,734	75,494	2,973,373	1,044,301	673,315	16,762	279,862	146,094
1991	4,993,063	3,364,663	156,888	3,521,551	418,864	75,448	3,178,135	1,076,824	738,104	17,385	287,202	147,147
1992	5,350,103	3,643,208	167,302	3,810,510	448,812	80,620	3,442,318	1,092,830	814,955	18,134	295,039	149,319
1993	5,719,888	3,898,324	165,973	4,064,297	478,793	91,194	3,676,698	1,163,198	879,992	18,865	303,205	154,522
1994	6,153,832	4,256,548	167,168	4,423,716	525,097	104,937	4,003,556	1,239,216	911,060	19,811	310,626	161,451
1995	6,571,977	4,464,915	145,375	4,610,290	555,451	133,190	4,188,029	1,368,800	1,015,148	20,690	317,638	165,842
1996	7,076,504	4,790,816	195,494	4,986,310	600,872	165,843	4,551,281	1,443,255	1,081,968	21,810	324,457	172,393
1997	7,381,912	4,957,525	208,048	5,165,573	622,115	198,268	4,741,726	1,522,306	1,117,880	22,256	331,688	176,546
1998	7,867,098	5,327,165	204,477	5,531,642	661,041	213,815	5,084,416	1,582,255	1,200,427	23,257	338,269	178,320
1999	8,313,780	5,713,383	226,987	5,940,370	697,142	220,171	5,463,399	1,526,841	1,323,540	24,169	343,985	180,860
2000	8,745,805	6,060,167	179,599	6,239,766	732,875	267,610	5,774,501	1,630,590	1,340,714	25,131	348,007	183,285
2001	8,903,459	6,034,217	202,573	6,236,790	728,533	270,315	5,778,572	1,613,906	1,510,981	25,324	351,581	180,757
2002	9,178,896	6,446,203	179,260	6,625,463	773,865	244,785	6,096,383	1,514,359	1,568,154	25,735	356,668	182,890
2003	9,695,734	6,748,887	237,174	6,986,061	809,730	237,080	6,413,411	1,647,333	1,634,990	26,904	360,377	186,683
2004	10,128,322	7,069,327	249,093	7,318,420	857,044	236,656	6,698,032	1,720,543	1,709,747	27,847	363,708	190,921
2005	10,428,091	7,307,512	259,707	7,567,219	912,447	222,926	6,877,698	1,704,912	1,845,481	28,334	368,046	196,212
2006	11,271,708	7,754,054	315,459	8,069,513	987,179	218,247	7,300,581	1,989,827	1,981,300	30,113	374,317	201,152
2007	11,806,197	8,064,460	315,113	8,379,573	1,036,585	198,995	7,541,983	2,104,804	2,159,410	31,089	379,755	205,800
2008	12,571,445	8,441,715	248,588	8,690,303	1,066,314	162,767	7,786,756	2,221,814	2,562,875	32,732	384,075	204,945
2009	12,293,268	8,200,051	233,396	8,433,447	1,034,451	-54,671	7,344,325	2,065,880	2,883,063	31,657	388,323	197,502
2010	12,320,757	8,178,831	223,077	8,401,908	1,041,233	-186,431	7,174,244	1,997,084	3,149,429	31,472	391,487	194,351
2011	12,715,595	8,203,028	213,014	8,416,042	929,028	-144,169	7,342,845	2,142,219	3,230,531	32,284	393,863	192,728
2012	13,075,516	8,422,644	242,624	8,665,268	957,280	-89,355	7,618,633	2,257,313	3,199,570	32,991	396,339	192,132
2013	13,395,498	8,751,819	264,007	9,015,826	1,119,567	-135,049	7,761,210	2,317,257	3,317,031	33,586	398,846	194,981
2014	14,286,410	9,257,164	288,984	9,546,148	1,191,948	-180,049	8,174,151	2,412,807	3,699,452	35,360	404,026	201,507

Personal Income and Employment by Area: Salinas, CA

(Thousands of dollars, except as noted.)

Year	Personal income, total	Earnings by place of work			Less: Contributions for government social insurance	Plus: Adjustment for residence	Equals: Net earnings by place of residence	Plus: Dividends, interest, and rent	Plus: Personal current transfer receipts	Per capita personal income (dollars)	Population (persons)	Total employment
		Nonfarm	Farm	Total								
1970	1,366,000	911,120	109,573	1,020,693	58,549	-5,123	957,021	316,699	92,280	5,503	248,235	134,519
1971	1,539,385	1,029,347	131,596	1,160,943	69,434	-6,588	1,084,921	348,936	105,528	6,091	252,730	140,268
1972	1,645,379	1,082,335	166,158	1,248,493	75,630	-7,435	1,165,428	364,105	115,846	6,474	254,140	136,674
1973	1,840,584	1,209,351	195,923	1,405,274	93,659	-9,909	1,301,706	408,709	130,169	7,211	255,261	144,582
1974	2,050,368	1,305,349	253,541	1,558,890	105,254	-12,784	1,440,852	455,565	153,951	7,780	263,534	147,280
1975	2,187,900	1,424,189	209,655	1,633,844	116,540	-15,945	1,501,359	488,326	198,215	8,074	270,976	150,780
1976	2,288,158	1,498,264	201,272	1,699,536	125,264	-15,455	1,558,817	511,038	218,303	8,292	275,942	148,250
1977	2,519,001	1,657,955	220,800	1,878,755	140,007	-16,532	1,722,216	567,927	228,858	8,947	281,545	154,161
1978	2,901,439	1,863,202	299,584	2,162,786	158,312	-14,984	1,989,490	661,629	250,320	10,212	284,129	158,622
1979	3,123,667	2,022,763	273,706	2,296,469	179,348	-17,383	2,099,738	747,082	276,847	10,888	286,882	162,099
1980	3,499,574	2,152,320	343,054	2,495,374	186,039	-12,517	2,296,818	868,685	334,071	11,968	292,406	160,320
1981	4,028,170	2,370,557	427,400	2,797,957	221,564	-2,558	2,573,835	1,066,752	387,583	13,442	299,677	161,159
1982	4,259,115	2,540,048	432,145	2,972,193	239,417	-4,524	2,728,252	1,130,371	400,492	13,908	306,241	161,196
1983	4,748,927	2,722,449	634,627	3,357,076	264,304	1,885	3,094,657	1,220,063	434,207	15,139	313,698	164,668
1984	5,110,473	3,008,726	558,396	3,567,122	304,024	5,527	3,268,625	1,387,082	454,766	15,898	321,458	170,038
1985	5,403,505	3,309,754	482,151	3,791,905	338,448	3	3,453,460	1,459,215	490,830	16,469	328,102	175,384
1986	5,845,629	3,589,030	572,946	4,161,976	371,492	1,370	3,791,854	1,524,228	529,547	17,406	335,849	176,778
1987	6,261,949	3,914,060	614,300	4,528,360	408,957	4,230	4,123,633	1,593,781	544,535	18,349	341,268	183,254
1988	6,604,413	4,206,186	558,487	4,764,673	459,432	13,309	4,318,550	1,698,185	587,678	19,091	345,947	190,927
1989	6,984,564	4,417,522	490,591	4,908,113	489,334	21,054	4,439,833	1,898,675	646,056	19,963	349,872	194,992
1990	7,407,486	4,721,855	541,806	5,263,661	529,134	24,475	4,759,002	1,929,657	718,827	20,718	357,535	200,058
1991	7,562,859	4,957,883	414,620	5,372,503	560,997	29,025	4,840,531	1,922,369	799,959	20,731	364,805	200,838
1992	8,217,698	5,283,804	607,943	5,891,747	597,196	31,409	5,325,960	1,968,043	923,695	22,099	371,860	195,598
1993	8,356,598	5,148,128	779,971	5,928,099	582,410	51,541	5,397,230	1,984,728	974,640	22,524	371,002	191,239
1994	8,378,446	5,104,682	765,365	5,870,047	573,895	73,075	5,369,227	2,023,908	985,311	23,778	352,363	183,917
1995	8,929,380	5,312,500	888,082	6,200,582	586,631	99,405	5,713,356	2,182,142	1,033,882	25,119	355,486	187,617
1996	9,264,157	5,631,351	717,944	6,349,295	599,739	120,469	5,870,025	2,307,665	1,086,467	25,576	362,215	195,179
1997	10,006,401	5,957,199	980,677	6,937,876	622,887	148,991	6,463,980	2,435,243	1,107,178	26,557	376,794	197,557
1998	10,929,231	6,505,613	1,065,766	7,571,379	660,012	177,815	7,089,182	2,665,556	1,174,493	28,176	387,889	208,973
1999	11,638,405	7,116,901	1,115,255	8,232,156	722,511	221,268	7,730,913	2,668,497	1,238,995	29,370	396,267	218,615
2000	12,840,106	7,716,559	1,380,043	9,096,602	776,918	359,919	8,679,603	2,876,173	1,284,330	31,862	402,990	219,037
2001	13,049,874	8,250,194	1,101,566	9,351,760	881,643	266,595	8,736,712	2,907,772	1,405,390	32,057	407,082	217,956
2002	13,315,978	8,705,423	1,205,247	9,910,670	940,871	242,196	9,211,995	2,593,878	1,510,105	32,559	408,977	221,446
2003	14,041,691	9,193,842	1,335,311	10,529,153	1,012,469	224,819	9,741,503	2,717,764	1,582,424	34,271	409,725	225,063
2004	14,653,817	9,573,940	1,105,315	10,679,255	1,100,617	205,613	9,784,251	3,216,884	1,652,682	35,852	408,731	224,221
2005	15,227,369	9,923,928	1,179,777	11,103,705	1,136,579	183,480	10,150,606	3,346,843	1,729,920	37,586	405,139	224,270
2006	16,339,249	10,382,984	1,221,594	11,604,578	1,151,537	159,273	10,612,314	3,872,676	1,854,259	40,662	401,831	221,997
2007	16,748,707	10,615,948	1,128,682	11,744,630	1,158,527	132,354	10,718,457	4,089,645	1,940,605	41,625	402,376	226,953
2008	16,738,324	10,628,052	1,000,173	11,628,225	1,169,062	100,152	10,559,315	3,982,194	2,196,815	41,225	406,022	225,770
2009	16,596,190	10,255,446	1,499,834	11,755,280	1,153,327	54,261	10,656,214	3,527,888	2,412,088	40,453	410,263	220,002
2010	16,922,093	10,506,248	1,328,491	11,834,739	1,160,055	46,613	10,721,297	3,534,488	2,666,308	40,643	416,364	222,066
2011	17,522,589	10,761,186	1,109,923	11,871,109	1,073,289	73,383	10,871,203	3,943,878	2,707,508	41,583	421,393	223,032
2012	18,524,806	11,315,705	1,288,112	12,603,817	1,116,177	34,115	11,521,755	4,276,863	2,726,188	43,444	426,411	227,931
2013	19,184,636	11,490,724	1,714,086	13,204,810	1,277,575	55,667	11,982,902	4,366,391	2,835,343	44,707	429,123	232,801
2014	19,889,054	11,946,490	1,709,227	13,655,717	1,325,164	69,092	12,399,645	4,542,039	2,947,370	46,109	431,344	240,804

Personal Income and Employment by Area: Salisbury, MD-DE

(Thousands of dollars, except as noted.)

Year	Personal income, total	Earnings by place of work			Less: Contributions for government social insurance	Plus: Adjustment for residence	Equals: Net earnings by place of residence	Plus: Dividends, interest, and rent	Plus: Personal current transfer receipts	Per capita personal income (dollars)	Population (persons)	Total employment
		Nonfarm	Farm	Total								
1970	660,546	486,962	39,134	526,096	33,261	7,918	500,753	96,887	62,906	3,694	178,804	92,457
1971	714,864	528,099	34,025	562,124	37,313	9,196	534,007	106,868	73,989	3,875	184,503	94,642
1972	809,803	596,170	50,343	646,513	44,245	8,528	610,796	118,348	80,659	4,332	186,939	99,270
1973	957,010	667,264	108,938	776,202	57,552	7,785	726,435	136,678	93,897	5,010	191,029	102,800
1974	990,081	720,163	51,919	772,082	64,473	8,313	715,922	159,956	114,203	5,053	195,957	101,927
1975	1,134,172	764,740	102,351	867,091	67,220	8,613	808,484	177,043	148,645	5,673	199,933	99,153
1976	1,218,867	848,637	83,284	931,921	75,284	9,279	865,916	191,178	161,773	5,982	203,759	100,183
1977	1,288,788	912,758	55,376	968,134	81,243	10,837	897,728	214,515	176,545	6,232	206,805	101,923
1978	1,437,097	1,039,369	55,028	1,094,397	94,793	5,368	1,004,972	239,386	192,739	6,872	209,113	107,617
1979	1,553,599	1,122,510	42,052	1,164,562	107,333	2,110	1,059,339	270,829	223,431	7,328	212,004	108,124
1980	1,687,758	1,192,089	2,748	1,194,837	114,582	-1,830	1,078,425	338,363	270,970	7,932	212,780	106,381
1981	1,897,724	1,267,358	39,464	1,306,822	131,338	-3,187	1,172,297	411,099	314,328	8,910	212,984	107,068
1982	2,101,065	1,352,143	71,747	1,423,890	142,762	-4,241	1,276,887	482,362	341,816	9,842	213,485	108,398
1983	2,310,029	1,525,131	62,937	1,588,068	162,602	-9,335	1,416,131	524,450	369,448	10,694	216,011	116,348
1984	2,625,169	1,711,608	128,482	1,840,090	187,167	-7,836	1,645,087	587,369	392,713	11,912	220,383	121,778
1985	2,889,002	1,899,911	135,396	2,035,307	210,083	-7,980	1,817,244	646,992	424,766	12,836	225,063	127,936
1986	3,220,028	2,085,265	213,375	2,298,640	232,978	-1,762	2,063,900	706,792	449,336	14,026	229,583	132,093
1987	3,463,351	2,304,620	168,265	2,472,885	253,922	5,968	2,224,931	751,798	486,622	14,860	233,065	137,270
1988	3,801,429	2,495,013	239,183	2,734,196	284,726	17,196	2,466,666	804,597	530,166	15,938	238,509	141,970
1989	4,131,063	2,643,825	261,186	2,905,011	304,719	29,616	2,629,908	924,921	576,234	17,028	242,598	143,143
1990	4,293,866	2,851,488	168,364	3,019,852	326,817	42,920	2,735,955	913,912	643,999	17,339	247,645	146,525
1991	4,556,475	2,968,109	157,351	3,125,460	343,095	58,989	2,841,354	988,127	726,994	17,922	254,246	145,358
1992	4,791,141	3,119,141	134,066	3,253,207	356,750	76,024	2,972,481	1,010,996	807,664	18,376	260,733	145,227
1993	4,984,691	3,248,003	135,303	3,383,306	375,202	92,821	3,100,925	1,020,320	863,446	18,610	267,853	147,101
1994	5,329,830	3,442,990	144,446	3,587,436	402,859	112,306	3,296,883	1,103,547	929,400	19,408	274,618	150,301
1995	5,678,614	3,620,975	113,580	3,734,555	423,942	133,944	3,444,557	1,210,615	1,023,442	20,177	281,441	157,221
1996	6,137,832	3,787,323	166,396	3,953,719	437,629	156,738	3,672,828	1,323,870	1,141,134	21,270	288,563	160,039
1997	6,495,552	4,033,492	135,267	4,168,759	460,761	174,623	3,882,621	1,433,802	1,179,129	22,036	294,772	164,110
1998	6,989,336	4,310,528	176,581	4,487,109	487,859	204,859	4,204,109	1,511,094	1,274,133	23,195	301,328	166,882
1999	7,460,821	4,638,010	180,084	4,818,094	514,493	237,952	4,541,553	1,558,787	1,360,481	24,264	307,487	170,842
2000	7,997,669	4,948,343	170,508	5,118,851	540,211	274,098	4,852,738	1,689,107	1,455,824	25,491	313,744	175,958
2001	8,596,655	5,215,365	261,579	5,476,944	575,997	334,136	5,235,083	1,742,403	1,619,169	26,938	319,128	177,298
2002	8,861,209	5,526,944	90,838	5,617,782	610,766	355,003	5,362,019	1,754,447	1,744,743	27,260	325,063	180,843
2003	9,477,673	5,907,321	206,475	6,113,796	650,299	381,597	5,845,094	1,751,200	1,881,379	28,534	332,157	182,802
2004	10,391,799	6,396,058	305,187	6,701,245	713,003	426,924	6,415,166	1,950,522	2,026,111	30,697	338,528	190,148
2005	11,115,363	6,850,972	324,299	7,175,271	770,649	470,276	6,874,898	2,031,011	2,209,454	32,153	345,704	196,034
2006	11,862,431	7,352,721	224,477	7,577,198	827,635	523,913	7,273,476	2,225,537	2,363,418	33,526	353,828	201,796
2007	12,644,985	7,562,348	226,714	7,789,062	865,100	573,772	7,497,734	2,570,260	2,576,991	35,036	360,918	204,689
2008	13,425,004	7,668,940	303,046	7,971,986	888,697	596,417	7,679,706	2,789,109	2,956,189	36,603	366,772	202,123
2009	13,345,997	7,525,100	276,361	7,801,461	881,277	598,579	7,518,763	2,593,638	3,233,596	36,016	370,558	196,510
2010	13,660,597	7,636,079	250,038	7,886,117	910,573	607,171	7,582,715	2,575,724	3,502,158	36,451	374,762	194,685
2011	14,241,937	7,713,397	226,548	7,939,945	822,130	644,455	7,762,270	2,851,079	3,628,588	37,666	378,111	194,070
2012	14,765,074	7,880,526	277,936	8,158,462	848,394	682,987	7,993,055	3,034,549	3,737,470	38,712	381,407	196,567
2013	15,136,636	8,053,257	504,732	8,557,989	968,848	682,071	8,271,212	2,966,917	3,898,507	39,302	385,140	199,073
2014	15,898,833	8,476,924	537,118	9,014,042	1,015,045	693,882	8,692,879	3,108,288	4,097,666	40,774	389,922	202,365

Personal Income and Employment by Area: Salt Lake City, UT

(Thousands of dollars, except as noted.)

Year	Personal income, total	Derivation of personal income					Equals: Net earnings by place of residence	Plus: Dividends, interest, and rent	Plus: Personal current transfer receipts	Per capita personal income (dollars)	Population (persons)	Total employment
		Earnings by place of work			Less: Contributions for government social insurance	Plus: Adjustment for residence						
		Nonfarm	Farm	Total								
1970	1,874,873	1,631,043	6,530	1,637,573	109,178	-62,381	1,466,014	266,061	142,798	3,882	482,939	228,004
1971	2,084,889	1,792,132	6,465	1,798,597	124,888	-54,911	1,618,798	299,243	166,848	4,179	498,890	235,582
1972	2,326,082	2,016,093	8,087	2,024,180	147,664	-73,715	1,802,801	332,586	190,695	4,557	510,409	248,748
1973	2,575,674	2,267,643	11,838	2,279,481	192,936	-89,439	1,997,106	357,758	220,810	4,915	524,033	265,327
1974	2,906,929	2,570,735	7,010	2,577,745	225,365	-109,613	2,242,767	414,866	249,296	5,419	536,395	278,466
1975	3,253,863	2,835,956	5,609	2,841,565	244,183	-120,508	2,476,874	459,127	317,862	5,899	551,569	282,198
1976	3,652,518	3,223,615	6,480	3,230,095	282,242	-138,657	2,809,196	500,148	343,174	6,411	569,758	295,659
1977	4,134,172	3,695,942	4,582	3,700,524	323,489	-168,794	3,208,241	558,195	367,736	7,046	586,735	312,954
1978	4,736,851	4,270,804	4,779	4,275,583	381,656	-208,872	3,685,055	646,098	405,698	7,817	605,964	333,838
1979	5,306,586	4,806,519	5,104	4,811,623	452,551	-245,757	4,113,315	734,751	458,520	8,478	625,894	346,245
1980	5,939,811	5,328,622	3,846	5,332,468	505,939	-295,789	4,530,740	870,180	538,891	9,135	650,232	350,072
1981	6,704,200	5,937,994	3,152	5,941,146	608,290	-324,935	5,007,921	1,063,527	632,752	10,018	669,210	353,355
1982	7,303,610	6,347,065	-435	6,346,630	662,047	-354,734	5,329,849	1,247,159	726,602	10,665	684,802	359,618
1983	7,851,291	6,856,952	3,928	6,860,880	720,356	-436,650	5,703,874	1,364,627	782,790	11,209	700,444	367,055
1984	8,641,586	7,597,697	4,728	7,602,425	819,857	-485,935	6,296,633	1,537,769	807,184	12,121	712,930	388,686
1985	9,234,528	8,086,343	4,001	8,090,344	883,267	-522,182	6,684,895	1,670,256	879,377	12,810	720,877	403,373
1986	9,670,605	8,460,936	4,672	8,465,608	928,001	-558,094	6,979,513	1,743,257	947,835	13,248	729,985	409,417
1987	10,130,397	8,929,136	3,937	8,933,073	972,698	-633,976	7,326,399	1,815,482	988,516	13,765	735,973	423,933
1988	10,721,832	9,494,018	9,538	9,503,556	1,079,211	-678,994	7,745,351	1,942,812	1,033,669	14,460	741,463	438,149
1989	11,426,759	10,096,193	9,004	10,105,197	1,166,008	-729,587	8,209,602	2,072,262	1,144,895	15,324	745,687	451,777
1990	12,341,834	10,998,049	12,261	11,010,310	1,314,902	-882,468	8,812,940	2,273,329	1,255,565	16,312	756,611	470,479
1991	13,161,191	11,839,887	8,911	11,848,798	1,434,867	-1,000,023	9,413,908	2,357,804	1,389,479	16,910	778,307	481,251
1992	14,203,031	12,966,147	11,970	12,978,117	1,557,244	-1,190,343	10,230,530	2,451,393	1,521,108	17,704	802,260	489,997
1993	15,251,490	14,078,815	14,575	14,093,390	1,697,023	-1,350,576	11,045,791	2,583,061	1,622,638	18,450	826,621	518,184
1994	16,583,258	15,365,367	9,681	15,375,048	1,863,867	-1,496,609	12,014,572	2,918,378	1,650,308	19,542	848,617	547,370
1995	18,128,962	16,646,163	8,896	16,655,059	2,023,179	-1,644,210	12,987,670	3,361,906	1,779,386	20,926	866,353	571,123
1996	19,760,794	18,130,327	6,920	18,137,247	2,154,587	-1,851,055	14,131,605	3,758,486	1,870,703	22,343	884,440	602,150
1997	21,465,652	19,878,330	6,029	19,884,359	2,331,289	-2,097,211	15,455,859	4,074,535	1,935,258	23,729	904,628	624,849
1998	23,024,990	21,563,003	5,291	21,568,294	2,484,983	-2,329,330	16,753,981	4,266,222	2,004,787	25,104	917,191	645,106
1999	24,599,380	23,468,019	8,848	23,476,867	2,632,671	-2,568,397	18,275,799	4,214,414	2,109,167	26,474	929,195	655,738
2000	26,731,482	25,410,552	7,834	25,418,386	2,823,786	-2,761,402	19,833,198	4,634,493	2,263,791	28,361	942,537	676,338
2001	28,154,691	26,773,352	10,225	26,783,577	2,951,214	-2,883,643	20,948,720	4,736,780	2,469,191	29,510	954,081	676,181
2002	28,500,732	26,814,316	4,147	26,818,463	2,974,836	-3,052,305	20,791,322	5,009,922	2,699,488	29,591	963,150	670,141
2003	28,670,147	26,973,423	4,743	26,978,166	3,052,406	-3,229,126	20,696,634	5,116,230	2,857,283	29,513	971,454	669,061
2004	30,231,479	28,757,608	5,611	28,763,219	3,282,814	-3,560,954	21,919,451	5,308,326	3,003,702	30,785	982,034	684,080
2005	33,008,449	31,011,282	5,161	31,016,443	3,548,499	-3,916,722	23,551,222	6,190,809	3,266,418	33,100	997,221	712,869
2006	36,729,747	34,497,931	7,701	34,505,632	3,870,967	-4,419,230	26,215,435	6,920,637	3,593,675	36,070	1,018,281	746,373
2007	39,422,693	37,174,716	6,022	37,180,738	4,172,864	-4,922,587	28,085,287	7,468,532	3,868,874	37,996	1,037,540	783,504
2008	40,844,287	37,789,244	7,588	37,796,832	4,249,329	-5,159,410	28,388,093	7,955,606	4,500,588	38,698	1,055,462	782,517
2009	39,121,835	36,593,672	8,425	36,602,097	4,136,935	-5,127,934	27,337,228	6,792,514	4,992,093	36,426	1,074,013	755,447
2010	40,014,077	37,197,036	9,011	37,206,047	4,172,417	-5,351,196	27,682,434	6,811,219	5,520,424	36,662	1,091,432	746,883
2011	42,659,870	39,010,603	10,771	39,021,374	3,956,318	-5,764,423	29,300,633	7,611,700	5,747,537	38,514	1,107,634	767,095
2012	45,067,228	41,623,483	9,897	41,633,380	4,188,029	-6,358,971	31,086,380	8,306,736	5,674,112	40,087	1,124,222	787,387
2013	46,458,791	43,723,794	16,936	43,740,730	4,969,914	-6,549,892	32,220,924	8,354,622	5,883,245	40,697	1,141,584	810,125
2014	48,371,342	45,660,028	16,768	45,676,796	5,210,529	-6,849,916	33,616,351	8,713,262	6,041,729	41,940	1,153,340	827,483

Personal Income and Employment by Area: San Angelo, TX

(Thousands of dollars, except as noted.)

Year	Personal income, total	Earnings by place of work			Less: Contributions for government social insurance	Plus: Adjustment for residence	Equals: Net earnings by place of residence	Plus: Dividends, interest, and rent	Plus: Personal current transfer receipts	Per capita personal income (dollars)	Population (persons)	Total employment
		Nonfarm	Farm	Total								
1970	273,769	201,169	11,960	213,129	12,175	-93	200,861	49,082	23,826	3,782	72,383	33,632
1971	294,283	221,435	7,648	229,083	13,922	-596	214,565	52,388	27,330	3,964	74,244	34,481
1972	323,816	242,690	9,757	252,447	15,884	-1,024	235,539	57,972	30,305	4,398	73,632	35,458
1973	363,033	272,683	10,577	283,260	20,456	-1,599	261,205	65,739	36,089	4,781	75,927	37,376
1974	398,783	300,663	6,631	307,294	23,377	-2,090	281,827	74,764	42,192	5,184	76,932	38,027
1975	456,001	340,368	7,359	347,727	26,122	-872	320,733	84,635	50,633	5,795	78,694	39,156
1976	517,563	387,446	14,493	401,939	30,055	-3,329	368,555	92,999	56,009	6,479	79,880	40,777
1977	570,864	435,785	7,780	443,565	34,248	-4,700	404,617	106,396	59,851	7,087	80,554	43,162
1978	656,595	507,283	5,521	512,804	40,621	-5,448	466,735	123,388	66,472	8,008	81,991	45,910
1979	725,677	565,133	2,204	567,337	47,902	-6,473	512,962	137,216	75,499	8,613	84,252	46,828
1980	833,058	640,286	-4,482	635,804	54,785	-8,340	572,679	173,549	86,830	9,606	86,724	48,508
1981	1,006,896	733,737	20,265	754,002	67,730	-7,560	678,712	229,643	98,541	11,353	88,690	50,976
1982	1,125,814	813,251	16,104	829,355	77,391	-7,108	744,856	270,400	110,558	12,180	92,432	53,252
1983	1,207,170	859,056	21,544	880,600	81,255	-7,431	791,914	292,368	122,888	12,552	96,176	53,418
1984	1,295,471	902,543	22,545	925,088	87,329	-4,920	832,839	330,017	132,615	13,227	97,944	54,135
1985	1,317,767	927,917	-13,455	914,462	91,362	-3,070	820,030	353,454	144,283	13,413	98,243	54,124
1986	1,355,332	943,033	2,047	945,080	92,510	-4,077	848,493	349,855	156,984	13,685	99,036	52,823
1987	1,381,414	954,629	12,341	966,970	93,117	-3,084	870,769	345,241	165,404	13,918	99,256	54,435
1988	1,456,733	1,003,846	9,633	1,013,479	100,836	-655	911,988	364,052	180,693	14,537	100,211	55,049
1989	1,548,152	1,023,362	8,076	1,031,438	104,776	1,524	928,186	418,943	201,023	15,278	101,335	54,853
1990	1,608,986	1,074,999	17,952	1,092,951	108,626	5,765	990,090	402,221	216,675	16,102	99,924	54,813
1991	1,665,628	1,140,462	9,223	1,149,685	118,242	5,861	1,037,304	397,482	230,842	16,703	99,719	55,746
1992	1,766,522	1,206,299	13,004	1,219,303	124,399	5,777	1,100,681	399,421	266,420	17,471	101,111	55,914
1993	1,863,213	1,287,077	14,606	1,301,683	132,702	5,105	1,174,086	408,370	280,757	18,294	101,848	57,157
1994	1,933,428	1,319,968	17,100	1,337,068	137,890	5,397	1,204,575	434,563	294,290	18,741	103,167	58,121
1995	2,064,244	1,401,009	11,466	1,412,475	146,192	4,292	1,270,575	469,806	323,863	19,918	103,639	60,203
1996	2,141,071	1,442,282	7,661	1,449,943	149,427	4,480	1,304,996	489,096	346,979	20,474	104,574	61,413
1997	2,253,827	1,526,791	11,208	1,537,999	155,651	8,051	1,390,399	499,201	364,227	21,412	105,261	61,580
1998	2,392,042	1,669,301	5,120	1,674,421	166,783	6,652	1,514,290	508,373	369,379	22,612	105,787	62,569
1999	2,448,962	1,707,968	18,080	1,726,048	170,490	5,862	1,561,420	503,233	384,309	23,178	105,657	62,437
2000	2,568,682	1,769,924	12,314	1,782,238	175,511	7,644	1,614,371	554,437	399,874	24,269	105,841	63,562
2001	2,674,154	1,833,070	30,221	1,863,291	185,790	2,943	1,680,444	562,746	430,964	25,324	105,596	63,801
2002	2,748,498	1,904,785	20,054	1,924,839	191,185	7,227	1,740,881	537,966	469,651	25,995	105,732	64,031
2003	2,916,683	2,003,083	32,711	2,035,794	202,946	10,915	1,843,763	570,166	502,754	27,515	106,002	64,344
2004	3,021,271	2,106,025	31,358	2,137,383	213,530	16,956	1,940,809	554,300	526,162	28,403	106,373	64,092
2005	3,193,247	2,164,476	36,464	2,200,940	219,460	22,896	2,004,376	618,554	570,317	29,959	106,587	64,676
2006	3,319,203	2,269,590	15,920	2,285,510	223,855	31,822	2,093,477	623,386	602,340	30,798	107,774	65,609
2007	3,483,986	2,290,201	31,157	2,321,358	230,557	38,934	2,129,735	691,866	662,385	32,173	108,289	65,639
2008	3,878,154	2,469,122	12,421	2,481,543	245,231	46,371	2,282,683	869,807	725,664	35,511	109,210	66,502
2009	3,704,155	2,392,576	19,832	2,412,408	248,299	30,223	2,194,332	729,380	780,443	33,532	110,466	66,569
2010	3,926,997	2,517,636	37,528	2,555,164	261,293	28,603	2,322,474	750,804	853,719	34,974	112,283	67,299
2011	4,344,716	2,714,436	45,427	2,759,863	246,414	84,789	2,598,238	868,556	877,922	38,303	113,429	67,456
2012	4,600,534	2,894,449	25,404	2,919,853	259,220	54,653	2,715,286	1,017,212	868,036	39,971	115,097	69,314
2013	4,759,697	3,043,671	47,261	3,090,932	304,538	68,859	2,855,253	1,009,503	894,941	40,833	116,564	70,952
2014	5,006,724	3,221,603	41,425	3,263,028	320,556	87,158	3,029,630	1,048,403	928,691	42,365	118,182	71,877

Personal Income and Employment by Area: San Antonio-New Braunfels, TX

(Thousands of dollars, except as noted.)

Year	Personal income, total	Earnings by place of work			Less: Contributions for government social insurance	Plus: Adjustment for residence	Equals: Net earnings by place of residence	Plus: Dividends, interest, and rent	Plus: Personal current transfer receipts	Per capita personal income (dollars)	Population (persons)	Total employment
		Nonfarm	Farm	Total								
1970	3,672,218	2,811,906	33,294	2,845,200	159,637	-2,283	2,683,280	715,414	273,524	3,834	957,715	421,654
1971	4,091,336	3,142,077	20,888	3,162,965	186,884	-3,131	2,972,950	798,817	319,569	4,143	987,523	433,674
1972	4,504,432	3,456,873	35,480	3,492,353	213,133	-5,384	3,273,836	870,610	359,986	4,465	1,008,844	443,581
1973	5,022,855	3,817,198	64,331	3,881,529	266,226	-7,818	3,607,485	978,286	437,084	4,835	1,038,887	462,283
1974	5,541,503	4,165,556	47,989	4,213,545	302,457	-2,421	3,908,667	1,106,762	526,074	5,251	1,055,225	467,397
1975	6,045,845	4,457,026	47,328	4,504,354	326,809	11,873	4,189,418	1,188,927	667,500	5,680	1,064,486	461,538
1976	6,634,512	4,932,187	40,937	4,973,124	369,354	22,560	4,626,330	1,279,921	728,261	6,123	1,083,489	475,281
1977	7,245,760	5,441,698	20,951	5,462,649	409,680	3,452	5,056,421	1,419,981	769,358	6,554	1,105,551	493,057
1978	8,184,746	6,156,351	12,971	6,169,322	475,334	-3,727	5,690,261	1,645,920	848,565	7,282	1,123,898	515,788
1979	9,269,910	6,964,451	18,472	6,982,923	566,623	3,207	6,419,507	1,872,301	978,102	8,141	1,138,722	535,097
1980	10,611,497	7,931,887	-20,539	7,911,348	654,032	8,378	7,265,694	2,214,377	1,131,426	9,132	1,161,968	557,276
1981	12,152,567	9,025,719	12,971	9,038,690	797,533	22,544	8,263,701	2,616,848	1,272,018	10,237	1,187,117	575,836
1982	13,396,279	9,812,471	11,466	9,823,937	881,171	17,759	8,960,525	3,025,347	1,410,407	10,961	1,222,136	594,500
1983	14,621,685	10,659,947	39,080	10,699,027	976,871	13,081	9,735,237	3,342,975	1,543,473	11,660	1,254,044	611,333
1984	16,428,990	11,975,601	45,086	12,020,687	1,122,939	9,788	10,907,536	3,842,734	1,678,720	12,796	1,283,925	646,427
1985	18,027,686	13,148,210	6,805	13,155,015	1,253,018	11,561	11,913,558	4,322,773	1,791,355	13,684	1,317,439	676,534
1986	19,039,904	13,874,522	12,769	13,887,291	1,318,806	6,561	12,575,046	4,528,562	1,936,296	14,034	1,356,676	685,123
1987	19,482,775	14,201,475	12,077	14,213,552	1,340,468	4,367	12,877,451	4,536,242	2,069,082	14,037	1,387,997	702,912
1988	20,672,522	15,155,249	4,503	15,159,752	1,479,623	4,005	13,684,134	4,778,048	2,210,340	14,825	1,394,458	706,182
1989	21,926,181	15,731,310	31,683	15,762,993	1,567,489	6,827	14,202,331	5,204,430	2,519,420	15,647	1,401,286	713,903
1990	23,103,242	16,540,752	49,940	16,590,692	1,641,026	11,414	14,961,080	5,297,207	2,844,955	16,375	1,410,902	723,234
1991	24,301,662	17,499,046	47,919	17,546,965	1,782,762	15,845	15,780,048	5,397,455	3,124,159	16,946	1,434,060	736,292
1992	26,503,209	19,088,140	71,050	19,159,190	1,937,422	25,175	17,246,943	5,604,456	3,651,810	18,086	1,465,365	752,583
1993	28,154,556	20,460,391	84,225	20,544,616	2,082,417	34,233	18,496,432	5,823,383	3,834,741	18,791	1,498,269	780,913
1994	30,180,728	22,000,170	70,316	22,070,486	2,252,550	38,384	19,856,320	6,191,434	4,132,974	19,659	1,535,185	813,191
1995	32,457,840	23,485,087	61,379	23,546,466	2,412,352	48,216	21,182,330	6,771,341	4,504,169	20,673	1,570,083	847,156
1996	34,246,396	24,820,156	31,257	24,851,413	2,528,200	70,930	22,394,143	7,008,250	4,844,003	21,412	1,599,427	872,230
1997	36,763,983	26,538,158	69,316	26,607,474	2,710,985	92,054	23,988,543	7,682,063	5,093,377	22,573	1,628,676	908,164
1998	39,695,230	29,122,769	60,287	29,183,056	2,918,153	133,629	26,398,532	8,056,036	5,240,662	23,915	1,659,847	931,967
1999	42,215,846	31,607,660	76,900	31,684,560	3,125,684	165,409	28,724,285	8,100,070	5,391,491	24,994	1,689,009	954,950
2000	46,509,203	35,188,028	62,960	35,250,988	3,354,690	212,832	32,109,130	8,692,248	5,707,825	27,040	1,720,003	980,485
2001	49,115,116	37,454,317	71,646	37,525,963	3,542,785	265,371	34,248,549	8,617,535	6,249,032	28,096	1,748,123	995,671
2002	49,745,878	37,763,527	101,325	37,864,852	3,656,925	315,884	34,523,811	8,438,071	6,783,996	27,882	1,784,153	1,005,949
2003	52,187,915	39,377,412	112,181	39,489,593	3,893,069	344,326	35,940,850	8,863,875	7,383,190	28,740	1,815,846	1,015,236
2004	54,915,359	41,506,355	112,401	41,618,756	4,124,633	485,539	37,979,662	9,081,618	7,854,079	29,562	1,857,602	1,035,764
2005	59,400,811	43,859,154	94,886	43,954,040	4,357,257	695,933	40,292,716	10,397,559	8,710,536	31,324	1,896,328	1,069,828
2006	64,871,981	47,835,074	58,501	47,893,575	4,671,588	925,080	44,147,067	11,273,680	9,451,234	33,160	1,956,361	1,115,152
2007	69,406,279	50,054,341	60,335	50,114,676	4,957,843	1,207,140	46,363,973	12,571,792	10,470,514	34,504	2,011,543	1,153,622
2008	73,887,061	51,979,329	-22,414	51,956,915	5,139,453	1,524,676	48,342,138	13,616,605	11,928,318	35,845	2,061,275	1,184,270
2009	72,882,745	51,703,838	-20,807	51,683,031	5,283,617	1,174,715	47,574,129	12,215,112	13,093,504	34,613	2,105,672	1,177,035
2010	77,313,994	54,283,158	1,309	54,284,467	5,555,648	1,171,641	49,900,460	12,831,343	14,582,191	35,906	2,153,255	1,180,822
2011	84,583,865	57,757,211	8,318	57,765,529	5,191,782	1,268,478	53,842,225	15,507,586	15,234,054	38,548	2,194,231	1,208,815
2012	88,682,521	61,079,949	30,162	61,110,111	5,444,767	1,624,491	57,289,835	16,113,398	15,279,288	39,630	2,237,771	1,237,987
2013	91,071,886	63,536,201	60,167	63,596,368	6,379,216	1,757,805	58,974,957	16,264,257	15,832,672	39,905	2,282,201	1,273,402
2014	96,341,038	67,470,769	60,576	67,531,345	6,750,850	2,015,210	62,795,705	16,884,528	16,660,805	41,372	2,328,652	1,308,059

Personal Income and Employment by Area: San Diego-Carlsbad-San Marcos, CA

(Thousands of dollars, except as noted.)

Year	Personal income, total	Earnings by place of work			Less: Contributions for government social insurance	Plus: Adjustment for residence	Equals: Net earnings by place of residence	Plus: Dividends, interest, and rent	Plus: Personal current transfer receipts	Per capita personal income (dollars)	Population (persons)	Total employment
		Nonfarm	Farm	Total								
1970	7,027,210	5,215,816	55,543	5,271,359	329,024	-30,555	4,911,780	1,578,944	536,486	5,144	1,365,976	647,900
1971	7,547,152	5,573,490	53,571	5,627,061	365,323	-34,207	5,227,531	1,695,375	624,246	5,422	1,391,925	649,466
1972	8,393,784	6,208,689	66,676	6,275,365	420,493	-39,513	5,815,359	1,880,928	697,497	5,857	1,433,126	672,285
1973	9,255,088	6,806,397	93,067	6,899,464	512,722	-42,782	6,343,960	2,110,483	800,645	6,172	1,499,594	707,773
1974	10,339,947	7,459,267	90,285	7,549,552	581,140	-36,886	6,931,526	2,424,081	984,340	6,711	1,540,667	738,023
1975	11,558,686	8,153,257	127,474	8,280,731	639,535	-28,252	7,612,944	2,675,292	1,270,450	7,149	1,616,907	755,698
1976	12,897,277	9,142,549	140,674	9,283,223	732,001	-12,001	8,539,221	2,916,763	1,441,293	7,851	1,642,781	786,899
1977	14,411,369	10,278,473	145,540	10,424,013	838,401	-25,170	9,560,442	3,293,549	1,557,378	8,401	1,715,527	837,772
1978	16,567,665	11,881,282	121,391	12,002,673	985,703	-16,662	11,000,308	3,866,551	1,700,806	9,332	1,775,410	901,275
1979	18,782,466	13,506,726	115,005	13,621,731	1,180,474	2,029	12,443,286	4,426,542	1,912,638	10,277	1,827,602	951,199
1980	21,656,539	15,275,802	130,630	15,406,432	1,304,493	8,212	14,110,151	5,285,812	2,260,576	11,546	1,875,620	988,237
1981	24,671,169	16,928,364	136,921	17,065,285	1,565,424	137,631	15,637,492	6,326,590	2,707,087	12,803	1,927,018	994,581
1982	26,673,187	18,170,980	146,039	18,317,019	1,708,897	145,157	16,753,279	6,928,289	2,991,619	13,524	1,972,354	1,001,945
1983	28,836,446	19,607,043	152,031	19,759,074	1,909,343	173,856	18,023,587	7,600,054	3,212,805	14,289	2,018,133	1,036,404
1984	32,383,520	22,307,355	166,620	22,473,975	2,260,032	178,394	20,392,337	8,606,209	3,384,974	15,671	2,066,419	1,099,543
1985	35,547,583	24,764,333	197,066	24,961,399	2,545,445	196,941	22,612,895	9,268,483	3,666,205	16,720	2,126,090	1,160,801
1986	38,778,452	27,320,299	230,526	27,550,825	2,852,096	224,217	24,922,946	9,867,284	3,988,222	17,652	2,196,834	1,215,030
1987	41,940,187	30,050,593	212,305	30,262,898	3,156,587	260,548	27,366,859	10,337,817	4,235,511	18,433	2,275,309	1,277,030
1988	46,065,579	33,429,775	182,362	33,612,137	3,637,887	289,649	30,263,899	11,199,174	4,602,506	19,484	2,364,284	1,349,526
1989	50,096,085	35,665,029	230,526	35,895,555	3,928,936	332,004	32,298,623	12,756,289	5,041,173	20,494	2,444,380	1,396,314
1990	52,831,363	37,779,689	298,772	38,078,461	4,158,501	378,625	34,298,585	12,980,768	5,552,010	21,029	2,512,365	1,426,402
1991	54,998,942	39,738,396	241,204	39,979,600	4,392,379	335,231	35,922,452	12,918,036	6,158,454	21,542	2,553,122	1,436,665
1992	57,790,057	41,599,770	197,911	41,797,681	4,583,415	328,559	37,542,825	13,256,772	6,990,460	22,286	2,593,126	1,406,200
1993	59,097,869	42,174,494	211,031	42,385,525	4,664,660	312,510	38,033,375	13,677,199	7,387,295	22,732	2,599,776	1,402,948
1994	60,822,501	43,439,884	224,569	43,664,453	4,841,405	289,183	39,112,231	14,150,425	7,559,845	23,262	2,614,685	1,408,463
1995	63,655,348	44,948,076	246,325	45,194,401	4,935,671	282,076	40,540,806	15,153,712	7,960,830	24,262	2,623,697	1,440,496
1996	67,886,459	48,215,118	281,483	48,496,601	5,143,271	269,501	43,622,831	15,922,503	8,341,125	25,603	2,651,549	1,479,423
1997	72,619,451	52,176,142	320,278	52,496,420	5,531,639	249,412	47,214,193	16,940,426	8,464,832	26,970	2,692,600	1,521,768
1998	80,550,095	58,819,046	354,060	59,173,106	6,095,194	241,080	53,318,992	18,431,788	8,799,315	29,433	2,736,720	1,610,198
1999	87,189,995	65,445,933	362,330	65,808,263	6,740,517	181,220	59,248,966	18,674,762	9,266,267	31,255	2,789,593	1,659,154
2000	95,753,005	72,703,742	360,665	73,064,407	7,489,562	137,401	65,712,246	20,357,079	9,683,680	33,867	2,827,366	1,701,171
2001	100,173,186	76,403,514	347,422	76,750,936	7,988,047	138,007	68,900,896	20,626,676	10,645,614	34,908	2,869,672	1,723,786
2002	104,400,001	80,554,826	361,674	80,916,500	8,514,350	-77,867	72,324,283	20,867,099	11,208,619	35,996	2,900,355	1,759,032
2003	109,323,606	84,896,065	402,026	85,298,091	9,102,507	-312,681	75,882,903	21,621,624	11,819,079	37,508	2,914,702	1,797,021
2004	116,727,654	90,788,230	447,782	91,236,012	10,025,154	-591,776	80,619,082	23,691,139	12,417,433	39,839	2,930,007	1,822,367
2005	121,544,485	94,482,619	464,331	94,946,950	10,470,224	-889,541	83,587,185	24,838,913	13,118,387	41,365	2,938,375	1,851,248
2006	128,079,224	99,176,833	422,879	99,599,712	10,754,723	-1,214,597	87,630,392	26,341,267	14,107,565	43,457	2,947,289	1,877,852
2007	132,954,811	101,532,224	423,051	101,955,275	10,871,251	-1,557,757	89,526,267	28,514,628	14,913,916	44,680	2,975,742	1,908,466
2008	138,673,021	104,018,025	365,842	104,383,867	11,233,441	-1,897,493	91,252,933	30,379,425	17,040,663	45,886	3,022,116	1,901,372
2009	134,139,980	100,544,000	424,287	100,968,287	11,047,503	-1,957,145	87,963,639	27,412,069	18,764,272	43,819	3,061,203	1,843,540
2010	138,346,589	102,768,198	423,031	103,191,229	11,196,284	-2,038,008	89,956,937	27,428,518	20,961,134	44,563	3,104,543	1,820,818
2011	147,960,807	107,893,524	329,619	108,223,143	10,553,251	-2,139,180	95,530,712	31,091,250	21,338,845	47,095	3,141,768	1,846,720
2012	155,954,440	114,376,518	348,247	114,724,765	10,940,195	-2,166,760	101,617,810	32,823,045	21,513,585	48,990	3,183,413	1,895,595
2013	160,828,662	118,119,628	390,544	118,510,172	12,693,354	-2,135,644	103,681,174	34,697,531	22,449,957	49,907	3,222,558	1,939,119
2014	167,931,419	123,239,802	379,686	123,619,488	13,274,961	-2,169,717	108,174,810	36,217,983	23,538,626	51,459	3,263,431	1,977,874

Personal Income and Employment by Area: San Francisco-Oakland-Hayward, CA

(Thousands of dollars, except as noted.)

Year	Personal income, total	Derivation of personal income									Per capita personal income (dollars)	Population (persons)	Total employment
		Earnings by place of work			Less: Contributions for government social insurance	Plus: Adjustment for residence	Equals: Net earnings by place of residence	Plus: Dividends, interest, and rent	Plus: Personal current transfer receipts				
		Nonfarm	Farm	Total									
1970	17,763,961	14,398,587	54,040	14,452,627	913,367	-499,193	13,040,067	3,236,536	1,487,358	5,715	3,108,460	1,559,634
1971	18,929,528	15,168,583	50,566	15,219,149	990,697	-484,105	13,744,347	3,480,419	1,704,762	6,069	3,119,247	1,528,383
1972	20,554,234	16,531,472	63,355	16,594,827	1,138,293	-503,831	14,952,703	3,775,202	1,826,329	6,557	3,134,632	1,561,571
1973	22,041,047	17,754,914	67,268	17,822,182	1,416,533	-527,506	15,878,143	4,150,749	2,012,155	7,006	3,146,217	1,614,085
1974	24,279,970	19,331,927	72,533	19,404,460	1,598,559	-572,849	17,233,052	4,714,402	2,332,516	7,702	3,152,349	1,648,391
1975	26,837,928	21,150,404	78,432	21,228,836	1,711,748	-636,975	18,880,113	5,070,544	2,887,271	8,497	3,158,346	1,670,337
1976	29,391,378	23,374,420	72,610	23,447,030	1,923,331	-733,229	20,790,470	5,441,287	3,159,621	9,222	3,187,017	1,693,226
1977	32,161,989	25,811,745	63,551	25,875,296	2,148,081	-880,613	22,846,602	5,996,101	3,319,286	10,053	3,199,300	1,733,826
1978	36,037,555	29,159,735	78,859	29,238,594	2,486,580	-1,041,001	25,711,013	6,811,877	3,514,665	11,214	3,213,638	1,817,444
1979	40,239,337	32,590,310	103,502	32,693,812	2,921,238	-1,160,863	28,611,711	7,770,173	3,857,453	12,472	3,226,421	1,895,178
1980	45,490,922	36,233,878	116,289	36,350,167	3,213,774	-1,359,486	31,776,907	9,341,442	4,372,573	13,950	3,260,930	1,955,758
1981	51,323,015	39,756,284	110,412	39,866,696	3,829,807	-1,414,956	34,621,933	11,680,461	5,020,621	15,572	3,295,803	1,971,802
1982	54,868,168	42,188,302	116,698	42,305,000	4,161,149	-1,374,827	36,769,024	12,651,883	5,447,261	16,457	3,333,995	1,960,504
1983	59,766,579	45,877,442	118,991	45,996,433	4,603,045	-1,300,901	40,092,487	13,871,323	5,802,769	17,651	3,386,080	1,996,122
1984	66,297,374	50,587,296	117,042	50,704,338	5,269,289	-1,293,379	44,141,670	16,154,342	6,001,362	19,340	3,428,080	2,066,961
1985	71,053,616	54,475,804	123,645	54,599,449	5,757,939	-1,289,695	47,551,815	17,110,926	6,390,875	20,421	3,479,465	2,120,828
1986	75,689,035	58,940,279	129,897	59,070,176	6,299,596	-1,539,219	51,231,361	17,657,746	6,799,928	21,479	3,523,866	2,168,002
1987	80,110,430	63,046,620	135,832	63,182,452	6,724,025	-1,514,198	54,944,229	18,105,074	7,061,127	22,509	3,558,999	2,224,223
1988	87,617,772	69,201,167	133,159	69,334,326	7,541,660	-1,492,712	60,299,954	19,787,526	7,530,292	24,315	3,603,440	2,310,192
1989	93,831,021	72,684,829	136,327	72,821,156	8,025,216	-1,648,971	63,146,969	22,401,534	8,282,518	25,658	3,656,981	2,351,774
1990	99,228,480	76,927,158	145,811	77,072,969	8,454,059	-1,643,198	66,975,712	23,239,965	9,012,803	26,677	3,719,675	2,399,266
1991	103,552,049	81,167,069	114,587	81,281,656	8,945,022	-1,767,211	70,569,423	23,197,627	9,784,999	27,538	3,760,370	2,388,786
1992	109,622,552	85,877,169	130,332	86,007,501	9,380,097	-1,625,199	75,002,205	23,491,892	11,128,455	28,806	3,805,588	2,347,136
1993	113,817,811	88,768,718	133,073	88,901,791	9,675,635	-1,590,028	77,636,128	24,539,547	11,642,136	29,643	3,839,619	2,358,677
1994	118,092,038	91,930,421	141,876	92,072,297	10,085,835	-1,542,589	80,443,873	25,838,134	11,810,031	30,595	3,859,905	2,385,264
1995	126,513,532	97,379,827	120,170	97,499,997	10,529,578	-1,291,445	85,678,974	28,475,503	12,359,055	32,574	3,883,894	2,436,826
1996	136,987,101	104,490,130	128,917	104,619,047	11,013,515	-183,395	93,422,137	30,744,096	12,820,868	34,917	3,923,208	2,492,590
1997	146,324,444	112,350,919	192,729	112,543,648	11,797,194	285,287	101,031,741	32,422,368	12,870,335	36,712	3,985,694	2,550,128
1998	162,505,408	124,835,888	182,432	125,018,320	12,826,355	877,812	113,069,777	35,890,723	13,544,908	40,173	4,045,185	2,642,295
1999	177,895,500	138,235,157	194,668	138,429,825	14,132,346	2,763,836	127,061,315	36,794,571	14,039,614	43,499	4,089,620	2,702,952
2000	205,043,368	161,571,508	208,228	161,779,736	16,305,284	3,793,062	149,267,514	41,229,208	14,546,646	49,577	4,135,875	2,777,696
2001	205,510,308	163,654,928	218,362	163,873,290	16,764,733	1,594,214	148,702,771	40,866,900	15,940,637	49,227	4,174,788	2,755,341
2002	202,274,677	159,303,040	208,016	159,511,056	16,553,731	2,617,298	145,574,623	39,318,047	17,382,007	48,641	4,158,544	2,693,404
2003	205,205,360	160,718,735	231,442	160,950,177	16,893,224	2,545,857	146,602,810	40,495,299	18,107,251	49,495	4,145,965	2,668,106
2004	217,590,331	168,391,910	190,505	168,582,415	18,088,948	2,537,027	153,030,494	45,704,982	18,854,855	52,642	4,133,400	2,676,462
2005	231,352,393	175,839,604	178,379	176,017,983	18,774,260	1,872,808	159,116,531	52,446,390	19,789,472	55,911	4,137,858	2,701,161
2006	250,453,763	185,113,095	178,755	185,291,850	19,290,220	1,283,152	167,284,782	61,930,752	21,238,229	60,369	4,148,724	2,751,899
2007	260,222,261	192,513,551	169,105	192,682,656	19,823,197	561,379	173,420,838	64,486,807	22,314,616	62,200	4,183,637	2,818,296
2008	264,563,680	193,975,589	135,839	194,111,428	20,333,095	-46,546	173,731,787	65,683,383	25,148,510	62,339	4,243,932	2,816,506
2009	248,917,851	186,007,462	139,283	186,146,745	19,734,712	-908,618	165,503,415	55,582,499	27,831,937	57,850	4,302,830	2,722,531
2010	255,461,345	189,048,947	133,165	189,182,112	19,759,523	1,094,721	170,517,310	54,333,315	30,610,720	58,792	4,345,179	2,690,582
2011	278,037,608	200,298,482	151,193	200,449,675	18,549,996	2,564,347	184,464,026	63,015,491	30,558,091	63,188	4,400,182	2,743,652
2012	304,722,327	224,779,102	212,957	224,992,059	19,999,956	-2,744,151	202,247,952	71,803,761	30,670,614	68,290	4,462,179	2,864,997
2013	313,452,105	234,136,302	156,514	234,292,816	24,028,949	-749,444	209,514,423	72,083,637	31,854,045	69,200	4,529,654	2,972,289
2014	332,445,103	248,722,826	177,213	248,900,039	25,693,902	1,037,251	224,243,388	75,066,242	33,135,473	72,364	4,594,060	3,064,300

Personal Income and Employment by Area: San Jose-Sunnyvale-Santa Clara, CA

(Thousands of dollars, except as noted.)

Year	Personal income, total	Earnings by place of work			Less: Contributions for government social insurance	Plus: Adjustment for residence	Equals: Net earnings by place of residence	Plus: Dividends, interest, and rent	Plus: Personal current transfer receipts	Per capita personal income (dollars)	Population (persons)	Total employment
		Nonfarm	Farm	Total								
1970	5,536,032	4,229,084	48,867	4,277,951	284,629	370,321	4,363,643	766,044	406,345	5,080	1,089,674	465,696
1971	5,959,025	4,528,366	51,593	4,579,959	314,099	360,317	4,626,177	850,727	482,121	5,325	1,119,155	468,263
1972	6,613,245	5,123,502	57,898	5,181,400	376,492	346,550	5,151,458	940,436	521,351	5,712	1,157,841	500,625
1973	7,379,516	5,860,694	78,728	5,939,422	498,849	313,457	5,754,030	1,052,330	573,156	6,235	1,183,576	544,854
1974	8,272,357	6,604,198	81,853	6,686,051	577,197	276,445	6,385,299	1,214,262	672,796	6,982	1,184,823	576,125
1975	9,179,697	7,152,008	82,909	7,234,917	609,197	308,690	6,934,410	1,349,494	895,793	7,563	1,213,688	578,145
1976	10,234,525	8,167,885	68,233	8,236,118	711,958	284,419	7,808,579	1,458,637	967,309	8,330	1,228,572	616,284
1977	11,467,468	9,421,177	82,006	9,503,183	839,279	198,841	8,862,745	1,609,561	995,162	9,142	1,254,396	654,919
1978	13,184,224	11,051,239	83,357	11,134,596	1,015,006	120,714	10,240,304	1,880,149	1,063,771	10,268	1,284,003	708,398
1979	15,260,930	13,105,167	94,626	13,199,793	1,259,754	-7,878	11,932,161	2,188,593	1,140,176	11,778	1,295,698	770,291
1980	17,595,046	15,020,071	104,694	15,124,765	1,422,650	-121,117	13,580,998	2,691,175	1,322,873	13,262	1,326,709	814,696
1981	19,966,896	16,975,646	84,949	17,060,595	1,738,311	-297,409	15,024,875	3,389,672	1,552,349	14,783	1,350,627	832,437
1982	21,843,763	18,890,514	95,526	18,986,040	1,976,945	-554,070	16,455,025	3,722,631	1,666,107	15,922	1,371,955	848,645
1983	24,133,636	21,271,713	99,450	21,371,163	2,276,316	-901,404	18,193,443	4,154,793	1,785,400	17,216	1,401,776	879,267
1984	27,008,344	24,154,159	118,983	24,273,142	2,692,042	-1,293,335	20,287,765	4,901,751	1,818,828	18,951	1,425,185	936,276
1985	28,694,042	25,870,783	125,325	25,996,108	2,910,080	-1,630,677	21,455,351	5,266,174	1,972,517	19,790	1,449,912	949,532
1986	29,829,418	26,953,836	141,408	27,095,244	3,039,145	-1,759,249	22,296,850	5,405,645	2,126,923	20,409	1,461,582	947,268
1987	31,721,957	29,238,212	148,800	29,387,012	3,265,043	-2,191,946	23,930,023	5,579,233	2,212,701	21,426	1,480,543	978,952
1988	34,724,533	32,579,903	141,139	32,721,042	3,735,748	-2,685,231	26,300,063	6,054,476	2,369,994	23,048	1,506,608	1,023,025
1989	37,306,597	34,697,307	138,039	34,835,346	3,967,946	-3,010,936	27,856,464	6,824,942	2,625,191	24,316	1,534,258	1,036,067
1990	39,146,214	36,910,002	126,958	37,036,960	4,200,371	-3,846,943	28,989,646	7,271,808	2,884,760	25,500	1,535,142	1,052,577
1991	40,702,820	38,471,043	112,918	38,583,961	4,407,707	-3,922,656	30,253,598	7,274,385	3,174,837	26,252	1,550,447	1,040,251
1992	43,783,227	41,402,176	120,834	41,523,010	4,650,377	-4,243,661	32,628,972	7,449,535	3,704,720	27,884	1,570,207	1,017,714
1993	44,624,031	42,073,598	155,773	42,229,371	4,779,377	-4,532,539	32,917,455	7,817,930	3,888,646	28,089	1,588,680	1,023,035
1994	46,487,323	43,952,811	169,310	44,122,121	5,055,694	-4,947,432	34,118,995	8,453,294	3,915,034	29,016	1,602,152	1,036,627
1995	51,253,601	48,634,205	197,267	48,831,472	5,521,021	-5,611,568	37,698,883	9,457,301	4,097,417	31,588	1,622,579	1,075,809
1996	55,791,894	54,152,217	178,138	54,330,355	6,075,691	-7,218,725	41,035,939	10,451,265	4,304,690	33,755	1,652,864	1,131,518
1997	61,899,794	61,318,571	193,098	61,511,669	6,782,567	-8,609,597	46,119,505	11,469,983	4,310,306	36,755	1,684,121	1,175,557
1998	67,149,396	67,031,962	198,397	67,230,359	7,313,028	-9,958,106	49,959,225	12,669,599	4,520,572	39,314	1,708,031	1,221,907
1999	75,296,430	78,559,040	223,355	78,782,395	8,408,638	-12,974,021	57,399,736	13,169,693	4,727,001	43,702	1,722,965	1,227,905
2000	93,909,845	100,615,109	324,311	100,939,420	10,266,029	-16,697,064	73,976,327	14,996,795	4,936,723	54,011	1,738,728	1,285,738
2001	85,569,962	88,552,816	249,241	88,802,057	9,300,955	-14,215,574	65,285,528	14,848,674	5,435,760	49,101	1,742,726	1,248,701
2002	78,809,886	78,656,752	221,472	78,878,224	8,404,181	-12,317,139	58,156,904	14,402,474	6,250,508	45,703	1,724,404	1,154,640
2003	79,538,160	78,069,289	229,963	78,299,252	8,380,877	-12,002,195	57,916,180	15,133,771	6,488,209	46,276	1,718,790	1,112,231
2004	84,086,300	82,584,286	243,269	82,827,555	8,954,510	-12,338,589	61,534,456	16,027,275	6,524,569	48,944	1,718,016	1,108,227
2005	89,047,729	85,350,818	230,207	85,581,025	9,176,419	-12,483,215	63,921,391	18,267,870	6,858,468	51,474	1,729,959	1,125,759
2006	98,346,897	92,067,780	226,461	92,294,241	9,657,447	-13,039,130	69,597,664	21,309,620	7,439,613	56,350	1,745,283	1,156,156
2007	106,829,167	98,748,109	207,604	98,955,713	10,137,146	-13,676,894	75,141,673	23,798,568	7,888,926	60,489	1,766,098	1,193,307
2008	107,165,424	98,289,966	168,582	98,458,548	10,403,403	-12,991,137	75,064,008	23,021,685	9,079,731	59,695	1,795,231	1,197,918
2009	100,131,564	91,750,092	229,441	91,979,533	9,937,756	-11,057,274	70,984,503	18,886,754	10,260,307	55,030	1,819,573	1,143,637
2010	108,321,089	100,159,492	205,574	100,365,066	10,421,076	-12,558,203	77,385,787	19,616,740	11,318,562	58,791	1,842,462	1,136,652
2011	119,126,335	109,233,784	166,179	109,399,963	9,892,017	-14,888,188	84,619,758	23,259,384	11,247,193	63,694	1,870,279	1,170,608
2012	134,089,564	115,946,556	188,852	116,135,408	10,363,580	-10,448,287	95,323,541	27,549,011	11,217,012	70,649	1,897,969	1,216,071
2013	135,934,181	123,058,832	235,525	123,294,357	12,801,691	-13,563,036	96,929,630	27,469,200	11,535,351	70,480	1,928,701	1,261,708
2014	144,290,968	134,648,893	246,589	134,895,482	13,958,311	-17,290,962	103,646,209	28,685,224	11,959,535	73,887	1,952,872	1,304,271

Personal Income and Employment by Area: San Luis Obispo-Paso Robles-Arroyo Grande, CA

(Thousands of dollars, except as noted.)

Year	Personal income, total	Derivation of personal income					Plus: Dividends, interest, and rent	Plus: Personal current transfer receipts	Per capita personal income (dollars)	Population (persons)	Total employment
		Earnings by place of work			Less: Contributions for government social insurance	Plus: Adjustment for residence	Equals: Net earnings by place of residence					
		Nonfarm	Farm	Total								
1970	410,207	252,677	17,638	270,315	15,461	13,420	268,274	86,166	55,767	3,860	106,280	38,922
1971	455,185	285,152	17,908	303,060	17,896	13,976	299,140	95,452	60,593	4,165	109,301	40,811
1972	512,853	324,290	23,147	347,437	21,631	14,931	340,737	106,845	65,271	4,441	115,484	43,478
1973	578,886	362,023	27,270	389,293	27,430	17,833	379,696	125,069	74,121	4,830	119,843	45,667
1974	671,161	403,459	40,083	443,542	31,590	21,582	433,534	146,210	91,417	5,346	125,535	48,387
1975	764,092	455,495	33,698	489,193	34,937	27,226	481,482	169,373	113,237	6,042	126,456	50,574
1976	870,098	526,877	33,850	560,727	40,546	33,059	553,240	187,042	129,816	6,481	134,260	53,644
1977	970,882	590,124	27,105	617,229	46,332	41,799	612,696	215,917	142,269	7,003	138,635	56,552
1978	1,150,446	700,189	44,864	745,053	56,581	48,043	736,515	257,497	156,434	7,884	145,914	60,728
1979	1,309,989	797,489	41,414	838,903	68,104	59,289	830,088	304,558	175,343	8,684	150,850	65,290
1980	1,482,034	849,038	45,673	894,711	70,417	72,537	896,831	378,555	206,648	9,453	156,786	66,956
1981	1,664,100	928,814	49,536	978,350	86,313	66,954	958,991	461,340	243,769	10,279	161,886	68,339
1982	1,781,982	960,465	62,286	1,022,751	92,552	74,658	1,004,857	511,914	265,211	10,699	166,563	68,574
1983	2,155,938	1,282,447	68,083	1,350,530	129,499	50,117	1,271,148	602,800	281,990	12,581	171,365	75,005
1984	2,373,876	1,414,006	53,564	1,467,570	146,826	68,296	1,389,040	679,589	305,247	13,369	177,566	79,834
1985	2,543,293	1,482,443	53,258	1,535,701	151,712	88,677	1,472,666	736,843	333,784	13,729	185,248	84,089
1986	2,770,921	1,629,177	72,418	1,701,595	168,011	95,206	1,628,790	782,931	359,200	14,395	192,497	87,984
1987	3,016,373	1,832,572	84,857	1,917,429	189,690	94,069	1,821,808	816,591	377,974	15,131	199,345	92,685
1988	3,309,458	2,025,552	88,696	2,114,248	216,497	103,087	2,000,838	902,610	406,010	16,202	204,261	98,930
1989	3,667,941	2,187,015	91,975	2,278,990	237,718	108,068	2,149,340	1,072,345	446,256	17,195	213,314	103,273
1990	3,828,138	2,351,778	72,761	2,424,539	253,857	111,634	2,282,316	1,062,757	483,065	17,538	218,276	106,051
1991	3,992,542	2,493,873	47,156	2,541,029	268,926	124,129	2,396,232	1,069,044	527,266	18,157	219,895	110,470
1992	4,232,319	2,644,684	63,697	2,708,381	283,637	130,122	2,554,866	1,080,319	597,134	19,078	221,848	110,178
1993	4,379,996	2,705,372	77,927	2,783,299	289,840	135,409	2,628,868	1,115,143	635,985	19,609	223,370	109,848
1994	4,552,480	2,804,440	70,575	2,875,015	302,014	143,053	2,716,054	1,178,355	658,071	20,123	226,228	112,959
1995	4,817,977	2,985,024	74,240	3,059,264	314,827	151,103	2,895,540	1,232,398	690,039	21,005	229,370	116,952
1996	5,195,413	3,227,508	76,942	3,304,450	327,594	159,532	3,136,388	1,328,080	730,945	22,300	232,976	120,730
1997	5,655,546	3,516,333	125,149	3,641,482	350,168	173,504	3,464,818	1,441,914	748,814	23,903	236,601	125,634
1998	6,122,952	3,851,517	101,643	3,953,160	376,232	189,968	3,766,896	1,570,651	785,405	25,510	240,020	132,120
1999	6,484,638	4,135,641	109,017	4,244,658	405,052	210,476	4,050,082	1,618,074	816,482	26,633	243,480	138,230
2000	7,041,288	4,422,578	166,160	4,588,738	434,991	250,533	4,404,280	1,771,760	865,248	28,411	247,839	138,984
2001	7,487,822	4,729,062	130,155	4,859,217	484,293	284,575	4,659,499	1,877,931	950,392	29,777	251,462	140,319
2002	7,800,239	5,091,896	131,445	5,223,341	526,891	308,577	5,005,027	1,795,085	1,000,127	30,821	253,083	143,960
2003	8,152,391	5,368,300	133,469	5,501,769	560,787	332,764	5,273,746	1,840,987	1,037,658	32,011	254,674	144,948
2004	8,746,789	5,788,131	122,720	5,910,851	625,412	371,877	5,657,316	2,012,717	1,076,756	34,055	256,842	148,297
2005	9,187,325	6,053,937	124,047	6,177,984	661,609	402,502	5,918,877	2,118,470	1,149,978	35,525	258,615	151,584
2006	9,926,022	6,354,207	125,739	6,479,946	669,618	447,148	6,257,476	2,429,716	1,238,830	38,104	260,498	154,129
2007	10,456,752	6,480,795	126,190	6,606,985	674,378	496,715	6,429,322	2,720,891	1,306,539	39,794	262,770	157,261
2008	10,441,864	6,508,284	63,983	6,572,267	686,242	530,384	6,416,409	2,529,518	1,495,937	39,202	266,358	155,039
2009	10,229,839	6,245,404	125,144	6,370,548	674,368	518,398	6,214,578	2,380,700	1,634,561	38,150	268,145	149,936
2010	10,473,063	6,317,857	146,899	6,464,756	675,189	528,008	6,317,575	2,363,345	1,792,143	38,809	269,860	148,369
2011	11,232,403	6,682,790	134,000	6,816,790	642,989	558,710	6,732,511	2,687,882	1,812,010	41,423	271,165	151,749
2012	11,908,742	7,016,166	219,122	7,235,288	658,826	589,129	7,165,591	2,908,525	1,834,626	43,379	274,528	156,153
2013	12,337,936	7,260,983	292,852	7,553,835	770,031	587,301	7,371,105	3,064,489	1,902,342	44,657	276,284	159,767
2014	12,823,005	7,579,652	250,292	7,829,944	812,107	620,778	7,638,615	3,191,552	1,992,838	45,947	279,083	164,042

Personal Income and Employment by Area: Santa Cruz-Watsonville, CA

(Thousands of dollars, except as noted.)

Year	Personal income, total	Derivation of personal income								Per capita personal income (dollars)	Population (persons)	Total employment
		Earnings by place of work			Less: Contributions for government social insurance	Plus: Adjustment for residence	Equals: Net earnings by place of residence	Plus: Dividends, interest, and rent	Plus: Personal current transfer receipts			
		Nonfarm	Farm	Total								
1970	557,769	313,428	19,379	332,807	21,290	48,118	359,635	127,157	70,977	4,470	124,788	49,358
1971	622,630	340,388	21,178	361,566	23,486	60,134	398,214	141,141	83,275	4,794	129,886	50,838
1972	706,925	386,890	24,048	410,938	27,969	75,281	458,250	156,201	92,474	4,983	141,878	55,131
1973	818,075	437,814	35,687	473,501	35,970	94,488	532,019	176,578	109,478	5,628	145,347	58,086
1974	934,983	487,195	35,625	522,820	41,200	117,750	599,370	205,162	130,451	6,240	149,828	61,601
1975	1,059,658	534,622	31,297	565,919	43,817	146,919	669,021	229,858	160,779	6,680	158,622	64,137
1976	1,212,624	625,758	36,258	662,016	51,254	175,600	786,362	251,105	175,157	7,217	168,026	68,940
1977	1,393,020	727,668	43,947	771,615	61,410	212,788	922,993	284,580	185,447	7,954	175,132	73,750
1978	1,610,006	843,184	50,910	894,094	72,810	257,819	1,079,103	330,333	200,570	9,207	174,865	77,918
1979	1,836,287	933,821	62,176	995,997	84,913	324,197	1,235,281	383,025	217,981	9,978	184,041	81,923
1980	2,131,864	1,041,201	65,159	1,106,360	92,424	393,676	1,407,612	471,542	252,710	11,262	189,305	84,798
1981	2,416,460	1,149,581	77,394	1,226,975	111,963	428,072	1,543,084	585,095	288,281	12,482	193,590	87,088
1982	2,578,528	1,216,911	80,138	1,297,049	121,970	465,908	1,640,987	631,428	306,113	13,066	197,353	87,797
1983	2,905,151	1,384,908	127,879	1,512,787	140,239	504,123	1,876,671	701,440	327,040	14,388	201,921	93,297
1984	3,228,588	1,572,482	129,453	1,701,935	165,942	557,359	2,093,352	796,099	339,137	15,675	205,964	97,417
1985	3,425,599	1,698,789	98,634	1,797,423	181,636	591,635	2,207,422	852,159	366,018	16,148	212,143	102,627
1986	3,677,604	1,852,660	135,321	1,987,981	200,846	606,260	2,393,395	894,036	390,173	16,974	216,661	103,042
1987	3,950,509	2,066,262	152,067	2,218,329	225,078	642,008	2,635,259	913,273	401,977	17,859	221,202	108,605
1988	4,322,999	2,337,117	160,563	2,497,680	263,877	686,688	2,920,491	979,594	422,914	19,154	225,700	117,109
1989	4,591,637	2,436,147	154,686	2,590,833	280,376	723,761	3,034,218	1,076,454	480,965	19,837	231,463	119,693
1990	4,982,189	2,740,707	187,277	2,927,984	311,448	749,437	3,365,973	1,105,729	510,487	21,698	229,616	125,068
1991	5,167,907	2,939,124	174,555	3,113,679	338,849	773,487	3,548,317	1,090,587	529,003	22,476	229,935	129,334
1992	5,525,426	3,127,471	214,771	3,342,242	359,790	824,381	3,806,833	1,109,687	608,906	23,723	232,912	126,162
1993	5,737,055	3,192,307	225,216	3,417,523	365,365	854,082	3,906,240	1,182,680	648,135	24,373	235,386	128,059
1994	5,962,931	3,316,594	211,314	3,527,908	379,550	891,778	4,040,136	1,276,061	646,734	25,084	237,714	129,313
1995	6,368,398	3,528,755	214,646	3,743,401	396,919	990,027	4,336,509	1,357,557	674,332	26,610	239,324	133,854
1996	6,859,912	3,772,812	227,894	4,000,706	407,504	1,112,232	4,705,434	1,460,469	694,009	28,445	241,168	136,690
1997	7,406,407	4,012,622	239,582	4,252,204	423,999	1,286,724	5,114,929	1,587,984	703,494	30,188	245,344	136,897
1998	8,039,359	4,426,362	216,759	4,643,121	454,569	1,425,611	5,614,163	1,708,755	716,441	32,043	250,889	145,426
1999	8,850,149	4,719,198	374,571	5,093,769	487,483	1,734,619	6,340,905	1,763,760	745,484	34,889	253,667	146,451
2000	10,259,913	5,532,220	295,963	5,828,183	556,332	2,270,082	7,541,933	1,952,539	765,441	40,104	255,835	146,510
2001	10,026,075	5,647,211	263,624	5,910,835	587,477	2,017,140	7,340,498	1,842,033	843,544	39,157	256,045	145,207
2002	9,960,710	5,697,294	241,362	5,938,656	588,256	1,864,033	7,214,433	1,833,314	912,963	39,134	254,531	142,986
2003	10,043,393	5,719,108	290,995	6,010,103	599,380	1,768,816	7,179,539	1,901,582	962,272	39,694	253,021	141,999
2004	10,518,330	5,943,122	310,341	6,253,463	644,904	1,747,283	7,355,842	2,171,251	991,237	41,681	252,356	142,442
2005	10,669,019	6,089,421	289,482	6,378,903	668,027	1,709,190	7,420,066	2,201,925	1,047,028	42,442	251,377	142,750
2006	11,460,367	6,461,307	250,203	6,711,510	683,038	1,757,567	7,786,039	2,552,077	1,122,251	45,547	251,616	143,513
2007	11,910,387	6,483,034	279,091	6,762,125	680,096	1,742,458	7,824,487	2,884,879	1,201,021	47,020	253,304	146,137
2008	11,940,819	6,265,899	269,170	6,535,069	670,339	1,633,776	7,498,506	3,064,645	1,377,668	46,549	256,520	143,090
2009	11,080,626	5,870,052	358,980	6,229,032	652,948	1,534,471	7,110,555	2,425,351	1,544,720	42,616	260,009	139,736
2010	11,267,634	5,934,746	368,869	6,303,615	645,367	1,603,701	7,261,949	2,296,915	1,708,770	42,808	263,213	138,820
2011	12,125,514	6,275,556	315,139	6,590,695	611,030	1,757,116	7,736,781	2,682,423	1,706,310	45,770	264,923	138,540
2012	13,116,916	6,479,415	338,248	6,817,663	614,221	2,030,741	8,234,183	3,151,389	1,731,344	49,195	266,632	140,550
2013	13,456,565	6,767,114	394,503	7,161,617	721,001	2,108,236	8,548,852	3,103,589	1,804,124	49,942	269,444	144,724
2014	14,209,814	7,110,027	375,020	7,485,047	762,244	2,360,421	9,083,224	3,241,717	1,884,873	52,280	271,804	148,684

Personal Income and Employment by Area: Santa Fe, NM

(Thousands of dollars, except as noted.)

Year	Personal income, total	Earnings by place of work			Less: Contributions for government social insurance	Plus: Adjustment for residence	Equals: Net earnings by place of residence	Plus: Dividends, interest, and rent	Plus: Personal current transfer receipts	Per capita personal income (dollars)	Population (persons)	Total employment
		Nonfarm	Farm	Total								
1970	204,576	139,648	1,931	141,579	7,853	11,367	145,093	40,660	18,823	3,718	55,026	22,514
1971	228,540	158,493	1,472	159,965	9,362	11,158	161,761	45,589	21,190	4,018	56,874	24,070
1972	261,017	182,638	1,202	183,840	11,241	14,047	186,646	51,316	23,055	4,406	59,243	26,263
1973	294,574	207,260	2,590	209,850	14,970	15,967	210,847	57,222	26,505	4,810	61,246	28,068
1974	337,523	234,870	3,170	238,040	17,567	18,093	238,566	66,800	32,157	5,334	63,278	29,166
1975	377,798	261,162	2,160	263,322	19,143	22,044	266,223	71,121	40,454	5,730	65,930	29,184
1976	428,000	296,353	1,583	297,936	21,533	27,178	303,581	80,382	44,037	6,195	69,090	30,690
1977	485,224	340,227	1,087	341,314	25,169	32,259	348,404	91,150	45,670	6,776	71,604	33,009
1978	565,773	394,854	2,639	397,493	30,115	37,122	404,500	109,950	51,323	7,786	72,669	35,227
1979	633,342	434,144	2,461	436,605	34,969	42,332	443,968	130,237	59,137	8,405	75,353	36,981
1980	714,488	480,937	533	481,470	39,903	46,239	487,806	155,650	71,032	9,417	75,872	37,378
1981	824,499	534,200	557	534,757	47,544	55,158	542,371	201,840	80,288	10,677	77,222	38,104
1982	927,398	584,834	1,011	585,845	53,555	62,284	594,574	246,898	85,926	11,575	80,118	40,035
1983	1,016,157	658,000	-385	657,615	60,722	69,156	666,049	259,625	90,483	12,354	82,250	42,732
1984	1,136,444	732,785	1,292	734,077	68,491	82,151	747,737	291,703	97,004	13,512	84,106	44,481
1985	1,259,563	798,580	3,175	801,755	76,060	97,226	822,921	331,461	105,181	14,701	85,676	46,724
1986	1,376,415	888,372	1,874	890,246	85,081	101,249	906,414	356,382	113,619	15,442	89,134	48,864
1987	1,456,363	929,383	1,061	930,444	88,325	119,401	961,520	372,268	122,575	15,775	92,323	50,998
1988	1,564,701	997,012	2,567	999,579	101,409	118,745	1,016,915	414,929	132,857	16,556	94,507	54,052
1989	1,721,290	1,098,556	1,094	1,099,650	113,378	129,447	1,115,719	455,122	150,449	17,752	96,962	56,683
1990	1,871,945	1,209,561	2,134	1,211,695	132,417	131,997	1,211,275	497,047	163,623	18,797	99,587	58,372
1991	2,027,918	1,351,207	4,009	1,355,216	149,873	116,115	1,321,458	526,783	179,677	19,778	102,536	63,309
1992	2,232,352	1,485,559	3,207	1,488,766	162,910	139,672	1,465,528	565,371	201,453	21,054	106,030	65,129
1993	2,451,428	1,657,480	2,611	1,660,091	180,393	122,405	1,602,103	625,885	223,440	22,301	109,927	68,364
1994	2,660,388	1,768,588	3,931	1,772,519	197,199	132,225	1,707,545	713,966	238,877	23,348	113,944	70,827
1995	2,955,721	1,915,845	2,885	1,918,730	214,154	134,436	1,839,012	848,737	267,972	24,951	118,462	75,227
1996	3,109,664	1,955,093	3,345	1,958,438	219,165	132,915	1,872,188	942,423	295,053	25,693	121,031	75,777
1997	3,296,298	2,092,117	2,042	2,094,159	231,305	129,598	1,992,452	995,193	308,653	26,546	124,172	77,163
1998	3,599,150	2,266,490	3,024	2,269,514	247,506	162,413	2,184,421	1,091,215	323,514	28,575	125,956	78,600
1999	3,746,943	2,354,725	6,992	2,361,717	258,012	183,700	2,287,405	1,107,271	352,267	29,281	127,966	79,078
2000	4,222,705	2,661,141	5,937	2,667,078	275,145	212,157	2,604,090	1,239,386	379,229	32,554	129,713	80,857
2001	4,549,751	2,959,416	7,524	2,966,940	297,647	192,357	2,861,650	1,270,075	418,026	34,716	131,057	79,912
2002	4,771,825	3,286,005	6,380	3,292,385	322,251	178,707	3,148,841	1,160,626	462,358	35,729	133,555	80,993
2003	4,779,027	3,283,473	4,934	3,288,407	334,573	158,374	3,112,208	1,173,035	493,784	35,344	135,213	83,493
2004	5,077,595	3,420,028	4,476	3,424,504	353,560	143,312	3,214,256	1,330,833	532,506	37,228	136,391	85,634
2005	5,480,294	3,595,686	5,191	3,600,877	373,996	124,577	3,351,458	1,551,525	577,311	39,825	137,610	87,701
2006	5,917,791	3,841,280	9,255	3,850,535	406,104	104,049	3,548,480	1,734,302	635,009	42,640	138,786	90,069
2007	6,282,341	4,016,891	3,069	4,019,960	437,126	80,010	3,662,844	1,921,540	697,957	44,807	140,210	93,603
2008	6,424,581	4,059,768	1,913	4,061,681	452,681	47,709	3,656,709	1,948,123	819,749	45,338	141,704	92,689
2009	6,084,336	3,768,838	186	3,769,024	431,745	123,071	3,460,350	1,712,625	911,361	42,487	143,205	88,457
2010	6,146,831	3,780,717	-1,659	3,779,058	436,227	166,163	3,508,994	1,629,447	1,008,390	42,538	144,503	86,606
2011	6,488,609	3,820,774	-819	3,819,955	393,820	176,056	3,602,191	1,851,878	1,034,540	44,612	145,447	86,347
2012	6,784,735	3,861,072	-2,136	3,858,936	396,978	244,614	3,706,572	2,025,583	1,052,580	46,349	146,385	85,862
2013	6,855,283	3,909,447	192	3,909,639	462,623	224,202	3,671,218	2,082,412	1,101,653	46,538	147,306	86,778
2014	7,155,057	3,980,477	15	3,980,492	472,077	282,201	3,790,616	2,149,205	1,215,236	48,291	148,164	86,905

Personal Income and Employment by Area: Santa Maria-Santa Barbara, CA

(Thousands of dollars, except as noted.)

Year	Personal income, total	Earnings by place of work			Less: Contributions for government social insurance	Plus: Adjustment for residence	Equals: Net earnings by place of residence	Plus: Dividends, interest, and rent	Plus: Personal current transfer receipts	Per capita personal income (dollars)	Population (persons)	Total employment
		Nonfarm	Farm	Total								
1970	1,339,453	923,672	35,407	959,079	57,439	-5,170	896,470	335,712	107,271	5,049	265,291	116,626
1971	1,430,987	975,750	38,675	1,014,425	62,342	-4,302	947,781	361,172	122,034	5,301	269,930	117,818
1972	1,571,280	1,064,038	53,455	1,117,493	71,039	-3,343	1,043,111	393,088	135,081	5,673	276,957	121,263
1973	1,743,168	1,178,354	66,679	1,245,033	89,770	-4,769	1,150,494	439,879	152,795	6,284	277,414	129,723
1974	1,919,940	1,280,431	69,400	1,349,831	101,120	-6,187	1,242,524	497,541	179,875	6,896	278,431	134,399
1975	2,117,353	1,410,540	68,732	1,479,272	109,335	-8,334	1,361,603	534,167	221,583	7,492	282,626	138,012
1976	2,344,045	1,590,961	68,134	1,659,095	124,424	-11,070	1,523,601	575,764	244,680	8,194	286,075	141,699
1977	2,579,954	1,764,219	74,682	1,838,901	142,811	-16,170	1,679,920	641,178	258,856	8,885	290,381	149,056
1978	2,954,821	2,044,273	80,906	2,125,179	169,465	-20,540	1,935,174	744,334	275,313	10,003	295,397	160,992
1979	3,318,640	2,285,344	94,856	2,380,200	201,716	-26,534	2,151,950	863,156	303,534	11,234	295,423	168,561
1980	3,774,305	2,507,885	132,061	2,639,946	218,303	-35,134	2,386,509	1,036,337	351,459	12,573	300,191	168,218
1981	4,300,536	2,754,170	123,347	2,877,517	261,988	-40,413	2,575,116	1,307,953	417,467	14,073	305,588	171,396
1982	4,638,392	2,949,083	149,116	3,098,199	288,319	-51,372	2,758,508	1,428,391	451,493	14,816	313,073	172,644
1983	5,030,596	3,208,441	170,756	3,379,197	318,948	-48,600	3,011,649	1,538,092	480,855	15,609	322,294	176,829
1984	5,670,480	3,728,276	133,162	3,861,438	386,614	-76,632	3,398,192	1,769,171	503,117	17,229	329,133	185,802
1985	6,106,961	4,092,433	134,969	4,227,402	429,120	-95,131	3,703,151	1,864,725	539,085	18,038	338,569	192,555
1986	6,508,720	4,409,198	154,335	4,563,533	465,447	-103,593	3,994,493	1,936,900	577,327	18,830	345,651	197,339
1987	6,892,885	4,692,849	180,566	4,873,415	492,651	-99,225	4,281,539	2,008,848	602,498	19,581	352,021	200,745
1988	7,446,137	5,065,140	204,678	5,269,818	546,178	-108,354	4,615,286	2,186,553	644,298	20,927	355,810	207,750
1989	8,063,009	5,406,235	217,498	5,623,733	590,598	-124,848	4,908,287	2,449,103	705,619	22,048	365,695	212,536
1990	8,334,826	5,612,657	239,916	5,852,573	617,345	-136,304	5,098,924	2,459,685	776,217	22,492	370,565	214,939
1991	8,787,077	6,041,238	205,414	6,246,652	661,817	-153,003	5,431,832	2,498,610	856,635	23,438	374,910	220,855
1992	9,151,357	6,236,356	170,978	6,407,334	676,349	-158,274	5,572,711	2,615,013	963,633	24,210	378,003	214,252
1993	9,340,249	6,266,267	239,029	6,505,296	679,869	-161,156	5,664,271	2,653,412	1,022,566	24,575	380,064	215,117
1994	9,668,554	6,264,723	219,509	6,484,232	690,911	-169,974	5,623,347	3,004,607	1,040,600	25,164	384,226	216,284
1995	9,880,073	6,392,488	276,876	6,669,364	699,257	-182,681	5,787,426	2,999,821	1,092,826	25,690	384,582	221,933
1996	10,339,668	6,640,294	281,121	6,921,415	707,335	-195,123	6,018,957	3,176,765	1,143,946	26,779	386,108	225,153
1997	10,738,571	6,968,054	330,822	7,298,876	737,354	-220,282	6,341,240	3,232,630	1,164,701	27,444	391,290	226,970
1998	11,725,435	7,578,945	318,447	7,897,392	782,538	-241,658	6,873,196	3,644,629	1,207,610	29,704	394,738	236,161
1999	12,354,432	7,981,204	352,135	8,333,339	828,761	-268,289	7,236,289	3,855,156	1,262,987	31,127	396,906	240,323
2000	13,480,888	8,876,635	389,498	9,266,133	925,326	-325,292	8,015,515	4,135,902	1,329,471	33,703	399,990	244,899
2001	13,565,995	9,131,308	303,985	9,435,293	975,063	-345,445	8,114,785	4,009,057	1,442,153	33,649	403,164	243,953
2002	13,536,828	9,485,152	345,774	9,830,926	1,026,637	-384,533	8,419,756	3,603,381	1,513,691	33,410	405,178	245,256
2003	14,282,590	10,098,083	382,290	10,480,373	1,109,838	-440,729	8,929,806	3,772,657	1,580,127	35,109	406,810	250,558
2004	15,859,153	10,821,792	377,519	11,199,311	1,224,905	-498,622	9,475,784	4,736,561	1,646,808	38,939	407,284	255,030
2005	16,871,037	11,430,193	410,993	11,841,186	1,286,890	-560,726	9,993,570	5,145,180	1,732,287	41,343	408,079	258,637
2006	18,308,614	11,782,951	408,846	12,191,797	1,284,361	-603,884	10,303,552	6,137,868	1,867,194	44,865	408,085	257,931
2007	18,723,624	12,089,568	402,345	12,491,913	1,300,746	-657,847	10,533,320	6,229,995	1,960,309	45,529	411,243	262,375
2008	18,808,064	12,364,505	386,337	12,750,842	1,337,122	-699,278	10,714,442	5,872,902	2,220,720	45,227	415,859	260,025
2009	18,000,151	11,922,160	648,233	12,570,393	1,320,046	-680,301	10,570,046	5,019,577	2,410,528	42,821	420,356	252,298
2010	18,374,133	12,069,789	542,783	12,612,572	1,310,653	-687,533	10,614,386	5,126,992	2,632,755	43,301	424,331	247,443
2011	19,878,720	12,721,069	449,770	13,170,839	1,241,423	-732,193	11,197,223	6,012,033	2,669,464	46,667	425,974	252,530
2012	21,237,984	13,558,251	541,087	14,099,338	1,297,813	-778,362	12,023,163	6,535,393	2,679,428	49,307	430,728	258,570
2013	21,404,955	13,725,132	714,477	14,439,609	1,476,235	-778,928	12,184,446	6,438,475	2,782,034	49,085	436,076	262,523
2014	22,263,835	14,312,639	716,341	15,028,980	1,547,900	-809,498	12,671,582	6,702,446	2,889,807	50,523	440,668	269,772

Personal Income and Employment by Area: Santa Rosa, CA

(Thousands of dollars, except as noted.)

| Year | Personal income, total | Derivation of personal income | | | | | | | | Per capita personal income (dollars) | Population (persons) | Total employment |
| | | Earnings by place of work | | | Less: Contributions for government social insurance | Plus: Adjustment for residence | Equals: Net earnings by place of residence | Plus: Dividends, interest, and rent | Plus: Personal current transfer receipts | | | |
		Nonfarm	Farm	Total								
1970	956,208	511,515	24,485	536,000	33,046	137,519	640,473	199,453	116,282	4,642	206,003	74,003
1971	1,062,453	567,667	18,145	585,812	37,911	160,964	708,865	222,646	130,942	5,002	212,402	76,798
1972	1,204,730	647,458	25,319	672,777	45,213	187,354	814,918	249,191	140,621	5,376	224,091	82,982
1973	1,367,687	734,899	33,869	768,768	58,484	213,180	923,464	285,447	158,776	5,748	237,957	88,869
1974	1,548,697	818,444	27,524	845,968	67,227	247,684	1,026,425	331,129	191,143	6,373	243,028	93,352
1975	1,768,677	904,980	29,681	934,661	72,373	288,200	1,150,488	373,061	245,128	6,984	253,255	96,964
1976	2,016,288	1,059,068	33,457	1,092,525	85,201	325,247	1,332,571	410,395	273,322	7,677	262,654	103,354
1977	2,282,361	1,203,281	41,600	1,244,881	98,747	373,439	1,519,573	467,883	294,905	8,355	273,175	109,903
1978	2,662,480	1,428,851	46,255	1,475,106	119,776	438,287	1,793,617	549,522	319,341	9,460	281,442	118,796
1979	3,042,177	1,646,630	45,489	1,692,119	145,843	495,130	2,041,406	640,736	360,035	10,423	291,859	127,676
1980	3,472,888	1,806,013	39,817	1,845,830	157,277	581,299	2,269,852	783,616	419,420	11,515	301,586	133,637
1981	3,954,335	1,985,696	67,446	2,053,142	190,125	641,558	2,504,575	955,724	494,036	12,813	308,609	137,159
1982	4,210,872	2,102,454	57,548	2,160,002	206,395	691,113	2,644,720	1,036,645	529,507	13,383	314,636	138,573
1983	4,628,915	2,346,093	42,214	2,388,307	234,250	742,553	2,896,610	1,174,640	557,665	14,394	321,580	145,902
1984	5,204,458	2,728,326	54,957	2,783,283	284,108	805,004	3,304,179	1,320,188	580,091	15,922	326,863	155,144
1985	5,655,749	3,000,498	58,263	3,058,761	316,596	854,629	3,596,794	1,435,399	623,556	16,865	335,355	161,324
1986	6,120,959	3,296,074	60,464	3,356,538	350,908	919,906	3,925,536	1,522,968	672,455	17,728	345,270	166,384
1987	6,579,248	3,632,998	72,134	3,705,132	389,242	967,981	4,283,871	1,592,066	703,311	18,475	356,111	174,046
1988	7,214,272	4,037,187	81,747	4,118,934	445,051	1,040,590	4,714,473	1,742,788	757,011	19,610	367,893	186,395
1989	8,070,693	4,417,715	110,172	4,527,887	493,549	1,116,899	5,151,237	2,081,427	838,029	21,203	380,633	193,548
1990	8,685,211	4,848,666	101,673	4,950,339	539,375	1,262,867	5,673,831	2,105,547	905,833	22,242	390,495	204,435
1991	9,057,992	5,147,924	117,482	5,265,406	579,206	1,241,242	5,927,442	2,130,433	1,000,117	22,762	397,937	207,198
1992	9,578,469	5,486,157	112,314	5,598,471	609,300	1,252,211	6,241,382	2,200,025	1,137,062	23,642	405,151	207,086
1993	10,045,302	5,764,430	93,382	5,857,812	638,111	1,314,598	6,534,299	2,317,370	1,193,633	24,460	410,687	210,765
1994	10,535,135	6,094,663	93,567	6,188,230	672,974	1,359,454	6,874,710	2,428,365	1,232,060	25,316	416,152	218,474
1995	11,012,702	6,296,947	82,049	6,378,996	691,325	1,387,596	7,075,267	2,643,676	1,293,759	26,079	422,286	221,033
1996	11,875,927	6,859,173	108,322	6,967,495	724,907	1,395,210	7,637,798	2,879,800	1,358,329	27,722	428,399	232,015
1997	12,984,861	7,643,290	168,525	7,811,815	797,979	1,511,126	8,524,962	3,082,375	1,377,524	29,704	437,141	242,030
1998	14,112,723	8,638,910	133,803	8,772,713	879,204	1,528,019	9,421,528	3,258,450	1,432,745	31,650	445,901	254,499
1999	14,948,280	9,384,656	125,170	9,509,826	957,492	1,545,895	10,098,229	3,363,568	1,486,483	32,968	453,421	263,927
2000	17,043,725	10,667,718	191,965	10,859,683	1,091,252	2,012,329	11,780,760	3,707,288	1,555,677	37,018	460,421	268,621
2001	17,305,730	10,938,225	176,019	11,114,244	1,164,544	2,002,690	11,952,390	3,640,956	1,712,384	37,193	465,293	273,682
2002	17,292,440	11,217,106	166,578	11,383,684	1,202,374	1,842,487	12,023,797	3,451,196	1,817,447	37,164	465,298	273,233
2003	17,550,632	11,386,017	114,610	11,500,627	1,236,680	1,693,795	11,957,742	3,667,441	1,925,449	37,623	466,489	270,576
2004	18,144,859	11,948,422	137,273	12,085,695	1,346,980	1,627,098	12,365,813	3,780,947	1,998,099	38,870	466,809	274,967
2005	18,839,106	12,369,247	198,617	12,567,864	1,403,431	1,539,040	12,703,473	4,022,669	2,112,964	40,433	465,938	276,676
2006	20,033,058	12,822,825	120,403	12,943,228	1,415,629	1,460,691	12,988,290	4,737,768	2,307,000	43,064	465,188	278,545
2007	20,511,416	12,960,762	137,806	13,098,568	1,417,619	1,367,505	13,048,454	5,022,592	2,440,370	43,888	467,356	282,795
2008	20,408,986	12,870,023	91,359	12,961,382	1,428,734	1,210,120	12,742,768	4,889,133	2,777,085	43,140	473,091	278,884
2009	19,472,412	11,920,247	175,849	12,096,096	1,351,561	1,394,129	12,138,664	4,257,189	3,076,559	40,612	479,479	266,092
2010	19,781,404	12,159,297	125,445	12,284,742	1,363,015	1,159,771	12,081,498	4,296,148	3,403,758	40,815	484,666	262,750
2011	21,026,736	12,757,296	113,616	12,870,912	1,285,737	1,155,040	12,740,215	4,856,873	3,429,648	43,112	487,722	266,123
2012	22,194,538	13,005,919	292,687	13,298,606	1,281,934	1,532,812	13,549,484	5,172,552	3,472,502	45,218	490,838	269,458
2013	23,269,688	13,594,842	320,832	13,915,674	1,512,018	1,740,523	14,144,179	5,548,842	3,576,667	46,968	495,432	279,431
2014	24,606,709	14,371,627	324,269	14,695,896	1,606,375	1,970,367	15,059,888	5,799,734	3,747,087	49,185	500,292	289,314

Personal Income and Employment by Area: Savannah, GA

(Thousands of dollars, except as noted.)

Year	Personal income, total	Derivation of personal income								Per capita personal income (dollars)	Population (persons)	Total employment
		Earnings by place of work			Less: Contributions for government social insurance	Plus: Adjustment for residence	Equals: Net earnings by place of residence	Plus: Dividends, interest, and rent	Plus: Personal current transfer receipts			
		Nonfarm	Farm	Total								
1970	744,206	615,405	3,000	618,405	39,518	-8,488	570,399	104,526	69,281	3,600	206,709	96,506
1971	789,159	640,055	3,745	643,800	42,696	-6,835	594,269	110,499	84,391	3,882	203,279	94,486
1972	842,222	686,073	3,687	689,760	48,026	-5,975	635,759	112,006	94,457	4,123	204,260	93,250
1973	920,081	750,416	5,257	755,673	60,968	-3,970	690,735	119,502	109,844	4,492	204,809	96,053
1974	1,017,230	814,840	5,277	820,117	68,884	-2,373	748,860	135,550	132,820	4,964	204,936	96,696
1975	1,188,778	934,062	4,551	938,613	76,871	-6,188	855,554	166,911	166,313	5,595	212,479	100,738
1976	1,350,133	1,042,451	3,848	1,046,299	87,331	32,894	991,862	177,257	181,014	6,174	218,664	103,097
1977	1,505,407	1,152,686	2,004	1,154,690	96,166	61,481	1,120,005	196,764	188,638	6,699	224,727	104,468
1978	1,706,013	1,303,262	6,907	1,310,169	111,123	77,803	1,276,849	224,973	204,191	7,546	226,093	108,230
1979	1,862,801	1,410,637	8,823	1,419,460	125,085	90,384	1,384,759	249,083	228,959	8,119	229,430	108,522
1980	2,097,617	1,557,204	2,042	1,559,246	138,005	95,990	1,517,231	309,232	271,154	9,054	231,691	109,966
1981	2,403,164	1,725,620	8,243	1,733,863	164,800	138,519	1,707,582	386,428	309,154	10,222	235,102	112,942
1982	2,603,477	1,854,716	10,972	1,865,688	182,852	142,215	1,825,051	442,901	335,525	10,888	239,114	114,351
1983	2,780,603	1,978,291	9,157	1,987,448	197,362	133,287	1,923,373	487,183	370,047	11,569	240,354	114,335
1984	3,034,448	2,171,378	7,643	2,179,021	223,190	132,241	2,088,072	553,746	392,630	12,515	242,463	118,390
1985	3,271,785	2,359,578	5,621	2,365,199	247,098	133,337	2,251,438	602,868	417,479	13,376	244,606	122,010
1986	3,535,878	2,616,042	4,027	2,620,069	277,737	100,433	2,442,765	650,071	443,042	14,294	247,365	126,772
1987	3,761,479	2,786,967	4,794	2,791,761	292,431	107,965	2,607,295	687,555	466,629	14,973	251,216	130,214
1988	4,025,149	2,984,055	5,151	2,989,206	323,058	100,483	2,766,631	764,410	494,108	15,843	254,061	134,151
1989	4,371,221	3,184,434	6,282	3,190,716	347,577	76,555	2,919,694	903,662	547,865	17,110	255,475	137,367
1990	4,630,722	3,491,178	4,147	3,495,325	380,911	-32,251	3,082,163	946,558	602,001	17,868	259,160	142,254
1991	4,834,478	3,535,486	5,417	3,540,903	388,474	25,684	3,178,113	980,351	676,014	18,404	262,690	138,590
1992	5,265,362	3,836,419	6,243	3,842,662	414,264	93,060	3,521,458	999,423	744,481	19,658	267,853	143,404
1993	5,476,467	4,019,783	3,211	4,022,994	433,637	34,549	3,623,906	1,050,871	801,690	20,069	272,886	145,860
1994	5,830,185	4,225,288	5,350	4,230,638	463,608	22,363	3,789,393	1,180,629	860,163	21,004	277,581	150,429
1995	6,168,019	4,455,948	2,922	4,458,870	487,444	29,291	4,000,717	1,248,313	918,989	21,940	281,126	155,080
1996	6,544,413	4,755,844	3,820	4,759,664	518,847	-10,637	4,230,180	1,347,771	966,462	23,086	283,480	158,374
1997	6,770,326	4,875,517	3,409	4,878,926	531,790	-17,300	4,329,836	1,460,337	980,153	23,615	286,697	162,397
1998	7,330,565	5,315,618	1,265	5,316,883	576,338	-15,960	4,724,585	1,620,775	985,205	25,414	288,441	164,869
1999	7,619,841	5,639,786	4,163	5,643,949	606,481	-50,869	4,986,599	1,594,542	1,038,700	26,130	291,618	168,258
2000	8,047,333	5,888,520	4,140	5,892,660	630,301	-22,964	5,239,395	1,705,525	1,102,413	27,398	293,721	172,650
2001	8,415,299	6,160,581	6,424	6,167,005	647,337	21,144	5,540,812	1,684,434	1,190,053	28,322	297,133	174,197
2002	8,694,500	6,290,742	4,949	6,295,691	666,641	45,919	5,674,969	1,674,335	1,345,196	28,824	301,644	175,076
2003	9,183,872	6,658,442	6,950	6,665,392	699,550	71,725	6,037,567	1,794,023	1,352,282	30,152	304,585	179,467
2004	9,844,598	7,196,815	7,335	7,204,150	774,078	102,317	6,532,389	1,881,708	1,430,501	31,700	310,553	187,047
2005	10,490,390	7,657,614	8,605	7,666,219	818,624	183,015	7,030,610	1,935,617	1,524,163	33,353	314,528	194,605
2006	11,487,055	8,348,121	9,424	8,357,545	891,004	241,542	7,708,083	2,161,325	1,617,647	35,667	322,065	202,627
2007	12,321,224	8,796,891	8,587	8,805,478	929,203	309,390	8,185,665	2,403,869	1,731,690	37,343	329,943	211,504
2008	12,756,847	9,000,931	7,196	9,008,127	980,784	350,110	8,377,453	2,390,947	1,988,447	38,059	335,185	208,981
2009	12,693,247	8,848,102	4,894	8,852,996	969,747	374,822	8,258,071	2,255,523	2,179,653	36,897	344,017	201,701
2010	13,137,980	8,900,963	6,341	8,907,304	988,139	553,001	8,472,166	2,237,757	2,428,057	37,662	348,843	199,282
2011	14,209,720	9,282,311	3,884	9,286,195	916,081	590,993	8,961,107	2,678,415	2,570,198	39,925	355,913	203,017
2012	14,284,139	9,587,573	8,759	9,596,332	948,419	557,740	9,205,653	2,569,290	2,509,196	39,427	362,293	205,615
2013	14,583,278	9,928,492	11,607	9,940,099	1,107,603	536,846	9,369,342	2,625,470	2,588,466	39,840	366,049	210,984
2014	15,131,390	10,407,590	8,065	10,415,655	1,158,142	436,583	9,694,096	2,723,329	2,713,965	40,599	372,708	216,195

Personal Income and Employment by Area: Scranton—Wilkes-Barre—Hazleton, PA

(Thousands of dollars, except as noted.)

| Year | Personal income, total | Derivation of personal income | | | | | | | | Per capita personal income (dollars) | Population (persons) | Total employment |
| | | Earnings by place of work | | | Less: Contributions for government social insurance | Plus: Adjustment for residence | Equals: Net earnings by place of residence | Plus: Dividends, interest, and rent | Plus: Personal current transfer receipts | | | |
		Nonfarm	Farm	Total								
1970	2,146,604	1,643,717	5,903	1,649,620	123,705	46,086	1,572,001	269,425	305,178	3,600	596,204	255,288
1971	2,342,907	1,758,687	6,397	1,765,084	137,169	44,449	1,672,364	291,972	378,571	3,898	601,087	253,153
1972	2,588,081	1,936,495	5,327	1,941,822	156,322	43,267	1,828,767	316,008	443,306	4,268	606,331	258,007
1973	2,865,576	2,138,478	6,904	2,145,382	197,262	43,203	1,991,323	359,551	514,702	4,729	605,941	266,382
1974	3,077,028	2,235,725	6,496	2,242,221	213,816	45,201	2,073,606	412,473	590,949	5,074	606,407	260,623
1975	3,355,001	2,356,360	10,455	2,366,815	218,479	40,981	2,189,317	444,549	721,135	5,518	608,007	251,998
1976	3,641,367	2,574,358	10,704	2,585,062	243,952	37,585	2,378,695	473,527	789,145	6,031	603,751	251,764
1977	3,978,015	2,839,056	14,436	2,853,492	267,387	35,059	2,621,164	528,065	828,786	6,583	604,269	254,824
1978	4,392,106	3,183,696	11,739	3,195,435	306,458	36,728	2,925,705	581,552	884,849	7,277	603,524	261,329
1979	4,849,702	3,449,758	15,603	3,465,361	342,349	32,947	3,155,959	645,643	1,048,100	8,061	601,656	265,502
1980	5,235,937	3,570,458	14,502	3,584,960	360,355	33,160	3,257,765	802,189	1,175,983	8,770	597,021	259,934
1981	5,728,169	3,796,582	16,908	3,813,490	411,740	34,638	3,436,388	991,494	1,300,287	9,640	594,227	257,840
1982	6,194,209	3,960,511	13,128	3,973,639	435,352	32,269	3,570,556	1,187,989	1,435,664	10,479	591,104	252,572
1983	6,584,764	4,194,392	12,266	4,206,658	464,791	34,820	3,776,687	1,257,758	1,550,319	11,203	587,760	252,296
1984	6,958,699	4,442,249	19,731	4,461,980	510,173	51,277	4,003,084	1,388,487	1,567,128	11,912	584,185	254,756
1985	7,399,332	4,736,689	20,804	4,757,493	550,929	49,254	4,255,818	1,536,811	1,606,703	12,763	579,742	259,357
1986	7,768,643	5,008,785	18,539	5,027,324	585,406	40,662	4,482,580	1,615,958	1,670,105	13,430	578,457	263,798
1987	8,136,602	5,383,828	17,082	5,400,910	623,406	46,396	4,823,900	1,621,727	1,690,975	14,124	576,085	269,274
1988	8,732,746	5,878,961	12,117	5,891,078	695,825	34,854	5,230,107	1,739,810	1,762,829	15,163	575,917	278,326
1989	9,486,431	6,358,602	17,620	6,376,222	742,276	25,504	5,659,450	1,994,810	1,832,171	16,473	575,871	283,746
1990	9,962,793	6,716,461	19,382	6,735,843	785,695	27,661	5,977,809	2,019,979	1,965,005	17,294	576,090	288,238
1991	10,363,255	6,890,801	14,794	6,905,595	818,681	6,979	6,093,893	2,015,324	2,254,038	17,923	578,212	284,245
1992	10,863,618	7,370,601	24,814	7,395,415	874,837	-44,551	6,476,027	2,005,426	2,382,165	18,743	579,606	285,358
1993	11,175,034	7,683,215	19,231	7,702,446	930,539	-80,261	6,691,646	1,985,925	2,497,463	19,256	580,330	286,290
1994	11,566,584	8,027,522	15,462	8,042,984	986,521	-72,671	6,983,792	2,057,276	2,525,516	19,984	578,788	289,245
1995	12,078,424	8,358,080	8,860	8,366,940	1,025,416	-92,231	7,249,293	2,228,485	2,600,646	20,934	576,980	293,803
1996	12,595,008	8,566,326	14,813	8,581,139	1,026,072	-68,257	7,486,810	2,380,275	2,727,923	21,947	573,886	294,639
1997	13,140,294	8,999,380	10,638	9,010,018	1,064,932	-75,803	7,869,283	2,493,286	2,777,725	23,078	569,384	297,412
1998	13,604,862	9,315,826	13,112	9,328,938	1,088,701	-59,944	8,180,293	2,626,826	2,797,743	24,028	566,216	296,543
1999	14,115,206	9,826,260	11,506	9,837,766	1,128,434	-62,151	8,647,181	2,567,307	2,900,718	25,064	563,157	300,333
2000	15,076,682	10,530,330	19,596	10,549,926	1,187,544	-52,425	9,309,957	2,770,606	2,996,119	26,928	559,879	307,768
2001	15,561,678	10,983,970	12,887	10,996,857	1,246,863	-101,490	9,648,504	2,727,225	3,185,949	27,915	557,476	306,431
2002	15,708,769	11,046,916	11,874	11,058,790	1,260,597	-56,824	9,741,369	2,629,802	3,337,598	28,268	555,702	301,625
2003	16,147,864	11,348,251	19,732	11,367,983	1,288,590	-9,992	10,069,401	2,645,149	3,433,314	29,070	555,483	302,248
2004	17,035,169	12,017,465	16,075	12,033,540	1,359,671	41,689	10,715,558	2,701,047	3,618,564	30,667	555,495	305,708
2005	17,632,339	12,502,157	13,472	12,515,629	1,442,904	97,390	11,170,115	2,615,459	3,846,765	31,676	556,652	309,351
2006	18,426,961	12,891,607	15,140	12,906,747	1,491,368	156,317	11,571,696	2,796,416	4,058,849	33,045	557,626	312,556
2007	19,444,744	13,320,344	7,107	13,327,451	1,553,317	222,663	11,996,797	3,153,702	4,294,245	34,721	560,032	316,867
2008	20,078,327	13,281,857	8,544	13,290,401	1,575,029	286,262	12,001,634	3,308,373	4,768,320	35,755	561,548	318,745
2009	20,059,115	13,054,851	9,741	13,064,592	1,562,095	296,918	11,799,415	3,082,714	5,176,986	35,633	562,933	311,154
2010	20,534,929	13,335,563	12,659	13,348,222	1,602,022	326,976	12,073,176	3,010,126	5,451,627	36,432	563,655	310,396
2011	21,309,076	13,726,303	11,191	13,737,494	1,494,653	325,589	12,568,430	3,231,641	5,509,005	37,788	563,913	312,878
2012	21,832,116	13,958,284	22,532	13,980,816	1,510,369	299,455	12,769,902	3,596,182	5,466,032	38,700	564,134	313,707
2013	21,750,657	14,274,234	16,781	14,291,015	1,736,610	246,528	12,800,933	3,498,164	5,451,560	38,713	561,838	316,000
2014	22,486,330	14,824,070	26,375	14,850,445	1,802,469	227,645	13,275,621	3,648,429	5,562,280	40,177	559,679	319,427

Personal Income and Employment by Area: Seattle-Tacoma-Bellevue, WA

(Thousands of dollars, except as noted.)

Year	Personal income, total	Earnings by place of work			Less: Contributions for government social insurance	Plus: Adjustment for residence	Equals: Net earnings by place of residence	Plus: Dividends, interest, and rent	Plus: Personal current transfer receipts	Per capita personal income (dollars)	Population (persons)	Total employment
		Nonfarm	Farm	Total								
1970	8,691,769	7,026,051	26,946	7,052,997	559,723	17,835	6,511,109	1,418,853	761,807	4,737	1,834,990	824,119
1971	8,898,715	7,029,258	28,446	7,057,704	580,348	14,455	6,491,811	1,508,731	898,173	4,849	1,835,190	786,245
1972	9,377,801	7,480,343	33,366	7,513,709	653,159	9,370	6,869,920	1,570,444	937,437	5,192	1,806,099	789,860
1973	10,417,751	8,425,627	49,155	8,474,782	840,240	467	7,635,009	1,737,351	1,045,391	5,784	1,800,981	834,401
1974	11,763,519	9,456,405	47,977	9,504,382	969,872	19,850	8,554,360	2,007,370	1,201,789	6,414	1,833,981	869,673
1975	13,330,296	10,587,167	50,176	10,637,343	1,076,303	64,065	9,625,105	2,211,701	1,493,490	7,143	1,866,276	887,648
1976	14,793,690	11,850,370	51,174	11,901,544	1,233,342	99,924	10,768,126	2,402,627	1,622,937	7,843	1,886,242	919,384
1977	16,463,147	13,450,844	54,295	13,505,139	1,428,946	51,706	12,127,899	2,671,397	1,663,851	8,589	1,916,683	968,408
1978	19,277,523	16,031,394	49,467	16,080,861	1,756,897	29,678	14,353,642	3,124,976	1,798,905	9,780	1,971,129	1,046,539
1979	22,351,805	18,854,006	56,541	18,910,547	2,138,583	-14,839	16,757,125	3,624,902	1,969,778	10,999	2,032,131	1,123,231
1980	25,551,410	21,096,478	44,721	21,141,199	2,359,828	-40,461	18,740,910	4,414,544	2,395,956	12,134	2,105,824	1,159,283
1981	28,713,379	23,191,542	55,977	23,247,519	2,781,762	-29,841	20,435,916	5,458,957	2,818,506	13,345	2,151,691	1,167,540
1982	30,671,728	24,280,081	47,955	24,328,036	2,960,991	-14,823	21,352,222	6,159,174	3,160,332	14,083	2,177,909	1,160,929
1983	32,251,857	25,235,967	54,058	25,290,025	3,113,281	-18,508	22,158,236	6,602,424	3,491,197	14,740	2,188,099	1,179,085
1984	34,858,155	27,300,625	55,652	27,356,277	3,469,223	-65,847	23,821,207	7,416,917	3,620,031	15,730	2,216,022	1,236,653
1985	37,700,064	29,701,375	62,125	29,763,500	3,803,822	-116,982	25,842,696	7,981,016	3,876,352	16,696	2,258,026	1,290,615
1986	40,717,658	32,464,318	70,168	32,534,486	4,169,389	-193,680	28,171,417	8,417,937	4,128,304	17,695	2,301,024	1,346,586
1987	43,604,428	35,081,212	75,522	35,156,734	4,481,173	-265,549	30,410,012	8,832,768	4,361,648	18,506	2,356,263	1,422,816
1988	48,029,903	38,870,477	77,155	38,947,632	5,073,602	-300,152	33,573,878	9,623,809	4,832,216	19,795	2,426,393	1,505,432
1989	53,268,368	42,828,321	91,413	42,919,734	5,572,027	-361,832	36,985,875	10,958,266	5,324,227	21,365	2,493,214	1,587,002
1990	58,741,700	47,604,867	94,275	47,699,142	6,338,121	-574,089	40,786,932	12,104,117	5,850,651	22,779	2,578,807	1,653,020
1991	62,401,454	50,840,291	89,714	50,930,005	6,838,627	-632,431	43,458,947	12,382,058	6,560,449	23,720	2,630,705	1,661,101
1992	67,183,718	55,569,803	117,051	55,686,854	7,472,269	-793,283	47,421,302	12,595,236	7,167,180	24,967	2,690,858	1,669,827
1993	69,768,875	57,357,281	110,486	57,467,767	7,697,913	-964,380	48,805,474	13,308,654	7,654,747	25,460	2,740,325	1,687,223
1994	73,254,299	59,630,731	105,935	59,736,666	8,113,596	-1,022,947	50,600,123	14,619,622	8,034,554	26,406	2,774,159	1,728,057
1995	77,712,047	62,597,829	95,132	62,692,961	8,532,250	-1,103,460	53,057,251	16,108,184	8,546,612	27,610	2,814,630	1,750,246
1996	83,907,451	67,735,211	100,263	67,835,474	9,072,695	-1,224,343	57,538,436	17,463,404	8,905,611	29,371	2,856,795	1,807,825
1997	91,646,917	75,064,171	91,990	75,156,161	9,785,287	-1,655,380	63,715,494	18,705,489	9,225,934	31,407	2,918,071	1,887,996
1998	102,605,666	85,394,985	116,423	85,511,408	10,958,770	-1,997,452	72,555,186	20,495,724	9,554,756	34,446	2,978,761	1,956,810
1999	111,806,009	94,548,104	121,949	94,670,053	11,579,454	-2,145,927	80,944,672	20,776,073	10,085,264	37,026	3,019,651	1,995,691
2000	119,289,923	100,757,763	91,390	100,849,153	12,562,561	-2,595,631	85,690,961	22,998,619	10,600,343	39,083	3,052,187	2,049,460
2001	120,433,089	101,302,654	107,779	101,410,433	12,083,472	-2,820,103	86,506,858	21,956,791	11,969,440	38,938	3,092,927	2,034,839
2002	122,758,777	101,935,938	91,828	102,027,766	12,187,433	-2,829,033	87,011,300	22,854,600	12,892,877	39,367	3,118,302	1,996,024
2003	126,457,152	104,263,616	130,222	104,393,838	12,628,454	-3,018,431	88,746,953	24,363,921	13,346,278	40,363	3,133,021	1,998,052
2004	137,288,892	109,482,799	113,676	109,596,475	13,372,101	-2,929,979	93,294,395	30,747,379	13,247,118	43,460	3,158,967	2,040,482
2005	141,952,085	115,113,252	104,596	115,217,848	14,169,065	-3,037,549	98,011,234	30,126,694	13,814,157	44,384	3,198,265	2,098,548
2006	155,556,326	124,255,169	93,001	124,348,170	15,108,508	-3,376,238	105,863,424	34,944,290	14,748,612	47,759	3,257,081	2,170,670
2007	168,822,933	132,818,612	86,594	132,905,206	15,968,170	-3,409,080	113,527,956	39,376,751	15,918,226	51,089	3,304,467	2,255,195
2008	175,370,651	136,820,703	67,372	136,888,075	16,330,784	-3,713,799	116,843,492	40,055,765	18,471,394	52,271	3,355,042	2,273,330
2009	167,015,537	131,962,483	67,705	132,030,188	16,024,712	-3,492,441	112,513,035	33,426,584	21,075,918	48,909	3,414,797	2,184,387
2010	171,255,147	135,314,664	74,671	135,389,335	16,440,150	-3,326,507	115,622,678	32,208,425	23,424,044	49,665	3,448,234	2,148,419
2011	182,038,694	142,259,587	90,331	142,349,918	15,549,191	-3,360,999	123,439,728	35,459,108	23,139,858	52,040	3,498,020	2,184,338
2012	197,669,457	151,977,338	86,829	152,064,167	16,209,392	-3,462,838	132,391,937	42,272,911	23,004,609	55,622	3,553,831	2,251,703
2013	201,248,544	158,055,562	103,039	158,158,601	19,137,659	-3,580,445	135,440,497	42,428,885	23,379,162	55,692	3,613,621	2,303,802
2014	213,700,152	168,297,959	116,339	168,414,298	20,074,506	-4,017,856	144,321,936	44,125,727	25,252,489	58,205	3,671,478	2,365,079

Personal Income and Employment by Area: Sebastian-Vero Beach, FL

(Thousands of dollars, except as noted.)

Year	Personal income, total	Earnings by place of work			Less: Contributions for government social insurance	Plus: Adjustment for residence	Equals: Net earnings by place of residence	Plus: Dividends, interest, and rent	Plus: Personal current transfer receipts	Per capita personal income (dollars)	Population (persons)	Total employment
		Nonfarm	Farm	Total								
1970	148,822	85,921	5,816	91,737	5,485	-402	85,850	45,283	17,689	4,112	36,192	15,206
1971	175,319	100,832	8,454	109,286	6,783	-1,554	100,949	52,887	21,483	4,661	37,617	16,339
1972	210,916	123,830	12,145	135,975	8,814	-2,688	124,473	61,241	25,202	5,199	40,570	18,541
1973	252,860	152,370	12,463	164,833	12,477	-4,275	148,081	74,483	30,296	5,791	43,668	21,051
1974	284,089	162,647	14,098	176,745	14,028	-4,165	158,552	89,474	36,063	6,200	45,818	21,271
1975	308,972	170,028	12,033	182,061	14,352	-4,375	163,334	99,710	45,928	6,538	47,259	21,020
1976	353,975	197,137	12,234	209,371	16,601	-5,973	186,797	114,979	52,199	7,348	48,176	22,091
1977	408,380	222,718	15,598	238,316	19,349	-6,614	212,353	137,102	58,925	8,089	50,485	23,515
1978	492,366	265,516	20,580	286,096	23,668	-8,389	254,039	171,663	66,664	9,236	53,309	25,884
1979	582,046	305,568	21,828	327,396	28,335	-8,008	291,053	209,832	81,161	10,051	57,912	27,380
1980	703,256	336,785	34,903	371,688	30,950	-4,187	336,551	266,417	100,288	11,580	60,728	28,130
1981	851,975	397,703	24,184	421,887	39,720	-8,432	373,735	357,137	121,103	13,323	63,946	29,823
1982	895,434	388,723	26,785	415,508	40,811	-2,715	371,982	374,052	149,400	13,266	67,499	30,005
1983	1,009,807	417,057	47,608	464,665	43,849	-1,127	419,689	423,181	166,937	14,340	70,419	31,067
1984	1,157,599	480,841	43,885	524,726	51,911	-5,601	467,214	509,089	181,296	15,687	73,792	33,139
1985	1,325,263	535,292	55,544	590,836	59,593	-7,141	524,102	601,530	199,631	17,465	75,879	35,176
1986	1,464,084	610,912	56,815	667,727	69,320	-7,272	591,135	652,131	220,818	18,585	78,776	37,595
1987	1,642,421	683,787	74,750	758,537	76,745	-5,522	676,270	727,580	238,571	20,234	81,171	37,686
1988	1,898,226	769,794	113,426	883,220	89,616	-8,205	785,399	855,052	257,775	22,629	83,885	41,082
1989	2,125,384	886,457	88,911	975,368	105,385	-14,951	855,032	974,697	295,655	24,278	87,542	43,275
1990	2,341,879	944,952	63,267	1,008,219	109,887	-14,211	884,121	1,135,926	321,832	25,702	91,115	44,005
1991	2,471,350	922,855	75,091	997,946	109,893	-3,161	884,892	1,233,631	352,827	26,405	93,593	43,445
1992	2,615,410	989,190	61,340	1,050,530	116,950	1,396	934,976	1,275,081	405,353	27,237	96,023	42,812
1993	2,730,433	1,043,094	54,148	1,097,242	122,579	4,800	979,463	1,321,829	429,141	27,985	97,566	43,672
1994	2,918,775	1,120,606	49,310	1,169,916	133,668	2,031	1,038,279	1,414,613	465,883	29,229	99,858	45,180
1995	3,218,049	1,196,186	46,581	1,242,767	142,418	2,754	1,103,103	1,620,644	494,302	31,571	101,929	47,392
1996	3,447,350	1,307,237	32,527	1,339,764	152,074	-2,017	1,185,673	1,734,758	526,919	33,281	103,583	49,354
1997	3,702,063	1,376,206	30,739	1,406,945	160,700	-781	1,245,464	1,902,867	553,732	34,830	106,291	51,903
1998	4,005,176	1,482,304	48,696	1,531,000	170,936	-1,486	1,358,578	2,068,458	578,140	36,758	108,961	53,888
1999	4,211,116	1,643,721	39,333	1,683,054	185,469	-5,547	1,492,038	2,123,398	595,680	37,838	111,294	54,789
2000	4,484,088	1,743,385	42,957	1,786,342	194,772	3,412	1,594,982	2,253,736	635,370	39,569	113,323	55,763
2001	4,740,408	1,767,979	35,762	1,803,741	203,604	4,037	1,604,174	2,450,139	686,095	41,058	115,456	56,312
2002	4,892,341	1,849,287	41,017	1,890,304	212,746	46,507	1,724,065	2,431,633	736,643	41,410	118,144	57,420
2003	5,215,757	2,065,305	35,579	2,100,884	236,420	98,883	1,963,347	2,474,388	778,022	43,302	120,450	61,498
2004	6,228,730	2,301,944	42,218	2,344,162	261,934	158,599	2,240,827	3,139,282	848,621	49,829	125,001	63,372
2005	6,819,207	2,447,138	59,698	2,506,836	283,232	226,161	2,449,765	3,507,386	862,056	53,294	127,955	66,598
2006	7,849,777	2,654,450	60,984	2,715,434	311,383	306,553	2,710,604	4,214,273	924,900	59,711	131,463	70,308
2007	8,216,809	2,744,813	41,812	2,786,625	326,327	391,006	2,851,304	4,375,555	989,950	61,062	134,564	70,842
2008	8,422,557	2,708,808	35,976	2,744,784	328,474	456,506	2,872,816	4,429,424	1,120,317	61,805	136,277	68,962
2009	7,202,124	2,489,125	41,657	2,530,782	310,390	474,958	2,695,350	3,270,165	1,236,609	52,564	137,016	65,706
2010	7,343,458	2,441,660	46,296	2,487,956	305,857	371,772	2,553,871	3,457,705	1,331,882	53,123	138,235	65,372
2011	8,184,138	2,467,121	47,030	2,514,151	282,435	490,440	2,722,156	4,074,972	1,387,010	58,890	138,973	65,714
2012	8,518,530	2,629,710	51,521	2,681,231	299,242	564,967	2,946,956	4,167,387	1,404,187	60,584	140,608	66,456
2013	8,700,335	2,667,378	49,326	2,716,704	340,280	711,918	3,088,342	4,164,413	1,447,580	61,261	142,021	67,253
2014	9,139,902	2,832,942	50,838	2,883,780	362,279	760,462	3,281,963	4,310,451	1,547,488	63,140	144,755	68,968

Personal Income and Employment by Area: Sebring, FL

(Thousands of dollars, except as noted.)

Year	Personal income, total	Earnings by place of work			Less: Contributions for government social insurance	Plus: Adjustment for residence	Equals: Net earnings by place of residence	Plus: Dividends, interest, and rent	Plus: Personal current transfer receipts	Per capita personal income (dollars)	Population (persons)	Total employment
		Nonfarm	Farm	Total								
1970	104,675	51,440	14,987	66,427	3,500	861	63,788	26,040	14,847	3,501	29,898	10,437
1971	118,873	58,069	16,873	74,942	4,108	827	71,661	29,280	17,932	3,723	31,931	10,970
1972	133,899	63,685	19,949	83,634	4,775	752	79,611	32,987	21,301	3,948	33,912	11,766
1973	156,749	75,662	20,943	96,605	6,415	407	90,597	39,779	26,373	4,362	35,937	12,899
1974	176,214	86,812	19,001	105,813	7,790	36	98,059	46,866	31,289	4,403	40,025	13,681
1975	201,071	93,810	21,470	115,280	8,307	150	107,123	54,283	39,665	4,896	41,070	13,811
1976	223,376	103,118	25,706	128,824	9,181	-216	119,427	59,135	44,814	5,372	41,584	13,930
1977	255,205	115,391	32,067	147,458	10,338	-755	136,365	68,670	50,170	6,082	41,962	14,676
1978	306,810	136,042	43,977	180,019	12,224	-1,599	166,196	83,887	56,727	7,039	43,588	16,021
1979	351,211	153,945	45,732	199,677	14,574	-2,613	182,490	100,753	67,968	7,664	45,828	16,722
1980	423,092	173,058	61,071	234,129	16,722	-3,096	214,311	126,068	82,713	8,796	48,102	17,930
1981	459,286	192,177	41,125	233,302	20,064	-7,003	206,235	153,737	99,314	9,128	50,315	18,584
1982	515,269	198,655	45,893	244,548	21,532	-6,815	216,201	182,543	116,525	9,855	52,286	19,097
1983	588,691	224,075	66,188	290,263	24,163	-7,761	258,339	203,758	126,594	10,969	53,670	20,205
1984	645,782	255,864	48,537	304,401	28,196	-8,215	267,990	241,177	136,615	11,607	55,636	21,386
1985	730,481	288,541	54,179	342,720	32,660	-9,179	300,881	276,899	152,701	12,702	57,508	22,542
1986	806,972	320,364	55,851	376,215	37,136	-9,584	329,495	308,525	168,952	13,591	59,375	23,609
1987	868,608	348,877	62,912	411,789	39,969	-7,272	364,548	320,992	183,068	13,983	62,119	23,712
1988	981,096	383,802	100,182	483,984	46,333	-6,802	430,849	349,031	201,216	15,252	64,325	24,811
1989	1,087,264	420,622	75,559	496,181	52,740	-5,261	438,180	415,392	233,692	16,391	66,334	25,945
1990	1,142,723	453,062	65,763	518,825	55,544	-3,630	459,651	423,561	259,511	16,504	69,238	27,382
1991	1,191,465	480,313	78,212	558,525	59,256	-4,016	495,253	407,998	288,214	16,637	71,614	28,117
1992	1,251,566	513,104	67,731	580,835	63,165	-3,223	514,447	406,241	330,878	16,961	73,790	28,451
1993	1,318,862	544,916	70,537	615,453	67,327	-3,107	545,019	416,187	357,656	17,285	76,301	28,985
1994	1,400,511	585,031	65,487	650,518	73,382	-2,255	574,881	430,241	395,389	17,790	78,724	30,386
1995	1,483,810	608,342	70,553	678,895	76,868	-179	601,848	461,213	420,749	18,366	80,792	30,952
1996	1,543,638	626,989	54,005	680,994	77,797	2,644	605,841	492,486	445,311	18,663	82,713	31,677
1997	1,612,380	660,932	55,855	716,787	81,299	5,145	640,633	509,095	462,652	19,119	84,334	32,801
1998	1,716,552	672,016	97,735	769,751	82,931	8,613	695,433	540,466	480,653	20,065	85,551	34,212
1999	1,754,624	706,875	99,398	806,273	85,461	10,975	731,787	523,809	499,028	20,260	86,604	35,618
2000	1,821,592	736,258	75,621	811,879	87,493	16,857	741,243	552,680	527,669	20,838	87,417	33,020
2001	1,933,615	818,648	56,153	874,801	99,964	22,404	797,241	563,639	572,735	21,846	88,510	32,696
2002	2,033,184	888,104	61,274	949,378	108,958	27,032	867,452	556,175	609,557	22,606	89,939	34,164
2003	2,120,000	961,059	50,251	1,011,310	116,835	32,151	926,626	554,171	639,203	23,311	90,943	36,312
2004	2,238,726	1,043,105	56,143	1,099,248	128,009	38,399	1,009,638	543,076	686,012	24,052	93,079	36,679
2005	2,383,854	1,102,475	80,088	1,182,563	139,921	45,100	1,087,742	563,255	732,857	24,932	95,614	37,703
2006	2,576,097	1,189,763	103,353	1,293,116	153,063	53,180	1,193,233	600,097	782,767	26,344	97,788	39,364
2007	2,709,916	1,213,227	76,094	1,289,321	159,666	60,234	1,189,889	690,746	829,281	27,367	99,023	40,866
2008	2,764,634	1,155,063	83,959	1,239,022	156,362	64,276	1,146,936	706,848	910,850	27,766	99,568	39,240
2009	2,722,134	1,136,986	96,179	1,233,165	157,752	54,693	1,130,106	603,470	988,558	27,509	98,956	38,125
2010	2,832,608	1,152,393	99,795	1,252,188	160,329	56,711	1,148,570	635,655	1,048,383	28,698	98,703	37,835
2011	2,908,259	1,167,922	92,807	1,260,729	149,620	53,742	1,164,851	671,008	1,072,400	29,567	98,360	38,116
2012	2,904,967	1,186,225	121,684	1,307,909	152,560	55,737	1,211,086	617,051	1,076,830	29,616	98,087	38,352
2013	2,918,725	1,200,612	111,207	1,311,819	171,022	59,019	1,199,816	618,341	1,100,568	29,808	97,919	37,869
2014	3,010,925	1,226,646	100,255	1,326,901	174,717	63,514	1,215,698	644,193	1,151,034	30,650	98,236	38,876

Personal Income and Employment by Area: Sheboygan, WI

(Thousands of dollars, except as noted.)

| Year | Personal income, total | Derivation of personal income | | | | | | | | Per capita personal income (dollars) | Population (persons) | Total employment |
| | | Earnings by place of work | | | Less: Contributions for government social insurance | Plus: Adjustment for residence | Equals: Net earnings by place of residence | Plus: Dividends, interest, and rent | Plus: Personal current transfer receipts | | | |
		Nonfarm	Farm	Total								
1970	381,301	298,213	11,237	309,450	22,448	-368	286,634	62,734	31,933	3,942	96,726	44,180
1971	405,514	313,378	11,680	325,058	24,438	911	301,531	67,476	36,507	4,177	97,081	44,145
1972	450,092	350,998	12,363	363,361	28,890	2,697	337,168	72,542	40,382	4,614	97,541	45,544
1973	496,845	387,728	14,081	401,809	36,779	5,112	370,142	80,243	46,460	5,029	98,803	47,761
1974	549,308	423,804	13,011	436,815	42,015	7,663	402,463	91,432	55,413	5,495	99,963	48,662
1975	595,609	437,992	17,304	455,296	42,067	9,023	422,252	101,045	72,312	5,934	100,372	47,393
1976	668,215	504,312	17,416	521,728	49,220	11,830	484,338	107,360	76,517	6,692	99,858	49,028
1977	753,043	573,131	22,151	595,282	55,830	14,460	553,912	119,073	80,058	7,493	100,495	51,286
1978	846,081	655,156	18,225	673,381	65,778	18,462	626,065	131,378	88,638	8,437	100,282	53,344
1979	957,905	740,306	22,579	762,885	77,325	23,594	709,154	146,880	101,871	9,510	100,727	55,367
1980	1,049,352	775,558	22,940	798,498	80,593	24,963	742,868	179,563	126,921	10,399	100,907	54,206
1981	1,148,885	837,961	16,912	854,873	93,101	20,710	782,482	222,814	143,589	11,426	100,554	54,019
1982	1,182,588	837,590	14,448	852,038	93,595	18,046	776,489	241,096	165,003	11,736	100,770	52,305
1983	1,236,408	883,393	2,021	885,414	98,920	14,936	801,430	259,531	175,447	12,291	100,592	51,763
1984	1,369,521	994,416	9,803	1,004,219	114,462	10,056	899,813	291,931	177,777	13,552	101,060	54,410
1985	1,421,056	1,026,245	12,451	1,038,696	118,610	7,297	927,383	306,011	187,662	14,066	101,028	54,488
1986	1,495,684	1,090,051	17,831	1,107,882	125,483	2,566	984,965	317,796	192,923	14,809	100,995	54,967
1987	1,574,943	1,165,658	21,558	1,187,216	131,329	-282	1,055,605	323,401	195,937	15,540	101,347	56,142
1988	1,689,575	1,282,415	10,271	1,292,686	148,829	-8,486	1,135,371	348,906	205,298	16,562	102,018	58,606
1989	1,849,911	1,387,087	28,321	1,415,408	160,340	-17,978	1,237,090	389,072	223,749	17,955	103,032	60,778
1990	1,917,493	1,443,590	22,717	1,466,307	172,766	-22,065	1,271,476	403,879	242,138	18,413	104,137	62,116
1991	1,969,975	1,491,629	17,541	1,509,170	180,485	-21,100	1,307,585	399,107	263,283	18,813	104,714	62,581
1992	2,144,455	1,627,744	22,572	1,650,316	194,811	-23,079	1,432,426	431,228	280,801	20,302	105,627	63,543
1993	2,281,614	1,767,673	16,296	1,783,969	213,150	-27,446	1,543,373	450,029	288,212	21,378	106,729	65,899
1994	2,440,442	1,910,854	20,155	1,931,009	232,315	-27,945	1,670,749	479,150	290,543	22,577	108,093	68,711
1995	2,572,206	1,985,823	15,082	2,000,905	242,258	-27,603	1,731,044	532,886	308,276	23,454	109,672	70,153
1996	2,683,754	2,053,193	25,566	2,078,759	249,268	-24,010	1,805,481	554,739	323,534	24,235	110,737	69,931
1997	2,782,533	2,151,581	18,727	2,170,308	259,090	-19,301	1,891,917	560,995	329,621	24,947	111,536	70,790
1998	2,993,174	2,300,466	29,875	2,330,341	276,439	-19,775	2,034,127	619,140	339,907	26,731	111,973	72,094
1999	3,128,625	2,484,469	30,048	2,514,517	299,481	-27,966	2,187,070	591,893	349,662	27,912	112,088	74,189
2000	3,327,436	2,641,278	21,819	2,663,097	314,423	-30,659	2,318,015	639,645	369,776	29,515	112,739	75,850
2001	3,467,026	2,745,111	29,747	2,774,858	319,405	-31,707	2,423,746	635,248	408,032	30,675	113,023	74,929
2002	3,562,953	2,838,131	28,973	2,867,104	324,981	-31,965	2,510,158	612,851	439,944	31,461	113,251	73,876
2003	3,667,173	2,933,756	34,092	2,967,848	335,381	-32,124	2,600,343	614,200	452,630	32,329	113,433	74,267
2004	3,867,704	3,134,741	33,645	3,168,386	358,594	-32,495	2,777,297	626,187	464,220	33,977	113,832	75,150
2005	4,040,040	3,281,112	28,441	3,309,553	373,708	-32,423	2,903,422	640,663	495,955	35,298	114,454	77,332
2006	4,292,490	3,445,446	24,059	3,469,505	390,084	-31,475	3,047,946	715,519	529,025	37,399	114,775	77,881
2007	4,505,819	3,558,121	43,025	3,601,146	403,583	-30,818	3,166,745	766,027	573,047	39,120	115,178	78,639
2008	4,987,000	3,895,222	32,474	3,927,696	426,476	-29,459	3,471,761	868,406	646,833	43,121	115,652	78,343
2009	4,689,092	3,613,585	11,271	3,624,856	401,503	-32,377	3,190,976	735,849	762,267	40,576	115,562	74,118
2010	4,570,307	3,445,844	22,880	3,468,724	399,976	-26,507	3,042,241	721,159	806,907	39,598	115,418	72,600
2011	4,964,916	3,685,645	51,685	3,737,330	379,029	-14,341	3,343,960	849,012	771,944	43,056	115,312	72,569
2012	5,230,832	3,779,874	63,356	3,843,230	388,836	-24,974	3,429,420	1,026,895	774,517	45,504	114,952	72,820
2013	5,093,681	3,779,942	64,670	3,844,612	444,733	-37,183	3,362,696	942,841	788,144	44,344	114,868	74,470
2014	5,341,196	3,979,892	74,376	4,054,268	467,315	-43,564	3,543,389	979,889	817,918	46,328	115,290	75,968

Personal Income and Employment by Area: Sherman-Denison, TX

(Thousands of dollars, except as noted.)

Year	Personal income, total	Earnings by place of work			Less: Contributions for government social insurance	Plus: Adjustment for residence	Equals: Net earnings by place of residence	Plus: Dividends, interest, and rent	Plus: Personal current transfer receipts	Per capita personal income (dollars)	Population (persons)	Total employment
		Nonfarm	Farm	Total								
1970	286,485	230,416	1,806	232,222	15,720	-4,430	212,072	44,771	29,642	3,466	82,644	38,706
1971	280,085	218,391	2,094	220,485	15,732	-2,781	201,972	43,334	34,779	3,470	80,725	35,761
1972	307,958	241,072	4,397	245,469	18,457	-3,844	223,168	46,884	37,906	4,001	76,977	36,851
1973	349,488	267,174	9,335	276,509	23,650	-3,728	249,131	54,986	45,371	4,529	77,168	37,720
1974	387,032	299,539	-1,537	298,002	27,275	-3,273	267,454	66,257	53,321	4,888	79,176	38,648
1975	420,744	308,038	-1,624	306,414	27,180	-662	278,572	72,794	69,378	5,116	82,243	36,797
1976	472,902	345,938	7,204	353,142	30,962	-335	321,845	77,121	73,936	5,624	84,093	37,567
1977	525,644	397,595	-981	396,614	35,971	-631	360,012	85,136	80,496	6,251	84,089	39,578
1978	620,164	479,806	2,139	481,945	44,532	-2,774	434,639	96,118	89,407	7,315	84,776	42,554
1979	728,359	575,007	6,745	581,752	55,802	-4,092	521,858	108,025	98,476	8,324	87,500	45,113
1980	820,254	628,541	1,175	629,716	61,252	-973	567,491	137,635	115,128	9,102	90,118	44,931
1981	915,249	684,187	798	684,985	71,476	-67	613,442	168,456	133,351	10,042	91,140	45,027
1982	989,846	698,657	2,306	700,963	74,483	4,060	630,540	207,454	151,852	10,776	91,857	44,236
1983	1,074,394	752,909	5,191	758,100	79,010	4,394	683,484	225,234	165,676	11,607	92,562	44,445
1984	1,184,366	828,679	6,602	835,281	89,718	6,760	752,323	258,326	173,717	12,637	93,722	45,965
1985	1,280,704	885,426	9,291	894,717	96,420	8,906	807,203	289,206	184,295	13,506	94,827	47,323
1986	1,332,829	932,116	561	932,677	101,066	6,703	838,314	297,172	197,343	13,771	96,787	47,263
1987	1,349,642	948,427	-1,165	947,262	102,795	6,115	850,582	292,626	206,434	14,100	95,717	48,538
1988	1,407,997	1,009,306	-1,424	1,007,882	112,486	4,611	900,007	294,001	213,989	14,783	95,246	48,810
1989	1,460,269	1,023,171	-1,238	1,021,933	114,886	6,457	913,504	320,764	226,001	15,291	95,499	48,602
1990	1,526,755	1,084,065	919	1,084,984	118,312	6,568	973,240	304,367	249,148	16,051	95,120	49,556
1991	1,573,097	1,119,030	2,127	1,121,157	124,164	5,191	1,002,184	302,081	268,832	16,356	96,178	49,176
1992	1,631,816	1,142,910	6,504	1,149,414	125,335	9,444	1,033,523	292,766	305,527	16,933	96,370	48,581
1993	1,680,922	1,185,856	1,366	1,187,222	131,527	11,977	1,067,672	290,096	323,154	17,245	97,474	48,917
1994	1,763,661	1,238,572	5,219	1,243,791	138,241	13,185	1,118,735	304,451	340,475	17,841	98,857	50,201
1995	1,873,264	1,307,160	-1,279	1,305,881	146,903	14,478	1,173,456	328,008	371,800	18,669	100,342	52,249
1996	2,004,788	1,392,105	1,164	1,393,269	155,227	19,270	1,257,312	351,088	396,388	19,465	102,993	53,694
1997	2,153,810	1,509,514	2,126	1,511,640	164,401	26,142	1,373,381	365,907	414,522	20,489	105,122	56,132
1998	2,279,892	1,609,364	784	1,610,148	173,399	36,926	1,473,675	378,647	427,570	21,303	107,020	55,293
1999	2,402,061	1,715,007	6,374	1,721,381	182,997	39,778	1,578,162	380,376	443,523	22,002	109,173	56,301
2000	2,608,345	1,863,205	1,090	1,864,295	194,642	47,202	1,716,855	420,807	470,683	23,512	110,939	57,538
2001	2,661,523	1,831,865	-563	1,831,302	195,915	86,537	1,721,924	427,392	512,207	23,694	112,330	56,379
2002	2,716,574	1,823,285	4,998	1,828,283	193,941	115,831	1,750,173	410,332	556,069	23,990	113,239	56,194
2003	2,857,433	1,878,300	9,846	1,888,146	203,927	150,789	1,835,008	429,770	592,655	24,973	114,421	56,728
2004	2,976,883	1,933,206	13,472	1,946,678	211,188	188,912	1,924,402	435,348	617,133	25,886	114,998	57,331
2005	3,150,599	2,004,641	6,479	2,011,120	219,654	231,402	2,022,868	454,897	672,834	27,239	115,666	57,761
2006	3,375,227	2,119,751	4,136	2,123,887	225,184	284,808	2,183,511	471,089	720,627	28,805	117,174	58,622
2007	3,632,499	2,170,837	9,910	2,180,747	231,535	335,636	2,284,848	561,417	786,234	30,698	118,331	58,711
2008	3,865,068	2,189,844	-4,136	2,185,708	236,037	382,312	2,331,983	662,493	870,592	32,525	118,834	58,836
2009	3,776,058	2,167,767	-9,037	2,158,730	238,974	321,179	2,240,935	585,415	949,708	31,449	120,069	57,926
2010	3,837,375	2,221,339	-5,490	2,215,849	248,251	286,764	2,254,362	550,484	1,032,529	31,691	121,086	57,171
2011	4,056,065	2,316,712	2,413	2,319,125	228,737	301,380	2,391,768	602,526	1,061,771	33,443	121,283	58,242
2012	4,262,467	2,397,466	6,335	2,403,801	234,513	359,043	2,528,331	668,887	1,065,249	35,044	121,631	58,317
2013	4,368,870	2,529,901	18,384	2,548,285	278,927	327,486	2,596,844	652,364	1,119,662	35,710	122,343	59,827
2014	4,575,002	2,570,294	9,635	2,579,929	285,128	431,805	2,726,606	677,625	1,170,771	37,034	123,534	60,557

Personal Income and Employment by Area: Shreveport-Bossier City, LA

(Thousands of dollars, except as noted.)

Year	Personal income, total	Earnings by place of work			Less: Contributions for government social insurance	Plus: Adjustment for residence	Equals: Net earnings by place of residence	Plus: Dividends, interest, and rent	Plus: Personal current transfer receipts	Per capita personal income (dollars)	Population (persons)	Total employment
		Nonfarm	Farm	Total								
1970	1,246,755	999,844	20,875	1,020,719	64,683	-24,628	931,408	194,623	120,724	3,477	358,599	156,510
1971	1,346,000	1,069,260	24,297	1,093,557	70,745	-25,167	997,645	207,647	140,708	3,706	363,150	156,487
1972	1,460,080	1,162,275	28,537	1,190,812	80,267	-27,501	1,083,044	222,178	154,858	3,974	367,392	158,719
1973	1,613,428	1,288,643	33,249	1,321,892	101,687	-32,216	1,187,989	250,114	175,325	4,363	369,828	166,046
1974	1,823,609	1,455,101	17,995	1,473,096	118,454	-36,273	1,318,369	302,529	202,711	4,891	372,886	171,606
1975	2,041,598	1,613,704	16,932	1,630,636	129,900	-39,643	1,461,093	331,771	248,734	5,358	381,019	174,633
1976	2,252,750	1,792,437	26,541	1,818,978	147,346	-44,381	1,627,251	351,723	273,776	5,822	386,919	178,905
1977	2,503,215	2,014,901	27,547	2,042,448	163,843	-49,066	1,829,539	384,052	289,624	6,420	389,881	184,422
1978	2,826,226	2,285,155	24,296	2,309,451	189,172	-59,023	2,061,256	447,616	317,354	7,179	393,685	189,618
1979	3,172,012	2,554,425	36,753	2,591,178	220,088	-67,174	2,303,916	507,790	360,306	7,971	397,929	192,590
1980	3,614,789	2,856,654	14,678	2,871,332	245,946	-77,605	2,547,781	635,269	431,739	8,952	403,812	197,589
1981	4,155,087	3,292,688	16,314	3,309,002	303,614	-130,278	2,875,110	796,349	483,628	10,177	408,275	205,422
1982	4,481,442	3,424,155	9,175	3,433,330	321,100	-90,416	3,021,814	905,464	554,164	10,811	414,540	206,376
1983	4,756,302	3,561,579	13,518	3,575,097	333,114	-92,635	3,149,348	996,465	610,489	11,376	418,102	204,949
1984	5,158,528	3,877,338	16,055	3,893,393	375,108	-101,004	3,417,281	1,103,356	637,891	12,279	420,125	211,853
1985	5,438,723	4,017,958	17,067	4,035,025	392,953	-98,264	3,543,808	1,196,347	698,568	12,848	423,310	212,767
1986	5,479,152	3,946,083	22,942	3,969,025	380,780	-86,015	3,502,230	1,207,408	769,514	12,875	425,565	201,775
1987	5,556,044	4,030,106	30,791	4,060,897	381,700	-78,839	3,600,358	1,175,805	779,881	13,215	420,448	198,273
1988	5,762,721	4,176,817	31,384	4,208,201	412,353	-76,474	3,719,374	1,221,290	822,057	13,932	413,628	197,372
1989	6,024,804	4,303,361	26,206	4,329,567	427,417	-63,255	3,838,895	1,289,276	896,633	14,743	408,649	195,216
1990	6,405,039	4,525,168	21,652	4,546,820	460,477	-52,656	4,033,687	1,393,969	977,383	15,963	401,238	196,252
1991	6,625,150	4,649,404	15,054	4,664,458	487,954	-55,666	4,120,838	1,389,735	1,114,577	16,557	400,139	196,602
1992	7,134,159	5,008,582	16,400	5,024,982	520,687	-70,644	4,433,651	1,430,154	1,270,354	17,714	402,750	198,843
1993	7,585,758	5,282,344	15,535	5,297,879	553,634	-85,861	4,658,384	1,500,502	1,426,872	18,687	405,929	204,276
1994	7,983,698	5,586,056	18,448	5,604,504	595,226	-97,650	4,911,628	1,560,155	1,511,915	19,557	408,225	207,412
1995	8,278,557	5,814,733	13,126	5,827,859	620,327	-124,940	5,082,592	1,671,780	1,524,185	20,120	411,451	214,651
1996	8,553,942	6,019,865	17,880	6,037,745	638,629	-122,457	5,276,659	1,735,320	1,541,963	20,695	413,330	217,592
1997	8,943,317	6,319,503	12,491	6,331,994	666,707	-138,554	5,526,733	1,840,611	1,575,973	21,496	416,050	221,717
1998	9,313,034	6,572,281	7,325	6,579,606	699,583	-150,258	5,729,765	1,947,864	1,635,405	22,441	414,997	224,328
1999	9,554,144	6,840,254	18,878	6,859,132	721,284	-163,657	5,974,191	1,886,270	1,693,683	22,928	416,699	226,629
2000	10,064,573	7,221,160	16,595	7,237,755	749,151	-170,721	6,317,883	2,016,720	1,729,970	24,087	417,850	228,304
2001	10,633,806	7,622,577	19,816	7,642,393	788,449	-184,185	6,669,759	2,007,187	1,956,860	25,463	417,622	227,523
2002	10,983,523	7,980,543	15,691	7,996,234	815,524	-208,069	6,972,641	1,929,100	2,081,782	26,279	417,953	225,392
2003	11,478,612	8,448,042	23,380	8,471,422	849,869	-245,834	7,375,719	1,967,373	2,135,520	27,445	418,234	228,683
2004	12,247,299	9,075,004	28,479	9,103,483	899,131	-278,497	7,925,855	1,968,295	2,353,149	29,043	421,695	233,451
2005	13,217,739	9,676,261	18,867	9,695,128	941,952	-292,663	8,460,513	2,245,383	2,511,843	31,152	424,302	238,784
2006	14,368,352	10,475,043	22,160	10,497,203	1,012,622	-321,921	9,162,660	2,543,211	2,662,481	33,349	430,852	247,082
2007	14,746,897	10,697,050	21,325	10,718,375	1,046,195	-322,391	9,349,789	2,589,304	2,807,804	34,176	431,496	251,863
2008	16,689,334	11,853,803	-19,623	11,834,180	1,113,220	-328,969	10,391,991	3,129,878	3,167,465	38,490	433,607	256,090
2009	15,746,309	10,991,648	-3,287	10,988,361	1,081,964	-316,149	9,590,248	2,805,470	3,350,591	36,117	435,976	252,515
2010	16,651,268	11,729,036	356	11,729,392	1,137,171	-354,785	10,237,436	2,877,324	3,536,508	37,744	441,161	254,484
2011	17,905,959	12,381,074	220	12,381,294	1,063,474	-392,580	10,925,240	3,410,482	3,570,237	40,236	445,021	260,328
2012	18,449,627	12,511,928	11,931	12,523,859	1,060,443	-356,616	11,106,800	3,687,800	3,655,027	41,147	448,379	260,450
2013	18,110,824	12,350,892	23,439	12,374,331	1,191,198	-331,353	10,851,780	3,492,373	3,766,671	40,532	446,825	257,691
2014	18,589,003	12,769,911	10,817	12,780,728	1,235,843	-337,601	11,207,284	3,614,624	3,767,095	41,760	445,142	259,202

Personal Income and Employment by Area: Sierra Vista-Douglas, AZ

(Thousands of dollars, except as noted.)

Year	Personal income, total	Derivation of personal income								Per capita personal income (dollars)	Population (persons)	Total employment
		Earnings by place of work			Less: Contributions for government social insurance	Plus: Adjustment for residence	Equals: Net earnings by place of residence	Plus: Dividends, interest, and rent	Plus: Personal current transfer receipts			
		Nonfarm	Farm	Total								
1970	257,515	203,450	6,493	209,943	11,329	-5,862	192,752	48,038	16,725	4,103	62,770	26,150
1971	309,697	244,557	9,400	253,957	14,297	-7,268	232,392	57,574	19,731	4,612	67,149	28,259
1972	349,636	271,548	11,193	282,741	16,344	-6,159	260,238	66,674	22,724	4,929	70,938	29,255
1973	392,076	298,396	14,483	312,879	19,246	-5,891	287,742	76,423	27,911	5,259	74,558	30,088
1974	420,365	318,108	13,649	331,757	21,768	-6,308	303,681	83,303	33,381	5,519	76,165	30,429
1975	441,430	322,606	13,448	336,054	22,551	-6,650	306,853	87,878	46,699	5,739	76,922	29,245
1976	483,089	345,565	21,298	366,863	24,075	-6,599	336,189	94,344	52,556	6,119	78,946	29,568
1977	524,288	382,336	11,603	393,939	26,597	-7,075	360,267	108,249	55,772	6,498	80,688	30,807
1978	596,041	427,274	16,333	443,607	30,254	-7,202	406,151	127,473	62,417	7,167	83,160	32,605
1979	641,996	454,192	10,252	464,444	33,640	-3,166	427,638	142,994	71,364	7,442	86,268	32,952
1980	726,959	506,881	8,623	515,504	38,656	-913	475,935	167,899	83,125	8,436	86,172	34,124
1981	807,944	551,647	11,386	563,033	45,082	-1,365	516,586	192,497	98,861	9,177	88,036	33,576
1982	853,108	567,191	13,785	580,976	46,391	-1,759	532,826	210,315	109,967	9,653	88,373	33,110
1983	929,834	613,035	18,706	631,741	52,544	-2,639	576,558	232,412	120,864	10,463	88,872	33,925
1984	1,026,511	683,424	14,677	698,101	59,650	-4,572	633,879	261,139	131,493	11,288	90,937	35,381
1985	1,075,355	713,180	10,723	723,903	65,788	-4,481	653,634	282,066	139,655	11,792	91,192	36,956
1986	1,143,598	749,220	16,665	765,885	70,853	-4,455	690,577	303,917	149,104	12,154	94,093	38,102
1987	1,220,944	799,723	18,986	818,709	75,676	-7,573	735,460	322,499	162,985	12,627	96,690	38,917
1988	1,285,659	830,875	30,623	861,498	83,964	-7,720	769,814	338,102	177,743	13,348	96,316	39,320
1989	1,351,110	859,043	19,773	878,816	91,079	-8,833	778,904	367,325	204,881	13,850	97,551	39,979
1990	1,430,797	921,786	18,913	940,699	100,318	-13,082	827,299	377,329	226,169	14,612	97,918	40,361
1991	1,515,676	978,320	19,896	998,216	107,427	-13,176	877,613	382,290	255,773	15,301	99,058	39,034
1992	1,641,710	1,058,159	28,782	1,086,941	118,797	-13,443	954,701	395,050	291,959	16,182	101,453	40,872
1993	1,707,638	1,080,288	26,738	1,107,026	123,757	-9,983	973,286	418,461	315,891	16,356	104,403	42,304
1994	1,803,984	1,139,864	9,385	1,149,249	130,616	-7,030	1,011,603	455,385	336,996	16,501	109,323	44,449
1995	1,872,952	1,157,724	6,900	1,164,624	129,596	-3,903	1,031,125	483,183	358,644	16,651	112,480	44,987
1996	1,971,892	1,193,959	23,873	1,217,832	136,244	-867	1,080,721	511,130	380,041	17,469	112,880	46,281
1997	2,056,321	1,247,261	30,516	1,277,777	141,091	894	1,137,580	517,966	400,775	17,896	114,907	47,434
1998	2,205,809	1,327,761	27,404	1,355,165	148,324	3,684	1,210,525	575,718	419,566	19,001	116,091	47,859
1999	2,295,646	1,372,930	34,146	1,407,076	152,174	8,874	1,263,776	585,106	446,764	19,700	116,530	48,411
2000	2,468,437	1,500,327	38,324	1,538,651	164,620	10,068	1,384,099	621,972	462,366	20,896	118,132	50,646
2001	2,666,118	1,597,161	46,986	1,644,147	174,953	14,947	1,484,141	653,934	528,043	22,442	118,798	51,597
2002	2,800,817	1,709,797	33,433	1,743,230	188,855	11,643	1,566,018	645,752	589,047	23,370	119,847	51,393
2003	3,017,278	1,862,883	35,140	1,898,023	204,416	8,199	1,701,806	662,649	652,823	25,011	120,638	53,365
2004	3,307,529	2,018,048	42,968	2,061,016	223,545	4,258	1,841,729	742,971	722,829	26,839	123,234	55,197
2005	3,641,132	2,229,571	68,941	2,298,512	247,823	-459	2,050,230	773,424	817,478	28,947	125,786	57,420
2006	3,851,706	2,399,405	34,759	2,434,164	262,963	-5,955	2,165,246	787,973	898,487	30,271	127,241	58,680
2007	4,138,495	2,539,500	45,068	2,584,568	282,843	-12,383	2,289,342	864,053	985,100	32,280	128,206	60,632
2008	4,281,853	2,621,827	26,609	2,648,436	299,545	-19,417	2,329,474	831,445	1,120,934	33,187	129,023	59,015
2009	4,471,211	2,664,518	25,196	2,689,714	310,010	-27,303	2,352,401	835,495	1,283,315	34,373	130,081	58,422
2010	4,570,411	2,739,342	26,116	2,765,458	321,463	-31,648	2,412,347	816,485	1,341,579	34,659	131,868	58,050
2011	4,736,361	2,786,808	46,386	2,833,194	294,581	-29,167	2,509,446	895,228	1,331,687	35,596	133,058	57,758
2012	4,678,914	2,726,639	49,174	2,775,813	289,506	-21,047	2,465,260	897,211	1,316,443	35,468	131,919	56,470
2013	4,593,193	2,600,105	52,569	2,652,674	311,191	-6,936	2,334,547	915,635	1,343,011	35,402	129,744	54,674
2014	4,679,941	2,575,955	44,780	2,620,735	307,325	-1,197	2,312,213	941,268	1,426,460	36,720	127,448	53,527

Personal Income and Employment by Area: Sioux City, IA-NE-SD

(Thousands of dollars, except as noted.)

Year	Personal income, total	Derivation of personal income					Equals: Net earnings by place of residence	Plus: Dividends, interest, and rent	Plus: Personal current transfer receipts	Per capita personal income (dollars)	Population (persons)	Total employment
		Earnings by place of work			Less: Contributions for government social insurance	Plus: Adjustment for residence						
		Nonfarm	Farm	Total								
1970	597,278	424,204	48,259	472,463	31,052	1,793	443,204	94,255	59,819	3,783	157,876	72,833
1971	642,912	456,174	50,410	506,584	34,480	1,859	473,963	102,904	66,045	4,028	159,627	73,517
1972	730,554	498,504	85,119	583,623	39,538	1,484	545,569	113,230	71,755	4,573	159,765	75,422
1973	871,709	557,980	151,976	709,956	51,321	1,425	660,060	129,091	82,558	5,444	160,131	79,574
1974	882,225	629,548	69,123	698,671	60,531	-736	637,404	148,364	96,457	5,503	160,327	82,025
1975	1,005,014	702,658	83,071	785,729	66,143	-2,673	716,913	170,308	117,793	6,208	161,899	82,537
1976	1,058,429	795,832	29,894	825,726	74,913	-4,207	746,606	182,356	129,467	6,463	163,760	84,198
1977	1,174,018	845,278	66,679	911,957	78,691	-3,938	829,328	205,300	139,390	7,123	164,822	83,528
1978	1,333,904	933,259	117,995	1,051,254	89,994	-7,470	953,790	222,084	158,030	8,191	162,857	84,631
1979	1,389,233	996,119	79,542	1,075,661	100,511	-6,201	968,949	243,207	177,077	8,593	161,674	84,150
1980	1,443,658	1,061,714	364	1,062,078	106,764	-6,707	948,607	292,472	202,579	8,995	160,495	82,883
1981	1,705,124	1,161,039	88,028	1,249,067	124,067	-11,415	1,113,585	364,352	227,187	10,590	161,009	82,444
1982	1,730,946	1,154,646	36,541	1,191,187	125,121	-9,917	1,056,149	421,930	252,867	10,838	159,718	79,728
1983	1,762,894	1,219,095	-22,461	1,196,634	131,102	-9,651	1,055,881	436,612	270,401	11,109	158,696	80,852
1984	1,934,121	1,281,123	56,366	1,337,489	140,345	-8,340	1,188,804	462,593	282,724	12,221	158,265	83,017
1985	2,037,680	1,329,369	86,220	1,415,589	149,234	-8,742	1,257,613	477,194	302,873	13,012	156,606	82,318
1986	2,087,168	1,375,630	84,161	1,459,791	158,678	-9,331	1,291,782	480,315	315,071	13,478	154,861	82,879
1987	2,236,938	1,493,548	132,283	1,625,831	173,110	-11,024	1,441,697	472,847	322,394	14,570	153,535	84,732
1988	2,307,700	1,590,366	95,614	1,685,980	189,694	-10,029	1,486,257	484,901	336,542	14,930	154,564	86,760
1989	2,488,802	1,713,158	129,645	1,842,803	204,509	-10,682	1,627,612	510,433	350,757	16,135	154,246	90,853
1990	2,659,107	1,813,611	141,578	1,955,189	222,806	-12,867	1,719,516	562,641	376,950	17,150	155,053	93,372
1991	2,747,869	1,890,678	126,810	2,017,488	235,120	-16,493	1,765,875	576,019	405,975	17,549	156,583	92,809
1992	3,006,810	2,086,040	169,772	2,255,812	256,340	-21,373	1,978,099	594,005	434,706	19,005	158,214	94,798
1993	3,079,838	2,220,036	113,321	2,333,357	273,323	-23,573	2,036,461	595,171	448,206	19,205	160,369	98,232
1994	3,305,955	2,401,268	161,436	2,562,704	298,461	-27,949	2,236,294	603,780	465,881	20,372	162,280	101,761
1995	3,527,276	2,602,088	108,218	2,710,306	323,908	-35,931	2,350,467	688,371	488,438	21,501	164,052	105,716
1996	3,902,142	2,779,334	234,945	3,014,279	331,924	-41,112	2,641,243	750,694	510,205	23,527	165,859	107,604
1997	3,969,515	2,885,269	176,123	3,061,392	352,903	-41,309	2,667,180	783,215	519,120	23,893	166,138	108,743
1998	4,203,268	3,110,567	139,568	3,250,135	374,958	-47,837	2,827,340	851,372	524,556	25,236	166,559	108,445
1999	4,297,161	3,236,796	114,663	3,351,459	386,445	-46,886	2,918,128	828,814	550,219	25,632	167,651	109,130
2000	4,520,897	3,383,178	115,223	3,498,401	399,733	-47,155	3,051,513	877,764	591,620	26,948	167,762	108,910
2001	4,629,827	3,425,813	129,271	3,555,084	403,301	-68,256	3,083,527	917,078	629,222	27,717	167,040	108,115
2002	4,710,895	3,442,848	107,711	3,550,559	404,184	-38,685	3,107,690	910,165	693,040	28,286	166,544	105,672
2003	4,823,340	3,511,580	155,168	3,666,748	413,138	-22,753	3,230,857	908,418	684,065	29,016	166,232	104,696
2004	5,090,309	3,628,864	257,725	3,886,589	422,091	-492	3,464,006	920,134	706,169	30,632	166,178	103,619
2005	5,235,113	3,734,230	225,046	3,959,276	439,101	21,132	3,541,307	935,537	758,269	31,759	164,840	104,713
2006	5,398,206	3,858,489	132,488	3,990,977	457,660	28,536	3,561,853	1,004,556	831,797	32,648	165,345	105,810
2007	5,867,554	4,068,462	184,997	4,253,459	481,844	41,806	3,813,421	1,177,008	877,125	35,431	165,607	108,708
2008	6,330,812	4,312,445	299,640	4,612,085	506,519	46,726	4,152,292	1,187,081	991,439	38,092	166,196	109,739
2009	6,199,546	4,295,198	216,970	4,512,168	507,920	56,931	4,061,179	1,092,752	1,045,615	37,001	167,549	108,016
2010	6,441,029	4,427,987	249,924	4,677,911	522,958	53,886	4,208,839	1,108,243	1,123,947	38,159	168,793	106,522
2011	6,888,013	4,584,580	438,177	5,022,757	476,576	76,052	4,622,233	1,129,642	1,136,138	40,772	168,940	106,603
2012	7,058,519	4,661,842	341,459	5,003,301	481,692	76,297	4,597,906	1,322,634	1,137,979	41,817	168,796	107,269
2013	7,325,512	4,771,202	679,471	5,450,673	563,884	58,446	4,945,235	1,230,340	1,149,937	43,401	168,785	109,250
2014	7,456,159	5,079,162	448,509	5,527,671	597,529	49,739	4,979,881	1,281,196	1,195,082	44,170	168,806	110,568

Personal Income and Employment by Area: Sioux Falls, SD

(Thousands of dollars, except as noted.)

| Year | Personal income, total | Derivation of personal income | | | | | | | | Per capita personal income (dollars) | Population (persons) | Total employment |
| | | Earnings by place of work | | | Less: Contributions for government social insurance | Plus: Adjustment for residence | Equals: Net earnings by place of residence | Plus: Dividends, interest, and rent | Plus: Personal current transfer receipts | | | |
		Nonfarm	Farm	Total								
1970	465,838	345,258	37,216	382,474	23,339	-3,948	355,187	70,055	40,596	3,752	124,171	60,271
1971	510,235	372,448	44,678	417,126	25,680	-3,975	387,471	76,031	46,733	4,079	125,075	60,995
1972	578,044	407,271	68,995	476,266	29,026	-4,124	443,116	82,923	52,005	4,584	126,094	61,395
1973	692,464	471,033	110,766	581,799	39,254	-4,514	538,031	94,131	60,302	5,456	126,920	65,595
1974	751,010	534,032	84,047	618,079	45,948	-4,909	567,222	112,852	70,936	5,867	128,011	67,350
1975	840,755	588,299	91,591	679,890	49,977	-4,594	625,319	130,274	85,162	6,516	129,032	68,274
1976	884,349	678,530	34,355	712,885	57,694	-4,656	650,535	140,966	92,848	6,748	131,050	71,764
1977	1,008,787	763,122	55,482	818,604	63,196	-5,262	750,146	160,559	98,082	7,590	132,916	75,138
1978	1,180,604	887,412	86,077	973,489	75,500	-5,961	892,028	182,114	106,462	8,845	133,481	79,276
1979	1,298,837	980,929	89,002	1,069,931	89,215	-5,515	975,201	203,345	120,291	9,599	135,312	80,201
1980	1,362,166	1,046,862	22,147	1,069,009	95,428	-5,101	968,480	252,635	141,051	9,787	139,185	79,520
1981	1,574,768	1,124,290	81,250	1,205,540	109,346	-7,768	1,088,426	320,397	165,945	11,318	139,142	78,983
1982	1,647,224	1,177,794	36,974	1,214,768	116,631	-9,112	1,089,025	373,199	185,000	11,703	140,747	79,169
1983	1,753,200	1,288,067	19,856	1,307,923	128,284	-11,864	1,167,775	386,534	198,891	12,257	143,042	82,261
1984	1,942,026	1,409,481	55,064	1,464,545	143,639	-14,313	1,306,593	424,826	210,607	13,294	146,081	86,170
1985	2,062,037	1,481,284	82,031	1,563,315	155,526	-16,153	1,391,636	443,793	226,608	13,939	147,929	88,138
1986	2,158,811	1,569,659	73,364	1,643,023	169,658	-18,095	1,455,270	463,946	239,595	14,607	147,796	89,382
1987	2,286,864	1,661,179	111,179	1,772,358	181,315	-20,092	1,570,951	467,415	248,498	15,382	148,672	93,682
1988	2,476,516	1,817,702	121,128	1,938,830	203,015	-23,970	1,711,845	499,811	264,860	16,351	151,460	97,090
1989	2,669,894	1,988,253	86,492	2,074,745	223,376	-26,547	1,824,822	560,162	284,910	17,537	152,240	100,812
1990	2,945,686	2,222,111	102,230	2,324,341	263,351	-30,327	2,030,663	610,573	304,450	19,109	154,148	105,115
1991	3,121,357	2,395,291	100,859	2,496,150	286,241	-32,939	2,176,970	617,535	326,852	19,890	156,928	109,696
1992	3,387,172	2,596,598	139,119	2,735,717	305,620	-37,737	2,392,360	640,666	354,146	21,071	160,753	113,135
1993	3,527,010	2,756,059	71,005	2,827,064	322,600	-42,381	2,462,083	692,858	372,069	21,495	164,088	116,256
1994	3,907,746	2,999,334	189,709	3,189,043	353,167	-48,626	2,787,250	729,145	391,351	23,262	167,987	122,281
1995	4,065,397	3,173,833	66,490	3,240,323	372,509	-53,037	2,814,777	827,547	423,073	23,816	170,698	125,850
1996	4,467,458	3,352,755	222,166	3,574,921	392,473	-59,112	3,123,336	894,011	450,111	25,681	173,960	129,330
1997	4,632,059	3,565,262	147,579	3,712,841	417,713	-69,346	3,225,782	937,098	469,179	26,355	175,756	132,805
1998	5,060,255	3,937,612	150,351	4,087,963	454,543	-82,000	3,551,420	1,022,159	486,676	28,275	178,964	136,833
1999	5,446,789	4,359,647	98,544	4,458,191	500,361	-96,532	3,861,298	1,075,644	509,847	29,741	183,138	142,266
2000	5,918,171	4,712,189	121,897	4,834,086	535,492	-111,880	4,186,714	1,176,066	555,391	31,428	188,310	146,439
2001	6,298,936	5,083,429	87,506	5,170,935	562,488	-122,175	4,486,272	1,210,396	602,268	32,859	191,693	149,153
2002	6,602,508	5,437,294	59,398	5,496,692	593,668	-155,231	4,747,793	1,202,754	651,961	33,956	194,442	150,748
2003	6,924,690	5,662,907	121,804	5,784,711	624,145	-178,433	4,982,133	1,265,155	677,402	35,006	197,813	151,689
2004	7,368,778	5,940,996	182,814	6,123,810	654,792	-191,192	5,277,826	1,360,436	730,516	36,420	202,328	155,488
2005	7,830,761	6,226,109	123,403	6,349,512	691,066	-163,826	5,494,620	1,528,360	807,781	37,902	206,605	159,768
2006	8,309,140	6,500,785	105,396	6,606,181	746,915	-184,131	5,675,135	1,738,588	895,417	39,273	211,576	164,522
2007	8,952,614	6,803,326	163,316	6,966,642	794,625	-160,950	6,011,067	1,986,781	954,766	41,267	216,943	169,868
2008	9,644,388	7,164,916	212,955	7,377,871	831,765	-157,852	6,388,254	2,136,798	1,119,336	43,465	221,887	173,157
2009	9,544,238	7,259,238	245,436	7,504,674	833,146	-161,411	6,510,117	1,854,208	1,179,913	42,247	225,913	171,707
2010	10,127,285	7,615,843	208,543	7,824,386	863,753	-156,448	6,804,185	2,037,921	1,285,179	44,205	229,099	170,260
2011	10,845,087	7,905,907	441,966	8,347,873	789,413	-171,757	7,386,703	2,138,823	1,319,561	46,615	232,650	173,723
2012	11,626,017	8,829,472	203,041	9,032,513	851,706	-183,572	7,997,235	2,298,755	1,330,027	48,901	237,748	177,659
2013	11,643,004	8,730,973	398,485	9,129,458	979,368	-184,905	7,965,185	2,289,381	1,388,438	47,791	243,622	182,008
2014	12,067,800	9,292,753	168,494	9,461,247	1,049,453	-195,573	8,216,221	2,388,310	1,463,269	48,592	248,351	186,596

Personal Income and Employment by Area: South Bend-Mishawaka, IN-MI

(Thousands of dollars, except as noted.)

Year	Personal income, total	Derivation of personal income									Per capita personal income (dollars)	Population (persons)	Total employment
		Earnings by place of work			Less: Contributions for government social insurance	Plus: Adjustment for residence	Equals: Net earnings by place of residence	Plus: Dividends, interest, and rent	Plus: Personal current transfer receipts				
		Nonfarm	Farm	Total									
1970	1,106,775	853,000	7,575	860,575	57,910	62,432	865,097	152,144	89,534		3,842	288,051	115,959
1971	1,180,445	884,747	9,614	894,361	62,256	73,060	905,165	163,556	111,724		4,106	287,489	113,550
1972	1,315,195	994,606	13,150	1,007,756	74,400	90,659	1,024,015	174,307	116,873		4,541	289,656	118,965
1973	1,466,971	1,106,066	23,862	1,129,928	95,536	103,062	1,137,454	193,428	136,089		5,068	289,459	125,314
1974	1,578,707	1,190,240	15,973	1,206,213	106,729	96,566	1,196,050	221,071	161,586		5,472	288,497	126,842
1975	1,706,061	1,238,018	32,921	1,270,939	109,135	95,642	1,257,446	246,120	202,495		5,917	288,309	123,186
1976	1,870,915	1,371,638	25,181	1,396,819	122,910	124,715	1,398,624	260,109	212,182		6,516	287,124	125,452
1977	2,060,503	1,523,857	14,792	1,538,649	137,336	151,059	1,552,372	286,397	221,734		7,154	288,007	129,758
1978	2,301,658	1,701,129	23,147	1,724,276	158,574	176,247	1,741,949	319,060	240,649		7,932	290,181	134,190
1979	2,517,737	1,863,282	19,796	1,883,078	179,831	182,475	1,885,722	356,855	275,160		8,633	291,639	135,847
1980	2,722,334	1,933,602	5,766	1,939,368	184,702	174,738	1,929,404	447,398	345,532		9,356	290,984	130,558
1981	2,990,062	2,071,104	8,387	2,079,491	213,252	176,394	2,042,633	558,042	389,387		10,317	289,810	129,347
1982	3,116,994	2,122,780	8,766	2,131,546	222,222	177,359	2,086,683	599,350	430,961		10,833	287,735	126,263
1983	3,317,858	2,236,843	2,936	2,239,779	235,260	215,139	2,219,658	637,092	461,108		11,576	286,626	127,770
1984	3,676,188	2,502,413	20,435	2,522,848	269,474	233,454	2,486,828	713,113	476,247		12,755	288,222	135,669
1985	3,851,988	2,631,211	14,099	2,645,310	288,088	238,778	2,596,000	752,049	503,939		13,311	289,373	137,736
1986	4,094,087	2,801,406	24,678	2,826,084	307,980	259,332	2,777,436	783,544	533,107		14,146	289,411	141,018
1987	4,361,178	3,037,156	36,483	3,073,639	329,889	274,531	3,018,281	797,612	545,285		14,989	290,952	146,392
1988	4,625,229	3,255,719	19,540	3,275,259	365,775	282,872	3,192,356	852,250	580,623		15,799	292,757	149,826
1989	4,929,085	3,409,336	41,183	3,450,519	384,833	276,101	3,341,787	960,720	626,578		16,681	295,488	151,731
1990	5,119,351	3,558,188	42,019	3,600,207	413,195	250,984	3,437,996	996,187	685,168		17,226	297,187	153,679
1991	5,241,828	3,668,047	25,953	3,694,000	432,884	244,369	3,505,485	980,337	756,006		17,548	298,719	153,036
1992	5,653,534	3,941,302	35,995	3,977,297	461,096	281,628	3,797,829	1,003,301	852,404		18,788	300,909	155,304
1993	6,009,694	4,205,674	30,101	4,235,775	494,335	294,628	4,036,068	1,079,630	893,996		19,723	304,704	158,330
1994	6,390,558	4,479,565	29,192	4,508,757	537,635	335,961	4,307,083	1,151,077	932,398		20,802	307,216	163,946
1995	6,699,603	4,726,532	18,038	4,744,570	571,583	334,503	4,507,490	1,241,525	950,588		21,607	310,072	168,659
1996	6,998,067	4,898,457	29,566	4,928,023	584,745	332,914	4,676,192	1,321,839	1,000,036		22,421	312,119	169,345
1997	7,345,297	5,136,330	31,633	5,167,963	613,750	328,865	4,883,078	1,428,417	1,033,802		23,424	313,574	172,747
1998	7,925,242	5,588,261	18,794	5,607,055	649,324	331,364	5,289,095	1,591,315	1,044,832		25,195	314,556	175,616
1999	8,267,375	5,940,464	10,400	5,950,864	680,449	369,718	5,640,133	1,527,556	1,099,686		26,179	315,804	174,965
2000	8,629,947	6,151,978	22,140	6,174,118	698,951	363,067	5,838,234	1,630,589	1,161,124		27,225	316,991	176,954
2001	8,796,104	6,242,269	24,146	6,266,415	697,393	302,579	5,871,601	1,643,045	1,281,458		27,757	316,897	172,278
2002	9,172,780	6,558,387	10,675	6,569,062	724,063	334,639	6,179,638	1,648,911	1,344,231		28,966	316,678	170,490
2003	9,395,765	6,791,085	28,835	6,819,920	752,423	375,387	6,442,884	1,560,503	1,392,378		29,682	316,545	170,826
2004	9,873,374	7,172,855	57,949	7,230,804	793,453	448,036	6,885,387	1,527,354	1,460,633		31,163	316,831	172,746
2005	10,093,032	7,242,838	37,172	7,280,010	816,573	495,067	6,958,504	1,564,340	1,570,188		31,817	317,221	173,180
2006	10,692,215	7,540,154	32,372	7,572,526	854,681	520,551	7,238,396	1,762,566	1,691,253		33,647	317,778	173,782
2007	11,121,861	7,687,454	38,644	7,726,098	881,760	572,489	7,416,827	1,927,229	1,777,805		34,901	318,668	174,814
2008	11,527,422	7,837,838	33,809	7,871,647	912,288	610,061	7,569,420	1,910,271	2,047,731		36,027	319,966	172,438
2009	10,941,677	7,484,020	27,158	7,511,178	878,398	331,631	6,964,411	1,728,233	2,249,033		34,280	319,189	163,778
2010	11,119,835	7,436,809	45,365	7,482,174	870,030	413,702	7,025,846	1,700,868	2,393,121		34,860	318,981	162,533
2011	11,678,372	7,705,495	108,837	7,814,332	798,410	397,981	7,413,903	1,886,746	2,377,723		36,584	319,222	165,353
2012	12,023,157	7,830,442	57,783	7,888,225	809,238	465,261	7,544,248	2,049,765	2,429,144		37,735	318,625	164,231
2013	12,104,372	7,871,256	74,839	7,946,095	921,221	640,685	7,665,559	1,991,999	2,446,814		38,000	318,532	164,031
2014	12,740,124	8,265,266	38,318	8,303,584	963,505	776,936	8,117,015	2,072,362	2,550,747		39,909	319,226	166,972

Personal Income and Employment by Area: Spartanburg, SC

(Thousands of dollars, except as noted.)

Year	Personal income, total	Derivation of personal income								Per capita personal income (dollars)	Population (persons)	Total employment
		Earnings by place of work			Less: Contributions for government social insurance	Plus: Adjustment for residence	Equals: Net earnings by place of residence	Plus: Dividends, interest, and rent	Plus: Personal current transfer receipts			
		Nonfarm	Farm	Total								
1970	646,100	581,830	7,033	588,863	42,161	-22,373	524,329	63,957	57,814	3,173	203,598	95,324
1971	708,536	636,825	8,587	645,412	47,844	-24,382	573,186	70,713	64,637	3,411	207,746	97,322
1972	792,059	718,860	4,674	723,534	56,420	-25,261	641,853	78,210	71,996	3,686	214,876	102,291
1973	903,190	818,604	9,843	828,447	73,332	-26,884	728,231	89,627	85,332	4,142	218,059	108,377
1974	998,949	889,166	8,428	897,594	82,767	-26,397	788,430	104,074	106,445	4,527	220,651	109,521
1975	1,086,183	925,150	13,616	938,766	83,413	-34,382	820,971	115,459	149,753	4,886	222,317	104,514
1976	1,223,280	1,077,829	6,180	1,084,009	99,800	-38,706	945,503	125,136	152,641	5,525	221,399	112,098
1977	1,322,838	1,162,849	4,676	1,167,525	107,962	-37,481	1,022,082	139,876	160,880	5,839	226,538	112,592
1978	1,492,268	1,319,860	6,481	1,326,341	126,129	-40,255	1,159,957	157,935	174,376	6,529	228,545	116,562
1979	1,665,459	1,461,071	7,135	1,468,206	143,708	-38,672	1,285,826	178,373	201,260	7,220	230,660	118,727
1980	1,877,254	1,609,708	3,485	1,613,193	157,816	-43,887	1,411,490	222,599	243,165	8,002	234,585	119,546
1981	2,087,444	1,743,034	5,909	1,748,943	182,659	-43,578	1,522,706	278,968	285,770	8,807	237,011	119,197
1982	2,179,175	1,754,633	166	1,754,799	186,510	-40,479	1,527,810	327,663	323,702	9,140	238,425	115,589
1983	2,363,154	1,899,901	850	1,900,751	205,296	-40,236	1,655,219	368,203	339,732	9,863	239,608	116,366
1984	2,632,869	2,134,576	11,636	2,146,212	238,004	-44,288	1,863,920	416,257	352,692	10,854	242,564	121,852
1985	2,804,249	2,268,757	-2,360	2,266,397	256,019	-37,171	1,973,207	451,955	379,087	11,423	245,495	123,771
1986	2,980,530	2,407,606	516	2,408,122	278,219	-25,492	2,104,411	478,672	397,447	12,093	246,475	125,105
1987	3,212,239	2,627,135	6,225	2,633,360	298,691	-24,227	2,310,442	495,852	405,945	12,927	248,494	128,824
1988	3,513,582	2,885,810	10,271	2,896,081	337,263	-17,991	2,540,827	541,960	430,795	13,980	251,333	134,930
1989	3,787,342	3,073,928	8,263	3,082,191	363,429	-12,512	2,706,250	598,421	482,671	14,840	255,211	140,069
1990	4,056,789	3,250,035	5,417	3,255,452	391,771	2,362	2,866,043	656,698	534,048	15,731	257,888	141,738
1991	4,219,756	3,345,691	9,759	3,355,450	408,488	-11,543	2,935,419	671,956	612,381	16,156	261,183	138,353
1992	4,472,061	3,646,595	9,165	3,655,760	440,454	-107,868	3,107,438	692,173	672,450	16,964	263,625	141,135
1993	4,772,966	3,883,549	10,793	3,894,342	474,297	-88,102	3,331,943	726,802	714,221	17,966	265,660	144,593
1994	5,042,433	4,117,820	9,902	4,127,722	509,446	-123,970	3,494,306	781,847	766,280	18,779	268,510	150,032
1995	5,348,150	4,390,919	7,790	4,398,709	544,512	-148,934	3,705,263	819,582	823,305	19,688	271,652	154,425
1996	5,639,879	4,560,944	3,877	4,564,821	555,383	-134,047	3,875,391	881,269	883,219	20,535	274,644	156,444
1997	5,942,709	4,806,337	5,730	4,812,067	582,934	-156,281	4,072,852	950,203	919,654	21,447	277,093	159,044
1998	6,211,786	5,053,935	6,290	5,060,225	614,698	-207,090	4,238,437	1,010,098	963,251	22,234	279,388	159,680
1999	6,572,413	5,330,521	8,679	5,339,200	637,626	-151,438	4,550,136	994,843	1,027,434	23,319	281,850	159,782
2000	7,021,486	5,577,222	9,537	5,586,759	662,930	-132,685	4,791,144	1,119,404	1,110,938	24,688	284,414	160,874
2001	7,240,998	5,726,569	6,480	5,733,049	686,060	-166,529	4,880,460	1,117,184	1,243,354	25,293	286,282	157,133
2002	7,465,750	5,879,191	5,354	5,884,545	702,177	-201,813	4,980,555	1,136,737	1,348,458	25,908	288,166	154,401
2003	7,535,650	6,007,156	11,080	6,018,236	717,247	-234,492	5,066,497	1,057,783	1,411,370	26,008	289,742	154,487
2004	7,924,361	6,238,825	1,416	6,240,241	740,429	-271,188	5,228,624	1,188,056	1,507,681	27,221	291,107	154,879
2005	8,334,657	6,429,195	11,794	6,440,989	763,733	-298,884	5,378,372	1,335,438	1,620,847	28,376	293,722	156,389
2006	8,974,246	6,846,705	13,000	6,859,705	832,814	-345,869	5,681,022	1,539,399	1,753,825	30,100	298,146	159,792
2007	9,554,993	7,157,022	16,561	7,173,583	865,971	-387,425	5,920,187	1,772,532	1,862,274	31,506	303,275	163,719
2008	10,146,755	7,448,275	19,533	7,467,808	900,792	-425,336	6,141,680	1,871,522	2,133,553	32,854	308,845	162,573
2009	9,781,152	7,020,864	22,125	7,042,989	854,711	-315,994	5,872,284	1,527,837	2,381,031	31,306	312,435	152,818
2010	9,956,398	7,128,140	23,921	7,152,061	861,701	-361,152	5,929,208	1,499,178	2,528,012	31,741	313,676	150,762
2011	10,529,360	7,366,674	14,848	7,381,522	804,627	-383,451	6,193,444	1,821,999	2,513,917	33,453	314,747	154,939
2012	11,303,416	7,840,325	15,654	7,855,979	832,896	-438,612	6,584,471	2,190,655	2,528,290	35,698	316,643	158,200
2013	11,019,327	8,045,743	21,767	8,067,510	969,294	-559,548	6,538,668	1,901,946	2,578,713	34,565	318,800	164,131
2014	11,537,824	8,474,991	17,945	8,492,936	1,020,589	-611,691	6,860,656	1,968,462	2,708,706	35,897	321,418	167,900

Personal Income and Employment by Area: Spokane-Spokane Valley, WA

(Thousands of dollars, except as noted.)

| Year | Personal income, total | Derivation of personal income | | | | | | | | Per capita personal income (dollars) | Population (persons) | Total employment |
| | | Earnings by place of work | | | Less: Contributions for government social insurance | Plus: Adjustment for residence | Equals: Net earnings by place of residence | Plus: Dividends, interest, and rent | Plus: Personal current transfer receipts | | | |
		Nonfarm	Farm	Total								
1970	1,198,281	909,252	23,387	932,639	73,775	-16,155	842,709	211,500	144,072	3,833	312,662	129,507
1971	1,309,992	987,981	23,187	1,011,168	83,296	-13,771	914,101	231,977	163,914	4,084	320,760	130,877
1972	1,447,721	1,094,489	31,408	1,125,897	96,852	-12,869	1,016,176	251,854	179,691	4,460	324,588	135,558
1973	1,599,973	1,208,691	44,486	1,253,177	123,183	-16,469	1,113,525	281,405	205,043	4,839	330,672	140,777
1974	1,833,404	1,363,643	69,245	1,432,888	142,743	-19,880	1,270,265	323,962	239,177	5,427	337,833	147,280
1975	2,025,990	1,483,117	61,514	1,544,631	152,627	-19,275	1,372,729	363,780	289,481	5,946	340,737	145,992
1976	2,267,380	1,710,256	45,867	1,756,123	179,804	-20,154	1,556,165	393,999	317,216	6,534	346,996	154,184
1977	2,514,022	1,924,977	35,768	1,960,745	203,587	-20,183	1,736,975	444,015	333,032	7,127	352,737	160,857
1978	2,874,092	2,236,492	35,661	2,272,153	242,846	-23,109	2,006,198	509,469	358,425	7,938	362,077	171,110
1979	3,233,525	2,505,443	49,342	2,554,785	281,438	-25,413	2,247,934	579,408	406,183	8,732	370,294	176,121
1980	3,617,080	2,721,165	41,158	2,762,323	305,563	-30,182	2,426,578	695,521	494,981	9,501	380,713	177,638
1981	3,989,768	2,934,167	44,896	2,979,063	353,372	-40,044	2,585,647	841,346	562,775	10,357	385,240	176,434
1982	4,172,397	2,969,883	34,231	3,004,114	363,285	-46,482	2,594,347	947,670	630,380	10,806	386,115	173,325
1983	4,497,893	3,188,484	53,286	3,241,770	396,794	-52,358	2,792,618	1,033,650	671,625	11,607	387,506	178,995
1984	4,808,522	3,426,046	38,570	3,464,616	443,708	-62,395	2,958,513	1,145,489	704,520	12,244	392,732	185,944
1985	4,984,034	3,508,032	29,999	3,538,031	458,758	-63,456	3,015,817	1,207,077	761,140	12,615	395,083	187,899
1986	5,204,442	3,652,420	46,683	3,699,103	482,390	-69,723	3,146,990	1,255,844	801,608	13,214	393,851	191,101
1987	5,406,403	3,852,409	18,018	3,870,427	503,753	-75,934	3,290,740	1,273,306	842,357	13,756	393,013	196,927
1988	5,728,165	4,113,566	32,933	4,146,499	555,534	-86,979	3,503,986	1,309,408	914,771	14,578	392,929	201,707
1989	6,234,391	4,370,225	37,217	4,407,442	589,953	-94,550	3,722,939	1,516,890	994,562	15,761	395,554	205,459
1990	6,694,241	4,809,402	30,216	4,839,618	655,359	-101,709	4,082,550	1,514,574	1,097,117	16,609	403,054	213,149
1991	7,265,556	5,225,056	23,257	5,248,313	713,978	-106,186	4,428,149	1,579,232	1,258,175	17,563	413,678	219,425
1992	7,863,534	5,723,889	31,939	5,755,828	777,562	-120,713	4,857,553	1,622,057	1,383,924	18,465	425,854	224,934
1993	8,356,791	6,130,716	38,158	6,168,874	838,582	-130,644	5,199,648	1,693,753	1,463,390	19,104	437,440	229,463
1994	8,853,524	6,529,021	23,304	6,552,325	897,619	-147,254	5,507,452	1,829,745	1,516,327	19,890	445,129	242,655
1995	9,219,786	6,732,251	33,186	6,765,437	927,248	-160,611	5,677,578	1,934,869	1,607,339	20,361	452,821	245,905
1996	9,693,502	7,046,335	34,719	7,081,054	945,083	-178,442	5,957,529	2,065,422	1,670,551	21,181	457,647	250,642
1997	10,253,837	7,462,374	26,485	7,488,859	961,234	-196,906	6,330,719	2,189,767	1,733,351	22,271	460,412	254,871
1998	10,881,686	8,039,718	25,052	8,064,770	1,016,575	-223,517	6,824,678	2,269,302	1,787,706	23,441	464,219	258,164
1999	11,356,475	8,477,983	20,554	8,498,537	1,033,737	-244,063	7,220,737	2,220,580	1,915,158	24,338	466,608	260,510
2000	12,266,284	9,194,550	25,998	9,220,548	1,132,572	-218,555	7,869,421	2,381,866	2,014,997	26,060	470,685	267,786
2001	12,499,178	9,218,087	22,594	9,240,681	1,151,227	-230,907	7,858,547	2,394,635	2,245,996	26,318	474,933	265,817
2002	12,824,709	9,380,473	32,277	9,412,750	1,175,516	-230,402	8,006,832	2,458,749	2,359,128	26,753	479,375	263,980
2003	13,325,837	9,738,026	48,245	9,786,271	1,231,013	-228,287	8,326,971	2,535,739	2,463,127	27,571	483,328	267,815
2004	13,975,213	10,328,976	32,855	10,361,831	1,317,239	-223,641	8,820,951	2,622,605	2,531,657	28,606	488,534	273,313
2005	14,517,596	10,917,728	21,482	10,939,210	1,411,797	-226,420	9,300,993	2,507,211	2,709,392	29,364	494,408	280,542
2006	15,590,532	11,634,486	15,048	11,649,534	1,495,745	-221,449	9,932,340	2,730,510	2,927,682	31,022	502,564	290,283
2007	16,833,712	12,253,795	17,084	12,270,879	1,563,771	-213,366	10,493,742	3,161,076	3,178,894	32,876	512,037	299,480
2008	18,033,221	12,584,040	2,011	12,586,051	1,592,704	-194,476	10,798,871	3,601,497	3,632,853	34,770	518,646	300,185
2009	17,788,362	12,224,142	9,719	12,233,861	1,588,720	-235,559	10,409,582	3,320,205	4,058,575	33,894	524,826	288,535
2010	18,128,498	12,355,205	25,670	12,380,875	1,612,611	-260,880	10,507,384	3,171,490	4,449,624	34,302	528,493	281,662
2011	18,923,793	12,719,464	37,850	12,757,314	1,514,571	-332,178	10,910,565	3,572,375	4,440,853	35,716	529,837	282,799
2012	19,586,369	13,242,399	24,351	13,266,750	1,547,240	-454,542	11,264,968	3,859,041	4,462,360	36,795	532,312	287,624
2013	19,759,139	13,574,180	37,769	13,611,949	1,786,159	-431,184	11,394,606	3,841,095	4,523,438	36,886	535,684	291,707
2014	20,800,635	14,122,417	14,026	14,136,443	1,845,317	-471,563	11,819,563	4,016,557	4,964,515	38,452	540,953	297,124

Personal Income and Employment by Area: Springfield, IL

(Thousands of dollars, except as noted.)

Year	Personal income, total	Earnings by place of work			Less: Contributions for government social insurance	Plus: Adjustment for residence	Equals: Net earnings by place of residence	Plus: Dividends, interest, and rent	Plus: Personal current transfer receipts	Per capita personal income (dollars)	Population (persons)	Total employment
		Nonfarm	Farm	Total								
1970	793,778	659,339	24,255	683,594	38,683	-26,888	618,023	116,822	58,933	4,620	171,806	90,195
1971	888,733	739,992	30,181	770,173	44,476	-32,927	692,770	127,197	68,766	5,063	175,525	92,866
1972	965,293	797,125	34,982	832,107	49,801	-36,297	746,009	140,849	78,435	5,467	176,557	93,833
1973	1,073,265	860,257	58,475	918,732	61,209	-39,774	817,749	160,725	94,791	6,009	178,605	96,418
1974	1,195,912	957,900	61,155	1,019,055	70,797	-46,494	901,764	185,002	109,146	6,661	179,531	99,017
1975	1,349,871	1,050,242	80,270	1,130,512	77,368	-51,938	1,001,206	208,062	140,603	7,338	183,947	100,341
1976	1,439,600	1,144,914	59,592	1,204,506	86,496	-54,092	1,063,918	219,910	155,772	7,684	187,362	101,727
1977	1,545,591	1,224,502	65,617	1,290,119	93,099	-56,788	1,140,232	242,829	162,530	8,203	188,410	103,960
1978	1,700,795	1,373,796	50,614	1,424,410	107,116	-65,353	1,251,941	271,898	176,956	9,054	187,846	107,229
1979	1,819,672	1,442,422	54,873	1,497,295	116,210	-66,494	1,314,591	309,159	195,922	9,706	187,471	106,604
1980	1,955,347	1,525,293	23,097	1,548,390	119,965	-73,796	1,354,629	364,934	235,784	10,413	187,780	103,610
1981	2,178,817	1,631,364	60,846	1,692,210	138,179	-85,662	1,468,369	435,677	274,771	11,621	187,489	102,830
1982	2,352,962	1,727,774	39,850	1,767,624	147,959	-91,011	1,528,654	526,910	297,398	12,593	186,844	103,591
1983	2,442,285	1,819,708	-1,026	1,818,682	156,440	-96,506	1,565,736	558,664	317,885	13,018	187,611	104,656
1984	2,668,166	1,960,788	42,698	2,003,486	173,027	-104,190	1,726,269	610,358	331,539	14,211	187,747	106,763
1985	2,806,251	2,082,297	44,712	2,127,009	188,037	-114,602	1,824,370	633,083	348,798	14,919	188,104	110,181
1986	3,007,935	2,291,349	38,283	2,329,632	208,804	-135,252	1,985,576	661,006	361,353	16,058	187,316	115,910
1987	3,204,964	2,506,162	43,335	2,549,497	228,130	-154,559	2,166,808	664,548	373,608	17,085	187,591	117,958
1988	3,382,662	2,715,862	13,684	2,729,546	256,930	-171,824	2,300,792	691,544	390,326	17,943	188,519	120,710
1989	3,693,795	2,863,957	57,818	2,921,775	272,199	-174,812	2,474,764	803,716	415,315	19,549	188,954	122,213
1990	3,905,456	3,145,439	43,726	3,189,165	295,285	-197,179	2,696,701	757,406	451,349	20,575	189,818	125,747
1991	4,020,708	3,250,604	26,475	3,277,079	314,837	-210,999	2,751,243	785,257	484,208	20,882	192,544	125,206
1992	4,324,776	3,489,498	54,624	3,544,122	335,407	-240,307	2,968,408	813,291	543,077	22,110	195,599	126,634
1993	4,466,446	3,637,160	31,549	3,668,709	352,481	-254,448	3,061,780	840,158	564,508	22,499	198,516	125,314
1994	4,729,216	3,854,074	62,712	3,916,786	381,048	-269,788	3,265,950	884,904	578,362	23,513	201,132	128,409
1995	4,929,409	3,996,694	11,303	4,007,997	395,249	-279,624	3,333,124	972,673	623,612	24,452	201,598	130,309
1996	5,225,936	4,176,281	74,866	4,251,147	411,568	-297,249	3,542,330	1,031,709	651,897	25,855	202,123	131,736
1997	5,378,056	4,273,075	69,524	4,342,599	419,173	-310,974	3,612,452	1,095,903	669,701	26,639	201,884	131,819
1998	5,630,193	4,533,773	42,802	4,576,575	443,107	-335,202	3,798,266	1,159,739	672,188	27,911	201,722	133,297
1999	5,789,668	4,763,438	31,317	4,794,755	456,341	-357,358	3,981,056	1,127,929	680,683	28,755	201,347	134,289
2000	6,161,365	5,034,298	57,620	5,091,918	471,676	-382,954	4,237,288	1,196,623	727,454	30,558	201,628	137,920
2001	6,456,219	5,336,674	60,375	5,397,049	495,002	-404,510	4,497,537	1,181,264	777,418	31,894	202,427	137,101
2002	6,654,582	5,571,094	44,001	5,615,095	517,678	-418,646	4,678,771	1,151,027	824,784	32,736	203,281	135,022
2003	6,674,397	5,432,955	75,311	5,508,266	513,771	-389,042	4,605,453	1,202,385	866,559	32,734	203,901	131,796
2004	6,801,390	5,500,213	129,650	5,629,863	524,783	-376,439	4,728,641	1,163,805	908,944	33,254	204,526	131,729
2005	6,876,854	5,621,816	61,778	5,683,594	554,489	-375,746	4,753,359	1,138,205	985,290	33,548	204,988	132,355
2006	7,104,464	5,718,274	78,192	5,796,466	559,693	-357,788	4,878,985	1,208,291	1,017,188	34,507	205,887	131,607
2007	7,437,920	5,857,542	138,005	5,995,547	582,705	-338,804	5,074,038	1,247,519	1,116,363	35,972	206,771	131,556
2008	7,779,658	5,985,464	172,811	6,158,275	601,639	-327,274	5,229,362	1,313,471	1,236,825	37,425	207,874	129,557
2009	7,918,793	6,049,169	115,412	6,164,581	604,580	-359,693	5,200,308	1,354,560	1,363,925	37,907	208,900	128,392
2010	8,069,363	6,141,788	93,722	6,235,510	621,556	-378,449	5,235,505	1,334,299	1,499,559	38,330	210,526	127,991
2011	8,491,662	6,324,672	167,359	6,492,031	575,398	-367,496	5,549,137	1,471,983	1,470,542	40,124	211,634	129,353
2012	8,588,211	6,390,884	94,037	6,484,921	583,676	-378,235	5,523,010	1,577,993	1,487,208	40,519	211,956	128,030
2013	8,763,670	6,404,992	233,391	6,638,383	659,647	-356,772	5,621,964	1,598,959	1,542,747	41,407	211,645	126,442
2014	8,924,866	6,650,686	106,834	6,757,520	692,890	-382,523	5,682,107	1,656,150	1,586,609	42,185	211,567	128,560

Personal Income and Employment by Area: Springfield, MA

(Thousands of dollars, except as noted.)

Year	Personal income, total	Derivation of personal income								Per capita personal income (dollars)	Population (persons)	Total employment
		Earnings by place of work			Less: Contributions for government social insurance	Plus: Adjustment for residence	Equals: Net earnings by place of residence	Plus: Dividends, interest, and rent	Plus: Personal current transfer receipts			
		Nonfarm	Farm	Total								
1970	2,381,796	1,804,569	13,029	1,817,598	113,961	53,942	1,757,579	375,969	248,248	4,078	584,006	249,926
1971	2,525,340	1,893,316	11,044	1,904,360	123,208	52,082	1,833,234	395,793	296,313	4,315	585,290	247,098
1972	2,720,837	2,048,189	9,290	2,057,479	139,561	61,325	1,979,243	416,755	324,839	4,592	592,484	250,911
1973	2,968,521	2,244,121	12,735	2,256,856	175,238	74,359	2,155,977	445,643	366,901	4,991	594,809	259,342
1974	3,191,107	2,356,512	16,997	2,373,509	190,893	91,663	2,274,279	482,869	433,959	5,377	593,517	260,953
1975	3,485,351	2,427,927	12,688	2,440,615	189,414	102,628	2,353,829	517,459	614,063	5,884	592,358	250,085
1976	3,702,814	2,642,864	14,052	2,656,916	210,688	114,041	2,560,269	539,942	602,603	6,274	590,171	251,721
1977	4,047,069	2,919,174	14,935	2,934,109	233,761	131,323	2,831,671	591,001	624,397	6,897	586,804	259,644
1978	4,473,605	3,259,586	17,019	3,276,605	269,317	160,156	3,167,444	645,841	660,320	7,667	583,481	270,979
1979	4,985,737	3,620,172	13,837	3,634,009	311,234	199,946	3,522,721	719,188	743,828	8,559	582,523	278,090
1980	5,575,600	3,917,108	17,596	3,934,704	336,772	244,358	3,842,290	882,783	850,527	9,569	582,692	281,837
1981	6,118,097	4,187,162	17,961	4,205,123	386,304	267,453	4,086,272	1,067,071	964,754	10,462	584,790	278,651
1982	6,621,417	4,380,939	14,274	4,395,213	410,648	280,116	4,264,681	1,289,464	1,067,272	11,402	580,705	274,230
1983	7,078,663	4,739,684	17,120	4,756,804	450,363	288,168	4,594,609	1,336,758	1,147,296	12,167	581,778	278,420
1984	7,836,112	5,264,596	23,012	5,287,608	517,994	321,448	5,091,062	1,535,238	1,209,812	13,443	582,893	290,483
1985	8,385,895	5,684,947	22,469	5,707,416	561,195	347,238	5,493,459	1,619,730	1,272,706	14,385	582,962	298,323
1986	8,976,125	6,135,865	24,049	6,159,914	618,070	381,519	5,923,363	1,704,239	1,348,523	15,385	583,433	306,741
1987	9,746,008	6,784,745	27,143	6,811,888	674,299	409,597	6,547,186	1,797,194	1,401,628	16,516	590,082	311,695
1988	10,629,733	7,454,390	34,057	7,488,447	756,072	436,891	7,169,266	1,949,740	1,510,727	17,806	596,967	320,757
1989	11,482,722	7,811,881	28,154	7,840,035	791,004	456,456	7,505,487	2,241,317	1,735,918	19,067	602,229	319,997
1990	11,607,000	7,878,905	30,490	7,909,395	789,880	474,010	7,593,525	2,092,965	1,920,510	19,224	603,765	313,127
1991	11,835,838	7,794,955	27,645	7,822,600	796,793	476,949	7,502,756	2,061,456	2,271,626	19,632	602,886	298,962
1992	12,172,135	8,145,784	23,653	8,169,437	823,938	481,684	7,827,183	2,016,536	2,328,416	20,205	602,439	301,351
1993	12,478,541	8,392,175	21,645	8,413,820	853,670	467,799	8,027,949	2,064,145	2,386,447	20,694	602,990	302,284
1994	13,007,934	8,723,886	21,970	8,745,856	890,633	484,958	8,340,181	2,124,498	2,543,255	21,532	604,128	304,888
1995	13,561,211	8,937,699	21,449	8,959,148	923,240	477,178	8,513,086	2,371,203	2,676,922	22,455	603,922	305,322
1996	14,130,137	9,362,142	22,172	9,384,314	949,610	501,582	8,936,286	2,469,523	2,724,328	23,420	603,331	308,475
1997	14,791,935	9,821,329	21,429	9,842,758	996,891	522,777	9,368,644	2,590,156	2,833,135	24,463	604,675	312,467
1998	15,293,553	10,240,579	15,080	10,255,659	1,033,468	562,746	9,784,937	2,670,402	2,838,214	25,245	605,809	317,047
1999	15,877,105	10,780,517	17,201	10,797,718	1,070,795	615,248	10,342,171	2,585,108	2,949,826	26,150	607,147	322,396
2000	16,961,418	11,504,002	23,243	11,527,245	1,130,345	687,387	11,084,287	2,758,207	3,118,924	27,856	608,897	329,831
2001	17,753,332	12,091,147	20,194	12,111,341	1,211,126	683,831	11,584,046	2,749,353	3,419,933	29,148	609,075	330,495
2002	18,305,546	12,515,802	22,712	12,538,514	1,253,845	683,781	11,968,450	2,598,753	3,738,343	29,899	612,241	328,173
2003	18,898,474	12,843,840	20,119	12,863,959	1,281,326	669,678	12,252,311	2,646,967	3,999,196	30,715	615,294	326,141
2004	19,561,863	13,461,126	21,228	13,482,354	1,375,459	671,978	12,778,873	2,581,778	4,201,212	31,763	615,860	329,351
2005	20,369,090	13,924,227	21,027	13,945,254	1,459,723	666,981	13,152,512	2,609,802	4,606,776	33,038	616,530	330,822
2006	21,366,625	14,439,029	15,343	14,454,372	1,494,663	651,063	13,610,772	2,958,837	4,797,016	34,598	617,576	331,809
2007	22,302,217	14,868,043	13,032	14,881,075	1,539,925	660,200	14,001,350	3,336,405	4,964,462	36,072	618,276	336,242
2008	23,330,965	15,302,998	7,208	15,310,206	1,596,035	649,317	14,363,488	3,310,139	5,657,338	37,651	619,668	334,776
2009	23,371,676	15,016,852	6,182	15,023,034	1,585,192	582,199	14,020,041	3,165,170	6,186,465	37,655	620,687	326,241
2010	23,847,838	15,311,002	9,115	15,320,117	1,592,115	608,238	14,336,240	3,045,467	6,466,131	38,253	623,426	326,344
2011	24,968,046	15,820,208	4,377	15,824,585	1,487,381	653,398	14,990,602	3,427,148	6,550,296	39,880	626,075	328,377
2012	26,196,314	16,619,295	8,714	16,628,009	1,541,863	654,624	15,740,770	3,780,875	6,674,669	41,788	626,890	338,147
2013	26,305,512	16,925,952	9,009	16,934,961	1,765,172	655,863	15,825,652	3,763,881	6,715,979	41,862	628,384	342,437
2014	27,159,515	17,494,003	6,949	17,500,952	1,832,267	669,161	16,337,846	3,906,246	6,915,423	43,172	629,100	346,134

Personal Income and Employment by Area: Springfield, MO

(Thousands of dollars, except as noted.)

| | | Derivation of personal income | | | | | | | | | | |
| | | Earnings by place of work | | | Less: Contributions for government social insurance | Plus: Adjustment for residence | Equals: Net earnings by place of residence | Plus: Dividends, interest, and rent | Plus: Personal current transfer receipts | Per capita personal income (dollars) | Population (persons) | Total employment |
Year	Personal income, total	Nonfarm	Farm	Total								
1970	700,276	556,602	16,899	573,501	38,236	-15,137	520,128	102,723	77,425	3,324	210,653	97,284
1971	768,286	608,024	17,126	625,150	42,946	-15,943	566,261	114,131	87,894	3,524	218,024	100,075
1972	863,745	685,550	22,901	708,451	50,738	-17,440	640,273	126,086	97,386	3,826	225,777	105,645
1973	975,811	767,871	35,536	803,407	65,543	-19,178	718,686	143,030	114,095	4,218	231,356	110,471
1974	1,060,940	827,520	21,499	849,019	72,837	-19,919	756,263	168,185	136,492	4,504	235,542	109,821
1975	1,174,526	877,792	25,039	902,831	75,374	-20,213	807,244	189,940	177,342	4,965	236,572	107,489
1976	1,330,406	1,016,306	30,991	1,047,297	88,263	-23,237	935,797	208,389	186,220	5,518	241,105	113,331
1977	1,477,784	1,145,056	24,874	1,169,930	99,859	-25,927	1,044,144	238,419	195,221	5,979	247,152	119,130
1978	1,690,253	1,316,317	35,266	1,351,583	118,477	-29,880	1,203,226	271,963	215,064	6,682	252,970	125,953
1979	1,888,784	1,472,338	27,809	1,500,147	137,093	-33,228	1,329,826	314,138	244,820	7,377	256,053	130,864
1980	2,139,921	1,608,438	29,827	1,638,265	149,283	-39,261	1,449,721	393,579	296,621	8,245	259,555	131,378
1981	2,395,840	1,745,375	47,968	1,793,343	174,136	-44,687	1,574,520	481,173	340,147	9,176	261,087	132,649
1982	2,585,730	1,861,066	21,229	1,882,295	189,951	-46,696	1,645,648	572,850	367,232	9,857	262,312	134,650
1983	2,805,215	2,025,886	14,861	2,040,747	206,065	-50,772	1,783,910	622,947	398,358	10,510	266,915	139,611
1984	3,124,391	2,266,281	19,031	2,285,312	236,219	-58,871	1,990,222	719,311	414,858	11,502	271,631	147,471
1985	3,342,687	2,432,421	19,928	2,452,349	258,740	-64,548	2,129,061	766,732	446,894	12,073	276,883	153,042
1986	3,595,665	2,635,501	21,354	2,656,855	282,259	-70,529	2,304,067	812,768	478,830	12,782	281,312	158,763
1987	3,797,979	2,823,853	18,293	2,842,146	297,371	-73,501	2,471,274	825,059	501,646	13,232	287,040	161,311
1988	4,062,090	3,037,158	21,912	3,059,070	329,698	-79,043	2,650,329	879,014	532,747	13,931	291,591	168,214
1989	4,414,210	3,272,772	40,960	3,313,732	357,176	-85,048	2,871,508	958,312	584,390	14,972	294,823	172,646
1990	4,668,754	3,469,369	33,517	3,502,886	390,859	-92,370	3,019,657	1,002,909	646,188	15,544	300,354	177,682
1991	5,039,732	3,720,775	24,062	3,744,837	422,921	-104,732	3,217,184	1,067,764	754,784	16,413	307,066	179,784
1992	5,515,642	4,088,525	19,502	4,108,027	459,248	-118,934	3,529,845	1,168,270	817,527	17,533	314,578	184,602
1993	5,946,506	4,421,559	16,398	4,437,957	497,639	-120,890	3,819,428	1,231,038	896,040	18,384	323,461	194,731
1994	6,411,953	4,803,031	2,814	4,805,845	545,153	-125,013	4,135,679	1,344,514	931,760	19,260	332,908	204,646
1995	6,760,492	5,111,036	76	5,111,112	578,151	-135,577	4,397,384	1,353,744	1,009,364	19,828	340,951	211,443
1996	7,159,342	5,391,320	700	5,392,020	601,227	-147,989	4,642,804	1,435,572	1,080,966	20,672	346,324	215,750
1997	7,603,053	5,672,782	3,120	5,675,902	628,281	-161,806	4,885,815	1,564,405	1,152,833	21,556	352,705	221,150
1998	8,109,616	6,092,443	7,993	6,100,436	668,653	-161,374	5,270,409	1,655,237	1,183,970	22,623	358,461	224,735
1999	8,514,255	6,548,067	-3,520	6,544,547	711,314	-170,220	5,663,013	1,615,273	1,235,969	23,398	363,882	229,508
2000	8,972,975	6,796,273	-2,353	6,793,920	739,578	-181,067	5,873,275	1,758,043	1,341,657	24,257	369,920	234,518
2001	9,605,806	7,264,147	8,422	7,272,569	782,869	-170,942	6,318,758	1,773,774	1,513,274	25,601	375,215	235,355
2002	9,721,395	7,383,652	7,416	7,391,068	802,235	-208,808	6,380,025	1,693,380	1,647,990	25,547	380,529	236,930
2003	10,339,229	7,851,924	21,639	7,873,563	847,602	-241,644	6,784,317	1,802,091	1,752,821	26,714	387,040	241,451
2004	10,957,626	8,366,493	64,486	8,430,979	897,086	-233,292	7,300,601	1,759,104	1,897,921	27,765	394,660	247,293
2005	11,583,084	8,909,024	47,603	8,956,627	963,157	-239,549	7,753,921	1,778,656	2,050,507	28,750	402,883	255,681
2006	12,396,462	9,421,387	23,086	9,444,473	1,030,768	-206,297	8,207,408	1,997,287	2,191,767	29,960	413,765	262,540
2007	13,236,109	9,790,874	4,985	9,795,859	1,091,201	-178,958	8,525,700	2,347,360	2,363,049	31,282	423,127	270,261
2008	14,117,878	10,006,128	18,943	10,025,071	1,125,834	-177,551	8,721,686	2,699,739	2,696,453	32,887	429,289	267,358
2009	13,838,350	9,913,207	-10,842	9,902,365	1,105,209	-203,646	8,593,510	2,295,797	2,949,043	31,869	434,220	258,853
2010	13,956,834	9,932,639	-2,716	9,929,923	1,103,792	-174,934	8,651,197	2,158,827	3,146,810	31,905	437,444	253,871
2011	14,530,497	10,084,285	29,832	10,114,117	1,026,141	-183,047	8,904,929	2,354,003	3,271,565	32,996	440,365	258,171
2012	15,371,911	10,682,081	1,134	10,683,215	1,064,029	-197,327	9,421,859	2,585,193	3,364,859	34,568	444,681	262,578
2013	15,574,647	10,904,684	43,359	10,948,043	1,234,679	-208,205	9,505,159	2,626,728	3,442,760	34,699	448,852	265,128
2014	16,251,347	11,396,325	95,486	11,491,811	1,293,116	-242,470	9,956,225	2,748,513	3,546,609	35,931	452,297	270,547

Personal Income and Employment by Area: Springfield, OH

(Thousands of dollars, except as noted.)

| Year | Personal income, total | Derivation of personal income | | | | | | | | | Per capita personal income (dollars) | Population (persons) | Total employment |
| | | Earnings by place of work | | | Less: Contributions for government social insurance | Plus: Adjustment for residence | Equals: Net earnings by place of residence | Plus: Dividends, interest, and rent | Plus: Personal current transfer receipts | | | |
		Nonfarm	Farm	Total								
1970	624,892	401,825	8,847	410,672	26,066	110,188	494,794	83,438	46,660	3,964	157,639	55,081
1971	701,547	463,560	8,279	471,839	31,270	111,832	552,401	93,135	56,011	4,384	160,007	57,561
1972	735,725	485,353	7,107	492,460	34,671	116,340	574,129	98,824	62,772	4,659	157,903	57,769
1973	802,004	531,558	13,268	544,826	43,832	121,066	622,060	106,805	73,139	5,096	157,377	59,907
1974	860,098	554,515	17,001	571,516	47,645	127,525	651,396	118,560	90,142	5,520	155,828	59,056
1975	915,861	556,041	23,663	579,704	46,403	134,778	668,079	131,918	115,864	5,922	154,645	55,640
1976	988,505	606,841	18,344	625,185	51,447	143,550	717,288	139,587	131,630	6,514	151,748	56,507
1977	1,078,580	682,030	13,125	695,155	58,395	154,926	791,686	154,804	132,090	7,155	150,753	58,103
1978	1,191,767	770,301	13,498	783,799	68,507	165,755	881,047	172,279	138,441	7,909	150,681	60,630
1979	1,305,459	838,876	17,051	855,927	77,425	178,556	957,058	191,387	157,014	8,658	150,789	61,472
1980	1,413,246	866,263	12,589	878,852	78,966	196,978	996,864	224,855	191,527	9,412	150,149	59,719
1981	1,476,439	890,436	946	891,382	86,067	182,671	987,986	264,309	224,144	9,878	149,463	58,312
1982	1,521,173	857,375	3,414	860,789	83,835	188,364	965,318	292,505	263,350	10,291	147,821	54,398
1983	1,610,210	928,089	-3,750	924,339	92,758	189,281	1,020,862	309,728	279,620	10,943	147,142	54,481
1984	1,798,015	1,078,475	12,321	1,090,796	110,922	195,680	1,175,554	340,796	281,665	12,223	147,100	57,693
1985	1,901,674	1,144,253	17,380	1,161,633	120,282	199,789	1,241,140	359,870	300,664	12,930	147,075	59,175
1986	2,001,358	1,227,966	12,845	1,240,811	132,919	198,981	1,306,873	375,286	319,199	13,577	147,403	60,508
1987	2,072,844	1,300,305	16,410	1,316,715	142,395	194,256	1,368,576	375,395	328,873	14,052	147,514	62,208
1988	2,257,057	1,456,769	23,751	1,480,520	165,889	195,795	1,510,426	397,091	349,540	15,251	147,992	63,505
1989	2,384,460	1,499,833	28,153	1,527,986	173,317	205,766	1,560,435	452,990	371,035	16,142	147,720	65,358
1990	2,518,782	1,536,251	26,221	1,562,472	180,739	249,940	1,631,673	470,138	416,971	17,065	147,596	65,336
1991	2,591,297	1,575,343	13,086	1,588,429	190,486	261,104	1,659,047	482,724	449,526	17,539	147,747	64,309
1992	2,746,179	1,710,633	32,470	1,743,103	206,264	240,378	1,777,217	477,938	491,024	18,608	147,584	64,709
1993	2,835,861	1,759,724	20,648	1,780,372	214,468	281,966	1,847,870	479,106	508,885	19,234	147,442	64,554
1994	2,971,579	1,843,333	21,952	1,865,285	225,275	309,522	1,949,532	498,069	523,978	20,166	147,355	65,631
1995	3,120,336	1,919,539	25,776	1,945,315	236,632	339,509	2,048,192	523,663	548,481	21,185	147,289	67,425
1996	3,224,196	1,945,399	23,535	1,968,934	234,640	363,614	2,097,908	550,948	575,340	21,916	147,116	67,183
1997	3,409,988	2,043,513	32,666	2,076,179	238,006	392,805	2,230,978	585,037	593,973	23,313	146,268	67,932
1998	3,582,810	2,247,192	17,576	2,264,768	249,198	338,844	2,354,414	616,535	611,861	24,583	145,742	70,721
1999	3,663,072	2,345,425	10,374	2,355,799	258,724	336,198	2,433,273	608,527	621,272	25,235	145,159	71,332
2000	3,795,322	2,366,671	15,167	2,381,838	252,859	391,586	2,520,565	608,607	666,150	26,246	144,605	72,310
2001	3,888,574	2,388,647	22,811	2,411,458	264,612	414,943	2,561,789	604,835	721,950	27,041	143,803	69,677
2002	3,823,969	2,308,982	16,542	2,325,524	248,932	397,202	2,473,794	585,279	764,896	26,698	143,229	68,062
2003	3,858,802	2,288,160	20,326	2,308,486	249,772	395,761	2,454,475	595,567	808,760	27,221	141,758	67,521
2004	3,924,616	2,339,548	38,510	2,378,058	260,740	410,076	2,527,394	554,407	842,815	27,759	141,380	66,922
2005	3,966,505	2,358,520	35,060	2,393,580	266,638	419,185	2,546,127	537,933	882,445	28,058	141,367	66,391
2006	4,160,386	2,467,752	36,949	2,504,701	281,252	448,019	2,671,468	572,029	916,889	29,576	140,668	66,851
2007	4,261,669	2,445,348	35,290	2,480,638	281,099	459,903	2,659,442	625,449	976,778	30,478	139,829	66,833
2008	4,429,889	2,497,452	25,852	2,523,304	293,678	480,415	2,710,041	637,769	1,082,079	31,777	139,404	66,337
2009	4,382,888	2,426,409	27,418	2,453,827	293,230	421,970	2,582,567	610,007	1,190,314	31,582	138,778	63,735
2010	4,434,825	2,417,154	21,678	2,438,832	288,035	431,066	2,581,863	598,348	1,254,614	32,084	138,227	62,256
2011	4,664,194	2,535,004	33,143	2,568,147	274,160	412,965	2,706,952	656,383	1,300,859	33,863	137,738	63,383
2012	4,755,020	2,622,435	19,283	2,641,718	279,228	437,453	2,799,943	680,863	1,274,214	34,659	137,194	63,398
2013	4,817,790	2,670,787	30,032	2,700,819	307,546	418,267	2,811,540	693,318	1,312,932	35,217	136,803	63,740
2014	4,995,211	2,737,748	16,770	2,754,518	318,286	463,984	2,900,216	720,759	1,374,236	36,580	136,554	64,488

Personal Income and Employment by Area: State College, PA

(Thousands of dollars, except as noted.)

Year	Personal income, total	Earnings by place of work			Less: Contributions for government social insurance	Plus: Adjustment for residence	Equals: Net earnings by place of residence	Plus: Dividends, interest, and rent	Plus: Personal current transfer receipts	Per capita personal income (dollars)	Population (persons)	Total employment
		Nonfarm	Farm	Total								
1970	310,133	276,529	3,052	279,581	18,156	-17,274	244,151	40,959	25,023	3,117	99,495	40,640
1971	336,955	301,391	2,130	303,521	20,603	-19,965	262,953	45,064	28,938	3,328	101,263	41,670
1972	375,255	332,238	2,779	335,017	23,205	-20,052	291,760	50,238	33,257	3,609	103,971	43,904
1973	423,948	372,789	4,835	377,624	29,201	-19,567	328,856	56,527	38,565	4,036	105,034	46,470
1974	470,537	410,728	5,993	416,721	33,778	-22,725	360,218	64,410	45,909	4,359	107,957	47,629
1975	525,036	442,428	4,983	447,411	35,719	-23,176	388,516	73,607	62,913	4,883	107,533	47,752
1976	584,475	495,200	6,455	501,655	41,155	-26,029	434,471	80,194	69,810	5,311	110,048	50,025
1977	650,395	556,345	5,645	561,990	46,198	-30,237	485,555	91,003	73,837	5,759	112,939	51,750
1978	717,075	615,573	3,635	619,208	52,860	-32,542	533,806	102,985	80,284	6,442	111,315	53,267
1979	809,943	689,707	8,034	697,741	61,587	-37,419	598,735	118,188	93,020	7,202	112,459	55,133
1980	898,373	742,833	8,177	751,010	67,291	-42,263	641,456	144,486	112,431	7,941	113,131	56,510
1981	979,705	788,761	9,782	798,543	77,473	-38,886	682,184	175,809	121,712	8,565	114,390	55,794
1982	1,058,941	841,116	7,119	848,235	83,543	-43,528	721,164	203,282	134,495	9,232	114,706	55,674
1983	1,151,447	910,674	3,508	914,182	91,290	-50,321	772,571	226,923	151,953	9,909	116,203	56,956
1984	1,255,155	1,008,590	10,481	1,019,071	105,966	-58,360	854,745	250,913	149,497	10,878	115,390	59,461
1985	1,330,890	1,065,687	9,944	1,075,631	114,220	-61,113	900,298	271,496	159,096	11,417	116,567	60,583
1986	1,414,980	1,142,830	7,686	1,150,516	124,833	-65,994	959,689	292,882	162,409	12,022	117,697	63,132
1987	1,534,784	1,261,160	9,246	1,270,406	136,786	-78,102	1,055,518	305,199	174,067	12,847	119,468	66,110
1988	1,701,193	1,410,023	13,392	1,423,415	159,173	-88,769	1,175,473	335,853	189,867	14,121	120,473	68,862
1989	1,912,212	1,582,639	16,006	1,598,645	174,932	-111,518	1,312,195	396,285	203,732	15,668	122,049	71,931
1990	2,023,930	1,692,971	12,166	1,705,137	188,121	-121,473	1,395,543	404,199	224,188	16,162	125,231	74,221
1991	2,153,919	1,810,837	5,159	1,815,996	203,343	-133,374	1,479,279	420,859	253,781	17,025	126,518	75,902
1992	2,297,079	1,923,990	16,831	1,940,821	213,848	-139,217	1,587,756	435,125	274,198	17,963	127,881	76,642
1993	2,367,974	1,994,221	9,622	2,003,843	223,580	-144,181	1,636,082	444,683	287,209	18,225	129,930	78,826
1994	2,496,040	2,113,541	11,365	2,124,906	237,988	-149,619	1,737,299	476,487	282,254	19,076	130,847	80,708
1995	2,620,178	2,210,827	4,197	2,215,024	248,937	-163,273	1,802,814	516,545	300,819	19,857	131,951	84,000
1996	2,778,827	2,316,684	15,646	2,332,330	254,534	-177,073	1,900,723	553,686	324,418	20,722	134,102	85,877
1997	2,942,892	2,478,333	8,575	2,486,908	271,755	-195,459	2,019,694	582,587	340,611	21,824	134,849	87,914
1998	3,095,383	2,605,326	16,825	2,622,151	278,440	-209,598	2,134,113	602,040	359,230	22,987	134,657	90,551
1999	3,261,746	2,765,091	12,458	2,777,549	291,179	-231,658	2,254,712	640,788	366,246	24,105	135,315	93,085
2000	3,422,788	2,935,494	18,951	2,954,445	305,990	-258,957	2,389,498	637,811	395,479	25,174	135,965	95,809
2001	3,681,682	3,166,951	13,825	3,180,776	319,946	-245,491	2,615,339	620,359	445,984	26,753	137,620	97,891
2002	3,795,847	3,344,659	8,268	3,352,927	340,702	-290,544	2,721,681	593,085	481,081	26,955	140,821	101,280
2003	3,928,652	3,453,267	16,267	3,469,534	344,884	-331,971	2,792,679	637,915	498,058	27,487	142,926	101,403
2004	4,233,583	3,735,235	20,795	3,756,030	367,240	-387,780	3,001,010	710,319	522,254	29,351	144,238	103,089
2005	4,380,084	3,943,108	15,852	3,958,960	391,784	-439,522	3,127,654	699,943	552,487	30,095	145,543	104,786
2006	4,687,230	4,204,099	12,465	4,216,564	410,751	-499,071	3,306,742	784,178	596,310	31,514	148,734	106,312
2007	4,914,045	4,372,133	11,745	4,383,878	431,717	-552,834	3,399,327	866,807	647,911	32,870	149,498	107,874
2008	5,147,509	4,542,069	4,286	4,546,355	448,765	-611,629	3,485,961	905,881	755,667	33,944	151,645	109,152
2009	5,189,638	4,565,926	-2,131	4,563,795	452,961	-639,654	3,471,180	903,532	814,926	33,908	153,052	109,287
2010	5,450,173	4,807,848	7,479	4,815,327	479,611	-681,355	3,654,361	909,017	886,795	35,349	154,182	109,448
2011	5,800,601	5,042,585	19,381	5,061,966	448,358	-730,484	3,883,124	1,012,178	905,299	37,460	154,847	111,626
2012	5,938,713	5,146,415	22,732	5,169,147	453,770	-754,535	3,960,842	1,086,704	891,167	38,171	155,582	111,693
2013	6,084,018	5,289,895	30,646	5,320,541	523,749	-761,896	4,034,896	1,124,126	924,996	38,544	157,847	113,480
2014	6,345,418	5,544,424	35,515	5,579,939	548,049	-830,128	4,201,762	1,150,995	992,661	39,973	158,742	114,463

Personal Income and Employment by Area: Staunton-Waynesboro, VA

(Thousands of dollars, except as noted.)

| Year | Personal income, total | Derivation of personal income | | | | | | | | | Per capita personal income (dollars) | Population (persons) | Total employment |
| | | Earnings by place of work | | | Less: Contributions for government social insurance | Plus: Adjustment for residence | Equals: Net earnings by place of residence | Plus: Dividends, interest, and rent | Plus: Personal current transfer receipts | | | |
		Nonfarm	Farm	Total								
1970	299,133	259,083	6,640	265,723	16,761	-8,531	240,431	38,135	20,567	3,492	85,665	41,054
1971	316,138	269,566	6,450	276,016	18,116	-8,679	249,221	42,383	24,534	3,604	87,707	40,415
1972	346,748	295,078	8,144	303,222	21,001	-10,256	271,965	46,969	27,814	3,920	88,454	41,457
1973	392,764	331,949	13,216	345,165	27,310	-11,951	305,904	53,336	33,524	4,459	88,087	43,253
1974	434,814	370,423	9,811	380,234	31,707	-14,984	333,543	61,364	39,907	4,889	88,941	45,156
1975	469,236	379,230	9,283	388,513	31,546	-12,901	344,066	69,090	56,080	5,207	90,122	42,447
1976	519,069	428,929	7,125	436,054	36,294	-14,840	384,920	75,055	59,094	5,747	90,316	44,035
1977	570,892	476,709	1,262	477,971	40,483	-16,069	421,419	84,160	65,313	6,305	90,541	45,245
1978	630,116	524,423	1,061	525,484	45,569	-15,631	464,284	95,324	70,508	6,951	90,646	46,008
1979	698,184	574,290	2,405	576,695	51,953	-11,658	513,084	103,617	81,483	7,682	90,886	46,584
1980	773,341	639,308	971	640,279	58,333	-26,502	555,444	121,303	96,594	8,495	91,031	47,059
1981	855,339	685,716	-160	685,556	67,467	-27,636	590,453	150,836	114,050	9,368	91,309	47,007
1982	907,907	690,609	161	690,770	69,050	-17,651	604,069	176,571	127,267	9,901	91,701	45,701
1983	982,684	731,650	1,047	732,697	73,617	-9,645	649,435	194,997	138,252	10,701	91,828	45,092
1984	1,106,151	808,190	12,191	820,381	83,645	-9,459	727,277	233,393	145,481	12,054	91,764	46,741
1985	1,173,256	842,754	14,542	857,296	88,637	-5,219	763,440	252,996	156,820	12,774	91,846	47,500
1986	1,258,351	895,212	19,478	914,690	96,820	2,184	820,054	271,337	166,960	13,637	92,272	48,454
1987	1,352,776	981,645	17,277	998,922	105,404	5,930	899,448	280,090	173,238	14,432	93,737	51,201
1988	1,472,894	1,074,215	23,989	1,098,204	118,561	12,080	991,723	300,686	180,485	15,502	95,015	52,603
1989	1,610,369	1,136,759	32,172	1,168,931	126,228	22,599	1,065,302	351,256	193,811	16,683	96,527	53,093
1990	1,706,204	1,198,230	35,524	1,233,754	135,103	31,101	1,129,752	367,836	208,616	17,393	98,096	54,582
1991	1,735,324	1,204,910	32,799	1,237,709	136,997	37,341	1,138,053	366,775	230,496	17,509	99,110	53,191
1992	1,830,890	1,262,840	35,482	1,298,322	142,180	44,115	1,200,257	370,210	260,423	18,297	100,067	52,582
1993	1,915,869	1,327,524	32,834	1,360,358	149,082	50,107	1,261,383	381,470	273,016	18,938	101,163	53,648
1994	2,006,327	1,389,651	36,185	1,425,836	155,087	54,956	1,325,705	393,746	286,876	19,619	102,263	54,075
1995	2,095,647	1,424,192	32,039	1,456,231	158,982	59,640	1,356,889	427,962	310,796	20,209	103,697	54,791
1996	2,202,432	1,493,937	32,012	1,525,949	165,165	61,681	1,422,465	453,772	326,195	20,977	104,994	56,133
1997	2,329,982	1,619,181	15,239	1,634,420	177,963	63,193	1,519,650	472,517	337,815	21,983	105,988	58,271
1998	2,495,686	1,737,807	20,077	1,757,884	186,716	73,302	1,644,470	499,786	351,430	23,351	106,879	59,946
1999	2,539,781	1,762,472	16,353	1,778,825	191,470	85,352	1,672,707	497,293	369,781	23,484	108,150	60,822
2000	2,700,862	1,846,675	26,915	1,873,590	198,410	95,786	1,770,966	534,044	395,852	24,749	109,129	61,747
2001	2,838,510	1,924,088	32,894	1,956,982	211,687	106,377	1,851,672	543,457	443,381	25,898	109,602	61,169
2002	2,901,129	1,990,352	19,368	2,009,720	218,396	122,096	1,913,420	514,210	473,499	26,270	110,436	61,703
2003	3,061,334	2,080,356	8,571	2,088,927	226,134	142,231	2,005,024	550,088	506,222	27,444	111,549	61,120
2004	3,288,444	2,213,873	27,747	2,241,620	243,079	167,429	2,165,970	586,841	535,633	29,166	112,751	62,687
2005	3,485,026	2,346,870	36,403	2,383,273	261,882	195,815	2,317,206	581,173	586,647	30,548	114,085	64,733
2006	3,662,298	2,410,651	15,178	2,425,829	272,940	218,218	2,371,107	642,984	648,207	31,500	116,262	65,297
2007	3,861,247	2,457,691	20,387	2,478,078	281,182	249,757	2,446,653	729,498	685,096	32,804	117,708	66,603
2008	4,064,196	2,560,714	14,283	2,574,997	292,572	279,155	2,561,580	733,822	768,794	34,320	118,420	66,269
2009	4,007,578	2,445,151	11,738	2,456,889	282,401	302,410	2,476,898	696,454	834,226	33,793	118,593	63,870
2010	4,023,107	2,419,926	21,380	2,441,306	285,729	297,653	2,453,230	680,646	889,231	33,985	118,378	62,470
2011	4,221,373	2,450,830	46,851	2,497,681	262,231	318,210	2,553,660	745,540	922,173	35,502	118,904	62,799
2012	4,394,130	2,565,540	32,935	2,598,475	272,756	327,195	2,652,914	823,513	917,703	37,041	118,629	63,149
2013	4,473,499	2,640,468	54,518	2,694,986	316,650	317,080	2,695,416	829,595	948,488	37,466	119,403	63,737
2014	4,620,405	2,727,248	60,508	2,787,756	325,861	310,570	2,772,465	862,901	985,039	38,579	119,766	64,319

Personal Income and Employment by Area: Stockton-Lodi, CA

(Thousands of dollars, except as noted.)

Year	Personal income, total	Derivation of personal income								Per capita personal income (dollars)	Population (persons)	Total employment
		Earnings by place of work			Less: Contributions for government social insurance	Plus: Adjustment for residence	Equals: Net earnings by place of residence	Plus: Dividends, interest, and rent	Plus: Personal current transfer receipts			
		Nonfarm	Farm	Total								
1970	1,277,481	904,987	103,228	1,008,215	57,368	-12,677	938,170	187,410	151,901	4,383	291,488	125,639
1971	1,389,625	988,585	104,415	1,093,000	64,732	-12,422	1,015,846	205,921	167,858	4,692	296,167	127,686
1972	1,526,878	1,081,669	123,592	1,205,261	74,689	-10,268	1,120,304	225,183	181,391	5,086	300,221	132,230
1973	1,700,645	1,181,111	167,599	1,348,710	94,184	-9,755	1,244,771	254,660	201,214	5,596	303,896	135,549
1974	1,932,221	1,313,909	209,817	1,523,726	108,589	-10,543	1,404,594	290,835	236,792	6,301	306,658	139,715
1975	2,124,107	1,427,148	190,228	1,617,376	114,863	-12,699	1,489,814	328,782	305,511	6,857	309,750	141,773
1976	2,311,342	1,585,975	171,009	1,756,984	131,092	-10,507	1,615,385	349,827	346,130	7,276	317,671	144,612
1977	2,546,964	1,751,067	186,272	1,937,339	148,224	-8,747	1,780,368	389,830	376,766	7,938	320,840	147,548
1978	2,863,084	2,002,624	171,395	2,174,019	172,720	-5,601	1,995,698	451,630	415,756	8,606	332,685	153,412
1979	3,239,418	2,245,026	212,841	2,457,867	204,375	-6,333	2,247,159	521,906	470,353	9,573	338,384	162,770
1980	3,682,201	2,408,009	287,853	2,695,862	216,497	-649	2,478,716	641,775	561,710	10,511	350,304	165,174
1981	4,061,172	2,631,371	212,959	2,844,330	258,346	18,327	2,604,311	789,935	666,926	11,235	361,462	167,276
1982	4,321,514	2,758,521	187,057	2,945,578	276,531	36,088	2,705,135	865,403	750,976	11,571	373,479	167,744
1983	4,556,058	2,895,796	123,438	3,019,234	295,460	68,032	2,791,806	949,350	814,902	11,812	385,721	169,304
1984	5,129,731	3,243,433	201,377	3,444,810	343,445	98,162	3,199,527	1,068,748	861,456	12,865	398,731	176,594
1985	5,560,046	3,530,547	203,962	3,734,509	377,886	130,972	3,487,595	1,138,140	934,311	13,364	416,042	181,855
1986	6,005,195	3,862,083	197,371	4,059,454	418,264	162,322	3,803,512	1,201,641	1,000,042	13,940	430,786	186,320
1987	6,541,486	4,230,774	297,989	4,528,763	459,197	199,370	4,268,936	1,227,537	1,045,013	14,676	445,726	195,501
1988	7,061,406	4,558,158	347,160	4,905,318	514,983	247,227	4,637,562	1,293,139	1,130,705	15,447	457,138	205,322
1989	7,654,819	4,879,802	317,769	5,197,571	553,852	303,120	4,946,839	1,472,635	1,235,345	16,396	466,863	209,243
1990	8,125,990	5,207,723	297,728	5,505,451	588,295	357,962	5,275,118	1,481,561	1,369,311	16,785	484,131	214,261
1991	8,504,783	5,484,295	261,403	5,745,698	627,167	377,378	5,495,909	1,481,338	1,527,536	17,262	492,694	216,618
1992	9,111,820	5,734,090	327,706	6,061,796	648,449	426,417	5,839,764	1,481,832	1,790,224	18,214	500,278	212,460
1993	9,500,647	5,956,625	374,500	6,331,125	674,849	454,137	6,110,413	1,521,529	1,868,705	18,762	506,385	214,476
1994	9,860,805	6,213,040	377,300	6,590,340	703,132	476,389	6,363,597	1,604,587	1,892,621	19,251	512,212	220,269
1995	10,192,241	6,329,264	351,001	6,680,265	709,225	548,170	6,519,210	1,695,550	1,977,481	19,679	517,923	224,933
1996	10,773,600	6,564,630	421,581	6,986,211	712,840	626,633	6,900,004	1,796,403	2,077,193	20,535	524,657	228,643
1997	11,500,953	7,142,667	449,033	7,591,700	761,852	702,853	7,532,701	1,900,076	2,068,176	21,622	531,908	233,118
1998	12,257,582	7,646,887	376,442	8,023,329	794,828	836,087	8,064,588	1,975,360	2,217,634	22,688	540,257	239,165
1999	13,066,296	8,178,439	408,932	8,587,371	853,915	992,419	8,725,875	2,015,885	2,324,536	23,653	552,424	249,905
2000	14,244,298	8,939,560	384,507	9,324,067	923,931	1,287,235	9,687,371	2,159,914	2,397,013	25,083	567,885	255,096
2001	14,951,527	9,455,239	423,313	9,878,552	1,045,259	1,177,838	10,011,131	2,226,766	2,713,630	25,290	591,207	260,808
2002	15,856,840	10,233,131	417,688	10,650,819	1,135,068	1,256,057	10,771,808	2,179,303	2,905,729	26,036	609,041	267,244
2003	17,004,045	10,962,784	508,148	11,470,932	1,234,590	1,365,200	11,601,542	2,291,055	3,111,448	27,129	626,778	273,510
2004	18,144,620	11,734,315	573,314	12,307,629	1,366,439	1,494,590	12,435,780	2,420,164	3,288,676	28,223	642,898	279,510
2005	18,893,369	12,218,977	578,482	12,797,459	1,428,859	1,594,882	12,963,482	2,482,004	3,447,883	28,758	656,985	282,627
2006	19,981,861	12,737,318	449,452	13,186,770	1,442,027	1,731,658	13,476,401	2,785,665	3,719,795	30,147	662,812	285,696
2007	21,147,791	13,089,195	592,936	13,682,131	1,454,673	1,895,011	14,122,469	3,064,366	3,960,956	31,655	668,080	291,806
2008	21,541,612	12,960,860	506,039	13,466,899	1,463,549	1,981,496	13,984,846	3,107,777	4,448,989	32,071	671,692	286,119
2009	21,106,628	12,388,254	552,718	12,940,972	1,427,826	1,804,677	13,317,823	2,858,388	4,930,417	31,143	677,736	275,502
2010	21,347,380	12,320,371	435,407	12,755,778	1,398,061	1,623,706	12,981,423	2,827,462	5,538,495	31,050	687,513	268,849
2011	22,376,580	12,704,916	532,363	13,237,279	1,305,667	1,724,145	13,655,757	3,149,675	5,571,148	32,174	695,479	271,655
2012	23,518,295	13,251,051	859,053	14,110,104	1,336,635	1,646,556	14,420,025	3,417,041	5,681,229	33,519	701,635	278,389
2013	24,470,917	13,617,881	934,644	14,552,525	1,543,348	2,018,614	15,027,791	3,564,599	5,878,527	34,709	705,027	286,279
2014	25,859,136	14,198,920	908,221	15,107,141	1,611,030	2,493,013	15,989,124	3,741,158	6,128,854	36,136	715,597	294,674

Personal Income and Employment by Area: Sumter, SC

(Thousands of dollars, except as noted.)

Year	Personal income, total	Earnings by place of work			Less: Contributions for government social insurance	Plus: Adjustment for residence	Equals: Net earnings by place of residence	Plus: Dividends, interest, and rent	Plus: Personal current transfer receipts	Per capita personal income (dollars)	Population (persons)	Total employment
		Nonfarm	Farm	Total								
1970	236,197	198,102	8,070	206,172	12,920	-16,725	176,527	41,152	18,518	2,963	79,727	36,298
1971	256,823	215,941	7,350	223,291	14,916	-16,635	191,740	43,226	21,857	3,137	81,867	36,617
1972	288,217	241,207	9,756	250,963	17,055	-17,900	216,008	47,487	24,722	3,421	84,259	37,059
1973	312,778	260,724	8,984	269,708	20,429	-18,383	230,896	52,172	29,710	3,762	83,151	37,868
1974	347,550	277,030	14,233	291,263	22,726	-16,854	251,683	57,891	37,976	4,172	83,313	37,426
1975	381,855	300,634	9,449	310,083	24,951	-18,583	266,549	65,302	50,004	4,472	85,380	37,204
1976	418,122	333,738	8,919	342,657	28,667	-19,302	294,688	69,281	54,153	4,905	85,241	37,621
1977	453,860	363,990	7,882	371,872	31,105	-20,286	320,481	77,558	55,821	5,242	86,589	38,477
1978	512,399	411,554	6,443	417,997	35,512	-22,478	360,007	90,660	61,732	5,902	86,824	39,864
1979	562,185	446,926	9,548	456,474	40,200	-23,446	392,828	98,657	70,700	6,421	87,556	40,248
1980	617,634	486,279	555	486,834	43,263	-24,414	419,157	112,294	86,183	6,960	88,736	40,098
1981	682,762	525,507	4,277	529,784	50,062	-23,645	456,077	128,164	98,521	7,551	90,420	40,072
1982	741,028	568,274	2,676	570,950	53,926	-27,701	489,323	145,653	106,052	8,068	91,845	39,657
1983	801,293	615,803	113	615,916	60,094	-27,679	528,143	158,731	114,419	8,647	92,663	40,634
1984	904,629	681,243	20,031	701,274	68,582	-28,684	604,008	179,335	121,286	9,557	94,657	42,253
1985	969,907	736,024	13,053	749,077	75,166	-31,485	642,426	195,490	131,991	10,065	96,362	43,248
1986	1,022,362	779,275	8,303	787,578	81,799	-29,624	676,155	207,659	138,548	10,423	98,084	43,739
1987	1,094,479	835,064	13,242	848,306	87,275	-29,448	731,583	221,419	141,477	11,009	99,420	44,627
1988	1,174,214	902,013	16,398	918,411	98,520	-31,797	788,094	236,051	150,069	11,768	99,777	45,935
1989	1,279,572	950,883	18,564	969,447	106,153	-29,794	833,500	269,586	176,486	12,553	101,933	46,844
1990	1,409,771	1,027,138	16,575	1,043,713	117,375	10,114	936,452	281,693	191,626	13,921	101,271	48,598
1991	1,453,413	1,055,550	20,191	1,075,741	122,604	-14,640	938,497	290,014	224,902	14,162	102,630	47,713
1992	1,548,713	1,109,123	18,333	1,127,456	129,044	-911	997,501	300,260	250,952	15,010	103,179	48,403
1993	1,613,063	1,186,621	12,573	1,199,194	139,899	-36,441	1,022,854	324,926	265,283	15,330	105,224	50,751
1994	1,711,105	1,233,057	16,496	1,249,553	145,939	-26,561	1,077,053	341,057	292,995	16,213	105,542	51,597
1995	1,784,775	1,300,859	7,866	1,308,725	153,396	-37,926	1,117,403	358,050	309,322	16,861	105,852	53,220
1996	1,873,185	1,347,452	22,158	1,369,610	157,072	-42,212	1,170,326	373,223	329,636	17,682	105,938	53,549
1997	1,963,107	1,426,094	13,541	1,439,635	165,684	-50,017	1,223,934	392,126	347,047	18,612	105,475	54,482
1998	2,049,430	1,496,176	9,515	1,505,691	174,517	-62,798	1,268,376	416,534	364,520	19,432	105,468	54,786
1999	2,137,979	1,553,027	11,628	1,564,655	179,458	-40,629	1,344,568	410,966	382,445	20,395	104,827	55,028
2000	2,242,541	1,643,851	11,876	1,655,727	189,347	-66,159	1,400,221	433,510	408,810	21,398	104,802	56,030
2001	2,288,318	1,646,715	20,433	1,667,148	192,993	-79,232	1,394,923	441,021	452,374	21,871	104,629	53,869
2002	2,428,760	1,729,275	9,134	1,738,409	201,021	-68,968	1,468,420	463,983	496,357	23,048	105,380	53,479
2003	2,545,700	1,815,942	15,758	1,831,700	209,556	-56,954	1,565,190	462,209	518,301	24,219	105,112	53,259
2004	2,702,890	1,908,254	25,023	1,933,277	220,779	-42,825	1,669,673	469,108	564,109	25,475	106,099	54,011
2005	2,816,674	1,970,799	29,945	2,000,744	226,876	-26,763	1,747,105	465,492	604,077	26,552	106,082	54,372
2006	2,969,384	2,060,946	14,253	2,075,199	243,712	-9,576	1,821,911	500,895	646,578	28,025	105,953	54,064
2007	3,107,727	2,113,588	14,981	2,128,569	249,545	8,472	1,887,496	531,768	688,463	29,314	106,014	54,400
2008	3,235,094	2,099,893	10,036	2,109,929	248,711	26,507	1,887,725	565,042	782,327	30,387	106,463	52,556
2009	3,201,789	2,046,338	10,792	2,057,130	243,591	27,075	1,840,614	515,906	845,269	29,922	107,004	50,267
2010	3,285,120	2,090,896	9,029	2,099,925	250,537	9,105	1,858,493	515,657	910,970	30,536	107,581	50,341
2011	3,481,843	2,219,373	6,382	2,225,755	241,057	-6,563	1,978,135	582,787	920,921	32,434	107,350	51,754
2012	3,752,190	2,455,338	25,585	2,480,923	263,992	-24,495	2,192,436	641,679	918,075	34,723	108,060	52,913
2013	3,784,560	2,467,121	37,292	2,504,413	295,194	-19,378	2,189,841	647,450	947,269	35,042	108,002	53,018
2014	3,893,440	2,535,460	16,651	2,552,111	302,264	-20,370	2,229,477	669,807	994,156	36,077	107,919	53,712

Personal Income and Employment by Area: Syracuse, NY

(Thousands of dollars, except as noted.)

Year	Personal income, total	Derivation of personal income					Equals: Net earnings by place of residence	Plus: Dividends, interest, and rent	Plus: Personal current transfer receipts	Per capita personal income (dollars)	Population (persons)	Total employment
		Earnings by place of work			Less: Contributions for government social insurance	Plus: Adjustment for residence						
		Nonfarm	Farm	Total								
1970	2,567,947	2,145,636	25,826	2,171,462	159,044	-33,000	1,979,418	334,213	254,316	4,028	637,540	270,461
1971	2,784,239	2,319,553	24,874	2,344,427	177,611	-38,156	2,128,660	355,807	299,772	4,350	640,019	274,853
1972	2,994,976	2,526,447	22,314	2,548,761	203,519	-42,604	2,302,638	379,181	313,157	4,666	641,826	278,450
1973	3,249,695	2,760,457	28,770	2,789,227	257,308	-45,621	2,486,298	415,446	347,951	5,059	642,407	289,236
1974	3,552,883	2,996,631	26,392	3,023,023	287,568	-51,691	2,683,764	466,812	402,307	5,526	642,995	294,880
1975	3,808,425	3,050,457	21,614	3,072,071	287,290	-49,427	2,735,354	512,005	561,066	5,894	646,105	283,301
1976	4,078,274	3,320,248	22,888	3,343,136	320,529	-54,565	2,968,042	535,759	574,473	6,298	647,543	286,493
1977	4,478,064	3,701,403	16,810	3,718,213	355,778	-64,652	3,297,783	590,089	590,192	6,919	647,200	295,258
1978	4,896,198	4,085,512	24,111	4,109,623	402,548	-69,689	3,637,386	628,112	630,700	7,570	646,806	304,167
1979	5,463,653	4,595,224	31,021	4,626,245	468,697	-82,012	4,075,536	705,319	682,798	8,475	644,646	311,104
1980	6,088,859	4,984,913	31,312	5,016,225	507,669	-88,754	4,419,802	863,332	805,725	9,473	642,764	307,311
1981	6,694,081	5,389,809	35,167	5,424,976	586,156	-106,484	4,732,336	1,055,107	906,638	10,448	640,720	308,076
1982	7,300,833	5,806,392	28,946	5,835,338	637,151	-128,021	5,070,166	1,211,966	1,018,701	11,400	640,442	308,937
1983	7,912,330	6,332,754	21,258	6,354,012	698,934	-151,223	5,503,855	1,333,131	1,075,344	12,306	642,984	314,098
1984	8,842,755	7,131,790	30,728	7,162,518	805,381	-177,772	6,179,365	1,521,899	1,141,491	13,679	646,469	327,908
1985	9,427,725	7,695,827	34,666	7,730,493	878,188	-200,545	6,651,760	1,571,431	1,204,534	14,496	650,383	340,140
1986	9,943,787	8,106,529	40,575	8,147,104	935,677	-208,840	7,002,587	1,654,687	1,286,513	15,330	648,635	346,353
1987	10,253,745	8,377,337	43,463	8,420,800	957,853	-210,316	7,252,631	1,688,833	1,312,281	15,855	646,725	348,298
1988	11,013,181	9,068,806	33,579	9,102,385	1,056,380	-229,217	7,816,788	1,797,576	1,398,817	16,960	649,352	359,990
1989	12,106,792	9,804,592	46,201	9,850,793	1,126,184	-258,393	8,466,216	2,121,014	1,519,562	18,488	654,842	367,410
1990	12,763,237	10,365,855	47,141	10,412,996	1,142,377	-298,076	8,972,543	2,132,737	1,657,957	19,294	661,505	374,714
1991	13,027,802	10,468,814	39,919	10,508,733	1,182,353	-302,787	9,023,593	2,158,834	1,845,375	19,572	665,618	368,948
1992	13,770,447	11,091,347	38,854	11,130,201	1,228,735	-325,134	9,576,332	2,130,806	2,063,309	20,599	668,488	367,160
1993	14,039,474	11,263,443	49,706	11,313,149	1,254,905	-333,855	9,724,389	2,156,458	2,158,627	20,945	670,309	367,707
1994	14,377,785	11,491,796	39,718	11,531,514	1,295,587	-343,495	9,892,432	2,208,133	2,277,220	21,540	667,499	369,006
1995	14,842,281	11,692,565	27,362	11,719,927	1,319,060	-360,323	10,040,544	2,376,304	2,425,433	22,340	664,389	365,912
1996	15,160,567	11,859,381	41,231	11,900,612	1,316,545	-392,604	10,191,463	2,440,099	2,529,005	22,957	660,384	367,025
1997	15,677,398	12,325,728	24,415	12,350,143	1,350,626	-390,304	10,609,213	2,537,041	2,531,144	23,927	655,229	366,983
1998	16,316,182	12,745,327	47,463	12,792,790	1,385,454	-367,123	11,040,213	2,584,569	2,691,400	25,044	651,499	366,129
1999	16,944,675	13,448,703	54,512	13,503,215	1,430,906	-385,469	11,686,840	2,535,126	2,722,709	26,057	650,297	373,572
2000	17,772,364	14,029,214	59,323	14,088,537	1,494,854	-362,635	12,231,048	2,668,593	2,872,723	27,344	649,961	377,457
2001	18,087,432	14,262,340	72,027	14,334,367	1,568,261	-384,925	12,381,181	2,624,988	3,081,263	27,797	650,697	373,813
2002	18,423,513	14,719,834	48,840	14,768,674	1,642,649	-423,529	12,702,496	2,430,099	3,290,918	28,246	652,241	369,540
2003	19,122,833	15,169,774	54,099	15,223,873	1,694,784	-452,430	13,076,659	2,595,339	3,450,835	29,191	655,091	370,543
2004	19,839,889	15,797,857	68,050	15,865,907	1,758,561	-442,947	13,664,399	2,524,867	3,650,623	30,237	656,149	375,258
2005	20,599,647	16,290,458	66,966	16,357,424	1,829,842	-462,015	14,065,567	2,751,463	3,782,617	31,449	655,021	379,192
2006	21,581,741	17,009,774	51,597	17,061,371	1,882,260	-456,908	14,722,203	2,861,680	3,997,858	32,933	655,321	379,405
2007	22,784,279	17,690,316	87,382	17,777,698	1,950,535	-440,330	15,386,833	3,229,389	4,168,057	34,721	656,209	384,369
2008	24,005,269	18,226,369	86,320	18,312,689	2,024,480	-378,290	15,909,919	3,455,201	4,640,149	36,432	658,913	384,542
2009	24,252,854	18,212,428	44,634	18,257,062	2,010,439	-366,740	15,879,883	3,252,298	5,120,673	36,699	660,857	375,481
2010	24,902,788	18,654,994	77,830	18,732,824	2,056,627	-330,911	16,345,286	3,071,082	5,486,420	37,562	662,976	372,404
2011	25,952,597	19,060,596	100,673	19,161,269	1,896,717	-351,999	16,912,553	3,419,671	5,620,373	39,167	662,609	375,666
2012	26,871,083	19,653,098	89,737	19,742,835	1,943,180	-355,388	17,444,267	3,782,276	5,644,540	40,636	661,256	377,436
2013	26,855,388	19,902,913	118,604	20,021,517	2,227,537	-346,222	17,447,758	3,663,897	5,743,733	40,514	662,861	378,296
2014	27,617,279	20,453,705	131,611	20,585,316	2,303,758	-339,477	17,942,081	3,795,397	5,879,801	41,751	661,478	380,126

Personal Income and Employment by Area: Tallahassee, FL

(Thousands of dollars, except as noted.)

Year	Personal income, total	Earnings by place of work			Less: Contributions for government social insurance	Plus: Adjustment for residence	Equals: Net earnings by place of residence	Plus: Dividends, interest, and rent	Plus: Personal current transfer receipts	Per capita personal income (dollars)	Population (persons)	Total employment
		Nonfarm	Farm	Total								
1970	491,632	404,376	18,424	422,800	23,566	-14,200	385,034	70,612	35,986	3,106	158,300	68,040
1971	566,806	469,326	17,662	486,988	28,966	-15,576	442,446	81,865	42,495	3,435	165,004	71,779
1972	667,969	558,740	16,968	575,708	35,850	-18,152	521,706	95,519	50,744	3,847	173,644	77,730
1973	780,045	653,437	20,466	673,903	48,662	-20,107	605,134	112,868	62,043	4,298	181,470	83,485
1974	877,779	726,234	18,682	744,916	56,903	-21,304	666,709	135,245	75,825	4,638	189,245	86,579
1975	971,998	789,129	17,403	806,532	62,054	-21,666	722,812	150,946	98,240	5,198	186,999	87,284
1976	1,052,149	855,112	18,407	873,519	70,559	-21,601	781,359	160,357	110,433	5,551	189,529	88,025
1977	1,147,449	934,668	12,405	947,073	78,583	-20,740	847,750	177,751	121,948	5,894	194,690	90,724
1978	1,291,516	1,049,486	16,526	1,066,012	92,922	-22,126	950,964	206,750	133,802	6,455	200,091	94,497
1979	1,470,104	1,191,796	20,378	1,212,174	111,764	-24,067	1,076,343	238,070	155,691	7,202	204,111	99,612
1980	1,684,325	1,336,138	19,914	1,356,052	122,191	-25,469	1,208,392	289,274	186,659	7,901	213,167	104,810
1981	1,901,563	1,492,615	15,531	1,508,146	148,207	-27,211	1,332,728	354,903	213,932	8,732	217,765	107,359
1982	2,069,361	1,598,272	23,265	1,621,537	162,314	-30,518	1,428,705	406,796	233,860	9,339	221,584	108,947
1983	2,293,824	1,760,160	24,597	1,784,757	177,507	-33,066	1,574,184	462,300	257,340	10,186	225,185	112,794
1984	2,514,741	1,934,017	26,125	1,960,142	198,603	-35,047	1,726,492	513,224	275,025	10,962	229,399	117,358
1985	2,737,695	2,110,640	26,093	2,136,733	219,344	-38,931	1,878,458	561,145	298,092	11,744	233,106	123,662
1986	3,037,817	2,372,341	29,076	2,401,417	250,568	-43,671	2,107,178	614,724	315,915	12,881	235,840	131,759
1987	3,316,546	2,622,087	29,532	2,651,619	270,086	-51,292	2,330,241	650,716	335,589	13,760	241,026	135,906
1988	3,681,959	2,942,005	34,484	2,976,489	316,599	-56,081	2,603,809	710,083	368,067	14,921	246,756	143,371
1989	4,124,822	3,223,485	39,370	3,262,855	345,890	-62,911	2,854,054	846,171	424,597	16,257	253,724	150,382
1990	4,483,239	3,533,190	37,538	3,570,728	374,634	-68,572	3,127,522	889,420	466,297	17,165	261,192	156,015
1991	4,751,839	3,769,857	47,278	3,817,135	401,885	-76,060	3,339,190	884,260	528,389	17,502	271,509	158,565
1992	5,061,810	4,033,622	47,474	4,081,096	429,302	-82,230	3,569,564	888,786	603,460	18,338	276,025	161,167
1993	5,401,770	4,310,588	47,845	4,358,433	453,609	-88,617	3,816,207	944,577	640,986	18,992	284,421	166,471
1994	5,756,919	4,607,384	45,320	4,652,704	489,181	-99,384	4,064,139	1,012,533	680,247	19,667	292,713	172,345
1995	6,253,870	4,945,338	46,894	4,992,232	523,725	-108,236	4,360,271	1,152,617	740,982	20,947	298,563	179,081
1996	6,584,741	5,234,805	44,556	5,279,361	551,490	-118,384	4,609,487	1,203,621	771,633	21,736	302,943	181,936
1997	6,921,692	5,521,348	53,182	5,574,530	583,043	-128,279	4,863,208	1,253,310	805,174	22,443	308,414	188,091
1998	7,457,529	5,983,493	55,076	6,038,569	629,110	-145,220	5,264,239	1,355,266	838,024	23,850	312,685	191,881
1999	7,901,660	6,419,758	58,888	6,478,646	673,894	-160,395	5,644,357	1,377,171	880,132	24,940	316,825	196,296
2000	8,316,042	6,756,266	55,879	6,812,145	707,268	-170,859	5,934,018	1,445,904	936,120	25,880	321,336	201,729
2001	8,999,670	7,359,374	59,649	7,419,023	761,440	-179,974	6,477,609	1,484,860	1,037,201	27,744	324,386	204,514
2002	9,002,286	7,405,876	53,469	7,459,345	774,908	-260,744	6,423,693	1,441,087	1,137,506	27,451	327,940	201,705
2003	9,429,421	7,678,278	44,572	7,722,850	802,278	-276,085	6,644,487	1,563,816	1,221,118	28,207	334,289	203,223
2004	10,087,449	8,112,357	49,312	8,161,669	850,231	-286,523	7,024,915	1,788,905	1,273,629	29,741	339,179	207,917
2005	10,817,163	8,590,801	49,166	8,639,967	900,995	-298,998	7,439,974	1,983,745	1,393,444	31,422	344,257	214,522
2006	11,461,144	9,014,500	49,672	9,064,172	956,953	-289,725	7,817,494	2,189,603	1,454,047	32,692	350,580	219,468
2007	12,047,681	9,414,724	37,757	9,452,481	1,004,535	-281,751	8,166,195	2,305,584	1,575,902	33,713	357,357	223,276
2008	12,322,744	9,468,931	45,403	9,514,334	1,016,928	-281,275	8,216,131	2,280,720	1,825,893	34,113	361,238	220,694
2009	12,098,515	9,195,673	37,242	9,232,915	998,211	-265,832	7,968,872	2,174,470	1,955,173	33,175	364,690	214,096
2010	12,725,497	9,338,306	41,917	9,380,223	1,012,557	-278,274	8,089,392	2,455,023	2,181,082	34,442	369,475	212,124
2011	13,395,387	9,296,328	32,491	9,328,819	901,312	-283,687	8,143,820	2,958,404	2,293,163	36,091	371,156	214,264
2012	12,980,332	9,408,737	43,320	9,452,057	910,726	-286,194	8,255,137	2,490,503	2,234,692	34,566	375,523	213,468
2013	13,027,796	9,520,884	50,446	9,571,330	1,040,063	-275,040	8,256,227	2,442,339	2,329,230	34,873	373,583	214,836
2014	13,646,794	9,939,549	60,450	9,999,999	1,086,622	-284,587	8,628,790	2,507,477	2,510,527	36,319	375,751	219,577

Personal Income and Employment by Area: Tampa-St. Petersburg-Clearwater, FL

(Thousands of dollars, except as noted.)

| Year | Personal income, total | Derivation of personal income | | | | | | | | Per capita personal income (dollars) | Population (persons) | Total employment |
| | | Earnings by place of work | | | Less: Contributions for government social insurance | Plus: Adjustment for residence | Equals: Net earnings by place of residence | Plus: Dividends, interest, and rent | Plus: Personal current transfer receipts | | | |
		Nonfarm	Farm	Total								
1970	4,366,121	2,837,956	43,720	2,881,676	186,697	25,907	2,720,886	1,090,730	554,505	3,908	1,117,227	439,739
1971	4,912,143	3,181,926	50,731	3,232,657	217,856	28,600	3,043,401	1,213,088	655,654	4,160	1,180,716	460,528
1972	5,713,081	3,780,403	64,599	3,845,002	271,412	32,836	3,606,426	1,346,637	760,018	4,563	1,251,917	509,052
1973	6,677,844	4,458,444	72,983	4,531,427	369,372	42,451	4,204,506	1,552,596	920,742	5,008	1,333,538	565,986
1974	7,538,324	4,945,638	65,798	5,011,436	427,349	49,067	4,633,154	1,821,800	1,083,370	5,406	1,394,490	581,774
1975	8,313,694	5,192,506	78,963	5,271,469	438,549	53,030	4,885,950	2,050,055	1,377,689	5,831	1,425,848	564,107
1976	9,012,578	5,618,664	84,829	5,703,493	481,335	55,787	5,277,945	2,214,715	1,519,918	6,205	1,452,426	567,011
1977	10,233,881	6,428,842	91,282	6,520,124	544,288	65,668	6,041,504	2,523,952	1,668,425	6,923	1,478,254	597,815
1978	11,800,018	7,476,110	102,214	7,578,324	649,760	75,123	7,003,687	2,944,456	1,851,875	7,775	1,517,764	644,879
1979	13,569,434	8,588,765	103,451	8,692,216	783,780	87,625	7,996,061	3,439,374	2,133,999	8,625	1,573,352	679,429
1980	15,982,005	9,791,284	137,091	9,928,375	903,469	98,875	9,123,781	4,323,344	2,534,880	9,823	1,626,975	717,538
1981	18,453,844	11,017,345	113,744	11,131,089	1,099,800	92,431	10,123,720	5,374,768	2,955,356	11,001	1,677,405	753,441
1982	20,078,126	11,808,311	159,858	11,968,169	1,223,135	71,068	10,816,102	5,918,425	3,343,599	11,655	1,722,726	776,167
1983	22,500,655	13,351,606	199,741	13,551,347	1,389,413	44,452	12,206,386	6,659,934	3,634,335	12,681	1,774,374	821,026
1984	25,076,463	15,137,522	161,407	15,298,929	1,623,627	19,305	13,694,607	7,586,623	3,795,233	13,735	1,825,777	883,678
1985	27,500,974	16,676,072	152,397	16,828,469	1,820,009	-1,607	15,006,853	8,413,372	4,080,749	14,651	1,877,018	932,733
1986	29,612,662	18,135,185	159,092	18,294,277	2,026,789	-29,854	16,237,634	8,990,288	4,384,740	15,394	1,923,591	969,125
1987	31,538,963	19,803,521	152,513	19,956,034	2,189,286	-56,082	17,710,666	9,202,548	4,625,749	16,032	1,967,197	983,589
1988	34,202,789	21,752,923	191,645	21,944,568	2,476,417	-89,067	19,379,084	9,820,502	5,003,203	17,054	2,005,545	1,029,281
1989	38,114,851	23,357,695	194,477	23,552,172	2,694,922	-109,596	20,747,654	11,761,908	5,605,289	18,690	2,039,321	1,052,726
1990	39,815,178	24,884,515	174,027	25,058,542	2,834,510	-158,539	22,065,493	11,703,034	6,046,651	19,162	2,077,857	1,074,649
1991	40,824,282	25,801,349	196,034	25,997,383	2,967,945	-172,194	22,857,244	11,295,000	6,672,038	19,339	2,110,974	1,060,636
1992	42,971,954	27,774,413	198,060	27,972,473	3,181,096	-233,606	24,557,771	10,899,755	7,514,428	20,125	2,135,204	1,062,769
1993	45,758,994	29,545,400	193,303	29,738,703	3,365,925	-211,244	26,161,534	11,550,013	8,047,447	21,146	2,163,912	1,093,939
1994	47,926,850	31,669,445	175,092	31,844,537	3,642,030	-241,759	27,960,748	11,427,315	8,538,787	21,842	2,194,294	1,137,326
1995	51,594,534	33,840,791	184,475	34,025,266	3,880,882	-171,061	29,973,323	12,528,448	9,092,763	23,178	2,226,036	1,178,494
1996	54,682,959	36,407,794	169,905	36,577,699	4,126,777	-424,609	32,026,313	13,121,041	9,535,605	24,234	2,256,460	1,230,493
1997	58,187,489	38,943,359	192,798	39,136,157	4,419,312	-540,837	34,176,008	14,183,439	9,828,042	25,329	2,297,251	1,275,654
1998	62,349,638	42,762,571	243,392	43,005,963	4,787,973	-771,620	37,446,370	14,972,867	9,930,401	26,681	2,336,822	1,343,513
1999	65,280,911	46,396,486	237,000	46,633,486	5,155,970	-1,132,687	40,344,829	14,739,479	10,196,603	27,555	2,369,105	1,400,105
2000	70,569,100	50,324,600	239,638	50,564,238	5,519,893	-1,001,107	44,043,238	15,824,578	10,701,284	29,355	2,404,013	1,452,647
2001	72,689,074	51,936,590	258,564	52,195,154	5,752,566	-1,231,421	45,211,167	15,910,178	11,567,729	29,742	2,444,015	1,417,909
2002	75,501,032	54,654,111	260,988	54,915,099	6,027,442	-1,226,363	47,661,294	15,484,973	12,354,765	30,353	2,487,445	1,446,574
2003	79,671,487	57,486,034	227,281	57,713,315	6,300,906	-1,037,311	50,375,098	16,223,785	13,072,604	31,495	2,529,652	1,460,010
2004	85,630,950	61,682,865	237,839	61,920,704	6,801,141	-849,337	54,270,226	17,386,265	13,974,459	33,091	2,587,771	1,518,405
2005	92,340,830	66,140,352	274,044	66,414,396	7,311,899	-603,644	58,498,853	18,788,718	15,053,259	34,825	2,651,580	1,567,351
2006	99,569,004	70,160,415	278,606	70,439,021	7,873,178	-126,899	62,438,944	20,906,556	16,223,504	36,878	2,699,935	1,599,488
2007	103,284,052	71,441,949	241,015	71,682,964	8,098,558	63,082	63,647,488	22,295,110	17,341,454	37,878	2,726,780	1,614,051
2008	104,664,402	70,783,261	253,708	71,036,969	8,096,807	422,267	63,362,429	21,769,704	19,532,269	38,102	2,746,981	1,552,563
2009	101,259,652	67,533,900	254,926	67,788,826	7,878,598	389,810	60,300,038	19,787,480	21,172,134	36,636	2,763,937	1,483,580
2010	107,071,966	68,585,617	240,356	68,825,973	7,993,910	408,829	61,240,892	22,632,016	23,199,058	38,386	2,789,334	1,458,864
2011	114,993,863	70,343,420	202,103	70,545,523	7,383,824	418,821	63,580,520	27,220,629	24,192,714	40,647	2,829,104	1,478,932
2012	113,716,527	74,126,083	222,425	74,348,508	7,766,562	393,923	66,975,869	22,954,806	23,785,852	39,929	2,848,003	1,509,561
2013	114,816,039	76,610,843	224,102	76,834,945	9,002,776	433,970	68,266,139	22,032,256	24,517,644	39,948	2,874,154	1,551,034
2014	120,400,728	80,208,870	199,180	80,408,050	9,433,274	444,428	71,419,204	22,965,202	26,016,322	41,296	2,915,582	1,590,096

Personal Income and Employment by Area: Terre Haute, IN

(Thousands of dollars, except as noted.)

Year	Personal income, total	Earnings by place of work			Less: Contributions for government social insurance	Plus: Adjustment for residence	Equals: Net earnings by place of residence	Plus: Dividends, interest, and rent	Plus: Personal current transfer receipts	Per capita personal income (dollars)	Population (persons)	Total employment
		Nonfarm	Farm	Total								
1970	601,500	483,981	10,413	494,394	33,374	-6,721	454,299	82,714	64,487	3,427	175,500	72,023
1971	644,869	497,512	19,716	517,228	35,422	-3,413	478,393	90,220	76,256	3,642	177,082	71,460
1972	685,884	526,028	16,170	542,198	39,329	599	503,468	96,638	85,778	3,883	176,637	71,698
1973	788,642	583,513	39,723	623,236	49,979	-20	573,237	110,076	105,329	4,493	175,537	73,710
1974	845,647	634,723	23,053	657,776	57,249	-1,212	599,315	126,776	119,556	4,894	172,796	74,911
1975	940,742	679,085	37,641	716,726	60,382	-2,006	654,338	144,087	142,317	5,440	172,939	73,605
1976	1,032,218	757,970	36,068	794,038	68,053	-1,474	724,511	155,153	152,554	5,943	173,680	74,743
1977	1,130,549	847,934	26,421	874,355	75,704	-3,181	795,470	174,848	160,231	6,477	174,548	76,933
1978	1,255,451	958,370	25,441	983,811	87,664	-7,735	888,412	194,390	172,649	7,191	174,590	79,642
1979	1,392,999	1,075,611	20,467	1,096,078	101,665	-16,603	977,810	218,093	197,096	7,987	174,406	82,452
1980	1,525,662	1,145,304	14,757	1,160,061	108,436	-25,170	1,026,455	267,090	232,117	8,649	176,395	81,575
1981	1,639,178	1,187,887	8,823	1,196,710	121,289	-24,550	1,050,871	325,616	262,691	9,353	175,255	78,331
1982	1,709,883	1,195,170	9,136	1,204,306	124,639	-25,935	1,053,732	366,182	289,969	9,783	174,781	75,509
1983	1,759,354	1,220,097	-11,604	1,208,493	126,947	-21,798	1,059,748	386,600	313,006	10,133	173,625	74,293
1984	1,909,068	1,308,945	19,567	1,328,512	139,476	-20,708	1,168,328	417,969	322,771	11,055	172,695	75,547
1985	1,989,270	1,363,670	18,956	1,382,626	148,066	-17,208	1,217,352	435,656	336,262	11,566	172,000	76,009
1986	2,078,048	1,429,969	17,126	1,447,095	155,779	-14,357	1,276,959	452,423	348,666	12,182	170,581	76,417
1987	2,140,481	1,494,404	15,205	1,509,609	160,498	-12,678	1,336,433	449,960	354,088	12,650	169,209	77,280
1988	2,224,398	1,561,742	8,188	1,569,930	174,291	-10,302	1,385,337	470,895	368,166	13,226	168,190	78,360
1989	2,434,865	1,666,851	25,585	1,692,436	187,755	-10,736	1,493,945	539,164	401,756	14,558	167,248	80,505
1990	2,549,127	1,782,304	17,295	1,799,599	205,463	-15,343	1,578,793	544,696	425,638	15,300	166,606	82,626
1991	2,657,361	1,903,317	-555	1,902,762	222,826	-26,519	1,653,417	545,744	458,200	15,918	166,943	83,969
1992	2,873,350	2,056,250	32,077	2,088,327	238,135	-30,486	1,819,706	537,504	516,140	17,090	168,127	86,041
1993	2,988,053	2,147,959	28,252	2,176,211	250,731	-37,056	1,888,424	553,714	545,915	17,621	169,575	87,972
1994	3,115,996	2,233,890	28,139	2,262,029	264,485	-34,634	1,962,910	580,254	572,832	18,332	169,975	89,740
1995	3,222,112	2,310,455	12,029	2,322,484	275,891	-39,440	2,007,153	635,257	579,702	18,851	170,921	91,712
1996	3,314,951	2,326,222	27,565	2,353,787	275,537	-38,866	2,039,384	664,583	610,984	19,309	171,682	90,589
1997	3,396,983	2,377,065	26,266	2,403,331	281,254	-42,081	2,079,996	688,205	628,782	19,788	171,665	89,365
1998	3,621,890	2,544,834	12,911	2,557,745	294,177	-37,761	2,225,807	741,512	654,571	21,151	171,237	89,182
1999	3,751,877	2,683,513	19,203	2,702,716	306,347	-41,124	2,355,245	704,434	692,198	21,911	171,235	89,809
2000	3,918,591	2,767,916	30,455	2,798,371	313,598	-44,379	2,440,394	756,765	721,432	22,935	170,855	90,905
2001	4,024,959	2,800,528	33,880	2,834,408	315,851	-43,646	2,474,911	756,649	793,399	23,607	170,497	89,447
2002	4,096,704	2,912,887	11,772	2,924,659	329,358	-58,628	2,536,673	726,691	833,340	24,090	170,055	88,475
2003	4,301,801	3,074,133	40,950	3,115,083	348,271	-63,667	2,703,145	738,679	859,977	25,240	170,438	89,613
2004	4,453,374	3,186,311	61,465	3,247,776	361,638	-57,210	2,828,928	717,383	907,063	26,196	170,001	89,828
2005	4,483,968	3,256,106	32,224	3,288,330	377,113	-68,850	2,842,367	659,955	981,646	26,278	170,634	89,399
2006	4,682,174	3,379,761	19,157	3,398,918	393,926	-69,436	2,935,556	696,062	1,050,556	27,265	171,730	90,113
2007	4,882,954	3,475,795	45,326	3,521,121	407,293	-75,811	3,038,017	758,935	1,086,002	28,391	171,987	90,996
2008	5,158,888	3,536,968	53,643	3,590,611	419,816	-78,312	3,092,483	827,037	1,239,368	29,999	171,967	89,576
2009	5,070,932	3,407,045	44,433	3,451,478	412,793	-76,025	2,962,660	768,201	1,340,071	29,450	172,190	87,587
2010	5,230,283	3,543,734	54,255	3,597,989	426,231	-95,737	3,076,021	736,256	1,418,006	30,353	172,314	86,957
2011	5,464,271	3,612,120	83,611	3,695,731	385,609	-92,139	3,217,983	820,197	1,426,091	31,662	172,581	86,982
2012	5,621,862	3,738,519	43,537	3,782,056	397,090	-100,794	3,284,172	858,377	1,479,313	32,567	172,626	87,488
2013	5,673,105	3,703,796	176,260	3,880,056	448,811	-92,706	3,338,539	858,820	1,475,746	32,945	172,201	87,079
2014	5,763,026	3,793,800	84,604	3,878,404	458,383	-89,478	3,330,543	891,138	1,541,345	33,608	171,480	87,105

Personal Income and Employment by Area: Texarkana, TX-Texarkana, AR

(Thousands of dollars, except as noted.)

Year	Personal income, total	Earnings by place of work			Less: Contributions for government social insurance	Plus: Adjustment for residence	Equals: Net earnings by place of residence	Plus: Dividends, interest, and rent	Plus: Personal current transfer receipts	Per capita personal income (dollars)	Population (persons)	Total employment
		Nonfarm	Farm	Total								
1970	375,649	324,856	11,436	336,292	18,697	-30,308	287,287	50,468	37,894	3,312	113,411	51,614
1971	400,527	336,246	9,817	346,063	19,670	-25,777	300,616	56,115	43,796	3,475	115,276	49,646
1972	450,613	374,743	13,100	387,843	22,977	-24,329	340,537	61,197	48,879	3,906	115,364	50,603
1973	499,708	405,615	17,198	422,813	28,914	-23,472	370,427	70,641	58,640	4,335	115,273	51,600
1974	556,874	442,061	16,765	458,826	32,689	-24,186	401,951	83,689	71,234	4,781	116,487	51,969
1975	610,932	469,968	10,204	480,172	33,445	-22,523	424,204	97,393	89,335	5,075	120,390	50,601
1976	686,677	528,881	11,390	540,271	38,716	-21,033	480,522	108,612	97,543	5,638	121,802	52,595
1977	756,029	584,560	9,404	593,964	43,510	-20,227	530,227	123,144	102,658	6,153	122,871	54,507
1978	851,367	660,613	10,235	670,848	51,017	-19,819	600,012	138,395	112,960	6,887	123,622	56,842
1979	973,112	771,173	21,406	792,579	63,966	-38,741	689,872	154,697	128,543	7,683	126,658	59,580
1980	1,058,310	800,261	6,746	807,007	64,733	-21,290	720,984	187,961	149,365	8,310	127,351	57,931
1981	1,186,665	876,655	11,872	888,527	75,730	-22,106	790,691	226,413	169,561	9,246	128,345	57,646
1982	1,275,694	937,922	10,523	948,445	82,646	-29,625	836,174	255,370	184,150	9,864	129,332	58,212
1983	1,367,235	1,003,997	7,881	1,011,878	92,070	-32,321	887,487	278,352	201,396	10,400	131,460	59,156
1984	1,517,767	1,111,015	21,099	1,132,114	105,168	-34,765	992,181	313,923	211,663	11,481	132,198	61,554
1985	1,610,103	1,173,207	16,009	1,189,216	114,106	-36,856	1,038,254	345,963	225,886	12,080	133,288	62,566
1986	1,660,149	1,203,483	21,265	1,224,748	118,805	-37,889	1,068,054	355,107	236,988	12,423	133,636	61,580
1987	1,698,821	1,242,932	19,495	1,262,427	122,375	-39,513	1,100,539	352,741	245,541	12,688	133,889	62,892
1988	1,773,916	1,290,930	31,411	1,322,341	133,327	-37,087	1,151,927	361,910	260,079	13,175	134,645	62,821
1989	1,900,676	1,374,191	34,858	1,409,049	144,821	-44,983	1,219,245	397,329	284,102	14,206	133,795	64,410
1990	2,012,541	1,488,690	29,284	1,517,974	161,227	-60,793	1,295,954	400,833	315,754	14,963	134,497	67,025
1991	2,100,461	1,534,271	32,544	1,566,815	168,449	-35,239	1,363,127	388,158	349,176	15,530	135,250	66,542
1992	2,215,565	1,579,317	32,928	1,612,245	173,066	-21,228	1,417,951	395,657	401,957	16,272	136,162	65,220
1993	2,292,920	1,636,336	32,845	1,669,181	179,675	-16,006	1,473,500	402,998	416,422	16,664	137,598	66,853
1994	2,404,371	1,692,079	36,552	1,728,631	188,346	-10,836	1,529,449	425,582	449,340	17,297	139,004	67,344
1995	2,538,131	1,770,120	32,753	1,802,873	196,885	-4,667	1,601,321	455,485	481,325	18,149	139,853	69,282
1996	2,671,878	1,847,860	40,961	1,888,821	202,969	-60	1,685,792	482,592	503,494	18,902	141,353	70,753
1997	2,822,587	1,964,054	49,125	2,013,179	213,780	5,691	1,805,090	492,533	524,964	19,892	141,893	71,877
1998	2,910,592	2,022,170	38,110	2,060,280	217,250	16,019	1,859,049	517,334	534,209	20,451	142,322	71,017
1999	3,044,414	2,146,067	51,550	2,197,617	228,061	9,283	1,978,839	527,170	538,405	21,282	143,051	72,581
2000	3,203,516	2,246,373	44,351	2,290,724	237,004	9,575	2,063,295	580,062	560,159	22,370	143,205	73,735
2001	3,352,394	2,301,561	51,415	2,352,976	245,488	23,260	2,130,748	607,180	614,466	23,463	142,882	73,775
2002	3,425,820	2,399,942	39,721	2,439,663	255,578	9,926	2,194,011	573,103	658,706	23,932	143,149	73,589
2003	3,528,027	2,525,063	54,254	2,579,317	271,134	-4,125	2,304,058	524,453	699,516	24,572	143,582	73,834
2004	3,773,617	2,677,362	69,144	2,746,506	286,375	-14,366	2,445,765	583,263	744,589	26,206	143,996	74,725
2005	3,918,240	2,822,333	39,289	2,861,622	302,252	-33,939	2,525,431	589,050	803,759	27,109	144,534	76,615
2006	4,120,129	2,980,824	26,413	3,007,237	317,467	-47,851	2,641,919	612,466	865,744	28,210	146,051	77,675
2007	4,407,651	3,115,476	44,173	3,159,649	337,097	-66,227	2,756,325	709,541	941,785	30,133	146,273	79,411
2008	4,611,125	3,238,373	13,718	3,252,091	356,524	-96,428	2,799,139	761,833	1,050,153	31,263	147,495	80,636
2009	4,581,501	3,213,972	5,621	3,219,593	360,228	-111,191	2,748,174	709,978	1,123,349	30,801	148,743	79,127
2010	4,716,717	3,242,192	10,364	3,252,556	365,449	-68,388	2,818,719	683,819	1,214,179	31,589	149,315	78,424
2011	4,922,279	3,310,021	14,244	3,324,265	333,141	-61,977	2,929,147	761,023	1,232,109	32,912	149,561	79,412
2012	5,059,921	3,367,503	26,036	3,393,539	336,107	-73,510	2,983,922	843,692	1,232,307	33,821	149,610	79,016
2013	4,933,465	3,232,966	40,556	3,273,522	364,563	-61,226	2,847,733	809,869	1,275,863	32,986	149,563	77,693
2014	5,100,055	3,296,350	56,035	3,352,385	371,323	-54,251	2,926,811	835,134	1,338,110	34,175	149,235	77,588

Personal Income and Employment by Area: The Villages, FL

(Thousands of dollars, except as noted.)

Year	Personal income, total	Earnings by place of work			Less: Contributions for government social insurance	Plus: Adjustment for residence	Equals: Net earnings by place of residence	Plus: Dividends, interest, and rent	Plus: Personal current transfer receipts	Per capita personal income (dollars)	Population (persons)	Total employment
		Nonfarm	Farm	Total								
1970	40,113	25,247	3,231	28,478	2,089	1,293	27,682	6,196	6,235	2,680	14,967	4,545
1971	46,122	27,618	4,346	31,964	2,296	2,017	31,685	7,136	7,301	2,920	15,797	4,724
1972	54,427	30,630	5,783	36,413	2,573	3,117	36,957	8,309	9,161	3,061	17,780	5,092
1973	65,361	35,084	7,313	42,397	3,208	4,629	43,818	10,235	11,308	3,414	19,143	5,413
1974	72,169	37,617	6,521	44,138	3,671	5,947	46,414	12,067	13,688	3,529	20,453	5,460
1975	82,460	40,950	7,113	48,063	3,978	6,863	50,948	13,868	17,644	3,927	20,999	5,497
1976	90,550	43,798	7,752	51,550	4,320	8,266	55,496	14,790	20,264	4,105	22,056	5,668
1977	100,225	47,895	7,901	55,796	4,774	10,181	61,203	16,723	22,299	4,490	22,324	5,961
1978	118,356	56,108	9,951	66,059	5,571	12,411	72,899	21,482	23,975	5,183	22,835	6,565
1979	139,412	63,202	12,223	75,425	6,433	14,688	83,680	26,705	29,027	5,979	23,318	6,841
1980	160,400	68,562	10,541	79,103	7,014	18,397	90,486	34,781	35,133	6,563	24,439	6,802
1981	177,624	75,061	7,351	82,412	8,335	19,538	93,615	42,683	41,326	7,087	25,063	6,847
1982	197,251	83,109	9,983	93,092	9,516	19,667	103,243	47,062	46,946	7,639	25,822	6,869
1983	222,689	93,372	11,107	104,479	10,554	20,707	114,632	55,849	52,208	8,379	26,577	7,337
1984	245,474	104,107	9,452	113,559	12,037	23,968	125,490	64,079	55,905	8,971	27,362	7,732
1985	268,848	115,535	7,785	123,320	13,666	26,101	135,755	71,443	61,650	9,496	28,313	8,285
1986	290,574	121,769	8,230	129,999	14,984	29,886	144,901	77,949	67,724	9,945	29,217	8,497
1987	313,268	129,491	6,940	136,431	15,473	35,060	156,018	81,656	75,594	10,523	29,771	8,769
1988	341,890	140,931	9,304	150,235	17,523	39,455	172,167	84,524	85,199	11,335	30,161	9,022
1989	376,671	151,261	11,156	162,417	18,903	43,427	186,941	100,675	89,055	12,155	30,990	9,138
1990	393,022	152,595	10,551	163,146	18,907	46,860	191,099	103,520	98,403	12,327	31,882	9,144
1991	412,731	157,649	14,012	171,661	19,853	45,938	197,746	104,261	110,724	12,559	32,863	9,069
1992	447,652	169,978	16,043	186,021	21,429	48,268	212,860	104,099	130,693	13,243	33,804	9,142
1993	469,680	179,178	14,259	193,437	22,370	51,176	222,243	105,092	142,345	13,511	34,764	9,427
1994	501,834	190,987	11,644	202,631	24,206	53,350	231,775	112,108	157,951	13,882	36,149	9,665
1995	548,600	217,979	8,772	226,751	26,925	50,463	250,289	121,154	177,157	14,271	38,441	10,357
1996	610,327	256,843	7,118	263,961	30,351	45,131	278,741	135,279	196,307	14,236	42,871	11,189
1997	660,112	278,876	9,589	288,465	32,739	45,325	301,051	144,526	214,535	14,162	46,611	11,587
1998	715,628	294,824	9,849	304,673	34,567	48,965	319,071	163,533	233,024	14,674	48,767	12,027
1999	781,345	322,750	13,432	336,182	37,446	48,976	347,712	164,719	268,914	15,106	51,725	12,239
2000	834,099	341,452	13,387	354,839	39,667	49,060	364,232	169,351	300,516	15,522	53,738	12,713
2001	947,691	415,556	14,965	430,521	47,238	34,107	417,390	167,362	362,939	16,986	55,793	13,385
2002	1,035,029	438,000	9,662	447,662	50,594	39,115	436,183	189,262	409,584	17,384	59,539	14,619
2003	1,194,015	532,822	11,025	543,847	61,302	50,182	532,727	216,340	444,948	19,279	61,934	17,054
2004	1,374,316	594,986	11,594	606,580	68,542	58,705	596,743	278,414	499,159	21,322	64,456	18,600
2005	1,638,384	739,269	13,834	753,103	84,648	76,958	745,413	308,753	584,218	23,655	69,261	21,532
2006	1,933,988	854,110	13,228	867,338	115,961	93,697	845,074	373,384	715,530	25,380	76,202	24,015
2007	2,157,063	921,369	9,908	931,277	128,261	107,949	910,965	420,836	825,262	26,273	82,101	24,763
2008	2,418,279	938,151	8,926	947,077	138,001	116,314	925,390	490,947	1,001,942	27,979	86,433	24,965
2009	2,511,533	978,603	8,133	986,736	148,656	14,463	852,543	473,800	1,185,190	27,708	90,643	25,660
2010	2,752,350	1,048,803	8,267	1,057,070	161,573	-26,512	868,985	569,537	1,313,828	29,191	94,287	26,711
2011	3,246,798	1,177,017	5,780	1,182,797	166,719	-33,448	982,630	799,575	1,464,593	32,930	98,598	28,222
2012	3,629,631	1,222,425	10,575	1,233,000	177,703	39,846	1,095,143	967,298	1,567,190	35,300	102,823	29,389
2013	3,957,619	1,357,029	9,824	1,366,853	215,754	36,463	1,187,562	1,101,183	1,668,874	36,481	108,483	31,607
2014	4,294,751	1,403,007	19,475	1,422,482	228,277	118,520	1,312,725	1,139,841	1,842,185	37,558	114,350	33,008

Personal Income and Employment by Area: Toledo, OH

(Thousands of dollars, except as noted.)

Year	Personal income, total	Earnings by place of work			Less: Contributions for government social insurance	Plus: Adjustment for residence	Equals: Net earnings by place of residence	Plus: Dividends, interest, and rent	Plus: Personal current transfer receipts	Per capita personal income (dollars)	Population (persons)	Total employment
		Nonfarm	Farm	Total								
1970	2,607,681	2,245,253	25,167	2,270,420	149,493	-85,747	2,035,180	361,227	211,274	4,293	607,493	277,346
1971	2,800,768	2,399,086	23,873	2,422,959	164,761	-84,850	2,173,348	385,754	241,666	4,563	613,790	277,628
1972	3,061,796	2,639,872	29,887	2,669,759	191,302	-92,364	2,386,093	410,928	264,775	4,952	618,239	283,180
1973	3,394,790	2,939,963	42,449	2,982,412	247,426	-103,331	2,631,655	455,404	307,731	5,464	621,256	295,425
1974	3,679,062	3,126,185	46,183	3,172,368	273,112	-110,719	2,788,537	518,255	372,270	5,906	622,934	294,935
1975	3,961,578	3,251,105	52,973	3,304,078	276,446	-112,848	2,914,784	554,605	492,189	6,382	620,746	285,579
1976	4,376,155	3,683,803	43,836	3,727,639	321,732	-139,407	3,266,500	589,268	520,387	7,115	615,085	292,558
1977	4,786,699	4,081,443	31,635	4,113,078	359,684	-169,749	3,583,645	650,390	552,664	7,798	613,830	299,282
1978	5,242,028	4,520,345	23,588	4,543,933	410,320	-199,193	3,934,420	722,014	585,594	8,578	611,100	307,404
1979	5,749,398	4,904,270	35,520	4,939,790	459,250	-223,446	4,257,094	816,507	675,797	9,344	615,273	312,170
1980	6,271,049	5,064,777	45,147	5,109,924	467,971	-228,272	4,413,681	973,492	883,876	10,161	617,164	301,227
1981	6,775,383	5,415,361	8,078	5,423,439	535,686	-241,225	4,646,528	1,176,527	952,328	10,982	616,977	298,217
1982	7,115,603	5,535,291	13,079	5,548,370	555,664	-240,952	4,751,754	1,302,386	1,061,463	11,570	614,991	289,638
1983	7,589,599	5,930,052	-8,666	5,921,386	605,550	-273,244	5,042,592	1,421,394	1,125,613	12,403	611,930	291,994
1984	8,409,147	6,643,354	52,912	6,696,266	695,246	-334,705	5,666,315	1,580,861	1,161,971	13,772	610,582	305,313
1985	8,960,930	7,179,345	40,848	7,220,193	764,196	-376,367	6,079,630	1,656,885	1,224,415	14,687	610,137	312,850
1986	9,352,431	7,487,625	33,956	7,521,581	818,123	-372,845	6,330,613	1,719,843	1,301,975	15,280	612,073	321,095
1987	9,779,129	7,871,118	40,103	7,911,221	856,486	-388,377	6,666,358	1,757,065	1,355,706	15,950	613,093	328,662
1988	10,390,942	8,439,666	51,846	8,491,512	948,667	-421,085	7,121,760	1,851,810	1,417,372	16,841	616,985	338,504
1989	11,112,939	8,894,334	65,124	8,959,458	1,003,995	-446,510	7,508,953	2,102,357	1,501,629	18,053	615,560	342,926
1990	11,539,765	9,121,728	84,577	9,206,305	1,042,490	-411,826	7,751,989	2,113,875	1,673,901	18,775	614,637	340,445
1991	11,610,614	9,127,372	72,457	9,199,829	1,072,849	-403,251	7,723,729	2,064,734	1,822,151	18,891	614,606	334,188
1992	12,416,776	9,849,311	77,652	9,926,963	1,151,801	-476,662	8,298,500	2,125,492	1,992,784	20,165	615,755	336,874
1993	12,898,415	10,340,389	68,729	10,409,118	1,219,918	-560,842	8,628,358	2,207,000	2,063,057	20,952	615,629	344,665
1994	13,532,498	11,042,544	76,590	11,119,134	1,318,073	-692,497	9,108,564	2,279,901	2,144,033	21,974	615,841	359,308
1995	14,143,676	11,451,959	62,893	11,514,852	1,377,170	-723,888	9,413,794	2,448,257	2,281,625	22,949	616,304	364,582
1996	14,656,696	11,816,283	85,339	11,901,622	1,410,734	-782,706	9,708,182	2,615,636	2,332,878	23,775	616,468	370,314
1997	15,404,640	12,398,799	106,693	12,505,492	1,438,838	-828,331	10,238,323	2,781,662	2,384,655	24,933	617,850	374,438
1998	16,028,813	12,990,997	73,878	13,064,875	1,453,723	-881,552	10,729,600	2,893,841	2,405,372	25,916	618,484	378,037
1999	16,562,948	13,764,479	56,004	13,820,483	1,535,697	-975,815	11,308,971	2,797,123	2,456,854	26,785	618,371	384,075
2000	17,215,056	14,180,169	74,432	14,254,601	1,526,540	-989,036	11,739,025	2,894,662	2,581,369	27,847	618,207	388,041
2001	17,593,029	14,606,611	54,884	14,661,495	1,582,496	-1,128,939	11,950,060	2,862,882	2,780,087	28,420	619,037	386,029
2002	17,916,603	14,877,741	26,924	14,904,665	1,582,894	-1,126,840	12,194,931	2,742,188	2,979,484	28,957	618,721	378,845
2003	18,478,627	15,335,663	49,454	15,385,117	1,645,480	-1,140,438	12,599,199	2,780,177	3,099,251	29,852	619,006	376,274
2004	18,991,092	15,824,219	87,403	15,911,622	1,723,183	-1,133,975	13,054,464	2,697,114	3,239,514	30,721	618,181	377,826
2005	19,476,134	16,146,486	82,719	16,229,205	1,763,541	-1,118,776	13,346,888	2,687,090	3,442,156	31,575	616,819	378,217
2006	20,584,776	16,872,013	82,255	16,954,268	1,839,626	-1,111,112	14,003,530	2,946,567	3,634,679	33,494	614,581	380,209
2007	21,280,414	17,116,533	73,095	17,189,628	1,869,825	-1,074,745	14,245,058	3,183,338	3,852,018	34,683	613,567	379,069
2008	21,603,322	16,987,658	61,522	17,049,180	1,875,058	-1,018,337	14,155,785	3,120,225	4,327,312	35,302	611,964	370,596
2009	21,038,584	16,086,191	80,630	16,166,821	1,794,118	-926,714	13,445,989	2,812,356	4,780,239	34,448	610,734	351,133
2010	21,671,651	16,509,812	60,402	16,570,214	1,809,707	-932,935	13,827,572	2,832,162	5,011,917	35,516	610,201	347,597
2011	22,994,079	17,339,426	133,233	17,472,659	1,718,402	-991,831	14,762,426	3,112,680	5,118,973	37,720	609,596	354,413
2012	23,557,826	17,987,138	89,866	18,077,004	1,771,234	-1,058,810	15,246,960	3,334,350	4,976,516	38,711	608,551	357,250
2013	23,715,985	18,248,163	124,812	18,372,975	1,966,735	-1,055,053	15,351,187	3,280,829	5,083,969	38,979	608,430	360,257
2014	24,684,223	19,099,731	78,209	19,177,940	2,088,687	-1,130,350	15,958,903	3,395,158	5,330,162	40,635	607,456	365,359

Personal Income and Employment by Area: Topeka, KS

(Thousands of dollars, except as noted.)

Year	Personal income, total	Earnings by place of work			Less: Contributions for government social insurance	Plus: Adjustment for residence	Equals: Net earnings by place of residence	Plus: Dividends, interest, and rent	Plus: Personal current transfer receipts	Per capita personal income (dollars)	Population (persons)	Total employment
		Nonfarm	Farm	Total								
1970	801,696	642,425	11,624	654,049	48,295	-8,111	597,643	131,679	72,374	4,055	197,701	95,350
1971	885,447	702,445	17,642	720,087	54,401	-7,666	658,020	143,187	84,240	4,455	198,772	96,314
1972	983,813	778,532	26,766	805,298	63,058	-8,180	734,060	156,973	92,780	4,850	202,849	98,653
1973	1,086,905	859,904	32,617	892,521	79,969	-5,213	807,339	171,232	108,334	5,367	202,528	102,182
1974	1,137,350	885,562	24,742	910,304	86,911	-1,049	822,344	189,439	125,567	5,858	194,147	100,477
1975	1,246,205	953,557	16,367	969,924	91,905	1,281	879,300	210,466	156,439	6,387	195,125	100,810
1976	1,364,072	1,056,861	7,967	1,064,828	103,140	5,146	966,834	223,543	173,695	6,901	197,659	102,988
1977	1,536,803	1,190,353	17,253	1,207,606	115,875	10,179	1,101,910	248,012	186,881	7,722	199,010	106,791
1978	1,712,931	1,337,140	8,779	1,345,919	133,652	16,850	1,229,117	277,493	206,321	8,550	200,351	110,694
1979	1,881,987	1,474,479	3,293	1,477,772	153,257	19,800	1,344,315	311,357	226,315	9,333	201,651	112,914
1980	2,089,200	1,591,686	-23,286	1,568,400	165,791	24,822	1,427,431	387,805	273,964	10,236	204,099	113,888
1981	2,373,653	1,721,268	14,567	1,735,835	192,745	22,479	1,565,569	494,320	313,764	11,613	204,404	113,415
1982	2,536,911	1,799,202	7,732	1,806,934	207,240	21,883	1,621,577	576,522	338,812	12,383	204,869	111,566
1983	2,656,382	1,915,352	-10,998	1,904,354	219,580	17,365	1,702,139	596,248	357,995	12,920	205,608	112,196
1984	2,887,352	2,097,053	4,394	2,101,447	245,738	15,516	1,871,225	651,634	364,493	14,016	206,005	116,313
1985	3,086,903	2,207,771	52,017	2,259,788	262,712	4,501	2,001,577	698,352	386,974	15,035	205,319	116,597
1986	3,211,500	2,331,670	24,206	2,355,876	277,956	-528	2,077,392	736,260	397,848	15,605	205,805	117,515
1987	3,339,149	2,452,688	19,201	2,471,889	287,955	-1,698	2,182,236	749,940	406,973	16,105	207,337	123,311
1988	3,545,952	2,631,645	10,724	2,642,369	321,779	-4,296	2,316,294	798,146	431,512	16,865	210,255	125,741
1989	3,706,092	2,762,747	11,434	2,774,181	338,489	-9,778	2,425,914	810,913	469,265	17,665	209,794	127,498
1990	3,872,683	2,887,672	27,169	2,914,841	366,944	-11,635	2,536,262	829,930	506,491	18,389	210,598	128,053
1991	3,985,049	2,975,092	8,296	2,983,388	380,201	-11,591	2,591,596	848,115	545,338	18,755	212,479	127,916
1992	4,251,674	3,143,943	50,149	3,194,092	397,767	-11,521	2,784,804	861,494	605,376	19,866	214,014	128,684
1993	4,438,129	3,336,146	9,926	3,346,072	422,500	-15,403	2,908,169	887,862	642,098	20,523	216,252	131,257
1994	4,682,460	3,523,671	25,671	3,549,342	450,040	-15,477	3,083,825	937,557	661,078	21,421	218,593	133,525
1995	4,864,278	3,650,950	321	3,651,271	458,512	-16,601	3,176,158	987,509	700,611	22,107	220,036	137,625
1996	5,138,084	3,793,858	54,404	3,848,262	471,846	-15,591	3,360,825	1,048,477	728,782	23,223	221,246	139,732
1997	5,313,116	3,911,899	24,545	3,936,444	486,895	-5,394	3,444,155	1,098,476	770,485	23,899	222,316	139,357
1998	5,654,027	4,201,327	8,265	4,209,592	514,149	-8,199	3,687,244	1,172,987	793,796	25,291	223,555	142,286
1999	5,831,023	4,406,749	-5,895	4,400,854	534,130	-3,928	3,862,796	1,132,632	835,595	26,058	223,772	142,662
2000	6,206,624	4,651,898	-11,832	4,640,066	557,998	1,282	4,083,350	1,224,935	898,339	27,602	224,859	145,296
2001	6,421,691	4,832,207	13,557	4,845,764	587,635	-11,462	4,246,667	1,187,956	987,068	28,529	225,090	145,189
2002	6,531,534	4,907,160	-9,185	4,897,975	595,742	-18,677	4,283,556	1,179,405	1,068,573	28,983	225,355	142,171
2003	6,662,355	4,922,501	11,998	4,934,499	599,297	-4,580	4,330,622	1,208,932	1,122,801	29,460	226,153	140,597
2004	6,849,734	5,108,999	48,045	5,157,044	618,810	-5,405	4,532,829	1,139,258	1,177,647	30,154	227,155	139,552
2005	7,048,113	5,272,985	16,054	5,289,039	640,080	7,381	4,656,340	1,158,262	1,233,511	30,885	228,208	139,227
2006	7,403,217	5,402,505	-4,639	5,397,866	654,328	19,555	4,763,093	1,324,358	1,315,766	32,353	228,825	138,251
2007	7,894,559	5,653,981	12,984	5,666,965	683,419	40,255	5,023,801	1,450,799	1,419,959	34,320	230,025	141,875
2008	8,384,379	5,929,518	28,281	5,957,799	707,121	85,141	5,335,819	1,468,946	1,579,614	36,253	231,272	142,030
2009	8,413,794	5,900,319	42,536	5,942,855	712,564	65,390	5,295,681	1,400,905	1,717,208	36,181	232,548	139,285
2010	8,490,471	5,977,587	7,585	5,985,172	728,206	60,065	5,317,031	1,352,292	1,821,148	36,252	234,209	138,591
2011	9,009,808	6,191,539	60,716	6,252,255	666,173	64,235	5,650,317	1,464,641	1,894,850	38,393	234,671	139,510
2012	9,190,180	6,344,019	45,711	6,389,730	683,790	65,260	5,771,200	1,521,072	1,897,908	39,200	234,444	139,305
2013	9,314,546	6,449,477	111,282	6,560,759	787,242	72,658	5,846,175	1,541,259	1,927,112	39,824	233,894	140,526
2014	9,518,655	6,627,519	58,266	6,685,785	813,134	72,572	5,945,223	1,593,843	1,979,589	40,720	233,758	142,859

Personal Income and Employment by Area: Trenton, NJ

(Thousands of dollars, except as noted.)

Year	Personal income, total	Earnings by place of work			Less: Contributions for government social insurance	Plus: Adjustment for residence	Equals: Net earnings by place of residence	Plus: Dividends, interest, and rent	Plus: Personal current transfer receipts	Per capita personal income (dollars)	Population (persons)	Total employment
		Nonfarm	Farm	Total								
1970	1,503,648	1,259,654	2,577	1,262,231	91,907	-13,171	1,157,153	235,649	110,846	4,929	305,091	153,757
1971	1,652,688	1,385,297	2,044	1,387,341	103,732	-22,836	1,260,773	257,769	134,146	5,354	308,680	153,733
1972	1,837,927	1,564,032	1,821	1,565,853	122,267	-38,251	1,405,335	282,466	150,126	5,844	314,505	161,814
1973	2,026,130	1,741,432	3,496	1,744,928	156,710	-39,651	1,548,567	305,634	171,929	6,428	315,209	166,704
1974	2,219,282	1,886,619	4,524	1,891,143	174,351	-39,790	1,677,002	340,327	201,953	6,998	317,113	169,496
1975	2,380,222	1,958,325	2,056	1,960,381	177,714	-26,653	1,756,014	359,526	264,682	7,544	315,506	163,246
1976	2,590,297	2,148,115	2,226	2,150,341	198,027	-35,480	1,916,834	384,150	289,313	8,276	313,004	166,848
1977	2,817,853	2,359,582	3,160	2,362,742	217,095	-61,333	2,084,314	425,121	308,418	9,048	311,427	169,701
1978	3,085,563	2,621,571	2,722	2,624,293	248,692	-94,171	2,281,430	469,582	334,551	9,897	311,764	175,837
1979	3,369,086	2,868,618	2,358	2,870,976	282,105	-123,542	2,465,329	527,121	376,636	10,868	309,998	180,281
1980	3,732,054	3,127,942	1,841	3,129,783	303,717	-167,504	2,658,562	635,035	438,457	12,125	307,796	182,263
1981	4,126,608	3,407,845	3,817	3,411,662	354,146	-208,563	2,848,953	796,413	481,242	13,444	306,944	182,845
1982	4,485,930	3,612,375	2,934	3,615,309	375,836	-231,253	3,008,220	942,803	534,907	14,570	307,882	181,854
1983	4,805,541	3,950,859	4,158	3,955,017	424,102	-280,924	3,249,991	982,783	572,767	15,449	311,052	185,431
1984	5,326,542	4,427,282	5,850	4,433,132	496,621	-339,886	3,596,625	1,132,756	597,161	17,123	311,067	194,000
1985	5,749,474	4,836,980	6,502	4,843,482	548,585	-390,150	3,904,747	1,214,539	630,188	18,303	314,133	199,290
1986	6,188,451	5,311,401	6,626	5,318,027	609,722	-452,381	4,255,924	1,272,792	659,735	19,427	318,557	207,145
1987	6,715,428	5,836,525	7,909	5,844,434	663,175	-509,697	4,671,562	1,359,365	684,501	20,837	322,280	212,933
1988	7,474,245	6,537,350	7,184	6,544,534	759,501	-583,449	5,201,584	1,545,794	726,867	22,916	326,162	218,832
1989	8,155,879	6,924,516	6,396	6,930,912	795,994	-667,382	5,467,536	1,904,067	784,276	24,999	326,246	219,559
1990	8,675,417	7,392,995	4,926	7,397,921	825,938	-715,191	5,856,792	1,958,491	860,134	26,573	326,477	219,736
1991	8,831,537	7,673,874	3,058	7,676,932	875,035	-915,902	5,885,995	1,960,022	985,520	26,869	328,694	216,604
1992	9,489,721	8,191,581	1,990	8,193,571	926,148	-871,433	6,395,990	1,965,184	1,128,547	28,698	330,674	217,454
1993	9,636,103	8,416,041	2,576	8,418,617	949,432	-949,815	6,519,370	1,917,576	1,199,157	28,912	333,292	219,615
1994	9,970,294	8,736,128	3,174	8,739,302	1,003,177	-1,017,141	6,718,984	2,041,050	1,210,260	29,742	335,229	220,293
1995	10,465,601	9,006,281	1,973	9,008,254	1,040,468	-1,056,985	6,910,801	2,262,552	1,292,248	31,011	337,476	222,501
1996	11,004,797	9,232,920	2,899	9,235,819	1,065,133	-871,973	7,298,713	2,379,225	1,326,859	32,449	339,146	220,840
1997	11,604,508	9,990,428	1,436	9,991,864	1,142,036	-1,115,995	7,733,833	2,513,322	1,357,353	34,055	340,755	224,588
1998	12,391,815	10,446,088	1,258	10,447,346	1,182,889	-971,646	8,292,811	2,735,585	1,363,419	36,021	344,013	225,215
1999	12,983,686	10,980,536	1,311	10,981,847	1,241,658	-919,353	8,820,836	2,745,799	1,417,051	37,263	348,435	228,566
2000	14,350,042	12,166,261	3,867	12,170,128	1,359,025	-1,024,862	9,786,241	3,046,641	1,517,160	40,829	351,465	241,693
2001	14,752,864	12,815,452	2,799	12,818,251	1,443,242	-1,364,317	10,010,692	3,044,188	1,697,984	41,696	353,816	246,334
2002	15,416,220	13,386,995	3,850	13,390,845	1,498,272	-1,457,648	10,434,925	3,102,049	1,879,246	43,312	355,935	248,253
2003	16,016,657	14,049,575	4,146	14,053,721	1,545,397	-1,549,939	10,958,385	3,229,961	1,828,311	44,649	358,724	252,094
2004	16,491,774	14,728,313	5,918	14,734,231	1,606,110	-1,654,570	11,473,551	3,208,344	1,809,879	45,652	361,248	256,862
2005	17,094,478	15,283,144	5,006	15,288,150	1,681,416	-1,751,683	11,855,051	3,324,292	1,915,135	47,220	362,015	258,376
2006	18,707,520	16,464,794	5,182	16,469,976	1,786,657	-1,890,675	12,792,644	3,821,177	2,093,699	51,559	362,840	264,993
2007	19,351,785	16,933,910	4,712	16,938,622	1,874,613	-1,957,236	13,106,773	4,043,249	2,201,763	53,298	363,088	264,533
2008	20,068,179	17,521,272	3,639	17,524,911	1,959,873	-2,078,449	13,486,589	4,090,095	2,491,495	55,114	364,119	265,987
2009	19,418,705	17,300,609	3,232	17,303,841	1,921,381	-2,321,709	13,060,751	3,615,899	2,742,055	53,145	365,388	260,387
2010	20,095,282	18,112,814	3,190	18,116,004	2,001,666	-2,516,346	13,597,992	3,530,191	2,967,099	54,600	368,043	260,050
2011	20,962,094	18,428,998	6,307	18,435,305	1,841,326	-2,604,788	13,989,191	3,966,944	3,005,959	56,971	367,941	261,984
2012	21,961,791	19,236,940	7,129	19,244,069	1,906,807	-2,716,218	14,621,044	4,381,931	2,958,816	59,508	369,057	263,172
2013	21,269,782	19,678,113	8,037	19,686,150	2,227,299	-3,352,557	14,106,294	4,148,583	3,014,905	57,323	371,052	266,841
2014	22,245,842	20,331,832	5,116	20,336,948	2,288,510	-3,215,107	14,833,331	4,297,245	3,115,266	59,875	371,537	271,817

Personal Income and Employment by Area: Tucson, AZ

(Thousands of dollars, except as noted.)

Year	Personal income, total	Derivation of personal income									Per capita personal income (dollars)	Population (persons)	Total employment
		Earnings by place of work			Less: Contributions for government social insurance	Plus: Adjustment for residence	Equals: Net earnings by place of residence	Plus: Dividends, interest, and rent	Plus: Personal current transfer receipts				
		Nonfarm	Farm	Total									
1970	1,442,740	1,028,149	9,121	1,037,270	69,598	14,507	982,179	333,588	126,973	4,053	355,962	144,257
1971	1,662,951	1,191,782	8,350	1,200,132	83,587	17,225	1,133,770	376,172	153,009	4,373	380,255	153,910
1972	1,891,480	1,367,847	12,649	1,380,496	100,346	15,926	1,296,076	419,402	176,002	4,641	407,515	165,820
1973	2,151,284	1,555,574	21,896	1,577,470	129,373	23,543	1,471,640	469,740	209,904	5,020	428,558	177,412
1974	2,399,946	1,713,183	16,922	1,730,105	148,097	27,344	1,609,352	540,039	250,555	5,408	443,741	181,576
1975	2,617,370	1,805,612	14,095	1,819,707	156,145	27,369	1,690,931	590,483	335,956	5,693	459,738	180,791
1976	2,868,036	1,973,069	18,384	1,991,453	171,550	33,077	1,852,980	636,231	378,825	6,082	471,596	185,903
1977	3,173,674	2,201,521	11,834	2,213,355	191,389	36,129	2,058,095	713,738	401,841	6,564	483,484	193,919
1978	3,661,080	2,521,085	15,924	2,537,009	223,517	34,526	2,348,018	852,911	460,151	7,356	497,687	206,946
1979	4,301,153	3,013,516	16,282	3,029,798	280,713	43,863	2,792,948	998,776	509,429	8,219	523,341	224,813
1980	4,950,869	3,399,077	16,831	3,415,908	322,646	39,634	3,132,896	1,214,886	603,087	9,240	535,780	234,354
1981	5,753,090	3,842,070	14,326	3,856,396	392,153	79,196	3,543,439	1,504,202	705,449	10,410	552,627	240,604
1982	6,103,099	4,027,339	13,593	4,040,932	419,400	60,695	3,682,227	1,638,521	782,351	10,745	568,004	245,297
1983	6,628,832	4,369,314	14,128	4,383,442	462,151	45,758	3,967,049	1,811,846	849,937	11,386	582,172	253,316
1984	7,309,341	4,845,993	33,960	4,879,953	529,159	46,309	4,397,103	2,012,748	899,490	12,345	592,087	271,828
1985	7,984,023	5,328,441	25,642	5,354,083	589,883	48,793	4,812,993	2,206,098	964,932	13,248	602,647	291,177
1986	8,685,830	5,821,823	29,159	5,850,982	646,842	58,266	5,262,406	2,377,727	1,045,697	13,974	621,586	302,631
1987	9,226,712	6,173,692	27,872	6,201,564	679,503	64,512	5,586,573	2,495,717	1,144,422	14,407	640,419	308,273
1988	9,841,744	6,564,781	31,163	6,595,944	749,450	96,226	5,942,720	2,647,449	1,251,575	14,986	656,727	318,154
1989	10,591,885	6,725,335	24,366	6,749,701	789,955	91,194	6,050,940	3,100,267	1,440,678	15,947	664,200	318,020
1990	10,909,178	6,891,984	26,634	6,918,618	830,940	117,028	6,204,706	3,103,312	1,601,160	16,310	668,844	318,925
1991	11,520,165	7,444,175	23,808	7,467,983	906,595	111,630	6,673,018	3,077,189	1,769,958	16,946	679,813	323,434
1992	12,187,358	7,966,345	20,226	7,986,571	964,720	115,270	7,137,121	3,056,396	1,993,841	17,458	698,091	328,018
1993	13,318,954	8,666,054	28,241	8,694,295	1,044,436	106,084	7,755,943	3,403,837	2,159,174	18,509	719,598	343,969
1994	14,447,589	9,562,929	14,876	9,577,805	1,160,187	94,225	8,511,843	3,638,347	2,297,399	19,390	745,112	367,152
1995	15,376,424	10,099,382	12,521	10,111,903	1,180,975	109,244	9,040,172	3,895,974	2,440,278	20,016	768,212	381,587
1996	16,361,336	10,676,110	18,087	10,694,197	1,278,928	136,442	9,551,711	4,220,655	2,588,970	20,877	783,685	389,883
1997	17,297,488	11,354,346	18,217	11,372,563	1,338,365	116,873	10,151,071	4,447,030	2,699,387	21,662	798,521	399,857
1998	18,772,072	12,439,221	14,721	12,453,942	1,439,605	108,810	11,123,147	4,874,457	2,774,468	23,079	813,386	416,641
1999	19,825,003	13,400,669	21,443	13,422,112	1,550,888	97,336	11,968,560	4,913,243	2,943,200	23,917	828,905	425,999
2000	21,265,281	14,506,406	15,003	14,521,409	1,650,518	89,609	12,960,500	5,213,036	3,091,745	25,076	848,019	442,901
2001	22,086,854	14,934,767	11,258	14,946,025	1,690,986	98,908	13,353,947	5,231,621	3,501,286	25,704	859,280	442,597
2002	22,646,748	15,561,853	17,359	15,579,212	1,765,211	75,599	13,889,600	4,860,629	3,896,519	25,904	874,267	442,491
2003	23,753,399	16,219,686	22,294	16,241,980	1,827,507	52,861	14,467,334	5,038,190	4,247,875	26,813	885,893	450,151
2004	25,828,750	17,414,733	28,815	17,443,548	1,961,418	29,675	15,511,805	5,714,609	4,602,336	28,656	901,342	469,406
2005	28,463,062	18,733,416	32,852	18,766,268	2,117,906	2,688	16,651,050	6,683,247	5,128,765	30,928	920,298	485,364
2006	31,256,011	20,580,373	27,473	20,607,846	2,296,275	-29,438	18,282,133	7,376,775	5,597,103	33,218	940,930	507,497
2007	32,765,928	21,481,918	16,346	21,498,264	2,430,891	-66,122	19,001,251	7,716,506	6,048,171	34,279	955,869	523,757
2008	34,604,080	21,869,548	16,709	21,886,257	2,511,794	-103,939	19,270,524	8,338,920	6,994,636	35,756	967,778	510,759
2009	32,750,031	20,988,094	16,439	21,004,533	2,432,262	-83,834	18,488,437	6,607,371	7,654,223	33,570	975,580	491,410
2010	33,001,217	20,991,293	17,055	21,008,348	2,439,510	-67,898	18,500,940	6,285,662	8,214,615	33,608	981,935	484,012
2011	34,539,779	21,410,383	28,700	21,439,083	2,223,500	-39,959	19,175,624	7,186,200	8,177,955	34,955	988,125	485,081
2012	35,590,889	22,131,766	30,238	22,162,004	2,275,526	-28,616	19,857,862	7,596,400	8,136,627	35,838	993,094	491,482
2013	35,784,754	22,412,644	41,586	22,454,230	2,611,478	-17,175	19,825,577	7,652,391	8,306,786	35,855	998,050	496,329
2014	37,198,714	23,039,410	50,722	23,090,132	2,687,726	1,716	20,404,122	7,945,810	8,848,782	37,031	1,004,516	500,623

Personal Income and Employment by Area: Tulsa, OK

(Thousands of dollars, except as noted.)

| Year | Personal income, total | Derivation of personal income | | | | | | | | Per capita personal income (dollars) | Population (persons) | Total employment |
| | | Earnings by place of work | | | Less: Contributions for government social insurance | Plus: Adjustment for residence | Equals: Net earnings by place of residence | Plus: Dividends, interest, and rent | Plus: Personal current transfer receipts | | | |
		Nonfarm	Farm	Total								
1970	2,241,250	1,805,186	17,819	1,823,005	118,059	-13,801	1,691,145	339,757	210,348	3,910	573,235	253,693
1971	2,418,660	1,925,515	15,964	1,941,479	129,622	-11,065	1,800,792	374,155	243,713	4,154	582,203	255,389
1972	2,655,295	2,139,210	21,145	2,160,355	151,577	-12,560	1,996,218	392,949	266,128	4,485	592,055	270,578
1973	3,003,396	2,430,291	25,672	2,455,963	201,071	-12,450	2,242,442	456,249	304,705	4,988	602,108	286,825
1974	3,528,280	2,857,243	28,731	2,885,974	242,127	-8,805	2,635,042	535,687	357,551	5,765	611,968	301,297
1975	4,031,448	3,229,511	26,245	3,255,756	267,329	10,401	2,998,828	591,295	441,325	6,447	625,290	309,562
1976	4,483,048	3,622,815	27,581	3,650,396	307,343	19,697	3,362,750	634,645	485,653	7,022	638,395	324,739
1977	5,030,726	4,118,206	17,591	4,135,797	347,292	18,935	3,807,440	702,287	520,999	7,719	651,741	336,418
1978	5,721,887	4,738,923	5,321	4,744,244	412,300	16,768	4,348,712	814,447	558,728	8,616	664,120	356,285
1979	6,548,044	5,467,660	16,969	5,484,629	494,812	-27,075	4,962,742	941,572	643,730	9,490	690,017	372,697
1980	7,729,775	6,419,146	11,648	6,430,794	582,946	-42,794	5,805,054	1,177,605	747,116	10,800	715,729	396,414
1981	8,989,644	7,410,254	22,929	7,433,183	724,104	-57,896	6,651,183	1,486,782	851,679	12,302	730,726	416,102
1982	9,836,742	7,929,601	16,706	7,946,307	799,460	-57,720	7,089,127	1,766,844	980,771	13,032	754,809	420,399
1983	9,993,392	7,892,873	14,600	7,907,473	792,124	-47,839	7,067,510	1,841,103	1,084,779	12,932	772,780	406,405
1984	10,702,472	8,416,040	12,368	8,428,408	856,524	-36,842	7,535,042	2,050,953	1,116,477	13,819	774,500	416,659
1985	11,322,389	8,841,087	10,333	8,851,420	913,651	-45,131	7,892,638	2,240,880	1,188,871	14,643	773,203	421,361
1986	11,494,517	8,972,647	21,113	8,993,760	946,414	-49,191	7,998,155	2,222,143	1,274,219	14,816	775,798	409,752
1987	11,527,640	8,984,457	16,105	9,000,562	945,958	-44,906	8,009,698	2,186,806	1,331,136	14,957	770,713	411,356
1988	12,090,655	9,467,574	26,063	9,493,637	1,040,903	-51,206	8,401,528	2,282,373	1,406,754	15,937	758,652	413,701
1989	12,953,946	10,157,264	29,269	10,186,533	1,117,273	-79,173	8,990,087	2,453,760	1,510,099	17,104	757,345	418,975
1990	13,906,302	10,838,089	13,894	10,851,983	1,237,258	-48,664	9,566,061	2,716,158	1,624,083	18,223	763,119	430,763
1991	14,421,634	11,285,969	30,254	11,316,223	1,316,611	-50,775	9,948,837	2,699,906	1,772,891	18,614	774,765	437,718
1992	15,246,278	11,873,928	31,082	11,905,010	1,371,430	-66,965	10,466,615	2,796,267	1,983,396	19,403	785,755	438,214
1993	15,835,997	12,395,554	29,253	12,424,807	1,438,719	-88,368	10,897,720	2,821,668	2,116,609	19,916	795,139	444,889
1994	16,560,900	12,862,154	35,297	12,897,451	1,515,286	-101,285	11,280,880	3,054,512	2,225,508	20,689	800,473	453,942
1995	17,523,341	13,433,147	9,776	13,442,923	1,580,279	-110,961	11,751,683	3,354,039	2,417,619	21,749	805,725	466,011
1996	18,695,156	14,335,001	13,657	14,348,658	1,654,861	-125,313	12,568,484	3,577,323	2,549,349	22,903	816,284	481,882
1997	19,979,578	15,567,041	16,410	15,583,451	1,772,428	-167,107	13,643,916	3,638,437	2,697,225	24,089	829,391	499,806
1998	21,794,858	17,146,024	-13,911	17,132,113	1,913,769	-194,511	15,023,833	4,034,867	2,736,158	25,852	843,057	523,148
1999	22,435,302	17,580,842	7,294	17,588,136	1,948,957	-175,865	15,463,314	4,106,134	2,865,854	26,251	854,631	522,585
2000	24,629,382	19,152,422	121	19,152,543	2,060,589	-205,087	16,886,867	4,725,272	3,017,243	28,598	861,237	533,329
2001	26,832,125	21,254,477	5,015	21,259,492	2,224,219	-191,642	18,843,631	4,689,521	3,298,973	30,927	867,602	540,976
2002	27,075,353	21,361,563	29,248	21,390,811	2,253,661	-255,820	18,881,330	4,663,043	3,530,980	30,949	874,844	533,764
2003	27,369,426	21,437,433	761	21,438,194	2,240,243	-214,899	18,983,052	4,654,172	3,732,202	31,187	877,577	519,765
2004	28,817,879	22,558,361	38,223	22,596,584	2,380,855	-288,091	19,927,638	4,926,346	3,963,895	32,822	878,004	523,740
2005	31,607,023	24,615,160	54,926	24,670,086	2,551,992	-392,641	21,725,453	5,581,363	4,300,207	35,801	882,861	538,911
2006	35,010,513	26,856,352	25,596	26,881,948	2,732,336	-458,734	23,690,878	6,610,325	4,709,310	39,161	894,011	557,293
2007	36,111,725	26,748,039	31,217	26,779,256	2,856,915	-381,199	23,541,142	7,495,202	5,075,381	39,839	906,441	572,692
2008	40,467,586	30,151,830	15,351	30,167,181	2,980,875	-377,218	26,809,088	7,930,843	5,727,655	44,153	916,525	582,477
2009	36,332,434	26,567,073	-1,601	26,565,472	2,872,565	-261,163	23,431,744	6,760,166	6,140,524	39,075	929,824	564,391
2010	37,819,078	27,624,225	23,053	27,647,278	2,877,450	-125,771	24,644,057	6,562,720	6,612,301	40,239	939,858	553,200
2011	41,919,304	30,514,121	46,083	30,560,204	2,788,414	-125,131	27,646,659	7,582,309	6,690,336	44,316	945,927	558,844
2012	45,826,879	33,073,095	84,086	33,157,181	2,980,456	-109,863	30,066,862	8,907,272	6,852,745	48,095	952,836	572,952
2013	46,059,145	33,966,231	113,206	34,079,437	3,444,206	-108,974	30,526,257	8,562,313	6,970,575	47,857	962,424	581,467
2014	48,274,434	35,670,400	153,128	35,823,528	3,522,559	-139,660	32,161,309	8,879,782	7,233,343	49,807	969,224	592,340

Personal Income and Employment by Area: Tuscaloosa, AL

(Thousands of dollars, except as noted.)

Year	Personal income, total	Earnings by place of work			Less: Contributions for government social insurance	Plus: Adjustment for residence	Equals: Net earnings by place of residence	Plus: Dividends, interest, and rent	Plus: Personal current transfer receipts	Per capita personal income (dollars)	Population (persons)	Total employment
		Nonfarm	Farm	Total								
1970	419,170	329,040	8,305	337,345	24,241	5,495	318,599	49,342	51,229	2,748	152,542	57,595
1971	475,544	371,486	11,259	382,745	28,071	6,082	360,756	56,360	58,428	3,057	155,545	59,464
1972	530,055	416,153	12,425	428,578	33,056	6,921	402,443	62,759	64,853	3,339	158,760	62,219
1973	593,160	466,005	17,845	483,850	42,654	8,615	449,811	69,942	73,407	3,685	160,974	64,792
1974	665,605	523,479	11,386	534,865	49,216	10,520	496,169	82,072	87,364	4,077	163,262	65,272
1975	749,515	569,913	12,707	582,620	53,314	12,136	541,442	95,593	112,480	4,561	164,319	64,783
1976	820,160	631,057	12,343	643,400	60,378	13,217	596,239	102,619	121,302	4,925	166,525	66,406
1977	933,328	734,652	9,710	744,362	68,854	13,580	689,088	114,926	129,314	5,543	168,371	68,549
1978	1,045,356	811,636	16,161	827,797	76,533	18,009	769,273	133,570	142,513	6,081	171,898	68,430
1979	1,160,283	894,708	15,288	909,996	87,175	20,614	843,435	153,534	163,314	6,694	173,338	69,758
1980	1,240,349	931,712	2,427	934,139	93,719	20,419	860,839	185,567	193,943	7,088	174,982	69,209
1981	1,385,826	1,013,140	7,528	1,020,668	110,457	27,868	938,079	227,723	220,024	7,870	176,099	69,349
1982	1,482,065	1,068,871	3,663	1,072,534	119,558	24,963	977,939	259,925	244,201	8,486	174,646	68,387
1983	1,591,825	1,138,461	-850	1,137,611	126,420	34,623	1,045,814	279,686	266,325	9,089	175,147	68,723
1984	1,765,834	1,269,273	8,273	1,277,546	142,479	33,052	1,168,119	314,694	283,021	10,037	175,924	71,003
1985	1,918,145	1,371,406	11,303	1,382,709	153,836	33,883	1,262,756	347,022	308,367	10,775	178,012	72,404
1986	2,011,854	1,434,779	14,355	1,449,134	162,051	39,325	1,326,408	361,687	323,759	11,155	180,361	75,044
1987	2,168,117	1,577,683	14,976	1,592,659	173,297	47,243	1,466,605	371,245	330,267	11,881	182,481	78,163
1988	2,307,553	1,669,674	21,864	1,691,538	193,322	61,661	1,559,877	402,738	344,938	12,558	183,746	81,570
1989	2,563,862	1,800,898	22,661	1,823,559	207,101	69,737	1,686,195	482,309	395,358	13,839	185,270	83,909
1990	2,792,855	1,987,837	27,036	2,014,873	230,606	66,682	1,850,949	497,299	444,607	14,910	187,311	87,832
1991	2,928,211	2,071,597	33,430	2,105,027	240,550	67,734	1,932,211	508,006	487,994	15,412	189,990	87,718
1992	3,161,465	2,209,954	36,488	2,246,442	251,662	84,367	2,079,147	520,281	562,037	16,571	190,785	88,695
1993	3,344,429	2,359,862	38,419	2,398,281	271,523	79,747	2,206,505	539,895	598,029	17,367	192,574	92,593
1994	3,557,071	2,500,703	28,915	2,529,618	289,967	77,491	2,317,142	592,626	647,303	18,310	194,272	94,585
1995	3,769,494	2,631,689	21,336	2,653,025	306,908	70,148	2,416,265	656,107	697,122	19,079	197,577	96,915
1996	3,903,991	2,719,745	27,038	2,746,783	316,023	66,986	2,497,746	673,391	732,854	19,722	197,955	99,421
1997	4,120,865	2,889,195	32,316	2,921,511	336,479	52,015	2,637,047	711,119	772,699	20,632	199,727	102,688
1998	4,409,944	3,112,236	46,318	3,158,554	355,764	46,799	2,849,589	779,483	780,872	21,907	201,299	104,871
1999	4,662,514	3,341,854	66,118	3,407,972	377,914	33,413	3,063,471	774,960	824,083	23,033	202,429	105,800
2000	4,858,016	3,439,924	45,036	3,484,960	387,532	29,473	3,126,901	850,721	880,394	23,757	204,489	106,557
2001	5,125,969	3,711,311	54,419	3,765,730	411,041	14,397	3,369,086	847,676	909,207	24,921	205,692	107,147
2002	5,214,021	3,777,110	44,212	3,821,322	423,336	-11,022	3,386,964	849,079	977,978	25,266	206,365	108,033
2003	5,416,879	3,908,716	60,738	3,969,454	437,400	-36,577	3,495,477	903,687	1,017,715	26,122	207,368	108,403
2004	5,710,397	4,162,461	75,158	4,237,619	459,987	-59,190	3,718,442	917,285	1,074,670	27,309	209,105	111,566
2005	6,170,671	4,529,705	75,369	4,605,074	503,540	-93,036	4,008,498	1,013,305	1,148,868	29,032	212,545	115,305
2006	6,585,083	4,880,541	50,545	4,931,086	541,474	-131,119	4,258,493	1,106,703	1,219,887	30,215	217,938	120,157
2007	6,945,958	5,043,470	44,430	5,087,900	567,503	-160,382	4,360,015	1,239,137	1,346,806	31,464	220,757	123,501
2008	7,264,412	5,183,852	47,524	5,231,376	591,391	-196,320	4,443,665	1,317,662	1,503,085	32,386	224,304	122,819
2009	7,234,438	5,052,896	58,314	5,111,210	576,045	-240,534	4,294,631	1,295,458	1,644,349	31,642	228,631	117,899
2010	7,438,091	5,260,197	51,767	5,311,964	607,346	-308,999	4,395,619	1,256,329	1,786,143	32,271	230,489	117,650
2011	7,647,645	5,468,642	37,130	5,505,772	560,293	-324,380	4,621,099	1,232,839	1,793,707	33,049	231,400	119,639
2012	7,882,342	5,605,739	50,734	5,656,473	575,446	-329,577	4,751,450	1,369,115	1,761,777	33,775	233,377	121,461
2013	7,997,961	5,683,003	115,809	5,798,812	666,941	-297,014	4,834,857	1,361,023	1,802,081	33,971	235,438	123,221
2014	8,321,280	5,985,063	86,003	6,071,066	693,383	-341,244	5,036,439	1,407,316	1,877,525	34,999	237,761	126,876

Personal Income and Employment by Area: Tyler, TX

(Thousands of dollars, except as noted.)

Year	Personal income, total	Derivation of personal income					Equals: Net earnings by place of residence	Plus: Dividends, interest, and rent	Plus: Personal current transfer receipts	Per capita personal income (dollars)	Population (persons)	Total employment
		Earnings by place of work			Less: Contributions for government social insurance	Plus: Adjustment for residence						
		Nonfarm	Farm	Total								
1970	349,873	290,650	2,119	292,769	19,129	-11,077	262,563	55,281	32,029	3,592	97,390	46,609
1971	384,674	317,373	3,785	321,158	21,431	-11,863	287,864	60,279	36,531	3,853	99,839	47,754
1972	436,670	367,561	3,343	370,904	26,074	-15,358	329,472	66,454	40,744	4,207	103,794	51,083
1973	498,615	415,580	8,045	423,625	34,373	-17,538	371,714	77,631	49,270	4,715	105,758	53,832
1974	568,403	464,838	8,027	472,865	39,172	-19,193	414,500	93,854	60,049	5,226	108,766	54,925
1975	634,233	507,188	3,205	510,393	41,468	-19,675	449,250	108,166	76,817	5,680	111,662	55,398
1976	729,177	590,214	7,480	597,694	48,693	-21,937	527,064	118,548	83,565	6,382	114,264	57,952
1977	836,670	695,627	5,332	700,959	57,449	-29,081	614,429	133,901	88,340	7,143	117,127	62,480
1978	970,017	811,448	3,889	815,337	68,508	-34,536	712,293	158,734	98,990	8,039	120,667	66,707
1979	1,124,115	937,047	10,433	947,480	83,063	-41,524	822,893	188,295	112,927	8,928	125,905	70,277
1980	1,280,881	1,028,753	10,260	1,039,013	91,630	-42,913	904,470	240,846	135,565	9,905	129,316	71,788
1981	1,492,786	1,178,956	11,480	1,190,436	113,283	-47,623	1,029,530	311,668	151,588	11,246	132,734	75,129
1982	1,694,584	1,303,686	17,550	1,321,236	128,982	-54,386	1,137,868	384,884	171,832	12,338	137,348	79,688
1983	1,838,335	1,411,812	23,739	1,435,551	139,100	-60,793	1,235,658	411,072	191,605	13,015	141,243	81,358
1984	2,019,110	1,568,128	21,554	1,589,682	160,465	-70,814	1,358,403	456,798	203,909	13,922	145,030	85,052
1985	2,130,259	1,629,731	8,798	1,638,529	169,055	-69,861	1,399,613	506,764	223,882	14,299	148,975	85,608
1986	2,201,743	1,657,663	18,574	1,676,237	170,825	-69,153	1,436,259	514,638	250,846	14,528	151,554	82,811
1987	2,221,417	1,657,925	18,204	1,676,129	168,973	-70,104	1,437,052	513,944	270,421	14,577	152,388	84,446
1988	2,318,623	1,708,805	12,720	1,721,525	179,711	-67,631	1,474,183	556,147	288,293	15,238	152,164	84,113
1989	2,454,755	1,766,072	16,008	1,782,080	187,530	-70,758	1,523,792	618,716	312,247	16,270	150,876	84,412
1990	2,594,818	1,878,079	14,867	1,892,946	195,391	-73,294	1,624,261	621,851	348,706	17,122	151,550	85,724
1991	2,700,511	1,972,352	12,758	1,985,110	211,497	-86,152	1,687,461	631,537	381,513	17,569	153,705	87,981
1992	2,874,379	2,133,462	13,160	2,146,622	225,166	-99,839	1,821,617	611,954	440,808	18,504	155,336	88,955
1993	3,034,674	2,277,443	14,024	2,291,467	240,888	-116,022	1,934,557	630,554	469,563	19,120	158,717	91,518
1994	3,182,734	2,383,109	13,799	2,396,908	254,152	-125,892	2,016,864	665,168	500,702	19,781	160,898	94,519
1995	3,402,375	2,512,126	14,219	2,526,345	267,755	-134,525	2,124,065	737,296	541,014	20,817	163,440	97,351
1996	3,622,652	2,697,871	12,463	2,710,334	283,333	-148,281	2,278,720	756,069	587,863	21,812	166,087	99,975
1997	3,887,131	2,964,967	22,403	2,987,370	305,022	-167,009	2,515,339	753,526	618,266	23,065	168,531	104,160
1998	4,203,679	3,220,604	27,999	3,248,603	328,064	-194,521	2,726,018	835,041	642,620	24,578	171,033	105,992
1999	4,373,976	3,407,505	34,137	3,441,642	342,937	-215,200	2,883,505	834,351	656,120	25,319	172,758	107,123
2000	4,807,792	3,761,445	28,595	3,790,040	364,907	-242,850	3,182,283	926,920	698,589	27,370	175,658	110,526
2001	4,931,102	3,870,310	35,625	3,905,935	383,025	-248,410	3,274,500	892,092	764,510	27,728	177,836	110,615
2002	5,048,885	3,962,603	38,094	4,000,697	394,680	-252,994	3,353,023	864,331	831,531	27,878	181,107	111,382
2003	5,337,054	4,166,224	33,709	4,199,933	421,578	-259,738	3,518,617	913,928	904,509	28,966	184,254	113,959
2004	5,619,879	4,461,343	30,892	4,492,235	454,039	-272,090	3,766,106	905,124	948,649	30,005	187,300	117,429
2005	6,143,053	4,744,418	32,900	4,777,318	479,881	-280,197	4,017,240	1,081,042	1,044,771	32,102	191,362	121,590
2006	6,565,866	5,065,279	25,897	5,091,176	500,683	-286,690	4,303,803	1,145,616	1,116,447	33,478	196,124	124,641
2007	6,853,994	5,162,704	20,810	5,183,514	522,325	-285,646	4,375,543	1,254,949	1,223,502	34,278	199,953	128,075
2008	7,953,572	5,963,860	10,794	5,974,654	564,923	-289,869	5,119,862	1,456,103	1,377,607	39,129	203,263	131,270
2009	7,313,877	5,373,046	14,885	5,387,931	553,136	-286,513	4,548,282	1,269,452	1,496,143	35,314	207,111	128,656
2010	7,802,348	5,723,291	18,094	5,741,385	577,928	-287,135	4,876,322	1,306,195	1,619,831	37,074	210,455	128,979
2011	8,429,406	6,138,511	16,560	6,155,071	531,762	-270,901	5,352,408	1,402,624	1,674,374	39,618	212,765	130,974
2012	8,841,073	6,424,884	23,657	6,448,541	550,122	-262,936	5,635,483	1,534,485	1,671,105	41,133	214,941	133,398
2013	9,021,524	6,620,268	32,113	6,652,381	639,627	-275,731	5,737,023	1,532,353	1,752,148	41,637	216,670	136,405
2014	9,464,715	6,975,338	29,958	7,005,296	668,656	-290,680	6,045,960	1,589,499	1,829,256	43,249	218,842	139,114

Personal Income and Employment by Area: Urban Honolulu, HI

(Thousands of dollars, except as noted.)

Year	Personal income, total	Earnings by place of work			Less: Contributions for government social insurance	Plus: Adjustment for residence	Equals: Net earnings by place of residence	Plus: Dividends, interest, and rent	Plus: Personal current transfer receipts	Per capita personal income (dollars)	Population (persons)	Total employment
		Nonfarm	Farm	Total								
1970	3,638,544	2,961,804	33,864	2,995,668	183,236	4,750	2,817,182	661,060	160,302	5,833	623,756	366,968
1971	3,930,462	3,158,221	32,321	3,190,542	203,001	5,059	2,992,600	727,549	210,313	6,209	633,043	367,494
1972	4,332,294	3,485,411	32,143	3,517,554	236,141	4,641	3,286,054	796,892	249,348	6,516	664,830	381,276
1973	4,792,871	3,875,375	31,032	3,906,407	300,444	4,430	3,610,393	901,611	280,867	7,009	683,772	398,757
1974	5,278,618	4,223,131	39,362	4,262,493	343,985	4,350	3,922,858	1,023,209	332,551	7,562	698,033	407,738
1975	5,834,941	4,622,999	40,096	4,663,095	380,298	6,349	4,289,146	1,112,995	432,800	8,243	707,866	415,990
1976	6,279,933	4,976,847	41,097	5,017,944	413,473	6,519	4,610,990	1,160,097	508,846	8,760	716,911	417,620
1977	6,764,711	5,362,073	47,097	5,409,170	442,424	6,396	4,973,142	1,256,320	535,249	9,204	734,962	418,536
1978	7,504,034	5,930,071	40,954	5,971,025	502,998	5,119	5,473,146	1,459,716	571,172	10,134	740,505	431,484
1979	8,379,001	6,651,101	43,531	6,694,632	589,044	4,681	6,110,269	1,639,676	629,056	11,121	753,428	454,142
1980	9,404,699	7,382,661	63,826	7,446,487	653,607	5,005	6,797,885	1,888,427	718,387	12,313	763,820	467,461
1981	10,281,065	7,957,410	45,816	8,003,226	750,841	4,990	7,257,375	2,183,000	840,690	13,394	767,573	461,302
1982	10,824,165	8,448,679	50,452	8,499,131	787,253	4,625	7,716,503	2,203,060	904,602	13,947	776,075	457,679
1983	11,836,096	9,072,195	72,563	9,144,758	865,649	4,662	8,283,771	2,562,508	989,817	15,000	789,097	463,241
1984	12,743,137	9,720,883	51,884	9,772,767	946,084	3,625	8,830,308	2,864,495	1,048,334	15,973	797,791	467,189
1985	13,551,931	10,357,834	55,720	10,413,554	1,027,509	4,991	9,391,036	3,053,095	1,107,800	16,849	804,294	477,011
1986	14,307,395	11,036,434	59,639	11,096,073	1,119,586	5,661	9,982,148	3,176,946	1,148,301	17,654	810,444	486,861
1987	15,231,897	11,927,035	58,526	11,985,561	1,220,266	6,038	10,771,333	3,271,317	1,189,247	18,611	818,447	509,161
1988	16,640,304	13,165,286	75,279	13,240,565	1,393,149	6,236	11,853,652	3,511,728	1,274,924	20,193	824,072	525,017
1989	18,424,698	14,459,143	68,648	14,527,791	1,530,995	10,515	13,007,311	4,004,541	1,412,846	22,163	831,337	540,855
1990	20,002,934	15,952,555	76,424	16,028,979	1,760,671	12,396	14,280,704	4,197,019	1,525,211	23,855	838,534	558,346
1991	21,057,382	16,865,285	67,200	16,932,485	1,883,628	10,661	15,059,518	4,334,762	1,663,102	24,759	850,510	569,711
1992	22,662,997	18,055,894	52,140	18,108,034	2,010,281	6,762	16,104,515	4,681,375	1,877,107	26,232	863,959	570,015
1993	23,387,806	18,399,803	76,253	18,476,056	2,044,634	5,578	16,437,000	4,882,627	2,068,179	26,872	870,348	566,606
1994	23,828,975	18,486,169	64,023	18,550,192	2,070,314	1,803	16,481,681	5,105,049	2,242,245	27,122	878,591	560,810
1995	24,281,165	18,427,094	71,016	18,498,110	2,060,577	-2,171	16,435,362	5,316,198	2,529,605	27,548	881,399	556,670
1996	24,204,197	18,356,530	66,664	18,423,194	2,055,206	-4,008	16,363,980	5,255,764	2,584,453	27,398	883,443	553,469
1997	25,019,377	18,877,908	66,597	18,944,505	2,085,665	-7,094	16,851,746	5,554,286	2,613,345	28,216	886,711	550,825
1998	25,225,736	18,929,228	72,154	19,001,382	2,108,859	-9,085	16,883,438	5,700,256	2,642,042	28,442	886,909	551,302
1999	25,816,006	19,327,007	90,522	19,417,529	2,144,373	-9,361	17,263,795	5,806,939	2,745,272	29,373	878,906	545,759
2000	27,146,382	20,342,949	83,727	20,426,676	2,249,693	-11,548	18,165,435	6,063,265	2,917,682	30,967	876,629	555,034
2001	27,961,960	21,116,525	78,931	21,195,456	2,370,256	-19,032	18,806,168	6,002,201	3,153,591	31,676	882,755	553,779
2002	29,153,052	22,338,809	86,883	22,425,692	2,518,548	-18,411	19,888,733	5,872,285	3,392,034	32,739	890,473	555,532
2003	30,513,893	23,773,739	89,283	23,863,022	2,702,508	-17,600	21,142,914	5,877,997	3,492,982	34,120	894,311	566,559
2004	32,841,336	25,518,502	75,109	25,593,611	2,839,339	-16,706	22,737,566	6,399,815	3,703,955	36,169	907,997	581,589
2005	34,968,191	27,052,466	68,673	27,121,139	3,020,373	-15,506	24,085,260	6,905,451	3,977,480	38,084	918,181	594,708
2006	37,484,293	28,600,680	66,073	28,666,753	3,238,726	-13,780	25,414,247	7,874,344	4,195,702	40,438	926,954	609,505
2007	39,637,385	29,805,603	53,651	29,859,254	3,378,250	-11,805	26,469,199	8,584,829	4,583,357	42,836	925,335	623,361
2008	41,729,138	30,834,955	48,511	30,883,466	3,468,733	-9,352	27,405,381	9,006,994	5,316,763	44,693	933,680	621,799
2009	42,131,389	30,718,210	47,898	30,766,108	3,468,360	-12,846	27,284,902	9,222,747	5,623,740	44,670	943,177	607,546
2010	43,178,434	31,554,042	49,837	31,603,879	3,667,421	-12,921	27,923,537	8,968,498	6,286,399	45,150	956,336	603,263
2011	45,060,846	33,020,655	52,834	33,073,489	3,501,889	-18,807	29,552,793	8,971,841	6,536,212	46,620	966,559	612,366
2012	47,044,902	34,521,474	71,576	34,593,050	3,617,838	-19,557	30,955,655	9,626,631	6,462,616	48,165	976,746	621,904
2013	47,255,799	35,053,928	79,078	35,133,006	4,187,941	-20,886	30,924,179	9,653,723	6,677,897	47,877	987,019	633,837
2014	49,313,300	36,257,935	85,889	36,343,824	4,200,723	-22,589	32,120,512	10,130,145	7,062,643	49,722	991,788	642,271

Personal Income and Employment by Area: Utica-Rome, NY

(Thousands of dollars, except as noted.)

Year	Personal income, total	Derivation of personal income					Equals: Net earnings by place of residence	Plus: Dividends, interest, and rent	Plus: Personal current transfer receipts	Per capita personal income (dollars)	Population (persons)	Total employment
		Earnings by place of work			Less: Contributions for government social insurance	Plus: Adjustment for residence						
		Nonfarm	Farm	Total								
1970	1,327,270	1,067,293	20,517	1,087,810	77,266	-17,327	993,217	193,977	140,076	3,889	341,324	144,349
1971	1,416,594	1,118,014	20,540	1,138,554	83,159	-14,280	1,041,115	207,800	167,679	4,118	343,966	142,378
1972	1,497,124	1,173,939	19,851	1,193,790	91,493	-11,878	1,090,419	220,871	185,834	4,349	344,262	140,209
1973	1,617,026	1,271,291	22,213	1,293,504	113,937	-10,580	1,168,987	241,624	206,415	4,773	338,821	143,694
1974	1,734,789	1,342,526	18,273	1,360,799	124,340	-7,815	1,228,644	268,948	237,197	5,181	334,835	143,415
1975	1,879,111	1,396,364	14,400	1,410,764	127,841	-6,428	1,276,495	293,962	308,654	5,641	333,120	138,881
1976	1,989,323	1,480,500	16,023	1,496,523	138,815	-4,478	1,353,230	310,274	325,819	6,030	329,897	137,590
1977	2,116,642	1,571,772	10,130	1,581,902	147,764	-791	1,433,347	341,682	341,613	6,474	326,942	137,404
1978	2,300,620	1,728,857	14,066	1,742,923	166,510	854	1,577,267	366,614	356,739	7,067	325,540	141,015
1979	2,512,034	1,880,002	18,552	1,898,554	187,576	4,754	1,715,732	409,481	386,821	7,761	323,689	143,203
1980	2,797,224	2,027,903	18,482	2,046,385	201,409	7,986	1,852,962	494,404	449,858	8,735	320,223	142,202
1981	3,093,049	2,190,097	18,208	2,208,305	230,838	9,654	1,987,121	593,058	512,870	9,672	319,790	141,590
1982	3,359,214	2,314,259	18,059	2,332,318	243,903	9,520	2,097,935	681,341	579,938	10,505	319,788	140,336
1983	3,554,659	2,439,928	14,724	2,454,652	259,401	11,457	2,206,708	720,272	627,679	11,096	320,361	139,924
1984	3,914,849	2,710,248	19,088	2,729,336	294,788	8,676	2,443,224	818,847	652,778	12,230	320,097	144,968
1985	4,111,988	2,846,041	24,378	2,870,419	315,513	10,713	2,565,619	855,898	690,471	12,875	319,368	145,991
1986	4,305,926	2,988,283	29,378	3,017,661	336,839	9,698	2,690,520	888,103	727,303	13,586	316,950	148,023
1987	4,497,629	3,164,072	32,302	3,196,374	351,925	8,365	2,852,814	904,476	740,339	14,224	316,211	147,894
1988	4,781,164	3,425,545	25,449	3,450,994	389,858	5,072	3,066,208	928,211	786,745	15,162	315,341	152,786
1989	5,147,892	3,596,475	34,895	3,631,370	407,576	3,875	3,227,669	1,081,021	839,202	16,286	316,088	154,516
1990	5,422,819	3,806,820	35,831	3,842,651	414,062	1,343	3,429,932	1,088,724	904,163	17,103	317,074	156,491
1991	5,541,774	3,860,292	25,501	3,885,793	431,328	7,668	3,462,133	1,088,513	991,128	17,350	319,408	153,350
1992	5,872,325	4,090,050	32,105	4,122,155	449,332	6,332	3,679,155	1,081,743	1,111,427	18,327	320,421	154,175
1993	6,015,940	4,185,289	31,784	4,217,073	464,491	8,847	3,761,429	1,095,382	1,159,129	18,823	319,608	154,382
1994	6,157,424	4,276,209	31,234	4,307,443	481,799	9,781	3,835,425	1,099,749	1,222,250	19,363	318,002	156,706
1995	6,258,597	4,284,970	22,195	4,307,165	486,687	17,679	3,838,157	1,136,578	1,283,862	20,095	311,447	154,290
1996	6,312,231	4,285,094	37,531	4,322,625	480,426	22,792	3,864,991	1,137,377	1,309,863	20,648	305,700	151,768
1997	6,539,902	4,472,240	15,591	4,487,831	494,000	22,846	4,016,677	1,193,726	1,329,499	21,607	302,681	151,824
1998	6,778,236	4,597,122	35,434	4,632,556	504,407	24,728	4,152,877	1,190,124	1,435,235	22,548	300,619	153,376
1999	7,052,827	4,910,795	40,684	4,951,479	526,127	26,339	4,451,691	1,162,210	1,438,926	23,519	299,874	157,676
2000	7,337,924	5,141,023	36,270	5,177,293	553,118	22,655	4,646,830	1,200,337	1,490,757	24,493	299,597	160,325
2001	7,528,018	5,212,975	60,450	5,273,425	577,548	31,255	4,727,132	1,200,286	1,600,600	25,218	298,521	157,601
2002	7,534,540	5,324,276	44,138	5,368,414	598,249	27,890	4,798,055	1,037,287	1,699,198	25,280	298,049	157,027
2003	7,785,651	5,509,104	50,475	5,559,579	645,960	20,218	4,961,935	1,041,143	1,782,573	26,098	298,323	157,365
2004	8,230,746	5,772,938	61,310	5,834,248	645,960	20,848	5,209,136	1,129,835	1,891,775	27,529	298,986	158,422
2005	8,510,374	5,960,503	61,580	6,022,083	672,882	32,206	5,381,407	1,164,462	1,964,505	28,503	298,574	159,132
2006	8,830,854	6,255,219	47,195	6,302,414	702,072	27,904	5,628,246	1,138,357	2,064,251	29,608	298,258	160,137
2007	9,310,827	6,541,293	43,270	6,584,563	730,174	24,185	5,878,574	1,282,663	2,149,590	31,158	298,831	161,567
2008	9,923,506	6,785,301	40,686	6,825,987	760,632	36,646	6,102,001	1,425,039	2,396,466	33,202	298,886	161,770
2009	10,117,241	6,861,879	19,538	6,881,417	761,472	31,520	6,151,465	1,342,564	2,623,212	33,837	299,000	159,049
2010	10,466,897	7,070,778	40,213	7,110,991	789,495	35,323	6,356,819	1,313,159	2,796,919	34,971	299,301	158,554
2011	10,818,680	7,148,073	61,827	7,209,900	724,210	40,078	6,525,768	1,444,109	2,848,803	36,202	298,846	157,044
2012	11,111,778	7,283,105	54,812	7,337,917	730,794	45,108	6,652,231	1,608,234	2,851,313	37,219	298,553	155,865
2013	11,114,844	7,382,195	75,929	7,458,124	836,537	47,563	6,669,150	1,552,744	2,892,950	37,292	298,047	155,379
2014	11,251,064	7,418,046	83,213	7,501,259	844,314	66,180	6,723,125	1,595,589	2,932,350	37,932	296,615	155,432

Personal Income and Employment by Area: Valdosta, GA

(Thousands of dollars, except as noted.)

Year	Personal income, total	Earnings by place of work			Less: Contributions for government social insurance	Plus: Adjustment for residence	Equals: Net earnings by place of residence	Plus: Dividends, interest, and rent	Plus: Personal current transfer receipts	Per capita personal income (dollars)	Population (persons)	Total employment
		Nonfarm	Farm	Total								
1970	244,560	180,003	19,547	199,550	11,387	-1,290	186,873	34,568	23,119	3,203	76,347	33,764
1971	271,155	198,388	21,745	220,133	13,112	-1,304	205,717	37,681	27,757	3,420	79,276	34,576
1972	304,159	224,525	23,089	247,614	15,309	-1,032	231,273	41,867	31,019	3,702	82,156	35,735
1973	334,961	244,838	27,018	271,856	18,758	-536	252,562	47,414	34,985	3,995	83,842	36,556
1974	373,293	263,869	32,732	296,601	21,127	-193	275,281	53,583	44,429	4,371	85,407	36,861
1975	388,314	268,610	25,892	294,502	21,582	731	273,651	59,773	54,890	4,541	85,511	35,575
1976	433,727	311,079	22,508	333,587	25,533	701	308,755	65,190	59,782	4,987	86,971	37,112
1977	462,363	346,151	6,920	353,071	28,215	1,557	326,413	73,075	62,875	5,214	88,679	38,149
1978	541,218	398,048	19,856	417,904	32,940	1,979	386,943	86,011	68,264	6,116	88,498	39,447
1979	597,713	441,356	16,711	458,067	38,008	2,056	422,115	96,663	78,935	6,606	90,486	40,040
1980	639,913	465,290	7,118	472,408	40,379	2,511	434,540	111,514	93,859	7,001	91,402	39,351
1981	726,237	511,163	16,829	527,992	47,574	1,698	482,116	133,198	110,923	7,883	92,131	40,149
1982	796,725	547,937	28,295	576,232	51,781	388	524,839	155,256	116,630	8,583	92,821	40,795
1983	849,107	594,514	15,095	609,609	56,949	1,016	553,676	168,940	126,491	9,007	94,274	42,007
1984	943,353	658,124	25,259	683,383	64,715	2,241	620,909	184,346	138,098	9,880	95,477	43,709
1985	1,014,451	711,942	25,615	737,557	71,622	1,616	667,551	198,231	148,669	10,553	96,133	44,826
1986	1,061,290	752,930	19,569	772,499	77,044	2,046	697,501	205,098	158,691	10,935	97,055	45,440
1987	1,143,708	800,581	32,496	833,077	81,333	4,837	756,581	217,642	169,485	11,687	97,863	46,586
1988	1,237,750	874,248	36,353	910,601	92,508	4,040	822,133	233,976	181,641	12,664	97,741	48,109
1989	1,350,852	946,851	37,295	984,146	100,862	-1,807	881,477	267,638	201,737	13,710	98,530	49,838
1990	1,417,613	990,478	37,252	1,027,730	106,270	-3,939	917,521	276,800	223,292	14,219	99,699	50,334
1991	1,504,091	1,040,773	45,082	1,085,855	113,104	-7,764	964,987	284,002	255,102	14,848	101,299	50,477
1992	1,615,667	1,120,501	48,259	1,168,760	120,950	-8,315	1,039,495	294,815	281,357	15,698	102,922	51,055
1993	1,710,199	1,189,893	40,102	1,229,995	129,101	-9,375	1,091,519	320,633	298,047	16,002	106,877	53,803
1994	1,835,175	1,262,381	52,868	1,315,249	137,631	-8,487	1,169,131	345,429	320,615	16,795	109,267	54,857
1995	1,997,565	1,371,235	59,701	1,430,936	147,906	-8,916	1,274,114	382,193	341,258	17,935	111,381	57,874
1996	2,105,967	1,457,771	49,757	1,507,528	155,630	-9,592	1,342,306	406,876	356,785	18,552	113,514	59,607
1997	2,232,633	1,556,680	49,694	1,606,374	164,051	-11,559	1,430,764	436,223	365,646	19,346	115,406	60,998
1998	2,372,074	1,681,451	37,091	1,718,542	174,843	-13,606	1,530,093	463,235	378,746	20,293	116,892	62,413
1999	2,477,038	1,752,373	55,911	1,808,284	180,901	-13,032	1,614,351	457,020	405,667	20,890	118,574	63,239
2000	2,595,128	1,799,640	57,645	1,857,285	185,131	-14,925	1,657,229	502,984	434,915	21,675	119,729	63,876
2001	2,714,581	1,874,277	56,674	1,930,951	193,638	-22,233	1,715,080	529,391	470,110	22,671	119,736	64,073
2002	2,856,821	2,014,134	46,205	2,060,339	208,619	-38,554	1,813,166	510,994	532,661	23,551	121,305	65,853
2003	2,989,548	2,147,336	68,847	2,216,183	219,047	-57,039	1,940,097	516,889	532,562	24,535	121,850	67,595
2004	3,142,205	2,266,957	55,286	2,322,243	238,535	-60,760	2,022,948	541,264	577,993	25,262	124,387	69,908
2005	3,306,959	2,379,077	65,519	2,444,596	249,869	-63,794	2,130,933	556,510	619,516	26,160	126,411	71,897
2006	3,475,200	2,516,180	51,180	2,567,360	267,126	-66,149	2,234,085	577,104	664,011	26,872	129,323	73,269
2007	3,682,832	2,613,202	49,398	2,662,600	272,758	-70,560	2,319,282	652,081	711,469	28,105	131,036	75,309
2008	4,006,186	2,803,689	64,962	2,868,651	301,092	-76,638	2,490,921	710,942	804,323	29,696	134,907	75,494
2009	4,048,542	2,783,940	55,763	2,839,703	299,516	-97,877	2,442,310	722,973	883,259	29,384	137,780	73,666
2010	4,169,869	2,800,303	47,847	2,848,150	305,583	-92,118	2,450,449	753,967	965,453	29,763	140,104	72,669
2011	4,408,105	2,832,256	61,984	2,894,240	276,327	-96,950	2,520,963	871,771	1,015,371	30,953	142,414	71,353
2012	4,396,258	2,921,938	57,186	2,979,124	286,278	-110,710	2,582,136	808,965	1,005,157	30,400	144,614	72,476
2013	4,435,058	2,988,804	79,279	3,068,083	325,551	-119,280	2,623,252	784,678	1,027,128	31,052	142,828	73,634
2014	4,582,510	3,105,705	49,749	3,155,454	336,850	-120,925	2,697,679	813,929	1,070,902	31,975	143,317	74,717

Personal Income and Employment by Area: Vallejo-Fairfield, CA

(Thousands of dollars, except as noted.)

Year	Personal income, total	Derivation of personal income									Per capita personal income (dollars)	Population (persons)	Total employment
		Earnings by place of work			Less: Contributions for government social insurance	Plus: Adjustment for residence	Equals: Net earnings by place of residence	Plus: Dividends, interest, and rent	Plus: Personal current transfer receipts				
		Nonfarm	Farm	Total									
1970	784,824	670,131	24,217	694,348	33,699	-113,595	547,054	169,931	67,839		4,530	173,238	77,595
1971	872,400	727,923	25,921	753,844	38,930	-108,247	606,667	187,697	78,036		4,888	178,481	77,695
1972	957,984	765,935	32,944	798,879	43,151	-84,089	671,639	202,299	84,046		5,285	181,259	76,710
1973	1,058,262	812,354	44,398	856,752	50,092	-63,930	742,730	221,567	93,965		5,776	183,223	77,022
1974	1,211,150	903,422	62,197	965,619	56,838	-57,653	851,128	247,182	112,840		6,462	187,439	80,026
1975	1,377,083	1,035,114	47,257	1,082,371	66,408	-60,662	955,301	282,524	139,258		7,190	191,535	83,585
1976	1,516,225	1,135,298	34,330	1,169,628	74,654	-40,010	1,054,964	304,480	156,781		7,659	197,971	85,184
1977	1,702,639	1,252,918	38,937	1,291,855	83,752	-13,390	1,194,713	335,729	172,197		8,317	204,713	87,746
1978	1,959,214	1,423,089	36,523	1,459,612	96,231	11,402	1,374,783	393,918	190,513		9,172	213,619	91,583
1979	2,202,848	1,535,380	41,130	1,576,510	111,923	81,200	1,545,787	438,457	218,604		9,814	224,455	94,584
1980	2,519,886	1,615,020	77,487	1,692,507	118,992	183,456	1,756,971	502,848	260,067		10,612	237,456	98,216
1981	2,833,024	1,799,961	41,290	1,841,251	143,035	234,997	1,933,213	590,314	309,497		11,516	246,003	100,008
1982	3,107,445	1,972,768	25,536	1,998,304	158,852	278,952	2,118,404	651,341	337,700		12,217	254,348	101,168
1983	3,431,845	2,178,096	21,415	2,199,511	186,043	332,605	2,346,073	727,438	358,334		13,180	260,386	103,847
1984	3,812,882	2,379,332	37,790	2,417,122	213,053	438,082	2,642,151	794,005	376,726		14,420	264,416	107,070
1985	4,237,501	2,632,504	42,855	2,675,359	243,147	525,457	2,957,669	863,629	416,203		15,600	271,634	111,397
1986	4,632,338	2,833,536	34,113	2,867,649	270,906	668,258	3,265,001	912,820	454,517		16,333	283,617	115,639
1987	5,016,060	3,011,768	50,884	3,062,652	293,172	819,644	3,589,124	945,813	481,123		16,898	296,835	119,521
1988	5,481,315	3,251,802	53,296	3,305,098	332,043	950,295	3,923,350	1,029,896	528,069		17,679	310,048	125,976
1989	6,083,261	3,523,182	67,131	3,590,313	365,651	1,101,332	4,325,994	1,171,745	585,522		18,656	326,074	131,381
1990	6,795,512	3,801,462	48,216	3,849,678	399,232	1,489,281	4,939,727	1,202,428	653,357		19,785	343,463	136,860
1991	7,053,274	3,893,114	49,734	3,942,848	417,750	1,594,138	5,119,236	1,200,500	733,538		19,919	354,104	137,031
1992	7,448,412	4,191,536	41,478	4,233,014	450,932	1,597,296	5,379,378	1,224,543	844,491		20,695	359,919	137,870
1993	7,722,611	4,346,332	44,964	4,391,296	470,239	1,642,922	5,563,979	1,279,511	879,121		21,201	364,251	139,183
1994	7,748,340	4,161,656	52,911	4,214,567	463,244	1,789,605	5,540,928	1,315,728	891,684		21,166	366,072	141,061
1995	7,960,286	4,165,852	29,342	4,195,194	456,158	1,876,674	5,615,710	1,402,327	942,249		21,785	365,395	139,996
1996	8,285,262	4,257,404	55,611	4,313,015	454,390	1,951,067	5,809,692	1,481,717	993,853		22,538	367,608	141,128
1997	8,819,284	4,496,445	36,132	4,532,577	471,813	2,212,255	6,273,019	1,543,339	1,002,926		23,715	371,881	143,144
1998	9,443,482	4,833,781	34,552	4,868,333	501,325	2,393,501	6,760,509	1,620,233	1,062,740		24,939	378,657	146,922
1999	10,112,033	5,256,880	46,821	5,303,701	543,637	2,551,931	7,311,995	1,652,347	1,147,691		26,085	387,657	153,224
2000	11,214,013	5,933,783	39,972	5,973,755	612,463	2,917,127	8,278,419	1,741,886	1,193,708		28,249	396,974	157,999
2001	12,106,001	6,416,488	47,542	6,464,030	696,750	3,184,764	8,952,044	1,836,590	1,317,367		29,950	404,209	162,871
2002	12,530,034	6,845,562	62,906	6,908,468	748,688	3,097,788	9,257,568	1,845,891	1,426,575		30,694	408,226	166,948
2003	13,137,899	7,304,842	63,352	7,368,194	812,986	3,076,438	9,631,646	1,975,337	1,530,916		32,168	408,409	171,013
2004	13,621,985	7,759,757	66,397	7,826,154	896,900	3,042,342	9,971,596	2,029,758	1,620,631		33,281	409,301	172,336
2005	14,020,230	8,089,449	80,368	8,169,817	942,075	2,956,399	10,184,141	2,088,861	1,747,228		34,348	408,181	174,067
2006	14,553,747	8,442,093	76,904	8,518,997	952,680	2,887,850	10,454,167	2,179,336	1,920,244		35,636	408,402	174,430
2007	15,036,560	8,691,827	95,159	8,786,986	949,967	2,809,781	10,646,800	2,353,884	2,035,876		36,832	408,243	174,634
2008	15,513,943	8,904,832	102,966	9,007,798	981,107	2,666,485	10,693,176	2,488,422	2,332,345		37,934	408,972	174,548
2009	15,100,467	8,966,449	88,512	9,054,961	999,708	2,099,877	10,155,130	2,342,716	2,602,621		36,804	410,290	170,055
2010	15,088,748	8,915,866	67,006	8,982,872	995,895	1,861,864	9,848,841	2,328,090	2,911,817		36,437	414,101	168,460
2011	15,774,619	9,092,359	82,164	9,174,523	924,545	2,018,627	10,268,605	2,556,723	2,949,291		37,834	416,945	166,135
2012	16,271,664	9,606,501	110,355	9,716,856	956,879	1,865,773	10,625,750	2,677,110	2,968,804		38,675	420,724	169,488
2013	17,080,201	10,099,436	110,935	10,210,371	1,119,432	1,976,346	11,067,285	2,887,239	3,125,677		40,168	425,219	174,243
2014	18,138,958	10,472,258	101,703	10,573,961	1,166,330	2,434,163	11,841,794	3,019,818	3,277,346		42,073	431,131	177,011

Personal Income and Employment by Area: Victoria, TX

(Thousands of dollars, except as noted.)

Year	Personal income, total	Earnings by place of work			Less: Contributions for government social insurance	Plus: Adjustment for residence	Equals: Net earnings by place of residence	Plus: Dividends, interest, and rent	Plus: Personal current transfer receipts	Per capita personal income (dollars)	Population (persons)	Total employment
		Nonfarm	Farm	Total								
1970	192,129	137,580	5,536	143,116	8,455	14,343	149,004	28,444	14,681	3,273	58,707	22,879
1971	212,118	154,758	2,694	157,452	9,867	15,910	163,495	31,662	16,961	3,556	59,656	24,144
1972	243,734	178,752	6,459	185,211	12,060	16,036	189,187	35,460	19,087	4,059	60,041	25,600
1973	271,267	194,225	10,068	204,293	15,270	18,307	207,330	40,474	23,463	4,406	61,570	26,406
1974	316,349	225,650	8,577	234,227	18,457	23,447	239,217	48,354	28,778	5,070	62,400	27,270
1975	368,600	264,775	6,762	271,537	21,345	27,135	277,327	55,487	35,786	5,756	64,032	28,572
1976	418,210	308,351	3,980	312,331	24,951	31,445	318,825	60,223	39,162	6,392	65,422	30,041
1977	466,171	347,900	-664	347,236	28,383	36,575	355,428	67,756	42,987	6,997	66,629	31,787
1978	547,217	414,648	-118	414,530	34,835	40,707	420,402	78,418	48,397	7,944	68,884	34,333
1979	641,044	472,466	10,476	482,942	41,645	53,229	494,526	91,153	55,365	8,938	71,718	35,474
1980	743,652	551,939	-5,627	546,312	49,406	61,356	558,262	118,823	66,567	9,969	74,599	37,678
1981	911,402	691,056	4,127	695,183	66,595	47,096	675,684	158,922	76,796	11,871	76,778	42,135
1982	997,512	731,498	-1,881	729,617	72,563	51,884	708,938	201,050	87,524	12,513	79,719	42,578
1983	998,030	702,812	-1,652	701,160	68,468	56,911	689,603	208,989	99,438	12,335	80,912	40,499
1984	1,073,580	749,900	-1,332	748,568	75,429	54,777	727,916	242,820	102,844	13,206	81,297	41,815
1985	1,125,159	772,572	-3,108	769,464	79,155	60,750	751,059	265,209	108,891	13,773	81,693	42,553
1986	1,105,076	725,916	-1,442	724,474	73,158	67,379	718,695	263,336	123,045	13,419	82,351	40,072
1987	1,101,980	712,117	1,204	713,321	70,983	67,810	710,148	260,830	131,002	13,586	81,112	40,743
1988	1,141,317	740,460	-1,215	739,245	76,486	70,421	733,180	270,988	137,149	14,236	80,171	40,664
1989	1,231,117	773,960	999	774,959	80,873	81,522	775,608	303,534	151,975	15,473	79,568	40,838
1990	1,349,990	839,317	3,144	842,461	85,927	93,098	849,632	335,305	165,053	16,758	80,560	41,598
1991	1,429,399	908,439	8,144	916,583	95,634	87,633	908,582	333,810	187,007	17,476	81,791	43,505
1992	1,535,468	955,642	5,790	961,432	99,325	105,546	967,653	348,570	219,245	18,432	83,304	43,216
1993	1,609,704	997,890	5,748	1,003,638	103,446	112,981	1,013,173	364,830	231,701	19,024	84,614	44,707
1994	1,661,398	1,064,402	11,512	1,075,914	111,089	116,810	1,081,635	328,085	251,678	19,341	85,899	45,882
1995	1,776,019	1,106,403	8,849	1,115,252	115,541	133,330	1,133,041	369,678	273,300	20,460	86,805	46,454
1996	1,885,611	1,178,980	-8,717	1,170,263	121,382	154,894	1,203,775	390,170	291,666	21,454	87,891	47,280
1997	1,967,089	1,254,913	1,174	1,256,087	128,314	131,585	1,259,358	403,734	303,997	22,195	88,626	48,767
1998	2,136,449	1,391,459	-8,938	1,382,521	138,865	146,459	1,390,115	439,542	306,792	23,737	90,004	49,735
1999	2,209,744	1,427,160	13,270	1,440,430	141,712	150,588	1,449,306	436,893	323,545	24,343	90,775	49,915
2000	2,408,709	1,600,884	5,873	1,606,757	153,947	161,258	1,614,068	455,341	339,300	26,486	90,944	51,226
2001	2,480,026	1,655,852	2,103	1,657,955	163,638	149,697	1,644,014	466,412	369,600	27,101	91,511	51,626
2002	2,496,970	1,696,829	2,593	1,699,422	167,514	132,496	1,664,404	433,971	398,595	27,252	91,624	51,584
2003	2,618,845	1,756,856	17,711	1,774,567	173,144	122,517	1,723,940	464,662	430,243	28,525	91,809	51,248
2004	2,740,445	1,872,326	19,845	1,892,171	182,403	111,668	1,821,436	467,714	451,295	29,856	91,789	51,813
2005	2,896,312	1,992,267	17,262	2,009,529	194,336	101,458	1,916,651	491,246	488,415	31,646	91,523	53,481
2006	3,129,509	2,212,993	13,341	2,226,334	209,883	92,704	2,109,155	500,119	520,235	34,147	91,649	54,982
2007	3,249,205	2,250,224	4,233	2,254,457	218,687	73,473	2,109,243	570,122	569,840	35,163	92,403	56,301
2008	3,495,529	2,465,650	-20,157	2,445,493	230,368	60,263	2,275,388	590,569	629,572	37,616	92,926	56,872
2009	3,303,599	2,276,230	-22,606	2,253,624	221,974	69,985	2,101,635	515,474	686,490	35,223	93,792	54,337
2010	3,466,187	2,375,194	-12,711	2,362,483	233,300	93,727	2,222,910	500,664	742,613	36,847	94,070	54,463
2011	3,793,071	2,590,530	-16,470	2,574,060	221,408	102,651	2,455,303	564,811	772,957	40,075	94,650	55,378
2012	4,189,202	2,859,452	-9,073	2,850,379	240,872	89,540	2,699,047	722,445	767,710	43,360	96,614	57,939
2013	4,337,950	3,014,978	-3,754	3,011,224	289,696	98,068	2,819,596	731,030	787,324	44,450	97,592	59,421
2014	4,622,795	3,204,068	4,240	3,208,308	306,872	134,636	3,036,072	758,983	827,740	46,870	98,630	60,792

Personal Income and Employment by Area: Vineland-Bridgeton, NJ

(Thousands of dollars, except as noted.)

Year	Personal income, total	Derivation of personal income									Per capita personal income (dollars)	Population (persons)	Total employment
		Earnings by place of work			Less: Contributions for government social insurance	Plus: Adjustment for residence	Equals: Net earnings by place of residence	Plus: Dividends, interest, and rent	Plus: Personal current transfer receipts			
		Nonfarm	Farm	Total									
1970	484,625	404,561	13,534	418,095	32,227	-7,104	378,764	53,429	52,432	3,962	122,309	58,153
1971	525,258	437,343	11,888	449,231	35,964	-9,802	403,465	59,156	62,637	4,143	126,773	58,260
1972	577,044	484,689	11,364	496,053	41,434	-15,068	439,551	65,534	71,959	4,472	129,031	60,730
1973	638,654	540,160	15,511	555,671	52,644	-19,512	483,515	74,712	80,427	4,885	130,746	62,667
1974	692,167	570,604	16,967	587,571	57,877	-22,113	507,581	85,102	99,484	5,192	133,306	61,865
1975	740,792	589,739	12,184	601,923	57,820	-27,673	516,430	91,329	133,033	5,514	134,350	58,858
1976	812,212	657,221	13,483	670,704	65,384	-34,208	571,112	97,132	143,968	6,000	135,359	60,950
1977	881,413	722,940	10,309	733,249	72,169	-37,968	623,112	108,119	150,182	6,520	135,184	61,741
1978	972,403	799,117	16,199	815,316	82,212	-37,203	695,901	116,579	159,923	7,224	134,615	62,802
1979	1,050,513	860,756	14,331	875,087	91,443	-40,031	743,613	127,233	179,667	7,842	133,966	63,029
1980	1,155,752	932,692	10,718	943,410	98,721	-49,077	795,612	155,147	204,993	8,684	133,088	64,876
1981	1,280,720	989,098	15,914	1,005,012	111,934	-40,558	852,520	190,867	237,333	9,577	133,726	63,534
1982	1,381,506	1,019,298	18,554	1,037,852	115,792	-22,003	900,057	219,391	262,058	10,349	133,494	61,162
1983	1,477,498	1,068,230	21,825	1,090,055	124,355	-13,482	952,218	242,844	282,436	11,151	132,497	61,559
1984	1,586,349	1,128,208	20,777	1,148,985	137,114	4,676	1,016,547	269,539	300,263	11,826	134,138	60,966
1985	1,689,442	1,197,565	22,782	1,220,347	145,205	17,203	1,092,345	288,082	309,015	12,507	135,083	61,704
1986	1,804,579	1,315,375	23,603	1,338,978	161,160	-4,816	1,173,002	307,192	324,385	13,298	135,700	63,622
1987	1,925,124	1,437,795	26,414	1,464,209	174,820	-19,081	1,270,308	319,569	335,247	14,156	135,995	65,766
1988	2,102,910	1,581,880	29,398	1,611,278	196,079	-14,643	1,400,556	342,992	359,362	15,398	136,569	67,638
1989	2,307,180	1,685,842	30,139	1,715,981	206,273	-15,024	1,494,684	420,621	391,875	16,733	137,881	68,023
1990	2,463,476	1,768,408	32,104	1,800,512	209,624	6,029	1,596,917	434,700	431,859	17,804	138,366	68,415
1991	2,541,997	1,800,725	33,009	1,833,734	217,962	-8,121	1,607,651	433,424	500,922	18,092	140,503	66,700
1992	2,728,753	1,904,619	38,743	1,943,362	228,325	2,225	1,717,262	425,054	586,437	19,227	141,921	67,268
1993	2,798,349	1,951,351	45,932	1,997,283	233,458	9,319	1,773,144	424,062	601,143	19,523	143,334	65,632
1994	2,858,571	2,038,445	50,870	2,089,315	246,401	-3,902	1,839,012	422,968	596,591	19,776	144,544	66,357
1995	2,943,195	2,124,648	49,193	2,173,841	256,109	-60,027	1,857,705	460,101	625,389	20,322	144,829	67,555
1996	3,016,580	2,198,076	49,380	2,247,456	264,737	-75,116	1,907,603	474,032	634,945	20,742	145,430	68,018
1997	3,172,211	2,326,297	44,188	2,370,485	273,437	-70,737	2,026,311	503,490	642,410	21,756	145,811	68,540
1998	3,243,714	2,399,161	50,776	2,449,937	279,384	-82,011	2,088,542	517,094	638,078	22,229	145,924	68,904
1999	3,327,173	2,457,455	34,717	2,492,172	282,815	-47,284	2,162,073	502,207	662,893	22,743	146,293	68,956
2000	3,451,515	2,560,412	52,327	2,612,739	297,617	-72,892	2,242,230	515,777	693,508	23,598	146,263	70,815
2001	3,681,553	2,728,255	43,670	2,771,925	315,177	-74,118	2,382,630	535,673	763,250	25,138	146,451	70,220
2002	3,846,355	2,783,290	47,177	2,830,467	322,144	-80,025	2,428,298	549,740	868,317	26,113	147,294	70,240
2003	3,996,485	2,931,839	48,734	2,980,573	334,454	-87,518	2,558,601	577,581	860,303	26,924	148,437	71,496
2004	4,155,916	3,151,362	51,603	3,202,965	360,915	-95,722	2,746,328	563,007	846,581	27,736	149,837	73,659
2005	4,327,356	3,300,991	53,063	3,354,054	385,282	-101,432	2,867,340	526,666	933,350	28,465	152,022	76,004
2006	4,497,067	3,393,370	69,931	3,463,301	397,427	-104,786	2,961,088	515,330	1,020,649	29,321	153,371	75,877
2007	4,678,598	3,490,062	78,492	3,568,554	419,806	-109,035	3,039,713	572,588	1,066,297	30,284	154,489	75,496
2008	4,973,537	3,624,121	71,372	3,695,493	435,558	-112,979	3,146,956	634,927	1,191,654	31,935	155,738	74,889
2009	5,077,647	3,615,424	69,019	3,684,443	436,006	-176,132	3,072,305	664,231	1,341,111	32,439	156,531	73,708
2010	5,217,133	3,626,801	63,711	3,690,512	440,227	-164,153	3,086,132	660,598	1,470,403	33,188	157,200	72,730
2011	5,399,858	3,704,378	56,864	3,761,242	407,460	-178,523	3,175,259	721,641	1,502,958	34,262	157,607	72,428
2012	5,391,890	3,815,942	68,775	3,884,717	412,483	-293,861	3,178,373	740,718	1,472,799	34,170	157,794	72,368
2013	5,388,153	3,780,702	67,128	3,847,830	460,177	-231,245	3,156,408	750,153	1,481,592	34,286	157,153	72,686
2014	5,582,203	3,937,485	70,378	4,007,863	475,785	-265,429	3,266,649	777,836	1,537,718	35,468	157,389	73,154

Personal Income and Employment by Area: Virginia Beach-Norfolk-Newport News, VA-NC

(Thousands of dollars, except as noted.)

Year	Personal income, total	Earnings by place of work			Less: Contributions for government social insurance	Plus: Adjustment for residence	Equals: Net earnings by place of residence	Plus: Dividends, interest, and rent	Plus: Personal current transfer receipts	Per capita personal income (dollars)	Population (persons)	Total employment
		Nonfarm	Farm	Total								
1970	4,635,635	3,771,803	21,017	3,792,820	217,484	-34,204	3,541,132	839,054	255,449	4,214	1,099,964	535,553
1971	5,073,499	4,129,370	13,745	4,143,115	250,128	-44,800	3,848,187	913,436	311,876	4,557	1,113,297	536,524
1972	5,604,477	4,590,920	28,147	4,619,067	289,659	-86,702	4,242,706	997,579	364,192	5,027	1,114,977	549,094
1973	6,217,962	5,084,842	42,099	5,126,941	355,467	-98,478	4,672,996	1,116,296	428,670	5,466	1,137,655	573,774
1974	6,914,731	5,618,671	31,439	5,650,110	410,330	-113,577	5,126,203	1,280,716	507,812	5,972	1,157,946	590,240
1975	7,435,247	5,931,671	35,620	5,967,291	443,770	-94,277	5,429,244	1,374,019	631,984	6,375	1,166,228	578,056
1976	8,063,875	6,462,900	31,692	6,494,592	495,932	-113,971	5,884,689	1,477,345	701,841	6,840	1,178,977	588,816
1977	8,895,633	7,143,453	14,563	7,158,016	551,779	-122,702	6,483,535	1,663,756	748,342	7,428	1,197,552	610,259
1978	10,047,647	8,005,169	22,154	8,027,323	618,009	-135,890	7,273,424	1,953,519	820,704	8,304	1,209,942	637,636
1979	11,023,652	8,713,113	-626	8,712,487	702,054	-90,756	7,919,677	2,164,951	939,024	9,116	1,209,282	645,753
1980	12,475,738	9,708,921	-131	9,708,790	773,379	-112,097	8,823,314	2,525,189	1,127,235	10,254	1,216,639	656,174
1981	14,180,629	10,946,569	31,032	10,977,601	928,769	-122,805	9,926,027	2,961,741	1,292,861	11,423	1,241,360	663,306
1982	15,507,845	11,941,386	15,869	11,957,255	1,015,746	-145,360	10,796,149	3,327,444	1,384,252	12,411	1,249,538	669,437
1983	16,762,021	12,964,455	-2,463	12,961,992	1,156,992	-146,924	11,658,076	3,612,751	1,491,194	13,087	1,280,795	689,339
1984	18,478,739	14,286,502	32,938	14,319,440	1,318,729	-149,216	12,851,495	4,046,777	1,580,467	14,128	1,307,970	721,529
1985	19,931,054	15,507,922	23,121	15,531,043	1,477,408	-148,998	13,904,637	4,345,869	1,680,548	15,094	1,320,458	753,916
1986	21,426,829	16,737,299	32,703	16,770,002	1,654,924	-146,509	14,968,569	4,679,344	1,778,916	15,831	1,353,468	782,672
1987	22,875,049	17,975,851	37,185	18,013,036	1,788,218	-146,291	16,078,527	4,943,033	1,853,489	16,422	1,392,921	817,041
1988	24,548,002	19,206,258	51,267	19,257,525	1,987,602	-129,340	17,140,583	5,421,659	1,985,760	17,291	1,419,734	833,888
1989	26,198,825	20,110,629	54,124	20,164,753	2,112,360	-109,986	17,942,407	6,006,833	2,249,585	18,236	1,436,650	848,379
1990	27,446,336	21,164,595	68,270	21,232,865	2,260,134	-110,856	18,861,875	6,148,534	2,435,927	18,796	1,460,246	860,162
1991	28,749,455	22,113,261	58,239	22,171,500	2,392,292	-113,673	19,665,535	6,342,613	2,741,307	19,520	1,472,822	849,974
1992	30,535,353	23,377,259	64,619	23,441,878	2,534,937	-113,208	20,793,733	6,675,697	3,065,923	20,280	1,505,656	854,326
1993	31,812,940	24,111,969	55,054	24,167,023	2,632,263	-106,988	21,427,772	7,098,929	3,286,239	20,834	1,526,947	862,226
1994	32,978,752	24,824,744	71,222	24,895,966	2,735,453	-100,542	22,059,971	7,411,085	3,507,696	21,459	1,536,791	865,351
1995	34,189,940	25,418,416	59,147	25,477,563	2,787,761	-93,123	22,596,679	7,801,514	3,791,747	22,141	1,544,193	880,792
1996	35,658,584	26,381,653	70,365	26,452,018	2,893,713	-80,350	23,477,955	8,147,382	4,033,247	22,984	1,551,433	896,189
1997	37,417,013	27,754,951	47,100	27,802,051	3,041,482	-64,105	24,696,464	8,572,075	4,148,474	24,037	1,556,639	910,489
1998	39,428,124	29,414,325	38,563	29,452,888	3,197,512	-53,362	26,202,014	8,991,462	4,234,648	25,319	1,557,271	923,322
1999	41,276,091	30,987,780	27,959	31,015,739	3,373,024	-26,817	27,615,898	9,171,224	4,488,969	26,318	1,568,344	932,477
2000	44,117,238	32,987,747	46,510	33,034,257	3,547,625	1,230	29,487,862	9,847,713	4,781,663	27,838	1,584,803	952,139
2001	46,571,317	34,934,214	41,283	34,975,497	3,773,737	451	31,202,211	10,069,654	5,299,452	29,226	1,593,489	957,518
2002	48,752,526	37,280,338	36,067	37,316,405	4,017,774	-417,804	32,880,827	10,257,473	5,614,226	30,312	1,608,368	967,321
2003	52,117,510	40,081,860	58,006	40,139,866	4,293,855	-711,648	35,134,363	10,913,709	6,069,438	32,244	1,616,332	981,025
2004	55,421,943	42,689,711	64,278	42,753,989	4,611,175	-499,927	37,642,887	11,345,834	6,433,222	33,739	1,642,657	1,003,664
2005	58,335,576	44,738,647	81,533	44,820,180	4,862,191	-428,622	39,529,367	11,788,375	7,017,834	35,376	1,649,013	1,018,342
2006	62,306,751	47,120,631	64,536	47,185,167	5,190,513	-405,851	41,588,803	13,103,121	7,614,827	37,404	1,665,757	1,030,793
2007	65,339,804	48,918,678	50,155	48,968,833	5,380,990	-212,666	43,375,177	13,890,893	8,073,734	39,277	1,663,563	1,045,088
2008	67,493,462	49,693,073	48,084	49,741,157	5,502,599	-228,274	44,010,284	14,270,771	9,212,407	40,597	1,662,528	1,038,246
2009	67,313,300	49,622,226	44,272	49,666,498	5,517,606	-267,465	43,881,427	13,531,247	9,900,626	40,345	1,668,443	1,006,125
2010	68,937,440	50,316,550	31,458	50,348,008	5,651,851	-222,775	44,473,382	13,521,016	10,943,042	41,032	1,680,110	992,219
2011	72,254,162	51,412,211	48,196	51,460,407	5,206,579	-179,227	46,074,601	14,746,407	11,433,154	42,830	1,686,982	993,752
2012	74,956,432	52,913,320	60,418	52,973,738	5,373,877	-179,403	47,420,458	15,957,766	11,578,208	44,134	1,698,391	997,275
2013	75,290,628	53,383,252	65,098	53,448,350	6,104,828	-198,427	47,145,095	16,104,718	12,040,815	44,097	1,707,385	1,006,062
2014	77,722,591	54,877,334	37,357	54,914,691	6,248,073	-204,047	48,462,571	16,823,192	12,436,828	45,276	1,716,624	1,009,898

Personal Income and Employment by Area: Visalia-Porterville, CA

(Thousands of dollars, except as noted.)

Year	Personal income, total	Earnings by place of work			Less: Contributions for government social insurance	Plus: Adjustment for residence	Equals: Net earnings by place of residence	Plus: Dividends, interest, and rent	Plus: Personal current transfer receipts	Per capita personal income (dollars)	Population (persons)	Total employment
		Nonfarm	Farm	Total								
1970	698,524	413,218	113,102	526,320	28,188	1,717	499,849	94,678	103,997	3,692	189,191	81,225
1971	758,854	448,992	118,462	567,454	31,321	4,584	540,717	102,863	115,274	3,910	194,103	83,183
1972	860,505	508,590	143,143	651,733	37,299	7,676	622,110	115,128	123,267	4,354	197,643	89,111
1973	1,018,778	569,768	211,175	780,943	47,678	11,283	744,548	135,556	138,674	5,048	201,805	91,598
1974	1,182,497	652,195	253,948	906,143	56,364	14,371	864,150	154,036	164,311	5,724	206,589	97,440
1975	1,258,847	719,454	194,072	913,526	59,198	21,728	876,056	175,543	207,248	5,907	213,115	99,934
1976	1,408,289	828,629	204,721	1,033,350	69,023	26,030	990,357	187,271	230,661	6,427	219,123	102,675
1977	1,549,760	920,158	222,287	1,142,445	78,588	32,439	1,096,296	209,894	243,570	6,860	225,906	106,394
1978	1,771,427	1,057,835	246,952	1,304,787	91,309	38,619	1,252,097	246,613	272,717	7,596	233,220	109,228
1979	2,097,482	1,210,969	351,225	1,562,194	108,934	50,366	1,503,626	292,138	301,718	8,737	240,074	117,964
1980	2,318,884	1,292,067	361,928	1,653,995	115,117	60,173	1,599,051	360,374	359,459	9,372	247,426	119,326
1981	2,436,598	1,379,751	265,166	1,644,917	136,580	61,021	1,569,358	436,750	430,490	9,604	253,694	119,692
1982	2,620,065	1,427,756	327,810	1,755,566	144,281	63,778	1,675,063	485,773	459,229	10,087	259,759	117,129
1983	2,695,805	1,555,048	208,208	1,763,256	159,806	64,158	1,667,608	539,150	489,047	10,095	267,034	121,911
1984	2,966,944	1,684,028	259,756	1,943,784	179,315	70,497	1,834,966	602,001	529,977	10,858	273,255	120,368
1985	3,134,160	1,789,123	249,829	2,038,952	192,157	73,601	1,920,396	621,721	592,043	11,193	280,000	122,160
1986	3,352,252	1,952,745	260,994	2,213,739	213,750	74,196	2,074,185	639,342	638,725	11,731	285,767	125,690
1987	3,705,452	2,109,708	422,426	2,532,134	230,650	82,913	2,384,397	661,814	659,241	12,701	291,752	128,885
1988	3,959,973	2,263,208	433,579	2,696,787	256,968	99,279	2,539,098	711,957	708,918	13,285	298,075	133,959
1989	4,225,805	2,438,809	375,302	2,814,111	281,118	115,266	2,648,259	796,521	781,025	13,880	304,451	137,419
1990	4,665,215	2,723,163	437,819	3,160,982	308,435	124,797	2,977,344	814,005	873,866	14,854	314,062	140,864
1991	4,777,175	2,841,779	311,785	3,153,564	322,406	134,709	2,965,867	818,744	992,564	14,758	323,705	141,436
1992	5,326,856	3,104,717	510,977	3,615,694	352,148	125,211	3,388,757	797,957	1,140,142	16,047	331,956	146,844
1993	5,474,896	3,203,471	458,402	3,661,873	362,101	133,158	3,432,930	842,399	1,199,567	16,138	339,253	150,060
1994	5,741,444	3,397,223	495,073	3,892,296	379,094	134,135	3,647,337	874,988	1,219,119	16,610	345,668	153,457
1995	5,864,582	3,535,856	413,330	3,949,186	387,806	138,351	3,699,731	899,953	1,264,898	16,846	348,127	155,994
1996	6,320,365	3,683,017	628,641	4,311,658	386,605	141,165	4,066,218	930,947	1,323,200	18,020	350,732	158,687
1997	6,441,068	3,761,545	654,039	4,415,584	392,330	141,152	4,164,406	969,923	1,306,739	18,147	354,946	158,454
1998	6,919,804	4,138,323	658,687	4,797,010	415,659	139,839	4,521,190	1,018,307	1,380,307	19,229	359,854	165,810
1999	7,168,375	4,343,337	645,125	4,988,462	438,700	142,394	4,692,156	1,003,872	1,472,347	19,655	364,708	169,890
2000	7,376,234	4,634,512	530,086	5,164,598	471,925	150,672	4,843,345	1,041,059	1,491,830	20,010	368,627	172,516
2001	8,085,292	4,924,895	742,905	5,667,800	536,933	171,860	5,302,727	1,112,617	1,669,948	21,666	373,171	168,519
2002	8,318,291	5,296,429	498,027	5,794,456	588,431	213,381	5,419,406	1,113,562	1,785,323	21,915	379,568	175,974
2003	9,027,645	5,641,914	603,640	6,245,554	633,426	258,762	5,870,890	1,235,084	1,921,671	23,223	388,743	176,153
2004	10,112,534	6,043,304	1,093,861	7,137,165	696,609	314,403	6,754,959	1,309,970	2,047,605	25,394	398,226	175,019
2005	10,650,163	6,382,083	1,193,968	7,576,051	742,379	375,402	7,209,074	1,304,569	2,136,520	26,105	407,970	179,581
2006	10,894,381	6,906,154	583,437	7,489,591	775,583	453,090	7,167,098	1,419,940	2,307,343	26,257	414,921	184,223
2007	12,170,508	7,122,813	1,239,844	8,362,657	786,281	532,819	8,109,195	1,567,719	2,493,594	28,831	422,140	190,615
2008	12,297,505	7,265,409	849,227	8,114,636	804,892	608,202	7,917,946	1,609,596	2,769,963	28,647	429,283	191,045
2009	12,028,629	7,073,221	523,808	7,597,029	796,303	584,031	7,384,757	1,586,985	3,056,887	27,526	436,987	186,327
2010	12,819,638	7,145,506	836,154	7,981,660	786,132	621,438	7,816,966	1,598,808	3,403,864	28,919	443,292	186,016
2011	13,903,753	7,479,428	1,276,414	8,755,842	741,438	669,102	8,683,506	1,804,867	3,415,380	31,047	447,824	187,766
2012	14,400,560	7,660,100	1,276,066	8,936,166	748,615	724,011	8,911,562	2,023,502	3,465,496	31,895	451,499	186,612
2013	15,194,558	7,980,959	1,687,058	9,668,017	867,828	718,378	9,518,567	2,070,446	3,605,545	33,415	454,725	193,338
2014	16,147,060	8,259,993	2,080,381	10,340,374	900,862	799,443	10,238,955	2,158,632	3,749,473	35,240	458,198	195,901

Personal Income and Employment by Area: Waco, TX

(Thousands of dollars, except as noted.)

| Year | Personal income, total | Derivation of personal income | | | | | | | | | Per capita personal income (dollars) | Population (persons) | Total employment |
| | | Earnings by place of work | | | Less: Contributions for government social insurance | Plus: Adjustment for residence | Equals: Net earnings by place of residence | Plus: Dividends, interest, and rent | Plus: Personal current transfer receipts | | | |
		Nonfarm	Farm	Total								
1970	554,725	422,219	11,223	433,442	26,930	1,402	407,914	84,101	62,710	3,362	165,008	72,540
1971	601,868	456,415	9,907	466,322	29,812	1,111	437,621	92,920	71,327	3,594	167,456	73,644
1972	665,559	508,496	9,600	518,096	34,736	900	484,260	102,443	78,856	3,893	170,979	77,099
1973	759,241	563,949	28,280	592,229	44,501	495	548,223	117,413	93,605	4,365	173,928	79,469
1974	825,302	618,270	6,428	624,698	50,124	192	574,766	138,079	112,457	4,661	177,057	80,372
1975	928,704	670,276	12,442	682,718	52,795	308	630,231	158,384	140,089	5,271	176,185	79,429
1976	1,043,074	774,667	12,136	786,803	61,837	-979	723,987	170,612	148,475	5,799	179,868	83,034
1977	1,125,637	848,857	194	849,051	68,812	-1,567	778,672	189,518	157,447	6,209	181,301	85,832
1978	1,278,999	971,937	2,092	974,029	80,694	-2,002	891,333	214,277	173,389	6,969	183,520	88,769
1979	1,426,023	1,086,490	2,361	1,088,851	95,001	-4,265	989,585	241,025	195,413	7,645	186,539	90,348
1980	1,612,391	1,197,295	-661	1,196,634	105,683	-5,504	1,085,447	300,747	226,197	8,512	189,416	92,112
1981	1,813,523	1,319,077	12,322	1,331,399	126,025	-9,238	1,196,136	364,334	253,053	9,459	191,717	93,873
1982	1,990,246	1,407,886	6,866	1,414,752	135,902	-7,899	1,270,951	442,710	276,585	10,261	193,961	94,587
1983	2,169,419	1,539,631	7,796	1,547,427	148,539	-6,656	1,392,232	477,691	299,496	10,975	197,671	96,325
1984	2,388,029	1,691,136	22,318	1,713,454	167,904	-9,798	1,535,752	539,460	312,817	11,951	199,820	100,053
1985	2,550,128	1,783,694	29,299	1,812,993	179,818	-12,334	1,620,841	594,645	334,642	12,674	201,204	101,927
1986	2,630,439	1,824,877	25,818	1,850,695	182,776	-17,289	1,650,630	617,831	361,978	12,859	204,568	100,542
1987	2,629,731	1,793,126	30,248	1,823,374	178,822	-18,149	1,626,403	621,555	381,773	12,858	204,519	101,805
1988	2,728,795	1,894,547	27,381	1,921,928	195,826	-19,757	1,706,345	619,462	402,988	13,354	204,348	103,130
1989	2,877,653	1,960,326	33,052	1,993,378	206,704	-21,525	1,765,149	680,570	431,934	14,002	205,516	103,364
1990	3,034,739	2,100,205	24,028	2,124,233	216,084	-19,152	1,888,997	669,447	476,295	14,627	207,477	104,832
1991	3,213,054	2,238,351	36,439	2,274,790	235,258	-23,601	2,015,931	675,238	521,885	15,335	209,531	107,920
1992	3,389,302	2,397,193	33,751	2,430,944	250,109	-29,031	2,151,804	646,993	590,505	16,042	211,278	109,069
1993	3,595,764	2,584,847	40,623	2,625,470	269,180	-31,648	2,324,642	648,788	622,334	16,771	214,400	112,112
1994	3,847,331	2,800,890	46,152	2,847,042	295,042	-33,594	2,518,406	669,061	659,864	17,578	218,877	115,322
1995	4,123,185	3,018,151	30,004	3,048,155	319,808	-38,203	2,690,144	732,192	700,849	18,646	221,128	119,892
1996	4,299,080	3,152,346	6,873	3,159,219	331,015	-36,704	2,791,500	769,754	737,826	19,150	224,497	121,857
1997	4,550,114	3,377,626	27,792	3,405,418	350,842	-38,409	3,016,167	769,532	764,415	20,083	226,561	124,685
1998	4,807,488	3,614,857	6,001	3,620,858	371,038	-41,025	3,208,795	820,822	777,871	21,044	228,450	126,954
1999	5,051,665	3,859,300	22,804	3,882,104	394,313	-43,425	3,444,366	807,316	799,983	21,952	230,120	129,302
2000	5,261,705	3,960,946	14,886	3,975,832	399,702	-37,824	3,538,306	872,026	851,373	22,632	232,489	130,929
2001	5,396,524	4,034,961	4,333	4,039,294	411,419	-56,720	3,571,155	896,261	929,108	23,123	233,379	130,740
2002	5,544,898	4,178,723	18,066	4,196,789	428,706	-73,497	3,694,586	837,384	1,012,928	23,629	234,661	131,411
2003	5,892,990	4,451,110	32,360	4,483,470	465,396	-93,892	3,924,182	882,621	1,086,187	24,883	236,830	134,370
2004	6,039,052	4,627,669	41,917	4,669,586	483,866	-111,862	4,073,858	835,712	1,129,482	25,224	239,419	136,882
2005	6,408,517	4,842,489	32,934	4,875,423	508,712	-137,082	4,229,629	951,044	1,227,844	26,615	240,784	138,889
2006	6,731,083	5,079,915	22,319	5,102,234	521,777	-158,269	4,422,188	1,007,967	1,300,928	27,769	242,397	140,576
2007	7,070,657	5,248,395	24,592	5,272,987	546,538	-181,065	4,545,384	1,102,617	1,422,656	28,924	244,453	143,624
2008	7,398,415	5,381,243	6,684	5,387,927	563,213	-202,226	4,622,488	1,183,475	1,592,452	29,985	246,735	143,038
2009	7,561,888	5,546,664	-8,672	5,537,992	587,521	-214,803	4,735,668	1,114,872	1,711,348	30,315	249,441	142,514
2010	8,014,845	5,850,136	16,315	5,866,451	615,281	-216,632	5,034,538	1,109,360	1,870,947	31,575	253,837	141,644
2011	8,293,469	5,880,421	16,187	5,896,608	551,424	-208,253	5,136,931	1,228,722	1,927,816	32,431	255,729	142,925
2012	8,665,026	6,135,437	30,704	6,166,141	572,047	-214,046	5,380,048	1,366,193	1,918,785	33,701	257,111	144,450
2013	8,784,419	6,252,881	32,413	6,285,294	661,442	-204,097	5,419,755	1,401,618	1,963,046	33,904	259,099	146,510
2014	9,203,555	6,534,444	45,955	6,580,399	688,234	-189,233	5,702,932	1,453,941	2,046,682	35,340	260,430	148,690

Personal Income and Employment by Area: Walla Walla, WA

(Thousands of dollars, except as noted.)

Year	Personal income, total	Earnings by place of work			Less: Contributions for government social insurance	Plus: Adjustment for residence	Equals: Net earnings by place of residence	Plus: Dividends, interest, and rent	Plus: Personal current transfer receipts	Per capita personal income (dollars)	Population (persons)	Total employment
		Nonfarm	Farm	Total								
1970	189,580	123,283	24,354	147,637	9,432	-6,076	132,129	36,073	21,378	4,071	46,570	21,692
1971	200,006	132,123	21,337	153,460	10,491	-6,496	136,473	39,791	23,742	4,301	46,500	21,679
1972	230,265	144,296	34,890	179,186	12,046	-6,498	160,642	43,933	25,690	4,892	47,071	22,024
1973	281,896	156,217	66,895	223,112	15,114	-6,313	201,685	51,159	29,052	6,006	46,936	22,869
1974	299,338	174,767	58,480	233,247	17,652	-7,064	208,531	56,686	34,121	6,345	47,175	24,001
1975	332,178	196,279	58,327	254,606	19,834	-7,287	227,485	63,530	41,163	6,829	48,641	24,622
1976	357,973	230,329	49,542	279,871	23,958	-10,594	245,319	68,131	44,523	7,286	49,130	25,952
1977	375,878	251,442	34,556	285,998	26,377	-9,899	249,722	78,664	47,492	7,622	49,317	25,164
1978	429,078	291,129	42,100	333,229	31,794	-12,008	289,427	87,843	51,808	8,709	49,269	26,012
1979	484,289	354,836	37,504	392,340	40,942	-25,330	326,068	99,292	58,929	9,637	50,254	28,027
1980	551,739	377,938	54,672	432,610	43,582	-25,637	363,391	118,662	69,686	10,695	51,590	27,566
1981	600,400	391,621	52,133	443,754	48,085	-15,600	380,069	143,699	76,632	11,571	51,889	27,391
1982	610,799	398,936	38,482	437,418	49,100	-18,511	369,807	157,954	83,038	11,572	52,781	26,940
1983	678,843	421,454	73,447	494,901	52,897	-23,799	418,205	171,360	89,278	12,781	53,114	27,297
1984	697,145	451,317	57,500	508,817	58,895	-31,534	418,388	184,129	94,628	13,193	52,843	27,723
1985	691,501	451,845	37,594	489,439	59,562	-32,421	397,456	191,064	102,981	13,173	52,495	27,577
1986	714,621	450,891	56,754	507,645	60,087	-33,852	413,706	192,836	108,079	13,686	52,215	27,147
1987	708,753	455,965	49,384	505,349	60,730	-35,521	409,098	187,190	112,465	13,721	51,656	26,419
1988	728,418	486,257	46,905	533,162	67,137	-41,132	424,893	184,012	119,513	14,184	51,354	26,831
1989	778,587	518,312	38,851	557,163	71,141	-46,824	439,198	211,190	128,199	14,909	52,223	27,198
1990	824,041	547,801	58,122	605,923	77,088	-50,192	478,643	207,468	137,930	15,680	52,554	28,459
1991	865,861	584,702	46,526	631,228	82,212	-53,089	495,927	212,184	157,750	16,022	54,041	28,184
1992	937,412	644,237	48,250	692,487	90,069	-57,076	545,342	217,946	174,124	17,062	54,941	28,961
1993	1,011,704	683,515	77,839	761,354	96,268	-58,300	606,786	222,664	182,254	17,944	56,381	29,896
1994	1,035,679	729,925	51,427	781,352	102,548	-58,052	620,752	227,889	187,038	18,074	57,303	31,079
1995	1,082,396	748,512	55,885	804,397	106,284	-59,472	638,641	245,878	197,877	18,696	57,895	31,720
1996	1,187,508	775,484	106,840	882,324	107,087	-61,238	713,999	263,735	209,774	20,373	58,287	31,769
1997	1,191,368	801,422	69,057	870,479	106,719	-60,703	703,057	275,136	213,175	20,360	58,515	32,279
1998	1,276,681	850,093	86,280	936,373	111,382	-59,509	765,482	284,497	226,702	21,769	58,648	32,369
1999	1,315,587	881,306	85,979	967,285	112,898	-58,699	795,688	281,116	238,783	22,348	58,867	32,461
2000	1,454,775	934,008	150,298	1,084,306	121,893	-61,896	900,517	297,665	256,593	24,554	59,247	33,405
2001	1,500,309	974,053	143,233	1,117,286	127,233	-77,245	912,808	310,671	276,830	25,383	59,106	33,457
2002	1,475,974	1,001,442	111,631	1,113,073	131,458	-77,300	904,315	284,851	286,808	24,739	59,661	33,697
2003	1,570,470	1,055,506	142,317	1,197,823	138,416	-78,395	981,012	291,157	298,301	26,126	60,111	34,180
2004	1,629,028	1,104,376	124,173	1,228,549	145,019	-76,159	1,007,371	307,106	314,551	26,847	60,679	34,136
2005	1,650,228	1,128,629	106,171	1,234,800	147,814	-73,224	1,013,762	303,616	332,850	27,257	60,543	34,080
2006	1,750,069	1,191,386	108,211	1,299,597	155,483	-70,444	1,073,670	320,130	356,269	28,879	60,600	34,458
2007	1,929,635	1,271,359	119,776	1,391,135	165,029	-68,322	1,157,784	387,951	383,900	31,770	60,737	35,187
2008	2,163,559	1,358,730	157,790	1,516,520	174,963	-67,968	1,273,589	461,447	428,523	35,342	61,218	36,309
2009	2,154,385	1,379,546	140,629	1,520,175	181,298	-63,062	1,275,815	412,979	465,591	34,703	62,080	36,111
2010	2,219,153	1,408,402	160,382	1,568,784	187,130	-66,537	1,315,117	394,938	509,098	35,208	63,029	36,147
2011	2,344,099	1,414,474	193,585	1,608,059	170,386	-59,685	1,377,988	455,136	510,975	36,889	63,545	35,889
2012	2,408,943	1,436,188	214,095	1,650,283	172,136	-62,156	1,415,991	474,465	518,487	37,961	63,459	36,300
2013	2,460,424	1,459,113	216,633	1,675,746	193,606	-61,678	1,420,462	511,948	528,014	38,642	63,673	36,937
2014	2,542,336	1,524,462	173,816	1,698,278	203,277	-68,330	1,426,671	532,915	582,750	39,830	63,829	37,482

Personal Income and Employment by Area: Warner Robins, GA

(Thousands of dollars, except as noted.)

Year	Personal income, total	Earnings by place of work			Less: Contributions for government social insurance	Plus: Adjustment for residence	Equals: Net earnings by place of residence	Plus: Dividends, interest, and rent	Plus: Personal current transfer receipts	Per capita personal income (dollars)	Population (persons)	Total employment
		Nonfarm	Farm	Total								
1970	365,213	409,923	8,740	418,663	13,918	-123,474	281,271	64,728	19,214	4,164	87,709	50,074
1971	407,268	448,085	12,977	461,062	15,605	-134,191	311,266	72,853	23,149	4,483	90,839	49,359
1972	435,149	473,406	12,390	485,796	17,126	-136,143	332,527	76,529	26,093	4,679	93,008	48,562
1973	485,784	504,362	22,145	526,507	20,801	-134,821	370,885	84,972	29,927	5,167	94,022	49,211
1974	539,353	549,496	19,024	568,520	24,984	-137,849	405,687	96,181	37,485	5,597	96,373	50,280
1975	585,086	587,893	13,946	601,839	28,511	-143,258	430,070	105,952	49,064	5,955	98,251	49,765
1976	624,044	617,215	15,433	632,648	31,081	-144,020	457,547	110,438	56,059	6,266	99,591	49,403
1977	687,624	692,482	9,667	702,149	34,496	-162,118	505,535	124,333	57,756	6,822	100,792	50,158
1978	758,662	736,780	13,054	749,834	37,615	-160,628	551,591	144,215	62,856	7,404	102,471	51,101
1979	827,143	781,535	16,258	797,793	42,341	-158,018	597,434	157,555	72,154	7,923	104,400	50,783
1980	897,765	818,748	3,229	821,977	46,563	-144,725	630,689	180,895	86,181	8,461	106,108	51,799
1981	1,024,191	929,446	12,003	941,449	54,760	-175,238	711,451	213,307	99,433	9,526	107,518	51,524
1982	1,127,747	1,001,737	17,051	1,018,788	59,939	-182,979	775,870	244,949	106,928	10,434	108,084	52,289
1983	1,224,326	1,074,130	9,749	1,083,879	73,789	-175,639	834,451	271,312	118,563	11,230	109,024	53,163
1984	1,341,431	1,142,535	21,412	1,163,947	80,165	-169,368	914,414	298,556	128,461	12,270	109,327	54,057
1985	1,441,625	1,219,593	18,046	1,237,639	92,824	-163,316	981,499	319,534	140,592	13,013	110,786	56,151
1986	1,532,620	1,259,578	14,747	1,274,325	101,092	-130,360	1,042,873	340,387	149,360	13,652	112,267	58,757
1987	1,611,647	1,278,059	16,142	1,294,201	106,204	-91,996	1,096,001	358,306	157,340	14,154	113,865	59,213
1988	1,747,396	1,365,719	22,354	1,388,073	120,056	-80,842	1,187,175	388,473	171,748	15,041	116,176	60,188
1989	1,897,289	1,469,943	17,675	1,487,618	133,812	-81,043	1,272,763	435,731	188,795	16,146	117,510	62,194
1990	2,041,428	1,549,350	18,200	1,567,550	145,229	-34,243	1,388,078	443,452	209,898	17,145	119,068	62,862
1991	2,137,699	1,583,839	31,245	1,615,084	152,282	-11,014	1,451,788	445,123	240,788	17,690	120,842	61,259
1992	2,295,014	1,716,634	31,823	1,748,457	165,575	-18,972	1,563,910	459,230	271,874	18,594	123,430	63,510
1993	2,411,454	1,771,483	30,667	1,802,150	174,589	2,566	1,630,127	492,247	289,080	19,121	126,114	65,146
1994	2,520,362	1,819,850	36,603	1,856,453	182,434	32,226	1,706,245	506,910	307,207	19,471	129,441	67,590
1995	2,696,650	1,937,576	30,847	1,968,423	194,686	33,536	1,807,273	559,065	330,312	20,590	130,968	69,161
1996	2,835,928	2,104,195	32,238	2,136,433	211,458	-40,089	1,884,886	592,413	358,629	21,247	133,473	70,825
1997	3,017,449	2,172,816	36,736	2,209,552	219,440	28,426	2,018,538	629,321	369,590	22,067	136,742	70,836
1998	3,193,831	2,328,606	24,095	2,352,701	232,417	18,753	2,139,037	669,311	385,483	22,899	139,475	71,504
1999	3,406,776	2,494,782	40,021	2,534,803	248,302	26,380	2,312,881	679,779	414,116	23,988	142,022	74,153
2000	3,592,132	2,662,140	32,684	2,694,824	265,538	-8,586	2,420,700	726,818	444,614	24,804	144,820	76,233
2001	3,874,038	2,795,004	34,741	2,829,745	283,205	-38,473	2,508,067	866,483	499,488	26,287	147,377	76,894
2002	4,158,832	3,041,759	23,142	3,064,901	309,555	-47,754	2,707,592	887,720	563,520	27,555	150,927	79,000
2003	4,452,377	3,252,584	41,815	3,294,399	329,174	-51,108	2,914,117	949,641	588,619	28,847	154,342	81,382
2004	4,602,130	3,433,338	34,764	3,468,102	356,597	-56,390	3,055,115	898,589	648,426	28,910	159,187	83,924
2005	4,940,755	3,680,026	47,928	3,727,954	379,360	-63,879	3,284,715	932,748	723,292	30,527	161,847	86,694
2006	5,264,953	3,931,873	44,754	3,976,627	409,265	-64,617	3,502,745	973,037	789,171	31,780	165,671	90,002
2007	5,650,610	4,118,694	47,800	4,166,494	425,011	-58,628	3,682,855	1,098,252	869,503	33,183	170,285	93,119
2008	5,973,581	4,213,761	31,986	4,245,747	453,372	-41,507	3,750,868	1,206,365	1,016,348	34,374	173,782	93,123
2009	5,927,281	4,309,267	17,277	4,326,544	467,179	-131,712	3,727,653	1,100,051	1,099,577	33,527	176,793	93,151
2010	6,174,633	4,465,677	27,782	4,493,459	487,569	-153,155	3,852,735	1,104,150	1,217,748	34,225	180,412	93,394
2011	6,571,805	4,588,487	39,502	4,627,989	445,972	-153,207	4,028,810	1,262,901	1,280,094	35,796	183,589	95,297
2012	6,656,340	4,659,716	40,790	4,700,506	456,394	-82,689	4,161,423	1,205,335	1,289,582	35,905	185,390	95,723
2013	6,720,994	4,639,344	52,017	4,691,361	507,960	-6,035	4,177,366	1,214,814	1,328,814	36,066	186,355	96,267
2014	6,969,114	4,731,748	34,478	4,766,226	517,083	65,780	4,314,923	1,263,302	1,390,889	37,165	187,516	96,363

Personal Income and Employment by Area: Washington-Arlington-Alexandria, DC-VA-MD-WV

(Thousands of dollars, except as noted.)

Year	Personal income, total	Earnings by place of work			Less: Contributions for government social insurance	Plus: Adjustment for residence	Equals: Net earnings by place of residence	Plus: Dividends, interest, and rent	Plus: Personal current transfer receipts	Per capita personal income (dollars)	Population (persons)	Total employment
		Nonfarm	Farm	Total								
1970	18,431,195	15,150,374	52,568	15,202,942	704,394	-26,273	14,472,275	3,210,861	748,059	5,806	3,174,781	1,635,996
1971	20,648,877	16,923,677	49,559	16,973,236	808,830	-162,149	16,002,257	3,733,043	913,577	6,396	3,228,473	1,676,874
1972	22,628,605	18,644,715	58,485	18,703,200	947,358	-271,579	17,484,263	4,077,622	1,066,720	6,861	3,297,994	1,728,072
1973	24,659,483	20,432,959	73,303	20,506,262	1,196,263	-379,913	18,930,086	4,475,278	1,254,119	7,433	3,317,553	1,785,895
1974	26,769,569	22,077,267	67,726	22,144,993	1,351,827	-511,200	20,281,966	4,998,318	1,489,285	8,041	3,329,115	1,820,202
1975	29,265,713	24,103,364	68,138	24,171,502	1,487,015	-688,145	21,996,342	5,407,777	1,861,594	8,723	3,354,959	1,837,675
1976	31,819,360	26,462,942	60,804	26,523,746	1,662,192	-850,671	24,010,883	5,814,847	1,993,630	9,430	3,374,253	1,868,791
1977	34,617,337	28,875,610	51,386	28,926,996	1,803,153	-1,025,371	26,098,472	6,419,574	2,099,291	10,235	3,382,257	1,919,713
1978	38,405,826	32,000,798	76,692	32,077,490	2,036,249	-1,287,646	28,753,595	7,384,832	2,267,399	11,258	3,411,506	2,000,343
1979	42,155,458	35,343,540	66,343	35,409,883	2,375,856	-1,645,641	31,388,386	8,203,472	2,563,600	12,331	3,418,637	2,061,280
1980	47,093,231	39,204,001	35,403	39,239,404	2,686,930	-1,994,786	34,557,688	9,559,482	2,976,061	13,678	3,442,968	2,096,829
1981	52,364,926	43,054,748	47,051	43,101,799	3,213,061	-2,187,408	37,701,330	11,225,667	3,437,929	14,956	3,501,294	2,118,775
1982	56,978,149	46,149,775	47,919	46,197,694	3,515,595	-2,249,052	40,433,047	12,706,506	3,838,596	16,079	3,543,649	2,120,432
1983	61,431,838	50,289,361	31,998	50,321,359	4,169,707	-2,316,920	43,834,732	13,460,490	4,136,616	17,084	3,595,901	2,185,742
1984	68,713,350	56,404,305	56,621	56,460,926	4,861,572	-2,557,340	49,042,014	15,212,248	4,459,088	18,711	3,672,371	2,319,314
1985	75,199,524	62,369,461	60,316	62,429,777	5,659,496	-2,786,787	53,983,494	16,548,173	4,667,857	20,038	3,752,795	2,449,391
1986	81,692,916	68,249,291	48,469	68,297,760	6,454,387	-2,812,836	59,030,537	17,741,743	4,920,636	21,239	3,846,429	2,578,468
1987	88,688,368	74,861,580	89,065	74,950,645	7,153,219	-3,036,170	64,761,256	18,771,227	5,155,885	22,466	3,947,690	2,713,726
1988	98,304,876	83,474,375	94,210	83,568,585	8,218,259	-3,329,808	72,020,518	20,735,505	5,548,853	24,299	4,045,716	2,823,319
1989	106,567,652	89,637,331	102,175	89,739,506	9,009,651	-3,543,107	77,186,748	23,448,512	5,932,392	25,856	4,121,547	2,898,376
1990	112,366,780	94,308,152	131,341	94,439,493	9,662,930	-3,609,935	81,166,628	24,696,782	6,503,370	26,925	4,173,328	2,930,896
1991	117,309,973	97,944,726	113,861	98,058,587	10,123,414	-3,577,313	84,357,860	25,683,869	7,268,244	27,699	4,235,129	2,864,621
1992	124,488,505	103,944,489	123,863	104,068,352	10,726,841	-3,755,767	89,585,744	26,674,687	8,228,074	28,950	4,300,061	2,851,903
1993	130,953,061	108,842,209	106,267	108,948,476	11,272,827	-3,996,910	93,678,739	28,497,683	8,776,639	30,021	4,362,043	2,898,087
1994	137,419,400	113,946,899	98,371	114,045,270	12,021,475	-4,250,483	97,773,312	30,420,505	9,225,583	31,076	4,422,005	2,933,968
1995	143,422,745	118,288,487	67,105	118,355,592	12,527,594	-4,307,295	101,520,703	32,194,256	9,707,786	32,041	4,476,203	2,984,951
1996	150,522,238	123,906,247	99,792	124,006,039	13,123,243	-4,600,923	106,281,873	33,810,537	10,429,828	33,177	4,536,908	3,030,891
1997	160,109,830	132,339,361	65,157	132,404,518	14,084,604	-5,058,860	113,261,054	36,168,716	10,680,060	34,791	4,602,056	3,098,310
1998	173,163,175	144,342,311	74,400	144,416,711	15,104,766	-5,380,239	123,931,706	37,851,473	11,379,996	37,061	4,672,330	3,169,549
1999	187,052,009	157,284,495	58,236	157,342,731	16,419,011	-5,089,364	135,834,356	39,243,087	11,974,566	39,267	4,763,645	3,254,595
2000	205,861,722	174,115,082	100,102	174,215,184	17,961,073	-5,920,389	150,333,722	42,702,578	12,825,422	42,329	4,863,388	3,399,433
2001	216,474,028	185,252,782	63,093	185,315,875	19,307,109	-6,232,577	159,776,189	42,630,961	14,066,878	43,553	4,970,350	3,452,265
2002	222,042,621	191,669,995	57,240	191,727,235	20,050,131	-7,599,397	164,077,707	42,700,077	15,264,837	43,918	5,055,829	3,488,336
2003	233,434,961	202,218,194	44,496	202,262,690	21,067,406	-8,330,176	172,865,108	44,325,929	16,243,924	45,552	5,124,633	3,536,901
2004	250,993,071	218,994,119	58,933	219,053,052	22,900,461	-8,726,802	187,425,789	46,516,721	17,050,561	48,269	5,199,870	3,639,717
2005	270,486,295	233,184,064	43,161	233,227,225	24,354,631	-8,887,880	199,984,714	52,124,946	18,376,635	51,291	5,273,577	3,722,735
2006	290,661,562	246,583,431	5,786	246,589,217	25,889,035	-8,816,760	211,883,422	59,319,946	19,458,194	54,647	5,318,889	3,790,273
2007	307,091,661	257,272,938	-11,212	257,261,726	27,124,927	-8,648,510	221,488,289	64,579,615	21,023,757	57,156	5,372,905	3,869,612
2008	321,524,020	269,043,711	9,065	269,052,776	28,522,483	-9,408,862	231,121,431	65,777,246	24,625,343	59,049	5,445,083	3,888,898
2009	317,220,857	271,552,365	11,133	271,563,498	29,010,126	-10,422,449	232,130,923	58,782,798	26,307,136	57,179	5,547,895	3,854,647
2010	330,371,604	282,803,979	8,074	282,812,053	30,428,141	-10,633,808	241,750,104	59,058,232	29,563,268	58,308	5,665,931	3,862,573
2011	352,120,886	294,223,289	45,290	294,268,579	27,989,213	-10,315,367	255,963,999	65,180,498	30,976,389	60,945	5,777,721	3,936,261
2012	366,624,979	301,479,307	98,082	301,577,389	28,773,119	-9,309,456	263,494,814	71,971,639	31,158,526	62,420	5,873,480	3,984,809
2013	366,309,397	304,371,411	116,456	304,487,867	33,137,747	-8,670,344	262,679,776	71,098,004	32,531,617	61,387	5,967,176	4,039,211
2014	379,973,588	313,853,503	64,989	313,918,492	34,067,150	-7,923,231	271,928,111	73,962,056	34,083,421	62,975	6,033,737	4,075,889

Personal Income and Employment by Area: Waterloo-Cedar Falls, IA

(Thousands of dollars, except as noted.)

| Year | Personal income, total | Derivation of personal income | | | | | | | | Per capita personal income (dollars) | Population (persons) | Total employment |
| | | Earnings by place of work | | | Less: Contributions for government social insurance | Plus: Adjustment for residence | Equals: Net earnings by place of residence | Plus: Dividends, interest, and rent | Plus: Personal current transfer receipts | | | |
		Nonfarm	Farm	Total								
1970	632,985	496,938	35,859	532,797	37,991	-21,159	473,647	101,472	57,866	3,727	169,857	76,398
1971	670,410	529,887	31,473	561,360	42,010	-23,548	495,802	109,624	64,984	3,937	170,283	75,817
1972	751,763	599,671	41,420	641,091	50,161	-27,432	563,498	119,319	68,946	4,433	169,595	77,925
1973	876,263	687,434	75,857	763,291	66,689	-33,754	662,848	133,998	79,417	5,150	170,158	83,267
1974	964,011	779,202	57,856	837,058	78,109	-39,946	719,003	152,720	92,288	5,665	170,178	85,777
1975	1,074,946	849,685	57,985	907,670	83,427	-43,864	780,379	174,813	119,754	6,287	170,987	85,435
1976	1,147,636	933,286	30,969	964,255	93,158	-47,238	823,859	189,173	134,604	6,671	172,038	86,484
1977	1,325,795	1,097,198	43,267	1,140,465	109,026	-60,490	970,949	214,792	140,054	7,673	172,797	91,066
1978	1,467,093	1,197,992	63,010	1,261,002	123,198	-67,387	1,070,417	240,616	156,060	8,411	174,425	92,582
1979	1,632,745	1,369,120	44,440	1,413,560	146,711	-81,993	1,184,856	273,122	174,767	9,336	174,893	95,443
1980	1,796,233	1,484,062	25,363	1,509,425	157,952	-90,945	1,260,528	328,151	207,554	10,138	177,172	95,288
1981	1,989,383	1,592,523	43,789	1,636,312	180,524	-98,354	1,357,434	400,686	231,263	11,248	176,866	93,456
1982	2,011,190	1,527,048	21,280	1,548,328	175,724	-89,815	1,282,789	452,369	276,032	11,463	175,444	88,697
1983	2,029,882	1,496,141	7,816	1,503,957	172,475	-82,709	1,248,773	480,686	300,423	11,673	173,893	86,524
1984	2,135,653	1,538,544	43,108	1,581,652	182,588	-83,379	1,315,685	520,353	299,615	12,447	171,586	85,792
1985	2,126,524	1,488,151	54,212	1,542,363	177,760	-75,283	1,289,320	521,508	315,696	12,731	167,036	82,930
1986	2,109,162	1,436,164	64,674	1,500,838	174,139	-65,221	1,261,478	519,160	328,524	13,001	162,232	80,235
1987	2,216,409	1,584,740	73,411	1,658,151	189,558	-80,876	1,387,717	500,977	327,715	13,944	158,953	82,491
1988	2,309,995	1,735,116	37,231	1,772,347	214,530	-94,317	1,463,500	507,642	338,853	14,691	157,238	85,872
1989	2,510,373	1,864,082	49,619	1,913,701	228,635	-104,611	1,580,455	565,018	364,900	15,881	158,077	88,775
1990	2,656,074	1,977,344	77,466	2,054,810	247,890	-113,249	1,693,671	568,305	394,098	16,702	159,026	91,900
1991	2,730,934	2,050,361	60,370	2,110,731	258,478	-114,803	1,737,450	571,710	421,774	17,016	160,489	93,283
1992	2,939,399	2,209,439	97,406	2,306,845	276,258	-125,297	1,905,290	578,215	455,894	18,228	161,261	94,400
1993	2,986,522	2,307,096	37,991	2,345,087	290,570	-129,677	1,924,840	577,712	483,970	18,412	162,204	95,937
1994	3,200,080	2,439,082	101,977	2,541,059	310,241	-134,800	2,096,018	599,564	504,498	19,705	162,400	96,870
1995	3,364,065	2,517,464	96,559	2,614,023	321,199	-137,045	2,155,779	676,150	532,136	20,719	162,363	99,104
1996	3,551,300	2,593,843	137,663	2,731,506	314,416	-142,184	2,274,906	719,991	556,403	21,786	163,010	100,755
1997	3,773,287	2,804,404	133,009	2,937,413	351,772	-156,890	2,428,751	777,112	567,424	23,163	162,902	103,664
1998	3,903,869	2,929,276	94,315	3,023,591	362,880	-160,099	2,500,612	808,545	594,712	23,900	163,342	105,571
1999	3,899,738	2,936,507	68,094	3,004,601	360,652	-155,462	2,488,487	795,996	615,255	23,849	163,516	104,795
2000	4,166,176	3,123,931	79,910	3,203,841	379,411	-173,152	2,651,278	865,496	649,402	25,450	163,699	106,141
2001	4,378,601	3,344,453	71,601	3,416,054	398,472	-177,890	2,839,692	827,562	711,347	26,766	163,590	105,555
2002	4,513,560	3,412,096	70,498	3,482,594	406,730	-203,114	2,872,750	863,106	777,704	27,753	162,634	105,353
2003	4,580,625	3,525,283	50,995	3,576,278	424,788	-221,447	2,930,043	869,602	780,980	28,208	162,388	105,129
2004	4,910,276	3,805,840	134,800	3,940,640	452,357	-247,697	3,240,586	861,950	807,740	30,163	162,793	106,911
2005	5,041,812	3,961,750	115,451	4,077,201	471,398	-262,643	3,343,160	847,339	851,313	30,882	163,260	108,259
2006	5,341,981	4,164,861	78,118	4,242,979	489,095	-269,898	3,483,986	929,720	928,275	32,578	163,976	109,445
2007	5,693,189	4,388,665	107,752	4,496,417	517,715	-283,640	3,695,062	1,024,214	973,913	34,649	164,310	111,251
2008	6,119,325	4,693,809	109,026	4,802,835	549,434	-304,343	3,949,058	1,088,314	1,081,953	36,925	165,724	111,912
2009	6,077,324	4,693,840	74,099	4,767,939	551,253	-315,170	3,901,516	1,031,863	1,143,945	36,342	167,225	110,909
2010	6,062,995	4,626,171	92,430	4,718,601	557,458	-323,330	3,837,813	1,005,571	1,219,611	36,113	167,888	110,114
2011	6,524,897	4,807,336	221,648	5,028,984	524,336	-350,402	4,154,246	1,110,007	1,260,644	38,781	168,250	112,244
2012	6,806,400	5,086,438	182,801	5,269,239	547,021	-375,368	4,346,850	1,213,375	1,246,175	40,383	168,547	113,983
2013	6,829,266	5,135,568	233,940	5,369,508	625,102	-376,222	4,368,184	1,200,582	1,260,500	40,296	169,479	114,569
2014	7,002,434	5,308,100	145,207	5,453,307	638,416	-377,881	4,437,010	1,244,955	1,320,469	41,192	169,993	114,961

Personal Income and Employment by Area: Watertown-Fort Drum, NY

(Thousands of dollars, except as noted.)

| Year | Personal income, total | Derivation of personal income | | | | | | | | Per capita personal income (dollars) | Population (persons) | Total employment |
| | | Earnings by place of work | | | Less: Contributions for government social insurance | Plus: Adjustment for residence | Equals: Net earnings by place of residence | Plus: Dividends, interest, and rent | Plus: Personal current transfer receipts | | | |
		Nonfarm	Farm	Total								
1970	314,674	234,618	13,226	247,844	17,886	1,363	231,321	44,512	38,841	3,544	88,789	36,388
1971	337,929	248,010	12,704	260,714	19,170	1,825	243,369	47,752	46,808	3,767	89,719	36,058
1972	355,018	259,917	12,596	272,513	21,020	1,194	252,687	51,305	51,026	3,911	90,773	36,058
1973	380,742	278,453	13,293	291,746	25,710	804	266,840	57,423	56,479	4,216	90,310	37,049
1974	412,170	299,159	10,516	309,675	28,471	-93	281,111	64,004	67,055	4,606	89,485	36,947
1975	450,961	317,405	7,626	325,031	29,592	-2,056	293,383	69,658	87,920	4,998	90,235	36,272
1976	480,109	338,080	10,448	348,528	32,046	-2,888	313,594	72,344	94,171	5,306	90,488	35,746
1977	507,582	362,626	5,744	368,370	34,443	-3,286	330,641	80,269	96,672	5,634	90,089	36,188
1978	561,107	408,567	10,688	419,255	39,685	-4,902	374,668	84,762	101,677	6,259	89,651	37,470
1979	617,995	456,114	11,220	467,334	45,747	-7,230	414,357	96,078	107,560	6,931	89,161	38,283
1980	685,670	496,493	8,382	504,875	49,402	-9,596	445,877	113,892	125,901	7,785	88,071	37,483
1981	747,255	528,878	7,048	535,926	55,388	-10,987	469,551	135,569	142,135	8,532	87,585	36,896
1982	820,364	556,147	9,497	565,644	58,787	-11,736	495,121	162,247	162,996	9,397	87,302	36,595
1983	876,137	598,906	7,740	606,646	63,922	-12,849	529,875	167,149	179,113	10,017	87,465	37,306
1984	972,689	675,108	9,639	684,747	73,089	-15,089	596,569	188,045	188,075	11,041	88,094	38,570
1985	1,055,091	742,892	12,640	755,532	81,387	-19,448	654,697	202,392	198,002	11,861	88,954	40,370
1986	1,165,027	843,051	15,534	858,585	92,370	-27,343	738,872	223,042	203,113	12,798	91,032	43,661
1987	1,371,880	1,061,259	17,406	1,078,665	114,820	-50,397	913,448	256,454	201,978	14,237	96,360	49,930
1988	1,578,234	1,281,900	12,875	1,294,775	143,014	-73,803	1,077,958	288,104	212,172	15,211	103,758	56,273
1989	1,784,665	1,425,049	19,483	1,444,532	156,679	-79,455	1,208,398	344,867	231,400	16,293	109,534	60,292
1990	1,846,592	1,459,276	20,830	1,480,106	156,051	-78,272	1,245,783	349,729	251,080	16,554	111,549	59,814
1991	1,939,900	1,516,852	13,645	1,530,497	165,526	-73,783	1,291,188	364,558	284,154	17,181	112,911	58,880
1992	2,050,066	1,576,385	18,860	1,595,245	172,555	-71,365	1,351,325	374,522	324,219	17,910	114,463	58,311
1993	2,051,712	1,558,393	17,626	1,576,019	173,235	-66,215	1,336,569	373,775	341,368	17,861	114,874	57,273
1994	2,111,367	1,602,980	15,834	1,618,814	177,783	-65,882	1,375,149	383,537	352,681	18,056	116,932	58,543
1995	2,195,929	1,647,383	9,650	1,657,033	180,459	-65,732	1,410,842	414,096	370,991	19,035	115,361	58,586
1996	2,253,654	1,677,352	20,720	1,698,072	182,095	-63,529	1,452,448	418,652	382,554	19,668	114,585	58,639
1997	2,310,841	1,738,788	8,033	1,746,821	186,017	-61,843	1,498,961	424,753	387,127	20,440	113,055	58,879
1998	2,417,342	1,810,589	8,949	1,819,538	192,984	-62,645	1,563,909	449,828	403,605	21,479	112,546	59,032
1999	2,516,030	1,889,572	8,964	1,898,536	197,607	-60,500	1,640,429	452,013	423,588	22,448	112,081	60,182
2000	2,644,792	1,982,132	7,704	1,989,836	207,614	-60,110	1,722,112	479,140	443,540	23,659	111,790	60,944
2001	2,760,335	2,044,123	11,694	2,055,817	218,985	-54,381	1,782,451	500,273	477,611	24,774	111,422	60,872
2002	2,867,493	2,140,984	15,476	2,156,460	231,978	-77,027	1,847,455	505,882	514,156	25,807	111,112	60,654
2003	3,060,206	2,308,710	24,436	2,333,146	247,022	-104,765	1,981,359	545,738	533,109	27,758	110,246	61,502
2004	3,260,724	2,487,040	37,617	2,524,657	268,370	-134,612	2,121,675	572,664	566,385	29,663	109,924	63,363
2005	3,586,366	2,823,212	38,792	2,862,004	303,851	-178,460	2,379,693	615,891	590,782	31,602	113,486	66,792
2006	3,923,520	3,201,967	25,778	3,227,745	342,401	-229,531	2,655,813	652,367	615,340	34,523	113,650	70,212
2007	4,130,940	3,356,498	38,487	3,394,985	356,660	-268,775	2,769,550	715,684	645,706	35,903	115,059	70,951
2008	4,428,262	3,574,979	40,334	3,615,313	383,090	-316,177	2,916,046	789,364	722,852	38,496	115,033	71,900
2009	4,618,333	3,725,042	19,223	3,744,265	402,116	-338,057	3,004,092	823,393	790,848	40,151	115,023	71,746
2010	4,897,920	3,956,274	40,484	3,996,758	432,324	-351,420	3,213,014	831,888	853,018	42,008	116,595	73,332
2011	5,133,742	4,086,165	66,217	4,152,382	408,624	-415,440	3,328,318	924,303	881,121	43,406	118,273	73,562
2012	5,171,233	4,029,414	55,630	4,085,044	404,777	-381,696	3,298,571	994,262	878,400	42,767	120,916	72,158
2013	5,092,344	3,966,237	77,176	4,043,413	438,890	-379,014	3,225,509	955,619	911,216	42,601	119,536	71,316
2014	5,167,172	3,959,999	96,168	4,056,167	436,187	-361,301	3,258,679	979,742	928,751	43,384	119,103	70,639

Personal Income and Employment by Area: Wausau, WI

(Thousands of dollars, except as noted.)

Year	Personal income, total	Earnings by place of work Nonfarm	Farm	Total	Less: Contributions for government social insurance	Plus: Adjustment for residence	Equals: Net earnings by place of residence	Plus: Dividends, interest, and rent	Plus: Personal current transfer receipts	Per capita personal income (dollars)	Population (persons)	Total employment
1970	336,176	255,780	21,015	276,795	18,854	499	258,440	47,572	30,164	3,439	97,762	42,507
1971	363,883	275,507	21,010	296,517	21,036	1,009	276,490	52,124	35,269	3,670	99,164	42,664
1972	406,522	312,029	22,947	334,976	25,095	758	310,639	56,872	39,011	4,060	100,135	44,356
1973	459,657	356,912	27,446	384,358	32,904	525	351,979	63,504	44,174	4,519	101,722	46,586
1974	501,520	390,089	22,355	412,444	37,292	1,439	376,591	72,090	52,839	4,860	103,197	47,168
1975	563,716	428,820	25,566	454,386	40,005	1,169	415,550	81,250	66,916	5,380	104,779	48,012
1976	637,549	493,788	28,919	522,707	46,867	1,497	477,337	86,578	73,634	6,065	105,124	50,209
1977	733,389	574,032	39,645	613,677	54,446	676	559,907	96,106	77,376	6,851	107,054	53,684
1978	827,451	647,842	45,564	693,406	63,114	1,445	631,737	109,161	86,553	7,618	108,618	55,887
1979	922,354	708,459	56,237	764,696	71,903	2,342	695,135	124,933	102,286	8,342	110,574	56,769
1980	1,007,423	743,919	54,780	798,699	75,229	4,037	727,507	152,832	127,084	9,056	111,246	55,624
1981	1,086,870	796,574	46,290	842,864	86,030	3,877	760,711	187,545	138,614	9,802	110,887	55,453
1982	1,138,753	808,757	41,897	850,654	88,085	8,373	770,942	211,704	156,107	10,257	111,023	54,768
1983	1,195,118	869,447	21,343	890,790	94,425	10,767	807,132	220,331	167,655	10,771	110,953	55,723
1984	1,304,142	929,711	37,255	966,966	102,992	14,546	878,520	252,776	172,846	11,724	111,241	56,858
1985	1,388,727	997,716	36,975	1,034,691	111,513	13,963	937,141	268,543	183,043	12,482	111,260	57,757
1986	1,474,734	1,065,099	41,993	1,107,092	118,954	15,454	1,003,592	286,317	184,825	13,231	111,458	59,211
1987	1,566,103	1,153,898	51,154	1,205,052	127,228	15,974	1,093,798	285,295	187,010	13,976	112,058	61,043
1988	1,662,748	1,261,137	39,761	1,300,898	144,204	16,400	1,173,094	297,197	192,457	14,688	113,201	62,564
1989	1,851,695	1,361,330	76,151	1,437,481	156,596	15,423	1,296,308	341,830	213,557	16,198	114,318	64,559
1990	1,977,323	1,479,088	69,842	1,548,930	177,127	19,275	1,391,078	356,788	229,457	17,084	115,743	66,554
1991	2,062,557	1,572,653	47,284	1,619,937	189,912	16,521	1,446,546	361,713	254,298	17,633	116,972	68,392
1992	2,232,794	1,709,762	54,597	1,764,359	203,981	17,389	1,577,767	379,877	275,150	18,855	118,417	69,877
1993	2,345,084	1,812,073	42,451	1,854,524	216,374	16,061	1,654,211	400,269	290,604	19,535	120,044	70,906
1994	2,476,331	1,927,584	49,367	1,976,951	232,626	14,572	1,758,897	415,670	301,764	20,506	120,760	72,786
1995	2,596,004	2,030,348	31,637	2,061,985	245,485	9,021	1,825,521	448,655	321,828	21,340	121,649	74,772
1996	2,770,536	2,140,684	52,741	2,193,425	256,810	4,105	1,940,720	494,736	335,080	22,606	122,560	76,066
1997	2,942,180	2,320,052	27,508	2,347,560	276,444	-5,602	2,065,514	529,394	347,272	23,807	123,583	78,232
1998	3,146,726	2,438,324	50,048	2,488,372	287,034	-2,059	2,199,279	594,564	352,883	25,255	124,597	80,849
1999	3,288,114	2,615,051	44,692	2,659,743	308,466	-11,604	2,339,673	580,147	368,294	26,220	125,404	83,243
2000	3,502,397	2,794,940	26,460	2,821,400	325,288	-21,524	2,474,588	632,219	395,590	27,798	125,995	84,761
2001	3,710,682	2,950,525	44,514	2,995,039	338,475	-14,879	2,641,685	625,127	443,870	29,343	126,459	85,581
2002	3,878,386	3,101,832	35,238	3,137,070	351,600	5,831	2,791,301	607,169	479,916	30,567	126,880	86,433
2003	4,000,776	3,174,406	52,944	3,227,350	360,678	27,704	2,894,376	617,352	489,048	31,425	127,311	86,454
2004	4,203,687	3,363,665	60,772	3,424,437	381,825	52,372	3,094,984	595,088	513,615	32,879	127,855	88,599
2005	4,429,995	3,542,016	52,551	3,594,567	404,339	79,551	3,269,779	609,784	550,432	34,352	128,958	90,843
2006	4,688,584	3,704,598	36,245	3,740,843	426,480	109,018	3,423,381	677,348	587,855	35,923	130,516	91,577
2007	4,971,356	3,816,128	63,953	3,880,081	441,605	142,462	3,580,938	753,167	637,251	37,727	131,773	92,397
2008	5,190,270	3,889,389	57,843	3,947,232	450,585	173,660	3,670,307	784,058	735,905	39,014	133,036	91,449
2009	5,124,757	3,733,343	19,182	3,752,525	432,913	216,076	3,535,688	736,062	853,007	38,304	133,793	87,307
2010	5,082,448	3,678,178	51,990	3,730,168	433,790	150,540	3,446,918	718,318	917,212	37,910	134,065	85,333
2011	5,349,598	3,783,040	102,980	3,886,020	404,014	199,107	3,681,113	782,926	885,559	39,765	134,531	86,098
2012	5,445,865	4,073,900	102,543	4,176,443	432,438	-26,103	3,717,902	835,833	892,130	40,433	134,689	87,295
2013	5,526,745	4,175,009	106,114	4,281,123	500,628	-38,719	3,741,776	881,156	903,813	40,828	135,365	88,691
2014	5,830,529	4,384,257	149,589	4,533,846	522,703	-33,885	3,977,258	916,794	936,477	42,941	135,780	90,479

Personal Income and Employment by Area: Weirton-Steubenville, WV-OH

(Thousands of dollars, except as noted.)

Year	Personal income, total	Earnings by place of work			Less: Contributions for government social insurance	Plus: Adjustment for residence	Equals: Net earnings by place of residence	Plus: Dividends, interest, and rent	Plus: Personal current transfer receipts	Per capita personal income (dollars)	Population (persons)	Total employment
		Nonfarm	Farm	Total								
1970	603,295	560,095	947	561,042	41,075	-43,325	476,642	68,862	57,791	3,624	166,471	67,336
1971	654,624	608,413	1,121	609,534	46,459	-50,605	512,470	73,946	68,208	3,916	167,161	68,528
1972	713,422	666,733	1,194	667,927	53,066	-56,435	558,426	78,483	76,513	4,297	166,032	68,997
1973	766,299	711,323	1,697	713,020	66,289	-58,535	588,196	87,023	91,080	4,614	166,066	70,056
1974	878,598	821,543	1,973	823,516	79,983	-71,140	672,393	101,361	104,844	5,338	164,593	71,072
1975	960,505	873,443	1,547	874,990	85,142	-72,663	717,185	115,578	127,742	5,787	165,977	69,428
1976	1,079,147	1,005,044	1,375	1,006,419	98,476	-92,612	815,331	123,590	140,226	6,554	164,666	71,679
1977	1,177,732	1,089,561	1,262	1,090,823	106,240	-96,496	888,087	136,863	152,782	7,191	163,770	71,144
1978	1,269,998	1,162,276	1,474	1,163,750	116,877	-98,152	948,721	149,837	171,440	7,846	161,867	70,906
1979	1,417,750	1,303,673	1,753	1,305,426	135,487	-113,378	1,056,561	167,883	193,306	8,773	161,602	72,151
1980	1,525,528	1,336,139	1,901	1,338,040	139,169	-121,391	1,077,480	209,770	238,278	9,339	163,345	68,618
1981	1,641,428	1,381,666	1,807	1,383,473	154,031	-110,170	1,119,272	255,265	266,891	10,162	161,525	66,467
1982	1,636,355	1,293,230	2,234	1,295,464	148,079	-104,331	1,043,054	285,386	307,915	10,196	160,486	60,765
1983	1,616,783	1,223,215	717	1,223,932	141,218	-95,588	987,126	305,254	324,403	10,303	156,918	57,943
1984	1,712,784	1,278,777	438	1,279,215	151,493	-101,165	1,026,557	346,039	340,188	11,076	154,644	58,635
1985	1,733,895	1,268,275	1,224	1,269,499	151,475	-92,327	1,025,697	349,456	358,742	11,409	151,981	57,275
1986	1,823,505	1,357,644	375	1,358,019	167,499	-101,287	1,089,233	363,460	370,812	12,227	149,132	58,845
1987	1,865,191	1,399,663	324	1,399,987	170,958	-100,804	1,128,225	354,819	382,147	12,708	146,776	59,897
1988	1,957,328	1,501,507	-1,417	1,500,090	190,200	-112,031	1,197,859	362,449	397,020	13,480	145,205	60,005
1989	2,102,192	1,619,323	748	1,620,071	207,340	-124,704	1,288,027	403,175	410,990	14,611	143,873	61,112
1990	2,226,551	1,682,092	757	1,682,849	218,628	-112,198	1,352,023	427,738	446,790	15,650	142,270	62,123
1991	2,218,571	1,620,547	-1,147	1,619,400	214,424	-71,613	1,333,363	399,321	485,887	15,641	141,845	60,857
1992	2,342,646	1,731,361	2,438	1,733,799	223,164	-102,337	1,408,298	399,374	534,974	16,613	141,012	60,156
1993	2,402,932	1,754,611	1,689	1,756,300	238,793	-72,360	1,445,147	392,389	565,396	17,078	140,704	59,913
1994	2,499,561	1,816,671	2,781	1,819,452	245,634	-69,332	1,504,486	401,938	593,137	17,854	140,001	60,141
1995	2,545,738	1,798,379	1,328	1,799,707	249,019	-33,179	1,517,509	411,328	616,901	18,243	139,547	60,826
1996	2,633,185	1,832,209	449	1,832,658	252,900	-36,584	1,543,174	441,002	649,009	19,043	138,275	60,868
1997	2,647,749	1,749,146	1,456	1,750,602	236,953	-4,339	1,509,310	470,644	667,795	19,381	136,619	59,452
1998	2,787,339	1,874,732	1,890	1,876,622	254,458	-9,700	1,612,464	497,729	677,146	20,697	134,675	61,693
1999	2,826,452	1,878,126	2,140	1,880,266	251,562	17,450	1,646,154	481,006	699,292	21,208	133,276	60,921
2000	2,977,485	1,981,019	3,796	1,984,815	268,544	23,379	1,739,650	509,453	728,382	22,611	131,681	60,674
2001	3,067,265	1,986,869	4,317	1,991,186	265,536	37,391	1,763,041	515,294	788,930	23,468	130,701	59,594
2002	3,160,024	2,061,782	4,491	2,066,273	269,092	40,378	1,837,559	487,810	834,655	24,355	129,750	59,634
2003	3,182,092	2,073,821	3,583	2,077,404	274,090	44,646	1,847,960	464,627	869,505	24,640	129,141	59,016
2004	3,241,920	2,090,731	3,127	2,093,858	274,439	50,685	1,870,104	491,868	879,948	25,280	128,241	57,524
2005	3,230,490	2,120,349	2,005	2,122,354	278,835	52,692	1,896,211	442,706	891,573	25,344	127,464	57,529
2006	3,348,265	2,175,507	1,639	2,177,146	277,134	51,020	1,951,032	447,710	949,523	26,506	126,321	57,081
2007	3,495,127	2,240,159	1,090	2,241,249	278,789	46,961	2,009,421	505,435	980,271	27,908	125,236	57,483
2008	3,739,387	2,399,325	-30	2,399,295	297,278	45,947	2,147,964	512,926	1,078,497	29,925	124,959	57,786
2009	3,741,569	2,177,693	891	2,178,584	277,981	195,669	2,096,272	473,613	1,171,684	29,996	124,734	54,465
2010	3,807,310	2,104,249	504	2,104,753	263,999	298,436	2,139,190	449,450	1,218,670	30,638	124,266	52,331
2011	4,023,496	2,188,521	1,188	2,189,709	246,410	356,756	2,300,055	495,003	1,228,438	32,625	123,324	52,259
2012	4,115,971	2,225,962	1,562	2,227,524	247,576	381,519	2,361,467	533,355	1,221,149	33,609	122,466	51,856
2013	4,152,521	2,212,837	8,412	2,221,249	270,628	429,044	2,379,665	524,590	1,248,266	34,053	121,942	51,349
2014	4,264,968	2,259,870	1,431	2,261,301	281,760	447,626	2,427,167	546,978	1,290,823	35,150	121,336	51,233

Personal Income and Employment by Area: Wenatchee, WA

(Thousands of dollars, except as noted.)

Year	Personal income, total	Earnings by place of work			Less: Contributions for government social insurance	Plus: Adjustment for residence	Equals: Net earnings by place of residence	Plus: Dividends, interest, and rent	Plus: Personal current transfer receipts	Per capita personal income (dollars)	Population (persons)	Total employment
		Nonfarm	Farm	Total								
1970	231,821	159,311	19,635	178,946	12,977	-215	165,754	39,840	26,227	4,003	57,905	28,819
1971	265,020	171,000	36,117	207,117	14,632	-198	192,287	43,027	29,706	4,555	58,182	28,335
1972	283,125	183,183	37,258	220,441	16,352	289	204,378	46,748	31,999	4,878	58,036	28,518
1973	327,152	203,593	53,433	257,026	21,005	1,099	237,120	54,172	35,860	5,610	58,318	29,659
1974	367,249	229,409	57,772	287,181	24,447	1,152	263,886	61,153	42,210	6,169	59,531	31,056
1975	429,693	261,233	72,111	333,344	27,982	1,108	306,470	71,121	52,102	7,071	60,767	32,893
1976	461,565	309,380	52,827	362,207	33,902	-110	328,195	76,369	57,001	7,392	62,443	35,350
1977	518,979	354,050	54,629	408,679	39,188	-204	369,287	87,418	62,274	8,067	64,337	36,078
1978	577,471	388,482	59,826	448,308	43,600	3,791	408,499	101,432	67,540	8,805	65,586	36,913
1979	626,841	424,160	52,683	476,843	48,920	4,541	432,464	117,542	76,835	9,458	66,273	38,625
1980	703,365	443,381	67,814	511,195	51,477	5,397	465,115	143,429	94,821	10,406	67,591	38,992
1981	758,176	473,908	59,802	533,710	58,946	5,325	480,089	173,924	104,163	10,987	69,004	39,690
1982	807,042	489,164	62,204	551,368	62,109	5,859	495,118	193,949	117,975	11,592	69,622	39,743
1983	883,594	530,372	72,443	602,815	68,509	6,593	540,899	215,177	127,518	12,448	70,983	41,521
1984	954,463	578,708	72,225	650,933	77,530	5,219	578,622	240,133	135,708	13,178	72,428	42,260
1985	979,106	609,607	47,732	657,339	82,939	5,962	580,362	251,117	147,627	13,306	73,586	42,158
1986	1,050,660	630,330	84,637	714,967	85,979	8,419	637,407	257,352	155,901	14,225	73,859	41,969
1987	1,145,231	667,696	133,123	800,819	90,570	9,205	719,454	263,272	162,505	15,427	74,236	43,915
1988	1,128,534	717,228	59,442	776,670	99,539	10,821	687,952	268,092	172,490	14,848	76,006	44,589
1989	1,245,413	761,497	87,670	849,167	107,926	12,693	753,934	302,791	188,688	16,069	77,504	45,586
1990	1,327,667	825,490	84,403	909,893	119,200	16,350	807,043	311,982	208,642	16,835	78,865	48,257
1991	1,480,172	909,966	125,219	1,035,185	131,365	17,801	921,621	324,350	234,201	18,224	81,220	48,854
1992	1,621,227	992,385	154,948	1,147,333	142,013	20,602	1,025,922	334,541	260,764	19,400	83,570	48,476
1993	1,717,689	1,071,594	142,267	1,213,861	153,062	23,060	1,083,859	357,692	276,138	19,967	86,027	49,733
1994	1,797,066	1,147,007	114,513	1,261,520	164,070	24,468	1,121,918	380,376	294,772	20,247	88,755	52,796
1995	1,870,561	1,168,092	113,796	1,281,888	167,817	26,928	1,140,999	419,093	310,469	20,404	91,676	53,327
1996	2,031,138	1,228,499	166,444	1,394,943	170,727	29,594	1,253,810	446,712	330,616	21,727	93,486	53,993
1997	2,126,903	1,321,555	121,829	1,443,384	174,799	32,838	1,301,423	485,269	340,211	22,361	95,118	54,720
1998	2,249,171	1,408,543	128,181	1,536,724	182,353	38,015	1,392,386	495,465	361,320	23,231	96,819	55,160
1999	2,292,200	1,468,345	106,281	1,574,626	185,982	41,841	1,430,485	478,444	383,271	23,310	98,336	56,029
2000	2,442,279	1,530,119	131,555	1,661,674	198,778	43,676	1,506,572	515,384	420,323	24,590	99,322	56,905
2001	2,532,164	1,619,768	101,423	1,721,191	207,465	42,900	1,556,626	508,428	467,110	25,484	99,361	56,618
2002	2,568,299	1,672,769	120,781	1,793,550	217,401	38,179	1,614,328	470,965	483,006	25,738	99,786	56,813
2003	2,738,594	1,772,606	147,711	1,920,317	227,319	36,749	1,729,747	497,614	511,233	27,208	100,654	57,482
2004	2,875,982	1,860,552	171,330	2,031,882	243,321	37,671	1,826,232	524,957	524,793	28,205	101,968	59,057
2005	2,966,979	1,953,870	137,110	2,090,980	260,910	44,578	1,874,648	528,873	563,458	28,703	103,369	61,192
2006	3,133,732	2,061,543	136,255	2,197,798	275,507	36,530	1,958,821	566,515	608,396	29,818	105,094	62,628
2007	3,390,745	2,159,223	128,853	2,288,076	288,359	44,700	2,044,417	687,946	658,382	31,773	106,717	64,292
2008	3,738,886	2,251,250	163,820	2,415,070	298,581	42,780	2,159,269	833,610	746,007	34,610	108,029	65,325
2009	3,690,208	2,216,722	165,868	2,382,590	304,588	40,940	2,118,942	747,270	823,996	33,665	109,614	64,749
2010	3,767,765	2,213,097	191,533	2,404,630	306,892	40,126	2,137,864	729,379	900,522	33,864	111,261	63,608
2011	3,994,374	2,264,509	236,002	2,500,511	287,501	41,525	2,254,535	831,705	908,134	35,635	112,091	63,880
2012	4,237,197	2,333,409	283,634	2,617,043	293,455	47,179	2,370,767	945,070	921,360	37,499	112,995	65,126
2013	4,280,491	2,437,161	252,538	2,689,699	339,335	47,381	2,397,745	946,193	936,553	37,715	113,496	66,216
2014	4,513,562	2,576,126	235,210	2,811,336	362,069	51,754	2,501,021	983,148	1,029,393	39,457	114,392	68,150

Personal Income and Employment by Area: Wheeling, WV-OH

(Thousands of dollars, except as noted.)

Year	Personal income, total	Earnings by place of work			Less: Contributions for government social insurance	Plus: Adjustment for residence	Equals: Net earnings by place of residence	Plus: Dividends, interest, and rent	Plus: Personal current transfer receipts	Per capita personal income (dollars)	Population (persons)	Total employment
		Nonfarm	Farm	Total								
1970	644,239	514,643	1,901	516,544	38,769	7,111	484,886	90,378	68,975	3,529	182,552	74,553
1971	687,701	542,866	2,345	545,211	42,239	7,189	510,161	96,887	80,653	3,694	186,174	74,644
1972	747,119	589,230	2,802	592,032	47,447	7,866	552,451	104,018	90,650	4,020	185,831	74,658
1973	816,072	642,810	3,185	645,995	60,044	7,233	593,184	115,138	107,750	4,406	185,230	76,692
1974	891,565	690,338	1,677	692,015	67,207	9,720	634,528	131,867	125,170	4,840	184,209	77,111
1975	990,217	757,814	2,702	760,516	71,683	4,398	693,231	144,366	152,620	5,349	185,114	76,968
1976	1,109,390	858,391	2,585	860,976	82,833	4,106	782,249	157,399	169,742	5,951	186,432	78,256
1977	1,228,976	958,686	1,932	960,618	92,719	2,996	870,895	176,056	182,025	6,619	185,683	79,725
1978	1,345,301	1,053,136	1,367	1,054,503	104,981	-834	948,688	192,124	204,489	7,262	185,256	81,408
1979	1,495,754	1,155,446	1,076	1,156,522	118,437	8,404	1,046,489	213,345	235,920	8,022	186,463	81,667
1980	1,616,804	1,176,802	732	1,177,534	121,537	16,358	1,072,355	269,173	275,276	8,723	185,340	78,635
1981	1,763,733	1,245,628	385	1,246,013	137,959	10,734	1,118,788	338,349	306,596	9,577	184,158	76,299
1982	1,845,270	1,255,715	-252	1,255,463	142,592	2,627	1,115,498	382,470	347,302	10,120	182,331	74,012
1983	1,879,389	1,219,375	-1,025	1,218,350	139,547	8,870	1,087,673	412,402	379,314	10,438	180,057	71,069
1984	1,982,890	1,276,572	501	1,277,073	148,814	14,911	1,143,170	451,638	388,082	11,217	176,777	70,504
1985	2,023,489	1,283,443	2,314	1,285,757	150,783	9,517	1,144,491	470,422	408,576	11,691	173,087	69,315
1986	2,066,244	1,296,869	1,747	1,298,616	156,896	7,953	1,149,673	490,686	425,885	12,246	168,724	68,607
1987	2,140,033	1,380,782	1,010	1,381,792	167,850	6,936	1,220,878	485,408	433,747	12,880	166,158	70,059
1988	2,222,993	1,457,133	-1,577	1,455,556	183,797	-7,539	1,264,220	504,039	454,734	13,576	163,741	71,434
1989	2,378,208	1,534,695	1,392	1,536,087	195,465	-7,079	1,333,543	565,936	478,729	14,711	161,663	71,939
1990	2,496,047	1,619,727	1,314	1,621,041	208,013	-2,158	1,410,870	577,178	507,999	15,702	158,961	72,385
1991	2,565,895	1,663,663	-2,791	1,660,872	219,889	-8,921	1,432,062	579,576	554,257	16,211	158,283	72,525
1992	2,730,354	1,733,822	2,101	1,735,923	230,546	20,623	1,526,000	585,584	618,770	17,223	158,525	71,690
1993	2,784,290	1,785,586	1,332	1,786,918	245,158	7,245	1,549,005	584,162	651,123	17,573	158,445	72,312
1994	2,901,681	1,889,763	1,625	1,891,388	258,848	3,384	1,635,924	598,819	666,938	18,372	157,944	74,195
1995	2,970,935	1,929,607	557	1,930,164	266,974	-8,946	1,654,244	629,047	687,644	18,983	156,502	75,761
1996	3,119,113	1,994,812	-1,726	1,993,086	274,725	8,586	1,726,947	667,029	725,137	19,822	157,354	76,900
1997	3,228,729	2,077,025	-1,875	2,075,150	279,854	1,578	1,796,874	690,106	741,749	20,684	156,100	77,888
1998	3,431,021	2,184,085	-532	2,183,553	293,381	12,371	1,902,543	737,279	791,199	22,056	155,562	79,949
1999	3,485,464	2,271,495	-492	2,271,003	303,693	10,064	1,977,374	707,237	800,853	22,599	154,230	79,773
2000	3,599,290	2,329,936	4,849	2,334,785	315,270	9,500	2,029,015	747,384	822,891	23,538	152,914	80,818
2001	3,708,441	2,385,551	4,463	2,390,014	312,643	-8,267	2,069,104	748,706	890,631	24,441	151,728	80,564
2002	3,826,745	2,474,038	2,081	2,476,119	317,555	-8,214	2,150,350	721,826	954,569	25,269	151,442	80,822
2003	3,928,327	2,568,653	234	2,568,887	334,256	-1,555	2,233,076	702,721	992,530	26,073	150,666	80,250
2004	4,050,269	2,692,179	7,648	2,699,827	347,513	-241	2,352,073	690,925	1,007,271	26,968	150,186	81,318
2005	4,128,512	2,808,579	5,930	2,814,509	364,995	-3,185	2,446,329	665,286	1,016,897	27,627	149,438	82,337
2006	4,360,659	2,937,520	448	2,937,968	370,732	673	2,567,909	714,716	1,078,034	29,225	149,208	82,735
2007	4,480,204	2,956,706	-3,632	2,953,074	361,218	10,666	2,602,522	757,548	1,120,134	30,124	148,727	83,137
2008	4,783,209	3,146,259	-6,111	3,140,148	372,417	9,901	2,777,632	798,313	1,207,264	32,303	148,073	83,199
2009	4,769,386	3,145,529	-6,963	3,138,566	379,733	-20,004	2,738,829	728,066	1,302,491	32,245	147,910	81,485
2010	4,875,895	3,235,007	-6,268	3,228,739	385,116	-27,842	2,815,781	704,485	1,355,629	32,983	147,829	81,106
2011	5,212,640	3,411,451	-4,524	3,406,927	357,531	-5,010	3,044,386	810,809	1,357,445	35,442	147,075	81,361
2012	5,513,457	3,664,610	-6,055	3,658,555	376,270	-6,027	3,276,258	867,486	1,369,713	37,669	146,364	81,804
2013	5,610,656	3,831,538	-1,829	3,829,709	438,896	-42,612	3,348,201	886,575	1,375,880	38,468	145,853	82,515
2014	5,867,763	4,018,738	-2,379	4,016,359	469,274	-42,284	3,504,801	921,930	1,441,032	40,410	145,205	83,120

Personal Income and Employment by Area: Wichita, KS

(Thousands of dollars, except as noted.)

Year	Personal income, total	Earnings by place of work			Less: Contributions for government social insurance	Plus: Adjustment for residence	Equals: Net earnings by place of residence	Plus: Dividends, interest, and rent	Plus: Personal current transfer receipts	Per capita personal income (dollars)	Population (persons)	Total employment
		Nonfarm	Farm	Total								
1970	1,806,603	1,466,984	38,013	1,504,997	104,731	-14,047	1,386,219	254,293	166,091	4,039	447,283	210,746
1971	1,909,327	1,516,032	53,110	1,569,142	111,656	-14,428	1,443,058	275,087	191,182	4,320	441,929	205,860
1972	2,119,024	1,711,203	70,116	1,781,319	133,326	-18,892	1,629,101	296,749	193,174	4,847	437,170	216,199
1973	2,371,365	1,904,407	112,894	2,017,301	170,583	-22,055	1,824,663	326,553	220,149	5,406	438,655	227,741
1974	2,669,102	2,175,288	84,732	2,260,020	201,772	-27,790	2,030,458	389,792	248,852	5,991	445,506	238,535
1975	3,013,776	2,442,881	69,542	2,512,423	222,988	-29,561	2,259,874	447,516	306,386	6,694	450,230	241,789
1976	3,300,416	2,729,571	37,217	2,766,788	253,687	-36,010	2,477,091	477,920	345,405	7,218	457,265	250,873
1977	3,558,225	2,950,838	28,271	2,979,109	278,608	-38,874	2,661,627	526,356	370,242	7,734	460,059	254,590
1978	4,048,288	3,407,424	18,230	3,425,654	333,735	-47,570	3,044,349	604,309	399,630	8,730	463,740	267,224
1979	4,672,263	3,980,437	39,032	4,019,469	405,815	-60,774	3,552,880	683,275	436,108	9,916	471,185	282,468
1980	5,291,078	4,450,067	-3,519	4,446,548	441,881	-72,106	3,932,561	838,902	519,615	11,061	478,352	287,480
1981	5,994,813	4,916,858	6,350	4,923,208	520,677	-74,776	4,327,755	1,058,089	608,969	12,343	485,677	291,074
1982	6,409,916	4,972,929	53,353	5,026,282	539,381	-71,464	4,415,437	1,268,203	726,276	13,085	489,883	279,479
1983	6,579,777	5,094,643	20,837	5,115,480	552,892	-67,818	4,494,770	1,313,264	771,743	13,437	489,678	280,797
1984	7,191,580	5,617,865	41,780	5,659,645	626,164	-73,830	4,959,651	1,448,300	783,629	14,598	492,652	291,814
1985	7,499,490	5,837,328	11,388	5,848,716	660,583	-72,553	5,115,580	1,561,648	822,262	15,115	496,168	292,297
1986	7,994,631	6,237,005	64,481	6,301,486	704,738	-78,885	5,517,863	1,609,696	867,072	16,041	498,385	292,210
1987	8,350,534	6,599,987	61,968	6,661,955	735,034	-79,753	5,847,168	1,611,485	891,881	16,571	503,923	302,541
1988	8,875,662	6,993,151	72,104	7,065,255	805,485	-82,292	6,177,478	1,747,017	951,167	17,424	509,395	307,398
1989	9,423,891	7,428,769	50,847	7,479,616	850,686	-84,646	6,544,284	1,825,736	1,053,871	18,255	516,224	314,218
1990	10,053,569	7,901,348	65,913	7,967,261	957,326	-85,394	6,924,541	1,978,816	1,150,212	19,317	520,465	320,176
1991	10,606,946	8,266,183	47,959	8,314,142	1,017,605	-93,294	7,203,243	2,140,505	1,263,198	20,094	527,868	325,468
1992	11,388,653	8,945,475	83,115	9,028,590	1,090,889	-104,074	7,833,627	2,159,289	1,395,737	21,169	537,981	327,396
1993	11,830,976	9,195,992	71,012	9,267,004	1,116,207	-104,642	8,046,155	2,292,413	1,492,408	21,722	544,645	329,318
1994	12,106,449	9,412,689	81,079	9,493,768	1,179,490	-106,537	8,207,741	2,351,850	1,546,858	22,083	548,229	332,894
1995	12,839,276	9,967,204	31,207	9,998,411	1,245,274	-114,772	8,638,365	2,573,862	1,627,049	23,265	551,873	339,959
1996	13,822,631	10,717,233	74,450	10,791,683	1,346,726	-125,690	9,319,267	2,821,045	1,682,319	24,795	557,473	349,157
1997	15,035,198	11,692,910	120,596	11,813,506	1,473,476	-144,685	10,195,345	3,075,964	1,763,889	26,617	564,862	361,796
1998	16,011,317	12,620,850	48,100	12,668,950	1,585,767	-162,921	10,920,262	3,341,614	1,749,441	27,872	574,469	372,834
1999	16,229,427	12,836,741	58,218	12,894,959	1,599,408	-163,494	11,132,057	3,279,016	1,818,354	28,050	578,580	371,016
2000	17,059,233	13,298,316	42,219	13,340,535	1,634,288	-163,884	11,542,363	3,501,297	2,015,573	29,366	580,911	370,992
2001	18,265,728	14,314,826	8,054	14,322,880	1,622,242	-180,134	12,520,504	3,520,005	2,225,219	31,275	584,043	376,551
2002	18,214,882	14,262,938	20,031	14,282,969	1,623,027	-227,747	12,432,195	3,354,085	2,428,602	30,940	588,719	371,001
2003	18,393,295	14,248,609	115,492	14,364,101	1,625,464	-236,811	12,501,826	3,319,510	2,571,959	31,138	590,712	365,596
2004	19,570,219	15,120,547	163,078	15,283,625	1,715,480	-272,770	13,295,375	3,650,013	2,624,831	33,002	593,004	368,485
2005	20,784,784	15,843,943	137,866	15,981,809	1,815,673	-286,647	13,879,489	4,152,970	2,752,325	34,858	596,270	373,408
2006	23,457,702	17,436,203	178,532	17,614,735	1,968,250	-333,604	15,312,881	5,198,792	2,946,029	38,999	601,501	382,079
2007	24,597,376	17,933,559	114,292	18,047,851	2,041,311	-296,598	15,709,942	5,724,096	3,163,338	40,402	608,816	392,731
2008	26,922,221	19,229,821	223,263	19,453,084	2,144,815	-285,089	17,023,180	6,297,607	3,601,434	43,624	617,142	398,751
2009	25,148,075	17,831,377	146,236	17,977,613	2,053,815	-267,759	15,656,039	5,451,440	4,040,596	40,095	627,215	385,203
2010	24,264,964	17,931,820	138,996	18,070,816	2,066,223	-251,123	15,753,470	4,211,355	4,300,139	38,398	631,936	375,803
2011	26,703,571	18,863,179	126,783	18,989,962	1,911,120	-264,267	16,814,575	5,553,021	4,335,975	42,168	633,266	376,715
2012	28,235,474	19,430,373	203,323	19,633,696	1,961,623	-244,902	17,427,171	6,573,429	4,234,874	44,399	635,942	380,517
2013	28,391,579	19,674,112	326,846	20,000,958	2,259,402	-247,149	17,494,407	6,614,739	4,282,433	44,483	638,259	386,788
2014	29,038,525	20,195,254	124,116	20,319,370	2,325,913	-222,671	17,770,786	6,837,655	4,430,084	45,297	641,076	391,977

Personal Income and Employment by Area: Wichita Falls, TX

(Thousands of dollars, except as noted.)

| Year | Personal income, total | Derivation of personal income | | | | | Per capita personal income (dollars) | Population (persons) | Total employment |
| | | Earnings by place of work | | | Less: Contributions for government social insurance | Plus: Adjustment for residence | Equals: Net earnings by place of residence | Plus: Dividends, interest, and rent | Plus: Personal current transfer receipts | | | |
		Nonfarm	Farm	Total								
1970	572,746	443,894	4,504	448,398	25,967	-1,805	420,626	112,273	39,847	4,257	134,547	68,460
1971	643,316	501,021	5,309	506,330	30,869	-2,728	472,733	125,241	45,342	4,733	135,914	71,202
1972	671,882	521,749	5,494	527,243	32,823	-3,516	490,904	130,541	50,437	5,006	134,213	69,547
1973	747,864	571,456	12,043	583,499	40,178	-4,530	538,791	148,826	60,247	5,633	132,776	72,373
1974	839,772	640,080	17,915	657,995	47,369	-7,073	603,553	166,511	69,708	6,187	135,739	74,009
1975	901,593	684,740	13,239	697,979	51,542	-7,945	638,492	178,475	84,626	6,627	136,058	73,601
1976	998,949	774,868	11,610	786,478	59,718	-10,337	716,423	190,701	91,825	7,186	139,008	76,059
1977	1,061,754	830,228	6,475	836,703	64,364	-12,150	760,189	204,338	97,227	7,672	138,389	77,471
1978	1,191,712	937,833	2,831	940,664	73,381	-15,529	851,754	233,550	106,408	8,688	137,175	79,811
1979	1,338,707	1,048,369	9,006	1,057,375	86,157	-18,541	952,677	266,235	119,795	9,744	137,384	82,264
1980	1,477,451	1,152,056	-1,816	1,150,240	96,220	-23,253	1,030,767	311,283	135,401	10,669	138,486	84,353
1981	1,730,287	1,332,440	11,081	1,343,521	119,850	-26,164	1,197,507	381,386	151,394	12,332	140,309	88,921
1982	1,822,575	1,366,899	13,655	1,380,554	126,246	-24,315	1,229,993	422,065	170,517	12,760	142,833	88,337
1983	1,887,549	1,380,052	19,283	1,399,335	127,419	-22,131	1,249,785	449,683	188,081	13,098	144,114	85,451
1984	2,031,929	1,470,262	25,273	1,495,535	140,483	-22,097	1,332,955	500,806	198,168	14,090	144,209	86,935
1985	2,093,201	1,508,284	12,272	1,520,556	146,573	-21,029	1,352,954	530,323	209,924	14,489	144,471	87,027
1986	2,103,792	1,482,404	22,374	1,504,778	144,488	-19,077	1,341,213	530,839	231,740	14,525	144,842	82,505
1987	2,104,899	1,476,220	23,056	1,499,276	142,864	-17,068	1,339,344	522,912	242,643	14,778	142,433	81,957
1988	2,199,040	1,532,525	28,040	1,560,565	155,736	-16,537	1,388,292	551,980	258,768	15,554	141,380	81,928
1989	2,279,404	1,594,917	23,736	1,618,653	163,580	-14,773	1,440,300	563,128	275,976	16,171	140,953	81,822
1990	2,405,439	1,658,604	42,191	1,700,795	167,913	-22,158	1,510,724	595,341	299,374	17,145	140,303	81,730
1991	2,394,186	1,627,221	30,069	1,657,290	170,544	-20,365	1,466,381	599,728	328,077	17,216	139,070	79,063
1992	2,519,110	1,713,417	37,065	1,750,482	177,837	-20,877	1,551,768	589,795	377,547	18,151	138,786	78,932
1993	2,644,853	1,832,631	24,050	1,856,681	190,835	-23,533	1,642,313	604,321	398,219	18,704	141,403	82,583
1994	2,772,879	1,911,509	24,431	1,935,940	199,539	-25,951	1,710,450	640,660	421,769	19,258	143,986	84,658
1995	2,982,345	2,046,919	21,702	2,068,621	213,216	-29,813	1,825,592	703,973	452,780	20,186	147,740	87,085
1996	3,112,278	2,139,723	21,286	2,161,009	219,448	-31,015	1,910,546	721,962	479,770	20,588	151,170	88,384
1997	3,288,231	2,312,550	22,113	2,334,663	230,928	-31,657	2,072,078	714,772	501,381	21,707	151,480	89,491
1998	3,438,667	2,408,362	33,661	2,442,023	236,305	-30,974	2,174,744	761,446	502,477	22,742	151,206	89,658
1999	3,581,513	2,506,475	43,076	2,549,551	245,036	-30,747	2,273,768	788,471	519,274	23,660	151,374	88,983
2000	3,755,903	2,636,132	34,176	2,670,308	254,255	-32,225	2,383,828	823,820	548,255	24,735	151,847	90,934
2001	4,044,870	2,860,190	41,788	2,901,978	271,936	-33,788	2,596,254	854,617	593,999	26,828	150,770	90,764
2002	4,142,243	2,949,369	41,868	2,991,237	282,737	-52,281	2,656,219	846,523	639,501	27,433	150,995	90,169
2003	4,368,060	3,103,341	48,835	3,152,176	297,344	-47,392	2,807,440	876,901	683,719	28,986	150,694	90,377
2004	4,461,649	3,205,335	48,643	3,253,978	305,816	-29,865	2,918,297	819,972	723,380	29,347	152,033	89,081
2005	4,650,906	3,329,007	34,332	3,363,339	315,370	-17,088	3,030,881	850,375	769,650	30,770	151,152	87,644
2006	5,083,885	3,643,705	17,244	3,660,949	338,224	-4,697	3,318,028	951,988	813,869	33,536	151,596	91,085
2007	5,188,929	3,629,034	13,126	3,642,160	349,042	10,588	3,303,706	995,599	889,624	34,446	150,641	91,472
2008	5,873,506	4,146,724	9,449	4,156,173	373,022	34,118	3,817,269	1,076,862	979,375	39,082	150,287	91,738
2009	5,275,598	3,556,073	-9,798	3,546,275	356,111	32,088	3,222,252	985,733	1,067,613	34,991	150,768	89,545
2010	5,460,138	3,691,593	-2,679	3,688,914	365,035	41,494	3,365,373	940,322	1,154,443	36,010	151,628	88,566
2011	5,915,750	3,952,373	3,824	3,956,197	334,106	50,728	3,672,819	1,058,256	1,184,675	39,351	150,332	87,319
2012	6,177,028	4,082,843	11,636	4,094,479	343,112	53,934	3,805,301	1,186,592	1,185,135	40,911	150,986	89,637
2013	6,099,507	4,071,164	13,804	4,084,968	385,729	57,294	3,756,533	1,110,265	1,232,709	40,253	151,529	89,287
2014	6,348,612	4,203,388	46,508	4,249,896	393,856	61,928	3,917,968	1,149,495	1,281,149	41,895	151,536	89,331

Personal Income and Employment by Area: Williamsport, PA

(Thousands of dollars, except as noted.)

Year	Personal income, total	Derivation of personal income								Per capita personal income (dollars)	Population (persons)	Total employment
		Earnings by place of work			Less: Contributions for government social insurance	Plus: Adjustment for residence	Equals: Net earnings by place of residence	Plus: Dividends, interest, and rent	Plus: Personal current transfer receipts			
		Nonfarm	Farm	Total								
1970	411,735	352,162	3,655	355,817	26,745	-13,974	315,098	51,080	45,557	3,626	113,547	53,041
1971	436,003	368,626	2,763	371,389	28,974	-13,624	328,791	54,362	52,850	3,777	115,429	52,143
1972	480,512	407,820	2,080	409,900	33,627	-14,757	361,516	59,270	59,726	4,162	115,443	53,343
1973	537,443	461,152	5,231	466,383	43,423	-16,036	406,924	64,554	65,965	4,612	116,542	56,253
1974	591,470	498,382	6,364	504,746	48,661	-16,805	439,280	72,581	79,609	5,040	117,354	56,294
1975	643,298	522,961	5,317	528,278	49,365	-18,297	460,616	78,646	104,036	5,452	117,985	54,271
1976	708,012	579,157	6,010	585,167	55,905	-19,319	509,943	85,144	112,925	5,966	118,684	55,204
1977	774,284	636,565	5,930	642,495	61,927	-21,493	559,075	95,525	119,684	6,566	117,927	55,790
1978	863,424	721,273	4,877	726,150	71,902	-23,633	630,615	105,432	127,377	7,300	118,274	58,649
1979	945,426	781,123	8,306	789,429	80,034	-24,902	684,493	116,774	144,159	7,906	119,588	58,472
1980	1,024,964	810,647	6,340	816,987	82,731	-25,910	708,346	144,986	171,632	8,666	118,271	56,384
1981	1,124,514	864,064	10,760	874,824	94,270	-28,967	751,587	180,573	192,354	9,574	117,455	55,670
1982	1,184,746	882,961	9,655	892,616	98,007	-31,752	762,857	206,165	215,724	10,095	117,354	54,240
1983	1,224,356	890,309	1,486	891,795	99,398	-29,694	762,703	224,478	237,175	10,457	117,083	52,384
1984	1,322,344	975,060	9,562	984,622	113,155	-34,398	837,069	253,336	231,939	11,338	116,627	54,551
1985	1,393,481	1,030,207	9,553	1,039,760	120,595	-39,284	879,881	272,573	241,027	12,035	115,787	54,780
1986	1,483,492	1,109,965	7,883	1,117,848	130,148	-43,577	944,123	285,705	253,664	12,832	115,613	56,188
1987	1,595,227	1,223,250	7,793	1,231,043	141,680	-51,784	1,037,579	298,776	258,872	13,664	116,750	59,376
1988	1,724,572	1,344,817	8,936	1,353,753	158,838	-56,401	1,138,514	311,580	274,478	14,645	117,756	61,254
1989	1,866,503	1,416,890	11,994	1,428,884	164,130	-60,078	1,204,676	367,456	294,371	15,728	118,673	61,947
1990	1,919,203	1,445,607	12,709	1,458,316	169,622	-64,507	1,224,187	372,531	322,485	16,145	118,876	62,293
1991	1,999,897	1,483,865	6,141	1,490,006	175,515	-62,246	1,252,245	379,479	368,173	16,656	120,068	61,029
1992	2,109,463	1,564,619	17,758	1,582,377	184,996	-61,233	1,336,148	380,807	392,508	17,390	121,303	61,727
1993	2,190,001	1,613,281	17,926	1,631,207	194,234	-55,641	1,381,332	394,675	413,994	17,930	122,141	61,763
1994	2,226,974	1,652,240	15,949	1,668,189	203,908	-52,749	1,411,532	400,048	415,394	18,213	122,273	62,543
1995	2,317,766	1,717,239	7,926	1,725,165	209,770	-51,290	1,464,105	418,360	435,301	19,025	121,825	63,196
1996	2,422,888	1,774,402	15,708	1,790,110	212,019	-52,878	1,525,213	439,567	458,108	19,969	121,333	64,164
1997	2,527,778	1,852,572	6,787	1,859,359	218,868	-50,181	1,590,310	467,325	470,143	20,894	120,983	64,890
1998	2,629,692	1,934,806	8,690	1,943,496	225,605	-49,447	1,668,444	497,893	463,355	21,807	120,590	64,864
1999	2,682,143	2,004,167	6,953	2,011,120	232,390	-49,351	1,729,379	476,070	476,694	22,317	120,182	65,349
2000	2,830,675	2,107,163	11,450	2,118,613	242,818	-52,829	1,822,966	504,509	503,200	23,618	119,851	67,186
2001	2,973,274	2,236,524	9,165	2,245,689	254,160	-64,248	1,927,281	503,367	542,626	25,000	118,930	67,611
2002	3,041,808	2,231,876	6,728	2,238,604	252,396	-60,704	1,925,504	537,194	579,110	25,703	118,344	66,556
2003	3,130,928	2,281,102	15,320	2,296,422	257,364	-58,740	1,980,318	544,254	606,356	26,509	118,108	66,380
2004	3,265,896	2,418,764	22,514	2,441,278	271,572	-57,255	2,112,451	520,125	633,320	27,698	117,911	66,986
2005	3,292,305	2,457,201	19,436	2,476,637	282,772	-53,680	2,140,185	475,312	676,808	28,012	117,530	66,915
2006	3,427,378	2,528,846	16,022	2,544,868	290,108	-49,649	2,205,111	513,718	708,549	29,298	116,983	67,239
2007	3,570,633	2,585,020	11,278	2,596,298	299,588	-45,671	2,251,039	561,594	758,000	30,643	116,524	67,883
2008	3,738,768	2,627,001	5,729	2,632,730	306,096	-41,227	2,285,407	603,843	849,518	32,190	116,147	67,557
2009	3,769,536	2,571,029	1,604	2,572,633	304,256	-34,588	2,233,789	598,784	936,963	32,473	116,081	65,778
2010	3,935,731	2,724,764	5,558	2,730,322	323,845	-35,152	2,371,325	582,663	981,743	33,878	116,173	66,653
2011	4,285,206	3,016,822	12,603	3,029,425	321,972	-62,298	2,645,155	658,220	981,831	36,730	116,669	69,407
2012	4,424,930	3,146,337	14,813	3,161,150	334,132	-83,434	2,743,584	693,274	988,072	37,724	117,296	70,511
2013	4,456,058	3,165,803	13,459	3,179,262	377,924	-69,397	2,731,941	709,336	1,014,781	38,173	116,732	69,834
2014	4,633,100	3,311,385	17,840	3,329,225	396,080	-81,297	2,851,848	738,637	1,042,615	39,766	116,508	70,600

Personal Income and Employment by Area: Wilmington, NC

(Thousands of dollars, except as noted.)

Year	Personal income, total	Derivation of personal income								Per capita personal income (dollars)	Population (persons)	Total employment
		Earnings by place of work			Less: Contributions for government social insurance	Plus: Adjustment for residence	Equals: Net earnings by place of residence	Plus: Dividends, interest, and rent	Plus: Personal current transfer receipts			
		Nonfarm	Farm	Total								
1970	325,930	263,540	10,504	274,044	18,307	-1,874	253,863	43,382	28,685	3,201	101,837	47,452
1971	357,622	289,713	9,525	299,238	20,660	-4,092	274,486	48,717	34,419	3,388	105,562	47,676
1972	415,877	340,647	9,578	350,225	25,410	-2,658	322,157	54,774	38,946	3,780	110,029	50,224
1973	477,415	395,618	11,934	407,552	34,045	-3,512	369,995	62,214	45,206	4,197	113,741	54,092
1974	527,366	425,086	10,382	435,468	38,188	1,376	398,656	72,771	55,939	4,527	116,500	54,463
1975	580,723	449,355	8,833	458,188	39,491	4,674	423,371	81,517	75,835	4,888	118,805	52,367
1976	648,504	502,930	8,679	511,609	44,899	7,329	474,039	89,189	85,276	5,379	120,568	54,105
1977	717,724	555,043	8,893	563,936	49,170	11,083	525,849	100,726	91,149	5,852	122,652	55,642
1978	805,675	625,943	10,567	636,510	56,948	12,644	592,206	116,407	97,062	6,598	122,115	57,773
1979	919,252	706,350	12,207	718,557	66,690	16,237	668,104	138,033	113,115	7,456	123,292	60,898
1980	1,043,558	780,324	13,609	793,933	73,770	18,297	738,460	169,967	135,131	8,266	126,245	61,704
1981	1,147,451	833,226	16,534	849,760	84,945	16,780	781,595	208,394	157,462	8,970	127,918	61,913
1982	1,221,214	869,467	12,260	881,727	90,921	20,875	811,681	232,467	177,066	9,366	130,392	61,420
1983	1,332,218	945,516	5,842	951,358	98,899	26,088	878,547	259,167	194,504	10,106	131,827	62,633
1984	1,484,484	1,051,285	10,013	1,061,298	111,780	25,934	975,452	304,529	204,503	11,086	133,911	66,887
1985	1,635,592	1,169,436	5,880	1,175,316	126,377	20,767	1,069,706	344,529	221,357	11,991	136,404	70,397
1986	1,816,156	1,329,895	5,593	1,335,488	146,475	5,891	1,194,904	378,210	243,042	13,022	139,471	74,836
1987	1,951,598	1,414,928	13,524	1,428,452	153,212	1,376	1,276,616	413,738	261,244	13,728	142,160	75,940
1988	2,148,935	1,559,961	12,586	1,572,547	174,672	-6,056	1,391,819	470,120	286,996	14,926	143,969	79,824
1989	2,338,466	1,705,830	13,925	1,719,755	191,849	-18,470	1,509,436	504,240	324,790	15,992	146,223	82,275
1990	2,556,656	1,830,936	18,259	1,849,195	211,044	-31,104	1,607,047	592,076	357,533	17,019	150,226	85,684
1991	2,758,496	1,939,412	27,367	1,966,779	226,430	-7,132	1,733,217	614,136	411,143	17,732	155,570	86,116
1992	2,998,706	2,125,133	30,177	2,155,310	244,477	-12,964	1,897,869	639,549	461,288	18,753	159,904	88,808
1993	3,250,108	2,278,429	32,573	2,311,002	262,179	-3,625	2,045,198	693,132	511,778	19,591	165,895	91,851
1994	3,563,543	2,481,715	32,810	2,514,525	290,622	2,302	2,226,205	806,322	531,016	20,690	172,233	96,120
1995	3,886,781	2,678,121	33,719	2,711,840	314,666	-1,677	2,395,497	889,609	601,675	21,696	179,144	101,327
1996	4,233,908	2,913,454	42,791	2,956,245	340,403	-23,430	2,592,412	987,814	653,682	22,825	185,496	106,945
1997	4,568,264	3,117,491	47,948	3,165,439	365,011	-39,919	2,760,509	1,122,230	685,525	23,899	191,148	113,067
1998	4,909,460	3,439,488	17,143	3,456,631	397,201	-66,793	2,992,637	1,195,751	721,072	24,980	196,533	116,078
1999	5,248,655	3,784,095	13,963	3,798,058	434,907	-90,330	3,272,821	1,211,607	764,227	26,334	199,312	119,878
2000	5,669,081	4,067,720	31,964	4,099,684	455,700	-93,578	3,550,406	1,303,759	814,916	28,051	202,099	121,763
2001	5,884,325	4,187,047	38,975	4,226,022	467,817	-65,651	3,692,554	1,276,700	915,071	28,565	205,996	122,727
2002	5,955,545	4,252,726	17,324	4,270,050	474,260	-81,053	3,714,737	1,241,360	999,448	28,284	210,563	124,643
2003	6,184,157	4,412,779	11,838	4,424,617	503,968	-96,381	3,824,268	1,312,844	1,047,045	28,780	214,877	126,953
2004	6,777,151	4,760,488	29,629	4,790,117	540,780	-109,176	4,140,161	1,508,881	1,128,109	30,459	222,498	132,998
2005	7,390,009	5,203,254	42,293	5,245,547	604,055	-146,425	4,495,067	1,680,726	1,214,216	32,006	230,897	139,468
2006	8,028,401	5,668,284	28,406	5,696,690	656,643	-169,789	4,870,258	1,848,512	1,309,631	33,694	238,272	145,383
2007	8,562,899	6,026,595	39,780	6,066,375	713,476	-200,615	5,152,284	2,007,151	1,403,464	35,163	243,520	152,541
2008	8,944,607	6,209,841	51,560	6,261,401	731,203	-216,157	5,314,041	2,044,734	1,585,832	36,029	248,260	152,300
2009	8,771,381	6,118,342	50,547	6,168,889	712,562	-280,104	5,176,223	1,822,168	1,772,990	34,833	251,814	145,323
2010	8,996,120	6,257,153	59,536	6,316,689	697,833	-255,612	5,363,244	1,736,862	1,896,014	35,178	255,734	143,138
2011	9,519,218	6,421,479	44,068	6,465,547	658,502	-234,963	5,572,082	1,973,163	1,973,973	36,706	259,334	146,674
2012	10,019,345	6,750,756	45,820	6,796,576	663,068	-204,350	5,929,158	2,065,807	2,024,380	38,082	263,101	148,329
2013	9,989,903	6,679,569	64,412	6,743,981	769,158	-224,681	5,750,142	2,144,486	2,095,275	37,234	268,301	151,844
2014	10,432,697	7,094,809	67,540	7,162,349	817,740	-322,680	6,021,929	2,230,985	2,179,783	38,278	272,548	156,378

Personal Income and Employment by Area: Winchester, VA-WV

(Thousands of dollars, except as noted.)

Year	Personal income, total	Derivation of personal income									Per capita personal income (dollars)	Population (persons)	Total employment
		Earnings by place of work			Less: Contributions for government social insurance	Plus: Adjustment for residence	Equals: Net earnings by place of residence	Plus: Dividends, interest, and rent	Plus: Personal current transfer receipts				
		Nonfarm	Farm	Total									
1970	181,265	142,879	2,873	145,752	9,607	4,393	140,538	24,510	16,217		3,261	55,578	27,231
1971	202,198	160,187	3,377	163,564	11,196	3,165	155,533	27,686	18,979		3,503	57,715	28,508
1972	223,563	177,354	4,151	181,505	13,030	3,031	171,506	30,918	21,139		3,842	58,191	29,150
1973	257,770	206,142	7,724	213,866	17,494	673	197,045	36,386	24,339		4,340	59,398	30,736
1974	292,361	234,658	9,152	243,810	20,715	-2,495	220,600	42,902	28,859		4,749	61,566	31,775
1975	308,818	246,155	6,299	252,454	21,065	-8,900	222,489	47,787	38,542		4,903	62,987	30,639
1976	346,648	285,217	4,398	289,615	24,797	-12,350	252,468	52,575	41,605		5,415	64,015	32,116
1977	386,880	322,239	4,078	326,317	28,167	-15,940	282,210	60,194	44,476		5,875	65,849	33,218
1978	446,237	371,245	12,744	383,989	33,036	-21,403	329,550	68,467	48,220		6,570	67,918	35,126
1979	488,238	407,195	13,121	420,316	37,630	-26,706	355,980	76,285	55,973		7,063	69,124	35,530
1980	530,617	439,649	3,881	443,530	40,757	-28,593	374,180	89,673	66,764		7,642	69,435	35,358
1981	598,861	478,805	5,750	484,555	47,696	-25,832	411,027	111,006	76,828		8,540	70,125	35,469
1982	644,048	499,513	5,584	505,097	50,636	-24,100	430,361	127,127	86,560		9,085	70,891	34,837
1983	701,981	541,472	3,724	545,196	55,310	-22,555	467,331	141,596	93,054		9,851	71,263	35,582
1984	796,007	608,482	7,330	615,812	63,192	-19,901	532,719	165,600	97,688		11,071	71,897	36,973
1985	877,607	672,707	4,858	677,565	71,095	-16,909	589,561	183,433	104,613		12,095	72,562	38,962
1986	983,190	761,981	11,008	772,989	82,865	-17,309	672,815	199,447	110,928		13,317	73,828	41,228
1987	1,089,375	856,716	12,518	869,234	92,881	-14,368	761,985	212,169	115,221		14,313	76,112	44,617
1988	1,210,944	946,085	10,723	956,808	104,280	-5,164	847,364	237,343	126,237		15,384	78,717	46,300
1989	1,342,298	1,020,831	8,936	1,029,767	114,050	7,323	923,040	280,771	138,487		16,479	81,456	48,563
1990	1,426,351	1,062,919	9,248	1,072,167	121,431	28,186	978,922	294,039	153,390		16,788	84,964	50,045
1991	1,458,925	1,074,465	12,241	1,086,706	124,789	25,579	987,496	298,477	172,952		16,773	86,981	49,180
1992	1,564,276	1,165,027	11,307	1,176,334	134,340	16,431	1,058,425	306,100	199,751		17,644	88,657	50,686
1993	1,668,476	1,251,942	9,805	1,261,747	144,156	15,908	1,133,499	326,856	208,121		18,405	90,652	52,047
1994	1,788,539	1,350,474	9,572	1,360,046	154,482	15,956	1,221,520	346,119	220,900		19,263	92,848	53,821
1995	1,913,391	1,423,529	12,342	1,435,871	162,475	17,084	1,290,480	382,585	240,326		20,205	94,698	55,672
1996	2,046,008	1,530,803	6,923	1,537,726	172,339	19,507	1,384,894	403,307	257,807		21,207	96,479	57,680
1997	2,144,720	1,609,999	5,293	1,615,292	180,788	29,409	1,463,913	411,683	269,124		21,840	98,202	58,997
1998	2,350,951	1,746,634	4,982	1,751,616	193,758	58,696	1,616,554	452,010	282,387		23,522	99,949	61,407
1999	2,486,103	1,858,666	5,783	1,864,449	206,135	80,951	1,739,265	449,318	297,520		24,511	101,429	62,092
2000	2,723,923	2,019,393	3,975	2,023,368	221,501	102,093	1,903,960	496,016	323,947		26,286	103,626	64,550
2001	2,845,508	2,082,177	6,665	2,088,842	237,137	104,031	1,955,736	525,040	364,732		26,781	106,252	65,440
2002	2,990,796	2,210,653	-989	2,209,664	251,997	141,998	2,099,665	495,377	395,754		27,452	108,945	66,699
2003	3,159,225	2,303,074	-637	2,302,437	261,889	177,630	2,218,178	513,917	427,130		28,343	111,464	66,949
2004	3,420,492	2,479,706	6,206	2,485,912	282,038	219,750	2,423,624	552,085	444,783		29,904	114,383	69,796
2005	3,705,174	2,692,523	2,223	2,694,746	308,608	268,513	2,654,651	568,347	482,176		31,441	117,847	72,529
2006	4,041,217	2,856,348	-4,986	2,851,362	330,041	326,343	2,847,664	660,696	532,857		33,335	121,229	74,892
2007	4,263,455	2,927,479	-14,414	2,913,065	336,494	379,910	2,956,481	743,119	563,855		34,421	123,863	75,394
2008	4,494,690	2,948,720	-2,062	2,946,658	340,445	430,762	3,036,975	787,147	670,568		35,749	125,728	73,995
2009	4,493,359	2,907,098	-2,184	2,904,914	336,931	477,808	3,045,791	717,816	729,752		35,288	127,333	71,189
2010	4,663,340	3,014,457	-4,401	3,010,056	352,111	494,127	3,152,072	717,804	793,464		36,227	128,726	71,063
2011	4,938,262	3,152,769	4,005	3,156,774	329,365	517,650	3,345,059	787,508	805,695		37,973	130,047	73,403
2012	5,164,864	3,278,340	13,984	3,292,324	340,852	517,187	3,468,659	870,347	825,858		39,421	131,017	74,119
2013	5,204,255	3,391,481	5,761	3,397,242	400,908	466,769	3,463,103	877,405	863,747		39,360	132,221	75,467
2014	5,396,907	3,516,685	4,445	3,521,130	414,124	469,874	3,576,880	915,626	904,401		40,456	133,403	76,536

Personal Income and Employment by Area: Winston-Salem, NC

(Thousands of dollars, except as noted.)

Year	Personal income, total	Earnings by place of work			Less: Contributions for government social insurance	Plus: Adjustment for residence	Equals: Net earnings by place of residence	Plus: Dividends, interest, and rent	Plus: Personal current transfer receipts	Per capita personal income (dollars)	Population (persons)	Total employment
		Nonfarm	Farm	Total								
1970	1,442,554	1,150,610	28,572	1,179,182	80,499	61,027	1,159,710	179,422	103,422	3,804	379,270	176,320
1971	1,570,262	1,245,327	30,541	1,275,868	90,286	67,587	1,253,169	194,448	122,645	4,045	388,244	178,777
1972	1,757,286	1,412,202	29,508	1,441,710	107,273	73,278	1,407,715	212,096	137,475	4,422	397,369	186,455
1973	1,984,531	1,606,923	45,796	1,652,719	140,746	75,731	1,587,704	238,303	158,524	4,927	402,778	197,084
1974	2,197,906	1,765,056	47,581	1,812,637	160,546	79,983	1,732,074	274,846	190,986	5,396	407,337	199,954
1975	2,402,509	1,883,767	43,895	1,927,662	168,190	78,566	1,838,038	299,594	264,877	5,836	411,650	193,474
1976	2,683,080	2,138,370	46,596	2,184,966	194,757	83,720	2,073,929	329,359	279,792	6,441	416,569	201,477
1977	2,978,740	2,402,627	40,238	2,442,865	217,575	88,006	2,313,296	371,827	293,617	7,055	422,231	210,239
1978	3,327,461	2,684,650	49,795	2,734,445	250,523	110,109	2,594,031	419,084	314,346	7,737	430,074	217,753
1979	3,684,308	2,988,275	33,880	3,022,155	290,181	121,007	2,852,981	471,892	359,435	8,414	437,876	224,330
1980	4,128,058	3,273,010	28,126	3,301,136	318,797	134,377	3,116,716	585,605	425,737	9,287	444,515	224,907
1981	4,672,030	3,608,820	54,839	3,663,659	377,432	154,981	3,441,208	742,665	488,157	10,399	449,284	228,321
1982	4,978,176	3,753,036	43,157	3,796,193	394,636	172,778	3,574,335	858,524	545,317	10,969	453,824	225,398
1983	5,397,420	4,075,442	24,697	4,100,139	430,034	208,607	3,878,712	930,521	588,187	11,801	457,356	229,151
1984	6,073,093	4,552,742	40,275	4,593,017	492,124	250,688	4,351,581	1,103,337	618,175	13,138	462,248	242,002
1985	6,603,405	4,963,679	40,881	5,004,560	543,113	268,506	4,729,953	1,209,299	664,153	14,105	468,149	251,201
1986	7,073,875	5,311,973	19,179	5,331,152	592,672	303,508	5,041,988	1,300,129	731,758	15,000	471,586	258,786
1987	7,675,404	5,823,159	22,124	5,845,283	637,994	352,507	5,559,796	1,377,893	737,715	16,019	479,157	268,061
1988	8,485,285	6,409,177	35,284	6,444,461	723,846	392,323	6,112,938	1,575,553	796,794	17,594	482,283	278,597
1989	9,168,555	6,777,489	42,576	6,820,065	763,725	440,469	6,496,809	1,783,959	887,787	18,889	485,397	281,675
1990	9,572,129	6,846,119	60,153	6,906,272	795,961	481,942	6,592,253	2,008,565	971,311	19,534	490,034	288,314
1991	9,782,827	7,000,797	70,763	7,071,560	823,931	464,330	6,711,959	1,970,114	1,100,754	19,705	496,463	283,093
1992	10,445,796	7,537,219	72,156	7,609,375	876,944	497,306	7,229,737	2,006,323	1,209,736	20,761	503,138	286,803
1993	11,037,437	7,904,976	63,196	7,968,172	931,080	571,140	7,608,232	2,103,057	1,326,148	21,555	512,062	294,537
1994	11,667,373	8,427,147	64,387	8,491,534	998,430	585,491	8,078,595	2,207,189	1,381,589	22,358	521,836	300,829
1995	12,539,112	8,894,819	48,271	8,943,090	1,057,655	679,827	8,565,262	2,428,756	1,545,094	23,628	530,693	308,135
1996	13,289,888	9,235,479	65,218	9,300,697	1,091,948	750,609	8,959,358	2,652,293	1,678,237	24,578	540,712	314,617
1997	14,124,706	9,890,067	56,926	9,946,993	1,158,297	771,870	9,560,566	2,811,949	1,752,191	25,701	549,576	320,761
1998	15,129,841	10,598,762	63,777	10,662,539	1,231,251	768,666	10,199,954	3,120,705	1,809,182	27,143	557,410	326,620
1999	15,745,404	11,119,199	69,647	11,188,846	1,278,203	828,342	10,738,985	3,096,260	1,910,159	27,921	563,928	330,998
2000	16,749,540	11,867,599	63,208	11,930,807	1,351,145	828,634	11,408,296	3,273,994	2,067,250	29,323	571,210	336,926
2001	16,846,833	11,912,272	61,806	11,974,078	1,368,395	739,365	11,345,048	3,212,364	2,289,421	29,137	578,186	332,403
2002	17,083,328	12,032,109	29,853	12,061,962	1,371,077	760,163	11,451,048	3,155,051	2,477,229	29,236	584,321	328,701
2003	17,651,870	12,405,578	36,726	12,442,304	1,437,301	766,847	11,771,850	3,260,619	2,619,401	29,971	588,964	328,512
2004	18,932,293	12,999,773	63,590	13,063,363	1,488,116	869,284	12,444,531	3,639,044	2,848,718	31,832	594,765	333,808
2005	19,700,787	13,434,094	69,777	13,503,871	1,572,347	942,448	12,873,972	3,752,092	3,074,723	32,682	602,805	341,262
2006	20,998,874	14,141,625	60,953	14,202,578	1,649,453	1,117,708	13,670,833	3,933,832	3,394,209	34,228	613,494	348,471
2007	22,025,856	14,501,519	57,814	14,559,333	1,729,831	1,232,531	14,062,033	4,301,122	3,662,701	35,351	623,068	355,307
2008	22,859,340	14,698,301	66,512	14,764,813	1,764,595	1,312,725	14,312,943	4,420,528	4,125,869	36,159	632,186	350,681
2009	22,041,141	14,222,984	59,443	14,282,427	1,710,717	1,119,617	13,691,327	3,739,114	4,610,700	34,564	637,688	338,454
2010	22,596,937	14,801,500	52,707	14,854,207	1,712,469	1,104,766	14,246,504	3,472,670	4,877,763	35,233	641,351	333,126
2011	23,477,615	14,983,389	43,209	15,026,598	1,601,273	1,108,980	14,534,305	3,954,701	4,988,609	36,419	644,651	336,547
2012	24,761,651	15,977,868	70,374	16,048,242	1,650,539	1,244,055	15,641,758	4,093,979	5,025,914	38,231	647,687	339,853
2013	24,072,097	15,511,044	87,161	15,598,205	1,875,687	1,256,974	14,979,492	3,957,800	5,134,805	36,948	651,520	344,479
2014	25,180,490	16,521,711	107,127	16,628,838	1,994,108	1,113,997	15,748,727	4,125,814	5,305,949	38,443	655,015	349,209

Personal Income and Employment by Area: Worcester, MA-CT

(Thousands of dollars, except as noted.)

Year	Personal income, total	Derivation of personal income								Per capita personal income (dollars)	Population (persons)	Total employment
		Earnings by place of work			Less: Contributions for government social insurance	Plus: Adjustment for residence	Equals: Net earnings by place of residence	Plus: Dividends, interest, and rent	Plus: Personal current transfer receipts			
		Nonfarm	Farm	Total								
1970	2,947,969	2,193,712	17,410	2,211,122	144,579	167,189	2,233,732	418,083	296,154	4,074	723,625	303,453
1971	3,134,177	2,283,136	17,035	2,300,171	155,062	193,730	2,338,839	440,004	355,334	4,296	729,613	299,766
1972	3,406,015	2,478,458	18,892	2,497,350	177,513	230,027	2,549,864	464,111	392,040	4,662	730,558	305,815
1973	3,766,609	2,767,830	23,340	2,791,170	228,772	267,769	2,830,167	499,693	436,749	5,120	735,701	320,736
1974	4,093,897	2,960,721	15,189	2,975,910	253,560	309,122	3,031,472	554,845	507,580	5,572	734,725	323,556
1975	4,443,444	3,026,229	15,877	3,042,106	249,893	343,154	3,135,367	592,485	715,592	6,060	733,288	309,349
1976	4,821,728	3,352,353	18,528	3,370,881	284,544	390,810	3,477,147	623,161	721,420	6,598	730,817	317,500
1977	5,256,380	3,642,292	16,555	3,658,847	311,374	480,539	3,828,012	684,095	744,273	7,195	730,608	324,246
1978	5,866,746	4,083,082	24,527	4,107,609	359,606	570,619	4,318,622	740,819	807,305	7,931	739,765	337,775
1979	6,542,103	4,527,073	20,310	4,547,383	417,250	683,547	4,813,680	817,263	911,160	8,823	741,446	348,159
1980	7,371,855	4,912,771	16,516	4,929,287	452,368	830,980	5,307,899	1,005,114	1,058,842	9,969	739,491	348,593
1981	8,201,946	5,370,539	20,046	5,390,585	523,478	908,165	5,775,272	1,222,070	1,204,604	11,067	741,103	347,686
1982	8,870,042	5,601,034	31,330	5,632,364	554,140	1,012,060	6,090,284	1,468,625	1,311,133	11,949	742,351	341,024
1983	9,505,276	5,949,586	27,918	5,977,504	596,891	1,148,139	6,528,752	1,602,761	1,373,763	12,820	741,465	343,763
1984	10,720,363	6,782,094	34,314	6,816,408	701,484	1,307,347	7,422,271	1,864,192	1,433,900	14,305	749,409	361,994
1985	11,578,936	7,409,844	29,516	7,439,360	772,509	1,434,687	8,101,538	1,968,301	1,509,097	15,282	757,692	374,819
1986	12,566,102	8,179,986	34,556	8,214,542	863,506	1,503,830	8,854,866	2,116,295	1,594,941	16,410	765,781	390,359
1987	13,692,215	9,139,778	29,315	9,169,093	950,689	1,593,891	9,812,295	2,234,077	1,645,843	17,598	778,071	397,657
1988	15,002,706	10,131,945	26,989	10,158,934	1,070,258	1,722,957	10,811,633	2,441,589	1,749,484	18,917	793,074	413,617
1989	15,916,190	10,596,980	25,262	10,622,242	1,110,459	1,770,852	11,282,635	2,657,860	1,975,695	19,693	808,224	410,592
1990	16,403,949	10,656,361	32,529	10,688,890	1,100,785	1,880,527	11,468,632	2,707,650	2,227,667	20,167	813,391	400,251
1991	16,512,882	10,587,503	32,476	10,619,979	1,110,664	1,806,464	11,315,779	2,664,229	2,532,874	20,324	812,492	382,147
1992	17,276,556	11,266,447	39,186	11,305,633	1,166,010	1,831,399	11,971,022	2,626,898	2,678,636	21,247	813,137	391,834
1993	17,883,816	11,899,178	36,463	11,935,641	1,240,207	1,731,404	12,426,838	2,702,273	2,754,705	21,874	817,597	401,887
1994	18,822,334	12,651,910	33,435	12,685,345	1,323,091	1,769,142	13,131,396	2,775,679	2,915,259	22,878	822,735	411,296
1995	19,678,142	13,002,766	23,408	13,026,174	1,367,831	1,981,102	13,639,445	2,950,365	3,088,332	23,834	825,647	415,200
1996	20,820,968	13,750,558	31,154	13,781,712	1,426,925	2,099,756	14,454,543	3,179,438	3,186,987	25,082	830,128	420,409
1997	22,363,777	14,608,003	31,150	14,639,153	1,506,638	2,549,852	15,682,367	3,390,848	3,290,562	26,726	836,766	429,799
1998	23,585,213	15,574,684	28,933	15,603,617	1,598,578	2,730,958	16,735,997	3,520,641	3,328,575	27,932	844,368	438,114
1999	24,868,436	16,335,037	37,691	16,372,728	1,661,576	3,261,210	17,972,362	3,468,586	3,427,488	29,143	853,319	442,867
2000	27,694,022	18,355,978	39,126	18,395,104	1,856,458	3,707,083	20,245,729	3,818,820	3,629,473	32,139	861,697	454,683
2001	28,937,798	18,734,046	30,865	18,764,911	1,921,262	4,234,285	21,077,934	3,913,692	3,946,172	33,221	871,081	456,983
2002	29,105,405	18,965,812	26,603	18,992,415	1,942,500	4,232,718	21,282,633	3,517,782	4,304,990	33,091	879,568	454,984
2003	30,215,072	19,568,847	29,041	19,597,888	1,993,983	4,405,417	22,009,322	3,662,480	4,543,270	34,059	887,129	456,270
2004	31,710,615	20,550,361	33,167	20,583,528	2,154,091	4,691,959	23,121,396	3,858,518	4,730,701	35,543	892,171	461,481
2005	32,628,330	21,013,939	26,842	21,040,781	2,252,818	4,860,218	23,648,181	3,934,015	5,046,134	36,379	896,901	465,550
2006	34,666,642	22,005,738	19,910	22,025,648	2,331,046	5,201,410	24,896,012	4,457,120	5,313,510	38,428	902,123	471,325
2007	36,487,618	22,742,505	23,300	22,765,805	2,401,826	5,590,127	25,954,106	4,935,474	5,598,038	40,294	905,524	478,386
2008	38,008,413	23,112,700	22,583	23,135,283	2,457,863	5,875,121	26,552,541	5,062,149	6,393,723	41,826	908,735	478,046
2009	37,592,719	22,623,410	17,694	22,641,104	2,422,962	5,613,462	25,831,604	4,702,083	7,059,032	41,159	913,363	465,985
2010	38,975,533	23,512,085	21,188	23,533,273	2,458,419	5,772,747	26,847,601	4,656,742	7,471,190	42,420	918,791	462,327
2011	40,585,494	24,341,884	22,875	24,364,759	2,307,696	5,847,933	27,904,996	5,206,444	7,474,054	44,008	922,224	469,504
2012	42,096,495	24,855,767	24,842	24,880,609	2,333,413	6,226,642	28,773,838	5,773,207	7,549,450	45,555	924,072	473,581
2013	42,162,385	25,643,542	34,696	25,678,238	2,722,703	5,844,665	28,800,200	5,776,659	7,585,526	45,431	928,050	485,284
2014	43,918,310	26,504,958	22,015	26,526,973	2,831,759	6,441,274	30,136,488	6,011,378	7,770,444	47,200	930,473	493,593

Personal Income and Employment by Area: Yakima, WA

(Thousands of dollars, except as noted.)

| Year | Personal income, total | Derivation of personal income | | | | | | | | Per capita personal income (dollars) | Population (persons) | Total employment |
| | | Earnings by place of work | | | Less: Contributions for government social insurance | Plus: Adjustment for residence | Equals: Net earnings by place of residence | Plus: Dividends, interest, and rent | Plus: Personal current transfer receipts | | | |
		Nonfarm	Farm	Total								
1970	512,508	330,775	45,375	376,150	27,791	8,440	356,799	80,145	75,564	3,520	145,600	63,707
1971	566,351	355,412	64,535	419,947	31,102	7,810	396,655	86,824	82,872	3,826	148,017	62,448
1972	626,208	391,044	76,739	467,783	35,780	8,723	440,726	94,717	90,765	4,160	150,541	64,284
1973	727,511	437,661	114,457	552,118	46,136	10,888	516,870	110,843	99,798	4,821	150,902	67,149
1974	835,444	495,912	137,963	633,875	53,685	13,815	594,005	125,647	115,792	5,382	155,229	69,450
1975	965,100	565,609	151,451	717,060	60,611	20,867	677,316	148,314	139,470	6,062	159,209	72,488
1976	1,010,526	649,149	101,320	750,469	72,029	23,221	701,661	157,840	151,025	6,235	162,074	77,178
1977	1,090,024	712,447	80,806	793,253	79,686	34,182	747,749	180,149	162,126	6,638	164,202	76,262
1978	1,285,926	816,139	134,548	950,687	92,894	44,331	902,124	207,979	175,823	7,726	166,436	78,991
1979	1,429,688	918,868	117,398	1,036,266	107,704	56,480	985,042	241,029	203,617	8,460	168,987	82,216
1980	1,564,107	975,146	116,390	1,091,536	114,788	58,756	1,035,504	284,873	243,730	9,035	173,118	82,688
1981	1,727,900	1,040,158	125,848	1,166,006	131,870	79,348	1,113,484	343,672	270,744	9,861	175,218	82,751
1982	1,814,116	1,057,635	133,228	1,190,863	135,778	69,715	1,124,800	384,315	305,001	10,259	176,825	81,334
1983	1,917,565	1,125,875	141,956	1,267,831	146,168	59,662	1,181,325	411,113	325,127	10,698	179,248	84,131
1984	2,065,643	1,195,693	177,018	1,372,711	161,293	48,872	1,260,290	456,309	349,044	11,462	180,209	84,048
1985	2,097,922	1,226,939	129,882	1,356,821	168,027	52,047	1,240,841	477,113	379,968	11,570	181,321	83,388
1986	2,238,538	1,272,269	195,348	1,467,617	175,992	53,292	1,344,917	496,244	397,377	12,370	180,961	84,095
1987	2,403,862	1,370,818	254,204	1,625,022	190,656	52,678	1,487,044	504,035	412,783	13,229	181,707	92,689
1988	2,473,071	1,470,667	211,266	1,681,933	210,961	55,533	1,526,505	505,670	440,896	13,335	185,454	96,178
1989	2,761,351	1,584,396	285,068	1,869,464	229,565	56,522	1,696,421	577,099	487,831	14,721	187,574	99,415
1990	3,022,771	1,749,246	266,181	2,015,427	257,487	63,337	1,821,277	657,040	544,454	15,955	189,454	101,956
1991	3,220,484	1,890,560	356,699	2,247,259	280,227	40,262	2,007,294	600,925	612,265	16,609	193,904	101,599
1992	3,505,565	2,075,084	382,568	2,457,652	307,326	40,154	2,190,480	624,268	690,817	17,617	198,983	102,197
1993	3,696,190	2,193,844	395,175	2,589,019	323,782	41,295	2,306,532	652,389	737,269	18,095	204,266	103,901
1994	3,854,525	2,337,214	358,599	2,695,813	341,767	42,898	2,396,944	702,150	755,431	18,446	208,963	108,409
1995	3,981,678	2,382,600	352,389	2,734,989	351,871	37,954	2,421,072	736,737	823,869	18,728	212,601	109,268
1996	4,250,769	2,477,185	427,577	2,904,762	352,463	33,694	2,585,993	801,344	863,432	19,776	214,951	111,266
1997	4,389,767	2,626,594	352,730	2,979,324	357,630	31,029	2,652,723	854,663	882,381	20,211	217,201	112,404
1998	4,652,651	2,825,088	407,411	3,232,499	376,419	25,976	2,882,056	875,492	895,103	21,173	219,748	112,061
1999	4,737,070	2,926,196	338,217	3,264,413	382,552	23,528	2,905,389	880,526	951,155	21,379	221,573	112,553
2000	5,007,004	3,046,631	409,258	3,455,889	405,190	19,248	3,069,947	922,699	1,014,358	22,492	222,615	112,886
2001	5,170,568	3,203,242	342,906	3,546,148	422,678	10,686	3,134,156	907,250	1,129,162	23,212	222,757	112,554
2002	5,247,172	3,311,547	366,550	3,678,097	438,007	10,219	3,250,309	843,788	1,153,075	23,488	223,402	112,407
2003	5,593,863	3,457,824	441,464	3,899,288	457,691	10,147	3,451,744	923,510	1,218,609	24,844	225,161	114,223
2004	5,857,908	3,620,257	522,253	4,142,510	482,778	10,138	3,669,870	932,947	1,255,091	25,774	227,280	113,376
2005	5,990,896	3,790,363	449,630	4,239,993	514,223	10,240	3,736,010	923,252	1,331,634	26,210	228,570	115,181
2006	6,256,093	3,990,553	416,144	4,406,697	539,596	10,212	3,877,313	962,345	1,416,435	27,128	230,617	118,089
2007	6,818,854	4,159,022	520,261	4,679,283	560,282	10,272	4,129,273	1,157,178	1,532,403	29,299	232,733	119,078
2008	7,435,817	4,316,011	577,088	4,893,099	586,437	10,503	4,317,165	1,375,377	1,743,275	31,605	235,272	122,245
2009	7,354,364	4,341,326	488,578	4,829,904	602,222	15,317	4,242,999	1,202,988	1,908,377	30,694	239,604	120,793
2010	7,782,490	4,448,219	631,943	5,080,162	620,567	19,797	4,479,392	1,189,476	2,113,622	31,876	244,146	119,329
2011	8,296,192	4,541,145	788,661	5,329,806	576,019	26,099	4,779,886	1,382,363	2,133,943	33,703	246,159	120,228
2012	8,802,854	4,770,126	900,359	5,670,485	601,232	16,181	5,085,434	1,574,945	2,142,475	35,679	246,721	124,835
2013	8,749,346	4,826,505	858,747	5,685,252	674,611	16,564	5,027,205	1,582,228	2,139,913	35,380	247,297	125,242
2014	9,320,512	5,029,590	934,438	5,964,028	710,401	15,302	5,268,929	1,644,821	2,406,762	37,630	247,687	127,286

Personal Income and Employment by Area: York-Hanover, PA

(Thousands of dollars, except as noted.)

Year	Personal income, total	Earnings by place of work Nonfarm	Farm	Total	Less: Contributions for government social insurance	Plus: Adjustment for residence	Equals: Net earnings by place of residence	Plus: Dividends, interest, and rent	Plus: Personal current transfer receipts	Per capita personal income (dollars)	Population (persons)	Total employment
1970	1,204,983	1,064,782	9,208	1,073,990	78,376	-31,556	964,058	150,678	90,247	4,407	273,427	139,933
1971	1,278,176	1,101,903	2,949	1,104,852	83,738	-11,769	1,009,345	164,749	104,082	4,581	278,991	137,875
1972	1,423,595	1,217,625	5,097	1,222,722	98,313	5,093	1,129,502	179,389	114,704	5,037	282,646	142,624
1973	1,586,968	1,332,160	14,619	1,346,779	123,335	29,689	1,253,133	203,768	130,067	5,546	286,122	147,199
1974	1,739,718	1,404,399	15,927	1,420,326	133,836	64,037	1,350,527	233,498	155,693	6,025	288,739	146,547
1975	1,895,206	1,458,070	13,416	1,471,486	133,920	89,929	1,427,495	260,344	207,367	6,473	292,808	140,987
1976	2,111,684	1,618,599	19,089	1,637,688	152,229	123,413	1,608,872	277,846	224,966	7,109	297,047	144,496
1977	2,356,683	1,806,525	15,226	1,821,751	170,638	161,572	1,812,685	309,464	234,534	7,839	300,642	148,395
1978	2,680,172	2,071,749	11,914	2,083,663	201,666	205,617	2,087,614	344,152	248,406	8,772	305,545	154,993
1979	3,031,779	2,316,540	22,491	2,339,031	233,864	255,645	2,360,812	392,592	278,375	9,771	310,297	160,882
1980	3,393,340	2,503,815	10,514	2,514,329	254,619	318,958	2,578,668	486,774	327,898	10,821	313,599	161,194
1981	3,722,740	2,695,589	19,911	2,715,500	293,384	324,369	2,746,485	597,385	378,870	11,808	315,266	159,431
1982	3,934,831	2,741,213	16,675	2,757,888	300,531	322,289	2,779,646	704,146	451,039	12,453	315,972	155,440
1983	4,117,981	2,844,123	2,225	2,846,348	317,874	350,067	2,878,541	753,000	486,440	13,026	316,125	154,109
1984	4,520,565	3,162,422	24,713	3,187,135	370,579	377,503	3,194,059	847,741	478,765	14,145	319,582	161,378
1985	4,834,505	3,385,528	20,956	3,406,484	400,621	389,217	3,395,080	928,753	510,672	15,101	320,150	165,404
1986	5,126,244	3,561,497	19,619	3,581,116	422,018	430,467	3,589,565	993,420	543,259	15,917	322,055	169,374
1987	5,476,652	3,889,562	19,581	3,909,143	455,167	440,358	3,894,334	1,023,052	559,266	16,804	325,922	176,386
1988	5,962,252	4,314,643	8,427	4,323,070	513,151	459,238	4,269,157	1,091,308	601,787	18,016	330,944	184,414
1989	6,473,651	4,588,065	20,529	4,608,594	535,963	474,400	4,547,031	1,272,523	654,097	19,263	336,068	188,133
1990	6,783,559	4,846,876	26,711	4,873,587	568,238	487,144	4,792,493	1,271,038	720,028	19,904	340,810	191,073
1991	7,091,536	5,022,061	13,380	5,035,441	594,220	520,784	4,962,005	1,304,660	824,871	20,483	346,209	188,389
1992	7,532,734	5,321,073	37,621	5,358,694	626,594	585,676	5,317,776	1,323,797	891,161	21,458	351,046	188,825
1993	7,926,787	5,525,421	24,733	5,550,154	665,066	640,476	5,525,564	1,468,497	932,726	22,257	356,156	190,523
1994	8,122,304	5,741,661	23,343	5,765,004	706,550	715,068	5,773,522	1,396,388	952,394	22,494	361,092	193,790
1995	8,567,407	6,028,437	11,880	6,040,317	739,924	772,733	6,073,126	1,485,100	1,009,181	23,408	365,997	198,685
1996	9,023,125	6,254,492	35,026	6,289,518	751,957	833,998	6,371,559	1,566,193	1,085,373	24,401	369,781	201,286
1997	9,491,032	6,602,508	12,813	6,615,321	783,393	868,834	6,700,762	1,665,363	1,124,907	25,465	372,706	204,054
1998	9,997,373	6,826,395	16,072	6,842,467	804,375	999,285	7,037,377	1,778,943	1,181,053	26,602	375,810	200,278
1999	10,389,088	7,127,511	9,216	7,136,727	833,055	1,096,142	7,399,814	1,741,870	1,247,404	27,419	378,905	204,186
2000	11,189,314	7,625,539	35,826	7,661,365	878,539	1,144,001	7,926,827	1,915,967	1,346,520	29,235	382,743	209,827
2001	11,350,100	7,681,548	26,391	7,707,939	889,550	1,178,284	7,996,673	1,852,966	1,500,461	29,422	385,773	207,242
2002	11,453,098	7,741,260	10,816	7,752,076	902,116	1,265,911	8,115,871	1,709,995	1,627,232	29,390	389,692	206,708
2003	12,124,775	8,079,532	65,878	8,145,410	932,611	1,394,776	8,607,575	1,780,909	1,736,291	30,688	395,093	207,217
2004	13,061,382	8,639,742	64,522	8,704,264	993,654	1,584,291	9,294,901	1,955,556	1,810,925	32,539	401,403	212,186
2005	14,016,263	9,326,572	45,104	9,371,676	1,083,004	1,811,113	10,099,785	1,915,762	2,000,716	34,264	409,066	218,227
2006	14,736,786	9,556,903	25,850	9,582,753	1,109,857	1,969,174	10,442,070	2,128,079	2,166,637	35,252	418,043	221,669
2007	15,776,511	9,906,035	37,370	9,943,405	1,151,404	2,192,015	10,984,016	2,477,069	2,315,426	37,128	424,919	226,550
2008	16,640,244	10,165,778	39,910	10,205,688	1,184,358	2,374,695	11,396,025	2,570,680	2,673,539	38,752	429,399	227,443
2009	16,876,419	10,067,704	26,086	10,093,790	1,163,220	2,484,357	11,414,927	2,459,919	3,001,573	38,974	433,022	218,827
2010	17,018,744	10,158,276	27,025	10,185,301	1,198,044	2,444,510	11,431,767	2,336,264	3,250,713	39,075	435,543	216,954
2011	17,930,210	10,598,289	33,390	10,631,679	1,128,078	2,557,364	12,060,965	2,592,299	3,276,946	41,043	436,868	219,622
2012	18,349,775	10,569,718	47,370	10,617,088	1,128,656	2,602,898	12,091,330	2,934,063	3,324,382	41,923	437,699	220,602
2013	18,369,673	10,719,472	53,447	10,772,919	1,297,277	2,688,661	12,164,303	2,777,773	3,427,597	41,807	439,393	221,557
2014	18,968,592	10,992,828	40,489	11,033,317	1,331,960	2,822,611	12,523,968	2,884,352	3,560,272	43,037	440,755	223,608

Personal Income and Employment by Area: Youngstown-Warren-Boardman, OH-PA

(Thousands of dollars, except as noted.)

Year	Personal income, total	Earnings by place of work			Less: Contributions for government social insurance	Plus: Adjustment for residence	Equals: Net earnings by place of residence	Plus: Dividends, interest, and rent	Plus: Personal current transfer receipts	Per capita personal income (dollars)	Population (persons)	Total employment
		Nonfarm	Farm	Total								
1970	2,585,295	2,243,237	8,172	2,251,409	154,468	-36,483	2,060,458	296,552	228,285	3,884	665,569	279,196
1971	2,755,612	2,368,294	7,656	2,375,950	167,755	-39,414	2,168,781	318,110	268,721	4,108	670,741	276,899
1972	3,044,654	2,641,542	8,730	2,650,272	197,250	-46,485	2,406,537	338,176	299,941	4,469	681,278	282,795
1973	3,433,860	3,022,132	14,941	3,037,073	263,301	-55,066	2,718,706	374,243	340,911	5,135	668,722	296,124
1974	3,754,035	3,257,666	15,570	3,273,236	294,955	-62,359	2,915,922	428,648	409,465	5,561	675,013	299,829
1975	3,973,422	3,300,071	17,575	3,317,646	292,039	-59,421	2,966,186	469,275	537,961	6,000	662,274	285,651
1976	4,367,054	3,636,608	20,754	3,657,362	325,744	-67,958	3,263,660	502,818	600,576	6,550	666,754	288,266
1977	4,833,214	4,071,437	17,270	4,088,707	366,240	-75,951	3,646,516	559,520	627,178	7,242	667,417	294,002
1978	5,309,770	4,480,789	12,833	4,493,622	416,924	-76,333	4,000,365	623,159	686,246	7,985	664,956	298,304
1979	5,852,528	4,914,328	13,963	4,928,291	474,007	-78,670	4,375,614	703,085	773,829	8,891	658,231	301,663
1980	6,358,839	5,045,258	8,081	5,053,339	481,906	-75,454	4,495,979	891,161	971,699	9,655	658,600	291,643
1981	6,935,237	5,385,775	12,046	5,397,821	552,630	-84,053	4,761,138	1,104,420	1,069,679	10,621	652,946	286,983
1982	6,917,816	4,928,297	9,375	4,937,672	509,401	-37,521	4,390,750	1,229,845	1,297,221	10,651	649,503	264,325
1983	7,234,570	5,127,894	1,050	5,128,944	538,677	-37,500	4,552,767	1,325,943	1,355,860	11,224	644,566	259,259
1984	7,860,143	5,652,890	17,182	5,670,072	611,304	-40,676	5,018,092	1,489,357	1,352,694	12,334	637,279	267,611
1985	8,219,409	5,888,856	19,729	5,908,585	645,607	-38,647	5,224,331	1,572,636	1,422,442	13,017	631,445	270,681
1986	8,460,695	5,986,494	16,567	6,003,061	667,252	-23,483	5,312,326	1,633,223	1,515,146	13,532	625,219	275,735
1987	8,648,435	6,139,905	22,379	6,162,284	684,431	-15,309	5,462,544	1,604,900	1,580,991	13,967	619,212	280,875
1988	9,358,451	6,778,999	29,579	6,808,578	774,338	-33,223	6,001,017	1,711,366	1,646,068	15,198	615,749	288,063
1989	10,062,333	7,242,465	35,429	7,277,894	835,789	-37,570	6,404,535	1,900,485	1,757,313	16,360	615,048	293,661
1990	10,431,923	7,390,497	33,616	7,424,113	870,435	-28,086	6,525,592	1,913,560	1,992,771	16,991	613,980	294,927
1991	10,689,891	7,561,176	19,772	7,580,948	915,357	-39,613	6,625,978	1,936,491	2,127,422	17,369	615,462	294,326
1992	11,275,690	7,982,710	38,592	8,021,302	955,817	-39,723	7,025,762	1,946,987	2,302,941	18,255	617,681	292,356
1993	11,613,993	8,261,895	25,312	8,287,207	1,010,873	-25,151	7,251,183	1,966,916	2,395,894	18,783	618,328	293,654
1994	12,181,090	8,757,471	26,268	8,783,739	1,081,577	-24,245	7,677,917	2,039,452	2,463,721	19,734	617,253	299,990
1995	12,681,224	9,005,270	21,431	9,026,701	1,121,436	4,330	7,909,595	2,185,346	2,586,283	20,600	615,595	309,477
1996	13,110,268	9,196,156	29,310	9,225,466	1,129,465	36,015	8,132,016	2,295,678	2,682,574	21,339	614,369	311,996
1997	13,698,008	9,581,248	22,530	9,603,778	1,139,752	42,386	8,506,412	2,444,260	2,747,336	22,386	611,902	315,429
1998	14,110,674	9,785,733	24,859	9,810,592	1,134,016	85,366	8,761,942	2,560,535	2,788,197	23,159	609,286	315,830
1999	14,471,084	10,161,346	21,568	10,182,914	1,166,620	91,389	9,107,683	2,504,381	2,859,020	23,881	605,978	317,159
2000	14,983,906	10,393,071	25,046	10,418,117	1,155,488	115,634	9,378,263	2,577,474	3,028,169	24,881	602,227	317,961
2001	15,242,517	10,377,958	18,625	10,396,583	1,174,707	183,121	9,404,997	2,562,052	3,275,468	25,442	599,116	308,929
2002	15,505,816	10,626,523	9,914	10,636,437	1,178,419	201,933	9,659,951	2,415,417	3,430,448	26,062	594,958	303,473
2003	15,976,906	10,940,428	17,966	10,958,394	1,223,271	226,271	9,961,394	2,449,872	3,565,640	26,987	592,016	301,429
2004	16,349,962	11,244,108	25,245	11,269,353	1,278,109	251,668	10,242,912	2,413,209	3,693,841	27,783	588,478	300,747
2005	16,769,730	11,505,390	18,611	11,524,001	1,320,855	278,614	10,481,760	2,384,298	3,903,672	28,704	584,222	302,901
2006	17,635,918	12,055,339	14,504	12,069,843	1,390,908	313,154	10,992,089	2,583,569	4,060,260	30,385	580,420	302,275
2007	18,173,232	12,004,230	22,646	12,026,876	1,392,345	340,199	10,974,730	2,934,265	4,264,237	31,576	575,543	300,216
2008	18,467,694	11,748,501	13,868	11,762,369	1,384,330	354,533	10,732,572	2,971,542	4,763,580	32,345	570,952	294,783
2009	17,823,785	10,892,506	7,551	10,900,057	1,303,675	384,546	9,980,928	2,619,630	5,223,227	31,371	568,156	279,696
2010	18,245,577	11,289,152	19,966	11,309,118	1,340,726	350,055	10,318,447	2,555,430	5,371,700	32,300	564,874	278,334
2011	19,434,512	12,017,786	48,879	12,066,665	1,283,138	357,010	11,140,537	2,827,369	5,466,606	34,551	562,487	282,651
2012	19,873,541	12,373,915	39,787	12,413,702	1,303,812	390,439	11,500,329	3,001,430	5,371,782	35,554	558,973	284,171
2013	19,942,173	12,406,207	39,278	12,445,485	1,434,691	435,352	11,446,146	2,987,473	5,508,554	35,859	556,129	284,250
2014	20,562,699	12,723,727	30,538	12,754,265	1,486,187	473,776	11,741,854	3,103,346	5,717,499	37,166	553,263	285,583

Personal Income and Employment by Area: Yuba City, CA

(Thousands of dollars, except as noted.)

Year	Personal income, total	Derivation of personal income									Per capita personal income (dollars)	Population (persons)	Total employment
		Earnings by place of work			Less: Contributions for government social insurance	Plus: Adjustment for residence	Equals: Net earnings by place of residence	Plus: Dividends, interest, and rent	Plus: Personal current transfer receipts				
		Nonfarm	Farm	Total									
1970	381,976	248,617	45,848	294,465	17,051	-1,153	276,261	66,199	39,516		4,385	87,104	38,704
1971	416,507	270,444	52,357	322,801	19,211	-1,042	302,548	70,179	43,780		4,715	88,345	39,301
1972	453,591	291,867	63,161	355,028	21,281	-1,474	332,273	74,935	46,383		5,184	87,505	39,903
1973	510,915	305,617	96,542	402,159	24,450	-1,970	375,739	83,188	51,988		5,678	89,980	39,333
1974	588,852	338,186	125,115	463,301	28,023	-3,563	431,715	93,100	64,037		6,445	91,363	40,753
1975	638,382	376,720	111,918	488,638	31,274	-4,413	452,951	106,984	78,447		6,877	92,830	42,061
1976	645,465	412,205	71,770	483,975	35,166	-5,570	443,239	112,753	89,473		6,725	95,979	42,261
1977	727,412	450,031	99,000	549,031	38,822	-6,273	503,936	124,773	98,703		7,502	96,962	42,971
1978	799,102	506,777	85,799	592,576	43,977	-6,726	541,873	146,383	110,846		8,127	98,325	44,298
1979	892,994	561,925	95,175	657,100	50,125	-6,096	600,879	166,977	125,138		8,876	100,611	45,882
1980	1,010,167	603,986	121,553	725,539	52,396	-7,124	666,019	193,019	151,129		9,866	102,388	45,871
1981	1,097,303	643,353	119,557	762,910	60,839	-8,645	693,426	226,170	177,707		10,568	103,831	45,667
1982	1,111,815	666,814	75,625	742,439	63,352	-5,935	673,152	243,849	194,814		10,449	106,405	45,349
1983	1,144,387	692,676	41,179	733,855	67,370	793	667,278	263,676	213,433		10,549	108,483	45,038
1984	1,300,988	741,943	100,198	842,141	74,996	10,570	777,715	294,535	228,738		11,930	109,052	45,505
1985	1,406,796	780,248	127,016	907,264	79,922	23,012	850,354	308,785	247,657		12,682	110,929	46,019
1986	1,467,166	843,911	94,718	938,629	87,883	32,618	883,364	319,057	264,745		13,070	112,256	46,253
1987	1,579,233	900,252	123,432	1,023,684	95,405	44,931	973,210	331,557	274,466		13,786	114,554	48,049
1988	1,679,425	980,487	106,519	1,087,006	108,154	56,153	1,035,005	346,836	297,584		14,364	116,916	50,737
1989	1,840,649	1,058,517	105,023	1,163,540	118,181	69,839	1,115,198	396,163	329,288		15,375	119,714	53,653
1990	1,932,338	1,122,577	79,553	1,202,130	125,191	89,535	1,166,474	400,009	365,855		15,647	123,499	54,925
1991	2,102,457	1,193,628	121,389	1,315,017	135,246	89,409	1,269,180	419,298	413,979		16,597	126,677	56,571
1992	2,251,036	1,249,005	135,722	1,384,727	141,628	94,186	1,337,285	433,549	480,202		17,331	129,886	56,076
1993	2,318,973	1,274,877	151,036	1,425,913	145,018	96,860	1,377,755	437,439	503,779		17,575	131,950	56,416
1994	2,419,498	1,329,408	173,133	1,502,541	149,882	106,186	1,458,845	452,963	507,690		17,986	134,518	57,920
1995	2,513,382	1,384,944	160,978	1,545,922	152,753	116,524	1,509,693	471,911	531,778		18,573	135,323	59,036
1996	2,611,464	1,426,837	160,395	1,587,232	152,746	127,057	1,561,543	495,119	554,802		19,179	136,160	60,320
1997	2,722,299	1,533,375	139,784	1,673,159	158,764	142,780	1,657,175	509,696	555,428		19,955	136,425	60,517
1998	2,892,439	1,659,278	102,002	1,761,280	165,942	161,929	1,757,267	541,080	594,092		21,110	137,016	61,867
1999	3,136,987	1,770,892	199,850	1,970,742	178,753	183,298	1,975,287	528,495	633,205		22,716	138,097	63,490
2000	3,269,747	1,875,687	170,056	2,045,743	189,415	213,790	2,070,118	552,161	647,468		23,428	139,564	63,507
2001	3,421,740	2,038,935	125,134	2,164,069	216,632	212,553	2,159,990	545,480	716,270		24,201	141,387	65,651
2002	3,640,424	2,216,797	116,136	2,332,933	235,409	245,626	2,343,150	529,543	767,731		25,235	144,262	66,758
2003	3,952,544	2,377,457	153,849	2,531,306	254,313	299,983	2,576,976	554,417	821,151		26,814	147,404	67,160
2004	4,268,307	2,536,743	158,886	2,695,629	280,762	374,613	2,789,480	624,400	854,427		28,413	150,226	68,597
2005	4,454,637	2,649,785	119,979	2,769,764	295,170	438,991	2,913,585	659,688	881,364		28,731	155,049	68,911
2006	4,843,725	2,832,170	141,898	2,974,068	304,498	529,231	3,198,801	687,861	957,063		30,201	160,384	70,229
2007	5,146,507	2,910,423	159,284	3,069,707	308,800	618,902	3,379,809	741,692	1,025,006		31,435	163,720	72,291
2008	5,442,170	2,892,255	255,907	3,148,162	310,871	678,696	3,515,987	768,364	1,157,819		32,858	165,628	70,243
2009	5,479,469	2,816,897	354,545	3,171,442	313,395	599,172	3,457,219	755,635	1,266,615		33,014	165,973	68,287
2010	5,485,692	2,827,257	269,394	3,096,651	310,326	556,191	3,342,516	742,469	1,400,707		32,808	167,204	67,905
2011	5,752,754	2,947,737	287,922	3,235,659	294,324	565,618	3,506,953	814,970	1,430,831		34,376	167,350	68,566
2012	5,850,085	3,094,583	220,243	3,314,826	304,548	529,507	3,539,785	865,849	1,444,451		34,902	167,614	70,074
2013	6,142,126	3,196,931	330,836	3,527,767	349,395	522,511	3,700,883	945,117	1,496,126		36,420	168,648	72,079
2014	6,313,643	3,334,895	254,411	3,589,306	364,181	538,314	3,763,439	993,443	1,556,761		37,180	169,813	73,262

Personal Income and Employment by Area: Yuma, AZ

(Thousands of dollars, except as noted.)

Year	Personal income, total	Earnings by place of work			Less: Contributions for government social insurance	Plus: Adjustment for residence	Equals: Net earnings by place of residence	Plus: Dividends, interest, and rent	Plus: Personal current transfer receipts	Per capita personal income (dollars)	Population (persons)	Total employment
		Nonfarm	Farm	Total								
1970	234,330	166,366	29,515	195,881	11,394	-7,687	176,800	41,293	16,237	3,816	61,415	29,730
1971	271,010	197,696	27,253	224,949	14,114	-8,118	202,717	48,942	19,351	4,179	64,853	31,172
1972	295,512	211,141	34,364	245,505	15,579	-8,968	220,958	52,196	22,358	4,401	67,150	31,018
1973	321,946	231,636	30,905	262,541	18,851	-9,354	234,336	60,527	27,083	4,687	68,685	31,328
1974	412,284	261,723	82,162	343,885	22,284	-11,233	310,368	69,875	32,041	5,775	71,396	32,675
1975	428,440	298,411	49,068	347,479	25,142	-14,724	307,613	78,043	42,784	6,170	69,434	33,614
1976	481,782	336,258	57,368	393,626	28,944	-16,505	348,177	84,001	49,604	6,300	76,476	35,033
1977	516,461	363,589	61,665	425,254	31,563	-21,030	372,661	91,864	51,936	6,500	79,454	36,573
1978	577,349	411,037	64,781	475,818	36,149	-28,504	411,165	108,808	57,376	7,156	80,680	38,692
1979	700,095	475,764	105,570	581,334	44,524	-33,477	503,333	128,192	68,570	8,383	83,512	39,541
1980	788,574	520,911	117,724	638,635	49,114	-37,875	551,646	151,668	85,260	8,628	91,393	40,634
1981	860,161	555,943	106,873	662,816	56,585	-22,605	583,626	174,381	102,154	9,366	91,834	40,844
1982	897,307	564,220	104,043	668,263	57,259	-20,903	590,101	195,481	111,725	9,558	93,878	40,449
1983	857,377	554,686	68,863	623,549	57,148	-17,389	549,012	198,726	109,639	10,204	84,027	38,578
1984	972,167	627,683	88,653	716,336	66,181	-18,183	631,972	228,656	111,539	11,387	85,373	40,324
1985	1,074,761	669,054	130,208	799,262	71,816	-16,754	710,692	250,238	113,831	12,273	87,572	41,031
1986	1,136,319	737,860	88,883	826,743	80,405	-14,366	731,972	275,413	128,934	12,555	90,505	42,571
1987	1,289,346	800,496	163,863	964,359	87,571	-11,799	864,989	283,007	141,350	13,911	92,684	45,954
1988	1,428,941	865,351	236,865	1,102,216	98,423	-7,060	996,733	279,215	152,993	14,722	97,064	48,117
1989	1,467,134	919,603	160,598	1,080,201	109,001	375	971,575	303,761	191,798	14,192	103,380	50,231
1990	1,527,144	972,570	137,633	1,110,203	118,736	4,809	996,276	313,343	217,525	14,132	108,063	50,626
1991	1,678,588	1,071,078	171,190	1,242,268	130,800	-4,893	1,106,575	320,557	251,456	14,992	111,967	53,294
1992	1,806,179	1,152,877	162,719	1,315,596	141,262	-2,293	1,172,041	326,904	307,234	15,221	118,660	54,781
1993	1,968,626	1,202,948	245,996	1,448,944	148,330	-3,235	1,297,379	336,953	334,294	15,763	124,892	55,460
1994	2,002,782	1,286,827	153,413	1,440,240	157,771	-6,984	1,275,485	370,921	356,376	15,650	127,975	57,080
1995	2,341,603	1,357,578	376,898	1,734,476	158,176	-9,182	1,567,118	395,928	378,557	17,770	131,776	59,415
1996	2,258,041	1,423,732	196,477	1,620,209	169,676	-10,834	1,439,699	418,890	399,452	16,452	137,248	63,061
1997	2,441,541	1,549,481	216,401	1,765,882	179,788	-14,385	1,571,709	453,124	416,708	16,967	143,896	63,462
1998	2,694,636	1,648,964	324,905	1,973,869	187,756	-13,551	1,772,562	478,395	443,679	18,077	149,065	66,606
1999	2,736,822	1,723,743	258,736	1,982,479	194,335	-10,984	1,777,160	481,603	478,059	17,581	155,665	67,016
2000	2,914,401	1,819,973	308,127	2,128,100	202,606	-11,098	1,914,396	507,238	492,767	18,150	160,576	68,052
2001	3,048,930	1,947,780	232,404	2,180,184	224,665	-9,357	1,946,162	540,413	562,355	18,720	162,873	70,219
2002	3,337,932	2,110,748	320,868	2,431,616	246,728	-6,872	2,178,016	532,923	626,993	20,181	165,398	72,220
2003	3,500,350	2,300,527	213,530	2,514,057	266,176	-4,060	2,243,821	569,857	686,672	20,835	168,003	73,936
2004	3,933,823	2,569,285	317,987	2,887,272	296,266	-704	2,590,302	607,582	735,939	22,762	172,824	77,576
2005	4,244,689	2,754,016	324,957	3,078,973	320,631	3,308	2,761,650	666,257	816,782	23,738	178,816	79,812
2006	4,502,769	3,045,977	229,644	3,275,621	347,414	8,251	2,936,458	680,795	885,516	24,492	183,848	82,816
2007	4,878,683	3,230,804	289,888	3,520,692	375,896	13,992	3,158,788	759,461	960,434	26,040	187,357	84,133
2008	5,095,721	3,295,394	220,532	3,515,926	387,375	19,754	3,148,305	813,074	1,134,342	26,651	191,202	83,439
2009	5,170,361	3,236,039	199,229	3,435,268	383,683	15,526	3,067,111	817,917	1,285,333	26,691	193,714	80,134
2010	5,323,706	3,220,840	294,867	3,515,707	385,795	18,681	3,148,593	763,623	1,411,490	27,009	197,105	79,764
2011	5,622,247	3,283,741	468,814	3,752,555	352,547	19,378	3,419,386	805,321	1,397,540	27,748	202,617	81,109
2012	5,586,005	3,391,142	295,616	3,686,758	364,059	23,198	3,345,897	867,327	1,372,781	27,617	202,264	82,392
2013	5,838,101	3,390,618	553,728	3,944,346	411,291	26,769	3,559,824	892,875	1,385,402	28,897	202,033	83,008
2014	5,841,652	3,519,714	349,486	3,869,200	425,558	29,001	3,472,643	927,950	1,441,059	28,742	203,247	83,391

PART B

GROSS DOMESTIC PRODUCT (GDP) BY REGION, STATE, AND AREA

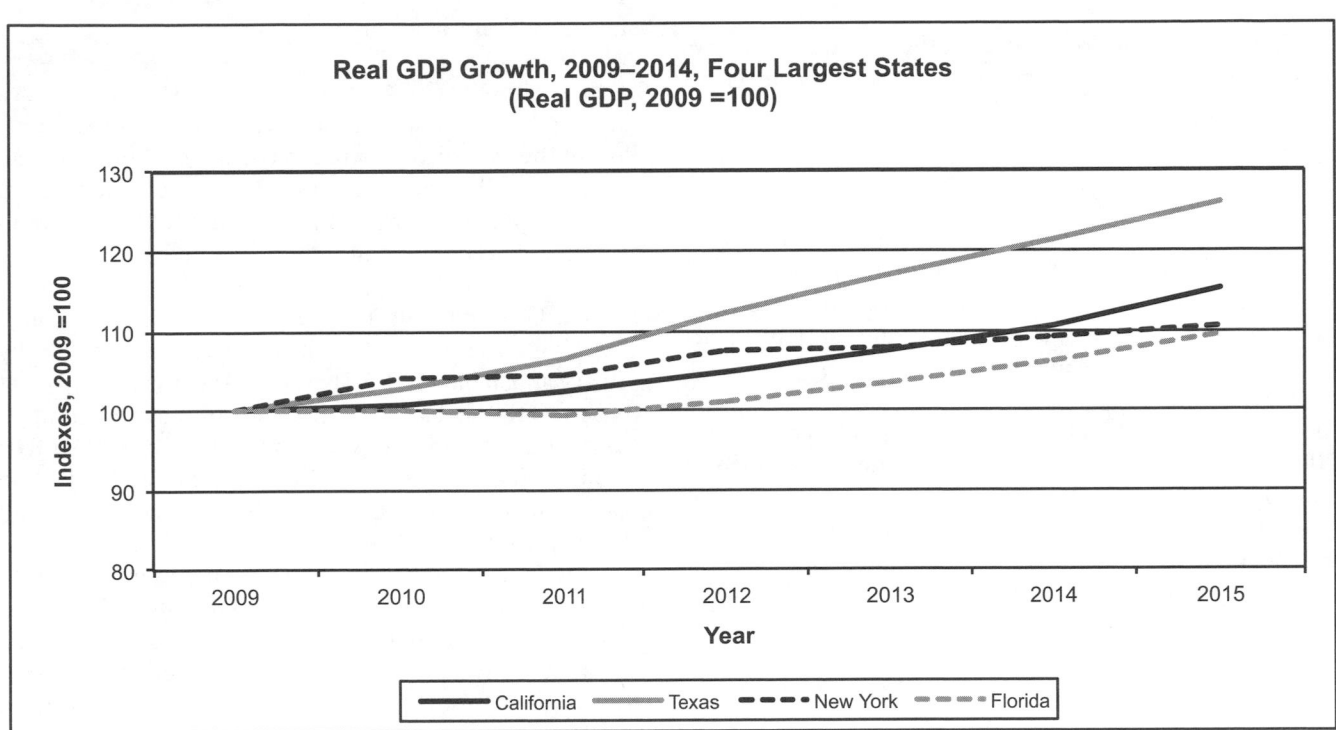

HIGHLIGHTS:

- The nationwide GDP increased 3.5 percent from 2014 to 2015. Oregon had the largest percent increase in production among the states (5.9 percent), followed by California and Florida, both at 5.7 percent.

- Alaska's GDP continued to decline for the third year in a row, with a decrease of 9.1 percent in 2015. Seven other states experienced a decrease in GDP from 2014 to 2015: North Dakota (5.8 percent), Wyoming (5.5 percent), Oklahoma (5.1 percent), New Mexico (2.7 percent), Louisiana (1.0 percent), Texas (1.0 percent), and West Virginia (0.9 percent).

- Midland, TX, experienced the largest growth in GDP in 2014 at 22.2 percent among all metropolitan statistical areas (MSAs), while Homosassa Springs, FL, suffered from the largest decline at 4.8 percent. GDP declined by one percent or more in 13 MSAs.

- New York-Newark-Jersey City, NY-NJ-PA, which had the largest GDP among all MSAs, made up 9.9 percent of the total U.S. metropolitan portion of GDP in 2014.

PART B. NOTES AND DEFINITIONS: GROSS DOMESTIC PRODUCT BY REGION AND STATE

Source: U.S. Department of Commerce, Bureau of Economic Analysis (BEA), http://www.bea.gov

The following definitions are from the BEA. In a following section, further detail and explanation of the concepts is provided.

BEA definitions

GDP by state is the state counterpart of the nation's gross domestic product (GDP), the Bureau's featured and most comprehensive measure of U.S. economic activity. GDP by state is derived as the sum of the GDP originating in all the industries in a state.

The statistics of real GDP by state are prepared in chained (2009) dollars. Real GDP by state is an inflation–adjusted measure of each state's gross product that is based on national prices for the goods and services produced within that state. The statistics of real GDP by state and of quantity indexes with a reference year of 2009 were derived by applying national chain–type price indexes to the current–dollar values of GDP by state for the 64 detailed NAICS–based industries for 1997 forward.

The chain–type index formula that is used in the national accounts is then used to calculate the values of total real GDP by state and of real GDP by state at more aggregated industry levels. Real GDP by state may reflect a substantial volume of output that is sold to other states and countries. To the extent that a state's output is produced and sold in national markets at relatively uniform prices (or sold locally at national prices), real GDP by state captures the differences across states that reflect the relative differences in the mix of goods and services that the states produce. However, real GDP by state does not capture geographic differences in the prices of goods and services that are produced and sold locally.

Relation of GDP by state to U.S. Gross Domestic Product (GDP). An industry's GDP by state, or its value added, in practice, is calculated as the sum of incomes earned by labor and capital and the costs incurred in the production of goods and services. That is, it includes the wages and salaries that workers earn, the income earned by individual or joint entrepreneurs as well as by corporations, and business taxes such as sales, property, and federal excise taxes—that count as a business expense.

GDP is calculated as the sum of what consumers, businesses, and government spend on final goods and services, plus investment and net foreign trade. In theory, incomes earned should equal what is spent, but due to different data sources, income earned, usually referred to as gross domestic income (GDI), does not always equal what is spent (GDP). The difference is referred to as the "statistical discrepancy."

Starting with the 2004 comprehensive revision, BEA's annual industry accounts and its GDP–by–state accounts allocate the statistical discrepancy across all private–sector industries. Therefore, the GDP–by–state statistics are now conceptually more similar to the GDP statistics in the national accounts than they had been in the past.

U.S. real GDP by state for the advance year, 2014, may differ from the Annual Industry Accounts' GDP by industry and, hence NIPA (National Income and Product Account) GDP, because of different sources and vintages of data used to estimate GDP by state and NIPA GDP. For the revised years of 1997–2012, U.S. GDP by state is nearly identical to GDP by industry except for small differences resulting from GDP by state's exclusion of overseas Federal military and civilian activity (because it cannot be attributed to a particular state). The statistics of GDP by industry are identical to those from the 2014 annual revision of the NIPAs, released in July 2014. However, because of revisions since July 2014, GDP in the NIPAs may differ from U.S. GDP by state.

 BEA's national, international, regional, and industry statistics; the Survey of Current Business; and BEA news releases are available without charge on BEA's Web site at www.bea.gov. By visiting the site, you can also subscribe to receive free e–mail summaries of BEA releases and announcements.

Further notes

The value of an industry's GDP is equal to the market value of its gross output (which consists of sales or receipts and other operating income, taxes on production and imports, and inventory change) minus the value of its intermediate inputs (which consist of energy, raw materials, semifinished goods, and services that are purchased from domestic industries or foreign sources). In concept, this definition is equal to the sum of labor and property-type income earned in that industry in the production of GDP, plus commodity taxes. Property-type income is the sum of corporate profits, proprietors' income, rental income of persons, net interest, capital consumption allowances, business transfer payments, and the current surplus of government enterprises less subsidies.

In practice, GDP by state, like GDP by industry, is measured using the incomes data rather than data on gross output and intermediate inputs, which are not available on a sufficiently detailed and timely basis.

Therefore, the *value* of *GDP by state* is defined as the sum of labor and property-type incomes originating in each of 63 industries in that state, plus commodity taxes, and plus the allocated value of the statistical discrepancy between national GDP and national gross national income.

Chained-dollar estimates. The effect of the "chained-dollar" deflation procedure that BEA uses is to combine the real, inflation-adjusted, quantity changes in output between two adjacent time periods for individual products and industries using, as weights for the individual products, their average prices in those two periods. The estimates for successive time periods are then "chained" each to the previous one to provide a continuous index of real quantities that is not distorted by using prices from a single base year.

GDP by state is now calculated on a North American Industry Classification System (NAICS) basis back through 1997. Data for earlier years, beginning with 1977, were calculated on the Standard Industrial Classification (SIC) basis. According to BEA (in a "Cautionary note" on the Web site, dated June 7, 2007), "There is a discontinuity in the GDP by state time series at 1997, where the data change from SIC industry definitions to NAICS industry definitions. This discontinuity results from many sources, including differences in source data and different estimation methodologies. In addition, the NAICS-based GDP by state estimates are consistent with U.S. gross domestic product (GDP) while the SIC-based GDP by state estimates are consistent with U.S. gross domestic income (GDI). This data discontinuity may affect both the levels and the growth rates of the GDP by state estimates. Users of the GDP by state estimates are strongly cautioned against appending the two data series in an attempt to construct a single time series of GDP by state estimates for 1963 to 2006."

Patterns of Economic Change nevertheless provides SIC-based data for 1980 to 1997 for those who require information about economic growth before 1997 by state.

Gross Domestic Product by Region and State

(Millions of dollars; index numbers)

Year	United States	New England	Mideast	Great Lakes	Plains	Southeast	Southwest	Rocky Mountain	Far West	Alabama	Alaska	Arizona	Arkansas
VALUE													
1980.............................	2,713,933	144,462	526,543	482,396	198,218	541,288	287,176	82,912	450,937	36,142	15,282	30,764	20,276
1981.............................	3,057,318	161,375	582,863	529,326	221,897	614,555	343,445	94,875	508,982	40,257	21,824	34,269	22,891
1982.............................	3,211,370	174,671	618,858	538,540	227,879	646,248	364,438	99,337	541,401	41,778	23,461	35,794	23,527
1983.............................	3,445,372	193,042	672,681	578,275	240,215	701,725	372,240	104,465	582,731	45,679	22,591	39,774	25,292
1984.............................	3,853,668	220,403	748,818	650,648	270,080	788,921	407,459	114,125	653,214	50,010	23,787	46,135	28,465
1985.............................	4,126,664	241,214	805,589	689,882	282,793	848,539	433,232	119,913	705,503	53,824	26,142	50,709	29,326
1986.............................	4,340,813	263,002	864,286	729,059	293,686	898,226	422,406	119,973	750,175	56,134	19,181	55,881	30,799
1987.............................	4,649,020	289,091	934,923	765,895	311,458	971,259	432,199	124,769	819,428	60,752	22,925	60,047	32,664
1988.............................	5,053,003	316,638	1,025,241	827,237	333,626	1,055,957	468,423	133,061	892,820	66,008	21,270	64,945	35,004
1989.............................	5,366,080	332,656	1,075,303	877,466	355,298	1,122,373	497,782	140,822	964,380	68,394	23,453	67,895	37,128
1990.............................	5,651,747	340,035	1,125,281	910,630	372,331	1,181,498	533,980	150,771	1,037,220	71,610	25,040	70,632	38,680
1991.............................	5,842,665	343,814	1,153,017	939,577	388,230	1,237,389	556,860	158,972	1,064,806	76,043	22,283	73,358	41,572
1992.............................	6,167,644	359,058	1,205,957	1,006,629	414,573	1,315,691	593,930	171,652	1,100,154	81,260	22,753	82,682	45,018
1993.............................	6,467,698	370,365	1,253,977	1,058,191	427,699	1,396,317	635,503	187,235	1,138,411	84,563	23,284	89,300	47,566
1994.............................	6,912,844	392,602	1,309,100	1,154,152	467,337	1,505,937	686,299	203,686	1,193,731	90,098	23,605	100,374	51,416
1995.............................	7,299,372	419,090	1,372,998	1,204,319	491,609	1,600,714	730,636	219,344	1,260,660	95,819	25,449	109,906	54,612
1996.............................	7,749,965	444,684	1,445,348	1,266,738	527,489	1,694,621	791,891	235,883	1,343,312	100,146	26,737	119,530	57,976
1997.............................	8,284,432	479,107	1,535,947	1,345,334	558,791	1,802,254	866,050	253,743	1,443,206	104,805	27,581	129,279	60,333
1997[1].............................	8,549,209	490,603	1,625,007	1,395,281	565,704	1,836,179	878,246	257,098	1,501,093	104,309	25,763	132,795	60,248
1998[1].............................	9,030,651	516,010	1,694,132	1,470,178	592,512	1,950,462	929,107	276,829	1,601,422	109,776	24,067	143,542	62,695
1999[1].............................	9,602,088	543,601	1,791,171	1,548,754	619,727	2,082,309	986,102	298,744	1,731,681	115,704	24,727	156,118	67,087
2000[1].............................	10,225,879	590,038	1,889,632	1,624,102	661,930	2,188,879	1,065,796	326,504	1,878,997	120,428	26,932	166,108	69,111
2001[1].............................	10,562,041	607,453	1,980,691	1,646,877	680,072	2,287,967	1,114,858	339,139	1,904,984	124,885	28,942	172,634	71,128
2002[1].............................	10,916,911	623,692	2,039,346	1,701,848	706,178	2,376,742	1,139,424	348,570	1,981,112	130,180	29,808	179,892	74,243
2003[1].............................	11,446,549	651,127	2,111,676	1,766,295	746,668	2,505,663	1,206,779	363,998	2,094,342	136,270	32,125	192,663	78,882
2004[1].............................	12,206,995	692,378	2,237,723	1,852,648	793,359	2,680,845	1,311,711	387,971	2,250,361	148,769	35,510	204,659	85,315
2005[1].............................	13,022,458	723,206	2,375,991	1,927,323	831,629	2,895,013	1,425,858	423,454	2,419,985	157,914	40,277	227,047	90,112
2006[1].............................	13,781,347	758,826	2,502,230	1,998,027	864,955	3,064,212	1,556,478	456,955	2,579,664	165,131	44,867	248,075	95,727
2007[1].............................	14,391,149	795,221	2,596,541	2,061,381	907,611	3,162,572	1,668,130	488,637	2,711,056	170,399	49,285	262,214	99,210
2008[1].............................	14,626,598	798,476	2,620,368	2,045,919	932,243	3,200,341	1,743,957	507,892	2,777,402	173,521	55,436	258,978	102,100
2009[1].............................	14,320,114	792,748	2,654,452	1,993,464	923,622	3,142,729	1,640,647	491,259	2,681,194	169,586	50,514	243,102	100,098
2010[1].............................	14,859,772	819,346	2,765,534	2,071,979	962,658	3,238,444	1,736,339	509,500	2,755,971	176,221	54,220	247,333	104,929
2011[1].............................	15,406,002	839,018	2,828,645	2,158,023	1,012,170	3,319,209	1,861,490	531,793	2,855,654	181,923	59,318	255,621	109,378
2012[1].............................	16,041,240	868,835	2,946,510	2,248,270	1,058,221	3,433,101	1,971,396	547,250	2,967,656	187,283	61,614	266,131	111,541
2013[1].............................	16,548,794	883,083	3,021,199	2,302,794	1,094,563	3,530,020	2,072,022	568,522	3,076,591	191,605	59,891	271,072	116,651
2014[1].............................	17,233,139	917,171	3,135,850	2,395,707	1,135,432	3,666,005	2,168,498	594,843	3,219,634	197,535	58,067	281,559	121,065
2015[1].............................	17,830,307	951,898	3,252,756	2,491,858	1,164,014	3,816,931	2,149,702	611,784	3,391,364	204,235	52,804	290,578	123,207

[1] NAICS basis, not continous with previous years.

Gross Domestic Product by Region and State—*Continued*

(Millions of dollars; index numbers)

Year	United States	New England	Mideast	Great Lakes	Plains	Southeast	Southwest	Rocky Mountain	Far West	Alabama	Alaska	Arizona	Arkansas
QUANTITY INDEX													
1997=100													
1980....................	59.3	56.6	65.9	63.5	61.6	54.2	55.6	56.5	57.2	61.6	81.4	43.0	57.6
1981....................	60.9	58.0	66.9	64.0	63.7	56.0	58.7	58.6	59.0	62.8	93.8	44.2	59.7
1982....................	60.1	58.6	66.5	61.1	62.1	55.4	58.9	58.0	58.9	61.2	96.2	43.1	58.1
1983....................	61.8	61.7	68.7	63.1	62.6	57.6	58.9	58.7	60.6	64.2	93.6	45.6	60.0
1984....................	66.2	67.3	73.0	68.1	67.3	61.9	62.5	61.7	64.9	67.3	97.4	50.5	64.7
1985....................	68.9	71.2	75.4	70.4	69.2	64.8	65.2	63.2	67.9	70.4	108.2	53.7	65.3
1986....................	70.3	74.7	77.6	71.5	69.5	66.8	64.2	62.4	70.0	71.1	90.5	56.9	66.6
1987....................	73.4	80.0	81.6	73.5	71.9	70.2	64.2	63.1	74.3	75.1	107.0	59.3	68.9
1988....................	77.2	85.0	86.4	77.0	74.6	73.9	67.8	65.4	78.4	78.7	101.0	62.1	71.5
1989....................	78.9	85.9	87.3	78.6	76.5	75.6	69.1	66.7	81.6	78.6	105.1	62.6	72.9
1990....................	80.1	84.5	88.0	79.0	77.6	76.7	70.9	68.9	84.4	79.9	104.3	63.1	73.8
1991....................	80.0	82.3	86.6	78.6	78.4	77.5	72.2	70.7	83.7	82.2	93.6	63.4	77.1
1992....................	82.4	83.7	88.1	82.3	81.8	80.4	75.6	74.7	84.4	85.7	94.8	69.8	81.6
1993....................	84.1	83.8	89.0	84.3	82.2	83.2	78.7	79.3	84.9	87.0	94.4	73.4	84.1
1994....................	88.0	86.8	90.9	89.7	87.8	88.1	83.6	84.5	87.0	90.5	94.9	80.5	88.9
1995....................	91.0	90.5	92.9	91.8	90.5	91.7	87.7	89.3	90.1	93.5	100.1	86.6	92.5
1996....................	95.0	94.4	96.1	95.4	95.3	95.5	93.0	94.3	94.5	96.7	98.9	93.5	96.7
1997....................	100.0	100.0	100.0	100.0	100.0	100.0	100.0	100.0	100.0	100.0	100.0	100.0	100.0
2009 =100													
1997 [1]....................	77.7	78.7	80.3	91.0	79.8	78.2	70.1	68.3	70.4	81.0	75.9	67.2	79.2
1998 [1]....................	81.1	81.7	82.3	94.2	82.2	81.6	74.7	72.8	74.6	83.9	73.1	72.9	80.9
1999 [1]....................	84.9	85.1	85.7	97.5	84.7	85.4	78.3	77.4	79.6	87.1	72.6	79.2	85.2
2000 [1]....................	88.2	90.9	88.4	99.9	88.5	87.3	81.3	82.6	84.7	88.5	71.4	83.3	85.8
2001 [1]....................	89.0	91.9	90.7	98.8	88.5	88.8	83.3	83.9	84.3	89.3	74.4	85.2	85.7
2002 [1]....................	90.6	92.6	91.6	100.6	90.4	90.7	84.8	84.8	86.4	91.7	76.5	87.4	88.3
2003 [1]....................	92.9	95.1	92.9	102.7	93.7	93.6	86.2	86.3	89.5	93.9	76.0	92.4	92.0
2004 [1]....................	96.2	98.5	95.6	104.9	96.6	97.2	90.1	89.0	93.5	99.3	79.2	95.7	96.2
2005 [1]....................	99.2	100.0	98.4	106.2	98.8	101.4	92.7	93.4	97.6	102.1	81.2	103.2	98.9
2006 [1]....................	101.9	102.1	100.5	107.2	99.9	104.0	97.7	97.4	101.1	103.5	86.5	109.2	101.9
2007 [1]....................	103.3	104.2	101.3	107.6	101.4	104.2	101.4	100.8	103.3	103.7	90.8	112.1	102.1
2008 [1]....................	102.8	102.9	100.3	105.0	102.3	103.4	101.6	101.8	104.0	103.4	91.9	108.9	102.7
2009 [1]....................	100.0	100.0	100.0	100.0	100.0	100.0	100.0	100.0	100.0	100.0	100.0	100.0	100.0
2010 [1]....................	102.2	102.4	102.9	102.9	102.7	101.6	102.3	101.3	101.3	102.2	98.5	100.7	103.2
2011 [1]....................	103.6	103.4	103.5	105.1	105.1	102.0	105.6	102.8	102.8	103.2	101.9	102.4	105.3
2012 [1]....................	105.6	104.8	105.4	106.8	107.3	103.2	110.4	104.0	104.8	104.2	107.5	104.5	105.3
2013 [1]....................	107.0	104.3	105.8	107.5	108.9	104.2	114.1	106.2	106.7	105.1	101.8	104.5	108.1
2014 [1]....................	109.3	106.1	107.4	109.6	111.1	106.1	118.0	109.4	109.6	106.0	98.3	106.4	110.4
2015 [1]....................	111.9	107.5	109.1	111.7	112.6	108.4	121.6	112.9	113.8	107.7	97.7	107.4	112.0

[1] NAICS basis, not continous with previous years.

Gross Domestic Product by Region and State—*Continued*

(Millions of dollars; index numbers)

Year	California	Colorado	Connecticut	Delaware	District of Columbia	Florida	Georgia	Hawaii	Idaho	Illinois	Indiana	Iowa	Kansas	Kentucky
VALUE														
1980..................	327,958	38,332	40,770	7,898	19,862	97,899	56,229	13,380	9,916	145,264	58,870	34,582	28,298	37,017
1981..................	368,808	43,974	45,642	8,839	21,740	112,167	63,751	14,640	10,677	159,649	64,724	38,272	31,978	41,068
1982..................	393,788	47,654	50,196	9,498	22,958	122,282	68,451	15,740	10,689	164,267	64,982	37,289	33,491	42,184
1983..................	426,143	50,718	55,528	10,611	24,573	136,768	76,738	17,260	11,834	173,119	69,335	37,481	35,257	44,092
1984..................	482,166	56,230	63,618	11,925	26,584	155,993	88,466	19,132	12,586	194,244	78,859	41,264	38,442	49,344
1985..................	523,906	59,641	69,231	13,092	28,534	170,894	98,223	20,722	13,044	206,281	82,011	42,431	40,658	51,893
1986..................	563,082	60,970	75,305	14,138	30,079	185,852	108,089	22,437	13,220	218,696	86,437	43,226	41,795	53,199
1987..................	615,359	63,920	82,984	15,568	32,129	204,816	117,033	24,273	13,996	231,210	91,650	45,283	44,164	56,282
1988..................	671,575	67,757	90,707	16,887	35,226	224,848	126,565	26,799	15,285	252,197	99,492	49,088	46,698	61,851
1989..................	722,979	71,179	95,831	18,900	37,469	241,633	133,794	29,427	16,909	266,608	107,199	52,907	48,814	65,525
1990..................	773,460	75,571	100,169	19,928	39,688	256,589	140,646	32,534	18,004	279,019	110,860	56,121	51,874	68,412
1991..................	790,046	79,766	101,475	21,746	41,430	267,669	147,760	34,357	18,852	288,473	114,637	57,944	53,981	71,679
1992..................	807,358	87,302	105,759	22,907	43,187	284,673	160,062	36,129	20,632	306,236	124,714	61,870	56,902	77,531
1993..................	826,447	95,659	107,680	23,509	45,356	304,403	171,659	36,732	23,100	320,079	132,108	63,386	58,953	81,618
1994..................	861,360	104,507	113,115	25,638	46,655	327,167	187,996	37,395	25,455	347,971	143,335	70,161	63,304	87,646
1995..................	911,577	112,708	123,212	27,721	47,094	346,951	203,397	37,763	27,762	364,451	150,404	73,137	65,282	91,915
1996..................	964,186	121,081	129,111	29,156	47,823	370,912	219,989	38,125	28,915	383,504	158,350	78,819	69,616	96,617
1997..................	1,037,091	133,204	140,280	31,450	49,702	393,074	235,200	39,064	30,312	408,048	167,366	83,113	74,147	103,621
1997[1]..................	1,082,051	136,296	140,127	33,911	51,682	403,677	242,669	37,915	29,686	422,741	172,949	83,743	75,239	105,103
1998[1]..................	1,158,822	149,057	147,616	35,955	53,891	431,374	264,225	37,627	31,152	443,392	187,005	85,833	79,114	109,859
1999[1]..................	1,258,697	162,273	153,781	39,053	58,088	459,431	287,670	39,177	34,390	465,795	195,668	88,936	82,944	115,931
2000[1]..................	1,377,014	178,331	166,995	41,677	60,458	490,538	304,942	41,247	38,416	492,922	205,807	95,021	87,446	115,126
2001[1]..................	1,394,863	185,264	172,336	43,314	65,400	519,024	316,351	42,789	37,812	503,969	207,104	96,093	90,269	118,975
2002[1]..................	1,449,536	189,464	174,856	43,046	69,608	550,486	323,644	45,185	39,185	514,227	214,788	100,359	92,953	123,928
2003[1]..................	1,535,202	195,704	181,750	46,092	73,846	585,729	335,367	48,559	41,125	531,957	225,933	106,935	97,651	128,804
2004[1]..................	1,643,908	205,347	198,921	50,618	79,564	637,113	353,025	53,306	44,445	561,117	240,428	118,710	101,343	135,994
2005[1]..................	1,760,508	222,415	208,154	52,901	83,968	700,222	376,626	58,123	47,990	588,847	247,048	124,021	106,864	144,174
2006[1]..................	1,868,969	233,142	220,994	55,826	88,502	748,021	393,920	61,684	51,821	623,535	258,525	128,346	113,738	152,394
2007[1]..................	1,951,997	245,169	235,299	56,805	93,695	773,682	411,730	64,775	55,010	648,647	271,444	137,377	122,276	155,486
2008[1]..................	1,993,589	255,213	231,486	54,303	98,399	754,278	410,778	66,304	55,927	645,447	275,017	136,871	126,343	158,732
2009[1]..................	1,913,674	250,082	226,076	56,374	98,938	721,928	402,728	64,986	53,832	639,965	263,380	136,596	122,431	156,113
2010[1]..................	1,960,935	258,148	230,357	57,674	104,044	729,761	407,999	67,539	55,420	653,164	283,111	141,382	128,589	165,787
2011[1]..................	2,031,348	266,796	232,271	59,763	108,029	735,244	418,917	69,689	57,081	679,269	291,890	149,402	137,654	172,255
2012[1]..................	2,121,602	277,647	238,322	60,774	109,760	764,646	434,978	72,100	58,545	712,604	299,906	159,096	141,600	178,210
2013[1]..................	2,215,232	288,809	242,417	61,424	111,816	797,344	450,934	74,012	61,111	720,495	310,669	163,495	142,774	182,696
2014[1]..................	2,324,995	305,367	250,764	65,485	116,539	835,578	471,879	76,425	63,364	742,028	324,289	170,715	146,562	188,518
2015[1]..................	2,458,535	314,878	258,532	68,071	122,510	882,798	495,727	79,745	65,242	775,007	336,411	174,103	147,765	194,643

[1] NAICS basis, not continous with previous years.

Gross Domestic Product by Region and State—*Continued*

(Millions of dollars; index numbers)

Year	California	Colorado	Connecticut	Delaware	District of Columbia	Florida	Georgia	Hawaii	Idaho	Illinois	Indiana	Iowa	Kansas	Kentucky
QUANTITY INDEX														
1997=100														
1980..................	57.8	52.9	56.1	51.3	91.9	47.6	43.8	68.5	54.2	63.4	61.1	67.8	67.0	60.8
1981..................	59.7	55.2	57.4	52.3	90.3	49.9	45.6	68.2	54.4	64.3	61.8	69.9	68.9	62.5
1982..................	59.7	56.3	58.8	52.9	87.6	51.1	46.3	68.8	52.2	62.0	58.4	65.3	68.3	60.3
1983..................	61.9	57.0	61.8	57.1	88.5	54.1	49.3	71.5	54.8	62.7	59.8	62.6	68.7	60.4
1984..................	66.8	60.3	67.5	61.3	90.3	58.6	54.1	74.2	55.7	67.2	65.3	66.0	71.8	64.9
1985..................	70.3	61.8	71.1	65.2	91.7	61.8	58.2	76.7	57.0	69.2	66.5	67.4	74.5	66.9
1986..................	72.9	61.4	74.3	67.0	92.2	64.5	61.6	79.3	55.9	70.7	67.6	66.5	74.8	65.9
1987..................	77.4	62.6	80.0	71.7	94.9	68.7	64.7	82.9	57.2	73.0	70.1	68.0	77.3	68.3
1988..................	81.8	64.5	84.9	75.0	99.0	73.0	67.6	88.5	60.3	77.1	73.6	71.6	79.4	72.9
1989..................	84.9	65.2	86.0	80.5	100.9	75.6	68.9	93.8	64.2	78.6	76.3	74.2	80.0	74.5
1990..................	87.4	66.8	86.4	82.3	103.0	77.4	70.2	100.3	66.5	79.4	76.6	76.4	81.8	75.5
1991..................	86.1	68.2	84.3	85.6	101.1	77.8	71.1	101.8	67.9	79.3	76.6	76.8	82.6	76.2
1992..................	86.0	72.9	85.4	86.4	101.8	80.8	75.1	104.5	72.7	82.4	81.5	80.4	85.1	80.4
1993..................	85.6	77.7	84.3	85.7	103.2	83.8	78.6	102.8	79.0	84.2	84.0	80.5	85.7	82.8
1994..................	87.2	83.0	86.3	91.4	103.2	87.9	84.2	102.6	85.3	89.4	89.1	87.2	90.0	87.9
1995..................	90.7	87.7	91.6	95.2	100.4	91.2	89.0	101.2	92.4	91.9	91.9	89.7	91.1	91.0
1996..................	94.3	92.4	94.0	97.0	99.1	95.9	94.9	100.2	95.4	95.5	95.6	94.9	94.9	94.4
1997..................	100.0	100.0	100.0	100.0	100.0	100.0	100.0	100.0	100.0	100.0	100.0	100.0	100.0	100.0
2009 =100														
1997 [1]............ ...	70.1	70.1	81.2	76.5	75.6	74.9	78.8	82.3	66.1	86.9	84.6	78.9	80.5	89.6
1998 [1]............ ...	74.7	76.0	83.9	80.1	76.7	78.6	84.2	79.7	69.0	89.6	89.8	79.6	83.3	92.1
1999 [1]............ ...	80.3	81.4	86.0	86.2	80.3	82.1	89.9	80.8	75.8	92.6	92.7	81.3	85.8	95.3
2000 [1]............ ...	86.4	87.5	91.5	89.3	80.8	85.4	93.0	82.3	84.6	95.7	95.5	85.4	88.2	92.6
2001 [1]............ ...	86.1	88.9	92.4	90.9	84.7	87.8	94.0	82.1	82.3	95.5	93.7	83.8	88.4	93.1
2002 [1]............ ...	88.2	89.4	92.1	88.7	86.9	91.2	94.5	84.5	84.4	95.8	95.9	86.2	89.8	95.5
2003 [1]............ ...	91.8	90.3	93.8	92.7	89.1	95.1	96.4	88.4	87.1	97.3	99.3	89.9	92.1	97.4
2004 [1]............ ...	95.6	91.9	99.9	98.8	92.6	100.4	98.9	94.1	91.3	99.7	102.9	97.0	92.8	99.8
2005 [1]............ ...	99.4	96.0	101.5	100.4	94.0	107.1	102.8	99.0	96.9	101.4	102.9	99.4	95.3	102.6
2006 [1]............ ...	102.6	97.7	104.9	102.9	96.0	110.8	104.4	101.5	102.1	104.1	104.9	100.5	98.7	105.2
2007 [1]............ ...	104.2	99.7	108.8	102.1	98.3	111.2	106.2	103.1	104.6	105.2	107.4	104.1	102.8	104.1
2008 [1]............ ...	104.7	101.1	104.9	96.2	101.2	106.7	104.2	103.7	104.7	102.8	106.7	101.8	104.1	104.0
2009 [1]............ ...	100.0	100.0	100.0	100.0	100.0	100.0	100.0	100.0	100.0	100.0	100.0	100.0	100.0	100.0
2010 [1]............ ...	100.9	101.3	100.9	100.6	103.0	100.1	100.3	102.7	101.3	100.9	106.3	102.2	103.3	104.6
2011 [1]............ ...	102.3	102.5	100.2	102.4	104.9	99.3	101.3	104.2	101.4	102.8	106.7	104.8	107.1	106.4
2012 [1]............ ...	104.7	104.9	100.4	101.4	104.9	101.1	102.8	105.5	101.8	105.1	106.9	108.7	107.7	107.6
2013 [1]............ ...	107.4	107.1	100.1	100.1	104.5	103.4	104.4	106.3	104.4	104.4	109.2	109.3	106.8	108.7
2014 [1]............ ...	110.7	111.5	101.3	104.4	106.4	106.1	107.0	107.2	106.5	105.4	111.6	112.4	108.1	109.9
2015 [1]............ ...	115.3	115.5	101.9	106.5	109.1	109.4	109.8	109.0	108.6	107.8	113.5	113.2	108.4	111.1

[1] NAICS basis, not continous with previous years.

Gross Domestic Product by Region and State—*Continued*

(Millions of dollars; index numbers)

Year	Louisiana	Maine	Maryland	Massachusetts	Michigan	Minnesota	Mississippi	Missouri	Montana	Nebraska	Nevada	New Hampshire	New Jersey
VALUE													
1980....................	63,925	10,263	47,522	69,684	104,134	50,219	21,353	52,420	8,925	18,294	11,633	9,263	88,334
1981....................	77,201	11,255	53,117	77,833	114,676	55,404	24,023	57,763	10,201	20,863	13,203	10,480	98,755
1982....................	78,067	12,115	56,339	83,777	115,166	57,472	24,614	60,699	10,206	21,265	13,885	11,407	105,759
1983....................	76,881	13,239	62,205	93,054	127,754	61,950	25,967	65,538	10,584	21,820	15,060	12,629	117,962
1984....................	82,623	14,897	69,920	106,425	143,678	71,369	28,744	74,539	11,010	24,631	16,514	14,767	133,572
1985....................	84,391	16,046	76,878	116,613	153,605	75,832	30,138	77,912	10,941	25,717	17,945	16,578	145,929
1986....................	77,107	17,382	83,744	127,155	163,458	79,450	30,996	83,330	10,979	26,045	19,731	18,369	158,836
1987....................	78,488	19,166	91,380	138,900	169,237	85,365	33,531	88,912	11,383	26,760	21,951	20,994	174,629
1988....................	83,196	21,371	101,280	151,625	180,621	91,896	35,534	95,760	11,703	29,262	24,987	22,937	194,709
1989....................	87,574	22,670	107,444	158,200	190,626	98,313	37,208	101,412	12,630	31,332	27,847	23,777	205,075
1990....................	95,177	23,256	112,835	159,505	193,103	102,757	38,757	103,566	13,242	33,734	30,980	23,768	214,357
1991....................	96,043	23,379	115,428	160,728	197,717	106,102	40,862	109,162	13,875	35,613	32,786	24,763	221,915
1992....................	90,890	24,329	119,535	167,435	212,057	114,518	44,012	115,288	14,937	38,214	36,052	26,332	230,774
1993....................	95,866	25,202	125,515	173,527	226,368	117,947	47,340	118,906	16,054	39,353	40,039	27,362	240,389
1994....................	105,119	26,543	133,311	185,710	251,484	128,167	51,602	130,567	17,062	43,504	45,173	29,190	251,573
1995....................	112,876	28,153	139,070	196,409	256,615	135,124	54,984	140,060	17,519	45,111	49,249	31,876	263,468
1996....................	118,807	29,256	145,023	210,630	270,320	145,880	57,460	148,257	18,119	49,007	54,419	34,561	278,191
1997....................	126,003	30,775	154,783	226,880	286,408	156,650	59,875	158,308	18,932	50,308	59,467	36,935	292,671
1997 [1]....................	118,073	30,675	160,965	237,390	301,805	157,206	58,657	163,749	19,196	50,719	59,468	37,992	308,631
1998 [1]....................	121,548	32,177	171,402	249,401	315,171	167,915	61,220	169,799	20,208	52,548	63,934	40,169	320,905
1999 [1]....................	127,230	34,350	181,987	264,906	338,889	176,966	64,142	177,924	20,834	54,427	70,376	41,229	336,975
2000 [1]....................	134,251	36,684	192,934	289,554	351,996	192,948	66,171	187,707	21,884	57,551	75,777	44,135	360,703
2001 [1]....................	140,264	38,317	206,296	296,348	351,014	198,343	67,662	191,750	23,063	60,217	80,134	45,163	373,205
2002 [1]....................	141,797	40,050	218,525	302,972	365,288	206,098	69,443	196,807	23,941	62,305	84,643	47,510	388,030
2003 [1]....................	157,562	41,858	229,840	315,339	377,462	218,061	73,982	205,338	25,788	67,656	90,419	50,276	404,905
2004 [1]....................	172,623	44,617	247,461	329,640	383,545	231,904	78,169	215,895	27,979	71,322	103,446	53,148	423,953
2005 [1]....................	200,436	46,052	264,729	344,145	396,268	244,800	82,274	225,268	30,425	74,415	116,764	56,123	444,973
2006 [1]....................	207,944	48,175	278,216	359,256	397,295	251,221	87,302	234,124	32,635	78,581	125,387	58,492	466,524
2007 [1]....................	209,676	49,269	290,139	377,987	402,390	259,493	91,919	241,909	35,676	82,918	131,137	59,958	481,936
2008 [1]....................	218,351	49,858	297,792	384,218	386,445	265,341	94,805	248,838	36,852	85,574	128,899	60,164	493,733
2009 [1]....................	209,507	50,222	303,265	382,747	366,401	259,460	92,182	249,574	35,605	86,694	119,482	60,681	484,185
2010 [1]....................	231,372	51,304	314,471	399,270	387,167	271,481	94,954	255,631	37,801	91,498	119,771	62,679	492,990
2011 [1]....................	236,958	51,481	323,942	413,673	401,360	284,491	96,840	256,996	40,842	99,050	122,744	64,098	497,571
2012 [1]....................	243,308	52,606	331,424	432,256	417,328	294,729	102,083	265,178	42,138	102,163	125,205	66,013	518,423
2013 [1]....................	238,308	53,300	337,422	438,641	431,112	307,216	103,270	274,540	43,223	107,188	126,935	67,307	530,091
2014 [1]....................	245,791	55,029	350,262	456,273	447,221	320,381	104,938	283,280	44,672	110,663	134,052	70,345	545,374
2015 [1]....................	243,317	56,600	363,845	476,743	466,536	333,267	107,100	293,378	45,933	113,998	141,282	72,573	568,155

[1] NAICS basis, not continous with previous years.

Gross Domestic Product by Region and State—*Continued*

(Millions of dollars; index numbers)

Year	Louisiana	Maine	Maryland	Massachusetts	Michigan	Minnesota	Mississippi	Missouri	Montana	Nebraska	Nevada	New Hampshire	New Jersey
QUANTITY INDEX													
1997=100													
1980......................	78.4	62.6	60.4	57.5	66.6	55.8	60.2	60.3	79.3	61.9	37.5	44.0	56.4
1981......................	80.5	63.0	61.6	58.9	66.5	57.3	62.2	61.1	82.4	65.5	39.1	45.8	57.9
1982......................	77.5	63.7	61.0	59.2	62.4	56.5	60.3	60.3	78.8	63.9	38.7	46.7	58.0
1983......................	76.6	66.5	64.0	62.6	66.6	58.4	61.6	62.3	78.9	62.3	39.9	49.7	62.1
1984......................	81.1	71.2	68.3	68.5	72.1	64.4	65.8	67.6	79.4	67.0	41.8	55.7	67.0
1985......................	82.6	74.3	72.2	72.5	75.1	67.0	67.6	68.6	77.3	69.3	43.5	60.7	70.5
1986......................	82.4	77.6	75.6	76.1	76.4	67.5	67.8	70.5	76.7	68.1	46.0	64.8	73.9
1987......................	82.8	82.6	79.6	81.0	77.3	70.8	72.2	73.3	77.2	68.3	49.0	72.2	78.9
1988......................	85.8	88.9	85.1	85.8	80.5	73.7	73.9	76.5	76.6	72.2	53.3	76.7	84.7
1989......................	85.8	90.6	87.0	86.2	81.8	75.9	74.6	78.1	79.7	74.3	57.4	76.6	85.9
1990......................	87.5	89.8	88.0	83.6	80.1	76.7	74.9	77.2	81.1	77.5	62.0	73.8	86.6
1991......................	87.3	87.2	86.4	81.1	78.8	76.6	76.6	78.4	83.1	80.0	63.4	74.2	86.3
1992......................	81.7	88.3	87.1	82.2	82.1	80.9	80.7	80.8	87.5	84.0	68.2	77.1	87.8
1993......................	83.6	88.8	88.5	82.8	84.6	81.1	84.2	81.0	91.3	84.3	74.0	78.1	88.8
1994......................	90.6	91.2	91.8	86.6	92.0	86.0	89.9	86.8	94.7	91.1	81.2	81.5	90.7
1995......................	95.5	93.5	93.3	89.6	92.2	88.6	94.4	91.2	95.3	92.5	85.9	87.7	92.9
1996......................	96.4	96.3	95.5	94.5	95.5	94.3	97.3	94.9	96.9	97.9	93.7	94.4	96.9
1997......................	100.0	100.0	100.0	100.0	100.0	100.0	100.0	100.0	100.0	100.0	100.0	100.0	100.0
2009 =100													
1997 [1]................	85.8	82.5	71.3	76.8	105.2	78.3	85.5	87.3	75.0	76.8	70.3	76.9	84.3
1998 [1]................	88.5	84.6	74.6	80.0	107.8	82.4	87.5	88.7	77.7	78.2	73.7	81.7	86.0
1999 [1]................	90.2	88.6	77.6	84.2	113.3	85.6	90.0	91.2	79.0	79.9	79.0	83.5	88.7
2000 [1]................	87.3	92.1	80.1	90.9	115.0	91.4	90.4	93.7	80.8	83.1	82.5	88.3	92.8
2001 [1]................	88.9	93.6	83.3	91.8	111.7	91.8	89.6	93.3	82.3	84.3	84.3	88.8	93.8
2002 [1]................	90.3	96.0	86.3	92.3	115.0	94.0	90.4	94.0	84.0	85.7	87.2	91.8	95.9
2003 [1]................	94.2	98.3	88.7	94.5	117.2	97.7	94.0	96.3	87.6	91.1	91.3	95.8	98.2
2004 [1]................	97.7	101.7	92.7	96.5	116.7	100.9	96.1	98.4	91.0	92.7	101.1	98.8	100.0
2005 [1]................	103.0	101.9	96.2	98.0	118.2	103.5	97.9	99.8	94.7	94.8	109.6	101.5	101.8
2006 [1]................	101.1	103.3	98.0	99.6	116.2	103.2	100.5	100.7	97.5	97.5	113.0	102.9	103.5
2007 [1]................	97.9	102.6	99.3	102.1	114.7	103.3	102.4	100.9	102.3	98.9	114.0	102.8	103.9
2008 [1]................	98.3	101.9	100.2	102.3	108.9	104.0	103.4	101.8	103.0	99.8	109.9	101.6	104.3
2009 [1]................	100.0	100.0	100.0	100.0	100.0	100.0	100.0	100.0	100.0	100.0	100.0	100.0	100.0
2010 [1]................	104.8	101.1	102.6	103.4	105.1	103.3	101.2	101.3	103.4	103.8	99.2	102.6	100.9
2011 [1]................	100.1	99.9	104.2	105.8	107.7	105.7	100.5	100.1	107.0	108.2	99.9	103.6	100.0
2012 [1]................	100.7	99.9	104.6	108.2	109.4	107.0	103.6	100.8	108.2	108.6	99.6	104.5	101.9
2013 [1]................	98.1	99.1	104.5	107.5	111.1	109.7	103.1	102.3	109.4	111.4	99.3	104.6	102.3
2014 [1]................	100.0	100.1	106.2	109.5	112.8	112.5	102.8	103.5	111.6	113.5	102.7	107.1	103.1
2015 [1]................	101.7	100.5	107.7	111.7	114.4	115.2	103.5	104.8	115.5	115.9	105.6	108.0	105.0

[1] NAICS basis, not continous with previous years.

Gross Domestic Product by Region and State—*Continued*

(Millions of dollars; index numbers)

Year	New Mexico	New York	North Carolina	North Dakota	Ohio	Oklahoma	Oregon	Pennsylvania	Rhode Island	South Carolina	South Dakota	Tennessee
VALUE												
1980	15,731	235,746	58,791	7,645	121,228	37,608	30,001	127,181	9,626	27,607	6,760	44,972
1981	18,511	261,840	65,869	9,954	132,782	45,430	31,590	138,573	10,729	31,048	7,661	50,265
1982	19,242	282,227	68,971	9,954	134,636	49,317	31,594	142,077	11,420	32,353	7,709	52,045
1983	19,882	305,288	77,543	10,045	144,897	47,701	33,727	152,042	12,323	35,850	8,123	57,073
1984	21,397	339,427	88,151	10,642	163,854	51,291	37,444	167,390	13,801	41,203	9,194	63,983
1985	22,534	364,281	96,535	10,655	174,165	52,765	39,446	176,873	15,222	43,988	9,588	68,426
1986	21,807	390,104	104,785	9,773	182,644	48,997	41,730	187,386	16,622	47,748	10,067	73,288
1987	22,429	418,306	113,262	10,306	191,784	49,055	44,594	202,910	17,891	52,688	10,669	80,715
1988	23,457	456,557	124,303	9,748	205,308	52,667	49,138	220,582	19,738	57,329	11,173	87,356
1989	24,927	473,252	133,866	10,729	217,817	55,007	52,610	233,162	21,059	61,347	11,790	91,579
1990	26,600	493,192	139,658	11,509	227,413	57,805	56,566	245,281	21,664	65,157	12,770	94,087
1991	30,295	497,336	146,367	11,691	233,975	59,632	59,441	255,163	21,738	68,000	13,736	101,208
1992	32,638	519,704	159,337	12,896	250,650	62,209	63,392	269,849	22,665	71,848	14,886	111,660
1993	36,876	537,504	168,006	13,049	259,612	65,552	69,409	281,704	23,566	76,158	16,105	119,568
1994	41,685	555,322	181,288	14,304	281,925	68,251	75,393	296,602	24,354	82,062	17,330	129,895
1995	42,146	582,656	193,467	14,842	297,538	70,859	81,554	312,989	25,550	87,248	18,054	137,061
1996	44,532	620,153	203,815	16,491	311,120	76,316	93,306	325,001	26,454	90,755	19,419	143,163
1997	48,683	664,679	221,259	16,501	332,476	81,106	100,363	342,662	28,717	96,465	19,765	152,687
1997 [1]	52,460	714,244	232,815	15,815	342,183	79,527	101,039	355,574	28,890	98,354	19,233	154,693
1998 [1]	50,519	739,583	244,146	16,858	360,273	81,533	105,525	372,396	30,529	104,676	20,445	167,243
1999 [1]	53,210	785,301	263,633	17,042	374,613	85,368	107,980	389,766	32,194	111,539	21,488	176,549
2000 [1]	55,597	824,386	276,963	17,991	391,503	92,083	118,086	409,473	34,405	116,812	23,267	182,844
2001 [1]	56,889	864,377	291,540	19,002	396,626	97,682	117,362	428,099	36,117	121,361	24,399	188,482
2002 [1]	58,845	879,623	301,781	20,322	411,997	99,532	121,998	440,514	38,231	126,044	27,334	197,724
2003 [1]	63,576	898,559	313,917	22,295	426,295	106,105	128,009	458,434	40,672	132,485	28,733	206,546
2004 [1]	70,121	954,249	332,598	23,396	450,842	114,160	142,516	481,879	43,513	136,875	30,789	220,543
2005 [1]	74,063	1,024,329	357,711	24,709	468,197	125,106	147,583	505,091	45,250	144,754	31,552	228,730
2006 [1]	77,536	1,083,194	386,354	26,491	482,227	136,804	163,033	529,969	47,659	152,802	32,455	239,425
2007 [1]	80,443	1,120,861	395,708	28,670	494,917	144,171	170,522	553,105	47,948	160,949	34,969	243,405
2008 [1]	86,209	1,109,994	412,889	32,263	493,813	155,015	180,251	566,147	47,447	162,676	37,014	250,558
2009 [1]	82,691	1,143,925	408,913	32,364	477,902	143,380	181,222	567,764	47,800	161,045	36,504	247,321
2010 [1]	86,195	1,208,079	417,375	36,033	494,736	151,318	191,393	588,276	49,329	165,237	38,044	254,343
2011 [1]	89,543	1,231,936	428,731	42,123	521,870	165,278	200,267	607,403	49,931	171,153	42,453	264,958
2012 [1]	90,535	1,299,814	439,332	52,197	544,552	173,911	196,982	626,316	51,492	175,434	43,258	280,843
2013 [1]	91,344	1,335,063	454,450	54,441	558,969	182,447	197,733	645,382	52,809	180,856	44,909	289,266
2014 [1]	94,792	1,385,776	474,355	58,230	588,827	190,171	203,328	672,413	55,098	189,656	45,600	300,016
2015 [1]	92,231	1,441,003	499,449	54,830	608,109	180,425	215,331	689,173	57,049	198,714	46,674	314,191

[1] NAICS basis, not continous with previous years.

Gross Domestic Product by Region and State—*Continued*

(Millions of dollars; index numbers)

Year	New Mexico	New York	North Carolina	North Dakota	Ohio	Oklahoma	Oregon	Pennsylvania	Rhode Island	South Carolina	South Dakota	Tennessee
QUANTITY INDEX												
1997=100												
1980......................	50.5	69.4	49.8	74.2	63.7	76.0	53.2	67.6	63.3	50.4	58.2	52.7
1981......................	51.2	70.7	51.5	85.4	64.4	80.5	51.7	67.9	64.8	52.2	61.7	54.2
1982......................	50.4	71.2	50.4	82.1	61.1	82.8	49.0	65.3	64.6	51.3	60.0	52.9
1983......................	51.3	72.7	53.0	80.5	63.6	78.9	49.5	67.1	66.5	54.6	59.6	55.8
1984......................	53.7	77.1	57.6	82.3	69.1	82.6	52.6	70.8	71.1	59.8	64.2	59.9
1985......................	55.7	79.2	61.2	82.8	71.6	84.0	53.9	72.5	75.8	62.0	66.7	62.2
1986......................	55.2	81.2	63.6	77.2	72.3	79.6	54.9	73.9	79.6	64.9	67.5	64.2
1987......................	55.3	84.7	66.6	79.2	74.4	78.3	56.8	77.9	83.1	69.7	68.9	68.7
1988......................	56.4	89.6	70.4	72.9	77.2	82.0	60.3	81.7	88.9	73.3	69.5	71.9
1989......................	57.6	89.4	72.7	77.2	78.9	82.3	62.1	83.1	91.3	75.7	70.6	72.6
1990......................	59.0	89.7	73.2	79.8	79.7	82.7	64.6	84.3	90.3	78.1	74.4	72.3
1991......................	65.7	86.9	73.3	79.5	79.1	83.1	65.7	84.5	87.1	78.8	78.0	74.8
1992......................	69.5	88.1	77.4	85.9	82.8	85.1	68.3	87.1	88.3	81.4	82.4	80.7
1993......................	77.0	88.5	79.9	84.8	83.5	87.2	72.3	88.4	89.3	84.3	87.1	84.2
1994......................	86.3	89.7	85.8	91.2	88.5	89.3	76.6	90.9	90.1	89.0	91.8	89.3
1995......................	87.8	91.6	90.0	92.9	91.7	91.1	81.6	93.9	92.5	92.3	93.7	92.2
1996......................	91.6	95.4	93.4	100.0	94.8	95.6	93.2	96.4	94.0	95.1	98.2	95.2
1997......................	100.0	100.0	100.0	100.0	100.0	100.0	100.0	100.0	100.0	100.0	100.0	100.0
2009 =100												
1997 [1]...................	77.7	80.0	73.8	64.1	93.2	76.1	62.1	83.6	81.0	81.8	62.8	82.0
1998 [1]...................	77.2	81.5	76.1	67.5	96.4	77.7	65.2	86.0	83.8	85.1	66.4	86.8
1999 [1]...................	81.9	85.5	80.8	67.5	98.6	79.8	66.7	88.6	86.7	88.9	69.7	89.7
2000 [1]...................	83.6	88.1	83.4	69.7	100.6	82.4	72.6	91.0	90.5	90.9	74.8	90.6
2001 [1]...................	84.6	90.8	85.5	71.1	99.4	85.1	71.5	92.7	92.5	91.7	76.6	91.1
2002 [1]...................	86.8	90.6	86.8	75.0	101.7	85.9	73.5	93.7	95.7	93.5	84.9	93.9
2003 [1]...................	89.6	90.8	88.8	79.8	103.4	87.6	76.3	95.6	99.7	96.8	87.3	96.7
2004 [1]...................	95.2	93.6	91.8	80.4	106.4	90.2	83.2	97.4	103.6	97.4	90.2	100.9
2005 [1]...................	95.7	97.7	96.1	82.8	107.4	93.1	84.9	98.7	104.4	100.0	91.3	101.9
2006 [1]...................	97.1	100.5	101.1	86.1	107.5	98.1	92.4	100.1	106.5	102.2	91.6	104.0
2007 [1]...................	97.3	100.8	101.0	88.9	107.3	99.6	95.3	101.4	104.1	104.6	94.9	103.0
2008 [1]...................	99.9	98.0	103.2	97.7	105.2	101.5	100.5	101.8	101.2	103.9	99.0	104.1
2009 [1]...................	100.0	100.0	100.0	100.0	100.0	100.0	100.0	100.0	100.0	100.0	100.0	100.0
2010 [1]...................	100.7	104.2	101.2	108.2	102.1	101.4	105.2	102.4	102.1	101.8	101.6	101.9
2011 [1]...................	101.1	104.6	102.2	120.7	105.3	106.4	109.6	103.8	101.8	103.9	108.8	104.7
2012 [1]...................	101.4	107.6	101.9	146.9	107.3	111.2	106.3	104.9	102.8	104.1	107.8	108.2
2013 [1]...................	100.5	107.8	103.2	149.9	108.3	114.1	104.7	106.2	103.4	105.2	109.3	109.4
2014 [1]...................	103.1	109.1	105.4	158.9	111.9	117.9	105.7	108.6	105.6	107.9	109.7	111.1
2015 [1]...................	103.8	110.6	108.2	155.6	113.9	119.5	110.0	110.4	106.8	110.0	111.6	113.3

[1] NAICS basis, not continous with previous years.

Gross Domestic Product by Region and State—*Continued*
(Millions of dollars; index numbers)

Year	Texas	Utah	Vermont	Virginia	Washington	West Virginia	Wisconsin	Wyoming
VALUE								
1980............................	203,073	15,311	4,856	58,669	52,682	18,408	52,899	10,428
1981............................	245,235	17,320	5,436	66,179	58,918	19,837	57,494	12,703
1982............................	260,085	18,365	5,755	71,465	62,933	20,511	59,488	12,422
1983............................	264,883	19,752	6,269	79,439	67,949	20,403	63,170	11,578
1984............................	288,637	22,147	6,895	89,768	74,170	22,172	70,013	12,152
1985............................	307,224	24,083	7,524	97,967	77,341	22,936	73,820	12,205
1986............................	295,721	24,282	8,169	107,348	84,015	22,880	77,824	10,522
1987............................	300,667	25,100	9,157	117,603	90,325	23,425	82,013	10,370
1988............................	327,354	27,325	10,259	128,088	99,051	25,876	89,620	10,991
1989............................	349,952	28,668	11,120	137,661	108,064	26,663	95,216	11,437
1990............................	378,943	31,249	11,674	144,971	118,640	27,754	100,236	12,705
1991............................	393,574	33,501	11,733	151,093	125,895	29,092	104,774	12,977
1992............................	416,401	35,602	12,538	158,990	134,469	30,410	112,972	13,179
1993............................	443,775	38,631	13,027	167,688	142,500	31,881	120,024	13,791
1994............................	475,990	42,591	13,689	177,057	150,805	34,592	129,437	14,070
1995............................	507,725	46,746	13,891	186,236	155,069	36,149	135,311	14,608
1996............................	551,513	52,016	14,672	197,756	166,540	37,224	143,444	15,752
1997............................	606,982	55,212	15,521	210,361	179,639	38,570	151,035	16,084
1997 [1]........................	613,463	57,159	15,529	218,905	194,856	38,677	155,603	14,760
1998 [1]........................	653,512	61,503	16,119	233,908	211,448	39,793	164,337	14,909
1999 [1]........................	691,405	65,525	17,141	251,671	230,725	41,720	173,789	15,721
2000 [1]........................	752,007	70,550	18,265	269,194	239,942	42,497	181,874	17,324
2001 [1]........................	787,653	74,191	19,172	284,595	240,894	43,700	188,164	18,809
2002 [1]........................	801,155	76,711	20,073	292,387	249,942	45,086	195,546	19,268
2003 [1]........................	844,435	80,130	21,232	309,648	260,027	46,471	204,649	21,251
2004 [1]........................	922,770	86,495	22,538	330,412	271,676	49,409	216,716	23,705
2005 [1]........................	999,641	94,876	23,483	358,730	296,731	53,331	226,963	27,748
2006 [1]........................	1,094,064	106,308	24,251	378,445	315,723	56,748	236,444	33,049
2007 [1]........................	1,181,302	116,019	24,759	391,842	343,339	58,564	243,982	36,763
2008 [1]........................	1,243,756	116,615	25,303	399,479	352,922	62,175	245,197	43,285
2009 [1]........................	1,171,474	114,525	25,222	409,823	351,316	63,485	245,815	37,214
2010 [1]........................	1,251,494	119,037	26,406	423,506	362,114	66,961	253,801	39,093
2011 [1]........................	1,351,048	125,497	27,565	431,961	372,287	70,891	263,635	41,578
2012 [1]........................	1,440,819	129,012	28,146	444,528	390,154	70,915	273,880	39,909
2013 [1]........................	1,527,158	134,922	28,611	451,877	402,789	72,763	281,549	40,457
2014 [1]........................	1,601,977	140,565	29,662	462,243	422,767	74,433	293,341	40,876
2015 [1]........................	1,586,468	147,108	30,401	479,809	443,665	73,741	305,795	38,624

[1] NAICS basis, not continous with previous years.

Gross Domestic Product by Region and State—*Continued*

(Millions of dollars; index numbers)

Year	Texas	Utah	Vermont	Virginia	Washington	West Virginia	Wisconsin	Wyoming
QUANTITY INDEX								
1997=100								
1980.........................	56.0	49.1	55.0	55.0	56.0	75.8	60.4	84.2
1981.........................	59.5	50.9	56.8	56.7	57.7	74.9	60.6	87.1
1982.........................	59.7	50.6	56.6	56.9	57.7	72.8	59.4	81.6
1983.........................	59.6	52.4	58.8	59.5	58.6	70.8	60.5	77.3
1984.........................	63.1	56.4	61.8	63.6	60.8	74.6	64.2	81.0
1985.........................	65.9	59.7	65.4	66.8	61.4	75.4	66.3	82.0
1986.........................	64.5	58.8	68.3	70.2	64.1	74.3	67.4	78.2
1987.........................	64.2	59.2	74.2	74.4	67.0	74.5	69.4	76.3
1988.........................	68.1	62.3	80.7	78.2	71.1	80.0	73.6	81.1
1989.........................	69.8	63.1	84.3	80.9	74.7	79.9	75.1	80.9
1990.........................	72.0	66.5	85.8	82.3	79.0	81.3	76.6	85.0
1991.........................	73.2	69.0	83.5	82.0	80.7	82.9	77.6	87.8
1992.........................	76.1	71.7	87.4	83.6	83.6	85.2	81.8	89.1
1993.........................	78.8	75.2	88.6	85.9	85.8	87.7	85.0	91.9
1994.........................	83.2	81.4	91.3	89.4	88.8	93.2	89.5	93.9
1995.........................	87.4	87.3	91.6	91.9	89.2	95.7	91.4	96.6
1996.........................	92.6	96.0	95.6	95.9	94.2	97.9	95.7	99.3
1997.........................	100.0	100.0	100.0	100.0	100.0	100.0	100.0	100.0
2009 =100								
1997[1].....................	69.6	66.0	77.4	71.8	74.2	87.2	83.1	61.4
1998[1].....................	74.6	69.8	79.6	75.2	78.9	88.4	85.9	62.6
1999[1].....................	77.8	73.0	83.7	79.1	84.1	91.6	89.2	65.0
2000[1].....................	80.6	76.4	87.9	82.3	85.1	91.0	91.4	67.3
2001[1].....................	82.7	78.3	90.4	84.7	83.0	90.8	92.1	71.2
2002[1].....................	84.0	79.4	93.3	85.1	84.5	91.8	94.2	72.3
2003[1].....................	84.6	81.2	97.2	88.3	85.9	92.1	97.1	74.3
2004[1].....................	88.7	84.9	100.7	91.7	87.3	93.8	100.1	77.1
2005[1].....................	90.3	89.9	102.2	96.6	92.7	96.2	102.1	80.5
2006[1].....................	95.5	97.1	102.8	98.8	95.6	97.7	103.6	90.2
2007[1].....................	99.8	102.8	102.2	99.4	101.0	97.4	103.9	95.3
2008[1].....................	100.3	101.3	102.7	99.5	102.2	99.9	102.7	102.7
2009[1].....................	100.0	100.0	100.0	100.0	100.0	100.0	100.0	100.0
2010[1].....................	102.9	101.7	103.8	102.4	101.8	102.8	102.5	98.0
2011[1].....................	106.4	104.5	106.7	103.1	102.6	105.3	104.8	97.9
2012[1].....................	112.2	105.4	106.7	103.8	105.3	103.7	106.3	93.6
2013[1].....................	117.0	108.5	106.3	103.6	106.7	105.2	107.0	94.0
2014[1].....................	121.4	110.9	107.9	103.8	109.9	105.9	109.3	94.5
2015[1].....................	126.0	114.6	108.1	105.3	113.1	106.0	111.3	94.9

[1] NAICS basis, not continous with previous years.

Gross Domestic Product by Metropolitan Statistical Area

(Millions of current dollars.)

Metropolitan Statistical Area	2001	2002	2003	2004	2005	2006	2007	2008	2009	2010	2011	2012	2013	2014
Abilene, TX	3,626	3,807	4,074	4,336	4,577	4,948	5,361	5,774	5,304	5,486	5,803	6,327	6,813	6,957
Akron, OH	21,684	22,781	23,777	25,340	26,785	27,550	28,386	28,792	27,882	28,660	29,544	30,601	31,317	32,509
Albany, GA	4,331	4,363	4,512	4,642	4,833	4,843	4,908	4,847	5,007	4,960	4,999	5,106	5,182	5,201
Albany, OR	2,376	2,504	2,506	2,859	2,962	3,225	3,197	3,264	3,090	3,078	3,163	3,309	3,412	3,593
Albany-Schenectady-Troy, NY	30,788	31,717	33,525	35,696	37,133	38,792	39,423	40,236	42,547	43,182	43,968	45,788	47,432	49,521
Albuquerque, NM	28,732	29,106	31,475	35,178	35,719	36,688	36,636	37,345	38,094	38,964	39,765	40,868	41,393	42,046
Alexandria, LA	3,386	3,568	3,698	4,080	4,379	4,844	5,139	5,301	5,373	5,518	5,210	5,298	5,300	5,290
Allentown-Bethlehem-Easton, PA-NJ	23,893	24,761	24,798	25,881	27,279	28,652	29,801	30,210	30,041	31,295	31,973	32,867	33,803	35,417
Altoona, PA	3,336	3,381	3,522	3,692	3,889	4,048	4,246	4,282	4,390	4,465	4,521	4,578	4,706	4,830
Amarillo, TX	6,469	6,700	7,138	7,631	8,095	8,798	9,305	9,980	9,821	10,203	10,532	11,147	11,750	12,227
Ames, IA	2,691	2,768	3,004	3,245	3,365	3,737	3,870	4,535	4,257	4,598	4,519	4,429	4,567	4,735
Anchorage, AK	15,373	16,090	17,357	19,250	21,960	23,676	25,650	28,875	26,620	28,328	29,955	30,656	30,756	30,714
Ann Arbor, MI	15,842	17,037	17,670	17,898	18,425	18,618	19,391	18,782	18,382	19,131	19,065	19,153	20,100	20,401
Anniston-Oxford-Jacksonville, AL	2,562	2,721	2,898	3,224	3,425	3,578	3,824	3,914	3,743	3,861	3,863	3,799	3,761	3,777
Appleton, WI	7,591	7,634	8,114	8,689	9,095	9,410	9,886	9,780	10,064	10,135	10,490	10,919	11,308	11,780
Asheville, NC	9,837	10,292	10,730	11,506	12,211	13,161	13,486	14,006	14,382	14,432	14,504	15,113	15,726	16,405
Athens-Clarke County, GA	4,788	4,887	5,146	5,417	5,770	5,982	6,262	6,528	6,686	6,771	6,899	7,171	7,358	7,648
Atlanta-Sandy Springs-Roswell, GA	213,325	219,133	226,130	236,920	253,679	266,298	280,293	280,241	273,465	277,639	286,108	296,059	309,059	324,881
Atlantic City-Hammonton, NJ	10,735	11,359	11,952	12,416	13,321	13,917	13,843	13,623	13,041	13,139	13,090	13,407	13,504	13,500
Auburn-Opelika, AL	2,322	2,469	2,607	2,905	3,138	3,358	3,519	3,697	3,725	3,909	4,159	4,285	4,590	4,866
Augusta-Richmond County, GA-SC	14,893	15,179	15,879	16,377	17,122	17,516	18,005	18,319	18,885	19,649	20,173	20,597	20,832	21,327
Austin-Round Rock, TX	53,915	54,597	57,517	62,703	68,185	74,931	78,148	82,997	81,540	87,368	92,763	100,273	106,981	115,262
Bakersfield, CA	16,977	18,489	20,067	22,406	25,325	28,206	31,121	33,284	30,988	33,770	35,933	38,350	39,586	39,989
Baltimore-Columbia-Towson, MD	102,843	108,173	112,907	121,624	129,363	136,460	141,835	144,020	146,909	152,899	157,416	162,670	167,871	173,516
Bangor, ME	4,223	4,398	4,486	4,791	4,958	5,208	5,342	5,329	5,379	5,396	5,431	5,584	5,711	5,764
Barnstable Town, MA	7,359	8,207	8,288	8,547	8,819	8,805	8,747	8,799	8,841	9,069	9,446	9,985	10,297	10,551
Baton Rouge, LA	23,159	25,152	28,180	31,122	38,153	39,143	39,427	40,449	40,549	44,869	46,964	50,232	49,561	51,149
Battle Creek, MI	4,175	4,569	4,693	4,800	4,928	4,851	4,864	4,935	4,870	5,237	5,085	5,316	5,573	5,710
Bay City, MI	2,550	2,679	2,720	2,735	2,790	2,860	2,865	2,900	2,928	2,985	2,987	3,059	3,165	3,136
Beaumont-Port Arthur, TX	10,886	11,564	12,619	14,863	15,390	16,957	19,145	17,403	18,267	20,641	21,858	22,193	23,114	23,795
Beckley, WV	2,716	2,813	2,836	3,028	3,342	3,594	3,660	3,914	3,851	4,307	4,669	4,484	4,597	4,756
Bellingham, WA	4,886	5,533	6,007	6,234	8,061	7,668	8,334	8,340	8,521	9,359	9,194	9,532	9,799	9,994
Bend-Redmond, OR	3,975	4,412	4,763	5,163	5,669	6,342	6,392	6,414	5,999	5,888	5,760	6,060	6,518	7,060
Billings, MT	4,552	4,640	5,111	5,643	6,246	6,708	7,674	7,432	6,666	7,361	8,493	8,990	9,123	9,455
Binghamton, NY	6,659	6,737	6,857	7,098	7,424	7,712	8,216	8,468	8,600	8,721	8,787	8,926	8,995	9,120
Birmingham-Hoover, AL	41,162	42,986	43,939	47,353	50,199	51,900	53,896	54,856	51,219	53,008	56,111	58,643	60,411	62,187
Bismarck, ND	3,108	3,261	3,580	3,844	4,086	4,287	4,456	4,695	4,845	5,176	5,588	6,360	6,691	7,283
Blacksburg-Christiansburg-Radford, VA	4,339	4,329	4,595	4,723	5,053	5,301	5,655	5,428	5,425	5,508	5,767	6,366	6,451	6,636
Bloomington, IL	7,176	7,358	7,769	8,351	8,361	9,143	9,319	9,157	9,549	9,835	10,105	10,587	11,356	11,126
Bloomington, IN	4,013	4,051	4,280	4,568	4,867	5,264	5,516	5,819	6,142	6,211	6,210	6,151	6,244	6,312
Bloomsburg-Berwick, PA	2,300	2,493	2,479	2,643	2,678	2,846	3,033	3,138	3,209	3,371	3,491	3,564	3,719	3,701
Boise City, ID	18,002	18,646	19,495	20,783	22,461	24,405	25,693	25,794	24,672	25,346	25,566	26,511	28,051	29,331
Boston-Cambridge-Newton, MA-NH	241,957	246,044	255,014	267,492	280,439	293,481	310,640	315,384	313,322	329,192	341,225	355,276	366,089	382,459
Boulder, CO	15,848	14,386	14,646	15,348	16,107	16,717	17,820	18,269	18,048	18,671	19,280	20,064	21,052	22,354
Bowling Green, KY	3,531	3,708	3,940	4,230	4,618	4,969	5,111	5,249	4,990	5,285	5,405	5,741	5,970	6,173
Bremerton-Silverdale, WA	6,325	7,076	7,441	7,661	8,083	8,641	8,856	9,037	8,996	9,050	9,177	9,286	9,365	9,627
Bridgeport-Stamford-Norwalk, CT	64,316	64,680	66,716	72,553	76,084	80,445	85,329	82,493	78,576	83,487	86,361	91,788	94,586	97,225
Brownsville-Harlingen, TX	5,332	5,577	5,840	6,105	6,417	6,872	7,272	7,577	7,795	8,059	8,221	8,667	9,020	9,285
Brunswick, GA	2,446	2,555	2,752	2,956	3,109	3,333	3,384	3,430	3,435	3,312	3,326	3,392	3,445	3,455
Buffalo-Cheektowaga-Niagara Falls, NY	36,053	38,065	39,256	41,099	42,299	44,035	44,545	45,241	47,185	48,404	49,852	51,881	53,230	54,942
Burlington, NC	3,789	3,949	3,834	4,050	4,217	4,498	4,479	4,488	4,316	4,465	4,613	4,967	5,088	5,158
Burlington-South Burlington, VT	7,887	8,166	8,712	9,196	9,545	9,910	10,038	10,363	10,483	11,194	11,827	12,349	12,418	12,704
California-Lexington Park, MD	3,096	3,390	3,728	3,949	4,103	4,431	4,663	4,782	5,072	5,466	5,758	5,765	5,846	5,892
Canton-Massillon, OH	11,505	11,776	12,002	12,566	13,183	13,180	13,335	13,560	12,817	13,308	14,197	14,959	16,354	17,126
Cape Coral-Fort Myers, FL	14,649	15,533	16,446	18,392	21,042	22,507	22,641	21,188	19,868	19,709	19,576	20,802	21,992	23,347
Cape Girardeau, MO-IL	2,528	2,622	2,738	2,823	2,980	3,168	3,348	3,424	3,557	3,553	3,531	3,588	3,734	3,774
Carbondale-Marion, IL	2,828	3,001	3,139	3,316	3,541	3,774	3,861	4,044	4,255	4,376	4,550	4,694	4,851	4,760
Carson City, NV	2,139	2,211	2,398	2,616	2,820	2,952	3,054	2,909	2,739	2,806	2,789	2,811	2,901	2,918
Casper, WY	2,931	3,086	3,462	4,124	5,306	6,292	6,489	9,090	5,783	6,221	6,900	6,626	6,871	7,340
Cedar Rapids, IA	9,672	9,540	10,446	11,396	12,115	12,042	13,423	12,990	15,186	15,671	16,127	16,508	17,181	17,738
Chambersburg-Waynesboro, PA	2,790	2,872	3,117	3,471	3,756	4,003	4,243	4,309	4,171	4,235	4,326	4,382	4,560	4,746
Champaign-Urbana, IL	6,477	6,847	7,111	7,439	7,675	8,182	8,536	9,163	9,447	9,630	9,712	10,030	10,532	10,394
Charleston, WV	9,185	9,421	9,555	10,003	10,695	11,436	11,959	12,749	12,789	13,337	14,159	13,478	13,569	14,642
Charleston-North Charleston, SC	17,527	18,682	20,006	21,390	23,314	24,765	26,664	27,703	27,790	28,751	30,388	31,877	33,032	34,428
Charlotte-Concord-Gastonia, NC-SC	78,853	85,720	89,136	95,890	105,716	114,039	112,998	116,379	112,075	116,164	124,937	129,239	137,680	143,628
Charlottesville, VA	6,193	6,541	6,951	7,556	8,238	8,752	9,093	9,393	9,581	10,069	10,552	11,005	11,523	11,734
Chattanooga, TN-GA	16,406	17,028	17,439	18,318	19,156	20,437	21,268	21,093	20,374	20,748	21,165	21,860	22,453	22,667
Cheyenne, WY	2,733	2,910	3,189	3,450	3,779	4,284	4,678	5,120	4,603	4,835	5,217	5,387	5,363	5,533
Chicago-Naperville-Elgin, IL-IN-WI	416,456	424,606	437,798	461,580	485,721	513,265	534,981	531,472	521,172	534,667	551,983	579,667	589,812	610,552
Chico, CA	4,381	4,797	5,071	5,413	5,782	5,972	6,237	6,226	6,237	6,348	6,395	6,392	6,683	6,891

Gross Domestic Product by Metropolitan Statistical Area—*Continued*

(Millions of current dollars.)

Metropolitan Statistical Area	2001	2002	2003	2004	2005	2006	2007	2008	2009	2010	2011	2012	2013	2014
Cincinnati, OH-KY-IN	79,634	82,509	85,739	90,101	95,018	97,604	101,142	102,365	100,311	104,120	108,189	112,971	116,671	121,407
Clarksville, TN-KY	5,453	5,755	6,406	6,847	7,739	8,300	8,546	9,051	9,288	9,749	10,498	10,777	10,795	10,866
Cleveland, TN	2,756	2,886	2,962	3,120	3,139	3,222	3,197	3,293	3,269	3,267	3,426	3,924	4,003	4,172
Cleveland-Elyria, OH	87,790	90,642	94,423	100,278	103,738	106,135	108,677	109,785	105,050	109,190	114,383	117,595	121,138	124,609
Coeur d'Alene, ID	2,598	2,739	2,994	3,293	3,698	4,089	4,395	4,431	4,316	4,343	4,416	4,410	4,665	4,901
College Station-Bryan, TX	4,362	4,278	4,684	5,005	5,397	5,837	6,162	6,583	7,071	7,355	7,488	8,012	8,532	9,026
Colorado Springs, CO	19,223	19,470	20,626	21,517	23,176	23,909	24,902	24,763	25,209	26,509	27,229	27,819	27,987	29,232
Columbia, MO	4,713	4,618	5,075	5,381	5,726	6,087	6,317	6,391	6,557	6,812	6,997	7,241	7,761	8,025
Columbia, SC	22,321	23,016	24,400	26,035	27,516	29,457	31,021	31,741	31,855	31,979	32,777	33,665	34,895	36,358
Columbus, GA-AL	8,548	8,522	8,979	9,376	9,985	10,487	11,168	11,344	11,693	12,193	12,745	13,070	13,413	13,729
Columbus, IN	3,102	3,054	3,163	3,440	3,570	3,888	4,203	4,382	3,965	4,430	4,651	5,100	5,251	5,446
Columbus, OH	74,181	77,949	80,349	84,722	87,662	91,352	94,397	94,299	93,017	96,482	101,556	107,992	113,487	117,824
Corpus Christi, TX	11,270	11,530	12,688	14,426	15,073	16,493	18,441	18,156	17,657	19,095	20,546	21,865	23,866	25,146
Corvallis, OR	2,740	3,098	3,448	4,057	3,972	4,466	4,587	5,034	5,190	5,400	5,281	4,996	4,709	4,733
Crestview-Fort Walton Beach-Destin, FL	6,850	8,664	9,331	10,116	11,773	12,513	12,638	11,771	11,528	11,010	11,455	11,532	11,803	12,002
Cumberland, MD-WV	1,962	2,065	2,127	2,180	2,324	2,444	2,467	2,545	2,695	2,818	2,862	2,899	2,958	3,003
Dallas-Fort Worth-Arlington, TX	256,467	265,837	273,223	293,669	315,419	340,870	358,514	375,846	355,756	375,940	402,824	430,109	461,320	504,358
Dalton, GA	4,486	4,655	4,680	5,350	5,697	5,805	5,979	5,513	5,335	4,941	5,260	5,364	5,514	5,768
Danville, IL	1,976	2,015	2,177	2,291	2,328	2,466	2,438	2,492	2,503	2,565	2,659	2,740	2,845	2,805
Daphne-Fairhope-Foley, AL	3,339	3,540	3,744	4,198	4,518	4,896	5,283	5,540	5,565	5,644	5,758	5,904	6,339	6,488
Davenport-Moline-Rock Island, IA-IL	12,128	12,762	13,405	14,603	15,435	16,073	16,794	17,228	17,001	17,717	18,533	19,336	19,780	19,707
Dayton, OH	29,657	30,682	31,419	32,910	34,076	35,328	35,558	34,997	33,377	34,348	35,969	36,594	37,396	38,178
Decatur, AL	3,658	3,648	3,913	4,371	4,446	4,699	4,893	5,023	4,879	5,064	5,045	5,242	5,422	5,498
Decatur, IL	4,328	4,202	4,436	4,775	5,035	5,189	5,488	5,775	5,641	5,607	5,782	5,776	5,754	6,220
Deltona-Daytona Beach-Ormond Beach, FL	10,412	10,811	11,445	12,281	13,201	14,012	14,588	13,902	13,364	13,484	13,166	13,499	13,878	14,579
Denver-Aurora-Lakewood, CO	110,683	114,793	118,217	123,716	134,786	141,184	147,169	154,820	150,035	155,391	160,492	167,964	175,635	187,111
Des Moines-West Des Moines, IA	24,090	25,346	27,817	31,142	34,101	34,423	38,679	35,807	35,543	36,462	38,422	41,760	43,222	45,226
Detroit-Warren-Dearborn, MI	190,916	196,302	202,858	204,408	212,050	209,490	212,695	202,513	186,325	197,789	206,508	217,418	226,926	236,500
Dothan, AL	3,289	3,573	3,772	4,069	4,366	4,521	4,586	4,441	4,426	4,566	4,565	4,658	4,947	5,017
Dover, DE	4,195	4,446	4,678	5,177	5,378	5,645	5,883	5,926	6,352	6,116	6,318	6,348	6,432	6,657
Dubuque, IA	2,971	3,175	3,326	3,712	3,938	4,100	4,245	4,209	4,212	4,475	4,604	5,289	5,267	5,410
Duluth, MN-WI	7,381	7,923	8,252	8,823	9,222	9,462	9,725	9,933	9,600	10,660	11,339	11,032	11,663	11,926
Durham-Chapel Hill, NC	22,307	23,758	25,312	25,848	27,566	32,865	35,571	36,852	39,073	39,931	38,047	38,666	41,883	43,484
East Stroudsburg, PA	3,598	3,807	3,884	4,227	4,596	4,923	5,285	5,501	5,586	5,615	5,402	5,357	5,338	5,238
Eau Claire, WI	4,389	4,701	4,970	5,286	5,796	6,005	6,157	6,115	6,241	6,512	6,663	7,002	7,225	7,594
El Centro, CA	3,012	3,485	3,572	3,716	3,963	4,347	4,481	4,850	4,865	4,880	5,383	5,235	5,477	5,655
Elizabethtown-Fort Knox, KY	3,338	3,496	3,779	4,049	4,206	4,504	4,511	4,690	4,724	5,437	5,776	5,904	6,026	5,980
Elkhart-Goshen, IN	7,822	8,486	9,398	9,962	10,342	10,689	11,085	9,704	7,945	10,143	10,236	11,347	12,166	12,987
Elmira, NY	2,290	2,305	2,360	2,469	2,660	2,708	2,791	2,925	2,930	3,139	3,240	3,320	3,339	3,361
El Paso, TX	18,701	19,601	20,102	20,617	21,493	23,693	24,877	24,086	24,464	25,191	25,979	27,075	27,959	28,526
Erie, PA	7,852	7,761	7,954	8,523	9,005	9,377	9,724	9,938	9,627	9,686	10,226	10,162	10,640	10,856
Eugene, OR	8,617	8,961	9,406	10,311	10,792	11,492	12,128	12,519	11,572	11,767	12,174	12,661	13,157	13,673
Evansville, IN-KY	11,528	12,194	12,617	13,202	13,487	14,151	14,525	15,331	15,203	15,924	16,744	16,656	16,628	16,634
Fairbanks, AK	3,536	3,473	3,789	4,069	4,403	4,930	5,276	5,381	5,070	5,187	5,410	5,446	5,400	5,426
Fargo, ND-MN	6,655	7,185	7,621	8,174	8,547	9,059	9,535	10,354	10,493	11,296	12,557	13,767	14,176	15,026
Farmington, NM	3,737	3,607	4,071	4,613	5,343	5,842	6,288	6,839	5,970	5,781	6,319	6,050	6,254	6,394
Fayetteville, NC	9,711	10,246	10,950	11,556	12,746	13,507	14,403	15,457	16,424	16,989	17,358	17,549	17,528	17,266
Fayetteville-Springdale-Rogers, AR-MO	10,909	11,946	13,223	14,868	16,134	17,178	17,660	18,603	18,473	20,194	21,646	22,472	24,006	25,105
Flagstaff, AZ	3,029	3,220	3,436	3,650	3,965	4,421	4,943	4,939	4,766	4,868	4,816	4,877	5,179	5,267
Flint, MI	12,300	12,940	13,325	13,284	13,233	13,127	12,872	11,902	11,297	11,900	12,043	12,411	12,990	13,200
Florence, SC	5,640	5,787	6,063	6,231	6,526	6,899	7,236	7,169	7,058	7,028	7,075	7,247	7,645	7,843
Florence-Muscle Shoals, AL	2,853	2,907	3,078	3,338	3,563	3,776	3,871	3,911	3,928	4,139	4,250	4,382	4,601	4,813
Fond du Lac, WI	3,044	3,045	3,195	3,398	3,534	3,684	3,806	3,818	3,648	3,734	3,936	4,079	4,285	4,503
Fort Collins, CO	8,478	9,136	9,277	9,630	10,113	10,513	11,038	11,197	11,232	11,711	12,061	12,595	13,285	14,323
Fort Smith, AR-OK	6,769	7,051	7,516	7,973	8,717	9,438	9,347	9,626	9,053	9,509	9,650	9,874	10,104	10,383
Fort Wayne, IN	14,436	14,750	15,110	15,613	16,295	17,197	17,753	17,360	16,750	17,860	18,304	19,142	19,612	20,046
Fresno, CA	20,616	22,665	24,411	26,115	27,534	29,431	30,480	31,097	31,177	32,024	34,060	34,616	36,287	37,149
Gadsden, AL	2,026	2,105	2,179	2,324	2,430	2,501	2,528	2,571	2,560	2,615	2,724	2,733	2,836	2,915
Gainesville, FL	6,723	7,007	7,350	8,326	8,768	9,350	10,121	10,292	10,374	10,651	10,631	10,800	11,171	11,557
Gainesville, GA	5,240	5,233	5,349	5,601	6,115	6,246	6,447	6,501	6,460	6,532	7,010	7,220	7,693	8,028
Gettysburg, PA	1,887	1,975	2,138	2,230	2,410	2,600	2,688	2,682	2,695	2,626	2,597	2,701	2,829	2,956
Glens Falls, NY	2,866	3,014	3,171	3,441	3,643	3,790	3,853	3,970	4,090	4,232	4,306	4,472	4,526	4,645
Goldsboro, NC	2,974	3,000	3,064	3,308	3,463	3,715	3,783	3,754	3,987	3,985	4,029	4,190	4,234	4,237
Grand Forks, ND-MN	2,605	2,735	3,035	3,035	3,070	3,196	3,481	3,652	3,903	3,824	3,993	4,042	4,472	4,578	4,788
Grand Island, NE	2,140	2,257	2,435	2,563	2,772	2,964	3,149	3,264	3,383	3,476	3,763	3,965	4,188	4,204
Grand Junction, CO	3,015	3,207	3,342	3,565	3,922	4,316	4,856	5,407	5,009	4,848	4,992	5,150	5,179	5,342
Grand Rapids-Wyoming, MI	35,232	37,022	38,243	39,761	41,480	42,276	42,030	40,780	39,484	41,093	42,752	46,180	48,809	51,921
Grants Pass, OR	1,307	1,389	1,484	1,631	1,724	1,856	1,848	1,840	1,813	1,785	1,797	1,839	1,847	1,987

Gross Domestic Product by Metropolitan Statistical Area—*Continued*

(Millions of current dollars.)

Metropolitan Statistical Area	2001	2002	2003	2004	2005	2006	2007	2008	2009	2010	2011	2012	2013	2014
Great Falls, MT	2,040	2,095	2,220	2,376	2,476	2,682	2,834	2,927	2,930	3,037	3,138	3,227	3,212	3,317
Greeley, CO	5,256	5,385	5,496	5,840	6,316	6,703	7,222	7,400	7,294	7,427	7,810	8,390	9,090	10,165
Green Bay, WI	11,609	11,887	12,487	13,199	13,680	14,146	14,600	14,430	14,749	15,307	15,860	16,590	17,341	17,599
Greensboro-High Point, NC	26,869	27,425	28,040	28,998	30,601	32,544	32,910	33,343	33,261	34,096	34,877	35,508	36,807	38,567
Greenville, NC	4,175	4,331	4,496	4,566	4,875	5,267	5,693	5,914	6,165	6,286	6,612	6,931	7,109	7,363
Greenville-Anderson-Mauldin, SC	24,750	25,085	26,223	25,737	27,179	28,236	29,985	30,605	30,135	31,250	32,766	33,411	34,727	36,498
Gulfport-Biloxi-Pascagoula, MS	10,481	10,535	11,626	11,736	13,214	13,906	15,018	16,020	15,270	15,577	15,850	17,504	16,044	15,841
Hagerstown-Martinsburg, MD-WV	5,557	5,822	6,082	6,474	6,991	7,468	7,502	7,561	7,520	7,652	7,977	8,241	8,391	8,643
Hammond, LA	1,739	1,847	2,013	2,263	2,615	3,303	3,322	3,471	3,309	3,688	3,800	3,670	3,615	3,721
Hanford-Corcoran, CA	2,753	2,985	3,453	3,879	4,042	4,133	4,783	4,731	4,236	4,519	5,238	5,148	5,192	5,275
Harrisburg-Carlisle, PA	21,893	22,516	23,407	24,835	25,850	27,172	28,264	28,312	28,782	29,141	29,824	30,630	31,565	32,213
Harrisonburg, VA	4,840	4,591	4,752	4,831	5,123	5,389	5,695	5,762	6,570	6,773	6,820	7,147	7,342	7,368
Hartford-West Hartford-East Hartford, CT	59,726	59,015	61,184	67,375	70,748	75,426	82,056	81,155	82,690	82,589	81,711	81,245	83,623	85,558
Hattiesburg, MS	3,095	3,278	3,454	3,697	3,901	4,328	4,535	4,687	4,831	4,973	5,061	5,335	5,432	5,519
Hickory-Lenoir-Morganton, NC	10,541	10,668	10,466	11,016	11,317	12,092	11,630	11,488	11,337	11,640	11,784	12,106	12,315	12,628
Hilton Head Island-Bluffton-Beaufort, SC	5,410	5,868	6,250	6,702	7,186	7,774	8,227	7,813	7,507	7,420	7,305	7,354	7,634	7,944
Hinesville, GA	1,712	1,778	2,014	2,168	2,429	2,566	2,745	3,082	3,166	3,448	3,680	3,572	3,576	3,615
Homosassa Springs, FL	2,086	2,179	2,382	2,515	2,825	3,029	3,140	2,955	3,182	3,261	3,168	3,085	3,092	2,943
Hot Springs, AR	1,952	2,010	2,097	2,241	2,405	2,533	2,572	2,643	2,592	2,745	2,959	3,165	3,377	3,420
Houma-Thibodaux, LA	6,217	5,694	5,987	6,228	6,932	8,476	9,446	10,395	10,567	11,247	11,265	12,230	13,124	13,198
Houston-The Woodlands-Sugar Land, TX	240,943	238,383	254,520	286,223	316,466	351,957	391,861	414,843	373,522	400,106	441,736	475,043	515,184	525,397
Huntington-Ashland, WV-KY-OH	8,309	8,659	9,016	9,624	10,311	10,963	11,455	12,073	12,154	12,569	12,913	13,269	14,016	14,376
Huntsville, AL	12,650	13,879	15,039	16,299	17,318	18,259	18,942	19,532	20,012	21,299	21,879	22,157	23,025	23,738
Idaho Falls, ID	3,082	3,313	3,478	3,758	3,991	4,370	4,705	5,007	5,064	5,141	5,312	5,423	5,550	5,755
Indianapolis-Carmel-Anderson, IN	78,008	80,217	83,654	90,062	93,913	99,184	103,465	107,369	106,578	110,943	113,463	116,839	122,508	125,864
Iowa City, IA	5,157	5,184	5,435	5,834	6,047	6,460	6,785	7,001	7,199	7,471	7,870	8,290	8,639	8,879
Ithaca, NY	2,901	3,054	3,291	3,410	3,549	3,662	3,797	4,023	4,183	4,284	4,339	4,513	4,621	4,677
Jackson, MI	4,191	4,344	4,374	4,577	4,792	4,848	4,942	4,794	4,698	5,001	5,143	5,168	5,551	5,808
Jackson, MS	17,081	17,898	18,866	20,164	20,961	22,301	23,603	24,653	24,200	25,344	26,421	27,316	28,041	28,620
Jackson, TN	3,827	4,042	4,257	4,444	4,678	4,820	4,744	5,017	4,990	5,080	5,327	5,768	5,888	5,978
Jacksonville, FL	40,443	42,762	46,417	49,812	53,873	58,774	60,554	58,696	56,396	57,490	57,611	59,964	61,983	65,085
Jacksonville, NC	3,781	3,757	4,109	4,642	5,095	5,396	6,009	6,711	7,406	7,987	8,044	8,073	8,004	7,947
Janesville-Beloit, WI	4,253	4,681	4,868	4,939	4,927	5,361	5,328	5,088	4,809	4,956	5,207	5,422	5,894	6,009
Jefferson City, MO	4,518	4,479	4,807	5,152	5,336	5,557	5,725	5,825	5,977	6,187	6,120	6,129	6,509	6,526
Johnson City, TN	4,105	4,361	4,659	5,061	5,259	5,440	5,516	5,788	5,896	5,649	5,846	6,124	6,188	6,322
Johnstown, PA	3,288	3,228	3,370	3,513	3,718	3,865	4,030	4,082	4,137	4,179	4,279	4,221	4,220	4,222
Jonesboro, AR	2,836	2,933	3,201	3,424	3,566	3,724	3,758	4,031	4,040	4,267	4,369	4,520	4,661	4,717
Joplin, MO	4,312	4,311	4,653	4,927	5,144	5,428	5,586	5,687	5,816	6,031	6,154	6,329	6,484	6,548
Kahului-Wailuku-Lahaina, HI	4,517	4,660	5,059	5,598	6,151	6,667	7,028	7,105	6,777	6,767	7,076	7,362	7,701	7,742
Kalamazoo-Portage, MI	9,938	10,906	11,385	11,515	11,524	11,911	12,441	12,520	12,534	12,734	13,032	13,247	13,903	14,271
Kankakee, IL	2,487	2,623	2,694	2,851	2,904	3,071	3,141	3,191	3,253	3,282	3,373	3,702	3,784	3,845
Kansas City, MO-KS	79,541	82,295	85,017	89,409	93,515	97,330	101,944	104,565	103,699	107,411	109,276	114,072	117,304	121,638
Kennewick-Richland, WA	6,207	6,772	7,244	7,559	7,971	8,140	9,041	9,593	10,346	11,207	11,339	10,950	11,301	11,544
Killeen-Temple, TX	8,075	8,532	9,273	9,909	11,144	12,450	13,578	14,670	15,268	15,322	15,709	15,924	15,898	16,221
Kingsport-Bristol-Bristol, TN-VA	7,861	7,735	7,880	8,673	8,662	9,375	9,581	9,734	9,839	10,196	11,066	11,556	11,512	11,458
Kingston, NY	3,575	3,734	3,987	4,187	4,411	4,765	4,869	4,880	4,995	5,153	5,097	5,238	5,336	5,460
Knoxville, TN	23,169	24,671	26,157	28,102	29,303	30,196	30,678	32,311	32,147	32,593	34,069	35,397	36,436	37,487
Kokomo, IN	3,552	3,882	4,356	4,142	3,998	4,140	4,397	3,566	2,574	3,647	3,749	3,908	4,152	4,246
La Crosse-Onalaska, WI-MN	4,030	4,264	4,545	4,699	4,935	5,112	5,297	5,560	5,745	5,902	6,062	6,289	6,585	6,740
Lafayette, LA	14,875	13,962	14,735	15,608	17,285	20,545	22,272	24,821	23,845	25,891	28,181	29,110	28,873	28,193
Lafayette-West Lafayette, IN	5,888	6,224	6,445	6,914	7,256	7,514	7,865	8,204	7,784	8,388	8,745	8,978	9,312	9,655
Lake Charles, LA	7,002	7,325	9,394	11,063	16,356	15,369	13,458	13,157	11,516	13,707	14,008	15,158	13,825	14,666
Lake Havasu City-Kingman, AZ	2,437	2,635	2,884	3,114	3,506	3,998	4,165	3,901	3,615	3,656	3,653	3,646	3,733	3,861
Lakeland-Winter Haven, FL	11,565	12,304	13,044	14,285	15,527	16,742	17,365	17,437	17,135	17,385	17,384	17,254	18,294	18,487
Lancaster, PA	15,606	16,104	16,612	17,486	18,383	19,038	19,471	19,643	19,664	20,773	21,660	22,454	23,180	24,125
Lansing-East Lansing, MI	15,858	16,774	17,428	17,486	18,165	18,738	19,192	18,512	17,882	19,304	19,215	19,240	20,331	21,096
Laredo, TX	3,920	4,164	4,469	4,725	5,233	5,609	5,817	6,424	5,873	6,199	6,660	7,072	7,478	7,882
Las Cruces, NM	3,398	3,789	4,142	4,564	4,876	5,081	5,411	5,669	5,924	6,187	6,227	6,216	6,402	6,564
Las Vegas-Henderson-Paradise, NV	57,038	60,535	64,783	74,890	85,479	91,532	95,598	93,320	85,694	84,447	85,173	86,924	90,502	94,521
Lawrence, KS	2,713	2,817	2,893	2,995	3,108	3,189	3,415	3,522	3,627	3,598	3,690	3,786	3,894	4,002
Lawton, OK	2,783	2,911	3,170	3,360	3,468	3,805	4,002	4,177	4,396	4,731	4,754	4,692	4,848	4,854
Lebanon, PA	2,720	2,786	2,973	3,178	3,309	3,483	3,661	3,830	3,915	4,126	4,226	4,342	4,406	4,449
Lewiston, ID-WA	1,476	1,509	1,596	1,664	1,734	1,817	1,900	1,923	1,922	1,983	1,967	2,016	2,071	2,160
Lewiston-Auburn, ME	2,782	3,028	3,150	3,326	3,391	3,585	3,752	3,820	3,810	3,824	3,876	4,027	4,094	4,172
Lexington-Fayette, KY	17,343	18,537	19,072	19,930	20,794	21,992	22,602	22,896	22,233	23,653	24,392	25,407	26,201	26,693
Lima, OH	3,865	3,933	4,032	4,260	4,484	4,604	4,626	4,337	4,810	5,029	5,486	5,387	5,673	5,771
Lincoln, NE	10,307	10,669	11,614	12,063	12,530	13,229	13,660	13,626	13,992	14,557	15,082	16,327	17,159	17,626
Little Rock-North Little Rock-Conway, AR	22,058	23,282	24,137	25,365	27,198	29,127	32,267	32,803	33,402	33,992	35,643	37,006	38,234	38,584

Gross Domestic Product by Metropolitan Statistical Area—*Continued*

(Millions of current dollars.)

Metropolitan Statistical Area	2001	2002	2003	2004	2005	2006	2007	2008	2009	2010	2011	2012	2013	2014
Logan, UT-ID	2,065	2,176	2,464	2,675	2,790	2,955	3,215	3,420	3,461	3,683	3,970	3,978	4,107	4,308
Longview, TX	5,547	5,608	6,033	6,652	7,481	8,489	9,181	10,593	9,428	10,396	10,484	11,142	11,874	12,407
Longview, WA	2,397	2,368	2,508	2,603	2,792	2,971	3,137	3,138	3,092	3,220	3,203	3,347	3,548	3,766
Los Angeles-Long Beach-Anaheim, CA	544,144	568,541	600,410	645,354	682,592	728,733	761,684	789,171	753,732	764,958	779,236	806,415	833,801	866,745
Louisville/Jefferson County, KY-IN	43,664	45,007	46,188	49,098	51,431	54,298	56,166	56,551	55,148	58,015	59,929	62,774	64,446	67,329
Lubbock, TX	6,797	7,231	7,659	8,228	8,667	9,169	9,462	9,808	9,904	10,441	10,400	11,419	12,569	13,145
Lynchburg, VA	6,438	6,354	6,606	6,924	7,374	7,866	8,059	8,147	8,441	8,611	8,539	8,634	8,874	8,944
Macon, GA	7,189	7,334	7,294	7,567	7,717	7,785	7,721	7,911	7,860	7,935	8,126	8,230	8,631	8,961
Madera, CA	2,197	2,459	2,694	3,221	3,378	3,538	3,764	3,746	3,469	3,910	4,304	4,462	4,699	4,729
Madison, WI	24,485	25,971	27,304	29,425	31,425	32,785	34,593	34,746	35,770	37,419	39,180	40,659	43,282	44,071
Manchester-Nashua, NH	15,417	16,429	17,972	18,846	20,100	20,622	21,204	21,539	21,590	21,567	22,700	23,193	23,786	24,870
Manhattan, KS	1,834	1,907	2,058	2,157	2,268	2,374	2,599	2,790	2,805	2,864	2,976	2,993	3,065	3,134
Mankato-North Mankato, MN	2,708	2,828	3,006	3,262	3,496	3,704	3,732	3,866	3,704	3,965	4,215	4,403	4,473	4,570
Mansfield, OH	3,626	3,797	3,914	4,156	4,238	4,303	4,166	4,052	3,559	3,682	3,823	3,895	3,997	4,118
McAllen-Edinburg-Mission, TX	8,448	8,900	9,674	10,554	11,473	12,490	13,196	13,796	14,186	14,911	15,514	16,457	17,454	18,226
Medford, OR	4,789	5,024	5,360	5,817	6,142	6,506	6,606	6,315	6,172	6,081	6,036	6,307	6,677	7,057
Memphis, TN-MS-AR	49,144	52,032	53,858	56,772	58,890	61,455	63,160	62,784	61,565	62,192	63,414	66,637	68,276	69,882
Merced, CA	3,971	4,427	4,980	5,655	5,731	5,922	6,664	6,290	6,131	6,226	6,920	6,789	7,180	7,225
Miami-Fort Lauderdale-West Palm Beach, FL	184,952	195,988	205,421	221,273	243,882	259,528	267,810	264,127	247,672	250,813	255,461	270,538	283,962	299,161
Michigan City-La Porte, IN	2,857	2,900	2,960	3,184	3,300	3,398	3,578	3,598	3,382	3,576	3,693	3,755	3,779	3,775
Midland, MI	2,892	3,108	3,064	3,394	3,188	3,253	3,446	3,483	3,564	3,712	3,897	3,790	3,816	4,028
Midland, TX	5,803	5,164	5,849	6,635	8,112	9,435	11,515	15,577	13,305	15,416	19,737	23,185	26,652	32,573
Milwaukee-Waukesha-West Allis, WI	65,033	66,622	69,439	72,763	76,907	80,972	83,337	84,939	84,966	86,779	89,668	91,862	94,840	97,307
Minneapolis-St. Paul-Bloomington, MN-WI	148,189	153,018	161,404	171,425	182,021	186,294	193,229	196,260	192,594	200,768	210,569	218,376	227,962	235,733
Missoula, MT	3,080	3,312	3,493	3,634	3,873	4,104	4,252	4,337	4,394	4,420	4,496	4,663	4,732	4,891
Mobile, AL	11,049	11,200	11,763	12,698	13,677	14,955	15,666	16,243	16,423	16,912	17,371	17,386	17,933	18,284
Modesto, CA	10,967	12,028	12,925	14,085	14,905	15,421	15,622	15,362	15,480	15,891	16,552	16,964	17,565	18,094
Monroe, LA	4,770	4,834	5,004	5,348	5,648	6,026	6,199	6,129	6,269	6,547	6,432	6,595	6,800	7,110
Monroe, MI	3,431	3,757	3,979	4,031	4,048	4,139	4,076	3,888	3,687	3,913	3,984	4,108	4,487	4,611
Montgomery, AL	11,255	11,911	12,531	13,441	14,205	14,924	15,147	15,268	15,168	15,518	15,842	16,042	16,667	16,703
Morgantown, WV	3,216	3,497	3,693	3,949	4,287	4,673	4,873	5,439	5,984	6,416	6,421	6,421	6,729	7,186
Morristown, TN	2,755	2,771	2,928	3,136	3,113	3,207	3,261	3,221	3,106	3,314	3,365	3,601	3,659	3,763
Mount Vernon-Anacortes, WA	3,308	4,012	4,068	3,935	5,682	5,005	5,182	5,032	4,954	5,374	5,068	5,128	5,273	5,449
Muncie, IN	3,221	3,242	3,356	3,314	3,300	3,435	3,408	3,424	3,274	3,371	3,439	3,620	3,723	3,759
Muskegon, MI	4,194	4,237	4,379	4,564	4,721	4,842	4,811	4,762	4,519	4,835	5,049	5,249	5,438	5,639
Myrtle Beach-Conway-North Myrtle Beach, SC-NC	9,367	9,865	10,438	11,096	12,079	12,781	13,553	13,676	13,458	13,639	14,122	14,480	15,100	15,569
Napa, CA	5,274	5,645	5,905	6,214	6,684	6,953	7,185	7,344	7,336	7,025	7,155	7,897	8,300	8,805
Naples-Immokalee-Marco Island, FL	9,910	10,049	11,073	12,432	14,176	14,837	14,862	13,452	12,098	12,414	12,635	13,633	14,738	15,910
Nashville-Davidson—Murfreesboro—Franklin, TN	58,239	60,885	64,198	69,122	71,927	76,354	77,939	81,986	81,475	84,728	89,229	96,223	101,006	106,695
New Bern, NC	3,149	3,151	3,364	3,642	3,911	4,079	4,285	4,460	4,671	4,715	4,684	4,863	4,858	4,887
New Haven-Milford, CT	30,764	32,494	33,743	36,942	37,968	39,834	41,480	41,334	40,498	41,222	41,438	42,390	43,909	44,858
New Orleans-Metairie, LA	52,021	52,281	58,284	63,771	72,620	70,822	70,801	72,780	69,298	77,938	79,309	81,497	79,552	80,278
New York-Newark-Jersey City, NY-NJ-PA	975,625	993,843	1,015,612	1,074,764	1,151,059	1,218,226	1,272,793	1,259,700	1,276,750	1,334,008	1,368,438	1,446,659	1,490,952	1,558,518
Niles-Benton Harbor, MI	4,628	4,841	4,872	4,991	5,102	5,415	5,722	5,635	5,582	5,939	5,731	5,636	6,097	6,285
North Port-Sarasota-Bradenton, FL	17,115	18,423	19,600	21,586	24,214	25,757	26,108	24,674	23,610	23,434	23,742	24,215	25,725	27,220
Norwich-New London, CT	10,192	11,271	12,269	13,884	14,670	16,154	16,965	17,294	16,053	16,043	15,280	15,106	15,107	15,536
Ocala, FL	4,835	5,092	5,603	6,229	6,984	7,769	7,951	7,636	7,017	7,020	6,995	7,069	7,319	7,741
Ocean City, NJ	2,944	3,240	3,541	3,808	4,089	3,982	4,017	4,207	4,319	4,308	4,397	4,530	4,657	4,653
Odessa, TX	3,157	3,162	3,321	3,537	4,115	4,868	5,819	6,270	5,574	6,019	7,371	8,752	9,581	10,342
Ogden-Clearfield, UT	12,822	13,673	14,454	15,617	16,724	18,617	19,655	19,502	19,464	20,715	21,577	21,499	22,704	23,862
Oklahoma City, OK	37,598	38,645	41,612	45,050	48,977	53,967	56,664	61,643	56,128	59,459	63,809	66,470	70,035	72,629
Olympia-Tumwater, WA	6,070	6,318	6,622	7,016	7,576	8,178	8,820	9,067	9,121	9,246	9,178	9,404	9,875	10,184
Omaha-Council Bluffs, NE-IA	32,043	33,829	35,928	38,298	40,220	42,916	44,775	45,470	46,419	47,975	49,934	52,675	55,371	57,885
Orlando-Kissimmee-Sanford, FL	66,644	71,167	76,542	83,959	93,761	100,920	105,951	103,406	99,970	101,460	101,781	105,142	109,756	115,927
Oshkosh-Neenah, WI	6,030	6,595	6,591	6,913	7,164	7,431	7,667	7,622	7,557	8,266	8,591	8,772	9,083	9,217
Owensboro, KY	3,162	3,375	3,548	3,643	3,787	4,181	4,121	4,307	4,364	4,560	4,781	5,138	5,518	5,550
Oxnard-Thousand Oaks-Ventura, CA	25,934	26,795	29,578	32,430	34,623	36,740	38,589	37,107	37,455	40,095	42,463	44,121	45,889	46,892
Palm Bay-Melbourne-Titusville, FL	12,460	13,251	14,302	16,164	17,384	18,100	19,023	18,802	18,397	18,539	18,539	17,781	17,655	18,087	18,583
Panama City, FL	4,400	4,765	5,212	5,681	6,365	6,751	6,997	7,094	7,025	7,221	7,064	6,877	7,170	7,674
Parkersburg-Vienna, WV	2,689	2,672	2,706	2,833	2,890	3,131	3,095	3,213	3,402	3,275	3,331	3,408	3,450	3,548
Pensacola-Ferry Pass-Brent, FL	10,229	10,490	11,105	12,386	12,920	13,947	14,329	13,963	13,832	14,330	14,632	14,697	15,238	15,916
Peoria, IL	11,720	11,957	12,601	13,934	15,185	16,587	17,553	18,170	17,857	18,068	20,071	22,113	20,300	20,462
Philadelphia-Camden-Wilmington, PA-NJ-DE-MD	249,671	258,713	272,733	287,484	301,412	315,681	329,680	338,704	340,442	348,104	355,652	367,916	379,899	391,118
Phoenix-Mesa-Scottsdale, AZ	129,939	135,842	145,257	154,126	171,217	186,767	195,909	193,132	179,833	183,554	191,158	200,989	207,193	215,214
Pine Bluff, AR	2,434	2,487	2,600	2,779	2,843	3,003	2,991	3,051	3,027	3,133	3,138	3,185	3,118	3,079
Pittsburgh, PA	88,768	91,158	94,742	98,945	102,527	106,845	110,681	112,499	110,915	116,554	121,635	125,133	129,857	135,662

Gross Domestic Product by Metropolitan Statistical Area—*Continued*

(Millions of current dollars.)

Metropolitan Statistical Area	2001	2002	2003	2004	2005	2006	2007	2008	2009	2010	2011	2012	2013	2014
Pittsfield, MA	4,391	4,783	5,040	5,281	5,440	5,430	5,272	5,319	5,433	5,260	5,529	5,925	6,049	6,198
Pocatello, ID	1,757	1,791	1,941	2,118	2,265	2,333	2,447	2,528	2,372	2,416	2,468	2,455	2,446	2,530
Portland-South Portland, ME	18,556	19,265	20,371	21,880	22,564	23,629	24,208	24,699	25,064	25,881	26,193	26,731	27,443	28,002
Portland-Vancouver-Hillsboro, OR-WA	80,731	82,424	86,087	96,635	100,598	112,776	119,721	128,506	130,972	140,954	149,423	150,750	150,590	159,328
Port St. Lucie, FL	6,937	7,543	8,176	9,518	10,938	11,792	12,336	11,446	11,099	11,170	11,152	11,170	11,380	11,776
Prescott, AZ	2,919	3,076	3,350	3,632	4,205	4,851	5,140	4,927	4,585	4,500	4,428	4,487	4,620	4,810
Providence-Warwick, RI-MA	49,996	52,667	56,080	59,495	61,598	64,977	65,472	65,618	65,792	67,705	68,959	70,897	73,449	75,940
Provo-Orem, UT	8,699	9,265	10,047	10,965	12,061	13,617	15,304	15,339	15,061	15,404	16,191	17,271	18,455	19,448
Pueblo, CO	3,263	3,291	3,366	3,662	3,582	3,725	3,939	4,093	4,178	4,224	4,383	4,509	4,540	4,785
Punta Gorda, FL	2,520	2,572	2,778	3,151	3,454	3,836	3,705	3,416	3,182	3,175	3,188	3,210	3,381	3,505
Racine, WI	5,805	5,951	6,142	6,423	6,426	6,754	6,777	6,536	6,559	7,105	7,106	7,493	7,488	7,526
Raleigh, NC	36,599	37,493	38,849	41,321	45,249	49,324	53,662	55,657	56,274	59,374	61,779	64,375	68,452	71,574
Rapid City, SD	3,516	3,981	4,102	4,297	4,499	4,696	4,938	5,120	5,141	5,410	5,640	5,823	5,902	6,117
Reading, PA	11,360	11,756	12,175	12,723	13,402	14,737	14,991	14,894	14,734	15,053	15,357	15,827	16,144	16,750
Redding, CA	3,970	4,498	4,815	5,088	5,383	5,541	5,560	5,271	5,035	5,103	5,216	5,223	5,369	5,592
Reno, NV	14,639	15,317	16,079	17,961	19,340	20,312	21,934	20,902	19,072	18,910	19,103	19,144	19,870	20,554
Richmond, VA	47,306	47,404	48,426	49,845	54,737	56,986	59,170	60,259	61,076	62,614	63,376	65,474	68,050	70,491
Riverside-San Bernardino-Ontario, CA	79,285	84,157	91,443	100,795	110,745	118,182	119,335	117,369	111,393	115,037	119,231	121,738	127,651	133,983
Roanoke, VA	10,012	10,191	10,549	11,026	11,693	12,369	12,865	13,047	13,208	13,067	13,081	13,323	13,796	14,249
Rochester, MN	6,736	7,353	8,125	8,522	8,638	8,835	8,991	9,045	9,130	9,850	9,808	10,095	10,341	10,561
Rochester, NY	38,218	39,697	41,190	43,102	44,886	46,595	46,273	46,258	48,118	49,167	49,676	51,578	52,868	53,279
Rockford, IL	10,337	10,624	10,860	11,295	11,819	12,578	13,033	12,733	12,244	12,621	13,229	14,058	14,010	14,410
Rocky Mount, NC	4,787	4,971	5,138	5,295	5,478	5,909	5,849	6,154	6,514	6,372	6,207	6,215	6,271	6,181
Rome, GA	2,727	2,787	2,877	3,112	3,018	3,112	3,151	3,221	3,229	3,243	3,230	3,291	3,368	3,466
Sacramento—Roseville—Arden-Arcade, CA	66,696	72,925	80,030	85,539	93,158	97,838	99,442	97,805	95,194	96,202	99,358	104,746	109,537	112,703
Saginaw, MI	6,807	6,891	7,122	7,114	7,266	7,386	7,193	6,709	6,580	6,991	7,132	7,150	7,430	7,587
St. Cloud, MN	5,601	5,917	6,235	6,817	7,104	7,279	7,374	7,499	7,459	7,693	7,916	8,167	8,443	8,737
St. George, UT	1,977	2,134	2,377	2,657	3,101	3,611	3,859	3,794	3,581	3,515	3,708	3,882	4,158	4,426
St. Joseph, MO-KS	3,169	3,261	3,386	3,633	3,711	4,044	4,360	4,457	4,716	4,861	4,933	5,322	5,490	5,684
St. Louis, MO-IL	102,382	106,338	110,806	115,499	120,653	123,947	127,873	133,060	131,905	134,290	137,258	142,033	145,036	149,951
Salem, OR	8,940	9,519	10,088	10,712	11,066	11,956	12,321	12,961	12,849	12,608	12,480	12,668	13,178	13,767
Salinas, CA	13,845	14,845	15,873	15,978	17,082	18,124	17,988	18,012	17,856	18,214	18,413	19,204	20,398	20,897
Salisbury, MD-DE	8,967	9,125	9,939	11,091	12,141	13,089	14,073	13,693	13,517	13,486	13,251	13,200	13,764	14,130
Salt Lake City, UT	42,438	43,542	44,391	47,440	52,013	58,042	63,580	63,287	61,547	63,681	67,006	69,327	72,881	75,672
San Angelo, TX	2,769	2,833	3,024	3,219	3,351	3,453	3,577	3,791	3,663	3,853	4,151	4,400	4,737	5,339
San Antonio-New Braunfels, TX	53,247	54,354	57,722	61,466	65,915	71,363	75,800	78,389	77,169	81,768	87,276	93,140	99,398	104,787
San Diego-Carlsbad, CA	121,885	131,560	140,086	150,710	161,031	168,789	175,653	178,066	174,640	176,461	183,453	193,090	200,249	206,817
San Francisco-Oakland-Hayward, CA	245,090	246,820	256,901	270,592	294,749	313,790	331,526	344,690	327,088	334,484	345,165	373,546	387,030	411,969
San Jose-Sunnyvale-Santa Clara, CA	125,036	117,286	120,705	126,873	135,528	144,908	155,651	156,885	149,513	164,457	176,780	183,558	198,066	213,819
San Luis Obispo-Paso Robles-Arroyo Grande, CA	7,216	8,177	8,900	9,670	10,465	10,829	11,078	10,868	10,608	11,140	11,496	11,926	12,557	13,121
Santa Cruz-Watsonville, CA	9,116	9,126	9,255	9,445	9,742	10,099	10,092	9,751	9,476	9,547	9,802	10,262	10,875	11,245
Santa Fe, NM	4,891	5,618	5,490	5,705	6,130	6,629	6,864	7,183	6,519	6,537	6,638	6,636	7,003	6,972
Santa Maria-Santa Barbara, CA	14,424	15,181	16,170	17,188	18,772	19,306	19,798	20,262	19,982	20,448	21,718	22,647	23,510	23,930
Santa Rosa, CA	16,692	17,529	17,973	18,627	19,895	20,363	20,362	20,522	19,654	20,268	21,177	21,521	22,582	23,804
Savannah, GA	9,261	9,490	9,905	10,749	11,673	12,747	13,256	13,193	13,238	13,553	13,880	14,463	15,010	15,905
Scranton—Wilkes-Barre—Hazleton, PA	15,775	15,890	16,539	17,563	18,238	18,914	19,572	19,281	19,551	20,281	20,538	20,756	21,393	21,980
Seattle-Tacoma-Bellevue, WA	166,308	170,943	176,427	183,981	200,021	214,643	235,437	242,806	240,144	248,859	257,729	273,087	285,501	300,827
Sebastian-Vero Beach, FL	2,761	2,938	3,307	3,856	4,153	4,372	4,662	4,485	4,216	4,080	4,066	4,244	4,334	4,677
Sebring, FL	1,284	1,401	1,526	1,686	1,786	1,967	1,983	1,844	1,809	1,865	1,872	1,873	1,904	1,908
Sheboygan, WI	4,124	4,304	4,482	4,791	4,935	5,154	5,304	5,553	5,507	5,397	5,592	5,802	6,023	6,278
Sherman-Denison, TX	2,521	2,582	2,699	2,899	3,020	3,232	3,260	3,314	3,300	3,416	3,540	3,624	3,873	3,958
Shreveport-Bossier City, LA	13,436	13,517	15,086	16,792	18,731	20,451	20,185	22,506	20,032	22,633	24,591	24,163	23,243	23,989
Sierra Vista-Douglas, AZ	2,542	2,604	2,794	3,019	3,342	3,556	3,826	3,907	4,073	4,273	4,320	4,136	4,004	3,957
Sioux City, IA-NE-SD	5,561	5,857	5,863	6,208	6,319	6,599	6,938	7,402	7,578	7,826	7,942	8,005	8,695	8,867
Sioux Falls, SD	9,364	11,156	11,371	11,969	12,515	13,056	13,797	14,306	14,176	14,741	15,904	16,894	17,582	18,301
South Bend-Mishawaka, IN-MI	9,287	9,805	10,440	11,160	11,331	11,771	12,138	12,355	11,863	12,423	13,009	12,978	12,996	13,337
Spartanburg, SC	8,781	9,202	9,575	9,684	10,048	10,661	11,099	11,270	10,678	11,364	12,001	12,346	12,897	13,372
Spokane-Spokane Valley, WA	13,736	14,055	14,704	15,516	16,773	17,963	19,062	19,493	19,341	19,636	20,069	20,645	21,325	22,213
Springfield, IL	7,591	7,667	7,658	7,844	8,043	8,304	8,612	8,673	9,000	9,074	9,356	9,380	9,682	9,892
Springfield, MA	17,004	17,471	18,206	19,026	19,800	20,494	21,342	21,897	22,021	22,443	22,927	23,535	24,196	24,937
Springfield, MO	10,912	11,015	11,909	12,716	13,685	14,262	14,695	14,969	15,213	15,628	15,859	16,371	16,997	17,582
Springfield, OH	3,476	3,424	3,380	3,558	3,622	3,780	3,730	3,680	3,553	3,580	3,795	3,990	4,098	4,094
State College, PA	4,270	4,478	4,644	5,000	5,365	5,650	5,968	6,134	6,381	6,579	6,820	6,961	7,328	7,755
Staunton-Waynesboro, VA	3,488	3,405	3,556	3,755	4,069	4,132	4,063	4,222	4,395	4,444	4,401	4,538	4,783	4,823
Stockton-Lodi, CA	13,992	15,299	16,633	17,915	18,991	19,840	20,645	20,284	20,190	20,423	21,116	22,108	22,972	23,491
Sumter, SC	2,349	2,462	2,584	2,726	2,858	2,982	3,056	3,011	3,003	3,026	3,163	3,486	3,530	3,679
Syracuse, NY	21,329	22,022	22,711	23,956	25,079	26,062	27,008	27,018	27,769	28,859	29,043	30,226	30,582	31,294
Tallahassee, FL	10,701	10,472	10,935	11,532	12,059	12,659	13,574	13,556	13,394	13,568	13,429	13,416	13,787	14,230

Gross Domestic Product by Metropolitan Statistical Area—*Continued*

(Millions of current dollars.)

Metropolitan Statistical Area	2001	2002	2003	2004	2005	2006	2007	2008	2009	2010	2011	2012	2013	2014
Tampa-St. Petersburg-Clearwater, FL ...	78,643	84,242	89,832	96,967	104,859	111,639	115,365	112,597	109,998	110,416	111,697	117,147	122,478	128,201
Terre Haute, IN	4,322	4,514	4,857	5,155	5,204	5,499	5,952	6,102	5,885	6,304	6,384	6,388	6,664	6,497
Texarkana, TX-AR	3,382	3,522	3,732	4,036	4,233	4,479	4,676	4,772	4,796	4,933	4,994	5,075	4,995	5,025
The Villages, FL	696	710	863	976	1,215	1,395	1,534	1,505	1,614	1,789	1,887	1,884	2,072	2,181
Toledo, OH	22,216	22,960	23,706	24,693	25,582	26,421	26,958	26,217	26,188	27,187	29,457	30,214	31,214	33,021
Topeka, KS	7,243	7,356	7,481	7,750	7,960	8,107	8,607	8,922	9,093	9,096	9,444	9,553	9,746	9,940
Trenton, NJ	17,311	18,315	19,911	20,984	22,203	23,635	24,014	24,670	24,603	25,843	26,228	28,036	29,387	29,809
Tucson, AZ	23,236	23,516	25,410	26,587	29,073	31,343	33,819	33,973	32,425	33,206	33,314	34,463	34,865	35,717
Tulsa, OK	31,126	31,494	32,625	35,026	39,495	43,257	45,292	50,956	44,977	46,548	49,832	51,814	53,380	55,959
Tuscaloosa, AL	5,560	5,786	6,257	6,917	7,641	7,945	8,566	8,739	8,720	9,363	9,938	9,851	10,217	10,359
Tyler, TX	5,679	5,747	6,132	6,833	7,445	7,907	8,289	9,739	8,489	9,169	9,914	10,267	10,993	11,754
Urban Honolulu, HI	32,265	34,066	36,522	40,123	43,427	45,837	48,409	50,180	49,506	52,388	53,935	55,764	57,453	59,271
Utica-Rome, NY	7,240	7,472	7,711	8,215	8,600	8,940	9,190	9,245	9,501	9,888	10,002	10,298	10,504	10,571
Valdosta, GA	3,142	3,097	3,329	3,441	3,644	3,835	4,008	4,328	4,480	4,400	4,393	4,480	4,655	4,894
Vallejo-Fairfield, CA	9,807	10,284	11,471	12,290	13,533	14,107	14,701	15,496	15,351	15,144	15,066	16,631	17,567	18,055
Victoria, TX	2,431	2,505	2,696	2,923	3,229	3,724	3,822	4,140	3,760	4,093	4,434	5,010	5,509	5,943
Vineland-Bridgeton, NJ	3,768	3,878	4,134	4,447	4,730	4,899	4,979	5,238	5,311	5,286	5,259	5,438	5,467	5,643
Virginia Beach-Norfolk-Newport News, VA-NC	54,039	57,371	61,728	65,401	70,441	74,945	78,942	80,175	82,143	83,123	84,661	87,362	89,050	90,772
Visalia-Porterville, CA	7,671	7,856	8,605	9,937	10,671	10,659	12,030	11,821	11,113	11,931	13,042	12,978	13,484	13,632
Waco, TX	5,728	5,925	6,415	6,906	7,339	7,737	8,022	8,252	8,604	9,092	9,141	9,725	10,223	10,637
Walla Walla, WA	1,605	1,621	1,760	1,791	1,836	1,986	2,157	2,347	2,358	2,425	2,466	2,480	2,536	2,582
Warner Robins, GA	4,106	4,438	4,715	4,920	5,283	5,553	5,828	5,898	6,195	6,438	6,622	6,693	6,687	6,690
Washington-Arlington-Alexandria, DC-VA-MD-WV	272,133	286,450	305,050	330,646	356,811	375,206	392,907	407,800	414,340	432,555	444,708	453,337	462,187	471,584
Waterloo-Cedar Falls, IA	5,239	5,649	5,746	6,561	6,916	7,078	7,511	7,684	7,771	7,831	7,828	9,293	9,458	9,572
Watertown-Fort Drum, NY	3,471	3,512	3,661	3,968	4,514	5,076	5,296	5,593	5,904	6,356	6,691	6,643	6,578	6,571
Wausau, WI	4,476	4,502	4,839	5,121	5,434	5,604	5,793	5,729	5,646	5,787	5,997	6,331	6,632	6,978
Weirton-Steubenville, WV-OH	2,967	3,150	3,129	3,276	3,530	3,466	3,669	3,875	3,544	3,518	3,534	3,760	3,731	3,842
Wenatchee, WA	2,458	2,675	2,888	3,082	3,206	3,403	3,527	3,743	3,684	3,642	3,738	3,920	4,107	4,338
Wheeling, WV-OH	3,590	3,750	3,951	4,226	4,535	4,795	4,975	5,345	5,629	5,824	6,026	6,191	6,649	7,362
Wichita, KS	21,187	21,294	21,580	22,007	23,270	26,510	29,099	29,041	26,682	28,149	29,948	31,082	29,315	30,267
Wichita Falls, TX	4,143	4,281	4,593	4,826	5,135	5,571	5,884	6,913	5,676	5,900	6,495	6,712	7,179	7,319
Williamsport, PA	3,121	3,124	3,190	3,366	3,485	3,604	3,662	3,676	3,695	3,938	4,368	4,645	4,848	5,128
Wilmington, NC	7,168	7,167	7,429	7,892	8,732	9,362	10,008	10,539	10,776	11,121	11,671	11,692	12,717	12,995
Winchester, VA-WV	3,496	3,553	3,812	4,033	4,440	4,711	4,671	4,599	4,904	5,124	5,243	5,440	5,681	5,725
Winston-Salem, NC	21,529	21,130	22,266	23,357	24,140	25,139	24,483	24,783	24,711	25,604	25,869	25,946	26,676	28,246
Worcester, MA-CT	26,633	27,143	28,659	29,478	30,416	31,710	32,697	33,232	32,811	34,108	34,915	35,380	36,751	37,993
Yakima, WA	5,117	5,370	5,731	6,091	6,447	6,667	7,128	7,503	7,359	7,628	7,903	8,287	8,603	8,762
York-Hanover, PA	10,933	11,091	11,937	12,699	13,917	14,488	15,072	15,773	15,729	16,155	16,088	15,944	16,473	16,891
Youngstown-Warren-Boardman, OH-PA	15,313	15,899	16,237	17,199	17,998	18,602	18,657	17,969	16,344	17,236	18,892	20,364	20,436	21,007
Yuba City, CA	3,161	3,478	3,832	4,098	4,273	4,538	4,645	4,866	4,898	4,854	5,051	5,138	5,354	5,472
Yuma, AZ	3,131	3,528	3,693	4,250	4,515	4,871	5,347	5,217	5,287	5,403	5,520	5,332	5,478	5,488

Quantity Indexes for Real GDP by Metropolitan Area

(2009 = 100.0)

Metropolitan Statistical Area	2001	2002	2003	2004	2005	2006	2007	2008	2009	2010	2011	2012	2013	2014
Abilene, TX	87.9	90.8	92.7	94.4	94.0	97.8	102.1	104.5	100.0	100.4	103.0	111.5	117.085	117.797
Akron, OH	95.4	98.7	101.3	104.8	107.4	107.1	107.2	106.7	100.0	102.2	103.8	105.1	105.558	107.961
Albany, GA	105.7	104.5	106.2	106.5	108.2	105.2	103.0	99.2	100.0	97.4	95.9	95.4	94.743	93.403
Albany, OR	91.3	95.3	93.6	101.5	102.6	107.4	102.7	103.0	100.0	97.0	97.5	101.1	102.847	105.49
Albany-Schenectady-Troy, NY	90.1	90.9	93.9	96.9	97.5	98.6	97.2	97.1	100.0	100.3	100.4	100.2	103.747	106.228
Albuquerque, NM	85.8	85.7	91.3	100.7	100.4	101.3	99.0	99.5	100.0	101.3	102.1	103.1	102.488	102.337
Alexandria, LA	79.6	82.3	83.3	88.7	92.0	98.3	100.9	101.6	100.0	101.4	93.6	93.0	90.852	88.771
Allentown-Bethlehem-Easton, PA-NJ	98.2	100.3	98.7	99.7	101.8	103.4	104.2	103.6	100.0	103.3	104.1	104.7	105.931	109.233
Altoona, PA	93.8	93.6	96.0	97.6	99.7	100.2	101.8	100.3	100.0	100.4	99.8	98.8	99.674	100.521
Amarillo, TX	83.4	85.4	87.7	90.1	90.9	95.5	97.3	99.6	100.0	101.2	101.3	105.3	108.395	111.016
Ames, IA	79.5	80.1	85.0	89.0	89.8	96.9	97.2	110.2	100.0	106.7	101.7	97.0	98.19	99.917
Anchorage, AK	74.1	77.4	77.0	80.7	83.7	86.7	89.9	91.1	100.0	98.5	99.6	102.9	100.102	98.656
Ann Arbor, MI	100.4	106.7	109.1	108.4	109.6	108.8	110.5	105.7	100.0	103.4	102.0	100.3	103.514	103.32
Anniston-Oxford-Jacksonville, AL	83.4	87.0	91.0	98.0	101.0	102.2	106.1	106.6	100.0	101.4	99.8	96.7	94.234	92.787
Appleton, WI	91.5	90.7	95.2	99.4	101.1	101.3	103.3	100.2	100.0	99.8	101.6	103.2	104.694	107.101
Asheville, NC	82.6	84.8	87.0	91.0	93.8	98.1	97.6	99.5	100.0	99.5	98.6	100.1	102.016	104.311
Athens-Clarke County, GA	89.3	89.3	92.0	93.9	97.3	97.8	99.1	100.6	100.0	100.0	99.8	101.0	101.61	103.631
Atlanta-Sandy Springs-Roswell, GA	92.3	93.2	94.8	97.0	101.3	103.3	106.1	104.5	100.0	100.6	102.3	103.4	105.805	109.025
Atlantic City-Hammonton, NJ	102.5	106.4	109.8	110.6	114.0	114.8	109.9	106.6	100.0	100.0	98.0	98.1	96.746	94.344
Auburn-Opelika, AL	76.6	79.9	82.8	89.7	93.8	97.1	98.8	101.9	100.0	104.1	109.3	110.0	115.715	120.365
Augusta-Richmond County, GA-SC	98.8	98.5	100.7	101.0	102.2	100.9	100.5	100.0	100.0	102.9	103.9	104.0	103.018	103.229
Austin-Round Rock, TX	73.5	73.9	77.2	82.8	88.0	95.0	97.7	102.2	100.0	105.8	110.8	117.8	123.344	130.861
Bakersfield, CA	68.9	74.9	76.0	80.0	85.0	90.9	94.7	95.5	100.0	101.3	99.9	106.4	107.375	108.138
Baltimore-Columbia-Towson, MD	86.1	88.5	90.3	94.5	97.4	99.6	100.6	100.3	100.0	102.9	104.4	105.8	107.148	108.643
Bangor, ME	96.5	98.8	98.9	102.5	102.9	104.6	104.1	101.8	100.0	99.0	97.9	98.4	98.59	97.545
Barnstable Town, MA	103.6	112.4	110.8	110.9	110.7	106.7	102.7	101.4	100.0	101.6	104.4	108.0	109.144	109.299
Baton Rouge, LA	76.6	82.9	89.1	93.9	105.0	101.5	98.5	99.1	100.0	106.3	103.2	106.9	105.099	108.633
Battle Creek, MI	99.8	107.5	109.3	110.3	111.5	108.7	106.4	106.2	100.0	107.3	103.7	105.1	108.227	108.794
Bay City, MI	101.8	106.1	106.2	105.0	104.9	105.2	102.8	102.3	100.0	101.4	99.9	100.0	101.476	98.619
Beaumont-Port Arthur, TX	78.2	84.4	87.6	97.8	91.3	94.9	102.9	92.2	100.0	105.5	98.6	96.3	101.553	107.35
Beckley, WV	96.3	97.2	95.4	97.3	101.6	104.0	101.8	104.6	100.0	108.2	113.0	107.3	109.298	112.056
Bellingham, WA	72.6	82.8	86.0	85.0	102.3	92.2	95.9	95.3	100.0	103.6	92.5	92.9	95.938	98.964
Bend-Redmond, OR	80.4	87.3	92.3	97.0	103.3	112.1	110.1	109.0	100.0	97.5	94.4	97.3	102.58	108.645
Billings, MT	88.8	90.3	95.4	100.4	103.1	105.4	115.7	109.7	100.0	106.8	115.3	118.1	120.428	126.827
Binghamton, NY	86.1	86.8	87.9	89.6	92.0	93.8	98.5	100.8	100.0	100.8	100.7	100.3	99.169	98.784
Birmingham-Hoover, AL	99.4	102.1	101.8	105.7	107.6	106.9	107.7	107.3	100.0	101.7	105.1	108.0	109.75	111.136
Bismarck, ND	80.9	83.6	89.2	92.2	93.9	94.8	94.8	97.9	100.0	104.2	108.2	120.6	124.677	134.125
Blacksburg-Christiansburg-Radford, VA	94.0	92.6	97.0	98.0	103.0	106.6	111.2	104.5	100.0	101.2	104.7	112.2	111.583	112.373
Bloomington, IL	90.8	91.9	94.6	97.8	95.6	102.0	100.6	98.1	100.0	101.8	102.3	104.9	110.398	106.73
Bloomington, IN	80.6	79.7	82.7	86.1	89.1	93.4	95.3	98.2	100.0	100.4	98.5	95.3	94.874	94.202
Bloomsburg-Berwick, PA	89.6	95.5	93.2	96.0	94.3	97.1	99.9	101.1	100.0	104.1	106.2	106.1	109.028	106.933
Boise City, ID	81.4	83.6	86.9	91.0	96.8	103.2	106.3	106.0	100.0	102.0	101.7	103.1	106.908	109.686
Boston-Cambridge-Newton, MA-NH	91.0	91.0	92.9	95.2	97.2	99.1	102.3	102.3	100.0	104.2	106.6	108.8	110.032	112.89
Boulder, CO	98.6	88.6	89.7	93.0	95.7	97.4	102.1	103.3	100.0	102.9	105.2	107.6	111.045	116.193
Bowling Green, KY	84.3	87.4	91.6	95.7	102.3	107.8	107.6	108.4	100.0	105.0	105.7	109.3	111.747	113.498
Bremerton-Silverdale, WA	90.8	98.0	99.2	98.6	100.0	103.2	102.2	102.2	100.0	98.8	98.6	98.2	97.258	98.309
Bridgeport-Stamford-Norwalk, CT	98.7	97.5	98.8	104.5	106.5	109.6	112.8	106.5	100.0	105.2	107.1	111.3	112.573	113.522
Brownsville-Harlingen, TX	84.3	86.6	88.7	89.8	91.8	95.5	97.5	99.5	100.0	101.8	101.8	104.9	107.045	108.114
Brunswick, GA	88.4	90.4	95.6	99.9	101.4	105.0	103.3	102.3	100.0	95.2	94.3	94.0	93.359	91.51
Buffalo-Cheektowaga-Niagara Falls, NY	91.8	95.4	96.7	98.6	98.7	100.0	98.5	98.1	100.0	101.4	102.8	104.2	104.869	106.24
Burlington, NC	106.0	108.5	104.3	107.2	108.3	112.2	108.7	107.1	100.0	102.7	104.8	110.2	110.649	109.86
Burlington-South Burlington, VT	84.9	87.1	92.4	96.0	97.9	99.8	98.9	100.7	100.0	105.9	110.6	113.2	111.692	112.178
California-Lexington Park, MD	78.5	83.0	87.8	89.9	89.8	93.6	95.1	95.7	100.0	105.6	109.2	108.0	107.509	106.933
Canton-Massillon, OH	109.1	109.9	110.4	112.2	113.7	110.1	108.1	107.3	100.0	102.4	106.9	109.8	118.492	123.053
Cape Coral-Fort Myers, FL	92.2	95.5	99.0	107.1	118.2	121.7	118.5	109.2	100.0	98.5	96.6	100.4	104.085	108.172
Cape Girardeau, MO-IL	83.7	85.6	88.0	88.6	91.5	94.5	97.6	97.9	100.0	98.1	96.2	95.7	97.575	96.927
Carbondale-Marion, IL	83.9	87.0	88.8	90.7	93.5	96.2	95.2	97.4	100.0	101.0	102.8	104.0	105.975	102.214
Carson City, NV	96.5	97.8	103.8	109.7	114.4	115.5	115.8	108.3	100.0	101.1	99.1	97.7	98.847	97.375
Casper, WY	71.5	76.5	76.2	83.5	92.1	103.6	101.6	123.8	100.0	99.2	103.8	100.3	101.402	107.516
Cedar Rapids, IA	72.1	70.3	76.0	81.6	85.2	83.3	91.5	87.8	100.0	103.0	104.7	105.0	107.185	108.603
Chambersburg-Waynesboro, PA	81.9	82.9	88.1	95.1	100.5	104.4	106.3	105.9	100.0	100.7	100.9	99.8	101.682	103.983
Champaign-Urbana, IL	83.6	86.7	88.0	89.2	89.7	93.1	93.8	98.5	100.0	100.4	98.7	99.5	102.399	99.283
Charleston, WV	96.5	96.8	95.4	95.6	96.5	98.5	99.2	101.3	100.0	101.3	103.9	97.3	96.443	102.592
Charleston-North Charleston, SC	77.7	81.0	84.9	87.9	92.6	95.0	99.1	101.2	100.0	100.2	106.5	109.5	111.397	113.635
Charlotte-Concord-Gastonia, NC-SC	83.5	89.1	91.3	95.7	102.7	107.7	104.0	105.3	100.0	102.7	109.0	109.8	114.614	117.054
Charlottesville, VA	80.0	82.9	86.2	90.8	95.7	98.4	99.1	100.2	100.0	103.8	107.3	109.6	112.587	112.332
Chattanooga, TN-GA	97.6	99.2	100.1	102.5	104.0	108.0	109.8	106.8	100.0	101.3	102.0	102.6	103.338	102.422
Cheyenne, WY	76.2	79.6	84.2	87.5	90.0	97.1	101.7	109.2	100.0	101.8	104.3	104.6	102.812	105.085
Chicago-Naperville-Elgin, IL-IN-WI	96.8	97.0	98.2	100.6	102.4	104.8	106.2	103.6	100.0	101.3	102.5	105.0	105.107	107.018
Chico, CA	86.6	92.9	95.8	98.8	102.8	103.0	103.7	101.3	100.0	100.0	97.8	95.6	97.767	98.77

Quantity Indexes for Real GDP by Metropolitan Area—*Continued*

(2009 = 100.0)

Metropolitan Statistical Area	2001	2002	2003	2004	2005	2006	2007	2008	2009	2010	2011	2012	2013	2014
Cincinnati, OH-KY-IN	96.8	98.5	100.6	102.6	104.9	104.4	105.1	104.4	100.0	102.6	104.6	106.5	108.197	110.927
Clarksville, TN-KY	73.1	75.2	80.9	84.0	91.9	95.6	95.1	98.8	100.0	103.3	109.5	110.3	108.935	107.631
Cleveland, TN	102.3	105.1	106.9	110.7	108.7	108.8	105.2	105.1	100.0	99.6	103.4	114.6	114.799	117.63
Cleveland-Elyria, OH	100.5	102.0	104.3	107.8	108.2	107.4	107.0	106.0	100.0	102.6	105.4	105.8	107.057	108.292
Coeur d'Alene, ID	73.3	75.8	81.3	86.6	94.0	100.4	104.8	103.9	100.0	99.2	99.2	97.3	101.231	104.015
College Station-Bryan, TX	77.3	74.5	79.0	81.3	84.2	88.0	89.8	92.7	100.0	101.9	101.4	106.5	111.02	115.503
Colorado Springs, CO	91.2	90.7	93.9	95.6	99.7	99.9	101.5	99.4	100.0	104.0	105.5	106.0	104.889	107.603
Columbia, MO	89.3	85.6	92.1	94.5	97.5	100.3	100.7	99.8	100.0	102.4	103.8	104.9	110.276	112.019
Columbia, SC	86.4	87.4	90.7	94.0	96.2	99.6	102.0	102.4	100.0	99.4	100.2	100.7	102.274	104.428
Columbus, GA-AL	89.5	87.0	89.5	90.8	93.4	94.9	98.2	98.1	100.0	102.5	105.7	105.9	106.716	107.026
Columbus, IN	89.9	87.5	89.9	96.8	98.4	106.0	112.4	116.2	100.0	112.7	118.2	124.8	125.234	127.15
Columbus, OH	95.1	98.2	99.4	102.2	103.0	104.6	105.2	103.4	100.0	102.8	106.6	110.7	114.071	116.204
Corpus Christi, TX	81.7	84.0	87.5	94.2	90.0	93.4	100.0	95.3	100.0	101.3	100.0	105.2	113.978	121.373
Corvallis, OR	45.9	52.6	59.7	71.3	71.1	81.8	85.9	96.9	100.0	104.6	103.2	97.1	90.173	89.568
Crestview-Fort Walton Beach-Destin, FL	74.7	91.6	95.5	100.5	112.8	115.8	113.6	103.9	100.0	94.6	97.1	96.0	96.614	96.322
Cumberland, MD-WV	92.0	94.7	95.5	94.9	97.6	98.9	96.8	97.6	100.0	103.4	103.5	102.4	102.255	101.725
Dallas-Fort Worth-Arlington, TX	84.9	87.4	87.3	91.2	93.9	98.7	101.3	102.6	100.0	103.1	107.4	113.2	119.183	129.345
Dalton, GA	96.3	99.0	101.0	114.3	117.8	117.0	118.7	108.3	100.0	92.2	94.0	95.0	96.653	99.429
Danville, IL	97.0	96.9	102.7	105.3	104.3	107.9	103.3	102.8	100.0	101.0	101.4	101.5	103.532	100.612
Daphne-Fairhope-Foley, AL	74.0	76.6	79.4	86.5	90.2	94.4	98.8	101.9	100.0	100.9	101.6	101.7	106.791	106.792
Davenport-Moline-Rock Island, IA-IL	88.0	90.9	93.7	98.5	101.0	101.7	102.9	103.7	100.0	103.2	106.1	108.4	108.782	106.484
Dayton, OH	105.0	106.9	107.5	110.1	111.2	112.6	110.5	107.3	100.0	101.8	104.9	104.5	104.77	105.057
Decatur, AL	91.6	90.2	95.6	103.4	101.9	103.3	104.5	103.9	100.0	102.0	98.6	100.4	102.341	101.768
Decatur, IL	93.0	88.4	91.8	97.3	99.9	100.8	104.4	106.9	100.0	99.1	101.6	98.0	95.525	100.715
Deltona-Daytona Beach-Ormond Beach, FL	96.6	98.0	101.6	105.7	110.1	113.0	113.9	106.7	100.0	100.0	96.2	96.5	97.18	100.016
Denver-Aurora-Lakewood, CO	88.2	89.9	90.3	91.7	96.1	97.8	99.1	101.4	100.0	101.4	102.5	105.6	108.266	113.638
Des Moines-West Des Moines, IA	80.4	82.9	88.8	96.6	103.0	101.5	111.6	102.3	100.0	101.5	105.1	111.4	112.815	115.72
Detroit-Warren-Dearborn, MI	118.3	120.3	122.8	121.4	123.6	120.0	118.9	112.2	100.0	105.8	109.6	112.6	115.449	117.999
Dothan, AL	90.6	97.5	100.7	105.4	110.1	110.8	109.0	103.5	100.0	102.5	100.6	100.6	104.501	103.617
Dover, DE	82.0	84.9	87.0	93.3	93.9	95.4	96.1	94.7	100.0	94.6	95.9	94.2	93.693	95.176
Dubuque, IA	84.6	89.0	91.7	100.1	103.5	105.3	106.2	103.5	100.0	106.0	107.5	120.3	116.999	117.732
Duluth, MN-WI	99.5	104.6	106.2	109.5	109.6	107.7	107.2	106.7	100.0	108.6	112.6	107.7	112.237	112.608
Durham-Chapel Hill, NC	64.1	67.5	71.1	71.5	74.6	87.9	95.0	96.9	100.0	101.7	95.0	94.0	99.997	102.12
East Stroudsburg, PA	81.2	84.1	84.1	89.1	93.6	96.9	101.2	101.8	100.0	99.6	93.4	90.4	88.357	85.18
Eau Claire, WI	82.1	86.6	90.4	93.7	100.8	102.4	102.6	100.5	100.0	103.6	104.3	107.1	108.339	111.986
El Centro, CA	75.4	87.0	85.6	84.5	89.8	96.4	92.8	98.0	100.0	96.7	100.3	95.5	97.695	99.243
Elizabethtown-Fort Knox, KY	86.2	88.1	92.5	96.7	97.5	101.7	99.1	101.4	100.0	113.8	119.3	119.6	120.013	117.012
Elkhart-Goshen, IN	104.2	113.0	124.9	131.7	136.9	143.3	147.7	129.3	100.0	129.1	130.8	140.3	147.695	154.395
Elmira, NY	93.4	92.7	93.6	95.7	100.2	99.0	99.4	102.6	100.0	106.2	108.3	108.4	106.767	105.246
El Paso, TX	94.1	97.0	97.2	96.8	97.2	103.4	105.3	100.1	100.0	101.2	101.6	103.6	105.657	106.382
Erie, PA	100.3	97.5	98.0	102.1	104.2	105.1	106.2	106.7	100.0	99.8	103.5	100.5	103.209	103.477
Eugene, OR	87.1	89.0	91.9	98.1	100.4	104.8	108.4	110.7	100.0	100.8	103.2	105.0	106.622	108.367
Evansville, IN-KY	96.4	100.6	102.2	102.7	100.3	100.6	100.1	102.3	100.0	102.5	102.0	98.7	98.23	97.776
Fairbanks, AK	91.5	88.3	93.4	96.7	99.1	105.0	108.0	108.5	100.0	99.3	100.2	99.1	97.214	96.4
Fargo, ND-MN	76.1	80.6	83.8	87.3	89.1	92.0	93.8	100.2	100.0	106.5	115.9	124.0	124.82	129.718
Farmington, NM	93.5	92.6	91.1	94.3	94.0	97.1	99.4	97.5	100.0	89.7	92.7	90.5	90.965	92.262
Fayetteville, NC	76.2	77.7	79.8	81.8	86.6	88.5	91.3	95.7	100.0	101.9	102.4	101.5	99.911	96.749
Fayetteville-Springdale-Rogers, AR-MO	72.4	77.9	84.9	92.4	97.6	100.9	100.3	103.5	100.0	108.5	115.2	116.3	121.948	125.768
Flagstaff, AZ	80.3	83.2	86.7	89.4	93.7	100.9	109.1	106.6	100.0	101.1	98.8	97.8	101.842	101.681
Flint, MI	118.5	124.2	126.9	125.5	124.3	123.1	118.5	108.9	100.0	104.8	105.5	105.8	108.669	108.215
Florence, SC	97.9	99.2	102.4	102.3	103.7	105.7	108.0	104.7	100.0	98.3	97.2	97.8	100.965	101.539
Florence-Muscle Shoals, AL	89.9	89.9	93.4	97.3	100.4	102.3	101.3	100.1	100.0	103.2	102.9	104.0	107.561	110.485
Fond du Lac, WI	101.1	99.4	102.9	107.1	108.4	110.2	110.5	108.5	100.0	101.8	105.0	105.7	108.531	111.794
Fort Collins, CO	88.3	93.9	94.4	95.9	97.9	99.2	101.7	101.8	100.0	103.6	105.6	108.1	111.894	118.503
Fort Smith, AR-OK	90.8	93.0	97.6	100.9	106.5	111.5	106.8	106.0	100.0	103.5	103.0	103.1	103.39	104.445
Fort Wayne, IN	99.0	99.9	101.2	102.3	104.5	108.2	109.5	106.1	100.0	106.1	107.5	110.0	110.874	111.289
Fresno, CA	81.0	87.7	91.8	94.2	97.4	101.5	100.1	100.0	100.0	100.5	103.0	102.3	104.918	105.399
Gadsden, AL	96.4	98.3	100.0	103.8	105.3	105.0	103.5	102.8	100.0	101.1	103.4	101.0	103.254	104.845
Gainesville, FL	82.2	83.5	85.3	93.2	94.9	97.8	102.4	102.0	100.0	101.4	99.7	99.3	100.719	102.193
Gainesville, GA	98.1	95.8	96.9	99.5	105.7	105.6	106.3	104.4	100.0	100.6	106.9	106.3	111.099	113.427
Gettysburg, PA	86.9	89.1	94.9	96.3	100.8	105.3	105.7	102.6	100.0	96.4	93.8	94.9	97.295	99.64
Glens Falls, NY	86.2	89.1	92.0	96.9	99.5	99.9	98.3	99.4	100.0	102.2	102.2	103.8	102.878	103.46
Goldsboro, NC	93.5	92.0	91.6	96.4	97.7	102.4	101.3	97.5	100.0	98.9	98.5	99.1	98.194	96.282
Grand Forks, ND-MN	85.8	88.1	94.8	92.3	93.3	98.6	98.7	103.1	100.0	102.5	100.6	108.5	108.669	111.467
Grand Island, NE	76.9	79.6	84.1	85.5	91.3	95.8	97.4	98.3	100.0	101.1	105.1	107.1	110.25	108.79
Grand Junction, CO	75.2	78.2	79.6	82.2	86.8	91.5	99.5	108.3	100.0	95.7	96.3	97.2	95.525	96.703
Grand Rapids-Wyoming, MI	104.5	108.5	110.9	113.2	115.4	115.3	111.8	107.0	100.0	103.7	106.6	112.0	116.217	121.478
Grants Pass, OR	84.9	88.7	93.2	99.9	102.8	107.9	105.4	103.9	100.0	97.9	97.7	97.9	96.315	101.515
Great Falls, MT	88.4	88.6	90.8	93.7	93.6	97.8	99.5	100.9	100.0	101.7	101.9	102.2	100.546	102.838
Greeley, CO	89.2	90.3	89.7	91.4	95.6	98.1	101.1	100.8	100.0	99.8	101.3	106.4	112.46	123.553

Quantity Indexes for Real GDP by Metropolitan Area—Continued

(2009 = 100.0)

Metropolitan Statistical Area	2001	2002	2003	2004	2005	2006	2007	2008	2009	2010	2011	2012	2013	2014
Green Bay, WI	96.4	97.4	100.5	103.4	104.2	104.4	104.5	101.4	100.0	103.0	105.2	107.5	109.92	109.581
Greensboro-High Point, NC	97.0	97.2	98.2	99.5	102.1	105.9	104.6	103.6	100.0	102.0	102.6	101.4	103.134	106.112
Greenville, NC	84.6	86.0	87.6	86.4	89.6	94.0	98.5	99.1	100.0	100.7	103.6	105.4	105.996	107.674
Greenville-Anderson-Mauldin, SC	98.4	98.3	101.8	98.0	100.6	101.4	104.9	105.2	100.0	103.4	106.9	106.3	108.339	111.744
Gulfport-Biloxi-Pascagoula, MS	86.7	85.3	90.9	88.6	94.3	94.6	98.4	103.9	100.0	99.1	96.3	103.4	94.382	92.102
Hagerstown-Martinsburg, MD-WV	89.5	92.1	94.4	98.0	102.7	106.4	103.8	102.7	100.0	100.7	103.3	104.1	103.836	105.011
Hammond, LA	66.1	69.3	73.5	79.4	86.7	104.2	100.5	103.8	100.0	107.7	105.1	99.0	97.098	99.787
Hanford-Corcoran, CA	83.0	88.3	97.4	103.7	107.0	106.6	115.3	111.3	100.0	103.6	112.5	107.6	106.501	106.72
Harrisburg-Carlisle, PA	93.8	94.4	96.1	98.8	99.7	101.6	102.5	100.8	100.0	100.2	101.1	101.7	102.96	103.365
Harrisonburg, VA	89.3	82.5	84.6	84.7	88.0	91.1	93.5	91.5	100.0	102.8	102.1	102.2	103.135	101.371
Hartford-West Hartford-East Hartford, CT	86.7	84.0	85.2	91.3	93.2	97.0	103.3	100.8	100.0	99.0	96.5	93.9	94.776	95.372
Hattiesburg, MS	79.1	82.2	84.9	88.1	90.2	96.6	98.1	99.2	100.0	101.6	101.8	104.9	104.533	103.986
Hickory-Lenoir-Morganton, NC	111.4	111.0	107.9	111.9	111.8	116.5	108.9	105.4	100.0	102.3	102.1	102.0	101.841	102.552
Hilton Head Island-Bluffton-Beaufort, SC	90.5	95.2	98.6	102.5	106.0	110.6	113.3	105.7	100.0	98.0	95.1	93.8	95.528	97.269
Hinesville, GA	72.9	72.5	77.5	80.6	85.8	86.9	89.5	98.0	100.0	106.6	111.7	106.7	105.599	104.934
Homosassa Springs, FL	85.1	88.4	93.3	95.3	102.6	105.0	105.7	98.1	100.0	102.6	98.5	95.5	93.495	86.45
Hot Springs, AR	93.6	94.3	96.3	99.7	103.5	105.1	103.5	104.3	100.0	104.8	111.4	116.5	121.758	120.828
Houma-Thibodaux, LA	72.9	66.9	66.1	65.9	68.4	80.1	86.6	92.2	100.0	101.8	99.4	107.4	112.586	110.602
Houston-The Woodlands-Sugar Land, TX	83.9	84.1	82.9	88.1	88.2	93.9	100.7	99.2	100.0	101.1	104.9	112.4	119.702	121.798
Huntington-Ashland, WV-KY-OH	85.6	88.8	89.7	91.7	92.8	94.1	95.0	98.5	100.0	99.4	96.9	97.5	102.818	105.592
Huntsville, AL	71.6	77.6	83.0	88.5	92.5	96.0	97.5	99.6	100.0	105.3	106.8	106.4	108.57	110.247
Idaho Falls, ID	73.7	78.2	80.2	83.9	86.9	92.3	95.3	99.7	100.0	99.8	100.1	99.7	99.997	101.958
Indianapolis-Carmel-Anderson, IN	89.4	90.4	92.6	97.3	98.5	101.1	103.0	104.2	100.0	103.4	103.1	103.4	106.497	107.493
Iowa City, IA	88.5	86.9	89.0	92.7	93.4	96.8	98.5	99.4	100.0	102.5	105.8	109.1	111.418	112.321
Ithaca, NY	86.4	88.8	93.4	94.0	95.1	95.1	95.4	99.0	100.0	100.7	100.2	101.5	101.537	100.315
Jackson, MI	108.8	111.7	110.3	112.7	114.7	112.7	112.2	107.1	100.0	106.3	108.0	107.0	112.842	115.089
Jackson, MS	85.5	88.0	90.5	93.5	94.1	97.4	100.0	101.7	100.0	102.9	105.2	106.7	107.213	107.298
Jackson, TN	94.3	98.1	101.5	102.9	104.5	104.4	99.6	102.8	100.0	100.3	102.6	108.1	108.735	108.546
Jacksonville, FL	88.2	91.2	96.7	100.7	105.4	111.3	111.3	106.0	100.0	100.7	99.6	101.4	102.771	105.743
Jacksonville, NC	68.1	64.9	67.2	73.2	76.4	77.7	83.2	90.9	100.0	105.6	104.6	103.4	101.386	98.85
Janesville-Beloit, WI	101.9	111.4	114.6	114.3	112.1	120.2	116.5	109.7	100.0	102.3	105.5	107.0	114.056	114.264
Jefferson City, MO	94.0	91.6	96.0	99.5	100.0	100.7	100.3	100.1	100.0	102.4	99.6	97.9	101.691	99.711
Johnson City, TN	81.1	84.8	89.6	95.5	97.1	98.3	97.6	100.8	100.0	95.1	97.1	99.2	98.285	98.715
Johnstown, PA	99.0	95.1	97.1	97.7	100.0	100.4	101.6	100.9	100.0	99.5	99.9	96.9	95.296	93.645
Jonesboro, AR	84.3	85.7	91.9	95.4	97.5	99.4	96.5	101.5	100.0	104.3	104.0	104.9	105.903	105.242
Joplin, MO	89.9	88.5	94.0	97.4	98.7	101.5	101.4	100.8	100.0	103.2	103.7	103.6	104.257	103.337
Kahului-Wailuku-Lahaina, HI	82.2	83.1	88.4	95.0	101.0	105.7	107.1	106.2	100.0	99.1	101.6	103.2	105.557	103.308
Kalamazoo-Portage, MI	95.4	103.2	105.7	104.6	102.2	103.0	104.5	103.0	100.0	100.9	101.5	100.5	103.31	103.866
Kankakee, IL	94.4	97.7	98.5	101.0	99.7	101.9	100.6	99.6	100.0	99.3	98.9	105.4	105.835	105.816
Kansas City, MO-KS	91.0	92.6	94.0	96.5	98.4	99.8	102.0	103.0	100.0	102.7	102.9	105.0	106.021	108.098
Kennewick-Richland, WA	73.4	78.8	81.8	82.2	85.5	85.2	89.6	92.9	100.0	105.9	103.5	97.7	98.664	98.757
Killeen-Temple, TX	68.7	70.2	73.2	75.5	81.2	87.1	91.7	96.9	100.0	98.4	99.1	98.7	97.235	97.524
Kingsport-Bristol-Bristol, TN-VA	98.6	95.7	96.1	103.4	100.0	104.8	104.6	102.8	100.0	102.8	108.6	110.1	108.046	105.887
Kingston, NY	88.3	90.6	94.8	96.5	98.5	102.8	101.7	99.8	100.0	101.9	99.2	99.6	99.378	99.569
Knoxville, TN	85.2	89.2	93.4	97.9	99.5	99.9	99.0	102.7	100.0	100.6	103.9	105.6	106.745	107.815
Kokomo, IN	127.9	142.3	160.6	154.8	153.5	165.4	175.3	145.1	100.0	143.1	149.4	151.6	159.266	158.738
La Crosse-Onalaska, WI-MN	86.5	89.8	93.9	94.3	96.3	96.9	97.4	100.2	100.0	102.2	103.5	104.6	107.228	107.567
Lafayette, LA	81.6	76.5	74.7	74.6	75.4	85.3	89.0	93.1	100.0	102.8	106.4	110.1	106.237	102.598
Lafayette-West Lafayette, IN	89.4	93.2	95.0	99.7	102.3	104.0	105.9	108.2	100.0	106.8	109.3	109.2	111.44	113.196
Lake Charles, LA	88.4	96.1	113.6	123.9	153.5	131.3	109.1	106.2	100.0	108.8	94.8	98.1	91.735	101.178
Lake Havasu City-Kingman, AZ	85.2	90.4	96.7	100.8	109.2	119.5	120.5	110.7	100.0	99.9	97.7	95.6	96.254	97.726
Lakeland-Winter Haven, FL	85.1	88.8	92.2	97.6	102.4	106.8	107.1	105.0	100.0	100.4	98.4	95.2	99.181	98.368
Lancaster, PA	96.9	98.4	99.9	101.9	104.1	104.4	103.2	102.1	100.0	104.7	107.0	108.3	109.841	112.1
Lansing-East Lansing, MI	104.6	108.9	111.1	108.8	110.6	112.0	111.8	106.5	100.0	107.1	105.3	103.0	106.825	108.616
Laredo, TX	84.7	88.5	91.3	92.5	97.1	100.3	100.3	105.6	100.0	102.5	107.3	112.4	115.749	120.048
Las Cruces, NM	69.6	75.9	80.9	86.3	90.6	92.1	94.3	97.0	100.0	102.5	100.5	98.5	99.389	100.118
Las Vegas-Henderson-Paradise, NV	82.7	85.9	90.2	101.1	111.0	114.4	115.3	110.7	100.0	98.0	97.5	97.1	99.009	100.974
Lawrence, KS	92.2	94.0	94.7	95.4	95.8	94.9	98.5	99.5	100.0	98.2	99.2	99.6	100.743	101.765
Lawton, OK	81.1	82.1	86.2	88.8	88.3	92.9	94.7	96.6	100.0	106.0	104.5	101.1	102.782	101.204
Lebanon, PA	86.6	87.5	91.2	94.1	94.7	96.8	98.4	100.3	100.0	103.9	103.8	103.8	103.425	102.784
Lewiston, ID-WA	96.1	96.7	100.0	100.5	101.6	103.0	103.9	102.9	100.0	101.7	98.6	98.9	99.198	101.417
Lewiston-Auburn, ME	88.9	95.1	97.1	99.4	98.4	100.7	102.4	102.3	100.0	99.3	99.3	100.5	99.986	99.731
Lexington-Fayette, KY	90.0	95.5	96.9	99.0	101.7	105.8	105.7	105.8	100.0	105.7	107.7	109.7	111.056	111.059
Lima, OH	94.7	96.2	96.5	99.7	100.9	100.7	98.4	90.7	100.0	99.4	98.5	93.0	98.84	103.247
Lincoln, NE	90.0	91.3	97.5	98.5	99.3	101.8	102.3	99.8	100.0	103.1	104.8	110.6	113.733	114.614
Little Rock-North Little Rock-Conway, AR	79.5	82.5	83.9	85.6	89.1	92.6	99.8	99.8	100.0	100.6	103.8	105.8	107.269	106.468
Logan, UT-ID	71.0	73.7	81.9	86.7	88.6	91.5	96.7	100.9	100.0	105.5	111.7	108.8	110.13	113.441
Longview, TX	74.3	74.9	76.6	80.8	84.7	92.1	96.4	104.4	100.0	106.3	102.9	108.9	113.195	116.922
Longview, WA	95.9	93.4	97.6	98.4	101.9	104.2	106.9	104.4	100.0	102.3	100.2	102.5	105.878	109.663
Los Angeles-Long Beach-Anaheim, CA	85.4	87.8	91.3	95.6	98.0	101.8	103.7	105.5	100.0	100.2	100.4	101.9	103.5	105.833

Quantity Indexes for Real GDP by Metropolitan Area—*Continued*

(2009 = 100.0)

Metropolitan Statistical Area	2001	2002	2003	2004	2005	2006	2007	2008	2009	2010	2011	2012	2013	2014
Louisville/Jefferson County, KY-IN	94.8	96.1	97.0	100.6	102.5	105.6	106.5	105.3	100.0	104.3	106.4	108.6	109.36	111.961
Lubbock, TX	82.7	86.6	89.6	93.2	96.0	99.1	98.9	100.0	100.0	103.6	100.7	108.5	116.876	120.184
Lynchburg, VA	92.9	90.3	93.1	95.3	98.3	101.9	101.7	100.5	100.0	101.8	99.9	97.9	98.61	97.536
Macon, GA	112.5	112.1	109.5	110.8	109.5	106.9	102.9	103.5	100.0	99.7	100.6	99.7	102.335	104.204
Madera, CA	76.7	84.9	90.3	102.8	108.1	110.7	110.0	107.2	100.0	109.2	111.2	112.7	115.677	114.496
Madison, WI	82.3	85.6	88.3	92.5	96.3	97.9	100.6	99.5	100.0	103.7	106.8	108.4	113.161	113.238
Manchester-Nashua, NH	80.9	85.2	92.5	95.4	99.7	100.2	101.2	101.7	100.0	99.4	103.5	103.9	104.762	107.777
Manhattan, KS	81.9	83.5	87.8	89.0	90.8	91.9	97.5	102.5	100.0	101.1	103.2	101.7	101.928	102.15
Mankato-North Mankato, MN	86.8	89.5	93.3	98.1	103.4	107.0	103.6	105.6	100.0	105.4	108.6	110.7	110.144	110.532
Mansfield, OH	111.2	116.0	118.9	124.6	125.7	126.3	120.1	116.1	100.0	102.3	104.5	104.5	105.689	106.753
McAllen-Edinburg-Mission, TX	74.3	76.8	81.4	85.6	90.0	94.9	96.6	98.5	100.0	103.2	105.2	109.2	113.44	116.265
Medford, OR	95.8	98.5	102.8	107.6	110.0	112.9	111.3	104.7	100.0	97.7	95.9	98.0	101.438	104.794
Memphis, TN-MS-AR	97.5	101.4	103.2	105.8	106.5	107.7	107.4	104.4	100.0	99.9	100.0	102.4	102.865	103.323
Merced, CA	78.2	86.4	94.2	101.8	103.8	105.5	110.5	101.8	100.0	98.8	103.0	98.3	101.626	100.587
Miami-Fort Lauderdale-West Palm Beach, FL	90.5	94.0	96.6	101.1	108.4	111.9	112.2	108.8	100.0	100.1	100.5	104.1	107.12	110.382
Michigan City-La Porte, IN	103.1	103.5	103.6	107.9	107.6	107.0	109.2	107.6	100.0	104.0	103.2	102.3	101.943	100.322
Midland, MI	106.1	112.4	108.3	115.9	104.6	102.2	104.4	101.8	100.0	103.5	105.0	99.3	98.284	102.654
Midland, TX	61.5	58.1	53.6	54.4	55.2	61.0	70.5	80.4	100.0	99.3	115.2	143.4	158.996	197.333
Milwaukee-Waukesha-West Allis, WI	91.3	92.0	94.6	96.6	99.4	101.9	102.4	102.8	100.0	101.6	103.7	103.9	105.181	105.991
Minneapolis-St. Paul-Bloomington, MN-WI	92.3	93.8	97.3	100.5	103.5	102.8	103.7	103.9	100.0	103.1	106.1	107.5	110.421	112.616
Missoula, MT	86.4	90.8	93.8	94.7	97.8	100.3	101.0	100.9	100.0	99.6	99.8	101.1	100.401	101.516
Mobile, AL	82.6	82.5	84.2	87.9	90.6	95.8	97.4	97.6	100.0	100.4	100.6	99.6	101.316	101.289
Modesto, CA	86.5	93.1	98.0	103.2	107.4	108.6	105.1	100.9	100.0	101.0	101.7	101.2	102.591	103.764
Monroe, LA	92.1	92.1	93.5	97.2	100.0	103.8	103.7	100.1	100.0	103.0	99.4	99.8	100.7	103.504
Monroe, MI	108.5	118.5	123.6	123.3	121.4	121.1	116.1	109.9	100.0	105.8	106.3	108.3	116.107	116.175
Montgomery, AL	91.6	94.6	97.1	101.0	103.4	105.5	103.9	102.9	100.0	101.2	101.9	100.9	102.851	100.983
Morgantown, WV	70.8	75.0	77.0	79.1	82.1	85.9	86.6	93.6	100.0	105.8	103.1	100.8	103.678	108.737
Morristown, TN	105.2	104.6	109.2	115.3	112.0	113.5	112.9	108.9	100.0	106.4	107.2	111.3	111.081	111.89
Mount Vernon-Anacortes, WA	86.3	107.4	102.5	93.9	123.1	101.9	100.4	97.1	100.0	100.1	82.8	80.8	84.024	88.959
Muncie, IN	115.7	114.9	117.3	113.4	110.5	112.3	108.1	107.0	100.0	101.8	102.3	105.4	106.413	105.442
Muskegon, MI	109.9	109.4	111.3	112.4	112.6	111.2	107.0	104.0	100.0	104.4	106.4	109.7	113.304	115.021
Myrtle Beach-Conway-North Myrtle Beach, SC-NC	85.3	87.9	91.2	94.3	99.5	101.7	104.9	104.1	100.0	101.1	103.4	103.8	105.875	106.451
Napa, CA	89.0	93.0	95.4	98.0	102.7	104.3	104.5	103.6	100.0	94.9	95.3	101.5	104.794	109.005
Naples-Immokalee-Marco Island, FL	102.1	101.0	108.7	117.8	130.1	131.2	126.5	112.6	100.0	101.6	101.3	106.7	112.946	119.244
Nashville-Davidson—Murfreesboro—Franklin, TN	84.3	86.6	90.0	94.9	96.5	100.1	99.7	103.3	100.0	103.1	107.5	113.1	116.619	120.855
New Bern, NC	85.1	82.7	85.4	89.4	92.8	93.8	94.9	96.6	100.0	99.0	96.4	98.2	96.278	95.171
New Haven-Milford, CT	92.2	95.6	97.5	104.1	104.0	106.0	107.7	105.0	100.0	100.8	99.8	99.9	101.52	101.777
New Orleans-Metairie, LA	100.1	101.3	105.1	108.4	110.9	102.0	97.9	96.9	100.0	105.2	98.3	99.4	96.647	98.246
New York-Newark-Jersey City, NY-NJ-PA	91.8	91.8	92.0	94.6	98.5	101.3	102.7	99.7	100.0	103.2	104.2	107.6	108.817	111.468
Niles-Benton Harbor, MI	99.8	103.8	103.0	103.1	102.7	105.6	108.1	104.6	100.0	106.0	100.9	97.0	103.042	104.141
North Port-Sarasota-Bradenton, FL	89.1	94.0	98.1	104.6	113.8	117.3	114.9	106.8	100.0	98.4	98.0	97.7	101.749	105.469
Norwich-New London, CT	81.1	88.0	92.9	102.3	104.2	110.6	113.2	111.4	100.0	98.8	92.4	89.6	88.102	88.729
Ocala, FL	83.8	86.9	93.8	101.2	110.0	118.7	118.1	111.6	100.0	99.3	97.8	96.6	98.098	101.601
Ocean City, NJ	85.3	91.4	97.4	101.6	105.5	99.1	96.8	99.5	100.0	99.1	99.8	100.6	101.293	98.821
Odessa, TX	73.5	73.1	73.0	74.2	80.2	90.7	104.5	106.5	100.0	105.0	124.7	145.8	155.15	164.911
Ogden-Clearfield, UT	79.3	82.7	85.3	89.3	92.3	99.2	101.5	99.2	100.0	103.4	104.5	102.4	106.807	110.958
Oklahoma City, OK	83.2	84.6	87.0	90.3	91.9	97.7	98.9	101.2	100.0	101.5	105.2	108.8	112.054	114.913
Olympia-Tumwater, WA	84.3	85.6	87.6	89.6	93.6	97.5	101.6	102.1	100.0	99.9	97.6	97.9	100.759	101.805
Omaha-Council Bluffs, NE-IA	84.9	87.8	91.4	94.6	96.2	99.4	100.8	100.3	100.0	102.5	104.7	107.8	110.898	113.596
Orlando-Kissimmee-Sanford, FL	81.1	84.8	89.6	95.6	103.6	108.0	110.1	105.8	100.0	101.0	100.1	101.0	103.313	106.82
Oshkosh-Neenah, WI	92.6	100.7	100.4	103.3	104.9	105.9	106.7	104.9	100.0	109.1	113.0	112.9	114.648	114.505
Owensboro, KY	88.7	93.2	97.1	95.3	96.5	102.2	97.1	99.1	100.0	101.9	104.0	109.4	116.165	114.509
Oxnard-Thousand Oaks-Ventura, CA	81.7	83.3	90.2	96.4	100.3	103.6	105.6	98.8	100.0	104.8	107.3	109.3	111.277	111.875
Palm Bay-Melbourne-Titusville, FL	77.1	80.9	86.3	95.6	100.4	102.2	105.6	104.0	100.0	100.3	95.4	93.1	93.706	94.667
Panama City, FL	78.1	82.5	87.8	92.7	100.3	102.6	103.1	102.7	100.0	101.6	98.0	93.7	95.785	100.274
Parkersburg-Vienna, WV	98.6	96.1	95.3	97.1	95.7	100.4	96.6	97.3	100.0	95.2	94.3	94.0	93.343	94.341
Pensacola-Ferry Pass-Brent, FL	93.9	93.7	96.3	103.8	104.4	108.6	108.0	103.1	100.0	102.3	102.8	101.3	103.054	105.466
Peoria, IL	80.2	80.4	83.2	89.5	94.6	100.6	103.2	105.3	100.0	101.1	110.7	118.7	106.369	105.133
Philadelphia-Camden-Wilmington, PA-NJ-DE-MD	89.0	90.6	93.5	95.8	97.2	98.7	100.3	101.3	100.0	101.1	101.6	102.8	104.12	105.295
Phoenix-Mesa-Scottsdale, AZ	85.0	87.7	92.8	96.3	104.2	110.3	112.8	109.6	100.0	101.2	104.0	107.0	108.166	110.091
Pine Bluff, AR	99.8	100.8	103.4	107.0	106.7	108.7	104.1	103.4	100.0	101.6	99.1	98.6	94.341	91.49
Pittsburgh, PA	99.1	99.9	101.6	102.4	102.2	102.5	102.9	102.7	100.0	103.5	105.9	107.1	109.286	112.496
Pittsfield, MA	100.8	107.3	110.8	113.0	112.6	108.4	102.2	100.8	100.0	96.0	99.4	103.9	103.84	104.074
Pocatello, ID	87.2	87.7	94.1	100.5	104.7	104.7	107.1	108.5	100.0	100.6	100.8	98.2	95.916	97.377
Portland-South Portland, ME	90.6	92.0	95.3	99.5	99.5	101.2	100.8	101.2	100.0	102.5	102.3	102.1	102.68	102.725
Portland-Vancouver-Hillsboro, OR-WA	66.2	67.0	69.5	76.9	79.0	87.4	92.1	99.0	100.0	107.5	113.9	113.6	111.673	116.525
Port St. Lucie, FL	78.4	83.8	88.6	99.8	111.0	115.2	116.6	106.4	100.0	99.9	98.1	96.6	96.325	97.394
Prescott, AZ	83.7	86.3	92.0	95.8	105.7	116.3	118.5	110.5	100.0	96.3	92.4	92.0	93.497	95.7
Providence-Warwick, RI-MA	92.6	95.5	99.8	103.0	103.4	105.7	103.4	101.9	100.0	101.8	102.2	103.0	104.717	106.304
Provo-Orem, UT	69.1	72.2	77.0	81.8	87.1	94.8	103.6	102.3	100.0	100.7	103.6	108.3	113.821	117.891

Quantity Indexes for Real GDP by Metropolitan Area—*Continued*

(2009 = 100.0)

Metropolitan Statistical Area	2001	2002	2003	2004	2005	2006	2007	2008	2009	2010	2011	2012	2013	2014
Pueblo, CO	99.0	97.6	97.6	101.4	95.3	94.8	97.0	98.5	100.0	99.2	100.8	102.1	101.431	104.615
Punta Gorda, FL	99.8	99.5	104.9	114.9	121.5	130.0	121.0	109.5	100.0	98.5	97.2	95.7	98.831	100.395
Racine, WI	108.2	109.3	111.3	114.1	110.7	113.2	110.8	104.1	100.0	108.1	105.9	108.1	105.756	104.319
Raleigh, NC	78.0	78.5	80.0	82.9	88.3	93.5	99.2	101.0	100.0	104.7	107.4	109.3	113.89	116.822
Rapid City, SD	81.6	90.8	91.4	92.9	94.6	95.7	97.7	99.8	100.0	103.5	106.2	106.9	106.003	107.407
Reading, PA	94.5	96.4	98.4	99.2	101.1	106.8	105.0	102.1	100.0	100.6	100.6	102.0	102.81	104.787
Redding, CA	99.0	109.9	114.7	116.9	119.5	118.8	115.4	107.2	100.0	100.1	100.8	98.9	99.38	101.222
Reno, NV	94.3	96.7	99.6	108.1	112.3	113.7	119.2	111.8	100.0	98.3	98.0	96.0	97.828	99.232
Richmond, VA	95.8	93.8	94.0	93.8	99.8	100.6	101.2	100.9	100.0	101.4	101.2	101.8	103.727	105.4
Riverside-San Bernardino-Ontario, CA	88.5	91.9	97.8	104.3	110.9	114.3	111.8	107.8	100.0	102.2	104.2	104.1	107.084	110.138
Roanoke, VA	92.6	92.5	94.3	95.8	98.5	101.2	102.5	102.0	100.0	98.3	97.2	96.5	97.8	99.078
Rochester, MN	83.4	90.3	99.1	102.3	102.0	102.8	101.8	101.2	100.0	106.6	104.3	105.1	105.914	106.518
Rochester, NY	96.1	98.5	100.5	102.8	104.1	105.1	101.7	99.3	100.0	101.4	100.5	101.7	102.135	101.1
Rockford, IL	100.4	101.8	102.8	105.0	106.8	111.4	112.7	108.7	100.0	103.1	106.9	110.4	107.822	108.896
Rocky Mount, NC	89.4	91.3	93.0	93.8	94.7	100.0	96.8	98.2	100.0	97.2	92.4	89.1	88.079	85.282
Rome, GA	101.5	101.9	104.3	110.3	104.0	104.4	103.2	103.3	100.0	99.4	97.7	97.4	97.83	98.583
Sacramento—Roseville—Arden-Arcade, CA	85.3	91.4	98.3	101.8	107.7	109.7	108.3	104.6	100.0	99.8	101.5	104.8	107.499	108.482
Saginaw, MI	115.7	116.5	119.3	116.6	117.7	118.2	112.6	104.4	100.0	105.7	107.0	104.9	107.201	107.195
St. Cloud, MN	92.0	96.1	99.1	104.9	105.7	104.9	102.4	102.4	100.0	102.0	102.9	103.5	104.684	106.157
St. George, UT	68.0	71.7	78.3	85.2	96.0	107.9	111.7	108.0	100.0	97.4	101.4	103.6	108.633	113.01
St. Joseph, MO-KS	83.0	83.9	85.6	89.4	89.0	94.3	98.6	97.8	100.0	102.3	101.5	105.7	106.833	108.606
St. Louis, MO-IL	95.0	97.0	99.1	100.1	101.3	100.7	100.8	102.9	100.0	100.5	100.8	101.8	102.239	103.999
Salem, OR	84.8	88.7	91.8	94.2	95.3	100.5	99.6	102.6	100.0	96.7	93.8	93.0	94.786	97.02
Salinas, CA	93.9	99.9	103.1	99.0	104.5	108.3	100.9	98.7	100.0	98.6	95.5	97.7	101.714	102.284
Salisbury, MD-DE	82.3	82.0	87.2	94.3	100.7	105.5	109.7	104.0	100.0	98.9	95.3	92.4	94.358	94.872
Salt Lake City, UT	82.5	83.2	83.1	86.2	91.2	98.3	104.7	102.2	100.0	101.4	104.3	105.7	109.252	111.607
San Angelo, TX	94.2	95.0	97.7	100.3	99.9	99.4	99.4	101.4	100.0	102.5	107.2	112.1	118.124	131.55
San Antonio-New Braunfels, TX	85.0	85.1	87.9	90.5	93.3	97.8	100.7	101.6	100.0	104.1	108.9	114.1	119.529	124.049
San Diego-Carlsbad, CA	84.0	88.8	92.5	96.9	100.6	102.5	103.9	103.7	100.0	100.1	102.7	106.0	107.898	109.392
San Francisco-Oakland-Hayward, CA	88.8	88.5	90.1	92.2	96.5	99.2	101.6	104.2	100.0	99.7	99.5	105.4	107.717	113.266
San Jose-Sunnyvale-Santa Clara, CA	84.1	79.3	82.3	86.5	91.7	97.7	105.1	106.3	100.0	110.1	118.2	121.3	129.094	137.776
San Luis Obispo-Paso Robles-Arroyo Grande, CA	86.0	96.3	101.8	106.7	110.8	110.0	108.5	104.5	100.0	103.3	103.6	105.4	108.861	111.613
Santa Cruz-Watsonville, CA	116.2	114.8	114.1	112.4	113.5	114.4	109.5	104.0	100.0	99.1	98.8	101.1	105.001	106.647
Santa Fe, NM	94.0	105.7	99.9	100.2	103.0	107.5	107.5	108.4	100.0	98.3	97.9	96.2	99.447	96.999
Santa Maria-Santa Barbara, CA	86.8	90.0	93.4	96.0	102.0	102.0	100.7	100.7	100.0	100.3	103.7	106.4	108.338	108.499
Santa Rosa, CA	101.5	104.8	105.8	107.1	111.5	111.1	108.0	106.9	100.0	102.4	105.8	104.8	107.792	111.38
Savannah, GA	87.0	87.6	89.4	94.2	98.6	104.0	104.9	102.3	100.0	101.0	101.8	103.6	105.174	109.117
Scranton—Wilkes-Barre—Hazleton, PA	97.9	97.2	99.4	103.0	103.8	104.4	105.4	101.9	100.0	102.9	102.9	102.0	103.084	103.941
Seattle-Tacoma-Bellevue, WA	82.8	83.4	84.4	86.0	91.0	94.9	101.7	103.4	100.0	102.9	105.3	109.4	112.197	116.001
Sebastian-Vero Beach, FL	81.1	84.6	93.0	105.0	109.7	111.8	114.7	108.4	100.0	95.6	93.4	95.1	95.076	100.412
Sebring, FL	87.5	94.3	99.9	106.2	110.3	117.9	112.4	102.3	100.0	100.7	97.0	95.0	94.579	93.006
Sheboygan, WI	92.3	94.9	97.9	101.9	101.4	102.8	103.0	105.0	100.0	97.5	98.1	98.6	101.045	104.384
Sherman-Denison, TX	84.8	86.1	89.3	94.1	95.9	101.0	100.8	101.7	100.0	102.7	105.4	105.8	111.039	111.414
Shreveport-Bossier City, LA	87.3	88.9	90.9	95.5	96.7	101.7	96.5	99.9	100.0	106.3	108.8	107.0	100.994	104.073
Sierra Vista-Douglas, AZ	80.3	80.1	82.5	85.8	91.7	94.0	97.3	97.4	100.0	103.0	101.8	96.1	91.538	88.976
Sioux City, IA-NE-SD	87.5	90.8	89.5	92.2	92.2	94.4	95.9	99.5	100.0	101.9	100.1	97.5	103.643	103.753
Sioux Falls, SD	74.5	87.4	87.6	89.9	92.1	93.8	96.5	99.0	100.0	102.1	108.0	111.3	112.968	114.911
South Bend-Mishawaka, IN-MI	93.3	97.2	101.9	106.2	105.2	106.6	107.1	107.2	100.0	104.0	106.9	103.6	101.726	102.435
Spartanburg, SC	96.3	99.9	103.6	103.1	104.6	108.4	110.3	110.3	100.0	106.3	111.2	111.2	113.877	115.75
Spokane-Spokane Valley, WA	87.1	87.4	89.6	91.7	96.0	99.4	102.5	103.0	100.0	100.3	100.9	101.7	103.095	105.243
Springfield, IL	103.7	102.6	99.9	98.7	98.4	98.6	98.8	97.8	100.0	99.0	99.7	97.6	98.855	99.326
Springfield, MA	95.9	96.4	98.3	99.7	100.5	100.8	101.9	102.6	100.0	101.0	101.7	102.1	102.88	104.05
Springfield, MO	86.6	85.7	91.2	95.0	99.4	100.8	101.0	100.9	100.0	101.8	101.9	102.4	104.305	105.969
Springfield, OH	114.7	111.8	108.6	111.7	111.7	115.0	110.1	107.0	100.0	100.0	104.5	106.9	107.669	105.671
State College, PA	82.9	85.2	86.5	90.0	93.7	95.5	97.7	98.4	100.0	101.8	104.1	104.2	107.717	111.892
Staunton-Waynesboro, VA	97.6	93.4	96.1	99.2	104.3	103.2	98.8	100.0	100.0	100.9	98.8	98.3	101.702	100.672
Stockton-Lodi, CA	85.6	92.1	97.7	101.3	104.9	106.4	106.3	102.2	100.0	99.7	100.5	102.8	104.517	104.832
Sumter, SC	97.0	99.1	101.4	104.3	106.1	107.9	107.2	103.4	100.0	100.0	103.2	110.9	110.357	112.963
Syracuse, NY	92.9	94.7	95.9	98.3	100.0	100.8	101.7	100.1	100.0	102.9	102.1	104.2	103.339	103.602
Tallahassee, FL	100.3	96.0	97.7	99.3	100.4	101.8	105.6	103.4	100.0	99.6	96.8	94.7	95.438	96.527
Tampa-St. Petersburg-Clearwater, FL	86.1	90.7	94.8	99.5	104.6	108.1	108.7	104.5	100.0	99.4	99.2	101.9	104.488	107.264
Terre Haute, IN	89.7	92.5	97.8	101.1	99.2	101.6	107.6	107.2	100.0	106.0	104.0	101.5	104.417	100.242
Texarkana, TX-AR	86.6	88.8	92.4	97.0	98.7	100.7	102.1	101.9	100.0	101.3	100.5	99.8	96.031	95.052
The Villages, FL	56.5	56.7	66.7	72.3	86.3	94.4	100.3	96.5	100.0	110.1	114.3	112.3	120.682	123.841
Toledo, OH	99.3	101.6	103.2	104.9	105.4	105.9	105.0	101.0	100.0	100.7	103.6	103.1	105.907	112.211
Topeka, KS	99.1	98.5	98.1	98.8	98.3	96.6	99.7	101.1	100.0	99.0	101.1	99.8	99.795	99.859
Trenton, NJ	86.7	89.7	95.5	97.6	100.2	103.4	101.7	102.4	100.0	103.8	103.6	108.5	111.684	111.324
Tucson, AZ	88.4	87.7	93.0	94.8	100.3	104.3	109.2	107.7	100.0	101.2	99.9	101.5	100.829	101.329
Tulsa, OK	85.4	85.9	85.1	87.6	92.3	97.4	98.6	104.6	100.0	99.1	102.0	105.4	106.146	110.03
Tuscaloosa, AL	78.0	80.5	84.6	90.0	95.1	96.0	100.3	99.9	100.0	103.9	105.4	102.4	105.613	106.098

Quantity Indexes for Real GDP by Metropolitan Area—*Continued*

(2009 = 100.0)

Metropolitan Statistical Area	2001	2002	2003	2004	2005	2006	2007	2008	2009	2010	2011	2012	2013	2014
Tyler, TX	81.5	82.2	83.6	89.1	90.7	92.8	93.8	103.3	100.0	102.6	106.2	110.5	115.432	122.638
Urban Honolulu, HI	81.4	83.6	87.1	92.7	96.9	98.7	101.1	102.9	100.0	104.4	105.6	106.9	108.147	109.256
Utica-Rome, NY	93.1	94.3	95.3	98.0	99.8	100.6	100.3	99.0	100.0	102.4	101.9	102.7	103.01	101.681
Valdosta, GA	87.1	84.0	87.9	88.1	90.6	92.3	93.2	98.5	100.0	97.0	95.0	94.6	96.281	99.304
Vallejo-Fairfield, CA	82.0	84.8	91.3	94.0	97.8	97.3	97.5	101.0	100.0	95.8	90.9	97.5	101.744	103.754
Victoria, TX	84.8	86.0	89.3	92.9	96.1	105.5	104.7	107.9	100.0	106.6	111.1	124.0	133.126	142.088
Vineland-Bridgeton, NJ	88.7	89.3	93.4	97.4	100.4	100.4	98.5	101.5	100.0	98.4	96.2	96.8	95.133	96.089
Virginia Beach-Norfolk-Newport News, VA-NC	82.1	84.6	88.3	90.9	94.6	97.5	99.8	99.3	100.0	99.9	100.5	101.5	101.709	101.564
Visalia-Porterville, CA	82.9	84.5	89.9	98.8	106.7	104.4	110.4	106.0	100.0	104.2	107.0	103.9	105.545	104.924
Waco, TX	80.3	81.6	86.6	90.8	93.6	96.2	97.6	98.6	100.0	104.7	103.1	107.1	110.558	113.311
Walla Walla, WA	83.2	83.2	87.5	85.4	86.6	91.5	93.9	99.8	100.0	100.3	97.4	95.5	95.166	95.191
Warner Robins, GA	83.6	87.6	90.3	91.4	95.1	97.2	98.7	97.7	100.0	102.2	103.6	102.5	100.373	98.701
Washington-Arlington-Alexandria, DC-VA-MD-WV	80.3	82.4	85.6	90.2	94.4	96.2	97.9	100.1	100.0	103.2	104.6	104.9	104.847	105.127
Waterloo-Cedar Falls, IA	81.3	86.1	86.2	96.6	99.4	99.7	102.6	103.0	100.0	100.6	98.6	113.5	112.689	111.805
Watertown-Fort Drum, NY	77.2	75.4	75.0	78.3	85.4	92.3	92.7	95.6	100.0	105.5	109.0	106.2	103.858	101.884
Wausau, WI	94.8	94.2	99.8	102.5	106.1	107.0	108.0	105.2	100.0	101.7	103.8	106.7	108.953	112.267
Weirton-Steubenville, WV-OH	108.5	115.1	111.0	108.8	110.0	100.7	103.0	107.0	100.0	96.4	93.1	98.7	97.229	97.867
Wenatchee, WA	81.1	87.0	91.3	93.2	95.5	98.3	96.8	100.6	100.0	96.2	94.7	97.4	100.22	103.924
Wheeling, WV-OH	85.6	87.6	89.9	92.2	93.7	94.2	94.3	97.9	100.0	100.9	100.3	100.8	107.206	117.381
Wichita, KS	97.0	96.2	94.7	93.8	95.5	105.5	112.5	110.1	100.0	103.8	107.2	108.7	101.05	103.276
Wichita Falls, TX	93.4	96.2	95.7	94.9	92.7	96.7	98.2	106.1	100.0	97.6	101.6	106.1	110.831	113.205
Williamsport, PA	102.8	101.2	101.6	104.2	104.7	104.5	103.3	101.5	100.0	105.2	114.4	119.0	121.75	126.46
Wilmington, NC	82.0	80.3	81.5	84.0	90.0	93.4	96.9	100.1	100.0	102.3	105.4	102.9	109.578	109.57
Winchester, VA-WV	86.4	86.1	91.5	95.2	101.7	104.8	101.6	97.7	100.0	104.2	105.6	105.8	108.35	107.193
Winston-Salem, NC	104.3	99.6	103.8	107.2	107.9	110.2	105.0	103.6	100.0	102.9	102.8	99.7	100.368	104.061
Worcester, MA-CT	97.0	97.3	101.4	101.9	102.3	103.6	104.4	104.4	100.0	103.3	104.4	103.6	105.508	107.158
Yakima, WA	84.1	87.7	90.7	91.9	96.6	97.7	98.0	100.9	100.0	100.6	98.5	100.7	102.18	102.462
York-Hanover, PA	85.4	85.4	90.5	93.8	99.5	100.2	101.3	104.1	100.0	102.2	100.7	97.7	98.973	99.637
Youngstown-Warren-Boardman, OH-PA	112.2	115.1	115.8	118.0	119.5	118.8	115.7	109.7	100.0	103.3	110.3	116.8	115.96	116.932
Yuba City, CA	79.8	86.0	91.3	93.6	94.9	97.6	95.2	97.3	100.0	95.9	95.0	94.7	96.752	97.111
Yuma, AZ	73.1	81.7	82.4	90.5	95.2	100.0	103.5	98.5	100.0	99.4	96.7	91.6	92.337	90.938

PART C
INCOME AND POVERTY BY STATE

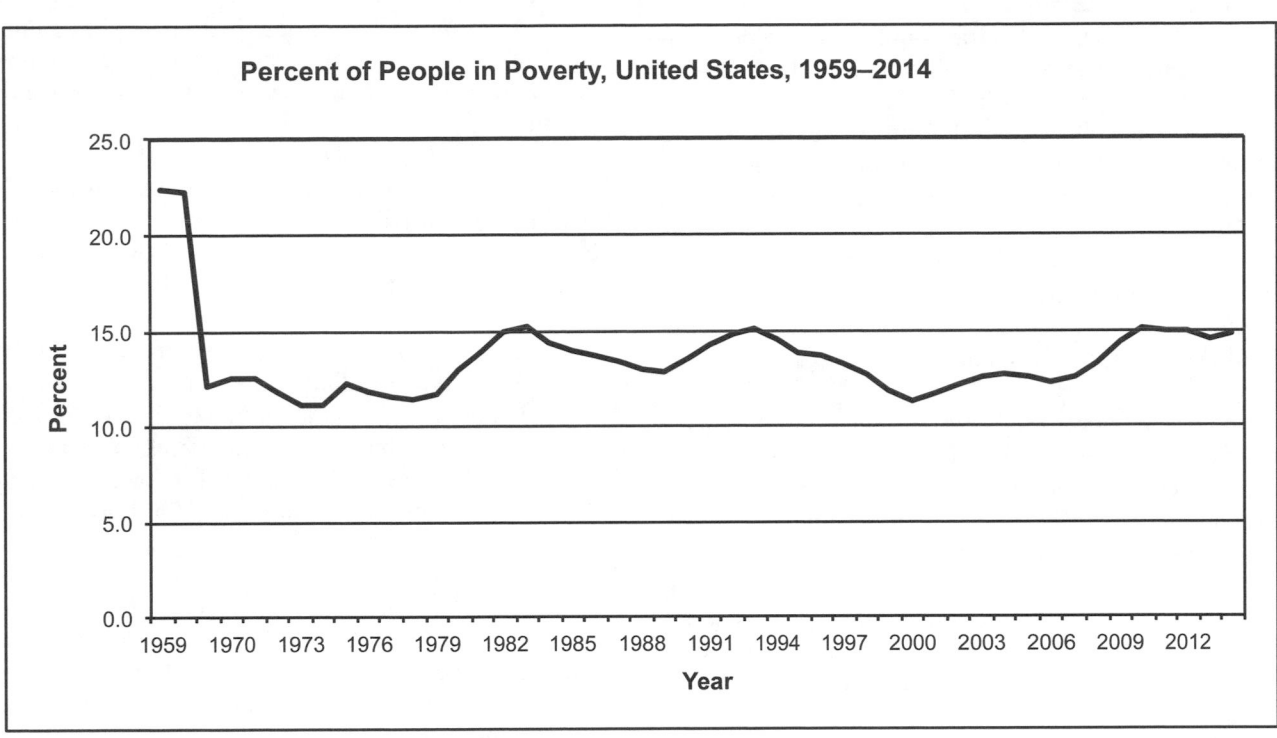

Percent of People in Poverty, United States, 1959–2014

HIGHLIGHTS:

- The percent of people in poverty in the United States increased slightly to 14.8 percent in 2014, up from 14.5 percent in 2013.

- The median household income in the United States increased 1.6 percent to $53,657 in 2014. The median income rose for the second year in a row, after declining for five consecutive years from 2008 through 2012.

- The South continued to have the highest poverty rate among U.S. regions at 16.5 percent, followed by the West at 15.2 percent, the Midwest at 13.0 percent, and the Northeast at 12.6 percent.

- In 2014 dollars, Maryland had the highest household median income at $76,165 in 2014, followed by New Hampshire at $73,397, Hawaii at $71,223, Connecticut at $70,161, and Washington, D.C., at $68,277. Mississippi and West Virginia had the lowest median household incomes at $35,521 and $39,552 respectively.

PART C NOTES AND DEFINITIONS: MEDIAN INCOME AND POVERTY

Source: U.S. Department of Commerce, Bureau of the Census, <http://www.census.gov>

These data are derived from the Current Population Survey (CPS), which is also the source of the widely followed monthly report on the civilian labor force, employment, and unemployment. In March of each year (with some data also collected in February and April), the households in this survey are asked additional questions concerning earnings and other income in the previous year. This additional information, informally known as the "March Supplement," is now formally known as the Current Population Survey Annual Social and Economic Supplement (CPS-ASEC). It was previously called the Annual Demographic Supplement.

The population represented by the income and poverty survey is the civilian noninstitutional population of the United States and members of the armed forces in the United States living off post or with their families on post, but excluding all other members of the armed forces. This is slightly different from the population base for the civilian employment and unemployment data, which excludes those armed forces households. As it is a survey of households, homeless persons are not included.

Definitions

A *household* consists of all persons who occupy a housing unit. A household includes the related family members and all the unrelated persons, if any (such as lodgers, foster children, wards, or employees), who share the housing unit. A person living alone in a housing unit or a group of unrelated persons sharing a housing unit as partners is also counted as a household. The count of households excludes group quarters.

Earnings includes all income from work, including wages, salaries, armed forces pay, commissions, tips, piece-rate payments, and cash bonuses, before deductions such as taxes, bonds, pensions, and union dues. This category also includes net income from farm and nonfarm self-employment. Wage and salary supplements that are paid directly by the employer, such as the employer share of Social Security taxes and the cost of employer-provided health insurance, are not included.

Income, in the official definition used in the survey, is money income, including *earnings* from work as defined above; unemployment compensation; workers' compensation; Social Security; Supplemental Security Income; cash public assistance (welfare payments); veterans' payments; survivor benefits; disability benefits; pension or retirement income; interest income; dividends (but not capital gains); rents, royalties, and payments from estates or trusts; educational assistance, such as scholarships or grants; child support; alimony; financial assistance from outside of the household; and other cash income regularly received, such as foster child payments, military family allotments, and foreign government pensions. Receipts not counted as income include capital gains or losses, withdrawals of bank deposits, money borrowed, tax refunds, gifts, and lump-sum inheritances or insurance payments.

Median income is the amount of income that divides a ranked income distribution into two equal groups, with half of the households having incomes above the median, and half having incomes below the median.

Historical income figures are shown in constant *2014 dollars*. All constant-dollar figures are converted from current-dollar values using the *CPI-U-RS* (the Consumer Price Index, All Urban, Research Series), compiled by the Bureau of Labor Statistics, which measures changes in prices for past periods using the methodologies of the current CPI-U.

The *number of people below poverty level,* or the number of poor people, is the number of people with family or individual incomes below a specified level representing the estimated cost of a minimum standard of living. These minimum levels vary by size and composition of family and are known as *poverty thresholds*. These poverty thresholds have been adjusted each year for price increases, using the percent change in the Consumer Price Index for All Urban Consumers (CPI-U).

The *poverty rate* for a demographic group is the number of poor people in that group expressed as a percentage of the total number of people in the group.

The data in this chapter were derived from the "Historical Income Tables" and "Historical Poverty Tables," which are available on the Census Web site.

A different set of estimates of median household income and poverty for states and smaller geographic units is also available. It is based on a different, more comprehensive Census survey, the American Community Survey (ACS); it is more precise but less timely, and it does not provide the historical record that is available in the CPS-ASEC data presented here. (The median household income data by state are available even farther back than shown here; they begin in 1984.) Further information on ACS and small-area statistics and on other research in measuring poverty can be found in the report referenced above and other reports posted on the Census website, under the subjects "Income" and "Poverty."

Median Household Income by State

(2014 dollars.)

State	1990	1991	1992	1993	1994	1995	1996	1997	1998	1999	2000	2001	2002
United States	52,623	51,086	50,667	50,421	51,006	52,604	53,345	54,443	56,445	57,843	57,724	56,466	55,807
Alabama	41,049	41,285	42,682	40,480	42,994	40,123	45,545	46,990	52,643	51,525	48,697	47,015	49,483
Alaska	69,064	68,868	69,133	69,287	71,721	74,028	79,328	70,610	73,584	73,051	72,649	76,705	69,447
Arizona	51,360	52,123	48,553	49,241	49,471	47,644	47,551	48,168	53,839	52,582	54,690	57,103	52,287
Arkansas	40,045	39,740	39,497	37,183	40,416	39,850	40,767	38,490	40,158	42,188	40,825	44,580	42,619
California	58,506	57,086	57,724	54,991	55,855	57,132	58,335	58,399	59,419	62,011	64,358	63,198	62,424
Colorado	54,012	53,415	53,723	55,661	59,811	62,839	61,549	63,606	67,642	68,476	66,316	66,053	63,551
Connecticut	68,312	71,483	67,544	63,776	64,971	62,124	63,306	64,712	67,510	71,909	68,972	71,334	70,253
Delaware	54,137	55,256	59,005	58,204	56,712	53,919	59,082	63,312	60,180	66,274	69,237	66,327	65,336
District of Columbia	48,140	50,678	50,023	44,067	47,611	47,466	48,046	46,874	48,531	54,963	56,668	55,050	51,413
Florida	46,898	46,213	45,231	46,077	46,311	45,918	46,054	47,749	50,673	50,928	53,415	48,701	50,037
Georgia	48,437	46,145	47,625	51,102	49,746	52,639	48,842	53,940	56,126	56,036	57,601	56,932	56,505
Hawaii	68,402	63,160	69,648	68,853	66,801	66,150	62,784	60,224	59,264	63,255	70,860	63,434	62,247
Idaho	44,472	44,286	45,818	50,048	49,856	50,443	52,168	49,145	53,244	50,884	51,704	51,135	49,630
Illinois	57,191	54,068	52,180	53,029	55,460	58,771	59,451	60,737	62,677	65,850	63,324	61,739	56,203
Indiana	47,325	45,936	47,184	47,570	44,041	51,537	52,827	57,215	57,673	58,044	56,177	53,994	54,015
Iowa	47,957	48,419	47,536	46,260	52,295	54,831	49,914	49,703	53,736	58,414	56,350	54,792	54,018
Kansas	52,578	49,677	50,187	48,046	44,775	46,838	48,976	53,657	53,289	53,084	56,444	55,379	56,084
Kentucky	43,550	40,298	38,840	39,341	42,044	46,018	48,718	49,216	52,623	47,953	49,854	51,397	48,376
Louisiana	39,376	42,901	42,072	42,465	40,591	43,145	45,485	48,933	46,066	46,412	42,228	44,557	44,752
Maine	48,267	47,257	48,981	44,283	47,927	52,267	52,149	48,215	51,735	55,236	51,230	48,957	48,496
Maryland	68,289	62,662	61,527	64,458	61,968	63,356	66,123	68,685	72,603	74,201	74,969	71,579	74,228
Massachusetts	63,702	60,562	60,132	59,818	64,027	59,547	59,360	61,826	61,467	62,546	64,272	69,872	65,606
Michigan	52,613	54,463	53,364	52,714	55,781	56,232	58,956	56,999	60,707	65,508	62,566	60,236	56,210
Minnesota	55,298	49,989	51,237	54,360	53,188	58,558	61,611	62,622	69,569	66,857	74,579	70,444	71,879
Mississippi	35,462	33,025	34,019	35,815	40,155	40,967	40,096	41,929	42,270	46,162	47,151	40,331	40,639
Missouri	48,035	47,356	45,250	46,290	47,728	53,760	51,501	53,778	58,355	58,819	61,995	55,278	56,290
Montana	41,080	42,101	43,868	42,720	43,682	42,849	43,113	42,978	45,837	44,115	45,059	42,958	45,840
Nebraska	48,298	50,108	49,694	50,044	50,263	50,833	51,124	51,040	52,857	54,900	57,394	58,316	56,316
Nevada	56,279	55,853	52,770	57,801	56,709	55,704	57,927	57,163	57,709	58,930	62,904	60,712	59,162
New Hampshire	71,713	61,102	65,220	61,271	55,719	60,469	59,230	60,318	65,260	65,459	70,008	68,639	72,799
New Jersey	68,073	67,913	64,499	65,364	66,841	67,806	71,346	70,650	72,327	70,689	69,292	69,227	71,808
New Mexico	44,005	45,005	42,768	43,185	42,534	40,123	37,705	44,264	45,787	46,298	48,242	44,293	46,659
New York	55,520	53,915	51,353	51,156	50,429	50,986	53,222	52,667	54,281	56,838	56,011	56,314	55,224
North Carolina	46,272	45,536	45,928	46,513	47,607	49,367	53,509	52,729	52,022	52,950	52,675	51,029	48,051
North Dakota	44,400	43,907	44,586	45,380	44,705	44,905	47,300	46,581	43,989	46,425	49,484	47,862	47,637
Ohio	52,746	50,517	51,937	50,492	50,360	53,939	51,208	53,162	56,503	56,127	59,060	55,874	56,169
Oklahoma	42,854	43,177	41,815	42,382	42,670	40,617	41,238	46,125	48,958	46,453	44,584	47,616	47,976
Oregon	51,460	51,195	52,802	53,482	49,729	56,151	53,345	54,799	56,709	57,733	58,424	55,189	55,008
Pennsylvania	50,975	51,495	49,420	50,023	50,693	53,295	52,454	55,196	56,634	53,667	57,979	58,166	55,924
Rhode Island	56,182	52,290	50,329	54,081	50,475	54,584	55,591	51,195	59,059	60,718	58,008	61,140	55,818
South Carolina	50,500	46,571	45,609	42,047	47,184	44,877	52,102	50,407	48,290	51,825	51,648	50,460	49,758
South Dakota	43,182	41,782	43,428	44,765	47,005	45,660	44,378	43,687	47,592	50,923	50,142	53,047	49,838
Tennessee	39,704	41,466	40,218	40,513	45,276	44,791	46,278	45,073	49,486	51,910	46,872	47,848	48,729
Texas	49,609	47,028	46,229	46,363	48,621	49,459	49,708	51,604	51,942	54,989	53,076	54,637	52,833
Utah	52,973	47,508	56,645	57,756	56,464	56,315	55,669	62,932	64,304	65,452	65,367	63,305	62,982
Vermont	54,653	49,440	54,171	50,136	56,600	52,215	48,635	51,571	57,152	59,105	54,430	54,549	56,584
Virginia	61,639	61,280	63,173	58,800	59,516	55,917	58,935	63,200	62,932	64,945	64,835	67,181	65,311
Washington	56,435	57,605	56,065	57,544	53,013	54,907	55,125	65,561	68,836	64,632	58,459	56,817	59,458
West Virginia	38,905	39,252	33,525	36,186	37,253	38,408	37,947	40,441	38,763	41,641	40,431	39,678	38,634
Wisconsin	53,973	52,794	55,086	51,268	55,945	63,223	60,123	58,254	59,990	64,908	61,983	60,636	60,405
Wyoming	51,775	49,262	49,960	47,517	52,391	48,672	46,523	49,173	51,168	52,942	54,478	53,111	52,325

Median Household Income by State—*Continued*

(2014 dollars.)

State	2003	2004	2005	2006	2007	2008	2009	2010	2011	2012	2013	2014
United States	55,759	55,565	56,160	56,598	57,357	55,313	54,925	53,507	52,690	52,605	52,789	53,657
Alabama	47,954	45,908	45,036	44,563	48,199	48,905	44,115	44,447	44,833	44,817	42,058	42,278
Alaska	66,724	69,012	67,755	66,246	71,927	70,362	67,975	62,814	60,456	65,629	62,137	67,629
Arizona	52,989	54,954	54,849	54,785	53,911	51,586	50,470	50,922	51,182	48,508	51,430	49,254
Arkansas	41,193	43,847	44,439	43,513	46,581	43,528	40,317	41,900	43,477	40,233	40,572	44,922
California	63,459	61,692	62,741	64,956	63,638	62,692	61,940	58,943	56,177	58,795	58,469	60,487
Colorado	64,283	63,777	61,158	65,400	69,812	67,012	61,715	65,404	61,717	59,037	64,408	60,940
Connecticut	70,751	69,059	68,899	73,275	73,238	71,124	71,558	71,665	68,860	66,247	68,890	70,161
Delaware	63,097	60,221	62,111	61,573	62,331	55,751	57,504	59,955	57,539	50,496	53,074	57,522
District of Columbia	57,980	54,459	54,544	56,922	57,985	61,126	58,637	61,816	58,161	67,277	61,668	68,277
Florida	50,165	50,804	52,115	53,633	52,289	49,324	50,350	47,850	47,480	47,505	48,670	46,140
Georgia	54,626	51,367	55,675	57,940	55,540	50,831	47,823	47,905	48,394	49,619	48,215	49,555
Hawaii	66,720	70,490	72,234	71,004	73,102	67,648	61,405	64,651	62,157	58,014	62,413	71,223
Idaho	54,541	55,595	53,553	54,264	56,160	52,143	51,616	51,090	49,958	49,414	52,614	53,438
Illinois	58,121	57,750	58,671	57,150	59,953	58,558	58,338	55,083	53,304	53,349	58,132	54,916
Indiana	54,609	53,052	51,445	53,317	54,183	51,153	48,887	50,101	46,786	47,595	51,380	48,060
Iowa	53,269	54,383	56,371	56,510	55,844	55,136	55,967	53,224	52,864	55,106	55,753	57,810
Kansas	56,935	51,469	50,948	53,487	55,375	52,645	49,342	50,008	48,577	51,560	52,328	53,444
Kentucky	47,544	44,631	44,489	46,364	45,047	45,246	47,077	44,633	41,955	42,365	42,848	42,786
Louisiana	43,130	45,658	45,140	42,844	47,172	43,503	50,132	42,675	42,799	40,302	40,270	42,406
Maine	47,772	51,799	53,246	53,593	54,687	51,931	52,415	52,046	52,310	50,688	50,941	51,710
Maryland	67,338	71,569	73,357	74,759	74,938	70,056	70,825	69,713	72,503	74,072	66,330	76,165
Massachusetts	65,589	65,197	67,908	64,969	66,755	66,327	65,514	66,165	66,647	65,638	63,993	63,151
Michigan	57,952	52,961	55,683	57,122	56,372	54,746	50,751	50,249	51,453	51,572	49,600	52,005
Minnesota	67,993	70,317	65,723	66,003	66,292	60,395	61,891	56,814	60,865	63,719	61,904	67,244
Mississippi	42,127	43,560	39,853	40,784	42,566	40,076	38,706	41,436	43,254	37,782	41,518	35,521
Missouri	56,330	52,812	52,111	52,345	52,530	50,623	53,813	49,750	48,185	51,313	51,134	56,630
Montana	43,904	42,558	45,233	48,266	49,846	47,172	44,619	44,824	42,398	46,492	44,854	51,102
Nebraska	56,603	54,878	58,096	56,532	56,148	55,780	54,724	57,012	58,545	53,821	54,654	56,870
Nevada	58,161	59,162	58,442	61,390	61,725	60,196	56,754	55,596	49,520	48,806	46,111	49,875
New Hampshire	71,526	71,208	69,080	72,766	77,160	72,766	70,764	72,354	69,349	69,930	72,489	73,397
New Jersey	72,141	69,278	76,819	79,915	69,090	71,810	71,477	68,374	65,621	68,768	62,793	65,243
New Mexico	45,187	49,584	47,214	47,001	50,647	46,295	48,045	49,010	44,193	44,776	42,816	46,686
New York	55,076	55,960	57,190	56,623	55,885	55,486	55,410	54,055	53,303	49,164	54,724	54,310
North Carolina	47,985	50,432	50,983	46,730	49,684	47,205	46,240	47,593	47,587	42,847	41,882	46,784
North Dakota	52,016	49,156	51,148	48,198	53,900	54,574	55,254	55,385	59,329	57,502	53,753	60,730
Ohio	56,019	53,962	53,586	53,896	56,062	51,608	50,624	49,825	46,999	45,756	47,157	49,644
Oklahoma	46,213	49,650	45,636	45,604	49,345	50,703	50,623	46,804	51,007	49,914	44,493	47,199
Oregon	53,596	51,379	53,533	55,295	57,361	56,878	54,176	54,946	54,240	53,387	57,228	58,875
Pennsylvania	55,263	55,280	56,128	56,922	55,307	56,521	53,154	52,462	52,538	53,520	54,835	55,173
Rhode Island	57,552	60,079	59,988	63,097	61,898	58,543	56,974	56,055	51,615	57,810	58,758	58,633
South Carolina	49,530	48,493	48,770	46,519	50,484	46,353	45,352	45,278	42,195	45,783	44,465	44,929
South Dakota	50,873	51,521	52,311	53,341	53,001	56,739	50,566	49,246	49,710	50,953	55,344	53,053
Tennessee	48,299	47,717	47,771	47,782	47,037	43,656	44,708	41,905	44,506	44,333	43,194	43,716
Texas	50,549	51,884	50,215	50,851	52,584	51,120	52,385	51,324	51,630	53,542	53,895	53,875
Utah	63,427	63,758	66,448	64,145	61,121	68,765	64,541	61,569	58,415	60,157	63,997	63,383
Vermont	55,685	59,319	61,467	61,036	54,111	55,756	57,729	60,730	54,593	57,312	55,739	60,708
Virginia	70,516	64,097	62,934	67,070	67,552	68,158	66,758	65,550	65,914	66,644	68,727	66,155
Washington	61,152	62,569	61,397	64,256	66,317	62,271	66,638	60,985	59,844	64,123	61,090	59,068
West Virginia	42,172	41,827	44,181	45,112	48,061	41,778	44,678	46,450	44,023	44,909	40,900	39,552
Wisconsin	59,557	57,317	54,128	60,697	58,549	56,299	56,536	54,674	54,800	54,731	56,162	58,080
Wyoming	54,777	56,898	54,210	55,236	55,657	58,649	57,897	56,683	57,380	59,302	56,612	55,690

Poverty Rate by State

(Percent of population.)

State	2000	2001	2002	2003	2004	2005	2006	2007	2008	2009	2010	2011	2012	2013	2014
United States	11.3	11.7	12.1	12.5	12.7	12.6	12.3	12.5	13.2	14.3	15.1	15.0	15.0	14.5	14.8
Alabama	13.3	15.9	14.5	15.0	16.9	16.7	14.3	14.5	14.3	16.6	17.2	15.4	16.2	16.7	17.8
Alaska	7.6	8.5	8.8	9.6	9.1	10.0	8.9	7.6	8.2	11.7	12.5	11.7	10.0	10.9	11.9
Arizona	11.7	14.6	13.5	13.5	14.4	15.2	14.4	14.3	18.0	21.2	18.8	17.2	19.0	20.2	21.2
Arkansas	16.5	17.8	19.8	17.8	15.1	13.8	17.7	13.8	15.3	18.9	15.3	18.7	20.1	17.1	18.4
California	12.7	12.6	13.1	13.1	13.2	13.2	12.2	12.7	14.6	15.3	16.3	16.9	15.9	14.9	15.8
Colorado	9.8	8.7	9.8	9.7	10.0	11.4	9.7	9.8	11.0	12.3	12.3	13.2	11.9	10.6	12.3
Connecticut	7.7	7.3	8.3	8.1	10.1	9.3	8.0	8.9	8.1	8.4	8.6	10.1	10.3	11.3	8.6
Delaware	8.4	6.7	9.1	7.3	9.0	9.2	9.3	9.3	9.6	12.3	12.2	13.7	13.5	14.0	11.0
D.C	15.2	18.2	17.0	16.8	17.0	21.3	18.3	18.0	16.5	17.9	19.5	19.9	18.4	21.3	19.0
Florida	11.0	12.7	12.6	12.7	11.6	11.1	11.5	12.5	13.1	14.6	16.0	14.9	15.3	14.9	16.7
Georgia	12.1	12.9	11.2	11.9	13.0	14.4	12.6	13.6	15.5	18.4	18.8	18.4	18.1	16.3	16.8
Hawaii	8.9	11.4	11.3	9.3	8.6	8.6	9.2	7.5	9.9	12.5	12.4	12.1	13.8	11.1	10.8
Idaho	12.5	11.5	11.3	10.2	9.9	9.9	9.5	9.9	12.2	13.7	13.8	15.7	14.4	12.9	12.4
Illinois	10.7	10.1	12.8	12.6	12.3	11.5	10.6	10.0	12.3	13.2	14.1	14.2	12.6	13.3	13.7
Indiana	8.5	8.5	9.1	9.9	11.6	12.6	10.6	11.8	14.3	16.1	16.3	15.6	15.2	11.6	14.6
Iowa	8.3	7.4	9.2	8.9	10.9	11.3	10.3	8.9	9.5	10.7	10.3	10.4	10.3	10.8	10.3
Kansas	8.0	10.1	10.1	10.8	11.4	12.5	12.8	11.7	12.7	13.7	14.5	14.3	14.0	13.2	12.1
Kentucky	12.6	12.6	14.2	14.4	17.8	14.8	16.8	15.5	17.1	17.0	17.7	16.0	17.9	20.0	20.0
Louisiana	17.2	16.2	17.5	17.0	16.8	18.3	17.0	16.1	18.2	14.3	21.5	21.1	21.1	19.2	23.1
Maine	10.1	10.3	13.4	11.6	11.6	12.6	10.2	10.9	12.0	11.4	12.6	13.4	12.8	12.3	14.6
Maryland	7.4	7.2	7.4	8.6	9.9	9.7	8.4	8.8	8.7	9.6	10.9	9.3	9.9	10.3	9.9
Massachusetts	9.8	8.9	10.0	10.3	9.3	10.1	12.0	11.2	11.3	10.8	10.9	10.6	11.3	11.9	13.6
Michigan	9.9	9.4	11.6	11.4	13.3	12.0	13.3	10.8	13.0	14.0	15.7	15.0	13.7	14.5	14.8
Minnesota	5.7	7.4	6.5	7.4	7.0	8.1	8.2	9.3	9.9	11.1	10.8	10.0	10.0	12.0	8.3
Mississippi	14.9	19.3	18.4	16.0	18.7	20.1	20.6	22.6	18.1	23.1	22.5	17.4	22.0	22.5	22.1
Missouri	9.2	9.7	9.9	10.7	12.2	11.6	11.4	12.8	13.3	15.5	15.0	15.4	15.2	13.7	10.4
Montana	14.1	13.3	13.5	15.1	14.2	13.8	13.5	13.0	12.9	13.5	14.5	16.5	13.4	14.5	12.0
Nebraska	8.6	9.4	10.6	9.8	9.5	9.5	10.2	9.9	10.6	9.9	10.2	10.2	12.2	11.0	11.8
Nevada	8.8	7.1	8.9	10.9	10.9	10.6	9.5	9.7	10.8	13.0	16.6	15.5	15.8	17.4	17.0
New Hampshire	4.5	6.5	5.8	5.8	5.5	5.6	5.4	5.8	7.0	7.8	6.5	7.6	8.1	9.0	7.2
New Jersey	7.3	8.1	7.9	8.6	8.0	6.8	8.8	8.7	9.2	9.3	11.1	11.4	9.3	11.1	11.3
New Mexico	17.5	18.0	17.9	18.1	16.5	17.9	16.9	14.0	19.3	19.3	18.3	22.2	20.4	21.7	20.0
New York	13.9	14.2	14.0	14.3	15.0	14.5	14.0	14.5	14.2	15.8	16.0	16.0	17.2	14.5	14.0
North Carolina	12.5	12.5	14.3	15.7	14.6	13.1	13.8	15.5	13.9	16.9	17.4	15.4	17.2	18.6	17.1
North Dakota	10.4	13.8	11.6	9.7	9.7	11.2	11.4	9.3	11.8	10.9	12.6	9.9	11.4	9.9	9.7
Ohio	10.0	10.5	9.8	10.9	11.6	12.3	12.1	12.8	13.7	13.3	15.4	15.1	15.4	13.7	15.6
Oklahoma	14.9	15.1	14.1	12.8	10.8	15.6	15.2	13.4	13.6	12.9	16.3	13.9	18.0	14.0	17.3
Oregon	10.9	11.8	10.9	12.5	11.8	12.0	11.8	12.8	10.6	13.4	14.3	14.4	13.5	15.1	14.4
Pennsylvania	8.6	9.6	9.5	10.5	11.4	11.2	11.3	10.4	11.0	11.1	12.2	12.6	13.9	12.4	12.5
Rhode Island	10.2	9.6	11.0	11.5	11.5	12.1	10.5	9.5	12.7	13.0	14.0	13.4	13.6	13.5	11.3
South Carolina	11.1	15.1	14.3	12.7	14.9	15.0	11.2	14.1	14.0	13.7	16.9	19.0	16.7	15.9	16.5
South Dakota	10.7	8.4	11.5	12.7	13.5	11.8	10.7	9.4	13.1	14.1	13.6	14.5	12.8	10.3	12.8
Tennessee	13.5	14.1	14.8	14.0	15.9	14.9	14.9	14.8	15.0	16.5	16.7	16.3	18.6	18.1	17.3
Texas	15.5	14.9	15.6	17.0	16.5	16.2	16.4	16.5	15.9	17.3	18.4	17.4	17.0	16.8	16.4
Utah	7.6	10.5	9.9	9.1	10.1	9.2	9.3	9.6	7.6	9.7	10.0	11.0	11.0	8.3	10.2
Vermont	10.0	9.7	9.9	8.5	7.8	7.6	7.8	9.9	9.0	9.4	10.8	11.6	11.2	8.7	9.3
Virginia	8.3	8.0	9.9	10.0	9.4	9.2	8.6	8.6	10.3	10.7	10.7	11.4	10.6	10.4	10.2
Washington	10.8	10.7	11.0	12.6	11.4	10.2	8.0	10.2	10.4	11.7	11.6	12.5	11.6	12.0	12.0
West Virginia	14.7	16.4	16.8	17.4	14.2	15.4	15.3	14.8	14.5	15.8	16.8	17.5	16.7	17.3	20.6
Wisconsin	9.3	7.9	8.6	9.8	12.4	10.2	10.1	11.0	9.8	10.8	10.1	13.1	11.4	11.0	10.9
Wyoming	10.8	8.7	9.0	9.8	10.0	10.6	10.0	10.9	10.1	9.2	9.6	10.7	9.6	11.8	9.7

Number and Percent of People in Poverty by Region

(Numbers in thousands, percent.)

Year	All Regions Below Poverty		Northeast Below Poverty		Midwest Below Poverty		South Below Poverty		West Below Poverty	
	Number	Percent	Number	Percent	Number	Percent	Number	Percent	Number	Percent
1959	39,490	22.4	...	...	...	...	19,116	35.4	...	...
1960	39,851	22.2	...	...	...	...	...	...	...	...
1969	24,147	12.1	4,108	8.6	5,424	9.6	11,090	17.9	3,525	10.4
1970	25,420	12.6	...	...	...	...	11,480	18.5	...	...
1971	25,559	12.5	4,512	9.3	5,764	10.3	11,182	17.5	4,101	11.4
1972	24,460	11.9	4,266	8.7	5,258	9.3	10,928	16.9	4,008	11.1
1973	22,973	11.1	4,207	8.6	4,864	8.6	10,061	15.3	3,841	10.5
1974	23,370	11.2	4,473	9.3	4,990	8.8	10,761	16.1	4,036	10.7
1975	25,877	12.3	4,904	10.2	5,459	9.7	11,059	16.2	4,454	11.7
1976	24,975	11.8	4,949	10.2	5,657	9.9	10,354	15.2	4,015	10.5
1977	24,720	11.6	4,956	10.2	5,589	9.8	10,249	14.8	3,927	10.1
1978	24,497	11.4	5,050	10.4	5,192	9.1	10,255	14.7	4,000	10.0
1979	26,072	11.7	5,029	10.4	5,594	9.7	10,627	15.0	4,095	10.0
1980	29,272	13.0	5,369	11.1	6,592	11.4	12,363	16.5	4,958	11.4
1981	31,822	14.0	5,815	11.9	7,142	12.3	13,256	17.4	5,609	12.7
1982	34,398	15.0	6,364	13.0	7,772	13.3	13,967	18.1	6,296	14.1
1983	35,303	15.2	6,561	13.4	8,536	14.6	13,484	17.2	6,684	14.7
1984	33,700	14.4	6,531	13.2	8,303	14.1	12,792	16.2	6,074	13.1
1985	33,064	14.0	5,751	11.6	8,191	13.9	12,921	16.0	6,201	13.0
1986	32,370	13.6	5,211	10.5	7,641	13.0	13,106	16.1	6,412	13.2
1987	32,221	13.4	5,476	11.0	7,499	12.7	13,287	16.1	6,285	12.6
1988	31,745	13.0	5,089	10.1	6,804	11.4	13,530	16.1	6,322	12.7
1989	31,528	12.8	5,061	10.0	7,043	11.9	12,943	15.4	6,481	12.5
1990	33,585	13.5	5,794	11.4	7,458	12.4	13,456	15.8	6,877	13.0
1991	35,708	14.2	6,177	12.2	7,989	13.2	13,783	16.0	7,759	14.3
1992	38,014	14.8	6,414	12.6	8,060	13.3	15,198	17.1	8,343	14.8
1993	39,265	15.1	6,839	13.3	8,172	13.4	15,375	17.1	8,879	15.6
1994	38,059	14.5	6,597	12.9	7,965	13.0	14,729	16.1	8,768	15.3
1995	36,425	13.8	6,445	12.5	6,785	11.0	14,458	15.7	8,736	14.9
1996	36,529	13.7	6,558	12.7	6,654	10.7	14,098	15.1	9,219	15.4
1997	35,574	13.3	6,474	12.6	6,493	10.4	13,748	14.6	8,858	14.6
1998	34,476	12.7	6,357	12.3	6,501	10.3	12,992	13.7	8,625	14.0
1999	32,791	11.9	5,814	11.0	6,250	9.8	12,744	13.2	7,982	12.7
2000	31,581	11.3	5,474	10.3	5,916	9.3	12,705	12.8	7,485	11.8
2001	32,907	11.7	5,687	10.7	5,966	9.4	13,515	13.5	7,739	12.1
2002	34,570	12.1	5,871	10.9	6,616	10.3	14,019	13.8	8,064	12.4
2003	35,861	12.5	6,052	11.3	6,932	10.7	14,548	14.1	8,329	12.6
2004	37,040	12.7	6,260	11.6	7,545	11.7	14,817	14.1	8,419	12.5
2005	36,950	12.6	6,103	11.3	7,419	11.4	14,854	14.0	8,573	12.6
2006	36,460	12.3	6,222	11.5	7,324	11.2	14,882	13.8	8,032	11.6
2007	37,276	12.5	6,166	11.4	7,237	11.1	15,501	14.2	8,372	12.0
2008	39,829	13.2	6,295	11.6	8,120	12.4	15,862	14.3	9,552	13.5
2009	43,569	14.3	6,650	12.2	8,768	13.3	17,609	15.7	10,542	14.8
2010	46,343	15.1	7,038	12.9	9,216	14.0	19,123	16.8	10,966	15.3
2011	46,247	15.0	7,208	13.1	9,221	14.0	18,380	16.0	11,437	15.8
2012	46,496	15.0	7,490	13.6	8,851	13.3	19,106	16.5	11,049	15.1
2013	45,318	14.5	7,046	12.7	8,590	12.9	18,870	16.1	10,812	14.7
2014	46,657	14.8	7,020	12.6	8,714	13.0	19,531	16.5	11,391	15.2

Metropolitan Statistical Areas, Metropolitan Divisions, and Components

Core based statistical area	State/County FIPS code	Title and Geographic Components
CBSA	FIPS	
10180		Abilene, TX
10180	48059	Callahan County
10180	48253	Jones County
10180	48441	Taylor County
10420		Akron, OH
10420	39133	Portage County
10420	39153	Summit County
10500		Albany, GA
10500	13007	Baker County
10500	13095	Dougherty County
10500	13177	Lee County
10500	13273	Terrell County
10500	13321	Worth County
10540		Albany, OR
10540	41043	Linn County
10580		Albany-Schenectady-Troy, NY
10580	36001	Albany County
10580	36083	Rensselaer County
10580	36091	Saratoga County
10580	36093	Schenectady County
10580	36095	Schoharie County
10740		Albuquerque, NM
10740	35001	Bernalillo County
10740	35043	Sandoval County
10740	35057	Torrance County
10740	35061	Valencia County
10780		Alexandria, LA
10780	22043	Grant Parish
10780	22079	Rapides Parish
10900		Allentown-Bethlehem-Easton, PA-NJ
10900	34041	Warren County
10900	42025	Carbon County
10900	42077	Lehigh County
10900	42095	Northampton County
11020		Altoona, PA
11020	42013	Blair County
11100		Amarillo, TX
11100	48011	Armstrong County
11100	48065	Carson County
11100	48359	Oldham County
11100	48375	Potter County
11100	48381	Randall County
11180		Ames, IA
11180	19169	Story County
11260		Anchorage, AK
11260	02020	Anchorage Municipality
11260	02170	Matanuska-Susitna Borough
11460		Ann Arbor, MI
11460	26161	Washtenaw County
11500		Anniston-Oxford-Jacksonville, AL
11500	01015	Calhoun County
11540		Appleton, WI
11540	55015	Calumet County
11540	55087	Outagamie County
11700		Asheville, NC
11700	37021	Buncombe County
11700	37087	Haywood County
11700	37089	Henderson County
11700	37115	Madison County
12020		Athens-Clarke County, GA
12020	13059	Clarke County
12020	13195	Madison County
12020	13219	Oconee County
12020	13221	Oglethorpe County
12060		Atlanta-Sandy Springs-Roswell, GA
12060	13013	Barrow County
12060	13015	Bartow County
12060	13035	Butts County
12060	13045	Carroll County
12060	13057	Cherokee County
12060	13063	Clayton County
12060	13067	Cobb County
12060	13077	Coweta County
12060	13085	Dawson County
12060	13089	DeKalb County
12060	13097	Douglas County
12060	13113	Fayette County
12060	13117	Forsyth County
12060	13121	Fulton County
12060	13135	Gwinnett County
12060	13143	Haralson County
12060	13149	Heard County
12060	13151	Henry County
12060	13159	Jasper County
12060	13171	Lamar County
12060	13199	Meriwether County
12060	13211	Morgan County
12060	13217	Newton County
12060	13223	Paulding County
12060	13227	Pickens County
12060	13231	Pike County
12060	13247	Rockdale County
12060	13255	Spalding County
12060	13297	Walton County
12100		Atlantic City-Hammonton, NJ
12100	34001	Atlantic County
12220		Auburn-Opelika, AL
12220	01081	Lee County
12260		Augusta-Richmond County, GA-SC
12260	13033	Burke County
12260	13073	Columbia County
12260	13181	Lincoln County
12260	13189	McDuffie County
12260	13245	Richmond County
12260	45003	Aiken County
12260	45037	Edgefield County
12420		Austin-Round Rock, TX
12420	48021	Bastrop County
12420	48055	Caldwell County
12420	48209	Hays County
12420	48453	Travis County
12420	48491	Williamson County
12540		Bakersfield, CA
12540	06029	Kern County
12580		Baltimore-Columbia-Towson, MD
12580	24003	Anne Arundel County
12580	24005	Baltimore County
12580	24013	Carroll County
12580	24025	Harford County
12580	24027	Howard County
12580	24035	Queen Anne's County
12580	24510	Baltimore city

Metropolitan Statistical Areas, Metropolitan Divisions, and Components—*Continued*

Core based statistical area	State/ County FIPS code	Title and Geographic Components	Core based statistical area	State/ County FIPS code	Title and Geographic Components
12620		Bangor, ME	14260	16001	Ada County
12620	23019	Penobscot County	14260	16015	Boise County
12700		Barnstable Town, MA	14260	16027	Canyon County
12700	25001	Barnstable County	14260	16045	Gem County
12940		Baton Rouge, LA	14260	16073	Owyhee County
12940	22005	Ascension Parish	14460		Boston-Cambridge-Newton, MA-NH
12940	22033	East Baton Rouge Parish	14460		Boston, MA Div 14454
12940	22037	East Feliciana Parish	14460	25021	Norfolk County
12940	22047	Iberville Parish	14460	25023	Plymouth County
12940	22063	Livingston Parish	14460	25025	Suffolk County
12940	22077	Pointe Coupee Parish	14460		Cambridge-Newton-Framingham, MA Div 15764
12940	22091	St. Helena Parish	14460	25009	Essex County
12940	22121	West Baton Rouge Parish	14460	25017	Middlesex County
12940	22125	West Feliciana Parish	14460		Rockingham County-Strafford County, NH Div 40484
12980		Battle Creek, MI	14460	33015	Rockingham County
12980	26025	Calhoun County	14460	33017	Strafford County
13020		Bay City, MI	14500		Boulder, CO
13020	26017	Bay County	14500	08013	Boulder County
13140		Beaumont-Port Arthur, TX	14540		Bowling Green, KY
13140	48199	Hardin County	14540	21003	Allen County
13140	48245	Jefferson County	14540	21031	Butler County
13140	48351	Newton County	14540	21061	Edmonson County
13140	48361	Orange County	14540	21227	Warren County
13220		Beckley, WV	14740		Bremerton-Silverdale, WA
13220	54019	Fayette County	14740	53035	Kitsap County
13220	54081	Raleigh County	14860		Bridgeport-Stamford-Norwalk, CT
13380		Bellingham, WA	14860	09001	Fairfield County
13380	53073	Whatcom County	15180		Brownsville-Harlingen, TX
13460		Bend-Redmond, OR	15180	48061	Cameron County
13460	41017	Deschutes County	15260		Brunswick, GA
13740		Billings, MT	15260	13025	Brantley County
13740	30009	Carbon County	15260	13127	Glynn County
13740	30037	Golden Valley County	15260	13191	McIntosh County
13740	30111	Yellowstone County	15380		Buffalo-Cheektowaga-Niagara Falls, NY
13780		Binghamton, NY	15380	36029	Erie County
13780	36007	Broome County	15380	36063	Niagara County
13780	36107	Tioga County	15500		Burlington, NC
13820		Birmingham-Hoover, AL	15500	37001	Alamance County
13820	01007	Bibb County	15540		Burlington-South Burlington, VT
13820	01009	Blount County	15540	50007	Chittenden County
13820	01021	Chilton County	15540	50011	Franklin County
13820	01073	Jefferson County	15540	50013	Grand Isle County
13820	01115	St. Clair County	15680		California-Lexington Park, MD
13820	01117	Shelby County	15680	24037	St. Mary's County
13820	01127	Walker County	15940		Canton-Massillon, OH
13900		Bismarck, ND	15940	39019	Carroll County
13900	38015	Burleigh County	15940	39151	Stark County
13900	38059	Morton County	15980		Cape Coral-Fort Myers, FL
13900	38065	Oliver County	15980	12071	Lee County
13900	38085	Sioux County	16020		Cape Girardeau, MO-IL
13980		Blacksburg-Christiansburg-Radford, VA	16020	17003	Alexander County
13980	51063	Floyd County	16020	29017	Bollinger County
13980	51071	Giles County	16020	29031	Cape Girardeau County
13980	51155	Pulaski County	16060		Carbondale-Marion, IL
13980	51933	Montgomery + Radford	16060	17077	Jackson County
14010		Bloomington, IL	16060	17199	Williamson County
14010	17039	De Witt County	16180		Carson City, NV
14010	17113	McLean County	16180	32510	Carson City
14020		Bloomington, IN	16220		Casper, WY
14020	18105	Monroe County	16220	56025	Natrona County
14020	18119	Owen County	16300		Cedar Rapids, IA
14100		Bloomsburg-Berwick, PA	16300	19011	Benton County
14100	42037	Columbia County	16300	19105	Jones County
14100	42093	Montour County	16300	19113	Linn County
14260		Boise City, ID	16540		Chambersburg-Waynesboro, PA

Metropolitan Statistical Areas, Metropolitan Divisions, and Components—*Continued*

Core based statistical area	State/ County FIPS code	Title and Geographic Components	Core based statistical area	State/ County FIPS code	Title and Geographic Components
16540	42055	Franklin County	17140	21023	Bracken County
16580		Champaign-Urbana, IL	17140	21037	Campbell County
16580	17019	Champaign County	17140	21077	Gallatin County
16580	17053	Ford County	17140	21081	Grant County
16580	17147	Piatt County	17140	21117	Kenton County
16620		Charleston, WV	17140	21191	Pendleton County
16620	54005	Boone County	17140	39015	Brown County
16620	54015	Clay County	17140	39017	Butler County
16620	54039	Kanawha County	17140	39025	Clermont County
16700		Charleston-North Charleston, SC	17140	39061	Hamilton County
16700	45015	Berkeley County	17140	39165	Warren County
16700	45019	Charleston County	17300		Clarksville, TN-KY
16700	45035	Dorchester County	17300	21047	Christian County
16740		Charlotte-Concord-Gastonia, NC-SC	17300	21221	Trigg County
16740	37025	Cabarrus County	17300	47125	Montgomery County
16740	37071	Gaston County	17420		Cleveland, TN
16740	37097	Iredell County	17420	47011	Bradley County
16740	37109	Lincoln County	17420	47139	Polk County
16740	37119	Mecklenburg County	17460		Cleveland-Elyria, OH
16740	37159	Rowan County	17460	39035	Cuyahoga County
16740	37179	Union County	17460	39055	Geauga County
16740	45023	Chester County	17460	39085	Lake County
16740	45057	Lancaster County	17460	39093	Lorain County
16740	45091	York County	17460	39103	Medina County
16820		Charlottesville, VA	17660		Coeur d'Alene, ID
16820	51029	Buckingham County	17660	16055	Kootenai County
16820	51065	Fluvanna County	17780		College Station-Bryan, TX
16820	51079	Greene County	17780	48041	Brazos County
16820	51125	Nelson County	17780	48051	Burleson County
16820	51901	Albemarle + Charlottesville, VA	17780	48395	Robertson County
16860		Chattanooga, TN-GA	17820		Colorado Springs, CO
16860	13047	Catoosa County	17820	08041	El Paso County
16860	13083	Dade County	17820	08119	Teller County
16860	13295	Walker County	17860		Columbia, MO
16860	47065	Hamilton County	17860	29019	Boone County
16860	47115	Marion County	17900		Columbia, SC
16860	47153	Sequatchie County	17900	45017	Calhoun County
16940		Cheyenne, WY	17900	45039	Fairfield County
16940	56021	Laramie County	17900	45055	Kershaw County
16980		Chicago-Naperville-Elgin, IL-IN-WI	17900	45063	Lexington County
16980		Chicago-Naperville-Arlington Heights, IL Div 16974	17900	45079	Richland County
16980	17031	Cook County	17900	45081	Saluda County
16980	17043	DuPage County	17980		Columbus, GA-AL
16980	17063	Grundy County	17980	01113	Russell County
16980	17093	Kendall County	17980	13053	Chattahoochee County
16980	17111	McHenry County	17980	13145	Harris County
16980	17197	Will County	17980	13197	Marion County
16980		Elgin, IL Div 20994	17980	13215	Muscogee County
16980	17037	DeKalb County	18020		Columbus, IN
16980	17089	Kane County	18020	18005	Bartholomew County
16980		Gary, IN Div 23844	18140		Columbus, OH
16980	18073	Jasper County	18140	39041	Delaware County
16980	18089	Lake County	18140	39045	Fairfield County
16980	18111	Newton County	18140	39049	Franklin County
16980	18127	Porter County	18140	39073	Hocking County
16980		Lake County-Kenosha County, IL-WI Div 29404	18140	39089	Licking County
16980	17097	Lake County	18140	39097	Madison County
16980	55059	Kenosha County	18140	39117	Morrow County
17020		Chico, CA	18140	39127	Perry County
17020	06007	Butte County	18140	39129	Pickaway County
17140		Cincinnati, OH-KY-IN	18140	39159	Union County
17140	18029	Dearborn County	18580		Corpus Christi, TX
17140	18115	Ohio County	18580	48007	Aransas County
17140	18161	Union County	18580	48355	Nueces County
17140	21015	Boone County	18580	48409	San Patricio County

Metropolitan Statistical Areas, Metropolitan Divisions, and Components—*Continued*

Core based statistical area	State/ County FIPS code	Title and Geographic Components	Core based statistical area	State/ County FIPS code	Title and Geographic Components
18700		Corvallis, OR	19820		Detroit-Warren-Dearborn, MI
18700	41003	Benton County	19820		Detroit-Dearborn-Livonia, MI Div 19804
18880		Crestview-Fort Walton Beach-Destin, FL	19820	26163	Wayne County
18880	12091	Okaloosa County	19820		Warren-Troy-Farmington Hills, MI 47664
18880	12131	Walton County	19820	26087	Lapeer County
19060		Cumberland, MD-WV	19820	26093	Livingston County
19060	24001	Allegany County	19820	26099	Macomb County
19060	54057	Mineral County	19820	26125	Oakland County
19100		Dallas-Fort Worth-Arlington, TX	19820	26147	St. Clair County
19100		Dallas-Plano-Irving, TX Div 19124	20020		Dothan, AL
19100	48085	Collin County	20020	01061	Geneva County
19100	48113	Dallas County	20020	01067	Henry County
19100	48121	Denton County	20020	01069	Houston County
19100	48139	Ellis County	20100		Dover, DE
19100	48231	Hunt County	20100	10001	Kent County
19100	48257	Kaufman County	20220		Dubuque, IA
19100	48397	Rockwall County	20220	19061	Dubuque County
19100		Fort Worth-Arlington, TX Div 23104	20260		Duluth, MN-WI
19100	48221	Hood County	20260	27017	Carlton County
19100	48251	Johnson County	20260	27137	St. Louis County
19100	48367	Parker County	20260	55031	Douglas County
19100	48425	Somervell County	20500		Durham-Chapel Hill, NC
19100	48439	Tarrant County	20500	37037	Chatham County
19100	48497	Wise County	20500	37063	Durham County
19140		Dalton, GA	20500	37135	Orange County
19140	13213	Murray County	20500	37145	Person County
19140	13313	Whitfield County	20700		East Stroudsburg, PA
19180		Danville, IL	20700	42089	Monroe County
19180	17183	Vermilion County	20740		Eau Claire, WI
19300		Daphne-Fairhope-Foley, AL	20740	55017	Chippewa County
19300	01003	Baldwin County	20740	55035	Eau Claire County
19340		Davenport-Moline-Rock Island, IA-IL	20940		El Centro, CA
19340	17073	Henry County	20940	06025	Imperial County
19340	17131	Mercer County	21060		Elizabethtown-Fort Knox, KY
19340	17161	Rock Island County	21060	21093	Hardin County
19340	19163	Scott County	21060	21123	Larue County
19380		Dayton, OH	21060	21163	Meade County
19380	39057	Greene County	21140		Elkhart-Goshen, IN
19380	39109	Miami County	21140	18039	Elkhart County
19380	39113	Montgomery County	21300		Elmira, NY
19460		Decatur, AL	21300	36015	Chemung County
19460	01079	Lawrence County	21340		El Paso, TX
19460	01103	Morgan County	21340	48141	El Paso County
19500		Decatur, IL	21340	48229	Hudspeth County
19500	17115	Macon County	21500		Erie, PA
19660		Deltona-Daytona Beach-Ormond Beach, FL	21500	42049	Erie County
19660	12035	Flagler County	21660		Eugene, OR
19660	12127	Volusia County	21660	41039	Lane County
19740		Denver-Aurora-Lakewood, CO	21780		Evansville, IN-KY
19740	08001	Adams County	21780	18129	Posey County
19740	08005	Arapahoe County	21780	18163	Vanderburgh County
19740	08014	Broomfield County	21780	18173	Warrick County
19740	08019	Clear Creek County	21780	21101	Henderson County
19740	08031	Denver County	21820		Fairbanks, AK
19740	08035	Douglas County	21820	02090	Fairbanks North Star Borough
19740	08039	Elbert County	22020		Fargo, ND-MN
19740	08047	Gilpin County	22020	27027	Clay County
19740	08059	Jefferson County	22020	38017	Cass County
19740	08093	Park County	22140		Farmington, NM
19780		Des Moines-West Des Moines, IA	22140	35045	San Juan County
19780	19049	Dallas County	22180		Fayetteville, NC
19780	19077	Guthrie County	22180	37051	Cumberland County
19780	19121	Madison County	22180	37093	Hoke County
19780	19153	Polk County	22220		Fayetteville-Springdale-Rogers, AR-MO
19780	19181	Warren County	22220	05007	Benton County

Metropolitan Statistical Areas, Metropolitan Divisions, and Components—*Continued*

Core based statistical area	State/County FIPS code	Title and Geographic Components	Core based statistical area	State/County FIPS code	Title and Geographic Components
22220	05087	Madison County	24580	55061	Kewaunee County
22220	05143	Washington County	24580	55083	Oconto County
22220	29119	McDonald County	24660		Greensboro-High Point, NC
22380		Flagstaff, AZ	24660	37081	Guilford County
22380	04005	Coconino County	24660	37151	Randolph County
22420		Flint, MI	24660	37157	Rockingham County
22420	26049	Genesee County	24780		Greenville, NC
22500		Florence, SC	24780	37147	Pitt County
22500	45031	Darlington County	24860		Greenville-Anderson-Mauldin, SC
22500	45041	Florence County	24860	45007	Anderson County
22520		Florence-Muscle Shoals, AL	24860	45045	Greenville County
22520	01033	Colbert County	24860	45059	Laurens County
22520	01077	Lauderdale County	24860	45077	Pickens County
22540		Fond du Lac, WI	25060		Gulfport-Biloxi-Pascagoula, MS
22540	55039	Fond du Lac County	25060	28045	Hancock County
22660		Fort Collins, CO	25060	28047	Harrison County
22660	08069	Larimer County	25060	28059	Jackson County
22900		Fort Smith, AR-OK	25180		Hagerstown-Martinsburg, MD-WV
22900	05033	Crawford County	25180	24043	Washington County
22900	05131	Sebastian County	25180	54003	Berkeley County
22900	40079	Le Flore County	25220		Hammond, LA
22900	40135	Sequoyah County	25220	22105	Tangipahoa Parish
23060		Fort Wayne, IN	25260		Hanford-Corcoran, CA
23060	18003	Allen County	25260	06031	Kings County
23060	18179	Wells County	25420		Harrisburg-Carlisle, PA
23060	18183	Whitley County	25420	42041	Cumberland County
23420		Fresno, CA	25420	42043	Dauphin County
23420	06019	Fresno County	25420	42099	Perry County
23460		Gadsden, AL	25500		Harrisonburg, VA
23460	01055	Etowah County	25500	51947	Rockingham + Harrisonburg, VA
23540		Gainesville, FL	25540		Hartford-West Hartford-East Hartford, CT
23540	12001	Alachua County	25540	09003	Hartford County
23540	12041	Gilchrist County	25540	09007	Middlesex County
23580		Gainesville, GA	25540	09013	Tolland County
23580	13139	Hall County	25620		Hattiesburg, MS
23900		Gettysburg, PA	25620	28035	Forrest County
23900	42001	Adams County	25620	28073	Lamar County
24020		Glens Falls, NY	25620	28111	Perry County
24020	36113	Warren County	25860		Hickory-Lenoir-Morganton, NC
24020	36115	Washington County	25860	37003	Alexander County
24140		Goldsboro, NC	25860	37023	Burke County
24140	37191	Wayne County	25860	37027	Caldwell County
24220		Grand Forks, ND-MN	25860	37035	Catawba County
24220	27119	Polk County	25940		Hilton Head Island-Bluffton-Beaufort, NC
24220	38035	Grand Forks County	25940	45013	Beaufort County
24260		Grand Island, NE	25940	45053	Jasper County
24260	31079	Hall County	25980		Hinesville, GA
24260	31081	Hamilton County	25980	13179	Liberty County
24260	31093	Howard County	25980	13183	Long County
24260	31121	Merrick County	26140		Homosassa Springs, FL
24300		Grand Junction, CO	26140	12017	Citrus County
24300	08077	Mesa County	26300		Hot Springs, AR
24340		Grand Rapids-Wyoming, MI	26300	05051	Garland County
24340	26015	Barry County	26380		Houma-Thibodaux, LA
24340	26081	Kent County	26380	22057	Lafourche Parish
24340	26117	Montcalm County	26380	22109	Terrebonne Parish
24340	26139	Ottawa County	26420		Houston-The Woodlands-Sugar Land, TX
24420		Grants Pass, OR	26420	48015	Austin County
24420	41033	Josephine County	26420	48039	Brazoria County
24500		Great Falls, MT	26420	48071	Chambers County
24500	30013	Cascade County	26420	48157	Fort Bend County
24540		Greeley, CO	26420	48167	Galveston County
24540	08123	Weld County	26420	48201	Harris County
24580		Green Bay, WI	26420	48291	Liberty County
24580	55009	Brown County	26420	48339	Montgomery County

Metropolitan Statistical Areas, Metropolitan Divisions, and Components—*Continued*

Core based statistical area	State/ County FIPS code	Title and Geographic Components	Core based statistical area	State/ County FIPS code	Title and Geographic Components
26420	48473	Waller County	27780		Johnstown, PA
26580		Huntington-Ashland, WV-KY-OH	27780	42021	Cambria County
26580	21019	Boyd County	27860		Jonesboro, AR
26580	21089	Greenup County	27860	05031	Craighead County
26580	39087	Lawrence County	27860	05111	Poinsett County
26580	54011	Cabell County	27900		Joplin, MO
26580	54043	Lincoln County	27900	29097	Jasper County
26580	54079	Putnam County	27900	29145	Newton County
26580	54099	Wayne County	27980		Kahului-Wailuku-Lahaina, HI
26620		Huntsville, AL	27980	15901	Maui + Kalawao, HI
26620	01083	Limestone County	28020		Kalamazoo-Portage, MI
26620	01089	Madison County	28020	26077	Kalamazoo County
26820		Idaho Falls, ID	28020	26159	Van Buren County
26820	16019	Bonneville County	28100		Kankakee, IL
26820	16023	Butte County	28100	17091	Kankakee County
26820	16051	Jefferson County	28140		Kansas City, MO-KS
26900		Indianapolis-Carmel-Anderson, IN	28140	20091	Johnson County
26900	18011	Boone County	28140	20103	Leavenworth County
26900	18013	Brown County	28140	20107	Linn County
26900	18057	Hamilton County	28140	20121	Miami County
26900	18059	Hancock County	28140	20209	Wyandotte County
26900	18063	Hendricks County	28140	29013	Bates County
26900	18081	Johnson County	28140	29025	Caldwell County
26900	18095	Madison County	28140	29037	Cass County
26900	18097	Marion County	28140	29047	Clay County
26900	18109	Morgan County	28140	29049	Clinton County
26900	18133	Putnam County	28140	29095	Jackson County
26900	18145	Shelby County	28140	29107	Lafayette County
26980		Iowa City, IA	28140	29165	Platte County
26980	19103	Johnson County	28140	29177	Ray County
26980	19183	Washington County	28420		Kennewick-Richland, WA
27060		Ithaca, NY	28420	53005	Benton County
27060	36109	Tompkins County	28420	53021	Franklin County
27100		Jackson, MI	28660		Killeen-Temple, TX
27100	26075	Jackson County	28660	48027	Bell County
27140		Jackson, MS	28660	48099	Coryell County
27140	28029	Copiah County	28660	48281	Lampasas County
27140	28049	Hinds County	28700		Kingsport-Bristol-Bristol, TN-VA
27140	28089	Madison County	28700	47073	Hawkins County
27140	28121	Rankin County	28700	47163	Sullivan County
27140	28127	Simpson County	28700	51169	Scott County
27140	28163	Yazoo County	28700	51953	Washington + Bristol, VA
27180		Jackson, TN	28740		Kingston, NY
27180	47023	Chester County	28740	36111	Ulster County
27180	47033	Crockett County	28940		Knoxville, TN
27180	47113	Madison County	28940	47001	Anderson County
27260		Jacksonville, FL	28940	47009	Blount County
27260	12003	Baker County	28940	47013	Campbell County
27260	12019	Clay County	28940	47057	Grainger County
27260	12031	Duval County	28940	47093	Knox County
27260	12089	Nassau County	28940	47105	Loudon County
27260	12109	St. Johns County	28940	47129	Morgan County
27340		Jacksonville, NC	28940	47145	Roane County
27340	37133	Onslow County	28940	47173	Union County
27500		Janesville-Beloit, WI	29020		Kokomo, IN
27500	55105	Rock County	29020	18067	Howard County
27620		Jefferson City, MO	29100		La Crosse-Onalaska, WI-MN
27620	29027	Callaway County	29100	27055	Houston County
27620	29051	Cole County	29100	55063	La Crosse County
27620	29135	Moniteau County	29180		Lafayette, LA
27620	29151	Osage County	29180	22001	Acadia Parish
27740		Johnson City, TN	29180	22045	Iberia Parish
27740	47019	Carter County	29180	22055	Lafayette Parish
27740	47171	Unicoi County	29180	22099	St. Martin Parish
27740	47179	Washington County	29180	22113	Vermilion Parish

Metropolitan Statistical Areas, Metropolitan Divisions, and Components—*Continued*

Core based statistical area	State/County FIPS code	Title and Geographic Components	Core based statistical area	State/County FIPS code	Title and Geographic Components
29200		Lafayette-West Lafayette, IN	31080	06059	Orange County
29200	18007	Benton County	31080		Los Angeles-Long Beach-Glendale, CA Div 31084
29200	18015	Carroll County	31080	06037	Los Angeles County
29200	18157	Tippecanoe County	31140		Louisville/Jefferson County, KY-IN
29340		Lake Charles, LA	31140	18019	Clark County
29340	22019	Calcasieu Parish	31140	18043	Floyd County
29340	22023	Cameron Parish	31140	18061	Harrison County
29420		Lake Havasu City-Kingman, AZ	31140	18143	Scott County
29420	04015	Mohave County	31140	18175	Washington County
29460		Lakeland-Winter Haven, FL	31140	21029	Bullitt County
29460	12105	Polk County	31140	21103	Henry County
29540		Lancaster, PA	31140	21111	Jefferson County
29540	42071	Lancaster County	31140	21185	Oldham County
29620		Lansing-East Lansing, MI	31140	21211	Shelby County
29620	26037	Clinton County	31140	21215	Spencer County
29620	26045	Eaton County	31140	21223	Trimble County
29620	26065	Ingham County	31180		Lubbock, TX
29700		Laredo, TX	31180	48107	Crosby County
29700	48479	Webb County	31180	48303	Lubbock County
29740		Las Cruces, NM	31180	48305	Lynn County
29740	35013	Dona Ana County	31340		Lynchburg, VA
29820		Las Vegas-Henderson-Paradise, NV	31340	51009	Amherst County
29820	32003	Clark County	31340	51011	Appomattox County
29940		Lawrence, KS	31340	51909	Bedford + Bedford City, VA
29940	20045	Douglas County	31340	51911	Campbell + Lynchburg, VA
30020		Lawton, OK	31420		Macon, GA
30020	40031	Comanche County	31420	13021	Bibb County
30020	40033	Cotton County	31420	13079	Crawford County
30140		Lebanon, PA	31420	13169	Jones County
30140	42075	Lebanon County	31420	13207	Monroe County
30300		Lewiston, ID-WA	31420	13289	Twiggs County
30300	16069	Nez Perce County	31460		Madera, CA
30300	53003	Asotin County	31460	06039	Madera County
30340		Lewiston-Auburn, ME	31540		Madison, WI
30340	23001	Androscoggin County	31540	55021	Columbia County
30460		Lexington-Fayette, KY	31540	55025	Dane County
30460	21017	Bourbon County	31540	55045	Green County
30460	21049	Clark County	31540	55049	Iowa County
30460	21067	Fayette County	31700		Manchester-Nashua, NH
30460	21113	Jessamine County	31700	33011	Hillsborough County
30460	21209	Scott County	31740		Manhattan, KS
30460	21239	Woodford County	31740	20149	Pottawatomie County
30620		Lima, OH	31740	20161	Riley County
30620	39003	Allen County	31860		Mankato-North Mankato, MN
30700		Lincoln, NE	31860	27013	Blue Earth County
30700	31109	Lancaster County	31860	27103	Nicollet County
30700	31159	Seward County	31900		Mansfield, OH
30780		Little Rock-North Little Rock-Conway, AR	31900	39139	Richland County
30780	05045	Faulkner County	32580		McAllen-Edinburg-Mission, TX
30780	05053	Grant County	32580	48215	Hidalgo County
30780	05085	Lonoke County	32780		Medford, OR
30780	05105	Perry County	32780	41029	Jackson County
30780	05119	Pulaski County	32820		Memphis, TN-MS-AR
30780	05125	Saline County	32820	05035	Crittenden County
30860		Logan, UT-ID	32820	28009	Benton County
30860	16041	Franklin County	32820	28033	DeSoto County
30860	49005	Cache County	32820	28093	Marshall County
30980		Longview, TX	32820	28137	Tate County
30980	48183	Gregg County	32820	28143	Tunica County
30980	48401	Rusk County	32820	47047	Fayette County
30980	48459	Upshur County	32820	47157	Shelby County
31020		Longview, WA	32820	47167	Tipton County
31020	53015	Cowlitz County	32900		Merced, CA
31080		Los Angeles-Long Beach-Anaheim, CA	32900	06047	Merced County
31080		Anaheim-Santa Ana-Irvine, CA Div 11244	33100		Miami-Fort Lauderdale-West Palm Beach, FL

Metropolitan Statistical Areas, Metropolitan Divisions, and Components—*Continued*

Core based statistical area	State/ County FIPS code	Title and Geographic Components	Core based statistical area	State/ County FIPS code	Title and Geographic Components
33100		Fort Lauderdale-Pompano Beach-Deerfield Beach, FL Div 22744	34820	45051	Horry County
33100	12011	Broward County	34900		Napa, CA
33100		Miami-Miami Beach-Kendall, FL Div 33124	34900	06055	Napa County
33100	12086	Miami-Dade County	34940		Naples-Immokalee-Marco Island, FL
33100		West Palm Beach-Boca Raton-Delray Beach, FL Div 48424	34940	12021	Collier County
33100	12099	Palm Beach County	34980		Nashville-Davidson--Murfreesboro--Franklin, TN
33140		Michigan City-La Porte, IN	34980	47015	Cannon County
33140	18091	LaPorte County	34980	47021	Cheatham County
33220		Midland, MI	34980	47037	Davidson County
33220	26111	Midland County	34980	47043	Dickson County
33260		Midland, TX	34980	47081	Hickman County
33260	48317	Martin County	34980	47111	Macon County
33260	48329	Midland County	34980	47119	Maury County
33340		Milwaukee-Waukesha-West Allis, WI	34980	47147	Robertson County
33340	55079	Milwaukee County	34980	47149	Rutherford County
33340	55089	Ozaukee County	34980	47159	Smith County
33340	55131	Washington County	34980	47165	Sumner County
33340	55133	Waukesha County	34980	47169	Trousdale County
33460		Minneapolis-St. Paul-Bloomington, MN	34980	47187	Williamson County
33460	27003	Anoka County	34980	47189	Wilson County
33460	27019	Carver County	35100		New Bern, NC
33460	27025	Chisago County	35100	37049	Craven County
33460	27037	Dakota County	35100	37103	Jones County
33460	27053	Hennepin County	35100	37137	Pamlico County
33460	27059	Isanti County	35300		New Haven-Milford, CT
33460	27079	Le Sueur County	35300	09009	New Haven County
33460	27095	Mille Lacs County	35380		New Orleans-Metairie, LA
33460	27123	Ramsey County	35380	22051	Jefferson Parish
33460	27139	Scott County	35380	22071	Orleans Parish
33460	27141	Sherburne County	35380	22075	Plaquemines Parish
33460	27143	Sibley County	35380	22087	St. Bernard Parish
33460	27163	Washington County	35380	22089	St. Charles Parish
33460	27171	Wright County	35380	22093	St. James Parish
33460	55093	Pierce County	35380	22095	St. John the Baptist Parish
33460	55109	St. Croix County	35380	22103	St. Tammany Parish
33540		Missoula, MT	35620		New York-Newark-Jersey City, NY-NJ-PA
33540	30063	Missoula County	35620		Dutchess County-Putnam County, NY Div 20524
33660		Mobile, AL	35620	36027	Dutchess County
33660	01097	Mobile County	35620	36079	Putnam County
33700		Modesto, CA	35620		Nassau County-Suffolk County, NY Div 35004
33700	06099	Stanislaus County	35620	36059	Nassau County
33740		Monroe, LA	35620	36103	Suffolk County
33740	22073	Ouachita Parish	35620		Newark, NJ-PA Div 35084
33740	22111	Union Parish	35620	34013	Essex County
33780		Monroe, MI	35620	34019	Hunterdon County
33780	26115	Monroe County	35620	34027	Morris County
33860		Montgomery, AL	35620	34035	Somerset County
33860	01001	Autauga County	35620	34037	Sussex County
33860	01051	Elmore County	35620	34039	Union County
33860	01085	Lowndes County	35620	42103	Pike County
33860	01101	Montgomery County	35620		New York-Jersey City-White Plains, NY-NJ Div 35614
34060		Morgantown, WV	35620	34003	Bergen County
34060	54061	Monongalia County	35620	34017	Hudson County
34060	54077	Preston County	35620	34023	Middlesex County
34100		Morristown, TN	35620	34025	Monmouth County
34100	47063	Hamblen County	35620	34029	Ocean County
34100	47089	Jefferson County	35620	34031	Passaic County
34580		Mount Vernon-Anacortes, WA	35620	36005	Bronx County
34580	53057	Skagit County	35620	36047	Kings County
34620		Muncie, IN	35620	36061	New York County
34620	18035	Delaware County	35620	36071	Orange County
34740		Muskegon, MI	35620	36081	Queens County
34740	26121	Muskegon County	35620	36085	Richmond County
34820		Myrtle Beach-Conway-North Myrtle Beach, SC-NC	35620	36087	Rockland County
34820	37019	Brunswick County	35620	36119	Westchester County

Metropolitan Statistical Areas, Metropolitan Divisions, and Components—*Continued*

Core based statistical area	State/ County FIPS code	Title and Geographic Components	Core based statistical area	State/ County FIPS code	Title and Geographic Components
35660		Niles-Benton Harbor, MI	37900	17179	Tazewell County
35660	26021	Berrien County	37900	17203	Woodford County
35840		North Port-Sarasota-Bradenton, FL	37980		Philadelphia-Camden-Wilmington, PA-NJ-DE-MD
35840	12081	Manatee County	37980		Camden, NJ Div 15804
35840	12115	Sarasota County	37980	34005	Burlington County
35980		Norwich-New London, CT	37980	34007	Camden County
35980	09011	New London County	37980	34015	Gloucester County
36100		Ocala, FL	37980		Montgomery County-Bucks County-Chester County, PA Div 33874
36100	12083	Marion County	37980	42017	Bucks County
36140		Ocean City, NJ	37980	42029	Chester County
36140	34009	Cape May County	37980	42091	Montgomery County
36220		Odessa, TX	37980		Philadelphia, PA Div 37964
36220	48135	Ector County	37980	42045	Delaware County
36260		Ogden-Clearfield, UT	37980	42101	Philadelphia County
36260	49003	Box Elder County	37980		Wilmington, DE-MD-NJ Div 48864
36260	49011	Davis County	37980	10003	New Castle County
36260	49029	Morgan County	37980	24015	Cecil County
36260	49057	Weber County	37980	34033	Salem County
36420		Oklahoma City, OK	38060		Phoenix-Mesa-Scottsdale, AZ
36420	40017	Canadian County	38060	04013	Maricopa County
36420	40027	Cleveland County	38060	04021	Pinal County
36420	40051	Grady County	38220		Pine Bluff, AR
36420	40081	Lincoln County	38220	05025	Cleveland County
36420	40083	Logan County	38220	05069	Jefferson County
36420	40087	McClain County	38220	05079	Lincoln County
36420	40109	Oklahoma County	38300		Pittsburgh, PA
36500		Olympia-Tumwater, WA	38300	42003	Allegheny County
36500	53067	Thurston County	38300	42005	Armstrong County
36540		Omaha-Council Bluffs, NE-IA	38300	42007	Beaver County
36540	19085	Harrison County	38300	42019	Butler County
36540	19129	Mills County	38300	42051	Fayette County
36540	19155	Pottawattamie County	38300	42125	Washington County
36540	31025	Cass County	38300	42129	Westmoreland County
36540	31055	Douglas County	38340		Pittsfield, MA
36540	31153	Sarpy County	38340	25003	Berkshire County
36540	31155	Saunders County	38540		Pocatello, ID
36540	31177	Washington County	38540	16005	Bannock County
36740		Orlando-Kissimmee-Sanford, FL	38860		Portland-South Portland, ME
36740	12069	Lake County	38860	23005	Cumberland County
36740	12095	Orange County	38860	23023	Sagadahoc County
36740	12097	Osceola County	38860	23031	York County
36740	12117	Seminole County	38900		Portland-Vancouver-Hillsboro, OR-WA
36780		Oshkosh-Neenah, WI	38900	41005	Clackamas County
36780	55139	Winnebago County	38900	41009	Columbia County
36980		Owensboro, KY	38900	41051	Multnomah County
36980	21059	Daviess County	38900	41067	Washington County
36980	21091	Hancock County	38900	41071	Yamhill County
36980	21149	McLean County	38900	53011	Clark County
37100		Oxnard-Thousand Oaks-Ventura, CA	38900	53059	Skamania County
37100	06111	Ventura County	38940		Port St. Lucie, FL
37340		Palm Bay-Melbourne-Titusville, FL	38940	12085	Martin County
37340	12009	Brevard County	38940	12111	St. Lucie County
37460		Panama City, FL	39140		Prescott, AZ
37460	12005	Bay County	39140	04025	Yavapai County
37460	12045	Gulf County	39300		Providence-Warwick, RI-MA
37620		Parkersburg-Vienna, WV	39300	25005	Bristol County
37620	54105	Wirt County	39300	44001	Bristol County
37620	54107	Wood County	39300	44003	Kent County
37860		Pensacola-Ferry Pass-Brent, FL	39300	44005	Newport County
37860	12033	Escambia County	39300	44007	Providence County
37860	12113	Santa Rosa County	39300	44009	Washington County
37900		Peoria, IL	39340		Provo-Orem, UT
37900	17123	Marshall County	39340	49023	Juab County
37900	17143	Peoria County	39340	49049	Utah County
37900	17175	Stark County	39380		Pueblo, CO

Metropolitan Statistical Areas, Metropolitan Divisions, and Components—*Continued*

Core based statistical area	State/County FIPS code	Title and Geographic Components	Core based statistical area	State/County FIPS code	Title and Geographic Components
39380	08101	Pueblo County	40580	37127	Nash County
39460		Punta Gorda, FL	40660		Rome, GA
39460	12015	Charlotte County	40660	13115	Floyd County
39540		Racine, WI	40900		Sacramento—Roseville—Arden-Arcade, CA
39540	55101	Racine County	40900	06017	El Dorado County
39580		Raleigh, NC	40900	06061	Placer County
39580	37069	Franklin County	40900	06067	Sacramento County
39580	37101	Johnston County	40900	06113	Yolo County
39580	37183	Wake County	40980		Saginaw, MI
39660		Rapid City, SD	40980	26145	Saginaw County
39660	46033	Custer County	41060		St. Cloud, MN
39660	46093	Meade County	41060	27009	Benton County
39660	46103	Pennington County	41060	27145	Stearns County
39740		Reading, PA	41100		St. George, UT
39740	42011	Berks County	41100	49053	Washington County
39820		Redding, CA	41140		St. Joseph, MO-KS
39820	06089	Shasta County	41140	20043	Doniphan County
39900		Reno, NV	41140	29003	Andrew County
39900	32029	Storey County	41140	29021	Buchanan County
39900	32031	Washoe County	41140	29063	DeKalb County
40060		Richmond, VA	41180		St. Louis, MO-IL
40060	51007	Amelia County	41180	17005	Bond County
40060	51033	Caroline County	41180	17013	Calhoun County
40060	51036	Charles City County	41180	17027	Clinton County
40060	51041	Chesterfield County	41180	17083	Jersey County
40060	51918	Dinwiddie, Colonial Heights + Petersburg, VA	41180	17117	Macoupin County
40060	51075	Goochland County	41180	17119	Madison County
40060	51085	Hanover County	41180	17133	Monroe County
40060	51087	Henrico County	41180	17163	St. Clair County
40060	51101	King William County	41180	29071	Franklin County
40060	51127	New Kent County	41180	29099	Jefferson County
40060	51145	Powhatan County	41180	29113	Lincoln County
40060	51149	Prince George County	41180	29183	St. Charles County
40060	51183	Sussex County	41180	29189	St. Louis County
40060	51570	Colonial Heights city	41180	29219	Warren County
40060	51670	Hopewell city	41180	29510	St. Louis city
40060	51730	Petersburg city	41420		Salem, OR
40060	51760	Richmond city	41420	41047	Marion County
40140		Riverside-San Bernardino-Ontario, CA	41420	41053	Polk County
40140	06065	Riverside County	41500		Salinas, CA
40140	06071	San Bernardino County	41500	06053	Monterey County
40220		Roanoke, VA	41540		Salisbury, MD-DE
40220	51023	Botetourt County	41540	10005	Sussex County
40220	51045	Craig County	41540	24039	Somerset County
40220	51067	Franklin County	41540	24045	Wicomico County
40220	51161	Roanoke County	41540	24047	Worcester County
40220	51770	Roanoke city	41620		Salt Lake City, UT
40220	51775	Salem city	41620	49035	Salt Lake County
40340		Rochester, MN	41620	49045	Tooele County
40340	27039	Dodge County	41660		San Angelo, TX
40340	27045	Fillmore County	41660	48235	Irion County
40340	27109	Olmsted County	41660	48451	Tom Green County
40340	27157	Wabasha County	41700		San Antonio-New Braunfels, TX
40380		Rochester, NY	41700	48013	Atascosa County
40380	36051	Livingston County	41700	48019	Bandera County
40380	36055	Monroe County	41700	48029	Bexar County
40380	36069	Ontario County	41700	48091	Comal County
40380	36073	Orleans County	41700	48187	Guadalupe County
40380	36117	Wayne County	41700	48259	Kendall County
40380	36123	Yates County	41700	48325	Medina County
40420		Rockford, IL	41700	48493	Wilson County
40420	17007	Boone County	41740		San Diego-Carlsbad, CA
40420	17201	Winnebago County	41740	06073	San Diego County
40580		Rocky Mount, NC	41860		San Francisco-Oakland-Hayward, CA
40580	37065	Edgecombe County	41860		Oakland-Hayward-Berkeley, CA Div 36084

Metropolitan Statistical Areas, Metropolitan Divisions, and Components—*Continued*

Core based statistical area	State/ County FIPS code	Title and Geographic Components	Core based statistical area	State/ County FIPS code	Title and Geographic Components
41860	06001	Alameda County	43900	45087	Union County
41860	06013	Contra Costa County	44060		Spokane-Spokane Valley, WA
41860		San Francisco-Redwood City-South San Francisco, CA Div 41884	44060	53051	Pend Oreille County
41860	06075	San Francisco County	44060	53063	Spokane County
41860	06081	San Mateo County	44060	53065	Stevens County
41860		San Rafael, CA Div 42034	44100		Springfield, IL
41860	06041	Marin County	44100	17129	Menard County
41940		San Jose-Sunnyvale-Santa Clara, CA	44100	17167	Sangamon County
41940	06069	San Benito County	44140		Springfield, MA
41940	06085	Santa Clara County	44140	25013	Hampden County
42020		San Luis Obispo-Paso Robles-Arroyo Grande, CA	44140	25015	Hampshire County
42020	06079	San Luis Obispo County	44180		Springfield, MO
42100		Santa Cruz-Watsonville, CA	44180	29043	Christian County
42100	06087	Santa Cruz County	44180	29059	Dallas County
42140		Santa Fe, NM	44180	29077	Greene County
42140	35049	Santa Fe County	44180	29167	Polk County
42200		Santa Maria-Santa Barbara, CA	44180	29225	Webster County
42200	06083	Santa Barbara County	44220		Springfield, OH
42220		Santa Rosa, CA	44220	39023	Clark County
42220	06097	Sonoma County	44300		State College, PA
42340		Savannah, GA	44300	42027	Centre County
42340	13029	Bryan County	44420		Staunton-Waynesboro, VA
42340	13051	Chatham County	44420	51015	Augusta County
42340	13103	Effingham County	44420	51790	Staunton city
42540		Scranton--Wilkes-Barre--Hazleton, PA	44420	51820	Waynesboro city
42540	42069	Lackawanna County	44700		Stockton-Lodi, CA
42540	42079	Luzerne County	44700	06077	San Joaquin County
42540	42131	Wyoming County	44940		Sumter, SC
42660		Seattle-Tacoma-Bellevue, WA	44940	45085	Sumter County
42660		Seattle-Bellevue-Everett, WA Div 42644	45060		Syracuse, NY
42660	53033	King County	45060	36053	Madison County
42660	53061	Snohomish County	45060	36067	Onondaga County
42660		Tacoma-Lakewood, WA Div 45104	45060	36075	Oswego County
42660	53053	Pierce County	45220		Tallahassee, FL
42680		Sebastian-Vero Beach, FL	45220	12039	Gadsden County
42680	12061	Indian River County	45220	12065	Jefferson County
42700		Sebring, FL	45220	12073	Leon County
42700	12055	Highlands County	45220	12129	Wakulla County
43100		Sheboygan, WI	45300		Tampa-St. Petersburg-Clearwater, FL
43100	55117	Sheboygan County	45300	12053	Hernando County
43300		Sherman-Denison, TX	45300	12057	Hillsborough County
43300	48181	Grayson County	45300	12101	Pasco County
43340		Shreveport-Bossier City, LA	45300	12103	Pinellas County
43340	22015	Bossier Parish	45460		Terre Haute, IN
43340	22017	Caddo Parish	45460	18021	Clay County
43340	22031	De Soto Parish	45460	18153	Sullivan County
43340	22119	Webster Parish	45460	18165	Vermillion County
43420		Sierra Vista-Douglas, AZ	45460	18167	Vigo County
43420	04003	Cochise County	45500		Texarkana, TX-AR
43580		Sioux City, IA-NE-SD	45500	05081	Little River County
43580	19149	Plymouth County	45500	05091	Miller County
43580	19193	Woodbury County	45500	48037	Bowie County
43580	31043	Dakota County	45540		The Villages, FL
43580	31051	Dixon County	45540	12119	Sumter County
43580	46127	Union County	45780		Toledo, OH
43620		Sioux Falls, SD	45780	39051	Fulton County
43620	46083	Lincoln County	45780	39095	Lucas County
43620	46087	McCook County	45780	39173	Wood County
43620	46099	Minnehaha County	45820		Topeka, KS
43620	46125	Turner County	45820	20085	Jackson County
43780		South Bend-Mishawaka, IN-MI	45820	20087	Jefferson County
43780	18141	St. Joseph County	45820	20139	Osage County
43780	26027	Cass County	45820	20177	Shawnee County
43900		Spartanburg, SC	45820	20197	Wabaunsee County
43900	45083	Spartanburg County	45940		Trenton, NJ

Metropolitan Statistical Areas, Metropolitan Divisions, and Components—*Continued*

Core based statistical area	State/ County FIPS code	Title and Geographic Components	Core based statistical area	State/ County FIPS code	Title and Geographic Components
45940	34021	Mercer County	47900	24021	Frederick County
46060		Tucson, AZ	47900	24031	Montgomery County
46060	04019	Pima County	47900		Washington-Arlington-Alexandria, DC-VA-MD-WV Div 47894
46140		Tulsa, OK	47900	11001	District of Columbia
46140	40037	Creek County	47900	24009	Calvert County
46140	40111	Okmulgee County	47900	24017	Charles County
46140	40113	Osage County	47900	24033	Prince George's County
46140	40117	Pawnee County	47900	51013	Arlington County
46140	40131	Rogers County	47900	51043	Clarke County
46140	40143	Tulsa County	47900	51047	Culpeper County
46140	40145	Wagoner County	47900	51059	Fairfax County
46220		Tuscaloosa, AL	47900	51061	Fauquier County
46220	01065	Hale County	47900	51107	Loudoun County
46220	01107	Pickens County	47900	51153	Prince William County
46220	01125	Tuscaloosa County	47900	51157	Rappahannock County
46340		Tyler, TX	47900	51177	Spotsylvania County
46340	48423	Smith County	47900	51179	Stafford County
46520		Urban Honolulu, HI	47900	51187	Warren County
46520	15003	Honolulu County	47900	51510	Alexandria city
46540		Utica-Rome, NY	47900	51600	Fairfax city
46540	36043	Herkimer County	47900	51610	Falls Church city
46540	36065	Oneida County	47900	51630	Fredericksburg city
46660		Valdosta, GA	47900	51683	Manassas city
46660	13027	Brooks County	47900	51685	Manassas Park city
46660	13101	Echols County	47900	54037	Jefferson County
46660	13173	Lanier County	47940		Waterloo-Cedar Falls, IA
46660	13185	Lowndes County	47940	19013	Black Hawk County
46700		Vallejo-Fairfield, CA	47940	19017	Bremer County
46700	06095	Solano County	47940	19075	Grundy County
47020		Victoria, TX	48060		Watertown-Fort Drum, NY
47020	48175	Goliad County	48060	36045	Jefferson County
47020	48469	Victoria County	48140		Wausau, WI
47220		Vineland-Bridgeton, NJ	48140	55073	Marathon County
47220	34011	Cumberland County	48260		Weirton-Steubenville, WV-OH
47260		Virginia Beach-Norfolk-Newport News, VA-NC	48260	39081	Jefferson County
47260	37053	Currituck County	48260	54009	Brooke County
47260	37073	Gates County	48260	54029	Hancock County
47260	51073	Gloucester County	48300		Wenatchee, WA
47260	51093	Isle of Wight County	48300	53007	Chelan County
47260	51095	James City County	48300	53017	Douglas County
47260	51115	Mathews County	48540		Wheeling, WV-OH
47260	51199	York County	48540	39013	Belmont County
47260	51550	Chesapeake city	48540	54051	Marshall County
47260	51650	Hampton city	48540	54069	Ohio County
47260	51700	Newport News city	48620		Wichita, KS
47260	51710	Norfolk city	48620	20015	Butler County
47260	51735	Poquoson city	48620	20079	Harvey County
47260	51740	Portsmouth city	48620	20095	Kingman County
47260	51800	Suffolk city	48620	20173	Sedgwick County
47260	51810	Virginia Beach city	48620	20191	Sumner County
47260	51830	Williamsburg city	48660		Wichita Falls, TX
47300		Visalia-Porterville, CA	48660	48009	Archer County
47300	06107	Tulare County	48660	48077	Clay County
47380		Waco, TX	48660	48485	Wichita County
47380	48145	Falls County	48700		Williamsport, PA
47380	48309	McLennan County	48700	42081	Lycoming County
47460		Walla Walla, WA	48900		Wilmington, NC
47460	53013	Columbia County	48900	37129	New Hanover County
47460	53071	Walla Walla County	48900	37141	Pender County
47580		Warner Robins, GA	49020		Winchester, VA-WV
47580	13153	Houston County	49020	51069	Frederick County
47580	13225	Peach County	49020	51840	Winchester city
47580	13235	Pulaski County	49020	54027	Hampshire County
47900		Washington-Arlington-Alexandria, DC-VA-MD-WV	49180		Winston-Salem, NC
47900		Silver Spring-Frederick-Rockville, MD Div 43524	49180	37057	Davidson County

Metropolitan Statistical Areas, Metropolitan Divisions, and Components—*Continued*

Core based statistical area	State/ County FIPS code	Title and Geographic Components	Core based statistical area	State/ County FIPS code	Title and Geographic Components
49180	37059	Davie County	49620	42133	York County
49180	37067	Forsyth County	49660		Youngstown-Warren-Boardman, OH-PA
49180	37169	Stokes County	49660	39099	Mahoning County
49180	37197	Yadkin County	49660	39155	Trumbull County
49340		Worcester, MA-CT	49660	42085	Mercer County
49340	09015	Windham County	49700		Yuba City, CA
49340	25027	Worcester County	49700	06101	Sutter County
49420		Yakima, WA	49700	06115	Yuba County
49420	53077	Yakima County	49740		Yuma, AZ
49620		York-Hanover, PA	49740	04027	Yuma County